The New Walford
Guide to Reference Resources

Volume 1
Science, Technology and Medicine

Editor-in-Chief

Ray Lester BSc PhD FCLIP FRSA

Published by
Facet Publishing
7 Ridgmount Street
London WC1E 7AE
www.facetpublishing.co.uk
Facet Publishing is wholly owned by CILIP: the Chartered Institute of Library and Information Professionals.

This book is the first volume of a series that succeeds *Walford's guide to reference material*, published in eight editions between 1959 and 2000 by Library Association Publishing.

First published 2005

British Library Cataloguing in Publication Data
A catalogue record for this book is available from the British Library.

ISBN 1-85604-495-5

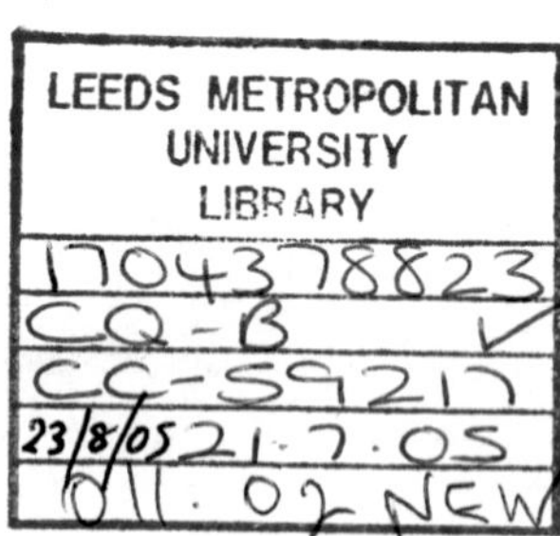

Text design by Studio 183
Database development and typesetting by York & Timberlake Partnership
Printed and made in Great Britain by Cromwell Press Ltd, Trowbridge, Wiltshire

This volume is dedicated to the memory of

John Walford MBE MA PhD FRHistS HonFLA FLA DipLib

1906–2000

Contents

Preface

Although *The new Walford: guide to reference resources* (TNW) has a broadly similar purpose to John Walford's classic *Guide to reference materials*, its structure and content are quite different. Developments on the internet and the web have ensured that. We have focused much more on the needs of newcomers to the various areas of science, technology and medicine (STM), simplifying the book's subject arrangement, but at the same time considerably widening the types of resource described. Above all, whilst hardly creating a book that is bedtime reading, we have aimed to make the guide easily browsable.

There is greatly increased emphasis on the *producers* of STM information, on the basis that these are less likely to change than the individual resources that they generate. This includes a wide range of stakeholders (sponsors, regulators, critics, etc.) who make up the landscape of STM research and practice. Distilling the volume and wealth of resources now accessible down to a 'starter pack' of a few thousand items not surprisingly has been rather challenging; and there is no doubt that we will have been more successful in some subject areas than in others. We shall welcome feedback on the resource choices we have made via the TNW dedicated e-mail address: newwalford@facetpublishing.co.uk. Most research for this volume was carried out mid-2004, however, **all URLs were checked in April 2005**.

It is not possible in a volume of this type and size to treat all the different viewpoints within each subject; especially in areas of controversy. The majority of the resources described reflect what the Editors perceive to be the currently dominant paradigms within STM. However, in a number of subject areas one or two works are cited which depart significantly from the mainstream in their treatments. These are included simply to remind the reader that such alternative viewpoints exist and should be pursued in any comprehensive survey.

I am very grateful to the subject specialists for their contributions, also to the editors' managers in the libraries where they work; to the staff of the various libraries we have all used in gathering information – particularly, in my case, those at the British Library at St Pancras, the University of Sheffield Library, and the Library of University College London, including its librarianship subject specialist, John Spiers; to Stephen York, for his commitment, responsiveness and persistence whilst we developed the new software and data environment; to Kathryn Beecroft and Helen Carley (and originally Janet Liebster) at Facet Publishing, for their cheerful patience and excellent professionalism throughout a project that took much longer than any of us thought it would at the outset; and, above all, to my children, Catherine, Richard and Joanna, and my wife, Professor Sheila Corrall, for all their love and support.

Ray Lester
May 2005

Quick-start guide

How TNW is organized

Entries are hierarchically classified by subject area to three levels:

- At the highest level are the *Subject Parts*, in the order Science, Medicine, Technology;
- At the next level are the twelve *Subject Groupings*, six in Science, three each in Medicine and Technology;
- Each Grouping is then sub-divided into around one hundred *Subject Fields*.
- There are also two generic collections of entries: one at the start, describing resources covering the whole of STM (and, in some cases, *all* disciplines) the other at the end, highlighting tools that are especially valuable for information professionals.

Within this structure, descriptions of resources are allocated to one of the subject areas and then placed within one of thirteen *Resource Categories*:

[1] Introductions to the subject
[2] Dictionaries, thesauri, classifications
[3] Laws, standards, codes
[4] Official & quasi-official bodies
[5] Research centres & institutes
[6] Associations & societies
[7] Libraries, archives & museums
[8] Portal & task environments
[9] Discovering print & electronic resources
[10] Digital data, image & text collections
[11] Directories & encyclopedias
[12] Handbooks & manuals
[13] Keeping up-to-date

For around a quarter of the resources, we have appended descriptions of associated or related resources (for example, additional items from the same producer or alternative views of the subject).

We do not duplicate or cross-reference entries within the set of resource categories for a specific subject area: if a resource description could equally well be placed within two (or more) categories, it will usually appear in the category earliest in the sequence. However, we do frequently cross-reference (but not duplicate) resource descriptions between different subject areas.

Entries, including cross-referenced entries, appear alphanumerically by title within each resource category. Where a resource has a particular area or country focus that is not apparent from its title, we have added a geographical indicator.

The Table of Contents lists all the subject parts, groupings and fields, as well as the two generic sections, in the order in which they appear in the volume.

The Topic Index provides alphabetical access to the subject headings used for the subject fields and groupings. It also lists more detailed and alternative subject headings to the ones chosen for the subject fields, indicating where commonly sought topics are located within our subject structure (for example, 'Global warming' takes you to entries located in Meteorology & Climatology).

The Title/Author Index lists the titles and authors for all resources listed, including both main entries and associated resources. For organizations, we have also often provided cross-references for commonly-used acronyms and cross-references linking parent and subordinate bodies.

How to find resources

- If you are looking for a known item, consult the Title/Author Index under the title of the work or the name of the author or organization associated with the resource.
- If you are looking for resources about a subject, browse the entries for the relevant subject part/grouping/field, using the Topic Index to target your search as necessary.

MEDICINE — subject part heading

Health — subject grouping heading

Environmental & Occupational Health — subject field heading

Handbooks & manuals — resource category heading

running number — **4290** **Hazardous chemicals desk reference** — title of resource

resource author — **R.J. Lewis** Wiley-InterScience, 2002, 1728pp. $199.95 (price*). ISBN 0471441651.

Contains safety profiles, synonyms, physical properties, standards, and recommendations of government agencies for approximately 5000 chemicals deemed both important and potentially hazardous by the international scientific community. Substances were chosen on the basis of meeting a variety of criteria, including: Having a US OCCUPATIONAL SAFETY AND HEALTH ADMINISTRATION standard; Having an American Conference of Governmental Industrial Hygienists Threshold Limit Value; Listed by the INTERNATIONAL AGENCY FOR RESEARCH ON CANCER. — main resource; cross references; explanatory detail of contents

review — 'of all the books I have on chemicals (and I have many), it is Lewis' book I most often turn to for information.' (*Journal of Hazardous Materials*)

■ **American Conference of Governmental Industrial Hygienists** (title of organization) www.acgih.org (URL). Have developed Threshold Limit Values and Biological Exposure Indices: 'determinations made by a voluntary body of independent knowledgeable individuals ... (They) are not standards (but) are health-based values established by various committees.' — additional resource

* Resources from primarily US-based publishers have been given US$ prices; from those primarily based in the UK (or Europe) UK£ (or €) prices

Topic Index entries:

hazardous chemicals *see* ENVIRONMENTAL & OCCUPATIONAL HEALTH **4222–4303**
industrial hygiene *see* ENVIRONMENTAL & OCCUPATIONAL HEALTH **4222–4303**

Title/Author Index entries:

ACGIH *see* American Conference of Governmental Industrial Hygienists

American Conference of Governmental Industrial Hygienists 4290

Hazardous chemicals desk reference 4290

Lewis, R.J.
Hazardous chemicals desk reference **4290**

Editor and subject specialists

Editor-in-Chief

Dr Ray Lester graduated in chemistry, took a PhD in chemical pathology, and then worked at the multinational company Unilever as an information scientist/systems analyst. He was a subject specialist in several academic libraries before becoming Head of the Library at the London Business School. Subsequently he became Director of Information Systems at LBS in charge of all of the School's IT, library, audio-visual and telephone services, before taking up the post of Head of Information Services at The Natural History Museum, with a remit to manage the institution's IT, library, archive, publishing, and collections databasing services, and to chair its Information Strategy Group. Dr Lester also served on the boards of SCONUL and the Research Libraries Group.

Subject specialists

Catherine Carr

AERONAUTICAL & AEROSPACE ENGINEERING, AUTOMOTIVE & AGRICULTURAL ENGINEERING, MARINE ENGINEERING & NAVAL ARCHITECTURE, MATERIALS SCIENCE & ENGINEERING

Catherine Carr has worked at Cranfield University's Kings Norton Library for over two years as an Information Specialist for Aerospace, Engineering and the Environment. During this time she has been involved with the development and maintenance of AERADE (Cranfield University's quality portal to aerospace and defence resources on the internet), academic liaison, student training and e-learning. After graduating with a degree in Physical Geography with Geology from Reading University she has also spent 21 years working in materials Research & Development Laboratory libraries (initially with TI Research Ltd, formerly Tube Investments Research, and then with Alcan International Ltd).

Jim Corlett

DESIGN, MANUFACTURING ENGINEERING, MICROENGINEERING & NANOTECHNOLOGY

Jim Corlett followed study at Cambridge University and North London Polytechnic with stints in the libraries at Imperial College and at The Nottingham Trent University. He was active within the SCITECH Group and worked with EEVL, the Internet Guide to Engineering, Mathematics and Computing. He has also produced and edited the Recent Advances in Manufacturing database for the past fifteen years. He now works for his own company.

Joanne Dunham

MEDICINE

Joanne Dunham is currently the Clinical Sciences Librarian at the University of Leicester where she has worked in a variety of roles within the Medical Library since 1991. She previously worked at Charing Cross and Westminster Medical School, having taken her postgraduate library qualification at Northumbria University. Joanne is currently on the Committee of the University Medical School Librarians Group. Her recent professional achievements have included the setting up of a Clinical Librarian Service and a Primary Care Outreach Library Service; developing information skills within the medical curriculum through eLearning and building a partnership with an Ethiopian College of Medicine library service.

Helen Hathaway

HYDROLOGY, OCEANOGRAPHY

Helen Hathaway is Faculty Team Manager for the Faculty of Science in Reading University Library. Over the years she has acted as liaison librarian for many Schools in the Science and Life Science faculties including Chemistry, Meteorology and Physics and has close links with Earth Sciences. In this capacity she has recommended, selected and managed the budget for reference material including datasets. Her other role as Information Skills Coordinator gives a pedagogic basis to understanding how students learn and considerable practical experience of helping them to identify their information need and to chose and evaluate resources – whether reference books, databases, or quality national and international websites.

Dr Jonathan Jeffery

PALAEONTOLOGY

Jonathan Jeffery read Biology at the University of Birmingham, and studied for his doctorate at the University of Cambridge Museum of Zoology. He wrote his thesis on rhizodonts, giant predatory fishes whose fossilized remains were first found near Edinburgh. His postdoctoral research was based at St George's Hospital Medical School and University College in London, and later at the University of Leiden in the Netherlands. His research included evolutionary biology, palaeontology and embryology. He now works at the International School of Amsterdam, where he teaches children about palaeontology using fossil mammoth and rhinoceros bones found in the nearby Wadden sea.

Gareth J. Johnson

MATHEMATICS, PHYSICS & ASTRONOMY

Gareth Johnson is currently working within the University of Warwick Library Research and Innovation Unit. Previous to this he was employed at the University of York Library as their Sciences Librarian. His particular professional interests are in the sciences, information literacy, teaching pedagogy and project management. He remains an active member of numerous CILIP branches and special interest groups, and as of 2005 is serving as the Honorary Secretary of the national University, College & Research Group of CILIP. He continues to write in various capacities, and is currently developing his first screenplay.

Nazma Masud
CHEMISTRY
Nazma Masud is one of the chemical information specialists, at the Library and Information Centre (LIC) of the Royal Society of Chemistry, who run the Chemical Enquiries Helpdesk. At the LIC there is a wealth of hard/electronic copy resources ranging from rare or unique books to latest journals covering cutting edge technology some of which are accessible remotely. Her job is to look after members' chemical information needs using any appropriate resources, including online commercial databases, or to point them in the right direction. She also runs tutorials and writes training materials in support of this and markets their services to membership.

Roger Mills
AGRICULTURE, FORESTRY, FISHERIES & FOOD
Roger Mills is Biosciences and Environmental Sciences Librarian and Oxford Forest Information Service Manager for Oxford University Library Services, UK. He is leader of the Bibliographic Information and Library Networks group of the International Union of Forest Research Organizations and active in the Aslib Biosciences Group and International Association of Agricultural Information Specialists. He is co-ordinator of the AgriFor (agriculture, forestry and food) section of the BIOME internet resource discovery service and works closely with CAB International, FAO and other international organizations.

Lorna Mitchell
BIOLOGICAL SCIENCES, BIOTECHNOLOGY
Lorna Mitchell is the Natural Sciences Librarian & E-Resources Co-ordinator at Queen Mary, University of London. Her current responsibilities include enabling access to high quality electronic resources and teaching science students how to find and use those resources. Following a biological sciences degree and postgraduate diploma in librarianship and information studies, her career in libraries began at The Natural History Museum, where she spent several years as the Assistant Librarian in the Entomology Library.

Dr David Newton
SCIENCE, TECHNOLOGY
David Newton is currently a patent information consultant and Associate Editor of the journal World patent Information having previously been Head of Patents Information at the British Library for almost twenty years. He has a BSc and PhD in Chemistry and is member of the Chartered Institute of Library and Information Professionals. He is a former Chairman of the Patent and Trade Mark Group.

Linda Norbury
CHEMICAL ENGINEERING & CHEMICAL TECHNOLOGY
Linda Norbury is currently an Academic Support Consultant for Engineering and Mathematics at the University of Birmingham, and this follows on from experience supporting engineering in similar roles at Aston University and the University of Nottingham. Before entering Higher Education she worked for the Institute of Energy in London, and for British Gas. She gained her Masters in Information Science from City University in 1989.

Bob Parry
SPATIAL TECHNOLOGIES
R. B. Parry is Honorary Fellow, Department of Geography, University of Reading. A Reading graduate in Geography, he was curator of that university's map collection for much of his career. His last appointment was Senior Research Fellow. He is co-author or editor (with C. R. Perkins) of several reference books on cartography, including *World mapping today* (Saur, 2000) and *The map library in the new millennium* (Facet Publishing, 2001).

Alison Sutton
METEOROLOGY & CLIMATOLOGY
Alison Sutton is Librarian in the Department of Meteorology, School of Mathematics, Meteorology and Physics at the University of Reading, where she manages an information service for the Department's undergraduate and postgraduate students and its world-leading research community. Prior to this she worked in university libraries in the Midlands.

Elizabeth Tilley
EARTH SCIENCES (excluding HYDROLOGY, METEOROLOGY & CLIMATOLOGY, OCEANOGRAPHY, PALAEONTOLOGY AND SPATIAL TECHNOLOGIES)
Elizabeth Tilley has been Principal Librarian at the Earth Sciences Department, University of Cambridge since January 2002. A degree in Geography led initially to teaching but a career change resulted in a job at the Earth Sciences Library. A Masters degree in Library and Information Studies, and a six-month secondment within the University paved the way for the appointment as Principal Librarian. She is now regarded as a subject specialist librarian, with additional roles on local, national (Education Librarians Group, CILIP) and international (Map and Geography Libraries Special Interest Group, IFLA) committees.

Dr Barry White

CIVIL ENGINEERING, CONSTRUCTION & BUILDING, ELECTRICAL & ELECTRONIC ENGINEERING, ENVIRONMENTAL ENGINEERING

Barry White has a first degree in chemistry and further degrees in the social aspects of science and technology. Prior to his current post as Faculty Librarian, Engineering and Physical Sciences, at the University of Manchester, he worked in industry and academia as well as the Library of the University of Nottingham. As a subject librarian he has held responsibilities at various times for mathematics, computer science, engineering, and the history of science and technology.

Fenella Whittaker

MECHANICAL ENGINEERING

Fenella Whittaker is an Information Officer at the Institution of Mechanical Engineers. She has ten years' experience working in specialist libraries, including previous engineering subject experience as an assistant librarian in London Underground's Engineering Library. She gained her postgraduate degree in Information Services Management at the University of North London in 2000 and last year achieved Chartered status with CILIP.

50 good websites to try first

SCIENCE, TECHNOLOGY & MEDICINE: GENERIC RESOURCES

American National Standards Institute
www.ansi.org

Max-Planck-Gesellschaft
www.mpg.de/english/portal

National e-Science Centre
www.nesc.ac.uk

Resource Discovery Network
www.rdn.ac.uk

Science Portal: Australia
www.science.gov.au

SCIENCE

National Science Teachers Association
www.nsta.org

Nobelprize.org
http://nobelprize.org

Mathematics

American Mathematical Society
www.ams.org

The MacTutor history of mathematics archive
www-history.mcs.st-andrews.ac.uk/history/index.html

Math Forum @ Drexel
www.mathforum.org

Physics & Astronomy

Centre National d'Etudes Spatiales
www.cnes.fr

Interactions.org: Particle physics news and resources
www.interactions.org

PhysicsWeb
http://physicsweb.org

Earth Sciences

Met Office
www.metoffice.com

Palaeontologia Electronica
www.palaeo-electronica.org

US Geological Survey
www.usgs.gov

Chemistry

ChemSoc
www.chemsoc.org

Chemistry Journals
www.ch.cam.ac.uk/ChemJournals.html

Reciprocal Net
www.reciprocalnet.org

Biological Sciences

ASIL Guide to Electronic Resources for International Law
www.asil.org/resource/env1.htm

National Center for Biotechnology Information
www.ncbi.nlm.nih.gov

The Tree of Life Web Project
http://tolweb.org

Agriculture, Forestry, Fisheries & Food

Sea Fish Industry Authority
www.seafish.org

WAICENT Portal
www.fao.org/waicent/index_en.asp

World Organisation for Animal Health
www.oie.int/eng/en_index.htm

MEDICINE

Health On the Net Foundation
www.hon.ch

The On-line Medical Dictionary
http://cancerweb.ncl.ac.uk/omd

Pre-clinical Sciences

The eSkeletons Project
www.eskeletons.org

Center for Devices and Radiological Health
www.fda.gov/cdrh

Pharmaceutical Research and Manufacturers of America
www.phrma.org

Clinical Medicine

Bandolier: Evidence-based thinking about health care
www.jr2.ox.ac.uk/bandolier

Communicable Disease Surveillance & Response
www.who.int/csr/en

National Institute for Health and Clinical Excellence
www.nice.org.uk

Health

Food and Nutrition Information Center
www.nal.usda.gov/fnic

The Merck manual of medical information
www.merck.com/mmhe/index.html

National Institute for Occupational Safety and Health
www.cdc.gov/niosh

TECHNOLOGY

British Library – Patents
www.bl.uk/collections/patents.html

Technology Review
www.technologyreview.com

Natural Resources & Energy

Commission on Sustainable Development
www.un.org/esa/sustdev

Los Alamos National Laboratory Library
http://lib-www.lanl.gov

Office of Energy Efficiency and Renewable Energy
www.eere.energy.gov

Engineering

International Maritime Organization
www.imo.org

Nanotechnology Now
www.nanotech-now.com

Royal Academy of Engineering
www.raeng.org.uk

Information & Communication Technology

bitpipe
www.bitpipe.com

NSF: Directorate for Computer & Information Science & Engineering [USA]
www.nsf.gov/funding/research_edu_community.jsp

World Wide Web Consortium: W3C
www.w3.org

TOOLS FOR INFORMATION PROFESSIONALS

Association of Learned and Professional Society Publishers
www.alpsp.org

D-Lib Magazine
www.dlib.org

Scholarly Societies Project
www.scholarly-societies.org

Introduction

This Introduction covers:

- Introducing TNW
- What's new about TNW?
- The new information universe
- Selection and description of resources
- Organization and arrangement of entries

Introducing TNW

The first volume of *The New Walford* (TNW) is a guide to reference resources in Science, Technology and Medicine (STM). It provides a collection of resources aimed particularly at helping people to research unfamiliar subject areas. It offers comprehensive coverage of the range of resources available in the networked world, but is necessarily selective in the set of items chosen for each subject field. Our aim is to get you started, to help you navigate uncharted territory and find the right types of resources to meet your needs.

This new guide builds on the reputation and concept of the classic *Walford's guide to reference material*, but we have made radical changes to the design, focus and layout. The internet and the world wide web have had a dramatic impact on the quantity and quality of information resources, especially in STM. The new information universe is diverse and complex with its mix of established and emergent media.

What's *new* about TNW?

TNW has been completely 're-engineered' for the hybrid information world. There are seven key changes from 'The Old Walford'.

- *Focus on the newcomer* – TNW has been specially designed to help the less-experienced user of STM resources, particularly people researching a field for the first time.
- *Simpler subject arrangement* – TNW has moved away from the Universal Decimal Classification (UDC) and adopted its own straightforward three-level scheme of subject parts, subject groupings and subject fields.
- *Navigation by topic* – TNW's new Topic index helps you to find your way quickly from a subject heading or an alternative sought term to the right place in the main sequence.
- *New resource categorization* – TNW has replaced the 40 or so 'form headings' used in the old Walford with a new simpler set of 13 resource categories.
- *Expansion of resource types* – TNW includes the full spectrum of resources now available to the internet user, with thousands of organizational websites and portals complementing its coverage of traditional reference tools.
- *Introductory essays* – TNW also helps the STM newcomer by offering fifteen short narrative introductions, highlighting key features of each subject part and subject grouping.
- *Improved visual layout* – TNW's new typographical design and use of the resource title as the lead term for each entry makes the volume easy to scan and quick to use.

The new information universe

The world wide web has revolutionized the world of reference. The number of host computers accessible via the internet has grown at an astonishing rate over the last ten years. At the time of writing, the leading search engine, Google, provides access to more than eight billion web pages. The proportion of that total that might be considered as 'reference resources' is debatable, but it must run into millions.

The later editions of the old *Walford* naturally recognized the gathering momentum of electronic information services and included a separate Online and Database Services Index in each volume, which covered both standalone CD-ROM and networked online services. It is now evident that the defining development of the electronic era was not the shift from print to digital resources, but the move to a digital format that is also networked – via the internet and the web. Five aspects of this revolution are significant for reference services.

1 *Networked versions of traditional reference resources*
This area has evolved from the abstracting and indexing services offered by online hosts using proprietary search systems to electronic versions of other resources – such as data compilations, dictionaries, directories and encyclopedias – provided by aggregators with web-based interfaces. It also includes networked versions of library online public access catalogues (OPACs).

In STM it is now rare to find a print-based reference resource that does not also have a web-based presence. CD-ROM and (especially) microform versions have been virtually eclipsed by web-based products. Many libraries now subscribe only to the networked version, which provides comprehensive access to their primary user group, but may have unfortunate consequences for other users for whom access to resources is either restricted or denied.

2 *Network availability of digital primary resources*
Following on from the networked versions of full-text secondary resources, such as encyclopedias, most of the primary journal literature in STM is now available

online, via an aggregator or direct from the publisher. Here again the trend is towards electronic-only access, controlled by licensing agreements which restrict access to members of the community, institution or corporation.

The *non-substitutability* of primary literature makes this a more serious concern than in the case of secondary resources, for which acceptable substitutes are often available. However, the 'open access movement' is starting to change this situation by encouraging scholarly authors to make their research papers and data publicly available through discipline-based or institutional repositories. This movement is now gaining high-level support within academic and official bodies, but it will take time for it to have full effect.

Web access is also being extended from 'born digital' to digitized 'legacy' artefacts, as a result of various local, national and international government-sponsored programmes. Such work encompasses a broad range of informational and other artefacts and the resulting resources frequently serve as an acceptable substitute for the 'real thing', which was formerly only accessible by visiting the relevant library, archive, museum, gallery, garden, laboratory, etc.

3 *Search engines, directories and resource discovery tools*

The creation of web search engines (such as Google) and research directories (such as Yahoo!) outside the traditional scholarly and scientific community is one of the most significant developments associated with the web. The success of such ventures is evident from the fact that large numbers of users – including students, academics and librarians – turn first to a tool like Google when seeking publicly available information.

Many other players have also tried to tame the web, producing both generic and domain-specific services, with the distinctions between 'engines', 'directories' and other tools becoming increasingly blurred. There have been numerous initiatives of this type in the academic world, with efforts at individual, institutional and national levels to develop 'subject gateways' and other resource discovery tools. These range from simple lists of web-page links to standardized descriptions of internet resources, but many of these services have proved unsustainable over time.

4 *Convergence and development of the information industry*

The new Google Scholar search engine and Google's digitization agreements with major research libraries are examples of the blurring of boundaries between the commercial and academic worlds. Within the information industry sector, established stakeholders are changing and expanding their roles and competing with new entrants to the field as other players develop their roles as information providers.

Traditional online hosts are now competing with booksellers, news agencies, broadcasting networks and software developers, as well as with subscription agents, document supply centres, information brokers and digital reference services. Many public sector and other non-profit organizations are also taking on significant roles as information providers through their websites. Linking technologies and partnerships enable users to move seamlessly from one resource to another, while portal and task environments offer a range of personalized services and facilities for online transactions.

5 *Dynamic resources and collaborative content creation*

Current awareness services have similarly been transformed by new technologies, which offer the STM information user various options for keeping up-to-date with literature and developments in the field. Automatic e-mail alerting of journal content pages is well established and has now been supplemented by the use of RSS feeds for new web-page content from organizational and personal websites, including feeds from specialist weblogs.

Dynamic resources are becoming the norm, with content continually updated as new information enters the public domain. People are moving beyond e-mail discussion lists to new forms of online communities, using technologies such as chat rooms, instant messaging and wiki software, which allows open access for users to create and edit content on the web. The classic example here is the Wikipedia, described as 'the free-content encyclopedia that anyone can edit'.

TNW helps you to negotiate the challenges of this new world in several ways:

- by identifying specific items on topics likely to be of interest
- by showing how the different subjects relate to each other
- by covering the full spectrum of print and digital resources
- by offering a pragmatic framework to structure your search.

Selection and description of resources

Selection policy

In line with our aim of helping the newcomer, we have concentrated our selection of resources on items suitable for entry to the field. These items are typically at the tertiary education level and are the kinds of resources likely to be found and used in academic and large public libraries.

The resources included aim to give international coverage, especially for organizations. The publications listed are predominantly from the UK and US and primarily in the English language, which reflects the nature of STM publishing activity.

Our policy is to include only those resources likely

to be maintained in the medium to long term. We have generally excluded personally maintained websites, but where such resources have been included, we have marked them as 'personal interest sites' in the annotation.

Resource descriptions
We have based our description of resources on the current edition of the Anglo American Cataloguing Rules. To aid the rapid scanning of entries, we have made the title the lead element for all descriptions.

Where an item has a particular area focus that is not obvious from its title, we have added a two- or three-letter Geographical Indicator. The codes cover Europe, the G8 countries, Australia and China, which are the leading producers of scientific papers.

Where possible, we have given indicative prices for resources, generally in the currency of the country where the publisher has its headquarters.

For practical reasons, we have often shortened URLs, which should reduce the impact of changed locators and broken links. This may require you to navigate to the specific item listed, but may also reveal additional items of interest in the process.

Resource annotations
Our annotations are intended to help you decide whether a particular resource will meet your needs. We have concentrated on providing factual information about the content and scope of resources and on highlighting any notable or unusual features. If there is a good description of the resource available from its producer, we have incorporated that in the annotation, enclosing it in single quotation marks ('…').

We have tried to make the book interesting to read by varying the style of annotation and allowing the editors to choose their own approach. The provision of in-depth reviews is beyond our scope, but we often quote from such reviews, where they usefully reinforce or extend our comments. If we mention the relationship of a resource to another resource which is included in the volume, its title is shown in SMALL CAPITALS.

Associated resources
For around a quarter of the main entries, we have appended related or associated resources, which have full descriptions and index entries, but usually shorter annotations. This practice has enabled us to include a larger number of resources in the volume than would otherwise have been possible. Examples of resources of this kind include:

- subsidiary organizations or units of an organization
- advocacy bodies associated with an organization's work
- additional resources produced by the same organization
- similar resources produced by another organization
- resources offering alternative treatments of a subject.

Organization and arrangement of entries

Subject parts
TNW Volume 1 is organized into three main Subject Parts matching the three parts of its title – Science, Technology and Medicine.

Generic resources
There is also a large section at the start of the sequence devoted to Generic Resources in STM.

Tools for information professionals
This is complemented by a smaller section at the end of the sequence devoted to Tools for Information Professionals, which covers both STM and generic resources in library and information science.

Subject groupings
The subject parts are organized into twelve Subject Groupings reflecting their main divisions:

Science
- Mathematics
- Physics & Astronomy
- Earth Sciences
- Chemistry
- Biological Sciences
- Agriculture, Forestry, Fisheries & Food

Medicine
- Pre-clinical Sciences
- Clinical Medicine
- Health

Technology
- Natural Resources & Energy
- Engineering
- Information & Communication Technology

Subject fields
The subject groupings are in turn organized into more than one hundred Subject Fields. The full list of subject fields is shown on the Contents page.

There are entries for resources at each level of this subject hierarchy, i.e.

Subject part (e.g. Medicine)
Subject grouping (e.g. Health)
Subject field (e.g. Environmental & Occupational Health)

The distribution of resources over the different levels of the hierarchy varies from subject to subject, reflecting the nature of the discipline and the judgement of the editors on the most useful balance.

Cross references
In order to maximize the number of resources included we have not duplicated resources between sections, but we have provided numerous cross-references for resources that are relevant to more than one subject field or grouping.

Introductory essays
Each subject part and each subject grouping is introduced by a short essay highlighting key points about the areas covered, including connections with other subjects in the volume.

Resource categories
All the resources listed in the different sections of the volume have been assigned to one of thirteen Resource Categories, which are shown in Figure 1 and listed below, with examples of the types included. These new categories replace the 'form headings' used in the old *Walford*. A table available at www. facetpublishing.co.uk/newwalford/index.shtml shows how the old form headings relate to these new categories.

Within each section, part, grouping or field, the categories are always arranged in the same order:

[1] Introductions to the subject.
Includes histories of the subject, academic course books, non-specialist overviews, alternative viewpoints.

[2] Dictionaries, thesauri, classifications
Includes abbreviations and acronyms, glossaries, quotations, taxonomies and ontologies.

[3] Laws, standards, codes
Includes intellectual property, patents and trademarks, regulations, nomenclatures, scientific laws and theories.

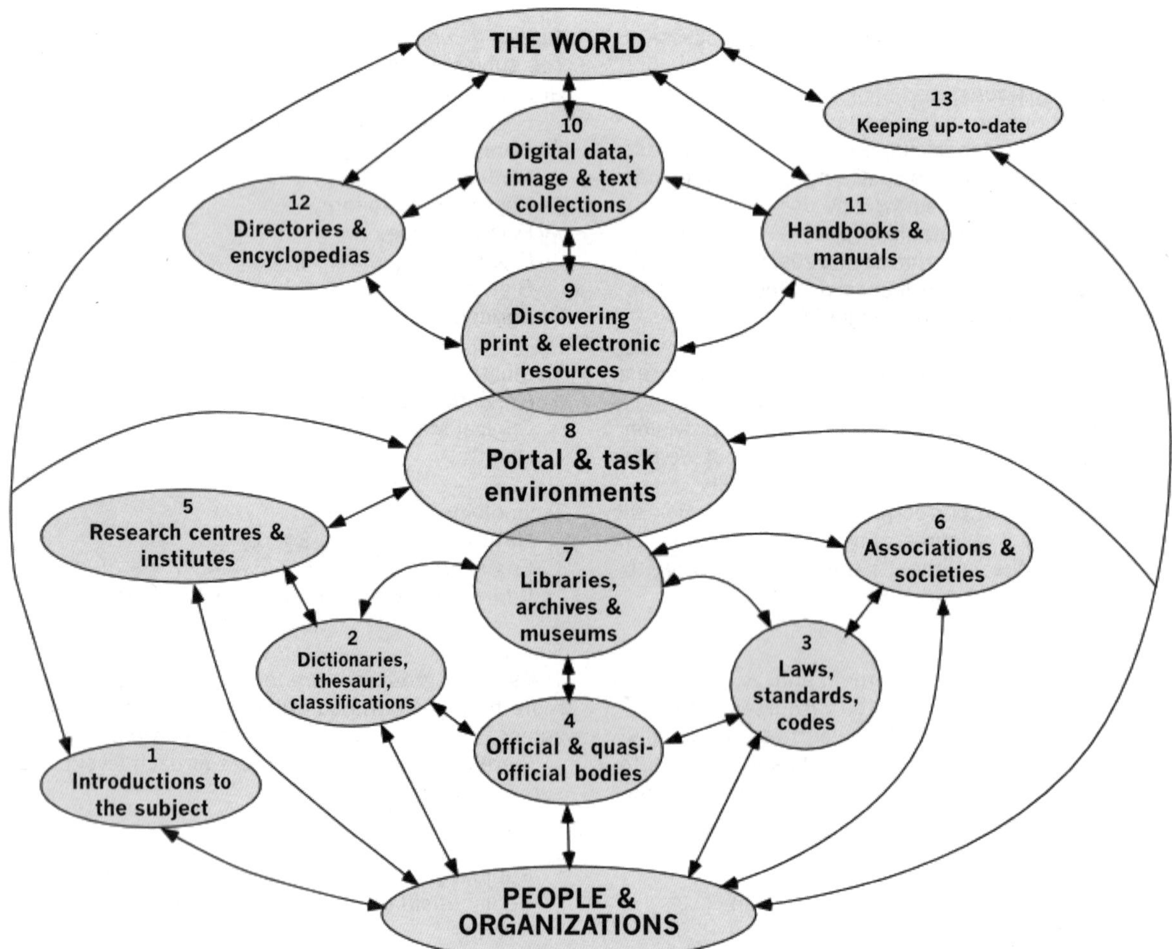

Figure 1 The Information Universe

[4] Official & quasi-official bodies
Includes government departments, international agencies, quasi-official government organizations, research councils.

[5] Research centres & institutes
Includes international centres of excellence, academic institutes, research foundations, commercially endowed non-profits.

[6] Associations & societies
Includes academies, scholarly societies, trade associations, advocacy and support bodies.

[7] Libraries, archives & museums
Includes national libraries, national archives, science museums, special collections.

[8] Portal & task environments
Includes aggregator/host services, e-type offerings (e-government, e-learning, e-science, etc), one-stop shops, virtual reference services.

[9] Discovering print & electronic resources
Includes abstracts and indexes, catalogues and bibliographies, finding tools, resource discovery services.

[10] Digital data, image & text collections
Includes science data banks, photograph sets, primary journal and book collections, statistical series.

[11] Directories & encyclopedias
Includes biographies, almanacs, chronologies, maps and gazetteers.

[12] Handbooks & manuals
Includes advanced textbooks, edited collections, field guides, technical compendia.

[13] Keeping up-to-date
Includes annual reviews, professional and trade magazines, current awareness services, discussion groups.

The categories are not mutually exclusive, so where a resource could be placed in more than one category, we have usually assigned it to the category that comes first in the sequence. The distribution of resources across the different categories naturally varies from subject to subject.

Indexes

The volume concludes with two indexes, offering access to the main sequence of entries by topic, resource title or author.

Topic Index

The Topic Index lists in a single alphabetical sequence all the terms used as subject headings for the subject groupings and subject fields, together with alternative terms for those headings as well as terms at a more detailed level than the subject fields. This index shows you where commonly sought terms are located in our subject structure and also helps you to navigate quickly to the right part of the main sequence.

Title/Author Index

The Title/Author Index lists the authors and titles for all resources listed, covering both main entries and associated resources. For organizations, it includes cross-references for commonly-used abbreviations and acronyms, in addition to cross-references linking parent and subordinate bodies. This index enables you to locate resource descriptions quickly when you already know the title or author.

Disclaimer

The inclusion of a resource in TNW in no way implies the publisher's and Editor's endorsement of the views contained within it.

SCIENCE, TECHNOLOGY & MEDICINE

Science, Technology & Medicine

This volume contains two collections of descriptions of generic resources. This section includes those likely to be used by researchers and practitioners within science, technology and medicine (STM); the final section within the book contains a selection of resources aimed more at the ifanformation professional. In both cases we have included many items that cover a wider subject canvas than just STM – and thus these will be of relevance also to the subject foci of the other two volumes of The New Walford (TNW) planned to follow this volume: Volume 2: The Social Sciences; Volume 3: Arts, Humanities & General Reference.

When using the later sections of this volume covering the individual subject fields, readers should always remember that there might well be an alternative good (or even better) resource listed within the field's relevant subject grouping; similarly regarding a subject grouping vis-à-vis its subject part; a subject part compared with this section. This is an obvious point, but one sometimes overlooked and these days given added force by the continuing consolidation within the industry towards just a small number of players offering integrated resources with very wide subject coverage.

Introductions to the subject

1 **Information: the new language of science**
H.C. Von Baeyer Weidenfeld & Nicolson, 2004, 192pp. Originally published 2003, £7.99. ISBN 0753817829.
'Today we live in the information age. Wherever we look it surrounds us, and with the help of ever more efficient devices, from the internet through to mobile phones, we are producing, exchanging and harnessing more than ever before. But information does far more than define our modern age – at a fundamental level it defines the material world itself, for it is through its mediating role that we gain all our knowledge, and everything derives its function, existence and meaning from it.

In twenty-five short chapters, von Baeyer takes us from the birth of the concept of information and its basic language, the bit, through to the coal-face of contemporary physics and beyond relativity; black holes; randomness; abstraction – explaining why it has the power to become the most fundamental concept in physics – as fundamental as mass and energy.'

'A sense of wonder is an essential prerequisite to an appreciation of the discoveries of science, and wonderment is the emotion that will be most pleasantly evoked in the reader of this book.' (*Times Higher Education Supplement*)

2 **The Oxford companion to the history of modern science**
J.L. Heilbron [et al.], eds Oxford University Press, 2003, 941pp. £67.00. ISBN 0195112296.
Outstanding introduction – not just to 'science', but also to large parts of 'technology' and 'medicine'. Perhaps most useful for those new to this arena are the entries relating to 'The Body of Knowledge': Epistemology and methodology; Cross-cutting concepts; Major subject divisions; Minor subject divisions; Theoretical constructs – with each article written in an approachable manner, stressing naturally the history, and appended with a short bibliography. Supplementing these entries for the 'basic' sciences are the ones for the 'applied' sciences.

But there are also considerable numbers of discussions relating to the historiography of science, the organization and diffusion of science, the apparatus and instruments it uses, as well as about 100 biographies of key current and past scientists.

Finally, there is a good Further Reading section, and a comprehensive Index.

3 **The science wars: debating scientific knowledge and technology**
K. Parsons, ed. Prometheus Books, 2003, 300pp. $21.00. ISBN 1573929948.
'Is science our most precious possession or has our culture elevated science into a false idol? Is technology a useful servant or a malign genie? These questions are at the center of the 'science wars' currently being waged over the role and future of science and technology in our society.' Good introductory anthology.
Series: Contemporary Issues.

4 **Servants of nature: a history of scientific institutions, enterprises and sensibilities**
L. Pyenson and S. Sheets-Pyenson HarperCollins, 1999, 496pp. £24.99. ISBN 000223842X.
'Tracing the establishment of institutions of higher learning, scientific societies and museums, the authors examine how the bodies that shape scientific tradition and guide innovation have acquired their authority. They proceed to consider how scientific goals have changed, as they analyze the relationship between scientists, militarists, and industrialists in modern times.'

5 **A short history of nearly everything**
B. Bryson Black Swan, 2004, 687pp. Originally published in Great Britain by Doubleday, 2003, £8.99. ISBN 0552997048.
The most enjoyable, well written, and informative introduction to science of recent times. A remarkable book.

6 **Sync: the emerging science of spontaneous order**
S. Strogatz Penguin, 2004, 352pp. £8.99. ISBN 014100763X.
An elegant, wide ranging layman's introduction to the study of synchrony: 'order in time' – where the same things happen at the same time, persistently, often with no obvious reason. Suggests that – following the fashions of cybernetics

(60s), catastrophe theory (70s), chaos theory (80s), complexity theory (90s), that – in this decade – it will be different: 'Even the most hard-boiled, mainstream scientists are beginning to acknowledge that reductionism may not be powerful enough to solve all the great mysteries we're facing.'

7 **A terrible beauty: the people and ideas that shaped the modern mind: a history**
P. Watson Phoenix Press, 2001, 847pp. Originally published by Weidenfeld & Nicolson, 2000, £16.99. ISBN 1842124447.
A masterly survey, with especial emphasis on the development and role of science in the 20th century. Excellent contextual explanations for the layman of critical advances, revolving around reviews of the lives of key figures. Two good indexes: Names, People, and Places; Ideas and Subjects. 3000 Notes and References plus a useful list in the Preface of the books 'whose pages I have pillaged, précised and paraphrased shamelessly'.

'Understanding this narrative, and the way that it was arrived at, involves a good appreciation of all the important sciences, the significant phases of history, the rise and fall of civilisations, and the reasons for the underlying patterns ... The evidence, at the end of the century, suggests that we are already living in what may be called a crossover culture. While people lament the effects of the mass media on our intellectual life generally, an inspection of the shelves in any good bookshop more or less anywhere in the Western world shows that, on the other hand, one of the greatest growth areas is in what is called popular science.'

'That phrase is in fact misleading, to the extent that many of these books are relatively difficult, examining for example the nature of matter, abstruse mathematics (Fermat's last theorem, longitude), the minutiae of evolution, the byways of palaeontology, the origin of time, the philosophy of science. But a growing number of people now accepts that one cannot call oneself educated unless one is up-to-date on these issues ...'

'All changed, changed utterly:
A terrible beauty is born.' W.B. Yeats

Dictionaries, thesauri, classifications

8 **Academic Press dictionary of science and technology**
C. Morris, ed. Academic Press, 1992, 2432pp. CD-ROM available, £67.99. ISBN 0122004000.
'Approximately 124,000 fully defined entries, not counting abbreviations – the largest range of vocabulary ever compiled in a science dictionary. Complete coverage of 124 fields of science and technology, including Computer science, Biotechnology, Engineering, Physics, Mathematics, Molecular biology, Ecology, Behaviour, Astronomy, Geology, and more.'

9 **Acronyms, initialisms and abbreviations dictionary**
Thomson Gale, Annual. $895.00 [Edition 34, 2004]. ISBN 078766667X.
www.gale.com/gvrl
'Here's a dictionary that will make you an expert on modern communications. Definitions of a wide variety of acronyms, initialisms, abbreviations and similar contractions enable you to quickly and easily translate terms into their full names or meanings. New terms from subject areas such as associations, education, the Internet, medicine and others are now included. Also a supplement including both by acronym and by meaning sections is included.'
Available online: see website.

- **Reverse acronyms, initialisms and abbreviations dictionary** Annual. $595.00 [Edition 34, 2004]. ISBN 078767348X. This volume provides the same data in reverse to enable users to look up the full abbreviation and retrieve the abbreviated form.

10 **Callaham's Russian-English dictionary of science and technology**
L.I. Callaham, P.E. Newman and J.R. Callaham 4th edn, Wiley, 1996, 848pp. $199.95. ISBN 0471611395.
Contains over 120,000 terms including some common non-technical terms. Entries give the field of use and a translation.

11 **Chambers dictionary of science and technology**
P.M.B. Walker Chambers, 1999, 1344pp. £20.00. ISBN 0550130020.
Contains short entries for words and expressions in science, technology, mineralogy, geology, computing and electronics. Full page panels for 100 entries give fuller explanations. Appendices include paper sizes, animal and plant classifications, amino acids, astronomical data, etc. 500 illustrations.

12 **Comprehensive Russian English polytechnic dictionary (Bolshoi russko–angliiskii politechnicheskii slovar)**
D.A. Russak and A.Yu. Ovsinskiy ETS, 1998, 2988pp. 4 v, $178.00. ISBN 5864550515.
www.ets.ru [DESCRIPTION]
Claims to be the first ever dictionary of its type published in Russia. Covers 500,000 scientific and technological terms.
See website for description also of electronic version of the dictionary.

13 **A dictionary of the European Union**
D. Phinnemore and L. McGowan 2nd edn, Europa, 2004, 419pp. £120.00. ISBN 1857432606.
Concise definitions and explanations on all aspects of the European Union, including details of the ten states which became full members of the EU in May 2004. 1000 entries.

14 **Elsevier's dictionary of technical abbreviations: English–Russian**
M. Rosenberg and S. Bobryakov Elsevier, 2005, 1184pp. £130.00. ISBN 0444515615.
www1.elsevier.com/homepage/sae/dictionaries/start.htm
65,000 entries listed as covering, for instance, space, agriculture, electronics, computer science, chemistry, thermodynamics, nuclear engineering, refrigeration, cryogenics, machinery, aviation, business, accounting, optics, radio electronics, military fields, etc.
Website is an easy to use gateway to details of approximately 200 Elsevier titles in print and in preparation – the majority of which cover areas of science, technology and medicine, and a number of which are referenced elsewhere in TNW. Browse through the detailed keyword index (but connection can sometimes be slow).

15 **EuroDicAutom**
http://europa.eu.int/eurodicautom/Controller
The European Commission's multilingual term bank, pleasant to use, but stated late 2004 soon to be 'integrated into a new interinstitutional terminology database, which will incorporate the contents of the databases already existing in

the various institutions and bodies of the European Union. The aim of this project is to meet the challenge of the forthcoming enlargement, which will extend the problems associated with terminological data to some twenty languages. The result will reflect Europe's linguistic diversity and richness. We will be examining the question of access to the new base keeping in mind the need for sound management of public funds'.

Currently records a daily average of 120,000 enquiries; and is 'particularly rich in technical and specialised terminology (agriculture, telecommunications, transport, legislation, finance) related to EU policy'.

'Entries are classified into 48 subject fields (ranging from medicine to public administration). A typical entry contains the term itself and its synonyms, together with definitions, explanatory notes, references, etc. At present the term bank contains about five and a half million entries (terms and abbreviations), subdivided into more than 800 collections.'

16 **German–English Dictionary**
Technische Universität Chemnitz
http://dict.tu-chemnitz.de
A simple – but powerful – German/English dictionary based on a wordlist containing over 179,000 entries. A nice feature is the series of Word Lists listing translated terms for: Occupations/professions/jobs; States/countries; Trees; Flowers; Animals; Tools; Natural disasters; Chemical elements; etc. There is also a Conversion of Units function.

17 **Illustrated scientific dictionaries**
Enchanted Learning.
www.allaboutspace.com/science/dictionary
Enjoyable engaging set of dictionaries designed for young people. Small annual subscription gives access to the whole of the site.

18 **International encyclopedia of abbreviations and acronyms in science and technology**
M. Peschke K.G. Saur, 1995–2000. 17 v, €2600.00. ISBN 3598229704.
680,000 entries in eight volumes covering the most important acronyms from diverse science fields. Also includes common vernacular abbreviations. There are two supplementary volumes containing an additional 170,000 entries. Covers organizations, journals, projects, systems, terms, etc. The remaining seven volumes are a reversed edition giving an alphabetical list of full names with their abbreviations.

19 **Longman glossary of scientific and technical terms: English-Chinese**
C. Lassure, comp. People's University of China Beijing, 2000, 1475pp. ISBN 7300034241.
www.chinabooks.com.au/language/Indictst_2.htm
'Contains 50,000 entries on fifty educational subjects, including biology, chemistry, physics, medicine, computer science, electronics, etc. A large number of new words and phrases, such as El Niño, avian flu, website, etc., are included.'
See (Australian) website for descriptions of other Chinese STM dictionaries.

20 **McGraw-Hill dictionary of scientific and technical terms**
6th edn, McGraw-Hill, 2003, 2380pp. $150.00. ISBN 007042313X.
Aimed at both scientist and general reader. 110,000 terms and 125,000 short definitions; 3000 illustrations. Each definition identified by field of use e.g. physics, engineering, acoustics, organic chemistry. Appendices include units, symbols, periodic table, mathematical notation, fundamental constants, particles, geological time scale and classification of organisms.
Various sub-sets of the dictionary are available, several referenced elsewhere.

21 **North American Industry Classification System: NAICS**
Bureau of the Census 2002.
www.census.gov/epcd/www/naics.html
Replacement for the US Standard Industrial Classification System (SIC). 'NAICS will reshape the way we view our economy.' There is a select list of new US industries being identified in NAICS (e.g. Cellular and other wireless communications; Hazardous waste collection; HMO medical centers; Diet and weight reducing centers) – with the economy now being grouped into 20 broad sectors, up from the 10 divisions of the SIC system. Of particular interest here is the new Information section which 'includes major components from Transportation, Communications, and Utilities (broadcasting and telecommunications), Manufacturing (publishing), and Services Industries (software publishing, data processing, information services, motion picture and sound recording)'.

- **North American Industry Classification System** Bernan Press, 2002, 1424pp. $45.00. ISBN 0890595666. www.bernan.com/General/About_Bernan.aspx [DESCRIPTION]. As well as publishing NAICS, Bernan is a leading distributor of a wide range of publications from the United States government and intergovernmental organizations, including many other classification schemes.

22 **OneLook dictionary search**
Datamuse.
www.onelook.com
A delightful service to use. A search for 'bilirubin' retrieved entries in 15 'General' dictionaries, 13 'Medicine' dictionaries, and 2 'Science' dictionaries; on 'nanotechnology', entries in 11 'General', 1 'Business', 6 'Computing' and 3 'Science' dictionaries; on 'genetic engineering', 18 'General', 1 'Art', 1 'Business', 3 'Medicine', 11 'Science', and 2 'Tech'. As of early 2005, more than 6 million words in 993 dictionaries were indexed. There is a list of the dictionaries with descriptive information about each. In addition: 'There are no pop-up advertisements on OneLook.com. We do not allow pop-up ads of any kind on this site and strongly object to them.' There is (thus) some sponsorship; but it is not intrusive.

23 **Routledge French technical dictionary: French-English (Dictionnaire technique anglais: anglais–français)**
Routledge, 1994. 2 v., £260.00. ISBN 0415056705.
Highly acclaimed set consists of some 100,000 keywords in both French and English, drawn from the whole range of modern applied science and technical terminology. Covers over 70 subject areas, from engineering and chemistry to packaging, transportation, data processing and much more.

24 **Science and technology encyclopedia**
University of Chicago Press (Distributed for the Octopus Publishing Group), 2000, 576pp. $22.50. ISBN 0226742679.
www.press.uchicago.edu [DESCRIPTION]

'Up-to-date, concise, and easy to use, the *Science and Technology Encyclopedia* is a reliable resource for a wide general readership – from high school students to undergraduates to all those with an interest in the comprehensive array of scientific fields it covers.

It includes: more than 6500 authoritative A–Z entries covering earth and life sciences (including natural history, physics, chemistry, medicine, information technology, and other disciplines; biographical entries for more than 850 famous scientists, detailing their careers and achievements; over 20,000 cross-references; more than 250 detailed illustrations, including schematic diagrams, representational natural history artwork, and technical cutaway diagrams.'

'Overall, I find the University of Chicago *Science and Technology Encyclopedia* to be a worthwhile addition for any general academic or science and technology library. I have no qualms recommending this book – the price is reasonable, the content coverage is pretty good for a book of this size, the publisher is reputable, and the illustrations are very well done. I just wish they called it a dictionary.' (*Issues in Science and Technology Librarianship*)

25 Scientific and technical acronyms, symbols, and abbreviations

U. Erb and H. Keller Wiley, 2001, 2114pp. $262.00. ISBN 0471388025.
www3.interscience.wiley.com/stasa

Contains 200,000 entries covering science, technology, medicine, including architecture, construction, geography, housing, nursing. Covers organizations, journals, projects, systems, etc. Gives the country of use, where appropriate. Appendices list units of measurement, mathematical and electrical symbols, chemical tables, ASCII codes, etc.

Available online: see website.

26 UNBIS Thesaurus

United Nations
http://unhq-appspub-01.un.org/LIB/DHLUNBISThesaurus.nsf

Online version of the 4th edn in all the UN's official languages: Arabic, Chinese, English, French, Russian, Spanish. 'It is multidisciplinary in scope, reflecting the Organization's wide-ranging concerns. The terms included are meant to reflect accurately, clearly, concisely and with a sufficient degree of specificity, matters of importance and interest to the United Nations.' Part of the United Nations Bibliographic Information System from the Dag Hammarskjöld Library.

27 Wörterbuch der exacten Naturwissenschaften und der Technik

A. Kucera 2nd edn, Oscar Brandstetter, 2002, 1460pp. Band II Deutsche-Englisch, €165.00. ISBN 3870971509.

The German-English volume contains about 220,000 entries covering 103 subject fields. Parts of speech are given for German and English words.

'This is a Rolls-Royce among polytechnical dictionaries' (*The Linguist*)

- **Wörterbuch der industriellen Technik R. Ernst, comp.** Oscar Brandstetter, 1984–2004. www.brandstetter-verlag.de/p16.html [DESCRIPTION]. Classic series of translating dictionaries between German and English, French, Spanish, and Portuguese, plus between French and English.

Laws, standards, codes

28 American National Standards Institute

www.ansi.org

Private, non-profit organization (501(c)3) that 'administers and coordinates the US voluntary standardization and conformity assessment system': founded in 1918 by five engineering societies and three government agencies. Wide range of information on standards activities, news, education and training, meetings and events. The eStandards Store is a catalogue that includes ANSI and foreign standards and which can be searched by keyword or publication number. Standards can be purchased online and other documents (some of which are available only to members) downloaded. There is a very useful *Internet Resources Overview*: 'a compilation of electronic assets and research materials available on the World Wide Web. The scope of this collection is research-oriented, and provides access to the websites of other organizations with missions of interest to the standardization and conformity assessment community.'

29 Association Française de Normalisation

www.afnor.fr/portail.asp?Lang=English

The French standardization body. Includes a searchable catalogue in French and English.

30 British Standards Institution

www.bsi-global.com

Organized into 5 'businesses': British Standards – the national standards body of the UK; BSI Management Systems – providing organizations with independent third party certification of their management systems, including ISO 9001:2000 (Quality), ISO 14001 (Environmental Management), OHSAS 18001 (Occupational Health and Safety) and BS 7799 (Information Security). In 2002 BSI 'purchased the North American Systems Assessment business of KPMG making BSI the largest management systems certification company in North America'; and in 2003 they became a major player in the Greater China certification market; BSI Business Information – adding value to business operations; BSI Product Services – helping industry develop new and better products and to make sure that products meet current and future laws and regulations; BSI Inspectorate – operating in Metals and Minerals, Oil and Petrochemicals and Agricultural Commodities, and having facilities in 110 countries, including 74 dedicated laboratories.

The website has an area Information for Students, including sections on environment, IT, and quality, as well as on information for teachers and lecturers and on access to standards. British Standards Online, updated daily, provides access to over 38,500 current, draft and historic British Standards – more than 16,000 of which are BSI adopted European and International standards, as well as to technical handbooks, codes of practice, guidelines, specifications, and glossaries. Registering gives FREE access to detailed bibliographic information and enables hardcopy ordering. Subscribers get instant unlimited online access to complete standards. The Library of Resources contains the helpful Directors' Briefings series of 164 four-page datasheets which provide clear, concise advice on various business issues: particularly use of IT.

31 **Canadian Standards Association**
www.csa-intl.org/onlinestore
'Not-for-profit membership-based association serving business, industry, government and consumers in Canada and the global marketplace.' The Site has a Consumers area including sections on, for instance: 'Why Standards Matter' and 'Who's Who Behind the Marks'; and their Info Update – published 8 times/year – gives important information about new and existing standards, and standards under development, as well as highlights of other activities and services. It is organized into 8 Program Areas: Communications/Information; Construction Products and Materials; Electrical/Electronics; Energy; Environment; Gas Equipment; Life Sciences; Quality/Business Management.

32 **Deutsches Institut für Normung**
www2.din.de/index.php?lang=en
The German Institute for Standardization. The easy-to-use site lists English language translations of DIN standards and publications. The DITR National and International Standards database contains references to British, US, German, Austrian, Swiss, French, Japanese and international standards and technical regulations.

DIN standards are a widely used European set of codes in engineering, with DIN's publishing arm, Beuth, producing a series of DIN handbooks bringing together basic standards in key areas.

- **Beuth** www.beuth.de/index_en.php. DIN subsidiary. One of the largest German publishing houses, differing from other such publishing houses in that the surplus income it earns is used to finance the standards work undertaken by DIN. Databases; handbooks; software; online services.

33 **Electronic Information System for International Law: EISIL**
American Society of International Law
www.eisil.org
'Designed as an open database of authenticated primary and other materials across the breadth of international law, which until now have been scattered in libraries, archives and specialized web sites ... EISIL offers the international law expert the depth of resources for sophisticated legal research. At the same time, EISIL can provide the novice researcher with the information needed to undertake a successful search.'

Categories include: International Organizations (e.g. United Nations; European Union); International air, space and water; International environmental law; International human rights (including: Women's human rights; Education; Health and human rights; Freedom of information and right to culture); Communications and transport.

- **EUR-Lex: The access to European Union law** http://europa.eu.int/eur-lex/lex/en/index.htm. Free access, daily updates. Now provides 1,400,000 documents in a number of languages. Good searching facility either via classification scheme or keyword (*EUROVOC*).
- **LawLinks: Legal information on the internet** S. Carter, comp.; University of Kent at Canterbury http://library.kent.ac.uk/library/lawlinks. Valuable portal to UK and international resources. 'Special legal topics' include: Environmental law; Information technology; Maritime law; Medical and mental health. Extensive entrée to European Union information.
- **Parry & Grant encyclopaedic dictionary of international law** J.C. Barker and J.P. Grant, eds 2nd edn, Oceana Publications, 2003, 641pp. $155.00. ISBN 0379214490. www.oceanalaw.com [DESCRIPTION]. 'Since 1948 Oceana has been the premier publisher of essential international legal information specifically designed for law librarians, practicing attorneys, business executives, academicians, and researchers worldwide'.

34 **Ente Nazionale Italiano di Unificazione**
www.uni.com/it
Italian official standards body; English language version of website 'under construction ... At present the only section available in English is the Catalogue online for UNI standards'.

35 **EuroAsian Interstate Council: for Standardization, Metrology and Certification** [RUS]
www.easc.org.by/english/english.php3
Easy to use, well designed site. 'The Interstate Council was created in accordance with the 'Agreement on realization of coherent policy in the field of standardization, metrology and certification of the 13 of March 1992 '... to coordinate the works in the field of standardization, metrology and certification and to define the main directions of the interstate standardization, metrology, certification and accreditation in stated fields of activities.' Represents Russia and the other 11 Interstate Council States on the quasi-official international bodies.

36 **European Committee for Standardization**
www.cenorm.be
'Contributes to the objectives of the European Union and European Economic Area with voluntary technical standards which promote free trade, the safety of workers and consumers, interoperability of networks, environmental protection, exploitation of research and development programmes, and public procurement.'

A March 2004 downloadable PDF CEN Compass – European standardization in a nutshell gives a good overview of their work – including listing the various CEN sectors (Chemistry; Building and civil engineering; Food; Information society; etc.). The Committee works in parallel with the INTERNATIONAL ORGANIZATION FOR STANDARDIZATION with more than 30% of the standards adopted being identical to ISO standards, and many more closely related.

There is also a good FAQ section answering questions, for instance, about CE marking and certification.

- **European Organisation for Conformity Assessment** www.eotc.be. Provides a range of services including registration of mutual recognition agreements, and the provision of information, advisory, educational and training services, thereby to facilitate free trade and to spread knowledge relating to Conformity Assessment.

37 **International Organization for Standardization**
www.iso.org
Network of the national standards institutes of 148 countries, on the basis of one member per country, with a Central Secretariat in Geneva, Switzerland, that co-ordinates the system. 'ISO standards are voluntary. As a non-governmental organization, ISO has no legal authority to enforce their implementation. A certain percentage of ISO standards – mainly those concerned with health, safety or the environment – has been adopted in some countries as part of their regulatory framework. (and) they may become a market requirement, as has happened in the case of ISO 9000 quality management systems, or of dimensions of freight containers and bank cards.'

Orders for ISO Standards and ISO publications should normally be addressed to the ISO member in your country (listed on the website); but shopping is also possible from the ISO Central Secretariat. The ISO Catalogue contains a complete listing of published standards, classified by subject.

The website specifically features the ISO 9000 (Quality Management) and ISO 14000 (Environmental Management) families of standards.

- **International Classification for Standards** www.iso.org/iso/en/catsupport/howcat.html. The classification used to organize the standards on the ISO site; the URL leads to a guide to the use of their catalogue, from which there is a link to the classification itself, and then via the fields, groups and subgroups to the standards of interest.

38 **Japanese Industrial Standards Committee**
www.jisc.go.jp/eng/index.html
Central co-ordinating body for Japanese standards activity; represents Japan on international committees. Clearly labelled site; easy to navigate. All newly established and revised standards are published by the Japanese Standards Association: www.jsa.or.jp/default_english.asp

39 **NSSN: a national resource for global standards**
www.nssn.org
Aims to become a leader in the provision of technical data and information about important developments in the global standardization arena. Their database now contains over 250,000 references to standards from more than 600 national, foreign, regional and international bodies. If a document is available electronically the user is seamlessly transferred to the shopping cart of the standards developer or designated information reseller. If a document is not available electronically then information is provided about how to obtain a hard-copy version of the text.

- **Standards Tracking and Automated Reporting Service** $99.00 [Annual]. Identifies new project proposals and automatically tracks changes in status of a development project or standard under maintenance. Covers more than 270,000 standards under development, revision and maintenance.

40 **Science and Technology Law** [USA]
American Bar Association
www.abanet.org/scitech/home.html
Section of the American Bar Association. 'Provides a forum for members to explore new and emerging topics such as electronic commerce and digital signatures, the scope of electronic notarial practice, online payment mechanisms such as smart cards and digital cash, scientific misconduct, law and the Internet, multimedia and interactive technology, information security and privacy, telecommunications law, biotechnology, scientific evidence and genetic engineering.'

Within the Section there are 4 Divisions (e-commerce; computer law; communications law; life and physical sciences), each of which has a number of component committees, plus Special Committees and Task Forces on: Opportunities For Minorities and Women; Dispute and Resolution; Nanotechnology; Scientific Evidence; Biometrics; the Health Insurance Portability and Accountability Act. E-mail contacts are given for most of these.

41 **Standardization Administration of China**
www.sac.gov.cn/english/home.asp
Established in April 2001 and authorized by the State Council 'to exercise the administrative functions and carry out centralized administration for standardization in China'. Represents China at the International Organization for Standardization, International Electrotechnical Commission and other international and regional standardization organizations. The English-language *Bulletin of national standards*, accessible from the site, announces newly approved national standards in the People's Republic of China.

- **China Association for Standardization** www.china-cas.com/english/index.htm. From January 2004 have produced the bimonthly English language magazine *China Standardization*.

42 **Standards Australia**
www.standards.org.au
'Established in 1922, Standards Australia is recognised through a Memorandum of Understanding with the Commonwealth Government as the peak non-government standards development body in Australia. It is a company limited by guarantee, with 72 Members representing groups with an interest in the development and application of standards and related products and services.' In 2003, the organization was restructured in recognition that 'the sale of standards and directly related documents has generated insufficient funds to operate a multidiscipline standards development body despite the tremendous and world leading marketing techniques developed within Standards Australia': interesting background in the first issue of *Consensus News*. PDF copies of their attractive and informative magazine *The Global Standard* (11 issues per year) can also be downloaded.

43 **Standards Council of Canada**
www.scc.ca
'Federal Crown corporation with the mandate to promote efficient and effective standardization.' The Council 'has the mandate to coordinate and oversee the efforts of the National Standards System, which includes organizations and individuals involved in voluntary standards development, promotion and implementation in Canada ... More than 15,000 Canadian members contribute to committees that develop national or international standards. As well, more than 400 organizations have been accredited by the Standards Council. Some of these develop standards, others are conformity assessment bodies which determine the compliance of products or services to a standard's requirements.'

44 **World Standards Service Network: WSSN**
www.wssn.net
Through the websites of its members, WSSN provides information on international, regional and national standardization and related activities and services.

Official & quasi-official bodies

45 **Bundesministerium für Bildung und Forschung**
www.bmbf.de/en/index.php
'Increasing Germany's innovative power, creating secure jobs, enhancing the quality of education – these are the goals pursued by the Federal Ministry of Education and Research. We also support international cooperation in education, science, research and technology.'

- **Deutsche Forschungsgemeinschaft** www.dfg.de/en/index.html. 'Central, self-governing research organisation that promotes research at universities and other publicly financed research institutions in Germany ... serves all branches of science ... by funding research projects and facilitating cooperation.'

46 **Canada Site**
Canada. Public Works and Government Services
www.canada.gc.ca
The primary internet portal for information on the Government of Canada, its programs, services, new initiatives and products, and for information about Canada. Features three audience-based gateways respectively for: Canadians; Non-Canadians; Canadian Business. Accessing the first of these reveals a series of Topics, including: Environment, Natural Resources, Fisheries and Agriculture; Health; and Science and Technology. The last of these then divides into: Energy; Environment; Food; Health; Space. And so on. A clear well organized site.

- **Science and Technology for Canadians** www.science.gc.ca. Targeted at the 'general public'. Major sections are: Energy; Environment; Food; Health; Security; Space.

47 **Consiglio Nazionale delle Ricerche**
www.cnr.it/sitocnr/Englishversion/Englishversion.html
The Italian National Research Council, whose 'primary function is to carry on, through its own organs, advanced basic and applied research, both to develop and maintain its own scientific competitiveness, and to be ready to effectively and timely take part in the strategic fields defined by the national planning system'.

English language website under development.

48 **CORDIS: Community Research and Development Information Service** [EUR]
www.cordis.lu/en
The European 'Community Research and Development Information Service'. The major source of information on EU funded research programmes. Not the most pleasant of sites to use; but persistence reveals a wealth of information about STM activity within the Union. Those new to the site can start with the Section CORDIS Guidance. There is also an interactive Help Desk.

- **European Research Area** www.cordis.lu/era. The idea 'grew out of the realisation that research in Europe suffers from three weaknesses: insufficient funding, lack of an environment to stimulate research and exploit results, and the fragmented nature of activities and the dispersal of resources'.
- **Sixth Framework Programme: FP6** http://fp6.cordis.lu/fp6/home.cfm. 'Whether you are a newcomer to EU-funded R&D programmes, or an experienced project participant, this service can direct you to all of your FP6 information and participation needs ...'

49 **Council for Science and Technology** [UK]
www.cst.gov.uk
The UK government's advisory body on strategic science and technology policy issues, organizing its work around five broad themes: research, science and society, education, science and government, and technology innovation. The website contains its reports and information on related developments.

50 **Department of Commerce** [USA]
United States. Department of Commerce
www.commerce.gov
The Department's strategic goals for 2004–2009 are: Provide the information and tools to maximize US competitiveness and enable economic growth for American industries, workers, and consumers; Foster science and technological leadership by protecting intellectual property, enhancing technical standards, and advancing measurement science; Observe, protect, and manage the earth's resources to promote environmental stewardship; Management Integration Goal: Achieve organizational management excellence.

51 **Department of the Interior** [USA]
United States. Department of the Interior
www.doi.gov
Bureaux managed by DOI include: National Park Service; US Fish and Wildlife Service; Office of Surface Mining; Minerals Management Service; and US Geological Survey: Major current DOI Initiatives are: 'Improving Our National Parks'; 'Promoting Healthy Forests'; 'Protecting Endangered Species and Wildlife Habitat'; 'Promoting Responsible Energy Policy'.

52 **Directgov** [UK]
www.direct.gov.uk
'The place to turn for the widest range of government information and services.'

Easy-to-use intuitive site providing a number of routes to relevant information. A good place to start is the section Browse government information by subject organized into 12 broad categories, including: Agriculture, environment and natural resources; Business and industry; Health, nutrition and care; Information and communication; Science, technology and innovation. The service replaced UK online.

More than 2000 websites use the gov.uk domain.

- **Office of the Deputy Prime Minister** www.odpm.gov.uk. UK Government Department responsible, among other matters, for policy on: Building regulations; Civil resilience; Devolution; Fire; Planning; Regions; Sustainable communities.

53 **ED.gov** [USA]
United States. Department of Education
www.ed.gov
Major sections grouped under: Students; Parents; Teachers; Administrators.

- **National Center for Education Statistics** http://nces.ed.gov. 'Primary federal entity for collections and analyzing data that are related to education in the United States and other nations.' Produce periodic *Trends in International Mathematics and Science Study* (TIMSS).
- **Gateway to Educational Materials: GEM** www.thegateway.org. Consortium membership organization whose 'goal is to improve the organization and accessibility of the substantial collections of materials that are already available on various federal, state, university, non-profit, and commercial Internet sites'.

54 **EUROPA: Gateway to the European Union**
http://europa.eu.int/index_en.htm
The home page has a section: What the European Union Does By Subject, with linked entries for 'Agriculture', 'Energy', 'Environment', 'Fisheries', 'Food Safety', 'Information Society', 'Public Health', and 'Research and Innovation'. At the introduction to the last of these, we read: 'The European Union produces almost one third of the world's scientific knowledge. The research and innovation underpinning this knowledge help deliver the prosperity and quality of life EU citizens expect. Joint programmes consolidate the work of EU countries. The main tool is the Sixth Framework Programme. This funds research in the member states and some other countries, and at the EU's own Joint Research Centre.' This is followed by links to relevant work of the European Commission, Parliament, Council, etc.

- **EurActiv.com: EU News, Policy Positions and EU Actors online** www.euractiv.com. 'An independent survey positions EurActiv as the first portal on EU policies, while a readership survey proves its strong influence, based on independence, neutrality and languages.' (May 2003).
- **Europe Unit** www.europeunit.ac.uk/home/index.cfm. Sector-wide body primarily funded by Universities UK [q.v.] and three UK higher education funding councils. Aims to raise awareness of European issues affecting UK HE. Good set of background briefings.
- **IDEA: the electronic directory of the European institutions** http://europa.eu.int/idea/en. Electronic directory presenting the organization charts of the EU institutions, bodies and agencies in the eleven official EU languages.

55 FirstGov.gov [USA]

www.firstgov.gov

'The official US gateway to all government information.' The Site's engine will search some 50 million federal and state web pages; 130,000 websites link to FirstGov.

Information by Topic includes Sections on: Environment, energy and agriculture; Health; Reference and general government; and Science and technology. Within the Reference Centre there are links to Government and other sites concerned with Abbreviations and acronyms, Contacts and directories, Data and statistics, Laws and regulations, Libraries, News, Publications from the US Government.

An excellent core resource.

- **RegInfo.Gov: Where to find Federal regulatory information US General Services Administration and US Office of Management and Budget.** www.reginfo.gov/public. Range of services including uniform reporting of data on regulatory and deregulatory actions under development throughout the Federal Government, covering over 60 departments, agencies, and commissions.
- **SciTechResources.gov: a catalog of government science and technology web sites** www.scitechresources.gov. Searchable catalogue of descriptions of websites that are entry points to government science and technology resources. A browsable list of links also provides a good starting point.
- **The United States government internet manual P. Garvin** Bernan Press, 2004. $59.00. ISBN 1886222185. www.bernanpress.com [DESCRIPTION]. 'Contains more than 2000 site records that provide descriptions and URLs for each site. Evaluations are given for the most important and frequently sought sites'.
- **US government on the web: getting the information you need P. Hernon, R.E. Dugan and J.A. Shuler** 3rd edn, Libraries Unlimited, 2003, 492pp. $50.00. ISBN 1591580862. Very clear and well laid out guide; good summary lists of URLs at the end of each chapter; helpful summary of government organization structure.
- **Using government information sources: electronic and print J.L. Sears and M.K. Moody** 3rd edn., Oryx Press, 2001, 550pp. £79.00. ISBN 1573562882.

56 GAO: Accountability Integrity Reliability [USA]

Government Accountability Office

www.gao.gov

Independent, non-partisan agency that works for Congress.

Very well structured website, easy to use, good search facility providing access to remarkable range and depth of information. A single example is the GAO Highlights issue of July 2004 (a one-page summary of the full Report GAO-04-639) entitled: 'Women's participation in the sciences has increased, but Agencies need to do more to ensure compliance with Title IX'.

57 GOST: a guide to the organisation of UK science, engineering and technology

British Council

www.britishcouncil.org/science/gost

The British Council 'connects people worldwide with learning opportunities and creative ideas from the UK and builds lasting relationships between the UK and other countries. We are the UK's international organisation for educational opportunities and cultural relations and are represented in 110 countries worldwide'.

GOST is an easily navigable set of pages, good for gaining a quick overview. It is accessible from the Council's Home Page Science Portal, which in turn has other useful information on 'UK Science', 'Research and collaboration', and 'Society and science', including downloadable copies of two monthly online news bulletins, Science Insight and European RTD Insight – the second produced in conjunction with UKRO (www.ukro.ac.uk): 'The UK's foremost information and advice service on EU research and higher education'.

58 GPO Access [USA]

US Government Printing Office

www.gpoaccess.gov

'Disseminates official information from all three branches of the Federal Government ... Provides online access to key Government publications.' GPO Access Resources by Topic includes the Sections: Environment; Food and Drugs; Health and Safety; Science and Technology. The page Federal Agency Internet Sites provides access to other Federal agency websites in partnership with Louisiana State University Libraries and the Federal Depository Library Program.

Users can securely buy official Federal publications online and locate a Federal Depository Library using a clickable map. A March 2004 meeting was the first activity in an initiative with the Federal depository library community to digitize the entire legacy collection of US government documents currently held in depositories. The Site also provides access to the Code of Federal Regulations, the Federal Register, and the United States Code.

There are details of GPO LISTSERV mailing lists; and – in conjunction with the University of North Texas libraries – a Cybercemetery of Former Federal Web Sites.

- **Catalog of US Government Publications** www.gpoaccess.gov/cgp. 'Index to print and electronic publications created by Federal agencies. When available, links are provided to the full-text of these publications. Additionally, the locate libraries feature enables users to find libraries by state or area code.'
- **Government Information Locator Service** www.gils.net. Pioneering decentralized service that uses 'an open, low-cost, and scalable standard so that governments, companies, or other organizations can help searchers find collections of information, as well as specific information in the collections'.

59 Her Majesty's Stationery Office [UK]

www.hmso.gov.uk

Delivers a wide range of services to the public, information industry and government relating to access and re-use of government information. Site includes the full text of all legislation enacted by the UK Parliament and delegated legislation (Statutory Instruments) whether this applies to the UK as a whole or only to its constituent parts (e.g. Scotland). The aim is to publish these documents on the internet simultaneously or at least within 24 hours of their publication in printed form. However, HMSO notes that documents which are especially complex may take longer to mount on the site. Full-text search facilities are available.

Access is also provided to Command Papers: Parliamentary Papers which derive their name from the fact they are presented to the United Kingdom Parliament nominally by 'Command of Her Majesty', but in practice generally by a Government Minister. Command Papers are published on Departmental websites. Their subjects may be major policy proposals (White Papers) and consultation documents (Green Papers), diplomatic documents such as treaties, Government responses to Select Committee reports, reports of major committees of inquiry or certain departmental reports or reviews.

- **Civil Service Year Book** Biannual. £110.00 [2004]. www.hmso.gov.uk/information/csyb.htm [DESCRIPTION]. Official reference for central government in the UK providing the most authoritative source of up-to-date information on the Civil Service. It is the essential guide to the work and structure of the Civil Service in the UK.
- **Official Documents** www.official-documents.co.uk. Contains a selection of Government titles covering a very broad range of topics including the economy, work and welfare, health, transport and the environment. Two main categories of document are Command (White or Green) and House of Commons Papers.
- **UK 2005: the official yearbook of the United Kingdom of Great Britain and Northern Ireland** www.statistics.gov.uk. 'The definitive overview of the United Kingdom in text, tables, charts, maps and (in the hardcopy version) colour photographs.' Very good readable summaries of activity in each economic sector: ideal as introductions, albeit from an 'official' standpoint.
- **UKOP** www.ukop.co.uk [FEE-BASED]. 'The official catalogue of UK official publications since 1980. Containing 450,000 records from over 2000 public bodies, it is the most comprehensive source of information on official publications available.'

60 Higher Education Academy [UK]

www.heacademy.ac.uk

Set up in 2004 incorporating – among other previous bodies – the UK Higher and Further Education's Learning and Teaching Support Network. The Network consists of a Generic Centre plus 24 Subject Centres, including (q.v.): Bioscience; Engineering; Geography, Earth and Environmental Sciences; Health Sciences and Practice; Information and Computer Sciences; Materials; Maths, Stats and OR Network; Medicine, Dentistry and Veterinary Medicine; Physical Sciences. (For the moment we have retained the prefix LTSN in the titles of these entries.) The Generic Centre sponsors work in a number of Project Areas (e.g. Curriculum; e-Learning; Learning and teaching portal; Problem and enquiry based learning; Research and scholarship) as well as providing a useful Glossary of terms in learning and teaching in higher education.

61 Higher Education Funding Council for England

www.hefce.ac.uk

'Promotes and funds high-quality, cost-effective teaching and research in universities and colleges in England.' Among much useful information regarding higher and further education in the UK, the site provides access to the results of the 2001 Research Assessment (RA) Exercise in which Institutions were able to submit research outputs in up to 69 subject areas (units of assessment) with each submission being given a quality rating, judged against standards of national and international excellence, on a seven-point scale: 5* (five star) being at the top. The range of outputs considered included publications, products, even artistic performances, assessed through peer review by panels of experts in the subject. (The next assessment is in 2008.)

There is also access to all the reports prepared during the 2003 RA Review: a valuable compendium of the challenges and problems of rating the quality of scientific and scholarly research.

- **HERO** www.hero.ac.uk. Aims to be 'the primary internet portal for academic research and higher education in the UK' and 'the natural entry point for enquiries about higher education in the UK'. Contains a very extensive wide-ranging and annotated Reference section.
- **Joint Academic Coding System: JACS** www.hesa.ac.uk/jacs/completeclassification.htm. Subject classification used for the UK's Higher Education Statistics Agency. Provides brief scope notes for each of the several hundred subjects categorized: a useful glossary.
- **UK Higher Education Research Yearbook** Evidence Ltd, 2004. £245.00. www.evidence.co.uk/yearbook.html [DESCRIPTION]. Directory 'for those looking where to invest in UK research, who has the most income, who has the best profile in any area of research'. Website also gives details of their *University Publications Database* based on ISI WEB OF KNOWLEDGE.

62 HM Treasury [UK]

Great Britain. HM Treasury

www.hm-treasury.gov.uk

'The strategy sets out a long term vision for science in the UK, including information on the Spending Review outcome, and the arrangements for working in partnership with other funders and users of research to ensure the UK science base is sustainable in the long term, and continues to contribute to productivity growth.'

Similarly accessible via HM Treasury's website is the cross-departmental Consultation Document issued in March 2004: Science and innovation: working towards a ten-year investment framework.

- **Investing in innovation: a strategy for science, engineering and technology** **Great Britain. Department of Trade and Industry and Great Britain. Department for Education and Skills** The Stationery Office, 2002. Long term vision for science in the UK; arrangements for working in partnership with other funders and users of research to ensure the UK science base is sustainable in the long term, and continues to contribute to productivity growth.
- **SET for Success** www.hm-treasury.gov.uk. The Roberts' Review into the supply of science and engineering skills in the UK, commissioned as part of the UK Government's productivity and innovation strategy. Accessible with other useful documents within the Enterprise and Productivity section.

63 Japan Science and Technology Agency

www.jst.go.jp/EN

Interesting source providing wide range of information under these headings: Creation of technological seeds; Creation of new industries backed by new technologies; Dissemination of scientific and technological information; Promotion of regional research activities; Public understanding of science and technology; Research exchanges at home and abroad. There is also an Organization Chart for the Agency – which became an independent administrative institution in October 2003.

JST, alongside CHEMICAL ABSTRACTS SERVICE in the USA and FIZ KARLSRUHE in Germany, is a partner in STN INTERNATIONAL: customers in Japan thereby having access to all the STN databases; JST providing the content of the bibliographic database JICST-Eplus. Many other database activities of the Agency are described under the heading 'Promotion of dissemination of science and technology information', supplementing the links from the Home Page. However, a number of the items listed were either out-of-date or unavailable when checked.

- **Database Promotion Center, Japan** www.dpc.or.jp/english/index.html. Publishes the annual *Databases in Japan*: see website.
- **Japan Science and Technology Information Aggregator, Electronic: J-STAGE** http://info.jstage.jst.go.jp/contents/eng/index.html. Supports the release of papers within Japanese science and technology electronic journals. Via the JST Link Center, research papers placed within J-STAGE are linked to worldwide systems such as ChemPort, PubMed and CrossRef: all [q.v.].
- **JST English Articles of Science and Technology: J-EAST** Monthly. http://j-east.tokyo.jst.go.jp. English citations and abstracts for documents published in Japan covering all fields of science, technology, and medicine. Sources include about 3000 journals and serials, conference proceedings, technical reports. 991,987 items: August 2004.
- **Science Council of Japan** www.scj.go.jp/en/scj/about/index.html. Founded 1949 'as a special agency ... to promote science in government, industry and everyday life. It represents Japanese scientists at home and abroad with the philosophy that science is the foundation upon which a civilized nation is built'.

64 National Audit Office [UK]

www.nao.org.uk

Although the Office does not have a great involvement with STM matters, when they do treat an issue, the (independent of government) results can be very valuable: e.g. Tackling cancer in England: saving more lives (March 2004); The British Library – Providing services beyond the Reading Rooms (July 2004); Reforming NHS Dentistry: ensuring effective management of risks (November 2004); Stopping illegal imports of animal products into Great Britain (March 2005).

65 National Research Council Canada

www.nrc-cnrc.gc.ca

'The Government of Canada's premier organization for research and development.' It is organized into three key areas: Physical Sciences and Engineering; Life Sciences and Information Technology; Technology and Industry Support – each of which encompasses a range of subject-based Institutes covering manufacturing technology, biotechnology, health, ICT, etc.

The Council is responsible for CISTI (see below) and in May 2004, they launched a new 'Student Science & Tech' whose aim is to 'foster understanding among young Canadians of the benefits of science and technology, both for their everyday lives and their future careers'.

- **Canada Institute for Scientific and Technical Information** cisti-icist.nrc-cnrc.gc.ca. The Library collection is one of the largest in North America and its material is available for document supply to registered users. Searches can be made in the catalogues of CISTI and its partner the Canadian Agricultural Library.

66 National Science Foundation [USA]

www.nsf.gov

The independent agency of the US Government established to promote the progress of science. It provides awards, contracts and grants. Wide-ranging website: a good place to start can be the well presented multimedia series of sections 'Overviews of NSF Research', early 2005 with headings: Arctic and Antarctic; Astronomy and space; Biology; Chemistry and materials; Computing; Earth and environment; Education; Engineering; Mathematics; Nanoscience; People and security; Physics.

A number of NSF Divisions are referenced elsewhere.

- **Coalition for National Science Funding** www.cnsfweb.org. Group of organizations 'supporting the goal of increasing the national investment in the National Science Foundation's research and education programs in response to the unprecedented scientific, technological, and economic opportunities facing the USA'.
- **National Science Board** www.nsf.gov/nsb. Governing Board of NSF with 24 part-time members, appointed by US President and confirmed by Senate. Publishes biennially *Science and Engineering Indicators*: latest volume, 2004.
- **Science and Engineering Statistics** www.nsf.gov/statistics. Division 'to provide a central clearinghouse for the collection, interpretation, and analysis of data on scientific and engineering resources, and to provide a source of information for policy formulation by other agencies of the Federal Government.'

67 Natural Sciences and Engineering Research Council of Canada

www.nserc.ca

Awards scholarships and research grants through peer-reviewed competition; builds partnerships among universities, colleges, governments and the private sector. The NSERC Newsbureau offers a service to the media which can 'rapidly put you in touch with the researchers, the work, the universities and, where relevant, the industrial partners' funded by NSERC' (about 65% of Canadian university researchers working in the natural sciences and engineering being NSERC-funded).

68 Office of Science [USA]

www.science.doe.gov

Located within the Department of Energy, and 'the single largest supporter of basic research in the physical sciences in the United States, providing more than 40 percent of total funding for this vital area of national importance. It oversees – and is the principal federal funding agency of – the Nation's research programs in high-energy physics, nuclear physics, and fusion energy sciences ... (It) manages fundamental research programs in basic energy sciences, biological and environmental sciences, and computational science ... (And it) is the Federal Government's largest single funder of materials and chemical sciences, and it supports unique and vital parts of US research in climate change, geophysics, genomics, life sciences, and science education.'

The Office of Science has overall responsibility for 10 national laboratories, amongst them Argonne, Brookhaven, Oak Ridge, as well as overseeing work at 6 others, including Lawrence Livermore and Los Alamos.

Within the Office, the Office of Scientific and Technical Information (OSTI) leads the Department of Energy's e-government initiatives for disseminating R & D information.

- **Facilities for the future of science: a twenty-year outlook** Downloadable PDF2003, 48pp. Proposes portfolio of 28 prioritized new scientific facilities and upgrades to current facilities spanning the scientific disciplines to ensure the US retains its primacy in critical areas of science and technology well into the next century.

69 Office of Science and Technology [UK]

www.ost.gov.uk

'The UK is second only to the United States in terms of the volume and influence of scientific publications and the number of major international science prizes won ... The Office of Science and Technology leads for Government in supporting excellent science, engineering and technology and their uses to benefit society and the economy.'

Good overview of UK Government activity including descriptions of the work of key departments and committees, budget allocations, strategic initiatives, policy issues, work on enterprise and innovation, and on science and society. Most sections have sets of external links listed.

- **Foresight** www.foresight.gov.uk. Aims to provide challenging visions of the future, to ensure effective strategies now. It does this by providing a core of skills in science-based future projects and unequalled access to leaders in government, business and science.
- **Promoting science, engineering and technology for women** www.set4women.gov.uk/set4women. Unit set-up to tackle women's under-representation in the SET community. 'Our aim is to improve the recruitment, retention and progression of women throughout SET education and employment and to increase their involvement in shaping SET policy.'
- **Sciencewise: Engaging society with science and technology** www.sciencewise.org.uk. New scheme, 2004, 'to support projects that build the capacity of scientists, policy-makers and citizens to engage in constructive dialogue on key issues arising from new developments in science and technology'.
- **Woman into Science, Engineering and Construction** www.wisecampaign.org.uk. Promotes science and engineering as a valuable and interesting career option for women.

70 Office of Science and Technology Policy [USA]

www.ostp.gov/index.html

'Congress established OSTP in 1976 with a broad mandate to advise the President and others within the Executive Office of the President on the effects of science and technology on domestic and international affairs. The 1976 Act also authorizes OSTP to lead an interagency effort to develop and to implement sound science and technology policies and budgets and to work with the private sector, state and local governments, the science and higher education communities, and other nations toward this end.'

- **Science for the 21st century** Downloadable PDF2004, 48pp. www.ostp.gov/nstc/21stcentury/Final_sm.pdf. Produced by the National Science and Technology Council: 'The principal means for the President to co-ordinate science, space, and technology to co-ordinate the diverse parts of the Federal research and development enterprise.'

71 Organisation for Economic Co-operation and Development

www.oecd.org

Group of now 30 Countries 'best known for its publications and statistics. Its work covers economic and social issues from macroeconomics, to trade, education, development and science and innovation'.

The clearly laid-out site provides – via the Statistics Portal – access to statistical data by topic, including for sub-fields of: Agriculture and fisheries; Energy; Environment; Health; Industry and services; Information and communication technology; Science, Technology and patents. There is a very extensive Glossary of Statistical Terms, including entries (with sources) for such as 'acid rain', 'biotechnology', 'cement', 'database', 'extinct species', 'farmstead', 'gene', and so on – as well as for all the standard statistical terms.

For Science and Innovation, OECD 'assesses how science, technology, innovation and education policies can efficiently contribute to sustainable economic growth and employment creation. It provides policy advice on coping with the challenges arising from developments in new science-based industries, notably biotechnology'. There are various sections, including one Measuring Science and Technology, OECD providing 'methodological guidelines, databases, indicators and policy-relevant analysis in this area, focusing mainly on R&D, patents, human resources and innovation'. An index to 'Information by Country' gives access to details of events, news releases, publications, working papers, etc related to each country.

- **OECD Science, Technology and Industry Outlook** www.oecd.org/document [DESCRIPTION]. 5th in biennial series, focusing on: Public/private partnerships for innovation; Innovation in the service sector; Human resources for science and technology; Contribution of multinational enterprises to productivity growth. Statistical annex.
- **Research and Development Statistics** www.oecd.org/document [DESCRIPTION]. Latest is 2003 edn. Wide range of data on resources devoted to R&D in OECD countries including: source of funds; type of costs; R&D personnel by occupation and level of qualification.
- **Science, technology and innovation for the 21st century** www.oecd.org/document. Report with useful background papers, e.g.: *Science and Innovation Policy: Key Challenges and Opportunities (2004)*; *Science and Technology Statistical Compendium (2004)*; *Patents and Innovation: Trends and Policy Challenges (2004)*.
- **SourceOECD** new.sourceoecd.org [FEE-BASED]. OECD's online library of statistical databases, books and periodicals. NEW SourceOECD launched December 2004: SourceOECDNews had article: 'Our public Beta launch, what it means for librarians.'

72 Research [EUR]

European Commission. Directorate for Research

http://europa.eu.int/comm/research/index_en.cfm

'The gateway to news and information about Scientific Research and Technological Development in the European Union.' Rather a busy site and there can be an unfortunate use of pop-ups. But a very rich source of information.

- **Science and society in Europe** http://europa.eu.int/comm/research/science-society/index_en.html. 'Advances in science drive European growth, but sometimes give rise to fears and scepticism among citizens.' Gathers policymakers, researchers, citizens to consider science and governance; ethics; scientific awareness; youth and science; women & science.

73 Research Councils UK

www.rcuk.ac.uk

Strategic partnership set up to champion science, engineering and technology supported by the seven UK Research Councils. These include: Biotechnology and Biological Sciences Research Council; Council for the Central Laboratory of the Research Councils; Engineering and Physical Sciences Research Council; Medical Research Council; Natural Environment Research Council; Particle Physics and Astronomy Research Council – all referenced elsewhere in this text.

Browsing the website is a good introduction to current UK research concerns: especially its political and social dimensions.

- **e-Science** www.rcuk.ac.uk/escience. Good overview of the UK's e-Science programme '... the large scale science that will increasingly be carried out through distributed global collaborations enabled by the Internet ...'
- **RESCOLINK** www.rcuk.ac.uk/rescolinc. Focal point of the library and information services of the UK Research Councils. Details of all the services.
- **A Vision for Research** 2003. www.rcuk.ac.uk/documents/vision_final.pdf. Sets out to describe the research challenges for the next ten to twenty years that will shape the world we live in.

74 **Science and Technology Network** [UK]
Great Britain. Foreign and Commonwealth Office
www.fco.gov.uk
Aims 'to inform British science policy by reporting on developments around the world, by communicating UK achievements to other countries, by encouraging international collaboration and by developing links and contacts for the benefit of the UK research community ... The network reports to a wide customer base and works with a range of UK organisations, including Government Departments, parliamentary bodies, Research Councils, British Council, learned societies, industry, universities and other public sector bodies.'

Also useful is the Section Environment: 'There are many international environmental issues that need urgent attention, such as Climate Change, Sustainable Development, Biodiversity, and Environmental Security. The FCO's Environmental Work, in co-operation with other government departments, consists in ensuring that the UK contributes to international responses in these areas to improve the global environment.'

75 **Science Portal** [AUS]
Australia. Department of Education, Science and Training
www.science.gov.au
One of a series of Australian Government customer focused websites whose aim is 'to provide you with easy online access to government information and services. This allows you to find what you are looking for without having to know the structure of government.' Entry points from the Home Page cover: My Research Field; Sectors; Research Grants and Programs; Science Policy; Awareness; Directories and Databases. The *Sectors* are: Agriculture; Construction; Defence; Environment; Health; Information and Communication Services; Manufacturing; Mining and Energy; Transport; Education and Training.

Separately accessible from australia.gov.au are portals headed: Australian Government Agriculture Portal, Environment Portal, and HealthInsite.

- **Federation of Australian Scientific and Technological Societies** www.fasts.org. 'We represent the interests of some 60,000 scientists and technologists in Australia.' Over 50 societies in membership.

76 **The United Kingdom Parliament**
Great Britain. Parliament
www.parliament.uk
Access – among much else – to the work and reports of the Select Committees of the House of Commons and House of Lords: Environment, Food and Rural Affairs; Health; Science and Technology; Trade and Industry. These can provide exceptionally useful overviews of current concerns, including the full texts of Reports and Oral and Written evidence. For instance, during May–June 2004, the Science and Technology Committee of the House of Commons considered (among other matters): government investment in nanotechnology; human reproductive technologies and the law; Within REACH – The EU's new chemicals strategy; work of the Council for the Central Laboratory of the Research Councils; and – controversially – the future of scientific publications.

The main site's 'What's On' page sets out various links to current and future business of the Houses of Parliament. There is a service 'Watch Parliament Online'.

- **Parliamentary Office of Science and Technology** www.parliament.uk/parliamentary_offices/post.cfm. Office of the two Houses of Parliament (Commons and Lords) providing 'independent and balanced analysis of public policy issues related to science and technology.'
- **Science and Technology Committee** www.parliament.uk/parliamentary_committees/science_and_technology_committee.cfm. 'Appointed by the House of Commons to examine the expenditure, administration and policy of the Office of Science and Technology and its associated public bodies'.

77 **United Nations**
www.un.org/english
Easily accessible from the Home Page of this very pleasant site – naturally among much else – are: the UN System Sites (which include the 'Official Web Locator for the UN System', the 'UN Information Centres', the 'UN System Pathfinder' – links to major publications and internet resources of the UN system, and the 'Depository Libraries'); Publications, Stamps and Databases; the file of Recent Additions; and the Daily Briefing.

Well worth spending time browsing around.

- **CyberSchoolBus** http://cyberschoolbus.un.org. The UN's lively global teaching and learning project. Curriculum areas include: Saving tomorrow's world; Health; Cleaner oceans; UN in space. Includes much other valuable material targeted at 12–18 year-olds: a well thought through service.
- **Inventory of International Economic and Social Classifications** http://unstats.un.org/unsd/cr/family1.asp. List of all classifications registered into the International Family of Classifications as of 1 January 2002.
- **Quantifying the world: UN ideas and statistics** M. Ward Indiana University Press, 2004, 256pp. $29.95. ISBN 0253216745. 'Explores the economic, social, and environmental dimensions of the UN's statistical work and how each dimension has provided opportunities for describing the well-being of the world community.'
- **UN News Centre** www.un.org/News. Good entrée to current concerns.
- **UN Statistics Division** http://unstats.un.org/unsd. Gateway to the full range of statistics produced by the Division including the generic *Statistical Yearbook* as well as in specialized fields such as energy, environment, industry, trade. Links to other international statistics and to national offices.
- **United Nations Shared Cataloguing and Public Access System: UNCAPS** http://uncaps.unsystem.org. 'Provides a single point of access to library catalogs, indexes and abstract databases, library holdings, links to full-text resources, and archives ... a Web interface to the electronic resources of the libraries of the UN system of organizations.'

78 **United Nations Economic Commission for Europe**
www.unece.org
'One of the five regional commissions of the United Nations. It is the forum where the countries of western, central and eastern Europe, central Asia and North America – 55 countries in all – come together to forge the tools of their economic cooperation. That cooperation concerns such areas as economics, statistics, environment, transport, trade, industry and enterprise development, sustainable energy, timber and habitat.' Wide range of information on activities.

79 **United Nations Educational, Scientific and Cultural Organization**
www.unesco.org
From the entry Natural Sciences on the Home Page, we are led to a series of Thematic Areas (e.g. Fresh water; People and nature; Oceans; Earth sciences; Basic and engineering sciences; Coastal regions and small islands; etc.) and Intergovernmental and international programmes (e.g. International Geological Correlation Programme (IGCP);

International Hydrological Programme (IHP); Intergovernmental Oceanographic Commission (IOC); Man and the Biosphere (MAB); etc.).

The UNESCO Libraries Portal is an international gateway to information for librarians and library users. There is a similar UNESCO Archives Portal. Also, a UNESCO Free Software Portal.

- **Encyclopedia of Life Support Systems** www.eolss.net. 'An integrated compendium of sixteen encyclopedias. It attempts to forge pathways between disciplines in order to show their interdependence and helps foster the transdisciplinary aspects of the relationship between nature and human society.'
- **Innovations in science and technology education** **E.W. Jenkins, ed.** 2003, 348pp. €16.50. ISBN 923103894X. www.unesco.org/science [DESCRIPTION]. 'Examines the state of science and technology education (STE) worldwide at a crucial time in human history ... it has been universally recognized that science and technology have a pivotal role to play ... the foundations of which are laid at school.'
- **International Association of Universities** www.unesco.org/iau/index.html. Site provides access to Universities of the world: the complete list: 9200 university level institutions from 184 countries; 8000 non-university level institutions of higher education are also included in their database.
- **UNESCO thesaurus** http://databases.unesco.org/thesaurus. 7000 English terms (8600 French/Spanish) covering education, culture, natural sciences, social and human sciences, communication and information.

80 United States House of Representatives

US House of Representatives

www.house.gov/Welcome.html

Access to the work and reports of the House Committees: Agriculture; Energy and commerce; Resources; Science. An efficient engine will 'Search all House Committee and Representative websites': mid-2004, some 180,000 documents in total. There are links to the websites of other parts of the Legislative Branch of Government, of the Executive and Judicial Branches, of State/Local Governments, and of course to the Library of Congress. A nice, clean site.

- **United States Senate** **US Senate**. www.senate.gov. Lists with links of Senate Committees – Standing; Special, select, and other; Joint. A Virtual Reference Desk 'organizes information by subject and provides links to related materials'.

Research centres & institutes

81 Centre for the History of Science, Technology & Medicine [UK]

University of Manchester

www.ls.manchester.ac.uk/research/centres

'Founded in 1986 to bring together the University's interest in history of science, technology and medicine, and to act as a focus for the discipline in the Manchester region and beyond.'

- **National Archive for the History of Computing** www.chstm.man.ac.uk/nahc. 'Opened in 1987 to provide a repository for the documents and images of computer history, and a centre to encourage its study. A rich collection is now available to scholars.'
- **Wellcome Unit for the History of Medicine** www.chstm.man.ac.uk/wellcome.htm. 'Focuses on the social, cultural and political history of medicine since the industrial revolution, and on the recent histories of biomedical sciences and technologies.'

82 Centre National de la Recherche Scientifique [FR]

www.cnrs.fr/index.html

'The French National Center for Scientific Research (CNRS) is a public basic-research organization that defines its mission as producing knowledge and making it available to society. The CNRS has 26,000 employees (among which 11,600 researchers and 14,400 engineers and technical and administrative staff). Its budget amounts to 2214 million euros for the year 2004. The 1260 CNRS service and research units are spread throughout the country and cover all fields of research.'

83 Chinese Academy of Sciences

http://english.cas.ac.cn

Comprises five academic divisions, 108 scientific research institutes, over 200 science and technology enterprises, and more than 20 supporting units including one university, one graduate school and five documentation and information centers. Well laid out English language website providing access to a large volume of information, relevant to activities within and outside the Academy. For instance, there is a daily newsletter CAS News, but one can also link to the website of the The Ministry of Science and Technology and thence to the texts of the China Science and Technology Newsletters, whose issues appear every 10 days or so. A good place to start when exploring scientific work in China.

- **National Natural Science Foundation of China** www.nsfc.gov.cn. 'Founded in February 1986 with the approval of the State Council. It is an institution for the management of the National Natural Science Fund, aimed at promoting and financing basic research and some applied research in China.'

84 Commonwealth Scientific and Industrial Research Organisation [AUS]

www.csiro.au

Australia's leading research organization has research interests in agribusiness, energy and transport, environment and natural resources, information, communication and services, manufacturing, mineral resources and health. The website has plans and reports of activities and policies, information sheets and education projects and resources.

85 Joint Research Centre [EUR]

www.jrc.cec.eu.int

'Europe faces public concern about complex issues such as food contamination, genetic modification, chemical hazards, global change, environment and health, and nuclear safety. The Joint Research Centre (JRC) supports EU policy makers in the conception, development, implementation and monitoring of policies to tackle such trans-national and global problems. In effect, the JRC is a research-based policy support organisation working for the EU policy-maker.'

The JRC consists of seven different institutes, each with its own focus of expertise, on five separate sites around Europe.

86 Kavli Foundation

www.kavlifoundation.org

'Dedicated to the goals of advancing science for the benefit of humanity and promoting increased public understanding of and support for scientists and their work. The Foundation has selected three areas in which to focus its activities: cosmology, neuroscience, and nanoscience. An international program of research institutes, prizes, symposia, and endowed professorships is being established to further these goals. '

The Foundation established its 10th Institute – at MIT – in August 2004.

87 **Max-Planck-Gesellschaft**
www.mpg.de/english/portal
Independent, non-profit research organization that primarily promotes and supports research at its own institutes. Very well structured site provides (English language) access to a fund of information.

- **Berlin Declaration on Open Access to Knowledge in the Sciences and Humanities** www.zim.mpg.de/openaccess-berlin/berlindeclaration.html. Produced at the conference on Open Access to Knowledge in the Sciences and Humanities, Berlin, October 2003. List of signatories.

88 **National e-Science Centre** [UK]
www.nesc.ac.uk
The best – and an excellent – entrée to the wide range of activities now taking place in the UK under the 'e-Science' umbrella. Provides access to the *NeSC Bibliographic Database* ('be patient') which, August 2004, had over 1000 entries. Useful sets of links to, for instance, work on the Grids planned to underpin much e-Science activity, including to a helpful glossary. There is a good Newsroom.

- **e-Science Community InfoPortal** http://tyne.dl.ac.uk/InfoPortal. Very rich set of resources 'designed to increase the effectiveness of users of HPC [high performance computing] resources on the Grid'.
- **Revolutionizing science and engineering through cyber-infrastructure** National Science Foundation. www.communitytechnology.org/nsf_ci_report. 'Overarching finding is that a new age has dawned in scientific and engineering research, pushed by continuing progress in computing, information, and communication technology, and pulled by the expanding complexity, scope, and scale of today's challenges'.

89 **National Institute of Advanced Industrial Science and Technology** [JAP]
www.aist.go.jp
The 'new' AIST was formed in 2001 and comprises 15 research institutes previously under the former Agency of Industrial Science and Technology (the 'former' AIST) in the Ministry of International Trade and Industry (and the Weights and Measures Training Institute). The Institute is Japan's largest public research organization with some 3200 employees.

90 **Science in Society Research Programme** [UK]
http://sbs-xnet.sbs.ox.ac.uk/scisoc
Goal 'to explore and facilitate the rapidly changing relations between science (including engineering and technology) and wider society. In so doing, it seeks to place British social science at the heart of international debates and practical interventions concerning the public understanding of science, science and technology policy, science studies, and the nature of citizenship and expertise within contemporary society.' Nice, clean, site: good entry point to UK work in this arena.

91 **Wellcome Trust** [UK]
www.wellcome.ac.uk
Leading biomedical research charity. Apart from their extensive scientific research programme (the *Site Index* reveals the extent of this), the Trust 'funds research and sponsors activities to: stimulate public interest in science; inform and facilitate public debate on science and its application; improve understanding of the social, ethical, historical and cultural context of science'. In support, a *Resources* section 'provides a wealth of resources and services for teachers in order to provide in-depth background, up-to-date information and ideas of how to make science come alive in the classroom'.

The Trust also has a wide-ranging involvement with study of the *History of Medicine* including maintaining world-class library facilities. The *Wellcome Library for the History and Understanding of Medicine* sustains a good set of resource guide and online bibliography pages and is also responsible for Psci-com.

- **Science policy and information news (SPIN)** www.wellcome.ac.uk/knowledgecentre/spin. Helpful weekly round-up of news relevant to science policy.

Associations & societies

92 **Association of American Colleges and Universities**
www.aacu.org
'The leading national association concerned with the quality, vitality and public standing of undergraduate liberal education.'

Helpful section Science and Health: 'AAC&U works to advance broad-based systemic innovation to connect science education, especially in general education, to large public questions where scientific inquiry and knowledge are essential. AAC&U also works to support educational leaders in developing an academic focus on health and HIV disease to improve student learning and our common health. AAC&U's work in these areas also focuses on improving science education for students who may never major in a scientific field; connecting science reform to more robust and relevant general education programs; encouraging curricular attention to issues of gender and science; and stimulating informed civic engagement with scientific questions.'

- **Higher Education Directory** www.hepinc.com/FrameHED.htm [DESCRIPTION]. Annual publication, the 2005 edn giving 'standardized profiles on 4364 institutions giving detailed information on highest offering, accreditations, date established, enrollment, IRS status and much, much more'.
- **National Faculty Directory** Thomson Gale. www.galegroup.com [DESCRIPTION]. Alphabetic listing of names and addresses of teaching faculty members at American colleges and universities – and at Canadian institutions that use instructional materials primarily in English.

93 **Association of American Universities**
www.aau.edu
'Founded in 1900 by a group of fourteen universities offering the PhD degree. The AAU currently consists of sixty American universities and two Canadian universities. The association serves its members in two major ways. It assists members in developing national policy positions on issues that relate to academic research and graduate and professional education. It also provides them with a forum for discussing a broad range of other institutional issues, such as undergraduate education.' Examples of Research Issues considered are 'Animals in Research', 'Cloning', 'Conflicts of Interest and Misconduct', 'Costs of Research'. There is access to the universities' views on many other key topics.

Association of British Science Writers
See entry no. 6333

94 **Council of Graduate Schools** [USA]
www.cgsnet.org
'Organization of institutions of higher education in the United States, Canada, and across the globe engaged in graduate education, research scholarship, and the preparation of candidates for advanced degrees.' Good coverage of research issues on attractive easy to navigate site: many valuable leads.

95 **Council on Undergraduate Research** [USA]
www.cur.org
Mission is 'to support and promote high-quality undergraduate student-faculty collaborative research and scholarship'. Divisions include: Biology; Chemistry; Geosciences; Math and Computer Sciences; Physics and Astronomy.

96 **European Science Foundation**
www.esf.org
'Promotes high quality science at a European level. It acts as a catalyst for the development of science by bringing together leading scientists and funding agencies to debate, plan and implement pan-European initiatives.' Early 2005 had 78 members from 30 European countries. Organize exploratory workshops, networks, and programmes including: EUROCORES European co-operative Research Projects; and Forward Looks Enabling Europe's scientific community to develop medium to long term views and analyses of future research developments in multidisciplinary topics, and interact with the policy makers from ESF Member Organizations.

97 **Foundation for Science and Technology** [UK]
www.foundation.org.uk
'Purpose is to provide a neutral platform for debate of policy issues that have a science, engineering or technology element.' Valuable Lecture and Dinner Discussion Summaries (e.g. 'The future of science publication – open access or library serials?': 23 June 2004), as well as downloadable PDF issues of the *FST Journal*. Also Register of Learned and Professional Societies (£15.00: nearly 400 entries).

98 **InterAcademy Council**
www.interacademycouncil.net
'Created by the world's science academies to mobilize the best scientists and engineers worldwide to provide high quality advice to international bodies – such as the United Nations and the World Bank – as well as to other institutions.' Good informative website.

- **Academy of Sciences for the Developing World** www.twas.org. '84 percent of the Academy's 768 members, the 645 'Fellows', are scientists living and working in 72 countries of the South. The 123 'Associate Fellows' are citizens of 17 advanced countries. 15 TWAS members are Nobel Laureates.' Formerly the Third World Academy of Sciences.
- **International Network for the Availability of Scientific Publications** www.inasp.info. 'Our mission is to enable worldwide access to information and knowledge with particular emphasis on the needs of developing and transitional countries.'
- **Inventing a better future: a strategy for building worldwide capacities in science and technology** Downloadable PDF2004, 161pp. ISBN 9069844028. www.interacademycouncil.net/report.asp?id=6258. Excellent IAC Report. Notes 'digital libraries of science and technology can bring knowledge to virtually everyone, everywhere' and proposes that STM resources should be made available on the web for free, or at modest cost, to all in developing nations.

99 **National Academies** [USA]
www.nationalacademies.org
'Advisers to the nation on science, engineering, and medicine.'

Comprises the National Academy of Sciences, theNational Academy of Engineering, the Institute of Medicine and the National Research Council. The expert members of these bodies advise the US federal government and the public.

The site is an excellent entrée to current work and thinking on STM in the USA. There are a number of good ways to navigate, including through 'Major Divisions', 'Quick Links', 'Topics'.

- **The Center for Education** www7.nationalacademies.org/cfe. Formed 1999 as locus for education activities of the National Academies. Its mission is to promote evidence-based policy analysis that is 'both responsive and anticipatory' – addressing critical national issues in education research, policy, and practice.
- **Interacademy Panel on International Issues** www.nationalacademies.org. 'Global network of the world's science academies, launched in 1993. Its primary goal is to help member academies work together to advise citizens and public officials on the scientific aspects of critical global issues.'
- **IP @ National Academies** http://ip.nationalacademies.org. 'From Internet content protection to human gene patenting, Intellectual Property (IP) in many forms [has] emerged from legal obscurity to public debate. This website serves as a guide to the Academies' extensive work on IP and a forum to discuss ongoing work.'
- **The National Academies Press** USA. www.nap.edu. Note especially The Discovery Engine which 'searches more than 500,000 book pages from nearly 3000 formal publications' plus 'more than 100,000+ web documents: current projects, testimony, press releases, news documents, etc'.
- **National Research Council** www.nationalacademies.org/nrc/. 'The principal operating agency of both the National Academy of Sciences and the National Academy of Engineering in providing services to the government, the public and the scientific and engineering communities.'

100 **Science Council** [UK]
www.sciencecouncil.org
'The Science Council is a leading independent body with a membership of over 25 professional institutions and learned societies, supported by their member networks of more than 300,000 scientists across the breadth of science and mathematics. The main purpose of the Science Council is to promote the advancement and dissemination of knowledge of and education in science, pure and applied.'

'The Science Council received its Royal Charter on 14 October 2003, Licensed Bodies on behalf of the Science Council can now award the prestigious designation of Chartered Scientist (Csci) to individual scientists who meet the high standards for the qualification.'

101 **Scientists for Global Responsibility** [UK]
www.sgr.org.uk
'Promotes ethical science and technology – based on the principles of openness, accountability, peace, social justice, and environmental sustainability. Our work involves research, education, lobbying and providing a support network for ethically-concerned scientists.'

'SGR is an independent UK-based membership organisation. We have around 600 scientist members, and are supported by some of the UK's top scientists, for example Prof. Sir Martin Rees and Prof. Stephen Hawking. Unlike many scientific bodies it is our policy to refuse funding from the military or large corporations involved in controversial science and technology – which means we depend for most of our finance on our members and supporters.'

- **International Network of Engineers and Scientists for Global Responsibility** www.inesglobal.com. Founded 1991. Efforts focus on disarmament and international peace, ethics, justice and sustainable development. INES is affiliated with the United Nations and with UNESCO as an NGO. Links to wide range of related organizations throughout the world.
- **Open Society Institute** www.soros.org. Serves as the hub of the Soros Foundations Network aiming to promote open societies by shaping government policy and supporting education, media, public health, and human and women's rights, as well as social, legal, and economic reform.

102 Union of Concerned Scientists [USA]

www.ucsusa.org

Founded in 1969 by faculty members and students at MIT, is 'an independent non-profit alliance of more than 100,000 concerned citizens and scientists. We augment rigorous scientific analysis with innovative thinking and committed citizen advocacy to build a cleaner, healthier environment and a safer world. UCS's programs are the means by which we accomplish this. They are the pressure points translating vision into action. Through them, we connect the best scientific insights with the knowledge and support of an astute citizenry and apply them to the machinery of government at all levels—with results that have set a standard for effective advocacy for decades'.

Current Programs – the pages of each leading to rich sets of resources – are: Clean Energy; Clean Vehicles; Food and Environment; Global Environment; Global Security.

103 Universities UK

www.universitiesuk.ac.uk

Promotes and supports the work of UK universities. Policy statements, publications, etc.

Libraries, archives, museums

104 24 Hour Museum [UK]

www.infoville.org.uk/culture/museums/culture_24hour.htm

A UK government-funded independent charity provides this gateway to details of some 3000 UK museums, galleries and heritage attractions – titled The National Virtual Museum – as well as much other useful information. An early 2005 database search for 'science' retrieved details of: 25 most relevant museums or galleries; 642 related museums or galleries; 211 articles; 23 trails; 52 events; 39 educational resources. Nice map search facility finds the location of particular types of collection. City Heritage Guides. Excellent entrée.

105 British Library

www.bl.uk

The UK's national library and 'the only organisation with a statutory public good remit to collect, preserve and provide long-term research information for the whole of the UK'. The BL's stocks include 150 million items, in most languages, with 3 million new items being incorporated every year; and it operates the world's largest document delivery service providing some 4 million items a year to customers all over the world.

The web page Resources for research provides links to resources within the British Library and selected links to other online resources. Sections include: Environment; Health; Patents; Science and Technology. An alternative approach is to start with the pages Collections, and then link through to the Sections headed: Patents, trademarks and designs; Reports, conferences and theses; Science, technology and business; Research resources. Two British Library services of especial value within STM are: BRITISH LIBRARY – PATENTS; and INSIDE.

- **The British Library Integrated Catalogue** http://catalogue.bl.uk. Describes over 12 million items held by the BL; can also be used to order items. An excellent resource; easy to use. Includes details of 60,000 serials to which the BL subscribes.
- **British National Bibliography** www.bl.uk/services/bibliographic/natbib.html [DESCRIPTION]. Listing of UK books and new serials, including forthcoming books and now electronic resources, UK and Irish publishers being obliged by law to send a copy of all new publications to the BL. Its records are available in the British Library Public Catalogue.
- **National Library Catalogues Worldwide University of Queensland**. www.library.uq.edu.au/natlibs. Excellent listing maintained within the University Library. Part of a more extensive gateway to library catalogues in Australia and elsewhere.
- **Research Libraries Network** www.rln.ac.uk [DESCRIPTION]. New body set up in autumn 2004, initially for three years up to the end of July 2007. It will be led by an executive unit, with a budget of up to £3 million, which will be based at the British Library and take strategic guidance from an advisory board.

106 Deutsche Bibliothek

www.ddb.de/index_e.htm

'The national library and national bibliographic information centre for the Federal Republic of Germany. It is responsible for the collection, processing and bibliographic indexing of all German and German-language publications issued since 1913. Die Deutsche Bibliothek co-operates closely with all national and international library institutions and organisations. Within this context, it has a leadership role in the development and application of common rules and standards for Germany.'

- **Bibliodata** www.ddb.de/index_e.htm [DESCRIPTION]. The largest literature database in Germany, contains bibliographic data on books, academic publications, maps, conference reports, periodicals, etc. in the collections of DDB. The database is updated weekly and is available on two online hosts.

107 Deutsches Museum

www.deutsches-museum.de/e_index.htm

'One of the biggest museums of technology and science in the world. It is not a state museum but an independent public institution. Under the terms of its constitution it has the right of self administration and functions under the protection and supervision of the Bavarian state government.'

Extensive interesting multimedia website.

108 Exploratorium [USA]

www.exploratorium.edu

Well presented, virtual science museum that contains over 15,000 web pages exploring hundreds of different topics. It is based on the museum of the same name in San Francisco. Many topics contain interactive, audio and visual material. Resources for educators include activities and photographs.

109 **Franklin Institute** [USA]
http://sln.fi.edu
Good range of learning resources, attractively presented.

110 **Intel International Science and Engineering Fair**
Intel Corporation.
www.intel.com/education/isef
'The world's largest pre-college science competition that provides an opportunity for the world's best young scientists and inventors to come together to share ideas, showcase cutting-edge science projects, and compete for more than US $3 million in awards and scholarships.' Part of Intel Innovation in Education.

111 **Library and Archives Canada**
www.collectionscanada.ca
Created from the *National Library of Canada* and the *National Archives of Canada* in 2004.

- **Amicus** www.collectionscanada.ca/amicus. 'Search over 28 million full records from 1300 Canadian libraries ... Access the entire database including National Library records ... The first place for items about Canada (#Canadiana).' Free of charge.
- **Canada's Digital Collections** http://collections.ic.gc.ca. 'One of the largest sources of Canadian content on the Internet. More than 600 collections are available, celebrating Canada's history, geography, science, technology and culture.'
- **Canadian Information by Subject** www.collectionscanada.ca/caninfo. Provide links to information about Canada from internet resources around the world. The subject arrangement is in the form of a 'Subject Tree', based on the structure of the Dewey Decimal Classification system.
- **Government Information** www.collectionscanada.ca/8/4. Selective collection of links to Canadian government sites and key federal documents, including a page of links to the news release pages of individual federal government departments.
- **Theses Canada** www.collectionscanada.ca/thesescanada. Central access point for Canadian theses and information about the Theses Canada program.

112 **Library of Congress** [USA]
www.loc.gov
'The nation's oldest federal cultural institution and serves as the research arm of Congress. It is also the largest library in the world, with nearly 128 million items on approximately 530 miles of bookshelves.' The Home Page link Global gateway: world culture and resources includes a section 'Portals to the world' which, for each of the world's countries, lists 'resources selected by Library of Congress experts'. Check out the link 'Science and technology' for the country of interest.

Alternatively, approach the wealth of accessible resources via the Librarians and archivists pages which has sections headed: Library functions (e.g. Building digital collections; Public service and reference; Standards); Services and other resources (e.g. Publications and products; Thesauri); Most requested topics (e.g. Digital reference).

- **Ask a Librarian: An online reference service from the Library of Congress** www.loc.gov/rr/askalib. 'Correspondents are encouraged to use local and online resources. For those seeking further assistance from the Library of Congress, the staff will respond to their reference and information needs to the extent possible.'
- **Classification Web: web access to LC classification and LC subject headings** www.loc.gov/cds/classweb.html [FEE-BASED]. Via an agreement with OCLC ONLINE COMPUTER LIBRARY CENTER, users can now enter a Dewey classification number and display a list of matches to LC subject headings or LC classification numbers as they have been applied in LC bibliographic records.
- **Encyclopedia of the Library of Congress: for Congress, the nation and the world** J. Aikin and J.Y. Cole Bernan Press, 2004, 400pp. $95.00. ISBN 0890599718. 'History of the Library of Congress that also provides users with official, current information about Library of Congress collections, services, and administrative units.'
- **Library of Congress Authorities** http://authorities.loc.gov. Forms of names (for persons, places, meetings, and organizations), titles, and subjects used on bibliographic records.
- **Library of Congress Classification** www.loc.gov/catdir/cpso/lcco/lcco.html. Letters and titles of the main classes of the LC Classification. Complete text of the classification schedules in printed volumes may be purchased from the Cataloging Distribution Service. Online access to complete text via Classification Web.
- **Library of Congress Online Catalog** http://catalog.loc.gov. Great resource – but can sometimes be difficult to get connection: 'Our peak usage is typically Tuesdays, Wednesdays, and Thursdays between 10:00am and 2:00pm (US Eastern Time)'.
- **Library of Congress subject headings** 28th edn 2005. http://www.loc.gov/cds/lcsh.html [DESCRIPTION]. Forthcoming: over 270,000 total headings and references. 'The only subject headings list accepted as the world wide standard. LCSH is the most comprehensive list of subject headings in print in the world. It's the one tool no librarian should be without.'
- **MARC code lists for relators, sources, description conventions** www.loc.gov/marc/relators/relahome.html. Lists of codes intended for use in MARC 21 Authority, Bibliographic, Classification, Community Information, and Holdings records. The lists contain over 500 discrete codes, several of which are obsolete.
- **Science Tracer Bullets Online** www.loc.gov/rr/scitech/tracer-bullets/tbs.html. Research guides that help locate information on science and technology subjects. Many are now rather old; but can still be valuable for historical research. The Library also has short Series Science reference guides and Everyday mysteries.
- **THOMAS: legislative information on the internet** http://thomas.loc.gov. Invaluable freely accessible compendium of Federal legislative information.

113 **Linda Hall Library of Science, Engineering and Technology** [USA]
www.lhl.lib.mo.us
Strong collections in mathematics, astronomy, physics, chemistry, and engineering as well as geology, life sciences and the history of science (including digitized material). The online library catalogue, LEONARDO, is a valuable resource, and there are useful listings of databases and websites.

The former New York-based Engineering Societies Library – originally founded by five leading US-based societies (AIME, ASCE, ASME, IEEE, AIChE) – consolidated all of its library services to the Linda Hall Library in Kansas City in 1998.

114 **Museum of Science, Boston** [USA]
www.mos.org
This major US museum has been displaying scientific and technological exhibits since 1830 and now also has a number of online exhibits that can be viewed on the web. The museum's library focuses on education resources.

115 National Archives [UK]
www.nationalarchives.gov.uk
'The National Archives, which covers England, Wales and the United Kingdom, was formed in April 2003 by bringing together the Public Record Office and the Historical Manuscripts Commission. It is responsible for looking after the records of central government and the courts of law, and making sure everyone can look at them. The collection is one of the largest in the world and spans an unbroken period from the 11th century to the present day.'

See also the entry elsewhere for Access to Archives; also that for the Archives Hub.

- **National Digital Archive of Datasets** http://ndad.ulcc.ac.uk. Preserves and provides online access to archived digital data and documents from UK central government departments.

116 National Archives and Records Administration [USA]
www.archives.gov
'Independent Federal agency that preserves our nation's history and defines us as a people by overseeing the management of all Federal records.' A good place to start is the web-accessible version of the *Guide to Federal Records in the National Archives of the United States* whereby 'comprehensive coverage of NARA's holdings of federal records, i.e., records that originated in the executive, judicial, and legislative branches of the federal government, is provided – at a very high level'. It is also well worth checking out the services of the NARA Archives Library Information Center (ALIC).

117 National Diet Library [JAP]
www.ndl.go.jp/en/index.html
The only national library in Japan.

- **Directory of Japanese Scientific Periodicals** www.ndl.go.jp/en/data/opac.html. Catalogue of almost 14,000 journals. There are subject listings and the entries for each title list secondary resources indexing that publication. In English.

118 National Library of Australia
www.nla.gov.au
The Library co-ordinates the activities of the Australian Subject Gateways Forum, 'a group of subject gateways owners, formed in February 2000, who have developed gateway services for the Australian Higher Education sector ... The ASGF includes a number of subject-specific gateways (covering areas such as agriculture, sustainable development, education, literature, law, music and performing arts) and non-subject specific gateways. The primary target audience for the gateways are under- and post-graduate students and lecturers in the HE sector, as well as professionals and researchers in the field. A subject gateway has been defined by the ASGF as: "a Web-based mechanism for accessing a collection of high quality, evaluated resources identified to support research and/or learning in a particular subject discipline".'

- **Australian Science and Technology on the Internet** www.nla.gov.au/oz/sciencew.html. Extensive links to universities, research institutes, government agencies, associations and societies, conferences, electronic journals and discussion lists. Subject listings for 28 topics plus sections on science for schools, libraries and archives.
- **Picture Australia** www.pictureaustralia.org. Excellent service allowing simultaneous search of several online pictorial collections. Clicking on a 'thumbnail' will send you to the website of the relevant agency to view the full-size version, where you can order a high-resolution copy if required.

119 National Museum of Science and Industry [UK]
www.nmsi.ac.uk
Comprises the National Museum of Photography, Film and Television, the National Railway Museum, and the Science Museum. 'NMSI is stepping out. It has to. Human invention, innovation and creativity have reached breakneck speed. Such is the avalanche of change in the fields that NMSI represents – science, technology, medicine. transport and the media – that it is imperative for everyone, staff and public, to try to make sense of these rapid and often confusing developments.'

- **Dana Centre** www.danacentre.org.uk. 'A stylish, purpose-built venue, complete with a cafébar, appealing to adults. It is a place for them to take part in exciting, informative and innovative debates about contemporary science, technology and culture.'

120 New York Public Library [USA]
www.nypl.org
The Library's 'research collections (for reference only, and organized as *The Research Libraries*, with four major centres) resemble the holdings of the great national and university libraries'.

The website of the *Science, Industry and Business Library (SIBL)* centre provides access to a well presented range of information about the Library's collections and services, including a good set of 'Research guides' ('Apparel and textiles'; 'Building and construction', 'Climatology and climatological data' etc. as well as more general topics such as 'Biographical resources'; 'Company information'; 'Government'; etc.), covering reference sources, indexes and abstracts, websites, and so on.

A good example of its type.

- **The New York Public Library desk reference** 4th edn, Hyperion Books, 2002, 1015pp. $34.95. ISBN 0786868465. The 'Science Desk Reference' version of this was last published 1996.

121 Radcliffe Science Library [UK]
www.bodley.ox.ac.uk/dept/rsl
Reference library and the science department of the Bodleian Library Oxford. Thus via the UK's official legal deposit scheme receives a free copy of all British scientific publications (including popular and children's publications). Also collects extensively overseas. Especially strong collections of older material.

- **Science information services in Oxford: a virtual tour** www.bodley.ox.ac.uk/users/millsr/science. Helpful pleasant facility.

122 Smithsonian Institution [USA]
www.si.edu
'The world's largest museum complex and research organization.' From the Research section of the website are links to quite detailed – but nicely accessible – descriptions of the work of the Smithsonian's many Science Centers (e.g. Astrophysical Observatory; Carrie-Bow Marine Field Station; Environmental Research Center; Migratory Bird Center; Natural History Museum Research and Collections).

The Smithsonian's Library Catalogues provide access to some 1.5 million volumes, including 15,000 journal titles, rare books and manuscripts. SIL collections are 'particularly strong in natural history, tropical biology, and Chesapeake Bay area ecology ... the history of science and technology; aerospace history, astronomy, and planetary sciences ...'

- **Encyclopedia Smithsonian** www.si.edu/resource/faq. '... helps answer frequently asked questions about the Smithsonian with links to resources on subjects from Art to Zoology'. Good opportunity to browse around a wide range of introductory resources.

- **Library and archival exhibitions on the web** www.sil.si.edu/SILPublications/Online-Exhibitions. Links to online exhibitions that have been created by libraries, archives, and historical societies, as well as to museum online exhibitions with a significant focus on library and archival materials.
- **National Museum of American History** http://americanhistory.si.edu. Includes the sections: Division of the History of Technology; Division of Information Technology and Society; Division of Science, Medicine, and Society.
- **Smithsonian Science Libraries** www.sil.si.edu/libraries/science.htm. Useful gateway to the various libraries.

Portal & task environments

123 AccessScience: McGraw-Hill encyclopedia of science and technology online

McGraw Hill.
www.accessscience.com [FEE-BASED]
Daily updated online versions of the encyclopedia and the McGraw-Hill dictionary of scientific and technical terms, as well as 'Research Updates' from the publisher's *Yearbook of Science and Technology* supplemented by late-breaking news from the magazine Science.

Also includes biographies of 2000 scientists from the *Hutchinson Dictionary of Scientific Biography* and much else: literature citations; links to evaluated related websites; learning resources and study guides; image banks; 'questions answered in our weekly Q&A'; and so on.

- **McGraw-Hill Education: showcase of online resources** www.mheducation.com/showcase.html. Entrée to range of services: AccessMedicine; AccessScience; ALEKS; GradeSummit; Harrison's Online; The McGraw-Hill Learning Network; McGraw-Hill eBookstore; PageOut; PassKey; PowerWeb; Primis Online; TechCONNECT. See also Digital Solutions below.
- **McGraw-Hill encyclopedia of science and technology** 9th edn2002, 15600pp. $2495.00. ISBN 0079136656. http://books.mcgraw-hill.com/ [DESCRIPTION]. 20 v. 7100 articles covering 97 fields of science; more than 5000 contributors including 30 Nobel Prize winners; 12,000 digitally prepared illustrations, including 90 full-colour plates.
- **McGraw-Hill yearbook of science and technology** 2005, 432pp. $175.00. ISBN 0071445048. Attractively presented articles on topics of current interest and concern. Good use of graphics and colour. 'An extensive subject index makes finding information a snap.' Worth seeking out.

124 Alacra: Aggregate – Integrate – Package – Deliver

www.alacra.com [FEE-BASED]
'Provides access to more than 100 premium commercial business databases that contain financial information, economic data, business news, and investment and market research. Alacra provides the requisite information in the appropriate format, gleaned from such prestigious content partners as Thomson Financial™, Barra, The Economist Intelligence Unit, Factiva, Mergerstat® and more.'

Although primarily aimed at the commercial marketplace, a very good example of trends in the publicly available information supply industry – recognizing the need to add significant value to the offerings of individual publishers such as Thomson (who themselves incorporate third-party content in their services). Apart from customers being able to 'select from a variety of options to integrate, display and access Alacra applications and premium content in their own environment', noteworthy is their Alacra Concordance Database: a 'master authority file of company and industry identifiers that are cross-indexed against all premium databases and content. Premium providers use various identifiers for a company or industry and in many cases, have assigned their own'.

125 Amazon

www.amazon.co.uk
'The leading online retailer of products that inform, educate, entertain and inspire.' Notable in this context not only for the breadth of its coverage of published resources; but also for its easily navigable subject catalogue. For instance, linking from 'Books' through 'Subject' to 'Scientific, Technical and Medical', and then to 'Engineering', 'Chemical and Biochemical Engineering', and finally 'Biosensors' displayed 50 items, ranging from the latest 'Advances' Volume to a now 'hard-to-find' market research report. Well worth browsing through is their 'Reference' section within 'Science and Nature' which is sub-classified by a score of STM subject areas.

Amazon continues to offer major innovations in its services, such as the A9 service referenced below.

- **Barnes & Noble** www.bn.com/library. Now have a 'comprehensive online bookstore for Library Professionals'. A good alternative to Amazon with a similarly useful subject tree.
- **Blackwell's Online Bookshop** http://bookshop.blackwell.co.uk. Good detailed browsable subject categorization based on the Book Industry Classification (BIC) system. Opportunity to include/exclude titles from the company's US catalogue.
- **Open Search** A9.com. www.a9.com. Amazon service bringing together diverse content in a single search interface. Early 2005, the service was extended to allow registered users to personalize their raft of content sources and resuts display. Could well become a major generic search service.

126 BBC

www.bbc.co.uk
Provides inter alia a very extensive compendium of current and archival STM information: especially tailored to the non-specialist. From the Home Page explore Health and Science and Nature, but also Learning with subheadings including 'Computers and IT', 'Geography', 'Maths', and 'Weather' as well as 'Health' and 'Science'. Or use the extensive and well structured A–Z index. An excellent professional service.

127 Blackwell Synergy

www.blackwell-synergy.com
As well as access to the content of most of Blackwell's 800 or so journals, including via a hierarchical subject tree, there is a link through this gateway to The Librarian Site which in turn leads to a series of potentially useful Subject Pages, each of which can contain as appropriate information for: Reading corner; E-mail alerts; Forthcoming books; Society partners; etc.

128 ConnectSciences

Institut de l'Information Scientifique et Technique
http://connectsciences.inist.fr
Provides free access to a full range of scientific and technical information resources and services: Article Catalog (access to 8.7 millions of journal articles held in INIST collections); New additions to the bibliographic database in Science,

Technology and Medicine – PASCAL – (current three months) and to the bibliographic database in Humanities and Social Sciences – FRANCIS – (current year). Easy to use search facility (English language interface). Especially worth checking for recent French language and European material.

- **PASCAL Institut de l'Information Scientifique et Technique.** www.inist.fr/en/PRODUITS/pascal.php [DESCRIPTION]. Multilingual, multidisciplinary database that covers the core scientific literature in Science, Technology and Medicine with special emphasis on European literature (45% of the indexed documents). Indexes some 15 million documents, 1973 to present.

129 CSA Illumina

CSA.
www.csa.com [FEE-BASED]

CSA is a privately-owned US information company, formerly in part trading under the name Cambridge Scientific Abstracts.

At the core of its activities CSA developed the Internet Database Service (IDS) providing access to 'more than 50 databases covering major areas of research, including materials science, environmental sciences and pollution management, biological sciences, aquatic sciences and fisheries, biotechnology, engineering, computer science, sociology, art history, and linguistics'. There were the usual search facilities, including an interactive Thesaurus feature. Lists of the primary journals covered by each database are freely accessible: many of the databases are cited elsewhere in TNW (noting that their titles and scopes seem to change relatively frequently).

However, in December 2004, CSA released their new platform for online bibliographic and full-text searching with the number of databases available for search having grown to over one hundred.

Meanwhile, a number of the collections are (still) available in print editions.

- **Biblioalerts** Monthly. www.biblioalerts.com. 1500 reports on detailed STM topics based on CSA's dataset. Each report includes up to 250 items, and is compiled by the editors at CSA. The reports can be ordered through any one of currently 16 publishing partners.
- **Conference Papers Index** www.csa.com/factsheets/cpi-set-c.php. Some 1.5 million records dating back to 1982. 'Subject emphasis since 1995 has been in the life sciences, environmental sciences and the aquatic sciences, while older material also covers physics, engineering and materials science'.
- **Sage Full-Text Collections** SAGE Publications. www.sagefulltext.com. In 2004 introduced two new collections: Materials Science; Nursing and Health Sciences, expanding their coverage of social sciences into STM. Accessible through CSA.
- **Science and Technology Digest** www.csa.com/factsheets/scitechdig-set-c.php [DESCRIPTION]. Abstracting and indexing database that covers selected articles from over 100 worldwide sources in the applied and theoretical sciences. Journals range from widely circulated, newsstand publications to academic journals.

130 Dialog

Thomson Dialog.
www.dialog.com [FEE-BASED]

'As part of the Deep Web, which is estimated to be 500 times larger than the content accessible via Web search engines, Dialog products offer unparalleled depth and breadth of content coupled with the ability to search with precision and speed. Our collection of over 900 databases handles more than 700,000 searches and delivers over 17 million document page views per month.'

Good to look at first are the 'Top 10 Most Frequently Downloaded Documents from dialog.com'. And to get a reasonably swift overview of the range of data accessible, browse through the Dialog Bluesheets, which 'contain detailed instructions on search techniques for the special features of each database, including file description, subject coverage, date range, update frequency, sources of the data, and the origin of the information'.

Dialog has a number of Portal and Technology Partners including: Autonomy; BEA WebLogic; IBM WebSphere; and Vignette.

- **Dialog DataStar** www.dialog.com/products/datastar [FEE-BASED]. Comprehensive European-based service acquired by Dialog in 1988. Particular emphasis on biomedical, pharmaceutical and health care information, especially within a European context.
- **Dialog eLinks** www.dialog.com/products/ejournal [FEE-BASED]. Partnership with over 100 publishers and aggregators to provide access to the full text of articles from more than 11,000 journals.
- **Dialog NewsRoom** www.dialog.com/sources/newsroom [FEE-BASED]. Single source covering more than 8000 separate periodical sources, approximately 80% in full text, from more than 100 countries.
- **Dialog Profound** www.dialog.com/products/profound [FEE-BASED]. Specializes in industry and market data sourced from market research reports; newspapers, magazines and trade journals; analyst reports; economic analyses and forecasts; statistical data; etc.
- **NewsEdge** www.dialog.com/products/productline/newsedge.shtml [FEE-BASED]. News delivered via a wide variety of formats and routes. 'Our editorial experts sift through the clutter, delivering only the stories and updates business people really need.' Highly recommended by INFORMATION ADVISOR.

131 Digital Solutions

McGraw-Hill.
http://mcgraw-hill.co.uk/readytolaunch

McGraw-Hill Europe, Middle East and Africa gateway to the wide range of 'digital solutions' offered by the company. Similar gateways were available for other geographical regions (though – as so often – sites and site maps frequently change). Details of the major services below.

- **Online Learning Centres** www.mcgraw-hill.co.uk/textbooks. Book-specific supporting websites, including resources for both lecturers and students, with a Website Gallery where text supporting websites can be browsed.
- **PageOut** http://mcgraw-hill.co.uk/pageout. 'Offers a wizard-style template that enables lecturers to create a professionally designed, structured website in less than an hour! ... Free to lecturers who adopt any McGraw-Hill textbook. In addition, we host your website from our server.'
- **PowerWeb** http://mcgraw-hill.co.uk/he/digital_solutions/powerweb. 'An expert for each discipline analyzes the day's news to show students how it is relevant to their field of study and to help them apply the concepts they are learning to real world events.' Newsfeeds used include: FT, BBC, ABC, Discovery Channel.
- **Primis** www.mhhe.com/primis. Service allowing course tutors to select chapters from existing McGraw-Hill textbooks – some 700,000 pages of content – and create customized learning tools, The service – inter alia – provides a useful list of the company's extensive e-book collection.

132 EBSCO Information Services

www.ebsco.com [FEE-BASED]

'The only vendor involved in selling print subscriptions, e-journals and online databases.' Operate the EBSCONET serials management system allowing administrators to order, search, claim and renew periodicals using their database of some 282,000 titles, including print and electronic formats. 50% of these are US titles, 50% non-US

But the company also – through EBSCOhost – provides access to the content of some 150 databases and over 10,000 e-journals (with title, ISSN, publisher details for each freely accessible). Using the EBSCO SmartLinks technology, EBSCOhost search results provide links to the full text of articles in other EBSCOhost databases and in e-journals on subscription through EBSCO or available from CrossRef member publishers.

There is also a freely-accessible Library Reference Center comprised of indexing and abstracts from more than 90 library trade magazines and journals.

133 European Information Network Services

www.eins.org [FEE-BASED]

From 1999, successor system to the former 'Information Retrieval Services' of the European Space Agency.

'The EINS (European Information Network Services) organisation provides GEM and the Complementary Services. GEM is a resource for scientific, technical and medical information. Complementary Services additionally provide news, business and legal information ... EINS is: a series of Service Providers (online host systems) working in co-operation with the British Library; a network of National Centres providing customer support; a Technological Centre, CINECA, providing computing, networking and Internet facilities; an Administration Centre, COBIDOC, providing statistical usage data, invoicing data and liaison with Service Providers. The organisation is co-ordinated by the British Library.'

The service providers are: CAS; CINECA; DIMDI; FIZ Karlsruhe; LexisNexis. National centres are located in: Austria; Belgium; France; Hungary; Italy; Netherlands; Norway; Spain; Sweden; UK. The overall service has a particularly strong set of chemistry-related databases – as well as of those related to space research.

- **GEM** www.eins.org/publications/price_list/pricelist-unitedkingdom.htm [FEE-BASED]. Offers access to a wide range of STM databases: the URL lists these with their prices for the UK. (There are price lists and other relevant information for other countries.).

134 Factiva

www.factiva.com [FEE-BASED]

News and archival service covering some 9000 sources from 118 countries in 22 languages, with access to more than 900 of the sources available on or before the date of publication.

There is an impressive range of types of source material covered: Newswires (e.g. Dow Jones, Reuters – the joint owners of the Service); Newspapers (e.g. *New York Times*, *Financial Times*); Television and radio transcripts (e.g. BBC, CNN); Magazines (e.g. *The Economist*, *BusinessWeek*); Pictures; Company reports; Historical market data; etc.

All this can be organized to provide 'knowledge at the point of decision': 'Our standards-based workflow products provide developers with tools and capabilities needed to embed content and functionality into applications such as portals, intranets or CRMs. Users get access to relevant and related information from all sources in their everyday applications. You get increased usage, productivity and better decision-making.'

- **Factiva Taxonomy** www.factiva.com/products/workflow. 'Whether just getting started with your taxonomy project, have design issues or are stalled, Factiva has a team of information professionals with the taxonomy skills, experience and products to help keep your knowledge solutions fresh and accurate'.

135 Find/SVP

www.findsvp.com [FEE-BASED]

Leading 'knowledge services company that offers a continuum of custom business intelligence, advisory, research and consulting solutions to address clients' critical business needs'. Although the thrust of the company's offerings is targeted at the business executive market, the wide mix of types and levels of service is well worth exploring as a good exemplar. These range from reference-type answering services, through in-depth research reports and current awareness, to full-blooded consultancy.

The Company's Quick Consulting Service uses more than 100 full-time research professionals and a network of 1700 technical and science experts who have access to a 'resource collection' containing: '3000 online databases and the Internet; 12,000 proprietary subject and company files; Current and back issues of 2000 periodicals; Hundreds of specialized directories and reference works'.

- **Information Advisor** Information TodayMonthly. $165.00 [Introductory]. www.informationadvisor.com. Newsletter providing information professionals with sources and strategies for conducting effective business research. Useful 'head-to-head analysis of the most popular information services'.
- **NERAC** www.nerac.com. US-based company which 'employs nearly 100 Information Specialists, all scientists, engineers or business professionals, to deliver customized search reports by Web account, email or print'. Specializes in science, technology, and intellectual property.

136 Google

http://labs.google.com

Currently, the world's leading web search engine.

The URL gives access to Google Labs which 'showcases a few of our favorite ideas that aren't quite ready for prime time. Your feedback can help us improve them. Please play with these prototypes and send your comments directly to the Googlers who developed them.' Includes Google Scholar which restricts searching to journal articles, abstracts and other scholarly literature.

Late 2004, Google announced a mass-digitization effort of documents held by libraries in Oxford, Harvard, Michigan, and Stanford universities together with those of the New York Public Library. This could transform the volume of – especially historical – material accessible online, and has led some to wonder whether physical libraries have a future. (They do.)

In a rapidly developing arena, perhaps also worth noting here are: the 'Sci/Tech' and 'Health' subsets of Google News – 4500 news sources updated continuously; Google Directory – with entries able to be viewed in Google PageRank order; and Google Catalog – 'applies Google's sophisticated search technology to thousands of scanned mail-order catalogs, from industrial adhesives to designer clothing and gourmet food'.

137 HighBeam Research

HighBeam Research Inc.

www.highbeam.com

'Runs an online research engine for individuals, filling the gap between free search engines and high-end research services ... Provides one place where you can access the free Web, online services to which you subscribe (both for-pay services and free services requiring registration) and our proprietary eLibrary archive of 32 million articles from 2800 respected publishers. We bundle this access with powerful tools to help you locate, organize and deliver your research – in short – to get you answers.'

Basic Membership is free and includes access to a number of research tools unavailable to casual visitors who do not sign up: 100, 000 'researchers' signed up within 20 days of the launch of the service in January 2004. Full Membership is $99.95 per annum [2005] allowing access to article full text and other benefits, including creating Research Groups, customized groupings of favourite sources.

This is a very interesting niche development, and should be pursued. The site is clearly organized, works well, and gives excellent background information. The company said at its launch: 'HighBeam wants to be the very best at providing customers with pretty good answers to serious business, educational, and personal questions. Our role is to serve the huge market that finds Google inadequate for its serious research needs and finds the high-end services overkill. With the launch of our new service, our biggest competitor will be Google and the perception that you can do serious research on it. Google is a wonderful service, but it is increasingly focused on facilitating ecommerce.'

- **Encyclopedia.com** www.encyclopedia.com. Free service 'providing users with more than 57,000 frequently updated articles from the Columbia Encyclopedia, Sixth Edition. Each article is enhanced with links to newspaper and magazine articles as well as pictures and maps'.

138 Infotrieve

www.infotrieve.com [FEE-BASED]

Well established company providing document delivery, table of contents, database searching, and other library-related services. The Table of Contents (TOC) Alert database is 'one of the largest aggregations of cross-disciplinary content, with specialization in science, technology and medicine. There are over 13,000 alert-able titles in the collection'.

Infotrieve provides a 'full-service' document delivery service, offering 'a single point of access to a wide variety of sources, tracking the statistics you need, and adapting the process to fit your workflow – we add value to the entire process. Our service is not limited to a particular collection or database, our 'Ends of the Earth' service will find your article anywhere in the world.'

Towards the end of August 2004, the company signed a content distribution agreement with John Wiley & Sons which they estimated 'will increase the total number of scientific, technical, and medical articles that it can deliver directly through publisher relationships to more than 18 million.' Subsequently, the company signed agreements enabling article distribution with a further ten leading STM publishers. 'As a result, Infotrieve can now electronically deliver articles from close to 5300 journal titles from over 130 publishers.'

Finally, early 2005, Infotrieve expanded its partnership with Ingenta enabling the company 'to provide full-text article searches via its discovery research portals, increasing the depth of discovery resources for Infotrieve customers and generating additional document delivery traffic for Ingenta-hosted publishers'.

- **Ingenta** www.ingentaconnect.com. Very successful document supply operation which now references over 6100 online, 28,500 fax and Ariel software delivered publications. However, in line with perceived changes in the marketplace, now is focusing more in development on tools and processes.
- **SciBASE** www.thescientificworld.com/DBProducts/sciBASE [FEE-BASED]. Access to 22 million citations and 13 million abstracts from over 35,000 scholarly journals and proceedings, thence to the full text of articles, supplied either by direct article delivery or through Infotrieve's document delivery service.

139 ISI Web of Knowledge

http://isiwebofknowledge.com [FEE-BASED]

'A unique research environment that connects researchers to a wealth of high quality content and powerful array of tools and technologies. ISI Web of Knowledge – one source for quickly and easily discovering essential research information ... A single session is maintained while searching, navigating, and browsing through the various content sources available in ISI Web of Knowledge.'

At the core are two long-standing offerings originally created by the Institute for Scientific Information. First, the citation indexes within Web of Science: 'Nearly 8500 authoritative, high impact journals covered by Science Citation Index Expanded, Social Sciences Citation Index, and Arts and Humanities Citation Index, plus two Chemistry editions: Index Chemicus, and Current Chemical Reactions'. Second, the CURRENT CONTENTS family of publications: 'Tables of contents from about 7600 journals and 2000 books; includes links to more than 4300 ISI-evaluated Web sites and over 400,000 searchable, full-text Web documents through Current Contents eSearch'.

This core has been supplemented by other Thomson ISI offerings – including now BIOLOGICAL ABSTRACTS and other BIOSIS offerings; by specialized content provided by various Partners (e.g. CAB ABSTRACTS, INSPEC, FOOD SCIENCE AND TECHNOLOGY ABSTRACTS); and by content from External Collections (e.g. PUBMED, AGICOLA, ARXIV.ORG). In addition, access is provided to a number of the wide range of tools produced by the ISI Research Services Group (www.isinet.com/rsg), exemplars of which are noted below.

- **Essential Science Indicators** www.isinet.com/rsg/esi [FEE-BASED]. 'Analyzes research performance of companies, institutions, countries, and journals; ranks top countries, journals, scientists, institutions and companies by field of research.'
- **High-Impact Papers** www.isinet.com/rsg/hip [FEE-BASED]. 'Database of the most influential papers in specific fields of the sciences and social sciences, 1981–2002, as reflected by citation counts tabulated from 1981 through 2003.'
- **In-Cites** http://in-cites.com/research/2005. Provides an interesting and useful range of 'behind-the-scenes' looks at the scientists, journals, institutions, nations and papers selected by ISI Essential Science Indicators. Updated weekly in SCI-BYTES – the summary of 'What's New in Research'.
- **ISI Proceedings** www.isinet.com/products/citation/proceedings. Abstracts of papers delivered at international conferences, symposia, seminars, colloquia, workshops, and conventions. Science and Technology edn indexes about 10,000 conferences a year; collectively gives access to some 2 million papers from 1990.
- **Journal Performance Indicators** www.isinet.com/rsg/jpi [FEE-BASED]. Rankings of over 10,000 of the world's most cited journals including *Citation Impact Statistics*: average citations per paper for all papers and for cited papers published in each journal.
- **Thomson Scientific Solutions** www.thomsonscientific.com. Excellent guide and gateway to the full range of services with news of developments.

140 LexisNexis

Reed Elsevier.

www.lexisnexis.com [FEE-BASED]

The flagship product most relevant to STM is labelled LexisNexis at nexis.com: the full text of over 4 billion documents in more than 35,000 individual publications or large groups of sources, subject indexed among 1200 topics in 36 categories, and delivering comprehensive coverage of all types of worldwide news and business sources, supplemented by in-depth coverage of legal sources.

But there are also a range of more specialized offerings, good examples being:

- LexisNexis environmental: Gathers 'content from sources not covered in competitive products which focus mainly on journals and newspapers, including: Conference papers and proceedings; Consumer and trade magazines; Newsletters; Law reviews; Environmental codes; Case law; Regulatory agency actions; Federal and state government reports'
- LexisNexis government periodicals index: 'A unique index to the full spectrum of US government periodicals to facilitate research'
- LexisNexis industry dossier: Provides 'in-depth information on more than 1000 US industries'
- LexisNexis patent and trademark solutions: Delivers 'copies of original US, EP, WO, and translated Japanese patent and trademark documents to your desktop'.

However, more recently the company have also developed a number of 'Integration Tools', examples being:

- LexisNexis Publisher: An 'advanced content management tool that offers an easy way to integrate crucial, comprehensive and on-point information to your website, portal, or intranet visitors ... With a single interface, LexisNexis Publisher allows you to tap into a full array of respected news sources'
- Total Search: Here 'a user can securely and confidentially search their firm's internal work product when searching any LexisNexis database or file. Users can then easily review and navigate between both internal and LexisNexis results'.

141 MadSci Network

Washington University

www.madsci.org

Free web-based Ask-A-Scientist service based at the University's Medical School in St Louis. 'Anyone may submit a question to be answered by people actively engaged in science education and research.' From 1995 to 2003 the network has received more than 200,000 questions, leading to an online archive of some 25,000 question/answer pairs, viewed during 2003 by more than 6 million people. More than 700 scientists are signed up to answer questions. Early in 2004 the service said that it did not have a critical mass of 'MadSci-entists' to answer questions in: anthropology, archaeology, entomology, meteorology, oceanography, palaeontology and psychology; but all other areas of STM seem well provided for.

When looked at 24 February 2005, the home page had been 'last modified February 30th, 1906'.

142 MetaLib

Ex Libris.

www.exlibrisgroup.com/metalib.htm

'Enables users to access their institution's e-collections, obtain relevant services, and work in a personalized environment. With MetaLib, an institution can manage today's hybrid information resources— be they local or remote— under one umbrella. Such resources include, for example, catalogs, reference databases, digital repositories, and subject-based Web gateways. Using the MetaLib portal, library patrons can conduct a MetaSearch™ across heterogeneous resources or link to the resources' native interface ... Incorporated in MetaLib is the award-winning SFX technology from Ex Libris. SFX, the OpenURL-compliant link server, provides users with context-sensitive linking to services that their institution has defined and customized on the basis of its e-collections and policies.'

143 National Information Services Corporation

www.nisc.com

'Publishes information products for access through BiblioLine, our Web search service, or on CD-ROM. Some of our abstract and index services are available in print. NISC's bibliographic and full-text databases cover a wide range of topics in the natural and social sciences, arts and humanities. Some titles provide comprehensive coverage of particular geographic regions, such as Latin America, Africa, South-East Asia or the Arctic and Antarctic.'

'NISC is dedicated to serving the public with top-quality products at reasonable rates. NISC is the consistent choice of thousands of users in a variety of research settings worldwide. Key to our success is an uncompromising zeal for quality throughout all phases of product production. NISC's search-and-retrieval software, ROMWright, brings related information from various sources together in a seamless interface – the results from years of listening carefully to what customers want. With a broad selection of titles, thorough data preparation, and one of the most advanced software technologies in the industry, NISC looks forward to becoming the 'household name' for both scholarly and lay users around the world.'

144 OCLC FirstSearch

OCLC Online Computer Library Center

www.oclc.org/firstsearch [FEE-BASED]

'Seamless electronic access to dozens of databases and more than 10 million full-text and full-image articles.' Covers a very wide range of databases, including versions of a number of major STM offerings: e.g. AGRICOLA; BIOLOGICAL ABSTRACTS; CHEMICAL ABSTRACTS; CSA; INSPEC; MEDLINE. These are underlaid by WORLDCAT, and its functionality can be extended to include other OCLC services such as NETLIBRARY and those below (or they can be subscribed to separately).

- **OCLC ArticleFirst** www.oclc.org/firstsearch/ordering/subscription [DESCRIPTION]. Index to the contents pages of some 15,000 journals: title list can be retrieved from this URL.
- **OCLC Electronic Collections Online** www.oclc.org/electroniccollections [DESCRIPTION]. Full text of more than 5000 titles in a wide range of subject areas, from over 70 publishers of academic and professional journals.

145 OpenCourseWare

Massachusetts Institute of Technology

http://ocw.mit.edu/OcwWeb/index.htm

'A free and open educational resource for faculty, students, and self-learners around the world. OCW supports MIT's mission to advance knowledge and education, and serve the world in the 21st century. It is true to MIT's values of excellence, innovation, and leadership.'

'MIT OCW: Is a publication of MIT course materials; Does not require any registration; Is not a degree-granting or certificate-granting activity; Does not provide access to MIT faculty.'

146 **OVID**
Wolters Kluwer.
www.ovid.com [FEE-BASED]
'An internationally recognized leader of electronic medical, scientific, and academic research information solutions. By providing a customizable suite of content, tools and services, Ovid supports the diverse research needs of its 13 million users worldwide – academic, medical, and corporate professionals and students seeking fast, accurate answers to important questions that help to fuel discoveries, explore topics, or research diagnoses.'

OVID is an especially strong aggregator in the health arena, being owned by WK Health, and 'used across the globe by librarians, researchers, clinicians and students from leading colleges and universities; medical schools; academic research libraries and library consortia; hospitals and healthcare systems; pharmaceutical and other corporate entities; HMOs; and clinical practices. In North America alone, Ovid is used by 93% of medical libraries, 97% of teaching hospitals, and 87% of US hospitals with more than 200 beds, as well as the top 30 pharmaceutical companies.'

- **SilverPlatter** www.silverplatter.com. Ovid and SilverPlatter became a single company in 2001. 'Future product innovations will focus on the Ovid platform, and customers who rely on SilverPlatter's ERL® and WebSPIRS® (versions 4.0 and higher) have our pledge to continue supporting their work.'

147 **PBS**
www.pbs.org
Companion websites for PBS television programs and specials, as well as original web content and real-time learning adventures. The Science and Nature Section is well structured; and topics such as 'Creatures', 'Earth and habitat', 'Technology and inventions' lead seamlessly to more detailed coverage. There is an efficient search mechanism; and PBS Teacher Source provides access to stories and lesson plans, with background resources.

A nice site.

- **Closer To Truth: Science, Meaning, and the Future** www.closertotruth.com. PBS program that 'brings together leading scientists, scholars and artists to debate latest discoveries and their impact on the human condition'.
- **NOVA** www.pbs.org/wgbh/nova. 'Seen in more than 100 countries, NOVA is the most watched science television series in the world and the most watched documentary series on PBS ... (It has) won every major television award, most of them many times over.'
- **SciTechDaily** www.scitechdaily.com. Intensive but well laid out coverage of breaking news together with excellent list of links to over 100 leading sci/tech publications and websites that are especially useful for keeping up-to-date.

148 **ProQuest Information and Learning**
www.il.proquest.com
ProQuest arose primarily from University Microfilms (then UMI), acquired by Bell & Howell in 1985, and then in 2001 becoming the ProQuest Company. In June 2004, the company was named one of the top 100 Fastest Growing Tech Companies by Business 2.0 Magazine.

'As a result of agreements with more than 9000 publishers worldwide, ProQuest Information and Learning provides access to information from periodicals, newspapers, out-of-print books, dissertations, and scholarly collections in various formats. Our archive includes more than 5.5 billion pages of information, spanning 500 years of scholarship, in formats that range from print to microform to digital.

'Disciplines covered include earth, life, physical, medical, and applied sciences. Coverage is front-to-back full-text, as well as full-page image and Text+Graphics to reproduce images and diagrams exactly as they appeared in the original publication.'

See also Online Dissertation Services and ProQuest Digital Dissertations.

- **ABI/INFORM** www.il.proquest.com/products/pt-product-ABI.shtml. The leading full-text, bibliographic database containing information on worldwide business and management issues including, for instance, for technology and engineering, environment, health care, information technology and communication, and so on.
- **Controlled Vocabulary of Subject Terms** Downloadable PDF, 498pp. www.umi.com/proquest/cv-controlled-vocabulary.shtml. Detailed regularly updated thesaurus-based (i.e. includes: broader terms; related terms; used for terms) listing of descriptors used for searching subject fields in ProQuest databases.
- **XanEdu** www.xanedu.com. Customized print and digital course packs.

149 **QuestionPoint**
OCLC Online Computer Library Center
www.oclc.org/questionpoint
Virtual reference service 'supported by global network of co-operating libraries worldwide, as well as an infrastructure of software tools and communications'. The member profile of each library indicates subject and language strengths, hours of service, number of questions can be responded to weekly, etc. Software then finds a best-match of institutions most likely to answer questions submitted. Users can submit questions by form or by talking to a librarian 'using interactive technology like chat, Voice over IP and video'.

150 **Reference Universe**
Paratext.
www.paratext.com/ru_intro.htm
'Reference Universe is the bridge between your library's printed reference collection and specialized online reference databases – a single search through more than 5000 authoritative subject encyclopedias, linked to each library's local holdings.'

'Highly recommended. All levels ... a rich source of information, providing unique access to print reference sources' (*Choice*)

'Paratext has taken its searching functionality to a new level of integration with local library catalogs ... Because each query against the library catalog occurs in real time, the holdings information is always current. Now that's pretty slick.' (*American Libraries*)

151 **Resource Discovery Network** [UK]
Joint Information Systems Committee
www.rdn.ac.uk
'A collaboration of over seventy educational and research organisations, including the Natural History Museum and the British Library. In contrast to search engines, the RDN gathers resources which are carefully selected, indexed and described by specialists in our partner institutions. You can be confident that your search results and browsing will connect you to Web sites relevant to learning, teaching and research.'

Four of the eight broad 'Hubs' of the RDN are germane to STM: BIOME; EEVL; Gesource; and PSIgate. Each has (competitively) developed its own identity with many services and products adding value to the basic directory.

Centrally, the Network has been an early adopter of newer technologies such as OAI, RSS, and SOAP. The pace of development has slackened recently: JISC, as many other similar funding bodies, is critically reviewing the long-term future of resource-intensive services such as the RDN within the evolving information universe. But at least for the foreseeable future the Network and its Hubs will continue to be major players in the e-learning landscape.

- **BUBL Information Service University of Strathclyde.** www.bubl.ac.uk. Good well established service providing resource descriptions categorized by DEWEY DECIMAL CLASSIFICATION. Not updated so frequently in the last year or so, as formerly. Now housed within the University's Centre for Digital Library Research.
- **The ePrints UK Project** www.rdn.ac.uk/projects/eprints-uk. Developing series of national, discipline-focused services through which the higher/further education community can access collective output of e-print papers available from compliant Open Archive repositories, especially in UK universities and colleges.
- **RDN Virtual Training Suite Institute for Learning & Research Technology.** www.vts.rdn.ac.uk. Generally excellent free online tutorials designed to help students, lecturers and researchers improve their internet information literacy and IT skills. UK Higher Education exemplars are referenced elsewhere; there is also a set for Further Education.

152 Science, Engineering and Technology Learning Information Portal: e-lip [UK]

LearnDirect and Science, Engineering, Manufacturing Technologies Alliance

www.elip.info

'Welcome to the one stop source of information and learning opportunities for the Science, Engineering and Manufacturing Technologies community in the UK! E-lip is brought to you by a partnership led by SEMTA and Learndirect, for information on the partnership please click on partners below.'

- **Science, Engineering, Manufacturing Technologies Alliance** www.semta.org.uk. UK Sector Skills Council covering 'some 100,000 companies employing 2,500,000 people in the UK.' Provide training and lifelong learning services; carries out sectoral research; oversees occupational standards and qualifications, etc. Extensive website.

153 ScienceDirect

Elsevier.

www.sciencedirect.com [FEE-BASED]

'Welcome to the world's largest electronic collection of science, technology and medicine full text and bibliographic information.'

Contains the full text with tables, figures and photographs of over 5 million articles from Elsevier and some other publishers' ranges of STM journals. Also gives access to encyclopedias and other reference works and some databases. Extensive search capabilities allow full text and bibliographic searching.

The service ContentsDirect (http://contentsdirect.elsevier.com) is a free e-mail alerting service which delivers directly to the desktop journal tables-of-contents and abstracts for Elsevier journals, and book tables-of-contents for forthcoming Elsevier books. 'All articles listed in the ContentsDirect email alerts, link directly to the article's abstract and full text in ScienceDirect. Please note that for full text you must either have an institute subscription to ScienceDirect or buy the article via Pay per View'.

- **Elsevier Science and Technology Books** http://books.elsevier.com. Useful subject-categorized gateway to full range of S & T titles under the imprints: Academic Press; Butterworth-Heinemann; Digital Press; Focal Press; Gulf Professional Publishing; Morgan Kaufmann; Newnes; Pergamon; Syngress – as well as Elsevier itself.
- **ScienceDirect Librarian Services Site** www.info.sciencedirect.com. Excellent guide and gateway to the full range of services with news of developments.
- **Scirus** www.scirus.com. Free of charge engine described as searching over 167 million science-specific web pages: not just scientific journals, but also unpublished research, university websites, corporate internet sites, conference agendas/minutes, discussion groups, etc.
- **SCOPUS** www.scopus.com. Launched late 2004 with 13,000 journals, 4000 publishers and 5 years of backfiles. 'We are aiming for the broadest content possible, with more journals than ISI and more types of document – conference proceedings, books, series and reference works.'

154 The Scout Report [USA]

Internet Scout Project and University of Wisconsin

http://scout.cs.wisc.edu/Reports/ScoutReport

'The Scout Report is the flagship publication of the Internet Scout Project. Published every Friday both on the web and by email, it provides a fast, convenient way to stay informed of valuable resources on the Internet. Our team of professional librarians and subject matter experts select, research, and annotate each resource.'

The premier US-based service within academia. It has very good evaluative descriptions of each new resource. The Archives 'is a searchable and browsable database to over nine years' worth of the Scout Report and subject-specific Scout Reports. It contains 16,969 critical annotations of carefully selected internet sites and mailing lists' (early 2005). Resource summaries are assigned detailed LIBRARY OF CONGRESS SUBJECT HEADINGS, supplementing 'keyword' and 'advanced' search facilities. However, it is not possible easily to browse among descriptions arranged in a subject hierarchy, and the search software seemed not the easiest to use.

Three enhanced subsets of the Report are currently available: NSDL SCOUT REPORT FOR PHYSICAL SCIENCES; NSDL SCOUT REPORT FOR LIFE SCIENCES; and NSDL SCOUT REPORT FOR MATH, ENGINEERING, AND TECHNOLOGY.

A number of the resources described in the database are now out-of-date or no longer accessible: as with other similar services, it is difficult to get the balance right between coverage of the new and updating of the old. Nevertheless, the Report is certainly well worth subscribing to (free of charge), and using.

155 Springer

www.springeronline.com

Good well structured and laid-out portal giving access to electronic and printed literature from Springer-Verlag plus a growing roster of other publishers, including Urban and Vogel, Steinkopff, Birkhäuser, and now Kluwer Academic. Free access is provided to search functions, tables of contents, as well as keyword and tables of contents alerts.

The online gateway SpringerLink now covers more than 1200 journals, with its content organized into a series of 'online libraries', each of which covers a separate subject category: Behavioural sciences; Biomedical and life sciences; Business and economics; Chemistry and material science; Computer science; Earth and environmental sciences; Engineering; Humanities, social sciences and law; Mathematics; Medicine; Physics and astronomy.

In a relatively new service Springer Open Choice, 'the author decides how he or she wants to be published in the leading and most respected journals in the scientific community. Springer still offers, and recommends, the traditional publishing model as a time-tested way of guaranteeing editorial quality and independence, but now also offers authors the option to pay to have their journal articles made available for free to anyone, anywhere in the world.'

156 STN International

www.stn-international.de [FEE-BASED]
A consortium of the AMERICAN CHEMICAL SOCIETY, JAPAN SCIENCE AND TECHNOLOGY AGENCY and FIZ Karlsruhe which provides access to a broad spectrum of fee-based bibliographic, factual and full-text databases in science and technology. Currently encompasses more than 220 electronic databases covering some 400 million documents with especial emphasis on patent-related information.

There are several interfaces available for the STN databases, including STN Express, a Windows-based, menu-driven software package that allows graphic structure input to assist the searcher; STN Easy, a forms-based interface; and STN on the Web, which combines STN command language functionalities with advanced web technology.

- **FIZ Karlsruhe** www.fiz-karlsruhe.de [FEE-BASED]. Operates STN in Europe. Also produces databases in energy, nuclear research and technology, crystallography, plastics, mathematics, computer science and physics – accessible via the internet, proprietary networks or in printed form.
- **NumeriGuide** http://info.cas.org/ONLINE/DBSS/numeriguidess.html. Information on all of the numeric properties available in each numeric file on STN, including: appropriate terminology for each property, property definition, files where the property may be searched, and default units for the property in each file.

157 T&F Informa

www.tfinforma.com
Company formed in May 2004 following the merger of Informa Group plc and Taylor & Francis Group plc and now publishing collectively more than 2000 journal and subscription products, and with a combined book backlist of over 35,000 volumes.

Some examples of environments offered by the two Groups at the time of merger are referenced below and elsewhere within TNW. Reviews of these sites reveals that Informa have been more active in this arena than Taylor & Francis – though with the T&F acquisition just prior to merger of CRC Press and Dekker during 2003 this was already no doubt set to change.

However, we must now anticipate development by the new conglomerate of the types of more sophisticated integrated environments typical of other large players in the marketplace such as those cited within this section from Elsevier, McGraw-Hill, Thomson, and Wiley.

- **CRCnetBASE** www.crcnetbase.com. URL leads to subject-focused searchable CRC full-text book collections: e.g. BIOTECHnetBASE, CivilENGINEERINGnewBASE, FOODnetBASE, NEUROSCIENCEnetBASE and so on. Generates PDF version of each book section retrieved.
- **Dekker.com** www.dekker.com. Rapid and relatively sophisticated access to the content of Dekker's books, journals and encyclopedias. Searching is free of charge; access to full-text charged. A pleasant service to use.
- **s@ra: Scholarly Articles Research Alerting** www.tandf.co.uk/sara. Free of charge e-mail alerting service of forthcoming articles, covering 950 journals published by the company.
- **Taylor & Francis eBookstore** www.ebookstore.tandf.co.uk. Includes imprints from Brunner-Routledge, Europa Publications, Garland, Spon Press, Psychology Press and Routledge as well as T&F itself. Covers over 7000 titles with a Library subscription package available.

158 Thomson Learning

www.thomson.com/learning [FEE-BASED]
One of the four Thomson Market Groups which 'is among the world's largest providers of tailored learning solutions'.

'In the academic marketplace, we serve secondary, post-secondary and graduate-level students, teachers, and learning institutions in both traditional and distance learning environments. In the professional and corporate training marketplaces, we offer adult education and certification materials for corporations, training centers and individuals.'

'For all of our customers, we help them find a total learning solution by offering courseware, test preparation, testing, assessment, and certification. Our products and services are sold throughout the world, through direct channels and via a worldwide network of distributors.'

- **Book Review Index Online Plus** Thomson Gale. www.galegroup.com [DESCRIPTION]. Product developed from the well established print and online Book Review Index which now includes more than 5 million review citations; it also includes more than 634,000 full-text reviews from Gale's InfoTrac family of products.
- **InfoTrac** http://infotrac.thomsonlearning.com [FEE-BASED]. 'Offers over 15 million full-text articles from over 5000 scholarly and popular periodicals. Articles cover a broad spectrum of disciplines and topics – ideal for every type of researcher.' Access is available 24/7 on any computer with internet access.
- **Thomson Delmar Learning** www.delmarlearning.com. Books, software, videos and online training materials focussed on the career education, healthcare, technology and trades markets.
- **Thomson Gale** www.galegroup.com/sitemap.htm. The well established provider of a range of reference and full-text products and services via libraries. The Site Map at the website provides access to details of each type of offering, many examples of which are referenced elsewhere in TNW.

159 The Virtual Reference Desk

www.vrd.org
'Digital reference, or 'AskA', services are Internet-based question-and-answer services that connect users with experts and subject expertise. Digital reference services use the Internet to connect people with people who can answer questions and support the development of skills.' The *VRD Network* supplements AskA services 'by accepting out-of-scope and overflow questions. When a subject specific service receives questions which are out of its stated scope area, it can forward those questions to the VRD Network for assistance.' Listed are about two dozen Network participants; but more useful is the extensive subject classified list of AskA services – 'a database of high-quality 'AskA' services designed to link students, teachers, parents and other K-12 community members with experts on the Internet' – and many with intriguing titles such as Ask a Hurricane Hunter (53rd Weather Reconnaissance Squadron, US Air Force Reserve), Ask Dr. SOHO (NASA's Solar and Heliospheric Observatory), Go Ask Alice! (Columbia University's Health Education Program), The Wild Ones (The Wildlife Preservation Trust International).

160 Wikipedia: The free encyclopedia

Wikimedia Foundation.
http://en.wikipedia.org
A brilliant free content encyclopedia being written collaboratively by contributors from around the world. The site is a wiki, which means that anyone can edit articles, simply by clicking on the edit link that appears at the top of each page ...

'Wikipedia began on January 15, 2001 by founders Jimmy Wales, Larry Sanger, and a few enthusiastic English-language collaborators. Four years later, as of December 2004, there were 13,000 active contributors working on over 1,300,000 articles in more than 100 languages. As of today [25 February 2005], there are 481,332 articles in English; every day hundreds of thousands of visitors from around the world make tens of thousands of edits and create thousands of new articles.'

161 **Wiley InterScience**
www3.interscience.wiley.com [FEE-BASED]
Web-based access to 'over 1000 journals, major reference works, online books, current protocols laboratory manuals, and databases as well as a suite of professional and management resources. The site was launched in 1997 and currently caters to over 12 million users in 87 countries'. There are a wide range of individual, institutional and society electronic licensing options plus the opportunity of pay-per-view.

For the online reference works, they offer the 'One Time Purchase Option': 'Take advantage of one-time funding and non-subscription funds to pay for permanent electronic access to titles and content your users need. The one-time purchase option includes archival access. This is consistent with traditional sources of funding for the print versions of these products.' Alternatively, an Annual Subscription License: 'Provides access to the active version of a reference work, plus to any content added or updated during the term of the subscription. The licensee must continue to subscribe each year in order to retain access to any of the content. Archival access will no longer be offered as a feature of the annual subscription license option.'

For the individual researcher, Wiley offers Roaming Access: 'Frees researchers from the confines of their institution's IP address range. Activated via a link in My Profile, it enables remote password access to full-text licensed content from any laptop or web-enabled computer in the world. Converting the global office into a working reality, Roaming Access is available exclusively to Registered Users affiliated with an Enhanced Access License Customer.'

These are just two examples of the very good range of facilities available within this extensive portal.

162 **WilsonWeb**
H W Wilson.
www.hwwilson.com [FEE-BASED]
Leading provider of traditionally library-based indexing and abstracting services, especially targeting the less specialist college, school and public library markets. But have now developed a range of valuable full-text databases, following a major overhaul in 2002, including the integration of SFX linking technology, OPAC links, and multifile searching.

A goodly number of Wilson databases are referenced elsewhere in TNW.

- **Book Review Digest Plus** www.hwwilson.com/databases/brdig.htm. Indexes and provides excerpts of reviews of current English-language fiction and non-fiction. In 2003 expanded its scope (from its former base of 109 periodicals) with entries drawn from thousands of periodicals covered by other WilsonWeb databases.

163 **World Book Online Reference Center**
World Book Inc.
www.worldbookonline.com [FEE-BASED]
'Encyclopedic database of more than 25,400 articles ... 248,000 definitions of words ... and a media database of 9300 audios, 11,000 illustrations including 1480 maps, 128 panoramic photographs, and 115 videos and animations.'

Based on the highly recommended 22 volume *World Book Encyclopedia*. Supporting online services include Parent Resource Center, School and Library Resource Center, and Student Resource Center.

The company produces a wide variety of well reviewed reference works, primarily aimed at the school educational marketplace, and examples of which are given below.

- **Biographical encyclopedia of scientists 2003** $339.00. 8 v. More than 1300 alphabetically arranged biographies are combined with over 700 photographs and illustrations.
- **Science Year in Review** Annual. $34.99 [2003]. Summary of the important research, discoveries, and breakthroughs during the year. *American Reference Books Annual* called the Volume 'an excellent addition to school and public libraries'.
- **World Book Research Libraries** Collection of more than 5000 complete books and some 175,000 documents across the whole of recorded knowledge, including from leading scientists: Darwin, Einstein, Newton, etc.

Discovering print & electronic resources

164 **About.com**
http://azlist.about.com/a.htm
'Each site in our unique network is run by a professional Guide who is carefully screened and trained by About. Guides build a comprehensive environment around each of their specific topics, including the best new content, relevant links, How-to's, Forums, and answers to just about any question.'

This is the well known service whose commercially intensive features can be intrusive, at least for some users. However, there are pleasant inviting page structures with good use of graphics and efficient search and navigation features. The subject entries on the Site A–Z clearly are 'consumer' rather than 'academically' driven; but About is worth remembering when access is needed to relatively less scholarly disciplines and material.

165 **Academic360.com**
Internet Employment Linkage, Inc.
www.academic360.com
'A meta-collection of Internet resources that have been gathered for the academic job hunter. It includes links to faculty, staff, and administrative announcements and is not restricted to teaching positions.' Useful.

166 **All that JAS: Journal Abbreviation Sources**
G. McKiernan, comp.; Iowa State University
www.public.iastate.edu/%7ECYBERSTACKS/JAS.htm
'Categorized registry of Web resources that list or provide access to the full title of journal abbreviations or other types of abbreviated publication titles (e.g., conference proceedings titles). Selected OPACs that offer abbreviated title searching have also been included. In addition ... Includes select lists and directories that provide access to the unabbreviated titles of serial publications.'

Good, regularly updated, and valuable compilation produced by University's Associate Professor and Science and Technology Librarian and Bibliographer.

- **LiveRef(sm): A Registry of Real-Time Digital Reference Services G. McKiernan, comp.** www.public.iastate.edu/~CYBERSTACKS/LiveRef.htm. Covers chat software, live interactive communications utilities, call centre management software, customer interaction management software, web contact centre software, bulletin board services, interactive customer assistance system, etc. Updated 2003.

- **Web Feeds from Electronic Journals** www.public.iastate.edu/~CYBERSTACKS/eFeeds.htm. Developing categorized registry of electronic journals that offer RSS/XML, Atom, or other web feeds. Publisher-specific and vendor web feeds are categorized in a separate category. Updated January 2005.

167 Alternative Press Index

Alternative Press Center, Quarterly. $400.00 [2005]. ISSN 0002662X.
www.altpress.org/api.html [DESCRIPTION]
'Subject index to over 250 alternative, radical and left periodicals, newspapers and magazines. Librarians consider the API to be the most comprehensive and up-to-date guide to alternative sources of information available today.' Contains nicely annotated list of sources plus links to other sources of 'alternative' material. Naturally stronger in social sciences and arts and humanities sources; but reasonable number of STM-related serials.
Available online: see website.

168 Bibliographic guide to conference publications

G.K. Hall, Annual. 2 v., $660.00 [2002]. ISBN 0783897987.
'Lists recent publications catalogued during the past year by The Research Libraries of the New York Public Library and the Library of Congress ... Contains proceedings, reports, and summaries of conferences, meetings, and symposia in all fields, as well as collections or partial collections of papers presented at conferences. Conference publications from all countries and in all languages are represented.'

169 China National Knowledge Infrastructure

East View Online Services.
http://online.eastview.com/cnki_login/index.jsp [FEE-BASED]
Gateway to a range of products and services.

- **China Scientific Book Services** Huayu Nature Book Trade Co. Ltd.. www.hceis.com. Commercial book supply service. Useful subject classified browsing of descriptions of titles.

170 Directory of Open Access Journals

Lund University
www.doaj.org
Compilation which covers 'free, full text, quality controlled scientific and scholarly journals': 1463 entries February 2005. Quite detailed subject browse structure: for instance, within Technology and Engineering there was 'Chemical Technology' (2 journals); 'Construction' (4); 'Materials' (4) and other small sub-categories (but with 'Computer Science' having 45 journals listed). The service is co-funded by the Open Society Institute and SPARC and is hosted at the University's Libraries Head Office.

'Open access journals' are defined as 'journals that use a funding model that does not charge readers or their institutions for access.'

- **Open Access News: News from the open access movement** P. Suber, comp. www.earlham.edu/~peters/fos/fosblog.html. 'The main purpose of this blog is to gather and disseminate news about the open-access movement, and to harness the energy and knowledge of a wide group of contributors in doing so ... Contributors to this blog speak as individuals ...'
- **Washington DC Principles for Free Access to Science** www.dcprinciples.org. 48 not-for-profit publishers and learned societies announced their partial commitment to open access.

171 Discovery.com

Discovery Communications Inc.
www.discovery.com
'Popular' Site, linked to the various Discovery TV Channels, with wide range of browsable content: e.g. 'Mission to Mars'; 'Dinosaurs on Parade'; 'Living World: What makes it tick?' were samples on the Science Channel in 2004. There is also Animal Planet and Discovery Health. References to lots of STM Resources tucked away; but there are generally more efficient, less commercialized (though for some less enjoyable) ways of getting at those than here.

172 ECHO: Exploring and Collecting History Online – Science, Technology, and Industry

George Mason University
http://echo.gmu.edu
'More than ninety percent of all scientists who have ever lived are alive today. It is the goal of ECHO to record their stories and the ever-expanding, ever-accelerating history of recent science and technology using a contemporary technology well suited to such a daunting yet critical task: the Internet.'

Attractive, engaging, well laid out resource. The Virtual Center incorporates the WWW Virtual Library for the History of Science, Technology and Medicine established in 1994. Maintained by the University's Center for History and the New Media.

173 EconLit

American Economic Association
www.econlit.org/accesslist.html [FEE-BASED]
As would be expected, there is a strong economic focus. But the subject categories include: Health, education and welfare; Economic development, technological change, and growth; Agricultural and natural resource economics.

Covers books, working papers and dissertations, as well as journal articles. The URL lists the companies which provide library and institutional subscriptions to EconLit, where it is noted that all offer the capability of linking its records to full-text electronic articles.

174 Fulltext Sources Online: For periodicals, newspapers, newsletters, newswires and TV/radio transcripts

Information Today, 2003/2004, Biannual. $219.50. ISBN 1573871826.
www.fso-online.com
Well established directory of periodicals accessible online in full text through about two dozen aggregators, and now listing over 22,000 newspapers, journals, magazines, newsletters, newswires, and transcripts. Each issue is complete and replaces previous issues. The aggregators whose products are included are a good checklist of leading players in this marketplace: Dialog, EBSCOhost, Eureka, Europresse, Factiva, FirstSearch, Fpinfomart, GBI, Genios, HeinOnline, InfoTrac, InSite, Lexis, NewsBank, Newscan, NewsLibrary, Nexis, NNI, Ovid, Pressed, Profound, ProQuest, Quicklaw, STN, Telecom21, Westlaw, and WilsonWeb – the majority of which are referenced elsewhere in this text.

Non-subscribers can search for free – a useful service in itself; but one has to be a registered user to display the full record resulting from a search. That full record includes for each title data on the aggregators and their specific databases which contain the publication online in full text, with: dates of coverage; ISSN, geographic location, language, and URL of the publication; notations for the frequency and lag times of the title appearing online; and whether or not coverage is 'Selected'.

An excellent service.

175 **Gale Directory of Databases**
Thomson Gale, 2004, Biannual. $515.00. ISBN 0787669040.
www.galegroup.com [FEE-BASED]
The premier established tool profiling thousands of databases available worldwide in a variety of formats. Entries include producer name and contact information, description, cost and more. Each edition is comprised of two volumes: v. 1. Online Databases; v. 2. CD-ROM, Diskette, Magnetic Tape, Handheld and Batch Access Database Products. Good descriptions and comprehensive indexes.
Also available online through DIALOG.

176 **Genamics JournalSeek**
Genamics/Openly Informatics.
www.journalseek.net
'The largest completely categorized database of freely available journal information available on the internet. The database presently contains 75,602 titles. Journal information includes the description (aims and scope), journal abbreviation, journal homepage link, subject category and ISSN. Searching this information allows the rapid identification of potential journals to publish your research in, as well as allowing you to find new journals of interest to your field. The database does not contain articles or abstracts.'

Very useful compilation, easy and efficient to use, with a good detailed subject categorization – though as so often in such compilations updating can be a problem.

Of particular interest here is the List of Publishers, each publisher name provided with a link to its website, and with the entries classified into 'Minor' (1–2 titles), 'Small' (3–29), 'Medium' (30–100) and 'Large' (more than 100 journals: 20 entries, with Elsevier Science scoring at the time of sampling 2036 titles, Kluwer Academic Publishers + Springer 1438, Taylor & Francis Group 1006, Blackwell's 792). The categorizations do not necessarily take account of the extensive ownership of imprints by such as Reed Elsevier (for instance, some of the other entries in the 'top 20' being owned by that conglomerate). Nevertheless, the database provides a valuable snapshot of the current state of the STM journal publishing market, and of that of journal publishing more generally.

- **Books and Periodicals Online** Library Technology Alliance Ltd. http://booksandperiodicals.com [DESCRIPTION]. Directory of sources available online: Alphabetical and keyword look up of over 146,000 titles; web links to over 4500 full text sources; Over 57,120 full text sources identified; Journals also included when only available in abstracts or citations.
- **New Jour** http://gort.ucsd.edu/newjour. Very useful listing of new e-journals and e-newsletters. Regularly updated. Archival searching (15,541 titles, 28 February 2005).

177 **GreyNet: Grey Literature Network Service**
TextRelease.
www.greynet.org
Good entrée to the grey literature field. The Network organizes the International Conference Series on Grey Literature, creates and maintains the list of web-based resources, and oversees a moderated Listserv. GreySource is a subject classified list of resources, and GreyText an in-house archive of documents, on grey literature. The term 'grey literature' was defined in 1997 at a Luxembourg Convention as 'information produced on all levels of government, academics, business and industry in electronic and print formats not controlled by commercial publishing'.

- **SIGLE** Multidisciplinary database, approximately 1/3 pure sciences, 1/3 technology, 1/3 economics, social sciences and humanities. Circa 900,000 records, 2004. Accessible via a range of Hosts.
- **Information sources in grey literature** P. Auger 4th edn, K G Saur, 1998, 177pp. €88.00. ISBN 3598244274. 'Fully revised to reflect all recent developments and expanded to include substantial amounts of new material, with sections on the Internet and the European Union.'
- **Managing Access to Grey Literature Collections: MAGiC** Cranfield University. www.magic.ac.uk/links/links1.html. Project that aimed to establish a new collaborative system for the collection, storage and utilization of engineering grey literature. Website gives still useful annotated list of related links.

178 **A guide to field guides**
D. Schmidt Libraries Unlimited, 1999, 304pp. $68.50. ISBN 1563087073.
www.library.uiuc.edu/bix/fieldguides/main.htm [COMPANION]
'Focusing on the North American continent, this book, the first of its kind, identifies and describes major field guides in all scientific subject areas (from plants, animals, and insects to astronomy and weather, geology and fossils, and man-made objects). Organized by topic, it offers complete bibliographic information and descriptions of more than 1300 field guides.' The companion website extends the international coverage of the print volume.

179 **Guide to reference books**
R. Balay, ed. 11th edn, American Library Association, 1996, 2040pp. $275.00. ISBN 0838906699.
www.haverford.edu/library/grb [DESCRIPTION]
The premier US-based guide, providing evaluative descriptions of 15,875 English- and foreign-language reference works organized within five major parts: general reference; humanities; social and behavioural sciences, history and area studies; science, technology, and medicine. The 12th edition – to be called *Guide to Reference Sources* to denote its format neutrality – is in preparation under the general editorship of Robert Kieft.

180 **Handbooks and tables in science and technology**
R.H. Powell 3rd ed, Oryx Press, 1994, 368pp. ISBN 0897745345.
A bibliography of older handbooks and other useful printed data sources in science, technology and medicine. Handbooks can be located by subject keyword and by author or editor. Entries give bibliographic information and a short annotation.
'Mr Powell's book will unlock many valuable sources of information lining the shelves of the average science reference collection ... Remarkably comprehensive and easy-to-use reference tool. It is also a valuable aid to collection development ... highly recommended.' (*Medical Reference Services Quarterly*)

181 **Index to Theses** [UK]
Expert Information, Quarterly. £400.00 (print + online). ISSN 09572724.
www.theses.com [FEE-BASED]
Bibliographic details of all theses produced by British and Irish universities, the earliest dated 1716. Each title is classified into one of over 300 subdivisions of eleven main subject areas. Author and subject indexes are also provided. The Index only includes abstracts; but full text of most

created since the early 1980s is available from the British Library's service.

- **British Thesis Service** British Library. www.bl.uk/britishthesis [FEE-BASED]. Access to the full text of more than 170,000 doctoral theses, mainly from the 1970s to the present day. Almost all UK universities make their theses available through the Service.

182 **Infomine**
University of California.
infomine.ucr.edu
Virtual library of internet resources designed for staff and students at university level. INFOMINE celebrated its tenth anniversary in 2004.

It was 'one of the first Web resources of any type offered by a Library. It was also one of the first Web-based, academic virtual libraries as well as one of the first to develop a system combining the advantages of the hypertext and multi-media capabilities of the Web with those of the organizational and retrieval functions of a database manager. We now include focused, automatic Internet crawling as well as automatic text extraction and metadata creation functions to assist our experts in content creation and users in searching. Many of INFOMINE's important features and services ... remain unique among Internet resource collections.'

The service provides access to records of resources such as databases, electronic journals, electronic books, bulletin boards, mailing lists, online library card catalogues, articles, directories of researchers, etc. Currently contains over 100,000 links (26,000 librarian created links and 75,000 plus robot/crawler created links).

183 **Information sources in science and technology**
C.D. Hurt 3rd edn, Libraries Unlimited, 1998, 346pp. $45.00. ISBN 1563085283.
'Introduces readers to the breadth of information sources in the fields of science and technology as well as to their applications.'
Series: Library and Information Science Texts.
'An extremely useful source for academic libraries and researchers, especially in choosing current resources in science and technology, including Internet resources.' (*Choice*)
'Would make an excellent textbook for a library school ... Or a good collection development guide for an academic science and engineering library ... A good compact guide to the current literature of science and engineering.' (*E-STREAMS*)

184 **International Bibliography of the Social Sciences**
www.lse.ac.uk/collections/IBSS [FEE-BASED]
Worth considering for STM queries that have more of a social science bias. The Subject Coverage section of the lists the relevant journals covered for: 'Agriculture'; 'Environment'; 'Health'; 'Psychology'; 'Science and Technology; and 'Statistics'. Note that 'all works included in the IBSS print volumes are analytical or theoretical, and make use of new ideas or new materials. Works such as textbooks, newspapers and news magazines are excluded, as are previously published works.'

185 **International government information and country information: a subject guide**
A.M. Morrison and B.J. Mann Greenwood Press, 2004, 312pp. $65.00. ISBN 1573564796.
'This is the only authoritative guide that offers a subject approach to the plentiful resources provided by international government organizations, national governments, and other foreign information sources. Although many of the resources described in this book are freely available on the Internet, finding or using them can be difficult.'

186 **The Internet Public Library**
www.ipl.org
Clearly organized and displayed descriptions of web-based resources, usefully separating out from other resources: newspapers; magazines, journals, E-zines, etc.; associations on the net. Good quite detailed subject categorization, including – e.g. within 'Science and Technology' – the categories 'Controversial', 'Science and Technology News' and 'Science and Technology Libraries' alongside the subject disciplines. Limited site search facilities.

Also, various other facilities such as a nice series of Pathfinders: 'Home-grown guides written by IPL staff which are intended to help you get started doing research on a particular topic, both online and at your local library': e.g. 'Endangered Species'; 'Medical Sources and Information'; and Ask a Question – with hundreds of the most popular questions and answers listed on the Frequently-Asked Reference Questions pages.

The site is 'a public service organization and a learning/teaching environment at the University of Michigan School of Information' – but they 'are actively seeking support, either in the form of funding, equipment, or help'.

187 **Japan Publications Guide Service: JPGSonline**
Japan Publications Guide Service.
http://jpgsonline.com
'Collects and catalogs information on currently available English books, periodicals, other publications and information products that are published in, on, or for Japan and East/Southeast Asia.'

188 **Librarians' Index to the Internet**
University of California, Berkeley
http://lii.org
Mission is 'to provide a well organized point of access for reliable, trustworthy, librarian-selected Internet resources, serving California, the nation, and the world'. LII is a 'searchable, annotated subject directory of more than 12,000 Internet resources selected and evaluated by librarians for their usefulness to users of public libraries'.

Very good, browsable collection for relatively high-level non-technical queries – with a nice feature: 'last updated on [Date]': 'An active weeding program keeps us current – while sites change and die all the time, LII almost never has more than 100 'dead' sites.'

The service – although still hosted at Berkeley – is 'funded through the (annual) Library Services and Technology Act, with additional funding from the Washington State Library, California Digital Library, and other sources'.

One can 'subscribe for free to LII New This Week, a weekly mailing of the most recent resources added to the Librarians' Index to the Internet. We have over 17,000 subscribers in 85 countries.'

- **Library Servers via WWW** **T. Dowling, comp.** http://sunsite3.berkeley.edu/Libweb. 'Updated daily at midnight, Pacific Time. Libweb currently lists over 7200 pages from libraries in over 125 countries.' Links to related sites, as well.

189 **Looksmart**

http://search.looksmart.com

Successful commercial service whose services 'reach Internet users worldwide through top portals, ISPs, and search services including Lycos, InfoSpace, CNET, and LookSmart.com'. There is good financial and operational information about the company within the About Us section of the website.

The core of the service is in three sections:

- Directory: Hand-picked websites organized into categories
- Web: Search engine referencing 1.2 billion web pages
- Articles: 5.5 million articles from over 900 publications.

The last is a non-specialist, general internet article abstract provider, part technical, part current awareness. It offers free searching, and its interface is very clearly laid-out, with excellent display features. And although the coverage is not extensive, it has a certain serendipitous quality, leading one to worthwhile material from unexpected sources – partly, of course, because of its relatively limited coverage.

A nice commercial service.

- **MagPortal** http://magportal.com. Browse or keyword search linking to the full text of magazine articles. Good for rapidly getting up-to-date introductions to a new topic.

190 **MarketResearch.com**

www.marketresearch.com

'Aggregator of global business intelligence representing the most comprehensive collection of published market research available on-demand.'

Very good coverage, including of Life Sciences (e.g. 24 Reports for 'Alternative and Complementary Medicine'; 16 for 'Enzymes') and Heavy Industry (e.g. 129 Reports for 'Agricultural Chemicals'; 194 for 'Natural Gas'). Easy search and browsing.

An excellent service with searching for reports freely available and normally leading to brief introductory descriptions of each (thereafter fee-based). There is also a free email alert service of new market research reports in each industry.

- **Market Research on the Web: MROW** IRN Research. www.marketresearchontheweb.com. Links to market data, company lists, statistics, and industry news on over 3000 regularly evaluated UK and European sites, including trade associations, professional bodies, trade journals, research companies, consultants, industry sites and portals.
- **Mindbranch** www.mindbranch.com. 'One-stop-shop for syndicated and custom industry research from 350 independent research firms'.
- **ResearchandMarkets** www.researchandmarkets.com. 'The world's largest market research resource – 373,202 live reports' (27 February 2005).

191 **MERLOT: Multimedia Educational Resource for Learning and Online Teaching**

www.merlot.org

Consortium of higher education institutions which collaboratively provide peer-reviewed links to online learning materials. At least two higher education faculty members conduct each review, the reviews being performed against evaluation standards in three dimensions: Quality of Content, Potential Effectiveness as a Teaching Tool, and Ease of Use. In addition, each resource is scored on a 1–5 scale, 5 stars being the highest. A review must average three stars (or textual equivalent) to be posted to the MERLOT site.

Mid-2004, there were almost 4500 science and technology entries (defined to include health science); over 700 for mathematics and statistics.

- **Canada's SchoolNet** www.schoolnet.ca/home/e. Access to details of over 7000 Learning Resources, as well as @SchoolNet Today – a daily information news service on the world of e-learning.

192 **Moving Image Gateway**

British Universities Film and Video Council

www.bufvc.ac.uk/gateway

'New service that collects together websites that relate to moving images and sound and their use in higher and further education. The sites are classified by academic discipline, some forty subjects from Agriculture to Women's Studies, collected within the four main categories of Arts and Humanities, Bio-Medical, Social Sciences and Science and Technology.'

- **Researcher's Guide Online** www.bufvc.ac.uk/databases/rgo.html. Entries for some 550 film, television, radio and related documentation collections in UK/Ireland. Includes national/regional archives, stockshot libraries/collections held by local authorities, museums, further/higher education, companies, individuals.

193 **National Grid for Learning** [UK]

www.ngfl.gov.uk

Gateway to educational resources on the internet – a 'network of selected links to websites that offer high quality content and information'. Primarily targets the UK schools market. Good, concise descriptions. Full A–Z site listing plus fortnightly series of guides to specific topics, often tied into national/international events: e.g. 'The NGfL guide to World Aids Day 2003'; 'The NGfL guide to European Science and Technology Week'.

- **National Learning Network** www.nln.ac.uk. National partnership programme set-up in 1999 designed to increase the uptake of information learning technology across the learning and skills sector in England. Currently undergoing major re-evaluation: instructive to review the website, e.g. the FAQs.
- **Qualifications and Curriculum Authority** www.qca.org.uk. UK non-departmental body that maintains and develops the national curriculum and associated assessments, tests and examination; accredits and monitors qualifications in colleges and at work. Useful descriptive information and links in the 'Subjects' pages.

194 **National Science Digital Library**

National Science Foundation

www.nsdl.org

Important educational resource for science, technology, engineering and mathematics at all levels funded by the US NATIONAL SCIENCE FOUNDATION. Aims to provide descriptions of and access to exemplary resource collections. The database can be searched or browsed, and the Library offers a range of ancillary services.

NDSL Portals 'provide specialized views of selected NSDL resources organized around the needs of specific audiences. These audiences may be defined by grade level, discipline, resource or data type, or some other designation ... (They) are developed and managed in partnership with organizations and institutions that have a history and expertise in serving the portal's target audience'.

- **Cornell Theory Center Math and Science Gateway** www.tc.cornell.edu/Edu/MathSciGateway. Award-winning US Gateway provides links to resources for educators and students in grades 9–12. Descriptions of useful websites on many topics within science, technology and medicine.

195 **NTIS** [USA]
National Technical Information Service
www.ntis.gov
'The largest central resource for government-funded scientific, technical, engineering, and business related information available today. Here you will find information on more than 600,000 information products covering over 350 subject areas from over 200 federal agencies.'

There is a concise Site Index, useful entrées therein including:

Datafiles 'NTIS offers access to a number of important US Government Databases. These databases include all types of information including: Bibliographic records of scientific, technical, and business information; Statistical databases; Databases developed from Government collected information'

Health 'NTIS is the central information source for more than 20,000 health and safety-related publications produced by US Government agencies since 1990.'

What's New Includes list of the 'Hot Topics Archives': bibliographies of NTIS products about subjects in the news.

- **Business and International Trade Online Bookstore** . http://tradecenter.ntis.gov. Collection of more than 20,000 titles specifically chosen with the business community in mind. Publications come from commercial publishers, non-profit organizations, and government organizations; it is possible to search each publisher's file separately.
- **Federal Research in Progress** http://grc.ntis.gov/fedrip.htm. Current federally funded projects in physical sciences, engineering, life sciences. Contributions from 12 US Agencies including Departments of Agriculture and Energy, EPA, NIH, NASA, NIST, NRC, NSF, USGS.
- **GOV.Research_Center: GRC** http://grc.ntis.gov. 'Partnership between NTIS and National Information Services Corporation to provide a single access point to valuable government information. This joint venture combines NISC's award winning technology and NTIS's valuable content'.

196 **OAIster**
University of Michigan
http://oaister.umdl.umich.edu/o/oaister
'Project of the University of Michigan Digital Library Production Services, originally funded through a Mellon grant ... Our goal is to create a collection of freely available, difficult-to-access, academically-oriented digital resources that are easily searchable by anyone.' Digital Resources are defined as including items such as: electronic books; online journals; audio files; images; movies. The service uses the University of Illinois's Metadata Harvester (http://uiliboai.sourceforge.net).

Early April 2005, the service offered access to 5,272,686 records from 458 institutions. Examples of STM-related collections come from: Advanced Knowledge Technologies Eprints Archive; arXiv.org Eprint Archive; BioMed Central; CERN Document Server; Chemical Preprint Server; Digital Library for Earth System Education, but also – more importantly – from several hundred individual institutions (such as the University of Tasmania ePrints Repository.

Good – and elegant – search and display system (though response time can be slow). An important service.

- **SAIL-eprints** http://eprints.bo.cnr.it. Collects metadata from OAI (Open Archives Initiative) data repositories all over the world publishing materials in a wide range of science and technology. List of sites with dates of last harvesting, numbers of records and sets.

197 **The Online Books Page**
J.M. Ockerbloom, ed.; University of Pennsylvania
http://onlinebooks.library.upenn.edu
Regularly updated listing of over 20,000 free books on the web plus 'News', 'Features', 'Archives', 'The Inside Story': a very useful facility.

198 **Online Dissertation Services** [USA]
ProQuest.
www.umi.com/hp/Products/Dissertations.html [FEE-BASED]
Clicking on the link 'Dissertation Services' leads to a useful summary page headed UMI Dissertation Services: 'Your map to UMI's many dissertation services and products. UMI publishes and archives dissertations and theses; sells copies on demand; and maintains the definitive bibliographic record for over 1.4 million doctoral dissertations and master's theses.' The page provides help for those 'preparing', 'finding', 'ordering', and 'using' dissertations and theses. In addition, there are links to: 'Digital Dissertations FAQ'; 'Dissertation Lore', and 'Related Web Sites', as well as to the service below and ProQuest Digital Dissertations. A really helpful site.

- **Dissertation Express** http://tls.il.proquest.com/hp/Products/DisExpress.html. 'Students, faculty, staff and researchers can now order their own unbound copies of dissertations and theses with express delivery to their home, school or office. Select from over one million titles available from UMI.' There is also a 'Library' service.

199 **ProQuest Dissertations & Theses** [USA]
ProQuest.
wwwlib.umi.com/dissertations
'Welcome to ProQuest Digital Dissertations! As a visitor, you will be able to freely access the most current two years of citations and abstracts in the Dissertation Abstracts database. To search the entire database of more than 1.6 million titles, you will need to connect from a subscription institution.'

One of ProQuest's Online Dissertation Services. Contains more than 2 million entries, culled from over 1000 graduate schools and universities, the first accepted in 1861. Full-text of 1.7 million of the publications is available in paper and microform format; there is online access to the complete file of dissertations in digital format starting with titles published from 1997 forward; the full text of over 450,000 dissertations is available at the website.

'Beginning with dissertations received in 2000, all titles will receive an ISBN (International Standard Book Number). Titles will be listed in the UMI Dissertation Abstracts database and other well known on-line and web-based book distributors and databases.'

- **Dissertation Abstracts Online** http://library.dialog.com/bluesheets/html/bl0035.html [DESCRIPTION]. Covers 'virtually every American dissertation accepted at an accredited institution since 1861'. Selected Masters theses since 1962. Also, from 1988, covers dissertations from 50 British universities plus some European works.

200 **Psci-com**
Wellcome Trust and Resource Discovery Network
www.psci-com.org.uk
Guide to quality Internet resources on public engagement with science and technology. Under headings such as associations, nature of science, communications, science education lists key websites and an annotation on each. Topics covered include astronomy and space science, consumer health, ethics, science and art, sociology of science and zoology. There is an electronic discussion forum associated with the website.

201 **Public Affairs Information Service**
CSA.
www.pais.org [FEE-BASED]
Publishes 'indexes and abstracts that help people identify and locate documents about important political, economic, and social issues'. Its 7000 Subject Headings Authority File is classified under 24 Broad Topics and 306 Subtopics.

Good source for periodical articles, books, government documents, serials, grey literature, pamphlets, reports of public and private organizations, etc. regarding: 'Agriculture, forestry, and fishing and agricultural policy'; 'Energy resources and policy'; 'Environment and environmental policy'; 'Health conditions and policy'; 'Manufacturing and heavy industry'; 'Media, telecommunications, and information policy'; and 'Science and technology policy'.
Acquired by CSA from OCLC.

202 **Repositories of Primary Sources**
T. Abraham
www.uidaho.edu/special-collections/Other.Repositories.html
An excellent, regularly updated geographically organized listing which is 'solely of web sites that describe physical collections of rare books, manuscripts, archives, historical photographs, oral histories, or other primary sources. The list focuses on actual repositories; therefore virtual collections and exhibitions are excluded. Others maintain lists of that sort, one is compiled by SMITHSONIAN INSTITUTION Libraries.' Over 5000 entries.

203 **SCRAN** [UK]
www.scran.ac.uk [FEE-BASED]
'The award winning learning image website with access to quality images, sounds, movies and learning resources. There are over 300,000 images from museums, galleries and archives.' Non-subscribers can search the whole resource base for free and see thumbnail images; subscribers gain access to full records, captions, large images, movies and learning resources. An excellent service. Entries have to have some relationship to Scotland; but do not have to be about Scotland – so there is a wealth of images about non-Scottish topics.

204 **The software encyclopedia: a guide for personal, professional and business users**
Bowker, 2004. 2 v., $300.00. ISBN 0835246353.
www.bowker.com/catalog/000103.htm [DESCRIPTION]
'Comprehensive, easy-to-navigate guide filled with detailed information on micro-computer software. Listings of over 40,100 software programs from 3845 publishers and distributors are fully annotated to facilitate research and acquisition.'

205 **Special Issues**
www.specialissues.com [FEE-BASED]
'Special issues are any regularly published special editorial content usually having an industry or company focus ... Examples of special issues include: industry outlooks, overviews, or surveys; statistical issues; company ranking lists; buyers guides; salary surveys; product/industry focus issues; membership directories; who's who registers; tradeshow specials; etc.'

Early 2005, there was coverage of an impressive c.3317 magazines: the titles of each listed on the website.

- **List of Lists G. Price** www.specialissues.com/lol. Very useful open access database of ranked listings of companies, people and resources freely available on the internet. Distinct from main SI Site, no password needed – but invitation to support endeavour, either through advertising or cash donation.

206 **VINITI: All-Russian Institute of Scientific and Technical Information** [RUS]
www.viniti.ru/Welcome.htm
'The leading information centre in Russia and CIS countries has been supplying the world community with scientific and technical information since 1952. The main task of VINITI is to provide information support to scientists and specialists of Russia in natural and technical sciences.' There is an excellent Library of Congress Science Reference Guide 'Russian Abstract Journals in Science and Technology' (No 32) at: www.loc.gov/rr/scitech/SciRefGuides/russian2.html.

- **Referativnyi Zhurnal** Monthly (Chemistry and Chemical Technology: Biweekly). www.viniti.ru/english/vinprint.html#VINIT [DESCRIPTION]. Also known as *VINITI Abstracts Journal*. Covers about one million documents annually including about 30% from Russian sources, the rest from all over the world. Entries for the latter are often in the original language of publication.

207 **Walford's guide to reference material**
Facet Publishing.
The precursor of the present work: *The New Walford*, providing evaluative descriptions of some 25,000 English- and foreign-language reference works organized into three volumes.

- **Universal Decimal Classification Universal Decimal Classification Consortium.** www.udcc.org [DESCRIPTION]. Consortium oversees scheme used to classify entries in Walford's Guide. Relatively small worldwide usage of the scheme elsewhere, but it is still being developed. Contains over 55,000 main numbers and 10,000 common auxiliaries. Strong on STM.
- **1. Science and technology M. Mullay and P. Schlicke, eds** 8th edn 1999, 704pp. £135.00. ISBN 185604341X.
- **2. Social and historical sciences, philosophy and religion A. Day and M.J. Walsh, eds** 8th edn 2000, 808pp. £135.00. ISBN 185604369X.
- **3. Generalia, language and literature, the arts A. Chalcraft, R. Prytherch and S. Willis, eds** 7th edn 1998, 1200pp. £135.00. ISBN 1856043002.

208 **The Web Library: building a world class personal library with free web resources**
N.G. Tomaiuolo CyberAge Books, 2003, 395pp. $29.95. ISBN 0910965676.
http://www.ccsu.edu/library/tomaiuolon/theweblibrary.htm [COMPANION]
A very useful guide. The author gives extensive contextual descriptions of hundreds of rich content sites which are free to use, supplementing the coverage within each chapter – Article and Indexes; News; Reference; Expert, AskA and Digital Reference; and so on – with a series of Insider's Viewpoint interviews with leading 'Web Library Professionals'. The writing is engaging – almost suitable for bed-time reading! – picking out all sorts of interesting facts.

Of course, not all the sites listed deliver the quality of content the user might need; and inevitably, being free resources, relatively they are more subject to change that fee-based ones. But, mid-2004, most of the entries in the companion website had been recently updated; and that in itself – freely accessible, of course! – is a valuable resource.

209 **WWW Virtual Library**
www.vlib.org.uk
Originally established by Tim Berners-Lee.

The service is run by a loose confederation of volunteers and the quality and currency of the various subject area sites is variable and the overall subject granularity uneven. However, 'the central affairs of the VL are now co-ordinated by an elected council, which took office in Jan 2000. Major decisions, including a set of bylaws are decided by the membership at large'.

Many good examples of libraries are cited elsewhere in TNW.

- **Dmoz Open Directory Project** http://dmoz.org. The largest, most comprehensive human-edited directory of the web. It is constructed and maintained by a vast, global community of volunteer editors.

210 **Yahoo! Directory**
http://dir.yahoo.com
Alongside its many other services, became a leading search directory, then used *Google* [q.v.] as its search engine, but early in 2004 started to use its own search facilities.

Yahoo's directory of websites is very large and the coverage of individual sections is often uneven. But: navigation down the subject tree is quick and easy; the subject classifications of the sites covered are usually fine; there is almost always a brief helpful description of each site; and it is normally clear which entries have been sponsored and which not. Certainly worth checking for out of the way topics where you just want to get a quick feel for what is going on. Note also the daily list of New Additions.

Digital data, image & text collections

211 **Australian Bureau of Statistics**
www.abs.gov.au
Australia's official statistical organization. The 'Themes' heading leads to pages labelled: 'Agriculture'; 'Building and Construction'; 'Environment'; 'Health'; 'Mining'; 'Science and Innovation' – each of which is clearly structured, and the last of which has questions such as: 'About ABS science and innovation statistics activities'; 'What's new in science and innovation statistics?'; 'Latest ABS science and innovation statistics'; and so on.

212 **California Digital Library**
www.californiadigitallibrary.org
Established in 1997 as a University of California (UC) Library, has become one of the largest digital libraries in the world. The URL provides a single point of access for the publicly available digital collections produced or managed by the UC.

The Subject Index includes entries such as: 'AIDS (Disease)'; 'Bacteria'; 'Coelacanth'; 'Diagnostic imaging'; etc. Includes access to the eScholarship Repository ('Scholar-led innovation in scholarly communication'), the Online Archive of California ('Provides access to and descriptions of over 6000 collections of primary source materials') and much else. The descriptions of the University of California digital collections are provided by the LIBRARIANS' INDEX TO THE INTERNET.

A model site of its type.

213 **Digital Curation Centre** [UK]
Joint Information Systems Committee and UK e-Science Programme
www.dcc.ac.uk
'Scientists and researchers across the UK generate increasingly vast amounts of digital data, with further investment in digitization and purchase of digital content and information. The scientific record and the documentary heritage created in digital form are at risk, by technology obsolescence and by the fragility of digital media. Working with other practitioners, the Digital Curation Centre will support UK institutions to store, manage and preserve these data to ensure their enhancement and their continuing long-term use. The aim of the Centre is to provide a national focus for research into curation issues and to promote expertise and good practice, both national and international, for the management of all research outputs in digital format.'

Centre was due to be formally launched towards end of 2004, its partners being: University of Edinburgh; University of Glasgow; UKOLN; Council for the Central Laboratory of the Research Councils.

- **DCC Associates' Network** www.dcc.ac.uk/network.html. Network of relevant UK data organizations, leading data curators overseas and supranational standards agencies, sectors of UK industry and commerce involved in digital curation, all being communities the Centre must engage with for it to be successful.
- **Dspace** www.dspace.org. Digital library system that captures, stores, indexes, preserves and redistributes the intellectual output of an organization's researchers in digital formats. Developed jointly by MIT Libraries and HP and now an open source system.

214 **ebrary**
www.ebrary.com [FEE-BASED]
Access to collections of more than 60,000 full-text books, reports, maps and other content from leading publishers and spanning multiple subject areas. Founded in 1999, ebrary is privately held and is funded by Random House Ventures LLC, Pearson plc and The McGraw-Hill Companies.

ebrary has recently expanded significantly and now has some 500 library subscribers in over 60 countries, each able to choose standard or custom-made groups of content. It also provides publisher branded databases, an example being SME SOURCE from the Society of Manufacturing Engineers.

But the company is also very actively developing its technology capabilities, announcing for instance early 2005 a new server-based technology code-named Isaac. This 'lets libraries create and share remote collections of PDF content and create virtual portals that seamlessly integrate PDF documents from any remote collection, their institutional repository or content management system, as well as existing subscription databases' (*Information Today*, January 2005).

215 **Eurostat**
European Commission
europa.eu.int/comm/eurostat
Website of the Statistical Office of the European Union providing links to statistical information about the Member States. 'Themes' include: Agriculture and fisheries; Environment and energy; Industry, trade and services; Population and social conditions; Science and technology – and there is easy navigation to documents and data treating quite specific aspects (e.g. Causes of death; operation of

nuclear power stations; broadband penetration rate), plus more general overviews.

- **RAMON: Eurostat's Classification Server** http://europa.eu.int/comm/eurostat/ramon. Includes index of international statistical classifications, general descriptions, hierarchical structure and explanatory notes.
- **Statistics on science and technology in Europe** 1991–2002, 173pp. €35.00. ISBN 9289468238. Published 25 February 2004. PDF version available.

216 **FedStats** [USA]
www.fedstats.gov
Gateway to statistics from over 100 US Federal agencies. The Topics A to Z has entries, for instance, for: AIDS/HIV; Breastfeeding; Coal ... Pollution; Research and development; Science and engineering; and so on. 'Data access tools' describes selected agency online databases; the 'Statistical reference shelf' and 'Additional links' provide concise lists of the most important other collections of statistics.

It is noted that: 'All of the statistical information available through FedStats is maintained and updated solely by Federal agencies on their own web servers.'

- **Bureau of the Census** www.census.gov. Access among much else to details of the *Statistical Abstract of the United States*: 1400 tables and charts with statistics from the most recent year or period available.
- **Statistics sources** 28th edn, Thomson Gale, 2004. $545.00. ISBN 0787674575. Guide to current sources of factual quantitative information on more than 20,000 specific subjects, incorporating almost 100,000 citations and more than 2000 sources. US and international coverage.

217 **Gale Virtual Reference Library**
Thomson Gale.
www.gale.com/eBooks [FEE-BASED]
Searchable collection of over 100 subject encyclopedias, handbooks, guides, etc. covering the humanities and social sciences as well as science and technology. Includes many leading Thomson Group titles, a number referenced elsewhere in TNW. Provides detailed search facilities and standard e-book navigation features such as browsing tables of contents and indexes, printing, e-mailing, and so on. Each library can customize the Virtual Library to fit its needs, selecting titles to serve children's, academic and general audience requirements.

- **Expanded Academic ASAP** www.gale.com/ExpandedAcademic [FEE-BASED]. 'Thomson Gale's premier database for research in all the academic disciplines. 3500 indexed and full-text titles – of which 2100 are peer-reviewed – in all disciplines with more than 20 years of backfile coverage'.
- **Gale Encyclopedia of Science K.A. McGrath and S. Blachford, eds** 3rd edn, Thomson Gale, 2003. $575.00. ISBN 0787675547. www.galegroup.com [DESCRIPTION]. Designed to cover the gap between introductory and high-level texts. Alphabetical by article title.
- **Gale's Ready Reference Shelf** www.galegroup.com/pdf/navguide/galerref_nvg.pdf [DESCRIPTION]. 14 of Gale's most popular reference titles, fully searchable across all files.
- **Science and its times** Thomson Gale, 2000. $650.00. ISBN 078763932X. www.gale.com/gvrl [FEE-BASED]. Eight-volume work covering different time periods with each volume featuring 25–30 essays of 1500 to 3000 words, 30 biographical entries of 500 to 1000 words and about 100 brief biographical profiles. Available online: see website.

218 **HighWire Press**
Stanford University HighWire Press.
highwire.stanford.edu
A division of Stanford's University Libraries which hosts 'over 15 million articles from over 4500 PubMed journals, including 851,711 free full text articles from 853 HighWire-hosted journals' (18 April 2005). Particularly strong in the biological and medical sciences, and so far including in its portfolio 42 of the 100 most frequently cited journals in the world: all 'available from the journals' own sites for complete and accurate representation of the research at its source including articles published online ahead of print'.

HighWire is committed to the principles of open access; and through its free back issues programme 'participating journals make all their research content free after a brief delay. Currently, 50 journals on HighWire offer content free within six months or less from the day of publication, another 161 titles after a wait of twelve months or more, and all offer immediate access for members, subscribers or those on an authorized institutional network'.

A particularly strong feature of the service is the Inter-Journal Link service whereby 'when one HighWire-hosted journal cites an article from another HighWire-hosted journal, hyperlinks have been created which allow you to move from the original article to the abstract of the cited article. Likewise, links have been created to allow users of other HighWire-hosted journals to quickly and easily access other HighWire-hosted articles. These Inter-Journal links take you to the abstract of the cited reference. Limited free access may be granted to allow you free use of the single article which was cited by the original article.'

- **CiteTrack** . www.highwire.org/help/citetrack. Provides alert by e-mail whenever new content in a participating journal is published that matches criteria based on the topics, authors and articles being tracked. Alerts include citations (authors, title, journal name, volume and page) and URLs.

219 **The Internet Archive**
www.archive.org
'Is building a digital library of Internet sites and other cultural artifacts in digital form. Like a paper library, we provide free access to researchers, historians, scholars, and the general public.'

The Archive's Wayback Machine currently contains over 300 terabytes of data and is growing at a rate of 12 terabytes per month. 'This eclipses the amount of text contained in the world's largest libraries, including the Library of Congress.'

220 **JSTOR**
www.jstor.org
A journal archival service – originally primarily designed to free up costly library shelving space – which delivers scanned page images to its users, while using raw text files (created using Optical Character Recognition (OCR) software) behind the images for search purposes.

On 1 December 2004, 2244 institutions were participating from 86 countries in collaboration with 272 participating publishers. 553 journals had become represented in the System, 457 accessible online.

JSTOR does not at present provide public access to its data: 'Access to the JSTOR archive is available only through affiliation with a participating institution (US or International) or through an individual account with a participating publisher.' However, they are continuing to review this policy.

221 **Knovel**
www.knovel.com
Search tool that aggregates over five hundred full-text engineering handbooks and conference proceedings from a

range of scientific-technical publishers. Abstracts and tables of contents can be retrieved freely but access to the full text requires a subscription. Books that can be browsed cover broad disciplines such as mechanical, electrical and chemical engineering alongside specialisms such as semiconductors, coatings and radar technology.

Very sophisticated service: especially good at handling data-sets. Originally targeted at companies, academic institutions and government organizations, but more recently single-user access has become available.

222 **NetLibrary**
OCLC Online Computer Library Center
http://legacy.netlibrary.com [FEE-BASED]
'We offer the only comprehensive approach to eBooks that integrates with the time-honored missions and methods of libraries and librarians. Our vision is one of enhancing the role of librarians as stewards of knowledge, supporting their crucial role in serving millions of people every day who seek information.'

Purchasers can choose from some 40,000 titles across all subjects, including – for instance within medicine and health – from major publishers such as McGraw-Hill Professional, John Wiley & Sons, BMJ Books, Kluwer, Taylor & Francis, Springer-Verlag, Karger, Health Administration Press, World Health Organization; and – for example, within IT – from Microsoft Press, Sybex, Elsevier, and so on. Recently, unlimited access to the entire catalogue of Kluwer e-books was introduced: the cost being 150% of list price plus Content Service and Support fees.

In the website's extensive Help system, we are reminded: 'Remember, netLibrary is not a subscription service. You own the eBooks.'

223 **Networked Digital Library of Theses and Dissertations: NDLTD**
http://scholar.lib.vt.edu/theses
Consortium of over 170 members, including 147 member universities (2 consortia), and 4 national libraries – 30 of which are 'Effective' members, the remainder 'Associated'. Useful gateway to activity in this arena.

- **Virginia Tech Electronic Theses and Dissertations** http://scholar.lib.vt.edu/theses. Leading developer of access to electronic theses and dissertations; early 2005 over 6300 titles (some of which are restricted or withheld). Part of the University's extensive Digital Library and Archives.
- **Australian Digital Theses Program** http://adt.caul.edu.au. Aims to 'create a distributed national database of digitised theses available via the web. Providing access via a central database will greatly enhance knowledge about Australian theses and research both nationally and internationally'.

224 **Occupational outlook handbook** [USA]
Bureau of Labor Statistics
www.bls.gov/oco
'Revised every two years, the Handbook describes what workers do on the job, working conditions, the training and education needed, earnings, and expected job prospects in a wide range of occupations.' Examples of occupations covered within the 'Professional and Related Service' sector are: mathematicians; atmospheric scientists; conservation scientists and foresters; pharmacists; materials engineers; librarians.

Complementing the Handbook is the equally valuable *Career Guide to Industries* which 'provides information on available careers by industry, including the nature of the industry, working conditions, employment, occupations in the industry, training and advancement, earnings and benefits, employment outlook, and lists of organizations that can provide additional information'.

The Guide discusses 42 industries, accounting for 3 out of every 4 wage and salary jobs in the USA in 2002, including those within: agriculture, mining and construction; manufacturing; information (broadcasting, ICT-based industries, publishing); government; and education and health services. 'As the largest industry in 2002, health services provided 12.9 million jobs ... With about 1 in 4 Americans enrolled in educational institutions, educational services is the second largest industry, accounting for 12.7 million jobs.'

There is also an 'Overview and Outlook' which provides an excellent summary of the present situation and outlook for the various industries and economy within the USA, as well as an essay 'Tomorrow's Jobs'.

225 **Office for National Statistics** [UK]
www.statistics.gov.uk
The government department that provides UK statistical and registration services. Browse by theme among: Agriculture, Fishing and Forestry; Commerce, Energy and Industry; Health and Care; Natural and Built Environment; etc.

- **Guide to official statistics** Downloadable PDF 2000. ISBN 011621161X. www.statistics.gov.uk/cci/advancedsearch.asp. An invaluable and comprehensive directory of all statistical censuses, surveys, administrative systems, publications and other services produced by government and a range of other organizations.
- **Sources of non-official UK statistics** D. Mort, comp. 5th edn, Gower, 2002, 358pp. £65.00. ISBN 056608449X. Details of c.1000 publications and services (including electronic publications) from trade associations, professional bodies, banks, consultants, employers' federations, forecasting organizations, etc., together with statistics appearing in trade sources.
- **Standard Occupational Classification 2000** www.statistics.gov.uk/methods_quality/ns_sec/soc2000.asp. Eight major groups including: 2. Professional occupations; 3. Associate professional and technical occupations; 5. Skilled trades occupations; 6. Personal service occupations; 8. Process, plant and machine operatives.
- **Statistics Commission** www.statscom.org.uk. Independent non-departmental public body set up to help ensure that official statistics are trustworthy and responsive to public needs. Operates openly independent of both Ministers and the producers of statistics, with all its papers normally made public.
- **United Kingdom Standard Industrial Classification of Economic Activities 2002: UKSIC (2003)** www.statistics.gov.uk. Downloadable PDF of complete classification. Introduction gives good background on relationship of current to previous versions, as well as to EU, international and other related classifications.

226 **Oxford Reference Online**
Oxford University Press. Individual annual subscription: £95.00 + VAT/$139.00. Institutional subscriptions available.
www.oup.com/online [FEE-BASED]
Core Collection of about 100 titles published by OUP, including bilingual, science and medical dictionaries, plus – within the Premium Collection – books from the Oxford Companion series and the *Oxford Dictionary of Quotations*. Includes cross-referencing within and across the included texts, as well as external links to additional sources of relevant information. An excellent compilation.

This is an example of a range of online services available from OUP. Others include: American National Biography; Oxford Dictionary of National Biography; Oxford Digital Reference Shelf; Oxford English Dictionary; Oxford Scholarship Online – as well as Oxford Journals. Check the website for details.

'the content is superb, and the design makes use of some of the best features we've seen in online reference publishing. Recommended for any and every library. This is a top-quality resource.' (*Library Journal*)

227 **Public Library of Science**
www.plos.org
Non-profit organization of scientists and physicians committed to making the world's scientific and medical literature a freely available public resource. Operates with the 'author-pays' open access publishing model. PLoS has published its own journals, beginning with *PLoS Biology* on October 13, 2003 and *PLoS Medicine* on October 19, 2004. PLoS is launching three new community journals in 2005 — *PLoS Genetics*, *PLoS Computational Biology*, and *PLoS Pathogens*.

228 **Statistics Canada**
www.statcan.ca
The site of Canada's central statistics agency. Several helpful features, including: First visit to our site?; a set of Learning Resources; Statistics Canada Thesaurus – list of subject terms used to describe the Agency's information resources; The Daily – free e-mailed bulletin which can be customized just to include 'hyperlinks to articles and product release announcements only on the subject(s) you have selected – and only on the days they appear in The Daily'.

229 **Xreferplus**
www.xreferplus.com [FEE-BASED]
Online reference library providing access to full text of 150 reference works including dictionaries, encyclopedias, thesauri, etc. Includes books on health, science and technology from publishers such as: A&C Black; Blackwell Publishing; Cambridge University Press; Collins; Columbia University Press; Elsevier; Harvard University Press; Houghton Mifflin; Macmillan; Oxford University Press; Philip's; Wiley; Woodhead Publishing.

The service is distinctive for its use of 'unique proprietary technology that integrates information through a network of intelligent, multi-dimensional cross-references'. The site provides exploratory access to The Research Mapper: 'a visual map that displays how search terms and topics are interconnected'. Well worth trying!

'The notable feature in xreferplus is its incredible cross-referencing capabilities ... A reliable, easy to use, fast and ready reference tool that can streamline your information search.' (*Library Quarterly*)

Directories & encyclopedias

230 **A to Z of STS scientists**
E.H. Oakes Facts On File, 2002, 372pp. $45.00. ISBN 0816046069.
'This is a comprehensive one-volume A-to-Z reference of past and present scientists who have contributed significantly to the new and growing field known as Science, Technology, and Society (STS). Those profiled include chemists, physicists, biologists, engineers, and mathematicians. The common element shared by these noted individuals is the way in which their scientific work was shaped by social setting. Designed for high school through early college students, this is an ideal reference of notable male and female scientists from antiquity to the present. The book contains approximately 200 entries and 62 black-and-white photographs.'

Other works in the 8-volume Notable Scientists *series cover: Biologists; Chemists; Computer Scientists; Earth Scientists; Marine Scientists; Physicists; Scientists in Weather and Climate.*

'Recommended for the science reference collections of high school, public, and undergraduate libraries.' (*E-STREAMS*)

231 **An atlas of cyberspaces**
M. Dodge; University College London
www.cybergeography.org/atlas
Fascinating full colour examples of maps and graphic representations of the geographies of the internet, world wide web and other emerging cyberspaces. Unfortunately, a number of the links need updating; but there is an active group and discussion list which can be joined.

232 **Biographical dictionary of scientists**
R. Porter and M. Ogilvie, eds 3rd edn, Oxford University Press, 2000, 1214pp. 2 v, $125.00. ISBN 0195216636.
Over 1280 biographies of key people (including 53 women) in science, mathematics, engineering and technology in two volumes written by 43 contributors. Each entry of 500 to 1200 words presents the contribution of the scientist. There is an extensive glossary and appendices listing Nobel Prize and Field Medal winners. Also contains a short section of essays on major science areas (astronomy, biology, chemistry, earth science, engineering and technology, mathematics and physics).

'The updated versions of the historical reviews, the new chronologies and other features as well as the inclusion of women are significant enough changes to warrant purchase.' (*E-STREAMS*)

233 **Encyclopædia Britannica Online**
£39.99 [2004].
www.britannica.co.uk [FEE-BASED]
Access to the online Britannica Premium Service includes: the 32-volume Encyclopaedia Britannica 2003; the new Britannica Student Encyclopedia, ideal for students age 10 upwards; the Britannica Internet Guide, over 165,000 of the web's best sites rated and reviewed by the editors. A wide range of other online as well as print services is available.

Within the USA, the URL: http://corporate.britannica.com/products.html gives an overview of Britannica products available for home, school, library or corporation.

- **Britannica Book of the Year** 904pp. £60.00 [2003]. ISBN 1593391005. Includes good coverage of STM developments.

234 **Encyclopedia of associations: international organizations**
41st edn, Gale, 2004. 3 v. Also available CD-ROM, $765.00. ISBN 0787668826.
www.galegroup.com
Provides addresses and descriptions of professional societies, trade associations, and other non-profit membership organizations worldwide. Entries are classified by subject. Related volumes cited below.

Available online through DIALOG.

- **National organizations of the US** 41st edn2004. $650.00. ISBN 0787668710. This is v. 1. Also available are two companion volumes: v. 2 *Geographic and Executive Indexes*; v. 3 *Supplement* (Updates contact information from the previous edition and provides coverage of new or newly identified associations and projects).

- **Regional, state and local organizations** 15th edn 2004. $695.00. ISBN 0787668850. Includes 30,000 primary websites plus an additional 42,000 websites for national affiliates of chapters listed.
- **Yearbook of international organizations** **Union of International Associations** 42nd edn, K G Saur, 2005. $1925.00. ISBN 3598245203. www.uia.org/organizations/pub.php [DESCRIPTION]. Current details of some 60,000 international non-governmental and intergovernmental organizations. Also available online: see website.

235 **Encyclopedia of ethics in science and technology**
N. Barber Facts on File, 2002, 386pp. $60.00. ISBN 0816043140.
Well reviewed book which 'features more than 400 entries that describe the varied ethical controversies in science and technology: laws, precedent-setting cases, regulations, agencies and organizations, ethical principles, concepts, people, and important events. Also covered are phenomena that are at the fringes of science but have important ethical implications, including voodoo deaths and experimental research into extrasensory perception (ESP)'.
'Well suited for the high school or multi-disciplinary undergraduate library where students will appreciate quick access to concise overviews of these terms and topics.' (*E-STREAMS*)

- **Encyclopedia of science, technology, and ethics** Macmillan Reference USA, 1800pp. $425.00. ISBN 0028658310. www.gale.com [DESCRIPTION]. Four-volume work announced for July 2005.

236 **Encyclopedia of physical science and technology**
R.A. Meyers, ed. 3rd edn, Academic Press, 2002, 15,453pp. 18 v., $4195.00. ISBN 0122274105.
www.sciencedirect.com/science/referenceworks
790 articles organized alphabetically by title. Each article is written to a standard format designed to make it useful to various readers with different levels of knowledge about the subject: Outline; Glossary; Defining statement; Main body of the article; Cross-references; Bibliography.

The Index volume is also well thought-out, including: A–Z list of the entries; List of contributors; Contents by subject area (44 broad headings); Relational index; Detailed subject index (c. 350 pp).

A valuable impressive work. Coverage is chemistry, molecular biology, biotechnology, physics, earth sciences, environment and atmospheric sciences, computers and telecommunications, electronics, mathematics, astronomy and space, energy, materials and engineering.
Available online: see website.

237 **Findout.tv**
Crystal Reference.
www.findout.tv [FEE-BASED]
'Findout.tv's content covers all popular areas of enquiry, such as plants and animals, technology, sports, history, geography, and the arts. Many entries are educational, providing an introductory account of major concepts in such fields as philosophy, economics, physics, and politics. You will also find a focus on international affairs, especially within Europe.'

'And there is more. A unique feature of Findout.tv is that, every day, our entries are updated with new information to track current affairs. When a significant event occurs, you can read the background to the story on Findout.tv.'

238 **Hutchinson Science Reference Suite**
Helicon, 1999. CD-ROM, Various pricings: see website.
www.rm.com/rmcomhome.asp [DESCRIPTION]
Suitable for school use: 19,500 entries; 1000 images covering difficult concepts; interactive quiz; quotations, fascinating facts, memory joggers, etc. Designed to interface with the UK National Curriculum.
'an all-round solid science reference.' (Daily Telegraph)

239 **The Nature yearbook of science and technology**
Nature Publishing, 2002, 1340pp. £150.00. ISBN 0333971477.
2nd edn whose core (800 pp) attempted systematically to describe the science systems and major scientific organizations of every country in the world. The aim was 'to provide, not a directory, but an easily navigated hierarchy of detailed profiles of the key players, beginning with science ministries and government bodies, followed by national research bodies, major research institutes, research universities, and so on'.

Supplementing this core was – potentially – a mass of useful information on happenings during the year, work of international bodies, progress within large scientific facilities, etc.: the whole enhanced by reprints from the periodical NATURE itself.

However, unfortunately, the book's typography, its use of monochromatic illustrations, and its general design created a rather dense, bland and uninviting appearance – which was a pity, as the concept behind the tome was excellent.

240 **Notable twentieth-century scientists**
E.J. McMurray, J.K. Kosek and R.M. Valade, eds Gale Research, 1995, 2397pp. 4 v. Supplement 1998. ISBN 0810391813.
1300 scientists active in the 20th century in all the natural, physical, and applied sciences. Includes for each entry: selected writings; sources (citations of biographies, interviews, obituaries, etc.). Subject index.

- **Scientists: their lives & works** UXL, 1997–2002. $350.00. ISBN 1414404875. 3 vols 1997 extended 7 vols by 2002, and aimed at middle school and above. 'The unique combination of accessible scientific information and fascinating personal details adds a human dimension to the presentation.' *School Library Journal*.
- **Women in science** Macmillan Reference USA, 2000, 421pp. $95.00. ISBN 0028655028. One of small series rewritten from the publisher's main offerings for students starting at middle school level. Other titles include: *Mathematicians & computer wizards*; *Scientists & inventors*; *Tycoons & entrepreneurs*.

241 **Prospects.ac.uk**
Graduate Prospects.
www.prospects.ac.uk
'Working in partnership with the most prominent official bodies in the field of Higher Education, Graduate Prospects has been bringing students, graduates and recruiters together for over 30 years. It is our close working relationships with HECSU (the Higher Education Careers Services Unit), AGCAS (Association of Graduate Careers Advisory Services), SCOP (the Standing Conference of Principals of Colleges) and Universities UK that allow us to maintain our status as the UK's official graduate careers support service.'

Good database search facility across all current UK undergraduate and postgraduate courses matching subject area, university/college, region, mode of study (full time, part time, distance learning) and optional keywords (e.g. management + technology).

- **GradSchools.com** Educational Directories Inc. www.gradschools.com. 'The leading online resource for graduate school information with over 58,000 programs listed on our site. The site contains a unique and comprehensive directory categorized by curriculum and subdivided by geography.'
- **Jobs.ac.uk** www.jobs.ac.uk. The UK's leading academic job site.

242 Science and technology firsts

L.C. Bruno, ed. Gale Research, 1996, 636pp. Foreword by Daniel Boorstin, $95.00. ISBN 0787602566.

Arranged into topics: agriculture and everyday life; astronomy; biology; chemistry; communications; computers; earth sciences; energy and weaponry; mathematics; medicine; physics; transportation. Entries are then chronological from the earliest human activities. Gives brief information on discoveries and other firsts focusing on science more than technology.

'A must-purchase for every science/technology collection.' (*American Reference Books Annual*)

243 Social issues in science and technology: an encyclopedia

D.E. Newton ABC-CLIO, 1999, 303pp. $75.00. ISBN 0874369207.

Alphabetical list of over 100 topics such as abortion, Bovine Somatotropin and Chernobyl giving the scientific and historical background. The entries provide a summary of differing views, possible impacts on society and results of government decisions. Each entry provides references and some are illustrated. Selected bibliography and general index.

244 Studying in France

Égide

www.egide.asso.fr/uk/guide

'Égide is a non-profit association employing a personnel of 210. It is not grant-supported, but costs its own operating and development budget by charging for its services. This drives a permanent quest for performance and innovation, which goes a long way to explaining the organisation's dynamic reputation ... Égide services include management of study and internship grants, organisation of conferences, reception of celebrity visitors, and arrangements for overseas missions by French experts. Services are provided under contract with the organisations responsible for financing incoming visits or outgoing expert missions. Égide's thus holds a portfolio of 800 partnership contracts with public and private organisations in France and worldwide: research laboratories, universities, schools, companies, foreign governments, state departments and local government organisations. Égide's biggest partnership contract is with the French Ministry of Foreign Affairs.'

An excellent site.

245 Van Nostrand's scientific encyclopedia

G.D. Considine, ed. 9th edn, Wiley-Interscience, 2002, 3898pp. 2 v., $375.00. ISBN 0471332305.

Contains over 8000 entries in two volumes on science, medicine, mathematics and technology. Entries start with a simple definition and continue with a detailed explanation and, in some cases, additional reading. Also contains 9000 cross-references, a comprehensive index and almost 5000 diagrams, tables and illustrations. Suitable as a very accessible introduction to many STM topics.

'. extensively updated since the last volume ... and it is an amazing accomplishment ... not only does it cover an enormous range of topics. it does so thoroughly and descriptively ... almost lyrical in its coverage.' (*Journal of the American Chemical Society*)

246 Whitaker's Almanack [UK]

A&C Black.

www.whitakersalmanack.com [DESCRIPTION]

The UK's 'ultimate single volume reference source'.

Available in several edns: see website.

- **Who's Who** A&C Black. www.ukwhoswho.com [DESCRIPTION]. Published annually since 1849 and the first biographical book of its kind. 32,000 short biographies, continually updated, of living noteworthy and influential individuals, from all walks of life, worldwide. c.1000 new entries added every year.

247 Who's who in science and engineering: 2005–2006

8th edn, Marquis Who's Who, 2004, 1400pp. $335.00. ISBN 0837957648.

www.marquiswhoswho.com/products/SCprodinfo.asp [DESCRIPTION]

Alphabetical list of 30,000 scientists, doctors and engineers predominantly from the USA. Entries give field of work, education and scientific achievements. There are also indexes by specialization and by geographic location.

248 The World Guide

New Internationalist; distributed by Carel, 2005. Includes CD-ROM, £55.00.

www.carelpress.co.uk/wguide03.htm [DESCRIPTION]

'An alternative reference to the countries of our planet ... Provides a wealth of information on the countries of the world from a refreshingly different perspective. It includes all the facts, history, political and economic analysis you would expect, but also offers information on the issues central to the lives of people in Africa, Asia, the Middle East, Latin America and the Caribbean.'

'I must congratulate everyone concerned. The layout is user-friendly, the text is clear and clean, and – most important of all – one can quote the statistics with confidence. The book is now an indispensable tool [on the previous edn].' (*Oxfam*)

- **The World Factbook Central Intelligence Agency.** www.cia.gov/cia/publications/factbook. The classic resource. '2004 marks the 57th anniversary of the establishment of the Central Intelligence Agency and the 61st year of continuous basic intelligence support to the US Government by *The World Factbook* and its two predecessor programs'.

249 World guide to scientific associations and learned societies

F. Kirchner, ed. 9th edn, K G Saur, 2003, 628pp. €298.00. ISBN 3598222645.

Provides descriptions of 17,500 international associations and learned societies involved in science, technology and culture. The primary arrangement is by country, then alphabetically. Indexes by association name, subject and personal names.

Series: Handbook of International Documentation and Information, v. 13.

- **World guide to trade associations M. Zils, comp.** 6th edn, K G Saur, 2002–2003, 1088pp. €548.00. ISBN 3598207360. 2 v.: v. 1 lists 23,641 associations covering every conceivable field of commercial, service and industrial activity; v. 2 contains details of all chambers of industry and commerce worldwide.

250 **The world of learning: the international guide to the academic world**
54th edn, Europa Publications, 2004, 2448pp. £395.00. ISBN 1857431820.
www.worldoflearning.com
The complete directory and guide to the organizations and institutions throughout the sphere of higher education and learning. Covers: 6200 Universities and colleges; 6600 Research institutes; 3000 Museums and art galleries; 5300 Learned societies; 3500 Libraries and archives; 26,000 Publications. Lists over 200,000 staff and officials.
Available online: see website.

Handbooks & manuals

A basis for scientific and engineering translation: German-English-German
M. Hann See entry no. 6393

The craft of scientific presentations: critical steps to succeed and critical errors to avoid
M. Alley See entry no. 6398

Keeping up-to-date

251 **AllConferences.Com**
www.allconferences.com
Covers conferences, conventions, exhibits, seminars, workshops, events, trade shows and business meetings, for each including calendar, dates, location, contact and registration information. Fairly detailed subject classification; good search facilities; relatively non-intrusive advertising.

- **CONF FIZ Karlsruhe**. www.fiz-informationsdienste.de/en/DB/conf [FEE-BASED]. Details of some 200,000 past, present and forthcoming conferences in science, technology, and medicine.
- **Forthcoming International Scientific and Technical Conferences** Emerald. £259.00. ISBN 00464686. www.emeraldinsight.com/fistc.htm [DESCRIPTION]. Main issue published February each year, followed by supplements in May, August and November. International and UK conferences are listed in chronological order giving date, title, location and contact. Indexes by subject, keyword, location, organization.
- **Mind: The Meetings Index** www.interdok.com/mind. Free access to locate future conferences, congresses, meetings, symposia. Categorized into four sections: Science/technology; Medical/life sciences; Pollution control/ecology; Social sciences/humanities.

252 **Annual Reviews**
Annual Reviews.
www.annurev.org
'Intelligent synthesis of the scientific literature.' Non-profit publisher of leading series of in-depth reviews. All have a title in the format 'Annual Review of ...', and many members of the series are referenced elsewhere in this Volume.

Individual titles are highly cited within the Institute for Scientific Information's JOURNAL PERFORMANCE INDICATORS service: 'Of the 5907 journals assessed by impact factor by the ISI, the Annual Review of Immunology is ranked #1, Annual Review of Biochemistry is ranked #2, and more than half of the Annual Reviews titles are in the top 100 regardless of category.'

When revisiting a topic, it is always worth checking if it has been recently reviewed by one of the Annual Reviews volumes. Perusal of the chapters in the relevant annual volume as it appears is also an excellent way of keeping abreast of broad developments in a discipline.

253 **The Chronicle of Higher Education** [USA]
The Chronicle of Higher Education, Weekly. $82.50. ISSN 00095982.
http://chronicle.com
Wide-ranging coverage with sections: News; Opinion and forums; Careers; Services – each divided into subsections (e.g. Research and Books). Daily updates at the website – which also gives subscribers access to every issue published since 1989, as well as the opportunity to sign-up for a daily news alert.

254 **Current Contents Connect**
Thomson ISI.
www.isinet.com/products/cap/ccc [DESCRIPTION]
'Access to complete bibliographic information of over 7000 of the world's leading scholarly journals and more than 2000 books.'

Available in 7 subject-area editions: Agriculture, Biology and Environmental Sciences; Arts and Humanities; Clinical Medicine; Engineering, Computing and Technology; Life Sciences; Physical, Chemical and Earth Sciences; Social and Behavioural Sciences.

An essay entitled *The ISI database: the journal selection process* was updated in January 2004: 'Recent citation analyses have shown that as few as 150 journals account for half of what is cited and one quarter of what is published. It has also been shown that a core of approximately 2000 journals now accounts for about 85% of published articles and 95% of cited articles. But this core is not static. Its basic composition changes constantly. The ISI editorial team's mission is to identify and evaluate promising new journals that will be useful to ISI subscribers, and to delete journals that have become less useful.'

255 **Inside**
British Library 2004. £750.00 [Single User].
www.bl.uk/services/current/inside.html [DESCRIPTION]
Current awareness service covering 20,000 journals giving titles and bibliographic details and abstracts for some journals. Provides access to electronically delivered articles and standard document supply. Now holds details of over 20 million articles, growing by two million new records each year, 8000 every day.

The site gives useful free access to the full list of titles, searchable by keyword, and providing title and ISSN (and BL shelfmark) but no other information.

- **Articles Direct** www.bl.uk/services/document/orddocs.html. Allows ordering of articles from the BL without the need to be a registered customer (such as a library). All articles incur a mandatory publication-specific copyright fee, details of which are given in entries in THE BRITISH LIBRARY PUBLIC CATALOGUE.
- **Inside Conferences** www.bl.uk/services/bibliographic/datalicensing.html. Daily updated file indexing papers published within comprehensive collection of some 14,000 conference proceedings per year received by the BL. Over 450,000 items/annum. Dataset accessible on several online hosts (and details here of other BL datasets).

256 **Nature**
Nature Publishing Group, 1869–, Weekly. £112.00. ISSN 00280836.
www.nature.com/nature
The leading UK-based periodical covering news of research,

science policy, peer-reviewed papers, book reviews and letters, and much more – including significant international coverage.

257 **New Scientist**
Reed Business Information, 1956–, Weekly. £114.00. ISSN 02624079.
www.newscientist.com
News, features and reviews well written by reporters and correspondents explain the latest developments in science, technology and medicine. UK-based but coverage is international.

Full content is available online for a charge, but – as with many other magazines and journals – there is a free web version which contains news items but often not access to the full-text of the feature articles, unless one is a subscriber. Nevertheless, even for non-subscribers, worth browsing is the section Explore by Subject which – early 2005 – was categorized: Info-tech; Being human; Life; Space; Mech-tech; Earth; Fundamentals; Sex and cloning; Health; Opinion.
Note Hot Topics

258 **NewsNow**
NewsNow Publishing Ltd.
http://newsnow.co.uk
'Breaking news in 15+ languages from thousands of the Internet's most important online publications, including international, national and regional titles, newswires, magazines, press releases and exclusively online news sources ... Automatically searching 19,845 news sources every 5 minutes.'

The basic service is free-of-charge; but the publishers 'occasionally add a site to NewsNow that requires users to register (free) or subscribe (paid) to their service in order to read stories ... More and more sites are moving to a registration business model to try and make money from their sites.'

NewsNow is exceptionally easy to use, with users readily able to choose newsfeeds relevant to specific topics: the more generic areas such as science, medical research, engineering; or quite specific topics, including 'Hot Topics' (e.g. Bird Flu; Climate Change). An RSS feed is available for subscribers.

A very good service.

- **The Globe and Mail** www.globetechnology.com. Good Canadian-based coverage of technology developments.
- **Moreover** www.moreover.com. Leading provider of sophisticated information management solutions whose technology 'continually scours the Internet to capture breaking news and business information from thousands of qualified, handpicked sources'. Used by many leading search services.
- **The New York Times** www.nytimes.com/pages/science. Relatively very good coverage of science, technology, health, etc. – though texts of articles generally only accessible to registered members of NYTimes.com.
- **Newswise** www.newswise.com [DESCRIPTION]. Primarily for journalists but able to be accessed more generally where the world's leading research institutions: universities, colleges, laboratories, professional organizations, governmental agencies, private research groups deliver research-based news.
- **SciCentral** www.scicentral.com. Good selective news service – with supporting resources – Editors using the criteria: Reliability; Timeliness of the information; Extent of daily coverage; Multidisciplinary coverage; Leads to follow up information; Presentation and general appeal.
- **SciDevNet: News, views and information about science, technology and the developing world** www.scidev.net. Sponsored by NATURE, SCIENCE, and ACADEMY OF SCIENCES FOR THE DEVELOPING WORLD, and funded by a range of agencies and foundations. Well structured and valuable gateway: good sets of briefing documents, as well as up-to-date news.
- **ScienceDaily** www.sciencedaily.com. 'Created by Canadian-American science writer/editor Dan Hogan and his wife Michele Hogan in December 1995 ... Produced from the couple's home office outside Washington, DC.' Well presented site, very detailed subject classification, interesting example.
- **WorldNews Network** www.wn.com. Aims to be 'the most comprehensive, one-stop news resource on the Internet. Today, WN has over 1500 thematic and regional news sites. It also includes the web's most comprehensive news search engine.' Very nice lively site with excellent use of graphics.

259 **Science**
American Association for the Advancement of Science 1883–, Weekly. $135.00. ISSN 00368075.
www.sciencemag.org
The leading US-based periodical covering news of research, science policy, peer-reviewed papers, book reviews and letters, and much more – including significant international coverage.

- **Science Books and Films American Association for the Advancement of Science**Bimonthly. $45.00. ISSN 0098342X. www.sbfonline.com. 'Every year, SB&F evaluates nearly 1000 books, A/V materials, and software packages for general audiences, professionals, teachers, and students from kindergarten through college.'

260 **Scientific American**
Scientific American, 1846–, Monthly. $24.97. ISSN 00368733.
www.sciam.com
Contains news items, feature articles, reviews and letters on science, technology and medicine. Explains science (with good illustrations) for the general reader. Substantially enhanced digital version.

261 **Times Higher Education Supplement** [UK]
TSL Education, Weekly. £54.00. ISSN 00493929.
www.thesis.co.uk
Excellent coverage of UK and some worldwide developments in higher and further education. Particularly good at tackling controversial topics in science, medicine and technology. Useful book review section. Free e-mailed 'Research' and 'Editor's' newsletters.

SCIENCE

Science

The sequencing here is similar to that in the widely used Dewey Classification scheme; but we have placed CHEMISTRY closer to the BIOLOGICAL SCIENCES and in turn EARTH SCIENCES closer to PHYSICS & ASTRONOMY – both these seeming to reflect better current research relationships. Also, AGRICULTURE, FORESTRY, FISHERIES & FOOD feels now well situated between BIOLOGICAL SCIENCES and the following subject part MEDICINE.

Introductions to the subject

262 The age of science: what scientists learned in the twentieth century
G. Piel Basic Books, 2001, 480pp. $40.00. ISBN 0465057551.
Engaging story by former Editor of SCIENTIFIC AMERICAN. Includes coverage of: fundamental forces of nature; subatomic world; cosmology; cell and molecular biology; earth history and evolution of life; human evolution. Useful end notes.
'Highly recommended for all libraries. All levels.' (*Choice*)

263 At the fringes of science: with a new epilogue
M.W. Friedlander Westview, 1998, 202pp. $31.00. ISBN 0813390605.
'What makes Friedlander's book especially useful is that he reviews conventional scientific method and shows how scientists examine the hard cases to determine what is science and what is pseudoscience. Emphasizing that there is no clear line of demarcation between science and non-science, Friedlander leads the reader through case after entertaining case, covering the favorites of 'tabloid science' such as astrology and UFOs, scientific controversies such as cold fusion, and those maverick ideas that were at first rejected by science only to be embraced later. There are many good stories here, but there is also much learning and wisdom.

Students of science and interested lay readers will come away from this book with an increased understanding of what science is, how it works, and how the non-scientist should deal with science at its fringes.'

- **The skeptic: encyclopedia of pseudoscience M. Shermer, ed.** ABC-CLIO, 2002, 903pp. $185.00. ISBN 1576076539. Editor and publisher of *The Skeptic* magazine provides comprehensive introduction to the most prominent pseudoscientific claims made in the name of 'science'.
- **Society for Scientific Exploration** www.scientificexploration.org. Professional forum for presentations, criticism, and debate concerning topics which are for various reasons ignored or studied inadequately within mainstream science. Quarterly journal. Useful set of Links (under *Young Investigators Program*.

264 Blackwell guide to the philosophy of science
P. Machamer and M. Silberstein, ed. Blackwell Publishing, 2002, 360pp. £18.99. ISBN 0631221085.
Good wide-ranging overview. 15 chapters ranging from *A brief historical introduction to the philosophy of science (and prognostications about its future)* to *Feminist philosophy of science.*

265 Chronology of science: from Stonehenge to the Human Genome Project
L. Rosner, ed. ABC-CLIO, 2002, 566pp. $85.00. ISBN 1576079546.
Chronologies divided into subject areas: astronomy, biology, chemistry, ecology, etc. 16 feature essays on critical scientific achievements. 800 brief biographies of scientists. Diagrams, illustrations, photographs.
'This will be a valuable reference for science and history students, as well as for the casual browser who is interested in science and/or history. Recommended.' (*Library Media Connection*)

- **Asimov's chronology of science and discovery I. Asimov** HarperCollins, 1994, 790pp. ISBN 0062701134. History of science, discovery, mathematics and some technologies from prehistory up to 1993. Readable account by the well known science fiction writer. Separate name and subject indexes.

266 Galileo's finger: the ten great ideas of science
P. Atkins Oxford University Press, 2003, 420pp. £20.00. ISBN 0198606648.
1. Evolution: the emergence of complexity; 2. DNA: the rationalization of biology; 3. Energy: the universalization of accountancy; 4. Entropy: the spring of change; 5. Atoms: the reduction of matter; 6. Symmetry: the quantification of beauty; 7. Quanta: the simplification of understanding; 8. Cosmology: the globalization of reality; 9. Spacetime: the arena of action; 10. Arithmetic: the limitation of explanation. Prologue – the emergence of understanding; Epilogue – the future of understanding. Further reading. An excellent introduction.

267 Higher superstition: the academic left and its quarrels with science
P.R. Gross and N. Levitt Johns Hopkins University Press, 1998, 328pp. $20.95. ISBN 0801857074.
Review of and engagement with criticism of science by humanists and social scientists on the 'academic left'. This edn has new afterword by the authors.
Originally published 1994.

268 History of modern science and mathematics
B. Baigrie, ed. Simon & Schuster, 2002, 920pp. 4 v., $425.00. ISBN 0684806363.
Emphasis is on natural rather than applied sciences. Overviews on biology, mathematics and physics and topical subjects. Bulk of work is essays on history of 23 scientific disciplines including their world-wide historical origins from about the 17th century. Extensive cross-indexing and bibliographies. Interdisciplinary timeline; name and subject indexes.
'If you have a keen interest and want to know anything about anyone who was anything in the history of science from Copernicus to the present day, then this four-volume set is for you; otherwise stay clear.' (*Reference Reviews*)

269 **How to win the Nobel prize: an unexpected life in science**
J.M. Bishop Harvard University Press, 2004, 271pp. Originally published 2003, $15.95. ISBN 0674016254.
Fascinating interweaving of science and biography by 1989 Nobel prize winner (for the discovery, with Harold Varmus, that normal genes under certain conditions can cause cancer). 'Affords us the pleasure of hearing about science from a brilliant practitioner who is a humanist at heart. Bishop's perspective will be valued by anyone interested in biomedical research and in the past, present, and future of the battle against cancer.'
'In these pages Bishop reveals himself as a good writer blessed with enviable clarity, someone sensible and levelheaded who likes people and is enamored of his science.' (*New York Times Book Review*)

270 **Magic universe: the Oxford guide to modern science**
N. Calder Oxford University Press, 2003, 756pp. £25.00. ISBN 0198507925.
Well written quite detailed A–Z guide to current science for general readers; c.150 entries cover physics, astronomy, earth sciences, chemistry, biological sciences. Good for browsing.
'The achievement of writing more than 100 engaging and accurate scientific essays is considerable and this is a great book to recommend to anyone who wants a wide introduction to science.' (*Times Higher Education Supplement*)

271 **The modern physical and mathematical sciences**
M.J. Nye, ed. Cambridge University Press, 2002, 678pp. £95.00. ISBN 0521571995.
Narrative and interpretative history of the physical and mathematical sciences from the early 19th century to the close of the 20th century. 33 chapters in 6 parts: I. The public cultures of the physical sciences after 1800; II. Discipline-building in the sciences: places, instruments, communication; III. Chemistry and physics: problems through the early 1900s; IV. Atomic and molecular sciences in the 20th century; V. Mathematics, astronomy and cosmology since the 18th century; VI. Problems and promises at the end of the twentieth century. Bibliography. Index.

Chapters represent a variety of investigative and interpretative strategies: 'The practice of history, like the practice of science, is a process that depends on conceptual reorientations and reinterpretations, as well as the invention of new research tools and the unearthing of new facts'.
Series: Cambridge History of Science, V. 5. Planned is V. 6. The modern biological and earth sciences, *and V. 8.* Modern science in national and international context.

272 **The politics of excellence: behind the Nobel Prize in science**
R.M. Friedman Times Books, 2001, 379pp. £19.99. ISBN 0716731037.
Based on more than 20 years of investigation into the extensive resources that have become accessible following the decision by the Nobel Foundation in 1974 to allow researchers to study archive material that is over 50 years old, plus work on a wide range of other archival sources. Insightful review of the frequently political context of great science.

273 **Real science: what it is, and what it means**
J. Ziman Cambridge University Press, 2002, 399pp. £18.99. ISBN 0521893100.
Excellent overview of how science really happens from experienced research scientist. Especially good discussion of the frequently subjective nature of peer review processes, and how these are changing as research becomes more collaborative and accountable.
Originally published 2000.

274 **Science: a history, 1543–2001**
J. Gribbin Penguin, 2003, 672pp. £8.99. ISBN 0140297413.
15 chapters in five volumes by experienced science writer 'from the perspective of someone who has been involved professionally in scientific research, not as a professional historian': 1. Out of the dark ages; 2. The founding fathers; 3. The enlightenment; 4. The big picture; 5. Modern times. Good bibliography. Index.

275 **Who wants to be a scientist?: choosing science as a career**
N. Rothwell Cambridge University Press, 2002, 176pp. £14.99. ISBN 0521520924.
'Scientific research is about discovering new things and applying them to improvements in life style for people and animals. But careers in science are now very demanding, requiring much more than a keen scientific mind and practical ability. If you are considering a career in research, have already embarked on your career and want to succeed, are uncertain which route to take, or advise, train or supervise scientists, this book should offer some helpful advice ... '
'. A valuable asset to anyone currently in, or contemplating, research, and should be recommended to all science undergraduates.' (*Biochemist*)

Dictionaries, thesauri, classifications

276 **Composition of scientific words: a manual of methods and a lexicon of materials for the practice of logotechnics**
R.W. Brown Smithsonian Institution Press, 2000, 882pp. $27.95. ISBN 1560988487.
Begins with text on the nature of English language and of Latin and Greek words and a discussion on the formation of words. Most of the book consists of an alphabetical list of words and parts of words in English, Latin, Greek and other languages giving origins, definitions and translations into other languages.
Reprint of the 1956 edn, which was a revision and update of previous editions, first of which published in 1927.
'A superb tool for composing scientific names ... And a fascinating work for anyone interested in words.' (*Taxon*)

277 **Dictionary of basic and general terms in metrology**
Tampere University of Technology
http://mit.tut.fi/dictionary
Multilingual dictionary, based on *International vocabulary of basic and general terms in metrology* (ISO, 1993), and covering a remarkable range of languages: Catalan, Chinese, Czech, Finnish, French, German, Hungarian, Italian, Latvian, Lithuanian, Portuguese, Romanian, Spanish, Swedish, Turkish, Russian. Last updated 2001.

278 **A dictionary of science**
A. Isaacs 4th edn, Oxford University Press, 2003, 864pp. £9.99. ISBN 0198607571.
Contains 9000 entries which give simple explanations. Covers biology, chemistry, physics, earth sciences and astronomy.
'The book will appeal not just to scientists and science students but also to the interested lay person. And it passes the most difficult test of any dictionary – it is well worth browsing.' (*New Scientist*)

Dictionnaire des techniques et technologies modernes: Anglais–Français (Modern dictionary of engineering and technology)
J.R. Forbes, ed. See entry no. 4501

279 **How many?: a dictionary of units of measurement**
R. Rowlett; University of North Carolina at Chapel Hill
www.unc.edu/%7Erowlett/units/index.html
Especially useful for describing and contrasting the INTERNATIONAL SYSTEM OF UNITS (SI) with the 'English traditional systems'.

Langenscheidts Fachwörterbuch Technik und Angewandte Wissenschaften: Deutsch–Englisch (Langenscheidt's dictionary technology and applied sciences: German–English)
P.A. Schmitt, ed. See entry no. 4503

280 **The new Penguin dictionary of science**
M.J. Clugston, ed. 2nd edn, Penguin, 2004, 752pp. £9.99. ISBN 0141010746.
Compact listing of about 7000 terms with diagrams and comprehensive cross-referencing. Covers chemistry, physics, mathematics, molecular biology, biochemistry, human anatomy and computing. Appendices list units, constants, periodic table and elements, amino acids, classification of organisms, derivatives and integrals, and the solar system.

281 **Scientifically speaking: a dictionary of quotations**
C. Gaither and A.E. Cavazos-Gaither, eds IOP Publishing, 2000, 496pp. £19.99. ISBN 075030636X.
http://bookmarkphysics.iop.org
Quotations are arranged in 87 broad categories and then by name of the person. The source of each quotation is given. Extensive bibliography, subject and author index. Suitable for general readers and for scientists wishing to use a quotation in classroom, presentation or paper.
Similar volumes available covering mathematics, physics, chemistry, etc.: see website.

Laws, standards, codes

282 **Bureau International des Poids et Mesures**
www.bipm.fr/en/home
The body which ensures world-wide uniformity of measurements and their traceability to the International System of Units. 'It does this with the authority of the Convention of the Metre, a diplomatic treaty between fifty-one nations, and it operates through a series of Consultative Committees, whose members are the national metrology laboratories of the Member States of the Convention, and through its own laboratory work.'

Well organized site (in English). Scientific work covers length, mass, time, electricity, ionizing radiation, chemistry – and there are collections of information for each of these areas, including excellent up-to-date bibliographies. Also links. A model facility.

- **Bureau National de Métrologie** www.bnm.fr/version_anglaise/index.english.htm. French national metrology body. Pleasant easy-to-use English language version of site.
- **The International System of Units: SI** (Le Système International d'Unités) www1.bipm.org/en/si. Base Units are a choice of seven well defined units which by convention are regarded as dimensionally independent: metre, kilogram, second, ampere, kelvin, mole, candela; Derived Units combine base units according to algebraic relations.

283 **Federal Agency for Technical Regulation and Metrology** [RUS]
www.gost.ru/sls/gost.nsf
Main directions; structure; standardization; metrology; certification; accreditation; standards catalogue; products and services; links; news. English language versions for much of the content.

284 **Institute for National Measurement Standards** [CAN]
http://inms-ienm.nrc-cnrc.gc.ca/main_e.html
Canada's national metrology institute. Useful briefing papers on accreditation, calibration, reference materials, etc. with the section on *Time Services* particularly helpful: web services; CBC daily time broadcasts; telephone talking clock; computer time and date; short wave broadcasts radio station; network time protocol; global positioning data; time zones and daylight saving time; frequency and time; FAQs.

285 **International Organization of Legal Metrology (Organisation Internationale de Métrologie Légale)**
www.oiml.org
Intergovernmental treaty organization whose membership includes Member States: countries that participate actively in technical activities, and Corresponding Members: countries that join the OIML as observers. *OIML Bulletin* (PDF), free access downloads, publications, etc.

286 **National Institute of Metrology, China**
http://en.nim.ac.cn/NIM.htm
'Founded in 1955, the National Institute of Metrology (NIM) is the highest state-level research center for metrology and the legal metrological technical center of the People's Republic of China, affiliated with the General Administration of Quality Supervision, Inspection and Quarantine (AQSIQ). Based on the constant efforts of about 800 staff for up to half a century, NIM has established 302 items of national primary standards and national standards of measurement, provided 586 verification services and 605 calibration services to the society, and participated in nearly 200 international comparisons. There are nearly 300 prize-winning R & D projects carried out by NIM, and 64 projects were awarded by state-level prizes. NIM will honor its commitment as the nation's leading metrological research body by working to provide the best technical support for trade, industry and society.'

National Institute of Standards and Technology
See entry no. 4523

287 **National Measurement Institute** [AUS]
www.measurement.gov.au
New institute, July 2004, formed from the National Measurement Laboratory (CSIRO), National Standards

Commission, and the Australian Government Analytical Laboratories, and continuing their work.

Questel.Orbit
See entry no. 4531

Official & quasi-official bodies

288 **Committee on Data for Science and Technology**
www.codata.org
Interdisciplinary scientific committee of International Council for Science, which works to improve the quality, reliability, management and accessibility of data resulting from experimental measurements, observations and calculations: including those in the physical sciences, biology, geology, astronomy, engineering, environmental science and ecology. It hosts databases of key values for thermodynamics, fundamental physical constants and a register of materials database managers.

Department of Energy
United States. Department of Energy See entry no. 4624

Engineering and Physical Sciences Research Council
See entry no. 4815

Homeland Security
United States. Department of Homeland Security See entry no. 4420

289 **House Committee on Science** [USA]
www.house.gov/science
Committee of US House of Representatives with Subcommittees on: Environment; Energy; Research; Space. Has jurisdiction over all non-defence federal scientific research and development. Hearings; Bills/publications; FAQs; Kids' page; etc. Winner of a Bronze Mouse in 2003 from the Congress Online Project.

290 **International Council for Science**
www.icsu.org
Non-governmental organization founded to bring together natural scientists in international scientific endeavour. Details of the work of its many committees, including a number of reports and reviews; international news on science policy; PDF downloadable copies of the newsletter *ICSU Insight*. A 'sensitive map' links through to the websites of ICSU's *National Members*; and amongst much other worthwhile information there are details of the 27 International Scientific Unions: many referenced elsewhere in this Volume.

- **Science international: a history of the International Council of Scientific Unions** **F. Greenaway** Cambridge University Press, 1996, 279pp. £40.00. ISBN 0521580153.

291 **United Kingdom Accreditation Service**
www.ukas.org
Accreditation is the 'procedure by which an authoritative body gives formal recognition that a body or person is competent to carry out specific tasks'; Certification is 'Procedure by which a third party gives written assurance that a product, process or service conforms to specified requirements'. UKAS is the sole national accreditation body recognized by government to assess, against internationally agreed standards, organizations that provide certification, testing, inspection and calibration services. Well designed trio of sites: Calibration; General; Testing.

- **American Association for Laboratory Accreditation** www.a2la.org. Nonprofit, non-governmental, public service membership society. Mission is 'to provide comprehensive services in laboratory accreditation and laboratory-related training. Services are available to any type of organization, be it private or government'.

Research centres & institutes

Belfer Center for Science and International Affairs
See entry no. 4550

292 **Council for the Central Laboratory of the Research Councils** [UK]
www.cclrc.ac.uk
'Owns and operates the Rutherford Appleton Laboratory in Oxfordshire, the Daresbury Laboratory in Cheshire and the Chilbolton Observatory in Hampshire.' Useful gateway to: Data, library and information services; large scale facilities; research activities; research highlights; the UK's laser, neutron and SR (synchrotron radiation) strategies – all with appropriate links. Educational service. Good site.

European Research Consortium for Informatics and Mathematics
See entry no. 6025

293 **German Academies of Science**
www.campus-germany.de/english/2.6.266.html [DESCRIPTION]
'Germany is a republic comprising 16 federal states. It therefore doesn't have one singular National Academy of Science but rather several different ones that are interconnected through the 'German Academy of Science' which is based in Mainz. There are 1400 active members in the academy, whose chief goal is to maintain and develop the study of science in Germany. It is particularly dedicated to the discipline of collaborative research.'

294 **Institute for Reference Materials and Measurements** [EUR]
www.irmm.jrc.be
European Commission body whose mission is 'to promote a common European measurement system in support of EU policies'. 'Competence' section of the website gives access to detailed information on: Reference materials; Isotopic measurements; Neutron data measurements; Radionuclide metrology; Food safety and quality. Similarly detailed descriptions of the Institute's Facilities and Research Areas. Events; news; publications.

International Institute for Applied Systems Analysis
See entry no. 4555

295 **National Center for Case Study Teaching in Science** [USA]
http://ublib.buffalo.edu/libraries/projects/cases/case.html
Aim is 'to promote the development and dissemination of innovative materials and sound educational practices for case teaching in the sciences. Our website provides access to an award-winning library of case materials ...' Includes reasonably up-to-date list of other case study sites on the

world wide web, plus links to science education related associations, discussions lists, journals, projects, reports, etc. There is also a subject-indexed dataset of contact details for US-based Case Study Teachers with, for each person, brief details of their use of the case study method.

296 **National Physical Laboratory** [UK]
www.npl.co.uk
UK national standards laboratory, maintaining world-class metrology facilities, and offering calibration services with the highest accuracy possible. Website gives information on its own activities and on measurement and standards generally. Learning Room provides range of resources for children and teachers.

- **National Measurement System** www.dti.gov.uk/nms/index.htm. The UK's national infrastructure of measurement laboratories.

297 **Nuffield Foundation** [UK]
www.nuffieldfoundation.org
'Our grants fund research and practical work in social policy, education and science. We also support the Nuffield Curriculum Centre and the NUFFIELD COUNCIL ON BIOETHICS.'

- **Nuffield Curriculum Centre** www.nuffieldcurriculumcentre.org. Leads and co-ordinates a range of school-based curriculum development projects and associated activities both within the Centre and in partnership with other institutions. Major work in science, mathematics and technology.

Online Ethics Center for Engineering and Science
Case Western Reserve University See entry no. 4819

298 **Science Learning Centres** [UK]
Great Britain. Department for Education and Skills and Wellcome Trust
www.sciencelearningcentres.org.uk
'The national network of *Science Learning Centres* will act as a catalyst for creating inspiring, intellectually stimulating and relevant science education. By mixing together teachers, technicians, advanced ICT, cutting-edge scientific thinking, industry expertise and high-quality professional development, the Science Learning Centres will provide the perfect conditions for innovation and inspiration.'

9 regional centres plus a recently established national centre. Comprehensive database of forthcoming courses with good search facility. Newsroom.

Associations & societies

299 **Académie des Sciences** [FR]
www.academie-sciences.fr
Part of the Insitut de France, the Académie develops science policy and international scientific relations, monitors teaching, contributes to the public understanding of science and supports the French scientific language. The website contains papers and reports and information on foundations and awards, membership, committees and links. Some pages in English.

300 **Accademia Nazionale dei Lincei** [ITA]
www.lincei.it
Founded in 1603. Aim is 'to promote, coordinate, integrate and spread scientific knowledge in its highest expression, in the unity and universality of culture'. The Academy is divided into two Classes: Physical, Mathematical and Natural Sciences and Moral, Historical and Philological Sciences. Each of the two Classes comprises 90 national members, 90 corresponding members and 90 foreign members. Limited English language resources accessible via the website; but an important science organization within Italy.

301 **American Association for the Advancement of Science**
www.aaas.org
Aim is to advance science and innovation throughout the world for the benefit of all people. Website provides extensive information on AAAS programmes, initiatives and policies and on careers and education. Additional information available for members. Publishes the leading periodical SCIENCE.

- **Commission on Professionals in Science and Technology** www.cpst.org. Founded in 1953 and is a participating organization within AAAS. Produces *Guide to Data on Scientists and Engineers*. Manages extensive and valuable *Clearinghouse for Information on Science, Engineering and Technology Disciplines*.
- **The establishment of science in America: 150 years of the** ***American Association for the Advancement of Science*** **S.G. Kohlstedt, M.M. Sokal and B.V. Lewenstein** Rutgers University Press, 1999, 272pp. $35.00. ISBN 0813527058.
- **EurekAlert!** www.eurekalert.org. Forum for research institutions, universities, government agencies and corporations to distribute science-related news to the media and provide public archive. International coverage. Registered reporters, freelances, journalists can access embargoed news.
- **Next Wave** http://nextwave.sciencemag.org. International career development magazine. Articles on research and non-research careers and employment are restricted to subscribers but other material is free. Gives news of factors affecting the science job market.
- **Science NetLinks** www.sciencenetlinks.com. Free internet-based content for K-12 science educators, including lesson plans and reviewed resources. All the site's content is organized around a set of *Benchmarks for Science Literacy* and classified against 12 broad themes and US grade level.

302 **Association for Science Education** [UK]
www.ase.org.uk
Professional association for UK teachers of science. 'Membership of the Association is now of the order of 20,000, with a broad spread of membership from primary and secondary teachers, to technicians, those involved in Initial Teacher Education, and also includes some 3500 student members. The Annual Meeting now attracts in excess of 3500 people and ASE has an enviable reputation worldwide.'

The Association publishes a range of journals and several books each year and the website has a useful *Resources* section covering: awarding and regulatory bodies; professional bodies, institutions and learned societies; scientific suppliers; publishers; industrial education liaison; other organizations. Monthly *ASE Newsletter* is freely available by e-mail.

303 **Association for Women in Science** [USA]
www.awis.org
Good source for links to statistics – and much else of value in this arena.

- **Women's history as scientists: a guide to the debates** **L.A. Whaley** ABC-CLIO, 2003, 252pp. $85.00. ISBN 1576072304. One of the *Controversies in Science Series* which *American Reference Books Annual* said was 'essential to understanding the exclusion of women throughout most of history from science, and the reluctance of women to enter science programs'.

304 Australian Academy of Science
www.science.org.au
Has defined four major program areas: recognition of outstanding contributions to science, education and public awareness, science policy, and international relations. Website gives information on these areas and includes pages on scientific, mathematical, health and environmental issues in the news, a science program for the seven years of primary school, and an electronic newsletter.

305 British Association for the Advancement of Science
www.the-ba.net
Dedicated to making science and its applications accessible to all. News of events and activities. Members have access to archives, e-mail alerts for events and online debates and surveys. Promotes *National Science Week*.

306 British Society for the History of Science
www.bshs.org.uk
Good news and events section. Quarterly PDF newsletter *Education Forum*. Guide to current history of science courses in UK and Ireland.

307 Campaign for Science & Engineering
www.sciencecampaign.org.uk
Object is 'to communicate to Parliament, Government and wider society, a proper appreciation of the economic and cultural benefits of scientific and technological research and development, and of the consequent importance to the nation of adequate funding of research by Government and industry'. Active *What's New* section – providing a good entrée to current issues and concerns. The links page has sub-headings: Academic institution members; Corporate members and sponsors; Scientific society members; Useful/interesting links.

Formerly named *Save British Science*.

- **Science for survival: scientific research and the public interest** **P. Cotgreave** British Library Publishing, 2003, 160pp. £14.95. ISBN 0712308911. Despite all the benefits of science to society, 'the public trusts the science and technology responsible for these benefits less and less. What a mess! Cotgreave's book is a valuable contribution to sorting it out.' *Times Higher Education Supplement*.

308 European Federation of National Academies of Sciences and Humanities
www.allea.org
Founded 1994 and federation of 52 academies of sciences and humanities in 39 European countries, whose member academies are self-governing communities of scientists and scholars.

'Allea seeks to: promote the exchange of information and experience between academies; offer European science and society advice from its member academies; strive for excellence in science and scholarship, high ethical standards and independence from political, commercial and ideological interests.'

Not a great deal on the website; but what is there is useful.

309 Euroscience
www.euroscience.org
Pan-European association of individuals interested in constructing scientific Europe 'from the bottom-up'. Members are scientists of all disciplines in the public sector, universities, research institutes as well as business and industry. Quarterly electronic newsletter *Euroscience news* contains short articles on science policy and association activities.

310 History of Science Society
www.hssonline.org
Site includes valuable *Guide to the History of Science*: 'Learn about people, institutions, organizations, and publications pursuing science history. Learn about history of science graduate programs. Contact more than 5000 scholars of science around the world. Discover a list of good places to start reading about the history of science ... which may be reproduced in whole of in part without further permission'.

The *HST Database* 'contains over 237,000 professionally collected entries from around the world ... (and is) ... the definitive international bibliography for the history of science, technology, and medicine'. However, this database is only accessible to members of the Society via the site (but is incorporated in RLG's HISTORY OF SCIENCE, TECHNOLOGY, AND MEDICINE database).

Institute of Measurement and Control
See entry no. 5437

311 Japan Society for the Promotion of Science
www.jsps.go.jp/english
'Independent administrative institution, established by way of a national law for the purpose of contributing to the advancement of science in all fields of the natural and social sciences and the humanities. JSPS plays a pivotal role in the administration of a wide spectrum of Japan's scientific and academic programs. While working within the broad framework of government policies established to promote scientific advancement, JSPS carries out its programs in a manner flexible to the needs of the participating scientists.'

Well organized (English-language) site with good news section and useful links.

312 National Academy of Sciences [USA]
www4.nationalacademies.org/nas/nashome.nsf
'Private, non-profit, self-perpetuating society of distinguished scholars engaged in scientific and engineering research, dedicated to the furtherance of science and technology and to their use for the general welfare ... Members and foreign associates of the Academy are elected in recognition of their distinguished and continuing achievements in original research; election to the Academy is considered one of the highest honors that can be accorded a scientist or engineer. The Academy membership is comprised of approximately 2000 members and 300 foreign associates, of whom more than 180 have won Nobel Prizes.'

The member listings are searchable by name, by scientific field, and by subject keyword, brief details of the work of each member being given – and collectively providing a fascinating overview of work in each subject in recent decades. Also, the listing of deceased members provides, when available, links to individual monographs of Biographical Memoirs.

- **Biographical memoirs** www.nap.edu/readingroom/books/biomems. Essays containing the life histories and selected bibliographies of deceased members of the Academy. They form a biographical history of science in

America: 'an important part of our nation's contribution to the intellectual heritage of the world'.

- **Marian Koshland Science Museum** www.koshlandsciencemuseum.org. Opened 2004: 'Uses engaging, interactive exhibits to bring to life the numerous reports conducted by the prestigious *National Academies* every year.
- **Proceedings of the National Academy of Sciences of the United States of America** Monthly. $275.00. ISSN 10916490. www.pnas.org. One of the world's most-cited multidisciplinary scientific serials. Publishes cutting-edge research reports, commentaries, reviews, perspectives, colloquium papers, and actions of the Academy.

313 National Science Teachers Association [USA]

www.nsta.org

Attractive wide-ranging site supporting NSTA's mission 'to promote excellence and innovation in science teaching and learning for all'. There is a very extensive links section 'Science Websites' recommended by NSTA members and non-members: good concise annotations against each entry. Also 'NSTA Recommends': 'Your best source for thoughtful, objective recommendations of science-teaching materials. Our panel of reviewers – top-flight teachers and other outstanding science educators – has determined that the products recommended here are among the best available supplements for science teaching. Why no negative reviews? They can be fun to read, even to write, but teachers are pressed for time – so only products that are reviewed favorably make their way into NSTA Recommends'.

Much else – some only accessible to NSTA members: an excellent resource.

314 New York Academy of Sciences

www.nyas.org

Wide ranging valuable site. Examples of offerings – some parts only accessible to members – include: *Academy eBriefings* Papers etc. from previous meetings; *Annals of the New York Academy of Sciences* Proceedings of a wide variety of international conferences; *Science Alliance* Consortium of 14 universities, teaching hospitals, and independent research facilities in the New York City metro area; *Science EduNet* Over 400 programs offered by science-rich institutions such as museums, universities, and non-profits in the New York and surrounding region.

315 Nobel Foundation

http://nobelprize.org/index.html

Clearly laid out and inviting site which offers information on all Prize winners to date, the Nobel Organization, Alfred Nobel, and Nobel events, as well as educational material and games. Consists of more than 9000 static documents, several databases and a number of multimedia productions with Nobel Prize connection.

316 Royal Institution of Great Britain

www.rigb.org

200-year-old institution that now concentrates on communicating scientific issues to the general public: especially through events for young people. Transcripts of talks and lectures; details of educational resources and activities.

317 Royal Society [UK]

www.royalsoc.ac.uk

Founded in 1660 and the UK national academy of science. Aims to be the champion of top quality science and technology in the UK. Critical policy advising role. Access to news of its activities, reports and statements on science policy, profiles of its fellows and scientists. Important *Library and Information Services*, especially strong in archival materials.

- **Catalogue of scientific papers** 1867–. 19 v. Cover the years 1860–1863, 1864–1873 and 1874–1900. Entries comprising bibliographic information are arranged by authors' names. Coverage is 1400 scientific and medical transactions of learned societies and reports of their committees.
- **International catalogue of scientific literature** Reprinted 1968 by Johnson Reprint Co, 1902–21. 17 v. – mathematics, mechanics, physics, chemistry, astronomy, meteorology, mineralogy, geology, geography, palaeontology, general biology, botany, zoology, human anatomy, anthropology, physiology, and bacteriology – within each annual volume.
- **Sc1** www.sc1.ac.uk. Created by the Society 'to interest and excite young people about modern scientific research, its significance for today's society, its complex history and the people involved in its development'.

318 Royal Society of Canada

www.rsc.ca

'The Royal Society of Canada, The Canadian Academy of the Sciences and Humanities, is the senior national body of distinguished Canadian scientists and scholars. Its primary objective is to promote learning and research in the arts and sciences. The Society consists of approximately 1700 Fellows: men and women from across the country who are selected by their peers for outstanding contributions to the natural and social sciences and in the humanities.'

In October 2004, the Canadian government announced the formation of a Canadian Academies of Science, modelled on the US National Academies.

319 Science Service [USA]

www.sciserv.org

'Founded in 1921 ... to advance public understanding and appreciation of science ... Through publications and programs, science fairs and scholarship competitions, Science Service helps young people utilize and strengthen their knowledge in science, math, and engineering. Many credit these experiences as a decisive factor in choosing a scientific career.' The Science Talent Search among its 3000 finalists includes three National Medal of Science winners, nine MacArthur Foundation Fellows, two Fields Medallists and five Nobel Laureates. The International Science and Engineering Fair is 'the world's largest pre-college celebration of science and the world's only international science competition for students in grades 9 through 12'.

- **Science News: the weekly newsmagazine of science** Weekly. $54.50 [2004]. www.sciencenews.org. Inviting design. A free e-mail newsletter each Saturday lists headline, summary, URL of each article published that week. Archives provides 'free access to the full text of articles that are available online (18 percent of all articles published)'.

Portal & task environments

320 Advanced Placement Digital Library [USA]

Rice University and National Science Digital Library

http://apdl.rice.edu [REGISTRATION]

Resources linked to AP content outlines published by the US College Board for biology, physics, and chemistry. The Advanced Placement Program allows high school students to take examinations for credit at college level.

321 **Community of Science**
www.cos.com [REGISTRATION]
Internet portal for scientists and researchers at universities, corporations and government agencies worldwide. Services include: *COS Expertise* Database of personal profiles of some 500,000 researchers from 1600 institutions worldwide; *COS Funding Opportunities* Source of grant information; *COS Abstract Management System* Online publishing system. Also provides host access to databases including US Patents, MEDLINE, AGRICOLA and GeoRef. Registration is free for individuals.

322 **Educational Realms: helping you find the pieces**
Ohio State University
www.stemworks.org
Educational REALMS (Resources for Engaging Active Learners in Mathematics and Science) also covers the environment. Useful material, freely available for reproduction, such as lesson plans, bulletins and digests suitable for teachers, parents and lifelong-learners. Links from lists of relevant journals, organizations, etc. New organization created in 2004 after the discontinuation of the federally funded *ERIC Clearinghouse for Science, Mathematics and Environmental Education.*

323 **ENC Online** [USA]
Eisenhower National Clearinghouse for Mathematics and Science Education
www.enc.org
Good resource for science and maths teachers sponsored by the US Department of Education. Provides curriculum resources, reference services and links to science and maths sites and newsletters. Many pages of projects, lesson topics and activities, professional development resources. ENC mission is 'to identify effective curriculum resources, create high-quality professional development materials, and disseminate useful information and products to improve K-12 mathematics and science teaching and learning'.

- **The Learning Matrix** http://thelearningmatrix.enc.org. Peer-reviewed digital resources for use in inquiry and problem-based learning in mathematics, science, and technology classes. Ranges from simulations and tutorials to research articles and video footage. Intended for student teachers.

324 **LESTER: Learning Science and Technology Repository**
Rice University
lester.rice.edu
Forum and clearinghouse for ongoing research and development efforts in educational technology and learning sciences. Data and analytical tools help the learning science and technology community in tracking emerging technologies and formulating informed future agenda.

325 **NSDL Scout Report for Physical Sciences**
University of Wisconsin, Internet Scout Project and National Science Digital Library Biweekly.
scout.cs.wisc.edu/Reports/ScoutReport/Current/
'The best new and newly discovered online resources in the physical sciences. Approximately 25 sites are reviewed in each report, covering materials of interest to everyone from kids to higher education, professionals to life-long learners.' Treats physics, astronomy, chemistry, geology and other physical science topics. First-rate service.

OSTI
Office of Scientific and Technical Information See entry no. 4584

326 **Planet Science** [UK]
National Endowment for Science, Technology and the Arts
www.planet-science.com
Designed 'for all children who study science and the teachers and other adults who support them ... Helping primary and secondary science teachers to teach inspirational science in the classroom is one of the key aims of Planet Science.'

Notable for the Library part of the site – 'the world's best science websites' – and its three newsletters designed respectively for adults, 10 years old and up, and primary school children.

327 **PSIgate**
University of Manchester and Resource Discovery Network
www.psigate.ac.uk
Access to some 11,000 high quality web resources in the physical sciences. Covers astronomy, chemistry, earth sciences, materials sciences, physics, and science history and policy. There is an excellent listing of the PSIgate browse headings, either A–Z alphabetical, or arranged by subject (showing top level headings then sub-levels). The current number of resources in each section is listed in brackets against each heading. Much other valuable information on this rich site.

Subsets of the site are cited elsewhere.

- **Science History/Policy Gateway** www.psigate.ac.uk/newsite/policy-gateway.html. Over 1000 resources evaluated and described relevant to histories of the constituent subject fields plus on scientific communication, ethics, philosophy, policy, public engagement, technology transfer.
- **Science Timelines** www.psigate.ac.uk/newsite/timelines.html. 'Notable events in the scientific world from prehistoric times to the present, broken down into separate subject areas. Each timeline contains dozens of key events which have shaped the world as we know it, together with suggested PSIgate searches.'
- **Spotlight** www.psigate.ac.uk/spotlight. 'Science articles and news features prepared exclusively for PSIgate by the award-winning science writer David Bradley.'

328 **Schoolscience** [UK]
www.schoolscience.co.uk
Biology, chemistry and physics resources for students and teachers arranged by pupil age: 11–14, 14–16 and 16–18 years. Includes written information, pictures, quick questions and some interactivity: all designed to support the UK curriculum and written by teachers. Sponsored by a range of leading institutes and companies.

'Schoolscience, supported by bodies such as the Association of the British Pharmaceutical Industry and the Institute of Petroleum, adds real colour to classroom theory by focusing on applications and processes ... Animation and questions keep you on your toes, although calling the resources 'e-sources' sounds a little highfalutin for what should be standard practice for the presentation of information on educational websites.' (*Sunday Times*)

329 **Science Enhancement Programme** [UK]
www.sep.org.uk
Gatsby Technical Education Project which aims 'to raise the achievement and motivation of secondary science students, particularly through practical activities. Its work is a continuing process of development, innovation, dissemination and influence. We are committed to

developing innovative resources that will support effective learning in science, and to providing courses and professional development opportunities for science teachers.'
Resources; Newsletter (PDF); Links; etc.

330 Science Resource Center
Thomson Gale.
www.gale.com/SciRC [DESCRIPTION]
New service launched Autumn 2004 providing one-stop shop for science classroom teaching. Includes: three core, proprietary reference titles, offering in-depth topic overviews from all science disciplines; 30 additional proprietary reference titles; 150 full-text science magazines; 8000 multimedia records; Links to 50 websites 'all chosen for their authoritative content and relevancy to the curriculum'. The results lists after searching organizes articles by content type – Reference; Magazines; Scholarly Journals; Newspapers and Newswires; Multimedia; Websites – giving for each item a reading level indicator and spotlighting topics of current high interest to students.

- **Macmillan Science Library** www.gale.com/pdf/facts/SciLib.pdf [DESCRIPTION]. Series of volumes intended for middle-school grades and up, now also accessible in the GALE VIRTUAL REFERENCE LIBRARY. Titles include: Animal sciences; Biology; Computer sciences; Mathematics; Plant sciences; Space sciences.
- **Opposing Viewpoints Resource Center** www.gale.com/OpposingViewpoints [DESCRIPTION]. Some 2000 articles from more than 170 titles in the print *Opposing Viewpoints* and other series plus: topic overviews; statistical tables, charts, and graphs; images; full-text periodicals and newspapers; and links to more than 1000 websites.
- **U X L** www.gale.com/uxl. Gale company whose 'goal is to make comprehensive reference books at a reading level of the average seventh grader, focusing on the curriculum topics they study in school and presenting that information in an attractive, inviting way'. Range of titles.

331 Science.gov: FirstGov for science [USA]
www.science.gov
Gateway provided by consortium of 17 US government science organizations within 12 federal agencies: primarily to websites and (often hard-to-access) scientific databases. Each agency selects its best science information for science.gov. Version 2.0 of the search software was launched in May 2004 and 'introduced real-time relevancy ranking to government science retrieval. This technology, funded by the Department of Energy, helps citizens sort through the government's reservoirs of research and return results most likely to meet individual needs'.

Discovering print & electronic resources

332 Bibliotheca Chemico-Mathematica: catalogue of works in many tongues on exact and applied science, with a subject index
H. C. Sotheran and H. Zeitlinger, comps H. Sotheran & Co, 1921–52.
53,489 annotated entries in five volumes (including supplements) compiled from Sotheran's sale catalogues. Details include author, full title, description, date and sale price. Records many old and rare books important in the history of science.

333 A catalogue of scientific and technical periodicals, 1665 to 1895
H.C. Bolton Reprint of 2nd edn, Johnson Reprint Corp, 1965, 1247pp. First published 1885.
A title catalogue in alphabetical order excluding transactions of learned societies. Part 1 is a corrected reprint of the 1st edn listing 4954 titles and Part 2 lists over 3600 new titles. There are cross-references from later titles, well known short titles and names of principal editors. Appended chronological table giving publication date of each volume of several hundred journals 1728–1895. Title index, general subject index and location list for titles in US libraries.

334 Catalogue of scientific serials of all countries, including the transactions of learned societies in the natural, physical and mathematical sciences, 1633–1876
S.H. Scudder Harvard University, 1879, 358pp. Reprinted New York, Kraus Reprints, 1965.
Lists over 4400 titles arranged by country and town of origin, with indexes of towns and titles and a brief subject index. Excludes serials devoted entirely to medicine, agriculture and technology. Complements H.C. Bolton's *Catalogue of scientific and technical periodicals*.

335 Frank Potter's Science Gems: great links to great science resources
F. Potter
sciencegems.com
This US website is designed for 'students, parents, teachers, scientists, engineers and mathematicians'. More than 12,000 science resources are listed by category, subcategory, and grade level. Entries have short annotations to help selection and links are kept reasonably up-to-date. Many useful snippets of information. Worth browsing around.

- **Martindale's 'The Reference Desk' J. Martindale** www.martindalecenter.com. Very wide-ranging resource discovery tool. Somewhat uneven in quality, but lots of useful leads, clearly presented – and with enthusiasm! Jim Martindale develops and maintains the Science Gems site with Frank Potter.

336 iFigure
www.ifigure.com
Links to very wide range of online calculators and worksheets. These are 'interactive, educational tools that provide information to help in planning, solving and making decisions for a multitude of problems and tasks that come up daily ...'

337 Index to physical, chemical and other property data
Arizona State University
www.asu.edu/lib/noble/chem/property.htm
Valuable A–Z index to selected library and internet resources that contain chemical, physical, thermodynamic, mechanical, toxicological, and safety data: compiled by the university's Science Reference Room within the Noble Science and Engineering Library.

Science and Technology Digest
See entry no. 4594

338 **Science experiments index for young people**
M.A. Pilger 3rd edn, Libraries Unlimited, 2002, 294pp. $65.00. ISBN 1563088991.
'Look no further to access the most appropriate science experiments and demonstrations for specific curricular needs. Updated with projects from the latest science books, this index is still the premier resource for tracking down excellent investigative activities perfect for science fairs, classroom presentations, or collaborative lab projects. Organized by subject. Modeling, math applications, social science work, and nutrition resources are just some of the thousands of areas explored. All Levels.'

Digital data, image & text collections

339 **arXiv.org e-Print archive**
Cornell University
http://arxiv.org
The 'e-print service in the fields of physics, mathematics, non-linear science, computer science, and quantitative biology'. Site includes Ginsparg's invited contribution to the Conference held at UNESCO HQ, Paris, 19–23 Feb 1996, given during the session *Scientist's View of Electronic Publishing and Issues Raised*: 'Winners and losers in the global research village'.

340 **iLumina**
University of North Carolina
http://turing.bear.uncw.edu
Digital library of thousands of sharable undergraduate teaching materials for chemistry, biology, physics, mathematics, and computer science. The resources range from images and video clips to entire courses. Resources are catalogued to capture technical and education-specific information. Searching and browsing provide access.

341 **Landolt-Börnstein Online**
Springer.
www.springeronline.com [FEE-BASED]
The major sets of chemistry, physics and technology data collections, now organized online into: Units and fundamental constants; Elementary particles, nuclei and atoms (Group I); molecules and radicals (Group II); Condensed matter (Group III); Physical chemistry (Group IV); Geophysics (Group V); Astronomy and astrophysics (Group VI); Biophysics (Group VII); Advanced materials and technologies (Group VIII).

The aim is a complete but critical compilation of all of the numerical data and functional relationships of science and technology resulting from physical, chemical, and technological research.

Available in print: see website.

MATLAB
See entry no. 4852

342 **NASA Technical Reports Server: NTRS**
National Aeronautics and Space Administration
http://ntrs.nasa.gov
Collects scientific and technical information from NASA's technical report servers and non-NASA sites using the OPEN ARCHIVES INITIATIVE Protocol for Metadata Harvesting (OAI-PMH). October 2004, announced provided access to full text PDF files.

November 2004, largest data subset was that which had replaced former *Center for AeroSpace Information Technical Report Server* database (c. 500,000 records); second largest was physics component of ARXIV.ORG E-PRINT ARCHIVE. Much smaller but significant collections also from BIOMED CENTRAL and the ENERGY CITATIONS DATABASE, as well as data harvested from a further 13 sites.

343 **The Open Science Project**
www.openscience.org
Project is 'dedicated to writing and releasing free and Open Source scientific software. We are a group of scientists, mathematicians and engineers who want to encourage a collaborative environment in which science can be pursued by anyone who is inspired to discover something new about the natural world'. Best populated subjects are: chemistry, mathematics, life sciences.

344 **Science Online**
Facts On File.
www.factsonfile.com [DESCRIPTION]
Highly visual resource making good use of hyperlink facilities, entries organized by the *National Science Education Standards* scheme for grades 6–12. Material within each feature – biographies, essays, definitions, diagrams, experiments, and the timeline – is arranged within 14 STM disciplines.

Publisher also offers Science Experiments On File, *as well as many other science resources online, in print or on CD-ROM: check the website.*

Directories & encyclopedias

345 **American men and women of science: a biographical directory of today's leaders in physical, biological and related sciences**
P.M. Kalte and K.H. Nemeh, eds 22nd edn, Gale, 2004, 9100pp. 8 v, $995.00. ISBN 0787673927.
www.galegroup.com [DESCRIPTION]
Includes approximately 120,000 living scientists, providing: birthdate; birthplace; field of specialty; education; honorary degrees; current position; professional and career information; awards; memberships; research information; addresses. Vol. 8 of the set is a comprehensive index listing scientists by field, and by state under field.

346 **Biographisch-literarisches Handwörterbuch der exakten Naturwissenschaften (Concise biographic-literary dictionary of the exact sciences)**
J.C. Poggendorff Wiley-VCH, 2000. 6 CD-ROM, €1399.00. ISBN 352740306X.
Dictionary first published in 1863 and containing biographic and literary data on around 29,000 natural scientists. This compilation contains its unabridged contents with hyperlinking between the entries. Search functions allow the user to look for people, places of birth and death, years, and subject areas. Pages from the original edition can be accessed from each individual entry.

347 **Black women scientists in the United States**
W. Warren Indiana University Press, 1999, 320pp. $35.00. ISBN 0253336031.
Lives and career paths of more than 100 scientists in the fields of anatomy, astronautics and space science, anthropology, biochemistry, biology, botany, chemistry,

geology, marine biology, mathematics, medicine, nutrition, pharmacology, psychology, physics, and zoology.

'The author writes in a lucid and clear manner. This biographical encyclopedia is a must for libraries serving high schools, the public and colleges.' (*E-STREAMS*)

348 A century of Nobel Prize recipients: chemistry, physics, and medicine
F. Leroy, ed. Marcel Dekker, 2003, 380pp. $150.00. ISBN 0824708768.
Arranged in three sections – physics, chemistry, medicine – each starting with an introduction to advances in that subject then listing the laureates by year, beginning in 1901 and ending with 2001. Entries include portrait, birth date and place, description of research carried out, and career development. Style varies slightly in the three sections. Well illustrated.

Translated from the French.

'One of the best introductions to the science that merited the Nobel Prize.' (*E-STREAMS*)

349 Collins biographical dictionary of scientists
T. Williams, ed. 4th edn, HarperCollins, 1995, 602pp. £25.00. ISBN 0004701097.
Standard biographical guide to the world's scientists and technologists. Contains 1300 entries, with subject-index, table of dates and reference-list of other scientists mentioned in the text.

350 Concise dictionary of scientific biography
American Council of Learned Societies 2nd edn, Scribner's, 2000, 1097pp. ISBN 0684806312.
Single volume abridgement of the 18 vol. *Dictionary of scientific biography* containing over 5400 entries arranged alphabetically by name of scientists who died before 1981. Portraits, lists by nationality and by field with a general index. For scientist bibliographies the reader must refer to the original Dictionary.

- **Dictionary of scientific biography C.C. Gillispie, ed.; American Council of Learned Societies** Scribner's, 1970–80. ISBN 0684147793. Contributed biographies with bibliographies of original works and secondary sources. Includes six essays on Indian, Babylonian, Assyrian, Egyptian, early Japanese and Mayan science. Index includes 40,000 names not the subject of articles.

351 Encyclopaedia of scientific units, weights and measures: their SI equivalences and origins
F. Cardarelli Springer, 2003, 848pp. £99.00. ISBN 185233682X.
Contains over 20,000 precise conversion factors and about 5000 definitions covering pure and applied science, technology, medicine and economics. Chapter 2 gives a brief history of the metric system and Chapter 3 details of other modern and ancient measuring systems. The bulk of the book (Chapter 4) is an alphabetical list of units giving a conversion to SI (Système International) equivalent followed by conversion tables by area of application. Chapter 5 gives fundamental constants.

Easy to use despite a confusing 'How to use this book' section – though some may find the relatively small typeface against a dark grey (and occasionally black) background difficult to peruse.

352 Eric Weisstein's World of Science
E. Weisstein Wolfram Research.
http://scienceworld.wolfram.com
Covers astronomy, physics, chemistry, and scientific biography with brief hyperlinked definitions and descriptions modelled on the highly successful format of *MathWorld* [q.v.]. However, most areas of the site outside mathematics not recently updated.

353 The history of science in the United States: an encyclopedia
M. Rothenberg, ed. Garland, 2001, 615pp. $150.00. ISBN 0815307624.
Coverage is science with some invention, technology, engineering and medicine. Many of the alphabetical entries are for individuals, organizations and bodies but there are also entries for topics such as public health, palaeontology and popularization of science. Two lengthy essays on science during the colonial period and science from 1789 to 1865. The encyclopedia is strong on discussion of explanations of past events.

Garland also publish History of astronomy *(1997) and* Instruments of science *(1998).*

354 The Hutchinson dictionary of scientific biography
R. Porter and M.B. Ogilvie, eds 3rd edn, Helicon, 2000, 1196pp. 2 v., £80.00. ISBN 1859863043.
Some 1300 biographies of scientists, mathematicians, engineers and inventors. Also contains short reviews of science and technology. Appendices give list of discoveries with dates, Nobel prize winners, chronology and index.

355 International encyclopedia of women scientists
E.H. Oakes Facts On File, 2002, 448pp. $82.50. ISBN 0816043817.
Alphabetical list of 500 women who have contributed significantly to their fields. Each entry has biographical details and an essay of about 750 words. Also contains a short general bibliography and indexes by field of specialization, country of birth, country of major scientific activity, and year of birth. General subject index; chronology.

Relatively strong US coverage; no reading lists with entries.

'It is a clearly written text with excellent detail and truly represents a wide range of scientific fields and accomplishments.' (*E-STREAMS*)

356 Notable scientists: 1900 to the present
B. Narins, ed. 2nd edn, Gale, 2001. This 5-volume set is considered the updated second edition of *Notable Twentieth-Century Scientists* published in 1995, $415.00. ISBN 0787617512.
Includes 1600 scientists active in the 20th century in all of the natural, physical, and applied sciences. Entries of 400 to 2500 words give name, birth/death dates, nationality and primary specialization, publications and further reading. Over 400 of the entries have photographs. Includes chronologies of scientific achievement as well as indexes in field of specialization, gender, nationality/ethnicity and subject.

357 Scientific laws, principles, and theories: a reference guide
R.E. Krebs Greenwood Press, 2001, 402pp. $77.95. ISBN 0313309574.
Alphabetical arrangement of theories, hypotheses and concepts giving explanations and subsequent developments. Examples include Aristotle's theories, Bernoulli's principle, Crick–Watson theory of DNA and Darwin's theory of evolution. There is a glossary of terms, a bibliography and a general index.

Wiley survey of instrumentation and measurement
S.A. Dyer, ed. See entry no. 5458

Handbooks & manuals

Electronic instrument handbook
C.F. Coombs, ed. See entry no. 5477

358 **Fundamentals of dimensional metrology**
R.H. Harlow, C. Dotson and R. Thompson 4th edn, Thomson Delmar Learning, 2003, 592pp. ISBN 0766820718.
www.delmarlearning.com [DESCRIPTION]
'Introduces the basic principles, techniques, and devices in the field of dimensional metrology, or the science of measurement. Topics include vernier and micrometer instruments, gage blocks, the dial indicator, calibration, and methods for angle measurement. The fourth edition updates the use of laser measurement technology and multisensor systems.'

359 **A guided tour of mathematical methods for the physical sciences**
R. Snieder 2nd edn, Cambridge University Press, 2004, 507pp. £19.95. ISBN 0521542618.
Interesting approach whereby all the material is presented in the form of problems. Topics covered include vector calculus, linear algebra, Fourier analysis, scale analysis, complex integration, Green's functions, normal modes, tensor calculus, and perturbation theory. 2nd edn contains new chapters on dimensional analysis, variational calculus, and the asymptotic evaluation of integrals
'a splendid book, quite a delight to see mathematical models from a different perspective ... treatment is so smooth that it is hard to know at any instant whether one is learning new tools or assimilating the applications to interesting examples ... excellent.' (*Astronomy & Geophysics*)

360 **Handbook of mass measurement**
F.E. Jones and R.M. Schoonover Chapman & Hall/CRC, 2002, 250pp. $99.95. ISBN 0849325315.
History of measurement, calibration, and maintenance of mass standards.

Instrumentation reference book
W. Boyes, ed. See entry no. 5497

361 **International critical tables of numerical data, physics, chemistry and technology**
E.W. Washburn [et al.], eds; National Academy of Sciences
Smithsonian Institution Press, 1926–1933.
www.knovel.com
Classic and widely-known reference. Contains vast amount of critical data on inorganic and organic compounds, and pure substances. Features physical, thermodynamic, mechanical, and other key properties – a major reference source used by those involved in chemistry, physics, and engineering.

In the online version, select tables are interactive and the entire content is full-text searchable. Additionally, the original 1000-page index is hyperlinked to each entry's appropriate page.

Mathematical techniques for engineers and scientists
L.C. Andrews and R.L. Phillips; SPIE – The International Society for Optical Engineering See entry no. 4858

Mathematics handbook for science and engineering
L. Råde and B. Westergren See entry no. 4859

362 **Measurement theory and practice: the world through quantification**
D.J. Hand Arnold, 2004, 320pp. £45.00. ISBN 034067783X.
Presents a unified overview of what measurement is, how it is done, how it has come to be, and what it is used for. Includes chapters on measurement in medicine and the physical sciences.

The measurement, instrumentation and sensors handbook
J.G. Webster, ed. See entry no. 5503

Statistical design and analysis of experiments: with applications to engineering and science
R.L. Mason, R.F. Gunst and J.L. Hess See entry no. 575

363 **Tables of physical and chemical constants**
G.W.C. Kaye and T.H. Laby, comps 16th edn, Longman, 1995, 611pp. Prepared under the direction of an Editorial Committee, £42.00. ISBN 0582226295.
Standard tool. Sections are: Units and fundamental constants; General physics (mass and mechanical quantities, materials, heat, acoustics, optics, electricity, astronomy and geophysics); Chemistry (elements, properties of compounds, electrochemistry, chemical thermodynamics); Atomic and nuclear physics (electrons, photon absorption, work function, particle absorption, radioactivity, fission, fusion, nuclei and particles); Miscellaneous engineering data.

Writing successful science proposals
C.L. Folt and A.J. Friedland See entry no. 6423

Keeping up-to-date

364 **American Scientist: the magazine of Sigma XI, the scientific research society**
Bimonthly. $65.00. ISSN 00030996.
www.americanscientist.org
Sigma Xi is a non-profit membership society of more than 70,000 scientists and engineers who were elected to the Society because of their research achievements or potential. It has more than 500 chapters at universities and colleges, government laboratories and industry research centres.

Good reflective magazine. Online features include: Site of the week; Author interview; Scientists' nightstand (a leading scientist's recent reading and favourite authors). Book reviews.

Full access to the site is provided without additional charge to Sigma Xi members and other individual magazine subscribers, and to institutional subscribers who arrange site licenses.

365 **FirstScience.com**
www.firstscience.com
Lively enjoyable site which 'offers science articles in various categories including space, physics, biology, earth science, and technology. As well as a science quiz, links, science and nature poems, games, webcams and comprehensive environmental, space and science news, its aim is to make science fun as well as accessible.'

366 **Public Understanding of Science**
SAGE Publications, 1992–, Quarterly. $534.00. ISSN 09636625.
http://pus.sagepub.com
'The only journal to cover all aspects of the inter-relationships between science (including technology and medicine) and the public. Topics Covered Include: surveys of public understanding and attitudes towards science and technology; perceptions of science; popular representations of science; scientific and para-scientific belief systems; science in schools; history of science education and of popular science; science and the media; science fiction; scientific lobbying; evaluative studies of science exhibitions and interactive science centres; scientific information services for the public; popular protest against science ('anti-science'); science in developing countries and appropriate technology.'

367 **ScienceWeek**
Science Week/Spectrum Press.
www.scienceweek.com
Specially written digests 'designed to provide researchers, policy makers, teachers, students, and science writers with access to scientific fields outside their own specialty. But anyone with some background in science will usually find material of interest in each issue ... The reports in ScienceWeek are selected to cross barriers between the sciences, to illuminate breakthroughs, ideas, concepts, policy, and historical aspects.' 18 reports per week.

368 **Scientific Computing World**
Europa Science, Bimonthly.
www.scientific-computing.com/main.html [REGISTRATION]
'Europe's only magazine dedicated to the computing and information technology needs of professional scientists and engineers ... written by European experts to meet the information requirements of an influential and loyal European audience.'

Mathematics

Five key types of reference resource can be characterized within mathematics:

- *Academic research* **The historical literature is very important – and very specialized; not just the scholarly journal literature but also collections of the works of eminent mathematicians with just a few exemplars referenced here.**
- *Learning/teaching* **Recent examples are given of maths textbooks, courseware, etc. for the subject fields covered.**
- *Policy issues* **Particularly because of the serious concern at the shortage of mathematicians, there is an important set of resources referenced.**
- *Popularizations* **There is considerable interest in mathematics as a recreational activity; nowadays resources of most interest to the non-specialist can be found online within encyclopedias, dictionaries, handbooks, and via the maths-specific web portals.**
- *Applied mathematics* **These resources generally are cited later within the section treating the relevant application.**

Traditionally mathematics is a very book-based discipline, with other resources such as journals, proving to be too specialised for anyone except experts of particular topics. However, thankfully for the student or eager amateur, the advent of the world wide web has provided an additional source of accessible, useful, and above all, quality sites. Fortunately, also, there are a number of excellent up-to-date print and electronic guides to the literature of mathematics available.

There is such a panoply of specialities in mathematics that it would be all too easy to break the subject down into dozens of groupings. However, as this book is principally intended for non-specialists who we trust will appreciate a somewhat broader brush, we have used only a limited number of subject fields. This has necessitated the drawing together of a few references that, in an ideal world, would perhaps be better suited to separate categories.

Those seriously interested in discovering more about mathematics should make themselves familiar with the *Mathematics Classification Scheme* **(MCS2000). This invaluable taxonomy, constructed by working mathematicians, is an excellent way to disentangle the interrelationships between the various mathematical fields. Mathematics also offers a range of exceptional subject-based encyclopedias, tables, and directories of formulas. These should be the key reference of any new student delving into the discipline. Naturally, the collections and tables will also be of prime importance to the working mathematician.**

Introductions to the subject

369 **1089 and all that: a journey into mathematics**
D. Acheson Oxford University Press, 2002, 184pp. £12.99. ISBN 0198516231.
http://home.jesus.ox.ac.uk/~dacheson [COMPANION]
A rewarding and enjoyable introduction.
'Parts of this book are extremely funny ... [It is] an ideal stocking filler ... An ideal present for friends and relatives who are not mathematicians, but have enough curiosity to spend a gentle afternoon trying to find out what mathematics is about ... Buy this book.' (*London Mathematical Society Newsletter*)
'There are a few mathematicians who succeed in writing popular accounts of their craft without being superficial or condescending. With this book Acheson has joined the best of them.' (*Times Higher Education Supplement*)

- **Mathematics: a very short introduction T. Gowers** Oxford University Press, 2002, 143pp. £6.99. ISBN 0192853619. A pleasant inviting read.

370 **The A to Z of mathematics: a basic guide**
T.H. Sidebotham Wiley, 2002, 474pp. $69.95. ISBN 0471150452.
'Makes math simple without making it simplistic'. Good reliable introductory guide for 'the millions of people who would love to understand math but are turned away by fear of its complexity'.

371 **Conversations with a mathematician: math, art, science and the limits of reason: a collection of his most wide-ranging and non-technical lectures and interviews**
G.J. Chaitin Springer, 2002, 158pp. £14.99. ISBN 1852335491.
'G. J. Chaitin is at the *IBM Thomas J. Watson Research Center* in New York. He has shown that God plays dice not only in quantum mechanics, but even in the foundations of mathematics, where Chaitin discovered mathematical facts that are true for no reason, that are true by accident. This book collects his most wide-ranging and non-technical lectures and interviews, and it will be of interest to anyone concerned with the philosophy of mathematics, with the similarities and differences between physics and mathematics, or with the creative process and mathematics as an art.'
'This book is wonderful in both senses of the word ... superlatively good and full of wonder. Nonmathematicians could read it, too, but as I read it I felt glad (and proud) to be a mathematician!' (*The American Mathematical Monthly*)

372 **Development of mathematics 1950–2000**
J.-P. Pier, ed. Birkhäuser, 2000, 1372pp. £147.50. ISBN 3764362804.
Follow-up to the editor's *Development of mathematics 1900–1950* (1994. 730pp. £75.50. ISBN 3764328215) which grew out of a colloquium organized by the Luxembourg Mathematical Society in 1992. Aims to provide both a history and a guide through the 'maze of mathematical theories' which have arisen over the last 50 years. Includes viewpoints of more than 40 mathematicians, most of them active researchers and renowned specialists in their fields. Statistics. Bibliography. 200 portraits of mathematicians.

373 **From here to infinity**
I. Stewart Oxford University Press, 1996, 310pp. £9.99. ISBN 0192832026.
Revised edition of the author's *The problems of mathematics* –

a layman's introduction to modern mathematics by a renowned mathematical communicator.

'An excellent account of what's going on in mathematics right now.' (*Guardian*)

- **What shape is a snowflake? I. Stewart** Weidenfeld & Nicolson, 2001, 224pp. £20.00. ISBN 0297607235. 'A masterpiece ... Not just a book to excite young people about science ... Should also spur their parents to encourage their offspring to pursue mathematics and science with a renewed enthusiasm and vigour.' *Times Higher Education Supplement*.

374 The heart of mathematics: an invitation to effective thinking

E.B. Burger and M. Starbird, ed. 2nd edn, Key College Publishing, 2005, 850pp. Includes CD-ROM, $84.95. ISBN 1931914419.
www.heartofmath.com [COMPANION]

'As you read this book, we hope you will discover the beauty and fascination of mathematics, admire its strength, and see its value to your life.'

'*The Heart of Mathematics* is a superb book (on the 1st edn).' (*The Mathematical Gazette*)

375 A history of mathematics: an introduction

V.J. Katz 2nd edn, Addison-Wesley, 1998, 864pp. $108.00. ISBN 0321016181.

Detailed survey very well written by leading authority – though needs a good grounding in basic mathematics for its full appreciation.

1st edn 1993.

- **Companion encyclopedia of the history and philosophy of the mathematical sciences I. Grattan-Guinness, ed.** Johns Hopkins University Press, 2003. V. 1. 864 pp. $49.95. ISBN 0801873967; V. 2. 976 pp. $49.95. ISBN 0801873975. Originally published Routledge, 1994. Companion to the author's *The Norton history of the mathematical sciences: the rainbow of mathematics*.
- **A concise history of mathematics D.J. Struik** 4th edn, Dover Publications, 1987, 288pp. $8.95. ISBN 0486602559. http://store.doverpublications.com [DESCRIPTION]. Good shorter introduction, concentrating on history, rather than on the nature of the mathematics itself.

376 The history of mathematics

J. Tabak Facts on File, 2004.

Based on the standards of the USA National Council of Teachers of Mathematics, covers key developments including 'discussions of certain narrowly framed but historically important problems ... to help convey the excitement of mathematical discovery to students'. Bibliography; chronology.

- **Algebra: sets, symbols, and the language of thought** $35.00. ISBN 0816049548.
- **Geometry: the language of space and form** $35.00. ISBN 081604953X.
- **Mathematics and the laws of nature: developing the language of science** $35.00. ISBN 0816049572.
- **Numbers: computers, philosophers, and the search for meaning** $35.00. ISBN 0816049556.
- **Probability and statistics: the science of uncertainty** $35.00. ISBN 0816049564.

377 The international review of mathematics

2004, 44pp. Downloadable PDF.
www.cms.ac.uk/irm

The UK Engineering and Physical Sciences Research Council (EPSRC) and Council for the Mathematical Sciences (CMS) jointly organized 'an international review of the standing, quality and potential of mathematics research in the UK. This review was the sixth in a series undertaken by EPSRC in collaboration with the relevant subject societies. The aim of the Review was to establish an independent assessment of the quality of UK research, compared with international standards'.

378 The language of mathematics: making the invisible visible

K.J. Devlin W H Freeman, 1998, 344pp. $10.00. ISBN 071673379X.

Successfully communicates for those already with some experience of the subject, the details of what maths is and what mathematicians do and why, using a series of topics as illustrations: number theory, logic, motion, geometry, tilings and packings, topology, probability and particle physics. Technically demanding in parts, however.

379 Making mathematics count: the report of Professor Adrian Smith's inquiry into post-14 mathematics education [UK]

A. Smith The Stationery Office, 2004, 180pp. PDF.
www.mathsinquiry.org.uk/report/MathsInquiryFinalReport.pdf

Report of more detailed follow-up to the Roberts' Review SET FOR SUCCESS. Terms of reference were: 'To make recommendations on changes in the curriculum, qualifications and pedagogy for those aged 14 and over in schools, colleges and higher education institutions to enable those students to acquire the mathematical knowledge and skills necessary to meet the requirements of employers and of further and higher education'.

380 A mathematician's survival guide: graduate school and early career development

S.G. Krantz American Mathematical Society, 2003, 222pp. $28.00. ISBN 082183455X.
www.ams.org/bookpages/gscm/index.html [COMPANION]

Describes the basic elements of a mathematical education, including choosing a program, gaining admission, exams, advisors, jobs. Krantz is a lively writer whose earlier books – such as *How to teach mathematics*, *A primer of mathematical writing* and *Techniques of problem solving* – all published by AMS, have been very favourably reviewed.

381 Mathematics in nature: modeling patterns in the natural world

J.A. Adam Princeton University Press, 2003, 360pp. $39.50. ISBN 0691114293.
http://pup.princeton.edu/math [DESCRIPTION]

Describes '*some* of the mathematics that lies behind *some* of the phenomena we encounter in the natural world around us'. Helpfully, limited to objects that can be seen with the naked eye: leaves, trees, spider webs, bubbles, waves, clouds, rainbows, etc. Partly for this reason, a highly engaging introduction to several areas of mathematics. Items in the substantial bibliography are annotated if they are recommended for general interest reading.

URL gives access to details of the range of current maths texts produced by Princeton.

382 Mathematics unlimited: 2001 and beyond

B. Engquist and W. Schmid, eds Springer, 2001, 1237pp. £30.50. ISBN 3540669132.

'What are the important developments in present-day mathematics? Where is mathematics headed? Our anthology attempts to shed light on these questions.'

64 stimulating chapters by leading experts 'ranging all the way from mathematical logic to applications of mathematics in the film industry'.

383 **Notable mathematicians: from ancient times to the present**
R.V. Young, ed. Thomson Gale, 1998, 612pp. $120.00. ISBN 0787630713.
300 of the world's leading mathematicians from the earliest times; includes individuals under-represented in previous resources such as women and minority group members. Each entry 450–1500 words; selected writings and further reading. Good introduction.
'The stories provide an insight ... into a sampling of individuals whose accumulated mathematical abilities have brought humanity to where it is today. This volume is a great read, and it is highly recommended for any reference collection.' (*American Reference Books Annual*)

384 **The philosophy of mathematics today**
M. Schim, ed. Oxford University Press, 2003, 656pp. £29.00. ISBN 0199262624.
Leading figures deal with 'foundational issues, from the nature of mathematical knowledge and mathematical existence to logical consequence, abstraction, and the notions of set and natural number. The contributors also represent and criticize a variety of prominent approaches to the philosophy of mathematics, including platonism, realism, normalism, constructivism, and formalism'.

Dictionaries, thesauri, classifications

385 **2000 mathematics subject classification**
American Mathematical Society Downloadable PDF.
www.ams.org/msc
Used to categorize items covered by MATHEMATICAL REVIEWS and ZENTRALBLATT MATH. Broken down into over 5000 two-, three-, and five-digit classifications, each corresponding to a discipline of mathematics (e.g. 11 = Number theory; 11B = Sequences and sets; 11B05 = Density, gaps, topology).

- **A gentle introduction to the Mathematics Subject Classification scheme** www.math-atlas.org. Intended for a person with approximately the training of an undergraduate mathematics student; links lead to pages at the MATHEMATICAL ATLAS website itself which assume somewhat greater familiarity with the sub-disciplines.

386 **Connecting mathematics**
University of Cambridge
http://thesaurus.maths.org
Brief explanations of mathematical terms and ideas in English, Danish, Finnish, Hungarian, Lithuanian, Polish, Slovak. Some Spanish. Thumbnail links to all the illustrated entries via a range of galleries (image, flash, cinderella, etc.): an attractive feature.

- **Core subject taxonomy for mathematical sciences education** Math NSDL Taxonomy Committee, 2002. http://people.uncw.edu/hermanr/MathTax. Arose out of work done by the *American Mathematics Metadata Task Force* (www.mathmetadata.org/ammtf) in 1999–2000.
- **Millennium Mathematics Project** http://mmp.maths.org. Members of the MMP team led the team which developed the thesaurus. The Project operates a wide range of maths education and outreach activities including the *NRICH* website offering free mathematics enrichment resources for ages 5–19.

387 **Dictionary of applied math for engineers and scientists**
E. Previato CRC Press, 2002, 168pp. $44.95. ISBN 1584880538.
Bridging the mathematical terminology gap for scientists, engineers and computer scientists, this text contains accessible definitions of terms often encountered in other disciplines.

388 **Earliest known uses of some of the words of mathematics**
J. Miller, ed.
http://members.aol.com/jeff570/mathword.html
Excellent resource, scholarly but well presented. There is a companion *Earliest uses of various mathematical symbols* and for both there is an extensive list of *Sources* – a valuable bibliography in its own right. Just slightly less serious are the pages headed *Ambiguously defined mathematical terms at the high school level*; and there is finally an enjoyable set of *Images of mathematicians on postage stamps*.

389 **HyperMath**
Georgia State University
http://hyperphysics.phy-astr.gsu.edu/hbase/hph.html
Fascinating hypertextual organization of concepts in applied mathematics with links to their applications to problems in physics and astronomy. 'It is not systematic or complete in any sense, but is a collection of foundation mathematics principles and applications which were collected as the need was encountered in developing the HYPERPHYSICS material.'

390 **Langenscheidt's dictionary of mathematics: English, German, French, Russian**
G. Eisenreich and R. Sube Langenscheidt, 1996, 1458pp. £175.00. ISBN 3861170744.
www.langenscheidt.de/english/catalogue/static/physik.html
35,000 words in each part. Covers fundamentals (incl. mathematical logic; set theory; combinatorial analysis; category theory); algebra; topology; analysis; stochastics; mathematical programming; theory of games; geometry; mathematical instruments; theory of automata.
Also published are dictionaries of acoustics and physics: see website.

- **Elsevier's dictionary of mathematics in English, German, French and Russian** **K. Peeva [et al.], comps** Elsevier, 2000, 996pp. £134.00. ISBN 0444829539. Contains 11,652 entries with more than 4750 cross-references (but there are no definitions).

391 **Mathematical quotations server**
M. Woodward; Furman University
math.furman.edu/~mwoodard/mquot.html
Maintained within the mathematics department at the university. 'Now, by popular demand, you may download the whole collection at once' (circa 80 printed pages).

392 **Mathematics dictionary**
R.C. James and A.A. Alchian, ed. Van Nostrand Reinhold, 1992, 548pp. ISBN 0442012411.
Now out-of-print but good short definitions, with appendices covering some French, German, Russian and Spanish equivalent terms.

393 **A maths dictionary for kids**
J. Eather
www.amathsdictionaryforkids.com
Animated, interactive, highly colourful and engaging

dictionary explaining over 500 common mathematical terms in simple language.

394 **PRIME: platonic realms interactive mathematics encyclopedia**
Math Academy Online/Platonic Realms.
www.mathacademy.com/pr/prime
Excellent easily browsable offering with options to search the whole or specific areas of mathematics; to work at elementary or advanced level or both. Very good cross-referencing within definitions. Many entries in the A–Z sequence supported by background reading – and there is much else to discover on the parent site. Discreet commercial sponsorship.

395 **Russian–English dictionary of the mathematical sciences**
R.P. Boas, ed.; American Mathematical Society 2nd edn, 1990, 343pp. $40.00. ISBN 0821801333.
Well established reference text.
1st edn originally produced by A.J. Lohwater.

Official & quasi-official bodies

396 **International Mathematical Union**
www.mathunion.org
Non-governmental and non-profit organization promoting international co-operation in mathematics. The bi-monthly *IMU-Net* 'aims to improve communication between IMU and the worldwide mathematical community, by reporting decisions and recommendations of IMU, and highlighting issues that are under discussion ... In addition, IMU-Net will report on major international mathematical events and developments, and on other topics of general mathematical interest'.

Site also has a comprehensive list of links to worldwide mathematical societies, as well as to other maths sites; and there is an impressive *Electronic World Directory of Mathematicians* within which 709 persons were registered, early June 2004.

IMU is a scientific union of the INTERNATIONAL COUNCIL FOR SCIENCE.

- **The Abel Prize** www.abelprisen.no/en. IMU nominates members of the Committee for this international prize for outstanding scientific work in the field of mathematics, founded in 2003, and worth approximately €750,000.
- **Committee for Electronic Information Communication: CEIC** www.ceic.math.ca. Established in 1998 to advise IMU on electronic matters. Range of potentially valuable activities include a newssheet *IMU on the Web* plus a proposed *World Digital Mathematics Library*: see http://www.wdml.org/publications/comm-jackson.pdf.
- **Fields Medal** www.mathunion.org/medals/Fields/index.html. Awarded every four years on the occasion of the *International Congress of Mathematicians* to recognize outstanding mathematical achievement for existing work and for the promise of future achievement.
- **Mathematics: frontiers and perspectives V. Arnold [et al.], eds** American Mathematical Society, 2000, 459pp. $39.00. ISBN 0821826972. IMU sponsored volume for World Mathematical Year and planned to present the state-of-the-art of mathematics at the end of the 20th century.
- **Mathematics without borders: a history of the International Mathematical Union O. Lehto** Springer, 1998, 399pp. £27.00. ISBN 0387983589. Includes bibliography pp 329–366.
- **Math-Net: an international information and communication system** www.math-net.de. Aimed to be a global electronic information and communication system for mathematics providing: results of mathematical research and development; teaching material; information about working mathematicians and mathematical institutions. Limited to date.

International Union of Theoretical and Applied Mechanics
See entry no. 5885

397 **NSF: Directorate for Mathematical and Physical Sciences** [USA]
National Science Foundation
www.nsf.gov/funding/research_edu_community.jsp
Covers mathematics, astronomical science, physics, chemistry, and materials research, each of which is a Division with quite extensive pages covering current programs, research highlights, news, for kids only – including a set of links.

Research centres & institutes

398 **Centre for Innovation in Mathematics Teaching** [UK]
www.ex.ac.uk/cimt
Established in 1986, and is 'a focus for research and curriculum development in mathematics teaching and learning, with the aim of unifying and enhancing mathematical progress in schools and colleges'.

Projects include:

International progress in mathematical attainment Monitors the progress made in the mathematical attainments of pupils (starting in Year 1) in 17 countries worldwide, with the aim of making recommendations for the best practice in teaching mathematics;

Mathematics enhancement programme Wide range of material for the teaching of mathematics, covering Years 1 to 11, and aimed at enhancing and encouraging whole class interactive teaching.

- **British Society for Research into Learning Mathematics** www.bsrlm.org.uk.
- **Dictionary of units F. Tapson** www.ex.ac.uk/cimt/dictunit/dictunit.htm. Summary of most of the units of measurement to be found in use around the world today (and a few of historical interest), together with the appropriate conversion factors needed to change them into a 'standard' unit of the SI. Useful historical background.

399 **Clay Mathematics Institute** [USA]
www.claymath.org
Leading institute which – to celebrate the new millennium – named seven *Prize Problems*, focusing on 'important classic questions that have resisted solution over the years'. A $1 million prize has been allocated for the solution of each. On an interesting site also is offered for sale the CD of *Fermat's Last Tango*.

- **The millennium problems: the seven greatest unsolved mathematical puzzles of our time K.J. Devlin** Granta (Originally published Basic Books, 2002), 2004, 237pp. £20.00. ISBN 1862076863.

400 **Fields Institute for Research in Mathematical Sciences** [CAN]
www.fields.utoronto.ca
Leading institute whose 'mission is to enhance mathematical activity in Canada by bringing together mathematicians from Canada and abroad, and by promoting contact and collaboration between professional mathematicians and the increasing numbers of users of mathematics. Thus the Institute supports research in pure and applied mathematics, statistics and computer science, as well as collaboration between mathematicians and those applying mathematics in areas such as engineering, the physical and biological sciences, medicine, economics and finance, telecommunications and information systems.'

Established in 1994 with the *Centre de Recherches Mathématiques* the *CRM-Fields Prize* to recognize exceptional work in the mathematical sciences. Audio and/or slides available for talks given at the Institute. Education Programme resources: e.g. *On-line mathematics: visions and opportunities, issues and challenges, and recommendations* (2001, PDF).

- **International Mathematical Science Institutes** www.fields.utoronto.ca/aboutus/IMSI.html. International consortium of research institutes in the mathematical sciences that run thematic research programs and have large visitor programs. Meetings are normally held in conjunction with major international meetings.

401 **Institute for Mathematics and its Applications** [USA]
University of Minnesota
www.ima.umn.edu
Established in 1982 by the NATIONAL SCIENCE FOUNDATION, as a result of a national competition. Mission is 'to increase the impact of mathematics by fostering research of a truly interdisciplinary nature, linking mathematics of the highest caliber and important scientific and technological problems from other disciplines and industry'. Quarterly *Update* treats various areas of maths application, as well as reporting on the work of the Institute. Considerable details of papers etc. given at workshops accessible on website.

- **IMA volumes in mathematics and its applications** Springer-Verlag, 1986–. www.ima.umn.edu/springer/volumes.html [DESCRIPTION]. (V. 139, 2004).

402 **Isaac Newton Institute for Mathematical Sciences** [UK]
www.newton.cam.ac.uk
'Now firmly established as the UK's national research institute for mathematics.' Funded by the ENGINEERING AND PHYSICAL SCIENCES RESEARCH COUNCIL and a wide range of public and private sector donors, including the University of Cambridge, where it is based.

'From its inception, it was intended that the Institute should be devoted to the Mathematical Sciences in the broadest sense. In this respect the Institute differs significantly from similar institutes in other countries. A key criterion in the selection of scientific programmes is the extent to which they are interdisciplinary, bringing together research workers with very different backgrounds and expertise. Sometimes a single mathematical topic may attract a wide entourage from other scientific fields. In the first 10 years there have been 22 Fields Medallists and 8 Nobel Prize winners attending Institute programmes.'

403 **Mathematical Sciences Research Institute** [USA]
www.msri.org
Exists to 'further mathematical research through broad programs in the mathematical sciences and related activities. Founded in 1982 the Institute has been primarily funded by the NATIONAL SCIENCE FOUNDATION with additional support from other agencies and sponsors'. Site provides access to extensive series of lectures via *Streaming Video*, one of the main goals of this offering being to discover efficient uses of Internet technology for mathematical communication. Also has a *Journalist in Residence Program*.

404 **Mathematics Education Centre** [UK]
http://mec.lboro.ac.uk
Mission is 'is to become an internationally-recognised centre of excellence in the learning, teaching and support of mathematics and statistics in higher education'. Good example of UK-based work in this area. Provides access to *Mathcentre* which 'offers students quick reference guides, practice and revision materials, workbooks and online practice exercises on many branches of mathematics, including: Algebra, Arithmetic, Complex Numbers, Differentiation, Finance, Functions and Graphs, Geometry, Guides and Case Studies, Integration, Matrices, Numeracy Skills, Sequences and Series, Statistics, Trigonometry and Vectors'.

- **Gallery of Mathematical Images** http://info.lboro.ac.uk/departments/ma/gallery/index.html. Created by the university's mathematics department.

Associations & societies

405 **American Mathematical Society**
www.ams.org
'Founded in 1888 to further mathematical research and scholarship, the American Mathematical Society fulfils its mission through programs and services that promote mathematical research and its uses, strengthen mathematical education, and foster awareness and appreciation of mathematics and its connections to other disciplines and to everyday life.

'The Society has over 28,000 individual members and 550 institutional members in the USA and around the world. Programs and services for AMS members and the mathematical community include professional programs such as meetings and conferences, surveys, employment services; publications including *Mathematical Reviews* (a database of nearly 2 million items covering over 60 years of mathematics literature), journals, and over 3000 books in print; support for Young Scholars Programs and the Mathematical Moments program of the Public Awareness Office; resources such as *MR Lookup* for researchers and authors; and a Washington office that connects the mathematical community with the broader scientific community and with decision makers who determine science funding.'

Exceptionally clear and well structured website: a joy to use! (tempered only by *Google* and similar generic tools never being the best search engines for domain specific sites). Amongst a wealth of information, there is the extensive list of resources *Math on the Web* noted below, with detailed coverage of the scholarly journals of mathematics (but the updating schedule across the service is quite variable). The *What's New in Mathematics* pages are also worth highlighting.

- **AMS Bookstore** www.ams.org/bookstore. Includes much useful material apart from details of the Society's publications themselves; e.g.

Where to find AMS books; Titles recommended for classroom use; Book series distributed by the AMS (from other publishers).

- **Combined Membership List** www.ams.org/cml. Names/addresses of members of AMS, and Mathematical Association of America, Society for Industrial and Applied Mathematics, American Mathematical Association of Two-Year Colleges, Association for Women in Mathematics, Canadian Mathematical Society.
- **Directory of mathematics preprint and e-print servers** www.ams.org/global-preprints. Aims to provide URLs and e-mail contacts for all mathematical preprint and e-print servers throughout the world. Divided into *Umbrella*: covering all areas of maths; *Special subject*; *Institute and departmental*; *Retired*: no longer operating.
- **Math on the web** www.ams.org/mathweb. Extensive LINKS divided into: Guides; Online; Offline (document delivery, libraries, etc.); Organized (by classification; topics; history); People; Reference (dictionaries, handbooks, serials); Servers (institutions, associations); Related (tools etc.).
- **Mathematics Books Online** www.ams.org/online_bks/online-books-web.html. Aims to provide a comprehensive gateway.

406 **Association for Women in Mathematics** [USA]
www.awm-math.org
A non-profit organization 'encouraging and promoting females in the mathematical sciences'. Extensive website includes information on the Association's professional development and outreach programmes, as well as resources and opportunities for mathematical students to become involved with activities.

407 **Australian Mathematical Society**
www.austms.org.au
The 'national society of the mathematics profession in Australia, promoting and developing mathematical knowledge'. Good set of links to sites providing information about Australian mathematics.

408 **British Society for the History of Mathematics**
www.bshm.org
Unsophisticated site but including much valuable material – albeit not necessarily recently updated: for instance, a *Mathematical Gazetteer of the British Isles* providing 'information about where mathematicians were born, lived, worked, died, or are buried or commemorated'.

409 **Canadian Mathematical Society**
www.cms.math.ca
Pleasant easily used well laid out site with good sets of resource lists – especially *Links to Mathematical Societies around the world* – alongside news of activities of the society itself.

410 **Conference Board of the Mathematical Sciences** [USA]
www.cbmsweb.org
'Umbrella organization consisting of sixteen professional societies all of which have as one of their primary objectives the increase or diffusion of knowledge in one or more of the mathematical sciences. Its purpose is to promote understanding and cooperation among these national organizations so that they work together and support each other in their efforts to promote research, improve education, and expand the uses of mathematics.'

411 **Council for the Mathematical Sciences** [UK]
www.cms.ac.uk
Established in 2001 by the INSTITUTE OF MATHEMATICS AND ITS APPLICATIONS, the LONDON MATHEMATICAL SOCIETY and the ROYAL STATISTICAL SOCIETY to provide a forum for the three societies.

- **Careers in Mathematics** www.mathscareers.org.uk. Aims to provide 'comprehensive access to information on careers in mathematics and statistics, and on the role of mathematics and statistics in careers in many other sectors, from the sciences and engineering to business and finance'. [www.scenta.co.uk].
- **Institute of Mathematics and its Applications** www.ima.org.uk. UK professional and learned society for qualified and practising mathematicians. Its mission is 'to promote mathematics in industry, business, the public sector, education and research'. Now has over 5000 members. Useful website.
- **Mathematical Association** www.m-a.org.uk. UK organization which 'exists to bring about improvements in the teaching of mathematics and its applications, and to provide a means of communication among students and teachers of mathematics'.

412 **European Mathematical Society**
www.emis.de/ems-general.html
Seeks to 'further the development of all aspects of mathematics in the countries of Europe, in particular aiming to promote research in mathematics and assisting with problems of mathematical education'.

- **Electronic Library of Mathematics** www.emis.de/ELibM.html. Impressive portal to online journals, article collections, monographs, and other electronic resources. Access is generally free, except for some periodicals with a 'moving wall': a certain delay period after which resources become freely available.
- **Euler: your portal to mathematics publications** www.emis.de/projects/EULER. Originally funded by the EU; little activity since 2002.
- **Euro-Math-Job: vacant academic positions in the European departments of mathematics and statistics** www.maths.lth.se/nordic/Euro-Math-Job.html. Simple well designed gateway to job pages around Europe set up and maintained by the various member societies of the EMS.
- **European Mathematical Information Service** www.emis.de. Entrée to a wide range of services – beyond and including those listed here. Supported by EMS.
- **European Research Centres on Mathematics: ERCOM** www.crm.es/ERCOM. Committee under EMS consisting of Directors of European Mathematical Research Centres.
- **The Jahrbuch Project: electronic research archive for mathematics** www.emis.de/projects/JFM. Database of *Jahrbuch über die Fortschritte der Mathematik* – which reviewed more than 200,000 mathematical publications during the period 1868–1942 – together with a digital archive of the most important mathematical publications for the same period.

413 **European Women in Mathematics**
www.math.helsinki.fi/EWM/index.html
'Affiliation for women bound by a common interest in the position of women in mathematics.' Founded in 1986; office in Helsinki, Finland. Meetings, news, mentoring, etc. Early 2005 there were participating members from almost 30 European countries.

414 **London Mathematical Society**
www.lms.ac.uk
Founded in 1865 this Society is the major British learned society for mathematics. It was established for the 'promotion and extension of mathematical knowledge, undertaking various publications and holding regular

meetings, conferences and symposia', and provides financial and other support to a wide range of mathematical activities.

415 **Mathematical Association of America**
www.maa.org
Mission is to 'advance the mathematical sciences, especially at the collegiate level'. Its 27000 members include 'university, college, and school teachers; graduate and undergraduate students; pure and applied mathematicians; computer scientists; statisticians; and many others in academia, government, business, and industry'.

- **American Mathematical Monthly** www.maa.org/pubs/monthly.html. The most widely read mathematics journal in the world. Publishes articles, as well as notes and other features, about mathematics and the profession. Its readers 'expect articles to inform, stimulate, challenge, enlighten, and even entertain'.
- **Math Gateway: an NSDL pathway to undergraduate mathematics** www.maa.org/news/101404gateway.html. 4-year NSF grant awarded October 2004 to 'support the creation of a portal ... (that) will bring together collections with significant mathematical content and services of particular importance to the delivery and use of mathematics on the web'.
- **MathDL** www.mathdl.org. Component of *NSDL* providing access to: *Journal of Online Mathematics and its Applications*; *Digital Classroom Resources*; *Convergence*: online magazine for the history of mathematics; *OSSLETS*: open source, sharable mathlets.

416 **National Council of Teachers of Mathematics** [USA]
www.nctm.org
US and Canada-based organization providing 'guidance, support, and advocacy for mathematics teachers at all levels – from elementary to research'. While the site provides a range of information which can be accessed by anyone, certain portions of the site, most notably publications (e.g. *Principles and standards for school mathematics*), are restricted to members only.

- **The Young Mathematicians' Network: Serving the community of young mathematicians** www.youngmath.net. A loose organization of mathematicians in the junior part of their careers founded in 1993. Good useful website.

417 **Pi Mu Epsilon** [USA]
www.pme-math.org
Purpose is 'the promotion of scholarly activity in mathematics among the students in academic institutions'. Founded 1914 at Syracuse University; currently over 300 chapters at USA colleges and universities. Conferences, grants, journal.

418 **Society for Industrial and Applied Mathematics**
www.siam.org
Major professional society with emphasis on supporting methodology and personal development for mathematicians in the applied mathematics domain. The Society has a comprehensive publishing program in applied and computational mathematics. In addition to *SIAM News*, *SIAM Review*, and *Theory of Probability and Its Applications*, they publish 11 peer-reviewed research journals.

Libraries, archives, museums

419 **Mathematics Museum** [JAP]
http://mathmuse.sci.ibaraki.ac.jp/indexE.html
Interesting eclectic virtual museum with links to related museums in the world. English and Japanese (and a musical welcome!).

Portal & task environments

420 **EEVL: Mathematics**
Heriot-Watt University and Resource Discovery Network
www.eevl.ac.uk/mathematics/index.htm
The leading UK-based subject collection of evaluations of resources in mathematics (and engineering and computing), as well as a national focal point for online access to information in these subjects. EEVL's primary audience are students, staff and researchers in UK higher and further education, but their overall site has achieved worldwide recognition for its excellence.

As well as the core resource guide, EEVL offer a number of other valuable services including a list of their current *Top 100 sites*, access to lists of the websites of UK and worldwide maths institutions, news of events, a jobs and recruitment facility, and so on. A key reference resource.

- **Mathematics current awareness services** www.eevl.ac.uk/mathematics/currentawarenessmaths.htm. Key sites for keeping abreast of recent internet resources, books, articles, and conferences, symposia and conference papers.
- **Recommended news sources in mathematics and statistics** www.eevl.ac.uk/mathematics/newsfeed.htm. Links to core titles in: General mathematics; Probability and statistics; Mathematics education; etc. as well as some more specialist disciplines.

421 **LTSN Maths, Stats and OR Network** [UK]
University of Birmingham and Higher Education Academy
ltsn.mathstore.ac.uk/index.shtml
One of UK higher education's *Subject Centres*, based in Birmingham but in partnership with Glasgow and Nottingham Trent Universities and the RSS Centre for Statistical Education. Wide range of resources – check the *A–Z Contents* page – including: Etalk (Links within mailing lists); MathML ('A low-level specification for describing mathematics as a basis for machine to machine communication. It provides a much needed foundation for the inclusion of mathematical expressions in Web pages': see www.w3.org/Math); News; Publications; Resources. The last provides a link, for instance, to *Mathcentre*: 'Offers students quick reference guides, practice and revision materials, workbooks and online practice exercises on many branches of mathematics, including: Algebra, Arithmetic, Complex Numbers, Differentiation, Finance, Functions and Graphs, Geometry, Guides and Case Studies, Integration, Matrices, Numeracy Skills, Sequences and Series, Statistics, Trigonometry and Vectors'.

422 **The Math Forum @ Drexel**
Drexel University
www.mathforum.org
Mission is 'to provide resources, materials, activities, person-to-person interactions, and educational products and services that enrich and support teaching and learning in an increasingly technological world'. Participants include 'teachers, students, researchers, parents, educators, and citizens at all levels who have an interest in math and math education'.

Rich site providing access to a valuable set of services including:

- *Ask Dr. Math* Question and answer service for math students and their teachers;
- *Discussion groups* Archives of newsgroups, mailing lists, web-based discussions;
- *Internet Mathematics Library* Annotated catalog of mathematics and mathematics education websites;
- *Key Issues* Very useful short overviews;
- *Math resources by subject* Lists of 'what we believe are the best Internet resources for each topic': K-12; College; Advanced;
- *Mathematics education* World wide web resources for mathematics education;
- *Teacher2Teacher* Resource for teachers and parents who have questions about teaching mathematics
- *Teachers' Lounge* Participation in current math education discussions.

USA focused, but valuable more generally. Although initially funded by the NSF, the Forum 'now depends on contributions from users, sponsors, foundations, and other institutions to provide quality services'.

423 The Mathematical Atlas: a gateway to modern mathematics
D. Rusin
www.math-atlas.org
Collection of articles about 'aspects of mathematics at and above the university level, but (usually) not at the level of current research. The goal of this collection is to introduce the subject areas of modern mathematics, to describe a few of the milestone results and topics, and to give pointers to some of the key resources where further information is to be found. Like any good atlas, we try to present several ways to look at each area and to show its relationship with neighboring areas and sub-areas.'

Not apparently updated since 2002, but still good for browsing – especially for those relatively new to the subject. Note the introductory *Tour of the subfields of mathematics*.

424 MSPnet: the math and science partnership network [USA]
TERC Inc.
http://hub.mspnet.org
The MSP supports partnerships that unite K-12 schools, institutions of higher education and other stakeholders in activities that ensure that 'no child is left behind'. This hub facilitates the sharing of resources and tools by participants but – inter alia – also provides general access to a range of useful resources in this arena, including to over 400 articles of interest to leaders engaged in K-12 science and mathematics education reform.

425 NIST: Math, Statistics, and Computational Science
National Institute of Standards and Technology
http://math.nist.gov
Clearly laid-out gateway to NIST's activities in these arenas. Links for instance to the Institute's *Mathematical and Computational Science Division* and *Statistical Engineering Division* within its *Information Technology Laboratory*. However, note that several areas of the site had not recently been updated, late 2004.

- **Guide to Available Mathematical Software**
  http://gams.nist.gov. Cross-index and virtual repository of mathematical and statistical components of use in computational science and engineering. Includes extensive list of *Other Sources of Math Software Information*.

426 PlanetMath.Org
http://planetmath.org
'Virtual community which aims to help make mathematical knowledge more accessible. PlanetMath's content is created collaboratively: the main feature is the mathematics encyclopedia with entries written and reviewed by members. The entries are contributed under the terms of the GNU Free Documentation License (FDL) in order to preserve the rights of both the authors and readers in a sensible way.'

- **Nicolas Bourbaki**
  http://planetmath.org/encyclopedia/NicolasBourbaki.html. The collective pseudonym used by an informal corporation of French mathematicians, numbering from 10 to 20 at any one time. This anonymous society is writing a comprehensive treatise on mathematics: *Eléments de Mathématique*.

Discovering print & electronic resources

427 A bibliography of collected works and correspondence of mathematicians
S.W. Rockey, comp.
www.library.cornell.edu/math/collectedworks.php
'Through the nineteenth century only a relatively small group of people made almost all of the important advances in mathematics, and collected works volumes exist for most of them. By the twentieth century more people were producing mathematics and the number of collected works proliferated. Collected works allow the researcher, historian or librarian to have much of the important literature available in a convenient and compact form. Sometimes collected works are the only way to find articles which were originally published in titles that are scarcely held even in the most comprehensive libraries. Collected works are often very useful in deciphering obscure citations. The best collected works may also include unpublished papers, correspondence, commentaries, translations, biographies, bibliographies, etc. that are unavailable anywhere else.'

Marvellous compilation; over 1000 entries; invaluable.

CompuMath Citation Index
See entry no. 6051

428 The history of mathematics from antiquity to the present: a selective annotated bibliography
J.W. Dauben, ed.; American Mathematical Society Rev edn, 2000. CD-ROM version, $49.00. ISBN 0821808443.
Revised from the book version published in 1985. Most entries are annotated, several with links to reviews of the resource referenced.

'An impressive resource, it has 4,800 annotated bibliographic citations, twice the number of references included in the 1985 print version ... a great addition to the disc is a listing of Internet sites that pertain to the history of mathematics, complete with URL links. This fantastic program is a valuable resource for mathematicians, mathematics historians, teachers and students of mathematics, and any layperson interested in mathematics.' (*Choice* Outstanding Academic Title 2001)

429 International Reviews on Mathematical Education (Zentralblatt für Didaktik der Mathematik)
Bimonthly. 1997 to 2000 available as printed and electronic; from 2001 only electronic. Current issue and previous 5 issues only accessible to subscribers, €190.00. ISSN 1615679X.
www.fiz-karlsruhe.de/fiz/publications/zdm/zdmp1.html
Information service and reference tool in mathematics education and computer science education from pre-school

level to teacher training and adult education. Reviews circa 500 journals plus books, reports, conference papers, etc.

- **Mathematics education subject classification** www.fiz-karlsruhe.de/fiz/publications/zdm/zdmclass.pdf. Detailed classification also known as the *ZDM Subject Classification Scheme*.

430 **Mathematics and Statistics Links**
Heriot-Watt University
www.ma.hw.ac.uk/maths.html
The University's Department of Mathematics maintain a comprehensive list of URLs of *UK mathematics departments, centres and institutes* – with a separate list of those for *UK statistics departments*. They also provide a reasonably extensive and up-to-date set of *External Links*.

431 **Mathematics Web Sites**
Pennsylvania State University
www.math.psu.edu/MathLists/Contents.html
A relatively extensive as well as well structured list of worldwide mathematically-related websites. Maintained within the Mathematics Department. Divided into: General; Related topics; Mathematics department web servers; Societies and associations; Institutes and centres; Commercial pages (publishers and software providers); Mathematics journals; Mathematics preprints; Subject area pages (algebra, algebraic topology, analysis, categories, combinatorics, complexity theory, computer algebra, computer tomography, constants, and so on); Other archived materials; Mathematics software. The list can be searched by keyword.

No annotations and no indication of updating schedule (a number of links were no longer active); but good for gaining a rapid overview of the range of web resources available in this field.

432 **The Maths Internet Guide**
B. Handal
www.members.optusnet.com.au/~borishandal/MathsInternetGuide
Well designed entrée to a carefully chosen set of some 100 websites, notable for their interactivity. The sites can be grouped by curriculum topics or grade levels, or both. There is a particularly useful list of maths education journals and magazines, all of which offer full-text articles or abstracts. A nice clean site.

433 **MathSciNet**
American Mathematical Society
www.ams.org/mathscinet [FEE-BASED]
One of the two most important databases of current and recent scholarly mathematical literature (the other being ZENTRALBLATT MATH). Facts and figures October 2004 were: 72220 items added in 2004; 1799 journals covered; links to 449918 original articles; 10843 active reviewers; 417254 authors indexed. Corresponds to *Current Mathematical Publications* and *Mathematical Reviews*.

- **Current Mathematical Publications** 17/year. $642.00. ISSN 03614794. Subject index of recent and forthcoming mathematical publications selected and classified by the editors of *Mathematical Reviews*. Data is added daily to *MathSciNet*; AMS members can receive a free e-mail notification of newly added items.
- **Mathematical Reviews** 1940–, Monthly. $547.00. ISSN 00255629. Reviews of the world's current mathematical literature, classified according to the 2000 MATHEMATICS SUBJECT CLASSIFICATION. Over 60,000 reviews or abstracts are published each year.

NSDL Scout Report for Math, Engineering, and Technology
University of Wisconsin, Internet Scout Project and National Science Digital Library See entry no. 4593

434 **RDN Virtual Training Suite: Mathematician** [UK]
G. Fratus and S. Hewett; University of Birmingham and Resource Discovery Network
www.vts.rdn.ac.uk/tutorial/maths
One of the series of online internet orientation tutorials aimed at participants in UK further and higher education. Contains tour of key internet sites in mathematics.

435 **Using the mathematics literature**
K.K. Fowler Marcel Dekker, 2004, 389pp. $169.95. ISBN 0824750357.
Very good edited collection of contributions covering general tools and strategies for exploring the mathematical literature followed by a series of chapters on recommended resources in: History of mathematics; Number theory; Combinatorics; Abstract algebra; Algebraic and differential geometry; Real and complex analysis; Differential equations; Topology; Probability theory; Numerical analysis; Mathematical biology; Mathematics education. Many of these chapters provide – inter alia – excellent entrées to the state-of-the-art in the respective fields.
Series: Books in Library and Information Science, 66.

'. highly recommended for all math, science, and technology libraries at the undergraduate, graduate, and research institution level. This includes biology and life science collections as the book contains a chapter on mathematical biology, a fairly new area of research. Larger public libraries with science collections may find it useful to have this volume to identify materials for ILL retrieval or to support local math teachers.' (*E-STREAMS*)

- **Guide to information sources in mathematics and statistics** **M.A. Tucker and N.D. Anderson** Libraries Unlimited, 2004, 348pp. $65.00. ISBN 1563087014. 'Overall, this is a convenient and well structured distillation of a great deal of knowledge and it represents very good value for money.' *Library + Information Update*.

436 **WWW Virtual Library: Mathematics**
Florida State University
web.math.fsu.edu/Science/math.html
Concise listing; brief annotations; clearly laid out. When visited late 2004 had not been updated since September 2003, but was still worth perusing.

437 **Zentralblatt MATH**
European Mathematical Society FIZ Karlsruhe/Springer.
www.emis.de/ZMATH
Abstracting and reviewing service in pure and applied mathematics containing more than 2.0 million entries drawn from more than 2300 serials and journals. Now covers the period from 1868 to the present following integration of data from THE JAHRBUCH PROJECT. Similarly to MATHSCINET, entries are classified according to the 2000 MATHEMATICS SUBJECT CLASSIFICATION. Mirror sites.

Digital data, image & text collections

438 **Digital Library of Mathematical Functions**
http://dlmf.nist.gov
Project to develop a replacement for the Handbook cited below. Website has useful background and contextual

information though from the information given it seems doubtful mid-2004 that the target date for publication (early 2005) will be met.

- **Handbook of mathematical functions with formulas, graphs, and mathematical tables** **M. Abramowitz** 1972. First published by the National Bureau of Standards in 1964. Referred to as *AMS55*. Remains a technical best-seller and is among the most widely cited of all math reference compendia. Can be ordered from the US GPO and various commercial publishers.

439 Electronic Mathematical Archiving Network Initiative: EMANI
www.emani.org
Project started in 2002 to ensure long-term preservation and accessibility of mathematical information in digital form. Supported by leading mathematical societies, the scientific publisher Springer-Verlag and four major international academic libraries: Cornell University Library (Ithaca, New York), the State and University Library Göttingen (Germany), Tsinghua University Library (Beijing), and Orsay Mathematical Library (Paris).

440 The MacTutor history of mathematics archive
J.J. O'Connor and E.F. Robertson; University of St Andrews
www-history.mcs.st-andrews.ac.uk/history/index.html
Biographies of more than 1300 mathematicians as well as cross-referenced articles on development of mathematical ideas. Chronologies show the lives of the mathematicians as well as events for any day in history. Also a collection of articles on famous curves, giving their history and including pictures and associated concepts.

- **The history of mathematics** **D.R. Wilkins** www.maths.tcd.ie/pub/HistMath. Collections on the work of Berkeley, Boole, Cantor, Newton, Riemann and Rouse Ball plus a wide-ranging and well organized set of links to websites relevant to the history of mathematics.

441 MATHnetBASE
CRC Press.
www.mathnetbase.com [FEE-BASED]
Full-text searchable collection of, at October 2004, 87 mathematical works.

MATLAB
See entry no. 4852

442 Netlib Repository
AT&T Bell Laboratories, University of Tennessee and Oak Ridge National Laboratory
www.netlib.org
Collection of freely available mathematical software, papers, and databases of interest to the numerical, scientific computing, and other communities. The collection is replicated at several sites around the world, automatically synchronized.

Directories & encyclopedias

443 Biographies of women mathematicians
http://www.agnesscott.edu/lriddle/women/women.htm
Project maintained by students at Agnes Scott College, in Atlanta, Georgia, to 'illustrate the numerous achievements of women in the field of mathematics'. Contains biographical essays, comments, and some photographic images.

444 CRC concise encyclopedia of mathematics
E.W. Weisstein, ed. 2nd edn, Chapman & Hall/CRC, 2002, 3252pp. CD-ROM, $119.95. ISBN 1584883472.
Written in an informal style so as to make accessible to a broad spectrum of readers with a wide range of mathematical backgrounds and interests. The cross-referencing is especially helpful and of course particularly powerful in the electronic version. An excellent compilation (though the visual design of the print version is not so excellent).
Note that this encyclopaedia is a precursor of MATHWORLD.

445 Encyclopaedia of mathematics
I.M. Vinogradov and M. Hazewinkel, eds Reidel, 1988–. 2 supplementary vols. Updated and annotated translation of the *Soviet Mathematical Encyclopaedia*, £1550.00. ISBN 1556080107.
http://reference.kluweronline.com [FEE-BASED]
Major work covering the whole of mathematics with three kinds of articles: survey-type dealing with the various main directions of mathematics; medium-length contributions tackling more detailed concrete problems, results and techniques and requiring more background and expertise than the first kind; short reference definitions.

The aim is a 'completeness level whereby every theorem, concept, definition, lemma, construction which has a more-or-less constant and accepted name by which it is referred to by a recognizable group of mathematicians occurs somewhere and can be found via the index.'

The Preface to the third supplementary volume explains how this notion has been progressed noting – inter alia – that the final ultimate version of the encyclopaedia is likely to be electronic only.
Available online: see website.
'The online Encyclopaedia of Mathematics is an excellent resource for graduate-level students and for faculty in mathematics and computer science. It is also particularly valuable for computer science students and researchers who are focusing on computational subjects such as genetic algorithms or artificial intelligence.' (*Reference Reviews*)

446 Encyclopedia of mathematics education
L. Grinstein and S. Lipsey, eds Taylor & Francis, 2001, 880pp. £131.00. ISBN 081531647X.
400 alphabetically arranged entries. Useful for mathematics teachers of any level for background information, project inspiration, and research papers.

447 Encyclopedic dictionary of mathematics
K. Ito, ed.; Mathematical Society of Japan 2nd edn, MIT Press, 1993. 2 v. Originally published 1987, $125.00. ISBN 0262590204.
Standard work; 450 quite detailed articles covering the full spectrum of mathematics.

448 The mathematics genealogy project
North Dakota State University
www.genealogy.ams.org
An attempt to produce an inclusive catalogue of all professional mathematicians working in the world, including those working in computer science or operational research. There are 'some errors and omissions due to the difficulty in collecting the biographical data, but this remains an invaluable resource for tracing key researchers'.

449 **MathWorld**
E. Weisstein Wolfram Research.
mathworld.wolfram.com
The leading 'comprehensive and interactive mathematics encyclopedia intended for students, educators, math enthusiasts, and researchers. Like the vibrant and constantly evolving discipline of mathematics, this site is continuously updated to include new material and incorporate new discoveries'. Contributions to the site are encouraged: *What's New on MathWorld* is a daily bulletin. See also Eric Weisstein's World of Science.

450 **The universal book of mathematics: from Abracadabra to Zeno's Paradoxes**
D. Darling Wiley, 2004, 400pp. $40.00. ISBN 0471270474.
www.daviddarling.info/works/Mathematics/mathematics.html [COMPANION]
Welcome compilation following the author's success with similar ventures in related disciplines. The website provides a complete list of entries.

Handbooks & manuals

451 **CRC standard mathematical tables and formulae**
D. Zwillinger, ed. 31st edn, Chapman & Hall/CRC, 2003, 910pp. $49.95. ISBN 1584882913.
Core text with chapters: Analysis; Algebra; Discrete mathematics; Geometry; Continuous mathematics; Special functions; Probability and statistics; Scientific computing; Financial analysis; Miscellaneous. The last includes a list of professional mathematical organizations, a section of electronic mathematical resources, and brief biographical notes of 40 mathematicians ranging from Ah'mose (c1650 BCE) to Turing.

452 **Encyclopaedia of mathematical sciences**
Springer, 1989–. ISSN 09380396.
www.springer-sbm.com
With a coverage 'at times encyclopaedic and sometimes pedagogical', the 142 volumes (as of early 2004) in this series cover a vast range of topics in impressive depth, written by leading figures in each relevant subfield.
Through the URL review the wide range of companies now owned by Springer, *including* Birkhäuser Verlag, *a notable publisher of mathematical monographs, edited collections and collected works. Alternatively, approach Springer's* Mathematics *subject area offerings via their home page (www.springeronline.com), including their extensive series* Lecture Notes in Mathematics *– of which 1840 volumes had been produced, early 2004.*

Essential mathematical methods for physicists
H.J. Weber and G.B. Arfken See entry no. 618

A guided tour of mathematical methods for the physical sciences
R. Snieder See entry no. 359

453 **Handbook of mathematics**
I.N. Bronshtein [et al.], eds 4th edn, Springer, 2003, 1157pp. £46.00. ISBN 3540434917.
Based on the German 5th edn which was originally derived from a Russian text. The style is characterized – and, indeed, fulfilled – as 'short, easily understandable, comfortable to use, but featuring mathematical accuracy (at a level of detail consistent with the needs of engineers)'. 20 main sections ranging from Arithmetic to Computer algebra systems, with a final chapter of Tables. Detailed table of contents and subject index. An attractive volume.

454 **Handbook of writing for the mathematical sciences**
N.J. Higham; Society for Industrial and Applied Mathematics 2nd edn, 1998, 302pp. $44.50. ISBN 0898714206.
Overview of the entire publication process; also writing and defending a thesis, and giving a talk. TeX and LaTeX. Useful Appendices.

- **Comprehensive TeX Archive Network: CTAN** www.ctan.org/tex-archive/CTAN.sites. Provides access to TeX, BibTeX, LaTeX and related tools, as well as much other useful supporting material.
- **Handbook of typography for the mathematical sciences S.G. Krantz** Chapman & Hall/CRC, 2000, 173pp. $54.95. ISBN 1584881496. 'Focusing on TeX, today's medium of choice for producing mathematical documents, the author illuminates all of the issues associated with page design and seeing your manuscript smoothly and accurately through each step of its publication'.
- **Mathematics into type E. Swanson [et al.]; American Mathematical Society** Rev edn1999, 102pp. $24.00. ISBN 0821819615. 'While it includes information for copy editors, proofreaders, and production staff ... It is increasingly more useful to authors, who have become intricately involved with the typesetting of their manuscripts'.

455 **Mathematical constants**
S.R. Finch Cambridge University Press, 2003, 622pp. £65.00. ISBN 0521818052.
Very useful reference work: 136 essays, each devoted to a mathematical constant or class of constants, from the well known to the highly exotic. After an introductory chapter, series of chapters on constants associated with specific fields: number theory; analytic inequalities; approximation of functions; enumerating discrete structures; functional iteration; complex analysis; geometry. Numerical *Table of constants*. Author index; subject index.
Series: Encyclopaedia of Mathematics and its Applications. Other titles include: The theory of information and coding *(2002);* The foundations of mathematics in the theory of sets *(2001).*

Mathematical methods for physics and engineering: a comprehensive guide
K.F. Riley, M.P. Hobson and S.J. Bence See entry no. 623

Mathematical techniques for engineers and scientists
L.C. Andrews and R.L. Phillips; SPIE – The International Society for Optical Engineering See entry no. 4858

456 **Mathematics by experiment: plausible reasoning in the 21st century**
J. Borwein and D. Bailey A K Peters, 2004, 288pp. $45.00. ISBN 1568812116.
www.experimentalmath.info [COMPANION]
'This new approach to mathematics – the utilization of advanced computing technology in mathematical research – is often called experimental mathematics. The computer provides the mathematician with a 'laboratory' in which she can perform experiments – analyzing examples, testing out new ideas, or searching for patterns. This book presents the rationale and historical context of experimental mathematics, and includes a series of examples that best portray the experimental methodology.'

'Let me cut to the chase: every mathematics library requires a copy of this book (and its companion volume ... *Experimentation in mathematics* ... Every supervisor of higher education students requires a copy on their shelf. Welcome to the rich world of computer-supported mathematics!' (*MathSciNet*)

Mathematics handbook for science and engineering
L. Råde and B. Westergren See entry no. 4859

457 ### Mathematics unbound: the evolution of an international mathematics research community, 1800–1945
K.H. Parshall and A.C. Rice, eds; American Mathematical Society and London Mathematical Society 2002, 406pp. $85.00. ISBN 0821821245.
Detailed fascinating series of chapters: e.g. *International mathematical contributions to British scientific journals, 1800–1900*; *Languages for mathematics and the language of mathematicians in a world of nations*.

Maths for chemists
M.C.R. Cockett and G. Doggett See entry no. 1719

Methods of mathematical physics
R. Courant and D. Hilbert See entry no. 624

458 ### Oxford users' guide to mathematics
E. Zeidler, ed. Oxford University Press, 2004, 1312pp. Translated by B. Hunt, £27.50. ISBN 0198507631.
Intended as a comprehensive introduction to mathematics and its applications. Material is accessible at a basic level, but quickly progresses to dealing with more advanced concepts. Includes over 300 line diagrams.

459 ### Pocket book of integrals and mathematical formulas
R.J. Tallarida 3rd edn, Chapman & Hall/CRC, 1999, 304pp. $24.99. ISBN 0849302633.
A handily sized reference which contains concise discussions of concepts and formulas frequently utilized by professionals and students in the physical sciences. A particular feature is the 'comprehensive table of integrals organised to aid the speedy location of the right form'.

460 ### Principles of mathematical modelling: ideas, methods, examples
A.A. Samarskii and A.P. Mikhailov Taylor & Francis, 2002, 349pp. £40.00. ISBN 0415272815.
Covers the multi-disciplinary field of mathematical modelling, illustrating the principles and common approaches to build models from a range of subject areas. Favours 'concepts and examples, rather than a heavily mathematical approach'. Of use to specialists and advanced students in mathematics and computer science.
Series: Numerical Insights, V. 3.

461 ### Second international handbook of mathematics education
A.J. Bishop [et al.], ed. Kluwer Academic, 2003, 982pp. 2 v., £252.00. ISBN 1402010087.
A follow-up to the first handbook, which 'set benchmarks in many areas of mathematics education'. This text covers the changes and developments that have occurred since 1994. A useful resource for interested students, researchers, teachers and most importantly mathematics education policy makers.
Series: Kluwer International Handbooks of Education, V. 10.

Selected mathematical methods in theoretical physics
V.P. Krainov See entry no. 625

Keeping up-to-date

462 ### Electronic Newsgroups and Listservs
University of Tennessee
http://archives.math.utk.edu/news.html
Part of the Mathematical Archives site hosted at the university's Knoxville campus. The main site seems not recently updated, but this remains a useful list.

463 ### The Mathematical Intelligencer
Springer, Quarterly. €85.00. ISSN 03436993.
'Publishes articles about mathematics, about mathematicians, and about the history and culture of mathematics. Articles should inform and entertain a broad audience of mathematicians, including many mathematicians who are not specialists in the subject of the article. Articles might discuss a current fad or a past trend, theorems or people, history or philosophy, applications or theory.'

464 ### Mathforge
http://mathforge.net/index.jsp
Community message board for maths-related news and user initiated discussions, but with much more – including access to freely available set of online mathematics tools.

Calculus, Analysis & Differential Equations

analysis • complex numbers • differential calculus • differential equations • functional analysis • functions • integral calculus • integral equations • integrals • mathematical analysis

Introductions to the subject

Calculus for biology and medicine
C. Neuhauser See entry no. 1896

465 ### Differential and integral calculus
E. Landau; American Mathematical Society 2001, 372pp. $37.00. ISBN 0821828304.
Reprint of the classic 1965 text.
'And what a book it is! The marks of Landau's thoroughness and elegance, and of his undoubted authority, impress themselves on the reader at every turn, from the opening of the preface ... to the closing of the final chapter. It is a book that all analysts ... should possess ... to see how a master of his craft like Landau presented the calculus when he was at the height of his power and reputation.' (*Mathematical Gazette*)

466 **Foundations of differential calculus**
L. Euler Springer, 2000, 194pp. Translated by John Blanton, £42.50. ISBN 0387985344.
www.springer.com
'The positive response to the publication of Blanton's English translations of Euler's 'Introduction to Analysis of the Infinite' confirmed the relevance of this 240 year old work and encouraged Blanton to translate Euler's 'Foundations of Differential Calculus' as well. The current book constitutes just the first 9 out of 27 chapters. The remaining chapters will be published at a later time. With this new translation, Euler's thoughts will not only be more accessible but more widely enjoyed by the mathematical community.'
Available online: see website.

467 **Functions modeling change: a preparation for calculus**
E. Connally [et al.] 2nd edn, Wiley, 2004, 571pp. $116.95. ISBN 0471266191.
Update of the first edition produced by the *Calculus Consortium*, faculty at 10 US institutions, with support from the National Science Foundation. Goal is to provide students with a clear understanding of the idea of functions as a foundation for subsequent courses in mathematics and other disciplines.
1st edn 2000.

468 **An interactive introduction to mathematical analysis**
J. Lewin Cambridge University Press, 2003, 492pp. £28.00. ISBN 0521017181.
Provides a rigorous course in calculus and real analysis. While gentle in initial approach, making it appropriate for advanced undergraduates, the text develops into one more suitable for those studying at a graduate level. The CD-ROM links to exercises and external resources, expanding on the printed text considerably, and provides an invaluable reference in this area. Includes material suitable for adaptation by a tutor to include in a course on the subject matter.

469 **Understanding analysis**
S. Abbott Springer, 2001, 257pp. £34.50. ISBN 0387950605.
Good basic introduction whose philosophy is 'to focus attention on questions which give analysis its inherent fascination'.
Series: Undergraduate Texts in Mathematics.

Dictionaries, thesauri, classifications

470 **Dictionary of analysis, calculus, and differential equations**
D.N. Clark CRC Press, 1999, 288pp. $44.95. ISBN 0849303206.
In excess of 2500 definitions of terms in analysis, calculus and differential equations. Includes synonymous terms and related references for further reading on the topic. Ideal for any reader.
Series: CRC Comprehensive Dictionary of Mathematics.

Portal & task environments

471 **Calculus.org: the calculus page**
University of California, Davis
www.calculus.org
Links to a variety of resources of interest to students and researchers working with calculus. Maintained by the university's mathematics department.

Handbooks & manuals

472 **Calculus with complex numbers**
J.B. Reade Taylor & Francis, 2003, 100pp. £15.99. ISBN 041530847X.
Practical text on complex calculus covering its applications, not extending to real analysis. Topics covered include algebraic and geometric aspects of complex numbers, differentiation, contour integration, evaluation of finite and infinite real integrals, summation of series and the fundamental theorems of algebra. A working knowledge of calculus and complex numbers is required.

473 **A course in functional analysis**
J.B. Conway 2nd edn, Springer-Verlag, 1990, 415pp. Corrected 4th printing, 1997, £57.50. ISBN 0387972455.
Extremely useful introductory text in functional analysis, aimed at the graduate and professional researcher with a background in integration and measure theory. A large number of examples and exercises are included.
Series: Graduate Texts in Mathematics, V. 96.

474 **Distribution, integral transforms and applications**
W. Kierat and U. Sztaba Taylor & Francis, 2003, 184pp. £46.99. ISBN 041526958X.
Approachable introduction to the theory of distributions and integral transforms, emphasizing the connections of distribution theory with the classical analysis and the theory of differential equations. Gives practical hints on using the theory of distributions where classical analysis proves is insufficient.

475 **Gradshteyn and Ryzhik's table of integrals, series, and products**
A. Jeffrey and D. Zwillinger, eds 6th edn, Academic Press, 2000, 1163pp. £57.99. ISBN 0122947576.
www.mathtable.com/gr [companion]
'The major reference source for integrals in the English language. It is essential for mathematicians, scientists, and engineers, who rely on it when identifying and subsequently solving extremely complex problems.'

476 **Handbook of analysis and its foundations**
E. Schechter Academic Press, 1997, 883pp. £73.99. ISBN 0126227608.
Self-study guide intended for advanced undergraduates or beginning graduate students in mathematics. This is a detailed text, notable for its sophisticated design and insightful approach to existing literature: 'In compiling this book I have acted as a reporter, not an inventor or discoverer ... The book's goal is to enhance classical results by modernizing the exposition, arranging separate topics into a unique whole, and occasionally incorporating some recent developments. I have tried to give credit where it is due, but that is sometimes difficult or impossible. Historical inaccuracies tend to propagate through the literature. I have tried to weed out the inaccuracies by reading widely, but I'm sure I have not caught them all'.

30 chapters divided into: A. Sets and orderings; B. Algebra; C. Topology and uniformity; D. Topological vector spaces.

477 **Handbook of complex variables**
S.G. Krantz Birkhauser, 1999, 290pp. £48.50. ISBN 0817640118.
'Written to be a convenient reference for the working scientist, student, or engineer who needs to know and use basic concepts in complex analysis. It is not a book of mathematical theory. Instead, it is a book of mathematical practice.'
'This modern book can be warmly recommended to mathematicians as well as to users of applied texts in complex analysis; in particular it will be useful to students preparing for an examination in the subject.' (*Mathematical Reviews*)

478 **Handbook of differential equations**
D. Zwillinger 3rd edn, Academic Press, 1998, 801pp. CD-ROM, £81.99. ISBN 0127843957.
Covers ordinary and partial as well as stochastic and delay differential equations. Very well organized with an excellent section *How to use this book*. Assumes basic familiarity with differential equations, its aim being a handy reference to popular techniques.
2nd edn 1992.

479 **Handbook of exact solutions for ordinary differential equations**
A.D. Polyanin and V.F. Zaitsev 2nd edn, Chapman & Hall/CRC, 2003, 787pp. $119.95. ISBN 1584882972.
Almost 6200 ordinary differential equations and their solutions concentrating on:
- equations that have traditionally attracted the attention of many researchers;
- equations that are encountered in various applications.

For this 2nd edn, 1200 nonlinear equations with solutions have been added, there is a new introductory chapter, and the layout has been improved to help readers get faster access to the desired equations.
1st edn 1995.
- **Handbook of nonlinear partial differential equations**
A.D. Polyanin and V.F. Zaitsev Chapman & Hall/CRC, 2003, 814pp. $99.95. ISBN 1584883553. More than 1600 equations. The authors have also produced *Handbook of first-order partial differential equations*; *Handbook of integral equations*; *Handbook of linear partial differential equations for engineers and scientists*.

480 **Real mathematical analysis**
C.C. Pugh Springer, 2002, 437pp. £42.50. ISBN 0387952977.
Contents: Real numbers; A taste of topology; Functions of a real variable; Function spaces; Multivariable calculus; Lebesgue theory.
'The text is complemented by an excellent index and frequent suggestions for further reading. I can recommend this book to serious undergraduates.' (*The Mathematical Gazette*)

481 **Topics in matrix analysis**
RA Horn and CR Johnson Cambridge University Press, 1994, 615pp. £27.29. ISBN 0521467136.
Building on the foundations of the author's introductory text *Matrix analysis*, this book examines in detail several topics not covered in that volume. An advanced undergraduate level of understanding is required to make use of this book, which includes many examples and exercises of varying difficulty.

482 **Trigonometric series**
A. Zygmund 3rd edn, Cambridge University Press, 2003, 390pp. £40.00. ISBN 0521890535.
First published in 1935 and established as a classic text presenting a concise account of the main results then known. A greatly enlarged second edition published in two volumes in 1959 took full account of developments since the publication of the original edition. These two volumes are bound together, with Volume I containing the completely rewritten material of the original while Volume II provides much previously unpublished material.

483 **Visual complex analysis**
T. Needham Oxford University Press, 1998, 616pp. £28.50. ISBN 0198534469.
A broad and thorough development of complex analysis and related areas from a geometric point of view. Intended to be of use to those operating at an undergraduate level or greater.

Keeping up-to-date

484 **Calculus of Variations and Partial Differential Equations**
Springer. €718.00. ISSN 09442669.
www.springeronline.com
Detailed scholarly journal but 'offers an opportunity for communication among scientists working in the field through a section 'News and Views' which is open to discussions, announcements of meetings, reproductions of historical documents, bibliographies etc'.
One of a range of mathematics research journals produced by Springer: see the 'Mathematics' section on the website.

Discrete Mathematics

algebra • algebraic geometry • arithmetic • Boolean algebra • combinatorics • graph theory • linear algebra • logic • mathematical logic • number theory • set theory • symbolic logic

Introductions to the subject

485 **Basic linear algebra**
T.S. Blyth and E.F. Robertson 2nd edn, Springer, 2002, 232pp. £15.95. ISBN 1852336625.
Very good introductory textbook.

486 **Classic algebra**
P.M. Cohn Wiley, 2000, 442pp. $74.00. ISBN 0471877328.
Updates the author's classic three-volume set, *Algebra*, combining a fully updated Volume 1 with the essential topics from Volumes 2 and 3.

487 **Counting: the art of enumerative combinatorics**
G.E. Martin Springer, 2001, 250pp. £34.50. ISBN 038795225X.
Contents organized: Elementary enumeration; The principle of inclusion and exclusion; Generating functions; Groups; Actions; Recurrence relations; Mathematical induction; Graphs.
'He has written a splendid introduction that requires very few prerequisites yet soon delivers the reader into some highly

effective methods of counting. The book is highly recommended.' (*The Mathematical Gazette*)

488 **Discrete mathematics: elementary and beyond**
L. Lovász, J. Pelikán and K. Vesztergombi Springer, 2003, 290pp. £27.00. ISBN 0387955852.
Excellent inviting text, starting with a chapter 'Let's count' and moving through 15 chapters to end with 'A glimpse of complexity and cryptography'.
'I highly recommend this book for all budding mathematicians and computer scientists.' (*The American Mathematical Monthly*)

489 **Elementary algebra**
A.S. Tussy and R.D. Gustafson 3rd edn, Brooks/Cole-Thomson Learning, 2005, 792pp. Includes CD-ROM, $105.95. ISBN 0495014001.
www.brookscole.com/math_d
'Tussy and Gustafson's fundamental goal is to have students read, write, and talk about mathematics through building a conceptual foundation in the language of mathematics. Their text blends instructional approaches that include vocabulary, practice, and well defined pedagogy, along with an emphasis on reasoning, modeling, and communication skills. With an emphasis on the 'language of algebra,' they foster students' ability to translate English into mathematical expressions and equations.'
An example from the extensive range of mathematics textbooks produced by Brooks/Cole. The website gives access to details of the full set, including to the companion websites for this text and others.

490 **Elementary number theory with applications**
T. Koshy Harcourt/Academic Press, 2002, 716pp. $99.95. ISBN 0124211712.
Fundamentals; Divisibility theory; Canonical decompositions; Linear diophantine equations and congruences; Congruences applications; Systems of linear congruences; Three classical milestones; Multiplicative functions; Cryptology; Primitive roots and indices; Quadratic residues; Nonlinear diophantine equations.
'This book is a marvellous resource for anyone teaching or studying a course in number theory.' (*The Mathematical Gazette*)

- **A friendly introduction to number theory J. Silverman** 2nd edn, Prentice Hall, 2001, 386pp. $84.00. ISBN 0130309540. http://vig.prenhall.com/catalog [DESCRIPTION]. Very good engaging introduction.

491 **Graph theory**
R. Merris Wiley, 2000, 237pp. $110.00. ISBN 0471389250.
Contents: Invariants; Chromatic number; Connectivity; Planar graphs; Hamiltonian cycles; Matchings; Graphic sequences; Chordal graphs; Oriented graphs; Edge colorings.
'The author's intent to write a lean and lively invitation to graph theory designed to attract and engage students, is well met.' (*Zentralblatt MATH*)

492 **The higher arithmetic: an introduction to the theory of numbers**
H. Davenport 7th edn, Cambridge University Press, 1999, 241pp. £21.99. ISBN 0521634466.
1. Factorization and the primes; 2. Congruences; 3. Quadratic residues; 4. Continued fractions; 5. Sums of squares; 6. Quadratic forms; 7. Some Diophantine equations; 8. Computers and the theory of numbers.
'. the seventh edition of the well-known and charming introduction to number theory ... it can be recommended both for independent study and as a reference text for a general mathematical audience.' (*European Mathematical Society Journal*)

- **An introduction to the theory of numbers G.H. Hardy and E.M. Wright** 5th edn, Clarendon Press, 1979, 426pp. £28.50. ISBN 0198531710. Classic introduction.

493 **History of the theory of numbers**
L.E. Dickson American Mathematical Society, 1999.
V. 1. Divisibility and primality. 483pp. £32.50. ISBN 0821819348. V. 2. Diophantine analysis. 803pp. £42.50. ISBN 0821819356. V. 3. Quadratic and higher forms. 313 pp. £22.50. ISBN 0821819364.

494 **Introductory combinatorics**
R.A. Brualdi Prentice Hall, 2004, 640pp. $102.00. ISBN 0131001191.
'This, the best selling book in its market, emphasizes combinatorial ideas including the pigeon-hole principle, counting techniques, permutations and combinations, Pólya counting, binomial coefficients, inclusion-exclusion principle, generating functions and recurrence relations, and combinatortial structures (matchings, designs, graphs), flows in networks.'

495 **Modern algebra: an introduction**
J.R. Durbin 5th edn, Wiley, 2004, 368pp. $105.95. ISBN 0471433357.
Well established text. 'Durbin has two main goals: to introduce the most important kinds of algebraic structures, and to help students improve their ability to understand and work with abstract ideas.'

496 **Ones and zeros: understanding Boolean algebra, digital circuits, and the logic of sets**
J. Gregg IEEE Press, 1998, 279pp. $48.95. ISBN 0780334264.
'This book explains, in lay terms, the surprisingly simple system of mathematical logic used in digital computer circuitry. Anecdotal in its style and often funny, it follows the development of this logic system from its origins in Victorian England to its rediscovery in this century as the foundation of all modern computing machinery. ONES AND ZEROS will be enjoyed by anyone who has a general interest in science and technology.'
Series: Understanding Science and Technology.

497 **The prime numbers and their distribution (Nombres premiers)**
G. Tenenbaum and M.M. France; American Mathematical Society 1997, 115pp. Translated by Philip Spain, $17.00. ISBN 0821816470.
Very good introduction to analytic number theory.
Series: Student Mathematical Library, V. 6.

498 **The queen of mathematics: an historically motivated guide to number theory**
J.R. Goldman A K Peters, 1998, 525pp. $59.95. ISBN 1568810067.
'This book takes the unique approach of examining number theory as it emerged in the 17th through 19th centuries. It leads to an understanding of today's research problems on the basis of their historical development.' (It is a) 'contribution to cultural history and brings a difficult subject within the reach of the serious reader.' The book is based on the notion that 'understanding the evolution of ideas leading to many modern mathematical definitions and theorems gives great insight into their significance and even greater

insight into the goals and open questions of mathematical theories.'

- **Algebraic number theory and Fermat's last theorem I. Stewart and D.O. Tall** 3rd edn, A K Peters, 2001, 313pp. $38.00. ISBN 1568811195. A much more extended and advanced treatment but written by two distinguished mathematicians with a gift for exposition.
- **An invitation to the mathematics of Fermat-Wiles** (Invitation aux mathématiques de Fermat-Wiles) **Y. Hellegouarch** Academic Press, 2002, 381pp. $52.95. ISBN 0123392519. 'Assuming only modest knowledge of undergraduate level math ... Presents diverse concepts required to comprehend Wiles' extraordinary proof. Furthermore, it places these concepts in their historical context'.

499 Schaum's easy outline of discrete mathematics
M. Lipson, ed. McGraw-Hill, 2003, 144pp. $8.95. ISBN 0071398775.
www.schaums.com
Example from the well known series which offers a very wide variety of introductory but also not so introductory treatments. Often well worth checking out.
Series: Schaum's Outlines.

Dictionaries, thesauri, classifications

500 Dictionary of algebra, arithmetic, and trigonometry
S.G. Krantz CRC Press, 2001, 331pp. $44.95. ISBN 158488052X.
Offers around 2800 detailed definitions in these fields, complete with alternative meanings, working definitions and related references. Entries tend to be 'self-contained, eliminating the necessity for cross-referencing, unless the user wishes to develop a concept significantly'. A clear style that should ensure that this text is usable by professional scientists no matter their discipline, as well as the more advanced university student.
Series: CRC Comprehensive Dictionary of Mathematics.

Dictionary of algorithms and data structures
National Institute of Standards and Technology See entry no. 6107

Research centres & institutes

501 Center for Discrete Mathematics & Theoretical Computer Science [USA]
Rutgers University
http://dimacs.rutgers.edu
Founded as a National Science Foundation Science and Technology Center. Rich site; helpful alphabetical index of web pages.

Associations & societies

502 Association for Symbolic Logic [USA]
www.aslonline.org
'Logic is an ancient discipline that has undergone striking modern developments through the introduction of rigorous formal methods, stimulated largely by foundational problems in mathematics. 'Symbolic logic' is a term intended to encompass the entire field of logical inquiry, undertaken in this modern spirit.

'The Association was founded in 1936, at a time when great advances in logic were beginning to be made. Its first members were mainly mathematicians and philosophers who perceived a common ground and sought to strengthen it. Recent research in other areas such as computer science, linguistics, and cognitive science has also been inspired by logic, and the current membership and activities of the Association reflects such expanding interests.'

Portal & task environments

503 CoCoA System: Computations in commutative algebra
L. Robbiano [et al.]; University of Genova
http://cocoa.dima.unige.it
'CoCoA is a program to compute with numbers and polynomials. It is free. It works on many operating systems. It is used by many researchers, but can be useful even for 'simple' computations.'

504 Number Theory Web
K. Matthews, comp.
www.numbertheory.org/ntw/web.html
A collection of links to online information of interest to number theorists and linking to the websites of practitioners in the field. Encourages collaboration and contribution from workers in number theory field, and is mirrored currently in five locations worldwide, including at the University of Cambridge.

505 The World Combinatorics Exchange
www.combinatorics.org
In combination with access to *The Electronic Journal of Combinatorics*. Databases, software, contacts, events, etc.

Discovering print & electronic resources

506 Mathematical Logic around the World
University of Bonn and University of Vienna
www.uni-bonn.de/logic/world.html
Extensive structured list of links.

Digital data, image & text collections

507 On-line encyclopedia of integer sequences
N.J.A. Sloane AT & T.
www.research.att.com/~njas/sequences
Searchable database with an interface accessible in over 30 languages providing a portal to information based around integer sequences. Indicates articles to be read for further information, as well as extensive external links to relevant websites. Extremely limited assistance for first time users, but the simple design should ensure that users soon grasp the functionalities of this resource. Contained 99,261 sequences, October 2004

Handbooks & manuals

508 Contemporary linear algebra
H. Anton Wiley, 2003, 594pp. $113.95. ISBN 0471163627.
Meets the recommendations of the Linear Algebra Curriculum Study Group, which was formed in 1990 to address the concern that 'the linear algebra curriculum at

many schools does not adequately address the needs of the students it attempts to serve'. Specifically, there is more of an emphasis on applications, less on abstraction of concepts.

- **International Linear Algebra Society**
  www.math.technion.ac.il/iic. Founded in 1989 as the successor to the *International Matrix Group* which was established in 1987. The general goal of ILAS is to encourage activities in linear algebra.

509 **Discrete dynamical systems and difference equations with Mathematica**
M.R.S. Kulenovic and O. Merino Chapman & Hall/CRC, 2002, 360pp. $94.95. ISBN 1584882875.
Both an introductory text on the theory and techniques of discrete dynamical systems and difference equations and a users' manual for the software package Dynamica, developed by the authors (based on the MATHEMATICA software). The book includes exercises and research projects relevant to applications encountered in the life and economic science fields.

510 **Handbook of algebra**
M. Hzewinkel, ed. Elseiver, 1996–2003. 3 v. For details see website.
www.elsevier.com/wps/find [DESCRIPTION]
'Algebra, as we know it today, consists of many different ideas, concepts and results. A reasonable estimate of the number of these different 'items' would be somewhere between 50,000 and 200,000. Many of these have been named and many more could (and perhaps should) have a 'name' or a convenient designation. Even the nonspecialist is likely to encounter most of these, either somewhere in the literature, disguised as a definition or a theorem or to hear about them and feel the need for more information. If this happens, one should be able to find enough information in this Handbook to judge if it is worthwhile to pursue the quest ...'

511 **Handbook of combinatorics**
R.L. Graham, M. Grötschel and L. László, eds MIT Press, 2003, 2401pp. 2 v., $180.00. ISBN 0262571722.
'Covers combinatorics in graph theory, theoretical computer science, optimization, and convexity theory, plus applications in operations research, electrical engineering, statistical mechanics, chemistry, molecular biology, pure mathematics, and computer science.'

- **The CRC handbook of combinatorial designs C.J. Colbourn and J.H. Dinitz, eds** CRC Press, 1996, 753pp. $129.95. ISBN 0849389488. 'From experimental design to cryptography, this comprehensive, easy-to-access reference contains literally all the facts you need on combinatorial designs. It includes constructions of designs, existence results, and properties of designs'.

512 **Handbook of discrete and combinatorial mathematics**
K.H. Rosen [et al.], eds CRC Press, 2000, 1232pp. $119.95. ISBN 0849301491.
Well designed approachable text aiming to provide a comprehensive reference volume for computer scientists, engineers, mathematicians, and others such as 'students, physical and social scientists, and reference librarians'. Covers the many areas considered to be part of discrete mathematics, focusing on the information considered essential to its application in computer science and engineering.

513 **Handbook of graph theory**
J.L. Gross and J. Yellen, eds CRC Press, 2004, 1167pp. $119.95. ISBN 1584880902.
The Preface notes that, over the past 40 years, graph theory has been one of the most rapidly growing areas of mathematics with – since 1960 – more than 10,000 different authors publishing papers classified as graph theory by MATHEMATICAL REVIEWS, and – over the last decade – 1000 graph theory papers being published each year.

60 contributors; 11 chapters divided into 54 sections. Ready reference style of presentation emphasizing quick access for the non-expert. Major bibliographical coverage throughout.
Series: Discrete Mathematics and its Applications.

514 **An introduction to algebraic geometry and algebraic groups**
M. Geck Oxford University Press, 2003, 307pp. £39.00. ISBN 0198528310.
1. Algebraic sets and algebraic groups; 2. Affine varieties and finite morphisms; 3. Algebraic representations and Borel subgroups; 4. Frobenius maps and finite groups of Lie type.
Series: Oxford Graduate Texts in Mathematics
'The style of exposition in the book is very reader-friendly ... The proofs are clear and complete.' (*Mathematical Reviews*)

515 **Lectures in logic and set theory**
G.J. Tourlakis Cambridge University Press, 2003.
Intensive treatments but notable for the engaging conversational style; also for the detailed proofs given since 'as I know from experience that omitting details normally annoys students'.

- **V. 1. Mathematical logic** 340pp. £47.50. ISBN 0521753732.
- **V. 2. Set theory** 592pp. £65.00. ISBN 0521753740.

516 **Modern algebra with applications**
W.J. Gilbert 2nd edn, Wiley, 2004, 330pp. $94.95. ISBN 0471414514.
www.wiley.com/WileyCDA
Especially valuable underpinning of uses of algebraic methods in science and technology. Acts as a bridge between basic and advanced treatments.
Series: Pure and Applied Mathematics. The URL provides access to details of Wiley's full range of current mathematics and statistics titles.
'This book is clearly written and presents a large number of examples illustrating the theory. There is no other book of comparable content available. Because of its detailed coverage of applications generally neglected in the literature, it is a desirable if not essential addition to undergraduate mathematics and computer science libraries (of the 1st edn).' (*Choice*)

517 **A primer of analytic number theory: from Pythagoras to Riemann**
J. Stopple Cambridge University Press, 2003, 383pp. £22.99. ISBN 0521012538.
Number theory is 'the study of interesting properties of integers. Of course, what is interesting depends on your taste. This is a book about how analysis applies to the study of prime numbers. Some other goals are to introduce the rich history of the subject and to emphasize the active research that continues to go on'.

Well written. Bibliography divided into: Recreational – expository; Historical; Technical.

Geometry & Topology

differential geometry • Euclidean geometry • non-Euclidean geometry • topology • trigonometry

Introductions to the subject

518 **The changing shape of geometry: celebrating a century of geometry and geometry teaching**
C. Pritchard, ed.; Mathematical Association Cambridge University Press, 2003, 560pp. £65.00. ISBN 0521824516.
An enjoyable and readable introduction for anyone wishing to discover more about geometry and in particular developments over the past 100 years. Collects together a wealth of popular articles, classic essays, and key theorems from leading mathematicians and writers. 'If you are not sure about geometry (and if you are under 50 and educated in England you will have had a limited diet of geometry in your education) then this volume might open your eyes to geometry's attractions ... Definitely a book worth reading even if you are not a geometer'.

519 **A comprehensive introduction to differential geometry**
M. Spivak 3rd edn, Publish or Perish, 1999. ISBN is V. 1 of 5 vols. Publish or Perish Inc is at www.mathpop.com, $225.00. ISBN 0914098705.
An excellent text ideal as an introduction to the topic for advanced undergraduates or as a handbook for PhD students and professional researchers.

520 **Fractals, graphics, and mathematics education**
M. Frame and B.B. Mandelbrot, eds; Mathematical Association of America 2002, 206pp. $43.75. ISBN 0883851695.
'Fractal geometry is a recent addition to the collection of mathematical tools for describing nature and the works of Man. It made possible for the first time a national study of roughness. Fractals are encountered in mathematics and many natural sciences, but also in finance and in art, music and literature most often without being consciously included by anyone. Therefore, fractals interconnect the arts and the natural and social sciences in many intrinsic ways. Rarely, if ever, are students exposed to anything like this in mathematics and science classes ...'
'As a mathematics educator with an interest in fractals, this reviewer found this book an invaluable resource. Recommended for high school mathematics teaching upper-level courses and undergraduate mathematics instructors interested in fractals and chaos, and for high school and university libraries.' (*Choice*)

521 **Geometry**
R.A. Fenn Springer, 2001, 313pp. £15.95. ISBN 1852330589.
'Geometry is probably the most accessible branch of mathematics, and can provide an easy route to understanding some of the more complex ideas that mathematics can present. This book is intended to introduce readers to the major geometrical topics taught at undergraduate level, in a manner that is both accessible and rigorous.'
'. written in recognition of the diminished role of geometry in mathematics curricula, and it aims to have wide appeal. This is a very readable account, intended for undergraduates, though some of the material is suitable for advanced school pupils.' (*Times Higher Education Supplement*)

522 **Non-Euclidean geometry**
H.S.M. Coxeter; Mathematical Association of America 6th edn, 1998, 320pp. $33.95. ISBN 0883855224.
This is a reissue of Coxeter's classic text on non-Euclidean geometry and an essential read for anyone with an interest in geometry. Beginning with a historical introductory chapter, it then devotes space to surveying real projective geometry, elliptic geometry, and then Euclidean and hyperbolic geometries are built up as special cases of a more general descriptive geometry.

523 **The shape of space**
J.R. Weeks 2nd edn, Marcel Dekker, 2002, 382pp. $29.95. ISBN 0824707095.
www.dekker.com [DESCRIPTION]
23 chapters in four parts: Surfaces and three-manifolds; Geometries on surfaces; Geometries on three-manifolds; The Universe.
'. stimulating and mind-bending experience.' (*Mathematical Spectrum*)

524 **Trigonometric delights**
E. Maor, ed. Princeton University Press, 1998, 236pp. $10.95. ISBN 0691057540.
'Trigonometry has always been the black sheep of mathematics. It has a reputation as a dry and difficult subject, a glorified form of geometry complicated by tedious computation. In this book, Eli Maor draws on his remarkable talents as a guide to the world of numbers to dispel that view. Rejecting the usual arid descriptions of sine, cosine, and their trigonometric relatives, he brings the subject to life in a compelling blend of history, biography, and mathematics.'
'Should be required reading for anyone who teaches trigonometry and can be highly recommended for anyone who uses it.' (*The American Mathematical Monthly*)

Dictionaries, thesauri, classifications

Dictionary of algebra, arithmetic, and trigonometry
S.G. Krantz See entry no. 500

Portal & task environments

525 **Topology Atlas**
http://at.yorku.ca/topology
Extensive well designed entrée designed to be a comprehensive on-line resource for those mathematicians and those members of the general public with some interest in topology.

Directories & encyclopedias

526 **Encyclopedia of general topology**
K.P. Hart, J. Nagata and J.E. Vaughan, eds Elsevier, 2004, 526pp. €145.00. ISBN 0444503552.
Multi-authored text intended for a broad community of scholars and students working in mathematics and other areas who want quickly to become acquainted with the field's terminology and ideas. Assumes the reader has a

rudimentary knowledge of set theory, algebra, geometry and analysis. Comprehensive bibliographies append each article.

Handbooks & manuals

Computer vision: a modern approach
D. Forsyth and J. Ponce See entry no. 5715

527 **Fractal geometry: mathematical foundations and applications**
K.J. Falconer 2nd edn, Wiley, 2003, 337pp. $70.00. ISBN 0470848626.
'Since its original publication in 1990 ... has become a seminal text on the mathematics of fractals. It introduces the general mathematical theory and applications of fractals in a way that is accessible to students from a wide range of disciplines.'

The geometry of physics: an introduction
T. Frankel See entry no. 619

528 **Geometry, topology and physics**
M. Nakahara 2nd edn, Institute of Physics Publishing, 2003, 573pp. £34.99. ISBN 0750306068.
'Differential geometry and topology have become essential tools for many theoretical physicists. In particular, they are indispensable in theoretical studies of condensed matter physics, gravity and particle physics. Geometry, Topology and Physics introduces the ideas and techniques of differential geometry and topology at a level suitable for postgraduate students and researchers in these fields.'
1st edn 1989. Series: Graduate Student Series in Physics.

529 **Handbook of discrete and computational geometry**
J.E. Goodman and J. O'Rourke, eds 2nd edn, CRC Press, 2004, 1488pp. $139.95. ISBN 1584883014.
Provides a one-stop reference both for researchers in geometry and geometric computing and for professionals who use geometric tools in their work. Bibliographies.

530 **Handbook of geometric topology**
R.J. Daverman and R.B. Sher, eds Elsevier, 2001, 1133pp. $194.00. ISBN 0444824324.
'Geometric Topology is a foundational component of modern mathematics, involving the study of spacial properties and invariants of familiar objects such as manifolds and complexes. This volume, which is intended both as an introduction to the subject and as a wide ranging resource for those already grounded in it, consists of 21 expository surveys written by leading experts and covering active areas of current research. They provide the reader with an up-to-date overview of this flourishing branch of mathematics.'

- **Handbook of algebraic topology I.M. James, ed.** Elsevier, 1995, 1324pp. $213.00. ISBN 0444817794. 'Written for the reader who already has a grounding in the subject, the volume consists of 27 expository surveys covering the most active areas of research'.

An introduction to algebraic geometry and algebraic groups
M. Geck See entry no. 514

531 **Knot theory**
V.O. Manturov CRC Press, 2004, 384pp. $84.85. ISBN 0415310016.
A useful reference texts for postgraduates and professional researchers, and of some use to advanced undergraduates

532 **Topology of chaos: Alice in stretch and squeezeland**
R. Gilmore and M. Lefranc Wiley-Interscience, 2002, 495pp. $110.00. ISBN 0471408166.
'Suitable at the present time for analyzing "strange attractors" that can be embedded in three-dimensional spaces, this groundbreaking approach offers researchers and practitioners in the discipline a complete and satisfying resolution to the fundamental questions of chaotic systems.'

Statistical & Numerical Analysis

Bayesian statistics • computer algebra • data analysis • data distribution • data visualization • experimental design • graphs • information design • mathematical statistics • numerical analysis • probability • sampling • spatial data analysis • statistical analysis • statistical design • statistical graphics • statistical significance • statistics • symbolic computation • time series

Introductions to the subject

533 **Common errors in statistics (and how to avoid them)**
P.I. Good and J.W. Hardin Wiley, 2003, 212pp. $49.95. ISBN 0471460680.
'High-speed computers and prepackaged statistical routines would seem to take much of the guesswork out of statistical analysis and lend its applications readily accessible to all. Yet, as Phillip Good and James Hardin persuasively argue, statistical software no more makes one a statistician than a scalpel makes one a surgeon. Choosing the proper technique and understanding the analytical context is of paramount importance to the proper application of statistics. The highly readable *Common errors in statistics (and how to avoid them)* provides both newly minted academics and professionals who use statistics in their work with a handy field guide to statistical problems and solutions.'

534 **Data reduction and error analysis for the physical sciences**
P. Bevington and D.K. Robinson 3rd edn, McGraw-Hill, 2003, 336pp. $51.25. ISBN 0072472278.
Purpose is 'to provide an introduction to the concepts of statistical analysis of data for students at the undergraduate and graduate level, and to provide tools for data reduction and error analysis commonly required in the physical sciences. The presentation is developed from a practical point of view, including enough derivation to justify the results, but emphasizing methods of handling data more than theory. The text provides a variety of numerical and graphical techniques'.

535 **Introduction to numerical analysis**
A. Neumaier Cambridge University Press, 2001, 356pp. £27.00. ISBN 0521336104.
1. The numerical evaluation of expressions; 2. Linear systems of equations; 3. Interpolation and numerical differentiation; 4. Numerical integration; 5. Univariate nonlinear equations; 6. Systems of nonlinear equations.

'This is very strongly recommended reading for all undergraduate students whose courses require a serious understanding and implementation of numerical analysis.' (*The Mathematical Gazette*)

536 An introduction to numerical analysis
E. Süli and D. Mayers Cambridge University Press, 2003, 430pp. £65.00. ISBN 0521810264.
Containing exercises and theory, useful to undergraduates at a 2nd year level and beyond.

537 An introduction to numerical methods: a Matlab approach
A. Kharab and R.B. Guenther Interpharm/CRC, 2001, 356pp. $74.95. ISBN 1584882816.
While requiring an undergraduate appreciation of calculus, this text is an introduction to a wide range of useful and important algorithms. Along with the standard numerical analysis material, included are sections on interval arithmetic, phase plane analysis, chaotic differential equations, bifurcation in differential equations and the quadratic method.

MATLAB is 'a high-level technical computing language and interactive environment for algorithm development, data visualization, data analysis, and numerical computation'.

538 Introduction to the practice of statistics
D.S. Moore and G.P. McCabe 4th edn, W.H. Freeman, 2003, 828pp. CD-ROM, $119.30. ISBN 0716796570.
http://bcs.whfreeman.com/ips4e [COMPANION]
Excellent clearly written introduction. Very well designed and laid out. 'The first book to successfully combine attention to broader content and reasoning with comprehensive presentation of the most-used statistical methods.' 15 chapters within 3 parts: I. Data; II. Probability and inference; III. Topics and inference. Commonly used tables in an Appendix; CD-ROM includes version of an *Electronic encyclopedia of statistical examples and exercises*, plus much other data.
Details of the publisher's range of mathematics and statistics texts can be found at: www.whfreeman.com/mathematics.

539 John E. Freund's mathematical statistics
I. Miller and M. Miller, ed. 7th edn, Prentice-Hall, 2003, 624pp. $111.00. ISBN 0131427067.
A classic and comprehensive introduction to statistical theory and application, from a calculus basis. Current thinking, teaching approaches and use of computerized systems, as well as practitioner issues, are all covered in depth.

540 Weighing the odds: a course in probability and statistics
D. Williams Cambridge University Press, 2001, 547pp. £27.00. ISBN 052100618X.
1. Introduction; 2. Events and probabilities; 3. Random variables, means and variances; 4. Conditioning and independence; 5. Generating functions and the central limit theorem; 6. Confidence intervals for 1-parameter models; 7. Conditional pdfs and multi-parameter Bayesian statistics; 8. Linear models, ANOVA etc; 9. Some further probability; 10. Quantum probability and quantum computing.
'This is a wonderfully stimulating textbook.' (*The American Mathematical Monthly*)

Dictionaries, thesauri, classifications

541 Oxford dictionary of statistical terms
Y. Dodge, ed.; International Statistical Institute 6th edn, Oxford University Press, 2003, 498pp. £25.00. ISBN 0198509944.
Latest edition of standard text, with work already in progress within the Institute for follow-up edition: 'To realise future updates, we rely upon your assistance. We would very much welcome your input, either by providing us with: suggestions for new terms; recommendations for new definitions or references; or corrections to existing terms or references' (www.cbs.nl/isi/dictionarysubmitForm.htm).
Rev edn of A dictionary of statistical terms *prepared for the* International Statistical Institute *by F.H.C. Marriott (Longman/Wiley).*

Associations & societies

542 American Statistical Association
www.amstat.org
'Founded in 1839, ASA is the nation's leading professional association for statistics and statisticians.' Their *Center for Statistics Education* covers K12, Undergraduate, Graduate, Professional, and Continuing Education. Good Section on *Careers in Statistics*. Also a comprehensive 1999 document *Ethical Guidelines for Statistical Practice*.

- **American Statistician** Quarterly. $120.00. ISSN 00031305. www.amstat.org/publications/tas. Articles organized into the following sections: Statistical Practice, General, Teacher's Corner, Statistical Computing and Graphics, Reviews of Books and Teaching Materials, and Letters.
- **Current Index to Statistics** $400.00 (web; general). www.statindex.org/CIS. Jointly with INSTITUTE OF MATHEMATICAL STATISTICS. 162 core journals (as of 2003) that are fully indexed, non-core journals from which articles are selected that have statistical content, proceedings and edited books, and other sources.

543 Institute of Mathematical Statistics
www.imstat.org
Set up to 'promote the development and dissemination of research into statistics and probability', through the publication of learned journals and professional development events.

International Federation of Classification Societies
See entry no. 6347

544 International Society for Bayesian Analysis
www.bayesian.org
Bayes (1702–1761) was the 'mathematician who first used probability inductively and established a mathematical basis for probability inference (a means of calculating, from the number of times an event has not occurred, the probability that it will occur in future trials)'.

Well organized, pleasant site. Good resource section including up-to-date list of 45 books 'published by ISBA members on Bayesian inference together with a short synopsis or review'.

545 International Statistical Institute
www.cbs.nl/isi
One of the oldest international scientific associations functioning in the modern world, its first congresses being convened in 1853, being formally established in 1885. Comprehensive up-to-date *Directory of official statistical*

agencies and societies ranging from Afghanistan to Zimbabwe, and including details of the various United Nations statistical offices, as well as those of a dozen other international organizations. ISI sections include: Bernoulli Society; International Association of Survey Statistics; International Association for Statistical Computing; International Association for Official Statistics: International Association for Statistical Education.

- **International Statistical Review** (Revue Internationale de Statistique) 3/year. €75.00. ISSN 03067734. Original research papers of wide interest; integrated critical surveys of particular fields of statistics and probability; reports on recent developments in statistics, computer facilities, survey programmes, teaching methods and experience.

546 **Royal Statistical Society** [UK]
www.rss.org.uk
Founded in 1834; 7200 UK/overseas members of whom about 1500 are professionally qualified. Good well structured LINKS. Society sections include: Environmental Statistics; Medical; Official Statistics; Research; Statistical Computing. Access to *JRSS Books for Review*, JRSS being the major *Journal of the Royal Statistical Society* (3 Series) which – inter alia – provides a concise list of recently published statistics texts.

- **Significance** Blackwell Publishing, 2004–, Quarterly. £25.00. ISSN 17409705. Published for the Society. Aim is 'to communicate and demonstrate in an entertaining and thought-provoking way the practical use of statistics in all walks of life and to show how statistics benefit society'.

Portal & task environments

547 **Mathematica**
Wolfram Research.
www.wolfram.com
The integrated numeric and symbolic computational engine, graphics system, programming language, documentation system, and application connectivity suite of programs.

- **Maple** Maplesoft. www.maplesoft.com. Widely used software tools for solving mathematical and engineering problems.

548 **SAS**
www.sas.com
The business analytics software company. 'Our software provides one integrated process for analyzing data from every source and gaining the predictive power to drive change at every level'. SAS is the world's largest privately held software company.

549 **SISA: Simple Interactive Statistical Analysis**
D. Uttenbroek
http://home.clara.net/sisa
'SISA allows you to do statistical analysis directly on the Internet. Click on one of the procedure names below, fill in the form, click the button, and the analysis will take place on the spot. Study the user friendly guides to statistical procedures to see what procedure is appropriate for your problem.'

A good easily used facility.

550 **SPSS**
www.spss.com
Leader in the provision of predictive analytics technologies. 'Predictive analytics connect data to effective action by drawing reliable conclusions about current conditions and future events.'

551 **StatLib**
Carnegie Mellon University
lib.stat.cmu.edu
Community led system for distributing freely available statistical software, datasets, and information by electronic mail, FTP and WWW. 'Due to increased spam email activity, StatLib will no longer distribute software or data through email.'

552 **SymbolicNet**
Kent State University
www.symbolicnet.org
'The area of Symbolic and Algebraic Computation (SAC), also known as Computer Algebra (CA) in some circles, aims to automate mathematical computations of all sorts. The resulting computer systems, experimental and commercial, are powerful tools for scientists, engineers, and educators. SAC research usually combines mathematics with advanced computing techniques.'

Provides: Introduction; Systems; Links; Events; Research; Contacts. The *Symbolic Mathematical Computation Information Center* is based within the university's *Institute for Computational Mathematics*, established in 1980.

Discovering print & electronic resources

553 **Materials for the History of Statistics**
www.york.ac.uk/depts/maths/histstat
Clearly presented resources including much of current (rather than just historical) value. Well worth browsing.

554 **Statistical and statistical graphical resources**
M. Friendly, comp.; York University
www.math.yorku.ca/SCS/StatResource.html
'Annotated, topic-based collection of available resources for statistics, statistical graphics, and computation related to research, data analysis and teaching, now containing over 580 links.'

555 **WWW Virtual Library: Statistics**
www.stat.ufl.edu/vlib/statistics.html
Simple but very extensive lists of worldwide links categorized: Departments, divisions, and schools of statistics; On-line educational resources; Government statistical institutes; Statistical research groups, institutes, and associations; Statistical services; Statistical archives and resources; Statistical software vendors and software FAQs; Statistical journals; Mailing lists and archives; Statistics related news groups; Related fields. In October 2004 had, however, been last updated June 2003.

Digital data, image & text collections

556 **Milestones in the history of thematic cartography, statistical graphics, and data visualization: an illustrated chronology of innovations**
M. Friendly and D.J. Denis
www.math.yorku.ca/SCS/Gallery/milestone
An extensive resource covering the period 1600 to present day. The expansive introduction to the subject is greatly

enhanced with live links to relevant sites, documents, and resources scattered across the world.

Directories & encyclopedias

Encyclopedia of biostatistics
P. Armitage and T. Colton, eds See entry no. 3512

557 Encyclopedia of statistical sciences
S. Kotz, ed. John Wiley and Sons, 2003, 8811pp. $3,950.00. ISBN 0471465194.
www.wiley.com/WileyCDA/WileyTitle/productCd-0471465194.html [DESCRIPTION]
Comprehensive and regarded by many as the 'premier source of information for all matters statistical'. This extensive encyclopedia is accessible to students of all levels, and is of considerable use for the statistical practitioner and researcher as well. Volumes are arranged in an alphabetic arrangement of topics with cross referencing throughout. Available as the set, or as individual volumes. Coverage is wide-ranging and applicable to all fields that make significant use of statistical mathematics in their research or trade.

Handbooks & manuals

558 The analysis of time series: an introduction
C. Chatfield 6th edn, CRC Press, 2003, 352pp. $54.95. ISBN 1584883170.
This latest edition of a classic text is an introduction to analysing time series aimed at university students of all levels. A very readable and informative text within this field, though it should be noted that it does lack in terms of real world applications. However, this edition does include a new section on handling real data.
Series: Texts in Statistical Science, V. 59

559 Applied longitudinal data analysis: modeling change and event occurrence
J.D. Singer and J.B. Willett Oxford University Press, 2003, 644pp. £39.50. ISBN 0195152964.
Examples with explanation demonstrating how research questions about change and event occurrence can be addressed with longitudinal data. Uses wide variety of methods developed over last 20 years within modelling (hazard, hierarchical linear, individual growth, mixed, multilevel, random coefficient regression) and analysis (event history, failure time, survival).

560 The Chicago guide to writing about numbers
J.E. Miller University of Chicago Press, 2004, 304pp. $17.00. ISBN 0226526313.
1. Why write about numbers? Part I. Principles: 2. Seven basic principles; 3. Causality, statistical significance, and substantive significance; 4. Technical but important: five more basic principles. Part II. Tools: 5. Types of quantitative comparison; 6. Creating effective tables; 7. Creating effective charts; 8. Choosing effective examples and analogies. Part III. Pulling it all together: 9. Writing about distributions and associations; 10. Writing about data and methods; 11. Writing introductions, results, and conclusions; 12. Speaking about numbers.
Series: Chicago Guides to Writing, Editing, and Publishing.

561 Computer algebra handbook: foundations, applications, systems
J. Grabmeier, E. Kaltofen and V. Weispfenning, eds Springer, 2003, 637pp. £49.00. ISBN 3540654666.
A 'comprehensive snapshot of this field containing both theory, systems and practice of the discipline of symbolic computation and computer algebra, showing the state of research and applications at the end of the twentieth century. In addition the text describes 67 software systems and packages that perform tasks in symbolic computation and offers many pages on their applications'.

Accompanied by a CD-ROM, containing demo versions for most of the computer algebra systems treated in the book. Of use to graduate students and researchers in relevant fields.

562 Designing experiments and analyzing data: a model comparison perspective
S.E. Maxwell and H.D. Delaney 2nd edn, Lawrence Erlbaum, 2004, 1120pp. CD-ROM CD with SPSS and SAS data sets for many of the text exercises, as well as tutorials reviewing basic statistics and regression; Instructor's Solutions Manual; companion website, $89.95. ISBN 0805837183.
Written 'to serve as either a textbook or a reference book on designing experiments and analysing experimental data'. Focuses on the behavioural sciences 'but the methods introduced can be applied in a variety of areas of scientific research'.

16 chapters grouped into 4 sections: I. Conceptual bases of experimental design and analysis; II. Model comparisons for between-subjects designs; III. Model comparisons for designs involving within-subjects factors; IV. Alternative analysis strategies.
1st edn 1999.

563 Foundations of modern probability
O. Kallenberg, ed. 2nd edn, Springer, 1997. £61.50. ISBN 0387953132.
A now well established comprehensive handbook.
'This is an essential purchase for any serious probabilist (on the 1st edn).' (*The Mathematical Gazette*)
'Kallenberg's present book would have to qualify as the assimilation of probability par excellence. It is a great edifice of material, clearly and ingeniously presented, without any non-mathematical distractions. Readers wishing to venture into it may do so with confidence that they are in very capable hands (on the 1st edn).' (*Mathematical Reviews*)

564 Graph drawing software
M. Jünger and P. Mutzel, eds Springer, 2004, 378pp. £61.50. ISBN 3540008810.
'Graph drawing is the task of the design, analysis, implementation, and evaluation of algorithms for automatically generating graph layouts that are easy to read and understand.' After a substantial introductory chapter *Technical foundations*, presents reviews of state-of-the-art graph drawing software tools whose purpose is to generate layouts of objects and their relationships. Good use of colour printing.
Series: Mathematics and Visualization. Other titles include: Geometric modeling for scientific visualization *(2004);* Multimedia tools for communicating mathematics *(2002).*

565 **Handbook of means and their inequalities**
P.S. Bullen, ed. Kluwer Academic Publishers, 2003, 537pp. £114.00. ISBN 1402015224.
Provides a very full account of means. A variety of proofs given throughout. Extensive biographical and bibliographical references. Most suitable for graduates and researchers.

566 **Handbook of numerical analysis**
Elsevier, 1990–. 12 v: see website for bibliographic details.
www.info.sciencedirect.com/handbooks/coming/numerical
Covers the basic methods of numerical analysis, under the following general headings: Solution of equations in Rn; Finite difference methods; Finite element methods; Techniques of scientific computing; Optimization theory and systems science. Also covers the numerical solution of actual problems of contemporary interest in Applied Mathematics, under the following headings: Numerical methods for fluids; Numerical methods for solids; Specific applications – including meteorology, seismology, petroleum mechanics and celestial mechanics.
Announced to be available online: see website.

567 **Handbook of parametric and nonparametric statistical procedures**
D.J. Sheskin 3rd edn, Chapman & Hall/CRC, 2003, 1232pp. $139.95. ISBN 1584884401.
While limited introductory information on descriptive statistics and experimental design is included this is at heart an advanced reference text for graduate students or professionals, detailing in excess of 75 procedures and tests. Very much aimed at those wishing to apply statistical procedures to real-world problems and experimental analysis.

568 **Handbook of statistics**
C.R. Rao, ed. Elsevier, 1983–.
www1.elsevier.com/homepage/sac/P11
Series of self-contained reference books with each volume devoted to a particular topic in statistics. Recent titles are: 20. *Advances in reliability*; 21. *Stochastic processes: modeling and simulation*; 22. *Statistics in industry*; 23. *Advances in survival analysis*.
The URL provides an entrée to Elsevier's current products in mathematics and applied mathematics, and in statistics and probability – including to details of all the titles in this series.

569 **Kendall's advanced theory of statistics**
T. O'Hagan [et al.], eds Hodder & Stoughton Educational, 1994–. 3 v., £220.00. ISBN 0340814934.
www.kendallslibrary.com [COMPANION]
The classic text now comprising the main volume (6th edn. 1994. 0340614307) plus V. 2A. *Classical inference* (6th edn. 1998. 0340662301) and V. 2B. *Bayesian inference* (2nd edn. 2004. 034080752).
- **Kendall's library of statistics** www.kendallslibrary.com/pub.htm. 9 vols supplementing the core work.

570 **Modern computer algebra**
J. von zur Gathen and J. Gerhard 2nd edn, Cambridge University Press, 2003. £40.00. ISBN 0521826462.
From the Preface: 'In science and engineering, a successful attack on a problem will usually lead to some equations that have to be solved ... In principle, there are two ways of solving such equations: approximately or exactly. *Numerical analysis* is a well developed field that provides highly successful mathematical models and computer software to compute *approximate* solutions. *Computer algebra* is a more recent area of computer science, where mathematical tools and computer software are developed for the exact solutions of equations'.
After a brief introduction the chapters are organized into five sections: I. Euclid; II. Newton; III. Gauss; IV. Fermat; V. Hilbert – each of which opens with a biographical overview. Extensive bibliography; colour plates.
A delightful overview of an important area of mathematics and mathematical application, albeit technically demanding.
1st edn 1999.
'[of the 1st edn] ... this lively and exciting volume represents the state of the art in textbooks on computer algebra. Every student and instructor in this area will want a copy.' (*Mathematical Reviews*)

Practical statistics for astronomers
J. Wall and C. Jenkins See entry no. 684

571 **Probability theory: the logic of science**
E.T. Jaynes and G.L. Bretthorst Cambridge University Press, 2003, 727pp. £45.00. ISBN 0521592712.
http://uk.cambridge.org
'Long awaited graduate introduction' to the role of probability theory in real world scientific endeavours. Text is ideal for those scientists, from various disciplines, who require inference from incomplete information.
Range of mathematics and statistics texts available from Cambridge University Press can be browsed from the URL.

572 **Research design and statistical analysis**
J.L. Myers and A. Well 2nd edn, Lawrence Erlbaum, 2003, 760pp. CD-ROM contains several real and artificial data sets used in the book in SPSS, SYSTAT, and ASCII formats; *Instructor's Solutions Manual*, containing the intermediate steps to all of the text exercises, is available free to adopters., $79.95.
Overriding goals are, first, to provide a textbook from which graduate and advanced undergraduate students can really learn about data analysis; second, to provide a source book which will be useful for researchers.
Substantial text; good clear commentaries on the various statistical techniques; detailed index.
1st edn 1995.

573 **Spatial data analysis: theory and practice**
R.P. Haining Cambridge University Press, 2003, 432pp. £29.95. ISBN 0521774373.
Clearly written guide to techniques and models that 'explicitly use the spatial referencing associated with each data value or object that is specified within the system under study'. 11 chapters in five parts: A. The context for spatial data analysis; B. Spatial data: obtaining data and quality issues; C. The exploratory analysis of spatial data; D. Hypothesis testing and spatial autocorrelation; E. Modelling spatial data. Short appendix on software.
- **Center for Spatially Integrated Social Science** www.csiss.org. Access to spatial resources/tools including search engine 'developed for software tools related to spatially integrated approaches in the social sciences ... Currently, the *Spatial Tools Clearinghouse* references over 700 individual software titles'.

574 **Statistical analysis with missing data**
R.J.A. Little and D.B. Rubin 2nd edn, Wiley, 2002, 381pp. $105.00. ISBN 0471183865.
'Statistical analysis of data sets with missing values is a pervasive problem for which standard methods are of limited value. The first edition of Statistical Analysis with Missing Data has been a standard reference on missing-data methods. Now, reflecting extensive developments in Bayesian methods for simulating posterior distributions, this Second Edition by two acknowledged experts on the subject offers a thoroughly up-to-date, reorganized survey of current methodology for handling missing-data problems.'
'The book should be studied in the statistical methods department in every statistical agency.' (*Journal of Official Statistics*)

575 **Statistical design and analysis of experiments: with applications to engineering and science**
R.L. Mason, R.F. Gunst and J.L. Hess 2nd edn, Wiley, 2003, 760pp. $105.00. ISBN 0471372161.
'Practicing engineers and scientists often have a need to utilize statistical approaches to solving problems in an experimental setting. Yet many have little formal training in statistics. *Statistical design and analysis of experiments* gives such readers a carefully selected, practical background in the statistical techniques that are most useful to experimenters and data analysts who collect, analyze, and interpret data.'

576 **Statistical rules of thumb**
G. Van Belle Wiley-Interscience, 2002, 221pp. $62.95. ISBN 0471402273.
Provides easily applicable standard rules for applying key statistical concepts to procedures such as sampling and experimental design. Topic coverage is broad and accessible to all statistical practitioners whatever their level of expertise.

577 **The visual display of quantitative information**
E.R. Tufte 2nd edn, Graphics Press, 2001, 197pp. $40.00. ISBN 0961392142.
www.edwardtufte.com/tufte [COMPANION]
Classic text produced by former professor at Yale University where he taught courses in statistical evidence, information design, and interface design. *Amazon* chose the book as one of its best 100 books of the 20th century. The author 'writes, designs, and self-publishes his books on information design, which have received more than 40 awards for content and design'.

Physics & Astronomy

Physics is a timeless subject – as is astronomy. Whilst this is true of all academic disciplines it is notable that as a result, like mathematics, many physics and astronomy resources do not go quickly out of date. Concepts are refined, and rarely abandoned. However, there continues to be a rapid development in the area, which we have attempted to reflect through the selection of modern texts, alongside some of less recent origin. Unsurprisingly with the creation of the world wide web at CERN, physicists were early embracers of this new technological advantage. Thus quality sites are plentiful and there are well established resources for all those seeking information in this field.

Physics can be broadly subdivided in two: formula- and mathematics-based on one hand, with conceptual and theoretical on the other. While those using this text may well have a solid grasp of the latter, gaining an understanding of the former can be far harder. As such, it is advised that both this and the previous MATHEMATICS section be utilized together in the assistance of customers.

Since on a conceptual level key aspects of physics can be readily understood by anyone with a basic understanding of science, we have included a considerable range of introductions to the various subject areas. For those who wish to discover more about the applications of physics, you may well find more appropriate resources in sections elsewhere, particularly within the EARTH SCIENCES and ENGINEERING subject groupings.

Within that context, we have been quite restrictive in the 'physics' subject fields we have characterized, compensating however with two extensive fields treating 'astronomy'. The first of these tends to contain resources used more by the non-professional astronomer; the second those aimed at the research scientist.

Introductions to the subject

578 The Cambridge companion to Newton
I.B. Cohen and G.E. Smith, ed. Cambridge University Press, 2002, 514pp. £15.99. ISBN 0521656966.
In this text 'distinguished contributors examine the main aspects of Newton's thought', including not only his work in mathematics and physics, but also his other investigations into alchemy, theology, and prophecy.

- **The Newtonian moment: science and the making of modern culture M. Feingold; New York Public Library and University of Cambridge** Oxford University Press, 2005, 234pp. £25.00. ISBN 0195177355. www.nypl.org/research/newton [COMPANION]. Produced to accompany an exhibition at NYPL co-sponsored by the University of Cambridge Library: 8 October 2004 – 5 February 2005.

Cosmology and controversy: the historical development of two theories of the universe
H. Kragh See entry no. 698

579 The elements of physics
I.S. Grant and W.R. Phillips Oxford University Press, 2001, 789pp. £32.99. ISBN 0198518781.
www.oup.com/ephys [COMPANION]
Good reliable solid text in seven parts: Mechanics; Vibrations and waves; Quantum physics; Properties of matter; Electricity and magnetism; Relativity; Mathematical review.
'The new text is elegantly produced and maintains an excellent standard. It is well illustrated, but not as profusely as American texts; this economy is welcome.' (*Times Higher Education Supplement*)

580 Explorations in physics: an activity-based approach to understanding the world
D.P. Jackson, P.W. Laws and S.V. Franklin Wiley, 2002, 368pp. $59.95. ISBN 0471324248.
A valuable source of projects and topics for pre-degree and undergraduate students and their teachers. Well presented materials include various problems for the reader to tackle, if wished, to gain a greater depth of understanding of a topic.
'A useful, well researched and interesting book. an excellent source of inventive and fascinating teaching ideas.' (*Physical Sciences Educational Reviews*)

581 Fundamentals of physics: extended edition
D. Halliday, R. Resnick and J. Walker 7th edn, Wiley, 2004, 1328pp. $140.95. ISBN 0471232319.
http://he-cda.wiley.com/WileyCDA
Leading textbook available in a variety of offerings. This extended edition provides enhanced coverage of developments in physics in the last 100 years, including: Einstein and Relativity, Bohr and others and Quantum Theory, and more recent theoretical developments such as String Theory.
URL gives access to details of the full range of Wiley's higher education texts for physics – and for other subjects.

582 Newton's Principia for the common reader
S. Chandrasekhar Oxford University Press, 2003, 616pp. £52.50. ISBN 019852675X.
A comprehensive analysis of Newton's text, which serves as an invaluable aid for anyone wishing to delve into the original versions of his work. Despite its title, this scholarly text is very much intended for researchers or graduate students.
Originally published 1995.

583 Nobel Laureates and twentieth-century physics
M. Dardo Cambridge University Press, 2004, 540pp. £24.99. ISBN 0521540089.
Historical overview of the past hundred years in physics drawing on the words and work of the most pre-eminent scientists in this field – the Nobel Laureates. Useful as a biographical resource or as an entrée for those wanting to discover which key discoveries paved the way for modern physics.

584 On the shoulders of giants: the great works of physics and astronomy
S. Hawking, ed. Penguin Books, 2003. £10.39. ISBN 0141015713.
Hawking brings together the greatest works by Copernicus,

Galileo, Kepler, Newton and Einstein, showing how their pioneering discoveries changed the world. Biographical content also examines the life and times of these physicists. An excellent introduction to physics for any reader.

585 The physics companion
A.C. Fischer-Cripps Institute of Physics Publishing, 2003, 384pp. £12.99. ISBN 0750309539.
A student resource and revision aid that can be used to support understanding of material covered by other physics texts.

586 Physics for scientists and engineers: extended version
P.M. Paul, S. Gasiorowicz and S. Thornton 3rd edn, Prentice Hall, 2005, 1440pp. $140.00. ISBN 0130352993.
http://vig.prenhall.com/catalog
A calculus-based text aimed at the undergraduate student. Provides a solid conceptual explanation of the fundamental physical laws and how these laws can be applied.
URL gives access to Prentice Hall's academic catalogue.

587 Physics matters: an introduction to conceptual physics
J. Trefil and R.M. Hazen Wiley, 2003, 691pp. $102.95. ISBN 0471150584.
'Conveys the principles of physics in a manner that is understandable to the non-scientist. In a prose style that is clear, engaging, and contemporary, it pays particular attention to the relevance of physics in comprehending our modern technological society and the issues created by those technologies.'

588 Remarkable physicists: from Galileo to Yukawa
I. James Cambridge University Press, 2004, 406pp. £19.99. ISBN 0521017068.
Lives and work of 55 physicists profiled. 'Scientific and mathematical detail is kept to a minimum, so the reader who is interested in physics, but perhaps lacks the background to follow technical accounts, will find this collection an inviting and easy path through the subject's modern development.'

Dictionaries, thesauri, classifications

589 Dictionary of pure and applied physics
D. Basu, ed. CRC Press, 2001, 389pp. $59.95. ISBN 084932890X.
Over 3000 terms of practical use to mathematicians, physicists, engineers and all who work in the physical sciences.

590 HyperPhysics
http://hyperphysics.phy-astr.gsu.edu/hbase/hframe.html
'HyperPhysics is an exploration environment for concepts in physics which employs concept maps and other linking strategies to facilitate smooth navigation. For the most part, it is laid out in small segments or 'cards', true to its original development in HyperCard. The entire environment is interconnected with thousands of links, reminiscent of a neural network. The bottom bar of each card contains links to major concept maps for divisions of physics, plus a 'go back' feature to allow you to retrace the path of an exploration. The side bar contains a link to the extensive Index, which itself is composed of active links. That sidebar also contains links to relevant concept maps. The rationale for such concept maps is to provide a visual survey of conceptually connected material, and it is hoped that they will provide some answers to the question 'where do I go from here?'. Whether you need further explanation of concepts which underlie the current card content, or are seeking applications which go beyond it, the concept map may help you find the desired information.'

591 Oxford dictionary of physics
A. Isaacs 4th edn, Oxford University Press, 2003, 543pp. £8.99. ISBN 0198607598.
www.oxfordreference.com
3500 definitions. 'The most popular paperback dictionary of physics available.'
Available online: see website.

Laws, standards, codes

592 The Cambridge handbook of physics formulas
G. Woan Cambridge University Press, 2000, 219pp. £14.95. ISBN 0521575079.
radio.astro.gla.ac.uk/hbhome.html [COMPANION]
A quick reference aid for students as well as professional physicists covering over 2000 core formulas and equations. Well indexed and easy to navigate, a very useful book for exam revision or practical experimentation.

593 The laws list
E.M. Francis
www.alcyone.com/max/physics/laws
List of laws, rules, principles and other related topics in physics and astronomy: from aberration to Zeeman effect. Very well laid out and easy to navigate (though the colour combinations used are unusual).

Official & quasi-official bodies

594 International Union of Pure and Applied Physics
www.iupap.org
Seeks to 'promote and encourage global cooperation in physics, through a programme of sponsored meetings and education events'. Site links to details on the operations of the Union, news, conferences, etc.

Research centres & institutes

595 Center for History of Physics
American Institute of Physics
www.aip.org/history
Their research mission is to 'preserve and make known the history of modern physics and allied fields including astronomy, geophysics, optics etc'. The hope is that this helps to eliminate various misconceptions that the general public may hold about the nature and purpose of scientific endeavour.

- **Emilio Segrè Visual Archives** www.aip.org/history/esva. Collection of some 25,000 historical photographs, slides, lithographs, engravings, and other visual materials: part of the Center's Neils Bohr Library.

Associations & societies

596 American Association of Physics Teachers
www.aapt.org
'Established in 1930 with the fundamental goal of ensuring the 'dissemination of knowledge of physics, particularly by way of teaching'.' Publishes the *American Journal of Physics* – whose 'Statement of Editorial Policy' is a model of its kind. Also *The Physics Teacher*. The *Physical Sciences Resource Center* is a 'web-based databank that provides K-20 teachers links to a wide range of teaching and learning resources in the physical sciences' and contributes to *ComPADRE* which 'creates, houses, and maintains collections of resources focused on the needs of specific audiences in Physics and Astronomy Education'.

American Geophysical Union
See entry no. 1088

597 American Institute of Physics
www.aip.org
Federation of 10 Member Societies and 23 Affiliated Societies representing the spectrum of the physical sciences, each referenced elsewhere in this volume. Check out the section *Librarians*: 'Welcome! Your patronage as a librarian helps us publish more of the critical research your users need each year. We hope this site provides all the information you need about AIP and Member Society publications — plus a complete listing of AIP news, products, and services.' Also the extensive range of Publications, Services, Resources (especially data from the *Statistical Research Center*) and Communities. AIP has started making its content accessible via RSS.

- **AIP physics desk reference R.E. Cohen, D.R. Lide and G.L. Trigg, eds** 3rd edn, Springer, 2003, 888pp. $74.95. ISBN 0387989730. Major revision of the best-selling reference book and is a concise compilation of the most frequently used physics data and formulae with their derivations. Bibliography.
- **Physics Today** Monthly. $69.00. www.physicstoday.org. Lively wide-ranging magazine, some content of which is freely accessible on the website. Useful Events Calendar linking to dozens of meetings etc. each month.
- **Scitation** http://scitation.aip.org. 'The online home of more than 100 journals from AIP, APS, ASCE, ASME, SPIE, and a host of other prestigious science and engineering societies.' Includes SPIN Web, providing access to 1 million abstracts, updated daily.

598 American Physical Society
www.aps.org
Founded 1899; now 'represents actively its more than 40,000 members in the arena of national, international, and governmental affairs' and 'publishes the world's most prestigious and widely-read physics research journals'. Archival issues of *APS News* are freely accessible; the current issue protected by password and only for APS members. In 2005, the Society will take a lead role in US participation in the *World Year of Physics* (http://physics2005.org). There is an excellent extensive *Physics Internet Resources* marred only by lack of information on when last updated. (However, all the links tried worked.)

- **Physical Review Focus** http://focus.aps.org. Selections from APS journals *Physical Review* and *Physical Review Letters* explained for students and researchers in all fields of physics.
- **Physics and Astronomy Classification Scheme: PACS** www.aip.org/pacs. Widely used scheme prepared by AIP in collaboration with certain other members of the *International Council on Scientific and Technical Information* (ICSTI) [q.v.] having an interest in physics and astronomy classification.
- **Physics Central: learn how your world works** www.physicscentral.com. 'We'll answer your questions on how things work and keep you informed with daily updates on physics in the news. We'll describe the latest research and the people who are doing it and, if you want more, where to go on the web.' Well designed, lively.
- **Physics Internet Resources** www.aps.org/resources. Wide-ranging and useful list of links, including to: exhibitions and special events; physics by fields; publications; important physics organizations; education/scientific reference sites; scientific societies; physics hotlists; and APS resources.

American Society for Gravitational and Space Biology
See entry no. 1919

599 European Physical Society
www.eps.org
A not-for-profit organization seeking to 'promote the interests and activities of physicists working in Europe through publication of research, and professional development programmes'. The site contains information on the Society's remit, activities, and publications.

600 Institute of Physics [UK]
www.iop.org
'A leading international professional body and learned society with over 37,000 members, which promotes the advancement and dissemination of knowledge of and education in the science of physics, pure and applied.'

Very extensive book, magazine and journal publishing programme. Range of other useful services organized under headings such as: Learning physics; Physics policy; What's on in physics. An important active society.

- **PEERS** http://peers.iop.org/cgi-bin/PEERS/main. Free service providing 'a moderated global e-mail directory of people working in science; a place where you can search for peers, colleagues or any useful contacts in your chosen scientific field'.
- **Physics.Org** www.physics.org. Primarily aimed at those relatively new to physics. 'Using powerful natural language query software (EasyAsk) the site answers your question with a series of relevant and accurate web sites from its database of refereed resources'.
- **PhysicsWeb** http://physicsweb.org. Excellent site with access to wide range of news and resources. Subject organized *Best of Physics Web* 'brings together articles about the most exciting areas of modern physics in a single place', including from the magazine *Physics World*.
- **Tcaep.co.uk** www.tcaep.co.uk. Extensive set of data and facts in science, maths and astronomy.

601 National Society of Black Physicists [USA]
http://nsbp.org
Purpose and mission is 'to promote the professional well-being of African American physicists within the international scientific community and within society at large. The organization seeks to develop and support efforts to increase opportunities for African Americans in physics and to increase their numbers and visibility of their scientific work. It also seeks to develop activities and programs that highlight and enhance the benefits of the scientific contributions that African American physicists provide for the international community. The society seeks to raise the general knowledge and appreciation of physics in the African

American community.' Well laid out website offers Career Services for employers and job-seekers.

Portal & task environments

602 LTSN Physical Sciences [UK]
University of Hull and Higher Education Academy
www.physsci.ltsn.ac.uk/Home/Index.aspx
'Supporting learning and teaching in chemistry, physics and astronomy.' Hosted by the University of Hull with partner sites at the universities of Leeds, Liverpool and Surrey. Provides access to briefing papers, guides, toolkits, reports on projects and issues of the journal *Physical Sciences Educational Reviews*.

603 PhysLink.com: physics and astronomy online
www.physlink.com
Well structured rich site: Education; Reference; Directories; Community; Fun; eStore. Top destinations are listed as: Ask the experts; University departments; Discussion forums (see below); Online chat; Einstein eGreetings; Science eStore. Privately operated, sponsored site but with good precise information about privacy, copyright, and becoming a volunteer (unpaid) contributor to the site. An excellent gateway.

- **Physics and Astronomy Forums**
  www.physlink.com/Community/Forums/Index.cfm. Wide ranging and relatively active set, divided into: General physics and astronomy; High school students; Undergrad/college students; Grad students/postdocs; Professional/industrial; Special topics. Over 50,000 registered members.

604 PhysNet: the worldwide network of physics departments and documents
www.physnet.net
'PhysNet is a distributed information service. It uses the information which can be found on the web-servers of the worldwide distributed physics institutions and departments of universities seen as a distributed database. The restriction to those professional institutions which are accepted by the learned societies ensures the quality and relevance of the offered information. PhysNet serves only professional specific information posted by the scientists themselves. Therefore PhysNet complements the services of commercial providers.'

Covers departments, documents, journals, conferences, jobs, education, links, tools and services. A valuable compendium.

Mirrored at a dozen sites worldwide.

605 PSIgate: Physics
University of Manchester and Resource Discovery Network
www.psigate.ac.uk/newsite/physics-gateway.html
The service designed primarily for UK higher and further education members; now describes almost 4000 resources plus offers a range of other useful services. Within the Hub there is also an *Astronomy* Gateway

Discovering print & electronic resources

606 Guide to information sources in the physical sciences
D. Stern Libraries Unlimited, 2000, 227pp. $68.50. ISBN 1563087510.
Covers bibliographic sources, abstracting and indexing databases, journals, books, online sources, and other subject-specific non-bibliographic tools, 'physical sciences' for the purposes of this book principally being equated with 'physics'. Well informed detailed comments on key resources.

INSPEC
Institution of Electrical Engineers See entry no. 5445

607 The NASA astrophysics data system: the digital library for physics, astrophysics, and instrumentation
National Aeronautics and Space Administration and Harvard–Smithsonian Center for Astrophysics
http://ukads.nottingham.ac.uk/mirrors.html
Free access to four databases of some 4 million records covering: Astronomy and astrophysics, including abstracts from planetary sciences and solar physics journals; Instrumentation, including abstracts from conference proceedings of SPIE: INTERNATIONAL SOCIETY FOR OPTICAL ENGINEERING; Physics and geophysics, including abstracts from AMERICAN PHYSICAL SOCIETY journals; and all the papers published in the ARXIV.ORG E-PRINT ARCHIVE. Mirrored on several sites worldwide.

- **Core list of astronomy books**
  http://ads.harvard.edu/books/clab. Note also *Core list of astronomy and physics journals*.
- **Handbook of space astronomy and astrophysics**
  http://ads.harvard.edu/books/hsaa. Freely searchable full text of the 2nd edn of Zomberg's text, published in 1990 by Cambridge University Press.

608 Physics Abstracts
Institution of Electrical Engineers 24 per year. £6100.00. ISSN 00368091.
www.iee.org/Publish/inspec/ProdCat/abstracts.cfm [DESCRIPTION]
Together with ELECTRICAL & ELECTRONICS ABSTRACTS and COMPUTER & CONTROL ABSTRACTS forms IEE's *Science Abstracts* series of journals which are print equivalents of portions of the INSPEC database. Covers all areas of physics, including particle, nuclear, atomic, molecular, fluid, plasma and solid-state physics, biophysics, geophysics, astrophysics, measurement and instrumentation. Around 180,000 abstracts are published each year.

609 RDN Virtual Training Suite: Physicist [UK]
C. Gibson; University of Manchester and Resource Discovery Network
www.vts.rdn.ac.uk/tutorial/physics
One of a set of internet orientation tutorials within the suite, each created by subject-specialists from universities and professional organizations across the UK. Contains tour of key internet sites in physics.

Digital data, image & text collections

610 Contributions of 20th Century women to physics
http://cwp.library.ucla.edu
A biographical resource focusing on pioneering female physicists from the 20th century (up to 1976). A brief historical mention is made of women working in this field in the preceding centuries.

611 **CPC program library**
http://cpc.cs.qub.ac.uk/cpc
'Established in 1969, the CPC Program Library now contains almost 2000 programs in computational physics and chemistry. Papers describing the programs are published in the *Computer Physics Communications Journal* and are available online via ScienceDirect.'

612 **Physics Formulary**
J. Wevers
www.xs4all.nl/~johanw/index.html
Personal website providing extensive summary of equations in physics in LaTeX, Postscript and PDF, with a similar Mathematics Formulary and much other useful information.

Directories & encyclopedias

613 **2004 graduate programs in physics, astronomy, and related fields**
American Institute of Physics 28th ed, Springer, 2004, Annual, 852pp. $62.00. ISBN 0735401233.
'Provides information on nearly every US doctoral program in physics and astronomy, plus data on most major master's programs in these fields. Information on many major Canadian programs is also included. In addition ... lists a substantial number of related-field departments'.

614 **Dictionary of physics**
Nature Publishing Group, 2004, 2500pp. 4 v., £675.00. ISBN 0333912365.
http://npg.nature.com/npg/forms/04_cat.jsp [DESCRIPTION]
Major resource work planned to cater both for undergraduate and graduate student needs, and attempting to 'bridge the gap between primary literature and educational texts'. Extensive coverage of core physics will be coupled with many cross-disciplinary areas. Entries will vary in length and complexity from concise definitions, through short essay length descriptions, to topical articles.

615 **Encyclopedia of applied physics: the classic softcover edition**
G.L. Trigg, ed. Wiley-VCH, 2004, 14576pp. 12 v., $780.00. ISBN 3527404783.
C. 500 articles arranged alphabetically by title. Aimed at anyone who has a professional connection with the technical world, articles treat areas of physics which already have found technical application as well as those that promise to be industrially applicable in the future. Good well designed guide.
Originally published 1991–1998

616 **Macmillan encyclopedia of physics**
J.S. Rigden Simon & Schuster/Prentice Hall International, 1996, 1881pp. 4 v. ISBN 0028973593.
www.gale.com/gvrl
Clearly written articles at a level of medium complexity. Introductory Readers' Guide lists titles of articles under broad themes. Glossary. Index. Good for beginners.
See website for details of Building blocks of matter: a supplement to the Macmillan encyclopedia of physics.

617 **McGraw-Hill concise encyclopedia of physics**
McGraw-Hill, 2004, 500pp. $24.95. ISBN 0071439522.
http://books.mcgraw-hill.com
Concise edition of the classic, and considerably larger, encyclopedia. Useful as a handy sized reference for all those looking for an accessible starting point.
Based on content from the McGraw-Hill Concise Encyclopedia of Science and Technology. *Similar derivative volumes are available for bioscience, chemistry, earth science, engineering, geoscience: search at the URL.*

Handbooks & manuals

CRC handbook of chemistry and physics
D.R. Lide, ed. See entry no. 1717

618 **Essential mathematical methods for physicists**
H.J. Weber and G.B. Arfken 5th edn, Academic Press, 2003, 932pp. $89.95. ISBN 0120598779.
New adaptation of this best-selling text, providing a modern, comprehensive, and accessible text for using mathematics to solve physics problems. Explanations and examples make it useful to students, as well as researchers.

619 **The geometry of physics: an introduction**
T. Frankel Cambridge University Press, 2004, 720pp. £30.00. ISBN 0521539277.
An intriguing text that expresses core equations reinterpreted through geometry. The book also examines the more esoteric aspects of differential geometry, demonstrating how apparent complications further allow the extraction of the meaning of the physical theory from the mathematical process. A book useful to graduate and advanced undergraduate students of physics, engineering and mathematics.

Geometry, topology and physics
M. Nakahara See entry no. 528

620 **Handbook of physics**
W. Benenson [et al.] Springer, 2002, 1181pp. £35.00. ISBN 0387952691.
Well structured and presented; detailed table of contents. 29 chapters in five parts: I. Mechanics; II. Vibrations and waves; III. Electricity; IV. Thermodynamics; V. Quantum physics. Appendix covers measurement and gives background in calculus. Subject index.
Translated from the German.

621 **Handbuch der Physik**
Springer, 1955–84. ISSN 0085140X.
Systematic – now largely historical – encyclopedic treatise for all areas of physics. German, English and French are used, with the subject indexes in each volume serving as multilingual dictionaries. Vol. 55 is a subject index for the entire set.

622 **Landing your first job: a guide for physics students**
J. Rigden American Institute of Physics, 2003, 110pp. $24.95. ISBN 0735400806.
www.aip.org/careersvc/flrr3.pdf [DESCRIPTION]
This book is indispensable for all students of physics seeking to convert their degree into a professional post. Contains up-to-date information on preparing and conducting a job search for graduating students of all levels.

623 Mathematical methods for physics and engineering: a comprehensive guide
K.F. Riley, M.P. Hobson and S.J. Bence 2nd edn, Cambridge University Press, 2002, 1256pp. £75.00. ISBN 0521813727.
Revised and significantly updated edition of a highly acclaimed text.

624 Methods of mathematical physics
R. Courant and D. Hilbert Wiley, 1996, 1390pp. 2 v., $186.00. ISBN 0471557609.
Comprehensive coverage of standard tools.
Volumes can be purchased separately.

625 Selected mathematical methods in theoretical physics
V.P. Krainov CRC Press, 2002, 216pp. $49.95. ISBN 0415272394.
Aims to show how a scientist, knowing the answer to a problem intuitively or through experiment can develop a mathematical method to develop the required answer. Of use to university students of all levels.

626 Theoretical concepts in physics: an alternative view of theoretical reasoning in physics
M.S. Longair 2nd edn, Cambridge University Press, 2003, 569pp. £30.00. ISBN 052152878X.
Refreshing approach – very well written – which should be regarded 'as a supplement to the standard courses, but one which I hope may enhance your understanding, appreciation and enjoyment of physics'.
1st edn 1988.
'Longair's book is, as he says, for 'students who love physics and theoretical physics', not for amateurs. However, it gives great insight into the equations of modern physics, and I enjoyed it very much ... I would hope that parts could be used to enliven the standard course fodder.' (*Times Higher Education Supplement*)

Keeping up-to-date

Journal of Physical and Chemical Reference Data
American Institute of Physics and National Institute of Standards and Technology See entry no. 1730

Nanotechweb.org: the World Service for Nanotechnology
Institute of Physics See entry no. 6002

627 PhysOrg.com: the latest physics and technology news
www.physorg.com
Good service 'totally dedicated to scientific discussions on physics, including such areas as nano- and quantum physics, applied physics, and semiconductor technology. We also have the news section about the latest scientific achievements in these areas'. Well laid out, clearly presenting breaking news as well as much other information, and with opportunities to receive newsfeeds, participate in forum discussions, etc. However, no significant information on the site 'about us' could be found.

628 Reports on Progress in Physics
Institute of Physics Publishing, Monthly. £1276.00. ISSN 00344885.
www.iop.org/EJ/journal/RoPP
Covers all areas of physics, publishing review articles typically covering the past decade of research in a chosen field. 'Review articles are normally commissioned on behalf of the Editorial Board from leading international authorities in their respective fields.'

629 Reviews of Modern Physics
American Institute of Physics, Quarterly. $640.00. ISSN 00346861.
http://rmp.aps.org
Serving students and researchers this journal offers review articles, surveys of recent work, and introductions to subjects in all fields of physics. Bibliographies attached to each article ensure that further elucidation of a topic is possible. Short colloquia also provide bite-sized reports on current work of general interest.

Astronomy

astrobiology • aurora • celestial mechanics • celestial objects • comets • constellations • cosmos • dark sky • eclipses • exobiology • exoplanets • Moon, the • moons • night sky • northern lights • planetary astronomy • planets • Solar System • stars • Sun, the • telescopes • universe

Introductions to the subject

630 Astronomy: the evolving universe
M. Zeilik 9th edn, Cambridge University Press, 2002, 572pp. £30.00. ISBN 0521800900.
http://us.cambridge.org/astronomy/zeilik [COMPANION]
Latest edition of the 'award winning text which provides a comprehensive degree level introduction to astronomy. Material has been streamlined ensuring descriptions, concepts, and explanations are as clear as possible, with chapters ending in a concise summary of concepts'. Each chapter contains at least one Celestial Navigator (map) providing a visual guide to major concepts in the chapter and explicitly shows their inter-connections. Illustrated throughout. In 1997, the 8th edition won a Texty Award from the Text and Academic Authors Association, and then an award for 'Excellence in Introductory College Physics Teaching' from the AMERICAN ASSOCIATION OF PHYSICS TEACHERS.

631 Babylon to Voyager and beyond: a history of planetary astronomy
D. Leverington Cambridge University Press, 2003, 558pp. £65.00. ISBN 0521808405.
Comprehensive survey, covering both the discoveries and developments in the underlying theories. Discusses the failures as well as the successes.
' ... I shall be using this book extensively as a definitive text and recommending it wholeheartedly to my students.' (*Astronomy Now*)

632 The backyard astronomer's guide
T. Dickinson and T. Dyer 2nd edn, Firefly Books, 2002, 320pp. $49.95. ISBN 155209507X.
www.backyardastronomy.com [COMPANION]
Updated edition of established guide; 500 colour photographs and illustrations.

633 Giant telescopes: astronomical ambition and the promise of technology
W.P. McCray Harvard University Press, 2004, 320pp. $45.00. ISBN 0674011473.

'Every night, astronomers use a new generation of giant telescopes at observatories around the world to study phenomena at the forefront of science. By focusing on the history of the GEMINI OBSERVATORY – twin 8-meter telescopes located on mountain peaks in Hawaii and Chile – Giant Telescopes tells the story behind the planning and construction of modern scientific tools, offering a detailed view of the technological and political transformation of astronomy in the post-war era.'

634 An introduction to astrobiology

I. Gilmour and M.A. Sephton Cambridge University Press, 2004, 358pp. £29.95. ISBN 0521546214.

Edited text designed for introductory courses, and co-published with the Open University. Covers: 1. Origin of life; 2. A habitable world; 3. Mars; 4. Icy bodies: Europa and elsewhere; 5. Titan; 6. The detection of exoplanets; 7. The nature of exoplanetary systems; 8. How to find life on exoplanets; 9. Extraterrestrial intelligence. Useful appendices.

- **Astrobiology: Exploring the living universe Ames Research Center**. http://astrobiology.arc.nasa.gov. Well organized wide-ranging portal maintained by this NASA Centre.
- **Astrobiology Society of Britain** www.astrobiologysociety.org. Founded in 2003. Short introductions to the subject and other useful information on the website, including list of current members and their affiliations.
- **Faint echoes, distant stars: the science and politics of finding life beyond Earth B. Bova** Perennial, 2005, 335pp. $14.95. ISBN 0060750995. www.benbova.net [DESCRIPTION]. Originally published Morrow, 2004. Produced by popular writer who is President Emeritus of the National Space Society and a past President of Science Fiction Writers of America.
- **The Transatlantic Exoplanet Survey: TrES California Institute of Technology**. www.astro.caltech.edu/~ftod/tres/tres.html. Network of three small-aperture telescopes searching the sky for transiting planets located: Sleuth (Palomar Observatory, Southern California), the PSST (Lowell Observatory, Northern Arizona) and STARE (Observatorio del Teide, Canary Islands, Spain).

635 Introduction to comets

J.C. Brandt and R.D. Chapman 2nd edn, Cambridge University Press, 2004, 441pp. £35.00. ISBN 0521004667.

Excellent overview, including – apart from much on the underlying physics – comets in history, comets and solar winds, origins of comets, comet lore. Colour plates. Index of comets.

636 An introduction to the sun and stars

S.F. Green and M.H. Jones, eds Cambridge University Press, 2004, 380pp. £30.00. ISBN 0521546222.

Introductory text intended to support modern undergraduate stellar astronomical courses. Includes term glossaries, exercises with solutions, and potted biographies putting a human perspective into this field.

Co-published with The Open University.

637 Moons and planets

W.K. Hartmann 5th edn, Brooks/Cole, 2005, 456pp. $120.95. ISBN 0534493939.

Established text that organizes its material 'by physical topic rather than by planet. This unique approach promotes an understanding of the unifying principles and processes that cause similarities and differences among the moon and planets.' The author had Asteroid 3341 named after him in recognition of his research work, and in 1998 was named first recipient of the Carl Sagan medal of the AMERICAN ASTRONOMICAL SOCIETY for communicating planetary science to the public. In 2002 he was awarded a medal from the European Geophysical Society (now incorporated into the EUROPEAN GEOSCIENCES UNION for his work on planetary cratering.

Planetary mapping

R. Greeley and R.M. Batson See entry no. 1549

638 Recent advances and issues in astronomy

C.G. De Pree, K. Marvel and A. Axelrod Greenwood Press, 2003, 259pp. $49.95. ISBN 157356348X.

Designed for the general public or the beginning undergraduate this text takes an overview of current research, findings and people working within this field. Includes a lot of practical information about astronomy as a career, along with statistics on careers and research and development, and descriptions of professional organizations and journals.

639 Solar system

N. Hey Weidenfeld & Nicolson, 2002, 272pp. £20.00. ISBN 0304359947.

Well written introduction. 'As our exploration of the Solar System gathers momentum this book explores what we have discovered already, what we might discover next, and explains the technologies, from telescopes to robot probes, which gather this information.'

640 Universe

R. Freedman and W.J. Kaufmann 7th edn, W.H. Freeman, 2005. Available as a range of packages: see the website. http://bcs.whfreeman.com/universe7e [COMPANION]

Latest edition of leading textbook.

- **The universe in a nutshell S.W. Hawking** Bantam, 2001, 216pp. £20.00. ISBN 0593048156. Hawking's book is a delight to read ... It conveys the author's sense of wonder and awe at the cosmos, and – like a child stepping into the darkness – illustrates his tentative gropings towards the ultimate theory of everything' *PhysicsWeb*.

641 Visions of the cosmos

C.C. Petersen and J.C. Brandt, comps Cambridge University Press, 2003, 218pp. £25.00. ISBN 0521818982.

A 'multi-wavelength snapshot album that shows how the universe looks'. Beautifully produced. General introduction to the science and tools of astronomy, followed by views in turn on the solar system, stars, galaxies, Big Bang, and ending with a brief look at the tools future astronomers will use to study the cosmos. Good glossary and further reading: websites; books; magazines.

Dictionaries, thesauri, classifications

642 The astronomy thesaurus

R.M. Shobbrook and R.R. Shobbrook
http://msowww.anu.edu.au/library/thesaurus

Web version of well established thesaurus, originally created under the auspices of the INTERNATIONAL ASTRONOMICAL UNION.

643 Cambridge dictionary of astronomy

J. Mitton Cambridge University Press, 2001, 466pp. £14.99. ISBN 0521804809.

Over 3000 terms including all constellations, all planets and moons of the solar system, and many individual comets, stars and asteroids, observatories and spacecraft.

644 **Dictionary of minor planet names**
L.D. Schmadel; International Astronomical Union 5th edn, Springer, 2003, 992pp. £115.50. ISBN 3540002383.
In November 2002, the figure of numbered planets exceeded 50,000 objects; this volume covers slightly more than 10,000 named planets. Useful and interesting introduction covers evolution of naming rules – starting with names taken from classical mythology.
4th edn 1999.

645 **Facts On File dictionary of astronomy**
V. Illingworth and J.O.E. Clark 4th edn, Facts On File, 2000, 544pp. $55.00. ISBN 0816042837.
Latest edition includes c.3700 entries of lengths from 25 to 500 words about celestial bodies, observational techniques and instruments, and scientific and mathematical theories.
Series: Facts On File Science Dictionaries.

646 **Firefly astronomy dictionary: an illustrated A–Z guide to the universe**
J. Woodruff Firefly Books, 2003, 256pp. $14.95. ISBN 1552978370.
1000 entries; 200 colour illustrations; 35 tables.
Also published in the UK by Philip's.

647 **Space sciences dictionary: in English, French, German, Spanish, Portuguese, and Russian**
J. Kleczek and H. Kleczková Elsevier, 1990–1994. 4 v.
1. *Radiation and matter* 664pp. £127.50. ISBN 0444988726; 2. *Motion / Space Flight / Data* 808pp. £137.50. ISBN 0444988181; 3. *Space Technology / Space Research* 742pp. £139.50. ISBN 0444988173; 4. *Earth Sciences / Solar System / Deep Space* 894pp. £128.00. ISBN 0444988165.

648 **StarBriefs plus: a dictionary of abbreviations, acronyms and symbols in astronomy and related space sciences**
A. Heck Kluwer Academic, 2004, 1114pp. £207.00. ISBN 1402019254.
http://cdsweb.u-strasbg.fr/~heck/sbpres.htm [COMPANION]
Massive compilation – including physically – with about 200,000 entries for items encountered in the literature of astronomy and space sciences as well as in a very wide range of cognate disciplines.

Laws, standards, codes

Consultative Committee for Space Data Systems
See entry no. 4885

International Institute of Space Law
See entry no. 4887

Official & quasi-official bodies

649 **International Astronomical Union**
www.iau.org
Mission is 'to promote and safeguard the science of astronomy in all its aspects through international cooperation'. 12 scientific divisions and 37 more specialized commissions cover the full spectrum of astronomy, along with 86 working and program groups. News, briefing papers, etc. Online Membership Directory.

- **Astronomical Headlines** http://cfa-www.harvard.edu/cfa/ps/Headlines.html. Brief information on recent astronomical discoveries as reported in the *International Astronomical Union Circulars* and the *Minor Planet Electronic Circulars* as well as links to ephemerides and orbital elements for comets and minor planets.
- **Brown dwarfs** **Astronomical Society of the Pacific**2003, 561pp. $95.00. ISBN 158381132X. www.astrosociety.org. Proceedings of the 211th Symposium of the IAU, Hawaii, 2002. Good example of wide range of conference and symposia proceedings published by ASP: see website.

650 **Space Studies Board** [USA]
www7.nationalacademies.org/ssb
Provides 'an independent, authoritative forum for information and advice on all aspects of space science and applications. The Board conducts advisory studies and program assessments, facilitates international research coordination, and promotes communications on space science and science policy between the research community, the federal government, and the interested public'. News and reports (e.g. *Assessment of Mars science and mission priorities* (2003); *Solar and space physics and Its role in space exploration* (2004).

United Nations Office for Outer Space Affairs
See entry no. 4896

Research centres & institutes

Aerospace Corporation
See entry no. 4897

Office National d'Etudes et de Recherche Aerospatiale: ONERA
See entry no. 4902

Associations & societies

651 **American Astronomical Society**
www.aas.org
Amongst much else – including details of the Society's leading journals – the *Education Office* supports a well laid out and wide-ranging collection of links to resources. The *Public Policy* Section includes significant information about political and related developments. Also accessible from the site is the v. 36(1), 2004 issue of the *Bulletin of the American Astronomical Society* which provides links to the *Annual Reports of Astronomical Observatories and Departments*. And they have some useful FAQ pages starting off with 'Can I buy a star?'.

American Institute of Aeronautics and Astronautics
See entry no. 4907

652 **Astronomical Society of the Pacific**
www.astrosociety.org
'Has become the largest general astronomy society in the world, with members from over 70 nations.' Wide range of publications and educational resources – including, for instance, an extremely extensive list of links to Amateur Astronomy Clubs and Organizations – over 20 in the UK alone.

- **Astronomical League** www.astroleague.org. The world's largest federation of amateur astronomers.

653 **British Astronomical Association**
www.britastro.org/main
Lively association founded in 1890 providing well designed pleasant website and access to range of useful resources.

International Academy of Astronautics
See entry no. 4909

654 **International Dark-Sky Association**
www.darksky.org
'To protect and restore the natural nighttime environment and our heritage of dark skies.'

Libraries, archives, museums

National Air and Space Museum
See entry no. 4917

Portal & task environments

655 **Astronomydaily.com**
www.astronomydaily.com [REGISTRATION]
US-based retailer of astronomy goods who also offers free access to real-time sky information: 'Most of our pages contain real-time sky information customized to your viewing location and time zone. In order to build these pages we need to know your location on planet Earth and a couple of other details. The registration process is free, takes about 30 seconds, and we don't ask for any personal information. Your data is only used to customize our pages and is never used for marketing.'

656 **The Aurora Page**
Michigan Technological University
www.geo.mtu.edu/weather/aurora
'A source for information, links and images about the 'Northern Lights' – on-line since the Web began.'

657 **Students for the Exploration and Development of Space**
www.seds.org
Student-based organization which promotes the exploration and development of space ... SEDS believes in a space-faring civilization and that focusing the enthusiasm of young people is the key to our future in space.' Good informative wide-ranging website.

Discovering print & electronic resources

658 **ARIBIB: ARI bibliographical database for astronomical references**
www.ari.uni-heidelberg.de/aribib/index.htm
For literature from 1969 to 2000, based on information in *Astronomy and Astrophysics Abstracts*; for older literature from 1899 until 1968, based on *Astronomischer Jahresbericht*; for yet older literature from ancient epochs until about 1880, based on bibliographies published by Houzeau and Lancaster (1882) and by de Lalande (1803).

- **Astronomy and astrophysics abstracts** **Astronomisches Rechen-Institut Heidelberg**Springer. www.ari.uni-heidelberg.de/publikationen/aaa. Annual volumes produced in co-operation with the Fachinformationszentrum Karlsruhe and the Institution of Electrical Engineers, UK.

659 **Astronomy Links**
http://astronomylinks.com
Good clearly laid-out directory.

AstroWeb: Astronomy/Astrophysics on the Internet
AstroWeb Consortium See entry no. 737

660 **Information and on-line data in astronomy**
D. Egret and M.A. Albrecht Kluwer Academic, 1995, 291pp. £122.00. ISBN 0792336593.
http://cdsweb.u-strasbg.fr/data-online.html [COMPANION]
Although dated, still useful for its detailed coverage of this specialist area. 24 chapters. Note, however, the companion website was also last updated in 1995
Series: Astrophysics and Space Science Library, v. 203.

- **Astronomical resources on the internet** **J. Kraus and P. Banholzer** . www.istl.org/02-spring/internet2.html. *Issues in Science and Technology Librarianship* Spring 2002 (with several URLs later updated). Excellent review: Starting points; Article and preprint databases; Journals and Magazines; Books; Catalogs and Data Centers; Organizations; Software; etc.

Digital data, image & text collections

661 **Earth and Moon Viewer**
J. Walker
www.fourmilab.ch/earthview/vplanet.html
Digital images of the earth and moon are available via this website. Requires a graphical web browser with the ability to display GIF and JPEG images. Options for viewing: map of the Earth showing the day and night regions at any one time; the Earth from the Sun or the Moon; the night side of the Earth; above any location on the planet specified by latitude, longitude and altitude, from a satellite in Earth orbit; above various cities around the globe. Ability to pan or zoom in and out on each satellite image. Satellite data provided by The Living Earth® Inc./Earth Imaging.

This is a good example of an engaging and useful site. It was developed and is maintained by John Walker, founder of Autodesk, Inc. and co-author of AutoCAD. Much other relevant data is accessible from the author's home page.

662 **The nine planets: a multimedia tour of the solar system**
W.A. Arnett
www.nineplanets.org
'An overview of the history, mythology, and current scientific knowledge of each of the planets and moons in our solar system. Each page has text and images, some have sounds and movies, most provide references to additional related information.' Excellent collection of information; especially useful for the amateur astronomer.

663 **SIMBAD astronomical database**
Centre de Données Astronomiques de Strasbourg
http://simbad.u-strasbg.fr/Simbad
'The SIMBAD astronomical database provides basic data, cross-identifications and bibliography for astronomical objects outside the solar system.' In September 2004 Simbad contained: 3,320,556 objects; 8,701,970 identifiers; 148,975 bibliographical references; 4,544,438 citations of objects in papers.

- **The Aladin interactive sky atlas** http://aladin.u-strasbg.fr/aladin.gml. An interactive sky atlas allowing one to visualize digitized images of any part of the sky, to superimpose entries from astronomical catalogues, and interactively to access related data from SIMBAD and VizieR for all known objects in the field.
- **Dictionary of nomenclature of celestial objects** http://vizier.u-strasbg.fr/cgi-bin/Dic. Full references and usages for about 15,000 different acronyms.
- **The VizieR catalogue service** http://vizier.u-strasbg.fr/viz-bin/VizieR. Homogenous access to about 3000 astronomical data catalogues, published tables, observation logs.

664 **Sloan digital sky survey**
www.sdss.org
'Simply put, the Sloan Digital Sky Survey is the most ambitious astronomical survey project ever undertaken. The survey will map in detail one-quarter of the entire sky, determining the positions and absolute brightnesses of more than 100 million celestial objects. It will also measure the distances to more than a million galaxies and quasars ... The SDSS addresses fascinating, fundamental questions about the universe. With the survey, astronomers will be able to see the large-scale patterns of galactic sheets and voids in the universe. Scientists have varying ideas about the evolution of the universe, and different patterns of large-scale structure point to different theories of how the universe evolved. The Sloan Digital Sky Survey will tell us which theories are right – or whether we have to come up with entirely new ideas.'

Joint project of about a dozen leading US, German and Japanese research institutions, with funding provided by the Alfred P. Sloan Foundation and several US and foreign governmental bodies. A wondrous venture.

Directories & encyclopedias

665 **Cambridge University Press: Astronomy and Astrophysics**
http://titles.cambridge.org/search.asp
CUP is the largest publisher of astronomy and astrophysics texts in the world. Included in their list is a range of well illustrated and produced large format encyclopedias, recent examples of which are listed below. Generally, these provide excellent overviews of the topic.

'This book is highly accessible and affordable, setting out the big picture in a factual and comprehensive way. It is the perfect reference for students, because it will keep their feet on the ground while raising their sights and filling their heads with notions. (About *The Cambridge encyclopedia of space*.)' (*Times Higher Education Supplement*)

- **The Cambridge encyclopedia of amateur astronomy M.E. Bakich, ed.** 2003, 354pp. £35.00. ISBN 0521812984.
- **The Cambridge encyclopedia of meteorites O.R. Norton, ed.** 2002, 374pp. £35.00. ISBN 0521621437.
- **The Cambridge encyclopedia of space F. Verger [et al.], ed.** 2003, 428pp. £35.00. ISBN 0521773008. Translated by Stephen Lyle, Paul Reilly.
- **The Cambridge encyclopedia of the Sun K.R. Lang, ed.** 2001, 268pp. £30.00. ISBN 0521780934.

666 **Cometography: a catalogue of comets**
G.W. Kronk Cambridge University Press.
Planned as a 4 vol. catalogue of every comet observed throughout history with 2 vols. Issued to date: v. 1. *Ancient–1799* 2000. 579pp. £90.00. ISBN 052158504X; v. 2. [1800–1899 2004. 852 pp. £120.00. ISBN 0521585058.

667 **Compact NASA atlas of the solar system**
R. Greeley and R.M. Batson Cambridge University Press, 2001, 408pp. £39.95. ISBN 052180633X.
Visually stunning, large format. Cartographic products in the Atlas created by Astrogeology branch of the US Geological Survey. Not intended as a textbook on the solar system. 'Rather, text and illustrations are provided to give the reader sufficient background to place the maps in an overall context of the solar system and to gain some insight into the nature of mapped planetary bodies.'

Derived from The NASA atlas of the solar system.

668 **Encyclopedia of the solar system**
R. Smith, ed. Fitzroy Dearborn, 2000, 785pp. $184.00. ISBN 1579581870.
Basic format; black and white photographs. C.150 articles of 3000–3500 words written to a standard template: Overview; Applications; Methods of study; Knowledge gained; Basic bibliography; Current bibliography. Categorized list of essays; subject index.

669 **The great atlas of the stars**
S. Brunier Firefly Books, 2001, 111pp. $49.95. ISBN 1552096106.
'Created to give the lay-person and amateur astronomer a map of the principal constellations and grand stars seen in the whole Northern Hemisphere. It covers the 30 most important constellations of the 88 visible from Earth.' A gorgeous book.

'What makes it special, however, are the sumptuous color illustrations. This is the kind of book calculated to inspire even the most jaded urban dweller to look up at the night sky, and to make the brightest constellations more accessible to novice observers who will form the next generation of astronomers. Highly recommended for general readers and lower- and upper-division undergraduates.' (*Choice*)

670 **Millennium star atlas (an all-sky atlas comprising one million stars to visual magnitude eleven from the Hipparcos and Tycho catalogues and ten thousand nonstellar objects)**
R.W. Sinnott; European Space Agency Sky Publishing Corporation, 1997. 3 v. ISBN 0933346840.
www.rssd.esa.int/Hipparcos [COMPANION]
Large format elegant volumes containing 1548 charts based on the historic observations of ESA's Hipparcos satellite. Contains three times as many stars as in any previous all-sky atlas. Useful selective references and bibliography section.

671 **StarGuides plus: a world-wide directory of organizations in astronomy and related space sciences**
A. Heck, ed. Kluwer Academic Publishers, 2004, 1137pp. £207.00. ISBN 1402019262.
http://cdsweb.u-strasbg.fr/~heck/sf.htm [COMPANION]
Major tool containing 6000 entries listed alphabetically by country (100 countries covered), but there is also an exhaustive index including acronyms, different designations for the bodies, locations, significant terms in the names, as well as the official names themselves.

672 **Universal book of astronomy: from the Andromeda Galaxy to the Zone of Avoidance**
D. Darling Wiley, 2003, 576pp. $40.00. ISBN 0471265691.
3000 extensively cross-referenced entries to every noted star, planet, authority, and telescope.
'. A first-rate resource for readers and students of popular astronomy and general science. Highly recommended for public libraries and essential for high school and undergraduate college libraries supporting general science, astronomy, and physics courses.' (*Library Journal*)

Handbooks & manuals

673 **Astronomical algorithms**
J. Meeus 2nd edn, Willmann-Bell, 1998, 477pp. $24.95. ISBN 0943396611.
www.willbell.com/math/mc1.htm [DESCRIPTION]
Inventory of the key algorithms and computational techniques astronomical observers are likely to need. Covers co-ordinate transformations, the apparent place of a star, the positions of solar system bodies, eclipse predictions, etc. Clear explanations and examples of use.
Willmann-Bell specialize in the publication of books and software for astronomers: www.willbell.com.

- **Eclipse Home Page** **F. Espenak; Goddard Space Flight Center** http://sunearth.gsfc.nasa.gov/eclipse/eclipse.html.

674 **Astronomy communication**
A. Heck and C. Madsen, eds Kluwer Academic, 2003, 226pp. £88.00. ISBN 1402013450.
Interesting overview of recent developments in astronomy communication. 'The experts contributing to this book have done their best to write in a way understandable to readers not necessarily hyperspecialized in astronomy nor in communication techniques while providing specific detailed information, as well as plenty of pointers and bibliographic elements.'
Series: Astrophysics and Space Science Library, v. 290.

675 **The century of space science**
J.A.M. Bleeker [et al.], eds Kluwer Academic, 2001, 1846pp. 2 v, £399.00. ISBN 0792371968.
www.springeronline.com [DESCRIPTION]
Marvellous comprehensive survey of astronomy, cosmology, and space science: 90 world-class contributors.
'Some books are so big that they are hard to pick up, let alone put down. This magnificent two-volume reference work, which provides an authoritative overview of space science, weighs in at a whopping 7.5 kg! The vast size of this work is a sign of the many achievements in space science during the past century.' (*Physics World*)

676 **Fundamental astronomy**
H. Karttunen [et al.] 4th edn, Springer, 2003, 468pp. £42.00. ISBN 3540001794.
Excellent mathematically based introduction with good use of images and graphics; colour supplement. The mathematical background needed includes plane trigonometry, basic differential and integral calculus and (only in the chapter dealing with celestial mechanics) some vector calculus. However 'most of the book can be read with very little knowledge of mathematics'.

677 **How to use a computerized telescope**
M.A. Covington, ed. Cambridge University Press, 2002, 240pp. £19.99. ISBN 0521007909.
Also in a two-volume series: *Celestial objects for modern telescopes.*
'Author and publisher are to be congratulated: Michael Covington's guidance is both timely and skilful. No amateur astronomer should be without these two excellent books.' (*Times Higher Education Supplement*)

678 **Meteors in the earth's atmosphere: meteoroids and cosmic dust and their interactions with the Earth's upper atmosphere**
E. Murad and I.P. Williams, eds Cambridge University Press, 2002, 322pp. £70.00. ISBN 0521804310.
Multi-author work integrating astronomical observations and theories with geophysical studies.

679 **Methods of celestial mechanics: theory, applications and computer programs**
G. Beutler Springer, 2004. 2 v. Includes CD-ROM in each volume. For details see website.
www.springeronline.com
Designed as a 'coherent textbook for students as well as an excellent reference for practitioners.' v. 1. Physical, mathematical, and numerical principles; v. 2. Application to planetary system, geodynamics and satellite geodesy.

680 **Moon observer's guide**
P. Grego Firefly Books, 2004, 192pp. $14.95. ISBN 1552978885.
www.philips-maps.co.uk [DESCRIPTION]
'Offers practical guidance to amateur astronomers viewing Earth's only natural satellite. There is valuable advice for observing the Moon with the naked eye, binoculars and telescopes. Central to this book is a detailed 28-day guide to lunar features. Lunar geology and the various causes of physical features, such as craters and volcanoes, are described.'
Published in the UK by Philip's (2003. 176pp. £9.99. ISBN 0540084190). URL leads to details of all Philip's currently published astronomy texts.
'This is not a light read or an appropriate choice for the reader who seeks only basic knowledge about the moon. Rather, it is clearly aimed at the dedicated amateur astronomer with an interest in intimate knowledge of the moon. This would be a good choice for public libraries with significant science collections, and college and university science libraries' (*E-STREAMS*)

- **Discover the moon** (Découvrir la lune) **J. Lacroux and C. Legrand** Cambridge University Press, 2003, 143pp. £10.99. ISBN 0521535557. Translated from the French. 'Discover the Moon had me hooked from the moment I opened the book ... Beautifully produced in full colour and packed full of interesting information and photos.' *Astronomy & Space*.

- **Practical astronomy** S. Dunlop and W. Tirion Philip's, 2003, 208pp. £9.99. ISBN 0540079588. Published by Firefly in USA/Canada (2004. 208pp. $14.95. ISBN 1552978257). '... And this is certainly as good an introductory book as you would want ...' *E-STREAMS*.

681 **Navigating the night sky: how to identify the stars and constellations**
G. de Almeida Springer, 2004, 205pp. £18.95. ISBN 1852337370.
Step by step guide to viewing the night sky with the naked eye: recognize key constellations, identify stars and planets, and interpret changes in the overall appearance of the sky throughout the year.
Series: Patrick Moore's Practical Astronomy

682 **Night sky month by month: January to December 2005**
J.-L. Heudier Firefly Books, 2004, 240pp. $24.95. ISBN 1552979725.
Annual guide for observers in the Northern Hemisphere.

683 **The planetary scientist's companion**
K. Lodders and B. Fegley Oxford University Press, 1998, 371pp. £8.99. ISBN 0195116941.
Compact handbook providing physical and chemical data used in planetary science. References with the tables enable data to be traced back to original sources.

684 **Practical statistics for astronomers**
J. Wall and C. Jenkins Cambridge University Press, 2003, 250pp. £18.95. ISBN 0521456169.
One of the series 'aimed primarily at graduate students and researchers ... (but that) ... will be of interest to keen amateurs and undergraduate students'. 1. Decision; 2. Probability; 3. Statistics and expectations; 4. Correlation and association; 5. Hypothesis testing; 6. Data modelling: parameter-estimation; 7. Detection and surveys; 8. Sequential data – 1D statistics; 9. Surface distribution – 2D statistics.
Series: Cambridge Observing Handbooks for Research Astronomers, No 3.

685 **Star watch: the amateur astronomer's guide to finding, observing, and learning about over 125 celestial objects**
P.S. Harrington Wiley, 2003, 312pp. $16.95. ISBN 0471418048.
www.philharrington.net/swtchtoc.htm [COMPANION]
For relative newcomers to star gazing using binoculars and small to medium aperture telescopes. Begins with the moon, extends through the solar system, and then goes out into deep space, beyond our own system. Useful appendices, glossary, bibliography.
'So, is Star Watch the ideal companion for people starting out in this wonderful hobby, or indeed those with limited observing experience? Yes, it most certainly is!' (*Astronomy and Space*)

Keeping up-to-date

686 **Astrobiology Magazine**
National Aeronautics and Space Administration
www.astrobio.net
Exobiology, also known as astrobiology, is the search for life outside of Earth, i.e. in space. Regularly refreshed collections of articles; interviews with experts; large, searchable collection of images; good news service.

687 **Astronomy Magazine**
www.astronomy.com
The world's most popular astronomy magazine: circulation 145,000.

688 **Astronomy Now**
Monthly. £31.00. ISSN 09519726.
www.astronomynow.com
'The UK's best-selling astronomy magazine.'

689 **Sky and Telescope**
Sky Publishing Corp, Monthly. $42.95.
http://skyandtelescope.com
The leading US-based current awareness magazine. Useful resources section including a list of Astronomy-Related Newsgroups. Much other valuable information.

- **Name index to Sky and Telescope** K. Krisciunas . www.nd.edu/~kkrisciu/st.html. Vol. 1., No. 1 (Nov. 1941) to Vol. 104, No. 6 (December 2002).

690 **SPACE.com**
Imaginova Corp.
www.imaginova.com/ourbrands
Imaginova 'is an integrated multimedia content and commerce company capturing people's fascination with space, science and technological innovation across consumer, education and professional markets'. As well as this flagship product, they are now engaged in an 'expansion of our successful business model beyond the space category into other areas of science and technological innovation. This model integrates traditional and new media into eCommerce and marketing platforms'.

Website gives good clear descriptions of their three types of *Brands* – Consumer media; Consumer products & experiences; Trade publishing – with links to current products and services.

- **LiveScience** Imaginova Corp. www.livescience.com. 'Aimed at the intellectually curious, it covers news, views and scientific inquiry with an original, provocative point of view ... We're not just reporting the news, we're taking on common misconceptions that surround scientific discoveries'.

SpaceDaily: Your Portal to Space
See entry no. 4955

SpaceRef.com
See entry no. 4956

691 **Yearbook of astronomy**
P. Moore, ed. PanMacmillan, 2005. £14.99. ISBN 1405041714.
'This annual features an extensive range of specially commissioned articles by some of the world's top astronomers, an authoritative collection of charts and astronomical data, and a month-by-month guide to everything the stargazer can expect to see in the coming year.'

Astrophysics & Cosmology

almanacs • asteroids • astronomical winds • astrophysical formulas • big bang theory • black holes • brown dwarfs • cosmic radiation • cosmology • deep sky objects • extragalactic radio sources • galactic dust • galaxies • Hubble space telescope • infrared astronomy • Mars exploration • meteorites • naval observatories • near earth objects • nebulae • nothingness • observatories • planetary exploration • plasmas • quasars • radio telescopes • solar and stellar physics • solar winds • space agencies • space exploration • space physics • space research • space telescopes • steady state theory • string theory • ultraviolet astronomy • virtual observatories • weather in space • x-ray astronomy

Introductions to the subject

692 **Astronomy: a physical perspective**
M. Kutner 2nd edn, Cambridge University Press, 2003, 600pp. £35.00. ISBN 0521529271.
A calculus-based text that explains astronomical phenomena, as well as how astronomers collect and interpret information about stars and the solar system. Very much a more advanced introduction.

693 **Astronomy and astrophysics in the new millennium**
National Research Council National Academy Press, 2001, 246pp. $34.95. ISBN 0309070317.
Compilation of reports of panels charged with identifying the most important scientific goals in their respective areas: high-energy astrophysics from space; optical and infrared astronomy from the ground; particle, nuclear, and gravitational-wave astrophysics; radio and submillimetre-wave astronomy; solar astronomy; theory, computation, and data exploration; ultraviolet, optical, and infrared astronomy from space.

694 **Astrophysical techniques**
C.R. Kitchin 4th edn, Institute of Physics Publishing, 2003, 493pp. £35.00. ISBN 0750309466.
Straightforward introduction covering: Detectors (optical, infrared, radio, microwave, x-ray, gamma-ray, cosmic ray, neutrino, gravitational radiation); Imaging; Photometry; Spectroscopy; Other techniques (astrometry, polarimetry, solar studies, magnetometry, computers and the world wide web).
3rd edn 2002.
'The book is thorough and is accurately aimed at the undergraduate who likes a good long read ... It is a superb review of the plethora of complicated physical processes.' (*Times Higher Education Supplement*)

- **Exploration of the solar system by infrared remote sensing R.A. Hanel [et al.]** 2nd edn, Cambridge University Press, 2003, 518pp. £80.00. ISBN 0521818974. 'a valuable addition to the literature. As mentioned earlier, it would benefit a much wider readership than its title suggests.' *Optics and Photonics News*.
- **Extreme ultraviolet astronomy M.A. Barstow and J.B. Holberg** Cambridge University Press, 2003, 390pp. £70.00. ISBN 0521580587. This book is 'the first to give a complete overview of Extreme Ultraviolet astronomy, and comes at the end of a major phase of discovery in the field'.
- **Revealing the universe: the making of the Chandra X-ray Observatory W. Tucker and K. Tucker** Harvard University Press, 2001, 295pp. $27.95. ISBN 0674004973. 'Chronicles the technical feats, political struggles, and personal dramas that transformed an inspired vision into the world's supreme X-ray observatory'.

695 **Astrophysics update: topical and timely reviews on astrophysics**
J.W. Mason, ed. Springer, 2004, 314pp. £69.00. ISBN 3540406425.
13 contributed chapters presenting a good state-of-the-art overview. Over 100 illustrations. Although written at a level suitable for professional astronomers and postgraduate students 'may also attract the interest of advanced amateur astronomers seeking scientifically rigorous coverage'.

696 **Blowing bubbles in the cosmos: astronomical winds, jets and explosions**
T.W. Hartquist, J.E. Dyson and D.P. Ruffle Oxford University Press, 2004, 180pp. £30.00. ISBN 0195130545.
'Many astrophysical bodies produce winds, jets or explosions, which blow spectacular bubbles. From a nonmathematical, unifying perspective, based on the understanding of bubbles, the authors address many of the most exciting topics in modern astrophysics including supernovae, the production of structure in the Early Universe, the environments of supermassive black holes and gamma-ray bursts.'

697 **A concise history of solar and stellar physics**
J.L. Tassoul and M. Tassoul Princeton University Press, 2004, 344pp. $39.95. ISBN 069111711X.
www.pupress.princeton.edu/catalogs/subjects/ac.html [DESCRIPTION]
Comprehensive overview, concentrating especially on the development of astrophysical and cosmological theory, particularly in the second half of the 20th century.
URL gives access to all current astronomy and cosmology books available from the publishers.
'This is a fascinating story well told. A host of brief biographies, portraits and figures brings the text to life.' (*New Scientist*)

698 **Cosmology and controversy: the historical development of two theories of the universe**
H. Kragh Princeton University Press, 1996, 500pp. $27.95. ISBN 069100546X.
www.pupress.princeton.edu/physics
Now classic description of the rivalries between steady-state and big bang theories. Bibliography pp 447–486.
See website for description of the full range of the publisher's offerings in physics and astronomy.

- **Quantum generations: a history of physics in the twentieth century H. Kragh** Princeton University Press, 2002, 494pp. $24.95. ISBN 0691095523. Originally published 1999. 'A sweeping survey of the development of modern physics ... Wide-ranging, studiously researched, and comprehensive.' *The Economist*.

699 **Dust in the galactic environment**
D.C.B. Whittet 2nd edn, Institute of Physics Publishing, 2003, 390pp. £34.99. ISBN 0750306246.
Aims to provide an overview, covering general concepts, methods of investigation, important results and their significance, relevant literature, and some suggestions for promising avenues of future research.
1st edn 1992. Series: Astronomy and Astrophysics.
'The fact that dust is now at the forefront of modern astrophysical research owes much to this excellent textbook.' (*Times Higher Education Supplement*)

700 **The elegant universe: superstrings, hidden dimensions, and the quest for the ultimate theory**
B. Greene W.W. Norton, 2003, 448pp. Reprint with new preface of original published by Jonathan Cape, 1999, $19.95. ISBN 0393058581.
'A new edition of the *New York Times* bestseller – now a three-part Nova special: a fascinating and thought-provoking journey through the mysteries of space, time, and matter. Now with a new preface (not in any other edition) that will review the enormous public reception of the relatively obscure string theory – made possible by this book and an increased number of adherents amongst physicists – *The elegant universe* 'sets a standard that will be hard to beat' (*New York Times Book Review*). Brian Greene, one of the world's leading string theorists, peels away the layers of mystery surrounding string theory to reveal a universe that consists of eleven dimensions, where the fabric of space tears and repairs itself, and all matter—from the smallest quarks to the most gargantuan supernovas—is generated by the vibrations of microscopically tiny loops of energy.'

- **The fabric of the cosmos: space, time and the texture of reality** **B. Greene** Allen Lane, 2004, 592pp. £25.00. ISBN 0713996773. 'The long-awaited follow-up to his international bestseller *The elegant universe* ...'

701 **The extravagant universe: exploding stars, dark energy and the accelerating cosmos**
R.P. Kirshner Princeton University Press, 2002, 282pp. Originally published 2002, $19.95. ISBN 069111742X.
'One of the world's leading astronomers ... takes readers inside a lively research team on the quest that led them to an extraordinary cosmological discovery: the expansion of the universe is accelerating under the influence of a dark energy that makes space itself expand. In addition to sharing the story of this exciting discovery, Kirshner also brings the science up-to-date in a new epilogue. He explains how the idea of an accelerating universe – once a daring interpretation of sketchy data – is now the standard assumption in cosmology today.'

702 **The future of theoretical physics and cosmology: celebrating Stephen Hawking's 60th birthday**
G.W. Gibbons, E.P.S. Shellard and S.J. Rankin Cambridge University Press, 2003, 879pp. £40.00. ISBN 0521820812.
Lectures given at the 60th birthday symposium collectively provide an excellent overview of current state-of-the-art. 38 chapters covering: Spacetime singularities; Black holes; Hawking radiation; Quantum gravity; M theory and beyond; De Sitter space; Quantum cosmology; Cosmology. Volume opens with an introductory overview followed by five presentations given at the *Popular Symposium* (Rees, Hartle, Penrose, Thorne, Hawking).

703 **Galaxies and the cosmic frontier**
W.H. Waller and P.W. Hodge Harvard University Press, 2003, 334pp. $29.95. ISBN 0674010795.
http://cosmos.phy.tufts.edu/cosmicfrontier [COMPANION]
In three parts with an Epilogue:

I. *A galaxy primer* 1. Galaxies and the universe; 2. Form and function; 3. Galactic anatomy; 4. The missing mass; 5. Creation and evolution.

II. *Nearby galaxies* 6. The Milky Way; 7. The Clouds of Magellan; 8. Dwarfs of the Local Group; 9. The nearest Giants; 10. Interacting and starbursting galaxies; 11. The most powerful galaxies.

III. *Our galaxian universe* 12. Gauging the galaxies; 13. Clusters and superclusters, filaments and voids; 14. The expanding cosmos; 15. Scenarios of origin; 16. The cosmic frontier.

Companion website provides updates, corrections and an extensive set of technical notes, as well as a concise list of periodicals and websites.

704 **An introduction to galaxies and cosmology**
M.H. Jones and R.J. Lambourne, eds Cambridge University Press, 2004, 442pp. £29.95. ISBN 0521546230.
With very little mathematics, this book is aimed at an undergraduate or general readership. As such readers are able to quickly get to grips with cosmological theories, without becoming baffled by mathematical constraints.

705 **New perspectives in astrophysical cosmology**
M.J. Rees 2nd edn, Cambridge University Press, 2002, 158pp. £16.95. ISBN 0521642388.
Excellent introduction by the current Astronomer Royal.
1st edn 1995 (as Perspectives in astrophysical cosmology*).*
'I can highly recommend this small book to everybody who wishes to be introduced by an outstanding expert into cosmology, one of the most exciting branches of modern astrophysics.' (*General Relativity and Gravitation*)

- **Our cosmic habitat** Weidenfeld & Nicolson, 2001, 205pp. £14.99. ISBN 0297829017. A highly readable but scientifically rigorous more popular introduction, based on the first *Scribner Lecture* given at Princeton in 2000. First published by Princeton University Press.

The new quantum universe
T. Hey and P. Walters See entry no. 764

706 **Nothingness: the science of empty space**
H. Genz Basic Books, 2001. $22.00. ISBN 0738206105.
'Nothingness addresses one of the most puzzling problems of physics and philosophy: Does empty space have an existence independent of the matter within it? Is 'empty space' really empty, or is it an ocean seething with the creation and destruction of virtual matter? With crystal-clear prose and more than 100 cleverly rendered illustrations, physicist Henning Genz takes the reader from the metaphysical speculations of the ancient Greek philosophers, through the theories of Newton and the early experiments of his contemporaries, right up to the current theories of quantum physics and cosmology to give us the story of one of the most fundamental and puzzling areas of modern physics and philosophy.'
'A masterfully written book ... The Epilogue alone is worth buying the book, for it is difficult to imagine a better summary of modern cosmology ... But whosoever is interested should read the 372 pages that come before it, too.' (*Neue Zürcher Zeitung*)

The shape of space
J.R. Weeks See entry no. 523

707 **Space physics: an introduction to plasmas and particles in the heliosphere and magnetospheres**
M.B. Kallenrode 3rd edn, Springer Verlag, 2004, 480pp. €79.95. ISBN 3540206175.
An introduction to the physics of space plasmas and its applications to current research into heliospheric and magnetospheric physics. Explanations of phenomena are given, along with their limitation and how they interact with other related concepts.

708 **Space policy in the twenty-first century**
W.H. Lambright, ed. Johns Hopkins University Press, 2002, 272pp. $49.95. ISBN 0801870682.
Ten leaders in their field ponder the future for space policy in the USA. Winner of the Emme Award for Astronautical Literature given by the American Astronautical Society.

Dictionaries, thesauri, classifications

709 **Dictionary of geophysics, astrophysics and astronomy**
R.A. Matzner, ed. CRC Press, 2001, 536pp. $59.95. ISBN 0849328918.
Provides a comprehensive lexicon of over 4000 terms covering an array of related fields. Novices may find a need for frequent cross-referencing to fully understand all entries, but undergraduates and above will have no difficulty in making use of this resource.

710 **NASA thesaurus and related information**
National Aeronautics and Space Administration
www.sti.nasa.gov/thesfrm1.htm
Contains over 18,000 authorized subject terms, 4000 definitions, and 4400 USE references. Has been used for indexing and retrieval of documents in the *NASA Aeronautics and Space Database*, access to which 'is available to NASA employees and prime contractors, and other Federal government employees and prime contractors registered at the NASA Center for AeroSpace Information (CASI) with an authorized IP address'. (Note, however, that the CASI Technical Report Server was taken offline on September 24, 2003 and replaced by the NASA Technical Reports Server.)

Various formats of the thesaurus are available.

Laws, standards, codes

711 **Astrophysical formulae: a compendium for the astronomer, astrophysicist and physicist**
K.R. Lang 3rd edn, Springer, 1999. 2 v.
I. Radiation, gas processes and high-energy astrophysics. 1999. 614pp. £77.00. ISBN 354061267X. II. Space, time, matter and cosmology. 436 pp. £77.00. ISBN 3540646647. Standard handbook covering 4000 fundamental formulae of physics. Supplemented by list of more than 5000 journal articles: references to original source of material presented, together with citations of descriptions of more recent modifications and applications.

Official & quasi-official bodies

Committee on Space Research
See entry no. 4890

712 **European Southern Observatory**
www.eso.org
An intergovernmental, European organization for astronomical research. It has 11 member countries. ESO operates astronomical observatories in Chile and has its headquarters in Garching, near Munich, Germany.

Well organized website providing access to a wealth of information in the broad areas: Observing facilities and operations; Products and developments; Science activities; General information and services; Outreach activities; Information technology.

The section ESO Libraries is especially useful and includes, for instance, a Directory of astronomy libraries which had 215 entries, August 2004.

- **Annual Reports of Observatories** www.eso.org/gen-fac/libraries/reports.html. An alphabetical list of those observatories that are known to publish Annual Reports. If available, hyperlinks to electronic versions are provided.

713 **European Space Agency** [EUR]
www.esa.int
ESA's mission is to 'shape the development of Europe's space capability and ensure that investment in space continues to deliver benefits to the citizens of Europe'. ESA has 15 Member States, along with participation by Canada and Hungary in some projects. ESA is not a branch of the EU, but rather an organization to co-ordinate the financial and intellectual resources of its members, allowing the undertaking of programmes and activities beyond the scope of any single European country. ESA also works closely with space organizations outside to share the benefits of their programmes. While the ESA HQs are based in Paris the subdivisions are located throughout Europe. Space craft and associated technology are driven primarily by ESTEC, while ESRIN deal with data reception, distribution and exploitation of data. ESOC handle the control of spacecraft such as the ENVISAT project. EAC focuses on manned space flight and training, though to date (2004) no manned missions have been achieved. Competitive tenders for everything ESA related from spacecraft design to data exploitation through web design to catering facilities at ESRIN are issued on the Invitations to tender site. These websites link to a host of information of interest to researchers, graduates, and professional scientists and engineers working in a host of fields allied to space exploration and exploitation.

- **European Space Policy Institute** www.asaspace.at/index2.htm. 'At the end of December 2002 the European Space Agency and the ESA Council decided to set up a European Space Policy Institute in Vienna. After fifteen years of development this event represents a significant hour of birth for space policy in general'.
- **Hubble: European Space Agency Information Centre** www.spacetelescope.org. The Hubble Space Telescope is a collaboration between ESA and NASA and is a long-term, space-based observatory. The observations are carried out in visible, infrared and ultraviolet light.

714 **Japan Aerospace Exploration Agency** [JAP]
www.jaxa.jp/index_e.html
Japanese official space agency site including details of a wealth of resources on projects and research of use to advanced students and professionals in the field, as well as information for the interested school student, teacher, or member of the public. Searchable news articles, mission reports, and image archives.

715 **National Aeronautics and Space Administration** [USA]
www.nasa.gov
Gateway to the extensive series of websites providing information about and by the official US space agency, and its related research institutes and centres. NASA provides the most comprehensive series of interlinked domains on the web that guide users to resources suitable for use by schools, general public, students, and professional researchers alike. Information on the current status of

orbital, deep space, and geosciences research projects can easily be located through the main site, though people with a particular interest in a sub-domain of research may well find that one of the more specialized sites is more suited to their work. While NASA is a US-based organization, the information provided is very much of global interest.

The sites cited below are indicative of the wide range of information offered under the NASA umbrella; a number of other NASA sponsored sites are referenced elsewhere in this volume: see the entry for National Aeronautics and Space Administration in the Author/Title Index. Late 2004, the NASA websites were undergoing major reorganization.

- **Exploration Systems Mission Directorate** www.exploration.nasa.gov. From late 2004 includes content of the former SpaceResearch site from the Office of Biological and Physical Research.
- **High Energy Astrophysics Science Archive Research Center: HEASARC** http://heasarc.gsfc.nasa.gov. 'For scientists and astronomy enthusiasts seeking actual data from a multitude of space-based observatories ... The primary archive for high-energy astronomy missions, in the extreme ultraviolet, X-ray and gamma-ray wavelengths.
- **HumanSpaceFlight** http://spaceflight.nasa.gov. Covers the *Space Shuttle* and the *International Space Station*, as well as 'Behind the scenes of human space flight'. Also, a *Readers' Room* for 'important documents and information about NASA'.
- **Infrared Processing and Analysis Center: IPAC** www.ipac.caltech.edu. NASA's multi-mission centre of expertise for long-wavelength astrophysics. Develops and maintains data archives and access/analysis tools; offers scientific expertise; conducts education and outreach efforts aimed at the general public.
- **Jet Propulsion Laboratory** www.jpl.nasa.gov. Based at CalTech and offering wide range of resources, including details of the Mars Exploration Program. Named in 2004 Scientific American list recognizing outstanding acts of leadership in science and technology for the Mars robot work.
- **NASA Multimedia Gallery** www.nasa.gov/multimedia/highlights/index.html. Gateway to images, video, and interactive features.
- **Planetary Data System** http://pds.jpl.nasa.gov. Archives and distributes scientific data from NASA planetary missions, astronomical observations, and laboratory measurements.
- **Science@nasa: The Science Mission Directorate Website** http://science.hq.nasa.gov. 'Recently NASA began the transformation of its Earth and space science programs by combining them into an integrated Science Mission Directorate (which) will be closely involved in the Vision for Space Exploration through its support of science.'
- **Space Calendar** **R. Baalke** http://www2.jpl.nasa.gov/calendar. Covers space-related activities and anniversaries for the coming year. Included are over 1400 links to related home pages.
- **The universe 365 days** **R.J. Nemiroff and J.T. Bonnell; Goddard Space Flight Center** Thames and Hudson, 2003, 744pp. £24.95. ISBN 0500511217. http://antwrp.gsfc.nasa.gov/apod [COMPANION]. Based on the highly popular 'Astronomy Picture of the Day' website. 'This book is a joy, and certainly the most beautiful book on astronomy that I have ever seen'. *Sir Patrick Moore*.

716 **Particle Physics and Astronomy Research Council** [UK]
www.pparc.ac.uk
The 'strategic leader for coordinating education and research in particle and astrophysics'. The site includes information on research funding, collaborative work, as well as information and news. While large portions of the site are primarily for professional researchers, there is a lot of general information provided for members of the public with an interest in these areas.

717 **US Naval Observatory** [USA]
Astronomical Applications Department.
http://aa.usno.navy.mil
The Department's 'products – almanacs, software, and web services – provide precise astronomical data for practical applications, serving the defense, scientific, commercial, and civilian communities'.

The annual astronomical and navigational almanacs are prepared jointly with Her Majesty's Nautical Almanac Office.

- **The air almanac** 2005. $61.00. ISBN 008054002013. Contains the astronomical data required for air celestial navigation.
- **The astronomical almanac** 2005. $40.00. ISBN 008054001998. Contains a wide variety of both technical and general astronomical information and is a worldwide resource for fundamental astronomical data.
- **Astronomical phenomena** 2006. $8.50. ISBN 008054001980. Preprint of general interest data from The Astronomical Almanac. It is published two years in advance.
- **The nautical almanac** 2005. $43.00. ISBN 008054002005. Contains the astronomical data required for marine celestial navigation.
- **Time Service Department** http://tycho.usno.navy.mil/time.html. 'The Official Source of Time for the Department of Defense (DoD) and the Global Positioning System (GPS), and a Standard of Time for the United States'.

Research centres & institutes

718 **Anglo-Australian Observatory**
www.aao.gov.au
Notable for the gateway to a unique collection of wide-field astronomical photographs, mostly made with the telescopes of the Observatory. Quarterly newsletter.

- **Griffith Observatory Star Awards** www.griffithobs.org/StarAward.html. Weekly awards established to recognize excellence in websites that promote public awareness of astronomy. 'They present useful, thorough, and accurate information in a well organized and attractive way, making the sky more accessible'.

719 **Association of Universities for Research in Astronomy**
www.aura-astronomy.org
A US-based consortium of universities, and other non-profit institutions operating and developing world-class astronomical centres. AURA aims to 'advance astronomy, articulate policy, respond to the priorities of the astronomical community, and enhance the public understanding of science'.

- **Gemini Observatory** www.gemini.edu. The Gemini Observatory consists of twin 8-metre optical/infrared telescopes located on two of the best sites on our planet for observing the universe. Together these telescopes can access the entire sky.
- **National Optical Astronomy Observatory** www.noao.edu. National centre for ground-based night time astronomy in the United States.
- **Space Telescope Science Institute** www.stsci.edu/institute. Operates the *Hubble Space Telescope* as an international observatory. Access to a wealth of resources including star catalogues, spectras, and astronomical software, as well as a collection of education and museum resources and the *STScI Library*.

British National Space Centre
See entry no. 1573

720 **Centre National d'Etudes Spatiales**
www.cnes.fr
'The French space agency. It is a state-owned industrial and commercial organization, currently under the joint responsibility of the *Ministry of Research* and the *Ministry of Defence*. Created in 1961, CNES is responsible for shaping France's space policy, presenting it to the government, and implementing it.'

An excellent wide-ranging visually stunning site – all supported by both English and French text.

721 **Harvard–Smithsonian Center for Astrophysics** [USA]
http://cfa-www.harvard.edu
Combines the resources and research facilities of the Harvard College Observatory and Smithsonian Astrophysical Observatory under a single directorate to pursue studies of those basic physical processes that determine the nature and evolution of the universe. In addition to their six scientific divisions (Atomic and molecular physics; high energy astrophysics; optical and infrared astronomy; radio and geoastronomy; solar, stellar, and planetary sciences; theoretical astrophysics) the Centre has a Science Education facility which 'Creates and conducts programs designed to improve instruction of precollege science, including summer workshops and video teleconferences for teachers, and curriculum and computer software development'.

- **Astronomical data sources on the web** **Telescope Data Center**. http://tdc-www.harvard.edu/astro.html. An excellent compilation, last updated November 2003 when visited October 2004.
- **Chandra X-Ray Observatory** http://chandra.harvard.edu. Formerly called *AXAF*, Chandra was launched July 23, 1999, and is the largest and most sophisticated X-ray observatory to date.
- **The extrasolar planets encyclopedia** http://cfa-www.harvard.edu/planets. US mirror site of original site established in France in 1995. English language.

722 **Institute of Astronomy** [UK]
www.ast.cam.ac.uk
Formed in 1972 by the amalgamation of three institutions that had developed on the site. These were the Cambridge University Observatory, which was established in 1823, the Solar Physics Observatory (1912) and the Institute of Theoretical Astronomy (1967). Large amount of useful information accessible by purposeful navigation.

723 **Jodrell Bank Observatory** [UK]
www.jb.man.ac.uk
Part of the School of Physics and Astronomy of the University of Manchester. Home to the Lovell Radio Telescope and the MERLIN/VLBI National Facility operated by the University for the PARTICLE PHYSICS AND ASTRONOMY RESEARCH COUNCIL.

MERLIN is the 'the Multi-Element Radio Linked Interferometer Network, an array of radio telescopes distributed around Great Britain, with separations of up to 217km'. VLBI is 'an observing technique used by radio astronomers. Radio telescopes around the world can be linked together electronically to create a synthetic telescope called an interferometer. Such an instrument creates the effect of one giant telescope as large as the largest separation of the individual antennas. These enormously powerful telescopes can image astrophysical objects in better detail than any other astronomical technique.'

- **National Radio Astronomy Observatory** www.nrao.edu. 'Designs, builds and operates the world's most sophisticated and advanced radio telescopes.' The US-based NRAO is operated for the NATIONAL SCIENCE FOUNDATION by Associated Universities, Inc under a co-operative agreement.

NASA Centers
National Aeronautics and Space Administration See entry no. 4901

724 **National Virtual Observatory** [USA]
http://us-vo.org/index.cfm
'Astronomy faces a data avalanche. Breakthroughs in telescope, detector, and computer technology allow astronomical surveys to produce terabytes of images and catalogs. These datasets will cover the sky in different wavebands, from gamma- and X-rays, optical, infrared, through to radio. In a few years it will be easier to 'dial-up' a part of the sky than wait many months to access a telescope. With the advent of inexpensive storage technologies and the availability of high-speed networks, the concept of multi-terabyte on-line databases interoperating seamlessly is no longer outlandish. More and more catalogs will be interlinked, query engines will become more and more sophisticated, and the research results from on-line data will be just as rich as that from 'real' telescopes. Moore's law is driving astronomy even further: the planned Large Synoptic Survey Telescope will produce over 10 petabytes per year by 2008! These technological developments will fundamentally change the way astronomy is done. These changes will have dramatic effects on the sociology of astronomy itself ...'

In response, the objective of this Observatory is 'to enable new science by greatly enhancing access to data and computing resources. The NVO is developing tools that make it easy to locate, retrieve, and analyze astronomical data from archives and catalogs worldwide, and to compare theoretical models and simulations with observations.'

- **International Virtual Observatory Alliance** www.ivoa.net. Aim is the 'development and deployment of the tools, systems and organizational structures necessary to enable the international utilization of astronomical archives as an integrated and interoperating virtual observatory'. 15 members currently.

725 **Planetary and Space Sciences Research Institute** [UK]
http://pssri.open.ac.uk
Major UK centre – notable for its work on the nature and effects of interplanetary dust and its hypervelocity impacts, as well as with the Beagle2 British-led exploration of Mars.

726 **Rutherford Appleton Laboratory** [UK]
CCLRC Rutherford Appleton Laboratory
www.sstd.rl.ac.uk
'Carries out an exciting range of space research and technology development. With significant involvement in over 50 space missions in recent years, SSTD is in the forefront of UK space research.'

- **Her Majesty's Nautical Almanac Office** www.nao.rl.ac.uk. Responsible for producing various key almanacs – see the entry for US NAVAL OBSERVATORY – as well as astronomical data for professional and amateur astronomers, mariners, aviators, surveyors, the armed forces, lawyers, religious groups, architects etc.

727 **United Kingdom Astronomy Technology Centre**
www.roe.ac.uk/ukatc
Scientific establishment aiming to help 'keep the UK at the forefront of world astronomy by providing a focus for the

design, production and promotion of state of the art astronomical technology'. Its scientists also carry out observational and theoretical research into fundamental cosmological questions. Site includes information on the staff, research, and research funding opportunities.

728 **Universities Space Research Association** [USA]
www.usra.edu
'An entity in and by means of which universities and other research institutions may cooperate with one another, with the Government of the United States, and with other organizations toward the development of knowledge associated with space science and technology.' Good range of Education and Public Outreach programmes.

- **Lunar and Planetary Institute** www.lpi.usra.edu. Housed in the USRA Center for Advanced Space Studies. Useful resources section on website.

Associations & societies

729 **American Association of Variable Star Observers**
www.aavso.org
Founded in 1911 at Harvard College Observatory to co-ordinate variable star observations made largely by amateur astronomers. Wide range of data provided. 'Members and Observers contribute data to headquarters where about 300,000 observations are received a year from around the world. At the end of each month, incoming observations are sorted by observer and checked for errors. They are converted into computer-readable form and processed using computer systems at AAVSO Headquarters. These observations are added to the data files for each star and the corresponding computer generated light curves are brought up to date.'

730 **American Astronautical Society**
www.astronautical.org
Independent US-based group dedicated to the 'advancement of space science and exploration through meetings and publications'. Details of conferences and publications, plus links.

European Geosciences Union
See entry no. 849

731 **International Astronautical Federation**
www.iafastro.com
Encourages the 'advancement of knowledge and the development and application of space assets'. The Federation provides access to a worldwide network of experts in space development and utilization in 45 countries. Site details activities, committees and relevant Federation publications.

732 **Planetary Society**
www.planetary.org
'The largest non-profit, nongovernmental space advocacy group on Earth.' Good set of resources, many suitable as introductions for the non-specialist, covering, for instance: Exploring Mars; Search for extraterrestrial intelligence; Solar sailing; Near earth objects. Comprehensive worldwide Space Events Calendar. News, publications.

- **Mars Society** www.marssociety.org. Busy active society with a very lively fruitful website.
- **Near Earth Object Program** **National Aeronautics and Space Administration**. http://neo.jpl.nasa.gov. Useful gateway.

733 **Royal Astronomical Society** [UK]
www.ras.org.uk
UK-based body supporting professionals working in astrophysics, planetary sciences, and related areas. Site includes links to publications, news and updates, as well as information on the RAS Library and Archives.

734 **Royal Astronomical Society of Canada**
www.rasc.ca
Publish annual *Observer's handbook* which 'has come to be regarded as the standard North American reference for data on the sky'.

Portal & task environments

735 **SpaceWeather.com**
T. Phillips
www.spaceweather.com
Website devoted to monitoring activity of the Sun, as well as the effect upon the Earth from flares, sunspots, and coronal mass ejections. Articles and explanations of these phenomena are linked throughout the site. A well organized facility.

Discovering print & electronic resources

736 **Asteroids: overview, abstracts, and bibliography**
E.V. Blair, ed. Nova Science Publishers, 2002, 252pp. $49.00. ISBN 1590334825.
Selected abstracts and citations of relevant literature about asteroids and the research into them. Short introductory overview. Author index; detailed subject index.

737 **AstroWeb: Astronomy/Astrophysics on the Internet**
AstroWeb Consortium
www.cv.nrao.edu/fits/www/astroweb.html
Links to over 3000 broadly classified and annotated astronomical resources freely available on the web. Maintained by members of a worldwide consortium. An excellent service, categorized: Observing resources; Data resources; Publication-related resources; People-related resources; Organizations; Software resources; Research areas of astronomy; Various lists of astronomy resources; Astronomical imagery ('Pretty pictures'); Miscellaneous resources.

Meteorological and Geoastrophysical Abstracts
American Meteorological Society See entry no. 1214

The NASA astrophysics data system: the digital library for physics, astrophysics, and instrumentation
National Aeronautics and Space Administration and Harvard–Smithsonian Center for Astrophysics See entry no. 607

738 **WWW Virtual Library: Plasma Science and Technology**
T.E. Eastman
http://plasmas.org/resources.htm
Excellent compilation – especially the part of the site 'Perspectives on Plasmas'.

Digital data, image & text collections

739 **Cloudy & Associates: photoionization simulations for the discriminating astrophysicist since 1978**
www.nublado.org
'Most of the quantitative information we have about the cosmos comes from spectroscopy. Examples include absorption lines superimposed on distant quasars by intervening galaxies or the intergalactic medium, emission lines in nebulae, and the emission lines of the quasars themselves. In turn many of these observations involve low-density gas, where the detailed ionization or gas kinetic temperature is determined by a host of microphysical balances rather than by a single temperature. Analytical solutions to the coupled set of equations are seldom possible, and numerical solutions are an aid to understand their physical properties. Cloudy is designed to simulate these environments ...'

740 **NRL Plasma Formulary**
http://wwwppd.nrl.navy.mil/nrlformulary/nrlformulary.html
'Has been the mini-Bible of plasma physicists for the past 20 years. It is an eclectic compilation of mathematical and scientific formulas, and contains physical parameters pertinent to a variety of plasma regimes, ranging from laboratory devices to astrophysical objects.'

Directories & encyclopedias

741 **The chronological encyclopedia of discoveries in space**
R. Zimmerman Oryx Press, 2000, 410pp. $99.95. ISBN 1573561967.
The *Booklist* Editor's Choice in 2000, this text takes a chronological rather than alphabetic approach to advances in space exploration. Suitable for readers of all levels.

- **Space exploration reference library** UXL, 2004, 400pp. $110.00. ISBN 0787692093. www.gale.com/pdf/introduction/SpaceExpAlmIntro.pdf [DESCRIPTION]. Four-volume work announced for late 2004: see website.

742 **Concise catalog of deep-sky objects: astrophysical information for 500 galaxies, clusters and nebulae**
W.H. Finlay Springer, 2003, 248pp. £24.50. ISBN 1852336919.
Aims to summarize the more interesting astrophysical facts known about objects commonly observed by amateur astronomers. Arranged in order of their *New General Catalogue* (NGC) number. Includes all the Messier objects, Herschel 400 objects, and Royal Astronomical Society of Canada Finest 110 NG objects.

- **Planetary Nebulae Observer's Home Page D. Snyder** www.blackskies.com. Lively wide-ranging popular site aimed at the non-specialist.

743 **Encyclopedia of astronomy and astrophysics**
P. Murdin IoP Publishing, 2001, 3670pp. 4 v., £399.00. ISBN 0333750888.
http://eaa.iop.org [FEE-BASED]
'In a unique collaboration, Nature Publishing Group and Institute of Physics Publishing published the most extensive and comprehensive reference work in astronomy and astrophysics in both print and online formats. First published as a four volume print edition in 2001, the initial Web version went live in 2002, and contained the original print material and was rapidly supplemented with numerous updates and newly commissioned material. Since August 2004 the Encyclopedia is published solely by the Institute of Physics Publishing.'

744 **Encyclopedia of planetary sciences**
J.H. Shirley and R.W. Fairbridge, eds Kluwer Academic Publishers, 1997, 990pp. £277.00. ISBN 0412069512.
www.eseo.com
A highly regarded, comprehensive work. More than 450 short biographical entries and longer authoritative articles on major aspects of planetary sciences. Includes indexes, cross-references, extensive bibliographies. 1 CD-ROM of NASA images. Many line drawings, black and white photographs, and 63 colour illustrations.
Available online: see website.
'GSIST-Mary B. Ansari Best Reference Work Award 1999' (*Geoscience Information Society*)

The encyclopedia of solid earth geophysics
D.E. James, ed. See entry no. 1099

745 **Encyclopedia of space science and technology**
H. Mark, ed. Wiley, 2003, 1864pp. 2 v., $575.00. ISBN 0471324086.
www.gale.com/gvrl
Comprehensive resource on the past, present, and future of space technology providing a quick guide to a range of topics. 80 articles; black and white photographs; index, but – surprisingly – no list of article titles.

Principles used in compilation were: the encyclopedia would be written at a high technical level; it would contain articles that would describe the technology of space exploration as well as scientific results and their applications; the authors would be people who are, or have been, active participants in the enterprise of space exploration; coverage would be international with a broadly based editorial board.
Available online: see website.

746 **Firefly atlas of the universe**
P. Moore Firefly Books, 2003, 228pp. $45.00. ISBN 1552978192.
www.fireflybooks.com [DESCRIPTION]
Updated, revised and informative guide to the cosmos written by one of Britain's best-known and respected astronomers. As well as photographs from ground-based Hubble Space telescopes it includes images from robotic exploration of the planets, tables of data, and 22 star maps. Practical advice for beginners and more advanced astronomers is also included.
Available outside North America as Philip's atlas of the universe *(£30.00. ISBN 0540082422).*

Handbooks & manuals

747 **Allen's astrophysical quantities**
A.N. Cox, ed. 4th edn, AIP Press/Springer, 2000, 719pp. CD-ROM, £107.50. ISBN 038795189X.
Detailed tables of the most recent data on: General constants and units; Atoms, molecules, and spectra; Observational astronomy at all wavelengths from radio to gamma-rays, and neutrinos; Planetary astronomy: Earth, planets and satellites, and solar system small bodies; The Sun, normal stars, and stars with special characteristics; Stellar populations; Cataclysmic and symbiotic variables, supernovae; Theoretical stellar evolution; Circumstellar and interstellar material; Star clusters, galaxies, quasars, and active galactic nuclei; Clusters and groups of galaxies; Cosmology. Extensive bibliographies.

Designed to be used for quick information but also for key references to more detailed sources. Intended as companion to *A physicist's desk reference*. Detailed index.

The century of space science
J.A.M. Bleeker [et al.], eds See entry no. 675

748 **Cosmic rays at earth: researcher's reference manual and data book**
P.K.F. Grieder Elsevier, 2001, 1093pp. £133.50. ISBN 0444507108.
Intended for researchers and students but its background material will be useful to a wider audience. Major sections are: cosmic rays in the atmosphere; cosmic rays at sea level; cosmic rays underground, underwater and under ice; primary cosmic radiation; heliospheric phenomena.

749 **A first course in string theory**
B. Zwiebach, ed. Cambridge University Press, 2004, 558pp. £35.00. ISBN 0521831431.
String theory Is a notoriously difficult subject (some would write 'string theories') and thus, not surprisingly, this is a book full of complexities. As the author writes: 'I was intrigued by the idea of a basic string theory course, but it was not immediately clear to me that a useful one could be devised at this level'.

Nevertheless, this seems an excellent attempt; especially useful for the novice is the opening chapter explaining string theory's aim of providing a unified description of all fundamental interactions. There is also a helpful appendix *References* summarizing the major works of string theory.

750 **Handbook of isotopes in the cosmos: hydrogen to gallium**
D.D. Clayton Cambridge University Press, 2003, 326pp. £60.00. ISBN 0521823811.
Suitable for all professionals with an interest in this field this text looks at the origins of the material world through examining elemental and isotopic abundance and how this is interpreted within the theory of nucleosynthesis. For each isotope, there is an historical and chemical introduction, and data on nuclear properties, solar system abundance, nucleosynthesis in stars, astronomical observations, and isotopic anomalies in presolar grains and solar-system solids. Glossary of terms.

- **Nucleosynthesis Goddard Space Flight Center**. http://helios.gsfc.nasa.gov/nucleo.html. Entry in NASA's useful and reasonably up-to-date *Cosmicopia* – formerly the *Cosmic and Heliospheric Learning Center*.

751 **Meteorites: a petrologic, chemical and isotopic synthesis**
R. Hutchison Cambridge University Press, 2004, 506pp. £65.00. ISBN 0521470102.
Focuses on the study of gram-sized or larger meteorites in the laboratory – allowing inference of interrelationships, chronology and genesis of meteorites and their parent bodies. Extensive bibliography; index of meteorite names.
Series: Cambridge Planetary Science, 2.

Meteors in the earth's atmosphere: meteroids and cosmic dust and their interactions with the Earth's upper atmosphere
E. Murad and I.P. Williams, eds See entry no. 678

752 **Norton's star atlas and reference handbook: epoch 2000.0**
I. Ridpath 20th edn, Pi Press, 2004, 195pp. $30.00. ISBN 0131451642.
For professional and amateur stargazers. Standard work since 1910: now the most famous and widely used star atlas in the world. Covers visible objects as well as star clusters, galaxies, and other celestial objects, along with observation guidance and technical explanations. This edn completely redesigned, with new sections on computer-controlled telescopes and CCD imaging.
19th edn 1998.

753 **The physics of extragalactic radio sources**
D.S. De Young University of Chicago Press, 2002, 558pp. $45.00. ISBN 0226144151.
'Extragalactic radio sources are among the most unusual and spectacular objects in the universe, with sizes in excess of millions of light years, radiated energies over ten times those of normal galaxies, and a unique morphology. They reveal some of the most dramatic physical events ever seen and provide essential clues to the basic evolutionary tracks followed by all galaxies and groups of galaxies. In *The physics of extragalactic radio sources*, David De Young provides a clearly written overview of what is currently known about these objects.'

Science and ultimate reality: quantum theory, cosmology, and complexity
J.D. Barrow, P.C.W. Davies and C.L. Harper, eds See entry no. 774

754 **Statistics of the galaxy distribution**
V.J. Martinez and E. Saar Chapman & Hall/CRC, 2001, 456pp. $94.95. ISBN 1584880848.
Details the statistical methods and techniques that can be used to formulate cosmological models. In particular, emphasis is given to the study of large-scale structures. The text should be accessible to advanced undergraduates, or those already working in the field. It should be noted that despite the title, a considerable portion of this text is concerned with the statistics of clustering in general.

755 **The Sun: an introduction**
M. Stix Springer, 2004, 490pp. £35.00. ISBN 3540207414.
Thorough revision with about 100 new pages and many new illustrations. 1. Characteristics of the Sun; 2. Internal structure; 3. Tools for solar observation; 4. The atmosphere; 5. Oscillations; 6. Convection; 7. Rotation; 8. Magnetism; 9. Chromosphere, corona, and solar wind. Bibliographies.
1st edn 1989. Series: Astronomy and Astrophysics Library

Keeping up-to-date

756 **Annual Review of Astronomy and Astrophysics**
Annual Reviews. $227.00.
www.annurev.org/catalog/2004/aa42.asp [DESCRIPTION]
One of the academic research series offering 'comprehensive, timely collections of critical reviews written by leading scientists'. Examples of chapters in recent volumes are: Cool white dwarfs; Evolution of a habitable planet; Fine structure in sunspots; Neutron star cooling.

757 **Astronomical Newsletters**
S. Stevens-Rayburn; Space Telescope Science Institute
http://sesame.stsci.edu/lib/NEWSLETTER.htm
Reasonably frequently updated list of free newsletters of interest to the astronomical community.

758 **Space Science Reviews**
Kluwer Academic, Quarterly.
www.kluweronline.com/issn/0038-6308 [DESCRIPTION]
Contains invited review papers from worldwide authors with emphasis on scientific results in the fields of astrophysics, physics of planetary systems, solar physics, and magnetospheric physics. Does not publish original research papers as its purpose is to provide a contemporary synthesis of the situation in the various branches of the subject: e.g. 'The impact of space experiments on our knowledge of the physics of the universe' (2004).

Modern Physics

Brownian motion • Einstein • general relativity • gravitation • Heisenberg • molecular physics • quantum mechanics • quantum physics • quantum theory • relativity • space-time • special relativity • theoretical physics • time and space

Introductions to the subject

759 **Beyond measure: modern physics, philosophy, and the meaning of quantum theory**
J. Baggott 2nd edn, Oxford University Press, 2004, 379pp. £20.00. ISBN 0198525362.
Complete re-write of the first 1992 edn, the most significant change being the removal of the mathematics to appendices. Successfully provides a rigorously based text but one that newcomers will be able to approach and understand.
'Does for quantum theory what Hawking's *A brief history of time* did for astronomy and cosmology.' (*Chemistry World*)

760 **Developments in modern physics: a volume in honour of Werner Heisenberg's 100th anniversary**
G. Buschhorn and J. Wess Springer, 2004, 180pp. £38.50. ISBN 3540202013.
Two major essays and a set of articles developing key central areas of research in the field today. Readable by specialists, doctoral students, and the physics community at large. Also includes a short biography of Heisenberg.

761 **Einstein defiant: genius versus genius in the quantum revolution**
E.B. Bolles Joseph Henry Press, 2004, 348pp. ISBN 0309089980.
www.nap.edu/books/0309089980/html [COMPANION]
Interesting example of electronic book developed by *The National Academies Press*: 'The Open Book page image presentation framework is not designed to replace printed books. Rather, it is a free, browsable, non-proprietary, fully and deeply searchable version of the publication which we can inexpensively and quickly produce to make the material available worldwide.'

- **Handbook of Brownian motion: facts and formulae A.N. Borodin and P. Salminen** 2nd edn, Birkhauser, 2002, 672pp. $176.00. ISBN 3764367059. 'The purpose of this book is to give an easy reference to a large number of facts and formulae associated with Brownian motion. The collection contains more than 2500 numbered formulae.' One of Einstein's classic 1905 papers was on Brownian motion.

762 **From classical to quantum mechanics: an introduction to formalism, foundations and applications**
G. Esposito, G. Marmo and G. Sudarshan Cambridge University Press, 2004, 592pp. £45.00. ISBN 0521833248.
Mathematically challenging but very well written with good historical background and flowing explanations of key developments. Indeed, 'written for educated readers who need to be introduced to quantum theory and its foundations' (as well as for expert readers: graduate students, lecturers, research workers).

763 **Gravity from the ground up**
B.F. Schutz Cambridge University Press, 2002, 424pp. £30.00. ISBN 0521455065.
'This book invites the reader to understand our Universe, not just marvel at it. From the clock-like motions of the planets to the catastrophic collapse of a star into a black hole, gravity controls the Universe. Gravity is central to modern physics, helping to answer the deepest questions about the nature of time, the origin of the Universe and the unification of the forces of nature ...'

Information: the new language of science
H.C. Von Baeyer See entry no. 1

764 **The new quantum universe**
T. Hey and P. Walters 2nd edn, Cambridge University Press, 2003, 374pp. £55.00. ISBN 0521564182.
An update of the successful 1987 text, this is an accessible book for readers of all scientific levels. Details potentially baffling quantum concepts with ease and avoiding over-reliance on mathematics. The book looks at current theories and the sometimes fantastic applications that they may one day allow.

Quanta: a handbook of concepts
P.W. Atkins See entry no. 1866

765 **Quantum dialogue: the making of a revolution**
M. Beller University of Chicago Press, 1999, 365pp. $20.00. ISBN 226041824.
'"Science is rooted in conversations", wrote Werner Heisenberg, one of the twentieth century's great physicists. In *Quantum Dialogue*, Mara Beller shows that science is rooted not just in conversation but in disagreement, doubt, and uncertainty. She argues that it is precisely this culture of dialogue and controversy within the scientific community that fuels creativity.

'Beller draws her argument from her radical new reading of the history of the quantum revolution, especially the development of the Copenhagen interpretation. One of several competing approaches, this version succeeded largely due to the rhetorical skills of Niels Bohr and his colleagues. Using extensive archival research, Beller shows how Bohr and others marketed their views, misrepresenting and dismissing their opponents as "unreasonable" and championing their own not always coherent or well supported position as "inevitable".' Bibliography pp 327–354.

'[R]emarkable and original... . [Beller's] arguments are thoroughly supported and her conclusions are meticulously argued... . This is an important book that all who are interested in the emergence of quantum mechanics will want to read.' (*History of Physics Newsletter*)

766 Spacetime and geometry: an introduction to general relativity
S. Carroll Addison Wesley, 2004, 513pp. $85.60. ISBN 0805387323.
From the Preface: 'General relativity is the most beautiful physical theory ever invented. It describes one of the most pervasive features of the world we experience – gravitation – in terms of an elegant mathematical structure – the differential geometry of curved spacetime – leading to unambiguous predictions that have received spectacular experimental confirmation.

'Consequences of general relativity, from the big bang to black holes, often get young people first interested in physics, and it is an unalloyed joy to finally reach the point in one's studies where these phenomena may be understood at a rigorous quantitative level. If you are contemplating reading this book, that point is here.'

767 Twentieth century physics
L.M. Brown, A. Pais and A.B. Pippard, eds Institute of Physics Publishing, 1995, 2576pp. 3 v, £350.00. ISBN 0750303107.
Fascinating series of articles by renowned experts reviewing the history of the various sub-parts of physics through the 20th century. V. I covers materials up to mid-century, its chapters to large extent written by physicist-historians; Vs. II and III have a more specialist flavour and deal with topics more important in the second half of the century.

Dictionaries, thesauri, classifications

Dictionary of material science and high energy physics
D. Basu, ed. See entry no. 5792

Research centres & institutes

768 Kavli Institute for Theoretical Physics [USA]
University of California, Santa Barbara
www.itp.ucsb.edu
Aims to 'contribute to the progress of theoretical physics, especially in areas overlapping the traditional domains'. Of especial interest here is the access provided to an extensive collection of free online seminars in all aspects of physics, held from 1997 onwards: see *KITP Online* at http://online.itp.ucsb.edu/online; as well as the website section headed *Kavli ITP and the Community*.

The Director of the Institute, David Gross, was 'awarded the 2004 Nobel Prize in Physics for solving in 1973 the last great remaining problem of what has since come to be called 'the Standard Model' of the quantum mechanical picture of reality. He and his co-recipients discovered how the nucleus of atoms works.'

Associations & societies

769 International Society on General Relativity and Gravitation
www.maths.qmul.ac.uk/grgsoc
Formed in 1971 and is the professional society for all those working in the GR and gravity field.

- **HyperSpace** www.maths.qmw.ac.uk/hyperspace. Set of hypertext-based services for general relativity research sponsored by the Society.

Digital data, image & text collections

770 Einstein Papers Project
California Institute of Technology
www.einstein.caltech.edu
Will contain 14,000 documents and will fill 25 volumes. Now located and supported by CalTech, the project is sponsored by the Hebrew University of Jerusalem and Princeton University Press. The project was located at and supported by Boston University from 1986 to 2000.

Handbooks & manuals

771 Handbook of molecular physics and quantum chemistry
S. Wilson, P.F. Bernath and R. McWeeny, ed. Wiley, 2003, 2200pp. 3 v., $1200.00. ISBN 0471623741.
Comprehensive work bringing together the most important theoretical concepts and methods. The format allows the reader to progress from foundations to the most important areas of current research. Invaluable for both expert researchers and graduate students working in any relevant field. Seven parts in each volume: v. 1. Fundamentals; v. 2. Molecular electronic structure; v. 3. Molecules in the physico-chemical environment: spectroscopy, dynamics and bulk properties.

772 Quantum theory of fields
S. Weinberg Cambridge University Press, 2000, 1600pp. 3 v, £120.00. ISBN 0521780829.
Comprehensive overview of the arena. Starts with a historical outline before developing the text into the emergent discoveries and theories. The second volume looks more at the practical details and applications of the field, with the third volume examining supersymmetry. This is very much an advanced text suitable for the researcher or graduate student who needs a detailed guide into this realm. Very well reviewed.

773 Relativity: an introduction to special and general relativity
H. Stephani 3rd edn, Cambridge University Press, 2004, 416pp. £30.00. ISBN 0521010691.
Comprehensive and self-contained overview, but 'the reader is expected to have a basic knowledge of theoretical mechanics and electrodynamics.'

- **Exact solutions of Einstein's field equations H. Stephani [et al.]** 2nd edn, Cambridge University Press, 2003, 732pp. £80.00. ISBN 0521461367. ' ... will be an important source and guide for researchers working in Relativity and in Mathematical and Theoretical Physics and Astrophysics'.

774 **Science and ultimate reality: quantum theory, cosmology, and complexity**
J.D. Barrow, P.C.W. Davies and C.L. Harper, eds Cambridge University Press, 2004, 721pp. £38.00. ISBN 052183113X.
Often advanced volume aimed at the physics generalist, and based on a special programme in honour of the 90th birthday of theoretical physicist J.A. Wheeler. Aims 'to stimulate thinking and research among students, professional physicists, cosmologists, and philosophers, as well as all scholars and others concerned with the deep issues of existence. Authors were invited to be bold and creative by developing themes that are perhaps more speculative than is usual in a volume of this sort ...'
'One final note: the meeting was sponsored by the Templeton Foundation, which is dedicated broadly to the reconciliation of the spiritual and the scientific aspects of the human mind – religion and science, if you will. As such, I was wary of its provenance and did not attend. My suspicions, or prejudices if you like, were mistaken. The generous funding provided by the foundation has helped to produce an excellent book.' (*Times Higher Education Supplement*)

Nuclear & Particle Physics

accelerators • antimatter • atomic particles • atoms • baryons • dark matter • elementary particles • extradimensions • forces of nature • fundamental forces • fundamental particles • grand unified theories • hadrons • high-energy physics • isotopes • linear accelerators • neutrinos • nuclear data • nuclear physics • nuclear structure • particle detectors • particle physics • quantum chromodynamics • quantum electrodynamics • quantum field theories • quarks • subatomic particles • supersymmetry • x-ray data

Introductions to the subject

775 **The discovery of subatomic particles**
S. Weinberg 2nd edn, Cambridge University Press, 2003, 206pp. £18.99. ISBN 052182351X.
'In this absorbing commentary on the discovery of the atom's constituents, Steven Weinberg accomplishes a brilliant fusion of history and science. This is in effect two books, cleverly interwoven. One is an account of a sequence of key events in the physics of the twentieth century, events that led to the discoveries of the electron, proton and neutron. The other is an introduction to those fundamentals of classical physics that played crucial roles in these discoveries.'
1st edn Scientific American Library, 1983

776 **The evidence for the top quark: objectivity and bias in collaborative experimentation**
K.W. Staley Cambridge University Press, 2004, 343pp. £45.00. ISBN 0521827108.
Detailed but very readable account of the search for the last of the six quarks of the modern physics 'standard model'. Good introduction to the social complexities of high-energy physics research.
- **The quantum quark A. Watson** Cambridge University Press, 2004, 476pp. £19.99. ISBN 0521829070. 'A refreshingly new and attractive account of particle physics in general and QCD [quantum chromodynamics] in particular' *Donald Perkins, University of Oxford.*

777 **Facts and mysteries in elementary particle physics**
M.J.G. Veltman World Scientific, 2003, 348pp. $19.00. ISBN 981238149X.
www.worldscibooks.com/physics/5088.html [DESCRIPTION]
'Comprehensive overview of modern particle physics accessible to anyone with a true passion for wanting to know how the universe works.'
- **Antiparticle** PhysicsDaily.com. www.physicsdaily.com/physics/Antiparticle. One of a very large number of useful articles in *The Physics Encyclopedia*, a compilation where 'the content of each of the content pages here besides headers, footers and side bars is obtained and licensed from Wikipedia.org'.

778 **An introduction to particle physics**
CCLRC Rutherford Appleton Laboratory
http://hepwww.rl.ac.uk/Pub/Phil/ppintro/ppintro.html
Accessible introduction to the subject with links to various key terms. Intended to be of use to children in secondary education, or professionals from outside the field who wish to gain an insight into the arena. Includes images of key CCLRC facilities.
- **International Baryons Conferences** http://baryons04.in2p3.fr. This is the website for the 10th Conference, held in Palaiseau, France, 2004. Entrée to the detailed work still proceeding in this arena.

779 **Particles and nuclei: an introduction to the physical concepts**
B. Povh [et al.] 4th edn, Springer, 2004, 396pp. £27.00. ISBN 3540201688.
Translated into many languages, has become a standard introduction to the subject.

780 **The pleasure of finding things out**
R. Feynman, comp. Rev edn, BBC Horizon/PBS Nova, 2005. VHS Videocassette.
www.sykes.easynet.co.uk/pofto.html
'*The Pleasure of Finding Things Out* was filmed in 1981 and will delight and inspire anyone who would like to share something of the joys of scientific discovery. Feynman is a master storyteller, and his tales – about childhood, Los Alamos, and the Bomb, or how he won a Nobel Prize – are a vivid and entertaining insight into the mind of a great scientist at work and play.'
- **The pleasure of finding things out: the best short works of Richard P. Feynman J. Robbins, ed.** Basic Books, 2000, 269pp. $15.95. ISBN 0738203491. http://nobelprize.org/physics/laureates/1965/feynman-lecture.html. Check also the website 'The development of the space-time view of quantum electrodynamics' – Feynman's fascinating Nobel Prize lecture.

Dictionaries, thesauri, classifications

Elsevier's dictionary of nuclear engineering: Russian-English; English-Russian
M. Rosenberg and S. Bobryakov, comps See entry no. 4720

781 **Handbook of particle physics**
M.K. Sundaresan CRC Press, 2001, 464pp. $54.95. ISBN 0849302153.
Contains in dictionary format terms of interest to researchers and students of particle physics, alongside

appropriate technical and mathematical details. Aimed largely at non-specialists and invaluable for newcomers to this field.

Official & quasi-official bodies

National Nuclear Security Administration
See entry no. 4723

Nuclear Energy Agency
See entry no. 4724

Particle Physics and Astronomy Research Council
See entry no. 716

Research centres & institutes

782 **Brookhaven National Laboratory** [USA]
www.bnl.gov
'A multi-program national laboratory operated by Brookhaven Science Associates for the US Department of Energy (DOE). Six Nobel Prizes have been awarded for discoveries made at the Lab.' The Site Index quickly reveals the range of the Lab's activities: worth scanning are the pages of the Office of Intellectual Property and Sponsored Research.

- **Fusion Power United Kingdom Atomic Energy Authority and European Atomic Energy Community**. www.fusion.org.uk. Website of the EURATOM/UKAEA Fusion Association, at the Culham Science Centre, home of the UK fusion research programme funded jointly by the UK Engineering and Physical Sciences Research Council and by EURATOM.
- **National Nuclear Data Center** www.nndc.bnl.gov. 'Collects, evaluates, and disseminates nuclear physics data for basic nuclear research and for applied nuclear technologies. The NNDC is a worldwide resource for nuclear data'.
- **National Synchrotron Light Source: NSLS** www.nsls.bnl.gov. Well laid out website describing the history of the synchrotron, current facilities and uses, and links to other synchrotrons in the USA and internationally.

783 **CERN** [EUR]
www.cern.ch
European-based organization for nuclear research, birthplace of the world wide web, and the world's largest particle physics centre. An institute where physicists come to explore matter and the forces that hold it together. CERN exists primarily to provide them with the necessary tools such as accelerators. Site includes information on CERN's current research and facilities; also much of historical import: e.g. about the so-called 'bubble chamber era'.

- **CERN Document Server** http://cdsweb.cern.ch. Access to over 650,000 bibliographic records, including 320,000 fulltext documents, of interest to people working in particle physics and related areas. Covers preprints, articles, books, journals, photographs, etc.
- **The Large Hadron Collider Project** http://lhc-new-homepage.web.cern.ch. Accelerator which brings protons and ions into head-on collisions at higher energies than ever achieved before – allowing scientists to penetrate still further into the structure of matter and recreate the conditions prevailing in the early universe.

784 **Particle Data Group**
http://pdg.lbl.gov
International collaboration that reviews particle physics and related areas of astrophysics, and compiles/analyses data on particle properties. Includes links to key related information and resources available around the globe.

- **Nuclear data dissemination Lund University**. http://ie.lbl.gov/toi.html. Very useful gateway to wide variety of datasets – though not all are currently maintained.
- **The particle adventure** http://particleadventure.org. Award-winning interactive tour of quarks, neutrinos, antimatter, extradimensions, dark matter, accelerators and particle detectors. Good section 'Unsolved Mysteries' – including comments on Grand Unified Theory and String Theory.
- **Particle physics education sites** http://pdg.ift.unesp.br/particleadventure/other/othersites.html. Good annotated list coverng: Particle Physics Education and Information sites; National Laboratory Education Programs; Women and Minorities in the Sciences; Other Interesting Educational and Informational Sites. No indication of updating schedule, however.
- **Review of particle physics** http://pdg.lbl.gov/pdg_products.html. 1100-page biennial review summarizing much of particle physics. 2004 edn had 1726 new measurements from 512 papers plus data from previous editions compiled and evaluated in Particle Listings and Summary Tables. Most cited publication in particle physics.

785 **Stanford Linear Accelerator Center** [USA]
www.slac.stanford.edu
'A national laboratory that is both a School and a Department of Stanford University. SLAC's research is funded by the Department of Energy Office of Science. SLAC is home of the first US website.'

Visitors are invited to explore the Virtual Visitor Center; a good place to start for newcomers to the subject and the work of the laboratory.

- **SLAC Library** www.slac.stanford.edu/library. Excellent frequently updated gateway to range of relevant services. Includes list of free physics-related online journals and an Ask a Librarian! virtual reference service.
- **SPIRES** www.slac.stanford.edu/spires. Access to high-energy physics related articles, including journal papers, preprints, e-prints, technical reports, conference papers and theses, comprehensively indexed since 1974. First US database on the web. Much other useful information accessible here.

Portal & task environments

786 **Interactions.org: Particle physics news and resources**
InterAction.
www.interactions.org
Wide ranging site resulting from collaboration of over 20 worldwide research laboratories, supported by 19 funding agencies in Canada, France, Germany, Italy, Japan, The Netherlands, UK, USA. An excellent entrée to this field.

Discovering print & electronic resources

787 **Particle physics: one hundred years of discoveries: an annotated chronological bibliography**
V.V. Ezhela [et al.], eds AIP Press, 1996, 328pp. $64.95. ISBN 1563966425.
Presents key historical material, including excerpts from 500 of the most influential theoretical papers and experimental discoveries in particle physics, many of which have been cited for the Nobel Prize. A general introduction places

original articles in historical context and for each entry there is a short description explaining the importance of the discovery, followed by complete bibliographic information.

Directories & encyclopedias

788 **Q is for quantum: particle physics from A–Z**
J. Gribbin Weidenfeld & Nicolson, 1998, 645pp. £26.00. ISBN 0297817523.
'An easy-to-read dictionary of nuclear physics, with many biographical entries and a timeline containing scientists, key dates in physical sciences, and important world events within a scientific context.'

789 **Table of isotopes**
R.B. Firestone, C.M. Baglin and S.Y.F. Chu, eds 8th edn, Wiley, 1999, 216pp. CD-ROM, $244.00. ISBN 0471356336.
http://ie.lbl.gov/education/isotopes.htm [COMPANION]
Massive compilation of nuclear structure and decay data for c.3,700 isotopes and isomers, plus useful supplementary information. More than 25,000 references.

Handbooks & manuals

790 **Handbook of accelerator physics and engineering**
A. Chao and M. Tigner, eds World Scientific, 1999, 650pp. £34.00. ISBN 9810238584.
Information useful to professionals in design, construction, and operation of accelerators. More than 200 contributions from accelerator institutions. Bibliography at end of each section.

791 **Handbook of neutron activation analysis**
S.J. Parry Viridian Publishing, 2003, 243pp. £35.00. ISBN 095448911X.
Noted for comprehensive, concise and clear coverage of the topic this text provides a straightforward review of what neutron activation analysis can do, describing the applied technique. Intended for both undergraduates, graduates and professional researchers. Novices will find the text easily understandable with sufficient detail to give a thorough background of the principles involved.

792 **Quantum field theory in a nutshell**
A. Zee Princeton University Press, 2003, 536pp. $49.50. ISBN 0691010196.
http://pup.princeton.edu [DESCRIPTION]
'An esteemed researcher and acclaimed popular author takes up the challenge of providing a clear, relatively brief, and fully up-to-date introduction to one of the most vital but notoriously difficult subjects in theoretical physics. A quantum field theory text for the twenty-first century, this book makes the essential tool of modern theoretical physics available to any student who has completed a course on quantum mechanics and is eager to go on.'

793 **X-ray data booklet**
A. Thompson and D. Vaughan, eds; Berkeley Lab 2nd edn, 2001. PDF, Free on request.
http://xdb.lbl.gov
Organized: 1. X-ray properties of the elements; 2. Synchrotron radiation; 3. Scattering processes; 4. Optics and detectors; 5. Miscellaneous.

Keeping up-to-date

794 **Annual review of nuclear and particle science**
Annual Reviews, 2004. $232.00. ISBN 0824315545 ISSN 01638998.
www.annurev.org/catalog/2004/ns54.asp [DESCRIPTION]
Chapters in the 2004 volume include: Direct detection of dark matter; The status of gravitational wave astronomy; The strength of the weak iterations.

795 **High Energy Physics Libraries Webzine**
Biannual. ISSN 14242729.
library.cern.ch/HEPLW
Launched in March 2000. Aims 'to discuss issues relevant to high energy physics libraries from the point of view of both information workers and library clients. A secondary aim is to give librarians the opportunity to experience the world of electronic publishing from the inside.'

Optical & Wave Physics

atomic physics • atomic spectra • colours • electromagnetic spectrum • holography • image science • lasers • light • microscopy • nonlinear optics • optical engineering • optics • optoelectronics • photonics • plasma spectroscopy • spectroscopy • synchrotrons • wave physics

Introductions to the subject

796 **Atomic physics**
C.J. Foot Oxford University Press, 2004, 346pp. £22.95. ISBN 0198506961.
1. Early atomic physics; 2. The hydrogen atom; 3. Helium; 4. The alkalis; 5/ The LS-coupling scheme; 6. Hyperfine structure and isotope shift; 7. The interaction of atoms with radiation; 8. Doppler-free laser spectroscopy; 9. Laser cooling and trapping; 10. Magnetic trapping, evaporative cooling and BEC; 11. Atom interferometry; 12. Ion traps; 13. Quantum computing.
Series: Oxford Master Series in Atomic, Optical and Laser Physics.

797 **Black-body theory and the quantum discontinuity, 1894–1912**
T.S. Kuhn Rev edn, University of Chicago Press, 1987. Originally published Oxford University Press, 1978, $29.00. ISBN 0226458008.
Describes the evolution of quantum theory arising from Max Planck's work on the so-called black-body problem, usually known at the start of the 20th century as the problem of black radiation.
'A masterly assessment of the way the idea of quanta of radiation became part of 20th-century physics ... The book not only deals with a topic of importance and interest to all scientists, but is also a polished literary work, described (accurately) by one of its original reviewers as a scientific detective story' (*New Scientist*)

798 **Mapping the spectrum: techniques of visual representation in research and teaching**
K. Hentschel Oxford University Press, 2002, 562pp. £85.00. ISBN 0198509537.
History of spectroscopy in the 19th and early 20th centuries.
'The beautiful illustrations are a visual pleasure ... Mapping the Spectrum is a must for historians of science. In addition, it can be great fun for scientists who are interested in the sunny side of their field, before the computer transformed it to such an extent that its origins are almost unrecognizable.' (Angewandte Chemie)

■ **NIST Atomic Spectra Database National Institute of Standards and Technology**. http://physics.nist.gov/cgi-bin/AtData/main_asd. Contains data for radiative transitions and energy levels in atoms and atomic ions. Data are included for observed transitions of 99 elements and energy levels of 52 elements.

799 **Optics**
E. Hecht 4th edn, Addison Wesley, 2003, 680pp. $108.00. ISBN 0805385665.
An 'up-to-date, comprehensive, lively and precise introduction to optics' for degree level students. As well as covering the key principles, this edition addresses all of today's significant technological advances, as well as giving the classical background. Includes problems and solutions to challenge and develop the reader.

800 **Principles of plasma spectroscopy**
H.R. Griem Cambridge University Press, 1997, 366pp. £80.00. ISBN 0521455049.
A comprehensive introduction to the theory and experimental applications of spectroscopic methods. With over 1000 references to further resources, this text is an ideal starting point for an advanced student or researcher relatively new to this field seeking theoretical and experimental details.

801 **The science of color**
S.K. Shevell, ed.; Optical Society of America 2nd edn, Elsevier, 339pp. £63.50. ISBN 0444512519.
Collection of articles by recognized authorities updating the 'legendary original edition' of 1953. 1. The origins of modern color science; 2. Light, the retinal image, and photoreceptors; 3. Color matching and color discrimination; 4. Color appearance; 5. Color appearance and color difference specification; 6. The physiology of color vision; 7. The physics and chemistry of color: the 15 mechanisms; 8. Digital color reproduction. Extensive subject index. Many colour plates.
1st edn 1953 (Crowell).

Research centres & institutes

802 **European Synchrotron Facility**
www.esrf.fr
'Eighteen nations work together to use the extremely bright beams of light produced by the ESRF's high-performance storage ring to study a remarkably wide range of materials, from biomolecules to nanomagnets, from ancient Egyptian cosmetics to metallic foams.' Excellent, clearly laid out and well designed site giving useful background on synchrotrons ('supermicroscopes'), and much other useful information.

803 **Optoelectronics Research Centre** [UK]
www.orc.soton.ac.uk
'Optoelectronics is the merging of physical, optical, electronic, chemical and materials sciences to develop newer, faster and more efficient ways of exploiting the properties of light.' Mission of the Centre – based at the University of Southampton – is 'to blend focused, application led research with fundamental studies on the generation, transmission and control of light, with particular emphasis on optical telecommunications'; and it is now the largest university-based group entirely devoted to optoelectronics in the European Union.

Associations & societies

804 **Laser Institute of America**
www.laserinstitute.org
'Started in 1968 with the sole intention of turning the potential of a powerful new technology into an actual, viable industry. The LIA was forged from the heart of the profession – a network of developers and engineers – people who were actually using lasers. These were the first 'members' of the LIA, the people who decided that sharing new ideas about lasers is just as important as developing them. The belief, as it remains today, is to promote laser applications and their safe use through education, training, and symposia.'

805 **Microscopy Society of America**
www.microscopy.com
Non-profit organization 'dedicated to the promotion and advancement of the knowledge of the science and practice of all microscopical imaging, analysis and diffraction techniques useful for elucidating the ultrastructure and function of materials in diverse areas of biological, materials, medical and physical sciences'.

806 **Optical Society of America**
www.osa.org
'Promotes the generation, application, archiving and worldwide dissemination of knowledge in optics and photonics.' Access to *Optics InfoBase*, a 'web-based repository of optics research with added services'.

■ **Optics Classification and Indexing Scheme: OCIS** www.osa.org/pubs/ocis. Two-level hierarchical structure containing 36 main headers and approximately 700 sub-categories. Used by OSA authors, presenters and reviewers to classify and index journal articles, meeting abstracts and presentations.

807 **Royal Microscopical Society** [UK]
www.rms.org.uk
Founded 1839 as *The Microscopical Society of London* and now 'involved in current developments in the fields of light and electron microscopy, scanning probe microscopy and image recording techniques. The RMS is devoted to Education. It publishes the highest rated journal in microscopy, *The Journal of Microscopy*, and microscopy handbooks, as well as helping young scientists through bursaries.

808 **SPIE – The International Society for Optical Engineering**
www.spie.org
Not-for-profit international society for the 'exchange, collection and dissemination of knowledge in optics, photonics and imaging'. Site includes information for students, teachers, and professionals studying and working within this field. A wealth of information.
Formerly the Society for Photo-Optical Instrumentation Engineers.

■ **SPIE Digital Library** spie.org/store/dlhome. 90,000 full-text papers from SPIE Journals and Proceedings published since 1998; citations and abstracts for most SPIE papers published since 1995; by end 2004 should have an archive of nearly 200,000 papers back to 1990; 15,000 papers added each year.

Portal & task environments

809 **Molecular Expressions: Exploring the world of optics and microscopy**
M.W. Davidson; Florida State University
http://micro.magnet.fsu.edu
Main focus is the *Photo Gallery*: photographs available for licensing to commercial, private, and non-profit institutions, and one of the web's largest collections of colour photographs taken through an optical microscope. Also, however, good range of background information covering basic concepts, digital imaging, and virtual microscopy.

810 **Optics.Org**
Institute of Physics
optics.org
News and archival portal for all students and researchers with an interest in optical research and industrial applications.

811 **Photonics.com**
www.photonics.com
Good entrée to academic and industry developments. Useful range of publications, including free online access to the *Photonics Dictionary*, containing more than 5800 industry-related terms, along with acronyms, abbreviations and illustrations.

Directories & encyclopedias

812 **Encyclopedia of modern optics**
B. Guenther and D. Steel, eds Elsevier Academic Press, 2004, 2400pp. 5 v., $1435.00. ISBN 0122276000.
Covering optics from the beginning of the laser era in 1960; sets out to cover all advances in the field since and their modern applications. Lengthy articles detail different topics, with important and complex topics being further subdivided. While detailed, the text is intended to be accessible for readers at an undergraduate level and above.

813 **Encyclopedia of optical engineering**
R.G. Driggers, ed. Marcel Dekker, 2003, 3049pp. 3 v., $1500.00. ISBN 0824709403.
www.dekker.com
'Optical engineering is concerned with the engineering of a device or system in which light is involved, while Photonics is concerned primarily with the basic interaction of light and matter. But there is a large overlap between the two ...'

Purpose is to provide an optical engineering reference text that can be used by engineers, physicists, and other scientists. c.250 articles each of target length 6000 words. Excellent wide-ranging coverage. A–Z sequence; combined index.

Available online: see website. Online version has quarterly updates.

814 **Optics encyclopedia: basic foundations and practical applications**
T.G. Brown [et al.], eds Wiley-VCH, 2003, 3472pp. £590.00. ISBN 3527403205.
High quality articles 'provide dependable information on both theoretical and applied topics of current interest in industrial and academic research'. Articles are accompanied by a glossary of terminology and bibliography, ensuring the text is both user friendly and good for reference.

815 **Photonics rules of thumb: optics, electro-optics, fiber optics, and lasers**
E. Friedman and J.L. Miller 2nd edn, McGraw-Hill, 2004, 418pp. $59.95. ISBN 0071385193.
'Intended to allow any engineer, regardless of speciality, to make first guesses at solutions in a wide range of topics that might be encountered in system design, modeling, or fabrication, as well as to provide a guide for choosing which details to consider more diligently. Another distinguishing feature of this book is that it has few of the detailed derivations found in typical academic books. We are not trying to replace them but to provide an augmentation of what they provide.'

300 rules; appendix: Tables of useful values and conversions. Glossary. Index.

- **Optical communications rules of thumb J.L. Miller and E. Friedman** McGraw-Hill, 2003, 428pp. $65.00. ISBN 0071387781. 250 rules.

Handbooks & manuals

816 **Atomic, molecular, & optical physics handbook**
G.W.F. Drake, ed.; American Institute of Physics AIP Press, 1996, 1095pp. $208.00. ISBN 156396242X.
Over 100 contributory authors to almost 90 chapters covering the full range of theory and appiication.

CRC handbook of laser science and technology
M.J. Weber, ed. See entry no. 5470

Electro-optics handbook
R.W. Waynant and M.N. Ediger, eds See entry no. 5483

Field guide to digital color
M.C. Stone See entry no. 6173

817 **Foundations of image science**
H.H. Barrett and K.J. Myers Wiley, 2003, 1584pp. $148.00. ISBN 0471153001.
Principles, mathematics, and statistics needed to understand and evaluate imaging systems. Extensive, mathematically intensive treatment, but with useful Prologue: 'We begin by surveying and categorizing the myriad imaging systems that might be discussed and then suggest a unifying mathematical perspective based on linear algebra and stochastic theory. Next we introduce a key theme of this book, object or task-based assessment of image quality.'
'Containing a clear, detailed and general mathematical description of image formation, representation, and quality assessment, this book will be of great interest to researchers and graduate students ... highly recommended.' (*Medical Physics*)

818 **Handbook of laser technology and applications**
C.E. Webb and D.C. Jones, eds Institute of Physics Publishing, 2004, 2725pp. 3 v., £600.00. ISBN 0750306076.
Overview of optics with particular emphasis on laser technologies, starting with the principles, then moving on to the techniques and finally the practical applications. An essential handbook for the research engineer or anyone involved in the application of lasers within industry, this is also an invaluable text for students and scientists working in the research domain.

819 **Handbook of lasers**
M.J. Weber CRC Press, 2001, 1198pp. $149.95. ISBN 0849335094.
Authoritative compilation of lasers and their properties, arranged primarily according to the phase (solid, liquid, or gas) of the lasing medium. Derived from Volumes I and II and Supplement I of the *Handbook of laser science and technology* plus more recent literature.
'This is an indispensable reference for workers in the field.' (*Choice*)

Handbook of microwave and optical components
K. Chang, ed. See entry no. 5491

820 **Handbook of nonlinear optics**
R.L. Sutherland, ed. 2nd edn, Marcel Dekker, 2003, 971pp. $195.00. ISBN 0824742435.
The scope of nonlinear optics (NLO) 'includes all phenomena in which the optical parameters of materials are changed with irradiation of light. Generally, this requires high optical intensities, which is the main reason NLO matured in parallel with laser technology'.
Detailed coverage; extensive index; good use of tables.
1st edn 1996. Series: Optical Engineering, 82.

821 **Handbook of optical materials**
M.J. Weber Interpharm/CRC, 2002, 536pp. $149.95. ISBN 0849335124.
A successor to the 'much respected' *CRC handbook of laser science and technology*, providing reliable data on optical materials. Contains data tables of the physical properties of all types of optical materials and safety guidelines, as well as terminology and standard units.

822 **Handbook of photonics**
M.C. Gupta, ed. CRC Press, 1997, 812pp. $149.95. ISBN 0849389097.
Contains 18 self-contained chapters, covering the range of optoelectronics, arranged into three sections – Photonic materials (semiconductors as well as oxide and organic materials); Photonic devices and optics (lasers, photodetectors, etc.); and Photonic systems (optical communications, optical storage, electronic displays, etc.) Well illustrated.

823 **Laser doppler and phase doppler measurement techniques**
H.-E. Albrecht [et al.], eds Springer, 2002, 738pp. £100.00. ISBN 3540678387.
Good detailed treatment. 14 chapters within four parts: I. Fundamentals; II. Measurement principles; III. Data processing; IV. Application issues. Bibliography pp 689–721.
Series: Experimental Fluid Mechanics.

824 **Optical engineer's desk reference**
W.L. Wolfe; Optical Society of America 2003, 734pp. $125.00. ISBN 1557527571.
This weighty and up-to-date volume is an invaluable resources for the working optical engineer. This text details the various formulae, procedures, systems, and instrumentation that they will encounter.

825 **Optics, light and lasers: the practical approach to modern photonics and laser physics**
D. Meschede Wiley-VCH, 2004, 410pp. $86.00. ISBN 3527403647.
Links the central topics of optics established 200 years ago to the most recent research topics such as laser cooling or holography. Assumes the reader is familiar with the formal concepts of electrodynamics and basic quantum mechanics.

- **Handbook of holographic interferometry: optical and digital methods** **T. Kreis** Wiley-VCH, 2005, 542pp. $200.00. ISBN 3527405461. www.wiley.com/WileyCDA [DESCRIPTION]. Extensive treatment including detailed appendices.
- **Lasers and holograms** **F. DeFreitas, comp.** www.holoworld.com. Personal interest regularly updated website providing a wide spectrum of information including an extensive list of helpfully annotated links.
- **Practical holography** **G. Saxby** 3rd edn, Institute of Physics Publishing, 2004, 482pp. £80.00. ISBN 0750309121. Well established text; previous edn Prentice Hall, 1994.

The reproduction of colour
R.W.G. Hunt; Society for Imaging Science and Technology See entry no. 6178

Earth Sciences

Earth Sciences as a discipline is, literally, the study of our entire planet, including its evolution, its current activity, and its future. It is the most multidisciplinary of the natural sciences, covering a wide spectrum of subject fields, all of which contribute to our understanding and comprehension of the nature, origin, evolution and behaviour of the earth and its parts. Specifically, it is the study of the lithosphere, atmosphere, hydrosphere and biosphere; and it is the inevitable interactions between these that are of particular interest to the Earth Scientist.

Earth Sciences, typically, borrows techniques and methodologies from other scientific fields, most notably those of physics and chemistry. As a result of the interrelationship of subject matter, research methodologies, and the varied nature of current and historical publications there is an obvious diversity of resources described for the Earth Sciences with text, data, images, and maps and much more. Resources in Earth Sciences, whilst being varied because of the subject matter, will also show that there is often a bias towards journal-based resources, whether it is the actual journal references, or the bibliography that leads to journal resources. This is inevitable given that the subject is clearly scientific, and that current, up-to-date publication in the sciences is crucial. The joy of being an Earth Scientist, however, is that the historical can offer just us much as the current, and it is this that contributes to the diversity and range of resources that are offered here.

- Geochemistry Closely allied to geology, but on a microscopic level. Geochemists study the chemical components of the earth's crust and mantle, especially isotopes and related processes. One family of minerals – silicates – is crucial in understanding many geological processes. Geochemistry is, to put it rather simply, the chemistry of silicates. Resources for Geochemistry tend to gravitate to the handbook/manual and primary resources sections.
- Geology An interdisciplinary subject, whose component parts are interrelated, forming for many a subject that lies at the heart of the Earth Sciences. Studies focus on the solid earth, the processes forming and modifying it, with special emphasis on two aspects: firstly the earth's materials (minerals, rocks, soil, water, ice) and secondly the study of stratified rocks through geological time. Specific subject areas within this field include those of sedimentology, stratigraphy and structural geology. There is a wide variety of resources for the amateur and professional geologist ranging from the 'story' to image-based resources to technical handbooks. Many online resources are available for those interested in geology.
- Geomorphology The study of landscapes and their evolution. There are inevitable interactions with the plate tectonic geosystem and climatic studies, all of which continually improve the scientist's understanding of the shape and form of the land. Geomorphology has traditionally been a part of 'Geography' as a subject field but the inevitable links with other Earth Science subjects makes this a logical place to put its resource information. Resources for this subject are as varied as the world landscapes that are studied. There is potentially something here for all with an interest in the subject with a bias towards the undergraduate student.
- Geophysics Concerned with all aspects of the physical properties and processes of the Earth and planetary bodies, including their interpretation. Studies and research in geophysics draw on techniques and understanding from both geology and physics focusing on the exploration and measurement of the physical structure and dynamics of the earth. Specific subject fields include seismology, magnetism and geochronology. Resources on earthquakes and plate tectonics are included in this section.
- Hydrology This is the study of the characteristics and movement of water both on and under the earth's surface. This field of study has become increasingly important as demand on our limited water supplies increases.
- Meteorology & Climatology Meteorology involves the study of the atmosphere and its conditions and related phenomena. Climatology looks at climatic conditions, including actual climatic data, and the analysis of the causes of differences in climate, applying the data to the solutions that are adopted. There is an especial focus on items concerned with global warming.
- Mineralogy The study of the composition and structure and stability of minerals, their appearance and occurrence. Minerals are naturally occurring crystalline substances in rocks and are usually inorganic. Four key aspects of mineralogy are firstly the investigation of crystal composition, secondly the study of mineral association and occurrence in natural and synthetic systems, thirdly description of mineral properties and identification tools and, finally, mineral classification. Resources are biased towards handbooks and texts useful in laboratories where work is done in conjunction with minerals. There are also a number of glossy coffee-table book resource references with photographs of minerals. Note also the later section Mining & Minerals Processing within the subject grouping Natural Resources & Energy.
- Oceanography Deals with the physical, biological and chemical aspects of oceans, and their interrelationships. Almost anything that comes within the oceans' physical boundaries comes under this remit. Specific resources that may be cited will include charts and maps of the ocean floor and data from ocean floor drilling. Note particularly here the Marine & Freshwater Biology subject field within the grouping Biological Sciences.
- Paleontology Examines evidence of life in past geological ages. This includes the fossilized remains of plants and animals, from the largest dinosaur to the smallest pollen spores, as well more subtle evidence such as fossilized footprints and burrows, and the chemical make-up of rocks. Palaeontologists are interested in the same range of topics studied by biologists working on living organisms; for example anatomy, behaviour, reproduction, illnesses, and the way different organisms interact with each other in the environment. In fact, most biological disciplines have a 'palaeo' equivalent. The subject is intimately linked with evolutionary studies, because it provides the only direct evidence of the way organisms change over millions of years. However, bear in mind that, because the research

themes have so much in common, many 'regular' biological resources (particularly journals) include palaeontology alongside 'conventional' biology: see the grouping BIOLOGICAL SCIENCES.

- PETROLOGY The study of how rock is formed – specifically how it originates and evolves. Petrologists also classify and describe rocks. Resources for this subject field reflect the nature of the subject in having many handbooks and manuals to aid identification. Resources for those interested in volcanoes are included here.
- SPATIAL TECHNOLOGIES Includes remote sensing, image processing and the development and use of the Global Positioning System.

Introductions to the subject

826 Building planet earth: five billion years of earth history
P. Cattermole Cambridge University Press, 2000, 292pp. £30.00. ISBN 0521582784.
Illustrated and accessible account of earth's history, geology, and climate: a good overview of its evolution. 128 colour plates. Useful appendices: bibliography; glossary of terms; Data for the earth and planets; index. General and undergraduate readership.

827 The Cambridge guide to the earth
D. Lambert; Diagram Group Cambridge University Press, 1988, 256pp. ISBN 0521336430.
Still valuable introduction, especially helpful for those with no previous knowledge of the subject. 12 chapters: 1. Sizing up the earth; 2. The restless coast; 3. Fiery rocks ... 7. How rivers shape the land; 8. The work of the sea ... 11. The last 600 million years; 12. Rocks and man. 1-page bibliography. Index. Large typeface and many diagrams, figures.

828 The earth: an intimate history
R.A. Fortey Harper Collins, 2004, 501pp. £25.00. ISBN 0002570114.
An impressive blend of travel, history, reportage and science, creating a picture of the earth over the last four billion years. Descriptions of many of its parts are used to illustrate how geology informs our lives today in many varied ways. Clear and accessible scientific expositions. An important easy-to-read resource, making earth sciences accessible and relevant to the general public.
'This is not a book for people who like science books. It is a book for people who love books, and life. [Fortey] has written a wonderful book.' (*Guardian*)

829 The earth: its origin, history and physical constitution
H. Jeffreys 6th edn, Cambridge University Press, 1976, 574pp. ISBN 0521206480.
Classic text. 12 chapters: 1. The mechanical properties of rocks ... 3. Observational seismology; 4. The theory of the figures of the earth and moon ... 9. The age of the earth ... 11. The origin of the earth's surface features. Appendices A–H (G. Statistical methods). Bibliography and author index, pp 535–66. Undergraduate readership.
First published 1924.

830 Earth story: the forces that have shaped our planet
S. Lamb and D. Sington British Broadcasting Corporation, 2003, 240pp. £12.99. ISBN 0563487070.
Broad coverage of the topic. Describes the forces that formed and shaped the world from four billion years ago to the current time. A wide range of geological issues is tackled. Would appeal to a general readership.
Originally published 1998 to accompany the television series Earth Story.

831 Earth under siege: from air pollution to global change
R. Turco 2nd edn, Oxford University Press, 2002, 546pp. Foreword by Carl Sagan, £32.50. ISBN 0195142748.
14 chapters in three parts: Fundamentals; Local and regional pollution issues; Global-scale pollution issues.
'In my more dictatorial moments, I might say that this book should be compulsory undergraduate reading ... This book lives up to its title and is, I hope, the type of interdisciplinary book that would inspire students.' (*Times Higher Education Supplement*)

832 The Living Earth
Facts On File, 2000–2002. 10 v., $550.00. ISBN 0816051712.
www.factsonfile.com [DESCRIPTION]
A set of ten highly accessible reference books, some recently revised, aimed at upper secondary schools and general readership. Good introductions to the subject. Topics covered include: fossils and minerals; asteroids, comets and meteorites; making of the earth; plate tectonics; rock formations and unusual geologic structures. Lively writing style. Glossary in each volume. Bibliographies for further study.

833 Natural phenomena
Chambers, 2004, 128pp. £5.99. ISBN 0550101578.
Useful introductory guide with good use of colour photographs and diagrams to illustrate and explain the earth's catastrophic events such as earthquakes, tornados, and tsunami.
Series: Chambers World Library. Other titles include: Endangered species, Seas and oceans, Weather and climates.

834 The nature of the environment
A. Goudie 4th edn, Blackwell, 2001, 544pp. £25.99. ISBN 063120069X.
www.blackwellpublishers.co.uk/goudie [COMPANION]
Now well established standard text. 17 chapters in 5 parts: The global framework; Major world zones; Mountain and maritime environment; Landscape and ecosystems; Conclusion.

835 New views on an old planet: a history of global change
T.H. van Andel 2nd edn, Cambridge University Press, 1994, 457pp. £33.00. ISBN 0521447550.
Provides a well written, readable historical account of global change, good for those requiring an introduction to earth and environmental sciences. Six sections: Foundations; Climate past and present: the ice age; Drifting continents, rising mountains; Changing oceans, changing climates; The four-

billion-year childhood; Life, time and change. 180 line diagrams. Bibliography; Glossary; Index.

1st edn New views on an old planet: continental drift and the history of earth, *1985*.

'This book is certainly enjoyable to read and it covers the subject at the right pace and overall to exactly the depth needed for the reader for whom it is written ... It should be a necessity for any introductory earth science course. I thoroughly recommend it.' (Geoscientist)

Dictionaries, thesauri, classifications

836 Dictionary of earth sciences (Dictionnaire des sciences de la terre)
J.-P. Michel, R.W. Fairbridge and M.S.N. Carpenter 3rd edn, Wiley, 1998, 343pp. $130.00. ISBN 0471966037.
Important English–French, French–English dictionary. Defines widely used scientific, technical and general terms in geology, pedology, petrography, petroleum and mining geology, planetology, sedimentology, stratigraphy and tectonics.
2nd edn 1992.

837 A dictionary of earth sciences
A. Allaby and M. Allaby, eds 2nd edn, Oxford University Press, 2003, 640pp. £9.99. ISBN 0198607601.
Six thousand entries provide broad coverage of climatology, economic geology, geochemistry, oceanography, petrology and volcanology. A useful section of appendices including wind strengths and time scales. Numerous line drawings. Includes bibliographical references (pp 609–619). For the general reader as well as students of geology and earth sciences.
Rev. edn of The concise Oxford dictionary of earth sciences, *1990*.

838 Dictionary of geosciences: containing approximately 38,000 terms (Wörterbuch Geowissenschaften)
A. Watznauer, ed. Elsevier Scientific, 1982. V. 1 ISBN 0444997016; V. 2 ISBN 0444997024. First published in 1974 by Elsevier North Holland.
Useful dictionary for important geoscience terms. Omits hydrogeology and soil mechanics – the subject of two other Elsevier dictionaries.

839 Dictionnaire des sciences de la terre: anglais–français, français–anglais (Comprehensive dictionary of earth science: English–French, French–English)
M. Moureau and G. Brace; Institut Français du Pétrole Editions Technip, 2000, 1096pp. $168.00. ISBN 2710807491.
A stand-alone reference resource for students and professionals alike with more than 37,000 entries. Covers all fields of earth sciences from archaeology to volcanology. Explanations are in both languages and illustrated by examples of use. Abbreviations are also explained and where possible given their equivalence in the other language. Greek and Latin roots are given, as well as names of people and places. Appendices with additional tables and figures.
Series: Publications de l'Institut Français du Pétrole.

GeMPeT: the geoscience, minerals and petroleum thesaurus
See entry no. 4618

840 GeoRef thesaurus
B. Goodman, ed.; American Geological Institute 9th edn, 2000, 830pp. $124.00. ISBN 0922152551.
This edition contains approx. 28,000 terms, nearly 1500 new additions. About 400 Ocean Drilling Program (ODP) and Deep Sea Drilling Project (DSDP) site and Leg terms added to complete coverage through ODP Leg 186. Used with GEOREF database and the Bibliography and Index of Geology to obtain best results in literature searches. Each term includes: relevant hierarchical, synonymous, and other relationships; usage notes; dates of addition; indexing rules; geographic co-ordinates; and guidelines for searching. Term entries, cross-references arranged A–Z. Organized according to the American National Standard Guidelines for the Construction, Format, and Management of Monolingual Thesauri.

841 Geostatistical glossary and multilingual dictionary
R.A. Olea; International Association for Mathematical Geology Oxford University Press, 1991, 177pp. £39.50. ISBN 0195066898.
Contains a large number of definitions of geostatistical terms of varying levels of complexity. Cross-referenced text with lists of equivalent terms in Chinese, French, German, Greek, Portuguese, Russian and Spanish. Part 1. The glossary; Part 2. The multilingual dictionary. Bibliography.
Series: Studies in Mathematical Geology, V. 3

842 McGraw-Hill dictionary of earth science
2nd edn, McGraw-Hill, 2003, 468pp. $19.95. ISBN 0071410457.
Definitions of key words and phrases encountered in earth science topics. Contains approximately 11,000 entries, each accompanied by a pronunciation guide. Entries are also supplemented by conversion tables, explanations of notation, and other data. Includes synonyms, acronyms and abbreviations.
All text in this dictionary was published previously in the McGraw-Hill dictionary of scientific and technical terms, *6th edn, 2003.*

843 Multilingual thesaurus of geosciences: English–French–German–Italian–Spanish–Finnish–Russian–Swedish
http://info.gsf.fi/multhes/index_eng.html
Almost 6000 terms. Developed by the Commission for the Management and Application of Geoscience Information.

Official & quasi-official bodies

Department of the Environment and Heritage
Australia. Department of the Environment and Heritage See entry no. 2116

Global Environment Facility
See entry no. 5556

844 Natural Environment Research Council [UK]
www.nerc.ac.uk
Supports independent research and training in the environmental sciences (atmospheric, earth, terrestrial and aquatic) in universities and research centres. Aims to promote and support research in environmental and earth sciences-related subjects and to improve understanding and predict the behaviour of the natural environment and its resources. Post-graduate in focus. Web page in newspaper

style, easy to navigate. Links to NERC research centres and other related websites.

- **Data Assimilation Research Centre** http://darc.nerc.ac.uk. 'Assessment, combination and synthesis of Earth Observation data with numerical models in order to reproduce the evolution of the earth system and to forecast its behaviour.' NERC Centre of Excellence.

845 **NSF: Directorate for Geosciences**
www.nsf.gov/funding/research_edu_community.jsp
One of the seven directorates of the NATIONAL SCIENCE FOUNDATION. Its mission is to support research in the atmospheric, earth, and ocean sciences.

Research centres & institutes

846 **Bureau de recherches géologiques et minières**
www.brgm.fr
'France's major public institution in the Geoscience field. It fulfils the triple role of scientific research, public expertise and international cooperation.' Provides an excellent set of links to geological information in France with some international coverage. Mainly in French.

The Earth Institute
Columbia University See entry no. 4631

847 **GeoForschungsZentrum Potsdam**
www.gfz-potsdam.de/welcome_en.html
A non-university geoscientific research institute. Aims to combine all solid earth science fields including geodesy, geology, geophysics, mineralogy and geochemistry, in a multidisciplinary research centre. Links on website to departments, major research projects and news items. Good English language coverage.

- **Helmholtz Association of National Research Centres** www.helmholtz.de. 15 scientific-technical and biological-medical research centres pursuing long-term research goals on behalf of state and society in six core fields: Energy; Earth and Environment; Health; Key Technologies; Structure of Matter; Transport and Space.

International Geosphere-Biosphere Programme
See entry no. 2320

Associations & societies

848 **Committee of Heads of University Geosciences Departments** [UK]
www.chugd.ac.uk
The website provides a focal point and forum for discussion.

- **Directory of geoscience departments in the UK & Ireland** 5th edn, Geological Society Publishing House, 2000, 58pp. £4.00. ISBN 1862390525. www.chugd.ac.uk/institutions.php. The most up-to-date published listing of geoscience departments in the UK in print. Useful for quick reference. An online listing is also now available.

849 **European Geosciences Union**
www.copernicus.org/EGU/EGU.html
Founded in 2002 as a merger of the European Geophysical Society (EGS) and the European Union of Geosciences (EUG): aims to promote the sciences of the earth and its environment and of planetary and space sciences. Provides a series of online open-access journals plus a range of other publications and services.

850 **Geoscience Information Society** [USA]
www.geoinfo.org
Aims to facilitate the exchange of information in the geosciences through co-operation among scientists, librarians, editors, cartographers, educators, and information professionals. Useful information including free access to the Geologic Guidebooks of North America Database. Also: 'Many GSIS members develop and maintain web sites for their clientele. Here are some of those web sites. They are excellent places to begin your research.'

- **Directory of geoscience libraries** 5th edn,1997, 113pp. $35.00. ISBN 0934485259. Useful directory on c.400 US libraries. Entries are arranged A–Z by US states, then by Canadian provinces. Organization index.
- **Geoscience Information Society Annual Meeting** www.libraries.psu.edu/emsl/GSIS2004.html. Held alongside Annual Meeting of the ECOLOGICAL SOCIETY OF AMERICA. Schedule for 2004 Meeting given at URL – providing good overview of current initiatives and concerns.

Libraries, archives, museums

American Museum of Natural History
See entry no. 1944

Australian Museum
See entry no. 1945

851 **Branner Earth Sciences Library and Map Collections** [USA]
www-sul.stanford.edu/depts/branner
A very useful website covering major collections in the earth sciences, and links to research. Particularly good for general reference resource queries.

852 **Natural History Museum, Earth Sciences Library** [UK]
www.nhm.ac.uk/library/palminlib.html
Part of the NATURAL HISTORY MUSEUM, London, the Library contains three distinct collections – Palaeontology, Mineralogy and Anthropology Libraries – which together cover all earth science subjects and physical and biological anthropology. Web links to the library catalogue, and to other libraries' catalogues within the Museum.

853 **Sedgwick Museum of Earth Sciences** [UK]
www.sedgwickmuseum.org
Based in Cambridge, the Museum has a world class collection of fossils, rocks and minerals. Free admission; activities and events are provided primarily aiming to encourage people of all ages to learn about the earth and its history. Web page has links to exhibits, research, education and further resources for exploring the subject.

854 **US Geological Survey Library**
US Geological Survey
http://library.usgs.gov
Includes catalogue of the largest geological library in the world, intended to be as complete as possible in geology, palaeontology, petrology, mineralogy, ground and surface water, cartography and mineral resources. Mainly books and monographs individually catalogued, under authors, titles (including periodical titles) and subject. Some old/rare items. Links to USGS databases and further resources.

Portal & task environments

855 **Center for International Earth Science Information Network** [USA]
www.ciesin.org
A non-profit, non-governmental organization, part of the Earth Institute at Columbia University. Aims to provide global online data via an easy-to-navigate website that would help scientists, decision-makers, and the public better understand the changing world. Website provides interactive applications, metadata resources, other data resources and information systems. Enables users to identify databases, information systems, and other resources relevant to global environmental change and sustainable development.

856 **Columbia Earthscape**
Columbia University
www.earthscape.org [FEE-BASED]
Wide-ranging interdisciplinary resource, primarily for undergraduates, relating earth and environmental sciences 'with their social, political, and economic dimensions'. Articles from journals and conferences; multimedia resources and image banks; etc. The service 'brings to the Web important works not otherwise available online, including original and collaborative new-media projects and publications'.

857 **Digital Library for Earth System Education**
National Science Digital Library
www.dlese.org/dds/index.jsp
'A grassroots community effort involving educators, students, and scientists working together to improve the quality, quantity, and efficiency of teaching and learning about the Earth system at all levels.'

Includes digital library of websites to support teaching and learning in earth sciences. US-based, but excellent, wide-ranging set of resources, with good browsing facilities: start with the section New to DLESE?. Select from school, college, research or general interest levels. Many peer-reviewed resources.

Funded by the NATIONAL SCIENCE FOUNDATION and a collection of the NATIONAL SCIENCE DIGITAL LIBRARY.

858 **Earth & Planetary Sciences**
Elsevier.
http://earth.elsevier.com
Example of commercial publisher providing online access to details of a very wide range of journals, books, reference works, and wall charts. Covers Pergamon and Academic Press offerings, as well as those imprinted Elsevier. Especially useful if using in conjunction with a SCIENCEDIRECT subscription.

Earth & Planetary Sciences Update is a 'free e-mail service, bringing direct to your desktop the latest updates, news and highlights from the Elsevier earth & planetary sciences program'.

859 **Earth Observatory**
National Aeronautics and Space Administration
http://earthobservatory.nasa.gov
Data and images (e.g. satellite images showing global geohazards), features, news, experiments, etc. Reference section to atmosphere, oceans, land, life on earth, heat and energy, remote sensing, and pioneers in geoscience. Information on space missions. Glossary. Excellent site.

- **Destination Earth** www.earth.nasa.gov. Very attractive, easy-to-navigate set of web pages. Information for all ages and abilities. Educational links for teachers, research, news stories, technical reports, images and videos illustrating use of space technology.

860 **Earth Pages: earth sciences and news from the geological world**
Blackwell Publishing.
www.earth-pages.com
A good commercial publisher sponsored starting point for web exploration in the earth sciences. Resource centre organized by subject providing substantial numbers of links. News section updated monthly and written by an earth scientist. Very useful for undergraduates. Further links to books and journals published by Blackwell.

861 **GeoScienceWorld: GSW**
www.geoscienceworld.org
Collaboration launched in 2004 of seven geoscience membership organizations (each referenced elsewhere) delivering online their aggregated journal content, and planned to include that of other not-for-profit and independent earth science publishers, extending to material such as maps, books, geoscience digital data and ('when technically practical') non-English publications.

862 **Global Change Master Directory**
National Aeronautics and Space Administration
gcmd.nasa.gov/index.html
A portal to data sets and services relevant to global change and earth science research. The GCMD database holds more than 15,000 descriptions of earth science data sets and services covering all aspects of earth and environmental sciences, including agriculture, land use and environmental impact.

863 **LTSN Geography, Earth and Environmental Sciences** [UK]
University of Plymouth and Higher Education Academy
www.gees.ac.uk
UK and international hub in the exchange of knowledge on learning and teaching for geography, earth and environmental sciences. Aims to encourage good practice in the disciplines. Provides guidance for professional teachers and promotes collaboration at all levels. Links to resource database and *Planet* – their biannual publication.

864 **PSIgate: Earth Sciences** [UK]
University of Manchester and Resource Discovery Network
www.psigate.ac.uk/newsite/earth-gateway.html
PSIGATE is the physical sciences hub of the RDN. This gateway is one of six within the hub aiming to provide access to quality-assured internet-based resources for teaching, learning and research. Resources searchable by subject or resource type. Much other valuable information. A good place to start exploration of the subject area.

Discovering print & electronic resources

865 **Earth online: an internet guide for earth science**
M.E. Ritter Wadsworth Publishing, 1997, 278pp. ISBN 0534517072.
Written exclusively for the earth sciences in an easy-to-read, accessible style – albeit with the content now significantly out of date. Ten chapters: 1. Getting to know the Internet ... 4.

File transfer over the Internet ... 6. Searching the Internet ... 10. Internet resources (Astronomy – Wetlands). Glossary, references, index.

866 Earth science resources in the electronic age
J.A. Bazler Greenwood Press, 2003, 303pp. $49.95. ISBN 1573563811.
Many hundreds of the most reliable earth science-related websites are evaluated. Accuracy and usefulness of sites analysed. Useful summary for information on science museums, science centres, careers in the earth sciences, and supplies. Sites described in topic sections. US focus. Glossary. Page design could be improved.
Series: Science Resources in the Electronic Age.

867 Earth Science Resources on the WWW
University of Wales Aberystwyth
www.aber.ac.uk/iges/old_html/geores/earthsci.html
Helpful website that was created within the University's Institute of Geography & Earth Sciences. Distinctive for the frank comments on the usefulness of the wide range of web exploration and resource guides covered. Unfortunately seems, however, not recently updated.

868 Earth Sciences
Smartdevil Thumbshots.
http://open.thumbshots.org/Science/Earth_Sciences
An DMOZ OPEN DIRECTORY PROJECT site with some 6000 links to all key areas of the earth sciences and including associations, directories, museums, etc. Links can be translated into approximately 20 other languages, mainly European. Being maintained, mid-2004. (Thumbshots are 'screenshots of web pages to help you locate web sites quickly and easily. Thumbshots display exactly what you would get before visiting a link. Millions of people trust and rely on thumbshots to take control of their surfing.')

869 European Geoscience University Departments
www.uni-mainz.de/FB/Geo/Geologie/GeoInst/Europa.html
Current website providing links to all the main earth science university departments in Europe and further links to departments around the world. Access to other earth science resources.

870 GeoAfrica: directory of African earth-science resources
www.geoafrica.co.za
A useful commercially-sponsored listing with links to earth science professionals (geologists, geophysicists, etc.), exploration and mining companies, associations and products in Africa, listed by category. Good coverage, focus more towards South Africa. Some information provided alphabetically, some by country.

871 GeoArchive
Oxmill Publishing. Published on the web on behalf of Geosystems (UK).
www.oxmill.com/geoarchive [FEE-BASED]
A reference tool covering all types of information sources in geoscience, hydroscience and environmental science. Indexes more than 5000 serials, books from more than 2000 publishers, conferences, technical reports, geological maps and dissertations. Indexes material only if publicly available and has relevant information content. Information is provided as a series of data sets that can be searched individually or together. Range of printed bibliographies (e.g. *Geotitles*. Monthly. ISSN 09522700) derived from database.

872 GeoGuide
Lower Saxony State and University Library, Göttingen
www.geo-guide.de
A fairly comprehensive annotated index to earth sciences resources on the web, with abstracts and bibliographical information. The index can be browsed or searched by subject or type of resource. Currently (mid-2004) lists over 3000 records, new ones added regularly.

873 GeoIndex
Datasurge Company.
www.geoindex.com/geoindex/index.html
Commercially sponsored search engine for those in geo-environmental professions, covering companies, associations, educational establishments and governmental departments. Provides links to geotechnical, environmental, hydrogeology, geology, mining and petroleum resources.

874 Geological Surveys and Associations
University of California, Berkeley
www.lib.berkeley.edu/EART/surveys.html
Useful links to geological surveys, natural resources departments, associations and societies. Concentrates on links to USA websites, but includes many to notable non-US geological surveys, geological societies and associations. Regularly updated by the Earth Sciences & Map Library.

- **Web Geological Time Machine University of California, Berkeley**. www.ucmp.berkeley.edu/help/timeform.html. Attractive informative and easily navigable guide. Primarily created 1995 but updated to reflect the GEOLOGICAL SOCIETY OF AMERICA 1999 Geologic Timescale and published by Palmer and Geissman, 2002.

875 GeoRef
American Geological Institute
www.agiweb.org/georef [FEE-BASED]
Contains over 2.4 million records of North America since 1785, and other areas of the world since 1933; updated monthly. One of the most comprehensive geosciences databases, used extensively by students and researchers for discovering resources in the earth sciences. Corresponds to the print publications BIBLIOGRAPHY OF NORTH AMERICAN GEOLOGY, BIBLIOGRAPHY AND INDEX OF GEOLOGY EXCLUSIVE OF NORTH AMERICA, GEOPHYSICAL ABSTRACTS, and the BIBLIOGRAPHY AND INDEX OF GEOLOGY. Gain access online, via CD-ROM, or in print.

The GeoRef Preview Database 'highlights references to geoscience publications which have recently been added to our GeoRef production system. Each weekend, completed references are removed from the Preview database and transferred to GeoRef, new references are added, and changes are made in the remaining data.'

876 GEOSCAN Database [CAN]
Natural Resources Canada
www.nrcan.gc.ca/ess/esic/geoscan_e.html
Bibliographic database of more than 40,000 records covering all publications of the Geological Survey of Canada. Assistance of the NRC Earth Science Information Centre Reference Service available via the website. Good entry point to Canadian material.

877 **Geoscience Data Catalog**
US Geological Survey
http://geo-nsdi.er.usgs.gov
Catalogue of over 1600 collections of earth science data produced by the Survey. Gives documentation with links to the data files. To use the data needs access to scientific software such as GIS systems.

878 **Information sources in the earth sciences**
D.N. Wood, J.E. Hardy and A.P. Harvey 2nd edn, K G Saur, 1989, 524pp. €112.00. ISBN 3598244266.
Illustrated developments in information sources available in the earth sciences up to the end of the 1980s. Included new areas of interest such as remote sensing and soil science. Full coverage of data bank and database information sources as well as traditional textual resources. Clearly dated, but good for more historical material.
Series: Guides to Information Sources.

879 **RDN Virtual Training Suite: Earth Scientist** [UK]
University of Liverpool and Resource Discovery Network
www.vts.rdn.ac.uk/tutorial/earth
Good short introduction in the series primarily aimed at members of UK further and higher education institutions

880 **Virtual Earth**
P. Ingram; Macquarie University
http://teachserv.earth.ox.ac.uk/resources/v_earth.html
This introduction to information retrieval on the web for earth scientists and those interested in research in the earth sciences was created in the mid-1990s, but has not been updated since 1997. Thus many of the links are now defunct. However, it brought together in narrative form many hundreds of connections to all aspects of earth sciences; and thus for those who have opportunity is well worth browsing through to get an overview of the variety of relevant resource producers and sources active at that time, the majority of which, of course, are still active.

881 **World databases in geography and geology**
C.J. Armstrong, ed. K G Saur, 1995, 1272pp. €240.00. ISBN 3598243138.
Useful listing of relevant databases, now needing substantial updating. Two sections: Geography, pp 1–586; Geology, pp 587–882. Listing of databases within each subject area – details of master record, keywords, online and CD-ROM availability. Addresses pp 883–918. Includes indexes of database names and subjects, pp 919–1255.
Series: World Databases Series.

Digital data, image & text collections

882 **Earth Lab Datasite** [UK]
Natural History Museum
www.nhm.ac.uk/museum/earthlab
Data on over 2000 UK rocks, minerals and fossils. Educational resource for amateur geologists and students. User-friendly website. Links to online bookshop.

883 **Pangaea: Publishing Network for Geoscientific & Environmental Data**
www.pangaea.de
Public data library 'aimed at archiving, publishing and distributing georeferenced data with special emphasis on environmental, marine and geological research'. Data is stored with metainformation in a relational database, accessible through a client/server system. Links to other data centres and government and institutional organizations. It is expected that this site will be used for long-term archiving of scientific primary data.

'PANGAEA guarantees long-term availability of scientific primary data related to publications following the Recommendations of the Commission on Professional Self Regulation in Science for safeguarding good scientific practice. The system is operated in the sense of the Berlin Declaration on Open Access to Knowledge in the Sciences and Humanities. The policy of data management and archiving follows the Principles and Responsibilities of ICSU World Data Centers' (cf. www.icsu.org).

Directories & encyclopedias

884 **A to Z of earth scientists**
A.E. Gates Facts On File, 2002, 352pp. $45.00. ISBN 0816045801.
A reference resource on approximately 200 notable earth scientists from the 19th to the 21st century, in subject areas including climate change, geophysics, oceanography, palaeontology, planetary geology, sedimentology, stratigraphy, and tectonics. Examples include: John Dewey, Carl Sagan and Richard Tuttle. 89 B&W photographs. Index. Appendix. Bibliography. Chronology. Cross-references. Useful for schools and public libraries.
Series: Notable Scientists.

885 **Cambridge encyclopedia of earth sciences**
D.G. Smith, ed. Cambridge University Press, 1982, 496pp. ISBN 0521239001.
Classic text from 32 contributors. Concentrates on those aspects in which significant advances of the time were made. 'The aim is to provide ready access to the wealth of geological information which has been gleaned over the years and to show how it fits into the framework of plate tectonics' (Foreword). Six parts (27 chapters). Glossary, pp 468–78; Further reading, by chapters. Analytical index, pp 481–94.

886 **Directory of geoscience departments**
C.M. Keane, ed.; American Geological Institute 42nd edn, 2004, 578pp. $40.00. ISBN 0922152691 ISSN 03647811.
A useful and current directory of information about approximately 1000 US and non-US departments of geoscience. Includes addresses, phone/fax numbers, e-mail addresses, degrees offered, field-camp information; 15,000 faculty (indexed) are identified by geologic specialty. Includes college and university geoscience departments, research institutes, selected natural history museums, state geological surveys, federal agencies and national laboratories, and AGI and AGI member-society staffs.

887 **Directory of geoscience organizations of the world**
Geological Survey of Japan
www.gsj.jp/Intl/Dir/a.htm
Useful, accessible up-to-date information on worldwide organizations. Developed by the International Geoscience Cooperation Office. 440 organizations from 168 countries and areas as well as 15 international organizations. Addresses, phone and e-mail contacts. Browse by country – including, attractively, via country flag.

888 **Earth**
D. Palmer [et al.] Dorling Kindersley, 2003, 520pp. £30.00. ISBN 1405300183.
An impressive collection of several hundred of the earth's most beautiful and intriguing natural features with explanations for the processes behind their formation. Unusual places are included in the descriptions – such as the Atacama Desert, or the Antarctic ice-sheet. Key features are clearly illustrated, with locator maps. Topical issues such as future population growth and deforestation are also covered. Contains over 2000 full-colour photographs and 1200 maps and artworks that, combined with the jargon-free text, make this an accessible reference resource for all.
'The definitive visual guide to our planet' (*Times Educational Supplement*)

- **Earth: the definitive visual guide** **J.F. Luhr, ed.** Dorling Kindersley, 2004, 520pp. £20.00. ISBN 1405307056. Comprehensive and authoritative full colour coverage of key topics such as Planet earth, Ocean, Atmosphere and Tectonic earth. 3D atlas in last section. Many large format full colour pages. For age 9 to adult, with a wide level of interest in the earth.

889 **Earth and astronomical sciences research centres: a world directory of organisations and programmes**
4th edn, Cartermill International, 1995, 650pp. £295.00. ISBN 1860670180.
This was a worldwide guide to over 6000 academic, industrial and private laboratories in 147 countries conducting, promoting or funding research in earth sciences, astronomy and related subjects. Each entry contained full contact details including title of establishment in original language, acronym and English translation, telecommunication contact nos., senior staff; research expenditure; publications; research activities; affiliation. Arranged A–Z (Algeria – Zimbabwe). Broad subject coverage. Titles of establishments index. Subject index. Personal name and acronym index would have been useful (but the volumes of which this is an exemplar are no longer published).

890 **Earth Sciences Encyclopedia Online**
M.R. Rampino, ed.
www.eseo.com [FEE-BASED]
Comprehensive and authoritative collection of nearly 7000 entries by leading authorities, with illustrations, examples and reference lists. It will be constantly updated and supplemented with new material. Contains all entries originally published in Kluwer's 21-volume hardbound *Encyclopedia of Earth Sciences* series. Suitable for undergraduate upwards.
Series: Kluwer Online Reference Works.

891 **Encyclopedia of earth system science**
W.A. Nierenberg [et al.], ed. Academic Press, 1993, 2825pp. 4 v., £1,035.00. ISBN 0122267192.
Comprehensive coverage of all earth sciences-related topics. Alphabetically arranged articles; 15,000-entry subject index included in Volume 4; 1300 illustrations, 250 tables; 1300 glossary and 1600 bibliographic entries. Extensive cross-referencing. Coloured plates. Undergraduate, postgraduate readership level.

892 **The encyclopedia of solid earth sciences**
P. Kearey and P.A. Allen, eds Blackwell Scientific, 1993, 722pp. £49.99. ISBN 0632036990.
Provides a reference text for all sub-disciplines of earth sciences. Three formats: short entry definitions, longer articles of about 200 words, and detailed entries of up to 1500 words. Contains 2700 headwords and over 8000 index entries. Useful if unable to acquire larger encyclopedia sets. Undergraduate and postgraduate readership.

893 **Macmillan encyclopedia of earth sciences**
E.J. Dasch, ed. Macmillan Reference, 1996, 1273pp. 2 v, $295.00. ISBN 0028830008.
Ideal resource for public and academic libraries – accessible to both technical and layperson alike. 360 entries, many of them biographical and all followed by good lists of further reading. Cross-references and illustrations; 81-page index.
'this set provides in a single place a significant amount of information and offers some very interesting and well-written entries.' (*Choice*)

894 **The Oxford companion to the earth**
P.L. Hancock and B.J. Skinner, eds Oxford University Press, 2000, 1184pp. £45.00. ISBN 0198540396.
Coverage of all aspects of the earth sciences, including volcanoes, flood plains, diamonds, meteors, deserts and deep seas. Many well chosen entries and biographies of key figures. Over 900 entries, several as learned essays. Illustrated and easily accessible for all with a professional or academic interest in the arena.

895 **Sciences of the earth: an encyclopedia of events, people, and phenomena**
G.A. Good, ed. Routledge, 1998, 937pp. 2 v, £145.00. ISBN 081530062X.
Charts the intellectual progression in the evolving perception of the earth by surveying the history of geology, geography, geophysics, oceanography, meteorology, space science, and many other fields. More than 230 articles written by 135 contributors, biased towards Western science. Name and subject indexes. Listing of entries by subject. Of special interest to the historian, but useful to all those working in the relevant subject fields.
Series: Encyclopedias in the History of Science.
'Highly recommended for all academic libraries and larger public libraries' (*Reference Books Bulletin*)

Handbooks & manuals

896 **Earth Science on File**
Diagram Group Facts On File, 2004. CD-ROM, $185.00. ISBN 0816053391.
Comprehensive reference resource, useful for upper secondary schools, and covering topics such as: Earth and space; The restless rocks; Air and oceans; Shaping the surface; Earth history. Many maps and tables. Includes a glossary, and a chronology of major achievements in earth sciences. Charts and diagrams of over 1000 important concepts in geology, meteorology, and oceanography.

- **Facts On File earth science handbook** **Diagram Group** Facts On File, 2000, 224pp. $35.00. ISBN 0816040818. More than 1400 entries, biographies of more than 250 scientists, and a chronology spanning nearly 3700 years. Many tables, charts, and diagrams. Useful handbook with helpful index.

897 **Geosciences, environment and man**
H. Chamley, ed. Elsevier, 2003, 527pp. £46.50. ISBN 0444514252.
Part of a new series that aims to provide a means to publish in-depth works in the area of earth and environmental sciences. This volume provides a useful summary of the relationship of geology and the environment. Three sections: I. A consideration of the main natural geological processes interfering with and threatening the activities of man: II. An examination of the exploitation of earth's natural resources and the resulting consequences on solid earth balance and future: III. An assessment of the hold level reached by the activities of man on the planet's surface. Epilogue. References. Index.
Series: Developments in Earth and Environmental Sciences.

898 **Geostatistics for environmental scientists**
R. Webster and M. Oliver Wiley, 2001, 271pp. $121.00. ISBN 0471965537.
Useful guide to important area. 'Geostatistics is essential for modern environmental scientists. Weather and climate vary from place to place, soil varies at every scale at which it is examined, and even man-made attributes – such as the distribution of pollution – vary. The techniques used in geostatistics are ideally suited to the needs of environmental scientists, who use them to make the best of sparse data for prediction, and to plan future surveys when resources are limited.'

899 **Handbooks of physical constants**
T. Ahrens, ed.; American Geophysical Union 3rd edn, 1995, 1000pp. 3 v., $160.00. ISBN 0875908543.
www.agu.org/reference/mainrefshelf.html [DESCRIPTION]
Provides accessible selected critical data for professional and student solid earth and planetary geophysicists. Print versions can be ordered online. Text published in searchable PDF format. Subject index. 1. *Global earth physics*; 2. *Mineral physics & crystallography*; 3. *Rock physics and phase relations*.
Series: AGU Reference Shelf.

900 **On the rocks: earth science for everyone**
J.S. Dickey Wiley, 1996, 280pp. $16.95. ISBN 0471132349.
Describes the changes, both gradual and cataclysmic, that shape the Earth, the lives of scientists and their discoveries. Informative and enjoyable to read. Includes coverage of geophysics (earthquakes and volcanoes) and space science (the moon and the planets). Suits a general readership. Includes bibliographical references (pp 237–243).

901 **A student's guide to earth science**
Greenwood Press, 2004, 720pp. 4 v., $160.00. ISBN 031332901X.
Gives an overview of earth science from ancient peoples to discoveries of today's scientists. 1. Words and terms; 2. Important people; 3. Developments and discoveries; 4. Debatable issues. Includes timeline of earth science. Many illustrations included. Suitable for general interest.

Keeping up-to-date

902 **Annual Review of Earth and Planetary Sciences**
Annual Reviews, 1973–. $227.00 (print/online) [2004]. ISBN 0824320328 ISSN 00846597.
http://arjournals.annualreviews.org [FEE-BASED]
A well read current series, part of the more general annual review series of the sciences. Contains a subject index. Cumulative indexes of contributing authors and chapter titles, v. 14–31. Abstracts of papers available online three months before publication date. Full-text online available to subscribing institutions. Combines research on the solid earth with planetary, geological and biological perspectives to give a good overview of current earth sciences research.

Environmental Media Services
See entry no. 2364

903 **Geochemistry, Geophysics, Geosystems: an electronic journal of the earth sciences**
American Geophysical Union and Geochemical Society 1999–. ISSN 15252027.
www.agu.org/journals/gc [FEE-BASED]
Highly regarded online journal – often referred to as G-cubed – dedicated to publishing relevant research of broad interest regarding the 'understanding of Earth as a dynamic physicochemical system'. Access to full-text is based on subscription, although tables of contents and abstracts are available free of charge. Articles searchable by author, title or themes. In press items available. Mid-2004, the News and FAQ section had an interesting subsection 'New Developments'.

904 **Virtual Journal – Experimental Earth**
Elsevier, 2003–, Bimonthly.
www.experimentalearth.com [FEE-BASED]
Intended as a web conduit for journal articles in the multi-disciplinary area of experimental earth sciences. Published by Elsevier on behalf of a group of not-for-profit and commercial publishers which have agreed to participate on a strictly non-commercial basis. Each issue includes an overview of the articles covered in its table of contents with links to the articles' abstracts and full text. 'Scientists can subscribe to an alerting service that will alert them when a new issue has been added. The alerting service, the table of contents and abstracts are freely accessible. The full text is only accessible for individuals whose institute subscribes to the respective source journals.'

Mid-2004 20 journals were covered, just over half published by Elsevier themselves.

Geochemistry

chemical geology • chemical weathering • cosmochemistry • igneous geochemistry • marine geochemistry • petroleum geochemistry • rock analysis

Introductions to the subject

905 **Geochemistry: an introduction**
F. Albarède Cambridge University Press, 2003, 262pp. £24.99. ISBN 0521891485.
An essential, comprehensive, introductory text for undergraduates. Covers a wide range of topics. Emphasizes general principles and concentrates on the inorganic chemistry of the condensed part of our planet. Includes diagrams, tables and exercises for students. Written by the author of the authoritative and widely acclaimed *Introduction to geochemical modelling* (1995). Provides an easily accessible introduction for researchers working in related fields.

Dictionaries, thesauri, classifications

906 **Illustrated glossary of petroleum geochemistry**
J.A. Miles Clarendon Press, 1994, 137pp. £17.50. ISBN 0198548494.
Quick and easy access to the basic geochemical terminology. Part 1: summary in tables and diagrams; Part 2: general references; Part 3: glossary with self-contained explanations of terms. Many illustrations. Valuable to professionals, as well as to academics and students.
First published 1989.

Research centres & institutes

907 **Earth Science Division: Geochemistry**
Berkeley Lab
www-esd.lbl.gov/GEO
Offers expert analysis via four research groups: molecular geochemistry and nanoscience; isotope geochemistry; atmosphere and oceans; and geochemical transport. Summaries of research projects are available. Links to publications lists and further related resources. Good exemplar and helpful in providing an overview of current research in the subject field.

Associations & societies

908 **The Association of Applied Geochemists**
www.aeg.org
Founded in 1970, the Association's goals are to advance and foster research in geochemistry. Published *Journal of Geochemical Exploration* from 1972 until 2000, and GEOCHEMISTRY: Exploration, Environment, Analysis, starting in 2001. Links to latest news, conferences, publications from its up-to-date website. Regional sections promoted. Includes link to Geochemical Applications of Commonly-Analyzed Elements.

909 **Geochemical Society**
http://gs.wustl.edu
Private non-profit international scientific society 'founded to encourage the application of chemistry to the solution of geological and cosmological problems'. Website provides links to publications, events, educational sites of interest and other information.

The Society for Organic Petrology
See entry no. 1504

Portal & task environments

910 **Geochemistry of Igneous Rocks**
www.geokem.com
'An eText of Geochemical Data Interpretation'. Interactive text with hypertext links and with many regular updates. Information on all aspects of igneous geochemistry provided. Contents include: Ocean ridge basalts, ocean island basalts, continental flood basalts, organic and e-sites. A section on extraterrestrial geochemistry included.

Especially useful for students: 'With the amount of data being produced in the fields of Petrology and Geochemistry, we find that any statement or summary made more than two years ago is already greatly in need of revision. Nor can students be expected to read and remember the thousands of papers and publications produced annually. Approximately 4000 scientific papers likely to have some relevance to geochemistry were published in the last 12 months. GEOKEM aims at keeping at hand and referable to within seconds, a brief description of all volcanic and igneous centres world-wide (and some associated sediments) for which there is reasonable data, together with a regional variation diagram as well as a multi-element fingerprint and other relevant diagrams for single centres ...'

911 **The Geochemistry Portal**
www.geochemistry.com
A useful web page to bookmark. Provides links to worldwide universities and institutions, databases, libraries, museums, journals and all aspects of geochemistry. Aimed at higher education. Easy to navigate web page. Has search facilities and ability to submit links for inclusion.

Digital data, image & text collections

912 **Earthchem: advanced data management for solid earth geochemistry**
www.earthchem.org
An integrated information system for rock geochemistry, combining the efforts of *GEOROC* and two other data compilations: NAVDAT – a Western North American Volcanic and Intrusive Rock Database; and PetDB – a Petrological Database of the Ocean Floor. The earthchem system focuses on archiving data, comprehensive reporting and dissemination of future data, cross-database compatibility, and developing analytical tools for using geochemical data in geochemical, petrological and geological applications.

- **GEOROC: Geochemistry of Rocks of the Oceans and Continents Max-Planck-Institut für Chemie**. http://georoc.mpch-mainz.gwdg.de/georoc. Chemical and isotope data of igneous rocks and minerals, and the related metadata about samples and analytical procedures. Over 130,000 analyses of samples from different tectonic settings provided.

913 **Geochemical Earth Reference Model: GERM**
Scripps Institution of Oceanography
http://earthref.org/GERM
Website dealing with the 'chemical characterization of the earth, its major reservoirs and the fluxes between them'. Contains links to databases such as the GERM Reservoir database with summary data on the geochemistry of all reservoirs in the earth. Information free to download. Links also to events, tools and publications. Further links to databases and statistics.

- **EarthRef.org: the web site for earth reference data and models** http://earthref.org/index.html. Manages GERM. Access to the EarthRef Digital Archive (ERDA) containing 'any type of digital object associated with the Earth Sciences'. Also includes reasonably up-to-date extensive list of links: especially useful in tracing data collections.

Directories & encyclopedias

914 **Encyclopedia of geochemistry**
C.P. Marshall and R.W. Fairbridge, eds Kluwer Academic, 1999, 712pp. £250.00. ISBN 0412755009.
www.eseo.com

A comprehensive and useful resource. Text includes information on: organics; trace elements; isotopes; and ore deposits. The instruments used to refine geochemical techniques are described, and the chemical elements have separate entries, which include common mineralogical, petrological and sedimentological depictions. Undergraduate, postgraduate readership level. Cross-referencing to related articles. Entries are arranged alphabetically. Subject and citation indices are comprehensive and extensive.
Available online: see website.

915 Geochemical atlases [UK]
British Geological Survey
www.bgs.ac.uk/bookshop [DESCRIPTION]
The atlases provide a systematic picture of the geochemistry of Britain. They identify new sources of metalliferous minerals, and provide quantitative information on natural element levels for assessing contamination. Vols. 1–7 based on the point-source data plotted on geological maps at a scale of 1:250,000.

916 The Wolfson geochemical atlas of England and Wales
J.S. Webb, ed.; Imperial College of Science and Technology Clarendon Press, 1978, 69pp. £90.00. ISBN 0198911130.
A classic set of maps: 55 maps (48 in colour) plus three maps in back cover at a scale 1:2,000,000. The computer-produced maps depict data on 21 elements from the analysis of 50,000 stream samples. Introductory text provides examples of potential uses of the atlas in agriculture, ecology and public health, as well as mineral exploration. Bibliography.
Sponsored by the Wolfson Foundation.

Handbooks & manuals

917 A compendium of geochemistry: from solar nebula to the human brain
Y.-H. Li Princeton University Press, 2000, 475pp. $39.50. ISBN 0691009384.
Comprehensive, up-to-date guide to geochemistry. Focuses on compositional data and related references. Primary objective is to illustrate the principles and processes that explain observed changes in natural substances. A useful resource for researchers expanding into other fields, students and teachers, and a complement to traditional geochemistry textbooks. Illustrations and tables. References pp 429–464. Appendices.

918 Geochemical reference material compositions: rocks, minerals, sediments, soils, carbonates, refractories & ores used in research & industry
P.J. Potts, A.G. Tindle and P.C. Webb CRC Press, 1992, 313pp. $189.95. ISBN 0849377579.
Good handbook for geochemists or those involved in applied geochemistry such as the mining industry where raw materials are exploited. Covers information in subject areas of rocks composition, determinative mineralogy, and analytical geochemistry. Sections: 1. Reference materials indexed by sample name; 2. Reference materials indexed by sample description; 3. Compilation tables (pp 22–189); 4. Concentration ladders; 5. References to source data. Includes bibliographical references (pp 302–313) and indexes.

919 Geochemistry of sedimentary carbonates
J.W. Morse and F.T. Mackenzie Elsevier, 1990, 696pp. $85.00. ISBN 0444887814.
Valuable classic reference text for those with interest in carbonates. Deals with carbonate minerals and their interaction with aqueous solutions; modern marine carbonate formation and sediments; carbonate diagenesis; the global cycle of carbon and human intervention; and the role of sedimentary carbonates as indicators of stability and changes in the earth's surface environment. Bibliographic references (pp 609–679). Useful for non-specialists, but primarily for students and postgraduates.
Series: Developments in Sedimentology, V. 48.

920 Handbook of rock analysis
P.J. Potts Viridian Publishing, 2003, 622pp. £50.00. ISBN 0954489136.
A standard reference work for rock and mineral analysis and a useful laboratory handbook for students of analytical geochemistry. Includes practical details with parametric data including most sensitive lines, interference effects and detection limit data. Divided into 20 chapters, covering general concepts in analytical chemistry, procedures based on wet chemistry and optical spectroscopy; the techniques of arc and spark emission spectrometry and ion selective electrodes; x-ray and micro-beam procedures; nuclear techniques; ion exchange chromatography; and other more specialized procedures, including fire-assay, and geochemical applications of mass spectrometry.

921 Marine geochemistry
R. Chester 2nd edn, Blackwell Science, 2002, 520pp. £32.50. ISBN 1405101725.
New edition covers fundamental conceptual changes relating to trace metal speciation, carbon dioxide, climate change and the transport of particulate material to the interior of the ocean. Aimed at intermediate and advanced students of chemical oceanography, marine geochemistry and the earth sciences. Many illustrations supplement the text. Generally regarded as a key text in the subject.
1st edn 1990.

922 Treatise on geochemistry
H.D. Holland and K.K. Turekian, eds Elsevier, 2003, 5300pp. 10 v., £3216.50. ISBN 0080437516.
www.treatiseongeochemistry.com [DESCRIPTION]
Coverage of the full range of disciplines and topics in the field of geochemistry. Contents: v. 1 Meteorites, comets and planets, v. 2 The mantle and core, v. 3 The crust, v. 4 The atmosphere, v.5 Fresh water geochemistry, v. 6 The oceans and marine geochemistry, v. 7 Sediments, diagenesis and sedimentary rocks, v. 8 Biogeochemistry, v. 9 Environmental chemistry, v. 10 Indexes.
Available online: see website.

Keeping up-to-date

Reviews in Mineralogy and Geochemistry
Mineralogical Society of America and Geochemical Society See entry no. 1343

Geology

continental drift • earth evolution • economic geology • geological conservation • geological maps • geological periods • geological timescales • mathematical geology • physical geology • plate tectonics • quaternary research • radiocarbon dating • sedimentology • stratigraphy

Introductions to the subject

923 **Beneath our feet: the rocks of planet earth**
R. Vernon Cambridge University Press, 2000, 216pp. £25.00. ISBN 0521790301.
Useful and interesting introductory resource which uses non-technical language and is therefore highly appropriate for school libraries, as well as those interested in museums and/or natural history. Many impressive colour images help to explain how rocks and minerals are created.
'Excellent pictures and straightforward, informative text make Ron Vernon's *Beneath our Feet* almost a coffee-table book for the scientifically literature non-geologist – or anyone who's always curious.' (*Nature*)

924 **The dating game: one man's search for the age of the earth**
C. Lewis Cambridge University Press, 2002, 253pp. £12.99. ISBN 0521893127.
The story of Arthur Holmes and his vision for developing a geological timescale, the process of which transformed geology as an 'art' into geology as a science. Very accessible, readable account of Holmes' life and investigations. Suitable for all. Bibliography.
'an engaging book ... a good read for geologists ancient and modern who want to understand better the transformation of their discipline. It paints a picture of the life and surprisingly varied career ... of a great scientist, strangely unsung both within his science and elsewhere.' (*Geoscientist*)

- **Radiocarbon: An international journal of cosmogenic isotope research** **University of Arizona**3/year. $200.00. ISSN 00338222. www.radiocarbon.org. 'The main international journal of record for research articles and date lists relevant to 14C and other radioisotopes and techniques used in archaeological, geophysical, oceanographic and related dating.' See 'Radiocarbon-Related Information Sources'.

925 **The dynamic earth: an introduction to physical geology**
B.J. Skinner, S.C. Porter and J. Park 5th edn, Wiley, 2004. $112.20. ISBN 0471152285.
www.wiley.com/WileyCDA [COMPANION]
A useful introductory physical geology text. Accompanied by multimedia GeoDiscoveries CD-ROM and with instructors' presentation materials available online. Appendices, glossary and index. Selected references for each chapter provided. Many illustrations. Personal essays from authors.

926 **Earth: an introduction to physical geology**
E.J. Tarbuck, F.K. Lutgens and D. Tasa 8th edn, Prentice Hall, 2004, 736pp. GEODe III CD-ROM is automatically packaged with the text, $96.00. ISBN 0131148656.
www.prenhall.com/tarbuck [COMPANION]
Coverage of the most recent geologic events aiming to keep as current as possible. For the 8th edition: significantly revised discussions of erosional processes, metamorphism and metamorphic rocks, fossils and 100 pieces of new or substantially redesigned line art. Especially useful for students with end-of-chapter review quizzes. Each chapter is designed as a self-contained unit.

- **GEODe III CD-ROM** **D. Tasa, F.K. Lutgens and E.J. Tarbuck** . Animation, interactive activities, expanded text art explains concepts including: the rock cycle, hydrologic cycle, erosional forces, mountain building, plate tectonics, geologic time, deserts and winds, crustal deformation.
- **On the move: Continental drift and plate tectonics** **National Aeronautics and Space Administration**. http://kids.earth.nasa.gov/archive/pangaea. Part of NASA's lively and colourful 'For Kids Only: Earth Science Enterprise'.
- **Orogeny** www.global-climate-change.org.uk/2-6-1.php. Folding and deformation of the earth's crust to form mountain ranges. Excerpt from the wide-ranging online encyclopedia GLOBAL CLIMATE CHANGE, itself now part of an *Enviropedia* that arose from a unit formerly in Manchester Metropolitan University.

927 **The earth inside and out: some major contributions to geology in the twentieth century**
D.R. Oldroyd, ed.; Geological Society of London 2002, 369pp. £85.00. ISBN 1862390967.
Fourteen papers, including eight from the symposium 'Major contributions to geology in the twentieth century' from 'Section 27 of the International Geological Congress held at Rio de Janeiro in August 2000'.
Important developments in the earth sciences in the 20th century are covered in this volume. Secondary literature on 20th-century geology is reviewed. A useful reference tool for undergraduate and postgraduate readers, and for the historian.
Series: Geological Society Special Publications, No. 192.

928 **Evolution of the earth**
R.H. Dott Jr and D. Prothero 6th edn, McGraw-Hill, 2004, 576pp. $106.88. ISBN 0072528087.
Interesting historical approach to the development of ideas about geology. Based on: new concepts of time; the universality of irreversible evolutionary changes; and the importance throughout time of ecological interactions between life and the physical world. 17 chapters. Glossary. Index. Two appendices: 1. The classification and relationships of living organisms; 2. English equivalents of metric measures.
First published in 1971.

929 **The field guide to geology**
D. Lambert; Diagram Group Facts On File, 1998, 256pp. $30.95. ISBN 0816038406.
Illustrated geological field guide, written by an expert team. It includes details about the earth's origin, the shaping of the continents, the forming of rocks, erosion, earth's geological history, and the impact of the oceans and rivers on the earth; 500 two-colour illustrations, diagrams, charts, and maps. Comprehensive volume with clear, simple field-guide procedures.
'An innovative, clearly descriptive, and enjoyable introductory earth science book. Highly recommended for any library's collection.' (*American Reference Books Annual*)

930 **The geology of Britain: an introduction**
P. Toghill Crowood Press, 2003, 224pp. £16.99. ISBN 1840374047.
A useful introduction to the geological history of Britain from over 2000 million years ago to the present day. An introductory chapter covers basic geological principles, other

chapters describe the rocks, minerals and fossils of each period. Many photographs, a number from Landform Slides. Large format, interesting text. Small glossary. Suit anyone with a general interest in geology.

931 **Holmes' principles of physical geology**
P.McL.D. Duff, ed. 4th edn, Chapman & Hall, 1993, 791pp. £24.99. ISBN 041240320X.
This classic text introduces the topic of geology assuming no prior knowledge. It successfully tackles the science and the place of geology in the world we live in. It covers of all aspects of geology, starting with a broad view of the earth as a planet, and develops all the major themes of contemporary geology; 300 line drawings, 400 b/w photos, 16 pp col. plates. Undergraduate readership.

932 **Physical geology: exploring the earth**
J.S. Monroe and R. Wicander 4th edn, Brooks/Cole-Thomson Learning, 2001, 688pp. Includes CD-ROM and use of InfoTrac College Edition, providing purchasers with 24-hour access to full-text articles from journals and periodicals for 4 months, £37.00. ISBN 0534572227.
www.brookscole.com [COMPANION]
An extensive overview of Earth processes from a physical perspective. Student book companion website with interactive teaching and learning resources. Appendices, glossary, index.
This version not available in the USA; see website for alternatives.

933 **Teach yourself geology**
D. Rothery Hodder & Stoughton Educational, 2003, 256pp. £8.99. ISBN 0340867531.
Comprehensive guide to the nature and history of the earth, covering subjects such as volcanoes, and the implications of our limited natural resources. Includes a section on field work. Many black-and-white and colour illustrations. General readership, suitable for all.

934 **Understanding earth**
F. Press [et al.] 4th edn, W H Freeman, 2004, 567pp. $68.03. ISBN 0716796171.
http://bcs.whfreeman.com/understandingearth [REGISTRATION]
Very well structured attractive introductory physical geology textbook. To help students understand basics, covers all aspects of the subject with clear explanations and many diagrams. New features for this edition: Figure Stories drawing photographs, line drawings, and text together to explain processes; photographs and maps combined with schematics; many revisions and introduction of new topics such as Global Positioning System technology, global warming. Useful appendices include 'Properties of the most commonminerals of Earth's crust', and there is an extensive glossary. Bibliography. Index.

935 **William Smith's 1815 Map** [UK]
W. Smith; British Geological Survey Reproduction, British Geological Survey. 1330 x 930mm (portrait), £15.00.
www.bgs.ac.uk/education
A reproduction of William Smith's famous 1815 geological map of 'England and Wales with part of Scotland'. The map was the subject of Simon Winchester's bestselling book, *The map that changed the world* and was published in 15 sections, each folded into six 'panels'. The reproduction involved the scanning of the sections and the digital removal of the joins. The original would have been 8 feet long by 6 feet wide if published as a single sheet. The reproduction is published at half scale: ten miles to the inch, and is colour-matched to the original.
Original Title: A delineation of the strata of England and Wales with part of Scotland; exhibiting the collieries and mines, the marshes and fen lands originally overflowed by the sea, and the varieties of soil according to the variations in the substrata, illustrated by the most descriptive names.

An impressive website dedicated to scanned images of the original map is at: www.unh.edu/esci/wmsmith.html.

Dictionaries, thesauri, classifications

936 **Collins dictionary geology**
D.F. Lapidus, D.R. Coates and I. Winstanley New edn. rev. and updated by James MacDonald and Christopher Burton, HarperCollins, 2003, 480pp. £9.99. ISBN 0007147686.
An accessible and comprehensive reference tool revised and updated to include practical and economic applications. Covers all the major areas of geology and its current terminology in c.4500 entries A–Z. Length of entries varies from a few words to several pages. Many cross-references. Appendices and suggested further reading. Despite the number of references, it still retains the depth of explanation required by students.
First published as Facts On File dictionary of geology and geophysics *(Facts On File Publications, 1987).*

937 **Dictionnaire de géologie**
A. Foucault and J-F. Raoult 5e éd, Dunod, 2000, 380pp. £19.15. ISBN 210004690X.
A relatively simple resource intended for amateurs, students and professionals. Pocket-sized format. A–Z listing. Bibliographic references. Some illustrations.
Previous edn Masson, 1995.

938 **Geological nomenclature**
W.A. Visser, ed. 2nd edn, Martinus Nijhoff Publishers, 1980, 568pp. £158.00. ISBN 9024724031.
This later edition of Schieferdecker's *Geological nomenclature*, includes Spanish in the languages covered. 4876 numbered English-based terms, with equivalents in Dutch, French, German and Spanish. Thematic arrangement; 5 language indexes, 14 indexes.
Previous edn 1959 sponsored by the Royal Geological and Mining Society of the Netherlands.

939 **Glossary of geology**
J.A. Jackson, ed. 4th edn, Springer, 1997, 769pp. £115.50. ISBN 3540012753.
Nearly 100 experts have reviewed definitions, added new terms and cited references for this edition. New entries especially in fields of carbonate sedimentology, mineralogy and crystallography, coastal geology, plate tectonics, snow and ice, geophysics, economic geology, remote sensing and geographic information systems, engineering and environmental geology, and stratigraphic nomenclature. Expanded reference section, aids to pronunciation. Authoritative reference tool for professional geoscientists and students alike.

940 **International stratigraphic guide**
M.A. Murphy and A. Salvador, eds; International Commission on Stratigraphy

www.stratigraphy.org/guide.htm
An online short version of the 2nd edition of the *International stratigraphic guide* that omits history, explanatory text, and exemplification, the glossaries and the bibliography. Provides accurate and precise internationally acceptable terminology and procedures in the interest of improved accuracy and precision in international communication, co-ordination and understanding. For the full published guide (2nd edn) see ISBN 0813774012, obtainable from the GEOLOGICAL SOCIETY OF AMERICA.
1st edn 1976

941 **McGraw-Hill dictionary of geology and mineralogy**
McGraw-Hill 2nd edn, McGraw-Hill, 2003, 430pp. $19.95. ISBN 0071410449.
Excellent up-to-date definitions with approximately 9000 entries, each accompanied by a pronunciation guide. Entries are supplemented by conversion tables and other data. Includes synonyms, acronyms and abbreviations. Suitable for wide range of readership.
Based on the MCGRAW-HILL DICTIONARY OF SCIENTIFIC AND TECHNICAL TERMS, *6th edn.*

942 **The new Penguin dictionary of geology**
P. Kearey 2nd edn, Penguin, 2001, 327pp. £8.99. ISBN 0140514945.
Over 7500 fully updated definitions: an essential reference tool for terms and expressions used in the field of geology. Includes a full bibliography of up-to-date works covering all areas of geology. Terminology found in related fields of biology, geography and physics is also included. Clear, helpful format. Cross-referencing useful. Of general use to all students and amateurs alike.
1st edn 1996.

Laws, standards, codes

943 **Guidelines for the curation of geological materials** [UK]
C.H.C. Brunton, T.P. Besterman and J.A. Cooper, eds; Geological Society 1985. Loose-leaf format. ISBN 0903317303.
A first edition of a code for maintaining standards of geological curation. Helpful for undergraduates and postgraduates and those in museums. An important attempt to standardize and codify procedures.
Prepared by the GEOLOGICAL CURATORS' GROUP.

Official & quasi-official bodies

944 **British Geological Survey**
www.bgs.ac.uk
An important geological body in the UK providing a national centre for earth science information. Its primary functions are to maintain and revise geological information for the land and offshore areas of the UK and the nearby continental shelf. Its work relates directly to mineral, energy and groundwater resources, land use, geological hazards, and the protection of the environment. A directory to themed datasets is available. Two of the publications listed below chart the life of the Survey to date, but there are many further publications available. The BGS website provides links to geological information in the UK.

- **Britain beneath our feet: an atlas of digital information** **British Geological Survey** 2004, 114pp. £5.00. ISBN 0852724799. Provides a comprehensive listing of everything that the BGS does, including information on Britain's land quality, underground hazards, resources and geology.
- **British regional geology** Set of textbooks providing comprehensive overviews of the geology of regions of the United Kingdom. Explanatory text. Contain maps, diagrams, sections and photographs. Suitable for informed amateurs, geology students and professionals alike.
- **Down to earth: one hundred and fifty years of the British Geological Survey H.E. Wilson** Scottish Academic Press, 1985, 189pp. £10.50. ISBN 0707304733. BGS: 1835–1985.
- **A geological survey in transition P. Allen** 2003, 220pp. £18.00. ISBN 0852724268.

945 **The Geological Conservation Review (GCR)** [UK]
Joint Nature Conservation Committee
www.jncc.gov.uk/earthheritage/gcr/default.htm
Remit of the Review is to identify and describe the most important geological sites in Britain, a process begun in 1977. The results of the GCR programme are being published in a series of 42 volumes, the Geological Conservation Review Series. Provides a public record of features of interest and importance at 'Sites of Special Scientific Interest' (SSSIs). Publication will be completed in 2004. Website provides other conservation links as well as publication information.

946 **Geological Survey of Canada**
http://gsc.nrcan.gc.ca/index_e.php
The GSC is Canada's premier agency for geoscientific information and research, with world-class expertise focusing on geoscience surveys, sustainable development of Canada's resources, environmental protection, and technology innovation. Formed in 1842. Website provides links to the GSC bookstore, educational websites, libraries and other geoscience links. GSC's mandate is to 'provide Canada with a comprehensive geoscience knowledge base'.

947 **Geoscience Australia**
www.agso.gov.au
The national geoscience research and geospatial information agency for Australia. Originally Australia's Geological Survey organization: took its present name in 2001. Provides high-quality geoscience research and information and links to a wide range of national data collections. Webpage easy to navigate.

948 **International Union of Geological Sciences**
www.iugs.org
Scientific organization promoting the study of geological problems of worldwide significance. Facilitates international and interdisciplinary co-operation in the earth sciences. A member of the INTERNATIONAL COUNCIL FOR SCIENCE, the IUGS has more than 110 national members.

- **Energy and mineral resources for the 21st century, geology of mineral deposits, mineral economics: Proceedings of the 30th International Geological Congress, Volume 9** VSP, 1997, 514pp. $188.00. ISBN 9067642649. www.vsppub.com/search.html [DESCRIPTION].
- **International Geological Congress** www.32igc.org. Held every four years and organized in co-operation with, and under the sponsorship of, the IUGS. This is the 32nd, 2004 in Florence, Italy. Collection of abstracts and papers presented at each Congress are made widely available – an exemplar cited above.

949 Norges Geologiske Undersokelse
www.ngu.no
Founded in 1858 with the aim of improving knowledge of 'nature and the environment, economic growth in the mineral industry, better planning and land-use management, and cost-effective development aid'. This easy-to-use website – with a strong English language version – is a good exemplar of the wealth of information available from national geological survey sites. Inter alia, under its links section, it has a comprehensive worldwide list of such sites.

950 US Geological Survey
www.usgs.gov
US Government source for science about the earth, its natural and living resources, natural hazards, and the environment. Provides high-quality information, is easy to navigate, with several major subdivisions covering geology, mapping, water resources, and more. Along with extensive materials geared towards the specialist, the site also offers news, information and educational activities designed for the general public. Numerous data files are accessible and full-text is available for many recent publications. Many component pages such as the National Atlas of the United States, the National Geologic Map Database and the Earthquake Hazards Program.

- **Ask a Geologist** http://walrus.wr.usgs.gov/ask-a-geologist. 'Do you have a question about volcanoes, earthquakes, mountains, rocks, maps, ground water, lakes, or rivers? You can e-mail earth science questions to: Ask-A-Geologist@usgs.gov.
- **This dynamic earth: the story of plate tectonics** W.J. Kious and R.I. Tilling http://pubs.usgs.gov/publications/text/dynamic.html. Simple textbook describing the basics of plate tectonics. Useful for the general public. Originally published in paper form in February 1996.
- **US Geological Survey Library Classification System** http://pubs.usgs.gov/bul/b2010. Downloadable PDF revision of the original edition, first printed in 1992, and only available online, This is USGS Bulletin 2010.

Associations & societies

951 American Association of Petroleum Geologists [USA]
www.aapg.org
The purpose of the society is to advance the science of geology, in particular as it relates to petroleum, natural gas, and other mineral resources. It promotes relevant technology, disseminates information, endeavours to encourage high standards and attempts to include the public. A news-style web page with links to current news items, education, meetings, publications, services, and further related gateways.

952 American Geological Institute
www.agiweb.org
'A nonprofit federation of 43 geoscientific and professional associations that represents more than 100,000 geologists, geophysicists, and other earth scientists. Founded in 1948, AGI provides information services to geoscientists, serves as a voice of shared interests in our profession, plays a major role in strengthening geoscience education, and strives to increase public awareness of the vital role the geosciences play in society's use of resources and interaction with the environment.'

Website provides information services to geoscientists via many links, including statistical data. Promotes geosciences, particularly in relation to environmental issues. Attempts to reach all ages via its busy, newsy web pages. Educational links.

- **Earth Science World** www.earthscienceworld.org. Excellent gateway giving wide access to resources and up-to-date news on geologically related topics.

953 Geological Association of Canada
www.esd.mun.ca/~gac
Geoscience society, publisher and distributor of quality geoscience publications and journals. Aims to meet largely academic and professional needs, in Canada and worldwide.

954 Geological Curators' Group [UK]
www.hmag.gla.ac.uk/gcg
Affiliated to the Geological Society of London, and dedicated to improving the status of geology in museums. The GCG committee is made up of a group of professional individuals who work in the museum sector or in museum education. Map-based links to locations of UK geological collections.

955 Geological Society of America
www.geosociety.org
Established in 1888, GSA provides access to information for all levels of expertise and from all sectors: academic, government, business and industry. Website is easy to navigate and provides key information quickly and easily – though the GSA Bookstore part of the site, albeit rich in resource descriptions, has, to this reviewer, a rather curious structure.

- **Catastrophic events and mass extinctions: impacts and beyond** C. Koeber No. 3562003. £102.00. ISBN 0813723566. Good example of popular monograph series Special Papers. Proceedings of the fourth informal meeting on mass extinctions, global catastrophes, and the geological and biological consequences of large-scale impact events. More than 50 papers.

956 Geological Society of Australia
http://gsa.org.au
Established in 1952 as a learned, non-profit organization. Its objectives are to promote, advance and support the earth sciences within the scientific and wider communities. Is a member of the Australian Geoscience Council. Website provides news of events, a bookshop and further links.

957 Geological Society of London [UK]
www.geolsoc.org.uk
The national society for geoscience and one of the biggest societies in Europe; often known just as the 'Geol(ogical) Soc(iety)'. Exists 'to promote the geosciences and the professional interests of UK geoscientists'. Teaching resources, events and current news are all provided via links on the web page. The Society has a publishing house which publishes its journals and books – though the Geological Society Bookstore part of the overall site, albeit rich in resource descriptions, has to this reviewer a rather curious structure.

- **200 years of British hydrogeology** J.D. Mather, ed. No. SP2252004. £90.00. ISBN 1862391556. Example of popular, regularly produced monograph series *Special Publications*; 25 papers moving from the application, by William Smith, of stratigraphic principles to the sinking of wells through to the present ever-changing regulatory regime.

958 **Geological Society of New Zealand**
www.gsnz.org.nz
Founded in 1954, encourages the advancement of geology in New Zealand. Membership is open to all who are interested in the earth sciences. GSNZ Web Links page is an excellent concise entrée to geologically related activity in New Zealand: a good example of its type.

959 **Geologists' Association** [UK]
www.geologist.demon.co.uk
An organization serving both amateur and professional geologists within the UK. Promotes the study of geology, helps geologists to develop their knowledge. Links to publications, events, further links available via their website. Regular publication – *Proceedings of the Geologists' Association*.

960 **International Association for Mathematical Geology**
www.iamg.org
Aims to promote international co-operation in the application and use of mathematics in geological research. IAMG accepts as members geoscientists, statisticians, and other interested individuals or organizations. The website has many links of interest – educational, publications, research, events and much more.

961 **International Association of Sedimentologists**
www.blackwellpublishing.com/uk/society/ias/society.htm
Aim is to promote the study of sedimentology and the interchange of research at an international level. Over 97 countries represented in membership. Access to newsletters, publications, meetings and further sedimentology links from web page.

962 **Quaternary Research Association** [UK]
www.qra.org.uk
'Archaeologists, botanists, civil engineers, geographers, geologists, soil scientists, zoologists and others interested in research into the problems of the Quaternary. The majority of members reside in Great Britain, but membership also extends to most European countries, North America, Africa and Australasia.'

963 **Society for Sedimentary Geology**
www.sepm.org
An international society based in Tulsa, Oklahoma. Disseminates scientific information on sedimentology, stratigraphy, palaeontology, environmental sciences, marine geology, hydrogeology, and related subjects. Produces *Journal of Sedimentary Research* (JSR) and *PALAIOS* – a 'bimonthly journal dedicated to emphasizing the impact of life on Earth history as recorded in the paleontological and sedimentological records'. Links to (predominantly) USA regions, events, publications.

Society for the History of Natural History
See entry no. 1940

964 **Society of Economic Geologists**
www.segweb.org
For those interested in academic field of economic geology. Provides information on the meetings and publications of the society, contents of recently published issues of *Economic Geology* and the *Bulletin of the Society of Economic Geologists*, and some relevant links.

Libraries, archives, museums

Oxford University Museum of Natural History
See entry no. 1952

Portal & task environments

965 **Geologynet**
MinServ (Mineral Services), Australia.
www.geologynet.com
Very wide range of offerings on easy-to-navigate site. Maintained by commercial provider of products and services; but not commercially intensive: up to date, mid-2004. Emphasis on Australia, but much also from elsewhere. Particularly good coverage of data and software sources.

Content within the Geolbases Collection, available for purchase on CD-ROM, is accessible online free of charge, and contains the same information but with a simpler search interface and fewer features: databases for minerals, rock-forming minerals, economic minerals, rocks, geochemical, and XRD minerals. However, not easily browsable in this medium.

National Geospatial Data Clearinghouse
Federal Geographic Data Committee See entry no. 1600

Discovering print & electronic resources

966 **Bibliography and Index of Geology**
American Geological Institute and Geological Society of America
1969–, Monthly. ISSN 00982784.
Well regarded and useful resource. References photocomposed from citations in GeoRef, the AGI database; 29 fields of interest but omitting geography and meteorology. Profuse cross-references. Analytical author and subject indexes; annual cumulative index in 4 pts. Available also on microfiche, online, and CD-ROM. A major indexing service for geology.

967 **Bibliography and index of geology and allied sciences for Wales and the Welsh borders**
D.A. Bassett National Museum of Wales, 246pp. V. 1. *1536–1896*. ISBN 0720000610. V. 2. *1897–1958*. ISBN 0720000602.
Useful means of discovering geological resources relevant to Wales in the 16th–20th centuries. Includes publications of the Geological Survey and Museum, reference books, bibliographies, indexes, theses. Author and detailed analytical subject indexes. Updated in issues of *Geological Journal* and *Welsh Geological Quarterly*.

968 **British Geological Literature**
Brown's Geological Information Service Ltd, 1972–, Quarterly. Supersedes a publication with the same title published 1964–8. Not published 1969–71. New series begins NS1 (1972). ISSN 01407813.
A comprehensive and useful 'bibliography and index of geology (and related topics) of the British Isles and adjacent sea areas'. About 500 abstracts pa. The 26 sections include geomorphology and palaeontology. Quarterly author index; annual author, subject and locality indexes.

969 **Geologic Guidebooks of North America Database**
http://guide.georef.org/dbtw-wpd/guidens.htm
Online access to material that used to be available in hard copy only. The database contains the information in the print publication *The Union List of Geologic Field Trip Guidebooks of North America*, 6th edn, compiled and edited by the Geoscience Information Society Guidebooks Committee. References to geologic field trip guidebooks of North America mainly from the period 1940–88. Post-1988 guidebooks have been added to the database. From 2002, new guidebooks are firstly added to GeoRef and then added to the guidebook database.

970 **Geological Literature Search System of Japan**
Geological Survey of Japan
www.gsj.jp/HomePage.html
GEOLIS-JP is a bibliographic database on earth sciences, compiled by the Library of the Geological Survey of Japan, in the 'new' AIST. GEOLIS covers literature which is about Japan and its adjacent sea area and written by Japanese authors. Keyword searching. Searches available in English or Japanese. 213,375 records as of January 2004.

971 **Geologists and the history of geology: an international bibliography from the origins to 1978**
W.A.S. Sarjeant Macmillan, 1980. 5 v., £420.50. ISBN 0333293932.
Covers publications on the history of geology written in the Latin alphabet: over 1548 bibliographies of geologists and over 6630 indexed words. 1. Introduction ... Accounts of geological events; 2. The individual geologists, A–K; 3. The individual geologists, L–Z; prospectors, diviners and mining engineers; 4. Geologists indexed by country and specialty; 5. Index of authors, editors and translators. Appendix.
Series: Macmillan Reference Books.

- **Geologists and the history of geology: Supplement I : 1979–1984 and additions** Krieger, 1987. £148.50. ISBN 0898749395. 2 v. 1691p: v. 1. Bibliography; v. 2. Index.
- **Geologists and the history of geology: Supplement II : 1985–1993 and additions** Krieger, 1996. £292.50. ISBN 0894648802. 3 v. 2317p: v. 1 Bibliography; v. 2 Bibliography and Index; v. 3 Index.

972 **Geology emerging: a catalog illustrating the history of geology (1500–1850)**
D.C. Ward and A.V. Carozzi University of Illinois Library, 1984, 565pp. ISBN 0878450718.
Compiled from a collection in the Library of the University of Illinois at Urbana-Champaign. A useful reference tool for those interested in how the study of geology changed over time.
Series: Robert B. Downs Publication Fund, No. 8.

973 **The Herrington list: titles of research theses on the geology of the British Isles and offshore areas 1974–1984, including those in preparation**
D.J.C. Laming and A.V. Hodgson, comps 3rd edn, Herrington Geoscience (Exeter), 1985, 108pp. £10.00. ISBN 0951079107.
About 1350 titles of theses. Useful bibliographic tool. Chronological author list; classified subdiscipline list (arranged by year of award, then by authors A–Z); author index; 2-letter code for geological systems; 4-letter code for geophysical subdisciplines. With classified subdiscipline/regional list.
Previous edn published by Bibliographic Press, 1976.

Digital data, image & text collections

974 **Geology of Northern Ireland**
www.geographyinaction.co.uk
Online information on the geology of Northern Ireland. Created by Geography in Action for geography students and is part of their more general website. Brief notes on each rock type provided. Further geology resource links on web page.

975 **Geology of the Wessex Coast. Southern England**
I. West
www.soton.ac.uk/~imw/index.htm
A geological 'metadirectory'. Well organized and detailed geological information and links. Particularly interesting Virtual Field Trips and Field Trip Guides. This is one of the world's largest geological websites, with more than 200 web pages, comprising geological field guides, hundreds of full-screen colour photographs of varied geological features and associated geological bibliographies. Primarily provides information on the Wessex coast of England, but also links to information on the geology of the Pyrenees and on sabkhas or salt flats of desert regions. Excellent resource.

976 **Overseas Geology and Mineral Resources**
British Geological Survey HMSO, 1958–, Irregular. ISSN 00307467.
www.bgs.ac.uk/magazine/magazines/docs/15/33.pdf [DESCRIPTION]
Original series was entitled *Colonial Geology and Mineral Resources*. Volumes were published on specific regions. Range is now worldwide and covers main resource areas. Issues individually numbered from no. 41 (1973) onwards, but more recent work subsumed within the activities of BGS International: www.bgs.ac.uk/int/inthome.html.

Directories & encyclopedias

977 **Directory of British geological museums**
J.R. Nudds, ed. Geological Society of London, 1994, 142pp. £9.00. ISBN 189779908X.
Provides useful information about those museums in the UK which are of interest for their geological services. General readership.
Series: Geological Society Miscellaneous Papers, No. 18.

978 **The encyclopedia of applied geology**
C.W. Finkl, ed. Kluwer Academic Publishers, 1984, 672pp. £289.00. ISBN 0442225377.
www.eseo.com
Provides practical coverage of engineering geology, hydrology, rock structure monitoring, and soil mechanics. Explanations, analyses, well subheaded and documented. Valuable preface, with sections on abstracting and indexing services, computerized databanks, periodicals, text and reference works.
Available online: see website.

979 **Encyclopedia of European and Asian regional geology**
E.M. Moores and R.W. Fairbridge, eds Kluwer Academic Publishers, 1997, 825pp. £277.00. ISBN 0412740400.
www.eseo.com
Alphabetically organized by country. Multi-authored, with chapters written by experts containing information for each country about the stratigraphy, structure, tectonics and natural resources, and a history of geological exploration and other unique features. Assumes some prior geological

knowledge. A valuable resource for libraries, academics and students, professional industrialists as well as governmental agencies.

Available online: see website.

'The editors have done as well as they possibly could in condensing the output of an immense and rather intractable task to 804 pages, albeit large pages of small but quite clear print ... The book will make a valuable addition to libraries and as such is strongly recommended.' (*Geoscientist*)

980 Encyclopedia of field and general geology
C.W. Finkl, ed. Kluwer Academic Publishers, 1988, 936pp. £302.00. ISBN 0442224990.
www.eseo.com
Intended as a companion volume to the ENCYCLOPEDIA OF APPLIED GEOLOGY, this volume includes biogeochemistry, geoanthropology, and geobotany. As with the other volumes in the series, there are many cross-references. Good subject and author-citation index. A classic reference.
Available online: see website.

981 Encyclopedia of geology
R.C. Selley, R. Cocks and I.R. Plimer, eds Elsevier, 2004. 5 v., £775.00. ISBN 0126363803.
www.sciencedirect.com
A well publicized five-volume reference work to be published in November 2004. Approximately 350 cross-referenced articles on the theory and application of geology are proposed, making this one of the most comprehensive works on the subject. Colour used throughout in diagrams and photographs. Further references given with each topic.
Available online: see website.

982 Encyclopedia of sediments and sedimentary rocks
G.V. Middleton [et al.], eds Kluwer Academic Publishers, 2003, 821pp. £250.00. ISBN 1402008724.
www.eseo.com
Comprehensive, one-volume, authoritative collection of approx. 250 academic articles, arranged A–Z, covering all aspects of sediments and sedimentary rocks. Author and subject indexes. For students and academics in universities, for professionals in geology and related disciplines, as well as informed lay readers.
Available online: see website.

983 Encyclopedia of structural geology and plate tectonics
C.K. Seyfert Van Nostrand Reinhold, 1987, 876pp. ISBN 0442281250.
www.eseo.com
An integral part of the *Encyclopedia of Earth Sciences* series. Alphabetically arranged entries. Cross-references at the end of entries where required, as are additional readings. Covers much of the same information as the American Geological Institute glossary, but more extensive discussion on each entry. Useful for academics, students, professionals and the informed layperson.
Available online: see website.

984 The encyclopedia of world regional geology: Part 1: Western hemisphere (including Antarctica and Australia)
R.W. Fairbridge, ed. Dowden, Hutchinson & Ross, 1975, 704pp. ISBN 047025145X.
www.eseo.com
A major reference work of considerable value for all levels of interest; 88 contributors; c.150 signed entries, with references and cross-references. Entries are under countries A–Z. Author and subject indexes. Well illustrated. Further references given.
Available online: see website.

985 Geologist's directory [UK]
13th edn, Geological Society of London, 2003, 248pp. £79.00. ISBN 1862391408.
The leading reference guide for earth scientists describing resources in the UK and Ireland. Published annually. Six colour-coded sections with a comprehensive classification system. Includes listings of chartered geologists, a buyers' guide section, company data, associations and institutions and a section on geology information. Cross-referencing.

986 IAS directory of sedimentologists
International Association of Sedimentologists
http://paleoweb.net/ias
A database that aims to support co-operation between sedimentologists. Provides search facilities for searching for family name, city, country or study topic. Facility to add to the directory. Link to SedLink, a searchable database of categorized links to sedimentological web resources.

987 McGraw-Hill encyclopedia of the geological sciences
S.P. Parker, ed. 2nd edn, McGraw-Hill, 1988, 722pp. ISBN 0070455007.
This well regarded reference work has an integrated approach to the geological sciences, including geology, geochemistry, mineralogy, petrology, geophysics. Entries are alphabetically arranged; there is an extensive system of cross-references and a detailed analytical index. A classic reference text.
Previous edn 1987

988 The millennium atlas: petroleum geology of the central and northern North Sea
D. Evans [et al.]; Geological Society of London 2003, 389pp. Published by The Millennium Atlas Company, jointly owned by Geological Society of London, the Geological Survey of Denmark and Greenland, Norwegian Petroleum Society. Facsimile edition and Screen edition available on CD-ROM as replica of printed.
An impressive A2 size, full colour atlas. Details on the Danish, Norwegian and UK sectors of the hydrocarbon-producing regions of the North Sea. Some 100 contributors. For undergraduate and postgraduate readership.

Handbooks & manuals

989 Beiträge zur Regionalen Geologie der Erde (Contributions to the Regional Geology of the World)
G Borntraeger, 1961–, Annual. ISSN 05227038.
www.borntraeger-cramer.de [DESCRIPTION]
Each volume – most are in English – covers the regional geology of a particular region of the world (e.g. East Africa, South Pacific Islands, Hungary, etc.) using maps, providing syntheses and stratigraphic detail. Bibliography of available literature of the region is provided. Listing of published volumes and further information (synopses, tables of contents, reviews) via the website. Each volume is

comprehensive and an important contribution in its own right to the geology of specific world regions.

990 **Classic geology in Europe**
Terra Publishing, 2001–, Irregular.
A series of detailed guides to attractive geological regions of Europe. Experts write each volume. Based on itineraries that have been tested in the field, they are essential introductory reference volumes for those visiting the regions. Suitable for amateur and professional alike. Many colour illustrations.

- **1. Italian volcanoes C. Kilburn and B. McGuire** 2001, 166pp. £13.95. ISBN 1903544041.
- **2. Auvergne P. Cattermole** 2001, 168pp. £13.95. ISBN 190354405X.
- **3. Iceland T. Thordarson and A. Hoskuldsson** 2001, 200pp. £15.95. ISBN 1903544068.
- **4. The Canary Islands J.C. Carracedo and S. Day** 2001, 294pp. £15.95. ISBN 1903544076.
- **5. The North of Ireland P. Lyle** 2003, 160pp. £13.95. ISBN 1903544084.
- **6. Leinster C. Stillman and G. Sevastopulo** 2004, 192pp. £13.95. ISBN 1903544130.

991 **A colour atlas of carbonate sediments and rocks under the microscope**
A.E. Adams and W.S. MacKenzie Manson, 1998, 180pp. £29.95. ISBN 1874545847.
An essential atlas and laboratory manual, this book is an aid to identifying grain types and textures in carbonates. Contents include sections on: Coated grains, Peloids, Bioclasts, Diagenesis, Porosity, Limestone classification and Cathodoluminescence. Useful for undergraduate and postgraduates. Illustrated in full colour. Bibliography.
'An immensely useful book. It is the next best thing to being lead [sic] through a collection of slides by an experienced tutor ... It will appeal to geologists at every level ... Unlike many books written to be kept by the microscope, it opens flat.' (*Microscopy & Imaging News*)

992 **The Cretaceous world**
P.W. Skelton [et al.] Cambridge University Press, 2003, 360pp. Co-published with the Open University, £28.00. ISBN 0521538432. http://publishing.cambridge.org/resources [COMPANION]
Well illustrated interdisciplinary text on a wide range of Cretaceous rocks and fossils and explores the interactions between the physical, chemical and biological processes. Related environmental implications are considered. Numerous learning features including chapter summaries, focus boxes, and questions and answers. Support from a website hosting sample pages, selected illustrations and worked exercises enhances the resource.

993 **Field geology in the British Isles: a guide to regional excursions**
J.G.C. Anderson Pergamon, 1983, 324pp. ISBN 008022055X.
This classic guide describes 194 geological itineraries, complementing J.G.C. Anderson's and T.R. Owen's *The structure of the British Isles* (2nd edn, Pergamon) by providing more local data. Ten chapters (e.g. Precambrian terrains; Caledonian terrains; Hercynian terrains; Alpine terrains). Three appendices dealing with stratigraphical groupings of excursions, centres in alphabetical order and routes in alphabetical order. Detailed index.

994 **A field manual for the amateur geologist: tools and activities for exploring our planet**
A.M. Cvancara Rev edn, Wiley, 1995, 352pp. £12.50. ISBN 047104430X.
A pocket guide supplying clear explanations of the geological forces that continue to reshape the planet. Shows readers how to identify minerals, rocks and fossils, read geological maps and cross-sections, use mineral and landforms keys, and create rock collections. Approximately 200 photographs and drawings. Includes lists of geological museums, geological surveys, and further resources. General and undergraduate readership.
Previous edn Prentice-Hall, 1985.

995 **Geologic atlas of China: an application of the tectonic facies concept to the geology of China**
K.J. Hsü and C. Haihong Elsevier, 1999, 262pp. $258.00. ISBN 0444828478.
A useful starting point for investigating the geology of China. Covers basic aspects of tectonics and orogenesis before interpreting the geology of various regions of China in relation to these concepts. Provides details of the phanerozoic history of China summarizing the geological evolution of the regions covered; 24 atlas sheets and numerous text figures. Includes bibliographical references (pp 247–53) and author and subject indexes. Suitable mainly for postgraduate geologists, geophysicists and geographers.
Translated from the Chinese.

996 **A geologic time scale 2004**
F. Gradstein, J. Ogg and A. Smith Cambridge University Press, 2004, 384pp. £28.00. ISBN 0521786738.
Successor to the book *A geologic time scale 1989* by W. Brian Harland et al., which presented a comprehensive review of the ages, stages, epochs, periods, eras and eons of geological time. It gave up-to-date estimates on the dates of each division (based on various methods, such as radioactive dating), and comparative tables of the international standard divisions, and the plethora of more local equivalents. Although the divisions and estimates of dates were subsequently constantly being revised (see the ICS website), the 1989 book has since its publication been the first port of call to interpret the dates of fossils given in the literature.

This text presents an international stratigraphic framework for the Precambrian and Phanerozoic. Contributions by 40 experts. Includes a wallchart summarizing the whole time scale, with paleogeographic reconstructions throughout the Phanerozoic. A valuable reference source for academics, professionals and students; 164 line diagrams, 24 colour plates, 63 tables.

- **International Commission on Stratigraphy** www.stratigraphy.org. The largest scientific body within the nternational Union of Geological Sciences [q.v.]. It is also the only organization concerned with stratigraphy on a global scale.
- **A geologic time scale 1989** Cambridge University Press, 1990, 263pp. £47.50. ISBN 0521383617.

997 **Geological atlas of China**
Ma Lifang, comp. Geological Publishing House, Beijing, 2002, 348pp. $400.00. ISBN 7116022686.
A comprehensive work. Consists mainly of geological maps accompanied by a variety of supplementary maps, tables, figures, photos and text. Also includes a series of special-subject maps covering nationwide geology. Additional

stratigraphic tables, appended maps, tables and photos. - Further references.
Translated from the Chinese.

998 **Geological atlas of Western and Central Europe**
P.A. Ziegler 2nd edn, Shell Internationale Petroleum Maatschappij, 1990, 239pp. £20.00. ISBN 9066441259.
A standard work of the region providing earth scientists with an overview of the tectonic and stratigraphic framework of the area. A major revision, with 56 enclosures in this edition, compared with 40 in the previous; nine chapters of text. References, pp 195–233. Geographic index, pp 234–7. Geodynamic processes, pp 238–9. Ideal for undergraduates and postgraduates.
First published in 1982.

999 **Geological evolution of South-East Asia**
C.S. Hutchison Clarendon Press, 1989, 368pp. ISBN 0198544391.
A key text on the geology of this region. Covers all aspects of the geology of South-East Asia. Nine sections: 1. Introduction; 2. Late Mesozoic and Cainozoic tectonic features ... 5. Terrains of Cathaysian affinity (pp 133–200) ... 7. Ophiolites and sutures ... 9. Granite and associated plutonic rocks. Many maps and figures. References pp 318–49.
Series: Oxford Monographs on Geology and Geophysics, No. 13.

1000 **Geological history of Britain and Ireland**
N.H. Woodcock and R.A. Strachan, eds Blackwell Science, 2000, 423pp. £32.50. ISBN 0632036567.
A key text relating the geological story of Britain, Ireland, and their surrounding areas, with full coverage of the Precambrian and Early Palaezoic periods, as well as later events. Accessible for undergraduates, and postgraduates as well as professionals or informed amateurs. Multi-disciplinary approach. Many illustrations. Guides to further reading and full references to data sources provided. Includes bibliographical references at end of every chapter.

1001 **Geological maps: an introduction**
A. Maltman 2nd edn, Wiley, 1998, 264pp. ISBN 0471976962.
A practical introduction to geological maps and mapping. Covers fundamental principles with data on sources of geological maps, a short history, new techniques and forms of geology maps. Examples used are taken from real maps and real situations around the world. Included in the book are three-dimensional diagrams and a list of technical terms. For first year geology undergraduates but could also be useful for the more advanced student. A knowledge of rocks and geological processes is assumed.
Previous edn published by Open University Press, 1990.

1002 **Geological structures and maps: a practical guide**
R.J. Lisle 3rd edn, Butterworth-Heinemann, 2003, 128pp. £19.99. ISBN 0750657804.
A well illustrated student guide introducing the skills of interpreting a geological map and relating it to the morphology of important types of geological structure. Thoroughly revised, with more international examples, and suitable for use by students as a self-study textbook. Bibliography. Index.

1003 **The geology of Antarctica**
R.J. Tingey, ed. Clarendon Press, 1991, 680pp. Map in pocket, £74.50. ISBN 0198544677.
Comprehensive reference volume with each chapter produced by a specialist, reviewing a particular aspect of Antarctic geology. Arranged in five parts: The continent's geological and geophysical framework; Antarctica's Cainozoic glaciation; Antarctic palaeontology; Antarctica's resource potential; Recovery of meteorites from the Antarctic ice cap. Undergraduate, postgraduate readership. Detailed list of references.
Series: Oxford Monographs on Geology and Geophysics, No. 17.

1004 **The geology of Australia**
D. Johnson Cambridge University Press, 2004, 288pp. £27.99. ISBN 0521601002.
An important new resource. Recounts the 4400 million year history of Australia; 83 colour plates. Contents: 1. An Australian perspective; 2. The earth – a geology primer; 3. Building the core of Precambrian rocks; 4. Warm times – tropical corals and arid lands; 5. Icehouse – carboniferous and Permian glaciation; 6. Mesozoic warming – inland plains of the Triassic and Jurassic; 7. Birth of modern Australia – flowering plants, mammals and deserts; 8. Eastern highlands and volcanoes barely extinct; 9. Building the continental shelf and coastlines; 10. Great barrier reef; 11. Planets, moons, meteorites and impact craters; 12. Cycles in a continental journey. Useful for students, or professionals in the natural sciences, and the interested general public.

1005 **The geology of China**
Y. Zunya [et al.] Oxford University Press, 1986, 303pp. ISBN 019854460X.
A useful summary of geology in China. Sections: Background – Stratigraphy – Magnetic and metamorphic rocks of China since 1939 – Geotectonic development of China. Includes regional stratigraphical tables and other illustrations. Selected references. Bibliography pp 279–89. Stratigraphic index. Subject index.
Series: Oxford Monographs on Geology and Geophysics, No. 3.

1006 **Geology of England and Wales**
P.McL.D. Duff and A.J. Smith, eds Geological Society of London, 1992, 651pp. £34.00. ISBN 0903317710.
Comprehensive account of the geology of the UK, including recent advances in offshore drilling, plate tectonics, age dating, structure geology and sedimentary environments; 19 documented sections by 22 contributing authors. Many black-and-white illustrations and figures. Index pp 639–51, is in very small print. Essential reading for all students of geology.

1007 **The geology of Ireland**
C.H. Holland, ed. Dunedin Academic, 2001, 531pp. £55.00. ISBN 1903765072.
Useful summary of the geology of Ireland which is described as a physical whole. Specialist contributors deal with the area's long geological history, putting each period in its context. Additional chapters on the geology of offshore Ireland and a history of geology. References at the end of each chapter. Intended for professional geologists and students.
Previous edn Scottish Academic Press, 1981.

1008 **Geology of North America**
Geological Society of America 1986–.
www.lib.utexas.edu/geo/DNAG_GUIDE.html [DESCRIPTION]
Comprehensive set of volumes on North American geology.

The series has been prepared to mark the Centennial of the GEOLOGICAL SOCIETY OF AMERICA and is one of the Decade of North American Geology (DNAG) Projects (see URL). Comprises both volumes of text and related volumes of maps. Aims at integrating geological and geophysical knowledge of the continent; 28 volumes when complete, 19 on USA/Mexico and 9 on Canada. Examples include: V. H: *The Caribbean Region* 1990. ISBN 0813752124; V. P-1: *Geology of Canadian mineral deposit types* 1995. ISBN 0660131366. All include bibliographical references.

1009 The geology of Scotland
N.H. Trewin, ed. 4th edn, Geological Society of London, 2002, 576pp. £27.50. ISBN 1862391262.
Significantly expanded from the 3rd edition with 34 authors contributing to 20 chapters. Includes recent advances in offshore drilling, discovery of North Sea oil, plate tectonics, igneous and metamorphic petrology, age dating, structural geology and sedimentary environments. Colour section of 32 plates. Coloured geological map of Scotland. Essential reference work for postgraduates and all geoscientists conducting research in this area.
First published 1965.

1010 The geology of Spain
W. Gibbons and T. Moreno, eds Geological Society of London, 2002, 649pp. £27.50. ISBN 1862391270.
Key reference work of interest to researchers, teachers and students of SW European geology. Contributions from 159 mostly Spanish authors; provides a comprehensive account in English of mainland Spain, the Balearic and Canary Islands. Bibliography of over 4000 references.

1011 The geology of Svalbard
W.B. Harland [et al.] Geological Society of London, 1997, 521pp. £99.00. ISBN 1897799934.
A definitive study of the detailed geology of Svalbard based on some 50 years of research. (Svalbard is the archipelago in the Arctic Ocean, some 400 miles north of Norway, and includes the island of Spitsbergen.) The work meets the needs of specialists or geoscientists requiring information about this region, and is planned as an integrated synthesis: 1. Introduction including outline of main geological features; 2. Describes eight regions of Svalbard in detail; 3. Interprets historical events and environments; 4. Summary of economic aspects. Alphabetical lists of place names, stratigraphic names and general index. Extensive references. Bibliographical references (pp 477–514).
Series: Geological Society of London Memoirs, No. 17.

1012 Geology of the United Kingdom
CD Vision, 1997. Three CD-ROMS, $99.00. ISBN 0646317415.
Contains information provided by the British Geological Survey [q.v.], and the UK Onshore Geophysical Library (which manages the archive and official release of seismic data recorded over landward areas of the UK, and was established by the Department of Trade and Industry [q.v.] and the UK Onshore Operators Group). An introduction to earth sciences. Comprehensive illustrated guide to the geology of the UK. A useful resource for teaching of geology and earth sciences from secondary school to university level.

1013 The impact of geology on the United States: a reference guide to benefits and hazards
A.M. Gunn Greenwood Press, 2001, 261pp. $55.95. ISBN 0313314446.
The geological regions in the US are described one by one, exploring the processes that shape land surfaces. The kinds of rocks found are described and examined. Geologic and climatic activities that contribute to the reshaping of landscapes are described. The impact of those forces on the environment is assessed with suggestions for minimizing that impact. An accessible text. Ideal for students. Many further resources suggested.

1014 Lexique stratigraphique international
International Geological Congress Centre National de la Recherche Scientifique, 1956–77. 8v., each in fascicules (c.17,000 p.).
Contributions by c.100 specialists. Each country fascicule has a detailed description of stratigraphic formations (A–Z), followed by a list of references, a stratigraphic index and folding maps. The dictionary of stratigraphic terms (v.8) is particularly helpful. V. 1. Europe; V. 2. U.R.S.S.; V. 3. Asie; V. 4. Afrique; V. 5. Amérique Latine; V. 6. Océanie; V. 7. Amérique du Nord; V. 8. Terms stratigraphiques majeurs. A standard source of reference.
'Nouvelle Série', Pergamon Press, 1983–

1015 The ocean basins and margins
A.E.M. Nairn and F.G. Stehli, eds Plenum Press, 1973–1998. 9 v.
The substantial work on the subject of submarine geology and continental margins. Volumes divided geographically: 1. The South Atlantic (1973, 583 pp); 2. The North Atlantic (1974, 598 pp); 3. The Gulf of Mexico and the Caribbean (1975, 503 pp); 4a. The Eastern Mediterranean (1977, 503 pp); 4b. The Western Mediterranean (1978, 447 pp); 5. The Arctic Ocean (1981, 447 pp); 6. The Indian Ocean (1982, 796 pp); 7. The Pacific Ocean (1985, 733 pp); 8. The Tethys Ocean (1998, 552 pp).
The Tethys Ocean was an ocean that existed between the continents of Gondwana and Laurasia before the opening of the Atlantic Ocean. Its remnants today are the Black, Aral, and Caspian Seas. It was first proposed by the Austrian geologist Eduard Suess in 1893, and was named after the sea goddess Tethys. (WIKIPEDIA).

- **InterMARGINS: Continental margin research University of Southampton**. www.intermargins.org. Southampton Oceanography Centre initiative 'to encourage scientific and logistical co-ordination, with particular focus on problems that cannot be addressed as efficiently by nations or national institutions acting alone or in limited partnerships'.

1016 Putnam's geology
P.W. Birkeland and E.E. Larson 5th edn, Oxford University Press, 1989, 654pp. £37.50. ISBN 0195055179.
Includes developments in mineral and energy resources, and describes trends in their use; 19 chapters. References appended to each chapter. Conversion table and glossary. Analytical index, pp 635–46. A detailed textbook, with numerous black-and-white illustrations and photographs. Suitable for geology, environmental science, and geography students. Popular text.
First published 1964.

1017 The Reed field guide to New Zealand geology: an introduction to rocks, minerals, and fossils
J. Thornton Reed Books, 2003, 276pp. NZD $39.95. ISBN 0790008564.
Written for the general public and beginners in geology and

is now a standard reference for New Zealand's geology. Describes the geological history of New Zealand from its beginnings some 600 million years ago to its present landscape. Revised and updated. Includes a geological time chart and quick reference maps of North and South Island for travellers.

1018 **Regional geology of Africa**
S.W. Petters Springer-Verlag, 1991, 722pp. £60.50. ISBN 354054528X.
A comprehensive overview of geology, tectonics, and mineral resources of Africa from Archean to Quaternary geology, including aspects of plate tectonics evolution and geological history. Assembled data on igneous and metamorphic petrology, geochemistry, structures and tectonics, stratigraphy, historical geology, geomorphology, geophysics, mineral deposits and petroleum geology combine to make this a unique textbook. Includes bibliographical references (pp 685–722).
Series: Lecture Notes in Earth Sciences.

1019 **The sedimentary record of sea-level change**
A.L. Coe [et al.] Cambridge University Press, 2003, 288pp. Co-published with The Open University, £28.00. ISBN 0521538424. http://publishing.cambridge.org/resources [COMPANION]
A comprehensive student textbook describing how past changes in sea-level can be detected through an analysis of the sedimentary record. Special focus on the current sequence stratigraphy model explaining the basics and relevant applications. Full-colour with numerous features to help tutors and students alike: detailed case studies on the practical applications of sequence stratigraphy; set-aside boxes with supplementary, background information; questions and answers throughout the text encourage students to test their understanding of the material. The book is supported by a free companion website, with additional information, exercises and related links.
'not only a textbook, but also a compact and descriptive encyclopedia for every scientist enrolled in sea level history ... the paperback edition is still reasonable; there are no competitors to this excellent piece of work.' (*EOS*)

1020 **The tectonic evolution of Asia**
A. Yin and T.M. Harrison, eds Cambridge University Press, 1996, 666pp. £130.00. ISBN 0521480493.
Essential reference work on this region; 21 contributors; 10 pages of illustrations on plates. Divided in five parts: Geodynamic models of the Cenozoic Deformation in Asia; Seismotectonics; Geological evolution of the Himalaya-Karakoram ranges; Tectonics of the Cenozoic Indo-Asia collision; Mesozoic-paleozoic assembly of Asia. Postgraduate in focus.
Series: World and Regional Geology. Papers from a Rubey Colloquium held at the University of California, Los Angeles, February 26 and 27, 1994.

1021 **Thrust tectonics**
K.R. McClay Chapman & Hall, 1991, 447pp. £45.95. ISBN 041243900X.
Well regarded informative text covering multidisciplinary research in the study of thrust systems, incorporating field observations, conceptual models and analogue and numerical simulations, as well as geophysical studies of thrust belts. Undergraduate and postgraduate readership.
The papers presented in this volume were part of the Thrust Tectonics Conference held at Royal Holloway and Bedford New College, University of London 4–7 April 1990. Includes bibliographical references and index.

Geomorphology

arid zones • beaches • caves • coastal regions • denudation • deserts • drylands • erosion • glaciology • islands • karsts • landforms • mountains • physical geography • polar regions • rivers • savannahs • speleology • weathering

Introductions to the subject

1022 **Contemporary meanings in physical geography: from what to why?**
S.T. Trudgill and A. Roy Arnold, 2003, 292pp. £18.99. ISBN 0340806907.
Provides a useful guide to the contemporary debates in the philosophy of physical geography, and introduces the reader to its wider cultural significance. Includes thoughts on the future of the discipline. Undergraduate readership.

1023 **Deserts**
M.C. Stoppato and A. Bini Firefly Books, 2003, 256pp. $24.95. ISBN 1552976696.
'Examines the fascinating eco-systems of 49 major deserts. Studying the history of deserts improves our understanding of the climatic conditions that create hostile environments. Deserts are located on every continent – including Antarctica. The book covers each with concise descriptions and quick-reference symbols and charts that display vital statistics such as average rainfall and temperatures, and expanse.'

- **World savannas: ecology and human use** **J. Mistry** Prentice Hall, 2000, 344pp. $29.47. ISBN 0582356598. 'Interdisciplinary text on the world's savannas covering the geography, ecology, economics and politics of savanna regions. Savannas are a distinct vegetation type, covering a third of the world's land surface area, supporting a fifth of its population'.

1024 **Fundamentals of geomorphology**
R.J. Huggett Routledge, 2002, 386pp. £24.99. ISBN 0415241464.
A comprehensive introduction to geomorphology, exploring the world's landforms from a systems perspective, with emphasis on change. Considers the roles of geomorphic processes and historical events in understanding their development. Contents include: Structure: landforms resulting from, or influenced by the endogenic agencies of tectonic and volcanic processes, geological structures and rock types; Process and Form: landforms fashioned by the exogenic agencies of running water, flowing ice and meltwater, ground ice and frost, the wind and the sea; History: Earth surface history, giving a discussion of the origin of old plains; relict, exhumed and stagnant landscape features; cycles of landscape change, and the evolutionary aspects of landscape change.
Series: Fundamentals of Physical Geography.
'This refreshing text, aimed at undergraduates, is clearly structured and takes its well-presented examples from a wide range of sources ... The language is accessible to the target audience and a large number of maps and diagrams are used effectively ... certainly recommended.' (*Geography*)

1025 **Introducing physical geography**
A.H. Strahler and A.N. Strahler 3rd edn, Wiley, 2003, 684pp. CD-ROM, $93.95. ISBN 0471417416.
Coverage of developments in the discipline, as well as multimedia and pedagogy. Incorporates relevant developments in science, as well as newsworthy environmental events. Aimed at undergraduate readers and

written in a lively manner with all-colour illustrations and supporting GeoDiscoveries CD-ROM (Present-Interact-Assess framework) enabling interactive and instant assessment. US bias. Includes coverage of the earth as a rotating planet; atmospheric moisture and precipitation; weather systems; global climates; biogeography; global ecosystems; the lithosphere and plate tectonics; volcanic and tectonic landforms; landforms and rock structure; landforms made by waves and wind; glacial landforms and the Ice Age.
Previous edn 1998.

1026 **Rivers of the world: a social, geographical, and environmental sourcebook**
J.R. Penn ABC-CLIO, 2001, 379pp. eBook, $90.00. ISBN 1576075796.
Includes about 200 rivers arranged in A–Z format, from Aare to Ziz. Provides basic facts including river source, tributaries, outlet, and length, but also gives historical and cultural content. Good bibliographical coverage.

Dictionaries, thesauri, classifications

1027 **A dictionary of karst and caves**
D. Lowe and T. Waltham, comps; British Cave Research Association 2002, 40pp. £3.50. ISBN 0900265248.
A brief guide to the terminology and concepts of cave and karst science. This resource will suit all interested in the subject area.
Series: The BCRA Cave Studies Series, V. 10.

1028 **The dictionary of physical geography**
D.S.G. Thomas, A. Goudie and D. Dunkerley, eds 3rd edn, Blackwell Publishers, 2000, 610pp. £24.99. ISBN 0631204733.
Significantly updated 3rd edn of this comprehensive encyclopedic dictionary providing an essential reference for all students and researchers in geomorphology. Large amount of additional material has been added. Well illustrated and referenced. An international perspective on key topics is included. Bibliography. Index. Useful for academic or public libraries.
Includes bibliographical references and index
'The Dictionary is a remarkable collaborative effort and a valuable resource. It is a very worthwhile purchase for anyone studying or teaching physical geography.' (*Progress in Physical Geography*)

1029 **Dictionnaire de la géographie**
P. George and F. Verger, ed. 7th edn, Presses Universitaires de France, 2000, 512pp. €45.50. ISBN 2130479243.
More than 3000 clear definitions of terms used in French geography. About two-thirds concern physical geography. References are appended to lengthier entries.
Series: Grands Dictionnaires.

1030 **Elsevier's dictionary of glaciology**
V.M. Kotlyakov and N.A. Smolyarova, comps Elsevier, 1990, 336pp. £84.50. ISBN 0444886710.
In four languages: English (with definitions), Russian (with definitions), French and German. c.1200 terms, with French, German, and Russian equivalents and indexes.

1031 **The Penguin dictionary of physical geography**
J.B. Whittow 2nd edn, Penguin, 2000, 590pp. £9.99. ISBN 0140514503.
This comprehensive book explains over 5000 technical terms students need to know about physical geography. Completely up to date with associated topics such as botany and geology incorporated. Illustrations accompany the text. Very good cross-referencing enables full understanding of the terms described.
Previous edn 1984.

Official & quasi-official bodies

Arctic Council
See entry no. 2112

1032 **International Geographical Union**
www.igu-net.org
An important body aiming to promote and co-ordinate geographical research. It organizes the International Geographical Congresses and other similar conferences. The website provides links to worldwide geography departments; but most of the other information is rather sparse and lacks currency.

1033 **Scientific Committee on Antarctic Research**
www.scar.org
Committee of the INTERNATIONAL COUNCIL FOR SCIENCE. SCAR is charged with the initiation, promotion and co-ordination of scientific research in Antarctica. It is 'the single international, interdisciplinary, non-governmental organization which can draw on the experience and expertise of an international mix of scientists across the complete scientific spectrum. It is, therefore, the obvious source of advice on a wide range of scientific questions and it is ideally placed to provide the answers.'
Research groups; News; Events; Topical articles; Antarctic Treaty; Publications; etc.

Research centres & institutes

1034 **British Antarctic Survey**
www.antarctica.ac.uk
Part of the NATURAL ENVIRONMENT RESEARCH COUNCIL, managed from Cambridge, UK, and undertaking a programme of science in the Antarctic region. Aims to promote scientific research and to raise public awareness worldwide. Navigation around website is relatively simple, with detailed scientific and newsworthy information via good set of links.
- **Antarctic Environmental Data Centre** www.antarctica.ac.uk/Resources/AEDC/aedc_link_page.html. NERC designated data centre and gateway to Antarctic data. Uses the BAS Metadata Management System.

National Snow and Ice Data Center
See entry no. 1133

1035 **Scott Polar Research Institute** [UK]
www.spri.cam.ac.uk
Part of the University of Cambridge, UK. Research groups investigate a range of issues in the environmental sciences of relevance to the Arctic and Antarctica. The Polar Library, which includes the Shackleton Memorial Library, has comprehensive holdings of scholarly books and journals on polar research, with exceptional archival collections from the exploration of the Antarctic and Arctic. Extensive online

resources, including bibliographic and other information. An important resource for all interested in this subject field.

Associations & societies

Association for Geographic Information
See entry no. 1578

1036 Association of American Geographers
www.aag.org
A scientific and educational society founded in 1904 with currently 8400+ members. Appeals to both academics and professionals working in a wide variety of geographically related fields. The website provides links to career information, publications, education and events. Membership required for special online services.

1037 Australian Speleological Federation
http://www.caves.org.au
An association which aims to preserve and protect the cave and karst environment in Australia. Standards, including risk management and cave safety feature on their website, as does relevant map information. Links to publications of the association and descriptions of terminology used help provide extra information for the amateur and enthusiast alike.

1038 British Cave Research Association
www.bcra.org.uk
A registered charity promoting the study of caves and associated phenomena. It supports cave and karst research; encourages original exploration (both in the UK and on expeditions overseas); collects and publishes speleological information; maintains a library; and organises conferences and meetings. Links to all these via their website.

1039 British Geomorphological Research Group
www.bgrg.org
Professional organization for geomorphologists in the British Isles. Extensive well categorized set of links to geomorphological news and information. Useful Educational Resources section (e.g. 'What do Geomorphologists do?'; 'Topical Issues in Geomorphology'). A good site.
Free

1040 The Canadian Association of Geographers
www.cag-acg.ca/en
National organization representing geographers from public and private sectors and from universities. Links to information about publications, meetings and education and information on membership required to access further online services.

1041 Cave Research Foundation [USA]
www.cave-research.org
Private non-profit organization dedicated to: facilitating research, management and interpretation of caves and karst resources; forming partnerships to study, protect and preserve cave resources and karst areas; promoting the long-term conservation of caves and karst ecosystems.

1042 International Association of Geomorphologists
www.geomorph.org/main.html
Non-governmental organization promoting geomorphology as a discipline through international co-operation. Links to members of the academic community and to more specific working groups, such as those concerned with bedrock rivers, volcanoes, large rivers and geoarchaeology. Up-to-date news on conferences, events, publications. Glossary and image gallery. Further links to organizations, journals and mailing lists.

1043 National Geographic Society [USA]
www.nationalgeographic.com
Well known as the producer of *National Geographic* Magazine, which is especially held in high regard for the quality of its photographic images – these now also accessible on its attractive, newspaper-style website. The Magazine's purpose is to educate, increase and diffuse geographical knowledge. Links on the website to other related National Geographic magazines and lots of other information and resources for all ages and interest levels. A very rich site, meriting detailed browsing.

- **Xpeditions National Geographic Society and MarcoPolo: Internet Content for the Classroom Program.** www.nationalgeographic.com/xpeditions. 'Xpeditions is home to the US National Geography Standards – and to thousands of ideas, tools, and interactive adventures that bring them to life'.

1044 National Speleological Society [USA]
www.caves.org
Mainly focused on USA. It is a society intended for advancing the study, exploration and conservation of caves. Membership required. Links to businesses, safety, education, conservation and events. Many educational links will attract schools and public libraries to this resource.

1045 Royal Geographical Society (with The Institute of British Geographers)
www.rgs.org
Society formed from the merger in 1995 of the Royal Geographical Society and the Institute of British Geographers. Nineteen research groups. Aims to focus on research, education and training, but also to provide the wider public with relevant information. Attractive, easy-to-use web interface. Good section Geography in the News.

Unlocking the Archives: 'On 8 June 2004 the Royal Geographical Society (with IBG) opened its new facilities to the public, which provide access to one of the world's largest geographical collections containing over two million maps, photographs, books, artwork, artefacts and documents. Our collection tells the story of 500 years of geographical discovery and research.' This major project was supported by the UK Heritage Lottery Fund and other donors.

Portal & task environments

1046 Gesource [UK]
Consortium of Academic Libraries In Manchester and Resource Discovery Network
www.gesource.ac.uk
The geography and environment hub of the RDN. Aimed at staff, students and researchers in the UK's higher education and further education communities. A wide range of services is provided, including a core database of high-quality internet resources catalogued by subject specialists. A full description of each resource is provided, with direct access to the resource itself.

Much other useful and interesting information, including the Gesource World Guide for over 270 countries and territories, and a list of the last month's Top 50 Sites.

Discovering print & electronic resources

1047 Arctic & Antarctic Regions
NISC.
www.nisc.com/Frame/NISC_products-f.htm
Online host access to 'the world's largest collection of international polar databases'.

1048 Bibliographie géographique internationale
Centre National de la Recherche Scientifique Annual. ISSN 12749249.
www.inist.fr/en/PRODUITS/bgi.php [DESCRIPTION]
Useful reference resource, providing abstracts, bibliographies, and statistics. Covers all geographical information.
Text in French.

1049 Cold Regions Bibliography Project
American Geological Institute
www.coldregions.org/index.html
As of November 2004, contained over 200,000 bibliographic records, increasing by about a further 3000 items per year. The last two years' monthly updates to the database can be viewed for free. Provides access to the Antarctic Bibliography and other useful material.
In paper form available as the annual Bibliography on Cold Regions Science and Technology *(ISSN 0149-3825).*

1050 GeoBase
Elsevier Science Publishing Company.
www.elsevier.com [DESCRIPTION]
A database supplying bibliographic information and abstracts for human and physical geography, ecology, geology, oceanography, geomechanics and development studies. The database provides current coverage of over 1700 journals and archival coverage of several thousand additional titles. Contains over a million records from 1980, with 72,000 records added annually. Each record contains full bibliographic citation, indexing terms and codes and 99.5% of records contain abstracts. Useful resource for higher education.
Available online: see website.

1051 Geographical Abstracts: Physical Geography
Elsevier, 1960–, Monthly. $2,391.00. ISSN 09540504.
www.elsevier.com
References with abstracts from over 2000 journals relevant to earth studies. Divided into eight subjects: synoptic geography; landforms; the Quaternary; sedimentology; soils; hydrology; meteorology and climatology; remote sensing, mapping and GIS. International coverage.
Available online: see website.

1052 Keyguide to information sources on the polar and cold regions
W.J. Mills and P. Speak Mansell, 1998, 330pp. £85.00. ISBN 0720121760.
A comprehensive overview of the literature on polar and cold regions. Includes analysis of the nature of polar literature which exhibits unusual features – especially the role played by expedition reports. Contains a select international bibliography. Directory of international organizations. Part 1 Survey of the polar and cold regions and information sources relating to them, Part 2 Bibliography, Part 3 Directory of selected organizations.
This Series has now been discontinued.

1053 Online Geographical Bibliography: GEOBIB
American Geographical Society Library
http://geobib.lib.uwm.edu [FEE-BASED]
Bibliographical searching available from 1985 to date. Current issue of *Current Geographical Publications* freely available.

1054 Polar and glaciological abstracts
Scott Polar Research Institute Cambridge University Press, 1990–. £122.00 [2004]. ISSN 09575073.
www.spri.cam.ac.uk/resources/sprilib [DESCRIPTION]
Compiled by the Institute's Library and Information Service in association with the World Data Centre for Glaciology, Cambridge, UK. Useful for keeping up to date on current research. Each issue contains c.1300 abstracts of 30–100 words in length. Classified A–Z. Contains subject-geographic and author indexes. Annual cumulative index.
Available online: see website.

Directories & encyclopedias

1055 The encyclopedia of beaches and coastal environments
M.L. Schwartz, ed. Hutchinson Ross, 1982, 940pp. ISBN 0879332131.
www.eseo.com
An authoritative volume on coastal processes; 184 contributors. Articles A–Z, usually documented. Cross-references. Covers geomorphology; ecology; coastal engineering; continental; regional and specific examples of types of coast. Well illustrated.
Available online: see website.

1056 Encyclopedia of caves
D. Culver and W. White, eds Academic Press, 2004, 1000pp. $99.95. ISBN 0121986519.
International in focus, a comprehensive reference handbook of 107 in-depth articles on the geological and geomorphological evolution of caves, and life in caves. Many colour photographs and detailed illustrations. Alphabetical listings, cross references, suggestions for further reading, glossary and index. Would suit a wide variety of readers from academic to the general public.

1057 Encyclopedia of caves and karst science
J. Gunn, ed. Fitzroy Dearborn, 2003, 896pp. $195.00. ISBN 1579583997.
Comprehensive coverage of 350 alphabetically arranged entries grouped in themes such as biospeleology; cave and karst geoscience; cave archaeology and human use of caves; art in caves; cave and karst history; hydrology and groundwater; conservation and management; and exploration, equipment and rescue. Each entry is fully referenced, with suggestions for further reading and cross-references to related articles. Over 500 photographs, maps, diagrams, and tables. Thematic content lists and a

comprehensive index enable easy searching and browsing. Undergraduate, postgraduate readership.

1058 Encyclopedia of geomorphology
A Goudie, ed. Routledge, 2003, 1200pp. 2 v., £230.00. ISBN 041527298X.
An essential reference tool for physical geographers. International editorial team of contributors. Two volumes, containing approximately 700 alphabetically organized entries. 220 line figures, 100 black-and-white photos and 50 tables. Provides a comprehensive guide to specific landforms and to the major types of geomorphological processes that create them. Major new developments over past few years described.

1059 UXL encyclopedia of landforms
R. Nagel UXL, 2003, 624pp. $170.00. ISBN 078767611X.
www.gale.com/gvrl
General introduction to physical geography – looks at the structures and features of 48 of Earth's landforms, including features such as canyons, cliffs, valleys and volcanoes. Alphabetically arranged entries. Also included are 25 maps, charts and graphs; 180 full-colour photos and illustrations; bibliography; and comprehensive index. Useful for school and public libraries.
Available online: see website.

Handbooks & manuals

1060 Applied geomorphology: theory and practice
R.J. Allison, ed. Wiley, 2002, 492pp. $190.00. ISBN 0471895555.
Valuable practical reference tool: not only for postgraduates and researchers in geomorphology, but also for more applied disciplines such as civil engineering and those involved in risk management consultancy. Four sections: slopes & landslides, sediment transfer dynamics, hazards & risks, and coasts. Global case studies are used to show how geomorphological evidence helps to establish 'effective land utilization and hazard risk assessment'.
Series: International Association of Geomorphologists.

1061 Arid zone geomorphology: process, form, and change in drylands
D.S.G. Thomas, ed. 2nd edn, Wiley, 1998, 713pp. $160.00. ISBN 0471976105.
Comprehensive updated edition; covers geomorphological processes operating in arid zone environments, providing a balanced view of research and applications in the field. Includes new chapters on soils, the role of vegetation, and groundwater as a geomorphological agent; 34 contributors. Six sections, made up of 30 chapters: 1. Framework; 2. Surface processes and characteristics; 3. The work of water; 4. The work of the wind; 5. Geomorphology of the world's arid zones; 6. Extensions and change in the arid realm. References are appended to each chapter. Index (pp 697–713).
Previous edn Belhaven, 1989.

1062 Australia: land beyond time
R. Morrison Cornell University Press, 2002, 334pp. $35.00. ISBN 0801488249.
A companion book to the large-screen film of the same name. More than '300 stunning color photographs of the continent and its breathtaking landforms, plants, and animals'. Clearly presented with timelines and maps. Suitable for all.

1063 Beaches and coasts
R.A. Davis Jr and D.M. Fitzgerald Blackwell Publishers, 2003, 448pp. £35.00. ISBN 0632043083.
Comprehensive text that covers the processes and explanations for the varied coastlines of the world. Many examples and types of coastline used to describe the tectonic processes, climatic influences, and geological materials that have an effect on coastlines.

1064 Coasts: form, process and evolution
C.D. Woodroffe Cambridge University Press, 2002, 638pp. £35.00. ISBN 0521011833.
This key text aims at providing information for those who will be improving the management of coastal resources. Provides the necessary geomorphological background for those studying coastal systems. Plenty of global examples are used to illustrate the points made. Aimed at postgraduates or professionals in the field. Many diagrams and illustrations to supplement the text. An extensive reference section.

Desert meteorology
T.T. Warner See entry no. 1245

1065 The encyclopedia of the earth: oceans and islands
F.H. Talbot and R.E. Stevenson, eds Merehurst Limited, 1991, 240pp. £25.00. ISBN 1853911569.
A useful reference resource from 40 contributors, exploring ocean and island environments. Supplemented by 350 colour photos. Three sections: 1. The miracle of the sea; 2. Islands: worlds apart; 3. The future of oceans and islands. Facts about oceans and islands, pp 228–9. Glossary. Further reading and an index. For school and public libraries.

1066 Geomorphology
B.W. Sparks 3rd edn, Longman, 1986, 561pp. ISBN 0470206675.
University student classic text for physical geography; 17 chapters; references by chapter and pp 521–43. About 250 illustrations. Includes index.
Previous edn 1972.

1067 Geomorphology: critical concepts in geography
D.J.A. Evans, ed. Routledge, 2004, 3040pp. 7 v., £995.00. ISBN 041527608X.
http://search.tandf.co.uk [DESCRIPTION]
A key collection making available classic as well as more contemporary, 'essential benchmark papers' in the areas of geomorphology covering such topics as fluvial, slope, coastal, glacial and periglacial, arid lands and landscape evolution. Each of the seven volumes provides an overview of a particular field of study and its development as well as some idea of where current studies and research are leading. The whole represents the changes in perspectives over the last century in the study of geomorphology. Specialist editors provide introductions to each volume and have made careful selections in their subject fields. An essential reference tool for those needing access to key papers in their field.
Series: Critical Concepts in Geography.

1068 **Geomorphology and global tectonics**
M.A. Summerfield, ed. Wiley, 2000, 367pp. $225.00. ISBN 0471971936.
A key reference resource in this field. Concentrates on the analysis of large-scale tectonics and topography. Examines the ways in which geophysical data and modelling help to explain the development of large-scale landscape features. Up-to-date surveys of important research questions. Approx. 16 pages of colour plates. Includes bibliographical references at end of each chapter. Undergraduate, postgraduate text.
Includes bibliographical references at end of each chapter, and index.

- **Geographic information science and mountain geomorphology M.P. Bishop and J.F. Shroder, eds** Springer-Verlag, 2004, 486pp. £100.00. ISBN 354042640X. Use of advanced satellite sensors, high resolution satellite imagery and digital elevation to do quantitative analysis and modelling of mountain landscapes.

1069 **Geomorphology for engineers**
P.G. Fookes, M. Lee and G. Milligan, eds Rev. edn, Whittles Publishing, 2004, 544pp. £75.00. ISBN 1870325036.
For the postgraduate or professional. Three parts: Part 1 – Geomorphological Controls – concerned with major factors that control the materials, form and processes on the earth's surface; Part II – Geomorphological Processes – details processes that help shape land surfaces and influence their engineering characteristics; Part III – Environments and Landscapes – includes specialist chapters for areas such as glacial, temperate, volcanic and coastal environments. Authoritative, comprehensive overviews of the subjects by specialists in their fields.

1070 **Geomorphology in the tropics: a study of weathering and denudation in low latitudes**
M.F. Thomas Wiley, 1994, 460pp. $280.00. ISBN 0471930350.
For undergraduate and postgraduate students of tropical environments with some knowledge of geomorphology and related earth sciences. An important text in addressing the issues related to tropical ecosystems and associated problems. Examines the special characteristics of the tropics and impact on the balance of forces and materials within denudation systems. Four parts (e.g. 4. The evolution of tropical landscapes). References, pp 389–433. Six pages of plates. Author and subject indexes.

1071 **Glacial landsystems**
D.J.A. Evans, ed. Hodder & Stoughton Educational, 2005, 532pp. £24.99. ISBN 0340806664.
Comprehensive overview of glaciation from the perspective of glacial land systems. International specialists provide up-to-date summaries of land systems relevant to both modern and ancient glacier systems. Reconstruction and interpretation of former glacial environments also included. A handbook of glacial land system types for undergraduate and postgraduate students of glaciation.

1072 **Glaciers & glaciation**
D.I. Benn and D.J.A. Evans Arnold, 1998, 734pp. £29.99. ISBN 0340584319.
Covers the nature, origin and behaviour of glacier systems and geological and geomorphological evidence for their former existence. International case studies integrated throughout the text. Incorporates much recent research, and covers all aspects of glaciers. Many photographs bring the text alive. An 86-page bibliography. Excellent value. Undergraduate and postgraduate readership.

1073 **Landform monitoring, modelling, and analysis**
S.N. Lane, K.S. Richards and J.H. Chandler Wiley, 1998, 454pp. $110.00. ISBN 047196977X.
An essential reference tool for those requiring information about methodological and technological developments in terrain data acquisition and analysis, including developments on how terrain can be used to answer geomorphological questions. Two sections: 1. Technical issues, and 2. Applications. Comprises selected and full-refereed papers from a BGRG Annual Conference. Undergraduate and graduate readership level.
Series: British Geomorphological Research Group Symposia.

1074 **Natural hazards**
E. Bryant 2nd edn, Cambridge University Press, 2005, 336pp. £21.99. ISBN 0521537436.
The 1st edn was an accessible, readable, reference volume, well supported with more than 180 maps, diagrams and photographs. Interdisciplinary treatment of the full range of natural hazards. Three documented sections: Section 1 examines storms, wind, the oceans, drought and flood, precipitation, fires; Section 2 covers earthquakes, volcanoes, tsunami, land instability; Section 3 looks at responses to hazards. Glossary, pp 275–86.

1075 **The periglaciation of Great Britain**
C.K. Ballantyne and C. Harris Cambridge University Press, 1994, 330pp. £18.95. ISBN 0521310164.
All aspects and effects of the periglaciation of upland and lowland Great Britain covered in this undergraduate text. The landforms, deposits and sedimentary structures that developed during the Quaternary Era are described, as well as more recent features that have formed. Four parts (14 chapters): 1. Introduction and context; 2. The periglaciation of lowland Britain; 3. The periglaciation of upland Britain; 4. Periglacial environments. References, pp 299–323. Detailed index.
Includes bibliographical references and index

1076 **World atlas of desertification**
N. Middleton and D.S.G. Thomas, eds; United Nations Environment Programme 2nd edn, Arnold, 1997, 192pp. £159.99. ISBN 0340691662.
Essential reference for environmental scientists, climatologists and geologists. Revised and expanded to include the latest updated computer images of desertification, and fuller descriptions and explanations of the issues concerned. Colour maps and graphs illustrating the severity of global desertification. Double the length of the 1st edn. Includes a wide range of case studies. Fully referenced throughout. Bibliography pp 171–80.
Previous edn 1992.

Keeping up-to-date

1077 **Progress in Physical Geography**
Arnold, 1977–, 3/year. £247.00. ISSN 03091333.
www.arnoldpublishers.com/journals
Volumes contain documented articles and reviews of current research and theoretical developments in the natural and environmental sciences. International coverage. Each issue

now also includes web page reviews, highlighting the most beneficial websites on the internet and a review of a classic book or paper.

Geophysics

earthquakes • faults • geomagnetism • geophysical exploration • magnetic fields • petroleum geoscience • rock physics • seismology • tsunami

Introductions to the subject

1078 Earthshaking science: what we know (and don't know) about earthquakes
S.E. Hough Princeton University Press, 2004, 256pp. $17.95. ISBN 0691118191.
A resource that will be of enormous value to those with a general interest in the subject. Issues at the forefront of modern seismology are handled in such a way that they are clear and accessible for all. The author is an expert in the field and explains not only the facts, but 'the passion and excitement associated with research at the frontiers of this fascinating field'. Recent developments in critical issues such as earthquake prediction, seismic hazard assessment, and ground motion prediction are addressed.
'A reader with no background in earth science or seismology can easily absorb the material presented... . Hough's writing style is easy and engaging, and she makes the subject matter entertaining.' (*American Scientist*)
'Fascinating and clearly written' (*London Review of Books*)

1079 Introduction to geomagnetic fields
W.H. Campbell 2nd edn, Cambridge University Press, 2003, 337pp. £33.00. ISBN 0521529530.
Focuses on the basic concepts and physical processes necessary for understanding the earth's natural magnetic fields. Appendix B is an extensive review: Geomagnetic organizations, services, and bibliography.

1080 Introduction to seismology, earthquakes, and earth structure
S. Stein and M. Wysession Blackwell, 2002, 512pp. £39.99. ISBN 0865420785.
Written for advanced undergraduate and beginning graduate students. Introduces the necessary mathematical tools with numerous examples. Extensive bibliography.
'This outstanding book is without equal.' (*Choice*)

1081 The little book of earthquakes and volcanoes
R. Schick Copernicus Books, 2002, 164pp. £15.50. ISBN 038795287X.
General introduction to the topic, demonstrating how earthquakes and volcanoes are related, and what part they play in the Earth's structure. Contents: The dynamic earth; The view of ancients; Great earthquakes in history; Great volcanoes in history; The ring of fire; Current tectonic theory; Monitoring volcanoes; Predicting earthquakes; Earth's hotspots. Light, accessible text. General readership.
Originally published in German (1997, Verlag C.H. Beck oHG, München, Germany).

1082 Living on an active earth: perspectives on earthquake science
National Academies Press, 2003.
http://dels.nas.edu
Describes the growth and origins of earthquake science and identifies research and data collection efforts that will strengthen the scientific and social contributions of the new discipline of earthquake science.
Produced by the former Committee on the Science of Earthquakes within the Board on Earth Sciences and Resources, which is part of the Earth & Life Studies Division of the NATIONAL ACADEMIES.
'For anyone professionally involved in seismology, this book is to be recommended as a top-rank synopsis of the state-of-the-art of practically the whole discipline as it stands at the start of the new century.' (*Times Higher Education Supplement*)

1083 Solid earth: an introduction to global geophysics
C.M.R. Fowler 2nd edn, Cambridge University Press, 2004, 472pp. £32.99. ISBN 0521893070.
An essential student textbook. This fully updated edition introduces the study of modern physics of the solid earth to students and geologists. Ten chapters each with appended 'problems and bibliography': 1. Introduction; 2. Tectonics on a sphere: the geometry of plate tectonics; 3. Past plate motions; 4. Seismology: measuring the interior; 5. Gravity; 6. Geochronology; 7. Heat; 8. The deep interior of the earth; 9. The oceanic lithosphere: ridges, transforms, trenches and oceanic islands; 10. The continental lithosphere; Appendices; Glossary; Index.
Previous edn 1990.

Statistics for petroleum engineers and geoscientists
J.L. Jensen [et al.] See entry no. 4741

Dictionaries, thesauri, classifications

Dictionary of geophysics, astrophysics and astronomy
R.A. Matzner, ed. See entry no. 709

1084 Earthquake image glossary
US Geological Survey
http://earthquake.usgs.gov/image_glossary
Illustrated A–Z glossary of earthquake terminology covering most aspects of earthquake phenomena including seismology, geophysics and structural geology. Many diagrams used to illustrate definitions.

1085 Gravity/Magnetic Glossary
Integrated Geophysics Corporation.
www.igcworld.com/gm_glos.html
A useful short A–Z index of terms used in gravity and magnetic fields of research. Some 50 entries intended for readers not confident with potential fields terminology.

Official & quasi-official bodies

1086 International Union of Geodesy and Geophysics
www.iugg.org
Non-governmental scientific organization dedicated to promoting and co-ordinating studies of the earth (physical, chemical, and mathematical) and its environment in space.

One of 25 Scientific Unions within the INTERNATIONAL COUNCIL FOR SCIENCE (ICSU). Composed of seven semi-autonomous associations, each responsible for a specific range of topics or themes. Relatively up-to-date website with access to each association, publications and a wide-ranging list of Links to Associated Bodies.

- **International Association of Seismology and Physics of the Earth's Interior** www.iaspei.org. Aim is to promote and co-ordinate the study of earthquakes, seismic waves, and the internal structure, properties and processes of the earth. Up-to-date web page with links to further resources.

Research centres & institutes

1087 Incorporated Research Institutions for Seismology [USA]
www.iris.washington.edu
A university research consortium which collects and distributes seismographic data. Links to publications, earthquake data and current news, as well as to acronyms and vocabulary definitions. Education & Outreach programme.

Associations & societies

1088 American Geophysical Union
www.agu.org
'A worldwide scientific community that advances, through unselfish cooperation in research, the understanding of Earth and space for the benefit of humanity.'

Promotes the organization and dissemination of information in a range of fields, including: atmospheric and ocean sciences; solid-earth sciences; hydrologic sciences; and space science. Provides information for the public on what is known about the earth and how the geophysical sciences are advancing. More than 35,000 members in over 115 countries. Website links to events, publications, news in related fields.

- **EOS** Weekly. ISSN 00963941. www.agu.org/pubs/eos.html [DESCRIPTION]. Articles on current research and on the relationship of geophysics to social and political questions, news, book reviews, AGU journal and meeting abstracts, meeting programmes and reports, a comprehensive meetings calendar, etc.
- **Geophysical Monograph Series** www.agu.org/pubs/book_series.html#gm [DESCRIPTION]. Well regarded series, classified as individual monographs, comprising compilations of papers on a single topic. Frequently multi-disciplinary. Of primary interest to researchers, teachers, and graduate students.

1089 Canadian Geophysical Union
www.cgu-ugc.ca
Focuses on all aspects of the physical study of Earth and its space environment. Information on Annual Meetings provided on website. Links to specialist websites, especially conferences, are also provided.

Earthquake Engineering Research Institute
See entry no. 5191

1090 Environmental and Engineering Geophysical Society [USA]
www.eegs.org
Formed in 1992 to promote geophysics, especially as applied to environmental and engineering problems. Main activities are its annual meeting, distributing a peer-reviewed scientific journal, and quarterly newsletter. Publishes, markets and distributes books and CD-ROMs on the application and use of geophysical technologies. Links to Australian and European societies available from this website.

European Geosciences Union
See entry no. 849

1091 Seismological Society of America
www.seismosoc.org
Scientific society devoted to the advancement of earthquake science, founded in 1906 in San Francisco. Index to *Bulletin of the Seismological Society of America*, a major publication by the society, available on the website. Information about meetings, publications and education. Many further links to other sites of interest to seismologists.

1092 Society for Exploration Geophysicists
www.seg.org
More than 20,000 members working in 110 countries in a not-for-profit society to educate and promote geophysics. Encourages development of new technologies. The SEG Geoscience Center comprises: the Museum of Geophysical Exploration at the Geophysical Resource Center (GRC) in Tulsa, Oklahoma; Virtual Museum (www.mssu.edu/seg-vm); Travelling Museum, taken to professional meetings, schools, etc.

Digital Cumulative Index (32,000+ entries from 1936 to March 2003) of publications of SEG, the European Association of Geoscientists (EAGE), the Australian Society of Exploration Geophysicists (ASEG) and the Canadian Society of Exploration Geophysicists (CSEG). Much else on this rich site.

Society of Exploration Geophysicists
See entry no. 4686

Society of Petrophysicists and Well Log Analysts
See entry no. 4757

Libraries, archives, museums

National Information Service For Earthquake Engineering
See entry no. 5204

Portal & task environments

1093 Advanced National Seismic System
Northern California Earthquake Data Center
http://quake.geo.berkeley.edu/cnss
Worldwide earthquake catalogue created by merging earthquake catalogues from contributing ANSS institutions. A useful resource. Previously called the CNSS Earthquake Catalog. Consists of earthquake hypocenters, origin times, and magnitudes. Information on current earthquakes. Weekly maps of global earthquake activity. Links to more regional data.

1094 **Earthquakes**
British Geological Survey
www.earthquakes.bgs.ac.uk
A well organized and useful gateway. Covers a broad spectrum of research and information services concerned with earthquakes and man-made seismic disturbances. Attractive web page with links including recent events, hazards, monitoring, environment and archives. Link to the UK Seismicity Database. Many other data and reference links provided.

1095 **National Earthquake Information Center** [USA]
http://neic.usgs.gov
An extensive, global seismic database on earthquakes providing real-time information about seismic activity around the globe. Operates a 24-hour-a-day service to ensure accurate information. Continually updated. Fact sheets, information services, data, links to global catalogues. Easy-to-use web interface. Recommended by academics in the field.

1096 **National Geophysical Data Center** [USA]
www.ngdc.noaa.gov/ngdc
Links to data and information, educational resources and very wide range of geophysical datasets describing the solid earth, marine, and solar-terrestrial environment, as well as earth observations from space. Accessible website, links to data, easily navigable. More than 300 digital and analog databases. Much of the material advertised is available for purchase.

- **World Data Center System: WDC National Geophysical Data Center**. www.ngdc.noaa.gov/wdc. Originated in 1957–8 International Geophysical Year but now includes 52 Centers in 12 countries. Holdings include a wide range of solar, geophysical, environmental, and human dimensions data. These data cover timescales ranging from seconds to millennia.

Discovering print & electronic resources

1097 **Quakeline**
Multidisciplinary Center for Earthquake Engineering Research
http://mceer.buffalo.edu/utilities/quakeline.asp
Started in 1987, a bibliographic database covering earthquakes, earthquake engineering, natural hazard mitigation, and related topics. It includes about 40,000 records for journal articles, conference papers, technical reports, maps, and videotapes. The MCEER Information Service possesses copies of all documents cited in the database; it will either loan or photocopy requested material, and may provide recommendations for where to purchase materials directly.

Directories & encyclopedias

1098 **Encyclopedia of earthquakes and volcanoes**
D. Ritchie and A.E. Gates Checkmark Books, 2001, 306pp. $18.95. ISBN 0816045836.
Useful overview from the *Facts On File Science Library*. Explains the specific terms and concepts associated with seismology and volcanology (A–Z listing of c.800 terms), and covers the places of the world where earthquakes and volcanoes have occurred, giving names of individual volcanoes and chronology of earthquakes and eruptions. Short biographies of scientists working in the field. For school and public libraries.

Encyclopedia of planetary sciences
J.H. Shirley and R.W. Fairbridge, eds See entry no. 744

1099 **The encyclopedia of solid earth geophysics**
D.E. James, ed. Springer, 1989, 1328pp. Originally published Van Nostrand Reinhold, £384.00. ISBN 0442243669.
www.eseo.com [FEE-BASED]
A comprehensive reference source comprising 160 articles, arranged A–Z covering seismology, gravity, geodesy, tectonophysics, geomagnetism and related subjects. Short bibliographies and cross-referenced list of related entries. Subject and author citation indexes. Aimed at both the academic and layperson.
Accessible online: see website.

- **International Association of Geomagnetism and Aeronomy** www.iugg.org/IAGA. 'The premier international scientific association promoting the study of terrestrial and planetary magnetism and space physics'. Member of the INTERNATIONAL UNION OF GEODESY AND GEOPHYSICS.

1100 **Encyclopedic dictionary of applied geophysics**
R.E. Sheriff; Society of Exploration Geophysicists 4th edn, 2002, 429pp. CD-ROM, $75.00. ISBN 1560801182.
Comprehensive update of the 1991 edition incorporating new developments in the field, e.g. routine use of seismic data. This is an especially important resource describing the major advances in applied geophysics during the 1990s. The entries cover terms from 'a' (the SI symbol for year) to 'z-transform' (for representing time series). Includes excerpts from the preface to the first edition and supporting reference tables and figures (some in colour). Appendices include material on units and symbols; geological time; and the Prem model for spherically symmetric earth. Cross-references. It provides the standard for terms specific to geophysical technology and contains the preferred (SI) units and abbreviations for units.

1101 **Geophysical Directory**
59th edn, The Geophysical Directory, Inc., 2004, Annual. $125.00.
www.informationservices.com [DESCRIPTION]
Lists over 7000 companies providing geophysical equipment, supplies of services, plus mining and petroleum companies using geophysical techniques, as well as over 18,000 geophysicists and geologists involved with geophysical operations. Company name cross-reference section. Separate listings of the activities of national and international geophysical societies.

Handbooks & manuals

1102 **Advances in seismic event location**
C.H. Thurber and N. Rabinowitz, eds Kluwer Academic Publishers, 2000, 266pp. £67.00. ISBN 0792363922.
Essential information for academic and professional researchers and graduate students in seismology. An overview of the primary issues involved in seismic event location. Includes: seismic monitoring for a Comprehensive Nuclear-Test-Ban Treaty (CTBT); seismic event location in three-dimensional Earth models; methods for multiple-event location. Many references.
Series: Modern Approaches in Geophysics, V. 18.

1103 **Earthquakes**
B.A. Bolt 5th edn, W H Freeman, 2003, 378pp. $40.95. ISBN 0716756188.
www.whfreeman.com/earthquakes [COMPANION]
Essential reference tool for those with an interest in earthquake research. The companion website has chapter by chapter links to electronic instructional and learning tools. Further links to related resources. Text provides an overview of topics: geologic faults, intensity patterns, plate tectonics, side effects of earthquakes, and protection of people and property. Contains descriptions of the 1995 Sakhalin and 1997 Assisi earthquakes, as well as those at Northridge, California (1994), Kobe, Japan (1995), Chi Chi, Taiwan (1999) and Denali, Alaska (2003). Many graphs, diagrams and photographs.

1104 **Field geophysics**
J. Milsom 3rd edn, Wiley, 2003, 244pp. $40.00. ISBN 0470843470.
The emphasis in this useful handbook is on the practical applications for those involved in small-scale geophysical surveying. Useful for students and professionals alike. New sections on: use of hand-held GPS receivers, and Controlled Source Audiomagnetotellurics (CSAMT). Provides guidance on use of field instruments.
Series: Geological Field Guides

1105 **Fundamentals of geophysics**
W. Lowrie Cambridge University Press, 1997, 368pp. £30.00. ISBN 0521467284.
A comprehensive overview of the main areas of study of theoretical and applied geophysics. As a result it is especially useful for intermediate-level earth science students. Contents: 1. The earth as a planet; 2. Gravity and the figure of the earth; 3. Seismology and the internal structure of the earth; 4. Earth's age, geothermal and electrical properties; 5. Geomagnetism and paleomagnetism; 6. Geodynamics; Bibliography (pp 341–6).

1106 **International handbook of earthquake and engineering seismology**
W.K.H. Lee [et al.], eds Academic Press, 2002–2003. Part A: ISBN 0124406521; Part B: ISBN 0124406580. Two CD-ROMs containing additional material packaged with the text, $300.00.
A comprehensive overview of current knowledge of earthquakes and seismology; an authoritative reference work. Part A has sections covering: History of seismology; Theoretical and observational seismology; Earthquake geology and mechanics; Seismicity of the earth and earth's structure. Part B, with contributions from more than 100 leading researchers, features 34 chapters detailing strong-motion seismology, earthquake engineering, quake prediction and hazards mitigation, as well as detailed reports from more than 40 nations. Includes practical resources for seismologists, a compilation of earthquake catalogues around the world, a global earthquake database with search and display software, selected software for earthquake and engineering seismology, and digital imagery of faults, earthquakes, volcanoes and their effects. Technical glossary. Subject index; Author index.
Series: International Geophysics, V. 81 A/B.

1107 **Introduction to geophysical exploration**
P. Kearey, M. Brooks and I. Hill 3rd edn, Blackwell Science, 2002, 288pp. £29.99. ISBN 0632049294.
Comprehensive introduction to key, important methods and techniques of geophysical exploration. Methods are a primary tool for investigation of the subsurface and applicable to a wide range of problems. This new edition reflects important developments in geophysical methods. Extensively revised figures. Systematic description of major geophysical methods dealing with theory and then the practicalities and interpretation. Case histories used extensively. Relatively simple mathematics required in order to understand the text. Suitable for undergraduates, but of use to postgraduates and professionals.

1108 **The mechanics of earthquakes and faulting**
C.H. Scholz 2nd edn, Cambridge University Press, 2002, 471pp. £33.00. ISBN 0521655404.
Well revised second edition, covering all the major advances in fault analysis research. Two predominant themes: the connection between fault and earthquake mechanics, and the central role of the rate-state friction laws in earthquake mechanics. Especially useful for postgraduates and researchers; 219 line diagrams, 9 colour plates. References (pp 415–67); Index.
Previous edn 1990.

1109 **Petroleum geoscience**
J. Gluyas and R.E. Swarbrick Blackwell Publishing, 2003, 376pp. £37.50. ISBN 0632037679.
A comprehensive introduction to the application of geology and geophysics to the search for and production of oil and gas. Chapters on the sequential and cyclical processes of exploration, appraisal, development and production are illustrated by many case histories from around the world and from petroleum systems ranging in age from late-Pre-Cambrian to Pliocene. A practical guide. Covers all the key aspects of the subject. Important in its field. Many line diagrams. References (pp 337–49). Undergraduate and postgraduate in focus.

1110 **The rock physics handbook: tools for seismic analysis in porous media**
G. Mavko, T. Mukerji and J. Dvorkin Cambridge University Press, 2003, 339pp. £26.00. ISBN 0521543444.
Brings together both theoretical and empirical relations that form the foundations of rock physics. Special emphasis on seismic properties. Includes commonly used models and relations for electrical and dielectric rock properties; 76 articles. Topics summarize wave propagation, AVO-AVOZ, effective media, poro-elasticity, diffusion and more. Useful empirical results on reservoir rocks and sediments, granular media, tables of mineral data, and an atlas of reservoir rock properties. Useful to the geophysicist practitioner as well as to the researcher. Postgraduate in focus.
Series: Stanford-Cambridge Program.
'... an invaluable single volume reference of material otherwise widely scattered in the literature.' (Mineral Planning)

1111 **Seismic data analysis: processing, inversion, and interpretation of seismic data**
O. Yilmaz and S.M. Doherty; Society of Exploration Geophysicists 2001, 2027pp. 2 v., $289.00. ISBN 1560800941.
A comprehensive, authoritative reference work with complete coverage of the modern trends in the seismic industry – from time to depth, from 3-D to 4-D, from 4-D to 4-C, and from isotropy to anisotropy. Revised from the 1987 volume to include inversion and interpretation of seismic data. Bibliographies.
Series: Investigations in Geophysics, No. 10.

Keeping up-to-date

1112 **Advances in Geophysics**
Academic Press, 1952–, Irregular. $140.00 [2003, V. 46]. ISBN 0120188465.
An important serialized review journal in publication for the last 50 years. Useful for keeping students and researchers up to date in this and related fields. Contents of the most recent volume (46): 1.Mountain building, erosion and seismic cycle in the Nepal Himalaya; 2. Seismic traveltime tomography of the crust and lithosphere; 3. Assembly of Pangea: combined paleomagnetic and paleoclimatic approach; 4. Characteristics of dense nests of deep and intermediate-depth seismicity.

1113 **Earth Almanac: an annual geophysical review of the state of the planet**
N. Goldstein 2nd edn, Oryx Press, 2001, 568pp., $73.95. ISBN 1573564524.
Reference resource which documents recent changes in the atmosphere, oceans, fresh water, and land. Basic processes are reviewed, research summarized, and necessary background statistics provided. Recommended for public and academic libraries. More than 300 photos, charts, and statistical graphs. Appendices: I. Selected treaties and laws; II. Selected international and national scientific programs. Glossary, formulas, abbreviations. Geologic timeline and earth facts section. Index.
This is the latest edn, December 2004
'This is a very useful book a veritable treasure trove for the lecturer and researcher and I have no doubt it will be required reading from now on.' (*Teaching Earth Sciences*)

1114 **Geophysics**
Society of Exploration Geophysicists 1939–, Bimonthly. ISSN 00168033.
http://scitation.aip.org/geophysics [FEE-BASED]
A bimonthly technical publication. Subscription or membership required for full-text access or print copy. Subscribers to *Geophysics* also get copies of the monthly companion print journal *The Leading Edge*: 'The Society's non-technical, non-mathematical, editorial-style magazine. It contains a stimulating mix of geophysics and other earth sciences, along with the latest exploration news'.

Geophysics covers research in petroleum, mining, geothermal, groundwater, environmental and engineering geophysics. Website provides contents lists and abstracts, and subscription details. Individual articles may be purchased online. The web-based Geophysics Online supplements *Geophysics* itself by providing prepublication details of accepted papers: see www.geo-online.org.

Hydrology

floods • forest hydrology • freshwater • groundwater • hydrogeology • ice • permafrost • snow • water • water policy • water resources • water supply • watersheds

Introductions to the subject

1115 **Fundamentals of ground water**
F.W. Schwartz and H. Zhang Wiley, 2003, 583pp. $119.95. ISBN 0471137855.
http://jws-edcv.wiley.com/college [COMPANION]
Wide-ranging coverage in 24 chapters. Covers both theoretical and practical aspects with good use of computing techniques.

1116 **Fundamentals of hydrology**
T. Davie Routledge, 2003, 169pp. £19.99. ISBN 0415220297.
Good basic introduction: 1. Hydrology as a science; 2. Precipitation; 3. Evaporation; 4. Interception; 5. Storage; 6. Runoff; 7. Streamflow analysis; 8. Water quality; 9. Hydrology in a changing world.
Series: Fundamentals of Physical Geography.

Global environment: water, air and geochemical cycles
E. K. Berner and R. A. Berner See entry no. 2297

1117 **Groundwater management: the search for practical approaches**
Food and Agriculture Organization and United Nations Educational, Scientific and Cultural Organization 2003, 51pp. £12.50. ISBN 9251049084 ISSN 10201203.
www.fao.org/waicent [DESCRIPTION]
Concise but wide-ranging cross-institutional overview in useful series. Good use of examples and case studies. Raises issues on limits to what achievable in practice.
Series: Water Reports, 25.

1118 **Groundwater science**
C.R. Fitts Academic Press, 2002, 461pp. $83.95. ISBN 0122578554.
www.academicpress.com/groundwater [COMPANION]
Excellent coverage. Ten chapters: Groundwater: the big picture; Physical properties; Principles of flow; Geology and groundwater flow; Deformation, storage, and general flow equations; Modelling steady flow with basic methods; Modelling transient flow with basic methods; Computer-assisted flow modelling; Groundwater chemistry; Groundwater contamination.

1119 **The hydrology of the UK: a study of change**
M. Acreman, ed.; British Hydrological Society Routledge, 2000, 303pp. £22.99. ISBN 0415187613.
Useful background text looking at the environment for hydrological change in the UK, its particular impacts on water stocks and availabilities, the responses of official bodies to the need for better water management.

1120 **Introducing groundwater**
M. Price 2nd edn, Stanley Thornes, 1998, 278pp. £21.99. ISBN 0748743715.
Written to be accessible to those with no previous background in the subject, keeping technical terms to a

minimum and explaining them where they are used. Good for school and college use.

1121 **An introduction to water quality in rivers, coastal waters and estuaries**
D. Hammerton; Chartered Institution of Water and Environmental Management 1997, 89pp. £11.62. ISBN 1870752279.
Covers biological assessment of water quality in Great Britain but water pollution across Europe.
Series: CIWEM Booklets, 5.

1122 **Physical hydrology**
S.L. Dingman 2nd edn, Prentice Hall, 2001, 656pp. $103.00. ISBN 0130996955.
http://wps.prenhall.com/esm_dingman_hydrology_2new [COMPANION]
Wide-ranging coverage with the 1st edn having been very well reviewed. Ten chapters: Introduction to hydrologic science; Basic hydrologic concepts; Climate, the hydrologic cycle, soils and vegetation: a global overview; Precipitation; Snow and snowmelt; Water in soils: infiltration and redistribution; Evapotranspiration; Ground water in the hydrological cycle; Stream response to water-input events; Hydrology and water-resource management. Useful appendices include: Basic statistics; Hydrological information sources on the internet.
1st edn Macmillan 1994.

1123 **Principles of water resources: history, development, management, and policy**
T.V. Cech Wiley, 2002, 468pp. $93.95. ISBN 0471438618.
Straightforward text covering the basics of hydrology and then moving on to the specific characteristics of groundwater, lakes, rivers, etc. and the challenges in water management. US focus.

Water resources engineering
L.W. Mays See entry no. 5534

1124 **Water supply**
A.C. Twort, D.D. Ratnayaka and M.J. Brandt, eds 5th edn, Arnold, 2000, 676pp. £52.50. ISBN 0340720182.
A widely used and classic text. This edition significantly expanded. Contains coverage of WHO, European, UK and US standards and guidelines. 15 chapters cover all aspects of water supply, from surface and groundwater sources, to storage, disinfection, and distribution.
1st edn Arnold 1963 as A textbook of water supply, *authored by Twort alone. Since then authors and publishers have varied. Last edn 1994.*

Dictionaries, thesauri, classifications

Computational hydraulics and hydrology: an illustrated dictionary
N.G. Adrien, comp. See entry no. 5157

Dictionary of water and waste management
P.G. Smith and J.S. Scott, comps See entry no. 5540

Dictionary of water engineering
K.D. Nelson, C. Kerr and R. Legg See entry no. 5541

A dictionary of weather
S. Dunlop See entry no. 1174

1125 **Elsevier's dictionary of hydrology and water quality management: in five languages English, French, Spanish, Dutch and German**
J.D. van der Tuin, comp. Elsevier, 1991, 540pp. £130.50. ISBN 0444886729.
Translation from fuller English entries to the other languages. There are indices from each of the other languages. Covers water resources management and the freshwater environment, especially quality and environmental concerns, including international aspects.
Elsevier also publish: Tuin, J. D. Van der Elsevier's dictionary of water and hydraulic engineering in five languages, *1987, ISBN 0444427686; Pfannkuch, H.-O.* Elsevier's dictionary of environmental hydrogeology in English, French and German, *1990. ISBN 0444872698; Zilberberg, L.-J.* Elsevier's dictionary of marine pollution, *1998. ISBN 0444500677.*

ICID multilingual technical dictionary on irrigation and drainage
International Commission on Irrigation and Drainage See entry no. 5162

1126 **International glossary of hydrology (Glossaire international d'hydrologie)**
P.J.Y. Hubert; United Nations Educational, Scientific and Cultural Organization and World Meteorological Organization 2nd edn, 1992, 422pp. ISBN 9230027456.
www.cig.ensmp.fr/~hubert/glu/aglo.htm
Web edition includes 13 languages: for some languages you need a UNICODE implementation. Arranged clearly in subject groupings such as surface hydrology, snow and ice. Definitions are brief but there are see-also links too. Printed edition is in English, French, Russian and Spanish and has definitions, alphabetical indexes and classifications for hydrology in all four languages.

- **Lexique de l'eau: en 6 langues: Français, Anglais, Allemand, Italien, Espagnol, Portugais** Editions Johanet, 2001, 788pp. ISBN 2900086736. www.editions-johanet.com. Includes CD-ROM. See website for details of the publisher's 'set of publications and periodicals specialising in the domain of water, waste and the environment'.

1127 **Terminology of water supply and environmental sanitation (Terminologie de l'approvisionnement en eau et de l'assainissement du milieu)**
P.J. Biron; World Bank and UNICEF 1987, 176pp. £15.50. ISBN 0821305859.
English–French, French–English word list with no definitions. Old but not superseded. Useful annex covers origin and transmission of diseases related to deficiencies in water supply and/or sanitation.

Laws, standards, codes

1128 **Water Policy in the European Union**
European Commission. Directorate for Environment
http://europa.eu.int/comm/environment/water
Useful frequently updated site, bringing together the different pieces of water legislation (and related policies) in the European Community related to the delivery of clean water and prevention of water pollution.

Official & quasi-official bodies

1129 **Global International Waters Assessment**
www.giwa.net/index.phtml
Established 'to produce a comprehensive and integrated global assessment of international waters, the ecological status of and the causes of environmental problems in 66 water areas in the world, and focus on the key issues and problems facing the aquatic environment in transboundary waters'. Good explanations of the rationale for the body's existence; excellent access to data on the nine megaregions, 66 subregions; very useful links section Global Water Links providing descriptions of the relatives roles of all the organizations involved worldwide in water matters: UN agencies; Other international organizations; Global conventions, agreements and declarations; Action programmes and initiatives; Research institutes; Networks, NGOs and dedicated water information directories. A good place to start research in this politically sensitive arena.

International Commission on Irrigation and Drainage
See entry no. 5172

1130 **International Office for Water** [FRA]
www.oieau.fr/anglais/index.htm
Non-profit-making Association under the French Law formed in 1991. Objective is 'to gather public and private partners involved in water resources management and protection in France, Europe and in the world'. Now comprises 149 member organizations. Access to very wide range of resources – data banks, international networks, research institutions, commercial companies, etc. News service; events; documentation service. French emphasis – with significant proportions of the content and linked sites in French; but much of value from elsewhere.

- **International Association of Hydrological Sciences** http://iahs.info. Objective is 'to promote the study of Hydrology as an aspect of the earth sciences and of water resources'. Good range of resources including useful range of links (wherein there is a list of 'Others IAHS').
- **Water for life: water management and environmental policy** **J.L. Wescoat and G.F. White** Cambridge University Press, 2003, 322pp. £27.00. ISBN 0521369800.. a concise and erudite primer aimed at helping hydrologists and environmental managers to find a common language to talk about policymaking for rivers, lakes, wetlands and underground water reserves. *Times Higher Education Supplement*.

Office of Ground Water and Drinking Water
Environmental Protection Agency See entry no. 5557

1131 **Office of Water** [USA]
www.epa.gov/OW
Excellent overview of the water-related activities of the US Environmental Protection Agency including coverage of the Agency's Strategic Plan for 2004–8, organized around five key goals: Clean air and global climate change; Clean and safe water; Land preservation and restoration; Healthy communities and ecosystems; Compliance and environmental stewardship.

- **Watershed Information Network** www.epa.gov/win. Useful gateway to range of resources on watersheds – defined as 'the area that drains to a common waterway, such as a stream, lake, estuary, wetland, or ultimately the ocean'. Access to extensive Watershed Tools Directory.

1132 **Water Resources of the United States**
US Geological Survey
http://water.usgs.gov
The key site for information about the water resources of the USA. Provides extensive sets of data, both real time and historical, on surface water, ground water and water quality, including information about the sites where the data is collected; maps in the form of satellite images and photographs dating back to the 1930s; and free applications software for ground water, surface water, geochemical and general use, statistics and graphics.

There is a series of *Water Resources Glossaries* covering: Water basics; Hydrologic definitions; Water science; National water quality assessment; Water-quality monitoring; Water resources data. Also lists of its own and some major international research projects, as well as of recent *Water Supply Papers*, and other water related publications. Good links to other organizations.

- **National Water-Quality Assessment Program: NAWQA** **US Geological Survey**. http://water.usgs.gov/nawqa. 'Since 1991, USGS scientists have been collecting and analyzing data and information in more than 50 major river basins and aquifers across the Nation ... to support sound management and policy decisions'.

Research centres & institutes

Centre for Ecology and Hydrology
See entry no. 2318

International Water Management Institute
See entry no. 2985

1133 **National Snow and Ice Data Center**
http://eosims.colorado.edu
Established as a 'national information and referral center in support of polar and cryospheric research, NSIDC archives and distributes digital and analog snow and ice data. We also maintain information about snow cover, avalanches, glaciers, ice sheets, freshwater ice, sea ice, ground ice, permafrost, atmospheric ice, paleoglaciology, and ice cores.' Provides an impressive range of products and services in a welcoming user-friendly fashion. The Cryosphere is an especially good set of pages aimed at the non-scientist. An excellent service.

- **Permafrost: a guide to frozen ground in transition** **N. Davis** University of Alaska Press, 2001, 352pp. $35.95. ISBN 1889963194. 'Outstanding introductory book on seasonally frozen ground and permafrost for a broad audience; also an excellent reference book for students, permafrost scientists and engineers, and professionals.' *Arctic, Antarctic, and Alpine Research*.

The UK Environmental Change Network
Centre for Ecology and Hydrology and Natural Environment Research Council See entry no. 2324

Associations & societies

1134 **American Institute of Hydrology**
www.aihydro.org
Society for certification and registration of professional hydrologists concerned especially with standards of professional conduct and public service: details about activities in these areas. Downloadable PDF *Bulletin* (Fall

2004, 12 pp). Good set of links to other US organizations and less extensively to international ones.

1135 **British Hydrological Society**
www.hydrology.org.uk
Simple site with emphasis on education, training events and employment.

- **Chronology of British hydrological events F.M. Law [et al.], comps.** www.dundee.ac.uk/geography/cbhe. 'Attempt to bring into searchable view on the Web as much material as possible so that the spatial extent of events, and their relative severity, can be assessed.' Concentrates on text rather than data; is restricted to Great Britain; only covers to 1933.

Chartered Institution of Water and Environmental Management
See entry no. 5569

Freshwater Biological Association
See entry no. 2590

1136 **Global Water Partnership**
www.gwpforum.org/servlet/PSP
A working partnership among all those involved in water management, GWP's mission is to 'support countries in the sustainable management of their water resources', identifying critical knowledge needs and designing programmes to meet them. Site contains an information toolbox to assist users in the design of policy packages, with supporting references and organizations.

1137 **International Water Association**
www.iwahq.org.uk
Founded in 1999 by the merger of the International Association of Water Quality and the International Water Supply Association. Large number of Specialist Groups within five broad areas: Drinking water, wastewater and solid waste treatment processes (e.g. Anaerobic digestion; Odours and volatile emissions; Sludge management); Education, health, management and training (e.g. Hydroinformatics); Network management (e.g. Biofouling and biocorrosion); Source management (e.g. Groundwater remediation); Water quality management (e.g. Eutrophication; Urban drainage). Some of the information produced by the Groups is accessible only to IWA members.

Organizes and supports a range of conferences and publishes their proceedings, books and reports. *Water21* is a useful bimonthly newsletter which also provides access to an online directory of water industry products and services. Although much good content here is freely accessible, much else is fee-based accessible only to members.

1138 **National Ground Water Association** [USA]
www.ngwa.org
Founded in 1948 as the National Water Well Association; now has 15,000 members. Good Consumer Corner, the Association feeling it 'important to keep the owners and prospective buyers of private water systems up to date on the latest information about those systems, ground water, and ways to protect this valuable natural resource. After all, more than 76 billion gallons of ground water is withdrawn in the United States every day.' Very extensive links section with strong commercial content. Publications – including the fee-based Ground Water On-Line: a database containing over 90,000 citations with keywords, abstracts, chemical compounds, biological factors, geographic locations, etc.

Universities Council on Water Resources
See entry no. 5573

1139 **World Water Council**
www.worldwatercouncil.org
'The International Water Policy Think Tank dedicated to strengthening the world water movement for an improved management of the world's water resources and water services. Membership comprises 'more than 300 members including public and private sectors, NGO's, UN agencies; a unique network representing over 50 countries ... The Council is financed primarily through membership fees and the support provided by the hosting City of Marseilles. Specific projects and programs are financed through donations and grants from governments, international organizations and NGOs.'

- **World water actions: making water flow for all F. Guerquin; World Water Council** Earthscan, 2003, 208pp. £25.00. ISBN 1844070786. 'Provides a review of over 3000 initiatives in every field of water management and affecting all stakeholders. It clearly demonstrates that the World Water Movement envisioned by the World Water Council is well underway.' Includes CD-ROM.

Libraries, archives, museums

1140 **Water Resources Center Archives: everything but the water ...**
University of California, Berkeley
www.lib.berkeley.edu/WRCA
Founded 1957 and 'collects, preserves and provides access to historical and contemporary water-related materials that support the instructional and research programs of the University of California and the needs of the people of the State'. Collection has emphasis on freshwater quality, supply and development, wastewater treatment, wetlands and estuaries, climate, and coastal zone management. Materials cover a broad spectrum of municipal, industrial, agricultural, environmental, biological and engineering issues. Well laid-out site. Extensive set of listings of internet resources.

Portal & task environments

Foundation for Water Research
See entry no. 5577

Water
European Environment Agency See entry no. 5579

1141 **The Water Portal**
United Nations Educational, Scientific and Cultural Organization
www.unesco.org/water
This site is 'intended to enhance access to information related to freshwater available on the World Wide Web'. Designed to encourage the sharing of facts and experience by water-related organizations, government bodies and NGOs, with users invited to provide information on activities, useful links, news, content etc. Good entrée particularly to official international work in this arena. Two especially useful facilities are searchable listings of worldwide Water Events

and Water Links. A weekly e-mailed Newsletter provides the latest news, events and links added to the Portal.

- **International Hydrological Programme** www.unesco.org/water/ihp/index.shtml. UNESCO's intergovernmental scientific programme in water resources. Provides access to series of databases including a group concerned with World Water Resources and their Use which includes data on discharge of selected rivers of the world.
- **World water resources at the beginning of the 21st century I.A. Shiklomanov and J.G. Rodda, eds** Cambridge University Press, 2003, 435pp. £50.00. ISBN 0521617227. 'A significant milestone in our knowledge of the world's water resources ... Will doubtless form the major source book of the next decade and deserves to be on the shelves of every university library.' *The Eggs*.

Discovering print & electronic resources

1142 **Geraghty and Miller's groundwater bibliography**
F. Van der Leeden, comp.; Water Information Center 5th edn, CRC Press, 1991, 516pp. $149.95. ISBN 0873716426.
Classic work providing over 5500 references to all aspects of ground water, organized in a detailed classification.

The Ultimate Civil Engineering Directory
See entry no. 5223

1143 **Water Resources Worldwide**
NISC.
www.nisc.com/factsheets/qwrw.asp
Major compilation encompassing four water-resource databases; search uses the *WATERLIT Thesaurus*. Two data sets are current: WATERLIT, over 350,000 references to industrial and environmental aspects of water, wastewater and sanitation, with especially good coverage of Africa; Aquatic Subset of CAB Abstracts, almost 150,000 citations, concentrating particularly on agricultural aspects of water use and management. Two are archival: AQUAREF, 85,000 items focusing on North America; DELFT HYDRO, 60,000 records with emphasis on engineering and technology.

Digital data, image & text collections

1144 **Transboundary Freshwater Dispute Database**
Oregon State University
www.transboundarywaters.orst.edu
Project within the University's Department of Geosciences. Various useful data subsets created in co-operation with a range of partners, most listed as 'work in progress', including: Atlas of International Freshwater Agreements; International Freshwater Treaties Database; Water Conflict and Cooperation Bibliography.

Directories & encyclopedias

1145 **Encyclopedia of hydrology and water resources**
R.W. Herschy and R.W. Fairbridge, eds Kluwer Academic, 1998, 830pp. £306.00. ISBN 0412740605.
www.eseo.com
Straightforward volume (small print, no colour) providing wide-ranging coverage with most of the 300 entries – created by over 100 scientists from 17 countries – having useful bibliographies. Good historical treatment. List of major rivers with latitudes and longitudes. Author and subject indexes.
Available online: see website.

1146 **The encyclopedia of water**
D.E. Newton Greenwood Press, 2003, 417pp. $75.00. ISBN 1573563048.
Good basic reference work: 236 entries in A–Z format covering the cultural context of water and its availability and use, as well as the scientific and technical aspects.

- **Mineralwaters.org P.M. Geiser** www.mineralwaters.org. Interesting personal interest site offering information about and around bottled water. Over 2900 brands from more than 115 countries are presented with their contents.

1147 **Encyclopedia of water science**
B.A. Stewart and T.A. Howell Marcel Dekker, 2003, 950pp. $593.00. ISBN 0824742419.
www.dekker.com
Addresses challenges facing agricultural water engineering in the provision of safe, sanitary and affordable water supplies for the 21st century, including design concepts, methodologies, and solutions for enhanced performance in water quality, treatment, conservation and irrigation methods, as well as improved water efficiency in agricultural programmes.
Available online: see website.

1148 **Water: science and issues**
E.J. Dasch, ed. Macmillan Reference USA, 2003, 1474pp. 4 v, $415.00. ISBN 0028656113.
www.galegroup.com [DESCRIPTION]
Some 300 essays arranged in A–Z order by title. Glossary; subject index.
'displays a breadth and depth of coverage that makes it valuable to both nonspecialists and those knowledgeable about water science and policy ... a first-source reference ... should be contained in the reference section of all libraries.' (*American Reference Books Annual*)

- **UXL encyclopedia of water science** UXL, 2004, 510pp. $165.00. ISBN 0787676179. www.galegroup.com [DESCRIPTION]. Aimed at US reading level grades 7–10. International coverage of lakes, oceans, aquatic animals, climate, glaciers, wetlands, ecology, hydropower, fishing, acid rain, pollution, conservation, international water law, global warming, etc.

1149 **The water encyclopedia**
F. Van der Leeden, F.L. Troise and D.K. Todd, eds 2nd edn, Lewis Publishers, 1990, 820pp. $269.95. ISBN 0873711203.
www.crcpress.com [DESCRIPTION]
Substantially revised and expanded from previous 1970 edn aiming to reflect the shift of awareness of environmental problems, issues of contamination, water treatment and reuse, the projected rise in sea levels. Strong data content – albeit now significantly dated. Wide coverage: Climate and precipitation; Hydrological elements; Surface water; Groundwater; Water use; Water quality; Environmental problems; Water resources management; Agencies and organizations.

Emphasis on USA and Canada with the subject index appearing exhaustive but providing some difficulty in drawing non-US topics together (e.g. there are Australian dams mentioned in tables, but no cross-reference from Australia in the index).
CRC Press have announced a 3rd edn for 2005 of The water encyclopedia: hydrologic data and internet resources.

Handbooks & manuals

1150 **Floods**
D.J. Parker, ed. Routledge, 2000. 2 v., £350.00. ISBN 0415172381.
Major handbook in nine parts: Introduction; Flooding as a human problem; Measuring and evaluating the impacts of floods; Strategies for addressing flood hazards and disasters; Reducing vulnerability by managing residual risk through preparedness, warnings and insurance; Reducing exposure and vulnerability through regulation and other social processes; Examining the physical basis of flooding; Enhancing the predictability of floods; Lessons, directions and future challenges.

1151 **Forest hydrology: an introduction to water and forests**
M. Chang CRC Press, 2003, 387pp. $99.95. ISBN 0849313635.
Forests and forestry management practices can have major effects on the freshwater environment. This is a useful overview filling a gap in the literature of this increasingly important area.

Groundwater chemicals desk reference
J. H. Montgomery See entry no. 5616

1152 **Groundwater hydrology**
D.K. Todd and L.W. Mays 3rd edn, Wiley, 2004, 636pp. (UK version), £34.95. ISBN 0471452548.
Standard text first published 40 years ago, substantially revised for this edn and providing an excellent overview of the whole field from a US perspective. Good treatment of print and electronic resources in the introductory chapter.
2nd edn 1980.

- **Groundwater hydrology: conceptual and computational models** **K.R. Rushton** Wiley, 2003, 430pp. $125.00. ISBN 0470850043. http://eu.wiley.com/WileyCDA [DESCRIPTION]. Valuable manual treating well the difficulties of modelling the complex 3-D hydrologic environment. Provides range of case studies from variety of locations throughout England and Wales.

Handbook of weather, climate, and water
T.D. Potter and B.R. Colman, eds See entry no. 1250

Measuring the natural environment
I. Strangeways See entry no. 1253

1153 **Palaeohydrology: understanding global change**
K.J. Gregory and G. Benito Wiley, 2003, 396pp. $185.00. ISBN 0470847395.
22 chapters – the word 'palaeohydrology' it appears having first been used in 1954, but now coming into common parlance: representative of a discipline very much wrapped up with concerns about global climate change. The volume summarizes developments in global continental palaeohydrology research for the period 1991–2002, and provides a useful overview,

1154 **Principles of hydrogeology**
P.F. Hudak 3rd edn, CRC Press, 2004, 248pp. $79.95. ISBN 0849330157.
Useful teaching and reference manual with good coverage of data and reference sources. Glossary, Subject index.
2nd edn 1999.

1155 **Water Resources**
American Society of Civil Engineers
www.asce.org/bookstore/subject.cfm
The Society publishes a wide range and considerable quantity of texts on and related to hydrology: principally on the more applied aspects, but also including a number of more basic treatments. The website provides an excellent listing of the resources currently available, categorized: Dams and hydropower; Hydraulics and hydrology; Irrigation and drainage; Reservoirs and water supply. For each item there is a detailed description of its contents.

1156 **Water Science and Technology Library**
Springer, 1981–.
www.springeronline.com [DESCRIPTION]
Series of over 50 reference books and monographs encompassing 'a wide range of topics dealing with science as well as socio-economic aspects of water, environment, and ecology'. Recent titles include: *Hydrogeophysics* (2004); *Snow and glacier hydrology* (2001); *Artificial neural networks in hydrology* (2000); *Hydrogeology of crystalline rocks* (1999).

Keeping up-to-date

1157 **Water Resources Discussion Lists**
J.R. Makuch; Water Quality Information Center
www.nal.usda.gov/wqic/lists.html
Very useful compendium produced by this centre located within the NATIONAL AGRICULTURAL LIBRARY. November 2004 version briefly described 81 'topical electronic forums where list subscribers may post announcements, participate in discussions and pose and answer questions ... that are primarily concerned with topics related to water resources.' The list excludes many environmentally oriented lists that may periodically address water resource issues.

Meteorology & Climatology

air • atmospheric sciences • aviation meteorology • barometers • bioclimatology • climate change • climatology • clouds • cyclones • El Niño • geoastrophysics • global climate • global warming • greenhouse effect • hurricanes • Kyoto protocol • lightning • ozone layer • storms • tornados • typhoons • weather • weather forecasting • winds

Introductions to the subject

1158 **The atmosphere and ocean: a physical introduction**
N. Wells 2nd edn, Wiley, 1997, 394pp. $75.00. ISBN 0471962163.
Brings together meteorology, atmospheric physics and oceanography. Includes: the Earth within the solar system; composition and physical properties of the ocean and atmosphere; radiation...; water in the atmosphere; global budgets ...; observations ...; the influence of the Earth's rotation on fluid motion; waves and tides; energy transfer in the ocean-atmosphere system; climate variability and predictability. Glossary. General reading. Further reading and references. Figure sources. Appendices. Index. Emphasis on ideas and mechanisms, rather than mathematics. For university libraries.

1159 **Calculating the weather: meteorology in the 20th century**
F. Nebeker Academic Press, 1995, 255pp. $91.95. ISBN 0125151756.
Explains the 'transformation' of meteorology into a 'unified, physics based, highly computational' science. Thirteen chapters: 2. An empirical tradition; 3. A theoretical tradition; 4. A practical tradition; 5. Vilhelm Bjerknes's program; 6. Lewis Fry Richardson; 8... . Inter war period ; 9. Effect of World War II; John von Neumann ... ;10... .numerical meteorology; 12 Unification of meteorology; 13... . limits to weather prediction.
Series: International Geophysics, V. 60.

1160 **Climate: into the 21st century**
W. Burroughs, ed. Cambridge University Press, 2003, 240pp. £24.99. ISBN 0521792029.
Covers climate processes and the challenges posed to the international community by climate change. 1. Our perceptions of climate; 2. The climate system; 3. Impacts of varying climate; 4. Climate for a better society; 5. The century ahead. Appendices: Glossary; Acronyms and abbreviations; Maps; Chemical symbols and conversion factors. Two-page coverage of topics in a magazine-style layout. For school, public and academic libraries.

1161 **The discovery of global warming**
S.R. Weart Harvard University Press, 2004, 228pp. $14.95. ISBN 0674016378.
www.aip.org/history/climate [COMPANION]
'Weart lucidly explains the emerging science, introduces us to the major players, and shows us how the Earth's irreducibly complicated climate system was mirrored by the global scientific community that studied it.' Eight chapters: How could climate change; Discovering a possibility; A delicate system; A visible threat; Public warnings; The erratic beast; Breaking into politics; The discovery confirmed.

The companion website of c.250,000 words is a much more extended 'hypertext history of how scientists came to (partly) understand what people are doing to change the Earth's climate'.

Excellent text and website; great introduction to this contentious field.
'a terrific book ... balanced historically, beautifully written and, not least important, short and to the point.' (*Nature*)

1162 **Fundamentals of weather and climate**
R. McIlveen Nelson Thornes, 1991, 520pp. £31.00. ISBN 0748740791.
'An introduction to the behaviour and mechanisms of the lower atmosphere.' Includes descriptive and technical explanations. Thirteen chapters: 2. Observations; 3... . constitution of the atmosphere; 4. State and climate; 5. Atmospheric thermodynamics; 6. Cloud and precipitation; 7. Atmospheric dynamics; 8. Radiation ... 9. Surface and boundary layer; 10. Smaller-scale weather ... 11. Larger-scale ... Well illustrated. For academic libraries.

Global environment: water, air and geochemical cycles
E. K. Berner and R. A. Berner See entry no. 2297

1163 **Global warming: the complete briefing**
J.T. Houghton 3rd edn, Cambridge University Press, 2004, 351pp. £43.99. ISBN 0071160108.
Updated edition of widely praised introduction. Glossary. Index. Concludes with the quote from Edmund Burke: 'No one made a greater mistake than he who did nothing because he could do so little.'
2nd edn 1997.
'It is difficult to imagine how Houghton's exposition of this complex body of information might be substantially improved upon ... Seldom has such a complex topic been presented with such remarkable simplicity, directness and crystalline clarity ... Houghton's complete briefing is without doubt the best briefing the concerned citizen could hope to find within the pages of a pocketable book.' (*Bulletin of the American Meteorological Society*)

■ **Frozen earth: the once and future story of ice ages** **D. Macdougall** University of California Press, 2004, 267pp. $24.95. ISBN 0520239229. www.ucpress.edu [DESCRIPTION]. 'Offers a perspective on current debates over anthropogenic global warming and should be required reading for anyone interested in the future of the planet.' (*Times Higher Education Supplement*).

1164 **Lightning: physics and effects**
V.A. Rakov and M.A. Uman Cambridge University Press, 2003, 687pp. £160.00. ISBN 0521583276.
Excellent, wide-ranging, very well produced compendium.
'As well as being desirable for university libraries, despite its price ... is sufficiently complete and universal to be an attractive buy for a public library.' (*Times Higher Education Supplement*)

1165 **Meteorology at the millennium**
R.P. Pearce, ed. Academic Press, 2001, 333pp. $104.95. ISBN 0125480350.
Authoritative overview of modern meteorology and its 'interfaces with science, technology and society'. Five parts comprising articles written by leading academics from around the world: I. Weather prediction at the millennium; II. Climate variability and change; III. The atmosphere and oceans; IV. The biogeochemical cycle; V. Middle atmosphere and solar physics: other planets and epochs. Articles have an abstract, sub-headings and a list of references. For academic libraries.
An edited collection of papers presented on the occasion of the Royal Meteorological Society's 150th anniversary. (International Geophysics, Volume 83.)

1166 **Meteorology today: an introduction to weather, climate, and the environment**
C.D. Ahrens 7th edn, Thomson Brooks/Cole, 2003, 624pp. $97.95. ISBN 0534397719.
www.brookscole.com/pubco/pub_companion.html [COMPANION]
An introductory text: atmosphere, temperatures, optics, moisture, clouds, precipitation, atmosphere in motion, wind, air masses, mid-latitude cyclones, forecasting, thunderstorms, hurricanes, air pollution, global climate, climate change. Short summaries within chapters. Tables of units and conversions A1–A19. Additional reading R1–R3. Glossary G1–G16. Index I1–I12. College and undergraduate.
With InfoTrac and accompanying CD-ROM tied to downloadable real-time weather data.

1167 **The Ozone Hole Tour**
O. Garrett and G. Carver; Centre for Atmospheric Science 1988–2002.
www.atm.ch.cam.ac.uk/tour
Survey produced within the Cambridge UK Centre in four parts using graphics and simulations: The discovery of the ozone hole; Recent ozone loss over Antarctica; The science of

the ozone hole; Latest ozone hole research at Cambridge. There is a glossary and links to other websites and organizations. Last updated 2002 but: 'Visited over 3500 times a week!'.

1168 Philip's guide to weather
R. Reynolds Philip's, 1999, 192pp. £9.99. ISBN 054007456X.
Concise introduction: 1. The atmosphere; 2. Observing the weather; 3. Mapping the weather; 4. Global weather; 5. Explaining the weather; 6. Forecasting ...; 7. Hazardous weather; 8. Holiday weather around the world; 9. Environmental issues. Glossary pp 186–9. Further reading. Index. For a general readership.
'an excellent pocket guide book to weather and climate.' (*The Journal of Meteorology*)

- **The Cambridge guide to weather** Cambridge University Press, 2000, 192pp. $17.00. ISBN 0521774896. Published for the US market, includes conversions to US measurements for temperature etc.

1169 Protecting the ozone layer: science and strategy
E.A. Parson Oxford University Press, 2003, 377pp. £45.00. ISBN 0195155491.
Challenges the orthodoxy of how protection of the atmospheric ozone layer was achieved and argues that we can learn and apply to other environmental issues much more than has been recognized. Archival sources; detailed notes; bibliography; index.

1170 Recent advances and issues in meteorology
A.J. Stevermer Oryx Press, 2001, 296pp. $52.95. ISBN 1573563013.
An overview of the main topics, key individuals, notable occurrences and recent advances in the field of meteorology. Includes statistics, articles about weather hazards, new technologies that help predict the weather, and how the climate is changing, recommended print and electronic resources for further study, information about education and training and professional associations.

1171 The rough guide to weather
R. Henson Rough Guides, 2002, 416pp. £10.99. ISBN 1858288274.
Clear and very readable introduction to weather. Explains worldwide weather patterns, weather systems, climate change and understanding weather forecasts. Weather data for over 150 travel destinations. Special feature is the useful Resources section: Books pp 363–8; Websites pp 369–79; Weather and health p. 380; Weather safety tips p. 384; Conversions and heat and cold indices p 386; Glossary pp 387–96. Index pp 398–416. For the general reader, tourist and student new to meteorology.

Dictionaries, thesauri, classifications

1172 Climate glossaries and weather tools
Climate Diagnostics Center
www.cdc.noaa.gov/ClimateInfo/tools.html
Links to 13 climate and weather glossaries, generated from projects, weather services and academic departments. Typical of glossaries found on various organizations' web pages. Also included are a weather conversions calculator and a units converter.

1173 Dictionary of global climate change
W.J. Maunder Chapman & Hall, 1992, 240pp. £100.00. ISBN 041203901X.
http://legacy.netlibrary.com
Approximately 1500 entries, including cross-references, covering not only scientific terms, but also including details of organizations in the main A–Z sequence. Abbreviations and acronyms are contained in a five-page section. Intended for 'media, interpreters and translators, readers of IPCC Reports ... And the broader community of people interested in climate change'.
Available online: see website.

- **Worldwide Bioclimatic Classification System** **Phytosociological Research Center, Spain.** www.globalbioclimatics.org. Proposes five macrobioclimates – Tropical, Mediterranean, Temperate, Boreal and Polar – with each of them, and every one of their subordinate units or bioclimates, represented by a characteristic group of plant formations, biocenosis and plant communities.

1174 A dictionary of weather
S. Dunlop Oxford University Press, 2001, 266pp. £7.99. ISBN 0192800639.
www.oxfordreference.com
Over 1800 entries listing weather, forecasting and climate terms. Appendices: Weather records; Conversion tables; British climatic data; World climatic data. Also includes hydrology, climatology and oceanography with some vocabulary from astronomy, geomagnetism and geology. Biographical information on key players in the development of meteorology.
Available online: see website.

1175 Elsevier's dictionary of climatology and meteorology: in English, French, Spanish, Italian, Portuguese and German
J.L. de Lucca Elsevier, 1994, 334pp. £119.50. ISBN 0444815325.
Includes important terms used in weather bulletins and textbooks. Also terms from agrometeorology, climatology, hydrometeorology, environmental meteorology, aeronautical meteorology, marine meteorology and radiometeorology.

1176 The Facts On File dictionary of weather and climate
J. Smith Facts on File, 2001, 256pp. $44.00. ISBN 0816045321.
Over 2000 entries. Aimed at the student and general reader. Topics include jet stream, pollution, cloud formation, winds, ocean circulation, precipitation and marine ecosystems. Appendices include a chronology of developments on meteorology and conversion tables.

1177 Glossary of meteorology
T.S. Glickman, ed.; American Meteorological Society 2nd edn, 2001, 855pp. Includes CD-ROM with hyperlinked references, $95.00. ISBN 1878220349.
12,000 terms from 300 contributors and produced by an editorial board of 41 distinguished scientists. Includes references to newer meteorological concepts such as satellite meteorology and numerical weather prediction, and to the related sciences of oceanography and hydrology.
1st edn 1959 contained 7900 terms.

1178 Glossary of weather and climate
I.W. Geer, ed.; American Meteorological Society 1996, 272pp. $34.95. ISBN 1878220195.
Contains over 3000 terms, aimed at a general audience.

Includes related hydrologic and oceanographic terms. Produced under the Project ATMOSPHERE initiative.

1179 **International meteorological vocabulary**
World Meteorological Organization 2nd edn, 1992, 784pp. SFR 90.00. ISBN 9263021821.
Multilingual meteorological nomenclature, containing some 3500 terms; English, French, Spanish and Russian indexes, enabling the reader to find the equivalent term in any of the languages.
First published in 1966.
A volume incorporating the terms in Chinese is also available.

1180 **Meteorological glossary**
R.P.W. Lewis, comp.; Met Office 6th edn, HMSO, 1991, 335pp. £20.00. ISBN 0114003637.
Approximately 2300 technical terms used in meteorology are clearly explained in definitions up to several paragraphs in length, with profuse cross-references. Gives physical or mathematical theory behind the definitions and includes the official definitions used by the World Meteorological Organization.
The 3rd edn (1938–9) carried tables of equivalents in English, Danish, Dutch, French, German, Italian, Norwegian, Portuguese, Spanish and Swedish.

Official & quasi-official bodies

1181 **Bureau of Meteorology** [AUS]
www.bom.gov.au
Australian government meteorological office, providing forecasts and warnings, climate information, hydrological services, links to Australian regional weather services and resources, including weather and climate charts, radar and satellite images. The Learn about Meteorology section is an extensive alphabetical directory of explanations with links to illustrations and data.

Commission on Sustainable Development
See entry no. 4623

1182 **EUMETSAT** [EUR]
www.eumetsat.de
Europe's meteorological satellite organization contributes to a global observing system. Provides input into numerical weather prediction systems, diagnosis of hazardous weather developments and provides information for climate change studies. Access to technical publications, satellite images and information about programmes.

1183 **Global Atmosphere Watch**
World Meteorological Organization
www.wmo.ch/web/arep/gaw/gaw_home.html
Co-ordinates and reports 'comprehensive observations of the chemical composition and selected physical characteristics of the atmosphere on global and regional scales' to help scientists predict the future state of the atmosphere and governments formulate policy. Carried out within the WMO's Environment Division of its Atmospheric Research and Environment Programme. Links to reports, maps and data on ozone and other chemical components of the atmosphere.

- **Ozone Bulletins and Data** www.wmo.ch/web/arep/ozone.html. Access to good set of information from within the WMO and elsewhere.

1184 **Intergovernmental Panel on Climate Change**
www.ipcc.ch
Assesses scientific, technical and socio-economic information relevant for the understanding of climate change, its potential impacts and options for adaptation and mitigation. Links to full text of reports, including to that within the four volumes of the IPCC Third Assessment Report: *Climate change 2001*.

- **Climate change 2001: the scientific basis J.T. Houghton [et al.], eds** Cambridge University Press, 2001, 881pp. £34.95. ISBN 0521014956.
- **Climate change 2001: mitigation B. Metz [et al.], eds** Cambridge University Press, 2001, 752pp. £90.00. ISBN 0521807697.
- **Climate change 2001: impacts, adaptation, and vulnerability J. J. McCarthy [et al.], eds** Cambridge University Press, 2001, 1032pp. £90.00. ISBN 0521807689.
- **Climate change 2001: synthesis report R. T. Watson [et al.], eds** Cambridge University Press, 2002, 397pp. £75.00. ISBN 0521807700.

1185 **Met Office** [UK]
www.metoffice.com
UK government meteorological office, providing forecasts, weather and climate news, some climate charts and data, advice on recording the weather, careers information and educational material for teachers and students.

- **The Beaufort scale Met Office.** www.met-office.gov.uk/education/secondary/students/beaufort.html. One of a number of quite detailed useful treatments aimed at students produced by the Office. This is the scale of wind force, ranging from 0 to 12, now used worldwide.
- **Climate Models Hadley Centre for climate prediction and research.** www.metoffice.com/research/hadleycentre. Short introduction to the types of climate model used in the Centre including variants of the general circulation model.
- **Hadley Centre for climate prediction and research** www.metoffice.com/research/hadleycentre. Aims to monitor, model and predict climate change. Provides clear explanations of the climate system and links to other climate change organizations and data centres.

1186 **Meteorological Service of Canada**
www.msc-smc.ec.gc.ca
Canada's national meteorological service monitors water quantities, provides information and conducts research on climate, atmospheric science, air quality, ice and other environmental issues. Access weather forecasts, maps and climate data, educational sites and fact sheets.

1187 **National Hurricane Center**
www.nhc.noaa.gov
Part of the Tropical Prediction Center of the US National Weather Service, the National Hurricane Center maintains a continuous watch on tropical cyclones over the Atlantic, Caribbean, Gulf of Mexico, and the Eastern Pacific, providing forecasts and warnings. Satellite imagery and archive information available.

1188 **National Oceanic and Atmospheric Administration** [USA]
www.noaa.gov
Part of the US Department of Commerce, NOAA's overall mission is twofold:

Environmental assessment and prediction, while protecting public safety and the US economic and environmental security through accurate forecasting

Environmental stewardship of ocean, coastal and living marine resources while assisting their economic development.

Well organized site with a vast amount of current and archival weather, climate and marine information, charts, data, illustrations, etc., relevant to: weather forecasts, storm warnings, air quality, climate change, navigational charts, fisheries, marine products, satellite imagery.

- **International Ice Patrol** **US Coast Guard.** www.uscg.mil/lantarea/iip. Formed to warn shipping between Europe and the USA of icebergs, especially where the 'Labrador Current meets the warm Gulf Stream and the temperature differences between the two water masses of up to 20 degrees Celsius produces dense fog'.
- **Ocean Surface Currents** **University of Miami.** http://oceancurrents.rsmas.miami.edu. Web-based ocean current reference site. Each current has important links, summary text detailing velocity and hydrographic observations, and plots such as: average current speed and locations, drifting buoy positions, sea surface temperature maps.
- **A comprehensive glossary of weather terms for storm spotters** **M. Branick; National Weather Service** . www.srh.noaa.gov/oun/severewx/glossary.php. Weather-related terms that may be either heard or used by severe local storm spotters or spotter groups. 'The idea is to allow smooth and effective communication between storm spotters and forecasters, and vice versa'.
- **National Weather Service** www.nws.noaa.gov. Note NOAA's recently adopted Policy on Partnerships in the Provision of Environmental Information which strengthens the partnership among government, academia and the private sector that provides the nation with high quality environmental information.
- **Climate Monitoring and Diagnostics Laboratory** www.cmdl.noaa.gov. Records of atmospheric gases, aerosol particles, solar radiation are used to understand the atmospheric system controlling climate forcing, ozone depletion, baseline air quality, so as to develop improved environmental products and services.
- **El Niño** www.elnino.noaa.gov. The disruption of the ocean–atmosphere system in the Tropical Pacific having important consequences for weather and climate around the globe.
- **Hurricanes** http://hurricanes.noaa.gov. Good informative gateway.
- **Space Environment Center** www.sel.noaa.gov. The official source of space weather alerts, warnings, and forecasts.

Ozone Secretariat
See entry no. 2314

United Nations Framework Convention on Climate Change
See entry no. 2317

1189 **World Meteorological Organization**
www.wmo.ch
A specialized agency of the United Nations. Co-ordinates global scientific activity for weather information. Provides information on research, publications and news. Online links to worldwide weather forecasts and climatological data, environmental data and processing centres, national weather services and national hydrological services.

- **World Radiation Center** www.pmodwrc.ch/pmod.php?topic=wrc. Prime objective is to 'guarantee world-wide homogeneity of the meteorological radiation measurements by maintaining the World Standard Group (WSG) which materializes the World Radiometric Reference'. Also calibration, research and development, training.

Research centres & institutes

1190 **Climatic Research Unit** [UK]
www.cru.uea.ac.uk
Comprehensive links to research institutes and organizations for climatology and meteorology worldwide – some oceanography coverage. Information sheets aimed at the lay person provide introductory material on climate-related subjects. The Unit is based in the University of East Anglia.

1191 **ECMWF: European Centre for Medium-Range Weather Forecasting** [EUR]
www.ecmwf.int
Information about research activities, publications and jobs. Current and archive forecast charts and meteograms for medium range and seasonal forecasts and current global observations are available online. Data sets can be ordered, some freely available online. Full text of Technical Memorandum and Technical Reports series available. Good entrée to wide range and depth of information about weather and climate across Europe, the Centre being supported by 25 European countries.

National Snow and Ice Data Center
See entry no. 1133

1192 **NERC Collaborative Centres** [UK]
www.nerc.ac.uk/aboutus/researchcentres
Fifteen Centres funded by contract and managed from outside NERC. Distributed across many UK universities and related institutions. [The exemplars listed below carry out core strategic research programmes into the atmosphere and environment and bring together research findings from different disciplines and institutions in the academic community. A source of information for government. Also referenced is one of the eight NERC Designated Data Centres: see www.nerc.ac.uk/data/directory.shtml.

- **British Atmospheric Data Centre** http://badc.nerc.ac.uk/home. NERC's Designated Data Centre for the atmospheric sciences. Assists UK atmospheric researchers to locate, access and interpret atmospheric data. Allows access to its own and other organizations' data sets. Some data sets require registration.
- **Climate and Land Surface Systems Interaction Centre** classic.nerc.ac.uk. Consortium of four institutions, combining expertise in earth observation science, satellite-sensor technology, and environmental (hydrological, ecological and climatological) modelling and analysis. Includes two (CEH and Hadley) also referenced elsewhere.
- **NERC Centres for Atmospheric Science** ncas.nerc.ac.uk. Role is to provide the UK with national capability (i.e. stable, long-term and broad) in atmospheric science research. NCAS also provides research outcomes for government policy-making and for the wider UK science base.
- **Tyndall Centre for Climate Change Research** www.tyndall.ac.uk. Brings together scientists, economists, engineers and social scientists to develop sustainable responses to climate change.

Pew Center on Global Climate Change
See entry no. 2321

The UK Environmental Change Network
Centre for Ecology and Hydrology and Natural Environment Research Council See entry no. 2324

Associations & societies

American Geophysical Union
See entry no. 1088

1193 **American Meteorological Society**
www.ametsoc.org
'Promotes the development and dissemination of information and education on atmospheric and related oceanic and hydrologic sciences' for professionals, students and enthusiasts. Organizes print and online publications, conferences, education programmes and members' services.

1194 **Canadian Meteorological and Oceanographic Society**
www.cmos.ca
'Society of individuals and organizations dedicated to advancing atmospheric and oceanic sciences and related environmental disciplines in Canada' for meteorologists, climatologists, oceanographers, limnologists, hydrologists and cryospheric scientists. Lists meetings, conferences, awards, consultants and higher education courses. Extensive links to other societies, organizations and government agencies.

1195 **Climatological Observers Link** [UK]
www.met.rdg.ac.uk/~brugge/col.html
Amateur meteorologists' weather observation network for the UK. It also includes professional, corporate and a few international members. Links to UK weather data: climatological averages, past weather data, monthly diary of weather. Invites members and non-members to submit monthly summaries.

- **Climatological Observers Link Bulletin** Monthly. £24.00. ISSN 13502158. www.met.rdg.ac.uk/~brugge/col.html [COMPANION]. For the UK provides a synopsis of the previous month's weather, data from 300 reporting stations, daily data from at least 12 sites, articles on noteworthy weather events worldwide, details of meetings.

Greenpeace
See entry no. 4640

1196 **International Association for Urban Climate**
www.indiana.edu/~iauc
Members have scientific, scholarly and technical interests in: climatology and meteorology of built-up areas, exchange processes between the urban 'surface' and the overlying boundary layer, air quality, wind and turbulence, measurement, modelling and remote sensing of urban atmospheric and surface characteristics, micro-scale processes, building climatology, biometeorology and bioclimatology, urban atmospheric processes in design, and urban landscapes in models of climate at meso-scales. Membership is free. Newsletter is posted on website.

1197 **National Weather Association** [USA]
www.nwas.org
Serves individuals interested in operational meteorology and related activities. There are also student and corporate members. News of conferences, meetings, regional events and job announcements. Extensive links to other organizations and resources. NWA Electronic Journal of Operational Meteorology is published on this website.

- **National Weather Association Newsletter** 1976–, Monthly. $18.00. ISSN 02711044. www.nwas.org/newsletters/newsletter.html [DESCRIPTION]. Association news, lists of meetings and job announcements for members. Also covers new equipment and techniques.
- **National Weather Digest** 1976–, Quarterly. $25.00. ISSN 02711052. www.nwas.org/digest/digest.html [DESCRIPTION]. Articles, studies, technical notes, correspondence, official news, announcements and advertising.

1198 **Royal Meteorological Society** [UK]
www.royalmetsoc.org
Advances and promotes the science of meteorology (climatology, hydrology, physical oceanography and other related disciplines) through publications, meetings, conferences, professional accreditation, grants, awards, workshops and educational activities. Serves professional meteorologists, students, teachers, amateurs and those whose lives are affected by weather and climate. Online information sheets 'Climate on the web' and 'Weather on the web' provide guidance and links to finding a vast array of internet sites.

- **International Association of Meteorology and Atmospheric Sciences** www.iamas.org. 'One of the associations of the INTERNATIONAL UNION OF GEODESY AND GEOPHYSICS, and provides the scientific community with platforms to present, discuss and promote the newest achievements in meteorology, atmospheric science and related fields'.

1199 **Tornado and Storm Research Organization: TORRO** [UK]
www.torro.org.uk
A privately supported research body focusing on forecasting and study of severe weather (thunderstorms, hailstorms, coastal storms, tornadoes, etc.). Information on publications, meetings. Details of research, forecasting procedures and severe weather events in UK. Monthly online newsletter.

Libraries, archives, museums

1200 **National Meteorological Library** [AUS]
www.bom.gov.au/library
The national archive for meteorology books, periodicals, reports and images published in Australia. A 'pre-eminent collection of key meteorological books and journals' in the English language, mostly 20th century but with some data from the 19th century. Website gives access to the library catalogue and extensive lists of web resources and organizations

1201 **National Meteorological Library and Archive** [UK]
www.meto.gov.uk/corporate/library
The UK Met Office Library and Archive is 'one of the most comprehensive collections of literature on meteorology anywhere in the world'. Information about access to the collection, the scope of the stock and links to the online catalogue. The useful Monthly Accessions List 'gives details of books, papers and journal articles taken by the National Meteorological Library. It gives information about the last three months' additions, and is extracted from the library's catalogue of meteorological literature'.

1202 **NCAR Library** [USA]
www.ucar.edu/library
English language books, journals and reports. The focus is on research level materials for weather and climate but the library also collects in the following subject areas where

applicable to the atmospheric sciences: chemistry, computer science, maths, physics, fluid mechanics, and biology. Website allows access to the online library catalogue.

1203 **NOAA Central Library** [USA]
National Oceanic and Atmospheric Administration
www.lib.noaa.gov
Provides scientific, technical and legislative information to NOAA staff, the general public, academia, industry and other government agencies. Its major resources are research collections including: hydrographic surveying (from 1820); oceanography, meteorology, and hydrology (from 1870); and meteorological satellite applications (from 1960). Links to library catalogue, which combines the holdings of various NOAA centres.

- **WINDandSEA: The Oceanic and Atmospheric Sciences Internet Guide** www.lib.noaa.gov/docs/wind/windandsea.html. Built by Library staff in response to the many reference questions posed to the Library: designed to make internet searching more efficient for the Library's various constituencies. Over 1000 selected links organized in good hierarchical subject listing.

1204 **WMO Technical Library**
www.wmo.ch/web/arep/lib1/homepage.html
Its mandate is to provide scientific and technical information services and document delivery mainly to the WMO Staff Members, Delegates and Personnel of the Permanent Missions. With its collections of 40,000 volumes, the library supports research in the meteorological and atmospheric sciences, oceanography, environment, hydrology, geophysics and related disciplines. The online catalogue can be accessed from the website.

Portal & task environments

1205 **BBC Weather**
BBC and Met Office
www.bbc.co.uk/weather
For a wide audience. Forecasts and current news on weather for the UK and worldwide. Also, forecasts tailored to sports, coasts and allergies. Weatherwise includes games, a glossary and 'things to do'. Includes 'over 200 articles written to cover a whole range of subjects related to the weather, including meteorology, the work of the BBC Weather Centre, planets in our solar system and so on'. Also an 'alphabetical tour of all things meteorological'. Conversion calculators. FAQs. A good site.

Carbon Dioxide Information Analysis Center
See entry no. 4641

1206 **Climate Change**
United Nations Environment Programme
climatechange.unep.net
Access to substantive work and information resources mostly from the United Nations. Key issues: Introduction to climate change; Causes and Evidence; Environmental impact; Social and economic impact; Solutions and abatement; Conventions and Treaties. Resources include maps, graphs, models, policy documents and reports. Also search by theme: climate; freshwater; mountains; Geo Data portal; socio-economic; or by region. Major facility.

- **United Nations Framework Convention on Climate Change** unfccc.int. This site provides access to the full text of and information about the United Nations Framework Convention on Climate Change and the Kyoto Protocol.

1207 **Climate Timeline: exploring weather & climate change through powers of 10**
National Geophysical Data Center and National Oceanic and Atmospheric Administration
www.ngdc.noaa.gov/paleo/ctl
Climate history from one year to over 100,000 years back: explanations of the measurement of climate change; the relationship between human development and climate; palaeoclimatology. Different points on the timeline link to specific resources. Tutorials. Climate glossary. Links to climate data from NOAA and US government agencies.

1208 **ClimateArk: climate change portal**
www.climateark.org
Advocacy site 'dedicated to promoting public policy that addresses global climate change through reductions in carbon dioxide and other emissions, renewable energy, energy conservation and ending deforestation'. Associated with Forests.org [q.v.]. Well arranged extensive site.

1209 **Global warming** [USA]
Environmental Protection Agency
yosemite.epa.gov/oar/globalwarming.nsf/content/index.html
Debates, initiatives and publications relating to global warming and causes, impacts and mitigation. Set in an international context but with extensive coverage of the United States by region and state.

1210 **The GLOBE Program**
University Corporation for Atmospheric Research and Colorado State University
www.globe.gov/fsl/welcome.html
Worldwide hands-on, primary and secondary school-based education and science programme launched by then US Vice President Al Gore in 1994. 'Participants take regular observations of weather and other variables. As they collect data and post them on the Internet, the students learn about science and the environment. Their reports eventually provide a unique data set on the local atmosphere, hydrology, soils, and land cover.'

Rich inviting site; good selective set of links in the Resource Room.

1211 **US Global Change Research Information Office**
US Climate Change Science Program
www.gcrio.org
'Provides access to data and information on climate change research, adaptation/mitigation strategies and technologies, and global change-related educational resources on behalf of the various US Federal Agencies that are involved in the US Global Change Research Program'. The USGCRP together with UCCSP – which assumed operational responsibility for the Information Office in February 2004 – are located together in Washington DC.

The Information Office maintains an extensive annotated list of links: early 2005, last updated February 2004.

1212 **Weather Channel** [USA]
www.weather.com
Covers US weather forecasts, including pollen and air quality. Information on planning leisure pursuits, gardening and

vacations and on managing health in the light of forecast weather. Search for forecast maps via US cities or activities.

- **Weather Glossary** www.weather.com/glossary. Over 800 terms, each with a brief annotation. Good use of hyperlinked cross-references.

1213 **Weather Network** [CAN]
www.theweathernetwork.com
Weather forecasts for Canadian, US and international cities. Current and the recent week's weather maps showing precipitation, temperature and humidity for Canada. Also current satellite and radar maps of Canada. Advice on highway conditions, flooding, forest fires, air quality, pollen forecast, snow reports and marine conditions. Invitation to sign up for e-mailed weather forecast

Discovering print & electronic resources

Cold Regions Bibliography Project
American Geological Institute See entry no. 1049

1214 **Meteorological and Geoastrophysical Abstracts**
American Meteorological Society CSA, 1974–, Monthly. £2675.00 [2004].
www.csa.com/factsheets/mga-set-c.php [DESCRIPTION]
Contains abstracts from worldwide literature on: meteorology, climatology, atmospheric chemistry and physics, astrophysics, hydrology, glaciology, physical oceanography and environmental sciences. Summaries from some 600 journal titles, conference proceedings, books, technical reports and other monographs. Over 253,300 records as of January 2004.
Available online: see website.

1215 **Satellite-related World Wide Web Sites**
University of Dundee
www.sat.dundee.ac.uk/web.html
Also includes links to weather information, atmospheric sciences, aerial photographs, government departments and UK higher education research institutions in atmospheric sciences.

Digital data, image & text collections

1216 **Cloud Types for Observers**
Met Office
www.metoffice.com/bookshelf/clouds
Explains, using colour photographs, the World Meteorological Organization classification, based on ten main groups of clouds (divided into three levels, low, medium and high). Each level is accorded a section.

- Rev. edn, HMSO, 1982, 37pp. £23.00. ISBN 0114003343. Similar to the web guide, this illustrates and explains the classification of clouds, assisting observers with reporting cloud types.

1217 **National Climatic Data Center** [USA]
www.ncdc.noaa.gov/oa/ncdc.html
Access to current and historical weather data and climate information for USA and some worldwide. Includes reports, weather station data and websites. NCDC operates the World Data Center for Meteorology and the World Data Center for Paleoclimatology. Extensive variety of references available – one example cited below; but searches can be time consuming.

- **Monthly Climatic Data for the World** www7.ncdc.noaa.gov/SerialPublications/index.jsp [DESCRIPTION]. Mean temperature, pressure, precipitation, vapour pressure, and sunshine for approximately 2000 surface data collection stations worldwide; mean upper air temperatures, dew point depressions and wind velocities for approximately 500 observing sites.

1218 **Polar Meteorology**
Naval Postgraduate School
www.weather.nps.navy.mil/~psguest/polarmet
A module which describes polar climate and climate change and links to web resources. Relates to both the north and south pole. There is also the option to run a climate model over the web.

1219 **UK Climate and Weather Statistics** [UK]
Met Office
www.metoffice.com/climate/uk
Climate summaries: monthly from 1988; annually and seasonally from 2002. Assessments, contoured maps and regional averages, monthly and seasonally. Annual rainfall, temperature and sunshine graphs. Locations of weather stations. Averages and extreme weather. Brief descriptions of the climates of the UK.

1220 **Watching the weather: making your observations count** [UK]
Met Office
www.metoffice.com/bookshelf/observations
Explanation of the standards to be met when recording the weather for the observations to be entered into the National Meteorological Archive. Information booklets for manual and automatic weather stations and rules for rainfall observers.

1221 **Weatherbase**
www.weatherbase.com
Collected from a number of sources, provides weather averages for 16,439 cities worldwide, by region, city, state, province or country. The advertisements can be distracting.

1222 **Wetterzentrale** [EUR]
www.wetterzentrale.de
A very extensive collection of weather and climate charts from meteorological services and organizations. Includes current observations, forecasts and analyses as well as archives, some extending back 100 years. Mostly for Northern Europe and in particular Germany. Wide coverage includes environmental data, tropical storms, ozone distribution and charts of 30-year averages for world temperature, radiation, precipitation. Some data values are also included. All in German but logical organization of the site makes it accessible for the non-German speaker with a basic knowledge of meteorology.

1223 **WW2010** [USA]
University of Illinois at Urbana-Champaign Also available on CD-ROM, 2nd edn, 1999.
ww2010.atmos.uiuc.edu
Online guides: fronts; clouds; precipitation; el Nino; winds; hurricanes; hydrologic cycle; light; mid-latitude cyclones; storms; forecasting. Photographs and diagrams. Most guides updated 1999. 'Archives' of data and descriptions of memorable weather events in North America. 'Current weather' surface and satellite data and images are for North America.

Directories & encyclopedias

Atlas of the oceans: wind and wave climate
I.R. Young and G.J. Holland See entry no. 1375

1224 **Climate Atlas of the United States**
National Oceanic and Atmospheric Administration Version 2.0, 2002. CD-ROM, $175.00.
Climate maps of 50 states; 3023 colour maps of climatic elements: temperature, precipitation, snow, wind, pressure ... for average spatial patterns. Maps of extreme climate events also included. Weather station data for 7700 locations. Most data relates to 1961–90, and is sourced via NOAA. Number of stations used for different data vary from 230 to 8198.
Supersedes Climate atlas of the United States, *published 1968 and version 1.0 of the CD-ROM, published in 2000. Version 2.0 includes Alaska and Hawaii.*

1225 **Climatic atlas of Europe**
World Meteorological Organization and United Nations Educational, Scientific and Cultural Organization Cartographia, 1970, 27pp. Loose-leaf; page size 60 x 42cm, SFR 172.00.
Two sets of 13 maps (scale: 1:5,000,000 and 1:10,000,000). Each set shows distribution, monthly and annual, of the mean atmospheric temperature and precipitation, plus a map representing annual temperature ranges. Based on data collected 1931–60 from 7000 stations. English, French, Russian and Spanish.
Part of the WMO preparation of a world climatic atlas indicating the principal climatic features of each continent. Companion atlases covering Asia, North and Central America, South America.
Page size 60 x 42cm.

1226 **Encyclopedia of air**
D.E. Newton Greenwood Publishing Group, 2003, 256pp. $79.95. ISBN 1573565644.
Alphabetical arrangement of 162 entries. Subjects include: tornados, legal and political issues, scientists and aviators, technical topics, cultural references to air and wind, aerial sports. Also contains: Guide to selected topics (tracing broad themes); Bibliography; Index.

1227 **Encyclopedia of atmospheric sciences**
A.J. Holton, J. Pyle and J. Curry, eds Academic Press, 2002, 4000pp. 6 v., $1400.00. ISBN 0122270908.
www.sciencedirect.com
Contains 330 signed articles by leading experts, each approximately 4000 words, covering 'all aspects of the atmospheric sciences', cross-referenced and with suggestions for further reading. Appendices include tables of physical constants, units and their SI equivalents, periodic table, geologic time scale and 12 pages of abbreviations.
Available online: see website.
'authoritative and concise articles review such complex subjects as weather prediction, climate change and variability, and atmospheric chemistry. Beautifully illustrated with maps, charts, photos and illustrations.' (*Library Journal*)

1228 **Encyclopedia of climate and weather**
S.H. Schneider, ed. Oxford University Press, 1996, 929pp. 2 v., £170.00. ISBN 0195094859.
Contains more than 350 signed articles, alphabetically arranged by topic. Includes biographies of important meteorologists. Each article has a bibliography and there is also a lengthy glossary of terms, pp 853–74. Subject index.

1229 **Encyclopedia of hurricanes, typhoons, and cyclones**
D. Longshore Facts On File, 1998, 384pp. $55.00. ISBN 0816033986.
Over 200 entries: storms by name; storm locations; storm related terms; biographies; meteorological terms and instruments; folklore; hurricane tracking and analysis. Numerous cross-references. Appendices include: a list of the names, locations, and dates of events and a chronology of major storms; hurricane safety procedures.

1230 **Encyclopedia of the Atmospheric Environment**
Atmosphere, Climate and Environment Information Programme
www.doc.mmu.ac.uk/aric/eae
Online resource on atmospheric pollution and related issues created in 2000. Some 400 entries under: acid rain; air quality; atmosphere; climate; climate change; global warming; ozone depletion; sustainability; weather. Over 100 photographs and diagrams. Current information on government and international initiatives is updated in the monthly Newsletters section.
'*Encyclopedia of the atmospheric environment* has received over 30 Internet awards for design and content and has been judged by Air Quality Management (www.air-quality-management.co.uk/aweb2001a.htm) as the best non-local authority air quality website in the UK.'
However, early 2005: 'The Atmosphere, Climate & Environment Information Programme is no longer being supported by the Department for Environment, Food and Rural Affairs (DEFRA), and has therefore ceased operations. For information on global warming, climate change, air quality, acid rain, ozone depletion, sustainable development and the weather please go to: http://www.enviropedia.org.uk.'

1231 **Encyclopedia of weather and climate**
M. Allaby Facts On File, 2001, 832pp. 2 v., $150.00. ISBN 0816040710.
Aimed at a young adult audience. A–Z format with cross-references. Definitions and sources for further study. Weather processes, circulations of atmospheres, classification of climates, scientific concepts, history of atmospheric sciences, biographies, notable weather events.

1232 **The Facts On File weather and climate handbook**
M. Allaby Facts On File, 2002, 301pp. $17.95. ISBN 0816049610.
Over 2000 entries offering basic information on atmospheric processes, the sciences of climatology and meteorology. Biographical information on approximately 100 scientists. Chronology of key developments from 340 BC to 2001. Twenty tables of physical and meteorological facts.

1233 **Macmillan encyclopedia of weather**
P. Stein Macmillan Reference, 2001, 275pp. $150.00. ISBN 0028654730.
Short, alphabetically arranged articles, with cross-references, on a wide range of weather and climate issues. Aimed at the non-specialist. Glossary pp 267–78. Bibliography pp 278–80. Analytical index pp 281–91. List of US weather websites p. 280. For school and public libraries.

1234 Smithsonian meteorological tables
R.J. List, ed. 6th edn, Smithsonian Institution, 1966. Reprinted 1984. Reprint on demand available. ISBN 0874741157.
The most comprehensive set of tables available for meteorological calculations, including: Conversion; Wind and dynamical; Barometric and hypsometric; Geopotential and aerological; Standard atmosphere ... ; Thermodynamic; Hygrometric and psychometric. ; Radiation and visibility ... Index pp 521–7

1235 Tables of Temperature, Relative Humidity, Precipitation and Sunshine for the World
Met Office HMSO, 1958–.
Tables of monthly data (average and extremes) based on 30-year averages from thousands of weather stations around the world. Volumes also contain: maps locating places in the tables; conversion tables; bibliography of originating meteorological data; place names index.

Six vols: 1. North America and Greenland (including Hawaii and Bermuda) (2nd edn, 1980); 2. Central and South America, the West Indies and Bermuda (2nd edn, 1975); 3. Europe and the Azores (Rev. edn, 1973); 4. Africa; the Atlantic Ocean south of 35 degrees north and the Indian Ocean (Rev. edn, 1983); 5. Asia (2nd edn, 1966); 6. Australasia and the South Pacific Ocean including the corresponding sectors of Antarctica (2nd edn, 1975).
Vols 2, 5 and 6 published under the earlier series title: Tables of Temperature, Relative Humidity and Precipitation for the World

1236 Weather almanac: a reference guide to weather, climate, and related issues in the United States and its key cities
R. A. Wood 11th edn, Gale, 2004, 820pp. $175.00. ISBN 0787675156.
www.gale.com/gvrl
'in-depth weather reports in narrative and tabular form for 108 major US cities and a climatic overview of the country, including 33 US weather atlas maps.' Chapter on recent weather from the last two years. Includes explanations, safety rules and statistics for hurricanes and tornados. Glossary. Index. Guide to additional weather resources.
Available online: see website.

1237 Weather America: a thirty year summary of statistical data and weather trends
D. Garoogian 2nd edn, Grey House Publishing, 2000, 2013pp. Previously published 1996 by Toucan Valley Publications, $175.00. ISBN 1891482297.
www.greyhouse.com/weather.html [DESCRIPTION]
Climatological data for over 4000 places throughout the United States. Nationwide rankings for temperature, precipitation, fog, humidity and wind speed. Lists of major storms. Fifty state sections with city index, narrative descriptions, map and data tables. Aimed at the general reader.
Previously published 1996 by Toucan Valley Publications.

- **Understanding clouds and fog** USA Today. www.usatoday.com/weather/wcloud0.htm. Useful – albeit quite commercially intrusive – overview with good set of links.

1238 Weltkarten zur Klimakunde (World maps of climatology)
E. Rodenwald and H.J. Jusatz, eds Springer-Verlag, 1965, 28pp. Edited under the sponsorship of the Heidelberger Akademie der Wissenschaften.
This continues the maps in vols 1–3 of the *World atlas of epidemic diseases*. Five colour charts 79cm x 46cm, scale 1: 45,000,000, based approximately on data for 1951 to 1960: mean averages for sunshine, rainfall and totals; generalized isolines of global radiation; climates of the earth, colour coded chart with text key.

Older maps and charts from a variety of sources can be found in national collections and specialist libraries: this is just one good exemplar.

Handbooks & manuals

1239 Antarctic meteorology and climatology
J.C. King and J. Turner Cambridge University Press, 1997, 409pp. £80.00. ISBN 0521465605.
Seven chapters: 2. Observations and instrumentation; 3. Physical climatology; 4. The large-scale circulation of the Antarctic atmosphere; 5. Synoptic-scale weather systems and fronts; 6. Mesoscale systems and processes; 7. Climate variability and change. Two appendices list weather stations in the Antarctic and on sub-Antarctic islands. References, pp 383–404. Index. A comprehensive survey. For academic libraries.

1240 Atmospheric pollution: history, science, and regulation
M.Z. Jacobson Cambridge University Press, 2002, 399pp. £30.00. ISBN 0521010446.
Twelve chapters, with summaries: atmospheric chemistry, composition of atmosphere, urban air pollution, smog, effects of weather, indoor air pollution, ozone, global warming. 'A synthesis of chemistry, meteorology, radiative processes, particle processes, cloud physics, soil sciences, microbiology, epidemiology, economics, and law.' References pp 355–99. Analytical index pp 377–99. Key concepts are colour highlighted throughout text. Aimed at students of environmental, earth and atmospheric sciences. For academic and public reference libraries.
'An unbiased overview on atmospheric pollution that deals with gases and aerosol particles in all parts of the world.' (*Meteorologische Zeitschrift*)
'A general reference and sourcebook for anybody interested in the study of airborne pollutants.' (*Weather*)

- **Chemistry of atmospheres: an introduction to the chemistry of the atmospheres of earth, the planets and their satellites** **R.P. Wayne** 3rd edn, Oxford University Press, 2000, 775pp. £39.99. ISBN 019850375X. Introduction providing 'foundations for the study of atmospheric chemistry on which rational decisions will need to be based'. Multidisciplinary approach 'to highlight the interplay between the atmosphere of a planet and other parts of the environment'.

1241 Blame it on the weather: strange Canadian weather facts
D. Phillips Key Porter Books, 2000, 240pp. illus, CAN $26.95. ISBN 1552631761.
Chapter headings: Weatherwise; Canadian weather moments; Weather across Canada; Weather observing and forecasting; Weather – more than tomorrow's forecasting. A wide range of topics is covered with a focus on specific weather events. Bibliographical references. Index. For a general readership.

1242 **The climate of the arctic**
R. Przybylak Kluwer Academic, 2003, 270pp. £68.00. ISBN 1402011342.
Good synthesis of current state of knowledge, past climate periods, specific climate areas, scenarios for 21st century. 'All meteorological elements are described in detail for the first time and an up-to-date review of the available literature for each element is given ... This monograph is intended for all those with a general interest in the fields of meteorology, climatology, and with a knowledge of the application of statistics in these areas.'
Series: Atmospheric and Oceanographic Sciences Library, V. 26.
- **Encyclopedia of the arctic M. Nuttall** Routledge, 2004, 2380pp. $525.00. ISBN 1579584365. www.routledge-ny.com/ref/arctic [DESCRIPTION]. 3 vols. 'Over 1200 A–Z entries that range in length from 500 words to 5000 words for the longer thematic entries and survey articles. Leading specialists from 20 countries, including a large number of contributors native to the Arctic and Subarctic'.

1243 **Climates of South Asia**
G.B. Pant and K. Rupa Kumar Wiley, 1997, 344pp. $225.00. ISBN 0471949485.
Two sections (nine chapters): 1. Meteorological background (1. South Asia: an introduction to the region ... 4. Other meteorological features and systems of south Asia) 2. Climatic characteristics (5. Mean climatology of South Asia ... 9. The changing climate of South Asia: its environmental impact). Two appendices: 1. All-India monthly and seasonal rainfall (1871–1994); 2. Climatological tables of some stations in South Asia. Bibliography pp 299–314.
Series: Belhaven Studies in Climatology.

1244 **Climates of the British Isles: past, present and future**
M. Hulme and E. Barrow, eds Routledge, 1997, 454pp. £24.99. ISBN 0415130174.
Twenty-eight contributors. Four parts, comprising 16 chapters: 1. The British Isles climate; 2. Reconstructing the past; 3. Monitoring the present; 4. Forecasting the future. Four appendices (including Listings of climate datasets). Glossary; Name index; Index of place names; General index.
'much of value and interest to readers of all nationalities ... unreservedly recommends this volume to geographers, climatologists, professional scientists and the general public alike.' (*Progress in Geography*)

1245 **Desert meteorology**
T.T. Warner Cambridge University Press, 2004, 595pp. £80.00. ISBN 0521817986.
Chapters include: atmospheric dynamics of deserts; climates of the world deserts; atmospheric and surface energy budgets; surface physics of the unvegetated sandy desert landscape; vegetation effects; substrate effects; desert-surface physical properties; numerical modelling of desert atmospheres; boundary layers; microclimates; dynamic interactions among desert microclimates; rainfall; anthropogenic effects on the desert atmosphere; changes in desert climate; severe weather; effects of deserts on the global environment; desertification; bioclimatology; optical properties of desert atmospheres; Appendices; Index.

1246 **Handbook of applied meteorology**
D.D. Houghton, ed. Wiley, 1985, 1461pp. ISBN 0471084042.
Fifty-four contributors. Five parts: 1.Fundamentals 2. Measurements 3. Applications 4. Societal impacts 5. Resources (data, books and journals; education; research centers and libraries; directory sources). Appendices: A. Glossary and units. B. Climatic data. Useful lists of references. North American slant. Although intended for professionals it gives a good overview of the shape and sources of the subject for university students. An update would be timely to accommodate electronic sources of information.

1247 **Handbook of atmospheric science: principles and applications**
C.N. Hewitt and A.V. Jackson, eds Blackwell Publishing, 2003, 633pp. £150.00. ISBN 0632052864.
Part I is a current overview: Principles of Atmospheric Science, Part II looks at air pollution: Problems, Tools and Applications. There are 21 subdivided chapters, with references, by leading experts on the physical and chemical properties of the atmosphere and of air pollution.

1248 **Handbook of aviation meteorology**
Met Office 3rd edn, HMSO, 1994, 401pp. £25.00. ISBN 0114003653.
Five parts comprising 21 chapters: 1. Physical principles; 2. Meteorological observations; 3. Synoptic meteorology; 4. General circulation and world climate; 5. Meteorological information for aviators. Two appendices and an annex; index. 'An elementary knowledge of meteorology on the part of the reader would be an advantage.'
4th edn in preparation.

1249 **Handbook of meteorological instruments**
Met Office 2nd edn, HMSO, 1980–2. £12 each.
Seven booklets intended primarily for Met Office personnel about the instruments used at official stations: 'Particulars of some other types are used to illustrate different principles' (Introductions). 1. Measurement of atmospheric pressure; 2. Measurement of temperature; 3. Measurement of humidity; 4. Measurement of surface wind; 5. Measurement of precipitation and evaporation; 6. Measurement of solar and terrestrial radiation; 7. Measurement of visibility and cloud height. Each volume has a glossary and index.
Each volume has a glossary and index.
- **The history of the barometer W.E.K. Middleton** Johns Hopkins University Press, 2002, 512pp. $25.00. ISBN 0801871549. www.press.jhu.edu/books [DESCRIPTION]. 'This is an excellent book and an important one. It is recommended generally; in science collections it will become a standard work.' *Library Journal*.

1250 **Handbook of weather, climate, and water**
T.D. Potter and B.R. Colman, eds Wiley, 2003. 2 v., $275.00. ISBN 0471450308.
Comprehensive review of the atmospheric and hydrologic sciences. Chapters are written by individual subject specialists. One volume, subtitled *Dynamics, climate, physical meteorology, weather systems and measurements*, has five sections, covering: dynamic meteorology, the climate system, physical meteorology, weather systems and measurements. A second volume, subtitled *Atmospheric chemistry, hydrology, and societal impacts*, has four sections covering: physical and mathematical explanations for atmospheric dynamics, climate system, physical meteorology, weather systems, measurements, atmospheric chemistry, hydrology.

Aims to update existing accounts and to be a comprehensive reference work for scientists of atmospheric and hydrologic sciences. The section on societal impacts is for anyone interested in the history of floods, droughts.

1251 **International cloud atlas**
World Meteorological Organization V. 1. English, French and Spanish. 1975, reprinted in 1995. Loose-leaf. SFR 47.00. ISBN 9263104077; V. 2. English and French. 1987, 212pp. SFR 78.00. ISBN 9263124078. A set of 100 slides is also available at SFR 50.00.
Volume 1 is a manual on the observation of clouds and other meteors containing descriptive text on the general classification of meteors, clouds and meteors other than clouds. This is complemented by Volume 2, 196 photographs with detailed captions.

1252 **The marine observer's handbook**
Met Office TSO, 1995, 227pp. Met. 0. 1016, £40.00. ISBN 011400367X.
Four parts, comprising 14 chapters: 1. Instrumental observations; 2. Non-instrumental observations; 3. Phenomena; 4. Summary of meteorological work at sea. 'State of sea photographs, Force 0 to 12', p 40–7. Cloud pl. in col., p 63–93. Analytical index, p 222–7.

1253 **Measuring the natural environment**
I. Strangeways 2nd edn, Cambridge University Press, 2003, 534pp. £35.00. ISBN 0521529522.
Examines, past, present and future techniques and the quality of the data produced. 1. Basics; 2. Radiation; 3. Temperature; 4. Humidity; 5. Wind; 6. Barometric pressure; 7. Evaporation; 8. Precipitation; 9. Soil moisture and groundwater; 10. Rivers and lakes; 11. Data logging; 12. Telemetry; 13. Visibility; 14. Clouds; 15. Lightning; 16. Upper air; 17. Oceans; 18. Cold regions; 19. Remote sensing; 20. Atmospheric composition; 21. Forward look; Appendix; Index. For university students and professionals.

1254 **Mediterranean climate: variability and trends**
H.-J. Bolle, ed. Springer, 2003, 320pp. £69.00. ISBN 3540438386.
Analysis of climatological data from 500 BC to present day. Discusses climate variability, biosphere in the Mediterranean area, water cycle, desertification, climate models, remote sensing.
First volume in the planned series Regional Climate Studies.

1255 **The meteorology and climate of tropical Africa**
M. Leroux Springer, 2001, 548pp. CD-ROM, £168.50. ISBN 3540426361.
'Its perspective is both an African and a global one.' (Preface). Four parts: I Chronological factors; II. Aerological factors; III. Dynamics of circulation, disturbances; IV. Climate of tropical Africa. Bibliography pp 497–548; 350 charts: air flow, sea level pressure, rainfall and temperature. Based on mean values 1931–60, still 'representative of the modern picture'.
2nd edn of Le climat de l'Afrique Tropicale *published under the sponsorship of the World Meteorological Organization, 1983.*
'Technical mathematics and physics are avoided ... style is very clear and straightforward.' (*The Journal of Meteorology*)

1256 **Meteorology for mariners**
Met Office 3rd edn, HMSO, 1979, 215pp. diags., graphs. ISBN 0114003114.
A textbook of elementary theoretical meteorology for Merchant Navy officers which also presents the practical application of meteorology to safe and economic ship operations. Six parts: 1. The meteorological elements; 2. Climatology; 3. Weather systems; 4. Weather forecasting; 5. Ocean surface currents; 6. Ice and exchange of energy between sea and atmosphere. Appended bibliography of ten items.
A 4th edn is in preparation.

1257 **Observer's handbook**
Met Office 4th edn, HMSO, 1982, 220pp. ISBN 0114003297.
Eleven chapters of instructions on making weather observations, both instrumental and non-instrumental, at all types of stations: 1. Observational routine; 2. Clouds; 3. Visibility; 4. Weather; 5. Wind; 6 State of ground and concrete slab; 7. Atmospheric pressure; 8. Temperature and humidity; 9. Precipitation; 10. Sunshine; 11; Special phenomena (e.g. electrometeors). Three appendices (e.g. Recording of observations ...) Bibliography. Analytical index. For both amateur and professional meteorologists.

The oceans and climate
G.R. Bigg See entry no. 1389

Palaeohydrology: understanding global change
K.J. Gregory and G. Benito See entry no. 1153

Paleoclimatology: reconstructing climates of the Quaternary
R.S. Bradley See entry no. 1476

Principles of paleoclimatology
T.M. Cronin See entry no. 1478

1258 **Regional climates of the British Isles**
D. Wheeler and J. Mayes Routledge, 1997, 343pp. £26.50. ISBN 0415139317.
A comprehensive and 'up-to-date survey of the diverse climate of the British Isles'. Eleven regions, including Ireland and the Channel Islands. Includes summaries of recent events and climatic averages. Three parts: 1. The anatomy of regional climates in the British Isles; 2. The character of regional climates.; 3. Regional perspectives on climatic variability and change. Most statistics are from 1961 to 1990. References at the end of each chapter. General index. Index of places.

1259 **Storms**
R.A. Pielke and R.A. Pielke, ed. Routledge, 1999, 960pp. 2 v., £350.00. ISBN 041517239X.
Reviews storms, their prediction and mitigation. Specialist articles cover: storm science and societal vulnerability, tropical cyclones, extratropical cyclones, mesoscale convective systems and other storms, such as polar lows, monsoon, space weather and dust. Detailed accounts of storms including in the USA, Cuba, Australia, India, Russia and Mexico.
Series: Hazards and Disasters
'will become a major source of information for meteorologists, climatologists, and insurers alike.' (*Meteorologische Zeitschrift*)

1260 **The USA today weather book: an easy to understand guide to the USA's weather**
J. Williams 2nd edn, Knopf, 1997, 240pp. $20.00. ISBN 0679776656.
A guide for a general readership and featuring the full colour weather graphics of America's newspaper, *USA Today*. It also

includes an updated state-by-state guide to weather patterns and scientifically accurate records.

1261 **The weather and climate of southern Africa**
P.D. Tyson and A. Preston-Whyte 2nd edn, Oxford University Press, 2000, 396pp. £40.00. ISBN 0195718062.
Includes atmospheric processes, general circulation of the Southern Hemisphere, weather over southern Africa, ocean-atmosphere interactions, boundary layer phenomena, aerosols, climate change, future predictions. Units and conversions. Glossary. Bibliography. Focus is on South Africa and surrounding oceans.
Revised edition of Atmosphere and weather of southern Africa *1988.*
'Essential to South African students of meteorology and climatology but also of much wider interest to those who would like to expand their knowledge of weather systems' (*Weather*)

1262 **The weather of Britain**
R. Stirling 2nd edn, Giles de la Mare Publishers, 1997, 306pp. £19.99. ISBN 1900357062.
Twenty-four chapters: 1. The weather and sea around us ...10. Drought ...16. Some notable snow falls ... 22. City weather ... 24. Is our climate changing? Notes appended. Further reading pp 290–1. Some suppliers of meteorological instruments, p 292. Index. Highly readable account, crammed with facts and figures. For anyone interested in British weather.

1263 **World survey of climatology**
H. E. Landsberg, ed. Elsevier, 1969–.
A major survey of climates, by geographical area, and climatology. Each volume consists of contributions by specialists, with appended bibliography of references, plus author and subject indexes. However, only two volumes are so far in print.

- **16. Future climates of the world: a modelling perspective A. Henderson-Sellers, ed.** 1995, 634pp. US$349. ISBN 0444893229.
- **1C. General climatology: classification of climates O. M. Essenwanger, ed.** 2001, 126pp. US$129.50. ISBN 0444882782.

1264 **World Weather Records**
National Climatic Data Center 8th edn. 1981–90.
www.wmo.ch/web/wcp/wcdmp/wwr/html/wwr.html [DESCRIPTION]
Published since 1927. Includes monthly mean values of pressure, temperature and precipitation. Six vols: 1. North America; 2. Europe; 3. West Indies, South and Central America; 4. Asia; 5. Africa; 6. Islands of the world.

Earlier records appeared in the Smithsonian Institution's Miscellaneous collection publication no. 79 (1929, covering pre-1921 data), no. 90 (1934, covering 1921–30) and no. 105 (1947, covering 1931–40). The US Weather Bureau issued *World Weather Records*, 1941–50 (USGPO, 1959) and *World Weather Records*, 1951–60 (1965–8), while Environmental Data and Information published *World Weather Records*, 1961–70, (v. 1–3, 6), 1979–.

A ninth series for 1991 to 2000 is in preparation.

Keeping up-to-date

1265 **Bulletin of the American Meteorological Society**
American Meteorological Society Monthly. $70.00 [2004]. ISSN 00030007.
ams.allenpress.com [DESCRIPTION]
Articles aimed at a wide meteorological readership. News, letters, activities of the Society, conference summaries, product and book reviews, calendars of meetings, professional directory.
References to articles can be viewed on website, with full-text access planned for all users.

1266 **Journal of Meteorology** [EUR]
Tornado and Storm Research Organization Artetech Publishing, 10/year. £36.95 [2004]. ISSN 03075966.
www.journalofmeteorology.com [DESCRIPTION]
Articles on severe weather across Europe. News of recent weather events and projects. Monthly diary of tornados and thunderstorms. List of recent world weather disasters. Monthly list of British weather extremes. Book reviews. Focuses on the effect of extreme weather on man.

1267 **National Weather Association newsletter** [USA]
National Weather Association 1976–, Monthly. $18.00 [2004]. ISSN 02711044.
www.nwas.org/newsletters/newsletter.html [DESCRIPTION]
Association news, lists of meetings and job announcements for members. Also covers new equipment and techniques.

- **National weather digest** 1976–, Quarterly. $25.00. ISSN 02711052. www.nwas.org/digest/digest.html [DESCRIPTION]. Articles, studies, technical notes, correspondence, official news, announcements and advertising.

1268 **Weather** [UK]
Royal Meteorological Society Monthly. £45.00 print/online [2004]. ISSN 00431656.
www.royalmetsoc.org [DESCRIPTION]
Aimed at a wide readership. Articles on the scientific and general, historical aspects of meteorology and climatology. Readers' letters. News and photographs. Lists conferences, seminars and meetings. Weather Log section has weather maps for the UK and the North Atlantic and monthly averages for UK and European weather stations. Website offers a search facility for references to articles published since 1946.

1269 **Weatherwise** [USA]
Heldref Publications, Bimonthly. $80.00 [2004]. ISSN 00431672.
www.weatherwise.org [DESCRIPTION]
Weather news journal aimed at the enthusiast. Presented in a popular style with lavish illustrations. Short articles, news and book reviews. Features US weather issues and events. Current month, selected articles and e-mail weather queries facility available online.
Online access to selected recent feature articles.

1270 **WMO Bulletin**
World Meteorological Organization Quarterly. English, French, Russian and Spanish editions, SFR 85.00 [2004]. ISSN 00429767.
www.wmo.ch/indexflash.html [DESCRIPTION]
Articles on current weather and climate research and recent weather events. Includes news of WMO activities and lists meetings. Book reviews.

Mineralogy

diffraction data • gemmology • gemstones • minerals • precious stones

Introductions to the subject

1271 **The Audubon Society field guide to North American rocks and minerals**
C.W. Chesterman Knopf, 1979, 850pp. $19.95. ISBN 0394502698.
A classic pocket-sized guide aimed at rock collectors and those interested in minerals collections and preservation in North America. Some 230 mineral species and 40 types of rocks are described in four parts. Pt 1 (Minerals) and Pt 2 (Rocks) both include a guide to identification, a visual key, and colour plates: pp 1–702 and pp 703–94 respectively. These are followed by Pt 3 (Mineral collecting) and Pt 4 (Appendices). Glossary pp 785–97; Bibliography, pp 799–801; Index pp 831–50.

1272 **Introduction to mineral sciences**
A. Putnis Cambridge University Press, 1992, 457pp. £35.00. ISBN 0521429471.
A classic introduction to modern mineralogy for undergraduates. Deals with solid state transformations in minerals which take place in response to changes in temperature and pressure and also introduces the basic crystallography. Examples from a range of mineral groups are set within the context of earth sciences. Case histories. Many diagrams. Includes bibliographic references at the end of each chapter.

Mineral resources: a world review
J.A. Wolfe See entry no. 4665

1273 **Mineralogy for students**
M.H. Battey and A. Pring 3rd edn, Longman, 1997, 363pp. £32.99. ISBN 0582088488.
Good introductory text for undergraduates. Detailed account of minerals and how to identify them. Revised edition incorporates advances in techniques and methods for studying materials that have developed during the last two decades. Two sections in the book: principles and methods, and systematic mineralogy. New topics include X-ray power diffractometry and electron and neutron diffraction.
Previous edn 1981.

1274 **Minerals: their constitution and origin**
H.-R. Wenk and A. Bulakh Cambridge University Press, 2004, 656pp. £35.00. ISBN 0521529581.
Designed as an up-to-date, comprehensive mineralogy undergraduate text. Contains 62 colour plates with superb photographs, handy reference tables, glossary and tables. Includes the identification of minerals in hand specimen and under the microscope. Combines geological and economic interests. A key reference resource for university students.

1275 **Minerals: an illustrated exploration of the dynamic world of minerals and their properties**
G.W. Robinson and J.A. Scovil; Canadian Museum of Nature Weidenfeld and Nicolson, 1994, 208pp. £19.99. ISBN 0297833294.
Covers minerals and all their attributes but emphasizes the environments that form them. The text describes their complexity and aims to lead to an understanding of how continent-shaping forces combined to create minerals. Related to well known geological sites. Impressive full-colour photographs of mineral specimens from the *Canadian Museum of Nature* are included in the book. Section summaries but no glossary.
Series: Peter N. Nevraumont Book.

1276 **Rocks and minerals** [UK]
A.P. Jones Harper Collins, 2003, 244pp. £8.99. ISBN 0007177941.
A useful beginners' guide, relevant for those with a general interest in the topic, but also to first-year undergraduates and other students of geology and earth sciences. Covering 240 commonly found types of rock, mineral and gemstone throughout the world, this concise introduction is suitable for all. All types are illustrated with colour photographs and further artwork showing other identification features. The 'Where to see' and 'What next?' sections contain further advice and information.
Series: Collins Wild Guides.

Rocks and minerals
S. Parker See entry no. 1498

Dictionaries, thesauri, classifications

1277 **Dictionary of gems and gemology**
M. Manutchehr-Danai Springer, 2000, 565pp. £134.50. ISBN 3540674829.
Comprehensive dictionary of 16,000 entries for use by gemologists, mineralogists, geologists, jewellery dealers, industrialists and hobbyists. More than 250 diagrams and figures. Extended definitions. Combines all of the information usually listed in separate references to create a complete and functional lexicon. Bibliography.

Dictionary of mining, mineral, and related terms
American Geological Institute See entry no. 4666

Elsevier's dictionary of mining and mineralogy: in English, French, German and Italian
A.F. Dorian, comp. See entry no. 4667

1278 **Fleischer's glossary of mineral species 2004**
J.A. Mandarino and M. Back 9th edn, Mineralogical Record, Inc, 2004, 309pp. Spiral bound, $24.00.
A complete, A–Z listing of the names, symmetry, and chemical compositions of approved mineral species. Descriptions of over 250 new species since the 1999 edn are included. Type locality information and crystal structure references added in this edition. For each mineral the following information is given: chemical formula, crystal system, polymorphism and relationships to other minerals, type locality (if known), and the best English language reference. Useful resource for mineralogy students.
8th edn 1999.

1279 **Larousse field guides: rocks and minerals**
D. Cook and W. Kirk Kingfisher Books, 1998, 192pp. £12.99. ISBN 0752300512.
A fully illustrated guide for identification for more than 160 rocks and minerals found throughout the world. Features include handy fact panels providing complete checklists and detailed colour photographs. Includes index. General readership.
Originally published: London: Kingfisher, 1991.

1280 **Structural classification of minerals**
J. Lima-de-Faria Kluwer Academic Publishers, 2001–2004. 3 v., £37.00 per vol. ISBN 0792368932(SET).
A new structural classification of minerals, based on internal crystal structure, and its natural classification. Divided in three volumes, in which the minerals are ordered from the structurally simple to the more complex. Detailed and comprehensive. Suitable for postgraduates.
Series: Solid Earth Sciences Library, 11, 11A and 11B.

Laws, standards, codes

1281 **Commission on New Minerals and Mineral Names**
www.geo.vu.nl/users/ima-cnmmn
Established in 1959 for the purpose of controlling the introduction of new minerals and mineral names, and of rationalizing mineral nomenclature. Downloadable PDF list of some 4000 minerals and mineral names which the Commission has officially taken a decision since 1959 on their approval (A), discreditation (D) and/or redefinition (R).

Official & quasi-official bodies

Mineral Resources Program
See entry no. 4670

Research centres & institutes

1282 **International Centre for Diffraction Data**
www.icdd.com
'Non-profit scientific organization dedicated to collecting, editing, publishing, and distributing powder diffraction data for the identification of crystalline materials.' Notable for its Powder Diffraction File data, its mission is: 'To be the world center for quality diffraction data meeting the needs of the technical community. To promote the application of materials characterization methods in science and technology by providing a forum for the exchange of ideas and information and through publication of X-ray diffraction data.'

Valuable source of topics and material suitable for secondary school and undergraduate students or their teachers. Includes problems intended to be tackled to further illustrate key concepts.

Associations & societies

1283 **European Mineralogical Union**
www.univie.ac.at/Mineralogie/EMU/welcome.htm
An international scientific organization. Aims to increase European co-operation in the mineralogical sciences. Produces the *European Journal of Mineralogy*. Useful links to institutions and resources. Events publicized on website.

1284 **Gemmological Association and Gem Testing Laboratory of Great Britain**
www.gagtl.ac.uk/gagtl/index.htm
Laboratory services to the jewellery trade, promoting the study of gems and offering courses and training in gemmology. Links to information on courses offered. Gemmological instruments.

1285 **Gemological Institute of America**
www.gia.edu
Established in 1931, as an international, non-profit educational, research, and gemmological laboratory service aiming to provide accurate resources for the gem and jewellery industry. Includes information on distance learning, industry and consumer data from the GIA Gem Trade Laboratory, access to current and back issues of *Gems & Gemology*, as well as additional online publications, news, and events details.

International Zeolite Association
See entry no. 4679

1286 **Mineralogical Association of Canada**
www.mineralogicalassociation.ca
'To promote and advance the knowledge of mineralogy and the allied disciplines of crystallography, petrology, geochemistry and mineral deposits.' Links to proceedings, journals, publications and further information. Annual meetings and symposia advertised.

1287 **Mineralogical Society of America** [USA]
www.minsocam.org
A website for all ages, and all academic levels, promoting an interest in minerals. Web page in newspaper style, with well organized and easy-to-access links. Ask-a-Mineralogist link to a discussion board. Details of publications including the well regarded journal *American Mineralogist*.

- **American Mineralogist** Monthly. $650.00. ISSN 0003004X. www.minsocam.org/MSA/AmMin/AmMineral.html. Leading publication. Subscriptions include all *Reviews in Mineralogy and Geochemistry* volumes published during the year, as well as all numbers of *Elements*, a magazine that has succeeded the Society's quarterly newsletter.
- **American Mineralogist Crystal Structure Database** **Mineralogical Society of America and Mineralogical Association of Canada**. www.geo.arizona.edu/AMS/amcsd.php. Interface to crystal structure database that includes every structure published in *American Mineralogist*, *The Canadian Mineralogist*, *European Journal of Mineralogy* and *Physics and Chemistry of Minerals*; also from *Acta Crystallographica*.

1288 **Mineralogical Society of Great Britain and Ireland**
www.minersoc.org
Instituted in 1876, the society has as its objective the advancement of the knowledge of the science of mineralogy and its application to other subjects. Very clear, easy-to-access website. Good set of educational links.

1289 **Russell Society** [UK]
www.russellsoc.org/index.htm
Sustains an online resource for amateur and professional mineralogists encouraging the study, recording and conservation of mineralogical sites and material. An important society in the United Kingdom, focusing on topographical mineralogy (the study of minerals by geographic location). Images via the Mineral Gallery link. Nice site.

Libraries, archives, museums

1290 **Ecole des Mines de Paris, Mineralogy Museum**
www.ensmp.fr/Eng/Services/Musee/MUSEE-GeneralInfos.html
Mineral catalogue of the museum online. English text available. Catalogue accessible by author, mineral, date of

first publication, atoms in chemical formula and holotypes, cotypes, metatypes, author samples and dedicated samples. Catalogue of best samples contains drawings and photographs.

1291 **National Gem and Mineral Collection** [USA]
National Museum of Natural History
www.nmnh.si.edu/minsci/collect.htm
Based at the SMITHSONIAN INSTITUTION and one of the greatest collections of its kind in the world. Over 375,000 individual specimens. The Department of Mineral Sciences is 'dedicated to the study of minerals, gems, rocks, volcanoes, and meteorites: their origin and evolution'.

Portal & task environments

Bob's Rock Shop
B. Keller See entry no. 1505

1292 **Gemology World** [CAN]
Canadian Institute of Gemmology
www.cigem.ca
Interactive gateway website with many links. Courses and training sessions offered. Includes access to an electronic gemmology library, Gemmology Source, an online shopping facility; provides up-to-date developments and information for all interested in gems and jewellery. Information available in French, German, Italian, Spanish and Portuguese. Many colour images.

InfoMine
See entry no. 4692

1293 **The Mineral and Gemstone Kingdom**
Hershel Friedman.
www.minerals.net
A free, interactive, educational guide to minerals and gemstones. Extensive information has been researched and categorized. Material is arranged interactively, with an easy-to-use interface with hyperlinks and search capability. The content is geared for both amateurs and experts.

Some advertising and sponsorship; but its purpose clearly stated in a useful role model statement: 'We get reimbursement from a limited number of advertisers whose banners we post. This defrays our costs and enables us to remain free ... This site is an educational site and was not created with any commercial intentions other than banner advertising and page sponsoring. We make just enough money to keep this site up and running. Any donations will enable us to enhance this free service to the public and will be gladly accepted.'

1294 **ThamesValleyMinerals** [UK]
www.thamesvalleyminerals.com
Frequently updated and attractive commercial website with regular publications of new lists or collections. Minerals can be searched for by country, species, price range, size. Although geared to selling, provides notes and descriptions for minerals and colour photographs; and, as such, is a useful reference resource.

Discovering print & electronic resources

1295 **Annotated bibliographies of mineral deposits in Africa, Asia (exclusive of the USSR) and Australasia**
J.D. Ridge Pergamon, 1976, 547pp. English text; English, French, German, Spanish and Russian abstracts. ISBN 0080204597.
A classic bibliography similar to the *Europe* volume. Main parts: Africa (Morocco–Zambia), Asia (Burma–Turkey), Australasia (Australia, New Zealand, Papua, New Guinea, New Caledonia, Fiji). Appendix 1: Classification of ore deposits. Index of authors; A–Z list of deposits; Index of deposits (according to metals and minerals produced; age of mineralization; modified Lindgren classification). Many references not in English.
Second volume of a revised and expanded version of the author's Selected bibliographies of hydrothermal and magmatic mineral deposits, *published by the Geological Society of America, 1958.*

1296 **Annotated bibliographies of mineral deposits in Europe**
J.D. Ridge Pergamon, 1990. 2 v. Text in English; abstracts in German, Spanish, French & Russian, £220.00. ISBN 0080240224.
Generally useful annotated bibliography covering all areas of Europe. Pt.1 : Northern Europe – covers Ireland, Great Britain, Norway, Sweden, Finland, Poland, USSR; Pt 2 : Western and South Central Europe – covers Portugal, Spain, France, Belgium, Germany, Netherlands, Switzerland, Italy, Iran. Pt 2 only has an author index, thus greatly reducing its usefulness, while Pt 1 has an index to authors; A–Z index of deposits; index of deposits (according to metals and minerals produced; according to age of mineralization; according to the modified Lindgren classification).
Text in English, abstracts in German, Spanish, French and Russian.

1297 **Annotated bibliographies of mineral deposits in the Western Hemisphere**
J.D. Ridge Geological Society of America, 1972, 681pp. ISBN 0813711312 ISSN 00107053.
A useful, comprehensive bibliography for North and South America; arrangement, under country/US state/Canadian province, is by deposit. For each deposit the following are covered: minerals mined; age and position in the Lindgren classification, plus bibliography and notes. Indexes of authors and deposits (A–Z, by age, by metals and minerals produced, by Lindgren classification). Appendices provide a classification of ore deposits, and topics for consideration. Aimed, like the other two volumes, at the economic geologist in his study of specific deposits.
Series: Geological Society of America Memoirs *No. 131. Supplement 1974.*

1298 **Athena Earth Sciences Resources**
P. Perroud; University of Geneva
http://un2sg4.unige.ch/athena/mineral/minlinks_frame3.html
A useful starting point for mineralogy – and some other earth science – information online. Databases, journals, societies and organizations, museums, images, links for geoweb exploration (but some links not kept up-to-date). Extensive minerals database using International Mineralogical Association approved mineral and variety names. Includes an alphabetical list, systematic list, elements, sulphides, halides, oxides, carbonates, sulphates, phosphates, silicates, organic materials and varieties.

1299 **Gemology: an annotated bibliography**
J. Sinkankas Scarecrow Press, 1994, 1216pp. 2 v., $198.00. ISBN 0810826526.
A comprehensive bibliography of gems and precious stones suited to a general readership. Winner of the 1994 Mary B. Ansari Best Reference Work Award. Contains over 7500 entries, books and articles from 1500 up to 1985. All important works are described, collated, and assessed in terms of content, accuracy, and importance. Illustrations; subject index. Bibliography is based mainly on the Sinkankas Library, one of the largest and most complete collections of its kind, housed in the Gemological Institute of America, Santa Monica, CA.

1300 **Links for Mineralogists**
University of Würzburg
www.uni-wuerzburg.de/mineralogie/links.html
Extensive collection of annotated links to mineralogy and earth sciences resources. Section of 'what's new' useful for gaining an idea of current and recently added sites. Brief descriptions of each site aids those searching. The straightforward layout of the site features resources grouped by broad category with finer subdivisions in each. Many useful sites, with brief but informative annotations for all links. In addition to featuring resources in different areas of geology, information is also provided on research equipment, jobs, educational materials, imaging techniques, and more.
An excellent resource.

1301 **The literature of gemstones**
M. O'Donoghue British Library, Science Reference and Information Service, 1986, 75pp. ISBN 0712307389.
Precious stones bibliography. A list 'based largely on the collection of Science Reference and Information Service of the British Library'; 16 sections including encyclopedic works, journals, textbooks, bibliographies, gemstone prices. Useful resource.

1302 **Mineralogical Abstracts**
Mineralogical Society of Great Britain and Ireland 1920–. ISSN 37915002.
www.minabs.com [FEE-BASED]
Earlier (1920–58) published in the *Mineralogical Magazine*. About 5000 references each year in 17 sections, including: Age determination – apparatus and techniques – book notices ... Economic minerals and mineral deposits ... Experimental mineralogy ...geochemistry ...Meteorites and tektites – Mineral data ...Petrology. Index of authors per issue; annual author and subject indexes. From 2004 available online only as MINABS Online.

1303 **Mineralogy and Petrology Research on the Web**
University of Dayton
http://homepages.udayton.edu/~koziol/resminpet.html
Simple collection of links to journals, publishers, surveys, mineralogical databases, professional societies, laboratories, and research groups focused on mineralogy and petrology. Well organized web page, easy to navigate around. Kept reasonably up-to-date.

Digital data, image & text collections

1304 **Mindat.org: The Mineral Database**
www.mindat.org
Claims to be one of the largest mineral databases on the internet. Currently there are 23,990 different minerals, varieties and synonyms listed, and information on 194,069 mineral occurrences worldwide, from 39,987 different sites. Interactive website. Alphabetical index of minerals. Simple search capabilities.

1305 **Mineral Atlas of the World: Europe**
United Nations Educational, Scientific and Cultural Organization
http://publishing.unesco.org [DESCRIPTION]
Digital version of the 1:10,000,000 scale map of the *International metallogenic map of Europe* printed in 1997 under the auspices of the Commission for the Geological Map of the World in conjunction with the International Geological Congress.

1306 **Mineralogy Database**
D. Barthelmy
http://webmineral.com
An online mineral database containing 4339 individual mineral species descriptions with links. Includes definitions, classifications and photo index. Some technical knowledge or science background required. Highly recommended for undergraduate use.

1307 **Virtual Atlas of Opaque and Ore Minerals in their Associations**
R.A. Ixer and P.R. Duller; Society for Mining, Metallurgy, and Exploration
www.smenet.org/opaque-ore
Excellent visual resource. Full colour photomicrographs of major ore-forming associations and opaque minerals in non-mineralized rocks with examples. Listings of major primary ore minerals given for each associations with further information and references. Indexed by association, country, location, mineral name, mineralogy, texture, optical property, and plate descriptions. Image gallery. Sponsored by the Society. However, last updated October 1998.

Directories & encyclopedias

The collector's encyclopedia of rocks & minerals
A.F.L. Deeson, ed. See entry no. 1512

1308 **Concise encyclopedia of mineral resources**
D.D. Carr and N. Herz, eds Pergamon Press, 1989, 426pp. £99.00. ISBN 0080347347.
A useful classic encyclopedia with over 100 alphabetically-arranged articles by 90 world authorities. Primarily a compilation of articles from the *Encyclopedia of materials science and engineering* (Pergamon Press, 1986), arranged A–Z (Abrasives ... Zirconium and hafnium resources). Larger topics are subdivided, e.g. coal: geology; mining; world resources. Short bibliographies are appended to the articles. Subject index. Undergraduate, postgraduate readership.
Series: Advances in Materials Science and Engineering, V.8.

1309 **Directory of institutions active in research in mineralogy, petrology, geochemistry and their applications** [EUR]
R.O. Felius [et al.], eds; European Mineralogical Union E. Schweizerbart'sche Verlagsbuchandlung, 1993.
Government publication comprising a listing of major

institutions in Europe. A useful starting point, despite being somewhat out of date.
Supplement to European Journal of Mineralogy.

1310 **The encyclopedia of gemstones and minerals**
M. Holden and E.A. Mathez, eds Facts On File, 1991, 303pp. A Friedman Group book. ISBN 0816021775.
Over 200 rocks, jewels, stones and other mineral substances are described in terms of properties/values. Data on characteristic form, specific gravity, symmetry, system, refraction, location, use and commercial use are supplied. Useful general text.

1311 **The encyclopedia of mineralogy**
K. Frye, ed. Kluwer Academic Publishers, 1982, 815pp. £405.00. ISBN 0879331844.
www.eseo.com
An authoritative resource. Comprises 148 articles by over 100 specialists with an A–Z mineral glossary of 3000 entries. A comprehensive subject index, extensive cross-references, reference lists and technical detail. Primarily for professionals.
Available online: see website.

1312 **Hey's mineral index: mineral species, varieties, and synonyms**
A.M. Clark 3rd edn, Chapman & Hall/Natural History Museum, 1993, 859pp. £106.00. ISBN 0412399504.
Revision of a standard text. About 3500 mineral species, A–Z, with chemical formulas and literature references. Features information on all known mineral species, varieties, and synonyms. Includes an index which simplifies location of species by type: Elements, Sulfides, etc. Details of all mineral chemical compositions are included. Type locality for each mineral, and changes in the chemical formulation of each species, also included. Chemical classification (32 sections), pp 783–852.
Rev edn of An index of mineral species & varieties arranged chemically *Max H. Hey. 2nd edn, 1955. Now out of print; 4th edn planned by Cambridge University Press*

1313 **Inventaire minéralogique de la France**
Bureau de recherches géologiques et minières Éditions du BRGM, 1971–, Periodical. Maps.
Current information arranged by regions (e.g. 2. Hautes Alpes, 3. Finistère, 4. Alpes Maritimes ...). Details of mineralogical excursions, with maps, access points, types of deposit, and mineralogy. Each guide has general and mineral indexes, plus a bibliography.
Prepared by Roland Pierrot et al. Volume numbering begins at no. 3. The first 2 vols are identified by the mineralogical numbers of the départements covered, viz. 15, 05.

1314 **The Macdonald encyclopedia of precious stones**
C. Cipriani Macdonald, 1986, 384pp. £10.99. ISBN 0356122077.
English translation of the Italian (Milan, Mondadori, 1984). Three parts: Natural stones, Organic gems, and Synthetic and artificial products. Synoptic table. Glossary. Bibliography. Analytical index. Useful, small-format guide. Over 300 coloured illustrations. Limited availability.

The Macdonald encyclopedia of rocks and minerals
A. Mottana See entry no. 1518

1315 **Mineral atlas of India**
J. Banerjee, S. Ghosh and A. Mukherjee, comps Geological Survey of India, 2001. $305.00. ISSN 02540436.
India's current mineral inventory well illustrated through 77 map sheets. Projects the distribution as well as the potential of the country's mineral deposits. Minerals are grouped into nine categories, based on their end-use. Appendices with lists of deposit names, location, lithology, age of host rock, etc. A comprehensive reference work useful for geoscientists and industrialists alike.
Series: Special Publications, No. 60.

1316 **Photographic guide to minerals of the world**
O. Johnsen Oxford University Press, 2002, 439pp. £17.99. ISBN 0198515685.
Comprehensive guide to the minerals of the world, aimed primarily at serious amateur geologists. Written in non-technical English. A mineral-by-mineral guide, sections on crystallography, physical and chemical properties, and identification characteristics. References to mineral locations. Many photographs and colour line drawings.

1317 **World directory of mineral collections**
O.V. Petersen [et al.], eds; International Mineralogical Association 3rd edn, Mineralogical Record Inc, 1994, 293pp.
A handy guide to world collections the 2nd edition of which was published by the Commission on Museums of the International Mineralogical Association in 1977. Lists collections from around the world, providing for each: name of collection (in original and in English), address, name of person in charge, total number of specimens (usually divided into minerals, rocks, ores, gems, meteorites/tektites), uses of the collection, speciality, loan facilities, exchange arrangements, catalogue, times of admission.

Handbooks & manuals

21st century complete guide to minerals: comprehensive information from the US Geological Survey (USGS) including the full mineral yearbook, commodity summaries, industry surveys, and information on gemstones, rock and mineral collecting
US Geological Survey See entry no. 4708

1318 **The 22nd edition of the manual of mineral science: (after James D. Dana)**
C Klein and C.S. Hurlbut 22nd edn, Wiley, 2002, 653pp. CD-ROM, $119.95. ISBN 0471251771.
Classic reference resource continually updated. Extensive and authoritative coverage of mineralogy and crystallography. Mineral and subject indexes. Extensively illustrated. Sections cover crystallography (structure, chemistry, etc.) and minerals (physical and optical properties). Systematic mineralogy and determinative tables for some 200 common minerals. Subject index. Minerals index.
First published 1848.

1319 **An atlas of minerals in thin section**
D.J. Schulze Oxford University Press, 2004. CD-ROM, £24.00. ISBN 019516038X.
The images are shown using a polarizing microscope, and the minerals listed according to structure and composition based on the Dana system. Alphabetical index. Access

information via mineral or topic name. Seven fundamental optical properties, with 65 minerals and images of alteration textures. Includes mineral name, chemical formula, two to four images, and explanatory text. All images can be enlarged to near-screen size. Useful for undergraduate lab work.

1320 Dana's new mineralogy: the system of mineralogy of James Dwight Dana and Edward Salisbury Dana
R.V. Gaines [et al.] 8th edn, Wiley, 1997, 1864pp. With illustrations by Eric Dowty. Previous edn published as: *The system of mineralogy of James Dwight Dana and Edward Salisbury Dana*. C. Palache, H. Berman, C. Frondel. Chapman & Hall, 1944, $325.00. ISBN 0471193100.
A comprehensive and authoritative reference work with descriptions of all of the 3000-plus recognized mineral species. Features an emphasis on mineral structure, presenting descriptions of all the important species. Specially commissioned structure diagrams describing the important mineral groups. Includes indexes. Systematic and detailed description of minerals, with reference to related literature and authoritative classification.

1321 A field guide to rocks and minerals
F.H. Pough 5th edn, Houghton Mifflin, 1996, 396pp. ISBN 0395727774.
A handy guide to rocks and minerals revised and updated for this edition with information on identification and testing. More emphasis on minerals than rocks; 385 colour photographs of rocks, minerals, and geologic formations. Section describing tests and techniques for identification of minerals. Includes glossary, bibliography, index. General and undergraduate readership level.
Series: The Peterson Field Guides, No. 7. Previous edn 1976.

1322 Gemology
C.S. Hurlbut and R.C. Kammerling 2nd edn, Wiley, 1991, 336pp. $200.00. ISBN 0471526673.
A comprehensive reference resource which covers the occurrence, mineralogy, identification and fashioning of gemstones. This edition focuses on the methods and instrumentation which characterize and identify gems. Gem determinative tables. Chapter references and detailed analytical index.
First published 1979.

1323 Gems: their sources, descriptions and identification
R. Webster and P.G. Read 5th edn, Butterworth-Heinemann, 1994, 1054pp. £99.99. ISBN 0750616741.
An attractive and useful resource. The revised edition included new gem sources and the most recently introduced gem test equipment and techniques. There were extensive revisions, several chapters completely rewritten with opal now covered in a separate chapter. Descriptions and identification of gemstones. Appendices. Bibliography. Name and subject (partly analytical) indexes. Colour plates.
First published 1962.

1324 Gemstone & mineral data book: a compilation of data, recipes, formulas and instructions for the mineralogist, gemologist, lapidary, jeweler, craftsman and collector
J. Sinkankas Van Nostrand Reinhold, 1981, 352pp. Originally published New York: Winchester, 1972. ISBN 0442247095.
Data on c.1000 gems, stones and ornamental minerals, their characteristics and chemical properties. Twelve sections. Much use of tables. Useful in a mineralogical laboratory or museum.

1325 Gemstones of the world
W. Schumann Rev. & expanded edn, N.A.G. Press, 2001, 279pp. Translation of *Edelsteine und Schmucksteine# (BLV Verlagsgesellschaft mbH. Munich), £18.50. ISBN 0719803012.*
A concise pocket-sized reference tool with descriptions of approximately 1400 gemstones. Descriptive text faces colour plates in four sections: minerals, precious stones and gemstones, rocks, and ore deposits. Hints to collectors. Mineral identification tables. Aids to identification. Includes index.

Handbook of marine mineral resources
D.S. Cronan, ed. See entry no. 4713

1326 Handbook of mineralogy
J.W. Anthony [et al.] Mineral Data Publishing, Tucson, 1990–.
Set of comprehensive, systematic handbooks. An invaluable reference resource. Covers all minerals known. The minerals are arranged in alphabetical order, each on a single page that contains enough data to completely characterize the species for most purposes. The volumes contain more than adequate literature citations to guide readers towards whatever additional information is required.

- **1. Elements, sulfides, sulfosalts** 1990, 588pp. ISBN 0962209708.
- **2. Silica, silicates** 1995, 918pp. ISBN 0962209716. www.minsocam.org/MSA/Handbook. 2 v.
- **3. Halides, hydroxides, oxides** 1997, 637pp. ISBN 0962209708.
- **4. Arsenates, phosphates, vanadates** 2000, 689pp. ISBN 0962209732.
- **5. Borates, carbonates, sulfates** 2003, 822pp. ISBN 0962209708.

1327 Identification of gemstones
M. O'Donoghue and L. Joyner Butterworth-Heinemann, 2002, 384pp. £40.00. ISBN 0750655127.
http://books.elsevier.com/companions [COMPANION]
A comprehensive reference to gemmological materials and their identification; 60 full colour photographs. Chapter summaries. Contents: Introduction; Bibliography; Gem testing; Diamond ... Ruby and Sapphire ... Topaz ... Moonstone ... Amber ... Glass; Metals; Plastics; Composite gems; Rare gem species; Locality information. Glossary and index. Would suit students, jewellers, dealers, collectors and amateurs.

1328 Introduction to ore-forming processes
L.J. Robb Blackwell Publishing, 2004, 384pp. £32.50. ISBN 0632063785.
A senior undergraduate–postgraduate textbook, the aim of which is to focus attention on the many geological processes resulting in mineral deposit formation. Contains an overview of magmatic ore-forming processes; describes hydrothermal and sedimentary metallogenic environments; relates metallogeny to global tectonics by examining the distribution of mineral deposits in space and time. Many case studies and examples. Summaries and further references at end of each chapter.

1329 **The magic of minerals**
O. Medenbach and H. Wilk Springer, 1986, 204pp. Translation of *Zauberwelt der Mineralien*. Text in English and German, $60.00. ISBN 0387157301.
Superbly illustrated resource with 110 colour photographs, each with descriptive and explanatory text to accompany. Useful addition to academic libraries. Colours in photographs especially useful for mineral identification. Index included.

1330 **The Michelin field guide to minerals, rocks and fossils**
N. Curtis Michelin I-Spy, 1997, 192pp. £4.99. ISBN 1856711862.
A good and useful introduction to the identification of rocks, minerals, and fossils. Will suit all ages and abilities. Handy for practical work.
Cover title: Minerals, rocks and fossils.

Mineral deposits of Europe
S.H.U. Bowie [et al.], eds; Institution of Mining and Metallurgy and Mineralogical Society of Great Britain and Ireland See entry no. 4715

1331 **Mineral deposits of the world: ores, industrial minerals and rocks**
M. Vanecek Elsevier, 1994, 519pp. Three folded maps, £162.00. ISBN 0444986677.
A useful list of metallic and non-metallic mineral deposits according to continents, with chapters for each regional metallogenic zones. Chapter 12. Principal trends in exploiting the world's mineral wealth. Characteristics supplemented by basic data on the amount, extent and manner of using these mineral resources. Undergraduate and postgraduate readership. Includes bibliographical references (pp 454–78). Subject index and locality index.
Series: Developments in Economic Geology, V. 28.

1332 **Mineral reference manual**
E.H. Nickel and M.C. Nichols Kluwer Academic Publishers, 1991, 254pp. £23.75. ISBN 0442003447.
Alphabetical listing of all valid minerals. Includes the name, formula, current status, crystal system, classification and selected literature references for each species. Helpful for brief description of relevant data for each mineral. A comprehensive resource of more than 3700 species. Table of synonyms. Bibliography.
'An excellent reference addition to mineralogical collections in all libraries.' (*New Technical Books*)
'merely a listing allowing someone in mineralogy to put a few pieces of information onto a name.' (*Choice*, June 1991, p. 1620)

1333 **Mineralization in the British Isles**
R.A.D. Pattrick and D.A. Polya Kluwer Academic Publishers, 1993, 499pp. £142.00. ISBN 041231200X.
A key review of the major orefields and metallogenic provinces in the British Isles; 12 contributors. Each chapter includes a discussion of the mineralization characteristics in detail, a review of recent research and places the mineralization of the area in a local and worldwide context. Ample references. Detailed analytical index. Includes bibliographical references (pp 484–9). Many B/W photographs.

1334 **Mineralogy and geology of rare earths in China**
P. Zhang [et al.] Science Press, Beijing, 1996, 226pp. £43.00. ISBN 9067642207.
All rare earth minerals and rare earth ore deposits discovered in China and their related geological features are described. This includes huanghoite and baotite, as well as new species and varieties discovered in China. Systematic descriptions of classification are given, including chemical composition, crystallography and crystal structure, physical properties, and X-ray powder data. Bibliography pp 198–205. Useful for those interested in theoretical and practical studies of mineralogy.
Series: Solid Earth Sciences Research in China.

1335 **Minerals in thin section**
D. Perkins and K.R. Henke 2nd edn, Prentice Hall, 2004, 176pp. $45.00. ISBN 0131420151.
Essential reading for undergraduates in conjunction with laboratory work. Clear and concise text assists students as they look at thin sections focusing on the practical, need-to-know information necessary for work in the laboratory. Especially useful for courses in mineralogy, optical mineralogy and petrography. Two parts: Theoretical considerations; Identifying minerals in thin section. Appendices with additional information. More than 30 pages of colour photographs. Clear descriptions and explanations of some 60 of the most important rock-forming minerals. Bibliography.
Previous edn 1999.

1336 **Minerals of Scotland: past and present**
A. Livingstone National Museums of Scotland, 2003, 212pp. £35.00. ISBN 1901663469.
Details over 60 minerals native to Scotland. Glossary of 552 known species. Descriptions, historical background and occurrence; 118 colour illustrations, 82 black and white. Highlights pioneering roles of Scottish scientists in the development of mineralogy. Brief account of Scotland's geological history. A comprehensive approach.

1337 **Philip's guide to gems, stones & crystals**
C. Oldershaw Philip's, 2003, 256pp. £9.99. ISBN 0540083895.
Practical guide to identification and use of precious and semiprecious stones, novelty stones, agates and crystals. Includes visual identification key and many other practical details for collectors. Includes geology, chemistry and properties of gemstones. General readership level.

1338 **Philip's guide to minerals, rocks & fossils**
W.R. Hamilton, A.R. Woolley and A.C. Bishop Philip's, 1999, 336pp. £9.99. ISBN 0540074292.
Compact handbook for amateur collectors and specialists alike. More than 13,000 A–Z features; 150 colour illustrations and 100 line drawings; 150 special box features and 200 individual country features. A guide to identifying all minerals, rocks and fossils.
Rev. edn of The Hamlyn guide to minerals, rocks, and fossils *(1974). Published in association with The Natural History Museum [q.v.].*

1339 **A photographic guide to minerals, rocks and fossils**
J.L. Roberts New Holland, 2001, 144pp. £9.99. ISBN 1859749399.
This is a practical and useful guide identifying more than 240 minerals, rocks and major invertebrate fossils. There is information on how to distinguish between varieties, and

discussion of their various properties and characteristic features. Technical details and jargon are kept to a minimum. Bibliography; index. General and undergraduate readership.
Originally published 1998.

Practical handbook of physical properties of rocks and minerals
R.S. Carmichael, ed. See entry no. 1528

1340 **Quantitative data file for ore minerals**
A.J. Criddle and C.J. Stanley, eds 3rd edn, Kluwer Academic Publishers, 1993, 635pp. £180.00. ISBN 041246750X.
A useful reference source for mineralogists. Includes keys for identification and data tables. Produced under the auspices of the Commission on Ore Mineralogy of the International Mineralogical Association, with the support of The Natural History Museum, London. Contains reference data for 505 mineral species and 130 compositional or structural variants or varieties. Significant increase in size on 2nd edn (1986).

1341 **Rock-forming minerals**
W.A. Deer, R.A. Howie and J Zussman 2nd ed., Geological Society, London, 1979–.
Essential reference work for mineralogists, petrologists and geochemists. Comprises a number of volumes. This second edition summarizes the advances in research made since the first edition was published. Much of the second edition has been completely rewritten and expanded. Primarily for undergraduate and postgraduate readership.

- **1A. Orthosilicates W.A. Deer, R.A. Howie and J. Zussman** 1997, 919pp. £75.00. ISBN 1897799888.
- **1B. Disilicates and ring silicates** 1997, 629pp. £75.00. ISBN 1897799896.
- **2A. Single-chain silicates** 1997, 668pp. £75.00. ISBN 1897799853.
- **2B. Double-chain silicates** 1997, 764pp. £99.00. ISBN 1897799772.
- **3A. Micas M.E. Fleet** 2004, 780pp. £125.00. ISBN 1862391424.
- **4A. Framework silicates W.A. Deer, R.A. Howie and J. Zussman** 2001, 972pp. £115.00. ISBN 1862390819.
- **4B. Silica Minerals, Feldspathoids & Zeolites R R.A. Howie, ed.** 2004. £125.00. ISBN 1862391440.
- **5B. Non-silicates: sulphates, carbonates, phosphates, halides L.L.Y. Chang, R.A. Howie and J. Zussman** 1996, 383pp. £120.00. ISBN 0582300932.

Keeping up-to-date

1342 **The Mineralogical Record**
Mineralogical Record Inc, 1970–, Bimonthly. $55.00. ISSN 00264628.
www.minrec.org
Flagship publication, written by and for mineral enthusiasts worldwide. Aims especially to serve the needs of mineral collectors. Most issues of the magazine are devoted to a single topic, and can stand alone as reference works. The website – wholly on a black background – gives further details.

1343 **Reviews in Mineralogy and Geochemistry**
Mineralogical Society of America and Geochemical Society
Biannual. $40.00 (V. 56, 2004). ISBN 0939950685 ISSN 15296466.
www.minsocam.org/MSA/RIM [description]
A useful means of keeping up to date with research in mineralogy and geochemistry. Individual monographs with contributions from experts in relevant fields are published as part of a series. Especially useful for undergraduate and postgraduate research.

Oceanography

bathymetry • coasts • oceans • seas • survey vessels • tides • underwater technology • waves

Introductions to the subject

The atmosphere and ocean: a physical introduction
N. Wells See entry no. 1158

1344 **Biological oceanography: an introduction**
C.M. Lalli and T.R. Parsons 2nd edn, Butterworth-Heinemann, 1997, 334pp. £26.99. ISBN 0750633840.
http://www3.open.ac.uk/courses
Companion to an Open University third-level course in oceanography. Chapters are: The abiotic environment; Phytoplankton and primary production; Zooplankton; Energy flow and mineral cycling; Nekton and fisheries; Oceanography; Benthos; Benthic communities; Human impacts.
Website gives access to descriptions of the full range of Open University courses – many of which provide useful brief overviews of the subject, as well as recommended reading lists. This volume was listed for Course No. S330, a Level 3 Diploma within Earth Sciences, under Science.

1345 **The changing ocean: its effects on climate and living resources**
B. Voituriez; United Nations Educational, Scientific and Cultural Organization 2003, 176pp. €14.80. ISBN 923103877X.
Good concise introduction to the science and technology. Six chapters: A brief history of oceanography; Driving forces of the ocean currents; Oceanic variations, climatic variations; Ecosystem dynamics; Climate variation and fish; See, observe, measure and model, to understand and forecast.

1346 **Essentials of Oceanography**
A. P. Trujillo and H. V. Thurman 8th edn, Prentice Hall, 2005, 552pp. CD-ROM, $94.00. ISBN 0131447734.
www.prenhall.com/thurman [companion]
Clearly laid-out text with good use of typography and colour designed to answer the question: 'How do the oceans work?' Systems-based approach but suitable for those who have no formal background in science or mathematics.
7th edn 2002.

1347 **Exploring ocean science**
K. Stowe 2nd edn, John Wiley, 1996, 441pp. ISBN 0471543764.
Wide-ranging introduction assuming little or no background in science. Organized: History and tools of oceanography; Materials and motion; Planet earth; Plate motion and the ocean floor; Sediments; Sea water; The ocean and our climate; Ocean currents; Waves and tides; The coastal ocean; Life and the production of food; Marine organisms; Environments and lifestyles; Coastal development, pollution and food; Ocean resources and law. Glossary; further reading.
Rev. edn of Essentials of ocean science, *1987.*

1348 **Introduction to ocean remote sensing**
S. Martin Cambridge University Press, 2004, 426pp. £45.00. ISBN 0521802806.
Good wide-ranging introductory reference text. Remote sensing involved primarily the use of the electromagnetic spectrum to observe the ocean, and secondarily the use of gravity observations to observe ocean currents and tides. Because remote sensing involves many disciplines, the book provides the necessary background in electromagnetic theory, atmospheric and seawater properties, physical and biological oceanography, physical properties of the sea surface, and satellite orbital mechanics. As prerequisites the book requires only a basic knowledge of electromagnetic theory and differential equations.

1349 **Mapping the deep: the extraordinary story of ocean science**
R. Kunzig Sort Of Books, 2000, 345pp. Improved version of the volume published Norton, 1999: *The restless sea*, £8.99. ISBN 0953522717.
www.sortof.co.uk/Deep [DESCRIPTION]
Popular introduction by author whose enthusiasm keeps the book lively and interesting, albeit with often curious chapter titles; e.g. 'Where the water goes' treats currents and circulation. Treats both the familiar and relatively unfamiliar aspects of oceanography such as deep ocean studies. Despite the title, little cartographic content. Bibliography; index.

1350 **Oceans 2020: science, trends, and the challenge of sustainability**
J.G. Field, G. Hempel and C.P. Summerhayes, eds; Intergovernmental Oceanographic Commission, Scientific Committee on Oceanic Research and Scientific Committee on Problems of the Environment Island Press, 2002, 296pp. $30.00. ISBN 1559634707.
Sponsored volume presenting good overview of the major problems likely to arise in marine and oceanic science in the next 20 years. Includes coverage of: Basic ocean sciences; Pressures on the coastal zone; Climate change and the ocean; Fisheries and fishery science and their search for sustainability; Offshore industries including oil drilling, carbon sequestration, and manganese nodule mining.
(*Guardian*, 5 Sep 1996, p 7, by T. Radford. *Nature*, 385 (6615), p 408, P.G. Brewer)

1351 **Scientists and the sea 1650–1900: a study of marine science**
M.B. Deacon 2nd edn, Ashgate Publishing, 1997, 499pp. £57.50. ISBN 1859283527.
Presents the background to the 17th-century movement, then treats marine science in that century and the following two centuries, stressing the ebbs and flows of interest in, and involvement with, the sea. Although scholarly and quite densely packed remains accessible and readable. Good bibliographies. Index of persons; subject index,

1352 **Understanding the oceans: a century of ocean exploration**
A.L. Rice, M. Deacon and C.P. Summerhayes, eds UCL Press, 2001, 318pp. £95.00. ISBN 1857287053.
Wide-ranging and authoritative multi-authored text treating the last century's development in oceanographic science; 17 chapters in four sections: The historical context; Ocean basins; Ocean measurements; The ocean ecosystem.

Dictionaries, thesauri, classifications

A dictionary of weather
S. Dunlop See entry no. 1174

Encyclopedia of marine sciences
J.G. Baretta-Bekker, E.K. Duursma and B.R. Kuipers, eds See entry no. 2567

1353 **A glossary of oceanographic terms**
J.J. Powlik, ed.; University of British Columbia 2nd edn, Raggedtooth Press, 2000, 204pp. $9.95. ISBN 0967730422.
www.raggedtooth.com/books/rtpress.html [DESCRIPTION]
1700 terms from wide range of disciplines plus other useful material. Prepared by members of the University's Department of Earth and Ocean Sciences.

Laws, standards, codes

1354 **International oceanographic tables**
United Nations Educational, Scientific and Cultural Organization 1968–1987. 4 v.
Still standard texts prepared by the Organization's Joint Panel on Oceanographic Tables and Standards and the (former) National Institute of Oceanography of Great Britain. Culmination of international effort to standardize oceanographic measurements and conversions for conductivity, salinity, temperature and oxygen saturation of seawater.

Official & quasi-official bodies

Intergovernmental Oceanographic Commission
See entry no. 2570

International Hydrographic Organization
See entry no. 1568

International Maritime Organization
See entry no. 5752

1355 **National Ocean Service** [USA]
www.oceanservice.noaa.gov
Vision is to be the Global Leader in Integrated Management of the Ocean (GLIMO), meeting the challenge through five themes: observations; modelling; watersheds; partnerships; technology. Strategic framework forthcoming. Access to wide range of information categorized: Oceans (e.g. Marine protected areas; Oil and chemical spills); Coasts (e.g. Coastal ecosystem science; Training and capacity building); Charting and Navigation (e.g. Aerial photography and shoreline mapping; Marine navigation).

The useful NOS Data Explorer 'serves as a portal to obtain NOS spatial data. This site allows users to: search NOS data holdings; view metadata; link to and/or download specific data sets.' Educational programme. Some 800 publications, many available online and/or can be downloaded in PDF.

- **Tide and current glossary S.D. Hicks [et al.]** 1999, 34pp. http://co-ops.nos.noaa.gov/publications/glossary2.pdf. Authoritative listing with a history dating back to 1941. Contains short, exact notes on each entry with cross-references.
- **Office of Coast Survey** http://chartmaker.ncd.noaa.gov. Produces nautical charts for United States waters, including possessions, territories.

Oldest US scientific organization: Thomas Jefferson established the office in 1807 to encourage commerce and to support a growing economy in a safe and efficient manner.

National Oceanic and Atmospheric Administration
See entry no. 1188

1356 **NOAA Coastal Services Center** [USA]
www.csc.noaa.gov
Office within the National Oceanic and Atmospheric Administration [q.v.] devoted to serving the USA's state and local coastal resource management programmes. Useful data, publications and tools.

- **Glossary of coastal terminology B Voigt** Southwest Washington Coastal Erosion Study, 2001. www.csc.noaa.gov/text/glossary.html. Terminology used in coastal science, engineering, geology, management, nearshore oceanography and the technologies that characterize, measure, describe or quantify the physical properties, processes and changes of the coastal zone. Bibliography.

Office of Naval Research
See entry no. 5753

Research centres & institutes

1357 **British Oceanographic Data Centre**
www.bodc.ac.uk
Designated Data Centre of the Natural Environment Research Council [q.v.] for marine science. Manages data from large scale marine field experiments, developing software allowing its manipulation and querying, and producing a range of products and service. Site provides comprehensive set of links to oceanographic and other data resources on sites around the world: associations and societies, conferences, data and information resources, journals, libraries, documents, data format and code definitions.

- **GEBCO Digital Atlas** 2003. £230.00. www.bodc.ac.uk [DESCRIPTION]. BODC have issued a CD-ROM Centenary Edition of the data comprising the General Bathymetric Chart of the Oceans.

1358 **Florida State University, Department of Oceanography** [USA]
http://ocean.fsu.edu
Includes clearly laid-out and easy-to-navigate excellent set of links including very impressive lists of US and international organizations and institutions, data, mapping tools and careers in earth sciences.

1359 **Scripps Institution of Oceanography** [USA]
http://sio.ucsd.edu
A leading world-class institution – part of the University of California, San Diego – whose mission is: 'To seek, teach, and communicate scientific understanding of the oceans, atmosphere, Earth, and other planets for the benefit of society and the environment'.

The SIO Oceanographic Collections comprise significant collections of marine vertebrate, pelagic invertebrate, benthic invertebrates, cored sediment and dredged rock specimens. There is a very extensive Photogallery arranged chronologically from 1928. The Library includes manuscripts and archival materials that document the history of the Institution with correspondence, photographs, logbooks, diaries, films, audio recordings, drawings, blueprints and other materials. The collection also contains 19th- and 20th-century materials documenting oceanographic expeditions, ships and instrumentation, science policy, marine life, marine resources, marine policy and law.

1360 **Southampton Oceanography Centre** [UK]
www.soc.soton.ac.uk
Run in partnership by the University of Southampton and the NATURAL ENVIRONMENT RESEARCH COUNCIL, is 'one of the world's leading centres for research and education in marine and earth sciences, for the development of marine technology, and for the provision of large scale infrastructure and support for the marine research community'. Inviting portal giving access to wide range of research and education-related resources. The Centre has developed a set of Ocean and Earth Science Resources for Schools.

- **National Oceanographic Library** www.library.soton.ac.uk/nol. Comprehensive facility including a commercial Marine Information and Advisory Service. Access to a large searchable archive of images covering historic as well as current research. Much other valuable material. Good links section.

1361 **Woods Hole Oceanographic Institution** [USA]
www.whoi.edu
Founded in 1930 with a primary mission 'to develop and effectively communicate a fundamental understanding of the processes and characteristics governing how the oceans function and how they interact with Earth as a whole'. Colourful inviting website with good use of images: there are also numerous informative slide shows throughout the site. The Institution provides a set of K-12 Resources and it participates in WHSTEP, the Woods Hole Science and Technology Education Partnership.

The MBLWHOI LIBRARY is run jointly with the Woods Hole Marine Biological Laboratory.

- **Oceanus** Biannual. $15.00. ISSN 00298182. http://oceanusmag.whoi.edu. First published in 1952 as a 16-page typewritten document to provide 'a worthwhile reference to modern oceanographic exploration ... That is neither too technical nor too popular.' Now supplemented by regularly updated online version.

Associations & societies

American Society of Limnology and Oceanography
See entry no. 2581

Canadian Meteorological and Oceanographic Society
See entry no. 1194

International Society for Reef Studies
See entry no. 2593

National Ocean Industries Association
See entry no. 4755

Society for Underwater Technology
See entry no. 5762

Libraries, archives, museums

1362 **Fisheries-Oceanography Library**
University of Washington
www.lib.washington.edu/fish
Contains extensive collections of books, journals and reports in oceanography and hydrology. Series of subject guides point visitors in the direction of appropriate databases, books and journals. Titles include: Marine mammals, Endangered aquatic and marine species, Polar, Tides, Coasts – ecology and management. Historical 'Freshwater and Marine Image Bank' contains over 10,000 images taken from a variety of publications issued between 1735 and 1924. There is also a well constructed and informative K-12 Resource Guide. A good site.

1363 **National Maritime Museum** [UK]
www.nmm.ac.uk
Contains over two million objects related to seafaring, navigation, astronomy and measuring time. Collections Online provides good access to digital reproductions of over of 5700 objects and over 8000 images of objects from the collections including prints and drawings, quadrants, globes, charts, and medals. A selection of images of flags, ship models and uniforms is being added during 2004.

The Caird Library is 'the most comprehensive reference library of its kind in the world' and provides a range of useful services.

- **PORT** www.port.nmm.ac.uk. Links to evaluated high-quality web-based maritime resources. Searchable or browsable. Categories include conflicts at sea, exploration, fishing, marine engineering, current and historical perspectives.
- **Royal Observatory, Greenwich** www.rog.nmm.ac.uk. Founded 1675. The astronomers left Greenwich during the 1950s because London light and air pollution was affecting observations. Under the new title Royal Greenwich Observatory, they moved first to Herstmonceux Castle Sussex and then in 1990 to Cambridge.

NOAA Central Library
National Oceanic and Atmospheric Administration See entry no. 1203

Portal & task environments

1364 **National Oceanographic Data Center** [USA]
www.nodc.noaa.gov
Archives and provides public access to global oceanographic and coastal data, products, and information. Good entrée to range of often requested data. 'Popular Items' listed were: Beach temperatures; Coastal buoy data; Global ocean temperature and salinity data; Ocean data archive; Photo collection; World ocean atlas; World ocean database (as well as the NOAA Central Library).

Well laid-out site with good intuitive links, often to detailed sets of data, e.g. Parameters & Data Types: Provides excellent summaries and key links for: biology data; buoy data; chlorophyll; nutrients; ocean currents; oxygen; plankton; profile data; salinity; satellite data; sea level; temperature; waves. Overall, a very good facility.

Ocean Explorer
National Oceanic and Atmospheric Administration See entry no. 2620

The Ocean Project
See entry no. 2621

ReefBase: A Global Information System on Coral Reefs
WorldFish Center See entry no. 2623

1365 **UN Atlas of the Oceans**
United Nations
www.oceansatlas.org/index.jsp
Designed for use by 'policy makers who need to become familiar with ocean issues and by scientists, students and resource managers who need access to underlying databases and approaches to sustainability'. Four main categories:

About the Oceans: encyclopedic collection of information organized under headings such as: How oceans were formed; How oceans are changing; Maps and statistics and online databases; Monitoring and observing systems; The oceans of the future.

Issues: examples are: Climate variability and climate change; Food security; Human health; Pollution and degradation; Sustainable development.

Uses of the Oceans: covers various aspects of the main types of use of the ocean's living and non-living resources, including: Fisheries and aquaculture; Transportation and telecommunication; Offshore oil, gas and mining; Energy; Marine biotechnology.

Geography: is still under development (as is the image section) and will display material by geographic region.

The site also has a news section and an excellent searchable and alphabetic glossary from the FAO. The resources include diagrams and illustrations and the pages are very easy to use with context specific links to news, documents and websites.

Discovering print & electronic resources

Aquatic Sciences and Fisheries Abstracts: ASFA
See entry no. 2627

1366 **OceanBase**
Elsevier.
www.info.sciencedirect.com/content_coverage/databases/oceanbase.shtml [DESCRIPTION]
Access to the entire contents of *Oceanographic Literature Review*, including *Ocean Data News* together with material from *Fluid Abstracts*, *Civil Engineering*, *Ecological Abstracts* and *Current Awareness in Biological Sciences*.

1367 **Oceanic abstracts**
CSA, 1981–, Monthly. $1645.00. ISSN 07481489.
www.csa.com/factsheets/oceanic-set-c.php [DESCRIPTION]
One of the wide range of CSA offerings, accessible from 2005 via the new Illumina interface. Almost 300,000 records; 1200 added per month.
Available online: see website.

1368 **Oceanis**
National Oceanographic Library
www.library.soton.ac.uk/subjects/socsoes/oceaniswebcat.shtml [FEE-BASED]
Online access to records of not just the book stock of the Library, but also contents of the relevant journal literature as well as maps and data sources in a variety of formats, making it overall an extremely useful source in finding literature. Currently includes over 280,000 records.

OceanPortal
Intergovernmental Oceanographic Commission See entry no. 2630

1369 **Research Tools for Searching the Oceanography Literature**
R. Sathrum; Humboldt State University
http://library.humboldt.edu/~rls/oceanlit.htm
Extensive regularly updated subject guide to the literature, offering help and advice on doing a literature search and information about the different types of materials such as journals, conferences and US government publications whether available in print or online. Good example of university library subject guide to the literature.

Primary resource collections

1370 **Ocean Drilling Program**
Ocean Drilling Programme
www-odp.tamu.edu
Funded by US NATIONAL SCIENCE FOUNDATION and 22 international partners (JOIDES) to conduct basic research into the history of the ocean basins and the overall nature of the crust beneath the ocean floor using the scientific drill ship. Website offers access to substantial sets of data, plus information about partners in the programme. There is a useful 'Public & media information' section.

- CD-ROM. $10 per volume.

Digital data, image & text collections

1371 **General Bathymetric Chart of the Oceans: GEBCO**
Intergovernmental Oceanographic Commission, International Hydrographic Organization and National Geophysical Data Center
www.ngdc.noaa.gov/mgg/gebco/gebco.html [DESCRIPTION]
Aims to provide the most authoritative, publicly available bathymetry data sets for the world's oceans. Available in printed sheets or as CD-ROM: cf. GEBCO DIGITAL ATLAS.

- **GEBCO Gazetteer of Undersea Feature Names** Downloadable PDF2004, 374pp. www.ngdc.noaa.gov/mgg/gebco/underseafeatures.html#gazetteer. Selected by the GEBCO Sub-Committee on Undersea Feature Names, who are developing a uniform policy for the handling of geographical names and standardization of undersea feature names to achieve consistent naming on maps and charts.
- **World atlas of the oceans: with the General Bathymetric Chart of the Oceans (GEBCO) M. Leier; Canadian Hydrographic Services** Key Porter Books. (In the USA Firefly Books), 2000, 264pp. $50.00. www.fireflybooks.com/books/5851E.html [DESCRIPTION]. Translated from the German; 80 deep-sea charts, 80 relief maps, 40 thematic maps with 7 special charts of the North Sea and the Baltic Sea published for the first time.

1372 **Ocean Planet**
Smithsonian Institution
http://seawifs.gsfc.nasa.gov/ocean_planet.html
Travelling exhibition which premiered at the Institution's National Museum of Natural History from April 1995 to April 1996, where it attracted nearly two million visitors. This electronic online companion exhibition contains all of the text and most of the panel designs and images found in the travelling exhibition. Range of texts – creative writing about the sea, popular science.

1373 **Physical Oceanography Distributed Active Archive Center** [USA]
http://podaac.jpl.nasa.gov
Primarily responsible for archiving and distributing data relevant to the physical state of the ocean. Most of the products available were obtained from satellites and are intended for use in oceanographic and interdisciplinary scientific research. Good list of links to oceanography resources.

1374 **World Ocean Atlas**
National Oceanographic Data Center CD-ROM, 1994–1998.
www.nodc.noaa.gov/OC5/indprod.html [DESCRIPTION]
Now comprises a series of predominantly online data sets and products (though offline versions continue to be available). Includes access to a range of ocean data variables such as in-situ temperature, salinity, oxygen, dissolved inorganic nutrients (phosphate, nitrate, silicate) and chlorophyll at various depths – as well as other information including, importantly, temperature.

- **International Ocean Atlas and Information Series** www.nodc.noaa.gov/OC5/indprod.html. Currently nine volumes including coverage of biology, climate, exploration, hydrochemistry of the arctic seas – some online, some downloadable PDF, some in print, one out of print.

Directories & encyclopedias

1375 **Atlas of the oceans: wind and wave climate**
I.R. Young and G.J. Holland Pergamon, 1996, 241pp. CD-ROM version available, £136.00. ISBN 0080425194.
Provides global estimates of wind and wave conditions and is based on data from the GEOSAT satellite. Parameters such as monthly values of wind speed and wave heights are presented as contour fields in global and regional charts. Includes bibliographical references, glossary and index. CD-ROM version comes with a user guide.

1376 **Coasts and seas of the United Kingdom**
Joint Nature Conservation Committee, Construction Industry Research and Information Association and UK Offshore Operators Association 1996–1999. 16 v. CD-ROM version available. For pricing see website.
www.jncc.gov.uk/communications/pubcat/c_dirs.htm [DESCRIPTION]
The JNCC Coastal Directories project, which 'collated extensive baseline environmental and human use information, including fisheries, for the coastal and nearshore marine zone of the whole of the UK, including Northern Ireland, the Isles of Scilly, Shetland, Orkney and the Isle of Man'.

- **Directory of the Celtic coasts and seas A.J. Weighell, A.P. Donnelly and K. Calder** 292pp. ISBN 1861075081. Quality status report of physical chemical and biological conditions of coastal and marine ecosystems including coastal zone management, conservation, fisheries and aquaculture, geology and dunes.

1377 **Encyclopedia of Antarctica and the southern oceans**
B. Stonehouse, ed. Wiley, 2002, 398pp. $375.00. ISBN 0471986658.
Geographical features are described together with their latitudinal and longitudinal positions. Includes definitions and sections on explorers and animals. Generally brief entries with many of the further readings being old and travel and expedition oriented. Study Guide on information

sources directs the reader to other resources. Illustrated, well indexed, clear typeface.

1378 Encyclopedia of ocean sciences
J.H. Steele, S.A. Thorpe and K.K. Turekian, eds Academic Press, 2001, 3399pp. 6 v., $1545.00. ISBN 012227430X.
www.apnet.com/companions [COMPANION]
Covers the methodology and technology of studying oceans, law, marine ecology and pollution and submarine geology. Useful summaries at the beginning of each section, further readings and colour plates.
Also available online: see website.

1379 The Global Oceans Directory: a compendium of organizations dedicated to marine conservation
Office of Wetlands, Oceans and Watersheds 1992.
http://yosemite.epa.gov/water/owrccatalog.nsf
Covers USA, UN, Canada, non-governmental organizations and Policy Centres. Searchable by keywords. It gives an overview of each organization, examples of projects and contact details. Particularly useful for US agencies although, clearly, much information now dated.
Now online, but also available in print: see website.

1380 Mangone's concise marine almanac
G.J. Mangone 2nd rev. and expanded edn, Taylor & Francis, 1991, 207pp. $94.95. ISBN 0844816744.
Includes measurements of coastlines, sea areas, physical features and admiralty charts and other areas such as naval forces fisheries both marine and seabed and pollution. The largest oil spills up to 1989 only.

1381 Maritime and Naval Museums in Britain and Ireland
M.H. Evans and J. West, comps; Scott Polar Research Institute
www.cus.cam.ac.uk/~mhe1000/marmus.htm
Comprehensive regularly updated plain text list of c.300 museums and museum-ships. 'Not a detailed guide to collections. It is primarily a check-list with location and contact addresses, web links and terse summaries of the exhibits and facilities.' Nevertheless, a valuable facility. Other data includes general introduction, regional cross-index, set of sketch maps, links to other maritime websites, and a list of historic vessels – all with the files cross-linked.

1382 Philip's atlas of the oceans
J. Pernetta 2nd edn, Philip's, 1994, 208pp. Foreword by C. Summerhayes, £20.00. ISBN 0540060887.
Useful tables and diagrams. Information on oceanographic history, marine life and resources and currents. Photographs. Includes indexes.

1383 Survey vessels of the world
5th edn, Oilfield Publications, 2003/2004, 507pp. $195.00. ISBN 1902157362.
www.oilpubs.com [DESCRIPTION]
The world's fleet of dedicated survey vessels, including all seismic, hydrographic and general research vessels.

1384 The Times atlas and encyclopedia of the sea
A.D. Couper, ed. Revised edn, HarperReference, 1989, 272pp. £35.00. ISBN 0060162872.
As much an encyclopedia as an atlas as there is substantial textual content. It covers geography, both physical and human, of the oceans and seas. It deals with environmental issues and trade, with appendices on fishing quotas, shipping information and the law. It is inevitably out of date but for many must remain the first port of call.

1385 United Kingdom Digital Marine Atlas: UKDMAP
British Oceanographic Data Centre 3rd edn, 1998. CD-ROM, £140.00.
www.bodc.ac.uk [DESCRIPTION]
Contains over 1600 thematic charts displayed via a variety of presentation methods, including contoured plots of physical, chemical and geological parameters; colour-coded distribution charts of sea use; biological and fisheries information; oceanographic data catalogues; geo-referenced directories which present detailed information on demand.

Water: science and issues
E.J. Dasch, ed. See entry no. 1148

1386 World atlas of coral reefs
M.D. Spalding, C. Ravilious and E.P. Green; UNEP World Conservation Monitoring Centre University of California Press, 2001, 424pp. $55.00. ISBN 0520232550.
www.ucpress.edu/books [DESCRIPTION]
Detailed description of all of the world's coral reefs. Excellent collection of images including some taken during the NASA space shuttle flights. Publication was supported by a number of other international institutions, apart from WCMC: Marine Aquarium Council; International Coral Reef Initiative; ICLARM–The World Fish Center; Professional Association of Diving Instructors; Aventis Foundation.
'Unique in scope, this atlas provides cleanly rendered maps, colorful photos, and lots of solid information. Content is detailed enough to satisfy adults with a scientific background, yet remains accessible to high school students. This atlas covers all bases, making it a great resource for students and teachers alike.' (*School Library Journal*)

Handbooks & manuals

The encyclopedia of the earth: oceans and islands
F.H. Talbot and R.E. Stevenson, eds See entry no. 1065

Handbook of marine mineral resources
D.S. Cronan, ed. See entry no. 4713

1387 Jane's Underwater Technology
7th edn, Jane's Information Group, 2004–2005, Annual, 633pp. £365.00. ISBN 0710626398.
http://juwt.janes.com [DESCRIPTION]
Information on the vehicles, systems, sensors and instruments that enable the exploration, survey and management of the oceans.

The ocean basins and margins
A.E.M. Nairn and F.G. Stehli, eds See entry no. 1015

The ocean engineering handbook
F. El-Hawary, ed. See entry no. 5771

1388 Ocean politics and policy: a reference handbook
P. Jacques and Z.A. Smith ABC-CLIO, 2003, 267pp. $45.00. ISBN 1576076229.
Welcome guide to the complex set of issues and players involved with management of the world's oceans.

'An excellent compilation of material on issues affecting the oceans of the world ... Recommended for any library.' (*Reference & User Services Quarterly*)

1389 **The oceans and climate**
G.R. Bigg 2nd edn, Cambridge University Press, 2003. £28.00. ISBN 0521016347.
Excellent overview structured: 1. The climate system; 2. Physical interaction between the ocean and atmosphere; 3. Chemical interaction of the atmosphere and ocean; 4. Biochemical interaction of the atmosphere and ocean; 5. Large-scale air–sea interaction; 6. The ocean and natural climatic variability; 7. The ocean and climatic change. Appendices; Glossary; Bibliography; Index.
'This well written and richly illustrated book ... Provides a reasonably priced, lucid, and not too technical, survey of the complex system called "climate", with emphasis on the special role played by the worlds oceans, but not neglecting other pieces in a multifaceted puzzle.' (*Meteorology and Atmospheric Physics*)

1390 **Polar oceanography**
W.O. Smith, Jr, ed. Academic Press, 1990, 760pp. 2 v. ISBN 0126530300.
Good reference text. Part A covers: Meteorology; Sea ice in the polar regions; Remote sensing of the polar oceans; Large-scale physical oceanography of the polar regions; Mesoscale phenomena in the polar oceans; Small-scale processes; Models and their applications to polar oceanography. Part B covers: Chemical oceanography; Polar phytoplankton; Polar zooplankton; Upper trophic levels in polar marine ecosystems; Polar benthos; Particle fluxes and modern sedimentation in the polar oceans.
'(Part A) The text is easily accessible with a moderate amount of equations and numerous illustrations – my only reservation lies in the under-representation of Soviet data, theories and result. The present volume offers an outstanding ...text on polar oceanography.' (*Pure and Applied Geophysics, 1991* 137(1/2): 166–7)

Practical handbook of estuarine and marine pollution
M.J. Kennish See entry no. 5642

Practical handbook of marine science
M.J. Kennish, ed. See entry no. 2649

1391 **Recent advances and issues in oceanography**
C.R. Nichols, D.L. Porter and R.L. Williams Greenwood Press, 2001, 418pp. $49.95. ISBN 1573564060.
Survey of the field – and a fascinating field it is. The book is clearly aimed at high school and college students but it is not exactly a textbook nor is it a handbook. Candidate for the reference shelf owing to the many information resources included.
Series: Oryx Frontiers of Science.

1392 **The sea: ideas and observations on progress in the study of the seas**
M.N. Hill, ed. Wiley, 1962–1998. 12 v. ISBN 0471633933.
Some volumes are out of print but still being recommended and used so worth referencing here. 'As oceanography has matured over recent decades, the once separate interests of chemical, biological, and physical oceanographers have converged. The volumes of "The Sea" reflect the change in attitude in oceanography to a solid, interdisciplinary approach.'

- **Vol. 1. Physical oceanography M.N. Hill** 1962, 579pp. ISBN 0898740975.
- **Vol. 10. The global coastal ocean: processes and methods K.H. Brink and A.R. Robinson, eds** 1998, 616pp. ISBN 0471115444.
- **Vol. 11. The global coastal ocean: regional studies and syntheses** 1998, 1079pp. ISBN 0471115436.
- **Vol. 12. Biological-physical interactions in the sea A.R. Robinson, J.J. McCarthy and B.J. Rothschild, ed.** 2002, 647pp. ISBN 0471189014.
- **Vol. 2. The composition of sea water: comparative and descriptive oceanography** 1963, 569pp. ISBN 0898740983.
- **Vol. 3. The earth beneath the sea: history** 1963, 979pp. ISBN 0898740991.
- **Vol. 4. New concepts of sea floor evolution A.E. Maxwell, ed.** 1971. ISBN 0471579106. 2 v.
- **Vol. 5. Marine chemistry E.D. Goldberg, ed.** 1974, 895pp. ISBN 0471310905.
- **Vol. 6. Marine modeling** 1977, 1070pp. ISBN 0471310913.
- **Vol. 7. The oceanic lithosphere C. Emiliane, ed.** 1981, 1741pp. ISBN 0471028703. 2 v.
- **Vol. 8. Deep-sea biology G.T. Rowe, ed.** 1983, 570pp. ISBN 0471044024.
- **Vol. 9. Ocean engineering science B. Le Méhauté and D.M. Hanes, eds** 1990, 1329pp. ISBN 0471633933. 2 v.

1393 **Sea ice: an introduction to its physics, chemistry, biology and geology**
D. Thomas and G. Dieckmann, eds Blackwell Science, 2003, 402pp. £89.50. ISBN 0632058080.
Wide-ranging group of contributions providing a very good review of current knowledge of polar pack ice, 'the study of which is severely constrained by the logistic difficulties of working in such harsh and remote regions of the earth'. Sea ice covers up to 7% of the earth's surface and is a major driver of ocean circulation patterns and global climate.
'This very well presented book is a collection of papers describing some of the most valuable aspects of [sea ice] research. Sea Ice is a whole new frontier of opportunities for, among others the fisheries and aquaculture sectors. This excellent book provides considerable food for thought.' (*Fishing Boat World*)

1394 **Seas at the millennium: an environmental evaluation**
C.R.C. Sheppard, ed. Elsevier, 2000, 2415pp. 3 v., $895.50. ISBN 0080432077.
Major reference work containing over 130 contributions: in Part 1 surveying all the different geographical regions of the world – from 'The seas around Greenland' to 'French Polynesia'; in Part 2 tackling a wide range of general issues – from 'Global status of seagrasses' to 'The econological, economic and social importance of the oceans'.

Keeping up-to-date

1395 **Estuaries and Coastal Waters of the British Isles: an annual bibliography of recent scientific papers**
National Marine Biological Library 1979–. £45.00. ISSN 02610663.
www.mba.ac.uk/nmbl/publications/otherpub/british_waters.htm [DESCRIPTION]
Covers 56 sea areas. Includes an author index. Note also

links to the other publications of Library and to its collections and archives

Oceanography and Marine Biology: an annual review
See entry no. 2652

Palaeontology

amber • ammonites • Archaeopteryx • coelacanth fishes • crinoids • dinosaurs • eras • extinct organisms • fossils • human palaeopathology • invertebrate palaeontology • mass extinctions • palaeobiology • palaeobotany • palaeoclimatology • palaeoecology • paleontology • palynology • taphonomy • trilobites • vertebrate palaeontology

Introductions to the subject

1396 Amber: window to the past
D.A. Grimaldi Harry N Abrams, 2003, 216pp. $24.95. ISBN 0810926520.
Amber (fossilized tree resin) is a unique resource for palaeontologists, because it preserves specimens (most commonly insects) in microscopic detail. At the core of this book are the beautiful photographs of amber-encased fossils, and reconstructions of the living animals. However, these are well supported with a clear, non-technical text on the biology and social history of amber.

1397 At the water's edge: fish with fingers, whales with legs, and how life came ashore but then went back to sea
C. Zimmer Touchstone, 1999, 288pp. $14.00. ISBN 0684856239.
Aimed at non-specialists, Zimmer describes two related examples of major evolutionary transitions: the emergence of fish-like animals onto land over 350 million years ago, and the move by the ancestors of modern whales and dolphins from the land to the sea, nearly 50 million years ago. He uses these to discuss the relationship between macroevolution (obvious changes in body shape) and the processes that drive it, including microevolution (changes in DNA and proteins).

1398 Bones of contention
P. Chambers John Murray, 2003, 288pp. £7.99. ISBN 0719560594.
A lively, popular account of the controversies surrounding the most famous of all fossil animals, Archaeopteryx. The book, illustrated with some black-and-white photographs, follows the central role of Archaeopteryx in Victorian arguments about evolution, and more recent debates about creationism, and the relationship between birds and dinosaurs.

1399 Crucible of creation: the Burgess Shale and the rise of animals
S. Conway Morris Oxford University Press, 1999, 266pp. £8.99. ISBN 0192862022.
The Burgess Shale in British Columbia is one of the most important fossil beds in the world. Preserved in exquisite detail are the remains of an astonishing diversity of soft-bodied animals, documenting the sudden appearance of complex organisms half a billion years ago (an event known as the 'Cambrian Explosion'). Conway Morris gives a detailed but readable description of the Burgess Shale's bizarre and perplexing fauna, and puts forward his views on the nature of evolution. These views differ in many respects from those of S.J. Gould, author of another popular book on the Burgess Shale, WONDERFUL LIFE.

- **Life's solution: inevitable humans in a lonely universe**
  S. Conway Morris Cambridge University Press, 2003, 486pp. £18.99. ISBN 0521827043. 'Builds a forceful case for the predictability of evolutionary outcomes, their broad phenotypic manifestations ... I recommend the book to anyone grappling with the meaning of evolution and our place in the Universe.' *Nature*.

Deep time: cladistics, the revolution in evolution
H. Gee See entry no. 2847

1400 Dino-birds: from dinosaurs to birds
A. Milner; Natural History Museum 2002, 64pp. £5.95. ISBN 0565091743.
Many exquisitely preserved fossil birds have been discovered over the last ten years, and this book accompanied a special exhibition of them at the Natural History Museum in London (home to the original specimen of the fossil bird Archaeopteryx). Beautifully illustrated, the text (written by one of the museum's palaeontologists) describes the mounting evidence for the relationship between dinosaurs and modern birds.

1401 The dinosaur heresies
R. Bakker Penguin, 1988, 481pp. £5.00. ISBN 0140100555.
Palaeontologists have been arguing about the metabolism of dinosaurs for many years: were they sluggish, cold-blooded reptiles, or fast-moving and bird-like? This book, written during the peak of the debate in the 1980s, is a popular work by a leading advocate of active dinosaurs (a minority view at the time). In fact, since the book was published the consensus of scientific opinion has moved Bakker's way, but the book remains a gripping, rumbustious testament from one of the 'big personalities' in dinosaur palaeontology.

1402 The dinosaur hunters: a story of scientific rivalry and the discovery of the prehistoric world
D. Cadbury Fourth Estate, 2001, 384pp. £7.99. ISBN 1857029631.
This book follows the turbulent careers of the early dinosaur palaeontologists, brilliantly describing the rapidly social, religious and scientific change, in the first half of the nineteenth century. It also shows that the intellectual jealousies and rivalries between academics are nothing new!

1403 Dinosaurs past and present
S.J. Czerkas and E.C. Olson, eds University of Washington Press, 1987. 2 v.
This was written in association with a travelling exhibition of the same name. It covers the history of dinosaur research; how ideas about their biology, ecology, and (most interestingly) how they looked, have evolved over the last 150 years. Each chapter is an essay written by an expert in a particular field, illustrated with black-and-white and colour photographs, and line drawings.
V. 1. 161pp. ISBN 0938644246; V. 2. 149pp. ISBN 0295967080.

1404 Dinosaurs, spitfires and sea dragons
C. McGowan Harvard University Press, 1991, 378pp. $22.50. ISBN 067420770X.
Aimed at the non-specialist, this book explains the process by which palaeontologists start with the preserved remains,

but use comparisons with living animals and a knowledge of physics and materials to reconstruct the biology of extinct animals. Taking examples from dinosaurs, pterosaurs and marine reptiles, McGowan shows how we can gain surprising insights in palaeobiology, and how some theories are based on flimsy evidence.

Evolution and the fossil record
J. Pojeta and D.A. Springer; American Geological Institute and Paleontological Society See entry no. 2438

1405 **The first fossil hunters: paleontology in Greek and Roman times**
A. Mayor Princeton University Press, 2001, 361pp. $19.95. ISBN 0691089779.
Modern palaeontology has its origin in the 18th-century Enlightenment. However, the classical civilizations of Greece and Rome were well aware of fossil remains, and often wrote about them. In this popular but well researched account, Mayor reviews Classical literature in the light of Mediterranean geology, and the archaeological evidence for ancient fossil collection. She even makes a convincing case for the probable role of fossils in Classical mythology!

1406 **A fish caught in time: The search for the coelacanth**
S. Weinberg Fourth Estate, 1999, 239pp. £6.39. ISBN 1857029062.
A lively account of the discovery of Latimeria, the last surviving member of the coelacanth fishes, a group that first appeared over 375 million years ago. It follows the drama of the initial finds in South Africa and the Comoros Islands (and the intense scientific rivalries they sparked), through to modern conservation efforts and the recent discovery of Latimeria in Sri Lanka.

1407 **Fossil**
P.D. Taylor and C. Hibbert Dorling Kindersley, 2003, 72pp. £5.99. ISBN 075136486X.
Aimed at young adults, this book is superbly illustrated in the DK style. It is a captivating and wide-ranging introduction to palaeontology.
Series: Eyewitness Guides.

1408 **Fossils: the key to the past**
R. Fortey; Natural History Museum 3rd edn, 2002, 232pp. £16.95. ISBN 0565091638.
Aimed at the interested amateur, this book is a well illustrated introduction to fossils; what they are, how they are studied, and what they can tell us about the emergence and evolution of life on earth.

1409 **Gaining ground: the origin and early evolution of tetrapods**
J.A. Clack Indiana University Press, 2002, 376pp. $49.95. ISBN 0253340543.
The origin of the tetrapods (four-limbed land animals) is one of the 'hot' areas of palaeontology. Old ideas have been overturned by a wealth of new discoveries, and by an increased understanding of the genetics underlying embryonic development. Clack (herself responsible for many of the fossil discoveries) avoids an overly journalistic style, concentrating on the fascinating science.

1410 **How to keep dinosaurs**
R. Mash Weidenfeld & Nicolson, 2003, 96pp. £9.09. ISBN 0297843478.
Computer-generated beasts in domestic settings are central to this humorous guide to dinosaur husbandry. The accompanying text packs a lot of real palaeobiology into its droll advice for aspiring dino keepers.

1411 **Hunting dinosaurs**
L. Psihoyos and J. Knoebber Cassell, 1994, 238pp. £51.95. ISBN 0304344850.
The book is a spin-off of a *National Geographic* cover story on dinosaurs. The journalist and photographer involved became fascinated by the palaeontologists themselves, and so produced this book. It covers some early 'personalities' in palaeontology, such as Cuvier, Cope and Marsh, but the most fascinating parts cover contemporary scientists, their ideas, and what inspires them to spend hours working on fossil remains. The text is lively and amusing, and it is lavishly illustrated with colour photographs.

1412 **The illustrated encyclopedia of pterosaurs**
P. Wellnhofer Salamander Books, 1991, 192pp. $19.95. ISBN 0517037017.
This book is now out of print, but copies are easily available second-hand, or through interlibrary loan. It is recommended here because it is still by far the best popular work on pterosaurs, the flying reptiles of the Mesozoic. Wellnhofer provides a readable, in-depth account of all aspects of pterosaur palaeontology, while John Sibbick's illustrations are stunning.

1413 **Life on a young planet: the first three billion years of evolution on Earth**
A.H. Knoll Princeton University Press, 2003, 304pp. $18.95. ISBN 0691120293.
One of the few books (and probably the only non-technical book) to deal with the major part of the history of life: the three billion years prior to the 'Cambrian explosion' (the period, 500 million year ago, when complex life-forms emerged). The author integrates fossil and geological information with recent advances in molecular biology, investigates the origin of life, and the way life and environment have co-evolved (each constantly reshaping the other). There are few illustrations, but this is more than compensated for by the vivid and lively text.

1414 **Predatory dinosaurs of the world**
G.S. Paul Simon & Schuster, 1988, 464pp. ISBN 0671687336.
Little-known, but one of the most influential non-academic dinosaur books of recent years. Paul is a 'palaeoartist' specializing in dinosaurs, and this lavishly illustrated book includes his personal views on the biology and evolution of the meat-eating theropod dinosaurs and early birds (some more controversial than others). It includes data for every species known at the time of publication. This book influenced the descriptions of dinosaurs in Michael Crichton's novel *Jurassic Park*, and Paul's distinctive illustrations formed the basis of the reconstructions in the film version (thus influencing a new generation of palaeoartists).

1415 The rise of birds: 225 million years of evolution
S. Chatterjee Johns Hopkins University Press, 1997, 304pp. ISBN 0801856159.
Chatterjee has controversial views on the origin of birds, particularly the significance of his discovery, Protoavis. In this well written and illustrated book he elaborates these ideas, and discusses the less controversial area of Cretaceous and post-Cretaceous bird fossils.

1416 The rise of fishes: 500 million years of evolution
J.A. Long Johns Hopkins University Press, 1996, 224pp. $41.00. ISBN 0801854385.
This is a good non-technical introduction to fish palaeontology, packed with colour photographs and drawings. Long has worked on many fossil fish sites around the world, and his passion for the subject shows through.

1417 The Scientific American book of dinosaurs: the best minds in paleontology create a portrait of the prehistoric era
G.S. Paul, ed. St Martin's Press, 2000, 432pp. $19.95. ISBN 0312310080.
A collection of articles about dinosaurs from the last 25 years of the popular science magazine SCIENTIFIC AMERICAN, each authored by a leading palaeontologist. An interesting (if inadvertent) review of the tide of ideas and debates in dinosaur palaeontology over the last quarter century.

1418 T. rex and the crater of doom
W. Alvarez Penguin, 1998, 185pp. Originally published by Princeton University Press, 1997, £7.99. ISBN 014027636X.
Alvarez was one of the central figures in determining that a giant meteorite impact had occurred in Mexico 65 million years ago, coinciding with the extinction of the dinosaurs (and countless other species). This book is less about the impact itself, but more about the fascinating detective work which led to the discovery of the impact crater in 1991. Written in a clear style, it shows how experts from many different disciplines worked together, each contributing a small piece of the final picture.

1419 Tracking dinosaurs: a new look at an ancient world
M. Lockley Cambridge University Press, 1991, 238pp. £9.95. ISBN 0521425980.
The fossilized footprints of dinosaurs and other extinct animals have been known for centuries. However, it is only in the last few decades that they have been subject to serious scientific study. This popular, well illustrated account reveals the surprising amount of information about the biology of dinosaurs that can be gained by a careful study of fossil trackways.

1420 Walking on eggs: the astonishing discovery of thousands of dinosaur eggs in the badlands of Patagonia
L.M. Chiappe and L. Dingus Simon & Schuster, 2001, 219pp. $25.00. ISBN 0743212118.
This book recounts the discovery of the remains of a huge dinosaur nesting site in the Patagonian desert of South America. Some of the dinosaur eggs contained fossilized embryos, an extremely rare find. As much about the expedition itself as the analysis of the fossils, this enjoyable book shows how two palaeontologists used a discovery in the field to build up scientific hypotheses about the life of a dinosaur community.

1421 Walking with beasts: a prehistoric safari
T. Haines BBC Worldwide, 2001, 264pp. Also published as *Walking with prehistoric beasts*. Dorling Kindersley. $29.95. ISBN 0789478293, £13.99. ISBN 0563537639.
A follow-up to *Walking with dinosaurs*, this book looks at the evolution and diversification of mammals after the extinction of the dinosaurs. It follows a similar format to the first book and television series, concentrating on a few very specific times and locations, and using computer generated models to illustrate extinct animals in naturalistic settings. In response to criticisms of *Walking with dinosaurs*, this book takes greater care to explain the evidence underlying the reconstructions.

- **Walking with dinosaurs: a natural history T. Haines** BBC Worldwide, 1999. £13.99. ISBN 0563384492. Focuses on a small number of specific locations/times, each treated as if a contemporary environment visited by a *National Geographic* team. Thus it can be hard to distinguish fact from supposition or speculation. However, spectacular illustrations.

1422 Walking with cavemen: discovering our ancestors
J. Lynch and L. Barrett Hodder Headline, 2003, 224pp. £20.00. ISBN 0755311779.
Another in the BBC's lavish *Walking with ...* series, this book depicts the daily lives of eight different species from our hominid ancestry. The engaging text presents each species in a little drama together with the high-tech illustrations, but always keeps one eye on the evidence. It goes a long way to dispel the 'Freddy Flintstone' image of popular culture.

1423 When life nearly died: the greatest mass extinction of all time
M.J. Benton Thames and Hudson, 2003, 336pp. $29.95. ISBN 050005116X.
This book gives a readable account of a devastating mass extinction, nearly 200 million years before the event that annihilated the dinosaurs. The author reviews the geological and palaeontological evidence, and its interpretation. He goes on to show that it has important implications for our understanding of contemporary climate change and environmental destruction.

1424 Wonderful life: the Burgess Shale and the nature of history
S.J. Gould Vintage, 2000, 384pp. £8.99. ISBN 0099273454.
The Burgess Shale contains the remains of some of the earliest known complex animals. Gould described these diverse and bizarre fossils, and put forward his views on evolution and the nature of scientific investigation. While Gould's conclusions remain controversial (and opposed to those of Conway Morris, author of CRUCIBLE OF CREATION, his style of writing is enjoyable, and his excitement and enthusiasm shine through.

- **The structure of evolutionary theory S.J. Gould** Belknap Press of Harvard University Press, 2002, 1433pp. $45.00. ISBN 0674006135. 'The world's most revered and eloquent interpreter of evolutionary ideas offered here a work of explanatory force unprecedented in our time – a landmark publication, both for its historical sweep and for its scientific vision ...'

Associations & societies

1425 Micropalaeontological Society [UK]
www.nhm.ac.uk/hosted_sites/tms
This is the main society dedicated to micropalaeontology

(the study of microscopic fossils such as plant spores and pollen, invertebrates, and fragments of vertebrate skeletons). Micropalaeontology is often used to track palaeoenvironmental changes and to date sediments. The society hosts meetings (including an annual general meeting) and publishes the twice-yearly *Journal of Micropalaeontology*.

- **Micropaleontology Press** www.micropress.org. 'Division of the Micropaleontology Project, a nonprofit organization with the mission of promoting the stratigraphic sciences, through publications, education, exhibitions, service to the profession.' Produces *Bibliography & Index of Micropaleontology*.

1426 **Palaeontological Association** [UK]
www.palass.org
This is the main British society for palaeontologists, although it also has members all over the world. It hosts several seminars each year, a symposium for young researchers (Progressive Palaeontology) and an annual meeting in December. The annual meeting takes place over two to three days; talks cover a wide range of topics, from descriptions of new discoveries, to phylogenetics, and 'evolutionary developmental biology'. The society's main publication is the quarterly journal PALAEONTOLOGY.

- **Field Guides to Fossils** Series covering different British areas and species: e.g. *Fossils of the chalk*; *Dinosaurs of the Isle of Wight*; *The Jurassic flora of Yorkshire*; etc.

1427 **Paleontological Society** [USA]
www.paleosoc.org
The American equivalent of the UK's PALAEONTOLOGICAL ASSOCIATION, the Society has over 1500 members worldwide. It produces two journals, the JOURNAL OF PALEONTOLOGY and PALEOBIOLOGY. The society's website contains some information on palaeontological resources available on the internet.

Society for the History of Natural History
See entry no. 1940

1428 **Society of Vertebrate Paleontology** [USA]
www.vertpaleo.org
The biggest and most active of all palaeontological organizations, the SVP has grown beyond its American roots to become the *de facto* organization for vertebrate palaeontologists worldwide. Its website is divided into public and member-only areas. The most useful service on the public area is the Bibliography of Fossil Vertebrates (BFV), a searchable database of published works covering the years 1509–1993. The members' area has a useful directory of members, including contact details. The society produces the JOURNAL OF VERTEBRATE PALEONTOLOGY, and a symposium is held every October.

1429 **Symposium of Vertebrate Palaeontology and Comparative Anatomy** [UK]
www.svpca.org
The main meeting of vertebrate palaeontologists in the UK, it also boasts a high percentage of overseas delegates (particularly from mainland Europe). It is held over three days at the beginning of September. Unusually, it is an informal meeting, not associated with a society and with no regular organizing committee. Each year it is hosted by a different university or museum. The relaxed atmosphere makes it a very welcoming meeting for first-time delegates, professional and amateur. It is preceded by the annual meeting of the smaller SPPC.

- **Symposium of Palaeontological Preparation and Conservation** www.preparator.org. A friendly two-day meeting, covering all aspects of the preparation, conservation and display of fossil material.

Libraries, archives, museums

1430 **American Museum of Natural History: Paleontology** [USA]
www.amnh.org
One of the largest natural history museums in the world, the palaeontology galleries reopened in 1996 after a major renovation. There are a huge number of specimens on display, particularly early land vertebrates, dinosaurs and mammals (reflecting the history of research at the museum). Behind the scenes are very large store-rooms and an active research group. The website contains useful contact information and an online catalogue of specimens.

1431 **Dinosaur Isle** [UK]
www.dinosaurisle.com
The rapidly eroding cliffs of the Isle of Wight produce some of the finest dinosaur fossils in the world. In 2001 the Museum of Isle of Wight Geology moved to a spectacular new building, designed by local architects, in the shape of a pterodactyl. The interesting, child-friendly displays are complemented by a dedicated and well informed curatorial staff. The associated website is well designed and easy to navigate.

- **Dino Directory** **Natural History Museum**. http://flood.nhm.ac.uk/jdsml/dino. Guide to 129 of the best described dinosaurs, including over 600 images.

Field Museum
See entry no. 1948

1432 **Muséum National d'Histoire Naturelle** [FRA]
www.mnhn.fr
Located in beautiful parklands in the Latin Quarter of Paris, the original museum galleries are an old-style collection of mounted skeletons. However, the palaeontological displays include historically important specimens (such as the Maastricht mosasaur, studied by George Cuvier). The modern and magnificent Grand Galerie de l'Evolution is in a nearby building, and would appeal to all ages. The website is in French only, but carries basic information on opening times and costs.
Galeries d'Anatomie comparée et de Paléontologie2, rue Buffon, 75005 Paris.

1433 **Natural History Museum: Palaeontology** [UK]
www.nhm.ac.uk/palaeontology/index.html
The largest collection of fossil material in the UK. Besides the impressive fossil galleries, the museum houses a huge store of vertebrate fossils for study and comparison. The curatorial staff includes academic researchers and experts in preparation and conservation.

1434 **Oxford University Museum of Natural History: Geological Collections** [UK]
www.oum.ox.ac.uk
The Geological Collections comprise a palaeontology

collection of over 500,000 fossils. The database contains details of over 1400 types and many cited fossils in the collections. Actively acquiring more specimens. Of interest to the amateur as well as to the researcher. The Museum also has significant collections of entomology, mineralogy, petrology and zoological material.

Oxford University Museum of Natural History
See entry no. 1952

1435 **Paleontological Institute of the Russian Academy of Science** [RUS]
www.ucmp.berkeley.edu/pin/pin.html
Located in the southern suburbs of Moscow (near the Konkova Metro station) this huge building is a wonder of the Soviet era. The architecture is incredible, although in a state of some disrepair. Palaeontological motifs appear on every part of the building and there is a huge mural showing the evolution of life. But even this is outshone by the huge number of fossils on display, including many dinosaurs from Mongolia, and ice-age mammals.

1436 **Royal Museum of Scotland**
www.nms.ac.uk/royal
The Royal Museum in Edinburgh is an impressive building, with large geology and natural history galleries. The newly built annex (the Museum of Scotland) contains detailed dioramas depicting Scotland's ancient flora and fauna. There is also an internationally important collection of fossils in the store-rooms, particularly from the Palaeozoic Era.

1437 **Sedgwick Museum of Earth Sciences: Fossils** [UK]
www.sedgwickmuseum.org
This free museum is part of the Earth Sciences department of the University of Cambridge, and is one of the oldest geological museums in the world. It has been extensively renovated over the last few years, although the well conceived new displays successfully retain the museum's essential character: it is a practical research collection, with a great deal of its fossil material on display. This, coupled with the friendly and knowledgeable curatorial staff, makes it an ideal place to identify your fossil finds.

The Museum is temporarily closed until 2006 – partly to allow the dismantling and restoration of the large dinosaur that forms its centrepiece. However, meanwhile, the website maintains an excellent links section.

Portal & task environments

Climate Timeline: exploring weather & climate change through powers of 10
National Geophysical Data Center and National Oceanic and Atmospheric Administration See entry no. 1207

1438 **Fossils and palaeontology** [UK]
British Geological Survey
www.bgs.ac.uk/fossils/home.html
The BGS holds important collections of fossils from across the UK, including type material (specimens used to define particular species). They have up-to-date information about fossil-bearing strata throughout the UK (e.g. geological age and relationships to other strata). The website includes a useful 'Enquiries' section that channels your question to the most appropriate member of staff.

1439 **Palaeontologia Electronica**
Coquina Press, Biannual. ISSN 10948074.
www.palaeo-electronica.org
By far the most successful palaeontological venture in the emerging field of web publishing. The site currently receives about 200,000 hits per month. The journal, sponsored by many major palaeontological organizations, covers all aspects of palaeontology. It includes editorials, research articles and reviews. It also seeks to use all the unique benefits of web publishing, such as hyperlinks, many colour figures and movies, online databases, etc. The site, which includes an archive of past issues, is free to access and is generally easy to navigate around. However, an up-to-date browser and a fast internet connection are necessary to appreciate it fully.

1440 **Paleomap Project**
C.R. Scotese, ed.
www.scotese.com
This project, a collaboration of several geologists, aims to provide an accurate illustration of the tectonic plate movements over the last billion years. This will allow fossil finds to be placed in their correct palaeogeographical setting. To this end, the project has produced several powerful (but expensive) computer mapping programs. However, numerous free samples and demonstrations are available on the website, making it a useful resource for amateur enthusiasts.

Discovering print & electronic resources

Take the Subway to Other Resources
University of California, Berkeley See entry no. 1979

Digital data, image & text collections

1441 **Fossil Record 2**
M.J. Benton, ed. Chapman & Hall, 1993, 845pp. £259.00. ISBN 0412393808.
http://palaeo.gly.bris.ac.uk/frwhole/FR2.html
The Fossil Record 2 is an enormous compendium of the time-ranges of almost every known taxonomic family of fossil organisms. This allows a broad overview of evolutionary processes, such as extinction and diversification, over geological time. The data set is also available online (although the search functions do not always work properly). It is an essential tool for anyone interested in biodiversity in the fossil record.

1442 **PaleoBase**
N. Macleod; Natural History Museum Blackwell Publishing, 2003–. CD-ROM. Part I and Part II covering macrofossils; $130.00. ISBN 0632064277.
www.paleobase.com [DESCRIPTION]
Excellent compilation 'designed primarily as an educational resource for earth science undergraduates, but which will also appeal to amateur, and professional palaeontologists – indeed, anyone with an interest in fossils'. Uses innovative digital imaging techniques (developed by the NHM's PalaeoVision project) to illustrate fossil morphologies in the clearest and most accurate manner possible.

Where appropriate, records are cross-referenced to Clarkson's INVERTEBRATE PALAEONTOLOGY AND EVOLUTION, labelled figures from the text being included in the database as a guide to each fossil group's morphology. Also included is a full glossary of morphological and other technical terms used in the fossil descriptions.

Part III due 2005. An analogous microfossils product is 'at an advanced stage'.

Directories & encyclopedias

1443 The dinosauria
D.B. Weishampel, P. Dodson and H. Osmólska University of California Press, 2004, 880pp. $95.00. ISBN 0520242092.
Announced second edition of the most comprehensive encyclopedia of dinosaurs. Each chapter covers a subgroup of dinosaurs, and is written by an expert on that topic. The contents includes a review of the anatomy of the subgroup (with extensive illustrations), a discussion on their evolutionary relationships, and a list of known species.

1444 Dinosaurs: the encyclopedia
D.F. Glut McFarland, 1997, 1088pp. Almost 1500 illustrations. *Supplements* V. 1 (2000, 456pp, $95.00, ISBN 0786405910); V. 2 (2002, 696pp, $95.00, ISBN 078641166X); V. 3 (2003, 736pp, $95.00, ISBN 0786415185), $195.00. ISBN 0899509177.
Major work whose main volume is in five sections: I. History of fieldwork, laboratory studies and paleontological research, theories of dinosaur extinction; II. Dinosaurian systematics; III. Alphabetically arranged compilation of dinosaurian genera; IV. Doubtful genera; V. Excluded genera or taxa that had been previously regarded as dinosaurian. Includes depictions of life models constructed by experts in vertebrate palaeontology restoration and based on the original fossil material.
'A welcome resource for all libraries and individuals ... useful and informative ... superb supplementary volume(s) ... extensive bibliography ... recommended.' (*American Reference Books Annual*)

1445 Encyclopedia of dinosaurs and prehistoric life
D. Lambert Dorling Kindersley, 2003, 376pp. £14.99. ISBN 140530099X.
As with all Dorling Kindersley books this guide, aimed at young adults, has pages packed with colour photographs and diagrams. Predictably it skips plants altogether, and rushes through invertebrates and fishes in its haste to get to dinosaurs and pterosaurs. However, it redeems itself by including a large section on fossil mammals.

1446 Encyclopedia of paleontology
R. Singer Fitzroy Dearborn, 1999, 1550pp. $355.00. ISBN 1884964966.
General reference work with 350 entries explaining palaeontological concepts and techniques, examining evolutionary development of particular organisms and their biological features, profiling major discoveries and leading scientists. Bibliographies.
'Outstanding reference source, 2001.' (*American Library Association*)

1447 Palaeobiology II
D.E.G. Briggs and P.R. Crowther, eds Blackwell, 2001, 600pp. £44.95. ISBN 0632051477.
This is a clear, well illustrated introduction to the biological aspects of fossils. It covers a wide range of topics, arranged approximately by geological age, each in the form of a short essay by an acknowledged expert in the field.

Handbooks & manuals

1448 Ammonites
N. Monks and P. Palmer Natural History Museum, 2002, 160pp. £15.95. ISBN 0565091697.
The spiral shells of ammonites are among the most recognizable of fossils. This book is an introduction to the group, including up-to-date information on the current ideas about their ecology and biology.

1449 Basic palaeontology
M.J. Benton and D.A.T. Harper Prentice Hall, 1998, 357pp. $54.00. ISBN 0582228573.
This book is similar in style to Benton's VERTEBRATE PALAEONTOLOGY; it is a compact but surprisingly detailed introduction to the science of palaeontology, using examples from many different organisms. The book is aimed at university students, but the text is readable and well illustrated, and would be accessible to any enthusiastic reader.

1450 The Cambridge encyclopedia of human paleopathology
A.C. Aufderheide and C. Rodriguez-Martin Cambridge University Press, 1998, 496pp. £85.00. ISBN 0521552036.
A well illustrated, well ordered and concise reference for identifying wounds, malformations and sickness in human remains. Perhaps not ideal bed-time reading, but a comprehensive reference work for those trying to extract information about living people from dead bones.

1451 Dinosaurs: the textbook
S.G. Lucas 4tn edn, McGraw-Hill, 2003, 304pp. $92.50. ISBN 0072528052.
An introduction to the study of dinosaurs, and to vertebrate palaeontology in general. Chapters are laid out clearly and well illustrated, introducing all aspects of dinosaur palaeontology, including their anatomy, current ideas on their biology, and the history of dinosaur research.

1452 Dinosaurs and other mesozoic reptiles of California
R.P. Hilton University of California Press, 2003, 342pp. $39.95. ISBN 0520233158.
A lavishly illustrated book, concentrating on an area of rich fossil finds. Much of California was under a shallow sea during the Mesozoic Era, and this is reflected in the diversity of marine reptile fossils (from ichthyosaurs to turtles). However, there are also fossils of dinosaurs (washed into the sea after death). Hilton describes the biology of the preserved animals, as well as the more recent history of their discovery and collection. This regional view is a fascinating contrast to the more usual 'general' dinosaur books.

1453 Early vertebrates
P. Janvier Clarendon Press, 2003, 408pp. £115.00. ISBN 0198526466.
This book offers a wealth of detail on early vertebrates: Palaeozoic 'fish' of the sort found in many places around Britain and Northern Europe. Although the text is broken down into small sections, it is fairly dense and would be difficult to read from cover to cover. However, the numerous illustrations and, in particular, the detailed discussion of

evolutionary relationships, make it a useful reference work (especially for answering specific, detailed questions).
Series: Oxford Monographs on Geology and Geophysics.

1454 **Elements of palaeontology**
R.M. Black Cambridge University Press, 1989, 416pp. £28.00. ISBN 0521348366.
This is a group-by-group guide to the identification of fossil finds, giving the key features of each group. The bias towards invertebrate animals reflects the most common fossils that amateur collectors will come across (there are also good entries on several plant groups). A refreshingly practical guide for those unlikely to find a *T. rex* in their back gardens!

1455 **Evolutionary patterns: growth, form, and tempo in the fossil record**
J.B.C. Jackson, S. Lidgard and F.K. McKinney, eds University of Chicago Press, 2001, 416pp. $30.00. ISBN 0226389316.
With the great advances in studying evolution and development at the molecular level, it is easy to forget the unique data which the fossil record can provide. In this book, aimed at university students, various authors reveal what fossils can tell us about evolutionary history, from extinction and speciation rates, to the mechanisms driving large-scale morphological changes.

1456 **Exceptional fossil preservation: a unique view on the evolution of marine life**
D.J. Bottjer [et al.] Columbia University Press, 2002, 424pp. $45.00. ISBN 0231102550.
Fossils usually only consist of the hard parts of organisms (bones, shells, spores, etc.). However, in rare circumstances, conditions allow the preservation of all kinds of soft tissues, offering a glimpse of the biology of extinct plants and animals. This book contains 20 essays by various experts on the nature and significance of different sites around the world.

1457 **Fossil crinoids**
H. Hess [et al.] Cambridge University Press, 2003, 292pp. £30.00. ISBN 0521524407.
This is a comprehensive guide to crinoids, the graceful, plant-like marine animals known to all fossil collectors. It deals with the biology, evolution and fossil preservations of crinoids from their first appearance over half a billion years ago, ending with a chapter on the living groups. It is illustrated by a wealth of photographs and line drawings.

1458 **Fossils**
C. Walker and D. Ward Dorling Kindersley, 2000, 320pp. $20.00. ISBN 0789489848.
This book serves as a simple, pictorial field-guide for fossil collectors, assisting in identifying unfamiliar groups.
Series: Smithsonian Handbooks.

1459 **Fossils of the Burgess Shale**
D.E.G. Briggs, D.H. Erwin and F.J. Collier Smithsonian Books, 1995, 256pp. $24.95. ISBN 156098659X.
The Burgess Shale is one of the most celebrated fossil sites in the world, as it records the evolutionary explosion of complex animal life forms, five hundred million years ago. Some animals are clearly early members of groups still familiar to us today. Others have no obvious modern relatives, and arguments rage as to their evolutionary relationships. This book is a species-by-species guide to this key site. Each entry discusses what is known about the animal, and is accompanied by photographs of the fossils and life-reconstructions.

1460 **Genetics, paleontology, and macroevolution**
J.S. Levinton 2nd edn, Cambridge University Press, 2001, 634pp. £38.00. ISBN 0521005507.
The fossil record can tell us about macroevolution (large changes in morphology), the rate of evolution, speciation and extinction, and the levels of biodiversity across time. Molecular biology can tell us about microevolution (changes in genes and molecules), how mutations arise and how they are spread through populations. This book, aimed at university students, integrates data from both sources (using specific examples) to produce a broader understanding of the way life evolves across geological time.

1461 **The great dinosaur controversy: a guide to the debates**
K.M. Parsons, ed. ABC-CLIO, 2003, 294pp. $85.00. ISBN 1576079228.
Historical review of the most important scientific controversies that have shaped knowledge of dinosaurs since the discovery of important fossils in the 1820s. Covers Owen, Huxley, Bakker, etc.
Series: Controversies in Science.
'The text is accurate, and the presentation is well balanced ... A useful addition to public and college libraries. Recommended. General readers and undergraduates.' (*Choice*)

1462 **The history of British mammals**
D.W. Yalden T & A D Poyser, 1999, 305pp. £29.95. ISBN 0856611107.
Spanning palaeontology, archaeology and agricultural history, Yalden guides us through the changing mammalian fauna of the British Isles, from dormice to mammoths, from the Ice Age to the present. The causes of the varying fates of different species are recounted in a scholarly but readable text, aimed at students and amateur naturalists.

1463 **History of the coelacanth fishes**
P.L. Forey Chapman & Hall, 1997, 419pp. £124.00. ISBN 0412784807.
Coelacanth fishes were thought to be extinct for nearly 70 million years, until one was discovered in 1938. In this book Forey reviews the long and diverse coelacanth lineage, and investigates their evolutionary relationships. The descriptions are well illustrated with line drawings, and the text, although detailed, takes care to explain all technical jargon. A must for all fossil fish enthusiasts, but also a good practical example of how palaeontologists study a group of organisms.

1464 **The horned dinosaurs: a natural history**
P. Dodson Princeton University Press, 1998, 360pp. $26.95. ISBN 0691059004.
The ceratopians (Triceratops and its relatives) form one of the most successful groups of dinosaurs. This book reviews everything we know about them, from anatomy to reproduction and ecology, as well as the colourful history of ceratopian research. Beautiful illustrated, the volume's concentration on a particular group marks a refreshing change from 'general' dino books.

1465 **The human fossil record**
J.H. Schwartz [et al.] Wiley, 2004. 4 v., $649.00. ISBN 0471678643.
Archaeology and anthropology will be covered in Volume 3 of *The New Walford*. However, it is worth citing here this major compilation. The work 'provides a compendium of uniform descriptions and illustrations of fossils from all the major sites that document the human evolutionary past. It focuses on the documentation of morphology, the essential basis for all further analysis of human biological history.'

1466 **Interrelationships of fishes**
M.L.S. Stiassny, L.R. Parenti and G.D. Johnson Academic Press, 1998, 496pp. $78.95. ISBN 0126709513.
Each chapter covers a different group of fishes, and is authored by experts. They generally review previous studies on the relationships of the group, and then undertake their own analysis. Although technical, this book serves as a useful starting-off point for anyone interested in the evolutionary relationships of fishes.

1467 **Invertebrate palaeontology and evolution**
E.N.K. Clarkson 4th edn, Blackwell, 2003, 468pp. £32.50. ISBN 0632052384.
This is *the* standard introduction to invertebrate palaeontology. The fourth edition is completely updated, and several sections have been extensively rewritten. The text is clear, although fairly technical in places. However, it is well informed and up to date, and illustrated with good black-and-white diagrams and drawings.

1468 **Life history of a fossil: an introduction to taphonomy and paleoecology**
P. Shipman Harvard University Press, 1993, 222pp. ISBN 0674530861.
Taphonomy is the study of the processes that act on animal remains as they 'pass from the biosphere of bones and carcass into the lithosphere of fossils' (*Nature)*.

An understanding of these processes can reveal much about the biology and ecology of the animal when alive. Aimed at university students and interested amateurs, this book is a comprehensive introduction to the topic.

1469 **Major events in early vertebrate evolution**
P.E. Ahlberg Taylor & Francis, 2001, 418pp. £60.99. ISBN 0415233704.
This book is based on a conference at The Natural History Museum in London in 1999. It documents research in the emerging field of Evolutionary Developmental Biology ('Evo-Devo'), where evolutionary data (including fossils) are combined with data from embryonic developmental biology to gain a clearer understanding of the mechanisms through which life has evolved and diversified over time. Each chapter is a research paper on a different aspect of early vertebrate evolution. While this is by no means a 'popular' work, the diversity of the scientific audience at the original conference means that technical terms are usually explained for the non-specialist.

1470 **A manual of practical laboratory and field techniques in palaeobiology**
O.R. Green Kluwer Academic, 2001, 538pp. £86.00. ISBN 041258980X.
Up-to-date and comprehensive, this handbook covers all the techniques used to collect and document fossils in the field, and to prepare and conserve material in the lab. A vital reference work for professionals and serious amateurs alike.

1471 **Mesozoic birds: above the heads of dinosaurs**
L.M. Chiappe and L.M. Witmer, eds University of California Press, 2002, 536pp. $95.00. ISBN 0520200942.
The last 15 years has seen an explosion in our understanding of early bird evolution. A series of stunning new fossils have been discovered, and analytical techniques have improved. This book, aimed at university students, has a series of chapters authored by experts, covering different aspects of fossil bird evolution and morphology.

The Michelin field guide to minerals, rocks and fossils
N. Curtis See entry no. 1330

1472 **Numerical palaeobiology: computer-based modelling and analysis of fossils and their distribution**
D.A.T. Harper, ed. Wiley, 1999, 478pp. $160.00. ISBN 0471974056.
Powerful computer analyses are featuring more and more in palaeontology, processing large amounts of data to get a new perspective on ancient ecologies. Aimed at university students, this text uses practical examples to illustrate the application of statistical and modelling software. It includes a disk of sample software.

1473 **Palaeobiology of trace fossils**
S.K. Donovan Wiley, 1994, 316pp. $177.00. ISBN 0471948438.
Trace fossils are the preserved remains of the activities of ancient organisms, from roots systems, trackways and burrows, to eggs and faeces. This book contains 11 essays by experts on different aspects of trace fossils. It forms a wide-ranging, if technical, introduction to the discipline, and what it can tell us about the biology of extinct plants and animals.

1474 **Palaeoecology: ecosystems, environments and evolution**
P. Brenchley and D. Harper Taylor & Francis, 1998, 432pp. £36.95. ISBN 0412434504.
This well illustrated textbook covers both traditional aspects of the field (such as fossil reconstructions and population dynamics) and modern, broader-scale studies (linking populations and communities to biogeographical regions). It is a comprehensive, if technical, introduction to palaeoecology.

1475 **Paleobotany and the evolution of plants**
W.N. Stewart and G.W. Rothwell 2nd edn, Cambridge University Press, 1993, 535pp. £45.00. ISBN 0521382947.
This is one of the most thorough textbooks on palaeobotany, describing the evolution and diversification of plants, from single-celled algae to the emergence of modern trees. It is well illustrated with line drawings and sketches. Although aimed at specialists, this book would also make a useful reference work for interested amateurs.

1476 **Paleoclimatology: reconstructing climates of the Quaternary**
R.S. Bradley 2nd edn, Academic Press, 1999, 613pp. $73.95. ISBN 012124010X.
This is a thorough textbook, covering the whole range of techniques used to understand past weather-systems, and

how climates change over time. The topics range from fossil data, to computer modelling.

Series: International Geophysics, V. 68.

'This is an excellent compilation of figures and tables covering the entire subject. Many subtopics are of interest to casual readers.' (*Choice*)

Philip's guide to minerals, rocks & fossils

W.R. Hamilton, A.R. Woolley and A.C. Bishop See entry no. 1338

Plant resins: chemistry, evolution, ecology, and ethnobotany

J.H. Langenheim See entry no. 2260

1477 The primate fossil record

C.W. Hartwig, ed. Cambridge University Press, 2002, 544pp. £130.00. ISBN 0521663156.

A fully illustrated, comprehensive review of the current state of primate palaeontology. The chapters, each authored by an expert, move from the earliest primates to the origins of modern humans.

1478 Principles of paleoclimatology

T.M. Cronin Columbia University Press, 1999, 560pp. $34.00. ISBN 0231109555.

This book describes the sources of information on ancient weather systems; how this information is collated to reconstruct past climates. It also covers research into the mechanisms behind climate change, the reaction of life to shifts in climate, and what we can predict about the future climate. Thorough and up-to-date, the book is divided into nine sections, building up a complete picture of the discipline. This book would serve as an excellent primer for students.

1479 Quaternary environmental micropalaeontology

S.K. Haslett Hodder & Stoughton, 2002, 288pp. £25.99. ISBN 0340761989.

Microfossils (the remains of microscopic organisms, or the fragments from larger ones) provide one of the richest data sources for studies of ancient environments. This is especially relevant for studies of the Quaternary Period (from the start of the ice-ages to the present day), a period of tremendous environmental change. Each chapter of this book deals with a different fossil group and their uses in palaeoenvironmental studies.

1480 Systematics and the fossil record: documenting evolutionary patterns

A.B. Smith Blackwell Scientific, 1994, 223pp. £29.99. ISBN 0632036427.

This book is an introduction to the study of evolutionary relationships in the fossil record. It leads the reader through the basic principles and the importance of subject – systematics turns the fossil record from a collector's curiosity into a vital record of the evolution of life on earth. Later chapters introduce more complex ideas, and give practical examples.

1481 Taphonomy: a process approach

R.E. Martin Cambridge University Press, 1999, 524pp. £35.00. ISBN 0521598338.

The 'process approach' of the title refers to the analysis of taphonomy (how freshly dead remains eventually pass into the fossil record) as a series of processes: ecological, mechanical and chemical. It is aimed at university students, and reviews the behaviours of plant and animal remains in different environments, marine and terrestrial.

1482 Trilobite: eyewitness to evolution

R. Fortey Vintage, 2001, 320pp. £8.25. ISBN 0375706216.

The trilobites are group of marine invertebrates, a favourite of collectors, found all over the world in rocks spanning a 300 million year period. Their diversity (many hundreds of species are known) makes them an ideal test-case for theories on evolutionary mechanisms, as well as for dating rock strata. Fortey covers the anatomy, ecology and interrelationships of the group, along with autobiographical sections on his passion for these beautiful fossils. His very personal style has won both acclaim and criticism (you'll have to judge for yourself), but this book is undeniably the most comprehensive introduction for non-specialists.

1483 Understanding fossils: an introduction to invertebrate palaeontology

P. Doyle Wiley, 1996, 426pp. $70.00. ISBN 0471963518.

In many ways this is the invertebrate counterpart of Benton's VERTEBRATE PALAEONTOLOGY. Comprehensive yet concise, illustrated with clear figures and diagrams, it is an excellent introductory text.

1484 Vertebrate palaeontology

M.J. Benton 2nd edn, Blackwell Science, 2000, 452pp. £29.99. ISBN 0632056142.

This book is intended as an introduction to vertebrate palaeontology for university students. The text is readable and logically laid-out, using text-boxes to elaborate certain points without interrupting the main text. It is extensively illustrated with black-and-white photographs and line drawings. Although slightly less detailed than its main competitor, Carroll's VERTEBRATE PALEONTOLOGY AND EVOLUTION, it concentrates more on phylogenetics (evolutionary relationships). Overall it forms a useful general reference work, and a good starting-point for information on unfamiliar vertebrate groups.

1485 Vertebrate paleontology and evolution

R.L. Carroll W H Freeman, 1988, 698pp. £39.45. ISBN 0716718227.

One of the best general textbooks for vertebrate palaeontology (along with Benton's VERTEBRATE PALAEONTOLOGY). Aimed at university students, the text is clear, well ordered and well researched, and there are copious black-and-white illustrations. However, it has two shortcomings: firstly its age (much has been done since 1988!) and secondly the lack of cladograms (diagrams of evolutionary relationships). Despite this, it will give the reader a firm 'bedrock' of knowledge on which further, more specialist reading will build.

Keeping up-to-date

1486 DINOSAUR Mailing List

http://dml.cmnh.org/information.html

An internet discussion group dedicated to dinosaurs, hosted at the Cleveland Museum of Natural History. It has a higher proportion of amateur enthusiasts than the vrtpaleo discussion group [q.v.], and is perhaps more accessible for beginners. A searchable archive of the last ten years of postings to the list is available at the website.

1487 **Journal of Paleontology**
Paleontological Society Bimonthly. ISSN 00223360.
www.journalofpaleontology.org [FEE-BASED]
This journal specializes in fossil systematics (the classification and interrelationships of fossil organisms) and the application of systematic information in biology, geology and palaeontology. The research articles (10–20 per issue) are generally interesting, but quite technical.
Available online: see website.

1488 **Journal of Systematic Palaeontology**
Natural History Museum Cambridge University Press, Quarterly. £120.00 [2004]. ISSN 14772019.
www.nhm.ac.uk/services/publishing/det_syspal.html [DESCRIPTION]
This journal is a direct successor to the *Bulletin of The Natural History Museum London: Geology Series*. Each issue carries 1–5 research articles that describe the taxonomy and phylogenetic relationships of fossil organisms, or that use systematics to understand wider biological questions.

1489 **Journal of Vertebrate Paleontology**
Society of Vertebrate Paleontology Quarterly. $270.00 [2004]. ISSN 02724634.
www.vertpaleo.org [DESCRIPTION]
The main journal to be devoted entirely vertebrate palaeontology. Each issue carries 10–20 peer-reviewed articles, usually illustrated with black-and-white photographs and line drawings. Most articles describe newly discovered material, although some more theoretical topics are covered. There are also occasional supplements, presenting a longer monograph on a single topic.

1490 **Palaeontology**
Palaeontological Association Blackwell Publishing, Bimonthly. £360.00 [2004]. ISSN 00310239.
www.palass.org/pages/publications.html [DESCRIPTION]
This is the main journal produced by the UK Association. It covers all aspects of palaeontology, with 10–20 research or review articles in each issue. Articles are generally well illustrated with maps, line drawings and photographs. The journal is sent free to all members of the PALAEONTOLOGICAL ASSOCIATION.

1491 **Paleobiology**
Paleontological Society Quarterly. $90.00 [2004]. ISSN 00948373.
www.paleosoc.org/paleobio.htm [DESCRIPTION]
Each issue of this journal carries 5–10 research articles on biological aspects of palaeontology, including 'speciation, extinction, development of individuals and colonies, natural selection, evolution, and patterns of variation, abundance and distribution of organisms in space and time'.

1492 **Paleontological Journal (Paleontologicheskii Zhurnal)** [RUS]
Palaeontological Institute Nauka/Interperiodica, Bimonthly. Each issue comes with a supplement, $3,831.00 [2004]. ISSN 00310301.
www.maik.rssi.ru [DESCRIPTION]
This journal is a simultaneous translation of the Russian-language *Paleontologicheskii Zhurnal*, produced by the Palaeontological Institute of the Russian Academy of Sciences. It covers all aspects of palaeontology, but with an emphasis on Eastern Europe and Asia. The translated version has successfully addressed an acknowledged problem: that Western palaeontologists were often unaware of research published in Cyrillic text. The research articles are illustrated with black-and-white photographs and line drawings. A table of contents and abstracts are available online.

1493 **Review of Palaeobotany and Palynology**
Elsevier, Biweekly. $2212.00 [2004]. ISSN 00346667.
www.elsevier.com/wps/find/homepage.cws_home [DESCRIPTION]
This is the main journal dealing exclusively with fossil plants. It covers all types of plant (both aquatic and terrestrial) and all aspects of plant palaeontology, from descriptions of new material to the use of fossil plant data to answer wide-ranging questions in areas such as evolution, ecology and stratigraphy.

1494 **Vertebrate Palaeontology Internet Discussion Group**
www.vertpaleo.org/vrtpaleo/index.html
A lively internet discussion group dedicated to all aspects of vertebrate palaeontology. Its members include professionals and well informed amateurs, and it is a good place to seek answers to (or opinions on) even the most obscure questions. The list is available through the University of Southern California and is owned by Dr Sam McLeod.

Petrology

igneous rocks • metamorphic rocks • organic petrology • rocks • sedimentary rocks • volcanoes

Introductions to the subject

1495 **Igneous Rocks Tour**
E.L. Ambos
http://seis.natsci.csulb.edu/basicgeo/IGNEOUS_TOUR.html
A simple introduction to igneous rocks. Explains composition of main types, with images of rock outcrops in natural settings. Educational and interactive. Useful for basics. There are also links to: Metamorphic Rocks Tour and Sedimentary Rocks Tour.

1496 **Mind over magma: the story of igneous petrology**
D.A. Young Princeton University Press, 2003, 686pp. $69.95. ISBN 0691102791.
A well written, lively book that 'traces the development of igneous petrology from ancient descriptions of volcanic eruptions to recent work incorporating insights from physical chemistry, isotope studies, and fluid dynamics'. Presents the application of various scientific methods to the study of rocks, the discovery of critical data and the development of major petrological theories. Illustrated. Includes bibliographical references (pp 615–73) and name and subject indexes.
'Young's account is so well organized and written that, at least for a petrologist, it is a real page-turner.' (*Science*)

1497 **Petrology: the study of igneous, sedimentary & metamorphic rocks**
L. Raymond 2nd edn, McGraw-Hill, 2001, 736pp. $135.00. ISBN 0073661686.
www.mhhe.com/earthsci/geoscience/virtuality [COMPANION]
A broad introduction to how rocks are formed, covering

fundamentals and information on recent advances, with an overview of the field of petrology. Treats igneous, sedimentary and metamorphic rocks. Important terms are set in bold print. Website gives access to extensive set of references and slides used in text. Glossary is included. Undergraduate use mainly.

Rocks and minerals
A.P. Jones See entry no. 1276

1498 **Rocks and minerals**
S. Parker Heinemann Library, 2002, 32pp. £7.50. ISBN 0431143137.
A well illustrated resource on rocks and minerals. Describes their origin, extraction, and manufacture and examines properties of rocks and minerals and related technologies used to shape them into products. Includes photographs, illustrations and detailed technical artwork; technology boxes illustrate manufacturing processes; historical facts and future possibilities explored. Recommended for school and public libraries.

Dictionaries, thesauri, classifications

1499 **Dictionary of petrology**
S.I. Tomkeieff [et al.], eds Wiley, 1983, 680pp. ISBN 0471101591.
Classic useful dictionary for all terms relating to sedimentary, igneous and metamorphic petrology. Associated terms grouped to create a thesaurus. Alphabetical listing in addition.

1500 **Dictionary of rocks**
R.S. Mitchell Van Nostrand Reinhold, 1985, 228pp. ISBN 0442263287.
A useful established text. Has c.5000 definitions, categorized. Appended glossary, p. 219–28. Igneous-rock definitions published by the International Union of Geological Sciences are included. Claims to be 'the first dictionary in the English language devoted exclusively to the names of rocks'. A fitting companion to the earlier book, *Mineral names: what do they mean?*, by R.S. Mitchell, with J.R. Henry (Van Nostrand Reinhold, 1979).

1501 **Igneous rocks: a classification and glossary of terms**
R.W. Le Maitre [et al.], eds 2nd edn, Cambridge University Press, 2002, 236pp. £45.00. ISBN 052166215X.
http://publishing.cambridge.org/resources [companion]
Contains the International Union of Geological Sciences (IUGS) recommendations for igneous rock classification and nomenclature. 1. Introduction; 2. Classification and nomenclature; 3. Glossary of terms; 4. Bibliography of terms; Appendix A. Lists of participants; Appendix B. 21 line diagrams, 20 tables. Website with downloadable code for chemical classifications available.
Previous edn 1989.

Rock blasting terms and symbols: a dictionary of symbols and terms in rock blasting and related areas like drilling, mining and rock mechanics
A. Rustan, ed.; International Society for Rock Mechanics See entry no. 4668

1502 **Volcano and Hydrologic Hazards, Features, and Terminology**
US Geological Survey
http://vulcan.wr.usgs.gov/Glossary/framework.html
Includes an A–Z glossary of volcano and related terminology. Links to a wide range of resources including volcano sites worldwide, other hazards, and publications and research.

- **Photo Glossary of Volcano Terms**
  http://volcanoes.usgs.gov/Products/Pglossary/pglossary.html. For each term listed, there is a photograph from a named location, a short description, and further links to explore more examples and detail of the term. A–Z list, but cross-references showing the relationship among key terms.

Associations & societies

1503 **International Association of Volcanology and Chemistry of the Earth's Interior**
www.iavcei.org
An association that represents the primary international focus for volcanological and related research. The *Bulletin of Volcanology*, a regular periodical, publishes much of its research. Web-page links to meetings, publications and further links of interest. A useful gateway.

1504 **The Society for Organic Petrology**
www.tsop.org
Established in 1984 to rationalize work with coal and kerogen petrology, organic geochemistry and related disciplines. Promotes research, disseminates information, and provides educational opportunities via meetings, field trips, and short courses. Publishes a quarterly newsletter and research reports. Website carries information on the society, its activities including publications and links about organic petrology and geochemistry.

Portal & task environments

1505 **Bob's Rock Shop** [USA]
B. Keller
www.rockhounds.com/rockshop/table.shtml
Online portal in co-operation with the US-based *Rock&Gem* magazine. An attractive website, it covers every aspect of rock and mineral collection and identification. Up-to-date news items with links.

1506 **Cascades Volcano Observatory**
US Geological Survey
http://vulcan.wr.usgs.gov
Specific information for volcanologists on the volcanoes of the Cascades range of mountains in western USA and Canada. Also many other useful volcano-related links available from this web page, including glossaries, FAQs, news and current events, educational links and plenty of photographic images. List of other relevant USGS websites. A detailed and useful resource.

1507 **Global Volcanism Program: Worldwide Holocene Volcano and Eruption Information**
National Museum of Natural History
www.volcano.si.edu
A catalogue of all known young volcanoes. Major source of regular reports of volcanic activity around the world. Documents small and large eruptions during the past 10,000

years. Further links. Basic and advanced search options. Useful to undergraduates and researchers alike.

1508 Volcano World
University of North Dakota
http://volcano.und.nodak.edu
Website established in 1995 containing an index to web resources. Volcano listings sorted by world region, country/area, volcano name and volcano descriptions. Many images used. Especially suitable for children. Some links not always up to date.

Discovering print & electronic resources

Geomechanics Abstracts
See entry no. 4700

Mineralogy and Petrology Research on the Web
University of Dayton See entry no. 1303

Digital data, image & text collections

1509 Igneous Petrology Reference Series
S.A. Gibson [et al.], comps; University of Cambridge
http://www.esc.cam.ac.uk/new/v10/teaching/geology/ib-b/gibson/IP%20reference.htm
A useful, well illustrated image and text collection of hand specimens and thin sections, useful as a reference series for use in individual study/revision for undergraduates. The collection is divided on the basis of the International Union of Geological Sciences nomenclature (Le Maitre, 2002). Brief descriptions of all igneous rocks are provided. Developed in the University's Department of Earth Sciences.

1510 Natural Stones Worldwide
K. Borner and D. Hill Available as CD-ROM for purchase.
www.stone-database.com
Free access available to a database of over 24,000 commercial names for natural stones. Provides a description of the stones, their geologic period, technical and physical characteristics, origin, commercial suppliers. Keyword index. Search facilities.

Directories & encyclopedias

1511 Catalogue of meteorites
M.M. Grady 5th edn, Cambridge University Press, 2000, 689pp. CD-ROM, £120.00. ISBN 0521663032.
Essential major reference tool for all interested in meteorites: includes a searchable CD-ROM with expanded information. Data on each meteorite name: place where found (or place of impact), plus co-ordinates; chemical content (with citations to the original literature); weight; present owner; specimen number (if appropriate). The definitive list of all well documented meteorites known worldwide. Describes those represented in the collection of the Natural History Museum, London. Includes the 10,000 new specimens recovered since publication of the fourth edition.
Revised edn of: Catalogue of meteorites, *A.L. Graham and A.W.R. Bevan, 4th edn.*
'This book represents a prodigious amount of human endeavour, and the meteorite community owes Monica Grady an enormous debt of gratitude. If you are a serious amateur or a professional, you will want this book.' (*Meteorite*)

1512 The collector's encyclopedia of rocks & minerals
A.F.L. Deeson, ed. David & Charles, 1973, 288pp. ISBN 0715363301.
Well over 2000 different types (AA or Aphrolith ... Zussmanite). Data include composition, physical properties,distinguishing characteristics, methods of identification, environment, variety. 1000 small colour illustrations. Useful classic for the amateur collector.
A Carter Nash Cameron book.

1513 A colour atlas of rocks and minerals in thin section
W.S. MacKenzie and A.E. Adams Manson, 1994, 192pp. £17.95. ISBN 1874545170.
Comprehensive and helpful overview and introduction to the use of thin sections. Many colour thin section photographs. Explanations of how to observe mineral and rock samples under the microscope. Good general review of rock and mineral identification, covering all rock types. A concise and useful introductory teaching and learning tool for undergraduates. Index.

1514 A colour atlas of sedimentary rocks in the field
D.A.V. Stow Manson Publishing, 2004, 320pp. £17.95. ISBN 1874545693.
A handy, pocket-sized volume, especially useful for practical use in the field and useful to students and professional geologists alike. Colour images and diagrams accompany text covering field techniques, identification of rock types, recognition of sediment characteristics and preliminary interpretation.

1515 The encyclopedia of igneous and metamorphic petrology
D.R. Bowes, ed. Van Nostrand Reinhold, 1990, 666pp. ISBN 0442206232.
www.eseo.com
Key reference tool in the subject. Includes bibliographical references and indexes. Contributions of more than 100 earth scientists from 18 countries and more than 250 entries. Provides information on the mineralogical, chemical, and textural characters of rock types across the spectrum of igneous and metamorphic petrology. Includes lists of both commonly and little-used terms. Subject index.
Available online: see website.

Encyclopedia of sediments and sedimentary rocks
G.V. Middleton [et al.], eds See entry no. 982

1516 Encyclopedia of volcanoes
H. Sigurdsson [et al.], eds Academic Press, 2000, 1417pp. $104.95. ISBN 012643140X.
This comprehensive encyclopedia summarizes the present knowledge of volcanoes. Well used in academic institutions. Provides a comprehensive source of information on the multi-disciplinary influences of volcanic eruptions with more than 80 peer-reviewed articles; 3000 Glossary entries. Extensive cross-referencing system. 16 pp. of plates. Large page size, easy-to-read double-column format. Suits general to more academic readership. Includes bibliographical references and index.

1517 **A guide to common rocks**
C. Pellant and H. Pellant; Field Studies Council 2003. Occasional Publication 78, £3.25 (poster). ISBN 1851538887.
www.field-studies-council.org [DESCRIPTION]
A colour foldout chart containing illustrations and brief notes on more than 60 types of rock. Describes the formation of igneous, sedimentary and metamorphic rock, and discusses their composition and structure. Suitable for general and student use.
Series: Fold-out Charts.

- **Rocks, minerals and fossils of the world C. Pellant** Little Brown, 1990, 176pp. ISBN 0316697966. Enables the collector and enthusiast to identify rocks, minerals and fossils the world over. Covers collecting and conserving fossils, their major characteristics, details of where they are located. Index and further reading; 300 colour illustrations.

1518 **The Macdonald encyclopedia of rocks and minerals**
A. Mottana Macdonald, 1983, 607pp. ISBN 0356091473.
Concise descriptions of minerals and rocks. Part 1: Minerals; Part 2: Rocks. A lengthy introduction precedes each part. Symbols indicate grade of rarity (very rare; rare; common; very common). Over 1000 col. illus. Index of entries. Small format. A very cheap compendium.
Translation of a work published Milan, 1977.

1519 **Volcanoes**
M. Rosi [et al.] Firefly Books, 2003, 336pp. $24.95. ISBN 1552976831.
Comprehensive guide to 100 active volcanoes around the world, written and illustrated by experts. Each volcano's characteristics, structure and geology are described. Covers all main types of volcanoes. Includes review of the environmental benefits and detriments caused by volcanoes. Many colour illustrations and photographs. Bibliography, index. Well suited to general readership.
Series: Firefly Guides.
'A superb guidebook to the world's volcanoes ... can be used as both a teaching tool and a field reference ... well illustrated diagrams and color images provide a great visual aid complementing the text ... Informative maps, simple geological diagrams, and vivid photographs accompany the text on each volcano ... An excellent, comprehensive source ... Highly recommended.' (*Choice*)

1520 **Volcanoes of the world: a regional directory, gazetteer, and chronology of volcanism during the last 10,000 years**
T. Simkin and L. Siebert; Smithsonian Institution 2nd edn, Geoscience Press, 1994, 349pp. ISBN 0945005121.
www.volcano.si.edu/world/index.cfm [COMPANION]
Summarizes 1521 volcanoes active in the last 10,000 years, and carries over 7900 eruptions since 8000 BC, arranged in order of occurrence and explosive magnitude. Includes bibliographical references (pp 305–49).

Handbooks & manuals

1521 **A color guide to the petrography of carbonate rocks: grains, textures, porosity, diagenesis**
P.A. Scholle and D.S. Ulmer-Scholle; American Association of Petroleum Geologists 2003, 474pp. New edition of the AAPG 1978 classic *A color illustrated guide to carbonate rock constituents, textures, cements, and porosities*, $68.00 (hbk). ISBN 0891813586.
http://bookstore.aapg.org [DESCRIPTION]
Much expanded and improved edition. Contains a significant collection of colour photographs and diagrams to increase understanding of concepts. Used as the basis for a nine-module online course. General references. Glossary and index.
Series: AAPG Memoirs, No. 77.

A colour atlas of carbonate sediments and rocks under the microscope
A.E. Adams and W.S. MacKenzie See entry no. 991

1522 **CRC handbook of physical properties of rocks**
R.S. Carmichael, ed. CRC Press, 1982–4, 1089pp. 3 v. ISBN 0849302269.
Useful set of handbooks; 16 contributors. V.1: Mineral composition of rocks; Electrical and spectroscopic properties of rocks and minerals. V.2: Seismic velocities; Magnetic and engineering properties of rocks and minerals. V.3: Density of rocks and minerals; Elastic constants of minerals; Inelastic properties of rocks and minerals: strength and sheology; Radioactive properties of minerals and rocks; Seismic attenuation. All chapters have an appended bibliography. Each volume has an index. 'The intent is to bridge the gap between individual reports with only specific limited data, and massive assemblies of data which are uncritically presented.'

1523 **The field description of igneous rocks**
R.S. Thorpe and G.C. Brown Wiley, 1991, 160pp. $65.00. ISBN 0471932752.
A handy pocket-sized book ideal for fieldwork. Complements textbooks on igneous petrology dealing with observations from the small to large scale and the techniques required. References and further reading. Index and appendix. Part of a series of handbooks designed as practical guides to field geology.
Series: Geological Society of London Handbooks.

- **The field description of metamorphic rocks N. Fry** Wiley, 1991, 128pp. $65.00. ISBN 0471932213.

1524 **Igneous and metamorphic petrology**
M.G. Best 2nd edn, Blackwell Science, 2002, 768pp. £34.99. ISBN 1405105887.
Revised edition providing up-to-date comprehensive coverage of new advances in geochemistry, geochronology and geophysics, as well as a basic grounding in aspects of igneous and metamorphic petrology. Emphasis on latest experimental and field data.
Previous edn Oxford: Freeman, 1982.

1525 **Layered intrusions**
R.G. Cawthorn, ed. Elsevier, 1996, 542pp. $87.00. ISBN 0444825185.
Summarizes important aspects and includes detailed 1:20,000 geological colour map of the Skaergaard intrusion. Each chapter reviews a theme or specific geological intrusion. Widely used university textbook. Author index. Subject index. Bibliographical references at end of every chapter.
Series: Developments in Petrology, V. 15.

The Michelin field guide to minerals, rocks and fossils
N. Curtis See entry no. 1330

1526 **Petrography to petrogenesis**
M.J. Hibbard Prentice Hall, 1995, 608pp. ISBN 0023541458.
A useful comprehensive text on optical mineralogy, petrography and petrology. Focuses on the study of rock behaviour in response to geological processes. Covers all common igneous, metamorphic and sedimentary rocks, and weathered, hydrothermally altered and low-temperature precipitative and deformed rocks. Mainly B & W illustrations, only a few in colour. Includes bibliographical references (pp 533–73) and index. Undergraduate, postgraduate readership.

Philip's guide to minerals, rocks & fossils
W.R. Hamilton, A.R. Woolley and A.C. Bishop See entry no. 1338

1527 **Physical properties of rocks and minerals**
Y.S. Touloukian, W.R. Judd and R.F. Roy, eds Hemisphere, 1989, 548pp. ISBN 0891168834.
A handy resource with information by 31 contributors. Thirteen chapters (most of them with bibliographies appended). Chapters 3–12, on the physical, mechanical, electrical, magnetic and thermophysical properties of rocks. Chapter 13: Heat index. Emphasis is on data useful to geothermal applications. Postgraduate readership.
Series: CINDAS Data Series on Material Properties : v. II-2.

1528 **Practical handbook of physical properties of rocks and minerals**
R.S. Carmichael, ed. CRC Press, 1989, 760pp. ISBN 0849337038.
A practical, concise, easy-to-use handbook/manual, comprising technical data compiled to provide well organized and definitive presentations. Topics covered include the mineral composition of rocks, and densities of rocks and minerals. Undergraduate, postgraduate readership.
An abridged and updated edition of the CRC HANDBOOK OF PHYSICAL PROPERTIES OF ROCKS *published in 1982–4.*

1529 **Sedimentary petrology**
M.E. Tucker 3rd edn, Blackwell Science, 2001, 262pp. £29.99. ISBN 0632057351.
Provides a concise account of sediments and sedimentary rocks and their composition, mineralogy, textures, structures, diagenesis and depositional environments. Includes 16 plates with 74 colour photo-micrographs of sedimentary rocks in thin-section. Revised and updated, new tables added to aid description and interpretation. Includes bibliographical references (pp 231–49).
Previous edn 1991.

1530 **Sedimentary rocks in the field**
M.E. Tucker 3rd edn, Wiley, 2003, 234pp. $35.00. ISBN 0470851236.
This handy pocket-sized book describes how sedimentary rocks may be observed, recorded and mapped. Especially useful for fieldwork. Basic techniques clearly described with tables, illustrations and photographs. Includes sections on safety in the field, the use of GPS in sedimentary studies, core description, fossils as depth indicators, and facies models; 2nd and 3rd-year undergraduate, postgraduate readership. Useful supplement for professional geologists, physical geographers and engineers.
Series: Geological Field Guides.

1531 **Volcanoes**
P. Francis and C. Oppenheimer 2nd edn, Oxford University Press, 2004, 521pp. £28.99. ISBN 0199254699.
www.oup.com/uk/booksites [COMPANION]
An important comprehensive reference tool for those studying volcanoes. A new edition with 18 comprehensive new chapters including the importance of the impact of volcanic eruptions on the earth's environment. Contains contemporary research findings. Chapter specifically on volcanic hazards and risk mitigation. A core text for students across a range of disciplines. Clear, well illustrated text. Explains volcanic processes with 'immense clarity, engaging humour and excellent illustrations'. References (pp 511–13).
Previous edn Clarendon Press, 1993

Spatial Technologies

aerial photography • cartography • earth observation • geodesy • geographical information systems • geographical names • global positioning systems • hydrography • land surveying • maps • maritime navigation • nautical astronomy • navigation • photogrammetry • planetary mapping • remote sensing • satellite remote sensing • surveying • web cartography

Introductions to the subject

1532 **Elements of cartography**
A.H. Robinson [et al.] 6th edn, Wiley, 1995, 674pp. $93.95. ISBN 0471555797.
Standard introductory text, first published 1953, but substantially revised in subsequent editions, becoming a multi-author work. Sixth edition now somewhat dated, but still very useful. Combines classic cartographic principles with new production technologies including GIS. Covers nature and history of cartography; basic geodesy, map projections and co-ordinate systems; data collection, sampling and digitizing; data processing and management; cartographic design and map compilation; cartographic abstraction; map production. Appendices provide now rather dated information on digital data products, file formats, graphic arts photography, and sources of mapping software and remote sensing products in North America. Index.

1533 **The elements of navigation and nautical astronomy**
C.H. Cotter and H.K. Lahiry 2nd edn, Brown, Son and Ferguson, 1992, 463pp. ISBN 0851745431.
First edn by C. H. Cotter (1977); 2nd edn revised by H. K. Lahiry. Provides groundwork for professional examinations in navigation and nautical astronomy. Illustrated with line drawings and provided with exercises and worked examples. This edition includes chapter on satellite navigation, and all aspects of chartwork have been updated.

1534 **Flattening the earth: two thousand years of map projections**
J.P. Snyder University of Chicago Press, 1993, 365pp. $21.00. ISBN 0226767477.
Originally intended as a contribution to the History of Cartography project, but published as a stand-alone volume. Provides an illustrated history and description of map projections from the classical period to the 20th century. Extensively referenced and indexed.

1535 Geodesy
W. Torge 3rd edn, Walter de Gruyter, 2001, 416pp. £24.50. ISBN 3110170728.
Standard text on geodesy ('the branch of mathematics concerned with the shape and area of the earth or large portions of it'), first published in English in 1980 and thoroughly revised to reflect recent developments in space systems for positioning and gravity field determination. Also gives attention to developments in automated terrestrial techniques. Extensive reference list.

1536 Geographic Information Systems and science
P.A. Longley [et al.] Wiley, 2001, 472pp. $55.00. ISBN 0471892750.
www.wiley.co.uk/gis [COMPANION]
Extensively illustrated introductory student textbook. Book is divided into three sections. Principles covers representation, georeferencing, the nature of geographical data, uncertainty, generalization and metadata. Techniques includes GIS software, data modelling, data collection, creating and maintaining geographical databases, visualization and user interaction, query and analysis, and advanced spatial analysis. Practice includes GIS and management, G-business, operational aspects, and GIS partnerships. Complementary website provides learning resources for teachers and students and links to the GIS and mapping software company ESRI's Virtual Campus.

1537 Geographical Information Systems: principles and applications
P.A. Longley [et al.], eds 2nd edn, Wiley, 1999, 1296pp. 2 v., $400.00. ISBN 0471321826.
Definitive reference book for users of Geographical Information Systems. This edition completely restructured and rewritten by an international team of almost 100 GIS experts. First volume covers principles and methodology, second covers management and practical applications. Includes colour illustrations, cross-referencing, an extensive bibliography, and list of acronyms.

1538 Getting started with Geographic Information Systems
K.C. Clarke 4th edn, Prentice Hall, 2003, 340pp. $77.00. ISBN 0130460273.
www.prenhall.com/clarke [COMPANION]
Well illustrated and very readable basic-level textbook. Chapters cover: what is GIS? (definitions and a brief history); cartographic roots of GIS (scale, projections, co-ordinate systems); maps as numbers (data models and formats); getting the map into the computer (data collection, digitizing, scanning and editing); what is where? (database management, searching and the query interface); why is it there? (statistical and spatial analysis); making maps with GIS (map types and design); how to pick a GIS; GIS in action (case studies); the future of GIS.

Each chapter ends with a study guide, exercises, references and key terms and definitions. Interviews with GIS practitioners are also included. Extensive glossary. Index. Companion website provides resources for teachers and students. This edition packaged with demo copy of ArcVIEW 3.1.

1539 The history of cartography
J.B. Harley and D. Woodward, eds University of Chicago Press, 1987–.
www.geography.wisc.edu/histcart [COMPANION]
The History of Cartography Project is a major research, editorial and publishing venture, drawing on international scholarship. Its primary product is a multi-volume history of cartography projected to be in six volumes of which three (the third is in three books) had been published by 2004. Founded by the late J.B. Harley and by David Woodward, and subsequently edited by Woodward (deceased 2004) with other guest editors. Further volumes have been in preparation, and exploratory essays towards Volume 6 (20th Century) are available on the University of Wisconsin website.

- **Volume 1. Cartography in prehistoric, ancient and medieval Europe and the Mediterranean J. B. Harley and D. Woodward, eds** University of Chicago Press, 1987, 599pp. $175.00. ISBN 0226316335.
- **Volume 2, Book 1. Cartography in the traditional Islamic and South Asian societies** University of Chicago Press, 1992, 579pp. $195.00. ISBN 0226316351.
- **Volume 2, Book 2. Cartography in the traditional East and Southeast Asian societies** University of Chicago Press, 1994, 970pp. $195.00. ISBN 0226316378.
- **Volume 2, Book 3. Cartography in the traditional African, American, Arctic, Australian and Pacific societies D. Woodward and G. M. Lewis, eds** University of Chicago Press, 1998, 639pp. $150.00. ISBN 0226907287.

1540 How maps work: representation, visualization, and design
A.M. MacEachren The Guilford Press, 1995, 513pp. £65.00. ISBN 0898625890.
Unique and penetrating attempt to integrate cognitive and semiotic approaches to the understanding of maps as synthetic spatial representations. In the first part, the author explores how maps are physical perceived and cognitively understood. In the second part, a semiotic approach is used to explore how maps are imbued with meaning. The third section uses the geographical visualization model to investigate how maps are used and how they stimulate visual thinking. There is an extensive reference list and author and subject indexes.

1541 Images of the earth: a guide to remote sensing
S.A. Drury 2nd edn, Oxford University Press, 1998, 203pp. £79.99. ISBN 0198549989.
Second edition of former title *A guide to remote sensing: interpreting images of the earth*. Clearly written and colourfully illustrated introduction to remote sensing, supported by many practical examples. Chapters cover the problems which the technology helps to solve, how images are obtained, how they are interpreted in relation to atmosphere, land, sea, land cover and geology, how the information is used, and with operational issues. Appendices cover training opportunities and image sources. There is a glossary, guide to further reading and index.

1542 Introduction to geodesy: the history and concepts of modern geodesy
J.R. Smith Wiley, 1997, 240pp. $80.00. ISBN 047116660X.
Non-mathematical introduction. Revised edition of the author's *Basic geodesy*. Topics include: traditional survey positioning techniques; geodetic systems, including horizontal and vertical geodetic datums; physical geodesy; the world geodetic system; satellite geodesy; the Global Positioning System; gravity measures; electromagnetic distance measurement; projections; examples of modern projects. Bibliography and index.

1543 **An introduction to Geographical Information Systems**
I. Heywood, S. Cornelius and S. Carver 2nd edn, Prentice Hall, 2002, 295pp. $83.60. ISBN 0130611980.
www.booksites.net/heywood [COMPANION]
Well presented and illustrated introductory student textbook. Part 1 covers the fundamentals of GIS, including the nature of spatial data, spatial data models, database creation, data input and analysis, and output formats and delivery mechanisms. The second part deals with issues in GIS, with chapters on the history of geographical computing, data quality, organizational issues, project design, and future developments in GIS. Revision questions and suggestions for further study complete each chapter. There is a useful glossary and index. The companion website offers both student and lecturer resources, the latter requiring free registration.

1544 **Introduction to microwave remote sensing**
I. Woodhouse Taylor and Francis, 2004, 208pp. £29.99. ISBN 041527124X.
Technical introduction to active and passive microwave remote sensing systems. Chapters cover: why microwaves? history of microwaves; physical fundamentals; microwaves in the real world; detecting microwaves; passive microwave systems; non-imaging radar; imaging radar; interferometry; polarimetry; microwave measurements in context. Appendices provide technical glossary and summary of useful mathematics.

Introduction to ocean remote sensing
S. Martin See entry no. 1348

1545 **Introduction to remote sensing**
J.B. Campbell 3rd edn, Taylor and Francis, 2002, 522pp. £29.99. ISBN 0415282942.
Heavily illustrated, comprehensive introductory text providing an overview of the most widely used forms of remote sensing imagery and their applications in plant sciences, hydrology, earth sciences, and land-use analysis. This edn features new coverage of lidar technology, radar interferometry, and the present generation of satellite sensors, as well as other topics of current significance and includes 28 colour plates and more than 380 black-and-white images and figures.

1546 **Land registration and cadastral systems: tools of land information and management**
G. Larsson Longman Scientific, 1991, 240pp. £24.99. ISBN 0582089522.
Considers cadastral and land registration systems as tools for land information and management. Discusses the historical development of these systems and describes their application in Europe and English-speaking countries. Focuses on benefits and scope for improvement, current methods of survey and registration and the move to automated systems.

1547 **The map library in the new millennium**
R.B. Parry and C.R. Perkins, eds Facet Publishing and American Library Association, 2001, 267pp. £55.00. ISBN 1856043975.
Explores the role of the map library in the context of new developments in the format and distribution of spatial data and the changing needs of users. Issues covered include the changing profile of map users, organizational change, GIS in the map room, the effect of the internet and world wide web, metadata standards, digital conversion, access to spatial data, intellectual property rights, the new mapping industry, and map dealing. Contributors are drawn from the USA, Canada, The Netherlands, New Zealand and the UK.

1548 **Map use and analysis**
J. Campbell 4th edn, McGraw-Hill, 2001, 480pp. $86.87. ISBN 0073037486.
www.mhhe.com/earthsci/geography/campbell4e
Clearly written and well illustrated introductory textbook on the nature of maps and map use. Includes mental mapping, air photos and satellite imagery, digital cartography and GIS as well as traditional maps; 21 chapters cover basic mapping processes, map projection, locational systems, scale and generalization, measurement, route selection, terrain representation and interpretation, topographic features, qualitative and quantitative information, characteristics of map features, cartograms and special purpose maps, maps and graphs, map misuse, remote sensing, digital map applications and GIS. The companion website includes numerous web links for both instructors and students.

1549 **Planetary mapping**
R. Greeley and R.M. Batson Cambridge University Press, 1990, 296pp. £65.00. ISBN 0521307740.
Describes the history and process of mapping planets and satellites beyond the Earth. Begins with an introduction to the differences between terrestrial and planetary mapping and continues with a general discussion of the history of planetary mapping. The fundamentals of cartographic techniques are described in detail, followed by sections on planetary nomenclature, geodetic considerations, and topographic and geologic mapping. Includes appendices on map formats and projections, half-tone processes for planetary maps, and available mission data.

1550 **Practical surveying and computations**
A.L. Allan 2nd edn, Laxton's (Butterworth-Heinemann), 1997, 573pp. ISBN 0750636556.
Previous edition *Practical field surveying and computations* by A.L. Allan, J.R. Hollway and J.H.B. Maynes, 1963. This edition takes account of the profound changes in surveying methods resulting from electronic instrumentation and computerized data processing, and emphasizes understanding of instrument function, and quality control. Aimed at land and geodetic surveyors, civil engineers and field scientists. Brief references and bibliography. Index.

1551 **Principles of Geographical Information Systems**
P.A. Burrough and R.A. McDonnell 2nd edn, Oxford University Press, 1998, 346pp. £34.99. ISBN 0198233655.
Comprehensive and concise introduction to the theory and practice of GIS, replacing Burrough's previous *Principles of Geographical Information Systems for land resource assessment.* Chapters cover: data models, geographical data in the computer, data input, verification, storage and output, creating continuous surfaces from point data, optimal interpolation using geostatistics, analysis of discrete entities in space, spatial analysis using continuous fields, errors and quality control, error propagation in numerical modelling, fuzzy sets and fuzzy geographical objects, and current issues and trends in GIS. Appendices include glossary, listing of www geography and GIS servers, and example data sets.

1552 Remote sensing and image interpretation
T.M. Lillesand, R.W. Kiefer and J. Chipman 5th edn, Wiley, 2003, 704pp. $71.74. ISBN 0471451525.
Classic text providing comprehensive, and discipline-neutral, introduction to remote sensing and image interpretation. Includes the latest developments in digital image processing and new satellite systems. Stresses the close interactions with GIS, GPS, digital image processing and environmental modelling. Contents include: concepts and foundations of remote sensing; elements of photographic systems; principles of photogrammetry; visual image interpretation; multispectral, thermal and hyperspectral sensing; earth resource satellites operating in optical spectrum; digital image processing; microwave sensing. Appendices include listing sources of remotely sensed data, remote sensing periodicals and web resources.

1553 The Remote Sensing Tutorial
Open Geospatial Consortium
rst.gsfc.nasa.gov
Available on the web as a comprehensive introduction to sensor technology, image processing and remote sensing applications. It is updated monthly. Also available as an educational CD-ROM.

1554 Surveying
A. Bannister, S. Raymond and R. Baker 7th edn, Longman, 1998, 502pp. £39.99. ISBN 0582302498.
Concise, practical introduction to surveying techniques for students of civil and structural engineering and all courses containing an element of surveying. Chapters cover: tape and offset surveying; levelling, theodolite survey; electromagnetic distance measurement; satellite positioning; survey methods; analysis and adjustment; areas and volumes; setting out; curve ranging; hydrographic surveying; photogrammetry. Each chapter is followed by exercises. Index.

1555 Web cartography: developments and prospects
M.-J. Kraak and A. Brown, eds Taylor and Francis, 2000, 213pp. £24.99. ISBN 074840869X.
kartoweb.itc.nl/webcartography/webbook [COMPANION]
Introduction to the nature and uses of maps on the web. Chapters include brief reviews of the visualization trend in cartography, how maps are currently used on the web, user profiles, and the principles of web map design. Four chapters discuss a range of examples of web maps found on special interest websites. There are useful appendices describing file formats and plug-ins, and the practicalities of website design, internet colour, fonts and file sizes. The accompanying website provides a dynamic environment for demonstrating principles set out in the text, and provides access to a basic course on web cartography.

Dictionaries, thesauri, classifications

1556 Cartographical innovations: An international handbook of mapping terms to 1900
H.M. Wallis and A.H. Robinson, eds; International Cartographic Association Map Collector Publications, 1987, 353pp. £45.25. ISBN 0906430046.
Intended as a history of cartographic innovations and their diffusion. Arranged as a dictionary of terms used to describe different kinds of map, and different cartographic concepts and techniques. Terms are arranged into eight main groups, and each term is provided with a definition, a scholarly discussion of its origin and evolution, and a list of references. The work concludes with a list of almost 100 contributors and correspondents, a general index and an index to bibliographies.

1557 Enzyklopädisches Wörterbuch Kartographie in 25 Sprachen (Encyclopedic dictionary of cartography in 25 languages)
J. Neumann 2nd edn, K G Saur, 1997, 586pp. ISBN 3598107641.
This dictionary replaces the *Multilingual dictionary of technical terms in cartography* published in 1973. Organized into ten main thematic sections, the work includes 1351 terms with definitions in German, English, Spanish, French and Russian. Equivalent terms are given in a further 20 languages. Many definitions are unaltered from the 1973 edition, but many new terms have been added, especially in the realm of computer-aided cartography.

1558 The ESRI Press dictionary of GIS terminology
H. Kennedy, ed. ESRI Press, 2001, 128pp. $19.95. ISBN 1879102781.
Over 1000 terms, including some from associated fields of geography, cartography, mathematics and computer science. Gives definitions, field from which term is taken, and cross-references to other terms. A two-page list of acronyms is also included.

1559 Glossary of terms for the standardization of geographical names
N. Kadmon, ed.; United Nations Group of Experts on Geographical Names 2002, 262pp. £31.00. ISBN 9210611926.
http://unstats.un.org/unsd/geoinfo/glossary.htm
375 toponymic terms are stated and defined in English, French, Spanish, Russian, Japanese and Arabic.
Available online: see website.

1560 Glossary of the mapping sciences
American Society for Photogrammetry and Remote Sensing 1994, 594pp. Published jointly with the American Congress on Surveying and Mapping and the American Society of Civil Engineers, $50.00. ISBN 1570830118.
Provides 11,000 definitions of terms used in photogrammetry, remote sensing, cartography, land surveying, construction and engineering surveying, geodesy, hydrography, GIS, surveying law and metrology.

Laws, standards, codes

Consultative Committee for Space Data Systems
See entry no. 4885

Eurocontrol
See entry no. 4886

1561 Federal Geographic Data Committee
www.fgdc.gov
FGDC is a 19-member interagency committee tasked to develop the United States National Spatial Data Infrastructure (NSDI). The NSDI encompasses policies, standards and procedures for state, local and tribal governments, the academic community and the private sector to co-operate in producing and sharing geographic data. The very rich website includes information on metadata

standards (with a downloadable workbook), links to numerous online resources, a clearinghouse for geospatial data and a metadata entry system.

1562 Infrastructure for Spatial Information in Europe: INSPIRE
www.ec-gis.org/inspire
A European Commission initiative developed in collaboration with member states to improve the availability of relevant, harmonized and quality geographical information in support of any Community policies having a spatial dimension or impact. Addresses technical standards and protocols, organizational and co-ordination issues, and data policy issues. Supports data sharing and access, and the creation of seamless data across national boundaries.

1563 Open Geospatial Consortium
www.opengis.org
International industry consortium, founded 1994, with current membership of 257 companies, government agencies and universities participating in a consensus process to develop publicly available interface specifications. OpenGIS® Specifications support interoperable solutions that 'geo-enable' the web, wireless and location-based services, and mainstream IT. The specifications empower technology developers to make complex spatial information and services accessible and useful with all kinds of applications. Website provides extensive news, information and demonstrations. A log-in for subscribing members gives further access.

1564 United Nations Group of Experts on Geographical Names
unstats.un.org/unsd/geoinfo/ungegn.htm
The United Nations holds a conference every five years on the standardization of geographical names, and UNGEGN meets between conferences to follow up the implementation of resolutions made at the conferences. The aim is to provide toponymic guidelines for map editors on the standardization of geographical names for international use. Also addressed are issues concerning training courses, digital data files and gazetteers, romanization systems, country names, and terminology. Reports have been published in *World Cartography* and as a series of *Working Papers*, some of which are available on the website. The website now serves as a focal point for disseminating information about the activities of UNGEGN and of material relating to name standardization.

Official & quasi-official bodies

1565 ANZLIC: The Spatial Information Council
www.anzlic.org.au
The ANZLIC Council is a joint initiative of the Australian and New Zealand governments, with a membership representing the two national governments and the State and Territory governments of Australia. The mission is to develop nationally agreed polices and guidelines for management of spatial data, and to facilitate easy and cost effective access to the wealth of spatial data and services provided by a wide range of organizations in the public and private sectors. Operates with three standing committees covering, respectively, the development of the Australian Spatial Data Infrastructure (ASDI), land administration, and surveying and mapping.

EUMETSAT
See entry no. 1182

1566 European Umbrella Organization for Geographic Information
www.eurogi.org
European Union initiative to encourage greater use of geographical information in Europe, to work towards the development of strong national geographical information associations, and to facilitate development of the European Spatial Data Infrastructure. Membership comprises 22 national associations and three pan-European associations. Website includes members-only pages, and links to the home pages of member associations.

1567 Fédération Internationale des Géomètres (International Federation of Surveyors)
www.fig.net/figtree
Founded 1878. Non-government organization, comprising a federation of national organizations representing 100 countries, which supports collaboration in the progress of surveying in all fields and applications. Concerns include professional standards and promoting professional development. Holds an international congress every four years and a series of regional conferences. Ten commissions meet and report on technical issues.

1568 International Hydrographic Organization
www.iho.shom.fr
Founded 1921 as International Hydrographic Bureau; IHO since 1970. Intergovernmental consultative and technical organization which seeks to ensure the provision of adequate and timely hydrographic information for worldwide marine navigation and other purposes, through the endeavours of national hydrographic offices. A subsidiary mission is the application of hydrographic data to support science, and to promote its use in Geographic Information Systems, principally for the sustainable development of national maritime zones. Responsible for promoting uniformity in national chart specification, including digital charts, and promoting efficient methods of hydrographic survey. Numerous publications on standards downloadable from website. Website also includes International Hydrographic Dictionary, searchable online.

National Ocean Service
See entry no. 1355

National Oceanic and Atmospheric Administration
See entry no. 1188

NOAA Coastal Services Center
See entry no. 1356

1569 Ordnance Survey of Great Britain
www.ordnancesurvey.co.uk
Website for the National Mapping Authority of Great Britain. Includes information on products (digital spatial data and paper maps), copyright, business links, and a link to the National GPS Website. Mapzone provides online educational material, while Get-a-map provides free online access to

printable map extracts. There is also a 250,000-word place-name gazetteer, an online map shop, and much more.

1570 United Kingdom Hydrographic Office
www.ukho.gov.uk
Founded 1795 and operates as part of UK Ministry of Defence. Provides navigational products and services to the Royal Navy and Merchant Marine including worldwide cover of 3300 nautical charts, 220 nautical publications, electronic charts and leisure charts. Website includes online catalogue launched 2004.

- **Admiralty EasyTide** http://easytide.ukho.gov.uk/EasyTide/EasyTide/index.aspx. The most comprehensive tidal prediction service on the web, providing tidal data for over 6000 ports worldwide. The Office has long produced the *Admiralty Tide Tables*.
- **The mariner's handbook** 1999, Supplement 2002. £36.50. ISBN 0707711231. Data on charts and publications, coverage, usage, maintenance. Operational information and maritime regulations; tides, currents and characteristics of the sea; basic meteorology, navigation in ice, hazards and restrictions; IALA Maritime Buoyage System.

1571 US Geological Survey: Maps
www.usgs.gov/pubprod/maps.html
The Map Information subset of the USGS site. The Survey is the principal US federal mapping agency, created in 1879 originally to survey the public lands of the USA and collect data on geology and mineral resources. Today provides products and expertise on earth sciences, topography, water and biological resources and environmental hazards. Enormously rich, interactive website increasingly provides direct access to products and resources. Current Cooperative Topographic Mapping Program aims to develop web portal as single access point to seamless digital National Map.

Currently site provides links to commercial sites, such as Maptech, Topozone and Terraserver, some of which provide free online access to USGS mapping. Also access to the National Atlas of the United States, a learning web, and much more.

Research centres & institutes

1572 British Geological Survey: Maps
www.bgs.ac.uk/products/digitalmaps/home.html [FEE-BASED]
This is the part of the Survey's website concerned with Digital Maps. BGS is the National Geoscience Data Centre for the UK, concerned with surveying, monitoring and disseminating earth science information for the UK landmass and continental shelf. Mission includes a core programme of long-term strategic mapping with the production of a principal map series at 1:50,000 scale. Website provides information on activities and publications, and availability of maps, digital data and geoscience reports. Includes an online shopping facility.

1573 British National Space Centre
www.bnsc.gov.uk
Formed in 1985 as voluntary partnership of ten UK government departments and research councils to co-ordinate the UK civil space activity. Facilitates co-operation in space research at both national and international levels. Extensive web pages provide information about earth observation, space technology and exploration, news of the space industry, an image bank, space resource directory and a learning zone for teachers and students.

1574 Canada Centre for Remote Sensing
www.ccrs.nrcan.gc.ca
Receives, processes and archives remotely sensed data. Co-ordinates a national research programme to apply remote sensing techniques to sustainable development and environmental protection. Provides electronic access to spatial databases. The website provides links to CCRS Earth Observation Catalogue, to GeoGratis (for free download of Canadian geospatial data) and to the online (national) Atlas of Canada.

1575 Earth Resources Observation Systems Data Center
[USA]
edc.usgs.gov
The EROS Data Center at Sioux Falls, South Dakota serves as a data management, systems development and research centre for the *National Mapping Division* of the US Geological Survey. It also provides a gateway to the description and acquisition of remotely sensed data and products, such as Landsat. From 2004, the Center will distribute photographic products only in digital format.

Associations & societies

1576 American Congress on Surveying and Mapping
www.acsm.net
US-based, non-profit educational organization which seeks to advance the science of surveying and mapping, and to encourage the development of educational programmes for these disciplines. Membership drawn mainly from the USA but also Canada and South America. Comprises four member organizations, each with its own, more specialized interests, namely: American Association for Geodetic Surveying, the Cartography and Geographic Information Society, the Geographic and Land Information Society, and the National Society of Professional Surveys.

ACSM holds conferences and organizes educational and certification programmes. Publications include *ACSM Bulletin*, *Cartography and Geographic Information Science* and *Surveying and Land Information Science*.

1577 American Society for Photogrammetry and Remote Sensing
www.asprs.org
Founded in 1934 and now has a worldwide membership. Mission is to advance knowledge and improve understanding of mapping sciences to promote responsible applications of photogrammetry, remote sensing, Geographical Information Systems, and their supporting technologies. In 1998 the Society adopted the tagline 'The imaging and geospatial information society' to reflect its focus on contemporary technologies. Membership drawn from private industry, government and academia. Official, peer-reviewed journal is *Photogrammetric Engineering and Remote Sensing*. Publishes substantial handbooks in remote sensing and photogrammetry (see separate entries).

1578 Association for Geographic Information
www.agi.org.uk
Non-profit organization, founded 1989, to represent the interests of users and providers of geographical information

in the UK. Mission is to help maximize the use of geographical information for the benefit of all. Covers all interest groups including local and central government, utilities, academics, system and service vendors, consultants and industry. Holds an annual conference and trade exhibition with proceedings published on CD-ROM. A GIS Sourcebook also published annually on CD-ROM. Website includes online GIS dictionary and information on GI standards. Members can also download sourcebook from the web. Responsible for GIGATEWAY.

1579 British Cartographic Society

www.cartography.org.uk

UK-based society established in 1963 to promote cartography in all its aspects. Membership is open to organizations and individuals interested in cartography whether professionally or not. Special interest groups comprise a Map Curators' Group (MCG), Design Group, Teachers' Group and Military Mapping Group. Publications include the peer-reviewed *Cartographic Journal* and a newsletter, *Maplines*. The MCG has its own newsletter *Cartographiti*.

- **Directory of UK Map Collections** 3rd edn, Map Curators' Group, 1995, 324pp. £15.00. ISBN 0904482111. www.cartography.org.uk/Pages/Publicat/Ukdir. Details and contact information for about 400 UK map collections, including national collections, college and university collections, and local record office collections. 4th edn only on the web.

1580 Commonwealth Association of Surveying and Land Economy

www.casle.org

Federation of independent professional surveying and land economy societies in the Commonwealth, formed 1969. Currently 40 member societies in 32 countries. Mission is to foster 'the advancement of the profession of surveying in the Commonwealth, and the enhancement of the skills of surveyors in the management of the natural and built environments for the common good'.

CASLE achieves these objectives through conferences and seminars, lecture tours, publications, manpower studies and direct advice to governments, universities, other educational bodies and its own member societies. In the period 1969–2002 CASLE organized eight general assemblies and many regional conferences, seminars, workshops and lecture tours.

1581 Eurogeographics

www.eurogeographics.org/eng/01_about.asp [REGISTRATION]

Formed from the merger of CERCO and MEGRIN in 2000 to represent European national mapping and cadastral agencies. Currently 44 member organizations from 40 countries. Mission is to co-operate in development of European spatial products and services, and provide official voice for Europe's NMCAs. Building European Spatial Data Infrastructure to achieve harmonization and interoperability of European GI data.

Current products include SABE (Seamless Administrative Boundaries of Europe), Euroglobal Map (1: 1,000,000 scale topographic data set) and Euroregional Map (1: 250,000 topographic data). There is also an online Geographic Data Description Directory (GDDD) providing metadata for products of the member organizations.

1582 European Association of Remote Sensing Laboratories

www.earsel.org

Network of about 250 European remote sensing institutes, including both academic and commercial/industrial. Individual membership also allowed. Founded 1977 and supported by ESA, Council of Europe and European Commission. Aims to stimulate and promote training in remote sensing and earth observation, co-ordinate application-oriented research, facilitate networking of experts in the agencies, and provide a bridge to the wider community. Organizes workshops and symposia and hosts special interest groups.

1583 Geoscience and Remote Sensing Society

www.ewh.ieee.org/soc/grss

Promotes the advance of GIS and remote sensing science and technology through scientific, technical and educational activities. It produces the monthly IEEE *Transactions in Geoscience and Remote Sensing* and sponsors the annual IGARSS (International Geoscience and Remote Sensing Society Symposium).

1584 Global Spatial Data Infrastructure Association

www.gsdi.org

Non-profit global organization with members from more than 50 countries, established following a meeting in 1996. Promotes efficient processes for exchanging geospatial information across political boundaries. Promotes 'awareness and implementation of complementary policies, common standards, and effective mechanisms for the development and availability of interoperable digital geographic data'.

1585 Groupe des cartothécaires de LIBER [EUR]

www.maps.ethz.ch/gdc-education.html

Website of the Working Group for Education of the Groupe de Cartothécaires of LIBER (European Research Libraries Cooperation). The group holds an annual meeting and papers from the meetings are published in LIBER Quarterly, the journal of European Research Libraries. This became an electronically published journal in 2003 (www.igitur.nl). Website includes listing of 'Who is who in map librarianship', reports on the Group's meetings, and links to web-based tutorials and courses in cartography and map librarianship.

1586 Institute of Navigation

www.ion.org

Non-profit professional society dedicated to the art and science of navigation. US-based, but with an international membership. Embraces interests in air, space, marine and land navigation, and in position determination. Holds annual National Technical Meeting, Annual Meeting and ION GPS Meeting. Publishes quarterly journal *Navigation*.

1587 International Association of Geodesy

www.iag-aig.org

Scientific organization that promotes co-operation and research in the field of geodesy. Individual membership recently introduced. Organization offers a range of support services. Website includes a newsletter, listing of recently published papers in geodesy, and links to related sites.

1588 **International Cartographic Association**
www.icaci.org
International organization that aims 'to promote the discipline and profession of cartography in an international context'. Member nations are represented through national learned societies, mapping agencies or national cartographic committees. The organization sponsors a number of commissions and working groups on diverse aspects of cartography, which meet separately and produce reports and occasional publications. A newsletter is also published and available on the website. A general assembly is held every four years and an international cartographic conference every two years. The latter is notable for the wide range of academic papers presented and the mounting of a substantial international map exhibition.

1589 **International Society for Photogrammetry and Remote Sensing**
www.isprs.org
Professional non-government organization comprising over 100 national member organizations, and devoted to the development of international co-operation in the advancement of photogrammetry and remote sensing and their applications. The ISPRS Congress is convened every four years in one of the member countries, and the organization is responsible for the peer-reviewed *ISPRS Journal of Photogrammetry and Remote Sensing*, and a news bulletin, *ISPRS Highlights*.

1590 **North American Cartographic Information Society**
www.nacis.org
Founded in 1980 to bring together cartographic interests and share ideas between the private, academic, commercial and government sectors. Members are drawn mainly from North and Central America and include map makers, map librarians, teachers and map distributors. The Society holds an annual meeting and publishes a journal *Cartographic Perspectives*. Selected recent articles are placed on the website, which also includes a listing of university staff cartographers and cartographic, GIS and remote sensing laboratories in North America.

1591 **Remote Sensing and Photogrammetric Society** [UK]
www.rspsoc.org
Society resulting from merger of the formerly separate Remote Sensing and Photogrammetric Societies. Co-ordinates and promotes activities in these two convergent areas, and encourages commercial and government use of remote sensing and photogrammetric technologies. Supports education and training in these disciplines, and fosters links between commercial, industrial, academic and international organizations. Supports several special interest groups and convenes an annual conference and other meetings and events. Official society journals are the *Photogrammetric Record* and the *International Journal of Remote Sensing*.

1592 **Royal Institute of Navigation** [UK]
www.rin.org.uk
Learned society founded 1947. Brings together those concerned with all aspects of navigation including associated disciplines such as cartography. Aims to encourage creation and dissemination of knowledge, to provide a forum for professional scrutiny of new ideas and products, and to further education and communication. Initiates conferences and symposia, and publishes the *Journal of Navigation*. International work co-ordinated through the International Association of Institutes of Navigation (IAIN). Hosts a number of specialist groups including a Civil Aviation Group, Satellite Navigation Group and a Navigation on Foot Group.

- **Navigation Acronyms, Abbreviations and Definitions D. Broughton, comp.**
  www.rin.org.uk/SITE/UPLOAD/DOCUMENT/Glossary.pdf. Excellent comprehensive list, but not searchable.

1593 **Society of Cartographers** [UK]
www.soc.org.uk
Founded in 1964 under former name of Society of University Cartographers. Aims to 'support the practising cartographer and encourage and maintain a high standard of cartographic illustration'. Membership originally mainly of practising cartographers in educational institutions, but has broadened to include local authorities, public utilities and commercial map publishers. Publishes *SoC Bulletin* and holds an annual summer school. Supports a very useful CARTO-SoC listserv on which many practical problems, especially relating to desktop cartography, are discussed.

1594 **Urban and Regional Information Systems Association** [USA]
www.urisa.org
USA-based non-profit association for professionals using Geographical Information Systems within regional, state and local government agencies. Promotes the effective and ethical use of spatial technologies for managing urban and regional systems. Publishes a journal and newsletter, organizes conferences, and supports its members in networking and professional development.

Libraries, archives, museums

1595 **British Library, Map Library**
www.bl.uk/collections/maps.html
Primary national collection of cartographic materials for the UK. Over four million items comprising printed and manuscript maps, atlases, globes and topographic views. Collection is worldwide and includes materials from the 15th century to the present. As a legal-deposit library it receives all ORDNANCE SURVEY and other UK-published maps.

1596 **Library of Congress, Geography and Maps Division** [USA]
lcweb.loc.gov/rr/geogmap
The Division is the largest map collection in the world, comprising 4.6 million maps, 60,000 atlases, 6000 reference works, as well as globes, three-dimensional models, and cartographic materials in digital format. Collection exists to provide Congress, Federal agencies, state and local governments, academics and the general public with cartographic and geographical information from all parts of the world. Website includes *Geography and maps: an illustrated guide* (also available as printed booklet), and an extensive online collection of digitized, non-copyright protected maps ranging in date from 1500 to 2004.

Portal & task environments

1597 **Earth Observation Portal**
European Space Agency
www.eoportal.org [REGISTRATION]
Aims to bring together and provide a single access point for information and services from earth observation, including satellite imagery, a directory to locate data and resources, and direct access to earth-observing satellite data. Also includes links to map servers and cartographic resources. Sponsored and run by the ESA. Registration is mandatory, but free.

1598 **Galileo: European satellite navigation system**
European Commission. Directorate for Energy and Transport and European Space Agency
http://europa.eu.int/comm/dgs/energy_transport/galileo
An independent satellite navigation system for Europe. 'More and more often, it will become necessary to ascertain one's precise position in space and time in a reliable manner. In a few years time this will be possible with the GALILEO satellite radio navigation system, an initiative launched by the European Union and the European Space Agency. This worldwide system will ensure complementarity with the current GPS system.'

1599 **Map history/history of cartography**
A. Campbell
www.maphistory.info
Some 100 searchable pages providing information for map collectors and students of early maps. Site includes web articles and commentaries, information about journals, conferences and talks, discussion lists, exhibitions, map societies, map collecting and collections, and college courses. Links to other web resources including image sites and web articles. Also provides update of *Who's who in the history of cartography*.

1600 **National Geospatial Data Clearinghouse**
Federal Geographic Data Committee
http://clearinghouse1.fgdc.gov
Collection of over 250 spatial data servers, that have digital geographic data primarily for use in geographic information systems, image processing systems, and other modelling software. These data collections can be searched through a single interface based on their descriptions, or 'metadata'.

- **National Geologic Map Database US Geological Survey and Association of American State Geologists.** http://ngmdb.usgs.gov. Access to valuable range of tools including: Geoscience map catalogue (70,000 maps from over 300 publishers); Geologic map image library (over 2000 maps online); Geologic names of the United States.

Discovering print & electronic resources

1601 **County atlases of the British Isles: published after 1703** [UK]
D. Hodson, comp. Tewin Press/British Library Publishing Division, 1984–. First two volumes published by The Tewin Press.
A series of bibliographies which aims to provide a detailed reconstruction of the publication history of all county atlases published after 1703. The books are based on original research, from map and atlas advertisements in 18th-century newspapers. Three volumes so far published.

- **Volume 1. Atlases published 1704 to 1742 and their subsequent editions D. Hodson, comp.** The Tewin Press, 1984, 200pp. ISBN 0950914908.
- **Volume 2. Atlases published 1743 to 1763 and their subsequent editions** The Tewin Press, 1989, 193pp. ISBN 0950914916.
- **Volume 3. Atlases published 1764 to 1800 and their subsequent editions** British Library Publishing Division, 1997, 256pp. ISBN 0712345248.

1602 **Go-Geo!** [UK]
EDINA and UK Data Archive
www.gogeo.ac.uk
Online resource discovery tool for finding and retrieving spatial metadata records. Under development for the UK academic community by EDINA, University of Edinburgh and the UK Data Archive, University of Essex, and currently limited in scope to the UK. Supports geospatial searching by co-ordinates as well as topic and keyword searches. Retrieves records of data sets held by UK academic nodes and accesses non-academic resources via GIGATEWAY.

1603 **Geographic information**
J.M. Johnson Greenwood Press, 2003, 232pp. $65.00. ISBN 1573563927.
Provides an easy-to-use reference guide to a wide range of print and digital sources of spatial data. Includes web and GIS resources, and includes information on standards, organizations, and instructional resources.
'Recommended. Academic and public libraries.' (*Choice*)

1604 **Geographical data: characteristics and sources**
N. Walford Wiley, 2002, 290pp. $140.00. ISBN 0471970859.
Focuses on the principal sources of geographical data and provides an overview of their characteristics and analytical capabilities. Details the characteristics of spatial and thematic geographical data relating to both environmental and human domains. Data types include remotely sensed, cartographic, census/survey, and administrative.

The benefits and drawbacks of using geographical data are highlighted, with a focus on the availability of digital (rather than analogue) geo-referenced datasets. Includes a comparison of spatial data frameworks from countries in Australasia, Asia, Europe and North America. Discusses future developments of internet-based GIS, online access and potential new sources of geographical data.

The book is intended for professionals within the administrative, commercial, educational, governmental and voluntary sectors, and academic users of GIS technology.

1605 **Gigateway** [UK]
Ordnance Survey and Association for Geographic Information
www.gigateway.org.uk
Gigateway is an information service launched in 2002 to provide access to geospatial metadata in the UK. Funded through the Ordnance Survey's National Interest Mapping Services Agreement (NIMSA) (set up to support mapping activities that cannot be justified on commercial grounds), and managed by the AGI. It provides online access to metadata via three searching facilities: Data Locator, Data Directory and Area Search. In 2004 metagenie software became available for free download. This enables providers of geospatial data to create metadata compliant with Gigateway specifications, and make it available to this service.

1606 **GIS data sources**
D. Decker Wiley, 2001, 208pp. $110.00. ISBN 0471355054.
American-based guide to GIS resources. Gives guidance on how to find and evaluate GIS data for different purposes. Provides limited resource listings, including web sources. Information given on data formats, media, compression and downloading.

1607 **Oddens' Bookmarks: the fascinating world of maps and mapping**
R. Oddens
http://oddens.geog.uu.nl/index.php
The most comprehensive, and invaluable, guide to cartographic resources on the web (over 20,000 in April 2004). The list is classified and may be browsed by category or searched by keyword plus country/area and category using drop-down menus. The main categories are: maps and atlases, sellers of cartographic materials, map collections, carto- and geoservers, cartographic and geographical societies, departments of cartography, government cartography, libraries, literature, gazetteers, miscellaneous, and tourist sites.

The list was started in 1995 and is maintained by Roelof Oddens, curator of the map collection at the University of Utrecht.

Satellite-related World Wide Web Sites
University of Dundee See entry no. 1215

1608 **World mapping today**
R.B. Parry and C.R. Perkins 2nd edn, Bowker-Saur, 2000, 1064pp. £195.00. ISBN 1857390350.
Major reference source on the range and availability of maps and spatial data worldwide. The main part of the book provides descriptions of topographic and thematic mapping by country and provides users with access to information about the structure, policies and programmes of the mapping industry within each country. Selected catalogue data, graphic indexes, addresses, telephone numbers and websites are included. Also included are review chapters on the status of world mapping and on the problems and possibilities of map and digital data acquisition in the electronic age.

1609 **WWW Virtual Library: Remote Sensing**
VTT Remote Sensing Group.
www.vtt.fi/tte/research/tte1/tte14/virtual
This site provides extensive listings of websites of remote sensing organizations, sources of satellite data, societies, conferences, journals, online publications, news groups and other remote sensing sources. VTT are an independent Finnish research and development organization.

Primary resource collections

1610 **Geographic Names Information System (GNIS)**
[USA]
US Board on Geographic Names and US Geological Survey
geonames.usgs.gov/index.html
Online gazetteer of US domestic names approved by the US Board on Geographic Names. Includes almost two million geographic features with description of location, geographic co-ordinates to one second resolution, names of host state and county, elevation, and (for populated places) estimated population. Online version has links to USGS maps and orthophoto quads containing the location. The gazetteer is also available on CD-ROM.

Digital data, image & text collections

1611 **Alexandria Digital Library Project**
www.alexandria.ucsb.edu
Initiated in 1994 with National Science Foundation Funding, and hosted by the Davis Library, University of California Santa Barbara (UCSB), the ADL aims to develop a globally distributed georeferenced digital library using web access. Aims to provide access to georeferenced objects (not limited to maps) through searching by geographical location, and ultimately to provide GIS-like services for use of the data. Currently it provides access to a subset of the holdings of the Map and Imagery Library at UCSB and some other data sets.

As well as implementing these objectives, ADL is an ongoing research project. In its second stage it is seeking to create a digital learning environment based on ADL technology. It is also working with other ADL nodes throughout the world to develop a more distributed system of access to data.

1612 **GEO Data Portal**
United Nations Environment Programme
geodata.grid.unep.ch
Authoritative source for data sets used by UNEP and its partners in the Global Environment Outlook (GEO) report and other integrated environment assessments. Included are the GRID-Geneva global and European databases, providing online access to digital georeferenced environmental data. These consist of a wide variety of thematic layers, such as climate, soils, vegetation and water-related data sets, for use in geographical information systems, as well as infrastructural and socio-economic data sets on human population, boundaries, roads and railways. The data sets are fully documented in an electronic meta-database. Most of the UNEP/GRID data sets are freely available for download by users via the internet.

UNEP's GRID (Global and Regional Integrated Data Centres) is a global network of 11 environmental data centres facilitating the generation and dissemination of key environmental georeferenced and statistical datasets and information products, focusing on environmental issues and natural resources.

1613 **GEOnet Names Server (GNS)**
National Geospatial-Intelligence Agency
http://earth-info.nga.mil/gns/html
The most extensive worldwide database of geographical names, formerly published in printed volumes for each country by the American Defense Mapping Agency. Official repository of foreign place names approved by the United States Board on Geographic Names. Contains 3.97 million features with 5.45 million names. May be searched online, or may be downloaded by country or in total. Provides latitude and longitude locations to nearest second.

1614 **TerraServer.com**
www.terraserver.com [FEE-BASED]
Worldwide source for digital imagery and aerial photography. Images may be viewed online to 8-metre resolution free of

charge, but for a paid subscription all imagery may be viewed at full resolution. Purchase and download of imagery is available online.

Directories & encyclopedias

1615 **The British Library Map Catalogue**
British Library Primary Resource Media, 1998. CD-ROM, £1,495.00. ISBN 0753640112.
www.copac.ac.uk
Searchable CD-ROM-based catalogue derived from the retroconversion of the 19 printed volumes of the map catalogues, together with the post-1974 automated file, and current to 1997. Includes powerful search and sort facilities. The catalogue is also now available on COPAC; and a new experimental interface allows searching by scale and location, as well as by subject and author/title. The COPAC file is updated monthly and includes correction to records on the CD-ROM.
- **Catalogue of cartographic materials in the British Library 1975–1988** K G Saur, 1989. ISBN 0862917654. 3 v.

1616 **The Columbia gazetteer of the world**
S.B. Cohen Coumbia University Press, 1998, 3578pp. 3 v. ISBN 0231110405.
www.columbiagazetteer.org [FEE-BASED]
New edition of comprehensive world gazetteer, formerly *Columbia-Lippincott gazetteer of the world*. Includes names of administrative and political areas, settled places, physical features and special places. Location by latitude and longitude to nearest minute. Complementary website provides access to the same information by subscription.

1617 **The dictionary of land surveyors and local map-makers of Great Britain and Ireland 1530–1850**
S. Bendall, ed. British Library, 1997, 912pp. 2 v., £75.00. ISBN 0712345094.
Latest revision of earlier work edited by Peter Eden. Provides details of persons who measured and made large-scale local maps in Great Britain or Ireland between 1530 and 1850. The first volume discusses the history of the surveying profession based on an analysis of the mapmakers in the dictionary, together with lists of sources and comprehensive indexes. The second volume contains biographical entries for each surveyor. This edition lists nearly 14,000 surveyors and mapmakers chronologically, with an earlier starting date to incorporate local military surveyors who practised in the 1530s and whose importance is being recognized by scholars.

1618 **Guide to US map resources** [USA]
D.A. Cobb, comp. 2nd edn, American Library Association, 1990, 495pp. ISBN 0838905470.
Information on 974 map collections in academic, public, private, geoscience, federal and state libraries. Arranged alphabetically by state, city and institution. Entries include address and name of responsible person, size of holdings, chronological cover, special strengths, equipment, opening hours and availability to users. Appendices include addresses of Earth Science National Information Centers (ESICs), State Information Resources and State Mapping Advisory Committees. A copy of the survey form is also included. Indexes are by name of library/institution, collection strengths and names of curators. Although now seriously dated, a 3rd edition was in preparation in 2004.

International satellite directory
See entry no. 6241

1619 **Tooley's dictionary of mapmakers**
R.V. Tooley Batsford, 1987, 140pp. Identical to 6th edn published 1979 by Map Collector Publications. ISBN 0713413956.
Popular work organized into national/regional schools, and giving brief information on persons associated with the production of maps up to the year 1900. Gives name, dates of birth and death, titles of honour, working addresses, and main cartographic outputs with dates and editions where known. Heavily illustrated with examples of maps. Indexed.

1620 **Who's who in the history of cartography: the international guide to the subject**
M.A. Lowenthal, comp. Map Collector Publications, 1998, 204pp. ISBN 0906430186.
www.maphistory.info
Lists 630 people in 45 countries engaged in research in early cartography. Part 1, 'What's what', provides a guide to general works, bibliographies and other reference sources. Part 2, 'Who's who', lists researchers and their research interests. Updates are provided on the Map History website.

1621 **World directory of map collections**
O. Loiseaux, ed.; International Federation of Library Associations and Institutions 4th edn, K G Saur, 2000, 541pp. IFLA Publications 92/93. ISBN 3598218184.
Published under the auspices of IFLA, lists 714 collections in 121 countries. Data were collected by questionnaires mailed in 1997 to 1999 and revised to 2000. Includes national libraries and archives, plus some university and public libraries, geographical, geological and hydrographic institutes and museums. Entries include address of collection, person in charge and contact details, size of collection, geographical and/or thematic focus, methods of bibliographic control, and access arrangements. Appendices include copies of questionnaire in five languages, index of names and index of institutions.

Handbooks & manuals

1622 **Basic cartography for students and technicians**
R.W. Anson and F.J. Ormeling, eds 2nd edn, Butterworth-Heinemann, 1998, 176pp. V. 2 of a 3-v. series, £30.99. ISBN 0750649968.
International Cartographic Association-sponsored handbook in three volumes. This Volume 2 (2nd edn) covers the theory and techniques of map compilation and generalization together with chapters on topographic and thematic mapping and map marketing. Volume 1 (1984) is out of print and much of its content is out of date.
- **Vol 3. Basic cartography for students and technicians** **F.J. Ormeling and R.W. Anson, eds** Butterworth-Heinemann, 1996, 128pp. £34.99. ISBN 0750627026. Covers map revision, technical aspects of remote sensing, toponymy, the role of GIS in cartography, communication, design and visualization, desktop cartography, and map documentation.

1623 **Cartographic materials: a manual of interpretation for AACR2 2002 Revision**
E.U. Mangan, ed. 2nd edn, Facet Publishing, 2003, 336pp. £65.00. ISBN 1856045161.
Provides cartographic cataloguers and map librarians with authoritative guidance on cataloguing new formats of digital cartography and geospatial data. Also provides guidance on describing early materials, including atlases. The book is to be used in conjunction with the Anglo-American Cataloguing Rules 2002 Revision.

1624 **Cartography: thematic map design with ArcView GIS software**
B.D. Dent 5th edn, William C Brown/McGraw Hill, 1999, 417pp. ISBN 0679384950.
Updated edition of established primer. Covers the nature of maps, projections and geographical phenomena and the processing and classification of thematic data. There are separate chapters on thematic mapping techniques (choropleth, dot, proportional symbols, isarithms, cartograms, flow maps), a section on the design process (composition, typography, colour) and chapters on GIS, printing methods and desktop mapping. Each chapter is accompanied by notes, glossaries and further reading. Book is packaged with 120-day time-limited version of ArcView GIS software and exercises on CD-ROM. Index.

1625 **Cataloging sheet maps: the basics**
P.G. Andrew The Haworth Information Press, 2003, 240pp. $24.95. ISBN 0789014831.
Aimed at the inexperienced map cataloguer. Provides guidance on all aspects of cataloguing maps using MARC21 and AACR2R. Gives information on cataloguing tools in both hard copy and electronic format, and examines each area of the bibliographic record in detail. Classification using LC G-Schedule is also considered and there are chapters on historical maps and on special formats.

1626 **Computer processing of remotely sensed images: an introduction**
P.M. Mather 3rd edn, Wiley, 2004, 324pp. $60.00. ISBN 0470849193.
Deals with the mechanics of processing remotely sensed images. Contents include: basic principles of remote sensing; remote sensing platforms and sensors; hardware and software aspects of digital image processing; data pre-processing; and techniques of image enhancement, transformation, filtering and classification. Extensive list of references. Index. An accompanying CD-ROM provides MIPS software, colour illustrations, exercises and links to web resources.

1627 **Geography mark-up language: foundation for the geo-web**
R. Lake [et al.] Wiley, 2004, 432pp. $140.00. ISBN 0470871539.
Technical reference guide to GML, which is emerging as the standard language for internet GIS. Provides a broad coverage of the use of GML in different application areas, along with the technical means for building these applications. Covers basic concepts, and works through topics in both GML 2.0 and GML 3.0, with illustrations and worked examples.

Volume I introduces GML, and explains its use across a broad range of GIS projects. Deals with the basic concepts of XML and GML, and enables readers to make decisions on the utility of GML in their projects and software acquisitions.

Volume II is for the technical reader and answers questions on the meaning and structure of GML schema components, the development of GML application schemas, and the use of GML in connection with web services, legacy GIS and relational databases.

Geological maps: an introduction
A. Maltman See entry no. 1001

Geomorphology and global tectonics
M.A. Summerfield, ed. See entry no. 1068

1628 **The Global Positioning System and GIS: an introduction**
M. Kennedy 2nd edn, Taylor and Francis, 2002, 345pp. £39.99. ISBN 0415286085.
Practical manual for integrating GPS and GIS technologies in the collection of spatial data. Chapters provide both a theoretical overview and a practical component. The latter is tied specifically to Trible GPS hardware and ESRI's ArcGIS software. Data for exercises are provided on an accompanying CD-ROM. Contents include: basic concepts; automated data collection; examining GPS data; differential correction; ArcView, ArcData and GPS; integrating GPS data with GIS data; beyond the basics; the present and the future.

1629 **GPS for land surveyors**
J. Van Sickle Taylor and Francis, 2001, 284pp. £50.00. ISBN 1575040751.
Non-technical manual on use of GPS in land surveying and engineering survey. Covers the basics of GPS technology, survey design, observation, post-processing, and the real-time kinesmatic (RTK) method. Review questions and answers accompany the chapters. Glossary.

1630 **GPS satellite surveying**
A. Leick 3rd edn, Wiley, 2004, 464pp. $125.00. ISBN 0471059307.
Comprehensive introduction to the field. Written to help specialists get the most out of GPS surveying techniques and the resulting measurements. Covers the Russian GLONASS, the forthcoming European GALILEO, as well as the United States GPS satellite systems. Chapters cover: geodetic reference systems; satellite systems; least-squares adjustments; pseudorange and Carrier Phase observables; troposphere and ionosphere; processing pseudoranges and Carrier Phases; network adjustments; two-dimensional geodetic models. Appendices, references and indexes.

1631 **Manual of aerial survey**
R. Read and R. Graham Whittles Publishing, 2002, 408pp. £65.00. ISBN 1870325621.
Updated edition of the 1986 *Manual of aerial photography*. Theoretical and practical guide to aerial photographic survey. Provides a guide to air camera instrumentation, photographic materials, exposure, air film processing, photogrammetric requirements, and image quality. Also covers camera platforms, mission planning, and operational procedures. Concludes with chapters on differential GPS, oblique air photography, airborne laser terrain mapping, and on developments in digital imagery and storage. There is a glossary, appendices and index.

1632 **Manual of map reading and land navigation** [UK]
Ministry of Defence 2nd edn, Her Majesty's Stationery Office, 1989. £7.95. ISBN 0117726117.
Produced primarily to provide instructors in the Armed Services with a comprehensive source of reference for use in training. Basic introduction to scales and distance measurements, representation of data, relief, grids and geodetic information, and the measurement of direction. Also includes sections on compasses, and interpretation of air photographs, and also position fixing, but predates the use of GPS. Heavily illustrated including Ordnance Survey and military map extracts.

1633 **Manual of photogrammetry**
C. McGlone, ed.; American Society for Photogrammetry and Remote Sensing 5th edn, 2004, 1168pp. $125.00. ISBN 1570830711.
Thoroughly updated edition of established manual last published in 1980 (with an addendum published in 1996). Reflects the new structure of the discipline brought about by new positioning technologies and inertial navigation systems, and fully digital production lines. This edition emphasizes digital methods and products, and includes more mathematical content and discussion of digital image processing and computer vision algorithms.

1634 **Manual of photographic interpretation**
W. Philipson, ed.; American Society for Photogrammetry and Remote Sensing 2nd edn, 1997, 700pp. $95.00. ISBN 1570830398.
Replaces 1960 edition of standard work. Structured in four parts: background (covers the fundamentals); recognizing and assessing elements of the environment (geology and landforms, soils, vegetation, water, snow and ice, structures and cultural features); applications (in geology, land cover, agriculture, forestry, range management, wetlands, wildlife, urban analysis, cultural resources, environmental monitoring, and army applications). The fourth section comprises appendices.

1635 **Manual of remote sensing**
R.A. Ryerson, ed. ASPRS/John Wiley and Sons, 1997–.
Third edition of this established work now published as a series, of which four volumes have been published.

- **1. Earth observing platforms and sensors** **S.A. Morain and A.M. Budge, ed.** 3rd, American Society for Photogrammetry and Remote Sensing, 1997. $40.00. ISBN 1570830290. CD-ROM.
- **2. Principles and applications of imaging radar** **F.M. Henderson and A.J. Lewis, ed.** 3rd, John Wiley and Sons, 1998, 900pp. $198.00. ISBN 0471294063.
- **3. Remote sensing for the earth sciences** **A.B. Rencz, ed.** 3rd, John Wiley and Sons, 1999, 700pp. £198.00. ISBN 0471294055.
- **4. Remote sensing for natural resource management and environmental monitoring** **S. Ustin, ed.** 3rd, John Wiley and Sons, 2004, 848pp. $198.00. ISBN 0471317934. Includes CD-ROM.

1636 **Map librarianship: an introduction**
M.L. Larsgaard 3rd edn, Libraries Unlimited, 1998, 487pp. $72.00. ISBN 1563084740.
Standard text covering all aspects of map librarianship, though with a North American bias. Still useful although parts are now out of date. Chapters cover: selection and acquisition; classification; cataloguing; storage, care and repair; reference services; public relations and marketing; education. Appendices include extensive bibliographies, sampling of digital data on CD-ROMs, addresses of US publishers of globes and raised-relief maps, and of map library equipment manufacturers. Index.

1637 **Maps and related cartographic materials: cataloging, classification, and bibliographic control**
P.G. Andrew and M.L. Larsgaard, eds Haworth Information Press, 2000, 487pp. Co-published simultaneously as *Cataloging and Classification Quarterly* 27, Numbers 1/2 and 3/4, 1999, $39.95. ISBN 0789008130.
Multi-authored work on aspects of cataloguing all kinds of spatial data formats. After an overview of map cataloguing practices based on a survey in the USA and Canada, six papers deal with cataloguing specific material types, including sheet maps, globes, geological sections, printed atlases and remotely sensed images. Three papers are then devoted to handling early cartographic materials, four to digital cartographic materials, two to classification and subject access of cartographic materials, and three to retrospective conversion. A final chapter covers cataloguing cartographic materials in archives. Papers are heavily referenced and there is an extensive index.

1638 **Observation of the earth and its environment: survey of missions and sensors**
H.J. Kramer 4th edn, Springer, 2002, 1510pp. £161.00. ISBN 3540423885.
Major handbook now comprising – including its electronic-only chapters – more than 1900 pages. Remarkably wide coverage and detail. But the author announces that this 4th edn will be his last: 'Growing a few vegetables in the garden is more profitable than book-writing.'!

Keeping up-to-date

1639 **Bibliographia Cartographica: international documentation of cartographical literature**
W. Crom and L. Zögner, eds K G Saur, 1974–, Annual. ISSN 03400409.
Supersedes *Bibliotheca cartographica* (1958–1972). Lists recent literature in cartography alphabetically by author and arranged into sections by theme and region. Each volume lists approximately 2000 monographs and articles published in some 400 periodicals. These are selected by an international group of collaborating experts. Titles listed in their original language. Each volume includes an index of authors. In 2004, a two-volume *Kumuliertes autorenregister* (Cumulated author index) covering volumes 1–29, 1974–2002, edited by Wolfgang Crom, was published by Saur (ISBN 359820647X).

Chemistry

This is a traditional straightforward chemical classification. Note, however, that LABORATORY TOOLS & TECHNIQUES contains descriptions of a number of resources concerned with the wider aspects of laboratory work; and PHYSICAL CHEMISTRY is home to several items that many would have placed within PHYSICS: cf. chemical physics.

Introductions to the subject

1640 **The art of chemistry: myths, medicines, and materials**
A. Greenberg Wiley-Interscience, 2003, 357pp. $69.95. ISBN 0471071803.
'Employs 187 figures (including 16 full-color plates) to illuminate 72 essays on the mythical origins, wondrous experiments, and adventurous explorers in the annals of chemistry.'
'suitable as a gift for either a chemist or a ... student ... or as a reference book for a chemistry teacher ... A useful visual compendium ... captures the joy of collecting chemical images.' (*Journal of Chemical Education*)

1641 **Basics of chemistry**
R. Myers Greenwood Press, 2003, 373pp. $75.00. ISBN 0313316643.
Good introduction for those starting out with chemistry, developing principles and concepts from discussions of everyday experiences, historic scientific discoveries, and laboratory experiments,
Series: Basics of the Hard Sciences.

1642 **Candid science I: conversations with famous chemists**
I. Hargittai Imperial College Press, 2000, 528pp. £21.00. ISBN 1860942288.
35 famous chemists, including 18 Nobel Laureates, talk about their lives in science, their careers, aspirations, hardships, triumphs. Includes Pauling, Hoffman, Kroto, Olah.
Candid science II *is conversations with famous biomedical scientists.*
'István Hargittai ... is brilliant at drawing his subjects out, tactfully asking them the right questions and thus providing us with an insider view of what chemistry in the 20th century has been like ... these people are extraordinarily successful chemists, and enthusiasts for it. They make the book delightful to browse. Maybe it will, as it should, produce enthusiasts in its turn; it should be on everyone's bedside table.' (*Chemistry & Industry*)

- **Candid science III: more conversations with famous chemists** 2003, 520pp. £21.00. ISBN 1860943373.

1643 **Chemical explanation: characteristics, development, autonomy**
J.E. Earley; New York Academy of Sciences 2003, 370pp. $130.00. ISBN 1573314560.
Papers in this volume address: relations between macroscopic and microscopic description; essential roles of visualization and representation in chemical understanding; and historical questions involving chemical concepts, impacts of chemical ideas on wider cultural concerns.
Series: Annals of the New York Academy of Sciences, V. 988. Based on the sessions of the Sixth Summer Symposium of the International Society for the Philosophy of Chemistry.

1644 **The chemical tree: a history of chemistry**
W.H. Brock W.W. Norton, 2000, 784pp. $19.95. ISBN 0393320685.
Overview of chemistry from ancient to present times; well compiled index; bibliographic chapter includes numerous references for further study. Additionally, chapters or parts of chapters include history of teaching of chemistry, development of the laboratory, chemical societies and scientific journalism, environmental chemistry, industrial chemistry, the chemical bond.
Originally published under the title The Norton History of Chemistry *(1992).*

1645 **Chemistry and chemical reactivity**
J.C. Kotz and P.M. Treichel 5th edn, Brooks/Cole, 2003, 1184pp. Includes CD-ROM, $146.95. ISBN 003033604X.
www.brookscole.com/pubco/pub_companion.html [COMPANION]
Provides a broad overview of the principles of chemistry and the reactivity of the chemical elements and their compounds. Well written; useful historical context; good use of graphics.

1646 **Chemogenesis: the story of how chemical reactivity emerges from the periodic table of the elements**
M.R. Leach
http://www.meta-synthesis.com/webbook.html
Stimulating new approach to chemistry published by meta-synthesis, a 'scientific publishing house offering books, posters, databases, multimedia materials, web books, seminars and short courses which attempt to explain and demystify chemical reaction science'. Chemogenesis is offered as 'a part of the scientific story between the periodic table of the elements and established organic and inorganic chemistry; an area that is poorly covered by traditional texts'.

1647 **Chemoinformatics: a textbook**
J. Gasteiger and T. Engel, eds Wiley-VCH, 2003, 649pp. £45.00. ISBN 3527306811.
www2.chemie.uni-erlangen.de/publications/ci-book/index.html [COMPANION]
From the Foreword: 'While until 1960 the number of natural and laboratory-produced compounds had almost linearly increased to roughly one million in about 150 years, its growth expanded exponentially from then on, reaching 18 million in 2000'.

After an introductory chapter, detailed treatments of: 2. Representation of chemical compounds; 3. Representation of chemical reactions; 4. The data; 5. Databases and data sources in chemistry; 6. Searching chemical structures; 7. Calculation of physical and chemical data; 8. Calculation of structure descriptions; 9. Methods for data analysis; 10. Applications; 11. Future directions. Chapters conclude with further readings and lists of websites.

Limited information on companion website, late 2004; links 'under construction'.

- **Handbook of chemoinformatics: from data to knowledge** J. Gasteiger, ed. Wiley-VCH, 2003, 4 v. £315.00. ISBN 3527306803. www2.ccc.uni-erlangen.de. URL gives access to web pages describing services and software offered by the TORVS (Techniques for Organic Reactions, Visualization, and Spectroscopy) Research Team.

1648 The extraordinary chemistry of ordinary things
C.H. Snyder 4th edn, Wiley, 2003, 612pp. $102.95. ISBN 0471415758.
Distinguished by each chapter starting with a demonstration that can be performed with simple apparatus and common substances that lead to observations and conclusions about the chemistry of 'ordinary things'. Good for holding the interest of non-science students who need to engage with chemistry.

1649 From elements to atoms: a history of chemical composition
R. Siegfried; American Philosophical Society 2002, 278pp. $24.00. ISBN 0871699249.
'Seeking to enlarge an understanding of the nature of chemical science and explain how the concepts being taught in the classroom came to be, Robert Siegfried presents a simple, readable account of how in the eighteenth century chemical composition slowly abandoned the centuries-long tradition of metaphysical elements of earth, air, fire, and water. Through the work of such scientists as Lavoisier, Dalton, and Davy, chemical theory moved from metaphysical ELEMENTS to operationally functional ATOMS. The content of the book is based on chemical writings of seventeenth- and eighteenth-century chemists; references to recently published secondary works are intended for the benefit of readers who wish to enlarge their contextual perspectives on the development of early chemical thinking.'

1650 A history of chemistry
J.R. Partington Macmillan, 1961–70. v. 1 (pt. 1), v. 2–4.
Classic work providing comprehensive treatment of the history of chemistry from alchemy to the 20th century. Coverage is international, topographical and well referenced. V. 1 covers the period up to 1500 and was left incomplete when the author died in 1965. V. 2–4 concern the period thereafter, assessing the achievements and influences of individual chemists. Practically the whole text is based on primary sources and is profusely footnoted.
Publication of v.1 (pt. 2) abandoned.

1651 A history of chemistry (Histoire de la chimie)
B. Bensaude-Vincent and I. Stengers Harvard University Press, 1996, 305pp. Translated by Deborah van Dam, $47.50. ISBN 0674396596.
Very successfully meets the challenge of 'writing a panoramic, global history of chemistry, one that is not simply a list of facts and theories or an accumulation of anecdotes about individual chemists. Chemistry has been presented here as the real subject of a history that has developed through the constantly reiterated commitments of people, the knowledge they produce, and the meanings assigned to that knowledge'. Bibliography (pp 285–96); Index.

1652 An introduction to chemoinformatics
A.R. Leach and V.J. Gillet Kluwer Academic, 2003, 260pp. £52.00. ISBN 1402013477.
Introduction to the major techniques of chemoinformatics – which are drawn from many disciplines including computer science, mathematics, computational chemistry and data visualization.

1653 Molecular modelling for beginners
A. Hinchliffe Wiley, 2003, 410pp. $46.00. ISBN 0470843101.
Friendly – though mathematically thorough-going – text explaining modern molecular modelling, especially the basic chemical theory behind the process of modelling. Wide coverage. Appendix is 'A mathematical aide-memoire'.

1654 Nature's building blocks: an A–Z guide to the elements
J. Emsley Oxford University Press, 2003, 552pp. £12.99. ISBN 0198503407.
Lists all known elements, for each discussing: derivation of the name; presence in the human body and in the diet; possible role in medicine; history of its discovery; economic role; environmental impact; basic chemistry; and 'element of surprise' – unexpected aspects of the element.
'. astonishingly comprehensive survey of nature's fundamental ingredients.' (*New York Times*)

- **The elements** J. Emsley 3rd edn, Oxford University Press, 1998. ISBN 019855818X. www.ch.cam.ac.uk/misc/weii. Compilation of data, in alphabetical order, of all the main properties of the chemical elements under the headings chemical data, physical data, biological data, nuclear data, electron shell data, crystal data, geological data.

1655 The new chemistry
N. Hall, ed. Cambridge University Press, 2000, 493pp. £60.00. ISBN 0521452244.
17 self-contained chapters, each covering a different topic in chemistry, ranging from the discovery of new elements and synthetic techniques to the design of drugs and materials. Each chapter is written by one of the world's leading chemists in that particular field, including several Nobel Prize winners.
'Without a doubt, it is a carefully written and superbly produced work. It is truly a joy to read this book ... I enthusiastically recommend this book to students of science, regardless of their major, age, and area of expertise. This book should [be] on the shelf of every library, personal and institutional.' (*Journal of Food Biochemistry*)

1656 Nobel laureates in chemistry, 1901–1992
L.K. James, ed.; American Chemical Society and Chemical Heritage Foundation 1993, 798pp. $34.95. ISBN 0841226903.
Brief biographies (c.5–7pp.) of 116 Nobel laureates, each with references and bibliography. Information includes education, employment history, research interests. Arranged chronologically.
Series: History of Modern Chemical Sciences.

1657 The periodic table compendium: descriptions of 103 elements, their properties, occurrences and uses, plus a summary of periodic table patterns
H. Eccles, comp.; Royal Society of Chemistry 1994, 152pp. £10.00. ISBN 1870343271.
www.chemsoc.org/networks/learnnet/PTCompendium.htm [COMPANION]
Useful introduction from the RSC Education Department:

part of the Society's Learn Net initiative 'for the use of teachers and students of chemistry at all levels'.

- **A visual interpretation of the Table of Elements Royal Society of Chemistry** www.chemsoc.org/viselements/index.htm. Fascinating compilation; includes animations and soundtracks. Much supplementary detail, including historical. Element 110 *Darmstadtium* – discovered 1994 but only recently named by IUPAC [q.v.] – was added late 2004.

1658 A philatelic ramble through chemistry
E. Heilbronner and F.A. Miller Wiley, 2004, 274pp. First published 1998, $99.00. ISBN 3906390314.
'This is not a history of chemistry which uses stamps instead of the usual illustrations, but a collection of short essays and comments on such chemistry as can be found on postage stamps and other philatelic items. In other words, the choice of topics is dictated by the philatelic material available, with the necessary consequence that important parts of chemical history will be missing for the simple reason that they have not found their way onto postage stamps ...'

1659 Philosophy of chemistry: between the manifest and the scientific image
J. van Brakel Leuven University Press, 2000, 246pp. €17.35. ISBN 9058670635.
'It is argued that chemistry is primarily the science of manifest substances, whereas 'micro' or 'submicro' scientific talk, though important, useful, and insightful does not change what matters, namely the properties of manifest substances. These manifest substances, their properties and uses cannot be reduced to talk of molecules or solutions of the Schrödinger equation. If 'submicroscopic' quantum mechanics were to be wrong, it would not affect all (or any) 'microlevel' chemical knowledge of molecules. If molecular chemistry were to be wrong, it wouldn't disqualify knowledge of, say, water – not at the 'macrolevel' (e.g. its' viscosity at 50 °C), nor at the pre- or protoscientific manifest level (e.g. ice is frozen water).'
'This is an excellent book. It is based on a massive survey of the literature, done in such a way that the tie between philosophy in general, philosophy of science, and chemistry itself is managed convincingly. The author is bold enough to take positions himself on various controversial matters, inviting us to argue with him. This is just what a good philosophy book should do! If anyone doubted that there is a philosophy of chemistry, full of interesting issues, this book should convince the skeptic.' (*HYLE – International Journal for Philosophy of Chemistry*)

- **International Society for the Philosophy of Chemistry** http://ispc.sas.upenn.edu.

1660 Recent developments in the history of chemistry
C.A. Russell [et al.], eds; Royal Society of Chemistry 1985, 334pp. ISBN 0851869173.
12 chapters: 1. Introduction; 2. Chemical biographies; 3. Chemical education and chemical institutions; 4. Chemistry to 1800; 5. General and inorganic chemistry; 6. Organic chemistry; 7. Physical chemistry; 8. Analytical chemistry; 9. Biochemistry; 10. Instruments and apparatus; 11. Industrial chemistry; 12. Chemistry by location in Western and Central Europe (with 187 footnotes). Appendices: 1. Periodicals for the history of chemistry; 2. Some useful addresses. Author index; subject index – people; subject index – theories.

- **Recent developments in the history of chemistry: Volume II G.K. Roberts and C.A. Russell, eds** 2004, 320pp. ISBN 0854044647.

1661 A source book in chemistry, 1400–1900
H.M. Leicester and H.S. Klickstein McGraw-Hill, 1952, 554pp. Re-issued by Harvard University Press.
Traces the development of modern chemistry in the actual words of the men whose work led to its growth. Material illustrates development of chemical theory only. Therefore descriptions of the discovery of individual elements, compounds or processes are excluded unless some contribution to the theoretical development of chemistry resulted from such a discovery. Selections made according to importance to further developments.
Series: Source Books in the History of the Sciences.

- **Source book in chemistry, 1900–1950 H.M. Leicester** Harvard University Press, 1969, 432pp. ISBN 0674822315.

1662 Transforming matter: a history of chemistry from alchemy to the buckyball
T.H. Levere Johns Hopkins University Press, 2001, 256pp. $18.95. ISBN 0801866103.
Accessible and clearly written introduction.
'Levere's book is commendably up to date, and amazingly full of information ... His book can be recommended for students as readable and reliable. It is expository, didactic and clear.' (*British Journal for the History of Science*)

Dictionaries, thesauri, classifications

1663 A dictionary of chemistry
J. Daintith 5th edn, Oxford University Press, 2004, 608pp. £8.99. ISBN 0198609183.
4300 entries, 100 new to this edn. Includes single- or double-page feature articles on important topics; chronologies chart main discoveries.

1664 Dictionary of chemistry and chemical technology in Japanese, English, Chinese
C. Huimin and B. Wenchu, eds Elsevier Science, 1990, 1716pp. Also Chemical Industry Press, Beijing. ISBN 0444873716.
Provides complete coverage of all aspects of chemical science and technology and other relevant fields, such as environmental engineering, computer applications etc. Detailed English index enables location of Japanese and Chinese equivalents when working from English. Japanese kanji index provides easy, alternative access to Japanese terms appearing in kanji form. Comprises table of chemical elements in Japanese, English and Chinese; English alphabet with Japanese pronunciation; Greek alphabet with Japanese pronunciation; the original complex forms of selected kanjis and their simplified versions.

Dictionary of chemistry and chemical technology in six languages: English, German, Spanish, French, Polish, Russian
Z. Sobecka and W. Choinski, eds See entry no. 5071

English–Russian dictionary of chemistry and chemical technology
V.V. Kafarov See entry no. 5075

1665 Patterson's German–English dictionary for chemists
A.M. Patterson, J.C. Cox and G.E. Condoyannis 4th edn, Wiley, 1992, 890pp. $170.00. ISBN 0471669911.
Compact format tailored to requirements of English-speaking

readers of German technical literature in chemistry and allied fields. Includes richer general vocabulary than many other pocket dictionaries. Good 35pp editor's introduction to form, arrangement, and wise use of dictionary.
3rd edn 1950.

1666 **Russian–English chemical and polytechnical dictionary**
L.I. Callaham 3rd edn, Wiley-Interscience, 1975, 852pp. ISBN 0471129984.
Extends from chemistry into coverage of chemical engineering and industries and related technical fields within earth sciences and engineering. Lists of reference works categorized: published in USSR; published in USA and England.

1667 **The Usborne illustrated dictionary of chemistry**
J. Wertheim, C. Oxlade and C. Stockley Usborne, 2000, 128pp. £7.99. ISBN 0746037945.
A fact-packed and densely illustrated study guide with clear definitions and images to explain complexities of difficult science concepts. Covers periodic table, polymers and plastics, elements, compounds, mixtures, atoms and molecules.

Laws, standards, codes

1668 **CAS Registry**
American Chemical Society
www.cas.org/EO/regsys.html [DESCRIPTION]
The largest and most current database of chemical substance information in the world referencing – late 2004 – almost 25 million organic and inorganic substances and over 50 million sequences. Covers substances identified from the scientific literature from 1957 to the present with some classes (fluorine- and silicon-containing compounds) going back to the early 1900s. Each substance is identified by a unique numeric identifier called a CAS Registry Number.
Well organized site with helpful series of FAQs.

1669 **Chemical Nomenclature Advisory Service**
LGC Limited.
www.lgc.co.uk [FEE-BASED]
The former UK Laboratory of the Government Chemist has over 80 years of experience in chemical nomenclature. This service offers: Guidance on correct chemical nomenclature to be used in official documents; Checks of text of scientific publications for suitable chemical nomenclature; Verification of chemical names used in documents concerning import and export of chemical products.
- **LGC Promochem** www.lgcpromochem.com/home/home_en.aspx. Leading Reference Materials supplier – phrase here denoting material or substance one or more of whose property values are sufficiently homogeneous/well established to be used for apparatus calibration, measurement method assessment, assigning values.

1670 **Chemical Structure Association Trust**
www.csa-trust.org
Promotes education, research and development in the field of storage, processing and retrieval of information about chemical structures, reactions and compounds.

1671 **Compendium of chemical terminology: IUPAC recommendations**
A.D. McNaught and A. Wilkinson; International Union of Pure and Applied Chemistry 2nd edn, Blackwell Science, 1997, 450pp. ISBN 0865426848.
www.chemsoc.org/chembytes/goldbook
Popularly known as the *Gold Book* – after Victor Gold, who worked on the first edition. Covers all IUPAC recommendations published to the end of 1995, together with some significant material published in 1996. Terminology definitions were drafted by international committees of experts in appropriate chemistry sub-disciplines, then ratified by IUPAC's International Committee on Nomenclature and Symbols. Appendix lists source documents used in compilation – primarily articles in the journal *Pure and Applied Chemistry*.
For the freely accessible online version, some minor errors have been corrected, and the ROYAL SOCIETY OF CHEMISTRY is now working to bring the website up to date and maintain it thus.

Official & quasi-official bodies

1672 **International Union of Pure and Applied Chemistry**
www.iupac.org
Recognized as the world authority on chemical nomenclature, terminology, standardized methods for measurement, atomic weights and much other critically evaluated data. In more recent years, IUPAC has been pro-active in establishing a wide range of conferences and projects designed to promote and stimulate modern developments in chemistry; also in chemical education and the public understanding of chemistry.

Research centres & institutes

1673 **University of Oxford, Department of Chemistry** [UK]
www.chem.ox.ac.uk
The largest chemistry department in the western world. Virtual tour of the 2004 £60 million chemistry research laboratory plus much other useful information – including of the collaborative worldwide project being carried out by the University's Centre for Computational Drug Discovery, using 'screensaver time' to help find a cure for cancer.
- **Chemical and Other Safety Information** http://ptcl.chem.ox.ac.uk/MSDS. Remarkable range and depth of safety and related information – but stressing that is not an official site and data provided is *not* a definitive statement of hazards associated with any particular chemical or a reliable interpretation of safety law.

Associations & societies

1674 **American Chemical Society**
www.chemistry.org
World's largest scientific society with over 159,000 members; established 1876. Maintains and advances chemical knowledge and research through extensive publishing, scientific conferences, information resources for education and business, and professional development efforts. Education and communication interactions with public audiences creates awareness of important role of chemistry

in identifying new solutions, improving public health, protecting the environment, and contributing to the economy.

Comprehensive collection of high-quality information products and services that advance the practice of chemical and related sciences. Currently, over 30 peer-reviewed journals and magazines are published or co-published by the Publications Division, with approximately 140,000 pages of research material published annually both in print and on the web, 90,000 pages of supporting information just web-accessible.

The Division produces two buyer's guides, *CHEMCYCLOPEDIA* and *LabGuide*, updated online throughout the year. It is also involved in a number of ACS Books endeavours including production of the compilation *Reagent Chemicals*. Online job and employment services are available to ACS members through *Chemjobs*.

Among ACS's other important Divisions are Chemical Abstracts Service and the Division of Chemical Information. There is also a useful Librarian Resource Center providing 'tools for librarians and information specialists': see http://pubs.acs.org.

- **ACS Journal Archives** http://pubs.acs.org/archives [FEE-BASED]. Online archive containing all titles published by ACS from 1879 up to the current ACS Web Edition institutional subscription: over 3 million pages of original chemistry. Articles can be located via full-text searching.
- **Chemical Consultants Network** www.chemconsultants.org. Jointly supported with American Institute of Chemical Engineers.
- **Chemical research facilities: an international directory** 3rd edn1996, 1248pp. $199.95. ISBN 0841233012. Dated list of institutions and universities granting advanced degrees in a wide variety of chemical sciences. Contains listings for over 1925 different departments and information for over 17,000 faculty members.

1675 **Chemical Heritage Foundation**
www.chemheritage.org
Jointly founded by Center for the History of Chemistry, American Chemical Society and American Institute of Chemical Engineers and devoted to history of chemical and molecular sciences and industries. 29 organizations now affiliated with the Centre.

Elegant website has a series of good sections such as Explore Chemical History, Collections and Exhibits, Classroom Resources; there is a useful online Library catalogue; and the Publications area provides a number of Online Publications alongside details of the quarterly *Chemical Heritage* news magazine. Worthwhile resource.

1676 **Chemical Institute of Canada**
www.cheminst.ca
The umbrella organization for, and providing good gateway to activities of, Canadian Society for Chemistry, Canadian Society for Chemical Engineering, Canadian Society for Chemical Technology.

1677 **Chemical Society of Japan**
www.chemistry.or.jp/index-e.html
Good well laid out site: News; Events; Journals; Major Activities. Useful list within the Links section of *WWW servers on chemistry in Japan* (but this not updated since 2000).

1678 **Royal Society of Chemistry** [UK]
www.rsc.org
Largest chemical society in Europe with over 45,000 members. Activities include publishing, education, training, conferences, special interest groups, science policy, careers advice and promotion of chemical sciences to the public. Helps set standards on many aspects of chemical sciences including safety in industry.

- **The directory of consulting practices** www.chemsoc.org/networks/dcp_index.htm. Useful resource for locating experts in very specialized areas within and around the chemical sciences e.g. engineering, metallurgy, physics. Practices listed have professional membership of Society as principal/senior manager responsible for services.
- **European Association for Chemical and Molecular Sciences** www.chemsoc.org/networks/enc/fecs.htm. Site part of European Network for Chemistry providing also information about the Alliance for Chemical Sciences and Technologies in Europe (AllChemE): five organizations all concerned with the development of science and technology policy in Europe.
- **RSC Journals Archive** www.rsc.org/is/journals/retrodigitisation.htm [FEE-BASED]. Contains all articles published by the RSC (and its forerunner societies) from 1841 to 1996 in a single archive. Items can be located via full-text searching and there is reference linking for articles published after 1990.

Libraries, archives, museums

1679 **RSC Library and Information Centre** [UK]
www.rsc.org/lic/library.htm
Foremost source of chemical knowledge in Europe, and significant repository of comprehensive chemical information. Developed from the legacy of the Chemical Society, founded 1841. Unique collection of historical chemistry books from 16th to 19th centuries, including books by Boyle, Faraday and Dalton. 2000 periodicals (600 current). Information and other services for members, including from Chemical Enquiry Helpdesk, but also range of offerings for non-members.

Portal & task environments

1680 **CambridgeSoft**
www.cambridgesoft.com
'Leading supplier of Internet browser and web server based life science desktop software, enterprise solutions, chemical databases and consulting services to the biotechnology, pharmaceutical, and chemical industries. The Company, in addition, is the leading supplier of infrastructure products and services to information publishers and chemical suppliers.'

Provides well laid out and detailed information of wide range of company's products and services. But also, perusal of its Partners section reveals for those new to the area the sophistication of the chemical data- and information-based facilities now commercially available: ChemACX, structurally searchable index of chemicals that are commercially available for purchase from suppliers worldwide; Modeling, ChemInformatics & Computer Assisted Molecular Discovery; Information e.g. Beilstein, Chemical Abstracts Service, Derwent Information, MDL; Publishing e.g. Brooks/Cole, McGraw-Hill, Prentice Hall, Wiley; Integration software for graphing, data analysis, etc.

- **ChemClub.Com: World Chemistry Community** www.chemclub.com. Features: Chemistry search engine; Index of scientific publications; Index of scientific websites; Place to view and create humorous chemical structures; and *ChemNews.Com* serving over 250,000 scientists worldwide.

- **ChemFinder.Com: database & internet searching** http://chemfinder.cambridgesoft.com. Free chemical database of c.75,000 unique substances searchable by name, molecular formula, molecular weight, chemical structure and CAS Registry Number. ChemDraw Plug-in, required for structure searching and display, can also be freely downloaded.
- **ChemOffice** www.cambridgesoft.com. 'Transforms your PC into a chemical & biological publishing, modeling, and database workstation.' Academic site licenses are available and can include access to web accessible databases such as *ChemACX* and MERCK INDEX.

1681 Chemsoc
Royal Society of Chemistry
www.chemsoc.com
Provides a wide range of chemical resources, especially links to academic, educational and scholarly society websites. Daily science, industry and product news, access to major chemistry information providers, information about new publications, lists of forthcoming conferences and events. Link to careers and job centre with latest vacancies in industry and academia, plus advice on career-related topics such as effective job hunting, writing the perfect CV, improving interview technique etc.

1682 ChemSpy.com: The internet navigator for the chemical industry
www.chemspy.com
Aims to make the most important chemistry and chemical engineering related www databases readily accessible for professionals and students. Wide-ranging coverage, including good news section. Easily navigable. 'All databases included in this service are free of charge and available without login. Having problems remembering passwords? No problem, at ChemSpy.com there are no passwords ... '.

1683 FIZ CHEMIE Berlin
www.fiz-chemie.de
State-supported information centre for the chemical sciences. Organizes, categorizes and supplies scientific data and literature, some of which it originates, for other sets acts as host; examples below. Provides wide range of services including abstracting, consultation and marketing, and workshops on the use of databases by governments, academia, industry and the public in general.

The Service's Internet search engines *ChemGuide*, *MedPharmGuide* and *PublishersGuide – Science and Technology* are 'full-text databases which, contrary to other search engines, only cover and index evaluated Web sites. The databases target exclusively scientific and subject-related sites, thereby effectively preventing endless hit lists and also avoiding the otherwise relatively high (and usually arbitrary) exclusion of scientific Web sites'.

- **ChemInform** Wiley-VCH. www.wiley-vch.de/publish/en [FEE-BASED]. Abstracting service covering the latest publications emphasizing organic and element-organic synthesis (preparative, organometallic, physiochemical, theoretical). Covers c.200 journals; 17,000 abstracts per year.
- **DETHERM: thermophysical property database** www.fiz-chemie.de/katalog/engineering/dethermsammlung.html. World's largest numerical database of thermophysical property data and bibliographic information for the construction and optimization of chemical plants and technical equipment.
- **Dictionary of common names** (Trivialnamen-Handbuch) 2nd edn, Wiley, 2001, 4641pp. $3000.00. ISBN 3527302883. Five-volume set covering some 50,000 trivial names of more than 40,000 substances.

LTSN Physical Sciences
University of Hull and Higher Education Academy See entry no. 602

1684 MDL Information Systems
www.mdli.co.uk
Elsevier company providing range of sophisticated chemical and related products and services, examples of which are referenced below.

- **DiscoveryGate** www.discoverygate.com. 'Integrates, indexes, and links scientific information to give immediate access to compounds and related data, reactions, original journal articles and patents, and authoritative reference works on synthetic methodologies – all from a single entry point'.
- **MDL Integrated Major Reference Works** www.mdli.co.uk/products/knowledge/reference_works/index.jsp. Links between: MDL's synthetic methodology databases; specific chemical reference works describing scope/limitations of synthetic methods; MDL's LitLink Servers – access to primary and secondary literature references in synthetic methodology.
- **MDL ISIS: Integrated Scientific Information System** www.mdli.co.uk/products/framework/isis. 'Application development environment that allows you to extend the software beyond chemical drawing and databasing to managing chemical inventories, creating electronic lab journals, and managing therapeutic-level lead candidates'.

1685 PSIGATE: Chemistry
University of Manchester and Resource Discovery Network
www.psigate.ac.uk/newsite/chemistry-gateway.html
Access to descriptions of over 4000 resources plus to range of other useful services.

1686 SciFinder Scholar
Chemical Abstracts Service
www.cas.org/SCIFINDER/SCHOLAR
Electronic version of CHEMICAL ABSTRACTS providing access to more than 8000 journals and patent references (from over 32 patent-issuing organizations). Also includes more than 26 million substance records and CAS Registry Numbers. The database is updated daily and information about the amount of data added can be consulted. The 2004 version of the software introduced a number of refinements: check the excellent information on the website for details of these and all other features.

SciFInder Scholar can also be used to access US NATIONAL LIBRARY OF MEDICINE *MEDLINE* database.

- **Information retrieval: SciFinder and SciFinder Scholar** **D.D. Ridley** Wiley, 2002, 252pp. $60.00. ISBN 0470843519. *Issues in Science & Technology Librarianship* 'Excellent text, highly recommended for any scientist'; *Chemistry & Industry* 'Strongly recommend this book for the library and the laboratory ... Carefully written, very readable and packed with tips'.

1687 The Sheffield Chemdex: the directory of chemistry on the WWW since 1993
M. Winter; University of Sheffield
www.chemdex.org
Extensive entrée to all types of web-based chemistry data: currently over 7000 links. There are entries for companies, communication resources, databases, etc. as well as academic institutions and individuals.

■ **WebElements** www.webelements.com. From the same author. Excellent site and graphics. The first ever periodic table on the web. Covers each element's history and uses, data on its simple compounds, its electronic properties, physical properties, crystallography and nuclear properties.

Discovering print & electronic resources

1688 **About.com: Chemistry**
http://chemistry.about.com
Brings together a number of very practical websites in chemistry to provide a comprehensive resource, directed at students, teachers, professionals and anyone wishing to refresh or increase their knowledge. Site is easy to navigate and links are organized into sections e.g. Periodic table of the elements; How-to guide; Structures archive; Worked problems; Glossary; FAQs; History, News; Employment; Material safety datasheets; Databases; and so on. Worth exploring; advertisements not too intrusive.

BioChemHub: the online biology and chemistry education center
D.K. Schmidel and W.G. Wojcik, comps See entry no. 1961

1689 **Chemical Abstracts Service**
www.cas.org
The essential resource for chemists to stay abreast of worldwide chemical literature, giving the only systematic approach to tackling the immense array of patents, conferences, journals, research disclosures etc. that encompass this; provides tools which enable highly focused searching for the retrieval of specific items. In particular, assigns unique CAS Registry numbers to individual compounds, enabling consistent reference and avoiding pitfalls inherent in chemical nomenclature.

CAS offers a wide range of services and products, accessible via a variety of routes, including via SciFinder Scholar and CA Selects; and with its parent body is a major partner in the host STN International. However, its data-sets are also accessible through many other vendors: check the website.

■ **CAS Standard Abbreviations and Acronyms** www.cas.org/ONLINE/standards.html. Useful list for when searching CA issues and indexes and computer-readable services – especially for material published prior to 1982.

■ **CASREACT** www.cas.org/ONLINE/DBSS/casreactss.html. Specialized reaction database which is structure searchable, its deep indexing allowing a wide range of types of targeted search: e.g. functional group; reaction steps; solvent; etc.

■ **ChemPort** www.cas.org/chemport. Free links for users of SciFinder, STN, and other electronic CAS products to articles from more than 5400 electronic journals from 242 participating publishers; also to electronic patent documents from USPTO, esp@cenet, and MicroPatent.

1690 **CHEMINFO: Chemical Information Resources**
Indiana University
www.indiana.edu/~cheminfo
Recommended, regularly updated guide to world-wide chemical information resources on the web and elsewhere. Provides *SIRCh* Selected internet resources for chemistry, including a useful A–Z index of its chapter and section headings, leading to nicely laid-out and categorized lists of links; *CCIM*: Clearinghouse for chemical information instructional materials; Databases – range of databases compiled or maintained at Indiana (e.g. *Acronym Database#;* Chemical Reference Sources Database (2539 records of books and other reference material)), as well as links to other free chemistry databases on the web. An especially useful section is Listservs, Discussion Lists, and Newsgroups for Chemistry.

■ **CHMINF-L: Chemical Information Sources Discussion List** https://listserv.indiana.edu/archives/chminf-l.html. 'A virtual reference desk, staffed with some of the world's most knowledgeable people. Frequent announcements of new Chemistry reference products and services are also included'.

■ **Molecular Visualization Tools & Sites** www.indiana.edu/~cheminfo/ca_mvts.html. Good collection of links categorized as: Chemical MIME; Free viewer and plug-in software; Selected commercial software; Molecular rendering software; Visualization demonstration sites; GIF depictions; Java and JavaScript VRML.

1691 **Chemistry Citation Index**
Thomson ISI.
www.isinet.com/products/citation/specialty/chci [description]
Subset of ISI's citation indexing database (see ISI Web of Knowledge) allowing both backward and forward searching through the chemical literature.

■ **Index Chemicus** Thomson ISI. www.isinet.com/products/litres. Text- and substructure-searchable database reporting 200,000 new compounds each year; comprises over one million structures published in the literature since 1991. Also includes newly isolated natural products, reaction intermediates, revised structures.

1692 **Chemistry Journals**
University of Cambridge
www.ch.cam.ac.uk/ChemJournals.html
One of the world's most comprehensive and up-to-date lists of internet-linked chemistry-related journals. Journal titles, which are hyperlinked to their publishers' web pages, are easy to locate being listed by subject area, publisher, and alphabetically. Links checked regularly.

■ **Chemical Data** www.ch.cam.ac.uk/c2k/data.html. Regularly updated useful list of links.

■ **Chemists in the Academic World** www.ch.cam.ac.uk/c2k/people. Almost 14,000 entries, May 2003. List 'created automatically, so that it can be updated rapidly. It is not comprehensive, and it contains some errors'. Cambridge also sustain lists of links to worldwide *Chemistry Departments* and *Learned Societies*.

1693 **Chemistry resources in the electronic age**
J.A. Bazler Greenwood Press, 2003, 312pp. $49.95. ISBN 157356379X.
Selective list of reliable chemistry related websites with evaluations of the accuracy and usefulness of each resource.
Series: Science Resources in the Electronic Age.

ChemVillage
See entry no. 5100

1694 **Free full-text journals in chemistry**
A. Ragoisha; Belarusian State University
www.abc.chemistry.bsu.by/current/fulltext05.htm
Very useful regularly updated list. Part A: Permanently available chemical journals; Part B. Trials and temporarily available chemical journals. 'All links and comments had been verified in August 2004. It was a surprise to me that less than ten journals died or closed free access to full texts since August 2003. Moreover, every fourth journal of the list

has expanded in free cyberspace. As in the previous year, I plan to add new information to the site twice a month.'

1695 How to find chemical information: a guide for practicing chemists, educators, and students
R.E. Maizell 3rd edn, Wiley, 1998, 515pp. $99.95. ISBN 0471125792.
Provides a broad overview of the literature, important research tools, and data depositories or information centres providing chemical information. Appendixes include a summary of relevant online databases and a chart indicating which vendors carry databases produced by Chemical Abstracts.

1696 How to find information: chemistry
N. Lees; British Library 1995, 30pp. £5.00. ISBN 0712308067.
Useful introduction to searching key sources in chemical information, covering: guides to chemical nomenclature; general reference works; compilations of chemical data; abstracting and indexing services; and online and CD-ROM databases.

1697 Information sources in chemistry
R.T. Bottle and J.F.B. Rowland 4th edn, Bowker Saur, 1994, 341pp. ISBN 0408023007.
An important guide, which represents a systematic survey and analysis of relevant sources of information in the international chemistry industry. Contents include: The primary literature of chemistry; Abstracting and indexing publications; Online searching for chemical information; Chemical business information; Health and safety information for chemists; Agricultural chemistry information; Government publications. New edition planned.

1698 Periodic Tables: if you were thinking that the internet needed one more
www.chemistrycoach.com/periodic_tables.htm
Although when reviewed had not been updated since early 2003, a remarkable and thoroughly enjoyable compilation of links to hundreds of periodic table related websites.

1699 RDN Virtual Training Suite: Chemist [UK]
A. Neville; University of Manchester and Resource Discovery Network
www.vts.rdn.ac.uk/tutorial/chemistry
Easily used and well organized tour covering: Subject gateways; Bibliographic resources; Electronic journals and other full text resources; Data collections and databanks; Chemical nomenclature; Health, safety and environmental information; Educational resources; Mailing lists; Organizational websites.

1700 WWW Virtual Library: Chemistry
University of Liverpool
www.liv.ac.uk/Chemistry/Links
Well used discovery tool, but not updated as systematically as some other services. However, has a number of useful features which complement those in some of the more current offerings, including a simple, well constructed list of headings, and – for some of the headings – an excellent depth of coverage.

Digital data, image & text collections

1701 Chemguide
J. Clark
www.chemguide.co.uk
Very clear well structured site maintained by retired UK schoolteacher. The About This Site section is exemplary: 'This site is intended to cover the needs of UK A level chemistry students, although it is actually being used by students on equivalent (16 to 18 year old) courses worldwide. It is also being used by students at the beginning of university level courses. I started by concentrating on the bits that textbooks tend to do too quickly and that students often find difficulty with. My over-riding aim is to try to increase your understanding of these difficult bits so that you gain confidence. More recently I have been adding more and more factual content, but always with a concentration on understanding. I'm simply not interested in the 'learn this parrot fashion and you will pass' approach – it is much more of a slog than taking a bit of time to understand what is going on ...' First-rate.

1702 Chemical Database Service [UK]
CCLRC Daresbury Laboratory
http://cds.dl.ac.uk/cds
Access to databases covering aspects of crystallography, spectroscopy, synthetic organic chemistry, physical chemistry. Free of charge to all 'academics' at UK universities.

1703 CHEMnetBASE
www.chemnetbase.com [DESCRIPTION]
Full-text searchable combination of *Combined chemical dictionary*, *Handbook of chemistry and physics*, *Polymers: a property database* and *Properties of organic compounds*. 'Searching each Chemnetbase product is completely free of charge – you can browse, perform searches and view search hit lists. If you want to view or print the full product entries you will need a current subscription.'

1704 NIST: Chemistry WebBook
National Institute of Standards and Technology
webbook.nist.gov/chemistry
Chemical and physical property data from collections maintained by the NIST Standard Reference Data Program and outside contributors. Data organized by chemical species, with search by formula, name, CAS registry number, reaction, molecular weight. Includes gas phase ion, spectra, thermochemical, and other data on, collectively, almost 50,000 species.

- **Elemental Data Index** http://physics.nist.gov/PhysRefData/Elements/cover.html. Access to the holdings of NIST Physics Laboratory online data organized by element: intended to simplify the process of retrieving online scientific data for a specific element.

Directories & encyclopedias

1705 The combined chemical dictionary
J. Buckingham, ed. Chapman & Hall/CRC Press, 2004, 35,000pp. CD-ROM, $7995.00. ISBN 041282020X.
www.chemnetbase.com/help/ccdhelp/ccdindex.htm
450,000 compounds covering all areas of chemistry, containing all compounds published in the Chapman &

Hall/CRC databases, and originally taken from: *Dictionary of organic compounds* (245,000 records); *Dictionary of natural products* (155,000 records); *Dictionary of inorganic and organometallic compounds* (100,000 records); *Dictionary of pharmacological agents* (38,000 records); *Dictionary of analytical reagents* (14,000 records); *Dictionary of carbohydrates* (22,000 records). Includes descriptive and numerical data on chemical, physical and biological properties of compounds; systematic and common names of compounds; literature references; structure diagrams and their associated connection tables. Detailed search facilities.

A related Chapman & Hall Chemical Database (formerly HEILBRON), accessible through the DIALOG online service, is listed as having been used to produce print publications with these titles: *Amino acids and peptides*; *Carbohydrates*; *Dictionary of analytical reagents*; *Dictionary of alkaloids*; *Dictionary of antibiotics and related substances*; *Dictionary of drugs*; *Dictionary of inorganic compounds*; *Dictionary of natural products*; *Dictionary of organic compounds*; *Dictionary of organometallic compounds*; *Dictionary of organophosphorus compounds*; *Dictionary of pharmacological agents*; *Dictionary of steroids*; *Dictionary of terpenoids*; *The lipid handbook* and *Phytochemical dictionary of the Leguminosae*.

Available online: see website.

- **Dictionary of natural products** **J. Buckingham** Chapman & Hall, 1993, 8584pp. $6349.95. ISBN 0412466201. About 150,000 products grouped in 11 vols within some 40,000 entries. Data includes uses, physical properties, structures, references.
- **The lipid handbook** **F.D. Gunstone, J.L. Harwood and F.B. Padley** 2nd edn, Chapman & Hall, 1994, 551pp. £399.00. ISBN 0412433206. Covers structure, occurrence, isolation, identification, analysis, synthesis, metabolism. Dictionary/reference section provides physical properties and literature references for over 3000 lipids, with name, molecular formula, CAS Registry Number indexes.

1706 **Concise encyclopedia chemistry**
M. Eagleson, comp. Walter de Gruyter, 1994, 1201pp. Revised translation of German language *ABC Chemie*, edited by Hans-Dieter Jakubke and Hans Jeschkeit, €88.00. ISBN 3110114518.
Covers all fields of chemistry in one volume, including: general chemistry; inorganic chemistry; organic chemistry; physical chemistry; technical chemistry and chemical engineering. Entries comprise abundance sources, refinement and purification, applications, history. Descriptions of numerous compounds include physical data, major reactions, and important uses.

1707 **Dictionary of chemical names and synonyms**
P.H. Howard and M.W. Neal 2nd edn, Synapse Information Systems, 1998. CD-ROM, $225.00 (Single user). ISBN 189059508X.
www.synapseinfo.com [DESCRIPTION]
Enables location of chemicals by name, synonym, CAS Registry Number or SMILES (Simplified Molecular Input Line Entry System) Notation. Covers a 'limited number of significant chemicals (approximately 25,000 chemicals with approximately 122,000 synonyms) ... 95% of the chemicals that most individuals will need.'

1708 **Encyclopedia of the elements: technical data, history, processing, applications**
P. Enghag Wiley-VCH, 2004, 1243pp. £175.00. ISBN 3527306668.
Based on a trilogy published in Swedish in the late 1990s, but extended to cover the transuranium elements, and to provide fact tables at the beginning of each element chapter. Chapter 1 explains the structure of the book. Good volume to browse through, especially re the non-chemical aspects of each element; but also a valuable compendium with – generally – relatively up-to-date data.

1709 **Hawley's condensed chemical dictionary**
R.J. Lewis, ed. 14th edn, Wiley, 2001, 1248pp. CD-ROM version available, $162.00. ISBN 0471387355.
Valuable reference book providing technical data and descriptive information for chemical substances and phenomena. Description of chemicals and processes along with an expanded definition of chemical entities and terminology may include: Name, Synonyms, CAS Registry Number, Formula, Physical properties, Source or occurrence, Grade, Hazard, Use, and Derivation.

1710 **The Merck Index**
13th edn, Merck & Co Inc, 2001, 2198pp. CD-ROM version available, $65.00. ISBN 0911910131.
www.merckbooks.com/mindex
The concise authoritative quick reference work. Includes over 10,000 monographs covering wide variety of drugs, pharmaceuticals, organic chemicals, laboratory reagents, plants, agricultural chemicals, endogenous substances and biological agents.
Available online: see website.

Ullmann's encyclopedia of industrial chemistry
M. Bohnet [et al.], eds See entry no. 5112

Handbooks & manuals

1711 **The art of scientific writing: from student reports to professional publications in chemistry and related fields**
H.F. Ebel, C. Bliefert and W.E. Russey 2nd edn, Wiley, 2004, 608pp. $35.00. ISBN 3527298290.
Gathers together tools of successful scientific writing, taking into account recent developments in communication techniques.

Bretherick's handbook of reactive chemical hazards: an indexed guide to published data
P.G. Urben and M.J. Pitt, eds See entry no. 4282

1712 **Chemical properties handbook: physical, thermodynamic, environmental, transport, safety, and health related properties for organic and inorganic chemicals**
C.L. Yaws McGraw-Hill, 1998, 779pp. $99.95. ISBN 0070734011.
Provides access to known (experimental) physical and chemical properties of chemicals and compounds as a function of temperature. Covers both organic and inorganic substances. Appendices offer conversion tables and equations, and lists of compounds by chemical formula, CAS registry number, and name.

1713 **Chemistry: foundations and applications**
Macmillan Reference USA, 2004. 4 v., $395.00. ISBN 0028657217.
www.gale.com/pdf/facts/Chem.pdf [DESCRIPTION]
'Explores the myriad of ways in which chemistry plays an important role (both seen and unseen) in daily life – from the food we eat to the air we breathe.' Major new work intended for general library users as well as students and faculty.

1714 **Communicating chemistry**
P.D. Bailey and S. Shinton, comps Royal Society of Chemistry, 1999, 141pp. £14.95. ISBN 0854049045.
www.chemsoc.org/pdf/LearnNet/rsc/Comm_select.pdf [COMPANION]
Will appeal to lecturers requiring a ready made course in communicating chemistry, or for ideas to produce their own materials. The resources presented are well described, with the rationale for activities explained. They comprise: industrial roles plays, literature interpretation, computer-based exercises and writing for various purposes/audiences.

1715 **Comprehensive coordination chemistry II: from biology to nanotechnology**
J.A. McCleverty and T.J. Meyer, eds Elsevier Pergamon, 2004, 8000pp. 10 v., $5975.00. ISBN 0080437486.
www.info.sciencedirect.com/reference_works
Follow-up to the 1987 work. Surveys developments since 1982, aiming to provide readers with the 'most reliable and informative background information on particular areas of co-ordination chemistry based on key primary and secondary references'. V. 10 is subject index to the series.

Broadly defines co-ordination chemistry to include the synthesis and products of association of Brønsted bases with a Lewis acid, thus excluding most organometallic compounds. Coverage of supramolecular chemistry restricted to developments since 1990.

Available online: see website.

- **Comprehensive coordination chemistry: the synthesis, reactions, properties and applications of coordinate compounds G. Wilkinson, ed.** Pergamon Press, 1987. ISBN 0080262325. 7 vols: 1. Theory and background; 2. Ligands; 3. Main group and early transition elements; 4. Middle transition elements; 5. Late transition elements; 6. Applications; 7. Index.

1716 **Comprehensive supramolecular chemistry**
J.-M. Lehn [et al.], eds Pergamon, 1996. 11 v., £2963.50. ISBN 0080406106.
Supramolecular chemistry has been defined as 'chemistry beyond the molecule, referring to the organized entities of higher complexity that result from the association of two or more chemical species held together by intermolecular forces'.

Each of 10 vols contains between 10 and 27 chapters reviewing specific aspects. Vol 11 is a very good cumulative subject index covering: General types of supramolecular compound; Specific supramolecular compounds; General and specific compounds where their synthesis or use involves supramolecular chemistry; Types of reaction (insertion, oxidative, addition, etc.); Analytical techniques (NMR, IR, etc.); Applications of supramolecular compounds.

- **Encyclopedia of supramolecular chemistry J.L. Atwood and J.W. Steed, ed.** Marcel Dekker, 2004, 1648pp. $420.00. ISBN 082475056X. 2 v.

1717 **CRC handbook of chemistry and physics**
D.R. Lide, ed. 85th edn, CRC Press, 2004, 2712pp. Free facsimile of the 1913 first edition with each purchase of the 85th print edition. CD-ROM version available, $139.95. ISBN 0849304857.
http://208.254.79.26
Often known as the Rubber Handbook or Rubber Bible, a definitive reference resource for chemists, physicists and technologists. Sections are: Basic constants, units and conversion factors; Symbols, terminology and nomenclature; Physical constants of organic compounds; Properties of the elements and inorganic compounds; Thermochemistry, electrochemistry and kinetics; Fluid properties; Biochemistry; Analytical chemistry; Molecular structure and spectroscopy; Atomic, molecular and optical physics; Nuclear and particle physics; Properties of solids; Polymer properties; Geophysics, astronomy and acoustics; Practical laboratory data; Health and safety information; Mathematical tables.

Online version available: see website.

Handbook of molecular physics and quantum chemistry
S. Wilson, P.F. Bernath and R. McWeeny, ed. See entry no. 771

1718 **Lange's handbook of chemistry**
J. Speight 16th edn, McGraw-Hill, 2005, 1000pp. 70th Anniversary Edition, $150.00. ISBN 0071432205.
Classic reference covering the entire field of chemistry with state-of-the-art facts, figures, values, tables and formulas. Comprises listings of properties of approximately 4000 organic and 1400 inorganic compounds including physical properties; thermodynamic properties; spectroscopy; electrolytes.

The 15th Edition (1999) included new material on separation methods and analytical chemistry; statistical methods; polymers; rubbers, fats, oils, and waxes; new inorganic compounds; IUPAC nomenclature of organic compounds; updated lists of physical and chemical symbols; definitions and abbreviations; new tables, charts, and illustrations; with SI units used throughout (conversion tables supplied).

1719 **Maths for chemists**
M.C.R. Cockett and G. Doggett Royal Society of Chemistry, 2003. ISBN 0854046771.
www.rsc.org/tct/maths1.htm [DESCRIPTION]
V. I: Numbers, Functions and Calculus (180 pp, ISBN: 0854046771, £14.95) ; V. II: Power Series, Complex Numbers and Linear Algebra (132 pp, ISBN: 0854044957, £14.95).

Keeping up-to-date

1720 **Angewandte Chemie: International Edition**
Gesellschaft Deutscher Chemiker Wiley-VCH, 48/year. €3430.00. ISSN 14337851.
www.wiley-vch.de/publish/en/journals
'The only journal in the field delivering a stimulating mixture of Review Articles, Highlights and Communications weekly. The Reviews summarize the important results of recent research on topical subjects in all branches of chemistry, point to unresolved problems and discuss possible developments. The Highlights provide concise evaluations of current trends in chemical research. The Communications are critically selected and report on the latest research results, making the journal indispensable to the chemist who wants to stay well informed. Angewandte Chemie also regularly publishes Nobel lectures in chemistry and related fields.'

1721 **Annual Reports on the Progress of Chemistry**
Royal Society of Chemistry Range of access and pricing arrangements: see website.
www.rsc.org/is/journals/current/ctitles.htm [DESCRIPTION]
Three sections: A *Inorganic Chemistry* 'Every year, all the

elements are reviewed, as is progress in organometallic and co-ordination chemistry, inorganic materials science, inorganic mechanisms and bio-inorganic chemistry'; B *Organic Chemistry* 'The full range of research from theoretical organic chemistry through reaction mechanisms and synthetic methodology to natural products and bio-organic chemistry is included'; C *Physical Chemistry* 'Theoretical and spectroscopic work, materials and catalytic chemistry, thermodynamics and kinetics are covered, each in a vast array of approaches'.

1722 CA Selects

Chemical Abstracts Service Biweekly. $285.00 each.
http://caselects.cas.org/html/home.html
These are current awareness services available electronically or in print. Each issue contains several hundred abstracts taken from the main publication. Topics cover the whole of chemistry and chemical-related activity. Examples relevant, as an example for instance, to environmental engineering include:

Acid rain and acid air. ISSN 0885-0097.
Air pollution. ISSN 0895-5980.
Indoor air pollution. ISSN 1047-8213.
Environmental pollution. ISSN 1084-044.
Liquid waste treatment. ISSN 1084-2381.
Recovery and recycling of wastes. ISSN 1084-0087.
Solid and radioactive waste treatment. ISSN 1084-0095.
Water treatment. ISSN 1084-0109.

Chemical Engineering

See entry no. 5151

1723 Chemical Informatics Letters

J.M. Goodman, ed.; University of Cambridge Monthly.
www.ch.cam.ac.uk/MMRG/CIL
Valuable bulletin giving the 'latest news in chemical informatics, links to relevant web sites, analysis and discussion'. Useful glossary.

1724 Chemical Society Reviews

Royal Society of Chemistry 1972–, 9 issues per year. Price includes free online access, £295.00 [2004]. ISSN 03060012.
www.rsc.org/is/journals/current/chsocrev/csrpub.htm [DESCRIPTION]
Publishes short introductory overviews of topics of current interest across the chemical sciences. Introduces chemists not familiar with the field under discussion to the most recent thinking and developments. Reviews not aimed at the expert and are thus written in a friendly, informative style. Background and historical context to review given as well as clear but concise guide to current thought.

The journal in 2004 had the relatively high ISI *Impact Factor* of 9.569 (c.f. ISI WEB OF KNOWLEDGE), and was in the top three general chemistry journals.

1725 Chemistry World

Royal Society of Chemistry Monthly. Subscription includes site-wide online access, £455.00. ISSN 14737604.
www.rsc.org/chemistryworld
The RSC's new magazine for its members and other subscribing chemical scientists around the world. Launched in January 2004 to replace *Chemistry in Britain*; provides a mix of news and features covering all of the chemical sciences.

1726 Chemtracts

Data Trace Publishing Company. $645.00.
www.datatrace.com/chemistry
'Provides updates on the newest trends and developments in chemistry by summarizing and commenting on current and past research. Unlike other publications, internationally recognized scholars select, summarize, and comment on the outstanding current research in the field of chemistry and provide commentary in an easy-to-read and standardized format.'

Three versions: *Biochemistry and Molecular Biology*; *Inorganic Chemistry*; *Organic Chemistry* – each published quarterly.

1727 Computational Chemistry List

Ohio State University
www.ccl.net/chemistry
An 'e-mail exploder which allows computational chemistry researchers from around the world to exchange information and experiences. It was created to promote contact between researchers involved in chemistry-related computation. This list is not restricted to any particular chemistry software or methodology; anyone is welcome to subscribe.' Good example of this genre.

1728 Current Chemical Reactions

Thomson ISI, Monthly.
www.isinet.com/products/cap/ccr [DESCRIPTION]
Database covering synthetic methods reported in the world's leading synthetic chemistry journals and now providing access to over 400,000 reactions. For each reaction, CCR presents complete reaction diagrams, critical conditions, bibliographic data, and author abstracts.

1729 Journal of Chemical Education

American Chemical Society Monthly. $240.00 [2005]. ISSN 00219584.
http://jchemed.chem.wisc.edu
Detailed and lively coverage of classroom and laboratory issues, meeting reports, news and announcements, book and media reviews, etc.

Available online: see website.

- **Chemical Education Resource Shelf**
  www.umsl.edu/~chemist/books. Excellent well structured and wide-ranging listings of books, most web-linked to their publishers' websites. Book reviews located are also cited, with more recent JCE items also hyperlinked. Archive is source for Journal's annual *Buyer's Guide* (April).

1730 Journal of Physical and Chemical Reference Data

American Institute of Physics and National Institute of Standards and Technology 1972–, Quarterly. $795.00. ISSN 00472689.
www.nist.gov/srd/jpcrd.htm [DESCRIPTION]
Core publication. 'The Journal came into existence as part of an effort to distribute standard reference data to a wider audience. It provides a means of systematizing and compacting the major components of the primary research literature, bringing together the research reported in widely dispersed journals and distilling the essential information into a manageable package.'

1731 Reactive Reports: Chemistry WebMagazine

D. Bradley Advanced Chemistry Development.
www.reactivereports.com
Engaging publication 'providing the chemistry community

with cutting edge reports of exciting developments in the world of the chemical sciences and related fields'.

The author has provided a helpful note, inter alia listing URLs of websites of more general key sources of chemistry-related information: 'Articles that provide a link to a particular paper will usually take you directly to the paper, although you may need a subscription or have to 'pay-per-view' to the journal to access the full text. For more information on any of the publishers and how to subscribe to any journals cited in RR please go direct to the publisher's home page (www.rsc.org, pubs.acs.org, www.pnas.org, www.sciencemag.org, www.nature.com, www.emboj.org, www.sciencedirect.com, oem.bmjjournals.com, atvb.ahajournals.org, www3.interscience.wiley.com, jama.ama-assn.org, bjsm.bmjjournals.com, www.cell.com).'

1732 **Specialist Periodical Reports: reviews of the chemical literature**
Royal Society of Chemistry Available in print and online. Individual chapters from volumes published 1998 onwards are available electronically, on a pay per view basis.
www.rsc.org/is/books/spr.htm [DESCRIPTION]
Series providing – every 1–2 years – systematic and detailed reviews of 10 major areas of chemical research. Current titles are: Amino acids, peptides and proteins; Carbohydrate chemistry, monosaccharides, disaccharides and specific oligosaccharides; Catalysis; Chemical modelling: applications and theory; Electron paramagnetic resonance; Nuclear magnetic resonance; Organometallic chemistry; Organophosphorus chemistry; Photochemistry; Spectroscopic properties of inorganic and organometallic compounds.

Inorganic Chemistry

bioinorganic chemistry • high-temperature compounds • organometallic chemistry • precious metals • rare earth elements • silicon

Introductions to the subject

1733 **Advanced inorganic chemistry**
F.A. Cotton [et al.] 6th edn, Wiley, 1999, 1376pp. $119.00. ISBN 0471199575.
Has often been the first source that students and professional chemists have turned to for the background needed to understand current research literature in inorganic chemistry and aspects of organometallic chemistry. Organized around the periodic table of elements, provides a systematic treatment of the chemistry of all chemical elements and their compounds. Incorporates important recent developments with an emphasis on advances in the interpretation of structure, bonding, and reactivity.
'The standard by which all other inorganic chemistry books are judged.' (*Nouveau Journal de Chimie*)

1734 **From Coello to inorganic chemistry**
F. Basolo Wolters Kluwer, 2002, 266pp. £42.50. ISBN 0306467747.
Autobiography of leading inorganic chemist. 'Students and chemists with interests in bioinorganic chemistry, catalysis, nanoscience, new materials research, and organometallics can follow the emergence of inorganic chemistry as a rival to organic chemistry through the accomplishments of one of its most influential pioneers.'
Series: Profiles in Inorganic Chemistry.
'In short, this autobiography should be read by anyone who has experienced the joy of doing chemistry or is contemplating such a career path. You won't be disappointed.' (*Journal of Chemical Education*)

1735 **Inorganic chemistry**
D.F. Shriver and P.W. Atkins 3rd edn, Oxford University Press, 1999, 786pp. CD-ROM, £34.99. ISBN 019850330X.
Standard text. CD-ROM enables almost all the numbered molecular structures to be viewed 3-dimensionally, rotatably. Colour images used in the text are downloadable for use in presentations etc.

Dictionaries, thesauri, classifications

Glossary of terms used in bioinorganic chemistry
International Union of Pure and Applied Chemistry See entry no. 2041

Laws, standards, codes

1736 **Inorganic chemical nomenclature: principles and practice**
B.P. Block, W.H. Powell and W.C. Fernelius, eds; American Chemical Society 1990, 210pp. ISBN 0841216975.
Classic guide to correct naming of inorganic compounds according to INTERNATIONAL UNION OF PURE AND APPLIED CHEMISTRY and ACS rules.

1737 **Nomenclature of inorganic chemistry II: recommendations 2000**
J.A. McCleverty and N.G. Connelly; International Union of Pure and Applied Chemistry Royal Society of Chemistry, 2000, 130pp. Issued by the Commission on the Nomenclature of Inorganic Chemistry, £49.95. ISBN 0854044876.
www.iupac.org/publications/books/author/mccleverty.html [DESCRIPTION]
'Whilst Part I is mainly concerned with general inorganic chemistry, this volume, *Part II*, addresses such diverse chemistry as polyanions, isotopic modification, tetrapyrroles, nitrogen hydrides, inorganic ring, chain, polymer, and graphite intercalation compounds. The recommendations bring order to the nomenclature of these specialized systems, based on the fundamental nomenclature described in Part I and the organic nomenclature publications. Each chapter has been subject to extensive review by members of IUPAC and practising chemists in various areas.'

- **Nomenclature of inorganic chemistry: recommendations 1990 G.J. Leigh, ed.** Blackwell Science, 1990, 315pp. ISBN 0632024941. Thorough revision of the last edition of the *Red Book*. This is *Part I*, concerned with general inorganic chemistry.

Discovering print & electronic resources

1738 **Comprehensive organometallic chemistry II: a review of the literature 1982–94**
E.W. Abel, F.G.A. Stone and G. Wilkinson Pergamon, 1995. 14 v. ISBN 0080406084.
The original work is used as a basis for these volumes focusing on developments in organometallic chemistry

reported since 1982 with reference back to the original work if necessary. Aimed to be a pivotal reference in this area of chemistry. Topics covered include: the organic chemistry of main group and transition elements; compounds containing heteronuclear metal-metal bonds; main group and transition metal organometallic compounds in organic synthesis; and organometallic structures studied by diffraction methods. The volumes are arranged as follows: 1–9 organometallic chemistry of individual elements; 10 heteronuclear metal–metal bonds; 11–12 main-group metal and transition metal organometallics in organic synthesis; 13 structure index: structures determined by diffraction methods; 14 formula and subject indexes.

- **Comprehensive organometallic chemistry: the synthesis, reactions and structures of organometallic compounds** **G. Wilkinson, F.G.A. Stone and E.W. Abel** Pergamon, 1982. ISBN 0080252699. 9 v.

1739 Gmelin
MDL Information Systems.
www.mdli.com/products/knowledge/crossfire_gmelin [DESCRIPTION]
The major structural and factual database providing in-depth coverage of organometallic and inorganic compounds, alloys, glasses, ceramics and minerals. Includes reviewed literature (from the *Gmelin Handbook*) and more recent unreviewed literature references, chemical structure and more than 800 different chemical and physical properties for over 1.8 million compounds.

Records contain substance identifying information (e.g., structure image, GMELIN Registry Number, CAS Registry Number), numeric and non-numeric data about chemical and physical properties, and preparation and reaction information. Comprehensive references to primary literature. In online versions, powerful searching capabilities include searches by structure, physical property ranges, environmental data etc.

Directories & encyclopedias

1740 Encyclopedia of inorganic chemistry
R.B. King [et al.], ed. Wiley, 1994, 4819pp. 8 v., $4533.00. ISBN 0471936200.
Features reviews of: Chemistry of all elements of inorganic chemistry; Physical and theoretical methods; Organometallic chemistry: Main group elements; Solid state chemistry; Transition metals; Bioinorganic chemistry. Simple alphabetical sequence: about 260 main articles and 850 definition entries. Relatively brief cumulative index in V. 8.

1741 Handbook of inorganic chemicals
P. Patnaik McGraw-Hill, 2003, 1086pp. $150.00. ISBN 0070494398.
A–Z encyclopedia of 2000 of the best known chemicals providing for each: Synonyms; Molecular weight; Formula/structure and the type of compound based on functional group; CAS Registry Number; Occurrence; Uses and applications; Physical properties; Methods of preparation with chemical equations; Chemical reactions; Health chemical analysis.

Handbooks & manuals

The biological chemistry of the elements: the inorganic chemistry of life
J.J.R. Fraústo da Silva and R.J.P. Williams See entry no. 2076

1742 Chemistry of precious metals
S.A. Cotton Blackie Academic & Professional, 1997, 374pp. £172.00. ISBN 0751404136.
Covers the elements gold and silver, palladium, rhodium and iridium, ruthenium and osmium, providing information on their chemistry and the principles underlying their compounds, reactions, applications and use.

1743 A comprehensive treatise on inorganic and theoretical chemistry
J.W. Mellor, ed. Longman, 1922–80. Multi-volume plus supplements.
Surveys the elements in Periodic Table order, discusses their important reactions and compounds. Each element has its own section beginning with a detailed descriptive history from alchemical origins. Although this publication is out of print it is a frequently quoted source of data for inorganic chemistry and described as indispensable in all chemistry libraries.
'Apart from Gmelin, the most comprehensive source of data for inorganic compounds. Old, but still useful. Fifteen volumes with vol.16 as index. Some volumes (alkali metals, B,N,P) have supplements.' (*British Library*)

1744 Critical stability constants
A.E. Martell and R.M. Smith Plenum Press, 1974–1989. 6 v.
www.nist.gov/srd/nist46.htm
A growing interest in such fields as bioinorganic chemistry has fuelled an explosion in the demand for stability constants of ligands. These volumes represent a thorough guide to metal metal complex equilibrium constants. V. 1. Amino acids. V. 2. Amines. V. 3. Other organic ligands. V. 4. Inorganic complexes. V. 5. First supplement. Ligand name and formula indexes.
Enhanced version available online: see website.

1745 Handbook of high temperature compounds: properties, production, applications
T. Kosolopova Hemisphere, 1990, 933pp. $560.00. ISBN 0891168494.
Covers properties of borides, carbides, nitrides, silicides, sulphides, selenides and tellurides. Also contains most-used methods of powder preparation and manufacture of articles, data on explosibility, flammability and toxicity of refractory-compound powders. Provides crystal structures; chemical, electric, magnetic, mechanical, optical, thermodynamic, thermophysical properties.

1746 Handbook of inorganic compounds
D.L. Perry and S.L. Phillips CRC Press, 1995, 584pp. $199.95. ISBN 0849386713.
Physical and crystallographic data, nomenclature and reference information for approximately 4000 inorganic compounds selected on grounds of their frequent usage in laboratories.

Handbook of metalloproteins
A. Messerschmidt [et al.], eds See entry no. 2078

1747 **Handbook on the physics and chemistry of rare earths**
K.A. Gschneidner and L. Eyring, eds North Holland. Multi-volume: V. 33, 2003.
www.elsevier.com/wps/find/homepage.cws_home [DESCRIPTION]
Series covering the physics and chemistry of this group of seventeen elements and their use in a wide range of applications.

Inorganic chemicals handbook
J.J. McKetta, ed. See entry no. 5143

1748 **Inorganic materials chemistry desk reference**
D. Sangeeta and J.R. LaGraff 2nd edn, CRC Press, 2004, 384pp. $149.95. ISBN 0849309107.
Introduction to inorganic materials chemistry and the chemical processing techniques used to prepare solid state inorganic materials.

1749 **Inorganic reactions and methods**
J.J. Zuckerman [et al.] Wiley, 1999, 10904pp. 19 v set with indexes, $6395.00. ISBN 0471328375.
www.wiley.com/WileyCDA [DESCRIPTION]
In-depth treatment organized by types of chemical bonds formed. Assembles all the knowledge that constitutes modern inorganic chemistry.

1750 **Inorganic Syntheses**
Wiley, Annual, 260pp. E-Book available, $99.95 [V. 34, 2004]. ISBN 0471647500.
Published 'to provide all users of inorganic substances with detailed and foolproof procedures for the preparation of important and timely compounds'.

1751 **Organometallics in synthesis: a manual**
M. Schlosser Wiley, 2002, 1256pp. $190.00. ISBN 0471984167.
Coverage includes chemistry of: organoalkali; organozinc; organocopper; organotin; organoboron; organoaluminium; organotitanium; organozirconium; organochromium and -iron; organopalladium compounds.
'... a clear, readable and up-to-date reference work needs to be at hand. This book offers just that ...' (*Applied Organometallic Chemistry*)

1752 **Silicon chemistry: from the atom to extended systems**
U. Schubert and P. Jutzi, eds Wiley, 2003, 506pp. $165.00. ISBN 3527306471.
Essential reference for the silicon chemist presenting combined results from an international research project involving 40 interdisciplinary groups.

Keeping up-to-date

1753 **Advances in Inorganic Chemistry**
Academic Press, 1957–, Annual. £102.50 [V. 56, 2004]. ISSN 8988838.
Reviews current progress in all areas of inorganic chemistry ranging from bio-inorganic to solid state studies.
Formerly Advances in Inorganic Chemistry and Radiochemistry.

1754 **Advances in Organometallic Chemistry**
Academic Press, 1964–, Annual. £113.00 [V. 51, 2004]. ISBN 0120311518.
Contains authoritative reviews that address all aspects of organometallic chemistry.

Laboratory Tools & Techniques

analytical chemistry • chemical analysis • chemical laboratories • chemometrics • chromatography • crystallography • diffraction • electron microscopy • electrophoresis • elemental speciation • infrared spectroscopy • laboratory chemicals • laboratory robots • mass spectrometry • nuclear magnetic resonance spectroscopy • radioactivity analysis • Raman spectroscopy • reagent chemicals • scanning probe microscopy • separation science • solubility data • specimen microscopy • thermochemical data • thin-layer chromatography • ultraviolet spectroscopy • x-ray spectroscopy

Introductions to the subject

1755 **The basics of crystallography and diffraction**
C. Hammond 2nd edn, Oxford University Press, 2001, 348pp. £27.50. ISBN 0198505523.
Provides a clear and comprehensive introduction to the topics of crystallography and diffraction for undergraduate and beginning graduate students and lecturers in physics, chemistry, materials and earth sciences, but will also be of interest to the layperson who wishes to know more. Coverage includes: crystals and crystal structure; two-dimensional patterns, lattices and symmetry; bravais lattices and crystal systems etc.

Bioseparations science and engineering
R.G. Harrison [et al.] See entry no. 5008

1756 **Chemical analysis in the laboratory: a basic guide**
I. Mueller-Harvey and R.M. Baker; Royal Society of Chemistry 2002, 92pp. £18.95. ISBN 0854046461.
Provides basic training in the whole analytical process for students, demonstrating why analysis is necessary and how to take samples, before they attempt to carry out any analysis in the laboratory. Initially, planning of work, and collection and preparation of the sample are discussed in detail. This is followed by a look at issues of quality control and accreditation and the basic equipment (e.g. balances, glassware) and techniques that are required. Throughout, safety issues are addressed, and examples and practical exercises are given.

1757 **Classic chemistry demonstrations: one hundred tried and tested experiments**
T. Lister; Royal Society of Chemistry 2000, 322pp. £27.50. ISBN 1870343387.
Well presented collection of 100 classic chemistry demonstrations to inspire and intrigue students. Primarily for the use of teachers of chemistry, this book is an ideal way of captivating the next generation of chemists. The fun demonstrations show often spectacular experiments that students would otherwise not see as they are unable to perform them themselves.

1758 **Illustrated pocket dictionary of chromatography**
P.C. Sadek Wiley, 2004, 240pp. $54.95. ISBN 0471200212.
Provides concise definitions, illustrations, formulas, and

other information needed in a laboratory chromatography reference.

'Does a fine job of laying a 'foundation of facts' so that students of the discipline can begin to explore this very complex subject ... Is a remarkable teaching text, it will service the professional scientist equally well.' (*Electric Review*)

1759 Introduction to macromolecular crystallography
A. McPherson Wiley, 2002, 256pp. $83.95. ISBN 0471251224.
'Crystallography has become the keystone of rational pharmacology, protein engineering, structural genomics, proteomics, bioinformatics, and nanotechnology. By growing molecules in three-dimensional crystal forms, researchers can determine precise molecular structure, leading to major advances in biotechnology applications such as improved drugs and crops. *Introduction to Macromolecular Crystallography* provides a comprehensive, approachable summary of the field of crystallography, from the fundamental theory of diffraction and properties of crystals to applications in determining macromolecular structure.'

1760 Mass spectrometry: principles and applications
E. De Hoffmann and V. Stroobant 2nd edn, Wiley, 2001, 407pp. $74.00. ISBN 0471485667.
'Complete overview of the principles, theories and key applications of modern mass spectrometry. Extensively revised and updated, the second edition of this highly successful introductory textbook focuses on recent developments in techniques and applications. All instrumental aspects of mass spectrometry are clearly and concisely described, with tandem mass spectrometry introduced early on and then developed in more detail in its own chapter.'

'Due to the rapid development of new technologies, mass spectrometry is an explosively expanding field. This book ... is the best source of current methods and available instrumentation. Upper-division undergraduates through practising professionals will benefit from this book (on the 1st edn).' (*Choice*)

The role of the solvent in chemical reactions
E. Buncel, R.A. Stairs and H. Wilson See entry no. 1868

1761 Scanning electron microscopy and X-ray microanalysis
J. Goldstein [et al.] 3rd edn, Kluwer Academic/Plenum Publishers, 2003, 586pp. CD-ROM, £53.00. ISBN 0306472929.
Comprehensive manual – though suitable as introduction for those with no previous experience of the field. Based on course taught for 10 years at Lehigh Microscopy Summer School to students with wide range of backgrounds in physical and biological sciences and diverse technologies.

1762 Scanning probe microscopy: the lab on a tip
E. Meyer, H.J. Hug and R. Bennewitz Springer, 2004, 210pp. £46.00. ISBN 3540431802.
Provides a well written general introduction to all types of scanned probe microscopes, with significant detail on scanning tunnelling microscopy, scanning force microscopy, and magnetic force microscopy, and lesser coverage of other members of the family of scanning probe microscopes. Almost 500 references. Index.

1763 Vogel's textbook of quantitative chemical analysis
A.I. Vogel and J. Mendham 6th edn, Prentice Hall, 2000, 806pp. $170.00. ISBN 0582226287.
www.prenhall.com/divisions/esm/chem_central/chemcentral
Standard undergraduate text book of laboratory techniques which provides a basis for the teaching, learning and application of analytical chemistry. It covers rapidly developing areas with sections on calibration methods and the analysis of variance. Experimental design, optimization techniques and examples of multivariate analysis are also included.

Chem Central *is a gateway to Prentice Hall's chemistry publications: see website.*

Dictionaries, thesauri, classifications

1764 Illustrated chemistry laboratory terminology
H.W. Ockerman CRC Press, 1991, 211pp. ISBN 0849301521.
Intended for chemists whose first language is not English and who wish to expand their English vocabulary in the chemical laboratory area. Tables of contents and indices listed in Chinese, French, German, Polish, Spanish, and Turkish. Alternate spellings in American English and British English provided for applicable terms. Useful reference for non-English-speaking chemists planning to teach chemistry in English or required to write or communicate in English.

Laws, standards, codes

1765 Analytical Standards
Sigma-Aldrich Co.
www.sigmaaldrich.com [REGISTRATION]
Described as covering over 7000 standards, 5500 of them for chromatography. Sections include: Standards & reference materials; Customized standards; Certified reference materials; Chromatography standards; Electrophoresis standards; Physical property standards; Spectroscopy standards; Thermal analysis standards; Titrimetry water standards.

Sigma-Aldrich also offer access to major collections of spectral and other analytical data.

1766 Good laboratory practice regulations
S. Weinberg 3rd edn, Marcel Dekker, 2003, 244pp. $135.00. ISBN 0824708911.
Exploring the role of Good Laboratory Practices (GLP) in the assurance of safety, quality, and control in regulated arenas, details specific standards and general guidelines for the management of efficient and effective research environments – presenting essential principles for anticipating new and emerging interpretations of GLP in a variety of laboratory settings.

1767 Recommended reference materials for the realization of physicochemical properties
K.N. Marsh; International Union of Pure and Applied Chemistry Blackwell Scientific, 1987, 500pp. ISBN 063201718X.
Contains contributions from internationally renowned experts to provide a comprehensive review of various materials which can be used as references for checking correct operation or for the calibration of equipment used for physicochemical measurement.

1768 **WebInsight**
Ariel Research Corporation.
www.arielresearch.com/Solutions/Products/WebInsight [DESCRIPTION]
Over 400 searchable regulatory lists updated monthly in Asia-Pacific, Latin America, North America, Central and Eastern Europe and Western Europe, in addition to *Dangerous Goods*, *Global Inventories* and the US-based *RegsLink®* databases.

Official & quasi-official bodies

1769 **International Union of Crystallography**
www.iucr.org
The IUCr is a member of the INTERNATIONAL COUNCIL FOR SCIENCE and exists to serve the world community of crystallographers. Website supplies information on the Union, its Associates, its important series of journals and other publications. Includes online access to *World Directory of Crystallographers*. Also a helpful section *Data Activities in Crystallography*, links to book reviews and much else of value in this arena – including a gateway: *Crystallography Online*.

- **World directory of crystallographers: and of other scientists employing crystallographic mathods** Y. Epelboin, ed.; International Union of Crystallography 10th edn, Kluwer Academic, 1997, 298pp. £19.75. ISBN 0792342283. The Union produces a number of books on crystallography, in association with Oxford University Press and Kluwer Academic Publishers.

Research centres & institutes

1770 **Cambridge Crystallographic Data Centre** [UK]
www.ccdc.cam.ac.uk
Now a non-profit, charitable institution, self financing and self administering, whose objectives are 'the general advancement and promotion of the science of chemistry and crystallography for the public benefit'. Offers number of free services including *WebCite* – a database of published research applications of the *Cambridge Structural Database* and other CCDC products.

- **Cambridge Structural Database**
www.ccdc.cam.ac.uk/products/csd [FEE-BASED]. Records bibliographic, chemical and crystallographic information for organic molecules and metal-organic compounds whose 3D structures have been determined using X-ray or neutron diffraction. Data from open literature, private communication, data deposit.

International Centre for Diffraction Data
See entry no. 1282

Associations & societies

American Council of Independent Laboratories
See entry no. 4563

1771 **American Crystallographic Association**
www.hwi.buffalo.edu/ACA
Objective is 'is to promote interactions among scientists who study the structure of matter at atomic (or near atomic) resolution'. Downloadable from the site is the PDF version of their very attractive, informative and extensive *Newsletter* (the Summer 2004 issue running to 32 pages). Also link to information about the US National Committee for Crystallography as well as to lists of Officers for their various Special Interest Groups.

1772 **American Society for Mass Spectrometry**
www.asms.org
Formed 1969 and now has over 7000 scientists involved in research and development in membership. Tutorial What is mass spectrometry?; very wide range of Interest Groups but most web services limited to members.

1773 **Association for Laboratory Automation**
http://labautomation.org
Mission is 'to advance science and education related to laboratory automation by encouraging the study, advancing the science, and improving the practice of medical and laboratory automation ... As a worldwide, virtual organization, our focus is on the benefits and utilization of automation, robotics, and artificial intelligence in order to improve the quality, efficiency, and relevance of laboratory analysis'. Well designed simple site: Conferences; Education; Journal; Membership; News & Events; Search.

1774 **Coblentz Society**
www.coblentz.org
Purpose is to foster the understanding and application of vibrational spectroscopy. Publishes *Infrared Reference Spectra*. Good links section.

1775 **GAMBICA**
www.gambica.org.uk
'National organization representing the interests of companies in the instrumentation, control, automation and laboratory technology industry in the UK. The diverse nature of the industry is reflected in the five industry sectors represented by the Association: Industrial Automation Products and Systems; Process Measurement and Control Equipment and Systems; Environmental Analysis and Monitoring Equipment; Laboratory Technology; Test and Measurement Equipment for Electrical and Electronics Industries.

1776 **Laboratory Robotics Interest Group**
www.lab-robotics.org
Non-profit special interest group, sponsored by vendor members. Good well annotated links section; gateway to RSS newsfeeds from 10 organizations, late 2004.

1777 **Society for Applied Spectroscopy** [USA]
www.s-a-s.org
'The term spectroscopy as used in the title and body of this Constitution is understood to mean the science and art of absorption, emission, Raman, mass, and related forms of spectral study for determining the composition and structure of matter.' News, publications, links.

Portal & task environments

1778 **The Analytical Sciences Digital Library**
American Chemical Society Electronic Environmental Resources Library.
www.asdlib.org
Collects, catalogues, and links web-based information and discovery material pertinent to innovations in curricular

developments and supporting resources about chemical measurements and instrumentation.

1779 **Bio-Rad Laboratories**
www.informatics.bio-rad.com
Offer wide range of spectral software and data – including for academic licence: e.g. *IQ Academic Spectral Database* 'Students and teachers can access high-quality spectra used by major companies and research institutions throughout the world. The database includes IR and NMR spectra for over 1200 specially selected compounds that cover a broad range of chemical classes useful within the chemistry curriculum. Each compound contains cross-referenced spectral data for IR, 1H NMR, and 13CNMR and value-added information, such as technique, molecular formula, molecular weight, CAS Registry Number, melting point, and boiling point.'

1780 **FTIRsearch.com**
Thermo Electron Corporation.
https://ftirsearch.com [FEE-BASED]
Pay-per-use service offering access to Fourier Transform Infrared (FTIR) and Raman spectral libraries designed 'to provide cost effective access to spectral libraries for smaller labs, researchers involved in short term projects, educational institutions and anyone else who performs less frequent spectral searching. *FTIRsearch.com* is the only product that allows you to search for commercial quality spectra online and pay only for the searches you request.' Over 70,000 FTIR and 15,000 Raman spectra searchable.

1781 **Reciprocal Net**
Indiana University
www.reciprocalnet.org
Well designed and useful crystallography gateway providing news and access to distributed databases used by crystallographers at US and a few non-US research institutions to store information about molecular structures. Much of the data is also publicly available.

- **Common Molecules** www.reciprocalnet.org/edumodules/commonmolecules. Structural presentation of over 500 molecules studied in the classroom plus some of more general interest. Java applet allows view and rotation of each molecule.

1782 **SelectScience: The Scientists' Choice**
www.selectscience.net [REGISTRATION]
'An independent product information guide for applied chemists and life scientists. It also provides user's views online and the option for visitors to post their own experiences.' Access to data in the product directory and the community services requires (free) registration; but there is a freely accessible extensive set of links.

1783 **SpecInfo**
Wiley.
www.interscience.wiley.com/db/specinfo
Integrated infrared, nuclear magnetic resonance, and mass spectroscopy solution for viewing, predicting, and searching spectra. 'All the data included in *SpecInfo* are curated – databases are quality controlled at the point of data preparation and are sourced from reputable laboratories and peer-reviewed literature.' Includes over 600,000 spectra.

1784 **SpectroscopyNOW.com: the new online resource serving the spectroscopy community**
Wiley.
www.spectroscopynow.com
News and features; Discussion forums; Education; Training; Jobs; Library and Bookshop; Links – categorized: What's new; What's hot; Application areas; Companies; Conferences; Data sets; Hardware; Journals; and so on: most entries with a short annotation. *Spectral Lines* is a wide-ranging webzine covering advances across spectroscopy.

Discovering print & electronic resources

1785 **Analytical Abstracts**
Royal Society of Chemistry Monthly. £1455.00 [2004]. ISSN 00032689.
www.rsc.org/is/database/aahome.htm [DESCRIPTION]
The only abstracting service designed specifically to meet information needs of analytical scientists. Provides comprehensive coverage of new techniques and applications and unique indexing designed for the analyst, including for chromatography, electrophoresis, spectrometry and radiochemical methods. Inorganic, organic and organometallic analysis, with application to applied and industrial products. Clinical and biochemical analysis, covering proteomics and genomics. Pharmaceutical analysis, including drugs in biological fluids. Environmental, agricultural and food analysis.
Available online: see website.

- **Chromatography Abstracts** £1155.00. ISSN 02686287. www.rsc.org/is/database/chroabs.htm. Published by RSC for the *Chromatographic Society*: www.chromsoc.com.
- **Mass Spectrometry Bulletin** Monthly. £2095.00. ISSN 00254738. www.rsc.org/is/database/msbhome.htm [DESCRIPTION]. 500 new literature references published each month from over 900 sources, including journals, books, patents and conference proceedings.

Chemical Safety NewsBase
Royal Society of Chemistry See entry no. 4273

1786 **MS Links**
Scientific Instrument Services Inc.
www.sisweb.com/mslinks.htm
Extensive reliable list of links to mass spectrometry related sites; regularly updated.

Digital data, image & text collections

1787 **Inorganic Crystal Structure Database**
FIZ Karlsruhe
www.fiz-informationsdienste.de/en/DB/icsd [FEE-BASED]
Includes pure elements, minerals, metals, and intermetallic compounds (with atomic co-ordinates, published since 1913). 82,676 entries (November 2004); updated twice a year, each update comprising about 2000 new records.

1788 **IUPAC solubility data series**
International Union of Pure and Applied Chemistry
www.nist.gov/srd/jpcrd.htm [DESCRIPTION]
The IUPAC Solubility Data Commission was established in 1979, with the duties and responsibilities within IUPAC to publish critically evaluated solubility and related thermodynamic data by enlisting over 100 scientists from

more than 25 countries. Volumes 1 through 53 were published by Pergamon Press, and Volumes 54 through to 65 were published by Oxford University Press.

A co-operative agreement between the IUPAC Commission and the *Standard Reference Data Program* of the NATIONAL INSTITUTE OF STANDARDS AND TECHNOLOGY was then signed, resulting in the Series volumes becoming part of the JOURNAL OF PHYSICAL AND CHEMICAL REFERENCE DATA. These volumes are published four times a year within the six yearly issues of JPCRD. The numbering of the volumes continues the sequence established by the IUPAC Commission.

1789 **NIST: Analytical Chemistry**
www.nist.gov/srd/analy.htm
Comprehensive set of easy-to-use databases and online systems that help the analytical chemist identify unknown materials and obtain physical, chemical, and spectroscopic data about known substances.

- **NIST/EPA/NIH Mass Spectral Library** www.nist.gov/srd/mslist.htm. Product of a multiyear, comprehensive evaluation and expansion of the world's more widely used mass spectral reference library. Now includes 147,198 compounds with spectra. Website lists the database's current distributors.
- **Wiley registry of mass spectral data** **F. McLafferty** 7th edn, Wiley, 2000. $4375.00. ISBN 0471440973. Software combined with data from the 1998 NIST/EPA/NIH Mass Spectral Library.

1790 **NMRShiftDB**
www.nmrshiftdb.org
Database for c.12,000 organic structures and their nuclear magnetic resonance spectra. Allows for spectrum prediction (at the time of review only for carbon) as well as for searching spectra, structures and other properties. Peer-reviewed submission of datasets by users; open source, data being published under open content license.

Directories & encyclopedias

1791 **Encyclopedia of chromatography**
J. Cazes Dekker/CRC Press, 2001, 927pp. Online/print version, $593.00. ISBN 0824741234.
'Chromatographic techniques and methodologies for the solution of analytical and preparative problems applicable across many disciplines, including biotechnology, pharmaceuticals, environmental sciences, polymers, food additives and nutrients, pathology, toxicology, fossil fuels, and nuclear chemistry. High-performance, thin-layer, gas, affinity, countercurrent, supercritical fluid, gel permeation, and size exclusion chromatography, as well as capillary electrophoresis, field-flow fraction, hyphenated techniques, and more.'

1792 **The encyclopedia of mass spectrometry**
R. Caprioli and M. Gross, eds Elsevier, 2004, 6500pp. 10 v., $3825.00. ISBN 0080438504.
Will consist of nine vols, plus an index vol. Estimated to have 600 articles by 1000 authors. Included will be over 15,000 figures and 20,000 references. Articles are intended to be tutorial in nature, citing both advantages and disadvantages of a technique or method. Where possible, articles are divided into primary (basic) considerations, and advanced: first aimed at the novice, second to the experienced practitioner who is not necessarily an expert in that specific subject.

1793 **Encyclopedia of nuclear magnetic resonance**
D.M. Grant and R.K. Harris, eds Wiley, 1996–2002. V. 1–8, 1996; V. 9 *Advances in nuclear magnetic resonance*, 2002, $6753.00. ISBN 0470847840.
Comprehensive coverage in over 700 articles: V. 1 from historical perspective; V. 2–8 alphabetical sequence with subject index in the last; V. 9 supplementary vol.

1794 **Encyclopedia of spectroscopy and spectrometry**
J.C. Lindon, G.E. Tranter and J.L. Holmes, eds Academic Press, 2000, 2581pp. 3 v., $1075.00. ISBN 0122266803.
www.info.sciencedirect.com/reference_works
Covers the most important spectroscopic and related techniques together with their applications. Separate contents lists, one listing articles alphabetically (as in the vols), the other grouping article titles within specialities such as mass spectrometry, atomic spectroscopy, magnetic resonance, etc. Additionally, each article flagged as 'Theory', 'Methods and Instrumentation', or 'Applications'.

Excellent design; small number of colour plates; detailed index in V. 3.

Available online: see website.

1795 **LabGuide Online: the premier buyers guide for all scientific laboratories**
American Chemical Society
www.mediabrains.com/client/LabGuide/bg1
'The most comprehensive online source for analytical instruments, laboratory products, chemicals, equipment, services and supplies.'

Handbooks & manuals

1796 **Analytical chemistry: a modern approach to analytical science**
J.-M. Mermet, M. Otto and M. Valcárcel Cases 2nd edn, Wiley-VCH, 2004, 1181pp. £55.00. ISBN 3527305904.
Large format comprehensive volume with 36 chapters in eight parts. Each chapter concludes with recommended reading. Detailed table of contents and index. Appendix has brief 'key to literature'. Major source.
1st edn 1998.

Biochemical methods: a concise guide for students and researchers
A. Pingoud [et al.] See entry no. 2075

1797 **Chemical analysis of contaminated land**
K.C. Thompson and C.P. Nathanail, eds Blackwell, 2003, 290pp. £89.00. ISBN 1841273341.
Comprehensive UK-based treatment, including methods of interpreting results within the new risk-based legislative framework for contaminated land.

1798 **Chemometrics: data analysis for the laboratory and chemical plant**
R.G. Brereton Wiley, 2003, 489pp. $79.00. ISBN 0470849118.
'Chemometrics has been broadly defined as the application of mathematical, statistical and formal logic methods to chemistry. Increasingly, analytical chemists require training in mathematics and statistics to augment their professional knowledge of chemistry. Chemometric techniques provide a method of information extraction from data acquired through various media.'

'In short, this is the best book that I have seen covering the entire field of modern chemometrics both for the academic and industrial user ... I highly recommend it.' (*Technometrics*)

- **Chemometrics: from basics to wavelet transforms F.-T. Chau [et al.]** Wiley-Interscience, 2004, 316pp. $99.95. ISBN 0471202428.

1799 **Color atlas and manual of microscopy for criminalists, chemists, and conservators**
N. Petraco CRC Press, 2002, 320pp. $199.95. ISBN 0849312450.
Almost 500 colour images of the most commonly encountered materials for specimen comparison and identification, together with basic instruction on microscopy techniques for professionals without formal training. Covers wide range of materials such as synthetic and natural fibres, wood fragments, paint chips, pigments, soils, mineral grains, gemstones, and human and animal hair.

CRC handbook of laboratory safety
A.K. Furr See entry no. 4286

Current protocols in food analytical chemistry
R.E. Wrolstad [et al.], eds See entry no. 3185

1800 **Dean's analytical chemistry handbook**
P. Pradyot McGraw-Hill, 2004, 1160pp. $150.00. ISBN 0071410600.
Offers detailed coverage of the full range of analytical methods, including all the conventional wet and instrumental techniques. Advances in all types of analytical techniques are covered. 40% new material in this edn.

1801 **Eight peak index of mass spectra: the eight most abundant ions in 81,123 mass spectra, indexed by molecular weight, elemental composition and most abundant ions**
4th edn, Mass Spectrometry Data Centre, 1991. 3 v. ISBN 0851864171.
Classic compilation produced by the former Centre. V. 1 categorizes the spectra by molecular weight and then by the number of C, H, ... atoms; in V. 2 arrangement is by molecular weight and m/e ratio; in V. 3 in ascending order of m/e ratio.

1802 **Encyclopedia of analytical chemistry: applications, theory, and instrumentation**
R.A. Meyers, ed. Wiley, 2000, 14344pp. 15 v., $7905.00. ISBN 0471976709.
Integrated coverage of theory, instrumentation and techniques. 600 articles, arranged alphabetically by topic.
'Overall, this Encyclopedia is a very impressive and extremely well produced set of volumes. Its comprehensive coverage of most aspects of modern analytical chemistry means that it will be the definitive reference work for many years to come, and it should be in the library of any institution where analytical chemistry is undertaken.' (*The Alchemist*)

1803 **Encyclopedia of analytical science**
P.J. Worsfold [et al.] 2nd edn, Academic Press, 2005, 5000pp. 10 v., £2950.00. ISBN 0127641009.
www.elsevier.com/wps/find/homepage.cws_home
Revised edn of text providing detailed and comprehensive coverage of techniques used for the determination of specific elements, compounds and groups of compounds, in physical or biological matrices. Addresses applications of chemical analysis in all areas, including medicine, environmental science, geology and food science. Important characterization techniques, such as microscopy and surface analysis also included.
Elsevier also offer an extensive series of vols Comprehensive Analytical Chemistry*: see website.*

1804 **Encyclopedia of separation science**
I.D. Wilson [et al.], eds Academic Press, 2000, 4502pp. 10 v., £2065.00. ISBN 0122267702.
www.info.sciencedirect.com/reference_works/sd_refworks_fs.pdf [DESCRIPTION]
Major work presenting information on three levels. V. 1 *Level 1*, provides broad overview of theory of 12 main categories of separation techniques. V. 2–4 *Level 2* expand coverage with detailed theoretical and technical descriptions of particular techniques. V. 5–9 *Level 3* cover applications of these techniques from the micro to the macro, and also from the analytical laboratory bench to large-scale industrial processes. V. 10 consists mainly of the index.
Available online: see website.

1805 **The essence of chromatography**
C.F. Poole Elsevier, 2003, 925pp. €89.00. ISBN 0444501991.
Aims to present a comprehensive survey of modern chromatographic and capillary electrophoretic techniques. Suitable for courses in the separation sciences at post-graduate level; also as a self-study guide for professionals wishing to refresh their background. Well written but intensive text; substantial bibliographies (but with journal article titles omitted).

1806 **The experimental determination of solubilities**
G.T. Hefter and R.P.T. Tomkins, eds Wiley, 2003, 629pp. $324.00. ISBN 0471497088.
Codifies reliable procedures for the measurement of all types of solubility data, as assessed by experienced researchers in the various areas. 15 contributed chapters in five parts: 1. Fundamentals of solubility; 2. Gases; 3. Liquids; 4. Solids; 5. Special systems. Bibliographies. Index.
Series: Wiley Series in Solution Chemistry, 6.

Food analysis
S.S. Nielsen See entry no. 3186

1807 **Handbook of analytical techniques**
H. Günzler and A. Williams, eds Wiley-VCH, 2001, 1182pp. 2 v, $650.00. ISBN 3527301658.
All relevant spectroscopic, chromatographic, and electrochemical techniques are described including chemical and biochemical sensors, as well as thermal analysis, bioanalytical, nuclear or radiochemical techniques. Covers procedures including weighing and sample preparation and compares different techniques.

1808 **Handbook of aqueous solubility data**
S.H. Yalkowsky and Y. He CRC Press, 2003, 1512pp. $299.95. ISBN 0849315328.
Solubility data for over 4000 chemicals covering a wide variety of organic non-electrolytes and unionized weak electrolytes. Includes data for pharmaceuticals, pollutants, nutrients etc.

1809 **Handbook of basic tables for chemical analysis**
T.J. Bruno and P.D.N. Svoronos 2nd edn, CRC, 2003, 672pp. $99.95. ISBN 0849315735.

Four chapters on the different chromatography, electrophoresis and electroanalytical methods; five chapters covering the various spectrometry techniques; qualitative tests, solution properties, tables for laboratory safety, miscellaneous tables. Subject and chemical compound indexes. Citations appended to each table. Excellent reference work.

1st edn 1989.

1810 **Handbook of chemical health and safety**
R.J. Alaimo, ed.; American Chemical Society Oxford University Press, 2001, 652pp. £27.50. ISBN 0841236704.

Guidebook on maintaining safe work environments, acting as starting point for chemical safety studies, and giving information on chemical handling, purchasing, storage, use and disposal. Outlines safe use of specialized equipment. Provides answers to queries on environmental laws and regulations. Allows planning for most emergency situations. Includes spill prevention and cleanup plans. Additionally covers industrial hygiene issues, radiation safety practices, safe laboratory and facility design criteria and biosafety issues.

'comprises the most complete and comprehensive resource on chemical health and safety, replacing many earlier texts, and should be the first place chemists, chemical hygiene officers, and safety specialists will look for answers to both simple and complex problems.' (*SciTech Book News*)

'It should be compulsory reading for any serious student of chemical safety and will join a small collection of books that make a substantial contribution to the field.' (*Chemistry and Industry*)

1811 **Handbook of elemental speciation: techniques and methodology**
R. Cornelis [et al.], eds Wiley, 2003, 657pp. $278.00. ISBN 0471492140.

' "Speciation", a word borrowed from the biological sciences, has become a concept in analytical chemistry, expressing the idea that the specific chemical forms of an element should be considered individually ... The concept is concerned with the forms of an element defined as to isotopic composition, electronic or oxidation state, and/or complex or molecular structure.'

Almost 50 contributions covering: Sampling and sample preparation; Separation techniques; Detection; Direct speciation of solids; Calibration; Screening methods; Risk assessment/regulations. Detailed index.

'the reader can use this book as a reference book for the next 5 to 10 years.' (*Applied Organometallic Chemistry*)

1812 **Handbook of free radical initiators**
E.T. Denisov, T.G. Denisova and T.S. Pokidova Wiley-Interscience, 2003, 904pp. $315.00. ISBN 0471207535.

Gives an up-to-date account of the physicochemical data on radical initiators and reactions of radical generation. The initiators serve as reactive intermediates in synthetic methodologies such as organic and polymer synthesis as well as in technological processes, oligomerization, network formation, and kinetic research. 20 chapters in 3 parts: I. Initiators; II. Biomolecular reactions of free radical generation; III. Reactions of free radicals. Large number of comprehensive tables; detailed index – including of chemical names. Major text.

1813 **The handbook of infrared and Raman spectra of inorganic compounds and organic salts**
R.A. Nyquist [et al.] Academic Press, 1996, 1184pp. 4 v. CD-ROM supplement, 1998, $1499.95. ISBN 0125234449.

Provides an essential information resource for industrial chemists and researchers who require both a spectral database and specific routines for spectrum analysis. The CD is able to undertake spectra analogue searches to identify unknown entities and provide extensive reference information on spectral methods and conditions.

- **Interpreting infrared, raman, and nuclear magnetic resonance spectra R.A. Nyquist, ed.** Academic Press, 2001, 1068pp. $656.95. ISBN 0125234759. 2 v.

1814 **Handbook of metathesis**
R.H. Grubbs, ed. Wiley-VCH, 2003. 3 v., $350.00. ISBN 3527306161.

Metathesis (within chemistry) has been defined as 'the interchange of atoms or groups of atoms between two molecules'. Major text divided into three thematic volumes: Catalyst development; Applications in organic synthesis; Applications in polymer synthesis.

'can be nominated for the 'Best publication' of the year. 'A must-have for every organic and polymer chemist,' this information resource would be a valuable addition for research collections in academic and corporate libraries around the world.' (*E-STREAMS*)

1815 **Handbook of radioactivity analysis**
M.F. L'Annunziata, ed. 2nd edn, Academic Press, 2003, 1273pp. $185.00. ISBN 0124366031.

Principles and practical techniques for the accurate measurement of radioactivity from the lowest traces. 1. Nuclear radiation, its interaction with matter and radioisotope decay. 2. Gas ionization detectors ... 5. Liquid scintillation analysis: principles and practice ... 7. Radioactivity counting statistics ... 10. Radioisotope mass spectrometry ... 15. Radiation dosimetry. Table of radioisotopes.

1st edn 1998.

1816 **Handbook of spectroscopy**
G. Gauglitz and T. Vo-Dinh, eds 2nd edn, Wiley-VCH, 2003, 1168pp. 2 v., $520.00. ISBN 3527297820.

Designed to be not 'just another treatise on the theory of spectroscopy, but rather a practical day-to-day guide'. Covers all the main fields, treating both methods and applications (including bioanalysis; environmental analysis; process control). Final section *General data treatment: databases/spectral libraries* has three chapters: Optical spectroscopy; Nuclear magnetic resonance spectroscopy; Mass spectrometry. Detailed index to both vols.

'... very comprehensive treatment of spectroscopy ... highly recommended ...' (*Choice*)

1817 **Handbook of thin-layer chromatography**
J. Sherma and B. Fried, eds 3rd edn, Marcel Dekker, 2003, 1016pp. $249.95. ISBN 0824708954.

Major established resource; 40 contributors cover both principles and practice (13 chapters) and applications (19 chapters). One of the few books available with coverage of TLC applications by compound type, facilitates industrial adaptation through easy reference. Appendix *Directory of manufacturers and suppliers of plates, equipment, and instruments for thin-layer chromatography.*

Series: Chromatographic Science, V. 89.

Hazardous chemicals desk reference
R.J. Lewis See entry no. 4290

1818 **Hazardous laboratory chemicals disposal guide**
M.A. Armour 3rd edn, Lewis Publishers, 2003, 557pp. $129.95. ISBN 1566705673.
Straightforward ring-back volume, single A–Z sequence of c.300 compounds. Clearly laid-out entries. Index of compounds with some cross-referencing.
2nd edn 1996.

1819 **Introduction to conventional transmission electron microscopy**
M. De Graef Cambridge University Press, 2003, 718pp. £34.95. ISBN 0521629950.
http://ctem.web.cmu.edu/FrontPage.html [COMPANION]
Mathematically in-depth text with two introductory chapters providing foundations respectively in crystallography, and quantum mechanics. Supplementary website contains more than 30,000 lines of Fortran 90 source code; and there are online interactive modules allowing the reader to try out real-time simulations.

1820 **Modern crystallography**
B.K. Vainshtein [et al.], eds Revised edn, Springer, 1994–2000.
V. 1 Fundamentals of crystals, symmetry, and methods of structural crystallography (482 pp, £84.50, ISBN 3540565582); V. 2 Structure of crystals (520 pp, £130.50, ISBN 3540568484). 1st edn included V. 3 Crystal growth, and V. 4 Physical properties of crystals. The 4 volumes cover all aspects of crystallography.

1821 **Official methods of analysis of AOAC International**
W. Horwitz, ed. 17th edn, AOAC International, 2000. 2 v. 2nd revision, 2003. Also on CD-ROM, $175.00. ISBN 0935584676.
www.aoac.org/pubs/oma_revised.htm [DESCRIPTION]
Association of Official Analytical Chemists' peer reviewed and tested compilation of chemical and microbiological methods. V. 1 details agricultural chemicals, contaminants, and drugs. V. 2 continues with food composition, additives, and natural contaminants. The 2300 'methods' are referenced for locator ease, cite supplier addresses, specifications for laboratory, scientific basis, and references.

1822 **Purification of laboratory chemicals**
W.L.F. Armarego and C.L.L. Chai 5th edn, Butterworth-Heinemann, 2003, 609pp. £60.00. ISBN 0750675713.
Includes detailed descriptions of techniques together with the physical properties and purification procedures, taken from literature, of an extensive number of commercially available organic, inorganic and biochemical compounds.

1823 **Reagent chemicals**
P.A. Boius; American Chemical Society 9th edn, Oxford University Press, 1999, 768pp. £100.00. ISBN 0841236712.
pubs.acs.org/reagents/index.html [COMPANION]
Contains the new specifications for the ACS grade reagent chemicals, in force from the start of 2000. It covers approximately 450 reagents and includes features new to this edition, such as reagents suitable for ultra trace analysis. Website contains information on the work of *The Committee on Analytical Reagents* together with a *Supplement* to the 9th edn.

Sittig's handbook of toxic and hazardous chemicals and carcinogens
R.P. Pohanish See entry no. 4301

1824 **Solubilities of inorganic and organic compounds**
H. Stephen [et al.], eds Pergamon, 1963–79. 3 v. Translation of *Spravochnik po rastvorimosti*, Moscow and Leningrad, 1961–69. ISBN 0080235999.
V. 1 Elements, inorganic, organometallic, and organic compounds in binary systems: about 3500 compounds; V. 2 Ternary and multicomponent systems: about 5200 systems; V. 3 Inorganic ternary and multicomponent systems: about 5600 systems. Non-aqueous solvents are included. All three volumes have indexes.

1825 **Thermochemical data of elements and compounds**
E.M. Binnewies 2nd edn, Wiley-VCH, 2002, 936pp. $465.00. ISBN 3527305246.
Comprehensive collection of thermochemical data. Contains selected values of the thermochemical properties of over 3000 mostly inorganic substances. Values are given for enthalpy of formation and entropy at 298 K. Using the compiled fixed Cp values or the Cp/T functions in the form of a polynomial, the enthalpy, entropy, and Gibbs free energy values at other temperatures can be calculated. In many cases special equilibrium constants, for instance, for evaporation or decomposition reactions, are also given.

- **ThermoDex: index of selected thermodynamic and physical property resources** **University of Texas at Austin.** http://thermodex.lib.utexas.edu. Annotated records that describe compilations of thermodynamic and physical property data for chemical compounds and other substances. Most of the compilations included are printed books; some are freely available web-based databases.

1826 **Writing the laboratory notebook**
H.M. Kanare; American Chemical Society 1985, 150pp. ISBN 0841209332.
In many professional and academic lists as the definitive style for writing up experiments, this book describes, among other things the reasons for notekeeping and organizing and writing the notebook with examples. It also provides photographs from laboratory notebooks of famous scientists.

Keeping up-to-date

1827 **Advances in chromatography**
CRC Press, Annual, 352pp. $189.95 [V. 43, 2004]. ISBN 0824753410.
Latest advances in the field with contributions and current research from world-renowned leaders.

1828 **The analyst**
Royal Society of Chemistry Monthly. £885.00 [2004]. ISSN 00032654.
www.rsc.org/is/journals/current/analyst/anlpub.htm [FEE-BASED]
Since 1887 has been publishing original research papers on fundamental and applied aspects of the theory and practice of analytical chemistry including chemometrics/statistics, oceanography, chromatography, new techniques and instrumentation, detectors and sensors, etc.
Available online: see website.

Analytical Biochemistry
See entry no. 2087

1829 **Analytical Chemistry**
American Chemical Society Biweekly. £132.00. ISSN 00032700.
http://pubs.acs.org/journals/ancham
Leading journal. Alternate years are published *Fundamental Reviews* and *Application Reviews*: critical overviews of the literature of the previous two years in particular subject areas. Updated June 2004 was data-set giving free access to the journal's 75 most-cited publications, together with a 75-year milestones timeline.

1830 **Laboratory News**
Quantum Business Media, Monthly.
www.labnews.co.uk
Leading UK magazine, available free within the UK. 'Links producers and consumers of all types of scientific equipment with a mixture of news, comments, reviews and features. It is the biggest and most informative of all UK publications serving the laboratory sector.'

R&D Magazine
See entry no. 4611

Organic Chemistry

combinatorial chemistry • heterocyclic chemistry • name reactions • organic synthesis • reagents organic synthesis

Introductions to the subject

Alkaloids: nature's curse or blessing?
M. Hesse See entry no. 2028

1831 **A fragrant introduction to terpenoid chemistry**
C.S. Sell Royal Society of Chemistry, 2003, 410pp. £49.95. ISBN 08404681X.
www.rsc.org/is/books/books_organic.htm
Introduces terpenoid chemistry with emphasis on the lower terpenoids, but the basic principles taught are also applicable to the chemistry of the higher terpenoids. The group is wide-ranging including Vitamin A, and representatives of hormones, perfumes, pharmaceuticals, etc.
Society publishes wide-ranging collection of organic chemistry (and other subject category) texts: see website.

Industrial organic chemicals
H.A. Wittcoff, R.G. Reuben and J.S. Plotkin See entry no. 5057

1832 **Organic chemistry**
J. McMurry 6th edn, Brooks/Cole, 2004, 1376pp. $154.95. ISBN 0534389996.
http://chemistry.brookscole.com/mcmurry6e [COMPANION]
Leading US-based text giving comprehensive coverage of organic chemistry topics. Traditional functional group combined with mechanistic approach. Range of supporting resources including multiple choice quizzes with explained answers; active figures; molecular models.

1833 **Organic chemistry**
J. Clayden [et al.] Oxford University Press, 2000, 1536pp. £35.99. ISBN 0198503466.
Leading UK-based text which has an excellent, carefully measured approach: especially good for those new to the field who have some basic grounding in chemical principles.

Organic chemistry principles and industrial practice
M.M. Green and H.A. Wittcoff See entry no. 5061

1834 **Organic synthesis: concepts and methods**
J.-H. Fuhrhop and G. Li 3rd edn, Wiley, 2003, 517pp. $79.95. ISBN 3527302735.
Written for the advanced chemistry student and research chemist, with the methods chosen based on applicability, didactic value, future aspects. Last chapter is a useful *Seventy-seven conclusions in alphabetic order.*
2nd edn 1994.

1835 **Vogel's textbook of practical organic chemistry**
A.I. Vogel and B.S. Furniss 5th edn, Longman, 1989, 1376pp. ISBN 0582462363.
Classic one-volume reference text aimed at organic chemists throughout training and practice. Designed to integrate mechanistic theory with strategy and methodology of synthesis, and to reflect development of philosophy of organic synthesis.

Dictionaries, thesauri, classifications

Glossary of terms used in medicinal chemistry
International Union of Pure and Applied Chemistry See entry no. 3682

1836 **The vocabulary and concepts of organic chemistry**
M. Orchin [et al.] 2nd edn, Wiley, 2005, 862pp. $125.00. ISBN 0471680281.
'Basic reference providing concise, accurate definitions of the key terms and concepts of organic chemistry. Not simply a listing of organic compounds, structures, and nomenclatures, the book is organized into topical chapters in which related terms and concepts appear in close proximity to one another, giving context to the information and helping to make fine distinctions more understandable. Areas covered include: bonding, symmetry, stereochemistry, types of organic compounds, reactions, mechanisms, spectroscopy, and photochemistry.'

Laws, standards, codes

1837 **Nomenclature of organic chemistry Sections A, B, C, D, E, F, and H: Blue book**
J. Rigaudy and S.P. Klesney Pergamon Press, 1979, 550pp. ISBN 0080223699.
www.acdlabs.com/iupac/nomenclature
The website HTML reproduction of Sections A, B and C of the IUPAC 'Blue Book' – made available by the company Advanced Chemistry Development (Toronto) – is 'as close as possible to the published version'. It also includes copy of the 1993 Recommendations published by Blackwell, see: www.iupac.org/publications/books/author/panico.html.

1838 **Recommendations on organic & biochemical nomenclature, symbols & terminology**
International Union of Pure and Applied Chemistry and International Union of Biochemistry and Molecular Biology
www.chem.qmw.ac.uk/iupac
Rich gateway giving access to full text of IUPAC, Joint Commission on Biochemical Nomenclature (IUPAC/IUBMB), and other recommendations, bibliographic data, etc. Last update 1 June 2004.

Associations & societies

American Peptide Society
See entry no. 2047

European Peptide Society
See entry no. 2053

Portal & task environments

PEPSOC.COM: The Peptide Societies Network
European Peptide Society, American Peptide Society and Japanese Peptide Society See entry no. 2057

Discovering print & electronic resources

1839 **Beilstein**
www.beilstein.com
The major structure and factual database in organic chemistry. The organic substance records contain the critically reviewed and evaluated documents from the *Beilstein Handbook of Organic Chemistry* as well as data from 176 leading journals in organic chemistry covering the period from 1779 to the present. A substance record contains the BEILSTEIN Registry Number, the CAS Registry Number, structure diagram, molecular formula etc., all of which are searchable and displayable, as is information on physical, chemical, pharmacological and ecological data for each substance.
Available online: see website.

1840 **Comprehensive heterocyclic chemistry II: a review of the literature: the structure, reactions, synthesis, and uses of heterocyclic compounds**
A.R. Katritzky, C.W. Rees and E.F.V. Scriven, eds Pergamon, 1996, 11628pp. 12 v. CD-ROM version available, £4441.50. ISBN 0080420729.
Covers the synthesis of heterocyclic compounds, reactions of heterocyclic systems, and the use of heterocycles as synthetic precursors. Presents a comprehensive account of fundamental heterocyclic chemistry, with the emphasis on basic principles, on unifying correlations in the properties, chemistry and synthesis of different heterocyclic systems and the analogous carbocyclic structures.

Comprehensive organometallic chemistry II: a review of the literature 1982–94
E.W. Abel, F.G.A. Stone and G. Wilkinson See entry no. 1738

1841 **Organic Chemistry Resources Worldwide**
K. Van Aken
www.organicworldwide.net
Aimed at synthetic organic chemists involved in academic or industrial research. Very easy – intuitive – guide, well laid out and selective, with 75 sections categorized: The literature; Synthesis planning; Chemical and reaction media/conditions; Reaction set-up; Work-up and purification; Structural analysis; The Desk; Communication; Additional activities.

1842 **Theilheimer's synthetic methods of organic chemistry**
Karger, 1945–, Biannual. $632.00 [2004]. ISSN 0253200X.
Provides a research tool for accessing organic synthetic methods reported in the world-wide scientific literature back to 1945. Each volume consists of 500 abstracts which give clear depictions of typical reactions and comments on scope, limitation and any specific advantages. The volumes have heavily cross referenced indexes devised for functional group retrieval allowing for the location of reactions by product or starting material. Supplementary references provide updates on established procedures.
'Has an established place among the informational tools available to organic chemists, and no library that caters to their needs can claim to be adequate without it.' (*Journal of the American Chemical Society*)

Digital data, image & text collections

1843 **Journal of synthetic methods**
Thomson Derwent.
www.derwent.com/products/pca/jsyntheticmethods [DESCRIPTION]
A structure-searchable chemical reactions database, designed on the principles set out originally by W. Theilheimer. Provides key references to novel synthetic methods from worldwide patent and scientific literature. Strict selection criteria ensure only new or most synthetically useful modifications of known methods are abstracted. In addition, all references cross-referenced to relevant prior art and other similar reactions.

Directories & encyclopedias

1844 **Encyclopedia of reagents for organic synthesis**
L.A. Paquette Wiley, 1995, 6234pp. 8 v., $5105.00. ISBN 0471936235.
www.interscience.wiley.com
Exhaustive reference work represents an authoritative and systematic description of the use of all reagents in organic chemistry. Each reagent is assessed and compared with others capable of similar chemistry. The online *e-EROS* is database of around 50,000 reactions and around 3800 of the most frequently consulted reagents and is fully searchable by structure and substructure, reagent, reaction type, experimental conditions etc. and allows sophisticated full text searches.
Available online: see website.

1845 **Name reactions: a collection of detailed reaction mechanisms**
J.J. Li 2nd edn, Springer, 2003, 465pp. £61.50. ISBN 3540402039.
Covers some 300 reactions, graphically depicting each reaction and citing the relevant literature. Subject index.
1st edn 2002.

1846 **Name reactions and reagents in organic synthesis**
B.P. Mundy and M.G. Ellerd Wiley, 1988, 560pp. $110.00. ISBN 0471836265.
Compilation of most commonly used and widely known name reactions and reagents in modern synthetic organic chemistry. Each item listed alphabetically, giving structure, physical properties, major uses, preparation, commercial availability and secondary information.

Handbooks & manuals

1847 **Comprehensive organic chemistry: the synthesis and reactions of organic compounds**
D. Barton and W.D. Ollis, eds Pergamon Press, 1979. 6 v. ISBN 0080213197.
Major historical work. Covered all facets of organic chemistry judged most important at the time. Emphasis was given throughout to the properties of all the important classes or organic compounds, including the remarkable array of different compounds prepared by synthesis as well as natural products created by biosynthesis. Information was presented in a concise and logical manner with mechanistic organic chemistry being adopted to provide a constant and correlative theme.

1848 **Comprehensive organic synthesis: selectivity, strategy and efficiency in modern organic chemistry**
B.M. Trost and I. Fleming, eds Pergamon Press, 1991. 9 v. ISBN 0080359299.
Compendium that was a highly acclaimed overview of synthetic methodology. Organized by reaction type e.g. additions to C-X bonds; additions to and substitutions at C-C bonds etc. Contains 9000 references with clearly drawn structures and reaction schemes.

1849 **CRC handbook of organic photochemistry and photobiology**
W.M. Horspool and F. Lenci 2nd edn, CRC Press, 2003, 2500pp. 2 v., $495.00. ISBN 0849313481.
Emphasizes synthetic value of photochemistry and photobiology over conventional thermal methods. Provides coverage of broad areas of organic photochemistry and photobiology. Includes 66 new chapters reflecting recent developments, new applications, and emerging areas of interest. 145 critically reviewed chapters present fundamental concepts, cutting-edge research, and up-to-date tables of physical data.

Environmental organic chemistry
R.P. Schwarzenbach, P.M. Gschwend and D.M. Imboden See entry no. 5614

1850 **Fiesers' reagents for organic synthesis**
T-L. Ho, ed. Wiley, 2004. 22 v. with index to vs. 1–12, $2250.00. ISBN 0471714569.
Provides concise descriptions, good structural formulae and selected examples of applications giving references to new reagents as well as to reagents included in previous volumes. Thousands of entries abstract most important information on commonly used and new reagents, including preparation, uses, sources of supply, critical comments, references and more. Reagents are considered in alphabetical order by common usage names.

1851 **Handbook of combinatorial chemistry: drugs, calatysts, materials**
K.C. Nicolaou, R. Hanko and W. Hartwig, eds Wiley-VCH, 2002, 1114pp. 2 v, $545.00. ISBN 3527305092.
First-rate wide-ranging survey of 35 chapters in five parts: General aspects; Synthetic chemistry; Special synthetic topics; Molecular design and combinatorial compound libraries; Novel applications of combinatorial chemistry. Combinatorial chemistry is a technique for rapidly and systematically assembling a variety of molecular building blocks in many different combinations.
'it is an excellent reference book that most researchers in the field will want on their bookshelves and/or in their library.' (*Synthesis*)

1852 **Mechanism and synthesis**
P.G. Taylor, ed.; Royal Society of Chemistry 2002, 368pp. CD-ROM version available, £27.50. ISBN 085404695X.
Examines strategies for synthesizing mainly organic compounds, especially those of interest to the health sector and related industries.
Series: The Molecular World.

The organic chemistry of drug design and drug action
R.B. Silverman See entry no. 3749

1853 **Organic Reactions**
Wiley, 1942–, 634pp. $125.00 (V. 65, 2005). ISBN 0471682608.
Critical discussions of most important reactions used in chemical synthesis. Each chapter devoted to single reaction, or definite phase of reaction, of wide applicability; includes tables giving all examples found of use of the reaction, these with their accompanying bibliographies thus substituting for literature searches.

1854 **Organic Syntheses**
Wiley, 1921–. $55.50 (V. 80, 2003).
Annual publication of 'satisfactory methods' for the preparation of organic chemicals. Collective vols, with cumulative indexes, act as revised editions of V. 1–9, 10–19, etc.

The practice of medicinal chemistry
C.G. Wermuth, ed. See entry no. 3751

1855 **Reactive intermediate chemistry**
R.A. Moss [et al.], ed. Wiley-Interscience, 2004, 1072pp. $105.00. ISBN 0471233242.
Excellent resource comprising 22 invited contributions organized into 2 parts: Reactive intermediates; Methods and temporal regimes.
'Physical organic chemists will race to the library to check out this authoritative text ... This book, which is well organized and contains an extensive index, would be an indispensable resource for graduate students and professionals in academia or industry.' (*E-STREAMS*)

1856 **Science of synthesis: Houben–Weyl methods of molecular transformations**
5th edn, Georg Thieme Verlag, 2001–. 48 v. (planned; 16 published by September 2004).
www.science-of-synthesis.com [DESCRIPTION]
Entirely new edn of the classic reference work. Organized in a logical hierarchical system based on target molecule to be synthesized. Each section will take account of 'all published

results from journals, books, and patent literature from the early 1800s until the year of publication'.

Available online: see website.

- **Houben–Weyl methods of organic chemistry** (Methoden der organischen Chemie) 4th edn, Georg Thieme Verlag, 1988–. 146,000 product-specific experimental procedures, 580,000 structures, 700,000 references. Also available online: see website.

1857 **Structure determination of organic compounds: Tables of spectral data**
E. Pretsch, P. Bühlmann and C. Affolter 3rd edn, Springer, 2000, 421pp. CD-ROM, £39.95. ISBN 3540678158.
Successful work, intended as a short textbook and a hands-on guide for interpreting experimental spectral data and elucidating the chemical structure of the respective compound behind it.

1858 **The systematic identification of organic compounds**
R.L. Shriner [et al.] 8th edn, Wiley, 2004, 723pp. $105.95. ISBN 0471215031.
Well established text. Chapter 12 is a traditional review of Chemical literature. Appendix 1 has a collection of 'Handy tables for the organic laboratory'; Appendix 2 'Tables of derivatives' is an extensive listing of boiling/melting points of common organic compounds, arranged by class of compound.

Keeping up-to-date

1859 **Advances in heterocyclic chemistry**
Academic Press, 500pp. $176.00 [V. 87, 2004]. ISBN 0120207877.
Of interest to organic chemists, polymer chemists and biological scientists. Written by established authorities in the field, consists of reviews combining descriptive chemistry and mechanistic insights to yield an understanding of how the chemistry drives the properties.
V. 87 will include the chapter: 'The Literature of Heterocyclic Chemistry, Part VIII, 2000–2002' (L.I. Belen'kii and V.N. Gramenitskaya).

Physical Chemistry

catalysis • chemical kinetics • chemical physics • chemical thermodynamics • colloid chemistry • condensed matter • electrochemistry • gases • liquids • nuclear chemistry • quantum chemistry • radiation chemistry • solids • statistical mechanics • statistical physics • stereochemistry • surface chemistry • theoretical chemistry • thermodynamics

Introductions to the subject

1860 **100 years of physical chemistry: a collection of landmark papers**
Royal Society of Chemistry 2004, 384pp. £50.00. ISBN 0854049878.
www.rsc.org/is/books/landmark.htm [DESCRIPTION]
Compiled to celebrate the centenary of the founding of the Faraday Society in 1903. Presents some of the key papers published in Faraday journals, topics covered including: Intermolecular Forces; Ultrafast Processes; Astrophysical Chemistry; Polymers; Electrochemistry. Feature articles all written by leaders in their field, including a number of Nobel Prize winners.

1861 **Atkins' physical chemistry**
P.W. Atkins and J. de Paula 7th edn, Oxford University Press, 2001, 1180pp. £36.99. ISBN 0198792859.
www.oup.co.uk/best.textbooks/chemistry/pchem7 [COMPANION]
The world's best-selling physical chemistry textbook. New co-author Julio de Paula brings a new perspective from applications of physical chemistry to biology and other topical research areas. Written in clear readable style. Includes numerous worked examples, self-tests, 'Illustrations' which show how an equation is used, and checklists of key ideas at chapter ends – now expanded to include key equations.
6th edn 1998.

1862 **Basic concepts for simple and complex liquids**
J.-L. Barrat and J.P. Hansen Cambridge University Press, 2003, 296pp. £29.95. ISBN 0521789532.
After good introduction, 12 chapters in 4 parts: I. Thermodynamics, structure and fluctuations; II. Phase transitions; III. Interfaces and inhomogenous fluids; IV. Dynamics. Each chapter has further reading. Index.

1863 **Chemical thermodynamics of materials: macroscopic and microscopic aspects**
S. Stølen and T. Grande Wiley, 2004, 395pp. $139.00. ISBN 0471492302.
Complements other texts with the focus on cases from a variety of important materials, with the mathematical derivations deliberately kept relatively simple. Inter alia gives a good overview of thermodynamics.

Fundamentals of heat and mass transfer
F.P. Incropera and D.P. DeWitt See entry no. 5053

1864 **A gallery of fluid motion**
M. Samimy Cambridge University Press, 2003, 118pp. £20.00. ISBN 052153500X.
Attractive visual images of fluids in motion chosen in competition sponsored by the AMERICAN PHYSICAL SOCIETY. Two criteria used in selection were: 1. Artistic beauty and novelty of the visualization; 2. Contribution to a better understanding of fluid flow phenomena. Each image or set of images is accompanied by short description of the underlying physics. Keyword index.

Introduction to chemical engineering thermodynamics
J.M. Smith, H.C. Van Ness and M. Abbott See entry no. 5058

1865 **Introduction to statistical physics**
K. Huang Taylor & Francis, 2001, 288pp. £24.99. ISBN 0748409424.
Textbook aimed at undergraduate students with a firm grounding in mathematics. Introduced from a phenomenological view and presented in terms of thermodynamics. Later examples are drawn from other current fields of interest. Example problems and solutions are included.

Mapping the spectrum: techniques of visual representation in research and teaching
K. Hentschel See entry no. 798

Physical and chemical equilibrium for chemical engineers
N. De Nevers See entry no. 5062

1866 **Quanta: a handbook of concepts**
P.W. Atkins 2nd edn, Oxford University Press, 1991. £43.49. ISBN 0198555733.
www4.oup.co.uk/isbn/0-19-855573-3 [DESCRIPTION]
A non-mathematical and highly visual account of the concepts of quantum mechanics widely encountered in chemistry and related disciplines.
'His marriage of extraordinarily good English with a marvellous grounding in the physical sciences has produced a clear, simple (yet profound) work which will grace any science reference collection. The bibliography ... cannot be faulted; the index is a marvel.' (*The New York Public Library*)

1867 **Rheology for chemists: an introduction**
J.W. Goodwin and R.W. Hughes Royal Society of Chemistry, 2000, 290pp. £29.50. ISBN 085404616X.
Introduces basic terminology of rheology and discusses limiting, temporal, and non-linear behaviour. Aims to give understanding of mechanisms responsible for the elastic, viscous, or viscoelastic behaviour of systems.

1868 **The role of the solvent in chemical reactions**
E. Buncel, R.A. Stairs and H. Wilson Oxford University Press, 2003, 159pp. £29.00. ISBN 0198511000.
Good short semi-quantitative review. Assumes the reader has taken courses in essentials of thermodynamics and kinetics, but gives brief reviews of each. Appendix characterizes selected solvents. Substantial bibliography. Index.
Series: Oxford Chemistry Masters.

1869 **Statistical mechanics made simple: a guide for students and researchers**
D.C. Mattis World Scientific, 2003. £16.00. ISBN 981238166X.
www.worldscibooks.com/bookseries.shtml
Wide-ranging, well reviewed text.
The publishers offer a wide range of relevant publications in this and related subjects: see the URL.
'Daniel Mattis's *Statistical mechanics made simple* is an admirable piece of work by an outstanding expert in the field ... for advanced graduate students, researchers, and professors, it contains a wealth of valuable material and unusual insights.' (*Physics Today*)

1870 **Stereochemistry**
D.G. Morris; Royal Society of Chemistry 2001, 170pp. £14.95. ISBN 085404602X.
www.rsc.org/tct [COMPANION]
Introduces basic terminology e.g. chirality, enantiomers, diastereoisomers and racemization, examples given to illustrate key concepts.
Series: Tutorial Chemistry Texts.

1871 **The world of physical chemistry**
K.J. Laidler Oxford University Press, 1995, 488pp. £35.00. ISBN 0198559194.
A history of physical and theoretical chemistry covering the origins of physical chemistry; communications in the physical sciences; the growth of the physical sciences; thermodynamics; kinetic theory and statistical mechanics; chemical spectroscopy; electrochemistry; chemical kinetics; colloid and surface chemistry; quantum chemistry.
'Laidler has provided a masterly survey of the field, which will help to put the record straight in many backwaters of the subject and in not a few estuaries too.' (*Nature*)

Dictionaries, thesauri, classifications

Dictionary of colloid and interface science
L.L. Schramm See entry no. 5072

Laws, standards, codes

1872 **Quantities, units and symbols in physical chemistry**
I. Mills, ed.; International Union of Pure and Applied Chemistry 3rd edn, Royal Society of Chemistry, 2004. ISBN 0854044337.
www.iupac.org/publications/books/author/mills.html [DESCRIPTION]
Forthcoming revision of the IUPAC *Green Book*, whose 2nd edn incorporated recommendations from the Bureau International des Poids et Mesures, the International Union of Pure and Applied Physics and the International Organization for Standardization as well as IUPAC itself.
2nd edn published by Blackwell Science (1993).

Associations & societies

1873 **Electrochemical Society**
www.electrochem.org
'Founded in 1902, The Electrochemical Society has become the leading society for solid-state and electrochemical science and technology. ECS has 8000 scientists and engineers in over 75 countries worldwide who hold individual membership, as well as roughly 100 corporations and laboratories who hold corporate membership.'
Useful up-to-date section *ECS Resource Information*.

1874 **International Society of Electrochemistry**
www.ise-online.org
Currently has about '1100 individual members and more than 30 Corporate Members (teaching institutions, non-profit-making research organizations and learned societies) and Corporate Sustaining Members (industrial and commercial organizations). Its membership comes from more than 60 countries and is organized in over 40 regional sections'.
Limited information for non-members.

1875 **North American Catalysis Society**
www.nacatsoc.org
Founded in 1956 as a forum for science of catalysis and related disciplines. Provides educational services; organizes and participates in professional meetings to report, discuss and exchange information and viewpoints in the field of catalysis.

Discovering print & electronic resources

1876 **Electrochemical Science and Technology Information Resource**
http://electrochem.cwru.edu/estir
General and varied information about electrochemistry in

thirteen sections. Extensive plain text listing: regularly updated.

Digital data, image & text collections

CPC program library
See entry no. 611

Directories & encyclopedias

1877 **Catalysis from A to Z: a concise encyclopedia**
B. Cornilis, ed. 2nd edn, Wiley-VCH, 2003, 840pp. £145.00. ISBN 3527303731.
Preface to 2nd edn quotes Sheldon: 'The world of catalysis is divided into three camps – heterogeneous, homogenous, and enzymatic – that do not communicate well with each other and tend to speak in 'different languages'. Here also there is a pressing need for integration.'

C.4600 keywords explained by 190 authors and co-authors. Literature citations appended to significant proportion of entries; 7pp list of general references. Model of its kind.

1878 **Encyclopedia of catalysis**
I.T. Horvath, ed. Wiley, 2002. 6 v., $2095.00. ISBN 0471241830.
Provides comprehensive coverage of homogeneous, heterogeneous, asymmetric, biomimetic, and biological catalysis. Includes principles of catalysis, scope of catalytic reactions, preparation, characterization, and use of catalysis including catalytic technology, modelling of catalytic processes, and related reaction engineering techniques.

1879 **Encyclopedia of chemical physics and physical chemistry**
N.D. Spencer and J.H. Moore Institute of Physics, 2001, 2796pp. 3 v., £600.00. ISBN 0750303131.
Extensive coverage in the closely related areas of chemical physics and physical chemistry. Focusing on both disciplines as interrelated, the encyclopedia enables specialists in both fields to conduct interdisciplinary research. Features include definitions of the scope of each subdiscipline and instructions on where to go for a more complete and detailed explanation.

Table of isotopes
R.B. Firestone, C.M. Baglin and S.Y.F. Chu, eds See entry no. 789

Handbooks & manuals

1880 **Atomic and electronic structures of solids**
E. Kaxiras Cambridge University Press, 2003, 676pp. £34.95. ISBN 0521523397.
Mathematically-based text with a wide-ranging integrated coverage. Mostly addresses theoretical concepts and tools relevant to the physics of solids with no attempt to treat related experimental facts. Useful appendices include five covering in turn elements of: classical electrodynamics; quantum mechanics; thermodynamics; statistical mechanics; elasticity theory – all, except the third – with lists of further reading.

Catalyst handbook
M.V. Twigg See entry no. 5118

Chemical thermodynamics for industry
T. Letcher, ed.; Royal Society of Chemistry See entry no. 5126

1881 **Comprehensive chemical kinetics**
Elsevier, 1969–. £179.00 (V. 40, 2004). ISBN 0444516530.
Purpose is background reference work, covering in a reasonably critical way practice and theory of kinetics, as well as kinetics of inorganic and organic reactions in gaseous and condensed phases and at interfaces (but excluding biochemical and electrochemical kinetics, unless very relevant). V. 40 is titled *Kinetics of multistep reactions.*

1882 **Condensed matter physics: crystals, liquids, liquid crystals, and polymers**
G. Strobl, ed. Springer, 2004, 379pp. £30.50. ISBN 3540003533.
Well written introduction dealing with the key characteristics of condensed matter: structures, susceptibilities, molecular fields, currents, and dynamics.
Translation of the original German version.

1883 **CRC handbook of radiation chemistry**
Y. Tabata, Y. Ito and S. Tagawa CRC Press, 1991, 937pp. ISBN 0849329957.
18 chapters with much tabular data and some references

- **NDRL Radiation Chemistry Data Center**
  http://allen.rad.nd.edu. Dedicated to the collection, evaluation, and dissemination of data characterizing the reactions of transient intermediates produced by radiation chemical and photochemical methods. Printed compilations and bibliographies; online documents and databases.

1884 **Electrochemical systems**
J. Newman and K.E. Thomas-Alyea 3rd edn, Wiley, 2004, 647pp. $115.00. ISBN 0471477567.
Established manual covering all the major areas of electrochemistry, from the basics of thermodynamics and electrode kinetics to transport phenomena in electrolytes, metals, and semiconductors. Extensive bibliography.

1885 **Encyclopedia of electrochemistry**
A.J. Bard and M. Stratmann Wiley-VCH, 2002–2004. 11 v., £1870.00. ISBN 3527302506.
V. 1. Thermodynamics and electrified interfaces; V. 2. Interfacial kinetics and mass transport; V. 3. Instrumentation and electroanalytical chemistry; V. 4. Corrosion and oxide films; V. 5. Electrochemical engineering; V. 6. Semiconductor electrodes and photoelectrochemistry; V. 7. Inorganic electrochemistry; V. 8. Organic electrochemistry; V. 9. Bioelectrochemistry; V. 10. Modified electrodes; V. 11. Index.

1886 **Fundamentals of quantum chemistry: molecular spectroscopy and modern electronic structure computations**
M.R. Mueller Kluwer Academic, 2001, 280pp. £50.50. ISBN 0306465965.
http://ebooks.kluweronline.com
Designed as practical introduction to quantum chemistry which is applied to explain molecular spectroscopy. Coverage includes classical mechanics; rotational motion; techniques of approximation; atomic structure and spectra etc.
Available online: see website.
'Is an excellent introduction to the discipline for advanced undergraduate students ... The text is very clear and readable, but

the book is complete enough to serve as a good reference.' (*Chemistry in Britain*)

1887 **Handbook of nuclear chemistry**
A. Vértes, S. Nagy and Z. Klencsár, ed. Kluwer Academic, 2004, 2800pp. 5 v., £1000.00. ISBN 1402013051.
http://reference.kluweronline.com
48 chapters divided between five standalone volumes: 1. Basics of nuclear science; 2. Elements and isotopes; 3. Chemical applications of nuclear reactions and radiations; 4. Radiochemistry and radiopharmaceutical chemistry in life sciences; 5. Instrumentation, separation techniques, environmental issues. Well produced; high-quality contributions; valuable appendices throughout the series (e.g. in V. 3, Appendix 4: Reference materials).
Available online: see website.

1888 **Handbook of surface and colloid chemistry**
K.S. Birdi 2nd edn, CRC Press, 2002, 784pp. CD-ROM version available, $299.95. ISBN 0849310792.
Summarizes current knowledge and recent developments in the chemistry of surface and colloidal systems, and its many practical applications. Topics of the 16 chapters include interfacial tension, solubilization in surfactant systems, and thermally sensitive latex particles.

1889 **Measurement of the thermodynamic properties of single phases**
A.R.H. Goodwin, K.N. Marsh and W.A. Wakeham, eds; International Union of Pure and Applied Chemistry Elsevier, 2003, 558pp. €195.00. ISBN 0444509313.
Detailed handbook covering: Temperature; Pressure; Mixture preparation and sampling hydrocarbon reservoir fluids; Density; Speed of sound; Calorimetry; Properties of mixing; Relative permittivity and refractive index; Extreme conditions.
Series: Experimental Thermodynamics, V. 6.

The physics and chemistry of materials
J.I. Gersten and F.W. Smith See entry no. 5857

1890 **Physics of atoms and molecules**
B.H. Bransden and C.J. Joachain 2nd edn, Prentice Hall, 2003, 1114pp. $111.40. ISBN 058235692X.
Comprehensive, well written handbook, in this edn presenting a revised account of molecular structure and spectra, extending the material on electronic and atomic collisions, and including two new chapters providing 'an introduction to the exciting advances of recent years and to some of the many important developments of the subject'.
1st edn 1983 (Longman Scientific and Technical).

1891 **The properties of gases and liquids**
B.E. Poling [et al.] 5th edn, McGraw-Hill, 2001, 768pp. $115.00. ISBN 0070116822.
Comprehensive and comprehensible treatment of properties of gases and liquids stressing understanding of basic laws governing behaviour of liquids and gases instead of associated mathematics. Treatment of topics suitable for engineers since allows quick understanding of phenomena and provides wealth of correlations and methods for estimating properties. Appendixes contain basic information for applying correlations shown.
4th edn 1987.

1892 **Superconductivity: fundamentals and applications**
W. Buckel and R. Kleiner 2nd edn, Wiley-VCH, 2004, 461pp. $85.00. ISBN 3527403493.
www.wiley.com/WileyCDA
Now classic text covering theory and applications.
Translation of the 6th German edn.

1893 **The theories of chemistry**
J.C.A. Boeyens Elsevier, 2003, 555pp. €190.00. ISBN 0444514910.
Innovative advanced treatment aiming, not to reformulate theoretical physics, but to identify the theoretical ideas fundamental to chemistry and recast them in more familiar style. 1. Basic mathematics. 2. Group theory. 3. Particles and waves. 4. Space and time. 5. Quantum theory. 6. Quantum chemistry. 7. Atoms and molecules. 8. Macrosystems. 9. Chemical change.

Thermodynamics of biochemical reactions
R.A. Alberty See entry no. 2085

Keeping up-to-date

1894 **Annual Review of Physical Chemistry**
Annual Reviews. $220.00 [V. 56, 2004]. ISBN 082431056X.
www.annurev.org/catalog/catalog.asp [DESCRIPTION]
'Physical chemistry provides a considerable basis for the study of sensing applications, biological measurements, and the physical properties of nanomaterials. This volume of the *Annual Review of Physical Chemistry* is fully allied with these trends, including broad groups of interrelated topics on single molecule spectroscopies and theory, more complex systems, interface dynamics, colloids, liquid-phase dynamics, and nanostructures.'

Biological Sciences

Public awareness of the biological sciences has probably never been higher. Media coverage of issues raised by cloning, gene therapy and the Human Genome Project has been extensive. As a result of this interest, new resources covering all aspects of the biological sciences are appearing every day, making it more difficult to find good, high-quality information amongst the morass of resources that are available.

One of the most difficult tasks in preparing this grouping was trying to decide on the most appropriate subject fields to use. Many fields were merged, created and deleted along the road to the final selection of 17.

The majority of the subject fields (BOTANY, ENTOMOLOGY, MARINE & FRESHWATER BIOLOGY, MICROBIOLOGY & VIROLOGY, MYCOLOGY, ORNITHOLOGY, PARASITOLOGY, PROTISTOLOGY and ZOOLOGY) bring together resources on particular groups of organisms. In most cases the allocation of resources in each of these fields is straightforward but, in cases where there was any doubt, the classification used in the *Tree of Life* web-site was used as the basis for the decision. Therefore, for example, resources dealing with algae (seaweeds, etc.) have been included in the PROTISTOLOGY field rather than in BOTANY.

The nine fields listed above also usually took priority over the remaining fields when resources covered aspects of the biology of individual or groups of organisms. For example, resources that dealt with whale conservation were included in MARINE & FRESHWATER BIOLOGY rather than in BIODIVERSITY & CONSERVATION (and note that resources on water-based animals, including amphibians, have tended to be placed in that field rather than in ZOOLOGY).

We have not used the subject heading 'environment' or 'environmental science' within TNW. There is of course immense (and to us justifiable) concern about the effects on the environment of STM-based practice. We have included a number of generic resources treating this theme within the ECOLOGY subject field, though no doubt we will need to return to the arena in TNW Volume 2 (Social Sciences): the solutions seem to us to lie principally within the commercial, economic, political and social domains, rather than within science, technology and medicine *per se*. Also, it has seemed more helpful (and salutary) to cite within this volume resources treating the environmental effects of use of a particular STM-based technique alongside those discussing the activity itself, rather than separately.

Nevertheless, it was deemed sensible to concentrate resources relevant to efforts to contain and constrain such effects within particular subject fields: respectively, these are ENVIRONMENTAL & OCCUPATIONAL HEALTH (within the subject grouping HEALTH); and ENVIRONMENTAL ENGINEERING (within ENGINEERING).

Introductions to the subject

1895 Biology: the unity and diversity of life
C. Starr and R. Taggart 10th edn, Thomson Brooks/Cole, 2004, 933pp. Includes CD-ROM and access to INFOTRAC, $120.95. ISBN 0534274137.
www.info.brookscole.com/starr10 [COMPANION]
Good undergraduate textbook covering all areas of the biological sciences. Introduction followed by seven parts: Principles of cellular life; Principles of inheritance; Principles of evolution; Evolution and biodiversity; Plant structure and function; Animal structure and function; Ecology and behaviour. Glossary; Subject and Application indexes. Accompanying website includes links to related sites, quizzes, tutorials.

1896 Calculus for biology and medicine
C. Neuhauser 2nd edn, Pearson/Prentice Hall, 2004, 822pp. $128.00. ISBN 0131234412.
Written exclusively for students in the biological and medical sciences showing throughout how calculus can help understand phenomena in nature.
1st edn 2000.

1897 Experimenting with humans and animals: from Galen to animal rights
A. Guerrini Johns Hopkins University Press, 2003, 165pp. $18.95. ISBN 0801871972.
Seven chapters: Bodies of evidence; Animals, machines, and morals; Disrupting God's plan; Cruelty and kindliness; The microbe hunters; Polio and primates; Conclusion: Human rights, animal rights, and the conduct of science.
Series: Johns Hopkins Introductory Studies in the History of Science.

Five kingdoms: an illustrated guide to the phyla of life on earth
L. Margulis and K.V. Schwartz See entry no. 2848

1898 A history of molecular biology (Histoire de la biologie moléculaire)
M. Morange Harvard University Press, 1998, 336pp. Translated by Matthew Cobb, $22.95. ISBN 0674001699.
21 chapters in three parts: The birth of molecular biology; The development of molecular biology; The expansion of molecular biology. Appendix gives definition of terms. Well written – and well translated – volume. Good, rather different, introduction to this arena.
'Well-researched and clearly written ... Morange is critical of the triumphalist and reductionist claims of molecular biology, and ends the book by reflecting on its place in the life sciences. Writing from Paris, he is able to stand back from the orthodox story with its focus on 'les Anglo-Saxons', giving credit to others such as Nobel prize-winners André Lwoff, Jacques Monod and François Jacob.' (*New Scientist*)

Human molecular biology: an introduction to the molecular language of health and disease
R.J. Epstein See entry no. 3570

1899 **Life: the science of biology**
W.K. Purves [et al.] 7th edn, Sinauer, 2004, 1120pp. $119.95. ISBN 0716798565.
http://bcs.whfreeman.com/thelifewire [COMPANION]
Standard undergraduate biology textbook providing very good overview of the subject. Eight parts: The cell; Information and heredity; Development; Evolutionary processes; The evolution of diversity; The biology of flowering plants; The biology of animals; Ecology and biogeography. Glossary; Subject index. Suggested further readings on website.

1900 **Of flies, mice, and men (Souris, la mouche et l'homme)**
F. Jacob Harvard University Press, 1998, 158pp. Translated by Giselle Weiss, $14.95. ISBN 0674005384.
François Jacob received the Nobel Prize for Medicine and Physiology in 1965 for his work on the mechanisms of gene regulation in micro-organisms. Introduction; The importance of the unpredictable; The fly; The mouse; The erector set; Self and other; Good and evil; Beauty and truth; Conclusion.

Dictionaries, thesauri, classifications

1901 **BioABACUS: biotechnology abbreviation & acronym uncovering service**
M. Rimer, ed.; New Mexico State University
darwin.nmsu.edu/~molbio/bioABACUShome.htm
Useful site which – despite a focus on 'biotechnology' – can be used to search for acronyms or journal abbreviations across the biological sciences, including in biochemistry, cell biology and bioinformatics. Database can be searched with an abbreviation or acronym to find the full version or vice versa. Links for many of the terms; however, last updated 2000.

1902 **Biocomplexity Thesaurus**
National Biological Information Infrastructure CSA.
thesaurus.nbii.gov
Developed 2002–2003 through a partnership between the NBII and CSA Illumina, the bibliographic database provider). Created through the merger of five existing thesauri covering aquatic sciences and fisheries, life sciences, pollution, sociology, and the environment. Site is developed and maintained by CSA together with the Center for Biological Informatics of the US Geological Survey – the operating agent for NBII.

1903 **BioTech's Life Science Dictionary**
Indiana University
biotech.icmb.utexas.edu/search/dict-search.html
Contains brief definitions for more than 8000 terms covering subjects such as biochemistry, ecology, genetics, botany and cell biology. It is searchable but uses US spellings (e.g. color rather than colour) and will not find the alternative spellings. Maintained by the University's Indiana Institute for Molecular and Cellular Biology as part of its BioTech collection of life sciences resources and reference tools.

CAB Thesaurus
CAB International See entry no. 2926

1904 **Concise dictionary of biomedicine and molecular biology**
P.-S. Juo CRC Press, 2001, 1154pp. $149.95. ISBN 0849309409.
Very useful reference work that provides concise definitions for more than 30,000 terms across the fields of cell biology, microbiology, biochemistry, biomedical sciences and genetics. Definitions are generally only a line or two in length but those given for chemical substances usually include a drawing of the structure.

1905 **A dictionary of biology**
E. Martin and R.S. Hine, eds 4th edn, Oxford University Press, 2000, 641pp. £8.99. ISBN 0192801023.
www.oxfordreference.com
With over 4500 entries, a very useful dictionary providing quite detailed definitions of terms in all areas of biological sciences. Includes several biographical entries for scientists and many entries also include illustrations. Appendices cover SI units, overviews of animal and plant kingdoms and geological time scale.
Available online: see website.

1906 **Dictionary of biomedical sciences**
P.J. Gosling Taylor & Francis, 2002, 444pp. £15.99. ISBN 0415237238.
Concise definitions for more than 7000 terms from disciplines including anatomy, biochemistry, cytology, genetics and pharmacology. Appendices contain list of UK and US biomedical organizations, short bibliography, suggestions for further reading.

1907 **The Facts On File dictionary of biology**
R. Hine, ed. 3rd edn, Checkmark Books, 1999, 361pp. $44.00. ISBN 0816039070.
www.factsonfile.com
Good basic dictionary with definitions for more than 3000 terms used in all fields of biology. Includes some illustrations; appendices cover animal and plant kingdoms and amino acids chemical structures.
Series: Facts On File Science Dictionaries: 20 vols, see website.

1908 **Henderson's dictionary of biological terms**
E. Lawrence, ed. 12th edn, Prentice Hall, 2000, 719pp. $24.56. ISBN 0582414989.
Generally regarded as the 'standard' biological dictionary. With definitions for more than 23,000 terms its coverage of the subject is vastly superior to that of any of the comparable works. Appendices cover etymological origins of biological terms, virus families and overviews of the plant, animal, fungal, bacterial and protist groupings.

NAL Agricultural Thesaurus: NALT
National Agricultural Library See entry no. 2928

1909 **The Penguin dictionary of biology**
M. Thain and M. Hickman 10th edn, Penguin, 2000, 678pp. £7.99. ISBN 0140513590.
Very good dictionary that provides quite detailed definitions for more than 7500 terms across all fields of biology. There are some brief biographies and a number of entries also include illustrations.

Laws, standards, codes

1910 **Quantities, symbols, units, and abbreviations in the life sciences: a guide for authors and editors**
A. Kotyk, comp. Humana Press, 1999, 130pp. $39.50. ISBN 0896036499.
www.humanapress.com
Useful compilation providing definitions of, and recommendations for, use of units, symbols, acronyms and abbreviations. Arranged by subject rather than alphabetically so the reader may need to check several headings to find a particular item.

Official & quasi-official bodies

1911 **Biological Records Centre** [UK]
www.brc.ac.uk
Founded 1964, co-ordinates recording of species found in Britain (other than birds, which are dealt with by British Trust for Ornithology). Information about the Centre and its activities, including on the species atlases published as a result of the recording schemes, as well as about the schemes and their organizers themselves.

1912 **Biotechnology and Biological Sciences Research Council** [UK]
www.bbsrc.ac.uk
Leading funding agency for biological research in universities and research institutes within the UK. Areas covered are organized into seven research programmes: Agri-food; Animal sciences; Biochemistry and cell biology; Biomolecular sciences; Engineering and biological systems; Genes and developmental biology; Plant and microbial sciences. Each of these areas has its own quite detailed pages which can provide good overviews of current research priorities in the relevant disciplines.

Website gives information on grants available, how to apply for them, and allows access to Oasis database containing data on all research funded at the Council's eight strategic research institutes, their six structural biology centres and about another dozen centres and institutes they support. Much other helpful information including a What's New? section.

Global Environment Facility
See entry no. 5556

1913 **International Union of Biological Sciences**
www.iubs.org
Created in 1919, was founding member of body now known as International Council for Science and has a membership of about 80 societies from around the world.

1914 **National Biological Information Infrastructure** [USA]
www.nbii.gov
Collaborative programme aiming to provide increased access to data and information on the USA's biological resources. Well designed site giving access to very wide range and considerable depth of information, categorized: Current biological issues; Biological disciplines; Geographical perspectives; Teacher resources; Data and information resources – the last including, for instance, access to lists of expertise databases, to information about metadata initiatives and tools, to websites of museum collections, and so on. An impressive compilation – though some areas of the site have not recently been refreshed.

- **Center for Biological Informatics** http://biology.usgs.gov/cbi. Operating agent for NBII, but also develops, identifies, and provides access to tools that facilitate collection and use of biological information and data.
- **The CERES/NBII Thesaurus Partnership Project** http://ceres.ca.gov/thesaurus. Collaboration of NBII with CERES, the California Environmental Resources Evaluation System, aimed at developing an integrated environmental thesaurus and thesaurus networking tool set for metadata development and keyword searching.

Natural Environment Research Council
See entry no. 844

1915 **NSF: Directorate for Biological Sciences** [USA]
National Science Foundation
www.nsf.gov/funding/research_edu_community.jsp
Responsible for most NSF programmes in biology. However, the helpful site, providing data and leads about existing and prospective initiatives, notes that biologically relevant activities are supported by virtually all parts of the Foundation. Also, NSF does not normally support bioscience research with disease-related goals – such as work on etiology, diagnosis or treatment of physical or mental disease, abnormality, or malfunction in human beings or animals.

President's Council on Bioethics
See entry no. 3468

Research centres & institutes

CAB International
See entry no. 2938

1916 **Hastings Center** [USA]
www.thehastingscenter.org
Independent, non-partisan, non-profit institute founded in 1969 to explore fundamental and emerging ethical and related questions in health care, biotechnology, and the environment. Good descriptions of wide ranging research programme; publications; library; links.

Kennedy Institute of Ethics
See entry no. 3470

Nuffield Council on Bioethics
See entry no. 3472

1917 **Salk Institute for Biological Studies** [USA]
www.salk.edu
Founded 1963 by Jonas Salk, developer of the polio vaccine, it carries out research in molecular biology, genetics, neuroscience and plant biology. News releases, seminars and events, education and outreach, technology transfer – for the last the Office of Technology Management section of the site listing all the technologies that are available for licensing: 'Our mission is to maximize patent protection for Institute technology and facilitate the transfer of such technology to the private sector'. Good, well categorized set of links (in 'Biology Resources' within Faculty and Research website area).

Associations & societies

1918 **American Institute of Biological Sciences**
www.aibs.org
Founded 1947, umbrella organization representing more than 80 professional societies. Free access to Virtual Library containing plenary lectures by some of the world's most eminent biologists recorded at AIBS Annual Meetings from 2000 onwards; additional content includes presentations from AIBS National Roundtable series.

Website gives details of number of important policy and other initiatives, including IBCRS: Infrastructure for Biology at Regional to Continental Scales, which has a current special focus NEON: National Ecological Observatory Network.

- **ActionBioscience.org: promoting bioscience literacy** www.actionbioscience.org. Designed to encourage general public, students, teachers to find out more about biological sciences current issues. Peer-reviewed articles and teaching resources in: Biodiversity; Environment; Genomics; Biotechnology; Evolution; New Frontiers; Education.
- **BioScience** BioOne, 1964–, Monthly. $294.00. ISSN 00063568. www.aibs.org/bioscience [DESCRIPTION]. Important life sciences journal publishing research articles, reviews, new books lists, information on US policy as relates to biology. Articles written for wide readership. Access to cover article, book reviews, education column freely available.

1919 **American Society for Gravitational and Space Biology**
http://asgsb.indstate.edu
Founded in 1984. Good sets of educational and other resources, including a useful series of Fact Sheets.

1920 **American Society of Naturalists**
www.amnat.org
Established in 1883 the Society organizes meetings and publishes the journal *The American Naturalist*. Regularly updated directory of members (c.1100 records).

1921 **Association of Applied Biologists** [UK]
www.aab.org.uk
Founded in 1904, has as its objectives: 'To promote the study and advancement of all branches of Biology and in particular (but without prejudice to the generality of the foregoing), to foster the practice, growth and development of applied biology, including the application of biological sciences for the production and preservation of food, fibre and other materials and for the maintenance and improvement of earth's physical environment'. C. 1000 members. Publications.

1922 **Biosciences Federation** [UK]
www.bsf.ac.uk
Umbrella organization for some 30 UK societies involved with the life sciences; further 50 or so affiliated societies are represented by the INSTITUTE OF BIOLOGY: all these listed. Useful Science Policy Priorities documents: 2005–2009 version currently being formulated. Also work of the Animal Science Group whose web pages have helpful set of 30 links to 'Websites of Groups with a Related Interest in Animal Experiments'.

1923 **British Naturalists' Association**
www.bna-naturalists.org
Founded 1905 and one of the oldest UK natural history societies. Website provides good details of its activities (both nationally and especially locally), including of its BNA Young Naturalists subsection. Library area of the site presents range of resources including Phenological Reports (studies of seasonal changes in animals), simple identification guides for common British wildlife, BNA Guide to Practical Field Work with Small Mammals. Good resource.

European Federation of Biotechnology
See entry no. 5023

1924 **European Life Scientist Organization**
www.elso.org
Founded 2000 principally to organize cross-disciplinary meetings similar to the 'successful US meetings like the one organized by the AMERICAN SOCIETY FOR CELL BIOLOGY every year'. Details of their meetings, and also their involvements with EU policy issues. Late 2004 site had had limited development; but links section includes quite detailed descriptions of over 40 'journals on the net'.

1925 **European Molecular Biology Organization**
www.embo.org
Major organization formed in 1964 to promote and encourage the development of molecular biology in Europe – but now uses the by-line 'Promoting biosciences in Europe', denoting its perceived broader remit. Wide range of activities include organizing meetings and courses, publishing journals, promoting the biosciences to the public, and developing an electronic information programme. Well designed site with many useful links in its various sections.

- **E-BioSci** www.e-biosci.org. Software platform for access/retrieval of full text/factual data being developed owing to 'torrent of biological data, held in a plethora of genomic sequence, sequence-related and other types of databases and scattered across many thousands of articles'.

1926 **Federation of American Societies for Experimental Biology**
www.faseb.org
Founded 1912, FASEB now provides an umbrella organization for 14 member and 8 associate member life sciences and biomedical organizations. Good source of information – especially on careers. Also through its Office of Public Affairs pages which, for instance, provide access to Breakthroughs in Bioscience, a series of illustrated essays that explain recent breakthroughs in biomedical research and how they are important to society.

- **FASEB Journal** 1987–, 15/year. $798.00. ISSN 08926638. www.fasebj.org [DESCRIPTION]. One of the most important life sciences research journals, publishing original articles, research communications and review articles in all areas of the life sciences, with a particular emphasis on the molecular aspects of the subject.

1927 **Institute of Biology** [UK]
www.iob.org
Founded 1950, the professional body for biologists in the UK, currently with 14,000 members and 76 affiliated societies. Extensive education and training, publications, policy advice activities, and vibrant network of regional branches. As well as details of all these, site also includes careers information and a collection of fact sheets on topical issues such as stem cell research and foot-and-mouth disease. Good set of well categorized links

- **Biologist: Journal of the Institute of Biology** 1969–, Quarterly. £106.00. ISSN 00063347. Peer-reviewed journal that contains research articles, reviews, letters and book reviews on all aspects of the biological sciences. Content is written in a very straightforward style making it accessible to a wide readership.

- **Journal of Biological Education** Quarterly. £94.00. ISSN 00219266. Policy developments; research into biology teaching, learning, and assessment; advances relevant to biology syllabi; current opinion from world-renowned experts; Web Watch 'Guide to what's hot (and what's not) in biology education online'.

1928 **International Biometric Society**
www.tibs.org
Founded 1947, and 'devoted to the mathematical and statistical aspects of biology ... The terms 'Biometrics' and 'Biometry' have been used since early in the 20th century to refer to the field of development of statistical and mathematical methods applicable to data analysis problems in the biological sciences'. Publishes journal *Biometrics* and, jointly with American Statistical Association, the *Journal of Agricultural, Biological and Environmental Statistics*. Useful online newsletter. Annual conference.

1929 **International Organization of Biological Field Stations**
www.iobfs.org
Field stations provide biologists with an opportunity to carry out research outside of the laboratory and they are therefore particularly important for disciplines such as ecology and marine and freshwater biology. The IOBFS is based in the US but its membership includes field stations from around the world. Site includes an extensive directory of stations, a Listserv and a selection of international internet resources.

1930 **International Society for Biological and Environmental Repositories**
www.isber.org
Primary goal to provide information and guidance on the safe and effective management of specimen collections. Good introductory Bibliography with sub-sections: Establishing a tissue bank; Informed consent issues; Privacy and confidentiality issues; IBR review of tissue banking protocols; Pharmacogenics; Collection and use of samples from newborns; Commercial biobanks; International; Books. Site also provides quarterly downloadable PDF newsletter.

1931 **London Natural History Society** [UK]
www.users.globalnet.co.uk/~lnhsweb
Founded in 1858. Significant programme of events; specialist sections; scientific work; etc. Society's library is currently held in the Imperial College London Library.

1932 **National Association of Biology Teachers** [USA]
www.nabt.org
'The leader in life science education.' Well chosen selective and annotated set of links organized into a score of sections running from 'Animals & Insects' to 'Women in Science'. Publishes *American Biology Teacher* magazine every two months.

1933 **National Federation for Biological Recording** [UK]
www.nfbr.org.uk
Recording of the sighting of species is an important information source for many areas of biology. The NFBR is a membership society for individuals and organizations that are involved in biological recording. Website includes very detailed set of links to related sites including to database of UK Local Records Centres, its maintenance funded by the UK's National Biodiversity Network.

1934 **Natural Science Collections Alliance** [USA]
www.nscalliance.org
Network of natural science collections located in USA, Mexico and Canada that includes institutions such as the American Museum of Natural History and the National Museum of Natural History based at the Smithsonian. Much of the website is 'Under Construction' while other sections, e.g. 'Conferences & Events', are very out of date. However, the site is still useful for the list of members (with links to their websites), and the Biodiversity Informatics section, which includes a glossary, a list of databases and further links to related sites.

1935 **Nature CANADA**
www.cnf.ca
Formerly the Canadian Nature Federation whose mission is 'the protection of nature, its diversity and the processes that sustain it'. Good set of educational publications and other resources. Details of conservation work.

1936 **Society for Cryobiology**
www.societyforcryobiology.org
Cryobiology is the study of biological materials or systems (cells, tissues, etc.) at low temperatures. Founded in 1964, the Society is based in the USA but has an international membership of biologists, medics and physical scientists. Pleasant website including access to PDF current issue of the Society's newsletter.

- **Society for Low Temperature Biology** www.sltb.info. Also founded in 1964, the Society is based in the UK and draws the majority of its membership from Europe.

1937 **Society for Experimental Biology**
www.sebiology.org
Founded in 1923, the SEB is based in the UK but has an international membership of over 2000. Education & Public Affairs section of the site includes links to related resources, careers information, as well as to BUGS, a separate site aimed at undergraduates. Extensive Publications section.

1938 **Society for In Vitro Biology** [USA]
www.sivb.org
'In vitro' refers to the study of biological processes in artificial environments (as opposed to 'in vivo', the study of processes in living organisms). The SIVB was founded in 1946 and is based in the USA. Employment; Marketing; Meetings; Publications; etc. The Education section of the site includes a guide to Terminology associated with cell, tissue and organ culture, molecular biology and molecular genetics.

1939 **Society for Integrative and Comparative Biology**
www.sicb.org
Founded in 1902, the SICB is based in the USA but has an international membership of more than 2000 across most fields of biology. Lively society with good links to details of publications and other services.

1940 **Society for the History of Natural History**
www.shnh.org
Founded in 1936, the SHNH is an international society that is concerned with the history of all aspects of natural history, including expeditions, collections, art and

bibliography. Biannual international conference, publications, small collection of links to related websites.

- **Archives of Natural History** Science History Publications, 1981–, Biannual. £98.00. ISSN 02609541. www.shnh.org/PUB_ANH_main.htm [DESCRIPTION]. Results of bibliographic and historical research on all aspects of natural history. Recent topics include: Darwin's correspondence; publication history for the journal EVOLUTION; hummingbird nest from Cook's *Endeavour* voyage.

1941 **Society for the Preservation of Natural History Collections** [USA]
www.spnhc.org
Founded in 1985: supports development and preservation of natural history collections, including library, archive and related collections, in the US and Canada. In addition to general information about the Society's activities, site also includes electronic version of its Guidelines for the Care of Natural History Collections.

- **Federation for Natural Sciences Collections Research: FENSCORE University of Manchester**. fenscore.man.ac.uk. Founded 1980 to co-ordinate activities of natural science curators in the UK. Access to national/regional databases of holdings (specimens, collectors, dates, published/unpublished literature) of UK natural history collections. Last update 1999.

1942 **Society for the Study of Human Biology**
www-staff.lboro.ac.uk/~hungn/sshb/index.htm
Relatively new society but now has more than 150 members from around the world. Objective is 'general advancement and promotion of research in the biology of human populations in all its branches, including human variability and genetics, human adaptability and ecology, and human evolution'. Publishes journal *Annals of Human Biology*.

Libraries, archives, museums

1943 **Academy of Natural Sciences** [USA]
www.acnatsci.org
Founded in 1812, the Academy is based in Philadelphia and is composed of three main parts: Museum; Educational section; Research section – comprising the Environmental Research Group, the Center for Systematic Biology and Evolution, and the Academy Library. The website, with more than 2000 pages, is a rich source of information on each of these areas of the Academy's work, with good sections for families and kids.

- **Ewell Sale Stewart Library** www.acnatsci.org/library. More than 200,000 vols covering all aspects of natural history. Online catalogue plus access to several digital collections including images from rare natural history books.

1944 **American Museum of Natural History**
www.amnh.org
The Museum was founded in New York in 1869. It has research programmes in anthropology, physical sciences, vertebrate and invertebrate zoology and palaeontology as well as extensive work in biodiversity and conservation and the Institute for Comparative Genomics.

Website provides access to a rich fund of information. Particularly worth noting are: Ology, science-rich website for children; Resources for Learning, collection of over 800 activities, articles, evidence and analysis and more, for educators, families, students and anyone interested in teaching or learning about science; Science Bulletin, current topics in astrophysics, earth sciences and biodiversity, with feature stories, interactive data visualizations and weekly snapshots of news of the natural world.

The Museum also houses an important research library that has been in the forefront of providing innovative products and services in recent years.

- **Center for Biodiversity and Conservation** http://research.amnh.org/biodiversity. Interdisciplinary research in: Invertebrate conservation; Remote sensing / geographic information systems; Conservation genetics. Also collaboration with the Museum's Committee on Recently Extinct Organisms.

1945 **Australian Museum**
www.austmus.gov.au
Excellent site – especially strong on natural history. Of particular value is the section Online Science, giving access to a wide range of data, information and publications details.

1946 **CABI Bioscience Libraries**
CAB International
www.cabi-bioscience.org/Html/BioscienceLibraries.htm
Established jointly with Imperial College, the Michael Way Library at Silwood Park, Ascot, holds books, journals and reprints that deal with applied entomology, crop protection and related topics. The library holdings are included in the main Imperial College London Library catalogue which can be searched online (www.imperial.ac.uk/library/resources/cataccess.htm).

CAB also operates a Bioscience Library at Egham that specializes in mycology, plant pathology, plant nematology and biodeterioration.

The CABI Bioscience Library total holdings span four centuries of international agricultural publishing and include many rare or unique runs of journals or reports.

1947 **California Academy of Sciences**
www.calacademy.org
Founded in 1853, the Academy consists of the Steinhart Aquarium, a Natural History Museum, the Morrison Planetarium, a Library, and eight research departments (Anthropology, Aquatic Biology, Botany, Entomology, Herpetology, Ichthyology, Invertebrate Zoology & Geology, and Ornithology & Mammalogy).

Well laid-out site with excellent use of graphics and images reveal a wealth of resources.

1948 **Field Museum** [USA]
www.fieldmuseum.org
Very good clearly-laid-out site. 'The Museum's curatorial and scientific staff in the four departments of Anthropology, Botany, Geology, and Zoology conduct basic research in the fields of systematic biology and anthropology, and also have responsibility for collections management and collaboration in public programs with the Departments of Education and Exhibits. Since its founding the Field Museum has been an international leader in evolutionary biology and paleontology, and archaeology and ethnography.'

1949 **National Museum of Natural History** [USA]
www.mnh.si.edu
Extensive and well structured website providing information about this Smithsonian Museum's exhibitions, its educational resources and the research activities of its seven science departments: Anthropology, Botany, Entomology, Mineral sciences, Paleobiology, Zoology – Invertebrate, Zoology –

Vertebrate. Also access within the Research & Collections section of the site to a significant set of Databases, including: searchable lists of specimens, illustrations, anthropological collections, and information resources that support or are the products of taxonomic and nomenclatural research.

- **National Museum of Natural History Library** www.sil.si.edu/libraries/nmnh-hp.htm. One of 20 libraries within the Smithsonian Institution Libraries, consisting of a Main Location and 15 specialized collections throughout the Museum building.

1950 Natural History Museum, Library and Information Services [UK]

www.nhm.ac.uk/library

The Library of the Natural History Museum contains one of the finest collections of natural history literature and related materials in the world, with over 800,000 books, more than 20,000 journals and the third largest collection of watercolour drawings in Britain. It also houses the Museum archives.

The Library is actually made up of six separate collections: the Botany, Earth Sciences, Entomology, Zoology and General libraries are at the South Kensington site; there is also an ornithology library supporting the work of the Natural History Museum, Bird Group. All of the libraries are open to the public by appointment and the Library's important catalogue is available online. As well as more details of the Library's holdings, the website also provides access to digital copies of images within its Art Collections.

- **Natural Selection Resource Discovery Network**. nature.ac.uk. Extensive and well used gateway within the UK Resource Discovery Network's BIOME hub, whose descriptions of web-based resources are created and maintained by NHM Library staff.

1951 Natural History Museum [UK]

www.nhm.ac.uk

The NHM traces its history back to 1756 when the collection of Sir Hans Sloane moved to the British Museum where it was located until 1881 when the Museum opened at its current site in South Kensington. The Museum's collections – totalling some 70 million specimens – support major research programmes in botany, entomology, mineralogy, palaeontology, and zoology, which are organized into seven Themes: Animal and human health; Origins and history of the Earth; Ecology and conservation; The environment; Biodiversity; Evolution; Collections management.

Very well designed and structured website provides access to wealth of information about the science, exhibitions and educational activities of the Museum: check the excellent Site map – where, for instance, there are links to the Museum's collections and research Data Locator, as well as to its Collections Navigator, planned eventually to provide a collection-level description of every collection, of whatever form and format, in the institution. There is a good publications section with an online bookshop.

Relatively new are videos of some 200 presentations given by Museum scientists in its Darwin Centre on topics such as: DNA and genetics; Extreme environments; Fakes and forgeries; Parasites. There are live webcasts of the latest presentations.

- **Biodiversity and WORLDMAP** www.nhm.ac.uk/science/projects/worldmap. Arising from the Convention on Biological Diversity, aims 'to develop and apply appropriate, explicit and accountable methods to tackle problems in biogeography and in biodiversity assessment to meet conservation needs'. Uses innovative software.
- **Nature Navigator** www.nhm.ac.uk/naturenavigator. Elegant single access point to information on more than 8000 of the best-known species that occur in Britain. Includes reproductions of over 6000 original paintings and illustrations held in the libraries of the Museum.

1952 Oxford University Museum of Natural History

www.oum.ox.ac.uk

Founded in 1860, the Museum houses the University's natural history specimen collections and four scientific departments (Entomology, Geology, Mineralogy and Petrology). The website provides more information about the Museum, its collections (including searchable specimen collection databases), and provides a children's Learning Zone.

- **The Hope and Arkell Libraries** www.oum.ox.ac.uk/library.htm. C.14,000 books, 8000 of which deal with entomology, with the others covering geology, mineralogy and zoology. Also holds a large collection of journals and an important manuscript collection. Its catalogue is online, and it is open to all researchers.

Portal & task environments

1953 BEN: BiosciEdNet

American Association for the Advancement of Science

www.biosciednet.org/portal [REGISTRATION]

Relatively new resource aiming to bring together digital resources from variety of professional associations and societies and make them available to teachers and other educators. Database of resources can be searched or browsed by subject or type of resource (bibliography, database, laboratory manual, etc). Collaboration with currently about 30 USA-based organizations – with more participants sought who would like to make their materials 'more accessible to biological educators in undergraduate, graduate, and professional schools through the BEN Portal'.

BioethicsWeb

Wellcome Trust and Resource Discovery Network See entry no. 3490

1954 Biology Online: information in the life sciences

R. Lees

www.biology-online.org

Three main elements: online dictionary of biological terms; collection of tutorials; small collection of links to related websites. Dictionary provides brief definitions for about 3000 terms and can be either searched or browsed. Tutorials provide a brief introduction to a range of topics including cell biology, genetics and evolution and freshwater ecology. In 2004 a forum section was added. Good introductory site.

1955 Biology4all [UK]

University of Central Lancashire

www.biology4all.com

Really useful collection of resources aimed at biology teachers, school pupils and undergraduates maintained by the University's Department of Biological Sciences and endorsed by the Biosciences Federation. Provides information on UK higher education, teaching resources, careers information and much more. The Speakers Database holds details of over 400 university academics and researchers who are willing to visit schools and colleges to give talks on their subject specialities.

1956 **BiologyBrowser: free information from a trusted source**
Thomson BIOSIS.
www.biologybrowser.org
Access to large collection of links to web resources that are searchable by organism name (common or scientific), subject or geographical region; also to a number of free resources that have been produced by BIOSIS.

- **Index to organism names** www.biosis.org.uk/ion/search.htm. Brings together data on organism names from a number of different resources including ZOOLOGICAL RECORD and ALGAEBASE. Currently covers animals (all names reported in ZR since 1978), algae, fungi and mosses.

Global Change Master Directory
National Aeronautics and Space Administration See entry no. 862

1957 **LTSN Bioscience** [UK]
University of Leeds and Higher Education Academy
bio.ltsn.ac.uk
'One of 24 Subject Centres, funded by the four UK higher education funding bodies, to promote and support high quality learning, teaching and assessment in UK higher education.' Apart from general information on activities, site provides access to three useful collections of resources: Practical compendium – tried and tested practical exercises in the biological sciences; Knowledgebase – collection of evaluated resources, including book reviews; ImageBank.

- **ImageBank LTSN Bioscience**. bio.ltsn.ac.uk/imagebank. Collection of images across all fields of biology that have been copyright-cleared for educational uses. Includes valuable links section providing subject-grouped access to websites of wide range of other worldwide bioscience image collections.

National Center for Research Resources
See entry no. 3498

1958 **NHBS**
www.nhbs.com
Natural history, environment and science bookstore whose catalogue has become a comprehensive guide to natural history literature in its own right. Apart from the catalogue and its associated ordering facilities, the bookstore offers a range of useful current awareness and other services.

Discovering print & electronic resources

1959 **Bio Links Online Database**
Biozone International.
www.biozone.co.nz/links.html
Attractive access to large collection of links on a range of biological subjects including animal behaviour, biotechnology, evolution and space biology (exobiology). The entry for each link includes a brief description of the content of the site. Regularly updated.

1960 **Bio Netbook**
Institut Pasteur
www.pasteur.fr/recherche/BNB/bnb-en.html
Directory of more than 8000 web pages presented with simple but effective search screens. Covers all areas of biology but has a slight bias towards the molecular side of the subject (biochemistry, bioinformatics, etc). Can also be browsed.

1961 **BioChemHub: the online biology and chemistry education center** [USA]
D.K. Schmidel and W.G. Wojcik, comps
biochemhub.com
This site brings together a collection of links to sites that provide educational resources in biology and chemistry. Some of the categories – e.g. Colleges, Graduate schools, Science textbooks – only include links that have been paid for. However, very clearly laid out site.

Biological & Agricultural Index Plus
See entry no. 3025

1962 **Biological Abstracts**
Thomson BIOSIS, 1927–, Monthly. ISSN 01926985.
www.biosis.org/products/ba [DESCRIPTION]
The most comprehensive single guide to the biological literature available. Indexes more than 4000 journals as well as books, reports, patents, meetings, multimedia items and other sources, covering all aspects of the subject. The print version includes author, organism and subject indexes in each issue and as annual cumulative indexes.
Available online and in variety of versions: see website.

- **BIOSIS Controlled Vocabulary** www.biosis.org/support/bcv. Controlled vocabulary terms used in BIOSIS system: Major concepts; Super taxa; New taxon/fossil modifiers; Taxa note terms; Organ system modifiers; Disease modifiers; Drug modifiers; Sequence type affiliations; Geographic classifiers; Institution types.
- **BIOSIS Serial Sources BIOSIS**BIOSIS, 1995–, Annual. ISSN 10862951. www.biosis.org/products/bss [DESCRIPTION]. Listing of 5000 current titles, as well as the 13,000 archival titles reviewed by BIOSIS. Full title, frequency, history notes, ISSN, and publisher addresses. Includes review annuals, proceedings of conferences, research reports, etc.

1963 **Biological Journals and Abbreviations**
G. Patton, ed.
http://home.ncifcrf.gov/research/bja
Abbreviations, full titles, and links to some WWW pages for a large variety of biological and medical journals. Searchable and browsable.

1964 **Biology Digest**
Plexus Publishing, Monthly. $149.00 [2004]. ISSN 00952958.
http://books.infotoday.com/infoscience/BioDigest.shtml [DESCRIPTION]
Covers the whole of the life sciences; c.300 abstracts per month.
Available online: see website.
'Finally, an abstracting service for student scientists and their educators. *Biology Digest* is an impressive publication, gleaning timely information from about 350 technical journals and offering comprehensible digests at the high school and undergraduate level. Academic libraries will surely want it, as will high school or public libraries with life science orientation.' (*Library Journal*)

1965 **Biology Links**
Harvard University
http://mcb.harvard.edu/BioLinks.html
Very useful nicely structured and displayed site providing access to large collection of links to websites; maintained within the University's Department of Molecular and Cellular Biology. Sections include: Biochemistry and molecular

biology; Biomolecular & biochemical databases (sequences, structures, etc.); Educational resources; Evolution; Immunology; Jobs; Online biological journals & articles; Zebrafish links. Also links to genetic databanks and databases, software directories and biological search engines.

1966 **Biology resources in the electronic age**
J.A. Bazler Greenwood Press, 2003, 286pp. $49.95. ISBN 1573563803.
Helpful guide to biology resources on the internet although there is a US bias in the sites indexed. Begins with an overview of the different types of resources that are available and then lists the sites by subject. Subject categories used seem rather random, e.g. there are no entries for botany, ecology or conservation and there is an entry for 'Evolution – theories' and then a separate category for 'Natural selection'. However, there is a subject index.

1967 **Biology Web Site References for Students and Teachers**
K. House, comp.
www.kensbiorefs.com/index.html
This site, founded in 1998 by a retired biology teacher, brings together a collection of more than 5000 links to websites covering all aspects of the biological sciences including genetics, evolution, marine biology and plant biology. Good layout; no site descriptions; links regularly checked.

1968 **BIOME**
University of Nottingham and Resource Discovery Network
www.biome.ac.uk
Access to descriptions of more than 24,000 web resources in life and health sciences, all of which have been evaluated by experts. Organized into six subject-specific gateways, five of which are referenced elsewhere: AgriFor, Natural Selection, NMAP, OMNI, VetGate. The gateways can either be searched individually or simultaneously through the BIOME interface. Browsing facilities are available using classification schemes appropriate to each gateway.

In October 2004, introduced Hot Topics: 'Subject experts within the BIOME team will choose an area of interest or a current topic and provide links to key sites in our database for that theme'.

- **BioResearch** http://bioresearch.ac.uk. BIOME gateway covering the biological and biomedical sciences, including genetics, biotechnology, virology, biochemistry and molecular biology. New resources are added to the database on a weekly basis.

1969 **BIOVISA**
Z. Wang, comp.
biovisa.net
Links compiled by group of researchers in the neuroscience field useful for its lists of: Protocols – over 2000 online laboratory protocols; Journals – more than 1500 online journals. Also selection of eBooks that are freely accessible; discussion forums. (However, seems not recently updated, April 2005.)

1970 **British natural history books, 1495–1900: a handlist**
R.B. Freeman Dawson, 1980, 437pp. ISBN 0712909710.
List of the books, including children's books, published in the UK between 1495 and 1900. Main body of text has the books listed alphabetically by author, with bibliographic details including size, pagination, details of plates and different editions. Separate lists of the titles by date of publication and subject.

CAB Abstracts
CAB International See entry no. 2949

Chemical Abstracts Service
See entry no. 1689

1971 **CSA Biological Sciences**
CSA.
www.csa.com/factsheets/biolclust-set-c.php [DESCRIPTION]
Database bringing together records from 21 of CSA's abstracting services covering a wide range of topics including ecology, entomology, microbiology, biochemistry and genetics: many of the services are referenced elsewhere. Collectively indexes more than 6000 journals, plus conference proceedings, technical reports, monographs and selected books and patents.

- **Life Sciences Thesaurus** www.csa3.com/factsheets/supplements/lscthes.php. Almost 10,000 descriptors used in indexing documents for the CSA life sciences databases and corresponding printed abstract journals.

1972 **Elsevier BIOBASE**
http://www1.elsevier.com/homepage/sah/spd/site/index.html [DESCRIPTION]
Detailed online coverage of the literature of: Applied Microbiology & Biotechnology*; Cancer Research; Cell & Developmental Biology; Clinical Chemistry; Ecological & Environmental Sciences*; Endocrinology & Metabolism; Genetics & Molecular Biology*; Immunology & Infectious Diseases; Neuroscience; Plant Science*; Protein Biochemistry; Toxicology – based on the print *Current Awareness in Biological Sciences* series of bulletins. Records from the four disciplines denoted by an * include species indexing. Uses a comprehensive and detailed classification scheme containing approximately 2300 terms.

1973 **ENVIRONMENT Cluster**
STN International.
www.cas.org/ONLINE/CATALOG/CLUSTERS/environment.html [DESCRIPTION]
Grouping of some 60 STN datasets, including all of the online host major offerings (BIOSIS, Chemical Abstracts, Compendex, Medline, etc.) which contain biological sciences data, and searchable as a set.

Instructions to Authors in the Health Sciences
Medical College of Ohio See entry no. 3505

1974 **The internet for molecular biologists: a practical approach**
C.E. Sansom and R.M. Horton, eds Oxford University Press, 2004, 249pp. £42.50. ISBN 0199638888.
www.oup.com/uk/booksites [COMPANION]
Edited collection aiming to help those 'who are more at home at a laboratory bench than in front of a computer screen'. Six chapters cover guides to general information sources that biologists need to use increasingly often – bibliographic resources, sequence databases, and phylogeny sites; and specialist and subject-specific resources

concerned, for example, with medical genetics, agricultural biotechnology, developmental biology.

There are five chapters explaining 'why molecular biologists might want to become active contributors to the Internet, as well as passive users of it, and how they can best go about doing so' (covering Internet collaborative tools; laboratory websites; visualization; virtual reality; web scripting).

Good detailed treatments, well presented – although one has to go to the companion website for a compendium of the URLs referenced in each of the authored chapters.

1975 Natural history manuscript resources in the British Isles
G.D.R. Bridson, A.P. Harvey and V.C. Phillips, comps Mansell, 1980, 473pp. ISBN 0720115590.
Manuscripts are an extremely important resource in natural history. For example, collecting diaries can provide detailed information about the precise location and habitat that a specimen was found in. However, the fact that these resources are unpublished can also make them difficult to identify and locate. This volume lists the UK institutions that hold natural history manuscripts and provides brief details about their collections. The main text is arranged geographically with separate name and subject indexes.

1976 Natural History Reference Sources
Special Libraries Association Natural History Caucus.
www.lib.washington.edu/sla
Substantial regularly updated links section including lists of natural history libraries and museums (US and international), bibliographies and reference sources. A very good compilation produced under the auspices of the Caucus, which is a network of natural history libraries in the USA, founded in 1991. The website also provides information about the work of the Caucus.

1977 NSDL Scout Report for Life Sciences
University of Wisconsin, Internet Scout Project and National Science Digital Library Biweekly.
scout.cs.wisc.edu/Reports/ScoutReport/Current
Available on the web or via e-mail, this report provides well written evaluations of new and updated internet resources in biology, zoology, ecology, botany and related topics. Resources are listed in three main categories: Research; Education; General. Each report also includes a Topic In Depth that consists of a collection of resources on a specific subject. Access to archival issues. Excellent service.

1978 RDN Virtual Training Suite: Nature [UK]
A. Freeman, C. Gokce and P. Setterfield; Natural History Museum and Resource Discovery Network
www.vts.rdn.ac.uk/tutorial/nature
Helpful introductory tutorial including short descriptions of key internet resources in botany, zoology, palaeontology and natural history.

1979 Take the Subway to Other Resources
University of California, Berkeley
www.ucmp.berkeley.edu/subway/subway.html
Extensive collection of links to: Natural history museums; Museum collections; Societies & organizations; Natural history education; Natural history booksellers; Journals & newsletters; Palaeontology resources; Phylogenetics resources. Maintained by the University's Museum of Palaeontology.

- **Museum Collections** www.ucmp.berkeley.edu/collections/other.html. Attractively presented subject-categorized links to online collection catalogues of interest to natural historians plus to wide range of other relevant resources. Links had been tested and updated mid-2004 when evaluated late-2004.

1980 UK Wildlife Links
O. Tickell, ed.
wildfile.co.uk
A collection of links to websites on all aspects of natural history including sites on wildlife travel, photography and gardening. It also includes links to e-mail discussion groups and news sites. 'We are an independent website that aims to help internet users to reach information on UK wildlife and other environmental themes. We particularly want to help voluntary and individual sites to gain an internet presence.' Formerly The Unofficial Wildlife Trusts.

1981 Using the biological literature: a practical guide
D. Schmidt, E.B. Davis and P.F. Jacobs 3rd edn, Marcel Dekker, 2002, 474pp. $85.00. ISBN 0824706676.
www.library.uiuc.edu/bix/biologicalliterature [COMPANION]
Good guide, aimed at undergraduates and postgraduates. Main section of the text is arranged by subject and provides listings of resources under headings such as Associations, Dictionaries and encyclopedias, Directories, Guides to Internet resources. Subject index. Companion website contains all the book's URLs accompanied by useful commentary.

Digital data, image & text collections

1982 ARKive: images of life on earth
Wildscreen
www.arkive.org
Brings together an exceptional collection of photographs, films and information about endangered species (global) and British species of plants, animals and fungi. Database can be searched or browsed by common or scientific names. Entry for each species includes information on: Status, Description, Range, Habitat, Biology, Threats, Conservation – as well as several colour photographs and video footage.

ARKive's current aim is to compile audiovisual records, where such media exist, for the 12,000-plus species currently threatened with extinction, according to the IUCN Red List of Threatened Species. 'Work is well underway on this task, with more species being continually added to ARKive.'

- **Explore-At-Bristol** www.at-bristol.org.uk/explore. 'An awesome extravaganza of the intriguing, the topical and the bizarre, to delight and inform people of all ages. At-Bristol sets new standards for making science and technology both accessible and fun' (Paul Davies).

Bioethics Central: a guide to primary documents and resources
See entry no. 3509

1983 BioImages: the virtual field guide [UK]
M. Storey, comp.
www.bioimages.org.uk
This very simple but effective site provides access to a large and remarkable collection of images of British natural

history including animals, plants and fungi. Also includes links to related sites and discussion groups.

1984 **Bioline International**
University of Toronto and Reference Center on Environmental Information
www.bioline.org.br
Free access to content of scientific research journals, reports and newsletters that are published in the developing world and covering wide range of disciplines. 'Bioline International is a not-for-profit electronic publishing service committed to providing open access to quality research journals published in developing countries.'

1985 **The Biology Project**
University of Arizona
www.biology.arizona.edu
This site, aimed at undergraduates, provides access to a collection of online problem sets and tutorials covering: Biochemistry; Cell biology; Chemicals & human health; Developmental biology; Human biology; Immunology; Mendelian genetics; Molecular biology. Organized by the University's Department of Biochemistry and Molecular Biophysics.

1986 **BioMed Central**
www.biomedcentral.com
BMC is 'an independent publishing house committed to providing immediate free access to peer-reviewed biomedical research'. The website provides access to the content of more than 100 journals as well as providing substantial information and views about the open access publishing movement.

- **Faculty of 1000** www.facultyof1000.com [FEE-BASED]. Online research tool that highlights the most interesting papers in biology, based on the recommendations of over 1000 leading scientists.

1987 **BioOne**
www.bioone.org [FEE-BASED]
Currently provides (primarily) subscription-based access to a collection of some 70 full-text scientific journals from about 60 different publishers, principally US-based scientific societies and non-commercial publishers. Includes a number of key titles such as EVOLUTION and BIOSCIENCE.

CogPrints
University of Southampton See entry no. 3988

1988 **eNature.com** [USA]
National Wildlife Federation
www.enature.com
The main feature of this site is its collection of online field guides that cover all aspects of US natural history. These are searchable and contain a brief description of each species along with information on their biology, habitat, distribution and a photograph. The site also provides information on wildlife gardening, bird watching and national parks.

1989 **Kimball's Biology Pages**
J.W. Kimball
biology-pages.info
Designed as an online undergraduate textbook, providing good overview and containing huge amount of information on topics such as behaviour, ecology, biochemistry and microbiology. Site can be searched or browsed but, unlike a printed textbook, contents are arranged alphabetically by topic and this could make it difficult for someone with no background in the subject to find the best place to start.

1990 **Online Biology Book**
M.J. Farabee
www.emc.maricopa.edu/faculty/farabee/BIOBK/BioBookTOC.html
Online undergraduate textbook which, unlike KIMBALL'S BIOLOGY PAGES, presents its contents in a similar manner to that found in printed textbooks – moving from basic aspects of a topic to the more complex. Although most of the content has not been updated since 2001, still a useful freely accessible site.

1991 **Virtual Text**
Ergito.
www.ergito.com [FEE-BASED]
Service started 2000 with aim of providing alternative to scientific textbooks, and providing comprehensive coverage of entire life sciences. 'Virtual Text expects to have the same impact on book publishing that Cell Press had on journal publishing.' Access is available as an annual subscription – though some content is freely available.

Directories & encyclopedias

1992 **A directory of natural history and related societies in Britain and Ireland**
A. Meenan, ed. British Museum (Natural History), 1983, 407pp. ISBN 0565008595.
Although this directory is now more than twenty years old it has been included here as it is still the closest that we have to a comprehensive listing of Britain's natural history societies. The main section of the book provides an alphabetical listing of the societies and includes information on their aims, meetings, publications, affiliations and other relevant information, e.g. changes of name, etc. The book also includes a geographical categorization (English counties and separate lists for Scotland, Wales, Northern Ireland and the Republic of Ireland) and one by subject: Botany and horticultural; Entomology; Geology and palaeontology; Mineralogy and lapidary; Mining and caving; Ornithology; Zoology.

Encyclopedia of bioethics
S.G. Post, ed. See entry no. 3511

1993 **Frontiers of life**
D. Baltimore [et al.], eds Academic Press, 2002. 4 v., $1995.00. ISBN 0120773406.
Originally published in Italian, contains a collection of articles that cover selected aspects of biology and related subjects. It is arranged in nine parts over four volumes: V. 1. The origin and evolution of life (cosmology, physics, chemistry and evolution); Genetic language; V. 2. Cells and organisms; Immunological systems; V. 3. The brain of *Homo sapiens* (the senses, language, movement, etc.); Building blocks for intelligence systems; V. 4. Biology of behavior; Discovery and spoliation of the biosphere; Bioethics.

1994 **The naturalists' directory and almanac (International)**
P.W. Mallard II, ed. 48th edn, Sandhill Crane Press, 1998, 464pp. ISBN 188913001X.

International directory of naturalists listing their names, addresses, contact details and areas of interest. Entries are listed in 3 indexes, alphabetically, by subject, geographically (with, however, a strong US bias to the publication).

1995 **Nature encyclopedia of life sciences**
D. Atkins [et al.], eds Nature Publishing Group, 2001–. ISBN 0333947886.
www.els.net [FEE-BASED]
This online encyclopedia currently includes more than 3000 articles on topics covering the entire range of the biological sciences. The individual articles are of a very high quality and, in some cases, represent unique sources of information on a topic but, unfortunately, the indexing and search functionality of the encyclopedia are very poor. For example, a search on 'lake or pond' found articles on birdsong, homology and glutamergic synapses and an article on 'hummingbirds' was indexed under the heading 'Coevolution: insect life'. The articles are categorized as either 'Introductory', 'Advanced' or 'Keynote' but these headings can be misleading. For instance, the article that provided an overview of the topic 'Bioinformatics' was classed as 'Advanced'.

This should be a key reference resource but the indexing needs to be greatly improved before it can achieve this status.
'The Nature Publishing Group, a division of Macmillan Publishers Limited (Macmillan) and John Wiley & Sons, Ltd. (Wiley), announce that with effect from 3 December 2004, the Encyclopedia of Life Sciences (ELS) in both print and online formats has been purchased by Wiley from Macmillan.' (Now thus titled Encyclopedia of life sciences.*)*

Handbooks & manuals

1996 **Choosing and using statistics: a biologist's guide**
C. Dytham 2nd edn, Blackwell Science, 2003, 240pp. £22.95. ISBN 1405102438.
Good basic text.

1997 **Current Protocols**
Wiley. Available in updateable loose-leaf, CD-ROM and web-based formats.
www.interscience.wiley.com/c_p/index.htm [DESCRIPTION]
Well established suite of regularly updated volumes, individual series covering: Bioinformatics; Cell biology; Cytometry; Human genetics; Immunology; Magnetic resonance imaging; Molecular biology; Neuroscience; Nucleic acid chemistry; Pharmacology; Protein science; Toxicology.

Geostatistics for environmental scientists
R. Webster and M. Oliver See entry no. 898

1998 **Life in the frozen state**
B.J. Fuller, N. Lane and E.E. Benson CRC Press, 2004, 672pp. $89.95. ISBN 0415247004.
Comprehensive overview of how living cells and complex organisms survive very low temperatures. Covers both theory and practice across a wide range of species and applications, including benefits of cryobiology to humanity.

1999 **Practical skills in biomolecular sciences**
R. Reed [et al.] 2nd edn, Pearson, 2003, 538pp. £26.99. ISBN 0130451428.
Undergraduate text providing overview of the laboratory techniques, but also including information on a wider range of topics such as general study skills, using internet and library resources (including the citing of references), scientific communication (e.g. essay writing, posters, etc.).

Keeping up-to-date

Astrobiology Magazine
National Aeronautics and Space Administration See entry no. 686

Bioethics.net: The American Journal of Bioethics
See entry no. 3520

2000 **Biological Reviews**
Cambridge Philosophical Society Cambridge University Press, 1926–, Quarterly. £142.00. ISSN 14647931.
Publishes review articles on all aspects of the biological sciences. Articles are written in a style that makes them accessible to a wide audience and include substantial bibliographies, providing useful introductions to the subjects they cover.

2001 **Cell**
Cell Press, 1974–, Fortnightly. $997.00. ISSN 00928674.
www.cell.com [DESCRIPTION]
This is one of the most important biological journals, publishing original research articles and reviews on all areas of experimental biology.
Cell Press publishes a number of related titles: see website.

2002 **Current Awareness in Biological Sciences**
Elsevier, Monthly. €10,416.00.
Twelve sections (which can be subscribed to separately): Applied microbiology and biotechnology; Cancer research; Cell and developmental biology; Clinical chemistry; Ecological and environmental sciences; Endocrinology and metabolism; Genetics and molecular biology; Immunology and infectious diseases; Neuroscience; Plant science; Protein biochemistry; Toxicology. ' Over 1700 primary research journals are scanned by specialized scientific editors to add approximately 15,000 titles to the database each month.'

2003 **The Scientist**
The Scientist, 1986–, Biweekly. Pricing varies with size of institution. ISSN 08903670.
www.the-scientist.com [REGISTRATION]
This is currently a freely available online news journal that covers all aspects of the life sciences with an emphasis on the molecular side of the subject. As well as news (produced in association with BioMed Central), the journal also includes more detailed feature articles, letters and book reviews. (A print copy of the journal is also available by subscription.)

Animal Behaviour

behavioural ecology • ethology • migration • neuroethology • sociobiology

Introductions to the subject

2004 **Animal behavior: an evolutionary approach**
J. Alcock 7th edn, Sinauer Publishers, 2001, 543pp. $87.95. ISBN 0878930116.

www.sinauer.com/titles.php [DESCRIPTION]
Good undergraduate textbook that includes numerous colour illustrations, glossary, bibliography. Approaches the subject from an evolutionary point of view, examining how particular types of behaviour (feeding, communication, reproduction, etc.) have evolved.

2005 **Animal behaviour: psychobiology, ethology and evolution**
D. McFarland 3rd edn, Longman, 1999, 580pp. £37.99. ISBN 0582327326.
Textbook aimed at both biology and psychology undergraduates. Divided into three main sections: The evolution of behaviour; Mechanisms of behaviour; Understanding complex behaviour. Also includes short biographies of some of the leading figures in these areas, e.g. Pavlov, Lorenz and von Frisch.
2nd edn 1993.

2006 **An introduction to animal behaviour**
A. Manning and M. S. Dawkins 5th edn, Cambridge University Press, 1998, 450pp. ISBN 0521578914.
An undergraduate textbook whose seven chapters cover aspects of the subject by looking at examples within the natural world. Includes a bibliography.

The migration atlas: movements of the birds of Britain and Ireland
C. Wernham [et al.], eds; British Trust for Ornithology See entry no. 2746

2007 **Unravelling animal behaviour**
M.S. Dawkins 2nd edn, Longman, 1995, 183pp. ISBN 0582218756.
Concise textbook that aims to provide an overview of the most important topics in the subject. References for further reading are provided at the end of each chapter and the book also contains a more extensive bibliography (pp 167–76).

Dictionaries, thesauri, classifications

2008 **Animal behavior desk reference: a dictionary of animal behavior, ecology, and evolution**
E.M. Barrows 2nd edn, CRC Press, 2001, 922pp. $149.95. ISBN 0849320054.
Contains definitions for more than 5000 terms, arranged alphabetically. Also includes appendices with names of organisms, list of related organizations, substantial bibliography.

2009 **A dictionary of ethology**
K. Immelmann and C. Beer New edn, Harvard University Press, 1989, 336pp. ISBN 0674205073.
Useful basic dictionary that provides definitions for many of the standard terms that are used in the animal behaviour literature. Includes bibliography (pp 333–6).

Official & quasi-official bodies

2010 **Convention on Migratory Species**
www.cms.int
Aims to 'conserve terrestrial, marine and avian migratory species throughout their range': website has good coverage of its parties and procedures. FAQs section contains useful general information about animal migration.

Research centres & institutes

2011 **Center for the Integrative Study of Animal Behavior**
Indiana University
www.indiana.edu/%7Eanimal/index.html
Brings together researchers with an interest in animal behaviour from across the university. Information on its staff and programmes; newsletter *Animal Behavior Bulletin*. Also information on careers in animal behaviour, links to related societies and some resources aimed at teachers and children.

Associations & societies

2012 **Animal Behavior Society**
www.animalbehavior.org
Founded in 1964, international society based in the USA. Website, in addition to providing information about the Society and the journal *Animal Behaviour*, produced jointly with the ASSOCIATION FOR THE STUDY OF ANIMAL BEHAVIOUR, includes section on applied animal behaviour and information relating to how animal behaviour can be used in nature conservation. Other features include searchable database of books published by ABS members, educational resources and links to related sites.

2013 **Association for the Study of Animal Behaviour**
http://asab.nottingham.ac.uk
International society, founded in 1936, with membership primarily drawn from the UK and Europe. Site provides access to the Society's *Guidelines for the treatment of animals in behavioural research and teaching*, links to related European societies, announcements of jobs, meetings, etc. and lists of related resources including mailing lists.

- **Feedback Online** http://asab.icapb.ed.ac.uk. Material to help school teaching of animal behaviour; general advice on behavioural methods, statistics, ethics in animal behaviour teaching; rough guides to animals commonly used in behaviour work; careers resources.

2014 **International Society for Applied Ethology**
www.applied-ethology.org
Founded in 1966 and concerned with behaviour and welfare of animals on farms, in laboratories and zoos, and as pets. Activities include publication of the journal APPLIED ANIMAL BEHAVIOUR SCIENCE and organizing regular meetings. Website also provides information about the Society's regional groups, access to its newsletter and other related information, e.g. ethical guidelines.

2015 **International Society for Behavioural Ecology**
web.unbc.ca/isbe
Information about the Society and its journal *Behavioral Ecology*; also access to its *Newsletter* – containing useful book and other reviews – and information about its meetings.

2016 **International Society for Neuroethology**
www.neuroethology.org
Neuroethology is study of the role of the nervous system in animal behaviour. Information about the subject, newsletter,

details of meetings, job postings, an e-mail list, short links list.

Portal & task environments

2017 **Applied Ethology**
University of Saskatchewan
www.usask.ca/wcvm/herdmed/applied-ethology
Useful entrée to the field of applied animal behaviour, which is defined: 'Deals with the behaviour of domestic animals or other animals kept in captivity'. Includes an applied ethology e-mail discussion list and archive, links to related sites and information sheets on a small range of animal behaviour problems. Maintained by members of the University's Western College of Veterinary Medicine.

Discovering print & electronic resources

2018 **Animal Behavior Abstracts**
CSA, 1982–.
www.csa.com/factsheets/animal-behavior-set-c.php [DESCRIPTION]
Bibliographic database that provides an index to the journal literature, covering all aspects of animal behaviour. Electronic version updated monthly, print version quarterly. Annual index. 233 serials currently monitored.

Digital data, image & text collections

2019 **The Global Register of Migratory Species: GROMS**
K. Riede, comp.; Convention on Migratory Species
www.groms.de
Provides a summary of information about almost 3000 migratory species. Entries include common and scientific names, conservation information, bibliographic references (totalling over 5000 titles) and links to websites containing further information.

Directories & encyclopedias

2020 **Encyclopedia of farm animal behavior**
Agricultural Research Service
www.depts.ttu.edu/liru_afs/EFAB/default.asp
Online encyclopedia that uses definitions based on those in the dictionary published in 1995. Also includes video clips that illustrate some types of behaviour in cattle and pigs. Created by the Service's Southern Plains Area, Livestock Issues Research Unit, Multimedia Division.

- **Dictionary of farm animal behavior** **J.F. Hurnik, A.B. Webster and P.B. Siegel** 2nd edn, Iowa State University Press, 1995, 210pp. $29.99. ISBN 0813824648.

Handbooks & manuals

2021 **Behavioural ecology: an evolutionary approach**
J.R. Krebs and N.B. Davies, eds 4th edn, Blackwell Science, 1997, 456pp. £32.99. ISBN 0865427313.
Advanced textbook that builds on the information provided in the companion introductory volume. Contains a collection of papers that review the main topics within the particular field and highlight areas of current research.

- **An introduction to behavioural ecology** **J.R. Krebs and N.B. Davies** 3rd edn, Blackwell Scientific, 1993, 420pp. £27.99. ISBN 0632035463. Standard introductory undergraduate textbook that considers ecological influences on animal behaviour. Includes bibliography and many colour illustrations.

2022 **Handbook of ethological methods**
P.N. Lehner 2nd edn, Cambridge University Press, 1998, 672pp. £33.00. ISBN 0521637503.
Practical guide on how to carry out research into animal behaviour. Divided into three main sections: Getting started; Collecting the data; Analysing the results (including statistical analyses). Also includes a substantial bibliography (pp 617–63).
'An outstanding and ambitious volume. It should be on the shelf of everyone who wants to become a serious student of animal behaviour ... This handbook will serve for many years to come as the source book for the study of animal behaviour.' (*Ethology*)

2023 **The Oxford companion to animal behaviour**
D. McFarland, ed. Oxford University Press, 1981, 685pp. Foreword by Niko Tinbergen, £12.95. ISBN 0192819909.
Collection of articles, alphabetically ordered by title, on all aspects of animal behaviour. Articles vary in length from, for example, one paragraph on 'Gregariousness' to 13 pages on 'Vision'. Provides a useful source of background information on the topic, including a bibliography of further reading.

Parasites and the behavior of animals
J. Moore See entry no. 2817

Keeping up-to-date

2024 **Advances in the Study of Behavior**
Academic Press, 1965–, Annual, 520pp. $135.00 [V. 34, 2005]. ISBN 0120045346.
Monographic series (each volume has an individual ISBN) that publishes review articles on all aspects of animal behaviour. All of the articles include substantial bibliographies and each volume contains an index.

2025 **Applied animal behaviour science**
International Society for Applied Ethology Elsevier, 1975–, 20/year. €1781.00. ISSN 01681591.
www.elsevier.com/locate/issn/01681591 [DESCRIPTION]
Published on behalf of the ISAE, contains articles and reviews on the behaviour of farm, laboratory and domestic animals.

2026 **Behavioral Ecology**
International Society for Behavioral Ecology Oxford University Press, 1990–, Bimonthly. £322.00. ISSN 10452249.
beheco.oupjournals.org [DESCRIPTION]
Official journal of the Society, containing high-level research articles covering all aspects of behavioural ecology, but with a 'Lay Summary' for each of the articles published.

2027 **Behavioral Ecology and Sociobiology**
Springer, 1976–, Monthly. ISSN 03405443.
www.springeronline.com/journal/00265/about [DESCRIPTION]
Reviews and original research articles dealing with animal behaviour at the level of the individual, population or community.

Biochemistry & Biophysics

alkaloids • amino acids • biochemical pathways • biological chemistry • biological macromolecules • biological physics • biophysics • carbohydrates • enzymology • fats • inborn errors of metabolism • metabolism • metalloproteins • molecular biology • neurochemistry • nucleic acids • nucleotides • peptides • proteins • proteomics • steroids

Introductions to the subject

2028 Alkaloids: nature's curse or blessing?
M. Hesse Wiley, 2002, 426pp. $175.00. ISBN 3906390241.
'As numerous historical documents – on fireclay, papyrus, or paper – testify, alkaloids, nitrogen containing natural substances, have been companions of mankind from ancient time. Valued as drugs and stimulants, some species are also feared because of their addictive potential, and often it seems impossible to distinguish these effects unambiguously. The chemistry of alkaloids has been captivating chemists for ages and generations. This is the first comprehensive reference work providing a concise overview of structure, properties, and history of these unique and fascinating substances.' Fascinating work.
'The reviewer must confess that he could not put the book down ... most medicinal chemists would find it an appealing choice for pleasure reading ... highly recommended.' (*Journal of Medicinal Chemistry*)

2029 Biochemistry
C.K. Mathews, K.E. Van Holde and K.G. Ahern 3rd edn, Benjamin Cummings, 2000, 1186pp. $145.40. ISBN 0805330666.
www.aw-bc.com/mathews [COMPANION]
Aimed at students taking their first course in biochemistry. Five parts: The realm of biochemistry; Molecular architecture of living matter; Dynamics of life: catalysis and control of biochemical reactions; Dynamics of life: energy, biosynthesis, and utilization of precursors; Information. Each chapter includes a bibliography and there is a glossary.

2030 Biochemistry
J.M. Berg, J.L. Tymoczko and L. Stryer 5th edn, W H Freeman, 2002, 974pp. International version, $77.49. ISBN 0716746840.
bcs.whfreeman.com/biochem5 [COMPANION]
Standard undergraduate textbook providing good overview of the subject. Authors adopt an evolutionary approach so that while the content is similar to that of other textbooks the structure is quite different. Divided into four parts: The molecular design of life; Transducing and storing energy; Synthesizing the molecules of life; Responding to environmental changes. Accompanying website includes online tutorials as well as the figures from the book.

2031 Biochemistry and molecular biology
W.H. Elliott and D.C. Elliott 2nd edn, Oxford University Press, 2001, 586pp. £27.99. ISBN 0198700458.
www.oup.com/uk/booksites/content/0199271992 [COMPANION]
Introductory text written in a very readable style. Six parts: Introduction to the chemical reactions of the cell; Structure of proteins and membranes; Metabolism; Information storage and utilization; Transport of oxygen and CO2; Mechanical work by cells. Each chapter includes suggestions for further reading and the accompanying website includes all of the illustrations, errata and links to related sites.
3rd edn now available: see website.

Biochemistry of the eye
D.R. Whikehart See entry no. 4049

The cell: a molecular approach
G.M. Cooper and R.M. Hausman See entry no. 2270

2032 Fundamentals of enzymology: the cell and molecular biology of catalytic proteins
N.C. Price and L. Stevens 3rd edn, Oxford University Press, 1999, 478pp. £32.99. ISBN 019850229X.
An undergraduate textbook that provides a useful overview of the subject. The 11 chapters cover a range of topics including historical aspects, nomenclature, enzyme structure, mechanisms of enzyme action, clinical enzymology and the industrial use of enzymes. Each chapter includes a bibliography.

Giant molecules: essential materials for everyday living and problem solving
C.E. Carraher See entry no. 5055

2033 Harper's illustrated biochemistry
R.K. Murray [et al.] 26th edn, McGraw-Hill/Appleton & Lange, 2003, 693pp. $44.95. ISBN 0071389016.
Well established undergraduate textbook primarily aimed at medical students. Each chapter includes a bibliography and there is also an appendix listing references to relevant websites.

Introduction to glycobiology
M.E. Taylor and K. Drickamer See entry no. 2272

2034 Introduction to molecular biophysics
J.A. Tuszynski and M. Kurzynski CRC Press, 2003, 550pp. $139.95. ISBN 0849300398.
Introductory textbook providing useful overview. Contains ten chapters (plus three appendices). Topics include: Structures of biomolecules; Nonequilibrium thermodynamics and biochemical reactions; Molecular biological machines; Tissue and organ biophysics.
Series: Pure and Applied Physics, 4.

2035 Introduction to protein structure
C. Branden and J. Tooze 2nd edn, Garland Science, 1999, 410pp. $69.95. ISBN 0815323050.
www.bios.co.uk/textbooks/0815323042.asp [DESCRIPTION]
Standard undergraduate textbook providing good overview. Two main parts: Basic structural principles; Structure, function, and engineering. Each chapter includes a bibliography.

2036 Lehninger principles of biochemistry
D.L. Nelson and M.M. Cox 4th edn, W H Freeman, 2004, 1119pp. $134.95. ISBN 0716743396.
www.whfreeman.com/lehninger [COMPANION]
A standard undergraduate textbook, this provides a good overview of the subject. After an introductory section on the Foundations of biochemistry the book is divided into three main sections: Structure and catalysis; Bioenergetics and metabolism; Information pathways (including coverage of genetic information). The accompanying website includes the figures from the book, online tutorials and animations. It is freely accessible but registration is required.

Molecular mechanisms of photosynthesis
R.E. Blankenship See entry no. 2181

Pharmaceutical chemistry: therapeutic aspects of biomacromolecules
C.M. Bladon See entry no. 3677

2037 Proteins, enzymes, genes: the interplay of chemistry and biology
J.S. Fruton Yale University Press, 1999, 783pp. $65.00. ISBN 0300076088.
http://yalepress.yale.edu/YupBooks
Excellent overview tracing the development of biochemistry and molecular biology from antiquity to the present time, examining their institutional settings, and discussing their impact on medical, pharmaceutical and agricultural practice.
'Broad coverage and an extensive bibliography make this book of great value as a point of departure for anyone who is interested in a particular aspect of the history of biochemistry or molecular biology. I can recommend this book as a superb choice for anyone interested in biochemistry or molecular biology who wants to know where it came from.' (*New England Journal of Medicine*)

- **A documentary history of biochemistry: 1770–1940 M. Teich and D.M. Needham** Fairleigh Dickinson University Press, 1992, 579pp. ISBN 0838634877. Reprints brought together – in a few cases the whole paper is reprinted – to make available source materials on evolution of the study of the chemistry of life into modern biochemistry. Over half the reprints translated into English for the first time.

Textbook of biochemistry with clinical correlations
T.M. Devlin, ed. See entry no. 3764

Dictionaries, thesauri, classifications

2038 Dictionary of biochemistry and molecular biology
J. Stenesh 2nd edn, Wiley, 1989, 525pp. ISBN 0471840890.
Although this book is now 15 years old it is still a very useful reference work, providing concise definitions for more than 15,000 terms. Includes many cross-references to related terms and to full versions of common abbreviations.

Encyclopedic dictionary of genetics, genomics, and proteomics
G.P. Rédei See entry no. 2506

2039 The Facts On File dictionary of biochemistry
J. Daintith, ed. Checkmark Books, 2003, 247pp. $49.50. ISBN 0816049149.
Useful basic dictionary that provides definitions for more than 2000 words commonly used in biochemistry. Also appendices covering topics such as the periodic table and the Greek alphabet together with short list of relevant web pages (some of which are now out of date) and a bibliography.

2040 Glossary of biochemistry and molecular biology
D.M. Glick Portland Press, 1997, 214pp. £16.50. ISBN 1855780887.
www.portlandpress.com/pp/books/online/glick/default.htm [COMPANION]
Provides brief definitions for more than 2000 terms that are or have been used in the fields of molecular biology and biochemistry. Entries include cross-references to related topics and many also include references to publications for further reading. There is also a more general bibliography.
The online version in late 2004 had last been updated December 2003.

2041 Glossary of terms used in bioinorganic chemistry
International Union of Pure and Applied Chemistry
www.chem.qmw.ac.uk/iupac/bioinorg
Definitions and (where needed) explanatory notes for about 400 terms. The compilers 'have attempted to select terms which are directly relevant to bioinorganic chemistry, but which either a biochemist or an inorganic chemist might have difficulty to understand or define. This is particularly important where a term has different meanings in the two fields.'

Glossary of terms used in medicinal chemistry
International Union of Pure and Applied Chemistry See entry no. 3682

2042 Oxford dictionary of biochemistry and molecular biology
A.D. Smith [et al.], eds Rev. edn, Oxford University Press, 2000, 738pp. £39.95. ISBN 0198506732.
www.oup.co.uk/isbn/0-19-850673-2 [DESCRIPTION]
With more than 17,000 entries this is one of the most comprehensive reference works in the subject area. Entries are generally quite short but they are very informative and include cross-references to related terms. There are eight appendices in the book and these provide information on the Greek alphabet, publications that deal with biochemical nomenclature, a list of organizations and use of the internet. An essential reference work.

Laws, standards, codes

2043 Biochemical nomenclature and related documents
C. Liébecq, ed.; International Union of Biochemistry and Molecular Biology and International Union of Pure and Applied Chemistry
2nd edn, Portland Press, 1992, 347pp. £18.00. ISBN 1855780054.
www.chem.qmul.ac.uk/iupac/bibliog/white.html [COMPANION]
Attempted to standardize the use of nomenclature in biochemistry by bringing together previously published articles. Seven main sections: General; Amino acids, peptides and proteins; Enzymes; Nucleotides, nucleic acids and protein synthesis; Carbohydrates, etc.; Lipids, etc.; Miscellaneous. Website provides access to full texts of many of the articles.

2044 Enzyme nomenclature: recommendations of the Nomenclature Committee of the International Union of Biochemistry and Molecular Biology on the nomenclature and classification of enzyme-catalysed reactions
G.P. Moss, comp.; International Union of Biochemistry and Molecular Biology
www.chem.qmul.ac.uk/iubmb/enzyme
Contains contents of the book *Enzyme nomenclature 1992* and its supplements. Each entry includes the enzyme number, recommended name and details of the enzyme. The compilation has also started to indicate which pathways individual enzymes participate in, and it includes a glossary.

- **Enzyme nomenclature 1992 E.C. Webb, comp.; International Union of Biochemistry and Molecular Biology** 6th edn, Academic Press, 1992, 862pp. ISBN 0122271645.

Recommendations on organic & biochemical nomenclature, symbols & terminology
International Union of Pure and Applied Chemistry and International Union of Biochemistry and Molecular Biology See entry no. 1838

Official & quasi-official bodies

2045 **International Union for Pure and Applied Biophysics**
www.iupab.org [DESCRIPTION]
Founded in 1961, the IUPAB aims to 'support research and teaching in biophysics'. Activities include organization of a triennial conference and publication of their official journal. Site also includes links to the websites of member societies, a meetings calendar and job listings.

- **Quarterly Reviews of Biophysics** Cambridge University Press1968–. £250.00. ISSN 00335835. Forum for general and specialized communication between biophysicists working in different areas. Most reviews published are invited from authors who have made significant contributions to the field.

2046 **International Union of Biochemistry and Molecular Biology**
www.iubmb.unibe.ch
Promotes biochemistry and molecular biology, particularly through the standardization of methods, nomenclature and symbols. Relatively active site maintaining a useful list of recent changes.

- **Trends in Biochemical Sciences** Elsevier, 1976–, Monthly. €1171.00. ISSN 09680004. www.elsevier.com/locate/issn/09680004 [DESCRIPTION]. Research journal published for IUBMB which commissions review articles on all aspects of biochemistry and molecular biology.

Associations & societies

2047 **American Peptide Society** [USA]
www.americanpeptidesociety.com
Founded in 1990; has approximately 1000 members from the US and other countries. Basic well presented information about activities and relationships.

2048 **American Society for Biochemistry and Molecular Biology**
www.asbmb.org
Founded in 1906, and now has almost 12,000 members. Especially notable for its production of *Journal of Biological Chemistry*, one of the key journals in this field, publishing original articles and mini-reviews on all aspects of biochemistry and molecular biology. Site also includes information on biochemistry education and careers and there are links to related sites throughout: of particular value is the Public Affairs section.

In 2003, created an Undergraduate Affiliate Network in response to concerns of those teaching biochemistry and molecular biology at the nationwide decline in the number of students expressing interest in the biological sciences as researchers.

- **HighWire Library of Science and Medicine** http://highwire.stanford.edu. In 2004, the largest repository of full-text life science articles in the world, developed since 1995 with the launch of *Journal of Biological Chemistry*. More than 750,000 free full-text articles plus over 15 million articles from PubMed.

2049 **Australian Society for Biochemistry and Molecular Biology**
www.asbmb.org.au
Pleasant well organized website. Details of conferences and meetings. Two employment databases: CVs and Positions. Special interest groups. Good list of related societies. Links.

2050 **Biochemical Society** [UK]
www.biochemsoc.org.uk
Based in the UK, the Society has an international membership and is open to anyone with an interest in biochemistry. Wide-ranging website. The education section is particularly good with resources for students and teachers from primary schools to universities. Also includes the contact details of the UK universities that offer biochemistry degrees and a very extensive links section.

2051 **Biophysical Society** [USA]
www.biophysics.org
Founded in 1957, aims 'to encourage development and dissemination of knowledge in biophysics'. Publishes *Biophysical Journal*. Site provides general information about biophysics, careers information, educational resources (although its navigation system can be difficult to negotiate).

2052 **British Society for Proteome Research**
www.bspr.org
Formerly the British Electrophoresis Society and represents both the Human Proteome Organization and the European Proteomics Organization in the UK. Useful list of links to proteomics and electrophoresis societies as well as to a small list of databases and journals.

2053 **European Peptide Society**
www.eurpepsoc.com
Founded 1989 to promote 'the advancement of education and in particular the scientific study of the chemistry, biochemistry, and biology of peptides'. Good information about the Society and its activities, which include publication of the *Journal of Peptide Science*. Also, regularly updated collection of links to related sites.

2054 **Federation of European Biochemical Societies**
www.febs.unibe.ch
Founded in 1964, FEBS is now one of the largest life science organizations in Europe. They publish two journals, the *European Journal of Biochemistry* and *FEBS Letters*. Website provides the usual range of information and has a useful page of Recent Updates.

2055 **Protein Society**
www.proteinsociety.org
International society founded in 1986 with the aim of supporting research and development in protein science. Website includes job listings, lists of forthcoming meetings and an Education & Outreach section, which contains a range of useful resources, including lists of textbooks. 'Members have an opportunity actively to participate in the emerging fields of protein science such as proteomics, bioinformatics, structural biology, and computational biology as they pertain to proteins at the molecular and cellular level.'

2056 Society for the Study of Inborn Errors of Metabolism [UK]
www.ssiem.org.uk
A rather unsophisticated website. However, provides access to a number of useful resources (e.g. A Hierarchical Classification For Inborn Errors Of Metabolism), provides a newsletter, and maintains an extensive list of Inborn Errors Links – including sections on: Learned societies; Diagnostic centres and assay finder services; Databases, other information services and mailing lists.

Portal & task environments

The Bioluminescence Web Page
S.H.D. Haddock, C.M. McDougall and J.F. Case; University of California, Santa Barbara See entry no. 2280

2057 PEPSOC.COM: The Peptide Societies Network
European Peptide Society, American Peptide Society and Japanese Peptide Society
www.pepsoc.com
This new site aims to bring together information on peptide science and is supported by the three societies. The site currently includes news, a database of scientific meetings and a collection of links to related sites but its content should increase over time.

Protocol Online
L.-C. Li See entry no. 2526

Discovering print & electronic resources

CMS molecular biology resource
University of California, San Diego See entry no. 2527

2058 Molecular Biology Database Collection: 2004 update
M.Y. Galperin, comp. Oxford University Press. *Nucleic Acids Research*, V. 32, database issue D3-D22.
http://nar.oupjournals.org/cgi/content/full/32/suppl_1/D3
Exceptionally valuable freely accessible annual guide to databases of interest to molecular biologists. Categories used for the 548 databases in the 2004 version (162 more than the previous one) were: Nucleotide sequence databases; RNA sequence databases; Protein sequence databases; Structure databases; Genomics databases (non-vertebrate); Metabolic and signalling pathways; Human and other vertebrate genomes; Human genes and diseases; Microarray data and other gene expression databases; Proteomics resources; Other molecular biology databases.

Each database in the list comes with a recently updated brief description and hot-links are provided for all the databases included in the compilation.

Natural Products Alert
University of Illinois at Chicago See entry no. 3726

2059 The World's Neurochemistry Portal
International Society for Neurochemistry
www.neurochem.org
News from the American, Asian-Pacific, European neurochemical societies. List of relevant publications (with the note: 'The Journal of Neurochemistry's web address is 'www.jneurochem.ORG'. The www.jneurochem.COM address is a pirate site that is blackmailing Blackwell and JNC with pornographic content in hopes of selling the address. Do not mistake the two sites.'). Small set of links.

2060 WWW Virtual Library: Biochemistry and Cell Biology
G. Fenteany, ed.; University of Illinois at Chicago
http://vlib.org/Science/Cell_Biology
Comprehensive, well laid-out and frequently updated. 'While many of the resources listed on these pages are for scientists or advanced students, basic introductions and tutorials for beginners are also listed.'

Digital data, image & text collections

2061 Biochemical Pathways
Roche Applied Science.
www.expasy.org/cgi-bin/search-biochem-index
An online version of the wall chart of biochemical pathways that was originally produced by Boehringer in 1993: access now freely available on the ExPASy server for non-commercial use. Pathways contain links to the ENZYME enzyme nomenclature database.

Biomolecular Interaction Network Database: BIND
Samuel Lunenfeld Research Institute See entry no. 2534

2062 BRENDA: The Comprehensive Enzyme Information System
, ed.Cologne University
www.brenda.uni-koeln.de [REGISTRATION]
Major dataset produced by the University's Bioinformatics Center. Sections are: Nomenclature; Isolation and preparation; Stability; Reaction and specificity; Enzyme structure; Functional parameters; Organism-related information; Disease and references; Application and engineering.

2063 ENZYME: Enzyme Nomenclature Database
Swiss Institute of Bioinformatics
www.expasy.org/enzyme
Each entry includes Enzyme Commission number, recommended name, alternative names, catalytic activity, cofactors, together with links to any related diseases and to entries in the companion SWISS-PROT database.

- **Swiss Institute of Bioinformatics** www.isb-sib.ch. Mission is 'to promote research, the development of databanks and computer technologies, teaching and service activities in the field of bioinformatics, in Switzerland with international collaborations'. Offers range of databases and software tools.

2064 Enzyme Structures Database
European Bioinformatics Institute
www.ebi.ac.uk/thornton-srv/databases/enzymes
Database containing the enzyme structures that have been deposited in the RCSB PROTEIN DATA BANK. Almost 14,000 entries, late 2004.

2065 Image Library of Biological Macromolecules
Institute of Molecular Biotechnology
www.imb-jena.de/IMAGE.html
Wide-ranging site disseminating information on three-dimensional biopolymer structures with an emphasis on

visualization and analysis. Provides access to structure entries deposited at the Protein Data Bank or the Nucleic Acid Database. Aims to fulfil both scientific and educational needs.

Kyoto Encyclopedia of Genes and Genomes: KEGG
Kyoto University See entry no. 2539

2066 **The Medical Biochemistry Page**
M.W. King
www.dentistry.leeds.ac.uk/biochem/thcme/home.html
In effect a freely accessible online textbook containing an extensive subject-classified collection of topics relating to medical biochemistry.

2067 **The Nucleic Acid Database: a repository of three-dimensional structural information about nucleic acids**
Rutgers University
http://ndbserver.rutgers.edu
Goal of the project is to assemble and distribute structural information about nucleic acids. The Atlas contained over 2500 released structures, late 2004. There is a small but useful Education section, lists of Tools, and a concise Links listing. Pleasing site.

2068 **Protein Data Bank: PDB**
Research Collaboratory for Structural Bioinformatics
www.rcsb.org/pdb
International repository for the processing and distribution of 3-D biological macromolecular structure data. Excellent section PDB Documentation and Information with subdivisions: General information; PDB WWW user guides; File formats and standards; News and discussion; Publications and press releases – as well as connections to other information sources covering: Education; Related news groups; Software; and (especially extensive listings of) Links. All in all, a mine of valuable data.

2069 **Protein Explorer**
E. Martz; National Science Foundation and University of Massachusetts
http://molvis.sdsc.edu/protexpl/frntdoor.htm
Free easily used software for visualizing three-dimensional structures of protein, DNA, and RNA macromolecules, and their interactions and binding of ligands, inhibitors, and drugs. Designed to be suitable for high school and college students, but is also widely used by graduate students and researchers. Lively site provides access to wide range of related information: well worth browsing around.
'The *Protein Explorer* has revolutionized the teaching of biology at a molecular level. This site welcomes students to explore molecules visually in ways that had previously been only abstract concepts. Students can view and manipulate 3-D images of biological molecules from any computer with Internet access, allowing them to study any time, any place, in small groups or independently.' (*MERLOT*)

- **MDL Chime E. Martz** www.umass.edu/microbio/chime/whatis_c.htm. This is a freely downloadable (but registration is needed) software plug-in from Elsevier's MDL Information Systems. Site includes useful links to the author's World Index of Molecular Visualization Resources and other related sites.

2070 **Structural classification of proteins**
University of Cambridge
http://scop.mrc-lmb.cam.ac.uk/scop/index.html
Comprehensive ordering of all proteins of known structure according to their evolutionary, functional and structural relationships. The basic classification unit used is the protein domain. Domains are then hierarchically classified into species, proteins, families, superfamilies, folds, and classes: these terms are all defined in the original articles describing the system published in 1995.

UniProt: the universal protein resource
European Bioinformatics Institute, Swiss Institute of Bioinformatics and Protein Information Resource See entry no. 2540

Directories & encyclopedias

2071 **Biochemicals & Reagents**
Sigma-Aldrich Co.
www.sigmaaldrich.com/Brands/Sigma/Sigma_General_Catalog.html
[REGISTRATION]
Lists over 35,000 products with a series of application-specific indexes covering areas of biomolecular science. Good example of commercial product directory.

Directory of approved biopharmaceutical products
S. Spada and G. Walsh See entry no. 3734

2072 **Encyclopedia of biological chemistry**
W.J. Lennarz and M.D. Lane, eds Elsevier Academic Press, 2004, 3000pp. 4 v., £600.00. ISBN 0124437109.
books.elsevier.com [DESCRIPTION]
Pre-publication information on the website – late 2004 – states that this 'comprehensive encyclopedia covers all areas of biological chemistry written by more than 500 selected international experts. Articles are generously illustrated including more than 800 images in four-color. Each entry contains a clear, concise review of the topic along with illustrations, a glossary of technical terms and a section for additional reading.'

2073 **Encyclopedia of hormones**
H.L. Henry and A.W. Norman, eds Academic Press, 2003, 2750pp. 3 v, $699.95. ISBN 0123411033.
www.info.sciencedirect.com/reference_works/works_available/hormones/index.shtml
Useful work that covers the hormones of vertebrates, insects and plants. Contains almost 300 articles of varying length on a wide range of subjects arranged alphabetically by title. Each article includes a bibliography.
Available online: see website.

Encyclopedia of molecular biology
J. Kendrew [et al.], eds See entry no. 2283

2074 **Encyclopedia of molecular cell biology and molecular medicine**
R.A. Meyers, ed. 2nd edn, Wiley, 2004–2005, 9600pp. 16 v, $5920.00. ISBN 3527305424.
www.wiley.com/WileyCDA [DESCRIPTION]
Major sections are: Nucleic acids; Proteins, peptides and amino acids; Structural determination techniques (DNA, RNA and protein); Biochemistry; Cellular biology; Biomolecular interactions; Molecular biology of specific organs or systems; Molecular biology of specific organisms; Molecular biology of specific diseases; Pharmacology; Biotechnology;

'an authoritative reference source of the highest quality ... It is extremely well written and well illustrated (on the 1st edn).' (*American Reference Books Annual*)

'It goes without saying that no library can afford to be without this new edition. Everyone working in the areas of molecular biology, genome research, medical science, or clinical research needs to have access to these volumes.' (*Angewandte Chemie*)

Handbooks & manuals

2075 **Biochemical methods: a concise guide for students and researchers**
A. Pingoud [et al.] Wiley, 2002, 360pp. Includes CD-ROM, $110.00. ISBN 3527302999.
Provides a very useful introduction to biochemistry methods and techniques. Nine chapters: Biochemical literature; General laboratory procedures; Sample preparations; Separation methods; Analytical methods; Immunological methods; Biophysical methods; Mathematical methods; Quantitative analysis of biochemical data. Each chapter includes a bibliography and the book is accompanied by a CD-ROM that includes exercises based on the last chapter.

2076 **The biological chemistry of the elements: the inorganic chemistry of life**
J.J.R. Fraústo da Silva and R.J.P. Williams 2nd edn, Oxford University Press, 2001, 575pp. £44.95. ISBN 0198508484.
www.oup.co.uk/isbn/0-19-850848-4 [DESCRIPTION]
Aims to 'describe the functional value of the chemical elements in living organisms'. Two main parts: The chemical and physical factors controlling the elements of life; The roles of individual elements in biology. Each chapter includes a list of suggested further readings.
'A general overview of biological inorganic chemistry as well as a fascinating novel view of the nature of living systems and their evolution ... The authors have created a text that nicely complements the usual chapters found in advanced inorganic and biochemistry text books.' (*ChemBioChem*)

Comprehensive coordination chemistry II: from biology to nanotechnology
J.A. McCleverty and T.J. Meyer, eds See entry no. 1715

Comprehensive supramolecular chemistry
J.-M. Lehn [et al.], eds See entry no. 1716

CRC handbook of organic photochemistry and photobiology
W.M. Horspool and F. Lenci See entry no. 1849

Enzymes in industry: production and applications
W. Aehle See entry no. 5039

Fundamental neuroscience
L.R. Squire [et al.] See entry no. 3997

Genome, transcriptome and proteome analysis (Analyse de génomes, transcriptome et protéoms)
A. Bernot See entry no. 2548

2077 **Handbook of biological physics**
A.J. Hoff, ed. Elsevier, 1995–.
www1.elsevier.com/homepage/sak/hbbiophys [COMPANION]
Aims to bring together information on all of the diverse fields of biophysics. The contents of the first two volumes are freely available via the internet while volumes 3 and 4 are only available in print.

- **V. 1. Structure and dynamics of membranes R. Lipowsky and E. Sackmann, eds** 1995. ISBN 0444819754.
- **V. 2. Transport processes in eukaryotic and prokaryotic organisms W.N. Konings, H.R. Kaback and J.S. Lolkema, eds** 1996, 935pp. ISBN 0444824421.
- **V. 3. Molecular mechanisms in visual transduction D.G. Stavenga, W.J. DeGrip and E.N. Pugh, eds** 2000, 581pp. ISBN 0444501029.
- **V. 4. Neuro-informatics and neural modelling F. Moss and S. Gielen, eds** 2001, 1059pp. ISBN 044450284X.

2078 **Handbook of metalloproteins**
A. Messerschmidt [et al.], eds Wiley, 2001–2004, 2308pp. 3 v., $1330.00. ISBN 047086981X.
Detailed coverage including illustrations of three-dimensional structures as well as information on 'biological function, occurrences, amino acid sequences, metal content, and spectroscopic and functional properties of the protein'. First two volumes covered iron, nickel, manganese, cobalt, molybdenum, tungsten, copper and vanadium while the third volume covers zinc and calcium.
'It is a pleasure to use ... This excellent, authoritative and valuable text ... I regard this work as essential for library purchase.' (*Natural Products Report*)

2079 **Handbook of proteolytic enzymes**
A.J. Barrett, N.D. Rawlings and J.F. Woessner, eds 2nd edn, Elsevier, 2004, 2368pp. 2v. CD-ROM, £275.00. ISBN 0120796104.
http://books.elsevier.com [DESCRIPTION]
Latest edn not available for review but positive reception for the first edn suggests will continue to be an important reference work. Publisher's website states: 'Edited by world-renowned experts in the field, this comprehensive work provides detailed information on all known proteolytic enzymes to date ... Volume I covers aspartic and metallo petidases while Volume II examines peptidases of cysteine, serine, threonine and unknown catalytic type. A CD-ROM accompanies the book containing fully searchable text, specialized scissile bond searches, 3-D color structures and much more'.

The metabolic and molecular basis of inherited disease
C.R. Scriver [et al.], eds See entry no. 3631

Metabolic and therapeutic aspects of amino acids in clinical nutrition
L.A. Cynober See entry no. 4407

Nutrient metabolism
M. Kohlmeier See entry no. 4408

The organic chemistry of drug design and drug action
R.B. Silverman See entry no. 3749

Phytochemical dictionary: a handbook of bioactive compounds from plants
J.B. Harborne, H. Baxter and G.P. Moss See entry no. 3750

2080 Practical handbook of biochemistry and molecular biology
G.D. Fasman, ed. CRC Press, 1989, 574pp. ISBN 0849337054.
Although now old, this is still a useful work that provides basic chemical and physical data and information. Four sections: Amino acids and proteins; Nucleosides, nucleotides, and nucleic acids; Lipids; Physical-chemical data.

2081 Principles and techniques of practical biochemistry
K. Wilson and J. Walker, eds 5th edn, Cambridge University Press, 2000, 784pp. (A 6th edn is due to be published in 2005.). ISBN 052165873X.
Aimed at undergraduate students; provides introduction to the most commonly used biochemical techniques. The fifteen chapters cover: General principles of biochemical investigations; Molecular biology and basic techniques; Molecular cloning and gene analysis; Immunochemical techniques; Centrifugation techniques; Protein structure, purification and characterization; Enzymes; Cell surface receptors and transporters; Atomic and molecular electronic spectroscopy; Vibrational spectroscopy and electron and nuclear spin orientation in magnetic fields; Mass spectrometric techniques; Electrophoretic techniques; Chromatographic techniques; Radioisotope techniques; Electrochemical techniques. Each chapter includes a list of suggestions for further reading.

Principles of bone biology
J.P. Bilezikian, L.G. Raisz and G.A. Rodan, eds See entry no. 3563

2082 The protein protocols handbook
J.M. Walker, ed. 2nd edn, Humana Press, 1176pp. $125.00. ISBN 0896039412.
Provides detailed descriptions of some 200 techniques commonly used in laboratory work involving proteins and peptides. Eight parts: Quantitation of proteins; Electrophoresis of proteins and peptides and detection in gels; Blotting and detection methods; Chemical modification of proteins and peptide production and purification; Protein/peptide characterization; Glycoproteins; Immunological techniques; Monoclonal antibodies. Each chapter includes a bibliography.
Series: Methods in Molecular Biology.

2083 Proteomics: from protein sequence to function
S.R. Pennington and M.J. Dunn, eds BIOS Scientific, 2001, 313pp. £29.99. ISBN 1859962963.
This book brings together information on several aspects of proteomics, with a particular emphasis on methodologies. Each chapter includes a bibliography.

2084 Short protocols in molecular biology
F.M. Ausubel [et al.], eds 5th edn, Wiley, 2002, 1512pp. 2 v., $169.00. ISBN 0471250929.
www.wiley.com/legacy/cp/cpmb [DESCRIPTION]
Short descriptions of more than 600 laboratory protocols originally published in the four-vol. *Current protocols in molecular biology*. 23 chapters covering topics such as: Preparation and analysis of DNA; Construction of recombinant DNA libraries; DNA sequencing; Analysis of proteins. Includes four appendices: Reagents and solutions; Useful measurements and data; Commonly used techniques; Suppliers.

2085 Thermodynamics of biochemical reactions
R.A. Alberty Wiley-Interscience, 2003, 397pp. $79.95. ISBN 0471228516.
Aimed at advanced undergraduates and researchers; provides an overview of the thermodynamics of enzyme-catalysed reactions. Eleven chapters cover topics such as: Structure of thermodynamics; Systems of biochemical reactions; Oxidation-reduction reactions. Includes bibliography and glossary.
'Written by the most experienced authority in this field ... Well-written and -organized, and nicely produced.' (*Angewandte Chemie International Edition*)

Keeping up-to-date

2086 Advances in Enzymology and Related Areas of Molecular Biology
Wiley, 1941–, Irregular. ISSN 0065258X.
Well established monographic series (each volume has an ISBN) that publishes review articles on all aspects of enzymology. Each article includes a substantial bibliography.

2087 Analytical Biochemistry
Elsevier, 1960–, Fortnightly. €5676.00. ISSN 00032697.
Research journal that publishes original articles, but also reviews covering the techniques and methodologies used in biochemistry and related fields, as well as Notes and Tips 'Methods that can be summarized in a shorter format allowing more rapid publication, including helpful 'kitchen tricks'.'

2088 Annual Review of Biochemistry
Annual Reviews, 1932–, Annual. $244.00 [V. 74, 2005]. ISBN 0824308743 ISSN 00664154.
arjournals.annualreviews.org/loi/biochem [DESCRIPTION]
The leading review, publishing articles on all aspects of biochemistry. Each includes comprehensive bibliographies making them excellent starting points for research. Examples of chapter titles from the 2004 vol. include: Analyzing cellular biochemistry in terms of molecular networks; Crawling toward a unified model of cell motility: spatial and temporal regulation of actin dynamics; Directed evolution of nucleic acid enzymes; Incorporation of nonnatural amino acids into proteins; Mechanical processes in biochemistry; Role of glycosylation in development; The excitement of discovery.

2089 Annual Review of Biophysics and Biomolecular Structure
Annual Reviews, 1992–, Annual. $233.00 [V. 34, 2005]. ISBN 082431834X ISSN 10568700.
arjournals.annualreviews.org/loi/biophys [DESCRIPTION]
One of the established series of volumes. Previous title was *Annual Review of Biophysics and Biophysical Chemistry* and before that *Annual Review of Biophysics and Bioengineering*.
'What about the next fifty years of biophysics? Although there is no crystal ball to foretell the future, it is a safe bet that much of the excitement will build on our knowledge of the properties of individual and small assemblies of molecules to achieve an integrated, molecular-level understanding of the functioning in space and time of entire cells and organisms. This series will chronicle these adventures from the inevitable, but essential, wrong turns and dead ends, to the discovery of previously uncharted

territories. Enjoy the ride!' (From the Preface to the 2004 vol.).

2090 Biochemical Journal
Biochemical Society Portland Press, 1906–, Fortnightly. €2250.00. ISSN 02646021.
www.biochemj.org [DESCRIPTION]
Research journal that publishes original articles and also reviews which 'bridge the gap between mini-reviews and longer ''Annual Reviews''-type articles, covering a wide range of modern biochemistry, molecular and cell biology'.

- **Biochemist e-Volution** www.biochemist.org. Freely available e-only 'journal' that contains news features, a calendar of events, careers information and book reviews.

2091 Biochemistry
American Chemical Society 1962–, Weekly. $3427.00. ISSN 00062960.
pubs.acs.org/journals/bichaw/index.html [DESCRIPTION]
Advanced research papers but also includes Current Topics, review articles intended to familiarize the general reader with current knowledge in a biochemical field or topic of particular interest.

Clinical Reviews in Bone and Mineral Metabolism
See entry no. 3972

2092 Laboratory Techniques in Biochemistry and Molecular Biology
Elsevier, 1969–, Irregular.
Monographic series publishing overviews of laboratory techniques and methodologies. Each volume covers a specific technique or techniques relating to particular types of compounds. Topics covered in recent volumes have included: Cancer metastasis; Synthetic peptides as antigens; Ultrasensitive and rapid enzyme immunoassay.

2093 Metal Ions in Biological Systems
Dekker, 1974–, Irregular.
Monographic series (Volume 42 was published in 2004). Recent volumes have covered topics such as the lanthanides, molybdenum and tungsten, and metal ions in medication.

Biodiversity & Conservation

biological diversity • conservation • endangered species • extinction • invasive species • national parks • nature conservation • species survival • threatened species • wildlife conservation

Introductions to the subject

2094 Against extinction: the story of conservation
W.M. Adams Earthscan, 2004, 311pp. £16.95. ISBN 1844070565.
Interesting book providing overview of the history of wildlife conservation from the 19th century to date. Bibliography within the notes for each chapter and a subject index.

2095 The atlas of endangered species: threatened plants and animals of the world
R. Mackay, ed. Earthscan, 2002, 128pp. £12.99. ISBN 1853838748.
www.earthscan.co.uk [DESCRIPTION]
Illustrated and comprehensive guide to the world's endangered plants and animals.
'This slim text is an excellent example of what is needed ... Quite simply, every school and institution library should get a copy.' (*TEG News* (British Ecological Society))

2096 Biodiversity: a biology of numbers and difference
K.J. Gaston, ed. Blackwell, 1996, 396pp. ISBN 0865428042.
Useful overview of the basic principles of biodiversity. After an introductory chapter, 'What is biodiversity?', the book is divided into three parts: Measuring biodiversity; Patterns in biodiversity; Conservation and management. Each chapter includes a bibliography and the book is illustrated throughout (including four pages of colour plates).

- **Biodiversity: an introduction K. Gaston and J. Spicer** Blackwell, 2003, 208pp. £19.99. ISBN 1405118571.

2097 Biodiversity
E.O. Wilson and F.M. Peter, eds; National Forum on BioDiversity
National Academy Press, 1988, 521pp. ISBN 0309037395.
books.nap.edu/books/0309037395/html/index.html
This word 'biodiversity' was first used at a national forum held in Washington in 1986. This classic book contains some of the papers that were presented at the Forum and it provides a comprehensive view of the state of biodiversity knowledge and research at that time.
Available online: see website.

- **Biodoversity II: understanding and protecting our biological resources M.L. Reaka-Kudla, D.E. Wilson and E.O. Wilson, eds** Joseph Henry Press, 1997, 551pp. ISBN 0309055849. books.nap.edu/books/0309052270/html/index.html. Update organized: The meaning and value of biodiversity; Patterns of the biosphere: how much biodiversity is there?; Threats to biodiversity; Understanding and using biodiversity; Building toward a solution; Getting the job done; Conclusions.

2098 Biodiversity and conservation: a hypertext book
P.J. Bryant
darwin.bio.uci.edu/~sustain/bio65/Titlpage.htm
Interesting online undergraduate textbook, the main text having direct links to related resources. Sixteen chapters cover topics such as: History of life; Extinction and depletion from over-exploitation; Whaling and fishing; Global patterns of diversity; Human population growth.

2099 The changing wildlife of Great Britain and Ireland
D.L. Hawksworth, ed.; Systematics Association Taylor & Francis, 2001, 454pp. £125.00. ISBN 0748409572.
The editor describes this book as a 'stock-check' of the state of British and Irish wildlife. Contains 23 chapters that review the recording and conservation status of organisms from across all of the animal and plant kingdoms. Each chapter includes a bibliography. The first chapter reviews the last 50 years of nature conservation in Britain while the final two chapters look ahead to the future.
Series: Systematics Association Special Volumes, 62.

2100 Conservation
C. Hambler Cambridge University Press, 2004, 368pp. £18.99. ISBN 0521000386.
This useful textbook provides an overview of conservation biology, covering topics such as environmental impact assessment, species and habitat management and environmental economics. Lists of further reading are provided for each chapter.
Series: Studies in Biology.

2101 **Conservation biology**
A.S. Pullin Cambridge University Press, 2002, 345pp. £30.00. ISBN 0521644828.
Undergraduate textbook that provides a good overview of the subject. Structured in three parts. Part one deals with biodiversity and outlines the major ecosystems, Part two covers the threats to biodiversity, while the final part looks at conservation efforts, what can be done and the methodologies involved. Bibliography; subject index.

2102 **Conservation biology**
I.F. Spellerberg, ed. Longman, 1996, 242pp. ISBN 0582228654.
Aimed at undergraduates, provides an overview of some of the issues in conservation biology. The book is structured in three parts: Conservation biology issues (an introductory section); Conservation biology in perspective (political, legislative, educational and taxonomic views); Conservation biology in practice. The book also includes a glossary and an index.

2103 **Conserving living natural resources: in the context of a changing world**
B.J. Weddell Cambridge University Press, 2002, 426pp. £24.99. ISBN 0521788129.
Overview of the theory, history and techniques of natural resource management. Structured in three parts: Management to maximize production of featured species; Protection and restoration of populations and habitats; Management to maintain processes and structures. Each chapter includes a bibliography.

A fish caught in time: The search for the coelacanth
S. Weinberg See entry no. 1406

2104 **Global biodiversity assessment**
V.H. Heywood, ed.; United Nations Environment Programme Cambridge University Press, 1995, 1140pp. ISBN 0521564816.
www.dhushara.com/book/globio/ass.htm [DESCRIPTION]
Independent, critical peer-reviewed, scientific analysis of all the current issues, theories and views regarding biodiversity, viewed from a global perspective, and commissioned by the United Nations Environment Programme. It was written by 13 teams of experts involving some 300 authors from over 50 countries, with the advice in addition of several hundred scientists from more than 80 countries. Invaluable compendium.

2105 **Nature conservation: a review of the conservation of the wildlife in Britain 1950–2001**
P. Marren HarperCollins, 2002, 344pp. £19.99. ISBN 0007113064.
Provides a history of conservation activities in Britain but also attempts to evaluate how successful those activities have been. Following an introduction, the book is divided into three parts: Dramatis personae (review of the official bodies, associations and the legislation involved in conservation); Wildlife habitats; Living with wildlife. The book includes a glossary, bibliography and a subject index.
Series: The New Naturalist Library, 91

2106 **Nature Insight Biodiversity**
R. Howlett and R. Dhand, eds Nature Publishing Group, 2000.
dx.doi.org/10.1038/35012215
A freely available collection of six review articles that were published as part of the journal *Nature* (V. 405, 2000). The articles provide a useful overview of the biodiversity research arena at that time.

2107 **A primer of conservation biology**
R.B. Primack 3rd edn, Sinauer Associates, 2004, 280pp. $44.95. ISBN 0878937285.
A good undergraduate textbook that provides a thorough introduction to the subject. It consists of five chapters: Conservation and biological diversity; Threats to biological diversity; Conservation at the population and species level; Conserving biological communities; Conservation and sustainable development. The book also includes a list of environmental organizations, a bibliography and a subject index. 100 illustrations.

A primer of conservation genetics
R. Frankham, J.D. Ballou and D.A. Briscoe See entry no. 2498

Dictionaries, thesauri, classifications

2108 **Dictionary of natural resource management**
J. Dunster and K. Dunster CABI Publishing, 1996, 363pp. £55.00. ISBN 0851991483.
www.cabi-publishing.org [DESCRIPTION]
Provides definitions for more than 6000 terms drawn from the published literature. Also includes three appendices covering: Classification of organisms; Geological time scales; Conversion tables and other measurements.

Encompasses terminology from the traditional fields of forestry, silviculture, pest management, mycology, botany, fish and wildlife management, forest fire control, geology, pedology, engineering and resource planning, with many terms from the emerging disciplines of landscape ecology, conservation biology, conflict resolution and sustainable development planning.

CABI Publishing, a division of CAB International, *publish a wide range of works in ecology & environmental sciences and related fields: see website.*

Laws, standards, codes

2109 **Basic legal documents on international animal welfare and wildlife conservation**
M. Austen and T. Richards, eds Kluwer Law International, 2000, 696pp. £140.00. ISBN 904119780X.
Copies of the full text of the key international, regional and EU legislation relating to animal welfare and wildlife conservation. Appendix provides contact details for some of the organizations involved in the legislation.

Commission on Genetic Resources for Food and Agriculture
See entry no. 2929

2110 **Environmental Law Alliance Worldwide**
www.elaw.org
Founded in 1989, E-LAW is an international organization, based in the US, that provides legal advice on environmental matters to lawyers and scientists. Resources section of the site contains links to general and legal information on a wide range of topics including biodiversity, coral reefs and genetic resources.

- **Wildlife Interest Group** American Society of International Law. www.internationalwildlifelaw.org. Aims to strengthen international law on conservation of endangered species. Useful resource bringing together full-text copies of relevant legal documents from around the world including many of the major international treaties and conventions.

2111 **Nature conservation law** [UK]
C.T. Reid 2nd edn, W. Green / Sweet & Maxwell, 2002, 429pp. £40.00. ISBN 0414013557.
Very useful overview of the legal framework that shapes conservation policy and practice in Scotland, England and Wales. Begins with tables of all of the relevant cases, statutes, Statutory Instruments and European legislation. Main text is divided into eight sections: Introduction; Authorities responsible for nature conservation; Protection of wild animals; Exploitation and destruction of wildlife; Conservation of habitat; Plants; European and international aspects; Miscellaneous. Appendices list schedules to legislation (listing protected species), open seasons and relevant licences.

Official & quasi-official bodies

Advisory Committee on Protection of the Sea
See entry no. 2569

2112 **Arctic Council**
http://arctic-council.org
The Council, an intergovernmental body, is notable for its CAFF working group which has a membership of professionals, indigenous peoples and observer countries and organizations. Its main role is to 'advise the Arctic governments (Canada, Denmark/Greenland, Finland, Iceland, Norway, Russia, Sweden and the United States) on conservation matters and sustainable use issues of international significance and common concern'. The website provides more information about the forum, access to documents that it has generated and useful links to related sites.

- **Conservation of Arctic Flora and Fauna** www.caff.is.

2113 **ASEAN Regional Centre for Biodiversity Conservation**
www.arcbc.org.ph
Main biodiversity network both within South-East Asia and between the region and EU partner organizations. Website provides information about the organization, its national members and its research and training programmes. Also access to the Biodiversity Information Sharing Service (BISS), a searchable database that includes information (descriptions, photographs and distribution information) on the area's species and protected areas.

Biosafety Clearing-House
See entry no. 5016

2114 **Convention on Biological Diversity**
www.biodiv.org
Agreed at the 1992 Earth Summit in Rio de Janeiro, the Convention is a key international agreement on biodiversity. The website contains a huge amount of information, including the full text of the convention (in six languages) and links to national information related to it. It also contains directories of experts working in the field, a calendar of events and links to other related sites.

- **Handbook of the Convention on Biological Diversity** Earthscan, 2001, 690pp. £29.95. ISBN 1853837482. www.earthscan.co.uk [DESCRIPTION].
- **Cartagena Protocol on Biosafety** www.biodiv.org/biosafety. Designed to protect biological diversity from the potential risks posed by living modified organisms.

2115 **Convention on International Trade in Endangered Species of Wild Fauna and Flora**
www.cites.org
CITES came into force in 1975 and is an international agreement between governments that aims to preserve the world's biodiversity by controlling the trade in wild species, both dead and alive. 166 countries are currently Parties to the agreement which means that they are legally bound to implement it through their national legal framework. The website provides more information about the Convention, the countries involved and the species of plants and animals that it protects. It also includes a searchable database of the species, a glossary and details of current research programmes.

- **TRAFFIC** WWF International and IUCN – the World Conservation **Union**. www.traffic.org. Originally set up to assist implementation of CITES but mission now to monitor trade in wildlife more generally. Access to a collection of resources organized under four headings: Factfile; Briefings; Publications; Themes.

Convention on Migratory Species
See entry no. 2010

2116 **Department of the Environment and Heritage** [AUS]
Australia. Department of the Environment and Heritage
www.deh.gov.au
The DEH 'advises the Australian Government on policies and programs for the protection and conservation of the environment, including both natural and cultural heritage places'. Its portfolio includes the Great Barrier Reef Marine Park Authority, the Office of the Renewable Energy Regulator and the National Oceans Office. Website includes good range of information on Australian biodiversity.

- **Australian Antarctic Division** www.aad.gov.au. Antarctic Treaty came into force in 1961, Australia being one of the original parties (with Argentina, Belgium, Chile, France, Japan, New Zealand, Norway, Russian Federation, South Africa, UK, USA). Site provides good entrée to research, policy, etc.
- **Australian Biodiversity** www.deh.gov.au/biodiversity. Authoritative information on Australian biodiversity and legal framework put in place to try to protect it. Full text of relevant legal documents; Biodiversity Hotspots programme; information on invasive and threatened species, research work, etc.

2117 **DIVERSITAS: an international programme of biodiversity science**
www.diversitas-international.org
Founded in 1991 with the aim of developing an international non-governmental programme of biodiversity research. It currently operates three core programmes: bioDISCOVERY, assessing and monitoring current levels of biodiversity); ecoSERVICES, ecological implications of biodiversity loss; bioSUSTAINABILITY, sustainable use of biodiversity. It also has four Networks that cut across these programmes: Agriculture and biodiversity; Freshwater biodiversity; Global mountain biodiversity; Global invasive species programme.

Website provides more information about all these aspects of DIVERSITAS' work as well details of its publications and links to related sites.

2118 **English Nature**
www.englishnature.org
The starting point for research on nature conservation within England. Provides searchable database of national and local nature reserves, information on Sites of Special Scientific Interest (SSSI) and a range of useful publications and datasets that can also be freely downloaded. Contains a large collection of links to partner organizations and other subject-specific sites.

Environment Agency
See entry no. 5554

2119 **Environment Directorate-General** [EUR]
European Commission. Directorate for Environment
europa.eu.int/comm/environment/index_en.htm
Based mainly in Brussels, role is to develop and implement EU policies in various environmental areas. Policies are guided by an environmental action plan, the sixth of which (2001–2010) has four priority areas: Climate change; Nature and biodiversity; Environment and health and quality of life; Natural resources and waste. The EDG website contains information about the environment, policy documents, and much else.

- **Eco-Management and Audit Scheme: EMAS** http://europa.eu.int/comm/environment/emas/index_en.htm. Voluntary scheme for organizations willing to commit themselves to evaluate and improve their environmental performance.

2120 **Global Biodiversity Information Facility**
www.gbif.org
Purpose of GBIF is to 'make the world's primary data on biodiversity freely and universally available via the Internet'. It is potentially an important facility, primarily aimed at researchers, and its site includes links to relevant databases, software, events, news, etc. Good entrée to the arena.

- **Integrated Taxonomic Information System** www.itis.usda.gov. Taxonomic information on North American species, searchable by common/scientific names. Completeness of data varies, but all entries include name/taxonomic hierarchy; many also details of experts on the species/group and citations. Last updated 2002.

2121 **Global Invasive Species Programme**
www.gisp.org
The GISP was established in 1997 to 'to address global threats caused by Invasive Alien Species (IAS), and to provide support to the implementation of Article 8(h) of the CONVENTION ON BIOLOGICAL DIVERSITY'. Website provides access to information about invasive species, lists of relevant databases, a calendar of related scientific meetings and events and links to related sites.

International Plant Protection Convention
See entry no. 2197

International Whaling Commission
See entry no. 2572

2122 **IUCN – the World Conservation Union**
www.iucn.org
Founded in 1948, the IUCN has a membership drawn from more than 140 countries and it is one of the most authoritative sources of biodiversity and conservation information. It maintains a large website but the main area of interest is the Our Work section, which provides details of the IUCN programmes of research, information by region and information about the Commissions, including the SPECIES SURVIVAL COMMISSION that produces the IUCN RED LIST OF THREATENED SPECIES. The site also includes a searchable directory of IUCN members and a calendar of conservation events and meetings.

- **Biodiversity is life!** www.iucn.org/bil/main.html. This site provides a clear, authoritative introduction to the subject. Five sections: The foundation of life; In our lives; Effect of human activities; How to act; IUCN and biodiversity.
- **ECOLEX: a gateway to environmental law** www.ecolex.org. Gateway to environmental law operated jointly by IUCN with FAO [q.v.] and UNEP [q.v.].

2123 **Joint Nature Conservation Committee** [UK]
www.jncc.gov.uk
The 'UK Government's wildlife adviser, undertaking national and international conservation work'. The main content of the site is arranged under the headings: Earth heritage; Habitats; Species; Marine; International; Protected sites; UK biodiversity; Conventions & legislation.

Man and the Biosphere Programme
See entry no. 2313

National Marine Fisheries
See entry no. 2573

Natural Resources Conservation Service
See entry no. 3358

Ramsar Convention on Wetlands
See entry no. 2575

2124 **Species Survival Commission**
www.iucn.org/themes/ssc
The SSC is the largest Commission within the IUCN and it provides information and advice on species conservation to governments and conservation organizations. It includes more than 120 Specialist Groups that cover particular taxonomic groups or issues such as invasive species or conservation breeding. The most important activity of the SSC is the production of the IUCN RED LIST OF THREATENED SPECIES but it also produces SPECIES ACTION PLANS and carries out research projects.

- **Conservation Breeding Specialist Group** www.cbsg.org. Within the Commission aims to conserve natural populations of both plants and animals through both captive and in situ breeding programmes.
- **Global Zoo Directory** www.cbsg.org/directory/index.scd. Service of the Conservation Breeding Specialist Group which offers listings of zoos from all over the world. Also details of zoo associations.

2125 **UNEP World Conservation Monitoring Centre**
www.unep-wcmc.org
Initially founded in 1979 by the IUCN, the WCMC now operates as the 'world biodiversity information and assessment centre' for UNEP. The site includes a huge amount of information presented under the headings: Habitats; Species; Climate change; Protected areas; International agreements; Interactive Map Services (which includes the *World atlas of biodiversity*.

2126 **US Fish and Wildlife Service**
www.fws.gov
Founded in 1881, the FWS is responsible for the conservation of the US plants and animals and their habitats. Their responsibilities include the regulation of hunting and fishing and the joint administration of the Endangered Species Act (shared with NOAA). The website provides access to a substantial amount of information about all aspects of the FWS' activities and US wildlife more generally.

Research centres & institutes

2127 **Center for Biological Diversity** [USA]
www.sw-center.org
Campaigns for protection of the US flora and fauna through legal action and advocacy. Website is useful source of news and opinion, as well as providing information on more than 100 species that the CBD is trying to protect.

Center for Plant Conservation
See entry no. 2198

Centre for Plant Biodiversity Research and Australian National Herbarium
See entry no. 2199

2128 **Instituto Nacional de Biodiversidad**
www.inbio.ac.cr/en/default.html
INBio is a private research centre, based in Costa Rica, that carries out research in five main areas: Inventory and monitoring; Conservation; Communications and education; Biodiversity informatics; Bio-prospecting. Website contains searchable database of the Costa Rican species.

2129 **Northern Prairie Wildlife Research Center** [USA]
www.npwrc.usgs.gov
Part of the US Geological Survey, the Center carries out research into the conservation and management of the species and ecosystems in the US interior. Access, via the Biological Resources section, to a wide range of useful US and international resources (i.e. not just about the 'Northern Prairie') including identification keys, bibliographies, checklists and species accounts. The resources can be searched or browsed by resource type, taxonomic group (mammals, fish, etc.) or by geographical region.

Associations & societies

African Wildlife Foundation
See entry no. 2885

American Bird Conservancy
See entry no. 2757

American Zoo and Aquarium Association
See entry no. 2888

2130 **Association for Tropical Biology and Conservation**
www.atbio.org
Founded in 1963, the ATB aims to promote research in tropical biology and conservation and encourage co-operation among biologists working in tropical environments. The Society publishes the journal *Biotropica* jointly with Blackwell Publishing.

Bat Conservation International
See entry no. 2889

Bat Conservation Trust
See entry no. 2890

Birdlife International
See entry no. 2759

British Dragonfly Society
See entry no. 2384

Buglife – the Invertebrate Conservation Trust
See entry no. 2386

Butterfly Conservation
See entry no. 2387

Caribbean Conservation Corporation & Sea Turtle Survival League
See entry no. 2582

2131 **Conservation International**
www.conservation.org
US-based international conservation organization that works in Africa, the Asia-Pacific region, Mesoamerica and South America. Its three main strategies focus on the identification and protection of Biodiversity Hotspots, conserving Tropical Wilderness, and Key Marine Areas.

2132 **Defenders of Wildlife** [USA]
www.defenders.org
Works to protect the native animals and plants of the USA. The Wildlife section of the site provides information on some of the species and habitats that the organization is campaigning on behalf of.

2133 **Endangered Species Coalition**
www.stopextinction.org
The ESC represents a network of organizations and individuals that are concerned with the US Endangered Species Act (1973). Website provides information about the Act and the species that it is intended to protect as well as offering links to related resources.

Environmental Investigation Agency
See entry no. 2329

2134 **Fauna & Flora International**
www.fauna-flora.org
Founded in 1903, FFI is an international conservation organization. Its work is divided into five programmes, four of which are regional covering Africa, the Americas, Asia-Pacific and Eurasia while the final one covers issues that are not confined to a specific region.

Hawk Conservancy Trust
See entry no. 2762

International Bee Research Association
See entry no. 2390

International Coral Reef Action Network
See entry no. 2592

2135 **International Fund for Animal Welfare**
www.ifaw.org
IFAW was initially set up to campaign for the end of the hunting of seals in Canada but its interests have now expanded beyond this, both in their areas of activity and geographically. Site provides quite detailed information on a range of endangered species and downloadable fact sheets.

Lobster Conservancy
See entry no. 2594

Mammal Society
See entry no. 2899

Mammals Trust UK
See entry no. 2900

Marine Conservation Biology Institute
See entry no. 2595

Marine Conservation Society
See entry no. 2596

Marine Fish Conservation Network
See entry no. 2597

National Audubon Society
See entry no. 2763

National Council for the Conservation of Plants and Gardens
See entry no. 2219

2136 **National Parks Conservation Association** [USA]
www.npca.org
An advocacy organization that campaigns on behalf of the US national parks with the aim of educating the general public and influencing policy makers. Website provides brief information about the habitats and species found in the parks.
- **National Park Service** www.nps.gov. Interesting and informative set of pages about this part of the US Department of the Interior organized: Parks & recreation; History & culture; Nature & science; Interpretation & education.

2137 **National Wildlife Federation** [USA]
www.nwf.org
Founded in 1936, the NWF is one of America's oldest conservation organizations. It is involved at regional and national levels in the areas of: Land stewardship; Water resources; Wildlife conservation. As well as more general information, website includes brief information on some endangered species and information on wildlife gardening.

Natural Science Collections Alliance
See entry no. 1934

2138 **Nature Conservancy**
nature.org
Founded in 1951, a charity that works to preserve natural habitats and the species that live in them in Central, North and South America, the Caribbean and the Asia Pacific area. Their activities focus on five areas: Climate change; Fire management; Freshwater conservation; Invasive species; Marine conservation. Well designed website giving access to news of their work, as well as to a range of publications. There is an excellent Online Field Guide to The Nature Conservancy describing with delightful photographs where and how the organization works.

Ocean Conservancy
See entry no. 2599

Otter Project
See entry no. 2600

Peregrine Fund
See entry no. 2764

Plantlife International
See entry no. 2221

2139 **Rainforest Action Network**
www.ran.org
Founded in 1985, RAN campaigns for the protection of the world's rainforests. Description of work; quite brief information about rainforests along with a collection of fact sheets; link to Rainforestweb.org, list of resources that provide information about rainforests.
- **Rainforestweb.org: World Rainforest Information Portal** www.rainforestweb.org.

2140 **Ray Society** [UK]
www.books.free-online.co.uk
Founded 1844, and named after the 17th century naturalist John Ray; dedicated to the publishing of scientific works, primarily those concerned with the British fauna and flora. Has now published more than 160 books, listed on the site.

Royal Society for the Protection of Birds
See entry no. 2765

2141 **Royal Society of Wildlife Trusts** [UK]
www.rswt.org
The Society was founded in 1912 and has changed its name several times since then, the latest change coming in June 2004 when it changed from the Royal Society for Nature Conservation. Co-ordinates the activities of the Wildlife Trusts in the UK and also runs several schemes that provide grants for environmental projects.
- **Wildlife Trusts** www.wildlifetrusts.org. Network of 47 local Trusts covering all of the UK and managing more than 2500 nature reserves. As well as information about activities, also includes brief information about some of the species and habitats that the Trusts aim to conserve.

Seal Conservation Society
See entry no. 2602

SeaWeb
See entry no. 2603

Shark Trust
See entry no. 2604

2142 **Society for Conservation Biology**
www.conbio.org
International professional association with a membership of

more than 8000 individuals that have an interest in or work in conservation biology. Publication of the journal CONSERVATION BIOLOGY; educational resources; job vacancies; etc.

Wetlands International
See entry no. 2607

Whale and Dolphin Conservation Society
See entry no. 2608

2143 **Wildfowl & Wetlands Trust** [UK]
www.wwt.org.uk
Founded in 1946 by Sir Peter Scott, the WWT is concerned with the conservation of wetlands and their associated biodiversity, particularly water birds. Information about the organization, its research and the 9 centres they run, including the London Wetland Centre; also on threatened species of water birds.

- **Learn for life** www.wwtlearn.org.uk. Gateway to wide range of teaching and learning resources. Good annotated links section.

Woodland Trust
See entry no. 2225

World Chelonian Trust
See entry no. 2609

2144 **World Land Trust**
www.worldlandtrust.org
The WLT is an international conservation charity that is active in India, Belize, Costa Rica, the Philippines, South America and the UK. The Trust works with local experts in these areas to identify, purchase and therefore protect sites that are rich in biodiversity. Website includes a collection of reviews of conservation and natural history books.

2145 **WWF International**
www.panda.org
Founded as the World Wildlife Fund in 1961, the organization changed its name to WWF International in 2001 in recognition of the wider spectrum of its activities, which now include all aspects of nature conservation. Operates six main research programmes: Climate change; Forests for life; Living waters (water shortages); Endangered seas (conservation of fish stocks and marine habitats); Species; Toxics. Very active in the policy arena. Website includes a collection of images and a range of other resources.

2146 **Xerces Society**
www.xerces.org
The Society, founded in 1971, takes its name from an extinct US butterfly and is dedicated to the conservation of invertebrate biodiversity. Website provides more information about the Society and its activities, which focus on three main programmes: Pollinator conservation; Aquatic invertebrates; Endangered invertebrates.

Zoological Society of London
See entry no. 2904

Libraries, archives, museums

Botanic Gardens Conservation International
See entry no. 2226

2147 **The Conservation Collection** [USA]
Denver Public Library
www.denver.lib.co.us/whg/conservation.html
Established in 1960, this collection has become a major archive of conservation materials including manuscripts, books, journals and photographs. It provides an important resource for the study of the history of the conservation movement in the US.

Portal & task environments

EarthTrends: the environmental information portal
World Resources Institute See entry no. 2334

Forest Conservation Portal
See entry no. 3252

Forest, Dryland & Freshwater Programme
UNEP World Conservation Monitoring Centre See entry no. 3253

Global Trees Campaign
Fauna & Flora International and UNEP World Conservation Monitoring Centre See entry no. 3259

2148 **Invasivespecies.gov: a gateway to Federal and State invasive species activities and programs** [USA]
National Agricultural Library
invasivespecies.gov
Gateway to Federal efforts concerning invasive species, detailing the impacts of invasive species and the Federal government's response, together with select species profiles and links to agencies and organizations dealing with invasive species issues. Also the website for the National Invasive Species Council, which co-ordinates Federal responses to the problem.

MarLIN: The Marine Life Information Network for Britain & Ireland
Marine Biological Association of the United Kingdom See entry no. 2619

2149 **National Biodiversity Network** [UK]
www.nbn.org.uk
A project to build the UK's first network for biodiversity information. The site includes the NBN Gateway that enables searching across a large number of habitat, species and geographical datasets: in November 2004, over 17 million species records from 115 different datasets were accessible. The site also includes a link to the NBN Species Dictionary (hosted at the NATURAL HISTORY MUSEUM) which lists the names of plants and animals found in the UK. Much other valuable information about UK biodiversity matters, including about the opportunities to contribute locally gathered data. A site worth spending time exploring in detail.

2150 **Naturenet** [UK]
M. Chatfield, ed.
www.naturenet.net
Useful site providing information on all aspects of the UK countryside including nature conservation. Covers careers information, relevant legislation, biodiversity and rights of way. Site also includes good set of links to a wide range of other resources.

OceanLink
Bamfield Marine Sciences Centre See entry no. 2622

Species 2000
University of Reading See entry no. 2860

2151 **UK Biodiversity Action Plan**
Joint Nature Conservation Committee
www.ukbap.org.uk
In 1992, the UK Government signed the Convention on Biological Diversity. The BAP represents the Government's response to its commitments under the Convention. It describes the UK biodiversity and outlines a plan for the protection of species and their habitats and it also supports local initiatives. Provides access to the 391 Species Action Plans (current status, threats, action to be taken and related links), 45 Habitat Action Plans and 162 Local Biodiversity Action Plans that are currently available.

Discovering print & electronic resources

2152 **Endangered Species**
North American Association for Environmental Education
eelink.net/EndSpp
Collection of links to (mainly US) websites that deal with endangered species that was put together for an audience of teachers, students and other education professionals. Arranged under eight headings: Endangered species lists; Extinct species; Species facts, data, and pictures; Current news events and sources; Take action; Organizations; Laws and policy; Education and interactive kids stuff.

Forest History Society Databases
Forest History Society See entry no. 3266

2153 **National Parks Worldwide**
Z. Zwolinski, ed. Polish National Parks.
www.staff.amu.edu.pl/~zbzw/ph/pnp/swiat.htm
The IUCN defines a national park as a 'protected area managed mainly for ecosystem protection and recreation'. This site provides links to web pages that contain information on the world's national parks as well as to sites that provide more general information about parks and related sites. Hosted by *Polish National Parks*.

Sea Turtle Online Bibliography
University of Florida See entry no. 2631

Digital data, image & text collections

2154 **Biodiversity Explorer**
Iziko Museums of Cape Town
www.museums.org.za/bio
Good source of information on a wide range of organisms. While the site's content primarily relates to South African species there is also much of interest to an international audience. Main focus was originally on insects and spiders and so these areas of the site are particularly good.

2155 **Biodiversity Hotspots**
Conservation International
www.biodiversityhotspots.org
Biodiversity hotspots are priority conservation areas that have been identified by Conservation International. They contain a great diversity of endemic species (i.e. organisms that have a very restricted geographical distribution) but are also severely threatened by human activities. This website provides more information about the 25 hotspots that CI has identified and the vertebrate species that they contain. It also contains a bibliography and a glossary.

2156 **Biological Inventories of the World's Protected Areas**
Information Center for the Environment and Man and the Biosphere Programme
www.ice.ucdavis.edu/bioinventory/bioinventory.html
Biosphere reserves are areas that have been identified by the UNESCO Man and the Biosphere Programme as 'areas of terrestrial and coastal ecosystems promoting solutions to reconcile the conservation of biodiversity with its sustainable use'. The ICE site provides access to the lists of plants, birds, reptiles, mammals, amphibians and fish that have been found at the reserves. The database can be browsed by species' scientific or common names or by country.

EuroTurtle
Mediterranean Association to Save the Sea Turtles and Kings College Taunton See entry no. 2637

The Global Register of Migratory Species: GROMS
K. Riede, comp.; Convention on Migratory Species See entry no. 2019

2157 **IUCN Red List of Threatened Species**
Species Survival Commission
www.iucnredlist.org
The Red List is the definitive guide to the endangered species of animals and plants of the world. Species are evaluated against a set of categories and criteria and those that are judged to be at a high risk of global extinction are included in the list along with those that are already extinct, those that can not be evaluated as a result of insufficient data and those that are close to the inclusion thresholds. This site provides access to a searchable version of the list (the data for plants is incomplete and so both the Red List and the UNEP-WCMC Threatened Plants of the World database should be searched).

2158 **Practical Conservation Online** [UK]
British Trust for Conservation Volunteers
handbooks.btcv.org.uk/handbooks/index
Access to the full text of the BTCV Handbooks. Fourteen titles are available (as of August 2004) covering practical conservation topics such as fencing, wetlands, tree planting and dry stone walling. An excellent resource.

2159 **Species Information: Threatened and Endangered Animals and Plants** [USA]
US Fish and Wildlife Service
endangered.fws.gov/wildlife.html
This site provides information on the species that have been placed on the *Federal list of endangered and threatened wildlife and plants* and that are therefore protected under the US Endangered Species Act. It provides access to the Threatened and Endangered Species database System (TESS) that can be searched by species (common or scientific names) or browsed to find information by US state or country. It also provides information on species that have been proposed as additions to the list and those that have been removed from it.

Threatened Plants of the World
UNEP World Conservation Monitoring Centre See entry no. 2254

2160 **The Tree of Life Web Project**
D. Maddison and K.-S. Schulz, eds
http://tolweb.org
One of the most ambitious projects in the biological sciences as it aims to bring together information on every group of organism on a single site, using a tree structure to illustrate the evolutionary relationships between them. It already contains more than 3000 pages of information and it is continuing to grow but there are still many groups that are not represented or for whom only partial information is available. The site takes the form of an evolutionary tree, making it easy to navigate to a particular group of organisms, or simply to follow your curiosity. At each point along the tree there is a web page with an article on the group concerned (often authored by a recognized expert), along with a bibliography and a list of web-resources.

UNEP-WCMC Species Database: Trees
UNEP World Conservation Monitoring Centre See entry no. 3276

2161 **Viva Natura: illustrated database of Mexican biodiversity**
Conexion con la Vida Silvestre, A.C..
www.vivanatura.org
More than 65,000 species of plants and animals have been described from Mexico (although some estimate that it may actually be home to more than 200,000) which makes it one of the most important countries in the world in terms of its biodiversity. This attractive website provides an overview of Mexican biodiversity and information about its national parks, biosphere reserves and other conservation efforts. It also includes information about the flora and fauna, including a collection of photographs and short video clips of some species.

World Bird Database: WBDB
Birdlife International and Royal Society for the Protection of Birds
See entry no. 2783

Directories & encyclopedias

The atlas of European mammals
A.J. Mitchell-Jones [et al.]; Societas Europaea Mammalogica See entry no. 2918

2162 **Conservation directory 2003: the guide to worldwide environmental organisations**
B. Street, ed.; National Wildlife Federation 48th edn, Island Press, 2003, 766pp. $70.00. ISBN 1559639962.
www.islandpress.org/books [DESCRIPTION]
First published in 1955, the directory includes information on US, state and international government agencies, international, national, and regional organizations and commissions, non-governmental organizations and educational institutions. The 2003 volume includes more than 4000 entries but these have a very strong US and Canadian bias with quite poor coverage outside of these areas. Arranged in three parts: Introduction; Listings (arranged by organization type); Organization, keyword, staff name and geographic indexes.

2163 **Encyclopedia of biodiversity**
S. A. Levin [et al.], eds Academic Press, 2001. 5 v., $1495.00. ISBN 0122268652.
Collection of 313 long articles by subject experts arranged alphabetically by title. Each article includes a bibliography making this work a useful starting point for further research. However, the article titles are inconsistent in their use of scientific / common names, e.g. beetles and butterflies are listed as such but termites are listed under their scientific name (Isoptera). The index, included in volume 5, is the easiest way to find an article on a particular topic, but even this is inconsistent. For instance, the index entry for 'beetles' says 'see Coleoptera' but the term 'butterflies' isn't listed at all.

2164 **Encyclopedia of endangered species**
M. Emanoil, ed.; International Union for Conservation of Nature and Natural Resources Gale, 1994, 1230pp. $150.00. ISBN 081038857X.
Very general introduction to about 700 endangered species of plants and animals. Provides brief taxonomic information for each species as well as its conservation status and other information under the headings: Description and biology; Habitat and current distribution; History and conservation measures. Individual entries do not include bibliographies but a general list of further reading is provided, along with a list of conservation organizations, maps and geographical and species indexes.
V. 2, 1998 ($150.00. ISBN 0810393158) profiles a further 500 species.

2165 **Life on earth: an encyclopedia of biodiversity, ecology, and evolution**
N. Eldredge, ed.; American Museum of Natural History ABC-CLIO, 2002, 792pp. 2 v., $185.00. ISBN 157607286X.
www.abc-clio.com/academic
This work provides a useful reference source on biodiversity and the impact that humans are having on it. It begins with four longer essays (What is biodiversity?; Why is biodiversity important?; Threats to biodiversity; Stemming the tide of the sixth global extinction event: what we can do) that introduce the subject. These are followed by 200 entries, arranged alphabetically by title, that cover specific aspects of the subject. Each entry includes cross-references and a bibliography. Vol. 2 contains a bibliography for the whole work and a subject index.

2166 **NatureServe Explorer: an online encyclopedia of life**
NatureServe
www.natureserve.org/explorer
Good source of information on more than 55,000 species of plants and animals from the USA and Canada, with an emphasis on endangered species. It can be searched by species name (common or scientific) or by type of ecological community. Entries include information on the species' conservation status, biology and geographical distribution and a bibliography.

- **InfoNatura: birds, mammals, and amphibians of Latin America** www.natureserve.org/infonatura. 'Conservation and educational resource on the birds, mammals and amphibians of Latin America and the Caribbean. You can use InfoNatura to learn about more than 6000 common, rare and endangered species'.

2167 **World atlas of biodiversity: earth's living resources in the 21st century**
B. Groombridge and M.D. Jenkins; UNEP World Conservation Monitoring Centre University of California Press, 2002, 340pp. $54.95. ISBN 0520236688.
This book aims to 'provide an overview of the current state of global biodiversity'. Eight chapters: The biosphere; The diversity of organisms; Biodiversity through time; Humans, food and biodiversity; Terrestrial biodiversity; Marine biodiversity; Inland water biodiversity; Global biodiversity: responding to change. Six appendices covering topics such as: Biodiversity at country level; Important areas for freshwater biodiversity. Each chapter includes a bibliography and the book is fully illustrated in colour.

World atlas of coral reefs
M.D. Spalding, C. Ravilious and E.P. Green; UNEP World Conservation Monitoring Centre See entry no. 1386

World who is who and does what in environment and conservation
N. Polunin, ed.; Foundation for Environmental Conservation See entry no. 2351

Handbooks & manuals

2168 **Biodiversity: a reference handbook**
A. Becher ABC-CLIO, 1998, 275pp. $50.00. ISBN 0874369231.
Compilation of some of the reference resources available to assist in the study of biodiversity. Seven chapters: Biodiversity: an overview; Chronology; Biographical sketches (includes people such as Rachel Carson, E. O. Wilson and Stephen Jay Gould); Statistics, illustrations, and documents; Directory of organizations; Print resources; Non-print resources. There is a slight US bias in some of the sections but, overall, a very useful resource.

2169 **Biological diversity handbook series**
M.S. Foster, ed.; National Biological Survey and National Museum of Natural History Smithsonian Institution, 1994–.
A series of books published with the aim of establishing standard methodologies that can be used to measure biodiversity. Each volume focuses on a specific taxonomic group – which so far includes mammals, amphibians and ants – and begins with an overview of the group, followed by details of the relevant techniques.

- **Ants: standard methods for measuring and monitoring biodiversity** **D. Agosti [et al.], eds** 2000, 280pp. ISBN 1560988851.
- **Measuring and monitoring biological diversity: standard methods for amphibians** **W.R. Heyer [et al.], eds** 1994, 364pp. ISBN 1560982845.
- **Measuring and monitoring biological diversity: standard methods for mammals** **D.E. Wilson [et al.], eds** 1996, 409pp. ISBN 1560986379.

2170 **The conservation handbook: research, management and policy**
W.J. Sutherland Blackwell Science, 2000, 278pp. £27.99. ISBN 0632053445.
A practical guide to conservation biology techniques ranging from political and management aspects through to collecting techniques in order to assess biodiversity. Includes case studies that illustrate particular techniques and a substantial bibliography (pp 252–71).

Forest conservation policy: a reference handbook
V.A. Sample and A.S. Cheng See entry no. 3286

Marine monitoring handbook
J. Davies [et al.], eds; Joint Nature Conservation Committee See entry no. 2648

2171 **Measuring biological diversity**
A.E. Magurran Blackwell, 2004, 256pp. £32.50. ISBN 0632056339.
Aimed at students and researchers and providing a useful overview of the mathematical techniques and theoretical approaches that can be used to measure biodiversity. Includes worked examples to illustrate the techniques described. Bibliography; subject index.

2172 **Principles of conservation biology**
G.K. Meffe and C.R. Carroll 2nd edn, Sinauer Associates, 1997, 729pp. $86.95. ISBN 0878935215.
An advanced textbook divided into four main areas: Introductory concepts; Population-level considerations; System-level considerations; Practical applications and human considerations. Under each of these headings, in addition to the main text, is a collection of essays and case studies that illustrate and expand on each topic.

2173 **Species Action Plans**
Species Survival Commission
www.iucn.org/themes/ssc/pubs/sscaps.htm
This is a series of freely available publications that provide authoritative sources of information on the conservation status of animals and plants and their habitats. Each volume in the series deals with a particular group, e.g. orchids, cycads, cetaceans, antelopes, etc. They provide information on both the current situation and the conservation priorities for the future. Each book also includes a substantial bibliography.

The world list of threatened trees
S.F. Oldfield, C. Lusty and A. MacKinven See entry no. 3293

Keeping up-to-date

2174 **Animal Conservation: A Journal of Ecology, Evolution and Genetics**
Zoological Society of London Cambridge University Press, 1998–, Quarterly. £132.00. ISSN 13679430.
A research journal that publishes original articles on all aspects of the conservation of animals including population biology, wildlife diseases, management and genetics. It also publishes reviews of relevant books.

2175 **Conservation Biology**
Society for Conservation Biology Blackwell, 1987–, Bimonthly. £425.00. ISSN 08888892.
A research journal that publishes original articles as well as items on conservation education and reviews of relevant books.

Habitat
D. Brear See entry no. 2365

2176 **Journal of International Wildlife Law & Policy**
W. C. G. Burns [et al.], eds Taylor & Francis, 1998–, Quarterly. ISSN 13880292.
www.jiwlp.com [DESCRIPTION]
This journal publishes articles on the legal, political and ethical aspects of wildlife conservation. It also includes reviews of books in the same subject areas. Website has extensive Resources (links) section.

Botany

angiosperms • arboreta • botanical gardens • bryophytes • cacti • carnivorous plants • economic botany • ferns • flora • flowering plants • flowerless plants • gardens • gymnosperms • herbaria • marine botany • mosses • photosynthesis • physiology plants • phytopathology • plant genetic resources • plants • pollination • roots • roses • seed-bearing plants • succulent plants • systematics – plants • toxic plants • tropical plants • vascular plants

Introductions to the subject

2177 **Biology of plants**
P.H. Raven, R.F. Evert and S.E. Eichhorn 6th edn, W H Freeman, 1999, 944pp. $92.30. ISBN 1572590416.
Good undergraduate textbook that provides an illustrated overview of all aspects of the subject. Seven sections: The biology of the plant cell; Energetics (includes photosynthesis); Genetics and evolution; Diversity (includes overviews of prokaryotes, viruses, fungi, protists and plants); The angiosperm plant body; Physiology of seed plants; Ecology. Includes a list of further readings for each chapter, a glossary and an index.

2178 **Botany: an introduction to plant biology**
J.D. Mauseth 2nd edn, Jones and Bartlett, 1998, 794pp. ISBN 0763707465.
www.jbpub.com/botanylinks [COMPANION]
This is a nice, illustrated undergraduate textbook that covers all areas of plant biology. The book has four main parts covering: Plant structure; Plant physiology and development; Genetics and evolution (includes an overview of the diversity of prokaryotes, fungi, algae and plants); Ecology. The book does not include a bibliography but does have a glossary and subject index. The accompanying website provides an online glossary and links to related websites and organizations.

2179 **Botany online: the internet hypertextbook**
A. Bergfeld, R. Bergmann and P. von Sengbusch
www.biologie.uni-hamburg.de/b-online/e00/contents.htm
English translation of an online textbook originally published in German. It currently includes nine sections: Introduction (history of botany, identifying plants); Anatomy of cells and tissues; Classic genetics; Molecules and molecular reactions in plant cells; Intercellular communication; Interactions between plants and fungi, bacteria, viruses; Evolution; The plant kingdom: an overview; Ecology. The site also includes a collection of links to related sites.

Introduction to world forestry: people and their trees
J. Westoby See entry no. 3194

2180 **Marine botany**
C.J. Dawes 2nd edn, Wiley, 1998, 480pp. $120.00. ISBN 0471192082.
This book provides an overview of marine plants and their biology. The 12 chapters cover general topics, e.g. light, salinity, water movement, the impact of humans, etc. as well as looking at specific ecosystems, e.g. salt marshes, mangals and coral reefs. Two appendices cover techniques used in the study of marine plants and the uses of algae. A large bibliography is included along with taxonomic and subject indexes.

2181 **Molecular mechanisms of photosynthesis**
R.E. Blankenship Blackwell Science, 2002, 321pp. £32.50. ISBN 0632043210.
Introductory textbook aimed at advanced undergraduates and postgraduate students. Provides a good overview including chapters on the history of photosynthesis research as well as on the more complex areas. Each chapter includes a bibliography and the book is illustrated throughout (mainly black and white but with 4 pages of colour plates).

2182 **The natural history of pollination**
M.C.F. Proctor, P.F. Yeo and A. Lack New edn, HarperCollins, 1996, 479pp. £25.00. ISBN 0002199068.
This book provides an excellent overview of pollination. It includes information on the role of insects, vertebrates and other pollinators (wind, water, etc.) as well as topics such as ecology, plant breeding and the history of pollination. The book is illustrated throughout (including 8 pages of colour plates) and includes a substantial bibliography.

2183 **Plant biology**
L.E. Graham, J.M. Graham and L.W. Wilcox Prentice Hall, 2003, 497pp. $105.00. ISBN 0130303712.
www.prenhall.com/plantbio [COMPANION]
An undergraduate textbook with full colour illustrations. The book is divided into four parts: Introduction; Molecules, cells, and microbes (includes algae, fungi and lichens); Plant structure, diversity, and reproduction; Plant diversity and the environment. Also includes a glossary and a subject index. Accompanying website includes an image gallery and links to related sites.

2184 **Plant molecular genetics**
M.A. Hughes Longman, 1996, 236pp. £35.99. ISBN 0582247306.
Aimed at undergraduates and provides an introduction to the molecular genetics of higher plants. Four parts: Plant genome structure; Agrobacterium tumefaciens; Plant molecular biology; An introduction to plant biotechnology. Each chapter includes a list of suggestions for further reading.

2185 **Plant physiology**
L. Taiz and E. Zeiger 3rd edn, Sinauer Associates, 2002, 690pp. $107.95. ISBN 0878938230.
www.plantphys.net [COMPANION]
A standard undergraduate plant physiology textbook. After an initial chapter outlining the structure of a plant cell, the book is divided into three sections: Transport and translocation of water and solutes; Biochemistry and metabolism (includes photosynthesis); Growth and development. Each chapter includes a bibliography and the book also contains a glossary and author and subject indexes. The accompanying website includes lists of suggested readings for each chapter (not the same as the published bibliographies), plus two additional chapters: Energy and enzymes; Gene expression and signal transduction.

2186 **Plant systematics: a phylogenetic approach**
W.S. Judd [et al.] 2nd edn, Sinauer Associates, 2002, 576pp. $92.95. ISBN 0878934030.
This book updates and expands on the earlier work by Stace. The content is arranged in nine chapters: The science of plant systematics; Methods and principles of biological systematics; Classification and system in flowering plants: historical background; Taxonomic evidence: structural and biochemical characters; Molecular systematics; The evolution of plant diversity; An overview of green plant phylogeny; Lycophytes, ferns and their allies, and extant gymnosperms; Phylogenetic relationships of angiosperms. The book also includes a guide to botanical nomenclature. Each chapter includes a bibliography and there is also a glossary and subject and taxonomic indexes.

2187 **Plant taxonomy and biosystematics**
C.A. Stace 2nd edn, Edward Arnold, 1989, 264pp. ISBN 0713129557.
Good overview of plant taxonomy. Three sections: The basis of plant taxonomy (scope and development of plant taxonomy); Sources of taxonomic information (characteristics that can be used by plant taxonomists); Taxonomy in practice. Substantial bibliography (490 references); subject index.

2188 **Toxic plants dangerous to humans and animals (Plantes toxiques pour l'homme et les animaux)**
J. Bruneton Intercept, 1999, 545pp. Originally published Editions Tec & Doc; translated by Caroline K. Hatton, £99.00. ISBN 1898298629.
This book provides a useful overview of poisonous plants. The first section covers general topics such as the incidence of events, risks associated with herbal medicines and managing plant poisoning. The second part provides a listing of toxic plants, arranged alphabetically by family. The entry for each family includes a bibliography and the book also includes a glossary and index.

Dictionaries, thesauri, classifications

2189 **Angiosperm Phylogeny Website**
P. F. Stevens
www.mobot.org/MOBOT/Research/APweb/welcome.html
A set of characterizations of all orders and families of angiosperms (flowering plants), as well as many clades grouping families and orders and some lower-level clades within families. They are designed to help in teaching angiosperm phylogeny, filling the gap resulting from the lack of any printed comprehensive phylogeny-based treatment of angiosperms.

2190 **The Cambridge illustrated glossary of botanical terms**
M. Hickey and C. King Cambridge University Press, 2000, 208pp. £22.99. ISBN 0521794013.
This is a very useful book that provides an alphabetical list of terms that are commonly used in relation to vascular plants (chemical terms are not included). This is accompanied by a collection of drawings that illustrate the features described in the list, with cross-references between the two. The drawings are arranged according to their subject, e.g. leaves, flower structure, fruits, seeds and seedlings, etc.

2191 **CRC dictionary of plant names: common names, scientific names, eponyms, synonyms, and etymology**
U. Quattrocchi CRC Press, 2000, 2896pp. 4 v., $829.95. ISBN 0849326737.
This impressive work provides an A–Z listing of (mainly generic) plant names. Each entry includes information on the origins of the name along with a list of the species (common and scientific names) that are found in each genus. The work also includes a bibliography.

2192 **A dictionary of plant sciences**
M. Allaby, ed. 2nd edn, Oxford University Press, 1998, 508pp. £7.99. ISBN 0192800779.
www.oxfordreference.com
Very good dictionary that provides definitions for more than 5000 botanical terms. Many of the entries are quite detailed and some also include illustrations. Also includes a list of European endangered plant species.
Available online: see website.

2193 **The Facts On File dictionary of botany**
J. Bailey, ed. Checkmark Books, 2003, 250pp. $19.95. ISBN 0816049114.
Good basic dictionary that contains definitions for more than 2000 botanical terms, with some illustrations and a short bibliography.

Laws, standards, codes

2194 **Index Nominum Genericorum: ING**
International Association for Plant Taxonomy and Smithsonian Institution
ravenel.si.edu/botany/ing
The ING project began as a card index in 1954. The database is now available via the internet and aims to provide a complete list of the generic names of plants. For each generic name it provides information on the authority, the status of the name (valid, synonym, etc) and the original

reference. Can be searched by genus, family or authority names. Updated monthly.

2195 **International Code of Botanical Nomenclature: St Louis Code**
W. Greuter [et al.], eds; International Association for Plant Taxonomy
www.bgbm.fu-berlin.de/iapt/nomenclature/code/SaintLouis/0000St.Luistitle.htm
The Code contains the rules that govern the naming of plants, including fungi and algae. It is revised regularly at International Botanical Congresses and the current version was created following the 16th Congress which was held at St Louis. The printed version, not this web-based one, is the official version of the current code.

- **International Code of Botanical Nomenclature (St Louis Code) W. Greuter [et al.], eds** Koeltz Scientific Books, 2000, 474pp. €41.00. ISBN 3904144227. www.koeltz.com [DESCRIPTION]. 'KSB is not only a big international mail order bookseller for botanical and zoological books, but also a publisher in the same fields. Up to four hundred (mainly botanical) books have been published, including many important items' (e.g. this Code).

International code of conduct for plant germplasm collecting and transfer
Food and Agriculture Organization See entry no. 2930

Official & quasi-official bodies

2196 **International Organization for Plant Information**
plantnet.rbgsyd.gov.au/iopi/iopihome.htm
IOPI was set up in 1991 with the aim of providing accurate taxonomic and biological information on plants to users around the world. It is currently (August 2004) working on two projects. The Global Plant Checklist aims to provide a list of all of the vascular plant species (will eventually also include nonvascular plants as well). The Species Plantarum programme aims to bring together taxonomic information on the plants of the world as both published volumes and electronically under the title *Flora of the world*.

2197 **International Plant Protection Convention**
www.ippc.int
The IPPC is an international treaty, signed in Rome in 1951, that aims to control the spread of plant pests and plant products. The website provides more information about the organization, including access to the full text of the treaty. It also provides access to standards and other documents that have been produced by the IPPC and to national and regional information.

Research centres & institutes

2198 **Center for Plant Conservation** [USA]
www.centerforplantconservation.org
Network of US botanical institutions set up with the aim of conserving the native US flora. Information about the Centre and the National Collection of Endangered Plants that it maintains. Also links to related sites as well as a conservation directory of US state and regional contacts.

2199 **Centre for Plant Biodiversity Research and Australian National Herbarium**
www.anbg.gov.au/cpbr
Collaboration supported by the Department of the Environment and Heritage's Australian National Botanic Gardens and the Commonwealth Scientific and Industrial Research Organization's Division of Plant Industry. Site provides excellent range and depth of information about 'botanical research, conservation, management and use of the Australian flora'.

- **Australian National Botanic Gardens** www.anbg.gov.au/anbg/index.html. Founded in 1970, the ANBG aims to 'grow, study and promote Australian plants'. Website provides more information about the Gardens and the taxonomy and horticulture of Australian plants.

2200 **International Plant Genetic Resources Institute**
www.ipgri.cgiar.org
Founded in 1974, the IPGRI carries out research into the conservation and use of plant genetic resources. The website provides access to a large number of documents produced by the Institute on topics such as bananas, forest genetics and conservation.

- **European Forest Genetic Resources Programme: EUFORGEN** www.ipgri.cgiar.org/networks/euforgen/euf_home.asp. European collaborative mechanism promoting and co-ordinating conservation and sustainable use of forest genetic resources; also monitoring progress nationally and internationally in exchange of reproductive materials and methods of conservation.

Poisonous Plant Research Laboratory
See entry no. 3075

Associations & societies

2201 **American Association of Botanical Gardens and Arboreta**
www.aabga.org
'Dedicated to promoting people's appreciation and understanding of the irreplaceable value of plants.' Within Related Sites extensive set of links. Also a gateway Networking Guide to Historic Landscape Resources.

2202 **American Bryological and Lichenological Society**
www.unomaha.edu/~abls
One of America's oldest botanical organizations; has a membership that includes both amateurs and professionals. News, publications, resources, etc.

2203 **American Fern Society**
amerfernsoc.org
Founded in 1893, the AFS has more than 900 members worldwide. Website includes an illustrated introduction to ferns, information on growing ferns, collection of links to related sites, and details of its publication *Annual Review of Pteridological Research*.

2204 **American Phytopathological Society**
www.apsnet.org
Founded in 1908, the APS is based in the USA but has an international membership of professionals with an interest in the study and control of plant diseases. Access to a wide range of resources including the Common Names of Plant Diseases database, careers information, an excellent set of

Images of the Week illustrating plant diseases, and a first-rate categorized and annotated list of website links. Much else of value on this excellent site.

2205 **American Society of Plant Biologists**
www.aspb.org
Founded in 1924, a professional society that aims to promote the study of all aspects of plant biology. Provides resources for school children, university students and teachers among other offerings.

2206 **American Society of Plant Taxonomists**
www.aspt.net
The ASPT was founded in 1935 and aims to promote research and teaching in plant systematics, taxonomy and phylogenetics. The site provides helpful information on careers in biosystematics.

2207 **Botanical Society of America**
www.botany.org
Founded in 1906 and has a membership that includes both professional and amateur botanists. Site includes a general introduction to botany, job listings, a collection of images and links to related sites.

2208 **Botanical Society of the British Isles**
www.bsbi.org.uk
Founded in 1836 as the Botanical Society of London, the BSBI has a membership of both amateurs and professionals with an interest in the flora of Britain and Ireland. Activities include recording the distribution of vascular plants and stoneworts.

- **BSBI database** rbg-web2.rbge.org.uk/BSBI. Common and scientific vascular plant names and literature references.
- **Vice-county census catalogue** C. A. Stace [et al.], eds; **Botanical Society of the British Isles** . www.reticule.co.uk/flora/vccc. List of vascular plant species and the counties that they have been found in.

2209 **British Bryological Society**
rbg-web2.rbge.org.uk/bbs/bbs.htm
Based in the UK, the BBS has an international membership and aims to encourage interest in bryology (the study of liverworts and mosses (Bryophytes)). Includes general information on bryophytes, an image gallery and links to related sites.

- **International Association of Bryologists** www.bryology.org. Founded in 1969, the IAB aims to promote co-operation and communication between bryologists. Website includes a searchable directory of Association members and a small collection of links to related sites.

2210 **British Cactus and Succulent Society**
www.bcss.org.uk
The BCSS was founded in 1983 through the merger of two other societies and it now has a membership of more than 3500. Information on how to grow cacti and succulents as well as more general coverage.

2211 **British Plant Gall Society**
http://www.btinternet.com/~bpgs
Founded in 1985, the BPGS has a membership of both professional and amateur cecidologists (cecidology = the study of galls). Includes a good introduction to plant galls and their study and a collection of brief notes on galls and their causes.

2212 **British Pteridological Society**
www.nhm.ac.uk/hosted_sites/bps
The BPS was founded in 1891 and is open to anyone with an interest in ferns and their allies. General information about ferns and a guide to nurseries, gardens and collections that contain ferns. The site does not appear to have been updated recently and so, unfortunately, the Links section is not particularly helpful.

British Society for Plant Pathology
See entry no. 3329

2213 **Federation of European Societies of Plant Biology**
www.fespb.org
The FESPB aims to encourage research and education in plant biology, with a slight emphasis on plant physiology. It has a membership that consists of national Societies, corporate and individual members. The website provides more information about the Society and its activities along with job listings, a directory of members and links to related sites.

2214 **Garden History Society** [UK]
www.gardenhistorysociety.org
Based in the UK but with an international membership, the GHS aims to promote the study of the history of gardening and to protect historic parks and gardens. Website contains reviews of relevant books, suggested lists of reading for anyone interested in the subject and links to related sites.

2215 **International Association for Plant Taxonomy**
www.botanik.univie.ac.at/iapt
The IAPT was founded in 1950 with the aim of promoting botanical systematics and related international projects. Details of its activities including work on the International Code of Botanical Nomenclature and Index Nominum Genericorum.

- **Taxon** Quarterly. $225.00. ISSN 00400262. Journal of the Association devoted to systematic and evolutionary biology with emphasis on botany.

2216 **International Association for Sexual Plant Reproduction Research**
www.iasprr.org
Founded in 1990, the Association aims to promote research in the field of plant reproduction. Activities include the publication of the journal *Sexual Plant Reproduction*. Site also includes information about relevant conferences and scientific meetings and links to related sites.

2217 **International Society for Molecular Plant-Microbe Interactions**
www.ismpminet.org
The Society was founded in 1990 and now has members from 30 countries around the world. Among other activities, it publishes the journal *Molecular Plant-Microbe Interactions*.

2218 **International Society for Plant Molecular Biology**
www.uga.edu/ispmb/home.htm
Aims to 'disseminate worldwide new techniques, protocols, and news of general interest to plant molecular biologists'.

2219 **National Council for the Conservation of Plants and Gardens** [UK]
www.nccpg.com
The NCCPG was founded in 1978 with the aim of conserving

cultivated (garden) plants in Britain and Ireland. Information about the Council and its activities – which include organizing the National Plant Collection – as well as on growing rare plants and on botanical nomenclature. Links to related sites.

2220 National Gardens Scheme [UK]
www.ngs.org.uk
The NGS is a scheme to open gardens in the UK to the public, with money raised going to selected charities. The website provides more information about the scheme along with a searchable list of the gardens of England (there is a separate scheme in Scotland), information on gardens around the world, and links to related sites.

- **Scotland's Gardens Scheme** Scotland's Gardens Scheme. www.gardensofscotland.org.

2221 Plantlife International
www.plantlife.org.uk
Based in the UK, Plantlife is involved in the conservation of wild plants in the UK and internationally. Activities include co-ordinating the Important Plant Areas programme in Europe and managing 22 nature reserves within the UK. Site also provides detailed information on endangered plant species and information on a range of other issues (e.g. invasive species, habitat destruction, etc.) that affect plants.

Rainforest Action Network
See entry no. 2139

2222 Royal Horticultural Society [UK]
www.rhs.org.uk
From its foundation in 1804, the Royal Horticultural Society has grown to be the world's leading horticultural organization and the UK's leading gardening charity. Organizes the annual Chelsea Flower Show and other shows, runs four flagship gardens and provides over 1000 lectures annually across the UK. Some areas of site restricted to members.

- **RHS Horticultural Database** Royal Horticultural Society. www.rhs.org.uk/databases/summary.asp. Objective is to bring together into a single cohesive structure as much horticultural information as possible, based around a comprehensive index of garden plant names.
- **RHS Plant Finder** Royal Horticultural Society2004–2005. £12.99. ISBN 1405303484. www.rhs.org.uk/rhsplantfinder/plantfinder.asp. Exists to put enthusiastic gardeners in touch with suppliers of plants, many of them unusual. Covers 73,000 plants compiled and updated from 750 UK nurseries.
- **RHS Plant Selector** www.rhs.org.uk/rhsplantselector/index.aspx. Access – primarily for gardeners – to descriptions, cultivation information as well as advice and photographs of plants suitable for particular environments.

2223 Royal National Rose Society [UK]
www.rnrs.org
Founded in 1876, the RNRS aims to 'encourage, improve and extend the science, art and practice of rose growing'.

2224 Society for Economic Botany
www.econbot.org
Founded in 1959, the SEB is based in the US but has an international membership. The website provides more information about the Society and its activities. However, more resources are available on the website of the UK chapter of the Society which is based at the Centre for Economic Botany, Royal Botanic Gardens, Kew. These include lists of new books, a collection of leaflets and links to related sites.

- **Society for Economic Botany, UK Chapter** www.rbgkew.org.uk/SEB-UK.

2225 Woodland Trust [UK]
www.woodland-trust.org.uk
Charity dedicated to conserving native woodland in the UK. Information about the Trust's activities, the woods that it looks after, its publications, resources for children, parents, teachers and youth leaders.

Libraries, archives, museums

2226 Botanic Gardens Conservation International
www.bgci.org.uk
International network of botanic gardens formed to support plant conservation efforts through research and education. Includes searchable directory of gardens worldwide as well as information on plant conservation and plant physiology.

2227 Chelsea Physic Garden [UK]
www.chelseaphysicgarden.co.uk
Founded in 1673, the Garden was originally used for the study of botany in relation to medicine (hence the 'physic' in its name). Information about the garden and its plant collections; gallery of photographs; notes on weather monitoring; brief coverage of the animals that live in or use the garden.

2228 Council on Botanical and Horticultural Libraries
www.cbhl.net
The CBHL is an international network of individuals, organizations and institutions involved with botanical and horticultural libraries. Lists of libraries (including links to their online catalogues) and botanical publishers and booksellers. Also collection of 'Useful links for plant libraries and archives resources' with sections on online exhibits, electronic books and bibliographic databases.

- **European Botanical and Horticultural Libraries Group** www.kew.org/ebhl/home.htm. Promotes co-operation and communication between all of the European botanical and horticultural libraries. Includes a list of member libraries, arranged by country, as well as of affiliated libraries outside Europe.

2229 Lindley Library [UK]
www.rhs.org.uk/libraries/index.asp
There are five RHS libraries (located in London and at Wisley Garden, Hyde Hall Garden, Harlow Carr Garden and Rosemoor Garden) that are collectively known as the Lindley Library, one of the best horticultural libraries in the world. All of the libraries are open to the public and the website provides additional information about their holdings and opening hours. The Library catalogue does not appear to be available online.

2230 Mertz Library [USA]
library.nybg.org
Founded in 1899, the Mertz Library is one of the largest botanical libraries in the world with more than 800,000 books, journals and art works in its collection. It is open to the public and its catalogue is available online.

2231 **Missouri Botanical Garden** [USA]
www.mobot.org
Founded in 1859, the Garden is one of the oldest in the US. The Plant Science section of its website is an excellent source of resources on plant taxonomy, biodiversity and conservation. There is also access to a large collection of datasets including a Bryological glossary, Index to plant chromosome numbers, several bibliographies and checklists of plants from countries including Ecuador, China and Peru.

2232 **Museum of Garden History** [UK]
www.compulink.co.uk/~museumgh
The Museum was founded in 1977 and aims to raise public awareness and knowledge of the history of gardens and gardening in the UK. Website provides information about the Museum, its collections and its garden, and also includes a useful collection of links to related sites.

2233 **New York Botanical Garden** [USA]
www.nybg.org
The International Plant Science Center is the research section of the NYBG. It is made up of four main sections: Institute of Economic Botany; Institute of Systematic Botany; Mertz Library; Steere Herbarium. Website provides more information about all of these and also access to a wide range of resources including the Index to American Botanical Literature.

- **Index Herbariorum: a global directory of public herbaria and associated staff New York Botanical Garden and International Association for Plant Taxonomy**. sciweb.nybg.org/science2/IndexHerbariorum.asp. Database of more than 3000 herbaria in 165 countries.

2234 **Royal Botanic Garden Edinburgh** [UK]
www.rbge.org.uk
The RBGE was founded in 1670 as a 'Physic Garden' and it now holds the second richest collection of plant species in the world. The website provides more information about the gardens at Edinburgh, Benmore, Logan and Dawyck, the herbarium and the scientific research that these are used in. The scientists based at the Garden carry out research into systematics, biodiversity, conservation biology and cryptogamic plants and fungi. The site includes more information on these themes as well as a searchable 'Catalogue of plants' (in the living collections) and a range of other useful resources.

The RBGE Library, with collections of more than 90,000 books plus journals, art works and archives, is Scotland's reference library for botanical literature. It collects in the areas of plant systematics, biodiversity, conservation, gardening and plant collecting. The Library is open to the public and its catalogue is available online although it does not yet include all of the Library's holdings.

2235 **Royal Botanic Gardens, Kew, Library & Archives** [UK]
www.kew.org/library
The Library was founded in 1852 and it now represents one of the most important botanical library collections in the world with holdings of more than 500,000 books, journals, manuscripts, archive materials and art works. The main subject areas covered are taxonomy and horticulture but it also includes materials on mycology and economic botany. The Library is open to bona-fide researchers through a written application and the catalogue is available online. The website also includes a collection of links to related sites.

2236 **Royal Botanic Gardens, Kew** [UK]
www.kew.org
A botanic garden was first established at Kew in 1759 and it is now one of the most important sites, in terms of both the collections and the research, in the world. The website contains a huge amount of information, including a new section on the history of the gardens at Kew (in 2003 they were listed as a World Heritage Site by UNESCO). The main content on the site is listed under four headings: Science & horticulture; Collections; Conservation & wildlife; Data & publications (includes the ELECTRONIC PLANT INFORMATION CENTRE).

2237 **United States National Herbarium**
www.nmnh.si.edu/botany/colls.htm
Founded in 1848, this collection now contains more than four million specimens, including about 90,000 type specimens. Details about the collection and the research it supports as well as access to a number of useful reference sources including the Index Nominum Genericorum [q.v.], a large collection of images and a link to the Botany & Horticulture Library of the Smithsonian Institution [q.v.].

2238 **University of Oxford, Plant Sciences Library** [UK]
www.plantlib.ox.ac.uk
Founded in 1621, the Library has a collection of more than 200,000 books plus journals and pamphlets in the areas of botany, agriculture and forestry. The Library is open to bona-fide researchers and its catalogue is included within the Oxford University online library information system.

Portal & task environments

AlgaTerra Information System
Botanic Garden Berlin-Dahlem See entry no. 2830

2239 **The Cycad Pages**
K. Hill; Royal Botanic Gardens Sydney
plantnet.rbgsyd.gov.au/PlantNet/cycad
One-stop shop for information on cycads covering their taxonomy, history, ecology, genetics and distribution as well as their cultivation and uses. Site is based around the World List of Cycads database that includes all currently accepted cycad names.

2240 **Electronic Plant Information Centre: ePIC**
Royal Botanic Gardens, Kew
www.kew.org/epic
ePIC is intended to bring together all of the digital information that is produced and held at Kew into a single source. It currently includes plant names (the International Plant Names Index), bibliographies (including the RBG Library catalogue and *Kew Record*), collection and species-level information, floras and general information from the RBG website.

- **International Plant Names Index: IPNI Royal Botanic Gardens, Kew, Harvard University Herbaria and Australian National Herbarium**. www.ipni.org. Database of the names and associated basic bibliographical details of all seed plants. Its goal is to eliminate the need for repeated reference to primary sources for basic bibliographic information about plant names.

2241 **The Garden Web** [USA]
The Virtual Mirror.
www.gardenweb.com
Award winning US-based gateway: the most popular gardening site on the Web. 'While there are a number of gardening sites on the Web, GardenWeb stands apart by being the first to have established an actual community of users through our forums. Our forums constitute one of the largest, and one of the oldest, Web communities on any subject.' Hosts forums, garden exchanges, articles, contests, a plant database, online catalogues, and the web's largest garden-related glossary.

- **GardenWeb Glossary of Botanical Terms** glossary.gardenweb.com/glossary. Brief definitions for more than 4000 terms used in botany, gardening and horticulture.
- **The Rosarian** www.rosarian.com. Range of resources about roses: FAQ section (mainly questions about growing roses), links to discussion forums, images and an electronic copy of the book *Roses for English gardens* by Gertrude Jekyll. Links to rose gardens/societies.

Global Trees Campaign
Fauna & Flora International and UNEP World Conservation Monitoring Centre See entry no. 3259

2242 **Science & Plants for Schools** [UK]
www-saps.plantsci.cam.ac.uk
Initiative launched in 1990, which works with teachers to: develop new resources that support the teaching of plant science and molecular biology in schools and colleges; interest young people in plants and in molecular biology. Core funded by the Gatsby Charitable Foundation but with additional support from a range of UK-based organizations.

- **A key for identifying British trees and shrubs** F. Perring; Botanical Society of the British Isles . www-saps.plantsci.cam.ac.uk/trees. Information on 80 species of trees/shrubs commonly found in Britain. Includes descriptions of mature trees as well as information on identifying characteristics, photographs, distribution maps and glossary of botanical terms. Slow to load, but worthwhile.

The Seaweed Site
M.D. Guiry, comp.; National University of Ireland, Galway See entry no. 2835

Discovering print & electronic resources

2243 **APIRS Online: the database of aquatic, wetland and invasive plants**
University of Florida
plants.ifas.ufl.edu/search80/NetAns2
Bibliographic database that contains information about more than 63,000 published items on freshwater and wetland plants and aquatic and terrestrial invasive plants. Can be searched by keyword, scientific name, author, date, publication or subject category. Covers a wide timescale, including items published in the 18th century as well as current items. Maintained by the university's Center for Aquatic and Invasive Plants.

2244 **Catalog of Botanical Illustrations**
L. Dorr, E. Farr and A. Tangerini, eds; National Museum of Natural History
www.nmnh.si.edu/botart
Access to a database of 500 botanical images, part of the collection of more than 3000 illustrations held in the Museum's Department of Botany. At the moment, the online collection only covers three families, the Bromeliaceae, Cactaceae and Melastomataceae. Also contains brief biographical information on the artists who produced the images.

2245 **Dr. Duke's Phytochemical and Ethnobotanical Databases**
J. Duke; Agricultural Research Service
www.ars-grin.gov/duke
Database of information on plants and their uses, including medicinal uses. It can be searched for a particular plant, an active chemical or for a particular use, e.g. treating bruises. Also contains list of publications indexed in the database and links to related sites.

2246 **Guide to information sources in the botanical sciences**
E.B. Davis and D. Schmidt 2nd edn, Libraries Unlimited, 1996, 275pp. $62.00. ISBN 1563080753.
Parts of this volume, particularly those dealing with electronic resources, are now out of date but it is still useful as a guide to some of the key resources in the subject. Content is arranged by resource type.
Series: Reference Sources in Science and Technology.

2247 **Internet Directory for Botany**
A.R. Brach [et al.], comps
www.botany.net/IDB
Access to an internationally maintained huge collection of simple links to botanical websites which can either be viewed alphabetically by title or be searched by keyword. Not clear how frequently updated; but the links seem well maintained and there is a good introductory history of the site. Potentially, a useful rapid reference tool.

2248 **Kew Record of Taxonomic Literature**
Royal Botanic Gardens, Kew
www.kew.org/bibliographies/KR/KRHomeExt.html [REGISTRATION]
A bibliographic database that indexes journal articles and books on the taxonomy of flowering plants, gymnosperms and ferns, covering the period from 1971 to date. It also includes biographical items. The database is freely available but registration is required in order to access the advanced search features.

2249 **Plant Pathology Internet Guide Book**
T. Kraska; University of Bonn
www.pk.uni-bonn.de/ppigb/ppigb.htm
Access to a large collection of links to websites that deal with plant pathology and related topics, e.g. entomology, nematology, etc. The sites are arranged under subject headings and include societies, dictionaries, careers information and journals, books and other publications. The author of the site is based at the University's Institute for Plant Disease.

Digital data, image & text collections

The Arabidopsis Information Resource
National Center for Genome Resources, Arabidopsis Biological Resource Center and Carnegie Institution of Washington See entry no. 2533

2250 **The Carnivorous Plant FAQ**
B. Rice; International Carnivorous Plant Society
www.sarracenia.com/faq.html
This site is an excellent source of information on carnivorous plants. It is structured around FAQs and covers: General questions; Where? (where do plants live, where to find information, etc.); Venus flytraps; Growing carnivorous plants; Carnivorous plants and conservation; Carnivorous plant genera. The site also includes links to related resources and a large collection of images (the Galleria Carnivora).

2251 **Gymnosperm Database**
C.J. Earle; Rheinische Friedrich-Wilhelms-Universität Bonn
www.conifers.org
Includes c.1000 taxa, with full descriptions and references. Also has 'Topics' session with a variety of background information including a review of literature on gymnosperms.

Plant Viruses Online: descriptions and lists from the VIDE database
A.A. Brunt [et al.], eds See entry no. 2687

2252 **PLANTS database** [USA]
Natural Resources Conservation Service
plants.usda.gov
This database contains standardized information on the vascular plants, mosses, liverworts, hornworts and lichens of the USA. Includes information on the taxonomy, nomenclature, images and distribution of all of the plants as well as references to the original sources of the information. Can be searched by scientific or common names.

2253 **The Postcode Plants Database** [UK]
M. Sadka, D.-J. Cassey and C. Humphries, comps; Natural History Museum
www.nhm.ac.uk/science/projects/fff
This is a really nice database that contains a huge amount of information about the native British flora and fauna. The basic search allows you to identify an area of the UK using its postcode and obtain a list of the native plants that are found in that area (including historical records). You can also search for information on particular plant or animal species using either common or scientific names. For each species, the database includes information on the taxonomy, habitat, cultivation and conservation status as well as a colour photograph.

2254 **Threatened Plants of the World**
UNEP World Conservation Monitoring Centre
www.wcmc.org.uk/species/plants/overview.htm
This database contains information on the conservation status of more than 140,000 plants and includes data that was published in the *1997 IUCN red list of threatened plants*. For each species, the database provides the scientific name, the conservation status, information on geographical distribution and the CITES listing. It can be searched using scientific name or by geographical area.

2255 **Tropical Plant Database**
L. Taylor Raintree Nutrition Inc.
www.rain-tree.com/plants.htm
Contains information about plants that are found in the Amazon rainforest and their uses. Can be browsed by common and scientific names, ethnic uses or by action or disorder. The record for each plant species includes general information about the plant, details of active chemicals that have been isolated from it and quite detailed information on its uses. There is also a collection of images.

Directories & encyclopedias

Encyclopedia of plant and crop science
R.M. Goodman, ed. See entry no. 3108

Encyclopedia of rose science
A. Roberts, S. Gudin and T. Debener, eds See entry no. 3109

Medicinal plants of the world: an illustrated scientific guide to important medicinal plants and their uses
B.E. van Wyk and M. Wink See entry no. 4216

2256 **New atlas of the British & Irish flora: an atlas of the vascular plants of Britain, Ireland, the Isle of Man and the Channel Islands**
C.D. Preston, D.A. Pearman and T.D. Dines, eds Oxford University Press, 2002, 910pp. £65.00. ISBN 0198510675.
Atlas of the distribution of flowering plants and ferns in the United Kingdom and Ireland. Introductory chapters cover the history, scope and organization of the work, a brief overview of vascular plant biodiversity and the changes in the British flora. The main section is the taxonomically arranged species accounts that include a distribution map and a brief overview of the habitat of the species. Glossary, substantial bibliography and an index that includes both scientific and common names. An accompanying CD-ROM includes all of the species accounts plus brief descriptions of 942 additional taxa.

2257 **New flora of the British Isles**
C. Stace 2nd edn, Cambridge University Press, 1997, 1130pp. £35.00. ISBN 0521589335.
Aims to facilitate identification of plant species found in the wild in Britain. Begins with a section that introduces the use of identification keys, classification and nomenclature and related topics, and provides a bibliography. There follows the identification keys and species accounts which include information on biology, distribution and conservation status. The index includes both scientific and common plant names.

2258 **The plant-book: a portable dictionary of the vascular plants**
D.J. Mabberley 2nd edn, Cambridge University Press, 1997, 858pp. £40.00. ISBN 0521414210.
Alphabetical listing of all of the accepted family, generic and common names of flowering plants and ferns: covers every family and genus of seed-bearing plant (including gymnosperms) plus the pteridophytes. Over 20,000 entries include abbreviated information on the geographic distribution and biology of the plants. Also contains an overview of vascular plant taxonomy and a list of the sources used in the book.

Handbooks & manuals

Handbook of plant biotechnology
P. Christou and H.J. Klee, eds See entry no. 5043

The Hillier manual of trees & shrubs
J. Hillier and A. Coombes, eds See entry no. 3113

2259 **Illustrated handbook of succulent plants**
U. Eggli and H.E.K. Hartmann, eds Springer, 2001–4. 6 v.
www.springeronline.com [DESCRIPTION]
Major series covering over 9000 taxa of all succulents except the Cactaceas (cacti).

- **Etymological dictionary of succulent plant names U. Eggli and L.E. Newton** Springer, 2004, 266pp. €74.95. ISBN 3540004890. Explains the meanings of the scientific names given to all known succulent plants, including cacti.

Paleobotany and the evolution of plants
W.N. Stewart and G.W. Rothwell See entry no. 1475

Phytochemical dictionary: a handbook of bioactive compounds from plants
J.B. Harborne, H. Baxter and G.P. Moss See entry no. 3750

2260 **Plant resins: chemistry, evolution, ecology, and ethnobotany**
J.H. Langenheim Timber Press, 2003, 586pp. ISBN 0881925748.
www.timberpress.com [DESCRIPTION]
'Plant resin' – a term often vaguely defined – in this marvellous and fascinating handbook is here taken to be 'primarily a lipd-soluble mixture of volatile and non-volatile terpenoid and/or phenolic secondary compounds that are (1) usually secreted in specialized structures located either internally or on the surface of the plant and (2) of potential significance in ecological interactions'.

'This book is certainly a valuable addition to the library of anyone interested in the cultural history of plants and another example of the high quality ethnobotanical books published by *Timber Press.*' (*Journal of Ethnopharmacology*)

'A remarkable book on a unique subject.' (*The American Herb Association*)

2261 **Poisonous plants and fungi in Britain: animal and human poisoning**
M.R. Cooper and A.W. Johnson; Guy's & St Thomas' Hospital Trust and Royal Botanic Gardens, Kew 2nd edn, Stationery Office, 1998, 398pp. £55.00. ISBN 0112429815.
Provides a very useful guide to the poisonous plants, fungi and algae of Britain, as well as a section on Poisonous Principles covering the toxic compounds that are found in plants. Appendices on plants affecting milk, and advisory services; glossary; bibliography; index.

Poisonous plants and fungi in Britain and Ireland
E.A. Dauncey, ed.; Royal Botanic Gardens, Kew and Guy's & St Thomas' Hospital Trust See entry no. 4297

The Royal Horticultural Society encyclopaedia of gardening
C. Brickell, ed. See entry no. 3114

World weeds: natural histories and distribution
L. Holm [et al.] See entry no. 3351

Keeping up-to-date

2262 **Advances in Botanical Research**
Academic Press, 1963–, Annual, 260pp. $159.95 [V. 41, 2004]. ISBN 012005941X.
Monographic series (each volume has an individual ISBN) that publishes reviews on plant genetics, biochemistry, cell biology, ecology, physiology and molecular biology.

2263 **Annual Plant Reviews**
Blackwell, 1998–, Irregular. ISSN 14601494.
www.blackwellpublishing.com/series.asp?site=1 [DESCRIPTION]
A monographic series (each volume has an ISBN) that brings together review articles on particular aspects of plant biology, e.g. plant reproduction, the plant cell wall, plastids, etc.

Annual Review of Phytopathology
See entry no. 3352

2264 **Annual Review of Plant Biology**
Annual Reviews, 2002–, Annual. $208.00 [V. 55, 2004]. ISSN 10402519.
arjournals.annualreviews.org/loi/arplant [DESCRIPTION]
Monographic series that publishes review articles on all aspects of plant biology. Each article includes an extensive bibliography. Previously titled *Annual Review of Plant Physiology and Plant Molecular Biology*, and prior to that *Annual Review of Plant Physiology*

2265 **Current Advances in Plant Science**
Elsevier/CABS, 1972–, Monthly. €2398.00. ISSN 03064484.
www.elsevier.com/wps/find [DESCRIPTION]
Comprehensive subject-classified coverage of articles within some 2000 journals. Species and author indexes.
Available online: see website. The bulletin is a component of Current Awareness in Biological Sciences, a collection of 12 such bulletins which are also available online as part of ELSEVIER BIOBASE.

2266 **New Phytologist**
Blackwell, 1902–, Monthly. £976.00. ISSN 0028646X.
www.blackwellpublishing.com/journal.asp?ref=0028-646X&site=1 [DESCRIPTION]
A research journal that publishes original articles, reviews, letters and items on new methodology in all areas of plant science. Regular *Special Issues* highlight key areas of current research.

Review of Palaeobotany and Palynology
See entry no. 1493

2267 **Sheffield Annual Plant Reviews**
CRC Press, 1998–, Irregular.
Monograph series whose latest title *The plant cell wall* (2003. 381pp. $139.95. ISBN 084932811X) aimed to bridge 'the gap between the biochemistry-oriented cell wall literature and the new technology-driven approaches'.

2268 **Trends in Plant Science**
Elsevier, 1996–, Monthly. €1171.00. ISSN 13601385.
www.elsevier.com/locate/issn/13601385 [DESCRIPTION]
Contains useful Review and Opinion articles on basic research topics which allow researchers to follow trends and important developments outside their specialist area. Also provides Update sections featuring Research Focus articles

designed to highlight recent advances in particular research fields.

Cell Biology

biological membranes • bioluminescence • biomolecular structures • cell signalling • cells • cytochemistry • cytology • histochemistry • tissues

Introductions to the subject

Biochemistry and molecular biology
W.H. Elliott and D.C. Elliott See entry no. 2031

2269 **The birth of the cell**
H. Harris Yale University Press, 1999, 212pp. $24.00. ISBN 0300073844.
Stimulating history over three centuries of the development of the notion of the cell, based particularly on careful examination of original sources: 'Translating many of these documents into English for the first time, Harris uncovers an authentic version of events quite different from that described in conventional science textbooks.'
'*The Birth of the Cell* is the best single source for anyone seriously interested in learning about the history of the cell theory. It will remain the standard reference for some time to come.' (*Trends in Cell Biology*)

2270 **The cell: a molecular approach**
G.M. Cooper and R.M. Hausman ASM Press, 2004, 713pp. Includes CD-ROM, $104.95. ISBN 0878932143.
First-rate introduction: very well designed and presented.

Cells, aging, and human disease
M.B. Fossel See entry no. 3888

The double helix: a personal account of the discovery of the structure of DNA
J.D. Watson See entry no. 2482

2271 **Essential cell biology**
B. Alberts [et al.] 2nd edn, Garland Science, 2004, 740pp. $70.89. ISBN 0815334818.
www.garlandscience.co.uk/ecb2/default.asp [DESCRIPTION]
Provides a concise introduction to molecular biology (including genomics) that is aimed at the general public rather than advanced students. The book is illustrated in colour throughout and further illustrations are provided on the accompanying CD-ROM. Includes a glossary but there is no bibliography.

Fundamentals of enzymology: the cell and molecular biology of catalytic proteins
N.C. Price and L. Stevens See entry no. 2032

Genomes
T.A. Brown See entry no. 2491

A history of molecular bology (Histoire de la biologie moléculaire)
M. Morange See entry no. 1898

An introduction to astrobiology
I. Gilmour and M.A. Sephton See entry no. 634

2272 **Introduction to glycobiology**
M.E. Taylor and K. Drickamer Oxford University Press, 2003, 207pp. £21.99. ISBN 0199258686.
www.oup.co.uk/best.textbooks/biosciences/glycobiology [COMPANION]
Aimed at advanced undergraduates and graduate students; each chapter includes a bibliography of further reading. Website includes full contents listing and illustrations from the book.

2273 **Molecular biology of the cell**
B. Alberts [et al.] 4th edn, Garland Science, 2002, 1463pp. $120.00. ISBN 0815332181.
Standard undergraduate molecular biology textbook. Five sections: Introduction to the cell; Basic genetic mechanisms; Methods; Internal organization of the cell; Cells in their social context. Each chapter includes a bibliography. Glossary; subject index.

Molecular principles of animal development
A. Martinez Arias and A. Stewart See entry no. 2444

Oral cells and tissues
P.R. Garant See entry no. 3823

Synapses
W.M. Cowan, T.C. Sudhof and C.F. Stevens; Howard Hughes Medical Institute See entry no. 3977

Dictionaries, thesauri, classifications

Biopharmaceutical glossary and taxonomies
M. Chitty, ed. See entry no. 2503

Dictionary of biochemistry and molecular biology
J. Stenesh See entry no. 2038

2274 **The dictionary of cell and molecular biology**
J.M. Lackie and J.A.T. Dow, eds 3rd edn, Academic Press, 1999, 502pp. Formerly *Dictionary of cell biology*, $50.95. ISBN 0124325653.
www.mblab.gla.ac.uk/dictionary
With more than 7000 entries this is a very useful reference work. Definitions are concise and include cross-references to related topics and synonyms. Electronic version of the dictionary is freely available but usage is restricted to 'occassional [sic] use (1 day every 90)'.

The dictionary of gene technology: genomics, transcriptomics, proteomics
G. Kahl See entry no. 5013

Encyclopedic dictionary of genetics, genomics, and proteomics
G.P. Rédei See entry no. 2506

Glossary of biochemistry and molecular biology
D.M. Glick See entry no. 2040

Illustrated dictionary of immunology
J.M. Cruse and R.E. Lewis See entry no. 3572

Oxford dictionary of biochemistry and molecular biology
A.D. Smith [et al.], eds See entry no. 2042

Official & quasi-official bodies

International Union of Biochemistry and Molecular Biology
See entry no. 2046

National Center for Biotechnology Information
See entry no. 2507

Research centres & institutes

European Bioinformatics Institute
See entry no. 2509

European Molecular Biology Laboratory
See entry no. 2510

Associations & societies

American Association of Immunologists
See entry no. 3574

American Society for Biochemistry and Molecular Biology
See entry no. 2048

2275 **American Society for Cell Biology**
www.ascb.org
Founded in 1960, the ASCB now has more than 10,000 members in the US and internationally. Activities include the publication of the journal *Molecular Biology of the Cell* and the site also includes careers information.

Australian Society for Biochemistry and Molecular Biology
See entry no. 2049

2276 **British Society for Cell Biology**
www.kcl.ac.uk/kis/schools/life_sciences/biomed/bscb/top.html
Founded in 1965, the BSCB aims to 'promote the advance of research in all branches of cell biology and to encourage the interchange of information'. Includes an online cell biology tutorial 'softCELL' that provides an introduction to the subject, as well as links to related sites.

European Molecular Biology Organization
See entry no. 1925

2277 **Histochemical Society**
www.histochemicalsociety.org
Founded in 1950, the HCS is 'devoted to the study of cell and tissue biology with molecular and morphological techniques'. Among a range of activities, it publishes the *Journal of Histochemistry & Cytochemistry*.

2278 **International Federation of Societies for Histochemistry and Cytochemistry**
www.ifshc.org
Brings together histochemistry societies from around the world. Website includes a list of the member societies, giving contact details and links to websites (where available). Newsletter.

International Society for Plant Molecular Biology
See entry no. 2218

Protein Society
See entry no. 2055

2279 **Society for Histochemistry**
www.sfh.unizh.ch
Founded in 1952, the Society has an international membership. The website provides more information about the Society and its activities, which include publication of the journal *Histochemistry and Cell Biology*.

Society for Molecular Biology and Evolution
See entry no. 2457

Portal & task environments

2280 **The Bioluminescence Web Page**
S.H.D. Haddock, C.M. McDougall and J.F. Case; University of California, Santa Barbara
www.lifesci.ucsb.edu/~biolum
Bioluminescence refers to light that is produced by organisms, usually through a chemical reaction. This site provides a very useful introduction to the subject, with a list of organisms that produce light as well as sections covering the chemistry and physiology of bioluminescence.

The Bio-Web: resources for molecular and cell biologists
A. Cabibbo, comp. See entry no. 2521

Model Organisms for Biomedical Research
National Institutes of Health See entry no. 2524

Protocol Online
L.-C. Li See entry no. 2526

2281 **The Signaling Gateway**
Alliance for Cellular Signaling Nature Publishing Group.
www.signaling-gateway.org
Comprises: Molecule Pages, relational database of all significant published qualitative and quantitative information on cell signalling proteins; AfCS Data Center, public repository of primary data from the Alliance's own cellular signalling experiments; Signaling Update, weekly updates of the literature, with related news, jobs, conference details.

Discovering print & electronic resources

Computational Molecular Biology at NIH
National Institutes of Health See entry no. 2528

Entrez: the life sciences search engine
National Center for Biotechnology Information See entry no. 2529

WWW Virtual Library: Biochemistry and Cell Biology
G. Fenteany, ed.; University of Illinois at Chicago See entry no. 2060

Digital data, image & text collections

BRENDA: The Comprehensive Enzyme Information System
Cologne University See entry no. 2062

2282 **CELLS alive!**
J.A. Sullivan
www.cellsalive.com
Access to a collection of images and animations of cells and cell biology, e.g. mitosis. Each image is accompanied by brief explanatory text. The site is freely available for personal and educational use.

Protein Data Bank: PDB
Research Collaboratory for Structural Bioinformatics See entry no. 2068

UniProt: the universal protein resource
European Bioinformatics Institute, Swiss Institute of Bioinformatics and Protein Information Resource See entry no. 2540

Directories & encyclopedias

Basic histology: text & atlas
L.C. Junqueira and J. Carneiro See entry no. 3584

2283 **Encyclopedia of molecular biology**
J. Kendrew [et al.], eds Blackwell, 1994, 1165pp. £125.00. ISBN 086542621X.
A classic reference work that contains more than 5500 entries, arranged alphabetically, covering all aspects of molecular biology. It includes 217 longer review articles that provide more in-depth information and a bibliography for topics such as: Nucleic acid structure; Protein structure; Membrane structure. Many of the entries include illustrations and there are cross-references to related topics throughout the work.

Encyclopedia of molecular biology
T.E. Creighton, ed. See entry no. 2543

Handbooks & manuals

2284 **Bone research protocols**
M.H. Helfrich and S. Ralston, eds Humana, 2003, 448pp. $125.00. ISBN 1588290441.
Multi-author work; thorough treatment. 'A collection of the latest laboratory techniques for the study of bone and bone tissue. Described in step-by-step detail, these readily reproducible methods cover such topics as the isolation and culture of bone cells, the preparation of bone tissue for histological and ultrastructural analysis, methods for the measurement of bone strength and for mechanical studies, and how to use digital imaging techniques in the analysis of bone.'
Series: Methods in Molecular Medicine.

'Bone Research Protocols is a most welcome compilation of methods. In it, many of the most productive laboratories in some of the most challenging areas of cell biology reveal detailed protocols that have been used to solve key problems. Short of spending a sabbatical in one of the eminent laboratories that contributed, this volume provides the best possible introduction to these methods.' (*Trends in Endocrinology and Metabolism*)

Encyclopedia of immunology
P.J. Delves and I.M. Roitt, eds See entry no. 3922

2285 **Essential cell biology**
J. Davey and M. Lord, eds Oxford University Press, 2003. £79.00. ISBN 0198527640.
These two volumes provide an introduction to, and detailed protocols for, many of the techniques used in cell biology. Each chapter covers a different technique and includes a bibliography. Each volume also includes a list of suppliers and a subject index.
- **Volume 1. Cell structure: a practical approach** 398pp. ISBN 0199638314.
- **Volume 2. Cell function: a practical approach** 235pp. ISBN 0199638330.

Fundamental neuroscience
L.R. Squire [et al.] See entry no. 3997

2286 **Handbook of cell signaling**
R.A. Bradshaw and E.A. Dennis, eds Academic Press, 2004. 3 v., $449.95. ISBN 0121245462.
Detailed reference work with 350 chapters (articles) arranged in three parts (Initiation; Transmission; Nuclear and cytoplasmic events), and each chapter including a substantial bibliography.

The phylogenetic handbook: a practical approach to DNA and protein phylogeny
M. Salemi and A.-M. Vandamme, eds See entry no. 2471

Practical handbook of biochemistry and molecular biology
G.D. Fasman, ed. See entry no. 2080

Principles and techniques of practical biochemistry
K. Wilson and J. Walker, eds See entry no. 2081

2287 **The structure of biological membranes**
P.L. Yeagle, ed. 2nd edn, CRC Press, 2004, 540pp. $159.95. ISBN 0849314038.
This book, aimed at researchers, brings together 16 chapters that review and update the state of knowledge on lipids, the lipid bilayer and protein function and structure in membranes. Each chapter includes a bibliography and the book also includes an index.

Tissue engineering
B. Palsson and S. Bhatia, ed. See entry no. 4139

Keeping up-to-date

Advances in Enzymology and Related Areas of Molecular Biology
See entry no. 2086

2288 Annual Review of Cell and Developmental Biology
Annual Reviews, 1995–, Annual. $215.00 [V. 20, 2004]. ISBN 0824331206 ISSN 10810706.
arjournals.annualreviews.org/loi/cellbio [DESCRIPTION]
An important research journal that publishes review articles on aspects of the topic. Each article includes a substantial bibliography.

Biochemistry
American Chemical Society See entry no. 2091

2289 Cell Biology Education
American Society for Cell Biology Quarterly.
www.cellbioed.org
Publishes original, previously unpublished, peer-reviewed articles on life science education at the K-12 outreach, undergraduate and graduate levels.

All published articles are available freely online without subscription, as well as being made available through PubMed Central. 'The ASCB believes that learning in biology encompasses diverse fields, including math, chemistry, physics, engineering, computer science, and the interdisciplinary intersections of biology with these fields. Within biology, CBE is particularly interested in how students are introduced to the study of life sciences, as well as approaches in cell biology, developmental biology, neuroscience, biochemistry, molecular biology, genetics, genomics, bioinformatics, and proteomics.'

Excellent journal. Provides useful set of Electronic Resources, including archival access to each issue's review of 'Web sites of educational interest to the life science community'.

EMBO Reports
European Molecular Biology Organization See entry no. 2553

2290 Histochemistry and Cell Biology
Society for Histochemistry Springer, 1995–, Monthly. ISSN 09486143.
A research journal that publishes original articles on all aspects of cell biology and molecular histology.

Laboratory Techniques in Biochemistry and Molecular Biology
See entry no. 2092

Microbiology and Molecular Biology Reviews
American Society for Microbiology See entry no. 2705

2291 Nature Cell Biology
Nature Publishing Group, 1999–, Monthly. £715.00. ISSN 14657392.
www.nature.com/ncb [DESCRIPTION]
An important research journal that publishes original articles on all aspects of cell and molecular biology. It also includes news items and reviews of relevant books.

2292 Trends in Cell Biology
Elsevier, 1991–, Monthly. €1171.00. ISSN 09628924.
A research journal that publishes commissioned review articles on all aspects of cell biology.

Ecology

biogeography • biomes • biosphere • ecosystems • environmental biology • environmental change • environmental law • geosphere • global environment • sustainability

Introductions to the subject

2293 A companion to environmental philosophy
D. Jamieson, ed. Blackwell Publishing, 2003, 531pp. £19.99. ISBN 140510659X.
Good introductory volume comprising 31 articles in four parts: Cultural traditions; Contemporary environmental ethics; Environmental philosophy and its neighbours; Problems in environmental philosophy.
'simply the best "field-guide" to environmental philosophy anywhere. Dale Jamieson has assembled an insightful set of chapters – the topics are well chosen, the writing is crisp, and the thinking is compelling. The volume is also historically informed, theoretically rich, multicultural, and practical – all especially appreciated strengths.' (*The Hastings Center*)

Conserving living natural resources: in the context of a changing world
B.J. Weddell See entry no. 2103

2294 Ecology: individuals, populations and communities
M. Begon, J.L. Harper and C.R. Townsend 3rd edn, Blackwell Science, 1996, 1068pp. £34.99. ISBN 0632038012.
Standard undergraduate textbook divided into four parts: Organisms; Interactions; Three overviews (Life-history variation; Abundance; Manipulating abundance: killing and culling); Communities. The book also includes a glossary, bibliography and organism and subject indexes.

2295 Ecology
R.E. Ricklefs and G.L. Miller 4th edn, W H Freeman, 2000, 822pp. $102.95. ISBN 071672829X.
www.whfreeman.com/ricklefsmiller [COMPANION]
Undergraduate textbook that covers a wider range of topics than the book by Begon [q.v.]. Seven parts: Introduction; Organisms in physical environments (heat, water, etc); Energy and materials in the ecosystem; Population ecology; Population interactions; Community ecology; Evolutionary ecology. Glossary; bibliography; subject index.

2296 Ecology: principles and applications
J.L. Chapman and M.J. Reiss 2nd edn, Cambridge University Press, 1999, 330pp. £28.00. ISBN 0521588022.
Introductory undergraduate textbook. Includes a glossary (pp 303–10) and bibliography (pp 311–26).

The economics of the environment and natural resources
R.Q. Grafton [et al.] See entry no. 4613

Fundamentals of aquatic ecology
R.S.K. Barnes and K.H. Mann, eds See entry no. 2561

Fungal ecology
N.J. Dix and J. Webster See entry no. 2708

2297 **Global environment: water, air and geochemical cycles**
E. K. Berner and R. A. Berner Prentice Hall, 1996, 390pp. ill., maps. ISBN 0133011690.
A good introduction by established authors. Well used by students. It would be improved by the use of colour in diagrams. Contents: Introduction to the global environment; The water cycle and atmospheric and oceanic circulation; Air chemistry: The greenhouse effect and the ozone hole; Rainwater and atmospheric chemistry; Chemical weathering and water chemistry; rivers; lakes; Marginal marine environments: Estuaries; The oceans.

An introduction to marine ecology
R.S.K. Barnes and R.N. Hughes See entry no. 2562

2298 **Introductory ecology**
P. Cotgreave and I. Forseth Blackwell Science, 2002, 278pp. £21.99. ISBN 0632042273.
www.blackwellpublishing.com/cotgreave [COMPANION]
This is a good introductory textbook that provides an overview of the main topics in ecology including biodiversity, climate change and population biology. Each chapter includes suggestions for further reading and the book also includes a bibliography.

Limnology: lake and river ecosystems
R.G. Wetzel See entry no. 2563

Limnology: inland water ecosystems
J. Kalff See entry no. 2564

The Ozone Hole Tour
O. Garrett and G. Carver; Centre for Atmospheric Science See entry no. 1167

Parasitoids: behavioral and evolutionary ecology
H.C.J. Godfray See entry no. 2799

A primer of population genetics
D.L. Hartl See entry no. 2499

Protecting the ozone layer: science and strategy
E.A. Parson See entry no. 1169

Sharing the planet: population-consumption-species: science and ethics for a sustainable and equitable world
B. van der Zwaan and A. Petersen, eds See entry no. 4616

Dictionaries, thesauri, classifications

Concise dictionary of environmental terms
L. Theodore, J. Reynolds and K. Morris, comps See entry no. 5536

2299 **A dictionary of ecology**
M. Allaby, ed. 2nd edn, Oxford University Press, 1998, 440pp. £8.99. ISBN 0192800787.
www.oxfordreference.com
With more than 5000 entries covering all areas of the subject this is a very useful reference work. The definitions are concise and include cross-references to related topics. Some entries also include illustrations.
Available online: see website.

2300 **The dictionary of ecology and environmental science**
H.W. Art, ed. Henry Holt, 1993, 632pp. ISBN 0805020799.
With over 8000 entries this dictionary aims to provide a complete coverage of the terminology in these fields but there is a bias towards the ecological side of the subject. Entries are generally quite short but very clear and many include illustrations.

2301 **Dictionary of ecology and the environment**
P.H. Collin 4th edn, Peter Collin Publishing, 2001, 292pp. £9.95. ISBN 1901659615.
A useful basic dictionary that contains definitions for more than 8500 terms. It includes a Supplement that provides brief information on classification, geological time scale, human population growth, endangered species and natural and man-made disasters.

2302 **A dictionary of ecology, evolution and systematics**
R.J. Lincoln, G.A. Boxshall and P.F. Clark 2nd edn, Cambridge University Press, 1998, 360pp. £20.99. ISBN 052143842X.
Provides definitions for more than 11,000 terms across the fields of study that can perhaps now be said to make up the core of natural history including newer terms that have arisen from areas such as biodiversity. 29 appendices cover diverse topics such as geological time scales, abbreviations and plankton size categories.

2303 **Dictionary of environmental quotations**
B.K. Rodes and R. Odell, eds Johns Hopkins University Press, 1998, 335pp. $30.00. ISBN 0801857384.
Consists of over 3700 quotations arranged chronologically within 143 categories (e.g. Air, Conservation, Forests, Greenhouse effect, History, Nuclear energy, Water, Wildlife). Wide range of sources, including poems, proverbs, slogans, radio and television broadcasts, magazines and newspapers. Author and subject indexes.
1st edn Simon & Schuster 1992.
'Fascinating and original ... I cannot imagine a reference work so useful to those concerned with man's place in the natural world.' (*Wilderness*)

Dictionary of environmental science and engineering: English–Spanish/Spanish–English
H. Headworth and S. Stienes, comps See entry no. 5537

Dictionary of environmental science and technology
A. Porteous, comp. See entry no. 5538

Dictionary of natural resource management
J. Dunster and K. Dunster See entry no. 2108

Elsevier's dictionary of the environment: in English, French, Spanish and Arabic
M. Bakr, comp. See entry no. 5545

The environment dictionary
D.D. Kemp, comp. See entry no. 5546

2304 **The Facts On File dictionary of ecology and the environment**
J. Bailey, ed. Facts On File, 2004, 248pp. $49.50. ISBN 081604922X.
This is a good basic dictionary with more than 2000 entries

covering all aspects of the subject. It includes a list of web resources and a very short bibliography.

2305 Macmillan dictionary of the environment
M. Allaby 4th edn, Macmillan, 1994, 377pp. ISBN 0333616553.
A good dictionary that covers all aspects of environmental science including geology, mineralogy, ecology and technology. It includes a table listing some of the major environmental disasters that occurred between 1930 and 1993.

Terms of environment
Environmental Protection Agency See entry no. 5552

Laws, standards, codes

2306 ENTRI: Environmental Treaties and Resource Indicators
Socioeconomic Data and Applications Center
sedac.ciesin.columbia.edu/entri/index.jsp
Innovative site offering a comprehensive online service with tailorable downloads for accessing environmental treaty data, including status data for environmental treaties, treaty text and other related information. Searchable by treaty or country, with country profiles listing treaties signed, in force or denounced.

Environmental Law Alliance Worldwide
See entry no. 2110

2307 European Network for the Implementation and Enforcement of Environmental Law: IMPEL
European Commission. Directorate for Environment
http://europa.eu.int/comm/environment/impel
An informal network of the environmental authorities of the Member States and candidate countries of the European Union and Norway. Concerned with: effective implementation and enforcement of environmental legislation; sharing information and experiences; greater consistency of approach; mutual understanding; best practices. Useful entrée to activity in this arena.

2308 International Environmental Law
A. Burnett; American Society of International Law
www.asil.org/resource/env1.htm
Excellent guide to internet resources, CD-ROMs, library catalogues and subscription services relating to environmental law. Content arranged under seven headings: Introduction (to the site); Overview; General search strategies; Primary sources; Secondary sources; Other related sites; Online discussion lists.
Series: ASIL Guide to Electronic Resources for International Law.

Official & quasi-official bodies

Arctic Council
See entry no. 2112

2309 Canadian Council of Ministers of the Environment
www.ccme.ca
'The major intergovernmental forum in Canada for discussion and joint action on environmental issues of national and international concern.' Good entrée to work in this region.

Commission on Sustainable Development
See entry no. 4623

2310 Council on Environmental Quality [USA]
www.whitehouse.gov/ceq
'In enacting NEPA (National Environmental Policy Act), Congress recognized that nearly all federal activities affect the environment in some way and mandated that before federal agencies make decisions, they must consider the effects of their actions on the quality of the human environment. NEPA assigns CEQ the task of ensuring that federal agencies meet their obligations under the Act. The challenge of harmonizing our economic, environmental and social aspirations has put NEPA at the forefront of our nation's efforts to protect the environment.'

Department of Energy
United States. Department of Energy See entry no. 4624

Department of the Environment and Heritage
Australia. Department of the Environment and Heritage See entry no. 2116

2311 Environment Portal: your gateway to Australian environment resources on the internet
www.environment.gov.au
Access to online services and information provided by Australian, State and Local Governments organized by seven broad environmental themes: Atmosphere; Biodiversity; Coasts and oceans; Environment protection; Heritage; Inland waters; Land.

2312 European Environment Agency
www.eea.eu.int
The EEA aims to provide information to European decision-makers in order to protect the environment and support sustainable development. The website, which is available in several different languages, provides more information about the Agency and its activities. The site is searchable or it can be browsed by country or by one of the its 32 themes, which include: Air; Climate change; Transport; Waste; Water. Also accessible is the *EEA multilingual environmental glossary* which provides definitions for more than 1000 terms in 23 languages.

- **EEA multilingual environmental glossary**
  glossary.eea.eu.int/EEAGlossary.

Global Invasive Species Programme
See entry no. 2121

2313 Man and the Biosphere Programme
www.unesco.org/mab
'Develops the basis, within the natural and the social sciences, for the sustainable use and conservation of biological diversity, and for the improvement of the relationship between people and their environment globally.' The website provides more information about the programme and its activities which are listed under the headings: Capacity building; Different ecosystems; Research and monitoring; Sustainable development. Also information about more than 400 Biosphere Reserves that have been established around the world.

National Ocean Service
See entry no. 1355

Office of Water
See entry no. 1131

2314 **Ozone Secretariat**
www.unep.org/ozone/index.asp
Secretariat for the two main treaties that aim to protect the ozone layer. The Vienna Convention for the Protection of the Ozone Layer was adopted in 1985 and the Montreal Protocol on Substances that Deplete the Ozone Layer adopted in 1987. The website reviews these treaties and their ratification. It is also a useful source of information on the ozone layer with a section of the site aimed specifically at the general public.

2315 **Scientific Committee on Problems of the Environment**
www.icsu-scope.org
SCOPE was founded by the International Council for Science in 1969 as 'an interdisciplinary body of natural and social science expertise focused on global environmental issues'. Access to many of the Committee's publications, covering topics such as environmental impact assessment, the carbon cycle and invasive species, plus details of their work.

2316 **United Nations Environment Programme**
www.unep.org
UNEP was founded in 1972 and it is probably the most important environmental organization in the world. Many of the key environmental agreements, e.g. CITES and the Convention on Biological Diversity are supported by UNEP. Its research programmes encompass environmental assessment, biodiversity, marine and freshwater issues, climate change and sport and environment. Well designed and structured site offering from the home page a series of gateways aimed at specific constituencies: Governments; Scientists; Journalists; Children and youth; Business persons; Civil society.

- **Earthprint.com** www.earthprint.com. UNEP's official online bookshop, but also selling other key environmental publications – both from the major commercial publishers and smaller NGOs or organizations with a few environment titles. Excellent Topics categorization.
- **UNEP-Infoterra** www.unep.org/infoterra. Designed as the Programme's 'Global Environmental Information Exchange Network'. Potentially a valuable entrée – though currency and functionality showed considerable variation throughout the site when reviewed late 2004.

2317 **United Nations Framework Convention on Climate Change**
unfccc.int
This site provides access to the full text of and information about the United Nations Framework Convention on Climate Change and the Kyoto Protocol.

Research centres & institutes

Centre for Alternative Technology
See entry no. 4786

2318 **Centre for Ecology and Hydrology** [UK]
www.ceh.ac.uk
Funded by the Natural Environment Research Council, the CEH carries out scientific research in the 'terrestrial and freshwater environments'. Its research programmes are structured into: Biodiversity; Biogeochemistry; Climate change; Sustainable economies; Water. The Centre hosts two of NERC's eight Designated Data Centres: National Water Archive, responsible for NERC's hydrological data and for the UK Government's National River Flow and Groundwater Level archives; Environmental Information Centre, responsible for all NERC's terrestrial and freshwater ecological data, including that from the Biological Records Centre.

- **CEH Library Service** library.ceh.ac.uk. Actually consists of nine site libraries (Banchory, Bangor, Dorset, Edinburgh, Lancaster, Monks Wood, Oxford, Wallingford and Windermere), collectively providing extensive holdings in ecology, biology, land use and hydrology.

2319 **Eden Project** [UK]
www.edenproject.com
The highly successful venture in Cornwall, England whose mission is 'To promote the understanding and responsible management of the vital relationship between plants, people and resources leading to a sustainable future for all'.

2320 **International Geosphere-Biosphere Programme**
www.igbp.kva.se
Established in 1986 by the International Council for Science and aims to 'describe and understand the interactive physical, chemical and biological processes that regulate the total Earth System' by supporting research at a national and regional level. Downloadable PDF Newsletter (quarterly: No. 59, September 2004, 28 pp). IGBP Book Series published by Springer, recent titles including: *Atmospheric chemistry in a changing world, Paleoclimate, global change and the future, Vegetation, water, humans and the climate*.

NERC Collaborative Centres
See entry no. 1192

2321 **Pew Center on Global Climate Change** [USA]
www.pewclimate.org
Founded in 1998, the Center aims to 'provide credible information, straight answers, and innovative solutions in the effort to address global climate change'. Website provides quite detailed information on global warming and US state and federal and international policies on climate change.

2322 **Resources for the Future** [USA]
www.rff.org
Major institute founded in 1952 whose mission to improve 'environmental and natural resource policymaking worldwide through objective social science research of the highest caliber'. Wide range of Discussion Papers, RFF Reports, Issue Briefs, Resources, Reference Materials, and Congressional Testimony are available as downloadable PDFs. Books from their RFF Press can be ordered online. Each of their extensive list of Research Topics is supported by citations to projects, scholars, publications, etc. germane to the Topic.

2323 **Smithsonian Environmental Research Center** [USA]
www.serc.si.edu
Mission: 'Leads the Nation in research on linkages of land and water ecosystems in the coastal zone, and provides society with knowledge to meet critical environmental challenges in the 21st century'. Well laid-out website, each of the Research Labs (Avian ethology, Benthic ecology, Biocomplexity, Biogeochemistry, etc.) having informative sets of pages. K-12 Education section.

2324 **The UK Environmental Change Network**
Centre for Ecology and Hydrology and Natural Environment Research Council
www.ecn.ac.uk/index.html
Long-term, integrated environmental monitoring and research programme, gathering information about environmental change in physical, chemical and biological systems. Aims to establish and maintain a selected network of sites within the UK from which to obtain comparable long-term datasets through the monitoring of a range of variables; to integrate and analyse these data, so as to identify changes and improve understanding of the causes; to distinguish short-term fluctuations from long-term trends, and predict future changes.

2325 **World Resources Institute**
www.wri.org
The WRI is an environmental research and policy organization that was founded in 1982. The website provides more information about the organization and its activities. It also provides access to the valuable EARTHTRENDS portal.

Associations & societies

2326 **British Ecological Society**
www.britishecologicalsociety.org
Founded in 1913, the BES has an international membership and promotes the study of ecology. The Society publishes several journals, has a number of specialist groups, and its site includes details of meetings and public affairs activities, and links to the sites of other ecological societies worldwide. Especially useful are the extensive Education & Careers pages, each providing links to wide ranges of resources within a structured framework. A well developed facility.

2327 **Ecological Society of America**
www.esa.org
Founded in 1915, the Society has more than 8000 members and promotes the study of all aspects of ecology. They publish *Ecology* and several other journals. Site includes careers information, job listings and information about ESA's educational resources.

- **Ecology Education Network: EcoEdNet** www.ecoed.net. The ESA's portal to locate, contribute, and disseminate ecology education resources.

2328 **Environmental Defense** [USA]
www.environmentaldefense.org
Founded in 1967, this organization brings together scientists, economists and lawyers in order to tackle environmental issues in the US and internationally. Its programme of activities covers seven main areas: Climate & air; Ecosystem restoration; Environmental alliances; Health; International; Living cities; Oceans.

2329 **Environmental Investigation Agency**
www.eia-international.org
Founded in 1984 and is 'an international campaigning organization committed to investigating and exposing environmental crime'. Website provides more information about the organization and its three core campaign areas: Species in peril; Forests for the world; Global environment.

2330 **Friends of the Earth**
www.foe.co.uk
FE is an international network of environmental groups and is represented in more than 60 countries around the world. Apart from information about its work, the well designed and pleasant website includes a large collection of Links to related websites, arranged under headings such as: Biodiversity & Habitats; Climate change; Corporates; Courses; 'Easy Actions you can take'; etc.

International Association of Theoretical and Applied Limnology
See entry no. 2591

2331 **National Council for Science and the Environment** [USA]
www.ncseonline.org
Non-profit-making organization founded in 1990 with the aim of improving the scientific basis of environmental decisions. Activities include facilitating the work of the Council of Environmental Deans and Directors that aims to improve the quality of environmental programmes in US universities and colleges, as well as that of the National Commission on Science for Sustainable Forestry.

- **National Library for the Environment** www.ncseonline.org/NLE. Access to collection of official US documents and reports on environmental issues. Redistributes more than 1250 Congressional Research Service (CRS) reports and a valuable collection of CRS Briefing Books. News, announcements, extensive set of links, etc.

2332 **Natural Resources Defense Council** [USA]
www.nrdc.org
The NRDC aims 'to safeguard the Earth: its people, its plants and animals and the natural systems on which all life depends'. Site includes information on nine environmental topics: Clean air & energy; Global warming; Clean water & oceans; Wildlife & fish; Parks, forests & wildlands; Toxic chemicals & health; Nuclear weapons & waste; Cities & green living; Environmental legislation.

2333 **Society for Ecological Restoration International**
www.ser.org
Founded in 1987, the SER has more than 2000 members in 37 countries all of whom are involved in the management and repair of ecosystems. The Reading section of the website contains 'Guidelines for ecological restoration' and a PDF downloadable version of 'The SER primer on ecological restoration' as well as information about other SER publications. The site also includes information on educational programmes, including online courses, a directory of expertise, a calendar of events and information about employment in the sector.

WWF International
See entry no. 2145

Portal & task environments

Climate Change
United Nations Environment Programme See entry no. 1206

ClimateArk: climate change portal
See entry no. 1208

2334 **EarthTrends: the environmental information portal**
World Resources Institute
earthtrends.wri.org
This site is an exceptional resource, providing access to a huge amount of authoritative environmental data. Information is provided under ten headings: Coastal and marine ecosystems; Water resources and freshwater ecosystems; Climate and atmosphere; Population, health and human well-being; Economics, business and the environment; Energy and resources; Biodiversity and protected areas; Agriculture and food; Forests, grasslands and drylands; Environmental governance and institutions. For each heading there is a searchable database, data tables, country profiles (PDF files), maps and features (related articles).

2335 **Eco-portal: the environmentalsustainability.info source**
Ecological Internet, Inc..
www.eco-portal.com
Access to substantial collection of links to environmental websites. Also includes news items, an environmental blog and a discussion list.

2336 **EnviroLink: the onlineenvironmental community**
EnviroLink
www.envirolink.org
Large collection of environmental websites, with significant information about each site and with the entries arranged in a subject hierarchy. There is a good search facility. Also includes items of news and a discussion forum. US bias but includes web pages and news items from around the world. Useful service.

2337 **European Environment Information and Observation Network: EIONET**
European Environment Agency
www.eionet.eu.int
Collaborative network of over 600 environmental bodies and agencies, public and private research centres across Europe within the EEA and its Member Countries, connecting National Focal Points in the EU and accession countries, European Topic Centres, National Reference Centres, and Main Component Elements. 'These organizations jointly provide the information that is used for making decisions for improving the state of environment in Europe and making EU policies more effective. EIONET is both a network of organizations and a electronic network (e-EIONET)'.

There is a useful regularly updated presentation Data Flows on e-EIONET which can be downloaded (and reveals the considerable complexity of environmental data stocks and flows within Europe). The presentation is within the section About EIONET – getting started. Otherwise, one just needs to work through the not uniformly well designed and well functioning areas of this potential cornucopia.

- **General Multilingual Environmental Thesaurus: GEMET** www.eionet.eu.int/GEMET. Extensive thesaurus from 2004 made web-accessible. There is a detailed and helpful 'About page', especially useful on the history of the thesaurus.

Forestry and Land Use
International Institute for Environment and Development See entry no. 3255

2338 **Sierra Club** [USA]
www.sierraclub.org
'The Sierra Club's members are more than 700,000 of your friends and neighbors. Inspired by nature, we work together to protect our communities and the planet. The Club is America's oldest, largest and most influential grassroots environmental organization.' News, magazines, resources, etc.

US Global Change Research Information Office
US Climate Change Science Program See entry no. 1211

Discovering print & electronic resources

2339 **Ecological Abstracts**
Elsevier, 1974–, Monthly. €2379.00. ISSN 0305196X.
www1.elsevier.com/homepage/sah/spd/site/index.html
Index to the journal literature covering all aspects of ecology, including conservation. Articles are indexed under 12 sections that include marine ecology, freshwater ecology, microbial ecology, evolution and palaeoecology and economic ecology. Each issue includes subject, organism, regional and author indexes.
Available online within GEOBASE*: see website.*

2340 **Ecology Abstracts**
CSA, 1982–, Monthly. $1550.00. ISSN 01433296.
www.csa.com/factsheets/ecology-set-c.php [DESCRIPTION]
Bibliographic database that covers the literature on the interaction between organisms and their environments. Covers 300 journals.
Available online: see website.

2341 **Ecology WWW Page**
A.R. Brach, comp.
www.botany.net/Ecology
Brings together large collection of links to ecological websites which can be searched (by title only) or browsed alphabetically.

Information sources in environmental protection
S. Eagle and J. Deschamps, eds See entry no. 5585

2342 **Wildlife & Ecology Studies Worldwide**
NISC.
www.nisc.com/Frame/NISC_products-f.htm [DESCRIPTION]
'The world's largest index to literature on wild mammals, birds, reptiles, and amphibians — over 625,300+ bibliographic records, many include abstracts.' Based on *Wildlife Review Abstracts*, formerly *Wildlife Review*, which until 1996 was produced by the US National Biological Service, but supplemented by content from other worldwide sources.

Digital data, image & text collections

2343 **Australian Natural Resources Atlas**
National Land and Water Resources Audit
audit.ea.gov.au/ANRA/atlas_home.cfm
Provides access to data that was gathered as part of the National Land and Water Resources Audit (1997–2002) and is intended to support natural resource management in Australia. The Atlas can be searched by geographical area or

by topic: Agriculture; Coasts; Land; People; Rangelands; Water resources; Vegetation and biodiversity.

2344 Early classics in biogeography, distribution, and diversity studies
C.H. Smith, comp.
www.wku.edu/%7Esmithch/biogeog
Access to an online bibliography of articles on a range of subjects including ecology, conservation, biodiversity and systematics. The bibliography includes links to full text of many of the items (mainly journal articles) that are listed, either via a digital copy that is freely available on the site or via alternative sources, e.g. JSTOR [q.v.], some of which may require a subscription. This site covers the literature to 1950; a companion site treats 1951–1975.

2345 Major biomes of the world
S.L. Woodward; Radford University
www.runet.edu/~swoodwar/CLASSES/GEOG235/biomes/intro.html
'Biomes are the major regional groupings of plants and animals discernible at a global scale'. Site created to support teaching within the University's Geography Department, and providing an overview of some of the world's major biomes: Tundra; Boreal forest; Temperate broadleaf deciduous forest; Tropical broadleaf evergreen forest; Tropical savannah; Desert scrub; Temperate grasslands; Mediterranean scrub.

- **Biomes of earth: terrestrial, aquatic, and human-dominated S.L. Woodward** Greenwood Press, 2003, 456pp. £45.99. ISBN 0313319774.

Practical Conservation Online
British Trust for Conservation Volunteers See entry no. 2158

Directories & encyclopedias

2346 The encyclopedia of ecology & environmental management
P. Calow, ed. Blackwell Science, 1998, 805pp. £49.99. ISBN 0632055464.
This impressive work contains more than 3000 entries, ranging in length from a paragraph to several pages. The volume does not contain an index but the extensive cross-referencing makes it very easy to locate all of the relevant information on a topic. A very useful reference work.

Encyclopedia of environmental microbiology
G. Bitton [et al.], eds See entry no. 2690

2347 The encyclopedia of environmental studies
W. Ashworth Facts On File, 1991, 470pp. ISBN 0816015317.
This useful basic encyclopedia was written by a librarian, assisted by an editorial board of environmental professionals. Entries are generally quite short and include cross-references to related entries. It includes terminology, biographical entries and entries for environmental organizations (addresses are given for US organizations / branches).

Encyclopedia of global change: environmental change and human society
A.S. Goudie and D.J. Cuff, eds See entry no. 4654

2348 Encyclopedia of global environmental change
T. Munn, ed. Wiley, 2002, 3440pp. 5 v., $2650.00. ISBN 0471977969.
This work provides a useful overview of the subject. Each volume begins with a series of essays that provide an introduction to the topics covered in that volume. These are followed by shorter articles, arranged alphabetically, that cover specific topics. Each article and all of the essays include bibliographies. Each volume includes an alphabetical list of the articles from all five volumes while Volume 5 also includes a complete subject index, along with a very useful list of abbreviations and acronyms.

- **Volume 1. The earth system: physical and chemical dimensions of global environmental change M.C. MacCracken and J.S. Perry, eds** 773pp.
- **Volume 2. The earth system: biological and ecological dimensions of global environmental change H. A. Mooney and J. G. Canadell, eds** 625pp.
- **Volume 3. Causes and consequences of global environmental change I. Douglas, ed.** 753pp.
- **Volume 4. Responding to global environmental change M. K. Tolba, ed.** 567pp.
- **Volume 5. Social and economic dimensions of global environmental change P. Timmerman, ed.** 608pp.

2349 Encyclopedia of the biosphere: a guide to the world's ecosystems
R. Folch, ed. Gale, 2000. 11 v. ISBN 0787645060.
www.galegroup.com [DESCRIPTION]
Produced under the auspices of UNESCO's MAN AND THE BIOSPHERE PROGRAMME each volume of this work focuses on an individual biome (forests, lakes, oceans, savannahs and deserts), and covers environmental factors, plant and animal ecology, human influences and biosphere reserves.

While the encyclopedia contains much useful information, its layout does not always make finding this information very easy. Each volume includes a Thematic Index (basically a contents page but located at the end of the volume) and a species index. The Terminological Index included in the final volume lists the contents of all of the volumes.

'[An] amazing work. Highly recommended for general readers, undergraduates, graduate students, and faculty, and for all college and university libraries.' (*Library Journal*)

Encyclopedia of world environmental history
S. Krech, J.R. McNeill and C. Merchant, eds See entry no. 4655

2350 The National Environmental Directory [USA]
Harbinger Communications, 327pp.
www.environmentaldirectory.net
This online directory provides information on more than 13,000 environmental organizations in the US. It can be searched by geographical region, organization name or by subject / keyword. Searching can also be restricted to those organizations that have websites.

2351 World who is who and does what in environment and conservation
N. Polunin, ed.; Foundation for Environmental Conservation
Earthscan, 1997, 592pp. £75.00. ISBN 1853833770.
An alphabetical listing of individuals that are employed or otherwise involved (e.g. as patrons, etc.) with conservation and environmental activities. Each entry includes details of the person's present and past employment, their areas of expertise and their publications. Appendices listing the

entries geographically and by speciality are included along with a list of relevant abbreviations and acronyms.

Handbooks & manuals

Behavioural ecology: an evolutionary approach
J.R. Krebs and N.B. Davies, eds See entry no. 2021

2352 **Biogeography: an ecological and evolutionary approach**
C.B. Cox and P.D. Moore 7th edn, Blackwell, 2004, 448pp. £32.95. ISBN 1405118989.
Biogeography is the study of the geographical distribution of plants and animals. This book is an undergraduate textbook that provides a useful overview of the subject. Each chapter includes a bibliography.

2353 **Ecological methods**
T.R E. Southwood and P.A. Henderson 3rd edn, Blackwell Science, 2000, 575pp. £38.50. ISBN 0632054778.
www.blackwellpublishing.com/southwood [COMPANION]
Comprehensive overview of the techniques that are used to study animal populations, including field techniques as well as data handling. A bibliography is included at the end of each chapter and the book also has an index. The accompanying website provides an overview of each chapter, new references and links to related sites.

2354 **Ecosystems of the World**
D.W. Goodall, ed. Elsevier, 1977–.
www.elsevier.com/locate/series/ew
Monographic series that publishes reviews of the current state of knowledge on a range of terrestrial, aquatic and underground ecosystems. Individual chapters in each volume cover specific aspects of the topic and include bibliographies.

Field and laboratory investigations in agroecology
S.R. Gliessman See entry no. 3047

2355 **Handbook of ecotoxicology**
D.J. Hoffman [et al.], eds 2nd edn, Lewis Publishers, 2003, 1312pp. $199.95. ISBN 1566705460.
45 chapters covering all aspects of ecotoxicology and divided into five sections: Quantifying and measuring ecotoxicological effects; Contaminant sources and effects (lead, pesticides, etc.); Case histories and ecosystem surveys (primarily US examples); Methods for making estimates, predictability, and risk assessment in ecotoxicology; Special issues in ecotoxicology. Each chapter includes a bibliography.

Lake and pond management guidelines
S. McComas See entry no. 2646

Life history of a fossil: an introduction to taphonomy and paleoecology
P. Shipman See entry no. 1468

Palaeoecology: ecosystems, environments and evolution
P. Brenchley and D. Harper See entry no. 1474

Palaeohydrology: understanding global change
K.J. Gregory and G. Benito See entry no. 1153

Plant resins: chemistry, evolution, ecology, and ethnobotany
J.H. Langenheim See entry no. 2260

2356 **Scientific method for ecological research**
E.D. Ford Cambridge University Press, 2000, 564pp. £35.00. ISBN 0521669731.
Important text which presents a critique of the scientific method, stressing the importance of being explicit about the thought processes involved in designing and carrying out experiments.
'. should be owned, read thoroughly, discussed, and consulted frequently by every graduate student and ecological researcher ... should be required reading by anyone planning an ecological research project, or planning to advise one.' (*Ecology*)

2357 **The world's environments**
K. Hillstrom and L.C. Hillstrom, eds ABC-CLIO, 2003. 6 v.
www.abc-clio.com/products/series.aspx [DESCRIPTION]
This series of books, available in print and as e-books, provides an overview of environmental issues in the different regions of the world. Each volume includes chapters on: Population and land use; Biodiversity; Parks, preserves, and protected areas; Forests; Agriculture; Freshwater; Oceans and coastal areas; Energy and transportation; Air quality and the atmosphere; Environmental activism. Each chapter includes a bibliography and the volumes also include lists of relevant organizations.
- **Africa & the Middle East: a continental overview of environmental issues** 297pp. ISBN 157607692X.
- **Asia: a continental overview of environmental issues** 245pp. ISBN 1576076881.
- **Australia, Oceania, & Antarctica: a continental overview of environmental issues** 269pp. ISBN 1576076946.
- **Europe: a continental overview of environmental issues** 261pp. ISBN 1576076865.
- **Latin America & the Caribbean: a continental overview of environmental issues** 266pp. ISBN 1576076903.
- **North America: a continental overview of environmental issues** 296pp. ISBN 1576076849.

Keeping up-to-date

2358 **Advances in Ecological Research**
Academic Press, 1962–, Irregular, 228pp. $149.95 [V. 33, 2003]. ISBN 0120139332 ISSN 00652504.
Monographic series that publishes review articles on all aspects of ecology. For example, V. 33 published articles on: The evolutionary ecology of carnivorous plants, Trophic interactions in population cycles of voles and lemmings, Scale effects and extrapolation in ecological experiments. Each article includes a substantial bibliography.

2359 **The American Naturalist**
American Society of Naturalists University of Chicago Press, 1867–, Monthly. $470.00. ISSN 00030147.
www.journals.uchicago.edu/AN/home.html [DESCRIPTION]
A research journal that publishes original articles on ecology, evolution, animal behaviour and other aspects of natural history.

2360 **Annual Review of Ecology, Evolution & Systematics**
Annual Reviews, 2003–, Annual. $202.00 [V. 35, 2004]. ISBN 0824314352 ISSN 1543592X.
arjournals.annualreviews.org/loi/ecolsys [DESCRIPTION]
High quality review articles, each with substantial bibliographies.

Behavioral Ecology
International Society for Behavioral Ecology See entry no. 2026

Behavioral Ecology and Sociobiology
See entry no. 2027

Conservation Biology
Society for Conservation Biology See entry no. 2175

2361 **The Ecologist**
Ecosystems Ltd, 1970–, 10/year. £28.00. ISSN 02613131.
www.theecologist.org [DESCRIPTION]
This journal publishes articles and investigative reports on a wide variety of environmental and related issues. It also includes news items and a 'Green directory' of 'environmentally friendly' shopping alternatives.

2362 **ENN: Environmental News Network**
Environmental News Network.
www.enn.com
This US-based site brings together environmental news items from a variety of sources, providing a useful way of keeping up to date with current issues. 'We are not an activist publication; instead we try to present information from all sides, enabling our audience to make their own informed decisions.'

2363 **Environment News Service**
Environmental News Service. $24.00 [2004].
www.ens-news.com [FEE-BASED]
Based in the USA provides environmental news stories from around the world. The headlines are freely available but a subscription is required for access to the full stories.

2364 **Environmental Media Services** [USA]
www.ems.org
'Non-profit communications clearinghouse dedicated to expanding media coverage of critical environmental and public health issues. We build relationships with top scientists, physicians, and other experts to bring journalists the latest and most credible information.' Often quite critical coverage – especially of current US government actions. The Library has a very useful series of 'Backgrounders, links and sources for journalists covering the environment' categorized: Climate & air; Consumer; Energy; Environmental health; Government; Land & ecology; Oceans & water; Transportation & sprawl (though many sections have not recently been updated).

green@work Today
See entry no. 4661

2365 **Habitat** [UK]
D. Brear
www.habitat.org.uk
This delightful site brings together news stories about environmental issues and wildlife, primarily from the UK but it does also include some international stories. It also provides selective links to environmental and wildlife websites.

How to save the world
D. Pollard, ed. See entry no. 4662

2366 **Our Planet**
United Nations Environment Programme 1989–, Quarterly. $20.00. ISSN 10137394.
www.ourplanet.com
Magazine which 'reports on international developments and action. It reviews current thinking, suggests solutions, and debates the key issues of environmentally sustainable development'. Includes articles by world leaders (recently including Tony Blair and Nelson Mandela). Each issue deals with a single theme, e.g. Global waste challenge; Mountains and ecotourism. All issues from 1996 to date are freely available at the website.

2367 **Trends in Ecology & Evolution**
Elsevier, 1986–, Monthly. €1171.00. ISSN 01695347.
www.elsevier.com/locate/issn/01695347 [DESCRIPTION]
A research journal that publishes accessible review articles on all aspects of the subject. It also includes book reviews.

Entomology

ants • bees • beetles • bugs • butterflies • crickets • cultural entomology • Diptera • dragonflies • flies • grasshoppers • Hymenoptera • insects • leaf miners • Lepidoptera • locusts • mosquitoes • moths • Orthoptera • springtails • stick insects

Introductions to the subject

Amber: window to the past
D.A. Grimaldi See entry no. 1396

2368 **For love of insects**
T. Eisner Belknap Press/Harvard University Press, 2003, 448pp. $29.95. ISBN 0674011813.
A fascinating story. 'Imagine beetles ejecting defensive sprays as hot as boiling water; female moths holding their mates for ransom; caterpillars disguising themselves as flowers by fastening petals to their bodies; termites emitting a viscous glue to rally fellow soldiers – and you will have entered an insect world once beyond imagining, a world observed and described down to its tiniest astonishing detail by Thomas Eisner ...'

2369 **Imms' general textbook of entomology**
O.W. Richards and R.G. Davies 10th edn, Chapman & Hall, 1977, 1354pp. V. 1 *Structure, physiology and development* ISBN 0412152002; V. 2 *Classification and biology* ISBN 0412152207.
The classic entomology textbook, this work provides a good overview of insect biology. The work is structured in three parts: Anatomy and physiology; Development and metamorphosis; The orders of insects. More up-to-date versions of the content in the first two parts is available in the books by Chapman [q.v.] and Gullan and Cranston [q.v.]. However, the third part still provides one of the best overviews of insect classification (to Family level), covering the topic in more detail than any of the other textbooks.

2370 **The insects: structure and function**
R.F. Chapman 4th edn, Cambridge University Press, 1998, 770pp. £40.00. ISBN 0521578906.
An undergraduate text that covers the anatomy, morphology and physiology of insects. Structured in five parts: The head, ingestion, utilization and distribution of food; The thorax and locomotion; The abdomen, reproduction and development; The integument, gas exchange and homeostasis; Communication (including vision, smell and pheromones). Bibliography for each chapter.

2371 **The insects: an outline of entomology**
P.J. Gullan and P.S. Cranston 3rd edn, Blackwell Science, 2004, 486pp. £29.99. ISBN 1405111135.
Good undergraduate-level textbook. Provides an introduction to all aspects of the subject including anatomy, physiology, reproduction, systematics, behaviour and insects as pests (both medical and agricultural).

2372 **Insects of Britain and Northern Europe**
M. Chinery 3rd edn, HarperCollins, 1993, 320pp. ISBN 0002199181.
This is the standard field guide to the British and European insect fauna, providing general information on insect biology, taxonomy and field techniques (collecting, etc.) as well as identification keys for all of the insect orders. It includes a large number of wonderful colour illustrations and a bibliography.

The natural history of pollination
M.C.F. Proctor, P.F. Yeo and A. Lack See entry no. 2182

Parasitoids: behavioral and evolutionary ecology
H.C.J. Godfray See entry no. 2799

Dictionaries, thesauri, classifications

2373 **Common names of insects and related organisms** [USA]
M.B. Stoetzel, ed.; Entomological Society of America 1989, 199pp. ISBN 0938522345.
www.entsoc.org/pubs/books/common_names/index.htm
2018 common names for the insects, mites and spiders found in the USA and Canada. Four sections list the species alphabetically by common name, scientific name, taxonomic order, taxonomically by phylum – giving the common names for families of insects.

The list of names is now maintained electronically by the Society: 'The edition published in 1989 contained 2018 names. The final printed edition, published in 1997, added another 28 names to the list. This new online version has another 46 names added since 1997. From now on, new names will be added to the online database as they are approved by the Governing Board.'

2374 **A dictionary of entomology**
G. Gordh and D.H. Headrick, comps CAB International, 2003, 1050pp. £45.00. ISBN 0851996558.
Supersedes the The Torre-Bueno glossary of entomology and encompasses all the terms from that work plus new terms that have appeared in the published entomological literature since 1989. Gives taxonomic names to sub-family level as well as biographical entries for several eminent entomologists. There are entries for a number of species under their common names but with no cross-reference to their scientific names which, given the variation that occurs in the use of insect common names, is surprising and out of keeping with the high quality of the rest of the work.

2375 **Insectes, araignees & acariens: correspondances entre les dénominations scientifiques et anglo-saxonnes (Insects, spiders, mites and ticks: equivalences between scientific and common English names)**
R. Couilloud CIRAD, 1991, 681pp. ISBN 2876140586.
One of the most comprehensive listings of the scientific and common names of the insects and arachnids. Alphabetical listings by scientific and common name, along with an index to names of the authors who first used the scientific names. Introduction in French.

2376 **Invertebrates of economic importance in Britain: common and scientific names**
P.R. Seymour, comp.; Ministry of Agriculture, Fisheries and Food 4th edn, HMSO, 1989, 147pp. ISBN 0112428290.
Common names of animals, particularly insects, can vary enormously from region to region and from country to country. In order to try to ensure that names were used consistently, MAFF produced this guide to the common and scientific names of the British species of nematodes, platyhelminthes, annelids, arthropods (including insects) and molluscs.

2377 **Nomina Insecta Nearctica: a check list of the insects of North America** [USA]
R.W. Poole and P. Gentili, eds
www.nearctica.com/nomina/main.htm
Checklist of the insects of North America listing generic and specific names, authorities (authors of the species name), the date that the name was published, and the genus that the species was originally described under (if different from currently). Based on the fuller 4-vol. print version.
Note that the website unfortunately has intrusive pop-ups.

- **Volume 1. Coleoptera, Strepsiptera** Entomological Information Services, 1996, 827pp. ISBN 1889002011.
- **Volume 2. Hymenoptera, Mecoptera, Megaloptera, Neuroptera, Raphidioptera, Trichoptera** Entomological Information Services, 1996, 793pp. ISBN 188900202X.
- **Volume 3. Diptera, Lepidoptera, Siphonaptera** Entomological Information Services, 1996, 1143pp. ISBN 1889002038.
- **Volume 4. Non-holometabolous orders** Entomological Information Services, 1997, 731pp. ISBN 1889002046.

2378 **The Torre-Bueno glossary of entomology**
S.W. Nichols and G.S. Tulloch, comps Rev edn, New York Entomological Society, 1989, 840pp. ISBN 0913424137.
Until publication of the new dictionary by Gordh and Headrick [q.v.], this was the standard entomological dictionary and it still remains a very useful reference work. Includes terminology and taxonomic information above the level of Family.

Research centres & institutes

Bee Research Laboratory
See entry no. 3158

Center for Medical, Agricultural and Veterinary Entomology
See entry no. 3325

Insect Biocontrol Laboratory
See entry no. 3326

2379 **Systematic Entomology Laboratory**
www.sel.barc.usda.gov
Part of the US Department of Agriculture (USDA) and carries out research into the systematics of insects and mites (Acari). Brief information about the work of the Laboratory, along with links to a vast collection of related resources, including checklists, literature databases and general information about insects: all produced by SEL staff.

Associations & societies

2380 **Amateur Entomologists' Society** [UK]
www.amentsoc.org
One of the most important UK entomological societies, producing some very useful publications. When reviewed, website had been awaiting major revision for some time, with much of the content out of date. However, there is still much useful material here: e.g. the Caresheets section that provides information on keeping invertebrates as pets.

2381 **American Board of Forensic Entomology**
www.missouri.edu/~agwww/entomology
A relatively new organization with only a few members based in the USA and Canada. The website provides a nice overview of forensic entomology (also known as medicocriminal entomology) with sections on the history of the subject and case studies.

2382 **American Mosquito Control Association**
www.mosquito.org
Founded in 1935, the AMCA is based in the USA but has an international membership. Excellent Mosquito Info covering the life-cycle, mosquito-borne diseases and control, etc., as well as information about the Association, with free access to the journal *Wingbeats* and extensive links to related websites.

2383 **Association for Tropical Lepidoptera** [USA]
www.troplep.org
The ATL, founded in 1989, is based in the USA but has an international membership. Includes information on the classification of the Lepidoptera (butterflies and moths), a collection of images, and links to related sites.

2384 **British Dragonfly Society**
www.dragonflysoc.org.uk
Founded in 1983 with the aim of supporting the study and conservation of dragonflies, the website being an excellent source of information about both those and damselflies. An FAQs section provides general information while the UK species section contains more detailed information on species status and distribution as well as some colour photographs. Also links to wide range of other relevant sites.

2385 **British Entomological and Natural History Society**
www.benhs.org.uk
Founded in 1872, the BENHS includes both amateur and professional members. Basic information about membership, meetings, workshops, publications, etc.

2386 **Buglife – the Invertebrate Conservation Trust** [UK]
www.buglife.org.uk
The UK has more than 47,000 species of invertebrates and Buglife is active carrying out research and campaigning to ensure their conservation. About Invertebrates provides an overview, including a list of species, and more detailed information on the insects sub-set (with data on other invertebrates still being created as of August 2004). Includes more general information on conservation and links to related organizations.

2387 **Butterfly Conservation** [UK]
www.butterfly-conservation.org
Founded in 1968, aims to conserve the native British species of butterflies and moths. Useful source of information, with the Species section of the site including information on all UK native and migrant species of butterflies, including colour photographs. There is a similar smaller section on moths.

2388 **Coleopterists Society** [USA]
www.coleopsoc.org
US-based society with an international membership that is open to anyone with an interest in beetles (Coleoptera). Links to a wide range of related resources and to several freely available newsletters that deal with specific groups of beetles. Access to a searchable version of the Society's membership directory.

2389 **Entomological Society of America**
www.entsoc.org
The largest entomological society in the world. Much valuable information with the Education and Information section containing a useful FAQs section covering topics such as pest control, careers in entomology, and insect trivia.

2390 **International Bee Research Association**
www.ibra.org.uk
Founded in 1949, the IBRA is a registered charity that promotes bees and bee-keeping. The website provides information on IBRA publications, events and their large Library that is based in Cardiff. Well structured links section together with a useful FAQs section (although the questions there seem not to be organized very helpfully). The Association 'aims to increase awareness of the vital role of bees in the environment and encourages the use of bees as wealth creators'. It publishes three journals including *Apicultural Abstracts*.

2391 **Lepidopterists' Society** [USA]
alpha.furman.edu/~snyder/snyder/lep
US-based society with an international membership. Many of the resources on the website have a US bias; but there is a handy FAQ section – with the answer to the first question, (How are many specialized words defined?), leading to a very useful online dictionary.

- **A dictionary for Lepidopterists: some terms used to describe butterflies and moths**
  http://alpha.furman.edu/~snyder/snyder/lep/lep-dictionary.htm.

2392 **Orthopterists' Society**
www.orthoptera.org
International society that publishes some of the key literature relating to Orthoptera (grasshoppers, crickets and locusts). Orthoptera Resources area of the site contains links to related sites, a collection of photographs, information on the Society's discussion list, and a literature database (unavailable when reviewed). There is also a searchable database of the Society's members.

2393 **Phasmid Study Group**
www.stickinsect.org.uk
Group was founded in 1980 and now has an international membership of both amateur and professional entomologists. Website provides a useful starting point for finding information on stick and leaf insects and includes a diary of forthcoming events, a list of species (including some photographs), a collection of informal articles and a discussion forum.

2394 **Royal Entomological Society** [UK]
www.royensoc.co.uk
Founded in 1833, the RES is the most important entomological society in the UK. Details of scientific meetings, special interest groups and publications (both books and journals). Links to related sites. The RES Library, housed at the Society's building in central London, contains an important collection of entomological books, journals and manuscript materials. Access is available to the public by appointment only.

Xerces Society
See entry no. 2146

Libraries, archives, museums

2395 **California Academy of Sciences, Department of Entomology**
www.calacademy.org/research/entomology
Founded in 1862, the Department currently has 17 staff looking after a collection of more than 12 million specimens. Website provides more information about the Department and its collection, including a searchable type-specimen database. Other resources include several check-lists and catalogues.

2396 **Entomology Libraries and Information Network**
www.nhm.ac.uk/hosted_sites/elin/index.htm
Includes an international directory of libraries with good entomological collections. Last updated in 2002 but still a useful starting point.

2397 **Natural History Museum, Entomology Library**
Natural History Museum, Entomology Library
www.nhm.ac.uk/library/entlib.html
One of the most comprehensive collections of entomological literature in the world with over 90,000 volumes, including books, 1000 current journals, 350 manuscript collections and more than 40,000 original drawings. Library catalogue is searchable online. Access by appointment only.

2398 **Ohio State Insect Collection**
Ohio State University
iris.biosci.ohio-state.edu
Part of the University's Museum of Biodiversity, the collection contains approximately 3.5 million specimens and supports research, primarily on the Hymenoptera. Website includes links to a variety of databases and related resources produced as a result of research carried out on the collection.

Portal & task environments

2399 **Antbase.Org: Social Insects WWW Ant Pages**
D. Agosti and N.F. Johnson, comp.; American Museum of Natural History and Ohio State University
http://antbase.org
A one-stop shop for information on ants (Formicidae) providing access to taxonomic databases, images, bibliographies and a Directory of the World's Ant Taxonomists.

- **FORMIS: a master bibliography of ant literature D. P. Wojcik and S. D. Porter, comps; Agricultural Research Service** . cmave.usda.ufl.edu/formis. Composite of several ant bibliographic databases containing citations for a large fraction of the world's ant literature (about 32,000 references).

2400 **The Bumblebee Pages**
L. Smith
www.bumblebee.org
Excellent introduction to bumblebees, providing images, general information on their biology and behaviour and more detailed information on individual species. Also a list of books and journal articles and links to related sites.

2401 **Dragonflies and Damselflies: Odonata Information Network**
B. Mauffray, comp.; International Odonata Research Institute
www.afn.org/~iori
Aimed at researchers rather than the general public this site contains lots of useful information. Provides access to a directory of researchers, details of forthcoming meetings, information on discussion groups and links to related sites. Site also provides access to a very useful online Odonata Bibliography.

- **Odonata Bibliographic Information: based on my odonatological library R. J. Beckemeyer** . www.windsofkansas.com/odbib.html.

2402 **Insect Information**
Clemson University
entweb.clemson.edu/insectinfo/index.htm
Attractively presented range of resources produced by Clemson Entomology: the Division of Entomology in the University's Department of Entomology, Soils and Plant Sciences. Includes images and information on urban entomology as well as an Insect Information Series: a collection of PDF downloadable leaflets covering a wide range of topics.

Mosquito Genomics WWW Server
See entry no. 2525

2403 **PEST CABWeb**
CAB Publishing.
http://pest.cabweb.org [FEE-BASED]
Access to range of CAB journals and other products covering entomology, nematology, weed science, biological control,

plant pathology and many other aspects of pest management, plus news of new publications, events, links, etc. Includes: Crop Protection Compendium; Nematological Abstracts.

- **Review of Medical and Veterinary Entomology** 1990–, Monthly. £655.00. ISSN 09576770. pest.cabweb.org/Journals/Abstract/rmvemain.htm. Index to the primary journal literature on insects and their role as carriers of disease. Online version updated weekly.
- **Review of Agricultural Entomology** Monthly. £1140.00. ISSN 09576762. http://pest.cabweb.org/Journals/Abstract/raemain.htm. Index to the primary journal literature relating to insects as agricultural pests derived from the CAB Abstracts database. Online version updated weekly.

Discovering print & electronic resources

2404 Abstracts of Entomology
Thomson BIOSIS, 1970–, Monthly. ISSN 00013579.
www.biosis.org/products/aoe [description]
Sub-set of the Biological Abstracts *BIOSIS Previews database containing details of 20,000 new references each year covering most aspects of entomology.*

2405 Bibliotheca Entomologica: Die Litteratur über das ganze Gebiet der Entomologie bis zum Jahre 1862 (The literature over the whole area of entomology up to the year 1862)
H.A. Hagen Leipzig: Wilhelm Engelmann, 1862–3. V. 1. *A–M* 1862. 566 pp; V. 2 *N–Z*. 1863. 512 pp.
Comprehensive listing of early entomological published literature.

- **Index Litteraturae Entomologicae: Die Welt-Literatur über die gesamte Entomologie bis inklusive 1863 W. Horn and S. Schenkling** Berlin: Dr Walther Horn, 1928. Continuation of the Hagen work.

2406 Entomology: a guide to information sources
P. Gilbert and C.J. Hamilton 2nd edn, Mansell, 1990, 265pp. £65.00. ISBN 0720120527.
Although now out of date this is still a good starting point for the subject. Lists sources of information on taxonomy, nomenclature, specimen collections, literature and organizations.

2407 Entomology Abstracts
CSA, 1969–, Monthly. $1570.00. ISSN 00138924.
www.csa.com/factsheets/entomology-set-c.php [description]
Important index to the primary literature, providing details of more than 200,000 articles and covering the period from 1982 to date. Treats all aspects of entomology with the exception of applied research (e.g. insects as pests).
Available online: see website.

2408 Entomology on World-Wide Web
L. Bjostad, comp.; Colorado State University
www.colostate.edu/Depts/Entomology/links.html
Large collection of links to entomological websites arranged alphabetically. Site is not searchable, which makes it difficult to identify all of the relevant resources on a particular topic, but still a worthwhile resource. Maintained within the Department of Bioagricultural Sciences and Pest Management.

2409 Identifying British insects and arachnids: an annotated bibliography of key works
P.C. Barnard, ed. Cambridge University Press, 1999, 353pp. £60.00. ISBN 0521632412.
Produced by staff in the Department of Entomology at the Natural History Museum, provides a guide to the literature that can be used to identify all of the British species of insects and arachnids. Includes chapter written by the Entomology Librarian on use of the literature.

2410 Iowa State Entomology Index of Internet Resources: the directory and search engine of insect-related resources on the internet
J.K. VanDyk and L.B. Bjostad; Iowa State University of Science and Technology, Department of Entomology
www.ent.iastate.edu/list
This site, founded in 1996, is the primary guide to entomological information on the internet. It brings together an enormous collection of links and groups them under helpful headings: Bibliographies; Image galleries; Job opportunities; Online courses; and so on (as well as by taxonomic group). Site is searchable and also includes a Newest Additions section. An excellent resource.

Zoological Record
Zoological Society of London See entry no. 2913

Digital data, image & text collections

2411 AntWeb
California Academy of Sciences
www.antweb.org
Information on the ant faunas of California and Madagascar, and global coverage of all ant genera. Excellent guide with very good image collection.

2412 British Leaf Mining Fauna
B. Dickerson [et al.]
www.leafmines.co.uk
Leaf miners are a group of insects whose larvae live and feed between the epidermal layers of leaves. This site provides information on British leaf mines and mining fauna, including photographs. Also includes a selective bibliography and links to related sites.

2413 Bugbios: shameless promotion of insect appreciation
D. Sear
www.insects.org
Access to a nice collection of insect photographs in which each image includes information about the species pictured, plus useful information on cultural entomology (insects in human culture – art, mythology, etc.).

2414 Butterflies & Moths of the World: generic names & their type-species
B. Pitkin and P. Jenkins; Natural History Museum
www.nhm.ac.uk/entomology/butmoth
Interactive catalogue of the genus-group names of the Lepidoptera, including colour images of most families and sub-families. Database can be searched by genus and family name and can be browsed by family and author name. (Species names can be found in LepIndex.)

2415 Checklist of the Collembola
P.F. Bellinger, K.A. Christiansen and F. Janssens
www.collembola.org
This site contains a huge amount of information on Collembola (springtails). It includes introductory information, directory of researchers, glossary, images, bibliography. Also searchable taxonomic checklist of all Collembola species.

2416 Coleoptera World Wide Web Site
N.J. Vandenberg, comp.; Systematic Entomology Laboratory
www.sel.barc.usda.gov/coleoptera/col-home.htm
Access to three main resources dealing with leaf chafers (Coleoptera: Scarabaeidae: Rutelinae), palearctic flea beetles (Coleoptera: Chrysomelidae: Alticinae) and Elaphidiini (Coleoptera: Cerambycidae). Also information on the US national Coleoptera collection.

2417 LepIndex: the global lepidoptera names index
G. Beccaloni [et al.], ed.; Natural History Museum
www.nhm.ac.uk/entomology/lepindex
Aims to provide a comprehensive list of the names of all species of Lepidoptera (butterflies and moths). Includes information on the authority (i.e. the original author of the name) and the publication details of the original description. Generic names for the Lepidoptera are listed in BUTTERFLIES & MOTHS OF THE WORLD.

2418 Orthoptera Species File Online
D. Otte, D.C. Eades and P. Naskrecki; Orthopterists' Society
osf2.orthoptera.org
Developed for use by researchers working in this area, this database contains taxonomic information for more than 22,000 species of Orthoptera (grasshoppers, crickets and locusts). Also includes bibliographic citations, images and sound recordings (an important identification tool for this group).

The Postcode Plants Database
M. Sadka, D.-J. Cassey and C. Humphries, comps; Natural History Museum See entry no. 2253

2419 TaxoDros: the database on taxonomy of Drosophilidae
G. Bächli; University of Zurich
taxodros.unizh.ch
A huge database of information on the Drosophilidae (Diptera). As the name suggests the main content of the database is taxonomic information but it also contains an index to literature relating to the family and information on the geographical distribution of species. Produced within the Zoological Museum.

2420 UK Moths
I. Kimber
cgi.ukmoths.force9.co.uk
An excellent source of information on British moths, covering more than half of the recorded species so far with more being added regularly. Entries provide brief information on each species along with colour photographs. The site also includes details of useful books, identification keys and links to related sites.

Directories & encyclopedias

2421 Directory of Entomological Societies
Scientific Reference Resources.
www.sciref.org/links/EntSoc/index.htm
Useful list of entomological societies from around the world. Where available, the societies' websites are included.

2422 Directory of Entomology Departments and Institutes (DEDI)
Scientific Reference Resources.
www.sciref.org/links/EntDept/index.htm
Global listing of academic departments, government organizations and research centres with an interest in entomology. Includes websites where these are available. Does not appear to have been updated recently but still a useful starting point.

2423 Encyclopedia of insects
V.H. Resh and R.T. Cardé, eds Academic Press, 2003, 1266pp. $99.95. ISBN 0125869908.
This claims to be 'a complete source of information on the subject of insects' and while this is probably a slight overstatement it is a very thorough work. It includes articles on all of the insect groups as well as on subjects such as museum collections, cultural references to insects, and the history of entomology. Each article includes a bibliography and there is also a glossary and subject index including both scientific and common names. The quality of the work has been endorsed by such luminaries as: Paul Ehrlich, Lord Robert May, Peter Raven, Sir Richard Southwood, Edward O. Wilson.
'AAP/PSP Best Single Volume Reference/Sciences for 2003.' *(Association of American Publishers' Professional Scholarly Publishing Division)*

2424 Insect and Spider Collections of the World
N.L. Evenhuis and G.A. Samuelson
hbs.bishopmuseum.org/codens/codens-r-us.html
Based on a 1993 book, and one of the most comprehensive checklists of museums with entomological and arachnological collections available on the internet. Is searchable and includes some website links.
- **The insect and spider collections of the world R. H. Arnett, G. A. Samuelson and G. M. Nishida** 2nd edn, Sandhill Crane Press, 1993, 310pp.

2425 The millennium atlas of butterflies in Britain and Ireland
J. Asher [et al.]; Butterfly Conservation and Biological Records Centre Oxford University Press, 2001, 433pp. £30.00. ISBN 0198505655.
Publishes the results of the Butterflies for the New Millennium project which surveyed the distribution of butterflies from 1995 to 1999. Seven chapters: Background (about the project); Butterfly habitats; Recording and data collection; Interpreting the data; Species accounts (the main part of the book); The pattern and cause of change; Conserving butterflies in the new millennium. Colour illustrations and photographs as well as bibliography, glossary and nine appendices covering topics such as common and scientific names, climate summaries and details of relevant organizations. An attractive work.

2426 **The University of Florida Book of Insect Records**
T.J. Walker, ed.; University of Florida
ufbir.ifas.ufl.edu
Currently contains 39 chapters on topics such as: Largest; Longest; Fastest runner. Each chapter consists of an article, of varying length, and including references to further reading from the scientific literature, and is written as a volunteer to write it (and so coverage is not comprehensive). Prepared within the University's Department of Entomology and Nematology.

Handbooks & manuals

2427 **Handbooks for the Identification of British Insects**
D. Hollis, ed.; Royal Entomological Society 1949–, Irregular.
www.royensoc.co.uk/pubs.html [DESCRIPTION]
This ongoing monographic series provides the definitive guide to the British insect fauna. Each volume in the series deals with a specific group (usually at family or sub-family level), providing an introduction to the group's morphology, biology and distribution and an illustrated identification key. The series also includes check-lists of the British insects.

Medical entomology: a textbook on public health and veterinary problems caused by arthropods
B.F. Eldridge and J.D. Edman, eds See entry no. 4436

2428 **The Naturalists' Handbook Series**
Company of Biologists Richmond Publishing, 1983–, Irregular.
www.biologists.com/web/other/naturalist/naturalist.html [DESCRIPTION]
This series of books, aimed at students and amateur naturalists, provides an introduction to the biology and identification of insects and other organisms. Individual volumes focus either on a particular type of insect, e.g. weevils, mayflies, mosquitoes, etc., or on a wider group of organisms, e.g. insects on nettles, animals of sandy shores, etc. In addition to identification keys, each volume includes colour illustrations, a bibliography and information on techniques (e.g. collection, preservation, etc.).

Keeping up-to-date

2429 **Advances in Insect Physiology**
Academic Press, 1963–, Irregular, 312pp. $139.95 [V. 31, 2003]. ISBN 0120242311 ISSN 00652806.
A monographic series that contains review articles on all aspects of insect physiology. Each article includes a substantial bibliography.

2430 **Annual Review of Entomology**
Annual Reviews, 1956–, Annual. $202.00 [V. 49, 2004]. ISBN 0824301498 ISSN 00664170.
arjournals.annualreviews.org/loi/ento [DESCRIPTION]
The most frequently cited entomological journal and an important current awareness tool. Each volume contains a collection of reviews of the literature on different aspects of the subject.

Evolution & Development

adaptation • creationism • Darwinism • developmental biology • evolutionary biology • human evolution • human growth and development • human speciation • intelligent design • life • molecular evolution • natural selection • origin of life • Wallace

Introductions to the subject

2431 **Almost like a whale: the origin of species updated**
S. Jones Doubleday, 1999, 402pp. £6.99. ISBN 0385409850.
Taking its chapter structure and headings from the original, this volume attempts to update the arguments outlined in Darwin's *Origin of species* using the evidence from modern evolutionary genetics research. The book is accessible to all and includes suggestions for further reading.

Deep time: cladistics, the revolution in evolution
H. Gee See entry no. 2847

2432 **Developmental biology**
S.F. Gilbert and S.R. Singer 7th edn, Sinauer Associates, 2003, 838pp. $109.95. ISBN 0878932585.
www.devbio.com [COMPANION]
Standard undergraduate textbook, the focus of the book is developmental biology in animals but it also includes a chapter on plants. Four parts: Principles of developmental biology; Early embryonic development (looking at examples in particular groups of animals); Later embryonic development; Ramifications of developmental biology. Accompanying website includes updates to the book as well as supplementary materials.

2433 **Developmental biology**
R.M. Twyman BIOS Scientific, 2001, 451pp. £18.99. ISBN 1859961533.
An undergraduate textbook that provides a summary of developmental biology, focusing on embryonic development, in both plants and animals. It includes a glossary and a bibliography of further reading.

2434 **Essential developmental biology**
J.M.W. Slack Blackwell Science, 2001, 321pp. £24.99. ISBN 0632052333.
Undergraduate textbook that provides a good overview of developmental biology in animals. Arranged in three sections: Groundwork (covers some of the basic concepts and processes); Major model organisms; Organogenesis and regeneration (the development of individual organs and systems).

2435 **Evolution: an introduction**
S.C. Stearns and R.F. Hoekstra Oxford University Press, 2000, 381pp. £25.99. ISBN 0198549687.
www.oup.co.uk/best.textbooks/biology/evolution [DESCRIPTION]
This is a good undergraduate textbook on evolutionary biology. It covers all aspects of the subject in 15 chapters which include: The nature of evolution; The origin and maintenance of genetic variation; The evolution of sex; Speciation; Systematics; The history of life.
'the best undergraduate evolution textbook available.' (*Times Higher Education Supplement*)

2436 Evolution
M. Ridley 3rd edn, Blackwell, 2003, 751pp. £27.50. ISBN 1405103450.
www.blackwellpublishing.com/ridley [DESCRIPTION]
Describes itself as an 'introductory text', but the content is more technical than that of the books by Futuyma [q.v.] and Skelton [q.v.]. Includes colour plates, a glossary and a bibliography.

2437 Evolution: a biological and palaeontological approach
P. Skelton, ed. Addison-Wesley/Open University, 1993, 1064pp. £42.99. ISBN 0201544237.
An introductory textbook designed to form the basis for an OU third level science course. The book focuses on the principles of evolution, i.e. what it is and how it works, rather than how particular organisms have evolved.

2438 Evolution and the fossil record
J. Pojeta and D.A. Springer; American Geological Institute and Paleontological Society 2001, 36pp. $8.95. ISBN 0922152578.
www.agiweb.org/news/evolution
Electronic version of a booklet that provides an introduction to evolution for a general readership. The introduction is followed by chapters on: Fossil record; Change through time; Darwin's theory; Mechanism for change; Nature of species; Nature of theory; Palaeontology, geology & evolution; Dating the fossil record; Examples of evolution. Glossary; Bibliography and suggestions for further reading.

2439 The evolution wars: a guide to the debates
M. Ruse ABC-CLIO, 200 , 428pp. Foreword by E.O. Wilson, $75.00. ISBN 1576071855.
This very readable book provides an illustrated introduction to the history of evolutionary thought and the controversies that surround it. It includes a bibliography, glossary and a collection of copies of original documents, including letters to and from Charles Darwin.
Series: Controversies in Science.
'Outstanding Academic Title 2000' (*Choice*)

2440 Evolutionary biology
D.J. Futuyma 3rd edn, Sinauer Associates, 1998, 763pp. $96.95. ISBN 0878931899.
A standard undergraduate textbook providing a basic introduction to the subject. Includes a glossary and a bibliography.
'In short, the third edition of *Evolutionary Biology*, like its predecessors, virtually defines the field of evolutionary biology, and will no doubt find a place on the bookshelves of almost all practicing evolutionary biologists.' (*The Quarterly Review of Biology*)

2441 Human evolution: an illustrated introduction
R. Lewin 5th edn, Blackwell Science, 2004, 288pp. £19.99. ISBN 1405103787.
An undergraduate textbook that provides a useful overview of human evolution. The book is divided into nine parts: Human evolution in perspective; Background to human evolution; Humans as animals; Hominine beginnings; The Hominine adaptation; Homo erectus: biology and behaviour; Origin of modern humans; The human milieu; New worlds. Each chapter includes a listing of key references and the book also contains a glossary.

2442 Life evolving: molecules, mind, and meaning
C. de Duve Oxford University Press, 2002, 341pp. £17.99. ISBN 0195156056.
This book provides a very readable informal overview of the origins of life on earth and evolution, including the controversies that have accompanied scientific progress in this area.

2443 The making of a fly: the genetics of animal design
P.A. Lawrence Blackwell Scientific, 1992, 228pp. £27.99. ISBN 0632030488.
This book provides an overview of fruit-fly (Drosophila) developmental biology from a genetic point of view. It is aimed at students and 'other interested persons', rather than researchers.

2444 Molecular principles of animal development
A. Martinez Arias and A. Stewart Oxford University Press, 2002, 410pp. £32.99. ISBN 0198792840.
www.oup.co.uk/best.textbooks/biochemistry/martinez [COMPANION]
Advanced undergraduate / graduate textbook that considers the molecular aspects (e.g. genetic and cellular aspects) of developmental biology. Includes a bibliography at the end of each chapter.

2445 The origin of animal body plans: a study in evolutionary developmental biology
W. Arthur Cambridge University Press, 2000, 352pp. £22.99. ISBN 0521779286.
Throughout much of the last century there was little communication between developmental biologists and evolutionary biologists. However, recent years have seen the emergence of evolutionary developmental biology ('evo-devo'), combining data from both fields in order to understand how changes in embryonic development can drive evolutionary changes. Aimed at university students, this book is a good introduction to the concepts, challenges and goals of this new discipline.

2446 Out of Eden: the peopling of the world
S. Oppenheimer Constable, 2003, 440pp. £18.99. ISBN 1841196975.
This book provides a readable introduction to the 'Out of Africa' theory of human evolution, i.e. that all modern humans are descended from a common African ancestor. Seven chapters: Out of Africa; When did we become modern?; Two kinds of European; First steps into Asia, first leap to Australia; The early Asian divisions; The great freeze; The peopling of the Americas. The notes for each chapter include references and the book also includes a subject index.
'provides an enviably clear and readable account. This book can be strongly recommended.' (*Times Higher Education Supplement*)

2447 Principles of development
L. Wolpert [et al.] 2nd edn, Oxford University Press, 2002, 542pp. £32.99. ISBN 0198792913.
www.oup.co.uk/best.textbooks/biology/wolpert [COMPANION]
An undergraduate textbook that highlights the main principles of developmental biology in both plants and animals. Includes colour illustrations and a bibliography at the end of each chapter. The accompanying website includes a table of contents and links to other sites relating to each chapter of the book.

2448 **The speciation of modern *Homo sapiens***
T.J. Crow, ed.; British Academy Oxford University Press, 2002, 265pp. Proceedings of the British Academy, V. 106, £14.99. ISBN 0197262465.
This book is the result of a meeting that was held at the British Academy in March 2000 and it provides a useful overview of human speciation. The book has 13 chapters in three parts: The origin of the species; Language and the evolution of the brain; The search for a critical event. Each chapter includes a bibliography.

Dictionaries, thesauri, classifications

2449 **Dictionary of developmental biology and embryology**
F.J. Dye Wiley-Liss, 2002, 165pp. $95.00. ISBN 0471443573.
A useful dictionary covering all aspects of developmental biology in both animals and plants. It also includes brief biographical information on important historical figures in the field.

A dictionary of ecology, evolution and systematics
R.J. Lincoln, G.A. Boxshall and P.F. Clark See entry no. 2302

2450 **Facts On File dictionary of evolutionary biology**
E. Owen and E. Daintith, eds Facts On File, 2004, 248pp. $49.50. ISBN 0816049246.
www.factsonfile.com
A good basic dictionary that contains definitions for more than 1800 terms used in evolutionary biology. Includes some illustrations and a very short bibliography.
Series: Facts On File Science Dictionaries: 20 vols, see website.

Research centres & institutes

2451 **Center for Science and Culture** [USA]
www.discovery.org/csc
Discovery Institute program which: Supports research by scientists and other scholars challenging various aspects of neo-Darwinian theory; Supports research by scientists and other scholars developing the scientific theory known as intelligent design; Supports research by scientists and scholars in the social sciences and humanities exploring the impact of scientific materialism on culture; Encourages schools to improve science education by teaching students more fully about the theory of evolution, including the theory's scientific weaknesses as well strengths.

Joint Genome Institute
University of California See entry no. 2514

Associations & societies

2452 **British Society for Developmental Biology**
www.bms.ed.ac.uk/services/webspace/bsdb/welcome.htm
The professional society for developmental biologists in the UK. Includes job listings, details of forthcoming meetings and links to related organizations and websites.

2453 **European Society for Evolutionary Biology**
www.eseb.org
Founded in 1987 the objectives of the ESEB are to 'support the study of organic evolution and the integration of those scientific fields that are concerned with evolution'. This is primarily achieved through organizing meetings and publishing the Journal of Evolutionary Biology.

International Association for Sexual Plant Reproduction Research
See entry no. 2216

2454 **International Society of Developmental Biologists**
www1.elsevier.com/homepage/sah/isdb
The Society aims to promote the study of developmental biology by organizing regular scientific meetings and through its publications. The website, provided by Elsevier Science, provides further information about these activities as well as links to related sites.

2455 **National Center for Science Education** [USA]
www.natcenscied.org
A US-based organization that aims to keep the teaching of creationism out of formal education. The website provides information about the organization's activities as well as resources relating to the evolution v creationism debate and links to related sites.

2456 **Society for Developmental Biology** [USA]
www.sdbonline.org
A US-based society that produces the journal *Developmental Biology*, maintains the Virtual Library site for the subject, and provides access to the Interactive Fly website.

2457 **Society for Molecular Biology and Evolution**
http://kumarlab.net/smbe
International society that aims to improve communication between the fields of evolution and molecular biology and within the field of 'molecular evolution' itself.

Portal & task environments

Cyberinfrastructure for Phylogenetic Research: CIPRes
National Science Foundation See entry no. 2859

2458 **EvoNet.org: A Worldwide Network for Evolutionary Biology**
University of Oregon
evonet.sdsc.edu
A collection of resources and links to related sites listed under four headings: Research; Education; Search; Public Interest. Resources include a searchable directory of evolutionary researchers and teaching materials. Site sustained by the University's Ecology and Evolution Group within its Department of Biology.

Discovering print & electronic resources

2459 **Evolution Update: The Evolution Research Center for Students and Teachers of Biology**
S.C. Spencer, comp.
users.mstar2.net/spencersa/evolutus
A collection of links to web-based evolution resources including journals and books. It also includes links to news sites (mainly US), mailing lists and newsgroups.

2460 **WWW Virtual Library: Developmental Biology**
Society for Developmental Biology
www.sdbonline.org/Other/VL_DB.html
Includes an Organisms Index as well as subject and other standard indexes. When reviewed late 2004, last updated April 2003.

Digital data, image & text collections

2461 **AboutDarwin.com: a website devoted to the life and times of Charles Darwin**
D. Leff
www.aboutdarwin.com
Excellent resource, providing information about all aspects of the life and work of Charles Darwin. Includes large number of illustrations, including photographs of Darwin and the places in which he lived and worked. Also brief information on people linked to Darwin, e.g. Lamarck and Wallace, and lists of related websites.

2462 **The Alfred Russel Wallace Page**
C.H. Smith
www.wku.edu/~smithch/home.htm
Wallace developed a theory of evolution similar to that of Darwin's at around the same time but, for various reasons, is now much less well known than Darwin. This site attempts to redress that balance providing biographical information, a bibliography of Wallace's publications and electronic copies of many of his works.

2463 **Charles Darwin and his Writings**
University of South Carolina
www.sc.edu/library/spcoll/nathist/darwin/darwinindex.html
This site – based on the University's C. Warren Irvin, Jr. Collection – traces Darwin's life and research through both his own and other related publications. The site's novel approach highlights some of the people and publications that influenced Darwin and those that were influenced by him.

2464 **Evolution: selected papers and commentary**
D.R. Forsdyke
post.queensu.ca/~forsdyke/evolutio.htm
Access to electronic versions of some historical articles on evolution, accompanied by a commentary. The articles and commentary are quite technical and would require the reader to have some prior knowledge of the subject.

The Interactive Fly
T. B. Brody and J. Brody See entry no. 2537

2465 **Science and Creationism**
National Academy of Sciences
www.nationalacademies.org/attic/evolution/index.html
A collection of resources including statements from scientific organizations, lists of relevant books and other relevant material. Last updated in December 2002 but still of value.

2466 **The Talk.Origins Archive: exploring the creation / evolution controversy**
Talk Origins Archive.
www.talkorigins.org/origins/faqs-evolution.html
This is the evolution section of the Usenet newsgroup Talk.Origins archive. It includes a collection of articles and essays on miscellaneous aspects of evolution written by a variety of authors.

Directories & encyclopedias

2467 **Atlas of descriptive embryology**
G.C. Schoenwolf and W.W. Mathews 6th edn, Pearson, 2002, 280pp. £37.99. ISBN 0130909580.
A collection of labelled photomicrographs that illustrate the developmental processes in worms, echinoderms, chordates, amphibians, birds, mammals and humans. It also includes a glossary and index.

2468 **The Cambridge encyclopaedia of human growth and development**
S.J. Ulijaszek, F.E. Johnston and M.A. Preece, eds Cambridge University Press, 1998, 497pp. £85.00. ISBN 0521560462.
Comprehensive and accessible series of essays from 120 internationally renowned experts.
'The editors are to be congratulated on a splendid achievement. They have produced a wonderfully organized and illustrated text; to dip into it will be a continuing source of information and pleasure. No department that has anything to do with human biology should be without it.' (*Journal of Biosocial Science*)

2469 **The Cambridge encyclopedia of human evolution**
S. Jones, R. Martin and D. Pilbeam, eds Cambridge University Press, 1992, 506pp. Foreword by Richard Dawkins, £30.00. ISBN 0521323703.
This volume is not an encyclopedia in the traditional sense as it consists of a collection of short essays grouped together under ten subject-based headings. The book begins with an overview of evolution, followed by several sections on primate biology and leading on to early human behaviour and ecology.

2470 **Encyclopedia of evolution**
M. Pagel, ed. Oxford University Press, 2002, 1205pp. 2 v., £200.00. ISBN 0195122003.
A collection of 365 articles, published in two volumes, covering all aspects of evolution, from the fundamental concepts through to more specific topics. The work begins with nine Overview essays, written by renowned evolutionary scientists, that highlight topics of current research interest. These are followed by the main section of the work which consists of entries of varying length, each of which includes a bibliography. A subject index is included in volume 2. The coverage of the book is very good and the entries are written in a nicely accessible style.

Encyclopedia of reproduction
E. Knobil and J.D. Neill, eds See entry no. 4470

Handbooks & manuals

Biogeography: an ecological and evolutionary approach
C.B. Cox and P.D. Moore See entry no. 2352

The biological chemistry of the elements: the inorganic chemistry of life
J.J.R. Fraústo da Silva and R.J.P. Williams See entry no. 2076

The developing human: clinically oriented embryology
K.L. Moore See entry no. 4471

Evolutionary patterns: growth, form, and tempo in the fossil record
J.B.C. Jackson, S. Lidgard and F.K. McKinney, eds See entry no. 1455

Genetics, paleontology, and macroevolution
J.S. Levinton See entry no. 1460

The human fossil record
J.H. Schwartz [et al.] See entry no. 1465

Major events in early vertebrate evolution
P.E. Ahlberg See entry no. 1469

2471 **The phylogenetic handbook: a practical approach to DNA and protein phylogeny**
M. Salemi and A.-M. Vandamme, eds Cambridge University Press, 2003, 406pp. £40.00. ISBN 052180390X.
This book, aimed at advanced undergraduates and researchers, provides a guide to phylogenetic techniques. The first chapter provides an introduction to molecular evolution and the other 14 chapters introduce individual techniques with each of these 14 chapters being split into sections on theory and practice. Each chapter includes a bibliography.

The primate fossil record
C.W. Hartwig, ed. See entry no. 1477

Keeping up-to-date

Annual Review of Ecology, Evolution & Systematics
See entry no. 2360

2472 **Current Topics in Developmental Biology**
Academic Press, 1969–, Annual. $149.95 [V. 61, 2004]. ISBN 0121531619 ISSN 00702153.
A monographic series that publishes review articles, with colour illustrations, on all aspects of developmental biology. Each article includes a substantial bibliography and there is an index in each volume.

2473 **Development**
Company of Biologists, 1987–, Semi-monthly. £1865.00. ISSN 09501991.
dev.biologists.org [DESCRIPTION]
Contains primary research articles and reviews of meetings on all aspects of developmental biology, including related diseases. Formerly titled *Journal of Embryology and Experimental Morphology*.

2474 **Evolution: international journal of organic evolution**
Society for the Study of Evolution Allen Press, 1947–, Monthly. ISSN 00143820.
lsvl.la.asu.edu/evolution [DESCRIPTION]
A highly cited research journal that publishes articles on all aspects of evolution. It also includes book reviews and announcements.

2475 **Evolutionary Biology**
Kluwer Academic, 1967–, Irregular. ISSN 00713260.
www.springeronline.com [DESCRIPTION]
A monographic series (each volume has an ISBN) that publishes review articles on all aspects of evolutionary biology. Each article includes a substantial bibliography.

2476 **Journal of Evolutionary Biology**
European Society for Evolutionary Biology Blackwell Science, 1987–, Bimonthly. £1076.00. ISSN 1010061X.
www.eseb.org [DESCRIPTION]
This is a highly cited academic journal that publishes articles on all aspects of evolution. It also includes review articles and book reviews.

Trends in Ecology & Evolution
See entry no. 2367

Genetics, Genomics & Bioinformatics

bioinformatics • chromosomes • computational biology • conservation genetics • DNA • Drosophila • evolutionary genomics • fruit flies • gene sequences • genes • genethics • genomics • mutations • population genetics • RNA

Introductions to the subject

2477 **50 years of DNA**
J. Clayton and C. Dennis, eds Nature Publishing Group, 2003, 144pp. £19.99. ISBN 140391480X.
This book was published to mark the 50th anniversary of the publication of the article by Francis Crick and James D. Watson in which they described the structure of DNA. It provides a very readable introduction to genetics research leading up to Crick and Watson's discovery and the research that has followed it, including the recent work on genomics. Includes facsimile versions of the original article and of other related papers.

2478 **Bioinformatics: genes, proteins and computers**
C. Orengo, D. Jones and J. Thornton, eds BIOS Scientific, 2003, 298pp. £29.99. ISBN 1859960545.
Aimed at final-year undergraduates and researchers, this book contains 18 chapters that cover all aspects of bioinformatics, including topics such as: Gene finding; Function prediction from protein sequence; Experimental use of DNA arrays. Each chapter includes a bibliography and the book also includes a glossary.

2479 **Bioinformatics and genomes: current perspectives**
M.A. Andrade, ed. Horizon Scientific Press, 2003, 227pp. £65.00. ISBN 1898486514.
www.horizonpress.com
Twelve invited review articles, each of which covers a particular aspect of bioinformatics and the tools that it uses. Includes illustrations (some in colour) and bibliographies.
See website for current publications list from this publisher: 'The leading specialist publushers in molecular biology and microbiology'.

2480 **A companion to genethics**
J. Burley and J. Harris, eds Blackwell, 2002, 489pp. £75.00. ISBN 0631206981.
This book brings together a collection of chapters that review ethical and legal aspects of genetics. It is divided into five parts: Genetics: setting the scene; Genetic research; Gene manipulation and gene selection; Genotype, phenotype, and justice; Ethics, law, and policy. Each chapter includes a bibliography.

2481 **DNA from the Beginning**
J.D. Watson [et al.], eds Dolan DNA Learning Center.
www.dnaftb.org/dnaftb
This is an online tutorial that provides an excellent introduction to DNA, genes and heredity. It contains 41 chapters arranged into three sections: Classical genetics (Mendelian genetics); Molecules of genetics (DNA and RNA); Genetic organization and control (genomes). Each chapter contains seven elements: Concept; Animation; Gallery; Audio/video; Bio (biographical information); Problem; Links. Also includes a bibliography.

2482 **The double helix: a personal account of the discovery of the structure of DNA**
J.D. Watson Penguin, 1997, 189pp. £8.99. ISBN 0140268774.
Originally published in 1968 (Weidenfeld & Nicolson), this book recounts the story of the discovery of the structure of DNA by Francis Crick and James Watson from the latter's point of view.

Essential cell biology
B. Alberts [et al.] See entry no. 2271

2483 **Essential iGenetics**
P.J. Russell Benjamin Cummings, 2003, 614pp. $99.00. ISBN 080534697X.
www.aw-bc.com/websites [COMPANION]
This is a standard genetics textbook that aims to provide a less complex introduction to the subject. The 24 chapters cover most of the standard topics including: Mendelian genetics; DNA replication; Gene control of proteins; Genome analysis; Genetics of cancer; Molecular evolution. It also includes a glossary and a list of suggestions for further reading. The companion website contains 50 animations, 24 activities, and 600 practice questions.

2484 **Essentials of genomics and bioinformatics**
C.W. Sensen, ed. Wiley-VCH, 2002, 419pp. £55.00. ISBN 3527305416.
This book aims to provide 'comprehensive introductory level information about the methods used in genomics research, the model organisms studied, the bioinformatics approaches, which are used to analyze genomic data, and the ethical implications'. It has 19 chapters, each of which includes a bibliography.

Essentials of medical genomics
S.M. Brown, J.G. Hay and H. Ostrer See entry no. 3599

2485 **The GEEE! In GENOME**
Canadian Museum of Nature
www.nature.ca/genome/index_e.cfm
This site provides an introduction to the science of genomics, aimed at the general public. It is made up of five sections: We are all alike (introduction); The basics (cell biology and heredity); Using genomics; The researchers (history of genomics, careers information, etc); Try it (online activities).

2486 **Gene regulation: a eukaryotic perspective**
D.S. Latchman 4th edn, Nelson Thornes, 2002, 323pp. £30.00. ISBN 0748765301.
A textbook aimed at advanced undergraduates and researchers that provides a useful overview of 'the processes involved in gene expression and the mechanisms by which such expression is regulated'. Ten chapters that cover topics such as: Tissue-specific expression of proteins and messenger RNAs; Gene expression; Regulation at transcription; Gene regulation and human disease. Each chapter includes a bibliography.

2487 **Genes VIII**
B. Lewin 8th edn, Prentice Hall, 2004, 1027pp. $130.00. ISBN 0131439812.
www.prenhall.com/lewin [FEE-BASED]
Standard undergraduate genetics textbook. Six parts: Genes; Proteins; Gene expression; DNA; The nucleus; Cells. Each chapter includes a bibliography and the book is illustrated in colour throughout. The accompanying website is subscription-based and provides access to a continuously updated version of the text.

2488 **Genetic Science Learning Center**
University of Utah
gslc.genetics.utah.edu
Site aimed at the general public and provides a nice overview of genetics as well as information on topical issues including stem cell research and cloning. It also includes teaching resources. Maintained within the university's Eccles Institute of Human Genetics.

2489 **Genetics: analysis and principles**
R.J. Brooker 2nd edn, McGraw Hill, 2005, 842pp. ISBN 0072835125.
www.mhhe.com/brooker [DESCRIPTION]
A standard undergraduate textbook divided into six parts: Introduction; Patterns of inheritance; Molecular structure and replication of the genetic material; Molecular properties of genes; Genetic technologies; Genetic analysis of individuals and populations. It includes an appendix that briefly covers some standard experimental techniques and a glossary. Access to a companion website that contains additional learning resources is freely available with a copy of the printed book.

2490 **Genetics: from genes to genomes**
L.H. Hartwell [et al.] 2nd edn, McGraw-Hill, 2004, 865pp. $123.12. ISBN 0072462485.
http://catalogs.mhhe.com/mhhe/home.do [DESCRIPTION]
Wide-ranging introduction in four parts: Basic principles: how traits are transmitted; What genes are and what they do; Genomes; How genes travel. Also included are genetic portraits of five of the model organisms commonly used in genetics research: Saccharomyces cervisiae (yeast); Arabidopsis thaliana (flowering plant); Caenorhabditis elegans (nematode); Drosophila melanogaster (fruit fly); Mus musculus (the house mouse). Glossary.

2491 Genomes
T.A. Brown 2nd edn, Bios Scientific, 2002, 572pp. £31.99. ISBN 1859960294.
This is a good undergraduate textbook. It is divided into four parts: Genomes, transcriptomes and proteomes; Studying genomes; How genomes function; How genomes replicate and evolve. The book is illustrated in colour throughout and each chapter includes a bibliography and suggestions for further reading. It also includes a glossary.

2492 Instant notes in genetics
P.C. Winter, G.I. Hickey and H.L. Fletcher 2nd edn, BIOS Scientific, 2002, 374pp. £16.99. ISBN 1859962629.
Useful overview of genetics and genomics aimed at undergraduate students with seven sections: Molecular genetics; Genomes; Mechanisms of inheritance; Population genetics and evolution; Recombinant DNA technology; Human genetics; Genetics and society. Includes suggestions for further reading and information on related websites.

2493 Introduction to bioinformatics
A.M. Lesk Oxford University Press, 2002, 283pp. £23.99. ISBN 0199251967.
www.oup.co.uk/best.textbooks/biosciences/bioinf [COMPANION]
This textbook, aimed at students and researchers, provides an introduction to the use of bioinformatics data and tools. Five parts: Introduction; Genome organization and evolution; Archives and information retrieval; Alignments and phylogenetic trees; Protein structure and drug discovery. Each chapter includes a list of suggested further reading.

2494 Introduction to bioinformatics: a theoretical and practical approach
S.A. Krawetz and D.D. Womble, eds Humana, 2003, 746pp. CD-ROM, $135.00. ISBN 1588290646.
An introductory textbook aimed at undergraduate students and researchers. It is divided into five parts: Biochemistry, cell, and molecular biology; Molecular genetics; The UNIX operating system; Computer applications; Appendices (guide to the accompanying CD-ROM, bioinformatics tools and UNIX commands). Each chapter includes a bibliography and suggestions for further reading.

2495 Introduction to bioinformatics
T.K. Attwood and D.J. Parry-Smith Prentice Hall, 1999, 218pp. $53.60. ISBN 0582327881.
http://umber.sbs.man.ac.uk/dbbrowser/bioactivity/prefacefrm.html [COMPANION]
Useful introduction to bioinformatics, with an emphasis on genomic and protein sequence analysis. It begins with an overview of the subject before going on to provide more information on the various tools and techniques that are available. The companion website provides an online bioinformatics tutorial.

2496 Introduction to genetic analysis
A.J.F. Griffiths [et al.] 8th edn, W H Freeman, 2004, 782pp. $79.38. ISBN 0716749394.
www.whfreeman.com/iga8e [COMPANION]
Standard undergraduate textbook with six sections: Transmission genetic analysis; The relationship of DNA and phenotype; Genome structure and engineering; The nature of heritable change; From genes to processes; The impact of genetic variation. Also includes information on model organisms, a glossary and a list of bioinformatics websites. The companion resource includes online tutorials, animations and problem sets.

Introduction to macromolecular crystallography
A. McPherson See entry no. 1759

Introduction to protein structure
C. Branden and J. Tooze See entry no. 2035

The making of a fly: the genetics of animal design
P.A. Lawrence See entry no. 2443

Molecular biology of the cell
B. Alberts [et al.] See entry no. 2273

2497 One hundred years of chromosome research: and what remains to be learned
A. Lima-de-Faria Kluwer Academic, 2003, 219pp. £66.00. ISBN 1402014392.
This book provides a critical review of the chromosome research carried out from 1795 to 2001 and also looks forward to new areas of research for the future. It is divided into nine parts: Nine periods of chromosome research: 1795 to 2010; Technology...: 1900 to 2001; In search of the eukaryotic chromosome; The three unique regions of the eukaryotic chromosome; No chromosomes can function outside a cell; Specific types of chromosomes; The antithetical properties of the chromosome; Chromosome models and what they do not tell us; Epilogue. Bibliography.

Plant molecular genetics
M.A. Hughes See entry no. 2184

2498 A primer of conservation genetics
R. Frankham, J.D. Ballou and D.A. Briscoe Cambridge University Press, 2004, 220pp. £19.99. ISBN 0521538270.
http://consgen.mq.edu.au/Primer2.htm [COMPANION]
This book provides a useful and accessible introduction to the subject of conservation genetics, i.e. the conservation of genetic diversity within populations. It includes many illustrations and each chapter includes a list of suggestions for further reading. The book also includes a glossary.

2499 A primer of population genetics
D.L. Hartl 3rd edn, Sinauer, 2000, 221pp. $34.95. ISBN 0878933042.
Aims to provide a concise but comprehensive introduction to population genetics, a discipline that 'seeks to understand the causes of genetic differences within and among species'. Four chapters: Genetic variation; The causes of evolution; Molecular population genetics; The genetic architecture of complex traits. Further readings and bibliography.

- **Principles of population genetics D.L. Hartl and A.G. Clark** 3rd edn, Sinauer, 1997, 542pp. $87.95. ISBN 0878933069. More detailed introduction aimed at advanced undergraduate students. Nine chapters cover topics such as: Genetic and phenotypic variation; Population substructure; Darwinian selection; Quantitative genetics. Further readings; bibliography.

2500 Principles of genome analysis and genomics
S.B. Primrose and R.M. Twyman 3rd edn, Blackwell, 2003, 263pp. £29.99. ISBN 1405101202.
Designed to introduce advanced undergraduates to the key techniques and theories.

- **Principles of gene manipulation S.B. Primrose, R.M. Twyman and R.W. Old** 6th edn, Blackwell Publishing, 2001. £29.99. ISBN 0632059540. www.blackwellpublishing.com/primrose [COMPANION]. Complete re-write of the 1995 edn, final chapter now having six themes: Nucleic acids as diagnostic tools; New drugs and new therapies for genetic diseases; Combating infectious disease; Protein engineering; Metabolic engineering; Modern plant breeding.

Principles of molecular virology
A.J. Cann See entry no. 2659

Proteins, enzymes, genes: the interplay of chemistry and biology
J.S. Fruton See entry no. 2037

2501 **Rosalind Franklin: the dark lady of DNA**
B. Maddox HarperCollins, 2002, 380pp. £9.00. ISBN 0002571498.
A biography of Rosalind Franklin, the chemist whose key research results helped Francis Crick and James D. Watson establish the double-helix structure of DNA. Franklin's precise role in the discovery is the subject of some debate with particular controversy surrounding its treatment in Watson's book THE DOUBLE HELIX.

A student's guide to biotechnology
See entry no. 5010

2502 **What mad pursuit: a personal view of scientific discovery**
F. Crick Weidenfeld and Nicolson, 1988, 182pp. ISBN 029779535X.
Francis Crick, along with James D. Watson, discovered the double-helix structure of DNA in 1953. This book is basically Crick's autobiography but it focuses on the period 1953 to the mid-1960s and the discoveries that were made in the field of genetics over that period.

Dictionaries, thesauri, classifications

2503 **Biopharmaceutical glossary and taxonomies**
M. Chitty, ed. Cambridge Healthtech Institute.
www.genomicglossaries.com [REGISTRATION]
A collection of online glossaries that cover genetics, genomics and molecular cell biology. They are 'descriptive' in that they illustrate the way that terms are actually being used in the literature rather than always providing authoritative definitions. They are also a work in progress and are therefore not comprehensive.

2504 **Dictionary of bioinformatics and computational biology**
J.M. Hancock and M.J. Zvelebil, eds Wiley-Liss, 2004, 636pp. $99.95. ISBN 0471436224.
Definitions for more than 600 words and phrases that are commonly used in bioinformatics. Entries are written by a variety of authors and vary in length, from a single paragraph to several pages. Most also include links to related websites and a bibliography. Also list of synonyms, author index, index of entries.

The dictionary of gene technology: genomics, transcriptomics, proteomics
G. Kahl See entry no. 5013

2505 **A dictionary of genetics**
R.C. King and W.D. Stansfield 6th edn, Oxford University Press, 2002, 530pp. £47.50. ISBN 0195143248.
Very useful reference work that provides concise definitions for more than 6500 terms, including the names of species that are commonly used in genetics research. Many of the definitions include cross-references to related items and a small number also include illustrations. Contains a chronology of genetics (Appendix C, includes a bibliography), a list of relevant journals (Appendix D) and a list of related websites (Appendix E).

2506 **Encyclopedic dictionary of genetics, genomics, and proteomics**
G.P. Rédei 2nd edn, Wiley-Liss, 2003, 1379pp. $185.00. ISBN 0471268216.
A very good single-volume encyclopedia that contains clear and concise definitions for more than 25,000 terms covering biochemistry and cell biology as well as genetics. Many of the articles include references to primary literature sources and the book also includes a bibliography of further reading, arranged by subject.

Laws, standards, codes

Commission on Genetic Resources for Food and Agriculture
See entry no. 2929

International code of conduct for plant germplasm collecting and transfer
Food and Agriculture Organization See entry no. 2930

Official & quasi-official bodies

The Genomic Resource Centre
World Health Organization See entry no. 3607

2507 **National Center for Biotechnology Information**
[USA]
www.ncbi.nlm.nih.gov
Founded in 1988, the NCBI aims to 'develop new information technologies to aid in the understanding of fundamental molecular and genetic processes that control health and diseases'. It does this by developing and providing access to a wide range of databases including PUBMED (an index to the biomedical literature) and sequence databases such as GENBANK and OMIM (ONLINE MENDELIAN INHERITANCE IN MAN. Well structured rich site worth detailed exploration.
- **Bookshelf** www.ncbi.nlm.nih.gov/Entrez. A 'growing' – but currently rather eclectic – collection of full-text searchable biomedical books.

Research centres & institutes

2508 **Cold Spring Harbor Laboratory**
www.cshl.org
Founded 1889, a leading research centre. Section Genomics & Bioinformatics leads to useful list of genome resources. The Library & Archives, among much of value, provide access to the Cold Spring Harbor Laboratory Oral History Collection, history 'through the eyes of the scientists who have worked and regularly visited here'.

BioSupplyNet from the Cold Spring Harbor Laboratory Press, is 'a current, integrated information source for life science laboratory supplies'.

- **Dolan DNA Learning Center** www.dnalc.org. Entirely devoted to educating the general public about genetics, DNA science and biotechnology. Range of resources including online tutorials, e.g. DNA FROM THE BEGINNING, DNA Interactive, encyclopedias, images, etc. all freely available.

2509 European Bioinformatics Institute
www.ebi.ac.uk
Part of the EUROPEAN MOLECULAR BIOLOGY LABORATORY the EBI was founded in 1992 with the aim of creating and providing access to a range of molecular biology databases. These include the EMBL Nucleotide Sequence Database and the TrEMBL and SWISS-PROT protein sequence databases. The Institute also carries out research in the areas of bioinformatics and computational molecular biology.

2510 European Molecular Biology Laboratory
www.embl.org
Set up in 1974 by EMBO, the EMBL is now an independent organization, funded by 17 member states including the UK. The website provides information about the Laboratory's teaching and research activities as well as other facilities and services that it provides.

2511 HUSAR Bioinformatics Lab [GER]
http://genome.dkfz-heidelberg.de/menu/biounit
Based at the German Cancer Research Center (DKFZ, Heidelberg) 'provides cutting-edge bioinformatics support and training to the scientist of the (post-)genomic era. This includes the Heidelberg Unix Sequence Analysis Resources (HUSAR), a large collection of essential sequence analysis tools.' Well designed website covering: Tools and Databases; Research; Developments; Workshops. Very extensive links section (well over 100 titles), with the entries having brief, but informative, annotations, and organized into seven categories: Data submission; FTP repositories; Major research and genome centres; Access to remote databases and applications; Gene prediction tools; Resources for microarray analysis; Resources for protein analysis.

2512 Institute for Genomic Research [USA]
www.tigr.org
Not-for-profit research institute founded in 1992. Focuses on the 'structural, functional and comparative analysis of genomes and gene products from a wide variety of organisms' – including viruses and bacteria. Provides access to data generated within the Institute including Comprehensive Microbial Resource, a database of all currently available bacterial genome sequences.

- **Comprehensive microbial resource Institute for Genomic Research.** gnn.tigr.org/tigr-scripts/CMR2/CMRHomePage.spl.

International Plant Genetic Resources Institute
See entry no. 2200

2513 Jackson Laboratory [USA]
www.jax.org
Non-profit institution which is 'the world's largest mammalian genetic research facility'. Excellent source of mouse information, the mouse being 'recognized by the scientific community as the most important model for human diseases and disorders'.

2514 Joint Genome Institute [USA]
University of California
www.jgi.doe.gov
Combination of the expertise of four DOE-funded national laboratories – Lawrence Berkeley, Lawrence Livermore, Los Alamos, Oak Ridge – with the Stanford Human Genome Center. Wide range and depth of resources – including via the JGI Genome Portal which offers an interface to several bioinformatics tools for studying genomes. Much other valuable material – for instance, from the Department of Evolutionary Genomics: 'Textbooks describe the 'modern synthesis' period as being the merger of evolutionary biology with genetics in the first half of the 20th century—There is now a chance for a new synthesis appearing at the boundary of evolutionary biology and genome science, with potential for much greater understanding within each field.'

National Human Genome Research Institute
See entry no. 3611

2515 Wellcome Trust Sanger Institute [UK]
www.sanger.ac.uk
The Institute was founded in 1993 and is a major non-profit-making research institute carrying out biomedical research, primarily now the sequencing and analysis of genomes. Well laid-out website providing detailed coverage of their research programmes and services.

Associations & societies

British Society for Human Genetics
See entry no. 3613

European Molecular Biology Organization
See entry no. 1925

2516 Genetics Society [UK]
www.genetics.org.uk
Founded in 1919, the Society is a learned society and has a membership of more than 2000 professional geneticists, teachers and students. Activities include publication of the journals *Heredity* and *Genes and Development* and a programme of educational and other events.

2517 Genetics Society of America
www.genetics-gsa.org
Founded in 1931, the GSA is a learned society with a membership of more than 4000 researchers, teachers and students. They publish the journal *Genetics* and – apart from the normal range of professional society activities – provide a useful gateway to information for about two dozen Model Organisms. There is also a link to the combined Membership Directory of GSA and four other societies (American Society of Human Genetics, The American College of Medical Genetics, The American Board of Medical Genetics, and The American Board of Genetic Counseling). However, the website states that use of the directory is 'limited to personal and informative use by members' (of the five societies) 'and by granting agencies'.

Human Genome Variation Society
See entry no. 3616

2518 **International Society for Computational Biology**
www.iscb.org
The ISCB was founded in 1997 and now has a membership of more than 1000 computational biologists from around the world. The website provides more information about the Society and its activities, which include the publication of the journal *Bioinformatics*. The site also includes job listings and information on universities around the world that offer bioinformatics programmes.

Progress Educational Trust
See entry no. 4464

Protein Society
See entry no. 2055

Libraries, archives, museums

2519 **Mendel Museum of Genetics**
www.mendel-museum.org
The Museum is located in the Abbey of St Thomas at Brno in the Czech Republic, the abbey at which Gregor Mendel (1822–84) carried out his experiments. The website provides access to an online exhibition about Mendel and his genetics experiments.

Portal & task environments

Bio.com: Life on the Net
See entry no. 5026

2520 **Bioinformatics.org**
J.W. Bizzaro [et al.]
bioinformatics.org
This site is primarily aimed at the research community, providing a rich set of links to software, tools and datasets as well as providing news, mailing lists and job listings. However, the FAQs section includes more general information as well as reviews of relevant books, careers information and links to related sites and is therefore likely to be useful to a much wider user group.

Biotechnology@nature.com
See entry no. 5029

2521 **The Bio-Web: resources for molecular and cell biologists**
A. Cabibbo, comp.
cellbiol.com
A useful collection of links to molecular and cell biology websites along with news items, software tools and other relevant resources.

2522 **DOEgenomes.org**
United States. Department of Energy
http://doegenomes.org
As of December 2004, apparently last modified April 2003, but a well laid-out, inviting page to the wide range of genome programmes of the Department.

- **Genome Glossary**
  www.ornl.gov/sci/techresources/Human_Genome/glossary. Last updated January 2004; includes links to a selection of other glossaries as well as serving as an index to the Doegenomes.org site.

DOEgenomes.org: Genome programs of the US Department of Energy Office of Science
United States. Department of Energy See entry no. 3617

2523 **Genome Gateway**
Nature Publishing Group.
www.nature.com/genomics
This site brings together a collection of freely available genomics resources including the article in *Nature* (15 February 2001) in which the sequence of the human genome was first published. The site also includes a collection of links to related articles, sites and information on the human genome.

Hum-molgen: The HUMan MOLecular GENetics Portal Site
See entry no. 3620

I-Bio: UK Information Biotechnology
See entry no. 5031

Information System Genetic Resources: GENRES
German Centre for Documentation and Information in Agriculture
See entry no. 3012

2524 **Model Organisms for Biomedical Research**
National Institutes of Health
www.nih.gov/science/models
Links to resources on organisms, e.g. Drosophila melanogaster, Arabidopsis, that are commonly used in biomedical research, giving information about the research that is being carried out using the organisms, as well as about the organisms themselves. Many other related pointers.

2525 **Mosquito Genomics WWW Server**
mosquito.colostate.edu/tikiwiki
Aimed at researchers and brings together a collection of resources relating to mosquitoes and the related genome sequencing projects. Includes images, articles, blogs, discussion forums and a directory of related sites.

2526 **Protocol Online**
L.-C. Li
www.protocol-online.org
Very comprehensive, well structured database of laboratory protocols and methods for bioinformatics, molecular biology, immunology, microbiology, proteomics, and cell biology. Contains protocols contributed by worldwide researchers as well as links to web protocols hosted by worldwide research labs, biotech companies, personal websites.

Discovering print & electronic resources

2527 **CMS molecular biology resource**
University of California, San Diego
restools.sdsc.edu
Brings together a large collection of links to molecular biology websites organized under the headings: Protein analysis & biochemistry; Biomolecular modeling; General phylogeny resources; General bioscience resources; DNA analysis & molecular biology; Bioinformatics & computational biology; General biochemistry; Biotechnology.

2528 Computational Molecular Biology at NIH
National Institutes of Health
http://molbio.info.nih.gov/molbio
Excellent, regularly updated, selective listings covering: Sequence analysis (tools at NIH and around the world); Documentation and information (about sequence analysis tools and programs); Databases (for molecular biology); Molecular biology desk reference (collection of basic information); Software repositories (access to molecular biology and sequence analysis software); Other molecular biology resources (major websites for molecular biology).

2529 Entrez: the life sciences search engine
National Center for Biotechnology Information
www.ncbi.nlm.nih.gov/Entrez
Search tool for multiple NCBI gene-based resources at the same time. The resources searched by Entrez include PubMed (the freely available version of Medline), PubMed Central (an archive of freely available journal articles), Online Mendelian Inheritance in Man, Bookshelf, and a range of specialized gene, protein, nucleotide, molecular and genome databases. The search interface is very simple and so while Entrez is probably not recommended for carrying out complex searches it does enable the user to identify the most appropriate database in which to carry out a more detailed search.

2530 GENESEQ
Thomson Derwent.
thomsonderwent.com/products/patentresearch/geneseq [DESCRIPTION]
Specialized database, aimed at researchers, that provides an index to the genetic sequences that have been published in patents. It is an important resource as many of the sequences that it indexes are not included in any of the publicly available databases.

2531 Highveld.com: the internet directory of molecular biology and biotechnology
highveld.com
Access to a huge collection of links to molecular biology, genomics and molecular microbiology websites. Includes links to journals, recently published and forthcoming books, laboratory protocols, newsgroups and databases.

Molecular Biology Database Collection: 2004 update
M.Y. Galperin, comp. See entry no. 2058

2532 RDN Virtual Training Suite: Bioresearcher [UK]
S. Wilson; University of Nottingham and Resource Discovery Network
www.vts.rdn.ac.uk/tutorial/biores
One of the useful tutorials aimed at newcomers needing to practise their internet information skills in specific subject areas.

Digital data, image & text collections

2533 The Arabidopsis Information Resource
National Center for Genome Resources, Arabidopsis Biological Resource Center and Carnegie Institution of Washington
www.arabidopsis.org/index.jsp
Arabidopsis thaliana is a member of the mustard family of plants that is widely used as a model organism for molecular studies of flowering plants. This site brings together scientific resources relating to this species. Much of the site's content is aimed at researchers but the About Arabidopsis section provides a nice overview that is accessible to a much wider audience.

2534 Biomolecular Interaction Network Database: BIND
Samuel Lunenfeld Research Institute
http://bind.ca
Collection of records documenting molecular interactions – each record representing an interaction between two or more objects that is believed to occur in a living organism. A biological object can be a protein, DNA, RNA, ligand, molecular complex, gene, photon or an unclassified biological entity. Interactions can link together to form molecular complexes (collections of two or more molecules that associate to form a functional unit in a living organism) or pathways (collections of two or more interactions that occur in a defined sequence within a living organism). In December 2004, the BIND database contained records for over 120,000 interactions, for some 2300 complexes, and for 8 pathways.

Good example of bioinformatics resource with well organized site providing – inter alia – access to much other valuable material from within and outwith the Institute.

ENZYME: Enzyme Nomenclature Database
Swiss Institute of Bioinformatics See entry no. 2063

2535 FlyBase: a database of the *Drosophila* genome
National Institutes of Health and Medical Research Council
flybase.bio.indiana.edu
Fruit flies (insects from the Drosophilidae family) are probably the most famous of the model organisms that are used in genetics research. This database aims to provide a comprehensive source of genetic and molecular information for these insects. It includes bibliographic citations, data from the relevant genome projects and a directory of researchers working in the area.

GeneCards
Weizmann Institute of Science See entry no. 3624

GrainGenes: A Database for Triticeae and Avena
United States. Department of Agriculture See entry no. 3103

The Greek Vitis Database
F. Lefort and K.A. Roubelakis-Angelakis; University of Crete See entry no. 3104

2536 The Human Genome: special issue of *Science* magazine
American Association for the Advancement of Science
www.sciencemag.org/content/vol291/issue5507
This freely available issue of the journal Science contains the human genome sequence that was produced by Celera Genomics. (Another version of the sequence was published in the journal Nature; cf. Genome Gateway). The issue also contains a number of related articles that review the implications of the production of the human genome sequence.

2537 The Interactive Fly
T. B. Brody and J. Brody
www.sdbonline.org/fly/aimain/1aahome.htm
Extensive amount of information about Drosophila genes and their role in development. Much of the site has been put together as a resource for researchers but each section contains an overview that is suitable for a wider audience.

2538 The International Nucleotide Sequence Database Collaboration: INSD
National Center for Biotechnology Information, European Bioinformatics Institute and DNA Data Bank of Japan
www.ebi.ac.uk/embl/Contact/collaboration.html
The INSD collaboration is based on three databases: GenBank; DNA DataBank of Japan; EMBL Nucleotide Sequence Database. These collectively contain all publicly available DNA sequences (more than 30 million sequences as of February 2004). The same sequence data is available in each of the three databases but they provide different search interfaces and present the data in slightly different formats.

- **DNA DataBank of Japan (DDBJ) National Institute of Genetics.** www.ddbj.nig.ac.jp.
- **EMBL Nucleotide Sequence Database European Molecular Biology Laboratory and European Bioinformatics Institute.** www.ebi.ac.uk/Databases/nucleotide.html.
- **GenBank National Center for Biotechnology Information.** www.ncbi.nlm.nih.gov/Genbank/GenbankOverview.html.

2539 Kyoto Encyclopedia of Genes and Genomes: KEGG
Kyoto University
www.genome.jp/kegg
Aimed at researchers and provides access to information on genes, genomes and their related biochemical pathways. Research project within the Kanehisa Laboratory of the University's Bioinformatics Center.

- **Post-genome informatics M. Kanehisa** Oxford University Press, 2000, 148pp. £30.95. ISBN 0198503261. Good introduction to bioinformatics. Four main sections: Blueprint of life; Molecular biology databases; Sequence analysis of nucleic acids and proteins; Network analysis of molecular interactions. Bibliography for bioinformatics methodologies.

Online Mendelian Inheritance in Man: OMIM
National Center for Biotechnology Information and Johns Hopkins University See entry no. 3626

Protein Data Bank: PDB
Research Collaboratory for Structural Bioinformatics See entry no. 2068

2540 UniProt: the universal protein resource
European Bioinformatics Institute, Swiss Institute of Bioinformatics and Protein Information Resource
www.expasy.uniprot.org/index.shtml
Freely accessible database of protein sequences, bringing together data that was previously held in databases such as Swiss-Prot. Aims to be comprehensive in coverage.

Directories & encyclopedias

2541 Encyclopedia of genetics
S. Brenner and J. Miller, eds Academic Press, 2002, 2257pp. 4 v, $1095.00. ISBN 0122270800.
www.sciencedirect.com/science/referenceworks [FEE-BASED]
These four volumes bring together a collection of articles, arranged alphabetically by title, that cover all aspects of genetics. The articles vary in length from a single paragraph to several pages. Many, but not all of the articles include a bibliography and some include illustrations. There are cross-references to related articles throughout the volumes. Volume 4 includes a subject index to the entire work.
Available online: see website.

- Online, Science Direct.

2542 Encyclopedia of genetics
E.C.R. Reeve and I. Black, eds Fitzroy Dearborn, 2001, 952pp. $195.00. ISBN 1884964346.
Brings together 125 articles on a wide range of topics. The articles are arranged under 14 headings which include the history of genetics, biotechnology, model organisms, population genetics, human genetics and genetics of various organisms. The book includes a glossary, an index and a list of related websites.

2543 Encyclopedia of molecular biology
T.E. Creighton, ed. Wiley, 1999, 2856pp. 4 v., $1695.00. ISBN 0471153028.
Collection of articles, arranged alphabetically by title, that cover all aspects of molecular biology. The articles vary in length from a single paragraph to several pages but they all include a bibliography and cross-references to entries for related terms. Many of the articles include illustrations and each volume also contains several pages of colour plates. Volume 4 includes a cumulative subject index.

Encyclopedia of molecular cell biology and molecular medicine
R.A. Meyers, ed. See entry no. 2074

Nature encyclopedia of the human genome
D.N. Cooper, ed. See entry no. 3630

Handbooks & manuals

2544 Analysing gene expression: a handbook of methods: possibilities and pitfalls
S. Lorkowski and P. Cullen, eds Wiley-VCH, 2003, 950pp. 2 v., £180.00. ISBN 3527304886.
This book provides an overview of the techniques that are used to study gene expression. The two volumes contain seven chapters that cover topics such as: Basic concepts of gene expression; Protein expression analysis; Computational methods and bioinformatic tools. Each chapter includes a substantial bibliography.

2545 Bioinformatics: a practical guide to the analysis of genes and proteins
A.D. Baxevanis and B.F.F. Ouellette, eds 3rd edn, Wiley, 2005, 470pp. $79.95. ISBN 0471478784.
www.wiley.com/bioinformatics [COMPANION]
This book provides a useful overview of bioinformatics. It includes 17 chapters that cover a wide range of tools and topics including: Structure databases; Genomic mapping and mapping databases; Information retrieval from biological databases; Phylogenetic analysis; Sequence alignment and database searching. Each chapter includes a bibliography

and a list of internet resources and most also include problem sets.

2546 **Bioinformatics: sequence and genome analysis**
D.W. Mount 2nd edn, Cold Spring Harbor Laboratory Press, 2004, 692pp. $159.00. ISBN 0879696877.
www.bioinformaticsonline.org [COMPANION]
Aimed at 'biologists who want to learn about computational and statistical methods and for computational scientists who want to learn about biology, especially genetics and genomics'. It provides a useful overview of genomics and the methodologies that it uses. The accompanying website provides a summary of each chapter and an excellent set of links to web resources that are mentioned in the book.

2547 **Bioinformatics methods and protocols**
S. Misener and S.A. Krawetz, eds Humana Press, 2000, 500pp. $99.50. ISBN 0896037320.
www.humanapress.com
Useful review of the techniques used in bioinformatics. Five sections: Sequence analysis packages; Molecular biology software; Web-based resources; Computers and molecular biology: issues and constraints; Teaching bioinformatics and keeping up to date with the literature. Each chapter includes a bibliography.
Available eBook; : see website.
Series: Methods in Molecular Biology.

Genetics, paleontology, and macroevolution
J.S. Levinton See entry no. 1460

2548 **Genome, transcriptome and proteome analysis (Analyse de génomes, transcriptome et protéoms)**
A. Bernot Wiley, 2004, 231pp. $55.00. ISBN 047084955X.
This useful handbook, originally published in French (Dunod, 2001), provides an overview of genomics and the processes in which the genome is transcribed and translated into specific proteins (proteomics). Seven chapters: General introduction; Linkage maps; Physical maps; Genome sequencing; Sequencing cDNA and the transcriptome; The proteome; Identification of genes responsible for disease. Short list of suggested further readings and links to related websites.

2549 **Handbook of statistical genetics**
D.J. Balding, M. Bishop and C. Cannings, eds 2nd edn, Wiley, 2003, 1022pp. 2 v, $535.00. ISBN 0470848294.
Useful overview of statistical genetics. 35 chapters arranged in six parts: Sequence, structure and expression; Evolutionary genetics; Animal and plant breeding; Population genetics (includes conservation genetics and forensics); Genetic epidemiology; Applications. Glossary; bibliographies.

Managing global genetic resources: agricultural crop issues and policies
Committee on Managing Global Genetic Resources See entry no. 3050

Molecular genetics and breeding of forest trees
S. Kumar and N. Fladung, eds See entry no. 3289

Molecular genetics of bacteria
J.W. Dale and S.F. Park See entry no. 2698

Principles and techniques of practical biochemistry
K. Wilson and J. Walker, eds See entry no. 2081

Short protocols in molecular biology
F.M. Ausubel [et al.], eds See entry no. 2084

2550 **Structural bioinformatics**
P.E. Bourne and H. Weissig, eds Wiley, 2003, 649pp. $175.00. ISBN 0471202002.
This textbook, aimed at advanced undergraduates and researchers, provides a good overview of bioinformatics which is defined here as 'the development and application of algorithms and methods to turn biological data into knowledge of biological systems'. Eight sections: Introduction; Data representation and databases; Comparative features; Structure and functional assignment; Protein interactions; Proteins as drug targets; Structure prediction; The future. Suggestions for further reading; bibliography.

Keeping up-to-date

2551 **Advances in Genetics**
Academic Press, 1961–, Irregular. ISSN 00652601.
www.elsevier.com/locate/issn/00652660 [DESCRIPTION]
A monographic series (each volume has an ISBN) that publishes review articles on all aspects of genetics. For example, volume 49 included articles on: Drosophila neuropeptide signalling; Genetics of wheat gluten proteins. Each article includes a substantial bibliography.

2552 **Annual Review of Genetics**
Annual Reviews, 1967–, Annual. $208.00 [V. 38, 2004]. ISBN 0824312384 ISSN 00664197.
arjournals.annualreviews.org/loi/genet [DESCRIPTION]
This is an important research journal that publishes review articles on all aspects of the subject. Each article includes a bibliography.

Annual Review of Genomics and Human Genetics
See entry no. 3632

Current pharmacogenomics
See entry no. 3753

2553 **EMBO Reports**
European Molecular Biology Organization Nature Publishing Group, 2000–, Monthly. €122.00. ISSN 1469221X.
www.nature.com/embor [DESCRIPTION]
Rapidly published short papers and review articles in all areas of molecular biology. Includes Science & Society section.

2554 **Genetics@Nature.com**
Nature Publishing Group.
www.nature.com/genetics
One of the series of gateways which allows one to find all the Group's relevant resources in the field of genetics – and to keep up to date with developments.

2555 Nature Reviews Molecular Cell Biology
Nature Publishing Group, 2000–, Monthly. £750.00. ISSN 14710072.
www.nature.com/nrm [DESCRIPTION]
An important journal that publishes commissioned review articles on all aspects of cell and molecular biology.

Trends in Biotechnology
See entry no. 5046

2556 Trends in Genetics
Elsevier, 1985–, Monthly. ISSN 01689525.
www.trends.com/tig/default.htm [DESCRIPTION]
A research journal that publishes commissioned review articles on all aspects of genetics and genomics.

Marine & Freshwater Biology

alligators • amphibians • aquaculture • aquatic ecology • cnidarians • conchology • coral reefs • crocodiles • crustaceans • dolphins • estuaries • fishes • freshwater biology • ichthyology • inland waters • jellyfish • lakes • limnology • lobsters • marine conservation • marine ecology • molluscs • ocean conservation • octopuses • otters • ponds • river ecosystems • sea exploration • seals • seashores • sharks • shells • turtles • water ecosystems • wetlands • whales

Introductions to the subject

Biological oceanography: an introduction
C.M. Lalli and T.R. Parsons See entry no. 1344

2557 Biology of fishes
Q. Bone, N.B. Marshall and J.H.S. Blaxter 2nd edn, Blackie Academic, 1995, 332pp. ISBN 075140022X.
A standard undergraduate fish biology textbook, this covers all aspects of fish biology, including a brief chapter on fisheries and aquaculture. Also provides some general information on fish taxonomy.

2558 Biology of fresh waters
P.S. Maitland 2nd edn, Kluwer, 1990, 288pp. ISBN 0216929881.
Good overview of all aspects of freshwater biology. Chapters include: The aquatic environment; Plants and animals of fresh waters; Field studies; Adaptation to environment.

2559 Fish of Britain & Europe
P.J. Miller and M.J. Loates HarperCollins, 1997, 288pp. £16.99. ISBN 0002199459.
Provides brief information on the species of marine and freshwater fish that are found in European waters. Colour illustrations are included for many of the species. Includes brief information on fish biology but this is covered more comprehensively in the book by Bone, Marshall and Blaxter [q.v.].
Series: Collins Pocket Guides.

2560 Fishes of the world
J.S. Nelson 3rd edn, Wiley, 1994, 600pp. ISBN 0471547131.
This book is primarily a guide to the classification of fish. Includes a substantial bibliography (pp 467–540).

2561 Fundamentals of aquatic ecology
R.S.K. Barnes and K.H. Mann, eds 2nd edn, Blackwell Scientific, 1991, 270pp. ISBN 0632029838.
Standard undergraduate textbook. It is divided into five parts: Introduction; Aquatic ecosystems; Aquatic individuals and communities; Habitat types peculiar to aquatic systems (reefs and streams and rivers); Human effects. Each chapter includes a bibliography.

2562 An introduction to marine ecology
R.S.K. Barnes and R.N. Hughes 2nd edn, Blackwell Scientific, 1988, 351pp. ISBN 0632020474.
An undergraduate textbook that is aimed at students with a general knowledge of ecology. It provides a good overview of the subject with sections covering specific ecosystems, e.g. rocky shores, salt marshes, etc, as well as sections on topics such as speciation and the exploitation of the sea by humans.

2563 Limnology: lake and river ecosystems
R.G. Wetzel 3rd edn, Academic Press, 2001, 1006pp. $83.95. ISBN 0127447601.
A standard undergraduate textbook, this provides a more detailed overview of the subject than the book by Kalff [q.v.]. Looks in some detail at the individual elements of lake and river ecosystems, with chapters on topics such as: Water economy; Oxygen; Planktonic communities.

2564 Limnology: inland water ecosystems
J. Kalff Prentice Hall, 2002, 592pp. $102.00. ISBN 0130337757.
A useful overview of the science of limnology (the study of lakes and ponds). It includes chapters on: The development of limnology; Origin and age of lakes; Water movements; Fish and water birds. Also includes a substantial bibliography.

2565 Marine biology: an ecological approach
J.W. Nybakken 5th edn, Benjamin Cummings, 2001, 516pp. $100.00. ISBN 0321030761.
A textbook aimed at undergraduates with a general background in biology. It covers all aspects of marine biology including plankton, intertidal regions, estuaries, deep-sea biology and the impact of humans on the sea. Each chapter includes a bibliography and the book also includes a glossary.

Marine botany
C.J. Dawes See entry no. 2180

2566 Photographic guide to the sea and shore life of Britain and North-west Europe
R. Gibson, B. Hextall and A. Rogers Oxford University Press, 2001, 436pp. £15.95. ISBN 0198507097.
Aimed at a general readership, this book provides colour photographs and brief information (species description, distribution, habitat, ecology and identifying features) for species of plants and animals that are commonly found around the UK coast. It also includes a brief introduction to each of the taxonomic groups covered, including suggestions for further reading.

The rise of fishes: 500 million years of evolution
J.A. Long See entry no. 1416

Dictionaries, thesauri, classifications

Aqualex: a glossary of aquaculture terms
M. Eleftheriou, ed. See entry no. 3117

Elsevier's dictionary of marine pollution: English–Spanish, with English and Spanish indexes (Diccionario de contaminación del mar)
L.-J. Zilberberg, comp. See entry no. 5543

2567 Encyclopedia of marine sciences
J.G. Baretta-Bekker, E.K. Duursma and B.R. Kuipers, eds 2nd edn, Springer, 1998, 357pp. £19.00. ISBN 3540626751.
This pocket-sized book contains definitions and explanations for 1980 terms relating to biology, chemistry, geology and physical oceanography.

2568 The Facts On File dictionary of marine science
B. Charton, ed. Rev edn, Checkmark Books, 2001, 373pp. $44.00. ISBN 0816042926.
This dictionary contains more than 2500 entries covering all aspects of marine science, including oceanography, biographical entries, history and biology. It includes several appendices and a bibliography. A useful general dictionary.

Official & quasi-official bodies

2569 Advisory Committee on Protection of the Sea
www.acops.org
Non-governmental organization, founded in 1952, works at regional, national and global levels to promote strategies for sustainable marine and coastal development. Website includes information on pollution in UK waters and links to related sites.

Global International Waters Assessment
See entry no. 1129

2570 Intergovernmental Oceanographic Commission
ioc.unesco.org
The IOC, part of UNESCO, was founded in 1960 with the aim of creating a body that could carry out research throughout the world's oceans. Forty countries are members, including the UK, US, Canada, France, Germany and Russia. Information about the Commission and the research programmes it supports, covering topics ranging from algal blooms to climate research. Includes link to OceanPortal.

- **Ocean Expert** ioc3.unesco.org/oceanexpert. Global directory of marine and freshwater professionals.

2571 International Council for the Exploration of the Sea
www.ices.dk
ICES (also known as the Conseil International pour l'Exploration de la Mer / CIEM) 'coordinates and promotes marine research in the North Atlantic'. The website is a first-rate source of information on a wide range of topics such as fish stocks, marine pollution and the ocean climate. The Photo Gallery contains some excellent images although an index would make it more user friendly.

International Maritime Organization
See entry no. 5752

2572 International Whaling Commission
www.iwcoffice.org
The IWC was set up under the International Convention for the Regulation of Whaling which was signed in 1946 and is intended to conserve whale stocks and control the development of the whaling industry. It is responsible for setting and monitoring catch limits and it also supports scientific research into related areas. The website provides access to the full text of the Convention, and information on catch limits and on whale watching. It also contains information on the taxonomy, biology, ecology and populations of the cetaceans (including dolphins and porpoises).

2573 National Marine Fisheries [USA]
www.nmfs.noaa.gov
Responsible for the management, conservation and protection of living marine resources within the USA's Exclusive Economic Zone (water three to 200 miles offshore). Good set of Features (e.g. Bycatch; International interests; Recreational fisheries; Strandings) plus access to information on Managing Marine Ecosystems and an active Media Center.

NOAA Coastal Services Center
See entry no. 1356

2574 North Pacific Marine Science Organization
www.pices.int
An intergovernmental organization that was founded in 1992 to promote and co-ordinate research in the North Pacific and adjacent seas. Its present members are Canada, Japan, People's Republic of China, Republic of Korea, the Russian Federation, and the USA. The website provides more information about the organization, its activities and its good range of publications – many available as downloadable PDFs.

Office of Naval Research
See entry no. 5753

2575 Ramsar Convention on Wetlands
www.ramsar.org
The Convention on Wetlands, signed in Ramsar, Iran, in 1971, is an intergovernmental treaty which provides the framework for national action and international co-operation for the conservation and wise use of wetlands and their resources. The website contains links to key documents on wetlands conservation, including a list of the wetlands of international importance.

The Convention is not part of the UN or UNEP system of environmental treaties; but with many of the treaties' secretariats Ramsar has, however, established collaborative agreements.

- **Ramsar Sites Database Service Wetlands International and Ramsar Convention on Wetlands.** www.wetlands.org/RSDB/default.htm. Searchable database of information about wetlands designated as internationally important under the Convention. Contains very detailed information about the wetlands including biological, hydrological and ecological data.

Research centres & institutes

CEH Windermere
See entry no. 3124

Centre for Ecology and Hydrology
See entry no. 2318

2576 **Marine Biological Association of the United Kingdom**
www.mba.ac.uk
The MBA is a professional body for marine biologists and has an international membership. The site provides information about their research and educational programmes as well as links to projects such as MarLIN and the Marine Environmental Change Network.

- **National Marine Biological Library** www.mba.ac.uk/nmbl. Based in Plymouth, and is one of the major reference libraries for the marine life sciences. Access is permitted to registered visitors and the Library's serials catalogue can be searched online.

2577 **Marine Biological Laboratory** [USA]
www.mbl.edu
MBL, located at Wood's Hole, Massachusetts, is the oldest private marine laboratory in the USA and carries out a broad range of research including cell and developmental biology, ecology, microbiology, molecular evolution, global infectious disease, neurobiology, and sensory physiology. The site is an excellent well designed resource about the Laboratory's work (51 Nobel Laureates having taught, taken courses, or done research at MBL), as well as about marine biology more generally.

- **MBLWHOI Library** www.mblwhoilibrary.org. Library of the Laboratory and the Woods Hole Oceanographic Institution. Houses one of the most important collections in this area, coverage including biological, biomedical, ecological and oceanographic sciences. Online catalogue.

2578 **National Marine Mammal Laboratory** [USA]
nmml.afsc.noaa.gov
The NMML carries out research on marine mammals (whales, dolphins, porpoises, seals, sea lions, walruses) around the world but with an emphasis on the coasts of California, Oregon, Washington and Alaska. The website provides more information about the Laboratory and its research. It also includes information on marine mammal species, a collection of images, information on (US) marine mammal law and links to related sites.

NERC Collaborative Centres
See entry no. 1192

2579 **Plymouth Marine Laboratory** [UK]
www.pml.ac.uk
Founded in 1988, the PML is now an independent organization that carries out research into areas such as modelling marine systems, molecular science and environmental risk.

Associations & societies

2580 **American Cetacean Society**
www.acsonline.org
Founded in 1967, the ACS is the oldest whale conservation group in the world. The website is a good source of general information on the biology of cetaceans and the issues that are affecting their survival.

2581 **American Society of Limnology and Oceanography**
www.aslo.org
One of the leading professional organizations in the field of aquatic sciences. The website is particularly useful for people thinking of a career in this area as it includes links to university courses, careers advice and a collection of abstracts of relevant postgraduate theses. The site also includes a collection of links to related sites.

American Zoo and Aquarium Association
See entry no. 2888

British Dragonfly Society
See entry no. 2384

2582 **Caribbean Conservation Corporation & Sea Turtle Survival League**
www.cccturtle.org
Founded in 1959, the CCC carries out research and provides educational resources on sea turtles. The website contains detailed information about the biology and conservation of turtles and the projects being undertaken by the CCC, as well as links to related sites.

2583 **Center for North American Herpetology**
www.cnah.org
The CNAH was founded in 1994 and, as a service to the community, it maintains a collection of links to herpetological sites on its home page. The links are arranged under the categories: Taxonomy; Societies; Academic/research links; Online collections; Current research. The site also includes news, details of scientific meetings, announcements of new species, and lists of recently issued publications.

2584 **CoastNET** [UK]
www.coastnet.org.uk
Founded in 1995, CoastNET is a network of individuals and organizations that are involved in the conservation and management of the UK coastline. Includes links to related websites, plus FAQs and details of publications.

2585 **Conchological Society of Great Britain and Ireland**
www.conchsoc.org
Founded in 1876, the Society is one of the oldest devoted to the study of molluscs and their shells. The website provides more information about its activities and publications and also includes a discussion forum, information on recording schemes, and a small collection of links to related sites.

2586 **Conchologists of America**
www.conchologistsofamerica.org
Founded in 1972, the COA is an international society that is open to anyone with an interest in shells and molluscs. Its website, known as Conch-Net, provides more information about the Society, its activities and its publications. The site also contains a nice introduction to molluscs and shells, along with information on taxonomy, conservation, and the collection of shells. There is free access to articles reprinted from the COA journal *American Conchologist*.

2587 **Crustacean Society**
www.vims.edu/tcs
An international society that aims to 'advance the study of all aspects of the biology of the Crustacea'. Its publications include the *Journal of Crustacean Biology*, and there is also

site access to a copy of the Martin and Davis classification as well as links to related sites.

- **An updated classification of the recent crustacea J.W. Martin and G.E. Davis** Natural History Museum of Los Angeles County, 2001, 124pp. ISBN 1891276271. www.vims.edu/tcs/LACM-39-01-final.pdf. Science Series, no. 39.

2588 **Estuarine Research Federation** [USA]
erf.org
A US-based organization that promotes estuarine and coastal water research. One of the most useful areas of the site is the Estuarine Science Reference Series: downloadable PDF lists of the key references and classic papers on a wide range of topics. There is also a good links section.

2589 **EurAqua: network of EU freshwater research organisations**
www.euraqua.org
Founded in 1993, EurAqua brings together research institutions from across the EU in joint projects and other initiatives to encourage closer collaboration. Apart from descriptions of its work the website also includes a helpful collection of links to relevant EU legislation, both current and forthcoming.

2590 **Freshwater Biological Association** [UK]
www.fba.org.uk
Based in the UK but with an international membership the FBA aims 'to promote freshwater science through innovative research, scientific meetings and publications, and by providing sound, independent opinion'. Information about the Association and its publications that is likely to be of interest to both marine biologists and hydrologists.

- **FBA Library and Information Services** www.fba.org.uk/Library/Index.html. Houses one of the world's finest collections of information on freshwater science. The Library catalogue, containing details of materials acquired from 1985 to date, can be searched online.

2591 **International Association of Theoretical and Applied Limnology**
www.limnology.org
Founded in 1922, the Association aims 'to further the study and understanding of all aspects of limnology'. Its website provides links to a range of related sites including those for relevant scientific meetings and publications; also a Jobs section that lists current vacancies in the field as well as relevant academic courses.

2592 **International Coral Reef Action Network**
www.icran.org
Global partnership of coral reef experts who are working to halt and reverse the decline of the health of the world's coral reefs. Good range of PDF downloadable policy and educational material.

- **International Coral Reef Information Network** www.coralreef.org. Information on coral reefs and factors such as water pollution and fishing practices that threaten them. Tools & Resources section contains factsheets, lists of educational resources, directory of coral reef organizations, database of coral images.

2593 **International Society for Reef Studies**
www.fit.edu/isrs
Website provides good entrée to resources in the area.

- **Proceedings of the International Coral Reef Symposia** www.plando.co.jp/icrs2004. Premier forum for discussions of science, conservation, and management of global coral reefs. Symposia proceedings are key references to the development of coral reef science, management, and conservation and to the trends of global coral reefs.

2594 **Lobster Conservancy** [USA]
www.lobsters.org
The TLC is based in Friendship, Maine and aims to sustain the local lobster fisheries in that area through scientific research and education. The website is a very good source of information on the taxonomy, biology and conservation of lobsters.

Malacological Society of London
See entry no. 2898

2595 **Marine Conservation Biology Institute** [USA]
www.mcbi.org
The MCBI was founded in 1996 and works in four main areas: Marine Protected Areas; Destructive fishing practices; Endangered species; Advancing the science. Site provides a collection of images of marine organisms and links to related sites.

2596 **Marine Conservation Society** [UK]
www.mcsuk.org
The UK's national charity dedicated to the protection of the marine environment and its wildlife. The website provides information, aimed at a wide audience, about aspects of the marine world, e.g. species, habitats, pollution, etc. It also includes links to relevant sites and a list of events on marine and related topics.

2597 **Marine Fish Conservation Network** [USA]
www.conservefish.org
The Network is a coalition of more than 150 national and regional groups with an interest in marine fish. The site provides more information about the Network, its activities and links to the member organizations. It also provides more information on relevant (US) legislation and links to reports produced by the Network, the US government and other organizations.

2598 **National Association of Marine Laboratories** [USA]
www.naml.org
Organization that brings together more than 100 marine laboratories across the US. Includes a number of useful research and educational presentations.

2599 **Ocean Conservancy** [USA]
www.oceanconservancy.org
Produces information and runs programmes of activities to highlight conservation issues relating to the marine environment. Good, lively, site.

2600 **Otter Project** [USA]
www.otterproject.org
Based in California, this charity is active in the conservation of sea otters and their website provides a nice introduction to the biology and conservation of the otters. The Research section of the site includes a bibliography of useful scientific articles and the Photo Gallery (in the About Sea Otters section) contains some wonderful images.

2601 Ponds Conservation Trust [UK]
www.brookes.ac.uk/pondaction
Founded in 1988, the PCT provides a focus for pond conservation in the UK. The website contains a link to the National Ponds Database which will provide information on ponds throughout the UK (incomplete as of August 2004). The site also includes PDF downloadable information sheets on topics such as: Good wildlife ponds; Problem pond plants.

2602 Seal Conservation Society
www.pinnipeds.org
Based in the UK, the Society was formed in 1996 and works internationally to protect seals, sea lions and walruses. Its website provides an introduction to the biology of these animals as well as more detailed information, including photographs, of the individual species. It also includes a Library of further reading that provides a useful starting point for research.

2603 SeaWeb
www.seaweb.org
An organization that aims to raise public awareness of the issues relating to the conservation of the oceans. Their activities are based around a series of programmes covering issues such as aquaculture, marine reserves and conserving sturgeon. The site includes a resources section that includes links to related sites and the newsletter *Ocean Update*.

2604 Shark Trust
www.sharktrust.org
Founded in 1997, the Trust is 'dedicated to promoting the study, management, and conservation of sharks, skates and rays (elasmobranchs) in the UK and internationally'. Provides quite detailed information about the taxonomy, biology and conservation of sharks and the related species, as well as much other useful data.

2605 Society for the Study of Amphibians and Reptiles
www.ssarherps.org
Founded in 1958, the SSAR is an international organization, based in the US, that is dedicated to the study and conservation of amphibians and reptiles. Its publications include the *Journal of Herpetology*. The site also includes an overview of conservation issues facing selected species and information on careers in herpetology.

2606 Society of Wetland Scientists [USA]
www.sws.org
Based in the US with International Chapters around the world. The site includes information on wetland jobs, training courses, meetings and conferences. The Wetlands Concerns section includes papers written by SWS members on issues of concern: e.g. restoration of wetlands. The site also includes links to related web pages.

2607 Wetlands International
www.wetlands.org
An international organization, based in The Netherlands, that is concerned with the conservation of wetlands. The website provides more information about the organization and its activities and includes a large collection of downloadable PDF documents plus links to related sites.

2608 Whale and Dolphin Conservation Society
www.wdcs.org
WDCS is an international organization that campaigns for the conservation of whales and dolphins. The website provides more information about the Society, its campaigns and its publications, many of which are freely available. It also includes an illustrated guide to all of the cetacean species (encompassing: Description; Distribution and threats; Fascinating facts) as well as information on sightings and strandings of whales and dolphins.

2609 World Chelonian Trust
www.chelonia.org
The WCT aims to conserve the world's species of tortoises and freshwater turtles. The website is rather dense but it contains great amounts of useful information (over 1000 pages). Its main features are a gallery of images, a collection of articles (including the Complete Chelonian Taxonomy List), information on caring for tortoises, and links to related sites.

Libraries, archives, museums

2610 International Association of Aquatic and Marine Science Libraries and Information Centers
www.iamslic.org
IAMSLIC is 'an association of individuals and organizations interested in aquatic and marine information science'. Website contains information about the Association including details of their publications and links to lists of new books in member libraries.

- **IAMSLIC Z39.50 Distributed Library International Association of Aquatic and Marine Science Libraries and Information Centers.** library.csumb.edu/cyamus/ill/search.php. Project aimed at facilitating international resource sharing among – currently – about 70 marine and aquatic science libraries.

Portal & task environments

2611 Aquaculture Network Information Centre: AquaNIC [USA]
Mississippi-Alabama Sea Grant Consortium
aquanic.org
This US-based site provides access to a wide range of resources on aquaculture, including a searchable collection of links to related sites. It also has a collection of pages that provide information on several fish species, and it also includes access to discussion forums, careers information and an events calendar.

2612 Aquatic Network
Seacoast Information Services.
www.aquanet.com
This US-based site contains links to a wide range of marine and freshwater resources, including commercial products, job listings and relevant news stories. The site also includes a discussion forum.

2613 Canada's Aquatic Environments
University of Guelph
www.aquatic.uoguelph.ca
This attractive site provides quite detailed information on the aquatic plants, animals and habitats that are found in Canada. It also includes a section on Human interactions that covers topics such as fisheries, water management and

invasive species while the Research section provides information on research institutions and scientists. Produced by the University's CyberNatural Software Group.

2614 **The Cephalopod Page**
J.B. Wood; Dalhousie University
is.dal.ca/~ceph/TCP
This is a useful site that includes collections of links to websites that deal with cephalopods (octopus, squid and cuttlefish) and molluscs (although the 'ink blot' cursor can be rather annoying!) There is also a nice introductory article on the cephalopods, information on keeping them as pets, a searchable FAQs page, and a list of useful books and videos.

2615 **The Cnidaria home page**
University of California, Irvine
www.ucihs.uci.edu/biochem/steele/default.html
Information and links to websites that deal with cnidarians (jellyfish, corals, etc.). In addition to those dealing with particular groups of cnidarians, the links are arranged in categories that include: General information; Materials and methods; Genes and genomics; Books and software; History.

2616 **Crocodilians: Natural History & Conservation**
A. Britton; Crocodile Specialist Group
www.crocodilian.com
This site provides an excellent overview of the biology of crocodiles, alligators and caiman. There are four main sections: Crocodilian species list (detailed information on all 23 species); Crocodilian biology database (evolution, behaviour, conservation and morphology); Crocodilian communication (sound recordings); Crocodilian captive care FAQ. The site also includes images and links to related websites.

EarthTrends: the environmental information portal
World Resources Institute See entry no. 2334

2617 **FreshwaterLife**
Freshwater Biological Association, Ponds Conservation Trust and Environment Agency
www.freshwaterlife.info
The aim of this relatively new site is to bring together a comprehensive collection of materials relating to freshwater biology. The content is arranged under four main headings: Natural history & education; Policy & regulation; Research & methods; Region / country. Includes information on publications, meetings, organizations and websites.

The Harmful Algae Page
Woods Hole Oceanographic Institution and National Oceanic and Atmospheric Administration See entry no. 2832

Man and Mollusc/Mollusk
A. Bouquin, comp. See entry no. 2908

2618 **Marine Biology Web**
J. Levinton; Stony Brook University
http://life.bio.sunysb.edu/marinebio/mbweb.html
An educational resource primarily aimed at undergraduates. It contains lots of useful information although some of it does have a US bias.

- **Glossary of marine biology** J. Levinton
  life.bio.sunysb.edu/marinebio/glossary.html. Taken from Levinton's book *Marine biology* and providing some brief definitions of standard terms.

2619 **MarLIN: The Marine Life Information Network for Britain & Ireland**
Marine Biological Association of the United Kingdom
www.marlin.ac.uk
This excellent site contains a huge amount of information about the UK marine environment, aimed at a wide audience, from researchers to members of the general public. Information is arranged under 6 main headings: Biology & Sensitivity; Data Access; Education & Recording; MarLIN Services; Searches; Publications & Products. The site also includes a useful glossary of marine biological terms.

2620 **Ocean Explorer**
National Oceanic and Atmospheric Administration
oceanexplorer.noaa.gov
The aim of this exceptionally well laid-out and easily navigable educational site is to provide access to some of the data generated by NOAA activities in the marine environment. The site is huge, with more than 9000 pages, and contains lots of useful information including images and video clips. 'The site is built with contributions from a broad range of authors, including marine scientists, resource managers, educators, students, historians, artists, musicians, creative writers, policymakers, and others.' An excellent resource.

2621 **The Ocean Project**
www.theoceanproject.org
There is a very good Ocean Resource Center section of the site with links to related sites that provide news, information and images; also factsheets on a range of marine species and careers information. The Project is 'an international network of aquariums, zoos, museums, and conservation organizations working to create an understanding among their visitors and members of the significance of the oceans and the role each person plays in conserving our ocean planet for the future'.

2622 **OceanLink**
Bamfield Marine Sciences Centre
oceanlink.island.net
Friendly US-based site containing a large amount of information aimed at the general public. OceanInfo provides access to a collection of introductory articles on topics such as seaweed, seal evolution and marine biodiversity. Records contains brief information on the largest, fastest, deepest, etc. organisms. There is also a glossary as well as an Ask a scientist feature that includes an archive of answers.

2623 **ReefBase: A Global Information System on Coral Reefs**
WorldFish Center
www.reefbase.org
Gathers available knowledge about coral reefs into one information repository, intended to facilitate analyses and monitoring of coral reef health and the quality of life of reef-dependent people, and to support informed decisions about coral reef use and management. ReefBase is the official database of the Global Coral Reef Monitoring Network (GCRMN), and the International Coral Reef Action Network (ICRAN).

2624 **ReefBase**
WorldFish Center and International Coral Reef Action Network
www.reefbase.org
An excellent source of information on coral reefs, including a bibliography of more than 20,000 related publications. Registration is required for access to some parts of the site.

2625 **Sea slug forum**
Australian Museum
www.seaslugforum.net
This site provides an excellent introduction to sea slugs (Cephalaspidea). It includes a species list (providing distribution information and photographs), general information (behaviour, anatomy, physiology, care, etc.), reviews of relevant books, a discussion forum and links to related sites.

2626 **Seaturtle.org**
www.seaturtle.org
This site brings together a huge number of turtle resources, including a huge collection of links to related sites, online access to the *Marine Turtle Newsletter* and an international directory of individuals involved in turtle research.

UN Atlas of the Oceans
United Nations See entry no. 1365

Discovering print & electronic resources

APIRS Online: the database of aquatic, wetland and invasive plants
University of Florida See entry no. 2243

2627 **Aquatic Sciences and Fisheries Abstracts: ASFA**
CSA, 1971–. Contains several hundred records published before 1971.
www.csa.com/factsheets/aquclust-set-c.php [DESCRIPTION]
The primary indexing tools for aquatic sciences. The most up-to-date version of the database, incorporating all 5 of the printed products, is available by subscription via the CSA INTERNET DATABASE SERVICE.
- **Aquaculture Abstracts: ASFA** CSABi-monthly. www.csa.com/factsheets/aquaculture-set-c.php [DESCRIPTION].
- **Aquatic Pollution and Environmental Quality: ASFA 3** CSABi-monthly. www.csa.com/factsheets/asfa3-set-c.php [DESCRIPTION].
- **Biological Sciences and Living Resources: ASFA 1** CSAMonthly. www.csa.com/factsheets/asfa1-set-c.php [DESCRIPTION].
- **Ocean Technology, Policy and Non-Living Resources: ASFA 2** CSABi-monthly. www.csa.com/factsheets/asfa2-set-c.php [DESCRIPTION].
- **ASFA Thesaurus** www.csa.com/factsheets/supplements/asfathes.php. 10,000 terms.
- **Marine Biotechnology Abstracts: ASFA** CSAQuarterly. www.csa.com/factsheets/marine-set-c.php [DESCRIPTION].

2628 **Fish & Fisheries Worldwide**
NISC.
www.nisc.com/Frame/NISC_products-f.htm [DESCRIPTION]
Abstracts from a range of worldwide sources covering all aspects of ichthyology, fisheries, and related aspects of aquaculture. More than 13,500 records are added each year.
- **Marine, Oceanographic & Freshwater Resources** NISC. www.nisc.com/factsheets/qmof.asp [DESCRIPTION]. 'Exclusive combination of the world's premier bibliographic databases on marine, oceanographic, and related freshwater resources. Over 1,205,000 records on international marine and oceanic information and estuarine, brackishwater, freshwater environments'.

2629 **Freshwater mollusk bibliography**
K. Cummings [et al.], eds; Illinois Natural History Survey
http://ellipse.inhs.uiuc.edu:591/mollusk/default.html
A bibliographic database that contains the details of more than 11,000 publications, including journal articles, books and book chapters, theses and grey literature, on freshwater molluscs. Its scope is international but its coverage of the literature relating to the North American freshwater mussels is more comprehensive than that of other areas.

OceanBase
See entry no. 1366

2630 **OceanPortal**
Intergovernmental Oceanographic Commission
ioc.unesco.org/oceanportal
Very large hierarchically structured collection of links to marine biology and oceanography websites arranged in categories: Information resources; Data resources; Scientific topics; Agencies & institutions; Organizations, associations & societies; Administration, conservation & policy; Scientists & ships (includes careers information); Commerce & trade; Miscellaneous. The collection is searchable.

2631 **Sea Turtle Online Bibliography**
University of Florida
accstr.ufl.edu/biblio.html
Website of the Archie Carr Center for Sea Turtle Research provides access to a number of resources including this bibliography, a searchable database of scientific articles, and the CTURTLE e-mail discussion list.

Digital data, image & text collections

2632 **Amphibian Species of the World: an online reference**
D.R. Frost; American Museum of Natural History
research.amnh.org/herpetology/amphibia/index.html
This site represents the results of an on-going project to produce a comprehensive taxonomic database of the amphibians (frogs, newts and toads). The database can be browsed or searched by keyword, author, scientific and common name, by country or any combination of these. Entries include information on taxonomy, scientific and common names, geographical distribution, comments and external links.

2633 **AmphibiaWeb: information on amphibian biology and conservation**
University of California, Berkeley
elib.cs.berkeley.edu/aw
This is a freely available database that contains detailed information on the biology and conservation of the amphibians (frogs, toads and newts) of the world. The database can be searched by genus, species or vernacular (common) name, country, IUCN category or 'Reasons for decline'. The entry for each species includes a description plus information on: Distribution and habitat; Life history, abundance, activity, and special behaviors; Trends and

threats; Relation to humans. Also provided are photographs and bibliographies. An exceptional resource.

2634 Catalog of Fishes
California Academy of Sciences
www.calacademy.org/research/ichthyology/catalog/fishcatsearch.html
This is an updated and corrected electronic version of the *Catalog of fishes* that was first published in 1998 by the Academy's Department of Ichthyology. It aims to provide taxonomic information on all of the fishes that have been described to date: approximately 26,000 species with more than 200 new species being described each year. The database can be searched by genus or species name and searches can also be carried out on the cited literature.
Available in print: see website.

2635 CephBase
J.B. Wood and C.L. Day
www.cephbase.utmb.edu
Brings together a vast collection of data on cephalopods (octopus, squid, nautilus and cuttlefish) including more than 1600 images in a set of interlinked databases. The databases cover species names (including common names), images, videos, references, predators, prey and biogeography (distribution maps etc.) and a search on any one database will identify relevant data in the others. The site also includes a searchable list of cephalopod researchers and links to related sites.

2636 Check List of European Marine Mollusca: CLEMAM
J. Le Renard, S. Gofas and P. Bouchet, eds
www.somali.asso.fr/clemam
Access to a database of taxonomic information for the European species of molluscs. The database includes images for many of the species and a searchable bibliography. Maintained within the Museum's Department of Systematics & Evolution.

The EMBL Reptile Database
European Molecular Biology Laboratory and German Herpetological Society See entry no. 2914

2637 EuroTurtle
Mediterranean Association to Save the Sea Turtles and Kings College Taunton
www.euroturtle.org
This site provides a huge amount of information on sea turtles with particular emphasis on those species found in the Mediterranean. It includes information on turtle biology, conservation and details of the threats to their survival. The site also includes educational resources (it is part of the NATIONAL GRID FOR LEARNING) and links to related sites.

2638 FishBase
R. Froese and D. Pauly, eds
www.fishbase.org/search.cfm
This is a huge database that brings together information on all aspects of fish biology and taxonomy providing a one-stop shop for fish information. It can be searched by common or scientific name, by family, by country, by ecosystem or by topic (e.g. ecology, physiology, uses, etc.). It also includes a glossary and a collection of Tools (identification keys etc.) as well as a searchable bibliography. An essential reference tool now supported by a consortium of seven research institutions.

2639 Guide to the South American Cichlidae
S.O. Kullander; Swedish Museum of Natural History
www.nrm.se/ve/pisces/acara/welcome.shtml
Cichlids are a large group (more than 1600 species) of mainly freshwater teleost fish and this site provides a very nice introduction to their biology and taxonomy. The site also includes a very useful list of recent publications and links to related sites.

2640 Hexacorallians of the World
D.G. Fautin, ed.
hercules.kgs.ku.edu/hexacoral/anemone2/index.cfm
Brings together data on the taxonomy, biology and geographical distribution of sea anemones, corals and their allies. Database can be searched by: Bibliographic data (museum, author, title, year); Distributional data; Taxonomic data (scientific and common names); Environmental data. Also includes images of many of the species and links to molecular data.

Marine Flatworms of the World
W. Seifarth See entry no. 2815

2641 Shells Database
M. Yamada
shell.kwansei.ac.jp/~shell/pic_book/index.html
A Japanese site (in English and Japanese) that provides access to a database of information about shells. The database can be browsed by shell shape, species name or by browsing through the classification. Entries for each species include a photograph, taxonomic information and information on distribution, habitat and size.

Toxic & harmful algal blooms
A. deCharon and S. Etheridge; Bigelow Laboratory for Ocean Sciences See entry no. 2840

2642 World List of Marine, Freshwater and Terrestrial Isopod Crustaceans
B. Kensley, M. Schotte and S. Schilling, comps; National Museum of Natural History
www.nmnh.si.edu/iz/isopod
A searchable list of the species of the isopod crustaceans that provides taxonomic and brief habitat information for each species. It can be searched by family, genus, species or type locality. The list is accompanied by a searchable bibliography. From the Museum's Invertebrate Zoology Department.

Directories & encyclopedias

Encyclopedia of environmental microbiology
G. Bitton [et al.], eds See entry no. 2690

2643 Encyclopedia of the sea
R. Ellis Alfred A. Knopf, 2000, 380pp. $35.00. ISBN 0375403744.
An encyclopedia aimed at the general public that includes entries for marine plants and animals, geographical areas, biographical information and popular culture relating to the sea. It is fully illustrated, including eight pages of colour art works by the author.

Water: science and issues
E.J. Dasch, ed. See entry no. 1148

World atlas of coral reefs
M.D. Spalding, C. Ravilious and E.P. Green; UNEP World Conservation Monitoring Centre See entry no. 1386

Handbooks & manuals

Exceptional fossil preservation: a unique view on the evolution of marine life
D.J. Bottjer [et al.] See entry no. 1456

The freshwater algal flora of the British Isles: an identification guide to freshwater and terrestrial algae
D.M. John, B.A. Whitton and A.J. Brook, eds; British Phycological Society and Natural History Museum See entry no. 2842

Freshwater issues: a reference handbook
Z.A. Smith and G. Thomassey See entry no. 5615

Handbook of fish biology and fisheries
P.J.B. Hart and J.D. Reynolds See entry no. 3137

History of the coelacanth fishes
P.L. Forey See entry no. 1463

2644 **Ichthyology handbook**
B.G. Kapoor and B. Khanna, eds Springer, 2004, 1059pp. £229.00. ISBN 3540428542.
Collects information on all aspects of fish biology, including taxonomy, evolution, ecology, behaviour and molecular biology. It includes a large bibliography (pp 952–1056) but the subject index is quite poor.

Interrelationships of fishes
M.L.S. Stiassny, L.R. Parenti and G.D. Johnson See entry no. 1466

2645 **Keys to the freshwater fish of Britain and Ireland, with notes on their distribution and ecology**
P.S. Maitland; Freshwater Biological Association 2004, 245pp. £22.00. ISBN 0900386711.
www.fba.org.uk/fbapub.html
This useful book provides an identification key to the adults, eggs, larvae and scales of the 62 species of freshwater fish that are found in Britain and Ireland. It also includes information on the distribution and ecology of each species. The book is fully illustrated (including 48 colour plates) and includes a substantial bibliography.
Series: Scientific Publications, 62: see website for list of titles in the series and their other publications.

2646 **Lake and pond management guidelines**
S. McComas Lewis, 2003, 286pp. $89.95. ISBN 1566706300.
Information on projects and techniques that can be used to manage lake and pond ecosystems. Seven chapters: Shoreland projects; Algae control; Aquatic plant management; Fish topics; Small-scale dredging; On-site wastewater treatment systems; Pond problems and solutions. Fully illustrated with each chapter including a bibliography.

2647 **The marine fauna of the British Isles and north-west Europe**
P. J. Hayward and J. S. Ryland, eds Clarendon, 1990.
These two volumes provide an overview of the marine fauna of the region, 'providing dichotomous keys, illustrations, brief descriptions, and notes on distributions for the most frequently occurring intertidal and subtidal marine organisms'. The volumes are arranged taxonomically with Volume 1 covering the protozoans to the arthropods and Volume 2 covering the molluscs to chordates. A standard reference work.
Handbook of the marine fauna of north-west Europe *(P.J. Hayward and J.S. Ryland ed. Oxford University Press, 1995, 800pp. ISBN 0198540558) is a concise version. However, while the total number of species covered was reduced slightly it does contain some species that were not covered in the earlier volumes, and it was updated to take account of changes in taxonomy.*

- **Vol. 1. Introduction and protozoans to arthropods** P. J. Hayward and J. S. Ryland 656pp. ISBN 0198573561.
- **Vol. 2. Molluscs to chordates** 352pp. ISBN 0198575157.

Marine geochemistry
R. Chester See entry no. 921

2648 **Marine monitoring handbook**
J. Davies [et al.], eds; Joint Nature Conservation Committee UK Marine SACs Project, 2001, 405pp. ISBN 1861075243.
www.jncc.gov.uk/marine/marine_habitat/survey/mmh.htm
Provides advice and guidance on methods that can be used to monitor marine Special Areas of Conservation (SACs) and the species that live in them. The full text of the handbook is available online and updates will be made available electronically.

Practical handbook of estuarine and marine pollution
M.J. Kennish See entry no. 5642

2649 **Practical handbook of marine science**
M.J. Kennish, ed. 3rd edn, CRC Press, 2001, 876pp. $159.95. ISBN 0849323916.
Six chapters: Physiography; Marine chemistry; Physical oceanography; Marine geology; Marine biology; Marine pollution and other anthropogenic impacts. Each chapter contains an overview of the topic, a bibliography and then collections of relevant data. A very useful reference work.

2650 **A student's guide to the seashore**
J.D. Fish and S. Fish 2nd edn, Cambridge University Press, 1996, 564pp. £30.00. ISBN 0521468191.
This textbook is aimed at undergraduates but it is also accessible to a much wider readership. It contains information on the identification and the biology of the plants, protists and animals that are found on the shores of north-west Europe. It is arranged taxonomically and contains many illustrations, a glossary and a bibliography.

Synopses of the British Fauna (New Series)
R.S.K. Barnes and J. H. Crothers, eds; Linnean Society of London and Estuarine and Coastal Sciences Association See entry no. 2922

Keeping up-to-date

2651 **Advances in Marine Biology**
Academic Press, 1963–, Irregular.
A monographic series that publishes review articles on all aspects of the subject. Articles vary in length but they all include a substantial bibliography.

Marine Pollution Research Titles
National Marine Biological Library See entry no. 5657

2652 **Oceanography and Marine Biology: an annual review**
Taylor & Francis, 1963–, Irregular. ISSN 00783218.
A monographic series that publishes reviews on a wide range of topics in marine biology. Each article includes a substantial bibliography.

Microbiology & Virology

Archaea • bacteria • bacteriology • culture collections • extremophiles • microbes • microorganisms • molecular virology • prokaryotes • virology • viruses

Introductions to the subject

2653 **Basic virology**
E.K. Wagner and M.J. Hewlett 2nd edn, Blackwell Publishing, 2003, 440pp. £29.99. ISBN 1405103469.
www.blackwellpublishing.com/wagner [COMPANION]
A good basic molecular virology textbook, divided into four parts: Virology and viral disease; Basic properties of viruses and virus–cell interaction; Working with virus; Replication patterns of specific viruses. The accompanying website includes chapter outlines, artwork, a glossary and links to related sites.

2654 **Brock biology of microorganisms**
M.T. Madigan, J.M. Martinko and J. Parker 10th edn, Prentice Hall, 2003, 1019pp. $132.00. ISBN 0130662712.
wps.prenhall.com/esm_madigan_brockbio_10 [COMPANION]
The standard undergraduate textbook. The book is organized into six units covering: Principles of microbiology; Evolutionary microbiology and microbial diversity; Metabolic diversity and microbial ecology; Immunology, pathogenicity, and host responses; Microbial diseases; Microorganisms as tools for industry and research. Each chapter includes a Working Glossary of the key terms covered in that chapter. The companion website includes chapter reviews and animated tutorials.

2655 **Introduction to molecular virology**
E. Rybicki and L. Stannard; University of Cape Town
www.mcb.uct.ac.za//tutorial/virtut1.html
Access to an online tutorial that was written to support virology courses at the University within its Microbiology Department. It provides information on a range of topics including: What is a virus?; Viral genome diversity; Emerging viruses. Also provides access to the Virus Ultrastructure site, a collection of electron micrographs of viruses.

2656 **Microbe Zoo**
Michigan State University
commtechlab.msu.edu/sites/dlc-me/zoo/index.html
This site offers an accessible introduction to microbial ecology. Information is listed under five headings: DirtLand; Animal pavilion; Snack bar; Space adventure; Water world. Created by the Common Tech Lab and Center for Microbial Ecology within the university.

2657 **Microbiology**
L.M. Prescott, J.P. Harley and D.A. Klein 5th edn, McGraw Hill, 2002, 1026pp. $128.75. ISBN 0072829052.
highered.mcgraw-hill.com/sites/0072320419 [COMPANION]
A good undergraduate textbook. Arranged in 11 parts: Introduction to microbiology; Microbial nutrition, growth, and control; Microbial metabolism; Microbial molecular biology and genetics; DNA technology and genomics; The viruses; The diversity of the microbial world; Ecology and symbiosis; Nonspecific resistance and the immune response; Microbial diseases and their control; Food and industrial microbiology. Glossary; subject index.

2658 **Milestones in microbiology: 1546 to 1940**
T.D. Brock, ed. ASM Press, 1999, 266pp. $34.95. ISBN 1555811426.
Contains text of key articles written by authors such as Pasteur, Lister, Koch and Fleming, edited to make them accessible to an undergraduate audience. Divided into six parts: Spontaneous generation and fermentation; The germ theory of disease; Immunology; Virology; Chemotherapy; General microbiology. Within each part the articles are arranged chronologically.

2659 **Principles of molecular virology**
A.J. Cann 3rd edn, Academic Press, 2001, 339pp. Includes CD-ROM, $44.95. ISBN 0121585336.
A standard undergraduate textbook that aims to outline the main principles of the subject in a comprehensible manner. The book contains eight chapters: Introduction; Particles; Genomes; Replication; Expression; Infection; Pathogenesis; Subviral agents. A glossary is included in the appendices along with a brief history of virology.

2660 **Principles of virology: molecular biology, pathogenesis, and control of animal viruses**
S.J. Flint [et al.] 2nd edn, ASM Press, 2004, 918pp. £109.95. ISBN 1555812597.
This is a good undergraduate textbook that introduces the basic principles of animal virus biology and aims to be 'readable, rather than comprehensive'. Each chapter includes a bibliography and suggestions for further reading.

Dictionaries, thesauri, classifications

2661 **A dictionary of microbial taxonomy**
S.T. Cowan and L.R. Hill, eds Cambridge University Press, 1978, 285pp. ISBN 052121890X.
Although now very old, this dictionary is still a useful source of definitions for standard microbiological terms. It also includes four short introductory essays on: Codes of nomenclature of microbes; Source material for taxonomy; Philosophy of classification; Early history of bacterial classification.

2662 **Dictionary of microbiology and molecular biology**
P. Singleton and D. Sainsbury 3rd edn, Wiley, 2001, 895pp. $110.00. ISBN 0471490644.
An excellent dictionary containing 18,000 entries covering both pure and applied microbiology. Entries vary in length and many include references to further reading.

2663 **A dictionary of virology**
B.W.J. Mahy 3rd edn, Academic Press, 2001, 418pp. $55.95. ISBN 0124653278.
An updated edition of a standard reference work, incorporating the new rules for virus taxonomy that were defined in the 7th report of the ICTV VIRUS TAXONOMY). This volume covers viruses of vertebrates but excludes those that only infect bacteria, fungi, invertebrates or plants. It includes references to relevant review articles for many of the topics that are covered.
'this dictionary proves a well-timed reference source, excellent for researching not only virus species and genera, but also the latest techniques used in the laboratory today.' (*Microbiology Today*)

Laws, standards, codes

2664 **International code of nomenclature of bacteria, and Statutes of the International Committee on Systematic Bacteriology, and statutes of the Bacteriology and Applied Microbiology Section of the International Union of Microbiological Societies: bacteriologi**
S.P. Lapage [et al.], eds; American Society for Microbiology, International Committee on Systematic Bacteriology and International Union of Microbiological Societies American Society for Microbiology, 1992, 189pp. $109.95. ISBN 155581039X.
The code specifies the criteria that must be used to identify valid bacterial taxonomic nomenclature.

2665 **International Committee on Systematics of Prokaryotes**
www.the-icsp.org
Formerly the International Committee on Systematic Bacteriology (ICSB), is the body that oversees the nomenclature of prokaryotes, determines the rules by which prokaryotes are named and whose Judicial Commission issues Opinions concerning taxonomic matters, revisions to the Bacteriological Code, etc.

2666 **International Committee on Taxonomy of Viruses**
www.danforthcenter.org/iltab/ictvnet
The ICTV is the body responsible for the development and maintenance of a single, universal taxonomic scheme for viruses. They maintain The International Code of Virus Classification and Nomenclature and publish regular reports on the current state of virus taxonomy (the most recent report, the 7th, was published in 2000 as VIRUS TAXONOMY).
- **ICTV Newsletter**
  www.danforthcenter.org/iltab/ictvnet/pdf/ICTVNewsletter103.pdf. Designed 'to provide useful information to all those involved in the work of the International Committee on Taxonomy of Viruses.

2667 **List of bacterial names with standing in nomenclature**
J.P. Euzeby; Société de Bactériologie Systématique et Vétérinaire
www.bacterio.cict.fr
Bacterial nomenclature is controlled by the INTERNATIONAL CODE OF NOMENCLATURE OF BACTERIA. The LBSN brings together all of the names that have been validly published under the terms of this code providing a central resource for bacterial nomenclature. The entry for each name includes details of the publication that the name was first published in and the collection that the type specimens was deposited in.

2668 **Virus taxonomy: classification and nomenclature of viruses: seventh report of the International Committee on Taxonomy of Viruses**
M.H.V. van Regenmortel [et al.], eds; International Committee on Taxonomy of Viruses and International Union of Microbiological Societies Academic Press, 2000, 1162pp. $185.95. ISBN 0123702003.
The most recent report of INTERNATIONAL COMMITTEE ON TAXONOMY OF VIRUSES on the state of viral taxonomy. The book is divided into four parts of which part 3, 'The viruses', is by far the largest, describing the taxa and individual viruses whose characterization has been approved by the Commission between 1970 and 1999. The remaining three sections cover 'The species concept', the ICTVDB and the work of the ICTV itself.

Official & quasi-official bodies

2669 **International Union of Microbiological Societies**
www.iums.org/index.html
The IUMS was founded in 1927 and aims to 'promote the study of microbiological sciences internationally'. Publish the journals *International Journal of Systematic and Evolutionary Microbiology* (jointly with the International Committee on Systematics of Prokaryotes) and *Journal of Food Microbiology* (jointly with the International Committee on Food Microbiology and Hygiene).
- **Resources for Systematists**
  http://ijs.sgmjournals.org/misc/related.shtml. Extensive recently updated list of links under the headings: Systematics; Culture collections; Online journals; Databases and other online resources; Genomics; International societies; Patent organizations; Meetings.

2670 **United Kingdom National Culture Collection**
www.ukncc.co.uk/index.htm
Provides access to a searchable database of microbial culture collections within the UK. Also provides information about the UK national service collections, i.e. other organizations with culture collections.

2671 **World Federation for Culture Collections**
www.wfcc.info
The WFCC is a Multidisciplinary Commission of the INTERNATIONAL UNION OF BIOLOGICAL SCIENCES and a Federation within the INTERNATIONAL UNION OF MICROBIOLOGICAL SOCIETIES. It works to promote and support 'the collection, authentication, maintenance and distribution of cultures of microorganisms and cultured cells'. Biannual downloadable PDF newsletter, various other papers and reports, details of workshops and conferences.

Research centres & institutes

2672 Deutsche Sammlung von Mikroorganismen und Zellkulturen (German Collection of Microorganisms and Cell Cultures)
www.dsmz.de/index.html
Provides the most comprehensive European resource centre for biological materials including bacteria, Archaea, fungi and phages. Website provides access to the collection catalogues, links to related organizations, and Bacterial Nomenclature Up-to-Date, a compilation of the valid bacterial names that have been published since January 1 1980.

Institute for Genomic Research
See entry no. 2512

Associations & societies

2673 American Society for Microbiology
www.asm.org
The world's largest microbiological society, the ASM has an international membership. The website provides a range of information about the Society and its activities as well as information about careers in microbiology, conferences and sources of funding. The site also includes links to three sites produced by the ASM: for children (www.Microbe.org); teachers (www.MicrobeLibrary.org); for general public (www.MicrobeWorld.org).

2674 American Society for Virology
www.mcw.edu/asv
Based in the USA but membership is open to anyone who is actively involved in virology research. Includes a searchable directory of members and a link to a History of Virology website.

2675 Federation of European Microbiological Societies
www.fems-microbiology.org
FEMS encourages co-operation and communication among its membership of 44 European microbiological societies. The website provides information about the Federation, links to the websites of the member societies and a calendar of international microbiological events. It also includes information on the FEMS journals including *FEMS Microbiology Reviews*.

2676 International Society for Extremophiles
extremophiles.org
Based in Japan but with an international membership, this Society is open to all researchers interested in extremophiles (Archaea). The site mainly contains information about the Society and its journal *Extremophiles*, but it does also include information on relevant scientific meetings and a small number of links to related websites.
(Website under construction, April 2005.)

International Society for Molecular Plant-Microbe Interactions
See entry no. 2217

2677 Society for Applied Microbiology [UK]
www.sfam.org.uk
Founded in 1931, and 'the UK's oldest microbiological society'. Six Interest Groups: Bioengineering; Educational development; Environmental; Food safety and technology; Infection, prevention and treatment; Molecular biology. Useful collection of book reviews reproduced from the monthly *Microbiologist* magazine. Publications. Links.

2678 Society for General Microbiology [UK]
www.socgenmicrobiol.org.uk
The largest microbiological society in Europe. Information about the Society and its activities and publications, as well as topics such as careers, scientific meetings, sources of research and study funding. Full text of all articles (and book reviews) from *Microbiology Today*, the Society's magazine, from 1999 to date is freely available.

- **Bioscience@Work** www.biocareers.org.uk. Information about careers in microbiology for school leavers (including lists of UK universities that offer microbiology degrees), graduates and researchers. Includes links to careers pages provided by other professional societies, and to related sites.
- **Microbiology On-line** www.microbiologyonline.org.uk. Resources for teachers and learners in schools and colleges. The section on Safety is particularly useful.

Society for Industrial Microbiology
See entry no. 5025

Portal & task environments

2679 All the Virology on the WWW
D.M. Sander
www.tulane.edu/~dmsander/garryfavweb.html
Founded in 1995, this site aims to be 'the best single site for Virology information on the Internet' and it certainly comes close. It contains links to a wide range of web-based virology resources arranged under headings that make it easy to find relevant resources. It also includes a link to the Big Picture Book of Viruses, a separate site that catalogues illustrations of viruses on the internet.

2680 ArchaeaWeb: the web's premier archaea and extremophile information resource
University of New South Wales
www.archaea.unsw.edu.au
This site contains information on Archaea and extremophiles, i.e. organisms that live in extreme environments. Much of the content is aimed at scientists working in the field but the Web Links section of the site provides a good starting point for anyone looking for information on the subject.

2681 Microbes.info: the microbiology information portal
A. Chan, comp.
www.microbes.info
The Resources section of this site contains links to more than 3500 microbiological and related sites. The site also contains a searchable news page, images, an FAQs section, and it also hosts several discussion forums.

2682 MicrobeWorld
American Society for Microbiology
www.microbeworld.org
This site, created by the ASM, is aimed at the general public and contains a substantial amount of high quality information. It is arranged under eight headings: Types of microbes (including fungi and protista); Microbe gallery; Timeline of microbiology; Who are microbiologists?; Tools

microbiologists use; More about microbes; Antibiotic resistance; Water quality. A very helpful site.

2683 The Microbial World: Microorganisms and Microbial Activities
J. Deacon; University of Edinburgh
helios.bto.ed.ac.uk/bto/microbes
Developed as a resource to support teaching by member of the University's Institute of Cell and Molecular Biology, provides a well designed, selective overview of microbiology. Topics covered include fungi, viruses, environmental processes and biological control.

2684 WFCC-MIRCEN World Data Centre for Microorganisms
World Federation for Culture Collections
wdcm.nig.ac.jp
This site aims to provide 'a comprehensive directory of culture collections, databases on microbes and cell lines, and the gateway to biodiversity, molecular biology and genome projects'. The collection of links is searchable but it can also be browsed under headings such as: Search engines and portal sites; Nomenclature and phylogeny; Genome projects. There are also links to websites of other national and international culture collections.

Discovering print & electronic resources

Highveld.com: the internet directory of molecular biology and biotechnology
See entry no. 2531

2685 Microbiology Abstracts
CSA, Monthly.
www.csa.com/e_products/databases-collections.php [DESCRIPTION]
The main abstracting and indexing tool in this area, published in three sections: A. Industrial and Applied Microbiology; B. Bacteriology; C. Algology, Mycology & Protozoology Abstracts.
Available in print and online: see website.

- **Virology and AIDS Abstracts** CSA, 1982–, Monthly. www.csa.com/factsheets/virology-set-c.php [DESCRIPTION]. Originally called *Virology Abstracts*, now expanded to include coverage of issues relating to AIDS.

2686 Virology: an information profile
R. Nicholas and D. Nicholas Mansell, 1983, 236pp. ISBN 0720116732.
Although now rather out of date this is still a useful work, providing an overview of the basic virology information sources.

Digital data, image & text collections

2687 Plant Viruses Online: descriptions and lists from the VIDE database
A.A. Brunt [et al.], eds
image.fs.uidaho.edu/vide
This database, while not comprehensive, is an excellent source of information on plant viruses. Each entry contains information under the headings: Nomenclature; Host range, transmission and symptoms; Physical and biochemical properties; Taxonomy and relationships; Comments and references. The database can be browsed by virus species, viral acronym, viral genera or by host plant.

2688 The Prokaryotes: an evolving electronic resource for the microbiological community
M. Dworkin [et al.], eds 3rd edn, Springer-Verlag, 1999–2004.
http://141.150.157.117:8080/prokPUB/index.htm
An excellent now online-only publication of the major established work, content being made available incrementally in 16 releases over 4 years. Interesting Preface and very good series of FAQs. Full text search facility; direct citation querying of PubMed database.

2689 The Universal Virus Database of the International Committee on Taxonomy of Viruses: ICTVdB
C. Buechen-Osmond, comp.; International Committee on Taxonomy of Viruses
phene.cpmc.columbia.edu
Database of viral information (partly based on the information in the book Virus taxonomy) arranged in two main sections. The Index of Viruses contains information about the taxonomy of viruses while more detailed information is found in the Descriptions section. Also contains a collection of images of viruses.

Directories & encyclopedias

2690 Encyclopedia of environmental microbiology
G. Bitton [et al.], eds Wiley, 2002, 3527pp. 6 v., $2095.00. ISBN 0471354503.
Multi-volume encyclopedia that contains 320 detailed articles, arranged alphabetically by title. Covers 14 main areas: Groundwater; Freshwater; Marine and estuarine waters; Biofilms; Soil microbiology; Environmental biotechnology; Aeromicrobiology; Wastewater microbiology; Drinking water microbiology; Methodology; Bacterial pathogens; Protozoan parasites & viruses; Biodegradation; Extreme environments. Each article includes a bibliography and many also include illustrations (and the book includes 44 pages of colour plates).

Encyclopedia of food microbiology
R.K. Robinson, C.A. Batt and P.D. Patel, eds See entry no. 3179

2691 Encyclopedia of microbiology
J. Lederberg [et al.], eds 2nd edn, Academic Press, 2000. 4 v., $925.00. ISBN 0122268008.
http://books.elsevier.com [DESCRIPTION]
The new edition of this standard reference work contains 298 articles, arranged in alphabetical order, that provide an overview of the subjects covered rather than comprehensive coverage of microbiology as a whole. Each article includes a bibliography and a glossary and subject index are included in v. 4.

2692 Encyclopedia of virology
A. Granoff and R.G. Webster, eds 2nd edn, Academic Press, 1999, 1997pp. 3 v., $1125.00. ISBN 0122270304.
A standard reference work containing articles of varying length, arranged in alphabetical order, that provide an overview of various aspects of virology. Each article includes a bibliography of further reading. Each of the 3 volumes contains a full contents list, an alphabetical listing of general topics (i.e. non-taxonomic entries), an alphabetical listing of

taxa, an Appendix listing the updated ICTV virus name index and a complete subject index. Volume 1 also includes 2 short essays on Tobacco mosaic virus and Foot-and-mouth virus.

2693 The Springer index of viruses
C.A. Tidona, G. Darai and C. Büchen-Osmond, eds Springer, 2001, 1511pp. £245.50. ISBN 3540671676.
Contains a summary of the information that is available for each of the virus genera, listed under the headings: Virion; Genome; Replication strategy; History; Genus members; Nucleotide sequences; Proteins; Biology; Diseases; Vaccine strains; Vector constructs (but not all headings are included for all viruses). The entry for each genus also includes an illustration of the virus and a list of 'key references'.

Handbooks & manuals

2694 Bergey's manual of systematic bacteriology
J.G. Holt [et al.], eds 1st edn, Williams & Wilkins, 1984–1989. 4 v. www.cme.msu.edu/Bergeys [COMPANION]
This is a very detailed work that is primarily aimed at researchers. It includes diagnostic tools for identifying bacteria as well as descriptive and taxonomic information. Each volume contains articles that deal with individual genera, providing a description of the genus, information on relevant techniques, details of identifying features, a bibliography and a list of species.

- **The Archaea and the deeply branching and phototrophic bacteria G. Garrity, D.R. Boone and R.W. Castenholz, eds** 2nd edn, Springer, 2001, 721pp. £84.50. ISBN 0387987711.
- **The proteobacteria G. Garrity, ed.** 2nd edn, Springer, 2005. ISBN 0387950400. www.springeronline.com [DESCRIPTION]. Will culminate a four-year effort by Bergey's Manual Trust and more than 150 internationally recognized authorities to provide a comprehensive view of the Proteobacteria, the largest prokaryotic phylum: 72 families; 425 genera; 1875 named species.

2695 Collins and Lyne's microbiological methods
C.H. Collins [et al.], eds 8th edn, Arnold, 2004, 456pp. £45.00. ISBN 0340808969.
Guide to a wide range of microbiological techniques, with 52 chapters on topics such as: Cultural methods; Clinical material; Environmental microbiology; Food microbiology. Also includes identification keys and safety guidelines.

2696 CRC handbook of microbiology
A.I. Laskin and H.A. Lechevalier, eds 2nd edn, CRC Press, 1977–88.
This handbook, aimed at researchers rather than the general public, provides a detailed overview of aspects of microbiology. It begins with an overview of microorganisms, including fungi, algae and protozoa (but not Archaea), before looking at more specific topics in more depth. Each chapter includes a bibliography and there are taxonomic and subject indexes in each volume.

W.M. O'Leary Practical handbook of microbiology *(CRC Press, 1989. 681pp. $149.95. ISBN 0849337046) is a condensed version of the series, still in print.*

- **Volume 1. Bacteria** 1977, 757pp. ISBN 0849372011.
- **Volume 2. Fungi, algae, protozoa, and viruses** 1978, 874pp. ISBN 084937202X.
- **Volume 3. Microbial composition: amino acids, proteins, and nucleic acids** 1981, 987pp. ISBN 0849372038.
- **Volume 4. Microbial composition: carbohydrates, lipids, and minerals** 1982, 729pp. ISBN 0849372046.
- **Volume 5. Microbial products** 1984, 908pp. ISBN 0849372054.
- **Volume 6. Growth and metabolism** 1984, 375pp. ISBN 0849372062.
- **Volume 7. Microbial transformation** 1984, 606pp. ISBN 0849372070.
- **Volume 8. Toxins and enzymes** 1987, 425pp. ISBN 0849372089.
- **Volume 9. Part A. Antibiotics** 1988, 594pp. ISBN 0849372100.
- **Volume 9. Part B. Antimicrobial inhibitors** 1988, 226pp. ISBN 0849372119.

2697 Fields virology
D.M. Knipe and P.M. Howley, eds 4th edn, Lippincott Williams & Wilkins, 2001, 3087pp. 2 v. CD-ROM, $359.00. ISBN 0781718325.
An advanced textbook on virology, published in two volumes. The first Part of the book provides an introduction to virology while Part II covers specific virus families with a particular focus on their replication and medical significance. Each chapter includes a substantial bibliography and there is a subject index in both of the volumes.

Handbook of culture media for food microbiology
J.E.L. Corry, G.D.W. Curtis and R.M. Baird, eds See entry no. 5040

2698 Molecular genetics of bacteria
J.W. Dale and S.F. Park 4th edn, Wiley, 2004, 346pp. $50.00. ISBN 047085085X.
This is a useful introductory undergraduate textbook although it does assume that the reader will already have a basic knowledge of molecular biology. It has ten chapters that cover topics such as: Nucleic acid structure and function; Genetics of bacteriophages; Plasmids; Genetic methods for investigating bacteria; Gene mapping to genomics.

Molecular medical microbiology
M. Sussman, ed. See entry no. 3597

Keeping up-to-date

2699 Advances in Applied Microbiology
Academic Press, 1959–, Irregular. ISSN 00652164. www.sciencedirect.com/science/journal/00652164 [DESCRIPTION]
A monographic series with volumes being issued on an approximately annual basis, each containing a collection of review articles on all aspects of applied and molecular microbiology. Some volumes treat a particular theme: for example, Volume 50 was on 'Archaea'. All of the articles include bibliographies and each volume has a subject index.

2700 Advances in Virus Research
Academic Press, 1953–, Irregular. ISSN 00653527. www.sciencedirect.com/science/bookseries/00653527 [DESCRIPTION]
A monographic series (each volume has an individual ISBN) with volumes being issued on an approximately annual basis. Each volume contains a collection of review articles that cover all aspects of virology. Some volumes are themed, for example Volume 56 was on 'Neurovirology'. Each article includes a bibliography and a subject index is included in each volume.

2701 **Annual Review of Microbiology**
Annual Reviews, 1947–, Annual. $202.00 [V. 58, 2004]. ISBN 0824311582 ISSN 00664227.
arjournals.annualreviews.org/loi/micro [DESCRIPTION]
This is one of the most important journals in the field, publishing review articles on all aspects of the subject. Each article summarizes the research to date on a particular topic and includes a comprehensive bibliography. The volume also includes a subject index.

2702 **Current Opinion in Microbiology**
Elsevier, 1998–, Bimonthly. €1171.00. ISSN 13695274.
www.elsevier.com/locate/issn/13695274 [DESCRIPTION]
A review journal covering all aspects of microbiology.

2703 **International Journal of Systematic and Evolutionary Microbiology**
Society for General Microbiology, 2000–, Bimonthly. £485.00. ISSN 14665026.
ijs.sgmjournals.org [DESCRIPTION]
This journal publishes articles on all aspects of bacterial systematics and is the official journal of record for new bacterial taxa. Formerly *International Journal of Systematic Bacteriology*, and prior to that *International Bulletin of Bacteriological Nomenclature and Taxonomy*.

2704 **Methods in Microbiology**
Academic Press, 1969–, Irregular. ISSN 05809517.
www.sciencedirect.com/science/journal/05809517 [DESCRIPTION]
A monographic series (each volume has an individual ISBN) containing review articles on microbiological techniques.

2705 **Microbiology and Molecular Biology Reviews**
American Society for Microbiology 1997–, Quarterly. $376.00. ISSN 10922172.
mmbr.asm.org [DESCRIPTION]
The most highly cited microbiology journal in both 2002 and 2003. The journal publishes review articles in the areas of microbiology, immunology and cell and molecular biology. Previous titles were *Bacteriological Reviews* and then *Microbiological Reviews*.

2706 **Trends in Microbiology**
Elsevier, 1993–, Monthly. €1171.00. ISSN 0966842X.
www.elsevier.com/locate/issn/0966842X [DESCRIPTION]
Each issue contains a collection of relatively short review articles relating to molecular microbiology and virology, providing an overview of recent developments. Useful current awareness tool.

Mycology

fungal ecology • fungi • lichens • yeasts

Introductions to the subject

2707 **Fungal Biology**
University of Sydney
bugs.bio.usyd.edu.au/Mycology/contents.shtml
This site provides an online tutorial, aimed at students in higher education, but accessible to all. The content is arranged in ten chapters: Structure & function; Growth & development; Feeding; Fungal reproduction & dispersal; Taxonomy; Ecology; Habitats of fungi; Plant interactions; Animal interactions; Uses of fungi. Also includes a glossary and bibliography.

2708 **Fungal ecology**
N.J. Dix and J. Webster Chapman & Hall, 1995, 549pp. ISBN 0412641305.
A useful introduction to the subject, this book does not try to be comprehensive, but each of the areas included (e.g. Structure of fungal communities; Colonization and decay of wood; Aquatic fungi; Fungi of extreme environments) have been covered in some depth. It includes a substantial bibliography (pp 398–497).

2709 **Fungi**
R. Watling; Natural History Museum 2003, 96pp. £9.95. ISBN 0565091824.
www.nhm.ac.uk/services/publishing/det_fungi.html [DESCRIPTION]
This book provides a nice introduction to the subject, with a focus on the larger fungi (mushrooms, etc), and includes full-colour illustrations. There are seven chapters: How important are fungi?; What is a fungus?; The larger fungi; When and where?; Collecting and studying fungi; Fungi and humans; Conservation. Includes a subject index, a glossary and a bibliography that covers both printed and online sources.

2710 **The Fungi**
M.J. Carlile, S.C. Watkinson and G.W. Gooday 2nd edn, Academic Press, 2001, 588pp. $50.95. ISBN 0127384464.
A standard undergraduate textbook providing a good overview of the subject. Chapters cover topics such as classification, growth, reproduction, genetics and biotechnology and each includes a bibliography of further reading.

2711 **Lichens**
O. Gilbert HarperCollins, 2000, 288pp. £18.90. ISBN 0002200821.
http://www.collins.co.uk [DESCRIPTION]
An introduction to the British lichens, this book takes an ecological approach to the subject with chapters including: What is a lichen?; Lichens and air pollution; Trees, woods and people; Rivers and lakes. There is also an overview of some of the uses that man has made of lichens.
Series: New Naturalist.

Dictionaries, thesauri, classifications

2712 **Ainsworth & Bisby's dictionary of the fungi**
P.M. Kirk [et al.] 9th edn, CABI Publishing, 2001, 655pp. £55.00. ISBN 085199377X.
www.indexfungorum.org/Names/fundic.asp [COMPANION]
First published in 1943, this is the standard dictionary of mycology with more than 20,000 entries covering all aspects of the subject including moulds, lichens and yeasts. The Systematic Arrangement section (pp 569–655) lists the generic names included in the dictionary in their correct systematic position and a searchable version of this is available online. An essential reference work.

- **Index Fungorum** CABI Publishing.
  www.indexfungorum.org/Names/Names.asp. Index to the names of fungi (including lichens, yeasts and fossil forms) that contains more than 345,000 species and sub-species names. It is searchable by scientific names only.

- **Index of Fungi** CABI Publishing, 1940–, Biannual. £200.00. List of names of new genera, species and intraspecific taxa, new combinations and new names of fungi and lichens, compiled from world literature.

2713 **Recommended English Names for Fungi** [UK]
E. Holden, S. Evans and M. Harper Plantlife International, 2003, 23pp. PDF. ISBN 1872613993.
www.plantlife.org.uk/html/species_and_conservation/species_and_conservation_fungi.htm
This book contains lists of the scientific and English (common) names for about 1000 British species of fungi. It also includes a bibliography.

Laws, standards, codes

International Code of Botanical Nomenclature: St Louis Code
W. Greuter [et al.], eds; International Association for Plant Taxonomy See entry no. 2195

Associations & societies

American Bryological and Lichenological Society
See entry no. 2202

American Phytopathological Society
See entry no. 2204

2714 **Association of British Fungus Groups**
www.abfg.org
The Association is open to both professional mycologists and amateurs with an interest in the subject. It has a network of local groups across the UK and links to their websites are provided as well as other useful data.

2715 **British Lichen Society** [UK]
www.thebls.org.uk
Founded in 1958, the BLS was the first lichenological society in the world and it now has members from around the world. Access to several useful documents and collections including: Lichen references (a list of recent publications on British lichens); Grey literature (unpublished works on lichens); British Isles list of lichens and lichenicolous fungi.

2716 **British Mycological Society**
www.britmycolsoc.org.uk
Founded in 1896, the BMS has an international membership and aims to promote all aspects of mycology. The Resources section of the website contains a large collection of useful items, including links to related sites, information on databases and directories and, from their Library: *Recent Additions to the Society Library and Abstracts of Recent Journals*, a quarterly publication.

2717 **International Association of Lichenologists**
www.botany.hawaii.edu/cpsu/ial.htm
The Association's website provides access to a searchable directory of lichenologists, information on endangered lichen species and a useful list of lichen societies.

2718 **International Mycological Association**
www.biologi.uio.no/org/ima
The IMA was founded in 1971 and it now has over 30,000 members worldwide. Website includes lists of recently published books, links to related websites and a collection of resources on fungal gastronomy.

International Society for Mushroom Science
See entry no. 3090

2719 **Mycological Society of America**
www.msafungi.org
Founded in 1932, the Society is based in the USA but has an international membership. Information about the Society, its meetings and its publications which include the journal *Mycologia*, and downloadable PDF versions of its well produced bimonthly newsletter *Inoculum* (November 2004, 28 pp), each issue including an extensive 'Mycologist's Bookshelf' section.

2720 **North American Mycological Association**
www.namyco.org
The NAMA website contains a range of useful resources including information on mushroom poisoning, reviews of recent books and images of fungi. It also includes information on other mycological societies within the US.

Libraries, archives, museums

2721 **Lichen Herbarium**
Arizona State University
http://ces.asu.edu/ASULichens
Access to records of over 70,000 of the 90,000 specimens within the Herbarium. Also to preliminary version of a Glossary being prepared for publication as part of the University's Sonoran Desert Flora Project containing 'terms and definitions from glossaries found in numerous lichen floras': not comprehensive but a useful online tool.

2722 **Royal Botanic Gardens, Kew, Mycology Section**
www.rbgkew.org.uk/scihort/mycolexp.html
Kew houses one of the oldest, largest and most important mycological collections in the world with over 800,000 specimens. This site provides more information about the collection and the research that is carried out by the Mycology section at Kew.

Portal & task environments

2723 **Doctor Fungus**
J. H. Rex [et al.]; DoctorFungus Corporation DoctorFungus Corporation.
www.doctorfungus.org
Brings together a collection of resources on a range of mycological topics although the main emphasis is on medical mycology. The five main sections of the site cover: The fungi (includes an image bank); Mycoses (human, veterinary and environmental); Drugs; Laboratory; Education & tools (includes a glossary, a bibliography for the site, lists of recent books and an events calendar).

2724 **LichenLand**
Oregon State University
mgd.nacse.org/hyperSQL/lichenland
This is a nice site that introduces the user to lichen biology and identification in a very accessible way. It includes

photographs of lichens as well as information on their habitats and bibliographies for each species.

2725 Mycology Online
D. Ellis; University of Adelaide
www.mycology.adelaide.edu.au
Simple but effective site providing access to a range of medical mycology resources. It has four sections: Fungal jungle (links to related sites, lecture notes, a glossary and images); Mycoses (information on clinical conditions caused by fungi); Fungal descriptions (descriptions of species that cause diseases); Laboratory methods.

2726 MykoWeb
M. Wood
www.mykoweb.com
This site contains a large collection of links to mycological sites including societies, mushroom recipes, systematics and general sites. It also includes information on the Californian fungi, a collection of images, book reviews and electronic versions of two books, *California mushrooms: a field guide to the boletes* by H.D. Thiers (1975) and *Wild about mushrooms* by L. Freedman.

2727 Tom Volk's Fungi
T. Volk; University of Wisconsin
TomVolkFungi.net
Lively site including an online presentation which provides a good introduction to the fungi. Also includes 'Fungus of the month' with an archive back to 1997, images, links to related sites. An engaging presentation.

Discovering print & electronic resources

2728 Abstracts of Mycology
Thomson BIOSIS, 1967–, Monthly. ISSN 00013617.
www.biosis.org/products/aom [DESCRIPTION]
A subset of BIOLOGICAL ABSTRACTS, this database provides an index to the contents of more than 4000 journals, books and other mycological literature. It covers all aspects of the subject including taxonomy, genetics and medical mycology. Each issue includes author, organism and subject indexes and cumulative indexes are issued at the end of each year.

2729 Bibliography of Systematic Mycology
CABI Publishing, 1943–, Biannual. £220.00. ISSN 00061573.
www.indexfungorum.org/BSM/bsm.htm
Listing of new publications on fungal taxonomy, classification, nomenclature and phylogeny. Also includes book reviews and notices. Can be searched by author or genus. Full details of items published in the last five years are only available in the printed version.
Available online: see website.

2730 The Mycology.net
Bayerisches Staatsministerium für Wissenschaft, Forschung und Kunst and Staatliche Naturwissenschaftliche Sammlungen Bayerns
www.mycology.net
Easy and very well designed access to a large collection of links to mycological websites organized into seven categories: Contacts (organizations and discussion lists); Bibliography (journals, books and booksellers); Systematics; Identification; Collections; Biogeography (conservation and biodiversity); Resources (dictionaries, teaching resources and laboratory methodologies). The site also hosts its own discussion forum.

2731 Review of Medical and Veterinary Mycology
CABI Publishing, 1951–, Quarterly. £535.00. ISSN 00346624.
www.cabi-publishing.org/index.asp [DESCRIPTION]
An index to the medical mycological journal literature. It covers the areas of medical mycoses, asthma and other allergies, fungal poisoning and antifungal agents. Each issue also includes author, subject and serials cited indexes.
Available online: see website.

Digital data, image & text collections

2732 British Isles List of Lichens and Lichenicolous Fungi
B. Coppins, M. Seaward and J. Simkin
users.argonet.co.uk/users/jmgray/checklist.html
This site provides a list of all of the validly published genera and species of lichens that have been found in Great Britain and Ireland.

- **Checklist of lichens of Great Britain and Ireland B.J. Coppins, comp.** British Lichen Society, 2002, 87pp. £9.00. ISBN 0954041828.

2733 British Mycological Society Fungal Records Database
British Mycological Society
194.203.77.76/fieldmycology/BMSFRD/bmsfrd.asp
The database contains more than 1 million records of fungi that have been recorded in the UK. The web-based version currently contains only summary data. It can be searched by order or genus (via the associated Checklist of British Fungi), vice-county or by the organism that a fungus is associated with. Entries include taxonomic information, brief information about records for the species (i.e. where and when it has been found) and, in some cases, links to a distribution map.

2734 Fungal Databases
D.F. Farr [et al.], eds; Agricultural Research Service
http://nt.ars-grin.gov/fungaldatabases/index.cfm
Access to a collection of databases that includes the US national fungi collection, literature on plant-pathogenic fungal systematics, fungal names and fungi-host distributions. The databases can be searched individually or all together using scientific names of the fungi or the host. From the Service's Systematic Botany & Mycology Laboratory.

2735 Fungi Images on the Net
F.V. Larsen, ed.
www.in2.dk/fungi
Access to images of more than 1500 mushrooms and other fungi. The images can be browsed alphabetically by genus and species names. The site does not actually host the images but simply provides links to them on their original servers.

Directories & encyclopedias

Medically important fungi: a guide to identification
D.H. Larone See entry no. 3589

Handbooks & manuals

Handbook of fungal biotechnology
D.K. Arora, P.D. Bridge and D. Bhatnagar, eds See entry no. 5041

2736 **Lichens of North America**
I.M. Brodo, S.D. Sharnoff and S. Sharnoff Yale University Press, 2001, 795pp. $85.00. ISBN 0300082495.
http://yalepress.yale.edu/yupbooks [DESCRIPTION]
This book, illustrated in colour throughout, provides a helpful introduction to lichen biology and ecology as well as identification keys and descriptions for all of the North American species. It also includes a glossary and a bibliography.

2737 **The Mycota: a comprehensive treatise on fungi as experimental systems for basic and applied research**
K. Esser, ed. Springer-Verlag, 1994–.
www.springeronline.com [DESCRIPTION]
This monographic series aims to 'address three basic questions: what are the fungi, what do they do, and what is their relevance to human affairs?' Each volume in the series contains a collection of articles on aspects of a particular topic, for instance: Plant relationships; Human fungal pathogens; Systematics and evolution. Each article includes a substantial bibliography.

Poisonous plants and fungi in Britain: animal and human poisoning
M.R. Cooper and A.W. Johnson; Guy's & St Thomas' Hospital Trust and Royal Botanic Gardens, Kew See entry no. 2261

Poisonous plants and fungi in Britain and Ireland
E.A. Dauncey, ed.; Royal Botanic Gardens, Kew and Guy's & St Thomas' Hospital Trust See entry no. 4297

2738 **The yeasts**
A.H. Rose and J.S. Harrison, eds 2nd edn, Academic Press, 1987–95. 6 v.
These six volumes provide an excellent overview of all aspects of yeast science (zymology). Each volume contains a collection of articles by a range of authors that review aspects of the subject. Each article contains a bibliography and each volume includes an index to the authors that are cited in these.

- **Volume 1. Biology of yeasts** 1987, 423pp. ISBN 0125964110.
- **Volume 2. Yeasts and the environment** 1987, 309pp. ISBN 0125964129.
- **Volume 3. Metabolism and physiology of yeasts** 1989, 635pp. ISBN 0125964137.
- **Volume 4. Yeast organelles** 1991, 765pp. ISBN 0125964145.
- **Volume 5. Yeast technology** 1993, 620pp. ISBN 0125964153.
- **Volume 6. Yeast genetics** 1995, 660pp. ISBN 0125964161.

2739 **Yeasts: characteristics and identification**
J.A. Barnett, R.W. Payne and D. Yarrow 3rd edn, Cambridge University Press, 2000, 1139pp. £225.00. ISBN 0521573963.
An extremely useful reference book as it provides descriptions of more than 700 yeast species, along with identification keys and a register of names. It also includes information on the classification of yeasts, relevant laboratory methods, a glossary and a substantial bibliography.

Keeping up-to-date

2740 **Myconet**
O.E. Eriksson, ed. 1997–, Irregular. ISSN 14031418.
www.umu.se/myconet/Myconet.html
An online taxonomic journal that publishes a regularly updated review of ascomycete systematics and taxonomy with the note that other groups of fungi may be published in the future.

2741 **Mycotaxon**
1974–, Quarterly. $165.00. ISSN 00934666.
www.mycotaxon.com [DESCRIPTION]
A research journal that publishes articles on fungal systematics.

Ornithology

Audubon • bird conservation • bird migration • birds • birds of prey • birds' eggs • owls • raptors

Introductions to the subject

2742 **Biographies for birdwatchers: the lives of those commemorated in western palearctic bird names**
B. Mearns and R. Mearns Academic Press, 1988, 490pp. ISBN 0124874223.
Many species of birds are named after particular individuals and this volume brings together biographical information on some of those individuals. The work includes an index of the bird names, an index of the individuals, and a bibliography.

2743 **Birds' eggs**
M. Walters Dorling Kindersley, 1994, 256pp. ISBN 0751310107.
A basic introduction to the eggs of birds that includes full colour illustrations. A brief overview of eggs (shape, colour and size), breeding and nests is followed by illustrations of the eggs of more than 500 species from around the world.

2744 **A concise history of ornithology: the lives and works of its founding figures**
M. Walters Christopher Helm, 2003, 255pp. £30.00. ISBN 1873403976.
Written by a former curator at the NATURAL HISTORY MUSEUM this book outlines the history of the development of ornithology as a subject in it's own right. Includes a chapter: Ornithology and ornithologists in the twentieth century.

Dino-birds: from dinosaurs to birds
A. Milner; Natural History Museum See entry no. 1400

2745 **The Life of Birds**
G.H. Davies and D. Attenborough; BBC and Public Broadcasting Service
www.pbs.org/lifeofbirds
This site accompanies the television series of the same name. It provides quite basic information under five headings: Bird brains; Evolution; Champion birds; Parenthood; Bird songs. It includes many colour photographs and sound recordings of bird songs.

2746 **The migration atlas: movements of the birds of Britain and Ireland**
C. Wernham [et al.], eds; British Trust for Ornithology Poyser, 2002, 884pp. £65.00. ISBN 0713665149.
Based on results from the ringing scheme operated by the BTO along with other sources, provides comprehensive overview of movements of all British and Irish species of birds. Introductory chapter reviews bird migration more generally including information on the ringing scheme and how migration is studied.

2747 **Ornithology**
F.B. Gill 2nd edn, W H Freeman, 1995, 763pp. $101.95. ISBN 0716724154.
A good undergraduate textbook that covers all aspects of bird biology. Six parts: Origins (evolution and systematics); Form and function; Behaviour and communication; Behaviour and the environment; Reproduction and development; Population dynamics and conservation. Also includes an illustrated overview of the birds of the world, a bibliography and a subject index.
3rd edn announced.

2748 **Ornithology**
G. Ritchison; Eastern Kentucky University
www.biology.eku.edu/RITCHISO/ornitholsyl.htm
Online lecture notes for an introductory ornithology course provided at the EKU. Topics covered include the evolution of birds, physiology, vocal communication, breeding and reproduction and flight.

The rise of birds: 225 million years of evolution
S. Chatterjee See entry no. 1415

2749 **RSPB handbook of British birds**
P. Holden and T. Cleeves; Royal Society for the Protection of Birds Christopher Helm, 2002, 303pp. £9.99. ISBN 0713657138.
A very useful overview of the British bird. The book is arranged taxonomically with a species account on each page that provides information under the headings: Identification; Habits; Voice; Habitat; Food; Breeding; Movements and migrations; Population; Conservation. Each species entry also includes colour illustrations of the birds and a distribution map. There is an index, a short glossary and a list of all of the different common names that are used for each species.

Dictionaries, thesauri, classifications

2750 **BabelBird**
S. Tewinkel and R. Jahn
www.babelbird.de/index_e.html
This is a searchable database of bird names that includes scientific names and common names in German, English, French and Spanish. Also includes more general information about bird watching.

Multilingual Animal Glossary of Unveiled Synonyms: MAGUS
T. Bartol [et al.], eds; University of Ljubljana See entry no. 2877

2751 **Multilingual Birdsearch Engine**
www.knutas.com/birdsearch
A searchable database of bird names containing scientific names and common names in 18 European languages including Danish, Dutch, Finnish, Italian and Spanish.

Laws, standards, codes

2752 **Distribution and taxonomy of birds of the world**
C.G. Sibley and B.L. Monroe Yale University Press, 1990, 1111pp. ISBN 0300049692.
This volume and its supplement provide a key guide to bird taxonomy. Arranged taxonomically using scientific names, they include an entry for every species of bird providing information on habitat and geographical distribution as well as taxonomy. They also include maps, a substantial bibliography and an index that includes both scientific and common names. The supplement includes changes to the distribution and taxonomy as well as corrections to the original volume.

- **A supplement to *Distribution and taxonomy of birds of the world*** **C. G. Sibley and B. L. Monroe** Yale University Press, 1993, 108pp. ISBN 0300055498.
- **A world checklist of birds** **B.L. Monroe and C.G. Subley** Yale University Press, 1993, 393pp. ISBN 0300055471. Scientific and common names and abbreviated geographical distribution information for the 9702 species of birds included in the 1990 vol. Listing arranged taxonomically; includes alphabetic indexes for the common and generic names.

2753 **Zoonomen**
A.P. Peterson, comp.
www.zoonomen.net
This site provides access to two nomenclature resources. Birds of the World – Current Valid Scientific Avian Names is a browsable list of generic and specific scientific names along with brief details of the authors and the publications that the names first appeared in. The second resource provides graphical illustrations of taxonomic activity relating to birds.

Research centres & institutes

2754 **Cornell Lab of Ornithology** [USA]
www.birds.cornell.edu
This leading laboratory has a wide range of research interests including bird conservation, population studies and evolution as well as being involved in educational activities. Their excellent website contains a huge amount of information including an Online Bird Guide ('A dynamic online guide for bird species identifications and in-depth information, including sounds, video, and distribution maps') – part of its All about Birds section – as well as many other valuable resources.

2755 **Edward Grey Institute of Field Ornithology** [UK]
http://egizoosrv.zoo.ox.ac.uk/EGI/EGIHome.htm
Part of the Department of Zoology at the University of Oxford. Conducts research in behaviour, ecology, evolution and conservation of birds, with a strong emphasis on understanding organisms in their natural environments.

- **Alexander Library** http://users.ox.ac.uk/~zoolib. Specialist library aiming to maintain comprehensive collection of ornithological literature. Holds over 10,000 books and 500 current journals as well as manuscript and other unpublished materials. Books added to stock often reviewed in THE IBIS.

2756 **Raptor Center** [USA]
www.ahc.umn.edu/ahc_content/colleges/vetmed/Depts_and_Centers/Raptor_Center
Established in 1974, the Center specializes in the medical care, rehabilitation, and conservation of eagles, hawks, owls and falcons, with an international training programme. Site offers a range of data sheets on specific raptors.

Associations & societies

2757 **American Bird Conservancy**
www.abcbirds.org
Aims to conserve wild birds and their habitats throughout the Americas through a variety of research and education programmes. Has range of publications and the ABC Store has 'one of the largest nature product catalogs on the web'.

2758 **American Ornithologists' Union**
www.aou.org
Founded in 1883, the AOU has a membership drawn from both professional and amateur ornithologists. It organizes an annual scientific meeting and produces several publications including the journal The Auk and the book series *Ornithological Monographs*.

2759 **Birdlife International**
www.birdlife.net
An international organization made up of national conservation organizations. The UK partner is the Royal Society for the Protection of Birds, and the website provides access to the World Bird Database, developed with the RSPB, that contains information on endangered birds and important bird areas.

2760 **British Ornithologists' Union**
www.bou.org.uk
Founded in 1858, the BOU is one of the oldest ornithological organizations in the world. Activities include the publication of the journal Ibis and organizing scientific meetings. The Union also maintains The British List, the definitive list of the species of birds that have been recorded in Britain and Ireland, and which is accessible via the website.

2761 **British Trust for Ornithology**
www.bto.org
An independent research organization, founded in 1933, that investigates bird populations, movements and ecology in Britain and Ireland. The BTO co-ordinates the national ringing programme and organizes a wide range of surveys including the Garden BirdWatch project.

2762 **Hawk Conservancy Trust** [UK]
www.hawk-conservancy.org
Primarily a conservation organization, the Trust raises funds by opening its collections of raptors to the public. The website is a good source of information on birds of prey with detailed information on more than 200 species.

2763 **National Audubon Society** [USA]
www.audubon.org
Named after John James Audubon (1785–1851), a naturalist and artist famous for his book *Birds of America*, the Society aims to conserve natural ecosystems with a particular focus on birds. The website features a Birds & Science section that includes conservation information and an online version of Audubon's famous book.

2764 **Peregrine Fund** [USA]
www.peregrinefund.org
Founded in 1970, this US-based organization works both nationally and internationally to conserve birds of prey. The Explore Raptors section provides a good introduction and currently under development are a Global Raptor Info Network and a comprehensive database of raptor information.

2765 **Royal Society for the Protection of Birds** [UK]
www.rspb.org
Founded in 1889, the RSPB is a leading conservation organization and a key resource for anyone with an interest in ornithology. The website contains a huge amount of information structured under five headings: Birds (includes an A to Z of UK birds); Gardens (wildlife gardens); Countryside (farming, habitats, etc.); Reserves (detailed information on the RSPB reserves); About the RSPB. As well as its work in the UK the RSPB is active internationally through its involvement in BirdLife International.

Wildfowl & Wetlands Trust
See entry no. 2143

Libraries, archives, museums

2766 **Natural History Museum, Bird Group, Department of Zoology**
Walter Rothschild Zoological Museum
www.nhm.ac.uk/zoology/tring/birdgroup.html
The NHM bird collection, based at the Walter Rothschild Zoological Museum at Tring, is one of the most comprehensive in the world, with more than one million bird specimens. Information about the collection and the research that it supports; a useful list of reference books; access to the NHM Bird Type-Specimen database.

Portal & task environments

2767 **Birding.com** [USA]
www.birding.com
This US-based site is aimed at bird watchers. It includes links to many other relevant sites, including US and international organizations, mailing lists and discussion forums, as well as sections on identifying birds, bird taxonomy, reviews of binoculars among many other features.

2768 **Birdingonthe.Net: birding for the 21st century**
birdingonthe.net
Brings together a large collection of internet links that includes mailing lists, bird artists, bird watching equipment and links to bird sites around the world arranged geographically. The site also provides access to several species lists.

2769 **BIRDNET** [USA]
Ornithological Council
www.nmnh.si.edu/BIRDNET
An organization of 11 US professional ornithological societies. Provides information about the Council and

includes links to the member societies' home pages. Also access to a collection of ornithology resources and links to related resources.

2770 **Birdzilla.com** [USA]
www.birdzilla.com
This US site contains lots of useful information for bird watchers although the structure of the site is a little haphazard. One of the most useful parts of the site is the ABC's section, providing an introduction to bird watching and feeding. The site also has its own internet television and radio sites.

2771 **Interbirdnet Online** [UK]
www.birder.co.uk
An introduction to bird watching rather than ornithology as such, this site provides information about relevant books and magazines, accommodation and links to related sites. The site also includes a Featured Bird of the Month.

2772 **Ornithology: the science of birds**
R. Lederer
www.ornithology.com
Links to sites covering a wide range of topics including migration, conservation and taxonomy. Each section of links includes a brief introduction to the topic. Also provides information on careers in ornithology.

2773 **The Owl Pages**
www.owlpages.com
This site contains large amounts of information about owls arranged primarily under the headings: Owl species; Owl galleries (images); Physiology; Culture & art; Information (articles, links, discussion forums). The site is searchable.

2774 **WildBirds.com** [USA]
www.wildbirds.com
A US-based site that provides information on attracting and watching wild birds in domestic gardens. Includes information on feeding birds, bird boxes, identifying (US) birds and helping baby and / or injured birds as well as links to related sites.

Discovering print & electronic resources

2775 **Bird Links to the World**
Bird Studies Canada and Birdlife International
www.bsc-eoc.org/links
More than 18,000 links to bird sites around the world providing an outstanding resource. The site is searchable and can also be browsed by geographical region or by topic such as science or conservation. Includes on its home page a list of the top ten most visited links as well as selective compilations headed: The best bird websites; Checklists; Bird names and taxonomy; general web pages; Worldwide organizations and information; Other lists of Birdlinks.

2776 **Fatbirder**
R. Crombet-Beolens
www.fatbirder.com
A large collection of links to internet resources of interest to bird watchers. The site is searchable and links can also be browsed under the headings: World birding; UK birding; Miscellany & fun; Birdnews; Travel; Library; Bird families; Ornithology; Sight & sounds; Equipment / supplies.

2777 **Ornithological Worldwide Literature: OWL**
American Ornithologists' Union, British Ornithologists' Union and Birds Australia
egizoosrv.zoo.ox.ac.uk/owl
Index to scientific literature on ornithology covering both recent and older literature. Almost 700 items were added to the database in 2003 from a wide range of journals. The database especially aims to include grey literature items (e.g. reports, leaflets, annual reports, etc.) that are often not indexed in the standard bibliographic tools.
Formerly titled Recent Ornithological Literature.

2778 **Raptor Information System: RIS**
US Geological Survey
ris.wr.usgs.gov
Online catalogue of more than 30,000 references on birds of prey. Includes articles and grey literature on 'raptor management, human impacts on raptors, the mitigation of adverse impacts and basic raptor biology (with an emphasis on population dynamics and predation)'. The database's search engine is not that easy to use but online help is provided. Maintained by the Survey's Forest and Rangeland Ecosystem Science Center, Snake River Field Station.

Zoological Record
Zoological Society of London See entry no. 2913

Digital data, image & text collections

2779 **Avibase: the world bird database**
D. Lepage, ed.; Bird Studies Canada
www.bsc-eoc.org/avibase/avibase.jsp
This database includes more than 1.5 million records, providing information on more than 10,000 species of birds. It includes taxonomic information, common names in a range of languages, distribution information and links to the INTEGRATED TAXONOMIC INFORMATION SYSTEM database. The database can be searched by common or scientific names or it can be browsed by family.

2780 **Bird Families of the World**
D. Roberson
montereybay.com/creagrus/list.html
This site, now in its 6th edn, lists more than 200 bird families using several major publications as a taxonomic guide. The name of each family is listed along with the common name(s) and acts as a link to a page that provides further information and photographs of the members of the family. Each page also includes a bibliography.

2781 **Breeding Birds in the Wider Countryside** [UK]
British Trust for Ornithology and Joint Nature Conservation Committee
www.bto.org/birdtrends/index.htm
Detailed information on the population and conservation status of more than 100 species of British birds over the period from 1967 onwards. For each species information is provided on changes in the size of population, breeding performance and the possible causes of any observed changes. The site also includes information on how the data was gathered.

2782 **The British List: the official list of birds in Great Britain and the work of the BOU Records Committee** [UK]
British Ornithologists' Union
www.bou.org.uk/recgen.html
Access to a taxonomically arranged list of all of the species of birds that have been recorded in Great Britain. Each species is assigned to a category to indicate the history of the species, e.g. whether it is native or has been introduced. The list is not searchable but can be browsed by species or by category. The site also provides information on changes that have been made to the list including taxonomic changes that affect its arrangement.

2783 **World Bird Database: WBDB**
Birdlife International and Royal Society for the Protection of Birds
www.birdlife.org/datazone/index.html
A database of information relating to bird conservation with information on more than 10,000 species. It includes the conservation status of the species as well as information on, among other things, identifying features, population and range, ecology, threats and references to relevant literature. The database is searchable by species (common and scientific names), geographical areas and by category used by the IUCN RED LIST OF THREATENED SPECIES.

Directories & encyclopedias

2784 **Birds of the world: a checklist**
J.F. Clements 5th edn, Ibis Publishing, 2000, 867pp. £28.00. ISBN 0934797161.
www.ibispub.com/updates.html [COMPANION]
This volume contains a large amount of very useful information for anyone with an interest in birds. It lists over 9700 species of birds with details of their geographical ranges. It also includes a substantial bibliography, a key reference work for every bird family, and lists of the number of species found in every country of the world. There are scientific and common name indexes. Updates to the volume are provided on the companion website.

2785 **The Cambridge encyclopedia of ornithology**
M. Brooke and T. Birkhead, eds Cambridge University Press, 1991, 362pp. ISBN 0521362059.
Divided into 11 sections: Introduction; Anatomy and physiology; Movement; Birds, ancient and modern; The daily activities of birds; Distribution; Migration and navigation; Bird populations; Breeding; Behaviour; People and birds. Includes many colour illustrations, a bibliography of further reading and a glossary.

2786 **A dictionary of birds**
B. Campbell and E. Lack, eds; British Ornithologists' Union Poyser, 1985, 670pp. ISBN 0856610399.
In many ways this is closer to an encyclopedia than a dictionary as many of the entries are several pages in length and provide detailed information on aspects of the subject. Its coverage is excellent and many of the longer articles also include bibliographies making the book an excellent starting point for research.

2787 **The illustrated encyclopedia of birds: the definitive guide to birds of the world**
C.M. Perrins, ed.; International Council for Bird Preservation
Headline, 1990, 420pp. ISBN 074720277X.
The main section of the book provides a taxonomic listing of species with colour illustrations, followed by quite brief information. The book also includes short sections on bird biology, ecology and conservation but it does not include a bibliography.

2788 **The new encyclopedia of birds**
C.M. Perrins, ed. Oxford University Press, 2003, 656pp. £35.00. ISBN 0198525060.
This is a good general encyclopedia that is beautifully illustrated with colour photographs throughout. It is arranged taxonomically by family with each entry providing an overview of the biology, ecology and conservation status of the family members. It does not include a full list of all of the species in each family. It includes a glossary, a bibliography and a subject index.

Handbooks & manuals

2789 **Birds of Europe: with North Africa and the Middle East**
L. Jonsson Christopher Helm, 1999, 558pp. £16.99. ISBN 0713652381.
www.acblack.com [DESCRIPTION]
A guide to the bird species that are regularly found in Europe. An initial overview of the features that can be used to identify birds is followed by descriptions of individual species accompanied by colour illustrations.
Christopher Helm are 'the largest ornithology publisher in the world': see website.

Field manual of wildlife diseases: general field procedures and diseases of birds
M. Friend and J.C. Franson, eds See entry no. 3421

2790 **Handbook of the birds of Europe, the Middle East and North Africa: the birds of the Western Palearctic**
S. Cramp [et al.], eds Oxford University Press.
This is a standard reference work that provides a good overview of the birds of the Palaearctic region. Arranged taxonomically, the main section of the text provides information about individual species. Information is also provided on the morphology, distribution, habitat, population trends, behaviour and breeding biology of each bird family. Each volume includes many colour illustrations, including plates showing the eggs of each species, and a bibliography.

- **Volume I. Ostrich to ducks** 1977, 722pp. ISBN 0198573588.
- **Volume II. Hawks to bustards** 1980, 695pp. ISBN 019857505X.
- **Volume III. Waders to gulls** 1983, 913pp. ISBN 0198575068.
- **Volume IV. Terns to woodpeckers** 1985, 960pp. ISBN 0198575076.
- **Volume IX. Buntings and new world warblers** 1994, 488pp. ISBN 0198548435.
- **Volume V. Tyrant flycatchers to thrushes** 1988, 1063pp. ISBN 0198575084.
- **Volume VI. Warblers** 1992, 712pp. ISBN 0198575092.
- **Volume VII. Flycatchers to shrikes** 1993, 577pp. ISBN 0198575106.
- **Volume VIII. Crows to finches** 1994, 899pp. ISBN 0198546793.

2791 Handbook of the birds of the world
J. del Hoyo, A. Elliott and J. Sargatal, eds; Birdlife International Lynx Edicions.
www.hbw.com [DESCRIPTION]
This is an ambitious work that is still in production (it is planned to be completed in ten volumes). The arrangement of the book is similar to that of the work by Cramp [q.v.] but with more information being provided under the Family entry (systematics, morphology, habitat, calls / songs, reproduction and conservation) and briefer entries for the individual species. The volumes are lavishly illustrated with many colour photographs and each also includes a bibliography.

- **Volume 1. Ostrich to ducks** 1992, 696pp. ISBN 8487334105.
- **Volume 2. New world vultures to guineafowl** 1994, 638pp. ISBN 8487334156.
- **Volume 3. Hoatzin to auks** 1996, 821pp. ISBN 8487334202.
- **Volume 4. Sandgrouse to cuckoos** 1997, 679pp. ISBN 8487334229.
- **Volume 5. Barn-owls to hummingbirds** 1999, 759pp. ISBN 8487334253.
- **Volume 6. Mousebirds to hornbills** 2001, 589pp. ISBN 848733430X.
- **Volume 7. Jacamars to woodpeckers** 2002, 613pp. ISBN 8487334377. Includes an alphabetical and pictorial index to the Non-passerines as an insert.

2792 Manual of ornithology: avian structure & function
N.S. Proctor and P.J. Lynch Yale University Press, 1993, 340pp. ISBN 0300057466.
This useful book is a cross between an undergraduate textbook and a laboratory manual. It contains 12 chapters: Introduction; Systematics; Topography; Feathers; The skeleton; The musculature; The digestive system; The circulatory system; The respiratory system; The urogenital and endocrine systems; The nervous system; Field techniques. Each chapter supplements information on the topic with practical exercises and worksheets. The book contains many illustrations and a substantial bibliography, in addition to the references given at the end of each chapter.

Mesozoic birds: above the heads of dinosaurs
L.M. Chiappe and L.M. Witmer, eds See entry no. 1471

Keeping up-to-date

2793 The Auk
American Ornithologists' Union American Ornithologists' Union, 1884–, Quarterly. $60.00. ISSN 00048038.
www.aou.org/auk/index.php3 [DESCRIPTION]
A research journal, covering all aspects of bird biology, that publishes original peer-reviewed articles, reviews, biographical and historical items and book reviews. Available electronically via a subscription to BioOne.

2794 Current ornithology
Plenum Press, 1983–, Annual. ISSN 0742390X.
www.springeronline.com [DESCRIPTION]
A monographic series (each volume has an individual ISBN) that publishes review articles on all aspects of bird biology, including ecology, behaviour and genetics. Each article includes a bibliography and each volume includes a subject index. Latest volume published 2001.

2795 Ibis: the international journal of avian science
British Ornithologists' Union Blackwell Publishing, 1859–, Quarterly. £264.00. ISSN 00191019.
www.ibis.ac.uk [DESCRIPTION]
A research journal covering all aspects of ornithology but with a particular emphasis on ecology, conservation, behaviour and systematics. The journal publishes original peer-reviewed articles, short communications and notices from the BOU. Each issue also includes a section 'Recent ornithological publications', which is a collection of reviews of books received by the Alexander Library.

Parasitology

helminthology • marine flatworms • nematodes • parasites • parasitic worms

Introductions to the subject

2796 Nematology: advances and perspectives
Z.X. Chen, S.Y. Chen and D.W. Dickson, eds CABI Publishing, 2004.
www.cabi-publishing.org/ProductsAndServices.asp [DESCRIPTION]
A collection of chapters, written by experts, that brings together areas of nematology that are of current research interest. The first two chapters review the history of the discipline over the last century and look forward to its development over the next century. Other areas covered include developmental biology, morphology, ecology and marine nematodes. Each chapter includes a bibliography.

- **Volume 1. Nematode morphology, physiology, and ecology** 636pp. £85.00. ISBN 0851996450.
- **Volume II. Nematode management and utilization** 608pp. £75.00. ISBN 0851996469.

2797 Parasite rex: inside the bizarre world of nature's most dangerous creatures
C. Zimmer Touchstone, 2000, 298pp. $14.00. ISBN 074320011X.
www.carlzimmer.com/parasite_1.html [DESCRIPTION]
A very readable book that uses case studies to illustrate parasite biology. It includes a bibliography (pp 265–86) and photographic plates.
'Carl Zimmer's tome is really a great book ... He provides an unparalleled breadth of material.' (*Science*)

2798 Parasitism: the diversity and ecology of animal parasites
A.O. Bush [et al.] Cambridge University Press, 2001, 566pp. £35.00. ISBN 0521664470.
A textbook designed for use on an introductory level course, providing an overview of the subject with a particular focus on ecological aspects. Includes chapters on each of the major phyla of parasitic organisms as well as separate chapters on evolution and biogeography.

2799 Parasitoids: behavioral and evolutionary ecology
H.C.J. Godfray Princeton University Press, 1994, 473pp. $52.50. ISBN 0691000476.
www.pupress.princeton.edu/catalogs/series/mbe.html [DESCRIPTION]
Parasitoids are insects in which the larval forms feed on the bodies of other species, resulting in the death of the host organism. This book provides a useful introduction to this form of parasitism, treating the subject from an evolutionary point of view.
Series: Monographs in Behavior and Ecology: see website.

Laws, standards, codes

2800 Turbellarian Taxonomic Database
S. Tyler and L.F. Bush, comps
devbio.umesci.maine.edu/styler/turbellaria
A searchable database listing the taxonomic status of the turbellarian platyhelminths.

Associations & societies

2801 American Society of Parasitologists
asp.unl.edu
In addition to information about the Society, the helpful website provides brief coverage of careers in parasitology, announcements of jobs and scientific meetings, access to educational resources. The site also provides information on the *Journal of Parasitology* as well as online access to the Society's newsletter.

2802 British Society for Parasitology
www.mri.sari.ac.uk/bsp
Founded in 1962, the BSP now has over 1000 members including many from overseas. The website provides more information about the Society and its activities including online access to its Newsletter.

2803 International Federation of Nematology Societies
www.ifns.org
A useful site with information grouped under five headings: Membership (information about each of the societies that make up the IFNS); Community (reports, letters, obituaries, notice board); Resources (relevant books, journals, CD-ROMs and internet resources); Events (listing of forthcoming and past events); Industry (under development).

2804 Society of Nematologists [USA]
www.nematologists.org
The About Nematology section of this site provides a brief introduction to the subject and includes a downloadable ecology manual. The site also provides access to the Society's newsletter and information about its activities.

2805 World Federation of Parasitologists
www.parasitologists.org
The primary activity of the WFP is to organize the International Congress of Parasitology, held every four years. Information about the forthcoming and previous congresses as well as a list of the member societies and their websites.

Portal & task environments

2806 *Caenorhabditis elegans* WWW Server
L. Avery, comp.
elegans.swmed.edu
The nematode *C. elegans* is widely used in biological research programmes. This site brings together links to many of the key resources relating to this species including recently published journal articles and a directory of researchers. The site also includes a section titled Nematodes that provides a nice collection of links to sites dealing with nematodes other than *C. elegans*.

DPDx: Laboratory Identification of Parasites of Public Health Concern
Centers for Disease Control and Prevention See entry no. 3581

2807 Plant and Insect Parasitic Nematodes
nematode.unl.edu
Provides a great amount of information either on its own pages or via links to related sites and presents it with an unexpected touch of humour (e.g. the 'Imaginemas'). Covers topics ranging from the basic 'What are nematodes?' through to those treating agriculture and systematics. An excellent (and entertaining) site. Produced within the University's Institute of Agriculture and Natural Resources.

Discovering print & electronic resources

2808 Helminthological Abstracts
CABI Publishing, 1932–, Monthly. £790.00. ISSN 09576789.
www.cabi-publishing.org/hma [DESCRIPTION]
Index to the literature published in journals, books and conferences with approximately 4000 items per year. Ten sections: General; Monogenea and Aspidogastrea; Digenea; Cestoda; Acanthocephala; Nematoda; Hirudinea; Mixed groups; Techniques; Anthelmintics. Each issue includes author and subject indexes.

2809 Multi-Language Nematode Sites on the Internet
E. A. Flack, comp.
pppweb.clemson.edu/Nematode/NematodeSites.html
Provides a list of sites relating to nematodes arranged under the headings: Fun; Organizations; Management (i.e. management of nematode pests); Genetic and molecular; Universities; Commercial; Government; Non-English language sites.

2810 Nematological Abstracts
CABI Publishing, 1932–, Quarterly. £360.00. ISSN 09576797.
www.cabi-publishing.org/ProductsAndServices.asp [DESCRIPTION]
This subset of CAB ABSTRACTS contains approximately 1800 abstracts every year giving details of books, journals, reports, theses and conference proceedings relating to nematology, with an emphasis on areas of economic importance.

2811 Parasitology Related Links
Kansas State University
www.ksu.edu/parasitology/links
A collection of more than 300 links grouped under the headings: Cryptosporidium related; Journals and Societies; Miscellaneous. Produced by the University's Parasitology Laboratory.

2812 Parasitology Resources
M. Korkmaz, comp.
bornova.ege.edu.tr/~mkorkmaz/linkmk3.htm
A useful collection of parasitological resources grouped under seven headings including: Departments & institutes; Journals; Societies; Images; Resources. The site does not appear to have been updated since 2002 but most of the links checked in 2004 were still active.

2813 WWW Virtual Library: Parasitology
D. Gibson, comp.
dialspace.dial.pipex.com/town/pipexdsl/q/aqpa17/purls/?
Key resource including listings for more than 600 sites

organized under headings such as: Images; Meetings; Newsgroups.

Digital data, image & text collections

2814 **Ecological Database of the World's Insect Pathogens: EDWIP**
D.W. Onstad, comp. Illinois Natural History Survey.
cricket.inhs.uiuc.edu/edwipweb/edwipabout.htm
Offers information on fungi, viruses, protozoa, mollicutes, nematodes, and bacteria that are infectious in insects, mites and related arthropods. Includes associations (or lack thereof) between pathogenic organisms and insect, mite and other arthropod hosts, supported by bibliographic citations. All areas of the database are searchable. Last updated 2002.

2815 **Marine Flatworms of the World**
W. Seifarth
www.rzuser.uni-heidelberg.de/~bu6/index.html
This site provides access to a collection of images of flatworms and nudibranchs. It also provides a general introduction to their biology.

NEMABASE
University of California, Davis See entry no. 3338

2816 **Parasites and Parasitological Resources**
Ohio State University
http://www.biosci.ohio-state.edu/~parasite/home.html
Access to more than 500 images of parasites along with information about parasite biology including a useful section on parasites and pets. Some of the pages take a very long time to load.

Handbooks & manuals

2817 **Parasites and the behavior of animals**
J. Moore Oxford University Press, 2002, 315pp. £27.99. ISBN 0195146530.
After an introduction and followed by a conclusion, chapters are: 2. Life cycles: blueprints for Ro; 3. Behavioral alterations and parasite transmission; 4. Behavioral alterations and avoiding parasites; 5. Behavioral alterations and the fitness and longevity of infected hosts.
Series: Oxford Series in Ecology and Evolution.
'A gripping account of the sometimes spectacular behavioural (and morphological) alterations caused by parasites ... Everyone with a general interest in biology who can still be amazed by the awesome power of natural selection should look at this book.' (*Nature*)

Keeping up-to-date

2818 **Advances in Parasitology**
Academic Press, 1963–.
www.elsevier.com/locate/issn/0065308X [DESCRIPTION]
A monographic series that publishes review articles on all aspects of parasitology. Each article includes a substantial bibliography.

2819 **Trends in Parasitology**
Elsevier, 2001–. €1171.00. ISSN 14714922.
www.trends.com/pt/default.htm [DESCRIPTION]
This was ranked as the most highly cited parasitological journal in 2002 and 2003. It includes commissioned reviews, articles and correspondence, many of which are accessible to a non-specialist readership. Formerly titled *Parasitology Today*.

Protistology

algae • amoebae • diatoms • phycology • protists • protoctista • protozoology • seaweeds

Introductions to the subject

2820 **Algae**
L.E. Graham and L.W. Wilcox Prentice Hall, 2000, 640pp. $94.00. ISBN 0136603335.
A standard undergraduate textbook. The book is arranged in systematic order with introductory chapters covering topics such as: Algae in biotic associations; Algal diversity. Also includes a glossary and bibliography.

2821 **Diatoms: Ever Wonder?**
University of California, San Diego
www.earthguide.ucsd.edu/diatom/d1.html
A nice introductory site providing an online tutorial aimed at a very general audience. Provides information on all aspects of diatom life including habitat, morphology and ecology. Also includes links to related websites and articles in scientific journals.

Marine botany
C.J. Dawes See entry no. 2180

2822 **Phycology**
R.E. Lee 3rd edn, Cambridge University Press, 1999, 614pp. £35.00. ISBN 0521638836.
An introductory textbook. The book does not attempt to be comprehensive in its coverage, instead aiming to cover the species that are most likely to be referred to in an introductory course.

2823 **Seaweeds**
D.N. Thomas; Natural History Museum 2002, 96pp. ISBN 0565091751.
www.nhm.ac.uk/services/publishing/det_Seaweeds.html [DESCRIPTION]
A very accessible introduction to seaweeds, with lavish colour illustrations. Includes a 'Further information' section providing lists of recommended readings and websites.

Laws, standards, codes

2824 **Index Nominum Algarum**
P. Silva, comp.; University of California, Berkeley
ucjeps.berkeley.edu/INA.html
A searchable version of a printed card file of the scientific names of algae, maintained at the University of California. Provides information on the original reference for the name as well as any changes to the name. Aimed at researchers rather than the general public. Maintained within the University Herbarium.

Associations & societies

2825 **British Phycological Society**
www.brphycsoc.org
Founded in 1952, the main activities of the Society are in publishing and education. They edit the *European Journal of Phycology*, run training courses, and organize an annual meeting. Good links section.

2826 **International Society for Diatom Research**
www.isdr.org
The main activities of the Society are organizing scientific meetings and publishing the journal *Diatom Research*. Forum; links.

2827 **Phycological Society of America**
www.psaalgae.org
Useful entrée to phycology (the study of algae), including a section on Student Information, a link to the PSA Education Center, and a good set of links.

2828 **Society of Protozoologists**
www.uga.edu/protozoa
An international Society with a very nice website, the highlight of which is the PORTAL TO PROTISTOLOGY. In addition to this there is information on relevant jobs and scientific meetings as well as small sections aimed specifically at teachers and students. The For Fun section is also small but it may be the only place to find those essential songs about protists!

Portal & task environments

2829 **Algae**
National Museum of Natural History
www.nmnh.si.edu/botany/projects/algae/Alg-Menu.htm
Includes a short introduction to algae covering their classification and economic uses, including references to algae cookbooks! Also provides information on the Department's collections and research as well as information on algal collection and preservation techniques.

2830 **AlgaTerra Information System**
Botanic Garden Berlin-Dahlem
www.algaterra.org
Project – based on the Berlin Model – to build a 'comprehensive information system including a database on terrestrial micro-algae, integrating taxon, type, name and collection data as well as ecological and molecular information'. Pilot phase due to be completed February 2005. Good overview of algal data characteristics and challenges; bibliography; links.

- **The Berlin Taxonomic Information Model Botanic Garden and Botanical Museum Berlin-Dhalem.** www.bgbm.org/biodivinf/Docs/BGBM-Model/default.htm#. Implementation of the IOPI Model designed for the INTERNATIONAL ORGANIZATION FOR PLANT INFORMATION devised 'to avoid the widely made error of over-simplification of taxonomic data and the resulting loss of data accuracy and quality'.

2831 **The Amoebae**
S. Maciver; University of Edinburgh
www.bms.ed.ac.uk/research/others/smaciver/amoebae.htm
Brings together information on the amoebae, one of the most widely known groups of protists. It provides brief information on topics such as the ecology and classification of the amoebae and, unlike many websites, it includes references to sources of more detailed information throughout. Also includes a glossary.

2832 **The Harmful Algae Page**
Woods Hole Oceanographic Institution and National Oceanic and Atmospheric Administration
www.whoi.edu/redtide
This site's main audience is the scientific community but it contains information that will be of use to anyone interested in the topic. As well as basic information (what algal blooms are, how they occur, etc.) it includes information on human illnesses, maps of where blooms occur (US and global) and links to related sites. The site is updated regularly with announcements of relevant meetings, courses and news stories. Organized with the Woods Hole National Office for Marine Biotoxins and Harmful Algal Blooms.

2833 **The Phycology.Net**
Bayerisches Landesamt für Wasserwirtschaft, Botanische Staatssammlung München and University of Bayreuth
www.phycology.net
Describes itself as an 'Internet portal from scientists for scientists' but its audience deserves to be wider than that. The site is well laid out and provides links to sites on all aspects of phycology, providing an excellent starting point for anyone interested in the field.

2834 **Portal to Protistology**
Society of Protozoologists
www.uga.edu/protozoa/portal.html
This site is still being developed but it already provides an excellent resource. Containing a mixture of commissioned articles and links to other web resources, it provides information on topics such as genetics, ecology and economically important protists. (Sections on physiology, symbiosis and identification among others are due to follow.)

2835 **The Seaweed Site**
M.D. Guiry, comp.; National University of Ireland, Galway
seaweed.ucg.ie
A nice introduction to seaweeds excluding the phytoplankton and cyanobacteria, with excellent information provided including lots of illustrations and links to more detailed information.

Discovering print & electronic resources

2836 **Protozoological Abstracts**
CABI Publishing, 1977–, Monthly. £910.00. ISBN 03091287.
www.cabi-publishing.org/ProductsAndServices.asp [DESCRIPTION]
An index to the literature published in journals, books and conferences, with approximately 5000 new items being added each year. The abstracts are arranged by subject under headings such as: Leishmania; Amoebae; Malaria. Each issue also includes an author and subject index.

Digital data, image & text collections

2837 **AlgaeBase**
M. D. Guiry and E. Nic Dhonncha; National University of Ireland
www.algaebase.org/
One of the most important protist resources on the internet, this database contains a huge amount of information on algae. Records in the database include taxonomic information, with references to original descriptions, as well as further literature references and links to related databases such as INDEX NOMINUM ALGARUM. It is searchable by genus, species or common name and there are also specific literature and image searches. The database does not attempt to provide a comprehensive resource but it is an excellent place to begin a search on this topic.

2838 **Protist image data**
C. J. O'Kelly and T. Littlejohn, comps; University of Montreal
megasun.bch.umontreal.ca/protists/protists.html
This is a much wider resource than its name suggests. Images are used as a navigational tool enabling the user to find information on a group or genus of interest. The site provides information grouped under headings that include: Appearance; Reproduction and life history; References; Internet resources. It also provides a large collection of links to related web pages (with some parts also used in the PORTAL TO PROTISTOLOGY).

2839 **Protist Information Server**
Y. Tsukii, ed.
protist.i.hosei.ac.jp
A Japanese-based website which is primarily a collection of images of protists with over 40,000 available by the end of 2004. However, a number of other resources are provided including a list of over 70 Biodiversity Websites in Japan, most having English language versions.

2840 **Toxic & harmful algal blooms**
A. deCharon and S. Etheridge; Bigelow Laboratory for Ocean Sciences
www.bigelow.org/hab
This site covers much of the same ground as the HARMFUL ALGAE PAGE, but it aims at a more general audience. Information is listed under headings such as: Background; Toxic v harmful; Locations; Toxin/Ecology; and it is presented in a more graphical format than in the other site.

Handbooks & manuals

2841 **Algae: an introduction to phycology**
C. van den Hoek, D.G. Mann and H.M. Jahns Cambridge University Press, 1995, 623pp. ISBN 0521304199.
An advanced textbook. The focus of this book is the taxonomy, morphology and cytology of the algae. There is some overlap between this and the book by Graham and Wilcox [q.v.] but this generally provides more detailed information. Includes a glossary and a bibliography.

2842 **The freshwater algal flora of the British Isles: an identification guide to freshwater and terrestrial algae**
D.M. John, B.A. Whitton and A.J. Brook, eds; British Phycological Society and Natural History Museum Cambridge University Press, 2002, 702pp. CD-ROM, £75.00. ISBN 0521770513.
A user-friendly guide to the freshwater algae species of Britain. The volume does not attempt to be comprehensive in its coverage but it does provide information on a representative sample for all of the British genera. It also includes information on algal distribution, methodology and classification. The book is accompanied by a CD-ROM of images. An essential reference work.

2843 **Handbook of Protoctista**
L. Margulis [et al.], ed. Jones and Bartlett, 1990, 941pp. ISBN 0867200529.
A detailed reference work aimed at researchers and advanced students although the introduction provides a useful overview of this complex group. The book is arranged taxonomically with each chapter dealing with an individual phylum. Coverage includes morphology, relevant literature, ecology and economic importance of the phylum as well as brief information on each genus.

- **Illustrated glossary of Protoctista** **L. Margulis, H.I. McKhann and L. Olendzenski, eds** Jones and Bartlett, 1993, 288pp. ISBN 0867200812. Abbreviated version of the Handbook. Main part is the illustrated glossary which, at the time of publication, aimed to be comprehensive in its coverage. Also includes a section on protist classification and short essays on protist research.

2844 **Seaweeds of the British Isles: a collaborative project of the British Phycological Society and the British Museum (Natural History)**
P.S. Dixon [et al.]; British Phycological Society and British Museum (Natural History) Intercept, 1977–.
www.nhm.ac.uk/services/publishing/pubcbot.html#Seaweeds
[DESCRIPTION]
This monographic series aims, when complete, to provide a comprehensive review of the British marine algal flora. The structure of individual volumes varies but they generally provide a general overview, including information on cell structure, morphology, reproduction and ecology, as well as a taxonomic review.

Vols 5 *Cyanophyta*, 6 *Haptophyta*, 7 *Bacillariophyta* are to be published.

- **Volume 1, part 1. Rhodophyta: introduction, Nemaliales, Gigartinales** **P. S. Dixon and L. M. Irvine** 1977. ISBN 0113100000.
- **Volume 1, part 2A. Rhodophyta: Cryptonemiales (sensu stricto), Palmariales, Rhodymeniales** **L. M. Irvine** 1983. ISBN 0565008714.
- **Volume 1, part 2B. Rhodophyta: Corallinales, Hildenbrandiales** **L. M. Irvine and Y. Chamberlain** 1994. ISBN 0113100167.
- **Volume 1, part 3A. Rhodophyta: Ceremiales** **C. A. Maggs and M. H. Hommersand** 1993. ISBN 0113100450.
- **Volume 1, part 3B. Rhodophyta: Bangiophycidae** **J. A. Brodie and L. M. Irvine** 2003. ISBN 1898298874.
- **Volume 2. Chlorophyta** **E. M. Burrows** 1991. ISBN 0565009818.
- **Volume 3. Fucophyceae (Phaeophyceae): Part 1** **R. L. Fletcher** 1987. ISBN 0565009923.
- **Volume 4. Tribophyceae (Xanthophyceae)** **T. Christensen** 1987. ISBN 056500980X.

Systematics & Taxonomy

biological classification • biological species • biological systematics • cladistics • class • division • domains • family • genus • kingdoms • Linnaeus • morphology • order • organisms • phylogenetics • phylum • species • species names • taxonomy

Introductions to the subject

2845 **Biological nomenclature**
C. Jeffrey; Systematics Association 3rd edn, Edward Arnold, 1989, 86pp. ISBN 0713129832.
A useful overview of the principles and practice regarding the use of nomenclature in taxonomy, including an introduction to the Codes of nomenclature. New editions of the Codes have appeared since the publication of this book and while this has reduced the currency of the book it is still relevant.

2846 **Biological systematics: principles and applications**
R.T. Schuh Comstock Publishing, 2000, 236pp. £39.50. ISBN 0801436753.
This book provides an overview of systematic theory based around cladistics and is arranged in three sections. The first section provides background to the subject including information on biological nomenclature. Section two covers cladistics methods, while the final section looks at the applications of systematics in other disciplines including ecology and biodiversity. Each chapter includes a bibliography and a separate list of recommended reading.
'This is an excellent book. Written by a practising systematist with a keen interest in the theoretical development of systematics, it has a blend of theory and empiricism which results in a very authoritative treatment ... In total, I thoroughly recommend this book ... [It] demands to be read as much for its readability as its content.' (*The Paleontological Association Newsletter*)

2847 **Deep time: cladistics, the revolution in evolution**
H. Gee Fourth Estate, 2001, 262pp. £7.99. ISBN 1857029879.
An entertaining, lucid account of the nature of evolutionary relationships and the way scientists study them. Peppered with simple examples and illuminating anecdotes, this book is an excellent introduction for the non-specialist. The author, Henry Gee, has been an editor of the science journal NATURE and is a trained palaeontologist.

Fishes of the world
J.S. Nelson See entry no. 2560

2848 **Five kingdoms: an illustrated guide to the phyla of life on earth**
L. Margulis and K.V. Schwartz 3rd edn, W H Freeman, 1998, 520pp. $41.95. ISBN 0716730278.
Classic but still valuable overview of the conception now being superseded by the three domains paradigm.

- **World Diversity Database CD-ROM Series** **Expert Center for Taxonomic Identification**Springer. ISSN 14321521. www.springeronline.com [DESCRIPTION]. 50 titles in this series, including version of *Five Kingdoms*: More than 500 photographs and drawings, 37 video clips, glossary, links to relevant websites, etc.: Version 2.0. 2002. £30.50. ISBN 3540408665.

2849 **Milestones in systematics**
D.M. Williams and P.L. Forey, eds; Systematics Association CRC Press, 2004, 304pp. $99.95. ISBN 041528032X.
This book contains a collection of essays by historians and systematists on the evolution of aspects of systematic theory and practice. It includes a subject index and each essay includes a bibliography.

Plant systematics: a phylogenetic approach
W.S. Judd [et al.] See entry no. 2186

Plant taxonomy and biosystematics
C.A. Stace See entry no. 2187

2850 **Principles and techniques of contemporary taxonomy**
D.L.J. Quicke Blackie, 1993, 311pp. ISBN 0751400203.
An introductory textbook providing an overview of taxonomy, nomenclature and taxonomic methodology. Still very useful.

Dictionaries, thesauri, classifications

Angiosperm Phylogeny Website
P. F. Stevens See entry no. 2189

A dictionary of ecology, evolution and systematics
R.J. Lincoln, G.A. Boxshall and P.F. Clark See entry no. 2302

A dictionary of microbial taxonomy
S.T. Cowan and L.R. Hill, eds See entry no. 2661

Nomenclator zoologicus
S.A. Neave; Zoological Society of London See entry no. 2878

Laws, standards, codes

Distribution and taxonomy of birds of the world
C.G. Sibley and B.L. Monroe See entry no. 2752

Index animalium: sive, Index nominum quae ab A.D. MDCCLVIII generibus et speciebus animalium imposita sunt
C.D. Sherborn See entry no. 2879

International Code of Botanical Nomenclature: St Louis Code
W. Greuter [et al.], eds; International Association for Plant Taxonomy See entry no. 2195

International code of nomenclature of bacteria, and Statutes of the International Committee on Systematic Bacteriology, and statutes of the Bacteriology and Applied Microbiology Section of the International Union of Microbiological Societies: bacteriologi
S.P. Lapage [et al.], eds; American Society for Microbiology, International Committee on Systematic Bacteriology and International Union of Microbiological Societies See entry no. 2664

International code of zoological nomenclature
W.D.L. Ride [et al.], eds; International Commission on Zoological Nomenclature See entry no. 2880

International Commission on Zoological Nomenclature
See entry no. 2881

International Committee on Taxonomy of Viruses
See entry no. 2666

List of bacterial names with standing in nomenclature
J.P. Euzeby; Société de Bactériologie Systématique et Vétérinaire
See entry no. 2667

Turbellarian Taxonomic Database
S. Tyler and L.F. Bush, comps See entry no. 2800

Virus taxonomy: classification and nomenclature of viruses: seventh report of the International Committee on Taxonomy of Viruses
M.H.V. van Regenmortel [et al.], eds; International Committee on Taxonomy of Viruses and International Union of Microbiological Societies See entry no. 2668

Zoonomen
A.P. Peterson, comp. See entry no. 2753

Research centres & institutes

2851 **Expert Center for Taxonomic Identification**
www.eti.uva.nl
Produces computer-based taxonomic and biodiversity information systems. The website provides access to the World Biodiversity Database, a taxonomic database that aims to document all known species (also available as a collection of CD-ROMs). It also provides access to the World Taxonomist Database, an international directory of taxonomists searchable by name or specialism, as well as links to other online taxonomic databases.

Systematic Entomology Laboratory
See entry no. 2379

Associations & societies

American Society of Plant Taxonomists
See entry no. 2206

2852 **BioNet-International**
www.bionet-intl.org
Based in the UK, this organization aims to support sustainable development by providing taxonomic training and resources (literature, etc.) to developing countries. They work through the creation of Locally Organized and Operated Partnerships (LOOPs), several of which have their own websites that give further information about their activities. Lots of useful information on the site including a section Why Taxonomy Matters containing (October 2004) the texts of 35 case studies. There is also a monthly downloadable BioNET Bulletin. A very useful colourful site.

International Association for Plant Taxonomy
See entry no. 2215

2853 **Linnean Society of London**
www.linnean.org
Founded in 1788 and named after Carl Linnaeus, the Society is involved in all areas of natural history with a particular emphasis on taxonomy. Among other collections, within its historic building in central London it houses 40,000 of Linnaeus' original specimen collections and his personal library. The Society is an active publisher and is also involved in Project Linnaeus.

- **Linnean Society of London Library** www.linnean.org. Holds collections of biological literature from 1483 to date, including the personal library and manuscripts of Linnaeus. Also important collections of archives, manuscripts, portraits and photographs, etc. of Society Fellows and others.

2854 **Society of Australian Systematic Biologists**
www.sasb.org.au
The SASB was founded in 1996 and aims to encourage the study and use of systematics in Australia. The website was last updated in 2003 but it contains several resources that will remain useful for a long time, including an introductory essay 'What is biological systematics?'. The site also includes reviews of taxonomic books and a collection of Invited Contributions.

- **Introductory glossary of cladistic terms** M.D. Crisp. www.science.uts.edu.au/sasb/glossary.html. Useful online glossary covering some of the terms commonly used in cladistics.

2855 **Society of Systematic Biologists** [USA]
systbiol.org
A US-based international society whose object is the 'advancement of the science of systematic biology in all its aspects of theory, principles, methodology, and practice'. The Society's activities include the production of the journal *Systematic Biology*, and there is a range of useful information on their activities, as well as a collection of links.

- **Classic Cladistic Literature** http://systbiol.org/cladlita-c.html. Major bibliography organized alphabetically by author.

Systematic and Applied Acarology Society
See entry no. 2902

2856 **Systematics Association** [UK]
www.systass.org
Founded in 1937, the Association aims to further all aspects of systematic biology. It does this through organizing conferences and its publishing programme. The website provides information on forthcoming and past scientific meetings and online access to the current issue of the Association's Newsletter.

2857 **Taxonomic Databases Working Group**
www.tdwg.org
The TDWG, under the auspices of the International Union of Biological Sciences, 'develops, adopts and promotes standards and guidelines for the recording and exchange of data about organisms'. The website provides a list of the standards as well as other information about the Group's activities.

2858 **Willi Hennig Society**
www.cladistics.org
An international society, founded in 1980. devoted to the study of cladistics. It organizes meetings and produces the journal *Cladistics*. The website includes a list of some recently published books and software, and a few related web pages.

Portal & task environments

AlgaTerra Information System
Botanic Garden Berlin-Dahlem See entry no. 2830

BiologyBrowser: free information from a trusted source
See entry no. 1956

The Ciliate Resource Archive
D.H. Lynn See entry no. 2907

2859 **Cyberinfrastructure for Phylogenetic Research: CIPRes**
National Science Foundation
www.phylo.org
Important project (2003–8) to enable large-scale phylogenetic reconstructions on a scale that will enable analyses of huge datasets containing hundreds of thousands of biomolecular sequences. Aim is to create a national computational infrastructure for the international systematics community. The project will incorporate work previously carried out within the TreeBase initiative and involves 12 US universities, the AMERICAN MUSEUM OF NATURAL HISTORY and the *San Diego Supercomputer Center*.

2860 **Species 2000**
University of Reading
www.sp2000.org
This project, founded in 1996, aims to produce a 'uniform and validated quality index of names of all known species'. It provides a gateway to existing species databases and is supported by key organizations such as the NATURAL HISTORY MUSEUM and the ROYAL BOTANIC GARDENS, KEW. The site provides access to annual and dynamic versions of the checklist plus related links.

Discovering print & electronic resources

Animal identification: a reference guide
See entry no. 2910

2861 **Guide to internet resources for biological taxonomy & classification**
Montgomery College
mclibrary.nhmccd.edu/taxonomy/taxonomy.html
This site, compiled by the Reference Librarian at the College, provides a good starting point for a search for taxonomic information. As well as listing general taxonomic sites, e.g. the NCBI TAXONOMY BROWSER, it includes annotated links to sites that contain taxonomic information on specific groups of organisms. The whole is very clearly laid out and pleasant to use.

Kew Record of Taxonomic Literature
Royal Botanic Gardens, Kew See entry no. 2248

2862 **Key works to the fauna and flora of the British Isles and northwestern Europe**
G.J. Kerrich, D.L. Hawksworth and R.W. Sims, eds; Systematics Association Academic Press, 1978, 179pp. ISBN 0124055508.
Now out of print but still a key resource, listing scientific books and journal articles that can be used to identify UK plants, animals, fungi, bacteria and viruses.

Digital data, image & text collections

Amphibian Species of the World: an online reference
D.R. Frost; American Museum of Natural History See entry no. 2632

Butterflies & Moths of the World: generic names & their type-species
B. Pitkin and P. Jenkins; Natural History Museum See entry no. 2414

Catalog of Fishes
California Academy of Sciences See entry no. 2634

Check List of European Marine Mollusca: CLEMAM
J. Le Renard, S. Gofas and P. Bouchet, eds See entry no. 2636

The EMBL Reptile Database
European Molecular Biology Laboratory and German Herpetological Society See entry no. 2914

FishBase
R. Froese and D. Pauly, eds See entry no. 2638

2863 **Journey into Phylogenetic Systematics**
University of California, Berkeley
www.ucmp.berkeley.edu/clad/clad4.html
An online introductory tutorial on cladistics created by the Museum of Paleontology. Includes four modules that provide an introduction to the topic along with information on methodology and on the implications of, and the need for, cladistics.

2864 **Linné on line**
Uppsala Universitet
www.linnaeus.uu.se/online/index-en.html
This site, produced by the university at which Linnaeus was a Professor, provides an excellent resource on his life and work. Currently only The Life of Linnaeus and Plants and animals sections are available in English but more of the site is to be translated over time.

Mammal Species of the World (MSW)
American Society of Mammalogists and National Museum of Natural History See entry no. 2915

2865 **NCBI Taxonomy Browser**
National Center for Biotechnology Information
www.ncbi.nlm.nih.gov/Taxonomy/tax.html
This database provides taxonomic information on the species for which nucleotide or protein sequences have been added to the NCBI genetic databases. Entries include common and scientific names, details of the taxonomic lineage and links to relevant published literature. It also includes links to the nucleotide and protein data that is held for the species as well as to relevant articles in PUBMED CENTRAL.

2866 **Project Linnaeus**
T. Anfält, ed.; Swedish Linnaean Society, Royal Swedish Academy of Science and Linnean Society of London
www.c18.rutgers.edu/pr/lc/proj.lin.html
Founded in 1995, this project aims to publish correspondence written to and by Carl Linnaeus, to produce

a union catalogue of his publications and to make digital versions available electronically. A representative sample of the correspondence is accessible now but it is anticipated that it will take several years to fulfil the remaining aims of the project.

TaxoDros: the database on taxonomy of Drosophilidae
G. Bächli; University of Zurich See entry no. 2419

The Tree of Life Web Project
D. Maddison and K.-S. Schulz, eds See entry no. 2160

UNEP-WCMC Species Database: Trees
UNEP World Conservation Monitoring Centre See entry no. 3276

2867 **Universal Biological Indexer and Organizer (uBio)**
Marine Biological Laboratory
www.ubio.org
A project to create a comprehensive catalogue of species names and related taxonomic data by bringing together data from existing international projects such as Integrated Taxonomic Information System, Global Biodiversity Information Facility and Species 2000. As of December 2004, the database contains more than 1.7 million names and is searchable by scientific (1.4. million) and / or common (0.3 million) name.

The Universal Virus Database of the International Committee on Taxonomy of Viruses: ICTVdB
C. Buechen-Osmond, comp.; International Committee on Taxonomy of Viruses See entry no. 2689

World List of Marine, Freshwater and Terrestrial Isopod Crustaceans
B. Kensley, M. Schotte and S. Schilling, comps; National Museum of Natural History See entry no. 2642

The World Spider Catalog
N.I. Platnick; American Museum of Natural History See entry no. 2917

Directories & encyclopedias

The Springer index of viruses
C.A. Tidona, G. Darai and C. Büchen-Osmond, eds See entry no. 2693

Handbooks & manuals

Bergey's manual of systematic bacteriology
J.G. Holt [et al.], eds See entry no. 2694

2868 **Cladistics: the theory and practice of parsimony analysis**
I.J. Kitching [et al.] 2nd edn, Oxford University Press, 1998, 228pp. £27.50. ISBN 0198501382.
A clear and concise introduction to cladistics, the now most commonly used method for investigating phylogenetic relationships. It runs from basic principles through to more esoteric topics such as the treatment of missing data and tree-search techniques. A comprehensive glossary is included.

Series: Systematics Association Special Volume.

Interrelationships of fishes
M.L.S. Stiassny, L.R. Parenti and G.D. Johnson See entry no. 1466

The phylogenetic handbook: a practical approach to DNA and protein phylogeny
M. Salemi and A.-M. Vandamme, eds See entry no. 2471

Systematics and the fossil record: documenting evolutionary patterns
A.B. Smith See entry no. 1480

Keeping up-to-date

Annual Review of Ecology, Evolution & Systematics
See entry no. 2360

International Journal of Systematic and Evolutionary Microbiology
See entry no. 2703

Myconet
O.E. Eriksson, ed. See entry no. 2740

Mycotaxon
See entry no. 2741

Zoology

animals • Arachnida • bats • bears • centipedes • elephants • fauna • gorillas • herbivores • herpetology • invertebrates • lions • lizards • mammals • millipedes • mites • monkeys • primates • reptiles • rhinos • rodents • scorpions • slugs • snakes • spiders • ticks • tigers • vertebrates • wolves • woodlice • worms • zoos

Introductions to the subject

Crucible of creation: the Burgess Shale and the rise of animals
S. Conway Morris See entry no. 1399

2869 **Fauna Britannica: the practical guide to wild & domestic creatures of Britain**
D. Hart-Davis Weidenfeld & Nicolson, 2002, 415pp. £30.00. ISBN 0297825321.
Beautifully illustrated volume that provides brief information on some of the well known wild and domesticated British animals. Also includes a chapter on 'foreign bodies': animals that have been introduced (accidentally or deliberately), or reintroduced, to Britain.

Introduction to mammalian reproduction
D. Tulsiani, ed. See entry no. 4447

2870 **Invertebrate zoology: a functional evolutionary approach**
E.E. Ruppert, R.S. Fox and R.D. Barnes 7th edn, Brooks/Cole, 2004, 963pp. $116.95. ISBN 0030259827.
biology.brookscole.com [companion]
A new edition of a textbook first published in 1963. The book

takes a functional approach to the subject, covering for each group of invertebrates topics such as: Form; Nutrition; Reproduction. The companion website includes an online glossary and laboratory manual.

2871 The invertebrates: a synthesis
R.S.K. Barnes [et al.] 3rd edn, Blackwell Science, 2001, 497pp. £32.50. ISBN 0632047615.
This popular undergraduate textbook provides a good overview of the invertebrates including information on their functional biology (physiology, behaviour, reproduction, etc.) as well as details of each taxonomic group. Brief bibliographies.
' I can not recommend this book highly enough. It should be in the library of every school and university and I think all biologists would benefit from having a copy in their personal collection.' (*Journal of Biological Education*)

2872 Invertebrates
R.C. Brusca and G.J. Brusca 2nd edn, Sinauer, 2002, 936pp. $109.95. ISBN 0878930973.
A useful undergraduate-level textbook. Introductory chapters on evolution, classification and physiology are followed by chapters covering each of the invertebrate phyla in more detail.

2873 The life of vertebrates
J.Z. Young 3rd edn, Clarendon Press, 1981, 645pp. ISBN 0198571739.
Although now quite old, this remains a standard undergraduate textbook. Arranged around an evolutionary theme, the book provides information on physiology, behaviour and taxonomy for all of the vertebrates.

2874 Vertebrate life
F.H. Pough, C.M. Janis and J.B. Heiser 6th edn, Prentice Hall, 2002, 699pp. $110.00. ISBN 0130412481.
www.prenhall.com/pough [COMPANION]
A popular undergraduate textbook. The arrangement is similar to that of the book by Young [q.v.] but the authors take a slightly different approach with a greater emphasis on vertebrate ecology and conservation.

Dictionaries, thesauri, classifications

Common names of insects and related organisms
M.B. Stoetzel, ed.; Entomological Society of America See entry no. 2373

2875 A dictionary of zoology
M. Allaby, ed. 2nd edn, Oxford University Press, 2003, 597pp. Reissue of 1999 edn with extensive corrections, £8.99. ISBN 019860758X.
www.oxfordreference.com
This is a very good dictionary, providing definitions for more than 5000 terms across all fields of zoology, including animal behaviour, genetics and taxonomy. Many of the entries are quite detailed and a few also include illustrations. The dictionary also includes a list of endangered species.
Available online: see website.

Insectes, araignees & acariens: correspondances entre les dénominations scientifiques et anglo-saxonnes (Insects, spiders, mites and ticks: equivalences between scientific and common English names)
R. Couilloud See entry no. 2375

2876 The invertebrates: an illustrated glossary
M. Stachowitsch Wiley-Liss, 1992, 676pp. ISBN 0471561924.
This covers the invertebrates excluding insects, arachnids and myriapods. The main section of the book consists of collections of definitions brought together under taxonomic headings, e.g. Crustacea, Annelida, etc. In addition, there is an 'Adjective Section' that defines the descriptive terms used in the main section.

Invertebrates of economic importance in Britain: common and scientific names
P.R. Seymour, comp.; Ministry of Agriculture, Fisheries and Food
See entry no. 2376

2877 Multilingual Animal Glossary of Unveiled Synonyms: MAGUS
T. Bartol [et al.], eds; University of Ljubljana
www.informatika.bf.uni-lj.si/magus.html
This site provides an alphabetical list of the scientific and common names of about 100 common domestic and wild animals and birds in 53 European languages.

2878 Nomenclator zoologicus
S.A. Neave; Zoological Society of London 1939–96.
There are currently nine volumes of this work listing all of the published generic and sub-generic names of animals. The names are listed alphabetically along with details of the author that first used the name and the publication in which it first appeared. The data included in the most recent volume (volume IX) was extracted from ZOOLOGICAL RECORD.

Laws, standards, codes

2879 Index animalium: sive, Index nominum quae ab A.D. MDCCLVIII generibus et speciebus animalium imposita sunt
C.D. Sherborn C J Clay, 1902–33.
This major historical tome provides a list of all of the generic and specific animal names that were published between 1758 and 1850. Entries are listed alphabetically and include details of the original author and publication. The work by Neave [q.v.] contains amended information regarding some of the generic names listed here.

2880 International code of zoological nomenclature
W.D.L. Ride [et al.], eds; International Commission on Zoological Nomenclature 4th edn, International Trust for Zoological Nomenclature, 1999, 306pp. £40.00. ISBN 0853010064.
www.iczn.org/code.htm [DESCRIPTION]
Zoological nomenclature, i.e. the naming of animals, has to operate in a standard way in order to ensure that each animal has a unique and stable name. This is achieved through a set of rules that are published as the *International code of zoological nomenclature*. The Code, published in both French and English, contains 18 chapters that cover topics such as: The number of words in the scientific names of animals; Criteria of publication; Validity of names and

nomenclatural acts; Authorship; The type concept in nomenclature. There is also a glossary of the terms that are used in the book.

2881 International Commission on Zoological Nomenclature
www.iczn.org
The Commission was set up in 1895 and is responsible for ensuring that every animal (including fossils) has a unique and internationally accepted scientific name. This is primarily achieved through the publication of the INTERNATIONAL CODE OF ZOOLOGICAL NOMENCLATURE. When problems arise over the application of the code the details are published in the ICZN journal, *Bulletin of Zoological Nomenclature*, in order to give the scientific community an opportunity to comment on them before the ICZN give a formal ruling. The ICZN is based at the NATURAL HISTORY MUSEUM.

Official & quasi-official bodies

2882 Interagency Grizzly Bear Committee [USA]
United States. Department of Agriculture and United States. Department of the Interior
www.fs.fed.us/r1/wildlife/igbc
Committed to conserving the grizzly bear, the IGBC site contains detailed information about the organization's activities, information about the bears and links to related sites.

International Council for the Exploration of the Sea
See entry no. 2571

International Whaling Commission
See entry no. 2572

Research centres & institutes

2883 Institute of Zoology [UK]
www.zoo.cam.ac.uk/ioz/index.htm
The IoZ is the research division of the ZOOLOGICAL SOCIETY OF LONDON and its main research interest is in the conservation of animal species and their habitats. The Institute currently has seven research themes: Animal health & welfare; Behavioural & evolutionary ecology; Biodiversity & macroecology; Genetic variation, fitness & adaptability; Population & community ecology; Reproductive biology; Wildlife epidemiology (diseases in wildlife).

National Marine Mammal Laboratory
See entry no. 2578

Associations & societies

2884 Acarological Society of America
web.wm.edu/biology/mites
A society that is open to anyone with an interest in the study of the Acari (mites and ticks). Apart from details of the work of the Society, the website also includes the Directory of Acarologists of the World 2002, a listing of more than 2500 individuals who are involved in acarological research.

2885 African Wildlife Foundation
www.awf.org
Originally founded in 1961, works to conserve African wildlife, including gorillas, rhino and elephants.

2886 American Arachnological Society
www.americanarachnology.org
Founded in 1972, the AAS promotes the study of arachnids (spiders, mites and ticks, and scorpions). Its activities include publication of the *Journal of Arachnology*, and its website provides a collection of images, a list of the spiders found in the USA, links to related sites and information on the common and scientific names of spiders.

2887 American Society of Primatologists
www.asp.org
The Society aims to 'promote and encourage the discovery and exchange of information regarding primates'. Provides educational materials, including information in response to questions arising in non-human primate research.

2888 American Zoo and Aquarium Association
www.aza.org
Site contains a goodly amount of information, including a searchable directory of Association members – the AZA Zoo & Aquarium Directory – and information about conservation activities. Also job listings, collection of images of birds and animals, and factsheets.

2889 Bat Conservation International
www.batcon.org
The BCI was founded in 1982 and is based in the USA. Site provides information about bat biology, reading lists and a searchable database of bat publications. Also a large and well categorized collection of links to related sites.

2890 Bat Conservation Trust [UK]
www.bats.org.uk
The Trust is the 'only organization solely devoted to the conservation of bats and their habitats in the British Isles'. Activities include running the National Bat Monitoring Programme, and the site contains good background information on bats, including a section on the relevant UK legislation.

2891 British Arachnological Society
www.britishspiders.org.uk
The BAS was founded in 1958 and it now has more than 250 members in the UK as well as overseas members. The website includes a checklist and atlas of British spiders as well as many other useful leads for those really interested in this arena.

2892 British Myriapod and Isopod Group [UK]
www.bmig.org.uk
The BMIG aims to 'promote the study of myriapods (millipedes, centipedes, pauropods and symphylans) and isopods (woodlice) by providing information and support to members and holding field meetings'. Information about activities and publications as well as lists of the British species of centipedes, millipedes and woodlice.

British Society of Animal Science
See entry no. 3396

2893 **British Tarantula Society**
www.thebts.co.uk
The BTS was founded in 1985 and is 'dedicated to the conservation, enhancement and spread of knowledge in keeping tarantulas'. The website provides access to a large collection of images of tarantulas (including a small video gallery), discussion forums, a collection of articles and book reviews, links to related sites, and information about the activities and publications of the Society. A well designed site.

Caribbean Conservation Corporation & Sea Turtle Survival League
See entry no. 2582

Center for North American Herpetology
See entry no. 2583

Conchological Society of Great Britain and Ireland
See entry no. 2585

Conchologists of America
See entry no. 2586

Crustacean Society
See entry no. 2587

2894 **European Snake Society**
www.snakesociety.nl
Founded in 1979, the Society is based in the Netherlands but has an international membership. The website, available in Dutch and English, contains information about the Society, a collection of images and links to related sites.

2895 **International Association for Bear Research and Management**
www.bearbiology.com
The Association's site provides biological and conservation information about the eight species of bears, including the Giant Panda and Polar bear. It also includes information about the Association's journal *Ursus*, online access to the International Bear News Newsletter and links to related sites.

- **The Bear Den American Zoo and Aquarium Association** www.bearden.org. Four sections: Sounds from the den (collection of miscellaneous information about bears); Bear species (more detailed information about the eight species of bears); Bear Taxon Advisory Group; Fun & Games.

2896 **International Society of Arachnology**
www.arachnology.org
An international society that promotes research into all of the arachnids (spiders, scorpions, etc.) with the exception of the Acari (mites and ticks). The website provides more information about the Society and its activities and also includes the Arachnology Home Page, a large collection of links to arachnological websites.

2897 **International Wolf Center**
www.wolf.org
The Center aims to educate the public about wolves and its website is an excellent source of information on the subject, ranging from a 'fun facts' section for children through to copies of scientific articles.

Lobster Conservancy
See entry no. 2594

2898 **Malacological Society of London**
www.sunderland.ac.uk/MalacSoc
Founded in the 1800s, the Society has an international membership and is dedicated to the promotion of education and research on molluscs. The website provides more information about the Society and its activities. It also includes a useful list of books for further reading and brief information about the Society's Library (the Radley Library), which is currently located in the Library at University College London.

2899 **Mammal Society** [UK]
www.abdn.ac.uk/mammal/index.shtml
The Society is based in London and is involved in the study and protection of British mammals. The Activities section of the site includes a collection of free fact sheets that provide quite detailed information on the British mammal species. A collection of links to related sites can be found in the Fun Zone.

2900 **Mammals Trust UK**
www.mtuk.org
The MTUK is an organization that raises funds to support the conservation of the British mammal fauna. The website provides more information about the Trust and its activities which include the publication of the annual *State of Britain's Mammals* reports (freely available at the site). The Mammals Facts section of the site provides an illustrated overview of the UK mammals that includes information on and photographs of all of the British species.

Otter Project
See entry no. 2600

Seal Conservation Society
See entry no. 2602

2901 **Societas Europaea Mammalogica**
www.european-mammals.org
The SEM was founded in 1988 in order to carry out the EMMA (European Mammals on Maps) project which resulted in the publication of The Atlas of European Mammals in 1999. The Society's website provides access to the Mammal Database which contains data that was used in the atlas and can be used to generate species lists for the European countries.

Society for the Study of Amphibians and Reptiles
See entry no. 2605

2902 **Systematic and Applied Acarology Society**
www.nhm.ac.uk/hosted_sites/acarology/saas
A relatively new international society dedicated to the study of mites and ticks (Acari). The website provides more information about the Society, including a membership directory and information on its publications which include the journal *Systematic and Applied Acarology*.

Whale and Dolphin Conservation Society
See entry no. 2608

2903 Wildlife Society [USA]
www.wildlife.org
Mission is 'to enhance the ability of wildlife professionals to conserve diversity, sustain productivity, and ensure responsible use of wildlife resources for the benefit of society'. Policy statements and range of publications – which include the *Journal of Wildlife Management* and downloadable PDF copies of a useful *Wildlife Policy News*.

World Chelonian Trust
See entry no. 2609

2904 Zoological Society of London
www.zsl.org
Founded in 1826, the ZSL is dedicated to the conservation of animals and their habitats. It consists of five operating departments: London Zoo; Whipsnade Wild Animal Park; Institute of Zoology; Scientific Publications Department; Library and Fellowship Services.

- **Zoological Society of London Library** www.zsl.org/info/library. One of the most important zoological libraries in the world: more than 200,000 volumes and 1300 current journals. Online library catalogue not currently complete (excludes non-journal material 1861–1991). Library open to the public but there is a fee.

Libraries, archives, museums

2905 University of Cambridge, Museum of Zoology [UK]
www.zoo.cam.ac.uk/museum/index.htm
Founded in 1814, the Museum is part of the Department of Zoology at the University. Its collections are of historical and international importance and include vertebrates, invertebrates (particularly insects and molluscs), birds and fossil vertebrates. The website provides more information about the Museum, its collections, exhibitions and the research interests of the Museum staff. The Museum is open to the public and admission is free.

Portal & task environments

2906 BigCats.com
www.bigcats.com
This site is aimed at the general public and provides information on the taxonomy and geographical distribution of the big cats (lions, tigers, etc.) as well as providing a collection of links to related sites. It also includes a searchable bibliography of almost 2000 titles, but with a rudimentary search mechanism and no information about its scope.

2907 The Ciliate Resource Archive
D.H. Lynn
www.uoguelph.ca/~ciliates
This site, last updated in 2003, presents a collection of resources on the taxonomy of the ciliates. Includes sections on: Representative genera; Ciliate classification; Type species; References (bibliography and links to related sites). Also a glossary.

The Cnidaria home page
University of California, Irvine See entry no. 2615

Crocodilians: Natural History & Conservation
A. Britton; Crocodile Specialist Group See entry no. 2616

2908 Man and Mollusc/Mollusk
A. Bouquin, comp.
www.manandmollusc.net
This site brings together a large collection of links to websites that deal with molluscs and shells. It is aimed at a wide audience with sections aimed specifically at children and teachers. The site also includes a useful guide to edible molluscs.

2909 Primate Info Net
University of Wisconsin-Madison
pin.primate.wisc.edu
This site brings together a large collection of resources on non-human primates (monkeys, apes, etc.). The links are arranged under the headings: About the primates; Info services (mailing lists, meetings, directories of primatologists, etc.); Research resources; PIN resources (careers, conservation, educational resources etc.). The site is searchable and it also includes a link to PRIMATELIT, a bibliography of primate literature.

Primate Info Net is maintained by the Wisconsin Primate Research Center Library at the University.

Sea slug forum
Australian Museum See entry no. 2625

Seaturtle.org
See entry no. 2626

Discovering print & electronic resources

2910 Animal identification: a reference guide
British Museum (Natural History), 1980.
These three volumes provide a guide to the primary reference sources that can be used to identify animals. The volumes are arranged taxonomically and include general works, works covering specific taxa, and works covering individual geographical regions.

- **Vol. 1. Marine and brackish water animals** **R. W. Sims, ed.** 111pp. ISBN 0471277657.
- **Vol. 2. Land and freshwater animals (not insects)** 120pp. ISBN 0471277665.
- **Vol. 3. Insects** **D. Hollis, ed.** 160pp. ISBN 0471277673.

Freshwater mollusk bibliography
K. Cummings [et al.], eds; Illinois Natural History Survey See entry no. 2629

2911 Guide to reference and information sources in the zoological sciences
D. Schmidt Libraries Unlimited, 2003, 352pp. $75.00. ISBN 1563089777.
This book is primarily taxonomically arranged with chapters on general reference works, invertebrates, arthropods, vertebrates, fish, amphibians and reptiles, birds and mammals. Each chapter includes a list of reference sources drawn from categories that include indexes and abstracts, journals, guides to the literature, biographies and histories, dictionaries, textbooks and handbooks. It includes both printed and electronic resources. There is a slight US bias to some of the categories but, overall, it is a very useful work.

Series: Reference Sources in Science and Technology.

Identifying British insects and arachnids: an annotated bibliography of key works
P.C. Barnard, ed. See entry no. 2409

2912 **PrimateLit: a bibliographic database for primatology**
Wisconsin National Primate Research Center and Washington National Primate Research Center
primatelit.library.wisc.edu
This is a freely available database that provides an index to the primate literature (journals, books, dissertations, reports etc.) from 1940 to date. The database contains a vast amount of information: 8000 items were added to the database for 2003 alone. It can be searched by keyword, author, title, publication year, journal, taxonomic category, common name and geographic region. The website also provides access to Current Primate References and Books Received, searchable indexes to items published in the last six months.

Sea Turtle Online Bibliography
University of Florida See entry no. 2631

2913 **Zoological Record**
Zoological Society of London Thomson BIOSIS, 1871–.
www.biosis.org/products/zr [DESCRIPTION]
This is the most important source of information on zoology and zoological systematics. It aims to be comprehensive, providing an index to the contents of more than 4500 journals and more than 1000 books, conferences and reports. It is available in print, on CD-ROM and via the web.

- **Zoological Record Thesaurus** www.biosis.org/support/zr-thesaurus. Contains about 10,000 terms: 7000 taxonomic names of family level and above arranged phylogenetically in a hierarchical classification; 3000 subject terms arranged in hierarchies representing major subject areas.

Digital data, image & text collections

Amphibian Species of the World: an online reference
D.R. Frost; American Museum of Natural History See entry no. 2632

AmphibiaWeb: information on amphibian biology and conservation
University of California, Berkeley See entry no. 2633

Check List of European Marine Mollusca: CLEMAM
J. Le Renard, S. Gofas and P. Bouchet, eds See entry no. 2636

2914 **The EMBL Reptile Database**
European Molecular Biology Laboratory and German Herpetological Society
www.reptile-database.org
This is a taxonomic database that covers all of the reptiles (lizards, snakes, crocodiles, turtles, etc.). It can be searched by species name, distribution or family and includes references to the original literature. The site also includes links to information on keeping reptiles as pets, as well as to other related sites.

The eSkeletons Project
University of Texas at Austin See entry no. 3553

EuroTurtle
Mediterranean Association to Save the Sea Turtles and Kings College Taunton See entry no. 2637

2915 **Mammal Species of the World (MSW)**
American Society of Mammalogists and National Museum of Natural History
http://nmnhgoph.si.edu/msw
This site provides access to a database of information about mammals. Each entry includes the author of the species name, the reference for the original description, the scientific and common names, geographical distribution, conservation status and a distribution map (for species found in North America). The database can be searched by common and scientific names.
Available in print: see website.

2916 **North American Mammals** [USA]
R. Costello and A. Rosenberger, eds; National Museum of Natural History
web4.si.edu/mna
Access to a searchable database of information and images of all of the living mammals of North America. Can be searched by species name (scientific and common names), by geographical region or conservation status, or by browsing the mammalian family tree. The site also includes a glossary.

The Postcode Plants Database
M. Sadka, D.-J. Cassey and C. Humphries, comps; Natural History Museum See entry no. 2253

Shells Database
M. Yamada See entry no. 2641

World List of Marine, Freshwater and Terrestrial Isopod Crustaceans
B. Kensley, M. Schotte and S. Schilling, comps; National Museum of Natural History See entry no. 2642

2917 **The World Spider Catalog**
N.I. Platnick; American Museum of Natural History
research.amnh.org/entomology/spiders/catalog
A taxonomic catalogue of the spiders (Araneae) of the world. The catalogue can be browsed by family (arranged alphabetically and taxonomically) or by genus. It also includes a bibliography of spider literature that covers the period from 1757 to date.

Directories & encyclopedias

2918 **The atlas of European mammals**
A.J. Mitchell-Jones [et al.]; Societas Europaea Mammalogica
Academic Press, 1999, 484pp. ISBN 0856611301.
Distribution information for all of the mammal species within Europe. Entry for each species also includes the common name used in each of the different countries, brief information on habitat, population and conservation status, and a short bibliography.

2919 Encyclopedia of the world's zoos
C.E. Bell, ed. Fitzroy Dearborn, 2001, 1577pp. 3 v, $395.00. ISBN 1579581749.
Information on zoological gardens around the world. The work also includes entries for some of the animals that may be found in zoos, biographical information on individuals associated with zoos (e.g. Gerald Durrell) and information on issues that affect zoos (e.g. ethical considerations, conservation issues). Volume 3 provides details of national and international zoological associations and a subject index.

2920 Grzimek's animal life encyclopedia
M. Hutchins [et al.], eds 2nd edn, Gale, 2004. $1750.00. ISBN 0787653624.
www.gale.com/gvrl
One of the most comprehensive zoological encyclopedias. This immense work is arranged taxonomically and includes full colour illustrations. Each volume provides an overview of the group(s) that it covers, followed by a more detailed section on each order or phylum. Within each volume there is also a bibliography, a glossary, a list of relevant organizations, and a subject index.
Available online: see website.

- **Volume 1. Lower metazoans and lesser deuterostomes D. A. Thoney and N. Schlager, eds** 530pp. ISBN 0787657778.
- **Volume 2. Protostomes S. F. Craig, D. A. Thoney and N. Schlager, eds** 569pp. ISBN 0787657786.
- **Volume 3. Insects A. V. Evans, R. W. Garrison and N. Schlager, eds** 472pp. ISBN 0787657794.
- **Volume 4. Fishes I D. A. Thoney, P. V. Loiselle and N. Schlager, eds** 517pp. ISBN 0787657808.
- **Volume 5. Fishes II** 547pp. ISBN 0787657816.
- **Volume 6. Amphibians W. E. Duellman and N. Schlager, eds** 507pp. ISBN 0787657824.
- **Volume 7. Reptiles J. B. Murphy and N. Schlager, eds** 593pp. ISBN 0787657832.
- **Volume 8. Birds I J. A. Jackson, W. J. Bock and D. Olendorf, eds** 635pp. ISBN 0787657840.
- **Volume 9. Birds II** 653pp. ISBN 0787657859.
- **Volume 10. Birds III J. A. Jackson, W. J. Bock and D. Olendorf, eds** 705pp. ISBN 0787657867.
- **Volume 11. Birds IV** 691pp. ISBN 0787657875.
- **Volume 12. Mammals I D. G. Kleiman, V. Geist and M. C. McDade, eds** 448pp. ISBN 0787657883.
- **Volume 13. Mammals II** 664pp. ISBN 0787657891.
- **Volume 14. Mammals III** 574pp. ISBN 0787657905.
- **Volume 15. Mammals IV** 556pp. ISBN 0787657913.
- **Volume 16. Mammals V** 670pp. ISBN 0787657921.
- **Volume 17. Cumulative index M. C. McDade, ed.** 278pp. ISBN 0787665703.

Handbooks & manuals

2921 The handbook of British mammals
G.B. Corbet and S. Harris, eds; Mammal Society 3rd edn, Blackwell Science, 1991, 588pp. ISBN 0865427119.
A very useful book. A vast range of information is provided for each species including identifying characteristics, footprints, food, anatomical features, habitat, distribution and behaviour. The first four chapters provide an introduction to the subject, including an overview of relevant UK legislation. A bibliography is included at the end of each of the chapters.

The history of British mammals
D.W. Yalden See entry no. 1462

The marine fauna of the British Isles and north-west Europe
P. J. Hayward and J. S. Ryland, eds See entry no. 2647

2922 Synopses of the British Fauna (New Series)
R.S.K. Barnes and J. H. Crothers, eds; Linnean Society of London and Estuarine and Coastal Sciences Association Field Studies Council, 1970–.
Series of accessible guides covering individual groups of British animals, with a particular bias towards aquatic species. Each volume provides an overview of the group including information on taxonomy, feeding and ecology, as well as an identification key.

- **Field Studies Council** www.field-studies-council.org. Provides 'informative and enjoyable opportunities for people of all ages and abilities to discover, explore, be inspired by, and understand the natural environment'. Each year over 70,000 people attend courses at 17 Centres in the UK. Good website.

Keeping up-to-date

Annual review of physiology
See entry no. 3566

Agriculture, Forestry, Fisheries & Food

This is a diverse subject area, which casts a wide net for its information resources, in areas shading off into environmental studies, natural history, medicine and economics amongst many others, and ranging from 'pure', sometimes controversial science to very 'applied' technology. For this section we have taken the common element to be 'production' and included sources that assist in activities related to the creation of some form of product that supports human life. This is broadly the remit of the area's main international body, the Food and Agriculture Organization of the United Nations, a large and complex system with a simple mission: to defeat hunger.

Publishing in this field has traditionally been dominated by 'thin' publications rather than books: research reports, conference papers, institutional series, reflecting a relatively small commercial market but also its reliance on factual data: production statistics, results of trials, geospatial data etc., leading to a relatively reduced emphasis on peer-reviewed journal literature and much more on locality-based reports. This in turn leads to a very long 'half-life': studies of trees, for example, may need to be carried out over several generations for species which have life-spans longer than our own. Archival collections are thus of particular importance and many older printed materials will continue to be needed for the foreseeable future.

Conversely, current information dissemination has moved very heavily to the web: it is noteworthy how many resources listed in the previous editions of *Walford's Guide to Reference Material* no longer exist in print. This also means that access is more focused on the institution that holds the data: relevant information is often scattered throughout a website rather than concentrated in a single PDF of a formally published report, for example.

Resources listed in this section are therefore heavily weighted towards institutional and web-based sources; this carries the penalty of volatility with both URL and organizational name changes, the latter particularly rife over the past decade, leading to potential archiving problems. And, for generations brought up on Primrose McConnell's *Agricultural notebook* and Nix's *Farm management pocketbook*, it represents a major change.

But there are considerable benefits in currency and responsiveness and in the ability to track user demands and potentially at least come closer to meeting real needs. So the selections here – as in so many places elsewhere within TNW – are offered as 'jumping-off points' rather than ends in themselves: almost all will lead to more serendipitous discoveries and an enriched information retrieval experience.

Introductions to the subject

2923 World agriculture: towards 2015/2030: an FAO perspective
J. Bruinsma, ed.; Food and Agriculture Organization Earthscan, 2003, 432pp. £35.00. ISBN 1844070077.
www.fao.org/documents
Review assessing the worldwide prospects for food and agriculture, including fisheries and forestry, considering the issues at stake over the years to 2015 and 2030.
Available online: see website.

Dictionaries, thesauri, classifications

2924 Agricultural Ontology Service: AOS
Food and Agriculture Organization
www.fao.org/agris/aos/default.htm
Project to develop a tool to help structure and standardize agricultural terminology in multiple languages for use by any number of different systems around the world. Aims to provide a framework for better indexing and retrieval of resources, increased interaction within the agricultural information community, and to contribute to W3C's Semantic Web [q.v.] activities.

2925 Agrovoc
Food and Agriculture Organization
www.fao.org/agrovoc
Multilingual agricultural thesaurus maintained by FAO. The online version can be searched in seven languages and the whole thesaurus can be downloaded free. New terms can be suggested by e-mail.

Biotechnology from A to Z
W. Bains See entry no. 5012

2926 CAB Thesaurus
CAB International 5th edn, CABI Publishing, 1999. £150.00. ISBN 0851993664.
www.cabi-publishing.org
Widely used thesaurus for the applied life sciences, available in printed and electronic formats; the latter may be used by third parties under licence. An online version, in beta test in 2004, allows searching for individual terms.

2927 Elsevier's dictionary of agriculture: in English, German, French, Russian and Latin
T. Tosheva, M. Djarova and B. Delijska Elsevier, 2000, 786pp. €191.00. ISBN 0444500057.
Multilingual dictionary containing terms in: plant growing and cultivation, processing of agricultural products, soil science, mineral nutrition, fertilizing, plant protection, agrometeorology, biochemistry and physiological characters of plants and animals, forest management and organization, animal breeding, foodstuffs, animal nutrition, veterinary

medicine, farm implements and machinery, vehicles, economics and organization of agriculture.

2928 **NAL Agricultural Thesaurus: NALT**
National Agricultural Library 3rd edn, 2004.
agclass.nal.usda.gov/agt/agt.htm
Excellent online tool for browsing agricultural and biological concepts and terminology, containing some 62,000 terms. Also now available via a WEB SERVICES (SOAP) interface: there is a well written downloadable PDF NAL Thesaurus Web Services Reference Manual.

Laws, standards, codes

2929 **Commission on Genetic Resources for Food and Agriculture**
www.fao.org/WAICENT/FAOINFO/AGRICULT/cgrfa
A permanent inter-governmental forum aiming to ensure the conservation and sustainable utilization of genetic resources for food and agriculture, as well as the fair and equitable sharing of benefits derived from their use, for present and future generations. The Commission aims to reach international consensus on areas of global interest, through negotiations.

- **The international treaty on plant genetic resources for food and agriculture** www.fao.org/ag/cgrfa/itpgr.htm. Adopted 2001. Covers all plant genetic resources relevant for food and agriculture. In harmony with CONVENTION ON BIOLOGICAL DIVERSITY. Seeks to ensure continued availability of plant genetic resources countries will need to feed their people.

ENTRI: Environmental Treaties and Resource Indicators
Socioeconomic Data and Applications Center See entry no. 2306

2930 **International code of conduct for plant germplasm collecting and transfer**
Food and Agriculture Organization
www.fao.org/WAICENT/FAOINFO/AGRICULT/AGp/agps/pgr/icc/icce.htm
A voluntary code which aims to promote the rational collection and sustainable use of genetic resources, to prevent genetic erosion, and to protect the interests of both donors and collectors of germplasm. Negotiated through FAO, and adopted in 1993, the Code is based on the principle of national sovereignty over plant genetic resources and sets out standards and principles to be observed.

2931 **International Portal on Food Safety, Animal & Plant Health**
Food and Agriculture Organization, United States. Department of Agriculture and Standards and Trade Development Facility
www.ipfsaph.org
Developed by FAO, in association with the organizations responsible for international standard setting in sanitary and phytosanitary matters, this portal provides a single access point for authorized official international and national information across the sectors of food safety, animal and plant health. In December 2004, contained over 16,000 records. Section The Regulatory Framework within the Help pages gives a useful list of binding international legal instruments relevant to this arena.

2932 **Sanitary and Phytosanitary Measures**
World Trade Organization
www.wto.org/english/tratop_e/sps_e/sps_e.htm
Covers the work of the WTO's committee on sanitary and phytosanitary (SPS) measures. Includes text of the SPS agreement for trade between members, which directs member governments in applying food safety and animal and plant health measures, with related documents.

Official & quasi-official bodies

2933 **Agriculture and Agri-Food Canada**
www.agr.gc.ca
Government department mandated to provide information, research and technology, and policies and programs to achieve security of the food system, health of the environment and innovation for growth. This bi-lingual site offers news and comprehensive links in all the department's areas of interest.

2934 **Australian Government Agriculture Portal**
Australia. Department of Agriculture, Fisheries and Forestry
www.agriculture.gov.au
An expanding catalogue of Australian, State and Territory Government information and services for the agricultural, fisheries, processed food and forestry industries. Contains three main collection areas: Resource Management for the management of natural resources for sustainable agriculture; Products & Industries, including information on agricultural industries and products (commodities); Agribusiness Business, information specific to agricultural industries.

Biotechnology and Biological Sciences Research Council
See entry no. 1912

Biotechnology and Pharmaceuticals
Great Britain. Department of Trade and Industry See entry no. 5018

2935 **DEFRA** [UK]
Great Britain. Department for Environment, Food and Rural Affairs
www.defra.gov.uk
Created in 2001, Defra is the UK government department responsible for all aspects of the environment, rural matters, farming and food production. Its comprehensive site includes news, policy reports, legislation and background information in a series of sub-sites covering all its interests.

European Environment Agency
See entry no. 2312

2936 **Food and Agriculture Organization**
www.fao.org
Founded in 1945, the Food and Agriculture Organization of the United Nations – to use its official title – leads international efforts to 'build a world without hunger'. Serving both developed and developing countries, FAO acts as a neutral forum where all nations meet as equals to negotiate agreements and debate policy, as well as being a source of knowledge and information. Its four main areas of activity are: Putting information within reach; Sharing policy expertise; Providing a meeting place for nations; Bringing knowledge to the field.

- **Biological diversity in food and agriculture** www.fao.org/biodiversity/index.asp. Comments on the questions 'How does Biodiversity benefit natural and agricultural ecosystems?' and 'How does farming benefit Biodiversity?' plus useful links to various resources.
- **Integrated production systems** www.fao.org/prods. Involves horizontal/vertical integration of crops, livestock, trees and aquaculture. Site provides co-ordinating framework for publications, reports, databases and information systems on integrated activities within FAO and collaborating institutions.
- **Trade in agriculture, fisheries and forestry** www.fao.org/trade/index_en.asp. News, events, agreements, negotiations in progress, publications, statistics: to help developing/transition countries participate effectively in multilateral trade negotiations and integrate into food, agricultural, fishery, forestry global trade.

2937 USDA
United States. Department of Agriculture
www.usda.gov
Home page for USDA's very extensive site, in fulfilment of its mission to provide leadership on food, agriculture, natural resources, and related issues based on sound public policy, the best available science, and efficient management.

- **Agricultural Research Service** www.ars.usda.gov. Large operation with research carried out at some 100 locations and organized into 22 National Programs encompassing more than 1200 research projects. Extensive sets of Products & Services including NATIONAL AGRICULTURAL LIBRARY.
- **Economic Research Service** www.ers.usda.gov. Website redesigned in 2001 to offer improved online services including: More than 80 briefing rooms; 22 key topic areas; Access to around 9000 data sets; Hundreds of publications. *Amber Waves* is an e-zine covering the economics of food, farming, etc.
- **USDA Economics, Statistics and Market Information System Cornell University**. http://usda.mannlib.cornell.edu. Contains nearly 300 reports and datasets from USDA economic agencies. Managed within the University's Mann Library.

Research centres & institutes

2938 CAB International
www.cabi.org
CAB International is a global not-for-profit organization involved in the generation, dissemination and use of knowledge in the applied biosciences to enhance development, human welfare and the environment. CABI's work is carried out by its Publishing and Bioscience divisions and an international network of offices and centres.

- **CABI Bioscience** www.cabi-bioscience.org. Integrates four former international biological institutes: International Institute of Biological Control; International Institute of Entomology; International Institute of Parasitology; International Mycological Institute.

2939 Central Science Laboratory [UK]
www.csl.gov.uk
CSL is an Executive Agency of the UK Government Department for Environment, Food and Rural Affairs (DEFRA), specializing in the sciences underpinning agriculture for sustainable crop production, environmental management and conservation, and in food safety and quality.

2940 Consultative Group on International Agricultural Research
www.cgiar.org/index.html
Created in 1971, the CGIAR is an association of public and private members supporting a system of 15 Future Harvest Centres that work in more than 100 countries to achieve sustainable food security and reduce poverty in developing countries, through scientific research and research-related activities in the fields of agriculture, forestry, fisheries, policy, and environment. This CGIAR Secretariat website and those of the member Centres give full information on all activities.

2941 Deutsche Gesellschaft fuer Technische Zusammenarbeit (German Society for Technical Co-operation)
www.gtz.de/english
An important international co-operative enterprise for sustainable development with worldwide operations, supporting many projects in agriculture and related fields. Its website was being given a major restructuring, late 2004.

2942 French Agricultural Research Centre for International Development
www.cirad.fr/en/index.php
A French development-oriented agricultural research organization serving the tropics and subtropics, covering the life sciences and social sciences applied to agriculture, forestry, animal production, natural resource management, agrifoods, ecosystems and communities in developing countries.

Associations & societies

European Association for Bioindustries
See entry no. 5022

2943 European Federation for Information Technology in Agriculture, Food and the Environment
www.efita.net
EFITA's mission is to facilitate the exchange of information and experience, the development of knowledge and promotion of awareness in the area of ICT in agriculture in order to enhance the competitiveness of Europe. Details of projects, international meetings, publications and networks.

Greenpeace
See entry no. 4640

Libraries, archives, museums

2944 David Lubin Memorial Library
Food and Agriculture Organization
www.fao.org/library
Established in Rome at the 1952 FAO Conference, according to the decisions of the 1950 Conference. Named David Lubin Memorial Library by the Conference to honour the founder of the International Institute of Agriculture (IIA). The extensive IIA collection formed a solid base for the present-day Library which is considered one of the world's finest collections in food, agriculture and international development. Good subject categorized links and other sections within Virtual Library area.

Portal & task environments

2945 **Agriculture 21**
Food and Agriculture Organization
www.fao.org/ag
A searchable magazine with news and features which also provides a gateway to other FAO agricultural information sites. Access is provided by A–Z list and by subject (with links to more than 320 documents and databases organized in 11 subject categories and 26 subcategories). A separate listing is given for site-wide resources (software, databases, publications lists and e-mail conferences).

2946 **AgriFor** [UK]
University of Oxford, University of Reading and Resource Discovery Network
http://agrifor.ac.uk
The AgriFor gateway covers agriculture, forestry and food and is part of RDN's BIOME hub, providing access to evaluated, quality internet resources. There is a companion VetGate, and both gateways can be browsed using the CAB Thesaurus, and searched individually or collectively with the other BIOME gateways.

Biotechnology in Food and Agriculture
Food and Agriculture Organization See entry no. 5028

2947 **EARD-InfoSys+: The European Information System on Agricultural Research for Development**
European Initiative for Agricultural Research for Development
www.eiard-infosys.org
Aims at improving access to European web resources devoted towards development in the fields of agriculture, environment, forestry, fisheries, socio-economics, rural-transformation and many others; provides an information and communication platform for institutions and parties all over Europe involved in scientific development co-operation.

Eco-portal: the environmentalsustainability.info source
See entry no. 2335

Global Change Master Directory
National Aeronautics and Space Administration See entry no. 862

PJB Publications
See entry no. 3720

2948 **WAICENT**
World Agricultural Information Centre
www.fao.org/waicent/index_en.asp
FAO established WAICENT as a corporate framework for agricultural information management and dissemination, and a strategic effort to fight hunger with information. The framework integrates and harmonizes standards, tools and procedures for the efficient and effective management and dissemination of high-quality technical information, including relevant and reliable statistics, texts, maps, and multimedia resources.

Discovering print & electronic resources

2949 **CAB Abstracts**
CAB International
www.cabi-publishing.org [DESCRIPTION]
CAB Abstracts is CABI Publishing's main bibliographic database, covering wide swathes of the applied life sciences. Among much else, it indexes research and development literature in the fields of agriculture, forestry, aspects of human health, human nutrition, animal health and the management and conservation of natural resources. Over 4 million records from 1973 to present currently online, with some 180,000 new records added each year; back files to 1908 will be available from 2005.
Available in wide range of print versions and online: see website.

2950 **RDN Virtual Training Suite: Agriculture, Food & Forestry** [UK]
G. Petrokofsky and L. Williamson; CAB International and Resource Discovery Network
www.vts.rdn.ac.uk/tutorial/agrifor
Free, 'teach yourself' tutorial in internet information skills. Covers some key sites for the subject area, with guidance on effective searching, evaluation of websites and practical use in research. Regularly updated.

Digital data, image & text collections

2951 **Core Historical Literature of Agriculture: CHLA**
Cornell University
chla.library.cornell.edu
A core electronic collection of agricultural texts published between the early 19th and the middle to late 20th centuries, covering agricultural economics, agricultural engineering, animal science, crops and their protection, food science, forestry, human nutrition, rural sociology, and soil science. Titles selected for historical importance, based on the 7-volume series *The literature of the agricultural sciences* edited by Wallace C. Olsen. Maintained within the University's Albert R Mann Library with – mid-2004 – 743,919 pages within 1873 book and journal volumes online.

2952 **FAOSTAT**
Food and Agriculture Organization
faostat.fao.org
Online multilingual database currently containing over 3 million time-series records covering international statistics on production, trade, food balance sheets, producer prices, forestry trade flow, land use and irrigation, forest products, fishery products, population, food quality control, fertilizer and pesticides, agricultural machinery, food aid shipments, and exports by destination.

2953 **National Academies: Agriculture**
National Academies Press.
www.nap.edu
Offers executive summaries and some full-text versions of a number of significant reports in agricultural science published by the US National Academies, with print/PDF ordering service. Wide variety of topics including agricultural bioterrorism and genetic modification.
Similar collections of reports available for all this volume's subject groupings: see website.

Directories & encyclopedias

Agricultural and Mineral Commodities Year Book
See entry no. 4703

2954 **Agricultural information resource centers: a world directory 2000**
J.S. Johnson, R.C. Fisher and C. Boast; International Association of Agricultural Information Specialists 2000, 718pp. $105.00. ISBN 0962405221.
www.nisc.com/factsheets/qair.asp
Almost 4000 entries from 189 countries, including address, telephone, fax, e-mail, websites, and online public access catalogue addresses. Organized alphabetically by country, city and parent institution, with institution, city and subject indexes. An extensive key to the acronyms and abbreviations that appear in the Directory for databases, database vendors, institutions, and networks is also provided.
Available online: see website.

2955 **Dimensions of need: an atlas of food and agriculture**
T. Loftas, ed.; Food and Agriculture Organization 1995, 127pp. ISBN 925103737X.
www.fao.org/docrep/U8480E/U8480E00.htm
An e-book created to mark the 50th anniversary of the Food and Agriculture Organization of the United Nations. With over 600 photographs, maps, charts and diagrams, it reviews FAO's past and future challenges in protecting and conserving the planet's natural resources and environment.

2956 **Encyclopedia of agricultural science**
C. Arntzen, ed. 1st edn, Academic Press, 1994, 2744pp. 4 v., $995.00. ISBN 0122266706.
Provides alphabetically-arranged articles aiming to be comprehensible to high school and undergraduate students, but also beneficial to researchers and specialists. Topics include animal, plant, range, and soil science; food processing, storage, and distribution; agricultural economics, education, engineering, policy; pest management; rural sociology; water resources, and more.
New edn forthcoming.

Encyclopedia of the biosphere: a guide to the world's ecosystems
R. Folch, ed. See entry no. 2349

Handbooks & manuals

2957 **Sustainable food and agriculture**
I.G. Malkina-Pykh and Y.A. Pykh, eds Wit Press, 2003, 376pp. £118.00. ISBN 1853129372.
www.witpress.com
Compact, approachable text by authors based at the Center for International Environmental Conservation, Russian Academy of Sciences. Useful section Classification of food and agriculture models which gives an entrée to worldwide work on food and agriculture systems, resources, technology, economics, society, global environment.
Series: The Sustainable World, V. 4. The publisher has an extensive list in this and related fields in engineering and technology: check the website.
'provides valuable and useful information for agriculturists, environmentalists, socio-economists and policy makers, and also provides recent, well-explained and organized information for those working on food policy and security ... The book is a valuable reference for all researchers of sustainable food, agriculture and the environment.' (*Biological Agriculture & Horticulture*)

2958 **Yearbook of agriculture** [USA]
United States. Department of Agriculture USGPO, 1894–1993. Title varies. ISSN 00843268.
No longer produced but an important historical source, the Yearbook was effectively the annual report of the Department of Agriculture until 1936; thereafter, volumes concentrated on a single topic, addressed to the American public, especially farmers.

Keeping up-to-date

2959 **Commodity Market Review**
Food and Agriculture Organization Annual. PDF.
www.fao.org
This annual publication provides in-depth analysis of major issues that have been identified by FAO as crucial to world agricultural commodity market developments. Available in print and pdf formats.

2960 **Current Contents/Agriculture, Biology & Environmental Sciences**
Thomson ISI.
www.isinet.com/products/cap/ccc/editions/ccabes [DESCRIPTION]
Provides access to complete bibliographic information from articles, editorials, meeting abstracts, commentaries, and all other significant items in recently published editions of over 1040 of the world's leading agriculture, biology, and environmental sciences journals and books in a broad range of categories.
Available in a variety of electronic and print formats: see website.

2961 **FAO Electronic Forums**
Food and Agriculture Organization
www.fao.org
FAO operates a number of e-mail conference lists, covering all areas of its operations, many with membership open to anyone interested. One of the best ways of keeping up-to-date.

2962 **The state of food and agriculture**
Food and Agriculture Organization 2003–04, Annual. $65.00. ISBN 9251050791.
www.fao.org/es/english/index_en.htm
Authoritative publication produced annually since 1947. Examines key developments in food and agriculture at the world, regional and national levels, with in-depth analysis of important issues shaping global food and agriculture. Theme for the 2003–04 edition is the potential for agricultural biotechnology to address the needs of the world's poor and food-insecure.
Now available in print and online.

2963 **State of the world**
L.R. Brown, ed. Worldwatch Institute, 2004, Annual, 245pp. $16.95. ISBN 0393325393.
www.worldwatch.org/pubs/sow [DESCRIPTION]
The 2004 volume was a special edition of this annual survey of key environmental, social, and economic trends, marking the 30th anniversary of the Institute. Examines the consumer society and steps that could be taken to build markets for

less-hazardous products, including fair-traded foods, green power, and fuel-cell vehicles.
Available online: see website.

- **Vital signs: the trends that are shaping our future L.R. Brown, ed.** Worldwatch Institute, 2003, 158pp. $14.95. ISBN 0393324400. Annual survey complementing *State of the world* with graphs and statistics. Well sourced data presented in a user-friendly way, this is a good starting point for reviewing broad trends in the agricultural and other sectors.

Agriculture

agribusiness • agricultural development • agricultural economics • agricultural policy • agronomy • countryside • farmers markets • farming • organic agriculture • rural development • sustainable agriculture • tropical agriculture

Introductions to the subject

2964 Agriculture: the science and practice of farming [UK]
J.A.S. Watson 11th edn., Oliver and Boyd, 1962, 818pp.
Classic textbook which ran to 11 editions from 1924–1962, giving a thorough overview of the development of UK agricultural science through the mid-twentieth century. It covered soil management, crops, livestock and farm organization.

Farm machinery
C. Culpin See entry no. 4960

Dictionaries, thesauri, classifications

2965 CRC dictionary of agricultural sciences
R.A. Lewis CRC Press, 2001, 680pp. $99.95. ISBN 0849323274.
Covers all areas of agriculture and related activities, including traditional farming, environmental sciences, biotechnology and genetics. C.15,000 terms with extensive cross-referencing of closely related entries, and definitions listing often-used variants of the principal meanings.

Laws, standards, codes

2966 Agricultural Metadata Elements Project: AgMES
Food and Agriculture Organization
www.fao.org/agris/agmes/default.htm
Set up to promote the use of metadata in description of all agricultural information resource types. Using semantically meaningful metadata elements and schemes will make it much easier to share and find information about agricultural resources. AgMES works closely with ontologies, in the effort to promote mutually agreed norms, and vocabularies to control the content of some of the metadata terms defined in AgMES.

2967 Agriculture
World Trade Organization
www.wto.org/english/tratop_e/agric_e/agric_e.htm
Background notes and progress news on WTO agricultural trade negotiations, with full texts and analysis of the Agricultural Agreement.

2968 Technical conversion factors (TCF) for agricultural commodities
Food and Agriculture Organization
www.fao.org/WAICENT/FAOINFO/ECONOMIC/ESS/tcf.asp
Contains technical conversion factors and ancillary information used to compile commodity balances and supply/utilization accounts for nearly all the countries in the world. The main scope is ultimately to arrive at approximate estimates of the total availability of food in each country, expressed in terms of quantity as well as in terms of calories, protein and fat. Updates two earlier printed versions of the publication produced in 1960 and revised in 1972, by the Statistics Division of FAO.

Official & quasi-official bodies

2969 Australian Centre for International Agricultural Research
www.aciar.gov.au
ACIAR is 'an Australian Government statutory authority that operates as part of Australia's Aid Program within the portfolio of Foreign Affairs and Trade. It contributes to the aid program objectives of advancing Australia's national interest through poverty reduction and sustainable development'. Site includes details of programs, publications and funding opportunities.

2970 Countryside Agency [UK]
www.countryside.gov.uk
Established by the UK Government in 1999, the statutory champion and watchdog working to make the quality of life better for people in the countryside, and the quality of the countryside better for everyone, including the conservation and management of landscape and biodiversity. Evidence and Analysis section provides well organized leads to wide range of relevant resources.

2971 England Rural Development Programme
Great Britain. Department for Environment, Food and Rural Affairs
www.defra.gov.uk/erdp/default.htm
The ERDP provides a framework for the operation of 10 separate but integrated schemes which provide new opportunities to protect and improve the countryside, to develop sustainable enterprises and to help rural communities to thrive. Gives details of the schemes and the benefits offered. Links to similar programmes for Northern Ireland, Scotland, Wales.

2972 FASonline [USA]
Foreign Agricultural Service
www.fas.usda.gov
FAS has primary responsibility for USDA's overseas activities, including market development, international trade agreements and negotiations, and the collection and analysis of statistics and market information. It also administers USDA's export credit guarantee and food aid programs, and helps increase income and food availability in developing nations by mobilizing expertise for agriculturally led economic growth.

2973 International Fund for Agricultural Development
www.ifad.org
Set up in 1977 to finance agricultural development projects primarily for food production in the developing countries,

IFAD's mandate is to fight rural poverty. Project details, disclosed documents and a photo and video gallery are available on this site.

2974 **World Agricultural Outlook Board** [USA]
www.usda.gov/agency/oce/waob
Created in 1977 to serve as the focal point for economic intelligence on the outlook for US and world agriculture, the Board co-ordinates USDA's outlook analysis and assures its accuracy, timeliness and objectivity, reviewing and approving the Department's commodity and farm sector forecasts and distributing information quickly to farmers, policymakers and the public.

Research centres & institutes

2975 **ADAS** [UK]
www.adas.co.uk
Former UK government agency now private company providing research and consultancy for agriculture and horticulture, the development of business management, diversification and socio-economic services, plus environmental, economic and community-based services for rural land-based industries with significant involvement in the food chain and European projects.

2976 **Agricultural Economics Research Institute**
www.lei.dlo.nl/lei_engels/HTML/home.htm
LEI is the leading institute in the Netherlands for social and economic research on agriculture, horticulture, fisheries, forestry and rural areas. LEI's focus at both national and international level is the increasing integration of agriculture and agribusiness with the social environment.

2977 **Centre for Novel Agricultural Products** [UK]
www.york.ac.uk/org/cnap/home.htm
Based at the University of York, CNAP conducts gene research directed at the use of plants and microbes as cell factories for the production of novel industrial products.

2978 **Food and Agricultural Policy Research Institute** [USA]
www.fapri.iastate.edu
With its research centres the Center for Agricultural and Rural Development (CARD) at Iowa State University and Center for National Food and Agricultural Policy (CNFAP) at the University of Missouri–Columbia, FAPRI provides economic analysis of trade and agricultural policy for decision makers and stakeholders in world agriculture.

2979 **Global Forum on Agricultural Research**
www.egfar.org/home.shtml
GFAR – whose Secretariat is based at the FAO – is a multi-stakeholder initiative that contributes to eradicating poverty, achieving food security, and conserving and managing natural resources. It enhances national capacities to generate, adapt and transfer knowledge and provides a forum to address issues of global concern. Extensive documentation in Knowledge Building section of site.

2980 **Institute of Grassland and Environmental Research** [UK]
www.iger.bbsrc.ac.uk
BBSRC-funded research institute founded in 1990, but originating in 1919 as the Welsh Plant Breeding Station. Covers forage-related plant breeding, plant biology and genetics, animal science and nutrition, organic dairying, soil science and agro-ecology. Site includes publications database, online information sheets and posters.

2981 **International Center for Agricultural Research in the Dry Areas**
www.icarda.org
A CGIAR Center, whose main research station and offices are based in Aleppo, Syria, ICARDA's mission is to improve the welfare of poor people and alleviate poverty through research and training in dry areas of the developing world, by increasing the production, productivity and nutritional quality of food, while preserving and enhancing the natural resource base.

2982 **International Center for Tropical Agriculture**
www.ciat.cgiar.org
A CGIAR Future Harvest Centre based in Colombia aiming to reduce hunger and poverty in the tropics through collaborative research that improves agricultural productivity and natural resource management, leading to competitive agriculture, healthy agro-ecosystems, and rural innovation. Well designed website gives ready access to variety of useful resources.

2983 **International Development Research Centre**
web.idrc.ca
IDRC is a Canadian public corporation that works in close collaboration with researchers from the developing world. Many projects have an agricultural focus. Site gives access to the IDRC Library Catalogue, a database of project information, and the IDRC photo library. An increasing number of titles in the collection are available in electronic format.

2984 **International Institute for Tropical Agriculture**
www.iita.org/index.htm
IITA is a CGIAR Centre with a mandate to improve food production in the humid tropics and to develop sustainable production systems, including crop improvement, plant health, and resource and crop management within a food systems framework, targeted at the identified needs of four major agro-ecological zones: the dry, moist, and mid-altitude savannah, and the humid forests.

2985 **International Water Management Institute**
www.iwmi.cgiar.org
Headquartered in Sri Lanka and works on the sustainable use of water and land resources in agriculture and on the water needs of developing countries. Co-operates with a variety of partners to develop tools and methods to help the countries eradicate poverty through more effective management of their water and land resources. Wide-ranging Publications section; good set of Tools & Resources.

Associations & societies

Agricultural Engineering Association
See entry no. 4969

American Society of Agricultural Engineers
See entry no. 4970

2986 **American Society of Agronomy**
www.agronomy.org
Founded in 1907, ASA is dedicated to the development of agriculture enabled by science, in harmony with environmental and human values, supporting scientific, educational and professional activities to enhance communication and technology transfer among agronomists and those in related disciplines on topics of local to international significance. Free access to abstracts of articles in its journals.

Council for Biotechnology Information
See entry no. 5021

European Committee of Associations of Manufacturers of Agricultural Machinery
See entry no. 4974

2987 **European Foundation of Landscape Architecture (EFLA)**
www.efla.org/default.htm
Aims to promote the profession of landscape architecture at a European level, provide an active framework for disseminating information both within and outside the profession, and particularly to ensure high and comparable standards of education and professional practice.

2988 **Future Harvest**
www.futureharvest.org
Charitable and educational organization created in 1988 by the 16 Future Harvest Centres and supported by 58 governments, private foundations, and international and regional organizations in the Consultative Group on International Agricultural Research. Aims to advance debate and catalyse action for a world with less poverty, a healthier human family, and a better environment. In 2001 Future Harvest UK was established in the United Kingdom.

Global Water Partnership
See entry no. 1136

2989 **International Association of Agricultural Information Specialists**
www.iaald.org
Facilitates professional development of, and communication among, members of the agricultural information community worldwide, aiming to enhance access to and use of agriculture-related information resources by promoting the agricultural information profession; supporting professional development activities; fostering collaboration; and providing a platform for information exchange.

International Commission of Agricultural Engineering (Commission Internationale du Génie Rural)
See entry no. 4978

2990 **International Federation of Agricultural Producers**
www.ifap.org/index.html
IFAP was established in 1946 to secure the fullest co-operation between organizations of agricultural producers in meeting the optimum nutritional and consumptive requirements of the peoples of the world. It works to improve the economic and social status of all who live by and on the land.

2991 **International Federation of Organic Agriculture Movements**
www.ifoam.org
Founded 1972 to promote 'the worldwide adoption of ecologically, socially and economically sound systems that are based on the principles of Organic Agriculture'. Range of useful information including IFOAM Positions, Declarations and Dossiers.

2992 **International Food and Agribusiness Management Association**
www.ifama.org/index.asp
A worldwide leadership forum bringing together top food and agribusiness executives, academics, policy makers and other concerned stakeholders to stimulate strategic thinking across the food chain. IAMA is a knowledge association, dedicated to achieving an efficient food system that is sensitive to the needs of consumers, safe, and environmentally responsive, is sustainable and has a high level of business integrity.

2993 **Landscape Institute** [UK]
www.l-i.org.uk
The chartered institute in the UK for landscape architects, incorporating designers, managers and scientists, concerned with enhancing and conserving the environment

2994 **National Association of Farmers Markets** [UK]
www.farmersmarkets.net
Set up to promote farmers' markets and assist in the formation of new ones; enable them to expand and remain self-sustaining; to define and accredit the farmers' market concept; to represent the interests of farmers' markets and lobby for measures that would help them; and to seek support of a range of regional, national and European agencies. 'A farmers' market is one in which farmers, growers or producers from a defined local area are present in person to sell their own produce, direct to the public. All products sold should have been grown, reared, caught, brewed, pickled, baked, smoked or processed by the stallholder.'

2995 **Royal Agricultural Society of England**
www.rase.org.uk
Founded in 1840, the RASE is grounded in science and technology transfer, organizing the annual Royal Show and a technical events programme. It also engages in policy development work, high level influence on Government and significant education effort in schools. It is currently developing The Open Country Initiative as a multifaceted national resource that will serve as a focus for all aspects of rural development and help shape a sustainable future for rural communities.

2996 **Tropical Agriculture Association**
www.taa.org.uk
A professional association of individuals and corporate bodies concerned with the role of agriculture for development throughout the world. Offers visits and meetings, a newsletter, travel funds, organizes conferences, runs a discussion forum and other activities.

2997 United States Agricultural Information Network
www.usain.org
An organization for information professionals that provides a forum for discussion of agricultural issues, takes a leadership role in the formation of a national information policy as related to agriculture, makes recommendations to the NATIONAL AGRICULTURAL LIBRARY on agricultural information matters, and promotes co-operation and communication among its members.

Libraries, archives, museums

CABI Bioscience Libraries
CAB International See entry no. 1946

2998 Museum of English Rural Life
www.ruralhistory.org/index.html
Built over the last 50 years, the Museum's collections are the most extensive of their type in England, including artefacts, books, archives, photographs, film and sound recordings, all related to the history of food, farming and country life. Online database offering the catalogue of all the main collections: library, archives, photographs and objects, and access to Bibliography of Rural History, which includes references to material not held at MERL. Innovative INTERFACE (Internet Farm and Countryside Explorer) presents selected images and details for children, general and advanced audiences.

2999 National Agricultural Library
www.nal.usda.gov
As the USA's primary source for agricultural information, NAL has a mission to increase the availability and utilization of agricultural information for researchers, educators, policymakers, consumers of agricultural products, and the public. Site describes all services with access to online resources including the Library's catalogue, its article citation database AGRICOLA, and the AGNIC portal.

3000 Wageningen UR Library
library.wur.nl
Major agricultural library dating from 1873. Now serving the whole of the life sciences, the Library moves to new premises in 2006, and offers extensive online facilities.

Portal & task environments

3001 AgBiotechNet: the online service for agricultural biotechnology
CAB International
www.agbiotechnet.com [FEE-BASED]
Subscription service on agricultural biotechnology and biosafety for researchers, policy makers and industry world-wide, providing access to research developments in genetic engineering, transgenic plants and animals, in vitro culture and molecular genetics with updates on economic and social issues. Includes review articles and abstracts database derived from CAB ABSTRACTS.

3002 AgNIC: The Agriculture Network Information Center
National Agricultural Library
www.agnic.org
A voluntary alliance of the NAL, land-grant universities and other agricultural organizations, in co-operation with citizen groups and government agencies. Members take responsibility for small vertical segments of agricultural information (including basic, applied, and developmental research, extension and teaching activities in the food, agricultural, renewable natural resources, forestry, and physical and social sciences), developing websites and reference services in specific subject areas, searchable and browsable via AgNIC.

3003 Agra-net.com
Agra Group.
www.agra-net.com/NASApp/cs/ContentServer?pagename=agra/home
[FEE-BASED]
Agra Group specializes in providing high value information on food, agriculture, soft commodities, fisheries and seafood. It produces over 50 separate publications and organizes high level conferences and seminars world-wide. The online archive is available to subscribers of printed publications, and contains over 20,000 articles.

3004 Agribusiness Online
Fintrac Inc.
www.agribusinessonline.com
A free market intelligence and technical information service for agribusiness professionals, with sections on crops, regulations, statistics and market prices for USA, Canada, Mexico and Europe.

3005 Agriculture in the Europe of 25
European Commission. Directorate for Agriculture and Rural Development
europa.eu.int/comm/agriculture/eu25/index_en.htm
Series of reports on the agricultural situation in the 10 new Member States who joined the European Union on 1 May 2004, as well as studies on specific topics, a glossary and documents relating to the pre-accession period.

3006 AgriSeek: World's Largest Marketplace [USA]
www.agriseek.com
An online marketplace for equipment, livestock, real estate, jobs, farm-related products and services, mainly aimed at North America, with worldwide news feeds.

3007 Common Agricultural Policy [EUR]
European Union
europa.eu.int/pol/agr/index_en.htm
Key texts, news and documentation on the CAP, including links to all relevant EU institutions, publications and statistics, full texts of important legislation, summaries of policy and future plans. Excellent starting point for CAP information.

3008 CTA
Technical Centre for Agricultural and Rural Cooperation ACP-EU
www.cta.int
CTA's programmes in agricultural and rural development aim to increase access to and awareness of information sources, to promote information exchange, and to increase the capacity to generate and manage information, in ACP countries. Site includes a wide range of downloadable documents. The Centre was established in 1983 under the Lomé Convention.

3009 Eldis Agriculture Resource Guide
Institute of Development Studies
www.eldis.org/agriculture/index.htm
Part of the well organized and extensive Eldis Gateway to Development Information, which collectively featured 14,850 online documents, 4500 organizations and 15,000 e-mail messages, late 2004. Offers summaries and full-text links to research reports and web resources, profiles of developing countries and other background information. A very useful service.
Similar Eldis Guides available for: Ageing populations; Biodiversity; Food security; Forestry; Health; Health systems; HIV/AIDS.

3010 Farmingsolutions: Success Stories for the Future of Agriculture
Greenpeace, Oxfam and Centre for Information on Low External Input and Sustainable Agriculture
www.farmingsolutions.org
Features success stories in environmentally sustainable agricultural projects worldwide, with background data. Created with the support of *Pesticide Action Network – Africa*.

3011 Health and Safety in the Agriculture Industry [UK]
Health and Safety Executive
www.hse.gov.uk/agriculture/index.htm
Home page for HSE's involvement in agriculture, identified as a priority because its high fatal accident rate is the worst in any UK industry. Includes downloadable interactive software to help farmers carry out a comprehensive health and safety assessment of their farms and to raise the levels of health and safety awareness in the industry.

3012 Information System Genetic Resources: GENRES
German Centre for Documentation and Information in Agriculture
www.genres.de/genres-e.htm
Provides an overview of relevant documents, facts, projects and other measures for the conservation and sustainable utilization of genetic resources for food, agriculture, forestry and fisheries in Germany, Europe and internationally.

3013 Introduction to Farming [UK]
Great Britain. Department for Environment, Food and Rural Affairs
www.defra.gov.uk/farm/farmindx.htm
Defra's farming pages contain comprehensive links to policy, environmental and sectoral issues affecting British farming.

- **Industrial Crops** www.defra.gov.uk/farm/acu/acu.htm. Source for information on non-food uses of crops, including energy, fibres and other industrial uses. Includes growing guides and aid scheme details.

3014 National Ag Safety Database: NASD [USA]
National Institute for Occupational Safety and Health and United States. Department of Agriculture
www.cdc.gov/nasd/index.html
NASD is an information clearinghouse for agricultural safety-related documents. It provides a national resource for the dissemination of information, educating workers and managers about occupational hazards associated with agriculture-related injuries, deaths and illnesses, providing prevention information, promoting consideration of safety and health issues and the sharing of educational and research materials.

3015 NFUonline [UK]
National Farmers' Union
www.nfu.org.uk
Founded in 1908, the National Farmers' Union is the largest farming organization in the UK, representing the farmers and growers of England and Wales. Its central objective is to promote successful and socially responsible agriculture and horticulture, while ensuring the long-term viability of rural communities.

3016 Organic Agriculture at FAO
Food and Agriculture Organization
www.fao.org/organicag/default.htm
Gateway to FAO's information on organic agriculture, with links to key external sites. Includes discussion fora, photos and videos, and country data.

Pew Initiative on Food and Biotechnology
Pew Charitable Trusts and University of Richmond See entry no. 5032

3017 Sustainable Agriculture and Rural Development: SARD
Food and Agriculture Organization
www.fao.org/wssd/SARD/index-en.htm
SARD is a capacity-building initiative to assist sustainable agriculture and rural development, including forestry and fisheries, to meet the nutritional requirements and other human needs of present and future generations, provide durable and decent employment, maintain and, where possible, enhance the productive and regenerative capacity of the natural resource base, reduce vulnerability and strengthen self-reliance.

3018 UK Agriculture
Living Countryside Ltd.
www.ukagriculture.com/index.html
Aims to advance the education of the public in all aspects of agriculture, the countryside and the rural economy; to promote greater public understanding of the role of agriculture in the countryside; and to conserve and protect the countryside as a whole for the benefit of the public. Site designed to be of general use to anyone interested in food, farming and the countryside.

Discovering print & electronic resources

3019 AGDEX
Scottish Agricultural College
edina.ac.uk/agdex [FEE-BASED]
Bibliographic references from farming and agricultural periodicals, aimed at UK higher and further education institutions. Covers non-academic titles often not covered in other services, from 1971 onwards, and includes new products and trials. Provided by the EDINA JISC-funded national data centre, who also give access to agcensus: grid square agricultural census data for England, Scotland and Wales.

3020 AGRICOLA: AGRICultural OnLine Access
National Agricultural Library
agricola.nal.usda.gov
Bibliographic database created by NAL and its co-operators. Covers materials in all formats, including printed works from the 15th century, encompassing all aspects of agriculture and allied disciplines. Site provides free searching of the NAL Online Public Access Catalogue and its Article Citation

Database. Links to full-text sources included where available.
Available though several online hosts: see website.

- **Journals indexed in AGRICOLA National Agricultural Library.** www.nal.usda.gov/indexing/jia.html. Searchable and downloadable database including details of all titles currently or previously indexed in AGRICOLA.

3021 **Agricultural history in Great Britain and western Europe before 1914: a discursive bibliography**
G.E. Fussell Pindar Press, 1983, 157pp. £75.00. ISBN 0907132049.
Useful survey of the history of the evolution of writing on agricultural history, from pre-medieval times to the First World War.

3022 **AGRIS/CARIS: International Information System for the Agricultural Sciences and technology**
Food and Agriculture Organization
www.fao.org/agris
Created by FAO in 1974 to facilitate information exchange and to bring together world literature dealing with all aspects of agriculture. AGRIS is a co-operative system in which participating countries input references to the literature produced within their boundaries and, in return, draw on the information provided by the other participants. Involves some 240 national, international and intergovernmental centres.

3023 **AgriSurf!: the farmers' search engine**
www.agrisurf.com
Claims to be the world's largest searchable agricultural WWW index. All sites are hand picked by agricultural experts. Includes a 'top-ten' listing based on click-throughs. The search engine accepts Boolean commands and can be limited by country.

3024 **AgriWeb Canada**
Agriculture and Agri-Food Canada
www.agr.gc.ca/agriweb
A national directory of Canadian agriculture and agri-food information resources available via the internet, produced by librarians and information professionals and regularly updated. Searchable by subject, author, keyword and geographic region, or by new additions in the past four weeks.

3025 **Biological & Agricultural Index Plus**
H W Wilson.
www.hwwilson.com/Databases/bioag.htm [DESCRIPTION]
Online bibliographic database indexing English-language periodicals published in the USA and elsewhere. Includes abstracts and full-text coverage for selected journals. Periodical coverage includes both popular and professional scientific journals; about 45% of the focus is on agriculture.

3026 **International union list of agricultural serials**
National Agricultural Library, CAB International and Food and Agriculture Organization CAB International, 1990, 767pp. £120.00. ISBN 0851986617.
A checklist of serials indexed in the databases AGRICOLA, AGRIS and CAB Abstracts. Although now out-of-date for current publishing, it forms a very useful tool for archival searching. Entries give full bibliographic details for each title and indicate in which database it is indexed.

3027 **WWW Virtual Library: Agriculture**
Center for Integrated Pest Management
cipm.ncsu.edu/agVL
Agriculture section of the WWW Virtual Library, maintained by CIPM at North Carolina State University. Can be browsed by region, type of site and subject area.

Digital data, image & text collections

3028 **AgEcon Search: Research in Agricultural and Applied Economics**
University of Minnesota
agecon.lib.umn.edu
A disciplinary archive collecting, indexing, and electronically distributing full text copies of scholarly research in agricultural economics, including agribusiness, food supply, natural resource economics, environmental economics, policy issues, agricultural trade, and economic development. Authors and organizations are encouraged to deposit appropriate scholarly materials in this permanent archive.

3029 **AGORA: Access to Global Online Research in Agriculture**
Food and Agriculture Organization
www.aginternetwork.org/en/index.php
Provides access to over 500 journals from major scientific publishers in the fields of food, agriculture, environmental science and related social sciences. AGORA is available to students and researchers in qualifying not-for-profit institutions in eligible developing countries. The goal is to increase the quality and effectiveness of agricultural research, education and training in low-income countries, and in turn, to improve food security.

3030 **Agricultural Science and Technology Indicators: ASTI**
Consultative Group on International Agricultural Research
www.asti.cgiar.org
Compiles, processes, and makes available internationally comparable data on institutional developments and investments in agricultural R&D worldwide, and analyses and reports on these trends in the form of occasional policy digests for research policy formulation and priority-setting purposes. Searchable database and country profiles.

3031 **Agriculture in the UK 2002**
Great Britain. Department for Environment, Food and Rural Affairs
The Stationery Office, 2003, Annual, 129pp. £19.00. ISBN 0112430708.
www.statistics.gov.uk
Annual statistical survey of UK agriculture, covering key events, farming income, industry, prices, commodities, accounts, productivity, subsidies, public expenditure and environment.
Accessible online: see website.

3032 **Farm Accountancy Data Network: FADN** [EUR]
European Commission. Directorate for Agriculture and Rural Development
europa.eu.int/comm/agriculture/rica/index_en.cfm
Instrument for evaluating the income of agricultural holdings and the impacts of the COMMON AGRICULTURAL POLICY. Derived from national surveys, the FADN is the only source of micro-economic data that is harmonized across Europe.

3033 Farmphoto.com
www.farmphoto.com/photography/forum.asp
A forum for agricultural photography enthusiasts to show and share their work. Begun in 1999, it now contains thousands of photographs listed by topic. Gives contact details for photograph owners, whose permission is required for reproduction.

3034 National Agricultural Statistics Service [USA]
www.usda.gov/nass
Gateway to extensive range of agricultural statistics, charts, maps and historical data for US agriculture. Searchable by commodity, keyword, data and specialists. Includes the developing Agricultural Statistics Data Base containing US and State data, together with county-level data for crops, livestock and farm numbers.

3035 PHYLLIS: the composition of biomass and waste
Energy Research Centre of the Netherlands
www.ecn.nl/phyllis
A database containing information on the composition of biomass and waste. Offers the possibility to obtain the average composition of any combination of groups and/or subgroups, answering queries such as: What is the average sulphur content of wood? What is the ash content of willow? What is the average calorific value of chicken manure?

3036 SAC Farm Diversification Database [UK]
Scottish Agricultural College
www1.sac.ac.uk/management/external/diversification
Series of information sheets on a range of topical alternative enterprises. Each sheet includes a general description of the enterprise, the market, physical requirements, capital and operating costs, possible returns, legal requirements and constraints, grants, training and further reading.

3037 TEEAL: The Essential Electronic Agricultural Library
Cornell University $16,500 (starter pack, 1993–2001).
http://teeal.cornell.edu/index.htm
Available only to developing countries, this CD-ROM library is updated annually and contains over 140 journals, together with a complex bibliographic search engine. In 2004 included the complete text and images from the 1993–2002 journals; annual updates are released one year following the original year of publication. Produced by the University's Albert R Mann Library.

3038 World Census of Agriculture
Food and Agriculture Organization
www.fao.org/ES/ESS/census/default.asp
The Programme for the World Census of Agriculture (WCA) is aimed at encouraging countries to carry out an agricultural census during every decade and provides for the basic concepts, definitions and methodological issues. Produced by the Statistics Division within the FAO's Economic and Social Department.

Directories & encyclopedias

3039 Agricultural Research Organizations on the Web
International Service for National Agricultural Research
www.isnar.cgiar.org/arow/index.htm
A worldwide directory of organizations and universities working in agricultural research that have a home page on the web. Continuously updated and searchable by institution name, acronym, country or region.

3040 Agriculture Fact Book 2001–2002 [USA]
United States. Department of Agriculture US Government Printing Office, 2003, Annual, 174pp. $26.00. ISBN 1000047094.
www.usda.gov/factbook
Annual review of USDA's policies and programs. Topics highlighted in the 2001–2002 edition include homeland security, conservation measures, biotechnology, organic farming and energy policy. Food consumption, American farms and rural America are also featured. The publication is aimed at the general public and encourages use of USDA web resources.
Available online: see website.

3041 Agrilink: Online Rural Enterprise [UK]
www.agrilink.co.uk
Online agricultural directory designed as a central source of information for agricultural and rural organizations, mainly in the UK. Contains over 800 listings for a broad range of agricultural service providers, farmers, manufacturers and suppliers.

3042 Directory of Chinese agricultural and related organizations
Q. Zhang, ed. CAB International, 1994, 368pp. £65.00. ISBN 0851987893.
980 entries covering agriculture in its broadest sense, with full contact and subject coverage information.

3043 Encyclopedia of agricultural, food and biological engineering
D.R. Heldman, ed. Marcel Dekker, 2003, 1184pp. $593.00. ISBN 0824742664.
www.dekker.com
Examines the role of engineering in the production of materials with agricultural origin, including food and non-food consumer goods. Covers the development and design of procedures, equipment, and systems utilized in the production and conversion of raw materials ranging from forest and aquaculture products to biological materials and energy sources.
Available online: see website.

Encyclopedia of biodiversity
S. A. Levin [et al.], eds See entry no. 2163

Encyclopedia of water science
B.A. Stewart and T.A. Howell See entry no. 1147

3044 Environmental management for agriculture 2004 [UK]
British Crop Protection Council 2004. CD-ROM, £40.00.
One of the most comprehensive sources of environmental management advice and assistance, now covering England, Wales and Scotland. Contains over 230 documents (over 3500 pages) of information including government codes of practice, industry guidelines, legislation summaries, contacts directory and information and topic sheets, with decision support modules.

3045 Worldwide agricultural machinery and equipment directory
Agmachine.com Ltd.
www.agmachine.com
Largest specialized directory of agricultural machinery and farm equipment manufacturers on the internet with over 3200 company listings in 63 countries worldwide, including over 2200 direct links to company websites.

Handbooks & manuals

3046 The agrarian history of England and Wales
J. Thirsk and H.P.R. Finberg, eds Cambridge University Press, 1967–2000. 8 v. in 11.
Major scholarly study, published over 33 years, covering prehistory to the outbreak of the Second World War.

3047 Field and laboratory investigations in agroecology
S.R. Gliessman CRC Press, 1999, 336pp. $49.95. ISBN 1566704456.
Laboratory manual providing the theoretical and conceptual framework for the study and analysis of sustainable agro-ecosystems. Investigates 24 topics in sections covering: Environmental factors; Population dynamics in soil systems, Interspecific interactions in cropping, farm and field systems; Food system studies.

- **Agroecology: ecological processes in sustainable agriculture S.R. Gliessman** CRC Press, 1997, 384pp. $69.95. ISBN 1575040433.

3048 Fream's principles of food and agriculture [UK]
C.R.W. Spedding 17th edn, Blackwell Scientific, 1992, 308pp. £25.00. ISBN 0632029781.
Classic work first published in 1892 as *Fream's elements of agriculture*. Earlier editions are of historic interest, painting a picture of the development of UK agriculture throughout the 20th century. This latest and probably final edition is rather thinner than its predecessors.
Rev. edn of Fream's agriculture, 16th edn, 1983 (816p.).

3049 A history of agricultural science in Great Britain 1620–1954
Sir E.J. Russell George Allen & Unwin, 1966, 493pp.
Written by the former director of Rothamsted Experimental Station shortly before his death, this classic account considers agriculture only as husbandry and science only as biology and chemistry, but within those boundaries is comprehensive.

3050 Managing global genetic resources: agricultural crop issues and policies
Committee on Managing Global Genetic Resources National Academies Press, 1993, 480pp. $49.95. ISBN 0309044308.
books.nap.edu/catalog/2116.html [DESCRIPTION]
Anchor volume to the series *Managing global genetic resources* examines the structure that underlies efforts to preserve genetic material, including the worldwide network of genetic collections; the role of biotechnology; and issues surrounding management and use. Other volumes cover livestock, plant germplasm and forest trees.

3051 Practical handbook of agricultural science
A.A. Hanson CRC Press, 1990, 544pp. $160.00. ISBN 0849337062.
A quick reference guide to a variety of topics pertaining to soils, and to the production and use of plants and animals. Emphasis has been devoted to basic considerations in plant adaptation, soils, seeds, major field crops and selected aspects of animal science.

3052 Primrose McConnell's The agricultural notebook [UK]
R.J. Soffe, ed. 19th edn, Blackwell Scientific, 1995, 646pp. ISBN 0632036435.
Primrose McConnell compiled the first edition of *The agricultural notebook* in 1883, since when it has become a standard text on British agriculture, covering crop production, animal production, farm equipment and farm management.

3053 Statistical methods for environmental and agricultural sciences
A.R. Hoshmand 2nd edn, CRC Press, 1997, 464pp. $100.00. ISBN 0849331528.
Shows the relevance of statistical techniques in the fields of agronomy, animal science, plant science, horticulture, agricultural engineering, agricultural business and economics, and environmental sciences. Uses simple, non-mathematical language requiring only a familiarity with elementary algebra and mathematical notations to understand and apply the concepts described.

3054 Statistical methods in agriculture and experimental biology
R. Mead, R.N. Curnow and A.M. Hasted 3rd edn, Chapman and Hall/CRC, 2003, 472pp. £34.99. ISBN 1584881879.
Popular introductory text, including all the basic statistical methods needed by undergraduate and graduate students of agriculture and experimental biology, together with more advanced topics to help develop an appreciation of the breadth of statistical methodology now available. The emphasis is not on mathematical detail, but on ensuring students understand why and when various methods should be used.

3055 Tropical agriculturalist series
R. Coste and A.J. Smith, eds Macmillan, 1987–. Published in association with CTA. French editions are available from Maissoneuve & Larose, Paris.
A comprehensive series of practical field guides and textbooks on many aspects of agricultural production in the tropics, covering both crops and livestock. The books are aimed at extension agents and development workers. They are also used in training and secondary education. The concise texts and small format make them ideal for use in the field.

Keeping up-to-date

3056 AgriCentre [UK]
BASF plc.
www.agricentre.co.uk/site/agricentre.taf [REGISTRATION]
Provides exclusive farm and crop management tools for farmers' day-to-day work, including the latest seasonal pest and disease alerts, comprehensive product technical information, local and national weather and the latest agricultural news. Free service requiring registration.

3057 **Agricultural Policies in OECD Countries**
OECD, 2003, Annual. £43.00. ISBN 9264102299.
www.oecd.org [DESCRIPTION]
Annual providing a comprehensive description and assessment of agricultural and related policy developments in OECD countries, with data on the level and composition of farm support and protection. Evaluates efforts by countries to reform their agricultural policies, and highlights areas needing improvement in OECD countries, notably the continuing wide differences in support levels across countries and among commodities.
Available online: see website.

3058 **FAO Production Yearbook**
Food and Agriculture Organization 2002, no. 56, 2004, Annual, 261pp. £34.00. ISBN 9250049854.
Compilation of statistical data on basic agricultural products for all countries and territories of the world. This edition includes data series on area, yield and production of crops; on livestock numbers and products; and on population, land use, irrigation and farm machinery, for the years 1999–2001.
Series: FAO Statistics Series, 176

3059 **Farm Management Pocketbook** [UK]
J. Nix; Imperial College of Science and Technology 35th edn, 2005, Annual. £15.00.
www.thepocketbook.co.uk [DESCRIPTION]
Widely used and respected yearbook on farm management, containing up-to-date data on gross margins of all the main farm enterprises, together with overhead cost analysis according to farm size and type. It is intended for farmers, managers, advisers, and agents, bankers, accountants and everyone involved with the business of farming. Produced with the Wye College campus of Imperial College.

3060 **OECD Agricultural Outlook 2004/2013**
10th edn, 2004, Annual, 244pp. £35.00. ISBN 926402008X.
www.oecd.org [DESCRIPTION]
Analyses world market trends and medium-term prospects for the main agricultural products, showing how these are influenced by government policies. Detailed commodity projections for production, consumption, trade, stocks and prices in OECD countries and selected information on other countries, including China, Argentina, Russia and Brazil. This edition also analyses how global and domestic forces are shaping agricultural markets over the medium term.
Available online: see website.

Crops & Horticulture

animal feed • arable farming • bamboo • cereals • cocoa • economic plants • fodder • forages • fruit • gardening • grains • herbs • horticulture • industrial crops • maize • mushrooms • non-food crops • plant breeding • potatoes • rattan • rice • seeds • sugar • vegetables • wheat

Introductions to the subject

Plant biotechnology: the genetic manipulation of plants
A. Slater, N.W. Scott and M.R. Fowler See entry no. 5009

Laws, standards, codes

Intellectual property law and the life science industries: a twentieth century history
G. Dutfield See entry no. 5015

Official & quasi-official bodies

3061 **British Potato Council**
www.potato.org.uk
The British Potato Council (BPC) is a non-departmental public body (NDPB) funded by statutory levies, paid by producers and trade purchasers of potatoes. It funds research and development, transfers technology, collects and disseminates market information, and promotes potatoes, at home and in export markets. Free access to British Seed Variety Handbook Online. Market information restricted to members.

3062 **Home Grown Cereals Authority** [UK]
www.hgca.co.uk
HGCA is a non-departmental public body established under the Cereals Marketing Act 1965, with the purpose of improving the production and marketing of cereals and oilseeds grown in the United Kingdom. Excellent set of well presented resources and links covering: Crop research; Varieties; Markets; Exports; Education; Health and nutrition; Non-food.

3063 **International Cocoa Organization**
www.icco.org/index.htm
The Organization was established in 1973 to administer the International Cocoa Agreement (full text of the latest Agreements online), and is the main world forum for the gathering and dissemination of information on cocoa, for the promotion of cocoa research and studies of the economics of cocoa production, consumption and distribution and for the encouragement of development projects.

International Coffee Organization
See entry no. 3155

3064 **International Network for Bamboo and Rattan (INBAR)**
www.inbar.int
An international organization created by 28 Member States of the United Nations, with headquarters in Beijing, China. Through a growing Network of participating organizations and individuals from all continents, INBAR develops and assists in the transfer of appropriate technologies and solutions to benefit the peoples of the world and their environment.

3065 **International Sugar Organization**
www.sugaronline.com/iso
Devoted to improving conditions on the world's sugar market through debate, analysis, special studies and transparent statistics. Administers the 1992 International Sugar Agreement (ISA) (full text online), the objectives of which are: to ensure enhanced international co-operation; to provide a forum for intergovernmental consultations; to facilitate trade by collecting and providing information; and to encourage increased demand for sugar, particularly for non-traditional uses.

Research centres & institutes

3066 Arable Group [UK]
www.arable.co.uk
TAG – The Arable Group – is a company formed by the merger of Arable Research Centres and Morley Research Centre, creating the UK's largest independent agronomy organization, which provides information and advice to arable farmers. Full access limited to members.

3067 Brogdale Horticultural Trust [UK]
www.brogdale.org
Brogdale, in Kent, is the site of the UK National Fruit Collections, a 'living' collection of temperate fruit varieties of great scientific, horticultural and historic importance. The Apple Collection is thought to be the most comprehensive authenticated collection of varieties anywhere and is therefore an internationally recognized genetic resource.

3068 International Consortium for Agricultural Systems Applications
www.icasa.net/index.html
Promotes systems-oriented methodologies in agriculture and natural resources, to advance national and international agricultural systems research through the development and application of compatible and complementary systems analysis tools and methodologies, including the use of crop simulation models.

3069 International Crops Research Institute for the Semi-Arid Tropics
www.icrisat.org/web/index.asp
ICRISAT focuses on the farming systems of the semi-arid tropical areas of the developing world, aiming to help developing countries apply science to increase crop productivity and food security, reduce poverty, and protect the environment. It conserves the seeds of 113,000 lines of crops of dietary importance, breeding them for higher productivity, resistance to pests, diseases, and other stresses.

International Feed Resources Unit
See entry no. 3297

3070 International Maize and Wheat Improvement Center
www.cimmyt.cgiar.org
Headquartered in Mexico, CIMMYT (its acronym in Spanish) conducts research on maize and wheat, in conjunction with partners worldwide. These crops provide about 25% of all food calories consumed in poor countries, and the aim is to help people overcome hunger and poverty and to grow crops without harming the environment.

3071 International Potato Center
www.cipotato.org/index2.asp
The International Potato Center (known worldwide by its Spanish acronym, CIP) seeks to reduce poverty and achieve food security on a sustained basis in developing countries through scientific research and related activities on potato, sweet potato, other root and tuber crops, and on the improved management of natural resources in the Andes and other mountain areas.

3072 International Rice Research Institute
www.irri.org
This CGIAR Institute's main goal is to find sustainable ways to improve the well being of present and future generations of poor rice farmers and consumers while at the same time protecting the environment. Site has comprehensive links to major rice resources, including world statistics, networks, genetic resources, training, media resources and publications.

3073 National Non-Food Crops Centre [UK]
www.nnfcc.co.uk/index.cfm
The NNFCC's remit includes the use of all plant-derived materials, derivatives and by-products for commercial non-food purposes, with the exception of plants grown for ornamental purposes and forestry grown solely for timber. Builds on the activities of the Plant Protein Club and the Alternative Crop Technology Interactive Network (ACTIN) which previously promoted scientific and technological advance in the use of non-food crops and their uptake by industry.

3074 NIAB [UK]
www.niab.com
NIAB is an independent plant sciences company providing a range of technical, research and consultancy services based in Cambridge. Produces the journal *Plant Genetic Resources: characterization and utilization*, published by CABI.

3075 Poisonous Plant Research Laboratory [USA]
www.pprl.ars.usda.gov
Aims to identify toxic plants, isolate and identify plant toxins, determine the mechanism of toxicity, document toxin metabolism and clearance from tissues, develop diagnostic and prognostic procedures, identify conditions of poisoning, and develop management strategies, antidotes, treatments and other recommendations to reduce losses, insure product quality and promote animal and human health.

3076 Processors and Growers Research Organisation [UK]
www.pgro.co.uk
UK centre for applied research on temperate peas and beans. Studies the agronomy and harvesting of new varieties and new ideas on usage, helping to underpin the expansion of pulse crops and improve the reliability, ease of growing and value of peas, beans and lupins.

3077 Rothamsted Research [UK]
www.rothamsted.ac.uk
The largest land-focused institute in the UK and the oldest in the world, Rothamsted's scientific research ranges from studies of genetics, biochemistry, cell biology and soil processes to investigations at the ecosystem and landscape scale. Its library is one of the oldest specialist agricultural collections in the UK. Very well structured website offering good sets of resources 'for the public' as well as for fellow research scientists.

3078 Scottish Crop Research Institute
www.scri.sari.ac.uk
Aims to increase knowledge in the basic biological sciences; to improve crop quality and utilization by the application of conventional and molecular genetical techniques and novel agronomic practices; and to develop environmentally benign

methods of protecting crops from depredations by pests, pathogens and weeds.

3079 **Warwick HRI** [UK]
www2.hri.ac.uk
Warwick HRI, formerly Horticulture Research International, now a devolved department of the University of Warwick, is the principal UK organization tasked with carrying out horticultural research and development and transferring the results to industry. Site offers background articles browsable by commodity or research theme.

3080 **World Cocoa Foundation**
www.chocolateandcocoa.org
A comprehensive program which aims to 'take science into the field', improving production efficiency, increasing farmer yields, and using cocoa to promote production reforestation of degraded tropical lands in a sustainable, environmentally responsible manner. Site offers a document resource centre and overview of all aspects of the industry.

Associations & societies

3081 **American Feed Industry Association**
www.afia.org/index.html
AFIA represents the business, legislative and regulatory interests of the animal feed and pet food industries and their suppliers in the US. It monitors and influences state and federal legislative and regulatory actions on issues such as genetically modified organisms (GMOs), bovine spongiform encephalopathy (BSE), dioxin, clean water, environmental activism, and industrial ergonomics, aiming to provide reasonable, science and fact-based responses.

3082 **American Society for Horticultural Science**
www.ashs.org/index.html
Founded in 1903, ASHS promotes horticultural science through research and education. It publishes several highly-cited journals and the site offers career advice and an extensive resources section including web links and video interviews, some of which require membership for full access.

3083 **Crop Science Society of America**
www.crops.org
An educational and scientific organization composed of more than 4700 members dedicated to the advancement of crop science, including crops in relation to seed genetics and plant breeding; crop physiology; crop production, quality and ecology; crop germplasm resources; and environmental quality.

3084 **CropLife International**
www.croplife.org
A global network representing the plant science industry, which aims through balancing environmental, economic and societal concerns to contribute to promoting sustainable agriculture, fundamental to food production and poverty alleviation. Useful set of links and other resources in the Library section of the website.

European Biomass Association
See entry no. 4792

3085 **Grain and Feed Trade Association**
www.gafta.com
The only worldwide trade association for the grain and feed industry, comprising international grain and feed traders, has been in existence for 125 years and currently has members in 80 countries. Its aim is to promote and protect the interests of its members in the trade of grain, animal feed, pulses and rice worldwide.

3086 **Horticultural Trades Association** [UK]
www.the-hta.org.uk/index.asp
Trade association representing the UK garden industry. Founded over 100 years ago, it promotes the profitable growth of its retail and grower members through a comprehensive range of business support initiatives. It provides a forum for identifying and dealing with key garden industry issues and opportunities, represents the views of the industry to Government and is its voice in the media.

3087 **Institute of Horticulture** [UK]
www.horticulture.org.uk
Represents all those professionally engaged in horticulture in the UK and Ireland. Arranges meetings and events, and gives advice on training. Publishes *The Horticulturalist*, with indexes and book reviews online.

3088 **International Herb Association**
www.iherb.org
Professional trade association providing educational, service and development opportunities for those involved in herbal endeavours. Provides newsletters, publications and conferences and strives to provide the latest information on growing, marketing and using herbs.

3089 **International Society for Horticultural Science**
www.ishs.org
The ISHS, originated in 1864, formally established in 1959 and with members in 128 countries, is the leading independent organization of horticultural scientists in the world. Publication series *Acta Horticulturae* available online, including over 30,000 articles, also online directory of international horticultural research.

3090 **International Society for Mushroom Science**
www.hri.ac.uk/isms
Seeks to further the cultivation of edible (including medicinal) macrofungi. It is non-political and non-profit making. The objectives of ISMS are the dissemination of information on new developments and the science of mushrooms and to stimulate exchange of new ideas between growers and scientists around the world.

Royal Horticultural Society
See entry no. 2222

Portal & task environments

3091 **BioMatNet: biological materials for non-food products** [EUR]
European Commission. Directorate for Research CPL Press.
www.nf-2000.org/home.html
This site makes available results of projects supported by the European Commission in the area of Biological Materials for Non-Food Products (Renewable Bioproducts), including

bulk chemicals and biofuels, integrated crop protection, cosmetics, drugs and vaccines, bioplastics, polymers and packaging, biocomposites/boards, wood products, speciality chemicals and other products.

3092 British Sugar: the portal site for sugar users
British Sugar plc.
www.britishsugar.co.uk/index.htm
This commercial site for British Sugar includes useful information on the history and processes of sugar production, and position statements by the British beet sugar industry.

CropBiotech.Net
International Service for the Acquisition of Agri-biotech Applications
See entry no. 5030

3093 FAO Crop and Grassland Service: AGPC
Food and Agriculture Organization
www.fao.org/WAICENT
Intended to help FAO member countries achieve sustainable increases in production of crops and grasslands, through plant improvement, application of plant biotechnology, development of integrated production systems, and rational grassland management. Site provides information about crop groups, themes, services and resources.

- **Grassland index** www.fao.org/ag/AGP/AGPC/doc/crops/4d.html. Basic information in this index was taken from two FAO publications published in 1988 and 1990 and continues to be updated. Obtains information on habitat, distribution, uses, etc. with references.

3094 Forage Information System: FIS
Oregon State University
forages.oregonstate.edu
FIS WWW is a global forage information resource envisioned to become a comprehensive information system for all aspects of forages, providing links to peer-reviewed worldwide information.

The Garden Web
See entry no. 2241

3095 Interactive European Network for Industrial Crops and their Applications: IENICA
European Commission. Directorate for Research
www.ienica.net
The IENICA project is an overarching network linking otherwise independent organizations and initiatives which are involved in the development of renewable materials from crops throughout Europe, and its accessing and associated states.

3096 International Crop Information System
Consultative Group on International Agricultural Research
www.icis.cgiar.org
A database system designed to provide integrated management of global information on genetic resources, crop improvement and evaluation for individual crops, being developed by genetic resource specialists, crop scientists and information technicians in several CGIAR and other research centres.

3097 International Rice Information System: IRIS
International Rice Research Institute
www.iris.irri.org
IRIS is the rice implementation of the International Crop Information System (ICIS) providing integrated management of global information on genetic resources and crop cultivars. This includes germplasm pedigrees, field evaluations, genetic (QTL) maps, structural and functional genomic data (including links to external plant databases) and environmental (GIS) data.

3098 Introduction to Horticulture [UK]
Great Britain. Department for Environment, Food and Rural Affairs
www.defra.gov.uk/hort/hortindx.htm
Home page for Defra's information on horticulture, covering quality standards helping free trade both in Europe and internationally, monitoring of the quality of fresh fruit and vegetables and advice on efficient growing and marketing.

- **Database of UK public research on non-food uses of crops** http://aims.defra.gov.uk/default.asp. Website established to provide a focal point for information on the UK funding bodies and R&D relevant to non- food crops.

3099 Plant Varieties & Seeds [UK]
Great Britain. Department for Environment, Food and Rural Affairs
www.defra.gov.uk/planth/pvs/default.htm
The UK Plant Variety Rights Office & Seeds Division of DEFRA provides: *Plant Breeders Rights* Offers legal protection for the investment plant breeders make in breeding and developing new varieties; *National Listing* Ensures no new variety can be marketed unless it is genuinely new and an improvement on varieties already being sold; *Seed Certification* Quality assurance process which ensures that seed is not marketed unless it meets specified standards.

Digital data, image & text collections

3100 Animal Feed Resources Information System: AFRIS
Food and Agriculture Organization
www.fao.org/WAICENT
Interactive searches, comments and contributions including feed safety, quality control and country profiles. Access by common and Latin names, with additional graphic interface by category – fodder, grasses, roots, etc. – under development. Bibliographic details of source references provided.

3101 Basic Horticultural Statistics [UK]
Great Britain. Department for Environment, Food and Rural Affairs and Office for National Statistics
statistics.defra.gov.uk/esg/publications/bhs
Annual publication designed to provide easy-to-reference, comprehensive statistics on the production and value of horticultural crops grown in the United Kingdom. Also includes some statistics on potatoes and hops and overseas trade data. Covers an 11-year period. Five issues online, in pdf and Excel formats.

3102 Country Pasture/Forage Resource Profiles
Food and Agriculture Organization
www.fao.org/ag/AGP
The FAO Grassland and Pasture Crops Group is developing a series of country profiles providing a broad overview of relevant general, topographical, climatic and agro-ecological information with a focus on livestock production systems and the pasture/forage resource, plus information concerning key

institutions, personnel, current research interests and selected references.

3103 **GrainGenes: A Database for Triticeae and Avena**
United States. Department of Agriculture
wheat.pw.usda.gov/index.shtml
GrainGenes is a compilation of molecular and phenotypic information on wheat, barley, rye, triticale, and oats. Searchable genetic database with additional information covering genomics, mapping, germplasm, pathology and taxonomy.

3104 **The Greek Vitis Database**
F. Lefort and K.A. Roubelakis-Angelakis; University of Crete
www.biology.uch.gr/gvd
A multimedia web-backed genetic database for germplasm management of Vitis resources in Greece. It attempts to present all the possible information about Greek cultivars including genetic data and ampelographic data. The databases will be upgraded permanently along with the production and publication of new data.

Directories & encyclopedias

3105 **Chemical dictionary of economic plants**
J.B. Harborne and H. Baxter Wiley, 2001, 236pp. $310.00. ISBN 0471492264.
Alphabetically arranged compilation listing plant substances found to be essential and invaluable in man's life and well being. Entries grouped as follows: medicinal plants; food plants; essential oils; oils and fats; dyestuffs; tannins; plant biocides; hallucinogenics; gums and rubbers; waxes and resins; plant fibres.

3106 **Encyclopedia of applied plant sciences**
B. Thomas, D.J. Murphy and B.G. Murray, ed. Elsevier Academic Press, 2003. 3 v, $995.00. ISBN 0122270509.
Covers the application of advances in biological sciences, especially advances in cell and molecular biology, to the production of sustainable, low pesticide food, feed and food ingredients, and renewable raw materials for industry and society, together with continuing advances in the areas of ecology, plant pathology, plant genetics, plant physiology, plant biochemistry, and biotechnology, addressing core knowledge, theories, and techniques and applications in research and industry.

3107 **Encyclopedia of grain science**
C. Wrigley, H. Corke and C.E. Walker, eds Elsevier Academic Press, 2004, 1700pp. 3 v, $795.00. ISBN 0127654909.
Stressing the paramount role of cereals as a global food source, coverage ranges from the genetics of grains to commercial, economic and social aspects, plus the biology and chemistry of grains, the applied aspects of grain production and processing into various food and beverage products.

3108 **Encyclopedia of plant and crop science**
R.M. Goodman, ed. Marcel Dekker, 2003, 950pp. $593.00. ISBN 0824742680.
www.dekker.com/servlet/product/productid/E-EPCS [DESCRIPTION]
Covers every aspect of plant breeding, including classic and modern studies in plant biology in conjunction with research, applications, and innovations in crop science. Topics range from the fundamentals of plant growth and reproduction to developments in agronomy and agricultural science, including genetics, genomics and genetic engineering.
Available online: see website.

3109 **Encyclopedia of rose science**
A. Roberts, S. Gudin and T. Debener, eds Elsevier Academic Press, 2003, 1200pp. 3 v, $640.00. ISBN 0122276205.
Ranges over 35 subject areas from the history of rose cultivation to discoveries in rose genetics, for researchers and students, as well as commercial rose growers and breeders, and avid amateurs. Incorporates *Modern roses XI*, published by the American Rose Society as International Cultivar Registration Authority for Roses, the most comprehensive list of roses of historical and botanical importance. Extensive illustration and exhaustive indexing.

3110 **The New York Botanical Garden illustrated encyclopedia of horticulture** [USA]
T.H. Everett Garland, 1980–1982, 3601pp. 10 v., available separately, $1000.00.
Comprehensive reference work covering over 26,000 species, entered under botanical name and cross-referenced from common names. Well illustrated, mostly in black-and-white.

The plant-book: a portable dictionary of the vascular plants
D.J. Mabberley See entry no. 2258

3111 **World economic plants: a standard reference**
J. H. Wiersema and B. Leon CRC Press, 1999, 792pp. $150.00. ISBN 0849321190.
Covers almost 10,000 vascular plants of commercial importance throughout the world. For each plant the accepted scientific name, synonyms, common names, economic uses, and geographical distribution are provided. Offers a means for international standardization in nomenclature of economic plants.

Handbooks & manuals

3112 **Fertiliser recommendations for agricultural and horticultural crops** [UK]
Great Britain. Department for Environment, Food and Rural Affairs 7th edn, The Stationery Office, 2000, 175pp. ISBN 0112430589.
www.defra.gov.uk/environ/pollute/rb209
First published in 1973, the recommendations are based on the latest research and intended to be of practical value to the agricultural industry, giving the best financial return for the farmer. Covers: Principles; Organic manures; Using the tables; Arable and forage crops; Vegetables and bulbs; Fruit, vines and hops; Grass.
Available online: see website.

Handbook of plant biotechnology
P. Christou and H.J. Klee, eds See entry no. 5043

3113 **The Hillier manual of trees & shrubs** [UK]
J. Hillier and A. Coombes, eds 8th edn, David & Charles, 2002, 511pp. £19.99. ISBN 0715310739.
Classic handbook describing over 9000 plants representing more than 650 genera, including sections on nomenclature and classification, planting, pruning and planning, an illustrated glossary and notes on horticultural awards.

3114 **The Royal Horticultural Society encyclopaedia of gardening**
C. Brickell, ed. Bicentenary edn, Dorling Kindersley, 2004, 751pp. £35.00. ISBN 1405303530.
http://uk.dk.com/static/cs/uk/11/features/rhs [DESCRIPTION]
Offers expert RHS advice on the entire range of gardening techniques, aimed at both amateur and professional gardeners. Over 3000 colour illustrations and step-by-step guides.

Keeping up-to-date

3115 **Feed Situation and Outlook Yearbook** [USA]
United States. Department of Agriculture and Cornell University 2004, Annual.
usda.mannlib.cornell.edu/reports/erssor/field/fds-bby
This annual report examines world and US production, consumption, trade, stocks, and prices for feed grains (focusing on corn). Includes special articles related to the feed grain industry. A supplement to *Feed Outlook*, available online at the same URL.

Fisheries

marine fish stocks • sea fisheries

Introductions to the subject

Biology of fishes
Q. Bone, N.B. Marshall and J.H.S. Blaxter See entry no. 2557

Fish of Britain & Europe
P.J. Miller and M.J. Loates See entry no. 2559

3116 **Fisheries ecology and management**
C. Walters and S.J.D. Martell Princeton University Press, 2004, 448pp. $45.00. ISBN 0691115451.
'Quantitative modeling methods have become a central tool in the management of harvested fish populations. This book examines how these modeling methods work, why they sometimes fail, and how they might be improved by incorporating larger ecological interactions. Fisheries Ecology and Management provides a broad introduction to the concepts and quantitative models needed to successfully manage fisheries.'
'This book is the next major contribution to the field of fisheries science. Walters and Martell provide fresh and non-intuitive perspectives on a variety of issues. Their merciless slaughtering of cherished sacred cows is supported by sound scholarship, and cogent, well-reasoned arguments. This will become a landmark work.' (*Jeffrey Hutchings, Dalhousie University*)

Oceans 2020: science, trends, and the challenge of sustainability
J.G. Field, G. Hempel and C.P. Summerhayes, eds; Intergovernmental Oceanographic Commission, Scientific Committee on Oceanic Research and Scientific Committee on Problems of the Environment
See entry no. 1350

Dictionaries, thesauri, classifications

3117 **Aqualex: a glossary of aquaculture terms**
M. Eleftheriou, ed. Aqualex Multimedia Consortium Ltd, 1997, 397pp. €50.00.
www.feap.info/home/aqualex_en.asp
Four-language glossary of 2750 aquaculture terms, with separate indexes for English, French, German and Greek. A CD-ROM edition includes instant definition and translation, and sound recordings of native-speaker pronunciation.
Available online: see website.

Elsevier's dictionary of marine pollution: English–Spanish, with English and Spanish indexes (Diccionario de contaminación del mar)
L.-J. Zilberberg, comp. See entry no. 5543

Laws, standards, codes

3118 **Code of Conduct for Responsible Fisheries**
Food and Agriculture Organization
www.fao.org/fi/agreem/codecond/codecon.asp
The Code sets out principles and international standards of behaviour for responsible practices with a view to ensuring the effective conservation, management and development of living aquatic resources, with due respect for the ecosystem and biodiversity. Full text of the Code and explanatory documentation.

Official & quasi-official bodies

3119 **The Common Fisheries Policy** [EUR]
European Commission. Directorate for Fisheries
europa.eu.int/comm/fisheries/policy_en.htm
Website of the European Commission's Directorate-General for Fisheries and of the Common Fisheries Policy (CFP). Aimed at practitioners and the general public, it contains news, factsheets, legislation, publications, press releases and other materials giving a comprehensive briefing on the CFP.

3120 **Fisheries Research Services** [UK]
www.marlab.ac.uk
An agency of the Scottish Executive Environment and Rural Affairs Department (SEERAD). FRS provides expert scientific and technical advice to Government on marine and freshwater fisheries, aquaculture and the protection of the aquatic environment.

National Marine Fisheries
See entry no. 2573

3121 **Sea Fish Industry Authority** [UK]
www.seafish.org
Works across all sectors of the UK seafood industry to promote good quality, sustainable seafood, conducting research and projects aimed at raising standards, improving efficiency and ensuring viable development of the industry. Established in 1981 as a non-departmental public body (NDPB) sponsored by the four UK government fisheries departments and funded by a levy on seafood. Good Resources section including a valuable Photo Gallery and an extensive Links section.

Research centres & institutes

3122 **AKVAFORSK**
www.akvaforsk.no/english/index.html
AKVAFORSK is an international research institution for aquaculture, specializing in breeding and genetics, product quality and marine species. It also conducts research related to fish health, environment and operational optimalization. Its objectives are to acquire and publish aquaculture expertise, thereby contributing to a strong and profitable industry with social benefit.

3123 **Alaska Fisheries Science Center**
www.afsc.noaa.gov/default.htm
The Centre generates scientific information necessary for the conservation, management, and utilization of the living marine resources in the coastal oceans off Alaska and parts of the west coast of the United States. Site offers news, information on programs and issues, datasheets on species and searchable databases on fishery, oceanography, marine mammal, and environmental research, plus publications and images.

3124 **CEH Windermere** [UK]
www.ceh.ac.uk/aboutceh/lancaster.htm
CEH Windermere (formerly the Institute of Freshwater Ecology) conducts research to develop an integrated theory for the science and management of fresh and estuarine waters. Research is carried out in four sections: Fish biology, Microbial ecology, Aquatic processes; Phyto-Limnology.
Early 2005 undergoing reorganization following the formation of a new Lancaster Environment Centre.

3125 **Centre for Environment Fisheries and Aquaculture Science** [UK]
www.cefas.co.uk/homepage.htm
Founded in 1902, CEFAS is an internationally renowned scientific research and advisory centre working in fisheries management, environmental protection and aquaculture. Four public online databases provide environmental and fisheries data for the UK shelf and beyond, real time wave data, spatial data for contaminants, and a range of physico-chemical and environmental variables in the southern North Sea.

3126 **Federal Research Centre for Fisheries** [GER]
www.bfa-fish.de/index-e.html
Institution within the administration of the German Federal Ministry of Food, Agriculture and Forestry. The Centre is composed of 5 research institutes; the Institute for Fishery Technology; Institute for Biochemistry and Technology; Institute for Fishery Ecology; Institute for Baltic Sea Fisheries; and the Institute for Sea Fisheries. Includes information and documentation service.

3127 **WorldFish Center**
www.worldfishcenter.org
Is a 'unique international research center involved in research on fisheries and other living aquatic resources, aiming to improve productivity; protect the environment; save biodiversity; improve policies; and strengthen national programs'. Formerly known as ICLARM. Includes Ian R. Smith Memorial Library and Documentation Center, with online catalogue.

Associations & societies

3128 **American Fisheries Society**
www.fisheries.org
Founded in 1870, AFS promotes scientific research and enlightened management of resources for optimum use and enjoyment by the public. It also encourages a comprehensive education for fisheries scientists and continuing on-the-job training. Its well respected fisheries research journals are available online to AFS members.

3129 **Fisheries Society of the British Isles**
www.le.ac.uk/biology/fsbi
Learned society catering for the interests of professional fish biologists and fisheries managers. It promotes and supports all branches of fish biology and fisheries science and conservation, and produces the *Journal of Fish Biology*.

Marine Fish Conservation Network
See entry no. 2597

Portal & task environments

3130 **Aquaculture compendium**
CAB International, University of Stirling and Asian Institute of Technology 2005.
www.cabi.org/compendia/ac
Forthcoming compendium in CABI's well respected series, covering aquaculture and aquatic resource management in the broader context, including information on all cultured species in freshwater, brackish and marine cultured systems, their production and health.

Aquaculture Network Information Centre: AquaNIC
Mississippi-Alabama Sea Grant Consortium See entry no. 2611

3131 **Fish Information & Services: FIS**
fis.com
Global seafood industry information site founded in 1995. It aims to deliver reliable, timely, comprehensive worldwide fishing, seafood, and aquaculture information in English, Spanish, Japanese, and Russian. Some sections, including market reports and prices, restricted to members.

3132 **Fisheries**
Food and Agriculture Organization
www.fao.org/fi/default_all.asp
FAO's Major Programme on Fisheries aims to promote sustainable development of responsible fisheries and contribute to food security, including global monitoring and strategic analysis of fisheries. Includes access to the Fisheries Information Center.

3133 **Introduction to Fisheries** [UK]
Great Britain. Department for Environment, Food and Rural Affairs
www.defra.gov.uk/fish/fishindx.htm
Home page for DEFRA's fisheries information, including the UK fishing industry, grants and financial assistance, conservation, aquaculture and fish health, marine environment, e-commerce, Restrictive Licensing System for Fishing Vessels, Fishing Vessel Decommissioning Scheme, and the Centre for Environment, Fisheries and Aquaculture Science (CEFAS).

3134 **OneFish**
Support unit for International Fisheries and Aquatic Research
www.onefish.org/global/index.jsp
A fishery projects portal and participatory resource gateway for the fisheries and aquatic research and development sector. Includes Fish Technology Knowledge Base. Covers donors/projects, aquaculture, marine and coastal fisheries, stakeholder/organizations, freshwater fisheries, utilization and technology.

ReefBase: A Global Information System on Coral Reefs
WorldFish Center See entry no. 2623

Discovering print & electronic resources

Aquatic Sciences and Fisheries Abstracts: ASFA
See entry no. 2627

Fish & Fisheries Worldwide
See entry no. 2628

Digital data, image & text collections

FishBase
R. Froese and D. Pauly, eds See entry no. 2638

3135 **Marine Stocks at Risk of Extinction** [USA]
American Fisheries Society
www.fisheries.org
The first-ever list of marine fish stocks and species at risk of extinction (MSRE) identifies 82 species or populations vulnerable, threatened, or endangered in North American waters. Twenty-two species are categorized as vulnerable, threatened, or endangered to global extinction.

Directories & encyclopedias

3136 **Encyclopedia of aquaculture**
R.R. Stickney Wiley, 2000, 1088pp. $425.00. ISBN 0471291013.
A comprehensive reference to the science, technology, and economics of aquaculture, containing over 150 entries covering: primary species being cultured worldwide, and under development; echinoderms, molluscs, crustaceans, and finfishes; aquaculture for food, research, bait, aquariums, and endangered species recovery; management techniques; aquaculture systems; environmental issues; business plans, marketing, and sales. Includes photographs, illustrations, graphs and extensive references.
'This impressive volume is the first work of its kind to cover the growing field ... in an encyclopedic format ... Public libraries ... and academic libraries with aquaculture programs ... will want to invest in this important and unique resource.' (*American Reference Books Annual*)

Handbooks & manuals

3137 **Handbook of fish biology and fisheries**
P.J.B. Hart and J.D. Reynolds Blackwell Publishing, 2002, 849pp. 2 v., £130.00. ISBN 0632064838.
Aims to provide the biological knowledge required to understand how fish stocks respond to exploitation, including evolutionary relationships, morphological diversity, behaviour and ecology. V. 1. *Fish biology*; V. 2. *Fisheries*.

Ichthyology handbook
B.G. Kapoor and B. Khanna, eds See entry no. 2644

3138 **Ken Schultz's fishing encyclopedia: worldwide angling guide**
K. Schultz Wiley, 1999, 1936pp. $60.00. ISBN 0028620577.
Aimed at both freshwater and saltwater anglers at all levels of experience, over 2000 detailed entries and over 1400 colour illustrations and photos cover every aspect of fishing today, including fish species, equipment, places, techniques, and a wide array of other information.

3139 **The State of World Fisheries and Aquaculture: SOFIA**
Food and Agriculture Organization 2002, Biennial, 150pp. PDF. ISBN 9251048428.
www.fao.org/sof/sofia/index_en.htm
The FAO Fisheries Department's premier advocacy document. Published every two years with the purpose of providing policy-makers, civil society and those who derive their livelihood from the sector a comprehensive, objective and global view of capture fisheries and aquaculture, including associated policy issues.

Food Science & Technology

bee-keeping • beer • beverage industry • brewing • butter • cheese • coffee • dairy sciences • drinks industry • eggs • fair trade • food additives • food analysis • food inspection • food microbiology • food policy • food programmes • food safety • food security • food standards • food supply • food technology • meat sciences • wine

Introductions to the subject

3140 **Cambridge world history of food**
K.F. Kiple and K.C. Ornelas, eds Cambridge University Press, 2000, 1958pp. 2 v., £150.00. ISBN 0521402166.
Exceptional work encapsulating much of what is known of the history of food and nutrition. Covering the full spectrum of foods that have been hunted, gathered, cultivated, and domesticated; their nutritional makeup and uses; and their impact on cultures and demography, including food fads, prejudices, taboos, food toxins, additives, labelling, and entitlements. Provides a dictionary offering brief histories of plant foods mentioned in the text – over 1000 in all – with common names and synonyms.
'A magisterial achievement. Food has long been central to humankind's relationship to the earth, and anyone interested in that relationship will find here an endless source of knowledge and insight. The book's perspective is sweeping, its ecological and cultural significance is profound.' (Donald Worster, University of Kansas. titles.cambridge.org/catalogue.asp?isbn=0521402166 [27/08/04])

3141 **A history of beer and brewing**
I.S. Hornsey Royal Society of Chemistry, 2003, 632pp. £39.95. ISBN 0854046305.
A comprehensive account of the history of beer covering a

time-span of around 8000 years, considering how, and why, the first fermented beverages originated. It establishes some of the parameters that encompass the diverse range of alcoholic beverages assigned the generic name 'beer' and considers the dissemination of early brewing technologies from their Near Eastern origins. Aimed at both an enthusiast and scholarly readership.

3142 Introduction to food biotechnology
P. Johnson-Green CRC Press, 2002, 312pp. $89.95. ISBN 0849311527.
Undergraduate-level text providing comprehensive coverage of food biotechnology issues, including case studies, consumer issues and regulatory concerns. Discusses gene-cloning strategies, applications of transgenic research to crops and food animals, and diagnostic methods based on the use of DNA, antibodies, and biosensors.

3143 Introduction to food engineering
R.P. Singh and D.R. Heldman 3rd edn, Academic Press, 2001, 682pp. $77.95. ISBN 0126463840.
http://books.elsevier.com [DESCRIPTION]
Now standard wide-ranging introduction.

Dictionaries, thesauri, classifications

Benders' dictionary of nutrition and food technology
D.A. Bender and A.E. Bender See entry no. 4382

3144 Epicurious wine dictionary
R. Herbst and S.T. Herbst CondéNet.
eat.epicurious.com/dictionary/wine
This dictionary from Epicurious, a food portal, contains more than 3500 terms related to wine and its production, which can be searched (with truncation) or browsed. Each record gives a phonetic spelling of the term and a definition, with cross-references to other entries. The source is the book *Wine lover's companion* by Ron Herbst and Sharon Tyler Herbst. There is a companion online food dictionary.

Laws, standards, codes

3145 Codex Alimentarius Commission
www.codexalimentarius.net
The Commission was created in 1963 by FAO and WHO to develop food standards, guidelines and related texts such as codes of practice under the Joint FAO/WHO Food Standards Programme, which aims to protect consumer health, ensure fair trade practices in the food trade, and promote co-ordination of all food standards work undertaken by international governmental and non-governmental organizations.

- **Understanding the Codex Alimentarius Food and Agriculture Organization and World Health Organization**1999. ISBN 9251042489. www.fao.org/docrep/w9114e/W9114e00.htm.

3146 Fairtrade Labelling Organizations International
www.fairtrade.net
FLO is the worldwide Fairtrade Standard setting and Certification organization. It permits more than 800,000 producers, workers and their dependants in more than 45 countries to benefit from labelled Fairtrade. FLO guarantees that products sold anywhere in the world with a Fairtrade label marketed by a National Initiative conforms to Fairtrade Standards and contributes to the development of disadvantaged producers.

3147 Food and Drug Law Institute [USA]
www.fdli.org
The Food and Drug Law Institute is committed to providing high quality education and a neutral forum for the generation of ideas and discussion of law and public policy in the US for its legal, policy and regulatory communities.

3148 Foodlaw-Reading
D.J. Jukes; University of Reading
www.foodlaw.rdg.ac.uk
Information on food law affecting the UK, designed for students but suitable for other interested parties. Content includes news on UK and EU food law, lecture material, information on UK regulations and standards (subject and chronological listings), example court cases, and information on EU legislation and international food law.

3149 International Office of Vine and Wine
www.oiv.int
Intergovernmental organization established 1924. Has particular role in international harmonization of practices and standards but the website – translated into English – is a good entrée to resources about vine and wine.

3150 NetRegs: Food and Drink Manufacture [UK]
Environment Agency
www.environment-agency.gov.uk/netregs
The UK Environmental Agency's guidance for small- and medium-sized enterprises (SMEs) on environmental legislation. NetRegs aims to provide practical advice on how to comply with environmental legislation and reduce the impact of a business on the environment.

Official & quasi-official bodies

3151 Canadian Food Inspection Agency
www.inspection.gc.ca
The Canadian Food Inspection Agency delivers all federal inspection services related to food; animal health; and plant protection. Extensive site contains many guidance documents and full-text legislation.

3152 European Food Safety Authority
europa.eu.int/comm/food/efsa_en.htm
EFSA provides the European Commission with independent scientific advice on all matters with a direct or indirect impact on food safety. It is a separate legal entity, independent from the other EU institutions. EFSA's work covers all stages of food production and supply, from primary production to the safety of animal feed, right through to the supply of food to consumers.

- **Gateway to Government Food Safety Information** www.foodsafety.gov. Wide-ranging US government site covering news, consumer advice, children and teenagers, illnesses, pathogens, the industry, food safety programmes, food agencies.

3153 Food and Drug Administration
www.fda.gov
FDA's mission is: to promote and protect the public health by

helping safe and effective products reach the market in a timely way; to monitor products for continued safety after they are in use, and to help the public get the accurate, science-based information needed to improve health. Comprehensive site gives detailed information on all these areas.

3154 **Food Standards Agency** [UK]
www.food.gov.uk
An independent food safety watchdog set up by an Act of Parliament in 2000 to protect the public's health and consumer interests in relation to food. Covers diet and health, safety, hygiene, labelling, BSE, GM and novel foods, with latest news and alerts.

- **The BSE Enquiry** www.bseinquiry.gov.uk. Archive site containing the full text of the *Report of the BSE Inquiry* set up by UK Parliament in 1998 and published in 2000, together with all supporting evidence.

Home Grown Cereals Authority
See entry no. 3062

3155 **International Coffee Organization**
www.ico.org
Set up in London in 1963 under the auspices of the United Nations, ICO is the main intergovernmental organization for coffee, bringing together producing and consuming countries to tackle the challenges facing the world coffee sector through international co-operation. Site contains text of the 2001 International Coffee Agreement and supporting documentation.

3156 **International Union of Food Science & Technology**
www.iufost.org/index.cfm
The sole global food science and technology organization: a voluntary, non-profit association of national food science organizations linking food scientists and technologists. Full scientific member of the INTERNATIONAL COUNCIL FOR SCIENCE. Aims to: Support international progress, co-operation and exchange of ideas in all areas of food science; Advance technology in the processing, manufacturing, preservation, storage and distribution of food products; Stimulate appropriate education and training; Foster professionalism and professional organization.

Meat and Livestock Commission
See entry no. 3296

3157 **World Food Programme**
www.wfp.org
Set-up in 1963, WFP is the United Nations frontline agency in the fight against global hunger, providing emergency relief, operating food-for-growth programmes using food aid as preventative medicine, and self-reliance through food-for-work programmes. Site includes extensive news coverage and downloadable background documents.

Research centres & institutes

3158 **Bee Research Laboratory** [USA]
www.barc.usda.gov/psi/brl
The 'Beltsville Bee Lab', as it is often referred to, founded over a century ago, conducts research on bee diseases and pests. It uses biological, molecular, chemical and non-chemical approaches to ensure an adequate supply of bees for pollination and honey production, and provides a bee diagnostic service. Searchable Beekeeping Bibliography covering 1905–1973 (for later coverage see AGRICOLA.)

3159 **Campden & Chorleywood Food Research Association** [UK]
www.campden.co.uk
CCFRA Group is the UK's largest independent membership-based organization carrying out research and development for the food and drinks industry worldwide, providing industry with the research, technical and advisory services needed to ensure product safety and quality, process efficiency and product and process innovation. Includes links to food legislation sites, news, factsheets and online shop for CCFRA publications.

Center for Veterinary Medicine
See entry no. 3388

Food and Agricultural Policy Research Institute
See entry no. 2978

3160 **Global Salm-Surv: GSS**
World Health Organization
www.who.int/salmsurv/en
A World Health Organization project, Global Salm-Surv is a global network of laboratories and individuals involved in surveillance, isolation, identification and antimicrobial resistance testing of *Salmonella*. Includes a country databank and background information.

3161 **Hannah Research Institute** [UK]
www.hri.sari.ac.uk
Founded in 1928 to support the dairy industry, HRI now covers all levels of biological organization from whole animals, through organs, tissues and cells, to the molecular, operating in two research divisions: Hannah Biomedical and CHARIS Food Research. The Directorship of the Institute is a joint appointment with the University of Glasgow.

Institute of Food Research
See entry no. 4383

3162 **International Food Policy Research Institute**
www.ifpri.org
Aims to identify and analyse policies for sustainably meeting the food needs of the developing world. Research at IFPRI concentrates on economic growth and poverty alleviation in low-income countries, improvement of the well being of poor people, and sound management of the natural resource base that supports agriculture.

3163 **Research Centre for the History of Food and Drink** [AUS]
arts.adelaide.edu.au/centrefooddrink
The primary purpose of the Research Centre is the promotion of research in the history of food and drink in both an Australian and a global context from their production to consumption, in their relationship to national and international politics, society, and economy, and in their environmental and medical effects and cultural meanings.

Vaccine and Infectious Disease Organization
See entry no. 3390

Associations & societies

3164 **British Beekeepers' Association**
www.bbka.org.uk
BBKA, founded in 1874, works to promote bees and beekeeping and to provide a range of services to its members. Non-members can access support boards, news, events, courses, sales and background documents. Aimed at both beginners and professionals.

3165 **British Egg Industry Council**
www.britegg.co.uk/home.html
The British Egg Information Service (BEIS) has been set up by the British Egg Industry Council (BEIC) to provide information and answer questions about eggs, including news, nutrition, safety and recipes for the consumer.

Council for Biotechnology Information
See entry no. 5021

European Dairy Association
See entry no. 3303

3166 **European Food Information Council**
www.eufic.org/gb/home/home.htm
EUFIC is a non-profit organization which provides science-based information on food and food-related topics to the media, health and nutrition professionals, educators, and opinion leaders. Includes articles from *Food Today*, reviews and mini-guides on safety and quality, nutrition and health, and technology and science.

3167 **Fairtrade Foundation**
www.fairtrade.org.uk/index.htm
The Fairtrade Foundation exists to ensure a better deal for marginalized and disadvantaged third world producers. The Foundation awards a consumer label, the FAIRTRADE Mark, to products which meet internationally recognized standards of fair trade. Useful Resources section.

3168 **Food and Drink Federation** [UK]
www.fdf.org.uk/home.aspx
The Food and Drink Federation (FDF) is the voice of the UK food and drink manufacturing industry. FDF promotes the industry's views and works to build consumer confidence in the food chain as a whole.

3169 **Food Marketing Institute** [USA]
www.fmi.org
Provides news, facts and figures on food safety and security, consumer issues, regulations, etc. of interest to producers, as well as other topics relating to retailing.

3170 **Institute of Masters of Wine** [UK]
www.masters-of-wine.org
Exists to promote the highest level of educational achievement for the wine industry, culminating in the internationally recognized qualification of Master of Wine (MW). Site gives guidance on educational requirements, provides support to students and members (restricted areas), and offers a series of lecture notes and reading lists, available to all.

3171 **International Association of Food Industry Suppliers**
www.iafis.org
Developed for the international food processing and supply industry, including an online suppliers directory and buyers guide, industry news and other resources.

International Bee Research Association
See entry no. 2390

International Food and Agribusiness Management Association
See entry no. 2992

International Food Information Council
See entry no. 4388

National Association of Farmers Markets
See entry no. 2994

Royal Society for the Promotion of Health
See entry no. 4428

3172 **UK Food Group**
www.ukfg.org.uk
The leading UK network for non-governmental organizations (NGOs) working on global food and agriculture issues. It seeks to promote sustainable and equitable food security policies; to balance corporate power by providing a public interest perspective to issues affecting global food security; and to strengthen the capacity of civil society to contribute effectively to international consultations on food security.

World's Poultry Science Association
See entry no. 3309

Libraries, archives, museums

Museum of English Rural Life
See entry no. 2998

Portal & task environments

Biotechnology@nature.com
See entry no. 5029

Food and Nutrition Information Center
National Agricultural Library See entry no. 4392

3173 **Food Science Central**
International Food Information Service
www.foodsciencecentral.com
Produced by IFIS Publishing, Food Science Central is a gateway to free and subscription-based information relating to the world of food science, food technology and food-related human nutrition. Some areas require free registration.

- **Food science and technology abstracts** Monthly. €2400.00. ISSN 00156574. www.foodsciencecentral.com [DESCRIPTION]. The leading service providing abstracts prepared from the world's food science, food technology and food-related human nutrition literature. C.2000 new records per month.

3174 **FoodlineWeb**
Leatherhead Food International.
www.foodlineweb.co.uk/FoodWeb
FoodlineWeb is a resource intended for companies needing to keep up-to-date with published information in the global food and drinks industry. Foodline is a collection of databases, produced by Leatherhead Food International and available to members, which brings together technical, market and legal information in one source.

3175 **Gender and Food Security**
Food and Agriculture Organization
www.fao.org/Gender/gender.htm
Gender issues are crucial in achieving global food security. This multilingual site from FAO includes documents, projects, statistics and multimedia resources in topic areas including forestry, environment, nutrition, population, rural economics, fisheries, and division of labour.

3176 **Global Information and Early Warning System on Food and Agriculture: GIEWS**
Food and Agriculture Organization
www.fao.org/giews/english/index.htm
The System aims to provide policy-makers and policy-analysts with the most up-to-date information available on all aspects of food supply and demand, warning of imminent food crises, so that timely interventions can be planned. Includes analysis tools, online databases, publications and satellite images.

Pew Initiative on Food and Biotechnology
Pew Charitable Trusts and University of Richmond See entry no. 5032

UK Agriculture
See entry no. 3018

Discovering print & electronic resources

Nutrition Abstracts and Reviews
See entry no. 4395

3177 **Nutrition and Food Sciences**
CABI Publishing.
www.nutritionandfoodsciences.org [FEE-BASED]
Offers access to the nutrition, food science and food technology subset of *CAB abstracts*, currently totalling more than half a million records, together with specially commissioned reviews and other resources for specialists in nutritional science, sports nutrition, clinical nutrition, food science and food technology.

Digital data, image & text collections

AGORA: Access to Global Online Research in Agriculture
Food and Agriculture Organization See entry no. 3029

FOODnetBase
See entry no. 4397

Directories & encyclopedias

Encyclopedia of agricultural, food and biological engineering
D.R. Heldman, ed. See entry no. 3043

Encyclopedia of common natural ingredients: used in food, drugs, and cosmetics
A.Y. Leung and S. Foster See entry no. 4213

3178 **Encyclopedia of dairy sciences**
H. Roginski, P. Fox and J. Fuquay, eds Academic Press, 2002, 3000pp. 4 v, $995.00. ISBN 0122272358.
www.sciencedirect.com/science/referenceworks [FEE-BASED]
Covers the core theories, methods and techniques employed by dairy scientists. It enables readers to access basic information on topics peripheral to their own areas, provides a repository of the core information in the area that can be used to refresh the researcher's own memory, and aids teachers in directing students to areas relevant to their course work.
Available online: see website

3179 **Encyclopedia of food microbiology**
R.K. Robinson, C.A. Batt and P.D. Patel, eds Academic Press, 1999, 2372pp. 3 v, $1075.00. ISBN 0122270703.
www.sciencedirect.com/science/referenceworks [FEE-BASED]
Claiming to be the largest, most comprehensive resource available in its field, covering the entire subject of food microbiology in 348 articles, containing tables, line drawings, black-and-white photographs or electron micrographs, and colour plates. Purchasers of the print edition can register for initial access to the online version of the Encyclopedia, which has many additional features. Aimed at a wide audience of academic and professional microbiologists in the food industry.
Available online: see website.
'Essential for any library supporting the food industry or related research fields; larger public libraries that have the budget should also acquire.' (*Library Journal*)

Encyclopedia of food sciences and nutrition
B. Caballero, L. Trugo and P. Finglas, eds See entry no. 4402

3180 **Encyclopedia of meat sciences**
W.K. Jensen, C. Devine and M. Dikeman, eds Elsevier Academic Press, 2004, 2000pp. $795.00. ISBN 012464970X.
Prepared by an international team of experts and aimed at both practitioners and students, this reference work covers all important aspects of meat science from stable to table, including animal breeding, physiology and slaughter, meat preparation, packaging, welfare, and food safety. Also includes food microbiology, meat in human nutrition, and biotechnological advances in breeding.

3181 **Food safety: a reference handbook**
N.E. Redman ABC-CLIO, 2000, 317pp. $45.00. ISBN 1576071588.
Presents laws, facts and figures about current and historical issues in food safety, illustrated with real-life examples. Includes a chronology of key events, movements and legislation, biographies of influential figures, a directory of organizations and resources for access to further study.

Foodborne Pathogenic Microorganisms and Natural Toxins Handbook: the 'bad bug book'
Center for Food Safety and Applied Nutrition See entry no. 3587

3182 **Oxford companion to food**
A. Davidson Oxford University Press, 1999, 908pp. £40.00. ISBN 0192115790.
A–Z encyclopedia of foods and prepared dishes from all over the world, together with entries on national and regional cuisines, food preparation and preservation, culinary terms and techniques, food science and diet, cookery books and their authors, and food in culture and religion. Extensive bibliography.

3183 **Wiley encyclopedia of food science and technology**
F.J. Francis, ed. 2nd edn, Wiley, 1999, 2816pp. 4 v, $1650.00. ISBN 0471192856.
www.knovel.com [FEE-BASED]
Features A-to-Z coverage of all aspects of food science, including: the properties, analysis, and processing of foods; genetic engineering of new food products; and nutrition. Contains information useful to food engineers, chemists, biologists, ingredient suppliers, and other professionals involved in the food chain.
Available online: see website.

Handbooks & manuals

3184 **Cheese: chemistry, physics, and microbiology**
P.F. Fox, ed. 2nd edn, Kluwer, 2001. 2 v, £237.50. ISBN 0834213397.
Authoritative technical study aimed at the cheese manufacturer. Vol. 1 covers general aspects and vol. 2 the major cheese groups.

CRC handbook of medicinal spices
J.A. Duke See entry no. 4219

3185 **Current protocols in food analytical chemistry**
R.E. Wrolstad [et al.], eds Wiley, 2001. Loose-leaf. Also available CD-ROM, $555.00. ISBN 0471176095.
www.does.org/masterli/cpfac.html [DESCRIPTION]
Entire chapters on water, proteins, enzymes, lipids, carbohydrates, colours and flavours. Each protocol includes detailed step-by-step annotated instructions as well as comprehensive lists of required materials, critical parameters, complete recipes, allotted time, and safety considerations.

3186 **Food analysis**
S.S. Nielsen 3rd edn, Kluwer Academic/Plenum Publishers, 2003, 536pp. £51.00. ISBN 0306474956.
Covers compositional analysis; chemical properties and characteristics of foods. A new chapter is included on agricultural biotechnology (GMO) methods of analysis. Includes large sections on spectroscopy, chromatography, and physical properties. All topics covered contain information on the basic principles, procedures, advantages, limitation, and applications.

Handbook of culture media for food microbiology
J.E.L. Corry, G.D.W. Curtis and R.M. Baird, eds See entry no. 5040

3187 **Handbook of food additives**
M. Ash and I. Ash, eds 2nd edn, Synapse Information Resources, 2002, 1100pp. CD-ROM version available, $350.00. ISBN 1890595365.
www.synapseinfo.com [DESCRIPTION]
Over 8000 trade name and generic chemicals used worldwide in manufacture and processing of foods. Information on additives indexed by trade name; chemical names; chemical synonyms; functions/applications; manufacturers/distributors; CAS numbers; EINECS/ELINCS numbers; FEMA numbers; e/ins numbers; FDA numbers.

3188 **Handbook of nutrition and food**
C.D. Berdanier CRC Press, 2001, 1600pp. $289.95. ISBN 0849327059.
Concisely presents the quantitative and qualitative data and information needed by nutritionists, dieticians, and health care professionals, covering human development to body systems and disease to micro/macro nutrients, concluding with nutrition counselling and community nutrition. Includes extensive bibliographic entries and tables, and website links.

3189 **McCance and Widdowson's The composition of foods**
Food Standards Agency and Institute of Food Research 6th edn, Royal Society of Chemistry, 2002, 537pp. £45.00. ISBN 0854044280.
www.rsc.org/is/books/comp_food.htm [DESCRIPTION]
Provides authoritative and comprehensive nutrient data for over 1200 most commonly consumed foods in UK. The official source of information for food composition data, aimed at students and professionals in all food and health disciplines

Nutrient metabolism
M. Kohlmeier See entry no. 4408

Keeping up-to-date

3190 **Advances in Food and Nutrition Research**
Academic Press, 2005, 336pp. $149.95. ISBN 0120164493.
Chapters in this volume of the series established in 1948 are: Re-inventing the food guide pyramid to promote health; Plant pigments: properties, analysis, degradation; Chitin, chitosan and co-products: chemistry, production, applications and health effects; A review of the application of sourdough technology to wheat breads; Detection of insect infestation in stored foods; Compression and compaction characteristics of selected food powders.

3191 **FoodNavigator.com: Breaking News on Food & Beverage Development**
Novis.
www.foodnavigator.com
A free news service providing information on food ingredients, science and nutrition, legislation, food safety and markets for the food and drink manufacturing industries.

3192 **Library of Food and Nutrition Listservs**
Center for Food Safety and Applied Nutrition
www.cfsan.fda.gov
Useful list of mailing lists run by this Centre, based within the US FOOD AND DRUG ADMINISTRATION. Much other valuable information at the website.

Forestry

agroforestry • arboriculture • dendochronology • forest products • paper industry • pulp industry • rainforests • shrubs • timber • tree preservation • tree rings • trees • tropical forestry • wood products • woodlands • woods

Introductions to the subject

3193 **A brief introduction to global forest policy**
International Institute for Sustainable Development
www.iisd.ca/process/forest_desertification_land-forestintro.htm
Useful summary of deliberations in various fora which have led to the development of global forest policy. Supported by links to official documents in full-text and daily summaries of current meetings.

3194 **Introduction to world forestry: people and their trees**
J. Westoby Blackwell, 1989, 228pp. ISBN 0631161341.
Summarizes the past, present and future of the world's forests in layman's language. Already a classic. Westoby, who died shortly after completing this work, was a senior director of FAO's Forestry Department, but originally a statistician and economist, and his book concentrates on the interactions between trees and humans, from pre-Roman times to the present. Includes country reviews and a critique of development policies as they affect forests.

3195 **State of the world's forests**
Food and Agriculture Organization 2003, Biennial. PDF.
www.fao.org/forestry/site/21407/en
The State of the World's Forests (SOFO) reports on the status of forests, recent major policy and institutional developments and key issues concerning the forest sector. It makes current, reliable and policy-relevant information widely available to facilitate informed discussion and decision-making with regard to the world's forests. Published biennially in Arabic, Chinese, English, French and Spanish.

Dictionaries, thesauri, classifications

Angiosperm Phylogeny Website
P. F. Stevens See entry no. 2189

3196 **The dictionary of forestry**
J. Helms; Society of American Foresters CABI Publishing, 1998, 224pp. Jointly published with the Society of American Foresters, £35.00. ISBN 0851993087.
Replaces the 1971 *Terminology of forest science, technology, practice, and products* edited by F.C. Ford-Robertson under the authorization of the Joint FAO/IUFRO Committee on Forest Bibliography and Terminology. Substantial changes in the forestry profession – from a focus on multiple use and sustained yield of forest products to a broader, more complex context of sustaining diverse forest uses and values – have modified the use of existing terms and introduced new ones, included in the 4500 defined here.

3197 **Directory of paper**
M. Kouris, ed. 5th edn, Tappi Press, 1996, 450pp. CD-ROM version available, $108.00. ISBN 0898520592.
Standard reference defining over 5300 terms commonly used in the pulp and paper industry.

3198 **Forest decimal classification: trilingual short version**
R. Schenker, ed.; International Union of Forest Research Organizations 1990, 147pp. ISBN 3704010626 ISSN 10163263.
http://iufro.boku.ac.at [DESCRIPTION]
Revised short edition of the earlier and widely used ODC, in English, French and German. No full English edition was published, but a completely revised classification to be known as the *Global Forest Decimal Classification* is under development and will be published online. Recognized as an official extension of the UNIVERSAL DECIMAL CLASSIFICATION.
Series: IUFRO World Series, 2

- **Forstliche Dezimal-Klassifikation: FDK D. Voshmgir and R. Schenker, ed.** 2nd edn, IUFRO, 1992, 131pp. ISBN 3704011347 ISSN 10163263. IUFRO World Series, 3.
- **The Oxford system of decimal classification for forestry: ODC CAB International**1954, 115pp. ISBN 0851983723.

3199 **An historical dictionary of forestry and woodland terms** [UK]
N.D.G. James Blackwell, 1991, 235pp. £50.00. ISBN 0631176365.
Unique compilation describing the special words used by those working or hunting in England's woodlands and forests from the early Middle Ages until the present. Includes definitions, descriptions of related customs and practices, and quotations from contemporary sources.

3200 **SilvaTerm Database**
International Union of Forest Research Organizations
http://iufro-down.boku.ac.at/iufro/silvavoc/svdatabase.htm
Terminological database for forestry being built by SilvaVoc, IUFRO's project on forest terminology. Based mainly on terms and equivalent terms of a trilingual forestry vocabulary produced by T.B. Yerke, USA. This basic stock of terms is regularly improved with definitions and additional terms provided by IUFRO Units in English, French, Spanish, German, Italian, Portuguese, Hungarian, Swahili, and Japanese.

3201 **World dictionary of trees**
M.M. Grandtner; Université du Québec à Rimouski
www.wdt.qc.ca
A work in progress, to comprise 5 volumes (North America, South America, Eurasia, Africa, Oceania), presenting information on the diversity of the trees of the world, their names, distribution, ecology, potential uses and threats of extinction. Currently contains only data on North America. Each section will be published in print when complete. Comprehensive search capability.

Laws, standards, codes

3202 **Forest Stewardship Council**
www.fsc.org/fsc
An independent, not for profit, non-government organization based in Bonn, Germany, that provides standard setting, trademark assurance and accreditation services for companies and organizations interested in responsible forestry. Founded in 1993, FSC's mission is to promote environmentally appropriate, socially beneficial and economically viable management of the world's forests. FSC

forest management standards are based on FSC's 10 Principles and Criteria of responsible forest management.

Official & quasi-official bodies

3203 Canadian Forest Service
www.nrcan.gc.ca/cfs-scf/index_e.html
Promotes the sustainable development of Canada's forests and competitiveness of the Canadian forest sector. Includes link to Canada's National Forest Inventory, presenting authoritative national statements on the distribution and structure of Canada's forests; catalogue of the CFS Library Network; and selected online publications.

3204 Collaborative Partnership on Forests
www.fao.org/forestry/site/2082/en
A innovative partnership of major forest-related international organizations, institutions and convention secretariats, established in April 2001 to support the work of the United Nations Forum on Forests. Documents a growing number of initiatives, including an online sourcebook on funding for sustainable forest management.

3205 Forestry Commission of Great Britain
www.forestry.gov.uk
The Forestry Commission is the UK Government Department responsible for forestry policy throughout Great Britain. It adopted a devolved structure with separate Commissions for England, Scotland and Wales in 2003. Site covers all the Commission's activities nationwide, and is aimed mainly at the public. Contains searchable catalogue of publications, some available for free download.

3206 Global Fire Monitoring Center
www.fire.uni-freiburg.de
A fire documentation, information and monitoring system, including: early warning of fire danger; near-real time monitoring; interpretation and synthesis; global information archive; facilitation of institutional links; policy support; and emergency assistance. Hosted by Max-Planck-Institut für Chemie.

3207 International Tropical Timber Organization
www.itto.or.jp
An intergovernmental organization promoting the conservation and sustainable management, use and trade of tropical forest resources. Its 59 members represent about 80% of the world's tropical forests and 90% of the global tropical timber trade. Established under the auspices of the United Nations in 1986, it develops internationally agreed policy documents and collects, analyses and disseminates data on the production and trade of tropical timber.

3208 Joint FAO/ECE/ILO Committee on Forest Technology, Management and Training
Food and Agriculture Organization, United Nations Economic Commission for Europe and International Labour Organization
www.unece.org/trade/timber/joint-committee
Assists countries to develop their forestry activities within the context of sustainable development. It fosters international co-operation on technical, economic and organizational aspects of forest management and forest working techniques and of the training of forest workers in logging and forest operations.

3209 Ministerial Conference on the Protection of Forests in Europe
www.mcpfe.org
A high-level political initiative for co-operation, addressing common opportunities and threats related to forests and forestry and promoting sustainable management of forests in Europe. Launched in 1990, it is the political platform for the dialogue on European forest issues. Site contains documentation issued by the process, some downloadable.

3210 National Agroforestry Center [USA]
www.unl.edu/nac
A partnership between the USDA Forest Service and the Natural Resources Conservation Service, NAC conducts research on how to design and install forested buffers to protect water quality and develops and delivers technology on a broad suite of agroforestry practices to natural resource professionals who directly assist landowners and communities. Includes downloadable publications and other information.

3211 United Nations Forum on Forests
www.un.org/esa/forests/index.html
Established in 2000 by the UN Economic and Social Council, to address all issues related to forests in a coherent and comprehensive manner and provide a forum to facilitate the exchange of experiences in the implementation of sustainable forest management practices by governments and stakeholders. Continues the work of the Intergovernmental Panel on Forests (IPF) set up after the Earth Summit in 1992 and its successor the Intergovernmental Forum on Forests (IFF), and is supported by the Collaborative Partnership on Forests (CPF) also set up in 2000. Site gives access to all official documentation.

3212 USDA Forest Service
www.fs.fed.us
Established in 1905, the Forest Service is an agency of the US Department of Agriculture, mandated to manage public lands in national forests and grasslands. This home page gives an overview of activities, aimed at the general public, but also linking to all FS research sites.

- **Forest Products Laboratory** www.fpl.fs.fed.us. Leading wood research institute concentrating on pulp and paper products, housing and structural uses of wood, wood preservation, wood and fungi identification, and finishing and restoration of wood products.

Research centres & institutes

3213 Center for International Forestry Research
www.cifor.cgiar.org
A CGIAR Center, CIFOR is an international research and global knowledge institution committed to conserving forests and improving the livelihoods of people in the tropics, through collaborative, strategic and applied research and by promoting the transfer and adoption of appropriate new technologies and social systems for national development. Large site with comprehensive background information.

3214 Chinese Academy of Forestry
www.caf.ac.cn/newcaf/english/main.htm
Major research institution affiliated to the State Forestry Administration, comprising 9 research institutes, 4 experimental centres and 3 research and development

centres, located in 10 provinces of China. It is principally engaged in applied forest research, covering all forestry-related subjects, including new and advanced technologies.

3215 **CSIRO Forestry and Forest Products** [AUS]
www.ffp.csiro.au
Strategic research is focused around six central themes: wood quality solutions; smart wood and fibre products; improved germplasm and breeding support tools; precision plantation solutions; commercial environmental forestry; and bushfire behaviour prediction systems, reflecting major industry trends.

3216 **European Forest Institute**
www.efi.fi
An independent non-governmental organization conducting European forest research. Site includes a number of online databases, information services and downloadable maps. Extensive publications programme, with selected titles available as PDFs.

- **Certification Information Service source book** A. Cullum 2001, loose-leaf. €25.00. Basic facts and information on the essential elements of certification and related issues and guidance on where to find more detailed information (with emphasis on material that is available electronically through the internet).

3217 **European Tropical Forest Research Network**
www.etfrn.org/etfrn
The ETFRN seeks to promote the involvement of European research expertise towards the conservation and wise use of forests and woodlands in tropical and subtropical countries. Site includes information on climate change; forests and water; biodiversity; non-timber forest products and related topics.

- **UK Tropical Forest Forum** www.forestforum.org.uk. ETFRN national node. Aims to strengthen the coherence and effectiveness of British-based actions in sustainable use and conservation of tropical forests, for benefit of their peoples and for the forests' global environmental values.

3218 **Forest Engineering Research Institute of Canada**
www.feric.ca
A private, non-profit research and development organization whose goal is to improve Canadian forestry operations related to the harvesting and transportation of wood, and the growing of trees, within a framework of sustainable development. Extensive publications database.

3219 **Forest Products Research Centre** [UK]
Buckinghamshire Chilterns University College
www.fprc.co.uk
The largest UK academic department specializing in wood science. Research covers wood protection, wood materials and forestry, and training and consultancy services are also offered, including identification services and production appraisal. Wood Information Library incorporates the collections of the Timber Research and Development Association (TRADA).

3220 **Forestry Research Institute Malaysia**
www.frim.gov.my
FRIM was established in 1929 and offers research, consultancy, technology, information and testing services for forestry and forest products industry. The Forestry Division provides data, standards and guidelines for sustainable management of natural forests. The Product Development Division focuses on the development of forest-based industries. The Biotechnology Division covers creating new planting material through genetic engineering.

3221 **Institute of Paper Science and Technology** [USA]
www.ipst.gatech.edu
Now integrated with Georgia Tech, IPST is a world-class centre for pulp and paper research and graduate education. Its William Haselton Library and Knowledge Center is one of the largest and most comprehensive sources for technical information for the pulp and paper industry, while the Robert C. Williams American Museum of Papermaking is recognized internationally as the world's most complete collection on the history of papermaking.

3222 **International Institute of Tropical Forestry**
www.fs.fed.us/global/iitf
Part of the USDA Forest Service but dedicated to tropical forestry on an international level. Its mission is to develop and exchange knowledge critical to sustaining tropical ecosystem benefits for humankind. Focuses on the scientific basis of tropical forest management and the ecological complexity of native tropical forests in Puerto Rico and throughout Latin America.

International Plant Genetic Resources Institute
See entry no. 2200

3223 **International Research Group on Wood Protection**
www.irg-wp.com
Wood-based products are important materials in many countries, and their loss or deterioration is economically serious. Consequently protection against biodeterioration is indispensable if these materials are to be used economically and effectively. More extensive use of the technology of wood preservation and improvements in that technology can also play a highly significant role in conserving forest resources. IRG promotes discussion and research with an extensive publications programme.

3224 **Rural Development Forestry Network**
www.odi.org.uk/fpeg/network
Influential network founded in 1985 to ensure that forestry focused more on people than on timber. Disseminates information on key issues in tropical forestry to 2900 members around the world; complete series of *Network Papers* available to download in English, French and Spanish. Future role of the Network under review in 2004 by ODI Forest Policy and Environment Group (FPEG).

3225 **Timber Research and Development Association** [UK]
www.trada.co.uk
TRADA is an internationally recognized centre of excellence on the specification and use of timber and wood products, originating in the 1930s. Membership encompassing the entire wood supply chain, from producers, merchants and manufacturers, to architects, engineers and end users. 'AskTRADA' website provides three levels of access: anonymous users can access suppliers directory and bookshop, free registration allows use of timber species database and members can access design software.

3226 Wood Supply Research Group [UK]
www.abdn.ac.uk/wsrg
Active for over 30 years in research for the UK and world forestry industry. Site gives access to tools and publications which are publicly available, mainly in the area of harvesting.

3227 World Agroforestry Centre
www.worldagroforestry.org
Founded in 1978 as the International Council for Research in Agroforestry (ICRAF), joined the CGIAR in 1991 and adopted its present name in 2002. It focuses on: agroforestry systems that restore soil fertility and regenerate degraded lands, and that enhance watershed protection, biodiversity conservation, and carbon sequestration; market-driven tree cultivation systems that help relieve rural poverty and improve health and nutrition; and capacity building for agroforestry research and development.

Associations & societies

3228 Arboricultural Association [UK]
www.trees.org.uk
UK professional association for all involved in the care of trees, with a remit to foster public interest in trees and assist in training. Site provides access to news and publications, and directories of registered consultants and approved contractors ('tree surgeons').

3229 Commonwealth Forestry Association
www.cfa-international.org
The world's longest established international forestry organization, founded in 1921. 1200 members in 78 Commonwealth and non-Commonwealth countries unite in a unique international network aiming to promote sustainable management, use and conservation of forests and forest lands throughout the world for socio-economic advancement and maintaining the natural environment. Publishes *International Forestry Review*, available online.

- **Commonwealth Forestry Conference** www.cfa-international.org/CFC2005.html. Approximately every four years, each now focusing on specific themes. Publication arrangements vary, but all reported in *International Forestry Review*. 1920–1980 proceedings available on microfilm from OXFORD FOREST INFORMATION SERVICE.

3230 Forest Products Association of Canada
www.cppa.org
Formerly the Canadian Pulp and Paper Association, FPAC's extensive site is aimed at the general public as well as members and contains background material, teaching resources and publications, news and statistics.

3231 Forestry and Timber Association [UK]
www.forestryandtimber.org/index.html
Representative body for all those with an interest, or a professional involvement, in the growing and management of trees. The FTA is the independent voice of UK forestry and acts as an information gateway for members and the wider community.

3232 Institute of Chartered Foresters [UK]
www.charteredforesters.org/intro.html
The Institute is the professional body for foresters and arborists throughout the UK. It sets and maintains the standards for the profession and safeguards the public interest in matters relating to forests, woodlands and trees; regulates the standards of entry to the profession; offers examinations for professional qualifications and keeps under review the status of Chartered Foresters and the profession.

3233 International Association of Wood Anatomists
www.kuleuven.ac.be/bio/sys/iawa
Founded in 1931 to: create awareness of wood anatomy; exchange ideas and information; facilitate collection, storage and exchange of research materials; provide rational bases for the consistent use of terminology; encourage publications and the study and teaching of wood anatomy and related fields; and to promote research. Publishes *IAWA Journal*, with abstracts (from 2000) available free online.

3234 International Society of Arboriculture
www.isa-arbor.com
A worldwide professional organization founded in 1924 and dedicated to fostering a greater appreciation for trees and to promoting research, technology, and the professional practice of arboriculture. Works to foster a better understanding of trees and tree care through research and the education of professionals as well as global efforts to inform tree care consumers.

3235 International Society of Tropical Foresters
www.istf-bethesda.org
Founded by the noted tropical forester Tom Gill, ISTF is a non-profit organization dedicated to providing a communications network for tropical forestry disciplines. Publishes *ISTF News* in English and Spanish and runs an extensive programme of training courses and meetings.

3236 International Union of Forest Research Organizations
www.iufro.org
IUFRO is a non-profit, non-governmental international network of forest scientists. Its objectives are to promote international co-operation in forestry and forest products research. IUFRO's activities are organized primarily through its 274 specialized Units in 8 technical Divisions. Quinquennial World Congress, extensive publications list and some online services.

- **International directory of forest information services: libraries, documentation centres, and subject specialists** iufro.andornot.com. Online directory aiming to facilitate contacts and networks between information centres and specialists both internationally and regionally for information and document exchange; also to help identify forest information collections within wider context.
- **IUFRO Research Series** CABI Publishing; available in the Americas through Oxford University Press. www.oup.com/us/catalog/general/series [DESCRIPTION]. Major series of handbooks covering a wide variety of forest-related topics.

3237 International Wood Products Association
www.iwpawood.org
Founded in 1956, the International Wood Products Association is the only association in the USA committed to the promotion and enhancement of trade in the imported hardwood and softwood products industry.

3238 National Community Forest Partnership [UK]
www.communityforest.org.uk
Community forestry is an environmental regeneration scheme, run by Community Forest Partnerships which work

together to deliver a comprehensive package of urban, economic and social regeneration. This shared vision is creating high-quality environments for millions of people by diversifying land-use, revitalizing derelict land and landscapes, enhancing biodiversity and providing new opportunities for leisure, recreation, cultural activity, education, healthy living and social and economic development.

3239 National Urban Forestry Unit [UK]
www.nufu.org.uk
The NUFU is a charitable organization which champions urban and community forestry to those tackling such issues as public health, leisure and recreation, land reclamation, built development, heritage and education. Main feature of the site is an online forum for the discussion about the many issues surrounding trees and woods in towns together with links to other sites of interest, including urban and community forestry projects throughout the UK.

Rainforest Action Network
See entry no. 2139

3240 The Rainforest Foundation
www.rainforestfoundationuk.org
Aims to support indigenous people and traditional populations of the world's rainforests in their efforts to protect their environment and fulfil their rights, through practical projects in tropical rainforest areas, all of which work with local indigenous peoples or non-governmental organizations, and by running advocacy campaigns that seek to address the underlying causes of the destruction of tropical rainforests.

3241 Royal Forestry Society [UK]
www.rfs.org.uk
The Royal Forestry Society of England, Wales and Northern Ireland was founded in 1882 and is open to anyone. Membership includes woodland owners, land managers, foresters, students, keen amateurs, arborists, landscapers, timber merchants, and ecologists. Publishes *Quarterly Journal of Forestry*. Site includes extensive background information on trees including 'Tree of the Month' and 'Topical Topics' features.

3242 Small Woods Association [UK]
www.smallwoods.org.uk
Lively UK-wide charity which aims to stimulate best practice in woodland management by organizing conferences and events, by networking and promoting initiatives. Well designed website; useful publications and Links sections.

- **WoodNet: The On-line Service for Wood Producers and Users** www.woodnet.org.uk. Provides networking and news for local wood producers and users in south-east England, including a directory and local timber marketing listings, links and an online forum.

3243 Technical Association of the Pulp and Paper Industry
www.tappi.org
TAPPI is the leading technical association for the worldwide pulp, paper and converting industry, founded in 1915. Extensive technical information, especially *TAPPI Standard Test Methods* and *Technical Information Papers*, available in print, cd-rom or online with licence.

3244 Timber Trade Federation [UK]
www.ttf.co.uk
Official voice of the UK timber trade, representing timber importers, agents, distributors and other suppliers and users of wood and wood products. The Federation aims to create the best conditions for its members to trade successfully and to ensure the long-term sustainability of the industry.

3245 Tree Advice Trust [UK]
www.treehelp.info
An independent charity providing practical information and guidance on the cultivation, maintenance and care of trees grown for amenity. The Trust is responsible for the work of the Arboricultural Advisory and Information Service (AAIS) at the Forestry Commission Forest Research Station, Farnham. Weekly alerting service *Assistance with Arboricultural Reading*.

3246 Tree Council [UK]
www.treecouncil.org.uk
Aims to improve the environment in town and country by promoting the planting and conservation of trees and woods throughout the UK; to disseminate knowledge about trees and their management; and to act as a forum for organizations concerned with trees, to identify national problems and to provide initiatives for co-operation.

3247 Tree Register of the British Isles [UK]
www.tree-register.org
A unique record of over 125,000 notable and ancient trees in Britain and Ireland. Full data and photo gallery available to members only, sample entries unrestricted. Also includes background information on tree measurement and recording. Fascinating.

3248 Tropical Forest Resource Group [UK]
www.tfrg.co.uk
A voluntary association of institutions and organizations based in the UK that have a demonstrated capacity in tropical forestry research, project management and consultancy. The consortium was established in 1992 and exists to foster collaboration and to mobilize the resources of the member organizations towards forestry research, management and education, offering training courses, project management and consultancy.

Woodland Trust
See entry no. 2225

Libraries, archives, museums

3249 Oxford Forest Information Service [UK]
www.plantlib.ox.ac.uk
Offers a worldwide service based on the collections of the former Imperial Forestry Institute and its successors, working in close collaboration with CAB International, who abstract the collections for FORESTSCIENCE.INFO. The collections are now maintained and developed by Oxford University Library Services.

Portal & task environments

3250 **Canadian forests: your internet gateway to forestry and forest products**
J. Roper and E. Ruiz, eds
www.canadian-forests.com
Privately-run gateway offering quick access to all the internet sites of the federal and provincial governments, the forest industries, service and supply companies, associations and NGOs, consultants, education and research, forestry news, employment opportunities, and more.

3251 **Forest Certification Resource Center**
Metafore.
www.certifiedwood.org
Comprehensive resource for information on forest management and product certification worldwide, including certified products, forests, businesses and approved certifiers, and background information on certification and systems, forest products policy and procurement.

3252 **Forest Conservation Portal**
Forests.org, Inc.
forests.org
Large news and information site offering ecological science-based forest conservation advocacy. Forests.org is committed to ending deforestation, preserving old-growth forests, conserving all forests, maintaining climatic systems and commencing the age of ecological restoration.

3253 **Forest, Dryland & Freshwater Programme**
UNEP World Conservation Monitoring Centre
www.unep-wcmc.org/forest/homepage.htm
Offers information, analysis and capacity building at regional, national and international levels for the conservation, protection and restoration of the world's forests and their biodiversity. Site includes data sets and maps, trends and indicators, regional and collaborative projects and certification information.

3254 **Forestry**
Food and Agriculture Organization
www.fao.org/forestry/index.jsp
Home page for FAO's very extensive forestry site, covering forest management, forest products and services, environment, people and forests, policy and institutions, sector analysis, assessment and monitoring, and interdisciplinary issues. Also links to events, processes and publications, including the journal *Unasylva*, available free online.

- **FAO Forestry Papers** www.fao.org/icatalog/inter-e.htm. Authoritative series of papers (143 issued to 2004) covering all areas of FAO's forestry activity. Many are state-of-the-art reviews.
- **Forestry Education Institutions Database** www.fao.org/forestry/site/12228/en. Contains contact information on 356 forestry education institutions from 78 countries. The inclusion of additional information is planned. The database was last updated during 2000–2001 on the basis of information sent by the institutions.
- **Forestry Research Institutions Database** www.fao.org/forestry/site/12248/en. Worldwide information on institutions involved in all aspects of forestry research such as agroforestry, biodiversity, forest fires, forest health, genetics, marketing, policy and wildlife. Can be queried by country, institution, area of research.
- **Global Forest Resources Assessment** www.fao.org/waicent. Has been carried out every 5–10 years since 1946, and is the most authoritative record of global forest cover. The main report of the 2000 Assessment is available free; and there are details of the 2005 Assessment procedures.
- **World Forestry Congress** www.fao.org/forestry/index.jsp. First held in Rome in 1926; generally every six years; XII Congress in Canada, 2003, and its Proceedings are available on this site. Forum for governments, universities, civil society, private sector to exchange views, formulate recommendations.

3255 **Forestry and Land Use**
International Institute for Environment and Development
www.iied.org/forestry/index.html
The programme seeks to improve people's livelihoods from forest and land use on the basis of equity, efficiency and sustainability, by working with communities, government, private sector and NGOs, mainly in the South, but increasingly aiming to evaluate and shape northern institutions, values and processes which impact on southern partners. Links to publications, partners and strategies.

3256 **Forests and Forestry**
World Bank Group
www.worldbank.org/html/extdr/thematic.htm
The World Bank Forests Team takes a multi-sectoral approach to forest management that takes into account impacts on forests and forest people of activities, policies and practices outside the forest sector. Details the Bank's strategy, projects and programmes.

3257 **Forests for Life**
WWF
www.panda.org/about_wwf/what_we_do/forests/index.cfm
A programme to provide solutions to the threats facing the world's forests which could potentially undermine forest conservation, including illegal logging and forest crime, conversion of forests to plantation crops of palm oil and soy, forest fires and climate change.

3258 **Global Forest Watch**
World Resources Institute
www.globalforestwatch.org/english
Aims to promote 'transparency and accountability into the decision making processes that determine how forests are managed and for whom' in order to slow forest degradation. Site offers interactive maps showing forest cover, logging concessions and administrative boundaries, downloadable publications and media centre. Extensive GIS data is also available for download from a Data Warehouse (requires free registration).

3259 **Global Trees Campaign**
Fauna & Flora International and UNEP World Conservation Monitoring Centre
www.globaltrees.org
This is a joint campaign by FFI and UNEP-WCMC that aims to conserve the world's endangered tree species. The campaign focuses on trees as flagship species for conservation of ecosystems and landscapes, and enables local people to carry out rescue and sustainable-use operations.

The site contains detailed information profiles on some of the most endangered species along with information on conservation projects taking place around the world (including in the UK). It also provides access to the UNEP-WCMC tree conservation database which contains information on more than 7000 endangered tree species. Other resources at the site include downloadable leaflets, and a list of useful publications.

- **Tree Conservation Information Service UNEP World Conservation Monitoring Centre**. www.unep-wcmc.org/trees/GTC/gtc_front.htm.

3260 **IUCN Forest Conservation Programme**
www.iucn.org/themes/fcp
Actively engages with governments, local communities, non-governmental organizations and the private sector around the world to improve forest conservation and management on the ground. Through its field research, project implementation, policy development and advocacy work at the national, regional and intergovernmental levels, the Programme promotes innovative approaches to create opportunities for positive change.

3261 **Ultimate Tree-Ring Web Pages**
H.D. Grissino-Mayer; University of Tennessee
web.utk.edu/~grissino/default.html
Comprehensive source for information on the science of dendrochronology, including databases, bibliographies, picture gallery, employment opportunities, etc.

3262 **Woodweb: woodworking industry information** [USA]
Woodweb Inc.
www.woodweb.com
Extensive portal for woodworking professionals, including resources, knowledge base, forums, exchanges and a product directory.

Discovering print & electronic resources

3263 **The Bradley bibliography: a guide to the literature of the woody plants of the world published before the beginning of the twentieth century**
H. Rehder Riverside Press, 1911–18. 5 v.
Definitive guide to literature on trees and forestry published up to 1900. Volumes cover dendrology, arboriculture, economic properties of woody plants and forestry.

3264 **Dictionary catalogue of the Yale Forestry Library**
Yale University G K Hall, 1962. 12 v. ISBN 0816106312.
Cumulative catalogue of the oldest 'continuous' forestry library in the United States covering forestry literature from the early 18th century to 1962. 217,000 card entries, including periodical articles.

3265 **Directory of selected tropical forestry journals and newsletters**
C. Haugen and P.B. Durst 2nd edn, FAO-RAP, FORSPA, and Green Horizons International, 1997, 130pp.
Lists and describes 450 periodicals focusing on tropical forestry, ranging from scientific journals to informal newsletters. The directory is organized by region, and within regions by country. E-mail addresses and internet sites are given whenever possible.

3266 **Forest History Society Databases**
Forest History Society
www.lib.duke.edu/forest/Research/databases.html
The *Environmental History Bibliography*, first published in print, contains over 30,000 annotated citations to books, articles and dissertations published from 1633 onwards relating to forestry, conservation and environmental history, updated quarterly online and searchable by keyword. Other databases are: a guide to archival collections in forestry, conservation and environmental history; a catalogue of the holdings of the US Forest Service Headquarters History Collection at the Forest History Society; a catalogue of 'Forests in Fiction'; and a bibliography relating to vegetation change in South and South-East Asia.

3267 **ForestryGuide**
Göttingen State and University Library
www.forestryguide.de/index.html
An internet-based subject gateway to scholarly relevant information in forestry, catalogued by subject and source type.

3268 **ForestScience.info**
CABI Publishing.
www.forestscience.info [FEE-BASED]
Web access to the forestry sections of CAB Abstracts [q.v.], including Forestry Abstracts, Forest Products Abstracts (both also available in print) and Agroforestry Abstracts (electronic only). Covers published research from 1939 to date, updated weekly. Also available on CD-ROM as TREECD.

- **Forestry Abstracts CAB International**CABI Publishing, 1939–, Monthly. £1065.00. ISSN 00157538. www.cabi-publishing.org/ProductsAndServices.asp [DESCRIPTION].
- **Forest Products Abstracts** CAB International, 1978–, Monthly. £585.00. ISSN 00157538. www.cabi-publishing.org/ProductsAndServices.asp [DESCRIPTION].

3269 **PaperChem**
Elsevier Engineering Information.
www.ei.org/eicorp/paperchem.html
Comprehensive bibliographic database covering international journal literature related to pulp and paper technology. Includes abstracts of articles, conference papers and technical reports with more than 480,000 records on hemicellulose, carbohydrates, lignin, wood extractives, engineering and processes, graphic arts, corrosion, packaging, and more.
Available online: see website

3270 **Tree and shrub field guides**
D. Schmidt
door.library.uiuc.edu/bix/fieldguides/trees.htm
Useful online bibliography of field guides covering all parts of the world except North America, for which see the companion printed volume A GUIDE TO FIELD GUIDES.

3271 **Urban Forestry Database**
University of Minnesota
forestry.lib.umn.edu/bib/urban.phtml
Valuable index of publications from the Minnesota Forestry Library relating to the history of urban forestry; urban forest legislation; the benefits of urban forests; selection and planting of trees; maintenance of the urban forest; planning and management; and urban forestry programs.

Digital data, image & text collections

3272 **Agroforestree Database**
World Agroforestry Centre
www.worldagroforestrycentre.org/Sites/TreeDBS/AFT/AFT.htm
A species reference and selection guide for agroforestry trees, allowing field workers and researchers to make rational decisions regarding the choice of candidate species for defined purposes. Coverage includes species identity, ecology and distribution, propagation and management, functional uses, pests and diseases and a bibliography. Over 500 species are included.

3273 **Forestry Commission Picture Library** [UK]
www.forestry.gov.uk/pictures
The Forestry Commission's picture library is one of the most comprehensive records of life in Britain's forests and woodlands. Incorporate images from The Forest Life Picture Library and the Forest Research Photo Library. Includes: tree species and woodland types; research and scientific projects; fungi and insects; landscapes throughout Britain; tree harvesting and woodland management; sports and leisure; wildlife and conservation

Gymnosperm Database
C.J. Earle; Rheinische Friedrich-Wilhelms-Universität Bonn See entry no. 2251

3274 **National Forestry Database Program** [CAN]
Canadian Council of Forest Ministers
nfdp.ccfm.org
A partnership between the Canadian federal government and provincial and territorial governments, the NFDP was created in 1990 to describe forest management and its impact on the forest resource, develop a public information programme based on the database, and provide reliable, timely information to the provincial and federal policy processes. Site offers statistics, frameworks and terminology.

PHYLLIS: the composition of biomass and waste
Energy Research Centre of the Netherlands See entry no. 3035

3275 **Tropical Forestry Papers**
Oxford Forestry Institute, 1968–. Price varies. ISSN 01419668.
www.plantlib.ox.ac.uk
Important series of technical papers, many reporting on UK forest research projects, with extensive literature reviews.
Available online from 2005: see website.

3276 **UNEP-WCMC Species Database: Trees**
UNEP World Conservation Monitoring Centre
sea.unep-wcmc.org/isdb/trees
Searchable by family/genus/species or by country, Red List category or assessor, this database contains information on threatened trees and other trees of conservation concern, and was used to generate The World List of Threatened Trees.

The UNEP-WCMC's Species Database collectively includes data on over 70,000 animals and almost 90,000 plants of conservation interest as well as some 9000 sub-species, stocks or synonyms. Subsets of the overall database which are searchable in addition to this 'Trees' subset are: Plants of global conservation concern; CITES-listed species; EU Wildlife Trade Regulation listed species; AEWA-listed species; Arctic Birds; Marine Aquarium Species in Trade; Coral Disease Mapping Service. Details of all these accessible via the website.

3277 **The Wood Collection**
Smithsonian Institution
ravenel.si.edu/botany/wood
Catalogue and other details for the Wood Collection of the US National Herbarium at the Smithsonian Institution. Contains c.42,500 specimens representing almost 3000 genera, and 5000 microscope slides.

Directories & encyclopedias

3278 **The Commonwealth forestry handbook 2001–2005**
Commonwealth Forestry Association 13th edn, CFA, 2001, 5-yearly, 218pp.
www.cfa-international.org/Handbook_index.html
Classic source of information for Commonwealth Forestry Association members and foresters in general, with sections covering the history of the Association, addresses of institutions and members, a list of journals, timber nomenclature and conversion tables for foresters. Originally published in hard-copy, this edition is now only available free online.

Encyclopedia of biodiversity
S. A. Levin [et al.], eds See entry no. 2163

3279 **Encyclopedia of forest sciences**
J. Burley, J. Evans and J. Youngquist, ed. Elsevier, 2004, 2400pp. £569.00. ISBN 0121451607.
www.sciencedirect.com/science/referenceworks [FEE-BASED]
Summarizes recent advances in forest science techniques, plus basic information vital to comprehensive understanding of the important elements of forestry. Includes relevant biology and ecology, different types of forestry (e.g. tropical forestry and dryland forestry), scientific names of trees and shrubs, and applied, economic and social aspects of forest management.
Available online: see website

3280 **Forestry compendium**
CAB International 2003. Online and CD-ROM versions available.
www.cabi.org/compendia/fc [FEE-BASED]
Global encyclopedia on forestry for practical decision-making. Includes information on trees, seed suppliers, pests and countries; detailed datasheets on over 1200 species worldwide of economic importance and basic data on c.20,000; and aids for species selection for planning trials. Statistics, maps and illustrations supplement a bibliography and selected full-text documents.

3281 **The Wood Explorer.com**
The Wood Explorer. CD-ROM also available.
www.thewoodexplorer.com [FEE-BASED]
The Wood Explorer Web Portal and The Wood Explorer CD provide search tools for identifying wood species based on 50 physical, mechanical and woodworking properties; finding the best types of wood for specific woodworking projects, and offers solutions for selecting substitutes for species that are endangered or unavailable. Free registration entitles access to details of 20 species, membership or CD purchase required for full access. Formerly *Woods of the world.*

Handbooks & manuals

3282 The arboriculturalist's companion: a guide to the care of trees
N.D.G. James 2nd edn, Blackwell, 1990, 244pp. £17.99. ISBN 0631167749.
Covers the growing and maintenance of trees from the point of view of ornament and amenity, whether in the town or the countryside. Includes spacing, transplanting, pruning, protection and safety.

3283 The EU tropical forestry sourcebook
G. Shepherd, ed.; Overseas Development Institute 1998, 362pp. £10.00. ISBN 0850033187.
Examines EC Directorates-General with forestry interests and Member States' policies and activities in tropical forestry with conclusions about effective aid delivery, an assessment of the totality of Europe's experience in tropical forestry and discussion of trends and issues for the future.

3284 A field guide to trees of Britain & Northern Europe
A. Mitchell 2nd edn, Collins, 2001, 420pp. Reprint of 1978 edn, £25.00. ISBN 0002192136.
Classic field guide covering 800 species, ordered by Families, with notes on English and scientific names, natural distribution, physical appearance, and date of introduction to Britain. Identification key based mainly on leaf features.

3285 The forest certification handbook [UK]
C. Upton and S. Bass Earthscan, 1995, 240pp. £35.00. ISBN 1853832227.
Essential text giving practical advice on developing, selecting and operating a certification programme which provides both market security and raises standards of forestry management. Covers commercial benefits, policy mechanisms required, the interpretation and implementation of forestry management standards, and the process of certification itself, with directories of currently certified forests, international and national initiatives, and active certification programmes.

3286 Forest conservation policy: a reference handbook
V.A. Sample and A.S. Cheng ABC-CLIO, 2003, 322pp. $45.00. ISBN 1576079910.
Introduction to the major issues and controversies in US forest policy, chronicling its dramatic history, current status, and global influence, from the foundations of early forest law during the colonial period through the rise of the Conservation Movement in the wake of 19th-century massive forest exploitation, to present-day environmental challenges and future policy directions.

Forest hydrology: an introduction to water and forests
M. Chang See entry no. 1151

3287 The forester's companion
N.D.G. James 4th edn, Basil Blackwell, 1989, 301pp. Out of print in UK, $79.95. ISBN 0631167242.
Classic guide to all aspects of forestry, including sections on the Woodland Grant Scheme, air pollution, and the Forestry Training Council. Changes over the four editions from the first publication in 1955 chart the development of UK post-war forestry.

3288 Measuring trees and forests
M.S. Philip 2nd edn, CAB International, 1994, 310pp. £30.00. ISBN 0851988830.
Forest mensuration provides quantitative data on aspects of length, mass and time of areas of forest, individual trees or parcels of felled timber This standard text covers: measuring single trees and tree crops; forest inventory; statistical principles in forest inventory; site assessment and forest growth models.

3289 Molecular genetics and breeding of forest trees
S. Kumar and N. Fladung, eds Food Products Press, 2004, 436pp. $59.95. ISBN 1560229594.
Concise but comprehensive review of all areas of research on the molecular biology of forest trees, integrating tree transgenesis, functional and structural genomics and including genome mapping and the molecular biology of wood formation.

Timber designers' manual
J.A. Baird and E.C. Ozelton, eds See entry no. 5279

3290 Tree preservation orders: a guide to the law and good practice [UK]
Great Britain. Office of the Deputy Prime Minister PDF. www.odpm.gov.uk
Sets out the Government's policy advice, outlining the law as it currently stands in England. Aimed at local planning authorities but a helpful source of advice for others interested in the tree preservation order system.

3291 Trees and shrubs hardy in the British isles
W.J. Bean and D.L. Clarke 8th edn, J Murray, 1970–1988. 4 v. plus supplement. ISBN 0719544432.
Leading reference source for British trees and shrubs, first appearing in 1914. Concise descriptions with details of distribution, history, distinctive characteristics and cultivation. New species, advances in taxonomy and notes on pests and diseases included in the Supplement together with a bibliography and index.
'Should long stand as an authoritative work ... there is no other published work equal to this.' (*RHS Journal*)

Wood handbook: wood as an engineering material
Forest Products Laboratory See entry no. 5283

3292 Weltforstatlas / World Forestry Atlas / Atlas des forêts du monde / Atlas Forestal del Mundo
C. Wiebeck; Bundesforschungsanstalt für Forst- und Holzwirtschaft Paul Parey, 1951–. 2 v. ; loose-leaf.
Loose-leaf mapping showing tree species distribution, forest ownership, timber production, and locations of forest industries. Publication appears to have ceased but the work is of historical significance.

3293 The world list of threatened trees
S.F. Oldfield, C. Lusty and A. MacKinven World Conservation Press, 1988, 650pp. £26.75. ISBN 189962810X.
WCMC, in association with the IUCN Species Survival Commission and a network of experts, identified over 8000 tree species which are threatened with extinction at a global level. This survey, supported by the Government of the Netherlands as part of the Conservation and Sustainable Management of Trees project, was the first of its kind to

assess the conservation status of tree species worldwide. Includes summary information on individual species.

Keeping up-to-date

3294 **FOREST Mailing List on Forest Research and Studies**
Finnish University and Research Network
www.listserv.funet.fi/archives/index.html
One of the best-known forestry mailing lists, covering a wide range of research interests with a large membership. However, announced 30.1.2005 that was closing down, but 'for your convenience we have provided links to some of the lists or their archives'.

Livestock

animal production • cattle • cows • dairy farming • deer • goats • pigs • poultry • sheep

Official & quasi-official bodies

3295 **FAO Animal Production and Health Division**
www.fao.org/ag/againfo/home/en/home.html
Programme and project details, resources and subject reports on the role of the fast expanding and changing global livestock sector in food security and food safety, in poverty alleviation and in sustainable use of the natural resource base. Includes multimedia resources and software downloads.

3296 **Meat and Livestock Commission** [UK]
www.mlc.org.uk
The MLC works with the British meat and livestock industry to improve its efficiency and competitive position, maintains and stimulates markets for British meat at home and abroad, while taking into account the needs of consumers. Includes news, headline prices and research.

Research centres & institutes

Institute for Animal Health
See entry no. 3389

3297 **International Feed Resources Unit**
www.mluri.sari.ac.uk/IFRU
Remit to conduct basic nutritional science research geared toward the needs of ruminant industry both in the UK and abroad. The unit has actively engaged in overseas rural development through advice to international and national agencies. The unit also provides training for students and scientists from many countries.

3298 **International Livestock Research Institute**
www.ilri.cgiar.org
ILRI brings high-quality science and capacity-building to bear on poverty reduction and sustainable development for poor livestock keepers and their communities, seeking to alleviate constraints on improving livestock livelihoods resulting from inappropriate policies, scarce feeds, devastating diseases, degraded lands, and poor access to markets.

Roslin Institute
See entry no. 5020

Vaccine and Infectious Disease Organization
See entry no. 3390

3299 **Wageningen University of the Life Sciences, Animal Sciences Group**
www.asg.wur.nl/english
Created in 2003 as the primary organization in the Netherlands with the expertise on animals, the entire animal product chain and the responsible use of animals. Site links to member organizations covering animal sciences, animal resources development, experimental animal services, infectious diseases, applied research, fisheries and nutrition and food.

Associations & societies

American Feed Industry Association
See entry no. 3081

3300 **American Society of Animal Science**
www.asas.org
A professional organization for animal scientists established in 1908, designed to help members provide effective leadership through research, extension, teaching and service for the livestock and meat industries, aiming to discover, disseminate and apply knowledge for sustainable use of animals for food and other human needs.

3301 **British Deer Farmers Association**
www.deer.org.uk
Represents deer farmers and farmed venison producers. Site provides information about deer farming and the activities of the Association, including background notes, publications and events, quality assurance and standards.

3302 **British Goat Society**
www.allgoats.com
Aims to act as the focal point for all goat-keeping activities in the United Kingdom, including close liaison with relevant Government departments. Site includes profiles of major breeds, advice on feeding, health, housing and breeding, and details of BGS publications. Similar societies exist for most farm animals.

3303 **European Dairy Association**
eda.euromilk.org
Represents the interests of the European dairy industry to the European administrative and political authorities and international bodies, aiming to assist decision making by relaying information and co-ordinating and stimulating consensual and coherent approaches. Online documents and links.

3304 **Farm Animal Welfare Council** [UK]
www.fawc.org.uk
An independent advisory body established by the UK Government in 1979, to keep under review the welfare of farm animals on agricultural land, at market, in transit and at the place of slaughter; and to advise the Government of any legislative or other changes that may be necessary.

3305 International Committee for Animal Recording
www.icar.org
Promotes the development and amelioration of performance recording for farm animals and their evaluation, establishing standards and guidelines, including the International Agreement on Recording Practices, available online.

3306 National Sheep Association [UK]
www.nationalsheep.org.uk
Founded in 1892 to represent the interests of UK sheep farmers. Site includes descriptions with photographs of British sheep breeds, and background information on the industry.

3307 Royal Association of British Dairy Farmers
www.rabdf.co.uk
The only independent organization dedicated to representing the interests of British dairy farmers, the Association strives to improve the status and wellbeing of British dairy farmers and the British dairy industry through the provision of information, training and lobbying activities.

3308 Royal Jersey Agricultural and Horticultural Society [UK]
www.royaljersey.co.uk
The representative organization for the Jersey Dairy Industry, promoting the benefits of agriculture to the Island community. Arranges regular agricultural shows, maintains studbook records and administers sire testing schemes and production trials. Also includes Jersey Island Genetics, official exporter of island genetics for the industry.

3309 World's Poultry Science Association
www.wpsa-uk.com
Strives to advance knowledge and understanding of all aspects of poultry science and the poultry industry. Founded in 1912, it organizes the World Poultry Congress and many other meetings and publishes the World's Poultry Science Journal.

Portal & task environments

Animalscience.com
See entry no. 3410

Pighealth.com
See entry no. 3412

3310 ThePigSite.com
5M Enterprises Ltd.
www.thepigsite.com/default.asp
ThePigSite.com is a free information resource for the global pig industry, supported by many of the main key pig industry players. News, directories, forum and technical advice.

VetGate
Royal College of Veterinary Surgeons, Royal Veterinary College and Resource Discovery Network See entry no. 3413

Discovering print & electronic resources

3311 Alternative Farming: an annotated database
Animal Welfare Institute
www.awionline.org/farm/altfrm.htm
Regularly updated searchable database of references to published and online information for farmers, consumers, students, and educators concerned about factory farming and seeking for humane alternatives. Covers various sustainable systems of livestock production as well as research articles on animal behaviour.

Nutrition Abstracts and Reviews
See entry no. 4395

3312 Virtual Livestock Library
Oklahoma State University
www.ansi.okstate.edu/library
Covers beef, dairy, sheep, goats, swine, horses and other livestock, including software, magazines, academic information and animal welfare.

Digital data, image & text collections

Animal Feed Resources Information System: AFRIS
Food and Agriculture Organization See entry no. 3100

3313 Animal Health and Welfare in Organic Farming: Compendium [UK]
University of Reading
www.organic-vet.reading.ac.uk
Compendium intended as a resource material and training tool for farmers, advisors, inspectors, veterinarians, organic sector bodies and policy makers on issues related to general and specific animal health and welfare aspects of organic livestock production. Covers sheep, cattle, pigs and poultry with a quick reference section on veterinary management of organic livestock. Produced by the Organic Livestock Research Group at the Veterinary Epidemiology and Economics Research Unit in the University's Department of Agriculture.

Directories & encyclopedias

3314 Animal health and production compendium
CAB International 2004. available on CD-ROM and the internet, from £70.
www.cabi.org/compendia/ahpc [FEE-BASED]
An encyclopedic and interactive database that draws together a range of scientific information on all aspects of animal health and production, including information on diseases, breeds, nutrition, husbandry and treatment of livestock and poultry. Contains bibliographic records, images, mapping and statistical tools.

Encyclopedia of meat sciences
W.K. Jensen, C. Devine and M. Dikeman, eds See entry no. 3180

3315 Mason's world dictionary of livestock breeds, types, and varieties
V. Porter, ed. 5th edn, CABI Publishing, 2002, 380pp. £60.00. ISBN 085199430X.
This is a new edition of a standard reference text, and contains key breed information about cattle, sheep, pigs, goats, horses, asses and buffalo. It contains approximately 9000 entries and cross-references on breeds, sub-breeds,

types, varieties, strains and lines of these species. The aim is to include all the livestock names that may be encountered in international literature.

Keeping up-to-date

3316 **Dairy-L**
University of Maryland
www.wam.umd.edu/~markv/Dairy-L.html
An electronic forum for the seeking and dissemination of factual-based information relating to the managing of dairy cows and dairy herds for people advising the dairy industry. This moderated list has a worldwide membership and an established reputation: a good example of its kind.

Plant & Crop Protection

crop protection • pest control • pesticides • plant pathology • plant protection • plant viruses • weeds

Dictionaries, thesauri, classifications

3317 **Compendium of pesticide common names**
A. Wood, comp.; International Organization for Standardization
www.hclrss.demon.co.uk
For purposes of trade, registration and legislation, and for use in popular and scientific publications, pesticides need names that are short, distinctive, non-proprietary and widely accepted. ISO has approved over 1000 standard names of chemical pesticides, listed here together with approved names from national and international bodies for pesticides without ISO names.

3318 **A dictionary of plant pathology**
P. Holliday 2nd edn, Cambridge University Press, 1998, 560pp. £80.00. ISBN 0521594537.
Standard reference source including over 11,000 entries for pathogens, including fungi from over 500 genera, 800 viruses, bacteria, mollicutes, nematodes and viroids, with supporting references, together with names of diseases and disorders, crops and their pathology, fungicides, taxonomic groups, terminology, toxins, vectors and past plant pathologists.

Laws, standards, codes

3319 **International code of conduct on the distribution and use of pesticides**
Food and Agriculture Organization
www.fao.org/WAICENT
The worldwide guidance document on pesticide management for all public and private entities engaged in, or associated with, the distribution and use of pesticides. Adopted in 1985 and revised in 2002, the full text is available for download in five languages in Word and pdf format, with guidance notes.

3320 **Plant health guide for importers** [UK]
Great Britain. Department for Environment, Food and Rural Affairs
2003, 30pp. PDF.
www.defra.gov.uk
Sets out restrictions on the import of plants, plant produce, plant pests, soil and growing medium from non-European Community (EC) countries into Great Britain. These restrictions are laid down in EC legislation with the aim of protecting plant health.

3321 **Plant Passports** [UK]
Great Britain. Department for Environment, Food and Rural Affairs
www.defra.gov.uk/planth/pass.htm
A limited range of plant material which hosts the most serious 'quarantine' pests and diseases requires a plant passport to facilitate its movement within the European Union. This site gives a full explanation of plant passporting requirements, including the 'Growers Guide': *Plant health guide to plant passporting and marketing requirements.*

Official & quasi-official bodies

Animal and Plant Health Inspection Service
See entry no. 3383

3322 **European and Mediterranean Plant Protection Organization**
www.eppo.org
An intergovernmental organization responsible for international co-operation in plant protection in the European and Mediterranean region, aiming to protect plants, to develop international strategies against the introduction and spread of dangerous pests and to promote safe and effective control methods

International Plant Protection Convention
See entry no. 2197

3323 **Pesticides Safety Directorate** [UK]
www.pesticides.gov.uk
The principal functions of PSD are to evaluate and process applications for approval of pesticide products for use in Great Britain and provide advice to Government on pesticides policy. Home page also contains information for all users, including the food industry and farmers and growers.

Research centres & institutes

3324 **Center for Integrated Pest Management** [USA]
cipm.ncsu.edu
Based at North Carolina State University, CIPM aims to serve a lead role in technology development, program implementation, training, and public awareness for integrated pest management at the state, regional, and national level in the US.

3325 **Center for Medical, Agricultural and Veterinary Entomology** [USA]
cmave.usda.ufl.edu
The Center conducts research aimed at reducing or eliminating the harm caused by insects to crops, stored products, livestock and humans. Research is directed not only at the insects themselves but at pathogens they may transmit and at identifying inherent protective mechanisms in plants.

3326 Insect Biocontrol Laboratory [USA]
www.barc.usda.gov/psi/ibl
The Insect Biocontrol Laboratory conducts research to develop selective and environmentally compatible methods for controlling insect pests of agricultural importance, developing naturally derived pest control agents, decreasing the amounts of chemical insecticides utilized, reducing adverse effects of chemical pesticides, and delaying the development of resistance to environmentally friendly insect control measures.

Associations & societies

American Phytopathological Society
See entry no. 2204

3327 APSnet: Plant Pathology Online [USA]
www.apsnet.org
An international scientific organization that promotes the study of plant diseases and their control through publications, meetings, symposia, workshops, and the world wide web. Wide-ranging site includes searchable abstracts of APS journals, with full-text access for subscribers; news and public affairs section; datasheets and images; teaching resources and careers details.

3328 BCPC [UK]
www.bcpc.org
BCPC (formerly known as the British Crop Protection Council) aims to promote the development, use and understanding of effective and sustainable crop production practice, by producing factual strategy reports on key topics for decision makers and by holding international conferences and seminars. Online bookshop.

3329 British Society for Plant Pathology
www.bspp.org.uk
BSPP was founded in 1981 for the study and advancement of plant pathology. It supports the professional interests of plant pathologists worldwide and provides a newsletter, website and regular scientific meetings, edits three international pathology journals and makes funds available to members for travel, short-term visiting fellowships, student bursaries and innovation projects.

3330 Crop Protection Association [UK]
www.cropprotection.org.uk
The Crop Protection Association represents those companies engaged in manufacture, formulation and distribution of Crop Protection products for agriculture, forestry, horticulture, gardening, industrial, amenity and Local Authority uses in the UK. The Association's members account for over 95% of the crop protection market at manufacturer level.

3331 European Crop Protection Association
www.ecpa.be
The pan-European voice of the crop protection industry. Its membership includes both national associations and companies throughout Europe, including Central and Eastern Europe, aiming to raise awareness about the industry's contribution to sustainable agriculture.

3332 European Weed Research Society
www.ewrs.org/index.html
The EWRS is an international organization which promotes and co-ordinates scientific research into all aspects of weed science. Publishes *Weed Research*, available online. Proceedings of Symposia and other publications available in print only.

3333 International Association for the Plant Protection Sciences
www.plantprotection.org
Provides a global forum for the purpose of identifying, evaluating, integrating and promoting plant protection concepts, technologies and policies which are economically, environmentally and socially acceptable. *Crop Protection*, published by Elsevier, is its official journal.

3334 International Society for Plant Pathology
www.isppweb.org
The ISPP promotes the worldwide development of plant pathology and the dissemination of knowledge about plant diseases and plant health management, and sponsors a quinquennial congress. Newsletter online.

- **World Directory of Plant Pathologists**
  www.scisoc.org/ispp/world_directory. Data combined from the records of about a dozen national plant pathology societies plus from a small number of regional and international societies working in the area.

Portal & task environments

Invasivespecies.gov: a gateway to Federal and State invasive species activities and programs
National Agricultural Library See entry no. 2148

PEST CABWeb
See entry no. 2403

3335 Prevention, Pesticides, and Toxic Substances [USA]
Environmental Protection Agency
www.epa.gov/opptsmnt/index.htm
Links to information about the work of the Agency's Office of Prevention, Pesticides and Toxic Substances, and within that its Office of Pesticide Programs, Office of Pollution Prevention and Toxics and Office of Science Coordination and Policy. The site includes a variety of resources including laws, regulations, test methods and guidelines.

Discovering print & electronic resources

3336 EXTOXNET: the EXtension TOXicology NETwork [USA]
Oregon State University and University of California, Davis
extoxnet.orst.edu
Provides a variety of information about pesticides, including Pesticide Information Profiles, Toxicology Information Briefs, news, technical information and other resources. Aims to offer objective, unbiased information in a form understandable by the non-expert, and to make that information fully searchable and selectively retrievable.

Plant Pathology Internet Guide Book
T. Kraska; University of Bonn See entry no. 2249

Digital data, image & text collections

3337 **National Pesticide Information Retrieval System: NPIRS** [USA]
Purdue University
http://aboutnpirs.ceris.purdue.edu [FEE-BASED]
Collection of pesticide-related databases available by subscription, and under the administration of the Center for Environmental and Regulatory Information Systems within the University.

3338 **NEMABASE**
University of California, Davis
www.ipm.ucdavis.edu/NEMABASE
The NEMABASE database gives fast, easy access to the host status of plants to plant-parasitic nematodes throughout the world, and helps with rotation and cover cropping decisions for nematode management. Entire database can be downloaded for advanced searching, and simple searches can be done on the Web. Part of the *University of California Statewide Integrated Pest Management Program* hosted within the University's *Agriculture and Natural Resources* Division.

Plant Viruses Online: descriptions and lists from the VIDE database
A.A. Brunt [et al.], eds See entry no. 2687

Directories & encyclopedias

3339 **Crop Protection Compendium**
2003. available on CD-ROM and the internet, from £70.
www.cabi.org/compendia/cpc [FEE-BASED]
A global compilation of crop protection knowledge for practical decision-making. Including information on crops, countries, pests, diseases and weeds and their natural enemies, with maps, bibliography, phytosanitary and economic data, taxonomic and common names.

Encyclopedia of agrochemicals
J.R. Plimmer, D.W. Gammon and N.R. Ragsdale, eds See entry no. 5107

3340 **Encyclopedia of pest management**
D. Pimentel, ed. Marcel Dekker, 2002, 903pp. $593.00. ISBN 0824708474.
www.dekker.com
Contains over 300 entries and 800 cited works, drawings, tables and photographs, describing sophisticated, scientifically-based issues and management techniques for pest control, including biotechnology, genetically modified foods, public health, soil science, GIS and GPS, with detailed index.
Available online: see website.

Handbooks & manuals

3341 **Ashgate handbook of pesticides and agricultural chemicals**
G.W.A. Milne, ed. Wiley, 2004, 226pp. $150.00. ISBN 0566083884.
www.wiley.com/WileyCDA [DESCRIPTION]
Includes data on over 1800 substances, including mixtures of agricultural importance. Pure chemicals largely indexed by CAS Registry Number associated EINECS Number. All chemicals which also appear in 12th edition of Merck Index have Merck Index Number provided. Index of 5000 chemical synonyms and trade names with cross referencing to their main entry.

3342 **CRC handbook of pest management in agriculture**
D. Pimentel 2nd edn, CRC Press, 1990. 3 v.
Discusses all aspects of insect, plant pathogen, and weed pest management, including pesticide resistance, biological control, and IPM on crops. Chapters on environmental aspects of pest management and new technologies for pest control.

3343 **Guide to Pesticides: 'The Blue Book'** [UK]
Pesticides Safety Directorate
www.pesticides.gov.uk
Formerly published on paper with a blue cover, hence its familiar name, but now only available electronically, this lists agricultural and non-agricultural pesticides products whose uses hold full or provisional approval in the UK. Describes legislation and the approvals process and is supplemented by the PSD's Product Information database accessible from the same site.

3344 **Handbook of pesticide toxicology**
R.I. Krieger, ed. 2nd edn, Academic Press, 2001, 1908pp. 2 v, $545.95. ISBN 0124262600.
A comprehensive examination of the critical issues related to the need, use and nature of chemicals used in modern pest management. Establishes context for important pesticide uses in agriculture, residential pest control and public health; 'emerging issues' section covers topics likely to be of special relevance in future.

3345 **Handbook of residue analytical methods for agrochemicals**
P.W. Lee, ed. Wiley, 2003, 1552pp. 2 v., $965.00. ISBN 0471491942.
Comprehensive overview of current global regulatory requirements, and applications of analytical technologies (chromatographic and non-chromatographic) to residue analysis. Reviews best practices to conduct crop residue and field monitoring studies, detailed method procedures for determination of major classes of agrochemicals, as well as of 40 key individual compounds.

3346 **The pesticide manual: a world compendium**
C.D.S. Tomlin 13th edn, BCPC, 2003, 1344pp. Also available CD-ROM, £195.00. ISBN 1901396134.
www.pesticidemanual.com [DESCRIPTION]
Published for over 35 years, now including 1469 profiles. Of these 858 are comprehensive main entries, with 611 abbreviated entries covering superseded products. Contains more than 8000 current and over 2000 discontinued names, with additional information on superseded substances.

3347 **Radcliffe's IPM World Textbook**
E.B. Radcliffe and W.D. Hutchison, eds; University of Minnesota
ipmworld.umn.edu
Electronic textbook of Integrated Pest Management featuring contributed chapters by internationally recognized experts, attempting to deliver 'state of the art' information, with extensive web links.

3348 The UK Pesticide Guide 2004
R. Whitehead, ed. 17th edn, BCPC / CAB International, 2004, Annual, 600pp. Also available CD-ROM, £33.95. ISBN 0851997376.
www.ukpesticideguide.co.uk [DESCRIPTION]
Valuable information on 1400 pesticide products and adjuvants for UK agriculture, horticulture, forestry and amenity use. Includes details of the 2004 Dangerous Preparations Directive which requires changes to the packaging and labelling of crop protection products. CD-ROM version contains additional information.

3349 Weed control methods handbook: tools and techniques for use in natural areas [USA]
M. Tu, C. Hurd and J.M. Randall; Nature Conservancy 2001.
tncweeds.ucdavis.edu/handbook.html
Online handbook, continuously revised. Available for free download in pdf or Word/Excel formats. Covers grazing, fire, biocontrol and herbicide use.

3350 Weed management handbook [UK]
R.E.L. Naylor, ed. 9th edn, BCPC, 2002, 432pp. ISBN 0632057327.
This definitive reference book (formerly *Weed control handbook*) has been rewritten by a team of crop protection specialists. The change in title reflects the changing emphasis on producing crops in a sustainable manner and the resulting new challenges. Covers biology through to management with case studies.

3351 World weeds: natural histories and distribution
L. Holm [et al.] Wiley, 1997, 1152pp. $325.00. ISBN 0471047015.
Comprehensive information on over 100 weeds. Each entry contains a full botanical description, plus details on habitat requirements and distribution, seed production, ecology, physiology, crop impact, and more. Illustrations and species distribution maps covering over 100 countries, extensive multilingual index of common names, and a bibliography with over 3000 references.

Keeping up-to-date

3352 Annual Review of Phytopathology
Annual Reviews, 1963–. $208.00. ISBN 0824313429 ISSN 00664286.
www.annurev.org/catalog/2004/py42.asp [DESCRIPTION]
Authoritative, analytic reviews synthesizing literature on the science of plant disease. Available in print and online to subscribers.

Soil Science

conservation agriculture • fertilizers • land use • pedology • soil surveys

Dictionaries, thesauri, classifications

3353 The Australian soil classification
R.F. Isbell; Commonwealth Scientific and Industrial Research Organisation Rev. edn, 2002, 144pp. £19.50. ISBN 0643068988.
Providing a framework for organizing knowledge about Australian soils and a means of communication among scientists and land managers, this revised classification is a good example of its type.
Series: Australian Soil and Land Survey Handbook, 4.

3354 Elsevier's dictionary of soil science: in English (with definitions), French, German and Spanish
A. Canarache, I.I. Vintila and I. Munteanu Elsevier, 2004, 950pp. $175.00. ISBN 0444824782.
Multilingual dictionary covering: soil physics, soil chemistry, soil biology, soil fertility, plant nutrition, soil genesis, soil classification, soil cartography, soil geography, soil technology, soil mineralogy, soil micromorphology, soil pollution, soil conservation, and related terms in physiography, geology, physics, chemistry, biology, agronomy, forestry, agricultural engineering, environmental sciences, computer sciences, etc.

3355 Internet Glossary of Soil Science Terms
Soil Science Society of America
www.soils.org/sssagloss
The SSSA has published definitions or glossaries of soil science terms since 1956. This 2001 revision replaces the 1997 edition and includes major revisions and additions. None of the terms listed are considered 'official' by the SSSA; they are published in an effort to provide a foundation for common understanding in communications covering soil science.

3356 Keys to soil taxonomy
Natural Resources Conservation Service 8th edn, USDA, 1998. PDF version incorporates amendments.
http://soils.usda.gov/technical
Intended both to provide the taxonomic keys necessary for the classification of soils in a form that can be used easily in the field, and to acquaint users of the taxonomic system with recent changes in the classification of soils. Provides information on what a soil is, the differences between mineral and organic soils, horizons and characteristics diagnostic for these soils, determining the taxonomic class of a soil, and the taxonomic keys for most soil types.

Official & quasi-official bodies

3357 International Union of Soil Sciences
www.iuss.org
The global union of soil scientists and member of the INTERNATIONAL COUNCIL FOR SCIENCE. Objectives are to foster all branches of the soil sciences and their applications, and to give support to soil scientists in the pursuit of their activities. Good list of forthcoming meetings, conferences, congresses; reviews of over 440 soil science books since 1999 (updated June 2004); much other useful information.

3358 Natural Resources Conservation Service [USA]
soils.usda.gov
The *Soils* website is part of the National Cooperative Soil Survey in the USA aiming to deliver scientifically based soil information to geographers, soil scientists, land use managers, teachers and students. Links to technical references, photo gallery, education resources, glossaries, and global information on soils.

- **World Soil Resources** soils.usda.gov/use/worldsoils. Encourages and promotes the free exchange of natural resource data for the continued evolution of soils knowledge for sustainable uses and management of this life-supporting resource. Learning materials, maps, technical references, organizations, etc.

Research centres & institutes

3359 International Fertilizer Development Center
www.ifdc.org
IFDC is a public, non-profit, international organization, which was founded in 1974 to assist in the quest for global food security, through the development and transfer of effective, environmentally sound plant nutrient technology and agricultural marketing expertise. Training and publications programmes.

3360 Macauley Institute [UK]
www.mluri.sari.ac.uk
Carries out research to meet the needs of sustainable rural development in Scotland, in Europe and elsewhere internationally, focusing on: quality of life, public good and wealth creation issues; the impact of land use on the quality of the environment; and evaluating the trade-offs between environmental, economic and social objectives for land use.

3361 National Soil Resources Institute [UK]
www.silsoe.cranfield.ac.uk/nsri
Originating as the Soil Survey of England and Wales (founded in 1945) and the National College of Agricultural Engineering (founded in 1960), NSRI was established in 2001 in order to create a unified Institute with the scientific expertise and research capability to focus on the long-term development of the sustainable management of soil and land resources both in the UK and around the world.

Associations & societies

3362 Agricultural Industries Confederation [UK]
www.fma.org.uk
AIC represents the views and interests of the fertilizer industry to governments and to appropriate organizations and bodies, and aims to promote the proper and responsible use of fertilizers. Site includes a range of booklets, leaflets and reference works for free download, including statistics, nutrient management, and health and safety notes.

3363 British Society of Soil Science
www.soils.org.uk
BSSS aims to raise both public and scientific community awareness of the importance of soil science, through the promotion of soil science related information in a wide variety of formats. Includes Soils Information Gateway, containing a good range of links to teaching materials, lecture notes, maps, etc., and some online editions of classic texts.

3364 European Conservation Agriculture Federation
www.ecaf.org
Brings together eleven national associations which promote among Europe's farmers the soil management 'best practice' aspects of conservation agriculture. A non-profit making association subject to Belgian law, it encourages discussion of any issue focused on maintaining the agrarian soil and its biodiversity in the context of sustainable agriculture.

3365 European Fertilizer Manufacturers Association
www.efma.org
The mission of the European Fertilizer Industry is to respond to the needs of agriculture and society by providing, in accordance with the principles of Responsible Care, a dependable and competitive supply of high quality mineral fertilizers. Site includes documents on all aspects of the industry.

3366 Institute of Professional Soil Scientists [UK]
www.soilscientist.org
The Institute of Professional Soil Scientists (IPSS), founded in 1991, is a professional body that aims to promote and enhance the status of soil science and allied disciplines. The website is basic [in 2004], but has a searchable database of experts who can be contacted for advice on a variety of soil-related issues.

3367 International Fertiliser Society
www.fertiliser-society.org
Founded in 1947 for individuals who have a professional interest in any aspect of fertilizer production, marketing and use. Membership is personal and is open to all; it currently covers almost 50 countries world-wide. Searchable catalogue of published Proceedings of the Society Meetings, a major source of information on fertilizer production and use, and on crop nutrition.

3368 Soil Science Society of America
www.soils.org
Aims to advance the discipline and practice of soil science by acquiring and disseminating information about soils especially in relation to crop production, environmental quality, ecosystem sustainability, bioremediation, waste management and recycling, and wise land use. Links to congresses, publications, glossary, and education resources.

Portal & task environments

3369 Canadian Soil Information System: CanSIS
Agriculture and Agri-Food Canada
sis.agr.gc.ca/cansis
Since 1972, the Canadian Soil Information System (CanSIS) has supported the research activities of Agriculture and Agri-Food Canada by building the National Soil DataBase, and acting as a source of GIS products and expertise through its personnel, GIS systems, and operating procedures.

3370 International Soil Reference and Information Centre
International Union of Soil Sciences and Wageningen University of the Life Sciences
www.isric.nl
ISRIC is a foundation for documentation, training and research on soils of the world. It is the World Data Centre for Soils of the INTERNATIONAL COUNCIL FOR SCIENCE. Site includes many downloadable datasets, covering soil profile data, soil and terrain data, soil degradation, soil conservation and derived products. Also gives background information, publications and links.

3371 Soil Action Plan [UK]
Great Britain. Department for Environment, Food and Rural Affairs
www.defra.gov.uk/environment
Published in May 2004 after extensive consultation, the Action Plan encompasses ongoing work on soils in England and identifies 52 actions for Government and others to take forward to improve the protection and management of soils

within a range of land uses. It is complemented by an Environment Agency report on the state of soils in England and Wales. Work on a European Thematic Soil Strategy is being progressed by the EU Commission. All documents accessible from this site.

3372 Soil Resources Mapping and Classification Portal
Food and Agriculture Organization
www.fao.org/WAICENT
Includes Digital Soil Map of the World; Global Soil and Terrain Database (SOTER); Key to the FAO Soil Units (1974); ProSoil – Problem Soils Database; Terrastat – land resource potential and constraints statistics at country and regional level; World Reference Base for Soil Resources; and Soil Events – Meetings, Courses, Conferences.

- **World Reference Base for Soil Resources**
  www.fao.org/WAICENT. Main objective is to provide scientific depth and background to the 1988 *FAO Revised Legend*, incorporating the latest knowledge relating to global soil resources and their interrelationships.

3373 Worldwide Portal to Information on Soil Health
Tropical Soil Cover and Organic Resource Exchange Consortium
mulch.mannlib.cornell.edu
Extensive database of annotated English and Spanish language web resources; a subject-specific browsing library; an online resource reference service; and classified resource listings for products, services, organizations, databases, and literature. Also offers archives of soil health electronic discussion groups and online learning modules keyed to discussions occurring on English, Spanish and French electronic discussion groups.

Discovering print & electronic resources

3374 A compendium of on-line soil survey information
D.G. Rossiter
www.itc.nl/personal/rossiter/research/rsrch_ss.html
Frequently updated virtual library attempting to bring together online information on soil survey activities, institutions, datasets, research, and teaching materials worldwide, including digital soil survey maps available free.

Digital data, image & text collections

3375 ProSoil: Problem Soils Database
Food and Agriculture Organization
www.fao.org/ag/AGL/agll/prosoil
A multimedia kit including a database and an electronic archive, allowing the user to get an overview of selected types of problem soils (by exploring their definitions); to search on literature sources which treat problem soils; to identify relevant tables, figures and case studies; to retrieve them from the electronic archive; and to use the retrieved files in projects.

3376 Soil & Water Assessment Tool: SWAT
Agricultural Research Service
www.brc.tamus.edu/swat/index.html
SWAT is a public domain river basin scale model developed to quantify the impact of land management practices in large, complex watersheds, aiming to predict the effect of management decisions on water, sediment, nutrient and pesticide yields with reasonable accuracy on large, ungauged river basins. Supported by the Service at the Grassland, Soil and Water Research Laboratory in Temple, Texas.

Directories & encyclopedias

3377 Encyclopedia of soil science
R. Lal, ed. Marcel Dekker, 2003, 1450pp. $593.00. ISBN 0824708466.
www.dekker.com
Provides detailed information on chemistry, analysis, and evaluation of soils and geography and focuses on agricultural development in the third world, particularly through research on sustainable management of natural resources, soil productivity and environmental quality. Includes around 400 entries with over 1000 illustrations.
Available online: see website.

3378 Encyclopedia of soils in the environment
D. Hillel, ed. Elsevier Academic Press, 2004, 2900pp. 4 v, $875.00. ISBN 0123485304.
www.sciencedirect.com/science/referenceworks
Encompasses the present knowledge of the world's variegated soils, their origins, properties, classification, and roles in the biosphere. Over 250 entries cover soil biology, ecology, chemistry and physics, together with cross-disciplinary subjects, such as the history of soil utilization for agricultural and engineering purposes and soils in relation to the remediation of pollution and the mitigation of global climate change.
Available online: see website.

Handbooks & manuals

3379 Russell's soil conditions and plant growth
E.W. Russell and A. Wild, eds 11th edn, Longman, 1988, 991pp. ISBN 0582446775.
One of the most influential books in agricultural science, this classic work was first published in 1912. A comprehensive survey of all aspects of soil as a medium for plant growth, emphasizing quantitative effects of soil and climate on farm crops, but also relevant to forest crops and natural vegetation. Well illustrated with extensive references and detailed index.

3380 Soil survey manual [USA]
Natural Resources Conservation Service 1993. PDF.
soils.usda.gov/technical/manual
Covers the major principles and practices needed for making and using soil surveys and for assembling and using data related to them. Primarily intended for use by soil scientists engaged in the classification and mapping of soils and in the interpretation of soil surveys, but also useful for students. Out of print but available for download.
Series: USDA Handbook, 18.

Veterinary Science

animal diseases • animal health • animal infections • animal protection • animal welfare • anthrax • bovine spongiform encephalopathy • cruelty to animals • foot-and-mouth disease • guide dogs • paratuberculosis • veterinary medicine • veterinary nursing • veterinary surgery • wildlife diseases

Introductions to the subject

The second creation: the age of biological control by the scientists who cloned Dolly
I. Wilmut, K. Campbell and C. Tudge See entry no. 4449

Dictionaries, thesauri, classifications

3381 **Black's veterinary dictionary**
E. Boden, ed. 20th edn, A. & C. Black, 2001, 585pp. £25.00. ISBN 0713650621.
Encyclopedic dictionary, first published in 1928, offering practical help and reference material. Covers bacteria, viruses, carriers and diseases, including causes, diagnoses, signs and treatment, and variations in different animals. Reflects latest legislation and scientific advances.

Laws, standards, codes

Basic legal documents on international animal welfare and wildlife conservation
M. Austen and T. Richards, eds See entry no. 2109

3382 **Terrestrial Animal Health Code**
World Organization for Animal Health 12th edn, OIE, 2003, Annual. €55.00. ISBN 9290445831.
www.oie.int/eng/Normes/mcode/A_summry.htm
The objective of this periodically updated volume is to prevent the spread of animal diseases, while facilitating international trade in live animals, semen, embryos and animal products. The OIE Code is a reference document for use by authorities of veterinary departments, import/export services, epidemiologists and all those involved in international trade.
Available online: see website.

Official & quasi-official bodies

3383 **Animal and Plant Health Inspection Service** [USA]
www.aphis.usda.gov
APHIS is responsible for protecting and promoting US agricultural health, administering the Animal Welfare Act, and carrying out wildlife damage management activities. Information on APHIS programmes, news and 'hot issues', plus online publications.

- **Animal Care** www.aphis.usda.gov/ac. Leads in establishing acceptable standards of humane animal care and treatment and in monitoring and achieving compliance with the Animal Welfare Act through inspections, education, and co-operative efforts. Downloadable *Animal Care Policy Manual*.

3384 **Animal Health Service**
www.fao.org/ag/AGA/AGAH
AGAH is responsible for helping FAO Member Countries develop strategies for the economic control of animal diseases. It operates through a series of sub-groups including infectious, parasitic, and insect vector diseases and veterinary services.

3385 **European Commission for the Control of Foot-and-Mouth Disease**
www.fao.org/ag/againfo/commissions/en/eufmd/eufmd.html
Established under the auspices of FAO (not the European Commission) in 1954, EUFMD is primarily a forum to foster co-operation between member countries and to co-ordinate their efforts to prevent and control foot-and-mouth disease. It also provides technical expertise, epidemiological information and advice to member countries.

FAO Animal Production and Health Division
See entry no. 3295

Food Standards Agency
See entry no. 3154

3386 **Veterinary Medicines Directorate** [UK]
www.vmd.gov.uk
An Executive Agency of the Department for Environment, Food and Rural Affairs protecting public health, animal health, the environment and promoting animal welfare by assuring the safety, quality and efficacy of veterinary medicines in the United Kingdom. Includes information on adverse reactions, residues surveillance, product recalls and unauthorized products.

3387 **World Organisation for Animal Health**
www.oie.int/eng/en_index.htm
The OIE is an intergovernmental organization created in 1924, with a remit to report on animal disease, to collect, analyse and disseminate veterinary scientific information, support animal disease control and develop sanitary rules for international trade in animals and animal products.

Research centres & institutes

Center for Medical, Agricultural and Veterinary Entomology
See entry no. 3325

3388 **Center for Veterinary Medicine** [USA]
www.fda.gov/cvm/default.html
CVM regulates the manufacture and distribution of food additives and drugs that will be given to animals, including those from which human foods are derived, as well as food additives and drugs for companion animals. Site includes regulatory and guidance documents on antimicrobial resistance, biotechnology, aquaculture, food safety, BSE, etc.

3389 **Institute for Animal Health**
www.iah.bbsrc.ac.uk
An international research centre on three sites, working to improve the health of farm animals worldwide. Its aims are: to carry out and provide training in fundamental and applied research on infectious diseases of farm animals; to advance knowledge and understanding of existing and new infectious diseases; to develop disease control measures; and to improve food quality and safety.

- **The Foot-and-Mouth Disease Home Page**
www.iah.bbsrc.ac.uk/virus. Good entrée to information on a wide range of viral diiseases including foot-and-mouth.

Raptor Center
See entry no. 2756

3390 **Vaccine and Infectious Disease Organization** [CAN]
www.vido.org
Founded in 1975, VIDO is a public research institute, owned by the University of Saskatchewan in Canada, dealing with food animal infectious disease research and the development of livestock vaccines. It aims to deliver leading-edge technology for disease solutions, to benefit livestock producers, the food industry and society as a whole.

3391 **Veterinary Laboratories Agency** [UK]
www.defra.gov.uk/corporate/vla
The Veterinary Laboratories Agency (VLA) is an Executive Agency of DEFRA, providing a specialist veterinary resource to the UK Government for veterinary public health and the development of sustainable agriculture and food industries. Located on 17 sites across the UK, including the former Central Veterinary Laboratory (CVL).

Associations & societies

3392 **American Society for the Prevention of Cruelty to Animals**
www.aspca.org
Aims to provide effective means for the prevention of cruelty to animals throughout the United States, offering national programmes in humane education, public awareness, government advocacy, shelter support, and animal medical services and placement.

Extensive ranges of well presented resources under the headings: Fight animal cruelty; Animal poison control centre; National shelter outreach; Pet care and nutrition; Human education; Animal precinct (TV programme); Legal information.

3393 **American Veterinary Medical Association**
www.avma.org
Established in 1863, and is a not-for-profit association representing veterinarians working in private and corporate practice, government, industry, academia, and uniformed services. Site offers a range of resources available to the public plus some limited to members.

Americans/Europeans/Japanese for Medical Advancement
See entry no. 3475

3394 **Animal Health Information Specialists (UK and Ireland)**
www.ahis.org
A group of library and information professionals working in the area of animal health. Holds an annual conference, produces a newsletter and runs a discussion list.

3395 **Animal Health Trust** [UK]
www.aht.org.uk
Provides specialist veterinary clinical, diagnostic and surgical services and research for dogs, cats and horses. Harris Library available for use by veterinary surgeons, veterinary nurses and students and others by appointment.

3396 **British Society of Animal Science**
www.bsas.org.uk
The Society's aim is to enhance the understanding of animal sciences and their integration into animal production, with a meetings and publication programme including the leading journal *Animal Science*.

3397 **British Veterinary Association**
www.bva.co.uk
The national representative body for the British veterinary profession, with three main functions: policy development in areas affecting the profession; promoting and protecting the profession; and provision of services to members.

3398 **British Veterinary Nursing Association**
www.bvna.org.uk
Website designed for future and current veterinary nurses and practice staff. Includes career and professional development information, annual congress, news and campaign details.

Coalition for Medical Progress
See entry no. 3480

3399 **Federation of Veterinarians of Europe**
www.fve.org
An umbrella organization of veterinary organizations from 35 European countries. Offers up-to-date information on public health (meat and food hygiene, zoonoses, BSE, European Food Safety Authority), education (recognition of veterinary degrees, postgraduate education), medicinal products (availability of medicines, antibiotic resistance), animal health (foot-and-mouth disease, classical swine fever) and welfare, and EU enlargement.

3400 **Guide Dogs for the Blind Association** [USA]
www.guidedogs.com
Founded in 1934 and now the world's largest breeder and trainer of working dogs, the Association is a UK-based charity and aims to provide guide dogs, mobility and other rehabilitation services that meet the needs of blind and partially sighted people.

3401 **International Association for Paratuberculosis**
www.paratuberculosis.org/index.htm
The Association is devoted to the advancement of scientific progress on paratuberculosis (Johne's Disease), a chronic, debilitating disease that affects the intestines of all ruminant animals, including cattle, sheep and goats. Site contains a directory of active researchers worldwide, and links to other sites with comprehensive information on the disease.

3402 **International Federation for Animal Health**
www.fedesa.be
IFAH is the international federation representing manufacturers of veterinary medicines, vaccines and other animal health products in both developed and developing countries. Aims to promote a harmonized, science-based regulatory and trade framework, contributing to a healthy and safe food supply as well as a high level of animal health and welfare.

International Fund for Animal Welfare
See entry no. 2135

International Society for Applied Ethology
See entry no. 2014

3403 **National Office of Animal Health** [UK]
www.noah.co.uk
Represents the UK animal medicines industry: its aim is to promote the benefits of safe, effective, quality medicines for the health and welfare of all animals. Lists withdrawal periods for animal medicines, during which the animal or its products must not be used for human consumption, and gives extensive background information.

RDS: Understanding Animal Research in Medicine
See entry no. 3482

3404 **Royal College of Veterinary Surgeons** [UK]
www.rcvs.org.uk
The regulatory body for veterinary surgeons in the United Kingdom. Ensures that standards within the veterinary profession are maintained, safeguarding the health and welfare of animals and the interests of the public. Comprehensive information about the profession in separate sections for surgeons, nurses and visitors to the site.

3405 **Royal Society for the Prevention of Cruelty to Animals** [UK]
www.rspca.org.uk
RSPCA Online is an extensive public information site including details of campaigns, educational resources, scientific studies, farm assurance and food labelling, animal care advice, publications and an extensive commercial photo library (which requires registration).

3406 **Universities Federation for Animal Welfare** [UK]
www.ufaw.org.uk
UFAW aims to use scientific knowledge and established expertise to improve the welfare of animals kept as pets, in zoos, laboratories and on farms, and of wild animals. It funds research, holds symposia, gives advice to Government and others and produces publications on animal welfare. Website provides information about the organization, links to related organizations and access to several electronic publications.

3407 **World Society for the Protection of Animals**
www.wspa.org.uk
A UK charity working with more than 460 member organizations to raise the standards of animal welfare throughout the world, and encourage effective legislation. Site includes details of current campaigns and teaching resources.

Portal & task environments

3408 **Animal Health and Welfare** [UK]
Great Britain. Department for Environment, Food and Rural Affairs
www.defra.gov.uk/animalh/animindx.htm
Defra is the UK government department responsible for protecting and improving livestock and controlling and eradicating disease. Its Animal Health and Welfare pages are divided into various subject areas including strategy, diseases surveillance and control, regulations on trade and livestock movement control.

- **Bovine Spongiform Encephalopathy: BSE** www.defra.gov.uk/animalh/bse. Sometimes known as 'mad cow' disease, first identified within cattle in 1986. These pages provide authoritative information in seven topic areas: Public health; Eradication; Beef industry; Europe; Science; Statistics; Publications.
- **BSEInfo.org: the source for Bovine Spongiform Encephalopathy information** **Cattlemen's Beef Board and National Cattlemen's Beef Association**. www.bseinfo.org. News and updating site on the presence of BSE in North America, with links to information sources around the world, including fact sheets and press releases.

3409 **Animal Welfare Information Center**
National Agricultural Library
www.nal.usda.gov/awic
Provides information for improved animal care and use in research, teaching, and testing. Extensive link lists including coverage of alternative medicine and zoo and circus animals.

3410 **Animalscience.com**
CABI Publishing.
www.animalscience.com [FEE-BASED]
Portal for information on all aspects of veterinary science including parasitology and zoonotic disease, animal nutrition, equine science, animal production and animal genetics, and aquaculture and fisheries. Includes database of over one million abstracts drawn from CAB Abstracts.

Applied Ethology
University of Saskatchewan See entry no. 2017

3411 **International Veterinary Information Service**
www.ivis.org/home.asp [REGISTRATION]
IVIS provides free access on registration for veterinarians, veterinary students and animal health professionals worldwide to a wide range of resources including electronic books, proceedings of veterinary meetings, short courses, continuing education (lecture notes, manuals, autotutorials and interactive websites), calendar of veterinary events, image collections, etc.

LTSN Medicine, Dentistry and Veterinary Medicine
University of Newcastle and Higher Education Academy See entry no. 3495

3412 **Pighealth.com** [UK]
Pig Disease Information Centre Ltd.
www.pighealth.com
Portal for pig health matters, particularly training and IT-related materials, presented in popular style. Includes news and lecture notes.

3413 **VetGate** [UK]
Royal College of Veterinary Surgeons, Royal Veterinary College and Resource Discovery Network
http://vetgate.ac.uk
One of the BIOME hubs, covering veterinary science and animal health, and providing access to evaluated descriptions of internet resources.

Discovering print & electronic resources

3414 **The NORINA Database: audiovisual alternatives to the use of animals in teaching**
Norwegian School of Veterinary Science
oslovet.veths.no/NORINA
English-language database of audiovisuals and other alternatives for use in the biological sciences, offering an overview of possible alternatives or supplements to the use of animals in student teaching, at all levels from schools to university. 30 searchable categories. Separate TextBase for textbooks addressing laboratory animal science.

3415 **RDN Virtual Training Suite: Internet Vet** [UK]
L. Williamson; University of Nottingham and Resource Discovery Network
www.vts.rdn.ac.uk/tutorial/vet
Free, 'teach yourself' tutorial in internet information skills. Covers some key sites for the subject area, with guidance on effective searching, evaluation of websites and practical use in research. Regularly updated.

Review of Medical and Veterinary Mycology
See entry no. 2731

3416 **Veterinary Medical Database**
Purdue University
www.vet.purdue.edu/depts/prog/vmdb.html
Located at the University since 1988, VMDB contains more than 6 million records on animal diseases, problems and procedures. No online access (in 2004) but searches, chargeable outside participating universities, can be submitted by post, e-mail, fax or phone.

3417 **The 'Virtual' Veterinary Center**
J. Martindale
www.martindalecenter.com/Vet.html
Large collection of annotated links to web resources on all aspects of veterinary and animal science.

Digital data, image & text collections

Animal Health and Welfare in Organic Farming: Compendium
University of Reading See entry no. 3313

3418 **Image Data Base**
Washington State University
imagedb.vetmed.wsu.edu
Extensive collection of high-quality animal images from the University's College of Veterinary Medicine, provided for educational, non-commercial use only. Many show animals with naturally occurring diseases; an image filter can be used to filter these if required.

3419 **World Anthrax Data Site**
World Health Organization
www.vetmed.lsu.edu/whocc/mp_world.htm
Clickable maps lead to statistical tables on anthrax occurrence throughout the world, compiled from FAO-WHO-OIE sources covering 1988–2001. Produced by the WHO Collaborating Center for Remote Sensing and Geographic Information Systems for Public Health at the Department of Pathobiological Sciences, School of Veterinary Medicine, Louisiana State University.

Directories & encyclopedias

Animal health and production compendium
CAB International See entry no. 3314

Encyclopedia of farm animal behavior
Agricultural Research Service See entry no. 2020

Encyclopedia of reproduction
E. Knobil and J.D. Neill, eds See entry no. 4470

Handbooks & manuals

3420 **The early history of veterinary literature and its British development**
F. Smith Baillière, Tindall and Cox, 1919–1933. 4 v.
Classic account of the development of veterinary literature from the earliest period to 1900. Numerous footnotes.

3421 **Field manual of wildlife diseases: general field procedures and diseases of birds** [USA]
M. Friend and J.C. Franson, eds USGPO, 1999, 400pp. ISBN 0607880961.
www.nwhc.usgs.gov/pub_metadata/field_manual/field_manual.html
Comprehensive manual including general field procedures; bacterial diseases; fungal diseases; viral diseases; parasitic diseases; biotoxins; chemical toxins; and miscellaneous diseases.

3422 **Foreign Animal Diseases: 'The Gray Book'** [USA]
United States Animal Health Association 6th edn, Pat Campbell and Associates and Carter Printing Company, 1998. Available in print, html, PDF and handheld versions.
www.vet.uga.edu/vpp/gray_book/FAD/index.htm
Aims to provide latest information on those foreign animal diseases considered to be the greatest threat to the livestock and poultry industries in the United States, including up-to-date information on the diseases; how they are diagnosed; how they are spread, and how they may be prevented, controlled and eradicated.

3423 **Handbook of laboratory animal science**
J. Hau and G.L. Van Hoosier, eds 2nd edn, CRC Press.
www.crcpress.com
These volumes bring together information on all aspects of laboratory animal science. Each chapter includes a bibliography.

- **Volume I. Essential principles and practices** 2003, 556pp. $139.95. ISBN 0849310865.
- **Volume II. Animal models** 2003, 269pp. $99.95. ISBN 0849310849.

3424 **Infectious diseases in livestock: scientific questions relating to the transmission, prevention and control of epidemic outbreaks of infectious disease in livestock in Great Britain** [UK]
Royal Society 2002. £25.00. ISBN 0854035796.
www.royalsoc.ac.uk/inquiry [COMPANION]
An independent scientific review on preventing and combating invasions of highly infectious livestock diseases.

Chaired by Sir Brian Follett, the strategic and wide-ranging review focused on the current state of relevant scientific knowledge and its policy implications, and highlighted gaps in that knowledge and the work required to fill them.
Series: Royal Society Policy Document, 15/02

3425 A manual for the primary animal health care worker
Food and Agriculture Organization 1994. ISBN 9251032580.
www.fao.org/docrep/T0690E/T0690E00.htm
A field manual for primary animal healthcare workers in developing countries, offering a working guide for diagnosing, treating and preventing common food animal diseases, for proper feeding of food animals and for useful husbandry practices for raising healthy and productive food animals. It also contains guidelines addressed to primary animal healthcare workers' trainers and supervisors and for adapting the manual to different conditions in various countries.

3426 Manual of diagnostic tests and vaccines for terrestrial animals
World Organization for Animal Health 5th edn, 2004, 1178pp. €140.00. ISBN 9290446226.
www.oie.int/eng/normes/mmanual/A_summry.htm
The purpose of the Terrestrial Manual is to contribute to the international harmonization of methods for the surveillance and control of the most important animal diseases. Standards are described for laboratory diagnostic tests and the production and control of biological products (principally vaccines) for veterinary use across the globe.
Available online: see website

Medical entomology: a textbook on public health and veterinary problems caused by arthropods
B.F. Eldridge and J.D. Edman, eds See entry no. 4436

3427 Merck veterinary manual: MVM
S.E. Aiello, ed. 8th edn, Merck & Co., Inc., 1998, 2305pp. $37.00. ISBN 0911910298.
www.merckvetmanual.com/mvm/index.jsp
First produced in 1955, this comprehensive manual is currently published in English, Spanish, Italian, Japanese, French and Portuguese. Covers all aspects of animal health and veterinary medicine, with over 12,000 indexed topics and over 1200 illustrations.
Available online: see website.

3428 Prions and mad cow disease
B.K. Nunnally and I.S. Krull, eds Marcel Dekker, 2004, 428pp. $179.95. ISBN 0824740831.
Multi-author text reviewing the state of the art.

3429 The veterinary formulary
Y. Bishop, ed. 5th edn, Pharmaceutical Press, 2001, 692pp. £69.95. ISBN 0853694516.
Published in association with the British Veterinary Association. Enables effective and safe prescribing for animals by providing an essential reference to all medicines for veterinarians, pharmacists and those involved with animal healthcare. Extensively revised in each edition.

3430 Veterinary medicine: a textbook of the diseases of cattle, sheep, pigs, goats and horses
O.M. Radostits [et al.] 9th edn, Saunders, 2000, 1881pp. $159.00. ISBN 0702026042.
Highly successful, definitive book on large animal medicine. All large animal species are covered – cow, horse, sheep, goat and pig – and every medical condition that could be encountered worldwide is discussed in detail. Fully revised and redesigned for this edition.

Keeping up-to-date

3431 Animal Health: Report of the Chief Veterinary Officer [UK]
Great Britain. Department for Environment, Food and Rural Affairs Annual.
www.defra.gov.uk/corporate/publications/pubcat/cvo/2003/index.htm
Comprehensive annual survey comprising a strategic overview followed by sections on the protection of public health, disease surveillance, prevention and control of disease, and animal welfare in the UK.

Applied animal behaviour science
International Society for Applied Ethology See entry no. 2025

Dairy-L
University of Maryland See entry no. 3316

3432 Theriogenology: An International Journal of Animal Reproduction
Elsevier, 1974–, 18/year. €1054.00. ISSN 0093691X.
www.elsevier.com/locate/issn/0093691X [DESCRIPTION]
Contains original research articles on all aspects of animal reproduction biology.

- **International Embryo Transfer Society** www.iets.org. Research and procedures associated with the 'follicle, ovulation, superovulation, gonadotropins, the embryo, the oocyte, the sperm cell, IVF, IVM, embryonic developmental stages, oocyte cryopreservation, lactation, and embryo transfer/cloning'.

3433 World Animal Health
World Organization for Animal Health 2003, Annual, 785pp. €100.00. ISBN 9290445882 ISSN 10173102.
www.oie.int/eng/info/en_sam.htm
Presents a synthesis of animal health information from 196 countries/territories and provides a unique tool for all those involved in the development of animal production, international trade in animals and animal products and the epidemiology and control of animal diseases, including zoonoses.
Available online: see website.

MEDICINE

Medicine

There is an excellent range of medical resources readily available, and an equally excellent set of library and information professionals supporting provision of access to such resources. For those new to the arena, an intensive examination of one or two of the generic tools listed at the outset of each of the three subject parts should prove highly rewarding.

We should stress, however, the need to be vigilant: much bogus information is produced – especially on the web. Fortunately, there are a number of valuable services evaluating the quality of the various offerings (we have made especial use here of those offered by HON: Health On the Net Foundation, whose mission is 'to guide lay persons or non-medical users and medical practitioners to useful and reliable online medical and health information'). But we would strongly stress that the content below is provided for general information only, and should not be treated as a substitute for professional medical advice.

Introductions to the subject

3434 **Biomedical platforms: realigning the normal and the pathological in late-twentieth-century medicine**
P. Keating and A. Cambrosio MIT Press, 2003, 544pp. $55.00. ISBN 0262112760.
Interesting sociologically-based review of the coming together of biological and medical approaches to form 'biomedicine'. Useful offset to dichotomies underpinning science/technology, basic/applied, as well as biology/medicine itself. Notes and references pp 341–525.

Calculus for biology and medicine
C. Neuhauser See entry no. 1896

3435 **Dicing with death: chance, risk and health**
S. Senn Cambridge University Press, 2003, 251pp. £14.99. ISBN 0521540232.
Explanation of how statistics determines many decisions about medical care, from allocating resources for health, to determining which drugs to license, to cause-and-effect in relation to disease.
'[a] remarkable achievement ... In a slim paperback that is best read cover to cover. Stephen Senn has attempted to do for medical statistics what Stephen Hawking did for physics in *A Brief History of Time* ... And Simon Singh did for pure mathematics in *Fermat's Last Theorem*. I think he has succeeded.' (*British Medical Journal*)

- **Medical statistics from A to Z: a guide for clinicians and medical students** **B.S. Everitt** Cambridge University Press, 2003, 230pp. £20.99. ISBN 0521532043. Aims to provide non-technical definitions; with most entries having background reading which – where possible – involves 'medical rather than statistical journals and introductory statistical texts rather than those that are more advanced'.

3436 **Essential medical statistics**
B.R. Kirkwood and J.A.C. Sterne 2nd edn, Blackwell Science, 2003, 501pp. £22.95. ISBN 0865428719.
Successfully builds on the strength of the 1st edn by 'keeping the emphasis on enabling the reader to know which method to apply when'. Responds to growth in use of IT-based techniques by covering methods formerly considered too advanced for an introductory text. Very well written and laid-out.
'the breadth of coverage of the book is excellent ... a rather different approach to teaching medical statistics.' (*Statistics in Medicine*)
'This book is statistically correct. That is enough to distinguish it from most of its competitors.' (*British Medical Journal*)

- **The Cambridge dictionary of statistics in the medical sciences** **B.S. Everitt** Cambridge University Press, 1995, 274pp. £20.99. ISBN 0521479282. 2000 simple definitions and explanations of statistical concepts, especially those used in biomedicine.

Experimenting with humans and animals: from Galen to animal rights
A. Guerrini See entry no. 1897

3437 **The Fontana history of the human sciences**
R. Smith Fontana, 1997, 1036pp. ISBN 0006861784.
After an introduction to the project, comprehensive overview in four sections covering the 16th/17th centuries, the 'long' 18th century, the 19th century – narrower in scope, the 20th century, focusing on psychology. Good for the sociological context to current medical research and practice.

3438 **Learning medicine: an informal guide to a career in medicine** [UK]
P. Richards and S. Stockill 16th edn, BMJ Books, 2003, 149pp. Foreword by HRH The Prince of Wales, £15.95. ISBN 0727917129.
Designed to help students decide whether a course in medicine is the right career path for them. As well as information on courses, schools and making an application, students will find out what to expect from life as a medical student and doctor.

3439 **A manual of English for the overseas doctor**
J. Parkinson 5th edn, Churchill Livingstone, 1999, 282pp. £22.95. ISBN 044306136X.
Good practical book for overseas doctors which addresses difficulty that can affect people from abroad working in the UK medical sector. Includes descriptions of the National Health Service and of the postgraduate medical training system as well as covering communication skills and use of colloquial English.

3440 **The Oxford illustrated companion to medicine**
S. Lock [et al.], eds 3rd edn, Oxford University Press, 2001, 891pp. £42.50. ISBN 0192629506.
Covers the main fields of medicine as well as medicine and art, literature, music, folk medicine, notable patients. Offers a stimulating, wide-ranging account of the current state and past history of the medical, nursing, and allied health sciences.

'This detailed and comprehensive book describes almost every medical condition and disease known to humanity.' (*Choice*) 'Tremendous ... Highly recommended.' (*Library Journal*)

- **Encyclopedia of folk medicine** **G. Hatfield** ABC-CLIO, 2003, 392pp. $85.00. ISBN 1576078744. 'Would be as much at home in folk culture collections as in a library's medical section. Public libraries with patron interest or academic libraries with collections in traditional medicine would profit from the author's historical approach' *Booklist*.
- **Western medicine: an illustrated history** **I. Loudon, ed.** Oxford University Press, 2001, 362pp. £20.00. ISBN 0199248133. 19 chapters in multi-author text in 2 sections: From the Hippocratic corpus to twentieth-century medicine; Medicine in context. 'An excellent book ... The selection of illustrations is first-class.' *History Today*.

Dictionaries, thesauri, classifications

3441 Black's medical dictionary
G. Macpherson, ed. 40th edn, A&C Black, 2002, 733pp. £25.00. ISBN 0713654422.
Gives over 5000 definitions of medical terms and concepts, with appendices on important subjects. Includes a list of professional organizations.
39th edn, 1999.

3442 Concise colour medical dictionary
E.A. Martin, ed. 3rd edn, Oxford University Press, 2003, 754pp. Uses the text of the 6th edn of the *Concise medical dictionary*, 2002, £12.99. ISBN 0198607547.
www.oxfordreference.com
Over 10,000 entries covering all medical and surgical specialties, plus coverage of all new drugs in clinical use. Clearly laid out and jargon free, accessible and informative.
Available online: see website.

3443 Dictionary of medical acronyms and abbreviations
S. Jablonski, ed. 4th edn, Hanley & Belfus, 2001, 440pp. $29.95. ISBN 1560534605.
www.elsevier-international.com/medicaldictionaries
One of the best acronym books available, the revised edn has over 5000 new entries.
See website for details of all the Elsevier medical dictionaries.

- **Elsevier's dictionary of abbreviations, acronyms, synonyms, and symbols used in medicine** **S.A. Tsur** 2nd edn, Elsevier, 2004, 843pp. $195.00. ISBN 0444512659. Contains over 30,000 entries used in the various medical disciplines.

3444 Dictionary of medicine: French-English with English-French glossary (Dictionnaire de médecin: Français-anglais avec glossaire anglais-français)
S.P. Djordjevic Schreiber Publishing, 2000, 1149pp. (2nd edn 2004), $179.50. ISBN 1887563539.
www.schreiberpublishing.com [DESCRIPTION]
French-English with English-French glossary: 104,500 terms in all areas of medicine; 10,217 acronyms and abbreviations; 12,819 eponyms; 1440 proprietary drugs; 2200 adverbial phrases. Largest number of terms in fields clinical and laboratory medicine, but covers also terms from relevant biological and engineering disciplines.

- **Dictionary of medical and biological terms and medications: English–French** (Dictionnaire des termes médicaux et biologiques des médicaments: français–anglais) **G.S. Hill** Flammarion Medecine Sciences, 2005, 1024pp. €75.00. ISBN 2257101693. 60,000 entries, in colour.
- **Dictionnaire médical** **J. Quevauvilliers, A. Somogyi and A. Fingerhut** 3rd edn rev, Masson, 2004, 1590pp. €32.00. ISBN 2294020553. www.masson.fr/catalogue.htm [DESCRIPTION]. 35,000 terms. E-book.

3445 Dorland's illustrated medical dictionary
D.M. Anderson, ed. 30th edn, W B Saunders, 2003, 2140pp. $49.95. ISBN 0721601464.
www.dorlands.com [COMPANION]
First published in 1900, now in its 30th edition with colour illustrations. Over 123,000 entries from all fields of healthcare, with over 3000 new entries, many from complementary and alternative medicine. Fully searchable online access available.
Website also provides access to the extensive set of more specialized print and electronic dictionaries, wordbooks and medical transcription products marketed by Elsevier under the Dorland brand name.

3446 Medical Online Glossaries and Resources
A. Fairchild, comp.
www.geocities.com/med_dictionary
Extensive and intensive personal interest site containing 'over 1745 links to useful and informative medical and health-related websites and medical dictionaries in eighteen languages'. A fascinating compendium.

3447 Medical Subject Headings
National Library of Medicine
www.nlm.nih.gov/mesh/MBrowser.html
This is the MeSH Browser: an online vocabulary look-up aid for use with the Library's controlled vocabulary thesaurus. Reveals descriptors and their hierarchical position, together with scope notes, annotations, entry vocabulary, history notes, allowable qualifiers, etc. The browser will search in chemical data fields including those for CAS REGISTRY Number. Updated weekly.

3448 MediLexicon
Pharma-Lexicon International.
www.pharma-lexicon.com
Previously known as Pharma-Lexicon, this excellent resource includes a dictionary of over 200,000 medical, pharmaceutical, biomedical and healthcare acronyms and abbreviations, plus medical news and services for the medical, pharmaceutical or healthcare professional. A good gateway whose producers subscribe to the HONcode principles.

3449 Melloni's illustrated dictionary of medical abbreviations
B.J. Melloni and J.L. Melloni Parthenon, 1998, 485pp. $34.95. ISBN 1850707081.
'The only illustrated dictionary in its field.' Contains over 17,000 medical abbreviations and acronyms commonly used in both the medical literature and the spoken language of medicine.

- **Melloni's pocket medical dictionary** **J.L. Melloni [et al.]** Parthenon, 2004, 632pp. $34.95. ISBN 1842140515. Very nicely presented. Excellent use of diagrams. Useful list of plates and tables. 17,000 definitions.

3450 The On-line Medical Dictionary
G. Dark; University of Newcastle upon Tyne
http://cancerweb.ncl.ac.uk/omd
Freely accessible marvellous compendium of over 46,000

definitions 'relating to biochemistry, cell biology, chemistry, medicine, molecular biology, physics, plant biology, radiobiology, science and technology. It includes: acronyms, jargon, theory, conventions, standards, institutions, projects, eponyms, history, in fact anything to do with medicine or science ... The dictionary is stored as a single source file in a simplified, easy-to-edit, human-readable form of mark-up which is converted to HTML on the fly by a Perl CGI script originally developed by Denis Howe at Imperial College for the FREE ON-LINE DICTIONARY OF COMPUTING.'

3451 Stedman's: The Best Words in Medicine
www.stedmans.com
Online medical dictionary plus details of the wide range of print and electronic dictionaries and related works marketed under the Stedman's brand.

- **Stedman's abbreviations, acronyms and symbols** 3rd edn, Lippincott Williams & Wilkins, 2004. $29.95. ISBN 0781744083. PDA version of the print version. Appendices include: professional associations; chemotherapy and other drug regimens; clinical trials. 78,000 terms. For Palm OS, Windows CE, and Pocket PC handheld devices.

3452 Thieme Leximed: medizinisches Wörterbuch (Thieme Leximed medical dictionary German–English)
P. Reuter and C. Reuter, eds Thieme, 1996, 841pp. €109.00. ISBN 3131004916.
www.thieme.com [DESCRIPTION]
This is the 2nd volume of a two-volume work with more than 55,000 entries and some 125,000 translations dealing with the relevant clinical vocabulary; the appendix contains numerous anatomical plates with a bilingual legend. There is a companion English-German volume, and related products from the same publisher: see website.

- **English-Russian and Russian-English medical dictionary A.Y. Bolotina and E.O. Yahusheva** Russo, 2001, 541pp. £26.95. ISBN 5887212071. www.eastview.com. About 24,000 terms. Listed as out-of-print at EastView Information Services: see website.

3453 Unified Medical Language System
National Library of Medicine
www.nlm.nih.gov/research/umls
Project to develop multi-purpose computer systems that behave as if they 'understand' the meaning of the language of biomedicine and health: as used, for instance, in patient records, scientific literature, guidelines, public health data.

Currently, there are three UMLS Knowledge Sources:

Metathesaurus – A very large, multi-purpose, and multi-lingual vocabulary database that contains information about biomedical and health-related concepts, their various names, and the relationships among them

Semantic Network – To provide a consistent categorization of all concepts represented in the metathesaurus and to provide a set of useful relationships between these concepts

SPECIALIST Lexicon – Natural language processing system intended as a general English lexicon, and containing commonly occurring words and biomedical vocabulary.

These tools are freely available, but can require a licence to use.

3454 Units, symbols and abbreviations: a guide for medical and scientific authors
D.N. Baron, ed.; Royal Society of Medicine 5th edn, 1994. £13.00. ISBN 185315217X.
Introduction; Metrication and SI units; Symbols and nomenclature; Layout of references; Proof correction.

3455 Vera Pyle's current medical terminology
V. Pyle 9th edn, Lippincott Williams & Wilkins, 2003, 822pp. $44.00. ISBN 0934385424.
www.hpisum.com
Latest edn of well established resource features 3000 new entries, c.100 pages new material, thousands of updated entries. New edn announced for 2005 of glossary specializing in 'new, difficult, and hard-to-find medical terms that are not yet appearing in major medical dictionaries ... Has long been a favorite reference among quality-conscious transcriptionists'.
See website for details of further resources from Health Professions Institute.

- **Medical dictionary in six languages B. Spilker** Lippincott Williams & Wilkins, 1994, 688pp. $139.00. ISBN 0781701821. English, French, Spanish, Italian, German, Japanese. 7500 commonly used words and phrases from medical and clinical trials literature.
- **Medical terminology: an illustrated guide B.J. Cohen** 4th edn, Lippincott Williams & Wilkins, 2004. $72.00. ISBN 0781762944. www.lww.com. Available in range of edns: see website. This version includes Blackboard course cartridge plus access to Smartthinking online tutoring service.

3456 The words of medicine: sources, meanings, and delights
R. Fortune Charles C Thomas, 2001, 440pp. $65.95. ISBN 0398071330.
History of medical vocabulary presented in topical (rather than dictionary) form. It is 'written primarily for physicians, biomedical scientists, and medical students, but should also appeal to anyone in the health professions or biological sciences with a "feel" for medical history and the English language'.

Laws, standards, codes

3457 Medical ethics today: the BMA's handbook of ethics and law [UK]
V. English [et al.], eds 2nd edn, BMJ Books, 2004. Includes CD-ROM, £60.00. ISBN 0727917447.
Well produced: an excellent survey. Lists of statutes, regulations, and cases. Each chapter has an extensive bibliography.

3458 Medical Litigation Online [UK]
G.M. Hall and C.J. Lewis, eds
www.medneg.com
Wide-ranging, well structured site. 'The largest online database of medical cases. Free access to patients and charities.' Also covers articles, books, links, news, and texts – the last a 'database which plans to provide a single source for important medico-legal texts and materials'.

3459 MediRegs
www.mediregs.com
'Leading provider of regulatory and compliance databases to regulatory professionals throughout the health, life science, medical and food industries in the US, Europe and other parts of the world. MediRegs' dedicated staff of editors and software professionals has developed and maintains over 2000 collections of regulatory data. MediRegs has over 600

clients and more than 12,000 users, including top global drug companies, medical device makers, Fortune 50 consumer product companies, nationally recognized providers, a long list of Blue Cross Blue Shield plans, 15 federal agencies, and more than three dozen leading health-care law firms and compliance consultants.'

Questel.Orbit
See entry no. 4531

Official & quasi-official bodies

3460 Canadian Institutes of Health Research
www.cihr-irsc.gc.ca/e/193.html
The major federal agency responsible for funding health research in Canada, created in 2000. 'CIHR integrates research through a unique interdisciplinary structure made up of 13 'virtual' institutes. CIHR's Institutes are not buildings or research centres, but networks of researchers brought together to focus on important health problems. Unconstrained by bricks and mortar, the Institute's virtual structure encourages partnership and collaboration across sectors, disciplines and regions.'

3461 Department of Health [UK]
Great Britain. Department of Health
www.dh.gov.uk/Home/fs/en
Portal 'providing health and social care policy, guidance and publications' with access to a wide range of resources, including links to the work of the Chief Medical Officer and Chief Nursing Officer as well as to other nationally important sites of health and social care information: Directgov; NHS; NICE; and so on.

Of particular value is the section of the website headed Publications and statistics – including, for instance, downloadable PDFs of the Department's three main annual reports: that of the Department of Health itself, of the Chief Medical Officer (*On the state of public health*), and of the Chief Inspector of Social Services; also the Annual Report of the NHS Modernization Board.

- **Department of Health thesaurus of health and social care terms: the DH-data thesaurus** Stationery Office, 2001, 1487pp. £90.00. ISBN 0113225601. V. 1. Alphabetical listing of terms; V. 2. Hierarchical listing of terms. Contains the entire Health Management Information Consortium thesaurus, with all terminology updated, new terms added, and defunct ones removed.
- **DHSS/DHZZ – DH-DATA** www.dialog.com/products/datastar [FEE-BASED]. Online database jointly produced by the Department's Library and Information Service, and its Protection of Health Information Unit. Articles indexed from c.2000 mainly English-language journals plus books, reports, official publications, etc.

3462 Department of Health and Ageing [AUS]
Australia. Department of Health and Ageing
www.health.gov.au
Mission statement is: 'To lead the development of Australian's Health and Ageing system'. Well laid-out guides 'For Consumers' and 'For Health Professionals'.

- **Health and Ageing Thesaurus** www.health.gov.au/thesaurus.htm. Produced by the Department's Library and based on NLM's MEDICAL SUBJECT HEADINGS.

3463 Department of Health and Human Services [USA]
United States. Department of Health and Human Services
www.os.dhhs.gov
The US Federal Government's principal agency for protecting the health of all Americans and providing essential human services, especially for those who are least able to help themselves. Its motto is: 'Leading America to better health, safety and well-being'.

DHHS Agencies include: National Institutes of Health; Food and Drug Administration; Centers for Disease Control and Prevention; Indian Health Service; Substance Abuse and Mental Health Services Administration; Centers for Medicare and Medicaid Services; Administration for Children and Families; Administration on Aging – many of which are separately described within *The New Walford*.

- **Agency for Healthcare Research and Quality** www.ahrq.gov. Mission is 'to improve the quality, safety, efficiency, and effectiveness of health care for all Americans'. Wide-ranging site: includes a helpful What's New section covering items posted in the last 30 days.
- **Health Resources and Services Administration** www.hrsa.gov. DHHS body directing 'programs that improve the Nation's health by expanding access to comprehensive, quality health care for all Americans'. Its Goal reads: 'Moving toward 100 percent access to health care and 0 health disparities for all Americans'.

3464 General Medical Council [UK]
www.gmc-uk.org
Established under the *Medical Act* of 1858, with legal powers designed to maintain the standards the public have a right to expect of doctors. Doctors must be registered with the GMC to practise medicine in the UK, and this includes people who are: Working in the National Health Service; Prescribing drugs, the sale of which is restricted by law; Signing medical certificates required for statutory purposes (death certificates, etc.). Useful links section – including to the websites of regulators in other countries.

- **Medical Register** Annual. ISSN 00720763. www.gmc-uk.org/register. List of all doctors registered to practise medicine in the UK.

3465 Institut National de la Santé et de la Recherche Médicale
www.inserm.fr
Created in 1964, the French Institute of Health and Medical Research 'overseen jointly by the French Ministries of Research and Health. INSERM's vocation is to promote health for all'. Encompasses 366 research units and 21 clinical research centres; employs 13,000 research professionals, of whom some 6000 are designated researchers – including 2500 clinicians. Well structured website, mostly in French.

3466 Medical Research Council [UK]
www.mrc.ac.uk
One of seven UK government funded Research Councils, the MRC promotes 'research into all areas of medical and related science with the aims of improving the health and quality of life of the UK public and contributing to the wealth of the nation'. Access to the 40 or so MRC research centres plus links to the sites of a range of other bodies concerned with medical research. The Public Interest part of the website includes overviews of topical issues (e.g. chronic fatigue syndrome/ME), news, ethics policy, etc.

- **National Centre for the Replacement, Refinement and Reduction of Animals in Research** www.nc3rs.org.uk.

- Established 2004 implementing recommendation of House of Lords Select Committee.

3467 National Institutes of Health [USA]
www.nih.gov
'The steward of medical and behavioral research for the Nation.'

It is an Agency within the US DEPARTMENT OF HEALTH AND HUMAN SERVICES aiming to conduct and fund research which will lead to better health for all. Comprehensive website including links to the 27 separate Institutes within the NIH umbrella – most referenced elsewhere. In 2003, the whole organization employed 18,000 people and had a budget of £27 billion.

- **The Ad Hoc Group for Medical Research Funding** www.aamc.org/research/adhocgp/start.htm. Coalition in support of increased funding for NIH.
- **NIH Roadmap: Accelerating Medical Discovery to Improve Health** http://nihroadmap.nih.gov. 'Integrated vision to deepen our understanding of biology, stimulate interdisciplinary research teams, and reshape clinical research to accelerate medical discovery and improve people's health.'

3468 President's Council on Bioethics [USA]
www.bioethics.gov
'Advising the President on ethical issues related to advances in biomedical science and technology.' Topics listed as being of Council concern during 2004 included: Age-retardation (life extension); Aging and end-of-life; Beyond therapy (enhancement); Biotechnology and public policy; Bioethics in literature; Cloning; Drugs, children and behaviour control; Memory boosting/suppression; Mood control; Neuroethics; Organ transplantation; Property in the body; Research ethics; Sex selection; Stem cells.

- **Bioethics Resources on the Web** National Institutes of Health. www.nih.gov/sigs/bioethics. Very extensive well categorized collection; but many parts of the site not recently updated. Still, provides a good overview of the range of issues and bodies germane to this complex arena.
- **Human cloning and human dignity: the report of the President's Council on Bioethics** L.R. Kass, ed. PublicAffairs, 2002, 350pp. $14.00. ISBN 1586481762. www.publicaffairsbooks.com [DESCRIPTION]. 'A council of leading scientists and philosophers offers wise and provocative insights into the ethical implications of one of the most momentous developments of all – cloning'.
- **Scientific and medical aspects of human reproductive cloning** National Academy Press, 2002, 272pp. $35.00. ISBN 0309076374. www.nap.edu [DESCRIPTION]. Produced by the Committee on Science, Engineering, and Public Policy, National Academy of Sciences, National Academy of Engineering, Institute of Medicine. Also available as downloadable PDF. The Report contains a very useful *Glossary of cloning terms*.

Research centres & institutes

3469 Howard Hughes Medical Institute [USA]
www.hhmi.org
'A revolution is taking place in biology, one that promises to transform our understanding of the living world and produce major advances in medical care. Among its leaders is the Howard Hughes Medical Institute (HHMI). The Institute is a non-profit medical research organization that employs hundreds of leading biomedical scientists working at the forefront of their fields. In addition, through its grants program and other activities, HHMI is helping to enhance science education at all levels and maintain the vigor of biomedical science worldwide. The Institute is one of the world's largest philanthropies, with laboratories across the United States and grants programs throughout the world.'

- **Becoming a Scientist** www.hhmi.org/becoming. 'What qualities do you need to succeed in biomedical research? Some of the world's most prominent biomedical researchers may surprise you with their answers.'

3470 Kennedy Institute of Ethics [USA]
http://kennedyinstitute.georgetown.edu/site/index.htm
The world's oldest and most comprehensive academic bioethics foundation. Wide-ranging programme of events, publications, teaching, research, affiliations. Good entrée to the field: 'Bioethics became a field of discourse, not just about religious links, but about problems all people face ... It's really an international field now that covers everything from fertilization to death.'

- **International Network on Feminist Approaches to Bioethics** www.fabnet.org. Approximately 350 individual members in 28 countries. Useful bibliography of books by members; newsletter; links.
- **National Reference Center for Bioethics Literature** http://www.georgetown.edu/research/nrcbl/nrc/index.htm. 'The world's largest collection related to ethical issues in medicine and biomedical research. This collection functions both as a reference library for the public and as an in depth research resource for scholars from the US and abroad.'

3471 National Institute for Medical Research [UK]
www.nimr.mrc.ac.uk
Four major subject groups – Genetics and development; Infections and immunity; Neurosciences; Structural biology – at the Institute contain 19 Divisions with over 200 scientists, 100 post-doctoral fellows, and approximately 100 postgraduate students. It is thus the largest of the research establishments of the MEDICAL RESEARCH COUNCIL; but early 2005 its future location and status were under discussion.

3472 Nuffield Council on Bioethics [UK]
www.nuffieldbioethics.org
Examines ethical issues raised by new developments in biology and medicine. Established by the NUFFIELD FOUNDATION in 1991, the Council is an independent body, funded jointly by the Foundation, and by the MEDICAL RESEARCH COUNCIL and the WELLCOME TRUST. The Council's wide-ranging and valuable publications – Discussion Papers, Reports and Annual Reports – are available for PDF download or can be purchased.

Associations & societies

3473 Academy of Medical Sciences [UK]
www.acmedsci.ac.uk
Established in 1998 to act as an authoritative body to promote medical science across traditional disciplinary boundaries: serving the medical sciences 'in the same way that the Royal Society serves the natural sciences, the British Academy serves the humanities and the Royal Academy of Engineering serves engineering science. The Academy of Medical Sciences draws its authority from its elected Fellowship of 803 leading medical scientists in the UK. Fellows are designated FMedSci'.

Useful policy papers and other publications and briefings.

- **Academy of Medical Royal Colleges** www.aomrc.org.uk. Objectives are to co-ordinate the work of the Medical Royal Colleges and Faculties.

3474 American Medical Association
www.ama-assn.org
The national professional organization for all physicians, founded in 1847, and 'always working to improve America's healthcare system'; they are 'advocates for physicians and their patients'. Wide range of publications – including a set of reference consumer publications.

- **AMA Physician Select**
http://dbapps.ama-assn.org/aps/amahg.htm. Basic professional information on virtually every licensed physician in the United States and its possessions, including more than 690,000 doctors of medicine (MD) and doctors of osteopathy or osteopathic medicine (DO).
- **Atlas of the Body** www.ama-assn.org/ama/pub/category/7140.html. Freely accessible; areas well labelled.
- **Complete Medical Encyclopedia** 2003, 1400pp. $45.00. ISBN 0812991001. Coverage of diseases and disorders, injuries, treatments, and preventive medicine. Special features include symptom charts, first aid, atlas of the body, and a full-colour section on genetics and other medical news.
- **Journal of the American Medical Association** 48/year. €485.00. http://jama.ama-assn.org. One of the world's leading medical journals. Subscribers have access to the interactive Users' guides to the medical literature: a manual for evidence-based practice.

3475 Americans/Europeans/Japanese for Medical Advancement
www.curedisease.com
Advocacy body which 'promotes human wellness by exposing the lost opportunities for cures and the life-threatening results of animal-modeled biomedical research. We educate the public, showing how government and charities misspend medical research dollars and place us at grave risk'.

3476 Association of American Medical Colleges
www.aamc.org
Non-profit association of medical schools, teaching hospitals, and academic societies. Represents 125 accredited US M.D.-granting medical schools and the 17 accredited Canadian medical schools; the principal source of hospital and health system input to AAMC is via the Council of Teaching Hospitals and Health Systems (COTH); and there is a useful list with links of the almost 100 academic society members.

3477 Association of Medical Research Charities [UK]
www.amrc.org.uk
Membership organization of the leading UK charities that fund medical and health research, founded in 1972. Good briefing, policy and position papers about medical research issues: especially on such as use of animals, stem cell research, patenting, and so on.

3478 British Medical Association
www.bma.org.uk
Professional association of doctors, founded in 1832, representing their interests and providing services for some 130,000 members, including almost 80% of UK practising doctors.

There is an extensive Public/Patients area of the website, with sections headed: A – Z of queries and useful sites; BMA health publications and policy reports; Clinical trials in the UK; Doctors' fees; Doctors' training and qualifications; Finding a self-help or patient organization; Health information on the internet; Information on specialists; Other useful websites; You and your doctor.

The BMA Library has a good range of services. There is a nice 'Online tour of the library'; a very useful range of Factsheets (e.g. Complementary and alternative medicine; Clinical audit; Genetically modified food; National medical journals; Statistics); and much else, both freely available and priced. An excellent resource.

- **British Medical Journal** Weekly.
http://bmj.bmjjournals.com/aboutsite/index.shtml [DESCRIPTION]. The leading journal with four paper editions with the same content but different advertising: General practice; clinical research; international; compact (for retired BMA members); range of online offerings.

3479 Canadian Medical Association
www.cma.ca
Founded in 1867, to serve and unite the physicians of Canada and to be the national advocate, in partnership with the people of Canada, for the highest standards of health and health care. Represents more than 55,000 practising physicians across the country, who are also represented through 12 provincial and territorial divisions.

3480 Coalition for Medical Progress [UK]
www.medicalprogress.org
Role is to help explain the case for medical progress and the benefits brought about by animal research. Membership is drawn from organizations representing: Science and scientists; Veterinary and animal welfare; Charities; Commercial sector; Research funders; Patients; Medical research and education.

3481 Institute of Medicine [USA]
www.iom.edu
One of the four organizations comprising the US National Academies – the others being the National Academy of Sciences, the National Academy of Engineering, and the National Research Council. The Institute is charged with providing unbiased, evidence-based, and authoritative information and advice concerning health and science policy to policy-makers, professionals, leaders in every sector of society, and the public at large. Copies of each of its often extensive reports (e.g. Immunization Safety Review: Vaccines and Autism, 2004) can be accessed via the website.

Medical Library Association
See entry no. 6349

3482 RDS: Understanding Animal Research in Medicine [UK]
www.rds-online.org.uk
Funded by its members, most of whom are medical researchers, doctors and vets, with corporate members including research institutes, university departments, medical research charities, learned societies and pharmaceutical companies. Membership is currently about 5000. 'RDS believes that research using animals should be well regulated, conducted humanely and only when there is no alternative. We work with welfare groups and government to promote good practice in laboratory animal welfare and the development of non-animal replacement methods.'

Good links section including lists of Groups campaigning to abolish animal research and Organizations explaining the need for animals in research.

UK Health Informatics Society
See entry no. 4159

World Association of Medical Editors
See entry no. 6356

3483 **World Medical Association**
www.wma.net/e
Founded 1947 and funded by annual contributions of its members, now some 80 National Medical Associations. Have an Ethics Unit, created in 2003, and a helpful Human Rights section, with a list of links. The *Handbook of WMA Policy* 'is issued as a record of the World Medical Association's stance on a variety of ethical and social issues'.

- **World Health Professions Alliance** www.whpa.org. Alliance of the Association with International Council of Nurses and International Pharmaceutical Federation. Aims to facilitate collaboration with key medicine and health stakeholders.

Libraries, archives, museums

3484 **Directory of health libraries and information services in the United Kingdom and the Republic of Ireland: 2002–3**
J. Ryder, ed. 11th edn, Facet Publishing, 2001, 288pp. £39.50. ISBN 1856043789.
The most comprehensive directory of its kind. Lists libraries wholly concerned with medicine and nursing, as well as libraries of veterinary, pharmaceutical and occupational medicine, and information services run by medical charities. Arranged by library or organization name in alphabetical order, the directory includes three detailed indexes: town; personal name; and hospital.

3485 **Medical/Health Sciences Libraries on the Web**
University of Iowa
www.lib.uiowa.edu/hardin
A service of the University's Hardin Library for the Health Sciences, the Library in turn being a very good example of its type in the range of services and products offered. The Libraries list itself is frequently updated, and provides international coverage.

3486 **National Library for Health** [UK]
www.library.nhs.uk
'A work in progress to develop an integrated library service for the NHS ... This website is the first phase in the development of the National Library for Health, and integrates electronic content from the national collections. Later developments include plans to add electronic resources from regional and local collections, so that ultimately, NHS staff can use the NLH website as the gateway to all the resources that are available to them.

Other plans include links to individual libraries, so that NHS staff can move seamlessly between electronic resources and the skilled library staff who can help them with their information needs. In addition, it is envisaged that the NLH will be the interface to engage with key national developments such as the National Programme for IT and NHSU, ensuring that the best available evidence is integrated wherever it is needed.'

The website has a useful section For Librarians, stressing, for instance, that the NLH is 'a programme of practical co-ordination, innovation and change, based on a reappraisal of how library services are led, developed and delivered in NHS England ... It is not simply a website'.

The National electronic Library for Health is now part of the NLH.

- **National electronic Library for Health** www.nelh.nhs.uk. Gives clinicians access 'to the best current know-how and knowledge to support healthcare-related decisions. Patients, carers and the public are welcome to use this site but NHS Direct Online provides the best public gateway to health information'.

3487 **National Library of Medicine** [USA]
www.nlm.nih.gov
Established in 1836 and based on the campus of the National Institutes of Health [q.v.] in Bethesda, Maryland. Is the world's largest medical library, collecting materials and providing information and research services in all areas of biomedicine and health care.

Offers a very wide range of general and specialized services: especially the 'Medline' suite, but including also such as consumer health information and human genome resources. Collections span the whole gamut from 11th-century manuscripts to electronic journals.

- **DIRLINE: Directory of Information Resources Online** www.nlm.nih.gov/pubs/factsheets/dirlinfs.html [DESCRIPTION]. 8000 regularly reviewed records, focused primarily on health and biomedicine, giving location and good descriptive information about wide variety of organizations, research resources, projects, databases, etc. Can search by keyword and MeSH Headings.
- **Guide to Finding Health Information** www.nlm.nih.gov/services/guide.html#five. Brief and excellent overview, explaining the relationship between the Library's services and services elsewhere, and giving good starting points for information from other government and health-related organizations as well as on the web.
- **History of Medicine** www.nlm.nih.gov/hmd. Valuable entrée: not just to the NLM's rich holdings of books and journals, archives and manuscripts, prints and photographs, films and videos; also to 'Doing research on the History of Medicine Web Site' and details of the Digital Manuscripts Program.
- **Lister Hill National Center for Biomedical Communications** http://lhncbc.nlm.nih.gov/lhc/servlet/Turbine. Research in high quality imagery, medical language processing, high-speed access to biomedical information, intelligent database systems development, multimedia visualization, knowledge management, data mining and machine-assisted indexing.
- **MedlinePlus: Trusted Health Information for You National Institutes of Health**. http://medlineplus.gov. Valuable service providing information on over 650 diseases/conditions, lists of hospitals and physicians, encyclopedia, dictionary, drug data, health information from the media, links to thousands of clinical trials, etc. No advertising or sponsorship.
- **NLM Classification** wwwcf.nlm.nih.gov/class. Classification used in the Library itself and in many other medical libraries. Good keyword searching facilities.
- **NLM Gateway** http://gateway.nlm.nih.gov/NewGatewayIntro.html. Web-based simultaneous search of MEDLINE/PubMed, TOXLINE Special, NLM Catalog, MedlinePlus, ClinicalTrials.gov, DIRLINE, Genetics Home Reference, Meeting Abstracts, HSRProj, OMIM, and HSDB. New Gateway April 2005: see website.
- **Specialized Information Services** http://sis.nlm.nih.gov. Information resources and services in toxicology, environmental health, chemistry, HIV/AIDS, and specialized topics in minority health. Includes TOXNET [q.v.] and ChemIDplus Lite, a very easy to use cross-database search system for chemical data.
- **The Visible Human Project** www.nlm.nih.gov/research/visible/visible_human.html. Complete, anatomically detailed, 3-D representations of the normal male and female human bodies. Long-term goal is system of knowledge structures that will

transparently link visual knowledge forms to symbolic knowledge formats such as body parts names.

3488 National Network of Libraries of Medicine [USA]
http://nnlm.gov
Programme co-ordinated by the NATIONAL LIBRARY OF MEDICINE whose 5482 Members and Affiliates provide a range of services for librarians, health professionals and the public.

- **Ejournals and Open Access** http://nnlm.gov/libinfo/ejournals. Useful gateway to the substantial developments currently taking place in this arena.

Portal & task environments

3489 Amedeo.com: The Medical Literature Guide
Amedeo Group.
www.amedeo.com
'Created to serve the needs of healthcare professionals, including physicians, nurses, pharmacists, administrators, other members of the health professions, and patients and their friends. They can easily access timely, relevant information within their respective fields ... All AMEDEO services are free of charge. This policy was made possible thanks to generous unrestricted educational grants provided by AMGEN, AstraZeneca, Berlex, Boehringer Ingelheim, Novartis, Pfizer, Roche, Schering AG.'

AMEDEO's core components include weekly emails with bibliographic lists about new scientific publications, personal web pages for one-time download of available abstracts, and an overview of the medical literature published in relevant journals over the past 12 to 24 months.

A good straightforward service.

- **FreeBooks4Doctors!** www.freebooks4doctors.com. Dedicated to promotion of free access to medical books over the internet. Currently provides access to content of 650 books. E-mail Book Alert available.
- **FreeMedicalJournals.com: Promoting free access to medical journals** www.freemedicaljournals.com. 1380 journals which can be sorted by speciality (as well as A–Z). There is a similar service of free books: 600, early 2005. For both e-mail alert service available.

3490 BioethicsWeb
Wellcome Trust and Resource Discovery Network
http://bioethicsweb.ac.uk
Gateway to evaluated, quality internet resources relating to biomedical ethics, including ethical, social, legal and public policy questions arising from advances in medicine and biology, issues relating to the conduct of biomedical research and approaches to bioethics.

- **MedHist Wellcome Trust and Resource Discovery Network**. http://medhist.ac.uk. Similar gateway to history of medicine resources on the internet, early 2005 describing and indexing over 900 records.
- **Medical Journals Backfiles Digitization Project Wellcome Trust, Joint Information Systems Committee and National Library of Medicine**. http://library.wellcome.ac.uk. Project to digitize the complete backfiles of number of important and historically significant medical journals. The digitized content will be made freely available on the internet via PUBMED CENTRAL, augmenting content already available there.

3491 ElsevierHealth
http://intl.elsevierhealth.com
Gateway to Elsevier's wide range of medical and health print, online and CD-ROM offerings, including under their imprints: Baillière Tindall; BC Decker; Butterworth-Heinemann; Churchill Livingstone; GW Medical Publishing; Hanley and Belfus; Mosby; Saunders.

3492 Health InterNetwork Access to Research Initiative: HINARI
www.healthinternetwork.org
Launched by the Secretary General of the UNITED NATIONS in 2000 'to bridge the 'digital divide' in health, ensuring that relevant information – and the technologies to deliver it – are widely available and effectively used by health personnel: professionals, researchers and scientists, and policy makers'. It provides free or very low cost online access to the major journals in biomedical and related social sciences to local, non-profit institutions in developing countries.

3493 Health On The Net Foundation
www.hon.ch/HomePage/Home-Page.html
Not-for-profit portal to medical information on the internet founded in 1996, and operated by Swiss foundation, supported by local Geneva authorities, and co-operating closely with the University Hospitals of Geneva and the Swiss Institute of Bioinformatics. In 2002 was granted consultative status to the Economic and Social Council of the UNITED NATIONS, which 'will facilitate HON participation with the WORLD HEALTH ORGANIZATION and other UN bodies, and reinforce its consultative role with government ministries in several countries where HON has contacts'.

The resources identified by HON are searchable using an extremely smart and intuitive software system. But the organization is particularly distinctive for its now widely recognized and used HONCode: a code of conduct for medical and health websites whose guidelines encompass eight principles: authority; complementarity; confidentiality; attribution; justifiability; transparency of authorship; transparency of sponsorship; honesty in advertising and editorial policy. Sites conforming to these principles are allowed to display the HONCode logo: 'Some 3000 sites are now formal HONcode subscribers, that is, they have a unique ID number and are indexed by us. About 80% of these are US sites, but the proportion of European and other non-US sites is growing. The HONcode now exists in 17 language versions, in addition to English'.

Much else of value on this excellent site including: Latest health news from selected trustworthy sources; Search the full text of over 80,000 medical documents; Top selection of illustrations representing over 1400 subjects.

- **Quackwatch: Your Guide to Quackery, Health Fraud, and Intelligent Decisions S. Barrett; Health On The Net Foundation** . www.quackwatch.org. Non-profit corporation 'whose purpose is to combat health-related frauds, myths, fads, and fallacies'. One of a number of similar and respected sites maintained with the help of volunteers.

3494 Knowledge Finder
Aries Systems Corporation.
www.kfinder.com/newweb/home.html
Automatically reviews, filters and synthesizes primary research to identify the principal contributions in the field of medicine, tailored to individual needs. The Company's mission is 'to provide technical innovations that empower all of the participants in the knowledge retrieval chain: publishers, database developers, librarians and knowledge workers. We believe that each of these participants has an essential role to play in the creation, dissemination and use of knowledge. Our technical solutions enhance each of their

roles and empowers them to take full advantage of the new opportunities created by the Internet'.

3495 **LTSN Medicine, Dentistry and Veterinary Medicine** [UK]
University of Newcastle and Higher Education Academy
www.ltsn-01.ac.uk
One of the centres established to promote high quality learning and teaching in UK higher education through the development and transfer of good practices. Good Resources section including a list of academic publications of relevance to learning and teaching in the sector, and an extensive set of web courseware links, organized by subject area.

3496 **MDLInx: Your Speciality is Our Speciality**
MDLinx Inc.
www.mdlinx.com [REGISTRATION]
'MDLinx's proprietary content aggregation technology is the industry leader in the health care vertical market. Currently, MDLinx owns and operates a network of 34 Websites and over 700 different, daily e-mail newsletters that provide highly focused content to 255,000 physicians and healthcare professionals, as well as to a growing number of patients.'

Good sets of resources – especially useful for some of the medical speciality areas. The organization subscribes to the HONCode principles.

3497 **MedBioWorld**
Healthnostics Inc.
www.medbioworld.com
'The largest medical and bioscience reference and resource directory on the Internet. The site is ranked #1 for medical and bioscience directories by GOOGLE. Includes 8200 journals within 80 subspecialties, the home pages of 7000 medical and bioscience associations, and links to over 2000 bioscience companies. Other research tools include medical glossaries, disease databases, clinical trials and guidelines, and medical journals offering full-text articles.

Despite the quantity – and indeed, wealth – of information, a well laid out and easily navigable site, with the commercial links clearly separate. The search and results display facilities need some improvement, however.

3498 **National Center for Research Resources** [USA]
www.ncrr.nih.gov
Component of the NATIONAL INSTITUTES OF HEALTH which 'supports primary research to create and develop critical resources, models, and technologies'. The heading Access to Scientific Resources leads through to often extensive website sections categorized: Biomedical technology resource centres; General clinical research centres; National gene vector laboratories; Human tissues and organs resources; Human islet cell resource centres; Non-human primates resources; Rodent resources; Fish resources; Invertebrate models and stocks; Biological materials; Comparative medicine information sources; Genetic and genomic resources.

3499 **OMNI** [UK]
University of Nottingham and Resource Discovery Network
www.omni.ac.uk
OMNI (Organizing Medical Networked Information), the gateway to high quality internet resources in health and medicine, was the precursor of the RDN's wider BIOME service. It is primarily aimed at students, researchers, academics and practitioners in the health and medical sciences: especially in the UK further and higher education sector. It is separately searchable, as are the other gateways within BIOME.

3500 **Thomson Healthcare**
www.thomson.com/healthcare
Gateway to the medicine and health-related products and services of Thomson; part of the company's Scientific and Healthcare principal global market groups, the other three such groups, in increasing order of employees and revenues being: Financial; Learning; and Legal and Regulatory. There is a Products and Solutions A–Z which lists all Thomson Healthcare offerings.

3501 **Unbound Medicine**
Unbound Medicine Inc.
www.unboundmedicine.com
Produce a range of handheld, wireless, and web-based technology products and services for healthcare professionals: for instance, PDA versions of: *CURRENT CONSULT Medicine 2005* (integrated medical reference suite covering 850+ disorders linked with 550 differential diagnoses); *Davis's Drug Guide* (covering several thousand brand name and generic drugs); *Taber's Cyclopedic Medical Dictionary*; and the MERCK MANUAL OF DIAGNOSIS AND THERAPY.

Discovering print & electronic resources

3502 **A bibliography of medical and biomedical biography**
L.T. Morton and R.J. Moore 3rd edn, Ashgate, 2005, 560pp. £85.00. ISBN 075465069.
Forthcoming edition of text detailing readily available sources of information in the English language on significant figures in the history of medicine and the biomedical sciences.
2nd edn 1994.
'a remarkable achievement, and a must for medical historians (of the 2nd edn).' (*British Medical Journal*)

Biological Journals and Abbreviations
G. Patton, ed. See entry no. 1963

3503 **EMBASE**
Elsevier, 1974–.
www.embase.com [FEE-BASED]
Contains over 9 million references from 1974 onwards covering the world's biomedical and pharmacological literature. Indexes over 4000 journals. Comprehensive in drug-related literature. Uses the EMTREE Thesaurus, with 37,000 drug and medical terms organized in a tree-like structure ranging from very broad to very specific concepts.

3504 **Finding and using health information on the Internet**
S Welsh, B Agnostelis and A Cooke ASLIB, 2000, 320pp. £29.99. ISBN 0851423841.
Focuses on the different uses and applications of biomedical information resources available on the internet. It explains not only how to find the best information resources quickly and effectively, but also how to customize Internet tools to your own personal requirements. Detailed evaluation of key resources: e.g. PUBMED. A well written guide.

Global Health
See entry no. 4179

3505 **Instructions to Authors in the Health Sciences**
Medical College of Ohio
www.mco.edu/lib/instr/libinsta.html
An excellent set of links to the information/instructions given to prospective authors for over 3000 journal titles. Useful additional links to more generic statements and reports on medical publishing. Produced by the College's Raymon H. Mulford Library.

The internet for molecular biologists: a practical approach
C.E. Sansom and R.M. Horton, eds See entry no. 1974

3506 **Medical information on the internet: a guide for health professionals**
R. Kiley 3rd edn, Churchill Livingstone, 2003, 185pp. £22.99. ISBN 0443072159.
www.medinfolinks.com [COMPANION]
Good concise guide in four major sections: Connecting, browsing and communicating; Medical databases on the web; Searching the web; The medical web. The URLs of the resources covered can be found at the companion website.

The Medical Library Association encyclopedic guide to searching and finding health information on the web
P.F. Anderson and N.J. Allee See entry no. 4181

3507 **PubMed**
National Library of Medicine and National Center for Biotechnology Information
http://nnlm.gov/nnlm/online/pubmed/pmtri.pdf [DESCRIPTION]
PubMed was developed by NCBI within NLM to provide access to citations from biomedical literature. Publishers participating in PubMed electronically submit their citations to NCBI prior to or at the time of publication. If the publisher has a website that offers full-text versions of its journals, PubMed provides links to that site as well as biological resources, consumer health information, research tools, and more. There may be a charge to access the text or information.

PubMed provides access to bibliographic information that includes that present in MEDLINE, but also covers citations out-of-scope for MEDLINE itself, citations that precede the date a journal was selected for MEDLINE coverage, and some additional life science journals that submit full text to PubMed Central and receive a qualitative review by NLM.

PubMed now includes over 15 million citations. Free access was announced in 1997 with approximately 9 million citations. More than 2.2 million searches are conducted each day on PubMed.

- **Entrez** www.ncbi.nlm.nih.gov/Database. Integrated, text-based search and retrieval system used at NCBI for their major databases, including PubMed, Nucleotide and Protein Sequences, Protein Structures, Complete Genomes, Taxonomy and others.
- **Index Medicus** Monthly. $620.00 [2003]. The original print listing of references to current articles from some 3700 biomedical journals. Included: *Bibliography of Medical Reviews*; *Medical Subject Headings*; *List of Journals Indexed in Index Medicus*. Publication ceased end 2004.
- **MEDLINE** http://omni.ac.uk/medline. Title of the original online version of Index Medicus whose content is now offered by a range of aggregators, as well as by NLM themselves: see website for useful summary.
- **PubMed Central** www.pubmedcentral.nih.gov/about/intro [DESCRIPTION]. Non-exclusive digital archive of life sciences journal literature launched in February 2000. All the content is free access – though some journals may delay submission from the date of their publication of the articles.

3508 **Super searchers on health and medicine: the online secrets of top health and medical researchers** [USA]
S.M. Detwiler CyberAge Books, 2000, 208pp. $24.95. ISBN 0910965447.
www.infotoday.com/supersearchers/ssmed.htm [COMPANION]
One of a series of texts featuring revealing interviews with 8–12 top online searchers in the discipline. The Companion has a list of almost 200 key websites.

- **Detwiler's directory of health and medical resources** **S.M. Detwiler, ed.** 9th edn, Information Today, 2002–3, 839pp. $195.00. ISBN 1573871559. Covers some 2000 corporations, associations, state and federal agencies, publishers, licensure organizations, healthcare market research firms, foundations, institutes, etc.

Digital data, image & text collections

3509 **Bioethics Central: a guide to primary documents and resources**
J Craig Venter Institute.
www.genomenewsnetwork.org/resources/bioethics [DESCRIPTION]
Valuable 'guide to the primary materials – landmark documents, legislation, and religious views – that have shaped the field of bioethics and to the academic centers, organizations, and government agencies that, along with the public, will do so in the future'. Hosted within the Genome News Network site (noting, however, that: 'In November 2004, Genome News Network suspended bi-weekly publication while staff reporters undertake some new writing projects. GNN's news and features will continue to be online, and we will continue to update the Guide to Sequenced Genomes').

Bioline International
University of Toronto and Reference Center on Environmental Information See entry no. 1984

BioMed Central
See entry no. 1986

Directories & encyclopedias

3510 **Companion encyclopedia of the history of medicine**
W.F. Bynum and R. Porter, eds Routledge, 1997, 1848pp. £60.00. ISBN 0415164184.
Comprehensive reference work which surveys all aspects of the history of medicine, both clinical and social, and reflects the complementary approaches to the discipline.
'It is both intelligent and discursive, and anyone with an interest in medicine past or present should have it on their shelves.' (*Daily Telegraph*)

3511 **Encyclopedia of bioethics**
S.G. Post, ed. Macmillan Reference USA, 2004, 3000pp. 5 v., $630.00. ISBN 0028657748.
www.galegroup.com [DESCRIPTION]

'Complete revision of the Dartmouth Medal-winning set first published in 1995.'

3512 **Encyclopedia of biostatistics**
P. Armitage and T. Colton, eds Wiley, 1998. 6 v, $4550.00. ISBN 0471975761.
The term 'biostatistics' is used to denote 'statistical methods in medicine and health sciences' ('biometry' being defined as 'the use of statistics in biology').

1208 articles in A–Z sequence, including treatments of many topics relevant in any branch of medicine and health: design of experiments and observational studies; problems associated with data collection; technical aspects of statistical inference, etc. Also articles about specific fields of medicine, research organizations, professional societies, journals, people, and so on.

An excellent, rewarding resource: start with the listing *Review articles*, which highlights important branches of the subject and areas of application.

3513 **Gale encyclopedia of medicine**
3rd edn, Thomson Gale, 2005. 5 v., $625.00. ISBN 1414403682.
www.galegroup.com [DESCRIPTION]
New edn announced for September 2005 of well established resource which 'fills a gap between introductory resources, such as single-volume family medical guides, and highly technical professional materials. Consult this authoritative, comprehensive in-depth medical guide for information on medical topics in language accessible to laypersons.'
Available online: see website.
'Outstanding Reference Source (on the 1st edn).' (*American Library Association*)

- **Encyclopedia of medical organizations and agencies** 14th edn, Thomson Gale, 2004, 1953pp. $360.00. ISBN 0787669008. Access to US public and private agencies concerned with medical information, funding, research, education, planning, advocacy, advice and service. See also the publisher's *Medical and Health Information Directory*.

3514 **RDInfo** [UK]
Great Britain. Department of Health and University of Leeds
www.rdinfo.org.uk
Provides the latest information on health-related research funding opportunities, including social care. The information supplied is gathered from a wide range of sources, and early-2005 their database held data gathered from over 1200 funding bodies offering some 4500 different awards. Produced by the University jointly with the Leeds Teaching Hospitals NHS Trust.

- **RDDirect** www.rddirect.org.uk. 'A friendly, professional signposting service for all researchers working in health and social care settings. This website contains information relevant to health research, whether you are an experienced researcher or a beginner.'
- **RDLearning** www.rdlearning.org.uk. Direct access to health-related training courses, conferences, workshops and short courses in the UK.

3515 **Women in medicine: an encyclopedia**
L.L. Windsor ABC-CLIO, 2002, 259pp. $85.00. ISBN 1576073920.
250 A–Z entries focusing primarily on women pioneers and mentors in medicine; additional entries on organizations and legislative acts.

- **Women and medicine B. Levin** 3rd edn, Scarecrow Press, 2002, 205pp. $45.00. ISBN 0810842386. 'Provides a comprehensive and definitive history, from early riots in medical schools when women tried to enroll, to women finally overcoming obstacles, making medical breakthroughs and enjoying brilliant medical careers'.
- **Women in medicine: career and life management M.A. Bowman, E. Frank and D.I. Allen** 3rd edn, Springer, 2002, 187pp. £20.50. ISBN 0387953094. Good basic coverage of the major issues.

Handbooks & manuals

3516 **Exploiting knowledge in health services**
G. Walton and A. Booth, eds 2nd edn, Facet Publishing, 2004, 274pp. £49.95. ISBN 1856044793.
Completely revised edition providing a snapshot of what health library and information professionals need to know now for today's demanding healthcare environment.
'New librarians will find this an extremely succinct and practical starting guide, and practicing librarians will find it an excellent refresher (on 1st edn).' (*Medical Reference Services Quarterly*)

3517 **Information retrieval: a health and biomedical perspective**
W.R. Hersh 2nd edn, Springer, 2003, 517pp. £54.00. ISBN 0387955224.
11 often rather technical chapters divided into three parts: basic concepts; state of the art; research directions. Chapter 2 'Health and biomedical information' is, however, an excellent overview of current trends and concerns.
Series: Health Informatics.

3518 **Peer review in health sciences**
F. Godlee and T. Jefferson, eds 2nd edn, BMJ Books, 2003, 367pp. £40.00. ISBN 0727916858.
2nd edn of this valuable edited collection reveals 'a definite lack of consensus on the aims of peer review ... Although most scholars and editors would agree that peer review is aimed at screening good submissions or good grant applications from bad ones, there seems little consensus on what 'good' and 'bad' mean'.

Keeping up-to-date

3519 **Annual Review of Medicine**
$207.00 [V. 55, 2004]. ISBN 0824305558 ISSN 00664219.
www.annurev.org/catalog/2004/me55.asp [DESCRIPTION]
Examples of chapters from the 2004 volume are: The impact of the completed human genome sequence on the development of novel therapeutics for human disease; Toward Alzheimer therapies based on genetic knowledge; The scientific basis for the current treatment of Parkinson's Disease; Lead poisoning; Basic advances and new avenues in therapy of spinal cord injury; Clinical management of tuberculosis in the context of HIV infection.

3520 **Bioethics.net: The American Journal of Bioethics**
Taylor & Francis.
www.bioethics.net
The most read source of information about bioethics, visited millions of times every month by readers from around the world and every walk of life. Mission is 'to provide the clinical, legal, academic, scientific, religious and broad community-at-large with a rapid but comprehensive debate of issues in bioethics'.

3521 Health News Daily [USA]
FDC Reports.
www.healthnewsdaily.com [FEE-BASED]
Coverage of a broad spectrum of healthcare issues including prescription pharmaceuticals, medical devices and diagnostics, over-the-counter pharmaceuticals and dietary supplements, biomedical research, federal health policy, Medicare/Medicaid, technology reimbursement and cost containment. Special emphasis is placed on regulatory and legislative developments.

3522 The Lancet
Elsevier, 1823–, Weekly. ISSN 01406736.
www.thelancet.com
Classic, long established journal which publishes clinical papers, state-of-the-art reviews, letters and news. Its electronic version includes back issues to 1996, some articles are free (upon registration); others by subscription.

3523 MediConf
www.mediconf.com
Lists 9000 future events in the fields of medicine, healthcare, pharmacology and biotechnology. Time range is currently from 1999 to 2013. Input is obtained by direct contact with over 3000 conference organizers.

3524 News-Medical.Net: medical news from around the world
www.news-medical.net
Clear, clean and well laid out site. Nice search and display facility. However, note also the information in their extensive section Terms and Conditions under 'Legals'.

3525 NewsRx
NewsRx.
www.newsrx.com [FEE-BASED]
Over 40 weekly reports (e.g. AIDS Vaccine Week, AIDS Weekly, Angiogenesis Weekly, Anti-Infectives Week, Biotech Business Week, Biotech Week, Bioterrorism Week, Blood Weekly, Cancer Gene Therapy Week, Cancer Vaccine Week, Cancer Weekly, Cardiovascular Week, Clinical Oncology Week, Clinical Trials Week, Diabetes Week, Drug Week ...) produced from data culled from a wide range of internet and news information sources (e.g. EBSCO Publishing, Factiva/Dow Jones, Gale Group, iSyndicate, Inc., MarketResearch.com, Medispecialty.com, Mindbranch, NewsEdge, ScreamingMedia.com.).

NewsRx is a private company originally operated under the name of its founder, CW Henderson, 'an acknowledged pioneer in the health reporting field'. The company subscribes to the HONCode principles.

Public Understanding of Science
See entry no. 366

Pre-clinical Sciences

Pre-clinical Sciences are traditionally those that someone who plans to be professionally trained and accredited as a medical doctor must become competent in before they begin their clinical training. We use the label here as a convenient shorthand even though the topics we cover and the Subject Field headings within which those topics are gathered are both partial and to some degree non-traditional.

Some of the partiality results from treatments in other subject areas, especially within the Subject Groupings CHEMISTRY and BIOLOGICAL SCIENCES: the Subject Fields LABORATORY TOOLS & TECHNIQUES, ORGANIC CHEMISTRY, BIOCHEMISTRY & BIOPHYSICS, CELL BIOLOGY, and GENETICS, GENOMICS & BIOINFORMATICS are especially pertinent in this regard – each containing much material complementing and in some cases overlapping what is presented here. As a rule of thumb, where a resource is wholly or predominantly concerned with the human organism, we have placed it here, rather than in an another Grouping or Field.

The major subject fields occurring later in the volume that are directly related to those here (apart, obviously, from the fields within the CLINICAL MEDICINE and HEALTH Subject Groupings) are: BIOTECHNOLOGY re the techniques it uses relevant to HUMAN GENETICS (and that subject area justified its own field by the sheer volume of material currently being generated: see also GENETICS, GENOMICS & BIOINFORMATICS); MATERIALS SCIENCE & ENGINEERING re MEDICAL TECHNOLOGY (the emphasis in the latter being on 'biomaterials' rather than 'biochemicals'); and CHEMICAL ENGINEERING re the industrial aspects of PHARMACOLOGY & PHARMACY. Note that toxicological resources appear mainly within ENVIRONMENTAL & OCCUPATIONAL HEALTH.

We should also comment on the label BIOMEDICAL SCIENCES: a narrower but increasingly common denotation than its words might suggest to the novice; and encompassing a number of services which would still in many places fall within the domain of a pathology laboratory. The realignment thus implied principally results from advances in molecular-based techniques at the expense of morphologically based ones.

Notwithstanding, clinically based pathological examination continues to have an essential role – particularly with regard to the causes of death, including within a forensic context. However, where the pathological process extends to 'the laboratory examination of samples of body tissue for diagnostic or forensic purposes' (*Oxford Dictionary of English*) the relevant reference resources will generally be found here under BIOMEDICAL SCIENCES; pathology resources concerned primarily with personal examination of the human body then being appropriately located alongside those treating human anatomy and physiology.

Introductions to the subject

3526 Basic medical sciences for MRCP Part 1
P. Easterbrook 3rd edn, Churchill Livingstone, 2005, 448pp. £25.99. ISBN 0443073260.
Forthcoming new edn organized: Recommended Reference Books; 1. Genetics and molecular medicine; 2. Microbiology; 3. Immunology; 4. Anatomy; 5. Physiology; 6. Biochemistry and clinical chemistry; 7. Statistics and epidemiology; 8. Clinical pharmacology.
2nd edn 1999.

3527 Cells, tissues, and disease: principles of general pathology
G. Majno and I. Joris 2nd edn, Oxford University Press, 2004, 1005pp. £120.00. ISBN 0195140907.
Excellent well presented overview. 34 chapters in five parts: Cellular pathology; Inflammation; Immunopathology; Vascular disturbances; Tumours.
1 st edn Blackwell Science, 1996.

3528 Clinical laboratory medicine
K.D. McClatchey, ed. 2nd edn, Lippincott Williams & Wilkins, 2002, 1693pp. $99.00. ISBN 0683307517.
Very useful wide-ranging overview. 11 major sections: General laboratory; Molecular pathology; Clinical chemistry; Medical microbiology and urinalysis; Cytogenetics; HLA typing; Haematology; Coagulation; Microbiology; Immunopathology; Blood bank transfulsion medicine.

Dictionaries, thesauri, classifications

Biotechnology from A to Z
W. Bains See entry no. 5012

Concise dictionary of biomedicine and molecular biology
P.-S. Juo See entry no. 1904

Dictionary of biomedical sciences
P.J. Gosling See entry no. 1906

Research centres & institutes

3529 National Institute of General Medical Sciences
[USA]
www.nigms.nih.gov
'Primarily supports basic biomedical research that lays the foundation for advances in disease diagnosis, treatment, and prevention. The Institute's training programs help provide the most critical element of good research: well prepared scientists.'

Four Divisions: Bioinformatics and computational biology; Cell biology and biophysics; Extramural activities; Genetics and developmental biology; Minority opportunities in research; Pharmacology, physiology and biological chemistry.

- **Coriell Cell Repositories** http://locus.umdnj.edu/ccr. NIH funded and maintained by the Coriell Institute for Medical Research. Provides 'essential research reagents to the scientific community by establishing, verifying, maintaining, and distributing cells cultures and DNA derived from cell cultures'.

Associations & societies

American Council of Independent Laboratories
See entry no. 4563

European Federation of Biotechnology
See entry no. 5023

GAMBICA
See entry no. 1775

Portal & task environments

3530 **Deutsches Institut für Medizinische Dokumentation und Information: DIMDI (German Institute of Medical Documentation and Information)**
www.dimdi.de/en/dimdi
Host offering access to wide range of online databases concentrating on medicine, drugs, and toxicology. Includes major internationally available offerings but especially useful for their German region datasets. They act as an officially designated central information system for drugs used in Germany, and are developing an eHealth service, and data systems for Health Technology Assessment and Medical Devices.

3531 **Knowledge Express**
Knowledge Express Data Systems.
www.knowledgeexpress.com [FEE-BASED]
Example of sophisticated commercial service providing tools for biotechnology, pharmaceutical, life sciences, and technology transfer activities. The website offers free access to a selection of latest updates.

Discovering print & electronic resources

Elsevier BIOBASE
See entry no. 1972

WWW Virtual Library: Biotechnology
See entry no. 5036

Digital data, image & text collections

LANGE Educational Library
See entry no. 3800

Directories & encyclopedias

Encyclopedia of molecular cell biology and molecular medicine
R.A. Meyers, ed. See entry no. 2074

Handbooks & manuals

Current Protocols
See entry no. 1997

Keeping up-to-date

Current Awareness in Biological Sciences
See entry no. 2002

R&D Magazine
See entry no. 4611

Anatomy, Physiology & Pathology

anaesthesiology • body • human anatomy • human pathology • human physiology • pain • pathology • physiology • skeleton

Introductions to the subject

3532 **Basic pathology**
V. Kumar, R.S. Cotran and S.L. Robbins 7th edn, W B Saunders, 2005, 750pp. $73.95. ISBN 1416025340.
www.studentconsult.com
Core textbook offering a balanced, accurate, and up-to-date picture of the central body of knowledge on human pathology, with a strong clinicopathologic orientation. Wherever possible, the impact of molecular pathology on the practice of medicine is highlighted.
A STUDENT CONSULT edn: 'Each time you purchase a STUDENT CONSULT title, you will receive full online access + numerous interactive extras – at no additional cost. The more STUDENT CONSULT titles you buy, the more resources you can access online! Build your own online library and search across all of your titles with speed.'

See website for details.

Cells, aging, and human disease
M.B. Fossel See entry no. 3888

3533 **Human anatomy: color atlas and text**
J.A. Gosling [et al.] 4th edn, Mosby, 2002, 377pp. $59.95. ISBN 0723431957.
www.fleshandbones.com [COMPANION]
Well established and designed introductory textbook.
The website – offering Companions to a range of Elsevier texts – is 'for medical students and instructors and aims to provide you with a service that you will find both genuinely useful and entertaining! Here are some of the features on offer:
- For students: Test yourself on over 1000 free MCQs; Download our Survival Guides to clinical rotations; Access websites supporting the world's leading textbooks; Play games and win prizes by entering competitions.
- For lecturers: Download free images and buy others from our Image Bank containing over 30,000 images; Preview sample chapters from new textbooks.'

Human body systems
M. Windelspecht, ed. See entry no. 3761

3534 **Human physiology: the basis of medicine**
G. Pocock and C.D. Richards 2nd edn, Oxford University Press, 2004, 734pp. £35.00. ISBN 0198585276.
Concise handbook of essential physiology with integrated clinical references, relevant explanations of anatomy and histology, and clear illustrations. Includes key objectives for each topic, frequent summary boxes, a self-test section on objectives and annotated further reading. Good introductory overview.

Oral cells and tissues
P.R. Garant See entry no. 3823

3535 **The Oxford companion to the body**
C. Blakemore [et al.], eds Oxford University Press, 2001, 753pp. £40.00. ISBN 019852403X.
A concise and readable account of the structures of all major systems of the body, their processes and the diseases which affect them. An approachable reference to the human body.
'this book is a hugely good read ... This volume is perfect for browsing, simultaneously comprehensive and eclectic, and great fun!' (*British Medical Journal*)

3536 **Physiology**
R.M. Berne [et al.] 5th edn, Mosby, 2004, 1014pp. $89.95. ISBN 0323022251.
A comprehensive, authoritative, and up-to-date textbook of human physiology that emphasizes fundamental mechanisms and concepts. Uses an organ system-based approach to clearly describe all of the mechanisms that control and regulate bodily function.

Physiology for health care and nursing
S. Kindlen See entry no. 4341

3537 **Principles of anatomy and physiology**
G.J. Tortora and S.R. Grabowski 10th edn, Wiley, 2003, 1104pp. Includes CD-ROM, $134.95. ISBN 0471415014.
Very well structured and presented. 29 chapters organized into five units: Organization of the human body; Principles of support and movement; Control systems of the human body; Maintenance of the human body; Continuity. Good introductory overviews of the function of each body system. And there is a unifying homeostatic theme running through the text, with ten Focus on Homeostasis pages, describing how various feedback mechanisms work to maintain physiological processes within the narrow range compatible with life.

3538 **Rethinking homeostasis: allostatic regulation in physiology and pathophysiology**
J. Schulkin MIT Press, 2003, 296pp. $52.00. ISBN 0262194805.
'Homeostasis, a key concept in biology, refers to the tendency toward stability in the various bodily states that make up the internal environment.' Text especially useful for its extensive bibliography: pp 175–277.

3539 **Review of medical physiology**
W.F. Ganong 22nd edn, Lange Medical Books/McGraw-Hill, 2005. $49.95. ISBN 0071440402.
Announced edn of well established text giving current and concise overview of mammalian and human physiology, providing examples from clinical medicine which have been integrated throughout the chapters to illuminate important physiologic concepts.

- **Vander's human physiology: the mechanisms of body function H. Raff, E. Widmaier and K. Strang** 10th edn, McGraw-Hill, 2005, 864pp. ISBN 0071116788. New edn also announced from the publisher of this classic work.

3540 **Textbook of medical physiology**
A.C. Guyton and J.E. Hall 10th edn, W B Saunders, 2000, 1064pp. $79.95. ISBN 072168677X.
Well established physiology textbook providing comprehensive coverage of basic physiology and its relation to clinical medicine.

Associations & societies

3541 **American Physiological Society**
www.the-aps.org
A non-profit organization, with over 10,500 members, founded in 1887, devoted to fostering education, scientific research, and dissemination of information in the physiological sciences: 'Integrating the Life Sciences from Molecule to Organism'.
Content-rich site. The Society publishes 14 scholarly journals and a good range of books jointly with Oxford University Press. They have very good Careers/Mentoring and Education sections including an Archive of Teaching Resources. Useful for getting into the subject.

American Society for Clinical Pathology
See entry no. 3575

3542 **American Society of Anesthesiologists**
www.asahq.org
Educational, research and scientific association of physicians organized to raise and maintain the standards of the medical practice of anaesthesiology and improve the care of the patient. Wide range of useful patient information, clinical information, continuing education, etc. resources – many directly accessible via the website. Useful links section.

3543 **Anatomical Society of Great Britain and Ireland**
www.anatsoc.org.uk
'A learned society for teachers and researchers of anatomical subjects, including morphological aspects of cell biology, neuroscience and embryology as well as traditional medical and veterinary anatomy. Although based in the United Kingdom and Republic of Ireland there are members in many other countries world wide.'

3544 **Association of Anaesthetists of Great Britain and Ireland**
www.aagbi.org
The Association was founded in 1932 to promote the development and study of anaesthesia as a specialized branch of medicine. The website presents links for members, trainees and the public to useful publications and resources – including The Anaesthesia Heritage Centre.

3545 **College of American Pathologists** [USA]
www.cap.org/apps/cap.portal
Founded in 1922 as the principal organization of board-certified pathologists, to serve and represent the interest of patients, pathologists, and the public by fostering excellence

in the practice of pathology and laboratory medicine. Has a helpful Patient and Public Resources section, including: About pathologists and pathology; resources for your health; about autopsies; media centre

- **SNOMED International** www.snomed.org. Aims to be the 'leader in clinical terminology for encoding the medical record through the Systematized Nomenclature of Medicine'. Early 2005, CAP licensed the National Library of Medicine mappings from SNOMED to the nursing taxonomy NANDA.

3546 **European Society of Anaesthesiology**
www.euroanesthesia.org
Resulted from the amalgamation of the former *European Society of Anaesthesiologists*, the *European Academy of Anaesthesiology*, and the *Confederation of European National Societies of Anaesthesiologists*.

3547 **International Association for the Study of Pain**
www.iasp-pain.org
Founded 1973. 'Membership in IASP is open to scientists, physicians, dentists, psychologists, nurses, physical therapists, and other health professionals actively engaged in pain research and to those who have special interest in the diagnosis and treatment of pain. Currently IASP has 6744 individual members from 107 countries.'
Good, wide-ranging sets of relevant resources.

3548 **Physiological Society** [UK]
www.physoc.org
Founded in 1876 and now has approximately 2500 members drawn from over 50 countries. The majority of members are engaged in research, in universities or industry, into how the body works. Website gives good insight into their work and preoccupations, and gives useful leads.

3549 **Royal College of Anaesthetists** [UK]
www.rcoa.ac.uk
The professional body for anaesthesia throughout the UK, founded in 1948. Its principal responsibility is to ensure the quality of patient care by educating, training, and setting standards in anaesthesia, critical care and pain management. The website provides useful links to training opportunities and information, standards, resources and publications.

3550 **Royal College of Pathologists** [UK]
www.rcpath.org
Founded in 1962 to promote excellence in the practice of pathology, and high standards of professional training and practice. Good overview of the work of pathologists including well presented sections for Education – with descriptions of the pathology specialities; and for Patient resources – with an extensive list of disease information websites. Much else of value.

3551 **Royal College of Pathologists of Australasia**
www.rcpa.edu.au/public/default.cfm
The College is Australasia's leading medical diagnostic organization and promotes the science and practice of pathology, with members in Australia, New Zealand, Hong Kong, Singapore and Malaysia. There is a useful section What is pathology?, providing therein Pathology – Discipline by Discipline: Anatomical pathology; Chemical pathology; Genetics; Haematology; Immunology; Microbiology; General pathology. Also, access to an extensive RCPA Public Document Library and the *RCPA Manual*, whose purpose is 'to provide useful guidelines for the selection of pathology tests and to facilitate interpretation of results'.

Portal & task environments

3552 **A.D.A.M.**
www.adam.com
Commercial company providing effective multimedia educational tools for teaching and learning about the human body. Covers human anatomy and physiology within medicine.

Digital data, image & text collections

3553 **The eSkeletons Project**
University of Texas at Austin
www.eskeletons.org
'Devoted to the study of human and primate comparative anatomy. It offers a unique set of digitized versions of skeletons in 2-D and 3-D in full color, animations, and much supplemental information. The user can navigate through the various regions of the skeleton and view all orientations of each element along with muscle and joint information. eSkeletons enables you to view the bones of both human and non-human primates ranging from the gorilla to the tiny mouse lemur. All of the large apes are represented as well as other species from different parts of the world. Many of these primates are rare or endangered species.'

Directories & encyclopedias

3554 **Anaesthesia and intensive care A–Z: an encyclopaedia of principles and practice**
S.M. Yentis, N.P. Hirsch and G.B. Smith 3rd edn, Butterworth-Heinemann, 2003, 564pp. £55.00. ISBN 0750687770.
Excellent, detailed encyclopedia of anaesthesia and intensive care for the trainee and the trainer. Easily searched entries and illustrations help to explain difficult concepts. Terminology summaries are bite-sized, succinct, yet comprehensive and very practical.

3555 **Anesthesia: atlas of regional anesthesia procedures**
R.D. Miller, ed. 5th edn, Churchill Livingstone, 1999, 3168pp. 2 v. plus CD-ROM, £210.00. ISBN 0443079889.
Provides both the essential basic science as well as the state of the art in clinical management. The CD-ROM demonstrates video clips of key techniques.

3556 **Atlas of human anatomy**
F.H. Netter and J.T. Hansen 3rd edn, Icon Learning Systems, 2003. $94.95. ISBN 1929007175.
http://store.netterart.com [COMPANION]
'Almost two-thirds of health science instructors in the United States choose Netter's *Atlas of human anatomy* to train their students in anatomy. And with very good reason – because Netter's incomparable medical art and artistry, the foundation of the *Atlas of human anatomy*, reflects his personal belief in the power of the visual image to teach without overwhelming the student with dense, confusing text. 'To clarify rather than intimidate' remains the distinctive and

effective Netter approach – and it's been working since the publication of the first edition in 1989.'

- **Wolf Heidegger's atlas of human anatomy** (Wolf-Heideggers Atlas der Anatomie des Menschen) **P. Kopf-Maier and G. Wolf-Heidegger** 6th edn, Karger, 2004. €89.00. ISBN 3805576641. www.karger.com. V. 1. Systemic anatomy, body wall, upper and lower limbs; V. 2. Head and neck, thorax, abdomen, pelvis, CNS, eye, ear. Website gives access to details of several publications related to this excellent offering.

An atlas of reproductive physiology in men
E.S.E. Hafez See entry no. 4467

3557 **Color atlas of the autopsy on CD-ROM**
S.A. Wagner CRC Press, 2004. $199.95. ISBN 0849330599.
'This is the CD-ROM version of the first full-color atlas to show the basics of autopsy and how it is used in death investigation. Different from other atlases, which concentrate on specific injury topics, this book focuses on autopsy protocol. More than 500 photographs display all the elements of the procedure ...'

Neuroanatomy: text and atlas
J.H. Martin See entry no. 3994

3558 **World of anatomy and physiology**
Thomson Gale, 2002, 600pp. 2 v, $180.00. ISBN 0787656844.
650 entries in A–Z format, written for the general enquirer. Subject index.
'Most valuable are the historical chronology and the numerous biographical sketches of pioneers in the field ... Recommended, primarily for its biographical information, for undergraduate and graduate students, community college through university libraries.' (*Choice*)

Handbooks & manuals

Anatomy of orofacial structures
R.W. Brand See entry no. 3842

Bone research protocols
M.H. Helfrich and S. Ralston, eds See entry no. 2284

Clarke's analysis of drugs and poisons: in pharmaceuticals, body fluids and postmortem material
A.C. Moffat [et al.], eds See entry no. 4283

The developing human: clinically oriented embryology
K.L. Moore See entry no. 4471

3559 **Grant's atlas of anatomy** [USA]
A.M.R. Agur and A.F. Dalley 11th edn, Lippincott Williams & Wilkins, 2004, 848pp. 1600 illustrations, $99.00. ISBN 0781742560.
First published in 1943, this classic atlas provides accurate anatomical images presented in a pedagogically effective, clinically relevant manner. Includes a student CD-ROM version with dynamic human anatomy including 800 images, 8 video clips and 100 USMLE (United States Medical Licensing Examination: www.usmle.org) questions.

3560 **Gray's anatomy: the anatomical basis of clinical practice**
S. Standring [et al.] 39th edn, Churchill Livingstone, 2004, 1600pp. 2260 ill, £99.00. ISBN 0443066752.
www.bartleby.com/107
The classic textbook on anatomy has been completely redesigned, and is now organized by body region. The online version of the 1918 publication available from Bartleby.com features 1247 engravings, as well as a subject index with 13,000 entries.

Handbook of death and dying
C.D. Bryant, ed. See entry no. 4318

Handbook of fingerprint recognition
D, Maltoni [et al.] See entry no. 6206

3561 **Handbook of physiology**
American Physiological Society Oxford University Press, 1977–.
www.the-aps.org/publications/books/handbooks.htm [DESCRIPTION]
Major treatise with each section typically having several volumes: Section 1: The nervous system; Section 2: The cardiovascular system; Section 3: The respiratory system; Section 4: Environmental physiology; Section 5: Adipose tissue; Section 6: The gastrointestinal system; Section 7: The endocrine system; Section 8: Renal physiology; Section 9: Reactions to environmental agents; Section 10: Skeletal muscle; Section 11: Aging; Section 12: Exercise: Regulation and integration of multiple systems; Section 13: Comparative physiology; Section 14: Cell physiology.

Knight's forensic pathology
P.J. Saukko and B. Knight See entry no. 3594

Maternal-fetal medicine: principles and practice
R.K. Creasy and R. Resnik, eds See entry no. 4017

3562 **McMinn's colour atlas of human anatomy**
P.H. Abrahams, S.C. Marks and R. Hutchings, eds 5th edn, Mosby, 2003, 378pp. Includes CD-ROM with anatomical animations, $62.95. ISBN 0723432120.
Maps out the structures of the human body and puts these structures into a clinical context. An outstanding guide to the human body, ideal for exam preparation, self-study and as a primer for laboratory work. Over 1000 illustrations.

Physiology of sport and exercise
J.H. Wilmore and D.L. Costill See entry no. 4487

3563 **Principles of bone biology**
J.P. Bilezikian, L.G. Raisz and G.A. Rodan, eds Academic Press, 2002, 1696pp. 2 v, $419.95. ISBN 0120986523.
Four parts: Basic principles (Cell biology; Biochemistry; Bone remodelling and mineral homeostasis; The hormones of bone; Other systemic hormones that influence bone metabolism; Local regulators); Molecular mechanisms of metabolic bone diseases; Pharmacologic mechanisms of therapeutics; Methods in bone research.

3564 **Robbin's and Coltrans pathologic basis of disease**
V. Kumar, N. Fausto and A.K. Abbas, eds 7th edn, W B Saunders, 2004. 1600 illustrations, $99.00. ISBN 0721601871.
Remains an authoritative and readable pathology text. Has a strong emphasis on pathophysiology and uses morphology boxes to summarize important pathologic features.

Skandalakis' Surgical anatomy: the embryologic and anatomic basis of modern surgery
J.E. Skandalakis and G.L. Colborn, eds See entry no. 4138

Textbook of work physiology: physiological bases of exercise
P.-O. Astrand See entry no. 4489

Wheeler's dental anatomy, physiology, and occlusion
M.M. Ash and S.J. Nelson See entry no. 3845

3565 **Wylie and Churchill-Davidson's a practice of anaesthesia**
T.E.J. Healy and P.R. Knight, eds 7th edn, Arnold, 2003, 1435pp. £155.00. ISBN 0340731303.
Fully revised and updated new edition with an increased international relevance. The book presents both the basic science underlying modern anaesthetic practice and up-to-date clinical anaesthetic management techniques in a comprehensive, but concise and accessible, style.

Keeping up-to-date

3566 **Annual review of physiology**
$213.00 [V. 66, 2004]. ISBN 0824303660 ISSN 00664278. www.annurev.org/catalog/2004/ph66.asp [DESCRIPTION]
Covers human and non-human physiology. Reviews in the current volume include: Some early history of membrane molecular biology; field physiology: physiological insights from animals in nature; oral rehydration therapy: new explanations for an old remedy.

Biomedical Sciences

antibodies • blood • blood products • blood tests • chemical pathology • clinical chemistry • clinical microbiology • fingerprints • forensic sciences • histology • immunology • laboratory medicine • medical microbiology • pathogens • urine tests

Introductions to the subject

3567 **Clinical chemistry: principles, procedures, correlations**
M.L. Bishop, E.P. Fody and L.E. Schoeff 5th edn, Lippincott Williams & Wilkins, 2004, 704pp. $76.95. ISBN 0781746116.
33 chapters in four parts: 1. Basic principles and practice of clinical chemistry; 2. Critical correlations and analytic procedures; 3. Assessment of organ system functions; 4. Specialty areas of clinical chemistry.

- **Clinical chemistry: concepts and applications S.C. Anderson and S. Cockayne, eds** McGraw-Hill, 2003, 723pp. $79.95. ISBN 0071360476. Treats the theory, concepts, correlations, and applications of clinical laboratory science, focusing especially on the principles of the analytical techniques used in medical investigations.

3568 **Four centuries of clinical chemistry** [UK]
L. Rosenfeld Marston, 1999, 592pp. £40.00. ISBN 9056996460.
Traces the impact of the development of analytical chemistry and biochemical knowledge on the emergence of clinical chemistry as an important adjunct of medical practice.

Harper's illustrated biochemistry
R.K. Murray [et al.] See entry no. 2033

3569 **Histology: a text and atlas**
M.H. Ross, G.I. Kaye and W. Pawlina 4th edn, Lippincott Williams & Wilkins, 2003, 875pp. $62.95. ISBN 0683302426.
Well presented leading introductory text, with – in this edn – increased coverage of cell and molecular biology.

3570 **Human molecular biology: an introduction to the molecular language of health and disease**
R.J. Epstein Cambridge University Press, 2003, 623pp. £35.00. ISBN 052164481X.
'Good health is a matter of having the right molecules in the right place at the right time. This may seem self-evident, but the idea that health is determined *mainly* by molecules has only gained acceptance in recent years ... All biology is about molecules. Molecular biology is little more than a buzzword from a bygone age in which technical change outpaced human understanding ... The biological basis of health and disease has become inescapably linked.'

Superb introduction to biomedical science 'from the molecules up rather than from the diseases down'. Each chapter ends with a short enrichment reading, divided into: Bedtime reading; Cheap 'n' cheerful; Library reference.

Textbook of biochemistry with clinical correlations
T.M. Devlin, ed. See entry no. 3764

Dictionaries, thesauri, classifications

A clinician's dictionary of pathogenic microorganisms
J.H. Jorgensen and M.A. Pfaller See entry no. 3926

Encyclopedia and dictionary of medicine, nursing, and allied health
M.T. O'Toole, ed. See entry no. 4346

3571 **Forensic science: an illustrated dictionary**
J.C. Brenner CRC Press, 2003, 296pp. $79.95. ISBN 0849314577.
2000 words and terms with nearly 170 photographs and drawings of forensic laboratory equipment and processes, aiding in the illustration of key concepts. Author and publisher have also produced *Forensic science glossary* (1999).

3572 **Illustrated dictionary of immunology**
J.M. Cruse and R.E. Lewis 2nd edn, CRC Press, 2002, 675pp. $99.95. ISBN 0849319358.
Helpful guide to often complex arena; 1200 illustrations including computer-generated figures, line-drawings, and illustrations.

- **Atlas of immunology J.M. Cruse and R.E. Lewis** 2nd edn, CRC Press, 2003, 835pp. $99.95. ISBN 0849315670. Coverage ranges from photographs of historical figures to molecular structures of recently characterized cytokines, major histocompatibility complex molecules, immunoglobulins, and molecules of related interest.
- **Immunology guidebook J.M. Cruse, R. Lewis and H. Wang** Elsevier Academic, 2004, 502pp. $125.00. ISBN 012198382X. 18 chapters, especially concentrating on nomenclatural issues.

Laws, standards, codes

3573 Clinical and Laboratory Standards Institute

www.clsi.org

'Global, non-profit, standards-developing organization that promotes the development and use of voluntary consensus standards and guidelines within the healthcare community. We are recognized worldwide for the application of our unique consensus process. CLSI is based on the principle that consensus is an efficient and cost-effective way to improve patient testing and services.

'The Harmonized Terminology Database is a compilation of internationally accepted terminology and is a tool for CLSI volunteers, members, and anyone in the laboratory sciences and related healthcare industries. It has been made publicly available to encourage broad acceptance and usage of internationally accepted terminology.'

Health Professions Council

See entry no. 4144

National Institute for Biological Standards and Control

See entry no. 4415

Research centres & institutes

Global Salm-Surv: GSS

World Health Organization See entry no. 3160

Associations & societies

3574 American Association of Immunologists

www.aai.org

Founded in 1913, represents the professional interests of some 6500 scientists; member of the Federation of American Societies for Experimental Biology and International Union of Immunological Societies. Full-text access to newsletter and journal; educational section; links.

American Board of Forensic Entomology

See entry no. 2381

3575 American Society for Clinical Pathology

www.ascp.org

'Founded in 1922, is the largest medical laboratory organization with more than 140,000 members. It represents the entire medical laboratory team – pathologists, medical technologists, and all other medical laboratory professionals.'

Good website; well worth exploring – see, for instance: 'What is a Pathologist?'; 'What is a Medical Technologist?'.

Association for Laboratory Automation

See entry no. 1773

3576 Association of Medical Microbiologists [UK]

www.amm.co.uk

Founded in 1983, the AMM is the professional body for the UK and Republic of Ireland. In addition to providing more information about the Association its website contains a diary of forthcoming scientific meetings and links to related sites. The Have you seen? section contains a list of reports on a very wide range of topics that have been published in the UK since 1995, while the Publications section contains information on more than 20 subjects including MRSA, rabies and salmonella.

3577 British In Vitro Diagnostics Association

www.bivda.co.uk

An 'in vitro diagnostic medical device' means 'any medical device which is a reagent, reagent product, calibrator, control material, kit, instrument, apparatus, equipment, or system, whether used alone or in combination, intended by the manufacturer to be used in vitro for the examination of specimens, including blood and tissue donations, derived from the human body, solely or principally for the purpose of providing information: concerning a physiological or pathological state, or concerning a congenital abnormality, or to determine the safety and compatibility with potential recipients, or to monitor therapeutic measures' (EUR-Lex).

Founded 1992; very good range of information.

- **AssayFinder.com** www.assayfinder.com. Free service for laboratories registering as assay providers – especially useful for anyone trying to find unusual diagnostic assays/tests and the laboratories that provide them.

British Society for Immunology

See entry no. 3918

3578 European Association for Professions in Biomedical Science

www.epbs.net

Founded 1999 with membership 'open to professional bodies committed to developing the skills and knowledge of the Biomedical Scientist in order to become an effective member of the health care team'.

3579 Institute of Biomedical Science [UK]

www.ibms.org

Founded 1912; approximately 16,000 members employed mainly in public and private medical and veterinary laboratories, and UK government departments and agencies. In 2003, the Institute was licensed by the Science Council to award the designation Chartered Scientist to qualifying IBMS members which 'adds science to the now familiar list of chartered professions such as biologist, accountant or surveyor'.

Rather plain site; but one that turns out to be surprisingly rich in resources. Especially useful for gaining a quick overview of the sub-sections of 'biomedical science' – 'the term for the investigations carried out by biomedical scientists on samples of tissue and body fluids to diagnose disease and monitor the treatment of patients', which are labelled on the website as: Cellular pathology; Clinical chemistry; Haematology; Immunology; Medical microbiology; Transfusion science; Virology.

3580 International Federation of Clinical Chemistry and Laboratory Medicine

www.ifcc.org

Good entrée to this area of professional activity; well structured and presented information, including details of and links to the websites of the Federation's full, affiliate and corporate members.

Royal College of Pathologists of Australasia

See entry no. 3551

Portal & task environments

Doctor Fungus
J. H. Rex [et al.]; DoctorFungus Corporation See entry no. 2723

3581 **DPDx: Laboratory Identification of Parasites of Public Health Concern**
Centers for Disease Control and Prevention
www.dpd.cdc.gov/DPDx
This site provides access to detailed information on parasites, parasitic diseases and the related diagnostic procedures. Information on parasitic species can be found via an A–Z list or by category (blood-borne, intestinal or other). Each entry includes details of the causal agent, life cycle, geographical distribution, clinical features, laboratory diagnosis and treatment. The site also includes a large collection of images.

The Harmful Algae Page
Woods Hole Oceanographic Institution and National Oceanic and Atmospheric Administration See entry no. 2832

3582 **Lab Tests Online: a public resource on clinical lab testing from the laboratory professionals who do the testing** [USA]
American Association for Clinical Chemistry
www.labtestsonline.org
A peer-reviewed resource aimed at patients and caregivers that provides information relating to clinical lab tests that are part of routine care as well as diagnosis and treatment of a broad range of conditions and diseases. The site producers – a wide range of collaborating partners and site sponsors (useful links in their own right) – subscribe to the HONCode principles.

Mycology Online
D. Ellis; University of Adelaide See entry no. 2725

SelectScience: The Scientists' Choice
See entry no. 1782

Discovering print & electronic resources

Review of Medical and Veterinary Mycology
See entry no. 2731

Digital data, image & text collections

The Medical Biochemistry Page
M.W. King See entry no. 2066

Directories & encyclopedias

3583 **Atlas of hematology**
S.C. Anderson and K. Poulsen Lippincott Williams & Wilkins, 2003, 586pp. $53.95. ISBN 078172662X.
www.lww.com
'With four-color illustrations, this manual describes and identifies the maturation sequence of developing blood cells, as well as categorizing cell abnormalities. Coverage includes both normal and abnormal cells, and the format allows for benchtop reference.'
Available in a variety of formats: see website.

3584 **Basic histology: text & atlas**
L.C. Junqueira and J. Carneiro 11th edn, McGraw-Hill, 2005, 544pp. Includes CD-ROM, $54.95. ISBN 0071440917.
'Recognized as the leading medical histology text in the world.' A fine introduction with over 600 high-quality photomicrographs, electron micrographs and illustrations, 500 in full colour.
A Lange medical book.

3585 **The dictionary of immunology**
W.J. Herbert, P.C. Wilkinson and D.I. Stott, eds 4th edn, Academic Press, 1995, 171pp. $69.95. ISBN 0127520260.
Contains brief descriptions of the most commonly used immunological techniques, as well as definitions, useful in clinical immunology, of immunodeficiency states and autoimmune diseases. With clear illustrations and tables, and extensive cross-referencing.

3586 **Encyclopedia of forensic sciences**
J.A. Siegel, P.J. Saukko and G.C. Knupfer, eds Academic Press, 2000, 1904pp. 3 v, $995.00. ISBN 0122272153.
www.info.sciencedirect.com/reference_works
Over 200 articles providing comprehensive coverage of the core theories, methods, techniques and applications employed by forensic scientists. Although its coverage is naturally far wider than human pathology – embracing techniques and principles from chemistry, biology, physics and mathematics as well as medicine – this is a valuable compendium of relevant information normally spread widely. Detailed contents list; glossary; index. Colour plates. List of major forensic science journals.
Available online: see website.
'The value of the encyclopedia? Quite simply and plainly put – 'Extremely valuable.' This encyclopedia would be useful to researchers, students, professors – indeed everyone who is connected with forensic science in any way. In this reviewer's opinion, this encyclopedia should adorn the bookshelves of every person connected with forensic science. Highly recommended reading.' (*Internet Journal of Forensic Medicine*)

- **FORENSICnetBASE/LawENFORCEMENTnetBASE** CRC Press. www.forensicnetbase.com. Early 2005, access to the full-text of 103 titles.

3587 **Foodborne Pathogenic Microorganisms and Natural Toxins Handbook: the 'bad bug book'**
Center for Food Safety and Applied Nutrition
http://vm.cfsan.fda.gov
Basic facts regarding food-borne pathogenic micro-organisms and natural toxins from a range of US agencies and centres, brought together in one place.

3588 **Linscott's Directory of Immunological and Biological Reagents**
www.linscottsdirectory.com
More than 100,000 different listings for products and services available from more than 500 different commercial and governmental sources worldwide.

3589 **Medically important fungi: a guide to identification**
D.H. Larone 4th edn, ASM Press, 2002, 409pp. $79.95. ISBN 1555811728.
Classic work that 'helps laboratory workers readily identify fungi by following a step-by-step procedure that incorporates consideration of macroscopic, microscopic, and other identifiable features'.

3590 **MSRS Catalog of Primary Antibodies**
www.antibodies-probes.com
Records of 225,000 primary antibodies, each record including: antibody, host, antigen species, label, form, clone number, isotype, unit size, product number, specifications and supplier name. List of over 600 worldwide manufacturers, laboratories and suppliers; of over 5500 worldwide immunology, molecular biology and biotechnology companies.

Handbooks & manuals

Clarke's analysis of drugs and poisons: in pharmaceuticals, body fluids and postmortem material
A.C. Moffat [et al.], eds See entry no. 4283

3591 **Clinical laboratory management**
L.S. Garcia [et al.], ed.; American Society for Microbiology ASM Press, 2004, 864pp. $149.95. ISBN 1555812791.
Extensive text focusing on financial, personnel, organizational and leadership issues.

Collins and Lyne's microbiological methods
C.H. Collins [et al.], eds See entry no. 2695

Color atlas and manual of microscopy for criminalists, chemists, and conservators
N. Petraco See entry no. 1799

CRC handbook of laboratory safety
A.K. Furr See entry no. 4286

Encyclopedia of immunology
P.J. Delves and I.M. Roitt, eds See entry no. 3922

3592 **Fingerprints and other ridge skin impressions**
C. Champod [et al.] CRC Press, 2004, 285pp. $94.95. ISBN 0415271754.
Brings together the scientific and legal aspects of this discipline; co-authored by 'the world's foremost fingerprint expert with other leading specialists in the field'.
Series: International Forensic Science and Investigation, V. 11.

3593 **Handbook of toxicologic pathology**
W.M. Haschek, C.G. Rousseaux and M.A. Wallig, eds Academic Press, 2001, 1706pp. 2 v, $545.95. ISBN 0123302153.
Treats the two complementary disciplines giving an excellent integrated overview.

Immunobiology: the immune system in health and disease
C.A. Janeway [et al.] See entry no. 3923

3594 **Knight's forensic pathology**
P.J. Saukko and B. Knight 3rd edn, Arnold, 2004, 662pp. £155.00. ISBN 0340760443.
Definitive international postgraduate text.
'The book remains the standard modern text in forensic pathology (on the 2nd edn).' (*Bulletin of the Royal College of Pathologists*)

3595 **Manual of clinical microbiology**
P.R. Murray [et al.] 8th edn, ASM Press, 2003. 2 v, $189.95. ISBN 1555812554.
A comprehensive reference book, the definitive resource on the microbiology and epidemiology of all clinically significant bacteria, viruses, fungi and parasites.

3596 **Modern cytopathology**
K.R. Geisinger [et al.] Churchill Livingstone, 2004, 960pp. $279.00. ISBN 0443065985.
Excellent multi-colour image-rich volume 'which evolved from the authors' common beliefs that a void was waiting to be filled – namely, a need for a comprehensive, yet user-friendly source of diagnostic data for all types of cytologic samples'. 29 chapters in six sections: Gynecology; Fluids; Neurology; Thorax; Abdomen; Superficial body sites.

3597 **Molecular medical microbiology**
M. Sussman, ed. Academic Press, 2001, 2223pp. 3 v, $766.95. ISBN 0126775303.
Synthesizes the many new developments in both molecular and clinical research into a single comprehensive resource. Comprises over 100 chapters, organized into 17 major sections.
'without question this work is destined to be successful as a teaching and information resource ... Each chapter is well referenced should additional information be desired ... Indeed, this work deserves a place in medical libraries because it is leading the way to where medical microbiology is going.' (*Diagnostic Microbiology and Infectious Disease*)

Official methods of analysis of AOAC International
W. Horwitz, ed. See entry no. 1821

3598 **Physician's guide to the laboratory diagnosis of metabolic diseases**
N. Blau [et al.], eds 2nd edn, Springer, 2002, 716pp. Includes CD-ROM, £154.00. ISBN 354042542X.
Six chapters in Part One – Approach to diagnosis – reviewing the various techniques; 35 chapters in Part Two with extensive coverage of the various metabolic disorders. Part Three has three indices: Disorders; Signs and symptoms; Tests. Very useful compendium.

Russell, Hugo and Ayliffe's Principles and practice of disinfection, preservation and sterilization
A.D. Russell [et al.], eds See entry no. 4299

Yeasts: characteristics and identification
J.A. Barnett, R.W. Payne and D. Yarrow See entry no. 2739

Keeping up-to-date

Laboratory News
See entry no. 1830

Human Genetics

biometrics • DNA profiling • gene therapy • genetic disorders • genetic testing • human genome • human molecular genetics • medical genetics • medical genomics

Introductions to the subject

Brave new brain: conquering mental illness in the era of the genome
N.C. Andreasen See entry no. 4094

3599 **Essentials of medical genomics**
S.M. Brown, J.G. Hay and H. Ostrer Wiley-Liss, 2003, 274pp. $59.95. ISBN 047121003X.
An introductory work, aimed at medical students and doctors, that provides an overview of genomics and its implications for human medicine. The eleven chapters include coverage of the Human Genome Project, bioinformatics, genetic variation, genetic testing, gene therapy, microarrays, proteomics and ethical considerations. Each chapter includes a bibliography; glossary.

The GEEE! In GENOME
Canadian Museum of Nature See entry no. 2485

3600 **Gene mapping: using law and ethics as guides**
G.J. Annas and S. Elias, eds Oxford University Press, 1992, 291pp. £59.95. ISBN 0195073037.
Overview of the social, legal and ethical aspects considered as part of the Human Genome Project. Six parts: The Human Genome Project; Social policy implications; The Human Genome Project and the human condition; How changes in genetics change clinical practice; Legal and ethical frontiers; Conclusion. Glossary; subject index.

Genetic Science Learning Center
University of Utah See entry no. 2488

3601 **Guide to biometrics**
R.M. Bolle Springer, 2004, 364pp. £38.50. ISBN 0387400893.
'Biometric identification, or biometrics, refers to identifying an individual based on his or her distinguishing characteristics. More precisely, biometrics is the science of identifying, or verifying the identity of a person based on physiological or behavioral characteristics.'

17 chapters organized into four parts: Basics of biometrics; Performance and selection; System issues; Mathematical analyses. A good overview.
Series: Springer Professional Computing.

3602 **Human molecular genetics**
T. Strachan and A.P. Read 3rd edn, Garland Science, 2004, 674pp. $60.00. ISBN 0815341849.
Designed to provide a bridge between elementary textbooks and the research literature, so that people with relatively little background in the subject can appreciate and read the latest research. This edn takes into account the results arising from the Human Genome Project.

Excellent volume, opening with a characteristic short section entitled: Before we start – Intelligent use of the internet, noting that: 'We have just run a Google search for 'genetics'. It produced 3,630,000 hits. Some of these sites are key resources, many are secondary, some are deliberately misleading and inaccurate.' following which seven core sites are referenced: all cited elsewhere in TNW.

The second creation: the age of biological control by the scientists who cloned Dolly
I. Wilmut, K. Campbell and C. Tudge See entry no. 4449

3603 **The sequence: inside the race for the human genome**
K. Davies, ed. Phoenix, 2002, 322pp. £7.99. ISBN 0753813165.
Provides a very readable account of the Human Genome Project and the race that developed between the publicly funded and commercial sequencing projects. Subject index; notes to each chapter include citations.

Dictionaries, thesauri, classifications

Biopharmaceutical glossary and taxonomies
M. Chitty, ed. See entry no. 2503

A dictionary of genetics
R.C. King and W.D. Stansfield See entry no. 2505

3604 **Talking Glossary of Genetic Terms**
National Human Genome Research Institute
www.genome.gov/glossary.cfm
Really helpful site aimed at the general public rather than the research community. Contains definitions for more than 175 terms that are commonly used in genetics research. A short definition is provided for each term, along with a pronunciation guide and a more detailed audio explanation. Many definitions also include illustrations.

Laws, standards, codes

3605 **HUGO Gene Nomenclature Committee**
www.gene.ucl.ac.uk/nomenclature
The HGNC is responsible for approving a name and symbol for every human gene that has been identified. The approved symbols are stored in the *Genew* database and are used by other databases, e.g. GeneCards, to uniquely identify genes. As well as details of the system and the work of the committee, there is an extensive set of links.

Legal and ethical issues in human reproduction
B. Steinbock, ed. See entry no. 4452

Official & quasi-official bodies

3606 **Gene Therapy Advisory Committee** [UK]
www.advisorybodies.doh.gov.uk/genetics/gtac
Founded in 1993, the GTAC 'advises on the ethical acceptability of proposals for gene therapy research on humans taking account of the scientific merits and the potential benefits and risks, and provides advice to UK health Ministers on developments in gene therapy research'. Good collection of downloadable PDF documents; small but useful collection of links.

3607 **The Genomic Resource Centre**
World Health Organization
www.who.int/genomics/en

Established 'to provide information and to raise awareness on human genomics' to an audience of the general public, health care staff and policy makers. Website contains a section of information aimed at each of these groups as well as coverage of the ethical, legal and social implications of human genomics. A very useful resource.

3608 **Human Genetics Commission** [UK]
www.hgc.gov.uk
The UK Government's advisory body on issues relating to human genetics with a particular emphasis on the social and ethical issues. There is a very useful Map of the UK Regulatory and Advisory Framework for Human Genetics supplemented by a series of briefing notes, and links to websites of relevant bodies. The site also contains a helpful set of introductions to various Topics (e.g. Genetics and employment; Genetic profiling at birth; Paternity testing services) with the invitation to forward 'any comments on the human genetic issues we might cover'. An excellent resource in potentially a troublesome arena.

- **Genetics and Insurance Committee** www.advisorybodies.doh.gov.uk/genetics/gaic/index.htm. Non-statutory advisory committee. Mission is 'to develop and publish criteria for the evaluation of specific genetic tests, their application to particular conditions and their reliability and relevance to particular types of insurance'.

National Center for Biotechnology Information
See entry no. 2507

Research centres & institutes

3609 **Celera Genomics**
www.celera.com
A commercial research institution that was founded by Dr. J. Craig Venter in order to sequence the human genome. Their human genome paper was published in the journal *Science* in February 2001.

3610 **Genetics & Public Policy Center** [USA]
www.dnapolicy.org
Established as 'an independent and objective source of credible information on genetic technologies and genetic policies for the public, media and policymakers'. It is funded by The Pew Charitable Trusts, is a part of The Phoebe R. Berman Bioethics Institute at Johns Hopkins University. Its first focus was reproductive genetics and the website provides helpful information on this subject, covering topics such as: Reproductive cloning; Genetic testing; Gene transfer. Also present are a glossary, a detailed bibliography and links to related websites.

Jackson Laboratory
See entry no. 2513

3611 **National Human Genome Research Institute** [USA]
www.genome.gov
The NHGRI was founded in 1989 as the National Institutes of Health representative in the international Human Genome Project. This role has now been expanded to include research into the role of the genome in human health and disease, and the site includes good sets of information on genetic diseases, policy, ethics and so on.

Associations & societies

American Society for Histocompatibility & Immunogenetics
See entry no. 3915

3612 **American Society of Human Genetics**
www.ashg.org
Founded in 1948, the ASHG is a professional organization for human geneticists. Good range of resources – especially educational.

3613 **British Society for Human Genetics**
www.bshg.org.uk
Founded in 1996, the BSHG is an independent body that represents human genetics professionals in Britain. It is made up of four constituent organizations, referenced below The website includes a list of UK genetics centres as well as a useful section For Patients.

- **Association of Clinical Cytogeneticists** www.cytogenetics.org.uk.
- **Association of Genetic Nurses and Counsellors** www.agnc.co.uk.
- **Clinical Genetics Society** www.clingensoc.org.
- **Clinical Molecular Genetics Society** www.cmgs.org/new_cmgs.

3614 **Genetic Alliance** [USA]
www.geneticalliance.org
The Alliance, founded in 1986 and based in the US, is an international coalition of individuals with genetic conditions and the organizations that support them. It works to support the individuals in managing their conditions and to educate the general public and policy makers about genetic diseases.

Site provides access to an extensive Disease InfoSearch database, plus a wide range of other relevant resources: a number, however, only being accessible to members.

3615 **Genetic Interest Group** [UK]
www.gig.org.uk
'National alliance of patient organizations with a membership of over 130 charities which support children, families and individuals affected by genetic disorders." As well as providing a list with URLs of the charities, has a Directory of Genetic Centres and Services, provides various educational resources and maintains a substantial Links section.

Genetics Society of America
See entry no. 2517

3616 **Human Genome Variation Society**
www.hgvs.org
Founded in 2001, the Society promotes the 'discovery and characterization of genomic variations including population distribution and phenotypic associations'. Website includes information on the nomenclature of genes and mutations, links to related sites and resources, and a bibliography.

Progress Educational Trust
See entry no. 4464

Society for the Study of Human Biology
See entry no. 1942

Society for the Study of Inborn Errors of Metabolism
See entry no. 2056

Portal & task environments

DOEgenomes.org
United States. Department of Energy See entry no. 2522

3617 **DOEgenomes.org: Genome programs of the US Department of Energy Office of Science**
United States. Department of Energy
www.doegenomes.org
This well organized rich and inviting site was designed to provide information on the Human Genome Project to the general public. Founded in 1990 by the US Department of Energy and the National Institutes of Health, the project involved an international research effort and resulted in the publication of a draft of the human genome in February 2001, and its completion in 2003. Although work in the area has now moved on, the site is still a very useful introductory gateway.

- **Genome glossary**
  www.ornl.gov/sci/techresources/Human_Genome/glossary. Last updated January 2004; includes links to a selection of other glossaries as well as serving as an index to the Doegenomes.org site.

3618 **GeneTests**
University of Washington and National Institutes of Health
www.genetests.org
This site, aimed at medical professionals and researchers, aims to provide an authoritative source of current information on genetic testing. The main resource that it contains is GeneReviews, a searchable collection of detailed reviews of genetic diseases. It also includes an international directory of laboratories that carry out tests and a directory of US clinics.

Genome Gateway
See entry no. 2523

3619 **HumGen: International database on the legal, social and ethical aspects of HUMan GENetics**
B.M. Knoppers [et al.], eds; Université de Montréal
www.humgen.umontreal.ca/en
Rich wide-ranging site from the University's Centre de recherche en droit public.

3620 **Hum-molgen: The HUMan MOLecular GENetics Portal Site**
Zollmann & Garlipp Information Service GbR.
www.hum-molgen.de
This splendid site brings together a collection of links and other resources related to human molecular genetics. Resources are grouped under the headings: Genetic news; Bioinformatics; Biotechnology (a listing of companies); Literature; Journals; Ethics (a discussion forum); Positions (job listings); Events.

Discovering print & electronic resources

3621 **Bibliography on computational gene recognition**
W. Li
www.nslij-genetics.org/gene
Personal interest site with revealing background on the growth in the field – and the difficulty of deciding its scope – since the site was first created in 1996.

3622 **Chromosomal variation in man**
Wiley.
www.wiley.com/legacy/products/subject/life/borgaonkar/access.html
Database open to the public and freely accessible, started in 1974 and now containing over 24,000 entries.

Entrez: the life sciences search engine
National Center for Biotechnology Information See entry no. 2529

3623 **Information for Genetic Professionals**
University of Kansas
www.kumc.edu/gec/geneinfo.html
Primarily aimed at an audience of geneticists and genetics counsellors with the links arranged under headings focusing on conditions and support. However the FAQs section is quite useful as it brings together links on subjects that include the genetic aspects of physical traits: blood types, eye colour, colour blindness, alcoholism, etc.

Created within the Genetics Education Center of the University's Medical Center.

Digital data, image & text collections

3624 **GeneCards**
Weizmann Institute of Science XenneX Inc.
bioinfo.weizmann.ac.il/cards/index.shtml
This is 'a database of human genes, their products and their involvement in diseases'. The organizers of the site recognized that the 'sheer number of different data sources now web-accessible, and their high degree of heterogeneity, have created an 'information labyrinth'. Where you can easily lose your way on your quest for information'.

'To test new approaches for the efficient navigation of biomedical information, we have designed the GeneCards Encyclopedia. We use it as a model to develop computational tools that may help to establish an electronic encyclopedia of biological and medical information based on intelligent knowledge navigation technology and a user-friendly presentation of information that makes use of current Human-Computer Interaction research. A crucial aspect of the GeneCards strategy is to make use of standard nomenclature, esp. approved gene symbols. We want to promote the widespread use of such a standard nomenclature.'

3625 **Human Gene Mutation Database**
University of Cardiff
www.hgmd.org
Sustained by the University's Institute of Medical Genetics and 'an attempt to collate known (published) gene lesions responsible for human inherited disease. This database, while originally established for the study of mutational mechanisms in human genes ... has now acquired a much broader utility in that it embodies an up-to-date and comprehensive reference source to the spectrum of inherited human gene lesions. Thus, HGMD provides information of practical diagnostic importance to (i) researchers and diagnosticians in human molecular genetics, (ii) physicians interested in a particular inherited condition in a given patient or family, and (iii) genetic counsellors.'

The Human Genome: special issue of *Science* magazine
American Association for the Advancement of Science See entry no. 2536

3626 Online Mendelian Inheritance in Man: OMIM
National Center for Biotechnology Information and Johns Hopkins University
www.ncbi.nlm.nih.gov
A database, intended for use by doctors and genetics researchers, of human genes and genetic disorders that includes links to literature references, DNA sequences, maps and related databases. It is updated on a daily basis.

'OMIM is intended for use primarily by physicians and other professionals concerned with genetic disorders, by genetics researchers, and by advanced students in science and medicine. While the OMIM database is open to the public, users seeking information about a personal medical or genetic condition are urged to consult with a qualified physician for diagnosis and for answers to personal questions.'

- **Mendelian inheritance in man: a catalog of human genes and genetic disorders V.A. McKusick [et al.]** 12th edn, Johns Hopkins University Press, 1998, 3972pp. $299.00. ISBN 0801857422. 3 v.

3627 UK Biobank
Great Britain. Department of Health, Medical Research Council and Wellcome Trust
www.ukbiobank.ac.uk
'UK Biobank is a long-term national project to build the world's largest information resource for medical researchers. It will follow the health of 500,000 volunteers aged 45–69 in the UK for up to 30 years ... The project will help approved researchers to develop new and better ways of preventing, diagnosing and treating common illnesses such as cancer, heart disease, diabetes and Alzheimer's disease.'

It is funded by the three bodies listed plus the Scottish Executive.

Directories & encyclopedias

Encyclopedia of genetics
S. Brenner and J. Miller, eds See entry no. 2541

3628 European Directory of DNA Diagnostic Laboratories: EDDNAL
Institut de Pathologie et de Génétique
www.eddnal.com
This site is aimed at medical staff and provides a listing of European laboratories that carry out diagnostic DNA testing. The list can be searched by the name of a disease, by country or by the name of the laboratory.

3629 Gale encyclopedia of genetic disorders
2nd edn, Thomson Gale, 2005. 2 v., $340.00. ISBN 1414403658.
www.galegroup.com
Announced new edn of work which 'provides clear, complete information on genetic disorders, including conditions, tests, procedures, treatments and therapies, in articles that are both comprehensive and easy to understand in language accessible to laypersons'.

'Gale does well in bridging the gap between consumer health and the complexity of understanding genetics information. The general public will find this ready-reference tool easy to use and invaluable. This source will be a good addition to public libraries as well as health sciences libraries (on the 1st edn).' (*American Reference Books Annual*)

3630 Nature encyclopedia of the human genome
D.N. Cooper, ed. Nature, 2003. 5 v. ISBN 0333803868.
Very useful major treatise, with articles organized A–Z by title, each having lists of further reading and weblinks. The work was conceived with these conceptual headings, each indexed with the relevant entries: Structural genomics; Functional genomics; Chromosome structure and function; Evolution and comparative genomics; Genome mapping and sequencing; Genes and disease; Behavioural and psychiatric genetics; Mathematical and population genetics; Proteomics; Bioinformatics; Ethical, legal and social issues; History.

Handbooks & manuals

3631 The metabolic and molecular basis of inherited disease
C.R. Scriver [et al.], eds 8th edn, McGraw-Hill, 2001, 6338pp. 4 v, $575.00. ISBN 0079130356.
http://genetics.accessmedicine.com [COMPANION]
A reference guide for information in the field of molecular biology. It covers areas such as, the effects of genes, their location on the chromosomes and what treatment, if any, can be recommended to paediatricians and other clinicians whose patients show certain signs and symptoms.

Myelin biology and disorders
R.A. Lazzarini, ed. See entry no. 4002

Keeping up-to-date

3632 Annual Review of Genomics and Human Genetics
Annual Reviews, 2000–. $215.00 [V. 5, 2004]. ISBN 0824337050 ISSN 15278204.
arjournals.annualreviews.org/loi/genom [DESCRIPTION]
An important research journal that publishes review articles on all aspects of the subject. Each article includes a bibliography.

Current pharmacogenomics
See entry no. 3753

Genetics@Nature.com
See entry no. 2554

Trends in Biotechnology
See entry no. 5046

Medical Technology

bioengineering • biomechanics • biomedical engineering • biomedical photonics • biomedical technology • healthcare products • medical devices • medical equipment • medical imaging • medical physics • molecular imaging • nuclear medicine • radiology • smart materials • ultrasound

Introductions to the subject

Basic biomechanics of the musculoskeletal system
M. Nordin and V.H. Frankel See entry no. 3950

Biomaterials science: an introduction to materials in medicine
B.D. Ratner [et al.], eds See entry no. 5778

3633 **Biomechanics: mechanical properties of living tissues**
Y.C. Fung 2nd edn, Springer, 1993, 568pp. £77.00. ISBN 0387979476.
Classic introduction to biomechanics and presenting solutions to bioengineering problems. Its focus on applications is a particular strength.

Bionanotechnology: lessons from nature
D.S. Goodsell See entry no. 5006

3634 **The essential physics of medical imaging**
J.T. Bushberg [et al.] 2nd edn, Lippincott Williams & Wilkins, 2002, 933pp. $99.00. ISBN 0683301187.
Well written guide covering theory and applications of physics in radiology, nuclear medicine and radiobiology. Almost 1000 illustrations.
1st edn 1994.

3635 **Introduction to biomedical engineering**
J.D. Enderle, S.M. Blanchard and J.D. Bronzino, eds Academic Press, 1999, 1062pp. New edn announced for 2005, $89.95. ISBN 0122386604.
A text aimed at engineering students which gives an overview of biomedical engineering. Chapters provide information on fundamental principles such as design, analysis and modelling procedures. In addition to technical information, this handbook also provides a historical perspective on the evolution of biomedical engineering with discussion on moral and ethical issues.
Series: Biomedical Engineering.

3636 **An introduction to tissue-biomaterial interactions**
K.C. Dee, D.A. Puleo and R. Bizios Wiley-Liss, 2002, 228pp. $94.50. ISBN 0471253944.
Three introductory chapters covering molecular-level events that happen at the tissue-implant interface, followed by chapters exploring selected material, biological, and physiological consequences of these events. The importance of the body's wound-healing response is emphasized throughout. 'Provides a solid framework for understanding today's and tomorrow's implantable biomedical devices.'
'a concise, topical, and not overly technical hardbound ... the strengths of this book are its crisp information and condensed summaries. The jewels of this book are the diagrams and tables.' (*Annals of Biomedical Engineering*)

3637 **Medical imaging physics**
W.R. Hendee and E.R. Ritenour 4th edn, Wiley-Liss, 2002, 512pp. $145.00. ISBN 0471382264.
Covers all aspects of image formation in modern medical imaging modalities, from radiography, fluoroscopy, and computed tomography, to magnetic resonance imaging and ultrasound.

3638 **Naked to the bone: medical imaging in the twentieth century**
B. Kevles Rutgers University Press, 1997, 378pp. $60.00. ISBN 0813523583.
'A most timely and readable survey of the vast field of imaging research. It provides a rare, sweeping perspective.' (Antonio Damasio, author of *Descartes' error: emotion, reason, and the human brain*).

3639 **Squire's fundamentals of radiology**
R.A. Novelline 6th edn, Harvard University Press, 2004, 638pp. $85.00. ISBN 0674012798.
www.hup.harvard.edu [DESCRIPTION]
Classic text now updated with the new techniques and procedures developed since the previous 1997 edn.

A student's guide to biotechnology
See entry no. 5010

Virtual reality technology
G. Burdea and P. Coiffet See entry no. 6157

Dictionaries, thesauri, classifications

Glossary of electrotechnical, power, telecommunication, electronics, lighting and colour terms: BS4727
British Standards Institution See entry no. 5416

3640 **Universal Medical Device Nomenclature System**
Emergency Care Research Institute
www.ecri.org
Standard international nomenclature and computer coding system for medical devices whose purpose is 'to facilitate identifying, processing, filing, storing, retrieving, transferring, and communicating data about medical devices. The nomenclature is used in applications ranging from hospital inventory and work-order controls to national agency medical device regulatory systems and from e-commerce and procurement to medical device databases'.

The US National Library of Medicine incorporates UMDNS into its UNIFIED MEDICAL LANGUAGE SYSTEM.

- **Health Devices International Sourcebook** www.ecri.org/Products_and_Services. Online database of medical product manufacturers and distributors and the types of products they supply. One of a wide range of products and services provided by the organization; downloadable PDF catalogue available.

Laws, standards, codes

3641 **Global Harmonization Task Force**
www.ghtf.org
Voluntary group of representatives from national medical device regulatory authorities and the regulated industry. Since its inception, the GHTF has been comprised of

representatives from five founding members grouped into three geographical areas: Europe, Asia–Pacific and North America, each of which actively regulates medical devices using their own unique regulatory framework.

Chairmanship of the GHTF is rotated between the regulatory representatives of the five founding members. The European Commission (EC) is the current (2005) Chair.

International Commission on Radiological Protection
See entry no. 4233

3642 **International labeling requirements for medical devices, medical equipment, and diagnostic products**
C.B. Sidebottom 2nd edn, Interpharm/CRC, 2003, 580pp. $299.95. ISBN 0849318505.
Treats the labelling of medical devices in the major medical device markets, country by country, including: Australia, Canada (and Mexico), China (Korea and Thailand), European Union, Japan, United States. Appendices cover device classifications, as well as listing useful websites and providing a glossary. References. Extensive index.

3643 **Medicines and Healthcare Products Regulatory Agency** [UK]
www.mhra.gov.uk
'The executive agency of the Department of Health protecting and promoting public health and patient safety by ensuring that medicines, healthcare products and medical equipment meet appropriate standards of safety, quality, performance and effectiveness, and are used safely.'

Good news section supplemented by set of Current issues and other useful background information.

National Radiological Protection Board
See entry no. 4234

Research centres & institutes

3644 **Center for Devices and Radiological Health** [USA]
www.fda.gov/cdrh
Part of the US Food and Drug Administration. Wide-ranging website: splendid entry to the field.

3645 **National Institute of Biomedical Imaging and Bioengineering** [USA]
www.nibib1.nih.gov
The newest of the research institutes at the National Institutes of Health, created in December 2000. Its mission is 'to improve health by promoting fundamental discoveries, design and development, and translation and assessment of technological capabilities in biomedical imaging and bioengineering, enabled by relevant areas of information science, physics, chemistry, mathematics, materials science, and computer sciences'.

Well laid out fruitful site, including this definition: 'Bioengineering integrates physical, chemical, or mathematical sciences and engineering principles for the study of biology, medicine, behavior, or health. It advances fundamental concepts, creates knowledge for the molecular to the organ systems levels, and develops innovative biologics, materials, processes, implants, devices, and informatics approaches for the prevention, diagnosis, and treatment of disease, for patient rehabilitation, and for improving health.'

- **Biomedical Engineering Society** www.bmes.org. Aims to give equal status to representatives of both biomedical and engineering interests. Joined Accreditation Board for Engineering and Technology in 2003; is 'the lead society for the accreditation of biomedical and bioengineering programs'.

Associations & societies

3646 **Academy of Molecular Imaging** [USA]
www.ami-imaging.org
Lively colourful website, the Academy being comprised of four distinct components that are governed by their own councils: Institute for Molecular Imaging; Institute for Clinical PET; Society of Non-Invasive Imaging in Drug Development; Institute for Molecular Technologies.

3647 **Advanced Medical Technology Association** [USA]
www.advamed.org
'The world's largest medical technology association representing manufacturers of medical devices, diagnostic products and medical information systems. AdvaMed's more than 1300 members and subsidiaries manufacture nearly 90 percent of the $75 billion of health care technology purchased annually in the United States and more than 50 percent of the $175 billion purchased annually around the world.'

Currency on the site quite variable; but useful for leads – especially policy-related. Also, there is a good downloadable PDF promotional document: The medical technology industry at a glance 2004.

3648 **American Association of Physicists in Medicine** [USA]
www.aapm.org
Organization of more than 4700 medical physicists, medical physics being defined as: 'An applied branch of physics concerned with the application of the concepts and methods of physics to the diagnosis and treatment of human disease. It is allied with medical electronics, bioengineering, and health physics'. Good links list.

3649 **American College of Radiology**
www.acr.org
The College's 30,000 members include radiologists, radiation oncologists and medical physicists. For over 75 years the College has devoted its resources to making imaging safe, effective and accessible to those who need it. Good resources section – including, for instance, about disaster planning.

- **Radiological Society of North America** www.rsna.org. Access to good wide-ranging sets of resources, especially via the headings Education Portal, Technology, and For Patients – the last leading to RadiologyInfo: The radiology information resource for patients developed jointly with ACR.

3650 **Association of British Healthcare Industries**
www.abhi.org.uk
'The lead trade association for manufacturers and distributors of medical device technology in the UK. Member companies supply the NHS and global healthcare markets with a vast array of equipment that ranges from latex gloves

through to hi-tech life support machines.' Quite an amount of useful information can be found through navigation.

3651 **British Healthcare Trades Association**
www.bhta.com
Founded 1917; 350 companies employing 17,000 people in membership. List of members by sector; useful information, especially disability-related.

3652 **British Institute of Radiology**
www.bir.org.uk/content/html/index.htm
A multidisciplinary learned society, founded in 1897, whose aim is to forge links between medicine, science and industry to improve the detection and treatment of disease. The oldest radiological society in the world.

Publish two journals online through HighWire Press. The BIR Information Centre 'provides services to BIR Members and to members of the College of Radiographers, the Royal College of Radiologists and the British Medical Ultrasound Society. It incorporates a reference library available, 'upon request and at the Manager's discretion, to anyone with a need for information about radiology and its allied sciences.'

- **Royal College of Radiologists** www.rcr.ac.uk. College Fellows have first to become doctors, then train for a further seven years: most are employed by NHS hospitals n the medical specialties of Clinical Radiology (diagnostic imaging) and Clinical Oncology (cancer treatment). Publications, links.
- **Society of Radiographers** www.sor.org. 'Diagnostic radiographers employ a range of sophisticated equipment to produce high quality images to diagnose an injury or disease; Therapy radiographers are part of an oncology team that treat patients who have cancer.' Useful links, etc.

3653 **European Medical Technology Industry Association**
www.eucomed.be
Mission is 'to represent the Medical Technologies Industry in Europe, to generate a clear understanding of issues of importance to the industry and to ensure that such issues are raised appropriately at both European Union and national government level'.

Excellent wide-ranging gateway with a wealth of information and pointers. Very good place to start an engagement with the industry and its environment worldwide: check the Sitemap first.

European Society for Biomaterials
See entry no. 5808

3654 **IEEE Engineering in Medicine and Biology Society**
www.ieee.org/portal
One of 42 Technical Societies/Councils within the ambit of the Institute of Electrical and Electronics Engineers.

3655 **International Organization for Medical Physics**
www.iomp.org
Represents over 16,000 medical physicists worldwide and 74 affiliated national member organizations. Useful range of resources.

International Radiation Protection Association
See entry no. 4258

International Society for Fracture Repair
See entry no. 3960

Society for Biomaterials
See entry no. 5812

Society for Radiological Protection
See entry no. 4263

3656 **Society of Interventional Radiology** [USA]
www.sirweb.org
'Interventional radiologists are board certified physicians who specialize in minimally invasive, targeted treatments performed using imaging for guidance. Their procedures have less risk, less pain and less recovery time compared to open surgery.' Pleasant website; well presented section Patients and Public; very good range of other useful information and pointers.

3657 **Society of Nuclear Medicine** [USA]
http://interactive.snm.org
The Society's motto is 'Advancing molecular imaging'. Very good range of resources, well presented, and including a helpful Links section.

Portal & task environments

3658 **AuntMinnie**
IMV Ltd.
www.auntminnie.com
Extensive commercially sponsored portal to radiology web resources aimed at radiologists and professionals in the medical imaging industry. 'The staff of AuntMinnie includes executives, editors, and software engineers with years of experience in the radiology industry.'

Biomaterials Network
See entry no. 5816

3659 **BMEnet: The Biomedical Engineering Network**
Whitaker Foundation
www.bmenet.org
The Foundation principally supports biomedical engineering and this site is a very pleasant well laid out overview of the field and gateway to current activity.

Cambridge Healthtech Institute
See entry no. 3709

3660 **Medical Devicelink**
Canon Communications LLC.
www.devicelink.com
An easy-to-use portal for engineers in the medical devices industry. The site provides topical news, a discussion forum and a CareerCenter with free registration for job hunters and advertisers. Users can search by industry to access ResourceCenters which contain information on products and companies and give access to links and magazine articles. The site maintains a directory for suppliers and services to the device industry covering North America and Europe.

3661 **NucMed Links**
T. Smith, comp.
www.nucmedlinks.com
Personal interest site written, updated and maintained by a nuclear medicine technologist in South Australia.

3662 Radiology Web
Vertibrae Inc.
www.radiologyweb.com [REGISTRATION]
An independently produced e-publication created by and for practising, teaching and student radiologists as a comprehensive source of new information, practical knowledge, and educational resources pertinent to the evolving field of radiology. Supported by unrestricted grants from sponsors.

Discovering print & electronic resources

3663 IEEE Biomedical Library
Institute of Electrical and Electronics Engineers and Institution of Electrical Engineers OVID.
www.ovid.com [DESCRIPTION]
Announced December 2003 and comprising 40,000 full text documents supplied by both IEEE and IEE, the content being drawn from over 130 journals and periodicals, more than 350 conferences, and standards published by the IEEE since 1988.

3664 Radiology Education.com: a digital library of radiology education resources
M.P. D'Alessandro, comp.
www.radiologyeducation.com
'RadiologyEducation.com uses the following criteria for World-Wide Web site selection: 1) The site is selected by a process of peer review by accreditation, because accreditation models are designed for works that change over time. To become accredited, a site must clearly display four core quality standards: A. Authorship, including the author's name, affiliation, and credentials. B. Attribution of facts through the listing of references. C. Disclosure of site ownership and sponsorship. D. Currency of the site by listing dates of content posting and updating. 2) The site must be free to use, in part or in whole. 3) The site's information must be primarily in Hypertext Markup Language format (HTML) so that it can be read by users with the lowest common denominator World-Wide Web browser.'

The Site subscribes to the HONCode principles.

Digital data, image & text collections

Obstetric Ultrasound: A Comprehensive Guide
J. Woo See entry no. 4014

Directories & encyclopedias

3665 Encyclopedia of smart materials
M.M. Schwartz, ed. Wiley, 2002, 1176pp. 2 v, $795.00. ISBN 0471177806.
www.knovel.com
'Smart materials – materials and structures that can impart information about their environment to an observer or monitoring device – are revolutionizing fields as diverse as engineering, optics, and medical technology.' Very good coverage in A–Z format.
Available online: see website.
'The contents of this encyclopedia will not fail to meet expectations of readers ... I strongly recommend this encyclopedia to researchers.' (*Pharmaceutical Research*)

Handbooks & manuals

3666 The biomedical engineering handbook
J.D. Bronzino, ed. 2nd edn, CRC Press, 1999. 2 v, $209.95. ISBN 0849385946.
The 1st edn 'defined the discipline of Biomedical Engineering by bringing together the core of knowledge that made up this rapidly growing field' and to some became known as the 'Bible of biomedical engineering'. This extensively revised 2nd edn was winner of the Association of American Publishers Best New Professional/Scholarly Publication – Engineering.

Biomedical engineering principles in sports
G.K. Hung and J.M. Pallis, eds See entry no. 4484

3667 Biomedical photonics handbook
T. Vo-Dinh, ed. CRC Press, 2003, 1872pp. $199.95. ISBN 0849311160.
'Biomedical photonics' is defined as 'the science that harnesses light and other forms of radiant energy to solve problems arising in medicine and biology'.

65 chapters contributed by 150 scientists, engineers, clinicians organized into seven sections: Photonics and tissue optics; Photonic devices; Photonic detection and imaging techniques; Biomedical diagnostics; Biomedical diagnostics II – Optical biopsy; Intervention and treatment techniques; Advanced biophotonics for genomics, proteomics, and medicine.

Extensive valuable appendix: Spectroscopic data of biologically and medically relevant species and samples (136 pp), including a significant bibliography.

3668 Biomedical technology and devices handbook
J.E. Moore and G. Zouridakis, eds CRC Press, 2004, 840pp. $169.95. ISBN 0849311403.
32 chapters in eight sections. Extensive bibliographies. Subject index.

3669 Handbook of materials for medical devices
J.R. Davis, ed.; ASM International 2003, 341pp. $220.00. ISBN 087170790X.
www.asminternational.org [DESCRIPTION]
A definitive source for information concerning the use of implant materials. The handbook provides an overview of the types of biomaterials used in medical devices and gives examples of applications. Materials are then reviewed in detail, followed by a section dedicated to dental applications. The handbook is useful for material selection, corrosion and failure analysis and design considerations.

Handbook of radioactivity analysis
M.F. L'Annunziata, ed. See entry no. 1815

Handbook of zeolite science and technology
S.M. Auerbach, K.A. Carrado and P.K. Dutta, eds See entry no. 4714

Integrated biomaterials science
R. Barbucci, ed. See entry no. 5852

Principles of radiological health and safety
J.E. Martin and C. Lee See entry no. 4298

3670 **Standard handbook of biomedical engineering and design**
M. Kutz, ed. McGraw-Hill, 2002, 2000pp. $150.00. ISBN 0071356371.
A practical reference guide for the biomedical professional seeking information on engineering and design problems. The book enables users to link diagnosis and treatment with the development and manufacture of medical devices.

3671 **Textbook of radiology and imaging**
D. Sutton and P.J.A. Robinson, eds 7th edn, Churchill Livingstone, 2002, 1856pp. 2 v, £289.00. ISBN 0443071098.
A standard two-volume reference work on the scientific basis and clinical practice of radiology. Clearly written overview of the applications of the full spectrum of imaging modalities used in daily clinical practice. 5640 illustrations.
'the text should become the gold standard against which all others are measured' (*Journal of the American Medical Association*)

Tissue engineering
B. Palsson and S. Bhatia, ed. See entry no. 4139

Keeping up-to-date

3672 **Annual review of biomedical engineering**
Annual Reviews Inc, 2004. $202.00. ISBN 0824335066 ISSN 15239829.
www.annurev.org/catalog/2004/be06.asp [DESCRIPTION]
Examples of chapters in this Volume are: Biomaterials: where we have been and where we are going; Micro-computed tomography–current status and developments; Fluid mechanics of heart valves; Robotics, motor learning, and neurologic recovery.

3673 **Biomedical Engineering**
, ed. BioMed Central.
www.biomedical-engineering-online.com
Good example of open access journal from this publisher. Book reviews. Also publish *BMC Medical Imaging* 'an Open Access, peer-reviewed journal that considers articles on the use, development, and evaluation of imaging techniques to diagnose and manage disease'.

3674 **The Pharmaceutical and Medical Devices Knowledge Centre**
ESPICOM Business Intelligence.
www.espicom.com [DESCRIPTION]
Sophisticated commercial service providing access to: More than 500 detailed company reports; Statistical and analytical market reports for over 70 countries; Major therapy and technology-specific services; Industry news services; Comprehensive online services.

Pharmacology & Pharmacy

antibiotics • biomolecular screening • biopharmaceuticals • chemotherapy • designer drugs • drug discovery • drugs • essential medicines • excipients • formularies • generic medicines • medications • medicinal chemistry • medicines • natural products • pharmaceutical chemistry • pharmaceuticals • pharmacognosy • pharmacopoeias • pharmacovigilance • pharmacy • phytochemistry • therapeutics

Introductions to the subject

Alkaloids: nature's curse or blessing?
M. Hesse See entry no. 2028

3675 **In quest of tomorrow's medicines**
J. Drews Springer, 1999, 272pp. Translated from the German by David Kramer, £19.00. ISBN 0387955429.
'Jurgen Drews, an acclaimed leader in the pharmaceutical industry, tells the fascinating story of drug discovery and development from his years of successfully leading international research teams at Hoffman-LaRoche.'

3676 **Oxford textbook of clinical pharmacology and drug therapy**
D.G. Grahame-Smith and J.K. Aronson, eds 3rd edn, Oxford University Press, 2002, 641pp. £29.50. ISBN 0192632345.
Good well written standard introduction

3677 **Pharmaceutical chemistry: therapeutic aspects of biomacromolecules**
C.M. Bladon Wiley, 2002, 234pp. $55.00. ISBN 0471496375.
Provides broad introduction to pharmaceutical chemistry, exploring therapeutic use of peptides, proteins, nucleic acids and carbohydrates.
'a very good value ... a useful addition to the personal library of many biomedical and pharmaceutical scientists ... could serve as a textbook or as supplemental reading }}}. This book. should be in the holdings of academic and pharmaceutical industry libraries.' (*Journal of Medicinal Chemistry*)

Sexual chemistry: a history of the contraceptive pill
L. Marks See entry no. 4450

3678 **The truth about the drug companies: how they deceive us and what to do about it**
M. Angell Random House, 2004, 336pp. $24.95. ISBN 0375508465.
www.nybooks.com/articles/17244 [DESCRIPTION]
'During her two decades at *The New England Journal of Medicine*, Dr. Marcia Angell had a front-row seat on the appalling spectacle of the pharmaceutical industry. She watched drug companies stray from their original mission of discovering and manufacturing useful drugs and instead become vast marketing machines with unprecedented control over their own fortunes. She saw them gain nearly limitless influence over medical research, education, and how doctors do their jobs. She sympathized as the American public, particularly the elderly, struggled and increasingly failed to meet spiraling prescription drug prices. Now, in this bold, hard-hitting new book, Dr. Angell exposes the shocking truth of what the pharmaceutical industry has become – and argues for essential, long-overdue change.'
'Dr Angell's case is tough, persuasive, and troubling.' (*The New York Times*)

Understanding biotechnology
A. Borém, F.R. Santos and D.E. Bowen See entry no. 5011

Dictionaries, thesauri, classifications

3679 **An A–Z of medicinal drugs**
J. Hawthorn and E. Martin Oxford University Press, 2003, 662pp. £8.99. ISBN 0198607687.

A family guide to over-the-counter and prescription medicines. Over 4000 entries written in an accessible style, giving information about medicines in common usage. Aimed at patients and their families but also useful reference tool for paramedical workers and medical students.

3680 A dictionary of natural products
G.M. Hocking Plexus Publishing, 1997, 994pp. $139.50. ISBN 0937548316.
Subtitled: Terms in the field of pharmacognosy relating to natural medicinal and pharmaceutical materials and the plants, animals, and minerals from which they are derived, 'pharmacognosy' being ' the branch of knowledge concerned with medicinal drugs obtained from plants or other natural sources' (*Oxford Dictionary of English*). 18,000 entries.

3681 Dictionary of pharmacovigilance
A. Alghabban Pharmaceutical Press, 2004, 627pp. £39.95. ISBN 0853695164.
'Pharmacovigilance is, in essence, the process of monitoring the everyday use of medicines to identify previously unrecognized adverse drug reactions, thereby assessing their risk/benefit balance in order to determine what action, if any, is necessary to improve their safe use.'

3682 Glossary of terms used in medicinal chemistry
International Union of Pure and Applied Chemistry
www.chem.qmul.ac.uk/iupac/medchem
'Medicinal chemistry' is defined in this glossary as 'a chemistry-based discipline, also involving aspects of biological, medical and pharmaceutical sciences. It is concerned with the invention, discovery, design, identification and preparation of biologically active compounds, the study of their metabolism, the interpretation of their mode of action at the molecular level and the construction of structure-activity relationships'. The definitions used in the glossary are identical to those in the 1998 paper within the journal *Pure and Applied Chemistry*.

Lexicon of psychiatry, neurology, and the neurosciences
F.J. Ayd, ed. See entry no. 4098

3683 Pharmaceutical medicine dictionary
A. Alghabban Churchill Livingstone, 2001, 390pp. £35.99. ISBN 044306475X.
www.xrefer.com
'Aimed at all those that work within the pharmaceutical industry (or aspire to do so) and contains information that covers the gamut of pharmaceutical medicine from drug discovery, development, trials, regulatory approval and marketing.'
Available online: see website.

3684 Saunders pharmaceutical word book 2005
R. Drake and E. Drake W B Saunders, 2005, 784pp. $37.95. ISBN 1416002944.
www.us.elsevierhealth.com [DESCRIPTION]
New edn of work formulated especially for medical transcriptionists containing the correct spelling and capitalization of over 25,000 brand and generic name drugs.

Laws, standards, codes

3685 The British Pharmacopoeia
The Stationery Office, 2004. 5 v. Also CD-ROM version, £818.19. ISBN 0113226632.
www.britpharm.com
'The authoritative collection of standards for UK medicinal substances and an essential reference point for everyone involved in their research, development and manufacture.' Includes some 3000 monographs. In January 2005, the 2004 edn was updated to include data in the *European Pharmacopoeia* 5th edition, by way of an update CD and web access to the integrated data. An eBook format was also made available.
Available online: see website.

3686 Dale and Appelbe's pharmacy law and ethics
G.E. Appelbe and J. Wingfield 7th edn, Pharmaceutical Press, 2001, 677pp. £29.95. ISBN 0853694753.
www.pharmpress.com [DESCRIPTION]
Widely regarded as the established, authoritative and comprehensive guide to this subject.

Intellectual property law and the life science industries: a twentieth century history
G. Dutfield See entry no. 5015

3687 International Conference on Harmonisation of Technical Requirements for Registration of Pharmaceuticals for Human Use: ICH
www.ich.org
'A unique project that brings together the regulatory authorities of Europe, Japan and the United States and experts from the pharmaceutical industry in the three regions to discuss scientific and technical aspects of product registration.

'The purpose is to make recommendations on ways to achieve greater harmonization in the interpretation and application of technical guidelines and requirements for product registration in order to reduce or obviate the need to duplicate the testing carried out during the research and development of new medicines.'

Medicines and Healthcare Products Regulatory Agency
See entry no. 3643

National Institute for Biological Standards and Control
See entry no. 4415

Patents for chemicals, pharmaceuticals and biotechnology: fundamentals of global law, practice and strategy
P. Grubb See entry no. 5080

3688 United States Pharmacopeia
www.usp.org
Non-profit making, non-governmental, standards-setting organization 'that advances public health by ensuring the quality and consistency of medicines, promoting the safe and proper use of medications, and verifying ingredients in dietary supplements. USP standards are developed by a unique process of public involvement and are accepted worldwide. In addition to standards development, USP's

other public health programs focus on promoting optimal healthcare delivery.'

Apart from details of the pharmacopoeia itself – available online and as CD-ROM, as well as in print, several related publications are produced. There is also a good range of other useful drug-related information on the website.

- **United States Pharmacopeia and National Formulary: USP-NF** 2004, Annual. $665.00. ISBN 1889788252). Standards and test procedures via nearly 4000 monographs, more than 160 general chapters. USP provides end product standards for prescription/non-prescription drug products and dosage forms and medical devices; NF primarily for excipients.

Official & quasi-official bodies

Biotechnology and Pharmaceuticals

Great Britain. Department of Trade and Industry See entry no. 5018

3689 Center for Drug Evaluation and Research

www.fda.gov/cder/index.html

'The Center is a consumer watchdog in America's healthcare system. CDER's best-known job is to evaluate new drugs before they can be sold. The Center's review of new drug applications not only prevents quackery, but it provides doctors and patients with the information they need to use medicines wisely.'

The Center is part of the US Food and Drug Administration. Its website provides a useful entrée, both to its work, and to drug-related information more generally (although some parts of the site seem not to have been updated recently).

- **DIOGENES: FDA regulatory information online** FOI Service Inc. www.foiservices.com [FEE-BASED]. The full range of FDA information needed by the regulatory affairs community. 'Unlike other databases, which concentrate on published clinical information, gives you unpublished FDA documents online, as well as full-text news articles. 1 million records.

3690 European Directorate for the Quality of Medicines

www.pheur.org

Part of the administrative structure of the Council of Europe, the Directorate evolved as the 'European Pharmacopoeia Secretariat took on new responsibilities in setting up a European network of laboratories involved in the quality control of medicines for human and veterinary use. Consequently, the European Pharmacopoeia Secretariat changed its name to the European Directorate for the Quality of Medicines (EDQM) to cover these new activities in addition to its other activities'.

3691 European Medicines Agency

www.emea.eu.int

A decentralized body of the European Union, with its headquarters in London, whose 'main responsibility is the protection and promotion of public and animal health, through the evaluation and supervision of medicines for human and veterinary use'. A network of some 3500 European experts underpins the scientific work of the EMEA and its committees.

Food and Drug Administration

See entry no. 3153

3692 International Union of Pharmacology

www.iuphar.org

Independent body since 1966, and member of the International Council for Science. Useful set of resources, including The IUPHAR compendium of basic principles for pharmacological research in humans 2004.

National Institute on Alcohol Abuse and Alcoholism

See entry no. 4306

Associations & societies

3693 American Association of Pharmaceutical Scientists

www.aaps.org

A professional, scientific society of more than 10,000 members, founded in 1986. Aims to advance science through the open exchange of scientific knowledge, serves as an information resource, and contributes to human health through pharmaceutical research and development. AAPS Pharmaceutica is the Society's Web portal.

3694 American Pharmacists Association

www.aphanet.org

The national professional society of pharmacists, founded in 1852 and now the largest professional association of pharmacists in the United States, with over 50,000 members. The Association is a leader in providing professional information and education for pharmacists and an advocate for improved health of the American public through the provision of comprehensive pharmaceutical care. Extensive links section plus wide range of publications.

3695 American Society for Pharmacology and Experimental Therapeutics

www.aspet.org

Large, well organized and prestigious society of pharmacologists covering all scientific aspects of pharmacology. Has ten Divisions that represent the research and education interests of it membership and two Interest Groups for specific areas of research.

3696 American Society of Health-System Pharmacists

www.ashp.org

The 30,000-member national professional association that represents pharmacists who practise in hospitals, health maintenance organizations, long-term care facilities, home care agencies, and other components of healthcare systems. Very wide range of useful publications.

- **AHFSfirstWEB** www.ashp.org/ahfs/web. One of a range of offerings from AHFS Drug Information – others including handheld, desktop, and print solutions. In 2004, ASHP expanded the classes in their AHFS Pharmacologic-Therapeutic Classification by 2 secondary and 3 tertiary classes.
- **PharmSearch** www.ashp.org/IPA. Access to the complete International Pharmaceutical Abstracts – notable for its coverage of alternative and herbal medicine (over 10,000 references). Early 2005, IPA was purchased by Thomson Scientific Solutions.

3697 Association of the British Pharmaceutical Industry

www.abpi.org.uk

The trade association for about a hundred companies in the UK producing prescription medicines. Its member companies research, develop, manufacture and supply more than 90% of the medicines prescribed through the National Health Service. Very good set of information and statistics, publications, resources for schools, links, etc. together with access to details of the work of the Animals in Medicines Research Information Centre – 'an information office set up by the pharmaceutical industry to provide information about the role of animals in the development of medicines'.

- **ABPI Resources for Schools** www.abpischools.org.uk. 'To encourage student interest in science and to support teaching in Primary and Secondary schools ... Provides an invaluable link between science topics studied in school and their applications in industry and research.'
- **Electronic Medicines Compendium: eMC** http://emc.medicines.org.uk. Free, up-to-date information on UK medicines – both prescription and those that can be bought 'over-the-counter' in a Pharmacy. Includes Data Sheets, Summaries of Product Characteristics, Patient Information Leaflets. Also print and CD-ROM versions.

Association of the European Self-Medication Industry

See entry no. 4201

3698 British Pharmacological Society

www.bps.ac.uk

'We are the primary UK learned society concerned with research into drugs and the way they work. Our members work in academia, industry and the health services, and many are medically qualified. The Society covers the whole spectrum of pharmacology, including the laboratory, clinical and toxicological aspects.' Extensive Educational Resources and Links sections.

3699 Commonwealth Pharmaceutical Association

www.commonwealthpharmacy.org

A non-government organization representing professional pharmaceutical societies from over 40 Commonwealth countries. The 'combined membership of skilled and expert pharmacists, committed to serving their communities, enables CPA to work continually towards improving health outcomes for almost one third of the world's population'.

European Association for Bioindustries

See entry no. 5022

3700 European Generic Medicines Association

www.egagenerics.com

EGA is 'the official representative body of the European generic pharmaceutical industry, which is at the forefront of providing high-quality affordable medicines to millions of Europeans and stimulating competitiveness and innovation in the pharmaceutical sector'.

3701 International Federation of Pharmaceutical Manufacturers & Associations

www.ifpma.org

Non-profit, non-governmental organization (NGO) 'representing national industry associations and companies from both developed and developing countries. Member companies of the IFPMA are research-based pharmaceutical, biotech and vaccine companies.'

3702 International Pharmaceutical Federation

www.fip.org

A worldwide federation, founded in 1912, of national pharmaceutical (professional and scientific) associations, representing and serving more than a million pharmacists and pharmaceutical scientists around the world. Each year, FIP organises a World Congress of Pharmacy and Pharmaceutical Sciences and its website provides a good entrée to global activity and trends within this arena.

3703 Pharmaceutical Research and Manufacturers of America

www.phrma.org

'Represents the country's leading research-based pharmaceutical and biotechnology companies, which are devoted to inventing medicines that allow patients to live longer, healthier, and more productive lives. The industry invested an estimated $33.2 billion in 2003 in discovering and developing new medicines. PhRMA companies are leading the way in the search for new cures.'

Excellent website with especially informative sections covering The Issues, and New Medicines in Development.

- **European Federation of Pharmaceutical Industries and Associations** www.efpia.org. 'Represents the research-based pharmaceutical industry operating in Europe. Founded in 1978, its members comprise 29 national pharmaceutical industry associations and 43 leading pharmaceutical companies involved in research, development and manufacturing'.

3704 Pharmaceutical Services Negotiating Committee

[UK]

www.psnc.org.uk

The Committee 'is recognized by the Secretary of State for Health as representative of community pharmacy on NHS matters ... PSNC's main objective is to secure the best possible remuneration, terms and conditions for NHS pharmacy contractors in England and Wales.'

3705 Royal Pharmaceutical Society of Great Britain

www.rpsgb.org.uk

The regulatory and professional body for pharmacists in England, Scotland and Wales. The primary objective of the RPSGB is to lead, regulate and develop the pharmacy profession. As well as many resources related to the pharmacy professions, there is a helpful monthly What's new on this website, and access to information about the services of the Society's Library and information services.

- **PJ Online** www.pharmj.com. Website of *The Pharmaceutical Journal* (official journal of RPSGB) and its family of publications, including *Hospital Pharmacist* and *Prescribing and Medicines Management*.
- **Register of pharmaceutical chemists** www.rpsgb.org.uk/register.html. Official register of pharmacists in England, Scotland and Wales, accredited by the RPSGB.

3706 Society for Biomolecular Screening

www.sbsonline.org

Provides a forum for education and information exchange among professionals within drug discovery and related disciplines – growing 500% between 1995 and 2001. More than 2000 members represent more than 30 countries, 400 companies, and 40 universities, membership being unique in that 'it reflects the interests of end users and suppliers in equal partnership'.

Well designed and structured website giving access to very good range of resources in this relatively new field standing 'at a key interface with medicinal chemistry and biology in the drug discovery process'.

- **Glossary of terms used in biomolecular screening** International Union of Pure and Applied Chemistry www.iupac.org/divisions/VII/index.html. Joint project, due to be completed 2006, between SBS and IUPAC Chemistry and Human Health Division, recognizing the need for 'clear and consistent understanding and application of the terminology' of the new field of biomolecular screening.

Portal & task environments

3707 **AdisInsight**
Wolters Kluwer Health.
www.adisinsight.com
Portal to a range of established services, including: Clinical Trials Insight, PharmaNewsFeed, STEDMAN'S. The company also offers a range of newsletters which can be accessed through the leading online hosts.

Bio.com: Life on the Net
See entry no. 5026

BioSpace
See entry no. 5027

3708 **British National Formulary**
D.K. Mehta; British Medical Association and Royal Pharmaceutical Society of Great Britain Pharmaceutical Press, Biannual. Also available in CD-ROM and PDA formats, £19.50 [September 2004]. ISSN 0260535X.
www.bnf.org
Provides ready access to key information on the selection, prescribing, dispensing and administration of medicines. Drugs that are generally prescribed in the UK are included, with special reference to their uses, cautions, contra-indications, side-effects, dosage and relative costs.

Access to the online version is free of charge: 'It is important that health care professionals have readily available access to the BNF if medicines are to be properly prescribed and dispensed. Although it is widely available in printed form, there will be occasions when it may be more convenient to look up the BNF on the internet. The publishers feel that users should not be discouraged from doing so by the imposition of charges ... The CD-Rom and the intranet versions of the BNF have been developed specifically for the GP and the hospital markets. They have a number of features which are not available on the internet version and the publishers have to recover their development costs by selling these versions on a commercial basis.'

- **Nurse Prescribers' Formulary: For District Nurses and Health Visitors D.K. Mehta; Community Practitioners' and Health Visitors' Association and Royal College of Nursing** 2003–2005, Pharmaceutical Press, 2003, 880pp. £21.50. ISBN 0853695601. Details of preparations which nurses may prescribe for patients receiving NHS treatment. The book incorporates the BNF, giving access to information on medicines prescribed by physicians or those purchased by the patient.

3709 **Cambridge Healthtech Institute**
www.healthtech.com
The Institute is a commercial organization whose 'renowned conferences are the underpinning for all our other information resources. Each year, approximately 60 conferences are held throughout the US and Europe. Conference programs are designed to be a useful, timely, and effective supplement to specialized journals, newsletters, and other meetings'.

As well as details of the conferences (useful overviews of current industry preoccupations), site offers access to a range of newsletters, white papers and other resources, most needing registration; also to the BIOPHARMACEUTICAL GLOSSARY AND TAXONOMIES.

CambridgeSoft
See entry no. 1680

3710 **Campaign for Access to Essential Medicines**
Médecins Sans Frontières
www.accessmed-msf.org
MSF campaign for access throughout the world to essential medicines, with three basic pillars: Overcoming access barriers; Countering 'globalization'; Stimulating research and development for neglected diseases.

CenterWatch: Clinical trials listing service
See entry no. 3784

Chemie.De Information Service
See entry no. 5093

3711 **CombiChem.net**
Technology Networks.
www.combichem.net [REGISTRATION]
One of a series of well designed commercially sponsored portals offering generally free on registration access to news, events, vendors and resources. Other portals offered by the company include: ADMET.net: The world d of ADME (Absorption, Distribution, Metabolism, and Excretion) and Toxicology; HighThroughputExperimentation.com; HTScreening.net ('The main web information portal dedicated to biomolecular screening'); PharmacoGenomicsOnline.com.

3712 **Current Drugs**
Thomson Scientific.
www.current-drugs.com
Company founded in 1989, now part of the Thomson Group, and 'supplying publications and databases to over 90% of the world's leading pharmaceutical and biotechnology companies'. Their flagship system is the Investigational Drugs Database (Iddb), from which they generate a daily alerting service to all aspects of drug development worldwide: from first patent to eventual launch or discontinuation.

Thomson, through its Derwent subsidiary operation, also offer the Derwent Drug File, for which it is claimed that an estimated 20% of the data is not available in any other drug database.

- **Thomson Pharma** www.thomsonpharma.com. 'Dynamic information solution for the pharmaceutical and biotechnology industries. It features the best scientific, patent, and financial content offered by Thomson businesses. This premium content has been enhanced with powerful search tools ...'

3713 **Drug Discovery@Nature.com**
www.nature.com/drugdisc
'An entirely free information resource for everyone with an interest in drug discovery and development, bringing you regularly updated content from Nature Publishing Group titles.'

3714 **DrugDigest** [USA]
Express Scripts Inc.
www.drugdigest.org
'Non-commercial, evidence-based, consumer health and drug

information site dedicated to empowering consumers to make informed choices about drugs and treatment options.' The producers subscribe to the HONcode principles.

3715 Drugs.com: Drug Information Online [USA]
www.drugs.com
'Welcome to the most popular, comprehensive and up-to-date drug information resource online. Fast, easy searching of over 24,000 approved medications.'

The company's mission 'is to be the Internet's most trusted information resource for over-the-counter (OTC) and prescription medicines sold in the USA'. Their database primarily is sourced by three independent leading medical-information suppliers: Physicians' Desk Reference [q.v.], Cerner Multum, and Thomson Micromedex. 'Individual drug (or drug-class) information content compiled by these sources is delivered complete and unaltered by Drugs.com.' The producers also subscribe to the HONCode principles.

3716 eFacts
Wolters Kluwer Health.
www.factsandcomparisons.com
Based on the leading publication *Drug Facts and Comparisons*, ' a brand new way of looking at the world of drug information ... When it comes to drug information, essentially you need two things: 1) Accurate, comprehensive, timely and unbiased content, and 2) the appropriate answer reached easily and quickly. With eFacts, this is exactly what you get.'

- **A to Z drug facts** **D.S. Tatro, ed.** 4th edn, Facts & Comparisons, 2003, 1463pp. $52.95. ISBN 1574391321. Includes CD-ROM. Very pleasant to use, well designed print volume.

3717 Essential Drugs and Medicines Policy
World Health Organization
www.who.int/medicines
'Essential medicines are those that satisfy the priority health care needs of the population. They are selected with due regard to public health relevance, evidence on efficacy and safety, and comparative cost-effectiveness. Essential medicines are intended to be available within the context of functioning health systems at all times in adequate amounts, in the appropriate dosage forms, with assured quality and adequate information, and at a price the individual and the community can afford. The implementation of the concept of essential medicines is intended to be flexible and adaptable to many different situations; exactly which medicines are regarded as essential remains a national responsibility.'

Herbalgram.org
American Botanical Council See entry no. 4206

MDL Information Systems
See entry no. 1684

Nurse Prescriber
See entry no. 4359

3718 PDR.net
Thomson Healthcare.
www.pdr.net
Data on pharmaceuticals together with a range of medical information and education tools, as well as a 'medical marketplace' allowing purchase and subscription to books, journals, newsletters, etc.

- **PDR for nonprescription drugs and dietary supplements** Thomson Healthcare, 2004, 500pp. $59.95. ISBN 1563634783. Comprehensive reference for over-the-counter drugs and preparations. Each product includes data on ingredients, indications and drug interactions. Also includes information on nutritional supplements, vitamins and herbal medicines.
- **PDR nurse's drug handbook** **G. Spratto and A. Woods, eds** Delmar, 2003, 1536pp. $34.95. ISBN 1401835481. A comprehensive resource for nurses containing some 1000 detailed descriptions of drugs.
- **Physician's desk reference** 58th edn, Blackwell Science, 2003, 3538pp. £72.00. ISBN 1563634716. Identifies thousands of prescription drugs and provides information on ingredients, purpose, usage, precautions, side effects and dosages.

3719 PharmWeb
www.pharmweb.net
Internet site for high quality pharmaceutical information provided by international professional organizations for patients and health professionals. It is a well developed and structured site which has been designed to be fully interactive. PharmSearch is the specialized search engine they use. Now has over 30,000 self-registered users.

3720 PJB Publications
www.pjbpubs.com
Provides a wide range of products and services – including several groups of newsletters accessible via the leading online hosts – for the pharmaceutical, biotechnology, medical devices, diagnostics, instrumentation, crop protection, animal health and brewing industries. Their offerings include: Pharmaprojects which has data on over 31,000 drugs gathered since 1980, the company's in-house scientists monitoring over 7000 drugs in active development at any one time; and a range of directories from PJB Reference Services.

3721 Prous Science
www.prous.com [FEE-BASED]
Company that has been providing information and communication services on drug R&D, pharmacology, medicine and medicinal chemistry since 1958. Was one of the first companies to adopt the internet as a strategic option – being awarded the European Commission's European World Wide Web Business Award '96 for best site in the medium business category.

They provide a wide range of commercial services including DailyDrugNews.com, Drug R&D Backgrounders, and a relatively new publication *Environnner: Stimulating Creative Thinking for New Medicines*.

3722 RXList: the internet drug index [USA]
www.rxlist.com
Provides detailed data to the consumer and health professional about drugs, their side effects and interactions – as well as much other related information.

3723 UKMi: Welcome to UK Medicines Information
National Health Service
www.ukmi.nhs.uk
An NHS pharmacy-based service whose aim is 'to support the safe, effective and efficient use of medicines by the provision of evidence-based information and advice on the therapeutic use of medicines. The service has two broad functions: to support medicines management within NHS

organizations; to support the pharmaceutical care of individual patients.'

The Service is provided by a network of: 260 local medicines information centres based in the pharmacy departments of most hospital trusts; 16 regional centres; 2 national centres (Northern Ireland and Wales).

The portal provides access to a wide range of useful information – a good proportion, however, found on investigation only to be accessible to NHS members. Also, parts of the site have been awaiting further development for some time.

- **Medicines Partnership** www.concordance.org. An initiative supported by the UK Department of Health, aimed at enabling patients to get the most out of medicines, by involving them as partners in decisions about treatment and supporting them in medicine taking.
- **Pharm-line: Database for medicines management, prescribing and pharmacy** **Guy's & St Thomas' Hospital Trust**. www.pharm-line.nhs.uk [FEE-BASED]. Bibliographic database on pharmacy practice and the clinical use of drugs which now comprises about 155,000 abstracts from major English language pharmaceutical and medical journals. About 11,000 new records are added each year.

Discovering print & electronic resources

3724 Citeline.com
CiteLine Inc.
www.citeline.com [FEE-BASED]
Intensive service which has chosen some 2000 'invisible' websites (sites which, although often free of charge to use, each have their own individual search forms), and developed a single interface for cross-searching. The service is now very widely used by pharmaceutical and other health-related industries – where depth of information retrieval is highly prized.

3725 Iowa Drug Information Service
www.uiowa.edu/~idis/idistday.htm [FEE-BASED]
Articles selected from 200 peer-reviewed English language medical and pharmaceutical journals covering a wide range of topics. Among the areas covered are pharmacy and pharmacology, general and internal medicine, infectious disease and immunology, transplant, cardiovascular, rheumatology, microbiology, geriatrics, and endocrinology. Accessible in a range of formats.

- **Drug Vocabulary and Thesaurus** www.uiowa.edu/~idis/idisdvt.htm. 8000 drug terms in the Vocabulary, constantly updated as new drug terms appear in the literature and as drug names change; 22,000 entries in the Thesaurus including US/international drug synonyms and trade names cross-referenced to the Vocabulary.

3726 Natural Products Alert
University of Illinois at Chicago
www.cas.org/ONLINE/DBSS/napralertss.html [DESCRIPTION]
Bibliographic and factual data on natural products, including information on the pharmacology, biological activity, taxonomic distribution, ethno-medicine and chemistry of plant, microbial, and animal (including marine) extracts. In addition, the file contains data on the chemistry and pharmacology of secondary metabolites that are derived from natural sources and that have known structure. Contains records from 1650 to the present.

Produced by the University's Program for Collaborative Research in the Pharmaceutical Sciences.

- **NAPRALERT Classification Codes** **American Chemical Society** 1993, 103pp. www.cas.org/ONLINE/UG/napralert.pdf. Comprehensive set of codes designating pharmacological activities.
- **Natural Products Updates** **Royal Society of Chemistry** www.rsc.org/is/database/npuhome.htm. Graphical abstracts of new developments in natural product chemistry, selected from over 100 primary journals. Isolation studies, biosynthesis, new natural products, known compounds from new sources, structure determinations, new properties, activities.

3727 Pharmaceutical News Index
ProQuest Information and Learning.
www.proquest.co.uk/products
Bibliographic information and indexing for all articles published in 20 key international pharmaceutical, healthcare, biotechnology, medical device and cosmetic industry newsletters. Updated daily.

- **Proquest Health and Medical Complete** Proquest Information and Learning. www.proquest.co.uk/products/proquest_health.html [DESCRIPTION]. Combines the full-text clinical and academic journals in *ProQuest Medical Library* with additional consumer health and health administration titles. Covers over 750 periodicals, in full text/full image.

3728 PHARMACOLOGY Cluster
STN International.
www.cas.org/ONLINE/CATALOG/CLUSTERS/pharmacology. html
Combined searching of 57 files accessible on the online host.

3729 RDN Virtual Training Suite: Pharmacist [UK]
F. Farhan; LTSN Health Sciences and Practice and Resource Discovery Network Mediapharm.
www.vts.rdn.ac.uk/tutorial/pharmacist
Good introductory tutorial; regularly updated.

Digital data, image & text collections

3730 Comprehensive medicinal chemistry
MDL Information Systems.
http://mdl.com/products/knowledge
'Derived from the Drug Compendium in Pergamon's *Comprehensive Medicinal Chemistry* (CMC), the MDL Comprehensive Medicinal Chemistry database provides 3D models and important biochemical properties including drug class, logP, and pKa values for over 8400 pharmaceutical compounds (1900–present). MDL updates CMC annually with compounds identified for the first time in the United States Approved Names (USAN) list.'

A product within the MDL Discovery Knowledge component of Elsevier's MDL INFORMATION SYSTEMS*: see website.*

3731 MedicinesComplete
Pharmaceutical Press.
www.medicinescomplete.com
Integrated search across a set of leading texts from this publisher: British National Formulary; Clarke's Analysis of Drugs and Poisons; Dietary Supplements; Herbal Medicines; Martindale: The Complete Drug Reference; Pharmaceutical Excipients; Stockley's Drug Interactions.

- **Handbook of pharmaceutical excipients** **R.C. Rowe, P.J. Sheskey and P.J. Weller** 4th edn, Pharmaceutical Press, 2003, 776pp. £195.00. ISBN 0853694729. 4th edn completely revised and updated; Over 250 excipient monographs; 41 new excipient monographs including Acetic acid, Hexetidine, Monosodium glutamate, Olive oil and Propionic acid; Many more excipients included as 'related substances'.

Natural Medicines Comprehensive Database
See entry no. 4212

Directories & encyclopedias

3732 **BMA new guide to medicines and drugs**
British Medical Association 6th edn, Dorling Kindersley, 2004, 512pp. £16.99. ISBN 1405302631.
www.bma.org.uk/ap.nsf/Content/bmabooksonhealth
Home reference guide to 260 major prescription and over-the-counter drugs and medicines. User friendly. Drug finder index includes colour tablet identification guide. Main drug groups (e.g. Brain and nervous system; Respiratory system). A–Z arrangement of individual drugs.
One of a series of reference books published by the Association with Dorling Kindersley: see website.

Catalog of teratogenic agents
T.H. Shepard and R.J. Lemire See entry no. 4468

3733 **Chemist and Druggist Directory 2004/5** [UK]
CMP United Business Media, Annual. £90.00. ISSN 02625881.
www.dotpharmacy.com
A long established directory, over 135 years, that is the only guide available providing essential information on the entire pharmaceutical and healthcare industries. Contains over 11,000 entries. Comprehensively updated each year.
Available online: see website

Dictionary of renewable resources
H. Zoebelein, ed. See entry no. 4800

3734 **Directory of approved biopharmaceutical products**
S. Spada and G. Walsh CRC Press, 2004, 336pp. $159.95. ISBN 0415263689.
'Biopharmaceuticals, the term for genetically engineered therapeutic proteins, monoclonal antibodies, and nucleic acid-based products, have become an increasing part of the pharmaceutical armament. While this category of drugs accounts for approximately 25% of all new drugs coming to market, very few references exist that review these commercially available products. Until now, accessing data on the list of currently approved biopharmaceuticals has been laborious and patchy.'

Covers products approved both in the US and the EU.

- **Biopharmaceuticals: biochemistry and biotechnology G. Walsh** 2nd edn, Wiley, 2003, 570pp. $85.00. ISBN 0470843276. 'Contains just about everything that anyone would want to know about the subject ... It's all here in this easy-to-read textbook.' *Biochemistry and Molecular Education*. Appendix: Biopharmaceuticals thus far approved in the USA or EU.

Drug dictionary for dentistry
J.G. Meechan and R.A. Seymour See entry no. 3841

Drugs in nursing practice: an A–Z guide
A.M. MacConnachie [et al.] See entry no. 4365

Encyclopedia of addictive drugs
R.L. Miller See entry no. 4314

3735 **Encyclopedia of biopharmaceutical statistics**
S.-C. Chow, ed. 2nd edn, Marcel Dekker, 2003, 1055pp. $395.00. ISBN 082474263X.
www.dekker.com
'More than 5800 references, 150 contributors, and nearly 3000 equations, tables, and figures for thorough exploration of emerging technologies, concepts, and trends vital to the biopharmaceutical industry.' Good straightforward A–Z presentation in large format volume.
Available online: see website
'This book is an essential to those working in pharmaceutical fields. It would be an excellent addition to academic institutions with pharmacy programs.' (*E-STREAMS*)

Encyclopedia of common natural ingredients: used in food, drugs, and cosmetics
A.Y. Leung and S. Foster See entry no. 4213

3736 **Encyclopedia of pharmaceutical technology**
J. Swarbrick and J.C. Boylan, eds 2nd edn, Marcel Dekker, 2002, 3042pp. 3 v., $1350.00. ISBN 0824728254.
www.dekker.com
Major work which was supplemented in 2004 with an Update supplying 40 expert-authored articles and some 1900 new references, covering for instance: Pilot plant design and operation; Quality assurance of pharmaceuticals; Processes and coating of oral solid dosage forms; Innovations in dry powder aerosol technologies; Tablet manufacture and testing; Pulsatile drug delivery systems; Non-prescription drugs and alternative medicines.
Available online: see website.
'the value of the encyclopedia is in its tremendous breadth ... highly recommended. should be in the library of any company or institution involved in pharmaceuticals.' (*Organic Process Research and Development*)

3737 **Martindale: the complete drug reference**
S.C. Sweetman, ed. 34th edn, Pharmaceutical Press, 2004, 2784pp. Available online and on CD-ROM, £275.00. ISBN 0853695504 ISSN 02635364.
www.pharmpress.com
Provides reliable, unbiased and evaluated information on drugs and medicines used throughout the world. Encyclopedic facts about drugs and medicines including 5300 drug monographs, synopses of disease treatments. Includes herbal medicines. Very useful introductory overviews for each of the families of drugs.

Medicinal plants of the world: an illustrated scientific guide to important medicinal plants and their uses
B.E. van Wyk and M. Wink See entry no. 4216

3738 **The Merck index: an encyclopedia of chemicals, drugs and biologicals**
M J O'Neil [et al.] 13th edn, Merck, 2001. CD-ROM version available, $65.00. ISBN 0911910131.
www.merckbooks.com/mindex
The classic one-volume encyclopedia of chemicals, drugs and biologicals that contains more than 10,000 monographs – each 'monograph' being 'a concise description of a single substance or a small group of closely related compounds'. First published in 1889.
Accessible online: see website.

- **The Merck manual of diagnosis and therapy** 17th edn,1999, 2833pp. $40.00. ISBN 0911910107. www.merckbooks.com/mmanual. 'More than 10 million copies have been sold in 18 languages making it the most widely used medical reference in the world!' Also online as a 'free public service by Merck – committed to providing excellent medical information for over a century'.

3739 **MIMS: Monthly Index of Medical Specialties** [UK]
Haymarket Publishing. £125.00. ISSN 09579095.
www.emims.net
The well established and excellent drug information directory available free of charge to all registered UK doctors currently practising within the NHS. Lists over 4000 products.
Available online: see website.

3740 **Mosby's Drug Consult** [USA]
15th edn, Mosby, 2005, Annual, 3392pp. Also CD-ROM version, $79.95. ISBN 0323033938.
www.mosbysdrugconsult.com
Standard collection of 'the most current, unbiased, accurate, and reliable drug information available. It contains full prescribing information for thousands of US-approved pharmaceuticals indexed by generic name, trade name, international brand name, indication and drug class'.
Available online: see website.

3741 **Stephens' detection of new adverse drug reactions**
J.C.C. Talbot and P. Waller, eds 5th edn, Wiley, 2004, 745pp. $205.00. ISBN 047084552X.
Latest edn of now well established multi-author work which explores the methods used to investigate new adverse drug reactions, discussing all elements from the scientific background and animal toxicology through to worldwide regulatory and ethical issues.
'a key text in the area of pharmacovigilance ... extensively referenced and well-written ... a valuable resource.' (*The Pharmaceutical Journal*)

3742 **Stockley's drug interactions**
I. H. Stockley 6th edn, Pharmaceutical Press, 2002, 1096pp. Also available on CD-ROM, £95.00. ISBN 0853695040.
www.pharmpress.com
Complete revision of the previous edition. International source of drug interaction information, containing 13,000 references and over 2400 drug interactions. Divided alphabetically into 24 chapters.
Available online: see website.

3743 **UK Medicines Compendium 2003** [UK]
Association of the British Pharmaceutical Industry DataPharm Communications Ltd, 2003. Formerly ABPI compendium of patient information leaflets. Also available as CD-ROM, updated quarterly, £95.00. ISBN 0907102204.
www.medicines.org.uk/emc.aspx
Electronic version eMC is freely available, and updated daily. Provides comprehensive and reliable data on prescription and over-the-counter medicines in the UK. Lists 2586 summary of product characteristics and patient information leaflets about 2051 products. Appendix 'Code of practice for the pharmaceutical industry'; Directory of participant companies; index of drugs by participant.

Handbooks & manuals

3744 **Burger's medicinal chemistry and drug discovery**
D.J. Abraham, ed. 6th edn, Wiley, 2003, 5568pp. 6 v., $3044.99. ISBN 0471370320.
www.wiley.ca/WileyCDA [DESCRIPTION]
Internationally renowned reference work in medicinal chemistry with comprehensive coverage of drug therapies, taking into account work in a range of related disciplines including: proteomics, genomics, bioinformatics, combinatorial chemistry, high-throughput screening.

3745 **Chronotherapeutics**
P. Redfern, ed. Pharmaceutical Press, 2003, 426pp. £70.00. ISBN 0853694885.
'In nature, many physical processes are governed by the passage of time. The study of these processes, chronobiology, reveals rhythmic patterns which may be yearly, monthly, daily or more frequent. Novel drug delivery systems are currently being developed that will release varying quantities of a drug at optimum times to coincide with these rhythmic patterns. *Chronotherapeutics* considers the pharmaceutical and therapeutic implications associated with biological clocks., solely in relation to humans. Comprehensive discussion is given to specific diseases, which are time dependent, and the drugs and new drug formulations that can be used as treatments.'

3746 **Drug information handbook with international index**
C.F. Lacy [et al.] 12th edn, Lexi-Comp, 2004, 2181pp. $64.95. ISBN 1591950848.
www.lexi.com
Quick access to concisely stated, comprehensive data concerning the clinical use of medications. Based on the US edn which covered some 1300 drug monographs with up to 34 key fields of information per monograph, the international edition adds international brand names for almost 60 countries.
One of a very wide range of drug-related print and online products and services offered by the company: see website.

Handbook of cancer vaccines
M.A. Morse, T.M. Clay and H.K. Lyerly, eds See entry no. 4046

3747 **Handbook on injectable drugs**
L.A. Trissel; American Society of Health-System Pharmacists 13th edn, 2004. Available CD-ROM, $219.00. ISBN 1585281077.
Classic manual; large and detailed. Includes: Over 360 drug monographs, including 47 non-US drugs; 29 drugs new to the 13th Edition, including 6 non-US drugs; drugs listed alphabetically by generic name for efficient searching; brand names also listed.

Mosby's dental drug reference
T.W. Gage and F.A. Pickett See entry no. 3843

3748 **Neonatal formulary**
E. Hey and C. Hall 4th edn, Blackwell BMJ Books, 2003, 312pp. £19.50. ISBN 0727917382.
www.neonatalformulary.com [COMPANION]
Regularly updated reference on the prescribing of drugs and the safe, accurate administering of drugs during pregnancy and labour; and during the first year of life.

3749 **The organic chemistry of drug design and drug action**
R.B. Silverman 2nd edn, Elsevier Academic Press, 2004, 617pp. $80.00. ISBN 0126437327.
An organic chemist's perspective of how drugs are designed and function; teaches organic chemists and biochemists the fundamentals of drug design and drug action using drugs as examples.
'This book is a tour de force in the title area ... This book would be appropriate for advanced undergraduate students and graduate students ... strongly recommended to scientists who are seeking an efficient introduction to medicinal chemistry, background in a specific drug principle or category, or a dose of inspiration (on the 1st edn).' (*Journal of the American Chemical Society*)

3750 **Phytochemical dictionary: a handbook of bioactive compounds from plants**
J.B. Harborne, H. Baxter and G.P. Moss 2nd edn, Taylor & Francis, 1999, 976pp. £351.00. ISBN 0748406204.
Provides basic information, including structural formulae on plant constituents, with emphasis on biologically active ones. Covers over 3000 substances from phenolics and alkaloids through carbohydrates and plant glycosides to oils and triterpenoids.

3751 **The practice of medicinal chemistry**
C.G. Wermuth, ed. 2nd edn, Academic Press, 2003, 768pp. $174.95. ISBN 0127444815.
Aims to be a complete guide to the drug discovery process for those new to medicinal chemistry – such as organic synthetic chemists.
'an impressive book suitable for not only Medicinal Chemists of all experience levels but for anyone working in the field of drug discovery. It would be a welcome addition to any drug discoverer's book shelf.' (*British Journal of Clinical Pharmacology*)

Keeping up-to-date

3752 **Annual Review of Pharmacology and Toxicology**
Annual Reviews, 1961–. $208.00 [2004]. ISBN 0824304446 ISSN 03621642.
www.annurev.org/catalog/2004/pa44.asp [DESCRIPTION]
Reviews, filters and synthesizes primary research to identify the principal contributions in the fields of pharmacology and toxicology.

3753 **Current pharmacogenomics**
Bentham Science Publishers, Quarterly. $1100.00. ISSN 15701603.
www.bentham.org
Research journal, pharmacogenomics being the study of how genes affect a person's response to drugs. 'Accepted articles for publication can be published online for an immediate free open access for all to view. Bentham Open Access offers FREE full text article access to anyone via Internet without charge. This service is available to all authors who publish with Bentham. Authors who choose for open access of their published article must pay an open access fee.'
One of a very large number and wide range of Bentham journals: see website.

3754 **Drug and Therapeutics Bulletin: the independent review of medical treatment** [UK]
Which? Ltd.
www.dtb.org.uk
'Provides rigorous and independent evaluations of individual treatments and overall management of disease for doctors, pharmacists, nurses and other healthcare professionals. DTB also produces similar information for patients in the form of *Treatment Notes*. And there will soon be fully web-enabled versions of DTB and Treatment Notes too.'

3755 **Drug Discovery Today**
Elsevier, 1995–, 24/year. Available free on request.
www.drugdiscoverytoday.com [DESCRIPTION]
Peer-reviewed journal; wide-ranging coverage, including useful reviews of bio and medical informatics, systems biology, etc. From 2005 incorporates former *Drug Discovery Today: BIOSILICO* and *Drug Discovery Today: TARGETS*.

The Pharmaceutical and Medical Devices Knowledge Centre
See entry no. 3674

3756 **PharmaTimes**
www.pharmatimes.com
Well designed news and background information online magazine; also available free of charge on registration.

Clinical Medicine

Broadly, we have aimed to place within this Subject Grouping generic resources designed primarily for use by clinically trained professionals; those on the same subjects aimed more at non-clinicians appear within the Subject Grouping HEALTH.

The growth of evidence-based medicine – and evidence-based nursing – has had a major effect on the publicly available information system of medicine and health: review of resources concerned specifically with that approach provides a very good way in to resources covering the various recognized medical diseases and conditions. In this context, note particularly the extensive literature about diseases and conditions produced for nursing and related professionals: literature which is often inherently more approachable than that produced for clinicians.

Underpinned by the excellent and extensive freely accessible resources of the US National Institutes of Health/National Library of Medicine, reliable information at all levels of detail is easily available about the full spectrum of diseases and conditions. Also now freely accessible, however, is much information that is not so reliable, or is misleading, or is just plain wrong. Therefore, as elsewhere in this Part, we have made particular use of the HONCode in choosing resources to cite.

Especially in that context, the reference resources cited for the various Subject Fields are simply indicative of the types of tools produced for and used by clinicians and those undergoing clinical training. Further, although we have used a relatively large number of subject field headings, we have not felt it would be helpful in the space available to cite more than a few resources within each field. This segment of the publishing market is now dominated by a very small number of reference work producers who collectively make available a very large frequently updated literature. The dictionaries, directories, encyclopedias, handbooks and manuals cited below, for instance, are just good, recent, generally not too technical, exemplars of the wealth of material available: see the websites of the relevant publishers for many additional items.

Interestingly, although all the publishers in this marketplace are offering electronic versions of their products, this is still an area where print-on-paper versions also continue to appear in abundance.

Introductions to the subject

3757 Clinical communication handbook
M. Piasecki Blackwell Science, 2003, 107pp. £16.95. ISBN 0632046465.
'Communication is a critical skill in clinical practice and sometimes not emphasized in medical education. Effective communication skills ease the pressure in dealing with difficult or even 'typical' patients and will make your patients feel more comfortable with you. *Clinical Communication Handbook* can become an essential part of your physician-patient education. Learn how to be a better communicator through the use of vignettes, dialog boxes, and evidence-based information.'

3758 Clinical research coordinator handbook
D. Norris 3rd edn, Plexus Publishing, 2004, 150pp. $39.95. ISBN 0937548545.
New edition of established text provides expanded coverage of the CRC duties and regulatory requirements, including new sections on investigator responsibilities, data clarification, and adverse event reporting.

3759 Concise Oxford textbook of medicine
J.G.G. Ledingham and D.A. Warrell, eds Oxford University Press, 2000, 2007pp. Foreword by David Weatherall. CD-ROM version available, £39.95. ISBN 0192628704.
Although a very good, nicely produced introduction and overview, still a large format substantial text. Section headings are: Cardiology; Haematology; Respiratory disease; Gastroenterology; Metabolic disorders; Endocrine disease and the pituitary; Nutrition; Disorders of the skeleton; Rheumatology; Diseases of the skin; Nephrology; Neurology; Psychiatry; Palliative medicine; Infectious disease; Sexually transmitted disease; Chemical and physical injuries and environmental factors and disease; Geratology; Forensic medicine.

- **Oxford textbook of medicine D.A. Warrell [et al.], eds** 4th edn, Oxford University Press, 2003. £275.00. ISBN 0192629220. Major well written and presented multi-author text. 'It is an invaluable source of information, well written by experts in their respective fields. It will be the first reference source I choose when questions arise ...' *Doody's Journal.*

3760 Foundations of evidence-based medicine
M. Jenicek Parthenon, 2003, 392pp. $99.95. ISBN 1842141937.
Emphasizes the use of formal logic as applied to clinical problems; offers essential definitions, formulae, outlines, flow charts, and checklists useful in health measurement, case and occurrence studies, search for causes, clinical trials, and prognoses.

3761 Human body systems
M. Windelspecht, ed. Greenwood Press, 2004. 10 v, $399.95. ISBN 0313331197.
The circulatory system; The digestive system; The endocrine system; The lymphatic system; The muscular system; The nervous system and sense organs; The reproductive system; The respiratory system; The skeletal system; The urinary system.
'Recommended for advanced middle school grade levels all the way through college and into the public library system is the outstanding 'Human Body Systems' reference set.' (*MBR Bookwatch*)

3762 Medical error: what do we know? what do we do?
M.M. Rosenthal and K.M. Sutcliffe, eds Jossey-Bass, 2002, 325pp. $48.00. ISBN 078796395X.
Edited collection of 12 chapters organized into five parts: Setting the stage; Error from the perspective of providers and patients; Approaches to managing error; Systems

models for reducing error; Where do we go from here? Two useful appendices: A collection of definitions; A collection of website information.

'If you expected books on medical errors to be dull, dry and depressing, this outstanding book will change your mind.' (*Healthcare Collaborator*)

3763 Oxford handbook of clinical medicine
J.M. Longmore, I. Wilkinson and S. Rajagopalan 6th edn, Oxford University Press, 2004, 874pp. £21.95. ISBN 0198525583.
Concise, informative and easy to use, one of the best guides as to how to practise medicine as a junior doctor.

3764 Textbook of biochemistry with clinical correlations
T.M. Devlin, ed. 5th edn, Wiley-Liss, 2002, 1216pp. $120.00. ISBN 0471411361.
Outstanding text, notable for its detailed interweaving of short descriptions of clinical conditions within a detailed coverage of human and related biochemistry.

'A delightful book to read ... I would recommend this book highly ... for any who seek to understand the biochemical basis of disease.' (*Annals of Clinical Biochemistry*)

Dictionaries, thesauri, classifications

3765 Concise dictionary of modern medicine
J.C. Segen McGraw-Hill, 2005, 1300pp. $29.95. ISBN 0838515355.
Illustrated dictionary of modern medical terms includes the jargon commonly encountered in the healthcare professions. Includes 20,000 alphabetized entries for medical acronyms and terms. The entries also consist of encyclopedic definitions, clinical aspects of medical terms, and references to popular medical journals.

3766 Dictionary of medical eponyms
B.G. Firkin and J.A. Whitworth 2nd edn, Parthenon Publishing, 2001, 450pp. $44.95. ISBN 1850703337.
List of eponyms used in the practice of internal medicine. Each entry tells the meaning of the eponym and provides bibliographic information about the person.

3767 International classification of diseases and related health problems: ICD-10
World Health Organization 10th edn.
www.who.int/whosis/icd10 [DESCRIPTION]
Contains the classification at the three- and four-character levels, the classification of the morphology of neoplasms, special tabulation lists for mortality and morbidity, definitions, and the nomenclature regulations.

In three volumes: 1. Tabular list; 2. Instruction manual; 3. Alphabetical index.

3768 International classification of functioning, disability and health
World Health Organization
http://www3.who.int/icf
A relatively new member of the WHO suite, ICF is a classification of health and health-related domains that describe body functions and structures, activities and participation. The domains are classified from body, individual and societal perspectives. Since an individual's functioning and disability occurs in a context, ICF also includes a list of environmental factors.

■ **Classifications of diseases and functioning and disability National Center for Health Statistics.**
www.cdc.gov/nchs/icd9.htm. Useful gateway from NCHS which serves as the WHO Collaborating Center for the Family of International Classifications for North America and in this capacity is responsible for co-ordination of all official disease classification activities in the USA.

3769 The language of medicine
D.-E. Chabner 7th edn, W B Saunders, 2004, 1024pp. $51.95. ISBN 0721697577.
Now well established and used text which helps readers understand and learn complex medical terms by using simple, clear and non-technical explanations of medical terminology in common use.

3770 Medical terminology: the language of health care
M.C. Willis 2nd edn, Lippincott Williams & Wilkins, 2005, 576pp. $52.95. ISBN 0781745101.
www.lww.com [DESCRIPTION]
Revised edn of wide-ranging valuable text, also accessible within a variety of online learning environments: 'With this powerful resource, you will master the intricacies of applied medical terminology through the real-world context of the medical record, which will teach you exactly how terms are used in clinical practice settings.'

3771 Medical terminology made easy
J.T. Dennerll 3rd edn, Thomson/Delmar Learning, 2003, 482pp. $54.95. ISBN 0766826732.
Promotes learning through word building. Ideal for individuals who wish to teach themselves basic medical terminology or as a supplement to entry-level healthcare oriented courses.

3772 Mosby's medical, nursing and allied health dictionary
D.M. Anderson [et al.], eds 6th edn, Mosby, 2002, 2200pp. $38.95. ISBN 0323014305.
http://www3.us.elsevierhealth.com/MERLIN/Dictionary [COMPANION]
UK and US versions available. Contains over 2000 colour illustrations which are used to enhance the definitions of a wide range of medical terminology. Includes easy to read comprehensive definitions for key entries such as major diseases, disorders and procedures; detailed drug entries; colour atlas of human anatomy and a variety of practical reference information included in the appendices.

'Brimming with compact and concise information ... The right choice (of the 5th edn).' (*American Journal of Nursing*)

3773 Who Named It?: The world's most comprehensive dictionary of medical eponyms
O.D. Enerson
www.whonamedit.com
A biographical dictionary of medical eponyms. Presents a complete survey of all medical phenomena named for a person, with a biography of that person. Is eventually planned to include more than 15,000 eponyms and more than 6000 persons: early 2005 there were 7116 eponyms described in 3451 main entries, these eponyms linking to 2852 persons, 2765 male, but only 87 female.

Official & quasi-official bodies

Gene Therapy Advisory Committee
See entry no. 3606

Research centres & institutes

3774 **Centre for Reviews and Dissemination** [UK]
www.york.ac.uk/inst/crd
Aims to provide research-based information about the effects of interventions used in health and social care. Carries out reviews; engages with a number of dissemination activities on the findings of good quality research evidence, promoting use of them in practice and policy; maintains three databases: Database of Abstracts of Reviews of Effects; NHS Economic Evaluation Database; Health Technology Assessment Database – each being searchable and providing monthly lists of new additions.

3775 **National Institute for Health and Clinical Excellence** [UK]
www.nice.org.uk
Important body which 'works on behalf of the National Health Service and the people who use it. We make recommendations on treatments and care using the best available evidence'.

NICE produces three kinds of guidance: technology appraisals; clinical guidelines; interventional procedures. The clearly laid out website leads easily to the texts of their Published Appraisals from each of these headings. But there is also, for instance, an entrée via the heading: 'Want to read our guidance on an illness or condition?', with the texts being gathered under a score of headings: Behavioural (for example, smoking cessation); Cardiovascular (for example, heart disease); Dental, oral and facial; and so on.

A very good service.

'On 1 April 2005 NICE [National Institute for Clinical Excellence] joined with the HEALTH DEVELOPMENT AGENCY *to become the new National Institute for Health and Clinical Excellence (also to be known as NICE).'*

Associations & societies

3776 **American Board of Medical Specialties**
www.abms.org
'The umbrella organization for the 24 approved medical specialty boards in the United States. Established in 1933, the ABMS serves to co-ordinate the activities of its Member Boards and to provide information to the public, the government, the profession and its Members concerning issues involving specialization and certification in medicine.'

Links to the Boards (Allergy and Immunology; Anesthesiology; Colon and Rectal Surgery; etc), plus other relevant information – including Search for a Specialist.

3777 **American College of Physicians**
www.acponline.org
The largest medical specialty society in the USA, with some 115,000 members, including medical students. Produces the *Annals of Internal Medicine*: 'the most widely-cited medical specialty journal in the world'. Their ACP Journal Club (limited to ACP members and other subscribers) contains abstracts of research literature evaluated by experts in the relevant fields, and designed to keep practitioners up-to-date with developments.

Genetic Alliance
See entry no. 3614

Genetic Interest Group
See entry no. 3615

International Alliance of Patients' Organizations
See entry no. 4158

International Association for the Study of Pain
See entry no. 3547

3778 **Massachusetts Medical Society** [USA]
www.massmed.org
Founded in 1781, the MMS is the oldest continuously operating medical society in the United States.

- **The New England Journal of Medicine** Weekly. £365.00. ISSN 00284793. http://content.nejm.org. The leading journal with an emphasis on internal medicine and specialty areas including allergy/immunology, cardiology, endocrinology, gastroenterology, haematology, kidney disease, oncology, pulmonary disease, rheumatology, HIV, and infectious diseases.

3779 **National Organization for Rare Disorders** [USA]
www.rarediseases.org
Private charity, founded in 1983, which among other activities maintains a very large database of 'rare' diseases. The accompanying reports are written in 'understandable language'; abstracts of the reports and information about patient organizations are available free, and 'NORD encourages patients and family members to contact the organizations listed as resources for additional information'. Full-text versions can be downloaded from the website for a $7.50 processing fee. 'The fees charged for NORD reports and other publications support maintenance of this website and other services for individuals and families affected by rare disorders.'

- **Office of Rare Diseases** http://rarediseases.info.nih.gov. This member of the NATIONAL INSTITUTES OF HEALTH provides a list of names of more than 6000 rare diseases and related conditions with links to select government databases.
- **Rare Diseases** www.hon.ch/HONselect/RareDiseases. Substantial list, referencing HONCode accredited information, including in French, German, Spanish, Portuguese, and providing where available access to: Definition; Articles; Images; News; Conferences; Clinical trials; Websites. Excellent service.

3780 **Royal College of Physicians** [UK]
www.rcplondon.ac.uk
A professional body that (eligible) doctors choose to belong and subscribe to. It has its own exacting standards and examinations, exercising a direct influence on the quality of training and the appointment of consultants in all medical specialties.

'The College is also an academic institution, with a diverse educational programme helping physicians to keep abreast of the latest scientific and clinical knowledge. However, the College remit excludes undergraduate education, which is the responsibility of the postgraduate deanery.'

'The College is a registered charity and is not a trade union. It is not part of the NHS or a government department, although it works closely with both. It is concerned mainly with secondary and tertiary care, although the implications of changes to primary care are of increasing interest.'

Well designed website with very good collections of resources under headings such as Clinical standards, Hot topics, Patients and carers, Specialities, Strategic areas, etc. Also an extensive range of Publications.

3781 **Royal Society of Medicine** [UK]
www.rsm.ac.uk
Founded almost 200 years ago as an independent, apolitical organization. Provides a broad range of educational activities and opportunities and promotes an exchange of information and ideas on the science, practice and organization of medicine.

The RSM Library is the largest postgraduate biomedical library in Europe, with a total collection of half a million volumes dating back to the 15th century. Access is offered through a range of categories of membership. Their catalogue is accessible online.

The Society also has an extensive RSM Publishing operation.

Portal & task environments

3782 **AccessMedicine**
McGraw Hill.
www3.accessmedicine.com
'An innovative online resource that provides complete references and services for physicians, students, and health professionals who need immediate access to authoritative and current medical data – UPDATED DAILY!'

'With the full text, graphics, images and illustrations of the most recent editions of world-class medical references in internal medicine, cardiology, genetics, pharmacology, diagnosis and management, basic sciences, and patient care, and with daily content updates, AccessMedicine provides critical information needed for clinical decision making.'

3783 **Bandolier: Evidence based thinking about health care**
Bandolier.
www.ebandolier.com
'The impetus behind Bandolier was to find information about evidence of effectiveness (or lack of it), and put the results forward as simple bullet points of those things that worked and those that did not: a bandolier with bullets. Information comes from systematic reviews, meta-analyses, randomized trials, and from high quality observational studies.

'Each month PubMed and the Cochrane Library are searched for systematic reviews and meta-analyses published in the recent past. Those that look remotely interesting are read, and where they are both interesting and make sense, they appear in Bandolier, first in the paper version and, after two months or so, on the website.'

'The award winning electronic version of Bandolier ... now has over one million visitors each month from all over the world. Whilst many visitors are healthcare professionals, Bandolier is also a source of high quality information for many patients and their carers, as well as for organizations that commission and pay for healthcare.'

- **The Oxford Pain Internet Site** www.jr2.ox.ac.uk/bandolier. 'This site is for anyone with a professional or personal interest in pain and analgesia. It is firmly based in the principles of evidence-based medicine and has pulled together systematic reviews with pain as an outcome'.

3784 **CenterWatch: Clinical trials listing service** [USA]
Thomson Centerwatch.
www.centerwatch.com [FEE-BASED]
Founded in 1994 and 'currently includes listings of more than 41,000 active industry and government-sponsored clinical trials, as well as new drug therapies in research and those recently approved by the US Food and Drug Administration (FDA). Our site is designed to be an open resource for patients interested in participating in clinical trials and for research professionals.'

Two modes of entry: Patient and General Resources; Industry Professional Resources. Helpful background information on clinical testing.

3785 **Clinical Evidence (The international source of the best available evidence for effective health care)**
National Library for Health BMJ Publishing Group.
www.clinicalevidence.com
'We promote informed decision making by summarizing what's known – and not known – about nearly 200 medical conditions and over 2000 treatments.' Free access provided with the support of the NLH within the UK National Health Service.

3786 **ClinicalTrials.com** [USA]
Pharmaceutical Research Plus, Inc.
www.clinicaltrials.com
'An Internet resource for finding clinical trials in the United States and Canada. Our site also provides thousands of local and national organizations that are associated with specific illnesses. We hope to help educate potential trial volunteers on clinical trials as well as help researchers find new participants for their research.'

The site subscribes to the HONCode principles.

- **ClinicalTrials.gov** www.clinicaltrials.gov. Regularly updated information about federally and privately supported clinical research in human volunteers. Gives information about a trial's purpose, who may participate, locations, phone numbers for more details. Also useful FAQs on 'clinical trials'.
- **Current Controlled Trials BioMed Central**. www.controlled-trials.com. 'Allows users to search, register and share information about randomised controlled trials. Access to all the information on this site is free; charges for the registration services offered by Current Controlled Trials are available on request'.

3787 **Cochrane Collaboration**
www.cochrane.org
'International non-profit and independent organization, dedicated to making up-to-date, accurate information about the effects of healthcare readily available worldwide. It produces and disseminates systematic reviews of healthcare interventions and promotes the search for evidence in the form of clinical trials and other studies of interventions.'

Founded in 1993 and named for the British epidemiologist, Archie Cochrane. The major product of the Collaboration is the Cochrane Database of Systematic Reviews which is published quarterly as part of The Cochrane Library.

The website gives a very good summary of how the Collaboration operates: data in 2004 showed that there were more than 11,500 people working for the organization in over 90 countries, half of whom were authors of Reviews.

- **Cochrane Collaboration Policy on Commercial Sponsorship** www.cochrane.org/docs/sponsorshippolicy.htm. Useful document produced in 2004 after an extensive consultation and discussion process: 'As described below, for some questions, there was very clear consensus; for others, there was not'.
- **The Cochrane Library** Wiley Interscience. www.thecochranelibrary.com [FEE-BASED]. A regularly updated collection of evidence-based medicine databases, including The Cochrane Database of Systematic Reviews. Browse and search of abstracts of reviews free of charge.

3788 eMedicine: Instant Access to the Minds of Medicine
eMedicine.com Inc.
www.emedicine.com
Well laid out general portal to a wide range of clinical medicine resources. Especially extensive sets of articles and other information organized by medical condition. Much else of value.

However, there is the helpful cautionary note – which of course applies to all similar resources described in *The New Walford*: 'The site is designed primarily for use by qualified physicians and other medical professionals. The information contained herein should NOT be used as a substitute for the advice of an appropriately qualified and licensed physician or other health care provider. The information provided here is for educational and informational purposes only. In no way should it be considered as offering medical advice. Please check with a physician if you suspect you are ill.'

Meanwhile, the site subscribes to the HONCode principles.

3789 HealthGate: The Evidence-Based Medicine Company
www.healthgate.com [FEE-BASED]
Internet medical and health information provider, with two main sources of content:

Proprietary Developed using a number of medical sources: Newswire reports; Professional journals; Government health agencies; Academic departments; National healthcare associations.

Licensed Vendors used are: Drug Information/USP DI; Infotrieve; MEDLINE; Merriam-Webster's Medical Dictionary; NewRx; Personal Health Manager; Reuters Health eLine; RxChecker (MyDrug-Reax™).

The company provide good and detailed information on the website about their value-adding procedures and policies. Mid-2004 it announced that it had 'forged a worldwide distribution relationship with EBSCO Information Services that will extend HealthGate's reach into new and untapped markets'.

3790 MD Consult
Elsevier.
www.mdconsult.com [FEE-BASED]
Launched in 1997, a family of electronic information resources that aim to meet the clinical content needs of physicians and other health care professionals. It 'now serves over 280,000 users and is licensed by over 1700 healthcare organizations worldwide, including nearly 95% of US medical schools. Each month, subscribers conduct more than 1.5 million information searches and view over 8 million pages of clinical content, primarily during daytime practice hours.'

3791 National Guideline Clearinghouse [USA]
Agency for Healthcare Research and Quality
www.guideline.gov
Comprehensive database of evidence-based clinical practice guidelines and related documents. This AHRQ initiative was originally created in partnership with the American Medical Association and the American Association of Health Plans (now America's Health Insurance Plans).

An excellent service with very good search and browse facilities, and an extensive set of additional Resources, including: discussion list, FAQs, glossary (particularly useful for non-specialists), web developer tools – with a 'new and exciting' RSS feature – and so on. The What's New section is updated weekly with new content.

3792 Virtual Hospital: a digital library for health information
University of Iowa
www.vh.org
A useful portal providing current, authoritative medical information for healthcare professionals, patients and the public. Divided into a number of specialties and contains links to numerous internet resources, hundreds of patient booklets, scores of medical textbooks.

- **Illustrated encyclopedia of human anatomic variation** www.vh.org. Divided into 5 sections ('Opera'): muscular; cardiovascular; nervous; endocrine, gastrointestinal, genitourinary and respiratory; skeletal.
- **Virtual Children's Hospital: a digital library of pediatric information** www.vh.org/pediatric. Variant of the main site designed especially for paediatric health care providers and patients.

Discovering print & electronic resources

3793 Best BETS: Best Evidence Topics
Manchester Royal Infirmary
www.bestbets.org
Rapid access to the best current evidence on a wide range of clinical topics, using a systematic approach to reviewing the literature. Initially had an emergency medicine focus, now includes cardiothoracics, nursing, primary care and paediatrics.

3794 Diseases, disorders and related topics
Karolinska Institutet
www.mic.ki.se/Diseases
Easy to use and extensive set of links to external 'no-charge' internet resources: regularly updated and with all the links routinely checked. Produced by the Institute's University Library. No descriptions of the sites listed; but the service is notable for its detailed classification – using the NLM's Medical Subject Headings – and for its good information search and display system. A useful service to browse around, including to the Library's other offerings.

3795 Evidence Based Medicine Reviews
OVID.
www.ovid.com
Online host provision of combination of four services: ACP Journal Club (American College of Physicians); Cochrane Central Register of Controlled Trials (Cochrane Collaboration); Cochrane Database of Systematic Reviews (Cochrane Collaboration); Database of Abstracts of Reviews of Effectiveness (NHS Centre for Reviews and Dissemination).

Early 2005 had over 360,000 records – including links to full-text, with some 12,000 records added annually.

3796 **Netting the Evidence: a ScHARR introduction to evidence based practice on the internet**
A. Booth, ed.; University of Sheffield
www.shef.ac.uk/scharr/ir/netting
Produced within the University's School of Health and Related Research (ScHARR), a wide-ranging and useful set of links 'intended to facilitate evidence-based healthcare by providing support and access to helpful organizations and useful learning resources, such as an evidence-based virtual library, software and journals'.

Distinguished by its extensive and helpful descriptions of the resources.

3797 **RDN Virtual Training Suite: Medic** [UK]
J. Ross and L. Williamson; University of Nottingham and Resource Discovery Network
www.vts.rdn.ac.uk/tutorial/medic
'A free, 'teach yourself' tutorial that lets you practise your Internet Information Skills.'

Digital data, image & text collections

3798 **Books@Ovid**
Ovid.
www.ovid.com [DESCRIPTION]
Key medical, nursing, and pharmacy texts from a variety of publishers, the complete text of these sources being searchable in a highly interlinked and easily navigated graphical system, giving quick access to crucial diagnostic, research, and reference information.

- **SKOLAR MD** Wolters Kluwer Health. www.skolar.com. Integrated access to full text of a wide range of handbooks and textbooks, journals, drug information, evidence-based datasets, patient information, software tools, Medline, etc.

Human Gene Mutation Database
University of Cardiff See entry no. 3625

3799 **images.MD: The online encyclopedia of medical images**
Current Medicine LLC.
www.images.md
'Medicine is a visual science, as every physician knows. Images are an important aid to diagnosis and an essential component of every lecture and presentation. Images.MD compiles over 50,000 high-quality images spanning all of internal medicine, all derived from Current Medicine's renowned series of illustrated atlases. Each image is accompanied by detailed and informative text written by over 2000 contributing experts.'

3800 **LANGE Educational Library**
Lange Medical Publications.
www3.accessmedicine.com/public/learnmore_lange.aspx
'Since 1938, students, instructors, and physicians have regarded LANGE textbooks as the most readable, authoritative, and current guides to fulfilling basic science and clinical requirements. With AccessMedicine these references are brought into the 21st century with the content of their most recent published edition.'

Very popular and well respected series of texts. Within *Clinical Medicine* provides coverage of: Cardiology; Endocrinology; Obstetrics and gynaecology; Ophthalmology; Orthopaedics; Paediatrics; Psychiatry; Surgery; Urology; within *Pre-Clinical Sciences*: Biochemistry; Epidemiology; Histology; Microbiology; Neuroanatomy; Pathology; Pathophysiology; Pharmacology; Physiology.
Texts also available in print: see website.

Online Mendelian Inheritance in Man: OMIM
National Center for Biotechnology Information and Johns Hopkins University See entry no. 3626

UK Biobank
Great Britain. Department of Health, Medical Research Council and Wellcome Trust See entry no. 3627

Directories & encyclopedias

Gale encyclopedia of genetic disorders
See entry no. 3629

Handbooks & manuals

3801 **Cecil textbook of medicine**
L. Goldman and D. Ausiello 22nd edn, W B Saunders, 2004, 2672pp. 2 v. Text with continually updated online reference, $229.00. ISBN 0721645631.
www.us.elsevierhealth.com [DESCRIPTION]
Originally published in 1927, a classic text providing comprehensive coverage of the scientific foundations and biological basis of disease processes; an introduction to clinical practice protocols; current concepts of pathophysiology, diagnosis, and treatment. An excellent substantial volume.

3802 **Design and analysis of clinical trials: concepts and methodologies**
S.-C. Chow and J. Liu 2nd edn, Wiley, 2003, 729pp. $140.00. ISBN 0471249858.
Comprehensive handbook which assumes minimal mathematical and statistical background, emphasizes real-world examples, and provides an extensive bibliography.
1st edn 1988.

3803 **Human embryonic stem cells**
A.Y. Chiu and M.S. Rao, eds Humana Press, 2003, 461pp. $135.00. ISBN 1588293114.
http://stemcells.nih.gov
'Stem cells are unprogrammed cells in the human body that can be described as 'shape shifters.' These cells have the ability to change into other types of cells. Stem cells are at the center of a new field of science called regenerative medicine. Because stem cells can become bone, muscle, cartilage and other specialized types of cells, they have the potential to treat many diseases, including Parkinson's, Alzheimer's, diabetes and cancer. Eventually, they may also be used to regenerate organs, reducing the need for organ transplants and related surgeries.' (HOW STUFF WORKS).

The authors – respectively from the NATIONAL INSTITUTES OF HEALTH and the NATIONAL INSTITUTE ON AGING – 'invited leaders in the field to present their work in an unbiased way so that readers can assess the potential of stem cells and the current state of the science'.

Website is: 'The official National Institutes of Health resource for stem cell research'.

'This is an excellent compendium about human stem cells.' (*Biologist*)

- **Adult stem cells K. Turksen, ed.** Humana Press, 2004, 360pp. $135.00. ISBN 1588291529. www.humanapress.com/Index.pasp. Wide ranging multi-author collection reviewing current understanding of adult stem cell types and their regulation. Website gives details of the publishers' many related titles currently in print.
- **Stem cell research: new frontiers in science and ethics N.E. Snow, ed.** University of Notre Dame Press, 2003, 219pp. $25.00. ISBN 0268017786. Papers from a conference co-sponsored by the Archdiocese of Milwaukee, Marquette University, and the Wisconsin Catholic Conference. Wide-ranging coverage of scientific, ethical, and public policy issues.

Instruments for clinical health-care research
M. Frank-Stromborg and S.J. Olsen, eds See entry no. 4373

The metabolic and molecular basis of inherited disease
C.R. Scriver [et al.], eds See entry no. 3631

3804 **Oxford handbook of clinical specialities**
J. Collier, M. Longmore and P. Scally 6th edn, Oxford University Press, 2003, 852pp. £21.95. ISBN 0198525184.
Essential one-stop port of call for all the clinical specialties: Obstetrics and gynaecology; Paediatrics; Psychiatry; General practice; Ophthalmology; ENT, Skin diseases; Orthopaedics and trauma; Unusual eponymous syndromes; Pre-hospital immediate care.

Cardiovascular & Respiratory System

atherosclerosis • blood pressure • cardiology • haematology • heart • hypertension • lungs • pacemakers • respiratory system • strokes

Introductions to the subject

3805 **Cardiology**
D.G. Julian, J. Campbell-Cowan and J.M. McLenachan 8th edn, W B Saunders, 2005, 400pp. $34.95. ISBN 0702026956.
Forthcoming edition of essential classic guide introducing all aspects of clinical cardiology.

3806 **The respiratory system**
A. Davies and C. Moores Churchill Livingstone, 2003, 197pp. £18.99. ISBN 0443062315.
Introduction. Structure of the respiratory system. Elastic properties of the respiratory system. Airflow in the respiratory system. Ventilation in the respiratory system. Gas exchange between air and blood – diffusion. The pulmonary circulation – bringing blood and gas together. Carriage of gases by blood and blood ph. Chemical control of breathing. Nervous control of breathing. Lung function tests.
Series: Systems of the Body.

Dictionaries, thesauri, classifications

3807 **A–Z of haematology**
B.J. Bain and R. Gupta Blackwell, 2003, 233pp. £31.50. ISBN 1405103221.
Quick reference guide to definitions covering the entire spectrum of haematology. Includes descriptions of online resources.

Research centres & institutes

3808 **National Heart, Lung and Blood Institute** [USA]
www.nhlbi.nih.gov
Provides leadership for a national program in diseases of the heart, blood vessels, lung, and blood; blood resources; and sleep disorders. Supports research, training and career development. Good set of information for patients and the public.

National Institute of Neurological Disorders and Stroke
See entry no. 3981

Associations & societies

American Association of Blood Banks
See entry no. 4326

3809 **American Heart Association**
www.americanheart.org
A national voluntary health agency, founded in 1924 to reduce disability and death from cardiovascular diseases and stroke. The website provides access to a very wide range of resources including an extensive Heart and Stroke Encyclopedia.

3810 **American Lung Association**
www.lungusa.org
The oldest voluntary health organization in the United States, with a National Office and constituent and affiliate associations around the country. Founded in 1904 to fight tuberculosis, the American Lung Association today fights lung disease in all its forms, with special emphasis on asthma, tobacco control and environmental health.

3811 **Blood Pressure Association** [UK]
www.bpassoc.org.uk
Good up-to-date set of 'information papers' plus useful range of other resources for professionals and patients.

3812 **British Cardiac Society**
www.bcs.com
Founded 1922, with the majority of the membership now being UK cardiologists and cardiac surgeons, but also including other doctors and healthcare professionals. The Society is involved in education, the setting of clinical standards and research into heart and circulatory diseases.

Well designed website – BCS subscribes to the HONCode principles; but most of the useful information is only accessible on registration (and to BCS members).

3813 **British Heart Foundation**
www.bhf.org.uk
Established in 1961, the Foundation plays a vital role in funding heart research in the UK, provides support and information and educates the public and health professionals about heart disease, its prevention and treatment. Well designed website – especially for lay people.

- **Heartstats** www.heartstats.org. Comprehensive, regularly updated, source of statistics on the burden, prevention, treatment and causes of heart disease in the UK.

3814 **British Hypertension Society**
www.hyp.ac.uk/bhs/default.htm
A scientific organization, founded in 1981 to provide a forum to bring together research workers in the UK and the Republic of Ireland. Rewarding, well structured site.

3815 **European Society of Cardiology**
www.escardio.org
Represents more than 45,000 cardiology professionals across Europe and the Mediterranean. Its mission is 'to improve the quality of life of the European population by reducing the impact of cardiovascular disease'. Well organized rewarding site, including an extensive online *Knowledge Centre*.

3816 **Heart Rhythm Society** [USA]
www.hrsonline.org
Incorporated 1979 and has a membership of approximately 3500 physicians and associated professionals from the United States, Canada, Mexico and many other countries. It is 'the dominant professional group representing the allied specialties of cardiac pacing and cardiac electrophysiology in North America'.

3817 **Stroke Association** [UK]
www.stroke.org.uk
'Each year over 130,000 people in England and Wales have a stroke. Of all people who suffer from a stroke, about a third are likely to die within the first 10 days, about a third are likely to make a recovery within one month and about a third are likely to be left disabled and needing rehabilitation. Stroke has a greater disability impact than any other medical condition. A quarter of a million people are living with long-term disability as a result of stroke in the UK.'

Portal & task environments

3818 **BloodMed.com: The global source for haematology education, practice and research**
F. Cotter and C. Willman, eds; British Society for Haematology Blackwell Publishing.
www.b-s-h.org.uk [FEE-BASED]
Interesting joint professional society/commercial publisher venture. Subscription to the portal includes electronic access to the full text of the Society's *British Journal of Haematology*.

Directories & encyclopedias

Atlas of hematology
S.C. Anderson and K. Poulsen See entry no. 3583

Handbooks & manuals

3819 **Heart disease: a textbook of cardiovascular medicine**
E. Braunwald, D.P. Zipes and P. Libby, eds 6th edn, W B Saunders, 2001, 2400pp. 2 v, $155.00. ISBN 0721685498.
Encompasses all of today's essential knowledge in the field, everything from the newest findings in molecular biology and genetics to the latest imaging modalities, interventional procedures and medications.

3820 **Respiratory medicine**
G.J. Gibson [et al.], eds 3rd edn, W B Saunders, 2003, 2042pp. 2 v. Includes CD-ROM, $341.00. ISBN 0702026131.
Definitive postgraduate textbook combining applied science with recommended clinical practice. Gives general information about a particular technique, disease or treatment as well as specialist information about rare conditions. Contributions from over 150 clinicians. 1500 illustrations.

Dentistry

dental surgery • oral medicine • periodontics • teeth

Introductions to the subject

3821 **A colour handbook of oral medicine**
M.A.O. Lewis and R.C.K. Jordan Manson, 2004, 176pp. £29.95. ISBN 1840760338.
Uses a symptom-based approach to assist the clinician in the diagnosis and management of those conditions that fall into the speciality of oral medicine.
'A genuinely practical source of reference ... lavishly illustrated ... will appeal to dental undergraduates who are sure to find its well-planned layout and wealth of colour images of real value in their studies.' (*Dental Update*)

3822 **A consumer's guide to dentistry**
G.J. Christensen 2nd edn, Mosby, 2002, 214pp. $48.95. ISBN 0323014836.
A highly visual reference – some 600 illustrations – written specifically for the patient to provide practical information on dental health and treatment options.
1st edn 1994.

3823 **Oral cells and tissues**
P.R. Garant Quintessence Publishing, 2003, 430pp. $98.00. ISBN 0867154292.
www.quintpub.com [DESCRIPTION]
Excellent introduction. Chapters are: 1. Early tooth development; 2. Dentin; 3. Enamel; 4. Oral mucosa; 5. Gingiva; 6. Periodontal ligament; 7. Root formation and cementogenesis; 8. Bone; 9. Salivary glands; 10. Oral somatosensory systems; 11. Muscle; 12. Cartilage and temporomandibular joint; 13. Immune system; 14. Phagocytic cells.

Dictionaries, thesauri, classifications

3824 Dental terminology
C.M. Dofka Thomson Delmar Learning, 2000, 304pp. $37.95. ISBN 0827390688.
Concise reference of 1300 common dental terms. An easy to use comprehensive resource for dental professionals. Terms are grouped by speciality, and are supported by review questions, and an appendix on word elements.

3825 Mosby's dental dictionary
T. Zwemer [et al.], eds Mosby, 2004, 763pp. Includes CD-ROM, $44.95. ISBN 0323025102.
Over 9500 terms feature in this comprehensive glossary. Extensive appendices provide quick, easy-to-use resources for vital information used daily in the clinical setting. The accompanying CD-ROM contains the entire text in Adobe Acrobat, with an audio component that allows users to click on an icon and hear the correct pronunciation of the most complex terms (approximately 30% of all terms); also provides links to several URLs of relevant websites.

Official & quasi-official bodies

3826 Dental Practice Board [UK]
www.dpb.nhs.uk
The statutory body that administers the General Dental Services of the National Health Service and is accountable to the UK Department of Health and National Assembly for Wales. Site could be a useful entrée to data, statistics and other relevant information.

3827 General Dental Council [UK]
www.gdc-uk.org
Regulates dental professionals in the UK. Keeps up-to-date registers of dentists, dental hygienists and dental therapists who are qualified to practise dentistry in the UK. These are called The Dentists Register and the Rolls of Dental Auxiliaries.

3828 National Institute for Dental and Craniofacial Research [USA]
www.nidcr.nih.gov
Clearly laid out website covering: Health information; Clinical trials; News & reports; Funding for research & training; Research.

Research centres & institutes

3829 Centre for Evidence-Based Dentistry [UK]
www.cebd.org
Independent body, formed in 1994, whose aim is to promote evidence-based dentistry worldwide. The Centre is linked to the Institute of Health Sciences in the University of Oxford and by this link with a number of other initiatives designed to promote evidence-based clinical practice.

Excellent up-to-date sets of links to evidence-based organizations, books and journals, teaching and tools, plus more general dental and medical websites.

Associations & societies

3830 Academy of General Dentistry [USA]
www.agd.org
'The 'go to' dental resource for the general practitioner – and the organization for consumers to find reliable oral health information.' The Academy was founded in 1952 and has a current membership of 37,000: serving the needs and interests of dentists, promoting oral health, and providing quality continuing education.

The AGD Library provides a nice index of articles published in their journals (many with free full-text access), as well as a short webliography. There is also a good consumer information section.

- **American Academy of Pediatric Dentistry** www.aapd.org. Some 6000 members, representing the specialty of paediatric dentistry. Primary contributors to professional education programs and scholarly works concerning dental care for children. Good sets of dental health and other resources.

3831 American Academy of Periodontology
www.perio.org
'A 7900-member association of dental professionals specializing in the prevention, diagnosis and treatment of diseases affecting the gums and supporting structures of the teeth and in the placement and maintenance of dental implants.' Well structured and displayed site subscribing to the HONCode principles.

3832 American Dental Association
www.ada.org
Founded in 1859 as the professional association for dentists working in the United States: 7 out of 10 US dentists are ADA members. Useful Oral Health Topics A–Z among many other resources.

3833 British Dental Association
www.bda-dentistry.org.uk
The professional association and trade union for dentists in the UK, founded in 1880. With over 18,000 qualified members, develops policies to represent dentists working in every sphere, from general practice, through community and hospital settings, to universities and the armed forces. The BDA Information Centre provides a range of services – primarily for BDA members.

3834 British Dental Health Foundation
www.dentalhealth.org.uk
The leading UK-based independent oral health charity, which aims to help people improve their oral health through a range of project activities. The site provides access to a range of resources, including a good selective list of links. It also serves as the site for the International Dental Health Foundation.

3835 British Dental Trade Association
www.bdta.org.uk
Body which represents manufacturers, wholesalers and distributors of products and services to the dental industry in the UK.

3836 Faculty of Dental Surgery [UK]
www.rcseng.ac.uk/dental/fds
Founded in 1947, to maintain and develop the highest professional standards of care and training across the dental

specialties. It provides information for trainers and trainees, whether they are based in the UK or abroad, and it is made up of some 2500 fellows and members who hold one or more of the Faculty's diploma qualifications: MFDS, FDS, M Orth, MRD, MCCD, M Surg Dent, M Paed Dent, DDPH and LDS. The Faculty is housed within the ROYAL COLLEGE OF SURGEONS OF ENGLAND.

- **Faculty of General Dental Practitioners**
  www.rcseng.ac.uk/fgdp. Also based at the Royal College, the 'academic home for general dental practitioners ... Around 95% of the dental care in the UK is provided in the primary dental care setting': thus the importance of their professional development and training.

3837 FDI World Dental Federation
www.fdiworldental.org
Official name is Fédération Dentaire Internationale, but the 'corporate image of the organization shall be the 'FDI World Dental Federation''. Its objectives are: to be the authoritative, professional, independent worldwide voice of dentistry; to promote optimal oral and general health for all peoples; to promote the interests of its Members and to advance and promote the art, science and practice of dentistry.

Useful globally oriented sets of resources on dentistry and more general public health: e.g. in the section: 'National and International Guidelines, Statements, Position papers, Proceedings and Meta-analyses'.

Libraries, archives, museums

3838 National Museum of Dentistry [USA]
www.dentalmuseum.umaryland.edu
The official dental museum of the USA, a SMITHSONIAN INSTITUTION Affiliate, properly titled The Dr. Samuel D. Harris National Museum of Dentistry.

Portal & task environments

3839 The Dental Web [UK]
Internet Portal Solution Providers Ltd.
www.thedentalweb.org
'The site for all the dental team. If you work in or with the dental industry or profession – dentist, PCD, practice manager, receptionist, practice owner, corporate body, manufacturer, supplier, lecturer, student, academic, researcher, journalist, publisher, engineer, technician – it doesn't matter who you are or what you do, there is a place for you here. This is what makes The Dental Web unique – it is the ONLY online portal for everyone in dentistry'.

LTSN Medicine, Dentistry and Veterinary Medicine
University of Newcastle and Higher Education Academy See entry no. 3495

Digital data, image & text collections

3840 Dental Reference Library
Lexi-Comp.
www.lexi.com/web/index.jsp [DESCRIPTION]
Online access to drug information including: 35 fields of information for each drug; Effects on dental treatment; Local anesthetic vasoconstrictor precautions; Dental treatment of medically compromised patients; Treating patients with specific oral conditions Encompasses all eight of the Lexi-Comp dental-related databases.

Directories & encyclopedias

3841 Drug dictionary for dentistry
J.G. Meechan and R.A. Seymour Oxford University Press, 2002, 434pp. £21.95. ISBN 0192632744.
Offers quick and convenient access to essential information on the wide range of drugs a dentist may use or prescribe in their practice, indicating their use, dosage, and possible interactions with other drugs that the patient may be receiving.
'This handy little book contains all the information dentists are likely to need to know about the drugs they come across in their daily practice ... Definitely one to be kept within arm's reach.' (*Dental Practice*)

Handbooks & manuals

3842 Anatomy of orofacial structures
R.W. Brand 7th edn, Mosby, 2003, 567pp. $58.95. ISBN 0323019544.
http://evolve.elsevier.com [COMPANION]
Features coverage of dental anatomy and head and neck anatomy as well as oral histology and embryology.

3843 Mosby's dental drug reference
T.W. Gage and F.A. Pickett 7th edn, Mosby, 2004. $39.95. ISBN 0323032044.
User-friendly guide giving detailed coverage of over 2000 commonly used drug products, including the top 200 prescription drugs in the USA. A companion CD-ROM includes 950 customizable patient information sheets.

3844 Traumatic dental injuries: a manual
J.O. Andreasen [et al.] 2nd edn, Blackwell, 2003, 85pp. £24.99. ISBN 1405111089.
Revised edition of manual which enjoyed a 'phenomenal success', a unique feature being 'the electronically generated images of a "model tooth" subjected to various sorts of trauma. This allows the dentist to appreciate and compare the manifestations and treatment outcomes of typical trauma types.'

3845 Wheeler's dental anatomy, physiology, and occlusion
M.M. Ash and S.J. Nelson 8th edn, Saunders, 2003, 523pp. Includes CD-ROM, $79.95. ISBN 0721693822.
Classic work. 1. Introduction to dental anatomy; 2. Development and eruption of the teeth; 3. The primary (deciduous) teeth; 4. Forensics, comparative anatomy, geometries, and form and function; 5. Orofacial complex: form and function; 6. The permanent maxillary incisors; 7. The permanent mandibular incisors; 8. The permanent canines, maxillary and mandibular; 9. The permanent maxillary premolars; 10. The permanent mandibular premolars; 11. The permanent maxillary molars; 12. The permanent mandibular molars; 13. Pulp chambers and canals; 14. Dento-osseous structures, blood vessels and nerves; 15. The temporomandibular joints, teeth, and muscles and their functions; 16. Occlusion.

Dermatology

dermatitis • eczema • skin

Introductions to the subject

3846 ABC dermatology
P.K. Buxton 4th edn, Blackwell, 2003, 152pp. Includes CD-ROM, £25.95. ISBN 0727916963.
'This is an introduction to dermatology that assumes a general understanding of medicine, but no specialist knowledge. The book provides the essential core of knowledge to which more detailed information can be added. It can be used for reference by general practitioners and doctors in other specialties. The discussion of common conditions before introducing more complex diseases makes it very suitable for teaching medical and nursing students.'

Dictionaries, thesauri, classifications

3847 Dermatology Lexicon Project
University of Rochester
www.dermatologylexicon.org
Aims to produce 'a widely accepted and comprehensive dermatology terminology to support dermatology research, medical informatics and clinical care with a blueprint for future maintenance and sustainability'. Project hosted by the university's Medical Center.

3848 Dictionnaire de dermatologie
J. Civatte [et al.], ed.; Académie de Médecine Conseil International de la Langue Francaise, 2000, 508pp. £61.81. ISBN 2853192776.
More than 3500 terms, with English translations, definitions and encyclopedic comments. English-French index.
Series: Dictionnaire de L'Acade´mie de Me´decine.

Research centres & institutes

National Institute of Arthritis and Musculoskeletal and Skin Diseases
See entry no. 3956

Associations & societies

3849 American Academy of Dermatology
www.aad.org
Established in 1869 with a current membership of over 13,700, it represents virtually all practising dermatologists in the United States.

Dermatology A–Z is a 'resource based on common dermatological conditions, treatments and terminology. It includes definitions of dermatology terms, explanation of common dermatologic conditions and procedures, links to AAD press releases and pamphlets, articles in Dermatology Insights, AAD Guidelines of Care, and links to other associations'. Very useful.

3850 American Society for Dermatologic Surgery
www.asds-net.org
Founded in 1970. 'Dermatologic surgery is the discipline that deals with the diagnosis and surgical, reconstructive and cosmetic treatment of diseases of the skin, hair and nail, for example, skin cancer and rejuvenation of the aging skin.'

Information about the society, membership resources, fact sheets on procedures and techniques and a skin care corner. An excellent site.

3851 British Association of Dermatologists
www.bad.org.uk
Founded in 1920, the Association is the only professional organization representing skin specialists in the UK and Ireland. Promotes appropriate medical and scientific research into the causes, effects and treatment of skin disease and publishes the results; collects, collates and publishes information relevant to dermatology. Good entrée to UK-based activity in this arena.

3852 National Eczema Society [UK]
www.eczema.org
Founded 1975 and is 'the only organization in the UK and one of the most established organizations worldwide dedicated to the needs of people with eczema, dermatitis and sensitive skin'.

- **Skin Care Campaign** www.skincarecampaign.org. NES subsidiary which is 'an umbrella organization representing the interests of all people with skin diseases in the UK'. Website provides excellent overviews of 34 types of skin condition and disease.

Portal & task environments

3853 DermIS: The comprehensive online dermatology information service for healthcare professionals and patients
University of Heidelberg and University of Erlangen
http://dermis.multimedica.de
Extensive web portal that includes the Dermatology Online Atlas (DOIA) with over 4500 images and its paediatric equivalent (PEDOIA) with 2000 images – plus other relevant information on all dermatological conditions including case studies and lectures.

Digital data, image & text collections

3854 DermAtlas.org: Dermatology image atlas
B.A. Cohen and C.A. Lehmann; Johns Hopkins University
http://dermatlas.med.jhmi.edu/derm
Regularly updated collection, now containing over 7000 dermatologic images from some 250 contributors. Arranged by category, diagnoses and body site. Includes quizzes, case studies, etc. The producers – based in the University's School of Medicine – subscribe to the HONCode principles.

Directories & encyclopedias

3855 Dermatology therapy: A–Z essentials
N. Levine and C.C. Levine Springer, 2004, 639pp. £69.00. ISBN 3540008640.
Contains nearly 1000 entries on dermatologic definitions, differential diagnoses and therapeutic possibilities. Structured articles include succinct discussions of the signs, symptoms and therapeutic options, including designations of therapies of choice, where appropriate.

3856 **An illustrated dictionary of dermatological syndromes**
S.B. Mallory and S. Leal-Khouri Parthenon, 1994, 250pp. $89.95. ISBN 1850704589.
'A compendium of dermatologic syndromes, describing some 716 syndromes in crisp detail with lavish colour illustrations.'

Handbooks & manuals

3857 **Clinical dermatology: a color guide to diagnosis and treatment**
T.P. Habif, ed. 4th edn, Mosby, 2004, 900pp. Multimedia package, $225.00. ISBN 0323026192.
www.clinderm.com [COMPANION]
Includes 1000 illustrations covering 'virtually every common skin disorder ... Access a PowerPoint® slide image library featuring 2000 additional illustrations, medline links for all of the text's bibliographic references, a 'differential diagnosis mannequin', frequent content updates, case of the month and more!'.

Condensed handbook of occupational dermatology
L Kanerva [et al.], eds See entry no. 4285

3858 **European handbook of dermatological treatments**
A.D. Katsambas and T.M. Lotti, eds 2nd edn, Springer, 2003, 804pp. £77.00. ISBN 3540008780.
Easy-to-read format provides comprehensive information at a glance. The three main sections listed alphabetically define the different diseases, the drugs available, and the various methods of treatment used in dermatological practice.

3859 **Rook's textbook of dermatology**
T. Burns [et al.], eds 7th edn, Blackwell Science, 2004, 4568pp. 4 v. 2346 illustrations, £450.00. ISBN 0632064293.
The most comprehensive work of reference available to the dermatologist. Covers all aspects of skin disease from basic science through pathology and epidemiology to clinical practice and unparalleled coverage of diagnosis.
' ... one of the towering academic and clinical achievements of twentieth century dermatology ... no self-respecting dermatologist should even think of practising our specialty without a copy of this book close at hand ... a delight to hold, a delight to browse, and a delight to read ... As usual, Blackwell's designers have done a beautiful job.' (*Journal of the American Academy of Dermatology*)

Keeping up-to-date

3860 **Advances in Dermatology**
Mosby, 1986–, Annual, 424pp. $111.00 [2005]. ISBN 0323020968 ISSN 08820880.
Presents collections of fully referenced articles from experts in dermatology.

Digestive System

biliary system • gastroenterology • kidneys • liver • nephrology • urology

Introductions to the subject

3861 **Gastroenterology**
G.P. Butcher Churchill Livingstone, 2003, 119pp. £19.99. ISBN 0443062153.
Very well presented volume with double-page spreads, each covering a specific aspect.
Series: Illustrated Colour Text.
'This is a very pleasant book to glance through when you need to recall some fundamental aspects of gastrointestinal disease and will be especially useful to junior hospital doctors, motivated specialist nurses ... and general practitioners.' (*Digestive and Liver Disease*)

Research centres & institutes

National Institute of Diabetes and Digestive and Kidney Diseases
See entry no. 3878

Associations & societies

3862 **American College of Gastroenterology**
www.acg.gi.org
Formed in 1932 to advance the scientific study and medical treatment of disorders of the gastrointestinal tract: 'Digestive disease specialists committed to quality patient care'.

3863 **American Gastroenterological Association**
www.gastro.org
Founded in 1897, to advance the science and practice of gastroenterology. The AGA's 14,000 members include physicians and scientists who research, diagnose and treat disorders of the gastrointestinal tract and liver.
- **British Society of Gastroenterology** www.bsg.org.uk. Founded 1937; has over 2000 members drawn from the ranks of physicians, surgeons, pathologists, radiologists, scientists, nurses, dietitians, and others interested in the field. *Gut*, the Society's journal is Europe's highest ranked by impact factor.

3864 **American Society of Nephrology**
www.asn-online.org
Founded in 1967 as a non-profit corporation to enhance and assist the study and practice of nephrology, to provide a forum for the promulgation of research, and to meet the professional and continuing education needs of its members.

3865 **American Urological Association**
www.auanet.org
Founded in 1902, it is the professional association for the advancement of urologic patient care, and works to ensure that its more than 15,000 members are current on the latest research and practices in urology. The site offers access to an extensive UrologyHealth.org, an 'online patient information resource ... written and reviewed by urology experts in partnership with the American Foundation for

Urologic Disease. Visitors can search by choosing from adult or pediatric conditions, or by entering a condition using the search option. Content is accompanied by medical illustrations when appropriate'.

3866 Digestive Disorders Foundation [UK]
www.digestivedisorders.org.uk
National charity that covers the entire range of digestive disorders. It funds research, provides information and helps to increase the knowledge of the symptoms of digestive disorders. Useful set of Patient Information Leaflets. The Society's working name is *CORE*.

3867 World Gastroenterology Organisation (Organisation Mondiale de Gastro-Entérologie)
www.omge.org
Officially constituted in 1958, it is a federation of 93 national societies and associations of gastroenterologists, representing over 50 000 gastroenterologists worldwide. Sets global standards in education and training. Useful leads.

Directories & encyclopedias

3868 Encyclopedia of gastroenterology
L.R. Johnson, ed. Academic Press, 2004, 2448pp. 3 v, $999.95. ISBN 0123868602.
Contains over 450 articles describing all significant aspects of the discipline of gastroenterology. It covers topics such as: heartburn; ulcers; gallstones; colorectal cancer; hepatitis and irritable bowel syndrome.

3869 The encyclopedia of the digestive system and digestive disorders
A. Minocha Facts On File, 2004, 360pp. $75.00. ISBN 0816049939.
'The human digestive system is a complicated, elegant network of tubes and organs. This encyclopedia does a wonderful job of offering insight as to how it functions when healthy, as well as when things go terribly wrong. In addition to the entries, the reader will find very helpful appendixes, including contact information for U.S and Canadian health departments and organizations, U.S and Canadian poison-control centers, and reliable Web sites for information regarding digestive diseases.

'The entries, however, are where the real value is. There are more than 300 of them, ranging in length from just a paragraph or two to multiple pages. They cover topics such as Acid blocking agents, Contaminated food or water, Crohn's disease, Obesity, Steroids, and Vitamin deficiencies. The discussion of various cancers related to the digestive system is 21 pages long and includes entries on diseases such as anal, colorectal, esophageal, and stomach cancer. Causes, risk factors, symptoms, diagnoses, and courses of treatment are discussed.' (Review in *Booklist*)

Handbooks & manuals

3870 Clinical handbook of gastroenterology
J.L.H. Wong [et al.], eds BIOS Scientific Publishers, 2002, 249pp. £35.00. ISBN 1859960537.
Provides key information on: diagnosis; planning and implementation of treatment; patient education and resource management. 'Highly commended' in the *BMA Medical Book Competition 2003*.

- **Textbook of gastroenterology T. Yamada [et al.], eds** 4th edn, Lippincott Williams & Wilkins, 2003, 3309pp. $649.00. ISBN 0781747449. www.lww.com. The price was for a package including the 2-volume textbook, the 4th edn of the *Atlas of gastroenterology*, and a *Gasteroenterology CD-ROM*: see website.

3871 Diseases of the liver and biliary system
S. Sherlock and J. Dooley 11th edn, Blackwell Science, 2001, 736pp. £89.50. ISBN 0632055820.
Clear and lucid description of the very latest issues in this growing discipline. A classic text written in a very readable style.

- **Hepatology: a textbook of liver disease D. Zakin and T.D. Boyer, eds** 4th edn, Saunders, 2003, 1952pp. $349.00. ISBN 0721690513. Major two-volume treatise with over 100 contributors.

3872 Oxford textbook of clinical nephrology
A.M. Davison [et al.], eds 3rd edn, Oxford University Press, 2004, 2512pp. £395.00. ISBN 0198508247.
An authoritative, well written and comprehensive textbook of clinical nephrology combining the clinical aspects of renal disease important for daily clinical practice while giving extensive information about the underlying basic science and current evidence available.

3873 Sleisenger and Fordtran's gastrointestinal and liver disease: pathophysiology, diagnosis, management
M. Feldman, L.S. Friedman and M.H. Sleisenger, eds 7th edn, W B Saunders, 2002, 2336pp. 2 v, $239.00. ISBN 0721689736.
A complete reference work in this field which provides a balanced, detailed account of the basic science of the digestive system, as well as complete coverage of current diagnosis and management.

Endocrine System

diabetes • hormones • thyroid

Introductions to the subject

3874 ABC of diabetes
P.J. Watkins 5th edn, BMJ Books, 2003, 101pp. £16.95. ISBN 0727916939.
www.blackwellpublishing.com/medicine/bmj
One of the useful introductory overviews: 'Comprises a comprehensive view of the practical issues relating to diagnosis and treatment of diabetes together with very practical advice on the management of its complications. The entire emphasis relates to clinical practice.'
Website gives access to details of other titles in the series – Blackwell Publishing acquiring BMJ Books from BMJ Publishing Group in April 2004.

3875 Basic & clinical endocrinology
F.S. Greenspan and D.G. Gardner, eds 7th edn, McGraw-Hill, 2004, 976pp. $54.95. ISBN 0071402977.
'The best-selling reference in endocrinology! Authoritative, concise, and current, this 'all-in-one' text focuses on the pathophysiology, diagnosis, and treatment of endocrine disorders. Written by recognized authorities and featuring more than 350 two-color illustrations, the Seventh Edition has been updated to reflect the latest in diagnostic testing and molecular biology as well as new approaches to medical management.'

3876 **Diabetes mellitus: a practical handbook**
S.K. Milchovich and B. Dunn-Long 8th edn, Bull Publishing Company, 2002, 229pp. $14.95. ISBN 0923521720.
Helpful and user-friendly this practical guide addresses the everyday concerns of all diabetics. The authors clearly and thoroughly explain the basic survival skills – the balancing of diet, medication and exercise for optimal health – that will help to improve the management of the disease and the quality of life.

Endocrine and reproductive systems
S. Sanders and M. Debuse See entry no. 4445

Official & quasi-official bodies

3877 **International Diabetes Federation**
www.idf.org
A non-governmental organization acting as global advocate for people with diabetes and their healthcare providers. Established in 1950, evolving as an umbrella organization of 185 member associations in 145 countries. In official relations with the World Health Organization and the Pan American Health Organization.

Access to very good wide ranging sets of resources, including to the innovative Diabetes e-Atlas.

Research centres & institutes

3878 **National Institute of Diabetes and Digestive and Kidney Diseases** [USA]
www.niddk.nih.gov
One of the Institutes within the National Institutes of Health.

Associations & societies

3879 **American Diabetes Association**
www.diabetes.org
The nation's leading non-profit health organization, founded in 1940, providing diabetes research, information and advocacy. It funds research, publishes scientific findings, provides information and other services to people with diabetes, their families, health professionals and the public. 'Over the last year, more than 350,000 people contacted the Association with questions and concerns, or to seek support or direction regarding diabetes and its management.'

3880 **American Thyroid Association**
www.thyroid.org
'A close-knit, collegial group of physicians and scientists, the ATA is dedicated to the research and treatment of thyroid diseases. ATA's rich history dates back to 1923 and its members are respected worldwide as leaders in thyroidology.'

3881 **Diabetes UK**
www.diabetes.org.uk
The operating name of the British Diabetic Association. With over 170,000 members, 'the largest organization in the UK working for people with diabetes, funding research, campaigning and helping people live with the condition'.

Excellent well organized and presented website.

3882 **Endocrine Society** [USA]
www.endo-society.org
'The world's largest and most active professional organization of endocrinologists.' Publishes four major peer-reviewed journals about endocrinology and metabolism: *Endocrine Reviews*; *Endocrinology*; *The Journal of Clinical Endocrinology and Metabolism*; *Molecular Endocrinology*. Useful introduction to endocrine-related societies worldwide.

- **Hormone Foundation** www.hormone.org. The public education affiliate of The Endocrine Society: public education campaigns; forums; media roundtables; publications; etc.

3883 **Juvenile Diabetes Research Foundation International**
www.jdrf.org
'The leading charitable funder and advocate of type 1 (juvenile) diabetes research worldwide. The mission of JDRF is to find a cure for diabetes and its complications through the support of research. Type 1 diabetes is a disease which strikes children suddenly and requires multiple injections of insulin daily or a continuous infusion of insulin through a pump. Insulin, however, is not a cure for diabetes, nor does it prevent its eventual and devastating complications which may include kidney failure, blindness, heart disease, stroke, and amputation.'

National Osteoporosis Society
See entry no. 3961

Directories & encyclopedias

3884 **Encyclopedia of endocrine diseases**
L. Martini, ed. Elsevier Academic Press, 2004, 2400pp. 4 v, $1095.95. ISBN 0124755704.
www.sciencedirect.com/science/referenceworks
'An authoritative reference developed by 16 international experts who recruited the world's top scientists for contributions. This stellar reference work focuses on nearly 500 endocrine diseases addressing everything from acromegaly, diabetes, hypertension, osteoporosis, thyroid disease, Von Hippel-Lindau Disease, unexplained weight loss, to androgen-related disorders.'
Available online: see website.

- **The encyclopedia of endocrine diseases and disorders** **W. Petit and C. Adamec** Facts on File, 2005, 352pp. $75.00. ISBN 0816051356. Volume to be issued as part of the 36-volume *Library of Health and Living*.

Encyclopedia of hormones
H.L. Henry and A.W. Norman, eds See entry no. 2073

Handbooks & manuals

Exercise endocrinology
K.T. Borer See entry no. 4486

3885 **International textbook of diabetes mellitus**
R.A. DeFronzo [et al.] 3rd edn, Wiley, 2004. 2 v, $575.00. ISBN 0471486558.
'The most comprehensive reference on both the clinical and scientific aspects of diabetes, and is truly global in perspective with the inclusion of epidemiology and the nature and care of diabetes in different parts of the world.'

'the text and production are excellent. Recommended for diabetes and endocrinology clinics and medical libraries.' (*Paediatric Endocrinology Reviews*)

Osteoporosis
R. Marcus, D. Feldman and J. Kelsey, eds See entry no. 3968

3886 **Oxford textbook of endocrinology and diabetes**
J.A.H. Wass [et al.], eds Oxford University Press, 2002, 1504pp. £275.00. ISBN 0192630458.
Over 200 contributions organized into 12 sections: Principles of international endocrine practice; Clinical neuroendocrinology; The thyroid; Parathyroid, calcium and bone metabolism; The adrenal gland; The diffuse endocrine system and their hormones; Growth and development during childhood; Female endocrinology; Male endocrinology; Hormone associations of ageing and systemic disease; Metabolic disorders; Diabetes mellitus.

- **Williams textbook of endocrinology** P.R. Larsen [et al.] 10th edn, Saunders, 2003, 1927pp. $155.00. ISBN 0721691846. Hormones and hormone action; Hypothalamus and pituitary; Thyroid; Adrenal; Reproduction; Endocrinology and the life span; Mineral metabolism; Disorders of carbohydrate and lipid metabolism; Polyendocrine disorders; Paraendocrine and neoplastic syndromes.

3887 **Textbook of diabetes**
J.C. Pickup and G. Williams, eds 3rd edn, Blackwell Science, 2003, 1520pp. 2 v., £250.00. ISBN 063205915X.
Now definitive work offering comprehensive coverage of clinical diabetes with a strong scientific perspective throughout.
'What makes Pickup and Williams different from its equally heavy competitors is the beautiful layout with exceptionally clear figures and generous use of colour photographs. The general standard of all the chapters is high and several are outstanding (on the 2nd edn).' (*Journal of the Royal College of Physicians*)

Keeping up-to-date

Clinical Reviews in Bone and Mineral Metabolism
See entry no. 3972

Geriatrics & Chronic Diseases

ageing • Alzheimer's disease • chronic diseases • dementia • older people

Introductions to the subject

3888 **Cells, aging, and human disease**
M.B. Fossel Oxford University Press, 2004, 489pp. £43.00. ISBN 0195140354.
A fascinating volume. 'This is the first textbook to explain human aging from genes to clinical disease. With over 4000 references, it explores both the fundamental processes of aging and the resultant tissue-by-tissue clinical pathology, detailing both breaking research and current state-of-the art clinical interventions in aging and age-related disease. It is the only book on the market to emphasize the theory of aging as caused by cell senescence rather than the traditionally held wear-and-tear theory.'

Official & quasi-official bodies

3889 **Administration on Aging** [USA]
www.aoa.gov
Goal is 'to make sure that all older Americans and their families have the information and assistance they need to make informed decisions about their life choices now and in the future. Choices that help people maintain and improve their health as they age. Choices that help families care for their loved ones, and most importantly – choices that help older people stay at home and have care options other than nursing home care.'

Research centres & institutes

3890 **National Institute on Aging** [USA]
www.nia.nih.gov
Established in 1974 to provide leadership in aging research, training, health information dissemination, and other programs relevant to aging and older people. It aims to improve the health and well-being of older Americans through research.

Associations & societies

3891 **Age Concern** [UK]
www.ace.org.uk
'Supports all people over 50 in the UK, ensuring that they get the most from life. We provide essential services such as day care and information. We campaign on issues like age discrimination and pensions, and work to influence public opinion and government policy about older people.'

3892 **Alzheimer's Association** [USA]
www.alz.org
The Association, a world leader in Alzheimer research and support, is a voluntary health organization dedicated to finding preventions, treatments and, eventually, a cure for Alzheimer dementia.

3893 **Alzheimer's Society** [UK]
www.alzheimers.org.uk
Founded in 1979, the Society is the UK's leading care and research charity for people with dementia, their families and carers, and has over 25,000 members. Good, clearly laid-out website.

3894 **American Association of Retired Persons**
www.aarp.org
Useful set of resources within the website section Health and Wellness.

- **AgeLine** www.aarp.org/research/ageline. Database of over 60,000 descriptions of current English Language literature about aging from around the world. Also access to a first-rate database of over 700 internet resources on aging. Similarly excellent collection AgeSource Worldwide.
- **Thesaurus of aging terminology** 7th edn2002. $10.00. www.aarp.org/research/ageline/thesaurus.html. Controlled vocabulary of subject terms used in AgeLine. Updated every 3–4 years.

3895 **American Geriatrics Society**
www.americangeriatrics.org
A professional organization, founded in 1942, of health care providers dedicated to improving the health and well-being of

all older adults. Now has an active membership of over 6000 health care professionals. Good set of online resources well presented on the home page.

- **British Geriatrics Society** www.bgs.org.uk. The only professional association, in the United Kingdom, of doctors practising geriatric medicine.

3896 Global Action on Aging
www.globalaging.org
'International grassroots citizen group that works on issues of concern to older people. It reports on older people's needs and potential within the globalized world economy. And it advocates by, with, and for older people worldwide.' Useful entrée to perspectives worldwide.

Portal & task environments

3897 Alzheimer Research Forum
www.alzforum.org/dis/abo
Founded in 1996 to create an online scientific community dedicated to developing treatments and preventions for Alzheimer's disease. Web-based resources and discussion forums for researchers.

'Alzheimer disease is the leading cause of dementia among older people. An estimated 10 percent of Americans over the age of 65 and half of those over age 85 have Alzheimer's. More than four million Americans currently suffer from the disease, and the number is projected to balloon to 10–15 million over the next several decades. Alzheimer's is now the third most expensive disease to treat in the USA, costing society close to $100 billion annually.'

3898 Alzheimer's Disease Education and Referral Center: ADEAR [USA]
National Institute on Aging
www.alzheimers.org
Access to resources about Alzheimer's available from the Institute.

- **Alzheimer's Disease Thesaurus** 2002. $15.00. www.alzheimers.org/catalog/thesaurus.html [DESCRIPTION]. Contains more than 1000 descriptors. Gives descriptors 3 ways: in alphabetical order, in more than 20 broad subject categories, and as keywords in context. Also available online: see website.

3899 ElderWeb
K. Stevenson, comp.
www.elderweb.com
Over its eight years of existence, ElderWeb has grown to include thousands of reviewed links to long term care information, a searchable database of organizations, and an expanding library of articles and reports, news, and events. They subscribe to the HONCode principles.

3900 Health and Age: live well, live longer
Web-based Health Education Foundation
www.healthandage.com
WHEF is a non-profit corporation providing web-based, interactive health information for people as they move towards their senior years, and for those who take care of them. This excellent portal was created by the Novartis Foundation for Gerontology in 1998, and licensed to WHEF in January 2004 – receiving an inaugural grant from Novartis. It is organized effectively into two sites: Public and Professional.

3901 SAGE KE: Science of Aging Knowledge Environment
American Association for the Advancement of Science
http://sageke.sciencemag.org [DESCRIPTION]
The third in a series of Knowledge Environments developed by the Association with its magazine SCIENCE. Divided into four main sections: Literature and news; Community; Resources; Highlights. An annual subscription ($99.00; 2005) provides access to the complete Environment; registration provides a more limited access: see the useful Access Chart.

- **SAGE Crossroads Alliance for Aging Research.** www.sagecrossroads.net/public. Online forum for emerging issues of human aging.

Discovering print & electronic resources

3902 AgeInfo: Information for everyone concerned with older people
Centre for Policy on Ageing
www.cpa.org.uk
An information service about old age and ageing provided by the Centre's Library and Information Service. Includes bibliographic database of over 40,000 books, articles and reports from its specialist collection on social gerontology, as well as information about over 4000 organizations active in the field of old age and ageing in the UK, Europe and worldwide. CD-ROM and web-based access.

3903 Alzheimer's disease: overview and bibliography
T.V. Bennington, ed. Nova Science Publishers, 2003, 164pp. $49.00. ISBN 1590335465.
www.novapublishers.com [DESCRIPTION]
Introductory overview followed by substantial bibliography with author, title and subject indexes.

Directories & encyclopedias

3904 Encyclopedia of aging
D.J. Ekert, ed. Macmillan Reference USA, 2002. 4 v., $499.00. ISBN 0028654722.
www.gale.com [DESCRIPTION]
Excellent A–Z work which, when published, received the awards: Best Reference Source (Library Journal); Editor's Choice of Outstanding Reference Titles (Booklist/Reference Book Bulletin); Outstanding Reference Source Awards 2002 (American Library Association).

Available online in GALE VIRTUAL REFERENCE LIBRARY.

'The articles, informative and exceptionally well written, are enhanced by the excellent drawings, which are especially useful for health-related articles, and valuable charts and figures, which clearly indicate sources and dates. The encyclopedia overall is comprehensive, up-to-date, and well worth the cost.' (*American Reference Books Annual*)

3905 The encyclopedia of Alzheimer's disease
C. Turkington Facts on File, 2003, 286pp. $75.00. ISBN 0816048185.
Presents up-to-date information on the physical, emotional and intellectual conditions that affect an Alzheimer's sufferer. It also examines research on prevention, causes and treatments, and the social issues surrounding the disease.
Series: Library of Health and Living.

- **Encyclopedia of Alzheimer's disease** E.A. Moore and L. Moore McFarland, 2003, 413pp. $75.00. ISBN 0786414383. Includes US-based directories of research, treatment and care facilities. NEW YORK PUBLIC LIBRARY 'Outstanding Reference Book'.

Handbooks & manuals

3906 **Brocklehurst's textbook of geriatric medicine and gerontology**
R.C. Tallis and H.M. Fillit, eds 6th edn, Churchill Livingstone, 2003, 1568pp. £160.00. ISBN 0443070873.
Covers gerontology, clinical geriatric medicine, problem-based geriatrics and health systems and geriatric medicine, with an emphasis on clinical practice.

3907 **Geriatric medicine: an evidence-based approach**
C.K. Cassel [et al.], eds 4th edn, Springer, 2003, 1318pp. £105.00. ISBN 0387955143.
New edition of critically acclaimed text, completely revised and updated, offering practical and comprehensive coverage of the diseases, common problems, and medical care of older persons.

3908 **Handbooks of aging**
5th edn, Academic Press, 2001, 1758pp. $179.95. ISBN 0120445212.
Three-volume set including: *Handbook of psychology of aging* (Birren, J.E., Schaie, K.W., eds); *Handbook of the biology of aging* (Masoro, S.J., Austad, S.N., eds); *Handbook of aging and the social sciences* (Binstock, R.H. George, L.K., eds.).

3909 **The Merck manual of geriatrics**
M.H. Beers and M.D. Berkow 3rd edn, Merck Research Laboratories, 2000, 1507pp. $37.50. ISBN 0911910883.
www.merckbooks.com/mgeri
Offers a wealth of information in a concise, easy-to-use, and clinically relevant manner and specifically addresses the challenges of caring for the elderly.
Accessible online 'as a free public service by Merck'.

3910 **Oxford textbook of geriatric medicine**
J. Grimley Evans [et al.], eds 2nd edn, Oxford University Press, 2003, 1264pp. £75.00. ISBN 0198528094.
Covers all aspects of the medical care of older persons, providing detailed clinical information on every disease, with reference to the ageing process, and the resultant appropriate management and prevention in older patients.

3911 **Physiological basis of aging and geriatrics**
P.S. Timiras, ed. 3rd edn, CRC Press, 2002, 454pp. $129.95. ISBN 0849309484.
Focuses on the established facts of physiological aging to provide an essential reference book for a wide spectrum of readers with different levels of biological and educational backgrounds. Provides a complete profile of the aging of individuals and populations.

3912 **Principles and practice of geriatric medicine**
M.S.J. Pathy, ed. 3rd edn, Wiley, 1999, 1621pp. 2 v., $515.00. ISBN 0471963488.
www.wiley.com/WileyCDA [DESCRIPTION]
Now standard work having a remarkably wide scope.
'It is difficult to imagine one's staff having recourse to the departmental 'Pathy' without coming away fully armed with the required information (of the 2nd edn).' (*British Journal of Hospital Medicine*)

Immune System

allergies • antigens • asthma • bronchodilators • clinical immunology • histocompatibility • immunogenetics • pollen counts

Introductions to the subject

3913 **Roitt's essential immunology**
I. Roitt and P.J. Delves 10th edn, Blackwell Publishing, 2001, 496pp. £31.95. ISBN 0632059028.
www.roitt.com [COMPANION]
Highly readable very well presented classic text.
'Overall, *Essential Immunology* is the best of the immunology primers. It clearly outdistances other textbooks in this area by its scope, its organisation, its clarity, and its ability to convey a carefully balanced and up-to-date view of immunology. The medical student who first comes on the mysteries of immunology here, as well as the seasoned immunologist, will find it an adventure and joy to read.' (*The New England Journal of Medicine*)

Dictionaries, thesauri, classifications

Illustrated dictionary of immunology
J.M. Cruse and R.E. Lewis See entry no. 3572

Research centres & institutes

National Institute of Allergy and Infectious Diseases
See entry no. 3931

Associations & societies

3914 **American Academy of Allergy, Asthma, Immunology**
www.aaaai.org
Established in 1943, it is the largest professional medical specialty organization in the United States, representing allergists, asthma specialists, clinical immunologists, allied health professionals, and others with a special interest in the research and treatment of allergic disease. Very good set of resources including access to The Allergy Report, a component of the Academy's Allergic Disorders: Promoting Best Practice initiative, the goal of which is to improve the health and well being of allergy sufferers.

- **National Allergy Bureau** www.aaaai.org/nab. Section of AAAAI responsible for reporting current pollen and mould spore levels to the public. Provides the most accurate and reliable pollen and mould counts from approximately 75 counting stations in the USA, two in Canada.

American Association of Immunologists
See entry no. 3574

American Lung Association
See entry no. 3810

3915 **American Society for Histocompatibility & Immunogenetics**
www.ashi-hla.org
Professional society dedicated to 'advancing the science and practice of Immunogenetics and its impact on the quality of

human life ... The study of human histocompatibility has grown from a few modest research efforts studying human genetics in the 1950s to a broadly based science merging immunology and genetics, including transplantation of organs and tissues, susceptibility to disease, regulation of immune responsiveness, and molecular characterization of the unique supergene HLA.'

Very good and wide-ranging set of resources, nicely and simply presented. The Links section is especially useful.

3916 Asthma UK
www.asthma.org.uk
'The new name for the National Asthma Campaign. Asthma UK is the charity dedicated to improving the health and well-being of people in the UK with asthma by building and sharing expertise about asthma. Asthma is serious: one person dies every seven hours from asthma in the UK, yet 90% of these deaths are preventable. Asthma is widespread, 5.2 million people have asthma in the UK – 1 in 5 households is affected, and if you don't have asthma yourself, you will know someone who has. Asthma is controllable. 74% of people with asthma suffer symptoms needlessly.'

3917 British Society for Allergy and Clinical Immunology
www.bsaci.org
Founded to improve the management of allergic and related diseases in the UK. Promotes good clinical practice, hosts forums for postgraduate education, provides a curriculum for the training of allergy specialists and supports research into the causes and treatment of allergic disease. Provides a list of BSACI NHS Allergy Clinics in the UK.

3918 British Society for Immunology
immunology.org
Founded in 1956 to advance the science of immunology for public good, now with 4000 members, 3000 in the UK, the remainder throughout the world. Good section on studying immunology; publications; specialist affinity groups (Autoimmunity; Biochemical immunology; Cellular signalling; etc.); links.

- **International Union of Immunological Societies** www.iuisonline.org. Established 1971 as umbrella organization for 54 regional and national societies of immunology throughout the world. Member of the International Council for Science since 1976.

3919 Federation of Clinical Immunology Societies
www.focisnet.org/index.php
'Engenders cross-fertilization among the many specialty societies that are included in the broad field of clinical immunology. Today, FOCIS represents nearly 30,000 clinicians and scientists with 28 member societies.'

3920 World Allergy Organization
www.worldallergy.org
Among a range of useful resources, sustains an Allergic Diseases Resource Center, presented as a series of briefings covering allergies that affect: Eyes; Nose; Mouth and throat; Lungs; Skin; Whole body.

- **Allergy Glossary Health On The Net Foundation**. www.hon.ch/Library/Theme/Allergy/Glossary/allergy.html. Contains common as well as medical terms.

Directories & encyclopedias

The dictionary of immunology
W.J. Herbert, P.C. Wilkinson and D.I. Stott, eds See entry no. 3585

3921 The encyclopedia of allergies
M.A. Lipkowitz and T. Navarra 2nd edn, Facts on File, 2001, 340pp. $75.00. ISBN 0816044058.
Clear and accessible current information in more than 1000 entries.
Previous edn published 1994 as Allergies A–Z.

MSRS Catalog of Primary Antibodies
See entry no. 3590

Handbooks & manuals

3922 Encyclopedia of immunology
P.J. Delves and I.M. Roitt, eds 2nd edn, Academic Press, 1998, 2516pp. 4 v, $1185.00. ISBN 0122267656.
www.info.sciencedirect.com/reference_works
The largest comprehensive reference source of current immunological knowledge available: 700 authors from 22 countries. Arranged into 31 subject areas with extensive cross-referencing and subject indexes in each volume.
Available online: see website.

Handbook of cancer vaccines
M.A. Morse, T.M. Clay and H.K. Lyerly, eds See entry no. 4046

3923 Immunobiology: the immune system in health and disease
C.A. Janeway [et al.] 6th edn, Garland Science, 2005, 732pp. Includes CD-ROM, £39.99. ISBN 0443073104.
www.blink.biz/immunoanimations [COMPANION]
15 chapters in six parts: An introduction to immunobiology and innate immunity; The recognition of antigen; The development of mature lymphocyte receptor repertoires; The adaptive immune reponse; The immune system in health and disease; The origins of immune responses.
'This book provides authority, clarity, breadth and inspiration. Its high standards have blazed a trail. It is a monument to the coordinated work of the whole production team but, especially, the prime author. Go and get your own copy, and fill up that inviting white margin on every page with your own notations.' *(TRENDS in Immunology)*

Keeping up-to-date

3924 Clinical Reviews in Allergy & Immunology
Humana Press, Bimonthly. $555.00. ISSN 10800549.
'The development of clinical allergy as a vigorous discipline of scientific medicine has, until relatively recently, lagged behind that of other subspecialties in internal medicine and pediatrics. The discovery of immunoglobulin E, the development of standardized protocols for allergy skin testing and challenge procedures, and concurrent advances in cell biology have all led to a major thrust by new data in changing the approach to the clinical management of allergic disease ...'

Infectious Diseases

acquired immune deficiency syndrome • AIDS • communicable diseases • HIV • human immunodeficiency virus • immunization • pathogenic microorganisms • tropical diseases • vaccination • vaccines • venereal diseases

Introductions to the subject

3925 **Infectious diseases**
S.L. Gorbach, J.G. Bartlett and N.R. Blacklow 3rd edn, Lippincott Williams & Wilkins, 2004, 2515pp. $275.00. ISBN 0781733715.
Provides comprehensive guidelines on the diagnosis, treatment, and prevention of every infectious disease seen in current clinical practice.

World epidemics: a cultural chronology of disease from prehistory to the era of SARS
M.E. Snodgrass See entry no. 4413

Dictionaries, thesauri, classifications

3926 **A clinician's dictionary of pathogenic microorganisms**
J.H. Jorgensen and M.A. Pfaller ASM Press, 2004, 250pp. PDA format available, $29.95. ISBN 1555812805.
Portable volume covering pathogenic bacteria, mycobacteria, fungi, viruses, and parasites that affect humans, includes clinical symptoms, cross references old and new names for clinically significant organisms.

3927 **Encyclopedic dictionary of AIDS-related terminology**
J.T. Huber and M.L. Gillaspy Haworth Information Press, 2000, 246pp. $24.95. ISBN 0789012073.
Defines words, phrases, and medical terms associated with HIV and AIDS, and includes entries that discuss related legal, social, psychological and religious issues.

Official & quasi-official bodies

3928 **Immunisation** [UK]
Great Britain. Department of Health
www.immunisation.nhs.uk
Official UK government site, including: News; FAQs; Publications; Reference library; Media centre; Children's area. Also Hot topics.

3929 **Office of National AIDS Policy** [USA]
www.whitehouse.gov/onap/aids.html
'Focus on co-ordinating our continuing domestic efforts to reduce the number of new infections in the US, in particular in segments of the population that are experiencing new or renewed increases in the rate of infection. In addition, the Office will be working to co-ordinate an increasingly integrated approach to the prevention, care and treatment of HIV/AIDS. The Office will also emphasize the integration of domestic and international efforts to combat HIV/AIDS.'

Reproductive Health and Research
World Health Organization See entry no. 4454

Research centres & institutes

3930 **National Center for Infectious Diseases** [USA]
www.cdc.gov/ncidod
Mission is 'to prevent illness, disability, and death caused by infectious diseases in the United States and around the world'. Current organization structure includes these major functional sections: Arctic investigations; Bacterial and mycotic diseases; Bioterrorism preparedness and response program; Global migration and quarantine; Healthcare quality promotion; Minority and women's health; Parasitic diseases; Surveillance; Vector-borne infectious diseases; Viral hepatitis; Viral and rickettsial diseases.

- **Emerging Infectious Diseases** www.cdc.gov/ncidod/EID/index.html. A peer-reviewed journal tracking and analysing disease trends.

3931 **National Institute of Allergy and Infectious Diseases**
www.niaid.nih.gov
'Conducts and supports basic and applied research to better understand, treat, and ultimately prevent infectious, immunologic, and allergic diseases. For more than 50 years, NIAID research has led to new therapies, vaccines, diagnostic tests, and other technologies that have improved the health of millions of people in the United States and around the world.'

- **Focus on the Flu** www2.niaid.nih.gov/newsroom/focuson/flu04. News, research, publications, resources, links, etc.
- **NIAID Biodefense Research** www2.niaid.nih.gov/biodefense. Wide-ranging biodefence-related information for biomedical researchers, the public and the media.

3932 **Sabin Vaccine Institute** [USA]
www.sabin.org
Maintains a stimulating group of useful resources on vaccination including a US-based Lifespan Immunization Guide. Promotes the Open Statement on Vaccines, supporting immunization as 'the safest, most effective way to control and eradicate infectious diseases'.

Associations & societies

Association for Professionals in Infection Control and Epidemiology
See entry no. 4424

3933 **Infectious Diseases Society of America**
www.idsociety.org
Represents physicians, scientists and other health care professionals who specialize in infectious diseases. IDSA's purpose is 'to improve the health of individuals, communities, and society by promoting excellence in patient care, education, research, public health, and prevention relating to infectious diseases.'

Society for Applied Microbiology
See entry no. 2677

3934 **UK Vaccine Industry Group**
www.uvig.org
Works with the Association of the British Pharmaceutical Industry to promote the positive benefits of vaccination as a

key element in improving the health of the nation. Represents the UK vaccine industry to all interested parties.

Portal & task environments

3935 **AIDSInfo**
United States. Department of Health and Human Services
www.aidsinfo.nih.gov
A central resource for current information on federally and privately funded clinical trials and treatment for AIDS patients and others infected with HIV.

- **HIV Glossary** www.aidsinfo.nih.gov/ed_resources/glossary. Downloadable PDF; also available in print.

3936 **Aidsmap**
NAM Publications.
www.aidsmap.com
'NAM is an award-winning, community-based organization, which works from the UK. We deliver reliable and accurate HIV information across the world to HIV-positive people and to the professionals who treat, support and care for them ... NAM's publications are evidence-based and reviewed by two international medical panels and one of HIV-positive people, which ensure accuracy, balance, relevance, and accessibility.'

Excellent portal, with a wealth of background information, a very good news service, and access to a searchable database of 3300 AIDS organizations in 175 countries.

3937 **Canadian AIDS Treatment Information Exchange: CATIE**
Health Canada
www.catie.ca
'National, non-profit organization committed to improving the health and quality of life of all Canadians living with HIV/AIDS. CATIE provides treatment information not only for people living with the virus but also for their families, care providers, AIDS service organizations and health care intermediaries. It does so through a comprehensive website, three electronic mailing lists, various print publications and a bilingual, toll-free phone service.'

- **HIV/AIDS Treatment Thesaurus** www.catie.ca/thesaurus.nsf. Extensive collection of terms, used to index website and library catalogue content.

3938 **Communicable Disease Surveillance and Response**
World Health Organization
www.who.int/csr/en
Details of how the WHO is working towards global health security – epidemic alert and response. Vision 'Every country should be able to detect, verify rapidly and respond appropriately to epidemic-prone and emerging disease threats when they arise to minimize their impact on the health and economy of the world's population.'

- **WHO Infectious Diseases** www.who.int/health_topics/infectious_diseases/en.

3939 **HIV InSite: Gateway to AIDS Knowledge** [USA]
University of California, San Francisco
http://hivinsite.ucsf.edu
Launched in March 1997, as a source for comprehensive, in-depth HIV/AIDS information and knowledge by the University's Center for HIV Information (CHI) at the University. Hosts an extensive collection of original material, including the *HIV InSite Knowledge Base*, a complete textbook with extensive references and related links organized by topic.

Travelers' Health
National Center for Infectious Diseases See entry no. 4429

Discovering print & electronic resources

3940 **AIDSearch**
NISC.
www.nisc.com/Frame/NISC_products-f.htm [REGISTRATION]
Free access to searchable combination of three files: AIDSDRUGS; MEDLINE AIDS/HIV Subset; AIDSTRIALS.

Directories & encyclopedias

3941 **Encyclopedia of sexually transmitted diseases**
J. Shoquist and D. Stafford Facts On File, 2003, 326pp. $75.00. ISBN 0816048819.
'Provides more than 600 entries explaining the different types of STDs, how they function and how they are spread, what kinds of care and treatment are available, how to decrease the risk of becoming infected, how to recognize the symptoms, key groups at risk, education, clinical studies, etc.'
Series: Library of Health and Living.
'In A–Z format, entries present material in clear, succinct language ... appropriate for public and academic libraries. Currency of information and clarity of presentation make it an excellent choice.' (*Booklist*)

- **The encyclopedia of HIV and AIDS** **S.B. Watstein, S.E. Stratton and E.J. Fischer** 2nd edn, Facts on File, 2003, 660pp. $75.00. ISBN 0816048088. Previous edn *The AIDS dictionary*, 1998. Part of the Library of Health and Living. More than 3000 entries covering the basic biological, medical, financial, legal, political, and social issues and terms associated with HIV and AIDS.
- **Encyclopedia of sexually transmitted diseases** **E.A. Moore and L.M. Moore** McFarland, 2005, 296pp. $65.00. ISBN 0786417943. Notes that 'there are more than 30 different organisms that cause infection and disease when transmitted by venereal contact. Sexually Transmitted Diseases (STDs) represent 87 percent of all reported infections'.

Handbooks & manuals

Biological risk engineering handbook: infection control and decontamination
M.J. Boss and D.W. Day, eds See entry no. 4433

3942 **Hunter's tropical medicine: and emerging infectious diseases**
G.T. Strickland, ed. 8th edn, W B Saunders, 1999, 1192pp. $210.00. ISBN 0721662234.
Thoroughly revised and extensively rewritten since its previous edition, with 27 new chapters. A comprehensive and clinically detailed resource on tropical medicine.

3943 **Infectious diseases**
J. Cohen and W.G. Powderly 2nd edn, Mosby, 2004, 2150pp. 2 v. Includes CD-ROM, $325.00. ISBN 0323024076.
www.idreference.com [COMPANION]
Comprehensive handbook. The website 'contains complete

text of Infectious Diseases 2nd edition in a fully searchable format: Continuous content updates; Complete library of easily downloadable electronic images; Regularly updated disease outbreak map; Links to key society websites; And much more!'.

3944 Mandell, Douglas and Bennett's Principles and practice of infectious diseases
G.L. Mandell, J.E. Bennett and R. Dolin, eds 6th edn, Churchill Livingstone, 2005, 3661pp. 2 v. Also available on CD-ROM, $329.00. ISBN 0443066434.
www.us.elsevierhealth.com [DESCRIPTION]
Widely acknowledged as the definitive reference source in this subject, new to this edn are: New, extensive section on biodefence, with discussions of major pathogens; New chapters on hospital preparedness for infections such as SARS, infections in elderly patients, infections in returning travellers, nutrition and infection, alternative therapies for infection, the design and evaluation of clinical trials, etc.; New antibiotics, including Daptomycin, telithromycin, gemifloxacin, as well as new antifungal and antiviral agents; Fresh perspectives from a number of new contributors.
Online enhanced versions are available: see website.
'The standard against which all challengers are judged ... Thorough, even encyclopedic yet easily readable, PPID has served clinicians well (on the 5th edn).' (*Journal of the American Medical Association*)

3945 Manson's tropical diseases
G.C. Cook and A.I. Zumla 21st edn, W B Saunders, 2003, 1847pp. $185.00. ISBN 0702026409.
This resource for clinical tropical medicine advises on diagnosis and management of infectious and non-infectious tropical diseases. It covers conditions encountered in the tropics or in patients from these areas.

Manual of clinical microbiology
P.R. Murray [et al.] See entry no. 3595

3946 Molecular epidemiology of infectious diseases: principles and practices
L.W. Riley ASM Press, 2004, 348pp. $99.95. ISBN 1555812686.
'Designed to provide a background in the principles and practices of epidemiology that take advantage of new molecular biology tools to solve infectious disease problems.' Includes useful appendix: Annotated websites of databases useful for molecular epidemiologic investigations.

Molecular medical microbiology
M. Sussman, ed. See entry no. 3597

3947 Statistical handbook on infectious diseases
S.B. Watstein and J. Jovanovic Greenwood Press, 2003, 321pp. $64.95. ISBN 1573563757.
Includes coverage of: HIV/AIDS; Malaria; Sexually transmitted diseases; Tuberculosis; Food-borne diseases; Waterborne diseases; Vaccine-preventable diseases; Infectious disease eradication; Bioterrorism.
'*Statistical Handbook on Infectious Diseases* is an excellent reference source for statistical data about infectious diseases.This work conveniently collocates data in one handy volume and is clearly written and well referenced. This statistical goldmine for students of health and medicine has few rivals. A valuable and unique resource. Highly recommended. All public, community college, and university libraries.' (*Choice*)

3948 Travelers' vaccines
E.C. Jong and J.N. Zuckerman B C Decker, 2004, 440pp. Includes CD-ROM, $104.95. ISBN 1550092251.
Good comprehensive multi-author handbook. 20 chapters in four sections: Vaccine immunology; Immunization practices; Travellers' vaccines state-of-the-art; Immunizations for targeted populations. Reference tables and maps.

3949 The vaccine handbook: a practical guide for clinicians
G.S. Marshall Lippincott Williams & Wilkins, 2004, 415pp. $42.95. ISBN 0781735696.
'This book has a simple purpose – to draw authoritative information about vaccines into a simple, concise, practical resource that can be used in the office or on the wards.' Includes a helpful chapter Sources of information about vaccines (pp 349–65), which includes at its end a list of 16 websites with a 'vaccine protest orientation'. Further reading: pp 367–99.

Musculoskeletal System

arthritis • bones • kinesiology • muscles • orthopaedics • orthotics • osteoporosis • prosthetics • repetitive strain injury • rheumatology • spine

Introductions to the subject

3950 Basic biomechanics of the musculoskeletal system
M. Nordin and V.H. Frankel 3rd edn, Lippincott Williams & Wilkins, 2001, 496pp. $53.95. ISBN 0683302477.
http://www.lww.com/product/?0-683-30247-7 [DESCRIPTION]
Presents a working knowledge of biomechanical principles for use in the evaluation and treatment of musculoskeletal dysfunction.

3951 Gait analysis: an introduction
M.W. Whittle 3rd edn, Butterworth-Heinemann, 2002, 220pp. Includes CD-ROM, £27.99. ISBN 0750652624.
'Gait analysis is the systematic study of human walking, using the eye and brain of experienced observers, augmented by instrumentation for measuring body movements and body mechanics, and the activity of the muscles. In individuals with conditions affecting their ability to walk, such as cerebral palsy, gait analysis may be used to make detailed diagnoses and to plan optimal treatment.' Good, now well established, overview.

Dictionaries, thesauri, classifications

3952 A manual of orthopaedic terminology
C.T. Blauvelt and F.R.T. Nelson 6th edn, Mosby, 1998, 463pp. $44.95. ISBN 0815127871.
A compendium of terms created in a dictionary format for professionals in orthopaedics. Easy-to-use format enables the reader to find particular names related to disease processes, radiographic techniques, and surgical problems. Terms are divided according to orthopaedic subspecialty.

3953 **Melloni's illustrated dictionary of the musculoskeletal system**
B.J. Melloni Parthenon Publishing, 1998, 308pp. $44.95. ISBN 1850706670.
Designed primarily for physical therapy and occupational therapy students, covering more than 4600 terms. Lists each term by bone, with tabular columns for location, description and articulations.

3954 **Prosthetics and orthotics online definitions/dictionary**
International Society for Prosthetics and Orthotics
www.ispo.ca/lexicon
Contains more than 1000 clinical, technical and biomechanical terms that can be either browsed or searched. The dictionary is available in both German and English. Prepared by the Canadian branch of ISPO – a 'prosthetic device' being 'an artificial limb or other replacement of body segments'; 'orthoses' being 'braces, splints, devices replacing lost function'.

3955 **The spine dictionary: a comprehensive guide to spine terminology**
C.J. Centeno Hanley & Belfus, 1999, 290pp. $32.95. ISBN 156053270X.
Useful dictionary including definitions of disorders, tests, treatments, drug names, acronyms, abbreviations, and symbols from all disciplines caring for patients with spine disorders, including orthopaedic surgeons, neurosurgeons, therapists, chiropractors, and all those looking for a complete guide to spine terminology.

Research centres & institutes

3956 **National Institute of Arthritis and Musculoskeletal and Skin Diseases** [USA]
www.niams.nih.gov
Supports research into the causes, treatment, and prevention of arthritis and musculoskeletal and skin diseases, the training of basic and clinical scientists to carry out this research, and the dissemination of information on research progress in these diseases. Good A–Z listing of relevant health topics.

Associations & societies

3957 **American Academy of Orthopaedic Surgeons**
www.aaos.org
'The American Academy of Orthopaedic Surgeons, founded in 1933, is the pre-eminent provider of musculoskeletal education to orthopaedic surgeons and others in the world. Its continuing medical education activities include a world-renowned Annual Meeting, multiple CME courses held around the country and at the Orthopaedic Learning Center, and various medical and scientific publications and electronic media materials.'

- **American Association of Orthopaedic Surgeons** www.aaos.org. 'The American Association of Orthopaedic Surgeons, founded by the Academy Board of Directors in 1997, engages in health policy and advocacy activities on behalf of musculoskeletal patients and the profession of orthopaedic surgery.'
- **Essentials of musculoskeletal care** **W.B. Greene, ed.; American Academy of Orthopaedic Surgeons** 2nd edn 2001, 756pp. $105.00. ISBN 0892032170. Sections include: General orthopaedics; Shoulder; Elbow and forearm; Hand and wrist; Hip and thigh; Knee and lower leg; Foot and ankle; Spine; Pediatric orthopaedics. One of a range of useful publications produced by the Academy.

3958 **American College of Rheumatology**
www.rheumatology.org
'Professional organization of rheumatologists and associated health professionals who share a dedication to healing, preventing disability, and curing the more than 100 types of arthritis and related disabling and sometimes fatal disorders of the joints, muscles, and bones. Members include practising physicians, research scientists, nurses, physical and occupational therapists, psychologists, and social workers.'

- **Classification Criteria for Rheumatic Diseases** www.rheumatology.org/publications. Access to a number of tools used in the diagnosis and management of rheumatic diseases. The ACR has also developed an extensive frequently updated Bibliography of Criteria, Guidelines, and Health Status Assessments Used in Rheumatology.

American Orthopedic Society for Sports Medicine
See entry no. 4477

3959 **Arthritis Research Campaign** [UK]
www.arc.org.uk
Very wide-ranging well organized resource, covering both research and practice: check the detailed site Index.

3960 **International Society for Fracture Repair**
www.fractures.com
Dedicated to the advancement and interchange of science of fracture repair and its application to improvement of patient care.

3961 **National Osteoporosis Society** [UK]
www.nos.org.uk
'The only national charity dedicated to improving the diagnosis, prevention and treatment of this fragile bone disease ... 1 in 3 women and 1 in 12 men over the age of 50 will develop osteoporosis. Without treatment, osteoporosis can cause painful and disabling fractures, particularly in the wrist, hip and spine.' Good sets of leaflets and publications plus other resources accessible via the heading For Health Professionals.

3962 **Society of Orthopaedic Medicine** [UK]
www.soc-ortho-med.org
A registered charity, formed in 1979, whose purpose is to promote orthopaedic medicine through education and the funding of research.

Portal & task environments

3963 **Orthogate: The Orthopaedic Internet Gateway**
Internet Society of Orthopaedic Surgery and Trauma
www.orthogate.com
A project to facilitate access to orthopaedic information using the internet through this portal. Hosts a global orthopaedic mailing list; orthopaedic surgery education forum; large collection of orthopaedic-related links on the internet and multimedia guides for patient education. A good facility.

- **OWL: Orthopaedic Web Links** http://owl.orthogate.com. Co-operative project which 'strives to become the definitive catalog of the Orthopaedic Internet; the only major directory that is 100% free ... There is not, nor will there ever be, a cost to submit a site to the directory, and/or use the directory's data'.

Discovering print & electronic resources

PEDro: Physiotherapy Evidence Database
University of Sydney See entry no. 4362

3964 **RECAL Information Services**
University of Strathclyde
www.strath.ac.uk/Departments/NatCentre/recal.html
RECAL is located in the University's National Centre for Training and Education in Prosthetics and Orthotics. Four information products are available: RECAL Current Awareness; RECAL Bibliographic Database; RECAL Thesaurus; RECAL Custom.

Handbooks & manuals

3965 **Arthritis**
F. McKenna and L.S. Simon Elsevier Science, 2002, 152pp. £11.99. ISBN 0723433143.
http://intl.elsevierhealth.com/series/rapidreference
Covers diagnosis, prevention, treatment and management of the disease area. Contains drug listings, clinical trial information, future developments, FAQs and website listings to keep the reader up to date with the disease area.
Series: Rapid Reference. See website for other titles in the series.

Bone research protocols
M.H. Helfrich and S. Ralston, eds See entry no. 2284

3966 **Campbell's operative orthopaedics**
S.T. Canale, ed. 10th edn, Mosby, 2003, 4608pp. 4 v. plus 2 CD-ROMs, $499.00. ISBN 0323012477.
Definitive reference in orthopaedic surgery revised and updated to encompass the latest procedures, techniques, and instruments.

3967 **Kinesiology: the mechanics and pathomechanics of human movement**
C.A. Oatis Lippincott Williams & Wilkins, 2004, 899pp. $74.95. ISBN 0781719828.
Major handbook; very good use of visuals.

3968 **Osteoporosis**
R. Marcus, D. Feldman and J. Kelsey, eds 2nd edn, Academic Press, 2001, 1672pp. 2 v, $440.95. ISBN 0124708625.
Comprehensive, wide-ranging collection of contributed articles.

3969 **Oxford textbook of orthopedics and trauma**
C. Bulstrode [et al.], eds Oxford University Press, 2002, 2773pp. 3 v. Originally published 2002, £99.00. ISBN 0198567944.
Provides comprehensive coverage of the relevant background science, theory, practice, decision-making skills and operative techniques required to provide modern orthopaedic and trauma care. Well reviewed when first appeared.

3970 **Oxford textbook of rheumatology**
D.A. Isenberg [et al.], eds 3rd edn, Oxford University Press, 2004, 1278pp. £225.00. ISBN 0198509480.
Comprehensive multi-author work. Seven sections: Clinical presentation of rheumatic disease; Outcomes and issues in delivering rheumatological care; Pathophysiology of musculoskeletal disease; The process of inflammation; Investigation of the rheumatic diseases; The scope of rheumatic disease; Surgical intervention and sports medicine.

3971 **Wheeless' textbook of orthopaedics**
Duke University Data Trace Publishing Company.
www.datatrace.com
Interesting example of an online textbook of orthopaedics, presenting in depth chapters on trauma, fractures, joints, muscles, etc. Produced within the University's Medical Center in 1996.
See website for details of electronic and print texts from this publisher.

Keeping up-to-date

3972 **Clinical Reviews in Bone and Mineral Metabolism**
Humana Press, Quarterly. $225.00. ISSN 15348644.
www.humanapress.com [DESCRIPTION]
Each issue focuses on a single theme that integrates new information, both basic and clinical science, into the context of clinical practice.

Nervous System

brain • central nervous system • chronic fatigue syndrome • cognition • consciousness • epilepsy • multiple sclerosis • myelin • neuroanatomy • neurology • neuropathology • neurosciences • olfaction • Parkinson's disease • synapses

Introductions to the subject

Brave new brain: conquering mental illness in the era of the genome
N.C. Andreasen See entry no. 4094

3973 **The central nervous system: structure and function**
P. Brodal 3rd edn, Oxford University Press, 2004, 515pp. £49.50. ISBN 0195165608.
Excellent, clear introduction, intended primarily for students of medicine, physical therapy and psychology.

3974 **Merritt's neurology**
L.P. Rowlands 11th edn, Lippincott Williams & Wilkins, 2005, 1200pp. $110.00. ISBN 0781753112.
New edn of well established text, presenting in short chapters the essentials on signs and symptoms, diagnostic tests, and neurological disorders of all etiologies. Reflects recent breakthroughs in molecular genetics, imaging, and research on many diseases.

3975 **Neuroscience for Kids**
E.H. Chudler
http://faculty.washington.edu/chudler/neurok.html
A really good effort – though future funding for its maintenance seems uncertain.

3976 **The quest for consciousness**
C. Koch Scion, 2004, 432pp. Foreword by Francis Crick, £29.99. ISBN 0974707708.
www.questforconsciousness.com/ [COMPANION]
Introduction to the study of consciousness; Neurons, the atoms of perception; The first steps in seeing; The primary visual cortex as a prototypical neocortical area; What are the neuronal correlates of consciousness?; The neuronal correlates of consciousness are not in the primary visual cortex; The architecture of the cerebral cortex; Going beyond the primary visual cortex; Attention and consciousness; The neuronal underpinnings of attention; Memories and consciousness; What you can do without being conscious: the zombie within; Agnosia, blindsight, epilepsy, and sleep-walking: clinical evidence for zombie agents; Some speculations on the functions of consciousness; On time and consciousness; When the mind flips: following the footprints of consciousness; Splitting the brain splits consciousness; Further speculations on thoughts and the unconscious homunculus; A framework for consciousness; An interview.
'an ideal combination of exquisite prose and rigorous science.' (*Scientific American*)
'Exciting and compelling ... *The Quest for Consciousness* is a brave attempt to fuse the best scientific thinking with one of the central aspects of human existence.' (*Science*)
'From the start, the reader is taken on an in-depth exploration of the most recent developments in the biology of consciousness ... The outcome is, in my view, exceptional.' (*Nature*)

3977 **Synapses**
W.M. Cowan, T.C. Sudhof and C.F. Stevens; Howard Hughes Medical Institute Johns Hopkins University Press, 2001, 767pp. $49.95. ISBN 0801871182.
A great book! 'Top Honour in the Single Volume Reference in Science Category from the Association of American Publishers.'
'Comprehensive in its coverage. The quality of the writing and of the numerous beautiful color figures is excellent ... Cowan and Eric Kandel offer an engaging history of the study of synaptic transmission from the first hints of its existence in 1791 through the 1970s ... For both seasoned neurobiologists and interested newcomers to the field, this book is a worthwhile introduction to the wonders of synapses and the many opportunities for future study that they offer.' (*Science*)

Dictionaries, thesauri, classifications

3978 **Application of the International Classification of Diseases to neurology: ICD-NA**
World Health Organization 2nd edn, 1997, 585pp. $163.80. ISBN 924154502X.
A detailed and authoritative instrument for coding virtually all recognized neurological conditions. Both neurological diseases and neurological manifestations of general diseases and injuries are included in this comprehensive coding tool. A good example of 'a growing family of specialty-based adaptations of ICD-10 which retain the 'core' codes of the parent classification while providing extended detail at the fifth character and beyond'.

3979 **Dictionary of multiple sclerosis**
L.D. Blumhardt and X. Lin, eds Martin Dunitz, 2004, 254pp. Includes CD-ROM, $69.95. ISBN 1853178667.
Defines over 600 terms and includes some 850 related references from clinical neurology, genetics, molecular biology, biochemistry, immunology, pathology, radiology, pathogenesis, clinical trial methodology, therapeutics and epidemiology.

Lexicon of psychiatry, neurology, and the neurosciences
F.J. Ayd, ed. See entry no. 4098

Research centres & institutes

3980 **Institute of Neurology** [UK]
www.ion.ucl.ac.uk
Established in 1950 it 'provides teaching and research of the highest quality in neurology and the neurosciences, and professional training for clinical careers in neurology, neurosurgery, neuropsychiatry, neuroradiology, neuropathology and clinical neurophysiology'.

The Institute is now part of University College London; is attached to the National Hospital for Neurology and Neurosurgery at Queen Square, London; and it contains the Rockefeller Medical Library – whose website provides access to a useful set of resources including, for instance, a Patient Support Database: details of support groups for over 200 neurological conditions.

3981 **National Institute of Neurological Disorders and Stroke** [USA]
www.ninds.nih.gov/index.htm
'The nation's leading supporter of biomedical research on disorders of the brain and nervous system.' Part of the NATIONAL INSTITUTES OF HEALTH.

Associations & societies

Alzheimer's Association
See entry no. 3892

Alzheimer's Society
See entry no. 3893

3982 **American Academy of Neurology**
www.aan.com
Founded in 1948 as an international professional association with more than 18,000 members, and provides valuable resources for medical specialists worldwide who are committed to improving the care of patients with neurological diseases. Useful entrée to the discipline under the Public Education part of the website, presented jointly with the American Academy of Neurology Foundation.

- **The Brain Matters** www.thebrainmatters.org. Good, interestingly designed site prepared by neurologists 'to help you better understand common disorders of the brain, as well as learn about people living with the disorders'.

3983 **American Association of Neurological Surgeons**
www.aans.org
Founded in 1931 as a scientific and educational association, now with over 6500 members worldwide 'dedicated to

advancing the specialty of neurological surgery and serving as the spokesorganization for all practitioners of the speciality of neurosurgery, in order to provide the highest quality of care to our patients'.

3984 **Parkinson's Disease Society** [UK]
www.parkinsons.org.uk
The UK's only charity dedicated to supporting all people with Parkinson's, their families, friends and carers.

3985 **Society for Neuroscience**
web.sfn.org
Non-profit membership organization of basic scientists and physicians who study the brain and nervous system. Founded 1970, and now has worldwide membership of 36,000. 'Neuroscience includes the study of brain development, sensation and perception, learning and memory, movement, sleep, stress, aging and neurological and psychiatric disorders. It also includes the molecules, cells and genes responsible for nervous system functioning.'

Extensive and wide-ranging set of publications – including downloadable PDF *Brain Facts*, a 52-page primer on the brain and nervous system: 'In addition to serving as a starting point for a lay audience interested in neuroscience, the book is used at the annual *Brain Bee*, which is held in conjunction with *Brain Awareness Week*.' Also a good set of Links – very usefully categorized for different audiences, from 'experts and specialists' to 'young people'.

A well thought through service.

Stroke Association
See entry no. 3817

Portal & task environments

Alzheimer Research Forum
See entry no. 3897

Alzheimer's Disease Education and Referral Center: ADEAR
National Institute on Aging See entry no. 3898

3986 **Neuroanatomy and Neuropathology on the Internet**
University of Debrecen
www.neuropat.dote.hu
Colourful inviting regularly updated website providing links to a number of neurology resources including an Internet Handbook of Neurology, images, knowledge tests and a wide range of useful resources. Produced within the University's Department of Neurology, in Hungary.

Discovering print & electronic resources

Alzheimer's disease: overview and bibliography
T.V. Bennington, ed. See entry no. 3903

3987 **Neurosciences on the Internet**
N.A. Busis, comp.
www.neuroguide.com
Lively, frequently updated 'searchable and browsable index of neuroscience resources available on the Internet: neurobiology, neurology, neurosurgery, psychiatry, psychology, cognitive science sites and information on human neurological diseases'.

The World's Neurochemistry Portal
International Society for Neurochemistry See entry no. 2059

Digital data, image & text collections

3988 **CogPrints**
University of Southampton
http://cogprints.ecs.soton.ac.uk
'An electronic archive for self-archive papers in any area of psychology, neuroscience, and linguistics, and many areas of computer science (e.g., artificial intelligence, robotics, vison, learning, speech, neural networks), philosophy (e.g., mind, language, knowledge, science, logic), biology (e.g., ethology, behavioral ecology, sociobiology, behaviour genetics, evolutionary theory), medicine (e.g., psychiatry, neurology, human genetics, imaging), anthropology (e.g., primatology, cognitive ethnology, archeology, paleontology), as well as any other portions of the physical, social and mathematical sciences that are pertinent to the study of cognition.'

Developed at the University's *Department of Electronics and Computer Science* and uses the Eprints.org open archive software.

Directories & encyclopedias

3989 **The brain atlas: a visual guide to the human central nervous system**
T.A. Woolsey, J. Hanaway and M.H. Gado 2nd edn, Wiley, 2003, 249pp. $55.00. ISBN 0471430587.
Easy-to-use spiral bound volume organized into five parts: Introduction; The CNS and its blood vessels; Brain slices; Histological sections; Pathways.
'an essential requirement for the library of any individual who works in the field ... if you buy only one atlas, this is the one to buy.' (*Journal of Neurosurgery*)

The encyclopedia of Alzheimer's disease
C. Turkington See entry no. 3905

3990 **Encyclopedia of neurological sciences**
M. Aminoff and R.B. Daroff, eds Academic Press, 2003, 3474pp. 4 v, $1495.00. ISBN 0122268709.
http://info.sciencedirect.com/reference_works
A–Z format entries covering topics in neurology, neurosurgery, psychiatry and the related neuroscience. Designed for those who are relatively non-specialist.
Available online: see website.

3991 **Encyclopedia of neuroscience CD-ROM**
G. Adelman and B.H. Smith 3rd edn, Elsevier, 2004. £47.00. ISBN 0444514325.
Broad scope and interdisciplinary coverage, has become an essential reference and learning tool for everyone involved in the study of the brain and how it mediates behaviour. Makes neurosciences readily accessible to both the specialist and non-specialist reader.

Encyclopedia of stress
G. Fink [et al.], eds See entry no. 4280

3992 Encyclopedia of the human brain
V.S. Ramachandran, ed. Academic Press, 2002, 3454pp. 4 v, $995.00. ISBN 0122272102.
350 worldwide experts contributed to this major treatise.

3993 The Gale encyclopedia of neurological disorders
Thomson Gale, 2004, 1000pp. 2 v., $325.00. ISBN 078769150X.
www.galegroup.org [DESCRIPTION]
Major guide targeted at patients, their families, and allied health students.

3994 Neuroanatomy: text and atlas
J.H. Martin 3rd edn, McGraw-Hill, 2003, 532pp. $54.95. ISBN 007138183X.
Good overview. 'The most comprehensive approach to neuroanatomy from both a functional and regional perspective! With over 400 illustrations, this thoroughly updated Third Edition examines how parts of the nervous system work together to regulate body systems and produce behavior. The illustration program features brain views produced by MRI and PET imaging technology, 2-color line illustrations, and myelin-stained sections as well as an 80-page atlas of key views of the surface anatomy of the central nervous system.'

Handbooks & manuals

3995 Chronic fatigue syndrome: a biological approach
P. Englebienne and K. De Meirleir CRC Press, 2002, 312pp. $99.95. ISBN 0849310466.
Includes advances in virology, bacteriology, immunology, protein chemistry and biochemistry, physiology and metabolism, pharmacology, clinical biology, and epidemiology. Presents diseases eventually acquired by CFS patients such as cancer, aging, and cell death. Sheds new light and insights for the specialist biomedical scientist and physician. Describes new molecular aspects of the biochemistry involved, pointing to the implications for the diagnosis and treatment of the disease.

- **Chronic fatigue syndrome: overview, abstracts, and bibliography K. Bondi, ed.** Nova Science Publishers, 2003, 236pp. $49.00. ISBN 1590335740. Useful introduction.
- **Handbook of chronic fatigue syndrome and other fatiguing illnesses L. Jason, P. Fennell and R.R. Taylor, eds** Wiley, 2003, 794pp. $90.00. ISBN 047141512X. 'Highly recommended for all academic, medical, and hospital libraries as well as all who are concerned with this complex disease.' *Medical Reference Services Quarterly*.

3996 The cognitive neurosciences
M.S. Gazzaniga [et al.] 3rd edn, MIT Press, 2004, 1385pp. $145.00. ISBN 0262072548.
http://mitpress.mit.edu [DESCRIPTION]
Now the standard treatise with, in this latest edition, some 70 new chapters and over 100 new authors.
'A hugely impressive volume ... a breathtaking achievement (on an earlier edn).' (*Times Higher Education Supplement*)

3997 Fundamental neuroscience
L.R. Squire [et al.] 2nd edn, Academic Press, 2003, 1426pp. Includes CD-ROM, $99.95. ISBN 0126603030.
Massive treatise. Excellent overview. 'With over 300 training programs in neuroscience currently in existence, demand is great for a comprehensive textbook that both introduces graduate students to the full range of neuroscience, from molecular biology to clinical science, but also assists instructors in offering an in-depth course in neuroscience to advanced undergraduates.'
'this remarkable textbook is laid out in seven sections, covering in turn cellular and molecular neuroscience, nervous system development, sensory systems, motor systems, regulation of the body by the brain, and finally, behavioral and cognitive aspects of higher brain function. The origin of the book is significant ... remarkable collection of both color and black-and-white illustrations ... a considerable achievement ... (on 1st edn).' (*Nature Neuroscience*)

- **From molecules to networks: an introduction to cellular and molecular neuroscience J.H. Byrne and J.L. Roberts, eds** Academic Press, 2004, 583pp. $79.95. ISBN 0121486605. 'Excellent book that has succeeded in its primary mission: to convey our understanding of the basic information regarding cellular and molecular biology of the nerve cell.' *Journal of Chemical Neuroanatomy*. CD-ROM included.

3998 The handbook of brain theory and neural networks
M.A. Arbib [et al.], eds 2nd edn, MIT Press, 2002, 1290pp. $195.00. ISBN 0262011972.
http://mitpress.mit.edu
'Dramatically updating and extending the first edition, published in 1995, the second edition of *The Handbook of Brain Theory and Neural Networks* presents the enormous progress made in recent years in the many subfields related to the two great questions: How does the brain work? And, How can we build intelligent machines? Once again, the heart of the book is a set of almost 300 articles covering the whole spectrum of topics in brain theory and neural networks.
The publishers have a very long list of neuroscience texts: see website.

3999 Handbook of olfaction and gustation
R.L. Doty, ed. 2nd edn, Marcel Dekker, 2003, 1121pp. $250.00. ISBN 0824707192.
www.dekker.com [DESCRIPTION]
Large format handbook. 80 of world's leading researchers: 'Examines the biochemistry, physiology, and anatomy of the olfactory, gustatory, and trigeminal chemosensory systems; Explores the role of olfactory assessment in disease diagnosis and provides an up-to-date review of the latest chemosensory research in the medical, food, beverage, flavor, perfume, and energy industries'.
Series: Neurological Disease and Therapy.

4000 Handbook of Parkinson's disease
R. Pahwa, K.E. Lyons and W.C. Koller, eds 3rd edn, Marcel Dekker, 2003, 597pp. $195.00. ISBN 0824742427.
Features the latest discoveries and breakthroughs in the diagnosis and management of Parkinson's disease. A good general text on the disease.

4001 The human nervous system
G. Paxinos and J.K. Mai, eds 2nd edn, Academic Press, 2004, 1366pp. $229.95. ISBN 0125476264.
Completely updated from the 1990 1st edn. Contents are organized: Section I: Evolution and development; Section II: Peripheral nervous system and spinal cord; Section III: Brainstem and cerebellum; Section IV: Diencephalon, basal ganglia and amygdala; Section V: Cortex; Section VI: Systems. Large, impressive presentation.

4002 **Myelin biology and disorders**
R.A. Lazzarini, ed. Elsevier Academic Press, 2004, 1600pp. 2 v, $495.00. ISBN 0124395104.
Brings together in one place, the recent advances in molecular and cellular biology along with visual data from MRI, confocal microscopy and high voltage EM techniques to provide new insights into disease mechanisms of myelin – 'the white matter coating our nerves, enabling them to conduct impulses between the brain and other parts of the body'.

4003 **Neurology in clinical practice**
W.G. Bradley [et al.] 4th edn, Butterworth-Heinemann, 2004, 2512pp. 2 v., £270.00. ISBN 0750674695.
www.nicp.com [COMPANION]
A comprehensive and practical book that covers all of the clinical neurosciences for neurologists in training and in practice. New edition has been completely revised and updated to include the plethora of new developments in the field.

4004 **Neuroscience in medicine**
P.M. Conn, ed. 2nd edn, Humana Press, 2003, 723pp. $135.00. ISBN 1588290166.
www.humanapress.com [DESCRIPTION]
Fine multi-author textbook. 32 wide-ranging chapters.

Prions and mad cow disease
B.K. Nunnally and I.S. Krull, eds See entry no. 3428

4005 **The synaptic organization of the brain**
G.M. Shepherd, ed. 5th edn, Oxford University Press, 2004, 719pp. £39.50. ISBN 019515956X.
Well reviewed, multi-author work, with each author having their own website: 'In this fifth edition, the results of the mouse and human genome projects are incorporated for the first time. Also for the first time, the reader is oriented to supporting neuroscience databases.'

The visual neurosciences
L.M. Chalupa and J.S. Werner, eds See entry no. 4067

Keeping up-to-date

4006 **Annual Review of Neuroscience**
Annual Reviews Inc, 2004. $202.00. ISBN 0824324277 ISSN 0147006X.
www.annurev.org/catalog/2004/ne27.asp [DESCRIPTION]
Strong coverage of the underlying cell biology, but includes, for instance, in this volume: Genetic approaches to the study of anxiety; The human visual cortex; How the brain processes social information: searching for the social brain.

Obstetrics & Gynaecology

childbirth • gynaecology • maternal health • maternal-fetal medicine • perinatology • pregnancy

Introductions to the subject

Before we are born: essentials of embryology and birth defects
K.L. Moore and T.V.N. Persaud See entry no. 4442

4007 **Essential obstetrics and gynaecology**
E.M. Symonds and I.M. Symonds 4th edn, Churchill Livingstone, 2004, 394pp. £27.99. ISBN 0443071470.
Notable for its friendly reading style – the whole book having been reviewed by a panel of advisors – including a nurse, midwife, and a panel of obstetric and gynaecologic 'referees.'

Dictionaries, thesauri, classifications

Reproductive medicine: from A to Z
H.E. Reiss [et al.], eds See entry no. 4451

Official & quasi-official bodies

Human Fertilisation and Embryology Authority
See entry no. 4453

Research centres & institutes

4008 **Perinatal Institute for Maternal and Child Health** [UK]
www.perinatal.nhs.uk
Set up in April 2000 to address the high rate of perinatal mortality and morbidity in the West Midlands Region of the UK, and to aid improvements in perinatal care. The website includes access to various projects and findings carried out by the Institute, and its resources include Pregnancy Notes, Birth Notes and Perinatal Reviews.

Associations & societies

4009 **American College of Obstetricians and Gynecologists**
www.acog.org
Founded in 1951, it is the association for the USA's professionals providing health care for women. It is a private, voluntary, non-profit membership organization with over 46,000 members. Amongst a range of useful resources there is an extensive section Women's Issues.

4010 **International Federation of Gynecology and Obstetrics**
www.figo.org
A worldwide organization, founded in 1954, representing obstetricians and gynaecologists in over one hundred countries. Aims to promote the well-being of women and raise the standard of practice in obstetrics and gynaecology. Four Committees are currently taking forwards the

Federation's priorities for the term 2003–2006: FIGO Committee for the Ethical Aspects of Human Reproduction and Women's Health; FIGO Committee on Gynecologic Oncology; FIGO Committee on Safe Motherhood and Newborn Health; FIGO Committee on Women's Sexual and Reproductive Rights.

- **Mother and Child Glossary** www.hon.ch/Dossier/MotherChild. Referenced information extracted from reliable, reviewed sources with links to further literature. Structured logically into the sections: Reproduction; Pregnancy; Birth; Postnatal; Childhood illnesses.

4011 National Childbirth Trust
www.nctpregnancyandbabycare.com/nct-online
The largest and best known childbirth and parenting charity in Europe, with over 40,000 members, set up over 40 years ago, run by parents for parents. Represents parents on antenatal, birth and post-natal issues and provides a range of quality educational and support services.

4012 Royal Australian and New Zealand College of Obstetricians and Gynaecologists
www.ranzcog.edu.au
Formally established in 1978 to provide postgraduate training and accreditation, support and assistance to its members, policy and research and dissemination of information. Well designed, clearly laid out website.

4013 Royal College of Obstetricians and Gynaecologists [UK]
www.rcog.org.uk
Founded in 1947, with its origins in the mid 19th century, to encourage the study and the advancement of the science and practice of obstetrics and gynaecology.

Portal & task environments

Imaginis: The Breast Health Resource
See entry no. 4039

MIDIRS: The definitive midwifery information service
See entry no. 4356

Midwivesonline.com
See entry no. 4357

Digital data, image & text collections

4014 Obstetric Ultrasound: A Comprehensive Guide
J. Woo
www.ob-ultrasound.net
Useful personal interest website with links to multimedia resources, including text, images, and audio about obstetric ultrasound.

Directories & encyclopedias

The Cambridge encyclopaedia of human growth and development
S.J. Ulijaszek, F.E. Johnston and M.A. Preece, eds See entry no. 2468

Catalog of teratogenic agents
T.H. Shepard and R.J. Lemire See entry no. 4468

Handbooks & manuals

4015 Danforth's obstetrics and gynecology
J.R. Scott [et al.], eds 9th edn, Lippincott Williams & Wilkins, 2003, 1099pp. $139.00. ISBN 0781737303.
Core reference concisely and completely covering the modern practice.

4016 Guide to effective care in pregnancy and childbirth
M. Enkin [et al.] 3rd edn, Oxford University Press, 2000, 625pp. £24.95. ISBN 019263173X.
This updated guide summarizes the most authoritative evidence available on the effects of care practices carried out during pregnancy, childbirth, and immediately after birth, in a clear and readily understandable format.

4017 Maternal-fetal medicine: principles and practice
R.K. Creasy and R. Resnik, eds 5th edn, W B Saunders, 2004, 1362pp. $149.00. ISBN 0721600042.
Provides comprehensive coverage of all of the basic and clinical sciences in maternal-foetal medicine including genetics and genetic testing, foetal and placental growth, and development to foetal evaluation.

- **Fetal and neonatal physiology R.A. Polin, W.W. Fox and S.H. Abman, eds** 3rd edn, Saunders, 2004, 2128pp. $389.00. ISBN 0721696546. www.us.elsevierhealth.com [DESCRIPTION]. 'Over 270 international authorities detail the unique characteristics that distinguish fetal and neonatal physiology from the physiology of adults and, where appropriate, address the pathophysiology and clinical management of selected neonatal diseases'.

4018 Maternal-newborn & child nursing: family-centered care
M.L. London [et al.] Prentice Hall, 2003, 1506pp. Includes CD-ROM, $98.00. ISBN 0130994065.
http://wps.prenhall.com/chet_london_maternal_1 [COMPANION]
'Co-written by maternity and pediatric nurses, this is the first combined book to thoroughly integrate maternal-newborn nursing and pediatric nursing into a single book. With an equal focus on community-based care and hospital-based care, this new textbook also incorporates complementary care, pain assessment and management, nutrition and health promotion, patient education and communication, research and evidence-based practice, and assessment as the core of the nursing proces.' Major volume; well written and presented.

4019 Novak's gynecology
J.S. Berek [et al.], eds 13th edn, Lippincott Williams & Wilkins, 2002, 1432pp. $135.00. ISBN 078173262X.
Comprehensive and general gynaecological textbook providing guidance for the management of specific gynaecological conditions.

4020 Textbook of gynecology
L.J. Copeland [et al.], eds 2nd edn, W B Saunders, 2000, 1539pp. $198.00. ISBN 0721655521.
Offers comprehensive, in-depth coverage of the entire field of gynaecology. Normal and abnormal, common and rare gynaecological problems are discussed.

Oncology

breast cancer • cancer • cancer vaccines • carcinogenesis • carcinogens • clinical oncology • leukaemia • malignant tumours • sarcomas • tumours

Dictionaries, thesauri, classifications

4021 **The cancer dictionary**
R. Altman and M.J. Sarg Rev edn, Facts on File, 1999, 387pp. $55.00. ISBN 0816039534.
'Provides clear and concise information that cancer patients and their families need to intelligently face their fears and concerns. It also guides readers through much of the confusion that surrounds the latest claims and media hype of this enigmatic disease.' More than 2500 definitions.

4022 **International classification of diseases for oncology: ICD-O-3**
World Health Organization 3rd edn, 2000, 240pp. $54.00. ISBN 9241545348.
Used for nearly 25 years as the standard tool for coding diagnoses of neoplasms in tumour and cancer registrars and in pathology laboratories.

4023 **TNM classification of malignant tumours**
L.H. Sobin and C. Wittekind, eds; International Union Against Cancer 6th edn, Wiley-Liss, 2002, 239pp. $24.95. ISBN 0471222887.
The TNM system is the most widely used means for classifying the extent of cancer spread. Provides the new internationally agreed standards to describe and categorize cancer stages and progression, agreed with the UICC.

- **UICC manual of clinical oncology R.E. Pollock [et al.], eds** 8th edn, Wiley-Liss, 2004, 917pp. $79.95. ISBN 0471222895. Produced in conjunction with the International Union and is a 'concise and accessible reference covering all aspects of clinical oncology and is of use to all who care for people with cancer'. It uses and contains copy of the revised TNM classification.

Research centres & institutes

4024 **Cancer Research UK**
www.cancerresearchuk.org
Established in February 2002 following the merger of Imperial Cancer Research Fund and The Cancer Research Campaign. The largest volunteer-supported cancer research organization in the world supporting the work of 3000 scientists working across the UK.

4025 **Gray Cancer Institute** [UK]
www.gci.ac.uk
A leading centre for research applied to cancer treatment, working in close collaboration with Mount Vernon Hospital, north of London.

4026 **Institute of Cancer Research** [UK]
www.icr.ac.uk
Established in 1909 to investigate the causes of cancer and develop new strategies for its prevention, diagnosis, treatment and cure. The Institute is part of the University of London and works closely with the Royal Marsden Hospital.

4027 **International Agency for Research on Cancer**
www.iarc.fr
Part of the World Health Organization, it co-ordinates and conducts research on the causes of human cancer, the mechanisms of carcinogenesis, and to develop scientific strategies for cancer control.

'The main emphasis of research is on epidemiology, environmental carcinogenesis and research training. This emphasis reflects the generally accepted notion that 80% of all cancers are, directly or indirectly linked to environmental factors, and thus are preventable; second, the recent recognition of the fact that epidemiology may play an important part in cancer prevention and in the evaluation of prevention measures; lastly, the fact that geographical variations in cancer incidence almost certainly reflect differences in the environment and are therefore particularly well suited for international research efforts.'

- **World Cancer Report B.W. Stewart and P. Kleihues, eds; World Health Organization** 2003, 362pp. $25.00. ISBN 9283204115. www.iarc.fr/WCR [DESCRIPTION]. 'Provides a comprehensive overview of cancer for all health care professionals and the general reader. Information is presented concisely, with more than 500 colour photographs, diagrams and tables.'

4028 **Memorial Sloan-Kettering Cancer Center** [USA]
www.mskcc.org
Provide good overviews of the different types of cancer. Amongst much else of value they also provide an information resource About Herbs, Botanicals and Other Products: Evidence-based information on herbs, botanicals, vitamins, and other supplements.

4029 **National Cancer Institute** [USA]
www.cancer.gov
Established under the National Cancer Act of 1937, is the Federal Government's principal agency for cancer research and training. Website gives access to a dictionary, statistics, details of clinical trials and much else. An excellent entry point to the subject.

- **Dictionary of Cancer Terms** http://cancernet.nci.nih.gov/dictionary. 3500 terms related to cancer and medicine.
- **Frederick/Bethesda Data and Online Services** http://cactus.nci.nih.gov. Includes access to the enhanced NCI database browser used to search the 'new and enlarged collection of open NCI database compounds (>250,000 structures) with all kinds of nifty output features and links to other services for continued processing'.
- **NCI Metathesaurus** http://ncimeta.nci.nih.gov/indexMetaphrase.html. Based on NLM's Unified Medical Language System Metathesaurus supplemented with additional cancer-centric vocabulary.

4030 **National Cancer Research Network** [UK]
www.ncrn.org.uk
Created in response to the need to improve the infrastructure within the National Health Service for clinical research in cancer and to ensure that research is better integrated with cancer care as outlined in the 2000 Report of the Science and Technology Committee on Cancer Research. Good map-based access to details of research networks, and much other useful information – including a well annotated Links section.

Associations & societies

4031 American Association for Cancer Research
www.aacr.org
Professional society of more than 24,000 laboratory and clinical scientists engaged in basic, translational, and clinical cancer research in the United States and more than 60 other countries. Founded 1907 and now publishes five major peer-reviewed scientific journals: *Cancer Research* – the most frequently cited cancer journal in the world; *Clinical Cancer Research*; *Molecular Cancer Therapeutics*; *Molecular Cancer Research*; *Cancer Epidemiology, Biomarkers and Prevention*.

4032 American Cancer Society
www.cancer.org
Founded in 1915, it is a nationwide community-based voluntary health organization dedicated to eliminating cancer as a major health problem by preventing cancer, saving lives, and diminishing suffering from cancer, through research, education, advocacy and service.

4033 American Society of Clinical Oncology
www.asco.org
Founded in 1964 and 'the world's leading professional organization representing physicians who treat people with cancer. ASCO's members set the standard for patient care worldwide and lead the fight for more effective cancer treatments, increased funding for clinical and translational research and, cures for the many different cancers that strike millions of people around the world every year'.

ASCO now has more than 21,500 members from over 100 countries. It produces a range of publications and has a useful worldwide news service.

British Institute of Radiology
See entry no. 3652

4034 European Organisation for Research and Treatment of Cancer
www.eortc.be
Founded in 1962 to conduct, develop, co-ordinate, and stimulate laboratory and clinical research in Europe; to improve the management of cancer and related problems by increasing survival but also patients' quality of life. Useful source of information on cancer-related research throughout Europe, including a very extensive Protocols Database.

4035 Leukaemia Research [UK]
www.lrf.org.uk
'Established in 1960 and is still the only national research charity devoted exclusively to leukaemia, the lymphomas, myeloma, aplastic anaemia, myelodysplasia, the myeloproliferative disorders and the related blood disorders in both children and adults.' Very good range of information and educational resources, details of science and research support.

4036 World Cancer Research Fund International
www.wcrf.org
'A global network of cancer charities dedicated to the prevention and control of cancer by means of healthy food and nutrition, physical activity and weight management.'

Portal & task environments

4037 Cancer BACUP [UK]
www.cancerbacup.org.uk
A charity founded in 1985 that is 'Europe's leading cancer information service, with over 4500 pages of up-to-date cancer information, practical advice and support for cancer patients, their families and carers'. Cancer BACUP is a Uk National Health Service 'Information Partner': see NHS DIRECT ONLINE for details of the current status of that programme.

4038 Cancerfacts.com
www.cancerfacts.com/
'Cancerfacts.com is owned and operated by NexCura, Inc. We are the first company to use scientific data from significant clinical studies to generate reports tailored to a patient's unique medical condition through the NexProfiler™ Tool for Cancer, a powerful database tool.' Also useful annotated Links and Resources section: the company subscribes to the HONCode principles.

4039 Imaginis: The Breast Health Resource
http://imaginis.com/index.asp
Excellent HONCode principles site: 'Our mission is to provide you with the most reliable, in-depth information on breast cancer and related women's health issues. Within our thousands of pages of physician-edited information, we explain complicated medical terms in everyday language to assist you in making informed decisions on prevention and treatment.'

4040 Macmillan Cancer Relief [UK]
www.macmillan.org.uk
A UK charity that works to improve the quality of life for people living with cancer. Good Cancer Information Centre and access to useful range of publications, including: Directory of information materials for people with cancer, produced in conjunction with the CENTRE FOR HEALTH INFORMATION QUALITY.

4041 OncoLink [USA]
University of Pennsylvania
www.oncolink.com
Comprehensive information about specific types of cancer, updates on cancer treatments and news about research advances. Updated daily it provides information at various levels, from introductory to in-depth. A nice service, provided by the University's Abramson Cancer Center.

Directories & encyclopedias

4042 Encyclopedia of cancer
J.R. Bertino 2nd edn, Academic Press, 2002. 4 v, $840.00. ISBN 0122275551.
Concise expositions on a broad range of topics, the encyclopedia is an excellent resource for those seeking information beyond their specific areas of expertise.

4043 The Gale encyclopedia of cancer: a guide to cancer and its treatments
Gale, 2005. 2 v., $340.00. ISBN 1414403623.
www.galegroup.com [DESCRIPTION]
Forthcoming revised edn of well received and reviewed

'comprehensive survey of 120 cancers, cancer drugs, traditional and alternative treatments and diagnostic procedures.'

Plants that fight cancer
S.E. Kintzios and M.G. Barberaki, eds See entry no. 4217

Handbooks & manuals

4044 Breast cancer sourcebook
S.J. Judd, ed. 2nd edn, Omnigraphics, 2004, 595pp. $78.00. ISBN 0780806689.
www.omnigraphics.com/sample/3.pdf
'Provides basic consumer health information about breast cancer, including statistics and risk factors, methods of prevention, screening and diagnostic methods, treatment options, complementary and alternative therapies, post-treatment concerns, clinical trials, special risk populations, and new developments in breast cancer research. A glossary and resources for additional help and information are included.'
Part of the publisher's Health Reference Series. The website provides a downloadable PDF Contents Guide to the 128 v. of the Series, containing more than 10,000 entries for the major topics, diseases and treatments included in the Series.

4045 The cancer handbook
M.R. Alison, ed. Wiley, 2002, 1772pp. 2 v, $575.00. ISBN 0470025069.
www.interscience.wiley.com
Over 100 chapters, 200 contributors, with contributions organized into six sections: The molecular basis of cell and tissue organization; The causation and prevention of cancer; Diagnostic imaging and image-guided intervention; Systemic oncology; Pre-clinical models for human cancer; The treatment of human cancer.

Early 2005, within Wiley InterScience, 'sophisticated 'All Product Searching' will allow the user to search across the extensive range of cancer and oncology journals, online books, reference works and databases ... Including *Cancer*, *Cancer Cytopathology*, *The Cochrane Library*, *TNM Online* and many, many more.'
Available online: see website.

4046 Handbook of cancer vaccines
M.A. Morse, T.M. Clay and H.K. Lyerly, eds Humana Press, 2004, 592pp. $185.00. ISBN 1588292096.
www.humanapress.com
'An authoritative survey of the scientific background for therapeutic cancer vaccines, the challenges to their development, and their current uses in treating cancer. The authors examine the basic issues that affect all vaccines (such as immune adjuvants and prime-boost strategies), describe the methods for antigen discovery, and review the preclinical development phases for each major vaccine strategy. They also spell out the clinical results for cancer vaccines now beginning to be used in the treatment of many common cancers.'
See website for details of the over 70 titles in the publisher's Series: Cancer Drug Discovery and Development.

4047 Head and neck surgery and oncology
J.P. Shah and S.G. Patel 3rd edn, Mosby, 2003, 732pp. $359.00. ISBN 0723432236.
An award winning atlas and text offering step-by-step guidance to every surgical procedure in head and neck surgery. Includes genetics of head and neck cancer, rehabilitation after surgery, implants and prostheses and orbital tumours.

Occupational toxicants
Deutsche Forschungsgemeinschaft See entry no. 4293

Ophthalmology

age-related macular degeneration • blindness • colour vision • eyes • glaucoma • optometry • vision impairment • visual sciences

Introductions to the subject

4048 ABC of eyes
P.T. Khaw, P. Shah and A.R. Elkington 4th edn, BMJ Books, 2004, 93pp. Includes CD-ROM, £26.00. ISBN 0727916599.
New edn includes recent development in the treatment of eye conditions, including for glaucoma and macular degeneration, the relative merits of laser treatment compared with surgery, and how to deal with refractive errors.

4049 Biochemistry of the eye
D.R. Whikehart 2nd edn, Butterworth-Heinemann, 2003, 319pp. £36.99. ISBN 0750671521.
Fine well written overview. General biochemistry is discussed in each chapter, with examples of biochemical pathology and disease processes such as age-related cataract formation and ocular diabetes.

Dictionaries, thesauri, classifications

4050 Dictionary of optometry and visual science
M. Millodot 6th edn, Butterworth-Heinemann, 2004, 370pp. £40.99. ISBN 0750688084.
Well established dictionary providing 'succinct understandable definitions, a wealth of tables and illustrations, and the practical clinical advice'.
- **Dictionary of ophthalmology M. Millodot and D. Laby** Butterworth-Heinemann, 2002, 313pp. £48.99. ISBN 0750647973. Contains over 4000 terms with contemporary definitions, and clinical advice. The information is presented in a A–Z format, with synonyms and cross references.

4051 Dictionary of visual science and related clinical terms
H.W. Hofstetter [et al.], eds 5th edn, Butterworth-Heinemann, 2000, 630pp. Includes CD-ROM, £58.99. ISBN 0750671319.
Comprehensive text 'completely updated to include more than 400 new terms on optics and refractive surgery. It contains a convenient appendix on key therapeutic drugs, listed by both generic and trade names to aid in the quick retrieval of information. Emphasis is placed on succinct definition rather than on encyclopedic elaboration.'

Official & quasi-official bodies

4052 General Optical Council [UK]
www.optical.org
'The statutory body which regulates dispensing opticians and optometrists and those bodies corporate carrying on business as optometrists or dispensing opticians. The GOC's main aims are to protect the public and promote high standards of professional conduct and education among opticians.'

Research centres & institutes

4053 Institute of Ophthalmology [UK]
www.ucl.ac.uk/ioo
Based in University College London, and in conjunction with Moorfields Eye Hospital, the largest ophthalmology research facility in the world. The website has information on eye science and health, research activities, courses and seminars, and the library. Extensive Links section. It works closely with the charity Fight for Sight.

4054 National Eye Institute [USA]
www.nei.nih.gov
Site includes: health information, details of research activities and funding, materials to order, including materials for children, visual resources (eye anatomy, eye disease simulation, eye charts, pictures of scenes as viewed by people with cataracts, glaucoma).

Associations & societies

4055 AMD Alliance International
www.amdalliance.org
'Age-related macular degeneration (AMD) is the leading cause of vision loss for people over the age of 50 in the Western world, affecting approximately 25–30 million people. However, vision loss should not be an inevitable consequence of aging. The AMD Alliance International is a global coalition of vision and seniors' organizations dedicated to raising awareness of AMD and the options available for prevention, early detection, treatment, rehabilitation and support services.'

4056 American Academy of Ophthalmology
www.aao.org
The largest membership organization in the USA for ophthalmologists. Details of professional and continual education, services for members, and some patient education materials. They have an extensive publications programme: see the website.

4057 Royal College of Ophthalmologists [UK]
www.rcophth.ac.uk
With its origins in the Ophthalmological Society founded in 1880, maintains standards and provides postgraduate and continuing education and guidelines for good practice.

4058 Royal National Institute of the Blind [UK]
www.rnib.org.uk
Resources and support for people with sight problems and their families. Also includes information on designing accessible websites, Braille and products for people with visual impairments.

Discovering print & electronic resources

4059 Glaucoma: a medical dictionary, bibliography, and annotated research guide to internet references
J.N. Parker and P.M. Parker ICON Health Publications, 2004, 360pp. $58.95. ISBN 0597839603.
www.icongrouponline.com/health/aboutus.html
'In March 2001, the National Institutes of Health issued the following warning: 'The number of Web sites offering health-related resources grows every day. Many sites provide valuable information, while others may have information that is unreliable or misleading.' Furthermore, because of the rapid increase in Internet-based information, many hours can be wasted searching, selecting, and printing. Since only the smallest fraction of information dealing with glaucoma is indexed in search engines, such as www.google.com or others, a non-systematic approach to Internet research can be not only time consuming, but also incomplete. This book was created for medical professionals, students, and members of the general public who want to conduct medical research using the most advanced tools available and spending the least amount of time doing so.'
One of an extensive range of texts from the publisher accessible via a variety of routes: see website.

Directories & encyclopedias

4060 The encyclopedia of blindness and vision impairment
J. Sardegna [et al.], eds 2nd edn, Facts on File, 2002, 352pp. $75.00. ISBN 0816042802.
'More than 500 detailed entries are written in clear, concise language with a minimum of technical jargon. The volume incorporates a history of blindness and vision impairment with an A–Z presentation of health issues, types of surgery, medications, medical terminology, social issues, myths and misconceptions, economic issues, and current research trends.'

Handbooks & manuals

4061 Adler's physiology of the eye: clinical application
P.L. Kaufman and A. Alm, eds 10th edn, Mosby, 2003, 876pp. $102.00. ISBN 0323011365.
Multi-author classic text; almost 700 illustrations.

4062 Clinical ophthalmology: a systematic approach
J.J. Kanski 5th edn, Butterworth-Heinemann, 2003, 733pp. £120.00. ISBN 0750655410.
This classic text has a broad coverage, systematic presentation and numerous full colour illustrations. It is a worldwide bestselling text, translated into eight languages.

4063 The epidemiology of eye disease
G.J. Johnson [et al.], eds 2nd edn, Arnold, 2003, 403pp. £49.99. ISBN 0340808926.
Good well produced volume.

4064 **The Lighthouse handbook on vision impairment and vision rehabilitation**
B. Silverstone [et al.] Oxford University Press, 2000, 1371pp. 2 v, £180.00. ISBN 0195094891.
'State-of-the-art guide to the scientific, clinical, rehabilitative, and policy aspects of vision impairment and blindness. More than 100 original contributions from physicians, therapists, rehabilitation specialists, and policy makers cover everything from the basic science of vision and its diseases to assistive technologies, treatment, and care.'

4065 **Normal and defective colour vision**
J.D. Mollon, J. Pokornv and K. Knoblauch, eds Oxford University Press, 2003, 456pp. £62.50. ISBN 0198525303.
Major contributed chapter survey of the field, integrating research findings from biology, genetics, neuroscience, physics, psychology – and ophthalmology.

4066 **Principles and practice of ophthalmology**
D.M. Albert [et al.], eds 2nd edn, W B Saunders, 2000, 5583pp. 6 v. CD-ROM included, $750.00. ISBN 072167500X.
Definitive treatise containing 7640 illustrations, 3585 of which are in full colour.

4067 **The visual neurosciences**
L.M. Chalupa and J.S. Werner, eds MIT Press, 2004, 1808pp. 2 v, $195.00. ISBN 0262033089.
Over 100 chapters cover the entire field of visual neuroscience, from its historical foundations to the latest research and findings in molecular mechanisms and network modelling. A very good overview.

Otorhinolaryngology

audiology • communication disorders • deafness • ear, nose & throat diseases • hearing • language • nose • otolaryngology • speech • voice

Dictionaries, thesauri, classifications

4068 **Terminology of communication disorders: speech-language-hearing**
L. Nicolosi, E. Harryman and J. Kresheck 5th edn, Lippincott Williams & Wilkins, 2003, 411pp. $48.00. ISBN 0781741963.
The leading dictionary/sourcebook of terms for speech, language, and hearing pathology. Terms are listed alphabetically and cross-referenced for synonyms and related terms, accommodating the sometimes complex classifications of speech, language, and hearing disorders.

Research centres & institutes

4069 **National Institute on Deafness and other Communication Disorders** [USA]
www.nidcd.nih.gov
Formed in 1988 to support and conduct research and research training in the normal and disordered processes of hearing, balance, smell, taste, voice, speech, language; 'Improving the lives of people who have communication disorders'.

Associations & societies

4070 **American Academy of Audiology**
www.audiology.org
The world's largest professional organization in the field, founded in 1988, with an active membership of more than 9600 audiologists.

4071 **American Academy of Otolaryngology Head and Neck Surgery**
www.entnet.org
The world's largest organization within the discipline, with more than 10,000 members, and representing specialists who treat the ear, nose, throat, and related structures of the head and neck. Useful, lively, wide-ranging website: a good introduction to the area for non-specialists. They include even a Virtual Museum.

- **ENT UK British Association of Otorhinolaryngologists-Head and Neck Surgeons.** www.entuk.org. Front name for the British equivalent body – which represents over 1000 medical practitioners including surgeons, trainees and audiologists. Useful range of Patient Information plus details of professional developments and involvements within the UK.

4072 **American Speech-Language-Hearing Association**
www.asha.org
Professional, scientific, and credentialing association for more than 115,000 members and affiliates who are audiologists, speech-language pathologists, and speech, language, and hearing scientists.

4073 **British Academy of Audiology**
www.baaudiology.org
Formed from the merged British Association of Audiological Scientists, the British Association of Audiologists, and the British Society of Hearing Therapists to become the largest UK audiology organization representing the views of audiologists. A Questions and Answers section of the website gives some helpful organizational and professional context.

- **British Society of Audiology** www.thebsa.org.uk. Founded 1966, and now the largest audiology society in Europe. It is multi-disciplinary and has members from all areas of audiology in the UK and throughout the world. It is open to suitable persons who have demonstrated an interest in audiology.

Council for Accreditation in Occupational Hearing Conservation
See entry no. 5570

4074 **Royal National Institute for Deaf People** [UK]
www.rnid.org
RNID's new website – launched March 2005 – ' aims to set a new standard for accessible websites: good looking and very accessible'.

Directories & encyclopedias

4075 **The encyclopedia of deafness and hearing disorders**
C. Turkington and A.E. Sussman 2nd edn, Facts on File, 2003, 294pp. $65.00. ISBN 0816056153.
Provides information for anyone concerned with hearing loss, their own or another's. Presents important and current information on hearing impairment and how it can be successfully treated. More than 600 entries cover parts of

the ear, clinical terms, specialists, devices and equipment, organizations, diseases and more.
Series: Library of Health and Living.

4076 The MIT encyclopedia of communication disorders
R.D. Kent, ed. MIT Press, 2003, 618pp. $95.00. ISBN 0262112787.
Almost 200 detailed entries, covering the entire range of communication and speech disorders in children and adults, from basic science to clinical diagnosis. Divided into four sections: Voice, Speech, Language and Hearing. Entries are then organized into three subsections: basic science, disorders and clinical management.

Handbooks & manuals

Head and neck surgery and oncology
J.P. Shah and S.G. Patel See entry no. 4047

4077 Otolaryngology
C.W. Cummings [et al.], eds 4th edn, Mosby, 2005, 4928pp. 5 v, $499.00. ISBN 0323019854.
www.us.elsevierhealth.com
A comprehensive, authoritative reference in the field of otolaryngology – head and neck surgery. Encompasses the body of core knowledge and cutting-edge developments within every otolaryngologic subspecialty.
See website for details of companion products to this work.

Paediatrics

child growth and development • child health • parenthood

Introductions to the subject

Before we are born: essentials of embryology and birth defects
K.L. Moore and T.V.N. Persaud See entry no. 4442

4078 Birth to five: your complete guide to parenthood and the first five years of your child's life
Great Britain. Department of Health
www.publications.doh.gov.uk/birthtofive
Available as a downloadable PDF file, designed to provide useful information and guidance to parents. Regularly updated.

Official & quasi-official bodies

4079 UNICEF
www.unicef.org
Created in 1946 by the United Nations, it is the driving force that helps build a world where the rights of every child are realized, with global authority to influence decision-makers, and the variety of partners at grass-roots level to turn the most innovative ideas into reality.
Wide range of valuable resources and pointers,

Research centres & institutes

4080 Institute of Child Health [UK]
www.gosh.nhs.uk
The leading British academic research institution for child health, which aims to define the scientific, epidemiological and clinical basis of childhood diseases and to promote child health across the country and internationally. Joint website with the Great Ormond Street Hospital for Children. Excellent set of resources.

4081 National Institute of Child Health and Human Development [USA]
www.nichd.nih.gov
Created by Congress in 1962, supports and conducts research on topics related to the health of children, adults, families, and populations. One of the National Institutes of Health.

Perinatal Institute for Maternal and Child Health
See entry no. 4008

Associations & societies

4082 American Academy of Pediatrics
www.aap.org
The Academy founded in 1930 and now is an organization of over 55,000 paediatricians, dedicated to the health of infants, children and teens. The official website provides general and specific information on all fields of child health, including access to an extensive publication programme.

4083 Royal College of Paediatrics and Child Health [UK]
www.rcpch.ac.uk
Established in 1928 for the advancement of the study of paediatrics and the promotion of friendship among paediatricians. Its 6000 members are mainly UK-based but overseas membership is continuing to grow.

Portal & task environments

4084 Children First [UK]
Great Ormond Street Hospital for Children NHS Trust and National Health Service
www.childrenfirst.nhs.uk
Health information for children and teenagers and their families, available in several languages.

4085 GeneralPediatrics.com
D.M. D'Alessandro, comp.
www.generalpediatrics.com
Very wide ranging personal interest site, notable not only for the breadth of its coverage and its functionality, but also for its clear statement of editorial policy. The site also subscribes to the HONCode principles.

4086 KidsHealth [USA]
Nemours Foundation.
www.kidshealth.org
Aims to provide families with accurate, up-to-date, and jargon-free health information that they can use. Has been on the web since 1995, and has separate areas for kids, teens,

and parents – each with its own design, age-appropriate content, and tone.

Midwivesonline.com
See entry no. 4357

Directories & encyclopedias

The Cambridge encyclopaedia of human growth and development
S.J. Ulijaszek, F.E. Johnston and M.A. Preece, eds See entry no. 2468

Handbooks & manuals

4087 **Forfar and Arneil's textbook of paediatrics**
N. McIntosh, P.J. Helms and R. Smyth 6th edn, Churchill Livingstone, 2003, 2112pp. Includes CD-ROM, £158.00. ISBN 0443071926.
The standard British and European text covering the entire specialty of paediatrics. Strong emphasis on evidence-based paediatrics and social and community paediatrics.

4088 **Manual of pediatric nutrition**
K.M. Hendricks, C. Duggan and W.A. Walker 3rd edn, B C Decker, 2000, 596pp. $38.95. ISBN 1550090917.
www.bcdecker.com
Provides an overview of nutritional care for children. In the third edition, coverage includes nutritional assessment, dietary intake methods, normal incremental growth rates, nutrition for the hospitalized child, and specific disease states and nutrition.
See website for details of wide range of medical texts offered by this publisher.

Maternal-newborn & child nursing: family-centered care
M.L. London [et al.] See entry no. 4018

4089 **Nelson textbook of pediatrics**
R.E. Behrman, R.M. Kliegman and H.B. Jenson 17th edn, W B Saunders, 2004, 2205pp. $129.00. ISBN 0721695566.
www.us.elsevierhealth.com/product.jsp?isbn=0721695566 [DESCRIPTION]
A classic text that provides state-of-the-art coverage of all medical and surgical disorders in children.
'Very comprehensive ... Carries on the long tradition of excellence that has sustained it as a standard in its field for many years (of the 15th edn).' (*Journal of the American Board of Family Practice*)

Neonatal formulary
E. Hey and C. Hall See entry no. 3748

4090 **Pediatric nursing: caring for children**
J.W. Ball and R.C. Bindler, ed. 3rd edn, Prentice Hall, 2003, 984pp. Includes CD-ROM, $74.95. ISBN 0130994057.
http://vig.prenhall.com/catalog [DESCRIPTION]
Well presented highly approachable text. 'Exceptionally user-friendly and up-to-date, it uses a unique body system approach rather than developmental stages, allowing faculty to teach pediatrics in integrated course or short course without redundancy. This approach also focuses students on nursing care. Features abundant four-color photos and drawings throughout, extensive marginal notes, chapter-opening vignettes and more plus a heavy emphasis on community nursing. This text details the core essentials of pediatric nursing practice while also providing the critical thinking skills necessary for future challenges.'

- **Wong's nursing care of infants and children M.J. Hockenberry [et al.]** 7th edn, Mosby, 2003, 1994pp. $82.95. ISBN 0323017223. http://evolve.elsevier.com [COMPANION]. Includes CD-ROM. 'Painstakingly accurate, up-to-date, and highly readable ... There's no question why this respected resource is pediatric nursing's foremost text.'

4091 **A reference manual of growth and development**
J.M.H. Buckler 2nd edn, Blackwell, 1997, 128pp. £27.50. ISBN 0865426805.
Very useful well reviewed text which covers the major aspects of child growth and development likely to be most frequently required by medical practitioners. The book's data is presented mainly in the form of charts and tables, which represent both the 'normal' value range as well as indications of the range that might be expected within a typical British population.

Keeping up-to-date

4092 **Advances in Pediatrics**
Mosby, 1942–, Annual. $110.00 [2004]. ISSN 00653101.
Presents collections of original, fully referenced clinical review articles in paediatrics.

Psychiatry

adolescent psychiatry • child psychiatry • clinical psychology • learning disabilities • mental disorders • mental health • mental illness • mental measurements • neuropsychology • post-traumatic stress disorder • psychology • psychopharmacology • psychotherapy

Introductions to the subject

4093 **The art and science of mental health nursing: a textbook of principles and practice**
I.J. Norman and I. Ryrie, eds Open University Press, 2004, 847pp. £24.99. ISBN 0335212425.
Well written; useful further reading.

4094 **Brave new brain: conquering mental illness in the era of the genome**
N.C. Andreasen Oxford University Press, 2004, 368pp. Originally published 2001, £10.50. ISBN 0195145097.
12 chapters in four parts: Broken brains and troubled minds; Mind meets molecule; The burden of mental illness; Brave new brain.
'Excellent introductions to neuroscience, brain imaging, and genetics. Outstanding overviews of what is known about the neuroscience and genetics of the major psychiatric disorders of schizophrenia, mood disorders, dementia, and anxiety disorders. The descriptions of the history and neuroscience of medication are especially good.' (*Nature*)
'A gripping account ... a truly outstanding book. Brave New Brain informs, provokes thought, conveys the excitement of science, indicates why science matters, and considers both the achievements with respect to clinical application and the difficulties involved. Quite an achievement!' (*Science*)

4095 Masters of the mind: exploring the story of mental illness from ancient times to the new millennium
T. Millon Wiley, 2004, 672pp. $34.95. ISBN 0471469858.
www.wiley.com/WileyCDA [DESCRIPTION]
14 chapters in seven parts: Philosophical stories; Humanitarian stories; Neuroscientific stories; Psychoanalytic stories; Psychoscientific stories; Sociocultural stories; Personologic stories. Prologue and Epilogue.

The quest for consciousness
C. Koch See entry no. 3976

Dictionaries, thesauri, classifications

4096 Dictionary of psychology and psychiatry: English–German (Wörterbuch der Psychologie und Psychiatrie (Englisch–Deutsch))
R. Haas 2nd edn, Hogrefe, 2003, 1112pp. 2 v, $169.00. ISBN 0889373027.
The most exhaustive bilingual compilation of terminology in these fields available. For new edn considerably expanded with c.4000 new terms. All the terms and vocabulary carefully reviewed and brought up to date by the inclusion of the terminology used in DSM-IV-TR and ICD-10.

4097 International classification of mental and behavioural disorders: ICD-10 Chapter V
World Health Organization and World Psychiatric Association 1992, 374pp. $45.00. ISBN 9241544228.
www.who.int/classifications/icd/en [DESCRIPTION]
Provides clinical descriptions, diagnostic guidelines, and codes for all mental and behavioural disorders commonly encountered in clinical psychiatry.

- **Lexicon of psychiatric and mental health terms World Health Organization** 2nd edn1994, 108pp. $22.50. ISBN 924154466X. Provides concise definitions for some 700 terms used in the diagnosis and classification of mental disorder. Each term where appropriate gives the code number of the ICD-10 category. Alternative names, synonyms, and near-synonyms are also included.

4098 Lexicon of psychiatry, neurology, and the neurosciences
F.J. Ayd, ed. 2nd edn, Lippincott Williams & Wilkins, 2000, 1104pp. $79.95. ISBN 0781724686.
Provides succinct, detailed and accessible definitions for the entire range of terms used in these fields, including drug categories, receptors, and the sites and mechanisms affected by pharmacologic treatments.

Laws, standards, codes

4099 DSM-IV-TR: diagnostic and statistical manual of mental disorders
American Psychiatric Association Rev. 4th edn, 2000, 992pp. $83.50. ISBN 0890420246.
www.appi.org/dsm.cfx [DESCRIPTION]
The most widely used psychiatric reference in the world. An essential up-to-date diagnostic tool, to promote effective diagnosis, treatment and quality of care.

Research centres & institutes

4100 Institute of Psychiatry [UK]
www.iop.kcl.ac.uk/iopweb
Founded in 1829, now with a worldwide reputation: provides postgraduate education and carries out research in psychiatry, psychology, and allied disciplines, including basic and clinical neurosciences. Associated with the Maudsley Hospital and part of King's College London.

The Institute Library is the largest psychiatric library in Western Europe, and provides an extensive set of well categorized links to mental health resources on the web.

4101 National Center for Post-Traumatic Stress Disorder [USA]
http://www.ncptsd.org/index.html
'Created within the Department of Veterans Affairs in 1989, in response to a Congressional mandate to address the needs of veterans with military-related PTSD. Its mission was, and remains: To advance the clinical care and social welfare of America's veterans through research, education, and training in the science, diagnosis, and treatment of PTSD and stress-related disorders.'

- **PILOTS Thesaurus** www.ncptsd.org/publications/pilots/Thesaurus_1.html. Used to help search the PILOTS Database itself – an electronic index to the worldwide literature on post-traumatic stress disorder and other mental-health consequences of exposure to traumatic events which, December 2003, contained c.25,000 entries.

4102 National Institute for Mental Health in England
www.nimhe.org.uk
Launched in 2002 to improve the quality of life for people of all ages who experience mental distress. Connects mental health research, development, delivery, monitoring and review. Section Information Resources provides 'an outline of all mental health policy, strategy and guidance launched in recent years' and includes Cases for Change: a 'literature view [which] collates evidence from over 650 documents published between January 1997 and February 2002 concerning adult mental health service delivery and/or policy in England'. The site is becoming a good introduction to official and quasi-official work in this arena.

4103 National Institute of Mental Health [USA]
www.nimh.nih.gov
Established in 1949 and 'provides national leadership dedicated to understanding, treating, and preventing mental illnesses through basic research on the brain and behavior, and through clinical, epidemiological, and services research'.

- **National Mental Health Information Center** www.mentalhealth.org. Centre within the Substance Abuse and Mental Health Services Administration (SAMHSA) of the US Department of Health and Human Services. Useful entrée to the more social aspects of 'Mental Health: The Cornerstone of Health'.

Associations & societies

4104 American Academy of Child and Adolescent Psychiatry
www.aacap.org
A non-profit membership-based organization, established in 1953, composed of over 6500 child and adolescent psychiatrists and other interested physicians. Its members actively research, evaluate, diagnose and treat psychiatric disorders.

4105 American Psychiatric Association
www.psych.org
A medical specialty society, founded in 1844 and recognized worldwide. Its has over 35,000 members who work together to ensure humane care and effective treatment for all persons with mental disorder, including mental retardation and substance-related disorders.

Apart from the wide range of helpful resources accessible via the website, the Association is notable for its wholly owned subsidiary American Psychiatric Publishing: 'The world's premier publisher of books, journals, and multimedia on psychiatry, mental health and behavioral science. We offer authoritative, up-to-date and affordable information geared toward psychiatrists, other mental health professionals, psychiatric residents, medical students and the general public'.

- **Practice guidelines for the treatment of psychiatric disorders: Compendium 2004** American Psychiatric Publishing, 1104pp. $67.00. ISBN 0890423768. www.appi.org [DESCRIPTION]. 'Has become an invaluable resource to help benchmark care strategies for 11 common mental disorders ... Provides convenient summaries of what we know about key mental disorders and the effectiveness of specific treatments.'

National Eating Disorders Association
See entry no. 4389

4106 Royal College of Psychiatrists [UK]
www.rcpsych.ac.uk/index.htm
The professional and educational body for psychiatrists in the UK and the Republic of Ireland, founded in 1841. Maintains a range of useful resources.

4107 Sainsbury Centre for Mental Health [UK]
www.scmh.org.uk
Charity that works to improve the quality of life for people with severe mental health problems. It carries out research, development and training work to influence policy and practice in health and social care. Useful well annotated Links section.

4108 World Federation for Mental Health
www.wfmh.org
The Federation, with members and contacts in 112 countries on six continents, was founded in 1948 to advance, among all peoples and nations, the prevention of mental and emotional disorders, the proper treatment and care of those with such disorders, and the promotion of mental health.

Portal & task environments

4109 Connects
Mental Health Foundation and Foundation for People with Learning Disabilities
www.connects.org.uk
'A worldwide, interactive website for the sharing of information by people interested in mental health problems and/or learning disabilities. We currently have 10,000 plus members. Connects contains more than 10,000 resources including details of news items, events, websites and organizations. You can tailor the information to suit your own interests using your Notice Board. Whenever you visit, we will tell you of any new resources which match those interests.'

- **Mental Health Foundation** www.mentalhealth.org.uk. Comprehensive website for mental health and illness in the UK. Lists a wide range of publications, patient information, programmes and other useful links. 'This is the biggest, most comprehensive website on mental health in the UK.'
- **Mind** www.mind.org.uk. The leading mental health charity in England and Wales.

4110 Internet Mental Health
P.W. Long, comp.
www.mentalhealth.com
A free encyclopedia of mental health information, first compiled in 1995 as a personal interest site by a Canadian psychiatrist, and continually updated since. Designed for anyone with an interest in mental health. Apart from access to a very wide range of reference resources, there is an extensive list of internet Links: 'We list only English-language sites providing more than 10 pages of free, scientifically sound mental health information. Whenever possible, sites are rated by popularity using asterisks (**).'

Discovering print & electronic resources

4111 PsycINFO
American Psychological Association Monthly. $1412.00. ISSN 00332887.
www.apa.org/psycinfo [DESCRIPTION]
The online version of a leading tool in this field, *Psychological Abstracts*, which contains summaries (abstracts, bibliographic information, and indexing) of English-language journal articles, technical reports, book chapters, and books in the field of psychology. 'PA is organized by subject area according to the PsycINFO Classification Codes for easy browsing, and monthly author, brief subject, and book title indices and annual author and subject indices are included with the subscription.'

APA offer a variety of products and services based on PA, as well as a range of other publications.

- **Psychoanalytical abstracts** www.apa.org/psycinfo/products/scan-analysis.html [DESCRIPTION]. Covers international literature in the field of psychoanalysis, including advances in psychoanalytic theory, therapy, and interpretation, as well as the history of psychoanalysis.
- **Thesaurus of Psychological Index Terms** www.apa.org/psycinfo/products/thesaurus.html. More than 7800 standard and cross-referenced terms; scope notes that define the terms; historical notes that include information about the historical usage of terms since their introduction; term hierarchies that show the relationship to other terms; etc.

Digital data, image & text collections

CogPrints
University of Southampton See entry no. 3988

4112 PsychiatryOnline
American Psychiatric Publishing.
www.psychiatryonline.com
'A powerful website that features DSM-IV-TR and The American Journal of Psychiatry as the cornerstones of an unsurpassed collection of psychiatric references, including books, journals, and self-assessment tools. Much more than individual titles, PsychiatryOnline features sophisticated

searching and indexing tools that enable you to quickly target all the information you need.'

Directories & encyclopedias

4113 **Campbell's psychiatric dictionary**
R.J. Campbell 8th edn, Oxford University Press, 2004, 700pp. £45.00. ISBN 0195152212.
An encyclopedic approach to the definition of many psychiatric terms, including new developments in the field. Use of cross-references between entries makes it easier to access the information.
'Although the volume is titled a dictionary, it serves nicely as an encyclopaedia for the more important terms which are not only defined but also described and explained. This makes the volume very convenient for the reader ... The definitions and accompanying information were clear, accessible, and authoritative ... Very useful to a variety of mental health specialists.' (*Contemporary Psychology*)

4114 **Encyclopedia of mental health**
H.S. Friedman [et al.], eds Academic Press, 1998, 2398pp. 3 v, $695.00. ISBN 0122266757.
Over 200 peer-reviewed entries providing a comprehensive overview of the many genetic, neurological, social, and psychological factors that affect mental health.

- **The encyclopedia of mental health A.P. Kahn and J. Fawcett** 2nd edn, Facts On File, 2001. $75.00. ISBN 0816040621. 'A good desktop reference: convenient size, high-quality paper, legibility, cross-references, adequate breadth of coverage, but most important, fine writing and language that is accessible but does not condescend to general readers' *Choice*.

Encyclopedia of mind enhancing foods, drugs and nutritional substances
D.W. Group See entry no. 4214

Encyclopedia of neurological sciences
M. Aminoff and R.B. Daroff, eds See entry no. 3990

4115 **Encyclopedia of psychology**
A.E. Kazdin, ed.; American Psychological Association Oxford University Press, 2000, 4128pp. 8 v., £452.50. ISBN 1557981876.
www.apa.org/books [DESCRIPTION]
Includes comprehensive coverage of mental health and mental disorders.

4116 **Encyclopedia of psychotherapy**
M. Hersen and W.H. Sledge, eds Academic Press, 2002, 1942pp. 2 v, $500.00. ISBN 0123430100.
www.info.sciencedirect.com/reference_works
'Psychotherapy is the dialogue between patient and therapist in the diagnosis and treatment of behavioral, crisis, and mental disorders. Psychoanalysis as formulated by Sigmund Freud is the first modern form of psychotherapy and this approach has given rise to several score of psychodynamic therapies ...'
Some 230 contributed articles arranged A–Z; good introduction to the field.
Available online: see website.

4117 **The Gale encyclopedia of mental disorders**
Thomson Gale, 2003, 1000pp. 2 v., $310.00. ISBN 0787657689.
www.galegroup.com
Some 400 entries arranged A–Z by title, providing in-depth coverage of the specific disorders recognized by the AMERICAN PSYCHIATRIC ASSOCIATION, as well as some disorders not formally recognized as distinct disorders.
'The articles are more accessible than those in a medical textbook or the DSM-IV-TR, but they still require a fairly high level of literacy. This is an excellent resource for public, academic, and consumer health libraries.' (*American Reference Books Annual*)

Handbooks & manuals

4118 **Cambridge handbook of psychology, health, and medicine**
A. Baum [et al.], eds Cambridge University Press, 1997, 660pp. £60.00. ISBN 0521436869.
Collates international and interdisciplinary expertise to form a unique encyclopedic handbook to this field which will be valuable for both medical practitioners and psychologists from trainee to professional level. Three parts: Psychological foundations; Psychology, health and illness; Medical topics.

The cognitive neurosciences
M.S. Gazzaniga [et al.] See entry no. 3996

4119 **Companion to psychiatric studies**
E. Johnstone [et al.], eds 7th edn, Churchill Livingstone, 2004, 836pp. £54.99. ISBN 0443072639.
A comprehensive textbook covering both basic sciences and the practice of psychiatry.

4120 **The fifteenth mental measurements yearbook**
B.S. Plake [et al.], eds 15th edn, 2003, 1143pp. $195.00. ISBN 0910674574.
www.unl.edu/buros [DESCRIPTION]
Contains original reviews of over 200 newly published or revised tests, and provides critical reviews and other information on instruments used in all areas of testing. Produced by the University's Buros Institute of Mental Measurements.

4121 **Handbook of clinical health psychology**
American Psychological Association
www.apa.org/books [DESCRIPTION]
Three volumes: 1. Medical disorders and behavioral applications. 2002. 654 pp. $69.95. ISBN 1557989095; 2. Disorders of behavior and health. 2004. 470 pp. $69.95. ISBN 1591470919; 3. Models and perspectives in health psychology. 2004. 641 pp. $69.95. ISBN 1591471060.
Part of the extensive range of related Association publications: see website.

- **Handbook of occupational health psychology J.C. Quick and L.E. Tetrick** 2002, 475pp. $59.95. ISBN 1557989273. Edited compilation from the APA offering 'tools to combat risks at their source'.

Handbook of eating disorders
J. Treasure, U. Schmidt and E. van Furth, eds See entry no. 4405

4122 **New Oxford textbook of psychiatry**
M. Gelder, J.J. Lopez-Ibor and N. Andreasen Oxford University Press, 2003, 2600pp. 2 v. Originally published 2000, £125.00. ISBN 0198528108.
Covers all areas of general psychiatry in depth, and includes sections on each of the subspecialties (for example child psychiatry and forensic psychiatry). It is designed to be used

by those in higher training, for continuing education and reaccreditation, and as a specialists' reference.

'even the most esoteric aspects of psychiatry have been made accessible ... there is something for everybody ... I treasure my own copy ... the general standard of writing is very high and printing, illustration, and indexing leave nothing to be desired ... this may be the foremost international textbook of psychiatry.' (*British Journal of Psychiatry*)

'accurate, comprehensive, accessible, and internationally authoritative ... For those seeking accreditation ... a treasure trove of information about contemporary thought and practice – better than many continuing-education courses.' (*New England Journal of Medicine*)

4123 **Psychiatry**
A. Tasman, J. Kay and J.A. Lieberman, eds 2nd edn, Wiley, 2003, 2552pp. 2 v, $389.00. ISBN 0471521779.
Wide-ranging edited compendium which 'takes a patient-centered approach, presenting information on normal development and then the behaviour, signs and symptoms of disordered behaviour. Its excellence of authorship, depth and breadth of coverage set it apart as a truly impressive reference that will be indispensable for all those involved in the treatment psychiatric disorders'.

'an extraordinary achievement ... the leading textbook in our field ... full of clinical vignettes, wonderful illustrations and is easy on the eyes.' (*Journal of Psychiatric Practice*)

Keeping up-to-date

4124 **Annual Review of Clinical Psychology**
Annual Reviews Inc, 2005. $203.00. ISBN 0824339010 ISSN 15485943.
www.annurev.org/catalog/2005/cp01.asp [DESCRIPTION]
Very good coverage of key aspects of the field in the planned contents of the first volume of this new series.

4125 **Clinician's Research Digest: Briefings in behavioral science**
American Psychological Association Monthly. $177.00. ISSN 87563207.
www.apa.org/journals/crd [DESCRIPTION]
'Clinicians don't have to read all the journals publishing research of interest to them – the Editor and staff of Clinician's Research Digest do it for them. CRD reviews over 100 journals each month and highlights the most relevant articles in this 6-page monthly newsletter.'

4126 **Psychiatric News**
American Psychiatric Association Biweekly. ISSN 00332704.
http://pn.psychiatryonline.org
'Keeps you up to the minute on everything from government and legislative activities that affect the world of psychiatry to the latest developments in the drug and therapy fields.'

4127 **Psychiatry Online**
Priory Lodge Education, 1994–. ISSN 13597620.
www.priory.com/psych.htm
'The International Forum for Psychiatry – the world's First Internet Medical Journal.' Approved for continuing professional development by the Royal College of Psychiatrists.
'3500 people read this medical journal every day.'
Website gives access to the publisher's other medical and health journals – the content of each of which is freely available, reflecting 'a belief that medical knowledge should not be parcelled up and sold to the highest bidder or available only to an academic elite'.

Surgery

clinical surgery • plastic surgery • tissue engineering

Introductions to the subject

4128 **Complications: a surgeon's notes on an imperfect science**
A. Gawande Profile, 2002, 269pp. Originally published Metropolitan, 2002, £7.99. ISBN 1861974981.
Lively, engaging account by author who 'is a staff writer on *The New Yorker*; was an adviser to President Clinton on American health policies; teaches surgery at Harvard Medical School; and uses his knife and scalpel in Boston hospitals. He has lectured in the UK and was a Rhodes Scholar at Oxford.'

'Gawande's book is a marvellous read, and is both thought-provoking and entertaining.' (*Times Higher Education Supplement*)

4129 **Oxford handbook of clinical surgery**
G. McLatchie and D.J. Leaper, eds 2nd edn, Oxford University Press, 2002, 930pp. £19.95. ISBN 0192626388.
Provides a succinct overview of the principles, techniques and procedures of surgery.

Associations & societies

American Academy of Orthopedic Surgeons
See entry no. 3957

American Academy of Otolaryngology Head and Neck Surgery
See entry no. 4071

American Association of Neurological Surgeons
See entry no. 3983

4130 **American College of Surgeons**
www.facs.org
A scientific and educational association of surgeons that was founded in 1913 to improve the quality of care for the surgical patient by setting high standards for surgical education and practice.

American Society for Dermatologic Surgery
See entry no. 3850

American Society of Anesthesiologists
See entry no. 3542

4131 **American Society of Plastic Surgeons**
www.plasticsurgery.org
'The largest plastic surgery specialty organization in the world. Founded in l93l, the society is composed of board-certified plastic surgeons who perform cosmetic and reconstructive surgery.'

Association of Anaesthetists of Great Britain and Ireland
See entry no. 3544

4132 **Association of Surgeons of Great Britain and Ireland**
www.asgbi.org.uk
Founded in 1920 it is 'the only organization covering general

surgery and all the specialties throughout the UK and Ireland'. Access to websites of the specialist bodies plus to information on the work of the Association.

European Society of Anaesthesiology
See entry no. 3546

Faculty of Dental Surgery
See entry no. 3836

International Society for Fracture Repair
See entry no. 3960

Royal College of Anaesthetists
See entry no. 3549

4133 **Royal College of Surgeons of England**
www.rcseng.ac.uk
Originating in 1540 it is an independent professional body committed to promoting and advancing the highest standards of surgical care for patients.

As well as having a leading Library and Archives and the newly refurbished Hunterian Museum, the College offers an online ImageBank – offering online access to, and purchase of, digital images of the wealth of its photographic resources.

Society of Interventional Radiology
See entry no. 3656

Portal & task environments

4134 **Surgical-Tutor**
www.surgical-tutor.org.uk
Very colourful HONCode principles site containing 'educational material aimed at those preparing for undergraduate and postgraduate surgical examinations. It includes clinical tutorials, a journal club, multiple choice questions, revision notes, slide library, discussion group and more ...'

Directories & encyclopedias

Anaesthesia and intensive care A–Z: an encyclopaedia of principles and practice
S.M. Yentis, N.P. Hirsch and G.B. Smith See entry no. 3554

Anesthesia: atlas of regional anesthesia procedures
R.D. Miller, ed. See entry no. 3555

4135 **Gale encyclopedia of surgery**
Thomson Gale, 2003, 1500pp. 3 v., $400.00. ISBN 0787677213.
www.galegroup.com [DESCRIPTION]
Another of the well established and well received series of Gale encylopedias written especially for patients and allied healthcare students by experts in the field. Approximately 450 entries.

'The *Gale Encyclopedia of Surgery* will help patients and their families by showing them what happens during the diagnosis, surgical procedure, and aftercare. It is very up-to-date, offering information on new techniques such as virtual colonoscopy, and will be accessible to lay readers with high school literacy levels. It is an excellent addition to public and consumer health libraries.' (*American Reference Books Annual*)

Handbooks & manuals

4136 **Bailey and Love's short practice of surgery**
R.C.G. Russell, N.S. Williams and C.J.K. Bulstrode, eds 24th edn, Arnold, 2004, 1522pp. £95.00. ISBN 0340808195.
Provides a comprehensive coverage of general surgery, with key information boxes in addition to core material. Includes extensive illustration to reinforce clinical messages, and aphorisms and biographies of prominent pioneers of surgery.

Campbell's operative orthopaedics
S.T. Canale, ed. See entry no. 3966

Head and neck surgery and oncology
J.P. Shah and S.G. Patel See entry no. 4047

4137 **Oxford textbook of surgery**
P.J. Morris and W.C. Wood, eds 2nd edn, Oxford University Press, 2000, 3992pp. 3 v., £425.00. ISBN 0192628844.
A reference book on all aspects of general surgery, that also offers substantial sections on subspecialties such as orthopaedics, paediatric surgery, neurosurgery and cardiac surgery.

4138 **Skandalakis' Surgical anatomy: the embryologic and anatomic basis of modern surgery**
J.E. Skandalakis and G.L. Colborn, eds Paschalidis Medical Publications, 2004, 1720pp. 2 v, £200.00. ISBN 9603990744.
Multi-author. Comprehensive coverage. Excellent clear diagrams. Extensive bibliographies.

4139 **Tissue engineering**
B. Palsson and S. Bhatia, ed. Pearson Education, 2004, 407pp. £35.99. ISBN 0130416967.
'Holds the promise to repair or replace damaged organs. As a discipline, the field has evolved dramatically from its origins in the late 1980s. In particular, the rapid advances in stem cell biology have rekindled the enthusiasm to use cell-based approaches for the treatment of disease.'

Four parts: Quantitative cell and tissue biology; Cell and tissue characterization; Engineering methods and design; Clinical implementation.

Wylie and Churchill-Davidson's a practice of anaesthesia
T.E.J. Healy and P.R. Knight, eds See entry no. 3565

Keeping up-to-date

4140 **Advances in Surgery**
Mosby, 1966–, Annual. $110.00. ISSN 00653411.
Presents a collection of original, fully referenced review articles in selected clinical topics important in all areas of surgery.

Health

We focus here on the individual and organizational contexts of clinical research and practice:

- HEALTH Public sector funding and regulation; generic resources aimed at the health consumer – with substantial reliance again on the HONcode.
- COMPLEMENTARY & ALTERNATIVE MEDICINE A range of specialities, some now accepted as worthwhile approaches complementary to established professional clinical medicine; others alternative treatments not (yet) accepted as having a mainstream scientific basis;
- ENVIRONMENTAL & OCCUPATIONAL HEALTH A large field, with particular emphasis on regulatory issues, and where we have concentrated on resources that focus specifically on hazardous materials and substances, and on toxicology. However, much of relevance to this high profile subject naturally appears in a wide range of other subject fields: METEOROLOGY & CLIMATOLOGY; CHEMISTRY; ECOLOGY; PLANT & CROP PROTECTION; PHARMACOLOGY & PHARMACY; INFECTIOUS DISEASES; PUBLIC HEALTH & PREVENTIVE MEDICINE; NUCLEAR ENERGY; OIL, GAS & COAL; BIOTECHNOLOGY; CHEMICAL ENGINEERING & CHEMICAL TECHNOLOGY; ENVIRONMENTAL ENGINEERING; MATERIALS SCIENCE & ENGINEERING. For a general comment on our treatment within TNW of 'environment' see the introduction to the BIOLOGICAL SCIENCES subject grouping.
- FAMILY & PERSONAL HEALTH Material on general (or family) practice; also on men's health and women's health.
- HOSPITALS & OTHER HEALTH FACILITIES Includes emergency medicine and associated facilities.
- NURSING, MIDWIFERY & ALLIED HEALTH Resources relevant to specific areas of nursing (e.g. surgical nursing) are normally placed within the specialist area (e.g. surgery).
- NUTRITION See also Food Science & Technology.
- PUBLIC HEALTH & PREVENTIVE MEDICINE Because of its importance, we have included here a number of more generic resources concerned with public safety.
- REPRODUCTIVE MEDICINE & HEALTH See also OBSTETRICS & GYNAECOLOGY and the subject fields concerned with genetics.
- SPORTS & EXERCISE MEDICINE Some coverage of physical education.

Introductions to the subject

The Oxford companion to the body
C. Blakemore [et al.], eds See entry no. 3535

Understanding biotechnology
A. Borém, F.R. Santos and D.E. Bowen See entry no. 5011

4141 War or health?: a reader
I. Taipale, ed. Zed Books, 2001, 672pp. Foreword by Kofi Annan, £16.95. ISBN 1856499510.
http://zedbooks.co.uk [DESCRIPTION]
70 articles specially commissioned by the organization now known as Physicians for Social Responsibility.

- **Physicians for Human Rights** www.phrusa.org. Founded 1986: promotes health by protecting human rights.
- **Physicians for Social Responsibility** www.psr.org. US-based organization 'committed to the elimination of nuclear and other weapons of mass destruction, the achievement of a sustainable environment, and the reduction of violence and its causes'.

Dictionaries, thesauri, classifications

International classification of functioning, disability and health
World Health Organization See entry no. 3768

4142 An introduction to medical terminology for health care: a self-teaching package
A. Hutton 3rd edn, Churchill Livingstone, 2002, 341pp. $19.99. ISBN 0443070792.
A very basic introduction, but well laid-out and surprisingly enjoyable to work through.

Medical terminology made easy
J.T. Dennerll See entry no. 3771

NAL Agricultural Thesaurus: NALT
National Agricultural Library See entry no. 2928

Laws, standards, codes

4143 American Health Lawyers Association
www.healthlawyers.org
'The nation's largest, nonpartisan, 501(c)(3) educational organization devoted to legal issues in the healthcare field.' Wide range of useful resources: News and analysis; Publications; Health law websites; etc.

4144 Health Professions Council [UK]
www.hpc-uk.org
'We are a new regulator and our job is to protect the health and wellbeing of people who use the services of the health professionals registered with us. At the moment, we register members of 13 professions. However, we may register members of other professions in the future. We only register people who meet our standards for their professional skills, behaviour and health.'

The 13 professions are: Arts therapists; Biomedical scientists; Chiropodists/podiatrists; Clinical scientists; Dietitians; Occupational therapists; Operating department practitioners; Orthoptists; Paramedics; Physiotherapists; Prosthetists and orthotists; Radiographers; Speech and language therapists. Details about all these.

- **Health Regulation Worldwide** www.hpc-uk.org/worldwide/index.html. Constructed and maintained by HPC to assist in identification of organizations throughout the world that regulate or control the practice of health care workers. Advanced Search facility nicely combines drop down lists of 'Country' and 'Profession'.

4145 **Health Web Site Accreditation**
URAC.
www.urac.org
'URAC, also known as the American Accreditation HealthCare Commission, is a 501(c)(3) (non-profit) charitable organization founded in 1990 to establish standards for the health care industry. URAC's broad-based membership includes representation from all constituencies affected by health care – employers, consumers, regulators, health care providers, and the workers' compensation and managed care industries. Member organizations participate in the development of standards and are eligible to sit on the Board of Directors.'

4146 **Health.cch.com: Print and electronic tools to meet the needs of today's healthcare environment** [USA]
CCH Incorporated.
http://health.cch.com
Commercial website from Wolters Kluwer providing a good link into resources for the American healthcare professional, including health law. Includes free (by registration) CCH Health NetNews, a weekly summary of news with the capability of linking to full text documents, court decisions, laws, and regulations; and a range of products and news relating to the specialty areas of: Medicare and Medicaid; Healthcare compliance; Managed care; Home health; Food, drugs and devices.

4147 **Joint Commission on Accreditation of Healthcare Organizations** [USA]
www.jcaho.org
Evaluates and accredits more than 15,000 health care organizations and programmes. It is an independent, not-for-profit organization, and is the nation's predominant standards-setting and accrediting body in health care.

Apart from details of its policies and procedures and database access to information on each of the accredited organizations, on an intensive site provides links to a wide range of related resources.

Official & quasi-official bodies

Center for Drug Evaluation and Research
See entry no. 3689

4148 **Commission for Patient and Public Involvement in Health** [UK]
www.cppih.org
Set up in January 2003 as an independent, non-departmental public body, sponsored by the UK Department of Health. Its remit is to ensure that the public is involved in decision making about health and health services. The Commission's Knowledge Management System is designed to be an 'open and transparent way of sharing knowledge and information across the Commission's Shaping Health network and with the general public. Everyone can access the KMS and view areas of interest. If you register you can contribute to all discussions'.

The Genomic Resource Centre
World Health Organization See entry no. 3607

4149 **Health and Consumer Protection** [EUR]
European Commission. Directorate for Health and Consumer Protection
europa.eu.int/comm/health/index_en.html
The European Commission's portal providing access to public health information across Europe.

4150 **Health Canada**
www.hc-sc.gc.ca
Well laid out gateway from the 'federal department responsible for helping the people of Canada maintain and improve their health'.

- **eHealth InfoSource cybersanté** www.hc-sc.gc.ca/ohih-bsi/pubs/bulletin/infosource_e.html. Free electronic awareness service alerting readers to new electronic information resources available in eHealth. It is published by the Health and the Information Highway Division within Health Canada.

Human Genetics Commission
See entry no. 3608

4151 **Medicare: The Official US Government Site for People with Medicare**
www.medicare.gov
Medicare is 'the federal health insurance program for: people 65 years of age or older, certain younger people with disabilities, and people with End-Stage Renal Disease (permanent kidney failure with dialysis or a transplant, sometimes called ESRD)'. Medicaid is 'A joint federal and state program that helps with medical costs for some people with low incomes and limited resources. Medicaid programs vary from state to state, but most health care costs are covered if you qualify for both Medicare and Medicaid.'

Through Medicare, Medicaid and SCHIP, about one in four Americans receive health care coverage.

- **America's Health Insurance Plans** www.ahip.net. National trade association representing nearly 1300 member companies. Well designed website providing access to detailed set of resources.
- **FamiliesUSA: The voice for health care consumers** www.familiesusa.org. US nonprofit, non-partisan organization 'dedicated to the achievement of high-quality, affordable health care for all Americans. We have earned a national reputation as an effective voice for health care consumers for over 20 years'.
- **Centers for Medicare & Medicaid Services** www.cms.hhs.gov. Formerly the Health Care Financing Administration. CMS administers the Medicare programme, and works with the States to administer Medicaid, the State Children's Health Insurance Program (SCHIP), and health insurance portability standards.

4152 **NHS Gateway** [UK]
National Health Service and Great Britain. Department of Health
www.nhs.uk
Very good entry point for information about the National Health Service in England; Scotland; Wales; Northern Ireland. 'The NHS search engine currently indexes over 600,000 web pages that provide NHS and health information.'

- **Healthcare Commission** www.healthcarecommission.org.uk. 'Promotes improvement in the quality of the NHS and independent healthcare. We have a wide range of responsibilities, all aimed at improving the quality of healthcare'. Work of The Commission for Health Improvement is now conducted by this Commission.
- **INVOLVE: Promoting public involvement in NHS, public health and social care research** www.invo.org.uk. National advisory group, funded by Department of Health. 'We believe that involving

members of the public leads to research that is: more relevant to people's needs and concerns; more reliable; more likely to be used.'

- **National Patient Safety Agency** www.npsa.nhs.uk. Special Health Authority created in July 2001 to co-ordinate the efforts of the entire country to report, and more importantly to learn from mistakes and problems that affect patient safety.
- **NHS Direct Online** www.nhsdirect.nhs.uk. The very successful website which provides 'high quality health information and advice for the people of England. It is unique in being supported by a 24-hour nurse advice and information helpline'. Backed up by extensive FAQs and self-help guide.

4153 **World Health Organization**
www.who.int
The United Nations specialized agency for health, established in 1948. WHO's objective is the attainment by all peoples of the highest possible level of health. List of WHO websites but also useful A–Z index of Health topics. Access to WHOLIS, which indexes all WHO publications from 1948 onwards and articles from WHO-produced journals and technical documents from 1985 to the present, and to the WHO online BookShop.

- **Council for International Organizations of Medical Sciences** www.cioms.ch. Set up 1949 by WHO and UNESCO. Full/associate membership 2005 was 49 international organizations, representing many of the biomedical disciplines, 18 national members mainly representing national academies of sciences and medical research councils.
- **WHO Regional Office for Europe** www.euro.who.int. Resources include WHO/Europe's statistical databases, country profiles – Atlas of health in Europe (2003), European health report (2002), etc., and the Health Evidence Network, primarily for public health and health care decision makers.
- **WHO Statistical Information System: WHOSIS** http://www3.who.int/whosis/menu.cfm. Wide range of data including: core health indicators from the *World Health Report* for each of the 192 countries; Burden of Disease activities; HIV/AIDS, drugs, immunization, micronutrients, alcohol, etc; and an excellent set of Links.
- **World Directory of Medical Schools** www.who.int/hrh/wdms/en. Updates printed list of institutions of basic medical education in 157 countries or areas. It also provides information on the conditions for obtaining the licence to practise medicine in 14 countries or areas that do not have medical schools.
- **The World Health Report** www.who.int/whr/en. First published 1995; WHO's leading publication. Each annual report combines an expert assessment of global health, including statistics relating to all countries, with focus on a specific subject. The 2004 edn called for a comprehensive HIV/AIDS strategy.

Research centres & institutes

Centre for Reviews and Dissemination
See entry no. 3774

Hastings Center
See entry no. 1916

4154 **King's Fund** [UK]
www.kingsfund.org.uk
Leading independent charitable foundation 'whose goal is to improve health, especially in London ... We carry out health policy research and analysis, working on our own, in partnerships, and through grants. We are a major resource to people working in health, offering leadership courses; seminars and workshops; an information and library service; and conference facilities. We promote our work widely through the media, events and publications, and we seek to influence Government and others to create change where we believe it is needed.'

The website is a significant source of useful generally free publications on health-related policy issues. There is also an extremely extensive and categorized list of website links collected, evaluated and maintained by the Fund's important Information and Library Service.

- **Health Management Information Consortium Database** www.ovid.com/site/products [FEE-BASED]. Data from the King's Fund Information and Library Service combined with data from the UK Department of Health Library and Information Services. Over 250,000 records.

National Institute for Health and Clinical Excellence
See entry no. 3775

4155 **Office of Health Economics** [UK]
www.ohe.org
Provides independent research, advisory and consultancy services on policy implications and economic issues within the pharmaceutical, health care and biotechnology sectors.

- **Compendium of Health Statistics** **P. Yuen, ed.** 16th edn 2004–2005. £798.00 + VAT. www.ohecompendium.org [DESCRIPTION]. Offers a wide range of statistical information on health and healthcare in the UK. Price includes single user web access as well as complimentary copy of the ring binder Compendium.
- **Health Economic Evaluations Database** www.ohe-heed.com [FEE-BASED]. Joint initiative between the Office and INTERNATIONAL FEDERATION OF PHARMACEUTICAL MANUFACTURERS & ASSOCIATIONS. Reports studies of cost-effectiveness and other forms of economic evaluation of medicines and other treatments and medical interventions.

Associations & societies

4156 **American Council on Science and Health**
www.acsh.org
Advocacy body 'founded in 1978 by a group of scientists who had become concerned that many important public policies related to health and the environment did not have a sound scientific basis. These scientists created the organization to add reason and balance to debates about public health issues and bring common sense views to the public ... The nucleus of ACSH is a board of 350 physicians, scientists and policy advisors – experts in a wide variety of fields – who review the Council's reports and participate in ACSH seminars, press conferences, media communications and other educational activities.'

Well organized website gives access to major collections of resources on a wide range of public and environmental health topics.

Genetic Alliance
See entry no. 3614

Genetic Interest Group
See entry no. 3615

4157 Global Health Council
www.globalhealth.org
'The world's largest membership alliance dedicated to saving lives by improving health throughout the world. Our diverse membership is comprised of healthcare professionals and organizations that include NGOs, foundations, corporations, government agencies and academic institutions that work to ensure global health for all.'

4158 International Alliance of Patients' Organizations
www.patientsorganizations.org
'A unique global alliance representing patients of all nationalities across all disease areas and promoting patient-centred healthcare around the world. Our members are patients' organizations working at the international, regional, national and local levels to represent and support patients, their families and carers. A patient is a person with any chronic disease, illness, syndrome, impairment or disability.'

Early 2005, it had a membership of 136.

4159 UK Health Informatics Society
www.ukhis.org.uk
Founded in 1986, to advance the knowledge and application of medical and health informatics, understood as the skills and tools that enable the sharing and use of information to deliver healthcare and promote health. Changed its name from British Medical Informatics Society in 2004 and new website to be 'officially launched early to mid 2005'.

- **American Medical Informatics Association** www.amia.org. Formed by the merger in 1990 of three predecessor societies. Its 3200 members include physicians, nurses, computer and information scientists, biomedical engineers, medical librarians, and academic researchers and educators. Very useful set of resources.
- **International Medical Informatics Association** www.imia.org. Not a very active website. But useful as a gateway to worldwide national informatics associations; and they have an impressive roster of 19 IMIA Working Groups and Special Interest Groups. Also publish *Yearbook of Medical Informatics* (Schattauer).
- **UK Council for Health Informatics Professionals** www.ukchip.org. Formed 2002 to promote professionalism in Health Informatics (HI). Operates a voluntary register of HI professionals who agree to work to clearly defined standards. Early 2005, 470 health informaticians had registered; 1500 had begun to register.

Libraries, archives, museums

4160 National Health Museum [USA]
www.nationalhealthmuseum.org
'The National Health Museum will educate, engage and inspire people to understand the past, present and future of health and health science and empower them to act upon that information to enhance their individual, family and community health.'

Concentrates especially on education resources including developing the initiative Access Excellence: 'a national educational program that provides high school health and biology teachers access to their colleagues, scientists, and critical sources of new scientific information via the World Wide Web'.

Portal & task environments

Bandolier: Evidence based thinking about health care
See entry no. 3783

4161 BBC Health
www.bbc.co.uk/health
Provides an excellent range and quality of services including substantial sections on: Healthy living; Help and advice; Illnesses and conditions; Your health.

4162 Binley's
www.binleys.com
The brand name given to the range of publications and services developed and marketed by Beechwood House Publishing, part of Wilmington Group Plc, a stock market listed company.

Leading provider of databases, directories, and online access covering the UK health system: especially the National Health Service, for which the website provides a range of useful freely accessible information, as well as the fee-based material. The site also has an extensive Glossary of abbreviations and acronyms.

- **Institute of Healthcare Management Yearbook: 2003–2004** Beechwod House Publishing, 2003, 582pp. £175.00. ISBN 011703147X. Formerly published by The Stationery Office. Lists all Health Authority NHS Trusts' Primary Care Trusts in England and their equivalents in Wales, Northern Ireland and Scotland. Gives information about the Institute, and news of recent developments.

Campaign for Access to Essential Medicines
Médecins Sans Frontières See entry no. 3710

Cochrane Collaboration
See entry no. 3787

4163 Dr Foster [UK]
www.drfoster.co.uk
'Dr Foster is an independent organization which collects and analyses information on the availability and quality of health services in the UK. Use Dr Foster to make the most informed decisions on how to access the right healthcare.'

'This is a truly remarkable resource. For the first time, I can find out what I want to know about local health services. It's the most authoritative measure of healthcare standards available anywhere in the world.' (*Claire Rayner, President, Patients Association*)

4164 Health [USA]
Federal Citizen Information Center
http://firstgov.gov/Citizen/Topics/Health.shtml
The health topic section within the US Government's official web portal FIRSTGOV.GOV.

4165 Health and Social Care Topics [UK]
Great Britain. Department of Health
www.dh.gov.uk/PolicyAndGuidance/HealthAndSocialCareTopics/fs/en
Valuable and extensive gateway to a very comprehensive range of topics in healthcare and social care within a UK context.

4166 Health and Wellness Resource Center
Thomson Gale.
www.galegroup.com [DESCRIPTION]
'Amid the chaos of the Internet, Gale has reserved places

just for students and library users. A Gale resource center is a safe haven, where research skills pay off. Far removed from the pitfalls of the open Web, resource centers allow users to determine search criteria, retrieve relevant results and find reliable information in a variety of formats.'

Integrated access to journals, pamphlets, encyclopedias, etc. Uses the InfoTrac interface. Subscribes to the HONCode.

'Because of the inclusion of worldwide literature in high school curricula, this is a much needed resource. This excellent set would benefit any high school library. It is reasonably priced and covers a lot of academic ground. Highly Recommended.' (*The Book Report*)

- **Nutrition and well-being A–Z** Macmillan Reference USA, 2004, 400pp. $195.00. ISBN 0028657071. www.gale.com/gvrl [FEE-BASED]. Two-volume set analysing how nutrition has, is and will affect quality of life, health and fitness in various countries. It defines the role nutrition plays in weight and height increases, and nutritional factors in diabetes and obesity.

4167 Health Information [USA]
National Institutes of Health
http://health.nih.gov
NIH gateway providing a useful range of approaches to US government and other health information: Browse categories; Health topics A–Z; Quick links; Related links; Search health topics. Good multi-faceted approach.

4168 HealthCentral: Information and products for a healthier life
www.healthcentral.com
Links to consumer health information, including a health encyclopedia and videos. Useful information, news and products. The producers subscribe to the HONCode principles.

HealthGate: The Evidence-Based Medicine Company
See entry no. 3789

4169 HealthInsite [AUS]
www.healthinsite.gov.au
Good example of government-sponsored site, conforming to the HONCode principles.

- **Health Thesaurus** www.healthinsite.gov.au/search/thesaurus_levels.cfm. 'The Health Thesaurus is used for subject terms in the resource metadata for HealthInsite. It has a hierarchical structure so that similar types of terms (e.g. names of diseases) are clustered together.'

HumGen: International database on the legal, social and ethical aspects of HUMan GENetics
B.M. Knoppers [et al.], eds; Université de Montréal See entry no. 3619

4170 LTSN Health Sciences and Practice [UK]
King's College London and Higher Education Academy
www.health.ltsn.ac.uk
Established by the UK higher education funding bodies to promote high quality learning and teaching in health sciences. The network supports the sharing of innovation and good practices in learning and teaching and the website has useful resources, links and reports that achieve this.

MD Consult
See entry no. 3790

4171 Medical Library
Medem Inc.
http://medem.com
Service from physician practice-patient communications network founded in 1999 by seven leading US medical societies; now encompasses 45 such societies.

The Library itself 'represents the full range of patient education information from our partner medical societies and other trusted sources, and is unsurpassed in quality, breadth and depth of health care information. Selected one of the top ten most useful websites by the Medical Library Association, our Medical Library provides patients with reliable health care information from introductory to advanced texts.

4172 Medicdirect [UK]
www.medicdirect.co.uk
'Provides a complete health information resource for both consumers and medical practitioners. The site is hosted by 26 leading National Health Service specialists in the field of medicine in the United Kingdom; these consultants also comprise the majority shareholders in the privately-owned company.'

4173 MedicineNet [USA]
MedicineNet Inc.
www.medicinenet.com
Patient-focused site covering over 400 conditions and diseases, more than 100 tests and procedures, and a medical dictionary of over 6500 terms. Original content provided from a network of over 40 doctors. One of the web's most highly regarded sources; HONCode certified.

- **MedTerms** www.medterms.com. Online medical dictionary: 15,000 terms.
- **Webster's new world medical dictionary** 2nd edn, Wiley, 2003, 456pp. £10.50. ISBN 0764524615. Definitions of 8000 medical terms produced by the MedicineNet.com team. 'Going beyond diseases and treatments, the book includes definitions of scientific terms, abbreviations, acronyms, and jargon – even institutions and research projects'.

4174 Mind, Body and Soul [UK]
www.mindbodysoul.gov.uk
Wired for Health site aimed at UK Key Stage 4 students (14–16 years). Covers: Alcohol; Drugs; Emotional health and wellbeing; Healthy eating; Physical activity; Safety; Sexual health; Smoking. There are related sites for Key Stages 1, 2, and 3.

- **Wired for Health** www.wiredforhealth.gov.uk. A series of websites managed by the UK Health Development Agency (now the National Institute for Health and Clinical Excellence) on behalf of its Department of Health and the Department for Education and Skills.

National Guideline Clearinghouse
Agency for Healthcare Research and Quality See entry no. 3791

4175 New York Online Access to Health: NOAH [USA]
www.noah-health.org
'NOAH provides access to high quality consumer health information in English and Spanish. The NOAH volunteer editors do not write this information. Instead, librarians and health professionals in New York and beyond find, select, and organize full-text consumer health information that is current, relevant, accurate and unbiased.'

4176 **Telemedicine and E-health Information Service: TEIS** [UK]
University of Portsmouth
www.teis.nhs.uk
'The objectives of TEIS are to bring together those working in the field of telemedicine, telecare and ehealth; to encourage them to share information and experience; and to provide an information resource on telemedicine activity in the UK.'

Virtual Hospital: a digital library for health information
University of Iowa See entry no. 3792

4177 **WebMD**
WebMD Corporation.
www.webmd.com
Wide-ranging highly-rated US-based site. The main site *WebMD Health* is accredited by HONCOde, as well as by URAC Health Web Site Accreditation and TRUSTe (www.truste.org), and there is a good well written section 'Our privacy commitment to you'. (See also the page 'How 'Sponsor Savvy' are you? Here's info you should know.')

- **Medscape** www.medscape.com [REGISTRATION]. WebMD offering. Personalization site providing specialists, primary care physicians, and other health professionals 'the Web's most robust and integrated medical information and education tools'.

Discovering print & electronic resources

CAB Abstracts
CAB International See entry no. 2949

4178 **The essential guide to the Internet for health professionals**
S.S. Chellen Routledge, 2003, 237pp. £19.99. ISBN 0415305578.
Introductory text written for health professionals and students following a course in health studies in a college of higher education. Attractive large format volume concentrating on the basics (getting online, the world wide web, e-mail, discussion groups, etc.), but with a well annotated selection of websites described.

4179 **Global Health**
CAB International.
www.cabdirect.org/globalhealth [FEE-BASED]
Specialist public health database with an emphasis on international health. 80% of the database coverage is from journal articles, but the database also covers books, conference proceedings, bulletins, reports and theses. 3500 journals, from more than 125 countries, are indexed; a total of 9500 journals are screened for relevant material.

4180 **Mapping health on the Internet: strategies for learning in an information age**
R. Scrivener Radcliffe Medical Press, 2002, 144pp. £21.95. ISBN 1857755936.
Useful introduction – though underlining each URL in the printed text makes for a more difficult transcription.
'This book is an invaluable tool for health care professionals.' (*Journal of the Royal Society for the Promotion of Health*)

- **Harnessing health libraries** **B. Madge** Radcliffe Medical Press, 2001, 112pp. £21.95. ISBN 1857754085. www.radcliffe-oxford.com. Designed to help the busy person find articles and other resources quickly – especially in the context of the increasing emphasis on evidence-based healthcare. Part of the Harnessing Health Information series: see website.

4181 **The Medical Library Association encyclopedic guide to searching and finding health information on the web**
P.F. Anderson and N.J. Allee Neal-Schuman, 2004, 824pp. 3 v., $395.00. ISBN 1555704948.
www.neal-schuman.com [DESCRIPTION]
Major comprehensive handbook. V. 1. *Search strategies*: 13 chapters; Quick reference guide: 7 parts; V. 2. *Diseases and disorders*: 293 sections within 32 parts; Mental health and mental disorders: 153 sections within 23 parts; V. 3. *Health and Wellness*: 164 sections within 11 parts; Life stages and reproduction: 114 sections within 11 parts.
'This impressive reference comprises an entire course in how to find consumer health information specifically through the use of Internet-only web sites and search engines. Even the most knowledgeable librarians will find something they don't know, or be reminded of a different way of searching the web.' (*Library Journal*)

- **Introduction to reference sources in the health sciences** **J.A. Boorkman, J. Huber and F. Roper, comps; Medical Library Association** 4th edn, Neal-Schuman, 2004, 300pp. $75.00. ISBN 1555704816. 'Now, after almost a decade, a new edition of THE standard guide to health science sources is available for students, librarians, and health professionals'.

Netting the Evidence: a ScHARR introduction to evidence based practice on the internet
A. Booth, ed.; University of Sheffield See entry no. 3796

4182 **Resources for Health Consumers** [USA]
Medical Library Association
www.mlanet.org/resources
Access to very useful compilation, focusing on US-based provision. There is a companion 'Resources for Medical Librarians', and a 'Consumer and Patient Health Information Section' (http://caphis.mlanet.org), as well as a helpful 'A user's guide to finding and evaluating health information on the web'. See also the entry for the Association itself in Tools for Information Professionals.

Digital data, image & text collections

4183 **ChildStats.gov: Forum on child and family statistics** [USA]
Federal Interagency Forum on Child and Family Statistics
www.childstats.gov
Easy access to federal and state statistics and reports on children and their families, including: population and family characteristics, economic security, health, behaviour and social environment, and education. Includes the annual *America's children: key national indicators of well-being.*

4184 **Health Education Assets Library: HEAL**
www.healcentral.org/index.jsp
Established 2000 'to provide free digital materials of the highest quality that meet the needs of today's health sciences educators'. In January 2005, HEAL began a 'rigorous peer review process of educational materials that have been submitted by authors. Until recently, few educators have received scholarly recognition for developing innovative teaching materials. HEAL is proud to initiate a process to

provide such recognition. Now educators can submit teaching materials to HEAL for peer review. Reviewers will systematically appraise the quality of the materials, which, upon acceptance, will be published permanently in HEAL.'

4185 Health Statistics [UK]
Office for National Statistics
www.statistics.gov.uk
Official statistics on: Abortions; Accidents and injuries; Ambulance service; Child health; Congenital anomalies and malformations notified; Deaths; Dental health; and so on.

4186 National Center for Health Statistics [USA]
www.cdc.gov/nchs
A rich source of information about America's health. USA's principal health statistics agency, compiling statistical information that guide actions and policies to improve the nation's health. Its parent body, Centers for Disease Control and Prevention, has a website section Data and Statistics providing access to a wide range of related information.

Directories & encyclopedias

4187 Complete reference guide to medicine and health
R.J. Wagman, ed. Facts On File, 2004, 1200pp. 4 v., $159.00. ISBN 0816061440.
General reference text aimed at US Grade 6 and upwards. Covers basic body functions, general nature of illnesses and probable course of corrective action, as well as matters of personal and social interest, such as drug and alcohol abuse, physical fitness and the stages of life.

4188 Encyclopedia of health and behavior
N.B. Anderson, ed. SAGE, 2004, 968pp. 2 v, $350.00. ISBN 0761923608.
www.sagepub.com
200 entries organized A–Z with a Reader's Guide grouping titles of entries by broad topic for easy browsing. Over 300 contributors.
See website for the current list of titles in health sciences, especially the social aspects, produced by SAGE.
'The encyclopedic title of Anderson's fine work signals its comprehensiveness and usefulness as a handbook for the discipline ... This encyclopedia's expert authors cover the key theories, ideas, and factors, that link psychology and health. An excellent organization facilitates multiple entry points. Highly recommended.' (*Choice*)

- **Encyclopedia of health care management M.J. Stahl** SAGE, 2003, 664pp. $150.00. ISBN 0761926747. 'This book would be of great use in reference collections at public, university, hospital, and corporate libraries.' E-STREAMS.

4189 The Merck manual of medical information
Merck Research Laboratories.
www.merck.com/mmhe/index.html
'Explains disorders, who is likely to get them, their symptoms, how they're diagnosed, how they might be prevented, and how they can be treated; also provides information about prognosis.

'Based on the world's most widely used textbook of medicine—*The Merck Manual*—but written in everyday language by 300 outstanding contributors.'

'Provided free of charge on the Internet by Merck & Co., Inc., as a public service on a non-profit basis.'
Also available in print for purchase.

4190 The Royal Society of Medicine health encyclopedia: the complete medical reference library in one A–Z volume
R.M. Youngson; Royal Society of Medicine Bloomsbury, 2001, 798pp. £30.00. ISBN 0747550506.
Guide to health and the surrounding issues. Entries are supported by clearly labelled and detailed diagrams where appropriate.

Keeping up-to-date

4191 Health Affairs [USA]
Project HOPE Bimonthly. ISSN 02782715.
www.healthaffairs.org
'Policy Journal of the Health Sphere' produced by US charitable organization founded 45 years ago to provide Health Opportunities for People Everywhere (HOPE). The charity's other current foci are: Infectious diseases (including HIV/AIDS and tuberculosis); Women's and children's health (including village health banks); Health professional education; Health systems and facilities; Humanitarian assistance.

4192 Health Service Journal [UK]
Emap.
www.hsj.co.uk
'The UK's leading weekly magazine for healthcare managers. With the latest health service news, views and issues, as well as job vacancies, HSJ is at the cutting edge of developments in the National Health Service.'
Also available for subscription.

4193 Reuters Health: The premier supplier of health and medical news on the Internet
www.reutershealth.com [FEE-BASED]
Providers of up-to-date medical and healthcare news. The news stories are written by a staff of dedicated journalists who produce some 100 news stories per day for three news wires: Reuters Health eLine, euters Medical News, and Reuters Health Industry Briefing. Reuters licenses these news wires for use on the Internet and as knowledge management tools for use on corporate intranets and extranets. However, sample stories are freely available at the website each day.

Complementary & Alternative Medicine

acupuncture • alternative medicine • Chinese herbal medicine • chiropractics • complementary therapies • healing • herbal medicines • homeopathy • medicinal plants • natural medicines • osteopathy • plant medicines • self-medication

Introductions to the subject

4194 ABC of complementary medicine
A.J. Vickers [et al.] BMJ Books, 2000, 56pp. £14.95. ISBN 0727912372.
A growing number of patients are using complementary therapies and practice is growing among conventional health professionals. This book takes an independent standpoint and provides a guide to decision making.

4195 **Alternative medicine: an objective assessment**
American Medical Association 1999, 656pp. $79.00. ISBN 1579470025.
Offers a balanced analysis of alternative medicine through a broad range of topics from the evaluation of treatment modalities to use of alternative medicine therapies.

4196 **Which? guide to complementary therapies**
B. Rowlands 2nd edn, Which? Books, 2002, 288pp. £10.99. ISBN 0852028938.
Offers an independent examination of a wide range of treatments ranging from acupuncture and chiropractic, through healing and reflexology, to yoga. It covers the history, theory and uses of each therapy including methods, efficacy and the possible side effects. It addresses common consumer concerns, discusses costs and availability on the UK National Health Service, and gives tips for finding a practitioner.

Dictionaries, thesauri, classifications

4197 **Churchill Livingstone's international dictionary of homeopathy**
J. Swayne, ed.; Faculty of Homoeopathy and Homeopathic Trust Churchill Livingstone, 2000, 251pp. £21.99. ISBN 0443060096.
An authoritative, up-to-date, international consensus on definition or interpretation of concepts necessary to the understanding of the principles and practice of homeopathy.

A dictionary of natural products
G.M. Hocking See entry no. 3680

Research centres & institutes

4198 **National Center for Complementary and Alternative Medicine** [USA]
http://nccam.nih.gov
'Dedicated to exploring complementary and alternative healing practices in the context of rigorous science, training complementary and alternative medicine researchers, and disseminating authoritative information to the public and professionals.' One of the 27 institutes and centres that make up the National Institutes of Health.

Associations & societies

4199 **Alternative Medicine Foundation** [USA]
www.amfoundation.org
501(c)(3) non-profit organization, formed to: respond to the public and professional need for responsible and reliable education, information, and dialogue about the integration of alternative and conventional medicine; conserve and respect the knowledge and practice of indigenous therapies and systems of healthcare; promote novel ways to blend ancient practice and modern science for the promotion of health; advance the ethical and sustainable development of alternatives to standard care.

The Foundation subscribes to the HONCode principles.

- **HerbMed** www.herbmed.org. 'Interactive, electronic herbal database – provides hyperlinked access to the scientific data underlying the use of herbs for health. It is an impartial, evidence-based information resource' (provided by the Foundation).

4200 **American Academy of Medical Acupuncture**
www.medicalacupuncture.org
Founded in 1987, to promote the integration of concepts from traditional and modern forms of acupuncture with Western medical training and thereby synthesize a more comprehensive approach to health care.

- **AcuBriefs** www.acubriefs.com. 'Purpose is to make available online the most comprehensive database of references on acupuncture in the English language. References on acupuncture in languages other than English will be incorporated contingent on time and resources'.

4201 **Association of the European Self-Medication Industry**
www.aesgp.be
Self-medication has been defined as 'a continuous process of caring for one's own health, starting with the recognition of a problem or the desire to prevent it up to the adoption of a series of interventions without calling upon the physician'. Range of useful information and pointers – though not always easy to navigate to the needed information.

4202 **British Complementary Medicine Association**
www.bcma.co.uk
'The leading authority in the field by helping therapists in all aspects of their work ... All applicants undergo an investigation to ensure that they have a satisfactory standard of education and training as part of the entry requirements ... Membership continues to grow and the current paid-up membership stands at 38 associations + independent and affiliated schools (representing approximately 25,000 practitioners). 50 basic therapies or variations of them are represented by 11 Therapy Groups. The first ever Government policy statement on Complementary Medicine in 1991 authorized the use of Complementary Medicine therapists in the National Health Service but reflected the General Medical Council's ruling that General Practitioners would remain in clinical control of their patients. This is in line with BCMA thinking.'

4203 **Complementary Medical Association** [UK]
www.the-cma.org.uk
Established in 1995, as a not-for-profit organization, to promote ethical, responsible, professional complementary medicine to the public and the medical profession.

4204 **Institute for Complementary Medicine** [UK]
www.i-c-m.org.uk
A registered charity formed in 1982 to provide the public with information on complementary medicine. The ICM administers the British Register of Complementary Practitioners which is a register of professional, competent practitioners whom have all been assessed individually.

International Herb Association
See entry no. 3088

4205 **Research Council for Complementary Medicine** [UK]
www.rccm.org.uk
'Founded in 1983 by a group of enthusiastic practitioners and researchers from both orthodox and complementary medicine. Today, our aim is to develop and extend the evidence base for complementary medicine in order to provide practitioners and their patients with information about the effectiveness of individual therapies and the

treatment of specific conditions.' Useful overview of Research Methods; Book reviews; Links.

Portal & task environments

Food and Nutrition Information Center
National Agricultural Library See entry no. 4392

4206 **Herbalgram.org** [USA]
American Botanical Council
www.herbalgram.org
'Established in 1988, the American Botanical Council is the leading independent, non-profit, international member-based organization providing education using science-based and traditional information to promote the responsible use of herbal medicine.' Educational resources; book catalogue, news, etc.

- **Chinese herbal medicine: modern applications of traditional formulas C. Liu, A. Tseng and S. Yang** CRC Press, 2004, 904pp. $89.95. ISBN 0849315689. More than 840 formulas categorized according to Traditional Chinese Medicine Zang-Fu syndrome differentiation; Includes 190 allopathic medical conditions or disorders; more than 640 single herbs and their characteristics.
- **The complete natural medicine guide to the 50 most common medicinal herbs H. Boon and M. Smith** 2nd edn, Firefly Books, 2004, 352pp. $19.95. ISBN 0778800814. 'Well written and will be easily understood by the lay reader as well as the health professional. It would be a good addition to the reference shelf of any library needing to provide information on medicinal herbs.' *American Reference Books Annual*.
- **CRC handbook of medicinal herbs J.A. Duke** 2nd edn, CRC Press, 2002, 896pp. $249.00. ISBN 0849312841. Catalogues more than 800 of the world's most important medicinal plant species.
- **Herbal medicines: a guide for healthcare professionals 2004 J. Barnes, L.A. Anderson and J.D. Phillipson, eds** Pharmaceutical Press, 2002, 530pp. £39.95. ISBN 0853694745. A reference work for pharmacists, doctors and other health care workers and to help them provide professional advice on the use of herbal remedies to members of the public. Also available on CD-ROM, and online.

Discovering print & electronic resources

4207 **Allied and Complementary Medicine Database: AMED**
British Library
www.bl.uk/collections/health/health.html [DESCRIPTION]
Database produced by the Health Care Information service of the BL, covers a selection of journals for professions allied to medicine, complementary medicine and palliative care. Many of the 600 journals are not covered by other indexing sources.

4208 **Alternative medicine: health care information resources for patients, their families, friends and health care workers**
T. Flemming; McMaster University
http://hsl.lib.mcmaster.ca/tomflem/altmed.html
This is a section within a very extensive regularly updated list of resources on health care in general, many with detailed annotations, created 'in the belief that the informed consumer is a more satisfied consumer of healthcare'. The author notes that 'The inclusion of a site in this list of resources is not an endorsement of its claims', and gives a link to a useful subsection Fraud in Healthcare Links within the 'Illness' section of the website.
The author is based within the University's Health Sciences Library.

4209 **The complementary and alternative medicine information sourcebook**
A.M. Rees Oryx Press, 2001, 240pp. $55.95. ISBN 1573563889.
Covers print and electronic sources for organizations, magazines and newsletters, pamphlets, professional literature, popular books (reviews of 355 titles).
'An exceptional resource for anyone interested in finding the best sources of information concerning any aspect of alternative health care. All levels.' (*Choice*)

4210 **Complementary therapies on the Internet**
W.M. Beckner and B. Berman Churchill Livingstone, 2003, 186pp. Includes CD-ROM, £20.99. ISBN 0443070679.
A clear and concise guide to accessing and assessing quality information about complementary medicine on the Internet. The CD-ROM gives immediate access to weblinks.

4211 **MANTIS: Manual Alternative and Natural Therapy Index System**
Action Potential Inc.
www.action-potential.com/MANTIS.asp [DESCRIPTION]
Access to over 60,000 records from over 1000 journals addressing all areas of alternative medical literature since 1900. It has become 'the largest index of peer reviewed articles for several disciplines including; chiropractic, osteopathy, homeopathy, and manual medicine'.

Natural Products Alert
University of Illinois at Chicago See entry no. 3726

Digital data, image & text collections

4212 **Natural Medicines Comprehensive Database**
Therapeutic Research Faculty.
www.naturaldatabase.com [FEE-BASED]
Now the leading database of natural medicines, containing over 1000 monographs with for each, as appropriate: name most widely used; also known as; scientific name; people use this for; evidence-based safety rating; effectiveness rating; mechanism of action and active ingredients; adverse reactions; interactions; drug influences on nutrient levels and depletion; dosage and administration; comments; references.
See website for details of other database versions and services from the company.
'The Natural Medicines Comprehensive Database, one of the most comprehensive and reliable natural medicine resources, is by Therapeutic Research Faculty, an impressive team of experts ... This reviewer highly recommends the Web version as a reference resource for all types of libraries.' (*Journal of the Medical Library Association*)

Directories & encyclopedias

Chemical dictionary of economic plants
J.B. Harborne and H. Baxter See entry no. 3105

4213 **Encyclopedia of common natural ingredients: used in food, drugs, and cosmetics**
A.Y. Leung and S. Foster 2nd edn, Wiley, 2003, 688pp. $160.00. ISBN 0471471283.
Expanded to twice the size of the 1st edn, includes 500 of the most commonly used ingredients, covering identification, processing, preparation, and manner of use for each. 'The inclusion of a new classification on Chinese medicinal herbs is particularly innovative, offering information that appears here for the first time in English. This classification draws on both classical and modern Chinese medicine and reflects the growing popularity of Chinese herbs in this country and in the rest of the world.'

4214 **Encyclopedia of mind enhancing foods, drugs and nutritional substances**
D.W. Group McFarland, 2001, 221pp. $55.00. ISBN 0786408537.
Foods and drugs believed to improve mental performance. Contains information on nearly 400 nutrients, herbs, and drugs, ranging from ancient plant compounds to the latest pharmaceuticals.
'Recommended ... accessible.' (*Public Library Quarterly*)

4215 **The Gale encyclopedia of alternative medicine**
2nd edn, Gale, 2004. 4 v., $425.00. ISBN 0787674249.
www.gale.com/pdf/facts/GEAM.pdf [DESCRIPTION]
Revised edition of major compilation containing some 750 entries, and exploring 275 diseases and conditions, 300 herbs and remedies, 150 therapies.

- **The encyclopedia of complementary and alternative medicine T. Navarra** Facts On File, 2004, 276pp. $75.00. ISBN 0816049971. 400 detailed descriptions of alternative practices, how they work, who developed them, anecdotal evidence, and what to look for when seeking a professional. 'Written for general readers but authoritative enough to be of use to the professional'.

4216 **Medicinal plants of the world: an illustrated scientific guide to important medicinal plants and their uses**
B.E. van Wyk and M. Wink Timber Press, 2004, 480pp. $39.95. ISBN 0881926027.
'Comprehensive and scientifically accurate guide to the best-known and most important medicinal plants. The book includes descriptions of more than 300 medicinal plants and their close relatives. Each entry gives a short summary with a description of the plant, the geographical origin, therapeutic category, historical and modern uses, active ingredients, and pharmacological effects. More than 500 full-color photographs assist in the identification of the plants. It is an essential reference guide for health care professionals — doctors, nurses, and especially pharmacists — or anyone with an interest in medicinal plants and their uses.'
'highly recommended for academic and public library botanical, gardening, holistic, and health science collections.' (*E-STREAMS*)

- **Medicinal plants of the world: chemical constituents, traditional and modern medicinal uses I.A. Ross** 2nd edn, Humana Press, 2003–2005. www.humanapress.com [DESCRIPTION]. Formerly in one volume, this major well reviewed text is now being published as three volumes.

4217 **Plants that fight cancer**
S.E. Kintzios and M.G. Barberaki, eds CRC Press, 2004, 296pp. $149.95. ISBN 0415298539.
Provides a modern review of plant species and genera with anticancer properties; Discusses conventional, advanced, and alternative treatments; Presents extensive, detailed information on more than 150 terrestrial plant genera and species; Includes numerous photographs, illustrations, and tables; Features extensive references and chemical structure and species indices.

Handbooks & manuals

4218 **Clinician's complete reference to complementary and alternative medicine**
D.W. Novey Mosby, 2000, 855pp. $53.95. ISBN 0323007554.
Each therapy includes a description/definition of treatment, its origins and history, biologic mechanism of action, and the therapy's practical application.

4219 **CRC handbook of medicinal spices**
J.A. Duke CRC Press, 2002, 360pp. $129.95. ISBN 0849312795.
Organized by scientific name provides the science behind the folklore of over 60 popular spices. Includes market and import data, culinary uses, ecology and cultural information, and discusses at length the use of spices as antiseptics and antioxidants.

4220 **Encyclopedic reference of traditional Chinese medicine**
X. Yang [et al.] Springer, 2003, 660pp. £38.50. ISBN 3540428461.
5000 terms with concise annotations and some colour pictures, running A–Z from abalone ('It is the meat of Haliotis Diversicolor Reeve or H. Gigantea Reeve (Haliotida)') to Zuxin (Ex-LE) ('An extra acupuncture point') and including, for instance, chickenpox, five emotions (joy, anger, anxiety, melancholy, fear), green tangerine orange peel, migraine, toad venom on the way.

Keeping up-to-date

4221 **Focus on Alternative and Complementary Therapies (FACT): An evidence-based approach**
Pharmaceutical Press, 1996–, Quarterly. £165.00. ISSN 14653753.
www.pharmpress.com [DESCRIPTION]
Review journal that aims to present the evidence on complementary and alternative medicine in an analytical and impartial manner.

Environmental & Occupational Health

accident prevention • aerospace medicine • burns • chemical hazards • chemical safety • environmental health • fire safety • hazardous chemicals • hazardous materials • health and safety • industrial hygiene • laboratory safety • material safety data • occupational dermatology • occupational health • occupational safety • poisons • radiological protection • safety at work • safety engineering • stress • toxic substances • toxicology • work-related illnesses

Introductions to the subject

Environmental, safety, and health engineering
G. Woodside and D.S. Kocurek See entry no. 5532

Introduction to weapons of mass destruction: radiological, chemical and biological
R.E. Langford See entry no. 4411

4222 **Life support: the environment and human health**
M. McCally, ed. MIT Press, 2002, 312pp. $22.00. ISBN 0262134144.
Sequel to a 1993 volume 'Critical condition' with three major underlying themes: that the habitat is an important determinant of human health, that prevention of human illness must involve protection of the environment, and that well informed physicians can and should communicate with the public and policymakers about environmental hazards. 'presents the evidence that humans, through our own actions, now threaten the global environment that we all need to survive.' (*Journal of the American Medical Association*)

4223 **Occupational health and safety management: a practical approach**
C.D. Reese Lewis, 2003, 532pp. $89.95. ISBN 1566706203.
Developed 'to provide safety professionals, students, and employers with the basic tenets for the initiation of an occupational health and safety initiative for those responsible for safety and health and their companies'. Aims to provide a management blueprint for occupational safety and health applicable for the smallest to the largest sized companies who see the need for improvements in this area.
US-based. Appendices include: 50 most cited violations by major industrial groups; the most common air pollutants and toxic chemicals; occupational safety and health resources. A very useful overview.

4224 **A small dose of toxicology: the health effects of common chemicals**
S.G. Gilbert CRC Press, 2004, 266pp. $35.95. ISBN 0415311683.
Good introduction: 'Exploring current toxicology concerns within a human context, this text discusses how toxicology affects our everyday lives while providing insight into the broader issues of public health and disease prevention. Environmental and public health professionals, as well as novices and students requiring a basic foundation in toxicology will find this resource incredibly useful.'

4225 **Theoretical basis of occupational therapy**
M.A. McColl [et al.] 2nd edn, Slack Incorporated, 2002, 195pp. $37.95. ISBN 1556425406.
www.slackbooks.com
Discussed the uses and applications of occupational therapy theory. Includes a substantial annotated bibliography.
See website for details of the publisher's list in: occupational and physical therapy; ophthalmology, and other eye-care professions; athletic training; nursing; gastroenterology; and other diverse fields of health care.

Toxic plants dangerous to humans and animals (Plantes toxiques pour l'homme et les animaux)
J. Bruneton See entry no. 2188

Dictionaries, thesauri, classifications

4226 **Australian occupational health and safety thesaurus**
National Occupational Health & Safety Commission 3rd edn, 2003, 236pp.
www.nohsc.gov.au/OHSInformation/LibraryServices/AOHST_e3.pdf
Developed by NOHSC for use by any Australian organization or individual with an interest in occupational health and safety. Covers: accidents and emergencies; education and training; hazards; health and safety management; occupational medicine; toxicology; workplace and industrial organization. Includes a list of changes between the 2nd and 3rd editions.

Concise dictionary of environmental terms
L. Theodore, J. Reynolds and K. Morris, comps See entry no. 5536

4227 **Dictionary of environmentally important chemicals**
D.C. Ayres and D. Heller Fitzroy Dearborn, 1999, 332pp. $55.00. ISBN 1579582060.
List of chemicals selected on whether they were listed by three of the following five regulatory agencies: the American Conference of Governmental Industrial Hygienists, the European Community Directive of Dangerous Substances, the German Commission for Investigation of Health Hazards of Chemicals in the Work Area, the International Agency for Research on Cancer, and the United States Environmental Protection Agency.

4228 **Health and safety at work: key terms** [UK]
J. Stranks Butterworth-Heinemann, 2002, 206pp. £19.99. ISBN 0750654465.
A–Z format, incorporating the principal legal, technical and practical terms derived from statutes, regulations, approved codes, case law and other appropriate publications.

4229 **Illustrated dictionary and resource directory of environmental and occupational health**
H. Koren 2nd edn, CRC Press, 2004, 712pp. $149.95. ISBN 1566705908.
More than 16,000 terms, supplemented with hundreds of additional synonyms, acronyms, and abbreviations; over 1000 illustrations; resources such as government agencies, professional and industrial organizations, and abstract services. 2nd edn includes over 8500 new terms.

4230 **Quick reference dictionary for occupational therapy**
K. Jacobs and L. Jacobs 4th edn, Slack Incorporated, 2004, 589pp. $26.95. ISBN 1556426569.
www.slackbooks.com
3600 terms defined with 60 appendices.

Laws, standards, codes

4231 **Chemical Hazards Communication Society** [UK]
www.chcs.org.uk
'Aims to provide information and training guidance to as many individuals as possible, regardless of whether they work in small or large companies, for associations or for government, involved with the ever increasing complexity of chemical hazards regulations and international codes.'

4232 **Government Institutes** [USA]
Scarecrow Press.
www.govinstpress.com
Since Spring 2004 part of the Rowman & Littlefield Publishing Group and continuing to focus on environmental and occupational health and safety law and related matters – with the former training activities remaining with ABS

Consulting. Produce the popular 'Occupational safety and health law handbook'.

4233 **International Commission on Radiological Protection**
www.icrp.org/index.asp
Independent Registered Charity, established to advance for the public benefit the science of radiological protection, in particular by providing recommendations and guidance on all aspects of protection against ionizing radiation. Educational area has downloadable PDF material aimed at promoting knowledge about radiological protection, initially focused primarily on radiation as used in medicine.

4234 **National Radiological Protection Board** [UK]
www.hpa.org.uk/radiation
Government agency created by the *Radiological Protection Act 1970*. It works to advance the acquisition of knowledge about the protection of mankind from radiation hazards, and to provide information and advice to persons (including Government Departments) with responsibilities in the UK in relation to the protection from radiation hazards – either of the community as a whole or of particular sections of the community.

Good sets of resources under the headings: Understanding radiation; Radiation topics.

On 1 April 2005 the National Radiological Protection Board merged with the Health Protection Agency forming its new Radiation Protection Division.

Sanitary and Phytosanitary Measures
World Trade Organization See entry no. 2932

4235 **Tolley's health and safety at work handbook 2005** [UK]
17th edn, LexisNexis UK, 2004. £74.95. ISBN 0754527530.
Standard annually produced volume in A–Z format covering key aspects of health and safety law and practice, as well as related environmental and employment information.

WebInsight
See entry no. 1768

Official & quasi-official bodies

4236 **Agency for Toxic Substances and Disease Registry** [USA]
www.atsdr.cdc.gov
An agency of the US Department of Health and Human Services that serves the public by using the best science, taking responsive public health actions, and providing trusted health information to prevent harmful exposures and disease related to toxic substances.

- **Managing hazardous materials incidents: medical management guidelines for acute chemical exposures** 2000, 57pp. www.atsdr.cdc.gov/mhmi-v3-p.pdf. Excellent downloadable PDF volume produced by the Agency.
- **National Toxicology Program** **United States. Department of Health and Human Services.** http://ntp-server.niehs.nih.gov. Interagency program whose mission is 'to evaluate agents of public health concern by developing and applying tools of modern toxicology and molecular biology'. 80,000 chemicals are registered for use in the USA, with an estimated 2000 new ones each year.

Biosafety Clearing-House
See entry no. 5016

4237 **Canadian Centre for Occupational Health and Safety**
www.ccohs.ca
Excellent detailed and comprehensive but very well designed home page. Amongst a wealth of resources includes access to the Web Information Service: portal providing one-step – generally fee-based – searching of all CCOHS database collections plus a growing number of third party datasets.

- **IPCS INCHEM: Environmental Health Criteria Monographs** www.inchem.org/pages/about.html. Co-operation between CCOHS and WHO International Programme on Chemical Safety (www.who.int/ipcs) consolidating current, internationally peer-reviewed chemical safety-related publications and database records from international bodies for public access.

Centers for Disease Control and Prevention
See entry no. 4416

Council on Environmental Quality
See entry no. 2310

Environment Directorate-General
European Commission. Directorate for Environment See entry no. 2119

Environmental Protection Agency
See entry no. 5555

4238 **Health & Safety Commission** [UK]
www.hse.gov.uk
The Commission is a body of up to ten people representing stakeholder interests in the UK; the Health and Safety Executive is a body of three people who advise and assist the Commission in its functions. The Executive's staff, approximately 400, include inspectors, policy advisers, technologists and scientific and medical experts – collectively known as the HSE. The two bodies are responsible for all work-related health and safety matters in the UK.

Wide-ranging website. Perhaps best to start with the Site map; but there is also an A–Z Index and a weekly What's new on the website.

- **HSE Science & Research Outlook** www.hse-scienceoutlook.com [REGISTRATION]. Quarterly newsletter plus interim news items in the website.

Health Protection Agency
See entry no. 4419

4239 **InFocus Programme on Safety and Health at Work and the Environment**
International Labour Organization
www.ilo.org/public/english/protection/safework
Well laid out inviting portal which readily leads also to other ILO work in this arena. Includes access to the *Encyclopaedia of occupational health and safety*.

- **International Occupational Safety and Health Information Centre** www.ilo.org/public/english/protection/safework/cis/index.htm. The 'knowledge management' arm of the InFocus Programme. Its goal is to ensure that workers and everyone concerned with their protection have access to the facts they need to prevent occupational injuries and diseases.

4240 International Commission on Occupational Health
www.icoh.org.sg
An international non-governmental professional society, founded in 1906, whose aims are to foster the scientific progress, knowledge and development of occupational health and safety in all its aspects. It is 'the world's leading international scientific society in the field of occupational health with a membership of 2000 professionals from 93 countries. The ICOH is recognized by the United Nations as a non-governmental organization.'

Mine Safety and Health Administration
See entry no. 4669

4241 National Center for Environmental Health [USA]
www.cdc.gov/nceh
Provides national leadership, through science and service, that promotes health and quality of life by preventing or controlling those diseases, birth defects, disabilities, or deaths that result from interactions between people and their environment.

Excellent entrée to the area, with an extensive list of Environmental Health Topics: e.g. Air pollution and respiratory health; Biomonitoring at-a-glance; Cancer clusters; Demilitarization of chemical weapons; Earthquakes; and so on. Very useful section: Emergency Preparedness Links.

Nuclear Energy Agency
See entry no. 4724

4242 Occupational Safety and Health Administration [USA]
www.osha.gov
Within the US Department of Labor, OSHA's mission is 'to assure the safety and health of America's workers by setting and enforcing standards; providing training, outreach, and education; establishing partnerships; and encouraging continual improvement in workplace safety and health'.

Well developed site including a MyOSHA facility: Choose content to personalize your own OSHA page; Arrange how content is laid out; Change your colour scheme; Choose from a list of pre-selected links to customize your page; Add any page within the OSHA website (except PDFs) to your own MyFavorites category.

- **The Safety Link** A.E. Michael, comp. Product Safety International. www.safetylink.com. Remarkable frequently checked very extensive list of links to Product Safety Resources (especially strong on standards organizations), Safety articles and other documents, and a wide range of other related resources.
- **SafetyInfo** www.safetyinfo.com. 'America's largest online OSHA COMPLIANCE Safety Library. Over 6000 printable/editable safety pages with essential safety information, and legal safety regulations. Online OSHA based Safety Library with safety tips and programs'.

4243 Office of Hazardous Materials Safety [USA]
Office of Hazardous Materials Safety
http://hazmat.dot.gov
An Office within the US Department of Transportation which 'formulates, issues and revises Hazardous Materials Regulations (HMR) under the Federal Hazardous Materials Transportation Law. The HMR cover hazardous materials definitions and classifications, hazard communications, shipper and carrier operations, training and security requirements, and packaging and container specifications'.

Office of Water
See entry no. 1131

Pesticides Safety Directorate
See entry no. 3323

United Kingdom Atomic Energy Authority
See entry no. 4726

4244 US Chemical Safety and Hazard Investigation Board [USA]
www.csb.gov
'The CSB is not a regulatory agency like the Occupational Safety and Health Administration or the Environmental Protection Agency. Indeed, the Congress designed the CSB to be independent of those agencies so that its investigations might, where appropriate, review the effectiveness of regulations and regulatory enforcement.'

4245 US Fire Administration
www.usfa.fema.gov
A rich well organized website 'working for a fire-safe America'.

- **Evaluation of fire safety** D. Rasbash [et al.] Wiley, 2004, 479pp. $175.00. ISBN 0471493821. 17 chapters in three parts: I. Structure of the fire problem; II. Quantifying fire safety (including 'Sources of statistical data'); III. Methods of measuring fire safety.

US Nuclear Regulatory Commission
See entry no. 4727

Research centres & institutes

Building and Fire Research Laboratory
See entry no. 5318

Center for Devices and Radiological Health
See entry no. 3644

4246 European Chemicals Bureau
http://ecb.jrc.it
Established by the European Commission in 1993 within the Joint Research Centre at Ispra, Italy. It provides scientific and technical support for developing and implementing European Union chemicals policies with the EC's Directorates for Enterprise and Industry, and Environment, by classifying, labelling and evaluating the risks of chemicals to humans and the environment.

Rather difficult site to navigate; but provides access to wide range and depth of resources.

The Commission is currently establishing a new European Chemicals Agency within Helsinki, Finland, under its REACH policy for chemicals: 'Registration, Evaluation, Authorization and Restriction of Chemicals'.

- **European chemical Substances Information System: ESIS** http://ecb.jrc.it/esis/esis. Compendium based on various European official chemicals inventories.

International Agency for Research on Cancer
See entry no. 4027

4247 National Institute for Occupational Safety and Health [USA]
www.cdc.gov/niosh
The US federal agency responsible for conducting research and making recommendations for the prevention of work-related injury and illness. Very well organized website, major headings, for instance, within its section Workplace Safety and Health Topics being: Chemical safety; Emergency response resources; Respirators; Traumatic injuries; Musculoskeletal disorders; Health care workers; Agriculture; Construction; Noise and hearing loss; Mining safety and health research.

- **NIOSH Manual of Analytical Methods** www.cdc.gov/niosh/nmam. Collection of methods for sampling and analysis of contaminants in workplace air, and in the blood and urine of workers who are occupationally exposed.

4248 National Institute of Environmental Health Sciences [USA]
www.niehs.nih.gov
'Human health and human disease result from three interactive elements: environmental factors, individual susceptibility and age. The mission of the National Institute of Environmental Health Sciences (NIEHS) is to reduce the burden of human illness and dysfunction from environmental causes by understanding each of these elements and how they interrelate. The NIEHS achieves its mission through multidisciplinary biomedical research programs, prevention and intervention efforts, and communication strategies that encompass training, education, technology transfer, and community outreach.'

- **Environmental Health Perspectives** Monthly. $414.00. ISSN 00916765. http://ehp.niehs.nih.gov. Peer-reviewed forum for the examination, discussion, and dissemination of news, scientific research, and ideas relating to issues and advances in environmental health. Content freely accessible online; print package includes special reports.

Poisonous Plant Research Laboratory
See entry no. 3075

Associations & societies

4249 Aerospace Medical Association [USA]
www.asma.org
'The largest most-representative professional organization in the fields of aviation, space, and environmental medicine.'

- **Fundamentals of aerospace medicine** R.L. DeHart and J.R. David 3rd edn, Lippincott Williams & Wilkins, 2002, 702pp. $159.00. ISBN 0781728983. Addresses all medical and public health issues involved in the care of crews, passengers, and support personnel.

4250 American Burn Association
www.ameriburn.org
Promotes and supports burn-related research, education, care, rehabilitation, and prevention. The ABA has more than 3500 members in the United States, Canada, Europe, Asia, and Latin America. Members include physicians, nurses, occupational and physical therapists, researchers, social workers, firefighters, and hospitals with burn centres.

4251 American College of Occupational and Environmental Medicine
www.acoem.org
Founded in 1916, ACOEM is 'the nation's largest medical society dedicated to promoting the health of workers through preventive medicine, clinical care, research, and education'. It represents more than 6000 physicians and other health care professionals. Range of useful resources, including a Recommended Library: 'A selection of suggested texts focusing on the field of occupational medicine and its major subdisciplines. The listings are divided into categories by subject, including a basic core section that identifies texts essential for the general practice of occupational and environmental medicine.'

- **A practical approach to occupational and environmental medicine** R.J. McCunney [et al.], eds 3rd edn, Lippincott Williams & Wilkins, 2003, 952pp. $79.95. ISBN 0781736749. Guide to diagnosis, treatment, and prevention of occupationally related disorders. Sponsored by the College.

American Council on Science and Health
See entry no. 4156

4252 American Occupational Therapy Association
www.aota.org
'The nationally recognized professional association of approximately 35,000 occupational therapists, occupational therapy assistants, and students of occupational therapy ... Therapy interventions occur in a wide range of settings including schools, hospitals, skilled nursing facilities, home health, outpatient rehabilitation clinics, psychiatric facilities, and community health programs.'

American Public Health Association
See entry no. 4423

4253 American Society of Safety Engineers
www.asse.org
'Founded in 1911, ASSE is the oldest and largest professional safety organization. Its more than 30,000 members manage, supervise and consult on safety, health, and environmental issues in industry, insurance, government and education.'

4254 British Safety Council
www.britishsafetycouncil.co.uk
The largest independent specialist occupational health and safety organization in Europe with around 10,000 member organizations.

4255 Chartered Institute of Environmental Health [UK]
www.cieh.org
Founded in 1883, an independent professional body and registered charity representing those who work in environmental health and related disciplines, whose primary function is to promote knowledge and understanding of environmental health issues.

- **Environmental Health Journal** www.ehj-online.com. The Institute's professional monthly magazine. Excellent survey of its current activities and of relevant developments in the UK and abroad. Good archival section.

Council for Accreditation in Occupational Hearing Conservation
See entry no. 5570

Flight Safety Foundation
See entry no. 4908

4256 Global Environmental Management Initiative
www.gemi.org
'Organization of leading companies dedicated to fostering global environmental, health and safety (EHS) excellence through the sharing of tools and information to help business achieve EHS excellence.'

4257 Institute of Occupational Safety and Health [UK]
www.iosh.co.uk
'Europe's leading body for health and safety professionals, represents 27,000 members in over 50 countries.'

4258 International Radiation Protection Association
www.irpa.net
Extensive website providing a good introduction to international and national activities in this arena.
- Online, Science Direct.

4259 National Environmental Health Association [USA]
www.neha.org
Incorporated in 1937 as a national professional society for environmental health practitioners. Now has 5000 members. Good news section; publications.

4260 National Safety Council [USA]
www.nsc.org
Vision is to be 'the recognized leader in providing safety and health solutions for reducing unintentional deaths and disabling injuries. The NSC will provide safety and health solutions to members, their employees and their families at home, at work, in communities, and in transportation'.
- **Fundamentals of industrial hygiene** B.A. Plog and P.J. Quinlan, eds 5th edn, National Safety Council Press, 2002, 1100pp. $150.95. ISBN 0879122161. www.nsc.org/public/catalog/nscCatalog.pdf [DESCRIPTION]. One of a wide range of publications produced by the Council: see website.

National Society for Clean Air and Environmental Protection
See entry no. 5571

4261 Professional Organisations in Occupational Health and Safety [UK]
www.poosh.org
Umbrella organization currently representing 14 organizations.

4262 Royal Society for the Prevention of Accidents [UK]
www.rospa.com
'A registered charity which was established over 80 years ago. Providing information, advice, resources and training, RoSPA is actively involved in the promotion of safety in all areas of life – at work, in the home, and on the roads, in schools, at leisure and on (or near) water. RoSPA aims to campaign for change, influence opinion, contribute to debate, educate and inform – for the good of all.'

4263 Society for Radiological Protection [UK]
www.srp-uk.org
Founded 1963; now has over 1100 members. Extensive and wide-ranging set of very useful documents accessible under Services: e.g. Bibliography of radiation protection legislation and standards; FAQs; Glossary of terms used in radiological protection; New legislation; Radioactive waste. Also a very good Links section: 'The SRP links to national and international organizations which work in the field of radiological protection, and to other pages with relevant content. In addition, where possible, the Society provides links to the sites of its Affiliate Members and Partner Societies. We will consider adding other links if formally approached. The SRP does not normally link to commercial organizations except those who are its Affiliate Members.'

Portal & task environments

4264 AirNow: Quality of Air Means Quality of Life [USA]
Environmental Protection Agency
www.epa.gov/airnow
Good cross-agency site, hosted by the EPA, but involving an extensive roster of US state and local, US tribal, US federal, international, and media (USA Today; The Weather Channel) partners.
- **Air quality compliance and permitting manual** R. Trzupek McGraw-Hill, 2003, 671pp. $125.00. ISBN 0071373349. Guide to applying for and staying compliant with US air quality regulations. Good sets of diagrams and tables. The Appendices – occupying over half the volume – reproduce the relevant regulations and guidance statements. Brief index.

Carbon Dioxide Information Analysis Center
See entry no. 4641

4265 Croner-i: Health, Safety & Environment [UK]
WoltersKluwer UK.
www.croner.co.uk [FEE-BASED]
Facts, news, advice, etc. on UK develpments.

4266 EnvironmentalChemistry.com
KLBProductions.com.
www.environmentalchemistry.com
'This site provides chemistry, environmental and hazardous materials educational resources including: a detailed periodic table of elements; chemical database; hazmat emergency response guides; hazmat placarding information; articles on environmental, hazardous materials and chemistry issues; and much more. At last count there were over 20,000 pages on this site that should keep you coming back for more.'

4267 European Agency for Safety and Health at Work
http://europe.osha.eu.int
Gateway set up by the European Union and providing access to a network of more than 30 occupational safety and health websites providing up-to-date and quality-assured information on safety and health issues from around Europe, with links also to key bodies outside of Europe.
- **Institute of Occupational Medicine** www.iom-world.org/index.html. 'The premier independent UK centre for research, consultancy and training in occupational and environmental health, hygiene and safety.' National Network Member of the Agency's UK Focal Point as well as a WHO Collaborating Centre for Occupational Health.

Fire on the Web
Building and Fire Research Laboratory See entry no. 5332

4268 Health and Safety [UK]
Trades Union Congress
www.tuc.org.uk/h_and_s/index.cfm
The UK trades unions' portal to their considerable health and safety involvements. Well laid out site with good list of topics to explore.

Health and Safety in the Agriculture Industry
Health and Safety Executive See entry no. 3011

4269 **Health, Environment and Work**
R. Agius
www.agius.com/hew/links/index.htm
Excellent wide-ranging portal. The author is Professor of Occupational and Environmental Medicine at the University of Manchester (though the site itself is self-funded). Subscribes to the HONCode principles.

4270 **MSDSonline** [USA]
www.msdsonline.com
'We develop unique Web-enabled services, which make it easier to access, manage and deploy material safety data sheets (MSDS). Our mission is to help you create a safer work environment, save you time, lower your costs, and reduce your risk/liability associated with meeting compliance standards set by OSHA, EPA, DOT, WHIMIS and the Joint Commission (JCAHO) as well as other health and safety regulatory organizations ... What makes us different is the fact that we add more than 10,000 new or updated documents to our database each week ...'

- **Where to find material safety data sheets on the internet R. Toreki** Interactive Learning Paradigms Inc. www.ilpi.com/msds. Excellent gateway – including to 100 free MSDS sites. Maintenance of the gateway is supported by Kelleher, Helmrich and Associates, Inc. who produce the Online-MSDS data sheet management software.

National Ag Safety Database: NASD
National Institute for Occupational Safety and Health and United States. Department of Agriculture See entry no. 3014

Offshore Engineering Information Service: OEIS
Heriot-Watt University See entry no. 4760

4271 **OSH WORLD**
Sheila Pantry Associates Ltd.
www.sheilapantry.com/oshworld
Relatively new, but clearly laid-out and useful gateway to a range of occupational safety and health resources. Some of the information was previously found in *Health and Safety World*, which Sheila Pantry edited for five and a half years.

Prevention, Pesticides, and Toxic Substances
Environmental Protection Agency See entry no. 3335

Discovering print & electronic resources

4272 **Chemical Information System**
NISC.
www.nisc.com/Frame/NISC_products-f.htm
34 databases brought together for online access, including from: Environmental Protection Agency, National Institute for Occupational Safety and Health, National Cancer Institute, National Institutes of Health, National Library of Medicine.

4273 **Chemical Safety NewsBase**
Royal Society of Chemistry
www.rsc.org/is/database/csnbhome.htm [DESCRIPTION]
Provides information on the hazardous effects of chemicals and processes encountered in industry and laboratories. Only covers well known hazards and commercial drugs when new information on these has been disclosed. Records contain abstracts and separately indexed chemicals with CAS Registry numbers where available.
Available online: see website.

Environment Abstracts
See entry no. 5581

EXTOXNET: the EXtension TOXicology NETwork
Oregon State University and University of California, Davis See entry no. 3336

4274 **RDN Virtual Training Suite: Health and Safety** [UK]
J. Corlett; Nottingham Trent University and Resource Discovery Network
www.vts.rdn.ac.uk/tutorial/healthandsafety
Tutorial concentrating on health and safety resources within the work setting.

4275 **Science Inventory**
Environmental Protection Agency
http://cfpub.epa.gov/si
Searchable inventory of EPA science activities and scientific/technical work products. Early 2005, contained over 5600 records.

4276 **TOXICOLOGY Cluster**
STN International.
www.cas.org/ONLINE/CATALOG/CLUSTERS/toxicology.html
Combined online access to 52 databases covering toxicological-related data and information.

4277 **TOXNET**
Specialized Information Services
http://toxnet.nlm.nih.gov
Cluster of database maintained by the National Library of Medicine's SIS. Includes: HSDB (Hazardous Substance Data Bank); CCRIS (Chemical Carcinogenesis Research Information System); GENE-TOX (Genetic Toxicology); and IRIS (Integrated Risk Information System).

Toxic Release Information (TRI) provides access to the US Environment Protection Agency's TRI (Toxic Chemical Release Inventory); and Toxicology Literature Search provides access to DART (Development and Reproductive Toxicology), EMIC (Environmental Mutagen Information Center), and TOXLINE. All these datasets can be searched together.

Worth also noting here is the SIS's Toxicology and Environmental Health gateway: http://sis.nlm.nih.gov/Tox/ToxMain.html.

- **Hazardous Substances Data Bank** www.nlm.nih.gov/pubs/factsheets/hsdbfs.html [DESCRIPTION]. Data file within TOXNET which focuses on the toxicology of potentially hazardous chemicals, and accessible free of charge via that gateway.
- **Tox Town** http://toxtown.nlm.nih.gov/index_content.html. A most enjoyable 'introduction to toxic chemicals and environmental health risks you might encounter in everyday life, in everyday places'.

Digital data, image & text collections

4278 **CHEMLIST**
Chemical Abstracts Service
www.cas.org/CASFILES/chemlist.html
Access to chemical regulatory data drawn from 13 national

inventories plus US and international regulatory lists. Early 2005, contained details of more than 235,000 substances with more than 50 additions/changes being made each week to the data-set.

Directories & encyclopedias

4279 **The dictionary of substances and their effects: DOSE**
S Gangolli, ed.; Royal Society of Chemistry 2nd edn, 1999. 7 v., £1295.00. ISBN 0854048030.
www.knovel.com
DOSE brings together all relevant data for over 4100 chemicals, making it a vital reference for all health, safety and environmental officers, toxicologists and regulatory bodies. All the information in DOSE is fully referenced and is presented in concise, easy-to-read summaries. Data include physical properties, occupational exposure limits, mammalian and avian toxicity, genotoxicity, ecotoxicity, environmental fate, plus regulatory requirements including risk and safety phrases.
Available online: see website.

Encyclopedia of agrochemicals
J.R. Plimmer, D.W. Gammon and N.R. Ragsdale, eds See entry no. 5107

Encyclopedia of energy technology and the environment
A. Bisio and S. Boots, eds See entry no. 4653

4280 **Encyclopedia of stress**
G. Fink [et al.], eds Academic Press, 2000, 2448pp. 3 v, $640.00. ISBN 0122267354.
Almost 400 articles on stressors, the biological mechanisms involved in the stress response, the effects of activating the stress response mechanisms, and the disorders that may arise as a consequence of acute or chronic stress.
'A fantastic endeavour and a very clear idea that manages to combine an academically relevant topic with a socially relevant issue. A really good combination of topics with scientific excellence and social relevance ... It is well-written, by many of the world authorities, and accessible, sexy and nicely cross-referenced with related topics and indexing ... There is really nothing like this book.' (*British Medical Awards*)

4281 **The encyclopedia of work-related illnesses, injuries, and health issues**
A.P. Kahn Facts On File, 2003, 448pp. $75.00. ISBN 0816048444.
A complete reference to the relationship between individual health and the workplace and the rights of employees.
Series: Library of Health and Living.
' ... an excellent overview of a timely topic ... interesting and concise ... an excellent reference source.' (*Reference Reviews*)

Handbook of environmental data on organic chemicals.
K. Verschueren See entry no. 5602

International encyclopedia of ergonomics and human factors
W. Karwowski See entry no. 5391

Handbooks & manuals

Atmospheric pollution: history, science, and regulation
M.Z. Jacobson See entry no. 1240

Biological risk engineering handbook: infection control and decontamination
M.J. Boss and D.W. Day, eds See entry no. 4433

4282 **Bretherick's handbook of reactive chemical hazards: an indexed guide to published data**
P.G. Urben and M.J. Pitt, eds 6th edn, Butterworth-Heinemann, 1999, 2100pp. 2 v. Includes CD-ROM, £220.00. ISBN 075063605X.
www.ei.org/eicorp/refxtitles.pdf
V. 1. Introduction; Reactive chemical hazards; Elements and compounds arranged in formula order; V. 2. Classes, groups and topics. Source title abbreviations used in references; tabulated fire-related data; Glossary of abbreviations and technical terms; Indexes.
Available online: see website.

Chemical process safety: fundamentals with applications
D.A. Crowl and J.F. Louvar See entry no. 5122

4283 **Clarke's analysis of drugs and poisons: in pharmaceuticals, body fluids and postmortem material**
A.C. Moffat [et al.], eds 3rd edn, Pharmaceutical Press, 2004. 2 v., £350.00. ISBN 0853694737.
www.medicinescomplete.com
V. 1. Analytical toxicology; V. 2. 1737 drug and poison monographs. Definitive source of analytical data for drugs and poisons, completely revised and expanded since previous edition.
Available online: see website.

4284 **Clay's handbook of environmental health**
W.H. Bassett, ed. 19th edn, Spon, 2004, 944pp. £160.00. ISBN 0415318084.
www.sponpress.com/series/CLoHE.htm [COMPANION]
The classic handbook in this field for the UK.

4285 **Condensed handbook of occupational dermatology**
L Kanerva [et al.], eds Rev edn, Springer, 2004, 528pp. £75.00. ISBN 3540443487.
Comprehensive coverage of all common chemicals and materials likely to be encountered in the working environment.

4286 **CRC handbook of laboratory safety**
A.K. Furr 5th edn, CRC Press, 2000, 774pp. $189.95. ISBN 0849325234.
Includes coverage of: OSHA laboratory safety standards; Guidelines for X-ray use in hospitals; Enforcement of the standard for dealing with blood-borne pathogens, including the Ryan White Act; DOT regulations on the packaging of hazardous materials; EPA action on the release of radioactive materials into the environment; OSHA actions covering hazardous waste operations and emergency response; CDC guidelines for research with microbiological hazards.

4287 **Fitness for work: the medical aspects**
R. Cox, F.C. Edwards and K. Palmer; Royal College of Physicians 3rd edn, Oxford University Press, 2000, 618pp. £55.00. ISBN 0192630431.
Now well established UK-based text: 'the bible of occupational medicine'. A publication of the College's Faculty of Occupational Medicine.

Groundwater chemicals desk reference
J. H. Montgomery See entry no. 5616

Handbook of chemical health and safety
R.J. Alaimo, ed.; American Chemical Society See entry no. 1810

Handbook of clinical health psychology
American Psychological Association See entry no. 4121

4288 **Handbook of environmental data on organic chemicals**
K. Verschueren 4th edn, Wiley, 2001, 2391pp. 2 v., CD-ROM version available, $525.00. ISBN 0471374903.
Provides comprehensive, in-depth coverage of organic compounds, mixtures, and preparations along with the control measures designed to reduce their destructive impact on the ecosystem. Data is categorized into: properties, air pollution factors (e.g. odour), water and soil pollution factors, biodegradation, biological effects (e.g. bioaccumulation).

4289 **Handbook of environmental health**
H. Koren and M.S. Bisesi 4th edn, CRC Press, 2002, 1560pp. 2 v., $270.00. ISBN 1566705487.
A standard reference for over 20 years, which provides a basis for understanding the interactions between humans and the environment and how such interactions affect the health and welfare of individuals. V. I. Biological, chemical, and physical agents of environmentally related disease; V. II. Pollutant interactions in air, water, and soil.

Handbook of pesticide toxicology
R.I. Krieger, ed. See entry no. 3344

Handbook of residue analytical methods for agrochemicals
P.W. Lee, ed. See entry no. 3345

Handbook of toxicologic pathology
W.M. Haschek, C.G. Rousseaux and M.A. Wallig, eds See entry no. 3593

4290 **Hazardous chemicals desk reference**
R.J. Lewis Wiley-InterScience, 2002, 1728pp. $199.95. ISBN 0471441651.
Contains safety profiles, synonyms, physical properties, standards, and recommendations of government agencies for approximately 5000 chemicals deemed both important and potentially hazardous by the international scientific community. Substances were chosen on the basis of meeting a variety of criteria, including: Having a US Occupational Safety and Health Administration standard; Having an American Conference of Governmental Industrial Hygienists Threshold Limit Value; Listed by the International Agency for Research on Cancer.
'of all the books I have on chemicals (and I have many), it is Lewis' book I most often turn to for information.' (*Journal of Hazardous Materials*)

- **American Conference of Governmental Industrial Hygienists** www.acgih.org. Have developed Threshold Limit Values and Biological Exposure Indices: 'determinations made by a voluntary body of independent knowledgeable individuals ... (They) are not standards (but) are health-based values established by various committees.'

Hazardous laboratory chemicals disposal guide
M.A. Armour See entry no. 1818

4291 **Hunter's diseases of occupations**
P.J. Baxter [et al.], eds 9th edn, Arnold, 2000, 1001pp. £165.00. ISBN 0340677503.
A classic text that provides information on diseases caused by work, outlining the assessment and treatment of patients. Covers environmental diseases arising from industrial and agricultural activity.

Indoor pollution: a reference handbook
E.W. Miller and R.M. Miller See entry no. 5632

4292 **Occupational and environmental health nursing: concepts and practice**
B. Rogers 2nd edn, Saunders, 2003, 750pp. $69.95. ISBN 0721685110.
'The only textbook on this topic ... Provides a comprehensive framework for occupational and environmental health nursing practice. The text presents an overview of the specialty and explores the knowledge, skills, and abilities that are needed to develop and manage occupational health services and programs. Issues that affect the health and safety of individuals in the work force are discussed, with an emphasis on contemporary strategies for improving and protecting the health of workers. Specific topics related to roles in occupational health, occupational health care, research, legal and ethical parameters, and health promotion are also presented.'
1st edn 1994.

4293 **Occupational toxicants**
Deutsche Forschungsgemeinschaft Wiley-VCH, 2004.
www.wiley-vch.de/books/info/dfg/index_en.html [DESCRIPTION]
The volumes of this series present about 400 indispensable toxicological evaluation documents on important occupational toxicants and carcinogens. They describe the toxicological database which determines the level of a MAK value (Maximum Concentrations at the Workplace).

4294 **Patty's industrial hygiene**
Wiley InterScience.
www3.interscience.wiley.com [DESCRIPTION]
'For over 50 years, Patty's has served as the standard reference for occupational health and toxicology professionals. Now in its 5th print edition, Patty's has been completely revised and updated. This landmark revision is now available online allowing you to access the information you need immediately in your library, office or lab. As with the latest print edition, this online edition has been logically organized into two discrete works – Patty's Industrial Hygiene and Patty's Toxicology.'

4295 **Patty's toxicology**
E. Bingham, B. Cohrssen and C.H. Powell, eds 5th edn, Wiley, 2001, 9008pp. 8 v. Also available as v. 9 is a cumulative index, $2395.00. ISBN 0471319430.
www.knovel.com
An important reference in the field of toxicology. Gives very detailed information on individual compounds. Provides CAS Registry numbers, RTECS numbers, physical and chemical properties, threshold limit values, permissible exposure limits, maximum workplace concentrations, and biological tolerance values for occupational exposures for compounds.
Available online: see website.

4296 **Physical and biological hazards of the workplace**
P.H. Wald and G.M. Stave, eds 2nd edn, Wiley-Interscience, 2002, 680pp. $165.00. ISBN 0471386472.
Multi-author text with very wide coverage, in two parts: Physical hazards (with chapters organized into three sections: Worker-material interfaces; The physical work environment; Energy and electromagnetic radiation); Biological hazards (e.g. Viruses; Envenomations; Prions; Wood dust).
1st edn Van Nostrand Reinhold, 1994.
'an ideal first reference text.' (*Journal of Occupational and Environmental Medicine*)

- **Biological hazards: an Oryx sourcebook J.R. Callahan** Oryx Press, 2002, 385pp. $65.00. ISBN 1573563854. 'Excellent and highly readable introduction to many aspects of the subject and extensive suggestions for further research ... covers a much broader range of topics within its scope than anything else I have seen.' *Reference & User Services Quarterly*.

Poisonous plants and fungi in Britain: animal and human poisoning
M.R. Cooper and A.W. Johnson; Guy's & St Thomas' Hospital Trust and Royal Botanic Gardens, Kew See entry no. 2261

4297 **Poisonous plants and fungi in Britain and Ireland**
E.A. Dauncey, ed.; Royal Botanic Gardens, Kew and Guy's & St Thomas' Hospital Trust Nightshade, 2000. CD-ROM, £39.95.
www.rbgkew.org.uk/data/poisplts.html [DESCRIPTION]
Question-based identification key with photographic images. Aimed at nurses or doctors treating a suspected poisoning case; parents, teachers or local authority workers wanting to provide a safe environment for children to play and learn in; or people who enjoy foraging food from the countryside and want to eat plants and fungi safely.

4298 **Principles of radiological health and safety**
J.E. Martin and C. Lee Wiley-InterScience, 2002, 624pp. $105.00. ISBN 0471254290.
Strong focus on the underlying physics leading to practical examples and policies.
'an excellent reference source on radiation protection theory, and provides a consolidated source of useful radiological data.' (*Health and Safety at Work*)

4299 **Russell, Hugo and Ayliffe's Principles and practice of disinfection, preservation and sterilization**
A.D. Russell [et al.], eds 4th edn, Blackwell Publishers, 2004, 678pp. £99.50. ISBN 1405101997.
Now established as a standard manual in the field.

4300 **Sax's dangerous properties of industrial materials**
R.J. Lewis, ed. 11th edn, Wiley, 2005, 4860pp. 3 v, $895.00. ISBN 0471701335.
Latest edn of classic comprehensive guide to hazard information on substances encountered in the workplace. Contains extensive data on approximately 26,000 substances, including 2000 new entries. Also includes Immediately Dangerous Life or Health (IDHL) levels for approximately 1000 chemicals. 'It is the only reference that combines, for so many substances, data on toxicological, fire, reactivity, explosive potential, and regulatory information.' (AMERICAN CONFERENCE OF GOVERNMENTAL INDUSTRIAL HYGIENISTS)

4301 **Sittig's handbook of toxic and hazardous chemicals and carcinogens**
R.P. Pohanish 4th edn, Noyes Publications, 2002, 2300pp. CD-ROM version available, $495.00. ISBN 081551459X.
www.williamandrew.com
Presents chemical, health and safety data for over 1500 chemicals in the plastics, pharmaceuticals/biotechnology, energy, cleaning solvents, agriculture and other industries.
See website for related texts from the same publisher.

- **International resources guide to hazardous chemicals S.A. Greene** Noyes Publications, 2002, 950pp. $205.00. ISBN 0815514751. Companion to Sittig: Manufacturers of Hazardous Chemicals; Chemical Industry organizations; Professional environmental health and industrial hygiene organizations; Federal agencies; Hot lines and useful websites.
- **Rapid guide to trade names and synonyms of environmentally regulated chemicals R.P. Pohanish** Wiley, 1998, 850pp. ISBN 0442025947. About 30,000 names and CAS registry numbers for hazardous chemicals regulated under US environmental laws. Cross-references to other data sources.
- **Wiley guide to chemical incompatibilities R.P. Pohanish and S.A. Greene** 2nd edn, Wiley-InterScience, 2003, 1278pp. £75.95. ISBN 0471238597. Covers 11,000 chemical compounds, 2000 more than in the 1st edn. Gives CAS registry nos. and glossary of general chemical terms.

Keeping up-to-date

Annual Review of Pharmacology and Toxicology
See entry no. 3752

Annual Review of Public Health
See entry no. 4439

4302 **Occupational and Environmental Medicine**
British Medical Association BMJ Publishing Group. (Price varies with size of educational institution), £412.00. ISSN 15260046.
http://oem.bmjjournals.com
International peer review journal.

4303 **Occupational Health** [UK]
Monthly. £87.00. ISSN 00297917.
www.ohmagazine.co.uk
Practitioner-oriented magazine offering practical advice, real-life professional dilemmas – and solutions, legal advice and a continuing professional development study programme.

Family & Personal Health

addictive drugs • consumer health • death • drugs of abuse • dying • family medicine • general practice • men's health • personal health • physical diagnosis • primary care • smoking • women's health

Introductions to the subject

4304 A textbook of general practice
A. Stephenson, ed. 2nd edn, Arnold, 2004, 321pp. £21.99. ISBN 0340810521.
Multi-author text; pleasant introduction; further reading at end of each chapter.

4305 Textbook of physical diagnosis: history and examination
M.H. Swartz 4th edn, Saunders, 2002, 826pp. Includes CD-ROM, $79.95. ISBN 1416024050.
Well established introductory manual which emphasises the 'old-fashioned doctor's approach'.

Laws, standards, codes

Legal and ethical issues in human reproduction
B. Steinbock, ed. See entry no. 4452

Official & quasi-official bodies

Centers for Disease Control and Prevention
See entry no. 4416

Health Development Agency
See entry no. 4418

4306 National Institute on Alcohol Abuse and Alcoholism
www.niaaa.nih.gov
Founded in 1971 to support and conduct biomedical and behavioural research on the causes, consequences, treatment, and prevention of alcoholism and alcohol-related problems. Provides leadership in the national effort to reduce the severe and often fatal consequences of these problems.

- **Drugs and alcohol** Reed Business Information, 2005. www.newscientist.com/channel/being-human. Special Report within the NEW SCIENTIST magazine: part of the 'Being Human' Channel.
- **Encyclopedia of drugs, alcohol & addictive behavior R. Carson-DeWitt** 2nd edn, Macmillan Reference USA, 2000, 1863pp. $499.00. ISBN 0028655419. www.gale.com/gvrl [FEE-BASED]. 4 volumes. Gale also a single volume *Drugs and controlled substances information for students*, with both works being available online through the *Gale Virtual Reference Library*: see website.

Research centres & institutes

Alan Guttmacher Institute
See entry no. 4455

National Center for Chronic Disease Prevention and Health Promotion
See entry no. 4421

Associations & societies

4307 Action on Smoking and Health
www.ash.org
The leading national antismoking and non-smokers' rights organization.

4308 American Academy of Family Physicians [USA]
www.aafp.org
A national, non-profit medical association with over 88,000 members. Extensive amount of information and web links. Special members-only areas. Online continuing medical education and course information. *American Family Physician* magazine online in full-text format. 'Family medicine is the medical specialty that provides continuing and comprehensive health care for the individual and family. It is the specialty in breadth which integrates the biological, clinical, and behavioral sciences. The scope of family medicine encompasses all ages, both sexes, each organ system, and every disease entity.'

- **FamilyDoctor.org** http://familydoctor.org. All of the information on this useful easy-to-use site 'has been written and reviewed by physicians and patient education professionals at the AAFP'. They subscribe to the HONCode principles.

American Public Health Association
See entry no. 4423

EngenderHealth
See entry no. 4459

Family Planning Association
See entry no. 4461

4309 Men's Health Forum [UK]
www.menshealthforum.org.uk
'News, info, events and discussion on all aspects of men's health policy.'

4310 Royal College of General Practitioners [UK]
www.rcgp.org.uk
'The word "College" is a little misleading because the RCGP doesn't have students or lectures in the normal sense of the word. Traditionally, medical organizations concerned with professional studies have been known as "colleges" – hence the use of the word. In practice, the Royal College of General Practitioners is a network of around 18,000 doctors who are committed to improving patient care, developing their own skills and developing general practice.'

A 'general practitioner' can be defined as 'a doctor based in the community who treats patients with minor or chronic illnesses and refers those with serious conditions to a hospital' (*Oxford Dictionary of Illness*). Wide-ranging very well laid out site. For its publications 'it now has the largest list with over 100 titles of any College or Academy of General Practice or Family Medicine in the world. All College publications are aimed at developing and promoting the interest of primary health care.' Good information and library services; also a research resources section. An excellent facility.

4311 Society for Women's Health Research [USA]
www.womenshealthresearch.org
'The nation's only non-profit organization whose mission is to improve the health of all women through research, education

and advocacy. The Society encourages the study of sex differences between women and men that affect the prevention, diagnosis and treatment of disease. The information provided on this site is designed to support, not replace, the relationship that exists between you and your doctor.'

Portal & task environments

Children First
Great Ormond Street Hospital for Children NHS Trust and National Health Service See entry no. 4084

Doctor Online
See entry no. 4330

KidsHealth
See entry no. 4086

4312 **Prodigy** [UK]
Great Britain. Department of Health
www.prodigy.nhs.uk
'PRODIGY guidance offers advice on the management of conditions and symptoms that are commonly seen in primary care. The guidance is advisory and has been developed to assist healthcare professionals, together with patients, make decisions about the management of the patient's health. It is intended to support discussion and shared decision-making, and is not a substitute for sound clinical judgment or seeking medical advice where appropriate. Should you require medical advice please contact your own general practice or NHS Direct.'

Discovering print & electronic resources

4313 **Consumer health information sourcebook**
A.M. Rees 7th edn, Greenwood Press, 2003, 325pp. $65.00. ISBN 1573565091.
Indexes more than 2000 popular and publicly available health information resources in both print and electronic formats.

Digital data, image & text collections

ChildStats.gov: Forum on child and family statistics
Federal Interagency Forum on Child and Family Statistics See entry no. 4183

Directories & encyclopedias

4314 **Encyclopedia of addictive drugs**
R.L. Miller Greenwood Press, 2002, 491pp. $75.00. ISBN 0313318077.
Describes more than 130 alphabetically arranged drugs of abuse, including both pharmaceutical and natural products.
'An outstanding example of the successful communication of complex and potentially controversial information ... [a]n eminently suitable book for public reference libraries. It could also be considered for college libraries, especially those catering for students in such subjects as social work, education and health studies, who are all likely to need basic information in this contentious area.' (*Reference Reviews*)

4315 **The encyclopedia of smoking and tobacco**
A.B. Hirschfelder Oryx Press, 1999, 480pp. $69.96. ISBN 1573562025.
Information relating to tobacco production, marketing, and consumption from the seventeenth century to the present. Includes essays on tobacco and health, union issues, product liability, and warning labels.

4316 **Encyclopedia of women's health issues**
K. Gay Oryx Press, 2002, 300pp. $78.95. ISBN 157356303X.
Provides information on 200-plus topics related to women's health problems and the social, political, economic, and ethical issues that affect their health decisions.

- **Encyclopedia of women's health S. Loue and M. Sajatovic, eds** Springer, 2004, 792pp. £158.00. ISBN 0306480735. 'This encyclopedia meets the need for a comprehensive, up-to-date reference work that incorporates social awareness with clinical knowledge. Summing Up: Highly recommended. All collections.' *Choice*.

Handbooks & manuals

4317 **Community/public health nursing: health for families and populations**
F.A. Maurer and C.M. Smith 3rd edn, Saunders, 2005, 848pp. $72.95. ISBN 0721603548.
http://evolve.elsevier.com [COMPANION]
33 chapters in eight units: The role and context of community/public health nursing practice; Core concepts for the practice of community/public health nursing; Family as client; Community as client; Tools foir practice; Contemporary problems in community/public health nursing; Support for special populations; Settings for community/public health nursing practice.

- **Community & public health nursing M. Stanhope and J. Lancaster** 6th edn, Mosby, 2004, 1129pp. $79.95. ISBN 0323022405. http://evolve.elsevier.com [COMPANION].

4318 **Handbook of death and dying**
C.D. Bryant, ed. SAGE Publications, 2003, 1088pp. 2 v., $350.00. ISBN 0761925147.
Major work with more than 100 contributors representing authoritative expertise in a diverse array of disciplines: Anthropology; Family studies; History; Law; Medicine; Mortuary science; Philosophy; Psychology; Social work; Sociology.
'Well researched with lengthy bibliographies ... The index is rich with See and See Also references ... Its multidisciplinary nature makes it an excellent addition to academic collections.' (*Library Journal*)

Handbook of family planning and reproductive healthcare
A. Glasier and A. Gebbie, eds See entry no. 4472

Maternal-newborn & child nursing: family-centered care
M.L. London [et al.] See entry no. 4018

4319 **Men's health**
R.S. Kirby [et al.], eds 2nd edn, Taylor & Francis, 2004, 522pp. Foreword by Anthony Clare, £55.00. ISBN 1841842583.
http://search.tandf.co.uk [DESCRIPTION]
'Men die younger than their female partners. When sick, they seek help later. Factors such as unemployment, marital and

family breakdown, the epidemic of AIDS and the changing roles of the sexes appear to significantly affect male health and life expectancy. Why, given the facts, is male health still so neglected? Despite the increasing profile of men's health as a specialization, few, if any, inroads have been made in terms of actually closing the gap between the sexes; hence the need for a second edition of Men's Health.'

A Martin Dunitz book. 1st edn Isis Medical Media, 1999.

'In summary, this is an indispensable book which every man has been waiting for.' (*Urology News*)

'Should be present in all men's health clinics as well as in all medical institutions, to be consulted by all physicians and more in particular by urologists interested in all aspects of quality of life in the ageing male' (*European Urology Today*)

4320 Oxford textbook of primary medical care
R. Jones [et al.], eds Oxford University Press, 2005, 1299pp. 2 v.; includes CD-ROM. Originally published as hardback, 2003, £99.00. ISBN 0198565801.

A splendid work. V. 1 *Principles and concepts* is a 'unique and exhaustive guide to the theory and principles underpinning primary care'; V. 2 *Clinical management* has more than 200 chapters that 'form a comprehensive clinical textbook on medical problems commonly seen in general practice worldwide. Here you will find detailed evidence-based guidance on diagnosis, investigation, and management.'

'Broad enough to establish a fundamental understanding of primary care, but detailed enough to use as a reference, the *Oxford Textbook of Primary Medical Care* is an impressive achievement and a useful tool for clinicians who practice primary care in today's environment. Its international and expert authorship ensures full coverage of the field from multiple disciplinary and cultural perspectives and reveals the global impact and importance of primary care for all nations. Highly recommended.' (*Dr James C. Martin, President, American Academy of Family Physicians*)

Pediatric nursing: caring for children
J.W. Ball and R.C. Bindler, ed. See entry no. 4090

Keeping up-to-date

4321 GP [UK]
Haymarket Medical, Weekly. £150.00. ISSN 02688417.

'The leading medical newspaper for 40,000 UK family doctors is read by around 70 per cent of GPs each week. GP is relied on to inform doctors about the latest medico-political and clinical news as well as helping them to run their practices on a day-to-day basis. With a strong campaigning element, GP is regarded as instrumental in bringing issues concerning doctors and the NHS as a whole to the forefront of the political agenda. In 2002 its website was launched at www.Gponline.com.'

4322 Journal of Family Practice [USA]
www.jfponline.com

'Now in its 29th year, JFP is published 12 times a year and, effective January 2003, will reach 86,000 MDs and Dos in family and general practice, as well as residents in family practice and educators and researchers within the family practice specialty.'

Hospitals & Other Health Facilities

blood banks • blood transfusions • first aid • health facilities • hospices • hospitals • intensive care • nursing homes • palliative care

Introductions to the subject

4323 ABC of resuscitation
M. Colquhoun, A.J. Handley and T.R. Evans; British Medical Association 5th edn, BMJ, 2004, 111pp. £19.95. ISBN 0727916696. www.bmjbookshop.com [DESCRIPTION]

Comprehensive coverage. 'The text is relevant for Europe, Australasia, South Africa, South America, Malaysia and the Middle East – especially Israel. Ireland is moving closer to the European position and away from the USA.'

4324 Mending bodies, saving souls: a history of hospitals
G.B. Risse Oxford University Press, 1999, 716pp. £24.99. ISBN 0195055233.

Thirteen chapters covering the whole spectrum from 'Pre-Christian healing places' to 'Towards the next milennium: hospitals as houses of technology'.

4325 Palliative care nursing: a guide to practice
M. O'Connor and S. Aranda, eds Radcliffe Medical, 2003, 388pp. £24.95. ISBN 1857758390.

Palliative care can be defined as 'specialized health care of dying people, aiming to maximize the quality of life and to assist families and carers during and after death'. Wide-ranging multi-author text; clearly laid out; detailed index. Very good introductory overview.

Official & quasi-official bodies

Emergency Management Australia
See entry no. 4417

Associations & societies

4326 American Association of Blood Banks [USA]
www.aabb.org

'International association of blood banks; hospital and community blood centers; and transfusion and transplantation services. Individual members include health-care professionals in blood banking, transfusion medicine and cellular therapy.' Extensive overview All About Blood. Publications, news, etc.

American Burn Association
See entry no. 4250

4327 American College of Emergency Physicians
www.acep.org/webportal

Exists 'to support quality emergency medical care, and to promote the interests of emergency physicians'.

4328 **American Hospital Association**
www.aha.org/aha/index.jsp
Originating in 1899 this is a national organization that represents and serves all types of hospitals, health care networks, and their patients and communities. It has about 5000 hospitals, health care systems, networks, other providers of care and 37,000 individual members.

Extensive Resource Center covering for instance: Fast facts; Statistics and studies; Ethical conduct for healthcare institutions. Also access to a good annotated list of Consumer Links. Major publishing operation, including, for example, the *AHA Guide* 'The leading directory of hospitals and health care systems'.

- **American Hospital Directory** www.ahd.com. Data for over 6000 US hospitals 'built from Medicare claims data (MedPAR and OPPS), hospital cost reports, and other public use files obtained from the federal Centers for Medicare and Medicaid Services'. Free summary data 'as a public service'.

4329 **National Hospice and Palliative Care Organization** [USA]
www.nhpco.org
'The largest non-profit membership organization representing hospice and palliative care programs and professionals in the United States. The organization is committed to improving end of life care and expanding access to hospice care.' Good entrée to this arena; includes annotated set of links: End-of-Life Care Resources.

Portal & task environments

CINAHL Information Systems: Leaders in delivering current and comprehensive health care information
See entry no. 4355

4330 **Doctor Online** [UK]
www.doctoronline.nhs.uk
'Your typical patient forgets half of what you tell them within five minutes and remembers only four points you make ... Our evidence-based, printable Patient Information Leaflets help keep patients informed of what they need, and want to know. These are revised by 154 clinical editors including 67 professors on a regular cycle.' Much else on this useful portal.

4331 **HospitalManagement.net**
International Hospital Federation
www.hospitalmanagement.net/ihf
The official website for the IHF: 'With membership encompassing over one hundred countries, we are recognized as the leading international centre for the cross-fertilization of ideas in health care policy, finance and management. We maintain an official relationship with the World Health Organization and close links with the World Medical Association and the International Council of Nurses. Our members range from architects to nursing administrators and government health planners – all of those involved in the health care industry recognize that we are the association to be involved with.'

NMAP
Royal College of Nursing, University of Sheffield and Resource Discovery Network See entry no. 4358

Discovering print & electronic resources

Best BETS: Best Evidence Topics
Manchester Royal Infirmary See entry no. 3793

Directories & encyclopedias

Anaesthesia and intensive care A–Z: an encyclopaedia of principles and practice
S.M. Yentis, N.P. Hirsch and G.B. Smith See entry no. 3554

4332 **The Care Directory** [UK]
www.nursing-home-directory.co.uk
Guide to care homes, nursing homes (care homes with nursing) and care agencies throughout England, Scotland, Wales and Northern Ireland.

Handbooks & manuals

4333 **Clinical information systems: a component-based approach**
R. van de Velde and P. Degoulet Springer, 2004, 294pp. £54.00. ISBN 0387955380.
Distinguishes hospital information systems (HISs) within broader community health information systems (CHIs) or networks (CHINs) and focuses on clinical information systems (CISs) 'considered as the subset of CHISs that are devoted to the direct management of the patient'. Good overview ending with examples of four real-life systems. Glossary.
Series: Health Informatics.

4334 **Emergency medicine: a comprehensive study guide**
J.E. Tintinalli [et al.], ed. 6th edn, McGraw-Hill, 2004, 2043pp. $175.00. ISBN 0071388753.
http://books.mcgraw-hill.com [DESCRIPTION]
Major treatise endorsed by the *American College of Emergency Physicians* [q.v.]; available in several versions.
'considered by most in the discipline to be a bible of emergency medicine.' (*Journal of Family Medicine*)

- **Clinical procedures in emergency medicine J.R. Roberts and J.R. Hedges, eds** 4th edn, Saunders, 2004, 1486pp. $165.00. ISBN 0721697607. 'If I am asked what is the best text on how to do procedures, there is only one answer, Roberts and Hedges. There are now four associate editors and 106 contributors, the list of whom is a whos who of Emergency Medicine.' *Journal of Emergency Medicine*.

4335 **First aid manual: the authorized manual of St John Ambulance, St Andrew's Ambulance Association, and the British Red Cross**
T. Lee [et al.], eds Dorling Kindersley, 2002, 288pp. £11.99. ISBN 0751337048.
Very useful manual; but no bibliography nor further resources.

4336 **Oh's intensive care manual**
A.D. Bersten and N. Soni, eds Butterworth-Heinemann, 2003, 1175pp. £51.99. ISBN 0750651849.
Excellent clearly laid-out work. Covers the full range of conditions and disorders, with the latest edn offering 13 new chapters: Ethics in intensive care; Common problems after ICU; Clinical information systems; Imaging the chest; Non-

invasive ventilation; Abdominal surgical problems; Pre-existing disease in pregnancy; Tropical diseases; Blast injury, gun shot wounds & stabbing; Biological warfare; Vasopressors & inotopes; Vasodilators; Paediatric cardiopulmonary resuscitation.

4337 **Oxford textbook of palliative medicine**
D. Doyle [et al.], eds 3rd edn, Oxford University Press, 2004, 1244pp. £150.00. ISBN 0198510985.
Established as the definitive book on the subject and is used in more than 8000 services in over 100 countries. Gives comprehensive coverage of all areas concerned with palliative care – 'care for the terminally ill and their families, especially that provided by an organized health service' (*Oxford Dictionary of English*).

Physician's guide to terrorist attack
M.J. Roy, ed. See entry no. 4438

Russell, Hugo and Ayliffe's Principles and practice of disinfection, preservation and sterilization
A.D. Russell [et al.], eds See entry no. 4299

Nursing, Midwifery & Allied Health

allied health professions • chiropody • health visiting • midwifery • nursing • palliative care nursing • physiotherapy • podiatry

Introductions to the subject

The art and science of mental health nursing: a textbook of principles and practice
I.J. Norman and I. Ryrie, eds See entry no. 4093

4338 **Introduction to research for midwives**
C. Rees 2nd edn, Butterworth-Heinemann, 2003, 264pp. £19.99. ISBN 0750653515.
An introductory text that explores and explains the world of research from the viewpoint of both those using it and those carrying it out. Includes chapter on Reviewing the literature.

4339 **Introductory medical-surgical nursing**
B.K. Timby and N.E. Smith 8th edn, Lippincott Williams and Wilkins, 2003, 1271pp. Includes CD-ROM, $54.95. ISBN 078173553X.
www.lww.com/promos1/timby [DESCRIPTION]
Good well established overview. Includes section on 'Nursing resources' containing list of relevant organizations with URLs.

Palliative care nursing: a guide to practice
M. O'Connor and S. Aranda, eds See entry no. 4325

4340 **Perspectives on nursing theory**
P.G. Reed, N.B.C. Shearer and L.H. Nicoll, eds 4th edn, Lippincott Williams & Wilkins, 2003, 658pp. $50.95. ISBN 0781747430.
Presents more than 60 of the most widely read and frequently cited articles that reflect seminal, current, and futurist thinking and perspectives on nursing theory.

4341 **Physiology for health care and nursing**
S. Kindlen 2nd edn, Churchill Livingstone, 2003, 582pp. $45.95. ISBN 0443071160.
'This UK book has a distinctive clear route from a cell to the complex human being. Beginning with cells and systems, it progresses to the cooperative activity of systems working together to maintain the internal environment; then to the predictable system responses to disturbance of the environment by injury and illness. This is extended to the application of the theory to the principles of selected therapies. The human is viewed not just as a whole body, but as a whole person, from conception to death; hearing, seeing, communicating and interacting with the external environment... .'

4342 **Theory and practice of nursing: an integrated approach to caring practice**
L. Basford and O. Slevin, eds 2nd edn, Nelson Thornes, 2003, 852pp. £27.00. ISBN 0748758380.
www.nelsonthornes.com
Best-sellIng textbook. Ten modules: Focus on care; The professional discipline of nursing; The philosophical and theoretical basis of nursing; Evidence-based practice; The social and human context of nursing care; Frameworks for practice; Therapeutic modes; The delivery of nursing care; Nursing perspectives; Into the future.
1st edn Campion, 1995. Nelson Thornes have an extensive list of nursing and related texts: see website.

Dictionaries, thesauri, classifications

4343 **Baillière's midwives' dictionary**
D. Tiran 10th edn, Baillière Tindall, 2003, 333pp. £8.99. ISBN 0702026824.
Offers clear and brief information on all key terms applicable to midwifery students and practitioners. Many new terms and fully revised appendices since the previous edition (1997).

- **Baillière's nurses' dictionary B.F. Weller; Royal College of Nursing** 23rd edn, Baillière Tindall, 2000, 568pp. £7.99. ISBN 0702025577. Essential pocket reference to meet the needs of today's nurses. Published in association with the RCN. Immense range of useful information covered in the appendices.

4344 **Churchill Livingstone's dictionary of nursing**
C. Brooker, ed. 18th edn, Churchill Livingstone, 2002, 527pp. £13.99. ISBN 0443064830.
Attractive two-colour format; wide coverage of issues of relevance to nursing.

4345 **A dictionary of nursing**
E.A. Martin 4th edn, Oxford University Press, 2003, 563pp. £8.99. ISBN 0198606915.
www.oxfordreference.com
10,000 entries provide comprehensive and authoritative coverage of the vocabulary of the nursing professions. Covers many other terms in medical and health-related areas.
Available online: see website.

4346 Encyclopedia and dictionary of medicine, nursing, and allied health
M.T. O'Toole, ed. 7th edn, W B Saunders, 2003, 2262pp. Includes CD-ROM, $35.95. ISBN 0721697917.
Multidisciplinary approach to current terminology in all facets of healthcare. Includes encyclopedic entries for significant topics – diseases, disorders and conditions. 3500 new terms since previous edition.

Includes 14 appendices: Diagnostic tools; Assessment; Anatomy tables; Nutrition; Tables of weights and measures; Chemical tables; Immunization schedules; Symbols, terms, and abbreviations; Dental caries and restorations; Reference intervals for the interpretation of laboratory tests; Patient advocacy and resources; Professional groups and boards; Research; Nursing vocabularies.

Compact, pleasant to use volume.

Previous edn published as Miller-Keane encyclopedia and dictionary of medicine, nursing, and allied health *(Miller, B.F., Keane, C.B., 1997).*

Mosby's medical, nursing and allied health dictionary
D.M. Anderson [et al.], eds See entry no. 3772

4347 NANDA International
www.nanda.org
'Committed to increasing the visibility of nursing's contribution to patient care by continuing to develop, refine and classify phenomena of concern to nurses ... For development of the discipline, the NANDA International Board believes that:

· Nursing diagnosis is seen as an essential component of any professional nursing/client interaction

· NANDA International is recognized as a major contributor to nursing knowledge development through the identification and use of concepts that are the building blocks of nursing science

· NANDA International is recognized as the leader in development and classification of nursing diagnoses.'

Laws, standards, codes

Health Professions Council
See entry no. 4144

4348 Legal aspects of nursing
B. Dimond 4th edn, Pearson/Longman, 2004, 746pp. £29.99. ISBN 0582822785.
Justifiably highly successful and well respected text, based on the UK environment.

Official & quasi-official bodies

4349 Nursing & Midwifery Council [UK]
www.nmc-uk.org
'An organization set up by Parliament to ensure nurses and midwives provide high standards of care to their patients and clients. The NMC is responsible for maintaining a live register of nurses, midwives and specialist community public health nurses. The NMC has the power to remove or caution any practitioner who is found guilty of professional misconduct. In rare cases (e.g. practitioners charged with serious crimes) it can also suspend a registrant while the case is under investigation.'

Research centres & institutes

Perinatal Institute for Maternal and Child Health
See entry no. 4008

Associations & societies

4350 American College of Nurse-Midwives
www.midwife.org
Established in 1929, the College is the oldest women's health care organization in the USA, and provides research, accredits midwifery education programmes, administers and promotes continuing education programmes, establishes clinical practice standards, and creates liaisons with state and federal agencies and members of Congress.

Well structured set of resources. The ACNM Resources and Bibliography Series 'is intended to facilitate the response of the national office to the many inquiries we have regarding a variety of topics': early 2005, covered over 40 topics ranging from 'Administration of midwifery practices' to 'Women and smoking'. Many other useful publications and data-sets freely accessible via the site.

4351 American Podiatric Medical Association [USA]
www.apma.org
Podiatry is 'a field of medicine that strives to improve the overall health and well-being of patients by focusing on preventing, diagnosing, and treating conditions associated with the foot and ankle'. Useful entrée to the area – though significant proportion of the website only accessible to Association members.

4352 Chartered Society of Physiotherapy [UK]
www.csp.org.uk
Very well developed site whose major sections are: Public information; Lifelong learning; Effective practice; Library and information; Media and government; Member groups; Workplace issues. 'The Society was founded in 1894 by four young nurses: Lucy Marianne Robinson, Rosalind Paget, Elizabeth Anne Manley and Margaret Dora Palmer. They set up the Society of Trained Masseuses to protect their profession from falling into disrepute as a result of media stories warning young nurses and the public of unscrupulous people offering massage as a euphemism for other services.'

4353 International Council of Nurses
www.icn.ch
Federation of national nurses' associations, representing nurses in more than 120 countries. Founded in 1899, ICN is the world's first and widest reaching international organization for health professionals.

National Hospice and Palliative Care Organization
See entry no. 4329

4354 Royal College of Nursing [UK]
www.rcn.org.uk
Founded in 1916 as the professional, regulatory body for nurses in the UK. It 'represents nurses and nursing, promotes excellence in practice and shapes health policies'.

Major Library and Information Services, with catalogue online. A number of the Services' bibliographical resources are only accessible via the website by members; but they are available to non-members through third-party vendors.

However, the RCN Publications section of the site has a full A–Z list of publications freely available to the public as downloadable PDFs.

Much else of value on this well organized site – including information about the work of an extensive range of Specialisms.

- **RCN Library thesaurus of nursing terms: a thesaurus of terms used in nursing, midwifery, health visiting and related subject areas** 4th edn, RCN Library and Information Services, 2003, 316pp. £20.00. ISBN 1904114067.

Portal & task environments

4355 **CINAHL Information Systems: Leaders in delivering current and comprehensive health care information**
EBSCO.
www.cinahl.com
Developed from the Cumulative Index to Nursing Literature into database that covers all aspects of nursing and allied health disciplines. More than 1200 publications are indexed, including books, pamphlets, dissertations, audiovisual material, etc. Selected full text and images are available. Some foreign language journals have been included since 1994.

Portal now gives access to range of other information services, including CINAHLsources – an extensive set of descriptions of selected websites of interest to nursing and allied health professionals, researchers and students, and others.

4356 **MIDIRS: The definitive midwifery information service**
www.midirs.org
Educational charity whose mission is: 'To be the central source of information relating to childbirth and to disseminate this information to midwives and others, both nationally and internationally, thereby assisting them to improve maternity care.'

4357 **Midwivesonline.com** [UK]
www.midwivesonline.com
Excellent commercially sponsored website bringing together relevant and up to date information for midwives and health professionals and new (and old) parents.

4358 **NMAP** [UK]
Royal College of Nursing, University of Sheffield and Resource Discovery Network
nmap.ac.uk
A searchable portal providing access to good quality, evaluated, internet resources within nursing, midwifery and the allied health professions. Part of the BIOME Hub within the RDN.

4359 **Nurse Prescriber** [UK]
Cambridge University Press.
www.nurse-prescriber.co.uk
A free online educational service and information resource devoted to all nurse prescribers and healthcare professionals in related fields.

Discovering print & electronic resources

Allied and Complementary Medicine Database: AMED
British Library See entry no. 4207

4360 **British Nursing Index: BNI**
Bournemouth University, Royal College of Nursing and Poole Hospital and Salisbury Health Care NHS Trusts
www.bniplus.co.uk
Covers over 220 of the most popular and important journal sources in the nursing and midwifery fields.

4361 **Intermid.co.uk: The online archive of peer-reviewed midwifery articles**
MA Healthcare Lts.
www.intermid.co.uk [FEE-BASED]
Also includes freely accessible healthcare news, bookshop, forum, jobs, book reviews, events.

- **Internurse** www.internurse.com [FEE-BASED]. Companion service providing continuously updated, fully searchable library of over 8000 peer-reviewed articles, plus similar range of other services.

4362 **PEDro: Physiotherapy Evidence Database**
University of Sydney
www.pedro.fhs.usyd.edu.au/index.html
Initiative of the Centre of Evidence-Based Physiotherapy based at the School of Physiotherapy at the University. Has been developed to give rapid access to bibliographic details and abstracts of randomized controlled trials, systematic reviews and evidence-based clinical practice guidelines in physiotherapy. Most trials on the database have been rated for quality.

4363 **RDN Virtual Training Suite: Nursing, Midwifery and Health Visiting** [UK]
R. Ward and L. Williamson; University of the West of England and Resource Discovery Network
www.vts.rdn.ac.uk/tutorial/nurse
Short tutorial designed especially for students within UK Further and Higher Education.

4364 **Resources for nursing research: an annotated bibliography**
C.G.L. Clamp, S. Gough and L. Land 4th edn, SAGE, 2004, 419pp. $99.95. ISBN 0761949917.
Comprehensive bibliography of sources on nursing research, including references for books, journal papers and internet resources.

- **Nursing research: principles and methods D. Polit-O'Hara and C.T. Beck** 7th edn, Lippincott Williams & Wilkins, 2003, 758pp. $66.95. ISBN 0781737338. http://connection.lww.com [COMPANION]. Very good approachable text. The companion: 'Connection's exclusive resource centers for faculty and students provide dynamic book-specific supplements such as content updates, web links, downloadable images, review questions and more!'.

Directories & encyclopedias

4365 **Drugs in nursing practice: an A–Z guide**
A.M. MacConnachie [et al.] 6th edn, Churchill Livingstone, 2002, 484pp. $29.95. ISBN 0443059462.
Nicely designed manual with clear indications of the 'nursing implications' for each drug.

4366 **Gale encyclopedia of nursing and allied health**
Thomson Gale, 2001, 4000pp. 5 v, $940.00. ISBN 0787649341.
www.gale.com/gvrl
850 entries covering topics in body systems and functions, conditions and common diseases, issues and theories, techniques and practices, and devices and equipment.
Available online: see website.

4367 **Nurse's 3 minute clinical reference**
J. Munden [et al.], eds Lippincott Williams & Wilkins, 2003, 1018pp. $49.95. ISBN 1582551790.
Highlights more than 300 acute and chronic disorders, 75 procedures, 55 treatments, and 150 diagnostic tests that nurses are likely to encounter in practice. Provides clear bullet-point information; and includes pointers to further resources.

4368 **Nursing procedures & protocols**
Lippincott Williams & Wilkins, 2003, 661pp. $45.95. ISBN 1582552371.
Very useful well presented guide 'designed to help nurses react to clinical situations appropriately with little or no guidance from colleagues. Protocols represent the framework for management of a specific disorder or clinical situation, while the procedures that compliment a specific protocol represent the numerous detailed steps for implementing that protocol. This book features over 300 major peer-reviewed protocols and nursing procedures on a wide range of clinical topics.'

Handbooks & manuals

4369 **Brunner & Suddarth's textbook of medical-surgical nursing**
S.C. Smeltzer [et al.], eds 10th edn, Lippincott Williams & Wilkins, 2004, 2315pp. CD-ROM version available, $99.95. ISBN 0781731933.
www.lww.com/product/?0-7817-3193-3 [DESCRIPTION]
Large format volume with comprehensive coverage; more than 50 contributors.

4370 **Clinical nursing skills: basic to advanced skills**
S.F. Smith, D. Duell and B.C. Martin 6th edn, Pearson/Prentice Hall, 2004, 1339pp. $72.00. ISBN 0130493716.
Well produced manual; very clearly structured with detailed learning objectives. Good use of images.

Community/public health nursing: health for families and populations
F.A. Maurer and C.M. Smith See entry no. 4317

4371 **Core skills for nurse practitioners: a handbook for nurse practitioners**
D. Palmer and S. Kaur Whurr, 2003, 223pp. £19.50. ISBN 1861562756.
www.whurr.co.uk
This handbook addresses professional issues that are part of the senior nurse's role in a clear and concise manner. It discusses leadership, change management and risk assessment and looks at evidence-based care.
Check website for the publisher's list in nursing and mental health nursing.

4372 **Handbook of art therapy**
C.A. Malchiodi, ed. Guilford Press, 2002, 449pp. $48.00. ISBN 1572308095.
www.guilford.com
Provides a complete and practical overview of art therapy: how it works, how it can be used, and with whom.
See website for details of the publisher's list of books, periodicals, software, and audiovisual programs in a wide range of mental health, behavioural science, and social science disciplines.

4373 **Instruments for clinical health-care research**
M. Frank-Stromborg and S.J. Olsen, eds 3rd edn, Jones and Bartlett, 2004, 713pp. $68.95. ISBN 0763722529.
Forty chapters providing detailed coverage in four areas. The first is an overview with chapters on specific issues regarding clinical research such as measurement issues with the elderly, with language translations, with children, etc. The rest of the sections discuss instruments by type of assessment: Health and Function, Health-Promotion Activities, and Clinical Problems.

Kinesiology: the mechanics and pathomechanics of human movement
C.A. Oatis See entry no. 3967

4374 **Medical-surgical nursing: assessment and management of clinical problems**
S.M. Lewis [et al.] 6th edn, Mosby, 2004. 2 v., $99.00. ISBN 0323016111.
http://www.us.elsevierhealth.com
Major reference work with a range of companion products: see website. 67 chapters in twelve sections.
5th edn, 2000.

- **Medical-surgical nursing: critical thinking in client care** **P. Lemone and K. Burke** 3rd edn, Prentice Hall, 2003, 1632pp. $92.95. ISBN 0130990752. www.prenhall.com/lemone [COMPANION]. Good example from the publisher's extensive list of nursing titles: the website leads to details of their full range of print and online offerings.

4375 **Myles textbook for midwives**
D.M. Fraser and M.A. Cooper, eds 14th edn, Churchill Livingstone, 2003, 1089pp. £35.99. ISBN 0443072345.
Leading international textbook for midwives. The focus is on the provision of woman-centred, midwife-friendly care.

4376 **Nursing diagnosis handbook: a guide to planning care**
B.J. Ackley and G.B. Ladwig, eds 6th edn, Mosby, 2004, 1099pp. $37.95. ISBN 032302551X.
'Nursing students and practicing nurses cannot possibly memorize the more than 1200 defining characteristics, related factors, and risk factors for the 169 diagnoses approved by the North American Nursing Diagnosis Council (NANDA). This book correlates suggested nursing diagnoses with what nurses know about clients and offers a care plan for each nursing diagnosis.' An excellent compilation.

Occupational and environmental health nursing: concepts and practice
B. Rogers See entry no. 4292

Pediatric nursing: caring for children
J.W. Ball and R.C. Bindler, ed. See entry no. 4090

4377 **The Royal Marsden hospital manual of clinical nursing procedures**
L. Dougherty and S. Lister 6th edn, Blackwell, 2004, 870pp. £26.50. ISBN 140510161X.
Excellent detail; very good sets of references and further reading. Helpful introductory 'Quick reference to the guidelines'.

Keeping up-to-date

4378 **Nursing Standard** [UK]
Royal College of Nursing RCN Publishing Company, Weekly. £210.00. ISSN 00296570.
www.nursing-standard.co.uk
News, professional development, courses, jobs, links, etc.

4379 **Nursing Times**
Emap, Weekly. £60.00. ISSN 09547762.
www.nursingtimes.net
'The UK's best-selling weekly magazine for nurses. News, clinical features, educational material and the widest selection of jobs of any of the UK's nursing press. The modern voice of nursing.'

Nutrition

additives • anorexia nervosa • bulimia nervosa • dietetics • dieting • eating disorders • food information • food ingredients • healthy eating • human nutrition • minerals • obesity • vitamins • weight management

Introductions to the subject

4380 **The complete illustrated guide to vitamins and minerals**
D. Mortimore Element, 2001, 192pp. £14.99. ISBN 0007122462.
Pleasant guide with each vitamin or mineral having its own entry, with the text supported by illustrations and diagrams, and good background information.

4381 **Principles of human nutrition**
M.A. Eastwood 2nd edn, Blackwell Science, 2003, 680pp. £39.50. ISBN 0632058110.
Comprehensive; well structured and designed.

Dictionaries, thesauri, classifications

4382 **Benders' dictionary of nutrition and food technology**
D.A. Bender and A.E. Bender 7th edn, Woodhead Publishing, 1999, 463pp. Also available from CRC Press, £45.00. ISBN 1855734753.
Definitions of over 5000 terms; nutrient composition data for 287 foods with reference tables for recommended nutrient intakes in the USA and EU included in appendix.

- **Nutritional biochemistry of the vitamins** D.A. Bender 2nd edn, Cambridge University Press, 2003, 488pp. £70.00. ISBN 0521803888. Good overview explaining the known biochemical functions of the vitamins; highlighting areas where our knowledge is lacking.

Research centres & institutes

4383 **Institute of Food Research**
www.ifrn.bbsrc.ac.uk
A not-for-profit company sponsored by the BIOTECHNOLOGY AND BIOLOGICAL SCIENCES RESEARCH COUNCIL. IFR is the UK's only integrated basic science provider focused on food, whose research is concerned with the safety and quality of food, and improving diet and health in people.

Straightforward clearly laid out website; useful series of: Information sheets; Science briefs; News releases. Access also to a score of websites designed by IFR on nutrition and food-related topics, as well as to descriptions of a select group of external sites.

National Center for Chronic Disease Prevention and Health Promotion
See entry no. 4421

Associations & societies

4384 **American Dietetic Association**
www.eatright.org/Public
Founded in 1917, the Association is the USA's largest organization of food and nutrition professionals: over 70,000 members. It promotes optimal nutrition, health and wellbeing. 'Dietetics' is defined as 'the integration and application of principles derived from the sciences of nutrition, biochemistry, physiology, food management and behavioral and social sciences to achieve and maintain people's health'.

Useful range of resources on clearly laid out site.

4385 **British Association for Parenteral and Enteral Nutrition**
www.bapen.org.uk
Founded in 1992 to advance clinical nutrition through research, education and training. Most BAPEN members hold their membership because they are members of one of the five 'Founder' organizations. Others can join as affiliates; but 'BAPEN needs new members to bring in new ideas and viewpoints and we are delighted to encourage this regardless of how they become members'.

An easily navigated but rather minimalist site. However, provides a goodly number of pointers to useful resources in this arena.

4386 **British Dietetic Association**
www.bda.uk.com
Established in 1936, the professional association of dietitians, with more than 5000 members, based in the UK. Wide-ranging, generally up-to-date sets of resources – including a Trade Union section.

4387 **British Nutrition Foundation**
www.nutrition.org.uk
A charitable foundation, set up in 1967, that promotes the nutritional wellbeing of society through the impartial interpretation and effective dissemination of scientifically based nutritional knowledge and advice.

Despite being rather a slow site when accessed, notable for its detailed briefing notes – under the heading Information – covering: Nutrition basics; Nutrition through life; Nutrition and health; Food commodities; Food science/labels. Also substantial education, projects, conferences, publications, and links sections – the last having a sub-section Member Companies, the charity raising its funds from the food industry, government and a variety of other sources.

4388 **International Food Information Council** [USA]
ific.org
'Purpose is to bridge the gap between science and communications by collecting and disseminating scientific information on food safety, nutrition and health and by working with an extensive roster of scientific experts and through partnerships to help translate research into understandable and useful information for opinion leaders and ultimately, consumers.' The IFIC Foundation – the designation used here – is 'supported primarily by the broad-based food, beverage and agricultural industries'.

Wide-ranging and well presented sets of resources: booklets; fact sheets; FAQs; glossary; newsletter; reviews; etc. – designed for different groups of stakeholders: Journalists; Health, nutrition, and agricultural professionals; Government officials; Educators; Consumers Students.

The Foundation subscribes to the HONCode principles.

4389 **National Eating Disorders Association** [USA]
www.nationaleatingdisorders.org
'The largest not-for-profit organization in the United States working to prevent eating disorders and provide treatment referrals to those suffering from anorexia, bulimia and binge eating disorder and those concerned with body image and weight issues.'

4390 **Nutrition Society** [UK]
www.nutritionsociety.org
Aims to advance the scientific study of nutrition and its application to the maintenance of human and animal health.

World Cancer Research Fund International
See entry no. 4036

Portal & task environments

4391 **Dietitians.co.uk** [UK]
www.dietitians.co.uk
Aims 'to support dietitians and dietetic departments at a local level by providing: useful and up to date information; a means for you to communicate with other Dietitians and local healthcare colleagues; a forum for you to sell your resources'. The site subscribes to the HONCode principles.

4392 **Food and Nutrition Information Center** [USA]
National Agricultural Library
www.nal.usda.gov/fnic
'Provides a directory to credible, accurate, and practical resources for consumers, nutrition and health professionals, educators and government personnel. Visitors can find printable format educational materials, government reports, research papers and more. FNIC nutrition information specialists review all site content to ensure top quality resources.'

- **Dietary supplements: toxicology and clinical pharmacology** **M.J. Cupp and T.S. Tracy, eds** Humana Press, 2003, 410pp. $115.00. ISBN 158829014X. Companion volume to *Toxicology and clinical pharmacology of herbal products*.
- **Dietary supplements** **P. Mason, ed.** 2nd edn, Pharmaceutical Press, 2001, 276pp. £39.95. ISBN 0853694591. 'I would not hesitate to recommend this book to health professionals interested in nutrition and those working in the field of complementay medicine.' *Complementary Therapies in Nursing and Midwifery*.
- **Food, Nutrition, and Consumer Services** **United States. Department of Agriculture**. www.fns.usda.gov/fncs. 'Ensures access to nutritious, healthful diets for all Americans ... Today, rather than simply providing food, FNCS works to empower consumers with knowledge of the link between diet and health, providing dietary guidance based on research'.
- **Office of Dietary Supplements** http://ods.od.nih.gov. In the USA dietary supplements 'are usually defined as including plant extracts, enzymes, vitamins, minerals, amino acids, and hormonal products that are available without prescription and are consumed in addition to the regular diet'.

4393 **NutritionData** [USA]
www.nutritiondata.com
Personal interest website which 'provides nutrition facts, calorie counts, and nutrient data for all foods and recipes ... ND obtains food composition data from a variety of published and unpublished sources, with the largest provider of data being the United States Department of Agriculture (USDA). While ND cannot guarantee 100% accuracy, we do our best to check or verify all data entries. For your reference, we also identify the data source for each individual food in the Footnotes section of every ND Analysis.'

Good selection of other useful information, including an extensive Glossary.

- **Bowes and Church's food values of portions commonly used** **J.A.T. Pennington** 18th edn, Lippincott Williams & Wilkins, 2005, 512pp. $56.95. ISBN 0781744296. 8500 common foods, plus supplementary tables for the less common. Includes calorie content, weight, water, protein, fat, cholesterol, carbohydrate, dietary fibre and major vitamins and minerals. Bibliography of sources for food composition data.

Discovering print & electronic resources

4394 **Ginseng: a medical dictionary, bibliography, and annotated research guide to internet references**
ICON Group International, 2004, 276pp. Downloadable PDF, $48.95. http://icon.ecnext.com
'In addition to offering a structured and comprehensive bibliography, this medical reference on ginseng will quickly direct you to resources and reliable information on the Internet, from the essentials to the most advanced areas of research. Public, academic, government, and peer-reviewed research studies are emphasized. Various abstracts are reproduced to give you some of the latest official information available to date. Abundant guidance is given on how to obtain free-of-charge primary research results via the Internet. E-book and electronic versions of this book are fully interactive with the Internet. For readers unfamiliar with the Internet, detailed instructions are offered on how to access electronic resources. For readers unfamiliar with medical terminology, a comprehensive glossary is provided. For readers without access to Internet resources, a directory of medical libraries, that have or can locate references cited here, is given. We hope these resources will prove useful to the widest possible audience seeking information on ginseng.'
One of a very extensive range of similar online offerings all described in similar vein: see website.

4395 Nutrition Abstracts and Reviews
CABI Publishing.
www.cabi-publishing.org [DESCRIPTION]
Fully searchable abstract database, marketed as two Series: A. Human and experimental: The latest information on all issues related to food and health – from food composition and safety to obesity, parenteral nutrition and allergies; B. Livestock feeds and feeding: The latest information on all aspects of commercially and environmentally important animal nutrition research, including methodology, feed processing and technology, feed production and composition, nutritional physiology and biochemistry, livestock, fish and shellfish performance, nutrition of companion and captive animals, nutritional disorders and diet treatment.
Also available in print: see website.

Nutrition and Food Sciences
See entry no. 3177

Digital data, image & text collections

4396 enLINK
Nestlé Foundation.
www.enlink.org
The Foundation has partnered with the online aggregator OVID to develop an electronic nutrition library for selected researchers working in the world's poorest countries.

4397 FOODnetBase
CRC Press.
www.foodnetbase.com [FEE-BASED]
A subscription service with over 100 online nutrition titles from the publisher, all fully searchable and browsable.

Directories & encyclopedias

4398 ABC of nutrition
A.S. Truswell 4th edn, BMJ Books, 2003, 140pp. £19.95. ISBN 0727916645.
Covers most aspects of nutrition in particular those which affect heart disease, blood pressure, chronic diseases and contains the most current nutritional recommendations for pregnancy and infant feeding as well as children and adults young and old.
'With the publication of this marvellous little book, there is no longer an excuse for any member of the health-care team not to be knowledgeable about nutrition.' (*American Journal of Clinical Nutrition*)

4399 An atlas of obesity and weight control
G.A. Bray Parthenon, 2003, 135pp. $99.95. ISBN 1842140493.
Colour illustrations of the etiology, development, and treatment of obesity. Clinical guidelines on assessment and treatment – including behaviour modification, diet, exercise, drugs and surgery. Bibliography.
Series: Encyclopedia of Visual Medicine, V. 56.

Chemical dictionary of economic plants
J.B. Harborne and H. Baxter See entry no. 3105

4400 Dictionary of food ingredients
R.S. Igoe and Y.H. Hui 4th edn, Kluwer Academic, 2001, 234pp. £36.00. ISBN 0834219522.
www.knovel.com
Defines and describes some 1000 food ingredients and additives, including natural ingredients, FDA-approved artificial ingredients, and compounds used in food processing. Definitions cover functionality, chemical properties, and applications.
Available online: see website.

4401 Encyclopedia of diet fads
M. Bijlefeld and S.K. Zoumbaris Greenwood Press, 2003, 264pp. $55.00. ISBN 0313322236.
Describes many of the health fads and fashions of the past, as well as current trends in weight loss, examining the pros and cons of different plans.
'[t]his useful and entertaining source is recommended for most public, consumer health, and academic library collections.' (*Library Journal*)

4402 Encyclopedia of food sciences and nutrition
B. Caballero, L. Trugo and P. Finglas, eds 2nd edn, Academic Press, 2003, 6500pp. 10 v, $2900.00. ISBN 012227055X.
www.sciencedirect.com/science/referenceworks
A substantial and up-to-date global source of information in the areas of food science and nutrition. It provides a complete understanding of the science of food, including a thorough and integrated analysis of nutrition.
Available online: see website.
'This is my 125th book review for FOOD TECHNOLOGY and this is indeed the jewel in the crown, the biggest and best work I've commented on so far ... Frankly, I'm impressed. I could not find a concept or word that was not listed ... (on the 1st edn).' (*Food Technology*)

- **Encyclopedia of human nutrition J. Strain, B. Caballero and M. Sadler, eds** Academic Press, 1998, 1973pp. $1075.00. ISBN 0122266943. www.academicpress.com [DESCRIPTION]. 3 v. 270 articles. Also accessible online through ScienceDirect. 4 v. new edn announced for 2005.

4403 Encyclopedia of nutrition and good health
R.A. Ronzio 2nd edn, Facts on File, 2003, 726pp. $71.50. ISBN 0816049661.
2500 references in A–Z guide to all aspects of nutrition and maintaining a healthy diet. New edition has 30% new material, including several new appendices.
Series: Library of Health and Living.
'The interested and perhaps confused health information consumer can turn with confidence to this encyclopedia ... a one-stop introduction to nutrition ... The book will be useful in all types of libraries serving sophisticated information consumers.' (*Booklist*)

Handbooks & manuals

4404 Clinical handbook of weight management
M.E.J. Lean 2nd edn, Martin Dunitz, 2003, 136pp. £21.50. ISBN 1841841048.
www.dunitz.co.uk
An up-to-date background on obesity and an understanding of weight management for health professionals. Offers outlines for management plans which can be instituted at a primary care level.
See website for range of titles published under the Martin Dunitz imprint via Taylor & Francis Medicine.

4405 **Handbook of eating disorders**
J. Treasure, U. Schmidt and E. van Furth, eds 2nd edn, Wiley, 2003, 479pp. $125.00. ISBN 0471497681.
Provides a clear, coherent, readable and authoritative overview.

Handbook of nutrition and food
C.D. Berdanier See entry no. 3188

4406 **Handbook of vitamins**
R.B. Rucker [et al.], eds 3rd edn, Marcel Dekker, 2001, 616pp. $175.00. ISBN 0824704282.
Presents a thorough examination of the fundamental characteristics, functions, and roles of vitamins in human health.
Series: Clinical Nutrition in Health and Disease.
'one of the best textbooks available in the field of vitamins; this was true for the First Edition ... and remains so for the Second. There are very few books [that] all nutritionists should have in their libraries, and [this] is certainly one of them. It is an outstanding desk reference [that] is well organized, concise, and as thorough as any single book on all vitamins can be.' (*Journal of Applied Nutrition* [of 2nd edn])

Manual of pediatric nutrition
K.M. Hendricks, C. Duggan and W.A. Walker See entry no. 4088

4407 **Metabolic and therapeutic aspects of amino acids in clinical nutrition**
L.A. Cynober 2nd edn, CRC Press, 2004, 755pp. $189.95. ISBN 0849313821.
'Covers amino acids in artificial nutrition; Provides up-to-date information, stimulating points of view, and selected ideas for future research; Presents the information in well organized format that avoids redundancies; Includes contributions from internationally respected experts.' Useful solid work.

4408 **Nutrient metabolism**
M. Kohlmeier Academic Press, 2003, 829pp. $119.95. ISBN 012417762X.
Chapters are: Introduction; Chemical senses; Intake regulation; Absorption, transport and retention; Xenobiotics; Fatty acids; Carbohydrates, alcohols and organic acids; Amino acids and nitrogen compounds; Fat-soluble vitamins and non-nutrients; Water-soluble vitamins and non-nutrients; Minerals and trace elements; Applications.
Very clearly laid-out; good use of tables and diagrams.
Series: Food Science and Technology International.
'One positive aspect of this book is its thoroughly and fully comprehensive coverage of its subject. This volume is highly recommended for academic libraries and those of practitioners.' (*American Reference Books Annual*)

- **Nutrition and metabolism M.J. Gibney, H.M. Roche and I. Macdonald; Nutrition Society** Blackwell Science, 2003, 385pp. £32.50. ISBN 0632056258. www.nutritiontexts.com. One of the Society's textbook series, other current titles being: *Introduction to human nutrition*; *Public health nutrition*; *Clinical nutrition*. See website.

Keeping up-to-date

Advances in Food and Nutrition Research
See entry no. 3190

4409 **Annual Review of Nutrition**
Annual Reviews Inc, 2004. $202.00. ISBN 0824328248 ISSN 01999885.
www.annurev.org/catalog/2004/nu24.asp [DESCRIPTION]
One of the major series of academic review publications.

Public Health & Preventive Medicine

bacteriological warfare • biological standards • biological warfare • chemical warfare • disease control • disease prevention • epidemics • epidemiology • health promotion • preventive medicine • public safety • public security • risk management • severe acute respiratory syndrome • travellers' health

Introductions to the subject

4410 **Health and disease in Britain: from prehistory to the present day**
C.A. Roberts and M. Cox Sutton, 2003, 476pp. £25.00. ISBN 0750918446.
An excellent review.

4411 **Introduction to weapons of mass destruction: radiological, chemical and biological**
R.E. Langford Wiley, 2004, 394pp. $95.95. ISBN 0471465607.
www.wiley.com/WileyCDA [DESCRIPTION]
Excellent and very wide-ranging entrée: check the Table of Contents at the website.
'its listings, compilation of data, brief technical histories and the sections dealing with containment are excellent.' (*Chemistry & Industry*)

4412 **Risk-benefit analysis**
R. Wilson and E.A.C. Crouch 2nd edn, Harvard University Press, 2001, 370pp. $25.00. ISBN 0674005295.
'Over the centuries, mankind has slowly reduced the risks and hazards that even as recently as a century ago kept life expectancy to a mere 45 years. Our average lifespan has improved to 77 years by remarkable progress in public health and safety. But with this improvement has come a demand for greater efforts to improve both life expectancy and the quality of life. The first edition of this book, published in 1982, was a pioneer in the development of logical, yet simple, analytic tools for discussion of the risks which we all face. This new edition, revised, expanded, and illustrated in detail, should be of value both to professionals in the field and to those who wish to understand these vital issues.'

4413 **World epidemics: a cultural chronology of disease from prehistory to the era of SARS**
M.E. Snodgrass McFarland, 2003, 479pp. $75.00. ISBN 0786416629.
A good resource guide; very useful appendices.

Dictionaries, thesauri, classifications

4414 **Dictionary of public health promotion and education: terms and concepts**
N. Modeste and T. Tamayose Jossey-Bass, 2004, 192pp. $45.00. ISBN 0787969192.
Definition of terms and concepts frequently used in public health education and promotion. Second section contains details of relevant health and professional organizations. Recommended reading.
- **The European multilingual thesaurus on health promotion in 12 languages European Commission.** www.hpmulti.net. Danish, Dutch, English, Finnish, French, German, Greek, Italian, Norwegian, Portuguese, Spanish and Swedish. Available as downloadable textfile and PDF.

Elsevier's dictionary of nuclear engineering: Russian-English; English-Russian
M. Rosenberg and S. Bobryakov, comps See entry no. 4720

Laws, standards, codes

International Portal on Food Safety, Animal & Plant Health
Food and Agriculture Organization, United States. Department of Agriculture and Standards and Trade Development Facility See entry no. 2931

4415 **National Institute for Biological Standards and Control** [UK]
www.nibsc.ac.uk
A multi-disciplinary scientific establishment whose purpose is to safeguard and enhance public health by standardizing and controlling biological substances used in medicine. NIBSC has a leading international role in preparing, evaluating and distributing International Biological Standards and other biological reference materials. It is a WHO International Laboratory for Biological Standards.

Official & quasi-official bodies

4416 **Centers for Disease Control and Prevention** [USA]
www.cdc.gov
The United States leading and 'lead federal agency for protecting the health and safety of people – at home and abroad, providing credible information to enhance health decisions, and promoting health through strong partnerships. CDC serves as the national focus for developing and applying disease prevention and control, environmental health, and health promotion and education activities designed to improve the health of the people of the United States'.
- **The DataWeb** www.thedataweb.org. A network of online data libraries. Topics include, census data, economic data, health data, income and unemployment data, population data, labour data, cancer data, crime and transportation data, family dynamics, vital statistics data.
- **Emergency Preparedness & Response Centers for Disease Control and Prevention.** www.bt.cdc.gov. Main coverage divided into: Bioterrorism agents; Chemical emergenices; Mass trauma; Natural disasters & severe weather; Radiation emergencies; Recent outbreaks & incidents – plus a section of Additional Topics & Resources.
- **Human Genome Epidemiology Network: HuGENet** www.cdc.gov/genomics/hugenet. Global collaboration of individuals and organizations committed to the assessment of the impact of human genome variation on population health and how genetic information can be used to improve health and prevent disease.

4417 **Emergency Management Australia**
www.ema.gov.au
Provides 'national leadership in the development of measures to reduce risk to communities and manage the consequences of disasters'.
- **Australian emergency management terms thesaurus** **Emergency Management Australia**Downloadable PDF1998, 128pp. www.ema.gov.au/agd/EMA/emaInternet.nsf/Page/EMA_Library. Regularly updated. Compiled by the staff of the Emergency Management Information Centre. To support the *International Decade for Natural Disaster Reduction* approved overseas organizations can reproduce the publication without payment of copyright fees.

European Aviation Safety Agency
See entry no. 4892

Global Fire Monitoring Center
See entry no. 3206

Health & Safety Commission
See entry no. 4238

4418 **Health Development Agency** [UK]
www.nice.org.uk
'The national authority on what works to improve people's health and reduce health inequalities.'
On 1 April 2005 the Health Development Agency joined with the National Institute for Clinical Excellence to become the new NATIONAL INSTITUTE FOR HEALTH AND CLINICAL EXCELLENCE *(to be known as NICE). The web address for the new organisation is that given.*

4419 **Health Protection Agency** [UK]
www.hpa.org.uk
Independent body – established in 2002 – that protects the health and wellbeing of everyone in England and Wales. 'The Agency plays a critical role in protecting people from infectious diseases and in preventing harm when hazards involving chemicals, poisons or radiation occur. We also prepare for new and emerging threats, such as a bio-terrorist attack or virulent new strain of disease.'
Extensive Topics A–Z; news, publications, links.
- **Centre for Emergency Preparedness and Response** www.hpa.org.uk/business. Based at Porton Down in Wiltshire. Formerly the *Centre for Applied Microbiology & Research*. Located within the HPA's Business Activities division.

4420 **Homeland Security** [USA]
United States. Department of Homeland Security
www.dhs.gov/dhspublic
The Department's Mission: 'We will lead the unified national effort to secure America. We will prevent and deter terrorist attacks and protect against and respond to threats and hazards to the nation. We will ensure safe and secure borders, welcome lawful immigrants and visitors, and promote the free-flow of commerce.'
- **Biological and chemical terrorism information for healthcare professionals R. Ramsey** 2004. www.istl.org/04-winter/internet.html. Valuable 'Science and Technology Resources on the Internet' in *Issues in Science and Technology Librarianship*: Overviews and news; Public health emergency preparedness; Agents, diseases, and threats; Treatment of diseases caused by biological weapons.

- **Federal Emergency Management Agency** www.fema.org. Former independent agency that became part of the new Department of Homeland Security in March 2003, and is tasked with 'responding to, planning for, recovering from and mitigating against disasters'. See also: www.hazardmaps.gov.
- **Research and Technology** www.dhs.gov/dhspublic/theme_home5.jsp. The Department's focus which 'harnesses our nation's scientific and technological resources to provide Federal, state, and local officials with the technology and capabilities to protect the homeland'.

Immunisation
Great Britain. Department of Health See entry no. 3928

National Center for Environmental Health
See entry no. 4241

National Institute on Alcohol Abuse and Alcoholism
See entry no. 4306

National Nuclear Security Administration
See entry no. 4723

Office of Ground Water and Drinking Water
Environmental Protection Agency See entry no. 5557

Railway Safety and Standards Board
See entry no. 5886

US Fire Administration
See entry no. 4245

Research centres & institutes

4421 National Center for Chronic Disease Prevention and Health Promotion [USA]
www.cdc.gov/nccdphp
'Chronic diseases—such as heart disease, cancer, and diabetes—are the leading causes of death and disability in the United States. These diseases account for 7 of every 10 deaths and affect the quality of life of 90 million Americans. Although chronic diseases are among the most common and costly health problems, they are also among the most preventable. Adopting healthy behaviors such as eating nutritious foods, being physically active, and avoiding tobacco use can prevent or control the devastating effects of these diseases.'

Associations & societies

American Burn Association
See entry no. 4250

American College of Occupational and Environmental Medicine
See entry no. 4251

4422 American College of Preventive Medicine
www.acpm.org
National professional society for physicians committed to disease prevention and health promotion: 2000 members.

4423 American Public Health Association
www.apha.org
'The oldest and largest organization of public health professionals in the world, representing more than 50,000 members from over 50 occupations of public health ... Brings together researchers, health service providers, administrators, teachers, and other health workers in a unique, multidisciplinary environment of professional exchange, study, and action.'

Very wide range of involvements, the Association having, for instance, 24 Sections (e.g. Alcohol, tobacco, and other drugs; Chiropractic health care; Community health planning and policy development; Environment; Epidemiology; Food and nutrition; etc.) – each with its own website, as well as seven Special Interest Groups. A rather intensive website; but gives access to lots of useful resources.

- **Encyclopedia of public health** Macmillan Reference USA, 2001, 2000pp. $499.00. ISBN 0028653548. www.gale.com/gvrl [FEE-BASED]. Four vols, also available online. 'Though other encyclopedias address more specific areas of public health, none provides such a global overview of the discipline. An outstanding addition to any academic or public library reference collection.' *Choice*.

4424 Association for Professionals in Infection Control and Epidemiology [USA]
www.apic.org
Multi-disciplinary voluntary international organization with over 10,000 members whose purpose is 'to influence, support and improve the quality of healthcare through the practice and management of infection control and the application of epidemiology in all health settings'.

4425 Association of Public Health Observatories [UK]
www.apho.org.uk
The notion of 'public health observatories' is relatively recent and they can be distinguished from related institutions such as disease registries and public health departments by their combination of academic and public, their more rapid response times, their more intensive data analysis and networking activities; and so on. This Association, established in 2000, has a main focus of facilitating collaborative working of the ten Public Health Observatories now existing in England and Wales.

4426 European Public Health Alliance
www.epha.org
Represents over 100 non-governmental and other not-for-profit organizations working on public health in Europe. It aims to promote and protect the health interests of all people living in Europe and to strengthen the dialogue between the EU institutions, citizens and NGOs in support of healthy public policies.

Access to news and resources under the headings: Environment; Food and agriculture; Society; Wealth. Also more general information about European developments.

4427 Faculty of Public Health [UK]
www.fphm.org.uk
Established in 1972 as the Faculty of Public Health Medicine within the Royal Colleges of Physicians of the United Kingdom. But changed in 2003 to its present name marking an 'official recognition that while doctors have an important contribution to make to improving the public's health, so too do other skilled specialists in the professional community.

What counts is each one's level of competence and skill to work in public health'.

Especially within that context, good introduction to current preoccupations and developments in the arena.

Federation of American Scientists
See entry no. 4730

4428 **Royal Society for the Promotion of Health** [UK]
www.rsph.org
'The Royal Society for the Promotion of Health is a charity. Since our foundation in 1876, our aim has been to promote continuous improvement in human health world-wide through education, communication and the encouragement of scientific research.'

- **Royal Institute of Public Health** www.riph.org. An independent organization promoting public health and hygiene through education and training, information, quality testing and policy development. Formerly the Royal Institute of Public Health and Hygiene and Society of Public Health.

Society for Radiological Protection
See entry no. 4263

Portal & task environments

Communicable Disease Surveillance and Response
World Health Organization See entry no. 3938

DPDx: Laboratory Identification of Parasites of Public Health Concern
Centers for Disease Control and Prevention See entry no. 3581

Jane's Information Group: Intelligence and Insight You Can Trust
See entry no. 4845

4429 **Travelers' Health**
National Center for Infectious Diseases
www.cdc.gov/travel
Very useful gateway from NCID providing links to all aspects of travel health and medicine, including data on the vaccinations required for worldwide destinations, and the latest information about many tropical diseases, including malaria.

Discovering print & electronic resources

4430 **Combined Health Information Database: CHID**
National Institutes of Health and Health Resources and Services Administration
www.chid.nih.gov
A bibliographic database, produced by health-related agencies of the Federal Government, which provides titles, abstracts, and availability information for health information and health education resources. CHID lists a wealth of health promotion and education materials and programme descriptions that are not indexed elsewhere.

Directories & encyclopedias

4431 **A dictionary of epidemiology**
J.M. Last; International Epidemiological Association 4th edn, Oxford University Press, 2001, 196pp. £17.95. ISBN 0195141695.
Covers common terms used in epidemiology and many from related fields such as biostatistics, infectious disease control, health promotion and medical ethics. Definitions accompanied by brief essays and discussions of the provenance of important items. Extensive bibliography.

4432 **Encyclopedia of primary prevention and health promotion**
T.P. Gullotta and M. Bloom, eds Kluwer Academic/Plenum, 2003, 1179pp. £176.00. ISBN 0306472961.
Large format multi-author work covering over 100 topics including strategies that work, strategies that might work, strategies that do not work.

- **Health promotion in the workplace M.P. O'Donnell, ed.** 3rd edn, Delmar Thomson Learning, 2001, 614pp. $86.95. ISBN 0766828662. www.delmarhealthcare.com. One of a wide range of relevant books, software, learning and training materials available via *DelmarHealthCare.com*: see website.

The encyclopedia of smoking and tobacco
A.B. Hirschfelder See entry no. 4315

Handbooks & manuals

4433 **Biological risk engineering handbook: infection control and decontamination**
M.J. Boss and D.W. Day, eds Lewis, 2003, 511pp. $159.95. ISBN 1566706068.
Compendium of biological risk management information. Introductory *Micro Dictionary* reviewing the major biological contaminants: bacteria; fungi; prions; viruses. Chapters covering sampling, toxicology, risk assessment, ventilation, maintenance control, decontamination, biocides, laws and regulations, security. Index.

4434 **Building better health: a handbook of behavioral change**
C.D. Jenkins; Pan American Health Organization 2003, 378pp. $40.00. ISBN 9275115907.
www.paho.org [DESCRIPTION]
The book is structured into five sections, which detail theoretical and practical aspects of health promotion. Blends tried-and-true disease prevention practices and behavioural science principles into a hands-on manual for health workers, community health promoters, nurses and family physicians.

Community/public health nursing: health for families and populations
F.A. Maurer and C.M. Smith See entry no. 4317

Emerging public safety wireless communication systems
R.I. Desourdis [et al.] See entry no. 6245

The epidemiology of eye disease
G.J. Johnson [et al.], eds See entry no. 4063

4435 **Evidence-based practice manual: research and outcome measures in health and human services**
A.R. Roberts and K.R. Yeager, eds Oxford University Press, 2004, 1050pp. £54.00. ISBN 0195165004.
www4.oup.co.uk [DESCRIPTION]
'Includes 104 original chapters, each specially written by the most prominent and experienced medical, public health, psychology, social work, criminal justice, and public policy practitioners, researchers, and professors in the United States and Canada. This book is specifically designed with practitioners in mind, providing at-a-glance overviews and direct application chapters.'

There is a helpful Appendix 'Internet resources on research and evaluation in healthcare and human service settings'

4436 **Medical entomology: a textbook on public health and veterinary problems caused by arthropods**
B.F. Eldridge and J.D. Edman, eds Rev. edn, Kluwer Academic, 2004, 659pp. £52.00. ISBN 1402017944.
Detailed authoritative text.

Molecular epidemiology of infectious diseases: principles and practices
L.W. Riley See entry no. 3946

4437 **Oxford handbook of public health practice**
D. Pencheon [et al.], eds Oxford University Press, 2001, 609pp. £24.95. ISBN 0192632213.
Nine broad sections: Public health assessment; Options and decisions; Policy; Direct action; Health care assessment; Health care assurance; Personal effectiveness; Organizational development; Case studies.

- **Oxford textbook of public health R. Detels [et al.], eds** 4th edn, Oxford University Press, 2004. £95.00. 3 v. 'A clear, consistent and easy read textbook ... This is an important book that should be found at every public health library and at the side of specialists in public health medicine.' *International Journal of Adolescent Medicine and Health.*

4438 **Physician's guide to terrorist attack**
M.J. Roy, ed. Humana Press, 2003, 420pp. $110.00. ISBN 158829207X.
www.humanapress.com [DESCRIPTION]
27 chapters covering the full spectrum of possibilities.
'Physician's Guide to Terrorist Attack is highly recommended for medical libraries and practices. As the content is presented in a clear, understandable way, this item may also be useful in a broader context such as defining various methods of biological and chemical warfare, methods of prevention and treatment, and other general information. These features make this book a viable collection addition for medical, academic, and public libraries.' (E-STREAMS)

- **Bioterrorism: guidelines for medical and public health management D.A. Henderson, T.V. Inglesby and T.J. O'Toole; American Medical Association** 2002, 244pp. $32.95. ISBN 157947280X. www.ama-assn.org [DESCRIPTION]. 'Ghastly though its subject is, this book teaches us that inaction is not an option because timely chemoprophylaxis or vaccination of appropriate populations could successfully limit catastrophic casualties and socioeconomic collapse.' *British Medical Journal.*

Statistical handbook on infectious diseases
S.B. Watstein and J. Jovanovic See entry no. 3947

Keeping up-to-date

4439 **Annual Review of Public Health**
Annual Reviews Inc, 2004. $215.00. ISBN 082432725X ISSN 01637525.
www.annurev.org/catalog/2004/pu25.asp [DESCRIPTION]
Chapters in the 2004 volume include: The current state of public health in China; Genetic testing in the workplace: ethical, legal, and social implications; International differences in drug prices; The public health workforce; The role of culture in health communication.

4440 **Public Health News Center**
, edsJohns Hopkins University
www.jhsph.edu/PublicHealthNews
Good attractively laid-out news and background information produced by the University's Bloomberg School of Public Health.

4441 **RiskWorld**
Ter-Com Inc.
www.riskworld.com
Wide-ranging well organized news and views service.

Reproductive Medicine & Health

abortion • birth control • contraception • embryology • family planning • fertility • human embryology • human fertilization • human reproduction • infertility • reproductive health

Introductions to the subject

4442 **Before we are born: essentials of embryology and birth defects**
K.L. Moore and T.V.N. Persaud 6th edn, W B Saunders, 2003, 448pp. $44.95. ISBN 072169408X.
An undergraduate textbook that provides an introduction to human embryology including a chapter on abnormal development. The book begins with a review of the processes that occur during development up to birth, followed by chapters dealing with the development of particular systems, e.g. the eye and ear, respiratory system, etc. It includes colour illustrations and a bibliography.

4443 **Biology of human reproduction**
R. Piñón University Science Books, 2002, 535pp. $72.00. ISBN 1891389122.
www.uscibooks.com
An undergraduate textbook that is aimed at students without an extensive background in biology. Structured in five parts: Introduction; The gonads; The H-P-G axis (hypothalamus-pituitary-gonadal axis); A new life (the processes from fertilization to birth); Societal issues (infertility, diseases, sexuality, etc).
See website for the current list from this publisher.

4444 **Contraception: your questions answered**
J, Guillebaud 4th edn, Churchill Livingstone, 2004, 588pp. £24.99. ISBN 0443073430.
'Serves as a primary source of information about reversible methods of contraception. Written in an informal – and yet highly informative – question-and-answer style, it represents a dialogue between general practitioner (asking the

questions) and a reproductive health specialist (providing the answers).'

4445 Endocrine and reproductive systems
S. Sanders and M. Debuse 2nd edn, Mosby, 2003, 278pp. $25.95. ISBN 0723432457.
One of the Crash Course series of books that present an overview of the core information on a particular subject in a format that is intended to facilitate rapid comprehension. A useful starting point although it would be even more useful if it included a bibliography.

4446 Essential reproduction
M.H. Johnson and B.J. Everitt 5th edn, Blackwell Science, 2000, 285pp. £27.50. ISBN 0632042877.
A good undergraduate textbook that covers all aspects of human reproduction. It has full colour illustrations and also includes suggestions for further reading.

- **Human reproduction at a glance L.J. Heffner** Blackwell Science, 2001, 119pp. £15.95. ISBN 0632054611. Provides an overview of human reproduction, including anatomy, physiology and genetics. Divided into two parts: Normal human reproduction; Human reproductive disorders (including sexually transmitted diseases).

4447 Introduction to mammalian reproduction
D. Tulsiani, ed. Kluwer Academic, 2003, 403pp. £119.00. ISBN 140207283X.
Provides an advanced introduction to this subject. 20 multi-author chapters in five parts: Male gamete: Female gamete; Early events of fertilization; Fusion of gametes; Medical implications. Each chapter includes a bibliography.

4448 Langman's medical embryology
T.W. Sadler 9th edn, Lippincott Williams & Wilkins, 2004, 534pp. Includes CD-ROM, $54.95. ISBN 0781743109.
Standard undergraduate textbook covering all aspects of embryology, the accompanying CD-ROM showing animations of embryological development. Divided into three parts. Part 1 covers general embryology, following the process through from gametogenesis to birth and including birth defects; Part 2 covers the development of individual systems and organs; Part 3 provides answers to the problems given in the first two parts. A bibliography of further reading is included at the end of each chapter.

4449 The second creation: the age of biological control by the scientists who cloned Dolly
I. Wilmut, K. Campbell and C. Tudge Headline, 2001, 362pp. Originally published 2000. Also available from Harvard University Press, £7.99. ISBN 0747259305.
'The cloning of Dolly in 1996 from the cell of an adult sheep was a pivotal moment in history. For the first time, a team of scientists, led by Ian Wilmut and Keith Campbell, was able to clone a whole mammal using a single cultured adult body cell, a breakthrough that revolutionized three technologies – genetic engineering, genomics, and cloning by nuclear transfer from adult cells – and brought science ever closer to the possibility of human cloning ...'

4450 Sexual chemistry: a history of the contraceptive pill
L. Marks Yale University Press, 2001, 372pp. $40.00. ISBN 0300089430.
'Heralded as the catalyst of the sexual revolution and the solution to global overpopulation, the contraceptive pill was one of the twentieth century's most important inventions. It has not only transformed the lives of millions of women but has also pushed the limits of drug monitoring and regulation across the world. This deeply-researched new history of the oral contraceptive shows how its development and use have raised crucial questions about the relationship between science, medicine, technology, and society.'
'Marks has produced a beautifully written, definitive history of the oral contraceptive pill. Every possible aspect of its development has been considered, ranging from the global population perspective to the impact of the pill on the lives of individual women... . [A] masterpiece... . The book is an invaluable reference source.' (*Nature*)

Dictionaries, thesauri, classifications

Dictionary of developmental biology and embryology
F.J. Dye See entry no. 2449

4451 Reproductive medicine: from A to Z
H.E. Reiss [et al.], eds Oxford University Press, 1997, 152pp. £27.50. ISBN 0192629018.
A dictionary of reproductive medicine providing definitions of around 800 terms. It is extensively cross-referenced, and explains the clinical relevance of each term.

Laws, standards, codes

4452 Legal and ethical issues in human reproduction
B. Steinbock, ed. Ashgate / Dartmouth, 2002, 484pp. £100.00. ISBN 0754620492.
www.ashgate.com/subject_area/law/library_medicine_series.htm
A collection of articles that were previously published in journals and that deal with the legal and ethical issues of reproduction, including genetic screening, cloning and assisted reproduction.
See website for other titles in the Series: International Library of Medicine, Ethics, and Law.

Official & quasi-official bodies

4453 Human Fertilisation and Embryology Authority [UK]
www.hfea.gov.uk
A non-departmental governmental body that regulates IVF clinics and licenses human embryo research in the UK. The site provides information on infertility, IVF and donor insemination (DI).

Human Genetics Commission
See entry no. 3608

President's Council on Bioethics
See entry no. 3468

4454 Reproductive Health and Research
World Health Organization
www.who.int/reproductive-health/index.htm
This site provides an authoritative source of information on topics relating to reproductive health including adolescence, family planning and sexually transmitted diseases (including HIV/Aids).

Research centres & institutes

4455 Alan Guttmacher Institute [USA]
www.guttmacher.org
A non-profit organization based in the US that aims to provide reliable, balanced, non-partisan information on sexual activity, contraception, abortion and childbearing. The Institute 'informs its various audiences – policymakers, activists, health care professionals, researchers, the media and the public – through its highly regarded journals, *Perspectives on Sexual and Reproductive Health* and *International Family Planning Perspectives*; its public policy review, *The Guttmacher Report on Public Policy*, and its website'.

Genetics & Public Policy Center
See entry no. 3610

Associations & societies

4456 American Society for Reproductive Medicine
www.asrm.org
Founded in 1944, the Society is 'devoted to advancing knowledge and expertise in infertility, reproductive medicine and biology'. Site content is divided under headings for all users, for patients, for professionals and for the media. Each of these headings contains lots of useful information including fact sheets, ethics reports and patient information booklets. The Society has 16 Specialty Societies. A good well constructed site: check the extensive Topic Index with some 60 entries.

4457 Association of Reproductive Health Professionals
www.arhp.org
This site, based in the US but with an international coverage, provides a huge amount of information (over 2000 pages) on all aspects of reproductive health. Information is provided under headings for healthcare providers, for patients, and for the media and includes news headlines and links to related sites. An excellent resource.

4458 British Fertility Society
www.britishfertilitysociety.org.uk
Founded in 1972, the Society produces the journal *Human Fertility* and organizes scientific meetings and training courses. Useful links section.

4459 EngenderHealth
www.engenderhealth.org
Founded in 1943, EngenderHealth is a non-profit organization that works internationally to support and strengthen reproductive health services for women and men worldwide. A good informative and well designed website, with a very extensive and useful list of Links.

4460 European Society of Human Reproduction and Embryology
www.eshre.com
Founded in 1985, the Society organises an annual meeting and publishes several journals including HUMAN REPRODUCTION UPDATE, one of the most highly cited journals in the field. The site provides information about the Society, a calendar of scientific meetings and useful links to descriptions of the activities of its Special Interest Groups.

4461 Family Planning Association [UK]
www.fpa.org.uk/about/index.htm
The only registered charity working to improve the sexual health and reproductive rights of all people throughout the UK.

4462 Infertility Network UK
www.infertilitynetworkuk.com
Formed by the merger of CHILD and ISSUE, the Network provides information on topics relating to infertility and links to support networks in the UK. It also provides access to factsheets, articles and an online video. 'We are now the largest network in the UK for those experiencing fertility problems, offering face-to-face and telephonic support and information at regional and national level.'

4463 International Federation of Fertility Societies
www.iffs-reproduction.org
Founded in 1968, the Federation organizes international meetings and publishes a regular newsletter. Short but useful links section, and especially good as an entrée to the sites of worldwide member societies ('affiliated societies').

4464 Progress Educational Trust [UK]
www.progress.org.uk
UK charity that aims to educate the general public on issues relating to human reproduction and genetics. They do this by organizing public debates and conferences and by producing literature for schools.

'Progress Educational Trust believes that reproductive and genetic technologies have much to offer. The development of IVF has already led to the birth of thousands of babies across the world. Genetic testing, carried out before or during pregnancy, has offered parents the chance to have children free from a particular genetic disease. Assisted reproduction and genetics offer an alternative to those who are unable – because of infertility or because they have a genetic disease in their family – to consider normal methods of having children.'

- **BioNews.org.uk** www.bionews.org.uk. 'News, information and comment in assisted reproduction and genetics.'

Portal & task environments

4465 ReproMED
University of Bristol
www.repromed.org.uk
'Since 1995 ReproMED has pioneered the use of the Internet to support collaborative clinical care, research and education in the field of Reproductive Medicine.' Inviting, very well designed website. Offered from the University's Centre for Reproductive Medicine, who subscribe to the HONCode principles. This is the gateway for professionals; there is also one for patients.

Digital data, image & text collections

4466 UNSW Embryology
M.A. Hill; University of New South Wales
http://embryology.med.unsw.edu.au
This site is effectively an online embryology textbook that includes animations, detailed notes and links to related web and print resources. It contains a huge amount of

information and is written in a style that makes it very accessible. A very good up-to-date example of its genre.

Directories & encyclopedias

Atlas of descriptive embryology
G.C. Schoenwolf and W.W. Mathews See entry no. 2467

4467 An atlas of reproductive physiology in men
E.S.E. Hafez Parthenon Publishing, 2004, 250pp. $169.95. ISBN 1842142356.
www.parthpub.com
Good exemplar of text in this extensive series of over 100 titles.

Series: Encyclopedia of Visual Medicine, V 67. (The publisher's website directs to that of CRC Press (now part of Taylor & Francis) for its books and CD-ROMs; unfortunately, there did not seem to be available there (nor elsewhere) a specifically organized online list of all titles in the Series.)

4468 Catalog of teratogenic agents
T.H. Shepard and R.J. Lemire 11th edn, Johns Hopkins University Press, 2004, 3166pp. $225.00. ISBN 0801879531.
This edition includes nearly 300 newly listed agents. 'As in previous editions, this volume emphasizes human data and covers pharmaceuticals, chemicals, environmental pollutants, food additives, household products, and viruses. A special effort has been made to obtain as much information as possible on drugs and other agents to which pregnant women may be exposed. Substances are listed alphabetically, and each entry briefly summarizes research procedures and results. In addition, a complete list of references is included for each agent.'

'High quality, well indexed, and up-to-date ... I would recommend this book for its breadth of entries and clarity of presentation (on a previous edn).' (*Journal of Medical Genetics*)

4469 Encyclopedia of birth control
V.L. Bullough [et al.], eds ABC-CLIO, 2001, 349pp. $85.00. ISBN 1576071812.
'A complete report on the historical development and efficacy of contraceptive practices around the world, both past and present.'

- **Encyclopedia of birth control M. Rengel** Oryx Press, 2000, 312pp. $65.95. ISBN 1573562556. '... an excellent book for those interested in the historical and social aspects of birth control ... Highly recommended for all collections.' *Library Journal*.

4470 Encyclopedia of reproduction
E. Knobil and J.D. Neill, eds Academic Press, 1998. 4 v, $765.00. ISBN 0122270207.
Provides an overview of reproduction in the animal kingdom, including humans. It consists of a collection of articles written by a range of authors, arranged alphabetically by subject title. Each article includes a glossary (all of the terms are brought together in an A–Z sequence in Volume 4) and a bibliography.

Handbooks & manuals

4471 The developing human: clinically oriented embryology
K.L. Moore 7th edn, Saunders, 2003, 560pp. $54.95. ISBN 0721694128.
A fine production; very good use of colour. 'This best-selling resource comprehensively covers human embryology and teratology, presenting all of the complex clinical and scientific concepts in an engaging, lucid, and practical way. Completely revised and updated, the 7th Edition consistently emphasizes the clinical aspects by using a wealth of case studies, clinical correlations, and hundreds of outstanding illustrations.'

4472 Handbook of family planning and reproductive healthcare
A. Glasier and A. Gebbie, eds 4th edn, Churchill Livingstone, 2000, 441pp. £37.99. ISBN 0443064504.
Practical handbook for daily reference by those working in reproductive health. All forms of contraception are covered in detail, giving guidance on practical prescribing, possible complications and the relative advantages and disadvantages of each method.

Maternal-fetal medicine: principles and practice
R.K. Creasy and R. Resnik, eds See entry no. 4017

Keeping up-to-date

Current Topics in Developmental Biology
See entry no. 2472

4473 Human Reproduction Update
European Society of Human Reproduction and Embryology Oxford University Press, 1995–, Bimonthly. ISSN 13554786.
http://humupd.oupjournals.org
'Aims to provide invited, comprehensive, authoritative, up-to-date critical and balanced reviews covering all areas of human reproduction including reproductive physiology and pathology, endocrinology, andrology, gonad function, gametogenesis, fertilization, embryo development, implantation, pregnancy, genetics, genetic diagnosis, oncology, infectious disease, surgery, contraception, infertility treatment, psychology and counselling, ethics and social issues.'

4474 Reproduction
Society for Reproduction and Fertility BioScientifica, 2001–, Monthly. £625.00. ISSN 14701626.
www.reproduction-online.org [DESCRIPTION]
Contains original research articles and reviews on all aspects of reproductive biology, with an emphasis on molecular and cellular aspects. Merger in 2000 of the *Journal of Reproduction and Fertility* and *Reviews of Reproduction*.

Theriogenology: An International Journal of Animal Reproduction
See entry no. 3432

Sports & Exercise Medicine

exercise medicine • physical education • physical fitness • sports injuries • work physiology

Dictionaries, thesauri, classifications

4475 **The Oxford dictionary of sports science and medicine**
M. Kent, comp. 2nd edn, Oxford University Press, 1998, 567pp. £26.95. ISBN 0192628453.
Comprehensive and authoritative dictionary for anyone interested in sport. Over 7500 cross-referenced terms and 165 illustrations.

Associations & societies

4476 **American College of Sports Medicine**
www.acsm.org
Founded in 1954 to advance and integrate scientific research to provide educational and practical applications of exercise science and sports medicine. Has developed a series of Current Comments: 'Proactive statements concerning sports medicine and exercise science-related topics of interest to the public at large. They are written in understandable language to be relevant and helpful to the general public'.

4477 **American Orthopedic Society for Sports Medicine**
www.sportsmed.org
Formed in 1972, as a national organization of orthopaedic surgeons specializing in sports medicine, including national and international sports medicine leaders. Works closely with many other sports medicine specialists and clinicians, including family physicians, emergency physicians, paediatricians, athletic trainers and physical therapists, to improve the identification, prevention, treatment and rehabilitation of sports injuries.

4478 **British Association of Sport and Exercise Medicine**
www.basem.co.uk
Founded in 1953, is the oldest sport and exercise medicine association in the UK, dedicated to the promotion of good health through physical activity, and the provision of sports medicine expertise to optimize athletic performance at all levels.

4479 **British Association of Sport and Exercise Sciences**
www.bases.org.uk
The UK professional body for all those with an interest in the science of sport and exercise. 'Sport and Exercise Science' is the application of scientific principles to the promotion, maintenance and enhancement of sport and exercise-related behaviours.

Chartered Society of Physiotherapy
See entry no. 4352

4480 **International Federation of Sports Medicine (Fédération Internationale de Médecine du Sport)**
www.fims.org
Comprised of individual members, national associations, and multinational groups, with a common involvement with sports medicine on all continents. FIMS aims primarily 'to promote the study and development of sports medicine throughout the world, and to assist athletes in achieving optimal performance by maximizing their genetic potential, health, nutrition, and high-quality medical care and training.'

- **Olympic Encyclopaedia of Sports Medicine** Blackwell Publishing. www.blackwellpublishing.com/medicine/sports.asp [DESCRIPTION]. 10 v. published in association with the Federation and the IOC MEDICAL COMMISSION, latest in 2002. Website provides details of all Blackwell's offerings in sports medicine and science, including the Olympic Handbook of Sports Medicine.

International Sports Engineering Association
See entry no. 5901

4481 **IOC Medical Commission**
www.olympic.org
'Created in 1967 in order to deal with the increasing problem of doping in the sports world. The initial goal of putting in place an anti-doping structure was rapidly widened to encompass the following three fundamental principals: Protection of the health of athletes; Respect for both medical and sport ethics; Equality for all competing athletes.'

World Cancer Research Fund International
See entry no. 4036

Discovering print & electronic resources

PEDro: Physiotherapy Evidence Database
University of Sydney See entry no. 4362

4482 **SportDiscus**
Sport Information Resource Centre
www.sportdiscus.com [FEE-BASED]
700,000 references from periodicals, books, e-journals, conference proceedings, theses, dissertations, and websites; direct links to full-text articles. 'Focuses on different areas involving sport, including: the arts and humanities, engineering and social sciences.'

- **Sport thesaurus: the thesaurus of terminology used in the SPORT database** Sport Information Resource Centre1994, 297pp.

Directories & encyclopedias

An atlas of obesity and weight control
G.A. Bray See entry no. 4399

4483 **The encyclopedia of sports medicine**
E.H. Oakes Facts On File, 2005, 322pp. $75.00. ISBN 0816053340.
150 articles arranged A–Z by title.
Series: Library of Health and Living.

Handbooks & manuals

4484 **Biomedical engineering principles in sports**
G.K. Hung and J.M. Pallis, eds Kluwer Academic/Plenum Publishers, 2004, 513pp. £80.60. ISBN 0306484773.
Edited collection bridging gaps between disciplines 'by providing the biomedical engineering student, the dedicated athlete, and the intelligent layperson, a book with the latest

advances in biomechanics and sports medicine in the sports they actively participate in or enjoy watching. This includes golf, tennis, baseball, football, soccer, and basketball'.

4485 **Essentials of research methods in health, physical education, exercise science, recreation**
K.E. Berg 2nd edn, Lippincott Williams & Wilkins, 2004, 292pp. $56.95. ISBN 0781738024.
Includes coverage of: Ethics in human subject research; Research writing – with short overview 'Getting started: information retrieval'; Statistics; Measurement and research design; Quality control and application of research. Glossary.

4486 **Exercise endocrinology**
K.T. Borer Human Kinetics, 2003, 273pp. $75.00. ISBN 0880115661.
www.humankinetics.com [DESCRIPTION]
Good overview; extensive bibliography pp 193–259.
The publisher has a very extensive list of titles in this arena: see website.

Kinesiology: the mechanics and pathomechanics of human movement
C.A. Oatis See entry no. 3967

4487 **Physiology of sport and exercise**
J.H. Wilmore and D.L. Costill 3rd edn, Human Kinetcis, 2004, 726pp. $79.00. ISBN 0736044892:.
www.humankinetics.com/physiologyOfSportAndExercise [COMPANION]
Excellent very clearly designed text. 21 chapters in seven parts: Essentials of movement; Energy for movement; Cardiovascular and respiratory function and performance; Environmental influences on performance; Optimizing performance in sport; Age and sex considerations in sport and exercise; Physical activity for health and fitness.

4488 **Sports injuries: their prevention and treatment**
L. Peterson and P. Renstrom 3rd edn, Martin Dunitz, 2000, 554pp. CD-ROM available, £34.50. ISBN 1853171190.
1. General principles; 2. Injuries to musculoskeletal tissues; 3. Mechanism and etiology of injuries; 4. Protective equipment; 5. Acute treatment principles; 6. Shoulder and upper arm; 7. Elbow; 8. Forearm, wrist and hand; 9. Back; 10. Groin and thigh; 11. Knee; 12. Lower Leg; 13. Ankle; 14. Foot; 15. Head and trunk; 16. Children and adolescents; 17. Environmental problems; 18. Specialized activities; 19. General risk factors; 20. Rehabilitation programs; 21. Glossary.

4489 **Textbook of work physiology: physiological bases of exercise**
P.-O. Astrand 4th edn, Human Kinetics, 2003, 656pp. $79.00. ISBN 0736001409.
Good straightforward text; over 600 references

Keeping up-to-date

4490 **British Journal of Sports Medicine**
British Association of Sport and Exercise Medicine BMJ Journals, Monthly. ISSN 03063674.
http://bjsm.bmjjournals.com
'An international peer review journal covering the latest advances in clinical practice and research. Topics include all aspects of sports medicine, such as the management of sports injury, exercise physiology, sports psychology, physiotherapy and the epidemiology of exercise and health. To ensure international coverage BJSM has dedicated North American editors, as well as Editorial Board members from countries including Canada, Australia, Scandinavia and South Africa.

Each issue includes selected summaries from *SportsMedUpdate*, an evidence-based journal watch service co-ordinated in South Africa; 2004 will see the launch of an education series that will encompass a core curriculum in sports medicine as well as interactive online case reports.'

TECHNOLOGY

Technology

The key difference from the former *Walford's Guide to Reference Material* in coverage is our decision for the most part to place resources concerned with companies, industries and markets in TNW Volume 2, alongside those treating business, economics and management, rather than here.

Introductions to the subject

4491 Global shift: reshaping the global economic map in the 21st century
P. Dicken Sage Publications, 2003, 632pp. £60.00. ISBN 0761971491.
Exceptionally good, very well presented and readable introduction. 'My basic argument is that globalization is not some inevitable kind of end-state but, rather, a complex, indeterminate set of processes operating very unevenly in both time and space ... It is vital to understand the long-term, underlying processes of global economic change.'

18 chapters in four parts: The shifting contours of the geo-economy; Processes of global shift (including *Technology: the 'great growling engine of change'*); Global shift: the picture in different sectors; Winners and losers in the global economy. 'It is utterly repellent that so many people live in such abject poverty and deprivation whilst, at the same time, others live in immense luxury. This is not an argument for levelling down but for raising up. The means for doing this are there. What matters is the *will* to do it ...'
'If there was a word beyond definitive, then that would be the word I would be using here.' (*Nigel Thrift, University of Bristol*)

4492 A history of engineering and technology: artful methods
E. Garrison 2nd edn, CRC Press, 1998, 347pp. $79.95. ISBN 084939810X.
From the earliest builders through antiquity, renaissance, industrial revolution, 20th century, to new technology and the future.

4493 History of technology
I. Inkster, ed. Continuum, 2004, 256pp. £75.00. ISBN 0826471870.
'The technical problems confronting different societies and periods and the measures taken to solve them form the concern of this annual collection of essays. It deals with the history of technical discovery and change and explores the relationship of technology to other aspects of life – social, cultural and economic – showing how technological development has shaped, and been shaped by, the society in which it occurred.'
Series: History of Technology, V. 25.

- **History of technology and science S. Collins; Carnegie Mellon University** . www.library.cmu.edu/Research/Humanities/History/hots.html. Very good example of briefly annotated resource list created by a university reference librarian (and updated January 2005). Well worth checking university library websites for such lists (though their quality and longevity varies considerably).

Introduction to weapons of mass destruction: radiological, chemical and biological
R.E. Langford See entry no. 4411

4494 MIT and the rise of entrepreneurial science
H. Etzkowitz Routledge, 2002, 173pp. $129.95. ISBN 041528516X.
Describes the evolution of the Massachusetts Institute of Technology. Especially covers the many difficult issues that arise in the development of a distinctive and mutually beneficial relationship between academia and industry: a relationship since emulated throughout the world.
'A fascinating volume.' (*Research Policy*)

4495 Society, ethics, and technology
M. Winston and R. Edelbach 2nd edn, Wadsworth, 2003, 352pp. $53.95. ISBN 053458540X.
'This anthology presents a variety of historical, social, and philosophical perspectives on technological change and its social consequences, stressing the manner in which technological innovation creates new ethical problems for human civilization ... A revised introduction and new readings highlight the most current issues and debates concerning ethics and technology, including climate change, nanotechnology, human cloning, globalization, innovation, and natural capitalism.'

Dictionaries, thesauri, classifications

4496 Abbreviations dictionary
D.A. Stahl and K. Kerchelich, comps 10th edn, CRC Press, 2001, 1552pp. $89.95. ISBN 0849390036.
Covers all sorts of abbreviations including acronyms, appellations, contractions, numbered abbreviations and other short forms: concentrating on technology, but also covering the underlying science, and including colloquial as well as technical terminology. 15,000 new references in the latest edn.

4497 Acronym Finder
www.acronymfinder.com
Searchable database of some 350,000 abbreviations and acronyms in the computers, technology, telecommunications, and military fields. Sponsored site, but: 'Your support of our sponsors helps keep Acronym Finder free!.'

4498 ASTM dictionary of engineering, science and technology
ASTM International 9th edn, 2000, 638pp. $129.00. ISBN 0803127456.
Contains all the 22,000 standard definitions referenced in all ASTM terminology standards. Formerly *Compilation of ASTM standard definitions.*

- Chinese Edition. $150.00.

4499 Defence terminology
G. Lee, ed. Brassey's, 1991, 225pp. ISBN 008041334X.
Useful entrée for those unfamiliar with the field.

- **DOD dictionary of military terms** **United States. Department of Defense.** www.dtic.mil/doctrine/jel/doddict. 'The *DOD Dictionary* and the *Joint Acronyms and Abbreviations* master database are managed by the Joint Doctrine Division, J-7, Joint Staff.

4500 **Dictionary of military terms**
R. Bowyer 3rd edn, Bloomsbury, 2004, 264pp. £9.99. ISBN 0747574774.
www.bloomsbury.com/reference
Good for those new to military matters. Topics covered include ranks, training, military personnel, manoeuvres, vehicles, tactics, commands, weapons and equipment. Encyclopedic notes expand upon the more complex terms.
See website for details of the publisher's other reference works.

- **Dictionary of military terms** **T.N. Dupuy [et al.]** 2nd edn, H W Wilson, 2003, 300pp. $90.00. ISBN 0824210255. 'Excellently conceived ... There is really nothing quite like it.' *American Reference Books Annual.*

4501 **Dictionnaire des techniques et technologies modernes: Anglais–Français (Modern dictionary of engineering and technology)**
J.R. Forbes, ed. 3rd edn, Editeur Technique & Documentation, 2003, 630pp. €87.00. ISBN 2743006560.
Contains 43,000 terms from scientific and technical fields including information technology, robotics, food processing, molecular biology and genetic engineering and ecology.

4502 **Dizionario tecnico (Technical dictionary)**
C. Crielesi and G. Landucci, comps Alinea, 1999, 1492pp. Vol. 1. English–Italian; Vol. 2. Italiano–Inglese; accompanying CD–ROM, €135.00. ISBN 8881253534.
This work includes fields such as acoustics, carpentry, ceramics, mechanics, mineral processing and welding. Over 45,000 entries in each volume.

4503 **Langenscheidts Fachwörterbuch Technik und Angewandte Wissenschaften: Deutsch–Englisch (Langenscheidt's dictionary technology and applied sciences: German–English)**
P.A. Schmitt, ed. Langenscheidt, 2002, 2155pp. €132.70. ISBN 3861171872.
250,000 entries covering technology from acoustics to waste disposal and science (chemistry, biochemistry, physics). Entries give the field of application and a translation.
'ideal for all but the most detailed specialist texts ... solid, fine and reliable reference source.' (*Irish Translators' & Interpreters' Association Bulletin*)

4504 **SYMBOLS.com**
www.symbols.com
Interesting compilation, based on the 'first comprehensive encyclopedia of Western ideograms ever published, unique in its search systems, that allows the reader to locate a symbol by defining just four of its visual characteristics. It is about our graphic cultural heritage as expressed in subway graffiti, fighter jets' signs and emergency exit symbols. It contains 2300 symbols, 1600 articles and streamlined reference functions. Ideograms carved in mammoth teeth by Cro-Magnon men 25,000 years ago, put on modern household appliances by their manufacturers or sprayed on walls by political activists, are all presented in dictionary form for easy reference. Symbols cover current designs used in advertising, logotyping, architecture, design, decoration, religion, politics and astrology.'

- **Thought signs: the semiotics of symbols – Western ideograms** **C. Liungman** IOS Press, 1995, 706pp. £41.00. ISBN 9051991975.

Laws, standards, codes

4505 **ASTM International**
www.astm.org
Originally known as the American Society for Testing and Materials, now operates internationally, its standards arising from the work of over 30,000 ASTM members representative of producers, users, consumers, government and academia from more than 100 countries. Currently there are over 12,000 standards, which are reproduced in the *Annual Book of ASTM Standards* (77 volumes, 2004: also available on CD-ROM).

Various web-based standards delivery services are offered – there is a good online standards search facility; and personal e-mails can alert when changes are made to standards and when new standards are under development. More generic news services are provided online and in print.

But the Society also 'publishes hundreds of technical publications in formats to meet your needs including Special Technical Publications (STPs), compilations, manuals, monographs, journals, data series, adjuncts, reference radiographs, handbooks and more' – a number of which are cited elsewhere in this Guide. A free print copy of the current ASTM Catalogue can be requested; or the catalogue can be examined online as a PDF file.

4506 **AvantIQ**
www.avantiq.com [FEE-BASED]
'Offers the widest range of trademark databases currently available online. Our 18 national and international trademark databases cover 75% of the EU, all of NAFTA, the European Community trademarks database, the WIPO database of International trademarks and the IMS Pharmaceuticals in-use file. AvantIQ® is the only company to offer online databases for Scandinavia and Mexico.'

Four Training Databases are freely available 'so that you can discover the unlimited possibilities of our Scan Search'.

4507 **British Library – Patents**
www.bl.uk/collections/patents.html
Features extensive information on library collections, databases and services; searching for patents, trade marks and registered designs; and other patent libraries. A comprehensive and well maintained list of links is given.

4508 **Canadian Intellectual Property Office**
http://cipo.gc.ca
Administers the intellectual property (IP) system in Canada and disseminates IP information. Contains links to the websites of related organizations in Canada, plus a set of International Intellectual Property Links where it is noted that 'some of these sites present information only in their respective national language'.

- **Canadian Patents Database** http://patents1.ic.gc.ca/intro-e.html. Contains bibliographic, text, and image data for Canadian patent documents filed or granted from 1920 to present. Intended 'for personal research and information purposes and should not be relied upon to make decisions'.

4509 **Defense Standardization Program** [USA]
http://dsp.dla.mil
Mission is to 'identify, influence, develop, manage, and provide access to standardization processes, products, and services for warfighters, the acquisition community, and the logistics community to promote interoperability, reduce total ownership costs, and sustain readiness'. Good entrée to the area.

- **Defense Advanced Research Projects Agency** www.darpa.mil. DoD central research and development organization. Manages and directs selected basic and applied research and development projects, and pursues research and technology 'where risk and payoff are very high and where success may provide dramatic advances'.

4510 **DEPATISnet**
Deutsches Patent- und Markenamt
www.depatisnet.de
Beginners, expert and family search interfaces to a free database from the German Patent and Trade Mark Office which covers the patents of several authorities. Provides bibliographic details and access to electronic copies of the full patent documents. English and German interfaces. Coverage not so extensive as ESP@CENET.

4511 **Derwent World Patents Index**
Thomson Derwent.
http://thomsonderwent.com/products [FEE-BASED]
Major database of 'intellectually enhanced' information from some 23 million patent documents issued by 40 patent-issuing authorities giving details of 11 million inventions. Key features include specially prepared English abstracts, indexing and organization into families. Apart from via the Hosts, the database – either in whole or in part – is accessible within a range of Thomson and some other environments. There are also a number of associated products such as: Chemistry Resource (chemical structure database for searching specific compounds), GENESEQ] (for nucleic and protein sequence information contained in patents), Merged Markush Service (offering unique coverage and graphical searching capabilities for searching chemical structures in patents).

- **Delphion Research** http://thomsonderwent.com/products/pca/delphionresearch. One of the wide range of Thomson services. Here, 'quick text search' of US and multinational patent numbers is free on registration; subscription enables advanced searching of over 35 million records from 70 patent offices worldwide.
- **Derwent Innovations Index** www.derwent.com/products/patentresearch/dii. Web-based resource merging *Derwent World Patents Index* with the *Derwent Patents Citation Index*.
- **Derwent Patents Citation Index** http://thomsonderwent.com/products/patentresearch/pci. 45 million examiner citations of patents and literature appearing in patents from the European Patent Office, Germany, United Kingdom, Japan, United States and Patent co-operation Treaty. Also integrated into Derwent Innovations Index.

4512 **European Patent Office**
www.european-patent-office.org
The EPO grants pan-European patents and provides information about them. Its web pages give official communications, applicant information, list of patent libraries in Europe, news and details of events and other web, print and CD-ROM products.

- **EPIDOS-INPADOC** www.european-patent-office.org/inpadoc/index.htm. Range of patent databases including PFS, which deals with all patent documents applied in 65 patent offices worldwide; and PRS, the legal status of patents (are they in force or not) in 22 patent offices.
- **Esp@cenet** http://ep.espacenet.com. Worldwide database of c.45 million records. Searching for bibliographic and classification information is simple but limited in flexibility. Many of the patent documents can be viewed and printed in full. An excellent first source for patent searching.
- **Patent Information on the Internet** www.european-patent-office.org/online. Frequently updated, wide-ranging list of links.
- **The PATLIB Network European Patent Office**. www.european-patent-office.org/patlib. Created by the national offices of the member states of the European Patent Organization (EPO) and their regional patent information centres. Currently there are about 280 information centres within the 27 EPO member states.

4513 **Federal Institute of Industrial Property** [RUS]
www.fips.ru/ruptoen/index.htm
Website of the organization *Rospatent*, an official Russian participant in work of the WORLD INTELLECTUAL PROPERTY ORGANIZATION. Well designed website with good English-language coverage.

ifi CLAIMS Patent Services
See entry no. 5079

4514 **Intellectual Property** [UK]
Patent Office
www.intellectual-property.gov.uk
UK Government-backed site aiming 'to bring you all the answers to your questions and all the resources you need to find your way through the IP jungle of Copyright, Designs, Patents and Trade Marks'. Very easy to navigate through a large set of clearly written sets of information. News section and A–Z indexes of the extensive lists of Copyright, Patent, Design and Trade Mark Links.

- **IP Menu** Phillips Ormonde Fitzpatrick. www.ipmenu.com. Excellent extensive gateway to international patent, intellectual property and related matters by Australian patent agents. News and information on rights and technology with well organized links.

4515 **Intellectual property law for engineers and scientists**
H.B. Rockman, ed. IEEE Press/Wiley, 2004, 544pp. $79.95. ISBN 0471449989.
27 fascinating chapters running from Overview of intellectual property law through, for example, Novelty, infringement, and other searches, Patentability of biotechnology inventions, The engineer and scientist as expert witness; and ethics to Cybersquatting. Between each chapter there are short essays on famous inventors with their patent drawings. Not, however, a how-to-do-it manual; more a guide to the promises and pitfalls of the arena.
'informative, interesting, and fun ... highly recommended for any library that counts inventors amongst its clientele.' (E-STREAMS)

- **Creative Commons** www.creativecommons.org. 'We use private rights to create public goods: creative works set free for certain uses. Like the free software and open-source movements, our ends are cooperative and community-minded, but our means are voluntary and libertarian.'
- **XrML: The Digital Rights Language for Trusted Content and Services** www.xrml.org. 'Provides a universal method for securely specifying and managing rights and conditions associated with all kinds of resources including digital content as well as services. Extensible and fully compliant with XML namespaces using XML schema technology.'

4516 **International classifications**
World Intellectual Property Organization
www.wipo.int/classifications/en
'Anyone applying for a patent or registering a trademark or design, whether at the national or international level, is required to determine whether their creation is new or is owned or claimed by someone else. To determine this, huge amounts of information must be searched. Four WIPO treaties ... Created classification systems which organize information concerning inventions, trademarks, and industrial designs into indexed, manageable structures for easy retrieval. Regularly updated to include changes and advances in technology and commercial practices, the classification systems are used voluntarily by many countries which are not member States of the related agreements.'

The treaties are:

- *Strasbourg Agreement* Concerning the International Patent Classification (IPC);
- *Nice Agreement* Concerning the International Classification of Goods and Services for the Purposes of the Registration of Marks;
- *Locarno Agreement* Establishing the International Classification for Industrial Designs;
- *Vienna Agreement* Establishing the International Classification of the Figurative Elements of Marks.

4517 **International Trademark Association**
www.inta.org
'Not-for-profit membership association of more than 4600 trademark owners and professionals, from more than 180 countries, dedicated to the support and advancement of trademarks and related intellectual property as elements of fair and effective national and international commerce.'

Very good well organized site. The Information Center part of the site has: FAQs; Basic fact sheets; Glossary and acronyms; Links – and 'if you still cannot find what you are looking for, please email the Information Resources Specialist'. A nice service.

4518 **Introduction to patents information**
S. Ashpitel, D. Newton and S. van Dulken 4th edn, British Library, 2002, 143pp. £34.00. ISBN 0712308628.
Detailed introduction to searching covering British, US, German, Japanese, European and Patent Co-operation Treaty (international) patent systems. Chapters on finding and using patent information and patent classification with appendices giving online resources, codes used in patent documents, bibliography and glossary. Illustrated with examples of search tools and patent documentation.

4519 **IP Australia**
www.ipaustralia.gov.au
The federal government agency responsible for granting rights in patents, trade marks and designs.

4520 **IPR Helpdesk** [EUR]
European Commission. Directorate for Research
www.ipr-helpdesk.org
European Commission sponsored programme run by University of Alicante and other bodies. It assists contractors carrying out EC-funded research and others in Intellectual Property Rights issues. News, information and advice. Another more global objective of the action is to raise awareness of the European research community on IPR issues, emphasizing their European dimension.

- **Office for Harmonization in the Internal Market (Trade Marks and Designs)** http://oami.eu.int/en. Promotes and manages trade marks and designs within the European Union.

4521 **Japan Patent Office**
www.jpo.go.jp
Clearly-laid out English language site with: What's new; Site map; Quick guide; Inquiries; etc.

- **Industrial Property Digital Library** www.ipdl.ncipi.go.jp/homepg_e.ipdl. Patent Abstracts of Japan database gives English-language abstracts of most Japanese patents issued since 1976. Gazette database allows retrieval of full patents/utility models and automatic translation into English.

4522 **MicroPatent**
www.micropat.com [FEE-BASED]
Patent database subscription service with daily and annual rates. PatentWeb full text and front page databases cover patents from major countries and authorities. Electronic copies of patent documents can be supplied. Aimed at end users. Aureka service enables analysis and mining of patent data.

4523 **National Institute of Standards and Technology** [USA]
www.nist.gov
Founded 1901, a non-regulatory federal agency within the US Department of Commerce TECHNOLOGY ADMINISTRATION. NIST's mission is 'to develop and promote measurement, standards, and technology to enhance productivity, facilitate trade, and improve the quality of life'.

NIST carries out its mission in four co-operative programs:

NIST Laboratories: Conduct research that advances the nation's technology infrastructure and is needed by US industry to continually improve products and services

Baldrige National Quality Program: Promotes performance excellence among US manufacturers, service companies, educational institutions, and healthcare providers; conducts outreach programmes and manages the annual Malcolm Baldrige National Quality Award which recognizes performance excellence and quality achievement

Manufacturing Extension Partnership: Nationwide network of local centres offering technical and business assistance to smaller manufacturers

Advanced Technology Program: Accelerates the development of innovative technologies for broad national benefit by co-funding R&D partnerships with the private sector.

There is an excellent A–Z Subject Index providing links to information about all the different NIST activities, products and services, including to a series of essays on various sectors of the form Aerospace Industry: How NIST Helps, Health Care Industry: How NIST Helps.

The NIST Virtual Library – among much other valuable information – has a series of regularly updated Resource Guides covering: Biotechnology; Chemistry; Computer Science; Engineering; Health Care; Homeland Security; Materials Science; Math/Statistics; Nanotechnology; Physics. It is a well laid out and inviting entrée to a very wide range of resources: well worth an intensive browse around.

- **Ceramics WebBook** www.ceramics.nist.gov/webbook/webbook.htm. Example of gateway giving access to both NIST and non-NIST data centres and sources, tools and resources.
- **Fire Research Information Services Building and Fire Research Laboratory**. www.bfrl.nist.gov/fris. Facility within NIST's Building

and Fire Research Laboratory providing information both to Laboratory staff as well as fire protection engineers, scientists, and fire service personnel around the world; c.f. FIREDOC.

- **NIST Data Gateway** http://srdata.nist.gov/gateway. Links to selected free online NIST databases as well as to information on NIST databases available for purchase. Search by specific keywords, properties and substances.
- **NIST Laboratories** www.nist.gov/public_affairs/labs2.htm. Very useful descriptive checklist of the seven NIST Laboratories – with their various sections, as well as the Technology Services Division.
- **NIST Materials Science and Engineering Laboratory** www.msel.nist.gov. Priority programmes are: Advanced manufacturing processes; Biomaterials; Materials for electronics; Nanometrology; Safety and reliability. Also more general data on ceramics, materials reliability, polymers, metallurgy.
- **Physical Reference Data** http://physics.nist.gov. As well as access to an invaluable collection of data, the site links to sections on Constants, Units and Uncertainty, and on Measurements and Calibrations.

4524 Patbase

RWS Group/Minesoft.
www.patbase.com [FEE-BASED]
Extensive international database organized by patent families, so that each invention is represented by one individual record and it is easy to see in which countries a filing for patent protection has been made. 75 countries are covered. Provides bibliographic information, abstract, and drawing with links to status, full text and statistical data. Alerting service available.

4525 Patent and trademark information: uses and perspectives

V. Baldwin, ed. Haworth Information, 2004, 217pp. $24.95. ISBN 0789004259:.
www.haworthpress.com [DESCRIPTION]
Reprint of the journal *Science and Technology Libraries*, V. 22, Nos. 1–2, 2004, which provides an introductory overview of searching international patents and trademark information for users of the library using the internet, databases, and other sources.

4526 Patent and Trademark Resources

Louisiana State University
www.lib.lsu.edu/sci/ptdl
Louisiana State University library is one of the US Patent and Trademark Depository Libraries. The website contains a short tutorial on searching US patents, information about trademarks, reading lists and links to other websites.

4527 Patent Information [USA]

University of Texas at Austin
http://www.lib.utexas.edu/engin/patent/uspat.html
Includes two well structured tutorials on online searching of US patents and on international intellectual property searching. Links to other key websites. Many pages of useful information for inventors – and, more generally, about engineering and other resources. Maintained by the University's Richard W. McKinney Engineering Library.

4528 Patent Information Users Group [USA]

www.piug.org
US-based organization with international membership and coverage. Authoritative and growing 'knowledge base' for patent searchers available on website. Includes bibliography and lists of events and links. Hosts an open discussion list piug-l which acts as the principal international patent information searching forum.

4529 PATENTS Cluster

STN International.
www.cas.org/ONLINE/CATALOG/CLUSTERS/patents.html
Cross-searchable gateway to 38 online databases containing patent-related information.

4530 Perinorm

www.perinorm.com [FEE-BASED]
'The world's leading bibliographic database of national, European and international standards from 18 countries: a total of more than 650,000 records ... Comes with a monthly update, meaning not only is Perinorm the only bibliographic database of standards with access to the source data, it is also the most current.'

A collaboration of Association Française de Normalisation, British Standards Institution and Deutsches Institut für Normung.

4531 Questel.Orbit

www.questel.orbit.com
Major science and technology host which specializes in patents and intellectual property materials. Databases designed both for expert searchers and end-users. Unique PlusPat database covering 50 million patent documents from over 75 patenting authorities: 'The Fruits of Human Innovation at your Fingertips'.

Overall mission is 'to provide the most comprehensive and accurate patent, trademark and domain name information so that companies can increase their value and grow their markets'. A PDF Miniguide can be used as an introduction for those new to the Service; Searching for patent and legal information provides greater detail. The Patent Delivery Service downloads PDF copies of patent documents from over 30 countries and international patent offices.

- **PATOLIS-e** www.patolis.co.jp/products/e-index.html. Comprehensive English-language subscription database of Japanese patents and other intellectual property information. Searching English word and other data returns machine translated text.

4532 The Standards Source

Information Handling Services.
www.ihsengineering.com/index.html
IHS is a leading worldwide 'One-Stop Provider' for more than a million technical documents, including engineering standards, military specifications, parts information, and regulations.

- **CatalogXpress** www.ihserc.com/catalogxpress. Web-based search of: More than 300,000 catalogs from over 16,000 manufacturers; Directory listings on an additional 500,000 manufacturers; More than 120 million part number references.
- **IHS Global** http://global.ihs.com. Entrée to all the companies of the wide-ranging Group, including the UK-based Technical Indexes subsidiary, also at: www.tionestop.com/ihsti.
- **Standards Infobase** ILI. www.ili.co.uk/en. 'The ILI standards database is the leading bibliographic standards database. It covers over 600,000 worldwide standards. Over 250 major Standards issuing authorities are covered from US, Europe, ISO, IEC, Japan, Australia ...'

4533 SurfIP

www.surfip.gov.sg/sip/site/sip_home.htm
Website run by the Intellectual Property Office of Singapore. Aggregates results of searches from a number of patent

databases (including some far-Eastern sources). Free registration required for most databases; additional value-added services are available. Covers biotechnology, IT, telecommunication, manufacturing industries, etc.

4534 Techstreet
Thomson Scientific.
www.techstreet.com
Major web-based ordering service for technical standards: provides a one-stop shop of bibliographic information and downloadable documents on more than 300,000 titles aggregated from over 350 leading standards developing organizations, the site bringing together the catalogues of the many engineering and technology interested publishers of codes, standards and specifications. These include larger concerns such as ISO, ASME, API and IEEE, but also some of the smaller and more specialized groups – the Hydraulic Institute, TAPPI and others. Access to some important but non-English language works, such as the DIN standards.

Helpful site with good organization by industry: Boilers and Vessels; Construction; Energy and Petrochem; etc.

4535 UK Defence Standardization Organisation
www.dstan.mod.uk
Offers a range of products and services including: Advice on the selection and use of appropriate standards; *Standards In Defence News* magazine; Access to external specialized support; Electronic and hard copy versions of all extant UK defence standards.

4536 The UK Patent Office
Patent Office
www.patent.gov.uk
Patents and other intellectual property information and resources. Databases for searching UK patents (see also the ESP@CENET database), patent status, trade mark searching etc. Manuals, brochures, history and links to other websites.

4537 United States Copyright Office
www.copyright.gov
'Provides expert assistance to Congress on intellectual property matters; advises Congress on anticipated changes in US copyright law; analyzes and assists in the drafting of copyright legislation and legislative reports and provides and undertakes studies for Congress; offers advice to Congress on compliance with multilateral agreements such as the Berne Convention for the Protection of Literary and Artistic Works; works with the State Department, the US Trade Representative's Office, and the Patent and Trademark Office in providing technical expertise in negotiations for international intellectual property agreements; provides technical assistance to other countries in developing their own copyright laws; and through its International Copyright Institute, promotes worldwide understanding and cooperation in providing protection for intellectual property.'

Well organized sets of information: NewsNet is a 'free electronic newsletter that alerts subscribers to hearings, deadlines for comments, new and proposed regulations, new publications, and other copyright-related subjects'.

4538 United States Patent and Trademark Office
www.uspto.gov
Complete searchable databases of US patents and published applications including copies of over six million US patents. Sections for first time visitors to the website and for those seeking local patent libraries in the USA. Other pages give details of how to get a patent, how to search, activities and education, addresses and contacts, and news and notices. A very extensive resource but largely devoted to US patents. The USPTO also produce information in print, CD-ROM and other media. Patent library facilities near Washington DC.

- **Office of Patent Classification** www.uspto.gov/web/offices/opc. Well classified informative site describing all aspects of the US patent classification system and providing links to related resources.
- **Trademarks** www.uspto.gov/main/trademarks.htm. USPTO service. 'The first step is to determine what type of intellectual property protection you need. There are three types of intellectual property: trademarks, patents and copyrights. The Trademark Office of the USPTO handles trademarks only.'

4539 World Intellectual Property Organization
www.wipo.int
'Intellectual property refers to creations of the mind: inventions, literary and artistic works, and symbols, names, images, and designs used in commerce ... (It) is divided into two categories: Industrial property Includes inventions (patents), trademarks, industrial designs, and geographic indications of source; Copyright Includes literary and artistic works such as novels, poems and plays, films, musical works, artistic works such as drawings, paintings, photographs and sculptures, and architectural designs. Rights related to copyright include those of performing artists in their performances, producers of phonograms in their recordings, and those of broadcasters in their radio and television programs.'

Among much other useful information, extensive website includes details of: Member states (currently 180); Treaties; Industrial property statistics; Publications (e-zines available). There is also an Intellectual Property Digital Library, as well as the WIPO Library – whose holdings are accessible through the UNITED NATIONS SHARED CATALOGUING AND PUBLIC ACCESS SYSTEM, and which is also accessible to external researchers.

- **Collection of Laws for Electronic Access: CLEA** www.wipo.int/clea/en. Bibliographic index of intellectual property laws and treaties in English linked with a full-text database available in English, French, Spanish.
- **Collection of National Copyright Laws** **United Nations Educational, Scientific and Cultural Organization.** http://portal.unesco.org/culture/en. Endeavours to provide access to national copyright and related rights legislation of UNESCO Member States. The collection currently comprises about 100 laws and is constantly being updated and completed.
- **Intellectual property: a power tool for economic growth** **K. Idris** WIPO, 2003, 377pp. 65 Swiss Francs [PDF download also available]. ISBN 9280511130. Seeks to demystify intellectual property, describing not only the 'what' but also the 'why' and the 'how' of the subject.
- **Katzarov's manual of industrial property** www.katzarov.com/manual.html [DESCRIPTION]. Comprehensive information on the protection of industrial property for 200 countries all over the world. 115 authors. Available in loose-leaf print and CD-ROM.
- **Patent Cooperation Treaty** www.wipo.int/pct/en/gazette. The PCT Electronic Gazette is major database of the texts of national and international laws. Also, details of activities, products and services.
- **PatentCafe** www.patentcafe.com. Well organized extensive portal providing patent research and intellectual property management services, news, information, etc. 'Each month delivers ... to nearly 1/2 million users.

4540 **World Patent Information**
Elsevier, 1979–, Quarterly. €586.00. ISSN 01722190.
Useful current awareness source containing papers, review articles, book reviews, conference and meeting reports, news and selective bibliography. Coverage is patents and other forms of industrial property information including patent classification, dissemination of information, international developments, chemical and other subject searching, trademarks and designs. The journal is aimed at the professional searcher.

Official & quasi-official bodies

4541 **Canadian Technology Network**
http://ctn-rct.nrc-cnrc.gc.ca/home_e.shtml
'Links federal and provincial government labs and agencies, universities, community colleges, industry associations, technology centres and economic development agencies. Together these organizations provide innovative Canadian companies with quick and personal access to expertise, advice and information about how to meet technology and related business challenges.'

Homeland Security
United States. Department of Homeland Security See entry no. 4420

4542 **NATO Research and Technology Organisation**
www.rta.nato.int
The Agency, a product of the merger between the Advisory Group for Aerospace Research and Development (AGARD) and the Defence Research Group (DRG), provides engineering information over a wide selection of fields in the military sphere. However, the data is relevant to non-military engineering. Technical panels exist on advanced vehicle technology; information systems technology; human factors and medicine; studies analysis and simulation; systems concepts and integration; and sensors and electronics technology. These sub-groups provide technical reports available as abstracts or full-text on a variety of topics of direct interest to the engineer. There is a strong interest in simulation, with a Modelling and Simulation Group.

- **NATO Science Series** www.nato.int/science-old/e/publications.htm. Results of NATO Advanced Study Institutes and Advanced Research Workshops published about one year after the meeting takes place, either by Kluwer Academic Publishers or IOS Press, and organized into five subject area sub-series.
- **Security Through Science Programme** www.nato.int/science. Aims to contribute to security, stability and solidarity among nations by applying cutting-edge science to problem solving. Research Topics supported are in areas of Defence Against Terrorism, or Countering Other Threats to Security.
- **STARNET: Science, Technology and Research Network** http://starnet.rta.nato.int. Access to organizational websites and internet-based resources in a series of subject nodes: Aerospace; Defence against terrorism; Environmental and biological sciences; Information science; Land and terrestrial; Naval, marine and sea; Research planning.

4543 **Science & Technology** [UK]
Great Britain. Department of Trade and Industry
www.dti.gov.uk/industries_science_technology.html
Excellent entrée to the various DTI science and technology initiatives: policy; innovation; exploitation; measurement and standards; science and society; and so on.

- **Standards and Technical Regulations Directorate** www.dti.gov.uk/strd. Represents UK government in a range of activities relating to EU Directives, UK standards and conformity assessment, safety of domestic gas and electric appliances, etc. Developing a National Standardization Strategic Framewortk with BSI and CBI.
- **World-Leading Innovation** www.britainusa.com/science. Vigorous promotion of the UK's science and technology base, including lists of leading websites for each of the key sectors covered: Biotechnology and life sciences; Energy and environment; Advanced engineering and materials; etc.

4544 **Technology Administration** [USA]
www.technology.gov
'The only Federal agency working to maximize technology's contribution to America's economic growth.' Oversees the work of National Institute of Standards and Technology and National Technical Information Service as well as an Office of Technology Policy – which 'fosters dialogue and develops and advocates national policies and initiatives that use technology to build America's economic strength.'

4545 **UK Trade & Investment**
www.uktradeinvest.gov.uk
The Government organization that supports both companies in the UK trading internationally and overseas enterprises seeking to locate in the UK. Its Engineering section, for instance, has contacts for mechanical, electrical and process engineering who can give free consultations, exporting advice and information on opportunities to small to medium-sized enterprises.

4546 **United Nations Conference on Trade and Development**
www.unctad.org
'Focal point within the UN for the integrated treatment of trade and development and related issues in the areas of investment, finance, technology, enterprise development and sustainable development.'

Provides a wide range of important statistical series relating to international trade, foreign direct investment and commodities. Provides a Digital Library, for which 'UNCTAD's Reference Service would be ready to assist readers in identifying printed or electronic publications ... Selected copies of UNCTAD´s publications can be provided ... upon request, subject to availability'.

- **Federation of International Trade Associations** www.fita.org. Links to 7000 international trade related websites. Really Useful Sites for International Trade Professionals is a free, bi-weekly newsletter that highlights important websites for professionals in import-export and international trade.
- **GlobStat** http://globstat.unctad.org. Online version of *Development and Globalization: Facts and Figures*, a 'compact statistical reference book which describes in a straightforward manner the evolution of developing countries, particularly in the context of globalization'.
- **Science and Technology for Development: StDev** **Commission on Science and Technology for Development**. http://stdev.unctad.org. Gateway to UN system-wide information on science and technology for development.
- **World Trade Organization** www.wto.org. 'The only global international organization dealing with the rules of trade between nations. At its heart are the WTO agreements, negotiated and signed by the bulk of the world's trading nations and ratified in their parliaments'.

4547 **United Nations Industrial Development Organization**
www.unido.org
Vision is 'to improve the living conditions of people and promote global prosperity through offering tailor-made solutions for the sustainable industrial development of developing countries and countries with economies in transition'. Information about developments in worldwide use of technology, particularly in 'developing countries and countries with economies in transition in their fight against marginalization in today's globalized world'.

Research centres & institutes

4548 **Agilent Technologies**
www.agilent.com
Good example of technology intensive commercial company – created in 1999 by Hewlett-Packard. Notable in this context for the section Key Library Information included in the web pages describing most of its products and services, and the industries the company serves. These typically comprise: Data sheets, demonstrations and catalogs; Application notes and technical papers; Manuals and guides; Product and safety notifications; Software and firmware; Downloads; Newsletters, articles and presentations; FAQs. Useful approach.

4549 **Battelle**
www.battelle.org
Global science and technology enterprise that develops and commercializes technology and manages laboratories for customers: oversees 19,000 staff members and $3 billion in annual R & D. In turn presents a rich site, describing in detail work carried out within: Energy and environment; Health and life sciences; National security; Transportation and space. The company manages four of the US Department of Energy national laboratories.

4550 **Belfer Center for Science and International Affairs** [USA]
http://bcsia.ksg.harvard.edu
Mission is 'to provide leadership in advancing policy-relevant knowledge about the most important challenges of international security and other critical issues where science, technology, environmental policy, and international affairs intersect'.

4551 **Defence Science and Technology Laboratory** [UK]
www.dstl.gov.uk
Created from the former *Defence Evaluation and Research Agency* (DERA) – as was QinetiQ. This part is still within the Ministry of Defence, and is notable for its collection of some three-quarters of a million research reports, both open access and restricted.

- **QinetiQ** www.qinetiq.com. Now one of the largest research companies in Europe covering for instance energy, health care, space, transport as well as defence.

4552 **Federal Laboratory Consortium for Technology Transfer** [USA]
www.federallabs.org
'Nationwide network of federal laboratories that provides the forum to develop strategies and opportunities for linking the laboratory mission technologies and expertise with the marketplace ... Technology transfer, the transfer of research results from universities to the commercial marketplace for the public benefit, is closely linked to fundamental research activities in universities. Although US universities were moving science from the laboratory to industrial commercialization as early as the 1920s, academic transfer as a formal concept is said to have originated in a report written by Vannevar Bush for the president in 1945, entitled Science, the endless frontier.'

4553 **Fraunhofer-Gesellschaft**
www.fraunhofer.de/fhg/EN
The largest organization for applied research in Europe which 'maintains roughly 80 research units, including 58 Fraunhofer Institutes, at over 40 different locations throughout Germany. A staff of some 12,500, predominantly qualified scientists and engineers, works with an annual research budget of over one billion euros'. Detailed English-language website, well organized; particularly useful is the page listing the names of the Fraunhofer Institutes in alphabetical order.

4554 **IBM Research**
www.research.ibm.com
Details of their work in a wide range of disciplines – Chemistry, Electrical Engineering, Materials Science, Mathematical Sciences, Physics – as well as in Computer Science.

4555 **International Institute for Applied Systems Analysis**
www.iiasa.ac.at
'IIASA's research scholars study environmental, economic, technological, and social developments. The research areas covered link a variety of natural and social science disciplines. The work is based on original state-of-the-art methodology and analytical approaches. The methods and tools generated are useful to both decision makers and the scientific community.'

4556 **MIT School of Engineering** [USA]
Massachusetts Institute of Technology
http://web.mit.edu/engineering
Gateway to MIT's extensive portfolio of departments and divisions; laboratories, centres and programmes; major alliances. Excellent bi-monthly newsletter *Engineering Our World* plus gateway to a wide range of other publications.

- **Invention Dimension** http://web.mit.edu/invent. Portal aiming 'to inspire and encourage tomorrow's inventors through outreach programs and awards and grants. Features an online inventor's handbook and information on past inventors.

4557 **Mitre Corporation** [USA]
www.mitre.org
Not-for-profit organization 'chartered to work in the public interest. As a national resource, we apply our expertise in systems engineering, information technology, operational concepts, and enterprise modernization to address our sponsors' critical needs ... MITRE manages three Federally Funded Research and Development Centers (FFRDCs) ... MITRE also has its own independent research and development program that explores new technologies and new uses of technologies to solve our sponsors' problems in the near-term and in the future.'

4558 Palo Alto Research Center: PARC [USA]
Xerox Corporation.
www.parc.com
'Conducts pioneering interdisciplinary research in physical, computational, and social sciences. Building on our three-decade tradition of innovation, PARC works with Xerox and other strategic partners to commercialize technologies created by our renowned scientists.

As the birthplace of technologies such as laser printing, Ethernet, the graphical user interface, and ubiquitous computing, PARC has an established track record for transforming industries and creating commercial value.'

4559 RAND Corporation [USA]
www.rand.org
Leading non-profit institution 'that addresses the challenges facing the public and private sectors around the world'. Research areas include: Energy and Environment; Health and Health Care; and Science and Technology. Since 1998, 'RAND books and publications can be purchased online, or downloaded for free in PDF format. RAND makes its research available for free as a public service. If you find a publication useful, please consider purchasing a copy to help support RAND's research efforts.' Their online database catalogues over 10,000 books and periodicals.

- **Knowledge Base: Research Gateway** Demos. www.demos.co.uk/knowledgebase/researchgateway. Valuable list of think tanks and research institutes, in the UK and abroad, accompanied by their descriptions of themselves. Maintained by a leading UK think tank: check *The Greenhouse* – the Demos weblog.

4560 Science and Technology Policy Research [UK]
www.sussex.ac.uk/spru
Mission is 'to deepen understanding of the place of science, technology and innovation in the global economy for the benefit of government, business and society'. Produces wide range of publications; the SPRU Library Internet Catalogue is indeed a 'good starting point for research on a broad range of science, technology and innovation policy issues' (though needs registration before use).

4561 SRI International
www.sri.com
'Since our beginnings in 1946, when we were called Stanford Research Institute, our strengths have been our staff's world-leading expertise and passion for working with clients on important challenges. SRI is well known for its innovations in communications and networks, computing, economic development and science and technology policy, education, energy and the environment, engineering systems, pharmaceuticals and health sciences, homeland security and national defense, and materials and structures.'

4562 State Science and Technology Institute [USA]
www.ssti.org
Non-profit organization dedicated to improving programmes that increase growth through application of science and technology. SSTI maintains current and historical information about tech-based economic development programs: current and archival weekly electronic newsletter accessible via the site. Distinctive here for its section S&T Resources in mid-2004 a collection of over 400 links arranged by eight groups: TBED (Science and tech-based economic development); Academic; Government; Congress; White House; Federal programs; Funding; Information.

Associations & societies

4563 American Council of Independent Laboratories
www.acil.org
Trade association representing independent, commercial scientific and engineering firms. Good well presented and up-to-date set of government website links; extensive lists of laboratories with detailed descriptions of their services.

4564 American Society for Quality
www.asq.org
Wide-ranging quality site with especially helpful sections organized by 'Industry' (e.g. 'Aerospace', 'Biomedical', 'Pharmaceutical', 'Software development') and 'Topics' (e.g. 'Benchmarking'; 'Environmental/sustainability'; 'Statistics').

4565 Council for Industry and Higher Education [UK]
www.cihe-uk.com
High-level body whose mission is 'to advance all kinds of learning through the fostering of mutual understanding, co-operation and support between higher education and business'. Current activities, news, publications. 'A government Minister usually attends Council meetings.'

- **Association for University Research and Industry Links** www.auril.org.uk. 'A growing network of professionals dedicated to the development of partnerships between higher education and industry to support innovation and competitiveness'. Have eight Professional Theme Groups, and a CPD for Knowledge Transfer Professionals website.
- **Business–Higher Education Forum** www.bhef.com. Formerly hosted American Council on Education, now independent US organization of leaders from American businesses, colleges and universities, museums, foundations. Aims to 'speak with one voice by issuing reports, white papers, policy positions', etc.

4566 Engineering and Technology Board [UK]
www.etechb.co.uk
'Aims to tackle the significant yet unaddressed needs of the UK's science, engineering and technology industry and to create a unified platform and voice ... We work in partnership with business and industry, Government, education and the profession to improve the perception of science, engineering and technology (SET) in the UK ... With more than 30 engineering institutions in the UK alone and equal numbers of science bodies, the etb aims to act as the voice for the sector.'

- **Scenta: The online gateway to the best in science, engineering and technology** www.scenta.co.uk. Very useful and well designed and presented gateway – initiated by the etb – to the best SET resources on the web. News, events, library, communities, careers, jobs, awards, relax, etc.
- **Science, engineering and technology learning information portal: e-lip** LearnDirect and Science, Engineering, Manufacturing Technologies Alliance. www.elip.info. 'The one stop source of information and learning opportunities for the Science, Engineering and Manufacturing Technologies community in the UK!'.
- **Science, Engineering, Technology, and Mathematics Network** www.setnet.org.uk. UK-wide charity that promotes Science Technology Engineering and Mathematics (STEM) awareness, especially among young people.

4567 Industrial Research Institute [USA]
www.iriinc.org
'The foremost business association of leaders in research and development (R&D) working together to enhance the effectiveness of technological innovation in industry.'

Founded 1938 by the NATIONAL RESEARCH COUNCIL, comprises about 225 industrial and service companies who collectively 'invest close to $90 billion annually in R&D, equivalent to more than 50% of the nation's privately funded effort'.

Most resources have restricted access; but through for instance their journal *Research-Technology Management* potentially a useful source of information on US developments, especially in the policy arena.

4568 International Federation of Inventors' Associations
www.invention-ifia.ch
Resources and links for inventors.

- **1000 Inventions** www.1000inventions.com. IFIA service sponsored by EUROPEAN PATENT OFFICE and other organizations offering for sale or licensing over 1000 inventions. Partnered by the United Inventors Association (UIA/USA).

4569 International Technology Education Association
www.iteawww.org
'Professional association for technology education teachers who teach a curriculum called 'technology education' which is problem-based learning utilizing math, science and technology principles.'

- **Innovation Curriculum Online Network: ICON Eisenhower National Clearinghouse for Mathematics and Science Education.** http://icontechlit.enc.org [REGISTRATION]. 'Electronic roadmap to connect users, such as teachers, professors, students, museum staff, and parents with information about the human built and innovated world ... Also provides a broad and deep collection of technological literacy resources.'

4570 National Academy of Engineering [USA]
www.nae.edu
'Mission is to promote the technological welfare of the nation by marshaling the knowledge and insights of eminent members of the engineering profession.' Under its charter the NAE, a private, independent, non-profit institution, and a member of the National Academies [q.v.], is directed 'whenever called upon by any department or agency of the government, to investigate, examine, experiment, and report upon any subject of science or art'. In addition, the NAE also conducts independent studies to examine important topics in engineering and technology.

Among a range of resources arising from that remit, also worth mentioning are the lively site Engineer Girl, and the section Engineering in the News, part of their Spotlight on Engineering, Technology, and Policy e-mail newsletter.

4571 Trade Association Forum [UK]
www.taforum.org
'Since its formation in 1997 ... has been encouraging the development and sharing of best practice among UK trade associations and promoting the role of effective trade associations to government, industry and the wider public.' The *Trade Association Directory* has brief descriptions with contact information for some 750 UK-based associations.

4572 United Kingdom Science Park Association
www.ukspa.org.uk
Mission is 'to be the authoritative body on the planning, development and the creation of Science Parks that are facilitating the development and management of innovative, high growth, knowledge base organisations'.

4573 Women in Technology International
www.witi.com
Founded 1989; mission is 'to empower women worldwide to achieve unimagined possibilities and transformations through technology, leadership and economic prosperity'. News, career development, community and business involvements, events, etc. Offer custom research services.

4574 World Transhumanist Association
www.transhumanism.org
Campaign for 'the ethical use of technology to extend human capabilities'. Transhumanism – a term coined by biologist Julian Huxley in 1957 is 'an interdisciplinary approach to understanding and evaluating the possibilities for overcoming biological limitations through technological progress. Transhumanists seek to expand technological opportunities for people to live longer and healthier lives and to enhance their intellectual, physical, and emotional capacities.' Extensive – and interesting – website.

- **Society for Philosophy and Technology** www.spt.org. Founded 1976, an 'independent international organization that encourages, supports and facilitates philosophically significant considerations of technology'. Journal, newsletter, useful links section.

Libraries, archives, museums

4575 Musée des Arts et Métiers
www.arts-et-metiers.net
Founded 1794 as a depository for the preservation of scientific instruments and inventions. Very well presented colourful website with good resources section.

4576 Tech Museum of Innovation [USA]
www.thetech.org
'The Tech is a cosmopolitan museum singularly focused on technology—how it works and the way that it is changing every aspect of the way we work, live, play and learn. Its people-and-technology focus and the integration of advanced technologies into visitor experiences and infrastructure, distinguishes it from other science centers.'

Portal & task environments

4577 BNP Media
www.bnpmedia.com
'Serves industry professionals by delivering useful, timely and accurate information through magazines, websites, conferences and events. We write, produce and publish more than 40 b-to-b publications, each one staffed with knowledgeable experts and industry veterans. The diverse industries we serve include manufacturing, security systems, architecture and construction, food and packaging, HVACR, industrial machinery and plumbing.'

Sophisticated but well organized intuitive website.

4578 CMP Media
www.cmp.com
Access to very wide range of 'technology'-related publications/websites/events: helpful introductory list of links to their current complete offerings. Classic print directories marketed within the CMP family – where still existing – now generally have their own websites.

- **CMP Computer Fulltext** http://library.dialog.com/bluesheets/html/bl0647.html [DESCRIPTION]. Full-text access via the host DIALOG to content of 12 CMP newspapers and magazines. Over 400,000 records (November 2003); circa 600 records added weekly.

- **CMPi Product Websites** www.cmpinformation.com. Useful checklist of websites, including for: Agriculture; Barbour Index; Builder Group; Directories; Entertainment Technology; Food Ingredients; Packaging; Pharmaceutical; Protection and Management.
- **The engineering industry buyers' guide** Comprehensive information on over 16,000 UK manufacturers and suppliers, covering over 5000 product and services. Formerly a priced publication, from 2004 available free of charge on a controlled circulation basis.
- **Kempe's engineers year-book** Compiled by Britain's top engineers, Kempe's is a 'unique source of information on the principles of engineering including facts, statistics, charts, graphs and illustrations in an impressive 2500-page publication'. Latest edn 2002.

4579 CMS Business Information
Chiltern Magazine Services.
www.biz-lib.com
'All the business intelligence you need at our "One-Stop Information Shop", from newsletters to e-mail bulletins, market studies, online services and management reports.' Promoted as an especially personal service; but their web catalogue includes 'a selection of the 15,000 reports, directories, newsletters and databases available for immediate purchase'.

4580 Defense Technical Information Center
www.dtic.mil
DTIC is the central facility for the collection and dissemination of scientific and technical information for the US Department of Defense (DoD).

Good clear access to a range of useful resources, including to: websites of the 11 Information Analysis Centers, several referenced elsewhere in TNW; some 100 websites hosted for other DoD programmes; news, job announcements, events.

- **Scientific and Technical Information Network: STINET** http://stinet.dtic.mil. Free of charge and provides access to citations to unclassified documents that have been entered into DTIC's Technical Reports Collection since December 1974 as well as some full-text reports for those citations.

4581 Forrester Research
www.forrester.com
The leading consultancy 'helping business thrive on technology change'.

4582 globalEDGE
Michigan State University
http://globaledge.msu.edu/index.asp
Created by the University's *Center for International Business Education and Research* a 'knowledge web-portal that connects international business professionals worldwide to a wealth of information, insights, and learning resources on global business activities'.

Impressive service, including: Academy (Extensive research and teaching resources); Community (Interactive forum for business professionals); Country insights; Diagnostic Tools (Decision-support tools for managers); Knowledge Room (Latest issues in international business – as well as access to descriptions of more than 2000 online resources).

4583 GlobalWatch Online [UK]
Great Britain. Department of Trade and Industry
www.globalwatchonline.com
'The website of the DTI's International Technology Service.'

Not the easiest site to navigate: somewhat over-designed. But of value are: Embassy Reports on STM developments around the world; lists of forthcoming events; descriptions of the various Government-sponsored UK technology networks (e.g. the Faraday Partnerships which 'promote improved interactions between the UK science, engineering and technology base and industry'); the DTI Technology Programme; and the *Global Watch Magazine* – available free of charge to organizations and individuals within the UK.

4584 OSTI [USA]
Office of Scientific and Technical Information
www.osti.gov
Office within the US Department of Energy (DOE) OFFICE OF SCIENCE.

A rich site providing entrées to a wide range of services. These include sites covering 'each of the three main ways by which scientists communicate their findings: R&D Results; E-print Literature; Journal Literature'; and a series of Subject Portals providing access to full-text DOE scientific and technical reports, links to journal literature, and other information sources, and including a distributed searching feature, which provides parallel searching across a select set of heterogeneous databases. Key examples follow.

- **Energy Citations Database** www.osti.gov/energycitations. Designed and developed with the science-attentive citizen in mind. Its creation is consistent with OSTI's objective to provide easier and faster access to the Department's scientific and technical information.
- **E-Print Network** www.osti.gov/eprints. Access to 10,000 servers in 35 countries housing 500,000 documents, and covering physics, mathematics, chemistry, and other topics of interest to the Department of Energy.
- **GrayLIT Network** www.osti.gov/graylit. The world's most comprehensive portal to over 130,000 full-text technical reports. Federal Agencies participating in this project are DoD, DOE, EPA, and NASA.
- **Information Bridge** www.osti.gov/bridge. Searchable and downloadable bibliographic records and full text of DOE research report literature from 1995 forward.
- **Subject pathways** www.osti.gov/energyfiles. Diverse resources hosted by a variety of agencies, organizations. Each pathway is preceded by a brief explanation of types of information found under that specific subject category, followed by: searchable resources; STI resources/tools; related resources.
- **Subject portals** www.osti.gov/subjectportals. Five sites currently for: Photovoltaics; Geothermal Energy; FreedomCAR and Vehicle Technology; Hydropower; and Wind Energy.

4585 Reed Business Information
www.reedbusiness.com
The business to business division of Reed Elsevier, providing a 'range of communication and information channels – magazines, exhibitions, directories, online media, marketing services – across five continents'.

4586 VertMarkets
www.vertmarkets.com
Industry specific online sales and marketing products and services to small and medium sized suppliers. 'VertMarkets continues to be the leader in e-commerce enablement, with marketplace solutions that attract and connect buyers and suppliers online through its 68 industry-specific marketplaces.' Sectors covered are classified: Electronics;

Energy; Environmental; Food/beverage; Information technology; Life sciences; Manufacturing; Services.

4587 The World Technology Network
www.wtn.net
'The World Technology Network (WTN) is a global meeting ground, a virtual think tank, and an elite club whose members are all focused on the business and science of bringing important emerging technologies of all types (from biotech to new materials, from IT to new energy sources) into reality. The WTN's membership is comprised of over 700 individuals and organizations from more than 50 countries, judged by their peers to be the most innovative in the technology world.'

Discovering print & electronic resources

4588 Abstracts in new technology and engineering: ANTE
CSA, 1993–, Bimonthly. $1865.00. ISSN 13679899.
www.csa.com/factsheets/ante-set-c.php [DESCRIPTION]
Abstracting and indexing service monitoring approximately 350 academic and trade publications from the UK and the US Coverage includes new technologies such as information technology and computing, electronics, biotechnology, medical technology, as well as engineering (including construction, electrical and chemical engineering) and allied subject areas.

4589 American Technical Publishers
www.ameritech.co.uk
Commercial operation 'formed to enhance the marketing and distribution requirements required in Europe and the Middle East of three US engineering societies'. Now distributes over 45,000 different information products for many of the major such societies, including their publications, standards, CD-ROMs and video training aids.

4590 Applied Science and Technology Full Text
H W Wilson.
www.hwwilson.com/Databases/applieds.htm [FEE-BASED]
'When you search Applied Science and Technology Full Text on WilsonWeb, you get seamless links to full text articles on any of your library's reference databases that are open-URL compliant—at no additional charge.'

Covers some 600 periodicals, including trade and industrial publications, journals issued by professional and technical societies, and specialized subject periodicals, as well as special issues such as buyer's guides, directories, and conference proceedings. Full text of approximately 100 of these.

Range of versions and vendors available: see website.

- **General Science Full Text** H W Wilson. www.hwwilson.com/Databases/gensci.htm [FEE-BASED]. Full text from 65 journals; abstracting and indexing of 224 periodicals back to 1984. '(For nonexpert searches), the most accessible and useful of all science databases.' *Online* (Information Today).

4591 Business & Industry
Thomson Gale.
www.gale.com/pdf/facts/busind.pdf [DESCRIPTION]
Covers 'more than 1700 of the world's most authoritative business publications, including premier trade and business journals, leading industry newsletters, plus a broad collection of regional, national and international newspapers'.

- **Predicast's Overview of Markets And Technology: PROMT** Thomson Gale. www.gale.com/pdf/facts/prom.pdf [DESCRIPTION]. Multiple-industry database providing information on companies, products, markets, and applied technologies for approximately 60 manufacturing and service industries including rubber, plastics, chemicals, paper.

4592 FIZ Technik
www.fiz-technik.de/en/index.html
'The German national centre for techno-scientific information and documentation for advanced research and science, in particular the industrial research and development in small and medium-sized companies. Apart from the techno-scientific area, FIZ Technik is also an important German supplier of technology-related economic, market and product information.'

Access to a range of bibliographic, patent, standard, trademark, company and business data.

4593 NSDL Scout Report for Math, Engineering, and Technology
University of Wisconsin, Internet Scout Project and National Science Digital Library
http://scout.wisc.edu/Reports/NSDL
Bi-weekly report covering the best new and newly discovered online resources in this area. 'Approximately 25 sites are reviewed in each report, covering materials of interest to everyone from kids to higher education professionals to life-long learners.' Service of the acclaimed Scout Report.

4594 Science and Technology Digest
CSA.
www.csa.com/factsheets/scitechdig-set-c.php
'Abstracting and indexing database that covers selected articles from over 100 worldwide sources in the applied and theoretical sciences. Journals range from widely circulated, newsstand publications, such as *Discover*, *Scientific American*, *Astronomy*, and *Weatherwise*, to such academic journals as *Science*, *Nature*, *Physics World*, *Chemical Innovation*, *Environmental Science and Technology*, and *Geophysical Research Letters*.' (many of these referenced elsewhere in TNW).

4595 The Virtual Technical Reports Center
University of Maryland
www.lib.umd.edu/ENGIN/techrpts.html
An exceptionally useful inventory of the University's Engineering and Physical Sciences Library listing websites of worldwide institutions which 'provide either full-text reports, or searchable extended abstracts of their technical reports on the world wide web. This site contains links to technical reports, preprints, reprints, dissertations, theses, and research reports of all kinds. Some metasites are listed by subject categories, as well as by institution.'

Planned to be updated monthly – though when reviewed early 2005 had apparently last been modified August 2004.

Digital data, image & text collections

4596 Applegate [UK]
www.applegate.co.uk
'Information on more than 140,000 companies cross-referenced to more than 34,000 products ... Receives around

55 million page impressions each year and is the most comprehensive and most used directory for UK industry, manufacturing and technology companies.'

- **ThomasNet** www.thomasnet.com. Comprehensive US-based company and product information.

4597 Business Monitor Online
Business Monitor International.
www.businessmonitor.com
Major publisher of specialist business information on global emerging markets. Offers 1900 reports on economics, politics and countries, as well as over 500 quarterly industry sector reports. In 2005 moved to target its services to academia, in addition to its commercial focus.

4598 How Stuff Works
Convex Group Inc.
www.howstuffworks.com
'Widely recognized as the leading source for clear, reliable explanations of how everything around us actually works. Through the flagship Web site *HowStuffWorks.com*, a popular series of books, an acclaimed kids' magazine, as well as many other ventures, the award-winning company has helped demystify the world for millions of curious people.'

4599 IBISWorld
www.ibisworld.com.au
'IBISWorld is fast becoming the world's leading strategic Business Information provider offering a wealth of powerful and comprehensive information on every industry, top 2000 companies and the business environment.' Although founded and owned within Australia, now has a major US presence.

4600 Plunkett Research
www.plunkettresearch.com
Provider of industry sector analysis and research, industry trends and industry statistics. Very well structured website typically giving free access to the introduction to their reports, the remainder being only accessible to subscribers. Produce also wide range of prnt publications: 'We experimented with many different types of data and analysis in various formats as we launched new books through the years. We eventually evolved the research methods and presentation that we rely on today. As a result, we had an eager audience for the 20 titles we published in 2004, expanding to 30 titles in 2005. In 2006, this will expand to 41 industry titles, and eventually about 150 titles in 2014 ...'

Directories & encyclopedias

4601 American women in technology: an encyclopedia
L. Zierdt-Warshaw, A. Winkler and L. Bernstein ABC-CLIO, 2000, 384pp. $80.00. ISBN 1576074048.
www.abc-clio.com/academic/index.aspx
'Tells the fascinating story of women's contributions to numerous fields, including aerospace, engineering, information technology, telecommunications, and medical technology. Entries focus on technological events that opened scientific areas to women, biographies of women who made important contributions to technology, and organizations that aided women to enter specialties ranging from astrophysics and aerospace to telecommunications and textiles.'
Available online: see website.
'These authors ... have done an outstanding job researching and writing their most current encyclopedia ... A good place to begin research for general readers and lower-division undergraduates.' (*Choice*)

4602 An encyclopaedia of the history of technology
I. McNeil, ed. Routledge, 1996, 1062pp. £45.00. ISBN 0415147921.
Comprehensive single volume work on the history of technology, with significant chapters on developments in the various engineering disciplines. Edited by a former Newcomen Society secretary with sectional topics written by individual authors.

Encyclopedia of applied physics: the classic softcover edition
G.L. Trigg, ed. See entry no. 615

4603 The encyclopedia of human ecology
J.R. Miller [et al.], eds ABC-CLIO, 2003, 760pp. 2 v., $255.00. ISBN 1576078523.
www.abc-clio.com/academic/index.aspx
'What knowledge, from what disciplines, is needed in order to understand the interdependence of humans with their physical-biological, social-cultural, and human-built environments? What information is needed to frame human decisions and actions that will enhance the quality of human life and the quality of the environment? What professions need to be consulted in order to find means to promote desirable behaviors and healthy development, to ameliorate already existing problems, and to optimize future life paths?'

'Once information about the ecology of human life has been gained, how do we use it to foster responsible citizenship, the prudent stewardship of the natural and the designed environment, social justice, and the institutions of civil society? How do we inform young people about these questions, and how answers to them affect their lives and those of their families and communities? How, through the delivery of this information, may we empower young people to contribute productively to society and culture? ...'
Available online: see website.
'Best Reference Source – 2003' (*Library Journal*)

4604 Encyclopedia of modern everyday inventions
D.J. Cole, E. Browning and F.E.H. Schroeder, eds Greenwood Press, 2003, 285pp. $49.95. ISBN 0313313458.
Articles such as ballpoint pens, coffee makers, electric guitars, hair dryer, the internet and zippers are included. Illustrated entries describe the history and how the inventions work.

4605 Encyclopedia of twentieth-century technology
C. Hempstead and W. Worthington, eds Routledge, 2004, 992pp. 2 v, $325.00. ISBN 1579583865.
www.routledge-ny.com/ref/20ctech [DESCRIPTION]
440 essays arranged alphabetically by title, focusing mostly on individual objects, artifacts, techniques, and products. Each entry has technical description, within historical narrative, of about 1000 words, plus illustrations and further reading. Also about 30 longer surveys addressing broad questions of technological systems.

Handbooks & manuals

CRC handbook of chemistry and physics
D.R. Lide, ed. See entry no. 1717

The handbook of brain theory and neural networks
M.A. Arbib [et al.], eds See entry no. 3998

International critical tables of numerical data, physics, chemistry and technology
E.W. Washburn [et al.], eds; National Academy of Sciences See entry no. 361

Keeping up-to-date

4606 **Business Week**
McGraw-Hill. $252.45. ISSN 00077135.
www.businessweek.com
The major US-based magazine.

4607 **Business Wire**
www.businesswire.com
'The leading source for full-text breaking news releases, multimedia and regulatory filings for companies and groups throughout the world.'

4608 **Financial Times**
http://news.ft.com/home/uk
The leading UK-based financial newspaper.
- **Wall Street Journal** http://online.wsj.com/public/us. The leading US-based financial newspaper.

4609 **International journal of technology transfer and commercialisation**
Inderscience Enterprises, 2002 –, Quarterly. €430.00. ISSN 14706075.
www.inderscience.com [DESCRIPTION]
Peer-reviewed journal covering knowledge and technology transfer, intellectual property rights, licensing, co-operation and commercial application of technology etc. Good international coverage.

4610 **Oligopoly Watch: the latest maneuvers of the new oligopolies and what they mean**
S. Hannaford
www.oligopolywatch.com
Personal interest site. 'This site is an attempt to make sense of the business pages in the newspaper, particularly the stories about mergers and acquisitions. I am developing a theory about how and why big companies keep growing bigger, and some of the dynamics behind their moves. This fits into a larger work I call 'Shelf Life, Shelf Space, Mind Space' that I am working on. In part, this blog is my way of keeping a diary of the many moves toward oligopoly that take place every day.

Are oligopolies sinister? Very possibly. But I think it's more useful to see how and why they work than simply rail against globalism and greed ...'

PhysOrg.com: the latest physics and technology news
See entry no. 627

Public Understanding of Science
See entry no. 366

4611 **R&D Magazine**
Reed Business Information.
www.rdmag.com
'Features new products for scientists, chemists, and research and development managers with buying responsibility in industry, government and university laboratories.' Useful Reference Guide to product, equipment and systems suppliers; also a Resources section listing associations and societies active in each field.

4612 **Technology Review**
Massachusetts Institute of Technology Bimonthly. ISSN 00401692.
www.technologyreview.com
MIT's 'magazine of innovation' since 1899. '*Technology Review* is at the center of the conversation on emerging technologies. No matter where the conversation takes place. With international editions recently launched in China, Italy, Germany and The Netherlands, the exposure of *Technology Review* magazine, combined with the our signature events, newsletters, and online businesses, reaches over two million business leaders throughout the world each month.'

Natural Resources & Energy

'Natural resources' we take here to be the non-living components of the earth. We focus especially on their use – or exploitation – to generate energy; on the concerns that we will run out of key sources of energy; on the undesirable effects of resource use on the natural environment; on the safety to humans and other living creatures of such use; and on the ensuing emphasis in many quarters on renewable (i.e. naturally replenished) and alternative sources of energy.

Mining – the extraction of the resources to be used from the earth – is a fundamental part of the overall energy-generating process. But it is also used to provide the metals and other chemical entities needed for industry and commerce. We have used the opportunity to gather together in the Mining & Minerals Processing subject field the resources we cite for all the metals that are covered specifically (apart from iron (and steel) and alumin(i)um), which seemed better treated in Materials Science & Engineering, its processing in Manufacturing Engineering, and its major uses in Civil Engineering and Construction & Building). Naturally, there are a number of more generic resources about the metals within the Chemistry subject grouping, and about minerals within the Mineralogy subject field.

Introductions to the subject

The discovery of global warming
S.R. Weart See entry no. 1161

Earth under siege: from air pollution to global change
R. Turco See entry no. 831

4613 **The economics of the environment and natural resources**
R.Q. Grafton [et al.] Blackwell Publishing, 2004, 520pp. £70.00. ISBN 0631215638.
Useful survey of the area. Four major parts: Economics of the environment; Resource economics; Environmental valuation; Global environment

4614 **Energy at the crossroads: global perspectives and uncertainties**
V. Smil MIT Press, 2005, 427pp. Originally published 2003, $16.95. ISBN 0262693240.
Excellent introductory overview. Bibliography pp 383–418.
'The most sober, thorough, and thoughtful integrated text on energy available, and it embodies core facts and some fundamental truths that any analyst of energy issues should ponder.' (*Nature*)

4615 **Energy, technology and directions for the future**
J.R. Fanchi Academic Press, 2004, 491pp. $69.99. ISBN 0122482913.
Introductory review of the energy sources that will be available in the 21st century energy mix, with useful background. Three major sections: The science of energy; Origins of energy sources; Energy technology.

Global warming: the complete briefing
J.T. Houghton See entry no. 1163

Life support: the environment and human health
M. McCally, ed. See entry no. 4222

Oceans 2020: science, trends, and the challenge of sustainability
J.G. Field, G. Hempel and C.P. Summerhayes, eds; Intergovernmental Oceanographic Commission, Scientific Committee on Oceanic Research and Scientific Committee on Problems of the Environment See entry no. 1350

Protecting the ozone layer: science and strategy
E.A. Parson See entry no. 1169

4616 **Sharing the planet: population–consumption–species: science and ethics for a sustainable and equitable world**
B. van der Zwaan and A. Petersen, eds University of Chicago Press, 2004, 264pp. Distributed for Eburon Publishers, Delft. Also available via University Presses Marketing (www.universitypressesmarketing.co.uk), $24.00. ISBN 9051669860. www.sharingtheplanet.org [COMPANION]
12 papers on sustainability submitted to the Pugwash Symposium, 2002, in two parts: Consumption, population and a sustainable economy; Biodiversity, globalization and sustainable governance. Appendix reproduces the Groningen Manifesto.
'The book is made available at distressing times, times when some with particularly large ecological footprints have decided to turn their backs on issues of sustainability. As the authors point out, it is awareness of the true nature of making choices that holds the potential for correcting our present trajectory. Highly recommended for anyone who is either truly concerned with or avoiding concern with the future of the planet while we are still here.' (*E-STREAMS*)

Dictionaries, thesauri, classifications

Dictionary of environmental quotations
B.K. Rodes and R. Odell, eds See entry no. 2303

Dictionary of environmental science and technology
A. Porteous, comp. See entry no. 5538

Dictionary of natural resource management
J. Dunster and K. Dunster See entry no. 2108

4617 **Energy glossary**
Energy Information Administration
www.eia.doe.gov/glossary/glossary_main_page.htm
Energy terms and definitions as used in EIA reports, presentations, and survey forms.

4618 **GeMPeT: the geoscience, minerals and petroleum thesaurus**
Charted Information Services, 2003. Various print and electronic pricings: see website.
www.chartedinfo.com.au/orders.html
9,000 terms covering the geoscience industries in a thesaural structure.

Laws, standards, codes

ENTRI: Environmental Treaties and Resource Indicators
Socioeconomic Data and Applications Center See entry no. 2306

4619 **North American Energy Standards Board**
www.naesb.org
'Serves as an industry forum for the development and promotion of standards which will lead to a seamless marketplace for wholesale and retail natural gas and electricity, as recognized by its customers, business community, participants, and regulatory entities.'

4620 **OGEL: global energy law portal**
Alexander's Gas & Oil Connections.
www.gasandoil.com/ogel
Oil, gas and energy law intelligence; newsletter published every two months.

Official & quasi-official bodies

4621 **Bureau of Land Management** [USA]
www.blm.gov
Agency within the US Department of the Interior, which 'administers 261 million surface acres of America's public lands, located primarily in 12 Western States. The BLM sustains the health, diversity, and productivity of the public lands for the use and enjoyment of present and future generations.'

- **Bureau of Reclamation** www.usbr.gov. Now largest wholesaler of water in the USA; also second largest producer of hydroelectric power in the western USA. Good 'Dataweb' presentation on their historic and current projects.

4622 **Cogent**
www.cogent-ssc.com
'Independent, employer-led organisation formed when Cogent, the trailblazer SSC [Sector Skills Council] for Oil and Gas Extraction, Chemicals Manufacturing and Petroleum Industries established in 2002, joined forces with the Polymer NTO. The Nuclear Industry, through the Nuclear Industry Association (NIA) was also actively involved in the development of Cogent.

Cogent is part of a network of better resourced, more influential SSCs established in 2001 to take over from National Training Organisations (NTOs). By the end of 2004, there will be around 25 SSCs in operation or in development covering all key UK industries. SSCs, together with the Sector Skills Development Agency (SSDA), form the Skills for Business (SfB) network, the purpose of which is to bring employers centre-stage in articulating their skills needs and delivering skills-based improvements to productivity.'

4623 **Commission on Sustainable Development**
www.un.org/esa/sustdev
Created in December 1992 to ensure effective follow-up of the Rio United Nations Conference on Environment and Development (the 'Earth Summit'); to monitor and report on implementation of the Earth Summit agreements at the local, national, regional and international levels.

4624 **Department of Energy** [USA]
United States. Department of Energy
www.energy.gov
'Overarching mission is to advance the national, economic and energy security of the United States; to promote scientific and technological innovation in support of that mission; and to ensure the environmental cleanup of the national nuclear weapons complex.' The Department's four strategic goals relate to : Defence; Energy; Environment; Science.

As would be expected, provides access to a wealth of information. However, note in particular that the National Nuclear Security Administration, the Office of Energy Efficiency and Renewable Energy, the Office of Nuclear Energy, Science and Technology, the Office of Science as well as its OSTI operation, are each given separate entries herein.

- **Energy Information Administration** http://eia.doe.gov. 'We provide policy-independent data, forecasts, and analyses to promote sound policy making, efficient markets, and public understanding regarding energy and its interaction with the economy and the environment.'
- **Environment, safety and health** www.eh.doe.gov. Extensive portal to the Department's involvements in this arena.
- **International Energy Annual** www.eia.doe.gov/iea. Presents information and trends on world energy production and consumption for petroleum, natural gas, coal, and electricity. 2002 edn issued mid-2004; 2003 edn to be released April-June 2005.
- **National Laboratories and Technology Centers** www.energy.gov. Checklist of DOE's laboratories and technology centres which house world-class facilities where more than 30,000 scientists and engineers perform cutting-edge research. Many have separate entries within TNW.

4625 **Energy** [EUR]
European Commission. Directorate for Energy and Transport
www.europa.eu.int/comm/energy
The Brussels-based Directorate-General for Energy and Transport implements European policies in the energy and transport field. Its energy section on the general EUROPA site takes in material on resources (coal, oil, gas, nuclear and renewable). The site provides news, conference details and the full text of policy documents, keynote and green papers on European energy positions. Useful documents of all types can be found – for example, a statistical pocketbook on energy matters – but also legal acts and nomenclatures.

4626 **Energy Group** [UK]
www.dti.gov.uk/energy
Details of the work of this Group within the UK Department

of Trade and Industry, with sections: Coal; Gas/electricity utilities; Nuclear; Oil and gas; Renewables.

Environmental Protection Agency
See entry no. 5555

4627 **International Energy Agency**
www.iea.org
An intergovernmental body within the ORGANISATION FOR ECONOMIC CO-OPERATION AND DEVELOPMENT for member countries to exchange energy information and to co-ordinate policies. It is the source for world-wide energy statistics, policy reports and country reviews. Pre-2000 publications, policy documents, factsheets and activities information are free to download. The IEA maintains a database of free statistics on renewables in OECD countries.

- **ETDEWEB** www.etde.org/etdeweb [REGISTRATION]. A database of worldwide energy literature, with over three million abstracted and indexed records, produced by the IEA's Energy Technology Data Exchange. References to journal papers, reports, conferences, books and miscellaneous documents.
- **World Energy Outlook** 2004, 550pp. €150.00. ISBN 9264108173. www.worldenergyoutlook.org [DESCRIPTION]. 'The most complete and authoritative energy publication and has received several prestigious awards from government and industry in recognition of its analytical excellence'.

Man and the Biosphere Programme
See entry no. 2313

National Agroforestry Center
See entry no. 3210

Ozone Secretariat
See entry no. 2314

United Nations Framework Convention on Climate Change
See entry no. 2317

4628 **World Bank**
www.worldbank.org
The World Bank produces financial and analytical overview information in support of its main function, that of channelling resources from rich nations to poor ones. Its website accesses many useful data resources and a library catalogue, *JOLIS*. Probably most interesting in this context are *Topics in Development*, containing project data on, for instance: Energy; Environment; Infrastructure; Mining; Transport; Water resources management; Water supply and sanitation.

- **Oil, Gas, Mining and Chemicals** www.worldbank.org/ogmc. Apart from much useful contextual material, contains substantial series of *Extractive Industries Review* reports issued at end of 2003 (and downloadable as PDFs).

4629 **World Energy Council**
www.worldenergy.org/wec-geis
'The foremost global multi-energy organisation in the world today. WEC has Member Committees in over 90 countries, including most of the largest energy-producing and energy consuming countries. The 81-year-old organisation covers all types of energy, including coal, oil, natural gas, nuclear, hydro, and renewables, and is UN-accredited, non-governmental, non-commercial and non-aligned.'

Research centres & institutes

4630 **Centre for Research, Education and Training in Energy** [UK]
www.create.org.uk
'CREATE motivates and educates people in businesses, communities, and schools to achieve more sustainable uses of energy and reduce carbon emissions.' Useful resources including news items and a links library containing over 200 annotated entries (though the method of display for both could be significantly improved).

4631 **The Earth Institute**
Columbia University
www.earthinstitute.columbia.edu
'Brings together talent from throughout the University to address complex issues facing the planet and its inhabitants, with particular focus on sustainable development and the needs of the world's poor. The Earth Institute is motivated by the belief that science and technological tools already exist, and could be expanded, to greatly improve conditions for the world's poor while preserving the natural systems that support life on Earth.'

4632 **Electric Power Research Institute**
www.epri.com
'Established in 1973 as an independent, non-profit center for electricity and environmental research. EPRI's collaborative science and technology portfolio now spans every aspect of power generation, delivery and end-use, drawing upon a world-class network of scientific, engineering and technical talent. EPRI's clients represent over 90% of the electricity generated in the US. International client participation represents over 10% of EPRI's program investment.'

4633 **Energy Research** [EUR]
European Commission. Directorate for Research
http://europa.eu.int/comm/research/energy/index_en.htm
Helpful gateway summarizing the involvements of the EU with energy research.

Resources for the Future
See entry no. 2322

4634 **Sustainable Development Research Network** [UK]
Policy Studies Institute
www.sd-research.org.uk
DEFRA initiative, co-ordinated by the PSI in London, which 'aims to facilitate and strengthen the links between providers of research and policymakers across government, in order to improve evidence-based policymaking to deliver the UK government's objectives for sustainable development'. Produce very useful 'Guide to research centres and evidence providers' (downloadable PDF, February 2005).

4635 **UK Energy Research Centre**
www.ukerc.ac.uk
Founded in April 2004, and 'is a distributed centre and will be at the heart of the UK's sustainable energy initiative, looking at new ways of reducing our reliance on fossil fuels by introducing an integrated whole systems approach to energy research, taking account of environmental, social, economic and technological factors. The UKERC research programme began in October and its activities will ramp up during the first quarter of 2005.'

World Resources Institute
See entry no. 2325

Associations & societies

4636 **Coalition for Affordable and Reliable Energy** [USA]
http://careenergy.com
'Formed in 2000 to advocate adoption of a comprehensive energy policy that will enable the United States to meet its energy needs, and strike a sensible balance among the nation's social, economic, national security, environmental and energy goals. Today, CARE is actively engaged in a wide variety of energy and environmental issues, but the coalition's fundamental mission has remained the same ... ensuring the availability of affordable and reliable supplies of energy for America's families and businesses.'

4637 **Edison Electric Institute** [USA]
www.eei.org
'The premier trade association for US shareholder-owned electric companies, and serves international affiliates and industry associates worldwide. Our US members serve more than 90 percent of the ultimate customers in the shareholder-owned segment of the industry and nearly 70 percent of all electric utility ultimate customers in the nation, and generate almost 70 percent of the electricity produced by US electric utilities.'

4638 **Energy Institute** [UK]
www.energyinst.org.uk
Leading professional body for the energy industries, representing 12,000 professionals internationally. EI publishes safety codes, industry standards, guidelines, measurement manuals and conference proceedings. The Institute was created in 2003 by the merger of the Institute of Petroleum and the Institute of Energy.

- **Fuel and Energy Abstracts** ElsevierBimonthly. €1816.00. ISSN 01406701. www.elsevier.com/wps/find/homepage.cws_home [DESCRIPTION]. 'Each issue contains more than 1500 abstracts and titles from more than 800 international publications, special reports, monographs, conference proceedings, surveys and statistical analyses.' Also available online through SCIENCEDIRECT.

4639 **European Association for the Promotion of Cogeneration**
www.cogen.org
'Cogeneration is the most efficient way to deliver heating, cooling and electricity. It is based on the simultaneous production of electricity and thermal energy, both of which are used. The central and most fundamental principle of cogeneration is that, in order to maximise the many benefits that arise from it, systems should be based according to the heat demand of the application.'

COGEN EUROPE is a Belgian not-for-profit organization, created in 1993, which promotes co-operation at a European level. Its membership includes cogeneration associations and suppliers in thirty countries. The website gives free access to reports, data, studies, briefings and position statements.

4640 **Greenpeace**
www.greenpeace.org
Founded in 1971, Greenpeace campaigns to: Stop climate change; Protect ancient forests; Save the oceans; Stop whaling; Say no to genetic engineering; Stop the nuclear threat; Eliminate toxic chemicals; Encourage sustainable trade. It is a non-profit body that operates in 40 countries around the world. Apart from information about the organization and its campaigns, the website also links to the Greenpeace Science Laboratory at Exeter University, which carries out research that can provide a basis for its campaigns.

Natural Resources Defense Council
See entry no. 2332

Society for Exploration Geophysicists
See entry no. 1092

Portal & task environments

4641 **Carbon Dioxide Information Analysis Center**
http://cdiac.esd.ornl.gov
The primary global-change data and information analysis centre of the US DEPARTMENT OF ENERGY. Includes the World Data Center for Atmospheric Trace Gases. Data on concentrations of carbon dioxide and other radiatively active gases in the atmosphere; role of terrestrial biosphere and oceans in the biogeochemical cycles of greenhouse gases; emissions of carbon dioxide to the atmosphere; long-term climate trends; effects of elevated carbon dioxide on vegetation; vulnerability of coastal areas to rising sea level.

4642 **Centre for Energy** [CAN]
www.centreforenergy.com
'The Centre for Energy was created to meet a growing demand for balanced, credible information about the energy sector and energy-related issues. An Executive Board provides strategy and direction for the Centre for Energy and independent advisors offer expert guidance related to information provided through our Web portal, interpretive centres and printed materials. A president manages the day-to-day operation and oversees the contract network charged with developing and maintaining the portal and publications.'

'We are committed to becoming your key resource for credible, up-to-date information that is supported by research and vetted by reputable, independent sources. Over time, our portal will cover the Canadian energy sector from the mainstays of oil, natural gas, coal, thermal and hydropower through to nuclear, solar and other alternative sources of energy. We aim to be your preferred source for energy news and to provide a forum for discussion. We will also serve as a research resource and offer links to a wide range of energy information sources.'

Climate Change
United Nations Environment Programme See entry no. 1206

ClimateArk: climate change portal
See entry no. 1208

4643 **CO_2 and Climate.org** [USA]
A service of the Greening Earth Society which is a 'not-for-profit membership organization comprised of rural electric cooperatives and municipal electric utilities, their fuel suppliers, and thousands of individuals ... CO_2 is required for life on earth. It cannot be reasonably construed to be a pollutant. With proper stewardship, the ability of earth's plant life to sequester carbon in soils can result in a host of

benefits. CO_2 and Climate.org provides sound information about CO_2 and climate to educators, students, business and media representatives, community leaders and policymakers alike.'

4644 erWEB: facilitating the environmental revolution
[USA]
http://erweb.org
'Comprehensive web utility that conveys current information about the Environmental Industry to all sectors of American society. In this way, erWEB is helping Americans understand and utilize the products and services of the emerging Environmental Industry.

erWEB is a product of the Earth Science Agency, LLC, which is a non-partisan, non-political, for-profit company whose mission is to increase the measure of quality in American communities through the proliferation of an idealized network of corporations that promote economic responsibility, financial growth, job creation, and environmental stewardship while providing essential services to consumers.'

4645 Platts
McGraw Hill.
www.platts.com
'The world's largest and most authoritative source of energy industry information and services.' Covers: Coal; Electric power; Metals; Natural gas; Nuclear; Oil; Petrochemicals. In 2001, incorporated *FT Energy*, from Pearson plc.

- **Electricity Bookmarks** www.platts.com. 'Free service providing links to the homepages of 1735 power producers, power distributors, power pools, electricity exchanges, traders, R&D organizations, and related associations, ministries, and agencies in 128 countries and territories.'

4646 Sustainability Knowledge Network [AUS]
University of Queensland
avel.edu.au
Aimed at pointing users toward engineering resources with a green, or sustainable edge. Broad subject categories 'hot topics', 'emerging technologies' and 'foundation topics' are subdivided by engineering discipline. Additional linked services include the usual jobs, institutional and other links. Of these, the most useful is the Australian Digital Theses database. There is a useful gateway to Engineering and Sustainable Systems Industry News.

UN Atlas of the Oceans
United Nations See entry no. 1365

US Global Change Research Information Office
US Climate Change Science Program See entry no. 1211

Water
European Environment Agency See entry no. 5579

Discovering print & electronic resources

4647 ENERGY Cluster
Questel Orbit.
www.questel.orbit.com [FEE-BASED]
Cross-searching access to eight files.

4648 Energy Databases
Dialog.
http://library.dialog.com/bluesheets/html/bloE.html#ENERGY
List of host Dialog databases covering various facets of 'energy', each able to be searched as a group. Similar lists available for other groupings: e.g. Ecology and conservation.

Environment Abstracts
See entry no. 5581

Information sources in environmental protection
S. Eagle and J. Deschamps, eds See entry no. 5585

Digital data, image & text collections

4649 Energy Statistics [UK]
Office for National Statistics
www.statistics.gov.uk
Energy is one of the themes within the UK's National Statistics site whereby users are able to browse amongst details of the key statistical series.

4650 Statistical Review of World Energy
www.bp.com
Key compilation produced annually by BP – as a public service – since 1951. Access via the Publications section of the website. There is a useful list of Links to contributors websites.

4651 World Markets Energy
World Markets Research Centre.
www.wmrc.com/wma_e.html
'The world's most sophisticated energy intelligence service. An integrated market awareness and market research service used by the world's largest oil, gas and power companies, financial institutions and professional services firms.'
World Markets Research Centre is part of the Global Insight group of companies.

Directories & encyclopedias

4652 Encyclopedia of energy
C. Cleveland, ed. Academic Press, 2004, 3600pp. 6 v, $1950.00. ISBN 012176480X.
www.info.sciencedirect.com/reference_works
Wide-ranging coverage within these broad themes: Basics of energy; Coal; Conservation and end use; Economics of energy; Electricity; Energy flows; Environmental issues; Global issues; History and energy; Material use and reuse; Measurement and models; Nuclear energy; Oil and natural gas; Policy issues; Public issues; Renewable and alternative sources; Risks; Society and energy; Sustainable development; Systems of energy.
Available online: see website.
'contains thorough and well-written summaries of a vast range of energy subjects ... it will prove an invaluable resource for people whose profession relates to the energy industry.' (*Petroleum Economist*)

4653 **Encyclopedia of energy technology and the environment**
A. Bisio and S. Boots, eds Wiley, 1995, 3024pp. 4 v., $955.00. ISBN 0471544582.
This set presents an A–Z reference of energy production technologies with an emphasis on environmental impact. Topics covered include air pollution, energy efficient systems, solar heating, waste management and water power. Dated; but useful if easily accessible.

4654 **Encyclopedia of global change: environmental change and human society**
A.S. Goudie and D.J. Cuff, eds Oxford University Press, 2002, 1200pp. 2 v., £180.00. ISBN 0195108256.
'Featuring over 320 original articles by leading scholars, this encyclopaedia captures the current knowledge of natural and anthropogenic changes in the physical, chemical, and biological systems and resources, and explores the effects of those on changes on human society.'

4655 **Encyclopedia of world environmental history**
S. Krech, J.R. McNeill and C. Merchant, eds Routledge, 2004. 3 v., £275.00. ISBN 0415937329.
www.routledge-ny.com/ref/eweh [DESCRIPTION]
520 articles arranged from A–Z within these general themes: Arts, literature, and architecture; Biomes, climate, and natural events; Economic systems; Energy sources; Eras and civilizations, ancient; Exploitation and processes; Key concepts and philosophies; Law and regulation; Nations and regions, modern; Nonliving resources; Organizations; People; Places and events; Plant and animal resources; Religion; Sociocultural resources; Technology and science.
Well presented compendium; detailed index.
'Recommended for school, public and undergraduate collections. It brings together a large, eclectic, interdisciplinary collection of articles related to environmental history that would be difficult to replicate any other way.' (*Reference & User Services Quarterly*)

4656 **Macmillan encyclopedia of energy**
J. Zumerchik, ed. Macmillan Reference USA, 2000. 3 v., $400.00. ISBN 0028650212.
www.gale.com/gvrl
250 articles arranged A–Z by title. Aimed at public, high school, and undergraduate libraries. Useful overview.
Available online: see website.

Handbooks & manuals

Combined heating, cooling and power handbook: technologies and applications: an integrated approach to energy resource optimization
N. Petchers See entry no. 5939

4657 **Energy: management, supply and conservation**
C. Beggs Butterworth-Heinemann, 2002, 284pp. £26.99. ISBN 0750650966.
Contents: Energy management in context; The utility companies and energy supply; Competition in energy supply; Energy auditing; Energy analysis techniques; Energy economics; Energy monitoring and targeting; Energy efficient heating; Waste heat recovery; Combined heat and power; Energy efficient air conditioning and refrigeration; Electrical services and lighting; Passive environmental control in buildings.

4658 **Energy management handbook**
W.C. Turner 5th edn, Marcel Dekker, 2004, 856pp. $179.95. ISBN 0824748123.
'Originally published two decades ago, the Energy Management Handbook has become recognized as the definitive stand-alone energy manager's desk reference, used by thousands of energy management professionals throughout the industry. Known as the bible of energy management, it has helped more energy managers reach their potential than any other resource.'

Handbook for cogeneration and combined cycle power plants
M.P. Boyce See entry no. 5950

Handbook of green chemistry and technology
J. Clark and D. Macquarrie See entry no. 5136

Modern power station practice: incorporating modern power system practice
See entry no. 5505

Observation of the earth and its environment: survey of missions and sensors
H.J. Kramer See entry no. 1638

Keeping up-to-date

4659 **Annual Review of Environment and Resources**
Annual Reviews, Inc, 2004. $233.00. ISBN 0824323297 ISSN 15435938.
www.annurev.org/catalog/2004/eg29.asp [DESCRIPTION]
Previously titled Annual Review of Energy and Environment. This volume has 12 reviews organized into three parts: Earth's life support systems; Human use of environment and resources; Management and human dimensions.

4660 **Environment Times** [UK]
Beckhouse Media.
www.environmenttimes.co.uk
Wide-ranging coverage of environmental issues.

Environmental Media Services
See entry no. 2364

4661 **green@work Today**
EnvironDesignWorks.
www.bondareport.com
'Portal for tracking environmental news for those who would like to stay informed but lack the time to peruse the ever-growing number of resources. Articles are gathered on every conceivable topic that deals with the environment.' Very useful list of 'Green Gateways' with links.

4662 **How to save the world**
D. Pollard, ed.
http://blogs.salon.com/0002007
Very well presented and informative (personal interest) blog: 'Dave Pollard's environmental philosophy, creative works, business papers and essays'.

State of the world
L.R. Brown, ed. See entry no. 2963

Mining & Minerals Processing

copper • exploration geophysics • explosives • geomechanics • gold • lead • metallurgy • metals • mine safety • mineral resources • minerals processing • mines • mining engineering • nickel • platinum group metals • rock mechanics • silver • tin • titanium • zeolites • zinc

Introductions to the subject

4663 **A concise history of mining**
C.E. Gregory Rev. edn, Balkema, 2001, 216pp. €88.40. ISBN 9058093476.
Four parts, dealing respectively with the history of man, the chronology of the mining industry, the conventions that govern the lives of those within the mining community, and the impact of mineral and metal production upon nations.

4664 **Introductory mining engineering**
H.L. Hartman 2nd edn, Wiley, 2002, 584pp. $125.00. ISBN 0471348511.
14 chapters: Introduction to mining; Mining and its consequences; Stages of mining: prospecting and exploration; Stages of mining: development and exploitation; Unit operations of mining; Surface mine development; Surface mining: mechanical extraction methods; Surface mining: aqueous extraction methods; Underground mine development; Underground mining: unsupported methods; Underground mining: supported methods; Underground mining: caving methods; Novel methods and technology; Summary of mining methods and their selection.

4665 **Mineral resources: a world review**
J.A. Wolfe Chapman and Hall, 1984, 293pp. £14.95. ISBN 0412251906.
A useful classic text on mines and mineral resources, along with mineral industries. Part 1 consists of short essays on various aspects of the mineral industries. Part 2 includes reports on 21 metals and 18 non-metals. Glossary. Briefly annotated bibliography: pp.283–4. Designed for those with an interest in the subject but not necessarily professionally trained.

Dictionaries, thesauri, classifications

4666 **Dictionary of mining, mineral, and related terms**
American Geological Institute 2nd edn, 1997, 646pp. $49.95. ISBN 0922152365.
Over 28,500 terms defined in an A–Z list. Cross-reference links. Includes standard mining terms, but also terms related to the environment, pollution, automation, health, and safety, many of which now have legal definitions. Includes current technological developments and environmental regulations. A useful resource.
Compiled by the staff of the former US Bureau of Mines.

4667 **Elsevier's dictionary of mining and mineralogy: in English, French, German and Italian**
A.F. Dorian, comp. Elsevier, 1993, 300pp. £115.50. ISBN 0444890394.
Provides translations and explanations of 3585 mining terms through brief definitions.

4668 **Rock blasting terms and symbols: a dictionary of symbols and terms in rock blasting and related areas like drilling, mining and rock mechanics**
A. Rustan, ed.; International Society for Rock Mechanics Balkema, 1998, 193pp. €121.00. ISBN 9054104414.
Compiled by a group of experts in co-operation with the Society's Commission on Fragmentation by Blasting. Contains 1980 terms, 316 symbols, 93 acronyms, abbreviations and shortened forms, 221 references, 31 figures, 32 formulas and 28 tables. Bibliography pp.185–93.

Laws, standards, codes

Commission on New Minerals and Mineral Names
See entry no. 1281

Official & quasi-official bodies

4669 **Mine Safety and Health Administration** [USA]
www.msha.gov
Mission 'is to administer the provisions of the Federal Mine Safety and Health Act of 1977 (Mine Act) and to enforce compliance with mandatory safety and health standards as a means to eliminate fatal accidents; to reduce the frequency and severity of nonfatal accidents; to minimize health hazards; and to promote improved safety and health conditions in the Nation's mines.'
- **Mining Safety and Health Research National Institute for Occupational Safety and Health.** www.cdc.gov/niosh/mining. Comprehensive and extensive A–Z mining site index; also FAQs, Links.

4670 **Mineral Resources Program** [USA]
http://minerals.usgs.gov
Program within the US Geological Survey which 'funds science to provide and communicate current, impartial information on the occurrence, quality, quantity, and availability of mineral resources'. Its Minerals Information website won the 2004 Shoemaker Award for Communication Product Excellence, established 'to recognize extraordinary examples of communicating and translating complex scientific concepts and discoveries into words and pictures that capture the interest and imagination of the American public'.
- **Minerals Information** http://minerals.usgs.gov/minerals. 'Statistics and information on the worldwide supply, demand, and flow of minerals and materials essential to the US economy, the national security, and protection of the environment.'

4671 **Minerals Management Service** [USA]
www.mms.gov
Bureau within the US Department of the Interior which 'manages the nation's natural gas, oil and other mineral resources on the outer continental shelf'. The Service's Library and Reading Room maintains a very useful wide-ranging set of links categorized: Congressional; Employee manuals and personnel information; Environmental; Freedom of Information Act; General; Leasing; Legal; News releases; Royalties and revenues; Scientific and technical. 'We want this Library to evolve into a solid resource for anyone with an interest in the Minerals Management Service and what we do. Your input is welcome and encouraged.' A good value-adding service.

4672 **Office of Surface Mining** [USA]
www.osmre.gov
US DEPARTMENT OF THE INTERIOR Bureau which has 'responsibility, in cooperation with the states and indian tribes, to protect citizens and the environment during coal mining and reclamation, and to reclaim mines abandoned before 1977.'

Associations & societies

Abrasive Engineering Society
See entry no. 5798

Aluminium Federation
See entry no. 5799

Aluminum Association
See entry no. 5800

4673 **Australasian Institute of Mining and Metallurgy**
www.ausimm.com
Extensive and well structured and presented site. Especially useful for those outside Australasia is the section Useful Links which includes full contact details, as well as the links themselves.

British Metals Recycling Association
See entry no. 5567

4674 **Canadian Institute of Mining, Metallurgy and Petroleum**
www.cim.org/mainEn.cfm
'11,000 members from industry, government and academia who are dedicated to the discovery, production, utilization and economics of minerals, metals and petroleum. Thousands more are also involved as CIM Branch members all across Canada. CIM periodicals also reach 2000 other subscribers across the world in various universities and libraries.'

4675 **Copper Development Association**
www.copper.org
Membership in CDA is open to copper producers worldwide and to brass mill, wire mill and foundry fabricators of copper and copper alloys with production facilities in the USA.

- **Copper News** www.coppernews.com. Subset of the WORLDNEWS NETWORK. Similar services available for: Aluminium and Coal.

European Aluminium Association
See entry no. 5806

Institute of Materials, Minerals and Mining
See entry no. 5809

4676 **International Council on Mining and Metals**
www.icmm.com/html/index.php
Good way in to international activity in this arena.

4677 **International Lead and Zinc Study Group**
www.ilzsg.org/ilzsgframe.htm
'An intergovernmental organisation which regularly brings together twenty-eight member countries in an international forum to exchange information on lead and zinc. ILZSG provides a unique and globally recognised source of industry statistics and organises twice yearly meetings between producing and consuming countries, industry and government representatives.'

4678 **International Society of Explosives Engineers**
www.isee.org
Founded 1974; 4500 members from 90 countries. Useful set of publications including *The Blasters Library*: 'Hundreds of publications including those produced by ISEE as well as books, videos and training materials produced by university presses and commercial publishers across the globe. Authors include the best in the explosives industry worldwide.'

4679 **International Zeolite Association**
www.iza-online.org
Aims to promote and encourage the development of all aspects of zeolite science and technology. Zeolites are a large group of minerals consisting of hydrated aluminosilicates of sodium, potassium, calcium, and barium.

The site has details of conferences, publications, structure type codes, links to other zeolite sites and to national associations. A database of zeolite structures has data on framework types, simulated XRD powder patterns, disordered structures and schemes for building zeolite framework models.

4680 **Minerals, Metals and Materials Society** [USA]
www.tms.org
'The vision of TMS is to be the professional society of choice for the worldwide minerals, metals, and materials community.' Very extensive set of resources – whose internal links are well displayed on the Site Map. Of especial value is the TMS Document Center which, for instance, has a useful online subject index to its book publications.

4681 **Mining and Metallurgical Society of America**
www.mmsa.net
'Professional organization dedicated to increasing public awareness and understanding about mining and why mined materials are essential to modern society and human well being.' The organization maintains an interesting 'library of published materials about many of the current issues that affect the minerals business. Links to the sources are provided. These materials are collected for you so that you don't have to do much research. Use them when you wish to speak or write to the public about their concerns regarding the minerals business'.

4682 **National Mining Association** [USA]
www.nma.org
'The voice of the American mining industry in Washington, D.C. NMA is the only national trade organization that represents the interests of mining before Congress, the Administration, federal agencies, the judiciary and the media.

'Our membership includes more than 325 corporations involved in all aspects of the mining industry including coal, metal and industrial mineral producers, mineral processors, equipment manufacturers, state associations, bulk transporters, engineering firms, consultants, financial institutions and other companies that supply goods and services to the mining industry.'

Apart from policy-related information, access to useful data on the industry.

4683 Nickel Institute
www.nidi.org
Well presented site covering wide range of valuable information organized: News; Nickel and its uses; Technical support; Human health & the environment; Recycling & sustainable development; Nickel Producers Environmental Research Association (NIPERA).

4684 Silver Institute
www.silverinstitute.org
'International association of miners, refiners, fabricators, and wholesalers of silver and silver products.' Good range of background information and other resources, attractively presented.

4685 Society for Mining, Metallurgy, and Exploration [USA]
www.smenet.org
'An international society of professionals in the minerals industry. The SME membership is more than 13,000 strong, with members in nearly 100 countries.' Attractive well laid out website – though significant proportions of the information only accessible to members. However, the SME Link List has more than 2500 freely accessible mining and mineral related web links.

4686 Society of Exploration Geophysicists
www.seg.org
'Founded in 1930, fosters the expert and ethical practice of geophysics in the exploration and development of natural resources, in characterizing the near surface, and in mitigating earth hazards. The Society, which has more than 23,000 members in 110 countries, fulfills its mission through its publications, conferences, forums, Web sites, and educational opportunities.'

This is a site rich in resources, to be explored in detail.

4687 Titanium Information Group
www.titaniuminfogroup.co.uk
An association of suppliers, design engineers and fabricators of titanium formed with the intention of promoting the use of titanium.

4688 World Gold Council
www.gold.org
Apart from concerns with the Value of gold, and its use in Jewellery, the Council's sits provides in its Discover section very good overviews of the use of gold in science and industry.

- **GOLDSHEET Mining Directory** B. Johnson www.goldsheetlinks.com. Extensive well structured personal interest site about gold. The author maintains a similar site about Oil and Natural Gas.

Libraries, archives, museums

4689 IMM Library and Information Services [UK]
www.iom3.org/MIS/index.htm
Service of the Institute of Materials, Minerals and Mining which provides 'a range of products and services developed from a unique collection of minerals industry publications. Covering the geology, mining and extraction of metalliferous and industrial minerals, these services are a highly cost-effective means of access to technical and scientific developments and descriptions of operations throughout the international industry'.

- **IMMAGE: Information on Mining Metallurgy And Geological Exploration** www.imm.org.uk/esales/iindex.htm [DESCRIPTION]. Bibliographic database that covers economic geology, mining and extraction technology and developments in the non-ferrous metals and industrial minerals fields. Available print and CD-ROM.

4690 The National Mining Hall of Fame and Museum [USA]
www.leadville.com/miningmuseum
'Located in the famous 1880's silver mining boomtown of Leadville, Colorado at the top of Colorado's Rocky Mountains ... The only federally-chartered non-profit national mining museum.'

Portal & task environments

4691 Ecomine
www.mineralinfo.org/cadres-ecom.htm
Provides an excellent set of links to mining and minerals information in France with some international coverage. Mainly in French.

4692 InfoMine
InfoMine Inc.
www.infomine.com
Access to the 'largest, fully integrated source of worldwide mining and mineral exploration information'. A key commercially sponsored mining information source. Links to mining news, commodity prices, publications, suppliers, equipment, consultants. News style webpage, with emphasis on current information.

- **The EduMine dictionary of mining, mineral and related terms** www.infomine.com/dictionary. Dictionary of more than 26,000 terms and definitions with extensive cross-referencing. Original content was compiled by the US Bureau of Mines. This XML version was translated and is supported by EduMine – a Division of InfoMine.

4693 Johnson Matthey
www.matthey.com
'Speciality chemicals company focused on its core skills in catalysts, precious metals and speciality chemicals.' Straightforward Site Map gives pointers to a range of useful resources.

- **Platinum Metals Review** www.platinummetalsreview.com. Free quarterly E-journal covering the science and technology of the six platinum group metals: platinum, palladium, rhodium, iridium, osmium and ruthenium.

4694 Metal Bulletin
www.metalbulletin.plc.uk
'Metal Bulletin plc takes its name from its principal title, *Metal Bulletin*, that was first introduced in 1913 some two years before incorporation as the Metal Information Bureau Ltd. Its mission then, as now, was to provide must have timely information, including price indications, for the global non-ferrous metals and steel markets.'

Provides information via a range of journals, newsletters, books, directories, and electronic products covering the production, processing, trade, pricing and markets for over 40 industrial minerals. IMI also organizes commercially focused conferences worldwide on many important and topical mineral and market-related subjects.

- **The Energy Information Centre** www.eic.co.uk. 'The UK's leading independent energy consultancy to industrial, commercial and public sector energy users. Established in 1975 to provide market intelligence on the oil industry, today we offer a complete range of integrated energy solutions.'

4695 Mineral Resources Forum
United Nations Conference on Trade and Development
www.natural-resources.org/minerals
'Information resource for issues related to mining, minerals, metals and sustainable development. It seeks to engage a diverse set of users from governments, mining, mineral and metal companies and other concerned civil society institutions, and to promote an integrated, inter-disciplinary approach to mineral issues and policies.'

Very well presented and informative website: particularly valuable for the access it provides to resources on the environmental and social implications of mining and minerals processing.

4696 The Northern Miner [CAN]
www.northernminer.com
Covers the worldwide mining activities of mining companies based in North America or listed on North American exchanges. Weekly and daily coverage supplemented by special reports on gold mining and other precious metals, base metals and diamonds. 'Unlike other mining journals and newsletters, *The Northern Miner*'s reports are written by geologists who know how to assess the technical details of a project and who have visited exploration sites firsthand.' Site includes Glossary of mining and financial terminology, a list of North American and Foreign mining associations and societies, and a searchable directory of mining company operations cross-referenced by country.

- **Canadian Mines Handbook** CANAnnual. CAN $89.00. Also available on CD-ROM. Concise snapshots of over 2400 Canadian and US mining companies, mines, and associated organizations such as smelters, refineries, and industry associations.

4697 TheBullionDesk
www.thebulliondesk.com
Very busy site aimed at the trading markets but full of fascinating background information.

4698 Tin Technology
www.tintechnology.biz
'Membership-based organisation involved in research, development, and marketing of tin based technologies. It is the world's foremost authority on tin with access to more than 60 years experience through its association with ITRI Ltd (formerly the International Tin Research Institute).'

Discovering print & electronic resources

4699 Aluminium Industry Abstracts
Aluminum Association and European Aluminium Association CSA.
www.csa.com/factsheets/aia-set-c.php [DESCRIPTION]
Coverage of the world's technical literature on aluminium, production processes, products, applications, and business developments. Includes information abstracted from approximately 2300 scientific and technical journals, government reports, conference proceedings, dissertations, books, and patents. About 230,000 records, September 2004.
Also available in print.

Annotated bibliographies of mineral deposits in Africa, Asia (exclusive of the USSR) and Australasia
J.D. Ridge See entry no. 1295

Annotated bibliographies of mineral deposits in Europe
J.D. Ridge See entry no. 1296

Annotated bibliographies of mineral deposits in the Western Hemisphere
J.D. Ridge See entry no. 1297

Athena Earth Sciences Resources
P. Perroud; University of Geneva See entry no. 1298

GeoAfrica: directory of African earth-science resources
See entry no. 870

4700 Geomechanics Abstracts
Elsevier, 1997–, Bimonthly. €631.00 2004. ISSN 13651617.
Provides coverage of papers published on rock and soil mechanics, and geotechnics taken from over 2000 journals. Each issue includes about 300–400 abstracts.

Also available online, and contents available electronically as part of GEOBASE. Supersedes in part *International Journal of Rock Mechanics and Mining Sciences and Geomechanics Abstracts* (ISSN 0148-9062) which was formed by the merger of *International Journal of Rock Mechanics and Mining Sciences* (ISSN 0020-7624) and *Rock Mechanics Abstracts* (ISSN 0035-7456).

4701 Mining History Network
www.ex.ac.uk/~RBurt/MinHistNet
Rather nice set of pages, not very current, but currency not so important in this area.

Digital data, image & text collections

ISSB
See entry no. 5829

4702 World Bureau of Metal Statistics
www.world-bureau.com
'Through regular publications – available on subscription in print and electronic format – we keep companies and organisations throughout the world up to speed on the production, consumption and trade in the major non-ferrous metals. As the leading independent supplier of statistical information to the global metals industry, we can save you the investment in time, money and resources that compiling such data demands.'

Directories & encyclopedias

4703 Agricultural and Mineral Commodities Year Book
Europa Publications, 2002, 384pp. £160.00. ISBN 1857431502.
Covers all major agricultural and mineral products including aluminium, coal, cotton, nickel, petroleum, bananas, rice, rubber, tea, coffee, tobacco, wheat, natural gas, soybeans, zinc, lead and phosphates.

4704 **Directory of mines and quarries** [UK]
D.G. Cameron [et al.], comps; British Geological Survey 6th edn, 2002. £65.00. ISBN 0852724454.
Comprehensive regularly updated directory containing location data and statistical information on minerals and their production for each of the 2368 mineral workings in the UK. Part 1: Major commodity products; Part 2: County list of mineral operators; Part 3: Alphabetical list of operators.
5th edn 1998.

Geophysical Directory
See entry no. 1101

4705 **United Kingdom minerals yearbook 2003**
J.A. Hillier [et al.]; British Geological Survey 2004, 106pp. £40.00. ISBN 085272473X.
'Comprehensive statistical data on minerals production, consumption and trade to 2002, estimates of production for major mineral commodities in 2003 and a commentary on the UK's minerals industry during 2003.'

4706 **Ure's dictionary of arts, manufactures and mines: containing a clear exposition of their principles and practice**
A. Ure and R. Hunt, eds Routledge/Thoemmes, 1999. 6 v. (Facsimile of 6th edn published in 3 v. by Longmans, Green and Co., 1867.), £995.00. ISBN 0415216311.
'Andrew Ure (1778–1857), Scottish chemist, scientific writer and professor at the University of Glasgow, was an enthusiast of the new manufacturing systems that were emerging in the nineteenth century ... His Dictionary is a well known and much-used work, which went to several editions ... (It) is alphabetically arranged and well illustrated with nearly 2000 wood engravings, plus numerous tables. Packed with thousands of useful technical and statistical information on material, chemical and machine processes, and industries, it covers an exceptional range of topics from manufacture and export figures of biscuits, cotton, steel or sugar, to descriptions of minerals, tools, machinery, elements, and organic chemistry.'

4707 **World mineral statistics: 1998–2002**
L.E. Taylor [et al.]; British Geological Survey 2004. £89.00. ISBN 0852724748.
www.bgs.ac.uk/mineralsUK/statistics/world/home.html [DESCRIPTION]
A fairly comprehensive volume of statistics on world minerals. Annual publication of the World Mineral Statistics commodity tables for a run of five years. Selected graphics. Single volumes containing data on 70 minerals. Include figures for production and trade, exports and imports, for the period. Many Eastern European countries can only be estimated for.
Series: Minerals Programme Publications, No. 16.

Handbooks & manuals

4708 **21st century complete guide to minerals: comprehensive information from the US Geological Survey (USGS) including the full mineral yearbook, commodity summaries, industry surveys, and information on gemstones, rock and mineral collecting**
US Geological Survey Progressive Management, 2002, 25165pp. CD-ROM, $29.95. ISBN 1592480403.
'This electronic book on CD-ROM presents comprehensive information from the US Geological Survey on minerals, including the very impressive *Mineral Yearbook* compiled by the USGS. There is detailed information about the production and use of every important mineral in the world – from abrasives to zirconium – with commodity summaries, nation surveys, state surveys, and industry surveys. Fascinating documents about rock and mineral collecting, gemstones, and gold round out this amazing collection.'

Chemistry of precious metals
S.A. Cotton See entry no. 1742

4709 **Explosion protection: electrical apparatus and systems for chemical plants, oil and gas industry, coal mining**
H. Groh Elsevier Butterworth-Heinemann, 2004, 524pp. £50.00. ISBN 0750647779.
Intended for engineers, scientists, plant safety personnel and for students in the field of electrical engineering to give an introduction to the basic principles of explosion protection and the relevant protection techniques. Diagrams, illustrations, tables, index.

4710 **Explosives**
R. Meyer, J. Köhler and A. Homburg 5th edn, Wiley, 2002, 434pp. $230.00. ISBN 3527302670.
'This world-famous reference work has been enlarged and updated without tampering with its tried and tested format. Around 500 alphabetically ordered, monographic entries consider the physicochemical properties, production methods and safe applications of over 120 explosive chemicals; discuss 70 fuels, additives and oxidizing agents; and describe test methods.'
'The objective of the book is to provide fundamental information on explosives to both the experts and the general public, making it of use to anybody working with explosives in the civil and military fields.' (*Mining Engineering*)

4711 **Extractive metallurgy of copper**
W.G. Davenport [et al.] 4th edn, Pergamon, 2002, 432pp. £80.00. ISBN 0080440290.
Detailed well established handbook, in this edn containing 'an even greater depth of industrial information, focussing on how copper metal is extracted from ore and scrap, and how this extraction could be made more efficient'.

Handbook of aluminum
G.E. Totten and D.S. Mackenzie, eds See entry no. 5843

4712 **Handbook of explosion prevention and protection**
M. Hattwig and H. Steen, eds Wiley-VCH, 2004, 699pp. Translated from the German, £150.00. ISBN 3527307184.
Major text. Seven sections: Explosion processes; Ignition processes; Properties of reactive gases and vapors; Properties of combustible dusts; Properties of flammable mists and foams; Measures of explosion protection and prevention; Fundamentals of understanding and judging explosion risks.

4713 **Handbook of marine mineral resources**
D.S. Cronan, ed. CRC Press, 2000, 406pp. $159.95. ISBN 084938429X.
Summarizes the main advances in our understanding of marine minerals and concentrates on the deposits of proven economic potential. Contributions made in the context of the recently agreed United Nations Law of the Sea.

4714 **Handbook of zeolite science and technology**
S.M. Auerbach, K.A. Carrado and P.K. Dutta, eds Marcel Dekker, 2003, 1184pp. $235.00. ISBN 0824740203.
Zeolites are extensively used in three applications: absorbents, catalysts, ion exchange. In addition, natural zeolites (there are about 40 of these) because of their lower cost are used in bulk mineral applications. More recently, they have become used in a range of health-related applications.

24 chapters in five parts: I. Introduction; II. Synthesis and structure; III. Characterization; IV. Host-guest chemistry; V. Applications.

Introduction to ore-forming processes
L.J. Robb See entry no. 1328

4715 **Mineral deposits of Europe**
S.H.U. Bowie [et al.], eds; Institution of Mining and Metallurgy and Mineralogical Society of Great Britain and Ireland 1978–1989. 5 v. in 4. ISBN 0900488441.
A comprehensive overview of the regions where mineral deposits are important in Europe. Clear descriptions given of classical and producing mining districts. A useful supplement to the map *Carte metallogenique de l'Europe 1:2,500,000*. Divided into 5 volumes. Bibliographies appended to each chapter in each volume. Name and subject indexes. General readership level.

Mineral deposits of the world: ores, industrial minerals and rocks
M. Vanecek See entry no. 1331

Physical metallurgy handbook
A.K. Sinha See entry no. 5856

Quantitative data file for ore minerals
A.J. Criddle and C.J. Stanley, eds See entry no. 1340

Remedial treatment for contaminated land
M.R. Harris, S.M. Herbert and M.A. Smith; Construction Industry Research and Information Association See entry no. 5645

4716 **SME Mining Reference Handbook**
R.L. Lowrie; Society for Mining, Metallurgy, and Exploration 2002, 464pp. $129.00. ISBN 0873351754.
Designed to serve as a practical field reference for mining and minerals engineers who spend time away from the office. 'With its comprehensive store of charts, graphs, tables, equations, and rules of thumb, the handbook is the essential technical reference for mobile mining professionals. It's also a convenient desk reference for in-office use ... . Covers all branches of mining – metal, coal, and non-metal – and all locales of mining – surface, underground, and hybrid.'

Although the main emphasis is US mining, numerous references are made to international practice, with more than 250 experts contributing to the text.

Keeping up-to-date

Geophysics
Society of Exploration Geophysicists See entry no. 1114

4717 **Mining Journal**
Mining Communications Ltd.
www.mining-journal.com
'The industry's leading weekly newspaper covering all aspects of the global mining industry, from grass-roots exploration, through financing and development, to production and marketing.' Founded in 1835.
The company offers a number of related publications: see website.

Nuclear Energy

atomic energy • nuclear engineering • nuclear fission • nuclear fusion • nuclear power • nuclear reactors • nuclear safety

Introductions to the subject

4718 **Nuclear power: a reference handbook**
H. Henderson ABC-CLIO, 2000, 250pp. $50.00. ISBN 1576074358.
This guide helps readers explore the science, technology, politics, and culture that surround nuclear energy.
'A compact, inexpensive, introductory guide to a wide variety of issues pertaining to nuclear energy and the industry that has arisen around it ... Recommended for readers looking for general information on this important environmental topic.' (*Choice*)

4719 **Nuclear renaissance: technologies and policies for the future of nuclear power**
W.J. Nuttall IOP, 2005, 322pp. £45.00. ISBN 0750309369.
11 chapters in three parts: The policy landscape; Nuclear fission technologies; Nuclear fusion technologies.
'For anyone seeking to take an informed position in the debate on the role – if any – of nuclear power in meeting our future energy needs, it is hard to imagine a better starting point than this comprehensive, meticulously reserched and thought-provoking book.' (*The Engineer*)

Dictionaries, thesauri, classifications

4720 **Elsevier's dictionary of nuclear engineering: Russian–English; English–Russian**
M. Rosenberg and S. Bobryakov, comps Elsevier, 2003. 2 v., €325.00. ISBN 0444510311.
50,000 terms covering: nuclear physics, thermonuclear research, nuclear reactors, nuclear fuel, isotopes, radiation, reliability and safety issues, environmental protection, emergency issues, radiation hazards. Terms from the military nuclear field are included, as well as names of nuclear power plants and nuclear societies worldwide. English-Russian volume also contains 6500 abbreviations.

4721 **Joint thesaurus: ETDE/INIS Joint Reference Series No. 1**
International Atomic Energy Agency 2004. Downloadable PDF.
www.etde.org/edb/download.html
Contains the controlled terminology for indexing all information within the subject scope of both INIS (International Nuclear Information System) and the

ETDEWEB information system. This December 2003 version contains 20,953 valid descriptors and 8600 forbidden terms. Supplements are available via the website.

Official & quasi-official bodies

4722 International Atomic Energy Agency
www.iaea.org
'The IAEA is the world's center of nuclear cooperation and works for the safe, secure, and peaceful uses of nuclear technologies. Three main pillars underpin the IAEA's mission: Safety and security; Science and technology; Safeguards and verification.' It is part of the UNITED NATIONS family.

The Site Index clearly indicates the Agency's range of activities, divided into six sections: About IAEA; Our work; News centre; Publications; Data centre; Resources. There is a wealth of resources under each of these headings; and this site is an excellent place to start for those new to the subject.

- **International Nuclear Information System** www.iaea.org/inis [FEE-BASED]. Maintains bibliographic database currently containing 2.5 million abstracts and over 600,000 full-text publications.: 'The world's most comprehensive and leading information source on the peaceful applications of nuclear science and technology.'

4723 National Nuclear Security Administration [USA]
www.nnsa.doe.gov
'The mission of the Administration shall be the following: To enhance United States national security through the military application of nuclear energy; To maintain and enhance the safety, reliability, and performance of the United States nuclear weapons stockpile, including the ability to design, produce, and test, in order to meet national security requirements; To provide the United States Navy with safe, militarily effective nuclear propulsion plants and to ensure the safe and reliable operation of those plants; To promote international nuclear safety and nonproliferation; To reduce global danger from weapons of mass destruction; To support United States leadership in science and technology.

- **Lawrence Livermore National Laboratory University of California**. www.llnl.gov. Operated by the University for NNSA. As Los Alamos, offers a wide and informative range of services to the community and the public more generally – subject to security considerations.
- **Los Alamos National Laboratory** http://lib-www.lanl.gov. Operated by the University for NNSA. Has a good innovative Research Library developing, for example, a Library Without Walls project. In February 2005, an external review said the Library was 'the best science research digital library in the world'.

4724 Nuclear Energy Agency
www.nea.fr/welcome.html
Specialized agency within the ORGANISATION FOR ECONOMIC CO-OPERATION AND DEVELOPMENT. Its main work areas – for each of which is offered a good range of resources – are: Legal affairs; Nuclear development; Nuclear energy and civil society; Nuclear safety and regulation; Nuclear science; Radiation protection; Radioactive waste management; Sustainable development.

The Agency also offers a range of nuclear data services.

4725 Office of Nuclear Energy, Science & Technology [USA]
www.ne.doe.gov
'We strongly encourage public involvement in our programs and seek to increase public knowledge about nuclear energy and related topics. On our site, you will find a wealth of information about our program's role in nuclear power research and development, space power systems, isotope production and distribution, facilities management, and science education. We have also provided numerous links to other sites on the Internet that we believe will be of interest to you.'

4726 United Kingdom Atomic Energy Authority
www.ukaea.org.uk
Responsible 'for managing the decommissioning of the nuclear reactors and other radioactive facilities used for the UK's nuclear research and development programme in a safe and environmentally sensitive manner. Our objective is to essentially restore the sites for conventional use'. Also 'for the UK's input to the European fusion research programme and for maximising the income from the land and buildings at our sites'.

4727 US Nuclear Regulatory Commission
www.nrc.gov
'NRC's primary mission is to protect the public health and safety, and the environment from the effects of radiation from nuclear reactors, materials, and waste facilities. We also regulate these nuclear materials and facilities to promote the common defense and security.' Among a range of resources germane to this remit, there is a particularly useful Glossary.

Research centres & institutes

Brookhaven National Laboratory
See entry no. 782

Associations & societies

4728 American Nuclear Society
www.ans.org
Not-for-profit, international, scientific and educational organization, established 1954. Members comprise some 10,500 engineers, scientists, administrators, and educators representing 1600 plus corporations, educational institutions, and government agencies.

Wide range of resources including for the public, teachers, students, and media. Important Standards activities. Links.

4729 European Nuclear Society [EUR]
www.euronuclear.org
Sophisticated resource intensive site from organization whose aims are 'to promote and to contribute to the advancement of science and engineering in the field of the peaceful uses of nuclear energy by all suitable means ... ENS was founded in 1975 and is the federation of 26 nuclear societies from 25 countries — stretching from the Atlantic to the Urals and on across Russia to the Pacific'.

- **NucNet** www.worldnuclear.org [FEE-BASED]. Non-profit organization founded 1990 by ENS which bills itself as The World's Nuclear News Agency. Available in eight languages including English, its database provides news on nuclear matters, including business and engineering material.

4730 **Federation of American Scientists**
www.fas.org/main/home.jsp
'The Federation of American Scientists is a nonprofit, tax-exempt, 501c3 organization founded in 1945 as the Federation of Atomic Scientists. Our founders were members of the Manhattan Project, creators of the atom bomb and deeply concerned about the implications of its use for the future of humankind. FAS is the oldest organization dedicated to ending the worldwide arms race and avoiding the use of nuclear weapons for any purpose.'

Very useful and wide range of briefing resources: especially about strategic security matters; but also concerning information technologies, and energy and the environment.

- **Bulletin of the Atomic Scientists** Bimonthly. www.thebulletin.org. Produced by organization whose mission is 'to educate citizens about global security issues, especially the continuing dangers posed by nuclear and other weapons of mass destruction, and the appropriate roles of nuclear technology.'

4731 **Nuclear Energy Institute** [USA]
www.nei.org
Excellent website from organization whose mission reads: 'The Nuclear Energy Institute is the policy organization of the nuclear energy and technologies industry and participates in both the national and global policy-making process. NEI's objective is to ensure the formation of policies that promote the beneficial uses of nuclear energy and technologies in the United States and around the world.'

4732 **World Nuclear Association**
www.world-nuclear.org
'Global industrial organisation that seeks to promote the peaceful worldwide use of nuclear power as a sustainable energy resource for the coming centuries. Specifically, the WNA is concerned with nuclear power generation and all aspects of the nuclear fuel cycle, including mining, conversion, enrichment, fuel fabrication, plant manufacture, transport, and the safe disposition of spent fuel.'

Extensive site includes sections entitled: Nuclear energy made simple; Information and issue briefs; Articles and opinion; Policy documents and treaties. Also, a sizeable Nuclear Portal with annotated links categorized under 34 headings.

A very useful resource.

- **World Nuclear Transport Institute** www.wnti.co.uk. Very useful set of facts sheets, reports of studies, information papers, FAQs, etc.

Libraries, archives, museums

4733 **National Museum of Nuclear Science and History** [USA]
www.atomicmuseum.com
New name for the *National Atomic Museum* – 'the nation's only Congressionally chartered museum of nuclear science and history. The museum was established in 1969 as an intriguing place to learn the story of the Atomic Age, from early research of nuclear development through today's peaceful uses of nuclear technology.'

Portal & task environments

4734 **NuclearMarket.com**
www.nuclearmarket.com
Products, jobs, links, etc. within the nuclear industry.

4735 **One Nuclear Place**
NAC International.
www.1nuclearplace.com
'1NuclearPlace provides you with breaking and daily news, a place to find answers to your nuclear questions, and a single location to obtain links to the world's nuclear firms, a place to interact with industry specialists, market your products, and a way to stay connected to the nuclear community.'

Discovering print & electronic resources

Waste Management Research Abstracts
International Atomic Energy Agency See entry no. 5586

4736 **WWW Virtual Library: Nuclear Engineering**
University of California, Berkeley
www.nuc.berkeley.edu/main/vir_library.html
Maintained within the university's Department of Nuclear Engineering. Compact well structured list.

Digital data, image & text collections

4737 **Alsos Digital Library for Nuclear Issues**
Washington and Lee University and National Science Digital Library
http://alsos.wlu.edu
Aims to provide a broad, balanced range of annotated references for the study of nuclear issues, including books, articles, films, CD-ROMs, and websites.

Handbooks & manuals

Handbook of nuclear chemistry
A. Vértes, S. Nagy and Z. Klencsár, ed. See entry no. 1887

Hazardous and radioactive waste treatment technologies handbook
C.H. Oh, ed. See entry no. 5631

Keeping up-to-date

4738 **Nuclear Engineering International**
Wilmington Publishing.
www.neimagazine.com
'For almost half a century, NEI has been the industry's leading independent provider of news, features and company data.'

Oil, Natural Gas & Coal

coal • coal mining • drilling • fossil fuels • gas technology • natural gas • offshore engineering • offshore oil • oilfields • petroleum • pipelines

Introductions to the subject

4739 **The golden century of oil 1950–2050: the depletion of a resource**
C.J. Campbell Kluwer Academic, 1991, 388pp. £110.00. ISBN 0792314425.
3 parts: 1. World assessment; 2. Regional assessment; 3. Production by country and giant oil fields. 'Units of measurement and conversion factors' precedes.
Series: Geojournal Library, V. 19.

4740 **Out of gas: the end of the age of oil**
D. Goodstein W W Norton, 2005. Originally published 2004, $13.95. ISBN 0393326470.
'Our rate of oil discovery has reached its peak and will never be exceeded; rather, it is certain to decline – perhaps rapidly – forever forward. Meanwhile, over the past century, we have developed lifestyles firmly rooted in the promise of an endless, cheap supply ...'
'A book that is more powerful for being brief ... [Goodstein] is no muddled idealist. And his argument is based on the immutable laws of physics.' (*New York Times Book Review*)

4741 **Statistics for petroleum engineers and geoscientists**
J.L. Jensen [et al.] 2nd edn, Elsevier, 2000, 338pp. $144.95. ISBN 0444505520.
Detailed treatment and mathematically demanding; but good introduction to the field.
'The introductory chapter ... is one of the best-written introductory/motivational chapters I have seen ... The book is enjoyable to read and served as an excellent primer. It contains an extensive bibliography of available literature on geostatistics ... I heartily recommend this book to fellow geoscientists [on the 1st edn].' (*The Leading Edge*)

Dictionaries, thesauri, classifications

4742 **Dictionnaire des sciences et techniques du pétrole: anglais–français, français–anglais (Comprehensive dictionary of petroleum science and technology)**
G. Brace and M. Moureau Editions TECHNIP, 1993, 1040pp. €163.00. ISBN 2710806487.
Nearly 70,000 terms, some with explanations (e.g. 'chemical': 1 1/3 columns). Includes abbreviations, technical names and colloquialisms. In between the two sequences, a list of symbols and conversion tables on tinted paper.

4743 **Elsevier's oil and gas field dictionary**
L.Y. Chaballe [et al.] Elsevier, 1980, 684pp. £158.00. ISBN 0444418334.
About 5000 terms in oil and gas drilling. Useful for all engaged in the industry or in associated research. It comprises English/American terms, their synonyms and variants in American spelling, followed by equivalents in French, Spanish, Italian, Dutch and German. Supplementary section of Arabic terms.

4744 **Glossary of coal preparation terms: BS 3552** [UK]
British Standards Institution 1994, 29pp. £80.00. ISBN 0580130878.
About 400 terms defined in 11 sections (e.g. 4. sizing; 5. cleaning; 11. automatic control). Appended: 'Bibliography of international standards defining terms for automatic control'.

Illustrated glossary of petroleum geochemistry
J.A. Miles See entry no. 906

4745 **Lexique des pipelines à terre et en mer (Glossary of onshore and offshore pipelines)**
Editions TECHNIP, 1979, 320pp. €97.00. ISBN 2710803569.
Classified into 57 categories. Includes abbreviations. List of sources.

4746 **The Oilfield Glossary**
Schlumberger Ltd.
www.glossary.oilfield.slb.com/Default.cfm
Launched in 1998 and now contains more than 3800 entries.

Official & quasi-official bodies

4747 **Coal Authority** [UK]
www.coal.gov.uk
Aims 'to facilitate the proper exploitation of the Nation's coal resources, whilst providing information and addressing liabilities for which the Authority is responsible, in a professional, efficient and open manner'. Information Resources section provides a very useful overview of the field.

Minerals Management Service
See entry no. 4671

Office of Surface Mining
See entry no. 4672

Research centres & institutes

4748 **Gas Technology Institute** [USA]
www.gastechnology.org
'GTI is the leading research, development and training organization serving the natural gas industry.' Resources include good series of reports, publications and software.

4749 **IEA Clean Coal Centre**
www.iea-coal.org.uk
'The world's foremost provider of information on efficient coal supply and use,' Access to a number of free and priced databases, especially on cleaner coal technologies: each well described and presented.

- **Major coalfields of the world S. Walker** 2nd edn, IEA Coal Research, 2000, 131pp. £100.00. ISBN 929029342X. www.iea-coal.co.uk/site/pdf/Newsletter32.pdf [DESCRIPTION]. One of a considerable number of reference reports produced by the Centre.

4750 **Institut Français du Pétrole**
www.ifp.fr/IFP/en/aa.htm
'Independent industrial research and development, training, and information center active in the oil, natural gas and automobile industries; its activities cover the entire oil and

gas chain: exploration, production, refining, petrochemicals, engines, and the utilization of petroleum products.'

Good set of resources with helpful English language site. Its publishing arm Editions TECHNIP has on its list original works in English as well as French texts and translations.

Associations & societies

American Association of Petroleum Geologists
See entry no. 951

4751 **American Gas Association**
www.aga.org
'Represents 192 local energy utility companies that deliver natural gas to more than 53 million homes, businesses and industries throughout the United States. AGA member companies account for roughly 83 percent of all natural gas delivered by the nation's local natural gas distribution companies.'

Good collection of well presented data and information – albeit significant proportions only directly accessible to AGA members.

4752 **American Petroleum Institute**
www.api.org
Major Institute whose website is clearly organized into three areas: Energy Consumer Site Information about oil and natural gas for the general public; Energy Professional Site Information for oil and natural gas professionals and policy makers; Media Center The latest news, reports, testimony, and journalists' resources.

API is notable for the extent and quality of its Industry Statistics; but its site provides access to, or at least details of, a very wide range of well presented publications, standards, and other resources.

A model site of its kind, and a good starting point for newcomers.

- **EnCompass** Elsevier Engineering Information. www.ei.org/eicorp/encompass.html [DESCRIPTION]. Formerly owned by API and 'designed to meet the demanding information requirements for the downstream petroleum, petrochemical, natural gas, energy and allied industries'. Access to worldwide scholarly literature, patents, business and economic news.

Canadian Institute of Mining, Metallurgy and Petroleum
See entry no. 4674

4753 **Coal Association of Canada**
www.coal.ca
Represents companies engaged in the exploration, development, use and transportation of coal. Its members include major coal producers and coal-using utilities, the railroads and ports that ship coal, and industry suppliers of goods and services. Much good and helpful information, and not just about Canada – including from a Coalblog.

4754 **International Association of Drilling Contractors**
www.iadc.org
Mission is to 'promote commitment to safety, preservation of the environment and advances in drilling technology ... Membership is open to any company involved in oil and gas exploration and production, well servicing, oil field manufacturing and other rig site services.' Well organized and presented website with very good range of data and statistics.

4755 **National Ocean Industries Association** [USA]
www.noia.org
'The only national trade association representing all facets of the domestic offshore petroleum and related industries.'

Society of Exploration Geophysicists
See entry no. 4686

4756 **Society of Petroleum Engineers** [USA]
www.spe.org
Site provides an extensive set of resources about oil and gas, and the technologies used to process them. There are useful guides to data and information – such as that to industry statistics. Well worth browsing around.

4757 **Society of Petrophysicists and Well Log Analysts**
www.spwla.org
'Nonprofit corporation dedicated to the advancement of the science of petrophysics and formation evaluation, through well logging and other formation evaluation techniques and to the application of these techniques to the exploitation of gas, oil and other minerals.'

- **Glossary of terms and expressions used in well logging** 1985, 116pp. $10.00. Nomenclature for well logging services used by service organizations. About 500 terms. List of sources.

Portal & task environments

4758 **Alexander's Gas and Oil Connections**
Alexander Wöstmann.
www.gasandoil.com
'Provides an extensive gathering of news on the global gas-, oil- and energy-developments open for all interested as well as several Special Information Services for subscribers.'

Geochemistry of Igneous Rocks
See entry no. 910

4759 **IHS Energy Group**
www.ihsenergy.com
A 'leading global provider of critical technical information, decision-support tools and related services for the energy industry. Our global experts placed strategically around the world, develop and deliver critical oil and gas industry data on exploration, development, production and transportation activities to major global energy producers and national and independent oil companies.'

4760 **Offshore Engineering Information Service: OEIS**
Heriot-Watt University
www.eevl.ac.uk/offshore
Information about publications and meetings dealing with: oil and gas exploration and production; offshore health, safety and environmental protection; resources of the seabed and renewable energy; and marine technology. Made available via EEVL and based in the University's Library.

4761 **Oil.com: Oil – Gas – Offshore**
http://oilsite.com
Highly informative wide-ranging subset of the WorldNews Network: excellent use of images.

4762 Rigzone: Your gateway to the oil and gas industry
www.rigzone.com [REGISTRATION]
Access to Online Oil and Gas Directory plus news, data, and information – especially about the offshore industry.

4763 WorldOil.com: The oilfield information source
WorldOil.com Inc.
www.worldoil.com
'The industry's preferred information source for news, technical and operating information, research and statistics, energy events, energy links, and the Composite Catalog Online. It is also the online presence of *World Oil* magazine, the magazine that delivers superior editorial content to more than 35,500 industry decision-makers around the globe.

The magazine is a flagship publication of the Gulf Publishing Company (www.gulfpub.com), the international publishing and events business dedicated to the energy sector. Founded in 1916, Gulf Publishing produces and distributes leading trade journals, industry research, databases, software, publications, conferences and events designed for the needs of the energy industry.'

Discovering print & electronic resources

4764 Petroleum Abstracts
University of Tulsa
www.pa.utulsa.edu [FEE-BASED]
'Provides bibliographic petroleum information products and services for the global petroleum exploration and production industry. These products cover the petroleum topic areas of geosciences, drilling, reservoir and production engineering, shipping and storage and other technologies relevant to the upstream petroleum industry.'

Two good search aids are provided: *Exploration and Production (E&P) Thesaurus* (16th edn, 2003); and *Geographic Thesaurus* (13th edn, 2002).

A very useful weekly bulletin based on the database contains from 400 to 600 items per issue.

4765 RDN Virtual Training Suite: Offshore Engineer [UK]
A. Myers; Heriot-Watt University and Resource Discovery Network
www.vts.rdn.ac.uk/tutorial/petroleum
Short tutorial in the RDN series.

4766 The Reference Database OIL
Norwegian Petroleum Directorate and Petroleum Safety Authority Norway
www.ptil.no/oil
60,000 references are taken from a wide variety of publications: research reports, government publications, journal articles, books, conference papers, standards and specifications, newspapers, articles, pre-prints and pamphlets. Freely searchable. Some material in Norwegian, but much in English.

Digital data, image & text collections

4767 Argus Online
Argus Media.
www.argusonline.com
Provider of price assessments, business intelligence and market data on the global oil, gas, electricity, coal, emissions and transportation industries. Large number of Newsletters and Market Reports: see 'Library'.

4768 Coal Information
International Energy Agency
http://new.sourceoecd.org/database/coal [FEE-BASED]
Details of the range of statistical series produced by the Agency.
Print versions are also available.

4769 OilTracers® Online Oil Library
OilTracers LLC.
https://oiltracers.com/library [REGISTRATION]
Online searchable database of 33,500 oils and other geological samples from 124 countries. Searching free, after registration.

Directories & encyclopedias

4770 Energy Sourcebook
CMP Information.
www.cmpdata.co.uk/energy [DESCRIPTION]
'Comprehensive coverage of the Oil and Gas Industry with a focus on the growing Renewables industry and reflects the world-wide supply chain of the energy sector covering Oil, Gas, Biomass, Hydro, Solar and Photovoltaics and Wave and Tidal.' Formerly *Oil and Gas Directory* and *Offshore Oil and Gas Directory*.
Also available in print: see website.

4771 International petroleum encyclopedia
PennWell, 2004, Annual, 332pp. Also available CD-ROM, $195.00. ISBN 1593700288.
www.pennwell.com
Worldwide data and statistics, country reports, industry trends on the oil and gas industry.
The publisher has an extensive list of publications in this and related field: see website for details.

The millennium atlas: petroleum geology of the central and northern North Sea
D. Evans [et al.]; Geological Society of London See entry no. 988

4772 Twentieth century petroleum statistics
59th edn, DeGolyer and MacNaughton, 2003. ISSN 10484825.
www.demac.com/index.htm [DESCRIPTION]
Collection of data 'culled from information published by the American Petroleum Institute, Oil & Gas Journal, WorldOil.com, the Energy Information Administration, and other government agencies. More than 100 charts and graphs accompany the tables to provide a visual sense of trends in the industry'.

First published in 1945 by the US Navy Department's Office of Naval Petroleum and Oil Shale Reserves.
Available on registration for nominal charge.

Handbooks & manuals

Chemistry of petrochemical processes
S. Matar and L.F. Hatch See entry no. 5127

4773 **Coal geology**
L. Thomas Wiley, 2002, 396pp. $200.00. ISBN 0471485314.
The 'first reference book to cover all aspects of coal geology in one volume'.

Explosion protection: electrical apparatus and systems for chemical plants, oil and gas industry, coal mining
H. Groh See entry no. 4709

Handbook of petrochemicals production processes
R.A. Meyers See entry no. 5139

4774 **Modern petroleum technology**
Wiley, 2000. 2 v, $880.00. ISBN 0471984116.
Produced by the UK Institute of Petroleum (now incorporated into the ENERGY INSTITUTE). Edited collection of contributions covering all the key areas, the first volume concerned with 'Upstream' processes; the second with 'Downstream'.
'It provides a comprehensive, authoritative and up-to-date review of technology across the whole of the oil and gas industry. This publication remains the essential information source for libraries and managers.' (*Petroleum Review*)

Petroleum geoscience
J. Gluyas and R.E. Swarbrick See entry no. 1109

4775 **United Kingdom oil and gas fields: commemorative millennium volume**
J.G. Gluyas and H.M. Hichens, eds; Geological Society of London
2003, 1006pp. £175.00. ISBN 1862390894.
The most comprehensive reference work on the UK's oil and gas fields available. 'The book is divided into nine parts covering the major petroleum provinces both offshore and onshore United Kingdom, from the Gas Basin in the southern North Sea to the Viking Graben in the northern North Sea, from the Atlantic Frontier to the Irish Sea and from the Wessex Basin to the East Midlands. Each part contains a reference map showing field locations. The introductory chapters reveal the stories behind the major plays and discoveries therein, and their tectonic and stratigraphic framework.'
Series: Geological Society Memoirs, No. 20.

Keeping up-to-date

4776 **Coal Trade**
www.coaltrade.com
WORLDNEWS NETWORK production.

4777 **Oil & Gas Journal**
PennWell, Weekly. Print subscription. Range of other subscription options available, $49.00. ISSN 00301388.
http://ogj.pennnet.com/home.cfm
'The world's most widely read and respected petroleum industry publication.'

4778 **Oil and Energy Trends**
Blackwell, 1976–, Monthly. £1540.00. ISSN 09501045.
www.oilandenergytrends.com [DESCRIPTION]
'The world's most comprehensive monthly source of energy information. Each issue gives up-to-date information for all major energy statistics, presented in a consistent format from a wide and constantly reviewed range of sources.'

4779 **Petroleum Economist**
Euromoney Institutional Investor, Monthly. £465.00. ISSN 0306395X.
www.petroleum-economist.com
Analyzes oil, gas and power developments worldwide.
'Petroleum Economist for Schools is working in partnership with governments, international and national oil companies, industry associations and the world's top 100 universities. We are aiming to provide a range of educational materials including wall maps, publications, and interactive CD-ROMs, for the use of teachers and their students, on a country-by-country basis.'

- **World Energy Atlas** Euromoney Institutional Investor, 2004. £415.00. ISBN 1861861931. The major: Oil and gas fields and pipelines; Gas processing and storage facilities; Deepwater fields; Oil refineries by capacity; Liquid natural gas facilities, including those under construction, planned or speculative; Tanker terminals.

Renewable & Alternative Energy

alternative energy • bioenergy • biomass energy • energy efficiency • fuel cells • geothermal energy • photovoltaics • renewable resources • solar energy • sustainable energy • wind energy

Introductions to the subject

4780 **The solar economy: renewable energy for a sustainable global future**
H. Scheer Earthscan Publications, 2002, 347pp. $29.95. ISBN 1853838357.
'The global economy and the way of life it has created are based on the exploitation of fossil fuels – coal, oil and, more recently, natural gas – that will be the engine of the collapse of that economy. Without fundamental change, it has no future. The alternative exists: renewable energy from renewable sources – above all solar ... '
'The most powerfully written book on the energy situation. Highly recommended!' (*Choice*)

4781 **Solar energy – the state of the art: ISES position papers**
J Gordon, ed. James & James, 2001, 720pp. £75.00. ISBN 1902916239.
A compilation of papers from leading scientists in the field. Each chapter examines a major sub-discipline covering areas such as solar radiation, water heating, solar collectors and photovoltaics. The book is aimed at students, researchers and practitioners. Theory and applications are studied in detail making this a comprehensive introduction to solar energy. ISES is the INTERNATIONAL SOLAR ENERGY SOCIETY.

4782 **Wind energy explained: theory, design and application**
J.F. Manwell, J.G. McGowan and A.L. Rogers Wiley, 2002, 590pp. $98.00. ISBN 0471499722.
After an introduction and historical context, sections are: Wind characteristics and resources; Aerodynamics of wind turbines; Mechanics and dynamics; Electrical aspects of wind turbines; Wind turbine design; Wind turbine control; Wind turbine siting, system design and integration; Wind

energy system economics; Wind energy systems: environmental aspects and impacts.

'Although there is a good sprinkling of equations, much of the text is accessible to non-mathematically inclined readers ... can be thoroughly recommended as a comprehensive introduction to the field for engineering students.' (*Times Higher Education Supplement*)

Dictionaries, thesauri, classifications

The CIMAC Lexicon
International Council on Combustion Engines See entry no. 5873

Dictionary of water engineering
K.D. Nelson, C. Kerr and R. Legg See entry no. 5541

Official & quasi-official bodies

4783 **International Geothermal Association**
http://iga.igg.cnr.it/index.php
Founded 1988; 2000 members in 65 countries. Non-political, non-profit, non-governmental organization in special consultative status with the Economic and Social Council of the UNITED NATIONS, and partner of the EU's Campaign for Sustainable Energy.

- **Geothermal Energy Association** www.geo-energy.org. 'Trade association composed of US companies who support the expanded use of geothermal energy and are developing geothermal resources worldwide for electrical power generation and direct-heat uses.'
- **Geothermal Resources Council** www.geothermal.org. US-based body which 'makes available the most comprehensive on-line geothermal library anywhere in the world, featuring over 30,000 individual bibliographic citations from books, articles, papers and other publications'.

4784 **Office of Energy Efficiency and Renewable Energy** [USA]
www.eere.energy.gov
One of the ten Program Offices of the US DEPARTMENT OF ENERGY: 'US Department of Energy Secretary Spencer Abraham has challenged the Office of Energy Efficiency and Renewable Energy (EERE) to revolutionize how we approach energy efficiency and renewable energy technologies, while we pursue the recommendations of the President's National Energy Policy. To meet this challenge, we intend to leapfrog the status quo and pursue dramatic environmental benefits. We know that our success in this mission could well be one of the greatest contributions to our nation's energy and national security for generations to come.'

Maintains an Energy Information Portal: 'A gateway to hundreds of Web sites and thousands of online documents on energy efficiency and renewable energy.'

Research centres & institutes

4785 **Carbon Trust** [UK]
www.thecarbontrust.co.uk
Independent company founded by Government to encourage awareness of a low carbon economy and to encourage commercial opportunities for renewable technologies. Information on energy efficiency and carbon management; short introductions to programmes such as the Marine Energy Challenge and field trials of small scale combined heat and power (CHP) plant. Useful set of interlinked PDF documents from Government (publications, briefings, speeches, etc.). Links.

- **Energy Saving Trust** www.est.org.uk. Funded by UK government and private sector to work with households, business and the public sector in the areas of energy efficiency, road transport and renewable energy. Good range of practical advice. Substantial Resources section. Links.

4786 **Centre for Alternative Technology** [UK]
www.cat.org.uk
'Environmental charity aiming to "inspire, inform, and enable" people to live more sustainably. A solutions driven organisation, offering practical solutions to environmental problems, our key areas of work are renewable energy, environmental building, energy efficiency, organic growing and alternative sewage systems. We have been in existence for 25 years.'

4787 **Centre for Analysis and Dissemination of Demonstrated Energy Technologies**
www.caddet.org
International information network on energy efficiency and renewable technologies. Among the web-based resources on offer in this INTERNATIONAL ENERGY AGENCY initiative are a database of technology demonstration projects on topics including renewables, cogeneration, fuel cells, and retrofitting of building services, all with engineering and environmental details. Free PDF brochures and expert reports are available. A linked and related network, GREENTIE, offers a directory of suppliers and services defined as sustainable and in mitigation of greenhouse gas emissions. Extensive links section of the website offers access to 'over 200 other relevant websites of organizations specializing in energy efficiency and renewable energy technologies'.

4788 **Centre for Sustainable Energy** [UK]
www.cse.org.uk
Organization 'entirely funded by project funding, grants and donations. At any one time, we have as many as 50–60 different and separately-funded projects under way, each contributing to the achievement of our mission. Funders and clients include national, regional and local government and associated agencies, energy companies and charitable sources ... Our mission as an independent charity is to advance sustainable energy policy and practice. We seek energy solutions that engage people and communities to meet real needs for both environmentally sound and affordable energy services.'

4789 **National Renewable Energy Laboratory** [USA]
www.nrel.gov
Originally established in 1974 and now 'the principal research laboratory for the DOE OFFICE OF ENERGY EFFICIENCY AND RENEWABLE ENERGY which provides the majority of its funding. Other funding comes from DOE'sOFFICE OF SCIENCE and Office of Electricity Transmission and Distribution.

Well organized set of pages under the rubric Clean Energy BASICS. Considerable detail on NREL's major R&D areas: Advanced vehicles and fuels; Basic sciences; Biomass; Buildings; Electric infrastructure systems; Energy analysis; Geothermal; Hydrogen and fuel cells; Solar; Wind. High-quality GIS-based renewable energy resource data for US and international locations.

- **National Wind Technology Center** www.nrel.gov/wind. One of the NREL Centres. Briefings, reports, news, etc. – including access to a useful Avian Literature Database 'of documents on the effects of wind energy development and towers, power lines and other wires, on birds'.

Associations & societies

4790 **American Solar Energy Society**
www.ases.org
'National organization dedicated to advancing the use of solar energy for the benefit of US citizens and the global environment. ASES promotes the widespread near- and long-term use of solar energy.'

- **Solar Energy Industries Association** www.seia.org. National trade association of solar energy manufacturers, dealers, distributors, contractors, installers, architects, consultants, and marketers.

4791 **American Wind Energy Association**
www.awea.org
Like its European and British equivalents, AWEA promotes wind power in the USA. General learned society material abounds on the website and the organization is an important publisher of conferences and handbooks in its field. Most usefully AWEA provides a resource library of downloadable documents and reports, factsheets, mini-databases and audio visual material.

Electric Drive Transportation Association
See entry no. 4973

4792 **European Biomass Association**
www.ecop.ucl.ac.be/aebiom
AEBIOM is a group of national biomass associations founded in 1990. The basic aim is the promotion of biomass production and application throughout Europe. Not an extensive nor sophisticated site, but useful entrée to Europe-based activity.

- **Bioenergy Information Network** **Oak Ridge National Laboratory** bioenergy.ornl.gov. Gateway to biomass information including about fast growing trees, grasses, and residues for fuels and power. Includes BibBib, a searchable Biomass Feedstock Research and Analyses Bibliography (last updated 2002), and a bioenergy Image Gallery.

European Natural Gas Vehicle Association
See entry no. 4975

4793 **European Wind Energy Association**
www.ewea.org
Established 1982; now 'the most powerful wind energy network and recognised voice of the wind industry – activity promoting the utilisation of wind power in Europe and worldwide'. Site gives access to extensive news and publications resources.

- **British Wind Energy Association** www.bwea.com. UK industry focus. Organizes and publishes proceedings for annual conferences on wind energy and wind energy conversion. With the equivalent US and European conference proceedings, these give very good reviews of technological advances in the field.

4794 **Forum for the Future** [UK]
www.forumforthefuture.org.uk
'Recognised as the UK's leading sustainable development charity. Our object as a charity is to educate different groups in sustainable development, in order to accelerate the building of a sustainable way of life, taking a positive solutions-oriented approach.

'We were founded in 1996 by environmentalists Jonathon Porritt, Sara Parkin and Paul Ekins out of a conviction that many of the solutions needed to defuse the environmental crisis and build a more sustainable society are already to hand. Our magazine *Green Futures* is a leading source of debate on those solutions. Our work with more than 150 companies, local authorities, regional bodies and universities to build their capacity to overcome the many barriers to more sustainable practice. We aim for nothing less than transformation-irreversible change.'

4795 **International Solar Energy Society**
www.ises.org
A global, non-governmental organization with a membership of 30,000 in over one hundred countries. ISES advises governments and organizations on policy and implementation and disseminates information concerning solar energy.

- **American Solar Energy Society** www.ases.org. Promotes the widespread near- and long-term use of solar energy. Publishes *Solar Today*, 'an award-winning bimonthly magazine that covers all renewable energy technologies'. Also a free online newsletter *Sunbeam*.
- **Solar Energy Society** www.thesolarline.com. UK-based society which maintains SOLEIL: 'aims to be a sophisticated and comprehensive on-line resource guide for UK solar and renewable energy information on the World Wide Web'.
- **World Wide Information System for Renewable Energy: WIRE** http://wire0.ises.org/wire/wire.nsf. Free portal which allows users to source web-based solar energy information. Users can also publish and share information about solar energy and locate books and articles on the subject. Service provided by ISES.

Portal & task environments

Advanced Buildings: Technologies & Practices
See entry no. 5330

4796 **Clear Zones**
Transport and Travel Research.
www.clearzones.org.uk
'a city where you can live without breathing-in polluted air; a city where you can travel with ease to work, to the shops, to a film, restaurant or bar; where your shopping is automatically delivered to your home, the train or bus station or your car; where zero-emission vehicles transport people from one location to another; and cyclists, pedestrians, elderly and disabled people can all move around freely and without fear.'

4797 **Fuel Cell Today**
Johnson Matthey plc.
www.fuelcelltoday.com/index
'Global internet portal which aims to accelerate the commercialisation of fuel cells ... Existing for the global fuel cell community, Fuel Cell Today is without bias towards any single organisation, fuel cell technology or application. It serves everyone who is or wants to be part of this dynamic new industry, from research scientists and marketers to journalists and end users.'

4798 **Fuel Cells UK**
Great Britain. Department of Trade and Industry
www.fuelcellsuk.org
An umbrella organization, funded by the DTI and guided by a

steering group. Provides free to access industry reports and news, and details the capabilities of companies within the fuel cell industry. Also provides links to other organizations and sector events.

Interactive European Network for Industrial Crops and their Applications: IENICA
European Commission. Directorate for Research See entry no. 3095

Discovering print & electronic resources

4799 **Alternative energy: facts, statistics, and issues**
P. Berinstein Oryx Press, 2001, 208pp. $77.95. ISBN 1573562483.
Overview of new techniques and advancements in the efficiency of various types of alternative energy sources such as: Biomass energy; Fusion power; Geothermal energy; Hybrid systems; Hydroelectric power; Hydrogen fuel cells; Photo-voltaic cells; Solar energy; Wind.
'Well organized and well written, with abundant tables and figures, a glossary, and a modest bibliography, this accessible work should appeal to general audiences as well as provide information to specialists. It is, moreover, mercifully free of the polemic and finger-pointing that too often characterizes books on this subject.' (*American Reference Books Annual*)

- **Statistical handbook on technology** **P. Berinstein** Oryx Press, 1999, 304pp. $77.95. ISBN 1573562084. An Oryx Statistical Handbook, designed to identify print and electronic public and private statistics within the various areas of technology application – including agriculture, medicine, and biotechnology.

Digital data, image & text collections

PHYLLIS: the composition of biomass and waste
Energy Research Centre of the Netherlands See entry no. 3035

Directories & encyclopedias

4800 **Dictionary of renewable resources**
H. Zoebelein, ed. Wiley-VCH, 2001, 408pp. £105.00. ISBN 3527301143.
The entries in this dictionary provide information on the natural sources of products, isolation techniques, the chemical products, derivatives, areas of application, economic significance and issues relating to further development of the products. 'In addition to the 'classical' use as raw materials of the chemical industry, the fields of energy/fuels, practical applications, e.g. as construction and insulation materials, the most important pharmaceutical agents, raw substances of cosmetics and aromas are treated. Not only modern methods are taken into account but also older, almost forgotten fields that stimulate new considerations.'
'especially useful to those readers working at the more basic chemical and biochemical levels of renewable resources.' (*American Reference Books Annual*)

Energy Sourcebook
See entry no. 4770

4801 **The Source for Renewable Energy**
Momentum Technologies LLC.
http://energy.sourceguides.com
Comprehensive online buyer's guide and business directory to more than 8000 renewable energy businesses and organizations worldwide.

Handbooks & manuals

4802 **Alternate energy: assessment and implementation reference book**
J.J. Winebrake Fairmont Publishing, 2004, 243pp. $125.00. ISBN 0881734365.
www.fairmontpress.com [DESCRIPTION]
Contains abridged technology 'road maps', with original contributions and commentary from the sustainable energy field. Uses these road maps to identify policy mechanisms needed to overcome technical and market barriers for sustainable energy technologies.
'written at an accessible level for researchers, industry officials, policy makers and all stakeholders. This book is recommended for large academic, government and research libraries that deal with alternative energy issues.' (*E-STREAMS*)

4803 **Fuel cell technology handbook**
G. Hoogers, ed. CRC Press, 2002. $99.95. ISBN 0849308771.
An up-to-date and comprehensive treatment. Arranged in two parts. Part 1 covers the technology, its history, thermodynamics and electrochemical kinetics, fuel cell components, fuel cell systems, catalysts, and the methanol fuel cell. Part 2 deals with applications – stationary power generation, portable systems, automotive applications, competing technologies for transportation, fuel cell fuel cycles, and a technology outlook.
'well-written and informative.highly recommended.' (*Choice*)

Green building handbook: a guide to building products and their impact on the environment
T. Wooley [et al.] See entry no. 5350

4804 **Handbook of fuel cells: fundamentals, technology, applications**
W. Vielstich, A. Lamm and H.A. Gasteiger, eds Wiley, 2003. 4 v., $1565.00. ISBN 0471499269.
170 chapters. V. 1. Fundamentals and survey of systems. V. 2. Electrocatalysis. V. 3/4. Fuel cell technology and applications. Detailed subject indexes.
'an awesome publication ... an excellent up-to-date source ... newcomers to fuel-cell technology will need look no further.' (*Chemistry & Industry*)

4805 **Handbook of photovoltaic science and engineering**
A. Luque and S. Hegedus, eds Wiley, 2003, 1138pp. $335.00. ISBN 0471491969.
'Photovoltaics is the technology that generates direct current (DC) electrical power measured in Watts (W) or KiloWatts (kW) from semiconductors when they are illuminated by photons ... When the light stops, the electricity stops. Solar cells never need recharging like a battery. Some have been in continuous operation on earth or in space for 30 years.'

24 chapters provide detailed coverage of the underlying technologies of the various types of cells, plus assessments of current usage and future prospects. Bibliography. Index.

Lightweight electric/hybrid vehicle design
R. Hodkinson and J. Fenton See entry no. 4999

4806 **Principles of solar engineering**
D.Y. Goswami [et al.], eds 2nd edn, Taylor & Francis, 2000, 666pp. £70.00. ISBN 1560327146.
A handbook which focuses on solar energy applications such as heating, cooling and daylighting and contains useful chapters on photovoltaics and biomass conversion. Engineering students are provided with information on the fundamental scientific principles behind radiation and energy conversion.

4807 **Wind energy handbook**
T. Burton [et al.] Wiley, 2001, 642pp. $150.00. ISBN 04711489972.
A comprehensive handbook that focuses on the use of wind energy for electricity generation. This text presents the theory and calculations required for wind turbine design and examines the practical and technical considerations behind the installation of a wind farm.

Keeping up-to-date

4808 **Renewable Energy World**
www.earthscan.co.uk [DESCRIPTION]
'Formed by the coming-together of two of the foremost publishers in environment science, technology and sustainable development, James & James/Earthscan is now becoming recognized as the most important specialist source of must-have information for all those around the world with a keen interest in a sustainable future.

'*Renewable Energy World* is an award winning, bimonthly, professional title with global coverage and circulation. The magazine accentuates the achievements and potential of all forms of renewable energy sources and the technologies being developed to harness them. In each issue, one or more of these gets the focus.'

The magazine is free of charge to qualifying professionals.

Engineering

The *Oxford Dictionary of English* defines an engineer as 'a person who designs, builds or maintains engines, machines, or public works'. An engine is 'a machine with moving parts that converts power into motion'; a machine is 'an apparatus using or applying mechanical power and having several parts, each with a definite function and together performing a particular task'; public works is 'the work of building such things as roads, schools, and hospitals, carried out by the state for the community'.

Explicit in those definitions are two of the four long-standing well established engineering disciplines – Civil Engineering and Mechanical Engineering; implicit is the third – Electrical & Electronic Engineering. Subject Fields for each of those three follow: their members and the resources those members produce and use are still of great importance.

But also now of great significance are engineering disciplines which focus on particular functions, especially 'motion' – or transport: Aeronautical & Aerospace Engineering; Automobile & Agricultural Engineering; Marine Engineering & Naval Architecture (the building of ships) – railway engineering here being given (limited) treatment within Mechanical Engineering. A more 'task'-based approach has in addition proved fruitful in recent decades, coalescing perhaps most notably in Manufacturing (or industrial) Engineering; also in Design – which seemed worth briefly highlighting as a separate Field. Similarly, we decided that resources relevant to Construction & Building worked best if given their own space.

Note that there is some treatment of artificial intelligence within Manufacturing Engineering; of ergonomics and human-computer interaction within Design; and of architecture within Construction & Building, but no doubt we will return to all these in later TNW volumes.

In addition to those foci there is currently great excitement within the disciplines – or technologies – concerned with 'stuff'. Chemical Engineering is the fourth of the long-standing well established engineering disciplines. Despite its rather negative public profile (true to some degree of all of engineering), it is an extremely important component of national and international economies, as increasingly is the more specialized Biotechnology. Mentioning 'biotechnology' here alongside 'chemical engineering' denotes our focus, which is on the development and production of 'biochemicals' – rather than of 'biomaterials' – for use in agriculture and especially medicine: thus much synergy with the subject fields Human Genetics and Pharmacology & Pharmacy.

Work on 'stuff' at a more granular level – the focus of Materials Science & Engineering – is generating equal excitement: as, even more so, is that at a micro-granular level: Microengineering & Nanotechnology. Descriptions of resources on biomaterials appear in those two subject fields; but many also have been posted in the field Medical Technology.

Introductions to the subject

4809 Engineers and their profession
J.D. Kemper and B.R. Sanders 5th edn, Oxford University Press, 2001, 346pp. $39.95. ISBN 0195120574.
Highly rewarding introduction based on the US environment. Very useful chapter *The branches of engineering* with quite detailed descriptions, as well as much other good background information. An ideal place to start for someone relatively unfamiliar with engineering's theories, practices, problems and prospects.

4810 Introduction to engineering ethics
R. Schinzinger and M.W. Martin McGraw-Hill, 1999, 272pp. $42.50. ISBN 0072339594.
In line with the guidelines of the US Accreditation Board for Engineering and Technology, provides an overview suitable as background within engineering courses. Six chapters: Professionalism; Moral reasoning and ethical theories; Engineering as social experimentation; Commitment to safety; Workplace responsibilities and rights; Global issues.

Dictionaries, thesauri, classifications

4811 Dictionary of engineering
2nd edn, McGraw-Hill, 2003, 642pp. $19.95. ISBN 0071410503.
Derived from the McGraw-Hill Dictionary of scientific and technical terms.

4812 The dictionary of engineering acronyms and abbreviations
U. Erb and H. Keller 2nd edn, Neal-Schuman, 1994, 878pp. $149.95. ISBN 1555701299.
65,000 terms: more than twice the first edition.

4813 Elsevier's dictionary of engineering
M. Bignami Elsevier, 2004, 1300pp. £196.50. ISBN 0444514678.
In English/American, German, French, Italian, Spanish and Portuguese/Brazilian. Contains terms for 14 main subject areas, described as: Architectural engineering and buildings; Civil engineering; Engineering; Geology; Geotechnical engineering; Hydraulics; Hydrogeology; Hydrology; Mechanical Engineering; Mechanics; Mining Engineering; Petroleum engineering; Science and technics; Surveying.

Laws, standards, codes

Deutsches Institut für Normung
See entry no. 32

Official & quasi-official bodies

4814 Accreditation Board for Engineering and Technology [USA]
www.abet.org
'In the United States, accreditation is used to assure quality in educational institutions and programs. Accreditation is a

voluntary, non-governmental process of peer review. It requires an educational institution or program to meet certain, defined standards or criteria. Accreditation is sometimes confused with certification. In general, institutions and programs are accredited, and individuals are certified.'

Four disciplinary areas are covered by ABET; Engineering; Engineering technology; Computing (including Information systems); Applied science (Health physics; Industrial hygiene; Industrial management; Safety; Surveying).

4815 Engineering and Physical Sciences Research Council [UK]
www.epsrc.ac.uk
The UK Government's leading funding agency for research and training in engineering and the physical sciences; one of currently seven such Research Councils. Well laid out inviting site with, for instance: Useful overview of International activity; Access to details of all current EPSRC funded research; Full list of publications including downloadable PDFs of issues of their magazines *Connect* and *Newsline*; Programme of Public Engagement with a website section Interesting links for young people and the public.

4816 Engineering Council UK
www.engc.org.uk
Mission is 'to set and maintain realistic and internationally relevant standards of professional competence and ethics for engineers, technologists and technicians, and to license competent institutions to promote and uphold the standards. Under its Royal Charter, the ECUK regulates the engineering profession in the UK and formally represents the interests of UK engineers abroad. It is a Designated Authority under the current General Systems Directives' (regulating professional bodies).

Provides good overview of the UK professional engineering framework.

4817 NSF: Directorate for Engineering [USA]
National Science Foundation
www.nsf.gov/funding/research_edu_community.jsp
National Science Foundation body whose research and related activities are principally organized into six subject areas: Bioengineering and environmental systems; Civil and mechanical systems; Chemical and transport systems; Design, manufacture, and industrial innovation; Electrical and communications systems; Engineering education and centers.

Cutting across these currently are six Thrust areas: Nanotechnology engineering and science; Information technology research; Cyberinfrastructure; Human and social dynamics; Sensors and sensor networks; Network for earthquake simulation.

United Kingdom Accreditation Service
See entry no. 291

US Fire Administration
See entry no. 4245

4818 World Federation of Engineering Organisations
www.unesco.org/wfeo
Body within the United Nations Educational, Scientific and Cultural Organization 'that brings together National Engineering Organisations from over 90 nations and represents some 8 million engineers from around the world. WFEO is the world wide leader of the engineering profession and co-operates with national and other international professional institutions in developing and applying engineering to the benefit of humanity.'

Research centres & institutes

4819 Online Ethics Center for Engineering and Science [USA]
Case Western Reserve University
http://onlineethics.org
Mission is 'to provide engineers, scientists, and science and engineering students with resources for understanding and addressing ethically significant problems that arise in their work, and to serve those who are promoting learning and advancing the understanding of responsible research and practice in science and engineering.'

Excellent range of resources; well set out.

- **Codes of Ethics Online** **Illinois Institute of Technology.** http://ethics.iit.edu/codes. Codes of ethics of professional societies, corporations, government, and academic institutions. Maintained by the Institute's Center for the Study of Ethics in the Professions.

Associations & societies

4820 American Association of Engineering Societies
www.aaes.org
'Multidisciplinary organization of engineering societies dedicated to advancing the knowledge, understanding, and practice of engineering. AAES member societies represent the mainstream of US engineering – more than one million engineers in industry, government, and academia.' Among various services and products provides – generally priced – data on US engineer enrolments, degrees, etc., and on the engineer workforce.

4821 American Council of Engineering Companies
www.acec.org
'Federation of 51 state and regional councils representing the great breadth of America's engineering industry. ACEC member firms employ more than 300,000 engineers, architects, land surveyors, scientists, and other specialists, responsible for more than $100 billion of private and public works annually. Member firms range in size from a single registered professional engineer to corporations employing thousands of professionals.'

4822 American Society for Engineering Education
www.asee.org
'Nonprofit member association, founded in 1893, dedicated to promoting and improving engineering and technology education. ASEE is more than 12,000 deans, professors, instructors, students and industry representatives.'

American Society of Safety Engineers
See entry no. 4253

4823 Association of Consulting Engineers [UK]
www.acenet.co.uk
The UK's leading trade association for engineering, technical and management consultancies. ACE represents over 700

member companies that cover the entire range of construction, environmental and infrastructure industry.

- **Institution of Incorporated Engineers** www.iie.org.uk. Representing the interests of approximately 40,000 Incorporated Engineers and Engineering Technicians, and now Chartered Engineers (CEng) IIE provides professional recognition and career development support for the modern practical professional'.

Campaign for Science & Engineering

See entry no. 307

4824 Canadian Council of Professional Engineers

www.ccpe.ca/e

'National organization of the 12 provincial and territorial associations/ordre that regulate the practice of engineering in Canada and license the country's more than 160,000 professional engineers.'

- **Engineering Institute of Canada** www.eic-ici.ca/english/home.html. Federation of nine Canadian engineering societies.

4825 Engineering Academy of Japan

www.eaj.or.jp/Welcome-e.html

'Non-profit, non-governmental organization to contribute to the advancement of engineering and technological sciences in Japan, whose members are in leading positions with outstanding achievements and extensive knowledge in engineering and related fields.' Useful entrée for those unfamiliar with the Japanese situation. Regularly updated.

4826 Engineering Employers Federation [UK]

www.eef.org.uk

Now simply known as EEF: The Manufacturers' Organisation, an important UK association which has a membership of 6000 manufacturing, engineering and technology-based businesses and represents the interests of manufacturing at all levels of government.

Extensive well structured site. Especially valuable is the What we do area of the site, leading to significant sections on: Education and skills; Environment; Health and safety; HR and legal; Information and research; Manufacturing matters; Training.

- **UK Steel** www.uksteel.org.uk. Trade association for the UK steel industry (and a subsidiary of EEF). All UK steel producing companies, and many steel processing companies, are members.

4827 Engineers Australia

www.ieaust.org.au

Site of The Institution of Engineers Australia, trading as Engineers Australia. Good well maintained site with sections covering: Awards; Careers; Events; Membership; Policy. The Information Resource Centre ('Library') provides access to: Institution publications; Technical papers; Virtual libraries; Resources; and Useful links.

4828 Fédération Européenne d'Associations Nationales d'Ingénieurs

www.feani.org

Organization of some 80 national engineering associations from 25 European countries. Useful data on developments in accreditation within Europe.

- **European Society for Engineering Education** www.ntb.ch/SEFI. Founded in 1973 as a non-profit organization, SEFI is presently the largest network of higher engineering institutions and individuals involved in engineering education in Europe.

4829 International Engineering Consortium

www.iec.org

'Committed to providing educational programs that will continue to help industry professionals and academics stay up-to-date with the substantial change occurring throughout the information industry. Widely recognized as an industry leader, the IEC brings its experience in providing high-quality education to the World Wide Web. The IEC's Web education program is a partnership between the IEC and an expanding number of industry-leading corporations.'

'More than 70 leading high-technology universities are IEC affiliates, and the IEC handles the affairs of the Electrical and Computer Engineering Department Heads Association.'

4830 Junior Engineering Technical Society [USA]

www.jets.org

National non-profit education organization that has served the pre-college engineering community for over 50 years. Through competitions and programs, JETS serves over 30,000 students and 2000 teachers, and holds programs on 150 college campuses each year. 'Opening the world of engineering to junior high and high school students, parents, and educators.'

4831 Royal Academy of Engineering [UK]

www.raeng.org.uk

'As Britain's national academy for engineering, we bring together the country's most eminent engineers from all disciplines to promote excellence in the science, art and practice of engineering. Our strategic priorities are to enhance the UK's engineering capabilities; to celebrate excellence and inspire the next generation; and to lead debate by guiding informed thinking and influencing public policy.'

Well designed, attractive and inviting site – good as an entrée to current academic, government, and professional preoccupations within UK engineering.

4832 Society of Women Engineers [USA]

www.societyofwomenengineers.org

Founded 1950 and 'is a not-for-profit educational and service organization. SWE is the driving force that establishes engineering as a highly desirable career aspiration for women. SWE empowers women to succeed and advance in those aspirations and be recognized for their life-changing contributions and achievements as engineers and leaders.'

- **Women in Engineering Programs and Advocates Network** www.wepan.org. Founded 1990. Membership of over 600 and led by a 16-person board of directors from academia and industry. Mission is 'to be a catalyst for change to enhance the success of women in the engineering profession'.
- **Women's Engineering Society** www.wes.org.uk. UK society 'formed 1919 when women engineers were a new breed in a male dominated environment. Because of their own sense of isolation, early members wanted to help women engineers to meet and exchange ideas on common interests, training and employment'.

Libraries, archives, museums

4833 Engineering Libraries on the Web [USA]

http://web.library.uiuc.edu/grainger

Comprehensive directory of links which can be browsed as a list geographically, or accessed graphically, via a US map.

Portal & task environments

4834 **E4 Network** [UK]
Centaur Communications.
www.e4engineering.com
UK-based group of sites 'dedicated to providing information and services to those working in industry and the engineering professions'. Includes *e4enginering.com* 'now become established as the leading website for the engineering industry. Professional engineers visit the site every month to get the latest industry news and views, product data and information, in depth features and analysis, details of forthcoming industry events, and to search our 5 year archive of content from all Centaurs engineering magazines.'

However, early 2005, 'e4engineering has been relaunched and rebranded as The Engineer Online'.

- **The Engineer Online: The News Magazine for Technology and Innovation** www.theengineer.co.uk. News magazine for technology and innovation. 35,000 circulation.

4835 **EEVL: Engineering**
Resource Discovery Network and Heriot-Watt University
www.eevl.ac.uk/engineering
The most important and extensive current gateway to web-based engineering resources. Also has substantial subsections EEVL: MATHEMATICS and EEVL: COMPUTING.

The core of the overall service remains the Internet Resource Catalogue, part of the RDN, and a collection of over 10,000 descriptions and links to quality internet websites. But the EEVL team has also developed an Ejournal Search Engine (EESE), which searches the content of over 250 freely available full text ejournals in engineering, mathematics and computing. There are also now a range of more specialized services, such as RECENT ADVANCES IN MANUFACTURING, a database of teaching and learning resources, an offshore engineering information service, the aggregation of jobs and industry news from a wide range of top sources to provide OneStep Jobs and OneStep News services, and so on.

Overall, an excellent service.

4836 **efunda**
www.efunda.com
'*eFunda* stands for engineering Fundamentals. Its mission is to create an online destination for the engineering community, where working professionals can quickly find concise and reliable information to meet the majority of their daily reference needs. eFunda is all about the basics, for most part, that means college level material covered in engineering schools. If you practice engineering, more often than not you would find yourself searching for something you knew but could not quite remember. eFunda wants to be your reminder of these formulas. Not only that, eFunda wants to tell you exactly under what conditions those formulas apply, so you don't have to read an entire chapter of the good old textbook.'

Useful wide-ranging service.

4837 **Engineering Information: Ei**
Elsevier Engineering Information.
www.ei.org/eicorp
The leading service which was developed primarily from the print *Engineering Index*, which commenced in 1986, the online Compendex service, launched in 1969, and the internet-based service Ei Village, live in 1995. After acquisition of all these services by Elsevier in 1998, there was further consolidation with the incorporation of PaperChem, and the American Petroleum Institute's EnCompass.

The website provides links to details of the current portfolio of print and electronic products and services marketed under the Ei umbrella, as well as to those of other databases within the overall Elsevier family.

- **Ei Thesaurus J.L. Milstead, ed.** 4th edn, Elsevier Engineering Information, 2001, 939pp. ISBN 0873942272. 18,000 terms, roughly half preferred, half non-preferred. 220 new descriptors and 200 new entry terms in this edn.
- **Engineering Village 2** www.ei.org/eicorp/ev2.html [DESCRIPTION]. Cross-searchable gateway with access to: Compendex; Engineering Index Backfile; Inspec; NTIS Database; Referex Engineering. See website for descriptions of each of these. There is a similar Paper Village 2, as well as a CHEMVILLAGE.

4838 **Engineering K12 Center** [USA]
American Society for Engineering Education
www.engineeringk12.org
Very well designed and enjoyable site which 'seeks to identify and gather in one place the most effective engineering education resources available to the K-12 community. From comprehensive data on outreach programs to profiles of 'cool' engineers to hundreds of links and readings related to engineering education, the ASEE Engineering K12 Center offers immediately useful, easily accessible materials specifically tailored to students' and educators' interests. The ASEE EngineeringK12 Center hopes to serve as a resource hub for stakeholders in engineering education.

- **Engineers Week** www.eweek.org. Lively site primarily designed to support the week's events taking place each in February; but providing throughout the year access to a good range of useful resources, particularly with respect to the young people.

4839 **The Engineering Tool Box**
www.engineeringtoolbox.com
Wide range of very useful resources, tools and basic information for engineering and design of technical applications.

4840 **Engineering.com**
www.engineering.com
'Being developed to become the ultimate resource tool for the global engineering community and to provide a leading business-to-business Internet marketplace for engineering products and services. ENGINEERING.com has been created by a group of experienced engineers who understand what their fellow professionals need to be more productive.'

4841 **Enginuity** [UK]
Science, Engineering, Manufacturing Technologies Alliance
www.enginuity.org.uk
Bright, busy, colourful site. 'Engineering is all about designing, making, and improving the everyday objects that we all take for granted. Mobile phones, cars, computers, trainers, and chairs will all have had engineers involved at some stage of their development. The Enginuity website has been developed in order to inform today's young people of the wide range of possibilities available in engineering, and how they can become involved.'

4842 EngNet: Engineering + Internet
EngNet Ltd.
www.engnetglobal.com
UK-based 'Directory/Search Engine/Buyers Guide Service aimed specifically at the Engineering Industry to enable Engineers, Technicians, Tradesmen, etc. to find information and communicate effectively with suppliers in the Engineering Industry'.

4843 GlobalSpec: the engineering search engine
www.globalspec.com
US 'Internet-based, 'media-model' business linking buyers and sellers in the $500 billion electrical, mechanical and optical products markets ... GlobalSpec currently has a registered user base of more than one million engineers and technical buyers, the world's largest registered community of its kind. And, GlobalSpec continues to add new registered users to its community at the rate of 14,000+ per week.'

4844 Graduate Engineer [UK]
Thomas Telford.
www.graduateengineer.com [REGISTRATION]
'Aimed at bringing together engineering students from all disciplines, providing a place to meet, exchange information and work collaboratively. Contains career, financial and general news items and offers the capability to manage an address book, calendar and project plans.' Supported by a range of the UK's professional engineering bodies.

4845 Jane's Information Group: Intelligence and Insight You Can Trust
Jane's Information Group.
www.janes.com
Well established key provider of directory information, now expanded into an extensive portfolio of products and especially (fee-based) online services: concentrating particularly on defence and security. Scan the product index within the section Products; there is also a Guide to janes.com.

- **Jane's Aero-Engines** http://jae.janes.com. Details of all civil and military gas-turbine engines (turbofans, turbojets, turboprops and turboshafts) currently in use worldwide for the propulsion of manned aircraft.
- **Jane's Chem-Bio Web** http://chembio.janes.com [FEE-BASED]. Registration allows viewing of headlines or headlines with abstracts, to gain an appreciation of the range of this service.
- **Jane's Citizen's Safety Guide** www.citizenssafetyguide.com. 'Information on how everyday people and families can protect themselves', focusing on the USA situation.
- **Jane's Marine Propulsion** http://jmp.janes.com. Specifications of transmissions, propellers and related systems, combined with imagery and drawings. Covers all diesel and gas turbine engine and propulsion systems over 370 kW.
- **Jane's World Railways** http://jwr.janes.com. Leading guide covering all aspects of railway systems and operators, manufacturers and services.

4846 LTSN Engineering [UK]
Loughborough University and Higher Education Academy
www.engsc.ac.uk
One of the range of Learning and Teaching Subject Network Centres, its three main areas of work being: Providing a national focus that is an accepted and essential point of contact for all involved in higher education engineering; Collating and disseminating good practice and innovation in learning and teaching in higher education engineering; Providing co-ordination and support for learning and teaching in engineering.
This site has been retitled 'Higher Education Academy – Engineering Subject Centre'.

NIST: Math, Statistics, and Computational Science
National Institute of Standards and Technology See entry no. 425

Sustainability Knowledge Network
University of Queensland See entry no. 4646

Discovering print & electronic resources

4847 ENGINEERING Cluster
STN International.
www.cas.org/ONLINE/CATALOG/CLUSTERS/engineering.html
63 databases cross-searchable in whole or in part as a cluster.

4848 Guide to information sources in engineering
C.R. Lord Libraries Unlimited, 2000, 345pp. $79.00. ISBN 1563086999.
1639 entries, concentrating on North America, each with a mostly short annotation, and organized into eleven chapters treating different categories of resource. Four of these (covering: Scholarly Journals, Trade Journals, and Newsletters; Handbooks, Manuals, and Tables; Internet Resources; and Professional and Trade Associations, Organizations, and Societies) are subdivided by about a dozen engineering disciplines. The other seven Chapters review: General Reference Sources; Information Access Tools; Grey Literature: Conference Literature, Research and Technical Reports; Buyer's Guides, Databooks, and Catalogs; Regulations, Standards, and Specifications; Government Resources; Education and Career Resources. There is a short introductory chapter 'How engineers use information', and each subsequent chapter has a brief preface. List of publishers' websites, and comprehensive index.

A very good easy to use overview of engineering information resources, almost all produced (or updated) less than 5 years before the book's publication.
Series: Reference Sources in Science and Technology.

4849 Information sources in engineering
R.A. Macleod and J. Corlett, eds K G Saur, 2005, 683pp. €148.00. ISBN 3598244428.
www.saur.de [DESCRIPTION]
A valuable overview of engineering information sources, which includes some excellent chapters.

After a reflective opening chapter 'Information and the engineer', 12 chapters treat different literature forms and formats: Journals and electronic journals; Reports, theses and research in progress; Conferences; Patent information; Standards; Product information; Electronic full-text services; Abstracting and indexing services; Bibliographies and reviews; Internet resources in engineering; Reference sources; Professional societies.

There are then a further 14 reviewing the various engineering and engineering-related disciplines: Aerospace and defence; Bioengineering/biomedical engineering; Chemical; Civil; Electrical, electronic and computer; Engineering design; Environmental; Manufacturing; Materials; Mechanical; Mining and mineral process; Nanotechnology; Occupational safety and health; Petroleum and offshore.

In each of the two main parts, the approach and structure of each chapter varies considerably: some are more successful than others. Also, a note of the criteria used to merit an entry in the book's index would have been helpful. But this is a book to be read rather than used as a quick reference tool: and some of the reading can be very good indeed. A core text.

Series: Guides to information sources.

NSDL Scout Report for Math, Engineering, and Technology
University of Wisconsin, Internet Scout Project and National Science Digital Library See entry no. 4593

Digital data, image & text collections

4850 **ENGnetBASE**
CRC Press.
www.engnetbase.com
One of the set of CRC full-text reference work databases, April 2005 featuring 284 titles online.

4851 **ESDU International**
IHS.
www.esdu.com [FEE-BASED]
Validated engineering data, methods and software for aerospace, chemical, mechanical, process and structural engineering. Important series supported by voluntary expert technical committees. Currently includes: 24 series; 1340+ data item design guides; 250+ programs. Also available in hard copy and CD-ROM.

- **ESDU Series Cranfield University**. http://aerade.cranfield.ac.uk/esdu [FEE-BASED]. Useful service from AERADE which has integrated 1300 ESDU abstracts.

4852 **MATLAB**
The MathWorks, Inc.
www.mathworks.com/products/matlab
'The MathWorks is the leading developer and supplier of technical computing software in the world ... Our customers are 1,000,000 of the world's leading technical people, in over 100 countries, on all seven continents. These technical people work at the world's most innovative technology companies, government research labs, financial institutions, and at more than 3500 universities. They rely on us because MATLAB and Simulink have become the fundamental tools for their engineering and scientific work.'

4853 **National Engineering Educational Delivery System: NEEDS**
National Science Foundation
www.needs.org
Digital library of learning resources for engineering education. Provides web-based access to a database of learning resources where the user (whether they be learners or instructors) can search for, locate, download, and comment on resources to aid their learning or teaching process.

An annual Premier Award, originally sponsored by publishers John Wiley, promotes successful courseware, recognizing academic developers who too often 'find little reward, either financially or institutionally, for their superb and time-demanding efforts. In addition, the use of multimedia technology in the classroom is expanding rapidly, yet many faculty integrating courseware into their classes are unsure of indications of quality.'

4854 **Referex Engineering**
Elsevier Engineering Information.
www.ei.org/eicorp/referexengineering.html [FEE-BASED]
Three full-text collections accessible via the ENGINEERING VILLAGE 2 platform combining content ranging from 'broad-based engineering titles to highly specialized professional reference texts, provided an extensive and detailed base of reference material to support researchers, academics, R&D engineers, technicians and corporate engineers alike in their diverse work processes. Each collection includes: Handbooks of engineering fundamentals; Highly specialized professional information; How-to guides; Scholarly monographs; Situational reference; Titles focused on technique and practice.'

The three services focus on: Chemical, petrochemical and process engineering; Electronics and electrical engineering; Mechanical and materials engineering.

Handbooks & manuals

4855 **Advanced systems thinking, engineering, and management**
D.K. Hitchins Artech House, 2003, 469pp. £62.00. ISBN 1580536190.
Succeeds in the objective of 'bringing systems theory, systems thinking, systems engineering, and systems management together into a single framework, and integrate them in such a way that systems engineering is seen as a distinct discipline, founded on a system-scientific basis.'

Series: Artech House Technology Management and Professional Development Library.

4856 **Communication patterns of engineers**
C. Tenopir and D.W. King Wiley-IEEE Press, 2003, 280pp. $79.95. ISBN 047148492X.
Chapters are: Communication models; An engineers' communication framework; The engineering profession and communication; Information seeking and use; Information output by engineers; Engineering education and communication skills; The engineering scholarly journal channel; Engineering communication patterns compared with science and medicine; The NASA/DoD Aerospace Knowledge Diffusion Research Project. Bibliography.

'this book is highly recommended for library and information science libraries and engineering special and academic libraries.' (E-STREAMS)

4857 **CRC handbook of engineering tables**
R.C. Dorf, ed. CRC Press, 2004. $99.95. ISBN 0849315875.
Purpose is 'to provide in a single volume a ready reference for the practicing engineer in industry, government, and academia ... The 450 tables and figures are compiled from 51 books [these are listed] and are inclusive of most ready available, important data widely used by the engineering practitioner'.

Organized: 1. Electrical and computer engineering; 2. Civil and environmental engineering; 3. Chemical engineering, chemistry and materials science; 4. Mechanical engineering; 5. General engineering and mathematics.

Detailed table of contents; index. First-class compendium.

Mathematical methods for physics and engineering: a comprehensive guide
K.F. Riley, M.P. Hobson and S.J. Bence See entry no. 623

4858 **Mathematical techniques for engineers and scientists**
L.C. Andrews and R.L. Phillips; SPIE – The International Society for Optical Engineering SPIE Press, 2003, 797pp. $88.00. ISBN 0819445061.
http://spie.org/app/Publications [DESCRIPTION]
Designed as a self-study text for practitioners and as a useful reference source to complement more comprehensive publications.

Attractively produced; well written; achieves its objectives. Special features include: introductory historical comments at the start of many chapters; clearly laid out exercises, most with answers; suggested further reading containing lists of textbooks generally providing deeper treatments than in the work itself.

4859 **Mathematics handbook for science and engineering**
L. Råde and B. Westergren 5th edn, Springer, 2004, 562pp. £38.50. ISBN 3540211411.
Concise coverage of definitions, results, formulae, graphs, figures and tables in the basic areas of mathematics, numerical analysis, probability and statistics and various applications. Cross references; extensive index.
4th edn 1999.

4860 **McGraw-Hill's engineering companion**
E.N. Ganic [et al.], eds McGraw-Hill, 2003. $99.95. ISBN 0071378367.
Includes essentials of engineering sciences, concise selection of engineering data, surveys for use in both design and everyday practice. Aims to be a compact but comprehensive source for both the 'old-school' and the new generation of engineers, working across traditional discipline lines.

Well presented; comprehensive index; good first source.

- **The Wiley engineer's desk reference: a concise guide for the professional engineer** S.I. Heisler 2nd edn, Wiley, 1998, 690pp. $100.00. ISBN 0471168270. 'No other book on the market covers the broad spectrum of engineering in as concise a fashion. So whether you're looking for a specific piece of data or general background knowledge, this ... puts the information you need right at your fingertips.'

Sax's dangerous properties of industrial materials
R.J. Lewis, ed. See entry no. 4300

Statistical design and analysis of experiments: with applications to engineering and science
R.L. Mason, R.F. Gunst and J.L. Hess See entry no. 575

4861 **System engineering management**
B.S. Blanchard 3rd edn, Wiley, 2004, 498pp. $110.00. ISBN 0471291765.
System engineering is 'a top-down process, which is life-cycle oriented, involving the integration of functions, activities, and organizations'. Good well written handbook, including nine-page select bibliography as appendix.

- **International Council on Systems Engineering** www.incose.org. Formed 1990 'to develop, nurture, and enhance the interdisciplinary approach and means to enable the realization of successful systems. Now 5000 member systems engineers; some 40 Corporate Advisory Board members from government, industry, and academia'.

4862 **What engineers know and how they know it: analytical studies from aeronautical history**
W.G. Vincenti Johns Hopkins University Press, 1990, 326pp. ISBN 0801845882.
Develops the theme that engineering knowledge – and technological knowledge in general – constitutes a discrete form of knowledge that is different from scientific knowledge.
'The biggest contribution of Vincenti's splendidly crafted book may well be that it offers us a believably human image of the engineer.' (*Technology Review*)
'"Must" reading for all thoughtful engineers and historians of technology, and even for those physical scientists who wonder why engineers frequently act and think differently than do basic scientists.' (*American Scientist*)

Keeping up-to-date

4863 **Engineering: For innovators in technology, manufacturing and management** [UK]
Gillard Welch.
www.engineeringnet.co.uk
'For over 135 years, ENGINEERING magazine has reported significant events from the world of manufacturing. Today the magazine continues to report progress in manufacturing techniques, information technology, product development, finance and distribution. This website represents an extension of that tradition. Explore the site to find a wealth of information, resources and editorial highlights from the print edition of the magazine.'

4864 **Engineeringtalk**
Pro-Talk Ltd.
www.engineeringtalk.com
Web-based newsletter service for engineering products and supplier information. News is dependent upon company press and product news releases and is therefore an uncritical source of information. Recent releases can be browsed by period, company or topic and therefore this is a useful supplement to standard directories.

4865 **Eng-Tips Forums**
Tecumseh Group Inc.
www.eng-tips.com
Extensive series of online forums. As is usual, the questions or issues posted are unpredictable and the quality of the discussions is variable; so hardly an area normally for solid technical information (there is some, but quality assessment judgements are entirely the user's own). As a resource for knowledge self-assessment and general amusement, worth dipping into.

Aeronautical & Aerospace Engineering

aerodynamics • aeroelasticity • aeroplanes • aerospace engineering • air traffic control • air transport • aircraft • aircraft design • aircraft structures • airships • airspace standards • astronautics • aviation • aviation safety • avionics • chemical propulsion • flight • flight safety • helicopters • jet engines • rockets • space flight • space law • space shuttle • space standards • space station • spacecrafts • vertical flight

Introductions to the subject

4866 Aerodynamics for engineering students
E.L. Houghton and P.W. Carpenter 5th edn, Butterworth-Heinemann, 2003, 590pp. £29.99. ISBN 0750651113.
www.ei.org/eicorp/refxtitles.pdf
Leading text, in this edition 'revised to include the latest developments in flow control and boundary layers, and their influence on modern wing design, as well as introducing recent advances in the understanding of fundamental fluid dynamics. Computational methods have been expanded and updated to reflect the modern approaches to aerodynamic design and research in the aeronautical industry and elsewhere, and the structure of the text has been developed to reflect current course requirements'.
Available online: see website.
'The book is clearly written and can be confidently recommended as a general and comprehensive aerodynamics text for the use of students of aeronautical engineering.' (*Journal of Aerospace Engineering*)

- **Aerodynamics for engineers J.J. Bertin** 4th edn, Prentice Hall, 2002. $118.00. ISBN 0130646334. http://vig.prenhall.com/catalog/academic [DESCRIPTION]. Merges fundamental fluid mechanics, experimental techniques, and computational fluid dynamics techniques to build a solid foundation for students in aerodynamic applications from low-speed flight through hypersonic flight.

4867 Aircraft design projects for engineering students
L.R. Jenkinson and J.F. Marchman; American Institute of Aeronautics and Astronautics Butterworth-Heinemann, 2003, 371pp. $74.95. ISBN 1563476193.
Comprehensive guide including a range of project case studies (e.g. scheduled long-range business jet; military training system).
Series: AIAA Education.

4868 Aircraft structures for engineering students
T.H.G. Megson 3rd edn, Butterworth Heinemann, 1999, 590pp. £38.99. ISBN 0340705884.
First published 1972 and now an established classic text.
'This is an excellent book and should find a place on the shelf of any student or practising engineer involved in aircraft structural analysis. I can recommend it to the aeronautical community without reservation.' (*The Aeronautical Journal*)

- **Aircraft structures and systems R. Wilkinson** 2nd edn, MechAero Publishing, 2001, 201pp. ISBN 095407341X. www.mechaero.co.uk [DESCRIPTION]. Taking a non-mathematical approach throughout, encourages an interest in the form and function of an aircraft and identifies the reasons for the major differences between various types of aircraft.

4869 The anatomy of the airplane
D. Stinton; American Institute of Aeronautics and Astronautics 2nd edn, Blackwell Science, 1998, 445pp. ISBN 1563472864.
Very successful, excellent introduction. Explains, without being too mathematical, the workings of aircraft and their operational and flying features. Good for the non-specialist.

- **The design of the aeroplane D. Stinton** 2nd edn, Blackwell Science, 2001, 720pp. £55.00. ISBN 0632054018. Now widely used classic textbook.

4870 Aviation century: the early years
R. Dick and D. Patterson Firefly Books, 2003, 240pp. $39.95. ISBN 1550464078.
www.fireflybooks.com [DESCRIPTION]
One of a planned series of five – v. 2 *The golden age* and v.3 *World War II* having also been published.

4871 Basic helicopter aerodynamics
J. Seddon and S. Newman; American Institute of Aeronautics and Astronautics 2nd edn, Blackwell Science, 2001, 160pp. £35.00. ISBN 063205283X.
Useful introduction. Contents are: Rotor in vertical flight: momentum theory and wake analysis; Rotor in vertical flight: blade element theory; Rotor mechanisms for forward flight; Rotor aerodynamics in forward flight; Aerodynamic design; Performance; Trim, stability and control.

4872 Elements of spacecraft design
C.D. Brown; American Institute of Aeronautics and Astronautics 2002, 610pp. $111.95. ISBN 1563475243.
Good overview: especially appropriate for self-taught students.
Series: AIAA Education.

4873 Introduction to aircraft design
J.P. Fielding Cambridge University Press, 1999, 263pp. £26.00. ISBN 0521657229.
Primarily concerned with the detailed design phase which follows preliminary design studies. Contains lots of valuable information that students will find useful in the layout stage of their design work. Good for getting an overview of the full range of types of aircraft and of aircraft project management.
Series: Cambridge Aerospace, 11.
'This book is very helpful for students and young design engineers as well as for aeronautical enthusiasts who intend to get a complete overview of all types of aircraft, their specific design considerations, the basic principles and why aircraft programmes in the past have been successful or failed.' (*Aircraft Design*)

4874 Introduction to avionics systems
R.P.G. Collinson 2nd edn, Kluwer Academic, 2003, 492pp. £80.00. ISBN 1402072783.
Chapters are: Introduction; Displays and man-machine interaction; Aerodynamics and aircraft control; Fly-by-wire flight control; Inertial sensors and attitude derivation; Navigation systems; Air data and air data systems; Autopilots and flight management systems; Avionic systems integration; Unmanned air vehicles.

- **Civil avionics systems I. Moir and A.G. Seabridge; American Institute of Aeronautics and Astronautics** Professional Engineering, 2003, 395pp. £79.00. ISBN 1860583423. Well reviewed handbook; good use of illustrations and diagrams.

4875 **Introduction to flight**
J.D. Anderson 5th edn, McGraw-Hill, 2004, 800pp. $83.16. ISBN 0071160345.
Good, straightforward, well established introduction with improved learning features in the latest edition. The author is notable for his engaging conversational style of writing.

- **Aircraft performance and design J.D. Anderson** McGraw-Hill, 1999, 580pp. £43.99. ISBN 0070019711. Integrates aircraft performance and design into one text.
- **Flight vehicle performance and aerodynamic control F.O. Smetana; American Institute of Aeronautics and Astronautics** 2001, 350pp. $127.95. ISBN 1563474638. Designed to serve as a text for either an 11-week or a 16-week course at the sophomore level. Includes 'time-tested computer programs that perform the analyses in a manner that reduces student error and improves result accuracy'.
- **Fundamentals of aerodynamics J.D. Anderson** McGraw-Hill, 2001, 792pp. £43.99. ISBN 0071181466. In four parts: Fundamental principles; Inviscid, incompressible flow; Inviscid, compressible flow; Viscous flow.

4876 **Introduction to structural dynamics and aeroelasticity**
D.H. Hodges and G.A. Pierce Cambridge University Press, 2002, 170pp. £40.00. ISBN 0521806984.
www.cambridge.org.uk [DESCRIPTION]
Designed as an up-to-date treatment for advanced undergraduate or beginning graduate aerospace engineering students.
Series: Cambridge Aerospace, No. 15.

4877 **The jet engine**
Rolls Royce plc, 1996, 278pp. £25.00. ISBN 0902121235.
www.rolls-royce.com/history/publications/tech.jsp
Simple and self-contained introduction from the leading aerospace manufacturers.
For details of other volumes produced by the manufacturer, see website.

4878 **Mechanics of flight**
A.C. Kermode 10th edn, Prentice Hall, 1996, 514pp. Revised and edited by R.H. Barnard and D.R. Philpott, $44.95. ISBN 0582237408.
Mathematically-based well organized overview of flight mechanics ('the science of predicting and controlling aircraft motion'). Assumes a prior understanding of the fundamentals of aerodynamics.

4879 **National aerospace technology strategy: implementation report** [UK]
Aerospace Innovation and Growth Team 2004, 40pp. Downloadable PDF.
www.aeigt.co.uk
A report on the Future of the UK Aerospace Industry (July 2003) recommended the establishment of a National Aerospace Technology Strategy (NATS) as a partnership between government, industry and academia. This follow-up report defines the processes and structures necessary for the implementation of AeGiT strategy. It is an excellent well produced and presented overview.

4880 **Persistent and critical issues in the nation's aviation and aeronautics enterprise** [USA]
American Society of Mechanical Engineers 2003, 30pp. Downloadable PDF.
www.asme.org/gric/ps/2003/ASMEPolicyPaper.pdf
Report prepared by a steering committee consisting of members of key US engineering and aerospace associations who had been asked by the Office of Science and Technology Policy to provide the engineering community's perspective on prioritizing technologies critical to the long-term health of the nation's civil and military aviation and aeronautics technology enterprise. Released by ASME's Aerospace Division. Appendices include useful data and statistics relating to the industry.

Space policy in the twenty-first century
W.H. Lambright, ed. See entry no. 708

4881 **Spacecraft systems engineering**
P. Fortescue, J. Stark and G. Swinerd, eds 3rd edn, Wiley, 2003, 678pp. $90.00. ISBN 0471619515.
Volume arose from a Southampton University course in the UK aimed at recent science and engineering graduates who wish to become spacecraft engineers. Now a well established text covering the full gamut of activities germane to spacecraft engineering: mechanics, propulsion, structures, power, telecommunications. This edn includes a new chapter on small satellite engineering and management; and it responds fully to the trend towards 'faster, better, cheaper' space missions.
Check the website for details of Wiley's extensive list of aeronautic and aerospace titles (listed within their section Mechanical Engineering).

Dictionaries, thesauri, classifications

4882 **Acronyms in aerospace and defense**
F.B. Morinigo and P. Landecker, eds; American Institute of Aeronautics and Astronautics 3rd edn, 2001, 303pp. Manufactured on demand, $400.00. ISBN 1563475367.
www.aiaa.org
More than 50,000 acronyms that have been found in aerospace defence industry publications and documents since 1982.
Available online: see website.

4883 **The Cambridge aerospace dictionary**
B. Gunston Cambridge University Press, 2004, 741pp. £45.00. ISBN 0521841402.
Excellent compilation – with a delightful foreword – based on the author's previous *Jane's Aerospace Dictionary*. c.15,000 new entries for this edn.

Laws, standards, codes

4884 **Airlines Electronic Engineering Committee**
www.arinc.com/aeec
International body of airline representatives that leads the development of technical standards for airborne electronic equipment – including avionics and in-flight entertainment equipment – used in commercial, military and business aviation.

4885 **Consultative Committee for Space Data Systems**
www.ccsds.org
Founded in 1993 by ten of the world's largest space agencies, and now also comprising 22 observer space agencies and over 100 industrial associates. 'To date, more than 300 space missions have chosen to fly with CCSDS-developed standards and the number continues to grow.'

Its Recommendations and Reports cover: Advanced orbiting systems; Information access and interchange systems; RF and modulation systems; Space communications protocol specifications; Telecommand systems; Telemetry systems; Tracking and navigation systems.

The website has a nice graphical feature displaying the Committee's organizational structure – including its Collaborative Workgroup Environment, its Engineering Steering Group, and its collaborative Working Groups (WG) and Birds of a Feather (BOF).

- **European Cooperation for Space Standardization: ECSS** www.ecss.nl. Initiative established to develop a coherent, single set of user-friendly standards for use in all European space activities.

4886 **Eurocontrol**
www.eurocontrol.int
'Autonomous organisation, established in the 1960s by six States (Belgium, France, Germany, Luxembourg, the Netherlands and the United Kingdom) with the intention of creating a single upper airspace. We now have 34 Member States (against currently 25 for the European Community). The European Community is a member of EUROCONTROL: on 8 October 2002, the Member States and the European Community signed a Protocol on the Accession of the European Community to the revised EUROCONTROL Convention.'

Extensive website; well structured; good site map. The EUROCONTROL Navigation Domain (www.ecacnav.com) is directed towards providing the means to improve air traffic control system capacity and to enable airspace changes to be implemented.

- **European Civil Aviation Conference** www.ecac-ceac.org. Objective is to promote the continued development of a safe, efficient and sustainable European air transport system.

4887 **International Institute of Space Law**
www.iafastro-iisl.com
Founded in 1960 by the International Astronautical Federation. 'The purposes and objectives of the Institute include the co-operation with appropriate international organizations and national institutions in the field of space law, the carrying out of tasks for fostering the development of space law and studies of legal and social science aspects of the exploration and use of outer space and the holding of meetings, colloquia and competitions on juridical and social science aspects of space activities.'

Official & quasi-official bodies

4888 **Aeronautics** [EUR]
European Commission. Directorate for Research
http://europa.eu.int/comm/research/aeronautics
News and information on aeronautics activities within the Aeronautics and Space priority thematic area of the European Commission's Sixth Framework Programme (FP6).

- **Advisory Council for Aeronautics Research in Europe** www.acare4europe.org. Arose from recommendation in January 2001 report European Aeronautics: A Vision for 2020, prepared by the Group of Personalities. Aims to develop and maintain a Strategic Research Agenda (SRA) for aeronautics in Europe.
- **Air Transport European Commission. Directorate for Energy and Transport**. www.europa.eu.int/comm/transport/air/index_en.htm. Site within the EU's Transport Sectors.
- **European Aeronautics Science Network** www.easn.net. Aims to bring European universities with aeronautics activities into an integrated network, operating in parallel with industry and the national research establishments. Its central element is an open, internet-based network.

4889 **Aviation** [UK]
Great Britain. Department for Transport
www.aviation.dft.gov.uk
Good gateway to details of UK government involvements.

- **Aerospace and Defence Great Britain. Department of Trade and Industry**. www.dti.gov.uk/sectors_aerospace.html. The DTI's site for this industrial sector.
- **Air Accidents Investigation Branch** www.aaib.gov.uk/home. Purpose is: 'To improve aviation safety by determining the causes of air accidents and serious incidents and making safety recommendations intended to prevent recurrence.' (It is not to apportion blame or liability).

4890 **Committee on Space Research**
www.cosparhq.org
Committee of International Council for Science which acts as a forum receiving contributions from most countries engaged in space research, with presentation of the latest scientific results, exchange of knowledge and discussion of space research problems. It also advises the UN and other intergovernmental organizations, prepares scientific and technical standards related to space research, and promotes research in space.

- **Advances in Space Research** Pergamon, 1981–, 27 issues per year. €3378.00 [2005]. ISSN 02731177. Proceedings of COSPAR symposia and other scientific meetings organized by this Committee. Subscription includes the *COSPAR Information Bulletin*.
- **International Heliophysical Year: 2007** http://ihy.gsfc.nasa.gov. An international program of scientific research to understand external drivers of the space environment and climate.

4891 **DOT Agencies**
United States. Department of Transportation
www.dot.gov/DOTagencies
Encompasses agencies for aviation, highway, maritime, motor carrier safety, railroad, traffic safety, and transit administration. Also the important Bureau of Transportation Statistics (BTS): www.bts.gov.

- **Directory of Transportation Libraries and Information Centers S.C. Dresley, comp.** 7th edn2002. http://ntl.bts.gov/tldir. Prepared for the Transportation Division of the Special Libraries Association and published by the BTS National Transportation Library. As well as being web-accessible, now includes libraries from outside the USA and Canada. c.140 entries.
- **Transportation Expressions 1996** www.bts.gov/publications/transportation_expressions. Transportation expressions and definitions used throughout the Federal government, private organizations, Canada and Mexico. Provides users of transportation information with a comprehensive inventory of expressions and their referents.

4892 **European Aviation Safety Agency**
www.easa.eu.int
Recently established agency modelled on the US Federal Aviation Administration, which moved in November 2004 to its permanent headquarters in Cologne, Germany. Its main tasks are certification, rulemaking, quality and standardization. Among a busy website full of useful content, there is a helpful Latest Website Updates within the section News and Events.

European Space Agency
See entry no. 713

4893 **Federal Aviation Administration** [USA]
www.faa.gov
Range of useful engineering-related resources accessible via the websites of a number of FAA organizations, including: Aircraft certification service offices; Airport traffic control towers; Air route traffic control centres; Flight standards district offices; Automated flight service stations; Automated international flight service stations; Terminal radar approach control facilities.

- **National Aviation Safety Data Analysis Center** www.nasdac.faa.gov. Access to several databases, including those for the: Air Registry; Aviation Safety Reporting System; Bureau of Transportation Statistics; FAA Incident/Accident Data System.
- **William J. Hughes Technical Center** www.tc.faa.gov. 'The nation's premier aviation research and development, and test and evaluation facility.' The centre's extensive Library is located within its Office of Knowledge Management.

4894 **International Civil Aviation Organization**
www.icao.int
Clean, simple home page leading to a range of useful material. Check the Site Index, for instance, for: Accident investigation and prevention; De-icing and anti-icing operation; Interesting websites; Persons with disabilities; Treaty collection; Web, Library and Archives.

- **Civil Aviation Authority** www.caa.co.uk. The Airspace website area has Sections on: Aeronautical charts and data; Airspace utilization; En-route airspace; Off route airspace; Surveillance and spectrum management; Terminal airspace; Met Authority.
- **Civil Aviation Authority of New Zealand** www.caa.govt.nz. Good example of alternative country agency website: well laid out easily navigable information.

National Aeronautics and Space Administration
See entry no. 715

4895 **National Transportation Safety Board** [USA]
www.ntsb.gov
Independent Federal agency charged by Congress with 'investigating every civil aviation accident in the United States and significant accidents in the other modes of transportation – railroad, highway, marine and pipeline – and issuing safety recommendations aimed at preventing future accidents.' Helpful section Resources for Journalists. Range of Data and Information Products. Enlightening is the area NTSB Most Wanted: critical changes needed to reduce transportation accidents and save lives.

4896 **United Nations Office for Outer Space Affairs**
www.oosa.unvienna.org
Responsible for promoting international co-operation in the peaceful uses of outer space. Good entrée to UN and Member State activities in this and related areas – especially the legal aspects. The good Links listings has an informative section: Space Technology and Disaster Management.

Research centres & institutes

4897 **Aerospace Corporation** [USA]
www.aero.org
Provides independent technical and scientific research, development, and advisory services to national-security space programmes. Among much technical information, there is an Education section, which includes primers for global positioning systems and space. Useful collection of books from the Aerospace Press.

4898 **Air Force Research Laboratory** [USA]
www.afrl.af.mil
There are Directorates concerned with: Air vehicles; Directed energy; Human effectiveness; Materials and manufacturing; Munitions; Propulsion; Sensors; Space vehicles – each of which will usually have several Divisions and other sub-sections. The Information Directorate (previously known as Rome Laboratory) is 'a vibrant confluence of information specialists; electrical and computer engineers, computer scientists, mathematicians, physicists and a supporting staff. We are dedicated to exploring, building, exploiting, and brokering the science and technology associated with meeting America's air and space information technology needs for the 21st century'.

British National Space Centre
See entry no. 1573

4899 **Central Aerohydrodynamic Institute** [RUS]
www.tsagi.ru/eng
'Founded on 1 December 1918 under the initiative and leadership of N. E. Zhukovsky, the father of Russian Aviation. Today's TsAGI is the largest scientific research center in the world.'

Information organized under a number of activity areas including; aerodynamics, flight dynamics, strength, hydrodynamics, measurements, and non-aerospace activities. Includes a brief history of the Institute and an image gallery. The Institute's test facilities are described, and there is a list of staff publications and news and contacts sections.

4900 **Institute for Aerospace Research** [CAN]
http://iar-ira.nrc-cnrc.gc.ca/main_e.html
Site of Canada's national aerospace laboratory whose core content is devoted to the four constituent IAR laboratories: Aerodynamics; Flight Research; Structures, Materials and Propulsion; Aerospace Manufacturing Technology.

4901 **NASA Centers** [USA]
National Aeronautics and Space Administration
www.nasa.gov/centers/hq/organization
Useful gateway to the ten research centres: Ames; Dryden; Glenn; Goddard; Jet Propulsion Laboratory; Johnson; Kennedy; Langley; Marshall; Stennis. See also the entry under NATIONAL AERONAUTICS AND SPACE ADMINISTRATION.

- **Human Space Flight** http://spaceflight.nasa.gov. Well designed gateway to information about the Space Shuttle, Space Station, and other related ventures.
- **NIX** http://nix.nasa.gov. Single point of entry to various photographic databases of six NASA centres. NIX searches return thumbnail sized images, textual descriptions, image numbers, links to higher resolution images, more information, and to the centres which store each image.
- **Selected Current Aerospace Notices: SCAN** www.sti.nasa.gov/scan/scan.html. Weekly electronic current awareness journal that announces recently issued report and journal literature from the NASA scientific and technical information knowledge base.

4902 **Office National d'Etudes et de Recherche Aerospatiale: ONERA**
www.onera.fr/english.html
The French national aerospace research establishment, reporting to the Minister of Defence. Site provides an overview of current research projects and services, as well as a searchable database of scientific publications, including journal articles, conference papers, theses, technical notes, etc. with some in full text format. Well laid out site available also, of course, in French.

Von Karman Institute for Fluid Dynamics
See entry no. 5890

Associations & societies

4903 **Aerius – International Association for Students of Aviation**
www.aerius.nl
Has two primary goals: (1) to establish and extend contacts between students and the world of aviation; (2) to bring students interested in aviation closer together. Lively well maintained site providing a wide range of resources. Very good entrée to the field.

- **Association of Aerospace Universities** www.aau.ac.uk. Focus for activities in the UK Higher Education sector relating to aerospace. Acts as a promotional and interactive forum for aerospace education and business in the UK.
- **StudentPilot.com** www.studentpilot.com. 'Established with the goal of becoming the number one online training aid for pilots. Currently over 30,000 aviation enthusiasts visit our site each month. Professional Pilots, Private Pilots and predominantly Student Pilots visit our site regularly'.

4904 **AeroSpace and Defence Industries Association of Europe**
www.asd-europe.org/main.html
Currently (early 2005) being formed in a merger of AECMA, the European Association of Aerospace Industries, EDIG, the European Defence Industries Group, and EUROSPACE, the association of the European space industry.

- **AECMA-STAN** www.aecma-stan.org. Portal for the preparation and promotion of European Standards (EN) for aerospace application. Membership includes national aerospace associations and large aerospace companies.

4905 **Aerospace Industries Association** [USA]
www.aia-aerospace.org
Trade association representing manufacturers of commercial, military and business aircraft, helicopters, aircraft engines and the like. The site provides a good collection of data and statistics on the industry, provides details of news and events, and reports on current issues and policy matters. Some of the information is available to paying members only but it is possible to sign up for a free email newsletter.

- **National Aerospace Standards** www.techstreet.com/aiagate.html. Partnership between AIA and TECHSTREET providing a one-stop shop for national aerospace and other relevant standards.

Aerospace Medical Association
See entry no. 4249

4906 **AHS International: The Vertical Flight Society** [USA]
www.vtol.org/index.html
'The world's premier professional vertical flight society', also known as the American Helicopter Society. Details of activities – including their quarterly *Vertiflite*, which contains 'commercial and military features, cutting edge technology articles, industry highlights, historical articles, and often a perspectives column by key industry leaders'.

4907 **American Institute of Aeronautics and Astronautics** [USA]
www.aiaa.org
The major professional society – with the aim of progressing engineering and science within aviation, space and defence. Large site providing wide range of resources for students and educators, news of events, information on professional development courses, and – for subscribers – access to full-text journal articles and technical meeting papers through their AIAA Electronic Library.

There is a good aerospace links section – among which is an extensive worldwide list of academic institutions pursuing aerospace teaching and research.

- **Aerospace America** Monthly. $163.00. ISSN 0740722X. www.aiaa.org/aerospace. Features items on design, electronics, materials, computer applications, propulsion, policy, products, and critical technologies affecting aviation, space, and defence.
- **AIAA Standards** www.aiaa.org. As part of the Institute's Publications & Papers section, provides access to a comprehensive listing of aerospace standards – from both AIAA and INTERNATIONAL ORGANIZATION FOR STANDARDIZATION.

4908 **Flight Safety Foundation**
www.flightsafety.org
Independent, non-profit, international organization engaged in research, auditing, education, advocacy and publishing to improve aviation safety, and founded in 1947. Its mission is 'to pursue the continuous improvement of global aviation safety and the prevention of accidents'. News, seminars, technical briefings, training materials, etc. Free access to a comprehensive publications collection – more than 12,000 pages of seven scheduled FSF periodicals (1988 to present) – which can be searched and downloaded as PDF documents, after registration.

- **Bureau d'Enquêtes et d'Analyses pour la Sécurité de l'Aviation civile** www.bea-fr.org. French organization responsible for investigating civil aviation flight incidents and accidents. Statistics; news; etc. English language version of site.

4909 **International Academy of Astronautics**
www.iaanet.org
Founded in 1960 during the 11th International Astronautical Congress. Regular meetings every two years. Six specialized commissions: Space physical sciences; Space life sciences; Space technology and system development; Space system operation and utilization; Space policy law and economy; Space and society, culture and education. Produce a valuable series of downloadable PDF Cosmic Studies and Position Papers: e.g. 'The next steps in exploring deep space: a cosmic study by the International Academy of Astronautics' (123 pp, July 2004).

4910 **International Air Transport Association**
www.iata.org
Brings together approximately 270 airlines, including the world's largest. Flights by these airlines comprise more than

95% of all international scheduled air traffic. Although much of the site is concerned with commercial aspects, the What We Do section gives a number of useful leads to resources concerning aircraft operations, safety, security and facilitation.

- **Air Transport Association** www.airlines.org. Represents the major US airlines. Good range of publications and excellent set of industry facts, figures and analyses.
- **Air Transport World** www.atwonline.com. Trade magazine for the industry.
- **Association of European Airlines** www.aea.be. Trade association representing airlines operating within Europe.
- **World Air Transport Statistics: WATS** www.iata.org/ps/publications. Comprehensive and up-to-date publication monitoring trends in the global airline industry.

4911 **International Council of the Aeronautical Sciences**
www.icas.org
Non-government, non-profit making, scientific organization established in 1957 to encourage the free interchange of information on aeronautical subjects. Thirty-two societies from as many countries are now in membership; in addition, the Council is supported by aerospace companies and scientific and technical institutions acting as associate members.

4912 **Royal Aeronautical Society** [UK]
www.raes.org.uk/homepage.asp
Promoted as 'the one multidisciplinary professional institution dedicated to the global aerospace community ... The RAeS is the world's only professional body which caters for the entire aerospace community ... Indeed, the RAeS is justifiably proud of its members' range of disciplines, not just engineers and pilots, but also doctors, legal specialists, bankers, air traffic controllers, cabin crew, marketers, journalists, etc. Anybody who is a professional within the aerospace industry can belong to the RAeS and indeed many of them do. The aerospace industry is global and The Royal Aeronautical Society reflects this. Although centred in the United Kingdom, it has members in almost 100 countries worldwide'.

Elegant access to a wide range of useful, especially archival, resources – albeit a sizeable proportion only directly accessible by society members. However, there is a freely downloadable and very nicely produced bimonthly bulletin entitled *Library Additions*.

SAE International
Society of Automotive Engineers See entry no. 4981

4913 **Society of British Aerospace Companies**
www.sbac.co.uk
National trade association of the UK Aerospace Industry representing the civil air transport, aerospace defence and space industry operating in the UK economy. Section Aerospace Today gives access to: UK aerospace facts and figures; Latest news; Climate change levy; Guided weapon tower of excellence (an initiative of the UK Ministry of Defence).

Launchpad for Learning is a recently launched initiative whose aim is 'to promote the education and innovative learning of young people for exciting careers in science, technology and engineering in the 21st century'.

- **Airports Intelligence Centre** **Society of British Aerospace Companies and UK Trade & Investment**. www.airportsintelligence.co.uk [REGISTRATION]. Range of useful information but most 'only available to UK nationals, firms and UK owned foreign subsidiaries' by registration.

Libraries, archives, museums

4914 **Airshipsonline** [UK]
www.aht.ndirect.co.uk
Houses the online archive of the Airship Heritage Trust, 'an extensive history relating to all of the British Airships from 1900 to the present day'.

4915 **Imperial War Museum**
www.iwm.org.uk
Well designed website giving access – among much else of interest in this arena – to the site of IWM Duxford: 'Europe's premier aviation museum – as well as having one of the finest collections of tanks, military vehicles and naval exhibits in the country.'

- **Museum of Flight** www.nms.ac.uk/flight. Part of the National Museums of Scotland and based in East Lothian. Good descriptions of items in their collection under Our Aircraft.

4916 **Museum of Aviation** [USA]
www.museumofaviation.org/home.htm
Multimedia rich site – and thus rewarding in that sense – of 'the fourth largest aviation museum in the United States with a collection of over 90 aircraft spanning a century of flight. It is also the home of the Georgia Aviation Hall of Fame'.

4917 **National Air and Space Museum** [USA]
www.nasm.si.edu
'Maintains the largest collection of historic air and spacecraft in the world. It is also a vital center for research into the history, science, and technology of aviation and space flight.' Easily navigable site organized into: Collections; Education; Exhibitions; Get involved; Museum; News and events; Research; Visit – with rich sets of resources under each heading.

- **International Women's Air & Space Museum** www.iwasm.org. Located at Burke Lakefront Airport in Cleveland, Ohio, USA and 'dedicated to the preservation of the history of women in aviation and space and the documentation of their continuing contributions today and in the future'.
- **Air & Space Magazine** Bimonthly. $24.00. ISSN 08862257. www.airandspacemagazine. Editorial goals are 'to evoke the various experiences of flight, to examine the received wisdom of aerospace history, and to delight a readership of enthusiasts with a wealth of information and entertainment'.
- **Wings: a history of aviation from kites to the space age** **T.D. Crouch** W.W. Norton for Smithsonian National Air and Space Museum, 2003, 725pp. $29.95. ISBN 0393057674. 'Wings contains an extensive bibliography of primary and secondary sources which for the most advanced reader would be a valuable source for further research. It is recommended for college, university and public libraries.' E-STREAMS.

Portal & task environments

4918 **AERADE: Your Quality Portal to Aerospace and Defence Resources on the Internet**
Cranfield University
http://aerade.cranfield.ac.uk
Provides well crafted descriptions of over 5000 quality-assessed internet resources (though the differing types of

resources could benefit from distinction at search), plus access to more than 10,000 historically significant, digitized reports from the Aeronautical Research Council (the principal agency in Great Britain with a major output of reports on matters aeronautical, which existed from 1909–1979, and published reports until 1980) and the National Advisory Committee for Aeronautics (chartered in 1915 and operational from 1917–1958). Access to full text or abstracts of several other related collections; ConferenceBrief is a list of forthcoming conferences and events within the fields of aerospace and defence.

AERADE contributes records to EEVL, the INTERNET GUIDE TO ENGINEERING, MATHEMATICS AND COMPUTING and provides, overall, a very useful service.

4919 **Aerospace Professional Network**
Institution of Electrical Engineers
www.iee.org/OnComms/sector [REGISTRATION]
Now has over 7000 members from a wide range of disciplines involved with aerospace. Access to electronic library of full text documents, plus to the resource discovery tool AERADE.

4920 **AviationNow**
McGraw-Hill.
www.aviationnow.com
Leading commercial service offering industry news and analysis organized around nine channels – military, commercial aviation, space, business aviation, eBiz, maintenance/safety, finance, tech, next century of flight. Subscriber only access to the content of a number of publications within the Aviation Week Intelligence Network such as *Aviation Week & Space Technology*, *World Aviation Directory*, *Homeland Security & Defense*. Careers section; Forthcoming events; Market data centre; Special reports; etc.

4921 **Chemical Propulsion Information Agency**
Johns Hopkins University
www.cpia.jhu.edu
National clearing house for worldwide information, data, and analysis on chemical, electrical, and nuclear propulsion for missile, space and gun propulsion systems; located in the University's Whiting School of Engineering. Provide a wide range of specialist services and products, and maintain 'the most comprehensive scientific and technical information (STI) and report collection in the world related to chemical propulsion, propellants, and explosives'. One of the Information Analysis Centers sponsored by the DEFENSE TECHNICAL INFORMATION CENTER.

- **Advances in chemical propulsion: science to technology** **G.D. Roy, ed.** CRC Press, 2001, 552pp. $159.95. ISBN 0849311713. Based on work carried out by the author at the US Office of Naval Research [q.v.]. Part of the CRC Environmental and Energy Engineering Series.

eFluids
See entry no. 5918

4922 **European Aeronautic Defence and Space Company**
www.eads.net
Formed from a merger between the French Aerospatiale Matra S.A., the Spanish Construcciones Aeronáuticas S.A., and the German DaimlerChrysler Aerospace AG. Covers aeronautics (military aircraft, helicopters, regional aircraft), military transport aircraft, defence and security systems and space. Site provides product information and specifications, a photo gallery, press releases, employment and financial information, etc. There is a link to a substantial subsite covering the new A380 Airbus.

Fluid Mechanics
M.S. Cramer See entry no. 5919

4923 **Landings.com**
www.landings.com
Very good entrée to news/forums, products and services covering the full range of aviation-related matters. The Directory gives an excellent overview of the site's departments, sections and categories/content. Non-intrusive commercial sponsorship.

4924 **National Space Centre** [UK]
www.nssc.co.uk
The Centre itself is 'the UK's largest attraction dedicated to space'. But the portal also gives access to a wide and useful collection of educational resources plus details of the centre's Creative Services division whose 'in-house creative team includes producers, directors, animators, graphic designers, IT and web designers, scriptwriters, musicians and exhibition fabricators. What makes us different from other design houses is not just the diversity of skills and talent under one roof, but also the understanding we have of science centres and similar attractions and, most importantly, of their public and schools audience. Our tried and tested audiovisual material is available for licence; we can supply a wide variety of excellent shows for a fraction of the cost of producing such material in-house. Or if you want to see an original creative idea turned into reality, we can help you all the way from concept to completion'.

- **British Interplanetary Society** www.bis-spaceflight.com. World's longest established organization devoted solely to supporting/promoting exploration of space and astronautics. Produce the monthly *Spaceflight*: 'a prime source of information on international space programmes and commercial space exploration'.
- **Space Now** www.spacenow.org.uk. The Centre's space news and information service divided into four sections: Into space; Exploring the universe; The planets; Orbiting earth.
- **UK Goes to the Planets** www.uk2planets.org.uk. Consortium of wide range of bodies involved with UK missions to the planets 'put together with the help of the scientists and engineers who carried out the work and are now awaiting the results'.

4925 **The Shephard Group**
www.shephard.co.uk
Publishes a range of handbooks and specialist magazines covering a wide spectrum of current events and latest developments in the aerospace and defence industry. 'The Portal has provided Shephard with huge traffic growth since its launch in April 2004, with an average of 2 million enquiries per month and over 25,000 visitors every week.'

- **Rotohub** www.shephard.co.uk/Rotorhub. 'The Hub of the Helicopter Industry.'
- **UV Online** www.shephard.co.uk/UVOnline. 'The most comprehensive, independent and up-to-date dedicated global news and business information reference source' for the Unmanned Vehicle (UV) industry.

Discovering print & electronic resources

4926 Aerospace and High Technology Database
American Institute of Aeronautics and Astronautics CSA, Monthly. $2260.00. ISSN 00205842.
www.csa.com/factsheets/aerospace-set-c.php
Major abstracting service now produced by CSA in co-operation with AIAA following its acquisition from the Institute. The print equivalent is *International Aerospace Abstracts*.

Provides bibliographic coverage of basic and applied research in aeronautics, astronautics and space sciences as well as covering technology development and applications in complementary and supporting fields such as chemistry, geosciences, physics, communications and electronics. The database includes coverage of reports issued by NASA, government agencies, international institutions and universities. Major subject coverage includes: aerodynamics, aircraft design, navigation, environmental pollution, fluid mechanics, heat transfer, materials, mechanical engineering, meteorology, thermodynamics, propellants and fuels, space sciences and spacecraft design.

4927 AEROTECH Cluster
STN International.
www.cas.org/ONLINE/CATALOG/CLUSTERS/aerotech.html
Combined access to a wide range of the host's databases, centred on the Aerospace and High Technology Database, and supplemented by STN's more generic science and technology offerings.

4928 Aviation Reference Desk: The One Stop Source for Aerospace Information
www.avrefdesk.com
Excellent site: 'We are aerospace professionals who initially designed the site for our own use, needing a business-oriented alternative to sites primarily for enthusiasts or with unmoderated link lists. The site is free, and all we ask is that you email us your best aerospace links so that we can continue to improve our site. We strive to have only the freshest, most relevant sources linked. If you want to suggest improvements, please do.'

4929 ERAU Virtual Libraries
Embry-Riddle Aeronautical University
www.erau.edu/libraries/virtual
Access to descriptions of over 2000 web resources divided into the Aerospace collection (advanced R&D with links to NASA resources, universities, manufacturers, etc), and the Aviation section (covering individual aircraft, airlines, pilot and military websites).

4930 Gale Group Aerospace/Defense Markets and Technology
Thomson Gale.
http://library.dialog.com/bluesheets/html/bl0080.html
Full-text articles and abstracts covering all aspects of the worldwide aerospace industry.

Global Mobility Database
Society of Automotive Engineers See entry no. 4990

4931 Military Science Index
Royal Military College of Science
www.rmcs.cranfield.ac.uk/infoserv [DESCRIPTION]
A unique index to the journal literature of military technology produced by the College's Information Service. It has an international reputation and is distributed widely. The printed version appears every two months.

4932 RDN Virtual Training Suite: Aviator [UK]
E. Turner and A. Maddison; Cranfield University and Resource Discovery Network
www.vts.rdn.ac.uk/tutorial/aviator
Tutorial for students, lecturers and researchers reviewing key: Databases; Educational resources; Organization websites; Gateways; Full-text documents; Mailing lists/Newsgroups; Library catalogues.

Digital data, image & text collections

4933 Advanced Topics in Aerodynamics
A. Filippone; University of Manchester
http://aerodyn.org
Very extensive excellent resource produced within the University's School of Mechanical, Aerospace and Civil Engineering. 'This website is an electronic media about aerodynamics, aeronautics and propulsion systems. The topics presented are of general interest, more or less advanced. The site is addressed to the expert and non-expert who have a prior knowledge of aerodynamics and fluid dynamics. There is no mathematics. Large use is made of graphics, figures, tables, summaries, reference to further reading.'

The Department will answer educational queries from around the world, but technical requests from non-educational institutions are dealt with as a professional service.

4934 Air University Research Web
Air University
https://research.au.af.mil
Service which 'offers a comprehensive approach to ePublishing that integrates with the time-honored missions and methods of the US Air Force. Our vision is one of enhancing the role of *Research* and supporting our crucial role in serving millions of people every day who seek information'. Access to over 2500 research studies in full text plus a range of other tools and services.

4935 Airliners.Net
www.airliners.net
'Biggest aviation site in the world! Over 100,000 visitors daily!'. Access, among much else of interest and enjoyment, to some 750,000 photographs online.

Directories & encyclopedias

4936 International directory of civil aircraft
G. Frawley Crowood Press, 2004, Biennial, 200pp. £16.99. ISBN 1875671587.
www.crowoodpress.co.uk/index.htm [DESCRIPTION]
Detailed descriptions of some 400 aircraft types in service or under development worldwide.

- **International directory of military aircraft** G. Frawley
  Crowood Press, 2002, Biennial, 220pp. £16.99. ISBN 1875671552.
  Features over 300 individual aircraft types currently in service or under development worldwide and a fleet inventory of the world's air arms, plus significant UAVs and aircraft carriers.

Handbooks & manuals

4937 **Aeronautical engineers' data book**
C. Matthews Butterworth-Heinemann, 2002, 271pp. £16.99. ISBN 0750651253.
This is an essential handy guide containing useful up-to-date information regularly needed by the student or practising engineer. Covering all aspects of aircraft, both fixed wing and rotary craft, this pocket book provides quick access to useful aeronautical engineering data and sources of information for further in-depth information.

4938 **Aerospace structural metals handbook**
http://www.cll.purdue.edu/extendeduniversity/selfdirected/ir/index.cfm?ir=aero
Surveys metals used in aerospace and their properties: covers over 200 alloys, many analysed especially for this service.

- **Structural alloys handbook**
  www.cll.purdue.edu/extendeduniversity/selfdirected/ir/index.cfm?ir=alloy [DESCRIPTION]. Wide coverage, including steels, aluminium, brass, bronze, copper, magnesium, titanium alloys.

4939 **Aircraft conceptual design synthesis**
D. Howe Professional Engineering Publishing, 2000, 448pp. £89.00. ISBN 1860583016.
Aircraft conceptual design synthesis means design by fitness-for-purpose. Very useful text covering the details of design and synthesis in a readable fashion. Concludes with four design examples.

4940 **Aircraft design: a conceptual approach**
D.P. Raymer; American Institute of Aeronautics and Astronautics 3rd edn, 1999, 923pp. $105.95. ISBN 1563472813.
An excellent resource, describing in detail the fundamental principles underpinning the initial design of aircraft. (It is the most popular aircraft design book used in undergraduate studies.) Particularly good for military aircraft projects, but also useful across the full range of types of aircraft. Includes two case studies: light sports plane; military fighter.
Series: AIAA Education.

4941 **Aircraft engine design**
J.D. Mattingly, W.H. Heiser and D.T. Pratt; American Institute of Aeronautics and Astronautics 2nd edn, 2002, 692pp. $95.95. ISBN 1563475383.
Significantly expanded and modernized version of the best-selling first edn. 'The AEDsys software that accompanies the text provides comprehensive computational support for every design step. The software has been carefully integrated with the text to enhance both the learning process and productivity, and allows effortless transfer between British engineering and SI units.'
'Most aircraft design books and textbooks do not include the entire product in one volume, instead they focus on different elements and besides Daniel Raymer's, Aircraft Design, 3rd edn, (AIAA, 1999) this is the best universal resource available for aircraft engine design. Highly recommended as a textbook and library resource.' (*E-STREAMS*)

4942 **Aircraft flight: a description of the physical principles of aircraft flight**
R.H. Bernard and D.R. Philpott 3rd edn, Prentice Hall, 2003, 376pp. £29.99. ISBN 0131200437.
Distinctive for providing accurate physical, rather than mathematical, descriptions of the principles of aircraft flight. The 14 chapters are titled: Lift; Wings; The Boundary layer and its control; Drag; High speed flow; Trust and propulsion; Performance; Supersonic aircraft; Transonic aircraft; Aircraft control; Static stability; Dynamic stability; Take-off and landing; Structural influences.

4943 **Aircraft performance: theory and practice**
M.E. Eshelby; American Institute of Aeronautics and Astronautics Butterworth-Heinemann, 2000, 288pp. £26.99. ISBN 034075897X.
Has the merit of linking fundamental analyses of both operational and airworthiness requirements. Particularly good coverage of civil aircraft design. The word 'performance' is 'taken to refer to tasks relating to the flight path of the aircraft rather than to those involving its stability, control, or handling quality'. Appendix on The International Standard Atmosphere Model.

4944 **Airplane Design I–VIII**
J. Roskam DAR Corporation. 8 v., $280.00. ISBN 1884885241.
www.darcorp.com/Textbooks/airplane_design_set.htm [DESCRIPTION]
Contains detailed design data used in undergraduate design courses.

4945 **Airplane stability and control: a history of the technologies that made aviation possible**
M.J. Abzug and E.E. Larrabee 2nd edn, Cambridge University Press, 2002, 391pp. £65.00. ISBN 0521809924.
An excellent well organized and written volume. Particularly useful for reference are two appendices: the first providing a series of short biographies of key stability and control figures; the second a very good References and Core Bibliography.
Series: Cambridge Aerospace Series, 14.
'This is a splendid book. The authors try to tell the whole story, starting with Cayley. With their immense background, practical as well as academic, the maths are all there but so are countless often fascinating references to actual aircraft ... How often do you find an erudite treatise that is truly un-put-downable?' (*Aerospace Magazine*)

4946 **Bramwell's helicopter dynamics**
A.R.S. Bramwell, D. Balmford and G. Done 2nd edn, Butterworth-Heinemann, 2001, 373pp. £67.50. ISBN 0750650753.
Comprehensive mathematically-based treatment and now a standard reference work.
'Professors Done and Balmford have retained the appeal of the original, while producing a truly modern text. The book is satisfying and in depth ... I commend it highly. It is an absolute must for practitioners in industry and academia.' (*The Aeronautical Journal*)

Flow around circular cylinders: a comprehensive guide through flow phenomena, experiments, applications, mathematical models, and computer simulations
M.M. Zdravkovich See entry no. 5945

Gas turbine performance
P.P. Walsh and P. Fletcher See entry no. 5949

Handbook of aviation meteorology
Met Office See entry no. 1248

Handbook of transportation engineering
M. Kurz, ed. See entry no. 4998

4947 **Space mission analysis and design**
J.R. Wertz and W.J. Larson, eds 3rd edn, Kluwer Academic, 1999, 969pp. £137.00. ISBN 0792359011.
Practical handbook for Space Mission Engineering: 'the process of defining mission parameters and refining requirements to meet the often fuzzy objectives of a space mission at minimum cost and risk'. Useful appendices, including for Astronautical and Astrophysical Data.
Series: Space Technology Library, V. 8.

4948 **Standard aircraft handbook for mechanics and technicians**
S. Leavell, S. Bungay and L.W. Reithmaier, eds 6th edn, McGraw-Hill Professional, 1999, 300pp. $24.95. ISBN 0071348360.
Well established practical manual covering: Aircraft structures; Tools and their uses; Materials and fabricating; Drilling and fabricating; Riveting; Bolts and threaded fasteners; Aircraft plumbing; Control cables; Electrical wiring and installation; Aircraft drawings; Non-destructive testing; Corrosion detection.

4949 **The standard handbook for aeronautical and astronautical engineers**
M. Davies, ed. McGraw-Hill, 2003. $175.00. ISBN 0071362290.
New text modelled on the successful series of *McGraw-Hill Standard Handbooks* – the author hoping that one day this volume will be as valuable as the century old MARKS' STANDARD HANDBOOK FOR MECHANICAL ENGINEERS.

Very wide coverage including, prior to the specifically aero-based content, reviews of underlying systems and technologies such as engineering, mathematics, units, symbols and constants, microprocessors, instrumentation and control. Also a section on earth's environment and space. The volume then covers intensively the full range of topics germane to aeronautics and astronautics. Relatively light coverage of military aspects. A major achievement.

What engineers know and how they know it: analytical studies from aeronautical history
W.G. Vincenti See entry no. 4862

Keeping up-to-date

4950 **Air International**
Key Publishing, Monthly. £35.00. ISSN 03065634.
www.airinternational.com
Apart from news, includes photo gallery, links and online shop.
The publisher offers a range of other relevant titles: see website.
- **Aviation Forum** http://forum.keypublishing.co.uk. Relatively active set of forums whose current order of popularity is: Modern military aviation; Commercial aviation; Historic aviation; General discussion – each of which, late 2004, had had over 100,000 posts and between 4000 and 11,000 threads.
- **Aviation News** www.airpictorial.com. Britain's longest established monthly aviation journal.

4951 **AV Web**
Aviation Publishing Group.
www.avweb.com [REGISTRATION]
Internet aviation magazine and news service, freely accessible on registration. Contains current aviation news stories, information on forthcoming events, feature sections on databases, classified advertisements, question of the week. There is a collection of articles arranged by subject including: Aeromedical, Airmanship, Aviation law, Avionics, Insurance, Maintenance, New aircraft, Reviews (new products and services for pilots and aircraft owners), Safety, Aviation training, Used aircraft. A good service, now with over 130,000 subscribers.

4952 **Aviation Today**
Access Intelligence. $2995.00 [2005].
www.aviationtoday.com/index.html
Intended to provide access to aviation market intelligence and business resources. Access to the content of several trade journals including *Air Safety Week*, *Aviation Maintenance*, *Rotor & Wing*. The site offers a searchable archive to its subscribers, as well as special reports, the latest accident information from the NATIONAL TRANSPORTATION SAFETY BOARD, industry links, listing of conferences and meetings, a forum for subscribers, and so on.

4953 **Flight International**
Reed Business Information, Monthly. £122.40. ISSN 00153710.
www.flightinternational.com
For over 90 years a leading reporter of the global information industry providing the latest technical and operational information from the defence, general aviation, business aviation, and technology and spaceflight sectors. 'No publication breaks as many stories or covers a wider cross-section of the aerospace industry.' The publisher compiles a series of complementary directories.
- **Air Transport Intelligence** Reed Business Information. www.rati.com [FEE-BASED]. Real-time data and news service for the aerospace and air transport industries.

4954 **Progress in Aerospace Sciences**
Elsevier, 1961–, Quarterly. €1443.00. ISSN 03760421.
www.elsevier.com/wps/find [DESCRIPTION]
Valuable generally specially commissioned reviews with coverage 'not only in the fields of aero- and gas-dynamics but also in other important aerospace areas such as structures, flight mechanics, materials, vibrations, aero-elasticity, acoustics, propulsion, avionics and occasionally also some related areas such as hydrodynamics'.

4955 **SpaceDaily: Your Portal to Space**
www.spacedaily.com
Commercial industry space news portal serving industry professionals, space scientists and policy makers. 'Monthly readership now regularly exceeds 500,000 unique readers generating over 2 million page views across our combined network of sites.'

4956 **SpaceRef.com**
SpaceRef Interactive Inc.
www.spaceref.com
Provides a wide range of services including an eclectic Space Directory – with links organized under a broad range of hierarchically arranged subject headings – as well as a section Commercial Space Watch.

Automotive & Agricultural Engineering

agricultural engineering • agricultural machinery • automobile engineering • bicycles • cars • farm machinery • motor vehicles • road transport • road vehicles • vehicles

Introductions to the subject

4957 **The automotive chassis: engineering principles: chassis and vehicle overall, wheel suspensions and types of drive, axle kinematics and elastokinematics, steering, springing, tyres, construction and calculations advice**
J. Reimpell, H. Stoll and J. Betzler 2nd edn, Butterworth-Heinemann, 2001, 444pp. Translated from the German, £57.50. ISBN 0750650540.
A good introduction to the engineering design of an automobile's fundamental mechanical systems covering: Types of accelerating and wheel suspension; Tyres and wheels; Dynamics of axle and flexible components; Steering linkage; Springs and damping; Chassis and centre of gravity.
'As with the first edition, material coverage is extensive and the current text also describes many recent innovations ... In fact, the density of information contained within the text is, quite simply, phenomenal ... The book contains a large number of very clear figures ... There is an exhaustive glossary of symbols and a bibliography ... This is a well presented, concise and comprehensive book ... Produced to a high standard.' (*Proceedings of the Institution of Mechanical Engineers*)

4958 **Automotive computer controlled systems: diagnostic tools and techniques**
A.W.M. Bonnick Butterworth-Heinemann, 2001, 252pp. £26.99. ISBN 0750650893.
Explains the fundamental principles of engineering that lie behind the operation of vehicle electronic systems, and how to apply the range of diagnostic equipment now available.

4959 **Bicycling science**
D.G. Wilson 3rd edn, MIT Press, 2004, 477pp. $22.95. ISBN 0262731541.
12 stylish chapters in three sections: I. Human power (including A short history of bicycling); II. Some bicycle physics; III. Human-powered vehicles and machines. Illustrations; diagrams; timeline; index.

4960 **Farm machinery**
C. Culpin 12th edn, Blackwell Scientific, 1992, 444pp. ISBN 063203159X.
Remains a leading work on agricultural engineering and farm mechanism for students, farmers, advisers and the agricultural engineering industry. This new edition was the most extensive revision undertaken and incorporated the rapid new developments that had occurred in recent years. Numerous new illustrations were included. The book's 1st edn appeared in 1938.

Introduction to internal combustion engines
R. Stone See entry no. 5866

4961 **The motor vehicle**
T.K. Garrett, K. Newton and W. Steeds 13th edn, Butterworth-Heinemann, 2001, 1214pp. £80.00. ISBN 0750644494.
First published in 1929 and an essential source, covering in its three parts all key aspects respectively of: The engine; Transmission; The carriage unit.
'As a reference book it has to be classed as one of the best! There should be a copy of it in every college library.' (*Association of Motor Vehicle Teachers' Newsletter*)

4962 **Road vehicle aerodynamic design: an introduction**
R.H. Barnard 2nd edn, MechAero, 2001, 276pp. £18.95. ISBN 0954073401.
www.mechaero.co.uk [DESCRIPTION]
Designed as a general purpose introduction with highly vehicle-specific information excluded. Useful bibliography.

Dictionaries, thesauri, classifications

4963 **Automotive A–Z: Lane's complete dictionary of automotive terms**
K. Lane Veloce Publishing, 2002, 352pp. $14.99. ISBN 1903706408.
www.veloce.co.uk
13,000 entries; includes English-American/American-English for 350 terms. Numerous appendices. Very useful reference work.
See website for details of the full range of the publisher's automotive books.

4964 **Automotive Terms Glossary**
AutoZone, Inc.
www.autozone.com
Freely accessible list of 6500 terms. Includes much other practical information about personal and commercial vehicles.

The CIMAC Lexicon
International Council on Combustion Engines See entry no. 5873

4965 **Dictionary for automotive engineering: English-French-German with explanations of French and German terms (Dictionnaire du génie automobile/Wörterbuch für Kraftfahrzeugtechnik)**
J. De Coster and O. Vollnhals 5th edn, K G Saur, 2003, 691pp. €128.00. ISBN 3598116241.
Handy volume organized alphabetically by English-language keywords, followed by respective translations and definitions in both French and German. New edn includes some 2500 newly entered keywords. Diagrams. Brief bibliography.

4966 **Dictionary of automotive engineering**
D.L. Goodsell 2nd edn, Butterworth-Heinemann, 1995, 265pp. Also published by SAE INTERNATIONAL, £25.99. ISBN 0750627956.
Contains over 3000 terms, including slang, US and UK terminology and over 100 detailed drawings used in automotive engineering worldwide. The second edition expands coverage of fuels, lubricants, materials, tyres, construction, off-road vehicles, testing and electronics.

Dictionary of materials and testing
J.L. Tomsic and R.S. Hodder, eds; Society of Automotive Engineers
See entry no. 5793

Official & quasi-official bodies

4967 **Automotive Industry** [EUR]
European Commission. Directorate for Enterprise and Industry
http://europa.eu.int/comm/enterprise/automotive/index_en.htm
Gateway to EU activity in this arena.

DOT Agencies
United States. Department of Transportation See entry no. 4891

National Transportation Safety Board
See entry no. 4895

4968 **Roads and Vehicles** [UK]
Great Britain. Department for Transport
www.dft.gov.uk
Gateway to UK government activity: there are similar offerings headed Freight Logistics, and Road Safety.

- **Automotive Industry Great Britain. Department of Trade and Industry**. www.dti.gov.uk/sectors_automotive.html. One of a series of DTI sites covering different industries.
- **Vehicle and Operator Services Agency** www.vosa.gov.uk. Aim is 'to contribute to the improvement of the road safety and environmental standards, and to the reduction of vehicle crime'. Merged from the former *Vehicle Inspectorate* and *Traffic Area Network* divisions of the Department for Transport.

Research centres & institutes

TRL
See entry no. 5183

Associations & societies

4969 **Agricultural Engineering Association** [UK]
www.aea.uk.com
Established in 1875 to promote the technical, trade and commercial interests of British manufacturers and suppliers of agricultural machinery. Since 1989 the association has also represented the interests of British outdoor power and machinery manufacturers and suppliers. Useful survey of United Kingdom Tractor Registrations. The News section has a much wider collection of information than its label connotes.

Aluminum Association
See entry no. 5800

American Gear Manufacturers Association
See entry no. 5892

4970 **American Society of Agricultural Engineers**
www.asae.org
An educational and scientific organization dedicated to the advancement of engineering applicable to agricultural, food, and biological systems, founded in 1907. Its membership is worldwide and its extensive range of technical publications and standards can be searched online with free abstracts: full-text is available to members.

4971 **Automotive Industry Action Group** [USA]
www.aiag.org
Founded 1982 and its 'more than 1600 member companies include North American, European and Asia-Pacific OEMs and suppliers to the automotive industry with combined annual sales of more than $850 billion. A not-for-profit association, AIAG's primary goals are to reduce cost and complexity within the automotive supply chain and to improve speed-to-market, product quality, employee health-and-safety and the environment'. Very wide range of resources; good intuitive website.

4972 **Consortium for Automotive Recycling** [UK]
www.caregroup.org.uk
Collaborative project involving the main UK motor vehicle manufacturers/importers and vehicle dismantlers. Its objective is 'to research and technically prove materials re-use and recycling processes with a view to reducing the amount of scrapped vehicle waste going to landfill from the disposal of End of Life Vehicles (ELVs)'. Very wide range of useful material and leads.

4973 **Electric Drive Transportation Association** [USA]
www.electricdrive.org
Industry association 'dedicated to the promotion of electric drive as the best means to achieve the highly efficient and clean use of secure energy in the transportation sector'. Wide ranging informative website, well laid out.

4974 **European Committee of Associations of Manufacturers of Agricultural Machinery**
www.cema-agri.org
'Agricultural Machinery' is defined to encompass 'agricultural tractors, agricultural machines, self-propelled machinery (such as harvesting machinery, sprayers, balers) as well as trailed and mounted machinery (such as ploughs, mounted sprayers, slurry spreaders), outdoor power machines and forestry and municipal equipment'. Founded in 1959, CEMA brings together 13 national associations active in this domain of agricultural machinery.

4975 **European Natural Gas Vehicle Association**
www.engva.org
Mission is 'to develop a sustainable and profitable market for NGVs throughout Europe by creating a favourable political and economic environment that encourages the development of NGV technology as well as a European fueling infrastructure'. Aims to attract membership from the natural gas industry and non-profit organizations as well as NGV product and service companies, and now has over 250 members.

4976 **Institute of Transportation Engineers**
www.ite.org
Founded in 1930, now has more than 16,000 members working in some 90 countries concerned with 'meeting society's needs for safe and efficient surface transportation through planning, designing, implementing, operating and maintaining surface transportation systems worldwide'. Good range of technical and professional information – though a sizeable proportion is only directly accessible to Institute members.

4977 **Intelligent Transportation Society of America** [USA]
www.itsa.org
'Intelligent transportation systems, or ITS, encompass a broad range of wireless and wireline communications-based information, control and electronics technologies. When

integrated into the transportation system infrastructure, and in vehicles themselves, these technologies help monitor and manage traffic flow, reduce congestion, provide alternate routes to travelers, enhance productivity, and save lives, time and money.'

Useful entrée.

4978 **International Commission of Agricultural Engineering (Commission Internationale du Génie Rural)**
www.cigr.org
International, non-governmental, non-profit organization, founded 1930, and 'regrouping, as a networking system, Regional and National Societies of Agricultural Engineering as well as private and public companies and individuals all over the world'. Its main aims are: To stimulate the development of science and technology in the field of Agricultural Engineering; To encourage education, training and mobility of young professionals; To encourage interregional mobility; To facilitate the exchange of research results and technology; To represent the profession at a worldwide level; To work towards the establishment of new associations, both at national and regional level, and to the strengthening of existing ones; To perform any other activity that will help to develop Agricultural Engineering and Allied Sciences.

CIGR's technical work is organized within seven areas: Land and water use; Farm buildings, equipment, structures and environment; Equipment engineering for plant production; Rural electricity and other energy sources; Management, ergonomics and systems engineering; Processing; Information systems.

- **CIGR Handbook of Agricultural Engineering** 1999. $194.00. Major reference work, 110 authors. Five v.: I. Land and water engineering; II. Animal production and aquacultural engineering; III. Plant production engineering; IV. Agro processing engineering; V. Energy and biomass engineering.
- **The CIGR-FAO Global Network on Agricultural Engineering** www.fao.org/ag/AGS/agse/GLOBNET.htm. Network of seven e-mail discussion lists corresponding to the seven sections of CIGR.

4979 **International Federation of Automotive Engineering Societies**
www.fisita.com
Independent world body representing over 167,000 automotive engineers through their membership of national automotive societies in 35 countries. Its mission is 'to help create efficient, affordable, safe and sustainable automotive transportation'. Very nicely designed website with good section on Automotive Sustainability. Link to extensive Technical Papers site (www.fisitatech.com) giving access to thousands of papers: (relatively small) subscription needed for full access. Diary of events. Good links section.

4980 **International Road Federation**
www.irfnet.org
Independent, not-for-profit federation of worldwide public and private entities involved in road planning, development, construction, management and usage.

4981 **SAE International**
Society of Automotive Engineers
www.sae.org
Based in the USA, this society aims to advance mobility engineering in land, sea, air and space worldwide. Very active society over a wide arena. The society sponsors and/or administers more than 25 international meetings and exhibitions each year that cover all aspects of technology related to the design, manufacture and life cycle technology for the automotive, aerospace and other related mobility industries: from these over 2000 papers are published per annum.

The SAE is heavily involved in technical standards development through the voluntary work of more than 7000 committee members and participants; and it maintains over 8300 technical standards and related documents. Much else to explore on this rich site – including an extensive array of print and electronic publications, both serial and non-serial. A good place to start for those new to the field.

- **Aerospace Engineering** www.sae.org/aeromag/current.htm. One of three magazines published by SAE, the others being AUTOMOTIVE ENGINEERING INTERNATIONAL and *SAE Off-highway Engineering*.

4982 **Society of Motor Manufacturers and Traders** [UK]
www.smmt.co.uk
Has provided services and support for the UK automotive industry since 1902. Represents the industry to the UK government and abroad on key industry issues. Delivers national and international events and exhibitions. Provides information and advice to any company whose business development relies on the success of the motor industry. Good source of data on the state of the industry.

Libraries, archives, museums

4983 **British Motor Industry Heritage Trust**
www.heritage-motor-centre.co.uk/archive
Contains 15,000 cubic feet of historic material ranging through: business records, sales and technical material, magazines and books, production and engineering records, plus a large collection of film, video and negatives which provide a photographic record of the development of the British motor industry from the 1900s to the present day.

- **Heritage Motor Centre** www.heritage-motor-centre.co.uk. Maintains the largest collection of classic, vintage and veteran British cars in the world, the 200 classic vehicles on display charting the history of the British car industry from the end of the 19th century to the present day.

4984 **Henry Ford Museum** [USA]
http://www.hfmgv.org
Interesting site with range of historical material.

Imperial War Museum
See entry no. 4915

Portal & task environments

Clear Zones
See entry no. 4796

4985 **Cosworth Technology**
www.cosworth-technology.co.uk
Good 'Library' section (within 'Information'). Cosworth is a manufacturer of integrated engine and powertrain solutions.

Fluid Mechanics
M.S. Cramer See entry no. 5919

4986 MotorBase
www.motorbase.com
Motorbase is an encyclopedia of motoring. The site is a motoring history containing: detailed profiles of every make and model of car, a comprehensive bibliography of books and articles, auction houses and their results; directories of related websites, car clubs, dealers and suppliers with a comprehensive shop selling books, models, restoration supplies, parts, biographical entries for all the key people and so on. A good site – especially for the motoring enthusiast.

4987 United States Council for Automotive Research: USCAR
www.uscar.org
The umbrella organization of DaimlerChrysler, Ford and General Motors, which was formed in 1992 to further strengthen the technology base of the domestic auto industry through co-operative research.

4988 Virtual Automotive Information Centre: VAIC
MIRA.
http://aic.mira.co.uk [FEE-BASED]
Provides a wide range of automotive information including: Technical and business news; Company profiles; Sector review reports; MIRA Technical Papers; Statistics; etc.

4989 WardsAuto.com
www.wardsauto.com
Excellent spectrum of products and services about the global automobile industry including newsletters, magazines, forums, suppliers' data.

Discovering print & electronic resources

CSA Mechanical and Transportation Engineering Abstracts
See entry no. 5926

4990 Global Mobility Database
Society of Automotive Engineers
http://store.sae.org/gmd [FEE-BASED]
Comprehensive database containing over 120,000 abstracts of international technical papers, standards, regulations, journals and reports of important new technologies, trends, innovations and research in sea, air, land and space vehicles.

ITRD
See entry no. 5217

Directories & encyclopedias

4991 Agmachine.com: Worldwide Agricultural Machinery and Equipment Directory
www.agmachine.com
The largest specialized directory of agricultural machinery and farm equipment manufacturers on the internet with over 3200 company listings in 63 countries worldwide, including over 2200 direct links to company websites. Also covers used farm machinery, replacement parts, news, publications, events, institutions, etc.

4992 The Beaulieu encyclopedia of the automobile
G.N. Georgano, ed. Fitzroy Dearborn, 2000, 1792pp. 2 v. Foreword by Lord Montagu of Beaulieu, $355.00. ISBN 1579582931.
Comprehensive guide to almost every make of car ever manufacutured and sold.

4993 The UK Motor Industry Directory
Society of Motor Manufacturers and Traders (SMMT)
www.smmt.co.uk/industrydirectory [FEE-BASED]
Detailed information on over 4500 companies including: component and vehicle manufacturers; research and development organizations; suppliers of production and garage machinery; business consultancies; agencies; trade and government bodies and providers of other services that support the industry.

Worldwide agricultural machinery and equipment directory
See entry no. 3045

Handbooks & manuals

4994 Advanced vehicle technology
H. Heisler 2nd edn, Butterworth-Heinemann, 2002, 654pp. £29.99. ISBN 0750651318.
Well written; comprehensive coverage. The wide-ranging contents are: Vehicle structure; Friction clutch; Manual gearboxes and overdrives; Hydrokinetic fluid coupling and torque converters; Automatic transmission; Transmission bearings and constant velocity joints; Final drive transmission; Tyres; Steering; Suspension; Brake system; Air operated power brake equipment and vehicle retarders; Antilock braking; Vehicle aerodynamics; Tyre tread design advances; Electronically controlled anti-vibration engine mountings; Transport refrigeration.
Previous edn Arnold, 1989.

4995 Automotive control systems
U. Kiencke and L. Nielsen; Society of Automotive Engineers 2nd edn, Springer, 2005, 512pp. £38.50. ISBN 3540231390.
Announced 2nd edn of book which 'enables control engineers to understand engine and vehicle models necessary for controller design and introduces mechanical engineers into vehicle-specific signal processing and automatic control. With only a few exceptions the approaches are close to some of those utilized in actual vehicles, rather than being purely theoretical. The authors have large experiences in industrial development (Bosch) as well as in academic research'.

4996 Automotive handbook
6th edn, Robert Bosch GmbH, 2004, 1232pp. £32.95. ISBN 0768006694.
www.bentleypublishers.com/bosch
Considered the most indispensable reference for automotive engineers, mechanics, students and anyone interested in automotive technical matters. Over 225 automotive subjects are covered including: vibration, acoustics, electronics, materials, corrosion, lubricants, fuels, engine management, steering, braking systems, chassis, lighting etc. New sections include topics that cover fuel filters, fuel cells, automatic cruise control, instrumentation, traffic telematics, etc.
See the website for the range of technical literature produced under the Bosch imprint. The Handbook itself is also available from SAE INTERNATIONAL

4997 Handbook of automotive body and systems design
J. Fenton Professional Engineering Publishing, 1998, 430pp. £79.00. ISBN 186058067X.
Detailed discussion of generic principles (creating and prototyping; ergonomics, seating and packaging; aerodynamics and air-conditioning; body trim and fittings interior trim basics; body electrical/electronic controls; body-electronics and telematics) following by application to a wide range of vehicle types (volume road-card; specialist cars; truck engineering; bulk-carrier vehicles; specialist commercial vehicles; specialist passenger vehicles).

4998 Handbook of transportation engineering
M. Kurz, ed. McGraw-Hill, 2003. $150.00. ISBN 0071391223.
Strategic planning, development, and maintenance of all varieties of public and private transportation systems, including freight, passenger, and mass transit air, rail, road, and water systems at the local, regional, national, and international levels.

Highway engineering handbook: building and rehabilitating the infrastructure
R.L. Brockenbrough and K.J. Boedecker, eds See entry no. 5264

The internal-combustion engine in theory and practice
C.F. Taylor See entry no. 5956

4999 Lightweight electric/hybrid vehicle design
R. Hodkinson and J. Fenton Butterworth-Heinemann, 2001, 253pp. £36.99. ISBN 0750650923.
Explores the 'rather dramatic departures in structural configuration necessary for purpose-designed electric vehicles including weight removal in the mechanical systems of the vehicle. It also offers a comprehensive review of design processes in the electric hybrid drive and energy storage systems'. Includes case studies and examples of practical applications.

5000 SAE handbook [USA]
Society of Automotive Engineers SAE, 2004. 3 v., $595.00. ISBN 0768013151.
www.sae.org
Standards, recommended practice and information reports on automotive mechanical, electrical and other components. The three volumes are: 1. Metals, materials, fuels, emissions, threads, fasteners and common parts; 2. Parts and components and on-highway vehicles; 3. On-highway vehicles and off-highway machinery. The ANSI-approved SAE standards development program has considerable relevance to the general mechanical engineer for materials, lubricants, fastenings, tubing and other fittings, power transmission, maintenance and repair, reliability, fuel cells and many other topics.

Keeping up-to-date

5001 Automotive Engineer [UK]
Professional Engineering Publishing, 11/year. £279.00. ISSN 03076490.
Technical and business information to the auto industry's directors, managers, engineers and analysts.

5002 Automotive Engineering International [USA]
Society of Automotive Engineers
www.sae.org/automag [DESCRIPTION]
Monthly magazine with useful coverage of the industry.

5003 International Journal of Vehicle Design
Inderscience Publishers, Monthly. €1155.00. ISSN 01433369.
www.inderscience.com [DESCRIPTION]
One example of the publisher's very wide range of journals serviing this sector: the website lists a further 13 titles subject classified as 'Automotive'.
See website for details of journals in other areas of technology, including: Product development, materials and manufacturing; Control and intelligent systems; Simulation, computing applications and cognitive science; Internet, information technology and communications.

5004 Just-Auto.com
Aroq Ltd.
www.just-auto.com
Automotive industry news, analysis and research.

Biotechnology

biocatalysis • bioindustries • bionanotechnology • bioprocess engineering • biosafety • bioseparations science and engineering • cell culture • cloning • gene technology • genetic engineering • genetically modified organisms • industrial microbiology • nanobiotechnology • recombinant DNA

Introductions to the subject

5005 Basic biotechnology
C. Ratledge and B. Kristiansen, eds 2nd edn, Cambridge University Press, 2001, 568pp. £35.00. ISBN 0521779170.
Good wide-ranging multi-author introduction.
'the book is well presented, with clear and instructive diagrams and useful glossaries for those subject matters that come with their own specific nomenclature. It will certainly be a good resource for anybody who wants to study biotechnology or move into the field from another discipline.' (*Chemistry in Britain*)

Biomaterials science: an introduction to materials in medicine
B.D. Ratner [et al.], eds See entry no. 5778

Biomechanics: mechanical properties of living tissues
Y.C. Fung See entry no. 3633

5006 Bionanotechnology: lessons from nature
D.S. Goodsell Wiley-Liss, 2004, 337pp. $88.50. ISBN 047141719X.
Introductory text in three parts. The first explores the properties of the nanomachines that are naturally available in cells. In the second, those natural machines are looked to for guidance in building our own machines. Finally, there are two chapters on applications: one surveying some of the applications of bionanotechnology currently being pursued; the final chapter looking to the future.

5007 Bioprocess engineering: basic concepts
M.L. Shuler and F. Kargi 2nd edn, Prentice Hall, 2002, 553pp. $115.00. ISBN 0130819085.
Leading textbook, reflecting 'advances that are transforming

the field – from genomics to cellular engineering, modeling to non-conventional biological systems. It introduces techniques with wide applicability in pharmaceuticals, biologics, medicine, environmental engineering, and beyond.'

Series: Prentice-Hall International Series in the Physical and Chemical Engineering Sciences.

5008 Bioseparations science and engineering
R.G. Harrison [et al.] Oxford University Press, 2003, 406pp. £44.99. ISBN 0195123409.
'Bioseparations involves the separation and purification of compounds of biological origin, which are derived from cells grown in bioreactors or from cells contained in animal or plant tissue ... Bioproducts – chemical substances or combinations of substances made by living things – range from methanol to whole cells. They are derived by extraction from whole plants or animals or by synthesis in bioreactors containing cells or enzymes.'

Very good overview, structured: Introduction to bioproducts and bioseparations; Analytical methods; Cell lysis and flocculation; Filtration; Sedimentation; Extraction; Liquid chromatography and adsorption; Precipitation; Crystallization; Drying; Bioprocess design; Laboratory exercises in bioseparations.

Series: Topics in Chemical Engineering.

Giant molecules: essential materials for everyday living and problem solving
C.E. Carraher See entry no. 5055

Introduction to biomedical engineering
J.D. Enderle, S.M. Blanchard and J.D. Bronzino, eds See entry no. 3635

Introduction to food biotechnology
P. Johnson-Green See entry no. 3142

Introduction to food engineering
R.P. Singh and D.R. Heldman See entry no. 3143

5009 Plant biotechnology: the genetic manipulation of plants
A. Slater, N.W. Scott and M.R. Fowler Oxford University Press, 2003, 346pp. £24.99. ISBN 0199254680.
www.oup.com/uk/best.textbooks/biochemistry/slater [COMPANION]
Twelve chapters: Plant genomes – the organization and expression of plant genes; Plant tissue culture; Techniques for plant transformation; Binary vectors for plant transformation; The genetic manipulation of herbicide resistance; The genetic manipulation of pest resistance; Plant disease resistance; Reducing the effects of viral diseases; Strategies for stress tolerance; The improvement of crop yield and quality; Molecular farming/'pharming'; Future prospects for GM crops.
'Quite simply this is a superb book and a valuable resource for all those with an interest in the genetic modification of plants, either as students of the science or potential consumers of the produce ... and I defy anyone not to be drawn to the one case study on the development of the flatulence-free baked bean! In short a great book, well worth the money.' (*Microbiology Today*)

Principles of genome analysis and genomics
S.B. Primrose and R.M. Twyman See entry no. 2500

5010 A student's guide to biotechnology
Greenwood, 2002. 4 v., $160.00. ISBN 0313322562.
Four v. designed for school grades 6 to 12 in the USA: Words and terms; Important people in biotechnology; The history of biotechnology; Debatable issues.
'This much-needed four-volume set offers readers a wealth of well researched and clearly written information ... this set will serve students and instructors well towards learning and understanding about a difficult and often emotional subject. Recommended.' (*Library Media Connection*)

5011 Understanding biotechnology
A. Borém, F.R. Santos and D.E. Bowen Prentice Hall PTR, 2003, 216pp. $34.99. ISBN 0131010115.
Good wide-ranging introduction concentrating on the medical and health aspects of biotechnology. Sixteen chapters: History: from biology to biotechnology; Genetic engineering; Transformation; Biotechnological products; Biosafety; Cloning; Gene therapy; Pharmacogenomics; Molecular markers; DNA forensic; Bioremediation; Biotechnology and biodiversity; Bioinformatics; Bioterrorism; Patents; Bioethics.

- **Understanding biotechnology: an integrated and cyber-based approach G. Acquaah** Prentice Hall, 2004, 432pp. $36.50. ISBN 0130945005. http://vig.prenhall.com/catalog [DESCRIPTION]. Wider ranging 25 chapters in 5 main parts: Brief review of the underlying science; Enabling technologies of biotechnology; Approaches of biotechnology; Specific applications (food, human health and diagnostics, industrial, environmental); Social issues.

Dictionaries, thesauri, classifications

5012 Biotechnology from A to Z
W. Bains 3rd edn, Oxford University Press, 2004, 413pp. £25.00. ISBN 0198524986.
www.biotech-atoz.com [COMPANION]
Designed as an extended glossary or mini-encyclopedia. 300 well written entries ranging from ADEPT (antibody-directed enzyme prodrug therapy) to Zoonosis. Inter alia, an excellent introduction to the subject: 'Biotechnology is the application of our knowledge of biological processes. As our knowledge of the natural world grows, so it is applied to the pressing problems of our society – health, food, a safe and clean environment.'
'William Bains is to be congratulated on producing a wonderfully lucid guide to an exciting but blindingly complex industry.' (*New Scientist*)

CRC dictionary of agricultural sciences
R.A. Lewis See entry no. 2965

5013 The dictionary of gene technology: genomics, transcriptomics, proteomics
G. Kahl 3rd edn, Wiley, 2004, 1290pp. 2 v., $220.00. ISBN 3527307656.
More than 2500 terms added to the 6500 of the 2nd edn. 'Multiple cross-references enable a broad readership, layman and expert alike, to form networks linking the various terms in context and to understand relationships between gene technology and genetics, molecular genetics, biochemistry, biotechnology, microbiology and applied sciences.'

- **The encyclopedia of cell technology R.E. Spier, ed.** Wiley, 2000, 1280pp. $835.00. ISBN 0471161233. Two v. work which CHOICE said was 'a fine example of an extensive ... collection of review articles'. Wiley also published in 1999 a 5 v. *Encyclopedia of bioprocess technology*.

Laws, standards, codes

5014 Encyclopedia of ethical, legal, and policy issues in biotechnology
T.H. Murray and M.J. Mehlman, eds Wiley, 2000, 1132pp. 2 v., $750.00. ISBN 0471176125.
www.wiley.com/legacy/products/subject/reference/murray_index.html [DESCRIPTION]
Major resource with 112 multi-author entries arranged A–Z by title.
'Dr. Murray and Professor Mehlman have succeeded admirably in creating a comprehensive reference work that should appeal to the novice as well as the scholar.' (*The Journal of Legal Medicine*)
'It will be a major reference source, and may influence policy making and the way science and media establishments communicate with the public ... Highly recommended for all research or science/technical libraries.' (*Choice*)

5015 Intellectual property law and the life science industries: a twentieth century history
G. Dutfield Ashgate, 2003, 298pp. £55.00. ISBN 0754621111.
Excellent overview, structured: Introduction; Intellectual property in the global economy: high stakes and propaganda warfare; Intellectual property and regulation theory; The emergence of modern patent law; Organic chemistry and the synthetic dyestuff industry; The pharmaceutical industry; Biotechnology, genomics and the new life science corporations; Plant breeding, the seed industry, and plant breeders' rights; Towards a global IP regime: trade and diplomacy; Forums of resistance?; Epilogue: the life science industries in a patent-free world; Bibliography; Indices.
'this is a fascinating account which must inform the debate about the value of intellectual property ... an interesting and rewarding work, which, as well as contributing to the TRIPs debate, should stimulate further studies of the history of intellectual property.' (*Bio-Science Law Review*)

Patents for chemicals, pharmaceuticals and biotechnology: fundamentals of global law, practice and strategy
P. Grubb See entry no. 5080

Official & quasi-official bodies

5016 Biosafety Clearing-House
http://bch.biodiv.org
An 'information exchange mechanism established by the *Cartagena Protocol on Biosafety* to assist Parties to implement its provisions and to facilitate sharing of information on, and experience with, living modified organisms (LMOs)'. An LMO is defined in the Glossary as 'any living organism that possesses a novel combination of genetic material obtained through the use of modern biotechnology'.
An exceptionally well structured and rewarding site. Particularly useful and interesting are the linked to website about the Protocol itself; and the latest additions section within the News part of this site. There is a very good Toolkit with 'five tutorial modules created to help you use and understand the BCH website'. Among much else of value there is also an extensive annotated list of Relevant Sites and Tools.

5017 Biotechnology
www.oecd.org
One of OECD's Topics: 'The content on our Web site has been organized in two ways: by department and by topic ... The content provided under each of the department headings. is limited to the work produced by that specific department ... Several OECD departments, however, work on the same topic, but from different angles. If you are more interested in OECD-wide work on a particular subject, you should enter the Web site via one of the TOPICS. The work from all the relevant departments will be provided on that topic.'

Biotechnology and Biological Sciences Research Council
See entry no. 1912

5018 Biotechnology and Pharmaceuticals [UK]
Great Britain. Department of Trade and Industry
www.dti.gov.uk/sectors_biotechnology.html
One of the DTI's industries and sectors foci. 'The UK is one of the best places in the world for bioscience. The UK boasts an excellent science base, with favourable economic and political conditions, and a clear and fair regulatory regime. The UK currently has around 480 specialist biotechnology companies estimated to employ more than 23,000 people with revenue in 2001 of over £2.8 billion. UK companies account for 43% (194 out of 456) of products in the pipeline by European public companies. Also, 43% of new biotechnology drugs in Phase 3 clinical trials in Europe are from the UK.'

- **Agriculture and Environment Biotechnology Commission Agriculture and Environment Biotechnology Commission.** www.aebc.gov.uk. UK strategic advisory body on biotechnology issues affecting agriculture and the environment, considering ethical and social issues as well as science. Publish reports and minutes of meetings. Early 2005, its future was being debated after critical review.

5019 Biotechnology Australia
www.biotechnology.gov.au
Agency comprising five Australian Government partner departments (Agriculture, Fisheries and Forestry; Environment and Heritage; Health and Ageing; Industry, Tourism and Resources; and Science Education and Training). It was created to assist in co-ordinating the Government's approach to biotechnology, and reports to the Australian Government's Biotechnology Ministerial Council on its progress and achievements.

Research centres & institutes

Centre for Novel Agricultural Products
See entry no. 2977

Hastings Center
See entry no. 1916

National Institute of Biomedical Imaging and Bioengineering
See entry no. 3645

5020 Roslin Institute [UK]
www.roslin.ac.uk
Centre based in Edinburgh, Scotland, whose research 'aims

to provide new opportunities for three industry sectors: animal breeding, biotechnology and animal production. This research also informs national and international policy on animal welfare, the environment and genetic diversity'. It is one of eight research institutes in the UK sponsored by the BIOTECHNOLOGY AND BIOLOGICAL SCIENCES RESEARCH COUNCIL, and is famous for 'Dolly the Sheep', the first mammal cloned from an adult cell 'by transferring the nucleus of a body cell into an egg from which the nucleus has been removed'.

Good background information on cloning and related topics.

Associations & societies

Association of Applied Biologists
See entry no. 1921

5021 **Council for Biotechnology Information**
www.whybiotech.com
'Communicates science-based information about the benefits and safety of agricultural and food biotechnology. Its members are the leading biotechnology companies and trade associations.' Very well constructed site, its home page for instance having sections directed at: 'Consumers'; 'Farmers'; 'Journalists'; 'Teachers and students'.

5022 **European Association for Bioindustries**
www.europa-bio.be
Represents about 40 member companies operating worldwide and 24 national biotechnology associations – thereby becoming also 'the voice of 1500 small and medium-sized enterprises involved in research, development, testing, manufacturing and commercialization of biotechnology applications ... The common denominator among all our members is the use of biotechnology at any stage of research, development or manufacturing.'

Wide ranging site among much valuable data and information making a helpful distinction between:

Green Biotech 'Mainly involves the introduction of foreign genes into economically important plant species, resulting in crop improvement and the production of novel products in plants.'

Healthcare Biotech 'Increasingly playing a role in conventional drug discovery as well as opening up new possibilities to prevent, treat and cure hitherto incurable diseases using novel methods of treatment and diagnosis. Biotech medicines such as proteins, antibodies and enzymes now account for 20% of all marketed medicines and 50% of those in clinical trials.'

White Biotech 'An emerging field within modern biotechnology that serves industry. It uses living cells like moulds, yeasts or bacteria, as well as enzymes to produce goods and services. Living cells can be used as they are or improved to work as 'cell factories' to produce enzymes for industry. Living cells can also be used to make antibiotics, vitamins, vaccines and proteins for medical use.'

5023 **European Federation of Biotechnology**
www.efbweb.org
'The association of European scientific institutes, societies, companies, biotechnology associations and personal members active or interested in biotechnology and its safe and beneficial applications ... More than 3000 scientists and students throughout Europe currently participate in EFB's Sections according to their special topical interests. In addition, the EFB has set up a number of Task Groups which deal with, for example, Public Perception of Biotechnology and formulate high-quality information about the use and application of biotechnology as well as with related ethical and safety aspects.

Useful gateway – especially to views from outside the industry itself.

5024 **Institute of Biological Engineering** [USA]
www.ibeweb.org
Uses the definition: 'Biological engineering is the biology-based engineering discipline that integrates life sciences with engineering in the advancement and application of fundamental concepts of biological systems from molecular to ecosystem levels'. Relatively small set of useful resources.

Society for Applied Microbiology
See entry no. 2677

5025 **Society for Industrial Microbiology** [USA]
www.simhq.org
Founded 1949 and 'promotes the exchange of scientific information through workshops, meetings and publications, in such areas as fermentation processes, bioremediation/biodeterioration, recombinant DNA technology, secondary metabolism, biotransformation, QA/QC, cosmetic microbiology, the environment and food, among others'. Includes information about careers in industrial microbiology and a Kids' Zone that contains links to relevant resources aimed at children.

Portal & task environments

AgBiotechNet: the online service for agricultural biotechnology
CAB International See entry no. 3001

5026 **Bio.com: Life on the Net**
www.bio.com
Founded 1992 and 'remains the premier information portal to the life sciences with over 200,000 registered users and over 100,000 subscribers to our weekly newsletter. Over 70% of our profiled users have a doctoral-level education – over 85% classify themselves as research scientists'. Subsets of the site are titled: Bioengineering; Bioinformatics; Biotherapeutics; Drug discovery; Genomics; Immunotech; Proteomics.

BioethicsWeb
Wellcome Trust and Resource Discovery Network See entry no. 3490

Biomaterials Network
See entry no. 5816

5027 **BioSpace**
www.biospace.com
An overtly commercial portal focusing on 'recruitment, investment, product, event and other life science industry messages'. Within a busy but well structured site there is a useful Glossary 'developed to keep pace with the ever-evolving language of biotechnology' and containing some 1800 terms of which 75 have been designated as 'Basic

Terms': essential to understanding the biotechnology industry and 'defined in simple, easy to understand language'. The site also has a Term of the day.

5028 Biotechnology in Food and Agriculture
Food and Agriculture Organization
www.fao.org/biotech/index.asp?lang=en
News, documents, background information and a forum provide for current awareness in the use of biotechnology in agriculture.

5029 Biotechnology@nature.com
Nature Publishing Group.
www.nature.com/biotech
Gateway to all relevant NPG resources in the field of biotechnology. Accessible from the gateway is a series of web focuses, covering: Biomanufacturing and bioprocessing; Proteomics; RNAi; GM crops; Stem cells; Food and the future; The mouse genome; Proteomics technology; The Y chromosome.

- **The Nature Biotechnology Directory** www.guide.nature.com. Global information resource listing over 8000 organizations, product and service providers in the biotechnology industry.

CambridgeSoft
See entry no. 1680

Chemie.De Information Service
See entry no. 5093

5030 CropBiotech.Net
International Service for the Acquisition of Agri-biotech Applications
www.isaaa.org/kc
Service is a 'not-for-profit organization cosponsored by the public and private sector with an international network of centres designed to contribute to the alleviation of hunger and poverty by facilitating transfer of crop biotechnology applications to developing countries'. The site itself is the home of Global Knowledge Center on Crop Biotechnology: 'an information service that provides regular updates and information about the global status of crop biotechnology, products and issues, regular news, communication materials, and links to other information sources'.

5031 I-Bio: UK Information Biotechnology
www.i-bio.gov.uk
This site, produced by the UK Government, aims to provide a comprehensive source of biotechnology information. Information and links to relevant sites are organized under the headings 'Industry information', 'Investment profile', 'Academic research', 'Government policy', 'General knowledge' and 'Absolute beginners' (contains a glossary and examples such as GMOs and cloning). It also provides access to the *UK biotechnology regulatory atlas* which provides a guide to the regulations that govern the biotechnology industry.

- **UK biotechnology regulatory atlas** **Great Britain. Department of Trade and Industry and LGC.** http://plus.i-bio.gov.uk/ibioatlas. 'Easy-access guide to the main technical regulation affecting biotech companies, particularly those starting out without access to a full time regulatory affairs department'.

Information System Genetic Resources: GENRES
German Centre for Documentation and Information in Agriculture
See entry no. 3012

5032 Pew Initiative on Food and Biotechnology
Pew Charitable Trusts and University of Richmond
http://pewagbiotech.org
'Established in 2001 to be an independent and objective source of credible information on agricultural biotechnology for the public, media and policymakers ... The Initiative advocates neither for, nor against, agricultural biotechnology. Instead, the Initiative is committed to providing information and encouraging debate and dialogue so that consumers and policymakers can make their own informed decisions.'

PJB Publications
See entry no. 3720

Discovering print & electronic resources

5033 Biotechnobase
Elsevier/Embase, Weekly.
www.elsevier.com/wps/find [DESCRIPTION]
1.5 million bibliographic citations and author abstracts from 1980 to the present, with items included on a cover-to-cover basis from a core list of 280 journals devoted exclusively to biotechnology, plus selective coverage of some 4000 relevant journals from related disciplines. Indexing supported by specially developed Biotechnobase Thesaurus containing over 2000 terms and 500 synonyms.

5034 Biotechnology and Bioengineering Abstracts
CSA.
www.csa.com/factsheets/biotclust-set-c.php [DESCRIPTION]
Entries culled from relevant CSA publications, including: *Agricultural & Environmental Biotechnology Abstracts*; *ASFA Marine Biotechnology Abstracts*; *Bioengineering Abstracts*; *Genetics Abstracts*; *Medical & Pharmaceutical Biotechnology Abstracts*; *Microbiology Abstracts Section A: Industrial & Applied Microbiology*.

Chemical Engineering and Biotechnology Literature Database: CEABA-VtB
See entry no. 5099

Citeline.com
See entry no. 3724

5035 Derwent Biotechnology Abstracts
Thomson Derwent. Print, CD-ROM, and online availability.
http://scientific.thomson.com/support/products/biotechnology [DESCRIPTION]
Information abstracted from over 1200 of the world's leading scientific and technological journals, patents from 40 patent-issuing authorities, and international conferences and meetings. 'More than 30% of the records in Derwent Biotechnology Abstracts contain important worldwide patent information.' Free downloadable PDF copy of the *Derwent Biotechnology Abstracts Thesaurus* is available.

GENESEQ
See entry no. 2530

Highveld.com: the internet directory of molecular biology and biotechnology
See entry no. 2531

5036 **WWW Virtual Library: Biotechnology**
Cato Research.
www.cato.com/biotech
Well organized and relatively up-to-date site including links to sites concerning: Clinical trials and regulatory affairs; Education; Employment, recruitment and contract staffing; Genomics and proteomics; Pharmaceutical companies; Product development and clinical trial support; Software – as well as more general products and services, and sources of information.

Directories & encyclopedias

Directory of approved biopharmaceutical products
S. Spada and G. Walsh See entry no. 3734

Encyclopedia of agricultural, food and biological engineering
D.R. Heldman, ed. See entry no. 3043

Wiley encyclopedia of food science and technology
F.J. Francis, ed. See entry no. 3183

Handbooks & manuals

5037 **Biocatalysis**
A.S. Bommarius and B.R. Riebel Wiley-VCH, 2004, 611pp. $175.00. ISBN 3527303448.
In a very rapidly moving arena, the book – as it planned – successfully fills the gap between the research front and the area beyond basic courses in biochemistry, organic synthesis, molecular biology, kinetics, and reaction engineering. It also addresses well the challenges arising from the inter-disciplinary nature of biocatalysis – spanning as it does chemistry, biology, chemical engineering and bioengineering.

Each of the 20 chapters starts with a helpful 1–2 page summary and ends with a significant bibliography.

5038 **Biotechnology**
Biotechnology, Wiley, 1996, 10942pp. 12 v., $3375.00. ISBN 3527283102.
www.wiley.com/WileyCDA [DESCRIPTION]
Major wide-ranging treatise, good for historical coverage.

Current Protocols
See entry no. 1997

DECHEMA corrosion handbook: corrosive agents and their interaction with materials
See entry no. 5840

5039 **Enzymes in industry: production and applications**
W. Aehle 2nd edn, Wiley-VCH, 2004, 484pp. £105.00. ISBN 3527295925.
Seven sections: Introduction; Catalytic activity of enzymes; General production methods; Discovery and development of enzymes; Industrial enzymes; Non-industrial enzyme usage; Enzyme safety and regulatory considerations.
'The quality ... is so great that there is no hesitation in recommending it as ideal reading for any student requiring an introduction to enzymes ... Enzymes in Industry—should command a place in any library, industrial or academic, where it will be frequently used.' (*The Genetic Engineer and Biotechnologist*)

5040 **Handbook of culture media for food microbiology**
J.E.L. Corry, G.D.W. Curtis and R.M. Baird, eds 2nd edn, Elsevier, 2003, 663pp. £166.00. ISBN 0444510842.
Written by the Working Party on Culture Media of the International Committee on Food Microbiology and Hygiene, this is 'a handy reference for microbiologists wanting to know which media to use for the detection of various groups of microbes in food, and how to check their performance'.
Series: Progress in Industrial Microbiology, 37.

5041 **Handbook of fungal biotechnology**
D.K. Arora, P.D. Bridge and D. Bhatnagar, eds 2nd edn, Marcel Dekker, 2004, 592pp. $229.95. ISBN 0824740181.
Covers molecular technologies, commercial fungal applications, medical mycology, culture collections, legal aspects, and biosafety. Agriculture, food and environmental biotechnology are treated in a companion volume: *Fungal biotechnology in agricultural, food, and environmental applications*.

5042 **Handbook of industrial cell culture: mammalian, microbial, and plant cells**
V. Vinci and S.R. Parekh, eds Humana Press, 2003, 536pp. $204.00. ISBN 1588290328.
www.humanapress.com
Major current and evolving technologies for improving the biocatalytic capabilities of mammalian, microbial, and plant cells.
Check the website for details of the publisher's wide range of other relevant reference texts.
'This book provides an updated, informative and practical knowledge of mammalian, microbial and plant cell culture methods for industrial use. The handbook can prove useful for students and experienced biotechnology professionals who are interested in industrial cell culture. The book is a great starting point and will be a useful addition to university libraries.' (*E-STREAMS*)

5043 **Handbook of plant biotechnology**
P. Christou and H.J. Klee, eds Wiley, 2004, 1420pp. 2 v, $830.00. ISBN 047185199X.
Valuable treatise whose chapters are organized into 11 parts: Introduction to plant biotechnology; Plant genetic modification: transgenes and transformation; Plant genetic modification: gene isolation; Agronomic traits; Quality and yield; Developmental traits; A production system for industrial and pharmaceutical proteins; Non-food crops; Risk assessment of transgeneic crops; Commercialization; Plant biotechnology in developing countries.

Managing global genetic resources: agricultural crop issues and policies
Committee on Managing Global Genetic Resources See entry no. 3050

5044 **Molecular biotechnology: principles and applications of recombinant DNA**
B.R. Glick and J.J. Pasternak; American Society for Microbiology 3rd edn, ASM Press, 2003, 784pp. $89.95. ISBN 1555812244.
Covers underlying scientific principles and industrial, agricultural, pharmaceutical, and biomedical applications of recombinant DNA technology.

5045 Nanobiotechnology: concepts, applications and perspectives
C.M. Niemeyer and C.A. Mirkin, eds Wiley-VCH, 2004, 469pp. £105.00. ISBN 3527306587.
Multi-authored text with 27 chapters organized into four parts: Interphase systems; Protein-based nanostructures; DNA-based nanostructures; Nanoanalytics.

Standard handbook of biomedical engineering and design
M. Kutz, ed. See entry no. 3670

Keeping up-to-date

Annual review of biomedical engineering
See entry no. 3672

Annual Review of Materials Research
See entry no. 5861

5046 Trends in Biotechnology
Elsevier, Monthly. €1171.00. ISBN 01677799.
http://www.trends.com/tibtech/default.htm [DESCRIPTION]
'As in the successful biotechnology companies and leading academic research groups, *Trends in Biotechnology* reflects the view that biotechnology is the integrated use of many biological technologies – from molecular genetics to biochemical engineering. This integration is essential for the effective translation of novel research into application.'

Chemical Engineering & Chemical Technology

adhesives • agrochemicals • chemical industry • chemical process technology • chemical products • chemical reactors • chemical technology • coatings • colloids • colour chemistry • cosmetic chemistry • dyes & dyeing • fine chemicals • green chemistry • industrial chemistry • mixing • oil chemistry • paints • petrochemicals • pigments • plastics • polymer chemistry • polymers • powders • process technology • rubber

Introductions to the subject

5047 Chemical engineering fluid mechanics
R. Darby 2nd edn, Marcel Dekker, 2001, 584pp. $75.00. ISBN 0824704444.
Good introduction for those new to chemical engineering.
'the author has succeeded in producing a pragmatic, wide-ranging, concise, and cohesive undergraduate textbook, replete with homework problems, on process fluid flows ... This specialized textbook on process flows is more comprehensive and effective than chapters in general books (on 1st edn).' (*Applied Mechanics Reviews*)

5048 The chemical industries 1900–1930: international growth and technological change
L.F. Haber Clarendon Press, 1971, 452pp. ISBN 0198581335.
A continuation of a volume on the 19th century, also from Clarendon Press. International survey but dwells particularly on Germany, Great Britain and USA. Emphasis is economic rather than technological.

5049 Chemistry of polymers
J.W. Nicholson; Royal Society of Chemistry 2nd edn, 1997, 190pp. £19.95. ISBN 0854045589.
A concise introduction to the subject which helps to give a rapid overview of the field. Covers synthesis, characterization, reaction kinetics and materials science, as well as important specialized topics such as polymer degradation, polymers and pollution, and a variety of technological developments.

5050 Chemistry, society and environment: a new history of the British chemical Industry
C.A. Russell, ed. Royal Society of Chemistry, 2000, 372pp. £70.00. ISBN 0854045996.
www.rsc.org/is/books/chemsocenviron.htm [DESCRIPTION]
Attempts to analyse effects of chemical industry on society in general. One of few publications to critically evaluate development of industrial chemistry in the UK in the context of its effects on the environment.

5051 The expanding world of chemical engineering
S. Furusaki, J. Garside and L.-S. Fan 2nd edn, Taylor & Francis, 2001, 352pp. £36.00. ISBN 1560329173.
Multi-authored text providing useful introduction to recent developments and future prospects.

5052 Fundamentals of chemical reaction engineering
M.E. Davis and R.J. Davs, ed. McGraw-Hill, 2003, 384pp. $126.25. ISBN 007245007X.
Well reviewed introduction.

5053 Fundamentals of heat and mass transfer
F.P. Incropera and D.P. DeWitt Wiley, 2002, 981pp. Includes software package, $141.95. ISBN 0471386502.
Standard well used manual giving comprehensive coverage with hundreds of problems to be solved.

5054 The fundamentals of polymer engineering
A. Ram Kluwer Academic, 1997, 264pp. £46.00. ISBN 0306457261.
Good basic introduction to the world of polymers, covering: The chemistry of polymers; Structure and characterization of polymers; Compounding and processing of plastics; Description of major plastics; Structure; Properties and utilization; Plastics and ecology.

5055 Giant molecules: essential materials for everyday living and problem solving
C.E. Carraher 2nd edn, Wiley-Interscience, 2003, 483pp. $120.00. ISBN 0471273996.
'Today, a scientific and technological revolution is occurring, and at its center are giant molecules. This revolution is occurring in medicine, communication, building, transportation, and so on. Understanding the principles behind this revolution is within the grasp of each of us and it is presented in this book.'
The text is truly written for the layman and seems to work well. Includes coverage of plastics, rubbers, paints, composites, as well as biological macromolecules. There is a short appendix: Electronic websites.
Rev. edn of Giant molecules *(R.B. Seymour, C.E. Carraher, 1990).*

5056 A history of the international chemical industry: from the early days to 2000
F. Aftalion Chemical Heritage Press, 2001, 442pp. Translated by Otto Theodor Benfey, $19.95. ISBN 0941901297.

A good short history of the chemical industry from the viewpoint of the chemicals produced with much interesting information on the contributions that chemistry has made to society.

5057 Industrial organic chemicals
H.A. Wittcoff, R.G. Reuben and J.S. Plotkin 2nd edn, Wiley, 2004, 662pp. $142.00. ISBN 0471443859.
www.wiley.com/WileyCDA [DESCRIPTION]
Excellent introduction to the whole field. Especially useful for newcomers to the area is the opening section 'How to use Industrial Organic Chemicals' giving a very helpful historical perspective.

The website – as well as leading to a good description of this text – is also an entrée to Wiley's extremely extensive set of texts in 'Chemical Engineering', 'Industrial Chemistry', 'Polymer Science and Technology', and so on.

- **Industrial organic chemistry K. Weissermel and H.-J. Arpe** 4th edn, Wiley-VCH, 2003, 491pp. $175.00. ISBN 3527305785. 'They have provided a book that is interesting reading as well as being an excellent reference. It is a highly recommended book, which I hope the authors will find the energy to continue updating on a regular basis.' *Chemistry in Britain*.

5058 Introduction to chemical engineering thermodynamics
J.M. Smith, H.C. Van Ness and M. Abbott 6th edn, McGraw-Hill, 2001, 816pp. $140.31. ISBN 0072402962.
http://books.mcgraw-hill.com
Well established comprehensive overview.

Website gives access to McGraw-Hill's wide range of chemical and biochemical texts – as well as their other offerings.

5059 An introduction to industrial chemistry
A. Heaton, ed. 3rd edn, Blackie Academic & Professional, 1996, 416pp. ISBN 0751402729.
Although now dated, a well crafted overview delivered by an experienced author and editor. Good historical background.

Introduction to materials engineering and science for chemical and materials engineers
B.S. Mitchell See entry no. 5781

5060 Inventing polymer science: Staudinger, Carothers, and the emergence of macromolecular science
Y. Furukawa University of Pennsylvania Press, 1998, 310pp. ISBN 0812233360.
Very good historical introduction to the subject.
Series: The Chemical Sciences in Society.

'Today we take for granted the existence of enormously long polymer molecules, which can be many millions of times larger than water, carbon dioxide and other so-called ordinary molecules. Yet as recently as the 1920s, the chemical community regarded with derision the idea that a single molecule could be so huge. This resistance to polymers had always been an enigma to me—until I read Yasu Furukawa's meticulously researched historiography.' (*American Scientist*)

5061 Organic chemistry principles and industrial practice
M.M. Green and H.A. Wittcoff Wiley, 2003, 341pp. $54.95. ISBN 3527302891.
Excellent introduction. Chapters are: What the experts say about this book; How petroleum is converted into useful materials: carbocations and free radicals are the keys; Polymerization, polypropylene and the principles of stereochemistry; The central role of electrophilic aromatic substitution; From nucleophilic chemistry to cross-linking, with a side trip to glycerol, in the synthesis of commercially important plastics; The nylon story; Competition for the best industrial synthesis of methyl methacrylate; Natural rubber and other elastomers; Ethylene and propylene: two very different kinds of chemistry; The demise of acetaldehyde: a story of how the chemical industry evolves; Doing well by doing good; An epilogue—the future.

'it is a fascinating presentation that is easy to read and keeps the reader alert by providing the historical details that put the industrial procedures into perspective.' (*Clinical Chemistry*)

5062 Physical and chemical equilibrium for chemical engineers
N. De Nevers Wiley, 2002, 474pp. $110.00. ISBN 0471071706.
Good coverage of the basic underlying physical chemistry.

5063 Polymers: the environment and sustainable development
A. Azapagic, A. Emsley and I. Hamerton Wiley, 2003, 219pp. $65.00. ISBN 0471877417.
In light of new regulations in the EU, America, and Japan, polymer producers have been forced to recycle. This book provides discussion on the impact of reusing polymers such as plastic and rubber on the environment.

5064 Polymers and the environment
G. Scott; Royal Society of Chemistry 1999, 132pp. £19.95. ISBN 0854045783.
www.chemsoc.org/networks/learnnet/poly-env.htm [DESCRIPTION]
Reviews properties and industrial applications of polymers in the context of environmental benefits compared with traditional materials. Covers polymer recycling processes for waste minimization and biodegradable polymers. Introduces non-specialist reader to benefits and limitations of polymeric materials from an environmental viewpoint.

5065 Principles of heat transfer
F. Kreith and M.S. Bohn 6th edn, Brooks/Cole, 2001, 864pp. $129.95. ISBN 0534375960.
Now standard overview.

5066 Principles of polymer systems
F. Rodriguez [et al.] 5th edn, Taylor & Francis, 2003, 760pp. £40.00. ISBN 1560329394.
Now produced by a team of authors, this standard text covers the whole of basic polymer science and technology. As well as the citations specific to each chapter's focus, there are also within most sets of more General references. Good subject index. Classic work.

5067 Reactor design for chemical engineers
J.M. Winterbottom and M.B. King CRC Press, 1999, 442pp. $54.95. ISBN 0748739920.
'Intended primarily for undergraduate chemical-engineering students, this book also includes material which bridges the gap between undergraduate and graduate requirements. The introduction contains a listing of the principal types of reactors employed in the chemical industry, with diagrams and examples of their use. There is then a brief exploration of the concepts employed in later sections for modelling and sizing reactors, followed by basic information on stoichiometry and thermodynamics, and the kinetics of homogeneous and catalyzed reactions. Subsequent chapters

are devoted to reactor sizing and modelling in some simple situations, and more detailed coverage of the design and operation of the principal reactor types.'

5068 Scaling up: the Institution of Chemical Engineers and the rise of a new profession
C. Divall and S.F. Johnston Kluwer Academic, 2000, 347pp. £104.00. ISBN 0792366921.
'Chemical engineering – as a recognised skill in the workplace, as an academic discipline, and as an acknowledged profession – is scarcely a century old. Yet from a contested existence before the First World War, chemical engineering had become one of the "big four" engineering professions in Britain, and a major contributor to Western economies, by the end of the twentieth century.'
Series: Chemists and Chemistry, V. 20.

5069 Seymour/Carraher's polymer chemistry
C.E. Carraher 6th edn, Marcel Dekker, 2003, 913pp. $84.95. ISBN 0824708067.
Standard comprehensive text, covering both theory and application. Useful introduction on Polymer nomenclature. Appendix K is a brief coverage of Electronic education – websites.

Dictionaries, thesauri, classifications

5070 Dictionary of chemical engineering: English, French, German, Spanish
A.L. Lydersen and I. Dahlø Wiley, 1992, 250pp. ISBN 0471933929.
'An expansion and up-to-date revision of a corresponding Norwegian dictionary by the same authors in 1988.' About 1200 English-base terms, with equivalents and indexes in the other languages. Includes word use in the manufacturing industries and skilled trades within chemical engineering.

5071 Dictionary of chemistry and chemical technology in six languages: English, German, Spanish, French, Polish, Russian
Z. Sobecka and W. Choinski, eds Pergamon, 1966, 1325pp. ISBN 0080116000.
11,987 numbered entries in English, with the five other language equivalents across the double page, and given index entries. Categorized terms, notes differences in meaning and gives genders of nouns. Omits English terms that have no corresponding expressions in one or other of the foreign languages.

5072 Dictionary of colloid and interface science
L.L. Schramm Wiley-Interscience, 2001, 218pp. $84.95. ISBN 0471394068.
300 terms, with tables, references, and a biographical section designed to put important developments in colloid and interface science into historical perspective.
Previous edn published as The language of colloid and interface science *(American Chemical Society, 1993).*

5073 Dictionary of named processes in chemical technology
A.E. Comyns Oxford University Press, 1993, 338pp. ISBN 0198553854.
About 5000 terms defined and occasionally explained. Some carry references to journal articles and patent numbers. Appendix Key to products, pp 309–338.

- **Encyclopedic dictionary of named processes in chemical technology A.E. Comyns** 2nd edn, CRC Press, 1999, 303pp. $139.95. ISBN 0849312051. Revised edn of the Dictionary.

5074 Dictionary of process technology in four languages: English, German, French, Russian
K. Hartman [et al.] Elsevier, 1989, 319pp. ISBN 0444988882.
Over 8000 English-base terms; indexes.

5075 English–Russian dictionary of chemistry and chemical technology
V.V. Kafarov Russo, 2002, 532pp. $103.50. ISBN 5887212136.
Contains about 65,000 terms.

5076 Gardner's chemical synonyms and trade names
G.W.A. Milne, ed. 11th edn, Ashgate, 1999, 1440pp. £185.00. ISBN 0566082195.
http://eu.wiley.com/WileyCDA [DESCRIPTION]
Covers over 35,000 chemicals, but not drugs. Gives name, CAS Registry Number, EINECS Number, formula, trade names, functions, applications and physical properties, with cross-reference entries from trade name to main name entry. One of the best known and most widely used sources of information on chemicals in commerce.
Now available from Wiley: see website.

- **Gardner's digital handbook of chemical synonyms and trade names** £195.00. ISBN 0566082195. Version 2.0. Includes 5300 drug compounds from the publisher's *Drugs: synonyms and properties* ISBN: 0566084910.

Lexique des pipelines à terre et en mer (Glossary of onshore and offshore pipelines)
See entry no. 4745

5077 Technological dictionary of plastics materials
W.V. Titow Pergamon, 1998, 398pp. £130.00. ISBN 0080418910.
Useful compendium. Three parts: Technical terms (Introduction; Definitions of terms); Abbreviated terms (letter symbols) for the base polymers and other components of plastics materials, and some miscellaneous abbreviations and acronyms of relevance to plastics; Trade names. Appendices (Official standards; References).

5078 The thesaurus of chemical products
M. Ash and I. Ash 2nd edn, Edward Arnold, 1992, 1200pp. v. 1 Chemical to tradename reference; v. 2 Tradename to chemical cross-reference and manufacturers' directory, £425.00. ISBN 0340583029.
Includes 40,000 international trade names by which more than 6000 generic chemicals are known and marketed worldwide. Also has a separate listing of trade name products containing the chemical entry as a major constituent.

Laws, standards, codes

Chemical Hazards Communication Society
See entry no. 4231

5079 ifi CLAIMS Patent Services [USA]
Wolters Kluwer Health.
www.ificlaims.com [DESCRIPTION]
Covers: All chemical patents since 1950; All utility patents since 1963; Complete collection of US patents issued from 1971–74, including 96,000 records that are missing from

the USPTO online database; All design and plant patents since December 1976.

5080 Patents for chemicals, pharmaceuticals and biotechnology: fundamentals of global law, practice and strategy
P. Grubb 4th edn, Oxford University Press, 2004. £59.00. ISBN 0199273782.
New edition of standard work which 'provides vital updating to take account of the latest legal developments, while retaining the focus upon the relevant technology and industry practices in this sector that sets it apart from more general books on patent law and procedure'. The author is European Patent Attorney and Intellectual Property Counsel at the pharmaceutical company Novartis, Switzerland.

WebInsight
See entry no. 1768

Research centres & institutes

5081 Paint Research Association [UK]
www.pra.org.uk
Known from 1971 by this title but in 2004 became the PRA Coatings Technology Centre. Is now 'the world's largest independent centre for coatings technology. Our membership of over 130 companies includes coatings manufacturers, raw material and equipment suppliers, applicators and end-users'.

- **British Coatings Federation** www.coatings.org.uk. Represents 130 companies, which produce about 90% of the UK output of coatings and printing inks. Useful resources, including downloadable PDF *The BCF Printing Ink Product Name Register*.
- **Federation of Societies for Coatings Technology** www.coatingstech.org. Nicely presented collection of useful resources including publications and links to the sites of the 27 constituent societies. List of North American universities/research facilities.

5082 Rapra Technology [UK]
www.rapra.net
Now Europe's leading independent plastics and rubber consultancy; formerly the Rubber and Plastics Research Association. Produce wide range of valuable resources, including books, journals, software, etc.

- **The polymer lexicon V. Beddoes, comp.** Rapra Technology, 1998, 202pp. £50.00. ISBN 1859571360. '5000+ references have been compiled from the journals, books, trade magazines, reports, data sheets and directories covering rubber and plastics, which are used to create abstracts for the Rapra Abstracts Database'.
- **Polymer Library** www.polymerlibrary.com [FEE-BASED]. 850,000 records dating back to 1972; approximately 32,000 new records added every year (roughly 1200 every two weeks). Was known as Rapra Abstracts.
- **Polymer Search on the Internet** www.polymer-search.com/home/default.asp. Free service. 'Only sites that offer considerable content directly related to rubber, plastics or adhesives are indexed. Each website submitted for inclusion in PSI will be vetted before inclusion in the search engine.'

Associations & societies

5083 American Institute of Chemical Engineers
www.aiche.org
Founded 1908; now has more than 50,000 members. Wide range of publications and other services. In 2004, entered into agreement with American Society of Mechanical Engineers for their delivery of AIChE's continuing education public seminars, on-site courses and e-learning CD-ROMs. More than 200 companies participate in four Industry Technology Alliances covering: Process safety, including safety and chemical engineering education; Sustainable development and environmental stewardship; Emergency relief systems; Thermophysical property data, evaluation of measurement.

- **Design Institute for Physical Properties** www.aiche.org/dippr. Mission is 'to develop the world's best source of critically evaluated thermophysical and environmental property data. Data and estimation methods developed are used by leading chemical, petroleum, and pharmaceutical companies throughout the world'.

5084 American Oil Chemists' Society
www.aocs.org
Mission is 'to be a global forum to promote the exchange of ideas, information, and experience, to enhance personal excellence, and to provide high standards of quality among those with a professional interest in the science and technology of fats, oils, surfactants, and related materials'. Pleasant nicely laid out site providing good range of up-to-date information.

5085 American Plastics Council
www.americanplasticscouncil.org
Much valuable background information in sections labelled: About plastics; Plastics in your life; Industry statistics; Classroom; Plastics and the environment; etc. These are supplemented by six Topics areas of the site: Child safety; Food safety; Medical uses; Automotive; Sports performance and safety; Home and garden. A well thought out site.

- **British Plastics Federation** www.bpf.co.uk. Leading trade association of the UK plastics industry – representing approximately 80% of turnover. Colourful website providing good entrée to information about the industry.
- **Society of Plastics Engineers** www.4spe.org. Founded 1942 and 'home to more than 20,000 plastics professionals in the United States and more than 70 countries around the world'. Good range of publications.
- **Society of the Plastics Industry** www.socplas.org. US-based plastics industry trade association. 'The US plastics industry employs 1.4 million workers and provides more than $310 billion in annual shipments.'

AVS Science and Technology Society
See entry no. 5804

5086 European Chemical Industry Council
www.cefic.org
Represents about 40,000 large, medium and small chemical companies which employ about two million people and account for more than 30% of world chemical production. Made up of the national chemical industry federations of 25 countries in Europe (including three associate member federations in Bulgaria, Estonia and Lithuania) as well as international corporate and business members. As an umbrella organization, Cefic has also recognized about 100 sector groups and affiliated associations.

Has useful information on issues such as education, the environment, research, energy, transport, international trade and economics accompanied by facts and figures.

5087 Institution of Chemical Engineers [UK]
www.icheme.org
Founded 1922, and now has membership approaching 25,000 in more than 80 countries. Apart from their publications they offer a useful portal to a wide range of different types of products and services.

5088 International Federation of Societies of Cosmetic Chemists
www.ifscc.org
Useful site about an organization which now represents activity in 44 countries and has over 14,000 individual members.

- **KOSMET** www.ifscc.org/kosmet. Bibliographic database which specializes in the scientific aspects of the cosmetics industry. Coverage includes trading and product development information in addition to formulations, analysis, toxicology and dermatology.

North American Catalysis Society
See entry no. 1875

5089 Society of Chemical Industry [UK]
www.soci.org
A 'unique international forum where science meets business on independent, impartial ground. It offers an exchange of information between sectors as diverse as food and agriculture, pharmaceuticals, biotechnology, environmental science and safety. Originally established in 1881, SCI (Society of Chemical Industry) is a registered charity with Members in over 70 countries.'

Very rich site, very well laid out. Wide range of publications; good news section; extensive range of Special Interest Groups – 23 groups including: BioActive sciences; Consumer and sensory research; Fine chemicals; Fire research; Materials chemistry; Oils and fats; Young chemists' panel. Well worth exploring.

- **Chemical Industries Association** www.cia.org.uk. Trade association and employers' organization representing member company interests both nationally and internationally. Advice on EU chemicals policy, best practice, profitability, health and safety, sustainable development, public image/perception, etc.
- **Chemistry & Industry** Biweekly. £412.00. ISSN 00093068. www.chemind.org/CI. Well established source of news, comment, analysis.

5090 Society of Dyers and Colourists [UK]
www.sdc.org.uk
The only international professional society specializing in all aspects of colour. Founded in 1884, granted a Royal Charter of Incorporation in 1963. The SDC is a registered charity and its aims and objectives are 'to advance the science of colour' in the broadest sense.

- **ColourClick** www.colourclick.org. Useful offering from the Society which is a 'simple, easy-to-use tool that keeps you up-to-date with all the latest trends and developments or, if you prefer, can provide you with a deeper understanding and insight into the fascinating world of colour'.

Portal & task environments

BioMatNet: biological materials for non-food products
European Commission. Directorate for Research See entry no. 3091

5091 Bulk-online: The Powder/Bulk Portal
www.bulk-online.com
Comprehensive well laid out site.

5092 Chemical Industry Education Centre [UK]
www.uyseg.org/ciec_home.htm
Joint initiative of the University of York and the Chemical Industries Association founded in 1988. Its aims are to: Enhance the effective teaching of science and technology; Create enthusiasm in school students and children for science and technology; Generate an improved level of understanding between schools and the chemical industry; Create a better understanding of the nature and role of the chemical industry within society. Well structured (and interestingly designed) website providing excellent entrée to the industry.

Chemical Propulsion Information Agency
Johns Hopkins University See entry no. 4921

5093 Chemie.De Information Service
www.chemie.de
Founded 1997 by Association for the Promotion of a German Research Network (DFN) with the aim of gathering and structuring chemical information from the Internet; incorporated as limited company, 2000. Now develops intelligent software systems for classification, evaluation, filtering, structuring and processing of digital content as well as innovative portal technology and retrieval systems.

The chemical news and product services accessible have strong German focus; but there are a number of website offerings worth exploring including a chemistry search engine and an extensive collection of specialized German/English dictionaries provided in conjunction with the publisher Langenscheidt.

Other information services marketed include similar Bionity.COM, oriented towards the biotechnology and pharmacy industries, plus recruitment services for the chemical, biotech and pharmaceutical industries.

5094 ChemIndustry.com
www.chemindustry.com
Comprehensive directory and search engine for chemical and related industry professionals. Provides access to over 45,000 chemical industry related entities which contain the full text of millions of pages. Specialized search services for chemical names, jobs, market research, consultants, etc. Valuable compendium which claims to be the most visited chemical industry-related site on the web.

ChemSpy.com: The internet navigator for the chemical industry
See entry no. 1682

FIZ CHEMIE Berlin
See entry no. 1683

Johnson Matthey
See entry no. 4693

5095 Plastics.com
www.plastics.com
Site produced by private US company which aims to 'embrace all materials, all processes and all plastics professionals worldwide'. Very well structured rich site

organized into three main areas: Plastics community; Plastics searches; Plastics resources.

5096 **Polysort: The Power of Many**
www.polysort.com
Online community for the plastics and rubber industry, providing news, links and networking opportunities.

Discovering print & electronic resources

5097 **APOLLIT: Applied Polymers Literature**
FIZ Karlsruhe, Fortnightly.
www.fiz-technik.de/en_db/d_dkii.htm [DESCRIPTION]
References to the production, applications, and technological properties of plastics, rubbers and fibres, the fundamental physical and chemical properties of polymers, and environmental and economic aspects of plastics. Abstracts in English or German are included for references from 1979 to 1996; those from 1997 to the present are in English.

5098 **CHEMENG Cluster**
STN.
www.cas.org/ONLINE/CATALOG/CLUSTERS/chemeng.html
A useful array of 22 major and less major databases which can be searched as a cluster.

Chemical Abstracts Service
See entry no. 1689

5099 **Chemical Engineering and Biotechnology Literature Database: CEABA-VtB**
DECHEMA Gesellschaft für Chemische Technik und Biotechnologie e.V.
www.dechema.de/ceaba_vtb-lang-en.html [DESCRIPTION]
Covers the international scientific and technical literature on chemical and process engineering and biotechnology comprising major aspects including analytics, processes and environment.

Chemical Safety NewsBase
Royal Society of Chemistry See entry no. 4273

5100 **ChemVillage**
Elsevier Engineering Information Inc..
www.chemvillage.org/c/s/C
Gateway access to a wide range of Elsevier and some other resources including: Beilstein Abstracts; Chemical Business NewsBase (700 trade magazines, financial reports, newspapers, etc.); Chimica (600 chemistry and chemical engineering journals); CRC handbooks (extensive set); Lexis-Nexis Chemical Industry News; Patents (US and European Patent Offices); Scirus.

5101 **International directory of chemical engineering URLs**
University of Karlsruhe
www.ciw.uni-karlsruhe.de/chem-eng.html#Research
Very useful checklist, recently updated; good categorization.

Digital data, image & text collections

5102 **Synapse Chemical Library**
M. Ash and I. Ash
www.synapseinfo.com/indexfr.htm [DESCRIPTION]
Comprehensive range of directories and handbooks, examples of which are listed below.

- **Chemical manufacturers directory of trade name products**
- **Handbook of adhesive chemical and compounding ingredients**
- **Handbook of cosmetic and personal care additives**
- **Handbook of fillers, extenders and diluents**
- **Handbook of green chemicals**
- **Handbook of industrial surfactants**
- **Handbook of paint and coating raw materials**
- **Handbook of plastic and rubber additives**
- **Handbook of solvents**
- **Specialty chemicals source book**

Directories & encyclopedias

5103 **Aldrich handbook of fine chemicals**
Sigma-Aldrich Co.
www.sigmaaldrich.com [REGISTRATION]
Well established directory listing over 40,000 products. Also includes section on laboratory equipment, books and computer products.
One of a wide range of directories available from the company. Similar publications are produced by other leading chemicals manufacturers.

5104 **Ashford's dictionary of industrial chemicals**
R.D. Ashford 2nd edn, Wavelength Publications, 2001, 1269pp. (Also CD-ROM: ISBN 0952267411; £230.00), £110.00. ISBN 095226742X.
http://home.btclick.com/wavelength [COMPANION]
Intended as a reference book to provide a concise source of information on industrial chemicals this dictionary has over 8360 different entries with information on virtually all of the industrial chemicals used today. It covers plastics, resins, solvents, lubricants, pesticides, drugs, dyes, explosives, curing agents, plastic additives and surfactants, as well as the intermediates used in their manufacture. Each entry has information on the manufacturing routes used industrially and the raw materials employed.

Cross-referencing allows a chemical's family tree to be traced back to the primary raw materials, to search for by-products and co-products, or to learn how a product is used in downstream applications.

5105 **Chem Sources chemical directory**
Chemical Sources International.
www.chemsources.com [FEE-BASED]
'Chem Sources was conceived in a small office on Wall Street in New York City in 1958. As a purchasing agent, it was a difficult and time consuming task to find available chemicals on the market, yet alone their manufacturers. Then there was the costly and often aggravating attempt to contact each company for order information. The need for an all-in-one directory was obvious. Chem Sources was thus created to meet that need. It has evolved into the most authoritative and widely recognized chemical source directory among purchasing agents, chemists, researchers and industrialists.'

5106 **Condensed encyclopedia of polymer engineering terms**
N.P. Cheremisinoff Butterworth-Heinemann, 2001, 362pp. £79.99. ISBN 0750672102.
An overview of the nature, manufacture, structure,

properties, processing and applications of commercially available polymers. Containing topics from both theory and practice, it should enable scientists to understand the commercial implications of their work.

'an excellent general reference resource for engineers, chemists, technologists, and technicians, as well as students. Working definitions and explanations are given for nearly four hundred terms typically encountered in the industry. Most terms are also cross-referenced to other terminology so the reader can locate other areas as well. A wealth of tables, graphs and figures are liberally sprinkled throughout the book.' (*SAMPE Journal*)

Dictionary of renewable resources
H. Zoebelein, ed. See entry no. 4800

5107 Encyclopedia of agrochemicals
J.R. Plimmer, D.W. Gammon and N.R. Ragsdale, eds Wiley-Interscience, 2003, 1638pp. 3 v., $1045.00. ISBN 0471193631.
www.knovel.com
Intended to serve principally as a source of chemical information, but toxicology, metabolism, biotechnology, regulatory and environmental aspects are also covered. Bibliography and further reading with each article. Good use of diagrams – including for chemical formulae. Detailed index.

Available online: see website.

'truly does provide whatever you want to know about agricultural chemicals and chemical technology.' (*Veterinary and Human Toxicology*)

5108 Encyclopedia of chemical processing and design
J.J. McKetta and W.A. Cunningham, eds Marcel Dekker, 1976–2002.
www.dekker.com
Now classic multi-volume encyclopedia, more restricted in scope than Kirk-Othmer. Each volume has 20–30 contributors, most recruited from industry. Many articles are reprinted from *Chemical Engineering* and other journals.

The publishers have announced a five volume 2nd edn Encyclopedia of chemical processing*: see website.*

Encyclopedia of pharmaceutical technology
J. Swarbrick and J.C. Boylan, eds See entry no. 3736

5109 Encyclopedia of polymer science and technology
J.I. Kroschwitz, ed. 3rd edn, Wiley-Interscience, 2003–2004. 12 v., $4200.00. ISBN 0471275077.
www3.interscience.wiley.com [FEE-BASED]
The purpose of the encyclopedia remains as for the 1st edn, which began publication in 1964, and the 2nd, published 1985–1990: 'To present authoritative articles, written and reviewed by specialists from all over the world, to serve as a unique source of reference to the entire field of polymer science and technology.' In this edn 'the growth of the importance of biological topics is reflected as well'.

Because of the opportunity of publishing online, the print schedule for this edn was changed: see the website.

Hawley's condensed chemical dictionary
R.J. Lewis, ed. See entry no. 1709

5110 Kirk-Othmer encyclopedia of chemical technology
J.I. Kroschwitz [et al.], eds 5th edn, Wiley-Interscience, 2004–. 27 v, $6075.00. ISBN 0471484946.
www.mrw.interscience.wiley.com/kirk
The major treatise in this arena, alongside Ullmann. Indexed by subject and CAS Registry Numbers, has substantial articles on wide variety of subjects including chemical substances, industrial processes, and pharmaceuticals. These have extensive bibliographies. A dependable resource for chemists, biochemists, and engineers at academic, industrial, and government institutions since publication of the first edition in 1949. Said to be used by lawyers and consultants for information on the 'state-of-the-art' in chemical technology for litigation or patent support.

Available online: see website.

5111 Plastics materials and processes
C.A. Harper Wiley-Interscience, 2003, 974pp. $135.00. ISBN 0471456039.
Useful compilation consisting of an extended glossary with an extensive range of some 50 appendices – some of which are reprinted from other works such as the *Modern plastics encyclopedia* (Chemical Week Associates, 1998). Still, good to have all the information brought together in an easily usable format.

- **Modern plastics handbook C.A. Harper, ed.** McGraw-Hill, 2000, 1298pp. $125.00. ISBN 0070267146. Guide to plastic product design, manufacture, and application, sponsored by the trade magazine *Modern Plastics*.

5112 Ullmann's encyclopedia of industrial chemistry
M. Bohnet [et al.], eds 6th edn, Wiley-VCH, 2003. 40 v., €5990.00. ISBN 3527303855.
www.wiley-vch.de/vch/software/ullmann/index.html
The other major treatise in this arena – alongside Kirk-Othmer. Over 800 articles written by 3000 experts in their field, more than 15,000 tables and innumerable literature sources and cross-references. Offers comprehensive and well structured information on all facets of industrial chemistry, process engineering, materials science, environmental chemistry, food science and biotechnology.

Available online: see website

- **Ullmann's processes and process engineering** Wiley-VCH, 2004, 2301pp. £415.00 (3 v.). ISBN 3527310967. Subset of the main encyclopedia 'for the many readers primarily interested in industrial chemical processes, process engineering, reactor design and optimization'.

5113 WWW Chemicals
CHEM.COM.
www.chem.com
Well organized searchable resource with links to distributors, equipment, services, suppliers, company listings. Extensive coverage with links to over 500 chemical suppliers. Users can perform structure searching by online drawing of molecular structures.

Handbooks & manuals

5114 Adhesion of polymers
R.A. Veselovsky and V.N. Kestelman McGraw-Hill, 2002, 397pp. $99.00. ISBN 0071370455.
Presents state-of-the-art methods for improving durability, sealing strength, etc between different materials.

5115 Analysis, synthesis, and design of chemical processes
R. Turton [et al.] 2nd edn, Prentice Hall PTR, 2003. Includes CD-ROM, $115.00. ISBN 0130647926.
Wide-ranging manual emphasizing real-world examples. This

edn contains extensive new coverage of environmental, health, and safety issues, green engineering, and engineering ethics.

5116 **BASF handbook on basics of coating technology**
A. Goldschmidt and H.-J. Streitberger Vincentz Network (Hannover), 2003, 792pp. Also from William Andrew Publishing, $225.00. ISBN 0815515030.
www.williamandrew.com/books.asp?id=1503 [DESCRIPTION]
English language edition of recently updated classic text. Organized into six sections: Coating materials; Coating technology; Safety, environmental protection and health; Principles of quality management; Coating industries; Standards, norms, appendix and index.

5117 **Basic principles and calculations in chemical engineering**
D.M. Himmelblau 7th edn, Prentice Hall PTR, 2004, 752pp. Includes CD-ROM, $149.33. ISBN 0131406345.
Now standard work with the 29 chapters forming the core of the work organized into four parts: Introduction; Material balances; Gases, vapours, liquids, and solids; Energy balances. Supplementary material on the CD-ROM. Many useful appendices.

Biocatalysis
A.S. Bommarius and B.R. Riebel See entry no. 5037

Bretherick's handbook of reactive chemical hazards: an indexed guide to published data
P.G. Urben and M.J. Pitt, eds See entry no. 4282

5118 **Catalyst handbook**
M.V. Twigg 2nd edn, Manson Publications, 1996, 608pp. £45.00. ISBN 1874545367.
Aims to bridge gap between theory and practice by dealing with principles of heterogeneous catalysis and the practicalities of catalysts and processes used in producing ammonia, hydrogen and methanol via hydrocarbon steam reforming.

5119 **Ceramic processing and sintering**
M.N. Rahaman 2nd edn, Marcel Dekker, 2003, 875pp. $229.95. ISBN 0824709888.
Completely rewritten 2nd edn with much new material. Clear presentation which, although has a detailed coverage, is suitable for those with little or no knowledge of the subject; good contextual introductions to each section.
Series: Materials Engineering, V. 23.

5120 **Chemical engineers' portable handbook**
R.G. Griskey McGraw-Hill, 2000, 422pp. ISBN 007024801X.
Pocket-sized handbook covering basic and practical chemical engineering knowledge. Includes facts, formulas, and methods; chapters on process operations, biochemical engineering, and environmental operations; hazmat procedures, equipment and regulations; and design factors.
Series: McGraw-Hill Portable Engineering.

5121 **Chemical process and design handbook**
J.G. Speight McGraw-Hill, 2002. $99.95. ISBN 0071374337.
Useful compendium divided into: Reaction types (akylation, amination, condensation and addition, etc.), and Manufacture of chemicals: details for about 400 common inorganics and organics.

■ **Perry's standard tables and formulas for chemical engineers J.G. Speight** McGraw-Hill, 2003, 653pp. $79.95. ISBN 0071387773. Based on *Perry's chemical engineer's handbook.*

5122 **Chemical process safety: fundamentals with applications**
D.A. Crowl and J.F. Louvar 2nd edn, Prentice Hall PTR, 2001, 625pp. $115.00. ISBN 0130181765.
Includes treatments of toxicology, industrial hygiene, toxic release and dispersion modelling, flammability, explosions, and relief sizing, with full coverage of hazard identification and risk assessment.

5123 **Chemical process technology**
J.A. Moulijn, M. Makkee and A. Van Diepen Wiley, 2001, 350pp. $75.00. ISBN 0471630624.
Useful comprehensive text.

5124 **Chemical product design**
E.L. Cussler and G.D. Moggridge Cambridge University Press, 2001, 229pp. £22.99. ISBN 0521796334.
www.cambridge.org/uk/catalogue/search.asp [DESCRIPTION]
'Until recently, the chemical industry has been dominated by the manufacture of bulk commodity chemicals such as benzene, ammonia, and polypropylene. However, over the last decade a significant shift occurred. Now most chemical companies devote any new resources to the design and manufacture of specialty, high value-added chemical products such as pharmaceuticals, cosmetics, and electronic coatings. Although the jobs held by chemical engineers have also changed to reflect this altered business, their training has remained static, emphasizing traditional commodities. This ground-breaking text.'
Series: Cambridge Series in Chemical Engineering.

5125 **Chemical reactor design, optimization, and scaleup**
E.B. Nauman McGraw-Hill, 2001, 589pp. $99.95. ISBN 0071377530.
A detailed examination of each type of major chemical reactor as well as their advantages and disadvantages for different applications. Examples are given of different reactor types and their purposes with an emphasis on the numerical techniques used to design, optimize and scaleup reactors.

5126 **Chemical thermodynamics for industry**
T. Letcher, ed.; Royal Society of Chemistry 2004, 276pp. £89.95. ISBN 0854045910.
Covers the latest developments in traditional areas such as calorimetry, microcalorimetry, transport properties, crystallization, adsorption, electrolyte systems and transport fuels. It highlights newly established areas such as multiphase modelling, reactive distillation, non-equilibrium thermodynamics and spectro-calorimetry. It also explores new ways of treating old technologies as well as new and potentially important areas such as ionic liquids, new materials, ab-initia quantum chemistry, nano-particles, polymer recycling, clathrates and the economic value of applied thermodynamics.

5127 **Chemistry of petrochemical processes**
S. Matar and L.F. Hatch 2nd edn, Gulf Publishing, 2001, 356pp. $95.00. ISBN 0884153150.
Useful overview of underlying reactions and applied processes.

Chemometrics: data analysis for the laboratory and chemical plant
R.G. Brereton See entry no. 1798

5128 **Color chemistry: syntheses, properties, and applications of organic dyes and pigments**
H. Zollinger and A. Iqbal 3rd edn, Wiley-VCH, 2003, 637pp. £105.00. ISBN 3906390233.
First-rate introduction. Proceeds from first principles (classification of colorants; history of dyes and pigments; production of colorants; basic concepts of colours; etc.) through to the different functional categories of dyes and pigments and then to applications across the full spectrum. Extensive bibliographies and very detailed subject index.

- **Industrial organic pigments: production, properties, applications** **W. Herbst and K. Hunger** 3rd edn, Wiley-VCH, 2004, 660pp. £150.00. ISBN 3527305769. Now the standard reference work covering the full range of synthetic organic pigments. Exceptionally well structured and presented. A model work.

5129 **Comprehensive desk reference of polymer characterization and analysis**
R.F. Brady, ed.; American Chemical Society Oxford University Press, 2003, 754pp. £200.00. ISBN 0841236658.
Intended as a first port of call for chemists new to the polymer industry: for an understanding of the work they do, how to do it, and how to interpret it. The book is 'not a research manual but, rather, a guide to performing and understanding polymer characterization, as well as an entrée to the specialized literature of the analytical chemistry of polymers'.

5130 **Comprehensive polymer science**
G. Allen [et al.], eds 2nd edn, Pergamon Press, 1996. 7 v. plus 2 supplements. ISBN 0080426816.
These volumes provided at the time an authoritative review of synthetic polymer science. Each volume covered different areas including polymer characterization, polymer properties, chain polymerization, step polymerization, polymer reactions, speciality polymers, polymer processing.

5131 **Coulson and Richardson's chemical engineering**
J.M. Coulson and J.F. Richardson Butterworth-Heinemann. 6 v.
This series of six books is a major text for undergraduate courses in the UK. The first volume was published in the 1950s and since then the series has been extended and updated on several occasions. The 6th edn of volume 1 was published in 1999.

DECHEMA corrosion handbook: corrosive agents and their interaction with materials
See entry no. 5840

5132 **Encyclopedia of industrial chemical analysis**
F.D. Snell, C.L. Hilton and L.S. Ettre, eds Interscience Publishers, 1963–1974. 20 v.
Major treatise which covered general techniques and analysis of specific techniques in articles which contain procedures, properties, uses, formulae and reactions to perform analyses.

Explosion protection: electrical apparatus and systems for chemical plants, oil and gas industry, coal mining
H. Groh See entry no. 4709

Explosives
R. Meyer, J. Köhler and A. Homburg See entry no. 4710

5133 **Handbook of adhesive technology**
A. Pizzi and K.L. Mittal, eds 2nd edn, Marcel Dekker, 2003, 1024pp. $249.95. ISBN 0824709861.
Multi-author. 50 chapters in four parts: Review topics – including a useful chapter 'Information Resources' prepared by Adhesives Information Services, Indiana; Fundamental aspects; Adhesive classes; Application of adhesives. Subject index.

5134 **Handbook of chemical and environmental engineering calculations**
J.P. Reynolds, J.S. Jeris and L. Theodore Wiley-Interscience, 2002, 948pp. $165.00. ISBN 0471402281.
55 sections organized into eight parts: Chemical engineering fundamentals; Chemical engineering principles; Air pollution control equipment; Solid waste; Water quality and wastewater management; Pollution prevention; Health, safety, and accident management; Other topics. Covers approximately 600 real-world, practical solutions to environmental problems that involve chemical engineering.

5135 **Handbook of chemical engineering calculations**
N.P. Chopey, ed. 3rd edn, McGraw-Hill, 2004. $125.00. ISBN 0071362622.
Outgrowth of the *Standard handbook of engineering calculations*. Almost the whole volume is populated with solved numerical illustrative examples – except in a few cases where an introduction to the technique seemed especially appropriate. Three new chapters in this edn: biotechnology; cost engineering; water-pollution control (reprinted from the publisher's *Wastewater engineering*). Subject index.

Handbook of chemical technology and pollution control
M.B. Hocking See entry no. 5618

Handbook of explosion prevention and protection
M. Hattwig and H. Steen, eds See entry no. 4712

5136 **Handbook of green chemistry and technology**
J. Clark and D. Macquarrie Blackwell Science, 2002, 540pp. £149.00. ISBN 0632057157.
An excellent volume with very wide coverage and especially good contextual information. 'Chemistry is having a difficult time. On the one hand the demand for chemical products is higher than ever ... However, there is unprecedented social, economic and environmental pressure on the chemical industry to "clean up its act" and make chemical processes and products more sustainable and environmentally compatible.'

5137 **Handbook of hard coatings**
R.F. Bunshah and C. Weissmantel, eds Noyes Publications, 2001, 550pp. $152.00. ISBN 0815514387.
www.knovel.com
Subjects covered are: Vapour deposition technologies; Thermal spraying and detonation gun processes; Structure/property relationships for hard coatings; Characterization of hard coatings; Macro- and micromechanical and tribological properties; Applications to cutting tools; Wear and corrosion resistant hard coatings for

non-cutting-tool applications; Cubic boron nitride and diamond-related thin films.

Available online: see website.

5138 **Handbook of industrial mixing: science and practice**

E.L. Paul, V.A. Atiemo-Obeng and S.M. Kresta Wiley, 2004, 1377pp. Includes CD-ROM, $165.00. ISBN 0471269190.

Volume sponsored by the North American Mixing Forum and written for the practising engineer who needs both to identify and solve mixing problems. In addition to a focus on industrial design and operation of mixing equipment, it contains summaries of the foundations on which these applications are based: most chapters pair an industrialist and an academic as co-authors.

Comprehensive coverage; well presented; good overview. Index.

'This is the most comprehensive of the mixing handbooks currently available ... I would rate this handbook as a must have for any company doing mixing at the industrial level. Similarly, any laboratory, college or university working on mixing research or that mixes its own reagents would benefit from keeping this book handy.' (*E-STREAMS*)

5139 **Handbook of petrochemicals production processes**

R.A. Meyers McGraw-Hill Professional, 2005, 1000pp. $125.00. ISBN 0071410422.

'Details the latest and most powerful chemical processes used to create the most economically important chemicals in the world.'

5140 **Handbook of plastics analysis**

H. Lobo and J.V. Bonilla, eds Marcel Dekker, 2003, 650pp. $199.95. ISBN 0824707087.

12 chapters covering both physical analysis ('evaluation of the physical behavior of the material') and chemical analysis ('to evaluate the compositional characteristics of the polymer'). Bibliographies and further reading. Appendix: ASTM methods for analysis of plastic and rubber materials. Good detailed handbook.

Series: Plastics Engineering, 68.

Handbook of zeolite science and technology

S.M. Auerbach, K.A. Carrado and P.K. Dutta, eds See entry no. 4714

Hazardous chemicals desk reference

R.J. Lewis See entry no. 4290

5141 **Industrial chemical process design**

D.L. Erwin McGraw-Hill, 2002, 722pp. Includes CD-ROM, $99.95. ISBN 0071376216.

Practical manual designed for the practising engineer.

5142 **Industrial dyes: chemistry, properties, applications**

K. Hunger, ed. Wiley-VCH, 2003, 660pp. £115.00. ISBN 3527304266.

Multi-author text giving intensive coverage of the full range of industrially produced dyes, including their syntheses, properties and main applications. Also treats toxicological, ecological and legal aspects. Subject index plus appendix listing examples of commercially available dyes, giving Colour Index and CAS Registry Nos.

- **Colour Index International Society of Dyers and Colourists and American Association of Textile Chemists and Colorists.** www.colour-index.org. First published 1925 and 'the definitive guide for anyone who needs to know details of which companies manufacture and distribute dyes and pigments, or for anyone looking for technical details of these products'.

5143 **Inorganic chemicals handbook**

J.J. McKetta, ed. Marcel Dekker, 1993, 1456pp. 2 v. ISBN 0824786866.

Has data in the form of diagrams, graphs and tables. Offers comprehensive coverage of the most common inorganic chemicals and provides complete information on manufacturing, design and operations.

5144 **Perry's chemical engineers' handbook**

R.H. Perry, D.W. Green and J.O. Maloney, eds 7th edn, McGraw-Hill, 1997. $150.00. ISBN 0070498415.

With over a million copies in print this is considered to be an essential reference book for the chemical engineer containing facts, figures, methods, and data relied on by people in that industry.

5145 **Plastics materials**

J.A. Brydson 7th edn, Butterworth-Heinemann, 1999, 920pp. £99.99. ISBN 0750641320.

Classic reference work which continues to provide a balanced and comprehensive overview of the nature, manufacture, structure, properties, processing and applications of commercially available plastics materials. The book aims to bridge the gap between theory and practice. Discussion of properties of plastics in general is followed by chapters each of which is devoted to a specific type of plastic, outlining sources, characteristics, past and present uses, and methods of handling and processing.

'One is dumbstruck with admiration and almost total disbelief on being presented with the new edition of *Plastics Materials*, or simply 'Brydson' as it is more popularly known. How can just one man know so much about the subject. Just about everything that could possibly be said about plastics or rubber material is there, which is why it has enjoyed a reputation and status as the Bible of the industry for many years.' (*British Plastics & Rubber*)

5146 **Polymer handbook**

J. Brandrup [et al.] Wiley, 2003, 2336pp. 2 v., $395.00. ISBN 0471479365.

Focuses on synthetic polymers, polysaccharides and derivatives and oligomers. Explores latest developments in field. Data tables logically divided into eight sections and include IUPAC nomenclature rules. Old data tables updated and new ones added.

5147 **Riegel's handbook of industrial chemistry**

J.A. Kent, ed. 10th edn, Kluwer Academic Plenum, 2003, 1373pp. £381.00. ISBN 0306474115.

Well established work with 48 subject experts presenting in 31 chapters up-to-date accounts of the chemistry and chemical engineering which underlies the major areas of the chemical process industry. New to this edn is a chapter on industrial cell culture. Bibliographies. Index.

5148 **Rules of thumb for chemical engineers**

C.R. Branan 3rd edn, Gulf Professional Publishing, 2002, 426pp. £69.99. ISBN 0750675675.

Standard handbook for chemical and process engineers.

Sittig's handbook of toxic and hazardous chemicals and carcinogens

R.P. Pohanish See entry no. 4301

Uhlig's corrosion handbook
R.W. Revie, ed. See entry no. 5860

Keeping up-to-date

5149 **Advances in Chemical Engineering**
Academic Press, 2004, 350pp. $189.00 [V. 29]. ISBN 0120085291.
www.info.sciencedirect.com/bookseries/packages/chemistry/index.shtml
Each volume focuses on one particular area; e.g. Volume 29 (2004) covered *Molecular and cellular foundations of biomaterials*.
Available online: see website.

5150 **Chemical & Engineering News**
American Chemical Society
pubs.acs.org/cen/index.html
Covers the latest news in science, technology, government policy, business and industry. Subscribers can access feature stories on cutting-edge research, careers and employment, and education – as well as other ACS resources. The Society also publish *Chemical Industry Notes*, which covers worldwide news on the chemical industry from approximately 90 national and international business and trade journals.
Also available in print.

5151 **Chemical Engineering**
Access Intelligence.
www.che.com [FEE-BASED]
'The best read publication in the chemical process industries.' The magazine's Media Kit provides a helpful and colourful overview of the seven major segments of the chemical process industries: chemicals and petrochemicals; food and beverages; non-ferrous metals; petroleum refining; pulp and paper; rubber and miscellaneous plastics; stone, clay, glass, ceramics.
- **Chemical Week** Access Intelligence. www.chemweek.com. 'The Worldwide News Source for Chemicals Makers and Processors'.

5152 **Chemical News and Intelligence**
International Chemical Information Service.
www.icis.com/ICIS_Portal/home/home.aspx [FEE-BASED]
The publisher, previously known as RBI Chemical Group, is 'the world's largest provider of information for the chemical industry. We have over 170 people working worldwide to ensure that our customers receive the best business-critical information available, when they need it.' They produce a range of other services and products in addition to this online news and analysis service.

5153 **European Chemical News**
Reed Chemicals Corporation.
www.europeanchemicalnews.com [FEE-BASED]
News weekly covering worldwide developments as they affect the European chemical industry. Provides industry news, features and analysis, including petrochemical and polymer prices, market trends, shipping rates, mergers and acquisitions, company results, new technologies, environmental issues, etc.

NanoFocus: Nanotechnology News for the Chemical World
American Chemical Society See entry no. 6000

Civil Engineering

bridges • cement • coastal engineering • concrete • dams • docks • drainage • dredging • earthquake engineering • foundations • geotechnical engineering • ground engineering • harbours • highways • hydraulic engineering • hydraulics • irrigation • ports • reservoirs • roads • rock engineering • soil engineering • soil mechanics • soil mechanics • steel construction • structural engineering • structures • surveying • traffic • transport • tunnels

Introductions to the subject

5154 **Civil engineering heritage** [UK]
Thomas Telford, 1981–.
www.thomastelford.com/books [DESCRIPTION]
A series of books that list and describe, with illustrations, sites in the UK selected for 'technical interest, innovation, durability or visual attraction'. Sites include bridges, reservoirs, lighthouses, docks, etc.
Eastern and Central England. 1994 ISBN 072771970X E.A. Labrum, ed. £17.50.*Ireland.* 1998. ISBN 0727726277 R.C. Cox and M.H. Gould, eds. £17.50.*London and the Thames Valley.* 2000 ISBN 0727728768 D. Smith, ed. £19.95.*Northern England.* 2nd edn. 1996 ISBN 0727725181 R.W. Rennison, ed. £17.50.*Wales and West Central England.* 2nd edn. 1997 ISBN 0727725769 R. Cragg, ed. £17.50.*Southern England.* 1994 ISBN 0727719718 R.A. Otter, ed. £17.50.

5155 **Civil engineering materials**
N. Jackson and R.K. Dhir, ed. 5th edn, Palgrave Macmillan, 1996, 549pp. £27.99. ISBN 033363683X.
A well regarded introductory textbook covering the most important construction materials. This edition thoroughly revised and extended. Arranged in seven parts: Metals; Timber; Concrete; Bituminous materials; Soils; Polymers; Bricks and blocks.
1st edn 1976 by Jackson alone; 4th edn 1988.

Dictionaries, thesauri, classifications

5156 **Arabic dictionary of civil engineering: English–Arabic, Arabic–English**
E. Kay, comp. Routledge, 1986, 272pp. ISBN 0710204299.
About 1500 terms covering civil engineering and the construction industry, from theory and planning through on-site requirements to office practices. Now out of print but still useful.

5157 **Computational hydraulics and hydrology: an illustrated dictionary**
N.G. Adrien, comp. CRC Press, 2003, 432pp. $199.95. ISBN 0849318904.
Contains definitions of more than 4000 basic terms, and includes nearly 100 illustrations, together with equations and formulas. Covers pertinent subjects such as wastewater disposal and stormwater management as well as general civil and environmental engineering. Also includes a list of sources for definitions.

5158 Dictionary geotechnical engineering: Wörterbuch GeoTechnik
H. Bucksch, comp. Springer, 1998. V. 1. *English–German/Englisch–Deutsch*. 1998. 688pp. ISBN 3540581642; V. 2. *Deutsch–Englisch/German–English* 1998. 591pp. ISBN 3540581634, £252.00.
The 2 volumes of this work contain between them about 140,000 entries, mainly short, covering all aspects of geotechnical engineering, including soil mechanics, foundation engineering, exploration geology, surveying, etc.
CD-ROM available.

5159 Elsevier's dictionary of civil engineering: Russian–English
K.P. Bhatnagar, comp. Elsevier, 1988, 694pp. £148.50. ISBN 0444429611.
Comprising about 36,000 terms in Russian with translations into English, covering civil, structural and, in particular, construction engineering. Includes trade names and abbreviations, with an appendix of personal names.

5160 Elsevier's dictionary of civil engineering in four languages: English, German, Spanish and French
M.F. Gutiérrez, comp. Elsevier, 1991, 392pp. Also available on CD-ROM (ISBN 0444827072), Print €159.00; CD-ROM €179.00. ISBN 04444889876.
Includes over 5500 terms. Wide coverage including applied geology, foundation engineering, construction, equipment, tunnels, hydraulic engineering, etc.

5161 Elsevier's dictionary of soil mechanics and geotechnical engineering in five languages: English, French, Spanish, Dutch and German
J.D. van der Tuin, comp. Elsevier, 1989, 508pp. €217.00. ISBN 0444704809.
Contains some 5800 terms covering soil and rock mechanics, groundwater hydraulics and pollution, construction, earthworks, tunnelling, surveying, and experimental methods.
Overlaps with, and replaces, the earlier Elsevier's dictionary of soil mechanics in four languages ... A.D. Visser, 1965.

5162 ICID multilingual technical dictionary on irrigation and drainage
International Commission on Irrigation and Drainage Rev. edn, 1996, 1262pp. $86.00. ISBN 8185068577.
www.icid.org/index_e.html [DESCRIPTION]
Contains over 10,000 terms with definitions covering irrigation, drainage, flood control, environmental impact, hydrology, hydraulic structures, and allied disciplines. More than 500 illustrative sketches. Indexes in English and French.
1st edn 1967. 2002 revised edn available on CD-ROM (ISBN 818506878X).

5163 Penguin dictionary of civil engineering
J.S. Scott and C. Bayliss 4th edn, Penguin, 1991, 560pp. £10.99. ISBN 0140512462.
Contains about 5000 terms concisely defined. Includes terms from all branches of civil engineering including soil mechanics, heavy construction and mining. US usage is covered. Mainly for the layman and non-specialist engineer.
1st edn 1958 as Dictionary of civil engineering; 3rd edn 1981.

Rock blasting terms and symbols: a dictionary of symbols and terms in rock blasting and related areas like drilling, mining and rock mechanics
A. Rustan, ed.; International Society for Rock Mechanics See entry no. 4668

Laws, standards, codes

5164 CESMM3 [UK]
Institution of Civil Engineers 3rd edn, Thomas Telford, 1991, 110pp. £25.00. ISBN 0727715615.
The *Civil Engineering Standard Method of Measurement* is the accepted standard for the preparation of bills of quantities in civil engineering work. This 3rd edn was revised to conform with the ICE CONDITIONS OF CONTRACT, 6th edn, and recent British Standards.
First published as Standard method of measurement of civil engineering quantities, 1965.

5165 Conditions of contract for works of civil engineering construction [EUR]
Fédération Internationale des Ingénieurs Conseils 4th edn, 1992, 100pp. 2 v., € 20.00. ISBN 2884320016.
www.fidic.org [DESCRIPTION]
FIDIC's famous Red Book. In two parts. Part I: General conditions with forms of tender, and agreement; Part II: Conditions of particular application, and guidelines for preparation of Part II clauses. Also available in electronic form, and in translation to a number of languages.
1st edn 1957; 4th edn 1987; with amendments, 1992.

Formulas for stress, strain, and structural matrices
W.D. Pilkey See entry no. 5882

5166 ICE conditions of contract [UK]
Institution of Civil Engineers, Association of Consulting Engineers and Civil Engineering Contractors Association Thomas Telford, 1999–2001. 6 v., £70.00. ISBN 0727730444.
This consists of a full set of relevant ICE documents which provide the standard for contracts for civil engineering work in the UK. Made up of:
- *ICE conditions of contract – measurement version*, 7th edn. 92 pp. ISBN 027727893. For instance, covers contract documents, general obligations, materials and workmanship, commencement time and delays, etc.
- *ICE conditions of contract – measurement version, 7th edn.: guidance notes.* 20pp. ISBN 0727728423.
- *ICE design and construct conditions of contract.* 2nd edn., 96pp. ISBN 0727730231.
- *ICE design and construct conditions of contract, 2nd edn.: guidance notes.* 40pp. ISBN 072773024X.
- *ICE conditions of contract for minor works.* 28pp. ISBN 0727729403.
- *Tendering for civil engineering contracts.* 32pp. ISBN 0727728539.

1st edn 1945, 6th edn 1991.

- **The ICE conditions of contract – seventh edition B. Eggleston** 2nd edn, Blackwell Science, 2001, 432pp. £59.50. ISBN 0632051965. Provides an explanatory commentary to the *ICE conditions of contract*, clause by clause, with reference to appropriate legal cases and legislation.

5167 **International handbook of earthquake engineering: codes, programs, and examples**
M. Paz, ed. Kluwer Academic, 1995, 545pp. £109.00. ISBN 0412982110.
In two parts. Part 1 presents the basic structural dynamic theory as regards earthquake resistant design. Part 2 presents and discusses the seismic design codes for 34 countries from active seismic regions.

5168 **Minimum design loads for buildings and other structures: ASCE 7-02** [USA]
American Society of Civil Engineers 2002, 404pp. $98.00. ISBN 0784406243.
A revision of ASCE 7-98, 7-02 provides current US structural requirements for dead, live, soil, flood, wind, snow, rain, ice, and earthquake loads, and their combinations, suitable for inclusion in building codes. With a detailed commentary.

5169 **Regulations for seismic design: a world list**
International Association for Earthquake Engineering First published 1996; Supplement 2000.
The 1996 compilation contains earthquake engineering design codes and regulations for 41 countries. Entries include scope, terminology, seismic design criteria, seismic zones, and seismic loads, and often maps and diagrams. The 2000 supplement contains seismic codes for 5 extra countries, plus revised and/or English translations of 11 of the 1996 codes.

5170 **Structural Eurocodes**
Comité Européen de Normalisation
The Structural Eurocodes, usually referred to as just the 'Eurocodes' and often by their number, for instance EC1, are a set of nine Euronorms containing common structural rules for the design of buildings and civil engineering structures. They are intended to harmonize methods of design across Europe by gradually replacing existing national codes. The prestandards (ENV) are available, and European Standards (EN) started to be published in 2002. They should all be published by the end of 2005, and replace national British standards and codes by the end of 2010. The Eurocodes are:

- EN 1990. *Basis of structural design.*
- EN 1991. *Actions on structures* (EC1).
- EN 1992. *Design of concrete structures* (EC2).
- EN 1993. *Design of steel structures* (EC3).
- EN 1994. *Design of composite steel and concrete structures* (EC4).
- EN 1995. *Design of timber structures* (EC5).
- EN 1996. *Design of masonry structures* (EC6).
- EN 1997. *Geotechnical design* (EC7).
- EN 1998. *Design of structures for earthquake resistance* (EC8).
- EN 1999. *Design of aluminium structures* (EC9).

Official & quasi-official bodies

5171 **Department for Transport** [UK]
Great Britain. Department for Transport
www.dft.gov.uk
The DfT's objective is 'to oversee the delivery of a reliable, safe and secure transport system that responds efficiently to the needs of individuals and business whilst safeguarding our environment'. Its website contains information about the Department's policies and activities, including information about railways, roads and vehicles, and its science and research programme.

- **Highways Agency** www.highways.gov.uk. Responsible for overall Government policy, planning, managing and operating of more than 5800 miles of motorways and trunk roads in England. News, travel information, road projects and other information about the Agency and its activities.

5172 **International Commission on Irrigation and Drainage**
www.icid.org
ICID was established in 1950 as a scientific, technical and voluntary not-for-profit non-governmental international organization with its headquarters in New Delhi. Its objective is to improve water and land management by the appropriate use of irrigation, drainage and flood management techniques. The Commission's website contains information about its work, events and publications.

5173 **International Commission on Large Dams**
www.icold-cigb.org
ICOLD was created in 1928 to advance 'the art and science of planning, designing, building, operating and maintaining dams to develop the world's water resources'. The non-governmental organization is now based in Paris, has National Committees from 82 countries, and approximately 7000 individual members. It pursues its work through a system of technical committees, three-yearly international congresses, and various lectures. Its website also provides a searchable glossary, and access to details of a wide range of publications – including the WORLD REGISTER OF DAMS.

- **The Dams Newsletter** 2003–, Quarterly. www.icold-cigb.org/PDF/newsletter2.pdf. 'To make dam's contributions to the well-being of humanity better known and to answer critics which appear groundless … '.

Roads and Vehicles
Great Britain. Department for Transport See entry no. 4968

5174 **World Commission on Dams**
www.dams.org
The WCD was established in 1998, following concerns about the role of large dams in development, with a mandate to review the development effectiveness of, and develop internationally acceptable criteria, guidelines and standards for, large dams. The WCD reported in 2000 and subsequently disbanded, but its website has been archived. Its report is available in English and Spanish, and overviews are available in a number of other languages. A great deal of supporting material is also freely available.

- **Dams and Development Project United Nations Environment Programme.** www.unep-dams.org. Information about follow-up initiatives around the world, reactions to the WCD Report and submissions on good practice.

Research centres & institutes

5175 **Coastal and Hydraulics Laboratory** [USA]
http://chl.erdc.usace.army.mil
Part of the US Department of Defense's Engineer Research and Development Center, the Laboratory is located in Vicksburg, Mississippi and is one of the world's foremost research organizations in its area. The subject content of the site is divided into five themes: Flood/Storm damage

reduction; Hydro-environmental; Integrated systems analysis (modelling of surface water, etc.); Military support; Navigation support (canals, dredging, etc.). Hydraulic software and datasets are available from the Technical Exchange and Data program, while full-text publications, including the Coastal Engineering Manual are also freely available.

5176 **Cold Regions Research and Engineering Laboratory** [USA]
www.crrel.usace.army.mil
CRREL is a research and engineering facility located in Hanover, New Hampshire and is part of the Engineer Research and Development Center, in turn part of the US Army Corps of Engineers. Its general aim is to gain knowledge of cold regions through scientific and engineering research. The Laboratory's current research programme has five major components: Military engineering; Battlespace environments; Infrastructure; Environmental quality; Civil works. As well as general information the website provides access to factsheets and the full text of all post-1995 CRREL reports.

5177 **Earthquake Engineering Research Center** [USA]
eerc.berkeley.edu
EERC is based at the University of California, Berkeley, and provides support for multidisciplinary research in earthquake engineering. Major projects include the Pacific Earthquake Engineering Research Center, the Network for Earthquake Engineering Simulation and the National Information Service for Earthquake Engineering.

5178 **Ecole Nationale des Ponts et Chaussées**
www.enpc.fr
Founded in 1747, Ponts et Chaussées is the oldest civil engineering university, or department, in the world. A major postgraduate research centre it has more than 1000 students and 300 staff, and a considerable library of 150,000 books and 30,000 photographs. Publisher of *Annales des Ponts et Chaussées*. Its website is mainly in French.

5179 **Institut National de Recherche sur le Transport et leur Securité (National Institute for Transport and Safety Research)**
www.inrets.fr/index.e.html
INRETS was established in 1985 as the French state-financed scientific and technological body to organize, conduct, and disseminate the results of research into traffic and transport systems, and safety. The INRETS website is available in English and French, and provides information about the Institute, its research activities, co-operative and partnership ventures, publications, and a set of links to other relevant web resources.

5180 **Multidisciplinary Center for Earthquake Engineering Research** [USA]
mceer.buffalo.edu
Established in 1986 as the US national centre in its area, MCEER is based at the University at Buffalo. Its research aims to improve seismic assessment and performance of buildings, highways and other infrastructure, as well as emergency response and recovery systems. The MCEER website provides free access to monthly newsletters and the Quakeline bibliographic database. Its set of links is especially useful, containing links to bibliographies, FAQs and an (untried) ask-a-geologist.

5181 **Steel Construction Institute** [UK]
www.steel-sci.org
Based in Ascot, Berkshire, the SCI is an independent organization, founded in 1986 to develop and promote the effective use of steel in construction. It has over 600 members in 30 countries. The Institute's website has details about the organization, news, information about projects and research, and library.

- **STEEL: a supra-national tool for enhancement of the Eurocodes online EContent Programme.** http://steel.steel-sci.org [DESCRIPTION]. SCI is one of 5 partners in this EU project whose goal is 'to enhance and create digital technical guidance and present this over the web in a way that overcomes the multi-lingual and multi-cultural barriers to practical application of EC3 and EC4'.

5182 **Transportation Research Board** [USA]
gulliver.trb.org
A division of the United States National Research Council. Its role is to promote advances in transportation through stimulating research, disseminating results and offering policy advice. The searchable TRB website provides information about the Board's activities, current research projects, news and recent publications.

5183 **TRL** [UK]
www.trl.co.uk
TRL is an independent research and development and consultancy organization specializing in all areas of land transport including road construction, structures, safety, traffic and materials. Based in Berkshire, TRL was founded in 1933 as the UK government's Transport Research Laboratory, later changing its name in 1994 upon privatization. TRL has a considerable library, publishes the *TRL Journal of Research*, and administers the ITRD database. Its website consists mainly of information about itself, but also lists TRL reports.

Associations & societies

5184 **American Concrete Institute**
www.concrete.org
Founded in 1904, the ACI is a technical and educational society, with 18,000 members, dedicated to improving the design, construction, maintenance and repair of concrete structures. It publishes two key journals, the *ACI Structural Journal* and *ACI Materials Journal*. Its searchable website contains information about the Institute, about its committees and events, and provides free access to a concrete research reports database and a bibliographic database of ACI publications.

5185 **American Institute of Steel Construction**
www.aisc.org
Established 1921 'to make structural steel the material of choice by being the leader in structural-steel-related technical and market-building activities, including: specification and code development, research, education, technical assistance, quality certification, standardization, and market development'.

Well structured website – see the Site Map – whose Resources section includes, for instance, a series of Top 10

Lists (steel gurus; steel resources; skyscrapers; codes and specifications for the design office; steel websites; significant steel buildings you might not know). There is a useful Engineering FAQs list and a range of downloadable publications – some of which are priced for non-members.

5186 American Society of Civil Engineers
www.asce.org
ASCE is the leading representative body for civil engineers in the United States, and one of the most important worldwide. Its website gives information about the Society, forthcoming events, jobs and careers, history of civil engineering in the USA, and publications. ASCE publishes some 30 journals, all leaders in their respective fields, and all of which are available in print and electronically.

5187 British Cement Association
www.bca.org.uk
Formerly the Cement and Concrete Association, the BCA is the trade and research organization representing the UK cement industry. Its website contains information about the Association, freely downloadable technical information sheets, statistical information, etc. It also provides access to various discussion forums, and to an online version of *Concrete Quarterly*, the BCA house magazine. The Association's long-established library produces the CONCRETE INFORMATION database.

5188 British Dam Society
www.britishdams.org
The British Dam Society was formed in 1990 and is an associated society of the INSTITUTION OF CIVIL ENGINEERS. Its aim is to advance the education of the public and the profession about dams by way of lectures and publications, and to participate at an international level on technical committees and working groups.

The clear and well organized BDS website provides information about forthcoming events, publications, current issues, best practice (with a bibliography), a summary of registered research projects, and pages of information about dams, reservoir safety, and the International Commission on Large Dams.

5189 British Geotechnical Association
www.britishgeotech.org.uk
With some 1400 members, the British Geotechnical Association (BGA) is the principal society specifically for geotechnical engineers in the UK. The BGA organizes educational events and lectures, and publishes for its members the magazine *Ground Engineering*. It is the UK member of the INTERNATIONAL SOCIETY FOR SOIL MECHANICS AND GEOTECHNICAL ENGINEERING, and an associate member of the INSTITUTION OF CIVIL ENGINEERS.

5190 Concrete Society [UK]
www.concrete.org.uk
Established in 1966, aims to encourage the use and development of concrete mainly by way of information exchange and dissemination, including the publication of *Concrete*. The Society's website offers information about the organization, details of publications, an Information & Advice section which includes details of regional activities, an advisory service, and a compendium of basic information called 'Concrete at your fingertips'. Some recent articles from *Concrete* are also available.

5191 Earthquake Engineering Research Institute [USA]
www.eeri.org
EERI is a national, not-for-profit, technical society of engineers, geoscientists, architects, planners, and others, based in the USA. Its objectives include reducing earthquake risk by advancing the science and practice of earthquake engineering. Its website includes a wealth of news, while the 'Learning from Earthquakes' section contains the texts of many reports on individual earthquakes.

5192 Fédération Internationale des Ingénieurs Conseils (International Federation of Consulting Engineers)
www1.fidic.org
Based in Geneva, FIDIC represents the international business interests of engineering-based consulting companies. Founded in 1913, FIDIC membership is made up of 65 national Member Associations, representing some 560,000 professionals, that follow the FIDIC code of ethics, policy statements, and statutes. FIDIC organizes an annual conference and publishes the Red Book: CONDITIONS OF CONTRACT FOR WORKS OF CIVIL ENGINEERING CONSTRUCTION.

5193 Fédération Internationale du Béton (International Federation for Structural Concrete)
http://fib.epfl.ch
fib is a non-profit organization based in Lausanne, created in 1998 from the merger of the Euro-International Concrete Committee (CEB – Comité Euro-International du Béton, founded 1953) and the International Federation for Prestressing (FIP – Fédération Internationale de la Précontrainte, founded 1952.) Its role is to develop, internationally, research into and study of concrete construction and structures. At present, fib has 37 National Member Groups as statutory members, and about 900 individual or corporate members in about 60 countries. fib publishes technical bulletins and the journal *Structural Concrete*, and organizes and supports conferences.

5194 Institution of Civil Engineers [UK]
www.ice.org.uk
Established in 1818, the Institution is the UK's professional association for civil engineers, with a worldwide membership of over 80,000. Its website has areas for news and events, education, knowledge and expertise, and members. ICE has a considerable library of more than 100,000 volumes whose catalogue is freely searchable. The Institution's publishing house, Thomas Telford, publishes eight professional journals plus a couple of magazines, and a range of books.

5195 Institution of Structural Engineers [UK]
www.istructe.org.uk
Established in 1980 the IStructE is the professional association representing structural engineers in the UK. It has three main functions: encouraging the exchange of information through meetings, technical reports, and its journal, the STRUCTURAL ENGINEER etc; setting and maintaining professional standards; and providing services to its 22,000 members. Its website contains information about the Institution, local branches and technical work, services, access to its Library catalogue, a membership directory services, events, jobs, and news posted on a bulletin board.

5196 **International Association for Bridge and Structural Engineering**
www.iabse.ethz.ch
Based in Zurich, IABSE is a non-profit scientific society established in 1929 to promote the international exchange of knowledge in the field of structural engineering. It has 4200 members in 100 countries. The IABSE website has information about the Association, publications and conferences. Part of the site is restricted to members only.

5197 **International Association for Earthquake Engineering**
www.iaee.or.jp
Established in 1963 and based in Tokyo, the purpose of the IAEE is to promote international co-operation among professionals in the field of earthquake engineering. The Association publishes the journal *Earthquake Engineering & Structural Dynamics* and organizes the four-yearly World Conference on Earthquake Engineering. Its website is in English.

5198 **International Association of Hydraulic Engineering and Research**
www.iahr.org
The IAHR, as the Association is usually known, is based in Madrid and promotes the advancement and exchange of knowledge on water resources, river and coastal hydraulics, industrial processes and related issues. Its website includes information about the association, its publications (contents and abstracts of recent journal volumes), and news.

International Road Federation
See entry no. 4980

5199 **International Society for Soil Mechanics and Geotechnical Engineering**
www.issmge.org
Based in London, the ISSMGE is the pre-eminent international professional body for ground engineers. It has a membership of 17,000 and 75 affiliated national organizations. It organizes conferences and oversees a system of technical committees to produce guidelines for geotechnical practice. The Society's website provides information about these activities, plus news. It can also be viewed in French or Spanish.

International Society of Explosives Engineers
See entry no. 4678

5200 **National Stone, Sand and Gravel Association** [USA]
www.nssga.org
Represents the crushed stone, sand and gravel (aggregates) industries, member companies producing more than 90% of the crushed stone and 70% of the sand and gravel consumed annually in the USA. Extensive Directory & Buyers Guide; good Links section; nice clean website.

5201 **Réunion Internationale des Laboratoires et Experts des Matériaux, Systèmes de Construction et Ouvrages (International Union of Testing and Research Laboratories for Materials and Structures)**
www.rilem.org
Established in 1947 and based in Geneva RILEM, as it's usually referred to, is a non-profit-making, non-governmental technical association which aims to stimulate progress in the design, manufacture, testing and use of building materials. Its website gives information about the organization, past and forthcoming events, RILEM publications, including the full text of RILEM Symposia, and RILEM Technical Committee reports. Part of the site is restricted to RILEM members.

5202 **Society for Earthquake and Civil Engineering Dynamics** [UK]
www.seced.org.uk
SECED is the UK national section of the international and European associations for earthquake engineering and is an associated society of the Institution of Civil Engineers. Its objective is to promote knowledge in earthquake engineering and civil engineering dynamics, including blast, impact and other vibration problems. The Society organizes meetings and lectures, publishes a newsletter and directories of members.

Libraries, archives, museums

5203 **Harmer E. Davis Transportation Library** [USA]
www.lib.berkeley.edu/ITSL/services.html
Based at the Institute of Transportation Studies at the University of California, Berkeley. Established in 1948, and is one of the pre-eminent transportation collections in the United States with over 176,000 monographs, 4700 serial titles and 146,000 microfiche. The Library maintains the PATH database.

5204 **National Information Service For Earthquake Engineering** [USA]
nisee.berkeley.edu
Based at the University of California, Berkeley, NISEE is part of the Earthquake Engineering Research Center. Its purpose is to provide access to technical research and development information in earthquake engineering and related fields, such as structural dynamics, etc. Among other facilities, NISEE provides free access to the Earthquake Engineering Abstracts database; and the Earthquake Image Information System, a database with 11,000 slides and photographs of earthquake damage.

- **Godden Structural Engineering Slide Library** http://nisee.berkeley.edu/godden. Online collection of 560 slides taken between 1950 and 1980 in order to illustrate structural systems in undergraduate teaching. The collection is arranged thematically, and each slide is accompanied by a short description of the structure.

5205 **National Transportation Library** [USA]
Bureau of Transportation Statistics
http://ntl.bts.gov
The NTL was established in 1998 as a 'virtual' library serving as a US repository of electronic materials from public, academic and private organizations. The Digital Collection is searchable and browsable by category (for instance, Highway/road transportation, Freight, etc.) The Reference Shelf consists of a set of links to US statistical sources, government and state websites, and the like. There is also an (untried) Ask-a-Librarian reference service.

Portal & task environments

5206 **Geoforum.com: the source for geotechnical information**
Webforum Europe AB.
www.geoforum.com
Intended to be an information and communication service for the geotechnical industry worldwide. The site is made up of a Market Guide (searchable directories of companies and organizations), an Events Guide, Geo Contacts (a directory of people and discussion forums), Geo Knowledge (an English/French/German/Swedish translating dictionary of over 700 geotechnical terms, some e-textbooks for subscription, and a unit converter), and a valuable selection of geophysical and pile information. The website is available in English, German and Swedish.

5207 **iCivilEngineer: the internet for civil engineers**
www.icivilengineer.com
Proclaims itself 'a knowledge portal specially designed for civil engineering professionals and students'. Offers news, access to free online magazines, careers opportunities, and IT, Tools, and Resource Centers, each containing useful links. Also has a web directory with links arranged by broad subject area – architectural engineering, construction, environmental engineering, etc.

A nice site – marred only by lack of information about its producers.

5208 **TrafficLinq**
TrafficLinq.
www.trafficlinq.com
A Netherlands-based site aimed at the professional consisting mainly of a directory of links to websites covering road traffic and transportation. It is searchable and browsable by categories such as Public transport, ITS (Intelligent transport systems), Maglev, etc. and also by institutions such as Ministries of Transport. Also contains sections 'Find Consultant', 'Find Job' and 'Find Pictures'. The site has over 1250 pictures which are available for purchase.

Discovering print & electronic resources

5209 **Bibliography on soil mechanics**
Institution of Civil Engineers 1950, 570pp.
Prepared by the Soil Mechanics and Foundations Committee of the Research Committee of the ICE. The first volume covers the years 1920–1946 with some earlier items. Arranged in four parts: UDC subject index with references to the author index, which contains about 3600 bibliographic entries, and classified and alphabetical subject indexes. A very useful guide to the early literature.
Annual supplements until 1959.

5210 **Civil Engineering Abstracts**
CSA, 1966–, 24/year.
www.csa.com/factsheets/civil-set-c.php [DESCRIPTION]
This electronic database provides citations to the serials literature in civil engineering and its complementary fields, monitoring of over 3000 periodical titles. All civil engineering specialities are covered, including Waste management, Storm water management and flood analysis, and Surface and groundwater hydrology. It is updated twice monthly, and as of September 2004, contained 366,000 records.

5211 **Civil Engineering Database**
American Society of Civil Engineers 1970–.
www.pubs.asce.org/cedbsrch.html
The CEDB is 'designed to provide easy bibliographic access to all ASCE publications'. It contains more than 100,000 records of ASCE documents – journal articles, conference proceedings, books, standards, manuals, magazines, etc. – published since 1970. Non-abstract journal records go back to the 1920s; book records are complete dating back to 1800. The simple interface is easy to use and has a browsable list of subject headings.

'A unique feature of the database is that it links discussions, closures, and erratas, back to the original records.'

5212 **Concrete Information**
British Cement Association and Concrete Society Also available on CD-ROM.
www.concrete-info.com [FEE-BASED]
Subscription online database containing nearly 120,000 records from 1976 onwards referring to the international literature on cement and concrete. It includes references to books, journal articles (over 400 current titles indexed), reports, translations, standards, and conference papers and proceedings. About 300 items are added each month.

5213 **Earthquake Engineering Abstracts**
National Information Service For Earthquake Engineering 1971–, Quarterly.
www.csa.com/factsheets/earthquake-set-c.php [DESCRIPTION]
Provided by NISEE and sponsored by the NATIONAL SCIENCE FOUNDATION, this free database contained about 100,000 records from 1971 to 2004 of journal articles, technical reports, conference proceedings, etc. related to earthquake engineering held in the NISEE library. It then became part of the CSA portfolio.

It indexes earthquake-related topics such as hazard mitigation, structural dynamics, and various types of engineering, and now increases by some 10–15,000 citations per year.

5214 **Earthquakes and the Built Environment Index**
NISC, 1971–, Biannual.
www.nisc.com/factsheets/Old_factsheets/ebei.asp [DESCRIPTION]
This database is made up of data from three otherwise separate databases: EARTHQUAKE ENGINEERING ABSTRACTS, QUAKELINE, and the Newcastle Earthquake Database (from Queensland, Australia) with duplicate records removed. Available on CD-ROM, it contained in late 2004 a total of over 140,000 records to the earthquake engineering literature.

Fluidex: The Fluid Engineering Abstracts Database
See entry no. 5927

Geomechanics Abstracts
See entry no. 4700

5215 **Geotechnical Abstracts**
Research Resources, 1990–, Biannual. $450.00. ISSN 10840656.
www.geoforum.com/marketguide [DESCRIPTION]
Accessible on CD-ROM, this service currently contains about

15,000 abstracts to the literature – mainly journal articles and conference papers – on soil mechanics, foundation engineering, rock mechanics, engineering geology and environmental geotechnology.

Also available in paper (ISSN 0016-8491). Continues the service previously supplied by Geodex International, 1970–, which was indexed by punched cards.

5216 International Civil Engineering Abstracts
Emerald, 1976–, Monthly. £2300.00 [2004]. ISBN 03324095.
The ICEA database provides selective rather than comprehensive coverage of the civil engineering literature. Abstracts are taken from 150 leading civil engineering journals, and as of September 2003 ICEA contained over 100,000 records going back to 1976.

5217 ITRD
TRL Limited, 1972–, Monthly.
www.itrd.org [FEE-BASED]
Sponsored by the OECD, the ITRD (International Transport Research Documentation) database contains more than 350,000 bibliographical references to the worldwide transport research literature – reports, books, journal articles, conference proceedings, etc. It covers all aspects of transport research – safety, accident studies, design, construction and maintenance of roads, drainage, traffic studies, finance, etc. Four languages are represented in the database – English, French, German, and Spanish – and records are linked by a quadrilingual thesaurus. About 1000 new records are added each month.

ITRD comprises part of the TRANSPORT *database.*

5218 PATH
Harmer E. Davis Transportation Library and Transportation Research Board
www.dcdata.com/path/path.htm
The PATH (Partners for Advanced Transit and Highways) database covers all aspects of intelligent transportation systems. It currently contains over 28,500 records with abstracts referring to monographs, journal articles, conference papers, technical reports, theses, websites, and selected media coverage.

PATH is also available as part of the TRIS *database.*

Quakeline
Multidisciplinary Center for Earthquake Engineering Research See entry no. 1097

5219 RDN Virtual Training Suite: Civil Engineer [UK]
R. Harrison and A. Ahearn; Imperial College of Science and Technology and Resource Discovery Network
www.vts.rdn.ac.uk/tutorial/civil
This is one of a set of tutorials within the RDN VIRTUAL TRAINING SUITE, created by experts based in UK universities and professional organizations. Although intended to introduce students, researchers and lecturers to finding and assessing material available on the internet, it is free to use, easy to follow, and thus a valuable starting point for anyone new to the internet, the subject, or both. It is divided into Tour, Discover, Review and Reflect sections, and contains as examples links to some key subject sites.

5220 Selective guide to literature on civil engineering
P.L. Anthony, comp.; American Society for Engineering Education
1995, 38pp. ISBN 0878231528.
One of a series of guides to the engineering literature produced under the aegis of the ASEE. Includes listings of bibliographies, indexes and abstracts, encyclopedias, dictionaries, handbooks, directories, standards and specifications, major periodicals, major conferences, important books, and yearbooks. Main focus is on US and Canadian materials but includes salient British resources. Very useful. An updated edition would be most welcome.

5221 TRANSPORT
OVID, 1968–, Quarterly.
www.ovid.com/site/catalog/DataBase [DESCRIPTION]
TRANSPORT is made up of two component bibliographic databases, ITRD and TRIS. It covers all aspects of transportation including highways construction, traffic, safety, and environmental effects. Altogether TRANSPORT contains over 650,000 references to books, journal articles, conference papers, etc. with some 12,000 or more added annually. Almost all references include abstracts which are predominantly in English, though 30% of the ITRD records are in French, German, or Spanish.

5222 TRIS
Transportation Research Board
www4.nationalacademies.org/trb/tris.nsf [DESCRIPTION]
The TRIS (Transportation Research Information Service) database at time of writing contains almost 500,000 records of references to books, technical reports, conference proceedings, journal articles (over 470 serial publications are indexed), and to ongoing research in the field of transportation. It covers all modes of transport – road, railways, aviation, etc. – and all disciplines – design and construction, safety, etc. It includes material provided by the US Transportation Research Board and other US transportation libraries, and also incorporates items from the PATH database, and English language items from the ITRD database.

5223 The Ultimate Civil Engineering Directory
TenLinks Inc.
www.tenlinks.com/engineering/civil
This site consists of a collection of more than 1000 web links arranged by discipline (geotechnical, hydrology, transportation), resources (standards, software, etc.) and structure. Useful 'top ten' listing of civil engineering sites, plus opportunity for e-mail news in certain areas.

5224 WWW Virtual Library: Geotechnical Engineering
The World Wide Web of Geotechnical Engineers.
www.ejge.com/GVL/index.htm
This award-winning site offers 'a comprehensive library of Internet resources about Geotechnical Engineering, including WWW, Gopher, and FTP servers, and newsgroups'. Its catalogue descriptions are divided into five areas – university departments, geotechnical goods and services (laboratories, consultancies, software resources, and soil testing), other internet resources, the Electronic Journal of Geotechnical Engineering and iGEM – The Internet Geotechnical Engineering Magazine.

Digital data, image & text collections

5225 ICE Virtual Library
Institution of Civil Engineers
www.iceknowledge.com [FEE-BASED]
Provides access to the digitized text of all peer-reviewed articles published by the Institution from 1836 onwards. Includes over 20,000 articles and 200,000 pages. Searchable by title, keyword, author, location and date. Pay per view or institutional access by IP address.

5226 Structurae: the international database and gallery of structures
N. Janberg
www.structurae.net
This free and gorgeous website offers information on works of structural engineering (and architecture) from around the world. At time of writing it contains information about more than 10,000 structures – from bridges, skyscrapers and towers to dams and off-shore structures. It is searchable (and browsable) by structure name, type or function, but also by personal name (engineers, architects, etc.) or company name. Entries often have associated web links and literature references. The site is available in English, French and German.

5227 Wind Engineering
ESDU. Available on subscription via the internet, on CD-ROM, and in loose-leaf folders.
www.esdu.com [DESCRIPTION]
This series consists of 46 data items arranged in 10 volumes. The items provide tested and validated methods and data, including software, for predicting the loads on, and the response of, buildings and structures to the wind.

Directories & encyclopedias

5228 Dolphin: Directory of Online Port and Harbour Information
Texas AandM University
dolphin.tamu.edu
Nicely displayed and categorized sets of website descriptions maintained within the University's Center for Ports and Waterways, housed within its Texas Transportation Institute. However, no information on updating schedule.

5229 Encyclopedia of bridges and tunnels
S. Johnson and R.T. Leon, eds Facts On File, 2002, 381pp. $21.95. ISBN 081604483X.
Made up of more than 200 jargon-free articles aimed at the layperson, describing the most notable bridges and tunnels from around the world. Each article mentions designers, engineers, and project managers, and the articles as a whole cover the evolution of bridge design and tunnelling techniques. More than 70 good photographs. Bias in selection toward the USA and early examples.
'enlightening ... readable ... This intriguing reference source is valuable on several levels from the historical and biographical to general engineering concepts. It is recommended for academic and public libraries.' (*American Reference Books Annual*)

5230 Reference guide to famous engineering landmarks of the world: bridges, tunnels, dams, roads, and other structures
L.H. Berlow Oryx, 1997, 250pp. $77.95. ISBN 0897749669.
Contains entries for about 600 structures arranged alphabetically. Entries include location, date of construction, size, and distinctive features. Appendices cover designs, biographies and chronology. Geographical and subject indexes, and also a list of relevant internet sites.

5231 Spon's civil and highway works price book [UK]
Davis Langdon 18th edn, Spon Press, Annual, 800pp. CD-ROM, £120.00 [2004]. ISBN 0415323665.
www.pricebooks.co.uk [DESCRIPTION]
Standard reference work for quantity surveyors and others that provides labour, plant and material costs. Arranged in 15 parts which include Unit costs, Land remediation, Oncosts and profits, Costs and tender price indices, Daywork, Professional fees, etc. and Tables and memoranda, which includes various conversion tables, formulas, design loadings, etc.
1st edn published 1984.

5232 World register of dams
International Commission on Large Dams 1998, 319pp.
Publishers' package includes book and searchable file on CD-ROM, €229.00.
www.icold-cigb.org/icoldorder.htm [REGISTRATION]
A 'who's who' of more than 25,000 dams worldwide. Entries include name of dam, dammed river, height of dam in metres, and some construction details, plus statistical summaries.

Handbooks & manuals

5233 ACI manual of concrete practice
American Concrete Institute 2003. 6 v. Also available online and on CD-ROM, $688.50.
A comprehensive concrete reference set containing the most widely used ACI concrete and masonry code requirements, specifications, guides and reports. Includes over 180 ACI documents arranged in six volumes by document number. Topics include the design and construction of structures and facilities, concrete mixes, formwork, inspection and testing, etc.

5234 Aluminum structures: a guide to their specifications and design
J.R. Kissell and R.L. Ferry 2nd edn, Wiley, 2002, 544pp. $140.00. ISBN 0471019658.
A comprehensive introduction to the use of structural aluminium, updated to include revised Specifications for Aluminum Structures of the *US 2000 Aluminum Design Manual*. It contains 11 chapters arranged in five parts: Introduction; Structural behaviour of aluminium; Design checks for structural components; Design of structural systems; Load and resistance factor design. Host of informative appendices.
1st edn published 1995.

5235 **Bridge engineering handbook**
W.-F. Chen and L. Duan, eds CRC Press, 1999. $179.95. ISBN 0849374340.
Wide-ranging, comprehensive and massive state-of-the-art reference work. More than 100 contributors to 67 chapters arranged in 7 sections: Fundamentals; Superstructure design; Substructure design; Seismic design; Construction & maintenance; Special topics; and Worldwide practice. Large number of charts, tables, and illustrations.
'Outstanding Title. any academic or technical library ... should have this handbook.' (*Choice*)

5236 **Civil engineering handbook**
W.-F. Chen and J.Y.R. Liew, eds 2nd edn, CRC Press, 2003, 2904pp. $189.95. ISBN 0849309581.
Well respected, this is a huge overview with more than 80 authors contributing 76 chapters arranged in eight sections: Engineering construction; Environmental engineering; Geotechnical engineering; Hydraulic engineering; Materials engineering; Structural engineering; Surveying; and Transportation engineering. This edition includes much new material and several new chapters. Good bibliographies.
Series: New Directions in Civil Engineering, v. 23. 1st edn 1992.

5237 **Civil engineer's reference book**
L.S. Blake, ed. 4th edn, Butterworth-Heinemann, 1994. £80.00. ISBN 0750619643.
Substantial and respected reference work, a little dated but still a valuable resource. 52 contributors to 45 chapters, which provide thorough overviews of their areas. Chapters cover basic background topics (Strength of materials, Theory of structures, Site investigation, etc.), materials (Aluminium, Load-bearing masonry, etc.), structures (Dams, Airports, etc.), and techniques (Tunnelling, etc.).
1st edn 1951 as Civil engineering reference book. 3rd edn 1975.

5238 **Coastal engineering manual**
US Army Corps of Engineers 2002. 6 v.
http://chl.erdc.usace.army.mil/Media/4/5/7/cem.pdf [DESCRIPTION]
CEM is a major source of guidance for coastal engineering projects about the world. Its purpose is 'to provide a single, comprehensive technical document that incorporates tools and procedures to plan, design, construct, and maintain coastal projects'. The six parts are: Introduction; Coastal hydrodynamics; Coastal sediment processes; Coastal geology; Coastal project planning and design; and Design of coastal project elements.
Free downloadable PDF version available. CEM is a replacement for the US Army's Shore protection manual, first published in 1974 and last updated in 1984.

5239 **Coastal, estuarial and harbour engineers' reference book**
M.B. Abbott and W.A. Price, eds Spon Press, 1994, 736pp. £185.00. ISBN 0419154302.
A comprehensive but concise overview of the fundamentals of the theory and practice in this area. 57 contributors to 51 chapters arranged in nine parts: Coastal, estuarial and harbour environment; Scientific background; Numerical models and their applications; Physical models and their applications; Coast, shoreline and beach management; Design, construction and maintenance of coastal structures; Materials for coastal structures; Cohesive sediments, estuaries and dredging; and Economics and management of coastal engineering works.

5240 **Comprehensive rock engineering: principles, practice & projects**
J.A. Hudson, ed. Pergamon, 1993. 5 v. ISBN 0080359310.
A truly comprehensive major work, dated now but a strong reference point in this subject's literature. Contains over 160 state-of-the-art chapters, most with substantial bibliographies.
- Vol.1. *Fundamentals*. Ed. E.T. Brown. 752pp.
- Vol.2. *Analysis and design methods*. Ed. C. Fairhurst. 843pp.
- Vol.3. *Rock testing and site characterization*. Ed. J.A. Hudson. 982pp.
- Vol.4. *Excavation, support and monitoring*. Ed. J.A. Hudson. 849pp.
- Vol.5. *Surface and underground project case histories*. Ed. E. Hoeck. 981pp.

5241 **Concrete construction engineering handbook**
E.G. Nawy, ed. CRC Press, 1998, 1232pp. $159.95. ISBN 0849326664.
Consists of 26 chapters covering most aspects of the use of concrete as a structural material, including concrete as a material – constituents, properties, etc., reinforced and specialized concrete construction, design recommendations for high performance, geotechnical and foundation engineering, and concrete repair, retrofit, and rehabilitation.

5242 **Concrete construction handbook**
J.A. Dobrowolski, ed. 4th edn, McGraw-Hill, 1998. ISBN 007017198X.
This edition revised throughout to incorporate the 1995 *ACI Concrete Building Code*. A thorough work, it includes 41 detailed chapters arranged in 13 parts: Materials; Properties; Mixes; Formwork; Batching; Placing; Finishing; Special concretes; Building construction systems; Specialized practices; Precast and prestressed concrete; Architectural concrete; and Repair.
1st edn 1968, 3rd edn 1993.

5243 **Concrete masonry designer's handbook**
J.J. Roberts, A. Tovey and A. Fried 2nd edn, Spon Press, 2000, 382pp. £75.00. ISBN 0419194401.
This edition has been considerably expanded and updated in line with British and European standards and codes, providing guidance on *Eurocode 6*, for instance. It is arranged in 22 chapters which include: Principles of limit state design; Types of block and brick; Walls under vertical load; Resistance of concrete masonry to rain penetration; Sound insulation; Fire resistance; and Specification and workmanship.
1st edn 1983 (Viewpoint).

5244 **Davis' handbook of applied hydraulics**
V.J. Zipparro and H. Hasen, eds 4th edn, McGraw-Hill, 1993. ISBN 0070730024.
A concise presentation of the fundamentals of hydraulic engineering. 29 authors in 28 sections cover all aspects of the subject including basic theory, canals and rivers, dams, gates and valves, locks, irrigation, drainage, water distribution and treatment, and wastewater conveyancing and disposal. Heavily illustrated.
1st edn 1952, 3rd edn 1969.

5245 **Design manual for roads and bridges**
Highways Agency 1992–, Quarterly. 15 v.; downloadable PDF.
www.official-documents.co.uk/document/deps/ha/dmrb/index.htm
This manual is composed of a set of 15 loose-leaf volumes

that contain all current standards, advice notes and other published documents relating to the design, assessment and operation of trunk roads and motorways in the UK. The manual is not a statutory or regulatory document but does represent a guide to good practice.

Volumes include: Highway structures (vols 1–3), Geotechnics and drainage, Assessment and preparation of road schemes, Road geometry, Pavement design and maintenance, Traffic signs and lighting, Networks – traffic control and communications, Environmental design and management, Environmental assessment, Traffic appraisal, and Economic assessment (vols 13–15).

5246 **Designers' handbook to Eurocode 2: Part 1.1. Design of concrete structures**
A.W. Beeby and R. Narayanan Thomas Telford, 1995, 256pp. £50.00. ISBN 0727716689.
This work aims to explain *Eurocode 2* by reference and comparison to the existing British Standard in this area, BS8110. Made up of 12 chapters: Introduction; Basis of design; Analysis of structure; Materials; Design data; Bending and axial load; Shear, punching shear and torsion; Buckling; Serviceability; Durability; Detailing; Construction; plus appendices.

5247 **Designers' guide to EN 1990: Eurocode: basis of structural design**
H. Gulvanessian, J.-A. Calgaro and M. Holický Thomas Telford, 2002, 192pp. £50.00. ISBN 0727730118.
This book provides some technical background to *EN 1990* which establishes for the Structural Eurocodes the principles and requirements for safety and serviceability of structures. Arranged in eight chapters – Principles of limit state design, Structural analysis and design assisted by testing, etc. – plus appendices.

5248 **Dredging: a handbook for engineers**
R.N. Bray, A.D. Bates and J.M. Land 2nd edn, Butterworth-Heinemann, 1997, 434pp. £105.00. ISBN 0340545240.
Considerably expanded since the first edition. A good and not overlong overview of the subject divided into 14 chapters, including Project implementation, Design of dredging works, Disposal of dredged material, and Estimating output. Well illustrated.
1st edn 1979.

5249 **Earthquake engineering handbook**
W.-F. Chen and C. Scawthorn, eds CRC Press, 2002, 1512pp. $199.95. ISBN 0849300681.
A comprehensive reference work covering the full spectrum of earthquake engineering topics. Some 36 authors contribute to 34 chapters arranged in five broad parts – Fundamentals; Geoscience aspects; Structural aspects; Infrastructure aspects; and Special topics. Well illustrated, extensive lists of references.
Series: New Directions in Civil Engineering, V. 24.

Environmental handbook for building and civil engineering projects
R. Venables [et al.]; Construction Industry Research and Information Association See entry no. 5347

Explosives
R. Meyer, J. Köhler and A. Homburg See entry no. 4710

5250 **Field engineer's manual**
R.O. Parmley, ed. 3rd edn, McGraw-Hill, 2001, 720pp. $54.95. ISBN 007135624X.
This portable format guide contains a wealth of basic technical information, arranged in 25 sections, such as Field inspection, Drainage, and Surveying. This edition includes new sections on sewage treatment, streets and roads, and rope tying and splicing.
1st edn 1981, 2nd edn 1996.

5251 **Foundation engineering handbook**
H.-Y. Fang, ed. 2nd edn, Van Nostrand Reinhold, 1990, 923pp. ISBN 0442224877.
A well regarded and still strongly recommended reference book. 30 authors contribute toward 26 chapters covering basic principles (Subsurface exploration and sampling, Bearing capacity of shallow foundations, etc.) and applications (Foundations in cold regions, Offshore structure foundations, etc.).
1st edn 1975.

Geomorphology for engineers
P.G. Fookes, M. Lee and G. Milligan, eds See entry no. 1069

5252 **Geotechnical and geoenvironmental handbook**
R.K. Rowe, ed. Kluwer Academic, 2001, 1088pp. £398.00. ISBN 0792386132.
Substantial and up-to-date overview of the ground engineering area. 50 contributors to 30 chapters organized in five broad sections: Basic behaviour and site characterization (Soil mechanics, Geosynthetics, etc.); Foundations and pavements; Slope, embankment and wall stability, and soil improvement; Special topics (Buried pipes and cold region engineering, etc.); and Geoenvironmental engineering (Contaminant hydrogeology, Barrier systems, etc.). Includes a significant 95-page bibliography.

5253 **Geotechnical engineering handbook**
U. Smoltczyk, ed. Wiley, 2003, 2175pp. 3 v, $675.00. ISBN 3433014523.
Massive new handbook offering a comprehensive overview of present-day geotechnical technology. 34 chapters in three volumes.

- V. 1. *Fundamentals.* ISBN 3433014493 808pp. Covers in 14 chapters the basic physical theories of rock and soil mechanics, geotechnical laboratory and field tests, etc.
- V. 2. *Procedures* ISBN 3433014507 701pp. In 14 chapters covers the realm of geotechnical procedures such as Grouting, Drilling, Ground freezing, etc.
- V. 3. *Elements and structures.* ISBN 3433014515 666pp. In 10 chapters covers mainly different kinds of foundations, including Spread foundations, Pile foundations, Caissons, etc.

5254 **Ground engineer's reference book**
F.G. Bell, ed. Butterworth, 1987, 1264pp. £105.00. ISBN 0408011734.
Ageing, but still a valuable and well organized compendium of information and data. Full of diagrams, tables, figures, etc. About 70 contributors to 59 chapters arranged in 5 parts: Properties and behaviour of the ground (Stability of soil slopes, Subsidence, etc.), Investigation in ground engineering (Surveying, Site investigation, etc.), Treatment of the ground (Grouts and grouting, Geotextiles, etc.), Construction in ground engineering (Caissons and

cofferdams, Embankments, etc.), and Numerical methods and modelling in ground engineering (Modelling in ground engineering, etc.) Most chapters have lengthy bibliographies.

5255 Guide to stability design criteria for metal structures

T.V. Galambos, ed. 5th edn, Wiley, 1998, 944pp. $160.00. ISBN 0471127426.

Sponsored and written by members of the Structural Stability Research Council. Well established guide to procedures, specifications, codes and standards regarding the stability of metal structures. This edition extensively revised and updated. Its 20 chapters include eight new ones, including Horizontal curved steel I-girders, Doubly curved shells and shell-like structures, and Stability analysis by the finite element method. Appendices include SSRC Technical Memorandums.

1st edn 1960, 4th edn 1988.

5256 Handbook of coastal engineering

J.B. Herbich, ed. McGraw-Hill, 2000, 1115pp. $125.00. ISBN 0071344020.

A compendium of information presented in 19 state-of-the art chapters written by 27 authors. Chapters include the more theoretical (for instance, Numerical solution of coastal water wave equations) with the more practical (for instance, Design of dikes and revetments – Dutch practice). Most chapters have good bibliographies. A long appendix details ACES Automated Coastal Engineering System), the programs for which are available via the world wide web.

5257 Handbook of dredging engineering

J.B. Herbich 2nd edn, McGraw-Hill, 2000, 992pp. $125.00. ISBN 0071343067.

An up-to-date guide to dredging practice and technology in 23 chapters covering such topics as: Dredge pumps; Dredge equipment; Pipeline transport of solids; Numerical methods for predicting the fate of dredged material; Subaqueous capping of contaminated sediments; Removal of contaminated sediment by dredging.

1st edn 1992.

5258 Handbook of hydraulics

E.F. Brater [et al.], eds 7th edn, McGraw-Hill, 1996. $77.00. ISBN 0070072477.

Packed with information, this is a standard reference work in its field. Arranged in 14 sections: Fluid properties and hydraulic units; Hydrostatics; Fundamental concepts of flow; Orifices, gates, and tables; Weirs; Pipes; Steady uniform flow in open channels; Open channels with non-uniform flow; High-velocity transitions; Wave motion and forces; Spatially variable and unsteady flow; Measurement of flowing water; Advances in hydraulics using computer technology; Applicable computer programs.

1st edn 1918, and well known as King's handbook of hydraulics, *6th edn 1976.*

5259 Handbook of port and harbor engineering: geotechnical and structural aspects

G.P. Tsinker, ed. Kluwer Academic, 1996, 1054pp. £203.00. ISBN 0412087014.

Comprehensive overview of the design, construction, and modernization of port and harbour structures. Organized in 10 sections: The marine environment and its effects on port design and construction; Port (harbor) elements – design principles and considerations; Design loads; Geotechnical aspects of soil-structure interaction design considerations; Gravity type quay walls; Sheet pile bulkheads; Piled waterfront structures; Offshore deep water terminals; Modernization of existing marine facilities; and Breakwater design.

5260 Handbook of road technology

M.G. Lay 3rd edn, Spon, 1999. 2 v., £160.00. ISBN 9056991590.

Revised and considerably enlarged, this major work covers most aspects of road use and road technology.

- V. 1. *Planning and pavements.* ISBN 9056991574. Deals with the design and construction of roads and pavements, from planning policies to the selection of materials. Chapters include Residential streets, Pavement design, Bridges, etc.
- V. 2. *Traffic and transport.* ISBN 9056991582. This volume covers road operating environments, and includes chapters on Driver behaviour, Traffic flow and capacity, and Speeds, as well as Lighting, Safety, etc.

Series: Transportation Studies. 1st edn 1986; 2nd edn 1990 (Gordon & Breach).

5261 Handbook of soil mechanics

Á. Kézdi, ed. Elsevier, 1974–90. 4 v. ISBN 044499890X.

Ageing a little but a well respected overview of soil mechanics.

- V. 1. *Soil physics.* ISBN 9630500884 294pp. 1974.
- V. 2. *Soil testing.* ISBN 0444997784. 260pp. 1980.
- V. 3. *Soil mechanics of earthworks, foundations and highway engineering.* ISBN 0444989293. 338pp. 1988.
- V. 4. *Application of soil mechanics in practice: examples and case histories.* ISBN 0444988432. 340pp. 1990.

Revised translation of Handbuch der Bodenmechanik, Budapest: Akadémiai Kiadó, 1969. Vols. 3 and 4 edited by A. Kézdi and L. Réthâti.

5262 Handbook of structural engineering

W.-F. Chen, ed. CRC Press, 1997, 1600pp. $149.95. ISBN 0849326745.

A very useful overview of many structural engineering topics. 37 contributors to 28 chapters organized in three sections: Fundamentals (for instance, Structural analysis), Special Structures (such as Aluminium structures, and Shell structures), and Special topics (for instance, Plate and box girders, and Structural reliability). Good bibliographies.

2nd edn expected 2005.

5263 Highway design and traffic safety engineering handbook

R. Lamm, B. Psarianos and T. Mailaender McGraw-Hill, 1999, 1088pp. ISBN 0070382956.

Aims to provide 'a comprehensive presentation about the relationships between highway design, driving behavior, driving dynamics, and traffic safety', particularly for the expert. 26 chapters arranged in three parts: Network; Alignment of non-built-up roads (Horizontal alignment, Vertical alignment, Sight distance, etc.); and Cross sections of non-built-up roads (Cross section design, etc.) Sometimes a little stilted in translation, it is still a massive accumulation of scientific and design data, aided by a 38-page list of international references.

5264 Highway engineering handbook: building and rehabilitating the infrastructure
R.L. Brockenbrough and K.J. Boedecker, eds 2nd edn, McGraw-Hill, 2003. $125.00. ISBN 007140080X.
US-based multi-authored text which is packed with detail. Each chapter is paginated separately, but there is an excellent cross-chapter subject index. Good use of tables and diagrams.

5265 Highway maintenance handbook
K. Atkinson, ed. 2nd edn, Thomas Telford, 1997, 576pp. £85.00. ISBN 0727725319.
This edition revised and greatly expanded. It concentrates on general maintenance and includes chapters on High profile maintenance; Carriageways maintenance; Footways; Street lighting and illuminated traffic signs; Traffic signal maintenance; Aids to movement; Road assessment and management systems; Accident prevention; Winter maintenance; and Maintenance of highway structures. Well illustrated.
1st edn 1990.

5266 Manual of bridge engineering
M.J. Ryall, G.A.R. Parke and J.E. Harding, eds Thomas Telford, 2000, 1012pp. £150.00. ISBN 0727727745.
Comprehensive overview of bridge engineering, with 29 contributors to 19 chapters, which include analytical topics (for instance, Loads and load distribution,) categories of bridge (for instance, Cable-stayed bridges), and more functional topics (such as Bridge management). Well illustrated and good chapter bibliographies.

5267 Manual of soil laboratory testing
K.H. Head 2nd edn, Wiley, 1992–98. 3 v.
A basic working manual, comprehensive in approach, covering most aspects of the topic.
- V. 1. *Soil classification and compaction tests*. 1992. 388pp. ISBN 0471964107. Covers the basics of soil classification. Seven chapters on Equipment; Techniques and safety; Moisture content and index tests; Density and particle density; Particle size; Chemical tests; Compaction tests; and Description of soils.
- V. 2. *Permeability, shear strength and compressibility tests*. 1994. 440pp. ISBN 0470233621. This volume covers standard laboratory tests and includes seven chapters: Equipment and laboratory practice; Preparation of test specimens; Permeability and erodibility tests; California bearing ratio test; Direct shear tests; Undrained compression tests; and Oedometer consolidation tests.
- V. 3. *Effective stress tests*. 1998. 428pp. ISBN 0471977950. Covers more complex tests. Eight chapters include Effective stress testing; Test equipment; Calibrations, corrections and general practice; Routine effective stress triaxial tests; Further triaxial shear strength tests; Triaxial consolidation and permeability tests; Stress paths in triaxial testing; and Hydraulic cell consolidation and permeability tests. Also includes Errata and Amendment for Vols. 1 and 2.

1st edn 1980–1992.

5268 Practical foundation engineering handbook
R.W. Brown 2nd edn, McGraw-Hill, 2001, 1208pp. ISBN 0071351396.
Substantial and comprehensive reference book aimed at the practitioner. 19 chapters by 12 authors arranged in nine parts: Foundation and civil engineering site development; Soil mechanics and foundation design parameters; Fundamentals of foundation construction and design; Reinforced concrete foundations; Residential and lightly loaded foundations; Soil improvement and stabilization; Foundation failure and repair (2 parts); and Miscellaneous concerns. Well illustrated and often lengthy bibliographies.
1st edn 1995.

5269 Reservoir sedimentation handbook: design and management of dams, reservoirs, and watersheds for sustainable use
G.L. Morris and J. Fan, eds McGraw-Hill, 1998, 805pp. $95.00. ISBN 007043302X.
A substantial overview with a practical approach to the subject. Divided into 25 chapters, covering reservoir limnology, sediment properties, erosion, modelling, hydraulics of sediment transport, decommissioning of dams, and seven chapter-length case-studies.

5270 Seismic design handbook
F. Naeim, ed. 2nd edn, Kluwer, 2001, 830pp. Accompanying CD-ROM carries the text of the handbook and various relevant building codes, £142.00. ISBN 0792373014.
22 authors of 16 chapters which deal with the science of seismic phenomena, general seismic design considerations (Design for drift and lateral stability, and Seismic design of floor diaphragms, for instance), and specific applications (Seismic design of steel structures, and Seismic upgrading of existing structures, for instance). Substantially revised and lengthened since the first edition. Contains a great deal of practical detail.
1st edn 1989.

5271 Standard handbook for civil engineers
F.S. Merritt, M.K. Loftin and J.T. Ricketts, eds 5th edn, McGraw-Hill, 2004, 1600pp. $150.00. ISBN 0071364730.
Major reference work covering the whole gamut of civil engineering. Over 30 contributors to 23 sections that include Systems design; Design management; Specifications; Construction management; Construction materials; Structural theory; Geotechnical engineering; Concrete design and construction; Structural steel design and construction; Cold-formed steel design and construction; Wood design and construction; Surveying; Earthwork; Community and regional planning; Building engineering; Highway engineering; Bridge engineering; Airport engineering; Rail-transportation engineering; Tunnel engineering; Water resources engineering; Environmental engineering; and Coastal and port engineering. Variable sectional bibliographies, good index.
1st edn 1968; 4th edn 1996.

5272 Standard handbook of heavy construction
J.J. O'Brien, J.A. Havers and F.W. Stubbs, eds 3rd edn, McGraw-Hill, 1996. ISBN 0070479712.
An overview consisting of 34 chapters contributed by 31 authors. Arranged in five parts: Construction/project management (Scheduling, Construction planning, etc.); Heavy construction equipment (Cranes, Excavators, etc.); Heavy construction materials (Conventional concrete, Reinforcing steel, etc.); Heavy construction types (Rock excavation/blasting, etc.); and Heavy construction projects (Airports, Highways, etc.)
1st edn 1959; 2nd edn 1971.

5273 **Steel designers' manual**
B. Davison and G.W. Owens, eds; Steel Construction Institute 6th edn, Blackwell Science, 2003, 1337pp. £89.50. ISBN 0632049251.
This is the classic work on structural steelwork design for the UK. This edition updated to include latest British Standards. 38 contributors to 36 chapters arranged in 7 sections: Design synthesis; Steel technology; Design theory; Element design; Connection design; Other elements; and Construction. Also includes substantial appendices of tabular and other data.
1st edn 1955; 5th edn 1992.

5274 **Steel detailers' manual**
A. Hayward, F. Weare and A.C. Oakhill 2nd edn, Blackwell Science, 2002, 248pp. £42.50. ISBN 0632055723.
Highly illustrated reference work showing a wide range of steelwork details. Updated to include material on computer-aided detailing and revisions to standards. Arranged in six sections: Use of structural steel; Detailing practice; Design guidance; Detailing data; Typical connection details; and Examples of structures.
1st edn 1989.

5275 **Stones of Britain: a pictorial guide to those in charge of valuable buildings**
B.C.G. Shore Leonard Hill, 1957, 302pp.
Thorough investigation of geological and chemical questions involved in the use of stone for building and in stone preservation. Four main sections: Care of ancient buildings; List of British stones, their occurrence and structure; Maintenance work using stone; New buildings of stone, and stone for sculpture. Lavishly illustrated with fine photographs and maps.

5276 **Structural engineering handbook**
E.H. Gaylord, C.N. Gaylord and J.E. Stallmeyer, eds 4th edn, McGraw-Hill, 1997, 1184pp. $125.00. ISBN 0070237247.
An authoritative and popular reference work. Updated to include latest US codes and specifications. 58 contributors to 32 chapters concerned with principles (e.g. Structural analysis; Fatigue), design of structural members (e.g. Plastic design of steel frames), and types of structures (e.g. Chimneys).
1st edn 1968, 3rd edn 1990.

5277 **Structural steel designer's handbook**
R.L. Brockenbrough and F.S. Merritt 3rd edn, McGraw-Hill, 1999, 1150pp. $125.00. ISBN 0070087822.
Provides data on the properties and uses of steel in structural settings. Contains 16 chapters including: Properties of structural steel, Fabrication and erection, General structural theory, Special structural theories, Connections, Design of building members, Floor and roof systems, Design of building members, Floor and roof systems, Lateral-force design, and five chapters on bridges.
1st edn 1972, 2nd edn 1994.
'proven handbook ... recommended.' (Hurt: *Information sources in science and technology* (about the 2nd edn).)

5278 **Tables for the hydraulic design of pipes, sewers and channels**
H.R. Wallingford and D.I.H. Barr 7th edn, Thomas Telford, 1998. 2 v., £85.00. ISBN 0727726390.
This updated edition presents tables of solutions to the Colebrook–White equation, which describes the transition between smooth and rough turbulent flows in full flowing pipes, for pipes of various diameters, roughnesses, gradients, at different temperatures, and for materials of various viscosities and densities.
V. 1. 291pp. ISBN 0727726374; V. 2. 292pp. ISBN 0727726382.
1st edn 1963, 6th edn 1994.

5279 **Timber designers' manual**
J.A. Baird and E.C. Ozelton, eds 3rd edn, Blackwell Science, 2002, 542pp. £85.00. ISBN 0632039787.
The manual covers the use of structural timber. Considerably revised since previous edition to include the latest revision of British Standard BS5268-2: 2002. Arranged in 30 chapters plus appendices of tables. Individual chapters cover beams, columns, joints, trusses, preservation, etc.
1st edn 1976, 2nd edn 1984.

5280 **Traffic engineering handbook**
J.L. Pline, ed.; Institute of Transportation Engineers 5th edn, 1999, 720pp. $110.00. ISBN 0935403329.
Long-established and respected handbook. 23 authors of 16 chapters cover the foundations of, and background to, traffic management (Road users, Vehicles, Community safety, etc.) as well as techniques (Geometric design of highways, Traffic signs and markings, etc.) This edition includes four new chapters: Probability and statistics for engineers; Effective public involvement; Traffic calming applications; Access management.
1st edn 1941, 4th edn 1992. Previous editors: J.E. Baerwald and H.K. Evans. Some edns entitled Transportation and traffic engineering handbook.

5281 **Tunnel engineering handbook**
J.O. Bickel, T.R. Kuesel and E.H. King, eds 2nd edn, Chapman & Hall, 1996, 544pp. ISBN 0412992914.
This edition includes eight new chapters covering rehabilitation and repair, stabilization and lining, difficult ground, deep shafts, water conveyance tunnels, small-diameter tunnels, fire line safety, and construction contracting. No index, but an annotated table of contents and extensive cross references.
1st edn 1982.

5282 **Wind loading: a practical guide to BS 6399-2**
N.J. Cook Thomas Telford, 1999, 243pp. £42.50. ISBN 0727727559.
Provides guidance on BS6399 with which new buildings in the UK must comply. Contents include Introduction; Commentary; Making BS 6399-2 work for you; Worked examples; Lattice structures; and Corrected factor tables.

5283 **Wood handbook: wood as an engineering material**
Forest Products Laboratory 1999, 463pp. ISBN 1892529025.
www.fpl.fs.fed.us
Consists of 19 chapters that describe the physical and mechanical properties of wood. These include: Fastenings, Structural analysis equations, Adhesive bonding, Composites and panel products, Glued structural members, Preservation, Finishing, and Fire safety. Useful glossary.
Available online: see website.

Keeping up-to-date

5284 Civil Engineering [USA]
American Society of Civil Engineers 1930–, Monthly. $225.00 [2004]. ISSN 08557024.
www.pubs.asce.org/ceonline/newce.html [DESCRIPTION]
ASCE's house membership magazine, reporting on projects and structures plus the societal context of civil engineering – markets, legal decisions, etc.

5285 Civil Engineering [UK]
Institution of Civil Engineers 1991–, 4 issues + 2 special issues pa. £92.00 [2004]. ISSN 0965089X.
www.ttjournals.com [DESCRIPTION]
The principal journal of the ICE. Contains refereed papers, short briefing articles, discussion and book reviews, covering the whole area of civil engineering. There are two special issues per year, each devoted to a major project or topical subject.
Formerly (1972–1991) the Proceedings of the Institution of Civil Engineers, Part 1 (ISSN 0307-8353) and Part 2 (ISSN 0307-8361).

5286 engineering-geotech [UK]
www.jiscmail.ac.uk/lists/engineering-geotech.html
With over 600 subscribers and an average of about 15 postings per month, this is one of the most popular engineering mailing lists in the UK. Postings consist mainly of technical questions, events, and jobs, especially UK academic. Mainly aimed at academics and researchers. The site has monthly archives of messages from September 1998 onwards.

5287 iGEM: the Internet geotechnical engineering magazine
The World Wide Web of Geotechnical Engineers.
www.ejge.com/iGEM/index.htm
iGEM is the magazine section of the Electronic Journal of Geotechnical Engineering. A good-looking, well designed site consisting of articles, both technical and popular, features (including book reviews and software information), and corners (jobs, events, etc.)

5288 Infoshare [UK]
Institution of Civil Engineers
www.ice.org.uk/knowledge/knowledge_newsletters.asp [REGISTRATION]
The ICE's weekly internet newsletter providing news and views on developments and projects within the profession. There are discussion forums on site and access to an archive of back issues.

5289 New Civil Engineer [UK]
EMAP Construct, 1972–, Weekly. £98.00. ISSN 03077683.
www.nceplus.co.uk
Popular weekly news and views and jobs magazine. Website provides access to a range of industry information – mostly for subscribers.

5290 Structural Engineer [UK]
Institution of Structural Engineers 1924–, Biweekly. £175.00. ISBN 14665123.
www.istructe.org.uk/thestructuralengineer
The Institution's house journal which contains news, reports, views, technical notes and papers, an events diary, and information about products and services.

Construction & Building

building construction • building materials • building services • buildings • floors • plumbing • timber construction

Introductions to the subject

5291 Building construction handbook
R. Chudley and R. Greeno 5th edn, Butterworth-Heinemann, 2004, 736pp. £19.99. ISBN 0750661968.
Comprehensive but concise summary of building practice intended mainly as a student textbook. Updated to take into account revised British and European Standards and changes to the Building Regulations. Divided into seven sections: General; Site works; Builders plant; Substructure; Superstructure; Internal construction and finishes; and Domestic services.
1st edn 1988, 4th edn. 2001.

5292 Building services handbook
F.E. Hall and R. Greeno Butterworth-Heinemann, 2003, 516pp. £19.99. ISBN 0750661437.
Good, cheap and cheerful introduction to the basics of building services, intended as a textbook. Updated to take into account revised British and European Standards and changes to the Building Regulations. Arranged in 16 parts, including appendices, covering Hot and Cold water supply, Heating systems, Air conditioning, Drainage and sewage systems, Sanitary fitments, Gas installations, Electrical supply and fittings, Mechanical conveyors, Fire prevention, Security, etc.
Based on Fred Hall's Essential building services and equipment, first published 1976.

Dictionaries, thesauri, classifications

5293 Building services thesaurus
G. Beale, comp.; Building Services Research and Information Association 5th edn, 1993, 208pp. £25.00. ISBN 0860223418.
Contains 5000 terms, with 5000 synonyms and cross-references for the mechanical and electrical services in buildings, including health and safety aspects of buildings. Constructed as an aid to searching BSRIA's library database, IBSEDEX, it consists of an alphabetical index of terms and a classified display of relationships.

5294 Construction glossary: an encyclopedic reference and manual
J.S. Stein, comp. 2nd edn, Wiley, 1993, 1137pp. $210.00. ISBN 047156933X.
Contains about 30,000 terms arranged in 16 sections: General requirements; Site work; Concrete; Masonry; Metals; Wood and plastics; Thermal and moisture protection; Doors and windows; Finishes; Specialities; Equipment; Furnishings; Special construction; Conveying systems; Mechanical; and Electrical. Also extra divisions for Professional services, Construction categories, and Scientific and technical and related data. Most definitions are 2–12 lines in length. US reference sources are listed. Appendices include abbreviations and weights and measures. Valuable 125-page index.
1st edn 1980.

5295 **Dictionary of architecture & construction**
C.M. Harris, comp. 3rd edn, McGraw-Hill, 2000, 1056pp. $69.95. ISBN 0071351787.
Prepared with the help of more than 50 contributors and 20 key associations. Contains more than 25,000 terms and 2500 illustrations, about 10% more than previous edition. Covers architectural design, construction, building trades, water supply, waste disposal, building preservation, etc.
1st edn 1975, 2nd edn 1993.

5296 **Dictionary of building and civil engineering (Dictionnaire du bâtiment et du génie civil)**
D. Montague, comp. Spon, 1996, 450pp. £58.00. ISBN 0419199101.
A dual language dictionary with over 20,000 entries in both English and French, with translations. Includes architecture and property terms as well as building and engineering ones.

5297 **Elsevier's dictionary of building construction**
J. Maclean, comp. Elsevier, 1989. 2 v., €154 per volume.
Covers 'the basic vocabulary of the industry with particular emphasis on mechanical and electrical services'. Differentiates between American and British English. Brief bibliography.
V. 1. *English–French*. 389pp. ISBN 0444429662.
V. 2. *French–English*. 345pp. ISBN 044442931X.

5298 **Elsevier's dictionary of building tools and materials in five languages: English/American, French, Spanish, German and Dutch**
L.Y. Chaballe and J.-P. Vandenberghe, comps Elsevier, 1982, 722pp. €245.00. ISBN 0444420479.
Contains 5853 English/American terms with synonyms and variants, plus equivalents and indexes, in the other four languages. Includes a bibliography of sources.

5299 **Glossary of building and civil engineering terms: BS6100**
British Standards Institution 1984–.
An important but usually forgotten reference work. Issued in, at time of writing, 53 current parts between 1984 and 2002. Each part is self-contained covering a specific topic – so, for instance, 4.1 covers Glazing, while 2.2.3 deals with the vocabulary of Tunnels. Each part is typically classified and includes an index. Entries are one sentence.
For ordering information see www.bsi-global.com.

5300 **An illustrated dictionary of building: an illustrated reference guide for practitioners and students**
P. Brett, comp. 2nd edn, Butterworth-Heinemann, 1997, 333pp. £21.99. ISBN 075063684X.
Contains about 3500 terms with generally concise definitions arranged in six thematic sections – Architectural style; Building construction; Documentation, administration, and control; General; Materials and scientific principles; and Services and finishes – linked by an index.
1st edn 1989 as Building terminology.

5301 **Illustrated dictionary of building terms**
T. Philbin, comp. McGraw-Hill, 1997, 249pp. $24.95. ISBN 007049729X.
Contains about 15,000 terms defined very briefly, normally a couple of lines, but occasionally up to a page in length. Includes US slang terms. Well illustrated.

5302 **Illustrated encyclopedia of building services**
D. Kut, comp. Spon, 1993, 355pp. £95.00. ISBN 0419176802.
More an encyclopedic dictionary than an encyclopedia, this work contains definitions of about 3000 terms mainly taken from the areas of air conditioning, heating and ventilating, hot and cold water supply, fire fighting and protection, drainage and sanitation, and electrical services.

International dictionary of heating, ventilating and air conditioning
Federation of European Heating, Ventilating and Air-conditioning Associations See entry no. 5875

5303 **McGraw-Hill constructionary: Spanish–English/English–Spanish construction dictionary**
L. Hager, comp.; International Conference of Building Officials McGraw-Hill, 2001, 210pp. $19.99. ISBN 0071375791.
A very basic translating dictionary aimed at the practising builder containing rather more than 1000 words and phrases. Includes phonic pronunciations, helpful construction terms, on-the-job phrases, a tools section, and practical tables.

5304 **Means illustrated construction dictionary**
J. Marchetti and M. Greene, comps Means, 2000, 691pp. CD-ROM, $99.95. ISBN 0876295383.
Standard US dictionary containing about 14,000 terms defined briefly and clearly. Excellent illustrations.

5305 **Multilingual dictionary of architecture and building terms**
C. Grech, ed. Spon, 1998, 453pp. £74.00. ISBN 0419199209.
Consists of over 2600 terms 'used most commonly in building design and construction', listed in English with French, German, Italian and Spanish equivalents. With four accompanying foreign language indexes.

5306 **Penguin dictionary of building**
J.S. Scott and J. Maclean 4th edn, Penguin, 1994, 516pp. £10.99. ISBN 014051239X.
A useful, clear dictionary that contains over 5000 terms covering the building trade, tools, and materials. Entries usually 3–20 lines long, are occasionally illustrated, and sometimes carry references to British or European standards, or Building Research Establishment publications. US usage is differentiated. Cross referenced to the Penguin dictionary of civil engineering. For both the professional builder and do-it-yourself enthusiast.
1st edn 1964, 3rd edn 1984.

5307 **Routledge German dictionary of construction: German–English/English–German (Wörterbuch bauwesen: Deutsch–Englisch/Englisch–Deutsch)**
H.D. Junge and D. Lukhaup, comps Routledge, 1997, 376pp. Also available on CD-ROM (ISBN 0415140293, £150.00.), £130.00. ISBN 0415112427.
Contains 25,000 words in each language in common use in the industry. Includes specialized technical words and phrases, cross-references and contexts of usage. Subjects covered include infrastructure and design, material properties, building accessories, structures, stone buildings, surface treatment, wastewater treatment, heating, ventilation and air conditioning, sound insulation, electrical engineering,

building machinery, architecture and building planning, environmental issues, and construction law.

5308 Wiley dictionary of civil engineering and construction
L.F. Webster, comp. Wiley, 1997, 688pp. $65.00. ISBN 0471181153.
Contains clear, concise definitions of about 30,000 terms. Strong coverage of construction, but its coverage of civil engineering is noted as less good.
Originally published as The contractors' dictionary of equipment, tools, and techniques for civil engineering, construction, forestry, open-pit mining, and public works, Wiley, 1995.
'Excellent dictionary of terminology used ... in construction engineering' (*Choice*)

5309 Wiley dictionary of civil engineering and construction: English–Spanish/Spanish–English
F. Kennedy, comp. Wiley, 1996, 553pp. $99.00. ISBN 0471122467.
Excellent translating dictionary containing about 50,000 terms (words and compound words) in each language, covering most aspects of architecture, construction, surveying, materials, environmental engineering, etc.

Laws, standards, codes

5310 Building Regulations [UK]
TSO, 2000–.
www.odpm.gov.uk [DESCRIPTION]
The Building Regulations apply to most new buildings in England and Wales, and also to extensions, alterations and to change of use of existing buildings. They are Statutory Instruments, approved by Parliament, and are thus legally binding. Their main purpose is to ensure reasonable levels of health and safety for people in and around buildings by providing mandatory functional requirements for building design. In addition, Building Regulations promote energy efficiency and contribute to meeting the needs of disabled people. They are arranged in sections, A (Structural Adequacy) – N (Glazing).
Available online: see website.

5311 The Building Regulations explained and illustrated [UK]
M.J. Billington, M.W. Simons and J.R. Waters 12th edn, Blackwell, 2003, 920pp. £39.95. ISBN 0632058374.
Long-established and straightforward introduction to the BUILDING REGULATIONS, arranged in two parts. Part 1 – Legal and Administrative – provides an overview of the Regulations. Part 2 – Technical – deals with the regulations and their import, section by section.
1st edn 1967, 11th edn 1999. Early editions by V. Powell-Smith and W.S. Whyte.

5312 Canadian Codes Centre
http://irc.nrc-cnrc.gc.ca/codes/home_E.shtml
Provides technical and administrative support to the Canadian Commission on Building and Fire Codes and its committees, responsible for development of national model construction codes for Canada.

5313 Code for lighting [UK]
Chartered Institution of Building Services Engineers and Society of Light and Lighting 16th edn, Butterworth-Heinemann, 2002, 192pp. £100.00. ISBN 0750656379.
Updated to include exterior as well as interior lighting, and to take into account the 2002 revision of Part L of the BUILDING REGULATIONS, as well as other new and forthcoming International and European Standards on lighting and ergonomics. In three sections: Visual effects of lighting; Recommendations (including schedule); and Lighting design.
1st edn 1949, last edn 1994.

5314 International Code Council [USA]
www.iccsafe.org
Established 1994 as a non-profit organization dedicated to developing a single set of comprehensive and co-ordinated national model construction codes within the USA. Founders were: Building Officials and Code Administrators International, International Conference of Building Officials and Southern Building Code Congress International.

Extensive website with wide range of useful resources, including publications, news, government information, standards development, etc.

Official & quasi-official bodies

5315 British Board of Agrément
www.bbacerts.co.uk
The British Board of Agrément is an organization partnered with Government which provides authoritative and independent information on the performance of building products. Every Agrément Certificate contains important data on durability, installation and compliance with Building Regulations. The BBA website contains information about its work, its testing procedures, and lists of approved products and installers.

5316 Building Regulations Division [UK]
Office of the Deputy Prime Minister
www.odpm.gov.uk
Through the Building Regulations Division, the Deputy Prime Minister's Office has overall responsibility for the BUILDING REGULATIONS, which ensure the safety of people in and around buildings, promote energy efficiency, and provide for the needs of people with disabilities by stipulating functional requirements in design and construction. This site contains a collection of recent relevant materials – discussion documents, legislation, etc. – and a good set of links to useful organizations.

5317 International Council for Research and Innovation in Building and Construction
www.cibworld.nl
Originally entitled Conseil International du Bâtiment – CIB, as the Council is usually known – was established in 1953 under the auspices of the United Nations, to stimulate and facilitate international co-operation between governmental research institutes in the building and construction sector. Based in Rotterdam, it now consists of a worldwide network of over 5000 experts from about 500 member organizations who co-operate in over 50 CIB Commissions covering all fields of building and construction related research.

The CIB website provides information about the Council, and its various Working Commissions and Task Groups, publications, membership, etc. Part of the site is restricted to members.

Research centres & institutes

5318 Building and Fire Research Laboratory [USA]
www.bfrl.nist.gov
A US National Institute for Standards and Technology laboratory, the BFRL carries out research in the areas of building materials, computer-integrated construction practices, fire science and fire safety engineering, and structural, mechanical, and environmental engineering as applied to building, with the intention of influencing building and fire standards and codes. The website includes a free online newsletter. *BFRL Publications Online* contains over 2300 document abstracts and complete publications produced by or for BFRL staff since 1993.

5319 Building Research Establishment [UK]
www.bre.co.uk
The UK's leading centre of expertise on buildings, construction, energy, environment, fire and risk. It is owned by the Foundation for the Built Environment, a registered charity, and offers a range of research and consultancy services. Its website has information about the Establishment and its services, and provides access to the BRE bookshop.

5320 Building Services Research and Information Association [UK]
www.bsria.co.uk
Based in Berkshire, BSRIA is a not-for-profit organization whose aim is to provide research, information and consultancy support to its members in the UK building services industry. It is one of the most reputable bodies in its area. The BSRIA website contains information about its products, services, research activities, and extensive range of publications. It is the producer of IBSEDEX. Much of the site is restricted to members.

5321 Centre Scientifique et Technique du Bâtiment [FRA]
www.cstb.fr
The CSTB is a state-owned industrial and commercial establishment under the administrative supervision of the French Ministry of Housing, and one of Europe's leading research centres in its field. Its aim is to improve well being and safety in buildings by research, advanced engineering, quality assessment and the dissemination of knowledge. The CSTB website is in French, although a reduced version in English is also available. The French site includes news, product evaluations, research project information, and a searchable catalogue of technical and regulatory documents.

5322 Construction Industry Research and Information Association [UK]
www.ciria.org.uk
CIRIA is an independent, not-for-profit private sector association in the UK which carries out research and disseminates information in construction and related areas. At present its research activities are concentrated in three broad categories: buildings and facilities; transport; and water and utilities. The CIRIA website has information about the Association, membership details, research activities, details of CIRIA publications, information about CIRIA networks – for instance, Construction Industry Environmental Forum – events, news, and links to other websites.

Associations & societies

5323 Chartered Institute of Building [UK]
www.ciob.org.uk
CIOB is the professional body for construction managers, and claims over 40,000 members in more than 90 countries. Its website includes information about its work, regional groups, etc. A Knowledge Centre includes downloadable booklets about choosing a builder, and various client guides. It also covers advice about construction as a career, continuing professional development, conferences, etc.

5324 Chartered Institution of Building Services Engineers [UK]
www.cibse.org
CIBSE is the professional body representing and providing services to the building services profession in the UK. It has 15,000 members, 20% of whom are based overseas, and was founded in 1976 following the amalgamation of the Institution of Heating and Ventilating Engineers (founded 1897) with the Illuminating Engineering Society (founded 1909).

The CIBSE website provides information about the Institution's publications, courses and meetings, and access to an electronic version of the *Building Services Journal*. It also has a register of consultants. Some of the site is restricted to members.

European Foundation of Landscape Architecture (EFLA)
See entry no. 2987

5325 Institute of Plumbing and Heating Engineering [UK]
www.plumbers.org.uk
Founded in 1906, the Institute is the UK's professional body for plumbers and others in the plumbing industry. It has about 11,000 members, and publishes the bimonthly magazine, *Plumbing*. The IoP website offers information about itself and the plumbing industry, a register of members, a register of industrial associates, consumer advice, events, news, discussion forums, and information about plumbing as a career.

The Institute's new titles – adding 'Heating Engineering' – was adopted in 2004 because 'corporate members agreed that the new title better reflects their scope of work and firmly identifies plumbing and heating as an engineering discipline'.

Landscape Institute
See entry no. 2993

5326 Royal Institution of Chartered Surveyors [UK]
www.rics.org.uk
RICS is a not-for-profit body dealing with all aspects of land, property, and construction with 110,000 members in 120 countries. The Institution's website provides information about the organization, a Public Zone which contains pages about surveyors' fees, auctions, consumer protection, etc., a directory of surveyors, regional activities, a set of discussion forums, faculties (subject arrangements), and a Career Zone.

Libraries, archives, museums

5327 Building Centre [UK]
www.buildingcentre.co.uk
Established in 1931, the Building Centre claims to be 'the worlds largest permanent exhibition and single source of information for the construction industry'. It is made up of a purpose-built exhibition centre, bookshop, internet bookshop, conference suites and market research facilities. Its web pages provide access to its Product Information Service (manufacturers' brochures) and online bookshop, as well as providing information about the Centre's own information services, market research activities, conference facilities, and exhibitions.

Portal & task environments

5328 4specs [USA]
C. Gilboy, comp.
www.4specs.com
Substantial links to over 400 construction-related associations and reference organizations ranging from the Academy of Certified Hazardous Materials Managers to the Woven Wire Products Association. Detailed directory of products and companies organized by the MasterFormat 2004 classification scheme maintained by the Construction Specifications Institute (www.csinet.org): an association of approximately 17,000 members representing all the disciplines engaged in non-residential building design and construction.

5329 Abacus Construction Index [UK]
www.construction-index.com
Abacus claims to be the most heavily used construction information website both in the UK and in Europe. It is aimed at UK construction professionals, including architects, engineers and surveyors, and consists primarily of a searchable directory of more than 1500 recommended websites – online documents, case studies and newsletters. The site is also browsable by resource type or topic, contains a weekly featured website, and highlights its most popular link and a selection of highly recommended websites.

5330 Advanced Buildings: Technologies & Practices [CAN]
www.advancedbuildings.org
Guide for architects, engineers and buildings managers to more than 90 environmentally-appropriate technologies and practices. The pleasant easy-to-use website is supported by a consortium of government and private organizations within Canada.

5331 aecportico [UK]
Royal Institute of British Architects
www.aecportico.co.uk
An internet gateway to architecture, engineering and construction resources maintained by the commercial arm of the Royal Institute of British Architects. Its searchable set of links is arranged by category, including Engineering, Building, Surveying, Environment, and Academic institution. It also features a list of organizations, a latest news section, a diary of forthcoming events, a site of the week, a list of recently added sites, and a book of the week (published by RIBA).

5332 Fire on the Web [USA]
Building and Fire Research Laboratory
www.fire.nist.gov
Divided into four sections: Fire tests/data – some with accompanying video sequences; Downloadable software/models; Publications; and Other. The publications section includes BFRL Publications Online, a collection of post-1993 publications available for free download, published by and for BFRL staff; Factsheets – a small number of short pamphlets about fire safety; and FIREDOC, a searchable database of publications in the Fire Research Information Services at BFRL. There is also a set of links to related sites.

Discovering print & electronic resources

5333 Construction and Building Abstracts
Arup; NBS, 1985–.
www.cbaweb.co.uk [FEE-BASED]
A joint venture between Arup and NBS – publisher of the *National Building Specification* and a part of RIBA Enterprises – this database contains over 100,000 bibliographic records of articles published in more than 125 journals. A wide range of topics is covered including civil and structural engineering, architecture, planning, building and the built environment, materials and energy. Items date back to 1985 and about 9000 articles are added per year. Access is by subscription only.

5334 FIREDOC [USA]
Building and Fire Research Laboratory
www.bfrl.nist.gov/fris/#FIREDOC
Free-to-use bibliographic database on fire research and engineering. Its 55,000 records of published reports, journal articles, conference proceedings, books, and audiovisual items reflects the holdings of the BFRL's Fire Research Information Services. The database is searchable by author, title, keyword, etc. and contains links to BFRL fire research publications for 2000 onwards.

The *FIREDOC Vocabulary List* (4th edn, 1997) is available in pdf at http://fire.nist.gov/bfrlpubs/fire97/art022.html.

5335 IBSEDEX [UK]
Building Services Research and Information Association 1960–.
www.einsgem.org
IBSEDEX contains over 130,000 references to the worldwide literature on mechanical and electrical services in buildings, including heating, ventilation, air conditioning, lighting and power, plumbing and sanitation, energy use, building structures, etc. It includes books, journal articles, conference papers, reports, and standards back to 1960. About 3000 items are added per year. It is equivalent to the BSRIA library catalogue and corresponds, in part, to INTERNATIONAL BUILDING SERVICES ABSTRACTS JOURNAL.
Available online: see website.

5336 ICONDA
Fraunhofer Information Centre for Regional Planning and Building Construction, International Council for Research and Innovation in Building and Construction and International Union of Building Centres 1976–, Monthly.
www.irbdirekt.de/iconda
ICONDA (International Construction Database) covers the worldwide technical literature on civil engineering, urban and regional planning, architecture, and construction. Sources,

including over 600 periodicals, are scanned by international organizations in 14 countries. It contained nearly 580,000 records as of November 2002. About 2500 new records are added each month.
Available online: see website.

5337 **Information sources in architecture and construction**
V.J. Nurcombe, ed. 2nd edn, Bowker-Saur, 1996, 489pp. £79.00. ISBN 1857390946.
22 contributors to 24 chapters covering the standard information sources (e.g. libraries, periodicals, trade literature, official publications, etc.), IT applications, management of the design process, contracts and liability, conservation, landscape, interior design, and architectural history.
1st edn 1983.

5338 **International Building Services Abstracts Journal**
Building Services Research and Information Association 1978–, Bimonthly. £100.00 [2004]. ISSN 01044237.
www.bsria.co.uk/bookshop/system/index.html [DESCRIPTION]
A bimonthly journal providing a survey of the literature on mechanical and electrical services of buildings from over 120 industry magazines. It contains about 200 items per issue.

Digital data, image & text collections

5339 **Barbour Index** [UK]
www.barbour-index.co.uk
Provides a range of free and subscription web-based information services in the fields of construction, facilities management, and health and safety. Subscription services include Construction Expert, a database of technical and product information, while free services include Facilities Management Expert and Opus Design File, as well as Building Product Expert. The Index also offers a telephone enquiry service, free other than the cost of the call.

- **Building Product Expert** http://bpe.barbour-index.co.uk. Information about some 100,000 products from over 10,000 UK manufacturers; collection of company profiles, case-studies, access to manufacturers' catalogues, links to manufacturers' websites. Searchable by product type or manufacturer/trade name.

5340 **Construction Information Service** [UK]
RIBA Enterprises; Technical Indexes.
www.tionestop.com/ihsti/index.html [FEE-BASED]
Available on CD-ROM and online, CIS is a browsable and searchable index and collection of several thousand UK construction-related documents – regulations, standards, technical documents, and some books – with their images in scanned or PDF format. It consists of a Core Service, plus supplements for Building, Civil and Structural Engineering, Mechanical and Electrical Engineering, and Construction Management.

As well as the BUILDING REGULATIONS, and relevant British Standards, CIS includes documents from BRE, BSRIA, CIBSE, CIRIA, DfEE, and HSE among other organizations, as well as books from Butterworth and the Architectural Press. A very useful and well behaved resource.

5341 **Specify-it: Building** [UK]
Technical Indexes.
www.tionestop.com/ihsti/index.html
This service consists of a collection of product full-text, catalogues, data sheets, selector guides and brochures, available in pdf or DjVu, from suppliers in the construction and civil engineering industries. It covers structural materials and elements, secondary elements and finishes, electrical fittings, plumbing equipment, etc. Searchable by product type, trade name, company name, address, etc. Various levels of service are available.

Directories & encyclopedias

5342 **Plumbing encyclopaedia**
R. D. Treloar, comp. 3rd edn, Blackwell, 2003, 592pp. £22.50. ISBN 1405106131.
More an encyclopedic dictionary consisting of over 1500 entries, including 200 new or revised, and more than 400 explicatory illustrations. Subject coverage includes water supply, sanitation, drainage, hot water heating, etc.
1st edn 1989 as Mechanical engineering services: a plumbing encyclopedia; 2nd edn 1996.

5343 **Spon's Architects' and Builders' Price Book** [UK]
Davis Langdon and Everest, ed. Spon, Annual, 1100pp. £120.00 [2004]. ISSN 03063046.
Long-standing and popular professional source of construction price information. Arranged in five parts: Fees and daywork (rates for professional services); Rates of wages; Prices for measured work; Approximate estimating; and Tables and memoranda, which includes various conversion tables, formulas, design loadings, etc. Useful set of addresses and index.
1st edn 1873, 129th edn 2004.

Handbooks & manuals

ASHRAE handbook
American Society of Heating, Refrigerating and Air-Conditioning Engineers See entry no. 5938

5344 **Building design and construction handbook** [USA]
F.S. Merritt and J.T. Ricketts, eds 6th edn, McGraw-Hill, 2000. $99.00. ISBN 007041999X.
Well established and comprehensive reference work with a US slant. New edition updated to include the *International Building Code 2000*, as well as the latest US fire and other codes. Aimed at the practitioner, it is arranged in 19 sections covering geotechnical and structural aspects (Structural theory, Soil mechanics and foundations, etc.), plus building materials (Structural steel construction, etc.), construction planning, and facilities (HVAC systems, electrical systems, etc.). Lavishly illustrated.
1st edn 1958, 5th edn 1994.

5345 **CIBSE guides** [UK]
Chartered Institution of Building Services Engineers 1998–.
An authoritative set of guides for service design in UK buildings.

- A: *Environmental design*. 1999. 336pp. ISBN 090093 969 £110.
- B1: *Heating*. 2002. 87pp. ISBN 1903287219 £90.
- B2: *Ventilation and air conditioning*. 2001. 160pp. ISBN 1903287162 £90.
- B3: *Ductwork*. 2002. 85pp. ISBN 1903287200 £90.

- B4: *Refrigeration and heat rejection*. 2003. 68pp. ISBN 1903287197 £90.
- B5: *Noise and vibration control for HVAC*. 2002. 55pp. ISBN 1903287251 £58.
- C: *Reference data*. 2001. 279pp. ISBN 0750653604 £100.
- D: *Transportation systems in buildings*. 2000. 256pp. ISBN 190328709X £80.
- E: *Fire engineering*. 2003. 180pp. ISBN 1903287316 £96.
- F: *Energy efficiency in buildings*. 1998. 204pp. ISBN 0900953861 £92.
- G: *Public health engineering*. 1999. 220pp. ISBN 090095387X £92.
- H: *Building control systems*. 2000. 200pp. ISBN 0750650478 £75.
- J: *Weather, solar and illuminance data*. 2002. (CD-ROM) £176.

An abridged version of the set is available as the CIBSE concise handbook, 2003, ISBN 1903287448, 248pp, £70.

5346 Construction materials reference book
D.K. Doran, ed. Butterworth-Heinemann, 1992. ISBN 0750610042.
Comprehensive overview made up of 51 chapters from 56 contributors covering all kinds of materials. Divided into two sections, Metals and their alloys, and Non-metals, the latter covering adhesives, asbestos, bituminous materials, ceramics, concrete, glass, paint and preservatives, polymers, stone, timber, etc. Each chapter includes a substantial selective bibliography. A little aged but still a very useful reference work.

Energy: management, supply and conservation
C. Beggs See entry no. 4657

5347 Environmental handbook for building and civil engineering projects [UK]
R. Venables [et al.]; Construction Industry Research and Information Association New edn, 2000. 3 v.
Intended to provide practical guidance and information on environmental issues likely to be encountered during building or civil engineering projects.

- Part 1. *Design and specification*. ISBN 086017512X 165pp. £80.00.
- Part 2. *Construction phase*. ISBN 0860175286 157pp. £80.00. This part covers Tendering, Project planning, Structural work, Landscaping, etc.
- Part 3. *Demolition and site clearance*. ISBN 0860175294 82pp. £90.00.

First produced in 1984.

5348 Faber and Kell's heating and air-conditioning of buildings: with some notes on combined heat and power [UK]
P.L. Martin [et al.], eds 9th edn, Architectural Press, 2001, 736pp. £69.99. ISBN 075064642X.
Long-established and respected comprehensive reference work which has become a standard in its field. This edition updated to include the requirements of the Building Regulations, Part L. Arranged in 24 chapters, including Electrical storage heating, Indirect heating systems, Principles of air-conditioning design, Refrigeration, Hot water supply systems, etc. Useful appendices.
1st edn 1936, last edn 1995. Formerly entitled Heating and air conditioning of buildings. Former editors include O. Faber and J.R. Kell.

5349 Floors and flooring: performance, diagnosis, maintenance, repair and the avoidance of defects
P.W. Pye and H.W. Harrison; Building Research Establishment 2nd edn, 2003, 303pp. £37.50. ISBN 1860816312.
Describes the materials, production methods and criteria used in the construction of floors. Organized in eight chapters: Basic function; Suspended floors and ceilings; Solid floors; Screeds, underlays, and underlayments; Jointless floor finishes; Jointed resilient finishes; Jointed hard finishes; and Timber and timber products. Includes references and suggestions for further reading.
Series: BRE Building Elements.

5350 Green building handbook: a guide to building products and their impact on the environment
T. Wooley [et al.] Spon, 1997–2000. 2 v., £69.99. ISBN 0419261508.
Essentially a guide to environment-friendly building products.
V. 1. 1997 ISBN 0419226907 224pp. Contents include, Part 1: How to set about green building; Examples of green building; and Part 2: Product analysis and materials specification; Energy; Insulation materials; Masonry; Timber; Composite boards; Timber preservatives; Window frames; Paints and stains for joinery; Roofing materials; Rainwater goods; Toilets and sewage disposal; and Carpets and floor coverings.
V. 2. T. Wooley and S. Kimmins, eds. 2000 ISBN 0419253807 192pp. Discusses green issues in building and considers eight building component types: Fencing products; Flat roofing membranes; Glazing products; Electrical wiring; Adhesives; Straw bale building; Interior decoration; Indoor air quality and ventilation.

Handbook of building materials for fire protection
C.A. Harper, ed. See entry no. 5844

5351 Handbook of glass in construction
J.S. Amstock McGraw-Hill, 1997, 584pp. $79.95. ISBN 0070016194.
A comprehensive guide to the specification, installation, manufacture and testing of glass units and windows used in construction. The 27 chapters include: Tempered, laminated, heat-treated, and heat-strengthened glass; Fire-rated, sound control, x-ray shielding, and bullet-resistant glass; Desiccants; Inert gases; and High-performance film. Much information is presented in tables and figures.

Handbook of heating, ventilation, and air conditioning
J.F. Kreider, ed. See entry no. 5951

5352 HVAC design data sourcebook
R.O. Parmley, ed. McGraw-Hill, 1994, 489pp. $49.50. ISBN 0070485720.
Compact collection of essential data arranged in 14 sections: Basic data and fundamentals; Heat loss estimating; Building material properties; Heating fuel data; Heating systems; Ventilating systems; Air conditioning piping design; Air distribution design; Attic ventilation; Sheet metal duct design; Energy conservation; Climatic data; Graphic standards and definitions; and Metric data and conversion. Extensive tables and graphs.

HVAC engineer's handbook
F. Porges See entry no. 5954

HVAC systems design handbook
R.W. Haines and C.L. Wilson See entry no. 5955

5353 Mechanical and electrical equipment for buildings
B. Stein and J.S. Reynolds 9th edn, Wiley, 2000, 1824pp. $120.00. ISBN 0471156965.
Comprehensive, long-standing and well respected work consisting of 28 chapters arranged in nine sections – Energy overview; Thermal control; Water and waste; Fire protection; Electricity; Illumination; Signal equipment; Transportation; and Acoustics – plus appendices. Well illustrated.
1st edn 1937, last edn 1992. Various authors along the way.

5354 Plumbing engineering services design guide [UK]
Institute of Plumbing 3rd edn, 2002, 240pp. £80.00. ISBN 1871956404.
Comprehensive and practical in approach. Consists of 14 sections, all updated or new: Hot and cold water services; Legionnaire's disease; Heating; Piped gas services; Sanitary plumbing and drainage; Pumps and pumping; Resources efficient design; Fire protection; Steam and condensate; Pipework expansion; Mechanical ventilation; Designing for the disabled; Domestic swimming pools; Electrical earthing and bonding; and Standards, codes and miscellaneous data.
1st edn 1977, 2nd edn 1988.

5355 SFPE handbook of fire protection engineering [USA]
Society of Fire Protection Engineers 3rd edn, National Fire Protection Association, 2002. $229.95. ISBN 0877654514.
A major set of over 60 overview chapters by more than 70 authors covering the science and technologies of fire protection. Arranged in five sections: Fundamentals; Fire dynamics; Hazard calculations; Design calculations; and Fire risk analysis. This edition incorporates a number of new chapters including Flammable liquid spill fires, Water mist systems, and Introduction to fire risk analysis. Chapters often include lengthy bibliographies. Good index.
1st edn 1988, 2nd edn 1995.

5356 Vertical transportation handbook
G.R. Strakosch, ed. 3rd edn, Wiley, 1998, 564pp. $140.00. ISBN 0471162914.
The standard work dealing with elevators, escalators, and the like, providing a comprehensive overview of the area. This edition has been completely revised. 20 chapters deal with the basics, traffic flow (Incoming traffic, Two-way traffic, etc.), requirements, different types of buildings (Commercial, Residential, etc.), special elevators (Service and freight, etc.), and the contexts (Specifying and contracting, Economics, maintenance and modernization, etc.)
1st edn 1967, 2nd edn 1983, both under the title Vertical transportation.

5357 Wall technology [UK]
B. Gillinson, ed.; Construction Industry Research and Information Association 1992. 7 v., £120.00. ISBN 0860173372.
A reference source covering structural and other aspects of walls.
- V. A: *Performance requirements.* ISBN 0860173380 262pp.
- V. B: *Loadbearing small units.* ISBN 0860173399 96pp.
- V. C: *Small units on framed buildings.* ISBN 0860173402 112pp.
- V. D: *Large lightweight units on framed buildings.* ISBN 0860173410 126pp.
- V. E: *Large heavy units on framed buildings and in-situ concrete.* ISBN 0860173429 68pp.
- V. F: *Glazing, curtain walls and cladding.* ISBN 0860173437 84pp.
- V. G: *Applied finishes.* ISBN 0860173445 48p.

5358 Wood engineering and construction handbook
K.F. Faherty and T.G. Williamson, ed. 3rd edn, McGraw-Hill, 1998, 912pp. $89.95. ISBN 0070220700.
Information, formulas, procedures and examples for the design of wood structures and structural components. 13 contributors to 12 chapters which include Columns, Trusses, Diaphragms and shearwalls, Arches and domes, Wood foundation structures, and Adhesives. Appendices include 11 tables of data.
1st edn 1989, 2nd edn 1995.

Keeping up-to-date

5359 Building Services Journal [UK]
Chartered Institution of Building Services Engineers 1978–, Monthly. £70.00. ISSN 13655671.
www.bsjonline.co.uk
CIBSE's official journal which is distributed free to members and is also available free, upon registration, in electronic form from the CIBSE website. The journal carries news, analysis, product information, job adverts, etc.
Former titles: 1985–1996, Building services ISSN 0951-9270; 1978–1985, Chartered Institution of Building Services. Journal ISSN 0142-3630, which was formed by the 1978 merger of Light and lighting and environmental design (ISSN 0307-5192) and Building services engineer (ISSN 0301-6536) formerly (until 1971) I.H.V.E. journal (ISSN 0018-9847).

5360 Engineering News-Record [USA]
McGraw-Hill, Weekly. $82.00 [2004]. ISSN 08919526.
www.enr.com
Covers the business and technical news of the global business and construction industry. The website provides access to the extensive and intensive McGraw Hill Construction portal: designed to connect 'people, projects and products across the design and construction industry. From project and product information to industry news, trends and forecasts, we provide industry players the tools and resources that help them save time, money, and energy'.

Design

accessibility • computer-aided design • concurrent engineering • design engineering • dimensioning • engineering design • ergonomics • human factors engineering • human-computer interaction • integrated product development • machine design • sustainable design

Introductions to the subject

Aircraft design projects for engineering students
L.R. Jenkinson and J.F. Marchman; American Institute of Aeronautics and Astronautics See entry no. 4867

Design of machinery: an introduction to the synthesis and analysis of mechanisms and machines
R.L. Norton See entry no. 5863

5361 Engineering design: a materials and processing approach
G.E. Dieter 3rd edn, McGraw-Hill, 2000, 816pp. $117.50. ISBN 0073661368.
www.mhhe.com/engcs/mech/dieter [COMPANION]
Well structured text – this third edition having been substantially reorganized resulting from 'the realization that engineering students need more structure to guide them through the design process. Thus, we have provided separate chapters on problem definition, concept generation and evaluation, the embodiment design process, and detail design'. Also treats several new topics – including the use of the internet in information gathering.

5362 Human factors methods for design: making systems human-centered
C.P. Nemeth CRC Press, 2004, 416pp. $99.95. ISBN 0415297982.
Overview of human factors and application of research to product and service development. Enables reader to define a design opportunity, develop product goals, and establish criteria for meeting these goals. Offers a road map for collecting and organizing information; applying information to the creation of solutions; evaluating potential solutions. Fifteen examples show how to apply the approach to software and product development.

5363 Human-computer interaction
A.J. Dix [et al.] 3rd edn, Pearson, 2004, 834pp. £39.99. ISBN 0130461091.
www.hcibook.com/e3 [COMPANION]
Very well produced and well structured introductory text. 21 chapters arranged within four parts: Fundamentals; Design process; Models and theories; Outside the box. Bibliography of c.400 references.
2nd edn 1998.

5364 Introduction to ergonomics
R.S. Bridger 2nd edn, Taylor & Francis, 2003, 548pp. £24.99. ISBN 0415273781.
Gives an introduction to ergonomics as the study of the relationship between people and their working environment and sets out the fundamental principles. New edition includes updated questions at the end of each chapter, new sections, more case studies, and glossary of scientific terms.

5365 Leonardo's laptop: human needs and the new computing technologies
B. Shneiderman MIT Press, 2002, 269pp. $16.95. ISBN 0262692996.
http://mitpress.mit.edu/main/feature/leonardoslaptop/index.html [COMPANION]
Ben Shneiderman 'dramatically raises computer users' expectations of what they should get from technology. He opens their eyes to new possibilities and invites them to think freshly about future technology. He also challenges hardware and software developers to build products that better support human needs and that are usable at any bandwidth. Shneiderman proposes Leonardo da Vinci as an inspirational muse for the 'new computing.' He raises the intriguing question of how Leonardo would use a laptop and what applications he would create. Shneiderman shifts the focus from what computers can do to what users can do . .'
'This book is an inspiration, a must read.' (*International Journal of Human-Computer Interaction*)

Dictionaries, thesauri, classifications

5366 Design Lexicon
Engineering Design Melbourne.
www.mame.mu.oz.au/eng_design/language
Part of research programme for a common design language at University of Melbourne, whose specific focus is the development of an internationally collaborative lexicon of design terms. Contains definitions of some 30 basic terms, with examples. Also has list of other design words, and words from BS 7000 and VDI 2221.

Laws, standards, codes

5367 Section 508 [USA]
www.section508.gov
'In 1998, Congress amended the *Rehabilitation Act* to require Federal agencies to make their electronic and information technology accessible to people with disabilities. Inaccessible technology interferes with an individual's ability to obtain and use information quickly and easily. Section 508 was enacted to eliminate barriers in information technology, to make available new opportunities for people with disabilities, and to encourage development of technologies that will help achieve these goals. The law applies to all Federal agencies when they develop, procure, maintain, or use electronic and information technology.'

Official & quasi-official bodies

5368 Access Board: a federal agency committed to accessible design [USA]
www.access-board.gov
Independent Federal agency devoted to accessibility for people with disabilities. Remit includes: Developing and maintaining accessibility requirements for the built environment, transit vehicles, telecommunications equipment, and for electronic and information technology; Providing technical assistance and training on these guidelines and standards; Enforcing accessibility standards for federally funded facilities.

Pleasingly well designed website. Publications, many downloadable PDFs; extensive list of links.

5369 Design Council [UK]
www.designcouncil.org.uk
Funded by the UK Department of Trade and Industry, exists to ensure the effective use of design in business, education and government. Offers information about design, the design process, markets and opportunities, and emerging issues. Publications (some available to download in PDF format), and case studies provided.

Research centres & institutes

5370 Centre for Sustainable Design [UK]
www.cfsd.org.uk
Aims to facilitate discussion research about eco-design and environmental, economic, ethical and social considerations in product and service development and design. Offers training and education, research, seminars, workshops, conferences, consultancy and publications. Also acts as an information

clearing house and focus for innovative thinking on sustainable products and services. Includes technical directory of PDF documents on relevant topics.

Associations & societies

5371 **British HCI Group**
www.bcs-hci.org.uk
Specialist Group of the British Computer Society. Provides an organization for 'all those working on the analysis, design, implementation and evaluation of technologies for human use'.

5372 **Ergonomics Society** [UK]
www.ergonomics.org.uk
Organization for professionals using knowledge of human abilities and limitations to design and build for comfort, efficiency, productivity and safety. Good introductory section on what ergonomics is, its uses and ergonomic design. Also news and information of use to practising ergonomists, a Consultancy Register and details of journals and books. well categorized Links section – including worldwide list of ergonomics societies.

5373 **Human Factors and Ergonomics Society** [USA]
http://hfes.org
Some useful publications; range of Technical Groups, some more active than others.

5374 **Institution of Engineering Designers** [UK]
www.ied.org.uk
Established in 1945, and 'is a professional body for designers who operate in widely diverse fields of design practice. In addition, there are members who operate in fields such as consultative practice, management and education'. Most services only directly accessible to members; but there is a useful online Database of Suppliers.

5375 **International Ergonomics Association**
www.iea.cc
Association of ergonomics and human factors societies around the world. Describes IEA's structure and activities, and includes a directory of educational programmes in ergonomics and list of IEA-endorsed journals.

Society for Experimental Mechanics
See entry no. 5907

5376 **Society of Concurrent Product Development** [USA]
www.scpdnet.org
Educational organization; objectives include disseminating knowledge to promote understanding of Concurrent Engineering (CE) and Integrated Product Development (IPD) concepts and processes, and providing a continuous forum for networking and sharing of ideas among professionals in all disciplines involved in product development.

Portal & task environments

5377 **CAD-Portal.com: the internet resource for engineering professionals**
www.cad-portal.com
Commercially focused site for computer-aided design with news, directory, bookstore, e-Weekly newsletter, forums, events, product reviews.

5378 **CADTutor: The Best Free Tutorials on the Web**
D. Watson
www.cadtutor.net
Personal interest engaging and well designed site which originated within the University of Greenwich, UK. Focused on the delivery of the best free AutoCAD tutorials on the web but provides much other useful and interesting information about computer-aided design and related matters. A nice site.

5379 **Design inSite**
T. Lenau Design Factory ApS.
www.designinsite.dk
Helpful designers' guide to manufacturing. Various manufacturing processes and materials are covered as well as the products in which they are used. Each product is described with text and photos or drawings and there are links to the relevant materials and processes. Environmental concerns also addressed. Links to useful websites included.

5380 **Design Surfer's Paradise**
University of Queensland
www.catalyst.uq.edu.au/designsurfer
Resource guide site providing links to sites and notes on specific design areas under headings: basics, teams, ideas, requirements, concepts, decisions, embodiment, communication and projects. Product and component catalogue (links to commercial pages illustrating the vast variety of products available to engineering designers) also offered. April 2005, last updated April 2003.

5381 **Design-engine.com** [USA]
DESIGN-ENGINE, Inc.
www.design-engine.com
Contains features on design topics from products and people to shows and software, as well as news and events. Offers a design registry which includes firms under various subject headings, engineering and design schools, non-profit organizations, online magazines, discussion forums, museums and contests, individuals' portfolios and an article archive. Identifies six hot designers. Has a training section.

5382 **Engineers Edge**
www.engineersedge.com
Lively well organized site. 'Our mission is to be the preferred online destination for designers, engineers and manufacturing professionals, where all can quickly find a variety of information to aid in the solution of typical and complex technical problems.'

5383 **Ergoweb**
Ergoweb, Inc.
www.ergoweb.com
Includes reference information on ergonomics and human factors engineering design, standards, case studies, buyers' guide, and a free registration-based discussion forum. Some elements of the site open to paid subscribers only.

5384 **Eureka** [UK]
Findlay Publications.
www.eureka.findlay.co.uk
Covers news and developments in engineering materials and

engineering design, highlighting new ideas in technology for engineers. Also offers search and browse facilities to look for UK suppliers of components, materials, equipment and services. Includes a reference library providing a range of information. Free registration required.

Evoweb: The online information service for everyone interested in evolutionary computing
Napier University and European Commission. Directorate for Information Society See entry no. 5703

5385 **HCI/Interactive Technologies**
Morgan Kaufmann.
www.mkp.com
Gateway to wide range of texts produced by the publisher in this field.

iCrank.com
See entry no. 5920

5386 **Usability.gov**
United States. Department of Health and Human Services
www.usability.gov
'Your resource for designing usable, useful and accessible Web sites and user interfaces.'

Discovering print & electronic resources

5387 **HCI Bibliography: Human Computer Interaction Resources**
G. Perlman
www.hcibib.org
A very good 'free-access online bibliographic database on Human-Computer Interaction. The basic goal of the Project is to put an electronic bibliography for most of HCI on the screens of all researchers, developers, educators and students in the field through the World-Wide Web and anonymous ftp access ... As of 2004-07-26, the HCI Bibliography has over 29,000 entries.' (However, overall site kept well up-to-date.)

5388 **HCI Index**
H. de Graaff
http://degraaff.org/hci
An excellent index of resources on human-computer interaction on the internet. Sections are: Books; Communication; Conferences; Groups; Organizations; Publications; Tools; Resources.

5389 **Mechanical Design Engineering Resources on the World Wide Web**
www.gearhob.com
Contains 14 main headings: associations, materials, CAD/CAM/CAE, newsgroups, components, patents, design information (including tables, charts and specifications), publications, safety, engineering sites, search tools, finite element, semiconductor, machine shop, standards, mailing lists. Mainly US-based, no information found about provenance, wide-ranging, reasonably up-to-date.

Digital data, image & text collections

Engineer-it
See entry no. 5451

Directories & encyclopedias

5390 **The Directory of Design Consultants** [UK]
European Design Innovations Ltd.
www.designdirectory.co.uk
Covers all design disciplines, including engineering design, product design and industrial design. Entries for consultants listed include brief descriptions, contact information, e-mail addresses, and where applicable, website information. Searchable and browsable. Design advice available. Noticeboard and showcase offered.

5391 **International encyclopedia of ergonomics and human factors**
W. Karwowski CRC Press, 2001, 1960pp. 3 v. Also available on CD-ROM. 2nd edn announced for 2005, $659.00. ISBN 0748408479.
Coverage: General ergonomics; Human characteristics; Performance related factors; Information presentation and communication; Display and control design; Workplace and equipment design; System characteristics; World design and organization; Health and safety; Social and economic impact of the system; Methods and techniques.

Handbooks & manuals

5392 **Bad Human Factors Designs**
M.J. Darnell
www.baddesigns.com
Scrapbook of illustrated examples of products that are hard to use because they do not follow human factors principles. Includes short descriptions and photos of examples of designs and suggestions on how problems could be avoided or resolved. New additions are highlighted.

Design for manufacturability handbook
J.G. Bralla, ed. See entry no. 5718

5393 **Dimensioning and tolerancing handbook**
P.J. Drake McGraw-Hill, 1999, 1280pp. $125.00. ISBN 0070181314.
www.knovel.com
Based on the Texas Instruments company course. Includes all phases of dimensional management, and developments in concurrent engineering, six sigma, statistical tolerancing, performance sigma and defect prediction for pieceparts and assemblies. Includes practical approaches to dimensioning and tolerancing, trade-offs between design and manufacturing, practical ways to inspect tolerances, new developments in the paperless environment, approaches used in tolerancing software and design by assembly.
Available online: see website.

5394 **Electromechanical design handbook**
R. Walsh and L. Ludewig 3rd edn, McGraw-Hill, 2000, 960pp. $125.00. ISBN 0071348123.
www.knovel.com
Sourcebook of engineering design data aimed at product engineers and designers whose work requires crossing the boundary between mechanical and electrical design. This

edition contains much updated material, including new discussions of engineering economics and elastomer springs, and new drawings.
Available online: see website.

Handbook of advanced materials: enabling new designs
J.K. Wessel See entry no. 5842

5395 Handbook of human factors and ergonomics methods
N. Stanton [et al.], eds CRC Press, 2004, 768pp. $99.95. ISBN 0415287006.
Account of methods that incorporate human capabilities and limitations, environmental factors, human-machine interaction and other factors into system design. Describes 83 methods in a standardized format, promoting use of methods that may have formerly been unfamiliar to designers. Six sections, each representing a specialized field of ergonomics with a representative selection of associated methods.

5396 Handbook of human systems integration
H.R. Booher, ed. Wiley-Interscience, 2003, 964pp. $130.00. ISBN 0471020532.
'The organizations for systems engineering and management are already well institutionalized in government, industry, and academia and have the common goal with human systems interaction to produce high performing, safe, and affordable systems. The major component currently missing from systems engineering and management is a detailed description of the principles and methods of human systems. The intent of the Handbook is to provide that.'
24 contributed chapters plus Afterword. Bibliographies. Index.

5397 Handbook of materials for product design
C.A. Harper, ed. 3rd edn, McGraw-Hill, 2001, 1000pp. $125.00. ISBN 0071354069.
www.knovel.com
14 chapters, appendices and glossary. Provides materials, data, information and guidelines for all who design, manufacture and use mechanical and electromechanical products, as well as those who develop and market materials useful for these products. Contains an extensive array of property and performance data, and explains fabrication trade-offs.
Available online: see website.

- **Handbook of ceramics, glasses and diamonds C.A. Harper, ed.** McGraw-Hill, 2001, 800pp. $110.00. ISBN 007026712X. Information and guidelines for all who design, manufacture and use products made from ceramics, glass and diamonds. Presents important aspects of application guidelines, fabrication methods, performance limits and basic material properties.
- **Handbook of plastics, elastomers and composites C.A. Harper** 4th edn, McGraw-Hill, 2002. $125.00. ISBN 0071384766. '... thorough sourcebook of practical design, manufacturing and data for all ranges of interests ... Highly recommended as a reference book.' *SAMPE Journal*.

5398 HCI models, theories, and frameworks: towards a multidisciplinary science
J.M. Carroll, ed. Morgan Kaufmann, 2003, 551pp. $59.95. ISBN 1558608087.
Aims to provide a pedagogical survey for the multidisciplinary science of human-computer interaction, bringing together a range of approaches to science in HCI, presenting them in a common format, at a middle level of detail. 'The goal is to provide enough detail on each approach, and enough comparative detail across the whole collection, to make primary sources more accessible.'

5399 The human-computer interaction handbook: fundamentals, evolving technologies, and emerging applications
J.A. Jacko and A. Sears, eds Lawrence Erlbaum, 2003, 1296pp. $295.00. ISBN 0805838384.
www.isrc.umbc.edu/HCIHandbook [COMPANION]
65 chapters in eight parts: The evolution of human-computer interaction: from Memex to Bluetooth and beyond; Humans in HCI; Computers in HCI; Human-computer interaction; application domains; The development process; Managing HCI and emerging issues; Perspectives on HCI,
'A 24-strong Advisory Board has guided the activities of 124 contributors, all admirably pulled together by Julie Jacko and Andrew Sears. The result is a landmark work; it would be difficult to find another on the same topic with equivalent breadth and coverage.' (*Institute of Electrical and Electronics Engineers*)

5400 Machine design databook
K. Lingaiah, ed. 2nd edn, McGraw-Hill, 2002, 1000pp. $150.00. ISBN 0071367071.
Provides hundreds of charts on material properties as well as the necessary equations, formulas, calculations, graphs, and data required to solve full range of machine design problems. 29 sections, plus glossary and index. New chapters on machine tool design, applied elasticity, locking machine elements, and retaining rings.

Machinery's handbook: a reference book for the mechanical engineer, designer, manufacturing engineer, draftsman, toolmaker and machinist
E. Oberg [et al.], eds See entry no. 5729

Mechanical engineering design
J.E. Shigley and C.R. Mischke See entry no. 5959

5401 Mechanisms and mechanical devices sourcebook
N. Sclater and N.P. Chironis 3rd edn, McGraw-Hill, 2001, 500pp. $89.95. ISBN 0071361693.
www.knovel.com
Provides encyclopedic collection of 2501 drawings and articles on mechanisms and mechanical devices and their practical application in modern products, machines and systems. Explains how various components work in machine tools, production and process plants, aircraft, automotive and construction equipment, instruments and consumer goods. This edition features more information on electromechanical devices.
Available online: see website.

Standard handbook of machine design
J.E. Shigley, C.R. Mischke and T. Brown, eds See entry no. 5966

Keeping up-to-date

5402 **Design Engineering**
Centaur Communications.
www.e4engineering.com
Information on applied technologies for design engineers. Offers news, analysis, product notes, comment, features and an event diary from the latest and previous issues. Part of the E4 NETWORK site for engineers.

5403 **Machine Design** [USA]
Penton Media, Fortnightly. Free subscriptions to US Residents.
www.machinedesign.com
Magazine for design engineers. Offers latest issue (features, applications), plus archives back to 2001. Also, supplier/product locator (mostly US), industry events, CD library and CAD library.
One of a very wide range of technology and industry magazines, newsletters and other publications produced by Penton: see www.penton.com.

5404 **Planet HCI**
http://planethci.org
'A web aggregator of feeds from HCI-related blogs, i.e., of those who care about how computers can serve users better.'

Tech Briefs: Engineering Solutions for Design and Manufacturing
National Aeronautics and Space Administration See entry no. 5745

Electrical & Electronic Engineering

acoustics • antenna engineering • audio engineering • batteries • cellular radio • chips • circuits • digital signals • electric cables & wires • electric motors • electric power • electrical technology • electronic circuits • electronic components • electronic engineering • electronics • electrotechnical engineering • filters • hi-fi equipment • illumination • instrumentation • insulators • integrated circuits • loudspeakers • magnetic recording • microchips • microelectronics • microwaves • power electronics • printed circuits • radar • radio frequency communication • radio science • semiconductors • signal processing • sound engineering • superconductivity • television engineering • thin film devices • transformers • video engineering

Introductions to the subject

5405 **Electric power systems**
B.M. Weedy and B.J. Cory 4th edn, Wiley, 1998, 563pp. $80.00. ISBN 0471976776.
This long-standing textbook provides a comprehensive account of power systems engineering covering generation, control, protection, operation, transmission and distribution. This edition contains extended coverage of power system components and a new chapter on power system economics and management issues.
1st edn 1967, 3rd edn 1979, both authored by Weedy alone.

5406 **Hughes electrical & electronic technology**
I. McKenzie Smith [et al.] 8th edn, Prentice Hall, 2001, 911pp. $115.00. ISBN 058240519X.
Voluminous and well tested introduction to the subject area. A textbook that covers all the basics. Arranged in 4 sections: Electrical principles (16 chapters); Electronic engineering (17 chapters); Power engineering (12 chapters); and Measurements (2 chapters).
1st edn 1960, 7th edn 1995.

5407 **Instrumentation and control systems**
W. Bolton Butterworth-Heinemann, 2004, 352pp. £21.99. ISBN 0750664320.
An introductory textbook aimed at first year undergraduates. The author presents the principles of instrumentation and control systems and gives examples of devices, techniques and applications. A section of the text is devoted to case studies and problem-solving exercises for self-assessment.

Introduction to avionics systems
R.P.G. Collinson See entry no. 4874

Materials science for electrical and electronic engineers
I.P. Jones, ed. See entry no. 5785

Nanoelectronics and information technology: advanced electronic materials and novel devices
R. Waser, ed. See entry no. 6076

Ones and zeros: understanding Boolean algebra, digital circuits, and the logic of sets
J. Gregg See entry no. 496

Dictionaries, thesauri, classifications

5408 **Authoritative dictionary of IEEE standards terms: IEEE Std 100-2000**
Institute of Electrical and Electronics Engineers 7th edn, 2000, 1352pp. $135.00. ISBN 0738126012.
This important dictionary includes nearly 35,000 technical terms and acronyms. Definitions are derived from over 800 IEEE and other standards. Each entry includes a reference to the standard carrying the explanation.
1st edn 1972, 6th edn 1997. Previously entitled IEEE standard dictionary of electrical and electronics terms.

Automation, systems, and instrumentation dictionary
Instrumentation Systems and Automation Society See entry no. 5669

5409 **Comprehensive dictionary of electrical engineering**
P.A. Laplante, comp. 2nd edn, CRC Press, 2005, 720pp. $69.95. ISBN 0849330866.
Contains almost 10,000 entries contributed by more than 100 authors. Areas covered include power systems, electric machinery, digital electronics, microelectronics, RF, radio and TV, communications, signal and image processing, circuits, control systems, electromagnetics, computer engineering, microwave systems, electro-optics, illumination, materials, and packaging. Includes acronyms, cross-references, and explanatory equations.
1st edn described.

5410 **Dictionary of acoustics**
C.L. Morfey Academic Press, 2001, 430pp. $79.95. ISBN 0125069405.
Aimed at undergraduates but equally as useful as a quick reference for research engineers. Covers topics in a wide range of disciplines, such as aerospace and medicine, giving in-depth definitions of terminology.

5411 **Dictionary of electrical engineering, power engineering and automation: Fachwörterbuch industrielle Elektrotechnik, Energie- und Automatisierungstechnik**
H. Bezner, comp. 5th edn, Wiley-VCH, 2003. 2 v., £60.00. ISBN 3895781932.
A standard and well established German/English translating dictionary covering power generation, transmission and distribution, drive engineering, automation, switchgear and installation engineering, power electronics, measurement, analysis and test engineering. This edition includes about 90,000 entries and 125,000 translations in Volume 1 (German–English) and 75,000 entries and 109,000 translations in Volume 2.
1st edn entitled Dictionary of power engineering and automation, 1985; 4th edn 1998. A CD-ROM identical to the 4th printed edn is also available (ISBN 3895781371).

5412 **Dictionary of electronics, computing, telecommunications and media: Wörterbuch der Elektronik, Datentechnik, Telekommunikation und Medien** [GER]
V. Ferretti, comp. 3rd rev. and enlarged edn, Springer, 2004, 2100pp. 2 v. Also available on CD-ROM, £230.00. ISBN 3540408312.
Much expanded since the first edition to include the computing/communications convergence and now media, this English–German dictionary now contains about 157,000 entries covering 102 subject fields, including abbreviations and acronyms. Entries are composed of short definitions plus references to synonyms, antonyms, general and derivative terms.
1st edn 1992.

Dictionnaire d'automatique de génie électrique et de productique: anglais–français, français–anglais (Systems and control dictionary: English–French, French–English)
P. Borne and N. Quayle, ed. See entry no. 5670

5413 **Electrical and computer engineering dictionary: English–Spanish, Spanish–English (Diccionario de ingenieria eléctrica y de computadoras: Inglés–Español, Español–Inglés)**
S.M. Kaplan, comp. Wiley, 1996, 792pp. $115.00. ISBN 0471010375.
Contains a total of about 50,000 entry terms in each half, with equivalents – usually a word or phrase – in the other.

5414 **Elsevier's dictionary of microelectronics: in English, German, French, Spanish and Japanese**
P. Nagy and G. Tarján, comps Elsevier, 1988, 944pp. €271.00. ISBN 0444426590.
Consists of 8521 English base terms with translations into the other four languages, with indexes in the other four languages referring back to the base terms. The Japanese is romanized.

5415 **Encyclopedic dictionary of electronics, electrical engineering and information processing: English–German, German–English (Enzyklopädisches Wörterbuch der Elektrotechnik, Elektronik und Informationsverarbeitung)**
P. Wennrich, comp. K G Saur, 1990–95. 8 v. ISBN 3598106815.
Vols.1–4, English–German, vols. 5–8, German–English. A definitive work with some 200,000 English entries and 600,000 German equivalents. It includes alternative uses, further explanations and differentiates between American and British English.

5416 **Glossary of electrotechnical, power, telecommunication, electronics, lighting and colour terms: BS4727**
British Standards Institution 1971–.
Excellent and definitive. There are presently 46 current documents in BS4727, which is arranged in 5 parts: Common terms; Power engineering terms; Telecommunications and electronics terms; Lighting and colour terms; and Electromedical equipment terms. Terminology is technically identical with terms appearing in the INTERNATIONAL ELECTROTECHNICAL VOCABULARY. Later published documents are identical, and also include definitions in French and Russian, together with translations of terms in German, Spanish, Italian, Dutch, Polish and Swedish.

5417 **IEC multilingual dictionary**
International Electrotechnical Commission 5th edn, 2002. CD-ROM, SF260.00.
This dictionary includes over 19,200 definitions in English and French. Equivalent terms, wherever available, are given in Arabic, Chinese, Dutch, German, Italian, Japanese, Polish, Portuguese, Russian, Spanish and Swedish. There are consolidated indexes in English, French, German and Spanish. It also includes all 74 parts of the IEC's INTERNATIONAL ELECTROTECHNICAL VOCABULARY. A free online database available at the IEC web pages contains some terms in English, French, German and Spanish

5418 **Illustrated dictionary of electronics**
S. Gibilisco, ed. 8th edn, McGraw-Hill, 2001, 800pp. $44.95. ISBN 0071372369.
This edition expanded to include more than 28,000 entries including abbreviations and acronyms. It covers wireless technology, lasers, television, radio, IC technology, audio and video, and communications. Entries are concise and generally aimed at the non-specialist. Extensively illustrated. An accompanying CD-ROM also carries the text in searchable pdf files.
1st edn 1980, 7th edn 1997. Earlier edns entitled McGraw-Hill dictionary of electronics.

5419 **International electrotechnical vocabulary**
International Electrotechnical Commission
With over 10,000 pages the IEV is the definitive electrotechnical terminology. It is available both on paper (IEC 60050) and on CD-ROM with the IEC MULTILINGUAL DICTIONARY. A limited selection of the IEV is also free from the IEC web pages.
Technically identical to British Standard BS4727, GLOSSARY OF ELECTROTECHNICAL, POWER, TELECOMMUNICATION, ELECTRONICS, LIGHTING AND COLOUR TERMS.

5420 **Modern dictionary of electronics**
R.F. Graf, comp. 7th edn, Newnes, 1999, 869pp. £47.50. ISBN 0750698667.
This well known dictionary now comprises about 28,000 terms – 3000 more than the last edition. Broad coverage includes consumer electronics, optics, microelectronics, computers, communications, and medical electronics. Also includes tables of units, etc.
1st edn 1962, 6th edn 1997.

5421 **Newnes dictionary of electronics**
S.W. Amos and R.S. Amos, eds 4th edn, Newnes, 1999, 394pp. £12.99. ISBN 0750643315.
Consists of about 3000 concise entries, usually 1–20 lines in length. New entries are largely from the fields of computing and data processing and are mainly acronyms and abbreviations, contained in appendices.
1st edn 1981, 3rd edn 1996.

5422 **The Penguin dictionary of electronics**
V. Illingworth, ed. 3rd edn, Penguin, 1999, 672pp. £10.99. ISBN 0140514023.
Substantially revised, this edition consists of some 4800 entries and almost 400 illustrations. Heavily cross-referenced. Entries are normally one line to two pages in length. Also contains definitions concerned with the related areas of computing, communications, electrical engineering, control, and music technology. Appended tables list graphical symbols, colour codes, etc.
1st edn 1979 as New Penguin dictionary of electronics; 2nd edn 1988. Previous editor, C. Young.

5423 **Routledge German dictionary of electrical engineering and electronics (Wörterbuch Elektrotechnik und Elektronik)**
P.-K. Budig, ed. Routledge, 1997–8. 2 v., £235.00.
V. 1. German–English. 5th edn. ISBN 0415171326
V. 2. English–German. 6th edn. ISBN 0415171318
Each volume contains about 67,000 terms with generally one-line translations. Terms are from all fields of electrical engineering, electronics, telecommunications, with special attention to modern developments in, for example, lasers, superconductivity, microelectronics, optoelectronics, and computing. Layman's terms and those formed by hyphenation are, for the most part, excluded.
Previous edn published as Fachwörterbuch Elektrotechnik, Elektronik (Dictionary electrical engineering, electronics), Berlin, Hatier, 1993.
'admirably comprehensive ... invaluable' (*Reference Reviews*)

5424 **Routledge German dictionary of microelectronics: English–German/German–English (Wörterbuch Mikroelektronik: Englisch–Deutsch/Deutsch–Englisch)**
W. Bindmann and H. Ryssel, eds 5th edn, Routledge, 1999, 699pp. £65.00. ISBN 041517340X.
Comprehensive, accurate and up to date, this translating dictionary contains 30,000 entries covering semiconductor electronics, microlithographic process components, microelectronic circuit technology, microprocessor technology, and software terminology.
Previous edn by Elsevier, 1984.
'reliable, user-friendly ... great value' (*Reference Reviews*)

5425 **Russian–English and English–Russian dictionary of radar and electronics**
S.A. Leonov and W.F. Barton, comps Artech House, 1993, 161pp. £53.00. ISBN 0890067058.
Consists of about 5000 entries in each language. Transliteration table.

Laws, standards, codes

Airlines Electronic Engineering Committee
See entry no. 4884

5426 **European Committee for Electrotechnical Standardization**
www.cenelec.be
The European Committee for Electrotechnical Standardization or CENELEC (Comité Européen de Normalisation Electrotechnique) as it is better known, is officially recognized as the European Standards Organisation in its area. It works with technical experts from 19 EC and EFTA countries to produce standards for the European market. Its website is available in English, French and German and contains a searchable catalogue of standards.

5427 **Letter symbols to be used in electrical technology**
International Electrotechnical Commission
Part 1, General (IEC 60027-1,6th edn, 1992–7); Part 2, Telecommunications and electronics (IEC 60027-2, 2nd edn, 2000); Part 3, Logarithmic and related quantities, and their units (IEC 60027-3, 3rd edn. 2002; BS7998-3:2002 is identical); Part 4, Symbols for quantities to be used for rotating electrical machines (IEC 60027-4, 1985).
Compatible with the US equivalent, ANSI/IEEE Std 280-1985, Letter symbols for quantities used in electrical science and electrical engineering.

- **Graphical symbols for diagrams** In 13 parts with identical British Standards (BS EN 6017: 2–13).

5428 **Requirements for electrical installations: BS 7621:2001** [UK]
Institution of Electrical Engineers 2001. £48.00. ISBN 0852969880.
The 16th edition of the IEE Wiring Regulations, was adopted as British Standard BS7671 in 1992. This amended version is the current national standard for wiring installations. The amendments include substantial changes to align with European documents.

Society of Motion Picture and Television Engineers
See entry no. 6164

Official & quasi-official bodies

5429 **Commission Internationale de l'Eclairage (International Commission on Illumination)**
www.cie.co.at/cie
Based in Vienna, the CIE was founded in 1900 as the International Commission on Photometry, and reorganized in 1913 to become the CIE. The Commission is a technical, scientific and cultural, non-profit autonomous organization devoted to international co-operation, including the development of standards, and exchange of information. Its website includes the text of its *News Bulletins*, abstracts of

CIE reports, sets of links, and information about the organization.

5430 **International Council on Large Electric Systems**
www.cigre.org
CIGRE (originally Conseil Internationale des Grands Réseaux Électriques) as it is better known, is a non-governmental and non-profit making international association based in France. It was founded in 1921 to facilitate and develop the exchange of information between countries regarding the generation and high voltage transmission of electricity. It is particularly concerned with the planning and operation of power systems equipment and plant. CIGRE holds conferences, publishes a journal *Electra*, and through a structure of study and technical committees issues technical brochures.

5431 **International Electrotechnical Commission**
www.IEC.ch
The IEC is the major world organization promoting co-operation and international standardization in the areas of electrical and electronic engineering. IEC standards often serve as the basis of national standards, and thus many British Standards are derived from or are identical to their IEC counterparts. The IEC website provides access to some documents, an online catalogue of publications, and a list of recently published IEC and ISO standards and draft standards.

5432 **International Union of Radio Science**
www.ursi.org
URSI (Union Radio-Scientifique Internationale) was founded in 1919 as the successor to the Commission Internationale de Télégraphie sans Fil which dated from 1913. Based in Ghent, and a non-governmental and non-profit organization operating under the International Council for Science, URSI is responsible for stimulating and co-ordinating, on an international basis, studies, research, applications, scientific exchange, and communication in the fields of radio science. Its website contains information about the organization, its publications, work and membership.

Research centres & institutes

Electric Power Research Institute
See entry no. 4632

Associations & societies

5433 **Acoustical Society of America**
http://asa.aip.org
Founded 1929; membership now almost 7000 from the US and abroad. Free access to quarterly *ARLO: Acoustics Research Letters Online*, a rapid publication journal accepting multimedia content; also to *Echoes* the Society's Newsletter 'which covers current and topical happenings of general interest and features articles about current research and personalities'. Wide-ranging links section plus other useful and interesting information.

5434 **Audio Engineering Society**
www.aes.org
The AES is the most important society in its specialist field worldwide and publishes the most prominent journal in its speciality, the *Journal of the AES*. Half a century old, the Society has a Standards Committee, a Technical Council, and a Historical Committee. The Society's website includes a set of relevant links.

5435 **European Association for Speech, Signal and Image Processing**
www.eurasip.org
EURASIP was founded in 1978 to improve communication in the signal processing field in Europe and elsewhere. Its intention is to provide a 'professional platform for dissemination and discussion of all aspects' of the subject. The Society publishes four peer-reviewed journals: *Applied Signal Processing*, *Image Communication*, *Signal Processing*, and *Speech Communication*.

GAMBICA
See entry no. 1775

5436 **Institute of Electrical and Electronics Engineers** [USA]
www.ieee.org/portal/index.jsp
Founded in 1963 upon the merger of the American Institute of Electrical Engineers (founded 1884) and the Institute of Radio Engineers (founded 1912), the IEEE is a non-profit, technical professional association. With more than 380,000 individual members in 150 countries, it is the prime professional body in its area.

The Institute publishes more than 100 journals, holds more than 100 conferences annually, produces a set of technical standards, and co-produces the INSPEC database. The Institution's website provides access to membership information, its publications (on subscription), IEEE online communities (forums, mainly technical subjects), careers and employment information, events, etc.

5437 **Institute of Measurement and Control** [UK]
www.instmc.org.uk
Founded in 1944 as the *Society of Instrument Technology* to cater for the growing body of instrument technologists whose interests transcended the fields of existing institutions. Subsequently encompassed control engineering: 'The theory and application of measurement and control characteristically require a multi-disciplinary approach and so do not fit into any of the single disciplinary professional institutes'. Useful set of resources including product/company directory based on *Instrument Engineer's Yearbook*.

5438 **Institution of Electrical Engineers** [UK]
www.iee.org
The IEE was founded in 1871 and has since incorporated the Institution of Radio and Electronic Engineers (1988) and the Institution of Manufacturing Engineers (1991) and is the main UK professional body for electrical and electronics engineers. It claims to be the largest professional engineering society in Europe, with a worldwide membership of just under 140,000.

IEE publishes several journals and books, co-produces the INSPEC database, issues regulations regarding the installation of electrical and electronic equipment, and helps formulate national and international standards.

- **IEE Professional Networks**
www.iee.org/oncomms/sector/index.cfm. Set of 35 professional networks covering industrial sectors (e.g. aerospace), academic disciplines (e.g.

antennas and propagation), and underlying activities (e.g. management). Not restricted to IEE members. News, academic articles, exchange of ideas, etc.

5439 **Instrumentation Systems and Automation Society**
[USA]
www.isa.org
The society caters for 38,000 members interested in the theory, design and manufacturing of systems for automation and control. The organisation has a strong manufacturing interest, but also acts as a professional or learned body for instruments, preventive maintenance and motion systems, including sensors and process automation. The website contains an online PDF library of technical papers accessible by subscription or by individual purchase.

- **Control Systems Society** www.ieeecss.org. Founded 1954 as a scientific, engineering and professional organization dedicated to the advancement of the theory and practice of systems and control in engineering. Now has more than 10,000 members around the world.

Orgalime
See entry no. 5905

5440 **Radio Society of Great Britain**
www.rsgb.org
The RSGB was founded in 1913 and incorporated in 1926. It is a not-for-profit organization that represents the interests of licensed radio amateurs in the UK. Its website includes technical information, news, links, and members-only pages.

Portal & task environments

5441 **EETimesUK: The Online Resource for the Electronics Industry in the United Kingdom**
www.eetuk.com
Part of the EE Times Network, EETimesUK offers news about the UK electronics scene. There are links to other parts of the Network (USA, China, etc), a job search, events calendar, a buyers guide, and a searchable library of white papers, case studies and research information. An online newsletter is available on registration, and a pdf version of the *EE Times* by subscription.

Fuel Cell Today
See entry no. 4797

Discovering print & electronic resources

5442 **Electrical and Electronics Abstracts: Science Abstracts, Section B**
Institution of Electrical Engineers and Institute of Electrical and Electronics Engineers 1898–, Monthly. £2120.00 [2004]. ISSN 00368105.
Covers the worldwide literature in all areas of electronics, radio, telecommunications, optoelectronics, and electrical power. Contains up to 105,000 abstracts per year arranged in classified order. Each issue contains indexes, plus a subject guide. Cumulated indexes are published separately twice a year and include subject, author and other indexes. The major abstracting service in electrical and electronic engineering, it is part of the INSPEC database.

5443 **Electronics: a bibliographic guide**
C.K. Moore, K.J. Spencer and L. Corbett, comps MacDonald, 1961–71.
A compilation and survey of reference works and bibliographies, from the journal literature and elsewhere. Worldwide coverage. V. 1 covers 1945–1959 (2877 entries), v. 2 1959–1964 (2880 entries), and v. 3 (by Corbett) 1965–1968 (4364 entries). It provides very useful coverage of the early literature of electronics.

5444 **Electronics and Communications Abstracts**
CSA, 1971–, Monthly.
www.csa.com/factsheets/electronics-set-c.php [DESCRIPTION]
This electronic databases contained over 270,000 records as of September 2004, culled from over 3000 serial titles and various non-serial publications. Produced in conjunction with Engineering Information, it covers circuits, components and materials, photonics, control and systems, telecommunications, power systems, theoretical electronics and communications milieux.
Formerly published as the print Electronics and Communications Abstracts journal, 1961–1994, ISSN 0013-5119.

5445 **INSPEC**
Institution of Electrical Engineers 1969–, Weekly.
www.iee.org/Publish/INSPEC [DESCRIPTION]
INSPEC is the most important and comprehensive English-language abstracting and indexing service for the worldwide literature in electrical engineering and electronics, as well as physics and computer science. It was formed in 1967, based on the *Science Abstracts* service which had been provided by the Institution since 1898.

The database now contains more than 8 million records. About 250,000 records are added to the database each year, principally from the 3400 journals and 2000 conferences as well as numerous books, reports and dissertations scanned. INSPEC is the electronic equivalent of ELECTRICAL AND ELECTRONICS ABSTRACTS, COMPUTER AND CONTROL ABSTRACTS, and PHYSICS ABSTRACTS.
Available online through variety of hosts: see website.

- **INSPEC classification** 1999. £30.00. ISBN 0852969678. Designed for use either with the database or its print equivalents.
- **INSPEC list of journals** 1983–, Annual. £23.00 [2003]. ISSN 02647508. www.iee.org/Publish/Support/Inspec/Document. Contains approximately 4000 journals and other serials, with abbreviated title, CODEN, ISSN, publisher's address, date of first issue covered, and any title changes. Free list of current titles at the website.
- **INSPEC thesaurus** www.iee.org/Publish/Support/Inspec/Document. Last published in paper form in 1999. The new revised thesaurus, 2003, is only available as part of the Inspec Search Aids CDROM (with classification and list of journals) or as part of the database.

5446 **RDN Virtual Training Suite: Electrical, Electronic & Communications Engineer** [UK]
N. Harrison; Heriot-Watt University and Resource Discovery Network
www.vts.rdn.ac.uk/tutorial/elec
This is one of a set of tutorials within the RDN VIRTUAL TRAINING SUITE, created by experts based in UK universities and professional organizations. Although intended to introduce students, researchers and lecturers to finding and assessing material available on the internet, it is free to use, easy to follow, and thus a valuable starting point for anyone new to the internet, the subject, or both. It is divided into Tour, Discover, Review and Reflect sections, and contains as examples links to some key subject sites.

Solid State and Superconductivity Abstracts
See entry no. 5827

5447 **WWW Virtual Library: Electrical and Electronics Engineering**
Monterrey Tech, State of Mexico Campus, Electrical and Electronics Engineering Department.
webdiee.cem.itesm.mx/wwwvlee
This is a good-looking site with over 600 links arranged in 5 sections: Academic and research institutions; Information resources; Journals and magazines; Products and services; and Standards. Searchable. Also hosts a discussion forum.

5448 **ZDE Elektrotechnik und Elektronik**
FIZ Technik, 1968–, Weekly.
www.fiz-technik.de/en/index.html [DESCRIPTION]
Online database containing more than 1.75 million references with abstracts – in English and German – to the worldwide literature in electrical and electronic engineering. Includes citations to journal articles, books, conference papers, etc.

Digital data, image & text collections

5449 **Chip Directory**
www.xs4all.nl/~ganswijk/chipdir/index.htm
This website contains numerically and functionally ordered chip lists, chip pinouts and lists of manufacturers, electronics books, CD-ROMs, magazines, WWW sites, etc. It is searchable by manufacturer and chip number and browsable. The site also hosts an associated mailing list and discussion group. It is updated only intermittently.

5450 **Circuits Archive**
University of Washington, Department of Electrical Engineering
www.ee.washington.edu/eeca
Formerly entitled Electrical Engineering Circuits Archive, this site is 'devoted to expanding the availability of circuit designs to engineering students, and... engineering professionals'. It contains a collection of circuit schematics grouped under the headings: Collection of ASCII circuit diagrams; Radio related; Computer related; Audio/music; Telephone related; and Miscellaneous. The site also includes supplementary information such as datasheets, text files, and software.

5451 **Engineer-it**
Technical Indexes.
www.ihsti.com/ihsti/a2z_engineer_it.html
Consists of three segments: Engineering design and manufacturing; Process engineering; and Electronic engineering. The last is a continually updated collection of data on electronic components and equipment, based on catalogues and data sheets from more than 4000 companies, available in pdf. Searches can be made by company name, product type or name, geographical location, or ISO 9000 status. Various levels of service are available.
Formerly known as info4engineering.

5452 **IEEE Xplore**
Institute of Electrical and Electronics Engineers
http://ieeexplore.ieee.org/Xplore [FEE-BASED]
IEEE Xplore provides full-text access to IEEE transactions, journals, magazines and conference proceedings published since 1988 plus selected content back to 1950, and all current IEEE Standards, together with all IEE journals and magazines. Tables of contents and abstracts are free to all. IEEE members have access to their personal online subscriptions. Institutional access is by combination of IP address and username/password. Over 950,000 full text documents. Easy to search and browse. Quick. High-grade content.
'search engine is excellent ... awesome power ... high quality information.' (*Reference Reviews*)

5453 **RS Online** [UK]
RS Components.
rswww.com [REGISTRATION]
RS Components Ltd is a well established UK distributor of electronic components. Its website includes a browsable and searchable catalogue of over 135,000 products. The associated Technical InfoZone includes 40,000 data sheets. Registration is required for full free access to the site.

Directories & encyclopedias

5454 **Encyclopedia of electronic circuits**
R.F. Graf and W. Sheets McGraw-Hill, 1985–. 7 v.
Not so much an encyclopedia, this is more an A–Z listing of electronic circuits. Each volume contains about 1000 circuit diagrams, each with a short description, listed alphabetically by type. Circuit type headings vary between volumes, but typically might include: Amplifier circuits, Logic circuits, White noise generator circuits, etc. Later volumes each include a detailed cumulative index.
'Overall, this is an excellent source for electronic circuits.it is highly recommended and is truly an invaluable storehouse.' (Hurt: *Information sources in science and technology* (about v. 6))

Photonics rules of thumb: optics, electro-optics, fiber optics, and lasers
E. Friedman and J.L. Miller See entry no. 815

5455 **Radar technology encyclopedia**
D.K. Barton [et al.], eds Artech House, 1997, 536pp. £102.00. ISBN 0890068933.
Contains approximately 5000 entries, alphabetical arranged, covering systems, components, targets, and performance features. Entries generally provide definitions, standard notation, evaluation formulas, relevant block diagrams, and performance summaries. It includes extensive bibliographies covering both literature in English and Russian.
(*Microwave Journal*, January 2000, 43(1), 258)

5456 **Semiconductor cross reference book** [USA]
5th edn, Sams, 2000, 857pp. Also available as CD-ROM, ISBN 0790611406, $43.95. ISBN 0790611392.
Provides a way of finding replacement semiconductors. Arranged in 2 sections. Section 1 lists device types in alphanumeric order by original equipment manufacturers' part number, type number, or other identification, and gives a replacement code. Section 2 lists replacements. Includes over 628,000 items and covers all major semiconductor types: bipolar transistors, FETs, diodes, rectifiers, ICs, SCRs, LEDs, modules, and thermal devices.
Also available as CD-ROM, ISBN 0790611406.

5457 Wiley encyclopedia of electrical and electronics engineering
J.G. Webster, ed. Wiley, 1999. 24 v. + supplements, $9675.00. ISBN 0471139467.
An important and immense reference work containing some 1300 reviewed articles covering all aspects of electrical and electronic engineering. Articles generally include excellent bibliographies. There is a one volume index. First supplementary volume published in 2001 contained 57 articles.
'Voted Outstanding Title. Highly recommended.' (*Choice*)

5458 Wiley survey of instrumentation and measurement
S.A. Dyer, ed. Wiley-IEEE Press, 2001, 1112pp. $220.00. ISBN 047139484X.
Contains 97 articles selected from the WILEY ENCYCLOPEDIA OF ELECTRICAL AND ELECTRONICS ENGINEERING, covering both general principles and specific forms of instrumentation. Useful in the absence of the full encyclopedia.

Handbooks & manuals

5459 AC power systems handbook
J.C. Whitaker 2nd edn, CRC Press, 1998, 608pp. $94.95. ISBN 0849374146.
All chapters have been updated since first edition, and there is now a chapter on grounding practices. Divided into the sections: Power distribution and control; Origins of AC line disturbances; Effects of transient disturbances; Power system components; Power system circuits; Facility-protection methods; Facility grounding; Standby power systems; and Safety and protection systems.
1st edn 1992.

5460 Antenna engineering handbook
R.C. Johnson, ed. 3rd edn, McGraw-Hill, 1993, 1392pp. $125.00. ISBN 007032381X.
A little dated, but still a definitive work. 64 contributors to 46 chapters arranged in four sections: Introduction and fundamentals; Types and design methods (for instance, Loop antennas, Small antennas, Microstrip antennas, etc.); Applications (for instance, Tracking antennas, Satellite antennas, etc.); and Associated topics.
1st edn 1961, edited by H. Jasik; 2nd edn 1984, editors Jasik and Johnson.

5461 ARRL Handbook for Radio Communications
American Radio Relay League 81st edn, Annual, 1216pp. CD-ROM available, $34.95 [2004]. ISBN 0872591964.
www.arrl.org/catalog [DESCRIPTION]
A standard US publication for the radio amateur and others. A heavily illustrated work – diagrams, graphs, circuits, etc. – covering all aspects of hobby radio use. It covers fundamentals, practical design and projects, construction techniques, operating practices, and wireless technology (pagers, cell phones, etc.).
1st edn 1926 under the title Radio Amateur's Handbook. Subsequently entitled ARRL Handbook for the Radio Amateur.

5462 Audio and hi-fi handbook
I. Sinclair, ed. 4th edn, Newnes, 2000, 464pp. £31.99. ISBN 0750649755.
This work has established itself now as a standard reference work in its area aimed at both the enthusiast and the professional. Contains 24 chapters covering all aspects of the subject, including Compact disc technology, MP3 – music on the internet (new chapter), Nicam and satellite radio, Analogue tape recording, the LP record, Valve amplifiers, Headphones, Public address, Interconnections, etc.
1st edn 1988 as Audio electronics reference book; 3rd edn 1998.

5463 Audio engineer's reference book
M. Talbot-Smith, ed. 2nd edn, Focal Press, 1999, 672pp. £55.00. ISBN 0240516850.
Contains 7 chapters: Basic principles; Acoustics and acoustic devices; Recording and reproduction; Digital equipment; Studios and their facilities; Distribution of audio signals; and Miscellaneous topics. This last chapter includes a useful section on international standards for sound systems and equipment.
1st edn 1994.

5464 Battery reference book
T.R. Crompton 3rd edn, Newnes, 2000, 752pp. £160.00. ISBN 075064625X.
A standard reference work in its field providing data on battery types from the very small to the very large. Its eight chapters include Guidelines to battery selection, Battery characteristics, Battery theory and design, Battery performance evaluation, Battery applications, Battery charging, and Battery suppliers. There is also a glossary and appendices, for instance, on battery standards.
1st edn 1990, 2nd edn 1995.

5465 The cellular radio handbook: a reference for cellular system operation
N.J. Boucher 4th edn, Wiley, 2001, 724pp. $158.00. ISBN 0471387258.
A comprehensive, although fairly basic and non-mathematical, introduction to, and overview of, cellular radio technology. Its 52 chapters cover both technological (Antennas, Noise and noise performance, etc.) and management (Marketing, Fraud, etc.) topics. It includes useful appendices and glossary and a good index, but its lack of a good bibliography restricts its utility.
3rd edn 1995.

5466 The circuits and filters handbook
W.-K. Chen, ed. 2nd edn, CRC Press, 2002, 2961pp. $139.95. ISBN 0849309123.
Substantial, comprehensive and advanced reference work stressing theoretical aspects. This edition much reorganized, and with 27 new chapters. Now more than 130 authors of 93 chapters arranged into 13 major sections, Mathematics; Circuit elements, devices and their models; Linear circuit analysis; Feedback circuits; Nonlinear circuits; Distributed circuits; Computer-aided design and optimization; Analog integrated circuits; VLSI circuits; Design automation; Passive filters; Active filters; and Digital filters. This edition includes 29 new chapters, mostly in the areas of computer-aided design, circuit simulation, VLSI circuits, design automation, and active and digital filters. Good bibliographies.
1st edn 1995.

5467 Complete guide to semiconductor devices
K.K. Ng 2nd edn, Wiley-IEEE Press, 2002, 768pp. $110.00. ISBN 0471202401.
An up-to-date handbook containing information – history, structure, characteristics and applications – on 74 major

semiconductor devices with 200 variants. Arranged in 13 broad subject groups: Diodes (four sections); Resistive and capacitive devices; Transistors (two sections); Non-volatile memories; Thyristors and power devices; and Photonics (four sections). Appendices cover physical properties and some selected non-semiconductor devices.

1st edn 1995.

5468 The complete handbook of magnetic recording

F. Jorgensen 4th edn, TAB Books, 1996, 806pp. ISBN 007033045X.

Covers the fundamentals of magnetic recording, aimed at the working engineer. Well illustrated and presented. Its 31 chapters include Design and performance of magnetic heads; Tape and disk materials; and Tribology and head/media interface.

3rd edn 1988.

5469 CRC handbook of electrical filters

J.T. Taylor and Q. Huang, eds CRC Press, 1997, 448pp. $129.95. ISBN 0849389518.

Introductory handbook and overview aimed at the non-specialist. 22 authors contribute to chapters on Approximation methods, CAD methods for filter design, LCR filters, Continuous time active RC filters, Digital filters, Switched capacitor filters, and Electromechanical filters.

5470 CRC handbook of laser science and technology

M.J. Weber, ed. CRC Press, 1985–93. 5 v. + 2 supplements.

Out of print now but this remains a standard-setting reference work in its field. Vols 1–2 (and Supplement 1) contain extensive tables of experimental data on all types of primary lasers with bibliographical citations. Later volumes and Supplement 2 cover physical properties of laser optical materials and fabrication techniques.

- V. 1. *Lasers and masers*. 1982. 552pp. ISBN 0849335019.
- V. 2. *Gas lasers*. 1982. 584pp. ISBN 0849335027.
- V. 3. *Optical materials...I: Nonlinear optical properties/radiation damage*. 1986. 480pp. ISBN 0849335035.
- V. 4. *Optical materials...II: Properties: fundamental properties*. 1986. 496pp. ISBN 0849335045.
- V. 5. *Optical materials...III: Applications, coatings and fabrication*. 1987. 544pp. ISBN 0849335051.
- Supp.1. *Lasers*. 1991. 560pp. ISBN 084933506x.
- Supp.2. *Optical materials*. 1993. 750pp. ISBN 0849335078.

Update and expansion of CRC handbook of lasers, with selected data on optical technology, 1971.

5471 Digital signal processing handbook

V.K. Madisetti and D.B. Williams, eds CRC Press, 1997, 1776pp. (CD-ROM version available: ISBN 0849321352; $149.95), $99.95. ISBN 0849385725.

Substantial and authoritative reference work that covers just about all aspects of digital signal processing, including both basic and advanced material.

Consists of 78 chapters by 139 authors arranged in 14 sections: Signals and systems; Signal representation and quantization; Fast algorithms and structures; Digital filtering; Statistical signal processing; Adaptive filtering; Inverse problems and signal reconstruction; Time frequency and multi-rate signal processing; Digital audio communications; Speech processing; Image and video processing; Sensor array processing; Nonlinear and fractal signal processing; and DSP software and hardware. Most chapters contain a useful bibliography.

5472 Electric cables handbook

G.F. Moore, ed. 3rd edn, Blackwell Science, 1997, 1120pp. £105.00. ISBN 0632040750.

Respected, comprehensive, authoritative. Arranged in seven parts – Theory; Wiring cables, flexible cables and cables for general industrial use; Supply distribution systems and cables; Transmission systems and cables; Submarine distribution and transmission; High-temperature superconductivity; Optical fibres in power transmission systems; and Cables for communication applications. Last two sections completely new. Appendix of data on commonly used cable types.

1st edn 1982; 2nd edn by E. Bungay and D. McAllister, 1990.

5473 Electric motor handbook

H.W. Beaty and J.L. Kirtley, eds McGraw-Hill, 1998, 404pp. $75.00. ISBN 0070359717.

Provides information about electric motors used in consumer, industrial, and commercial applications. It includes size and performance data, as well as electrical and mechanical parameters and protection information. Contains ten chapters including Terminology and definitions; Fundamentals of electromagnetic forces and loss mechanisms; Induction motors; Synchronous motors; Permanent magnet-synchronous (brushless) motors; Direct current motors; Other types of electric motors and related apparatus; Motor noise and product sound; and Servomechanical power-electronic motor drives.

5474 Electric power engineering handbook

L.L. Grigsby, ed. CRC Press; IEEE, 2000, 1430pp. $159.95. ISBN 0849385784.

Made up of 102 chapters by over 150 contributors, grouped into 15 sections: Electric power generation – non-conventional methods; Electric power generation – conventional methods; Transformers; Transmission systems; Substations; Distribution systems; Electric power utilization; Power system analysis and simulation; Power system protection; Power system transients; Power systems dynamics and stability; Power system operation and control; Power system planning (reliability); Power electronics; and Power quality.

Achieves aim of 'comprehensive coverage' but relies mainly on US standards and codes.

5475 Electrical engineering handbook

R.C. Dorf, ed. 2nd edn, CRC Press, 1998, 2752pp. Also available on CD-ROM (ISBN 0849397502), $134.95. ISBN 0849385741.

Massive, comprehensive, and popular, this is an important one-stop resource containing a collection of overviews that combine both underlying theory and practical data. Over 280 contributors to 118 chapters (subdivided into over 200 articles) arranged in 12 sections: Circuits; Signal processing; Electronics; Electromagnetics; Electrical effects and devices; Energy; Communications; Digital devices; Computer engineering; Systems; Biomedical systems; and Mathematics, etc. Each article includes definitions, references, and suggestions for further reading.

1st edn 1993.

'definitive handbook ... is a must for any reference library.' *(Choice)*

5476 Electrical engineer's reference book
M.A. Laughton and D.F. Warne, eds 16th edn, Newnes, 2003, 1376pp. £110.00. ISBN 0750646373.
A long-established and core reference book, substantially revised since the last edition. Some 39 chapters are new or updated. Now includes additional sections on control systems, PLCs, and microprocessors. The 49 chapters are arranged in nine sections: General principles (Units, Electrotechnology, etc.); Materials and processes (Conductors and Superconductors, etc.); Control (Industrial instrumentation, etc.); Power electronics and drives (Motors and actuators, etc.); Environment (Lighting, Environmental control, etc.); Power generation (Prime movers, Alternative energy sources, etc.); Transmission and distribution (Overhead lines, Cables, etc.); Power systems (Power quality, etc.); and Sectors of electricity use (Railways, etc.). Bibliographies generally short. Good index.
1st edn 1945, 15th edn by G.R. Jones et al., 1993.

5477 Electronic instrument handbook
C.F. Coombs, ed. 3rd edn, McGraw-Hill, 1999. $125.00. ISBN 0070126186.
A useful handbook covering the range of instrumentation, much extended since the last edition with ten new chapters, including a whole new part, dealing mainly with virtual and network-based instrumentation. 37 authors contribute 47 chapters organized in 12 parts that include Current and voltage measurement instruments; Signal and waveform generation instruments; Digital domain instruments; Microwave passive devices; Software and connectivity for instrumentation, etc.
1st edn 1972, 2nd edn 1995.

5478 Electronic materials and processes handbook
C.A. Harper, ed. 3rd edn, McGraw-Hill, 2003, 800pp. $125.00. ISBN 0071402144.
A major rewrite of the last edition, this work covers the materials and processes involved in electronic design and packaging. It contains ten substantial overview chapters: Development and fabrication of IC Chips; Plastics, elastomers, and composites; Ceramics and glasses; Metals; Solder technologies for electronic packaging and assembly; Electroplating and deposited metallic coatings; Printed circuit board fabrication; Materials and processes for hybrid microelectronics and multichip modules; Adhesives underfills and coatings in electronics assemblies; and Thermal management materials and systems.
1st edn entitled Handbook of materials and processes for electronics, 1970; 2nd edn 1993.

5479 Electronic packaging and interconnection handbook
C.A. Harper, ed. 3rd edn, McGraw-Hill, 2000, 1024pp. £91.99. ISBN 0071347453.
Covers all aspects of electronic packaging. Arranged in 13 chapters: Materials; Thermal management; Mechanical and thermomechanical stress; Connector and interconnection technology; Wiring and cabling; Soldering and solder technology; Integrated circuit packaging and ball grid arrays; Surface mount technologies; Hybrid microelectronic and multichip module packaging; Chip scale packaging and direct chip attach technologies; Rigid and flexible printed wiring boards; Packaging of high speed and microwave electronic systems; and Packaging of high voltage electronic systems.
1st edn 1991, 2nd edn 1997.

5480 Electronic packaging handbook
G.R. Blackwell, ed. CRC Press, 1999, 640pp. $139.95. ISBN 0849385911.
Contains 16 chapters covering the range of packaging concerns. Chapters include Fundamentals of the design process; Surface mount technology; Integrated circuit packages; Direct chip attach; Circuit boards; EMC and PCB design; Hybrid assemblies; Interconnects; Design for test; Adhesive and its application; Thermal management; Testing; Inspection; Package/enclosure; Electronics package reliability and failure analysis; and Product safety and third-party certification.

5481 Electronics engineers' handbook
D Christiansen [et al.], ed. 4th edn, McGraw-Hill, 1997. $150.00. ISBN 0070210772.
A substantial reference work containing a mass of information covering 'the entire range of electronics' from fundamentals to applications. 180 contributors to 31 chapters arranged in four sections: Principles and techniques (Basic phenomena, Circuit principles, Systems engineering, etc.); Materials and hardware (UHF and microwave devices, Transducers and sensors, etc.); Circuits and functions (Amplifiers and oscillators, Power electronics, etc.); and Systems and applications (Audio systems, Telecommunications, etc.)
1st edn 1975, 3rd edn 1989.

5482 Electronics handbook
J.C. Whitaker, ed. CRC Press; IEEE, 1996, 2575pp. $115.00. ISBN 0849383455.
A major handbook providing a comprehensive and definitive overview. Over 180 authors, and 156 chapters arranged into 24 sections covering all aspects of electronics. Sections include Fundamental electrical theory, Optoelectronics, Power supplies and regulation, Packaging electronic systems, Information recording and storage, Wireless communication systems, and Radar and radionavigation. Most chapters contain definitions, references, and recommended sources of further information.

5483 Electro-optics handbook
R.W. Waynant and M.N. Ediger, eds 2nd edn, McGraw-Hill, 2000. $125.00. ISBN 0070687161.
Extended considerably since the first edition, this reference work covers optical communications, electro-optic devices, and lasers. 43 authors provide 29 chapters dealing with fundamentals, types of lasers (Visible lasers, Infrared gas lasers, etc.), devices (Infrared detectors, Imaging detectors, etc.), and applications (Lasers in medicine, Material processing applications, etc.)
1st edn 1994.

Fuel cell technology handbook
G. Hoogers, ed. See entry no. 4803

5484 Handbook for sound engineers
G.M. Ballou [et al.], eds 3rd edn, Focal Press, 2002, 1568pp. £90.00. ISBN 0240804546.
Well presented and comprehensive work, packed with diagrams and practical information. Consists of 47 chapters by 27 authors arranged in seven parts: Acoustics (Psychoacoustics, Small room acoustics, etc.); Electronic components; Electroacoustic devices (Microphones, Loudspeakers, etc.); Audio electronic circuits and equipment

(Amplifier design, etc.); Recording and playback (MIDI, Compact discs, etc.); Design applications; and Measurement.

1st and 2nd edns published by Howard W. Sams & Co., 1987 and 1991 respectively.

5485 Handbook of advanced electronic and photonic materials and devices
H.S. Nalwa, ed. Academic Press, 2000. 10 v., $4050.00. ISBN 0125137451.
www.elsevier.com/wps/find/homepage.cws_home [DESCRIPTION]
Monumental work consisting of over one hundred review chapters, each with a major bibliography, written by more than 200 contributors.

- V. 1. *Semiconductors*. 316pp. ISBN 0125137516.
- V. 2. *Semiconductor devices*. 275pp. ISBN 0125137524.
- V. 3. *High Tc superconductors and organic conductors*. 375pp. ISBN 0125137532.
- V. 4. *Ferroelectrics and dielectrics*. 237pp. ISBN 0125137540.
- V. 5. *Chalcogenide glasses and sol-gel materials*. 267pp. ISBN 0125137559.
- V. 6. *Nanostructured materials*. 421pp. ISBN 0125137567.
- V. 7. *Liquid crystals, display and laser materials*. 322pp. ISBN 0125137575.
- V. 8. *Conducting polymers*. 354pp. ISBN 0125137583.
- V. 9. *Nonlinear optical materials*. 485pp. ISBN 0125137591.
- V. 10. *Light-emitting diodes, lithium batteries and polymer devices*. 313pp. ISBN 0125137818.
- **Silicon-based materials and devices H.S. Nalwa, ed.** Academic Press, 2001, 609pp. $657.95. ISBN 0125139098. http://books.elsevier.com [DESCRIPTION]. Subset of articles published in the 10 volume handbook.

5486 Handbook of batteries
D. Linden and T.B. Reddy, eds 3rd edn, McGraw-Hill, 2001. $150.00. ISBN 0071359788.
Over 80 contributors to 43 chapters arranged in six sections: Principles of operation; Primary batteries; Reserve batteries; Secondary batteries; Advanced batteries; and Portable fuel cells. Appendices include definitions etc. This edition includes 4 new chapters.

1st edn 1984 as Handbook of batteries and fuel cells; 2nd edn 1995

5487 Handbook of electric motors
R.H. Engelmann and W.H. Middendorf, eds Marcel Dekker, 1995, 801pp. $185.00. ISBN 0824789156.
Covers the fundamentals of electric motors, plus providing information on applications, design, testing, insulation, installation, and use. 47 authors provide 14 chapters: Principles of energy conversion; Types of motors and their characteristics; Motor selection; Induction motor analysis and design; Synchronous motor analysis and design; Direct current motor analysis and design; Testing for performance; Motor insulation systems; Motor control; Motor protection; Mechanical considerations; Environmental considerations; Reliability; and Maintenance.

5488 Handbook of electric power calculations
H.W. Beaty, ed. 3rd edn, McGraw-Hill, 2000, 600pp. $125.00. ISBN 0071362983.
www.knovel.com
This work provides an easy 'step-by-step approach' to common electric power calculations, arranged by topic. 17 authors contribute 20 sections: Network analysis; Instrumentation; DC motors and generators; Transformers; 3 phase induction motors; Single phase motors; Synchronous machines; Generation of electric power; Transmission lines; Electric power networks; Load flow studies; Power system control; Short circuit computations; System grounding; Power system protection; Power system stability; Cogeneration; Batteries; Economic methods; and Lighting design. Each section includes example calculations.

Available online: see website.

1st edn 1983, edited by A. Seidman and H. Mahrous; 2nd edn 1997, edited by Seidman, Beaty and Mahrous.

5489 Handbook of electrical and electronic insulating materials
W.T. Shugg 2nd edn, Wiley, 1995, 608pp. $99.95. ISBN 0780310306.
Easy-to-use source of information – technologies, manufacture, applications, properties, etc. – on almost all kinds of electrical insulating material. Arranged by type, for instance, thermoplastic moulding compounds, extrusion compounds, dielectric films, ceramic and glass insulations, etc.

1st edn VNR, 1985.

5490 Handbook of electrical installation practice
G. Stokes, ed. 4th edn, Blackwell Science, 2003, 688pp. £85.00. ISBN 0632060026.
Covers all aspects of domestic and non-domestic electrical power installations. UK orientation. Chapters include topics such as wiring cables, mains and submains cables and distribution in buildings, power supplies, transformers, switchgear, and electricity on construction sites. Revised to take account of changes in British and other standards, and the latest edition of the IEE Wiring Regulations (REQUIREMENTS FOR ELECTRICAL INSTALLATIONS.

1st edn 1983, 3rd edn 1996. 1st and 2nd edns edited by E.A. Reeves, 3rd edn by A. Smith.

Handbook of fuel cells: fundamentals, technology, applications
W. Vielstich, A. Lamm and H.A. Gasteiger, eds See entry no. 4804

Handbook of lasers
M.J. Weber See entry no. 819

5491 Handbook of microwave and optical components
K. Chang, ed. Wiley, 1989–91. 4 v.
Wide scope and coverage, an important but now rather dated overview of the area.

- V. 1. *Microwave passive and antenna components*. 1989. 907pp. ISBN 0471613665 £175. 13 chapters including Transmission lines, Transmission-line discontinuities, and Antennas IV: Microstrip antennas.
- V. 2. *Microwave solid-state components*. 1990. 635pp. ISBN 0471843652 £115. Includes chapters on Mixers and detectors, and Multipliers and parametric devices, for instance.
- V. 3. *Optical components*. 1990 616pp. ISBN 0471613673 £138. Includes chapters on Optical wave propagation, Infrared techniques, Optical lenses, Optical resonators, etc.
- V. 4. *Fiber and electro-optical components*. 1991. 484pp. ISBN 0471613657 £115. Eight chapters including Optical fibre transmission technology, and Optical channel waveguides and waveguide couplers

Handbook of photonics
M.C. Gupta, ed. See entry no. 822

Handbook of superconducting materials
D. Cardwell and D. Ginley, eds See entry no. 5849

5492 **Handbook of thin film devices**
C. Wood [et al.], eds Academic Press, 2000, 1412pp. 5 v., $2095.00. ISBN 0122653203.
Major and substantial overview of the area. Each volume separately edited.
- V. 1. *Hetero-structures for high performance devices*, ed. by C.E.C. Wood 352pp. ISBN 0127628703.
- V. 2. *Semiconductor optical and electro-optical devices*, ed. by A.G.U. Perera and H.C. Liu 372pp. ISBN 012550760.
- V. 3. *Superconducting film devices*, ed. by P. R. Broussard 233pp. ISBN 0124089526.
- V. 4. *Magnetic thin film devices*, ed. by J.D. Adam 220pp. ISBN 0121364607.
- V. 5. *Ferroelectric film devices*, ed. by D.J. Taylor 235pp. ISBN 0120440709.

5493 **Handbook of thin film materials**
H.S. Nalwa, ed. Academic Press, 2002, 3451pp. 5 v., $2780.00. ISBN 0125129084.
Comprehensive and up-to-date work containing 65 review articles written by 125 authors.
- V. 1. *Deposition and processing of thin films* 706pp. ISBN 0125129092.
- V. 2. *Characterization and spectroscopy of thin films* 773pp. ISBN 0125129106.
- V. 3. *Ferroelectric and dielectric thin films* 634pp. ISBN 0125129114.
- V. 4. *Semiconductor and superconductor thin films* 705pp. ISBN 0125129122.
- V. 5. *Nanomaterials and magnetic thin films* 633pp. ISBN 0125129130.

5494 **The industrial electronics handbook**
J.D. Irwin, ed. CRC Press; IEEE Press, 1997, 1686pp. $149.95. ISBN 0849383439.
Over 250 contributors. Arranged in two parts containing ten sections and 122 chapters. First part covers fundamentals – supporting technologies, data acquisition and management, power electronics, factory communications, system control, and factory automation. Part 2 is concerned with modern technologies affecting industrial systems – expert systems and neural networks, fuzzy systems and soft computing, evolutionary systems, and emerging technologies such as virtual reality and microelectromechanical systems.

5495 **Industrial power engineering and applications handbook**
K.C. Agrawal Newnes, 2001, 992pp. £110.00. ISBN 0750673516.
An in-depth treatment of power drives, their controls, power transfer and distribution, protection, and maintenance. Arranged in 5 parts: Electric motors; Switchgear assemblies and captive power generation; Voltage surges, over voltages and grounding practices; Power capacitors; and Bus systems.

5496 **Instrument engineers' handbook**
B.G. Lipták, ed. 4th edn, CRC Press, 2003, 1860pp. $169.95. ISBN 0849310830.
This is v. 1, Process measurement and analysis, of the updated edn, the 3rd edn v. 2 Process control having been issued in 1995, its v. 3 Process software and digital networks in 2002.
'Comprehensive, practical, and well-organized, this book is highly recommended for academic libraries and engineering company libraries. It can best serve as a teaching aid for students, or a reference manual for both new and experienced practicing engineers.' (*E-STREAMS*)

5497 **Instrumentation reference book**
W. Boyes, ed. 3rd edn, Butterworth-Heinemann, 2003, 1062pp. £80.00. ISBN 0750671238.
52 contributors to 44 overview chapters arranged in five parts: Mechanical measurements (Measurement of flow, etc.); Measurement of temperature and chemical composition; Electrical and radiation measurements; Instrumentation systems (Sampling, Telemetry, etc.); and Further scientific and technical information (Statistics, etc.). Well illustrated with photographs and drawings.
1st edn 1988; 2nd edn 1995, edited by B.E. Noltingk et al. Developed from Jones' Instrument technology, first published 1953–7.

5498 **The J & P transformer book: a practical technology of the power transformer**
M.J. Heathcote, ed. 12th edn, Newnes, 1998, 945pp. £125.00. ISBN 0750611588.
Long-established title with a firm reputation aimed at practitioners. This edition has been extensively rewritten and restructured, and is rather longer than the last edition (28 chapters, 815pp.) The ten chapters of this edition include: Transformer theory; Design fundamentals; Basic materials; Transformer construction; Testing of transformers; Operation and maintenance; Special features of transformers for particular purposes; and Transformer enquiries and tenders.
1st edn 1925, 11th edn 1983.

5499 **Loudspeaker handbook**
J.M. Eargle 2nd edn, Kluwer Academic Publishers, 2003, 432pp. £78.00. ISBN 1402075847.
Following the 'successful first edition' this updated and augmented text covers a rich array of examples and topics. Text is clear and while intended for loudspeaker engineers it is also accessible by supporting technicians and intermediate university students.

5500 **Magnetic fields: a comprehensive theoretical treatise for practical use**
H. Knoepfel Wiley, 2000, 619pp. $185.00. ISBN 0471322059.
Foundation of magnetic field theory; Magnetic potentials; Periodic fields and wave phenomena; Magnetic field diffusion and eddy currents; Electromagnetic and thermal energies; Magnetic forces and their effects; Magnetomechanical stresses; Magnetohydrodynamics and properties of matter; Numerical and analog solution methods.

5501 **Magnetic recording technology**
C.D. Mee and E.D. Daniel, eds 2nd edn, McGraw-Hill, 1996. $65.00. ISBN 0070412766.
Concerned with the underlying science and technology of magnetic recording. This edition thoroughly revised and updated with three new chapters. 14 authors of ten chapters: Introduction; Recording and reproducing processes; Particulate media; Film media; Micromagnetics of thin-film media; Recording heads; Tribology of the head-

medium interface; Recording limitations; Recording measurements; and Magnetooptical recording.

2nd edn of Part I of Magnetic recording handbook, 1990. Companion volume is MAGNETIC STORAGE HANDBOOK.

5502 Magnetic storage handbook

C.D. Mee and E.D. Daniel, eds 2nd edn, McGraw-Hill, 1996. $89.50. ISBN 0070412758.

Covers the more practical aspects and applications of magnetic recording. Revised and updated since the first edition, with five chapters new or almost entirely rewritten. 13 authors of ten chapters; Introduction; Data storage on rigid disks; Data storage on flexible disks; Data storage on tape; Analog video recording; Digital video recording; Analog audio recording; Digital audio recording; Instrumentation recording; and Signal and error-control coding.

2nd edn of Part II of Magnetic recording handbook, 1990. Companion volume is MAGNETIC RECORDING TECHNOLOGY.

5503 The measurement, instrumentation and sensors handbook

J.G. Webster, ed. CRC Press, 1999, 2608pp. $179.95. ISBN 0849383471.

A very substantial reference work with over 200 contributors to 104 chapters, organized according to measurement problem. Sections cover Measurement characteristics, Spatial variables measurement, Time and frequency measurement, Mechanical variables measurement (3 sections – solid, fluid, thermal), Electromagnetic variables, Radiation, Chemical variables, Biomedical variables, Signal processing, Displays, and Controls. Good index, plenty of useful illustrations.

Mechanical and electrical equipment for buildings

B. Stein and J.S. Reynolds See entry no. 5353

5504 Modern cable television technology: video, voice, and data communications

W. Ciciora [et al.] 2nd edn, Morgan Kaufmann, 2004, 1053pp. $84.95. ISBN 1558608281.

http://books.elsevier.com

Revision of highly praised 1st edn. 25 chapters in six parts: 1. Once over lightly (Introduction to cable television); 2. The signals; 3. Headends; 4. Broadband distribution systems; 5. System architecture; 6. Customer interface issues. Glossary. Index. Easily readable; limited mathematics.

Series: The Morgan Kaufmann Series in Networking. See website for other titles in the Series.

5505 Modern power station practice: incorporating modern power system practice

3rd edn, British Electricity International, 1991. 12 v. ISBN 0080164366.

A revised and expanded series of textbooks (in the broadest sense of the word) with exercises, covering all aspects of power station practice. The impact of privatization appears as a running theme. Volume indexes as well as a consolidated index enhance the value of this authoritative work.

- A. *Station planning and design.*
- B. *Boilers and ancillary plant.*
- C. *Turbines, generators and associated plant.*
- D. *Electrical systems and equipment.*
- E. *Chemistry and metallurgy.*
- F. *Control and instrumentation.*
- G. *Station operation and maintenance.*
- H. *Station commissioning.*
- J. *Nuclear power generation.*
- K. *EHV transmission.*
- L. *System operation.*
- M. *Index.*

1st edn 1963–4 in 5 vols; 2nd edn, 1971, 8 vols. Modern power system practice is a separate work, published by Pergamon, 1991.

5506 Modern wiring practice: design and installation

W.E. Steward and T.A. Stubbs 12th edn, Newnes, 1995, 340pp. £18.99. ISBN 0750621346.

Highly illustrated and with a practical approach this long-established work is aimed at the working electrician and designer. This edition takes into account the 16th edition of the IEE *Wiring regulations*, issued as BS7621, REQUIREMENTS FOR ELECTRICAL INSTALLATIONS. Arranged in two parts, Design of electrical installation systems, and Practical work, which covers conduit and trunking systems, switches, sockets, earthing, etc.

1st edn 1952; 11th edn 1992.

5507 Newnes electrical pocket book

M.J. Heathcote and E.A. Reeves, eds 23rd edn, Newnes, 2002, 499pp. £16.99. ISBN 0750647582.

A handy pocket book of information aimed at practitioners, covering most aspects of practical electrical engineering. The chapters on semiconductors, power generation, transformers, building automation systems, electric vehicles, hazardous areas, and electrical installation have all been updated, the last to bring it in line with the *IEE Wiring regulations*, 2001, or British Standard BS7621, REQUIREMENTS FOR ELECTRICAL INSTALLATIONS.

1st edn 1932, 22nd edn 1995. Various editors.

5508 Passive electronic component handbook

C.A. Harper, ed. 2nd edn, McGraw-Hill, 1997, 786pp. $89.50. ISBN 0070266980.

Provides a range of important practical data, performance curves, and guidelines on passive electronic components – resistors, capacitors, electrical transformers, electrically operated relays and manual operated switches, etc. Well illustrated and extensive bibliographies.

1st edn entitled Handbook of components for electronics 1977.

5509 The power electronics handbook

T.L. Skvarenina, ed. CRC Press, 2002, 664pp. $159.95. ISBN 0849373360.

Covers a wide range of topics, particularly concerned with applications. 53 authors contribute 23 chapters arranged in three parts: Power electronic devices (Diodes, Schottky diodes, etc.); Power electronic circuits and controls (DC–DC converters, Rectifiers, Inverters, etc.); and Application and systems considerations (DC motor drives, Step motor drives, etc.) Well illustrated.

'good resource ... selection of topics is excellent' (*Choice*)

5510 Power electronics handbook

M.H. Rashid, ed. Academic Press, 2001, 895pp. $149.95. ISBN 0125816502.

Wide-ranging coverage with an emphasis upon practical applications. More than 50 authors of 35 chapters, including eight on modern power semiconductor devices (MCTs, IGBTs, SIDs, power MOSFETs, etc.), 10 chapters on principles and types of power converters, 11 chapters covering applications

(Power supplies, Motor drives, Automotive applications, etc.), and four miscellaneous chapters covering Power quality issues, Active filters, Simulation, and Packaging of smart power systems.
'well written ... wealth of material' (*Choice*)

5511 **Printed circuit board materials handbook**
M.W. Jawitz, ed. McGraw-Hill, 1997, 784pp. $99.50. ISBN 0070324883.
A comprehensive work on the various processes and products used in the design and manufacture of printed circuit boards. 36 authors contribute 32 chapters arranged in three divisions – Properties, Manufacturing processes, and Performance and function.

5512 **Radio communication handbook**
D. Biddulph and C. Lorek, eds; Radio Society of Great Britain 7th edn, 2000, 820pp. £29.99. ISBN 1872309240.
Well tried and tested comprehensive guide to the theory and practice of radio communication for the amateur and enthusiast. All material has been updated and several chapters have been extensively rewritten. Made up of 23 chapters covering first principles, components (Passive components, Electronic tubes and valves, etc.), equipment (HF receivers, HF antennas, etc.), and practical background (Telegraphy and keying, Power supplies, etc.)
1st edn 1938, 6th edn 1994.

5513 **Radio handbook**
W.I. Orr 23rd edn, Butterworth-Heinemann, 1987, 672pp. £42.99. ISBN 0750699477.
A long-established and standard handbook aimed at engineer and amateur alike. It covers all aspects of radio theory and technology, including components and devices, design, interference, power supplies, mobile equipment, propagation and construction practices. Index lacks some expected terms. Little attention to audio and output stages.
22nd edn 1982.

5514 **Reference data for engineers: radio, electronics, computers and communications**
M.E. Van Valkenburg and W.M. Middleton, eds 9th edn, Newnes, 2001, 1672pp. £90.00. ISBN 0750672919.
This is a standard and well respected compendium of data containing a wealth of information, and packed with tables, illustrations, formulas, etc. 96 contributors to 49 chapters, including Attenuators, Scattering matrices, Antennas, and Electroacoustics. This edition has been updated particularly in the areas of satellite technology, space communication, microwave science, telecommunication, global positioning systems, frequency data, and radar.
1st edn 1942, 8th edn 1993.

5515 **The resource handbook of electronics**
J.C. Whitaker CRC Press, 2000, 512pp. $99.95. ISBN 0849383536.
One-stop source for essential information arranged mainly in tables, charts, formulas, equations, and definitions. Structured in 19 chapters each with a bibliography. Appendices include glossary, conversion tables, list of acronyms, etc.
Largely taken from the author's ELECTRONICS HANDBOOK.

5516 **Review of radio science**
W.R. Stone, ed.; International Union of Radio Science Wiley/IEEE Press, 1999–2002. $145.00. ISBN 0471268666.
A series of substantial reviews published every three years under the auspices of the International Union. The broad topic areas are (latest volume): Electromagnetic metrology; Fields and waves; Signals and systems; Electronics and photonics; Elecromagnetic noise and interference; Wave propagation and remote sensing; Ionospheric radio and propagation; Waves in plasmas; Radio astronomy; Electromagnetics in biology and medicine.
Earliest volumes published by URSI; later vols. By Oxford University Press; the most recent by Wiley.

5517 **The RF and microwave circuit design cookbook**
S.A. Maas Artech House, 1998, 267pp. £58.00. ISBN 0890069735.
Intended as a recipe book for the practising engineer. Contains chapters on Microwave circuits and circuit elements; Solid-state devices; Diode mixers; Diode frequency multipliers; Other diode applications; Active mixers; FET resistive mixers; and Active frequency multipliers.
Series: The Artech House Microwave Library.
'highly recommended.' (*Choice*)

5518 **The RF and microwave handbook**
M. Golio, ed. CRC Press, 2001, 1376pp. $159.95. ISBN 084938592X.
Substantial and comprehensive set of overviews. Over 100 contributors to nearly 80 chapters arranged in nine sections cover in detail: Microwave and RF product applications; System considerations; Microwave measurements; Circuits; Passive technologies; Active device technologies; CAD, simulation and modelling; and Underlying physics. Chapters include definitions and extensive bibliographies.
'Outstanding title ... highly recommended.' (*Choice*)

5519 **Semiconductors: data handbook**
O. Madelung 3rd edn, Springer, 2004, 691pp. £130.50. ISBN 3540404880.
Contains basic data for all known groups of semiconductors. CD-ROM included in this edn allows much greater data coverage than in previous editions. All the data is compiled from the 17 volumes of the New Series of LANDOLT-BÖRNSTEIN.

Sound synthesis and sampling
M. Russ See entry no. 6179

5520 **Standard handbook for electrical engineers**
D.G. Fink and H.W. Beaty, eds 14th edn, McGraw-Hill, 1999, 2304pp. $150.00. ISBN 0070220050.
Long-standing respected handbook that provides a comprehensive technical treatment of the generation, transmission, distribution, control, conservation, and application of electrical power. This edition includes much new material, for instance concerning energy conservation and alternative energy sources. Oriented towards practical issues. 63 contributors to 28 sections which include Generation, Prime movers, Direct current generators, Hydroelectric power generation, Transmission systems, Substations, etc. Bibliographies updated since last edition, when they were criticized.
1st edn 1907; previous edn 1993.

5521 **Standard handbook of audio and radio engineering**
J.C. Whitaker and K.B. Benson, eds 2nd edn, McGraw-Hill, 2001. $125.00. ISBN 0070067171.
www.tvhandbook.com [COMPANION]
A major reference work by 37 authors covering all aspects of audio engineering. Consists of 45 chapters arranged in 13 sections: Principles of sound and hearing; The audio spectrum; Architectural acoustics; Microphone devices and systems; Sound reproduction; Digital coding of audio signals; Compression technologies; Audio networking; Recording systems; Production standards and equipment; Broadcast transmission systems; Radio receivers; and Standards and practices. Good bibliographies.
1st edn 1988, edited by Benson alone.
An accompanying CD-ROM comes with diagrams, pictures, industry specifications and standards, and additional reference material.

5522 **Standard handbook of video and television engineering**
J.C. Whitaker and K.B. Benson, eds 4th edn, McGraw-Hill, 2003, 1300pp. $150.00. ISBN 0071411801.
www.tvhandbook.com [COMPANION]
Becoming a substantial reference work in this fast-paced area. This latest edition contains much new material. More than 100 articles arranged in 13 sections that cover fundamentals (Light, vision and photometry, for instance), basic technologies (Digital coding and signal processing, for instance), recording (Video cameras, for instance), and transmission and reception (Compression techniques for video and audio, Networking principles, protocols, and systems, etc.).
1st edn 1986, 3rd edn 1999. First two edns edited by Blair alone and entitled Television engineering handbook. *An accompanying CD-ROM contains the text of the book plus supporting material.*

Superconductivity: fundamentals and applications
W. Buckel and R. Kleiner See entry no. 1892

5523 **Switchgear and control handbook**
R.W. Smeaton and W.H. Ubert, eds 3rd edn, McGraw-Hill, 1998. $99.50. ISBN 0070584516.
Solid work, practical in approach. Over 50 contributors to 32 chapters arranged in four parts: Electrical systems, general considerations and standards; Switchgear and distribution equipment and accessories (AC switchgear, Substations, etc.); Motor and industrial systems, controls, control and protection devices; and Solid-state electronic, programmable, and microprocessor-based controls, controllers and logic systems (PLC control systems, for instance). The last part is new to this edition. Also includes a useful glossary of electrical and electronic terms.
1st edn 1976, 2nd edn 1987.

5524 **The VLSI handbook**
W.-K. Chen, ed. CRC Press, 1999, 1788pp. $159.95. ISBN 0849385938.
Aimed at practitioners, this large and comprehensive work covers VLSI circuit design, fabrication, and testing. It contains over 90 chapters including Devices and their models; Scaling of MOS circuits; Circuit simulations; Amplifiers; Logic circuits; Structured logic circuits; Memory, registers, and system timing; Analog and mixed signal circuits; Test and testability; GaAs technology; and Design automation.

Keeping up-to-date

5525 **Current Papers in Electrical and Electronics Engineering**
Institution of Electrical Engineers Monthly. £325.00 [2004]. ISSN 00113778.
An INSPEC current awareness service which has the same subject coverage as ELECTRICAL AND ELECTRONICS ABSTRACTS, but content is restricted to bibliographic citations only. Includes about 75,000 items per year, mainly journal articles and conference papers, arranged in classified order.
- **Inspec Current Awareness** www.iee.org/inspec/currentawareness [FEE-BASED]. 'Weekly email alert service to keep you abreast of global published literature in physics, electronic and electrical engineering, computer science, communications and information technology.'

5526 **Electronic Systems & Software**
Institution of Electrical Engineers 2003, Bimonthly. £175.00. ISSN 14798336.
www.iee.org/oncomms/sector/electronics
One of the IEE's suite of professional magazines 'covering issues in electronic system architecture and design'.
Continues Electronics & communication engineering journal (ISSN 0954-0695).

5527 **IEE Power Engineer**
Institution of Electrical Engineers 2003–, Bimonthly. £185.00. ISSN 14798344.
www.iee.org/oncomms/sector/power [DESCRIPTION]
'Written for professional engineers engaged in electrical power generation, transmission, distribution and applications.'
Part of one of the IEE PROFESSIONAL NETWORKS.

5528 **IEE Review** [UK]
Institution of Electrical Engineers 1988–, Monthly. £175.00 [2004]. ISSN 09535683.
www.iee.org/oncomms/sector/ieereview.cfm
IEE's monthly 'flagship' professional magazine, relaunched at the beginning of 2003, containing feature articles, columns, opinion, analysis, book reviews, and letters.
Formerly entitled Electronics and Power (1964–1987), and before that, the Journal of the Institution... (1955–63).

5529 **IEEE Spectrum** [USA]
Institute of Electrical and Electronics Engineers 1964–, 12 pa. $230.00 [2004]. ISSN 0018923.
www.spectrum.ieee.org
The IEEE's leading house magazine for its members containing news, views, and reviews. Most recent issue partially available online.
Formerly issued as a supplement to Electrical Engineering (ISSN 0095-9197).

5530 **Key Abstracts**
Institution of Electrical Engineers 1975–, Monthly. £235.00 each.
The Institution publishes a series of Key Abstracts in 22 specialized subject areas each month. Each issue contain about 250 abstracts selected from the INSPEC database. Relevant titles are: *Antennas and Propagation*, *Computing in Electronics and Power*, *Electronic Circuits*, *Electronic Instrumentation*, *Microelectronics and Printed Circuits*, *Microwave Technology*, *Optoelectronics*, *Power Systems and Applications*, *Semiconductor Devices*, and *Telecommunications*.

Environmental Engineering

acid rain • air pollution • air quality • bioremediation • chemical pollution • clean air • contaminated land • drinking water • environmental pollution • environmental protection • environmental technology • groundwater engineering • hazardous wastes • industrial pollution • marine pollution • municipal waste • noise pollution • odour control • pollution • pollution control • public health engineering • radioactive wastes • recycling • sewage engineering • solid waste management • waste management • wastewater treatment • water engineering • water pollution • water quality • water treatment

Introductions to the subject

5531 **Basic water treatment**
C. Binnie, M. Kimber and G. Smethurst 3rd edn, Thomas Telford, 2002, 291pp. £25.00. ISBN 0727730320.
A very basic introduction aimed at the non-professional. Updated to include latest water quality standards. Its 13 chapters discuss water demand and use, membrane processes, filtration, disinfection, water quality criteria, etc.
1st edn 1974, 2nd edn 1988.

Earth under siege: from air pollution to global change
R. Turco See entry no. 831

The economics of the environment and natural resources
R.Q. Grafton [et al.] See entry no. 4613

5532 **Environmental, safety, and health engineering**
G. Woodside and D.S. Kocurek Wiley, 1997, 580pp. $150.00. ISBN 0471109320.
Broad in scope, this introduction has sections on Regulation (US perspective); Environmental engineering – covering air pollution engineering, waste management, and water engineering; Safety engineering, covering safety management, fire and life safety, construction; and Industrial hygiene, covering chemical hazards, ventilation, noise, etc.

Life support: the environment and human health
M. McCally, ed. See entry no. 4222

Polymers: the environment and sustainable development
A. Azapagic, A. Emsley and I. Hamerton See entry no. 5063

Polymers and the environment
G. Scott; Royal Society of Chemistry See entry no. 5064

5533 **Wastewater engineering: treatment and reuse**
F. Burton [et al.] 4th edn, McGraw-Hill, 2003, 1819pp. $145.00. ISBN 0070418780.
A popular textbook and a mine of information with over 300 tables. Its 15 chapters include Physical unit operations, Chemical unit operations, Water reuse, etc.
1st edn 1972, last edn 1991.

5534 **Water resources engineering**
L.W. Mays Wiley, 2004, 842pp. $125.00. ISBN 0471705241.
Basic, easy-to-understand introduction to water engineering, covering water use and water excess, including water distribution systems, stormwater control, and flood storage systems.

Water supply
A.C. Twort, D.D. Ratnayaka and M.J. Brandt, eds See entry no. 1124

Dictionaries, thesauri, classifications

Computational hydraulics and hydrology: an illustrated dictionary
N.G. Adrien, comp. See entry no. 5157

5535 **Concise dictionary of environmental engineering**
T.M. Pankratz, comp. CRC Press, 1996, 416pp. $44.95. ISBN 1566702127.
Contains more than 5200 technical terms, abbreviations, trademarks and brand names, covering water and wastewater treatment, air pollution, solid waste disposal and hazardous waste remediation.

5536 **Concise dictionary of environmental terms**
L. Theodore, J. Reynolds and K. Morris, comps Spon Press, 1998, 392pp. £45.00. ISBN 9056996002.
Aimed at the non-specialist, this dictionary contains some 6000, mainly one-sentence, definitions of words and phrases which often include references for further reading. Has a separate list of about 700 organization and technical acronyms. An accompanying diskette contains the searchable text of the dictionary in Word Perfect and as an ASCII file.
'Its coverage is substantial, it is very well produced, clearly printed, and ... should be very useful.' (*Reference Reviews*)

Dictionary of environmental quotations
B.K. Rodes and R. Odell, eds See entry no. 2303

5537 **Dictionary of environmental science and engineering: English–Spanish/Spanish–English**
H. Headworth and S. Stienes, comps Wiley, 1998, 324pp. $70.00. ISBN 0471962732.
Contains 28,000 entries altogether – 14,000 in each language covering relevant vocabulary in the areas of chemistry, biology, ecology, geology, hydrogeology, water and waste engineering, waste management and pollution control. Includes some long entries. For instance, 'water' is allotted a full page, and 'waste' a half page. Good value.
Print-on-demand title.

5538 **Dictionary of environmental science and technology**
A. Porteous, comp. 3rd edn, Wiley, 2000, 732pp. $41.57. ISBN 0471634700.
Considerably expanded since first edition now containing more than 4000 cross-referenced entries. Also includes four appendices – a list of acronyms, updated references, a guide to further reading, and international case studies. This is a very useful dictionary that has a focus on environmental protection and resource management.
1st edn 1991 Open University Press, 2nd edn 1996.

5539 **Dictionary of water and sewage engineering: in German, English, French and Italian**
F. Meinck and H. Möhle 4th edn, Oldenbourg, 1994, 937pp. ISBN 3486353543.
Contains about 18,000 German base terms with English, French and italian equivalents and indexes. Genders are given in entries. Appendices include weights and measures tables.
1st edn 1963, 2nd edn 1977: both by Elsevier.

5540 **Dictionary of water and waste management**
P.G. Smith and J.S. Scott, comps 2nd edn, Butterworth-Heinemann, 2002, 439pp. £35.00. ISBN 0750646381.
This well regarded dictionary contains about 7000 concise entries, an increase of some 50% over first edition. Coverage now includes such areas as air pollution control, hazardous and solid waste management, and pipeline management. Many earlier entries revised. Cross-references. Some entries have accompanying graphs or charts.
1st edn 1981 as Dictionary of waste and water treatment.
'This is an important and timely dictionary that all libraries supporting programs in waste management, environmental studies, and hydrology should have in their collections. Highly recommended for all libraries.' (*Choice*)

5541 **Dictionary of water engineering**
K.D. Nelson, C. Kerr and R. Legg ITDG Publishing, 2004, 256pp. £35.00. ISBN 1853394904.
www.itdgpublishing.org.uk
3500 terms; good illustrations. Emphasis on needs of less-developed countries. 'It is a practical handbook of down-to-earth use for all those involved in sustainable development programmes from planners to field workers.'
ITDG Publishing is the publishing arm of the Intermediate Technology Development Group*: see website.*

5542 **The drinking water dictionary**
J.M. Symons, L.C. Bradley and T.C. Cleveland, eds McGraw-Hill, 2001, 656pp. $79.95. ISBN 0071375139.
Includes more than 15,000 definitions covering terminology from all areas of water supply, treatment, regulation, chemistry, health effects, microbiology, distribution, management, etc. Definitions of abbreviations, acronyms, hydraulic formulas, and mathematical models also included.
Previously published by the AMERICAN WATER WORKS ASSOCIATION, *2000.*

5543 **Elsevier's dictionary of marine pollution: English–Spanish, with English and Spanish indexes (Diccionario de contaminación del mar)**
L.-J. Zilberberg, comp. Elsevier, 2000, 732pp. €143.00. ISBN 0444504672.
Contains about 12,500 terms. Covers all aspects of marine pollution, including legalities, coastal pollution, effect on fishing, etc.

5544 **Elsevier's dictionary of noise and noise control: in English, French and German**
R. Serré, comp. Elsevier, 1989, 214pp. €124.00. ISBN 0444880739.
Covering aspects of noise and noise pollution. Contains nearly 1200 definitions in English, with synonyms and spelling variants, bibliographic sources, and a separate listing of acronyms and abbreviations. French and German indexes. Covers all aspects of noise and noise pollution.

5545 **Elsevier's dictionary of the environment: in English, French, Spanish and Arabic**
M. Bakr, comp. Elsevier, 1998, 474pp. €137.00. ISBN 0444829660.
Contains 4312 terms from the wide area of environmental science and technology, including air pollution, biological diversity, biomass energy, etc. through to sustainable development, tropical ecosystem, wetland ecosystem.

5546 **The environment dictionary**
D.D. Kemp, comp. Routledge, 1998, 480pp. £23.99. ISBN 041512753X.
Clear, well designed encyclopedic dictionary containing about 1600 entries, which usually include an explanation as well as a definition, and some with brief bibliographies. It covers the physical elements of the environment, as well as socio-economic, cultural, historical and political issues. Boxed entries highlight issues of particular importance or topicality. Name and subject indexes.

5547 **Environmental engineering dictionary** [USA]
C.C. Lee, comp. 3rd edn, Government Institutes, 1998, 682pp. $125.00. ISBN 0865876207.
Well regarded, this expanded edition contains many new or revised terms. Overall, it includes more than 14,000 technical and regulatory engineering definitions from areas including pollution control and monitoring, risk assessment, sampling and analysis, quality control, and environmental engineering and science. Many entries have citations to US legislation and government reports.
1st edn 1989, 2nd edn 1992.

5548 **Glossary of building and civil engineering terms ... Environmental engineering: BS6100:2.7** [UK]
British Standards Institution 1992, 30pp.
www.bsi-global.com/Building/Structural/index.xalter [DESCRIPTION]
Standard classified glossary, with index, covering solid waste, wet waste, and water supply. It contains about 300 short, one-sentence, definitions.

5549 **Routledge French dictionary of environmental technology: French–English/English–French (Dictionnaire anglais du génie de l'environnement: Français–Anglais/Anglais–français)**
T. Gordon, comp. Routledge, 1997, 261pp. £125.00. ISBN 041513918X.
Consists of some 25,000 headwords in both French and English giving wide coverage. Terms are drawn from all areas of environmental technology including air quality control, analysis, sampling and measurement, environmental policy and legal instruments, environmentally related safety engineering, general environmental management, marine pollution, noise pollution and control, soil contamination and remediation, water pollution and wastewater treatment, water supply and drinking water, and waste treatment and management.
'[Admirable for its] accuracy and completeness.' (*Reference Reviews*)

5550 **Routledge German dictionary of environmental technology: German–English/English–German (Wörterbuch Umwelttechnologie: Deutsch–Englisch/Englisch–Deutsch)**
Routledge, 1997, 272pp. Also available on CD-ROM (ISBN 0415142717), £125.00. ISBN 0415112435.
Fine translating dictionary containing 25,000 terms in each

language covering energy sources, air and water pollution, soil contamination, remediation methods, noise pollution and control, legal matters, water supplies, waste treatment, methodology, and safety issues.

5551 **Routledge Spanish dictionary of environmental technology: Spanish–English/English–Spanish (Diccionario Inglés de Tecnología Medioambiental: Español–Inglés/Inglés–Español)**
M.A. Gaspar Paricio Routledge, 1998, 261pp. Also available on CD-ROM, £140.00. ISBN 0415152658.
Typically admirable Routledge translating dictionary consists of about 25,000 words, phrases and acronyms in each language, covering energy sources, air and water pollution, soil contamination, remediation methods, noise pollution and control, legal matters, water supplies, waste treatment, methodology, and safety issues.

Terminology of water supply and environmental sanitation (Terminologie de l'approvisionnement en eau et de l'assainissement du milieu)
P.J. Biron; World Bank and UNICEF See entry no. 1127

5552 **Terms of environment** [USA]
Environmental Protection Agency 1997.
www.epa.gov/OCEPAterms
ToE 'defines in non-technical language the more commonly used environmental terms appearing in EPA publications'. It is made up of a few hundred concise definitions, plus abbreviations and acronyms. Easy to use, and well arranged.

Official & quasi-official bodies

Council on Environmental Quality
See entry no. 2310

5553 **Drinking Water Inspectorate** [UK]
www.dwi.gov.uk
The DWI was established in 1990 after the privatization of the water industry to regulate public supplies in England and Wales. It is responsible for assessing the quality of drinking water in England and Wales, taking enforcement action if standards are not being met, and appropriate action when water is unfit for human consumption. Its website contains consumer and technical information, and links to other sites.

5554 **Environment Agency** [UK]
www.environment-agency.gov.uk
Non-departmental public body, established by the Environment Act, 1995, answerable to the Department for Environment, Food and Rural Affairs (DEFRA). The Agency has the responsibility for protecting and improving the environment in England and Wales, working in the areas of air, land and water pollution, water resources, waste management, floods, fishing, conservation, and inland and coastal waterways. Its website includes links, news, and publications.

Environment Directorate-General
European Commission. Directorate for Environment See entry no. 2119

5555 **Environmental Protection Agency** [USA]
www.epa.gov
Its responsibility is 'to protect human health and to safeguard the natural environment – air, water, and land – upon which life depends'. The Agency has a huge, searchable gateway which provides information about itself and its policies, but also access to EPA technical documents, and databases of environmental software and information.

- **Envirofacts Data Warehouse** www.epa.gov/enviro. Single point of access to select US EPA environmental data, providing information about environmental activities that may affect air, water, and land anywhere in the United States.

5556 **Global Environment Facility**
www.gefweb.org
Established in 1991 to help developing countries fund projects and programmes that protect the global environment. Its grants – managed by the GEF Implementing Agencies (UNEP, UNDP, World Bank) – support projects related to biodiversity, climate change, international waters, land degradation, the ozone layer, and persistent organic pollutants. Wide range of useful documents covering both policy issues and the various work programmes.

Global International Waters Assessment
See entry no. 1129

5557 **Office of Ground Water and Drinking Water** [USA]
Environmental Protection Agency
www.epa.gov/safewater
'Together with states, tribes, and its many partners, protects public health by ensuring safe drinking water and protecting ground water. OGWDW, along with EPA's ten regional drinking water programs, oversees implementation of the Safe Drinking Water Act, which is the national law safeguarding tap water in America.'

Well laid out website with access to wide range of useful information. Good background in the downloadable OGWDW *Information strategic plan* (January 2004, 26 pp).

5558 **Royal Commission on Environmental Pollution** [UK]
www.rcep.org.uk
An independent standing body established in 1970 to advise the Queen, the Government, Parliament and the public on environmental issues. The site includes links to current and recent studies, to technical reports (some in full text), and agendas and minutes of meetings.

5559 **Waste and Resources Action Programme** [UK]
www.wrap.org.uk
WRAP is a not-for-profit company supported by funding from DEFRA, the Department of Trade and Industry, and the devolved administrations of Scotland, Wales and Northern Ireland for the period 2001 to 2004. Its aim is to promote sustainable waste management by creating stable and efficient markets for recycled materials and products. The website contains information about recycling process, materials, WRAP events and business services. There is also free access to WRAP publications and an e-newsletter.

Water Resources of the United States
US Geological Survey See entry no. 1132

Research centres & institutes

5560 **Air Quality Management Resource Centre** [UK]
www.uwe.ac.uk/aqm
Based in the Faculty of Applied Sciences at the University of the West of England in Bristol, the AQM aims to be a focal point for air quality management issues in the UK. Its website includes information about events, an electronic library of documents available on the internet, descriptions of dispersion models, newsletters, links to other sites, etc.

Centre for Alternative Technology
See entry no. 4786

5561 **Environmental Technology Centre** [CAN]
www.etcentre.org
Body under Environment Canada which 'provides specialized scientific support and undertakes research and development for Environmental Protection programs'. Four main areas: Technologies for measuring air pollutants in ambient air and from mobile and stationary sources; Analysis of a wide variety of organic and inorganic compounds in diverse samples; Assessments and clean-up of contaminated sites; Prevention of and response to pollution emergencies such as oil and chemical spills. Maintains a range of databases.

International Water Management Institute
See entry no. 2985

5562 **Syracuse Research Corporation** [USA]
www.syrres.com
Independent, not-for-profit research organization. 'For more than four decades, SRC has been a leader in technology programs of national significance. Historically, we have supported a broad range of federal government organizations, including the Departments of Defense (all Services), Energy, State, Transportation, Commerce, Labor, and Agriculture. The Corporation has also provided technical assistance to numerous agencies, such as the Environmental Protection Agency (EPA), National Library of Medicine (NLM), Occupational Safety & Health Administration (OSHA), National Science Foundation (NSF), and the United Nations (UN). Through these relationships, SRC has developed a trusted advisor reputation in a wide array of technology areas ranging from advanced sensor systems and signal processing design through information technology development to environmental chemistry and risk assessment.'

- **Environmental Fate Data Base** www.syrres.com/esc/efdb.htm [FEE-BASED].

5563 **WRc** [UK]
www.wrcplc.co.uk
The WRc is now a privately owned consultancy providing services to the water, wastewater and environmental industries, as well as working with government and regulatory bodies. It developed from the Water Pollution Research Board (later the Water Pollution Research Laboratory) founded in 1927, as the first central body to promote and supervise water pollution research in the UK. In the 1970s it merged with the Water Research Board and the Water Research Association to become the Water Research Centre, later privatized as the WRc. The WRc publishes the SEWERAGE REHABILITATION MANUAL. Its website consists mainly of information about the organization.

Associations & societies

5564 **Air and Waste Management Association** [USA]
www.awma.org
Based in Pittsburgh, USA, the AWMA is a not-for-profit professional organization claiming members in 65 countries worldwide. Its website includes news of events, its publications, etc. Full access to its house journal, the *Journal of the AWMA*, is restricted to members.

5565 **American Academy of Environmental Engineers**
www.aaee.net
Established in 1955 the AAEE is the prime US body in its field. Its website has information about the organization, *HighPoints* – a monthly news publication – details of events, a contents table of the latest *Environmental Engineer* magazine, a bookstore, and links to related organizations.

5566 **American Water Works Association**
www.awwa.org
Society founded in 1881, dedicated to the improvement of drinking water quality and supply, and now the largest organization of water supply professionals in the world. Almost 60,000 personal and 5000 utility members. Buyer's Guide to water industry products and services, magazines, newsletters, bookstore, etc.

5567 **British Metals Recycling Association**
www.recyclemetals.org
Acts as a hub for the sector, providing key support services and a forum for generating consensus on strategic issues. Useful resources including links to the (currently) 115 members' websites.

5568 **Chartered Institution of Wastes Management** [UK]
www.iwm.co.uk
With its headquarters in Northampton, the CIWM – formerly the Institute of Waste Management, is the UK professional body for the waste management industry. Its website has an events diary, jobs news, a discussion forum, news, and a list of publications for sale.

5569 **Chartered Institution of Water and Environmental Management** [UK]
www.ciwem.org.uk
CIWEM is an independent professional body for scientists, engineers, other environmental professionals in the UK. The website has membership information, plus information about jobs, some factsheets, and a professionals directory.

Consortium for Automotive Recycling
See entry no. 4972

5570 **Council for Accreditation in Occupational Hearing Conservation** [USA]
www.caohc.org
Mission is 'to promote the conservation of hearing by enhancing the quality of occupational hearing conservation programs'. Began with the Intersociety Committee on guidelines for noise exposure control in the mid 1960s and took its present name in 1973. Its Council comprises two representatives from nine audiology-related US organizations.

- **Hearing conservation manual** A.H. Suter and E.H. Berger, eds 2003, 312pp. $55.00. ISBN 097231430X. Set-up and maintenance of hearing conservation programme; regulatory and standards information; audiometric equipment and procedures; etc.

Environmental and Engineering Geophysical Society
See entry no. 1090

Global Water Partnership
See entry no. 1136

International Water Association
See entry no. 1137

5571 **National Society for Clean Air and Environmental Protection** [UK]
www.nsca.org.uk
Formerly, just the National Society for Clean Air – and still referred to as NASCA – the Society's objectives are to promote clean air and environmental protection through the reduction of air, water and land pollution, noise and other contaminants. Its website contains text of a number of leaflets and factsheets, plus FAQs, links to other useful sites, etc.

Natural Resources Defense Council
See entry no. 2332

5572 **Society of Environmental Engineers** [UK]
environmental.org.uk
Founded in 1959 SEE is the UK professional society for environmental engineers. The Society provides nominated representatives to a number of national and international committees, such as those concerned with design and test standards, and lobbies more generally on behalf of the interests of its membership. The Society website provides information about the Society and its technical groups, plus news and jobs. SEE's house journal is ENVIRONMENTAL ENGINEERING.

5573 **Universities Council on Water Resources** [USA]
www.ucowr.siu.edu
About 90 universities in the USA and a few worldwide are members. The site has collections of research and teaching information available to members, as well as news of events and jobs. Most information is restricted to members.

World Water Council
See entry no. 1139

Libraries, archives, museums

5574 **Wastes Management Library** [UK]
wmlibrary.northampton.ac.uk
The UCN Wastes Management Library consists of approximately 125,000 records and is widely regarded as the pre-eminent wastes management library in Europe. It is based on the library of the Waste Management Information Bureau, AEA Culham, originally formed in 1974, transferred to Northampton in 2001. As well as its catalogue the library website has a set of links to other organizations plus a useful Topic of the Month page.

Portal & task environments

5575 **Bioremediation Discussion Group**
www.bioremediationgroup.org
The 'BioGroup' has about 2400 members worldwide. The website includes Bioreferences – an archive of technical papers on bioremediation, BioTerms – a compilation of definitions, a set of links to other sites, and a Discussion Group.

5576 **Edie: environmental data interactive exchange**
www.edie.net
A site dedicated to water, waste and environmental engineering. Its search facility only collects websites in these areas. Features include an advanced search option, plus a useful Marketplace option which restricts searches to companies. The site also has a news section, a job centre, and a library of links to full text documents, including policy documents and glossaries.

5577 **Foundation for Water Research** [UK]
www.fwr.org
Based in Buckinghamshire, the Foundation is an independent, not-for-profit organization that shares and disseminates knowledge about water, wastewater and research into related environmental issues. Its website is divided into the sections: Reviews of Current Knowledge (ROCKs – free in PDF); Forums; Publications; Information; and News and events.

5578 **Introduction to Environmental Protection** [UK]
Great Britain. Department for Environment, Food and Rural Affairs
www.defra.gov.uk/environment
DEFRA's remit includes environmental protection and within that brief its website has sections on: Air quality; Land – soil and contamination; Pollution, prevention and control; Recycling and waste; Water issues. Each section has links to various policy and technical documents and information.

5579 **Water** [EUR]
European Environment Agency
http://themes.eea.eu.int/Specific_media/water
Based in Copenhagen, the EEA 'aims to support sustainable development and to help achieve significant and measurable improvement in Europe's environment' through the provision of information to policy makers and the public. Its well designed website offers access to the full text of commissioned reports, plus indicators, maps and graphs, and a useful glossary. The site is arranged by theme/topic and also by country. This is the entrée to resources concerned with 'Water'. There are similar gateways for 'Air', 'Nature', and 'Soil' as well as for a range of environmental issues, sectors and activities, and actions for improving the environment. A good user-friendly approach to website design.

The Water Portal
United Nations Educational, Scientific and Cultural Organization
See entry no. 1141

Discovering print & electronic resources

5580 Aqualine
CSA, 1960–, Monthly. £780.00 [2004]. ISSN 02635534.
www.csa.com [DESCRIPTION]
This database covers the scientific, technical and trade literatures in water supply, treatment, analysis, distribution, and pollution, as well as sewage and effluent treatment. References are to journal articles, conference papers, reports, books, etc, with about 300 journals covered. Corresponds to the bimonthly printed *Aqualine Abstracts*.

As of May 2004 the database contained about 240,000 records, and about 10,000 new records are added each year.

Until 1985 entitled WRC Information (ISSN 0306-6649) which superseded Water Pollution Abstracts (1949–73, ISSN 0043-1281).

CSA also compile other relevant collections: e.g. Environmental Engineering Abstracts; EIS: digests of environmental impact statements. Subfile 3 of CSA's Aquatic Sciences and Fisheries Abstracts database is Aquatic Pollution and Environmental Quality. Its coverage of aquatic pollution includes: Methods and instruments; Characteristics, behaviour, and fate; Effects on organisms; Prevention and control.

Chemical Information System
See entry no. 4272

5581 Environment Abstracts
Congressional Information Services, 1975 –, Monthly. ISSN 00933287.
www.lexisnexis.com/academic/3cis/cist/eanet [DESCRIPTION]
This abstracting service covers about 1000 sources published worldwide, including over 630 journal titles. Each monthly issue contains about 1600 new items. Subject, author, source and title indexes with annual cumulations. Covers air, water, and noise pollution; solid and toxic wastes; radiological contamination; toxicological effects; control technologies; resource management; population; endangered species; and geophysical and climatic change.

5582 Environmental information: a guide to sources
N. Lees and H. Woolston; British Library 2nd edn, Science Reference and Information Service, 1997, 271pp. £36.50. ISBN 0712308253.
Much expanded. A guide to (mainly) databases, essential journals, directories, and organizations. Arranged in 14 sections including General environmental information, Air pollution, Recycling, and Noise pollution, plus appendices. Most entries have a useful descriptive annotation. A new edition would be welcome.
1st edn 1992.

5583 Environmental Sciences & Pollution Management
CSA, 1981–, Monthly.
www.csa.com/factsheets/envclust-set-c.php [DESCRIPTION]
This multidisciplinary database provides coverage of the environmental sciences. Put together from 12 separate databases, including Environmental Engineering Abstracts, Pollution Abstracts, and Water Resources Abstracts, it includes citations to journal articles, conference papers, reports, books and government publications, back to 1981. Most citations have abstracts. The database includes material on all aspects of pollution and waste management, plus water resource issues. As of July 2004 it contained about 1.7 million records.

■ **Water Resources Abstracts** CSA1967–.
www.csa.com/factsheets/water-resources-set-c.php [DESCRIPTION].
Originally produced by the US Geological Survey, when it was generally known as *Selected Water Resources Abstracts*. As of September 2004 contained about 400,000 records, growing by about 1000 records per month.

5584 Environmental technology resources handbook
D.W. Gottlieb Lewis Publishers, 2003, 216pp. $159.95. ISBN 1566705665.
Intended to help users find an appropriate technology to deal with environmental problems. Lists mostly websites, grouped into 4 categories – Control, Remediation, Assessment, and Prevention. Expensive, likely to have a short life span, but useful while still newish.

5585 Information sources in environmental protection
S. Eagle and J. Deschamps, eds Bowker-Saur, 1997, 280pp. £67.00. ISBN 1857390628.
Attempts 'to provide a narrative introduction to the principal sources of information'. 20 contributors to 17 chapters arranged in four parts: The official and the unofficial (Government policies, national and international, etc.); Effects and the affected (The effects of pollutants on wildlife, Wastes management, etc.); Practicalities (Land use, etc.); and Controls and public awareness (Environmental law, etc). Very useful.
'great value.' (*Reference Reviews*)

5586 Waste Management Research Abstracts
International Atomic Energy Agency 1988–. Also available in printed form, free, from the IAEA, 1970–.
www.iaea.org/programmes/irais
WMRA is a collection of research summaries planned or in progress in the field of radioactive waste, including activities related to the decommissioning of nuclear facilities and environmental restoration.

Water Resources Worldwide
See entry no. 1143

5587 Waternet
American Water Works Association 1971–.
http://library.dialog.com/bluesheets/html/bl0245.html [DESCRIPTION]
Basically an online index to the publications – books and proceedings, journals, newsletters, standards, manuals, handbooks, and water quality standard test methods – of the Association, the AWWA Research Foundation, and some selected important journals in the field. Currently contains some 50,000 records.

5588 WWW Virtual Library: Wastewater Engineering
www.cleanh2o.com/ww
A browsable and searchable site of about 1500 links to resources, arranged by general subject area (Wastewater, for instance) or function (for example, Academic and Research Institutions). Good collection of links with brief descriptions.

Digital data, image & text collections

5589 E-Digest of Environmental Statistics
Great Britain. Department for Environment, Food and Rural Affairs
www.defra.gov.uk/environment/statistics/index.htm
Provides summary statistics on the environment in the

United Kingdom. Topic headings include Air quality, Coastal and marine waters, UK environmental protection expenditure by industry survey, Global atmosphere, Inland water quality and use, Land use and land cover, Noise, Public attitudes, Radioactivity, Waste and recycling, Wildlife, and Supplemental data. There are also links to electronic versions of *The environment in your pocket*, a compilation of key facts, *UK Environmental Protection Expenditure by Industry Survey*, and *Municipal Waste Bulletin*.

Replaces the previously printed Department of the Environment's Digest of Environmental Protection and Water Statistics, 1979–1994, and Digest of Environmental statistics, 1995–.

5590 **EnviroNetBase: Environmental Resources Online**
CRC Press.
www.environetbase.com [FEE-BASED]
This service consists, at time of viewing, of the digitized text of 123 environmental textbooks and reference works published by CRC Press, one of the core publishing groups in this field. New titles are added when published. The database is searchable as a whole, by individual title, or by one of 12 subject segments, which include: Environmental engineering; Water science, technology, and engineering. Access is by username and password.

5591 **National Atmospheric Emissions Inventory** [UK]
AEA Technology.
www.naei.org.uk
Funded by the Department for Environment, Food and Rural Affairs (DEFRA), and the national bodies of Wales, Scotland and Northern Ireland, the NAEI compiles estimates of emissions to the atmosphere from UK sources such as cars, trucks, power stations and industrial plant. Information is provided about national and international policy initiatives, about forms of pollution, and also specific pollutants. Emission data is available by map, and searchable by postcode. Some full text publications are also available. Easy-to-use and useful.

- **Air Quality Archive** www.airquality.co.uk. Essentially a database containing UK air quality information from the present back to 1960, collected from 1500 sites across the UK. The website also contains related databases of research reports and contracts, plus a useful glossary of terms.

5592 **OECD Environmental Data Compendium**
Downloadable PDF, 1985–.
www.oecd.org/publications
Published regularly but not annually, this is a compilation of data reported by the governments of member countries. The 2002 Compendium is in three parts: The State of the Environment, with sections on Air and climate, Inland waters, Waste, and Risks; Sectoral Trends – energy, transport, industry, and agriculture; and Managing the Environment, which includes the information about multilateral agreements and general data.

Transboundary Freshwater Dispute Database
Oregon State University See entry no. 1144

Directories & encyclopedias

5593 **Concise encyclopedia of environmental systems**
P.C. Young, ed. Pergamon, 1993, 769pp. ISBN 0080361986.
Intended as a comprehensive reference work covering all aspects of environmental systems, including non-engineering aspects, from 'Abiotic control mechanisms in terrestrial and freshwater environments' to 'Wind velocity determination using optical lasers'. It includes 184 signed articles from 138 contributors. Many entries are taken from *Systems and control encyclopedia*, but about 80 are new.

Encyclopedia of energy technology and the environment
A. Bisio and S. Boots, eds See entry no. 4653

5594 **Encyclopedia of environmental analysis and remediation**
R.A. Meyers, ed. Wiley, 1998. 8 v., $2850.00. ISBN 0471117080.
A major work, containing over 280 scholarly review articles, covering specific pollutants, analytical techniques, sampling methods, remediation of hazardous wastes, pollution of the biosphere, health effects, and socio-legal-economic frameworks. Extensive cross-referencing and bibliographies. Well designed, well written, good illustrations. A condensed version is available as *The Wiley encyclopedia of environmental pollution and cleanup*.

- **The Wiley encyclopedia of environmental pollution and cleanup** **R.A. Meyers and D.K. Dittrick, eds** Wiley, 1999, 1890pp. $295.00. ISBN 0471316121. 2v. Essentially an abridged version of the Encyclopedia, containing 230 highly condensed articles taken from the original 280. Well designed, good illustrations. The good bibliographies are retained. Useful, but not a replacement for the full work.

5595 **Encyclopedia of environmental science and engineering**
J.R. Pfafflin and E.N. Ziegler, eds 4th edn, Gordon & Breach, 1998, 1408pp. 2 v., $795.00. ISBN 9056996363.
A substantial, popular and established encyclopedia covering all aspects of environmental science and engineering with its main emphases on air, water and soil pollution issues.
1st edn 1976, 3rd edn 1992.

Encyclopedia of water science
B.A. Stewart and T.A. Howell See entry no. 1147

5596 **Environment industry yearbook**
Waterlow, 1993–.
www.eiy.co.uk
Arranged in three sections: Industry information & contacts; Buyers guide (29,500 entries in 10 specialisms); and an A–Z listing of some 5800 companies. The searchable online version has a listing of events and a few hyperlinks
Early yearbooks published by Macmillan.

5597 **Environmental contaminant reference databook**
J.C. Prager, comp. Wiley, 1998. 3 v. $550.00. ISBN 0471314595.
www.knovel.com
A quick reference compendium of data on over 1000 contaminants. Entries include information on physical and chemical properties, physical, chemical, and biological effects, CAS and SAX numbers, sampling, detection methods, common uses, manufacturers, etc. Also includes information about remediation techniques and preventative measures.
Also available on CD-ROM (ISBN 0471292869 $630.00) and online: see website.

5598 **Environmental encyclopedia**
W.P. Cunningham, ed. 3rd edn, Gale, 2002, 2000pp. $295.00. ISBN 0787654868.
www.gale.com/gvrl
Revised and extended, this multidisciplinary work contains over 1300 signed articles covering such issues as atmospheric pollution, water pollution, endangered species, green politics, and the environmental effects of war. Includes a chronology and many illustrations.
Available online: see website. 1st edn 1990.

5599 **The Facts On File dictionary of environmental science**
B. Wyman and L.H. Stevenson, comp. Facts On File, 2001, 458pp. $44.00. ISBN 0816042330.
Broad coverage, aimed at a general audience. Contains about 4000 entries, including some 3000 or so from the first edition which remain largely unchanged. Includes entries for place names and people as well as topics. Useful appendices of acronyms, chemical elements, recycling codes, and conversion factors.
Series: The Facts On File Science Dictionaries Set. 1st edn 1992.
'essential for most public and science libraries.' (*Library Journal*)

5600 **Formula handbook for environmental engineers and scientists**
G. Bitton Wiley, 1998, 290pp. $59.95. ISBN 047113905X.
Consists of an A–Z list of some 200 formulas and equations from 'Absorption coefficient' and 'Activated sludge: floc load' to 'Zeta potential' and 'Zooplankton'. Entries are typically 1–2 pages in length and include definition or introduction, formula, numerical values reported in the literature, references, and pertinent tables and charts.

5601 **Green Pages: the global directory for environmental technology**
http://eco-web.com
Set up in 1994 Green Pages is a global online gateway to environmental products and services. The directory is structured into 10 main chapters: Environmental information; Waste water treatment; Water supply & purification; Air pollution control; Waste management; Recycling; Soil preservation; Noise protection; Power generation; and Energy efficiency, with a total of 78 subdivisions.

The current edition of Green Pages features (a spooky) 6666 leading suppliers and environmental organizations from 140 countries. The site also has an interesting set of editorials. A well organized, easy-to-use site, if a bit heavy-handed with the green paintpot.

5602 **Handbook of environmental data on organic chemicals.**
K. Verschueren 4th edn, Wiley, 2001. 2 v, $550.00. ISBN 0471374903.
Contains property and environmental data for over 3000 organic chemicals listed in alphabetic order, including 230 compounds new to this edition and 600 revised and updated entries. Entries include information on chemical and physical properties; CAS registry number; data relating to air, water, and soil pollution factors; and biological effects. Toxicity is classified by organism and by type of test. 10,500 references. Remains highly recommended.
1st edn 1972, 3rd edn 1996.
'an excellent source of information on the behavior of organic chemicals in the environment.' (*SciTech Book News*)

5603 **Handbook of water treatment chemicals: an international guide to more than 3400 products by trade name, chemical, function and manufacturer**
M. Ash and I. Ash, comps Gower, 1996, 642pp. £250.00. ISBN 0566078015.
Entries for each chemical include chemical description, uses, properties, toxicology, precautions, storage, regulations, hazardous decomposition products, etc.

5604 **The Sitefile Digest** [UK]
Waterlow, 1987–, Annual. £209.00 [2004/05]. ISBN 1900105357.
www.eiy.co.uk/ourproducts.htm [DESCRIPTION]
A directory of licensed waste management facilities in Great Britain with some 8000 entries in 2003/04. Entries include full site address, details of approved wastes for each site, site rating by licensed waste type, and maximum licensed input rate.

Handbooks & manuals

5605 **Air pollution**
A.C. Stern, ed. 3rd edn, Academic Press, 1976–88. 8 v.
A comprehensive treatise, still important although a little dated.
- V. 1. *Air pollutants, their transformation and transport.* ISBN 0126666016.
- V. 2. *The effects of air pollution.* ISBN 0126666024.
- V. 3. *Measuring, monitoring, and surveillance of air pollution.* ISBN 0126666032.
- V. 4. *Engineering control of air pollution.* ISBN 0126666040.
- V. 5. *Air quality management.* ISBN 0126666059.
- Vols. 6–8 are later supplements. V. 6. ISBN 0126666067. V. 7. ISBN 0126666075. V. 8. ISBN 0126666083.

1st edn 1962 in 2 vols; 2nd edn 1968 in 3 vols.

5606 **Air pollution control handbook** [USA]
E.R. Alley, L.B. Stevens and W.L. Cleland, eds McGraw-Hill, 1998, 1008pp. $99.95. ISBN 0070014116.
Covers the available technologies for air pollution control, testing and regulations. 25 chapters arranged in four Parts: Theory and quantification of air pollution (Atmospheric dispersion models, Ambient air monitoring, Stack sampling, etc.); Air quality management (Air management programs, Air quality audit); Air pollution regulation (Hazardous air pollutants, Acid rain, Operating permits, etc.); and Pollutant control systems (Adsorption of gaseous compounds, Incineration of gaseous emissions, Biofiltration of gaseous compounds, etc.) 17 appendices include definitions and details of regulatory regimes. Strong US emphasis.

5607 **Air pollution control technology handbook** [USA]
K.B. Schnelle and C.A. Brown CRC Press, 2001, 408pp. $159.95. ISBN 0849395887.
24 chapters cover the background to air pollution legislation in the USA and discuss the various technologies used for control and their cost effectiveness. The technologies include absorption, adsorption, filtration, oxidation, condensation, membranes, etc.

5608 Air pollution engineering manual [USA]
W.T. Davis, ed.; Air and Waste Management Association 2nd edn, Wiley, 2000, 912pp. $175.00. ISBN 0471333336.
Sponsored by the Association and aimed at the professional engineer. Describes air pollution control measures and equipment. Contains general chapters on Gaseous pollutants, Particulate matter, etc. plus chapters on industries which are the source of pollution, such as Semiconductor manufacturing and Wood processing.
1st edn 1992.

Atmospheric pollution: history, science, and regulation
M.Z. Jacobson See entry no. 1240

5609 Bioremediation: principles and practice
S.K. Sikdar and R. L. Irvine, eds Technomic, 1998. 3 v., $199.95 per volume.
Massive multi-author comprehensive overview of advances in pollution treatment and reduction using biological means. Covers the removal of hazardous and non-hazardous contaminants from solid, liquid, and gaseous media.
- V.1 *Fundamentals and applications.* 765pp. ISBN 1566763088.
- V. 2 *Biodegradation technology developments.* 718pp. ISBN 1566765307.
- V. 3 *Bioremediation technologies.* 672pp. ISBN 1566765617.

5610 CRC handbook of incineration of hazardous wastes
W.S. Rickman, ed. CRC Press, 1991, 593pp. ISBN 0849305578.
Covers incinerator technology, regulatory requirements, siting issues and includes some case histories. 19 contributors to nine chapters, some exhaustively documented, including Market trends, Regulatory requirements and the permitting process, Siting issues and public acceptance, Established techniques, Innovative thermal destruction technologies, Combustion calculations, and Trial burn.

5611 Design of municipal wastewater treatment plants
American Society of Civil Engineers and Water Environment Federation 4th edn, 1998. 3 v., $338.00. ISBN 0784403422.
Longstanding and comprehensive, this work 'aims to be the principal reference of contemporary practice'.
- V. 1, chapters 1–8. *Planning and configuration of wastewater treatment plants.*
- V. 2, chapters 9–16. *Liquid treatment processes.*
- V. 3, chapters 17–24. *Solid processing and disposal.*

Also available on CD-ROM. 1st published in 1959 as Sewage treatment plant design *produced by a joint committee of ASCE and the Federation of Sewage and Industrial Wastes Association. 2nd edn 1977 under the title* Wastewater treatment plant design *and produced by ASCE and the Water Pollution Control Federation. 3rd edn 1991.*

5612 Encyclopedia of environmental control technology
P.N. Cheremisinoff, ed. Gulf Publishing, 1989–95. 9 v.
Monumental collection, now a little dated but still a core work. Less an encyclopedia than a related series of handbooks.
- V. 1. *Thermal treatment of hazardous wastes.* 1989. 828pp. ISBN 0872012417 £125.
- V. 2. *Air pollution control.* 1989. 1066pp. ISBN 087201245x £125.
- V. 3. *Wastewater treatment.* 1989. 684pp. ISBN 0872012476 £125.
- V. 4. *Containment and treatment.* 1990. 776pp. ISBN 0872012514 £125.
- V. 5. *Waste minimization and recycling.* 1992. 864pp. ISBN 0872012581 £125.
- V. 6. *Pollution reduction and containment control.* 1992. 712pp. ISBN 0872012859 £125.
- V. 7. *High-hazard pollutants.* 1994. 704pp. ISBN 08722012913 £125.
- V. 8. *Work area hazards.* 1995. 804pp. ISBN 0872013049 £125.
- V. 9. *Geotechnical and leak detection treatment operations.* 1995. 1137pp. ISBN 0872013278 £125.

5613 Environmental engineers' handbook
D.H.F. Liu, B.G. Lipták and P.B. Bouis, eds 2nd edn, Lewis Publishers, 1998, 1453pp. $139.95. ISBN 0849399718.
Clearly laid-out and written, this updated and expanded edition has 81 contributors to 11 sections: Environmental laws and legislation; Environmental impact assessment; Pollution prevention in chemical manufacturing; Standards; Air pollution; Noise pollution; Wastewater treatment; Removing specific water contaminants; Groundwater and surface water pollution; Solid waste; and Hazardous waste. Extensive use of diagrams and tables. Good bibliographies.
1st edn in 3 volumes in 1974 by Chilton Book Co., edited by Lipták.

Environmental handbook for building and civil engineering projects
R. Venables [et al.]; Construction Industry Research and Information Association See entry no. 5347

5614 Environmental organic chemistry
R.P. Schwarzenbach, P.M. Gschwend and D.M. Imboden Wiley, 2002, 1313pp. $94.50. ISBN 0471357502.
Focuses on environmental factors governing processes determining fate of organic chemicals in natural and engineered systems. Applies this to quantitatively assess environmental behaviour of organic chemicals.

5615 Freshwater issues: a reference handbook [USA]
Z.A. Smith and G. Thomassey ABC-CLIO, 2003, 281pp. $45.00. ISBN 1576076490.
'A compelling look at the challenges of freshwater conservation and management issues facing the United States at the start of the new millennium.'

Green building handbook: a guide to building products and their impact on the environment
T. Wooley [et al.] See entry no. 5350

5616 Groundwater chemicals desk reference
J. H. Montgomery 3rd edn, Lewis Publishers, 2000, 1380pp. $199.95. ISBN 1566704987.
Well established handbook emphasizing organic compounds found in groundwater, surface water, soil, air, and plants. Extensive bibliography (81 pages) and index

5617 Handbook of air pollution control technologies
N.P. Cheremisinoff Butterworth-Heinemann, 2002, 562pp. £75.00. ISBN 0750674997.
Concise and up-to-date overview of the technologies for preventing and managing industrial air pollution. Also includes material on environmental cost accounting. Includes

chapters on Industrial air pollution, Properties of pollutants, Ventilation and indoor air quality control, Air pollution dispersion, Prevention versus control, Prevention and control hardware, and Environmental cost accounting.

Handbook of chemical and environmental engineering calculations
J.P. Reynolds, J.S. Jeris and L. Theodore See entry no. 5134

5618 Handbook of chemical technology and pollution control
M.B. Hocking Academic Press, 1998, 777pp. $65.00. ISBN 012350810X.
Integrates environmental control technology with industrial chemistry. Arranged in 23 chapters, five covering air and water pollution in general, while the remainder consider the pollution stemming from major chemical commodities such as ammonia, metals, paper, fermentation products, petroleum and petrochemicals, and polymers.

5619 Handbook of chlorination and alternative disinfectants
G.C. White 4th edn, Wiley, 1998, 1592pp. $230.00. ISBN 0471292079.
A standard handbook on disinfectants for water purification. Its 17 chapters cover the use of chlorine and other disinfectants (chloramines, ozone, bromine, and ultraviolet radiation) in treating potable water and wastewater from various industrial processes.
1st edn 1972, 3rd edn 1992.

5620 Handbook of complex environmental remediation problems
J.H. Lehr [et al.], ed. McGraw-Hill, 2001, 800pp. $99.95. ISBN 0070276897.
Written for the professional engineer. Composed of 12 chapters covering most aspects of pollution remediation. Some are general in nature, such as those on Soil, Groundwater, and Oil spills and leaks, while others are more specialized such as Groundwater remediation at former manufactured-gas plant sites, and Innovative strategies in remediating mining wastes.

5621 Handbook of drinking water quality
J. De Zuane 2nd edn, Wiley, 1997, 575pp. $130.00. ISBN 047128789X.
Well regarded and practical work that includes discussion of US, WHO and EC drinking water guidelines and standards. Its 11 chapters cover Potable water, General or physical parameters, Chemical parameters – inorganics, Chemical parameters – organic compounds, Microbiological parameters, Radionuclide parameters, Carcinogens, etc. Deals in detail with water treatment, disinfection and fluoridation, common water distribution problems.
1st edn 1990 by Van Nostrand Reinhold.

Handbook of ecotoxicology
D.J. Hoffman [et al.], eds See entry no. 2355

5622 Handbook of environmental analysis: chemical pollutants in air, water, soil, and solid wastes
P. Patnaik Lewis Publishers, 1998, 608pp. $85.00. ISBN 0873719891.
Roughly divided into two: a discussion of analytical techniques and methods of determination – chromatography, spectroscopy, etc. – of chemical pollutants; and descriptions of the analysis of individual and groups of pollutants. The book covers pollutants in ambient air, groundwater, surface water, industrial wastewater, and soils and sediments. Appendices include information on formulae and statistics, characteristics of organic pollutants not listed, etc.

5623 Handbook of environmental engineering calculations
C.C. Lee and S.D. Lin McGraw-Hill, 2000, 1400pp. $125.00. ISBN 0070381836.
A substantial compendium of calculation procedures in 16 chapters divided into three parts: Calculations of water quality assessment and control (Basic science and fundamentals, Streams and rivers, Lakes and reservoirs, etc.); Solid waste calculations (Basic combustion and incineration, Practical design of waste incineration, etc.); and Air pollution control calculations (Air emission control, Particulate emission control, etc.) Descriptions accompanied by plentiful examples.

- **Water and wastewater calculations manual** **S.D. Lin and C.C. Lee** McGraw-Hill, 2001, 854pp. $89.95. ISBN 0071371958.

5624 Handbook of environmental management and technology
G. Burke, B.R. Singh and L. Theodore 2nd edn, Wiley, 2000, 824pp. $155.00. ISBN 0471349100.
Considerably expanded since the first edition. Contains 48 mainly practical chapters arranged in ten sections: Introduction; Air pollution; Water pollution; Solid and radioactive waste; Hazardous waste; Pollution prevention; Additional environmental concerns; New technologies; Risk related topics; and Recent developments.
1st edn 1993.

Handbook of green chemistry and technology
J. Clark and D. Macquarrie See entry no. 5136

5625 The handbook of groundwater engineering
J.W. Delleur, ed. CRC Press, 1998, 992pp. $139.95. ISBN 0849326982.
A substantial handbook authored by 44 contributors to 27 chapters arranged loosely about five broad themes: Introduction; Basic equations and analyses of seepage and infiltration; Well and aquifer hydraulics; Contaminant transport and modelling; Environmental, engineering and legal aspects. Some chapters have lengthy bibliographies. All supported by a wealth of diagrams, tables, etc.
'This excellent resource covers the field of groundwater from an engineering perspective ... It provides a practical treatment of the flow of groundwater, the transport of substances ... and remediation of groundwater pollution.' (*International Journal of Geosciences Environmental Geology*)

5626 Handbook of pollution control and waste minimization
A. Ghassemi, ed. Marcel Dekker, 2001, 536pp. $175.00. ISBN 0824705815.
Details the legal, organizational, hierarchal, and environmental components of pollution prevention and waste reduction. 30 authors of 20 chapters arranged in six sections: Legal/organizational/hierarchal requirements; Fundamentals; Methodology; Life cycle; Risk and decision;

and Case studies (from the mining, oil and chemical industries).

5627 **Handbook of pollution prevention practices**
N.P. Cheremisinoff Marcel Dekker, 2001, 440pp. $175.00. ISBN 0824705424.
Focuses on reducing manufacturing and environmental compliance costs by implementing policies and technologies for improved operational schemes, recycling and recovery, waste minimization, and energy efficiency policies. Describes major case-studies in the chemical, oil refining, and metallurgical industries.

5628 **Handbook of solid waste management** [USA]
G. Tchobanoglous and F. Kreith, eds 2nd edn, McGraw-Hill, 2002, 950pp. $125.00. ISBN 0071356231.
With 20 authors contributing towards 15 chapters, this work offers an integrated approach to solid waste disposal systems although with a US bias. Includes chapters on Source reduction, Recycling, Composting of municipal solid wastes, Waste to energy conversion, Landfilling, and Siting solid waste facilities. This edition contains new material on optical-separation techniques, weight-based collection systems, yard-waste management, collection cost and technologies, etc.
1st edn 1994.

5629 **Handbook of solid waste management and waste minimization technologies**
N.P. Cheremisinoff Butterworth-Heinemann, 2003, 477pp. £75.00. ISBN 0750675071.
Aimed at the practising engineer, this work describes technologies and procedures for dealing with solid wastes. Arranged in nine sections: What solid wastes are; Solid wastes handling methods and management; Technologies of incineration; Volume reduction; Sanitary landfilling; Pollution prevention for landfill operations; Pollution prevention technologies; and Environmental management plans.

5630 **Handbook of water and wastewater treatment technologies**
N.P. Cheremisinoff Butterworth-Heinemann, 2002, 576pp. £75.00. ISBN 0750674989.
An authoritative work aimed at the practising engineer. Contains ten sections dealing with the technologies and processes of water treatment: Overview; Chemical additives that enhance filtration; Filter media; Pressure- and cake-filtration; Cartridge and other filters; Sand filtration; Sedimentation, clarification, flotation, and coalescence; Membrane separation; Ion exchange and carbon adsorption; Water sterilization; and Treating the sludge.

5631 **Hazardous and radioactive waste treatment technologies handbook**
C.H. Oh, ed. CRC Press, 2001, 792pp. $99.95. ISBN 0849395860.
Composed of more than 30 chapters describing current technical approaches to the treatment of hazardous materials. Sections deal with in-situ remediation of contaminated soils, thermal technologies (incineration, vitrification, etc), non-thermal treatments (fluid extraction, etc), stabilization and solidification technologies, offgas control, and various decontamination techniques.

5632 **Indoor pollution: a reference handbook**
E.W. Miller and R.M. Miller ABC-CLIO, 1998, 330pp. ISBN 0874368952.
Intended for the general reader, this book contains sections on characteristics, health effects, standards, sources, and control. Sources offers more than 35 different chemical and biological entities that can cause human illness and discomfort. Extensive bibliographies and useful appendices which include glossary, acronyms, etc.

5633 **Industrial pollution prevention handbook**
H.M. Freeman, ed. McGraw-Hill, 1995, 935pp. $115.00. ISBN 0070221480.
78 contributors to 53 chapters covering processes and technologies from design to implementation. Includes numerous case-studies of specific industries. Distinguishes between legal requirements and voluntary programmes.

5634 **Industrial waste treatment handbook**
F. Woodard Butterworth-Heinemann, 2001, 528pp. £69.99. ISBN 0750673176.
Presents a practical approach to identifying waste types and their treatment. Includes general chapters on scientific fundamentals and the legal background, and on Wastes from industry; Management of industrial stormwater run-off; Wastes characterization; Pollution prevention; Treatment methods; Advanced, or tertiary treatment methods; Disposal of residuals; Ground and groundwater contamination; and Remediation of groundwater contamination.

5635 **Industrial wastewater systems handbook**
R.L. Stephenson and J.B. Blackburn Lewis Publishers, 1998, 495pp. $129.95. ISBN 1566702097.
A compilation of facts, formulas and other information necessary to design and operate industrial wastewater systems. Its 11 chapters include: Wastewater systems; Wastewater collection; Equalization and storage; Physical separation; Chemical treatment; Biological treatment; VOCs; Sludge and solid wastes, etc. as well material about US legislation. Good on discussions of treatments.

5636 **McGraw-Hill recycling handbook**
H.F. Lund, comp. 2nd edn, McGraw-Hill, 2000, 1152pp. $89.00. ISBN 0070391564.
Follows on from the highly regarded first edition, now a standard work. Composed of 36 chapters arranged in two sections. The Basics of Recycling covers the management of the process of recycling – collection, economics, etc, while the second section is divided into chapters on particular kinds of recyclable material, including electronic devices, paper, tyres, batteries, etc. Also contains case studies.
1st edn 1993.

5637 **Methods for the examination of waters and associated materials** [UK]
Standing Committee of Analysts 1976–.
www.environment-agency.gov.uk/science
A series of almost 200 published booklets – the *Blue Books* – intended to 'provide authoritative guidance on methods of sampling and analysis for determining the quality of environmental matrices'. Recent Blue Books are only available in electronic format, as downloadable PDF documents.
First booklets published by HMSO.

5638 Municipal solid waste factbook [USA]
Environmental Protection Agency
www.epa.gov/epaoswer/non-hw/muncpl
Easy-to-use electronic reference manual containing a wealth of well presented information about household waste management practice. Information is divided between the topics: Basic facts; Frequently asked questions; Reduce, reuse and recycle; Commodities; Disposal; Programs; State data; and Topics. Although very American in focus this site has a good general utility.

5639 Odor and VOC handbook
H.J. Rafson, ed. McGraw-Hill, 1998, 648pp. $105.00. ISBN 0070525234.
The only reference work to focus specifically on the control of odour and volatile organic compounds, as distinct from air pollution control. Deals with odours and vocs emanating from a variety of industrial sources, including wastewater, food, and chemical processes. 50 authors contribute towards 13 chapters, including Analytical methods, Modelling, Air pollution prevention, and a lengthy one on Emission control technologies.

5640 OECD Environmental Performance Reviews
1998–. www.oecdbookshop.org
A series of reviews on environmental conditions and progress in each member country. Efforts to meet both domestic objectives and international commitments are scrutinized. Recent volumes include sections on Environmental management and air, Water and waste management, etc.

The first cycle of 32 Reviews (all OECD countries and 3 non-OECD countries) was completed. A new cycle began in 2001.

5641 Practical design calculations for groundwater and soil remediation
J.-F. Kuo Lewis Publishers, 1998, 288pp. $94.95. ISBN 1566702380.
Aimed at the practising engineer or scientist. A 'cookbook' containing some 200 formulas, plus tables and figures, arranged in eight chapters: Introduction; Site assessment; Groundwater movement and plume migration; Mass balance concept and reactor kinetics; Soil remediation; Groundwater remediation; VOC-laden air treatment; and Other important design calculations.

5642 Practical handbook of estuarine and marine pollution
M.J. Kennish CRC Press, 1997, 524pp. $104.95. ISBN 0849384249.
Multidisciplinary – aimed at marine biologists and oceanographers as well as chemists and geologists. Looks at anthropogenic effects on estuarine and marine ecosystems, locally, regionally and globally. Lots of tables of pollution, case studies and references. The oil spill incidents are from USA and Canada only, but there is information on pollution in Europe specifically Netherlands, Denmark and Germany.

5643 Practical handbook of processing and recycling municipal waste
A.G.R. Manser and A.A. Keeling 1996, Lewis Publishing, 557pp. $129.95. ISBN 1566701643.
An overview of the practical considerations of recycling and reprocessing, based on an understanding of waste product characteristics, concentrating on composting, materials recovery, and the production of refuse-derived fuel. Its 11 chapters include: The nature of waste; Mechanical handling; Composting in waste management; Simple windrow composting systems; More sophisticated mechanical composting systems; Biological aspects of compost production and utilization; Material recovery facilities; Refuse-derived fuel (RDF) processes; Combined RDF/compost/recycling plants; and Markets for recycled products.

5644 Practical recycling handbook
Kindred Association Thomas Telford, 1994, 184pp. £32.50. ISBN 0727719904.
Offers practical advice and guidance on recycling and collection of domestic waste. Contains ten chapters that include Recyclable materials; Recycling centres; Storage and handling; Composting; etc.

5645 Remedial treatment for contaminated land [UK]
M.R. Harris, S.M. Herbert and M.A. Smith; Construction Industry Research and Information Association 1995–8. 12 v., £450.00.
Standard series of guides to UK practice.

- V. I: *Introduction and guide*. 1998 ISBN 0860173968.
- V. II: *Decommissioning, decontamination and demolition*. 1995 ISBN 0860173976.
- V. III: *Site investigation and assessment*. 1995 ISBN 0860173984.
- V. IV: *Classification and selection of remedial methods*. 1995 ISBN 0860173992.
- V. V: *Excavation and disposal*. 1995 ISBN 086017400x.
- V. VI: *Containment and hydraulic measures*. 1996 ISBN 0860174018.
- V. VII: *Ex-situ remedial methods for soils, sludges and sediments*. 1995 ISBN 0860174026.
- V. VIII: *Ex-situ remedial methods for contaminated groundwater and other liquids* 1995 ISBN 0860174034.
- V. IX: *In-situ methods of remediation*. 1995 ISBN 0860174042.
- V. X: *Special situations*. 1995 ISBN 0860174050.
- V. XI: *Planning and management*. 1995 ISBN 0860174069.
- V. XII: *Policy and legislation* By M. R. Harris et al. 1998 ISBN 0860174077.

5646 Sewerage rehabilitation manual [UK]
WRc 4th edn, 2001, 687pp. 2 v., £395.00. ISBN 1898920397.
Often referred to by its acronym, SRM, this manual is recognized as the standard reference work in the maintenance and development of sewerage systems in the UK.

- V. 1. *Rehabilitation planning*. Nine chapters covering Initial planning, Diagnostic studies, and Implementation and monitoring, plus appendices.
- V. 2. *Sewer renovation*. Ten chapters covering such topics as Renovation techniques, Specifications, Grouting, etc., plus appendices.

1st edn 1983, 3rd edn 1994.

5647 Standard handbook of environmental engineering
R.A. Corbitt, ed. 2nd edn, McGraw-Hill, 1998, 1532pp. $110.00. ISBN 0070131589.
A comprehensive reference work embracing the whole area of environmental engineering. It covers technical aspects of air and water quality, control and treatment, wastewater and solid waste management, and hazardous waste management. This edition includes new material on pollution prevention, drinking water standards, volatile organic compounds, indoor air quality and emissions monitoring. 47

authors contribute ten overview chapters including Air quality control; Water supply; Wastewater disposal; Solid waste, etc. Most chapters have extensive bibliographies.
1st edn 1990.

5648 **Standard handbook of hazardous waste treatment and disposal**
H.M. Freeman, ed. 2nd edn, McGraw-Hill, 1997. $195.00. ISBN 0070220441.
Heavily updated and comprehensive work covering hazardous waste management, site cleanup, and treatment alternatives. This edition includes new material on storage and transportation of hazardous wastes, hazardous waste spills and spill clean-ups, and low-level red waste management, and there is a greater emphasis upon waste minimization and pollution prevention technologies than in first edition. 99 authors contribute 71 sections arranged in 15 chapters which include Hazardous waste recovery processes; Physical and chemical treatment; Thermal processes; and Remedial action techniques and technology.
1st edn 1989.

5649 **Standard methods for the examination of water and wastewater** [USA]
L.S. Clesceri, A.E. Greenberg and A.D. Eaton, eds; American Public Health Association, American Water Works Association and Water Environment Federation 20th edn, 1998, 1205pp. Also available on CD-ROM, $200.00. ISBN 0875532357.
www.standardmethods.org
A standard US work with international application containing over 400 EPA approved tests of water properties and quality, covering: Physical and aggregate properties; Metals; Inorganic and organic compounds; Radioactivity; Toxicity; and Biological and microbiological examination.

In April 2004, an online version was released, leading to the work being 'forever current'.
1st edn 1905, 19th edn 1995.

5650 **The Wastebook: a free guide to recycling and sustainable waste management** [UK]
D. Oakley-Hill and L. Maxwell WasteWatch.
www.recycle.mcmail.com
Sponsored by Friends of the Earth, Building Research Establishment, the Environment Agency, and regional Government Offices, this site offers advice on recycling a wide range of materials. Although aimed mainly at businesses and organizations in South-East England, much of its advice is general. Divided into two sections: Specific waste options, a guide to solutions to particular waste problems; and Waste connections, a list of related subjects and aids to better practice.

5651 **Water quality and treatment: a handbook of community water supplies** [USA]
R.D. Letterman; American Water Works Association 5th edn, McGraw-Hill, 1999, 1232pp. $135.00. ISBN 0070016593.
Well respected manual for the US water supply industry that discusses water quality issues, sources of contamination, and in particular the physical and chemical technologies of water treatment, including disinfection and fluoridation. Its 18 chapters include for instance, Ion exchange and inorganic and adsorption; Chemical precipitation; Membrane processes; and Chemical oxidation.
1st edn 1940 under title Manual of water quality and treatment*; last published 1990.*

Water Resources
American Society of Civil Engineers See entry no. 1155

5652 **Water treatment handbook**
S.A. Degrémont 6th edn, Rueil-Malmaison, 1991, 1596pp. 2 v. ISBN 2950398413.
Comprehensive and well known work intended for the professional engineer. Well illustrated. V. 1 contains eight chapters covering the general aspects of water and water treatment. V. 2 contains 18 chapters on water treatment techniques, physical and chemical.
1st French edn 1950. Last English edn 1979. Translated from the French.

Keeping up-to-date

CA Selects
Chemical Abstracts Service See entry no. 1722

5653 **Croner's Waste Management** [UK]
Croner, 1991–, Quarterly. £356.33 [2004].
www.croner.co.uk [DESCRIPTION]
Aims to explain 'the complex field of waste legislation', both UK and EU, and provide practical advice on waste management. The paper version comes as a looseleaf file arranged in four chapters: Legal aspects of waste management; Practical waste management; Waste charts – charts showing disposal options, handling precautions, recycling potential and storage options and a Waste Management Directory.

The subscription also includes *Waste Management Briefing*, a monthly newsletter that records changes in waste management legislation, etc. and *Environment Magazine*, issued quarterly. Full package includes online access, CD-ROM, a telephone helpline, and various newsletters.
Available online: see website.

- **Environment-Centre** www.environment-centre.net [REGISTRATION]. Free daily news, legislation, feature articles, etc. for those involved in environmental management.

5654 **ENDS Report**
Environmental Data Services, 1978–, Monthly. £359.00. ISSN 09664076.
www.endsreport.com
Central UK news publication comprising a Bulletin section (technical and other news), Features, Marketplace (what's happening in the industry), Policy & Legislation, and In Court. It also contains listings of courses and events, and a substantial appointments section.

Very good on particular topics of interest to the engineer – landfill and waste disposal, chemical industry, water industry, emissions, recycling, renewable energy. Other related products are available from the Environmental Data Services company (recently acquired by Haymarket), including daily updates. This solid and well put-together report is consistently the best single resource around.

5655 **Environmental Engineering** [UK]
Society of Environmental Engineers Professional Engineering Publishing, 1972–, Quarterly. £109.00. ISSN 09545824.
The official magazine of the SEE. It generally includes news items, company news and profiles, technical notes, product information, letters, job advertisements, etc.
Formerly entitled Society of Environmental Engineers Journal, ISSN 0374-356X.

5656 **Journal of the Air & Waste Management Association** [USA]
Air and Waste Management Association 1951–, Monthly. ISSN 10962247.
www.awma.org/pubs/aboutjour.htm [FEE-BASED]
A premier technical journal in its field first published in 1951. Free to members of the A&WMA.
Feb. 1993–1995 entitled Air and waste *(ISSN 1073-161X). 1989–1993 entitled* Air and Waste Management Association Journal *(ISSN 1047-3289). 1986–1989 entitled* JAPCA – Journal of Air Pollution Control Association *(ISSN 0894-0630). 1956–1985 entitled* Air Pollution Control Association. Journal *(ISSN 0002-2470) 1951–1955 entitled* Air Repair *(ISSN 0096-6665).*

5657 **Marine Pollution Research Titles**
National Marine Biological Library 1974–, Monthly. £140.00 [2004]. ISSN 02048051.
A current awareness service which contains about 5000 abstracts per year on marine and estuarine pollution. Arranged in eight sections: General; Petroleum hydrocarbons; Metals; Radioactivity; Other chemicals; Biological wastes; Heat; and Solids.

5658 **Municipal Engineer**
Institution of Civil Engineers Thomas Telford, 1873–, Quarterly. £77.00. ISSN 09650903.
For the professional engineer, the journal is mainly concerned with engineering projects in the public sector, management issues, waste management and the environment.
1873–1982 entitled Chartered Municipal Engineer *(ISSN 0020-3505), then until 1991* Municipal Engineer *(ISSN 0263-788X). Part of the* Proceedings of the Institution of Civil Engineers.

5659 **Water & Waste Treatment** [UK]
Faversham House Group, 1950–, Monthly. £65.00. ISSN 09506551.
www.edie.net/magazines [DESCRIPTION]
Well known magazine aimed at professionals in the water and wastewater industry carrying news and technical reports. A selection of papers, etc. is available free from the publication's website each month.

Manufacturing Engineering

advanced manufacturing • artificial intelligence • automation • castings • cellular manufacturing • computer numerical control • computer vision • control engineering • control systems • foundries • furnaces • industrial engineering • intelligent manufacturing • logistics • machine tools • machining • manufacturing processes • manufacturing technology • mechatronics • metalworking • neural networks • plant engineering • production engineering • rapid prototyping • robotics • simulation modelling • supply chains • welding

Introductions to the subject

5660 **21st century manufacturing**
P.K. Wright Prentice Hall, 2001, 460pp. $117.00. ISBN 0130956015.
Covers current technologies and future of manufacturing. Gives details of product design process, rapid prototyping, a survey of manufacturing techniques relevant to production of consumer electronics or electromechanical devices, and biotechnology, as well as metal and plastic products manufacturing. Aims to offer broader appreciation of impact of manufacturing process, not just manufacturing per se. Includes workbook of 'ideas' for projects.

5661 **Castings**
J. Campbell 2nd edn, Butterworth-Heinemann, 2003, 335pp. £34.99. ISBN 0750647906.
Very well and engagingly written – though the volume's rather plain design and appearance belies this. 'What is presented is a new approach to the metallurgy of castings. Not everything in the book can claim to be proved at this stage. Ultimately, science proves itself by underpinning good technology. Thus, not only must it be credible but, in addition, it must really work. Perhaps we may never be able to say for certain that it is really true, but in the meantime it is proposed as a piece of knowledge as reliable as can now be assembled.'
'No foundry, and no foundry technologist, can afford to be without it (on the 1st edn).' (*Foundry Trade Journal*)

5662 **Exploring advanced manufacturing technologies**
S.F. Krar and A.R. Gill Industrial Press, 2003, 448pp. $49.95. ISBN 0831131500.
Ready reference introducing 45 new technologies. For each: brief description, where it is used; underlying theory/principles, how it works; where it can be used, what it may replace; requirements necessary to make it work, possible pitfalls; advantages/disadvantages; successful application areas. Includes: Internet sourcing, superabrasive technology, direct metal deposition, fineblanking, product design/development, Internet 2D/3D file transfer, open architecture CNC, immersive/virtual reality, machine diagnostics online, CNC manufacturing, lasers, robotics, rapid prototyping, e-manufacturing, STEP NC, nanotechnology, future manufacturing, etc.

5663 **Fundamentals of manufacturing** [USA]
P.D. Rufe; Society of Manufacturing Engineers 2nd edn, 2001, 411pp. $75.00. ISBN 0872635244.
Aims to provide a structured review for the Manufacturing Engineering Certification Institute examination and to present a comprehensive text on the fundamentals of manufacturing. Contains 47 chapters in 9 sections: Mathematical fundamentals; Physics and engineering sciences; Materials; Product design; Manufacturing processes; Production systems; Automated systems and control; Quality; Manufacturing management.

5664 **Introduction to manufacturing processes**
J. A. Schey 3rd edn, McGraw-Hill, 1999, 984pp. $99.38. ISBN 0070311366.
Emphasis remains on the physical principles and the application of these principles to processes. Key difference relative to the second edition is highlighting of interactions between process and design (concurrent engineering). Includes geometric and service attributes of manufactured products, materials processing, casting, forming, sheet metalworking, machining, joining, surface treatment, systems and competitiveness.

5665 **Manufacturing engineering and technology**
S. Kalpakjian and S.R. Schmid 4th edn, Prentice Hall, 2001, 1148pp. $118.00. ISBN 0201361310.
www.nd.edu/~manufact/backup_index.html [COMPANION]
Standard textbook. 40 chapters cover: Fundamentals of materials; Metal-casting and forming/shaping processes and

equipment; Material removal processes and machines; Joining processes and equipment; Surface technology; Common aspects of manufacturing; Manufacturing in a competitive environment. Offers review questions, qualitative and quantitative, and synthesis and design, problems.

Materials and processes in manufacturing
E.P. DeGarmo, J.T. Black and R.A. Kohser See entry no. 5782

5666 Measurement and control basics
T.A. Hughes; Instrumentation Systems and Automation Society 3rd edn, 2002, 375pp. $89.00. ISBN 155617764X.
www.isa.org [DESCRIPTION]
Best-selling text providing practical introduction to the technologies, systems, and strategies involved in industrial measurement and control.

5667 Rapid prototyping: principles and applications
C.K. Chua, K.F. Leong and C.S. Lim 2nd edn, World Scientific, 2003, 448pp. £43.00. ISBN 9812381171.
www.worldscibooks.com/engineering/engineering.shtml
Offers a comprehensive coverage of rapid prototyping and rapid tooling processes, data formats and applications. Includes a CD-ROM which presents RP and its principles in an interactive way to augment the learning experience.
URL gives access to details of publisher's extensive range of engineering (and then other STM subject area) titles.

5668 User's guide to rapid prototyping
T. Grimm; Society of Manufacturing Engineers 2004, 404pp. $89.00. ISBN 0872636976.
Twelve chapters, and appendices including case studies and glossary. Aims to give an understanding of how to apply rapid prototyping technologies (e.g. 3D printing, stereolithography, selective laser sintering, and fused deposition modelling) to the product development process. Rapid tooling and rapid manufacturing also discussed, along with in-house versus service provider issues. Justification, evaluation and implementation issues also outlined.

Dictionaries, thesauri, classifications

5669 Automation, systems, and instrumentation dictionary
Instrumentation Systems and Automation Society 4th edn, 2003, 600pp. Includes CD-ROM, $84.00. ISBN 155617778X.
www.isa.org [DESCRIPTION]
New edn of standard tool now includes references to relevant ISA and IEC standards throughout, along with illustrations to enhance the definitions of more difficult terms.

5670 Dictionnaire d'automatique de génie électrique et de productique: anglais–français, français–anglais (Systems and control dictionary: English–French, French–English)
P. Borne and N. Quayle, ed. Editions Technip, 1998, 509pp. ISBN 2710807319.
64,000 technical terms and expressions used in the fields of: automatic control, electronics, electrotechnics, mechanics, electrical engineering, mechanical engineering, chemical engineering, production engineering, robotics, energy production, production and processing industries.

5671 Embedded systems dictionary
J.G. Ganssle and M. Barr CMP, 2003, 291pp. $34.95. ISBN 1578201209.
'Of the 6.2 billion processors manufactured in 2002, less than 2% became the brains of new PCs, MACs, and Unix workstations. The other 6.1 billion went into embedded systems.' Circa 4500 entries; clear often substantial definitions. Nicely laid out.

5672 Glossary of metalworking terms
D. Pohanish, ed. Industrial Press, 2003, 384pp. $39.95. ISBN 0831131284.
Contains more than 4000 essential general and functional terms used in all areas related to metalworking and manufacturing technology. Also offers details of professional organizations and a list of manufacturers and addresses of proprietary alloys and processes. Each entry contains a cross-referencing system.

5673 Sheet Metal Forming and Stamping Glossary
Ohio State University
nsmwww.eng.ohio-state.edu/Stamping_Glossary
Created by the University's Engineering Research Center for Net Shape Manufacturing. Covers bending, flanging, hemming, deep drawing, stamping. Contains approximately 800 words and expressions, sorted A–Z. Includes references.

Laws, standards, codes

5674 Inch Fastener Standards [USA]
Industrial Fasteners Institute 7th edn, 2003.
www.industrial-fasteners.org
A simplified guide to, and compendium of, the various standards issued by the Institute and by the AMERICAN SOCIETY OF MECHANICAL ENGINEERS, the American Society for Testing and Materials (ASTM INTERNATIONAL), and the Society of Automotive Engineers (SAE INTERNATIONAL). Standard types of threaded fastener are covered (bolts, screws, nuts, pins) with rivets, washers and locking mechanisms. Elements of materials, quality assurance, threading, clearances and other basics are appended. References to original standards throughout.

5675 Manufacturing Engineering Laboratory [USA]
www.mel.nist.gov
NIST MEL works to satisfy the measurements and standards needs of US manufacturers in mechanical and dimensional metrology and in advanced manufacturing technology (AMT). Five divisions cover: Precision engineering; Manufacturing metrology; Intelligent systems; Manufacturing systems integration; Fabrication technology. Provides details of research areas and programmes, along with products and services.

5676 Standards of the Expansion Joint Manufacturers Association [USA]
Expansion Joint Manufacturers Association 8th edn, 2003, 230pp. $200.00.
http://ww3.ejma.org
Industry and manufacturers' standards for specialist expansion joints used to absorb dimensional changes in pipes, ducts and vessels caused by temperature variations. Contains definitions, safety recommendations, design criteria, manufacturing and testing data, shipping and

installation advice and standard specifications with supporting information.

5677 Standards of the Tubular Exchanger Manufacturers Association [USA]
Tubular Exchanger Manufacturers Association 8th edn, 1999, 294pp. $250.00.
www.tema.org
Practical material on shell and tube heat exchangers. Nomenclature, fabrication tolerances and performance, installation, operation and maintenance, standard heat exchangers, flow induced vibration and fluid properties. With recommended good practice guidelines for designers.

5678 Welding codes, standards, and specifications
J.D. Mouser McGraw-Hill, 1997, 608pp. $74.95. ISBN 0070435502.
One-stop guide to the welding codes and standards from American Welding Society, Uniform Building Code, American Institute of Steel Construction, Building Officials and Code Administrators International and other agencies.

Official & quasi-official bodies

5679 Manufacturing Advisory Service [UK]
www.mas.dti.gov.uk
Offers an integrated support service to UK industry via ten Regional 'Centres for Manufacturing Excellence', more than 290 'Centres of Expertise in Manufacturing' and the website. Provides free information and advice for all UK manufacturers. Search and browse facilities available on website, along with factsheets, case studies and FAQs.

- **Innovative Manufacturing Research Centres Engineering and Physical Sciences Research Council.** www.epsrc.ac.uk/ResearchFunding/Programmes. Aim to promote and support high quality research and masters level postgraduate training in manufacturing engineering and related topics, so as to help improve the performance of the UK manufacturing sector.

5680 Solutions for Advanced Manufacturing [CAN]
Industry Canada
http://strategis.ic.gc.ca/epic/internet/insam-sfp.nsf/en/Home
Website focused on advanced manufacturing technologies and the Canadian companies that produce these technology solutions.

Research centres & institutes

5681 Advanced Manufacturing Research Centre [UK]
www.amrc.co.uk
£15 million partnership building on the shared scientific excellence, expertise and technological innovation of the world's leading aerospace company, Boeing, and world-class research within the University of Sheffield's Faculty of Engineering. AMRC mission is to create a Centre of Excellence for aerospace manufacturing which will be the focus of a new Advanced Manufacturing Park.

5682 Center for Non Traditional Manufacturing Research [USA]
www.unl.edu/nmrc
Established in 1988. The only research facility in the USA dedicated solely to the examination of non-traditional manufacturing methods. Projects involve both basic and applied research on numerous non-traditional manufacturing processes.

5683 National Center for Manufacturing Sciences [USA]
www.ncms.org
Claims to be largest cross-industry collaborative research and development consortium in North America and only consortial effort in the US devoted exclusively to manufacturing technologies, processes and practices. Offers details of projects and success stories; also has copies of reports and other resources for sale.

5684 Pera [UK]
www.pera.com
Formerly known as the *Production Engineering Research Association*, now 'an international technology-based consulting and training group that provides businesses with the expertise to succeed by developing groundbreaking technological solutions and implementing world-class strategies'. Have a well developed 'Knowledge Centre' which spends 'hundreds of thousands of UK pounds on information sources every year, ensuring our experts are supported by the best resources available: combine this with our wide network of industry contracts and you can see why we have one of the most powerful sources of commercial and technical information in Europe'.

5685 TWI World Centre for Materials Joining Technology [UK]
www.twi.co.uk
Non-profit distributing company. Operating arm of The Welding Institute. Provides industry with engineering solutions in structures incorporating welding and associated technologies (surfacing, coating, cutting, etc.) via information, advice and technology transfer, consultancy and project support, contract R&D, training and qualification, software, and personal membership. Claims to be one of the foremost independent research and technology organizations and only single source of expertise in every aspect of joining technology for engineering materials – metals, plastics, ceramics and composites.

Associations & societies

Abrasive Engineering Society
See entry no. 5798

5686 American Association for Artificial Intelligence
www.aaai.org
The leading society in this arena. Rich website giving access to wide range of resources.

- **AI Topics: A dynamic library of introductory information about artificial intelligence** www.aaai.org/AITopics/aitopics.html. 'For students, teachers, journalists, and everyone who would like to learn about what artificial intelligence is, and what AI scientists do.' Limited number of exemplary non-technical resources, organized and annotated as basic introduction. Good resource.

5687 American Foundry Society
www.afsinc.org
Mission is 'to provide and promote knowledge and services that strengthen the metalcasting industry for the ultimate benefit of its customers and society'. Now has 10,000 members in 47 countries. AFS Library is 'the most complete

library of foundry/metallurgical technology available in the English language. Information is available through technical literature searches, information retrieval, videotapes and compiled literature series'. Publications (though the 'What's New' section had not recently been updated).

5688 **American Welding Society**
www.aws.org
Details of the extensive AWS Standards program within the Technical Services section; also safety and health fact sheets. Publications catalogue, including the important WELDING HANDBOOK. Relatively active AWS Forum – with, for instance, some 10,000 posts in each of the 'Shop Talk' and 'Technical' sections.

Association for Iron and Steel Technology
See entry no. 5803

5689 **Association for Manufacturing Technology** [USA]
www.amtonline.org
Founded 1902; represents and promotes the interests of American providers of manufacturing machinery and equipment. Good range of information on industry trends, standards and regulations, policy issues, etc. on pleasant and well structured website.

5690 **Chartered Institute of Logistics and Transport** [UK]
www.ciltuk.org.uk
The UK's professional body for transport, logistics and integrated supply-chain management, 'logistics' setting out 'to deliver exactly what the customer wants – at the right time, in the right place and at the right price'. 22,000 members.

5691 **Consortium for Advanced Manufacturing – International**
www.cam-i.org
Not-for-profit, co-operative membership organization established in 1972 to support research and development in areas of strategic importance to manufacturing industries. Provides details of programmes and resources, events and membership. Has its own bookstore. Impressive roster of members.

European Powder Metallurgy Association
See entry no. 5807

5692 **Global Alliance of Rapid Prototyping Associations**
www.garpa.org
GARPA and its annual meeting, the 'Global Summit', were formed to encourage the sharing of information on rapid prototyping and related subjects across international borders. Members include 17 national associations, with links to their sites.

5693 **Institute of Industrial Engineers** [USA]
www.iienet.org
'The world's largest professional membership society dedicated solely to the support of the industrial engineering profession and individuals involved with improving quality and productivity ... Many people are misled by the term 'industrial engineer'. The 'industrial' does not mean just manufacturing. It encompasses service industries as well. It has long been known that industrial engineers have the technical training to make improvements in a manufacturing setting. Now it is becoming increasingly recognized that these same techniques can be used to evaluate and improve productivity and quality in service industries.'

Much accessible directly just to members; but the Resource Library has a Reviewed Links section containing resources which 'represent a wide assortment of specialty material covering all aspects of industrial engineering practice. Member volunteers who review and select each site do so based on criteria that rate the material's relevance and usefulness to industrial engineers, its technical accuracy, and its alignment with IIE values and mission'.

- **IE terminology** 2001, 662pp. $75.00. ISBN 0898062055. Official standard of the AMERICAN NATIONAL STANDARDS INSTITUTE with over 12,000 definitions in 17 subject areas related to industrial engineering.
- **Maynard's industrial engineering handbook** **K.B. Zandin and H.B. Maynard, eds** 6th edn, McGraw-Hill, 2001. $175.00. ISBN 0070411026. http://books.mcgraw-hill.com [DESCRIPTION]. 133 chapters from 176 worldwide contributors.

Institute of Measurement and Control
See entry no. 5437

Instrumentation Systems and Automation Society
See entry no. 5439

5694 **International Federation of Automatic Control**
www.ifac-control.org
'Multinational federation of National Member Organizations, each one representing the engineering and scientific societies concerned with automatic control in its own country. The purpose of the Federation is to promote the science and technology of control in the broadest sense in all systems, whether, for example, engineering, physical, biological, social or economic, in both theory and application. IFAC is also concerned with the impact of control technology on society.'

'Scope' section has a helpful set of definitions of the Federation's 39 Technical Committees, which are organized into nine broad areas: Systems and signals; Design methods; Computers, cognition and communication; Mechatronics, robotics and components; Manufacturing systems; Industrial systems; Transportation systems and vehicles; Bio and ecological systems; Social systems.

5695 **International Federation of Robotics**
www.ifr.org
IFR promotes research, development, use and international co-operation in the entire field of robotics and acts as a focal point for organizations and governmental representatives in activities related to robotics. Site provides details of publications, statistics, robot types, fairs and exhibitions and conferences and symposia, and ISO information on robot standards.

5696 **International Institution for Production Engineering Research**
www.cirp.net
Aims include promoting international collaborative research into manufacturing processing methods: see the good introductory General Presentation. Lists publications, including dictionaries and journals for sale, and the text of a Unified Terminology on design, on manufacturing systems and on assembly systems. Offers details of meetings, seminars and conferences. Useful inventory of CIRP Members Research Laboratories.

5697 **Manufacturing Industries Division** [UK]
www.imeche.org.uk/manufacturing
Formerly the Institution of Manufacturing Engineers, now part of IMechE, the UK qualifying body for mechanical engineers. Holds regular conferences and lectures and has established manufacturing forums. Overall objective to allow manufacturing engineers to be updated on technological advances and to facilitate the exchange of information.

Responsible for major activities including Manufacturing Excellence Awards, Imagineering, Microsystems Manufacturing Association, Rapid Prototyping Manufacturing Association, the Midlands Manufacturing Centre. Also supports the Manufacturing Advisory Service.

5698 **National Association of Manufacturers** [USA]
www.nam.org
USA's largest industrial trade association. Mission is to enhance competitiveness of manufacturers and to improve American living standards by shaping a legislative and regulatory environment conducive to US economic growth and to increase understanding among policymakers, the media and the public about the importance of manufacturing to America's economic strength. Site includes good section of Manufacturing Statistics as well as other documents, video clips, etc.

5699 **Society of Manufacturing Engineers** [USA]
www.sme.org
Major international professional association for the manufacturing community, promotes increased awareness of manufacturing engineering, helps keep manufacturing professionals up-to-date on leading trends and technologies. Publishes books, journals, CD-ROMs, technical papers and videos; organizes conferences and training events; provides other support, e.g. e-newsletters, buyers' guide (US-biased), etc. Some services members only.

- **SME Source** http://corp.ebrary.com/collateral/ebrary-sme.pdf. The world's largest full-text database of publications in manufacturing engineering containing more than 4000 individual book chapters, journal articles and technical papers. Anchored by the nine-volume *Tool and Manufacturing Engineers Handbook* series.

United States Association for Computational Mechanics
See entry no. 5910

Portal & task environments

Advanced Materials and Processes Technology Information Analysis Center: AMPTIAC
See entry no. 5814

5700 **AgentLink III: European coordination action for agent-based computing** [EUR]
University of Southampton, University of Liverpool and European Commission. Directorate for Information Society
www.agentlink.org
'We view agent-based computing as consisting of three main constituent components:

Agents Encapsulated computer systems that are situated in some environment and are capable of flexible, autonomous action in that environment in order to meet their design objectives

Interactions Such agents invariably need to interact with one another in order to manage their inter-dependencies. These interactions involve agents co-operating, negotiating and co-ordinating with one another

Organisations Agent interactions take place within some organisational context (e.g. a marketplace or some other form of electronic institution).'

Entrée to a rapidly developing field.

5701 **AMR Research**
www.amrresearch.com
Commercial consultancy which 'provides practical, decisive research and actionable advice for more than 5000 executives who seek to improve business process performance and cut costs with technology. These companies rely on AMR Research to support their most critical business initiatives, including supply chain transformation, new product introduction, customer profitability, compliance and governance, and IT benefits realization'. Good exemplar of its type. Most resources fee-based, but some accessible on registration.

5702 **ARC Advisory Group: Thought Leaders for Manufacturing and Supply Chain**
www.arcweb.com
Provide a very wide range of services – some accessible on registration. There is a good Site Map and an excellent Website Tour.

Engineers Edge
See entry no. 5382

5703 **Evoweb: The online information service for everyone interested in evolutionary computing**
Napier University and European Commission. Directorate for Information Society
http://evonet.lri.fr
'Evolutionary computing harnesses the power of natural selection to turn computers into automatic optimisation and design tools. The three mechanisms that drive evolution forward are reproduction, mutation and the Darwinian principle of survival of the fittest. In the biological world these mechanisms enable lifeforms to adapt to a particular environment over successive generations. The camel's hump, the eagle's eye, the dolphin's sonar, the crafty human brain itself; all these solutions to environmental problems were generated by evolution. All bear witness to its power as a universal optimiser. Like evolution in nature, evolutionary computing also breeds progressively better solutions to a wide variety of complex problems.'

Entrée to a rapidly developing field.

5704 **Intelligent Manufacturing Systems**
IMS International Inc.
www.ims.org
Industry-led R&D initiative to develop next generation of manufacturing and processing technologies, supported by governments/public administrations of Australia, Canada, the EU, Norway, Switzerland, Japan and the US. Provides a framework for industrial companies, research institutes and universities worldwide to co-operate on R&D topics of mutual interest. Offers information on the initiative, its activities, technical themes, background, terms of reference. Includes glossary and newsletter.

5705 **Manufacturing.net**
Reed Business Information.
www.manufacturing.net
Well organized site containing content contributed by 23 magazines. Includes substantial news section, pages on the US and international economy, and a product supplier database (Manufacturing Yellow Pages). Has a marketplace for books, industry standards and market research. Provides search and browse facilities. Content also arranged by topic. Offers e-mail newsletter.

MATTER
University of Liverpool See entry no. 5820

5706 **Robotics Online** [USA]
Robotic Industries Association
www.roboticsonline.com
Free full-text articles, technical papers and case studies on robotics topics such as simulation, inspection and safety are available. The site contains a selection of helpful beginners' fact sheets and hosts an 'Ask the Experts' question and answer forum.

5707 **Worldwide Guide to Rapid Prototyping**
Castle Island Co.
home.att.net/~castleisland
Site contains a directory of services and equipment (including materials and software); access to tutorials; details of the RP industry; a bibliography, details of patents and a glossary; and links to applications. Site search facilities also available.

Discovering print & electronic resources

Computer & Control Abstracts
Institution of Electrical Engineers See entry no. 6052

Fluidex: The Fluid Engineering Abstracts Database
See entry no. 5927

5708 **R&M Library** [USA]
Reliability Analysis Center
http://rac.alionscience.com
The Centre is a US Department of Defense chartered Information Analysis Center which collects and disseminates scientific and technical information within the 'engineering disciplines of Reliability, Maintainability, Supportability, and Quality (RMSQ) to support accurate decision making and implement cost-effective solutions throughout all phases of a product or system life cycle'.

5709 **Recent Advances in Manufacturing: RAM**
J.R. Corlett, ed.
www.eevl.ac.uk/ram
Fully-searchable bibliographic database, 1990 to date, freely available on the web. Covers both engineering and management aspects of manufacturing and related areas (e.g. product development). Hosted on EEVL site; complements EEVL collection of manufacturing/product development web resources. Updated regularly, but not as thoroughly as in the past.

5710 **WWW Virtual Library: Control Engineering**
University of Cambridge Department of Engineering.
www-control.eng.cam.ac.uk
The work of the Department's *Control Group* – who maintain the Virtual Library – is dedicated to control theory and modelling as applied to, for example, the internal combustion engine, flight systems, air traffic control, telecommunications and submarines. This site is a good source of papers and technical reports in the field, with abstracts and pdf files for the period 1993–2004.

Digital data, image & text collections

Engineer-it
See entry no. 5451

Directories & encyclopedias

5711 **Encyclopedia of production and manufacturing management**
P.M. Swamidass, ed. Kluwer Academic, 2000, 1048pp. £362.00. ISBN 0792386302.
http://reference.kluweronline.com
Consists of 100 longer articles on key concepts and practices and over 1000 shorter entries on concepts, practices and principles. Identifies manufacturers and organizations discussed, for easy access to real-life examples. Provides alphabetical and topical bibliographies. Online version offers searching and browsing facilities.
Available online: see website.
'Overall, the editor Paul Swamidass and Kluwer did a very good job in organizing the book project.' (*OR News*)

Handbooks & manuals

BASF handbook on basics of coating technology
A. Goldschmidt and H.-J. Streitberger See entry no. 5116

5712 **Basic machining reference handbook**
A.R. Meyers and T.J. Slattery 2nd edn, Industrial Press, 2001, 299pp. $34.95. ISBN 0831131209.
www.industrialpress.com/en
Presents principles of basic machining, while summarizing major considerations involved. Includes speeds and feeds tables, and various checklists. Covers measurement standards, cut-off, turning, milling, presses, grinding, materials, NC and CNC and cost per cut.
The publisher announced early 2005 a collaboration with the SOCIETY OF MANUFACTURING ENGINEERS *'to provide enhanced authoritative manufacturing and engineering references and guides': see website*

5713 **CNC programming handbook**
P. Smid 2nd edn, Industrial Press, 2003, 600pp. $69.95. ISBN 0831131586.
Deals with CNC milling and CNC turning (CNC being 'computer numerical control'). Presents common programming subjects in depth as well as advanced subjects. More than one thousand illustrations, tables, formulas, tips, shortcuts and practical examples. CD-ROM included. 53 sections, plus appendix and index.

Comprehensive structural integrity
I. Milne, R.O. Ritchie and B. Karihaloo, eds See entry no. 5837

5714 **Computational intelligence in manufacturing handbook**
J.L. Wang and A. Kusiak, eds CRC Press, 2000, 577pp. $139.95. ISBN 0849305926.
Describes the use of computational intelligence (neural networks, fuzzy logic, genetic algorithms) in manufacturing system modelling and design, process planning and scheduling, manufacturing process monitoring and control, and quality assurance and fault diagnosis.

5715 **Computer vision: a modern approach**
D. Forsyth and J. Ponce Prentice Hall, 2003, 693pp. $98.00. ISBN 0130851981.
'We see computer vision ... As an enterprise that uses statistical methods to disentangle data using models constructed with the aid of geometry, physics and learning theory.'

Although mathematically intensive, this is an excellent overview addressed to those engaged in computational geometry, computer graphics, image processing, imaging in general, and robotics, as well as computer vision itself.

5716 **Control systems engineering**
N.S. Wise 4th edn, Wiley, 2003, 1008pp. $119.95. ISBN 0471445770.
Updated standard text on control matters for students and engineers, with material on the use of MATLAB for control system calculations and design.

5717 **Control systems theory with engineering applications**
S.E. Lyshevski Birkhauser, 2001, 416pp. Includes CD-ROM, £106.00. ISBN 081764203X.
Provides good coverage of the technical underpinnings and is designed 'to bridge the gap between theory and practice for students and engineers working in the fields of electrical, mechanical and aerospace engineering'.

5718 **Design for manufacturability handbook**
J.G. Bralla, ed. 2nd edn, McGraw-Hill, 1999, 1344pp. $135.00. ISBN 007007139X.
Written by over 70 experts in manufacturing and product design. Features new chapters on DFM for electronics, DFX (designing for all desirable attributes), DFM for low-quality production, and concurrent engineering. Covers economical use of raw materials, formed metal components, machined components, castings, non-metallic parts, assemblies. Includes glossary of terms.

5719 **Engineering formulas for metalcutting: presented in customary US and metric units**
E. Isakov, ed. Industrial Press, 2003, 240pp. $24.95. ISBN 0831131748.
Claims to be a 'unique' resource. Enables users to calculate necessary speeds, feeds, and required machining power in order to maximize the productivity of cutting. Sections cover: mechanical properties of work materials; milling; turning; boring; and drilling.

5720 **Expert systems**
C.T. Leondes, ed. Academic Press, 2001, 1947pp. 6 v., $1985.00. ISBN 0124438806.
'An "expert system" is a knowledge-based computer system that emulates the decision-making ability of a human expert. The primary role of the expert system is to perform appropriate functions under the close supervision of the human, whose work is supported by that expert system. In the reverse, this same expert system can monitor and double check the human in the performance of a task. Human-computer interaction in our highly complex world requires the development of a wide array of expert systems.'

Detailed coverage of principles and the full range of current applications.

- **AboutAI.net** www.aboutai.net. Extensive portal covering all aspects of artificial intelligence and its applications.
- **European Coordinating Committee for Artificial Intelligence** www.eccai.org. Established 1982 as a representative body for the European artificial intelligence community. Its aim is to promote the study, research and application of artificial intelligence in Europe.
- **WWW Virtual Library: Artificial Intelligence J. Bowen; London South Bank University** www.afm.sbu.ac.uk/ai. Organized into three sections: research sites and projects; Newsgroups; Other information.

5721 **Handbook of cellular manufacturing systems**
S.A. Irani, ed. Wiley, 1999, 776pp. $190.00. ISBN 0471121398.
Hands-on guide to implementing multi-cell manufacturing systems on a large scale. Aimed at industrial engineers and production managers. Looks at history and principles, methods for cell formation, setup time reduction, quality control, benchmarking, costs and benefits, human resources, and computer-aided tools and methods. Case studies included.

5722 **Handbook of fuzzy computation**
E.H. Ruspini, P.P. Bonissone and W. Pedrycz Institute of Physics Publishing, 1998, 1232pp. £350.00. ISBN 0750304278.
Large format, well designed compendium. Although a detailed and mathematically demanding treatment, the Editors have included much useful introductory comment to each section. And over half the volume is concerned with Applications (knowledge-based systems; control; machine learning; data and information management, etc.) and Practice (aerospace systems control, nuclear engineering, manufacturing, etc.)

5723 **Handbook of industrial engineering: technology and operations management**
G. Salvendy, ed.; Institute of Industrial Engineers 3rd edn, Wiley, 2001, 2796pp. $275.00. ISBN 0471330574.
Excellent volume: over 100 contributors; 1000 tables, graphs, figures, formulae. Detailed coverage of: technology; performance improvement management; management, planning, and design control; and decision-making methods.

5724 **Handbook of industrial robotics**
S.Y. Nof, ed. 2nd edn, Wiley, 1999, 1378pp. $250.00. ISBN 0471177830.
Based on contributions from 120 leading experts. Of 66 chapters, 33 are new. Places particular emphasis on applications and problem-solving technologies for industry rather than theoretical and research-based topics which formed most of the original edition. Features glossary with over 800 terms and CD-ROM illustrating the motions and intelligence of robots. Includes sections on development, design, control, intelligence, applications.

5725 **Handbook of machining and metalworking calculations**
R.A. Walsh, ed. McGraw-Hill, 2000, 400pp. $125.00. ISBN 0071360662.
Twelve sections. Covers most of the basic and advanced calculation procedures required for machining and metalworking applications. It includes recent ANSI and ISO specifications and calculations for machining operations, gears and sprockets, springs, linkages and more. Examples of solved problems given.

Handbook of materials for product design
C.A. Harper, ed. See entry no. 5397

Handbook of materials selection
M. Kutz, ed. See entry no. 5847

5726 **Handbook of metalforming processes**
H.G. Theis, ed. Marcel Dekker, 1999, 655pp. $225.00. ISBN 082479317X.
Written by over 30 experts from industry and academia. Provides information on flat-rolled sheet metal products. Eight sections cover: mechanical metallurgy; stamping systems; rollforming; non-traditional cutting and forming; traditional bending and shearing systems; machine vibration control; ISO 9000; and safety. Contains over 450 tables, drawings and photographs.

5727 **Handbook of metallurgical process design**
G.E. Totten, K. Funatani and L. Xie, eds Marcel Dekker, 2004, 966pp. $249.95. ISBN 0824741064.
Multi-author, multi-national work. 'While there are various texts which address a particular process design such as forging, casting, and rolling, there is a need for a single text that will provide an overview of these processes as they refer to metallurgical component design.'

22 chapters in five sections: Hot and cold forming; Casting; Heat treatment; Surface engineering; Machining. Good bibliographies at the end of each chapter; limited subject index.

5728 **Industrial furnaces**
W. Trinks 6th edn, Wiley, 2004, 473pp. $150.00. ISBN 0471387061.
Updated edn of standard reference text often referred to as 'the furnace man's bible'.

Instrument engineers' handbook
B.G. Lipták, ed. See entry no. 5496

5729 **Machinery's handbook: a reference book for the mechanical engineer, designer, manufacturing engineer, draftsman, toolmaker and machinist**
E. Oberg [et al.], eds 27th edn, Industrial Press, 2004, 2704pp. Includes CD-ROM + Handbook Guide, $149.95. ISBN 0831127279.
www.industrialpress.com/en/mh.asp#27279 [DESCRIPTION]
Comprehensive data book. Coverage includes mathematics, mechanics, materials, dimensioning and measuring, tooling and toolmaking, machining and manufacturing, fasteners and threads, machine elements, and measuring units.

Now includes INTERACTIVE MATH: 'With a simple Internet connection you'll be able to instantly calculate cutting speeds, dimensions of bevels, moments of inertia, the measurement of various screw threads, the center of gravity for any shape, hardness of material, volumes, taper angles, matrices, and much, much more.' Standard work.

First published 1914. Previous edn 2000 (accessible at: www.knovel.com). Range of versions available: see website.

5730 **Manufacturing engineering handbook**
H. Geng, ed. McGraw-Hill, 2004, 1088pp. $125.00. ISBN 0071398252.
http://books.mcgraw-hill.com
Includes conventional metalworking plus the latest manufacturing and automation technologies. Eight sections cover: Business management; Product development and design; Manufacturing automation and technologies; Heat treating, hot work, and metalforming; Metalworking and machine design; Surface preparation and coating; Robotics, machine vision and assembling; Manufacturing management.
Good example of a number of relevant Handbooks from McGraw-Hill currently in print: see website.

5731 **Manufacturing engineer's reference book**
D. Koshal, ed. Butterworth-Heinemann, 1993, 896pp. £155.00. ISBN 0750611545.
www.knovel.com
19 sections; materials and processes described, also management issues, ergonomics, maintenance and computers in industry. CAD, CAE, CIM and quality explored at length. Extensive reference lists provided. Detailed, analytical index. Still valuable.
Available online: see website.

5732 **Manufacturing handbook of best practices: an innovation, productivity and quality focus**
J.B. ReVelle, ed. CRC Press, 2001, 472pp. $99.95. ISBN 1574443003.
19 chapters. Describes new approaches to design, organization and quality control in manufacturing. Topics include agile and lean manufacturing, six sigma, ISO 9001:2000 and ISO 14000, process analysis and SQC/SPC, QFD and integrated product and process development, theory of constraints, TRIZ, supply chain management, design of experiments, measurement systems analysis and more.

Mechanical engineering design
J.E. Shigley and C.R. Mischke See entry no. 5959

5733 **Modern control engineering**
K. Ogata 4th edn, Prentice Hall, 2001, 970pp. $117.00. ISBN 0130609072.
'This comprehensive treatment of the analysis and design of continuous-time control systems provides a gradual development of control theory—and shows how to solve all computational problems with MATLAB. It avoids highly mathematical arguments, and features an abundance of examples and worked problems throughout the text.'

5734 **Modern Machine Shop Handbook for the metalworking industries**
W. Chapman, ed. Hanser Gardner Publications, 2002, 2368pp. Also available as CD-ROM, $55.00. ISBN 156990345X.
www.mmsonline.com/handbook [DESCRIPTION]
Addresses mathematics, measurement, materials, machining centres, machining, fasteners, machine components. Claims to be first machinist's reference to cover such topics as accuracy in machining centres, high speed machining, HSK tooling, co-ordinate measuring machines, encoders and probes, and waterjet machining. Other highlighted topics

involve machining techniques, exotic materials including superalloys and composites, adhesives, threading operations, CNC canned programs, balanced tooling, superfinishing, precision machining with lasers.

- **Modern Machine Shop** Gardner Publications. www.mmsonline.com. US-based magazine. Includes emphasis zones (metalworking topics, each containing details of suppliers, products, articles, forums, online marketplace and training and the like): also divided into industry news, research, manage, interact sections.

5735 Non-traditional machining handbook
C. Sommer Advance Publishing, 2000, 437pp. $79.95. ISBN 1575373254.
www.advancepublishing.com/mall/technical.asp [DESCRIPTION]
Contents include EDM, waterjet and plasma cutting, photochemical and electrochemical, abrasive flow and ultrasonic machining, rapid prototyping and manufacturing, laser applications, etc. Some management issues also covered.
'contains so much valuable information about new machining technologies, that no business or individual involved in industrial manufacturing can afford to be without it.' (*EDM Today*)

5736 Plant engineer's handbook
R.K. Mobley, ed. Rev. edn, Butterworth-Heinemann, 2001, 1189pp. £85.00. ISBN 0750673281.
Comprehensive guide to the role and responsibilities of the plant engineer with introductory essays on an impressive range of machinery, environmental matters and maintenance issues. Offers solid technical information but places this in the context of both UK and US health and safety regulations. Non-technical chapters on, for example, insurance, add to the conventional strengths of this volume.

5737 Simulation modeling handbook: a practical approach
C.A. Chung CRC Press, 2004, 608pp. $149.95. ISBN 0849312418.
Aims to insulate practitioners from uneccessary simulation theory; designed to be used independently of the particular software package being used for modelling. Well designed; good logical structure.
Series: Industrial and manufacturing engineering.

5738 Welding handbook
American Welding Society 9th edn. 5 v., published continuously from 1938 through 2004. ISBN 0871716577.
www.aws.org/handbook [DESCRIPTION]
Start of most recent edition of respected AWS Welding Handbook series. Volume 1 *Welding Science and Technology* reflects latest developments in field of welding from regenerated processes benefiting from the explosions in electronic technology, to most current information on robotics and best practice in manual arc welding. 17 chapters contain 530 illustrations and 168 tables. Provides panoramic view of welding technology.

Volume 2, the first part published 2004, covers *Welding Processes*.
Previous edition published 1987–98.

Keeping up-to-date

5739 Advanced Manufacturing
CLB Media, Bimonthly. $96.00 [2004].
www.advancedmanufacturing.com
Deals with AMT (automation, software, and manufacturing technology). Site includes full-text items and editorial from the magazine, along with industry news, a directory of collaborative software and services providers, research reports, etc. Search of archive items available. Emphasis on Canada, but worldwide coverage: good set of links.

5740 Control Engineering
Reed Business Information.
www.manufacturing.net/ctl
Covering control, instrumentation, and automation systems worldwide.

5741 Industry Week
Penton Media.
www.industryweek.com
Management resource magazine featuring articles and columns oriented to manufacturing business issues.

5742 Manufacturing Engineering [USA]
Society of Manufacturing Engineers
www.sme.org/manufacturingengineering
Online magazine issues contain full text of articles, plus shop solutions and newsdesk sections. Includes (mainly US) buyers' guide. Print version available. Access to other Society products and services, including the SME Online Library and its service: Ask the Librarian: 'Email the SME librarian with your reference and research questions.'

5743 Manufacturingtalk [UK]
Pro-Talk Ltd.
www.manufacturingtalk.com
Well organized colourful site of UK-based e-mail newsletter. Current news and archives available. Divided into news by date, by supplier and by product. Includes non-UK companies. Categories include machine tools, cutting tools, welding, finishing, automation, quality, software, metals processing, books/CDs/videos, motor sports manufacturing and others. Offers substantial listing of conferences, courses and exhibitions. An excellent service.

5744 Metalforming OnLine [USA]
Precision Metalforming Association
www.metalforming.com
Site of the Association. Includes buyers' guide, tradeshows and *MetalForming* magazine. Latter contains ten enterprise zones: specific topic sections within metalforming comprising suppliers, forums and articles in each section. Current issue and archive articles available to browse or search. Exclusive online articles offered. News section available.

5745 Tech Briefs: Engineering Solutions for Design and Manufacturing
National Aeronautics and Space Administration ABP International.
www.nasatech.com
Service primarily fulfilling the NASA charter mandate that 'its contractors must report to industry any new, commercially significant technologies developed in the course of their R&D, so that engineers, managers, and scientists could use this valuable information to improve their competitiveness and productivity'. Fascinating collection organized monthly within 12 categories: Bio-Medical; Computers/Electronics; Machinery-Automation; etc.

- **It came from outer space: everyday products and ideas from the space program M. Bijlefeld and R. Burke** Greenwood Press, 2003, 264pp. $55.00. ISBN 0313322228. Story of 67 of the most consumer-friendly products born of space-related research. 'Recommended for middle and secondary school libraries, particularly those focusing on the sciences'. (E-STREAMS).

5746 **Tooling & Production** [USA]
Nelson Publishing, Monthly. ISSN 00409243.
www.manufacturingcenter.com/tooling
Online monthly magazine dedicated to manufacturing in the metalworking industries. Archives back to October 1997. In addition to features and departments, offers a buyers' guide, daily news, and events calendar. Also machine tool searchable database, resource centre and e-mail newsletter.

Marine Engineering & Naval Architecture

hovercrafts • lifeboats • marine technology • maritime transport • naval architecture • naval technology • ocean engineering • shipbuilding • underwater technology

Introductions to the subject

5747 **Basic ship theory**
K.J. Rawson and E.C. Tupper 5th edn, Butterworth-Heinemann, 2001, 731pp.
Good standard textbook
- V. 1 *Hydrostatics and strength* £26.99, ISBN 0750653965
- V. 2 *Ship dynamics and design* £26.99, ISBN 0750653973
- **Introduction to naval architecture E.C. Tupper** 3rd edn, Butterworth-Heinemann, 1996, 361pp. £31.99. ISBN 0750625295. Updated edition of *Muckle's naval architecture for marine engineers*.

5748 **Introduction to marine engineering**
D.A. Taylor 2nd edn, Butterworth-Heinemann, 1996, 372pp. £31.99. ISBN 0750625309.
Comprehensive introduction, organized: Ships and machinery; Diesel engines; Steam turbines and gearing; Boilers; Feed systems; Pumps and pumping systems; Auxiliaries; Fuel oils, lubricating oils and their treatment; Refrigeration, air-conditioning and ventilation; Deck machinery and hull equipment; Shafting and propellers; Steering gear; Fire-fighting and safety; Electrical equipment; Instrumentation and control; Engineering materials; Watchkeeping and equipment operation; Appendix (SI units, engineering terms, power measurement, fuel estimation, engineering drawings); Index.

Dictionaries, thesauri, classifications

5749 **Dictionary of naval abbreviations**
D.W. Cutler and T.J. Cutler 4th edn, Naval Institute Press, 2005, 304pp. $26.95. ISBN 1591141524.
www.usni.org/press/press.html
Announced new edition of wide-ranging dictionary, covering both official and unofficial usages.
Check the website for details of the Press's many titles in the fields of naval, military and maritime history.

Laws, standards, codes

5750 **American Bureau of Shipping**
www.eagle.org
Develops and verifies standards for design, construction and operational maintenance of marine-related facilities. 'These standards are known as *Rules* and *Guides*. They are derived from principles of naval architecture, marine engineering and related disciplines. Currently, ABS has over 60 Rules and Guides available.'

The Bureau is a not-for-profit, non-governmental, self-regulating agency for the international marine industry, and is also one of the world's leading ship classification societies.

5751 **Ship Classification**
Det Norske Veritas (DNV).
www.dnv.com/maritime
'DNV is one of the world's leading classification societies, and helps the maritime industry manage risk in all phases of the ship's life, through ship classification, statutory certification, fuel testing and a range of technical, business risk, financial and competency related services.'

Within the Ship Types area of the site there is a 'selection of various ship types from our website. For each ship type you will find a presentation, links to relevant information and/or class notations'. Downloadable PDF publications list. Much other helpful information for those new to the intricacies of ship classification from this commercial site.
- **International Association of Classification Societies** www.iacs.org.uk. Classification societies, DNV is one of 10, 'establish and apply technical standards in relation to the design, construction and survey of marine related facilities including ships and offshore structures'. Straightforward website with good range of data.

Official & quasi-official bodies

DOT Agencies
United States. Department of Transportation See entry no. 4891

5752 **International Maritime Organization**
www.imo.org
The IMO's purposes are 'to provide machinery for co-operation among governments in the field of governmental regulation and practices relating to technical matters of all kinds affecting shipping engaged in international trade; to encourage and facilitate the general adoption of the highest practicable standards in matters concerning maritime safety, efficiency of navigation and prevention and control of marine pollution from ships.

First-rate, easily navigable website with wealth of resources and pointers: e.g. Bibliography of maritime literature (January 2005, 62 pp); Directory of maritime links; Hot topics; Maritime safety conventions; SeaLibrary Online; and so on.

An excellent portal – with a great opening page.

National Transportation Safety Board
See entry no. 4895

5753 **Office of Naval Research** [USA]
www.onr.navy.mil
'Coordinates, executes, and promotes the science and technology programs of the United States Navy and Marine Corps through schools, universities, government laboratories,

and non-profit and for-profit organizations. It provides technical advice to the Chief of Naval Operations and the Secretary of the Navy and works with industry to improve technology manufacturing processes.'

Rich sets of resources organized within headings of the Office's science and technology departments: Engineering, Materials and Physical Science; Human Systems; Industrial and Corporate Programs; Information, Electronics and Surveillance; Naval Expeditionary Warfare; Ocean, Atmosphere and Space.

5754 Shipping and Ports [UK]
Great Britain. Department for Transport
www.dft.gov.uk
Access to UK government work in this area.

- **Marine Accident Investigation Branch** www.maib.gov.uk/home. Examines and investigates all types of marine accidents to or onboard UK ships worldwide, and other ships in UK territorial waters.
- **Marine and Coastguard Agency** www.mcga.gov.uk. Useful source of guidance and regulations, survey and certification, environmental, seafarer and safety information.
- **Marine Unit Great Britain. Department of Trade and Industry.** www.dti.gov.uk/sectors_marine.html. Summarizes DTI engagements with this sector.

Research centres & institutes

5755 British Maritime Technology: BMT
www.bmt.org
Created in 1985 from the merging of the National Maritime Institute and the British Ship Research Association. Now is a 'leading international multi-disciplinary engineering, science and technology consultancy offering a broad range of services, particularly in the defence, energy, environment, shipping and general transportation sectors. Customers are served by a staff of around 1000 professionals located in a network of international subsidiary companies'.

5756 National Maritime Research Institute [JAP]
www.nmri.go.jp/index_e.html
Institute established in 2002 presenting a very wide range of valuable material on well structured site. Good gateway to Japanese involvement in the field.

Associations & societies

5757 American Society of Naval Engineers
www.navalengineers.org
Simple site giving access to (fee-based) *Naval Engineers Journal* and information about the work of the Society.

5758 Institute of Marine Engineering, Science and Technology [UK]
www.imarest.org
The Institute's Marine Information Centre is 'amongst the world's foremost marine library collections'. Their most substantial product is *Marine Technology Abstracts*, containing over 80,000 abstracts and web accessible via British Maritime Technology. Other services include the *The International Directory of Marine Consultancy* and the *IMarEST Maritime Links Directory*.

5759 Marine Technology Society [USA]
www.mtsociety.org
Founded 1963 'to allow members of academia, government and industry to have a common forum for the exchange of information and ideas, and to 'make real contributions in fostering progress in the marine sciences for the benefit of mankind' Useful range of information presented in a straightforward manner.

5760 Royal Institution of Naval Architects [UK]
www.rina.org.uk
Helpful page About the RINA Website, describing its layout and the planned purpose of each of its sections. The Institution was founded in 1860 to 'advance the art and science of Naval Architecture'. They publish a range of technical journals, conference proceedings, transactions and books, covering all aspects of naval architecture and the maritime industry.

SAE International
Society of Automotive Engineers See entry no. 4981

5761 Shipbuilders and Shiprepairers Association [UK]
www.ssa.org.uk
Represents the industry in the UK. Links to members' websites.

5762 Society for Underwater Technology
www.sut.org.uk
Founded 1966; now has members from more than 40 countries. Extensive list with links of Associated Firms and Organizations; Special Interest Groups (e.g. Diving and Marine Submersibles; Underwater Robotics Group). Useful site.

5763 Society of Naval Architects and Marine Engineers [USA]
www.sname.org
'Founded in 1893, the Society comprises over 10,000 individuals throughout the United States, Canada and abroad. Membership is open to all qualified applicants in or associated with the maritime, offshore, and small craft industries.' Good Site Index demonstrates the range and depth of activities: notable are the extensive set of Technical Committees and Special Committees (including a Banquet Committee); also the Publications section. However, some parts of the site (e.g. What's New) had not recently been updated when reviewed.

5764 Transportation Institute [USA]
www.trans-inst.org
Established in 1967 as a Washington-based, non-profit organization dedicated to maritime research education and promotion. Website has very good range of useful data – but use of its strictly hierarchical navigation structure can prove tiring.

- **Maritime Glossary** www.trans-inst.org/seawords.htm. Good A–Z listing supplemented by details of Signal Flags.

Libraries, archives, museums

Imperial War Museum
See entry no. 4915

National Maritime Museum
See entry no. 1363

5765 **Naval Historical Center** [USA]
www.history.navy.mil
'Official history program of the Department of the Navy. Its lineage dates back to 1800 with the founding of the Navy Department Library by President John Adams. The Center now includes a museum, art gallery, research library, archives, and curator as well as research and writing programs.' Among much of interest there is an extensive well categorized collection of Online Publications and Documents, as well as a substantial set of answers to FAQs.

Portal & task environments

Chemical Propulsion Information Agency
Johns Hopkins University See entry no. 4921

5766 **Infomarine**
www.infomarine.gr
Lively commercially sponsored gateway to a very wide range of serious and not so serious resources. Efficient search processes. Well worth browsing among all the advertisements.

5767 **Lifeboats** [UK]
Royal National Lifeboat Institution
www.rnli.org.uk
Details of the work of the charity that saves lives at sea. 'It provides, on call, the 24-hour lifeboat search and rescue service to 50 miles out from the coast of the UK and the Republic of Ireland, and a beach lifeguard service on 57 beaches in the south-west of England. The RNLI continues to rely on voluntary contributions and legacies for its income.'

5768 **Lloyd's Register**
www.lr.org/market_sector/marine/index.htm
Non-profit distributing organization – income derived from fees and sale of publications being used for research and development, training staff and improving services.

The Reference Library offers a range of useful services – including a set of Information Sheets 'covering the history of Lloyd's Register, the Register of Shipping, popular maritime subjects and sources for researching areas outside the scope of our records'.

The Register's Rules and Regulations 'set appropriate standards for the design, construction and lifetime maintenance of ships, offshore units and land-based installations – providing all the information you need for classification purposes'.

- **Sea-web** Lloyd's Register–Fairplay. www.lrfairplay.com. Web accessible version of the *Register of Ships* and *List of Shipowners*, containing over 140,000 ship and 154,000 ship owner and manager entries. Check the website for details of the very wide range of other offerings from the publisher.

5769 **Naval Technology**
SPG Media PLC.
www.naval-technology.com
One of a series of well laid out internet reference portals offering industry news, company indexes, listings of events, etc. There is a companion Ship Technology site.

Offshore Engineering Information Service: OEIS
Heriot-Watt University See entry no. 4760

Discovering print & electronic resources

CSA Mechanical and Transportation Engineering Abstracts
See entry no. 5926

Global Mobility Database
Society of Automotive Engineers See entry no. 4990

Directories & encyclopedias

Dolphin: Directory of Online Port and Harbour Information
Texas AandM University See entry no. 5228

Maritime and Naval Museums in Britain and Ireland
M.H. Evans and J. West, comps; Scott Polar Research Institute See entry no. 1381

Handbooks & manuals

Handbook of port and harbor engineering: geotechnical and structural aspects
G.P. Tsinker, ed. See entry no. 5259

Handbook of transportation engineering
M. Kurz, ed. See entry no. 4998

5770 **Marine structural design**
Y. Bai Elsevier, 2003, 606pp. €185.00. ISBN 0080439217.
Comprehensive but mathematically intensive handbook devoted to the 'modern theory for design and analysis of marine structures. The term 'marine structures' refers to ship and offshore structures'. Logically laid out with very detailed table of contents. However, very limited subject index.

5771 **The ocean engineering handbook**
F. El-Hawary, ed. CRC Press, 2001, 416pp. $99.95. ISBN 0849385989.
www.engnetbase.com
Five major sections: Marine hydro dynamics and vehicles control; Modelling considerations; Position control systems for offshore vessels; Applications of computational intelligence in the ocean's environment; Fibre optics in oceanographic applications.
Available online: see website.

5772 **Practical ship design**
D.G.M. Watson Elsevier, 1998, 531pp. £82.00. ISBN 0080429998.
Useful clearly written manual covering cargo ships and passenger ships, tugs, dredgers and other service craft. Deals with concept design, detail design, structural design, hydrodynamics design, the effect of regulations, the preparation of specifications and matters of costs and economics.

5773 **Practical ship hydrodynamics**
V. Bertram Butterworth-Heinemann, 2000, 270pp. £29.99. ISBN 0750648511.
Well received text giving a good survey of experimental and numerical methods. Bibliography. Subject index.
'Highly useful for graduate and postgraduate students, the book is also a professional reference work for naval architects and consulting engineers.' (*Maritime Journal*)

5774 **Ship construction**
D.J. Eyres 5th edn, Butterworth-Heinemann, 2001, 354pp. £29.99. ISBN 0750648872.
Excellent handbook, covering the full range of systems and processes involved in ship construction, including: design; materials; classification; construction; shipyards; structures; outfitting; regulations.
'This book has to be the ultimate in ship construction, very informative and in reviewing this volume I can say that during my studies I have come across other books on the subject, but in my opinion none as good as this. A must for all students and those of us who need a little refreshing now and again.' (*Nautical Magazine*)

5775 **Theory and design of air cushion craft**
L. Yun and A. Bliault Butterworth-Heinemann, 2000, 632pp. £88.99. ISBN 0340676507.
Covers both air cushion vehicles and surface effect ships. Historical introduction; Theoretical design features; Design methodology. Useful source of technical information as well as for teaching support.

Keeping up-to-date

5776 **Maritime Global Net**
Maritime Information Systems, Inc.
www.mgn.com
Access to products, services, news and other industry related data. Also includes details of over 80,000 maritime-related companies, industry associations, world ports, etc.

5777 **NSNet**
www.nsnet.com
Useful news site 'conceived in 1993 as an experiment in applying emerging information and communications technologies in the maritime industry'. In 1994, became a Defense Advanced Research Projects Agency project within the University of Michigan. 'Although no longer affiliated with the University, some of the original team members are still maintaining the site.'

Materials Science & Engineering

abrasives • alloys • aluminium • biomaterials • ceramics • composites • corrosion • elastic properties • engineering materials • iron • materials engineering • metal materials • non-destructive testing • physical metallurgy • powder metallurgy • solid state physics • steel • superconducting materials • surface engineering

Introductions to the subject

5778 **Biomaterials science: an introduction to materials in medicine**
B.D. Ratner [et al.], eds 2nd edn, Academic Press, 2004, 864pp. $95.00. ISBN 0125824637.
New edition of widely used text. Three parts: Materials science and engineering; Biology, biochemistry and medicine; Practical aspects of biomaterials

Castings
J. Campbell See entry no. 5661

5779 **The coming of materials science**
R.W. Cahn Pergamon, 2001, 568pp. £43.95. ISBN 0080426794.
www1.elsevier.com/homepage/saa/cahn [COMPANION]
Critical review dealing – among much else of detail and great value – with the core issues of: What is a scientific discipline?; How do disciplines merge and differentiate?; Can a discipline also be interdisciplinary?; Is materials science a real discipline? Two useful concluding chapters are: The management of data; The institutions and literature of materials science.
Series: Pergamon Materials, v. 5.

- **Materials science and technology: a comprehensive treatment – the classic softcover edition R.W. Cahn, P. Haasen and E.J. Kramer** Wiley, 2005, 14000pp. £415.00. ISBN 3527313958. http://catalogue.bl.uk. Planned 11 v. reissue of 18 v. treatise published 1990–1998. See website for bibliographic details of original.
- **Physical metallurgy R.W. Cahn and P. Haasen, eds** 4th edn, North Holland, 1996, 2740pp. £585.00. ISBN 0444898751. www.elsevier.com/wps/find/homepage.cws_home [DESCRIPTION]. Standard text in 3 v.

Engineering design: a materials and processing approach
G.E. Dieter See entry no. 5361

5780 **Foundations of materials science and engineering**
W.F. Smith 3rd edn, McGraw-Hill Education, 2003, 864pp. $134.06. ISBN 0072921943.
http://catalogs.mhhe.com/mhhe/home.do [DESCRIPTION]
Provides coverage of the full range of underlying science and technology starting with atomic structure and bonding, crystal characteristics, mechanical properties of metals, and so on through to ceramics, corrosion, and electrical, optical and magnetic properties.
Available online within the McGraw-Hill Online Learning Centres: see website.

- **Materials handbook: an encyclopedia for managers, technical professionals, purchasing and production managers, technicians and supervisors G.S. Brady, H.R. Clauser and J.A. Vaccari** 15th edn, McGraw-Hill, 2002, 1244pp. $99.95. ISBN 007136076X. Published for over 60 years. Contains over 15,000 generic, patented, and trade-name materials: includes concise descriptions of the materials, origin, physical appearance, composition and basic application.

5781 **Introduction to materials engineering and science for chemical and materials engineers**
B.S. Mitchell Wiley, 2004, 922pp. $125.00. ISBN 0471436232.
Well presented and designed text with treatment of a wide range of types of materials and organized: The structure of materials; Thermodynamics of condensed phases; Kinetic processes in materials; Transport properties of materials;

Mechanics of materials; Electrical, magnetic, and optical properties of materials; Processing of materials; Case studies in materials selection.

'I heartily recommend this book, primarily because of the unified presentation of topics across the materials classes. All of the important topics in an introductory materials science class are presented well, and covered by problems.' (*AIChE Journal*)

An introduction to tissue-biomaterial interactions
K.C. Dee, D.A. Puleo and R. Bizios See entry no. 3636

5782 Materials and processes in manufacturing
E.P. DeGarmo, J.T. Black and R.A. Kohser 9th edn, Wiley, 2003, 1154pp. $124.95. ISBN 0471033065.
www.wiley.com/college/degarmo [COMPANION]
Large format black and white comprehensive textbook. Good introductory overviews of: Materials; Properties of materials; Nature of metals and alloys; Equilibrium phase diagrams and the iron-carbon system; and so on – followed by chapters in sections headed: Inspection; Casting processes; Forming processes; Machining processes; Joining processes; Manufacturing systems design. Subject index.

5783 Materials research to meet 21st century defense needs
National Materials Advisory Board National Academies Press, 2003, 307pp. $69.50 (Paperback + PDF). ISBN 0309505747.
www.nap.edu/books/0309087007/html
An Open Book. ('The Open Book page image presentation framework is not designed to replace printed books. Rather, it is a free, browsable, non-proprietary, fully and deeply searchable version of the publication which we can inexpensively and quickly produce to make the material available worldwide.')

5784 Materials science and engineering: an introduction
W.D. Callister 6th edn, Wiley, 2003, 820pp. $69.85. ISBN 0471224715.
Standard now very well established text.

5785 Materials science for electrical and electronic engineers
I.P. Jones, ed. Oxford University Press, 2001, 339pp. £31.99. ISBN 0198562942.
Chapters are: Conductors, insulators, and semiconductors; An introduction to metals; Mechanical properties; Manufacturing conductors; Steel; Electrochemistry: electroplating and corrosion; Ceramics; Plastics; Semiconductors and the electronics industry; Magnetic materials; Superconductors and optical fibres.

'This book is suitable for those new to the subject. I have no hesitation in recommending it.' (*Times Higher Education Supplement*)

Mechanics of materials
J.M. Gere See entry no. 5870

5786 Navigating the materials world: a guide to understanding materials behavior
C. Baillie and L. Vanasupa, eds Academic Press, 2003, 242pp. $49.99. ISBN 0120735512.
High-level inviting entrée for students and others new to the field. Each chapter has an alternative title, such as: 'Visiting the travel agency'; 'The land of polymers'; 'Accident and emergency'. Designed to put the student at the centre of learning ... The guide is co-authored by the deputy director of the UK Centre for Materials Education.

5787 Physical foundations of materials science
G. Gottstein Springer, 2004, 502pp. Translated from the German, £46.00. ISBN 3540401393.
Detailed but highly approachable text. Enables those with little previous knowledge of solid-state physics to move on to the more specialized and fundamental literature of materials science. Very good explanations of key concepts.

Rheology for chemists: an introduction
J.W. Goodwin and R.W. Hughes See entry no. 1867

Dictionaries, thesauri, classifications

5788 A+ Materials Science and Engineering: Glossary of Terms
J. McCarthy
www13.brinkster.com/justinmc/glossary/index.html
Personal interest site providing comprehensive glossary of materials science and engineering terms as well as listings of key web-based and other resources.

5789 Concise dictionary of materials science: structure and characterization of polycrystalline materials
V. Novikov CRC Press, 2003, 272pp. $159.95. ISBN 0849309700.
Contains more than 1400 terms commonly used in modern literature, research, and practice; includes a German-English glossary, reflecting the large number of items of materials science literature published in German.

5790 Dictionary of composite materials technology
S.M. Lee, ed. Technomic Publishing, 2001, 160pp. $64.95. ISBN 0877626006.
http://composite.about.com/cs/compositedefns/l/blglossary.htm
Over 6000 definitions of terms used in both the scientific and engineering aspects of composite materials (in the broadest sense), from simple fibrous materials to the most advanced aerospace applications.

See website for an expanded version of the original print version published by CRC Press (and details of many other useful resources).

- **International encyclopedia of composites S.M. Lee, ed.** Wiley, 1997, 3293pp. $2200.00. ISBN 0471187062. Six v. originally published 1989–1991, and described as 'the only true encyclopedia on composite materials and related process technology ... The contributors came from such significant institutions as Boeing, Dupont, Ford, ICI, MIT and NASA'.

5791 Dictionary of engineering materials
U. Erb and H. Keller, eds Wiley, 2004, 1314pp. $238.00. ISBN 0471444367.
Detailed entries for some 25,000 generic, trade-named, and trademarked engineering materials.

'The dictionary is highly recommended for engineering libraries and recommended for any science library. The work will be of use to all levels of education and expertise working in engineering and to laypeople who want to know more about a material.' (*E-STREAMS*)

5792 Dictionary of material science and high energy physics
D. Basu, ed. CRC Press, 2001, 346pp. $59.95. ISBN 0849328896.
While the focus is on the title subjects this text does touch

upon aspects of all the physical sciences. Over 4000 terms, definitions, and alternative meanings make up the body of this book. Cross-referencing can be carried out, but individual entries are intended to be self-contained.

5793 **Dictionary of materials and testing**
J.L. Tomsic and R.S. Hodder, eds; Society of Automotive Engineers 2nd edn, 2000, 422pp. $39.95. ISBN 0768005310.
Covers: Metals; Welding materials; Composites; Polymers; Plastics; Adhesives; Lubricants.

5794 **English–German dictionary of materials and process engineering**
C.G. Goetzel and L.K. Goetzel, eds; Deutsche Gesellschaft für Materialkunde Hanser Publishers, 1995, 753pp. €149.90. ISBN 1569901481.
Published in association with the German Association for Materials Science, this excellent dictionary covers alloys, ceramics, composites, metals and polymers, and is notable for the efforts of the authors to 'interrelate the true sense of the individual terms with actual usage in both languages, German and English'.

Technological dictionary of plastics materials
W.V. Titow See entry no. 5077

Laws, standards, codes

5795 **Encyclopaedia of international corrosion standards**
G.S. Fomin, ed.; Institute of Materials, Minerals and Mining Maney Publishing, 2003, 442pp. Translated from the Russian by A.D. Mercer; Edited and revised by Paul McIntyre, £96.00. ISBN 1902653718.
One of a series of reference volumes on international standards in various fields prepared by the Russian National Institute for Standardization. Detailed coverage with valuable commentary; 11 appendices list the relevant standards. No index.

Official & quasi-official bodies

NSF: Directorate for Mathematical and Physical Sciences
National Science Foundation See entry no. 397

Research centres & institutes

Air Force Research Laboratory
See entry no. 4898

5796 **CERAM** [UK]
www.ceram.co.uk
Formerly British Ceramic Research, CERAM is an 'internationally renowned centre of technical excellence for the ceramics and other materials-based industries'. Weekly news service; expert witnesses; detailed descriptions of its industry services.

European Synchrotron Facility
See entry no. 802

5797 **Manchester Materials Science Centre** [UK]
http://www2.umist.ac.uk/material
Now part of the amalgamated University of Manchester Institute of Science and Technology and Victoria University of Manchester. Major centre, their Research in Progress area of the site demonstrating the breadth of their involvements. Produce the *Journal of Corrosion Science and Engineering* (www.jcse.org), Manchester also having a Corrosion and Protection Centre.

National Institute of Biomedical Imaging and Bioengineering
See entry no. 3645

Steel Construction Institute
See entry no. 5181

Associations & societies

5798 **Abrasive Engineering Society** [USA]
www.abrasiveengineering.com
'Dedicated to promoting technical information about abrasives minerals and their uses. That includes abrasives grains and products such as grinding wheels, coated abrasives (sandpaper) and countless other items made from synthetic minerals as well as the myriad of tools and products that serve as accessories.' Densely packed site, but full of useful and regularly updated information.

5799 **Aluminium Federation** [UK]
www.alfed.org
Trade association representing the UK aluminium industry. Its online Technical Library gives access to details of some 12,000 articles, copies of which can be ordered online. There a series of useful Fact Sheets. Other online services are promised – though access to these may be restricted to members.

5800 **Aluminum Association** [USA]
www.aluminum.org
Trade association for producers of primary aluminium, recyclers and makers of semi-fabricated aluminium products, as well as suppliers to the industry. Aims to promote aluminium as the 'material of choice'. This website, some of which is restricted to members, provides news, production figures, information on events, and details of publications which can be purchased from the online bookstore.

- **Automotive Aluminum** www.autoaluminum.org. Extensive and well presented collection of information related to the use and prospective use of aluminium within the automobile industry.

5801 **American Ceramic Society**
www.ceramics.org
Provides its members (7500) and subscribers in 80 countries with access to periodicals and books, meetings and expositions, and on-line technical information. Useful About Ceramics section. Ceramic Links now references over 600 resources. Important group of serial and non-serial publications. Good website.

- **Ceramic Properties Databases** www.ceramics.org/cic/propertiesdb.asp. Excellent inventory of free and fee-based databases.

American Foundry Society
See entry no. 5687

American Institute of Steel Construction
See entry no. 5185

American Plastics Council
See entry no. 5085

American Welding Society
See entry no. 5688

5802 **ASM International: The Materials Information Society**
www.asminternational.org
Formerly the American Society of Metals and founded in 1913, ASM International is a major society, publishing a wide range of standards-related, serial, and other resources, and providing news, organizing events, and co-ordinating the work of a number of affiliate societies: Electronic Device Failure Analysis Society, Heat Treating Society; International Metallographic Society, Society of Carbide and Tool Engineers, Thermal Spray Society.

The website section 'Materials Info' gives details of ASM Materials Information Online, which 'makes it easy to search across the world's most comprehensive collection of materials property, process, and performance information to find the answers you need. Materials Information Online consists of four collections: ASM Handbooks Online, ASM Alloy Center Online, ASM Micrograph Center Online, and the ASM Failure Analysis Center Online. Work has already begun on the fifth collection, the Phase Diagram Center Online, to be released in late 2005'.

Among much else, there is an Ask ASM section, providing access to a set of discussion groups.

- **ASM materials engineering dictionary** J.R. Davis, ed. 1992, 555pp. $174.00. ISBN 0871704471. 10,000 entries covering materials, processes, and concepts related to ferrous and non-ferrous metals, plastics, ceramics, composites, and adhesives. Also 64 Technical Briefs that provide encyclopedia-type coverage of key material groups.

5803 **Association for Iron and Steel Technology** [USA]
www.aistech.org
Established January 2004 from the merger of the Iron and Steel Society and the Association of Iron and Steel Engineers, with a goal of advancing the technical development, production, processing and application of iron and steel. Good news section; library; publications; etc.

- **International Iron and Steel Institute** www.worldsteel.org. Very good source for statistics on the industry, including a section Fast Track Statistics designed as an 'executive summary'. Much other helpful information on this nice clean site. See also MATTER.
- **SteelLinks.com** www.steellinks.com. Extensive list of hierarchically categorized resource descriptions; regularly updated.

5804 **AVS Science and Technology Society** [USA]
www.avs.org
Committee founded in 1953 following a forum to discuss problems and applications of high vacuum technology; formalized as a society in 1961. Its concerns have now widened out considerably with, for instance, its Divisions treating an extensive range of topics: Advanced surface engineering; Applied surface science; Biomaterial interfaces; Electronic materials and processing; Magnetic interfaces and nanostructures; Nanometer-scale science and technology; Plasma science and technology; Surface science; Thin films; Vacuum technology.

There are now over 6000 members and the website provides access to details of a fruitful spectrum of resources covering the gamut from high-level academic journals to buyers' guides for equipment, services, and resources.

5805 **British Institute of Non-Destructive Testing**
www.bindt.org
'Non-destructive testing is the branch of engineering concerned with all methods of detecting and evaluating flaws in materials. Flaws can affect the serviceability of the material or structure, so NDT is important in guaranteeing safe operation as well as in quality control and assessing plant life. The flaws may be cracks or inclusions in welds and castings, or variations in structural properties which can lead to loss of strength or failure in service.'

Basic site – but providing access to a good range of current resources.

- **American Society for Nondestructive Testing** www.asnt.org. Membership over 9000 including a corporate membership of more than 400 companies. Develops standards, issues publications, provides education, runs events, etc. Good site.

British Metals Recycling Association
See entry no. 5567

5806 **European Aluminium Association**
www.eaa.net
Represents the aluminium industry in Europe. Statistics and information on the uses of aluminium. Publications. Educational resources. News. Links.

- **International Aluminium Institute** www.world-aluminium.org. Publishes a very useful set of statistics and provides much other helpful information about the industry and its environment.

5807 **European Powder Metallurgy Association**
www.epma.com
'The world's most comprehensive website on powder metallurgy'. Busy site which, however, has good background information on the technology, and a helpful Site Map. Worth exploring.

- **Metal Powder Industries Federation** www.mpif.org. 'The world's most comprehensive resource for information about Powder Metallurgy (P/M) and Particulate Materials.' Also access to the details of the work of APMI International, and the Center for Powder Metallurgy Technology.

5808 **European Society for Biomaterials**
www.esb-news.org
Founded 1976; now has approximately 600 members from 27 countries. Limited information at present, but likely to expand. Note the list of Sister Societies.

5809 **Institute of Materials, Minerals and Mining** [UK]
www.iom3.org
Created from the merger of the Institute of Materials and the Institution of Mining and Metallurgy – and early 2005 is proposing a further merger with the Institute of Packaging. A leading international professional body for the advancement of materials, minerals and mining to governments, industry, academia, the public and the professions.

The Institute provides an extensive set of Information Services, and houses a valuable Library.

■ **Materials World** IOM Communications Ltd Monthly. £42.00. ISSN 09678638. www.iom3.org/materialsworld. News about: Analysis/microscopy; Environment/sustainability; Industry/innovation; R&D; Materials/minerals processing; Minerals exploration/Mining technology; Professional development; Testing/inspection; Thermal processing, surface engineering/coating.

5810 **Materials Research Society**
www.mrs.org
'Brings together scientists, engineers and research managers from industry, government, academia and research laboratories to share findings in the research and development of new materials of technological importance. Founded in 1973, MRS now consists of more than 12,600 members from the United States – as well as over 50 other countries. The Society is different from that of single discipline professional societies because it encourages communication and technical information exchange across the various fields of science affecting materials.'

Wide range of resources, though – although labelled The Materials Gateway – once one got beyond the home page it seemed not the easiest of sites to navigate. However, there is a clearly laid out Site Map.

Minerals, Metals and Materials Society
See entry no. 4680

5811 **NACE International: The Corrosion Society** [USA]
www.nace.org
Established in 1943 by eleven corrosion engineers in the pipeline industry but has now become the largest organization in the world committed to the study of corrosion. Useful sets of resources (under the heading Journals) – including Corrosion Abstracts, information on standards, and a downloadable PDF NACE glossary of corrosion-related terms.

■ **COR-SUR: Corrosion Survey Database** www.knovel.com. Documents the performance of 87 (37 metal and 50 non-metal) materials in more than 1500 different chemical environments, the database now contains approximately 28,000 unique records.

Orgalime
See entry no. 5905

5812 **Society for Biomaterials** [USA]
www.biomaterials.org
Vision is 'to promote the discipline of biomaterials and their uses in medical and surgical devices including synthetic, natural, and biologically sourced materials. It is the premier Society for biomaterials education, and the leader in dissemination of biomaterials research for the benefit of humankind'.

5813 **Society of Rheology** [USA]
www.rheology.org
Long-established society concerned with the deformation and flow of matter. Site contains information for members, but also links to resources for those interested in pursuing a career or research in this field.

Portal & task environments

5814 **Advanced Materials and Processes Technology Information Analysis Center: AMPTIAC**
amptiac.alionscience.com
One of the DEFENSE TECHNICAL INFORMATION CENTER Information Analysis Centers, operated by Alion Science and Technology. Covers five functional areas: Ceramics and ceramic matrix composites; Electronic, optical, and photonic materials; Environmental protection and special function materials; Metals, alloys, and metal matrix composites; Organic structural materials and organic matrix composites.

Provides literature searches of its bibliographic database, which covers the material in its Library (containing some 220,000 technical books and reports), as well as documents from two other Alion-operated IACs: Reliability Analysis Center; Manufacturing Technology Information Analysis Center. The quarterly newsletter *AMPTIAC Quarterly* is now distributed to over 23,000 people. Many other products and services – including Ask an Expert.

5815 **AZoM: Metals, Ceramics, Polymers, Composites – An Engineers Resource**
www.azom.com
'A totally new concept in the field of Material Science publishing and information provision – AZoM.com (the A to Z of Materials) was formed with the primary aim of increasing the use of Advanced Materials by the engineering and design community worldwide. Over 21 million engineers now use the internet as part of their daily lives, yet the vast majority of them are still unaware what can be achieved by the use of advanced ceramics, novel metallic alloys or state of the art composites. AZoM is here to change that.'

Lively, wide-ranging site; commercial presence reasonably under control; a very good up-to-date gateway.

5816 **Biomaterials Network** [EUR]
www.biomat.net
A biomaterials portal providing access to news, conference notices, funding opportunities, course details, research project listings, company details and links to articles on publishers' websites. The portal is sponsored by the EUROPEAN SOCIETY FOR BIOMATERIALS. The strength of this site is the comprehensive and up-to-date lists it provides, such as a list of the latest market reports that have been published in the biomaterials field.

5817 **Corrosion Source: The One Stop Corrosion and Materials Information Resource**
www.corrosionsource.com [FEE-BASED]
Commercially based site providing a very wide range and depth of resources organized under headings such as: Discussions; Handbook; Hot Topics; Learning Center; Reports Online; Tools; Technical Library; Training Center. Check the Premium Content Site Map.

Eureka
See entry no. 5384

5818 **Future Materials: Technology for Competitive Advantage** [AUS]
www.future.org.au
This is the marketing name for the Australian Materials Technology Network, which is sponsored by the Australian Government's AusIndustry, the Institute of Materials

Engineering Australasia, and a group of Australian university research institutes. The aim is to provide Australian companies with easy access to the kind of services and equipment previously difficult to attain.

Johnson Matthey
See entry no. 4693

5819 **Materials Information Solutions: Software – Data – Customization**
Granta Design Ltd.
www.granta.co.uk
'The leading materials information technology (IT) provider, supplying the world's first and only comprehensive materials IT system. The goal of everything we do is to help our customers unlock the potential of materials information. Our software enables design engineers, material and process professionals, and materials developers to get the most from engineering materials and manufacturing processes. Our enterprise-wide materials information systems help manufacturers realise multi-million dollar benefits in reduced product cost, enhanced performance, improved quality, and speedier time-to-market. Our educational packages are helping university and college professors to transform the effectiveness and popularity of course on materials and manufacturing processes.'

- **MatData.Net ASM International**. http://matdata.net. 'The fast way to find materials information. It focuses exclusively on information relating to the professional application of materials and processes. Only the highest quality information sources are included . .' An excellent search engine.

5820 **MATTER**
University of Liverpool
www.matter.org.uk
Non-profit consortium of UK academic materials science departments which develops and helps integrate computer-based learning materials into mainstream teaching. It is led by the University of Liverpool and was originally funded by the UK's Teaching and Learning Technology Programme. Since the end of that Programme they have developed a range of valuable teaching resources using an 'industry standard' software development protocol (see Guide for Storyboard Authors). Many other good resources on this very well designed site.

- **AluMATTER University of Liverpool and European Aluminium Association**. aluminium.matter.org.uk. Freely accessible website that aims to provide innovative and interactive e-learning tools for aluminium science and technology.
- **AluSELECT** http://aluminium.matter.org.uk/aluselect. Data about mechanical, physical and chemical properties of aluminium alloys to aide selection of an appropriate alloy and temper for an application. Also glossary of more than 450 definitions of technical terms with French/German translations.
- **Glossary of materials science** www.matter.org.uk/glossary. Originally developed to support Materials Science on CD-ROM. Since then, it has been converted to a web format, and has been continuously updated.
- **Materials Science on CD-ROM** www.matter.org.uk/matscicdrom. Award winning interactive learning tool which covers crystallography, defects, dislocations, phase diagrams, diffusion, nucleation, elasticity and aluminium alloys, composite materials and polymers.
- **SteelMATTER** www.matter.org.uk/steelmatter. Interactive website for ferrous metallurgy produced in conjunction with Corus (formerly British Steel).
- **Steeluniversity.org International Iron and Steel Institute**. http://ilsap.matter.org.uk. Co-operative venture with IISI which in 2004 was winner of the European Academic Software Award.

5821 **MatWeb: Material Property Data**
Automation Creations, Inc.
www.matls.com
A freely accessible valuable compendium of data sheets for over 45,000 metals, plastics, ceramics, and composites. 'The heart of MatWeb is a searchable database of material data sheets, including property information on thermoplastic and thermoset polymers such as ABS, nylon, polycarbonate, polyester, polyethylene and polypropylene; metals such as aluminum, cobalt, copper, lead, magnesium, nickel, steel, superalloys, titanium and zinc alloys; ceramics; plus semiconductors, fibers, and other engineering materials.' Other useful resources – including a set of MatWeb Forums.

Plastics.com
See entry no. 5095

Polysort: The Power of Many
See entry no. 5096

5822 **PSIgate: Materials Science**
University of Manchester and Resource Discovery Network
www.psigate.ac.uk/newsite/materials-gateway.html
At end 2004 had evaluative descriptions of over 1600 materials science resources. There are sub-sections Materials Lecture Notes and Materials Tutorials, as well as a listing of the latest additions to the section (available as an RSS feed).

5823 **Steel Works** [USA]
American Iron and Steel Institute
www.steel.org
Well designed rich site offered by the Institute – which 'is comprised of 31 member companies, including integrated and electric furnace steelmakers, and 118 associate and affiliate members who are suppliers to or customers of the steel industry. AISI's member companies represent approximately 75 percent of both US and North American steel capacity'. Good promotional sections on industry characteristics and initiatives but including also sets of AISI Statistics and Fact Sheets. An extensive Steel Links section. The Learning Center has a good glossary of terms, updated November 2004.

Tin Technology
See entry no. 4698

5824 **UK Centre for Materials Education**
University of Liverpool and Higher Education Academy
www.materials.ac.uk
One of the 24 subject centres promoting high quality learning and teaching through the development and transfer of good practices within UK higher and further education. Provides 12 guides for lecturers; materials awareness projects; database of resources (c.1000): lists new and recently updated resources; etc.

Discovering print & electronic resources

Aluminium Industry Abstracts
Aluminum Association and European Aluminium Association See entry no. 4699

5825 **Materials Science**
CSA.
www.csa.com/e_products/databases-collections.php
CSA provide integrated access to a wide range of materials science datasets, key exemplars of which are referenced below.

- **Aluminium Industry Abstracts** www.csa.com/factsheets/aia-set-c.php.
- **Ceramic Abstracts/World Ceramics Abstracts** www.csa.com/factsheets/wca-set-c.php.
- **Copper Data Center Database** http://oh1.csa.com/factsheets/copper-set-c.php.
- **Corrosion Abstracts** www.csa.com/factsheets/corrosion-set-c.php.
- **CSA Materials Research Database with METADEX** www.csa.com/factsheets/materials-set-c.php.
- **Engineered Materials Abstracts** www.csa.com/factsheets/emaclust-set-c.php. (Subsets are: Advanced Polymers Abstracts; Composites Industry Abstracts; Ceramics).
- **Materials Business File** www.csa.com/factsheets/mbf-set-c.php.
- **Materials Science: A SAGE Full-Text Collection** www.csa.com/factsheets/sagemat-set-c.php.
- **Weldasearch** www.csa.com/factsheets/weldasearch-set-c.php.

5826 **RDN Virtual Training Suite: Materials Engineering**
[UK]
J. Dagg; University of Sheffield and Resource Discovery Network
www.vts.rdn.ac.uk/tutorial/materials
One of the useful tutorials created by subject-specialists from universities and professional organizations across the UK.

5827 **Solid State and Superconductivity Abstracts**
CSA, 1981–. $1695.00. ISSN 08965900.
www.csa.com/factsheets/solid-state-set-c.php [DESCRIPTION]
Global coverage on all aspects of theory, production, and application of solid state materials and devices, as well as the new high- and low-temperature superconductivity technology. Circa 220,000 records, September 2004; 15–20,000 records added per year.
Available online: see website.

5828 **Worldwide Composites Search Engine**
Deltronix Enterprises.
www.wwcomposites.com
Frequently updated site: see Latest Site Additions. 'Our search engine only contains information on companies and products which we deem are relevant to the composites industry. All submissions to the database are reviewed by our staff ... As an example, associations, manufacturers, component fabricators, distributors and services involved with Advanced Composites (Kevlar, Graphite, Fiberglass) prepregs, fabrics, tow, braiding, film adhesives, potting compounds, core materials, autoclave, vacuum bonding, sandwich panels would all be acceptable additions to our database.'

Digital data, image & text collections

5829 **ISSB**
www.issb.co.uk
'Offers a wide range of publications and custom reports covering UK, European and Global trade in steel and raw materials. The company maintains a comprehensive database of international trade in steel and steelmaking products. There is currently no direct public access to the database.'

World Bureau of Metal Statistics
See entry no. 4702

Directories & encyclopedias

5830 **CASTI Metals Data Book Series**
Casti Publishing Inc.
www.casti.ca
Well established series, now available exclusively through ASM International. Access collectively to over one million data items, with comprehensive cross-referencing to national and international standards, as well as chemical compositions, mechanical and physical properties. There is a companion *CASTI Corrosion Series*. Available as print or CD-ROM or in combination (the binding of the print versions being rather poor).

5831 **Characterization of materials**
E.N. Kaufmann, ed. Wiley-Interscience, 2003, 1392pp. 2 v., $450.00. ISBN 0471268828.
www.mrw.interscience.wiley.com [FEE-BASED]
Major work containing about 150 commissioned articles, primarily grouped according to the measurement 'probe' upon which a method relies: electrons, ions, x-rays, heat, light, etc. However, it is recognized that 'the field is too complex for this not to be an oversimplification and indeed some logical inconsistencies are inevitable'. The Preface explains how the broad approach adopted has then been refined.
Available online: see website.

Condensed encyclopedia of polymer engineering terms
N.P. Cheremisinoff See entry no. 5106

5832 **Encyclopedia of materials: science and technology**
K.H.J. Buschow [et al.], eds Elsevier, 2001, 9913pp. 11 v., £3490.00. ISBN 0080431526.
www1.elsevier.com/emsat [FEE-BASED]
The only reference work to cover all aspects of the broad and interdisciplinary field of materials science. With more than 1800 articles written by over 1500 internationally recognized experts, each article provides a concise overview of a particular aspect of the field. The content is enhanced by over 11,000 tables and 7300 diagrams. All classes of materials and the phenomena related to them are covered, ranging from optical and dendritic phenomena to characterization of materials and crystalline polymers.
Available online: see website.

5833 **Encyclopedia of materials science and engineering**
M.B. Bever, ed. MIT Press/Pergamon, 1986. 8 v. ISBN 0262022338.
Major work which provided the first unified treatment of this emerging field. 1500 articles from scientists and engineers in more than 20 countries.

Encyclopedia of smart materials
M.M. Schwartz, ed. See entry no. 3665

5834 **Key to aluminium alloys (Aluminium-Schlüssel)**
J. Datta, ed. 6th edn, Aluminium-Verlag Marketing & Kommunikation, 2003, 284pp. €155.00. ISBN 3870172738.
www.alu-verlag.com/index_e.htm [DESCRIPTION]
A comprehensive guide to worldwide aluminium standards, designations and compositions. The book is particularly useful for quick comparison of alloy designations and for looking up standard designations and compositions in various countries and from international organizations. Also enables identification of unfamiliar alloy designations and of alloys by known chemical composition. Current and inactive/old designations and compositions for alloys are covered and older data has been retained in order to be able to interpret earlier literature and standards.
See website for details of much other relevant material (but often only in German).

Plastics materials and processes
C.A. Harper See entry no. 5111

Handbooks & manuals

Aerospace structural metals handbook
See entry no. 4938

Aluminum structures: a guide to their specifications and design
J.R. Kissell and R.L. Ferry See entry no. 5234

Atomic and electronic structures of solids
E. Kaxiras See entry no. 1880

BASF handbook on basics of coating technology
A. Goldschmidt and H.-J. Streitberger See entry no. 5116

The biomedical engineering handbook
J.D. Bronzino, ed. See entry no. 3666

5835 **Carbon alloys: novel concepts to develop carbon science and technology**
E. Yasuda [et al.], eds Elsevier, 2003, 569pp. £113.50. ISBN 0080441637.
The concept of 'carbon alloys' was initiated in Japan as a national project and is now recognized internationally. Five parts: Definitions and approaches to carbon alloys; Analyses of results in terms of controlling the locations of other alloying elements; Typical carbon alloys and their preparation; Characterization of carbon alloys; Development and application of carbon alloys. There is a companion *Carbon dictionary*, but in Japanese (and all the contributors are based in Japan). Good subject index.

Ceramic processing and sintering
M.N. Rahaman See entry no. 5119

5836 **Comprehensive composite materials**
A Kelly and C Zweben, eds Elsevier, 2000, 5300pp. £2035.00. ISBN 0080429939.
www1.elsevier.com/homepage/sai/compcomp [DESCRIPTION]
Major treatise in six volumes: Fibre reinforcements and general theory of composites; Polymer matrix composites; Metal matrix composites; Carbon/carbon, cement and ceramic matrix composites; Test methods, non-destructive evaluation and smart materials; Design and applications
Available online: see website.

5837 **Comprehensive structural integrity**
I. Milne, R.O. Ritchie and B. Karihaloo, eds Pergamon, 2003, 7750pp. 10 v., $4950.00. ISBN 0080437494.
www.sciencedirect.com/science/referenceworks [FEE-BASED]
'Structural integrity' is referred to by the UK Forum for Engineering Structural Integrity as 'safety, reliability, durability, integrity and life time evaluations of and improvements to engineering products'. Railways, automobiles, aircraft, roads and bridges, chemical plant, shipping, off-shore structures, computer software, energy production, transmission systems, etc. all require continuous surveillance and improvements to reduce the possibility of serious accidents due to lifetime deterioration.

This major work has nine volumes (plus an index volume): Structural integrity assessment – examples and case studies; Fundamental theories and mechanisms of failure; Numerical and computational methods; Cyclic loading and fatigue; Creep and high temperature failure; Environmentally-assisted fracture; Practical failure assessment methods; Interfacial and nanoscale failure; Bioengineering.
Available online: see website.

Condensed matter physics: crystals, liquids, liquid crystals, and polymers
G. Strobl, ed. See entry no. 1882

Construction materials reference book
D.K. Doran, ed. See entry no. 5346

5838 **The corrosion monitoring handbook**
N. Rothwell and M. Tullmin Coxmoor, 2000, 180pp. £39.00. ISBN 1901892034.
www.coxmoor.com/corrosionbook.html [DESCRIPTION]
One of a useful set of overviews within the publisher's *Machine and Systems Condition Monitoring Series.*

5839 **CRC materials science and engineering handbook**
J.F. Shackleford and W. Alexander 3rd edn, CRC Press, 2001, 1949pp. $199.95. ISBN 0849326966.
www.engnetbase.com
Latest edition of bestselling source of data on engineering materials. Excellent coverage and ease of use.
Available online: see website.

5840 **DECHEMA corrosion handbook: corrosive agents and their interaction with materials**
www.dechema.de/The_DECHEMA-lang-en.html
DECHEMA Gesellschaft für Chemische Technik und Biotechnologie e.V. (Society for Chemical Engineering and Biotechnology) is a non-profit-making scientific and technical society, founded in 1926 and based in Frankfurt on Main. Its aim is 'to promote research and technical advances in the areas of chemical engineering, biotechnology and environmental protection'.

This handbook – described within the Information Systems section of their website – is a major work whose new edition (from Wiley) will gradually replace the classic 14-volume handbook published 1987–1993. Check the site for the wide range of other key products and services offered by the Society.

Electronic materials and processes handbook
C.A. Harper, ed. See entry no. 5478

5841 Handbook of advanced ceramics
S. Somiya [et al.], eds Academic Press, 2003, 1320pp. 2 v.: V. 1. Materials science; V. 2. Processing and their applications, £255.00. ISBN 0126546401.

Invited experts cover the present state of advanced ceramics: from fundamental science and processing to application. Comprehensive bibliographies; diagrams; illustrations. Detailed indexes in each volume.

Handbook of advanced electronic and photonic materials and devices
H.S. Nalwa, ed. See entry no. 5485

5842 Handbook of advanced materials: enabling new designs
J.K. Wessel Wiley, 2004, 656pp. $130.00. ISBN 0471454753.

Multi-author work covering the full range of advanced ceramic, metal and polymer-based materials.

'*The Handbook of Advanced Materials* contains the most recent information designers and engineers need to know ... this outstanding monograph is an essential reference for engineers.' (*Polymer News*)

5843 Handbook of aluminum
G.E. Totten and D.S. Mackenzie, eds Marcel Dekker, 2003.

V. 1 (1403 pp, $250.00, ISBN 0824704940) covers *Physical metallurgy and processes*; V. 2 (736 pp, $195.00, ISBN 0824708962) *Alloy production and materials manufacture* with comprehensive coverage of all aspects.

'An indispensable acquisition for academic engineering libraries and industrial libraries ... Essential.' (*Choice*)

5844 Handbook of building materials for fire protection
C.A. Harper, ed. McGraw-Hill, 2003, 800pp. $125.00. ISBN 0071388915.

Completely devoted to building and construction materials in the field of fire engineering. Covers the typical properties of selected building materials and provides all the information and guidelines necessary to synthesize, manufacture and utilize materials.

5845 Handbook of elastic properties of solids, liquids and gases
M. Levy, H. Bass and R. Stern, ed. Academic Press, 2000, 1959pp. 4 v., $1750.00. ISBN 0124457606.

Comprehensive tabulated reference to information regarding the elastic properties of particular materials (solids, liquids, and gases) for physicists or materials scientists. Covers substances from the mundane (e.g. cork, food, cement), to the more esoteric (e.g. superfluid helium 3, two dimensional solids, fullerines etc.). Particular coverage is given to the propagation of sound in these various media.

Handbook of hard coatings
R.F. Bunshah and C. Weissmantel, eds See entry no. 5137

5846 Handbook of industrial materials
I. Purvis, ed. 2nd edn, Elsevier Advanced Technology, 1992, 803pp. $190.25. ISBN 0946395837.

Updated to include recent major advances made in ceramics and polymer technology, this handbook became the most up-to-date source of information on industrial materials. Packed with vital information for all industries. Excellent coverage of ceramics, composites, metals, polymers, etc.

Handbook of materials for medical devices
J.R. Davis, ed.; ASM International See entry no. 3669

Handbook of materials for product design
C.A. Harper, ed. See entry no. 5397

5847 Handbook of materials selection
M. Kutz, ed. Wiley, 2002, 1497pp. $250.00. ISBN 0471359246.

Multi-author text which – after an introductory review of quantitative methods of materials selection – covers in 13 chapters all the key variants of metals, plastics, ceramics and composites. There are then four very useful chapters on Finding and managing materials information and data: How to find materials properties data; Sources of materials data; Managing materials data; Information for materials procurement and disposal.

The remaining 28 chapters are organized into four parts: Testing and inspection; Failure analysis; Manufacturing; Applications and uses. A major achievement.

'will undoubtedly become a classic of its genre.' (*Journal of Materials Technology*)

Handbook of metallurgical process design
G.E. Totten, K. Funatani and L. Xie, eds See entry no. 5727

5848 Handbook of nondestructive evaluation
C.J. Hellier McGraw-Hill, 2001, 800pp. $110.00. ISBN 0070281211.

Good overview. Chapters are: Introduction to nondestructive testing; Discontinuities – origins and classification; Visual testing; Penetrant testing; Magnetic particle testing; Radiographic testing; Ultrasonic testing; Eddy current testing; Thermal infrared testing; Acoustic emission testing.

Handbook of plastics analysis
H. Lobo and J.V. Bonilla, eds See entry no. 5140

5849 Handbook of superconducting materials
D. Cardwell and D. Ginley, eds Institute of Physics Publishing, 2002, 1000pp. £399.00. ISBN 0750308982.

This is a guide to the techniques for fabricating and analysing superconducting materials. Intended for use by graduate and professional material scientists and electrical engineers who require easy access to practical standard reference information on fabrication and characterization techniques.

5850 Handbook of surface and nanometrology
D.J. Whitehouse Institute of Physics Publishing, 2002, 1100pp. £299.00. ISBN 0750305835.

Objective is to bring two metrologies together in the nano range (taken to be 100nm down to about 0.1nm): the engineer keen to jump down many scales of size from automotive type components to those of mm or even less; the physicist pushing up from even smaller scales anxious to build practical working devices.

Mathematically intensive text that recognizes the dearth of proven and tested facts; but which enhances such facts as there are with suggestions, new ideas and proceedings to help gel 'the new discipline'. Bibliographies. Glossary. Index.

5851 **Handbook of surfaces and interfaces of materials**
H.S. Nalwa, ed. Academic Press, 2001, 2911pp. 5 v, $2780.00. ISBN 0125139101.
http://books.elsevier.com/companions [COMPANION]
Major treatise. V.1. Surface and interface phenomena. V. 2. Surface characterization and properties; V. 3. Nanostructures, micelles, and colloids. V 4. Thin films and layers. V. 5. Biointerfaces and applications. 62 state-of-the-art review chapters written by 120 world-leading experts from 23 countries; more than 15,000 bibliographic citations and several thousand illustrations, figures, tables and equations.

Handbook of thin film materials
H.S. Nalwa, ed. See entry no. 5493

Inorganic materials chemistry desk reference
D. Sangeeta and J.R. LaGraff See entry no. 1748

5852 **Integrated biomaterials science**
R. Barbucci, ed. Kluwer Academic/Plenum, 2002, 1037pp. £130.50. ISBN 0306466783.
http://ebooks.springerlink.com/Details.aspx
Contributed chapters covering a very wide spectrum of applications within medical technology. Good entrée to the area.
Available online: see website.

5853 **Key to steel: Stahlschlüssel**
C.W. Wegst, ed. 20th edn, Verlag Stahlschlüssel, 2004, 720pp. In English, French and German, $165.00. ISBN 3922599206.
Latest edn includes more than 45,000 standard designations and trade names from approximately 250 steelmakers and suppliers. Materials covered include structural steels, tool steels, valve steels, high-temperature steels and alloys, non-magnetic steels, stainless and heat-resisting steels, stainless steel castings, heat-resistant steel castings, and welding filler materials. Standards and designations from 23 countries are cross-referenced.

Machine design databook
K. Lingaiah, ed. See entry no. 5400

5854 **The Materials selector**
N A Waterman and M F Ashby, ed. 2nd edn, Chapman & Hall, 1997, 2680pp. 3 v., $1272.25. ISBN 0412615509.
Standard reference work with V. 1 addressing the initial stages in solving a materials selection problem, providing the background to all aspects of materials behaviour, and discussing manufacturing processes; V. 2 detailing the performance of metals and ceramics; and V. 3 covering the performance of polymers, thermosets, elastomers, and composites.

5855 **Metallic materials: physical, mechanical, and corrosion properties**
P.A. Schweitzer, comp. Marcel Dekker, 2003, 702pp. $199.95. ISBN 0824708784.
Aims to provide all the data needed when choosing commercially available metallic materials to enable an optimal choice of construction material. Two introductory chapters with general treatments of physical and mechanical properties, and of corrosion of metallic materials, followed by 24 chapters reviewing the full range of currently available steels and alloys.
Series: Corrosion Technology, 19.

- **International metallic materials cross reference J.G. Gensure and D.L. Potts** 3rd edn, Genium Publishing, 1998. $199.00. http://www.genium.com/drafting/icd3.shtml [DESCRIPTION]. Comprehensive reference covering 45,000 materials designations classified into 59 systems.

5856 **Physical metallurgy handbook**
A.K. Sinha McGraw-Hill, 2003, 1100pp. $150.00. ISBN 0070579865.
'The most comprehensive single-source guide to the production of metals and minerals ever published. Despite the advent of 'high-tech' materials such as polymers, advanced ceramics, and graphite and boron fibre, the age of metals is far from over. The development of new alloys continues to be driven by the need for better, cheaper, more versatile engineering materials.'

5857 **The physics and chemistry of materials**
J.I. Gersten and F.W. Smith Wiley, 2001, 826pp. $125.00. ISBN 0471057940.
Five parts: Structure of materials, including crystal structure, bonding in solids, diffraction and the reciprocal lattice, and order and disorder in solids; Physical properties of materials, including electrical, thermal, optical, magnetic, and mechanical properties; Classes of materials, including semiconductors, superconductors, magnetic materials, and optical materials in addition to metals, ceramics, polymers, dielectrics, and ferroelectrics; Surfaces, thin films, interfaces, and multilayers; Synthesis and processing.
'an excellent text for advanced students and an excellent reference for more experienced chemists ... its range of coverage ... is certainly unmatched.' (*Journal of Chemical Education*)
'a fine addition to the library of material science ... Highly recommended' (*Choice*)

Plastics materials
J.A. Brydson See entry no. 5145

5858 **Smithells metals reference book**
W.F. Gale and T.C. Totemeier 8th edn, Elsevier Butterworth-Heinemann, 2004, 1856pp. £140.00. ISBN 0750675098.
Classic authoritative reference resource continually updated: very detailed compendium of information on the physical, electrical, mechanical and magnetic properties of metals. Up-to-date with all international standards. Relatively small typefaces; but the careful design makes the whole easy to navigate and use. There is a useful Bibliography of some sources of metallurgical information which, however, does not extend to web-based resources.

Elsevier also publish *Smithells light metals handbook* (1998).

5859 **Structure and properties of engineering materials**
D.P. Henkel and A.W. Pense 5th edn, McGraw-Hill, 2001, 512pp. £44.99. ISBN 0071201343.
www.mhhe.com/engcs/materials/henkel [COMPANION]
Well established manual providing detailed coverage of metals, metal alloys, polymers, ceramics and composites.

5860 **Uhlig's corrosion handbook**
R.W. Revie, ed. 2nd edn, Wiley, 2000, 1301pp. $265.00. ISBN 0471157775.
www.wiley.com/WileyCDA [DESCRIPTION]
Revised edn of the classic handbook published in 1948.
Series: Electrochemical Society.
'excellent handbook ... an excellent sourcebook on a wide range of corrosion topics.' (*Chemical Engineering Research & Design*)

Keeping up-to-date

5861 **Annual Review of Materials Research**
Annual Reviews Inc, 2004. $200.00. ISBN 0824317343 ISSN 15317331.
www.annualreviews.org
The 12 reviews in the 2004 volume all had the theme Bio and Nanobiomaterials.

Mechanical Engineering

air conditioning • bearings & shafts • boilers • cogeneration • combustion engineering • compressed air equipment • diesel engines • dynamics • engineering mechanics • engines • experimental mechanics • flow engineering • fluid dynamics • fluid engineering • fluid mechanics • fluid power • friction • gas turbines • gears • heating • internal combustion engines • locomotives • lubrication • machinery • mechanical stress and strain • mechanics • pneumatics • power plants • power transmission • pressure equipment • pumps • railways • refrigeration • rheology • sports engineering • statics • thermal technology • tribology • turbines • turbulence • vacuum technology • valves • ventilation • vibration

Introductions to the subject

5862 **Classical mechanics**
H. Goldstein, C.P. Poole and J.L. Safko 3rd edn, Addison-Wesley, 2002, 638pp. $110.00. ISBN 0201657023.
'For more than 30 years, Classical Mechanics has been the standard text for advanced and graduate level courses on the subject. This revision retains all the best features of the Second Edition while including new material reflecting advances in nonlinear dynamics, chaos, and fractal geometries.'

5863 **Design of machinery: an introduction to the synthesis and analysis of mechanisms and machines**
R.L. Norton 3rd edn, McGraw-Hill, 2004, 858pp. Reprint of 1998 edn, $140.31. ISBN 0073109444.
www.designofmachinery.com/DOM [DESCRIPTION]
Well established text whose foremost goal is 'to convey the art of the design process and the fundamentals of kinematics and dynamics in order to prepare students to successfully tackle genuine engineering problems encountered in practice'.
Series: McGraw-Hill Series in Mechanical Engineering.

5864 **Engineering mechanics**
J.L. Meriam and L.G. Kraige, eds 5th edn, Wiley, 2001.
General student text, summarizing basic concepts, with problem-solving exercises. There are many similar introductory volumes in print, each with their adherents. This has the advantage of crisp layout and illustrative material.
- **V. 1. Statics** 494pp. $122.95. ISBN 0471406465.
- **V. 2. Dynamics** 736pp. $122.95. ISBN 0471406457.

Fundamentals of heat and mass transfer
F.P. Incropera and D.P. DeWitt See entry no. 5053

5865 **History of tribology**
D. Dowson Professional Engineering Publishing Ltd, 1998, 768pp. £98.00. ISBN 186058070X.
The development of tribology – 'The study of friction, wear, lubrication, and the design of bearings; the science of interacting surfaces in relative motion' (*Oxford Dictionary of English*) – presented chronologically from the prehistoric era to the Millennium. Each chapter covers technical and industrial developments and presents the key pioneers of each time period. Detailed biographies appear in the appendix and the main organizations in the field of tribology are listed.

Instrumentation and control systems
W. Bolton See entry no. 5407

5866 **Introduction to internal combustion engines**
R. Stone 3rd edn, Macmillan, 1999, 664pp. £29.99. ISBN 0333740130.
Book aimed at undergraduates. Covers commercial and economic aspects of internal combustion engines as well as the key topics of thermodynamics and combustion. This edition provides further worked examples and problem-solving exercises with tables and calculations.

5867 **An introduction to mechanical engineering**
J. Wickert Brooks/Cole, 2004, 448pp. $77.95. ISBN 053439132X.
www.brookscole.com/pubco/pub_companion.html [COMPANION]
Eight chapters: The mechanical engineering profession; Problem-solving skills; Machine components and tools; Forces in structures and fluids; Materials and stresses; Thermal and energy systems; Motion of machinery; Mechanical design.

Introduction to structural dynamics and aeroelasticity
D.H. Hodges and G.A. Pierce See entry no. 4876

5868 **Mechanical engineering principles**
J. Bird and C. Ross Newnes, 2002, 290pp. £17.99. ISBN 0750652284.
A student-friendly introduction to core engineering topics which does not assume any background in engineering studies. Includes over 600 problems and 400 worked examples.

5869 **Mechanical science**
W. Bolton 2nd edn, Blackwell Scientific, 1998, 496pp. £22.50. ISBN 0632049146.
A single volume introduction to the subject, intended as a preparatory text for students of mechanical engineering. The volume discusses the broad themes and general principles of statics, dynamics, mechanics of materials and the mechanics of machines.

5870 **Mechanics of materials**
J.M. Gere 5th edn, Nelson Thornes, 2002, 944pp. £30.95. ISBN 0748766758.
Good overview structured: Tension, compression, and shear; Axially loaded members; Torsion; Shear forces and bending moments; Stresses in beams; Analysis of stress and strain; Applications of plane stress; Deflections of beams; Statically indeterminate beams; Columns; Review of centroids and moments of inertia. Appendices treat properties of various types of materials.

Principles of heat transfer
F. Kreith and M.S. Bohn See entry no. 5065

5871 **Railway engineering**
V.A. Profillidis 2nd edn, Ashgate, 2000, 291pp. Translated from Greek, £61.00. ISBN 0754612791.
Clear, concisely presented introduction with good use of graphics. Structured: Railways and transport; The track system; Railway subgrade; Mechanical behaviour of track; The rail; Sleepers – fastenings; Ballast; Transverse effects – derailment; Track layout; Switches and crossings; Track maintenance; Train dynamics; Diesel and electric traction.
'The reader must ... regard this book as a comprehensive base text on railway infrastructure ... it provides useful information on European practices that are seldom covered in similar British texts. It is well written, presenting information in a logical and compartmentalized manner' (*Journal of Rail and Rapid Transit*)

5872 **Various and ingenious machines: the early history of mechanical engineering**
B. Lawton Brill Academic Publishers, 2004. €225.00. ISBN 9004136096.
V.1. Power generation and transport; V.2. Manufacturing and weapons technology. 'Describes the early history of mechanical engineering from prehistory, when mining and agriculture first appear, to the beginnings of industrialization. The old definition that "if it moves it's mechanical" is used.'
Series: Technology and Change in History.

Dictionaries, thesauri, classifications

5873 **The CIMAC Lexicon**
International Council on Combustion Engines
www.cimac.com/cimaclexicon/index1_lexicon.htm
Helpful easy to use lexicon of technical terms used in the internal combustion engine and gas turbine industries translated into Dutch, English, French, German, Italian, and Spanish. Information about the work of the Council, including of its Working Groups: Exhaust Emission; Users; Fuels and Lubricants; Operation and Maintenance; Classification. Some information only accessible to CIMAC members.

5874 **Dictionary of mechanical engineering**
G.H.F. Nayler; Society of Automotive Engineers 4th edn, Butterworth-Heinemann, 1996, 454pp. $69.95. ISBN 1560917547.
Although there are perhaps far too many branches of mechanical engineering to produce a truly comprehensive guide to technical terms, this compact dictionary attempts to bring together terms in use for 'the production of, the means for, and the utilization of, mechanical power in engines, transport and mechanisms'.

Dictionnaire d'automatique de génie électrique et de productique: anglais–français, français–anglais (Systems and control dictionary: English–French, French–English)
P. Borne and N. Quayle, ed. See entry no. 5670

5875 **International dictionary of heating, ventilating and air conditioning**
Federation of European Heating, Ventilating and Air-conditioning Associations 2nd edn, Spon, 1994, 793pp. £140.00. ISBN 041915390X.
A multilingual dictionary consisting of some 4000 terms in English, with their translations, together with alphabetical indexes for the other 11 languages covered: French, German, Italian, Danish, Finnish, Dutch, Spanish, Swedish, Hungarian, Polish and Russian.
1st edn 1982.

5876 **The railway dictionary: with index of themes**
A.A. Jackson 3rd edn, Sutton, 2000, 368pp. £25.00. ISBN 075092554X.
A reference work for both enthusiasts and professionals to the often specialist language which has developed around railways over 200 years. International in scope, the dictionary covers all aspects of railway terminology, past and present, and includes real names, abbreviations and slang.

5877 **Railway Object Name Thesaurus**
MDA
www.mda.org.uk/railway
Valuable compilation produced by the Railway Terminology Working Group. Lists 4015 terms of which 3165 are preferred terms, 372 non-preferred, and 478 are Class terms, Grouping terms and Facet indicators.
- **Waterways Object Name Thesaurus MDA.** www.mda.org.uk/texts.htm [DESCRIPTION]. Produced by the *Waterways Terminology Working Group*.

5878 **Wörterbuch Maschinenbau und Tribologie: Deutsch–Englisch/Englisch–Deutsch (Dictionary machine engineering and tribology: German–English/English–German)**
F. Wunsch Springer, 2004, 1444pp. Includes CD-ROM, £164.50. ISBN 354067666X.
Covers approximately 75,000 English and American technical terms in mechanical engineering, including materials, metallurgy, tribology, etc.

Laws, standards, codes

5879 **ANSI/HI pump standards**
American National Standards Institute and Hydraulic Institute
2003, 1100pp. Print, CD-ROM and web-based formats available.
www.pumps.org
Standards overseen by this US-based non-profit industry association. Arranged by type, the website offers nomenclature, definitions, applications and operation for rotary pumps, centrifugal pumps, centrifugal/general/vertical, vertical pumps and reciprocating pumps.

5880 ASME boiler and pressure vessel code: an international code
American Society of Mechanical Engineers 2004. $10,600.00.
www.asme.org/bpvc
Heavily used international standard pertinent to all aspects of the power generation and process industries and beyond. Section 1 – Rules for construction of power boilers. 2 – Materials. 3 – Rules for construction of nuclear facility components. 4 – Rules for construction of heating boilers. 5 – Non-destructive examination. 6 – Recommended rules for the care and operation of heating boilers. 7 – Recommended guidelines for the care of power boilers. 8 – Rules for the construction of pressure vessels. 9 – Welding and brazing qualifications. 10 – Fiber-reinforced plastic pressure vessels. 11 – Rules for inservice inspection of nuclear power plant components. 12 – Rules for construction and continued service of transportation tanks. With associated Case Codes. So important are these standards that an entire sub-literature on their interpretation has grown up. This includes reference publications, notably handbooks, that are substantial resources in their own right.

- **Pressure vessels: design and practice** S. Chattopadhyay CRC Press, 2004, 185pp. $149.95. ISBN 0849313694. Volume in the publisher's Mechanical Engineering Series addressing the ASME Code with coverage of relevant international codes.

5881 ASME/ANSI codes and standards
American Society of Mechanical Engineers and American National Standards Institute
store.asme.org
AMSE, under the umbrella of ANSI, produce a raft of standards crucial to the mechanical engineering profession. These national standards include material in the areas of: chains, compressors, conveyors, cranes, fasteners, flow measurement, gauges, machine guarding, measurement, nuclear engineering, a performance test code (PTC) series, piping, pumps, screw threads, tools, turbines and valves.

5882 Formulas for stress, strain, and structural matrices
W.D. Pilkey 2nd edn, Wiley, 2004, 1520pp. $175.00. ISBN 0471032212.
A very useful and comprehensive compilation of formulae, arranged by topic in 19 sections. These include: Dynamic loading; Beams and columns; Torsion and extension of bars; Frames; Torsion of thin-walled beams; Cross-sectional stresses; Curved bars.

5883 International Institute of Refrigeration
www.iifiir.org
A 'scientific and technical intergovernmental organization enabling pooling of scientific and industrial know-how in all refrigeration fields on a worldwide scale'. Particularly useful here for its access to documents and information on regulations and standardization applying to the refrigeration sector at global or regional levels. Key themes covered are: Global warming; Ozone depletion; Refrigerating systems; Refrigerants; Refrigerated transport.

However, access also to much other valuable information – including a set of links to 200 websites containing 'high-quality information provided by the industry, universities, laboratories, associations, public organizations.'

Official & quasi-official bodies

5884 Federal Railroad Administration [USA]
www.fra.dot.gov
One of ten Department of Transportation agencies concerned with intermodal transportation whose purposes are to: promulgate and enforce rail safety regulations; administer railroad assistance programs; conduct research and development in support of improved railroad safety and national rail transportation policy; provide for the rehabilitation of Northeast Corridor rail passenger service; and consolidate government support of rail transportation activities.

Good wide-ranging set of resources on well organized site.

5885 International Union of Theoretical and Applied Mechanics
www.iutam.org
Mission is to 'promote cooperation in the field of mechanics, through publications and conferences'. Some publications freely available on the site.

5886 Railway Safety and Standards Board [UK]
www.rssb.co.uk
Set up in the wake of Lord Cullen's enquiry, the RSSB is a limited company charged with the continuous improvement of the UK's railway system. The Board manages Railway Group Standards used by the industry and these may be accessed via the main RSSB site. Additionally, there are PDF Research Reports on various aspects of rail safety. These are heavily skewed towards human factors topics, but also contain technical and engineering information on matters such as accident investigation, wheel profile design, rail vehicle braking, rolling stock design and train dynamics.

Research centres & institutes

5887 BHR Group [UK]
www.bhrgroup.co.uk
Independent research and consultancy provider in fluid engineering and process technology. The group publishes non-confidential technical reports on power stations, hydraulic equipment, flow measurement, mixing, pipeline systems, pumps, seals, valves, slurry transport, jet cutting and many other areas. BHR conference series form a valuable source of information on all aspects of fluid engineering from waste water treatment to the aerodynamics of vehicle tunnels.

5888 Center of Mechanics: Institute of Mechanical Systems
Swiss Federal Institute of Technology
www.ifm.mavt.ethz.ch
Good example of website providing basic details of research activities in this arena. Research project headings – vibration, multibody dynamics, material behaviour, experimental method in mechanics, micro- and nanomechanics, railway systems and biomechanics – provide the basis for a series of short review articles on main headings and sub-activities. These are useful topic introductions.

5889 Institute of Sound and Vibration Research [UK]
www.isvr.soton.ac.uk
The ISVR is an internationally recognized teaching, research and consulting centre for the study of all aspects of sound and vibration. Specializes in knowledge of the effects of noise and vibration from generation mechanisms, transmission and propagation effects. Strong focus on physical and physiological effects of vibration on people.

5890 Von Karman Institute for Fluid Dynamics [EUR]
www.vki.ac.be
The Institute specializes in fluid dynamics, aerospace engineering and turbomachinery matters, particularly for propulsion. The website is a useful general source for education in these areas (course details and syllabus are very complete). Additionally, it features current and archived lecture series. VKI publications are listed, particularly the Technical Notes, Technical Memoranda and Reprints 1997–2004. A selection of these may be downloaded as full text files.

Associations & societies

5891 Air-Conditioning and Refrigeration Institute [USA]
www.ari.org
Free online access to the full-text downloads of ARI standards and guidelines, covering topics such as pumps, exchangers and condensers. ARI also provides free reports on research and technology news important to the air-conditioning and refrigeration industry. *PrimeNet On-line Directories of Certified Equipment* is ARI's applied and unitary certified performance ratings directory database for air conditioners, heat pumps and other HVAC equipment.

5892 American Gear Manufacturers Association
www.agma.org
Founded 1916, now a 'strong, growing organization that began the 21st Century with over 400 members in more than 30 countries'. Useful range of information.

5893 American Railway Engineering and Maintenance of Way Association
www.arema.org
Formed in 1997 from the merger of the American Railway Bridge and Building Association, the American Railway Engineering Association and the Roadmasters and Maintenance of Way Association, along with functions of the Communications and Signal Division of the Association of American Railroads. There is a free full-text searchable collection of major association publications (including those of the predecessor organizations). The *AREMA Manual for Railway Engineering* has a companion *Portfolio of Trackwork Plans* consisting of 'plans and specifications of switches, frogs, turnouts and crossovers, crossings, rails and special trackwork'.

- **Practical guide to railway engineering** 2002. $179.95. www.arema.org/eseries/scriptcontent/custom/e_arema/practical_guide.htm l [DESCRIPTION]. 'Written by over 50 railroad professionals, representing over 1200 years of experience.' Website offers downloadable PDF chapter abstracts and preview summaries.

5894 American Society of Heating, Refrigerating and Air-Conditioning Engineers
www.ashrae.org
ASHRAE is a key publisher of standards and handbooks, together with the usual learned society production of Transactions and associated literature. ASHRAE is a producer of databases, for example CD-ROMs in duct-fitting and psychrometric analysis. The organizational website contains their range of publications, some password protected for members, but with significant tranches of free information. These include e-Newsletters, public review copies of draft standards and position documents. Title page information on learned journals, for example the *HVAC&R Research Journal* 1995–present, is available with pay-per-view downloads.
A model website.

5895 American Society of Mechanical Engineers
www.asme.org
Founded in 1880, ASME is the leading US-based mechanical engineering professional body, equivalent to the UK's IMechE and JSME in Japan. With around 120,000 members, it is significantly bigger than both and a major force in technical, educational and research issues for the engineering and technology community as a whole.
ASME conducts one of the world's largest technical publishing operations, holds numerous technical conferences worldwide, and offers hundreds of professional development courses each year. The organization oversees internationally recognized industrial and manufacturing codes and standards that enhance public safety.
Its 37 Technical Communities (Divisions and Groups) cover all sub-sets of activity within 'mechanical engineering' – many of which have been developed as separate Subject Fields within this volume.

- **Transactions of the American Society of Mechanical Engineers** www.asme.org/pubs/journals [DESCRIPTION]. Learned society multi-part journal on all aspects of mechanical engineering. Generally, formal technical papers and brief technology notes. Currently 20 titles published either bimonthly or quarterly.

American Welding Society
See entry no. 5688

AVS Science and Technology Society
See entry no. 5804

5896 British Mechanical Power Transmission Association
www.bga.org.uk
Trade association promoting research activity and manufacturers in the field of power transmission systems. Maintains a website containing a mix of free and commercial technical publications and training information. Codes of practice are available, as are bibliographies, a teaching pack and European language dictionaries and glossaries of technical terms. Links to useful industry technical and commercial data, including websites of companies active in gearing matters and offering products and services.
Formerly the British Gear Association.

5897 British Pump Manufacturers' Association
www.bpma.org.uk
Trade association representing the interests of UK suppliers of liquid pumps and pumping equipment. The BPMA provides a technical advisory service and gives advice on pump-related standards, technical best practice and codes of practice. The website contains a consultants' directory, a buyers' guide and a shop with selected reports that can be

downloaded free of charge. The site also contains a technical information resource which contains pages on a range of subjects such as cavitation, shaft seals and pump shaft power.

Chartered Institution of Building Services Engineers
See entry no. 5324

5898 European Association of Internal Combustion Engine Manufacturers
www.euromot.org
Trade association concerned with all kinds of internal combustion engines, including those applied in: agricultural tractors, harvesters, excavators, cranes, forklifts ... ; recreational craft, boats, seagoing vessels ... ; trucks, buses, locomotives; lawn mowers, chain saws, snow blowers ... ; generator sets, pumps, compressors ... Useful source of engine emission standards and legislation, as well as developments in the industry.

5899 European Pressure Equipment Research Council
www.eperc.bam.de
Promotes European co-operation in the arena of (non-nuclear) pressure equipment by co-ordinating RandD and organizing conferences and workshops centred on pressure vessel standards, plant maintenance, inspection, testing, and life assessment. Produces various free documents in PDF format including newsletters, bulletins, and current project notes.

5900 Institution of Mechanical Engineers [UK]
www.imeche.org.uk
Main UK-based, but internationally scoped, professional body for mechanical engineers with a current membership of 80,000. The organization has interests in the education and continuing professional development of working engineers, by accrediting courses and industrial employers.

In technical and research matters the IMechE covers all sectors of mechanical engineering, having sub-sections in main industry groupings: aerospace, automotive, combustion engines and fuels, construction and building services, energy environment and sustainability, fluid machinery, management, manufacturing, mechatronics informatics and control, medical engineering, power industries, pressure systems, process industries, railway, safety and reliability, structural technology and materials, thermofluids, tribology.

An organizer of seminars and conferences, with an independent publishing arm, Professional Engineering Publishing.

- **Engineers' data book** 2nd edn, Professional Engineering Publishing, 2000, 256pp. £9.95. ISBN 1860582486. Useful inexpensive pocket guide. (From 2005, all book titles previously published by Professional Engineering Publishing have been transferred to John Wiley & Sons).
- **Proceedings of the Institution of Mechanical Engineers** www.pepublishing.com/frm_journal.asp [DESCRIPTION]. Major series of academic journals now comprising 14 Parts. As well as the traditional disciplines, includes coverage of engineering as applied to: aerospace; maritime environments; materials; medicine; nanosystems; power and energy; rail and rapid transit.

5901 International Sports Engineering Association
www.sportsengineering.co.uk
Acts as a forum discussing the technology of sport. Essentially, a liaising body between the leisure industry, manufacturers and researchers. Apart from its journal, ISEA maintains a small database of the content of this and of related material – conference papers and other references – but access to this is exclusive to members. However, the website freely links to useful organizations, research institutes, university courses and events. List of all members.

- **Sports Engineering** Quarterly. £237.00 [2004]. ISSN 13697072. www.sportsengineering.co.uk/journal.php. Designed to 'to fill the niche area which lies between classical engineering and sports science and aims to bridge the gap between the analysis of the equipment and the athlete'.

5902 International Union for Vacuum Science, Technique, and Applications
www.iuvsta.org
Union of national member societies whose role is to stimulate international collaboration in the fields of vacuum science, techniques and applications and related multi-disciplinary topics including solid-vacuum and other interfaces.

5903 Japan Society of Mechanical Engineers
www.jsme.or.jp
The largest technology-based learned society of its type in Japan. A scientific publisher of *Transactions*, in Japanese, and *JSME International Journal*, in English, the organization also specializes in standards and codes, the latter particularly for power generation facilities, including nuclear engineering facilities, transportation etc. The website contains an e-Newsletter in English and JSME output in general has a part-English language component. Useful for general information on regional engineering and relations with China, Korea and other neighbours.

5904 National Fluid Power Association [USA]
www.nfpa.com
The Association deals with matters of hydraulic and pneumatic technology, representing, primarily, members in US industry. Publications include technical papers and standards (in association with ANSI) which can be searched for on the appropriate part of the organization's website. Other resources include industry facts and figures and brief market trends data, test standards report forms and an education section for students and others. NFPA is a conference organizer on fluid power topics.

5905 Orgalime
www.orgalime.org
European federation of national industry associations representing the European mechanical, electrical, electronic and metal articles industries – and thereby directly or indirectly representing some 130,000 companies of an industry which, as a whole, employs 7.3 million people. Useful set of *Positions* papers; news section.

5906 Railway Industry Association [UK]
www.riagb.org.uk
Trade association for 120 member companies, UK-based rail equipment and service providers. Not a particularly information-rich website, but useful for its industry-specific products and services guide.

5907 Society for Experimental Mechanics [USA]
www.sem.org
Professional society of engineers and designers involved in the validation of new designs and materials. The society is

committed to interdisciplinary application, research and development, education and active promotion of experimental methods. Conferences. Publications. Buyers' Guide. Free to download full text articles from SEM's publication *Experimental Techniques* on a wide range of subjects e.g. biomechanics, dynamic strain measurement and computational validation.

5908 Society of Tribologists and Lubrication Engineers [USA]
www.stle.org
The STLE is a US-based international society devoted to the promotion of best practice associated with the design and operation of modern machinery and equipment. In addition to its publications, the STLE maintains a research index containing more than fifty years of tribology and lubrication research.

STLE has collaborated with the Independent Lubrication Manufacturers Association to provide an online education resource called LubeLearn. Users can download courses on a variety of topics covering best practice, industrial skills and lubrication engineering. Registration is free and courses are individually priced.

5909 Union Internationale des Chemins de Fer (International Union of Railways)
www.uic.asso.fr
This worldwide, but Europe-based, organization for rail transport is engaged in all areas of rail development and interoperability. UIC is, importantly, a standards-issuing body, and the UIC codes have a heavy bias towards engineering topics such as passenger and freight traffic, rolling stock, operating, traction and technical specifications, but extending into all areas of rail company management.

In addition to these and other publications, the UIC website offers an exceedingly extensive set of useful links, as well as access to related databases. The latter includes a search facility which encompasses standard current topics, for example air pollution, energy, environment, high speed railways, noise and research and development. What is particularly useful in, for example, the 'Energy Efficiency Technologies for Railways' strand, is that it offers interactive information on evaluated technologies.

5910 United States Association for Computational Mechanics
www.usacm.org
'Computational Mechanics (CM) is concerned with the use of computational methods and devices to study events governed by the principles of mechanics. CM is a fundamentally important part of computational science and engineering, concerned with the use of computational approaches to characterize, predict and simulate physical events and engineering systems governed by the laws of mechanics ... Computational Mechanics has had a profound impact on science and technology over the past three decades. CM has transformed much of classical Newtonian theory into practical tools for prediction and understanding of complex systems. These tools are used in the simulation and design of current and future advances in technology throughout the developed and developing world. There has been a pervasive impact on manufacturing, communication, transportation, medicine, defense and many other areas central to modern civilization.'

Libraries, archives, museums

5911 Delft University of Technology Library
www.library.tudelft.nl
The largest technical library of the Netherlands with strong interests in civil, mechanical, aerospace and other branches of engineering. A freely available online catalogue may be consulted. Website resource guides and portals are a good source for useful sites and subject group information, including mechanical engineering.

Attached is *Tresor*, a historical library of full-text digital works, which includes *Transactions of the Dutch Royal Institution of Engineers*, 1848–1869 (Verhandlingen Koninklijk Institut van Ingenieurs), the works of Simon Stevin, etc. In December 2004, the Library of the OTB Research Institute merged with the Delft Technology, Policy and Management Library.

5912 Imperial College of Science and Technology, Mechanical Engineering Department Library [UK]
www.imperial.ac.uk/library
Specialist departmental library reflecting the research interests of this leading UK-based University. Subject coverage includes computational mechanics, dynamics, robotics, thermofluids, tribology and strength of materials. Usefully supplemented by the main University Library and the Science Museum collections.

5913 Institution of Mechanical Engineers, Information and Library Service [UK]
www.imeche.org.uk/library
157-year-old learned society/professional body library based in central London, specializing in enquiries on all aspects of mechanical engineering. Reading room services offered to the general public. Maintains a web-based library catalogue of 60,000 references to mechanical engineering publications, current and historic. This includes detailed technical abstracts of all Institution publications 1984–2004. A complementary archive catalogue presents 21,000 references to historical and manuscript material in mechanical engineering 1736–1997.

Produces web-based subject guides reviewing useful publications, websites and resources in specific branches of mechanical engineering.

5914 National Railway Museum [UK]
www.nrm.org.uk
The NRM in York is the largest railway museum in the world, responsible for the conservation and interpretation of the British national collection of historically significant railway vehicles and other artefacts. The Museum's Library and Archive contains important works on railway development in Britain and some titles on overseas railways, particularly in the USA, France and Germany. The Archive Collection contains over a million engineering drawings of locomotives, carriages and other rolling stock. Most have come from British Rail and its predecessors, and from private manufacturers, 1820 to the present day.

5915 UK Heritage Railways [UK]
Heritage Railway Association
www.heritagerailways.com
A guide to the entire heritage railway scene in the UK and Ireland, including details of special events, trains and operating days for all steam railways.

- **Railway Glossary** www.heritagerailways.com/glossary. Almost 1000 entries in this useful and interesting compilation.

Portal & task environments

5916 **CFD Online: an online center for computational fluid dynamics**
www.cfd-online.com
Discreetly sponsored online centre for computational fluid dynamics. Books, discussion forums, events, jobs, news and announcements, resources – the last having a clear hierarchically structured index providing links to data about organizations, software, hardware, references, documents, etc.

5917 **Diesel and Gas Turbine Publications**
www.dieselpub.com
Diesel and Gas Turbine Publications offer a range of published products on the topics of diesels, turbines, compressors and emissions. This is reflected in their website which offers versions of their longstanding output. Their catalogue is presented in searchable format giving basic specifications on key manufacturers' engines and associated equipment. The website has downloadable PDF files on marine propulsion and power generation order surveys.

A lively example of a specialist publisher's online offerings in this arena.

5918 **eFluids**
iCentral, LLC.
www.efluids.com
'Specialty web portal designed to serve as a one-stop web information resource for anyone working in the areas of flow engineering, fluid mechanics research, education and directly related topics. It is designed to become the first step on the path to solving problems in flow engineering and fluid mechanics research and development for the global fluid dynamics community by providing engineers, industry professionals, researchers, educators, and students with a consolidated, intelligently selected and organized database linking all aspects of the fluid flow specialization.'

Engineers Edge
See entry no. 5382

5919 **Fluid Mechanics**
M.S. Cramer Cambridge University Press.
www.fluidmech.net
Personal interest site currently sponsored by CUP. Major reorganization Summer 2004, but does not seem further work since then. However, good collection of resources – including a 'Gallery of Fluid Mechanics'.

5920 **iCrank.com**
iCrank.com Inc.
www.icrank.com
Mechanical engineering portal with an emphasis on design engineering tools and resources. Most reference materials are generally available, and these cover information under four headings: vendors of services and components, design tools, a knowledge centre and a computing resource. Design tool information includes data for standard components – taps, screw threads, springs, etc. Computing guides users to software products for CAD, FEA etc. Details of jobs, events, publications and discussion forums can be used, member registration required in some areas.

Cheerful and user-friendly.

5921 **Interactive Engineering Catalogue**
SKF Group.
www.skf.com/portal/skf/home/products
The online interactive engineering catalogue produced by the SKF Group and available on this site is intended as a sales tool. It incidentally provides a useful web-based encyclopedia of rolling bearings, bearing units and housings, plain bearings and seals with guidance on bearing selection criteria and some associated calculation tools. Brief and comprehensible explanations of the technology are supported by good technical details and data with general illustrations of devices under discussion.

MATTER
University of Liverpool See entry no. 5820

5922 **Ricardo plc Information Services** [UK]
www.ricardo.com
The engineering consultancy Ricardo is a world leader in internal combustion engine technology. The Information Service offers a library stock of technical papers in a variety of languages with access provided by a 200,000 reference library catalogue. This general service is supported by several specialist databases/resources, for example a Fuel Cell Engineering Library and Emleg, a summary of worldwide engine emissions regulations. Sample files of other Ricardo publications are available in pdf format. All services are charged.

5923 **Thermal Resource Center**
K&K Associates.
www.tak2000.com
Access to extensive range of thermophysical material properties plus well organized set of links and other relevant data.

5924 **X-Rail.net** [EUR]
H. Kyster-Hansen, M. Christiansen and T. Fach-Pedersen, eds
www.x-rail.net
Busy-looking railway current awareness website and e-mail alerting service, with much useful reference material. Content is European and organized into news, infobank, contacts and services. The site has some interesting features, including rail project tendering updates and latest useful document notifications.

Discovering print & electronic resources

5925 **Classic Collection: European Research Community on Flow, Turbulence and Combustion Database**
University of Manchester 1995–.
http://cfd.me.umist.ac.uk/ercoftac [REGISTRATION]
A fluid dynamics database which contains test cases, computational results and conclusions from the ERCOFTAC Workshops on Refined Turbulence Modelling. ERCOFTAC also supplies a database of experimental datasets and a flow visualization library. Now administered by the CFD research group in the School of Mechanical, Aerospace and Civil Engineering at the University.

5926 CSA Mechanical and Transportation Engineering Abstracts
CSA, 1966–, Biweekly.
www.csa.com/factsheets/mechtrans-set-c.php [DESCRIPTION]
Provides citations, abstracts, and indexing of the serials literature in mechanical and transportation engineering and their complementary fields, including forensic engineering, theoretical mechanics and dynamics, and mathematics and computation. This database provides in-depth, comprehensive coverage of the international engineering literature with the monitoring of over 2600 serial titles as well as numerous non-serial publications.

5927 Fluidex: The Fluid Engineering Abstracts Database
Elsevier, 1974–. Access also available on a range of online hosts.
www.info.sciencedirect.com/content_coverage/databases/fluidex.shtml [DESCRIPTION]
This online database provides coverage of the scientific and trade literature dealing with the management and control of fluids in engineering, including coastal engineering, offshore engineering, ports and harbours, etc. as well as hydraulic machinery. Useful for its cross-disciplinary coverage where databases covering the individual disciplines are not easily accessible.

5928 How to find out in mechanical engineering
R. MacLeod and C. Ure; Heriot-Watt University
www.hw.ac.uk/library/howtomecheng.html
A university-based listing of mechanical engineering resources. Very comprehensive, exploring all manner of finding aids from paper-based collections (dictionaries, books, periodicals, patents, theses, translations, etc) to databases and web-resources. Intended for the student, but generally useful. Original guide 1999, updated November 2004.

5929 RDN Virtual Training Suite: Mechanical Engineer [UK]
J. Corlett; Nottingham Trent University and Resource Discovery Network
www.vts.rdn.ac.uk/tutorial/mechanical
One of the useful 'teach yourself' tutorials aimed primarily at students in UK further and higher education. This one briefly describes about 80 web-based resources.

5930 Tribology Index
Federal Institute for Materials Research and Testing 1970–.
www.bam.de/english/service/databases/tribology_i.htm [DESCRIPTION]
An international literature database covering friction, lubrication and wear. A considerable portion of the database is made up of literature not published in journals, such as company reports and conference proceedings.

5931 WWW Virtual Library: Mechanical Engineering
Stanford University
dart.stanford.edu/vlme
An excellent university-based portal site combining vendor pages and free online services guides. The latter fall into the broad categories of general information, jobs, publications, online calculation facilities, catalogues and databases, free software and miscellaneous. The listings of free online services are very full and briefly annotated as to content. Maintained within the University's Department of Mechanical Engineering – though no information given on the updating schedule.

Directories & encyclopedias

5932 Encyclopedia of vibration
S.G. Braun, D.J. Ewins and S.S. Rao, eds Academic Press, 2001, 1645pp. 3 v., $995.00. ISBN 0122270851.
www.info.sciencedirect.com/reference_works [FEE-BASED]
Some 200 articles covering the whole spectrum of basic and applied aspects of vibration in buildings and equipment. Coverage of the medical aspects. A good starting point.
Available online: see website.
'Essential for any library supporting an engineering degree program.' (*Choice*)

5933 Guide to European pressure equipment: the complete reference source
S. Earland, D. Nash and B. Garden Professional Engineering Publishing, 2003, 228pp. £249.00. ISBN 1860583458.
This guide provides practical information and data for the design, selection and use of pressure vessels. Current legislation, directives and standards are covered and clear guidance is given concerning inspection, testing, erection and installation. Equipment types are classified and linked to suppliers. A section is given over to the translation of pressure vessel terms into French and German.

5934 Guide to European pumps and pumping: the practical reference book on pumps and pumping with comprehensive buyers guide to European manufacturers and suppliers
B. Nesbitt, ed. 2nd edn, Professional Engineering Publishing, 2001, 426pp. £175.00. ISBN 1860582869.
Companion volume to the *Guide to European valves*, this work illustrates and describes pump types with a classification system linked to manufacturers and suppliers. In addition to type, the volume covers issues of materials, installation, and maintenance. With chapters on technical elements such shaft couplings and motors. Concludes with a discussion of economics and case studies.

5935 Guide to European valves for control, isolation and safety: the practical reference book covering valves, their design, selection, applications, and uses. Including a comprehensive buyers' guide to European manufacturers and suppliers.
B. Nesbitt, ed. 2nd edn, Professional Engineering Publishing, 2001, 440pp. £199.00. ISBN 1860582915.
A systematic type-by-type descriptive summary of valves for isolation, safety, flow regulation and control, illustrated by diagrams and photographs for ease of recognition. The valves are defined by a classification system throughout, linked to a European manufacturer and supplier guide. Technical chapters are included on requisite considerations of use such as sealing and packing, actuation and piping systems. Practical issues of selection, installation and maintenance are treated briefly.

A companion volume to the editor's *Guide to European pumps and pumping*.

5936 Jane's world railways
K. Harris and J. Clarke, eds 44th edn, Jane's Information Group, 2003, Annual, 900pp. £419.00. ISBN 0710625669.
www.janes.com [DESCRIPTION]
The best overview publication for international railway systems, providing country-by-country snapshots of the organization, operation, infrastructure and rolling stock of

major rail operations. Coupled with outlines of manufacturers of motive power units and rolling stock, leasing companies, railway associations and agencies and consultants.

- **Jane's urban transport systems** **M. Webb, A. Pattison and J. Clarke, eds** 22nd edn, Jane's Information Group, 2003, Annual, 733pp. £419.00. ISBN 0710625650. http://juts.janes.com [DESCRIPTION].

5937 **Railway directory**
C. Bushell, comp. 109th edn, Reed Business Information, 2003, Annual, 589pp. £210.00. ISBN 0617010196.
www.railwaygazette.com [DESCRIPTION]
Comparable to *Jane's World railways* in scope, the directory collects information on worldwide railway organizations but combines this with elements of urban transport systems into a single volume. Manufacturers of rolling stock, components, traction and control, infrastructure and data control systems are listed, with support services and consultancy information.

Handbooks & manuals

5938 **ASHRAE handbook**
American Society of Heating, Refrigerating and Air-Conditioning Engineers 2000–2003. 4 v.
www.ashrae.org/template/Index [DESCRIPTION]
Volumes are updated, one volume per year, in a four-year cycle. Volumes available in SI or I-P (inch pound) units, on CD-ROM, and by individual chapter from the Society website. They comprise a detailed survey of US practice.

- *Systems and Equipment*. 2000. SI edition ISBN 1883413818 780pp 48 chapters describing equipment, components and assemblies.
- *Fundamentals*. 2001. SI edition ISBN 1883413885. 39 chapters covering the basic principles and containing HVAC & refrigeration design data.
- *Refrigeration*. 2002. SI edition ISBN 193186201X. 50 chapters, heavily revised since the last edition.
- *Applications*. 2003. SI edition ISBN 1931862230 868pp. 56 chapters arranged in five broad sections: Comfort applications, Industrial applications, Energy-related applications, Building operations and management, and General applications.

5939 **Combined heating, cooling and power handbook: technologies and applications: an integrated approach to energy resource optimization**
N. Petchers Fairmont Press, 2003, 875pp. $199.95. ISBN 0824742338.
Nine chapters organized into four parts: Theory and technology; Operating environment; Applications; Analysis and implementation.
'excellent reference source and is recommended for any library supporting an electric power engineering program.' (*E-STREAMS*)

5940 **Compressed air and gas handbook**
Compressed Air and Gas Institute 6th edn, 2003, 776pp. $69.00. ISBN 0974040002.
www.cagi.org/resources/edu.asp [DESCRIPTION]
One of a range of useful publications produced by the Institute: the website giving details of its technical article programme as well as of its educational, standards and other publications.

The corrosion monitoring handbook
N. Rothwell and M. Tullmin See entry no. 5838

5941 **CRC handbook of mechanical engineering**
F. Kreith, ed. CRC Press, 1998, 2624pp. $99.95. ISBN 084939418X.
A reference book for the practising engineer covering modern mechanical engineering topics as well as traditional themes. Manufacturing, robotics, project management and environmental engineering are presented in addition to the fundamental principles of mechanical engineering such as mechanics and thermodynamics.
Series: Mechanical Engineering Handbooks, v. 1.

5942 **Diesel-engine management**
H. Bauer [et al.], eds 3rd edn, Robert Bosch Gmbh, 2004, 489pp. Co-published in UK by Professional Engineering Publishing, £39.00. ISBN 1860584357.
Everything you might need to know about diesel engine operation, from basic principles to detailed views of particular operational parts and systems. Well illustrated and up-to-date, with the authority of one of the world's key diesel engineering companies.

5943 **Dudley's gear handbook**
D.P. Townsend, ed. 2nd edn, McGraw-Hill, 1992, 815pp. ISBN 0070179034.
A valuable resource for gear technology and design information. This edition contains updated information and data for materials, lubrication, vibration and noise. The handbook is written for the practising engineer.

5944 **Engineering tribology**
G.W. Stachowiak and A.W. Batchelor 2nd edn, Butterworth-Heinemann, 2001, 744pp. £69.99. ISBN 0750673044.
Good interdisciplinary handbook, accessible to non-specialists.
'This well illustrated textbook is a valuable source of information for anyone working and/or studying in the field of tribological and mechanical engineering, i.e. researchers, lecturers, engineers and students. Due to the excellent content of this book, it would even justify a price twice as high as demanded.' (*Tribology International*)

5945 **Flow around circular cylinders: a comprehensive guide through flow phenomena, experiments, applications, mathematical models, and computer simulations**
M.M. Zdravkovich Oxford University Press, 1264pp.
V. 1. *Fundamentals* 1997. 672 pp. £94.00. ISBN 0198563965; V.2. *Applications* 2003. £100.00. ISBN 0198565615. Highly regarded text that is a core reference text for any researcher working on fluid flow, and essential for those working on flows around circular cylinders.

5946 **Fluid mechanics**
F. Kreith, ed. CRC Press, 1999, 326pp. $89.95. ISBN 084930055X.
A guide to fluid mechanics that is useful as a quick reference resource. Examples of problems and their solutions are given throughout the text making the book a practical manual for engineers.

5947 **Fundamentals of fluid mechanics**
B.R. Munson, D.F. Young and T.H. Okiishi, ed. 5th edn, Wiley, 2005, 769pp. $122.95. ISBN 0471675822.
http://eu.wiley.com/WileyCDA/WileyTitle/productCd-0471675822.html [DESCRIPTION]
The best-selling fluid mechanics text. Extensive set of appendices.

5948 **Gas turbine engineering handbook**
M.P. Boyce 2nd edn, Gulf Professional Publishing, 2002, 799pp. $125.00. ISBN 0884157326.
A general treatment of the gas turbine as an industrial power unit, from design, to a breakdown of major components, fuel technology and installation, operation and maintenance.

5949 **Gas turbine performance**
P.P. Walsh and P. Fletcher 2nd edn, Blackwell Science, 2004, 648pp. £69.50. ISBN 063206434X.
Detailed handbook, covering all aspects of performance, and all gas turbine variants. 'Gas turbine performance' is defined as 'the thrust or shaft power delivered for a given fuel flow, life, weight, emissions, engine diameter and cost. This must be achieved while ensuring stable and safe operation throughout the operational envelope, under all steady state and transient conditions'.
Many useful charts, lists of formulae, tables. Very detailed subject index.

5950 **Handbook for cogeneration and combined cycle power plants**
M.P. Boyce ASME Press, 2002, 560pp. $140.00. ISBN 0791801691.
Provides a brief but comprehensive overview of power generation methods. Reviews US performance test codes produced by ASME, ANSI and API relating to combined cycle plant. Thereafter, plant elements, notably gas and steam turbines, pumps, heat recovery generators, condensers and cooling towers, generators, fuels, bearings and controls are accounted for chapter-by-chapter. Concludes with performance testing and maintenance of CC plant.

5951 **Handbook of heating, ventilation, and air conditioning**
J.F. Kreider, ed. CRC Press, 2000, 680pp. $179.95. ISBN 0849395844.
An up-to-date coverage of the area that combines a theoretical approach with practical consideration. Consists of 17 chapters arranged in seven sections: Introduction to the building sector; Fundamentals; Economic aspects of buildings; HVAC equipment and systems; Controls; HVAC design calculations (including chapters on Energy conservation in buildings, and Solar energy system analysis and design); and Operation and maintenance. Appendices cover properties of gases and vapours, liquids, solids, etc.
Series: Handbook Series for Mechanical Engineering, *v. 4.*

5952 **Handbook of mechanical engineering calculations**
T.G. Hicks, ed. McGraw-Hill, 1997, 1536pp. 500 illustrations, $140.00. ISBN 0070288135.
A handbook of the mathematics of mechanical engineering, grouped under the general activity headings of power generation, plant and facility engineering, environmental control (including areas such as solar energy) and mechanical systems design. An eclectic selection of topics but with straightforward calculation procedures for particular problems.

5953 **Handbook of mechanical in-service inspection: pressure systems and mechanical plant**
C. Matthews Professional Engineering Publishing, 2003, 704pp. £121.00. ISBN 1860584160.
A practical technical guide to the inspection of machinery and systems once installed. Generally, the guide focuses on the types of inspection procedure for common types of mechanical plant in the power and process environment – pressure vessels and pipework, heat recovery systems and heat exchangers, but also moving plant such as cranes, lifts and lifting tackle.
The guide is linked to in-force international standards and regulations and appends a good range of websites containing relevant technical information.

HVAC design data sourcebook
R.O. Parmley, ed. See entry no. 5352

5954 **HVAC engineer's handbook**
F. Porges 11th edn, Architectural Press, 2001, 320pp. £54.99. ISBN 0750646063.
Widely known, useful and comprehensive reference work aimed at the practitioner. Mainly tabular in approach. Includes updated data on natural ventilation, ventilation rates, free cooling and night-time cooling. 17 sections including Combustion; Heat and thermal properties of materials; Properties of steam and air; Heat losses; Cooling loads; Heating systems; Steam systems; Domestic services; Ventilation; Air conditioning; Pumps and fans; Sound; and Labour rates.
1st edn 1942, 10th edn 1996. Until 8th edn, entitled Handbook of heating, ventilating, and air conditioning.

5955 **HVAC systems design handbook** [USA]
R.W. Haines and C.L. Wilson 4th edn, McGraw-Hill, 2003, 513pp. $99.95. ISBN 0071395865.
Now becoming a standard US handbook in this field, dealing with residential, industrial and commercial installations. Consists of 21 chapters that cover HVAC engineering fundamentals, design procedures, equipment – cooling, heating, and air handling, and engineering fundamentals – fluid mechanics, heat transfer, etc.
1st edn by Haines alone 1988; by Tab, 3rd edn 1998.

5956 **The internal-combustion engine in theory and practice**
C.F. Taylor 2nd edn, MIT Press, 1985–1996.
An in-depth analytical treatise that is indispensable for designers of internal combustion engines and those working in the fields of power and machine design. This revised edition included the latest developments in fuel economy and the legal restraints on air pollution. Also, fuel, engine materials and the future of the internal-combustion engine.

- **1. Thermodynamics, fluid flow, performance.** 1996, 574pp. $48.00. ISBN 0262700263.
- **2. Combustion, fuels, materials, design.** 1985, 783pp. $60.00. ISBN 0262700271.

Laser doppler and phase doppler measurement techniques
H.-E. Albrecht [et al.], eds See entry no. 823

5957 **Lubrication fundamentals**
D.M. Pirro and A.A. Wessol 2nd edn, Marcel Dekker, 2001, 523pp. $125.00. ISBN 0824705742.
Introduction; Lubricating oils; Lubricating greases; Synthetic lubricants; Machine elements; Lubricant application; Internal combustion engines; Stationary gas turbines; Steam turbines; Hydraulic turbines; Nuclear power plants; Automotive chassis components; Automotive power transmissions; Compressors; Handling, storing, and dispensing; Lubricants; In-plant handling for lubricant conservation.
Series: Mechanical Engineering

Machinery's handbook: a reference book for the mechanical engineer, designer, manufacturing engineer, draftsman, toolmaker and machinist
E. Oberg [et al.], eds See entry no. 5729

5958 **Marks' standard handbook for mechanical engineers**
E.A. Avallone and T. Bauneister, eds 10th edn, McGraw-Hill, 1996. CD-ROM available, $150.00. ISBN 0070049971.
http://books.mcgraw-hill.com [DESCRIPTION]
The classic handbook, providing complete coverage – especially of the more practical aspects – of the discipline.

Mechanical and electrical equipment for buildings
B. Stein and J.S. Reynolds See entry no. 5353

5959 **Mechanical engineering design**
J.E. Shigley and C.R. Mischke 7th edn, McGraw-Hill, 2003, 1248pp. Includes CD-ROM, $139.06. ISBN 0072921935.
Well established handbook with 18 chapters in three parts: Basics; Failure prevention; Design of mechanical elements.

5960 **Mechanical engineering formulas pocket guide**
T.G. Hicks McGraw-Hill, 2003, 290pp. $39.95. ISBN 0071356096.
Useful spiral-bound compendium of thousands of formulas used in everyday work.

5961 **Mechanical engineers' handbook**
M. Kutz, ed. 2nd edn, Wiley, 1998, 2352pp. $275.00. ISBN 0471130079.
www.knovel.com
Handbook covering a broad spectrum of engineering topics with 26 new chapters, including seven on mechanical design, added to this edition. The text guides the mechanical engineer through topics such as concurrent engineering, virtual reality, advanced and composite materials, ergonomic design factors and packaging. In addition to technical topics, career and legal issues are also addressed.
Available online: see website.

Modern power station practice: incorporating modern power system practice
See entry no. 5505

5962 **Pneumatic handbook**
A. Barber 8th edn, Elsevier, 1997, 659pp. £174.00. ISBN 185617249X.
Basic principles volume, treating compressors and compressed air transmission. General chapters on energy efficiency and applications. Associated mechanical and electrical equipment is discussed: valves and sensors, actuators and seals. Some guidance to other sources of literature and symbols, but limited to British Standard recommended.

5963 **Roark's formulas for stress and strain**
W.C. Young and R.G. Budynas 7th edn, McGraw Hill, 2001, 832pp. 150 illustrations, $89.50. ISBN 007072542X.
Resource for designers who need to calculate loads and stresses, incorporating equations and diagrams of structural properties. This edition includes expanded coverage of joint bearing and shear stress, experimental stress analysis, and stress concentration. User-friendly page layout for quick reference use.

5964 **Rules of thumb for mechanical engineers: a manual of quick, accurate solutions to everyday mechanical engineering problems**
J.E. Pope Gulf Publishing Company, 1996, 406pp. $94.95. ISBN 0884157903.
A compendium of calculation examples in fluids, heat transfer, thermodynamics, seals, compressors, motors, gears, bearings piping and pressure vessels, tribology, materials with stress and fatigue, instrumentation and economic aspects of engineering. Slighter, but more user-friendly than Hicks' handbook, the volume is nevertheless referenced and sourced to original appearances of calculation methods in standards, technical datasheets, papers, etc.

5965 **Spon's mechanical and electrical services price book** [UK]
Mott Green and Wall, eds 35th edn, Spon Press, 2003, Annual, 664pp. Published with an integral CD-ROM, £120.00. ISBN 0415323681.
An annual price book with information on material costs and measured work pricing for HEVAC installations and other mechanical and electrical services. Cost indices, rates of wages and daywork rates are included.

5966 **Standard handbook of machine design**
J.E. Shigley, C.R. Mischke and T. Brown, eds 3rd edn, McGraw-Hill, 2004, 1200pp. 500 illustrations, $125.00. ISBN 0071441646.
Intended to be used by working designers as a manual, containing condensed formulae, tables, charts and graphs. This handbook addresses the introduction of new technology, such that the content will remain relevant to future developments in computer hardware and software.

5967 **Tribology handbook**
M.J. Neale 2nd edn, Butterworth-Heinemann, 1995, 640pp. £99.99. ISBN 0750611987.
Aims to provide easy access to key information on the performance of tribological components, and is aimed at the practising engineer. The text contains materials and design data and refers to relevant standards. Units and conversion factors are provided.

5968 **Turbulence: an introduction for scientists and engineers**
P.A. Davidson Oxford University Press, 2004, 678pp. £35.00. ISBN 019852949X.
'The study of turbulence is not easy, requiring a firm grasp of applied mathematics and considerable physical insight into the dynamics of fluids. Worse still, even after the various theoretical hypotheses have been absorbed, there are

relatively few situations in which we can make definite predictions ...'

This attempt to bridge the gap between the elementary treatments of undergraduate texts and accounts given in research monographs is demanding; but 'throughout we seek to combine the maximum physical insight with the minimum of mathematical detail'.

Keeping up-to-date

5969 Annual Review of Fluid Mechanics
Annual Reviews, 2004. $202.00. ISBN 0824307364 ISSN 00664189.
www.annurev.org/catalog/2004/fl36.asp [DESCRIPTION]
One of the well established series of reviewing volumes.

5970 Applied Mechanics Reviews
American Society of Mechanical Engineers Bimonthly. $560.00 [2004]. ISSN 00036900.
www.asme.org/pubs/amr [DESCRIPTION]
Short articles reviewing key publications within particular topics or themes, primarily in mechanical engineering, together with reviews of new, primary monographs. The latter tends to concentrate on traditional media, i.e. they are book reviews. The material under scrutiny is genuinely international in scope. Now available in a full-text version via the website, with a series of linked tools. These include the AMR classification scheme and standard abbreviations used in the journal.

Machine Design
See entry no. 5403

5971 Mechanical Engineering [USA]
American Society of Mechanical Engineers Monthly. $25.00 per issue. ISSN 00256501.
www.memagazine.org
Like its UK-based analogous publication *Professional Engineering*, this US news-and-features magazine looks at trends and topics within the field. Contains the usual jobs, products, services, and events listings. Also provides updates on the important ASME standards and Q&A technical enquiries based upon them. Full text is available via the website.

5972 Professional Engineering [UK]
Professional Engineering Publishing, 21/year. £79.00 [2004]. ISSN 09536639.
www.profeng.com
A general news, technology and features magazine nominally on general engineering matters but specializing in mechanical topics. Individual issues during the publishing year are generally themed, for example: engineering software, rail, medical, automotive, supply chain, design engineering, defence, etc. Notable for the size of recruitment pages for mechanical engineering jobs.

5973 Railway Gazette International
Reed Business Information Reed Business Information, Monthly. £68.50 [2004]. ISSN 03735346.
www.railwaygazette.com
The website provides access to the Gazette and sister publications, including the 2004 *Railway Directory*. Users have subscription/non-subscription versions of the site which contains worldwide news stories on railway matters, together with tendering information, company profiles and the like. There is also courses and conferences information, useful for practising mechanical engineers.

Microengineering & Nanotechnology

micro-electro-mechanical systems • molecular nanotechnology • nanoscience • nanostructures • nanotechnology

Introductions to the subject

Bionanotechnology: lessons from nature
D.S. Goodsell See entry no. 5006

5974 Exploring the Nanoworld
University of Wisconsin-Madison
www.mrsec.wisc.edu/edetc
Uses examples of nanotechnology and advanced materials to explore science and engineering concepts at the college level. Provides pictures and movies of technical processes as well as information on research programmes. Bibliography and information on other resources including presentations and links to other websites are given. Produced by the University's Materials Research Science and Engineering Center.

Introduction to macromolecular crystallography
A. McPherson See entry no. 1759

5975 Introduction to nanotechnology
C.P. Poole and F.J. Owens Wiley, 2003, 400pp. £47.50. ISBN 0471079359.
Thirteen chapters. Practical, general introduction to various aspects of nanotechnology. Uses representative examples of research results to illustrate important features of each individual area of investigation. Provides technical administrators and managers with a broad, practical overview of the subject and gives researchers in different areas an appreciation of developments in nanotechnology outside their own fields of expertise.

Nanoelectronics and information technology: advanced electronic materials and novel devices
R. Waser, ed. See entry no. 6076

5976 Nanotechnology: a gentle introduction to the next big idea
M.A. Ratner and D. Ratner Prentice Hall PTR, 2002, 208pp. £19.99. ISBN 0131014005.
Eleven chapters, resources list, glossary and index. Begins with brief introduction to nanotech science, then surveys the entire field (technology and business), covering nanobots, molecular electronics, quantum computing, biostructures, nanosensors and other breakthrough technologies, and investment opportunities. Ethical issues also discussed.
Preface and sample chapter available at http://vig.prenhall.com

5977 **Nanotechnology: basic science and emerging technologies**
M. Wilson [et al.], eds CRC Press, 2002, 271pp. £41.99. ISBN 1584883391.
Bridges gap between highly detailed specialist publications and generalities of speculative science books. Accessible to engineers and scientists outside the field and even to students at the undergraduate level. Explores molecular nanotechnology, nanomaterials and nanopowders, nanoelectronics, optics, photonics, solar energy, and nanobiomimetrics. Concludes with look at cutting-edge applications and prophecies for the future.

5978 **Recent advances and issues in molecular nanotechnology**
D.E. Newton, ed. Greenwood, 2002, 306pp. ISBN 1573563072.
Contents: Molecular nanotechnology today; The promise and threat of nanotechnology; Recent advances; Biographical sketches; Chronology; Documents; Molecular nanotechnology as a career; Data and statistics; Organizations and associations; Research organizations; Print resources; Non-print resources; Glossary.
Series: Oryx Frontiers of Science
'Newton offers a creditable survey; especially valuable is his list of journals and Web-based resources to which the reader may turn for the most recent information ... this is a good basic reference for students interested in pursuing the field, as well as scientifically curious general readers. Recommended. General readers; lower-division undergraduates through graduate students.' (*Choice*)

5979 **Self-assembled nanostructures**
J.Z. Zhang [et al.] Kluwer Academic/Plenum, 2003, 316pp. £86.00. ISBN 0306472996.
'Nanostructures refer to materials that have relevant dimensions on the nanometer length scales and reside in the mesoscopic regime between isolated atoms and molecules in bulk matter. These materials have unique physical properties that are distinctly different from bulk materials.'
Introductory-level text providing systematic coverage of basics of nanomaterials organized: Materials assembly and synthesis; Characterization; Application.
Series: Nanostructure Science and Technology.

5980 **Understanding nanotechnology**
Scientific American/Time Warner, 2003, 150pp. $12.95. ISBN 0446679569.
www.twbookmark.com [DESCRIPTION]
Part of *Science Made Accessible* series, by editors of *Scientific American* magazine. Collection of articles together providing overview, containing information on medicine, motors, nanobots, circuits, electronics, computing, etc., as well as more general articles.
Also available as e-Book from Franklin using the Mobipocket Reader: www.franklin.com.

Official & quasi-official bodies

5981 **Micro and Nanotechnology Manufacturing Initiative** [UK]
Great Britain. Department of Trade and Industry
www.microandnanotech.info
A '*UK Micro and Nanotechnology (MNT) Network* has been established by the DTI and the 12 Regional Development Agencies and Devolved Administrations working together, to provide a market-oriented focus for the facilities, people and organizations engaged in Micro and Nanotechnologies in the UK. The Network is helping to lower entry barriers and drive the widespread market development and exploitation of these technologies – building a prosperous, world-class MNT sector in the UK.'

5982 **Nanotechnology Service** [EUR]
European Commission
www.cordis.lu/nanotechnology
Provides an overview of nanotechnology-related activities across the European Community's programmes. This includes information on projects and funding opportunities, information about the European Research Area and the 6th Framework Programme.

- **Towards a European strategy for nanotechnology**
  Downloadable PDF 2004, 28pp.
  www.cordis.lu/nanotechnology/src/communication.htm. Useful review adopted by the Commission on 12 May 2004 [COM(2004) 338]. 'It seeks to bring the discussion on nanoscience and nanotechnology to an institutional level and proposes an integrated and responsible strategy for Europe.'

5983 **National Nanotechnology Initiative** [USA]
www.nano.gov
Major US Government initiative to support research and development in the area of nanoscience and nanoengineering. Contains nanotechnology facts, a news section, pages on research and funding, agencies and centres, and a resources area. Latter offers photo gallery, articles and other publications, acronyms, FAQs and links to other sites.

Research centres & institutes

5984 **Center for Nanotechnology** [USA]
ipt.arc.nasa.gov
Research focuses on experimental research and development in nano and bio technologies as well as on a strong complementary modelling and simulation effort which includes computational nanotechnology, computational nanoelectronics, computational optoelectronics, and computational modelling of processes encountered in nanofabrication.
Includes interesting Gallery of Images, Presentations, Report and a WebCast 'Introduction to nanotechnology'.

5985 **Interdisciplinary Research Collaboration in Nanotechnology** [UK]
www.nanoscience.cam.ac.uk/irc
Funded by the UK Research Councils EPSRC, BBSRC, and MRC together with the Ministry of Defence as a collaboration between the University of Cambridge, University College London and the University of Bristol. Core projects involve characterization of nanostructures by scanning probe microscopy, nanofabrication, computational methods for molecular nanotechnology, and smart biomaterials. Details of exploratory projects also given.

5986 **London Centre for Nanotechnology** [UK]
www.london-nano.ucl.ac.uk
Designed to act as focus for current interdisciplinary nanoscale materials and device research. Joint enterprise between University College London and Imperial College

London, the Centre will be housed in a new building offering eight levels of laboratory and office space for academics from electrical engineering, physics, chemistry, biology and medicine. Aims to bring together world-class infrastructure and leading nanotechnology research activities.

5987 **Nanotechnology Research Institute** [JAP]
unit.aist.go.jp/nanotech
Centre of diverse nanotechnology activities within the NATIONAL INSTITUTE OF ADVANCED INDUSTRIAL SCIENCE AND TECHNOLOGY (AIST), Japan. Aims for strategic advancement of methodology and concepts in nanomaterials and device technology, elucidation and utilization of novel physical, chemical and biological phenomena on the nanometer regime, and their extension to industrially relevant technologies. Describes research and gives details of events.

Associations & societies

5988 **Foresight Institute** [USA]
www.foresight.org
A non-profit organization based in the US promoting nanotechnology. Freely available information on the website includes a quarterly newsletter, *Foresight Update*, which aims to inform a wide audience about technical and non-technical developments in nanotechnology. Free text white papers, essays and briefing documents can be downloaded. Also links to free full-text nanotechnology books and conference abstracts, as well as to online discussion groups, Nanodot and sci.nanotech. Information concerning jobs, events, a nanotechnology FAQ and the history and future of nanotechnology. A good wide-ranging service.

5989 **Institute of Nanotechnology** [UK]
www.nano.org.uk
UK membership organization, created to foster, develop and promote all aspects of nanotechnology in those domains where dimensions and tolerances in the range 0.1nm to 100 nm play a critical role. Site contains details of the Board, news, images, events and publications sections, a glossary, and links to sites of related interest. Also, members-only services.

- **Nanoforum** www.nanoforum.org. EU sponsored Thematic Network aiming to provide a linking framework for all nanotechnology activity within the Community. The Network is led by the UK Institute.

Microscopy Society of America
See entry no. 805

Portal & task environments

5990 **AZoNano.com**
www.azonano.com
Includes news, information about new products, supplier and expert directories and details about conferences, courses, books and exhibitions. Articles and news items are also classified in terms of materials, applications and the industries they benefit. Focused on the requirements of industrial end-users of nanotechnology.

5991 **MEMSnet: MEMS and Nanotechnology Clearinghouse** [USA]
MEMS and Nanotechnology Exchange.
www.memsnet.org
Contains industry news, lists of jobs, events and resumés, along with pages on what MEMS is and a beginners' guide to the topic. Also features glossary and materials database, discussion groups hosted, and links to other sites.

5992 **NanoApex**
www.nanoapex.com
Provides sections on nanoscience news, nanobusiness news, nanoinvestor news, nanostudent, nano events, nanomagazine (mainly interviews). Also links to applications, business, MEMS information, microfabrication, microsystems, and nanotech news and information. Also has company profiles, forums, latest books.

5993 **Nanonet** [JAP]
Nanotechnology Researchers Network Center of Japan
www.nanonet.go.jp/english
Under auspices of the Ministry of Education, Culture, Sports, Science and Technology. Collects and evaluates information domestically and internationally, and supports workshops and symposiums. Offers links to each website of governmental organizations, institutes, universities, etc. which provide nanotechnology information. Also supplies a database of laboratories related to nanotechnology in Japan, and calendar of events.

Discovering print & electronic resources

5994 **Web of Nanotechnology**
Thomson Derwent.
www.derwent.com/products/patentresearch/won [FEE-BASED]
Searchable database bringing together all existing nanotechnology prior art in single, web-based repository. Features 50,000 nanotechnology and nanotechnology-related patents from 1963 onwards, 225,000 literature records, and relevant websites. Based on Derwent and ISI information held within the Thomson conglomerate.

Directories & encyclopedias

5995 **Encyclopedia of nanoscience and nanotechnology**
H.S. Nalwa, ed. American Scientific Publishers, 2004, 10,000pp. 10 v., $6992.00. ISBN 1588830012.
www.aspbs.com/enn [DESCRIPTION]
Claimed to be world's first encyclopedia ever published in the field of nanoscience and nanotechnology. Comprehensive coverage of all aspects of the nanoscale science and technology in all disciplines. Over 410 review chapters contributed by nearly 1000 leading scientists. Approximately 70,000 bibliographic citations. 6800 figures, 650 tables and hundreds of chemical structures and equations.
Available online: see website.
'Shortly after the American Scientific Publisher's Encyclopedia of Nanoscience and Nanotechnology was published, the Dekker Encyclopedia of Nanoscience and Nanotechnology was published ... When the two encyclopedic sets are compared in the context of writing structure and style, the nod has to go to American Scientific for following the World Book model. The consistency in providing basic explanations before plunging into minute details makes it an encyclopedia that is useful to a wider audience. The

glossary included in each chapter makes the information that much more user friendly.' (E-STREAMS)

- **Dekker encyclopedia of nanoscience and nanotechnology** J.A. Schwarz, C.I. Contescu and K. Putyera, eds
  Dekker, 2004, 3979pp. $3500.00. ISBN 0824750551.
  www.dekker.com/servlet/product/productid/E-ENN [DESCRIPTION]. 5 v.
  Available online: see website.

5996 **What is what in the nanoworld: a handbook on nanoscience and nanotechnology**
V.E. Borisenko and S. Ossicini Wiley, 2004, 429pp. $185.00. ISBN 3527404937.
Introductory work summarizing terms and definitions, regulations, and most important phenomena discovered in the physics, chemistry, technology and application of nanostructures. More than 1000 entries, from a few sentences to a page. Each entry interprets the term or definition, briefly presents main features of the phenomena behind it. Additional information in the form of notes supplements entries and gives historical retrospective with reference to further sources.

Handbooks & manuals

Comprehensive coordination chemistry II: from biology to nanotechnology
J.A. McCleverty and T.J. Meyer, eds See entry no. 1715

5997 **Handbook of nanoscience, engineering, and technology**
W.A. Goddard [et al.] CRC Press, 2003, 824pp. £104.00. ISBN 0849312000.
www.engnetbase.com [FEE-BASED]
Sets out the fundamentals of nanoelectromechanical systems (NEMS), studies their fabrication and explores their most promising applications. Provides information and references for nanoscale structures, devices and systems, molecular technology and nanoelectromechanical theory. Introduction plus four sections: molecular and nano-electronics: concepts, challenges and designs; molecular electronics: fundamentals and processes; manipulation and assembly; functional structures and mechanics.
Series: Electrical Engineering Handbooks, v. 27. Available online: see website.

Handbook of surface and nanometrology
D.J. Whitehouse See entry no. 5850

5998 **The MEMS handbook**
M. Gad-el-Hak CRC Press, 2001, 1368pp. £111.99. ISBN 0849300770.
www.engnetbase.com
Three parts cover background and fundamentals (14 chapters), design and fabrication (9 articles), and applications of MEMS (Micro-Electro-Mechanical Systems) (9 chapters). Includes over 900 figures and 16 pages of colour. Contains chapters on the electrical, structural, fluidic, transport, and control aspects of MEMS. Explores both existing and potential applications in a variety of fields, including instrumentation and distributed control.
Series: Handbook Series for Mechanical Engineering, v. 7. Available online: see website.

Nanobiotechnology: concepts, applications and perspectives
C.M. Niemeyer and C.A. Mirkin, eds See entry no. 5045

5999 **Springer handbook of nanotechnology**
B. Bhushan, ed. Springer, 2004, 1222pp. £191.50. ISBN 3540012184.
www.springeronline.com [DESCRIPTION]
Some 40 chapters written by about 100 experts from industry and academia. Covers basic concepts, theory, materials, properties and fabrication. Contains over 900 illustrations and numerous comprehensive materials data tables. Features exhaustive references to approved data. Detailed index and fully searchable CD-ROM. Very good design and production.

Keeping up-to-date

Annual Review of Materials Research
See entry no. 5861

6000 **NanoFocus: Nanotechnology News for the Chemical World**
American Chemical Society
http://pubs.acs.org/cen/nanofocus/
Useful subset of CHEMICAL & ENGINEERING NEWS with some archival material.

6001 **Nanotechnology Now: Your Gateway to Everything Nanotech**
www.nanotech-now.com
Good, well laid-out overview of current developments; minimal commercial presence on the website: 'We are committed to do an honest, informative, and constructive day's work, each and every day, and to provide you with the most comprehensive and informative website dedicated to transformative science, technology, and engineering.'

6002 **Nanotechweb.org: the World Service for Nanotechnology**
Institute of Physics
http://nanotechweb.org
Useful news service and archival material from the publishers of the journal *Nanotechnology*. Well designed.

6003 **Scientific American Channels: Nanotechnology**
Scientific American Inc.
www.sciam.com/nanotech
Nanotechnology part of Scientific American magazine site. Offers [almost all] full-text articles under three headings: current coverage, highlights and further articles.

6004 **Small Times: Big News in Small Tech**
Small Times Media.
www.smalltimes.com
Commercially focused magazine offering news and articles by section or application. Events are listed. Includes a glossary of terms and search facility.

Information & Communication Technology

The phrase 'information and communication technology' (ICT) has a somewhat old-fashioned feel to it, but it seemed the best one to capture the subject and topic areas we wished to reference here. Five groups of players are predominant within the overall arena:

- *Academic research and teaching* The label 'Computer Science' is still that most frequently used within universities and colleges for the more fundamental and scholarly study of the nature and uses of information technology (IT), or of ICT; 'Information Systems' is also common, especially within a more management and business oriented context. With such approaches, much will necessarily be drawn from MATHEMATICS, and also from ELECTRICAL & ELECTRONIC ENGINEERING.
- *Software development* There has been a massive growth in the amount of computer software being developed and maintained during the last 10–20 years. Of especial focus here are the internet-enabled programming environments, and within those the burgeoning open source movements.
- *IT industry* Although – as elsewhere in TNW's TECHNOLOGY Part – we are reserving a proper treatment of business and industry resources for TNW Volume 2, it would have been curious not to reference directly some examples of the leading IT industry commercial players which – moderated to some degree by the success of the open source movement – have come to dominate the field. The major theme within the industry has of course been the convergence of formerly separate industry segments within a single global digital network economy.
- *Information/knowledge systems and management* The innumerable applications of ICT are referenced within the appropriate subject sections, either within this volume, or in the forthcoming volumes. Here we focus on the technology itself, though there are a few more generic resources cited in the TOOLS FOR INFORMATION PROFESSIONALS.
- *Legal and regulatory frameworks* Given the now considerable mission-critical importance of ICT within all types of organization, both public and private, there is an inevitable considerable concern, fully reflected in the resources listed below, about delivery, performance, and security issues.

Introductions to the subject

6005 Chasing Moore's law: information technology in the United States
W. Aspray, ed. William Andrew, 2004, 208pp. $39.95. ISBN 1891121359.
Excellent introductory overview to major policy issues in the USA related to information technology. Chapters are: Research and development funding; Telecommunications and computing; Internet governance; Internet use; Computer security and critical infrastructure; Privacy; Intellectual property; Antitrust; Digital divide; Workforce.

6006 Computer: a history of the information machine
M. Campbell-Kelly and W. Aspray 2nd edn, Westview, 2004, 400pp. $35.00. ISBN 0813342643.
Excellent history now extended beyond the development of Microsoft Windows and the Internet, to include open source operating systems like Linux, and the rise again and fall and potential rise of the dot.com industries.
'Terrific! This is the best general history of computing yet written, by two of the field's most prominent historians. *Computer* is comprehensive, engaging, and a pleasure to read. Aspray and Campbell-Kelley paint the big picture of the information revolution that is affecting all of our lives.' (*David Mindell, MIT*)

Discrete mathematics: elementary and beyond
L. Lovász, J. Pelikán and K. Vesztergombi See entry no. 488

6007 Milestones in computer science and information technology
E.D. Reilly Greenwood Press, 2003, 392pp. $69.95. ISBN 1573565210.
'Using the same approach as the popular *Milestones in Science and Technology* and *Milestones in Health and Medicine*, this unique reference features more than 600 concise entries describing the most significant advances in the field of computer science and information technology. Arranged in a convenient A-to-Z format, entries explain topics in a wide variety of categories.'
'[A] very useful one-volume reference book for general readers, even high school students. While this is clearly a book heavy on history, it is not a dull tome of past events only, for the author carefully describes many basic terms and devices that are very much part of the scene today.' (*Communication Booknotes Quarterly*)

Dictionaries, thesauri, classifications

6008 The ACM Computing Classification System: 1998 Version
Association for Computing Machinery
www.acm.org/class/1998
'ACM's first classification system for the computing field was published in 1964. Then, in 1982, the ACM published an entirely new system. New versions based on the 1982 system followed, in 1983, 1987, 1991, and now 1998 ... The full CCS classification tree is available as a hypertext

document, as a single document, as an ascii file, or as an xml file.'

6009 BABEL: a glossary of computer oriented abbreviations and acronyms
I. Kind and R. Kind, comps
www.ciw.uni-karlsruhe.de/kopien/babel.html
First published 1989; updated three times per year; downloadable.

6010 The BCS glossary of ICT and computing terms
British Computer Society 11th edn, Pearson Education, 2004, 472pp. £18.99. ISBN 0131479571.
www.bcs.org/BCS/Products/Publications
Compiled by a working party of the BCS Schools Expert Panel. Over 3000 terms explained in classified sequence organized into four parts: How computer systems are used; What computer systems are made of; How computer systems are developed; How computers work.
See website for details of the Society's extensive range of academic journals, newsletters, magazines and books.

6011 The comprehensive Russian computer dictionary: Russian–English/English–Russian
P.Z. Druker and Y. Avrutin Wiley-IEEE Computer Society, 1999, 379pp. $44.95. ISBN 0769500749.
30,000 entries divided equally between the English and Russian languages.

6012 Computer Desktop Encyclopedia: The indispensable reference on computers
The Computer Language Company, Quarterly. CD-ROM, $45.00.
www.computerlanguage.com [DESCRIPTION]
'Defines every important computer concept, term and buzzword used in the world of computers from micro to mainframe.' 18,000 definitions; 2500 illustrations; phonetic entries.

6013 Dictionary of acronyms and technical abbreviations: for information and communication technologies and related areas
J. Vlietstra 2nd edn, Springer, 2001, 696pp. £73.00. ISBN 1852333979.
33,000 terms, with 10,000 new to this edn, and obsolete terms and less relevant acronyms deleted.

- **Information technology encyclopedia and acronyms E. Kajan** Springer, 2002, 684pp. £42.50. ISBN 3540417931. Resolves more than 4000 broadly used acronyms, with most entries for acronyms associated with organizations, corporations, conferences, etc. including web links to the respective home pages.

6014 Dictionary of computer science, engineering, and technology
P.A. Laplante, ed. CRC Press, 2000, 543pp. $99.95. ISBN 0849326915.
Written by team of over 80 contributors and contains more than 8000 terms.

6015 Dictionary of computing
V. Illingworth and I. Pyle, comps 5th edn, Oxford University Press, 2004, 608pp. £8.99. ISBN 0198608772.
www.oxfordreference.com
6,500 terms; highly successful dictionary, over 35,000 copies sold of previous edn.
Available online: see website.

Dictionary of electronics, computing, telecommunications and media: Wörterbuch der Elektronik, Datentechnik, Telekommunikation und Medien
V. Ferretti, comp. See entry no. 5412

6016 Dictionnaire des technologies de l'informatique: Français/Anglais (Dictionary of information technology: English/French)
J. Hildebert La Maison du Dictionnaire, 1998, 2702pp. 2 v. Also available CD-ROM, €75.00. ISBN 2856081053.
67,500 entries.

Electrical and computer engineering dictionary: English–Spanish, Spanish–English (Diccionario de ingenieria eléctrica y de computadoras: Inglés–Español, Español–Inglés)
S.M. Kaplan, comp. See entry no. 5413

6017 Elsevier's dictionary of cybernyms: abbreviations and acronyms used in telecommunications, electronics and computer science in English, French, Spanish, and German with some Italian, Portuguese, Swedish, Danish, and Finnish
T.R. Pyper and C.A.C. Stout Elsevier, 2000, 334pp. £82.95. ISBN 0444504788.
26,000 definitions drawn from some 16,000 individual cybernyms.

6018 Free On-Line Dictionary of Computing: FOLDOC
http://foldoc.doc.ic.ac.uk/foldoc/index.html
'Acronyms, jargon, programming languages, tools, architecture, operating systems, networking, theory, conventions, standards, mathematics, telecoms, electronics, institutions, companies, projects, products, history, in fact anything to do with computing.' Over 14,000 terms, early 2005. Also accessible at a score of websites worldwide.

Laws, standards, codes

6019 ECMA International
www.ecma-international.org
Industry association founded in 1961 and dedicated to the standardization of information and communication technology systems. Formerly ECMA – European Computer Manufacturers Association. Standards have primarily been developed for: Data communication; Data interchange by physical media; Data presentation; Software engineering and interfaces.

6020 Information Technology Industry Council [USA]
www.incits.org
Trade association representing the leading US providers of information technology products and services. 'ITI is the voice of the high tech community, advocating policies that advance industry leadership in technology and innovation; open access to new and emerging markets; promote e-commerce expansion; protect consumer choice; and enhance the global competitiveness of its member companies.'

- **InterNational Committee for Information Technology Standards: INCITS** www.incits.org. 1700 members/13 countries, sponsored by ITI. Primary focus of ICT standardization encompassing information storage, processing, transfer, display, management, organization, retrieval. Serves American National Standards Institute internationally.

LLRX.com
See entry no. 6311

6021 **Organization for the Advancement of Structured Information Standards: OASIS**
www.oasis-open.org
Not-for-profit, global consortium that drives the development, convergence and adoption of e-business standards. Produces worldwide standards for security, Web services, XML conformance, business transactions, electronic publishing, topic maps and interoperability within and between marketplaces. Has more than 600 corporate and individual members in 100 countries around the world.

OASIS and the United Nations jointly sponsor ebXML, a global framework for e-business data exchange; and it has Member Sections for: CGM Open, which 'works to make Web graphics standards easy to adopt and practical to use in real world, open systems applications'; DCML, which 'drives the development and adoption of the Data Center Markup Language for utility computing'; PKI which 'advocates the adoption of Public-Key Infrastructure as a foundation to enable secure e-business transactions'; and UDDI which 'advances a standard method for enterprises to dynamically discover and invoke Web services'.

- **The Cover Pages** www.oasis-open.org/cover. Comprehensive web-accessible reference collection supporting the SGML/XML family of (meta) mark-up language standards and their application. Principle objective of this knowledgebase is to promote and enable use of open, interoperable standards.
- **Universal Description, Discovery and Integration Protocol: UDDI** www.uddi.org. UDDI creates a standard interoperable platform that enables companies and applications to quickly, easily, and dynamically find and use web services over the internet.
- **XML.org** www.xml.org. 'XML, the next-generation of HTML, is now viewed as the standard way information will be exchanged in environments that do not share common platforms.' This portal to XML information and schemas receives some 17,000 page views, over 4000 visitors per day.

Official & quasi-official bodies

Accreditation Board for Engineering and Technology
See entry no. 4814

6022 **International Federation for Information Processing**
www.ifip.or.at
'Non-governmental, non-profit umbrella organization for national societies working in the field of information processing. It was established in 1960 under the auspices of UNESCO as an aftermath of the first World Computer Congress held in Paris in 1959. Today, IFIP has several types of Members and maintains friendly connections to specialized agencies of the UN system and non-governmental organizations. Technical work, which is the heart of IFIP's activity, is managed by a series of Technical Committees.'

6023 **NSF: Directorate for Computer & Information Science & Engineering** [USA]
National Science Foundation
www.nsf.gov/funding/research_edu_community.jsp
Organizations within the Directorate include: Computing & Communication Foundations; Computer & Network Systems; Information & Intelligent Systems; Shared Cyberinfrastructure. For each of these there are valuable overviews of current projects.

- **National Coordination Office for Information Technology Research and Development** www.hpcc.gov. Includes details of the work of the *President's Information Technology Advisory Committee* (PITAC).

Research centres & institutes

6024 **Center for Women and Information Technology** [USA]
www.umbc.edu/cwit
Located at the University of Maryland, Baltimore County. Good range of resources and initiatives – including books about women and IT, gender-related electronic forums, girl-related resources, women-related science and technology resources, and so on. Regularly updated.

6025 **European Research Consortium for Informatics and Mathematics**
www.ercim.org
Group of 18 leading European research institutes aiming to foster collaborative work within the European research community and to increase co-operation with European industry.

ERCIM News is the magazine of ERCIM. 'It reports on joint actions of the ERCIM partners, and aims to reflect the contribution made by ERCIM to the European Community in Information Technology. Through short articles and news items, it provides a forum for the exchange of information between the institutes and also with the wider scientific community. Quarterly; circulation 11,000.

Joint Information Systems Committee
See entry no. 6327

Palo Alto Research Center: PARC
See entry no. 4558

Associations & societies

American Association for Artificial Intelligence
See entry no. 5686

6026 **Association for Computing Machinery** [USA]
www.acm.org
Major US-based society with 78,000 members. A rich site, which – as well as its diverse headquarters activities – gives details of more than 170 professional and local special interest group (SIG) chapters and over 750 student chapters worldwide. These 'function as intellectual and geographical nodes of activity for both ACM members and the computing community at large, offering seminars, lectures, and the opportunity to meet peers and experts in many fields of interest'.

Wide range of educational, professional and policy involvements – as well as THE ACM PORTAL.

- **ACM Special Interest Groups** www.acm.org/sigs/guide98.html. Descriptions of the work and links to the websites of 34 SIGs: many of the Groups are important societies in their own right within their respective fields. The acronyms of each all start with the character string 'SIG': e.g. SIGART; SIGEVO; SIGGRAPH; etc.
- **Computing Reviews** 1985–, Daily. www.reviews.com [FEE-BASED]. Full-text reviews of computer science articles, books, reports, proceedings, theses, etc. judged to be of high quality and relevance in their fields. Reviews written by team of reviewers in conjunction with category editors. Print version available.
- **ACM Queue** www.acmqueue.org. Useful review of the latest computing trends; each issue tackles a specific theme. Free print subscriptions are available to US and Canadian Residents only unless you are an ACM member. Other useful magazines are offered by the Association.

6027 Association for Information Systems
www.aisnet.org
Professional organization whose purpose is 'to serve as the premier global organization for academics specializing in Information Systems'. AISWorld Net aims to 'provide information management scholars and practitioners with a single entry point to resources related to information systems technology and promote the development of an international information infrastructure that will dramatically improve the world's ability to use information systems for creating, disseminating, and applying knowledge'.

6028 Association for Women in Computing [USA]
www.awc-hq.org
Dedicated to the advancement of women in the technology fields.

6029 British Computer Society
www.bcs.org.uk
A leading industry body for IT professionals, as well as being a Chartered Engineering Institution for Information Technology. Very good range of resources about IT-related education, training and careers, as well as information and advice, news, and details of an extensive suite of publications.

6030 Computer Professionals for Social Responsibility
www.cpsr.org
'A public-interest alliance of people concerned about the impact of information and communications technology on society. We work to influence decisions regarding the development and use of computers because those decisions have far-reaching consequences and reflect our basic values and priorities. As experts on ICT issues, CPSR members provide realistic assessments of the power, promise, and limitations of computer technology. As concerned citizens, we direct public attention to critical choices concerning the applications of computing and how those choices affect society.'

Issues the Society is currently concerned with include: Computers and the environment; Free/libre open source software; Intellectual property; Internet governance; Participatory design; Privacy and civil liberties; Voting technology.

6031 Computing Research Association [USA]
http://cra.org
Association of 'more than 200 North American academic departments of computer science, computer engineering, and related fields; laboratories and centers in industry, government, and academia engaging in basic computing research; and affiliated professional societies'. Simple site providing on browsing, however, a very good snapshot of current activity in the discipline.

- **Computing Research News** ISSN 1069384X. Well produced downloadable PDF newsletter produced five times per year. Major source of job vacancies whose descriptions – inter alia – give an excellent overview of academic and related research activity in the field.

6032 Council of European Professional Informatics Societies
www.cepis.org
Unites 37 professional informatics societies over 33 European countries, representing more than 200,000 ICT professionals. A new service UPENET will 'republish selected scientific articles from national specialized Informatics journals and magazines of CEPIS member societies. Papers are chosen by editors of publications participating in UPENET and translated into English. The digital journal UPGRADE will republish the articles in English making them available to the ICT community in Europe and worldwide.'

EDUCAUSE: transforming education through information technologies
See entry no. 6341

6033 IEEE Computer Society
www.computer.org
Major provider of books, journals and other publications – especially through its Digital Library. The Society's Online Books programme gives access to a full text collection of up to 4000 books from BOOKS24X7. Co-ordinated by its Standards Activities Board, the Society develops standards over a wide range of ICT-related activity, drawing on the expertise of its membership (numbering over 100,000 worldwide: it is the largest of the IEEE technical societies), and co-operating with standards bodies both elsewhere within the Institute, as well as outside the body.

- **Computer** www.computer.org/computer. The Society's flagship magazine. Peer-reviewed technical content that covers all aspects of computer science, computer engineering, technology, and applications – edited to enhance readability for the general reader.
- **IEEE Standards Association** http://standards.ieee.org. 'Provides a standards program that serves the global needs of industry, government, and the public. It also works to assure the effectiveness and high visibility of this standards program both within the IEEE and throughout the global community.'

6034 Information Processing Society of Japan
www.ipsj.or.jp/english
Good well laid out English language pages. IPSJ is the largest IT society in Japan. IPSJ Digital Courier, a new online English journal, was first issued in January 2005 and published in electronic form via J-STAGE, operated by the JAPAN SCIENCE AND TECHNOLOGY AGENCY.

6035 National Computing Centre [UK]
www.ncc.co.uk
Founded 1966, originally funded by UK government, but since 1988 independent and today 'NCC is the UK's foremost independent Membership organisation for users of IT. Since 2002 NCC has been growing its portfolio of

membership activities through the acquisition of other IT focused membership organisations.'

NCC offer a wide range of publications through the NCC Shop: particularly useful are the benchmark series of IT spending patterns.

6036 Network and Systems Professionals Association
www.naspa.com
'Since 1986 NaSPA has been the official voice of the corporate computing technical professional. NaSPA has members in over 80 countries worldwide ... In the United States, NaSPA has members in all companies on the Fortune 500 list.'

6037 USENIX: The Advanced Computing Systems Association
www.usenix.org
'Since 1975, the USENIX Association has brought together the community of engineers, system administrators, scientists, and technicians working on the cutting edge of the computing world. The USENIX conferences have become the essential meeting grounds for the presentation and discussion of the most advanced information on the developments of all aspects of computing systems.'

- **SAGE** www.sage.org. USENIX Special Technical Group organized to advance the professional status of the computer system administrator – being a person 'who, as a primary job function, manages computer and network systems on behalf of another, such as an employer or client'.

Libraries, archives, museums

6038 Charles Babbage Institute [USA]
www.cbi.umn.edu
Historical archives and research center within the University of Minnesota. 'CBI is dedicated to promoting study of the history of information technology and information processing and their impact on society. CBI preserves relevant historical documentation in all media, conducts and fosters research in history and archival methods, offers graduate fellowships, and sponsors symposia, conferences, and publications.'

Excellent well designed and informative site – providing access also, via its Other Resources, to details of the cornucopia available elsewhere including, for instance, that used in the film industry: see Hollywood and computers.

6039 Computer History Museum [USA]
www.computerhistory.org
Established 1996, 'a public benefit organization dedicated to the preservation and celebration of computing history. It is home to one of the largest collections of computing artifacts in the world, a collection comprising over 4000 artifacts, 10,000 images, 4000 linear feet of cataloged documentation and gigabytes of software.' The first phase of new premises opened June 2003.

Portal & task environments

6040 The ACM Portal
http://portal.acm.org/portal.cfm [FEE-BASED]
Major gateway with two main sections:

- ACM Digital Library: Full text collection of every article published by ACM, including over 50 years of archives
- Guide to Computing Literature: Bibliographic collection from major publishers in computing with over 750,000 entries.

For both sections there are informative FAQs, and the portal also gives access to the range of other services from the ASSOCIATION FOR COMPUTING MACHINERY.

AgentLink III: European coordination action for agent-based computing
University of Southampton, University of Liverpool and European Commission. Directorate for Information Society See entry no. 5700

6041 Bitpipe
www.bitpipe.com [REGISTRATION]
'The leading destination for busy professionals who need technology white papers, webcasts, case studies and IT product information – all the IT information and resources you need to make smart enterprise IT purchasing decisions.'

Very good range and depth of data, information and documents. For instance, Bitpipe KnowledgeAlerts are 'free email newsletters that notify you when new white papers, webcasts, product information or case studies are available on the topics that most interest you'; AnalystViews is a fee-based service which 'indexes and syndicates information from over 90 top technology analyst firms including Gartner, IDC, Forrester and Current Analysis'.

Bitpipe was acquired by TechTarget in December 2004.

- **TechTarget** www.techtarget.com. Targeted IT content delivered via: Controlled qualified e-Newsletters; Technology-specific websites; Invitation-only conferences; webcasts featuring industry experts; In-depth magazines that deliver the end-user and decision makers' perspective.

6042 BRINT
BRINT Institute, LLC.
www.brint.com
'The Premier Business Technology Knowledge Portal and Global Community Network for E-Business, Information, Technology, and Knowledge Management. Recommended by Business Week, Fortune, Wall Street Journal, Fast Company, Business 2.0, Computerworld, Information Week, CIO Magazine, KM World, New York Times, and hundreds of other worldwide publications.'

- **WWW Virtual Library: Knowledge Management** www.brint.com/km. Extensive and rewarding gateway to data and information about KM businesses, processes, systems, technologies, etc. Registration needed for some facilities.

CMP Media
See entry no. 4578

6043 CNET
CNET Networks.
www.cnet.com
'Provides expert and unbiased advice on technology products and services to inform users and expedite purchasing. Integrating an extensive directory of more than 200,000 computer, technology, and consumer electronics products with editorial content, downloads, trends, reviews and price comparisons.'

- **IT Papers** http://itpapers.com. 'The Web's largest library of technical white papers, Webcasts, and case studies. We've changed our look and functionality to help you find what you're looking for faster. Registered users gain additional benefits.'
- **Silicon.com** www.silicon.com. Leading ICT news service/portal.

6044 **EEVL: Computing** [UK]
Heriot-Watt University and Resource Discovery Network
www.eevl.ac.uk/computing
The computing section of the leading RDN hub EEVL.

Evoweb: The online information service for everyone interested in evolutionary computing
Napier University and European Commission. Directorate for Information Society See entry no. 5703

6045 **Gartner**
www.gartner.com/Init
'The leading provider of research and analysis on the global IT industry. Our goal is to support enterprises as they drive innovation and growth through the use of technology. We help clients make informed technology and business decisions by providing in-depth analysis and actionable advice on virtually all aspects of technology.'

6046 **InfoWorld Media Group**
IDG Publishing Network.
www.infoworld.com/about
'Delivers in-depth coverage and evaluation of IT products for technology experts involved in major purchase decisions for their companies. InfoWorld reaches the most influential readers through its integrated online, print, events, and research channels.'

IDG also publish the leading magazines: *Computerworld*; *CIO*; *Network World*; *PC World* – as well as a number of more specialized offerings.

6047 **LTSN Information and Computer Sciences** [UK]
University of Ulster, Loughborough University and Higher Education Academy
www.ics.heacademy.ac.uk
Now to be known as the Higher Education Academy Subject Centre for Information and Computer Sciences, one of 24 Subject Centres based in higher educational institutions throughout the UK offering subject specific expertise and information on learning and teaching for the UK's higher education community.

6048 **Open Source Technology Group**
www.ostg.com
'The leading network of technology sites for today's IT managers and development professionals. OSTG sites provide a unique combination of news, original articles, downloadable resources, and community forums to help IT managers, development professionals, and end-users make critical decisions about information technology products and services.

OSTG's IT-focused sites include Slashdot.org, Linux.com, NewsForge.com and ITManagersJournal.com. Its development- and software-focused sites include freshmeat.net, DevChannel.org and SourceForge.net.

- **SourceForge.net** http://sourceforge.net. 'The world's largest Open Source software development website, with the largest repository of Open Source code and applications available on the Internet ... Provides free services to Open Source developers.'

Discovering print & electronic resources

6049 **A bibliographic guide to the history of computer applications: 1950–1990**
J.W. Cortada, comp. Greenwood Press, 1996, 278pp. $109.95. ISBN 0313298769.
'Covering over 40 industries and dozens of applications, this is the first bibliography on the history of computer applications. After an introductory essay on the history of applications, the volume is divided into two time periods and includes over 1600 entries, arranged by application and industry. Users will find sections on such fields as higher education, manufacturing, law enforcement, accounting, space travel, ATMs, artificial intelligence, banking, and trucking. Entries are annotated to describe their content and, when appropriate, their historical significance.'
Series: Bibliographies and Indexes in Science and Technology.
'Cortada's superb bibliography is organized in two periods, 1950–65 and 1966–90. In the 1950s, computers were first being introduced to business and by the early 1960s were going through the first stages of implementation ... Historians of computers and technology would find this an excellent research guide.' (*Choice*)

- **Second bibliographic guide to the history of computing, computers, and the information processing industry J.W. Cortada** Greenwood Press, 1996, 416pp. $109.95. ISBN 0313295425. 2500 citations covering all significant literature published since the late 1980s.

6050 **The collection of computer science bibliographies**
A.-C. Achilles
http://liinwww.ira.uka.de/bibliography
Very extensive invaluable collection which 'currently contains more than 1.4 million references (mostly to journal articles, conference papers and technical reports), clustered in about 1400 bibliographies ... More than 19,000 references contain crossreferences to citing or cited publications. More than 240,000 references contain URLs to an online version of the paper. Abstracts are available for more than 180,000 entries. There are more than 2000 links to other sites carrying bibliographic information'.

Not surprisingly, the site now receives very heavy use: in excess of 300,000 accesses per month.

- **CompuScience** www.zblmath.fiz-karlsruhe.de/COMP/about.html. Part of project FachInformationsSystem Informatik, 'bibliographic database covering literature in the field of Computer Science and Computer Technology with about 400 000 citations from 1972'. Covers journals, books, conference proceedings. Very quick.
- **Computer science bibliography M. Ley** http://dblp.uni-trier.de. Over 600,000 articles indexed from major computer science journals and proceedings as well as several thousand links to home pages of computer scientists. Originally focused on DataBase systems and Logic Programming (DBLP) but now expanded to other fields.
- **Computer science technical reports University of Waikato**. www.nzdl.org. Index to reports downloaded from selected internet sites. Currently covers over 45,000 reports located in some 300 sites worldwide. Almost 400 million words from 1.3 million pages are indexed; also nearly 30,000 figures are extracted from the reports.

6051 **CompuMath Citation Index**
Thomson ISI.
www.isinet.com [DESCRIPTION]
One of a range of Speciality Citation Indexes providing 'convenient, targeted access to current and retrospective bibliographic information and author abstracts from the

world's leading journals, books, and proceedings in a number of specialties. They also reach outside the core literature to provide coverage of related articles from the ISI database of over 16,000 scholarly publications in the sciences, social sciences, and arts and humanities'.

- **Computer Database** Thomson Gale, 1980–. www.galegroup.com [DESCRIPTION]. Useful wide-ranging service providing access to information within some 700 periodicals on computer, telecommunications and electronic industries accessible via INFOTRAC, web, or Z39.50 client interface.

6052 Computer & Control Abstracts
Institution of Electrical Engineers
www.iee.org/Publish/inspec/ProdCat/abstracts.cfm
Together with ELECTRICAL AND ELECTRONICS ABSTRACTS and PHYSICS ABSTRACTS forms IEE's *Science Abstracts* series of journals which are print equivalents of portions of the INSPEC database. Contains some 100,000 items in 12 monthly issues.

6053 Help-Site Computer Manuals
http://help-site.com
Links to some 18,000 documents on over 160 sites providing help and support for use of all the major operating systems. 'A new site is under development, which will eventually replace Help-Site. It will be called HelpSpy ...'

6054 How to find information: computer sciences
P. Allchin British Library, 2003, 106pp. £9.95. ISBN 0712308784.
Useful overview, related particularly to the British Library's holdings and to the UK situation more generally.

INSPEC
Institution of Electrical Engineers See entry no. 5445

6055 WWW Virtual Library: Museum of Computing
J. Bowen, comp.; International Council of Museums
http://vmoc.museophile.com
First-rate and 'eclectic collection of World Wide Web (WWW) hyperlinks connected with the history of computing and on-line computer-based exhibits available both locally and around the world'. Sections are: Galleries; Local virtual exhibits; Corporate history and overviews; History of computing organizations; General historical information; Computer-related museums; On-line exhibits and information; Personal collections; Selected newsgroups; Computer simulators.

Digital data, image & text collections

6056 Books24x7
SkillSoft.
www.books24x7.com
A 'leading provider of web-based digital technical and business reference content, containing thousands of digitized 'best-in-class' reference books, research reports, documentation and articles'. February 2005 contained the full text of over 7000 titles from more than 220 imprints: almost 3 million pages in total. Useful list with descriptions and links for each of the imprints.

Subsets of the overall collection – including ITPro and EngineeringPro – are available. An impressive service.

- **Safari Tech Books Online** http://safaribooksonline.com. Joint venture between business technology publishers O'Reilly and Pearson Technology Group providing enterprise or individual full-text access to some 2500 titles including from Addison-Wesley, Cisco Press, Peachpit Press/Adobe Press, Prentice Hall, etc.

6057 Computer Source
EBSCO.
www.epnet.com/academic/computersource.asp [DESCRIPTION]
Online database containing 'more than 300 full text journals and magazines covering topics such as computer science, programming, artificial intelligence, cybernetics, information systems, robotics, and software ... Provides a balance of full text technical journals and full text consumer computer titles.'

- **Computer Science Index** EBSCO. www.epnet.com/academic/computersci.asp [DESCRIPTION]. Formerly Computer Literature Index. Indexing and abstracting of almost 700 periodical titles.

6058 ITKnowledgeBASE
Auerbach Publications.
www.auerbach-publications.com [FEE-BASED]
A CRCNETBASE portal to the content of 'current and back issues of eight vital Auerbach journals and newsletters, and the Information Security Management Handbook — over 4000 articles, more than 40,000 pages of information expanded and updated every month'.

This website is a gateway to the full spectrum of offerings from Auerbach Publications (which was acquired by *CRC Press* in 1997), with a special emphasis on large-scale information systems management and security.

6059 Networked Computer Science Technical Reference Library: NCSTRL
www.ncstrl.org
Access to open archives of – early 2005 – some 90 digital report collections from around the world. Searching and browsing facilities.

Directories & encyclopedias

6060 Computing Directories [UK]
VNU Business Publications.
www.itdirectories.co.uk [DESCRIPTION]
Details of the range of print and online computing directories covering UK-based computing suppliers and sites. Formerly known as the Computer Users Year Book.

- **Computing** www.computing.co.uk. The leading UK-based magazine.

6061 Encyclopedia of computer science
A. Ralston, E.D. Reilly and D. Hemmendinger, eds 4th edn, Wiley, 2003, 2034pp. $200.00. ISBN 0470864125.
600 articles from 300 contributors organized around nine main themes: Hardware; Software; Computer systems; Information and data; Mathematics of computing; Theory of computation; Methodologies; Applications; Computing milieux.
Originally published Nature Publishing Group, 2000

6062 Encyclopedia of computer science and technology
A. Kent and J.G. Williams, eds Dekker, 2001. 43 v., $8775.00. ISBN 082472299X.
www.dekker.com [DESCRIPTION]
Major series published over the period 1975–2001: 15 original volumes, then a series of supplements.

6063 Encyclopedia of computers and computer history
R. Rojas Fitzroy Dearborn, 2001, 930pp. 2 v., $250.00. ISBN 1579582354.
Over 400 articles on the history of computers, from personal computing and mainframes to robotics and artificial intelligence; from the theoretical underpinnings of computers to the people and organizations that translate that theory into reality.
'Outstanding Reference Source, 2002.' (American Library Association)

6064 Encyclopedia of information systems
H. Bidgoli, ed. Academic Press, 2002, 2969pp. 4 v., $1250.00. ISBN 0122272404.
www.sciencedirect.com/science/referenceworks
200 topics alphabetically arranged by title addressing technical as well as managerial, social, legal and international issues in information system design, implementation, and utilization. Short glossary at the start of each clearly written article, collectively providing 2000 definitions; bibliography at each article end (though with few references later than 1999). Comprehensive subject index. Generally, a good starting point.
Available online: see website.

Handbooks & manuals

Expert systems
C.T. Leondes, ed. See entry no. 5720

Reference data for engineers: radio, electronics, computers and communications
M.E. Van Valkenburg and W.M. Middleton, eds See entry no. 5514

Keeping up-to-date

6065 Advances in Computers
Academic Press, 2005, 340pp. £87.50. ISBN 0120121646.
http://books.elsevier.com [DESCRIPTION]
Regularly produced volumes, each with a particular theme. This forthcoming volume will treat 'New programming paradigms'; recent volumes have reviewed: 'Parallel, distributed, and pervasive computing'; 'Advances in software engineering'; 'Architectural issues'; 'Information security'.

6066 Computer Weekly [UK]
Reed Business Information.
www.computerweekly.com
The leading UK-based magazine.

6067 ComputerWire
Datamonitor.
www.computerwire.com [REGISTRATION]
'The world's leading supplier of integrated news, opinion, research and analysis for the IT industry. Its focus is the 10 million + worldwide IT professionals, working in the $1 trillion IT market. Since its foundation in 1984, ComputerWire has gained a reputation for quality, independence, professionalism and responsiveness.'

The Data Administration Newsletter
R.S. Seiner See entry no. 6426

6068 Guardian Unlimited Online
www.guardian.co.uk/online
Excellent overview of current developments – especially for non-professionals, together with good set of reference resources.

6069 PC Magazine
Ziff Davis Publishing.
www.pcmag.com
'The world's largest computing print publication with over 6 million readers.'
See website for details of the wide range of other ICT magazines offered by the company.

6070 Red Herring: The business of technology
www.redherring.com
US privately held company 'whose mission is to cover innovation, technology, financing and entrepreneurial activity. Its staff of award-winning journalists tell readers what's first, what matters and most importantly, why.' Worth perusing is the company's detailed Ethics Policy: Policy goals and who is covered; Separation of advertising and editorial; Separation of marketing and editorial; Financial holdings; Standards for news gathering.

6071 The Register
Situation Publishing.
www.theregister.co.uk
Well presented and delivered news categorized: Enterprise; Software; Personal; internet; Mobile; Security; Management; Channel; Odds and Sods. UK-based, but international coverage.

6072 Wired [USA]
Lycos Inc.
www.wired.com
Prominent commentator on ICT-related issues. Covers: Technology; Culture; Business; Politics.

Computer & Networking Hardware

computer architecture • computer communications • computer engineering • computer hardware • computer networks • concurrent systems • data communications • data networks • hardware • high-performance computers • local area networks • microcomputers • networking hardware • parallel computing • personal computers • pervasive computing • small computer system interface • storage networks • supercomputers

Introductions to the subject

6073 The architecture of computer hardware and systems software
I. Englander 3rd edn, Wiley, 2003, 728pp. $93.95. ISBN 0471073253.
'Most computer architecture books are just too technical and complex. Focusing on specific technology, they often bypass the basics and are outdated as quickly as technology advances. Now, Irv Englander's gentle-but-thorough introduction to computer architecture and systems software

provides just the right amount of technical detail you'll need to make successful decisions in your future career.'

6074 **Chronology of Personal Computers**
K. Polsson
www.islandnet.com/~kpolsson/comphist
Personal interest site. Contains close to 3000 entries gathered from over 1000 sources. 'I have tried to keep it open-minded and unbiased, but the annoying fact is that 'the winners write the history books.'

Computer networking: a top-down approach featuring the internet
J.F. Kurose and K.W. Ross See entry no. 6264

6075 **Data and computer communications**
W. Stallings 7th edn, Prentice Hall, 2003, 847pp. $100.00. ISBN 0131006819.
www.williamstallings.com/DCC/DCC7e.html [COMPANION]
One of a series of leading texts produced by the author for this publisher. 'Emphasizing both the fundamental principles as well as the critical role of performance in driving protocol and network design, it explores in detail all the critical technical areas in data communications, wide-area networking, local area networking, and protocol design. It covers the material in the Computer Communication and Networking core course of the joint ACM/IEEE Computing Curricula 2001.'

- **Computer Engineering 2004: Curriculum guidelines for undergraduate degree programs in computer engineering IEEE Computer Society and Association for Computing Machinery** Downloadable PDF, 162pp. http://www.computer.org/education/cc2001. 'Computer engineering is a discipline that embodies the science and technology of design, construction, implementation, and maintenance of software and hardware components of modern computer systems and computer-controlled equipment.'

6076 **Nanoelectronics and information technology: advanced electronic materials and novel devices**
R. Waser, ed. Wiley-VCH, 2003, 1001pp. £55.00. ISBN 3527403639.
Attractively designed large-format volume in eight parts: I. Fundamentals; II. Technology and analysis; III. Logic devices; IV. Random access memories; V. Mass storage devices; VI. Data transmission and interfaces; VII. Sensor arrays; VIII. Displays.

Numerous diagrams and illustrations, many in colour. Concentrates on fundamental underlying principles and thus can serve as a very good general introduction to the information technologies.

6077 **PC hardware in a nutshell**
R.B. Thompson and B.F. Thompson 3rd edn, O'Reilly, 2003, 850pp. $39.95. ISBN 059600513X.
Well reviewed text that has made strenuous efforts to be accurate – and useful (rather than just interesting). Intended for 'anyone who buys, builds, upgrades or repairs PCs in a corporate, small-business, or home setting'.

6078 **Pervasive computing: the mobile world**
U. Hansmann [et al.] 2nd edn, Springer, 2003, 448pp. £29.50. ISBN 3540002189.
Wide-ranging detailed coverage of the era of Pervasive Computing: 'A new class of devices make information access and processing easily available for everyone from everywhere at any time. Users get enabled to exchange and retrieve information they need quickly, efficiently, and effortlessly, regardless of their physical location.'

Includes coverage of: information access devices; smart identification; embedded controls; entertainment systems; Java; operating systems; client middleware; security; internet protocols and formats; mobile internet; voice; web services; connectivity; service discovery; gateways; application servers; internet portals; device management; synchronization.

Each chapter concludes with a set of further reading and web addresses. A first-rate overview.

6079 **Storage networks explained: basics and application of fibre channel SAN, NAS iSCSI and InfiniBand**
U. Troppens Wiley, 2004, 400pp. $110.00. ISBN 0470861827.
Covers the concepts of storage networks and their basic techniques; usage options; proposed solutions for support of business processes; advantages of and new possibilities opened up by storage networks. Good glossary and short annotated bibliography.

Dictionaries, thesauri, classifications

Wireless A to Z
N.J. Muller See entry no. 6226

Laws, standards, codes

Data, networks, IP and the internet: protocols, design and operation
M.P. Clark, ed. See entry no. 6269

Research centres & institutes

6080 **EPCC** [UK]
University of Edinburgh
www.epcc.ac.uk
'EPCC was established during 1990 as a focus for the University of Edinburgh's work in high performance computing during the previous decade. The Centre's task is to accelerate the effective exploitation of high performance parallel computing systems throughout academia, industry and commerce. It houses an exceptional range of computers, with over 45 full-time staff committed to the solution of real-world problems. 'Good gateway, particularly to research activity in the UK.

6081 **National Center for Supercomputing Applications** [USA]
www.ncsa.uiuc.edu
Located at the University of Illinois campus at Urbana-Champaign and 'one of the five original units in the National Science Foundation's Supercomputer Network. It implements experimental super computing and high performance systems and networks.' Good way in to the field – especially via the facility 'Learn more about.' (Cluster computing; Cyberinfrastructure; Data analysis; Education; Grids; Visualization).

6082 **San Diego Supercomputer Center** [USA]
www.sdsc.edu
Founded in 1985, and 'enables international science and

engineering discoveries through advances in computational science and high performance computing'. Excellent website with revealing details about their wide range of work, categorized: Applications; Storage; Networking & Grids; High-Performance Computing; Data Technology & Databases; Software & Services; Visualization.

6083 **Standard Performance Evaluation Corporation** [USA]
www.specbench.org
Non-profit corporation formed 'to establish, maintain and endorse a standardized set of relevant benchmarks that can be applied to the newest generation of high-performance computers. SPEC develops suites of benchmarks and also reviews and publishes submitted results from our member organizations and other benchmark licensees.'

Associations & societies

6084 **Storage Networking Industry Association** [USA]
www.snia.org/home
Founded 1997 and 'dedicated to ensuring that storage networks become complete and trusted solutions across the IT community'. Good range of news, education and technology resources. Useful and extensive *Dictionary of storage networking terminology*.

Libraries, archives, museums

6085 **Museum of HP Calculators** [USA]
www.hpmuseum.org
'Displays and describes Hewlett-Packard calculators introduced from 1968 to 1986 plus a few interesting later models. There are also sections on calculating machines and slide rules as well as sections for buying and selling HP calculators, an HP timeline, collecting information and a software library.' Useful links to other sites, including for 'Other calculating and scientific instruments' and 'Old computers'.

Portal & task environments

6086 **Hewlett-Packard**
www.hp.com
Major sections are: Desktops and workstations; Notebooks and tablet PCs; Handheld devices; Monitors and projectors; Entertainment; Music; Printing and multifunction; Fax, copiers and scanners; Digital photography; Software products; Supplies and accessories; Servers; Storage; Networking; Management software; Business and IT services; Solutions.

- **Handhelds.Org** www.handhelds.org. 'Part of the Open Source Software movement, focused specifically on handheld and wearable computers. Goal is to encourage and facilitate the creation of open software solutions for use on handheld computing platforms.' Primary sponsor is HP.

6087 **TOP500 Supercomputer Sites**
www.top500.org
Started in 1993 to provide a reliable basis for tracking and detecting trends in high-performance computing.

6088 **WWW Computer Architecture**
University of Wisconsin
www.cs.wisc.edu/arch/www
'Computer Architecture is the science and art of selecting and interconnecting hardware components to create computers that meet functional, performance and cost goals. Computer architecture is not about using computers to design buildings.'

Good set of resources: What's new; Conferences; Tools, simulators and benchmarks; Groups and projects; People; Commercial; On-line publications; Organizations; Books; Awards; Newsgroups.

Discovering print & electronic resources

6089 **WWW Virtual Library: Concurrent Systems**
J. Bowen; London South Bank University
http://vl.fmnet.info/concurrent
Good annotated list of links to resources on concurrent, parallel and distributed systems. Last updated January 2004 in early 2005.

Directories & encyclopedias

6090 **Encyclopedia of microcomputers**
A. Kent and J.G. Williams, eds Marcel Dekker, 1988–2002. 21 v. + 7 supplements, $5460.00. ISBN 082472724X.
www.dekker.com [DESCRIPTION]
'Comprehensive compendium of reliable information on microcomputers from the history and indelible presence of this rapidly advancing technology throughout academe, business, government, as well as other aspects of daily life to its development and future impact.' Last supplement, 2002.

Handbooks & manuals

6091 **The indispensable PC hardware book**
H-P. Messmer 4th edn, Addison Wesley, 2001, 1296pp. $52.99. ISBN 0201596164.
'This is the completely revised and updated fourth edition of this bestselling and award-winning title. It is an essential resource for the relative newcomer to the field looking for expert advice on the basics, or for a systems engineer/hardware engineer looking for a detailed explanation that can't be found elsewhere.'

Internetworking technologies handbook
W. Briggs See entry no. 6286

6092 **iSCSI: the universal storage connection**
J.L. Hufferd Addison-Wesley, 2003, 346pp. $49.99. ISBN 020178419X.
Clearly written introduction, placing SCSI (Small Computer System Interface) technologies in context of related and competitive technologies. Useful appendices, including definitions, acronyms, references and web pointers.

6093 Mac manual: the step-by-step guide to upgrading, repairing and maintaining a Mac
K. Martin Haynes, 2003, 192pp. £19.99. ISBN 1859608892.
www.haynes.co.uk [DESCRIPTION]
'Following in the Haynes style of producing clear step-by-step guides, including the best-selling *Haynes Computer Manual*, this full-colour manual shows how easy it is to upgrade, maintain and repair a Mac. From adding more memory or upgrading the processor to installing a new DVD drive, it takes the reader through each stage using plain English and clear photographs. This jargon-free manual will save time and money and give the reader a basic understanding of all areas of Mac hardware and installation – without blinding them with science.'
'Without question, the *Mac Manual* should be on every Mac user's bookshelf.' (*Times Higher Education Supplement*)

Magnetic storage handbook
C.D. Mee and E.D. Daniel, eds See entry no. 5502

6094 Network consultants handbook
M. Castelli and S. Buker Cisco Press, 2001, 1008pp. $45.00. ISBN 1587050390.
http://safaribooksonline.com
Designed to help consultants and engineers to assess, audit, analyze, and evaluate any existing or future internetwork environment.
Available online: see website.

6095 Newnes data communications pocket book
M.H. Tooley and S. Winder 4th edn, Newnes, 2002, 246pp. £17.99. ISBN 0750652977.
LAN software; Networking; Operating systems; Bluetooth and wireless LANs; Fault-finding on RS-232 systems; Optical fibre technology and the IEEE interface standard; Multiplexing (TDM and FDM); Data compression; Digital line systems; On-line services; Digital radio systems; Glossary of data communications terms; Index.

6096 Practical industrial data networks: design, installation and troubleshooting
S. Mackay [et al.] Elsevier/Newnes, 2004, 421pp. £34.99. ISBN 075065807X.
17 chapters with five appendices: Glossary; Basic terminology; Practicals; Miscellaneous industrial protocols overview; Local services, regulations and standards.
'Because of its practical nature and accessible style, *Practical Industrial Data Networks* could be useful for almost anyone working with networked data on an industrial scale. It is the sort of book that any institute of higher learning, from a community college to a four year university, should have on hand to support its computer science, information technology, engineering and technology departments. Similarly, any business running an industrial data network will find this book a useful reference and guide.' (*E-STREAMS*)

6097 Sourcebook of parallel computing
J.J. Dongarra [et al.], eds Morgan Kaufmann, 2003, 842pp. $59.95. ISBN 1558608710.
Principal goal is to make it easy for newcomers to the field to understand the technologies available and how to apply them. Extensive treatment based on the work done at the Center for Research on Parallel Computation through 25 chapters organized: I. Parallelism; II. Applications; III. Software technologies; IV. Enabling technologies and algorithms; V. Conclusion. Over 1000 references; detailed index.

Tools and environments for parallel and distributed computing
S. Hariri and M. Parashar, eds See entry no. 6152

Keeping up-to-date

6098 NetworkWorldFusion
Network World Inc.
www.nwfusion.com/edge
Busy useful news and background briefing service. Research Centers currently listed are: Applications; Careers; Convergence; Data Center; LANs; Net/Systems Mgmt; NOSes; Outsourcing; Routers/Switches; Security; Service Providers; Small/Med. Business; Storage; WAN Services; Web/e-commerce; Wireless/Mobile.

6099 Primeur
www.hoise.com/primeur
'EnterTheGrid – Primeur is the premier Grid and Supercomputing information source in the world. With Primeur Monthly we provide you a free update with news and in-depth stories. Primeur is supported by a network of analysts, consultants and HPCN centres spread over Europe. Initially, Primeur was supported by the European Commission under the Esprit IV RTD in the Information Technologies work programme.'
- **EnterTheGrid** http://enterthegrid.com. The world's largest directory on Grid computing.

Computer Software & Programming

ADA • algorithmic techniques • C programming language • C# • C++ • computer programming • data compression • data mining • driver files • Fortran • free software • Java • Linux • middleware • open source programs • operating systems • Perl • PHP • programming • scripts • shareware • software development • software engineering • software testing • web services

Introductions to the subject

Human factors methods for design: making systems human-centered
C.P. Nemeth See entry no. 5362

6100 JAVA for engineers and scientists
G.J. Bronson Thomson/Brooks/Cole, 2003, 812pp. $49.95. ISBN 0534384536.
In a manner accessible to the beginning programmer, aims to introduce the four elements Java users need to be familiar with for object-oriented graphical-based programming: The concept of object-oriented program class code; The visual objects required in creating a graphical user interface; The input, output, and mathematical classes required for creating engineering and scientific programs; The concept of event-based programming, where the user, rather than the

programmer, determines the sequence of operations to be executed.

6101 **Programming in C++: lessons and applications**
T.B. D'Orazio McGraw-Hill, 2004, 954pp. $83.12. ISBN 0071194533.
Teaches the C++ language and object-oriented design to students with no previous programming experience.

6102 **Programming languages: principles and practice**
K.C. Louden 2nd edn, Thomson Brooks/Cole, 2003, 694pp. $97.95. ISBN 0534953417.
www.course.com/computerscience/catalog.cfm [DESCRIPTION]
Introduction, containing a general presentation of principles with considerable detail about many modern languages, including some of the newest functional and object-oriented frameworks. Major languages covered include C, C++, Java, ADA, ML, Haskell, Scheme, and Prolog. Although this becomes a fairly advanced treatment, the descriptions are excellent, and there are useful Notes and References appending each chapter.

6103 **Software development failures: anatomy of abandoned projects**
K. Ewusi-Mensah MIT Press, 2003, 276pp. $35.00. ISBN 0262050722.
Designed to help improve the science and practice of software development by making conspicuous the problem of software development failures in both public and private organizations of all types. 'It has been estimated that one-third of software development projects fail or are abandoned outright because of cost overruns, delays, and reduced functionality. Some consider this an acceptable risk – that it is simply the cost of doing business. Ewusi-Mensah argues that understanding the factors involved in development failures will help developers and businesses bring down the rate of software failure and abandoned projects.' Bibliography.

6104 **The success of open source**
S. Weber Harvard University Press, 2004, 320pp. $29.95. ISBN 0674012925.
'Weber argues that the success of open source is not a freakish exception to economic principles. The open source community is guided by standards, rules, decisionmaking procedures, and sanctioning mechanisms. Weber explains the political and economic dynamics of this mysterious but important market development.'

6105 **The Turing test: verbal behavior as the hallmark of intelligence**
S.M. Shieber, ed. MIT Press, 2004, 346pp. $35.00. ISBN 0262692937.
Collection of writings, each with a valuable introductory commentary, related to the famous test whether an artefact was indistinguishable from a person with regard to verbal behaviour. Contributors include Descartes, Sampson, Searle, Dennett, and Chomsky.

- **Turing Digital Archive** www.turingarchive.org. Reproductions of mainly unpublished personal papers and photographs of Alan Turing from 1923–1972. The originals are in the Turing archive in King's College Cambridge.

6106 **Web services: a technical introduction**
H.M. Deitel [et al.] Prentice Hall PTR, 2003, 494pp. $39.99. ISBN 0130461350.
'Web services' are software programs that use XML to exchange information with other software via common internet protocols. Concise, comprehensive, handbook including detailed coverage of the underlying technologies (XML, SOAP, WSDL, UDDI) followed by an overview of web services platforms, vendors and strategies, treatment of.NET and JAVA web services, and extended discussions of security issues.
An excellent manual.

- **WebServices.Org** Web Services Solutions Ltd. www.webservicessolutions.com [REGISTRATION]. 'Vendor-neutral organisation with the aim to offer comprehensive and focused reporting. It is privately owned, and while Sponsors help drive the website, no direct affiliation with any sponsor determines any agenda.'

Dictionaries, thesauri, classifications

6107 **Dictionary of algorithms and data structures**
National Institute of Standards and Technology
www.nist.gov/dads
Algorithms, algorithmic techniques, data structures, archetypical problems, and related definitions. 'We need help in automata theory, combinatorics, parallel or randomized algorithms, heuristics, and quantum computing. We do not include algorithms particular to business data processing, communications, operating systems or distributed algorithms, programming languages, AI, graphics, or numerical analysis: it is tough enough covering 'general' algorithms and data structures. However, if you want to tackle one of these areas, we'll consider including them.' (October, 2004)

6108 **The dictionary of standard C**
R. Jaeschke and D. Byrne Pearson, 2001, 150pp. £13.99. ISBN 0130906204.
Written by the former Chair of the ANSI C committee, this book is an alphabetized quick reference guide to the programming language C.

Laws, standards, codes

6109 **The C++ standard: incorporating Technical Corrigendum 1 : BS ISO/IEC 14882:2003**
British Standards Institution Wiley, 2003, 782pp. $70.00. ISBN 0470846747.
The international standard for the C++ programming language prepared under the auspices of the international C++ committee (Working Group 21 of Sub-Committee 22 of the Joint Technical Commission 1 between ISO and IEC: ISO/IEC JTSC1/SC22/WG21).

6110 **Liberty Alliance**
www.projectliberty.org
'Alliance of more than 150 companies, non-profit and government organizations from around the globe. The consortium is committed to developing an open standard for federated network identity that supports all current and emerging network devices.'

- **Microsoft.NET** www.microsoft.com/net.NET is the Microsoft web services strategy to connect information, people, systems, and devices through software.

Unicode
See entry no. 6319

Research centres & institutes

Center for Discrete Mathematics & Theoretical Computer Science
Rutgers University See entry no. 501

Associations & societies

6111 **Apache Software Foundation**
www.apache.org
Non-profit organization incorporated in the United States of America formed primarily to: Provide a foundation for open, collaborative software development projects by supplying hardware, communication, and business infrastructure; Create an independent legal entity to which companies and individuals can donate resources and be assured that those resources will be used for the public benefit; Provide a means for individual volunteers to be sheltered from legal suits directed at the Foundation's projects; Protect the 'Apache' brand, as applied to its software products, from being abused by other organizations.

Among now a wide range of projects, the Apache HTTP Server 'has been the most popular web server on the Internet since April of 1996. The February 2005 Netcraft Web Server Survey found that more than 68% of the websites on the Internet are using Apache, thus making it more widely used than all other web servers combined.'

6112 **Association of C & C++ Users** [UK]
www.accu.org
'Non-profit organisation devoted to professionalism in programming at all levels. Although primarily focussed on C and C++, we also have interests in Java, C# and Python.' Not a very active website; but maintain an extensive Book Reviews section which – early 2005 – had 2400 reviews dating back to 1991, from 94 publishers, broken down into 93 different subjects, and including a 'Highly Recommended Index'.

6113 **Association of Shareware Professionals**
www.asp-shareware.org
'ASP members are known world-wide for creating quality software at reasonable prices. If you are tired of buying retail software that isn't as good as the picture on the box, and that doesn't quite meet your needs, then discover the world of try-before-you-buy software. Whether you're looking for complete applications, utilities, games, development tools, or any other type of software, chances are good that an ASP member has developed the right software for you ...'

Federation Against Software Theft
See entry no. 6194

6114 **Free Software Foundation**
www.gnu.org/fsf/fsf.html
Founded 1985, and dedicated to promoting computer users' right to use, study, copy, modify, and redistribute computer programs.

6115 **Object Management Group**
www.omg.org
'An open membership, not-for-profit consortium that produces and maintains computer industry specifications for interoperable enterprise applications. Our membership includes virtually every large company in the computer industry, and hundreds of smaller ones. Most of the companies that shape enterprise and Internet computing today are represented on our Board of Directors.'

Very good website with extensive set of resources, including about the flagship specification Model Driven Architecture (MDA): 'An approach to software development that maintains the independence of software designs from the code in which the designs are implemented and from the infrastructure and middleware the application relies upon.'

6116 **Open Source Initiative**
www.opensource.org
'Non-profit corporation dedicated to managing and promoting the Open Source Definition for the good of the community, specifically through the OSI Certified Open Source Software certification mark and program.'

6117 **The Perl Foundation**
www.perlfoundation.org
'Dedicated to the advancement of the Perl programming language through open discussion, collaboration, design, and code.'

6118 **Software & Information Industry Association**
www.siia.net
'The principal trade association for the software and digital content industry.' Good range of programmes and resources; searchable membership directory.

6119 **Web Services Interoperability Organization**
www.ws-i.org
'An open industry organization chartered to promote Web services interoperability across platforms, operating systems and programming languages. The organization's diverse community of Web services leaders helps customers to develop interoperable Web services by providing guidance, recommended practices and supporting resources. All companies interested in promoting Web services interoperability are encouraged to join the effort.'

Are developing a series of Deliverables: 'Resources for Web services developers to create interoperable Web services and verify that their results are compliant with WS-I guidelines. Key WS-I deliverables include Profiles, Sample Applications and Testing Tools.'

Portal & task environments

6120 **Dev Shed**
www.devshed.com
'The Open Source Web Development Site.' Sections include: Administration; Apache; BrainDump; Flash; Java; JavaScript; Multimedia; MySQL; Oracle; Perl; PHP; Practices; Python; Reviews; Security; Style-Sheets; Web Services; XML; Zend; Zope.

6121 **DriverGuide.com**
www.driverguide.com
Searchable archive of over 100,000 driver files, manufacturer information, and links.

6122 **Eclipse Foundation**
www.eclipse.org
'As mainstream IS organizations begin implementing and deploying service-oriented architectures like J2EE and.NET into new computing environments, having standardized, integrated and interoperable technologies will become increasingly important to their success. Industry consortiums like Eclipse and NetBeans that implement tools based upon standards from groups like the Object Management Group and Java Tools Community are well suited to address these types of problems–especially if the groups can coordinate their efforts.' (Gartner)

6123 **Java Technology**
www.sun.com/java
Valuable overview of Sun's Java technology, now ten years old, with range of tools offered.

6124 **The JSP Resource Index**
InfoGenius, Inc.
www.jspin.com
'The definitive guide for JSP web applications, tag libraries, java beans, scripts, and other related resources for JavaServer Pages.'

6125 **Linux Central**
http://linuxcentral.com/_v3
Created and maintained for Linux users by Linux users.

6126 **MetaCollection**
STADTAUS.net.
www.metacollection.com
'This site is a guide for webmasters and developers who are in search of CGI or PHP script archives. As a webmaster you will find link directories where you can look for scripts and code snippets that power your interactive dynamic website. As a programmer you will find link directories where you can publish your own software and drive traffic to your website.'

6127 **Microsoft**
www.microsoft.com
Product Families are: Windows; Office; Windows server system; Developer tools; Business solutions; Games and Xbox; MSN; Windows Mobile.

- **C# Help** www.csharphelp.com. 'C# is a modern, object-oriented language that enables programmers to quickly build a wide range of applications for the new Microsoft.NET platform, which provides tools and services that fully exploit both computing and communications.'
- **Developers dex: Empowering Developers Worldwide** www.developersdex.com. 'One of the fastest growing developer sites on the net ... Over a million resources and unlimited access to over 75 live usenet feeds ... Almost 40,000 developers worldwide have chosen ... [it] for staying up to date on Microsoft web technologies.'
- **SQL Server Worldwide Users Group** www.sswug.org. 'At 219,100+ members, SSWUG is simply the largest group of database professionals, and lots of great help: 72,775 Articles/Summaries; 523 Scripts; 60,202 Discussion Archives; 219 FAQs.' Also covers Oracle, IBM DB2 and XML.
- **WindowSecurity.com** Internet Software Marketing Ltd. www.windowsecurity.com. One of a group of network administration websites, this one focusing on the Microsoft Windows environment. 'WindowSecurity.com is in no way affiliated with Microsoft Corp. Links are sponsored by advertisers.'

6128 **PHP**
http://uk.php.net
'PHP is a widely-used general-purpose scripting language that is especially suited for Web development and can be embedded into HTML ... Much of its syntax is borrowed from C, Java and Perl with a couple of unique PHP-specific features thrown in. The goal of the language is to allow web developers to write dynamically generated pages quickly.'

6129 **SYS-CON Media**
www.sys-con.com
'The world's leading i-technology magazine publisher.' Includes JDJ (Java Developer's Journal) 'ranked number 1 in the world in digital circulation delivery. JDJ's most recent six-month average circulation was 162,019 copies, of which 43% was requested by its subscribers to be delivered digitally. JDJ's monthly digital edition is an identical replica of its print edition.'

6130 **Tucows**
www.tucows.com
Over 40,000 shareware and freeware titles to download for Windows, Linux, Macintosh, and other operating systems.

6131 **UNESCO Free Software Portal**
United Nations Educational, Scientific and Cultural Organization
www.unesco.org/webworld/portal_freesoft
Access to documents and websites which are references for the free software/open source technology movement; also a gateway to resources related to free software.

6132 **Visualbuilder.com: Community for multi-skilled developers**
www.visualbuilder.com
Tech Channels currently include: Java; JSP and servlets; EJB;.NET; ASP.NET; VB.NET; C#; ASP; Visual Basic; Delphi; C++; Web Design; JavaScript; PHP / Perl; XML; Project Mgt; UML; Oracle; SQL Server; Wireless / PDA; CURL.

Directories & encyclopedias

6133 **Encyclopedia of software engineering**
J.J. Marciniak Wiley, 2001, 2076pp. 2 v., $725.00. ISBN 0471377376.
'Covering all aspects of engineering for practitioners who design, write, or test computer programs, this updated edition explores all the issues and principles of software design and engineering. With terminology that adheres to the standard set by The Institute of Electrical and Electronics Engineers, the book features over 500 entries in 35 taxonomic areas, as well as biographies of over 100 personalities who have made an impact in the field.'
'a landmark publication ... a model for other specialized encyclopedias ... highly recommended ... This is a superb reference source, which has no competitors.' (E-STREAMS)

Handbooks & manuals

6134 **The art of computer programming**
D. Knuth Addison Wesley, 1997–. Being issued in several volumes: see website for details.
www-cs-faculty.stanford.edu/~knuth/taocp.html [COMPANION]
'At the end of 1999, these books were named among the best twelve physical-science monographs of the century by AMERICAN SCIENTIST, along with: Dirac on quantum mechanics, Einstein on relativity, Mandelbrot on fractals, Pauling on the chemical bond, Russell and Whitehead on foundations of mathematics, von Neumann and Morgenstern on game theory, Wiener on cybernetics, Woodward and Hoffmann on orbital symmetry, Feynman on quantum electrodynamics, Smith on the search for structure, and Einstein's collected papers. Wow!'

6135 **The art of software testing**
G.J. Myers [et al.] 2nd edn, Wiley, 2004, 177pp. $100.00. ISBN 0471469122.
Revision of bestselling text.

6136 **C# in a nutshell**
P. Drayton 2nd edn, O'Reilly, 2003, 897pp. Includes CD-ROM, $44.95. ISBN 0596005261.
Desktop reference for the Microsoft programming language. Includes API quick reference: guide to 21 namespaces and more than 700 core types and their members.

- **Programming C#** **J. Liberty** 4th edn, O'Reilly, 2005, 689pp. $44.95. ISBN 0596004893. Tutorial on C# and on writing.NET applications with C#.

6137 **Code reading: the open source perspective**
D. Spinellis Addison-Wesley, 2003, 495pp. $49.99. ISBN 0201799405.
Uses more than 600 real-world examples to show how to identify good (and bad) code: how to read it, what to look for, and how to use this knowledge to improve one's own code.

6138 **Critical testing processes: plan, prepare, perform, perfect**
R. Black Addison-Wesley, 2004, 571pp. $49.99. ISBN 0201748681.
Designed for 'everyone who is interested in improving their work as a test professional ... Unlike most other books on software testing, which focus on nuts-and-bolts issues of performing specific tasks, this book will also help you understand the larger context in which and for which testing occurs.'

6139 **Data compression: the complete reference**
D. Salomon 3rd edn, Springer, 2004, 898pp. £54.00. ISBN 0387406972.
Excellent handbook, with an extensive bibliography and a useful glossary. Enlightened throughout by judicious quotations (e.g. 'Are no probabilities to be accepted, merely because they are not certainties?' Jane Austen *Sense and Sensibility*).
'A wonderful treasure chest of information; spanning a wide range of data compression methods, from simple text compression methods to the use of wavelets in image compression. It is unusual for a text on compression to cover the field so completely.' (*ACM Computing Reviews*)

6140 **Data mining: concepts, models, methods, and algorithms**
M. Kantardzic IEEE Press/Wiley, 2003, 345pp. $74.95. ISBN 0471228524.
A first-rate wide-ranging overview. After two introductory chapters covers: Data reduction; Learning from data; Statistical methods; Cluster analysis; Decision trees and decision rules; Association rules; Artificial neural networks; Genetic algorithms; Fuzzy sets and fuzzy logic; Visualization methods.

An extensive first appendix covers data mining tools, followed by one examining 'a few application domains illustrated by the results of data-mining systems that have been implemented'.

Database design and development: an essential guide for IT professionals
P. Ponniah See entry no. 6399

6141 **FORTRAN 95/2003 explained**
M. Metcalf 3rd edn, Oxford University Press, 2004, 416pp. £23.95. ISBN 0198526938.
The latest standard – Fortran 2003 – greatly extends the power of the language by introducing object-oriented concepts, interoperability with C, better integration with operating systems and many other enhancements detailed in this comprehensive and well written, well presented reference to a language which 'remains one of the principal languages used in scientific, numerical, and engineering programming'.

- **The Fortran Company** www.fortran.com. Products, services, and general information related to the Fortran programming language.

Handbook of data management in information systems
J. Blazewicz [et al.], eds See entry no. 6401

6142 **A handbook of software and systems engineering: empirical observations, laws, and theories**
A. Endres and H.D. Rombach Addison Wesley, 2003, 327pp. $55.80. ISBN 0321154207.
'Intended as a handbook for students and practitioners alike. The book is structured around the type of tasks that practitioners are confronted with, beginning with requirements definition and concluding with maintenance and withdrawal. It identifies and discusses existing laws that have a significant impact on the software engineering field. These laws are largely independent of the technologies involved, which allow students to learn the principles underlying software engineering. This also guides students toward the best practice when implementing software engineering techniques.'
Series: Fraunhofer IESE Series in Software Engineering, v. 1.

6143 **Linux in a nutshell**
E. Siever, S. Figgins and A. Weber 4th edn, O'Reilly, 2003, 928pp. $39.95. ISBN 0596004826.
Covers all substantial user, programming, administration, and networking commands for the most common Linux distributions.

6144 **Mathematical structures for computer science**
J.L. Gersting 5th edn, W H Freeman, 2003, 729pp. $103.95. ISBN 0716743582.
www.whfreeman.com/gersting [COMPANION]
Covers all the topics identified in Computing Curricula 2001

as the discrete structures 'foundational material for computer science', one of the set of knowledge units 'for which there is a broad consensus that the material is essential to an undergraduate degree in computer science'.

Includes: formal logic; proofs, recursion, and analysis of algorithms; sets, combinatorics, and probability; relations, functions, and matrices; graphs and trees; graph algorithms; Boolean algebra and computer logic; modelling arithmetic, computation, and languages.

- **ACM Special Interest Group on Computer Science Education: SIGCSE** www.sigcse.org/topics. 'SIGCSE Education Links is a collection of resources maintained and shared by SIGCSE members to support computer science education. You can borrow resources and learn from others ... Share your resources (takes about 10 minutes).'

6145 Metrics and models in software quality engineering
S. Kan 2nd edn, Addison-Wesley, 2003, 560pp. $64.99. ISBN 0201729156.
Provides practical guidelines in the practice of quality engineering in software development, as well as coverage of the various types of metrics and models in the emerging field of software quality engineering. Then attempts to focus on using, not just describing, the metrics, as well as on the more general aspects of quality process and control within the organization.

6146 Middleware for communications
Q.H. Mahmoud Wiley, 2004, 487pp. $130.00. ISBN 0470862068.
Aims to provide a state-of-the-art guide to middleware, covering all aspects and including chapters on concepts and fundamentals for beginners to get started, leading on to advanced topics, research-oriented treatments, and case studies.

6147 Perspectives on web services: applying SOAP, WSDL and UDDI to real-world projects
O. Zimmermann, M. Tomlinson and S. Peuser Springer, 2003, 648pp. £34.50. ISBN 3540009140.
A well written manual, primarily using a Java/IBM WebSphere framework, but – since similar architectural decisions need to be taken – valuable also for those using an alternative platform such as.NET rather than J2EE. Interestingly and – for many managers charged with deciding how to proceed with web services – helpfully organized as a series of perspectives covering, in turn: Business; Training; Architecture; Development; Operational; Engagement (the rear view on web services projects); Future.

6148 The SEI series in software engineering
Carnegie Mellon University Addison-Wesley.
www.awprofessional.com/series [DESCRIPTION]
Collaboration between the University's Software Engineering Institute and Addison-Wesley 'to develop and publish a body of work on selected topics in software engineering. The common goal of the SEI and Addison-Wesley is to provide the most current software engineering information in a form that is easily usable by practitioners and students.'
One of a considerable number of ICT-related series from the publisher: see website.

6149 Software design
D. Budgen 2nd edn, Pearson Addison-Wesley, 2003, 468pp. £35.99. ISBN 0201722194.
Seeks to describe the domain of software design in a scholarly and non-partisan manner. Covers the whole range of issues in its three parts: The role of software design; Transferring design knowledge; Design principles. Each of the 19 chapters concludes with Further Reading; and there is an extensive bibliography. A good book.
Series: International Computer Science.

6150 Software engineering: a practitioner's approach
R.S. Pressman 6th edn, McGraw-Hill, 2005, 880pp. $110.93. ISBN 007301933X.
http://catalogs.mhhe.com/mhhe/home.do [COMPANION]
'For over 20 years, *Software engineering: a practitioner's approach* has been the best selling guide to software engineering for students and industry professionals alike ...'

- **Software engineering resources** www.rspa.com/spi/index.html. Over 1000 software engineering resources assembled by the firm R S Pressman & Associates.

6151 Software engineering handbook
J. Keyes Auerbach, 2003, 874pp. $139.95. ISBN 0849314798.
Practical text. Section 1 contains 20 chapters on all facets of software engineering; Section II is concerned with metrics: productivity, quality, reliability methods; Section III is a series of 19 appendices giving guides, templates, forms, and filled-out examples from the real world.
'The *Software Engineering Handbook* is written for software developers; unlike many other texts, it is written to be used in developers' everyday work. Care has been taken to reference outside sources consulted for the text, easily leading readers to more detailed information when needed. This book is recommended for libraries that serve IT professionals or training programs.' (*E-STREAMS*)

6152 Tools and environments for parallel and distributed computing
S. Hariri and M. Parashar, eds Wiley, 2004, 212pp. $94.95. ISBN 0471332887.
'Covering a wide variety of approaches to parallel and distributed computing, with emphasis on such factors as tradeoffs between performance and cost, the authors present a thorough survey of today's most promising software applications, their strengths and limitations, including: Grid computing; Message-passing tools; Distributed shared-memory tools; Distributed object computing tools.'

Keeping up-to-date

6153 BetaNews
www.betanews.com
Provides news on what beta versions of software are available (and in some cases visitors can download them directly from the site), as well as the latest news and reviews. Members can post reviews of software, comment on articles, and take advantage of special member-only features.

Digital Multimedia

3D applications • computer graphics • digital audio • digital video • graphics • image management • image processing • multimedia • video databases • video electronics • virtual reality

Introductions to the subject

6154 **Digital multimedia**
N. Chapman and J. Chapman 2nd edn, Wiley, 2004, 698pp. $50.00. ISBN 0470858907.
www.digitalmultimedia.org [COMPANION]
First-rate very well written introduction with friendly well laid out companion site giving access to a Showcase of professional sites, student work and worldwide course-related information and other useful resources.

- **Digital media tools** **N. Chapman and J. Chapman** 2nd edn, Wiley, 2003, 646pp. $55.00. ISBN 047085748X. Common features; Photoshop bitmapped images; ImageReady web graphics; Flash: animation with interactivity; Illustrator vector graphics; Dreamweaver websites; Premiere video and audio; Colour, typography and Bézier curves; Optimizing images for the web.

6155 **Fundamentals of multimedia**
Z.-N. Li and M.S. Drew Pearson Education, 2004, 560pp. $75.00. ISBN 0130618721.
www.prenhall.com/li_drew [COMPANION]
Organized into three parts: Multimedia authoring and data representations; Multimedia data compression; Multimedia communication and retrieval.

Wide coverage reflects the definition of multimedia applications as those which 'use multiple modalities to their advantage, including text, images, drawings (graphics), animation, video, sound (including speech), and, most likely, interactivity of some kind'.

This is a mathematically-rich text, but valuable in emphasizing the important contributions that previously rather separate disciplines – graphics, visualization, HCI, computer vision, data compression, graph theory, networking, database systems – are making to multimedia at the present time. A very good overview.

6156 **The new media reader**
N. Wardrip-Fruin and N. Montfort, eds MIT Press, 2003, 823pp. Includes CD-ROM, $48.00. ISBN 0262232278.
'Collects the texts, videos, and computer programs – many of them now almost impossible to find – that chronicle the history and form the foundation of the still-emerging field of new media ... The texts are by computer scientists, artists, architects, literary writers, interface designers, cultural critics, and individuals working across disciplines.'
'*The New Media Reader* ... is my if-you-can-only-take-one pick for a computer history vacation suitcase-stuffer.' (*Dr Dobb's Journal*)

The science of color
S.K. Shevell, ed.; Optical Society of America See entry no. 801

6157 **Virtual reality technology**
G. Burdea and P. Coiffet 2nd edn, Wiley-InterScience, 2003, 444pp. Includes CD-ROM, $120.00. ISBN 0471360899.
www.caip.rutgers.edu/vrtechnology [COMPANION]
'Virtual reality is a very powerful and compelling computer application by which humans can interface and interact with computer-generated environments in a way that mimics real life and engages all the senses. Although its most widely known application is in the entertainment industry, the real promise of virtual reality lies in such fields as medicine, engineering, oil exploration and the military, to name just a few. Through virtual reality scientists can triple the rate of oil discovery, pilots can dogfight numerically-superior 'bandits', and surgeons can improve their skills on virtual (rather than real) patients.'
'a well written introductory book on the subject ... a fascinating book on a subject that everyone in medical technology will be using more of in coming years.' (*Biomedical Instrumentation & Technology*)

Dictionaries, thesauri, classifications

6158 **Elsevier's dictionary of computer graphics in English, German, French and Russian**
P. Manoilov and B. Delijska Elsevier, 2000, 792pp. £119.50. ISBN 0444500278.
'10,540 terms with more than 2600 cross-references that are commonly used in the theory and practice of computer graphics. Included are terms from all areas related to a) the theory of computer graphics – descriptive geometry, projective geometry, topology, fractal geometry, color science; and b) the practice of computer graphics – computer-aided design (CAD) systems, technical drawing, computer art, computer animation, business graphics, scientific visualization, virtual reality, graphical programming, image processing, graphical computer devices.'

6159 **IMCCA Glossary**
Interactive Multimedia Collaborative Communications Alliance
www.imcca.org/Glossary.asp
Extensive lists – usefully divided into general reference, and technical – 'elucidates the 'nitty-gritty' of the industry jargon'. Access to good collection of other relevant resources.

6160 **The Photoshop user's A–Z**
P. Cope Thames & Hudson, 2001, 266pp. £14.95. ISBN 050051061X.
'Every Photoshop term you're ever likely to need, see or use.' There is a companion *Digital photographer's A–Z*.
'The definitive guide to the terminology of the best image editing suite on the market. If you are serious about digital photography and want to maximise the potential of Photoshop, then this is a book worth adding to your digital library' (*Amateur Photographer*)

6161 **Thesaurus for graphic materials**
Library of Congress
www.loc.gov/rr/print/tgm1
Over 6300 terms for indexing visual materials as well as numerous cross references. Divided into: I. Subject terms; II. Genre and physical characteristic terms. Prepared by the Library's Prints and Photographs Division. Last revised 1995.

Laws, standards, codes

6162 **International Multimedia Telecommunications Consortium**
www.imtc.org
'Worldwide community of companies dedicated to the advancement of real-time, rich-media communications.

Interoperability through international standards is our core value. Member companies come together to ensure compatibility amongst their products and services, thus guaranteeing trouble-free operation for both end customers and service suppliers.'

6163 **Moving Picture Experts Group**
www.chiariglione.org/mpeg/index.htm
MPEG, the working group of the standards bodies ISO/IEC, established in 1988 and in charge of the development of standards for coded representation of digital audio and video.

- **MPEG Industry Forum** www.m4if.org. 'To further the adoption of MPEG Standards, by establishing them as well accepted and widely used standards among creators of content, developers, manufacturers, providers of services, and end users.' Useful set of resources.

6164 **Society of Motion Picture and Television Engineers**
www.smpte.org
Important standards body. Range of engineering committees. Useful list of websites of related bodies. Good 'motion imaging news' service.

6165 **Video Electronics Standards Association**
www.vesa.org
130 corporate members worldwide. 'VESA supports and sets industry-wide interface standards for the PC, workstation, and consumer electronics industries. VESA promotes and develops timely, relevant, open standards for the display and display interface industry, ensuring interoperability and encouraging innovation and market growth.'

Associations & societies

6166 **Association for Information and Image Management International**
www.aiim.org
'AIIM is the international authority on Enterprise Content Management (ECM), the tools and technologies that capture, manage, store, preserve, and deliver content in support of business processes.'

6167 **European Association for Computer Graphics**
www.eg.org
Very good cleanly-displayed website. Excellent sets of resources including the *Eurographics Bibliography Database*. 'Eurographics is the only truly Europe-wide professional Computer Graphics association. The association supports its members in advancing the state of the art in Computer Graphics and related fields such as Multimedia, Scientific Visualization and Human Computer Interfaces.'

European Association for Speech, Signal and Image Processing
See entry no. 5435

6168 **International Academy of Digital Arts and Sciences**
www.iadas.net
'Founded in 1998 to help drive the creative, technical, and professional progress of the Internet and evolving forms of interactive media.' Selects the nominees and winners for The Webby Awards, 'the leading honor for Web sites and individual achievement in technology and creativity'.

6169 **International Imaging Industry Association**
www.i3a.org
Merged from Digital Imaging Group (DIG) and Photographic and Imaging Manufacturers Association (PIMA) and 'dedicated to developing and promoting the adoption of open industry standards, addressing environmental issues and providing a voice for the industry'. Well designed and presented website with useful resources and excellent links section.

6170 **Visual Resources Association**
http://vraweb.org
'The international organization of image media professionals ... Our international membership includes: information specialists, digital image specialists; art, architecture, film and video librarians, museum curators; slide, photograph, microfilm and digital archivists, architectural firms, galleries, publishers, image system vendors, rights and reproductions officials, photographers, art historians, artists, and scientists.'

6171 **Web3D Consortium**
www.web3d.org
'Member-funded industry consortium committed to the creation and deployment of open, royalty-free standards that enable the communication of real-time 3D across applications, networks, and XML web services. The Consortium works closely with the ISO, MPEG and W3C standardization bodies to maximize market opportunities for its membership.'

Excellent set of resources on well structured website. X3D is an Open Standards XML-enabled 3D file format to enable real-time communication of 3D data across all applications and network applications. There is a useful '10 compelling reasons' for moving from the VRML standard to X3D.

Portal & task environments

CADTutor: The Best Free Tutorials on the Web
D. Watson See entry no. 5378

Molecular Expressions: Exploring the world of optics and microscopy
M.W. Davidson; Florida State University See entry no. 809

Discovering print & electronic resources

6172 **Graphbib**
Association for Computing Machinery
www.siggraph.org/publications/bibliography
15,500 references in easily searched basic database. Maintained by the ACM SIGGRAPH – the specialist interest group on graphics.

Handbooks & manuals

Computer vision: a modern approach
D. Forsyth and J. Ponce See entry no. 5715

Digital signal processing handbook
V.K. Madisetti and D.B. Williams, eds See entry no. 5471

6173 **Field guide to digital color**
M.C. Stone A K Peters, 2003, 326pp. $48.00. ISBN 1568811616.
Contents are: Color vision; Color appearance; RGB and brightness; Color in nature; Color reproduction; Color image capture; Additive color systems; Subtractive color systems; Color management systems; Color in computer graphics; Color selection and design; Color in information display.

- **International Color Consortium** www.color.org. Established 1993 by eight industry vendors for the purpose of creating, promoting and encouraging the standardization and evolution of an open, vendor-neutral, cross-platform colour management system architecture and components.

Foundations of image science
H.H. Barrett and K.J. Myers See entry no. 817

6174 **Handbook of video databases: design and applications**
B. Furht and O. Marques, eds CRC Press, 2004, 1211pp. $139.95. ISBN 084937006X.
Written 'to serve the needs of a growing community of researchers and practitioners in the fields of database systems, information retrieval image and video processing, machine learning, data mining, human-computer interaction, among many others, and provide them with a comprehensive overview of the state of the art in 'video databases and applications'.'

Over 100 contributors have provided generally good overviews of each of their fields. However, the book's basic black and white design and large-scale format are rather uninviting.

6175 **The image processing handbook**
J.C. Russ 4th edn, CRC Press, 2002, 744pp. $159.95. ISBN 084931142X.
Well established in its area. Organized in 14 chapters – Acquiring images; Printing and storage; Correcting imaging defects; Image enhancement; Processing images in frequency space; Segmentation and thresholding; Processing binary images; Global image measurements; Feature-specific measurements; Feature recognition and classification; 3d image acquisition; High resolution tomography; 3d image visualization; and Imaging surfaces.
1st edn 1992, 3rd edn 1998.

6176 **Multimedia databases: an object-relational approach**
L. Dunckley Addison-Wesley, 2003, 452pp. Includes CD-ROM, £37.99. ISBN 0201788993.
Comprehensive overview – suitable for those working in either multimedia or database areas. Includes a useful introduction to relational, object-oriented and object-relational databases. SQL, the standard language for interfacing with relational databases is covered in detail based on the SQL3 (or SQL: 1999) standard.

6177 **Professional content management systems: handling digital media assets**
A. Mauthe and P. Thomas Wiley, 2004, 314pp. $110.00. ISBN 0470855428.
Well structured, clearly written and wide-ranging volume including treatments of: Content-related workflows; Essence ('the physical representation of content in different forms and formats'); Content representation and metadata; File formats; Content management system architecture; Content management system infrastructure; System and data integration in CMS; Applications; Future trends.

6178 **The reproduction of colour**
R.W.G. Hunt; Society for Imaging Science and Technology 6th edn, Wiley, 2004. $155.00. ISBN 0470024259.
Now standard text. 37 chapters in six parts: Fundamentals; Colour photography; Colour television; Colour printing; Digital imaging; Evaluating colour appearance.

- **Society for Imaging Science and Technology** www.imaging.org. 'The first place technical professionals and users go for knowledge on techniques, processes, and systems for imaging.'

6179 **Sound synthesis and sampling**
M. Russ 2nd edn, Focal, 2004, 473pp. £29.99. ISBN 0240516923.
Excellent well produced non-mathematical introduction. Good reference section which includes: References; Glossary; Jargon; Index. The 'jargon' section is 'designed to try and prevent the confusion that often results from the wide variation in the terminology which is used in the field of synthesizers. Each entry consists of the term which is used in this book, followed by the alternative names which can be used for that term'.

6180 **SVG unleashed**
A. Watt [et al.] Sams, 2003, 1117pp. $49.99. ISBN 0672324296.
Scalable vector graphics (SVG) is an XML-based graphics standard from the World Wide Web Consortium which opens up new and powerful ways for programmers to generate graphics for display on a variety of devices.

Extensive and comprehensive handbook organized: SVG fundamentals; Programming SVG client-side; Producing SVG server-side; Case studies; Looking ahead. Extensive index.

Keeping up-to-date

6181 **Computer Graphics World**
PennWell Corporation.
http://cgw.pennnet.com
Covers graphics, 3D modelling, computer-aided design, visual computing, etc. 48,000 subscribers.

6182 **DigitalMediaEurope: Digital media news for Europe**
www.dmeurope.com
Online daily newswire and subscription service dedicated to covering continent-wide developments in digital media.

Information System Security

authentication • computer security • cryptography • cybercrime • cybersecurity • fingerprint recognition • firewalls • hacking • information security • public key infrastructure • smart cards • software theft • spam • viruses

Introductions to the subject

6183 **Computer security: art and science**
M. Bishop Addison-Wesley, 2003, 1084pp. $79.99. ISBN 0201440997.

A well designed and written theoretically-based text, beginning with the mathematical fundamentals and principles that provide boundaries within which security can be modelled and analyzed effectively. These are then applied to the challenges of expressing and analyzing the requirements of the security of a system. Bibliography of over 1000 entries.

6184 Cybercrime: a reference handbook
B.H. Schell and C. Martin ABC-CLIO, 2004, 247pp. $50.00. ISBN 1851096833.
'Documents the history of computer hacking from free long distance phone calls to virtual espionage to worries of a supposed 'cyber apocalypse,' and provides accessible information everyone should know.' Bibliography pp 209–222.

6185 Firewalls and Internet security: repelling the wily hacker
W.R. Cheswick, S.M. Bellovin and A.D. Rubin 2nd edn, Addison-Wesley, 2003, 433pp. $49.99. ISBN 020163466X.
An easy to read good introductory text. Although primarily intended for those charged with installing and maintaining secure systems, highly recommended reading for all those with significant managerial responsibility for information systems. Appendix B is an excellent overview of techniques for 'keeping up' with the subject.
Series: Addison-Wesley Professional Computing.

Guide to biometrics
R.M. Bolle See entry no. 3601

6186 Practical cryptography
N. Ferguson and B. Schneier Wiley, 2003, 432pp. $50.00. ISBN 0471223573.
'Much anticipated follow-up book to Schneier's seminal encyclopedic reference, *Applied Cryptography* ... which has sold more than 150,000 copies.'

Dictionaries, thesauri, classifications

6187 The information security dictionary: defining the terms that define security for e-business, internet, information and wireless technology
U.E. Gattiker Kluwer Academic, 2004, 411pp. £92.00. ISBN 1402078897.
Defines c.1200 of the most commonly used words in the field with particular attention to those terms used most often in forensics, malware ('encompasses all types of malicious or harmful software, such as viruses, Trojan horses, and worms'), viruses, vulnerabilities, and IPv6 ('the next generation internet').

Extensive definitions including – inter alia – 29 supplementary tables, and a very useful series of appendices: 'Suggestion for additional resources: Books or internet sites ... that are especially clearly written, and/or widely cited 'classical' accounts, and/or representative of some of the many (relevant) disciplines.'

An excellent volume, marred only by its less than excellent page design.
Series: Kluwer International Series in Engineering and Computer Science, V. 767.

6188 Virus glossary
McAfee.
http://us.mcafee.com/virusInfo
Useful glossary maintained by the provider of retail and online solutions designed to secure, protect and optimize the computers of consumers and home office users.

Laws, standards, codes

6189 Information security: BS 7799 [UK]
British Standards Institution
www.bsi-global.com/Global/bs7799.xalter
'There is a need to establish a comprehensive Information Security Policy within all organisations. You need to ensure the confidentiality, integrity, and availability of both vital corporate information and customer information. The standard for Information Security Management System (ISMS) BS 7799, has fast become one of the world's established biggest sellers.'

Official & quasi-official bodies

6190 Communications-Electronics Security Group [UK]
www.cesg.gov.uk
'The Information Assurance (IA) arm of GCHQ [Government Communications Headquarter] and we are based in Cheltenham, Gloucestershire, UK. We are the UK Government's National Technical Authority for IA, responsible for enabling secure and trusted knowledge sharing to help our customers achieve their business aims.

There are five key principles, essential for safe electronic transactions: Confidentiality – keeping information private; Integrity – ensuring information has not been tampered with; Authentication – confirming the identity of the individual who undertook the transaction; Non-repudiation – the individual who undertook the transaction cannot subsequently deny it; Availability – ensuring information is available when required.'

- **European Network and Information Security Agency** www.enisa.eu.int. New European Community body which 'assists the Commission, the Member States and, consequently, the business community in meeting the requirements of network and information security, including present and future Community legislation'.
- **MI5** www.mi5.gov.uk. Official website of service 'responsible for protecting the UK against threats to national security ... Provides information on the current major threats to UK security and practical advice to help businesses and organizations to protect against them'.

6191 Computer Security Resource Center [USA]
http://csrc.ncsl.nist.gov
The National Institute of Standards and Technology Computer Security Division works to improve information systems security by: Raising awareness of IT risks, vulnerabilities and protection requirements, particularly for new and emerging technologies; Researching, studying, and advising agencies of IT vulnerabilities and devising techniques for the cost-effective security and privacy of sensitive Federal systems; Developing standards, metrics, tests and validation programs: Promoting, measuring, and validating security in systems and services; Educating consumers; Establishing minimum security requirements for Federal systems; Developing guidance to increase secure IT planning, implementation, management and operation.

- **Computer Incident Advisory Capability: CIAC United States. Department of Energy and National Nuclear Security Administration**. www.ciac.org/ciac/index.html. Wide range of bulletins, documents, tools, and news. Detailed website index. 'The mission of CIAC is to apply cyber security expertise to prevent, detect, react to, and recover from cyber incidents for DOE/NNSA and other national stakeholders.'
- **National Security Agency/Central Security Service** www.nsa.gov. 'America's cryptologic organization. It coordinates, directs, and performs highly specialized activities to protect US information systems and produce foreign intelligence information.' Extensive multi-media site: sections for Responsible Citizens/Kids.

Research centres & institutes

6192 **CERT Coordination Center** [USA]
www.cert.org
Centre of internet security expertise, located at the Carnegie Mellon Software Engineering Institute. 'Our information ranges from protecting your system against potential problems to reacting to current problems to predicting future problems. Our work involves handling computer security incidents and vulnerabilities, publishing security alerts, researching long-term changes in networked systems, and developing information and training to help you improve security at your site.'

Associations & societies

6193 **Coalition Against Unsolicited Commercial Email** [USA]
www.cauce.org
Advocating legislation and now has affiliates in Europe, Canada, Australia, and India.

- **SPEWS.ORG: Spam prevention early warning system** www.spews.org. List of areas on the internet which several system administrators, ISP postmasters, and other service providers have assembled and use to deny e-mail and in some cases, all network traffic from. Now available for general public to use for e-mail filtering.

6194 **Federation Against Software Theft** [UK]
www.fast.org.uk
Set up in 1984 by the British Computer Society Copyright Committee and the first software copyright organization. Unique in being the only association in the world that represents both software publishers and end users.

6195 **International Association of Computer Investigative Specialists**
www.cops.org
'Volunteer non-profit corporation composed of law enforcement professionals dedicated to education in the field of forensic computer science.'

6196 **Open Web Application Security Project**
www.owasp.org
'All-volunteer group that produces free, professional-quality, open-source documentation, tools, and standards.'

6197 **SANS Institute**
www.sans.org
'The most trusted and by far the largest source for information security training and certification in the world. It also develops, maintains, and makes available at no cost, the largest collection of research documents about various aspects of information security, and it operates the Internet's early warning system – Internet Storm Center.'

Portal & task environments

6198 **The Information Warfare Site: IWS**
www.iwar.org.uk
Useful wide-ranging 'online resource that aims to stimulate debate on a variety of issues involving information security, information operations, computer network operations, homeland security and more. It is the aim of the site to develop a special emphasis on offensive and defensive information operations.' However, some parts of the site not developed or recently updated.

6199 **PKIForum.com**
www.pkiforum.com
Independent news, information and education organization focused on public key infrastructure.

- **Planning for PKI: best practices guide for deploying public key infrastructure** R. Housley and T. Polk Wiley, 2001, 327pp. $65.00. ISBN 0471397024. An in-depth technical guide on the security technology driving internet e-commerce expansion.

6200 **SNP: The security news portal for information system security professionals**
www.securitynewsportal.com
Includes detailed listings of latest security, virus, vulnerability, etc threats. Also more general extensive news service.

6201 **Sophos**
www.sophos.com
UK-headquartered company which aims to be a 'world leader in protecting businesses against viruses and spam. Over 35 million users from organizations of all sizes already benefit from our software and first-class 24/7 support.' Latest virus and spam information.

- **ActiveState** www.activestate.com. 'Leading provider of tools and services for dynamic languages such as Perl, PHP, Python, Tcl and XSLT. Over two million developers rely on ActiveState's professional development tools, high-quality language distributions and enterprise services.'

Digital data, image & text collections

6202 **infoSECURITYnetBASE**
CRC Press.
http://infosecuritynetbase.com
One of the series of searchable full-text collections of handbooks: 51 titles online, early 2005.

Handbooks & manuals

6203 **Authentication: from passwords to public keys**
R.E. Smith Addison-Wesley, 2001, 549pp. $49.99. ISBN 0201615991.
'Reviews every option for authentication, from passwords to biometrics, and virtually every application scenario – offering practical guidance on choosing the best option, implementing it, and managing it.'

6204 **Cryptography, error correction, and information theory: a handbook for the 21st century**
A.A. Bruen and M.A. Forcinito Wiley, 2005, 468pp. $99.95. ISBN 0471653179.
www.surengineering.com [COMPANION]
24 chapters offering a detailed coverage, organized into the three sections: I. Cryptography; II. Information theory; III. Error correction. Glossary. Bibliography. Index.

6205 **Cybersecurity operations handbook**
J.W. Rittinghouse and W.M. Hancock Elsevier Digital Press, 2003, 1267pp. $94.95. ISBN 1555583067.
Primarily US-based text systematically covering the underlying principles, followed by a detailed review of the range of issues that must be addressed in this critical field: e.g. Firewalls; Virtual Private Networks (VPNs) and remote access; Intrusion detection; Keys, signatures, certificates; Hacking; Cyberforensics ('the science of acquiring, preserving, retrieving, and presenting data that has been processed electronically and stored on computer media'); Business continuity; Outsourcing; Service Level Agreements.

There are a number of useful appendices, including a good list of 'Useful URLs'.

6206 **Handbook of fingerprint recognition**
D, Maltoni [et al.] Springer, 2003, 348pp. Includes CD-ROM, £56.00. ISBN 0387954317.
Chapters are: Introduction; Fingerprint sensing; Fingerprint analysis and representation; Fingerprint matching; Fingerprint classification and indexing; Synthetic fingerprint generation; Multimodal systems; Fingerprint individuality; Securing fingerprint systems.
Series: Springer Professional Computing.
'a useful reference for all biometric security professionals and researchers. The four co-authors have a distinguished combination of academic and professional experience ... Overall, readers will be pleased with the style and substance of this book.' (*Computing Reviews*)

6207 **Security in computing**
C.P. Pfleeger and S.L. Pfleeger 3rd edn, Prentice Hall PTR, 2003, 746pp. $79.00. ISBN 0130355488.
Detailed but readable handbook, notable for its good use of diagrams, and extended non-technical discussions of the issues.

6208 **Smart card handbook**
W. Rankl and W. Effing 3rd edn, Wiley, 2003, 1088pp. Translation by Kenneth Cox of the German 4th edn, $185.00. ISBN 0470856688.
Translation of the original (2002) German edn aiming to describe the subject in as much detail as possible: 'We have remained true to our motto: "Better one sentence too many, than one word too few."'

Nevertheless, this major compendium is well structured and presented with a useful appendix including an 85-page glossary and a 30-page 'Annotated directory of standards and specifications'.

The definitive work.

6209 **Writing information security policies**
S. Barman and M. Puckett Pearson Education, 2001, 240pp. £27.50. ISBN 157870264X.
13 chapters in three parts: I. Starting the policy process; II. Writing the security policies; III. Maintaining the policies. Useful Resources section encompassing: Incident response teams; Other incident response information; Virus protection; Vendor-specific security information; Security information resources; Security publications; Industry consortia and associations; Hacker and 'Underground' organizations; Health Insurance Portability and Accountability Act; Survivability; Cryptography policies and regulations; Security policy references.

Telecommunications

3G mobile communications • broadband networks • communications technology • digital subscriber line technology • fibre-optic communications • local loops • mobile communications • remote access networks • satellite communications • wireless communication

Introductions to the subject

Data and computer communications
W. Stallings See entry no. 6075

6210 **Fundamentals of telecommunications**
R.L. Freeman 2nd edn, Wiley, 2005, 675pp. $89.95. ISBN 0471710458.
Provides an overview of the broad area of telecommunications, written for those with only a limited technical understanding. Its 18 chapters cover all aspects including telephony, local area networks, data communications, television, and radio. Appendices give basic mathematical and circuit background.
'Very readable ... A very good introductory book (on 1st edn).' (*Choice*)

6211 **Guide to telecommunications technology**
T. Dean Thomson Course Technology, 2003, 840pp. $73.95. ISBN 0619035471.
www.course.com/catalog
Good introductory textbook. Chapters are: Telecommunications overview; Principles of telecommunications technology; The evolution of telecommunications technology and policy; The public network; Customer premise equipment and applications; Signalling and switching; Data networking fundamentals; Physical transmission media; Wireless transmission services; Network access and transmission methods; Data network connectivity; internet standards and services; Information security; Convergence of voice, video and data.

Extensive glossary (50 pp).
See website for details of extensive range of publisher's Course Technology *offerings: 'What started as 'helping people teach and learn* about *technology' has now evolved to 'helping people teach and learn* with *technology.'*

6212 **Introduction to 3G mobile communications**
J. Korhonen 2nd edn, Artech House, 2003, 544pp. £69.00. ISBN 1580535070.
Well organized and well written detailed information source explaining the principles and basic concepts of the third generation (3G) telecommunications systems, focusing on Universal Mobile Telecommunication System (UMTS)/Third Generation Partnership Project (3GPP). Appendix C is a set of useful web addresses; and Appendix E a descriptive list of standardization organizations and industry groups.
Series: Artech House Mobile Communications.

6213 **The second information revolution**
G.W. Brock Harvard University Press, 2003, 336pp. $39.95. ISBN 0674011783.
Brock's thesis is that there has been twice in history when information technology has dramatically changed daily life. The first 'information revolution' occurred with the advent of the telephone and telegraph, which made communication less expensive and more readily available. The second information revolution is currently in progress.

6214 **Telecommunications essentials: the complete global source for communications fundamentals, data networking and the internet, and next-generation networks**
L. Goleniewski Addison-Wesley, 2002, 582pp. $54.99. ISBN 0201760320.
www.telecomessentials.com [COMPANION]
'Providing a comprehensive, one-stop reference for anybody wanting to get up to speed on the $2.5 trillion telecommunications industry, this book not only covers the basic building blocks but also introduces the most current information on new technologies like wireless, broadband, and optical networking.'
The Companion site is very lively.

6215 **Wireless technician's handbook**
A. Miceli 2nd edn, Artech House, 2003, 292pp. £55.00. ISBN 1580533574.
Covers first generation analogue cellular and second generation digital cellular systems and then the 2.5G and 3G wireless technologies that deliver increased voice capacity and/or high-speed packet data services.

Dictionaries, thesauri, classifications

6216 **Anglo-russkii slovar' po telekommunikatsiiam (English–Russian dictionary of telecommunications)** [RUS]
A.V. Aleksandrov RUSSO, 2004, 480pp. $39.95. ISBN 5887212489.
www.eastview.com/search_book.asp
About 34,000 terms.
See website for details of further subject area dictionaries treating the Russian language.

6217 **Communications standard dictionary**
M.W. Weik, comp. 3rd edn, Kluwer Academic Publishers, 1995, 1100pp. Also available CD-ROM, £135.00. ISBN 0412083914.
This 'comprehensive compilation' has become a standard work in its area. Some 13,000 entries of definitions, abbreviations, and cross-references, ranging widely over the field of communications.
1st edn 1983, 2nd edn 1989

6218 **Dictionary of communications technology: terms, definitions, and abbreviations**
G. Held, comp. 3rd edn, Wiley, 1998, 692pp. $98.00. ISBN 0471975176.
Contains 18,000 entries for definitions, acronyms, trade names, events, and abbreviations. Comprehensive coverage with clear concise entries. There is some American bias, but UK topics are still well represented.
'Excellent value.' (*Reference Reviews*)

6219 **Elsevier's dictionary of communications: in English, German, French and Russian**
D. Delijska and P. Manoilov, comps Elsevier, 1997, 1045pp. £146.00. ISBN 0444824391.
12,908 terms with more than 4000 cross-references that are commonly used in communication theory, practice and education, including in the various areas germane to telecommunications.

6220 **German dictionary of telecommunications/ Fachwörterbuch Telekommunikation: English–German/German–English**
J.-P. Rehahn, comp. Routledge, 1998, 590pp. £110.00. ISBN 0415193729.
A very good technical translating dictionary containing about 24,000 terms and references in both languages. It covers all the major telecommunication areas, including networks, speech and picture digitization, mobile communications, and satellite communication.

Glossary of electrotechnical, power, telecommunication, electronics, lighting and colour terms: BS4727
British Standards Institution See entry no. 5416

6221 **McGraw-Hill illustrated telecom dictionary**
J. Clayton, ed. 4th edn, McGraw-Hill, 2002, 756pp. $34.95. ISBN 0071395083.
Wide-ranging, with 4000 definitions and 600 illustrations and seven appendices, this edition is substantially larger than its predecessor. New entries are mainly from new communication areas such as video streaming. The complete text is available on an accompanying CD-ROM which also includes an additional 1000 pages of material, all in searchable PDF format.
1st edn 1998, 3rd edn 2001.
'attractive ... A good reference source.' (*Choice*)

6222 **Newton's telecom dictionary**
H. Newton 20th edn, CMP, 2004, 923pp. $34.95. ISBN 1578203090.
Defines more than 21,000 terms: 'All the important terms are defined. No proprietary products, i.e. those made only by one firm, are defined. No proprietary terms are defined.'

6223 **Routledge French dictionary of telecommunications: French–English/ English–French (Dictionnaire anglais des télécommunications: Français–Anglais/ Anglais–Français)**
S. Wittering, comp. Routledge, 1997, 440pp. Also available CD-ROM, £110.00. ISBN 0415133483.
Consists of about 30,000 terms in each language. Its coverage includes the areas of television and video, radio, telephony and telegraphy, data transmission, signalling, switching, applications and service, terminal and peripheral apparatus, parts and materials, computing, control technology, testing procedures, and power systems.

6224 **Routledge Spanish dictionary of telecommunications: Spanish–English/ English–Spanish (Diccionario Inglés de telecomunicaciones: Español–Inglés/ Inglés–Español)**
E.G. Muniz Castro, ed. Routledge, 1998, 576pp. £110.00. ISBN 0415152666.

A standard translating dictionary containing about 30,000 terms in both languages. Covers applications and services, climate control, components and materials, computing, control technology, power systems, radio-based technologies, signalling, switching, television and video, and transmission.
'[To be praised for its] selection and comprehensiveness of vocabulary, as well as [its] currency, accuracy, and presentation.' (*Reference Reviews*)

6225 **The telecommunications illustrated dictionary**
J.K. Petersen, comp. 2nd edn, CRC Press, 2002, 1073pp. $69.95. ISBN 084931173X.
An encyclopedic dictionary, with good historical coverage, including entries for abbreviations, acronyms, people, and institutions. Contains over 10,000 entries. Has generally useful illustrations, although the photos are of lesser quality.
1st edn 1999, entitled Data and telecommunications dictionary.

6226 **Wireless A to Z**
N.J. Muller McGraw-Hill, 2003, 541pp. $29.95. ISBN 0071410880.
100 articles; 700 acronyms; detailed subject index.

Laws, standards, codes

6227 **Alliance for Telecommunications Industry Solutions** [USA]
www.atis.org
'Committed to rapidly developing and promoting technical and operations standards for the communications and related information technologies industry worldwide using a pragmatic, flexible and open approach ... Over 1100 industry professionals from more than 350 communications companies actively participate in ATIS' 22 industry committees and incubator solutions programs.'

- **Telecom Glossary 2000** www.atis.org/tg2k. Preparation co-ordinated by the Alliance and now an American National Standard. Contains over 6000 definitions with much other helpful information including an introduction and an extensive bibliography. Very useful compilation.

Data, networks, IP and the internet: protocols, design and operation
M.P. Clark, ed. See entry no. 6269

6228 **European Telecommunications Standards Institute**
www.etsi.org
Body which is 'officially responsible for standardization of Information and Communication Technologies (ICT) within Europe. These technologies include telecommunications, broadcasting and related areas such as intelligent transportation and medical electronics. ETSI unites 688 members from 55 countries inside and outside Europe, including manufacturers, network operators, administrations, service providers, research bodies and users – in fact, all the key players in the ICT arena.'

- **e-Standardization** http://portal.etsi.org. Very useful ETSI Portal providing access to a wealth of information.

6229 **Federal Communications Commission** [USA]
www.fcc.gov
'Independent United States government agency, directly responsible to Congress. The FCC was established by the Communications Act of 1934 and is charged with regulating interstate and international communications by radio, television, wire, satellite and cable. The FCC's jurisdiction covers the 50 states, the District of Columbia, and US possessions.'
Very good range of information targeted at different stakeholders.

International Multimedia Telecommunications Consortium
See entry no. 6162

6230 **International Press Telecommunications Council**
www.iptc.org
Originally established to safeguard the telecommunications interests of the world's press. Now primarily focussed on developing and publishing industry standards for interchange of news data. Currently membership is drawn mainly from the major news agencies around the globe but it also has a strong representation from newspaper publishers, system vendors and new media organizations.

Official & quasi-official bodies

6231 **International Telecommunication Union**
www.itu.int/home/index.html
Based in Geneva, the ITU is the international organization with the remit to co-ordinate telecom networks and services around the world. The ITU website describes its organization and work, and provides access to a wide range of data and documents: there are a useful series of site maps.

- **European Conference of Postal and Telecommunications Administrations** www.cept.org. With the European policy of separating postal and telecommunications operations from policy-making and regulatory functions, CEPT has became a body of policy-makers and regulators, and now has 45 members covering almost the whole of Europe.
- **World Summit on the Information Society** www.itu.int/wsis. 'Paradoxically, while the digital revolution has extended the frontiers of the global village, the vast majority of the world remains unhooked from this unfolding phenomenon.' Thus ITU has organized a Summit – in two phases: Geneva (2003); Tunisia (2005).

6232 **National Telecommunications and Information Administration** [USA]
www.ntia.doc.gov
'The President's principal adviser on telecommunications and information policy issues, and in this role frequently works with other Executive Branch agencies to develop and present the Administration's position on these issues. Since its creation in 1978, NTIA has been at the cutting edge of critical issues. In addition to representing the Executive Branch in both domestic and international telecommunications and information policy activities, NTIA also manages the Federal use of spectrum; performs cutting-edge telecommunications research and engineering, including resolving technical telecommunications issues for the Federal government and private sector; and administers infrastructure and public telecommunications facilities grants.'

6233 **Office of Communications** [UK]
www.ofcom.org.uk
The UK's 'independent regulator and competition authority for the UK communications industries, with responsibilities across television, radio, telecommunications and wireless communications services'.

Research centres & institutes

Optoelectronics Research Centre
See entry no. 803

Associations & societies

6234 **DSL Forum**
www.dslforum.org
Consortium of nearly 200 leading industry players covering telecommunications, equipment, computing, networking and service provider companies. 'We have global standardization of ADSL and SHDSL. VDSL and more will follow. These will provide a complete portfolio of digital subscriber line technologies designed to deliver ubiquitous broadband services for a wide range of situations and applications that will continue the transformation of our day-to-day lives in an on-line world.'

- **ATM Forum** www.atmforum.com. Formed 1991 with the objective of 'accelerating the use of ATM (Asynchronous Transfer Mode) products and services through a rapid convergence of interoperability specifications. In addition, the Forum promotes industry cooperation and awareness'.

6235 **Open Mobile Alliance**
www.openmobilealliance.org
Mission is 'to facilitate global user adoption of mobile data services by specifying market driven mobile service enablers that ensure service interoperability across devices, geographies, service providers, operators, and networks, while allowing businesses to compete through innovation and differentiation'.

Radio Society of Great Britain
See entry no. 5440

6236 **Telecommunications Industry Association** [USA]
www.tiaonline.org
'Represents providers of communications and information technology products and services for the global marketplace through its core competencies in standards development, domestic and international advocacy, as well as market development and trade promotion programs. The association facilitates the convergence of new communications networks while working for a competitive and innovative market environment.'

Discovering print & electronic resources

Electronics and Communications Abstracts
See entry no. 5444

6237 **ProQuest Telecommunications**
ProQuest Information and Learning.
www.proquest.co.uk/products/proquest_telecoms.html [DESCRIPTION]
'An online resource designed to keep you at the heart of this industry. Indexing over 100 key journals in telecommunications, it delivers the full text from almost 50 of these directly to your desktop. Whether you are looking for the latest news on WAP technology, following market penetration of the Internet or gathering information about the key players in this field, ProQuest Telecommunications™ helps you stay one step ahead.'

6238 **WWW Virtual Library: Telecoms**
Analysys.
www.analysys.com/vlib
Over 8000 links organized: Broadband technologies; Equipment, software or IT company; Fixed telecommunications company: IP service provider; Mobile telecommunications company; Other telecoms-related organizations; Related virtual libraries; Resources and issues; Satellite telecommunications company. Most categories sub-divided.

Directories & encyclopedias

6239 **Desktop encyclopedia of telecommunications**
N.J. Muller, ed. 3rd edn, McGraw-Hill, 2002, 1100pp. $59.95. ISBN 0071381481.
Contains about 300 articles, from 'Access charges' to 'World wide web', with a useful appended list of acronyms. Individual articles are usually 3–5 pages in length and are mainly illustrated. Some 50 articles are new to this edition. A US bias does not negate its usefulness.
1st edn 1998, 2nd edn 2000.
'excellent reference ... [on the 2nd edn].' (*Choice*)

6240 **Encyclopedia of wireless telecommunications**
F. Botto McGraw-Hill, 2002, 512pp. $59.95. ISBN 0071390251.
This work provides good coverage of wireless technologies, including 1G, 2G, 2.5G, and 3G wireless architectures. Wide range of topics includes physical principles, network infrastructures, handset technologies, protocols and standards. Alphabetically arranged, clear concise up-to-date entries.
'Recommended.' (*Choice*)

6241 **International satellite directory**
18th edn, Satnews Publishers, Annual, 1400pp. 2 v., $395.00. ISSN 10414541.
www.satnews.com/free/pubs/isd.html [DESCRIPTION]
Comprehensive guide to people, companies, products, and services. 25,000 entries.

- **The satellite communication applications handbook** **B.R. Elbert** 2nd edn, Artech House, 2004, 554pp. £90.00. ISBN 1580534902. www.artechhouse.com [DESCRIPTION]. Detailed coverage of: Systems considerations; Broadcast and multicast links to multiple users; Bidirectional and interactive networks for voice and data; Regulatory and business affairs. See website for details of a number of related texts.

Photonics rules of thumb: optics, electro-optics, fiber optics, and lasers
E. Friedman and J.L. Miller See entry no. 815

6242 **Telecommunications directory**
14th edn, Gale, 2004, Annual. $650.00. ISBN 0787656208.
Information on telecommunications companies providing a range of products and services from cellular communications and local exchange carriers to satellite services and internet service providers.

6243 **Wiley encyclopedia of telecommunications**
J.G. Proakis, ed. Wiley, 2003. 5 v, $1550.00. ISBN 0471369721.
www.mrw.interscience.wiley.com/eot
Authoritative and comprehensive work containing 275 articles spread over more than 3000 pages. Well illustrated. Includes coverage of both fundamentals and recent

technological advances. Topics include communication networks, optical communications, acoustic communications, multi-user communication, satellites, antennas, etc.
Available online: see website.
'an excellent reference resource ... recommended.' (*Choice*)

Handbooks & manuals

6244 **The communications handbook**
J.D. Gibson, ed. 2nd edn, CRC Press, 2002, 1616pp. $149.95. ISBN 0849309670.
A comprehensive reference work containing 102 chapters arranged in eight sections: Basic Principles; Telephony; Networks; Optical communications; Satellite communications; Wireless communications; Source compression; and Data recording. The new chapters focus on wireless technologies and next-generation networking. Includes the bulk, if not all, of *The mobile communications handbook*, 2nd edn.
1st edn 1997.

6245 **Emerging public safety wireless communication systems**
R.I. Desourdis [et al.] Artech House, 2002, 646pp. £79.00. ISBN 0890065756.
'With the increasing need for more effective and efficient responses to man-made and natural public safety threats, the necessity for improved private mobile and commercial wireless digital communication systems has become apparent. This one-of-a-kind resource describes today's public safety communication requirements and radio systems from a technical perspective, and shows you how communication systems are evolving to meet the growing demands of multimedia wireless applications.'

6246 **Emerging telecommunications networks**
G. Madden Edward Elgar Publishing, 2003, 296pp. £80.00. ISBN 1840642963.
www.e-elgar.co.uk [DESCRIPTION]
'The scope of this Handbook is simply awesome. Every technology (wireline, wireless, satellite, cable.), every service (internet, e-commerce, telephony, video.), every regulation (FCC, universal service, international settlements.), and both management and economic issues (development, pricing, demand, costs, innovation.), all written by the leading lights in this field. Every telecommunications scholar and executive should keep a copy within easy reach; it is indispensable.' (Gerald Faulhaber, University of Pennsylvania, USA).
Series: International Handbook of Telecommunication Economics.

6247 **Handbook of fiber optic data communication**
C. DeCusatis, ed. 2nd edn, Elsevier, 2002, 823pp. £75.00. ISBN 0122078918.
19 chapters in four parts: The technology; The links; The applications; The manufacturing technology. Six useful appendices; Acronyms; Glossary; Index. There is a companion volume: *Fiber optic data communication: technological advances and trends.*

6248 **Handbook of formulas and tables for signal processing**
A.D. Poularikas CRC Press, 1998, 864pp. $129.95. ISBN 0849385792.
Covers deterministic as well as statistical signal processing, and applications of signal processing in filtering, coding, transmitting, estimating, detecting, analysing, recognizing and reproducing signals. Some of the 44 chapters are devoted to a specific topic (e.g. Z transform), some to more general topics (matrices). Definitions and programs are also included.

Internetworking technologies handbook
W. Briggs See entry no. 6286

6249 **Local access network technologies**
P. France, ed.; Institution of Electrical Engineers 2004, 366pp. £59.00. ISBN 0852961766.
The access network, or local loop, based for more than 100 years on the twisted copper pair, is now being replaced or augmented by ADSL, optical fibre, radio, hybrid fibre-coaxial cable, wireless LAN, GSM or 3G, satellite, etc. This volume, primarily authored by people based or associated with the company BT's development facilities, reviews the major new access technologies that are finding their way into significant use. Acronym list.
Series: IEE Telecommunications, 47.

Modern cable television technology: video, voice, and data communications
W. Ciciora [et al.] See entry no. 5504

Newnes data communications pocket book
M.H. Tooley and S. Winder See entry no. 6095

6250 **Packet broadband network handbook**
H.H. Wang McGraw-Hill, 2003, 620pp. $65.00. ISBN 0071408371.
23 chapters in five parts: Packet network foundations; Broadband transport networks; Packet broadband access networks; Next-generation IP network infrastructure; Packet broadband network services. Three appendices: AP routing protocols; Wireless basics and history; Acronyms and abbreviations.
Series: McGraw-Hill Networking Professional.

6251 **Reference manual for telecommunications engineering**
R.L. Freeman 3rd edn, Wiley, 2002, 3648pp. 2 v., $695.00. ISBN 0471417181.
www.mrw.interscience.wiley.com/rmte
Revised, updated and very considerably expanded since the last edition. Contains wealth of tables, figures, formulas, statistics, standards, regulations, etc. It consists of 41 chapters covering all aspects of telecommunications including: Telephone traffic, Switching, Numbering, routing, and networks, and Noise, modulation, and other radio system parameters, etc.
1st edn 1985, 2nd edn 1994. Available online: see website.
'a necessary reference tool ... (about 2nd edn)' (*Choice*)

The RF and microwave handbook
M. Golio, ed. See entry no. 5518

6252 **Telecommunications engineer's reference book**
F.F. Mazda, ed. 2nd edn, Focal Press, 1998, 1120pp. £130.00. ISBN 0240514912.
70 contributors to 64 chapters organized in five parts: Mathematical techniques; Physical phenomena; Communications components (PABX and key systems,

Modems, Multiplexes, etc.); Communication fundamentals (Multiple access techniques, Coding; Digital modulation, etc.); and Communications applications (Voice processing; Electronic data interchange, etc.).

1st edn 1993 by Butterworth-Heinemann.

6253 Telecommunications handbook
K. Terplan and P. Morreal, eds CRC Press/IEEE Press, 2000, 424pp. $139.95. ISBN 0849331374.
Covers all forms of telecommunications, including the internet, taking a technical approach. Divided into four sections: Services, regulation, and standardization; Communication principles, focusing on telecommunication architectures; Communication technologies; Video communications and multimedia technologies.

6254 Telecommunications quality of service management: from legacy to emerging services
A.P. Oodan [et al.], eds; Institution of Electrical Engineers 2003, 602pp. £63.00. ISBN 0852964242.
28 chapters providing a detailed treatment of all the issues concerned with telecommunications QoS, defined as: 'Collective effort of the performance levels of all parameters considered pertinent to a service. The set of parameters for a given service may have different priorities and performance level requirements by different segments of users.' Acronym list.

Series: IEE Telecommunications, 48.

6255 Telecommunications technology handbook
D. Minoli 2nd edn, Artech House, 2003, 780pp. £83.00. ISBN 1580535283.
Major theme of this 2nd edn is introduction of broadband/Ethernet-based wireless transmission in enterprise networks. Detailed review of the technologies expected to be important including optical networking, Ethernet technology, customer-practical connectivity options, virtual private networks.

Series: Artech House Telecommunications Library.

6256 Telecommunications transmission handbook
R.L. Freeman 4th edn, Wiley, 1998, 1232pp. $185.00. ISBN 0471240184.
Substantially larger than the last edition, with new material especially on cellular and wireless communication systems, and cable and digital television. Its 16 chapters include: Introductory concepts; Telephone transmission; Multiplexing techniques; Digital networks; Line-of-sight microwave; Beyond line-of-sight tropospheric scatter and diffraction links; Satellite communications; Radio system design above 10ghz; High frequency radio; Meteor burst communication; Fibre optic communication links; Cellular radio and PCS; Transmission of digital data; Community antenna television (cable television); Video transmission – television; and Facsimile communication.

1st edn 1975, last edn 1991.

6257 Troubleshooting remote access networks
P. Nedeltchev Cisco Press, 2003, 864pp. $65.00. ISBN 1587050765.
After overviews of remote access and telecommunications basics, four parts covering: Dial; ISDN; Frame relay; VPN. Good design and index.

6258 Wireless data services: technologies, business models and global markets
C. Sharma Cambridge University Press, 2003, 361pp. £40.00. ISBN 0521828430.
'There are over 1.3 billion mobile subscribers around the world. It is interesting to note that wireless technologies have been adopted differently in key geographies such as Asia, Europe, and North America. Technologies such as i-mode in Japan, SMS in Europe, PDAs and Blackberry in North America point to the fact that wireless applications and services are not only unique to the culture and business models of a region but their success also depends on how services and technologies are introduced to consumers. This book takes a deeper look into why certain technologies, business models, and adoption strategies succeed while others fail, and how all these elements will impact the future of wireless communications.'

'This is a useful practical cookbook for those who are skilled in the art or who wish to be ... Wireless data is here to stay, and this is an invaluable source of basic information.' (*IEE Review*)

Wireless Internet handbook: technologies, standards, and applications
B. Furht and M. Ilyas See entry no. 6289

Keeping up-to-date

6259 3G Newsroom.com
www.3gnewsroom.com
News, discussion forums, events, background reading, etc.

6260 Communications Engineer
Institution of Electrical Engineers 2003–, Bimonthly. £185.00. ISSN 1479835.
www.iee.org/Publish/Journals/MagsNews [DESCRIPTION]
One of IEE's professional magazines intended for engineers in the communications sector.

6261 ComNews.com
www.comnews.com
News, buyers guides, events, recent books, etc.

6262 DIALOG Telecommunications Newsletters
Dialog.
http://library.dialog.com/bluesheets/html/bl0696.html [DESCRIPTION]
Online host access to collection of full-text newsletters from primary publishers in the field of telecommunications. Current sources include: TR Daily, Multimedia Daily, Interactive Services Report, Communications Today, Interactive Daily, Electronic Commerce News, Cable and Satellite Europe, Satellite Trader, Television Business International.

NetworkWorldFusion
See entry no. 6098

6263 Telecoms.com
www.telecoms.com
'This site provides potential advertisers with a dedicated portal providing the latest news, analysis and statistics to reach the decision makers within the increasingly complex ecology of international media markets, whether they work within broadcasting, programming and production, network development, or new media.'

Web & Internet

grid computing • internet • internet architecture • internet engineering • internetworking • interoperability • IP addresses • world wide web

Introductions to the subject

6264 **Computer networking: a top-down approach featuring the internet**
J.F. Kurose and K.W. Ross 3rd edn, Pearson/Addison Wesley, 2005, 821pp. $102.00. ISBN 0321227352.
www.aw-bc.com/kurose-ross [COMPANION]
Now well established text which 'broke new ground 4 years ago by treating networking in a top-down manner – that is, by beginning at the application level and working its way down towards the physical layer'. Focuses especially on the internet, primarily using its architecture and protocols as primary vehicles for studying fundamental computer networking concepts. Bibliography.
A splendid introduction.
2nd edn 2003.

Firewalls and Internet security: repelling the wily hacker
W.R. Cheswick, S.M. Bellovin and A.D. Rubin See entry no. 6185

6265 **The Grid: blueprint for a new computing infrastructure**
I. Foster and C. Kesselman 2nd edn, Morgan Kaufmann, 2004, 748pp. $59.95. ISBN 1558609334.
www.mkp.com/grid2 [COMPANION]
Edited by leaders in the development of grid computing. 'Many believe that by allowing all components of our information technology infrastructure – computational capabilities, databases, sensors, and people – to be shared flexibly as true collaborative tools, the Grid will have a similar transforming effect [to the electric power grid], allowing new classes of application to emerge.'
Goal of the book is to present an up-to-date view of Grids that both reports on real experiences and explains the technologies available today and emerging from labs, companies, and standards bodies. Most of the material in the books 1st edn has been placed on the web, allowing the second to focus on what is new. An excellent volume.

- **GridCafé: The place for everyone to learn about the Grid CERN.** http://gridcafe.web.cern.ch/gridcafe/index.html. Engaging introduction, well presented. Also, good set of links, including to Grid projects worldwide.

6266 **History of the internet: a chronology, 1843 to the present**
C.J.P. Moschovitis [et al.] ABC-CLIO, 1999, 312pp. ISBN 1576071189.
Examines the complex and intertwined strands of the internet's origins, evolution, and growth from the mid-19th century to the end of the 20th century. Organized into seven chronological chapters, each charts a different era of internet development. Each chapter opens with an essay and discusses the prevailing themes and trends.

- **The internet: a historical encyclopedia** ABC-CLIO, 2005. $285.00. ISBN 1851096590. www.abc-clio.com [DESCRIPTION]. Forthcoming 3-volume work: Biographies; Issues; Chronology.

6267 **Hobbes' Internet Timeline**
R.H. Zakon
www.zakon.org/robert/internet/timeline
The definitive reference work.

The internet under the hood: an introduction to network technologies for information professionals
R.E. Molyneux See entry no. 6290

Dictionaries, thesauri, classifications

6268 **Dictionary of internetworking terms and acronyms**
Cisco Systems, Inc, 2001, 412pp. CD-ROM also available, $12.95. ISBN 1587200457.
'A comprehensive reference to thousands of technical terms that networking students and professionals refer to on a daily basis. The book is organized in dictionary fashion, with alphabetized entries and concise, to-the-point definitions.'

- **Glossary of Internet terms M. Enzer** . www.matisse.net/files/glossary.html#index. Good personal interest compilation. Can be copied and redistributed via either a Creative Commons or an Open Content licence.
- **NetLingo.com** www.netlingo.com. Extensive and valuable dictionary of internet terms plus other related services and links.

Laws, standards, codes

6269 **Data, networks, IP and the internet: protocols, design and operation**
M.P. Clark, ed. Wiley, 2003, 848pp. $185.00. ISBN 0470848561.
www.wiley.co.uk/clarkdata [COMPANION]
Excellent detailed reference volume providing 'an explanation of the complex jargon of networking: putting the plethora of 'protocols' into context and providing a quick and easy handbook for continuing reference'. Very good contextual descriptions of the history and current status of the various contributory frameworks.
Extensive series of appendices cover the protocols, recommendations, standards, etc. of the various regulatory bodies. An 80 pp compilation *Abbreviations and standards quick reference* is especially valuable (and see also the companion website).
A first-rate resource.

GovTalk: Information on policies and standards for e-government
See entry no. 6304

6270 **Internet Corporation for Assigned Names and Numbers**
www.icann.org
'Internationally organized, non-profit corporation that has responsibility for Internet Protocol (IP) address space allocation, protocol identifier assignment, generic (gTLD) and country code (ccTLD) Top-Level Domain name system management, and root server system management functions. These services were originally performed under US Government contract by the Internet Assigned Numbers Authority (IANA) and other entities. ICANN now performs the IANA function.'

- **ICANNWatch** www.icannwatch.org. 'The Internet is a global resource of incalculable value, and nothing is of greater importance to its future than the way in which ICANN performs its role as manager of the Domain Name System.'

- **Internet Assigned Numbers Authority** www.iana.org.

6271 **Internet Society**
www.isoc.org
Professional membership society with more than 150 organization and 11,000 individual members in over 182 countries. 'It provides leadership in addressing issues that confront the future of the Internet, and is the organization home for the groups responsible for Internet infrastructure standards.'

Publications; Education and Training; Public Policy; Standards and Protocols; Chapters; Press Info; Conferences; Discuss.

- **Internet Architecture Board** www.iab.org. Committee of IETF and advisory body to ISOC. Responsibilities include architectural oversight of IETF activities, internet standards process oversight and appeal, and appointment of RFC Editor. Also manages IETF protocol parameter registries.
- **Internet Engineering Steering Group** www.ietf.org/iesg.html. With the Internet Architecture Board organizes and manages the internet standards process: see the useful document The Internet standards process (Revision 3, October 1996).
- **Internet Engineering Task Force** www.ietf.org. 'International community of network designers, operators, vendors, researchers concerned with the evolution of the internet architecture, smooth operation of the internet. Open to any interested individual.' Critical role in internet standards development.
- **Internet Systems Consortium** www.isc.org. 'Dedicated to supporting the infrastructure of the universal connected self-organizing Internet – and the autonomy of its participants – by developing and maintaining core production quality software, protocols, and operations'.
- **RFC Editor** www.rfc-editor.org. The Requests for Comments (RFC) document series is a set of technical and organizational notes about the internet (originally the ARPANET), beginning in 1969. The RFC Editor is the publisher of the RFCs and also maintains a master archival file.

Liberty Alliance
See entry no. 6110

6272 **Open Group**
www.opengroup.org
'Vendor-neutral and technology-neutral consortium, whose vision of Boundaryless Information Flow will enable access to integrated information, within and among enterprises, based on open standards and global interoperability.' Over 200 member organizations, with over 6000 participants in Open Group activities from 19 countries. 50% of members from North America, 25% from Europe, and 25% from Asia-Pacific.

6273 **World Wide Web Consortium**
www.w3.org
'The World Wide Web Consortium (W3C) develops interoperable technologies (specifications, guidelines, software, and tools) to lead the Web to its full potential. W3C is a forum for information, commerce, communication, and collective understanding. On this page, you'll find W3C news, links to W3C technologies and ways to get involved. New visitors can find help in Finding Your Way at W3C. We encourage organizations to learn more about W3C and about W3C Membership.'

A veritable cornucopia!

- **Designing with web standards** J. Zeldman New Riders, 2003, 436pp. $35.00. ISBN 0735712018. www.zeldman.com/dwws [COMPANION]. Well written rewarding book which. 'In Amazon's annual roundup of the 'Best Books of 2003', *Designing With Web Standards* ranked #4 in Editor's Picks and #7 in Customer's Picks'. Zeldman co-founded the Web Standards Project.
- **The Web Standards Project** www.webstandards.org. 'Grassroots coalition fighting for standards that ensure simple, affordable access to web technologies for all.' Useful briefings, comments, opinions, proposals, etc.

Research centres & institutes

6274 **Canarie**
www.canarie.ca
Mission is 'to accelerate Canada's advanced Internet development and use by facilitating the widespread adoption of faster, more efficient networks and by enabling the next generation of advanced products, applications and services to run on them'.

6275 **The Globus Alliance**
www.globus.org
Conducts research and development to create the fundamental technologies behind the Grid – which lets people share computing power, databases, and other online tools securely across corporate, institutional, and geographic boundaries without sacrificing local autonomy.

6276 **Internet2**
www.internet2.edu
'Led by more than 200 US universities, working with industry and government, Internet2 develops and deploys advanced network applications and technologies for research and higher education, accelerating the creation of tomorrow's Internet.'

Associations & societies

Apache Software Foundation
See entry no. 6111

6277 **Association of Internet Researchers** [UK]
http://aoir.org
'An academic association dedicated to the advancement of the cross-disciplinary field of Internet studies. It is a resource and support network promoting critical and scholarly Internet research independent from traditional disciplines and existing across academic borders. The association is international in scope.' Very useful well laid out gateway.

6278 **Global Grid Forum**
www.gridforum.org
'Community-initiated forum of 5000+ individual researchers and practitioners working on distributed computing, or 'grid' technologies. GGF's primary objective is to promote and support the development, deployment, and implementation of Grid technologies and applications via the creation and documentation of 'best practices' – technical specifications, user experiences, and implementation guidelines.'

International Academy of Digital Arts and Sciences
See entry no. 6168

6279 Internet Services Providers' Association [UK]
www.ispa.org.uk
'The UK's Trade Association for providers of Internet services ... ISPA's main activity is in making representations on behalf of the industry to Government bodies, such as the Home Office, the Department of Trade and Industry and Oftel. Government and political representatives often approach ISPA for its knowledge and expertise.'

SANS Institute
See entry no. 6197

Portal & task environments

6280 Internet FAQ Archives
www.faqs.org
Searchable archive containing Usenet FAQs postings in hypertext format and in FTP archive textual format. Also includes information about FAQ authoring and FAQ maintenance. Invaluable collection.

6281 JANET: The UK's education and research network [UK]
UKERNA.
www.ja.net
Private, government funded network for education and research. All UK further and higher education organizations are connected to JANET as are all its Research Councils. Range of useful resources including, for instance, about: Computer Emergency Response Team (CERT); Domain name registration; External peering; SuperJanet5.

6282 PEW/INTERNET: Pew internet and American life project
Pew Charitable Trusts
www.pewinternet.org
'Produces reports that explore the impact of the Internet on families, communities, work and home, daily life, education, health care, and civic and political life. The Project aims to be an authoritative source on the evolution of the Internet through collection of data and analysis of real-world developments as they affect the virtual world.'

Recent reports, early 2005, had covered: How the Internet has woven itself into American life; Search engine users; The state of blogging; The future of the Internet.

Goodly amount of other valuable information accessible via the site.

6283 W3 Schools
www.w3schools.com
'At W3Schools you will find all the Web-building tutorials you need, from basic HTML and XHTML to advanced XML, XSL, Multimedia and WAP. Our references cover all Web-building technologies, including W3C standards like HTML, XHTML, CSS, XML and other technologies like ASP and ADO plus much more.'

WWW Computer Architecture
University of Wisconsin See entry no. 6088

Discovering print & electronic resources

6284 Allwhois
Alldomains.com.
www.allwhois.com
Free service which 'is the most complete whois service on the internet. It automatically locates the appropriate 'whois' database server for a particular domain name, queries that database for information about that domain name, and returns all available data'.

Directories & encyclopedias

6285 The internet encyclopedia
H. Bidgoli, ed. Wiley, 2003, 2688pp. 3 v., $750.00. ISBN 0471222011.
200 essays, starting with 'Active server pages' and ending with 'XBRL (Extensible Business Reporting Language): Business reporting with XML'. The chapter list by subject area has the section headings: Applications; Design, implementation, and management; Electronic commerce; Foundation; Infrastructure; Legal, social, organizational, international and taxation issues; Marketing and advertising on the web; Security issues and measures; Supply chain management; Web design and programming; Wireless internet and e-commerce: thus indicative of the very wide scope of the resource.

This is a well designed suite of volumes, pleasant to use, and providing good state-of-the-art summaries of each topic covered.

Handbooks & manuals

6286 Internetworking technologies handbook
W. Briggs Cisco, 2003, 1128pp. $60.00. ISBN 1587051192.
Very comprehensive coverage of all aspects starting with: 'What is an internetwork?: A collection of individual networks, connected by intermediating networking devices, that functions as a single large network' – and then ranging in 59 chapters through, for instance, LAN protocols, WAN technologies, routing and switching basics, virtual private networks, voice/data integration, network protocols, network management, etc. to quality of service networking. Detailed index.

6287 LDAP directories
M. Rizcallah Wiley, 2003, 446pp. $60.00. ISBN 0470843888.
Aims to familiarize readers with the notion of directories and the contribution of LDAP (Lightweight Directory Access Protocol) using examples and case studies. Aimed at managers, IT decision makers, project managers, consultants and developers.

6288 Webmaster in a nutshell
S. Spainhour and R. Eckstein 3rd edn, O'Reilly, 2003, 561pp. $34.95. ISBN 0596003579.
Now classic text designed to provide all the major pieces of information needed by those creating and maintaining web-based content. 'By no means is this book a replacement for more detailed books on the Web. But when these books have been digested and placed on your bookshelves with pride, this one will remain on your desktop.'

6289 Wireless Internet handbook: technologies, standards, and applications
B. Furht and M. Ilyas CRC Press, 2003, 599pp. $99.95. ISBN 0849315026.
Multi-authored text. 24 chapters covering: Basic concepts; Technology and standards; Networks and architectures; Applications. Good bibliographies at end of most chapters; detailed volume index.

Keeping up-to-date

NetworkWorldFusion
See entry no. 6098

TOOLS FOR INFORMATION PROFESSIONALS

Tools for Information Professionals

This aide-memoire categorizes resources strictly according to the definitions of the 13 resource categories. Thus the *American Library Association* is placed within the 'Associations & societies' category, not the 'Libraries, archives & museums' one; and so on. Please bear that in mind.

Introductions to the subject

6290 The internet under the hood: an introduction to network technologies for information professionals
R.E. Molyneux Libraries Unlimited, 2003, 328pp. $40.00. ISBN 1591580056.
'Providing a clear and comprehensive introduction to network applications and concepts, this practical text covers the Internet; IP addresses; network operating systems; routing; domain names; servers; file formats; and more. It also includes information about the economics of the Internet, privacy, intellectual property, and legal issues.'
'Molyneux provides a readable and often engaging primer for setting up your library, organization, or home office network.a valuable guide for the information professional who either is new to networking or who seeks greater understanding of these technologies and their applications.' (*Public Libraries*)

6291 Science and technology research: writing strategies for students
T. Neville, D. Henry and B. Neville Scarecrow Press, 2002, 232pp. $24.95. ISBN 081084429X.
Contents are: Entering the library world; Getting focused; The first step: dictionaries, encyclopedias, and other ready-reference resources; Getting down to business; Composing your search strategy; Advanced on-line searching; Moving along: locating books; Locating information in journals, conference proceedings, and newspapers; Locating quality information on the World Wide Web; Government resources; What have I found?; Evaluating information; Where do I go from here? Appendices: Ten tips for efficient library research; Sample research strategy.
'The book is an excellent introductory textbook for library technicians and library staff being trained to provide research assistance services. The principles of research are concisely presented and the writing is very accessible. Those looking for in depth coverage of science and technology research sources and skills should look elsewhere.' (*E-STREAMS*)

6292 The semantic web: a guide to the future of XML, web services, and knowledge management
M.C. Daconta, L.J. Obrst and K.T. Smith Wiley, 2003, 281pp. $35.00. ISBN 0471432571.
An easily read introductory overview with very good coverage of: the semantic web as a concept; XML; web services; RDF (Resource Description Framework); taxonomies; ontologies. There is a helpful last chapter Crafting your company's roadmap to the semantic web.

6293 Web of deception: misinformation on the Internet
A.P. Mintz, ed. CyberAge Books, 2002, 278pp. Foreword by Steve Forbes, $24.95. ISBN 0910965609.
'Intentionally misleading or erroneous information on the Web can wreak havoc on your health, privacy, investments, business decisions, online purchases, legal affairs, and more. Until now, the breadth and significance of this growing problem for Internet users have yet to be fully explored. In *Web of Deception*, Anne P. Mintz (Director of Knowledge Management at Forbes Inc.) brings together 10 information industry gurus to illuminate the issues and help you recognize and deal with the flood of deception and misinformation in a range of critical subject areas. A must-read for any Internet searcher who needs to evaluate online information sources and avoid Web traps.'

6294 The weblog handbook: practical advice on creating and maintaining your blog
R. Blood Basic Books, 2002, 208pp. $14.00. ISBN 073820756X.
www.rebeccablood.net/handbook [COMPANION]
Useful introductory guide.
- **Blogs: The Internet Public Library University of Michigan.** www.ipl.org/div/blogs. Excellent 'library-related' gateway to categorized lists of blogs plus much else of value about blogging. 'We only add blogs with substantive content and that we deem useful to those searching for information.'

6295 Worlds of reference: lexicography, learning and language from the clay tablet to the computer
T. McArthur Cambridge University Press, 1986, 230pp. ISBN 052130637X.
Rewarding well written history. 20 chapters in six parts: Mind, word and world; The ancient world; The medieval world; The early modern world; The modern world; Tomorrow's world. The chapters Semantic fields and conceptual universes: the unshapeable lexis and Shaping things to come: the priests of High Technology are particularly insightful – especially given that they were written 20 years ago.
Notes, references and related reading pp.186–209; Bibliography pp.210–218; Index.

Dictionaries, thesauri, classifications

6296 Multilingual dictionary of knowledge management: English–German–French–Spanish–Italian
O. Vollnhals K G Saur, 2001, 402pp. €120.00. ISBN 3598115512.
Well produced volume with 3400 entries and cross-referencing indexes between each of the languages. KM

activities are divided into: Knowledge representation; Database technologies; Document management; Intelligent systems; Business applications.

6297 **Sears list of subject headings**
18th edn, H W Wilson, 2004, 804pp. $110.00. ISBN 0824209893.
www.hwwilson.com/print/searslst_18th.cfm [DESCRIPTION]
The classic list, especially designed for use in small and medium-sized libraries. A 23-page document *Principles of the Sears list* states its theoretical foundations and offers an introduction to subject cataloging in general.

Units, symbols and abbreviations: a guide for medical and scientific authors
D.N. Baron, ed.; Royal Society of Medicine See entry no. 3454

Laws, standards, codes

6298 **ConsortiumInfo.org: The source for standard-setting news and information**
Gesmer Updegrove LLP.
www.consortiuminfo.org
Excellent site maintained by Boston USA-based law firm that specializes in representing technology clients. As well as extensive information about the current situation and developments in standards generally, focuses particularly on Consortia: 'While standard setting has been an important aspect of industrial society for over a hundred years, the formation of unofficial, fast-acting standard setting and promotional consortia is a more recent phenomenon. Given that the first wave of consortia was not formed until the late 1980s, the consortium process has only recently begun to be seriously studied.'

The Consortium and Standards List is a regularly updated annotated and worldwide list of several hundred such organizations; subject and geographical categorizations are available.

6299 **Copyright Clearance Center** [USA]
www.copyright.com
'The largest licenser of text reproduction rights in the world, was formed in 1978 to facilitate compliance with US copyright law. CCC provides licensing systems for the reproduction and distribution of copyrighted materials in print and electronic formats throughout the world ... The company currently manages rights relating to over 1.75 million works and represents more than 9600 publishers and hundreds of thousands of authors and other creators, directly or through their representatives.'

6300 **CrossRef**
Publishers International Linking Association
www.crossref.org
Mission is to be 'the citation linking backbone for all scholarly information in electronic form'. CrossRef is a collaborative reference linking service that functions as a sort of digital switchboard. It holds no full text content, but rather effects linkages through Digital Object Identifiers (DOI), which are tagged to article metadata supplied by the participating publishers. The end result is an efficient, scalable linking system through which a researcher can click on a reference citation in a journal and access the cited article. The service is operated by a non-profit, independent organization: Publishers International Linking Association, whose Board of Directors 'comprises representatives from AAAS (Science), AIP, ACM, APA, Blackwell Publishers, Elsevier Science, IEEE, Kluwer, Nature, OUP, SAGE, Springer, and Wiley.'

CrossRef has been a great success story. Late in 2003, it announced that 'it will drop its DOI retrieval fees for all members and affiliates starting in January 2004. This move gives all CrossRef users unlimited access to DOIs, and is particularly significant for secondary publishers, as DOI links from citations and bibliographic databases to full text are expected to increase greatly as a result'. Then early in 2004 we read that 'the 10 millionth DOI registered was ... From the Japanese Society for Hygiene (and) among the other content types now included in CrossRef are the new Molecule Pages produced by Nature Publishing Group and the Alliance for Cellular Signaling.' By early April 2004, 300 publishers had signed up; and at the end of that month, there was the significant announcement of CrossRef Search, a collaboration with GOOGLE: 'Now, researchers and students interested in mining published scholarship have immediate access to targeted, interdisciplinary and cross-publisher search on full text using the powerful and familiar Google technology ... CrossRef Search is available to all users, free of charge, on the websites of participating publishers, and encompasses current journal issues as well as back files. The results are delivered from the regular Google index but filter out everything except the participating publishers' content, and will link to the content on publishers' websites via DOIs (Digital Object Identifiers) or regular URLs.' Nine organizations participated in the pilot, a mixture of professional society and commercial publishers.

Early 2005 CrossRef had 1408 participating publishers, 349 members, 34 affiliates, 6 agents and 490 library affiliates. There were over 15 million registered DOIs. Cf. DIGITAL OBJECT IDENTIFIER SYSTEM.

- **Distributed Systems** **A. Powell, comp.; UKOLN** www.ukoln.ac.uk/distributed-systems. Summary of range of projects which – inter alia – provides useful access to current work on OpenURL and related initiatives.
- **OpenURL** http://library.caltech.edu/openurl. Being developed by NATIONAL INFORMATION STANDARDS ORGANIZATION. Provides an architecture for context-sensitive reference linking in the web-based scholarly information environment. Now widely used since its introduction five years ago.
- **Publishing Requirements for Industry Standard Metadata: PRISM** www.prismstandard.org. 'Defines an XML metadata vocabulary for managing, aggregating, post-processing, multi-purposing and aggregating magazine, news, catalog, book, and mainstream journal content.' Recommends use of existing standards such as XML, RDF, Dublin Core.

6301 **Digital Object Identifier System**
International DOI Foundation
www.doi.org
System for 'identifying and exchanging intellectual property in the digital environment ... The DOI System provides a framework for managing intellectual content, for linking customers with content suppliers, for facilitating electronic commerce, and enabling automated copyright management for all types of media ... Several million DOIs have been assigned by DOI Registration Agencies in the US, Australasia, and Europe ... DOIs are names (characters and/or digits) assigned to objects of intellectual property (physical, digital or abstract) such as electronic journal articles, images, learning objects, e-books, images, any kind of content. They

are used to provide current information, including where they (or information about them) can be found on the Internet. Information about a digital object may change over time, including where to find it, but its DOI will not change.'

Excellent website: especially valuable are the FAQ section, the Glossary of Terms, and the 169 page DOI Handbook which contains an extensive bibliography. Cf. CROSSREF.

6302 Dublin Core Metadata Initiative

http://dublincore.org

Mission is 'to make it easier to find resources using the Internet through the following activities: Developing metadata standards for discovery across domains; Defining frameworks for the interoperation of metadata sets; Facilitating the development of community- or disciplinary-specific metadata sets that are consistent with items 1 and 2.' The Initiative created the Dublin Core metadata element set, a standard for cross-domain information resource description where an information resource is defined to be 'anything that has identity'.

- **The Dublin Core metadata element set International Organization for Standardization**ISO 15836:2003(E). www.niso.org/international/SC4/n515.pdf. 'The simplicity of Dublin Core can be both a strength and a weakness. Simplicity lowers the cost of creating metadata and promotes interoperability (but it) does not accommodate the semantic and functional richness supported by complex metadata schemes.'

6303 Freedom of Information Act 2000 [UK]

Great Britain. Department for Constitutional Affairs

www.foi.gov.uk

Came into force January 2005; supersedes 'Code of Practice on Access to Government Information'. Under the Act, 'anybody may request information from a public authority which has functions in England, Wales and/or Northern Ireland. The Act confers two statutory rights on applicants:

– To be told whether or not the public authority holds that information; and if so,

– To have that information communicated to them.'

- **The Freedom of Information Act: FOIA National Security Archive**. www.gwu.edu/~nsarchiv/nsa/foia.html. Gateway to resources relevant to the law ensuring public access to US government records. 'FOIA carries a presumption of disclosure; the burden is on the government – not the public – to substantiate why information may not be released.'
- **Your right to know: how to use the Freedom of Information Act and other access laws H. Brooke** Pluto Press, 2005, 272pp. £12.99. ISBN 0745322727. www.plutobooks.com [DESCRIPTION]. 'Even with my knowledge of Britain's secretive and undemocratic system of government, I found this book to be an eye opener. I will certainly be using the book myself.' David Shayler, former MI5 officer.

6304 GovTalk: Information on policies and standards for e-government [UK]

www.govtalk.gov.uk

'Purpose of this site is to enable the Public Sector, Industry and other interested participants to work together to develop and agree policies and standards for e-government.' The *Schemas and Standards* part of the site 'covers all aspects relating to the e-Government Interoperability Framework (e-GIF) and the e-Government Metadata Framework (e-GMF). It provides repositories for draft and agreed XML schemas, best practice and case studies, and also advice on toolkits and other relevant information.'

There is an extensive 'Library' of downloadable documents.

- **The Government Category List** www.govtalk.gov.uk/schemasstandards/gcl.asp. 'A structured list of categories for use with the Subject.category element of the e-GMS. The categories also help with website and portal directories, for instance, on DIRECTGOV.
- **Guidelines for UK government websites** TSO, 2003. £35.00. ISBN 0114301794. www.cabinetoffice.gov.uk/e-government/resources. Provide a comprehensive blueprint of best practices for building and managing well designed usable and accessible websites. Companion illustrated handbook also available.

6305 IMS Global Learning Consortium

www.imsglobal.org

'Develops and promotes the adoption of open technical specifications for interoperable learning technology ... IMS specifications and related publications are made available to the public at no charge ... No fee is required to implement the specifications.'

Some 50 Contributing Members come from every sector of the global e-learning community, including hardware and software vendors, educational institutions, publishers, government agencies, systems integrators, multimedia content providers, and other consortia.

6306 Information Commissioner [UK]

www.informationcommissioner.gov.uk

Independent supervisory authority reporting directly to the UK Parliament with an international role as well as a national one. Enforces and oversees the UK *Data Protection Act 1998* and the *Freedom of Information Act 2000*. Also responsible for enforcing the *Privacy and Electronic Communications (EC Directive) Regulations 2003* which came into force on 11 December 2003: the site provides a good section on 'spam' with a glossary of some 70 terms.

It is anticipated that the Commissioner will become responsible for enforcing the forthcoming new regulations obliging public authorities to provide access to information about the environment.

6307 International ISBN Agency

www.isbn-international.org

Promotes, co-ordinates and supervises the world-wide use of the ISBN system – the standard numbering system for 'books, software, mixed media etc. in publishing, distribution and library practices.' Their Users' Manual can be downloaded as a PDF file; and there is also a description of the Directory.

- **Publishers' international ISBN directory** 31st edn, K G Saur, 2004/2005, 5167pp. €448.00. ISBN 3598215843. 3 v. Edited by the Agency. CD-ROM version available.

International Press Telecommunications Council

See entry no. 6230

6308 ISSN International Centre

www.issn.org

'The ISSN (International Standard Serial Number) is an eight-digit number which identifies periodical publications as such, including electronic serials. More than one million ISSN numbers have so far been assigned ... It is managed by a world wide network of 77 National Centres coordinated by an International Centre based in Paris, backed by Unesco and the French Government.' The standard is currently being revised: completion expected by October 2006. ISSN Compact is a quarterly CD-ROM containing details of all currently assigned ISSNs plus a list of serial title word abbreviations: more than 54,000 words and their abbreviations in 70 languages. ISSN Online is the (fee-based) web version.

6309 **Librarian's guide to intellectual property in the digital age: copyright, patents, and trademarks** [USA]
T.L. Wheery ALA Editions, 2002, 170pp. $38.00. ISBN 083890825X.
'An authoritative, quick reference for the thorny issues of copyright, trademarks, and patents. With detailed explanations of the various types of intellectual property, how they differ, what they cover, and how the protections affect library work and services to customers, this is a book you will turn to every day for answers.'

'Though called a librarian's guide, this book will be useful to anyone who wishes to understand the basics about copyrights, patents, and trademarks.' (*Reference & Research Book News*)

- **Practical copyright for information professionals: the CILIP handbook S. Norman** Facet, 2004, 194pp. £24.95. ISBN 1856044904. 'As well as being an indispensable guide for library and information staff, the guide will also be essential for researchers, academics, teachers, reprographics staff and technicians – anyone who uses, or wants to learn about using, copyright material'.

6310 **Licensing digital content: a practical guide for librarians**
L.E. Harris ALA Editions, 2002, 152pp. $45.00. ISBN 0838908152.
Introduction; Note to Canadian and other non-US readers; Quick-starter tips for a successful agreement; 1. When to license; 2. Demystifying the licensing experience; 3. Learning the lingo; 4. Key digital licensing clauses; 5. Boilerplate clauses; 6. Unintimidating negotiations; 7. Questions and answers on licensing; 8. Go license!. Appendixes: A. Section 107 of the US Copyright Act on Fair Use; B. Section 108 of the US Copyright Act on Inter-library Loan. Glossary. Resources. Index

'very useful for academic and public librarians of information professionals who are, or will be, licensing digital content, especially licenses that may require negotiation ... well written and insightful.' (*Portal*)

6311 **LLRX.com**
Law Library Resource Xchange LLC.
www.llrx.com
'Unique, free Web journal dedicated to providing legal, library, IT/IS, marketing and administrative professionals with the most up-to-date information on a wide range of Internet research and technology-related issues, applications, resources and tools, since 1996.'

6312 **National Information Standards Organization** [USA]
www.niso.org
Non-profit association accredited by the American National Standards Institute, which 'identifies, develops, maintains, and publishes technical standards to manage information in our changing and ever-more digital environment. NISO standards apply both traditional and new technologies to the full range of information-related needs, including retrieval, re-purposing, storage, metadata, and preservation.'

The well designed website provides a Standards Quicklist (all the standard numbers having the prefix ANSI/NISO Z39) as well as information on standards in development, on trial, at ballot, etc; a section on NISO Initiatives (exchanging serials information; thesauri; metasearch; ISBN); and access to various white and briefing papers.

6313 **Open Archives Initiative**
www.openarchives.org
Develops and promotes interoperability standards that aim to facilitate the efficient dissemination of content. The Initiative 'has its roots in an effort to enhance access to e-print archives as a means of increasing the availability of scholarly communication'.

- **Eprints.org: Self-Archiving and Open Access Eprint Archives University of Southampton**. www.eprints.org. Dedicated to opening access to the refereed research literature online through author/institution self-archiving.

6314 **Open eBook Forum**
www.openebook.org
'International trade and standards organization for the electronic publishing industries. Our members consist of hardware and software companies, print and digital publishers, retailers, libraries, accessibility advocates, authors and related organizations whose common goals are to establish specifications and standards and to advance the competitiveness and exposure of the electronic publishing industries.'

6315 **Patent, trademark and copyright searching on the internet** [USA]
C.C. Sharpe McFarland, 2000, 240pp. $39.95. ISBN 0786407573.
First five chapters concern patent laws and applying for a patent. Patent searching is in chapters 6–10. Limited to law and searching US patents and inevitably some internet sources have now changed. Likewise Part II on trademarks is restricted to the USA. No content on searching for copyright records. Appendices give copies of official forms and documents.

'A gem ... a well-crafted and easy-to-use handbook.' (*Reference Reviews*)

- **Patent and Trademark Depository Library University of Maine**. www.library.umaine.edu/patents. Good facility within the University's Folger Library: Extensive links to US and international patent resources, databases, inventor resources. Includes a short tutorial on searching US patents.
- **Patent search tutorial Pennsylvania State University**. www.libraries.psu.edu/instruction/business/Patents/index.html. Detailed, illustrated tutorial on patents and searching the US patents system compiled by the University's Schreyer Business Library.

6316 **Privacy Rights Clearinghouse** [USA]
www.privacyrights.org
Non-profit consumer information, research, and advocacy program, based in San Diego, California. Their clearly-laid out site provides direct access to fact sheets and speeches and articles on, for example: Telephone and Communications; Internet Privacy; Public and Government Records; and Medical Records.

Quantities, symbols, units, and abbreviations in the life sciences: a guide for authors and editors
A. Kotyk, comp. See entry no. 1910

6317 **Thomson Legal and Regulatory**
www.thomson.com/corp/about/ab_home.jsp [DESCRIPTION]
The largest of the four Thomson Market Groups (the others being: Learning; Financial; Scientific and Healthcare). Apart

from its extensive legal, tax, accounting, intellectual property, and compliance activities, includes the DIALOG group of operations.

6318 **Understanding barcoding**
B. Williams Pira International, 2004, 428pp. £99.00. ISBN 1858029171.
www.pira.co.uk [DESCRIPTION]
Objective to present enough information to help a range of readers understand barcoding in ways that suit each of their needs. Well designed and presented manual that progresses from in Part 1, four overview chapters, through to Parts 2 and 3 which presents 8 chapters on the main codes, how they work, and how technology is developing. Part 4 is more detailed for those who really need to understand the technical details. Extensive glossary.

6319 **Unicode**
www.unicode.org
'Unicode provides a unique number for every character, no matter what the platform, no matter what the program, no matter what the language. The Unicode Standard has been adopted by such industry leaders as Apple, HP, IBM, JustSystem, Microsoft, Oracle, SAP, Sun, Sybase, Unisys and many others. Unicode is required by modern standards such as XML, Java, ECMAScript (JavaScript), LDAP, CORBA 3.0, WML, etc., and is the official way to implement ISO/IEC 10646. It is supported in many operating systems, all modern browsers, and many other products. The emergence of the Unicode Standard, and the availability of tools supporting it, are among the most significant recent global software technology trends.'

- **Unicode and multilingual support in HTML, fonts, web browsers and other applications A. Wood** www.alanwood.net/unicode. First-rate personal interest site – a superb cornucopia, frequently refreshed and renewed.

6320 **Who owns academic work?: battling for control of intellectual property**
C. McSheery Harvard University Press, 2003, 275pp. Originally published 2001, $16.95. ISBN 0674012437.
Introduction. 1. Building an epistemic regime; 2. An uncommon controversy; 3. 'University Lectures Are Sui Generis'; 4. Metes and bounds; 5. Telling tales out of school.
'The book provokes much thought about issues that most academic scientists likely do not consider in much depth – copyright, patent and data ownership, and the 'work-for-hire' exclusion of individual employee's rights in the US ... McSherry ably demonstrates that universities are going through a second revolution. Academics should be wary of what that revolution may bring.' (*New Scientist*)

6321 **Z39.50: International Standard Maintenance Agency**
Library of Congress
www.loc.gov/z3950/agency
Links to information about Z39.50 resources and about the development and maintenance of Z39.50 (existing as well as future versions) and the implementation and use of the Z39.50 protocol. The standard specifies a client/server-based protocol for searching and retrieving information from remote databases.

Official & quasi-official bodies

6322 **CENDI: Federal STI Managers Group** [USA]
www.cendi.gov
Interagency working group of senior scientific and technical information (STI) managers from 11 federal agencies whose mission is 'to help improve the productivity of federal science- and technology-based programs through effective scientific, technical, and related information-support systems. In fulfilling its mission, CENDI agencies play an important role in addressing science- and technology-based national priorities and strengthening US competitiveness'. The agencies' programmes collectively represent over 93% of the FY04 US federal research and development budget ($127 billion).

Priorities early in 2004 were: continued development of SCIENCE.GOV; permanent access to government STI; federal policy and legislation (including public domain in S & T data and information, homeland security, e-government, intellectual property and copyright, database protection, privacy, and IT security); review of technologies of interest, such as XML, persistent digital identifiers, and deep-web searching.

- **CENDI STI Manager** http://cendi.dtic.mil/sti_mgr/index.html. Reference collection providing access to high-quality materials (primarily web-based) related to the management of scientific and technical information, particularly within the US government.

6323 **Institute of Museum and Library Services** [USA]
www.imls.gov
'Independent federal agency of the Executive Branch of the US Government. The US Congress appropriates the funding for IMLS. For Fiscal Year 2004 the IMLS budget is $262,240,000 which includes $198.2 million for library services and $31.4 million for museum services ... IMLS invests federal funding in museums and libraries to enhance their unique resources and ensure broad community access to these vital educational institutions.'

6324 **International Council of Museums**
http://icom.museum
Non-governmental organization maintaining formal relations with UNESCO and having a consultative status with the United Nations' Economic and Social Council. Financed primarily by membership fees, but supported by various governmental and other bodies. 17,000 members. Hosts the extensive Virtual Library Museums Pages and this, rather than the search engine on the site itself, is usually the best place to start a search for detailed information.

- **Museums of the world M. Zils, comp.** 11th edn, K G Saur, 2004, 1277pp. €428.00. ISBN 359820616X.

6325 **Museums, Libraries and Archives Council** [UK]
www.mla.gov.uk
'The national development agency working for and on behalf of museums, libraries and archives and advising government on policy and priorities for the sector. MLA's roles are to provide strategic leadership, to act as a powerful advocate, to develop capacity and to promote innovation and change. Museums, libraries and archives connect people to knowledge and information, creativity and inspiration. MLA is leading the drive to unlock this wealth, for everyone.'

Research centres & institutes

6326 eContent Programme [EUR]
European Commission. Directorate for Information Society
www.cordis.lu/econtent
EU programme which ran from 2001–2004. Late January 2005, the European Parliament voted in favour of an eContentplus programme. 'The new programme will concentrate on those parts of the digital content market where there is clear fragmentation in Europe, and where market forces alone so far have been insufficient to drive growth. It targets three domains: spatial (or geographical) data, educational material and cultural content.'

- **eContentplus and Safer Internet programmes** www.cordis.lu/ist/directorate_e/ecsi/index.html. Both programmes are scheduled to run from 2005 to 2008.

6327 Joint Information Systems Committee [UK]
www.jisc.ac.uk
'JISC works with (UK) further and higher education by providing strategic guidance, advice and opportunities to use ICT to support teaching, learning, research and administration.'

JISC is notable here for its role in negotiating – on behalf of UK Higher and Further Education institutions – licensed access to wide range of high quality online research tools, learning materials and digital archives. A list of the collections – each with quite detailed descriptions and web links – gives a good overview of the range of STM resources currently being used within UK HE/FE.

JISC also manages a wide range of projects covering topics such as metadata, networking, ICT, content creation, content access, training, teaching and learning technologies, as well as funding JISCMAIL and the RESOURCE DISCOVERY NETWORK.

- **EDINA University of Edinburgh**. http://edina.ac.uk. Offers the UK tertiary education and research community networked access to a library of data, information and research resources. Hosted by the University's Data Library.
- **JISCMail** www.jiscmail.ac.uk. Provides extensive set of mailing (discussion) lists – primarily for UK Further and Higher Education; but many extend into, and are used by members of, many other sectors both in the UK and abroad. Valuable service.
- **MIMAS: Manchester Information and Associated Services University of Manchester**. www.mimas.ac.uk. Provides UK further and higher education and research community with networked access to key data and information resources to support teaching, learning and research across a wide range of disciplines.
- **Technical Advisory Service for Images** www.tasi.ac.uk. Provides advice and guidance to UK Further and Higher Education on the use of digital images in teaching and learning.
- **Technology and Standards Watch** http://www.jisc.ac.uk/index.cfm?name=techwatch_home. Helps keep track of developments in information and communication technologies that might have high impact on the core business of UK Further and Higher education in five to ten years' time. Commissions reports on specific technologies. Extensive Links.
- **UKOLN University of Bath**. www.ukoln.ac.uk. Centre of expertise in digital information management, providing advice and services to the library, information, education and cultural heritage communities. Primarily co-funded by JISC and MUSEUMS, LIBRARIES AND ARCHIVES COUNCIL.

6328 National Cataloguing Unit for the Archives of Contemporary Scientists [UK]
www.bath.ac.uk/ncuacs
Established in April 1987 'to locate, sort, index and catalogue the manuscript papers of distinguished contemporary British scientists and engineers'. Processed their 250th archive collection in 2004. A fascinating collection. Most of the catalogues compiled by the Unit can now be viewed in their entirety online through the ACCESS TO ARCHIVES website.

- **Cooperation on Archives of Science in Europe** EUR. www.bath.ac.uk/ncuacs/case.htm. 'Working group of archivists operating at a European level dedicated to the promotion and development of contemporary scientific archives.' Latest newsletter July 2004.

Associations & societies

6329 American Library Association
www.ala.org
'The oldest and largest library association in the world, with more than 64,000 members.' It has a number of important subsidiary associations, including the ASSOCIATION OF COLLEGE AND RESEARCH LIBRARIES and the REFERENCE AND USER SERVICES ASSOCIATION. ALA is very active in advocacy, diversity, intellectual freedom, and so on; and it has significant research and statistics activities. The ALA Online Store [www.alastore.ala.org] provides access to a large range and quantity of books, periodicals, and other library-related products.

- **American Libraries** 11 issues/year. $60.00 (North America); $70.00 (Foreign). ISSN 00029769. The official organ of the Association, but 'every opportunity shall be assured for expression of diverse views'. ALA members receive *American Libraries* as a perquisite of membership, but it is also available by paid subscription.
- **Booklist** 22 issues/year. $79.95 (USA); $95.00 (Outside USA). www.ala.org/booklist [DESCRIPTION]. 'For more than 90 years, *Booklist* magazine has been the librarian's leading choice for reviews of the latest books and (more recently) electronic media.' Reviews more than 500 reference books and electronic reference tools.
- **Library and Information Technology Association** USA. www.ala.org/ala/lita. Produce a valuable set of Resources: e.g. 'Top technology trends'; 'Tool kit for the expert web searcher' – as well as their journals *Information Technology and Libraries* and *Technology Electronic Reviews*.

6330 American Society for Information Science and Technology
www.asis.org
Established 1937, now with membership of 'some 4000 information specialists from such fields as computer science, linguistics, management, librarianship, engineering, law, medicine, chemistry, and education; individuals who share a common interest in improving the ways society stores, retrieves, analyzes, manages, archives and disseminates information, coming together for mutual benefit.'

Wide range of Special Interest Groups, some more active than others, including for: Bioinformatics; Human-computer interaction; Information architecture; International information issues; Medical informatics; Scientific and technical information systems; Technology, information and society; Visualization, images and sound.

'The most venerable of the LIS databases is Wilson's Library Literature & Information Science, introduced in 1921. A full-text version was introduced in 2000. This year [2003] the Library Literature Thesaurus became available to users of the new

WilsonWeb system. Wilson's database still leads the pack owing to its high-quality indexing, full text, complete coverage of the journals that are indexed, and participation of an advisory committee for journal title selection.'

- **Annual Review of Information Science and Technology** Information Today, 2004, 704pp. $99.95. ISBN 1573872091. www.asis.org/Publications/ARIST/index.php. Excellent series of volumes with definitive reviews of key fields in each.
- **ASIS thesaurus of information science and librarianship** **J.L. Milstead** 1998, 169pp. $39.95. ISBN 1573870501. www.asis.org/Publications/bookstore/home.html. Includes 1316 preferred terms (descriptors), 691 non-preferred terms (user references), and 37 facet indicators. Scope notes provide information about the use of terms in the thesaurus, as well as definitions of ambiguous terms.
- **Dictionary for library and information science** **J.M. Reitz** Libraries Unlimited, 2004, 788pp. $50.00. ISBN 1591580757. Last updated 2003 and now has 4000 terms and cross-references.
- **Harrod's librarians' glossary and reference book** **R. Prytherch** 10th edn, Ashgate, 2005, 768pp. £110.00. ISBN 0754640388. Directory of over 10,200 terms, organizations, projects and acronyms in the areas of information management, library science, publishing and archive management.
- **International encyclopedia of information and library science** **J. Feather and P. Sturges, eds** 2nd edn, Routledge, 2003, 736pp. £150.00. ISBN 0415259010. 'Easily accessible to the less initiated, with extensive reference and reading lists for those interested in delving further ... highly recommended for information science and library school collections.' *Library Journal*.
- **Library Literature and Information Science Full Text** H W Wilson. www.hwwilson.com/Databases/liblit.htm [FEE-BASED]. Indexes English and foreign-language periodicals, selected state journals, conference proceedings, pamphlets, books, and library school theses, plus over 300 books per year. Full-text articles from over a hundred select publications. An excellent service.

6331 American Society of Association Executives

www.asaenet.org/asae/cda/public_home

'To advance the value of voluntary associations to society and to support the professionalism of the individuals who lead them.' Includes gateway to details of over 6000 Associations searchable by name, interest area, or geographic location – with significant international coverage.

6332 Association of American University Presses

http://aaupnet.org

125 members located around the world. Interesting and useful set of resources including a scholarly publishing bibliography and descriptions of e-publishing initiatives among their membership.

Each year the Association works with the Public Library Association to recommend a list of notable books for public and high school libraries.

- **Association of American Publishers** www.publishers.org. Principal trade association of the publishing industry representing publishers of all sizes and types. Have active Professional and Scholarly Publishing Division concerned about Open Access and other related politically charged issues.
- **Online usage statistics: a publisher's guide** Association of American Publishers, 2004. $50.00. www.pspcentral.org/committees/electronic/UsageStatsGuide.doc [DESCRIPTION]. Series of contributed chapters in useful volume produced by the Electronic Information Committee of AAP's Professional and Scholarly Publishing Division.

6333 Association of British Science Writers

www.absw.org.uk

'Exists to help those who write about science and technology, and to improve the standard of science journalism in the UK.'

Excellent set of *Crib sheets* ('Reference material is the lifeblood of journalism, well some journalism. You might find these resources useful.'): Briefings; Bookmarks; Wire services; Find an expert; Books by members; On writing; Practical advice; PUSET and PEST ('See what is happening on the bandwagon called PUSET, the Public Understanding of Science, Engineering and Technology. (Our preferred acronym, Public Engagement with Science and Technology, PEST, has yet to catch on.)'). Much else – serious and not so serious – about science journalism on this lively site.

6334 Association of College and Research Libraries

[USA]

www.ala.org/ACRL

ALA's largest division with more than 12,000 members 'representing librarians working with all types of academic libraries—community and junior college, college, and university—as well as comprehensive and specialized research libraries and their professional staffs'. In 2002, the Association 'launched its Scholarly Communication initiative, with goals of creating increased access to scholarly information; fostering cost-effective alternative means of publishing, especially those that take advantage of electronic information technologies; and encouraging scholars to assert greater control over scholarly communications'. The website provides in-depth information about its work in this area and related resources.

- **Choice** 1964–, 11 issues/year. $270 (Print, North America. Many other packages available, including online versions). ISSN 00094978. http://www.ala.org/ala/acrl/acrlpubs/choice [DESCRIPTION]. Subject expert reviews of significant current books and electronic media of higher education interest. Subscribers rate it highest among sources used to select materials for academic libraries. Some 7000 reviews/year: strong coverage of reference titles.
- **College & Research Libraries** www.ala.org/ala/acrl/acrlpubs/crljournal/collegeresearch.htm [DESCRIPTION]. Scholarly articles. Columns of the companion *College & research libraries news* include: Washington Hotline, Grants and Acquisitions, People in the News, New Publications, internet Reviews and internet Resources: full text of the last accessible online.
- **Issues in Science and Technology Librarianship** Quarterly. ISSN 10921206. www.istl.org. Very useful, well produced and wide-ranging. An essential tool providing articles, surveys of science and technology resources on the internet, book reviews, conference reports, news, etc.

6335 Association of Learned and Professional Society Publishers

www.alpsp.org

'The international trade association for not-for-profit publishers and those who work with them; it currently has 272 members in 30 countries.' The site has an impressive list of Hot Topics (e.g. 'Developing Country Initiatives'; 'Linking'; 'Peer Review'; 'Science Citation Index'), with each topic being provided with Links to papers from the Association and other bodies. There are also many other good lists of sources of scholarly and scientific publishing related material, each regularly updated.

An excellent resource.

- **Learned Publishing** Quarterly. ISSN 09531513. www.alpsp.org/journal.htm [DESCRIPTION]. Useful articles on developments in the STM publishing marketplace. As of mid-2004, Volumes 10–16 (1997–2003) are freely available online to all. The current volume, Volume 17 (2004), is available online only to ALPSP Members.

6336 Association of Science-Technology Centers
www.astc.org
'Organization of science centers and museums dedicated to furthering the public understanding of science among increasingly diverse audiences.' Now has 550 members in 43 countries. The service Find a Science Center – although initially rather garish to this staid reviewer – is very quick and efficient. There is also a Resource Center and much other useful information. A good site.

6337 CILIP: the Chartered Institute of Library and Information Professionals [UK]
www.cilip.org.uk
Formed following the unification of the Institute of Information Scientists (IIS) and The Library Association (LA). Special interest groups include: Industrial and Commercial Libraries Group; Information Services Group (who produce a useful thrice-yearly bulletin *Refer* – a forum for news and views on all aspects of reference and information work); Multimedia Information and Technology Group. Desktop bulletins summarizing news relevant to the library and information sector are available daily, weekly and monthly.

- **CILIP: the Chartered Institute of Library and Information Professionals Yearbook 2004–2005** **K. Beecroft, Comp.** Facet Publishing, 2005. £44.95. ISBN 1856045285. ISSN 0075-9066. Annual. 'An invaluable source of contacts for all librarians and information professionals, this is the essential guide to the organization that aims to position the profession at the heart of the information society.'
- **Health Libraries Group** www.cilip.org.uk/specialinterestgroups [DESCRIPTION]. Largest special interest group in this field, with 2000 members. Range of useful information including up-to-date select list of links. Good for newcomers to the field.
- **Library + Information Update** Monthly. www.cilip.org.uk/publications/updatemagazine [DESCRIPTION]. Editorially independent of CILIP and 'covers everything from policy issues, the political landscape or changes in technology to what you need to know for your personal professional development'.
- **Patent and Trade Mark Group** www.cilip.org.uk/specialinterestgroups [DESCRIPTION]. Now a CILIP Special Interest Group. Website gives access to *Searcher* newsletter, events, conference papers and list of selected links.
- **UK eInformation Group** www.ukeig.org.uk. Formerly UKOLUG. Wide range of resources (factsheets, links) as well as details of activities – meetings, publishing, etc. Members can access the e-journal eLucidate.
- **University Science and Technology Librarians Group** www.leeds.ac.uk/library/ustlg. Independent informal group which tries to meet two or three times a year to discuss any topics of interest to members. The group uses the JISCMAIL *LIS-SCITECH* discussion list, and maintains a directory of members on the EEVL website.

6338 Consortium of University Research Libraries [UK]
www.curl.ac.uk
Consortium of UK university libraries with a national or international reputation plus the UK's legal deposit libraries and other major research information providers.

- **COPAC** www.copac.ac.uk. Free access to the merged online catalogues of 24 of the largest university research libraries in the UK and Ireland PLUS the British Library and the National Library of Scotland. Currently contains some 30 million records. Good search facilities.

6339 Directory and Database Publishers Association [UK]
www.directory-publisher.co.uk
Over 100 Members, commercial and non-commercial. Full list of members giving addresses, key personnel, basic operating details (no. of employees, established, turnover, parent company), together with the an A–Z list of the directories they produce: a valuable feature. Subject index. Useful source.

- **Current British directories** **G.P. Henderson, ed.** 14th edn, CBD Research, 2003. £165.00. ISBN 0900246936. www.cbdresearch.com [DESCRIPTION]. '2800 directories, yearbooks, guides, registers published in Britain in book, CD Rom, internet and list formats – in fact any publication with directory information and in any field of activity.'

6340 ECSITE-UK
www.ecsite-uk.net
'Represents over 80 science centres, museums and discovery centres in the UK. Ecsite-uk's purpose is to raise the profile of science centres, and to establish their role as a forum for dialogue between science specialists and the public and as an informal learning resource for learners of all ages.' UK affiliate of the European Collaborative for Science, Industry and Technology Exhibitions (ECSITE).

6341 EDUCAUSE: transforming education through information technologies [USA]
www.educause.edu
Non-profit association whose mission is 'to advance higher education by promoting the intelligent use of information technology. Membership is open to institutions of higher education, corporations serving the higher education information technology market, and other related associations and organizations. EDUCAUSE programs include professional development activities, print and electronic publications, strategic policy initiatives, research, awards for leadership and exemplary practices, and a wealth of online information services. The current membership comprises nearly 1900 colleges, universities, and education organizations, including more than 180 corporations, and more than 13,000 active member representatives.'

The Association has a good, interesting and current Resource Center including links to articles, books, conference sessions, contracts, effective practices, plans, policies, position descriptions and blog content. Early 2005, the 'Topical Resources' were categorized: Cybersecurity; Information systems and services; Technology management and leadership; Libraries and technology; Networking and emerging technologies; Policy and law; Teaching and learning.

6342 European Association of Science Editors
www.ease.org.uk
'Non-governmental and non-profit-making international organization operated for scientific and educational purposes.' The website reproduces The Editor's Bookshelf from the Association's *Journal* which 'lists and briefly describes articles and books likely to be of interest to editors of publications in the sciences'. Headings used in the listings include: 'Politics of Publishing'; 'Economics and Funding'; 'Ethical Issues'. A good current awareness source.

- **Council of Science Editors** www.cbe.org. US-based. Mission is 'to promote excellence in the communication of scientific information'. Recently approved document Guidelines for journals developing or revising policies on conflict of interest, disclosure, or competing financial interests.

- **European Science Editing** Quarterly. ISSN 02583127. www.ease.org.uk/publications.html#ESE [DESCRIPTION]. 'Publishes articles, reports meetings, announces new developments and forthcoming events, reviews books and software and calls attention to publications of interest to members.' Copies of back numbers are placed on the web 9 months after publication.
- **Science Editors' Handbook** £18.00. www.ease.org.uk/publications.html#Handbook [DESCRIPTION]. Sections on: Editing; Standards and Style; Nomenclature and Terminology (General, Chemistry, Medical Sciences, Biology, Earth Sciences); Publishing and Printing.

6343 Foundation Center [USA]
www.fdncenter.org
'Mission is to strengthen the nonprofit sector by advancing knowledge about US philanthropy.' Their Online Librarian service was developed 'to respond to your need for factual information on foundations, philanthropy, and other issues related to nonprofits, and to assist with your fundraising research'. The Foundation Finder provides 'basic information about foundations within the universe of more than 70,000 private and community foundations in the USA'.

- **Foundation Directory** USA. http://fdncenter.org/learn/classroom/fdoguidedtour [FEE-BASED]. Instant access to information on thousands of grant makers and their giving interests.
- **Foundation Grants Index** http://fdncenter.org/marketplace [DESCRIPTION]. Records describing grants that have been awarded to non-profit organizations by the larger independent, corporate, and community foundations (over 1000 in 1995) located in the United States. 1,157,705 records as of February 2004.
- **World Guide to Foundations M. Zils, comp.** 3rd edn, K G Saur, 2004. €418.00. ISBN 359822267X. 41,000 foundations in 115 countries. Two volumes: V. 1 Europe; V. 2 Africa / The Americas / Asia and Oceania.

6344 Information Access Alliance [USA]
www.informationaccess.org
'Over the past two decades, increased concentration in the publishing industry has been accompanied by significant escalation in the price of serials publications, eroding libraries' ability to provide users with the publications they need. Nowhere does this seem more troublesome than in the market for scientific, technical, and medical (STM) journals and legal serial publications where pricing, as well as marketing practices for electronic publications, threatens library budgets and ultimately the widespread availability of important writings to the public.

The Information Access Alliance believes that a new standard of antitrust review should be adopted by state and federal antitrust enforcement agencies in examining merger transactions in the serials publishing industry. When reviewing proposed mergers, antitrust authorities should consider the decision-making process used by libraries – the primary customers of STM and legal series publications – to make purchasing decisons. Only then will these mergers be subjected to the degreee of scrutiny they deserve and adequate access be preserved.'

- **The academic publishing industry: a story of merger and acquisition M.H. Munroe** www.niulib.niu.edu/publishers/index.htm. Useful review, early 2005 last updated June 2004, of ten leading STM publishing conglomerates: Blackwell; Bertelsmann; Candover and Cinven (Springer); Elsevier; Holtzbrinck; McGraw-Hill, Pearson; T&F Informa; Thomson; Wolters Kluwer.

6345 Institute of Translation and Interpreting [UK]
www.iti.org.uk
'Founded in 1986 as the only independent professional association of practising translators and interpreters in the United Kingdom. It is now one of the primary sources of information on these services to government, industry, the media and the general public.' ITI Subject Networks include: Construction; Information Technology; Medical and Pharmaceutical; Patents; Terminology. There is a free service that will help find a qualified provider of language services among the Institute's membership.

- **The translator's handbook M. Sofer** 4th edn, Schreiber Publishing, 2003, 500pp. $25.95. ISBN 188756375X. Coverage includes: translation techniques; using electronic media for translation; dictionaries in 39 languages; publications for translators; translation terminology.

6346 International Association of Scientific, Technical & Medical Publishers
www.stm-assoc.org
Represents roughly 200 publishing imprints – including all the large players – who collectively create an estimated 80% of the annual output of scientific research information. Members list with links.

6347 International Federation of Classification Societies
www.classification-society.org
Federation of national, regional, and linguistically-based classification societies; aims are to further classification research. among other activities, the IFCS organizes a biennial conference, publishes a newsletter, and supports the *Journal of Classification*. For its communications is starting to use the Class-L listserver, set up by the Classification Society of North America, and currently with about 50 members.

6348 International Federation of Library Associations and Institutions
www.ifla.org
'The leading international body representing the interests of library and information services and their users. It is the global voice of the library and information profession.' The page headed IFLA Electronic Collections links to lists of web-based 'Government Information and Official Publications Resources' prepared by the IFLA Section on Government Information and Official Publications. There are also reasonably up-to-date selective and interesting lists of resources about 'Digital Libraries', 'Information Policy', 'Internet and Networking', and 'Library and Information Science' – the last of these having a section 'Quotations about Libraries and Librarians' and even one headed 'Library Humour'!

- **Professional Associations in the Information Sciences San José State University**. http://slisweb.sjsu.edu/resources/orgs.htm. Useful comprehensive list of archive, computing, information science, library, media, and other related associations. Maintained within the University's School of Library and Information Science. Early 2005, last updated January 2004.
- **Survey of scientific and technological information needs in less-developed and developing countries** www.ifla.org/VII/s7/projects/litmain.htm. Website – updated July 2003 – which 'brings together journal articles, publications, reports, conference proceedings, research, and websites on the needs of scientific and technological libraries in less-developed and developing countries'.

6349 Medical Library Association [USA]
www.mlanet.org
A non-profit, educational organization, founded in 1898, of more than 1100 institutions and 3600 individual members in the health sciences information field, committed to educating health information professionals, supporting health information research, promoting access to the world's health sciences information, and working to ensure that the best health information is available to all.

Within a very good wide-ranging site, includes a helpful section Resources for Health Consumers: Deciphering Medspeak; 'Top Ten' useful websites; Consumer Health Library Directory; MLA User's Guide to Finding and Evaluating Health Information on the Web; etc.

6350 National Association of Science Writers [USA]
http://nasw.org
From the Cybrarian: 'The association was formally incorporated in 1955 with a charter to 'foster the dissemination of accurate information regarding science through all media normally devoted to informing the public.' Over the years, its officers have included both freelancers and employees of most of the major newspapers, wire services, magazines, and broadcast outlets in the country. Above all, NASW fights for the free flow of science news.'

- **Communicating science news: a guide for public information officers, scientists and physicians** www.nasw.org/csn. Valuable overview. Major sections are: Who are the media?; Telling your story; Media arrangements at scientific meetings; Some pitfalls in reporting science news.

6351 National Federation of Abstracting and Indexing Services
www.nfais.org
'Seeks to be recognized globally as the premier membership organization for groups that aggregate, organize and facilitate access to information.' Not a great deal on the site for non-members; but the descriptions of the work of the 50 or so Members of the Federation give a good overview of current foci in this area.

- **European Association of Information Services** www.eusidic.org. A similar European-based association – with about 80 members.
- **International Council for Scientific and Technical Information** www.icsti.org. Sponsored by the International Council for Science. Not an especially active body, but worth noting.

6352 Reference and User Services Association [USA]
www.ala.org/RUSA
'Responsible for stimulating and supporting excellence in the delivery of general library services and materials to adults, and the provision of reference and information services, collection development, and resource sharing for all ages, in every type of library.' Lively Association who, for instance, have produced an extensive set of Reference Guidelines (e.g. 'Definition of a reference transaction'; 'Guidelines for medical, legal, and business responses'; 'Professional competencies for reference and user services librarians'). The collection of Papers entitled 'The future of reference services', presented to the 2002 ALA Annual Conference are well worth perusing, as is the chronological bibliography 'Definitions of reference service', which was discussed in 2004.

RUSA organizes the production of each year's *Outstanding reference sources for small and medium-sized libraries* and supports The Virtual Reference Desk project.

- **Reference & User Services Quarterly** American Library Association. ISSN 10949054. http://www.ala.org/ala/rusa/rusapubs/rusq/referenceuser.htm [COMPANION]. Official journal of RUSA. Site provides useful listing of all books reviewed in and received by RUSQ since 1998: full texts of the reviews are accessible to RUSA members – their first members-exclusive service.

6353 Research Libraries Group
www.rlg.org
'International, not-for-profit membership organization of over 150 universities, libraries, archives, historical societies and other institutions with collections for research and learning.' The RLG Union Catalog provides access to 45 million titles with coverage across all subjects in almost 400 languages. The Catalog provides gateway access to the CURL's COPAC.

- **Cultural Materials Initiative** www.rlg.org/culturalres [DESCRIPTION]. 'Designed to provide greater access to primary sources and cultural materials – the rare and often unique works collected for their value to history and the humanities, to education and research.'
- **History of science, technology, and medicine** www.rlg.org [DESCRIPTION]. RLG online service which integrates four separate bibliographies to create the definitive international bibliography for the history of science, technology, and medicine and their influence on culture, from pre-history to the present.
- **RedLightGreen** www.redlightgreen.com. New project designed specifically for undergraduates using the web – and the libraries that support them. Delivers information from RLG members about more than 130 million books: links students back to their campus libraries for the books they select.
- **Russian Academy of Sciences Bibliographies** www.rlg.org [DESCRIPTION]. Covers more than 12,500 periodicals published primarily in Russia, the republics of the former Soviet Union, and countries in Eastern Europe. Cites and abstracts books, manuscripts, dissertations, and articles. Available online only as RLG database.

6354 Society of American Archivists
www.archivists.org
'North America's oldest and largest national archival professional association ... more than 3400 individual and institutional members concerned with the identification, preservation, and use of records of historical value.' There is a helpful A Code of Ethics for Archivists with Commentary plus access to details of extensive series of events and publications.

- **Society of Archivists** www.archives.org.uk. 'The Society exists to promote the care and preservation of archives and the better administration of archive repositories to advance the training of its members and to encourage relevant research and publication.'

Software & Information Industry Association
See entry no. 6118

6355 Special Libraries Association [USA]
www.sla.org
'Serves more than 12,000 members in 83 countries in the information profession, including corporate, academic and government information specialists.' Organized into 24 Divisions representing subject interests, fields, or types of information-handling techniques, and including: Biomedical and Life Sciences (with a Medical Section); Chemistry; Engineering (with an Aerospace Section); Environment and Resource Management (with a Forestry Section); Food,

Agriculture and Nutrition; Information Technology (with a range of sections); Materials Research and Manufacturing; Petroleum and Energy Resources; Pharmaceutical and Health Technology; Physics – Astronomy – Mathematics; Science – Technology. Most of these have their own sets of web pages providing lists of relevant events, people, organizations and resources: example below.

- **Physics-Astronomy-Mathematics Division of SLA** www.sla.org/division/dpam. Fosters co-operation between libraries and librarians working within these fields. Site includes information on members, membership, a freely available online bulletin newsletter, discussion groups, and periodically updated subject resource guides.

UK Health Informatics Society
See entry no. 4159

6356 **World Association of Medical Editors**
www.wame.org
Membership is free and open to all editors of peer-reviewed medical journals. January 2005 there were 1170 members representing 733 journals from 80 countries: lists with links both of the members and their journals. Also good extensive collection of 'Resources for Medical Editors' – including on ethics and peer reviewing.

Libraries, archives, museums

6357 **Association of Research Libraries** [USA]
www.arl.org
'Not-for-profit membership organization comprising the leading research libraries in North America.' Currently 123 members. The site provides efficient access to a very wide range of excellent resources relevant to the various ARL Programs: e.g. Access and Technology Program; Copyright and Intellectual Property; Federal Relations and Information Policy; Office of Scholarly Communication – and is well worth browsing through.

Particularly pertinent here is the Section Issues in Scholarly Communication: 'Over the past two decades, increased concentration in the publishing industry has been accompanied by significant escalation in the price of serials publications, eroding libraries' ability to provide users with the publications they need. Nowhere does this seem more troublesome than in the market for scientific, technical, and medical (STM) journals and legal serial publications where pricing, as well as marketing practices for electronic publications, threatens library budgets and ultimately the widespread availability of important writings to the public.'

The journal *ARL* – content accessible online – is 'the bimonthly report on research library issues and actions' from ARL, CNI, and SPARC.

- **Coalition for Networked Information** www.cni.org. 'Dedicated to supporting the transformative promise of networked information technology for the advancement of scholarly communication and the enrichment of intellectual productivity.' 200 institutional members from academia, publishing, ICT, libraries.
- **SPARC: the scholarly publishing and academic resources coalition** www.arl.org/sparc. Aims to stimulate the 'creation of better, faster, and more economically sustainable systems for distributing new knowledge. especially in science, technology, and medicine'. Very good range of resources cited: almost all freely accessible full-text.

Portal & task environments

6358 **KMCentral**
George Mason University
www.icasit.org/km/index.htm
'A dynamic central resource for practitioners and academics of all levels. The website includes materials that can be used for a general introduction to KM, overviews and links to KM technologies, emerging KM trends and best industry practices. A special section for KM Academics includes selected syllabi, recommended course textbooks and additional readings. Additionally the website highlights books, articles, conferences, events and presentations from leading KM scholars. The website also facilitates communication and interaction between academics and practitioners through a list-serv.'

Sustained by the University's International Center for Applied Studies in Information Technology.

LTSN Information and Computer Sciences
University of Ulster, Loughborough University and Higher Education Academy See entry no. 6047

6359 **Nielsen Norman Group**
www.nngroup.com
'The members of Nielsen Norman Group are user experience pioneers ... They advocated user-centered design and usability before it became popular to do so:

Jakob Nielsen, Ph.D. "The Guru of Web Page Usability" (New York Times)

Donald A. Norman, Ph.D. "The Guru of Workable Technology" (Newsweek)

Bruce 'Tog' Tognazzini "Leading Authority on Software Design" (HotWired)'

6360 **OCLC Online Computer Library Center**
www.oclc.org
'Founded in 1967, OCLC Online Computer Library Center is a nonprofit, membership, computer library service and research organization dedicated to the public purposes of furthering access to the world's information and reducing information costs. More than 45,000 libraries in 84 countries and territories around the world use OCLC services to locate, acquire, catalog, lend and preserve library materials.'

OCLC's site has an interesting Section Topics and trends ('issues on the minds of librarians around the world') which, mid-2004, was treating 'E-learning' and 'Virtual reference'. There is also the research laboratory ResearchWorks which 'demonstrates a few of our ideas for applying new technologies to organize information'. OCLC Research is 'one of the world's leading centers devoted exclusively to the challenges facing libraries in a rapidly changing information technology environment', and has a wide range of current projects and involvements: RSS feed available.

See also: OCLC FirstSearch.

- **Dewey Decimal Classification** www.oclc.org/dewey [FEE-BASED]. 'The world's most widely used library classification system.' The DDC 22 Edition encompassed significant updates in: computer science; mathematics; chemistry; medicine and health. WebDewey and Abridged Edition versions available.
- **OCLC PICA** www.oclcpica.org. A European library co-operative 'providing economical access to knowledge through innovation and collaboration'. Represents OCLC in Europe, the Middle East and Africa, as well as providing a number of products developed locally.

- **WorldCat** www.oclc.org/worldcat. The world's largest bibliographic database, the merged catalogues of thousands of OCLC member libraries, with over 50 million unique records. As well as providing co-operative library cataloguing and other services, underlies OCLC's FirstSearch service.

6361 Scholarly Societies Project
J. Parrott, ed.; University of Waterloo
www.scholarly-societies.org
'Facilitating access to information about scholarly societies across the world since 1994.'

A superb resource. It is very well laid out with good search and display facilities; and the Guidelines for Inclusion in the Scholarly Societies Project are exceptionally clear: the focus is on societies with scholarly, academic, or research goals; preference is given to membership-based societies (in which a qualified person may apply to become a member); societies must have the URL of their website in standard domain-name format (with some exceptions noted); preference is given to societies of an international or national scope (again with some exceptions); any country; all languages; all academic subjects; societies must have a website if the society was founded from 1900 to the present.

Project Entries include the society name, an English translation of the society name (if not originally in English), the URL and URL Stability Index of the website (if the society has a website), the language of the website, the subject pages in the Project where the website occurs, the founding year and notes about name changes (if any), and the geographical scope of the society. At 21 February 2005, the Project was describing 4066 societies and providing access to 3755 websites.

Much other good information is provided: e.g. Creating a society website: recommendations – which includes helpful advice on keeping the URL as stable as possible.

Discovering print & electronic resources

6362 Access to archives [UK]
www.a2a.org.uk
'Contains catalogues describing archives held throughout England and dating from the 900s to the present day.' In March 2004, the database contained 6.6 million catalogue entries from 348 record offices and other repositories. A Standard Search simply using the keyword 'science' retrieved records for 1322 catalogues: the earliest an 18th-century 'Volume of science and trade notes from the Norwich Castle Museum'. Within an Extended Search, it is possible among other search parameters to choose 'Theme'. The Theme 'Web of Science' retrieved details of 353 catalogues; the theme 'Muck and Brass', 1476 catalogues. A nice service.

- **European Archival Network** www.european-archival.net. Map of Europe provides access to contact details for archives within 49 European 'countries'. Covers over 200 archives.

6363 American reference books annual
Libraries Unlimited, Annual, 832pp. $125.00 [V. 35, 2004]. ISBN 1591581672.
www.arbaonline.com [FEE-BASED]
'ARBA has served as a trustworthy source of information for the library and information community for more than three decades. With more than 1800 descriptive and evaluative entries, ARBA 2004 continues its tradition as the most comprehensive and reliable review source available for recent reference publications. This important reference and research tool provides reliable reviews by subject experts of materials from more than 300 publishers and in nearly 500 subject areas. Having ARBA to refer to keeps you abreast of the most recent reference works in all fields while helping you to answer everyday reference questions. Of perhaps most importance, ARBA helps you maintain your library's quality standards by helping you make selections as you build your reference collection.'

ARBA introduced in 2004 ARBAonline featuring '12,000+ reviews of reference works published since 1997. Written by librarians for librarians, ARBAonline's reviews cover reference sources from more than 400 publishers in over 500 subject areas'

ARBA had already announced in September 2002: 'With the significant increase and interest in Web resources in the past several years, ARBA and ARBAonline are greatly expanding the coverage of this medium. Internet sites that will be useful to reference librarians in public, academic, and school library media centers are our top priority. We plan to expand the number of reviews of Websites in ARBAonline until coverage is as comprehensive for Websites as it is for print resources. When appropriate, Internet sites will be compared to their book counter part so that users can decide which format will best fit their needs.'

- **Recommended reference books for small and medium-sized libraries and media centers** Libraries Unlimited, 2003, 328pp. $70.00. ISBN 1591580552. Approximately 500 books selected as the best works for smaller libraries.

6364 Archives Hub [UK]
www.archiveshub.ac.uk
'A national gateway to descriptions of archives in UK universities and colleges.' Covers over 80 institutions. Detailed subject search facility: e.g. 13 archives concerned with 'trees' were listed in the 'Collections of the Month' for December 2003 (to which list were added 11 links to relevant websites).

6365 CataList
www.lsoft.com/lists/listref.html
The official catalogue of lists based on LISTSERV, the e-mail list management software, originally developed in 1986 and the first e-mail list management software available. February 2005 inventoried over 54,000 public lists. Range of search options available, including viewing lists with more than 10,000 or more than 1000 subscribers; viewing lists by host country.

- **Majordomo** Great Circle Associates. www.greatcircle.com/majordomo. 'Program which automates the management of Internet mailing lists. Commands are sent to Majordomo via electronic mail to handle all aspects of list maintenance. Once a list is set up, virtually all operations can be performed remotely by email'.
- **Syndic8** www.syndic8.com. Access to master list of over 100,000 syndicated news content feeds; reviews and pointers to syndicated tools and sites; much other useful information.
- **TILE.NET** http://tile.net. Inventories of: E-mail newsletters and e-zines; Usenet Newsgroups; Computer products vendors; internet and web design companies.

6366 The directory of online European information
3rd edn, Landmarks, 2000, 272pp. €115.00.
Covers almost 900 Sources described in 9 Chapters: A. Online European Union Databases; B. Online Commercial Databases; C. Internet; D. CD-ROMs; E. Diskettes; F. Reference Information; G. Index by Product; H. Index by

Subject; I. Index by Source. Although now somewhat out-of-date, a good browsable collection.

6367 The extreme searcher's Internet handbook: a guide for the serious searcher

R. Hock CyberAge Books, 2004, 272pp. Foreword by Gary Price, $24.95. ISBN 0910965684.
www.extremesearcher.com [COMPANION]
Excellent text: well written, authoritative, easy to use. Primarily designed to take those who have not gone far beyond using Google and Yahoo! and wish to explore the 'invisible web'. But there is lots also for experienced searchers to savour. All the sites included in the book are listed on the (freely-accessible) companion website: a great resource in itself – which also provides news and updates to the parallel volume *The extreme searcher's guide to web search engines*.

- **The invisible web: uncovering information sources search engines can't see C. Sherman and G. Price** CyberAge Books, 2001, 402pp. $29.95. ISBN 091096551X. www.invisible-web.net [COMPANION]. Now classic text. 'Many thanks to FreePint for hosting this site. We highly recommend their free newsletter as an exceptional resource for Invisible Web and other valuable information industry news and comment'.

6368 Finding information in science, technology and medicine

J. Lambert and P.A. Lambert Europa Publications, 2003, 127pp. ISBN 0851424627.
Short, readable introduction, concentrating on – primarily UK-based – process rather than content: 'How information is communicated'; ' Searching the web'; 'Using libraries'; and so on. The authors worked respectively as a librarian and an academic at Aston University; and although the book's copy was completed in August 2001, it anticipates some – though not all – of the major changes that have subsequently taken place in STM communication.

6369 Fundamental reference sources

J.H. Sweetland 3rd edn, ALA Editions, 2001, 384pp. $67.50. ISBN 0838907806.
'Completely updated and revised, this authoritative 'reference on reference' features the best available materials in all media for general library collections. Credible and comprehensive, this handy manual outlines what it takes to easily locate, evaluate, and select the best information sources for a wide variety of needs.'

Instructions to Authors in the Health Sciences

Medical College of Ohio See entry no. 3505

6370 Lexicool.com: Directory of bilingual and multilingual dictionaries

www.lexicool.com
Pleasant, easy-to-use site whose aim 'has been to create a complete and efficient search utility for linguists, especially translators and interpreters. The site is run by an international team of linguists and IT specialists based in France.'

The efficient dictionary search engine has links to over 3500 bilingual and multilingual dictionaries and glossaries freely available on the internet; with each dictionary classified against about 60 languages (Afrikaans to Yiddish) and 20 subject areas. An E-zine lists new dictionaries and glossaries referenced at the site.

6371 Reference Reviews

Emerald, 8 issues/year. £5795.29. ISSN 09504125.
www.emeraldinsight.com [DESCRIPTION]
'Choosing the most appropriate reference material can be a difficult decision for librarians and information service managers. With no guidelines to keep them on the right track, mistakes can prove costly. A subscription to Reference Reviews helps you to make informed decisions by offering comprehensive analyses of the latest and most significant reference material available today. Written for librarians by librarians, each in-depth review offers a comprehensive and unbiased appraisal by professionals who understand the criteria you use when purchasing a resource. Each issue also contains an editorial that outlines the key issues for reference librarians today and highlights some of the major developments for the future. With the advent of the World Wide Web, *Reference Reviews* also provides a regular commentary on the wealth of resources and material available online in its Internet Column. When using *Reference Reviews*, making key purchasing decisions has never been easier.'

- **Reference Services Review** EmeraldQuarterly. £238.16. ISSN 00907324. www.emeraldinsight.com [DESCRIPTION]. 'Dedicated to the enrichment of reference knowledge and the advancement of reference services'.

6372 Scholarly electronic publishing bibliography

C.W. Bailey
http://info.lib.uh.edu/sepb/sepb.html
'This bibliography presents selected English-language articles, books, and other printed and electronic sources that are useful in understanding scholarly electronic publishing efforts on the Internet. Most sources have been published between 1990 and the present; however, a limited number of key sources published prior to 1990 are also included. Where possible, links are provided to sources that are freely available on the Internet.'

Wide ranging, valuable service – available by e-mail or as a weblog. Good selective directory of related websites. Search facility.

6373 Search Engine Guide

K Clough, Inc.
www.searchengineguide.com
Good up-to-date subject categorized directory of search engines and directories: when reviewed the 'Science' category had some two-dozen 'generic' entries and about 80 more specialized tools listed, each given a brief description. News section and some background reading. Subscription newsletters.

- **Search Engine Watch** Jupitermedia Corporation. www.searchenginewatch.com. Lively comment on current industry developments – though many of the details often only accessible to members. Emphasis on search engine marketing. Interesting section: Getting covered in Search Engine Watch. Two free newsletters: one daily; one monthly.

6374 Ulrichsweb

Bowker.
www.ulrichsweb.com [FEE-BASED]
'Access to detailed and authoritative information for more than 250,000 serials worldwide, including electronic journals and other full-text resources.' Covers more than 80,000 publishers from over 200 countries. Range of related services and products.

- **American Book Trade Directory** 50th edn, Information Today, 2004–2005, 1800pp. $299.00. ISBN 1573871869. 'Profiles nearly 30,000 retail and antiquarian book dealers, plus 1000 book and magazine wholesalers, distributors, and jobbers – in all 50 states and US territories.'
- **BookWire: The book industry resource** Bowker. www.bookwire.com [FEE-BASED]. 'The most comprehensive online portal into the book industry'.
- **Directory of publishers and vendors** http://acqweb.library.vanderbilt.edu. Sister to ACQNET a forum for acquisitions librarians, now with over 1800 subscribers. Useful free source giving some 6000 URLs and e-mail addresses; also including an annotated subject classified list of publishers. However, intermittently updated.
- **Global Books in Print** Bowker. www.globalbooksinprint.com [FEE-BASED]. Over 9 million book, audio book, and video titles. Covers Australian, Canadian, USA, UK, New Zealand and South African bibliographic titles including full-text reviews and out-of-print selections.
- **Literary Market Place: the directory of the American book publishing industry** Information Today, 2004, Annual, 2200pp. $299.00. ISBN 1573871788. www.literarymarketplace.com. 'The ultimate insider's guide to the US book publishing industry.' Publishers, literary agents, industry services. Limited but useful information available online on free registration. International version also available.
- **Nielsen BookData** www.nielsenbookdata.co.uk. Merger in 2002 of Whitaker, first Edition and Book Data offering bibliographic data services to publishers, booksellers and libraries in over 110 countries worldwide.
- **Royal Swets & Zeitlinger** www.swets.com. 'The world's largest distributor and service provider of scientific and professional information. Our broad portfolio includes the provision and management of print and electronic information for the STM, government and corporate markets'.
- **Ulrich's Serials Analysis System** www.ulrichsweb.com/ulrichsweb/analysis/default.asp [DESCRIPTION]. 'A powerful tool for library professionals who need to identify, analyze, evaluate and create reports about their libraries' print and electronic serials holdings.'

6375 UNESCO Libraries Portal

United Nations Educational, Scientific and Cultural Organization
http://portal.unesco.org/en
Within the Communication and Information Theme, a collection of some 14,000 links to: Libraries; Professional groups; Training facilities; Preservation and access initiatives; Reference directories, portals, publications, blogs, catalogues; Conferences and meetings; Librarianship resources – each notable for their coverage beyond Europe and North America.

- **UNESCO Archives Portal** A similar portal covering: Primary sources online; Education and training; Preservation and conservation; International co-operation; Associations; Conferences, meetings and exhibitions; and internet resources.

6376 YourDictionary.com

www.yourdictionary.com
Access to more than 2500 dictionaries and grammars in over 300 languages. The section Speciality Dictionaries lists dictionaries and glossaries of specialized words in the English language, organized by subject area.

- **Specialist and technical dictionaries catalogue** Grant & Cutler, 2004. www.grantandcutler.com. Lists of bilingual and multilingual specialist and technical dictionaries, as well as books of interest to translators and other language professionals, organized into 29 sections, and produced by the UK's largest language bookseller.

Directories & encyclopedias

6377 American Library Directory

57th edn, Information Today, 2004, 3900pp. $299.00. ISBN 1573871907.
http://books.infotoday.com/directories [DESCRIPTION]
'Profiles for more than 30,000 public, academic, special and government libraries, and library-related organizations in the United States, and Canada — including addresses, phone and fax numbers, and e-mail addresses, network participation, expenditures, holdings and special collections, key personnel, special services, and more — over 40 categories of library information in all.'

- **Libraries and information services in the United Kingdom and the Republic of Ireland 2005** 31st edn, Facet Publishing, 2004, 568pp. £44.95. ISBN 1856045293. ISSN 1741-7120. Well established annuall directory listing nearly 3000 libraries and information services. 'The pre-eminent source for general information and contact detail on UK and Irish libraries, deserving a place in any serious reference collection.' (*Reference Reviews*)

6378 ASK Hollis: the directory of UK associations

4th edn, Hollis Publishing, 2003, 1150pp. £190.00. ISBN 1904193072 ISSN 14714256.
www.hollis-pr.com/publications/ask.htm [DESCRIPTION]
'Over 6000 associations, pressure groups, unions, institutes, societies and more are profiled, representing every interest area from abrasives through to zoos, from industrial, professional and business sectors to government, charities and the consumer.'

6379 The Aslib directory of information sources in the United Kingdom

K.W. Reynard, ed. 12th edn, Europa Publications, 2002, 1559pp. £350.00. ISBN 0851424724.
Listings of over 11,000 associations, clubs, societies, companies, educational establishments, institutes, commissions, government bodies, and other organizations which provide information freely or on a fee-paying basis.

6380 The Central Register of Charities [UK]

Charity Commission for England and Wales
www.charitycommission.gov.uk
Can provide useful financial and other information about STM associations, societies, etc officially registered as charities. There is a keyword search facility.

- **Britishcharities.com: The UK's definitive guide to charities** www.britishcharities.com. Subject categorization of charities: e.g. Animals and birds; Blind and partially sighted; Conservation and environment; Deaf and hard of hearing; etc.

6381 Councils, committees and boards: including government agencies and authorities: a handbook of advisory, consultative executive, regulatory and similar bodies in British public life

13th edn, CBD Research, 2004, 529pp. £163.00. ISBN 0900246952.
www.cbdresearch.com [DESCRIPTION]
Standard work giving access to details of some 2000 bodies.

- **Centres, bureaux and research institutes: the directory of UK concentrations of effort, information and expertise** **C.M. Edwards** 4th edn, CBD Research, 2000, 420pp. £125.00. ISBN 0900246855. 'Concentrations of effort and expertise, or which provide information to the general public and have 'centre', 'bureau' or 'institute' in their names, specialising in areas ranging from acupuncture to whisky and from gerontology to organic farming'.

6382 **Directories in print: a descriptive guide to print and non-print directories, buyer's guides and other address lists of all kind** [USA]
24th ed, Gale. 3 v., $625.00 [2004]. ISBN 078767415X.
www.galegroup.com [DESCRIPTION]
'The most comprehensive source in its field, Directories in Print describes approximately 15,500 active rosters, guides and other print and nonprint address lists published in the United States and worldwide. Hundreds of additional directories (defunct, suspended and directories that cannot be located) are cited, with status notes, in the title/keyword index.'

6383 **Directory of British associations**
17th edn, CBD Research, 2004, 833pp. Also available CD-ROM, £195.00. ISBN 0900246960.
www.cbdresearch.com [DESCRIPTION]
The leading tool: 'Covers ALL aspects of life; it includes over 1500 trade associations, over 1350 professional bodies, over 800 learned societies; the remaining 3170 organisations fall into 19 separate categories such as art, education, farming, hobbies, medical, sports, etc.'

- **Directory of European professional and learned societies** 6th edn, CBD Research, 2004, 720pp. £147.50. ISBN 090024691X. 'Over 6000 European professional, academic, scientific and technical societies covering areas such as agriculture, astronautics, criminology and robotics.' Except for Great Britain and the Republic of Ireland, covers the whole of Europe, not just EU.
- **Trade associations and professional bodies of the UK and Eire** 17th edn, Graham & Whiteside, 2003, 800pp. $290.00. ISBN 1860993656. www.galegroup.com/graham&whiteside [DESCRIPTION]. Information on more than 3700 trade associations and professional bodies. There is also a companion *Trade associations and professional bodies of the continental European Union*: see website.

6384 **Directory of museums, galleries and buildings of historic interest in the United Kingdom**
K.W. Reynard, ed. 3rd edn, Europa Publications, 2003, 656pp. £150.00. ISBN 0851424732.
'Covers all types and sizes of museums; galleries of paintings, sculpture and photography; and buildings and sites of particular historic interest. It also provides an extensive index listing over 3200 subjects. The directory covers national collections and major buildings, but also the more unusual, less well known and local exhibits and sites.'

- **The official museum directory** **American Association of Museums**. www.officialmuseumdir.com [DESCRIPTION]. US publication covering museums, historic sites, planetariums, technology centres, zoos, etc. of every size and type in all 50 states.

6385 **Directory of research grants**
Oryx Press, 2004, 744pp. $135.00. ISBN 1573565954.
'A treasure chest of information on more than 5100 current programs from 1880 sponsors, including US and foreign foundations, corporations, government agencies, and other organizations. Find grants for basic research, equipment acquisition, building construction/renovation, fellowships, and 23 other program types. Government grants include CFDA, NSF, and NIH program numbers.'

- **Annual register of grant support: a directory of funding sources** 37th edn, Information Today, 2004, 1500pp. $239.00. ISBN 1573871745. 'Guide to more than 3500 grant-giving organizations offering nonrepayable support'.
- **Directory of biomedical and health care grants** 18th edn, Oryx Press, 2004, 536pp. $84.50. ISBN 1573565946. Covers over 2300 funding sources from all levels of government, corporations, and foundations.
- **Illinois Research Information Service: IRIS** **University of Illinois at Urbana-Champaign**. www.library.uiuc.edu/iris. 'Funding opportunities in every field from agriculture to zoology.' Free of charge to Illinois community; subscriptions are available to other colleges and universities for a low annual subscription fee.

6386 **Directory of special libraries and information centers**
M. Faerber and M. Miskelly, eds 30th edn, Gale, 2004. Includes mid-year supplement, $1050.00. ISBN 0787668648.
'Covers thousands of special libraries and information centers associated with the general fields of science and engineering, medicine, law, art, religion, the social sciences and humanities, including international listings.' Separate Geographic and Personnel Indexes provide access to profiled libraries by geographic region, as well as by the professional staff that are cited in each listing.

6387 **Encyclopedia of international media and communications**
D.H. Johnston, ed. Academic Press, 2003, 2773pp. 4 v, $995.00. ISBN 0123876702.
Explores the ways that editorial content – from journalism and scholarship to films and infomercials – is developed, presented, stored, analyzed, and regulated around the world. 220 articles, all specially commissioned.

6388 **Guide to libraries and information services in government departments and other organisations**
P. Dale and P. Wilson, eds; British Library 34th edn, British Library, 2004, 192pp. £39.00. ISBN 0712308830.
'This comprehensive directory lists UK organisations which offer collections and services on your subject, identifying contacts, plus information on opening times and facilities, and free and charged services. Librarians and information officers, students and academics, politicians and lawyers, pressure groups, local authorities and planners, journalists, companies, consultants: everyone who needs an answer to a specific question or access to information for detailed research will find this an invaluable book. Since the publication of the 33rd edition UK government departments have continued to float off constituent units which have become separate agencies, and so a number of organisations now appear under new names or as separate entities. Elsewhere there have been many other reorganisations and mergers, which have led to changes of name. These are all reflected in this new edition. There is an organisational index and a subject index.'

6389 **Research centers directory** [USA]
32nd edn, Gale, 2004. $690.00. ISBN 0787671134.
www.dialog.com
Programs, facilities, publications, educational efforts and services of North America's leading non-profit research institutes. Related texts are cited below.
Available online: see website.

- **Government research directory** 18th edn, Gale, 2004. $625.00. ISBN 0787669059. More than 4800 research facilities and programs of the US and Canadian federal governments.
- **International research centers directory** 18th edn, Gale, 2004. $605.00. ISBN 0787669083. Government, university, independent, non-profit and commercial research and development activities in countries worldwide.

- **New research centers** 31st edn, Gale, 2004, 116pp. $465.00. ISBN 0787669490. 600 recently established or newly discovered centres.

6390 **World guide to special libraries**
W. van der Meer and P. Schmidt, eds 6th edn, K G Saur, 2003, 1322pp. 2 v., €348.00. ISBN 3598222610.
'35,450 libraries in locations scattered all over the world. 803 key words, structured alphabetically by country and name, comprise over 38,000 libraries worldwide. Including multiple entries, the World Guide to Special Libraries boasts a total of 47,513 records.'

The keyword headings are quite specific (e.g. abrasives, acoustics, acupuncture, aerodynamics, etc.) and the entries are sorted by country. Libraries can be listed under more than one subject. Can be useful in specialist fields, or less intensively researched countries – though the details for each library are minimal.

- **World guide to libraries W. van der Meer, ed.** 18th edn, K G Saur, 2003, 1302pp. €428.00. ISBN 3598207425. 2 v. '42,954 entries in 203 countries, covering every imaginable type of library, from smaller ones with collections amounting to only a few thousand volumes/media right up to the big libraries with several million volumes.'

Handbooks & manuals

6391 **The advanced internet searcher's handbook**
P. Bradley 3rd edn, Facet Publishing, 2004, 272pp. £34.95. ISBN 1856045234.
www.facetpublishing.co.uk
Coverage includes: Free text search engines; Index-based search engines; Multi/meta search engines; Resource or site-specific search engines; Searching the 'hidden' web; Finding images, sounds and multimedia information; Finding people; Weblogs; Virtual libraries and gateways; USENET newsgroups and mailing lists.
See website for details of other titles from the publisher.
'It is an invaluable guide that should be alongside anyone actively searching the Internet [about the 2nd edn].' (*Managing Information*)

6392 **Archival information** [USA]
S. Fisher Greenwood Press, 2004, 192pp. $69.95. ISBN 1573563897.
'This definitive guide shows novice and experienced researchers how to find archival information. It provides tips on how to use archival materials effectively and efficiently. Topics covered include: Government archives; Science and technology collections ... Also provided is an overview of the world of archives, including archival terminology, how to contact archives, and archival etiquette.'
Series: How to Find It, How to Use It.
'The ability to find and use archival information is important in the research process, yet few works provide practical, succinct introductions to the process. Fisher's book does so, supplying for general researchers a useful guide to archival sources ... Recommended. All libraries.' (*Choice*)

The art of scientific writing: from student reports to professional publications in chemistry and related fields
H.F. Ebel, C. Bliefert and W.E. Russey See entry no. 1711

6393 **A basis for scientific and engineering translation: German–English–German**
M. Hann John Benjamins, 2004, 250pp. Includes CD-ROM, $126.00. ISBN 158811483X.
www.benjamins.com [DESCRIPTION]
Attacks many of the most crucial difficulties encountered by both native and non-native English speakers when translating scientific and engineering material from German. The e-book is like a miniature encyclopedia dealing with the fundamental conceptual basis of science, engineering and mathematics, with particular regard to terminology; the handbook provides a useful introduction to the e-book, enabling readers proficient in two languages to acquire the basic skills necessary for technical translation by familiarity with fundamental engineering conceptions themselves.

6394 **Chat reference: a guide to live virtual reference services**
J.S. Ronan Libraries Unlimited, 2003, 240pp. $45.00. ISBN 1591580005.
'Functioning as a blueprint, this guide leads the reader through the many decisions and considerations involved in setting up a real-time reference service. Ronan introduces both basic and advanced real-time reference software, offers practical information about features, advantages, and disadvantages, and discusses human and organizational issues.'

6395 **The Chicago guide to communicating science**
S.L. Montgomery University of Chicago Press, 2003, 228pp. $15.00. ISBN 0226534855.
www.press.uchicago.edu [COMPANION]
Covers writing of papers, abstracts, proposals, reports and articles; using graphics; oral presentations; dealing with the press, internet publication; and using English as a foreign language. Along with extensive background and context on scientific communication there are practical recommendations, advice and examples to help the reader craft improved communications.
Companion website displays Chapter 14 The online world: using the internet.
'This guide is a superb one, well written, and a pleasure to read.' (*E-STREAMS*)

The Chicago guide to writing about numbers
J.E. Miller See entry no. 560

6396 **Chicago manual of style**
15th edn, University of Chicago Press, 2003, 984pp. $55.00.
http://www.press.uchicago.edu [COMPANION]
For this Edition, 'every aspect of coverage has been examined and brought up to date – from publishing formats to editorial style and method, from documentation of electronic sources to book design and production, and everything in between. In addition to books, the Manual now also treats journals and electronic publications. All chapters are written for the electronic age, with advice on how to prepare and edit manuscripts online, handle copyright and permissions issues raised by technology, use new methods of preparing mathematical copy, and cite electronic and online sources.'

Clinical information systems: a component-based approach
R. van de Velde and P. Degoulet See entry no. 4333

Communicating chemistry
P.D. Bailey and S. Shinton, comps See entry no. 1714

Communication patterns of engineers
C. Tenopir and D.W. King See entry no. 4856

6397 Content management bible
B. Boiko 2nd edn, Wiley, 2004, 1150pp. $39.99. ISBN 0764573713.
Revised edn of superb guide, very clearly written and presented. Five parts: What is content?; What is content management?; Doing content management projects; The logical design of a CMS; Building a CMS. 33 chapters. There is a companion website 'accessible only to owners of the book by entering specific facts from the book'.

- **CMS Review** www.cmsreview.com. Links to the top CM sites in the world. Directories with descriptions of over 350 proprietary CMS, open-source CMS, and CMS services hosted at application service providers. Lists of 'CMS-Lite' products such as forums, news portals, weblogs, wikis, etc.

6398 The craft of scientific presentations: critical steps to succeed and critical errors to avoid
M. Alley Springer, 2003, 241pp. £23.00. ISBN 0387955550.
'Unlike other books that discuss technical presentations, this book anchors its advice in the experiences of scientists and engineers, including such successful presenters as Robert Oppenheimer, Richard Feynman, Niels Bohr, and Rita Levi-Montalcini, as well as currently active laboratory directors, scientists, and engineers.'

Data compression: the complete reference
D. Salomon See entry no. 6139

Data mining: concepts, models, methods, and algorithms
M. Kantardzic See entry no. 6140

6399 Database design and development: an essential guide for IT professionals
P. Ponniah IEEE Press/Wiley, 2003, 734pp. $94.95. ISBN 0471218774.
Indeed designed for more general IT professionals – rather than database experts. Comprehensive; well written; logically organized. A good introductory text.

Exploiting knowledge in health services
G. Walton and A. Booth, eds See entry no. 3516

6400 The Guild handbook of scientific illustration
E.R.S. Hodges, ed. 2nd edn, Wiley, 2003, 623pp. $150.00. ISBN 0471360112.
Designed as a reference book for the scientific illustrator and scientists doing their own illustration or commissioning work. Chapter I gives the basics of the job: materials, tools, preservation. Chapters II, III and IV are on rendering, how to treat different subjects and advanced topics such as the microscope. The final part is on the business aspects. As one would expect, very well illustrated.
Sponsored by the Guild of Natural Science Illustrators.

6401 Handbook of data management in information systems
J. Blazewicz [et al.], eds Springer, 2003, 800pp. £84.00. ISBN 3540438939.
'Provides practitioners, scientists and graduate students with a good overview of basic notions, methods and techniques, as well as important issues and trends across the broad spectrum of data management. In particular, the book covers fundamental topics in the field such as distributed databases, parallel databases, advanced databases, object-oriented databases, advanced transaction management, workflow management, data warehousing, data mining, mobile computing, data integration and the Web.'
Series: International Handbooks on Information Systems.

Handbook of writing for the mathematical sciences
N.J. Higham; Society for Industrial and Applied Mathematics See entry no. 454

6402 How to write and publish a scientific paper
R.A. Day 5th edn, Oryx Press, 1998, 296pp. Co-published with Cambridge University Press, £23.99. ISBN 1573561649.
On the premise that a cornerstone of science is publication of research, the book sets out to be a practical manual on the writing of a scientific paper. The 35 chapters deal with every aspect of writing from preparing a title through writing results to ethics and rights. Seven appendices deal with topics such as abbreviations, errors in style and spelling and submission to an electronic journal.
'The only book about scholarly communication that this reviewer has ever wanted to read from cover to cover ... a valuable reference source for scientists in every discipline.' (*American Reference Books Annual*)

- **Committee on Publication Ethics** www.publicationethics.org.uk. Major objective to provide sounding board for editors who are struggling with how best to deal with possible breaches in research and publication ethics: Guidelines on good publication practice; Code of conduct for editors of biomedical journals.

6403 Information theory, inference, and learning
D.J.C. MacKay Cambridge University Press, 2003, 628pp. £30.00. ISBN 0521642981.
Comprehensive, well organized text unifying information theory and machine learning 'because they are two sides of the same coin. In the 1960s, a single field, cybernetics, was populated by information theorists, computer scientists, and neuroscientists, all studying common problems. Information theory and machine learning still belong together. Brains are the ultimate compression and communication systems. All the state-of-the-art algorithms for both data compression and error-correcting codes use the same tools as machine learning.'

6404 Intellectual freedom manual [USA]
Office for Intellectual Freedom 6th edn, ALA Editions, 2002, 434pp. $45.00.
'A lot has happened in the world of intellectual freedom since the publication of the fifth edition of this authoritative manual. The Internet and electronic access to information have changed the landscape dramatically, raising new questions and issues to consider. Information providers in all types of settings must be equipped to set guidelines and policies for new and fast-changing points of access, factoring in all of the traditional principles of intellectual freedom.'

'This completely updated new edition serves as a must-have guide for developing policy, responding to censorship challenges, developing a materials section program, dealing with pressure groups, and promoting access to all types of information for all types of users in the new millennium.'

6405 **Internet research: theory and practice**
N.L. Fielden 2nd edn, McFarland, 2001, 205pp. $25.00. ISBN 078641099X.
'Provides useful information for anyone who wants to broaden the range and scope of their research tools or anyone who wants to increase their knowledge about what is available electronically.'
'Fills an important niche.' (*Library Journal*)

- **Search engines handbook N.L. Fielden and L. Kuntz** McFarland, 2002, 115pp. $25.00. ISBN 0786413085. Looks at the way search engines are put together, how they run, and how they locate information and display it. 'Should be required reading ... most worthwhile ... fluent and readable ... this handbook is an absolute gem'. (Voya).

6406 **Introduction to indexing and abstracting**
D.B. Cleveland and A.D. Cleveland 3rd edn, Libraries Unlimited, 2000, 283pp. $47.50. ISBN 1563086417.
'Put your hands on the basic knowledge necessary to become a professional indexer. Based on new research and years of practical experience, the book introduces you to such fundamentals as the nature of information, the organization of information, vocabulary control, types of indexes and abstracts, evaluation of indexing, and the use of computers. A new chapter on indexing and the Internet has been added, as has a chapter that lists Web resources for indexers and abstractors.'

6407 **IssueWeb: a guide and sourcebook for researching controversial issues on the Web**
K.R. Diaz and N. O'Hanlon Libraries Unlimited, 2004, 304pp. $30.00. ISBN 1591580781.
'Provides instruction on techniques for researching controversial topics on the Web and evaluating Web information sources. Forty 'Issue Briefs' include background on the topic, outline key controversies, and suggest search terms for use in search engines and other databases.'
'They do an excellent job of taking readers through steps needed to evaluate each resource's value for the project, and then to put it all together with helpful instructions for citations and plagiarism avoidance ... This easy-to-use, easy-to-reference book is a godsend for those are able to incorporate controversial issues into their research instruction.' (*School Library Journal*)

6408 **Library web sites: creating online collections and services**
A.P. Wilson ALA Editions, 2004, 160pp. $35.00. ISBN 0838908721.
'Public and academic librarians, technology specialists, and all those front line staff responsible for creating, designing and updating the library's web site will find an all-encompassing user-friendly guide designed to help them make the library's vast resources accessible online.'

6409 **Manual of online search strategies**
C.J. Armstrong and A. Large 3rd edn, Ashgate, 2001. 3 v. [1] Sciences: agriculture, earth sciences, chemistry, biosciences, engineering and energy; [2] Business, Law and Patents: patents, business and economics, news and current affairs, law; [3] Humanities and Social Sciences, £240.00. ISBN 0566079909. www.ashgate.com [DESCRIPTION]
'Comprehensively updated, this three-volume edition of the *Manual of online search strategies* covers the whole range of Internet, CD-ROM and dial-up online services, and includes several new chapters. International experts on each subject area, selected from the UK and North America, describe in detail how to identify and exploit specialist bibliographic and non-bibliographic databases, the best search methods and delivery modes, and the relative merits of different services and online hosts in their different disciplines. Numerous examples of search results are used to illustrate different strategies and commands.'

Authoritative, well written reviews: the chapters on 'Chemistry' and 'Earth Sciences' in Volume 1 being especially extensive and intensive. Detailed index covering each database and producer mentioned in the text. Very good for getting an overview of how the (generally, more traditional part of the) online information industry operates in each discipline.

6410 **Mapping scientific frontiers: the quest for knowledge visualization**
C. Chen, ed. Springer, 2003, 240pp. £49.50. ISBN 1852334940. www.pages.drexel.edu/~cc345 [COMPANION]
'Examines the history and the latest developments in the quest for knowledge visualization from an interdisciplinary perspective, ranging from theories of invisible colleges and competing paradigms, to practical applications of visualization techniques for capturing intellectual structures, and the rise and fall of scientific paradigms.'
'Dr. Chen notes that continued progress in the ability to map science effectively will require the combined efforts of those from many disciplines including science philosophy, scientometrics, knowledge discovery, data mining, and visualization. To that list, I would add the domain experts in all branches of science that would benefit from insertion of knowledge beyond their own specialties. The work of Don Swanson on linking non-interactive literatures, which is given a brief overview in the final chapter, is a strong reminder that all scientists should be looking outside their specialties. It is my hope that Chen's final intent for the book, to stimulate interdisciplinary research, will indeed come to pass.' (*D-Lib Magazine*)

- **Visualizing the semantic web: XML-based Internet and information visualization V. Geroimenko and C. Chen** Springer, 2003, 202pp. £49.50. ISBN 1852335769. Methods for visualizing the 'second-generation web': the web created with XML documents enriched with semantic and structural features, where the visual appearance of a document is completely separated from its underlying content.

6411 **Museums of modern science**
S. Lindqvist, M. Hedin and U. Larsson, eds Science History Publications, 2000, 216pp. $24.95. ISBN 0881352993. www.shpusa.com/books/museums.html [DESCRIPTION]
17 chapters in 4 parts: 1. The issues: how to explain modern science and how to reach the indifferent; 2. The level of complexity: the middle way between the superficial and the repellent; 3. Virtual museums: the challenges of new technology; 4. Controversial science issues: neither apologetic glorification nor 'the science war'.
Series: Nobel Symposium, 112.
'This well-produced, well-illustrated volume is a very suitable contribution to the debate over exhibiting science, and I recommend it to anyone interested in the topic.' (*Isis*)

6412 **Ontological engineering: with examples from the areas of knowledge management, e-commerce and the semantic Web**
A. Gómez-Pérez, M. Fernández-López and O. Corcho Springer, 2004, 403pp. £55.00. ISBN 1852335513.
The title phrase refers to 'the set of activities that concern the ontology development process, the ontology life cycle, the methods and methodology for building ontologies, and the tool suites and languages that support them'.

Detailed but approachable and well laid out text covering theoretical foundations as well as practical procedures. 'We have paid special attention to the influence that ontologies have on the Semantic Web.' Each chapter ends with a well constructed Bibliographical Notes and Further Reading.

6413 **Ontologies: a silver bullet for knowledge management and electronic commerce**
D. Fensel 2nd edn, Springer, 2004, 162pp. £27.00. ISBN 3540003029.
Introduced the notion of ontologies for the non-expert reader. Covers languages (XML, RDF) and tools and then surveys a range of applications. Appendix contains a very useful survey of the different groups of relevant standards: Ontology; Agent; Software engineering; WWW; Text, video, and metadata; Electronic commerce (including web services).

- **International Society for Knowledge Organization** http://is.gseis.ucla.edu/orgs/isko. 500 members all over the world, from fields such as information science, philosophy, linguistics, computer science, as well as special domains such as medical informatics. Useful publications.
- **Networked Knowledge Organization Systems/Services: NKOS** http://nkos.slis.kent.edu. Group focusing on 'functional/data model for enabling knowledge organization systems such as classification systems, thesauri, gazetteers, ontologies as networked interactive information services for Internet description/retrieval of diverse information'.

6414 **Organizing scientific meetings**
A. Epple Cambridge University Press, 1997, 198pp. £17.99. ISBN 0521589193.
Practical manual covering whether to hold a meeting, types of event, the social programme, scheduling venues, choosing a date, publication of proceedings, participant selection, organizing committees, budgeting, fundraising, preparation and announcements. 18 appendices give examples and details.

'Epple leaves no detail about organising a meeting, small or large, international or home based, unaddressed ... I wish *The Lancet* had had this book when we started on our own conference programme.' (The Lancet)

Peer review in health sciences
F. Godlee and T. Jefferson, eds See entry no. 3518

Professional content management systems: handling digital media assets
A. Mauthe and P. Thomas See entry no. 6177

6415 **Publication manual of the American Psychological Association**
American Psychological Association 5th edn, 2001, 400pp. $26.95. ISBN 1557987912.
www.apastyle.org [COMPANION]
Style widely used beyond psychology. The website section Electronic References is particularly useful.

6416 **Reference and information services: an introduction**
R.E. Bopp and L.C. Smith 3rd edn, Libraries Unlimited, 2001, 617pp. $49.50. ISBN 1563086247.
Wide ranging handbook providing in Part I – albeit primarily from a North American perspective – a range of good reviews of reference work entitled 'Concepts and Processes' (history, ethics of reference service, the reference interview, user education, challenges of electronic resources, etc.), followed by, in Part II, a series of chapters on specific types of information source and their use: directories; almanacs, yearbooks, and handbooks; biographical sources; dictionaries; encyclopedias; geographical sources; indexes and abstracts; government documents and statistics sources. Each of these chapters helpfully provides a checklist of the sources discussed at its end together with a short bibliography of further reading. And there is a Subject Index to the whole work as well as a collated Author/Title Index.

The Chapter that starts Part II Selection and evaluation of reference sources, with its conclusion 'one impact of technology on reference is the need to think in new ways about reference sources, collections, and the services they support' is particularly germane to this present work.

6417 **Scholarly publishing: books, journals, publishers, and libraries in the twentieth century**
R.E. Abel [et al.], eds Wiley, 2002, 318pp. $34.95. ISBN 0471219290.
'Well rounded and accurate account of the amazing and unpredictable sequence of inter-related events experienced by the field of scholarly publishing in the 20th century.'

'provides a unique view into the world of scholarly publishing ... there are no works that treat so thoroughly the history, current situation, and future prospects of scholarly publishing.' (*College & Research Libraries*)

- **Society for Scholarly Publishing** www.sspnet.org. Founded 1978. Good sets of website resources including well laid out annotated and wide ranging list of interesting Links. Also a useful Calendar of forthcoming conferences, meetings, etc. Developing a Professional Services Directory.

6418 **Science in public: communication, culture, and credibility**
J. Gregory and S. Miller Basic Books, 2000, 304pp. $20.00. ISBN 0738203572.
'Does the general public need to understand science? And if so, is it scientists' responsibility to communicate? Critics have argued that, despite the huge strides made in technology, we live in a 'scientifically illiterate' society – one that thinks about the world and makes important decisions without taking scientific knowledge into account. But is the solution to this 'illiteracy' to deluge the layman with scientific information? Or does science news need to be focused around specific issues and organized into stories that are meaningful and relevant to people's lives? In this unprecedented, comprehensive look at a new field, Jane Gregory and Steve Miller point the way to a more effective public understanding of science in the years ahead.'

6419 **Scientific method in practice**
H.G. Gauch Cambridge University Press, 2002, 454pp. £29.95. ISBN 0521816890.
The book's purpose is to provide scientists with an understanding of the principles of scientific method. It discusses principles such as hypothesis generation and testing, deductive and inductive logic, parsimony and science's presuppositions, domains and limits. To aid the reading of this complex subject each chapter includes a summary and there is one chapter of case studies. The book is drawn from extensive sources listed at the end.

6420 **Scientific style and format: the CBE manual for authors, editors, and publishers**
Council of Science Editors 6th edn, 1994, 704pp. $60.00.
www.councilscienceeditors.org/publications/style.cfm [COMPANION]
Formerly the Council of Biology Editors Manual. Definitive text covering all scientific disciplines; technologic fields not closely related to experimental and observational science are generally not represented. Recommends how scientific papers, journals and books should be styled and formatted for publication.

33 chapters organized: 1. Introduction; 2. General style conventions; 3. Special style conventions (e.g. The electromagnetic spectrum; chemical names and formulas; cells, chromosomes, and genes; bacteria; the earth); 4. Journals and books; 5. The publishing process. Annotated bibliography. Detailed index.

The website includes corrections to the 6th edition, as well as preview items for the 7th edition, in preparation: Number Style; Citing the internet: Formats for Bibliographic Citation; Resources for Genetic and Cytogenetic Nomenclature.

6421 **Thesaurus construction and use: a practical manual**
J. Aitchison, A. Gilchrist and D. Bawden 4th edn, Europa, 2000, 240pp. £42.50. ISBN 0851424465.
An excellent work: clearly written and laid-out. Coverage includes: vocabulary control; specificity and compound terms; structure and relationships; auxiliary retrieval devices; thesaurus display; etc. Extensive bibliography.

- **Subject Analysis Systems Collection University of Toronto.** www.fis.utoronto.ca/resources/inforum/sas.htm. North American Clearinghouse for subject classifications and controlled vocabularies in many different subject areas. Included are: Subject heading lists; Thesauri; Classification schemes. Maintained by the University's Faculty of Information Studies.

6422 **The virtual reference librarian's handbook** [USA]
A.G. Lipow Neal-Schuman, 2004, 199pp. Includes CD-ROM. Foreword by Clifford Lynch, $85.00. ISBN 155570445X.
Very useful and practical guide. Three parts: The decision to go virtual; The process of moving to the virtual desk; Techniques for building a lively service.

Webmaster in a nutshell
S. Spainhour and R. Eckstein See entry no. 6288

What engineers know and how they know it: analytical studies from aeronautical history
W.G. Vincenti See entry no. 4862

6423 **Writing successful science proposals**
C.L. Folt and A.J. Friedland Yale University Press, 2000, 190pp. $16.00. ISBN 0300081413.
A short, practical guide that the authors recommend is read in full. The aim is to assist development of research ideas and provide guidelines for grant applications. Includes sections on timetables, sample budgets and common pitfalls to watch out for. Contains a bibliography and a listing of web addresses for funding agencies.

'This inexpensive book could prove to be your best investment of the year. It is a step-by-step guide to the preparation of a high-quality research proposal in the natural sciences.' (*Bioscience*)

Writing the laboratory notebook
H.M. Kanare; American Chemical Society See entry no. 1826

6424 **XML: a manager's guide**
K. Dick 2nd edn, Addison-Wesley, 2003, 298pp. £30.99. ISBN 0201770067.
Attractive introduction, each chapter starting with an executive summary. The last two chapters review, respectively, five XML applications for enterprises, and for vendors.

- **Cafe con Leche XML News and Resources** http://cafeconleche.org. Excellent gateway to XML news, tutorials, recommended reading, specifications, development tools, etc.

Keeping up-to-date

6425 **Cites & Insights: Crawford at large** [USA]
W. Crawford Monthly [circa]. Free. ISSN 15340937.
http://cites.boisestate.edu
Good example of a single expert's view of current issues around libraries and their environments. 'My primary aims in Cites & Insights are to point people in interesting directions and encourage them to think about certain issues. If, after thinking about them, they come to different conclusions than mine, that's as it should be. (If I've obviously overlooked issues and facts, I trust readers to let me know – and I publish reader feedback when given permission and when it's at all feasible.)' Among much always interesting comment and opinion, includes: Interesting and Peculiar Products ('Gadgets and gizmos, but also truly interesting new products'); The Library Stuff ('Annotated and argumentative citations of articles and other stuff directly related to libraries and librarians'); and Scholarly Article Access ('Events and articles related to access, including Open Access, alternative publishing models, and institutional archives').

6426 **The Data Administration Newsletter**
R.S. Seiner
www.tdan.com
'This is a web-based newsletter, published by consultant Robert Seiner. It contains a range of articles on data management and related topics. It also has listings of conferences, jobs, companies and related Web pages. An archive and a search engine are provided.' An excellent extensive compilation.

6427 **D-Lib Magazine** [USA]
11 issues per year.
www.dlib.org
Very valuable 'solely electronic publication with a primary focus on digital library research and development, including but not limited to new technologies, applications, and contextual social and economic issues'.

- **Corporation for National Research Initiatives** www.cnri.reston.va.us. US not-for-profit organization formed in 1986 to foster research and development for the National Information Infrastructure. Publisher of D-Lib Magazine and other useful documents.

6428 **E-STREAMS: Electronic reviews of Science and Technology References covering Engineering, Agriculture, Medicine and Science**
H.R. Malinowsky, ed. YBP Library Services, 1998–, Monthly.
www.e-streams.com
Valuable well respected newsletter containing about 50 subject arranged electronic reviews in each issue of newly published STM books from a range of publishers. E-mail

copies of the newsletter can be requested by registration. Text of the reviews and bibliographic details can be searched.

- **Reference sources in science, engineering, medicine, and agriculture** **H.R. Malinowsky** Oryx Press, 1994, 368pp. ISBN 0897747453.

6429 **FreePint** [UK]
www.freepint.com
Website of the leading UK-based network of information researchers globally, with over 70,000 registered users. Entrée to a very wide range of useful news, comment and evaluation of information work. The FreePint newsletter is e-mailed free of charge fortnightly, each issue including – among much other interesting and relevant material – concise reviews of information resources in a specific sector.

6430 **Information Today**
Information Today Inc, 11 issues/year. $69.95 [2004]. ISSN 87556286.
www.infotoday.com/it
US-based newspaper 'for users and producers of electronic information services'. Each monthly issue treats major developments in the industry by acknowledged experts – both in the public and private sectors. Useful are the sections Product News and Reviews and the various items entitled Report from the Field. The company produces and organizes a wide range of valued events, publications and services in addition to the four noted below.

For more emphasis on UK and European developments, see the similar Information World Review

- **Econtent: digital content strategies and resources** www.econtentmag.com [FEE-BASED]. 'Essential research, reporting, news, and analysis of content related issues (for) executives and professionals involved in content creation, management, acquisition, organization, and distribution in both commercial and enterprise environments.'
- **ITI Newslink** www.infotoday.com/newslink. Free weekly newsletter, with subscribers receiving each month a full-length issue with articles and reviews covering recent developments in the information industry.
- **Searcher** 10 issues/year. $83.95 [2004]. ISSN 10704795. 'Targeted to experienced, knowledgeable searchers and combines evaluations of data content with discussions of delivery media.'
- **Online** 6 issues/year. $112.00. ISSN 01465422. 'Practical articles, product reviews and comparisons, case studies, and informed opinions about selecting, using, manipulating, and managing digital information products.'

6431 **Information World Review**
VNU Business Publications, Monthly. ISSN 09509879.
www.iwr.co.uk
'Europe's leading newspaper for the information industry, covering both content and information management issues from the perspective of information professionals and managers responsible for intranets, extranets, portals and content management.'

[For more emphasis on US developments, see the similar Information Today. IWR's publisher is part of the multinational VNU Business Information Group, which includes in its portfolio the annual Online Information Conference and Exhibition, held each December in London and the leading global venture of its kind.

6432 **Internet Resources Newsletter**
R. Macleod, C. Ure and C. Ferguson, eds; Heriot-Watt University
www.hw.ac.uk/libwww/irn
Very useful and interesting – and free of charge. Current sections are: Comment (including an eclectic 'News items of interest'); A–Z new and notable websites; Nice (websites): 'In the course of finding sites of interest for this Newsletter, we sometimes come across Web sites which we feel deserve slightly more than a passing mention'; Press releases; Network news (principally UK); Recent internet books in the library (Heriot-Watt University); internet in print; Book reviews; Blogorama (News about weblogs, RSS, etc.); Get a life! Leisure time (in Edinburgh and Scotland).

- **Pinakes** www.hw.ac.uk/libWWW/irn/pinakes/pinakes.html. Colourful links to about 50 major subject gateways. ('As it became increasingly difficult to locate material in the Library of Alexandria, the poet Callimachus solved the problem by compiling a catalogue called *The Pinakes*'.)
- **RSSxpress: RSS channel editor and directory** **A. Powell; UKOLN** http://rssxpress.ukoln.ac.uk. Service to create, modify and register RSS news channels plus directory of RSS channels in the UK Higher Education/Further Education community, the UK cultural sector (galleries, libraries and museums) and in related organizations.

6433 **Library Journal** [USA]
Reed Business Information, 20 issues/year. $141.00 [USA]; $221.00 [International Air Delivery]. ISSN 03603113.
www.libraryjournal.com
'The oldest independent national library publication. Founded in 1876, this 'bible' of the library world is read by over 100,000 library directors, administrators, and others in public, academic, and special (e.g., business) libraries.' Wide ranging coverage, but with much of little relevance to STM. Nevertheless, although overtly commercial, it includes lively – indeed, often pungent – comment on current developments. And it has many sections well worth browsing through: e.g. the book review section covers nearly 7000 books each year with hundreds of reviews of audiobooks, videos, databases, systems, and software. Three Newsletters are available: Corporate Library Update; Library Hotline; and Academic Newswire.

Subscription includes immediate access to all of the Library Journal web site, as well as the electronic newsletters.

6434 **ResourceShelf: Resources and news for information professionals** [USA]
G. Price
www.resourceshelf.com
Free of charge daily electronic newsletter containing news and other resources of interest to the online researcher. Wide coverage, especially of US-based developments. Apart from news of movements and machinations in the online database industry, there are usually posted each day useful items in the sections Professional Reading Shelf and Resources, Reports, Tools, Lists, and Full Text Documents. Well worth scanning.

6435 **Science and Technology Libraries**
Haworth Press, 1980–, Quarterly. $300.00. ISSN 0194262X.
www.haworthpress.com/focus/Library
Scholarly journal for the academic STM librarian consisting of themed issues. Coverage includes collections and collection management, electronic sources and digitization, bibliometrics, subject resources, user needs and book reviews.

See website for gateway to the publisher's extensive range of titles in this and related fields.

Topic Index

This topic index references the more specific subject areas treated within each subject field, and includes names of topics that have been considered to be too specialized to be subject fields in their own right, plus a small number of subject synonyms. The list of topics for each subject field is reproduced in the body of the book at the start of the relevant field's resource descriptions.

The topic index also includes the names of the subject fields themselves and those of the subject groupings. For clarity, the subject grouping and subject field headings have been distinguished typographically thus: PRE-CLINICAL SCIENCES (subject grouping, followed by the entire range of entry numbers within the grouping); PRE-CLINICAL SCIENCES (generic resources for the grouping, appearing immediately following its heading, followed by the range of entry numbers of those generic resources); MEDICAL TECHNOLOGY (subject field, followed by the range of entry numbers within that field).

D

N

O

P

Q

R

S

T

U

V

W

X

Y

Z

Title/Author Index

All references are to entry numbers, not page numbers. Titles of resources and names of corporate bodies are in bold type.

B

C

D

E

F

H

J

K

M

N

P

U

X

Y

Z